A Concordance to the
Complete English Poems of
JOHN SKELTON

THE CORNELL CONCORDANCES

S. M. Parrish, *General Editor*

Supervisory Committee
M. H. Abrams
Donald D. Eddy
Ephim Fogel
Alain Seznec

POEMS OF MATTHEW ARNOLD, *edited by Stephen Maxfield Parrish* (out of print)
POEMS OF W. B. YEATS, *edited by Stephen Maxfield Parrish*
POEMS OF EMILY DICKINSON, *edited by S. P. Rosenbaum*
WRITINGS OF WILLIAM BLAKE, *edited by David V. Erdman* (out of print)
BYRON'S *DON JUAN*, *edited by Charles W. Hagelman, Jr., and Robert J. Barnes*
THÉÂTRE ET POÉSIES DE JEAN RACINE, *edited by Bryant C. Freeman* (out of print)
BEOWULF, *edited by J. B. Bessinger, Jr.*
PLAYS OF W. B. YEATS, *edited by Eric Domville*
POEMS OF JONATHAN SWIFT, *edited by Michael Shinagel*
PLAYS OF WILLIAM CONGREVE, *edited by David Mann*
POEMS OF SAMUEL JOHNSON, *edited by Helen Harrold Naugle*
FABLES AND TALES OF JEAN DE LA FONTAINE, *edited by J. Allen Tyler*
POEMS OF OSIP MANDELSTAM, *edited by Demetrius J. Koubourlis*
POEMS OF SIR PHILIP SIDNEY, *edited by Herbert S. Donow*
PLAYS AND POEMS OF FEDERICO GARCÍA LORCA, *edited by Alice M. Pollin*
PASCAL'S *PENSÉES*, *edited by Hugh M. Davidson and Pierre H. Dubé*
COMPLETE WRITINGS OF GEORGE HERBERT, *edited by Mario A. Di Cesare and Rigo Mignani*
THE ANGLO-SAXON POETIC RECORDS, *edited by J. B. Bessinger, Jr.* (out of print)
POEMS OF BEN JONSON, *edited by Mario A. Di Cesare and Ephim Fogel*
PLAYS, POEMS, AND TRANSLATIONS OF CHRISTOPHER MARLOWE, *edited by Robert J. Fehrenbach, Lea Ann Boone, and Mario A. Di Cesare*
COMPLETE ENGLISH POEMS OF JOHN SKELTON, *edited by Alistair Fox and Gregory Waite*

A Concordance to the Complete English Poems of
JOHN SKELTON

Edited by
ALISTAIR FOX
and
GREGORY WAITE

Cornell University Press

ITHACA AND LONDON

Copyright © 1987 by Cornell University

All rights reserved. Except for brief quotations in a review, this book, or parts thereof, must not be reproduced in any form without permission in writing from the publisher. For information, address Cornell University Press, 124 Roberts Place, Ithaca, New York 14850.

The concordance is based on *John Skelton: The Complete English Poems*, ed. John Scattergood (New Haven: Yale University Press, 1983), introductory matter, notes, and glossary copyright © 1983 by John Scattergood, by permission of Yale University Press.

First published 1987 by Cornell University Press.

International Standard Book Number 0-8014-1944-1
Library of Congress Catalog Card Number 87-47552
Printed in the United States of America
Librarians: Library of Congress cataloging information appears on the last page of the book.

The paper in this book is acid-free and meets the guidelines for permanence and durability of the Committee on Production Guidelines for Book Longevity of the Council on Library Resources.

CONTENTS

Preface	vii
Editorial Principles	ix
Acknowledgments	xi
Abbreviations	xiii
Concordance to the Complete English Poems of John Skelton	1
Appendixes	
A. Frequency Index	873
B. Modern Spelling Index	913
C. Index of Compounds	953
D. Transcript of *Collyn Clout*, British Library MS Harley 2252	961
E. Word Index to *Collyn Clout*, British Library MS Harley 2252	985

PREFACE

As recently as 1925 John Skelton, despite the intermittent attention of poets and editors, could still be described as "forgotten."[1] That is emphatically not true today. Together with Donne, Skelton (1460?–1529) exerted a potent influence on a whole generation of modern poets from Robert Graves and W. H. Auden to A. D. Hope and Robin Skelton.[2] The twentieth-century poetic sensibility was ripe for what Skelton had to offer: verbal dexterity, a delight in the intrinsic sound quality, vigor, and connotative power of a native English language felt to antedate the "liquidness of diction" and "divine fluidity of movement" (as Matthew Arnold described it) which had dominated English poetry from Chaucer onward.[3] Skelton was judged to be a master poet who wrote "from the back of the mind" with a spontaneity and a sense of the integrity of his poetic calling capable of reminding modern poets of possibilities closed to them for centuries.[4]

Once Skelton had been rediscovered by the poets, his significance in English literary history was soon revised. From being called the "beastly" rhymer of a barbarous doggerel (Pope),[5] Skelton was considered an important representative of late fifteenth-century humanism[6] and a poet of distinction who not only resuscitated medieval genres into a late flowering but also anticipated many of the radical techniques (disjunctions, rapid transitions of tone, wordplay, and calculated ambiguity) of modernist poetry.[7] More recently, Skelton's verse has attracted the attention of postformalist critical approaches. Arthur Heiserman, applying the assumptions of conservative fictionalism, found Skelton's poetry to constitute "manifest fictions"

---

1. L. J. Lloyd, "John Skelton: A Forgotten Poet," *English Review*, 40 (1925): 659–665.
2. See Robert S. Kinsman, *John Skelton, Early Tudor Laureate: An Annotated Bibliography, c. 1488–1977* (Boston: G. K. Hall, 1979), pp. xlii–xliii.
3. Matthew Arnold, *Essays in Criticism, Second Series* (London: Macmillan, 1888), p. 28.
4. Robert Graves, "The Dedicated Poet: The Oxford Inaugural Lecture," *Encounter*, 17 (1961): 11–18.
5. Alexander Pope, *The First Epistle of the Second Book of Horace Imitated (1731)*, quoted in *Skelton: The Critical Heritage*, ed. Anthony S. G. Edwards (London: Routledge & Kegan Paul, 1981), p. 75.
6. William Nelson, *John Skelton, Laureate* (New York: Columbia University Press, 1939).
7. Ian A. Gordon, *John Skelton, Poet Laureate* (Melbourne and London: Melbourne University Press, 1943).

through the metafictional manipulation of conventions and structural devices,[8] whereas Stanley Fish saw it as a psychobiographical dramatization of its author's quest to resolve the problem of moral action.[9] Building on these reassessments, the edition of Skelton published by John Scattergood in 1983 seems bound to ensure that interest in Skelton will continue, particularly given the renewed impetus imparted to Renaissance studies by the new historicism and so-called cultural poetics.[10]

It is timely, therefore, for a concordance to the poetical works of Skelton to appear. As a guide to the idiosyncratic stylistic and linguistic habits that make Skelton a unique genius, it should help consolidate the reassessment that has been formulating for half a century; even more important, it can be used as a tool to remedy a serious deficiency in approaches to Skelton and his contemporaries: relative ignorance of the state of the English language between 1480 and 1580.

Surprisingly, the standard modern bibliography of Skelton studies notes only two substantial entries on Skelton's language.[11] This fact is symptomatic of a wider problem: there has been very little systematic study of the English language between the Pastons and Shakespeare.[12] Such neglect is understandable: many of the texts of major writers of this period have not been published in modern editions—Sir Thomas Elyot is a notorious case in point, and even Sir Thomas More had to wait over 400 years for a reprint of many of his polemical works—and the language itself appears to have been in such a rapid and fluid state of change in the first four decades of the sixteenth century that even the most tentative conjectures have seemed foolhardy and premature. In short, the language of the early Tudor period still awaits systematic study, and Skelton is an obvious place to start. He has by far the greatest stylistic range of any early Tudor writer, moving from the most aureate diction and elevated literary genres to an unusually colorful and vigorous low style that is probably closer to popular oral traditions than is the case with other writers of the time who got into print. (More and Tyndale, in some of the more scurrilous passages of their polemics, are possible exceptions.) Even a passing glance at Skelton, such as that given by

8. Arthur P. Heiserman, *Skelton and Satire* (Chicago: University of Chicago Press, 1961), especially pp. 299–312.

9. Stanley Fish, *John Skelton's Poetry* (New Haven: Yale University Press, 1965).

10. As practiced, for example, by Stephen Greenblatt, *Renaissance Self-Fashioning from More to Shakespeare* (Chicago: University of Chicago Press, 1980).

11. See Kinsman, *John Skelton, Early Tudor Laureate*, pp. 98, 119. The works referred to are F. M. Salter, "John Skelton's Contribution to the English Language," *Transactions of the Royal Society of Canada*, 3d ser., sect. 2, 39 (1945): 119–217; and Hilkka Jalava, "The Language of John Skelton's Rhymes" (dissertation for the Licentiate in Philosophy, University of Helsinki, 1965).

12. For a recent exception, see Norman Davis, "Notes on Grammar and Spelling in the Fifteenth Century," in *The Oxford Book of Late Medieval Verse and Prose*, ed. Douglas Gray (Oxford: Clarendon Press, 1985), pp. 493–508.

N. F. Blake in his study of nonstandard literary English, suggests the vast untapped riches still to be mined by a systematic study.[13] Blake identifies a collocation of dialect words, invented words, loan words, onomatopoeic words, proverbial expressions, and reduplicating forms which not only testifies to linguistic virtuosity of a very high order but also suggests a world of language of which readers accustomed only to the more formalized utterances of the "courtly makers" and their Elizabethan successors are hardly aware. Moreover, our findings suggest that Skelton may have been a much more important lexical innovator than has hitherto been supposed. F. M. Salter, for example, noted 816 words and senses in Skelton's prose translation of *Diodorus Siculus* which are unrecorded or antedate the earliest citation in *The Oxford English Dictionary*,[14] and we have identified in his poetry 92 words or compounds unrecorded in the *OED* as well as 132 antedatings and at least 150 antedated senses. Indeed, of 47 unique compounds, the *OED* lists only 17. It appears that Skelton was a significant innovator and that the study of his language will prove indispensable for future historians of Renaissance English literature; systematic study of his language should reveal much about the dynamics of linguistic change in the early sixteenth century. This concordance has been compiled in the hope that it will provide a preliminary instrument for, and a modest impetus toward, such an endeavor.

EDITORIAL PRINCIPLES

The concordance is based on *John Skelton: The Complete English Poems*, ed. John Scattergood (New Haven: Yale University Press, and Harmondsworth: Penguin Books, 1983), which replaces the edition by Alexander Dyce, *The Poetical Works of John Skelton*, 2 vols. (London: Thomas Rodd, 1843), as the standard edition. Scattergood's text is printed verbatim except for occasional instances when we have restored original text forms in the copy text which were emended by Scattergood. Such restored readings are indicated by an asterisk (*). Editorial emendations of the copy text, whether Scattergood's or our own, are indicated by square brackets.

Variants

All significant lexical variants found in sixteenth-century printed or manuscript editions are recorded immediately following the line in which the preferred reading is cited. A closing square bracket follows the preferred

---

13. N. F. Blake, *Non-Standard Language in English Literature* (London: André Deutsch, 1981), pp. 40–46, 68–69.
14. Salter, "John Skelton's Contribution."

reading, and the variant is enclosed in single quotation marks (e.g. "that] 'so'"). A dagger (†) accompanying a reference for a variant indicates the reading in the copy text as contrasted with the reading Scattergood adopted. "Editions" following a variant reading indicates that this reading occurs in all sixteenth-century printed editions. Our readings are taken in the first instance from Scattergood, checked against Dyce. We have also in some instances made our own collations from microfilm copies of sixteenth-century editions and manuscripts. The version of *Collyn Clout* found in British Library MS Harley 2252 varies so radically from any of the printed texts that we thought it best to index this version separately. The word index to this version (Appendix E) is based on a fresh transcription of the text from MS Harley 2252 (Appendix D). The headwords in Appendix E are spelled and alphabetized according to the principles used for the concordance of Scattergood's edition (see "Spelling and Alphabetization" below). Following each headword is a listing of the line numbers in Appendix D in which the headword occurs.

Omissions

We have not concorded Latin, Greek, French, and other foreign-language words occurring in Skelton's verse, but because of their special linguistic and aesthetic interest, we have included those periphrastic titles, incipits, explicits, rubrics, and stage directions in English prose which seem likely to be Skelton's rather than an editor's. In the concordance these materials are identified in the third column with the abbreviations I (incipit or other material preceding a poem), R (rubric), E (explicit or other material at the end of a poem), or SD (stage direction). Proper names, whether English or not, that occur within an English context are included, but names that occur in a foreign-language context are excluded.

The following high-frequency words are not concorded: AND (2826x), THE (2267x), TO (2148x), OF (1935x), I (1596x), A (1500x), THAT (1264x), IN (1099x), FOR (973x).

Citations

Headwords are listed in alphabetic order, and homographs are not separated. There is, however, a lemmatized index of spelling forms in Appendix B. Citations normally consist of a complete line of verse, but for those passages written in short-line "Skeltonics," lines are often cited in pairs (separated by a slash) in order to create a more coherent sense-unit. Sources of the lines of verse are given by abbreviated title of the poem and the page and line numbers in Scattergood's edition.

Preface

Spelling and Alphabetization

Following Scattergood's edition, contractions have been expanded, *i/j* and *u/v* have been normalized according to modern usage, þ is rendered as *th* and ȝ (on the few occasions it occurs) as *gh* or *y*, and initial *ff* is rendered as *F*. Because the two letters *y* and *i* are often used interchangeably in early Tudor texts, *y* within a word is treated as an *i* alphabetically except that words with an internal *i* precede words with an internal *y* in the same position—for example, BITTER is followed by BY through BYTWENE, which precedes BLABER. Initial *y* follows *x*. In the version of *Collyn Clout* printed from MS Harley 2252, þ is rendered as *th*, contractions have been expanded, and both capitalization and word division have been regularized; *u* and *v*, however, are printed exactly as they occur in the manuscript.

Word Division

We have treated as compounds those words in Scattergood's edition which can form compounds yet were typeset in that edition as separate words. The second elements of all compounds are listed in Appendix C.

ACKNOWLEDGMENTS

We are indebted to the New Zealand University Grants Committee and the University of Otago for generous research and publication grants, without which this concordance would not have been possible, and to Mary Sullivan, Anaig Fenby, Penny Love, Jane Jones, Katherine Spears, and Signy Henderson, all of whom have offered invaluable assistance and labor. Our sincere thanks go also to the members of the User Services Section of the Computing Centre, University of Otago, for advice and attentiveness that went far beyond the call of duty.

ALISTAIR FOX
GREGORY WAITE

University of Otago

Abbreviations

TITLES OF POEMS

Ag Scottes	Agaynst the Scottes
Ag Scottes2	Unto Dyvers People that Remord this Rymyng . . .
Albany	Howe the Douty Duke of Albany . . .
Balettys	Dyvers Balettys and Dyties Solacyous
Balettys1	With 'Lullay, lullay', lyke a chylde
Balettys2	The auncient acquaintance, madam, betwen us twayn
Balettys3	Knolege, aquayntance, resort, favour, with grace
Balettys4	Though ye suppose all jeperdys ar paste [Cuncta licet . . .]
Balettys5	Go, pytyous hart, rasyd with dedly wo
Bowge	The Bowge of Courte
Calliope	Calliope
Collyn Clout	Collyn Clout
Couplet	A Couplet on Wolsey's Dissolution of the Convocation at St Paul's
Coystrowne	Agaynste a Comely Coystrowne
Coystrowne1	Of all nacyons under the hevyn
Coystrowne2	Contra alium cantitantem . . . sarcasmos
Coystrowne3	Uppon a deedmans hed
Coystrowne4	Womanhood, wanton, ye want
Dol Dethe	Upon the Dolorus Dethe and Muche Lamentable Chaunce of the Mooste Honorable Erle of Northumberlande
Dundas	Against Dundas
El Rummynge	Elynour Rummynge
Epitaphe	Epitaphe . . . of Two Knaves Sometyme of Dis
Epitaphe1	A Devoute Trentale for Old John Clarke
Epitaphe2	Adam Uddersale
Garlande	A Garlande or Chapelet of Laurell
Garlande2	Justyce now is dede
Garnesche	Agenst Garnesche
Garnesche1	Sithe ye have me chalyngyd, Master Garnesche
Garnesche2	How may I your mokery mekely tollerate
Garnesche3	I have your lewde letter receyvyd

Garnesche5	Garnyshe, gargone, gastly, gryme
Hauke	Ware the Hauke
Lawde	A Lawde and Prayse Made for Our Sovereigne Lord the Kyng
Magnyfycence	Magnyfycence
Man Margery	Manerly Margery Mylk and Ale
Phy Sparrow	Phyllyp Sparowe
Replycacion	A Replycacion Agaynst Certayne Yong Scolers Abjured of Late
Scot Kynge	A Ballade of the Scottysshe Kynge
Speke Parott	Speke Parott
Ven Tongues	Against Venemous Tongues
Why Come Ye	Why Come Ye Nat to Courte?
Why Come Ye2	Now mayster doctor, howe say ye

MANUSCRIPTS

MS Cotton Vitellius E.x	British Library, London, MS Cotton Vitellius E.x., ff. 208r–225v
MS Harley 367	British Library, London, MS Harley 367, ff. 101r–109r
MS Harley 2252	British Library, London, MS Harley 2252, ff. 133v–140r, 147r–154v
MS Lansdowne 762	British Library, London, MS Lansdowne 762, f. 71r
MS Rawlinson C. 813	Bodleian Library, Oxford, MS Rawlinson C. 813, ff. 36r–43v
MS Royal 18 D.ii	British Library, London, MS Royal 18 D.ii, ff. 165r–166v

PRINTED EDITIONS

Dates given are those established by R. S. Kinsman. Reference numbers are given for both *STC*² (see "Other Sources" below for full title) and Kinsman's annotated bibliography.

Day 1560	*Heare after Foloweth Certain Bokes* . . . (J. Day, 1560?). *STC*² 22600. Kinsman 1560.4.
Douce Fragment d.7	*Magnyfycence, a Goodly Interlude and a Mery* (P. Treveris for J. Rastell, 1530?). Bodleian Library copy, Oxford, Douce Fragments d.7. *STC*² 22607. Kinsman 1530.3.
Fakes 1513	*A Ballade of the Scottysshe Kynge* (R. Faques, 1513). *STC*² 22593. Kinsman 1513.4.
Fakes 1523	*A Ryght Delectable Tratyse vpon a Goodly Garlande or Chapelet of Laurell* (R. Faukes, 1523). *STC*² 22610. Kinsman 1523.3.
1521 Fragment	[*The Tunnyng of Elynour Rummyng*] (W. de Worde, 1521?). *STC*² 22611.5. Kinsman 1521.
Godfray 1531	*Here after Foloweth a Lytell Boke Called Collyn Clout* (T. Godfray, 1531?). *STC*² 22600.5. Kinsman 1531.2.

Abbreviations

Kele 1545.1	*Colyn Cloute* (R. Kele, 1545?). *STC*² 22601. Kinsman 1545.1.
Kele 1545.2	*Here after Foloweth the Boke of Phyllyp Sparowe* (R. Kele, 1545?). *STC*² 22594. Kinsman 1545.2.
Kele 1545.3	*Here after Foloweth a Lytell Boke, whiche hath to Name, Why Come Ye Not to Courte* (R. Kele, 1545?). *STC*² 22615. Kinsman 1545.3.
Kitson 1560.6	*Here after Foloweth a Litle Boke, of Phillip Sparow* (A. Kitson, 1560?). *STC*² 22596. Kinsman 1560.6.
Kitson 1560.7	*Here after Foloweth a Litle Boke, whyche hathe to Name, Whye Come Ye Not to Courte* (A. Kytson, 1560?). *STC*² 22617. Kinsman 1560.7.
Kynge & Marche 1554	*Here after Foloweth Certaine Bokes, Compyled by Mayster Skelton . . .* (J. Kynge and T. Marche, 1554?). *STC*² 22599. Kinsman 1554.
Lant 1545	*Here after Foloweth Certayne Bokes, Compyled by Mayster Skelton. Speke Parrot. The Deth of Kyng Edwarde the Fourth. A Treatyse of the Scottes. Ware the Hawke. The Tunnyng of Elynour Rummynge* (R. Lant, 1545?). *STC*² 22598. Kinsman 1545.
Marshe 1568	*Pithy Pleasaunt and Profitable Workes of Maister Skelton. Nowe Collected and Newly Published* (T. Marshe, 1568). *STC*² 22608. Kinsman 1568.
Pynson 1528	*Honorificatissimo, amplissimo, . . . A Replycacion Agaynst Certayne Yong Scolers Abjured of Late* (R. Pynson, 1528). *STC*² 22609. Kinsman 1528.2.
Rastell 1527	*Skelton Laureate Agaynste a Comely Coystrowne* (J. Rastell, 1527?). *STC*² 22611. Kinsman 1527.
Rastell 1527.1	*Here Folowythe Dyuers Balettys and Dyties Solacyous* (J. Rastell, 1527?). *STC*² 22604. Kinsman 1527.1.
Rastell & Treveris B 1530	*Magnyfycence, a Goodly Interlude and a Mery* (P. Treveris for J. Rastell, 1530?). British Library copy. *STC*² 22607. Kinsman 1530.3.
Rastell & Treveris C 1530	*Magnyfycence, a Goodly Interlude and a Mery* (P. Treveris for J. Rastell, 1530?). Cambridge University Library copy. *STC*² 22607. Kinsman 1530.3.
Scattergood	*John Skelton: The Complete English Poems*. Ed. John Scattergood (New Haven: Yale University Press, and Harmondsworth: Penguin Books, 1983).
Toy 1553	*Here after Foloweth a Little Boke . . . Whi Come Ye Not to Courte* (R. Toy, 1553?). *STC*² 22616. Kinsman 1553.3.
Wyght 1553	*Here after Foloweth a Litle Booke, of Phillyp Sparow* (J. Wyght, 1553?). *STC*² 22595. Kinsman 1553.2.
Wynkyn de Worde 1499	*Here Begynneth a Lytell Treatyse Named the Bowge of Courte* (W. de Worde, 1499?). *STC*² 22597. Kinsman 1499.2.
Wynkyn de Worde 1510	*Here Begynneth a Lytell Treatyse Named the Bowge of Courte* (W. de Worde, c. 1510). *STC*² 22597.5. Kinsman 1510.3.

OTHER SOURCES

Kinsman   Kinsman, Robert S. *John Skelton, Early Tudor Laureate: An Annotated Bibliography, c. 1488–1977*. Boston: G. K. Hall, 1979.

OED   *The Oxford English Dictionary*. Ed. James A. H. Murray and others. Oxford: Clarendon Press, 1933.

STC^2 *A Short-Title Catalogue of Books Printed in England, Scotland, and Ireland and of English Books Printed Abroad, 1475–1640*. First compiled by A. W. Pollard and G. R. Redgrave. 2d ed., revised and enlarged, begun by W. A. Jackson and F. S. Ferguson, completed by Katharine F. Pantzer. Vol. 2, I–Z. London: Bibliographical Society, 1976.

A Concordance to the
Complete English Poems of
JOHN SKELTON

ABACKE—ABJECTYD

	Page	Title	Line

ABACKE
Stande a lytell abacke, syr, and let hym come hyder. — 186, Magnyfycence, 1647

ABANDUNE
Fortune to her lawys can not abandune me; — 181, Magnyfycence, 1459

ABASHYTH
Abashyth me, albeit I have no nede. — 44, Balettys3, 35

ABASSHE
Abasshe you not, but hardely be bolde, — 48, Bowge, 87

ABASSHEMENT
Whiche maner of abasshement became her not yll; — 337, Garlande, 889

ABATE
Theyr courage to abate — 270, Collyn Clout, 973

ABATED
And theyr courage abated, — 283, Why Come Ye, 162

ABBEY
Of an abbey ye make a graunge − — 257, Collyn Clout, 419
  ye] 'they' Kele 1545.1, 'to' MS Harley 2252

ABBESSE
Dame Sybly our abbesse, — 256, Collyn Clout, 391

ABBOT
Hathe made himselfe abbot — 306, Why Come Ye, 1099

ABBROGATE
There is none that your name woll abbrogate — 240, Speke Parott, 317

A B C
Owur new-founde A. B. C. — 238, Speke Parott, 277
For drede and he lerne them there A B C to spell.' — 353, Garlande, 1476

ABELL
Lyke that untrue rebell /Fals Kayn agaynst Abell. — 121, Ag Scottes2, 20

ABHOMINACION
And in abhominacion /Of all maner of nacion, — 362, Albany, 141

ABHOMYNABLE
In their study abhomynable, — 375, Replycacion, 25

ABHOR
All flatringe faytors abhor and from the kast. — 34, Dol Dethe, 172

ABHORDE
Where trouth is abhorde, — 300, Why Come Ye, 847

ABHORE
For I abhore to smatter — 297, Why Come Ye, 714

ABHORRE
For I abhorre to wryte — 257, Collyn Clout, 437

ABYDE
That wyll abyde and never frome us fall. — 49, Bowge, 130
Wylt thou abyde by the wordes agayne? — 55, Bowge, 324
No broken galles /May there abyde — 83, Phy Sparrow, 474
  No] 'Nor' Kitson 1560.6
Perceyve you not howe lothe he was to abyde — 147, Magnyfycence, 241
I trowe it shall not nede to abyde. — 156, Magnyfycence, 571
Abyde. Lette me se. Take better hede. — 157, Magnyfycence, 595
Abyde, syr, quod he! Mary, so I do. — 162, Magnyfycence, 789
Where is he? Mary, I made hym abyde — 187, Magnyfycence, 1685
Abyde, syr, abyde. Let me holde your hede. — 189, Magnyfycence, 1727
Abyde, syr, abyde. Let me holde your hede. — 189, Magnyfycence, 1727
Thou must not abyde the dynt of my hande. — 193, Magnyfycence, 1879
Nay, thou false harted dastarde! Thou dare not abyde. — 202, Magnyfycence, 2193
Abyde, syr, abyde; I shall make hym to pysse. — 204, Magnyfycence, 2250
Abyde, syr, abyde; I shall make hym to pysse. — 204, Magnyfycence, 2250
Alarum, alarum! To longe we abyde! — 206, Magnyfycence, 2323
Then welthe with you myght in no wyse abyde. — 210, Magnyfycence, 2447
Syrs, I am agreed to abyde your ordenaunce − — 210, Magnyfycence, 2471
Abyde, abyde, /And to you shall be tolde — 218, El Rummynge, 156
Abyde, abyde, /And to you shall be tolde — 218, El Rummynge, 156
That no man may abyde — 261, Collyn Clout, 594
And his layser abyde, — 295, Why Come Ye, 636
And abyde the correctyon — 304, Why Come Ye, 1014
It was not for hym to abyde the tryall. — 315, Garlande, 98
  abyde] 'byde' MS Cotton Vitellius E.x
For ye dare nat abyde. — 363, Albany, 187
That durst abyde no reknyng; — 365, Albany, 249

ABYDEN
Nowe, by Cockes harte, well abyden! — 156, Magnyfycence, 576

ABYDES
That no man abydes, — 84, Phy Sparrow, 508
But, for the, Fansy, Magnyfycence abydes. — 176, Magnyfycence, 1305

ABYDYNGE
Why, under whom was he abydynge? — 166, Magnyfycence, 938

ABYDYTHE
For Tytus at Dover abydythe in the rode; — 239, Speke Parott, 284

ABYLEMENT
Where is nowe all my ryche abylement? — 198, Magnyfycence, 2059

ABYLYMENT
Take nowe upon you this abylyment, — 208, Magnyfycence, 2405
But to recounte her ryche abylyment, — 313, Garlande, 44

ABJECTE
And in maner as abjecte, /For evermore suspecte, — 380, Replycacion, 240

ABJECTIONS
All maner of abjections; — 268, Collyn Clout, 890

ABJECTYD
Fyrst, from your magnyfycence syn must be abjectyd; — 211, Magnyfycence, 2484

ABJURED — ABOWTE

	Page	Title	Line

ABJURED
A Replycacion Agaynst Certayne Yong Scolers Abjured of Late,	373	Replycacion	1
and rechelesse yonge heretykes lately abjured, etc.	373	Replycacion	1
Now of late abjured, /Most unhappely ured;	385	Replycacion	404

ABLE
By the masse, for ye are able to dystroy an hole lande.	154	Magnyfycence	513
Howe they are able to make /With theyr golde and treasure	250	Collyn Clout	143
But now to helpe myselfe I am not able.	321	Garlande	312
My name, I know well, beyonde that I am able,	324	Garlande	438
An hole reame he is able to set at devysion:	333	Garlande	758
That they juge them selfe able to be	374	Replycacion	7

ABOLETE
To practique suche abolete sciens.	297	Why Come Ye	713
practique] 'practyve' †Kele 1545.3			

ABOUNDE
What noblenesse dothe abounde,	369	Albany	424

ABOUT
Then ren they with lesinges, and blow them about,	139	Ven Tongues	69
By God, I have bene about a praty pronge -	154	Magnyfycence	501
Nowe let me se about	168	Magnyfycence	991
Upon her brayne-pan, /Lyke an Egypcyan /Lapped about.	216	El Rummynge	79
Lapped] 'Capped' Kynge & Marche 1554, Day 1560, Marshe 1568			
Some with a sho clout /Bynde theyr heddes about;	218	El Rummynge	144
In all her joyntes about;	226	El Rummynge	485
With a sory face /Whey-wormed about;	228	El Rummynge	553
Ye go about to amende, and ye mare all.	235	Speke Parott	154
This can nat be brought about	267	Collyn Clout	849
Some walke about in melottes,	268	Collyn Clout	864
Hangynge about the walles	270	Collyn Clout	940
With all our strength that we can brynge about,	324	Garlande	424
This hous envyrowne was a myle about;	326	Garlande	489
With alys ensandid about in compas,	330	Garlande	654
Were newly enbybid; and rownd about the same	331	Garlande	682
And ye coude bryng /The matter about	361	Albany	93
About your traytours throtes.	362	Albany	124
About hym a parke /Of a madde warke,	365	Albany	267
Shulde bring about that thing.	367	Albany	335
For you to bring about	368	Albany	391
I rede you, loke about;	371	Albany	500
Ye cobble and ye clout /Holy scripture so about,	380	Replycacion	223

ABOUTE
That were aboute hym, his awne servauntis of trust,	30	Dol Dethe	37
He was envyronde aboute on every syde	32	Dol Dethe	99
To all cuntreis aboute hym reporte me I dare:	33	Dol Dethe	136
Nor stand long wrestyng there aboute;	41	Coystrowne4	25
They thronge in fast and flocked her aboute.	49	Bowge	122
He wente aboute to take me in a fawte:	55	Bowge	318
Who deleth with shrewes hath nede to loke aboute!'	61	Bowge	525
But tell me where aboute ye go.	157	Magnyfycence	617
All this ye may easely brynge aboute.	158	Magnyfycence	655
Well rounde aboute.	163	Magnyfycence	831
It is wonder to se the worlde aboute,	177	Magnyfycence	1326
He can full craftely this matter brynge aboute.	187	Magnyfycence	1691
Theyr lockes aboute theyr face,	218	El Rummynge	146
And yf ye stande in doute /Who brought this ryme aboute,	248	Collyn Clout	48
As though they wolde flye /Aboute the sterry skye.	248	Collyn Clout	74
Aboute] 'Above' Kele 1545.1, Marshe 1568, MS Harley 2252			
Aboute the cattes necke,	250	Collyn Clout	164
As I go aboute,	253	Collyn Clout	286
Aboute churches and market.	255	Collyn Clout	326
But how that came aboute,	296	Why Come Ye	693
Let se, my syster, now spede you, go aboute.	319	Garlande	242
you] not in MS Cotton Vitellius E.x			
Enwallyd aboute with the stony flint,	328	Garlande	569
Then furthermore aboute me my syght I revolde,	330	Garlande	664
Castyng my syght the chambre aboute,	343	Garlande	1093
It must nedes after rin all the worlde aboute.'	353	Garlande	1483
'Triumpha, triumpha!' they cryid all aboute.	354	Garlande	1506

ABOVE
In thy palace above the orient,	34	Dol Dethe	202
Pray to thy son above the starris clere,	35	Dol Dethe	208
Above the sky /That is so hy,	40	Coystrowne3	55
To solfe above E-la - /Fa, lorell, fa, fa -	84	Phy Sparrow	487
Fa] 'Ga' †Kele 1545.2, Wyght 1553, Kitson 1560.6			
That Phyllyp may fly /Above the starry sky,	86	Phy Sparrow	599
An ynche above her kne,	225	El Rummynge	420
Above all other byrdis, set Parrot alone.	233	Speke Parott	112
An ynche above your eere,	263	Collyn Clout	674
Above threscore and ten.	288	Why Come Ye	373
Above all other inordinatly.	296	Why Come Ye	704
Desyring you above all thynge	299	Why Come Ye	828
Renownyd lady above the sterry hevyn,	313	Garlande	51
In our collage above the sterry sky,	323	Garlande	403
Above, in the top, a byrde of Araby,	330	Garlande	667

ABOWTE
They rangyd Hankyn Bovy /My churche all abowte.	65	Hauke	118
A bawdy dyscheclowte, /That bryngyth the worlde abowte	125	Garnesche3	37
Abowte my necke a cerculett lyke the ryche rubye,	231	Speke Parott	17

ABRODE — ACCORDE   Page   Title   Line

	Page	Title	Line
Some ranne the nexte way, sume ranne abowte.	319	Garlande	252
ABRODE			
That agaynst preesthode /Theyr malyce sprede abrode, agaynst] 'agayn' Marshe 1568	260	Collyn Clout	535
And sayle nat farre abrode,	277	Collyn Clout	1256
ABROGATE			
And that wolde abrogate	264	Collyn Clout	707
ABSENCE			
Syr, the longe absence of you, Sad Cyrcumspeccyon,	209	Magnyfycence	2424
ABSENS			
But absens, alas, wyth tremelyng fere and drede,	44	Balettys3	34
You I assure, absens is my fo,	44	Balettys3	36
But hatefull absens, to me so envyous,	45	Balettys3	45
ABSENT			
Where lyberte is absent, set welthe asyde.	142	Magnyfycence	80
Where measure is absent, ryot kepeth resydence;	144	Magnyfycence	123
Yet measure hath ben so longe from us absent,	146	Magnyfycence	221
ABSOLON			
In his goodly person /Lyke unto Absolon,	369	Albany	435
ABSOLUTE			
In there absolute consciens	297	Why Come Ye	712
ABSTRACT			
An abstract or a concrete, abstract] 'obstract' †Kele 1545.3	289	Why Come Ye	421
ABSTRACTE			
A false abstracte cometh from a fals concrete.	58	Bowge	439
ABULL			
Loke on this tabull, /Whether thou art abull	68	Hauke	236
ABUSAR			
Ye are a fals entrusar, /And a fals abusar,	364	Albany	228
ABUSE			
He doth abuse /Hym selfe to to;	164	Magnyfycence	871
ABUSED			
And I am a vyce where I am abused.	199	Magnyfycence	2102
But he abused so his free lyberte,	200	Magnyfycence	2113
ABUSION			
In realmes, in cities, by suche fals abusion.	139	Ven Tongues	56
ABUSIOUNS			
And by her abusiouns, /And damnable illusiouns	350	Garlande	1340
ABUSYD			
That be so far abusyd /They cannot be excusyd	62	Hauke	5
The church is thus abusyd, /Reproched and pollutyd;	66	Hauke	160
That never was /Abusyd before.	164	Magnyfycence	868
Helas! I lamente the dull abusyd brayne,	242	Speke Parott	383
ABUSYON			
She brought him in abusyon;	89	Phy Sparrow	708
And wenyst thow that I know not the, cankard Abusyon?	161	Magnyfycence	757
COURTLY ABUSYON alone in the place.	163	Magnyfycence	SD
Abusyon /Forsothe I hyght;	164	Magnyfycence	856
Here cometh in COURTLY ABUSYON, doynge reverence and courtesy.	182	Magnyfycence	SD
For suche abusyon I use nowe and than.	185	Magnyfycence	1625
It is none abusyon, syr, in a noble man.	185	Magnyfycence	1626
And your payntyd Pleasure, Courtly Abusyon,	192	Magnyfycence	1860
Alasse, that ever I occupyed suche abusyon!	200	Magnyfycence	2129
Ye, and beware of unhappy abusyon.	210	Magnyfycence	2452
Through suche abusyon, /And by suche illusyon,	279	Why Come Ye	19
Thus by demeryttes of their abusyon,	374	Replycacion	14
ABUSYONS			
And by her abusyons,	105	Phy Sparrow	1347
With other abusyons grete;	306	Why Come Ye	1086
ABUSYOUN			
And useth suche abusyoun,	290	Why Come Ye	456
With Courtely Abusyoun; who pryntith it wele in mynde	346	Garlande	1196
ACCESSARY			
Whiche shall be to you a sufferayne accessary,	326	Garlande	523
ACCOMPLYSSHE			
I can not myne appetyte accomplysshe and fulfyll	160	Magnyfycence	733
ACCOMPLYSSHEMENT			
In your servyce; and, to the accomplysshement	314	Garlande	61
ACCOMPTE			
Redresse sholde be at the rekenynge in every accompte,	208	Magnyfycence	2413
Syr, to accompte you, the contynewe of my consayte	209	Magnyfycence	2421
ACCOMPTYNGE			
Accomptynge them as fictyons.	249	Collyn Clout	114
ACCORD			
And the date of the Devyll dothe shurewlye accord.	244	Speke Parott	445
ACCORDE			
He sayth he can not well accorde with the.'	51	Bowge	185
To you no thyng it dyde accorde	113	Scot Kynge	3
To you nothing it dyd accorde	118	Ag Scottes	93
Thy wordes and my mynde odly well accorde.	185	Magnyfycence	1605
And howe may this accorde,	272	Collyn Clout	1029
But to his sentence must accorde.	287	Why Come Ye	343
Whiche shrewdly doth accorde!	294	Why Come Ye	621
And how his wordes with reason wyll not accorde.	314	Garlande	88
Of very dwte it may not well accorde,	318	Garlande	212
It may wele ryme, but shroudly it doth accorde,	346	Garlande	1210

ACCORDIS — ADEWE

	Page	Title	Line
ACCORDIS			
This shrewdly accordis /To be a cupborde for lordys!	302	Why Come Ye	913
ACCORDYNG			
Rebukyng and remordyng, /And nothing accordyng.	120	Ag Scottes2	12
ACCORDYNGE			
Accordynge to treuth they be well devysyd.	210	Magnyfycence	2470
ACCUSETH			
For the temporalte /Accuseth the spirytualte;	248	Collyn Clout	62
ACCUSTOMABLE			
Mayster Lidgate, of your accustomable	324	Garlande	436
Of your bounte the accustomable rate	344	Garlande	1130
ACCUSTOME			
But, good madame, the accustome and usage	314	Garlande	64
ACHADEMIOS			
His commedy, Achademios callyd by name;	346	Garlande	1184
ACHERONTES			
From the marees depe /Of Acherontes well,	73	Phy Sparrow	70
ACHEVE			
Helthe of body his besynesse to acheve;	207	Magnyfycence	2369
ACHILLIEDOS			
Lucan, with Stacius in Achilliedos;	321	Garlande	337
ACHYLLES			
Whom Achylles slew,	88	Phy Sparrow	675
ACOMBERYD			
Me thynke ye are not gretly acomberyd wyth wyt.	203	Magnyfycence	2215
ACON			
In Acon it was brought to pas,	296	Why Come Ye	706
ACONCYUS			
That of Aconcyus whan she founde the byll	337	Garlande	886
ACORD			
Demaundinge soche dutes as nedis most acord	31	Dol Dethe	66
ACORDE			
In whome dothe wele acorde	110	Lawde	12
ACOUNTYD			
Lyberte without measure is acountyd for a beste;	144	Magnyfycence	138
Laudable your consayte is to be acountyd,	145	Magnyfycence	191
Of Cato the counte, acountyd the cane,	181	Magnyfycence	1487
ACQUAINTANCE			
The auncient acquaintance, madam, betwen us twayn,	42	Balettys2	1
ACQUAYNTED			
Not acquaynted worth a fly /With honorable Haly,	292	Why Come Ye	520
ACQUAYNTYD			
Yet your problemes ar preignaunte and with loyalte acquayntyd.	240	Speke Parott	344
ACQUEINTAUNCE			
Of your acqueintaunce I was in tymes past,	327	Garlande	540
ACQUYTE			
In faythe, and your servyce ryght well shall I acquyte;	190	Magnyfycence	1794
ACTEON			
That plucked Acteon to the grounde,	79	Phy Sparrow	297
ACTES			
Of hardy merciall actes,	368	Albany	397
ACTIS			
Of noble actis auncyently enrolde	29	Dol Dethe	15
Whos noble actis shew worsheply his name,	33	Dol Dethe	143
ACTYON			
They put you to your actyon.	273	Collyn Clout	1060
ACTYS			
In Arturys auncyent actys nowhere ys provyd your pere;	123	Garnesche2	24
ACTYVITE			
So noble a prince as he /In all actyvite	368	Albany	396
ACTYVYTE			
Or what actyvyte /Is in you, beggars braules,	364	Albany	217
ADAM			
John Jayberd et Adam all a knave,	106	Epitaphe	I
ADAM UDDERSALE, ALIAS DICTUS ADAM ALL A KNAVE,	109	Epitaphe2	I
ADAM UDDERSALE, ALIAS DICTUS ADAM ALL A KNAVE,	109	Epitaphe2	I
ADAME			
Of one Adame all a knave, late dede and gone —	347	Garlande	1247
ADAUNTED			
With myghty corage /A[d]aunted the rage /Of a lyon savage; Adaunted] 'Auaunted' editions	104	Phy Sparrow	1310
ADAUNTID			
With myghty corrage /Adauntid the rage /Of a lyon savage;	349	Garlande	1303
ADDERS			
Yet is youre tong an adders tayle,	41	Coystrowne4	16
ADDICYON			
and her foloweth an addicyon made by Maister Skelton.	103	Phy Sparrow	R
ADDRESSYNG			
Addressyng your selfe, lyke a sadde messengere,	239	Speke Parott	303
ADEW			
Farewell Phyllyp, adew;	80	Phy Sparrow	331
Youre eye is out; adew, good nyght!	119	Ag Scottes	142
Adew Philosophia, /Adew Theologia.	284	Why Come Ye	213
Adew Philosophia, /Adew Theologia.	284	Why Come Ye	214
ADEWE			
Adewe tyll soone, we shall speke more of this.	60	Bowge	492
Adewe, for I wyll not come in his clokys.	193	Magnyfycence	1874
Adewe, syrs, for I thynke leyst that I come to late.	201	Magnyfycence	2152

ADIEU —ADVYSED   Page   Title   Line

Than have good daye. Adewe!   280   Why Come Ye   58
ADIEU
Adieu, Jayberd, adue. /I faith, dikkon, thou crue!   108   Epitaphel   62
Adieu, syr sumner, cast of your crowne! 117   Ag Scottes   64
ADYMENT
Enhardid adyment the sement of your wall! 320   Garlande   306
ADMYRALL
His sone the lorde admyrall is full good, ... 115   Scot Kynge   70
ADMYRELL
God save my Lorde Admyrell! 288   Why Come Ye   376
ADMYT
Put fro you presumpcyon and admyt humylyte, ... 207   Magnyfycence   2361
ADMYTTES
But suche as he admyttes, ... 287   Why Come Ye   327
ADONIS
Adonis of freshe colour, ...   111   Lawde   43
ADRASTUS
Adrastus wise and sage. 110   Lawde   14
ADRES
Adres the to me, whiche am bothe halt and lame, ...   29   Dol Dethe   10
And now to begyn I wyll me adres, ... 117   Ag Scottes   89
ADRESSE
And after his mynde herdely your selfe adresse, ... 144   Magnyfycence   151
And quyckely your appetytes to sharpe and adresse;   183   Magnyfycence 1549
And fumously adresse you with magnanymyte;   211   Magnyfycence 2497
A-DROPPYNGE
His nose a-droppynge, his lyppes were full drye;   56   Bowge   362
  a-droppynge] 'droppynge' Marshe 1568
ADUE
Adieu, Jayberd, adue. /I faith, dikkon, thou crue!   108   Epitaphel   62
Farewell, my frende. Adue tyll sone.   167   Magnyfycence   966
Fare well tyll sone; adue tyll to morowe. 192   Magnyfycence 1850
Adue, nowe, Sir Wrig-wrag! /Adue, Sir Dalyrag!   366   Albany   296
Adue, nowe, Sir Wrig-wrag! /Adue, Sir Dalyrag!   366   Albany   297
Adue, cowarde, adue! /Fals knight and mooste untrue, ...   366   Albany   314
Adue, cowarde, adue! /Fals knight and mooste untrue, ...   366   Albany   314
ADVERSARY
And his untrew adversary? 298   Why Come Ye   789
ADVERSYTE
Or ever we were ware, brought us in adversyte, ...   193   Magnyfycence 1863
Here cometh in ADVERSYTE. 193   Magnyfycence   SD
I am Adversyte, that for thy mysdede   193   Magnyfycence 1876
The stroke of God, Adversyte, I hyght.   193   Magnyfycence 1882
I counsayle them beware of adversyte. 194   Magnyfycence 1899
Wherfore, of adversyte loke ye be ware; 195   Magnyfycence 1936
And beware of adversyte by my counsell, ... 195   Magnyfycence 1945
And brynge you agayne out of adversyte. 196   Magnyfycence 1999
O dolorous herte, O harde adversyte!   198   Magnyfycence 2052
In welthe to beware of herde adversyte. 201   Magnyfycence 2159
Dyspare is my name, that adversyte dothe f[o]lowe;   205   Magnyfycence 2284
  folowe] 'felowe' †Rastell & Treveris C 1530, B,
  Douce Fragment d.7
Alas, syr! So I am lapped in adversyte   206   Magnyfycence 2331
Myxed with bytter alowes of herde adversyte.   207   Magnyfycence 2354
And hartely thanke God of your adversyte; 207   Magnyfycence 2362
Adversyte to hym therwith nowe and than;   207   Magnyfycence 2368
Is from adversyte Magnyfycence to unbynde.   209   Magnyfycence 2422
Caused me of adversyte to fall in subjeccyon. 209   Magnyfycence 2425
Of adversyte it is to stande in drede.   209   Magnyfycence 2428
I herde say that adversyte with Magnyfycence had fought. . .   210   Magnyfycence 2460
Ye, syr, with adversyte I have bene vexyd;   210   Magnyfycence 2461
Sodenly comfort, and sodenly adversyte; 212   Magnyfycence 2528
But now in welthe, now in adversyte.   312   Garlande   14
ADVERTENCE
It askyth lesure with good advert[ence].   141   Magnyfycence   42
  advertence] 'advertysment' †Rastell & Treveris C 1530, B
Who so to me gyveth good advertence 177   Magnyfycence 1333
Tenderly to consyder in your advertence - 186   Magnyfycence 1635
ADVERTYSEMENT
'Beholde and se in your advertysement 335   Garlande   808
Of Good Advertysement, ...   384   Replycacion   361
ADVERTYSYNG
Advertysyng you, madame, to warke more secretly, ...   43   Balettys2   39
ADVERTYSMENT
For I wyll use you by his advertysment. 146   Magnyfycence   196
ADVYSE
I advyse yow beware of thys war, rannge yow in aray.   123   Garnesche2   33
Mary, Lusty Pleasure, by myne advyse, ... 167   Magnyfycence   964
Be it ryght or wronge, by the advyse of me, ... 185   Magnyfycence 1597
By myne advyse, with you in fayth he shall not rest.   186   Magnyfycence 1660
But use your largesse by the advyse of me, ...   189   Magnyfycence 1765
Your comfortable advyse and wyt excedyth all gladnesse; . . . 210   Magnyfycence 2477
ADVYSED
A parson benyfyced /But nothynge well advysed.   62   Hauke   37
No; for or we stryke, we wyll be advysed twyse. 163   Magnyfycence   810
And surely, as I am nowe advysed, ... 186   Magnyfycence 1657
They mought be better advysed 261   Collyn Clout   579
But sodeynly at ones, as I me advysed, ...   313   Garlande   36

ADVYSEMENT —AFTER | | Page | Title | Line

ADVYSEMENT
Yet, syr, reserved your better advysement,	187	Magnyfycence	1661
And to that I say gyve good advysement.	208	Magnyfycence	2406
Item Good Advysement, that brainles doth blame;	346	Garlande	1186

ADVYSEMENTE
To worke me this chapelet by goode advysemente.	334	Garlande	807

ADVYSID
'The sum of your purpose, as we ar advysid,	314	Garlande	78

ADWE
Your pryd is paste, adwe, good nycht.	114	Scot Kynge	43

AFAR
That semyth from afar	97	Phy Sparrow	1046
They must stande all afar	286	Why Come Ye	301

AFERD
Nor no man on molde can make me aferd.	182	Magnyfycence	1505

AFERDE
Whan I loked on hym, my purse was half aferde.	52	Bowge	238

AFFABILITE
His affabilite, /His humanyte,	370	Albany	451

AFFECCYON
This wrytynge is welcome with harty affeccyon!	149	Magnyfycence	313
To rayne, for all his marcyall affeccyon;	181	Magnyfycence	1470
Nay, syl. That affeccyon ought to be reserved,	186	Magnyfycence	1643
Good Hope, I pray you with harty affeccyon	208	Magnyfycence	2399

AFFECTION
But with scornefull affection	379	Replycacion	190
Somtyme for affection,	385	Replycacion	389

AFFECTIONS
But they have no affections	268	Collyn Clout	893
affections] 'afflictions' Kele 1545.1, 'affeccions' Harley 2252			

AFFECTYON
Of his wylfull affectyon.	304	Why Come Ye	1015
his] 'him' Toy 1553, Kitson 1560.7, Marshe 1568			
The thirde, with hole affectyon	307	Why Come Ye	1125

AFFERDE
'Be mirry,' she sayd, 'be not afferde a whit,	344	Garlande	1145

AFFYAUNCE
Set not all your affyaunce in Fortune full of gyle;	211	Magnyfycence	2501

AFFYAUNSYNGE
Affyaunsynge her myne hole assuraunce	327	Garlande	555

AFFYNITE
In your divynite /Of Luthers affynite,	381	Replycacion	266

AFFYNYTE
With other foure of theyr affynyte:	50	Bowge	139
Of one affynyte /Consent and agre	259	Collyn Clout	497
That wolde God everychone /Of his affynyte	300	Why Come Ye	835

AFFLICTYONS
Through temporall afflictyons.	249	Collyn Clout	111

AFFLYCCYON
Afflyccyon and trouble to prove his pacyence;	207	Magnyfycence	2371

AFFORCE
Sith ye must nedis afforce it by pretence	335	Garlande	817

AFFRAY
Let never negarshyp your noblenesse affray;	211	Magnyfycence	2493

AFFRYC
In Affryc tongue byrsa is a thonge of lether;	233	Speke Parott	80

AFYRE
That the premenyre /Is lyke to be set afyre	249	Collyn Clout	109

AFLOTE
That was sometyme aflote,	78	Phy Sparrow	250

AFORCE
I was sore moved to aforce the same,	46	Bowge	17

AFORE
To fysshe afore the nette and to drawe polys.	243	Speke Parott	427
With a flap afore his eye,	308	Why Come Ye	1169
afore] 'before' Kitson 1560.7, Marshe 1568, MS Rawl. C. 813			
He plucked hym backe, and he went afore.	319	Garlande	254

AFORESAYD
By Lewes the kyng aforesayd,	297	Why Come Ye	730

AFORSE
Herein I wyll aforse me to shewe you my mynde:	211	Magnyfycence	2483

AFRAYD
In her bosome, lorde, how she was afrayd!	337	Garlande	887
how] not in MS Cotton Vitellius E.x			
Why shulde she be afrayd?	348	Garlande	1276
With that I stode up, halfe sodenly afrayd,	353	Garlande	1477
For the moost recrayd /Cowardes afrayd,	362	Albany	116

AFRAYDE
Ageynste you hardely; therefore be not afrayde.	51	Bowge	174
But for I am a mayde, /Tymerous, halfe afrayde,	87	Phy Sparrow	608
Why shuld she be afrayde?	103	Phy Sparrow	1283
Mary, syr, ye were afrayde.	150	Magnyfycence	362
Some sayde they were afrayde	285	Why Come Ye	254

AFRAYE
Whom Theseus dyd afraye,	74	Phy Sparrow	86

AFTER
Of thy bounte after the usuall rate	29	Dol Dethe	19

AFTER-CLAPPES —AGAINST

	Page	Title	Line
Thus after her cold she cought a hete.	42	Balettys1	19
After ceremoniallys;	66	Hauke	173
And lerned after my scole	74	Phy Sparrow	117
And seke after small wormes,	74	Phy Sparrow	122
Lord, how he wolde pry /After the butterfly!	75	Phy Sparrow	135
Lorde, how he wolde hop /After the gressop!	75	Phy Sparrow	137
Nowe, after my dome,	75	Phy Sparrow	147
Oft tyme after pleasaunce,	81	Phy Sparrow	368
Wryteth after an hyer rate;	91	Phy Sparrow	805
Pride gothe before and schame commyth after.	133	Garnesche5	165
Skelton laureat /After this rate	135	Dundas	20
Of that may come after; experyence trewe and playne,	141	Magnyfycence	11
Howe after a drought there fallyth a showre of rayne	141	Magnyfycence	12
And after a hete oft cometh a stormy colde.	141	Magnyfycence	13
And after his mynde herdely your selfe adresse,	144	Magnyfycence	151
If ye lyst to lyve after your fre lyberte.	146	Magnyfycence	208
And rule hym after the rule of your scole.	146	Magnyfycence	231
From whens come you, syr, that no man lokyd after?	147	Magnyfycence	255
I folow even after your noble grace.	151	Magnyfycence	395
In bastarde ryme, after the dogrell gyse,	151	Magnyfycence	408
But I wyll be ruled after your counsell.	157	Magnyfycence	615
Ye, so I can devyse my gere after the cowrtly maner.	161	Magnyfycence	766
So I am poynted after my consayte.	167	Magnyfycence	961
And within an houre after,	169	Magnyfycence	1031
And next come I after, Crafty Conveyaunce.	177	Magnyfycence	1332
Inpurtured with fetures after your purpose,	183	Magnyfycence	1552
To do you servyce after your appetyte.	190	Magnyfycence	1793
That nonnes wyl leve theyr holynes and ryn after me;	201	Magnyfycence	2146
Syr, after your message I hyed me hyder streyght,	209	Magnyfycence	2419
Truth it is, syr; for after he wrought me moch shame,	209	Magnyfycence	2444
Well, syr, after your counsell my mynde I wyll set.	210	Magnyfycence	2457
Where every thyng is ordenyd after your noble porte.	214	Magnyfycence	2568
Wrythen in wonder wyse /After the Sarasyns gyse,	216	El Rummynge	74
in] 'in a' Day 1560, Marshe 1568			
For, after all our sport,	220	El Rummynge	231
Pronownsyng my purpose after my properte,	231	Speke Parott	30
Every man after his maner of wayes,	233	Speke Parott	90
Yf it were cond perfytely, and after the rate,	234	Speke Parott	143
Let every man after his merit take his parte;	236	Speke Parott	199
Ar mete for a swyne herde to hunte after hogges.	240	Speke Parott	321
After olde seygnours, /And the lernynge of Lytelton Tenours	256	Collyn Clout	369
For after gloria, laus,	258	Collyn Clout	449
After gloria, laus, /May come a soure sauce.	258	Collyn Clout	482
After this maner rates;	264	Collyn Clout	709
After suche a rate,	271	Collyn Clout	1014
Though I wryte after this facyon;	273	Collyn Clout	1080
And after this rate	276	Collyn Clout	1180
They play their olde pranckes /After Huntley Bankes.	285	Why Come Ye	267
After the sectes of heretykis!	306	Why Come Ye	1082
Garnysshed fresshe after my fantasy,	313	Garlande	39
Where I sawe come after, I wote, full lytell lake	320	Garlande	285
All famous poetis ensuynge after me	321	Garlande	321
The monke of Bury then after them ensuyd,	323	Garlande	390
In maner and forme as ye shall after here.	323	Garlande	399
That ever more after by it they were aspyid;	329	Garlande	627
Dasyng after dotrellis, lyke drunkardis that dribbis;	330	Garlande	641
'How say ye? Is this after your appetite?	331	Garlande	707
Ornatly pullysshid after your faculte.	335	Garlande	816
Commensyng your proces after there degre,	335	Garlande	819
After all duly ordred obeisaunce,	335	Garlande	836
After the Aprill showre.	340	Garlande	987
And after conveyauns as the world goos,	347	Garlande	1238
Dyvysed by Skelton after the funerall rate;	348	Garlande	1256
Whereupon he metrefyde after his mynde;	353	Garlande	1464
It must nedes after rin all the worlde aboute.'	353	Garlande	1483
Though I you wrate /After this rate	355	Garlande	1537
After the auncient manner	360	Albany	62
After myne allegyaunce	369	Albany	405

AFTER-CLAPPES

And such after-clappes.	366	Albany	278

AFTER-DELE

So myche forcastyng, and so farre an after-dele;	244	Speke Parott	463

AFTERNONE

I shall come to you myselfe, I trowe, this afternone.	149	Magnyfycence	322

AFTERWARDE

The one was a tumblar, that afterwarde againe	330	Garlande	634

AFTYR

Yet, aftyr the sagacite of a popagay,	243	Speke Parott	419

AGAIN

Whose skales ensilvred again the son beames	330	Garlande	662

AGAINE

The one was a tumblar, that afterwarde againe	330	Garlande	634

AGAINST

Against odyous Envi,	94	Phy Sparrow	905
Against Venemous Tongues	136	Ven Tongues	I
Thus eche of other blother /The tone against the tother.	248	Collyn Clout	67
And against his lorde soverayn!	297	Why Come Ye	738
Against the churche doth ryse.	306	Why Come Ye	1071

AGAYN —AGAYNE

	Page	Title	Line
Against their wylles, God wot.	306	Why Come Ye	1100
Against our st[r]onge captaine;	365	Albany	245
stronge] 'stonge' †Marshe 1568			

AGAYN

	Page	Title	Line
What willfull foly made you to ryse agayn	30	Dol Dethe	53
What movyd you agayn hym to war or to fight?	31	Dol Dethe	62
Whan I remembre agayn /How mi Philyp was slayn,	72	Phy Sparrow	17
From her to hym agayn;	88	Phy Sparrow	687
Agayn Dundas, /That Scottishe asse.	135	Dundas	23
Nowe, Parott, my swete byrde, speke owte yet ons agayn,	244	Speke Parott	447
When thei agayn thyder shal come,	268	Collyn Clout	883
He must pay agayn	302	Why Come Ye	943

AGAYNE

	Page	Title	Line
Agayne the kingis plesure to wrastel or to wringe.	31	Dol Dethe	82
And lyke marciall Hector he faught them agayne	31	Dol Dethe	88
Agayne rebellyonns arme the to make debate;	33	Dol Dethe	166
That is agayne you, you shall have wetynge;	54	Bowge	278
Wylt thou abyde by the wordes agayne?	55	Bowge	324
I hate this wayes agayne you that they take!	59	Bowge	471
this] 'these' Wynkyn de Worde 1510			
As I shall tell ycu, yf ye wyll harke agayne:	61	Bowge	520
But nothynge it avayled /To call Phylyp agayne	72	Phy Sparrow	26
And playe with me agayne.	77	Phy Sparrow	207
Agayne me for to kyll!	77	Phy Sparrow	223
Alas, I say agayne,	80	Phy Sparrow	328
Of fresshe youth agayne;	85	Phy Sparrow	546
And there agayne /Envy doth complayne, /And hath disdayne;	95	Phy Sparrow	963
To loke on her agayne.	97	Phy Sparrow	1010
on] 'to' Marshe 1568			
And welthe ar com agayne,	111	Lawde	41
The amense therof is far to call agayne;	140	Magnyfycence	9
And that I sayd ones yet I say agayne:	147	Magnyfycence	266
That I shall have you agayne my good lorde.	149	Magnyfycence	310
For Cockys harte, tary whylyst that I come agayne.	159	Magnyfycence	685
By Cockys harte, and call shall agayne!	162	Magnyfycence	783
Put on thy gowne agayne, for thou hast lost nowe.	173	Magnyfycence	1203
thou ... nowe] 'nowe thou hast lost' †Rastell & Treveris C 1530, B			
Nowe put on, fole, thy cote agayne.	173	Magnyfycence	1205
Nor Hanyball, agayne Rome gates that ranne,	182	Magnyfycence	1511
Yet ones agayne I shall fall on my kne	188	Magnyfycence	1708
What! Woldest thou, lurden, with me brawle agayne?	188	Magnyfycence	1722
Mary, I wene he wolde not be glad to come agayne.	189	Magnyfycence	1740
That may restore you agayne to felycyte,	196	Magnyfycence	1998
And brynge you agayne out of adversyte.	196	Magnyfycence	1999
Ye, syr, yesterday wyll not be callyd agayne.	197	Magnyfycence	2031
They cast up theyr obedyence to cache me agayne;	201	Magnyfycence	2148
And agayne thy maker thou hast made suche warre,	205	Magnyfycence	2302
But let us turne playne, /There we lefte agayne.	219	El Rummynge	188
But we wyll turne playne /Where we left agayne.	220	El Rummynge	243
Besy, besy, besy, and besynes agayne!	232	Speke Parott	57
O Esebon, Esebon, to the is cum agayne	234	Speke Parott	120
Turne ons agayne to me;	237	Speke Parott	237
Nowe torne agayne to me.	237	Speke Parott	245
My propyr Besse, /To turne agayne to me.	237	Speke Parott	251
I pray the, Besse, unfayned, /Yet com agayne to me!	238	Speke Parott	256
My propyr Besse, /And torne agayne to me!	238	Speke Parott	262
And the cokkes begyn to crowe agayne the day;	239	Speke Parott	286
Agayne all remordes arme yow with paciens.	239	Speke Parott	298
Wherfor he may now come agayne as he wente,	240	Speke Parott	338
Vouchesafe to defend yow agayne the brawlyng scolde	241	Speke Parott	361
Agayne Frentike Frenesy there dar no man sey nay,	243	Speke Parott	422
The spirytualte agayne	248	Collyn Clout	63
Relyggyous men are fayne /For to tourne agayne	256	Collyn Clout	375
Agayne all suche rebelles	259	Collyn Clout	492
And reherse them agayne,	266	Collyn Clout	775
One agayne another.	274	Collyn Clout	1106
Who dare say there agayne,	276	Collyn Clout	1214
We shulde nat ryse agayne	277	Collyn Clout	1232
To come to court agayne.	279	Why Come Ye	39
With, 'Tourne all home agayne!'	282	Why Come Ye	151
Ones yet agayne /Of you I wolde frayne	289	Why Come Ye	399
And agayne all reason /Commyted open trayson	297	Why Come Ye	736
'To make repugnaunce agayne that ye have sayde,	318	Garlande	211
To Occupacyon I wyll agayne resorte,	354	Garlande	1492
Who redyth it ones wolde rede it agayne;	354	Garlande	1501
Nor to derayne /Batayle agayne /Scornfull disdayne,	356	Garlande	1564
They can not come agayne.	358	Garlande2	15
False and false agayne,	362	Albany	133
Twyt, Scot, yet agayne ones,	362	Albany	149
'Twyt, Scot,' agayne I saye,	363	Albany	157
Sende him to F[r]aunce agayne	363	Albany	173
Fraunce] 'Faunce' †Marshe 1568			
But thou ran home agayne	365	Albany	246
That dare nat turne agayne,	366	Albany	306
And never tourne agayne.	368	Albany	372
Ye shulde take further payne /To resorte agayne	379	Replycacion	202

AGAYNST —AGEINE

	Page	Title	Line

AGAYNST

	Page	Title	Line
Agaynst my mynde and wyll	64	Hauke	98
Skelton laureate Agaynst The Scottes	115	Ag Scottes	I
Agaynst the prowde Scottys claterynge,	115	Ag Scottes	1
Agaynst you gave so sharpe a shower,	119	Ag Scottes	133
AGAYNST THE SCOT JEMMY	120	Ag Scottes	R
Agaynst this my makyng, /Their males therat shakyng,	120	Ag Scottes2	7
Agaynst whom he dyd fyght /Falsly agaynst all right,	120	Ag Scottes2	17
Agaynst whom he dyd fyght /Falsly agaynst all right,	120	Ag Scottes2	18
Lyke that untrue rebell /Fals Kayn agaynst Abell.	121	Ag Scottes2	20
What ellys? For otherwyse it were agaynst kynde;	144	Magnyfycence	132
As in that I wyll not be agaynst your pleasure.	148	Magnyfycence	276
A rebellyon agaynst nature –	155	Magnyfycence	522
No stormy rage agaynst me can pervayle.	181	Magnyfycence	1465
No man so hardy to worke agaynst my wyll.	181	Magnyfycence	1479
And yf you se ony thynge agaynst your mynde,	185	Magnyfycence	1599
It is foly to grudge agaynst his vysytacyon.	196	Magnyfycence	1990
It is foly agaynst God for to plete.	197	Magnyfycence	2035
Thyselfe that thou wolde sloo agaynst nature and kynde.	206	Magnyfycence	2326
Agaynst all [s]autes of your goostly foo.	206	Magnyfycence	2329
sautes] 'fautes' †Rastell & Treveris C 1530, B, Douce Fragment d.7			
His rumpe also he frygges /Agaynst the hye benche.	219	El Rummynge	179
Agaynst the spirytual contradictyons,	249	Collyn Clout	113
Agaynst the communewell,	255	Collyn Clout	359
Agaynst the churche to be,	259	Collyn Clout	499
To maynteyne argumentes /Agaynst the sacramentes.	259	Collyn Clout	518
That agaynst preesthode /Theyr malyce sprede abrode,	260	Collyn Clout	534
agaynst] 'agayn' Marshe 1568			
Agaynst the sely preest.	261	Collyn Clout	576
Agaynst curates, they repyne,	268	Collyn Clout	873
They] not in Kele 1545.1, Marshe 1568, 'They' MS Harley 2252			
Agaynst holy churche estate,	269	Collyn Clout	915
They renne agaynst the steple,	271	Collyn Clout	983
Agaynst all spirytuall men.	272	Collyn Clout	1054
Agaynst me to be gr[am]ed,	274	Collyn Clout	1114
gramed] 'greved' †Godfray 1531, Kele 1545.1, Marshe 1568, MS Harley 2252			
Agaynst us of the counsell?	275	Collyn Clout	1163
Agaynst us dothe prate.	276	Collyn Clout	1181
Agaynst Englande to fyght.	364	Albany	231
Agaynst the lyon white,	366	Albany	309
To rayle agaynst his grace	368	Albany	365
A Replycacion Agaynst Certayne Yong Scolers Abjured of Late,	373	Replycacion	I
Agaynst whiche erronyous errours,	375	Replycacion	I
Agaynst this horryble heresy	375	Replycacion	21
Agaynst her grace disputed	375	Replycacion	30
Agaynst her excellence, /Agaynst her reverence,	375	Replycacion	40
Agaynst her excellence, /Agaynst her reverence,	375	Replycacion	41
Agaynst her preemynence, /Agaynst her magnifycence,	375	Replycacion	42
Agaynst her preemynence, /Agaynst her magnifycence,	375	Replycacion	43
Your sysmaticate sawes /Agaynst Goddes lawes,	377	Replycacion	123
agaynst Skelton laureate, devyser of this Replycacyon, etc.	382	Replycacion	R
To answere or reply /Agaynst suche heresy.	383	Replycacion	313
Agaynst these frenetykes, /Agaynst these lunatykes,	385	Replycacion	400
Agaynst these frenetykes, /Agaynst these lunatykes,	385	Replycacion	401
Agaynst these sysmatykes, /Agaynst these heretykes,	385	Replycacion	402
Agaynst these sysmatykes, /Agaynst these heretykes,	385	Replycacion	403

AGAYNSTE

	Page	Title	Line
Skelton Laureat Agaynste a Comely Coystrowne	36	Coystrowne	I
and madly in hys musykkys mokkyshly made agaynste	36	Coystrowne	I
So hote hatered agaynste the Chyrche, and cheryte so colde;	245	Speke Parott	500

AGASPE

	Page	Title	Line
Galba, whom his galantys garde for agaspe,	182	Magnyfycence	1508

AGAST

	Page	Title	Line
Of that aventuris, whiche made me sore agast.	330	Garlande	649

AGE

	Page	Title	Line
O yonge lyon, bot tender yet of age,	33	Dol Dethe	162
Savyng that olde age	85	Phy Sparrow	544
Alexis yonge of age,	110	Lawde	13
Whan ye war yonger of age	124	Garnesche3	24
By God, syr, ye se but fewe wyse men of myne age.	148	Magnyfycence	289
And they never thryve in theyr age, it shall not gretly skyll.	200	Magnyfycence	2138
And well worne in age,	214	El Rummynge	8
For age is a page	279	Why Come Ye	32
For age can nat rage,	279	Why Come Ye	34
But whan age seeth that rage	279	Why Come Ye	36
Than wyll age have a corage	279	Why Come Ye	38
That age for dottage /Is reconed nowadayes.	279	Why Come Ye	43
reconed] 'recovered' Toy 1553, Kitson 1560.7, Marshe 1568			
Thus age, (a graunt domage)	280	Why Come Ye	45
a] not in Kitson 1560.7, Marshe 1568			
How dotynge age wolde jape with yonge foly;	322	Garlande	361
Of womanly feturis, whos florysshyng tender age	336	Garlande	869
But, as I sayd, your florisshinge tender age	337	Garlande	876

AGEINE

	Page	Title	Line
Wordes be swordes, and hard to call ageine.'	328	Garlande	567

	Page	Title	Line
AGEINST			
Skelton Laureate Defendar Ageinst Lusty Garnyshe	129	Garnesche5	1
With Salusty ageinst Lucius Catelyne,	321	Garlande	331
Of what charge so ever ye lay ageinst me;	344	Garlande	1138
The Recule ageinst Gaguyne of the Frenshe nacyoun;	346	Garlande	1187
AGEYN			
Thorow treson, ageyn hym compassyd and wrought,	29	Dol Dethe	6
What aylde you to slo your lord ageyn all right? slo] 'sle' Marshe 1568	31	Dol Dethe	63
AGEYNE			
Till the chaunce ran ageyne hym of Fortuns double dyse.	33	Dol Dethe	140
Wherfore I wryght ageyne	124	Garnesche3	8
Went with the pecok ageyne the fesaunt;	315	Garlande	103
Ageyne whom he cowde make no contradiccyoun?'	316	Garlande	133
And we shall se you ageyne or it be pryme.'	326	Garlande	525
And turne home ageyne, for they cam al to late.	329	Garlande	605
He is not wyse ageyne the streme that stryvith.	352	Garlande	1432
Ageyne envy, /And obloquy. /And wote ye why?	355	Garlande	1558
Not for to fyght /Ageyne dispyght,	356	Garlande	1562
AGEYNST			
Ageynst a stormy shouer.	127	Garnesche3	147
Ageynst all infeccyons with cancour enflamyd, cancour] 'rancour' Marshe 1568	331	Garlande	672
Ageynst all baratows broisiours of olde,	331	Garlande	673
For he was ever ageynst Goddis hows;	347	Garlande	1251
Ageynst Holy Chyrche, the preste, and the clarke.	347	Garlande	1253
AGEYNSTE			
Ageynste you hardely; therefore be not afrayde.	51	Bowge	174
AGENYST			
Skelton Lawryate Defender Agenyst Lusty Garnyche	124	Garnesche3	1
AGENNE			
Wyth, 'Knave, syr, knave, and knave agenne',	130	Garnesche5	19
AGENNST			
Agennst me for to make,	126	Garnesche3	93
AGENST			
Skelton Lauriate Defender Agenst Master Garnesche Chalenger,	121	Garnesche1	1
Skelton Lauryate Defender Agenst Master Garnesche Chalangar,	122	Garnesche2	1
Your stondarde, Syr Olifranke, agenst me for to splay;	123	Garnesche2	30
Agenst hys poysond infeccioun,	128	Garnesche3	153
Agenst ye now I bynde;	128	Garnesche3	160
Agenst a poyet lawreat	132	Garnesche5	90
AGERDOWS			
With wordes devoute and sentence agerdows,	347	Garlande	1250
AGO			
(A proverbe longe ago.)	293	Why Come Ye	584
AGRE			
Playne delynge and I can never agre.	159	Magnyfycence	699
What the devyll! Can ye agre no better?	162	Magnyfycence	795
Of one affynyte /Consent and agre	259	Collyn Clout	498
To well they do agre,	286	Why Come Ye	278
No better they agre!	288	Why Come Ye	375
Than must we agre /With poverte;	300	Why Come Ye	864
All his subjectes and he /Moost lovyngly agre	371	Albany	481
To this ye nedes must agre.	381	Replycacion	284
And infallibly agre /Of necessyte,	384	Replycacion	363
AGREABYLL			
I truste your grace wyll be agreabyll	179	Magnyfycence	1417
And also prophytabyll, /Yf ye be agreabyll,	237	Speke Parott	249
AGREABLE			
In faythe, and I wyll be to reason agreable.	203	Magnyfycence	2205
That but if my warkes therto be agreable,	324	Garlande	439
And to our faithe moche agreable,	382	Replycacion	290
AGREAMENT			
Of all our hooll collage by the agreament,	324	Garlande	417
AGREDE			
Yf ye coude be otherwyse agrede;	59	Bowge	480
Unto that same I am ryght well agrede,	144	Magnyfycence	128
Both worde and dede /Should be agrede /In noblenes:	357	Garlande	1600
AGREE			
What the devyll ayleth you? Can you not agree?	158	Magnyfycence	636
What! Can ye agree thus and appose?	180	Magnyfycence	1425
With Dowche, with Spaynyshe, my tonge can agree;	231	Speke Parott	32
AGREED			
How be it, mayden Meed /Made theym to be agreed;	65	Hauke	150
Why, were not your selfe agreed to the same,	147	Magnyfycence	233
Syrs, I am agreed to abyde your ordenaunce –	210	Magnyfycence	2471
Now Neptune and Eolus ar agreed of lyclyhod,	239	Speke Parott	283
AGRIPPINA			
Dame Agrippina also I may reherse	336	Garlande	859
AY			
Ay, beshrewe yow! Be my fay	35	Man Margery	1
And ay he sange, 'In fayth, Decon, thou crewe.'	56	Bowge	360
'Ay,' quod he, 'in the devylles date,	56	Bowge	375
Ay, in my pouche a buckell I have founde;	57	Bowge	397
I am not happy, I renne ay on the losse!	57	Bowge	399
They wandred and stode styll in no stede.	58	Bowge	423
Ay to contynewe and styll to endure.	141	Magnyfycence	15
Ay warre and warre /In every place.	166	Magnyfycence	914

AYE—ALAS   Page   Title   Line

	Page	Title	Line
Immoysturid with mislyng and ay droppyng dry,	331	Garlande	698
And here to inhabite and ay for to dwell!	332	Garlande	719
Intentyfe ay /And dylygent, /No tyme myspent;	338	Garlande	942

AYE

With her aye to remayne.	97	Phy Sparrow	1013

AYLDE

What aylde you to slo your lord ageyn all right?	31	Dol Dethe	63
slo] 'sle' Marshe 1568			

AYLE

What ayle them to deprave /Phillip Sparowes grave?	103	Phy Sparrow	1274
Plucke up your mynde, syr, what ayle you to muse?	148	Magnyfycence	283
For who loveth God can ayle nothynge but good.	207	Magnyfycence	2365
Alas, what ayle you to be so overthwhart,	320	Garlande	307
What ayle them to deprave /Phillippe Sparows grave?	348	Garlande	1267

AYLETH

What the devyll ayleth you? Can you not agree?	158	Magnyfycence	636

AKE

Your fansy maketh myne elbowe to ake.	156	Magnyfycence	559
A, my bonys ake! My lymmys be sore!	195	Magnyfycence	1955

AKED

Ones hed wold have aked /To se her naked.	226	El Rummynge	478

AKERS

And at Saynt Thomas of Akers	276	Collyn Clout	1188

AKUSE

He dothe mysse use /Eche man to [akuse],	164	Magnyfycence	874
akuse] 'take a fe' †Rastell & Treveris C 1530, B			

AL

Of al good praiers God send him sum!	86	Phy Sparrow	584
Al floodes that ever was	93	Phy Sparrow	878
Regent is she, /Of poetes al,	112	Calliope	4
Al maters wel pondred and wel to be regarded,	137	Ven Tongues	1
1 thyngys contryvyd by mannys reason,	140	Magnyfycence	1
Al of pleasure /My hose strayte tyde;	164	Magnyfycence	851
Though al his conquestys were brought to rekenynge,	181	Magnyfycence	1468
For al his pompe, for all his ryall trone,	181	Magnyfycence	1475
And turne home ageyne, for they cam al to late.	329	Garlande	605

ALAYD

Avaunt, cowarde recrayed! /Thy pride shalbe alayd,	371	Albany	496

ALARUM

Alarum, alarum! To longe we abyde!	206	Magnyfycence	2323
Alarum, alarum! To longe we abyde!	206	Magnyfycence	2323

ALAS

Of hym that is gone, alas, withoute restore,	29	Dol Dethe	3
Your naturall lord? Alas, I kan not fayne.	30	Dol Dethe	54
Alas, ye madmen, to far ye did excede.	31	Dol Dethe	60
Alas his golde, his fee, his annuall rente,	32	Dol Dethe	97
Alas for routhe, what thouthe his mynde wer goode,	32	Dol Dethe	102
All left alone, alas, he fawte in vayne!	32	Dol Dethe	104
Alas for pite that Percy thus was spylt,	32	Dol Dethe	106
To slo suche a lord, alas, it was grete shame.	33	Dol Dethe	154
slo] 'sle' Marshe 1568			
But absens, alas, wyth tremelyng fere and drede,	44	Balettys3	34
'Alas,' quod I, 'how myghte I have her sure?'	49	Bowge	118
Alas, a connynge man ne dwelle maye	58	Bowge	445
Alas, I coude not dele so with a [J]ew.	59	Bowge	462
a Jew] 'on yew' †Wynkyn de Worde 1499, 'a yew' Wynkyn			
de Worde 1510, Marshe 1568			
Alas, it wyll me slo,	75	Phy Sparrow	141
Alas, I was evyll at ease!	75	Phy Sparrow	144
Alas, I wolde ryde and go	76	Phy Sparrow	186
And sayd, 'Alas, alas,	77	Phy Sparrow	231
And sayd, 'Alas, alas,	77	Phy Sparrow	231
Alas, I say agayne,	80	Phy Sparrow	328
Alas, my face waxeth pale,	80	Phy Sparrow	341
Alas, my hert it styngs,	80	Phy Sparrow	349
Alas, myne hert it sleth	80	Phy Sparrow	351
Alas, for dolefull desteny!	86	Phy Sparrow	593
Alas, what shuld I fayne?	97	Phy Sparrow	1011
Alas, that goodly mayd,	103	Phy Sparrow	1282
Alas, dere harte, loke that we be not perseyvyd!'	177	Magnyfycence	1349
Alas! My stomake fareth as it wolde cast.	188	Magnyfycence	1726
Alas, wh[o] is yonder that grymly lokys?	193	Magnyfycence	1873
who] 'why' †Rastell & Treveris C 1530, B			
Alas! Of Fortune I may well complayne.	197	Magnyfycence	2030
Alas, myn owne servauntys to shew me such reproche!	205	Magnyfycence	2277
Alas, dere sone, sore combred is thy mynde,	206	Magnyfycence	2325
Alas, syr! So I am lapped in adversyte	206	Magnyfycence	2331
Alas, I am dysdayned, /And as a man halfe-maymed,	237	Speke Parott	252
Alas, they make me shoder,	248	Collyn Clout	68
Alas, for very shame,	253	Collyn Clout	275
Alas, why do ye nat handle	255	Collyn Clout	332
Alas, it is great ruthe!	255	Collyn Clout	343
Alas, and wellaway, /What eyles them thus to say?	261	Collyn Clout	577
Alas, for Goddes wyll,	263	Collyn Clout	687
Alas, what ayle you to be so overthwhart,	320	Garlande	307
Unto me; alas, that herbe nor gresse	321	Garlande	314
gresse] 'gras' †Fakes 1523			
Alas, that goodly mayd,	348	Garlande	1275

ALASSE—ALE

	Page	Title	Line
With frowarde frostis, alas, was all to-fret!	352	Garlande	1450

ALASSE

	Page	Title	Line
Alasse! Where is my botes and my spores?	156	Magnyfycence	569
The case requyreth. Alasse, alasse, an hevy metynge!	192	Magnyfycence	1847
The case requyreth. Alasse, alasse, an hevy metynge!	192	Magnyfycence	1847
Alasse, syr, ye are undone with stelyng and robbynge!	192	Magnyfycence	1852
Gone? Alasse, ye have undone me!	192	Magnyfycence	1858
Alasse, I have the cyatyca full evyll in my hyppe!	195	Magnyfycence	1956
Alasse, where is youth that was wont for to skyppe?	195	Magnyfycence	1957
Alasse! Where is nowe my golde and fe?	196	Magnyfycence	1967
Alasse, I say, where to am I brought?	196	Magnyfycence	1968
Alasse, alasse, alasse! I dye for thought.	196	Magnyfycence	1969
Alasse, alasse, alasse! I dye for thought.	196	Magnyfycence	1969
Alasse, alasse, alasse! I dye for thought.	196	Magnyfycence	1969
Alasse that ever I sholde be so shamed!	196	Magnyfycence	1982
Alasse that ever I Magnyfycence was named!	196	Magnyfycence	1983
Alasse that ever I was so harde happed	196	Magnyfycence	1984
Alasse that I coude not myselfe no better gyde!	196	Magnyfycence	1986
Alasse in my cradell that I had not dyde!	196	Magnyfycence	1987
Alasse! I wote not what I sholde pray.	196	Magnyfycence	1994
Alasse! With colde my lymmes shall be marde.	197	Magnyfycence	2004
Alasse my foly! Alasse my wanton wyll!	198	Magnyfycence	2062
Alasse my foly! Alasse my wanton wyll!	198	Magnyfycence	2062
Alasse, that ever I occupyed suche abusyon!	200	Magnyfycence	2129
Of worldly welthe, alasse, who can be sure?	201	Magnyfycence	2155
Alasse, alasse, syrs, ye are to blame!	204	Magnyfycence	2245
Alasse, alasse, syrs, ye are to blame!	204	Magnyfycence	2245
Alasse! To lyve longer I have no delyght;	205	Magnyfycence	2281
Alasse, my wyckydnesse, that may I wyte!	205	Magnyfycence	2304

ALBANY

	Page	Title	Line
Of the Duke of Albany,	288	Why Come Ye	357
Howe the Douty Duke of Albany	359	Albany	1
This Duke so fell /Of Albany, /So cowardly	359	Albany	7
Duke of Albany, /Than shamefully	360	Albany	50
But now must I /Your Duke ascry /Of Albany	361	Albany	74
By your Duke of Albany.	363	Albany	162
Sir Duke of Albany, /Right inconvenyently	363	Albany	188
With the Duke of Albany,	371	Albany	513

ALBEIT

	Page	Title	Line
Abashyth me, albeit I have no nede.	44	Balettys3	35

ALBERTUS

	Page	Title	Line
Albertus De modo significandi	235	Speke Parott	169

ALBION

	Page	Title	Line
From Brytons Albion /To the towre of Babilon. To] 'Bo' †Kele 1545.2	94	Phy Sparrow	887
The brutid Britons of Brutus Albion,	323	Garlande	405

ALBYAN

	Page	Title	Line
Arthur of Albyan, for all his brymme berde,	182	Magnyfycence	1502

ALBONS

	Page	Title	Line
Saint Albons, to recorde,	306	Why Come Ye	1097

ALBUMASAR

	Page	Title	Line
Nor with royall Ptholomy, /Nor with Albumasar,	292	Why Come Ye	523
And though Albumasar can the enforme and ken	352	Garlande	1428

ALBUMAZER

	Page	Title	Line
By Albumazer /The astronomer,	84	Phy Sparrow	501

ALCHEUS

	Page	Title	Line
Or Fraucys Petrarke, /Alcheus or Sapho, Or] 'Or of' Kitson 1560.6, Marshe 1568	90	Phy Sparrow	759
Lyke unto Alcheus, he dothe hym magnify.	383	Replycacion	335

ALCUMYN

	Page	Title	Line
To copper, to tyn, /To lede, or alcumyn?	301	Why Come Ye	907

ALDAYE

	Page	Title	Line
Thou muste swere and stare, man, aldaye longe,	57	Bowge	381

ALDERBEST

	Page	Title	Line
It was nat heled alderbest,	308	Why Come Ye	1188

ALE

	Page	Title	Line
With manerly Margery Mylk and Ale.	35	Man Margery	7
With manerly Margery Mylk and Ale.	36	Man Margery	14
With manerly Margery Mylk and Ale.	36	Man Margery	21
With manerly Margery Milk and Ale.	36	Man Margery	28
With manerly Margery Mylk and Ale.	36	Man Margery	30
A bolde man in a bole of newe ale in cornys.	162	Magnyfycence	772
Tushe! These maters that ye move are but soppys in ale;	203	Magnyfycence	2233
She breweth noppy ale,	217	El Rummynge	102
Howe hyr ale is solde /To mawte and to molde.	218	El Rummynge	158
For theyr ale to pay;	218	El Rummynge	162
Ye shall not bere awaye /Myne ale for nought, myne] 'my' Kynge & Marche 1554, Day 1560, Marshe 1568	218	El Rummynge	166
The donge of her hennes /And the ale togyder,	219	El Rummynge	203
This ale shal be thycker,	219	El Rummynge	205
And all for the good ale. ale] 'all' †Lant 1545	221	El Rummynge	265
Bycause the ale is good;	221	El Rummynge	284
And ye wyll gyve me a syppet /Of your stale ale,	223	El Rummynge	368
And blessed her with a cup /Of newe ale in cornes.	224	El Rummynge	378
Of thyne ale let us assaye,	224	El Rummynge	397
Elynour made the pryce /For god ale eche whyt.	224	El Rummynge	411
And smelled all of ale.	226	El Rummynge	487

ALE BARME —ALL	Page	Title	Line
For the good ale sake.	228	El Rummynge	534
'This ale,' sayd she, 'is noppy;	228	El Rummynge	557
And so with ale stuffed,	229	El Rummynge	571
Of Manerly Margery Maystres Mylke and Ale;	346	Garlande	1198
Margery Maystres] 'maistres Margery' Marshe 1568			
ALE BARME			
And with good ale barme /She could make a charme	226	El Rummynge	455
ALECTO			
And from foule Alecto,	73	Phy Sparrow	74
ALE DRYNKERS			
And all good ale drynkers,	217	El Rummynge	106
ALE HOUSE			
Dronken as a mouse /At the ale house,	266	Collyn Clout	802
ALE-JOUST			
For they go to roust, /Streyght over the ale-joust,	219	El Rummynge	192
ALE-POLE			
To offer to the ale-pole.	227	El Rummynge	525
ALE POLE			
Powle hatchettis, that prate wyll at every ale pole,	329	Garlande	613
wyll] 'well' Marshe 1568			
ALERYCUS			
Nor Alerycus, that rulyd the Gothyaunce by swerd,	182	Magnyfycence	1504
ALES			
Than thydder came dronken Ales	223	El Rummynge	351
Ales founde therin no thornes,	224	El Rummynge	379
ALE SOPPE			
Whan the good ale soppe /Dothe daunce in theyr foretoppe;	260	Collyn Clout	530
ALE STAKE			
Howe some synge letabundus /At every ale stake,	253	Collyn Clout	249
ALE TAP			
To offer to the ale tap,	221	El Rummynge	286
ALE TAPPE			
At the good ale tappe,	266	Collyn Clout	804
ALE TUNNES			
And donge, whan it commes, /In the ale tunnes.	219	El Rummynge	194
ALEXANDER			
Of Kyng Alexander; /And of Kyng Evander	90	Phy Sparrow	745
Alexander, of Macedony kynge,	181	Magnyfycence	1466
Alexander, a gander of Menanders pole,	235	Speke Parott	173
In exemplyfyenge /Great Alexander the kynge,	292	Why Come Ye	544
Of Alexander; and Macrobius that did trete	322	Garlande	367
ALEXIS			
Alexis yonge of age,	110	Lawde	13
ALY			
Your lege ye layd and your aly,	118	Ag Scottes	103
ALYDE			
Measure with noblenesse sholde be alyde.	145	Magnyfycence	194
ALYE			
To be so scornefull to your alye	113	Scot Kynge	13
ALYS			
With alys ensandid about in compas,	330	Garlande	654
ALL			
Fulfilled with honour, as all the world dothe ken,	30	Dol Dethe	30
world] 'wold' Marshe 1568			
What aylde you to slo your lord ageyn all right?	31	Dol Dethe	63
slo] 'sle' Marshe 1568			
The welle concernyng of all the hole lande,	31	Dol Dethe	65
Whiche kyndelde the wyld fyre that made all this smoke.	31	Dol Dethe	77
Bot all they fled from hym for falshode or fere.	31	Dol Dethe	91
All left alone, alas, he fawte in vayne!	32	Dol Dethe	104
All merciles in the ys no pite!	32	Dol Dethe	122
O homycide, whiche sleest all that thou kan,	32	Dol Dethe	123
Sourmountinge in honour all erlis he did excede;	33	Dol Dethe	135
To all cuntreis aboute hym reporte me I dare:	33	Dol Dethe	136
With my rude pen enkankerd all with rust,	33	Dol Dethe	142
With trowth to medelle was all his hole delight,	33	Dol Dethe	152
As all his kuntrey kan testefy the same:	33	Dol Dethe	153
In me all onely wer sett and comprisyde,	33	Dol Dethe	156
To me also all thouthe yt wer promysyde	33	Dol Dethe	159
All were to litill for his magnyficence.	33	Dol Dethe	161
Right to maynten and to resist all wronge.	34	Dol Dethe	171
All flatringe faytors abhor and from the kast.	34	Dol Dethe	172
All gyf Englond and Fraunce wer thorow sought.	34	Dol Dethe	179
All kingis, all princis, all dukis, well thei ought	34	Dol Dethe	180
All kingis, all princis, all dukis, well thei ought	34	Dol Dethe	180
All kingis, all princis, all dukis, well thei ought	34	Dol Dethe	180
And all other gentelmen with hym enterteynd	34	Dol Dethe	184
That with one worde formd all thing of nought;	34	Dol Dethe	191
All mankynd, whom thou ful dere hast boght,	34	Dol Dethe	194
The sowle of this lorde from all daunger of hell,	34	Dol Dethe	200
Of all women O floure withouten pere,	35	Dol Dethe	207
With all the hole sorte of that glorious place,	35	Dol Dethe	212
Thorow bounte of hym that formed all solace,	35	Dol Dethe	214
Yet, for his love that all hath wrought,	36	Man Margery	25
Of all nacyons under the hevyn,	36	Coystrownel	1
These frantyke foolys I hate most of all;	36	Coystrownel	2
Of Martyn Swart and all hys mery men.	37	Coystrownel	18
For all oure pamperde paunchys,	39	Coystrowne3	25

ALL — ALL

	Page	Title	Line
For all your 'Draffe' yet and your 'Dreggys',	40	Coystrowne4	6
All those by whom ye have avayle.	41	Coystrowne4	18
Holde youre tong, now, all beshrewde!	41	Coystrowne4	28
All drowsy, dremyng, drouned in slepe,	41	Balettys1	6
He had forgoten all dedely syn.	42	Balettys1	11
He trusted her payment and lost all hys pray.	42	Balettys1	13
Ye may be countyd comfort of all corage.	42	Balettys2	7
Of all your feturs favorable to make tru discripcion,	42	Balettys2	8
Ye cast all your corage uppon such courtly haggys!	43	Balettys2	19
Theyre browys all to-brokyn, such clappys they cach;	43	Balettys2	32
Ask all your neybours whether that I ly.	43	Balettys2	35
Let not all the world make an owtcry;	43	Balettys2	40
Transendyng plesure, surmountyng all dysporte;	43	Balettys3	7
Of my trew hart, to love her best of all!	45	Balettys3	49
Though ye suppose all jeperdys ar paste,	45	Balettys4	1
And all is done ye lokyd for before,	45	Balettys4	2
That when ye thynke all daunger for to pas,	45	Balettys4	6
I am content so all partys be pleasyd:	45	Balettys5	11
Amonge all other I put myselfe in prece.	47	Bowge	44
Amonge all other was wrytten in her trone,	47	Bowge	65
Fortune gydeth and ruleth all our shyppe.	49	Bowge	111
Whome she loveth, of all plesyre is ryche	49	Bowge	113
She promysed to us all she wolde be kynde;	49	Bowge	124
We wante no wynde to passe now over all;	49	Bowge	128
All erthely tresoure it is surmountynge.	50	Bowge	154
For by that Lorde that bought dere all mankynde,	50	Bowge	163
Els, I prayed hym with all my besy cure,	52	Bowge	221
And of his mynde he shewed me all and some.	52	Bowge	226
Me thoughte his gowne was all furred wyth foxe.	52	Bowge	234
Me] 'My' †Wynkyn de Worde 1499			
His gawdy garment with Scornnys was all wrought;	54	Bowge	285
Scornnys] 'storunys' †Wynkyn de Worde 1499, 1510, 'scornes' Marshe 1568			
With scornfull loke mevyd all in moode.	55	Bowge	317
scornfull] 'scorfull' Marshe 1568			
Wyth that came Ryotte, russhynge all at ones,	56	Bowge	344
'Nowe have at all, by Saynte Thomas of Kente!'	56	Bowge	348
His rumpe, he wente so all for somer lyghte;	56	Bowge	355
And wake all nyghte and slepe tyll it be none.	57	Bowge	382
Now have at all that lyeth upon the burde.	57	Bowge	391
To her wyll I nowe all my poverte lege.	57	Bowge	412
But, what, a strawe! I maye not tell all thynge.	59	Bowge	459
For all our courte is full of dysceyte.	59	Bowge	469
All that he wereth, it is borowed ware;	60	Bowge	489
Sterte all at ones, I lyked no thynge his playe,	60	Bowge	502
His hode all pounsed and garded lyke a cage.	60	Bowge	508
hode] 'body' Marshe 1568			
Syth all in substaunce of slumbrynge doth procede.	61	Bowge	536
All grace is far hym fro.	62	Hauke	16
He shoke downe all the clothys,	63	Hauke	51
Boke, bell and candyll, /All that he myght handyll;	64	Hauke	113
They rangyd Hankyn Bovy /My churche all abowte.	65	Hauke	118
And all for lacke of grace.	66	Hauke	163
Nor Sardanapall, /Unhappyest of all;	67	Hauke	201
And for all sparowes soules	72	Phy Sparrow	11
But all without redresse;	72	Phy Sparrow	33
Reportynge the vertues all	75	Phy Sparrow	157
All the flees blake	76	Phy Sparrow	180
But all this is in vayne	77	Phy Sparrow	208
All sparowes of the wode	78	Phy Sparrow	267
On all the hole nacyon	78	Phy Sparrow	275
Myght tere out all thy trypes!	79	Phy Sparrow	308
That all the world may gase	79	Phy Sparrow	316
All maner of byrdes in your kynd;	81	Phy Sparrow	388
Plinni sheweth all /In his Story Naturall,	85	Phy Sparrow	536
The kestrell in all this warke	86	Phy Sparrow	569
And all the hole warke	87	Phy Sparrow	642
That made the Romaynes all /For-drede and to quake;	88	Phy Sparrow	666
That] 'What' †Kele 1545.2, Wyght 1553			
That was all theyr joye,	88	Phy Sparrow	674
Wherfore all Troy dyd rew;	88	Phy Sparrow	676
And all that was in vayne,	89	Phy Sparrow	694
Mournyng all alone,	89	Phy Sparrow	704
And mar all they warke;	91	Phy Sparrow	799
And of all pleasaunt thynges,	93	Phy Sparrow	868
That passeth all erthly good;	93	Phy Sparrow	876
all] 'all the' Wyght 1553, Kitson 1560.6, Marshe 1568			
All other of whom we rede,	93	Phy Sparrow	884
His foule semblaunt /All displesaunt;	95	Phy Sparrow	937
foule] 'feule' †Kele 1545.2, Wyght 1553			
All the goodly sort /Of her fetures clere,	96	Phy Sparrow	999
Ennewed all with grace,	96	Phy Sparrow	1003
all with] 'with al' Wyght 1553, Kitson 1560.6, Marshe 1568			
All with favour fret,	98	Phy Sparrow	1048
To serve for all ententes,	101	Phy Sparrow	1182
Dame Venus of all pleasure,	102	Phy Sparrow	1227
All the wyttes they have.	103	Phy Sparrow	1273
By Chemeras flames, /And all the dedly names	105	Phy Sparrow	1331

ALL —ALL

	Page	Title	Line
I pray you all,	108	Epitaphe1	68
Exclude now all dolowrs.	110	Lawde	7
That wont wer over all	111	Lawde	38
Kynge Jamy, Jomy your joye is all go.	113	Scot Kynge	1
God save kynge Henry and his lordes all	115	Scot Kynge	72
Slew all the floure /Of theyr honoure.	116	Ag Scottes	27
To face, to brace, /All voyde of grace,	116	Ag Scottes	34
A mad rekenynge, /Consydrynge all thynge,	116	Ag Scottes	46
It shameth all your noughty nacyon.	117	Ag Scottes	56
Of all our royall Englysh nacyon.	117	Ag Scottes	76
All have ye lost and cast away.	119	Ag Scottes	163
Agaynst whom he dyd fyght /Falsly agaynst all right,	120	Ag Scottes2	18
Yor moth etyn mokkysh maneres, they be all to-myryd.	123	Garnesche2	12
Is voyd of all good grace;	124	Garnesche3	10
But sche of all men	125	Garnesche3	65
And grow all oute of kynde,	126	Garnesche3	102
Ye rayle all out of seson.	127	Garnesche3	130
Your chorlyshe chauntyng ys all o lay.	129	Garnesche5	6
Ye, syr, rayle all in deformite:	129	Garnesche5	7
Of all prowde knavys thow beryst the belle,	130	Garnesche5	27
Lythe and lystyn, all bechrewde!	131	Garnesche5	86
That all the warlde wyll spye your shame.	132	Garnesche5	111
They wolde the wryght, all with one stevyn,	133	Garnesche5	144
Presumptuous pride ys all thyn hope;	133	Garnesche5	160
Defendeth with his pen /All Englysh men	135	Dundas	22
But men take upon theim nowe all the shame	139	Ven Tongues	61
And all is not worth a couple of nut shalis.	139	Ven Tongues	66
And you knew all ye would be ill apayd'.	139	Ven Tongues	72
And so dysordereth this worlde over all,	141	Magnyfycence	20
Lyberte to let from all maner offence;	141	Magnyfycence	45
It is so swete in all maner of kynde.	142	Magnyfycence	51
With all my herte intere.	143	Magnyfycence	113
All trebyllys and tenours be rulyd by a meyne.	144	Magnyfycence	137
But plenarly all thought from you must be dyschargyd,	146	Magnyfycence	207
All delectacyons aquayntyd is with me;	146	Magnyfycence	209
By me all persons worke what they lyste.	146	Magnyfycence	210
All that ye say is as trewe as the crede.	146	Magnyfycence	218
That all men laugh at lyberte to scorne.	146	Magnyfycence	222
That all is without measure and fer beyonde the mone.	146	Magnyfycence	224
Largesse, that all lordes sholde love, syr, I hyght.	148	Magnyfycence	270
Largesse is he that all prynces doth avaunce;	148	Magnyfycence	279
Why have ye hym named and all other refused?	148	Magnyfycence	281
For largesse stynteth all maner of stryfe.	150	Magnyfycence	367
Thus am I occupyed at all assayes.	152	Magnyfycence	428
What so ever I do, all men me prayse,	152	Magnyfycence	429
Of all lewdnesse I kyndell the brande.	152	Magnyfycence	437
All the newe gyse, fresshe and gaye,	153	Magnyfycence	463
Your counterfet countenaunce is all of nysyte,	153	Magnyfycence	478
A plummed partrydge all redy to flye.	153	Magnyfycence	479
Why, shall we dwell togyder all thre?	154	Magnyfycence	509
So he ruleth over all our place.	155	Magnyfycence	545
For all these japes yet that [y]e make - ye] 'we' †Rastell & Treveris C 1530, B	156	Magnyfycence	558
What! Shall we jangle thus all the day styll?	156	Magnyfycence	565
In all this hast whether wyll ye ryde?	156	Magnyfycence	570
That all this matter must under grope.	157	Magnyfycence	600
By God, we wolde gete us all thyder,	157	Magnyfycence	618
Ye. But he spendeth it all in mesure.	157	Magnyfycence	621
Ye. And he hath rule of all his tresure.	158	Magnyfycence	632
Craftely all thynges upryght to save:	158	Magnyfycence	642
All this ye may easely brynge aboute.	158	Magnyfycence	655
Hem! That lyke I nothynge at all.	158	Magnyfycence	664
All thre, I say. Shall I go? Whyder?	158	Magnyfycence	666
Double delynge and I be all one;	159	Magnyfycence	696
By the menys of myschyef to bryng all thynges to nought.	159	Magnyfycence	702
And tolde all the myschyef I coude behynde theyr backe,	160	Magnyfycence	718
I wolde begyn all myschyef, but I wolde bere no lacke.	160	Magnyfycence	720
My speche is all pleasure, but I stynge lyke a waspe.	160	Magnyfycence	730
I laughe at all shrewdenes, and lye at lyberte.	160	Magnyfycence	735
To flater and to flery is all my pretence	161	Magnyfycence	738
Amonge all suche persones as I well understonde	161	Magnyfycence	739
By God, syr, what nede all this waste?	161	Magnyfycence	754
Dusty! Nay, syr, ye be all of the lusty;	161	Magnyfycence	760
Wyll ye se this gentylman is all in his skornys?	162	Magnyfycence	773
Properly drest /All poynte devyse,	164	Magnyfycence	843
My persone prest /Beyonde all syse	164	Magnyfycence	845
That all men it founde /Through out Englonde.	165	Magnyfycence	882
All this nacyon /I set on fyre; /In my facyon	165	Magnyfycence	884
Spende all his hyre	165	Magnyfycence	907
All is out of harre	165	Magnyfycence	912
Cockes bones! This is all of Johnn de Gay.	167	Magnyfycence	960
Eche thynge is fayre when it is yonge; all hayle, owle!	167	Magnyfycence	970
She is furred for the hete /All to the fete;	167	Magnyfycence	978
In all this rowte	168	Magnyfycence	992
All that I make forthwith I marre;	169	Magnyfycence	1036
In faythe, ellys is there none in all Englonde.	170	Magnyfycence	1099
For all that my name hyght Foly,	171	Magnyfycence	1110
Where the devyll gate he all these hurtes?	171	Magnyfycence	1127

ALL—ALL	Page	Title	Line
Ye, for all thy mynde is on owles and apes.	171	Magnyfycence	1134
What! Canest thou all this Latyn yet,	172	Magnyfycence	1143
To pyke theyr fyngers all the day longe;	174	Magnyfycence	1222
That wyll syt ydyll all the day	174	Magnyfycence	1229
Nay, beyonde all other set hym alone.	174	Magnyfycence	1235
All that he dothe muste be alowde;	175	Magnyfycence	1247
All men beware of suche folys!	175	Magnyfycence	1265
But all that he dothe, and yf he reken well	175	Magnyfycence	1274
So is all the remenaunt, I make God avowe;	175	Magnyfycence	1283
And whan foly cometh, all is past.	176	Magnyfycence	1289
But all is foly that I can se.	176	Magnyfycence	1291
Howe frantyke fansy fyrst of all	176	Magnyfycence	1294
All mesure and good rule is gone quyte.	176	Magnyfycence	1315
Foly and fansy all where every man dothe face and brace.	177	Magnyfycence	1330
Theyr conveyaunce weltyth the worke all by wyll;	178	Magnyfycence	1363
Tyll all theyr conveyaunce is turnyd into madnesse.	178	Magnyfycence	1367
For all hokes unhappy to me have resorte.	178	Magnyfycence	1374
All that ye say, syr, is reason and skyll.	178	Magnyfycence	1381
At ones, and let hym not tary all day.	179	Magnyfycence	1400
What! All by mesure, good syr, and none excesse?	180	Magnyfycence	1422
I say it is foly to gyve all welth away.	180	Magnyfycence	1430
For welth without largesse is all out of kynde.	180	Magnyfycence	1441
All honour to me must nedys stowpe and lene.	181	Magnyfycence	1462
I have wynde and wether over all to sayle;	181	Magnyfycence	1464
That all the oryent had in subjeccyon,	181	Magnyfycence	1467
To rayne, for all his marcyall affeccyon;	181	Magnyfycence	1470
For al his pompe, for all his ryall trone,	181	Magnyfycence	1475
Surely it is I that all may save and spyll,	181	Magnyfycence	1478
I drede no daunger; I dawnce all in delyte:	182	Magnyfycence	1492
For of all barones bolde I bere the bell;	182	Magnyfycence	1498
Of all doughty I am doughtyest duke as I deme;	182	Magnyfycence	1499
To me all prynces to lowte man bese[m]e.	182	Magnyfycence	1500
beseme] 'be sene' †Rastell & Treveris C 1530, B			
Arthur of Albyan, for all his brymme berde,	182	Magnyfycence	1502
Nor Basyan the bolde, for all his brybaunce,	182	Magnyfycence	1503
At your commaundement, syr, wyth all dew reverence.	182	Magnyfycence	1515
Poynt devyse, all pleasure is your porte.	183	Magnyfycence	1540
Money maketh marchauntes, I tell you, over all.	184	Magnyfycence	1574
A, howe my stomake wambleth! I am all in a swete.	185	Magnyfycence	1617
All that I can his matter for to spede.	187	Magnyfycence	1664
But for all that he is lyke to have a glent.	187	Magnyfycence	1668
So it is all the maner nowe a dayes	187	Magnyfycence	1677
That he shall lyke the worse all this woke.	187	Magnyfycence	1682
I set not a flye and all go to all.	188	Magnyfycence	1710
I set not a flye and all go to all.	188	Magnyfycence	1710
That day I se hym I shall be worse all nyght.	188	Magnyfycence	1724
With Mesure. Where as all noblenes is, there I have past:	189	Magnyfycence	1749
Out of all measure themselfe to enryche;	189	Magnyfycence	1751
With pollynge and pluckynge out of all measure,	189	Magnyfycence	1753
It is the gyse nowe, I say, over all –	189	Magnyfycence	1759
And let all your fansyes upon them rest.	190	Magnyfycence	1770
And as for all other, let them trusse and packe;	190	Magnyfycence	1774
Let them have all, and the other go without;	190	Magnyfycence	1780
A knave and a carle and all of one kynde?	191	Magnyfycence	1820
What! Is all your myrthe nowe tourned to sorowe?	192	Magnyfycence	1849
And had robbyd you quyte from all felycyte.	193	Magnyfycence	1864
What? Yes, by the rode, syr. It was I all this whyle	193	Magnyfycence	1870
and spoylyd from all his goodys and rayment.	193	Magnyfycence	SD
Ly there, losell, for all thy pompe and pryde;	193	Magnyfycence	1880
All worldly welth for hym to lytell was;	193	Magnyfycence	1892
Lo, syrs, thus I handell them all	194	Magnyfycence	1896
An all is for theyr ungracyous lyfe.	194	Magnyfycence	1915
I am Poverte that all men doth hate.	195	Magnyfycence	1960
Syr, all this wolde have bene thought on before.	196	Magnyfycence	1970
All that God sendeth, take it in gre;	196	Magnyfycence	1979
Ye, syr, ye; leve all this rage,	196	Magnyfycence	1988
Howe be it of all synne he was innocent,	196	Magnyfycence	2002
Nowe all in welth, forthwith in poverte;	197	Magnyfycence	2027
All her delyte is set in doublenesse.	197	Magnyfycence	2029
Where is nowe all my servauntys that I had here a late?	198	Magnyfycence	2057
Where is nowe all my ryche abylement?	198	Magnyfycence	2059
Where is nowe all my pleasure and my worldly good?	198	Magnyfycence	2061
She is the bote of all my bale.	199	Magnyfycence	2070
Welthe without lyberte gothe all to wrake.	199	Magnyfycence	2086
That nowe he hath loste all his felycyte;	200	Magnyfycence	2114
A prynce to use with all his hole intent,	200	Magnyfycence	2118
That they lose theyr lyberte and all that there is.	200	Magnyfycence	2128
Tyll, as ye se many tymes, they shame all theyr kynne.	201	Magnyfycence	2144
At lyberte to wander and walke over all,	201	Magnyfycence	2149
For to be wyse all men may lerne of me,	201	Magnyfycence	2158
What a very vengeaunce nede all these wordys?	202	Magnyfycence	2198
Now let us be all one, and let us lyve in rest;	202	Magnyfycence	2202
For there be horys there at all assayes.	204	Magnyfycence	2275
All grace and pyte I lay in the duste.	205	Magnyfycence	2290
Agaynst all [s]autes of your goostly foo.	206	Magnyfycence	2329
sautes] 'fautes' †Rastell & Treveris C 1530, B,			
Douce Fragment d.7			
And have you banyshed from you all dyspare?	208	Magnyfycence	2393

	Page	Title	Line
Determyne to amende all your wanton excesse;	208	Magnyfycence	2409
All that he sayth of trouthe dothe procede;	209	Magnyfycence	2426
Cyrcumspeccyon inhateth all rennynge astray,	209	Magnyfycence	2430
Your comfortable advyse and wyt excedyth all gladnesse;	210	Magnyfycence	2477
In all your warkys more grace shall ye fynde;	211	Magnyfycence	2485
And not all the nygarde nor the chyncherde to play.	211	Magnyfycence	2492
And knowe your selfe mortal for all your dygnyte;	211	Magnyfycence	2499
Set not all your affyaunce in Fortune full of gyle;	211	Magnyfycence	2501
Today it is well, tomorowe it is all amysse;	213	Magnyfycence	2541
There to indeuer with all felycyte.	214	Magnyfycence	2569
Her face all bowsy,	215	El Rummynge	17
And all good ale drynkers,	217	El Rummynge	106
Wyth theyr heles dagged, /Theyr kyrtelles all to-jagged,	217	El Rummynge	124
Theyr smockes all to-ragged, /Wyth tytters and tatters,	217	El Rummynge	125
With all theyr myght runnynge /To Elynour Rummynge,	217	El Rummynge	128
A sorte of foule drabbes /All scurvy with scabbes.	218	El Rummynge	140
Theyr tresses untrust, /All full of unlust;	218	El Rummynge	148
Take up dyrt and all, /And bere out of the hall.'	219	El Rummynge	183
dyrt] 'drit' Kynge & Marche 1554, Day 1560, Marshe 1568			
For, after all our sport,	220	El Rummynge	231
And all for the good ale.	221	El Rummynge	265
ale] 'all' †Lant 1545			
She ran in all the hast /Unbrased and unlast,	222	El Rummynge	319
Amonge all the blommer,	224	El Rummynge	407
But of all this thronge /One came them amonge,	225	El Rummynge	445
All foggy fat she was;	226	El Rummynge	483
In all her joyntes about;	226	El Rummynge	485
And smelled all of ale.	226	El Rummynge	487
But yet, for all that,	226	El Rummynge	490
What nede all this be spoken?	227	El Rummynge	499
And all this shyfte they make	228	El Rummynge	533
To make all thynge cleane;	229	El Rummynge	578
But, syr, amonge all /That sate in that hall,	229	El Rummynge	580
'Parott hathe not dyned of all this long day;'	231	Speke Parott	23
To lerne all langage and hyt to speke aptlye.	232	Speke Parott	45
Dyscrecion ys modyr of nobyll vertues all;	232	Speke Parott	51
Above all other byrdis, set Parrot alone.	233	Speke Parott	112
Ye go about to amende, and ye mare all.	235	Speke Parott	154
Parrot sayth playnly, shall tourne all to dust.	236	Speke Parott	224
Agayne all remordes arme yow with paciens.	239	Speke Parott	298
And shewe hym that all the world dothe conjecte,	240	Speke Parott	327
For he wantythe of hys wyttes that all wold rule alone;	240	Speke Parott	329
To bryng all the see into a cheryston pytte,	240	Speke Parott	331
To nombyr all the sterrys in the fyrmament,	240	Speke Parott	332
God amend all, /That all amend may!	241	Speke Parott	353
God amend all, /That all amend may!	241	Speke Parott	354
How thys prosses I prate of, hyt ys not all for nowghte.	242	Speke Parott	389
O manles manhod, enfayntyd all with fere,	242	Speke Parott	391
Wylfulnes and Braynles no[w] rule all the raye.	243	Speke Parott	421
now] 'no' †MS Harley 2252			
He caryeth a kyng in hys sleve, yf all the worlde fayle;	243	Speke Parott	429
He facithe owte at a flusshe with, 'Shewe, take all!'	243	Speke Parott	430
He tryhumfythe, he trumpythe, he turnythe all up and downe,	244	Speke Parott	432
Paregall with all prynces, farre passyng hys estate;	244	Speke Parott	436
Sette asyde all sophysms, and speke now trew and playne.	244	Speke Parott	448
So royall a kyng, as reynythe uppon us all –	245	Speke Parott	468
So myche crossyng and blyssyng and hym all be shrewde;	246	Speke Parott	516
I purpose to shake oute /All my connynge bagge,	248	Collyn Clout	51
They gaspe and they gape /All to have promocyon:	248	Collyn Clout	86
For sothe, they are to lewde /To say so, all beshrewde!'	249	Collyn Clout	91
Of the clergye all, /Bothe great and small.	249	Collyn Clout	117
I speke nat nowe of all,	252	Collyn Clout	244
Of suche paternoster pekes /All the worlde spekes.	253	Collyn Clout	263
A chaplayne of trust, /Layth all in the dust.	253	Collyn Clout	284
With golde all betrapped,	254	Collyn Clout	309
And them all to-mangle?	255	Collyn Clout	333
to-mangle] 'mangle' †Godfray 1531, Kele 1545.1, Marshe 1568			
And all the faute they lay	256	Collyn Clout	402
the faute] not in Kele 1545.1, Marshe 1568			
And all that they have elles.	257	Collyn Clout	411
With all his false lore –	257	Collyn Clout	430
To redeme us with all.	258	Collyn Clout	455
And rule all thynges alone.	258	Collyn Clout	475
Agayne all suche rebelles	259	Collyn Clout	492
Ye wyll brynge all to nought,	261	Collyn Clout	606
And that is all your thought.	261	Collyn Clout	607
Almoost nothynge at all.	261	Collyn Clout	610
And ruleth so over all	262	Collyn Clout	633
I am lothe to tell all;	262	Collyn Clout	636
All this is out of mynde.	263	Collyn Clout	660
All] 'Alas' Kele 1545.1, Marshe 1568, 'All' MS Harley 2252			
That all the worlde myght say,	263	Collyn Clout	669
Yet over all that,	263	Collyn Clout	671
And suffre all this yll?	263	Collyn Clout	689
And all wayes to chase	264	Collyn Clout	699
Then all the freres letter.	265	Collyn Clout	762
And through all the worlde thei go	268	Collyn Clout	885
All maner of abjections;	268	Collyn Clout	890

ALL —ALL   Page   Title   Line

	Page	Title	Line
With all solempnyte, /For theyr indempnyte;	269	Collyn Clout	926
All is fysshe that cometh to the net:	269	Collyn Clout	933
to the net] 'to net' Marshe 1568, 'to nett' MS Harley 2252			
Howe all the worlde stares	270	Collyn Clout	960
And all suche holynesse.	271	Collyn Clout	977
With all temporall people	271	Collyn Clout	982
To governe over all	271	Collyn Clout	991
All that ever they ken	272	Collyn Clout	1053
Agaynst all spyrytuall men.	272	Collyn Clout	1054
And let be all your motynge,	273	Collyn Clout	1073
Is all my hole wrytynge;	274	Collyn Clout	1108
Howe we wyll rule all at wyll	276	Collyn Clout	1190
For all maister Doctour of Cyvyll	277	Collyn Clout	1219
And let take all the rest!	277	Collyn Clout	1224
All noble men of this take hede,	278	Why Come Ye	1
of this] not in MS Rawlinson C. 813			
All noble men of this take hede,	279	Why Come Ye	15
Than the devyll take all!	279	Why Come Ye	26
All noble men of this take hede,	279	Why Come Ye	27
With all good myndes.	280	Why Come Ye	56
Our talwod is all brent,	281	Why Come Ye	82
Our fagottes are all spent.	281	Why Come Ye	83
And trouthe is all to-torne;	281	Why Come Ye	93
For Wyll dothe rule all thynge,	281	Why Come Ye	105
All that he dothe is ryght.	281	Why Come Ye	116
To weve all in one lome	282	Why Come Ye	130
All is warse and warse.	282	Why Come Ye	135
And all nat worth a flye,	282	Why Come Ye	148
With, 'Tourne all home agayne!'	282	Why Come Ye	151
With all the power he may.	282	Why Come Ye	156
Lyke cankerd cowardes all,	283	Why Come Ye	165
They shote all at one marke:	283	Why Come Ye	174
They shote all at that!	283	Why Come Ye	176
They] 'Thy' †Kele 1545.3			
All maters there he marres,	283	Why Come Ye	189
For he hathe all the sayenge /Without any renayenge.	283	Why Come Ye	192
He ruleth all the roste	283	Why Come Ye	201
They have layde all in the myre.	285	Why Come Ye	251
For all theyr crack and bost,	285	Why Come Ye	256
crack] 'crake' †Kele 1545.3, Toy 1553, Marshe 1568			
For all this worldly wonder,	285	Why Come Ye	258
They make us all sottes,	285	Why Come Ye	263
Lost all his father wan.	285	Why Come Ye	271
all his] 'al that his' Toy 1553, Kitson 1560.7, Marshe 1568			
Bryngeth all thynges under cure.	286	Why Come Ye	284
They must stande all afar	286	Why Come Ye	301
For all their noble blode,	286	Why Come Ye	303
That all our lerned men	287	Why Come Ye	322
All men must folow his desyre.	287	Why Come Ye	345
must] not in Marshe 1568			
I trow all wyll be nought,	287	Why Come Ye	353
And all Scotlande owers	288	Why Come Ye	360
For all youre amyte,	288	Why Come Ye	374
To whose magnifycence /Is all the conflewence,	289	Why Come Ye	413
Embassades of all nacyons.	289	Why Come Ye	415
That he ruleth them all.	290	Why Come Ye	436
That all is but nutshales.	290	Why Come Ye	443
Now yet all this myght be	290	Why Come Ye	446
But all he bringeth to nought,	290	Why Come Ye	450
But he laythe all in the dyche,	290	Why Come Ye	455
All commeth to confusyon.	290	Why Come Ye	458
He ruleth all at wyll	291	Why Come Ye	487
Of all this prelacy,	291	Why Come Ye	503
Ye recrayed ruffyns all ragged!'	294	Why Come Ye	606
All noble men shulde outface,	294	Why Come Ye	623
And yet, for all that,	296	Why Come Ye	680
Above all other inordinatly.	296	Why Come Ye	704
To make all or to mar,	297	Why Come Ye	733
And agayne all reason /Commyted open trayson	297	Why Come Ye	736
Lo, yet for all that	297	Why Come Ye	742
To put all the governynge,	298	Why Come Ye	761
All the rule of this lande,	298	Why Come Ye	762
I have told you part, but nat all.	299	Why Come Ye	822
Desyring you above all thynge	299	Why Come Ye	828
All ryvers and wellys,	303	Why Come Ye	959
All waters that swellys;	303	Why Come Ye	960
Without all good reason.	304	Why Come Ye	997
And all out of season!	304	Why Come Ye	998
They play nat all clene,	304	Why Come Ye	1006
But all must be tryde,	304	Why Come Ye	1013
Shavyn and shorne, /And all threde bare worne!	304	Why Come Ye	1029
Now all is out of facion, /Almost in desolation.	305	Why Come Ye	1041
So braggynge all with bost	306	Why Come Ye	1074
All maner of flesshe mete	306	Why Come Ye	1084
For all privileged places	306	Why Come Ye	1089
All placis of relygion	306	Why Come Ye	1091
All this he dothe deale	306	Why Come Ye	1101
'Thys now he dothe meale' MS Rawlinson C. 813			

ALL —ALL

	Page	Title	Line
Pyked out of all good lawe,	306	Why Come Ye	1106
of] not in Marshe 1568			
All justyce he pretended:	307	Why Come Ye	1110
All thynges sholde be amended,	307	Why Come Ye	1111
All wronges he wolde redresse,	307	Why Come Ye	1112
All injuris he wolde represse,	307	Why Come Ye	1113
All perjuris he wolde oppresse.	307	Why Come Ye	1114
That all his trust hangis	308	Why Come Ye	1183
trust] 'harte' MS Rawlinson C. 813			
All other transcendyng, of very congruence	313	Garlande	52
To whos astate all noblenes most leven,	313	Garlande	54
leven] 'lene' †Fakes 1523, MS Cotton Vitellius E.x			
Them selfe to embesy with all there holl corage,	314	Garlande	66
With helpe of the ram, ley all in the dust.	315	Garlande	105
All be it grete parte he hath surrendred	316	Garlande	150
Whiche passid all other; wherfore I may	316	Garlande	159
Amonge the thickeste of all the hole rowte,	319	Garlande	240
'Make rowme,' sayd another, 'ye prese all to sore,'	319	Garlande	256
The dredefull dinne drove all the rowte on a rowe;	319	Garlande	264
Anone all was whyste, as it were for the nonys,	319	Garlande	267
Sterte all at ones an hundrethe fote backe.	320	Garlande	282
But Phebus was formest of all that cam theder;	320	Garlande	287
I helpe all other of there infirmite,	321	Garlande	311
That profytith all other is nothynge profytable	321	Garlande	313
All famous poetis ensuynge after me	321	Garlande	321
But blessyd Bachus, that bote is of all bale,	322	Garlande	376
How all that I do is under refformation,	323	Garlande	411
Of all our hooll collage by the agreament,	324	Garlande	417
That bounde ar we with all deu reverence,	324	Garlande	423
With all our strength that we can brynge about,	324	Garlande	424
Of Fames court, by all our holl assent	324	Garlande	433
All orators and poetis shulde thider go before,	325	Garlande	454
With all the prese that there was lesse and more.	325	Garlande	455
That all the worde, I trowe, and it were sought,	325	Garlande	462
worde] 'worlde' Marshe 1568			
Unto this place all poetis there did sue,	325	Garlande	481
All other transcendynge, the most rychely besene,	325	Garlande	483
Fret all with orient perlys of garnate,	325	Garlande	485
Encrownyd as empresse of all this wordly fate,	325	Garlande	486
wordly] 'worldly' Marshe 1568			
There were, I say, of all maner of sortis,	326	Garlande	512
And all tyme wandred I thus to and fro,	326	Garlande	516
Welcome to me with all my hole desyre!	327	Garlande	548
Be issuis and portis from all maner of nacyons';	328	Garlande	580
Sum dysdanous dawcokkis that all men dispyse,	329	Garlande	618
Bowns, bowns, bowns! that all they out cryde.	329	Garlande	624
For a gun stone, I say, had all to-jaggid his cap,	329	Garlande	629
to-jaggid] 'to lagged' Marshe 1568			
And, sir, amonge all me thought I saw twaine,	329	Garlande	633
That all the dayes of ther lyfe shall styck by ther rybbis.	330	Garlande	638
Ageynst all infeccyons with cancour enflamyd,	331	Garlande	672
cancour] 'rancour' Marshe 1568			
Ageynst all baratows broisiours of olde,	331	Garlande	673
It passid all bawmys that ever were namyd,	331	Garlande	674
All frutis and flowris grew there in there kynde.	331	Garlande	678
and] not in †Fakes 1523			
And formest of all dame Flora, the quene	331	Garlande	685
This joy excedith all wordly sport and play,	332	Garlande	716
wordly] 'worldly' Marshe 1568			
Of your questyon ye make all this whyle	333	Garlande	738
To tell his all his towchis it were to grete wonder;	333	Garlande	764
Of ladys a beve with all dew reverence:	334	Garlande	771
a beve] 'aboue' †Fakes 1523			
For all ladyes he hath the library,	334	Garlande	780
Of all gentylwomen he hath the scruteny,	334	Garlande	782
With vertu enbesid all tymes and howris;	334	Garlande	805
How theis ladys and gentylwomen all	335	Garlande	809
Committyth all to God, and lettyth his shyp ryde;	335	Garlande	834
After all duly ordred obeisaunce,	335	Garlande	836
Of all your bewte I suffyce not to wryght:	336	Garlande	875
Madame regent /I may you call /Of vertuows all.	339	Garlande	953
All good and no badnes,	341	Garlande	1010
I wyll that ye shall be /In all benyngnyte	341	Garlande	1047
Where all the sayd poetis sat in there degre.	343	Garlande	1104
All other besyde were counterfete they thought	343	Garlande	1106
All ... counterfete] 'that they ware were counterfettis' MS Cotton Vitellius E.x			
In famous glory all other transcendyng,	344	Garlande	1129
To all that to reason is condiscendyng,	344	Garlande	1132
To all that to] 'to all tho that' †Fakes 1523			
The margent was illumynid all with golden railles	345	Garlande	1157
to reherse all by name that he hath compylyd, &c.	345	Garlande	R
All the demenour of princely astate,	347	Garlande	1231
Of one Adame all a knave, late dede and gone -	347	Garlande	1247
All his delight was to braule and to barke	347	Garlande	1252
But what of that? Hard it is to please all men;	348	Garlande	1259
All the wittis they have.	348	Garlande	1266
By Chemeras flamys, /And all the dedely namys	349	Garlande	1324

19

ALL A KNAVE —ALL THYNGE

	Page	Title	Line
But, lorde, how the parker was wroth with all.	351	Garlande	1386
But yet for all that, be as be may,	352	Garlande	1415
And all overcast with cloudis unkynde,	352	Garlande	1444
With frowarde frostis, alas, was all to-fret!	352	Garlande	1450
It must nedes after rin all the worlde aboute.'	353	Garlande	1483
All orators and poetis, with other grete and smale,	354	Garlande	1504
'Triumpha, triumpha!' they cryid all aboute.	354	Garlande	1506
Under the banner /Of all good manner,	356	Garlande	1573
With all his hoost	359	Albany	9
For all theyr boost,	359	Albany	11
Your chefe cheftayne, /Voyde of all brayne,	360	Albany	49
And brake up all his hoost.	360	Albany	67
For all his crake and bost,	360	Albany	68
Suche trechery /And traytory /Is all your cast.	361	Albany	101
Whose name over all	361	Albany	108
And in abhominacion /Of all maner of nacion,	362	Albany	142
And byrne you all to colles,	362	Albany	152
Ye Scottes all the rable,	363	Albany	177
And of all maner vyce?	364	Albany	221
For all your comly crackes.	367	Albany	350
All out of joynt ye jar.	368	Albany	378
So noble a prince as he /In all actyvite	368	Albany	396
Fortunate in all his *faytes.	368	Albany	398

    *faytes] 'faycates' Scattergood

	Page	Title	Line
Devoyde of all nobles,	369	Albany	410
All the roiall sorte /Of his nobilyte,	370	Albany	445
For to recount them all.	370	Albany	458
He rules his cominalte /With all benignite.	370	Albany	464
As all men can reporte.	370	Albany	474
All his subjectes and he /Moost lovyngly agre	371	Albany	480
At all houres to be redy	371	Albany	485
With hym in all dystresse, /Alway in redynesse	371	Albany	489
Over all the world[e] to sprede.	371	Albany	511

    worlde] 'worlds' †Marshe 1568

	Page	Title	Line
Of all trewe Englyshemen,	372	Albany	521
shall evermore be, with all obsequious redynesse,	373	Replycacion	I
For all that they preche and teche	374	Replycacion	12
Of all pure clennesse virgynall,	375	Replycacion	32
All men can testifye.	376	Replycacion	64
That ye dawns all in a sute	379	Replycacion	168
Of all good Christen order.	380	Replycacion	226
Than all your lytterature.	380	Replycacion	233
With heresy all infecte.	380	Replycacion	237
From all honest company,	380	Replycacion	243
to all waywarde or frowarde altercacyons	382	Replycacion	R
Poete of poetes all, /And prophete princypall.	383	Replycacion	321
Nor solempne Serenus, for all his armony	383	Replycacion	337

ALL A KNAVE

	Page	Title	Line
John Jayberd et Adam all a knave,	106	Epitaphe	I
ADAM UDDERSALE, ALIAS DICTUS ADAM ALL A KNAVE,	109	Epitaphe2	I

ALLBEIT

	Page	Title	Line
For allbeit that this longe not to me,	59	Bowge	456

ALLE

	Page	Title	Line
Barons, knightis, squyers, one and alle,	31	Dol Dethe	92
For alle your proude prankyng, yor pride may apayere.	122	Garnesche1	19
As ar brystlyd on the bake for alle your gay gere.	122	Garnesche1	26
Brynges yow out of favyr with alle femall teggys:	122	Garnesche1	31
That mastres Punt put yow of, yt was nat alle causeles;	122	Garnesche1	32
I sey, ye solem Sarson, alle blake ys yor ble;	122	Garnesche1	36
[Your] pride ys alle to peviche, your porte importunate;	123	Garnesche2	3
For alle your carpet cousshons	124	Garnesche3	11
For alle ys nat worthe a myteyng,	127	Garnesche3	115
Fusty bawdyas, I sey nat alle.	131	Garnesche5	76
If thow war aquentyd with alle	133	Garnesche5	138

ALLECTYUES

	Page	Title	Line
solacyous and ryght pregnant allectyues of syngular pleasure,	312	Garlande	I

ALLECTUARY

	Page	Title	Line
Allectuary arrectyd to redres	44	Balettys3	8

ALLEGYAUNCE

	Page	Title	Line
After myne allegyaunce	369	Albany	405

ALLELUYA

	Page	Title	Line
With, 'Trompe up!' 'Alleluya!'	284	Why Come Ye	205

ALL HALLOWE

	Page	Title	Line
I swere by all hallowe	222	El Rummynge	323

ALLYGATE

	Page	Title	Line
Allygate the gospell	275	Collyn Clout	1162

ALLMYGHTY

	Page	Title	Line
Allmyghty God, I trust,	298	Why Come Ye	750

ALLONE

	Page	Title	Line
And as I stode redynge this verse myselfe allone,	48	Bowge	68

ALL THYNG

	Page	Title	Line
Ye, all thyng mortall shall torne unto nought	236	Speke Parott	214
Frantiknes dothe rule and all thyng commaunde;	243	Speke Parott	420
So ys all thyng wrowghte wylfully withowte reson and skylle.	245	Speke Parott	496
Thus all thyng ye disorder	380	Replycacion	227

ALL THYNGE

	Page	Title	Line
I[n] ponder, by number, by measure all thynge is wrought,	143	Magnyfycence	118

    In] 'I' †Rastell & Treveris C 1530, B

ALLWAY —ALSO Page Title Line

	Page	Title	Line
Where measure lackyth, all thynge dysorderyd is;	144	Magnyfycence	122
For defaute of measure all thynge dothe excede.	146	Magnyfycence	217
All thynge is worse whan it is worne.	153	Magnyfycence	451
How all thynge passyth as doth the somer flower,	312	Garlande	9
All thynge compassyd, no perpetuyte,	312	Garlande	13
All thynge convenable here is contryvyd	332	Garlande	712
convenable] 'convenably' Marshe 1568			

ALLWAY

This wanton clarkis be nyse allway.	35	Man Margery	2
Ye syng allway the kukkowe songe.	129	Garnesche5	4
Fye on this wynnyng allway!	302	Why Come Ye	929
this] not in MS Rawlinson C. 813			

ALL WAY

All way to have pleasure.	81	Phy Sparrow	371

ALMANAK

Makynge his almanak for the new yere;	354	Garlande	1516

ALMESSE

It is great almesse the hung[re] to fede,	177	Magnyfycence	1344
hungre] 'hunger' †Rastell & Treveris C 1530, B			

ALMIGHTY

The flayle, the scourge of Almighty God.	308	Why Come Ye	1165
The flayle] not in MS Rawlinson C. 813			

ALMON

Then Parot moste have an almon or a date.	231	Speke Parott	7
An almon now for Parott, delycatelye dreste;	232	Speke Parott	48

ALMONDE

Ye, syr, a blaunched almonde is no bene.	151	Magnyfycence	381

ALMOOST

Whan that he was even at me almoost,	58	Bowge	432
Almoost two or three, /Of that dygnyte,	250	Collyn Clout	148
Almoost nothynge at all.	261	Collyn Clout	610

ALMOST

That every man almost groweth out of kynde.	175	Magnyfycence	1285
Now all is out of facion, /Almost in desolation.	305	Why Come Ye	1042
That no prechour almost	306	Why Come Ye	1075

ALMOSTE

Then noblenesse, I se well, is almoste undone,	146	Magnyfycence	225
So myche consultacion, almoste to none entente;	244	Speke Parott	453

ALOES

That with myxture of aloes and bytter gall	117	Ag Scottes	81

ALOFT

Upon my fynger aloft!	80	Phy Sparrow	356

ALOFTE

He set up fresshely upon his hat alofte.	56	Bowge	367

ALONE

All left alone, alas, he fawte in vayne!	32	Dol Dethe	104
Behold, thou lyeste, luggard, alone!	42	Balettys1	25
And yet there is none /But one alone;	84	Phy Sparrow	517
Mournyng all alone,	89	Phy Sparrow	704
COURTLY ABUSYON alone in the place.	163	Magnyfycence	SD
What, Fansy! Arte thou alone?	169	Magnyfycence	1044
Nay, beyonde all other set hym alone.	174	Magnyfycence	1235
CRAFTY CONVEYAUNCE alone in the place.	177	Magnyfycence	SD
MAGNYFYCENCE alone in the place.	181	Magnyfycence	SD
God gyve hym a myscheffe! Nay, nowe let me alone.	189	Magnyfycence	1730
and leveth MAGNYFYCENCE alone in the place.	190	Magnyfycence	SD
Above all other byrdis, set Parrot alone.	233	Speke Parott	112
For he wantythe of hys wyttes that all wold rule alone;	240	Speke Parott	329
And rule all thynges alone.	258	Collyn Clout	475
Alone, and make rekenynge	271	Collyn Clout	990
That ruleth the rest alone.	272	Collyn Clout	1019
That hathe the strokes alone;	281	Why Come Ye	114
That ruleth but he alone,	304	Why Come Ye	996
In place alone then musynge in my thought	312	Garlande	8
But that princesse alone,	381	Replycacion	259

ALOWDE

Your harte ys to hawte, iwys, yt wyll nat be alowde.	123	Garnesche2	26
By the masse, odly well alowde.	155	Magnyfycence	533
All that he dothe muste be alowde;	175	Magnyfycence	1247

ALOWED

His Englysh well alowed	91	Phy Sparrow	792
And so little learning, so lewdly alowed,	138	Ven Tongues	40

ALOWES

Myxed with bytter alowes of herde adversyte.	207	Magnyfycence	2354

ALSO

And were not thei to blame, I say also,	30	Dol Dethe	36
To me also all thouthe yt wer promysyde	33	Dol Dethe	159
Devysed and also wrate /Uppon a lewde curate,	62	Hauke	34
In lyke maner also	74	Phy Sparrow	112
The spynke and the martynet also;	82	Phy Sparrow	407
And also the mad coote,	82	Phy Sparrow	410
The storke also,	83	Phy Sparrow	469
Also the noble fawcon, /With the gerfawcon,	85	Phy Sparrow	556
Troylus also hath lost	89	Phy Sparrow	714
Also John Lydgate	91	Phy Sparrow	804
Also by Ecates bower	104	Phy Sparrow	1322
The wolvis, the beris also,	111	Lawde	23
Thalya, my muse, for you also call I,	117	Ag Scottes	85

21

ALTERACYON — AM

	Page	Title	Line
Also nat fare from Bowgy Row,	130	Garnesche5	47
Mary, so wyll we also.	157	Magnyfycence	616
Counterfet Countenaunce to have also,	158	Magnyfycence	645
Yes, yes. He fell with me also at debate.	166	Magnyfycence	944
With the also? What! He playeth the state?	166	Magnyfycence	945
Why, shall I not have Foly with me also?	176	Magnyfycence	1306
Thefte also and pety brybery	177	Magnyfycence	1354
To be supervysour, and on Largesse also;	190	Magnyfycence	1785
For in Pleasure and Surveyaunce and also in the,	190	Magnyfycence	1787
For Lyberte is gone, and also Felycyte.	192	Magnyfycence	1857
For to understande your pleasure and also your mynde.	209	Magnyfycence	2420
And caused me also to use to moche lyberte,	209	Magnyfycence	2445
And made also mesure to be put fro me.	209	Magnyfycence	2446
And also theyr fete /Hardely full unswete;	217	El Rummynge	121
His rumpe also he frygges /Agaynst the hye benche.	219	El Rummynge	178
She had also the gout	226	El Rummynge	484
'With Kateryne incomporabyll, owur royall quene also,	231	Speke Parott	36
Parot can say, 'Cesar, ave,' also;	233	Speke Parott	110
And also prophytabyll, /Yf ye be agreabyll,	237	Speke Parott	248
Your rudeness to pardon and also that they wolde	241	Speke Parott	360
And also gratyfyed /By holy synodalles	264	Collyn Clout	715
Another Clementyne also:	268	Collyn Clout	880
And also dame Prudence, /With sober Sapyence.	279	Why Come Ye	13
The Gommoryans also /Were brought to deedly wo,	291	Why Come Ye	472
Also, to furnisshe better his excuse,	314	Garlande	92
For men to loke on? Aristotille also,	315	Garlande	127
He sange also how, the tre as he did take	320	Garlande	300
That wrote the history of Jugurta also;	321	Garlande	332
Orace also with his new poetry;	322	Garlande	352
Poggeus also, that famous Florentine,	322	Garlande	372
Of Dertmouth, of Plummouth, of Portismouth also;	326	Garlande	513
To Mercury also hertely prayed I then,	335	Garlande	826
Thamar also wrought with her goodly honde	336	Garlande	852
Dame Agrippina also I may reherse	336	Garlande	859
Of Vertu also the soveraynne enterlude;	345	Garlande	1177
Also the Tunnynge of Elinour Rummyng,	347	Garlande	1233
The Balade also of the Mustarde Tarte.	347	Garlande	1245
Also by Hecates powre	349	Garlande	1315
powre] 'bowre' Marshe 1568			
Also the Murnyng of the Mapely Rote;	351	Garlande	1377
Murnyng] 'murmyng' †Fakes 1523			
Also a Devoute Prayer to Moyses Hornis,	351	Garlande	1381
And Sainct Williams also.	360	Albany	64

ALTERACYON

	Page	Title	Line
Of the same facyon /Without alteracyon,	85	Phy Sparrow	543

ALTERCACYONS

	Page	Title	Line
to all waywarde or frowarde altercacyons	382	Replycacion	R

ALTHOUGH

	Page	Title	Line
Although he made it never so tough,	139	Ven Tongues	77

ALTRYCACYON

	Page	Title	Line
Cryst you assyste in your altrycacyon!	142	Magnyfycence	81

ALUMBEK

	Page	Title	Line
Alumbek sodyldym syllorym ben!	37	Coystrowne1	16

ALWAY

	Page	Title	Line
That I may say /Honour alway /Of womankynd!	96	Phy Sparrow	975
And I so lytell alway styll.	170	Magnyfycence	1070
In good hope alway for to indure.	208	Magnyfycence	2396
But answere that I may, /For myselfe alway	266	Collyn Clout	786
He ruleth alway styll.	281	Why Come Ye	107
With hym in all dystresse, /Alway in redynesse	371	Albany	490
Protestacion alway canonically prepensed, professed,	373	Replycacion	I

ALWAYE

	Page	Title	Line
Me thoughte alwaye Dyscymular dyde devyse;	58	Bowge	424
But ye have crafte your selfe alwaye to save.	59	Bowge	452

AM

	Page	Title	Line
Adres the to me, whiche am bothe halt and lame,	29	Dol Dethe	10
Bot ther was fals packinge or els I am begylde,	31	Dol Dethe	71
I am no hakney for your rode;	35	Man Margery	11
I am insuffycyent to make such enterpryse;	42	Balettys2	9
For your jentyll husband sorowfull am I;	43	Balettys2	37
I am content so all partys be pleasyd:	45	Balettys5	11
Nay, naye, be sure, whyles I am on your syde	50	Bowge	169
For now am I plenarely dysposed	52	Bowge	216
And ever he sange, 'Sythe I am no thynge playne'.	52	Bowge	235
Syr, pardone me, I am an homely knave	53	Bowge	264
I have grete scorne and am ryghte evyll apayed.'	54	Bowge	298
I tell the, I am of countenaunce.	55	Bowge	330
I am not happy, I renne ay on the losse!	57	Bowge	399
But I am lothe for to reyse a smoke,	59	Bowge	479
And I am your, syr, so have I blys,	60	Bowge	495
Heu, heu, me, /That I am wo for the!	73	Phy Sparrow	65
So urgently I am brought /Into carefull thought.	74	Phy Sparrow	106
But for I am a mayde, /Tymerous, halfe afrayde,	87	Phy Sparrow	607
Yet I am nothyng sped,	90	Phy Sparrow	754
I am but a yong mayd,	91	Phy Sparrow	770
In Chauser I am sped,	91	Phy Sparrow	788
But enforsed am I /Openly to askry	94	Phy Sparrow	902
I am now constrayned, /With wordes nothing fayned,	120	Ag Scottes2	1

Text	Page	Title	Line
I am laureat, I am no lorell.	124	Garnesche3	14
I am laureat, I am no lorell.	124	Garnesche3	14
And eyther I am dysseyved, or ye be the same.	141	Magnyfycence	25
Unto that same I am ryght well agrede,	144	Magnyfycence	128
Well, I am content your wayes to take.	144	Magnyfycence	155
Surely I am joyous that ye be myndyd thus;	144	Magnyfycence	156
And I am Lyberte, made of in every nacyon.	145	Magnyfycence	172
Ye wene that I am dronken bycause I loke pale.	147	Magnyfycence	259
For Counterfet Countenaunce knowen am I.	152	Magnyfycence	410
Thus am I occupyed at all assayes.	152	Magnyfycence	428
And mekyll am I made of nowe adays.	152	Magnyfycence	430
And I am made a knyght.	155	Magnyfycence	521
I am sure ye wolde have me excused.	156	Magnyfycence	581
And I, am counterfet of one mynde and thought,	159	Magnyfycence	701
In faythe, yet am I occupyed with the best;	160	Magnyfycence	705
I am never glad but whan I may do yll,	160	Magnyfycence	731
And never am I sory but whan that I se	160	Magnyfycence	732
Howe sayst thou, man? Am not I a joly rutter?	161	Magnyfycence	752
For thou shalt well knowe I am nother durty nor dusty.	161	Magnyfycence	759
I am of fewe wordys. I love not to [crake].	162	Magnyfycence	775
crake] 'barke' †Rastell & Treveris C 1530, B			
I am so lyght /To daunce delyght;	164	Magnyfycence	840
Mary, I am come for the. For me?	166	Magnyfycence	929
So I am poynted after my consayte.	167	Magnyfycence	961
But, in faythe, I am so occupyed	168	Magnyfycence	1019
I daunce up and downe tyll I am dyssy.	169	Magnyfycence	1040
Cockys harte! Thou lyest; I am no [h]ogge.	170	Magnyfycence	1083
hogge] 'dogge' †Rastell & Treveris C 1530, B			
Yet gyve me thy dogge, and I am content;	171	Magnyfycence	1112
Yes, yes! I am yet as full of game	172	Magnyfycence	1140
By the masse, I am glad I came hyder	176	Magnyfycence	1286
I am content so it in measure be.	179	Magnyfycence	1390
Syr, I am here at your pleasure.	179	Magnyfycence	1409
I am here redy. What! Shall we	179	Magnyfycence	1414
So it be by mesure I am ryght well content.	180	Magnyfycence	1421
For nowe, syrs, I am lyke as a prynce sholde be;	181	Magnyfycence	1457
For I am prynce perlesse, provyd of porte,	181	Magnyfycence	1471
I am the dyamounde dowtlesse of dygnyte.	181	Magnyfycence	1477
Were never halfe so rychely as I am drest.	181	Magnyfycence	1483
Of all doughty I am doughtyest duke as I deme;	182	Magnyfycence	1499
As I be saved, with pleasure I am supprysyd	183	Magnyfycence	1529
Truste me, with you I am hyghly pleasyd;	183	Magnyfycence	1535
Syr, I am the better of your noble reporte;	183	Magnyfycence	1541
A, howe my stomake wambleth! I am all in a swete.	185	Magnyfycence	1617
Yet I am not harte seke, but that me lyst.	185	Magnyfycence	1621
I am forthwith as hole as a troute.	185	Magnyfycence	1624
And surely, as I am nowe advysed,	186	Magnyfycence	1657
Nay, I tell you, I am not wonte to fode	188	Magnyfycence	1698
For I am panged ofte tymes in this same facyon.	189	Magnyfycence	1734
Nowe Measure is gone, I am the better pleased.	189	Magnyfycence	1738
Thus, I say, I am envyronned with solace.	190	Magnyfycence	1797
I am Adversyte, that for thy mysdede	193	Magnyfycence	1876
From God am sente to quyte the thy mede.	193	Magnyfycence	1877
I am Goddys preposytour; I prynt them with a pen;	195	Magnyfycence	1941
I am lowsy and unlykynge and full of scurffe;	195	Magnyfycence	1958
I am Poverte that all men doth hate.	195	Magnyfycence	1960
I am baytyd with doggys at every mannys gate;	195	Magnyfycence	1961
I am raggyd and rent, as ye may se;	195	Magnyfycence	1962
Alasse, I say, where to am I brought?	196	Magnyfycence	1968
I am desyred with hyghest and lowest degre.	199	Magnyfycence	2079
I am presydent of prynces; I prycke them with pryde.	199	Magnyfycence	2082
For I am a vertue yf I be well used,	199	Magnyfycence	2101
And I am a vyce where I am abused.	199	Magnyfycence	2102
And I am a vyce where I am abused.	199	Magnyfycence	2102
I am Magnyfycence, that somtyme thy mayster was.	200	Magnyfycence	2107
For where I am occupyed and usyd wylfully,	200	Magnyfycence	2131
I am so lusty to loke on, so freshe, and so fre,	201	Magnyfycence	2145
Ha, ha, ha! For laughter I am lyke to brast.	201	Magnyfycence	2160
Ha, ha, ha! For sporte I am lyke to spewe and cast.	201	Magnyfycence	2161
Goddys fote! I warant you I am a gentylman borne;	203	Magnyfycence	2216
I am the better yet in a bowget. And I the better in a male.	203	Magnyfycence	2232
I am wery of the worlde, for unkyndnesse me sleeth.	205	Magnyfycence	2283
In tyme of dystresse I am redy at hande;	205	Magnyfycence	2285
And I, Myschefe, am comyn at nede,	205	Magnyfycence	2309
Alas, syr! So I am lapped in adversyte	206	Magnyfycence	2331
Good Hope, your potecary, assygned am I,	207	Magnyfycence	2351
Ye, syr, now am I armyd with good hope,	207	Magnyfycence	2378
Now, surely, Magnyfycence, I am ryght well apayed	208	Magnyfycence	2402
And be ruled by me, whiche am called Redresse.	208	Magnyfycence	2410
Redresse my name is, that lytell am I used	208	Magnyfycence	2411
As the worlde requyreth, but rather I am refused.	208	Magnyfycence	2412
Syr, in good hope I am to amende.	210	Magnyfycence	2454
Syrs, I am agreed to abyde your ordenaunce -	210	Magnyfycence	2471
I am content, my frendys, that it so be.	214	Magnyfycence	2570
How bright I am of ble!	220	El Rummynge	218
Ich am not cast away, /That can my husband say,	220	El Rummynge	219

AMALEC —AMENDE   Page   Title   Line

I am a mynyon to wayte apon a quene;   231   Speke Parott   19
  a (2)] 'the' Lant 1545, Kynge & Marche 1554, Day 1560,
  Marshe 1568
Alas, I am dysdayned, /And as a man halfe-maymed, ...   237   Speke Parott   252
Be love I am constreyned /To be with yow retayned, ...   238   Speke Parott   257
For lothe I am to offende   251   Collyn Clout   186
I am sory for your sake!   253   Collyn Clout   252
Sory therfore am I, ...   258   Collyn Clout   484
I am lothe to tell all;   262   Collyn Clout   636
I am forcebly constraynd /At Juvynals request   309   Why Come Ye   1210
Therto am I full insuffycyent;   313   Garlande   46
I am content that he be not exylide   318   Garlande   224
But now to helpe myselfe I am not able.   321   Garlande   312
Whiche glad am to please, and loth to offende'   324   Garlande   427
'So am I preventid of my brethern tweyne   324   Garlande   428
My name, I know well, beyonde that I am able, ...   324   Garlande   438
I am elles rebukyd of that I intende, ...   324   Garlande   440
Which glad am to please, and lothe to offende.'   324   Garlande   441
So am I supprysyd with pleasure and delyght   327   Garlande   537
I am not woundid but that I may be cured.   332   Garlande   732
I am not ladyn of liddyrnes with lumpis, ...   332   Garlande   733
To be your remembrauncer, madame, I am bounde, ...   336   Garlande   864
Though insufficient am I   369   Albany   401
AMALEC
And ye were disloyall Amalec.   118   Ag Scottes   116
AMALECKE
But this madde Amalecke, ...   291   Why Come Ye   478
AMALOCH
Now Geball, Amon and Amaloch - 'Harke, harke, ...   234   Speke Parott   118
AMASED
She made me sore amased   99   Phy Sparrow   1103
They make him so amased, ...   283   Why Come Ye   180
As people halfe amased, ...   379   Replycacion   194
AMASID
As a mariner that amasid is in a stormy rage, ...   335   Garlande   829
  amasid] 'masid' MS Cotton Vitellius E.x
My mynde of the grete din was somdele amasid.   354   Garlande   1512
AMBER
But my bedes of amber.   229   El Rummynge   603
AMBICIOUS
He is so ambicious, /So elate and so vicious, ...   308   Why Come Ye   1176
AMBICYOUS
He is so ambicyous, ...   290   Why Come Ye   461
AMBYCYON
With covytous ambycyon /And other superstycyon, ...   269   Collyn Clout   901
  ambycyon] 'and ambycyon' Kele 1545.1, Marshe 1568,
  'ambyssyon' MS Harley 2252
AMBROSE
Saynt Gregorie and saynt Ambrose, ...   381   Replycacion   275
AMBROSIUS
As Jerome, in his preamble Frater Ambrosius, ...   316   Garlande   162
AMEN
Amen.   40   Coystrowne3   60
Amen, say ye with me!   74   Phy Sparrow   94
Amen, amen, amen!   86   Phy Sparrow   602
Amen, amen, amen!   86   Phy Sparrow   602
Amen, amen, amen!   86   Phy Sparrow   602
God save him in his right! /Amen   112   Lawde   57
Amen, for saynt charyte   115   Scot Kynge   E
AMEN.   214   Magnyfycence   2573
Amen, quod Parott, /The royall popagay.   241   Speke Parott   355
Amen, amen, say ye   300   Why Come Ye   837
Amen, amen, say ye   300   Why Come Ye   837
Amen, /Of your inward charyte.   300   Why Come Ye   839
AMEND
But suche dawes to amend, ...   62   Hauke   26
No man that can amend   91   Phy Sparrow   809
Is to discommende /That they cannot amend, ...   103   Phy Sparrow   1271
He is not lyvynge your maners can amend;   183   Magnyfycence   1537
And sette to a D, /And then hyt ys 'Amend', ...   238   Speke Parott   276
  to] not in †MS Harley 2252
God amend all, /That all amend may!   241   Speke Parott   353
God amend all, /That all amend may!   241   Speke Parott   354
AMENDE
I trowe she coude not amende   75   Phy Sparrow   156
And to amende her tale, ...   99   Phy Sparrow   1116
Your awne lewdnes to amende.   124   Garnesche3   18
But largesse may amende your name.   151   Magnyfycence   389
And yf I se therby they wyll not amende, ...   194   Magnyfycence   1926
And I truste to ratyfye and amende your fame.   208   Magnyfycence   2398
Determyne to amende all your wanton excesse;   208   Magnyfycence   2409
Syr, in good hope I am to amende.   210   Magnyfycence   2454
Ye go about to amende, and ye mare all.   235   Speke Parott   154
Amende whan ye may, ...   251   Collyn Clout   189
To amende the gospell, ...   267   Collyn Clout   821
Themselfe to amende;   274   Collyn Clout   1126
To rectyfye and amende   278   Collyn Clout   1263
How no man can him amende!   292   Why Come Ye   531

24

AMENDED —AMONGE   Page   Title   Line

	Page	Title	Line
Nowe God amende that is amys;	308	Why Come Ye	1162
Who list amende it, let hym set to his penne.	348	Garlande	1260
Is to discommende /That they can not amende,	348	Garlande	1264
AMENDED			
And now men wold have amended	91	Phy Sparrow	797
All thynges sholde be amended,	307	Why Come Ye	1111
AMENDIS			
Amendis maye be of that is now amys;	60	Bowge	494
AMENDYD			
I pray you it may be amendyd	102	Phy Sparrow	1246
Syr, is your pacyent any thynge amendyd?	208	Magnyfycence	2387
AMENDYS			
But yf therof the soner amendys be made;	146	Magnyfycence	226
AMENDMENT			
So myche nobyll prechyng, and so lytell amendment;	244	Speke Parott	452
AMENSE			
The amense therof is far to call agayne;	140	Magnyfycence	9
AMIS			
With your reformacion, if I say amis,	316	Garlande	145
AMYABYLL			
My vyolet amyabyll, /My joye inexplicabill,	237	Speke Parott	243
AMYABLE			
This jelofer amyable;	98	Phy Sparrow	1053
AMYS			
Amendis maye be of that is now amys;	60	Bowge	494
This worke devysed is /For suche as do amys,	61	Hauke	2
For sure he wrought amys	62	Hauke	41
And whyles the heedes do this, /The remenaunt is amys	249	Collyn Clout	116
But my recountynge is /Of them that do amys	274	Collyn Clout	1102
Thynges that are amys,	278	Collyn Clout	1264
No shame to do amys;	305	Why Come Ye	1051
Nowe God amende that is amys;	308	Why Come Ye	1162
AMYSSE			
In theyr amysse of gray;	85	Phy Sparrow	560
Where measure is ruler, there is nothynge amysse.	144	Magnyfycence	124
But so longe they rekyn with theyr reasons amysse	200	Magnyfycence	2127
they] 'theyr' †Rastell & Treveris C 1530, B			
Today it is well, tomorowe it is all amysse;	213	Magnyfycence	2541
Somwhat there is amysse!	272	Collyn Clout	1050
AMYTE			
For all youre amyte,	288	Why Come Ye	374
AMMAS			
Those wordes his grace dyd saye /Of an ammas gray.	372	Albany	531
AMON			
Now Geball, Amon and Amaloch – 'Harke, harke,	234	Speke Parott	118
AMONG			
To ask wher he fyndyth among hys monacordys	37	Coystrownel	20
Among the Nones Blake.	72	Phy Sparrow	9
That right dwelt us among,	111	Lawde	20
Among this prese – /Even a hole mese –	168	Magnyfycence	995
Lucina she wadythe among the watry floddes,	239	Speke Parott	285
Le tonsan de Jason is lodgid among the shrowdes;	239	Speke Parott	287
Spent among wanton lasses;	257	Collyn Clout	424
Among my recordes suffer hym namyd,	316	Garlande	160
Among the scabbed skyes /Of Wycliffes flesshe flyes.	378	Replycacion	165
Among the Grekes most relucent of lyght,	383	Replycacion	332
AMONGE			
For cruell[y] amonge them ther he was slayne.	32	Dol Dethe	105
cruelly] 'cruell' †MS Royal 18 D.ii, Marshe 1568			
Amonge all other I put myselfe in prece.	47	Bowge	44
Amonge all other was wrytten in her trone,	47	Bowge	65
'And, syr, in fayth, why comste not us amonge	57	Bowge	379
Amonge huswyves bolde,	87	Phy Sparrow	621
Sepultus est amonge the wedes;	107	Epitaphel	18
When Garnyche cummyth yow amonge	128	Garnesche3	150
Yet amonge noble men I was brought up and bred.	147	Magnyfycence	261
And have you not amonge you Lyberte?	157	Magnyfycence	625
I muster, I medle amonge these grete estates;	160	Magnyfycence	736
Amonge all suche persones as I well understonde	161	Magnyfycence	739
That fell amonge us this same day?	166	Magnyfycence	933
Not amonge noble men, as the worlde gothe.	189	Magnyfycence	1747
Cryst be amonge you, and the Holy Goste!	208	Magnyfycence	2385
Amonge all the blommer,	224	El Rummynge	407
But of all this thronge /One came them amonge,	225	El Rummynge	446
Than began the sporte /Amonge that dronken sorte.	229	El Rummynge	575
But, syr, amonge all /That sate in that hall,	229	El Rummynge	580
To dwell amonge ladyes, Parrot, is mete.	233	Speke Parott	105
And remembre amonge how Parrot and ye	236	Speke Parott	221
And better shulde remayne /Amonge the people playne,	265	Collyn Clout	773
Well-syghted when /He is amonge blynde men?	292	Why Come Ye	535
Amonge the Burgonyons	302	Why Come Ye	923
For amonge us is none	304	Why Come Ye	995
Amonge the thickeste of all the hole rowte,	319	Garlande	240
Forthwith there rose amonge the thronge	319	Garlande	246
Mustred ther amonge them with many a mad tale.	322	Garlande	373
And as I thus sadly amonge them avysid	323	Garlande	386
And, sir, amonge all me thought I saw twaine,	329	Garlande	633
Moche mischefe, I hyght you, amonge theem ther happid.	330	Garlande	643

AMONGEST —AN   Page   Title   Line

	Page	Title	Line
Cause me to cese, /Amonge this prese,	339	Garlande	958
Amonge the byrdes smale,	340	Garlande	998
There was amonge them no worde then but mum,	344	Garlande	1118
amonge them no worde] 'not a worde amonge them' MS Cotton Vitellius E.x			
AMONGEST			
Unneth they leve a locke /Of wolle amongest theyr flocke.	248	Collyn Clout	81
Amongest the sely nonnes.	256	Collyn Clout	389
Amongest you everychone	258	Collyn Clout	477
Amongest the hole rout	273	Collyn Clout	1082
AMOUNT			
With maters that amount the Romayns in substaunce;	321	Garlande	346
AMPHION			
Weth Amphion, and other musis of Archady	320	Garlande	273
AMPLE			
If he to the ample encrease of his name	318	Garlande	222
Over this, for a more ample processe	374	Replycacion	1
AMPLYFY			
Bycause that ye encrese and amplyfy	323	Garlande	404
ye] not in †Fakes 1523			
AMRELL			
Whan he herde tell /That my Lorde Amrell	360	Albany	55
Of my Lorde Amrell,	365	Albany	237
AN			
And I love you an hole cart lode.'	35	Man Margery	9
An holy water clarke a ruler of lordys.	37	Coystrowne1	21
He fumblyth in hys fyngeryng an ugly good noyse;	37	Coystrowne1	31
It semyth the sobbyng of an old sow!	37	Coystrowne1	32
An ussher of the hall fayn wold I get	37	Coystrowne1	40
from an honorable Jentyllwoman for a token,	39	Coystrowne3	1
Yet is youre tong an adders tayle,	41	Coystrowne4	16
I wys he hath an hevy hed,'	42	Balettys1	21
Let not all the world make an owtcry;	43	Balettys2	40
She kyste an anker, and there she laye at rode,	47	Bowge	39
kyste] 'keste' Wynkyn de Worde 1510, 'kast' Marshe 1568			
But, an he can Bone aventure take,	48	Bowge	102
an] 'and' Wynkyn de Worde 1510, Marshe 1568			
Ye be an apte man, as ony can be founde	50	Bowge	155
Syr, pardone me, I am an homely knave	53	Bowge	264
An eestryche fedder of a capons tayle	56	Bowge	366
An] 'And' Marshe 1568			
Had I as good an hors as she is a mare,	57	Bowge	407
And by my trouthe, but yf an ende they make,	59	Bowge	473
I have an errande to rounde in your ere.	60	Bowge	513
He semeth a sysmatyke /Or els an heretike,	62	Hauke	18
Pater noster qui, /With an Ave Mari,	72	Phy Sparrow	14
Whan he saw an ant;	75	Phy Sparrow	133
It were worth an hundreth pound	76	Phy Sparrow	189
Was chaunged to an harte:	79	Phy Sparrow	301
An horshowe so great,	83	Phy Sparrow	479
An epytaphe I wold have /For Phyllyppes grave.	86	Phy Sparrow	605
An ouche or els a ryng,	88	Phy Sparrow	686
Wryteth after an hyer rate;	91	Phy Sparrow	805
An epytaphe to wryght	92	Phy Sparrow	822
And to make an outcri	94	Phy Sparrow	904
an] 'a' †Kele 1545.2			
It were an hevenly blysse	97	Phy Sparrow	1039
and her foloweth an addicyon made by Maister Skelton.	103	Phy Sparrow	R
An hart was slayne /With hornes twayne	104	Phy Sparrow	1298
A subtyll sysmatyke, /Ryght nere an heretyke,	121	Ag Scottes2	28
Howkyd as an hawkys beke, lyke Syr Topyas.	122	Garneschel	40
Nosyd lyke an olyfaunt,	126	Garnesche3	71
Ye ar an eldyr steke;	126	Garnesche3	79
Of harlottes to use soche an harres,	131	Garnesche5	77
Prickyd lyke an unicorne.	133	Garnesche5	132
Ye be nat cawte in an hempen snare.	133	Garnesche5	163
I made, he said, a windmil of an olde mat.	137	Ven Tongues	13
It were a shame, to God I make an othe,	144	Magnyfycence	145
Without an antetyme or a stole;	150	Magnyfycence	359
An olde barne wolde be underset.	153	Magnyfycence	454
As longe as I lyve, thou haste an heyre parent.	154	Magnyfycence	507
By the masse, for ye are able to dystroy an hole lande.	154	Magnyfycence	513
Here is a leysshe of ratches to renne an hare!	156	Magnyfycence	586
What the devyll hast thou on thy fyste? An owle?	166	Magnyfycence	922
Torde! Man, it is an hawke of the towre.	166	Magnyfycence	925
And within an houre after,	169	Magnyfycence	1031
Plucke downe an house and set up a rafter,	169	Magnyfycence	1032
What is this, an owle or a glede?	169	Magnyfycence	1047
I have an hole armory of suche haburdashe in store;	175	Magnyfycence	1279
I have an hoby can make larkys to dare;	177	Magnyfycence	1342
A byll of recorde for an annuall rent.	187	Magnyfycence	1667
An honest person, I tell you, and a sad.	187	Magnyfycence	1690
Plucke from an hundred, and gyve it to thre;	190	Magnyfycence	1775
Flewe, I sholde say - in to an olde barne	191	Magnyfycence	1808
The case requyreth. Alasse, alasse, an hevy metynge!	192	Magnyfycence	1847
Nowe hath he ryght nought, naked as an asse.	193	Magnyfycence	1893
And some for to hange themselfe in an halter;	194	Magnyfycence	1911
An all is for theyr ungracyous lyfe.	194	Magnyfycence	1915

ANACREON — ANALETICALL

	Page	Title	Line
For totum in toto is not worth an hawe –	199	Magnyfycence	2089
Shall I myselfe hange with an halter? Nay,	206	Magnyfycence	2320
Upon her brayne-pan, /Lyke an Egypcyan /Lapped about.	216	El Rummynge	78
Lapped] 'Capped' Kynge & Marche 1554, Day 1560, Marshe 1568			
As wyse as an hare!	217	El Rummynge	112
An huswyfe of trust /Whan she is athrust,	220	El Rummynge	253
And thyder came an hepe /Of mylstones in a route.'	223	El Rummynge	361
thyder] 'there' †Lant 1545, Kynge & Marche 1554, Day 1560, Marshe 1568			
'Lo, here is an olde typpet,	223	El Rummynge	366
An ynche above her kne,	225	El Rummynge	420
She was somwhat foule, /Crokenebbed lyke an oule;	225	El Rummynge	427
Crokenebbed] 'Croke necked' †Lant 1545, Kynge & Marche 1554, Day 1560, Marshe 1568			
Of the vertue of an unset leke;	225	El Rummynge	451
Like an onyon syded, /Lyke tan ledder hyded.	226	El Rummynge	470
There came an old rybybe;	227	El Rummynge	492
Lyke an honest dame.	227	El Rummynge	511
Necked lyke an olyfant;	227	El Rummynge	519
Then Parot moste have an almon or a date.	231	Speke Parott	7
An almon now for Parott, delycatelye dreste;	232	Speke Parott	48
In Popering grew peres, whan Parrot was an eg.	232	Speke Parott	70
A narrow unfethered and without an hed,	232	Speke Parott	74
A trym-tram for an horse-myll it were a nyse thyng,	234	Speke Parott	128
So myche forcastyng, and so farre an after-dele;	244	Speke Parott	463
Was nevyr suche a fylty gorgon, nor suche an epycure,	246	Speke Parott	510
Moche herted lyke an hen.	251	Collyn Clout	168
An holy anker call	254	Collyn Clout	303
An] 'a' †Godfray 1531, Kele 1545.1, Marshe 1568			
For coverynge of an olde cottage	255	Collyn Clout	364
Out of theyr cloyster and quere /With an hevy chere,	256	Collyn Clout	395
Of an abbey ye make a graunge –	257	Collyn Clout	419
ye] 'they' Kele 1545.1, 'to' MS Harley 2252			
But hunte and blowe an horne,	262	Collyn Clout	621
An ynche above your eere,	263	Collyn Clout	674
But it is an olde sayd sawe	268	Collyn Clout	862
it] not in Kele 1545.1			
They have an evyll name,	275	Collyn Clout	1143
An ende of an olde song:	281	Why Come Ye	88
An ende of an olde song:	281	Why Come Ye	88
Stronge-herted lyke an hen.	285	Why Come Ye	276
Wold wyrry them lyke an hogge.	286	Why Come Ye	299
Lyke an oxe or a bull;	286	Why Come Ye	308
He is but an yonglyng,	287	Why Come Ye	348
An abstract or a concrete,	289	Why Come Ye	421
abstract] 'obstract' †Kele 1545.3			
That in a fume or an hete,	289	Why Come Ye	424
How an one-eyed man is	292	Why Come Ye	533
To make within an hower,	293	Why Come Ye	566
An hunderd pounde and more,	302	Why Come Ye	947
An] 'And' †Kele 1545.3			
Whiche madly he dothe apply /Unto an extravagancy,	306	Why Come Ye	1105
How oftyn fortune varyeth in an howre,	312	Garlande	11
Of an oke, that somtyme grew full streyghte,	312	Garlande	18
As one in a trans or in an extasy,	313	Garlande	37
Displease not an hundreth for one mannes pleasure.	314	Garlande	90
Of suche an endarkid chapiter sum season.	315	Garlande	108
Sterte all at ones an hundrethe fote backe.	320	Garlande	282
Ye have deservyd to have an enplement	323	Garlande	402
An hundred steppis mountyng to the halle,	325	Garlande	471
'A slipper holde the taile is of an ele'	326	Garlande	501
In an herber I saw, brought where I was,	330	Garlande	652
An hole reame he is able to set at devysion:	333	Garlande	758
And, 'Wynde me that botowme of such an hew',	334	Garlande	799
an] 'a' MS Cotton Vitellius E.x			
It were an hevenly helth,	340	Garlande	994
It were an endeles welth,	340	Garlande	995
He wrate an Epitaph for his grave stone,	347	Garlande	1249
An hart was slayne	348	Garlande	1291
An hynde unhurt hit by casuelte, not bled	351	Garlande	1406
with an hundred thousande tratlande Scottes	359	Albany	I
As an hoost royall	360	Albany	61
What an army were ye?	364	Albany	216
And an untrewe knyght.	364	Albany	229
And lurke there lyke an as	366	Albany	289
Gyve it up, and cry, 'creke', /Lyke an huddy peke.	366	Albany	301
Of suche an horne keke	366	Albany	304
Of suche an bolde captayne	366	Albany	305
Those wordes his grace dyd saye /Of an ammas gray.	372	Albany	531
For it is an auncyent brute,	378	Replycacion	156
They saye howe latria is an honour grete,	381	Replycacion	282
A confutacion responsyve, or an inevytably prepensed answere	382	Replycacion	R
Of suche an industry /And suche a pregnacy,	384	Replycacion	370

ANACREON

Anacreon and Arion, /Sophocles and Philemon, ... 90 Phy Sparrow 763

ANALETICALL

analeticall, topicall, and logycall: .... 375 Replycacion I

ANALOGY —ANKER   Page   Title   Line

ANALOGY
  In theology, /Nor analogy, ...   383   Replycacion   309
ANDREWE
  Twit, Andrewe! Twit, Scot!   282   Why Come Ye   125
    Scot] 'scote' †Kele 1545.3
ANDROMACH
  Like Andromach, Hectors wyfe, ...   74   Phy Sparrow   108
ANGELYK
  Though angelyk be youre smylyng, ...   41   Coystrowne4   15
ANGER
  His lyver, his longe /With anger is wronge;   94   Phy Sparrow   919
    longe] 'longes' Wyght 1553, Kitson 1560.6, Marshe 1568
  Frete yourselfe for anger and for dyspyte;   185   Magnyfycence   1602
  Why than /Wreke ye your anger on me?   273   Collyn Clout   1091
ANGERLY
  That frownyd on me full angerly and pale;   322   Garlande   375
ANGGRE
  At Orwelle hyr havyn your anggre was laules.   122   Garnesche1   33
ANGLEA
  'What yate call ye this?' And she sayd, 'Anglea'.   328   Garlande   588
    yate] 'gate' Marshe 1568
ANGRE
  I shall the angre ones in every vayne!   55   Bowge   326
  That shall them angre, I holde thereon a grote, ...   59   Bowge   475
  With angre and yre, ...   95   Phy Sparrow   932
  To angre the Scottes and Irysh keterynges withall, . . .   117   Ag Scottes   83
ANGRY
  A red angry man, but easy to intrete.   37   Coystrowne1   39
  Nay, and you be angry and overwharte, ...   156   Magnyfycence   562
  A man may beshrowe your angry harte.   156   Magnyfycence   563
  Art thou so angry as thou semyst?   162   Magnyfycence   794
  But, Lorde, as she was testy, /Angry as a waspy!   222   El Rummynge   330
ANIMOSITE
  His magnanymyte, /His animosite, ...   370   Albany   448
ANY
  Of formar writinge by any presidente   30   Dol Dethe   23
  Hys hart is to hy to have any hap;   37   Coystrowne1   12
  If any such might be found!   76   Phy Sparrow   188
  Any of the ofsprynge   76   Phy Sparrow   199
    ofsprynge] 'sprynge' Kitson 1560.6, Marshe 1568
  Or any of the blode.   76   Phy Sparrow   200
  Any of my sparowes kynde, ...   78   Phy Sparrow   261
  For any bodely lust, ...   90   Phy Sparrow   731
  It wold make any man   98   Phy Sparrow   1080
  And any man convert   99   Phy Sparrow   1101
  Of any sorowfull lamentacyon, ...   117   Ag Scottes   74
  Than to be founde in any such faute.   137   Ven Tongues   25
  Any such foly to rest or to be.   138   Ven Tongues   35
  Then any poysoned tode, or any serpent.   138   Ven Tongues   54
  Then any poysoned tode, or any serpent.   138   Ven Tongues   54
  Syr, yf any worde have past   143   Magnyfycence   92
  Convenyent persons for any prynce ryall.   145   Magnyfycence   173
  For no dyscorde that any man can sawe;   145   Magnyfycence   187
  Syr, without any longer delyaunce, ...   147   Magnyfycence   237
  Beryst thou any rome? Or cannyst thou do ought?   162   Magnyfycence   776
  Forsothe, tell on. Hast thou any mo?   175   Magnyfycence   1262
    mo] 'more' †Rastell & Treveris C 1530, B
  But, I say, let se and yf thou have any more.   175   Magnyfycence   1278
  Ne by non other that any man can rehersse.   181   Magnyfycence   1490
  Why, is there any store of rawe motton?   204   Magnyfycence   2265
  Then yf any there be   274   Collyn Clout   1117
  Any man to offende.   274   Collyn Clout   1128
  Of any vertuous wrytynge;   274   Collyn Clout   1136
  Nor rede in any scrolles, ...   277   Collyn Clout   1241
  For he hathe all the sayenge /Without any renayenge. . .   283   Why Come Ye   193
  They are fel as any fyre!   285   Why Come Ye   249
  That any other sayth, ...   290   Why Come Ye   444
  To any good ende were brought.   290   Why Come Ye   449
  To treate of any star   292   Why Come Ye   524
  Any man shulde be /In perplexyte /Of dyspleasure;   300   Why Come Ye   843
  Than any other a thousand folde.   310   Why Come Ye2   16
    any] 'yn any' MS Rawlinson C. 813
  To put any man in lack   310   Why Come Ye2   25
  That any man under supportacyon   318   Garlande   220
  Can lay any werkis that he hath compylyd, ...   318   Garlande   223
  Any worde defacid /That myght be rasid, ...   356   Garlande   1581
  or to make oblacions to any ymages of sayntes, ...   375   Replycacion   I
  To preche in any clawes, ...   375   Replycacion   38
ANY THYNG
  And if there be in it any thyng ment, ...   332   Garlande   723
ANY THYNGE
  Any thynge to do that myght be to your pleasure.   183   Magnyfycence   1528
  Syr, is your pacyent any thynge amendyd?   208   Magnyfycence   2387
ANKER
  Gayne dangerous stormys theyr anker of supporte, ...   44   Balettys3   26
  She kyste an anker, and there she laye at rode, ...   47   Bowge   39
    kyste] 'keste' Wynkyn de Worde 1510, 'kast' Marshe 1568

ANNE —AN OTHER

	Page	Title	Line
An holy anker call	254	Collyn Clout	303
An] 'a' †Godfray 1531, Kele 1545.1, Marshe 1568			
Shote anker, and lye at rode,	277	Collyn Clout	1255
From the anker he kuttyth the gabyll rope,	335	Garlande	833

ANNE
Good mastres Anne, there ye do shayle!	41	Coystrowne4	19
To mastres Anne, that farly swete,	41	Coystrowne4	29
To my Lady Anne Dakers of the Sowth	337	Garlande	R
To fayre maistres Anne that shuld have be sent,	347	Garlande	1241

ANNEX
Unto your rule I wyll annex my mynde.	144	Magnyfycence	142

ANNEXYD
I trowe good fortune hath annexyd us together,	146	Magnyfycence	198
And sad cyrcumspeccyon to me they have annexyd.	210	Magnyfycence	2463

ANNOT
And Annot wolde be nyce, and laughes, 'tehe wehe.'	153	Magnyfycence	477

ANNUALL
Alas his golde, his fee, his annuall rente,	32	Dol Dethe	97
A byll of recorde for an annuall rent.	187	Magnyfycence	1667

AN ODYR
Soche an odyr chalyngyr cowde me no man wysch,	121	Garneschel	3

ANOYANCE
To no mannes anoyance.	385	Replycacion	396

ANOYNTED
A kynge anoynted, and ye be non.	114	Scot Kynge	26
Unto our prince, anoynted kyng.	117	Ag Scottes	58
Anoynted kyng, and ye were none.	118	Ag Scottes	118
Gently joynted, /Gresed and anoynted /Up to the knockles:	215	El Rummynge	43

ANONE
There was moche noyse, anone one cryed, 'Cese!'	47	Bowge	46
Anone ther mette with him, as me thoughte,	54	Bowge	282
Anone Dyscymular came where I stode.	58	Bowge	427
Anone he waxyth so hy and prowde,	174	Magnyfycence	1244
Anone cometh another, /As drye as the other,	221	El Rummynge	276
Anone, I sey, this trumpet were founde out,	319	Garlande	243
Anone all was whyste, as it were for the nonys,	319	Garlande	267
A cry anone forthwith she made proclame,	325	Garlande	453

ANOTHER
To whome there came another gentylwoman.	48	Bowge	84
And sende the Frensshe kynge suche another fall.	115	Scot Kynge	73
And another bade put out myne eye;	150	Magnyfycence	353
Another wolde myne eye were blerde;	150	Magnyfycence	354
Another bade shave halfe my berde;	150	Magnyfycence	355
Cockys bonys! Herde ye ever syke another?	170	Magnyfycence	1090
But wylte thou make another on Gryme?	172	Magnyfycence	1151
Nay, nay. Thou shalt fynde hym another maner of man.	173	Magnyfycence	1189
I have another maner of sorte	174	Magnyfycence	1238
And let the other another [time] awayte.	180	Magnyfycence	1454
time] not in †Rastell & Treveris C 1530, B			
If ever I herde syke another, God gyve me shame.	192	Magnyfycence	1833
Cockes bones! Harde ye ever suche another?	192	Magnyfycence	1841
Somtyme to fall, another tyme to beware:	207	Magnyfycence	2374
Anone cometh another, /As drye as the other,	221	El Rummynge	276
Another brought her his cap	221	El Rummynge	285
Another there was that ran /With a good brasse pan -	222	El Rummynge	316
Another brought a spycke /Of a bacon flycke;	223	El Rummynge	335
Nowe in cometh another rabell;	224	El Rummynge	382
Another with a cradell,	224	El Rummynge	384
Another brought a skommer,	224	El Rummynge	408
Another sorte of sluttes:	225	El Rummynge	436
Another brought two goslynges	226	El Rummynge	459
In came another dant, /With a gose and a gant.	227	El Rummynge	515
Another brought her garlyke heddes;	227	El Rummynge	522
Another brought her bedes /Of jet or of cole,	227	El Rummynge	523
They wolde pype you another daunce.	262	Collyn Clout	618
Another Clementyne also:	268	Collyn Clout	880
One agayne another.	274	Collyn Clout	1106
I wyll no further ryme /Tyll another tyme;	284	Why Come Ye	231
Tyll another tyme etc.	284	Why Come Ye	232
That is another thyng.	287	Why Come Ye	347
Now he is gone to another stede	299	Why Come Ye	797
Another manes mynde diffuse is to expounde;	315	Garlande	111
'Nay, holde thy tunge,' quod another, 'let me have the name.'	319	Garlande	255
'Make rowme,' sayd another, 'ye prese all to sore,'	319	Garlande	256
A murmer of mynstrels, that suche another	320	Garlande	270
One of jasper, another of whalis bone;	325	Garlande	472
Another tolde how shyppes wente to wrak.	326	Garlande	507
So was there never another,	381	Replycacion	258

AN OTHER
And this an other, I have but smale substaunce.'	48	Bowge	94
And] 'But' Marshe 1568			
Ye never dwelte in suche an other place,	51	Bowge	201
But my learning is of an other degree	138	Ven Tongues	28
Than cometh an other gest;	221	El Rummynge	270
An other than dyd hyche her,	224	El Rummynge	401
hyche] 'hye' 1521 Fragment			
Suche an other there coude no man fynde;	325	Garlande	463

ANOTHERS —APON	Page	Title	Line

ANOTHERS
I have not sene suche anothers page — . . . . 60 Bowge 506
ANOTHYR
Get ye anothyr where ye may. 131 Garnesche5 62
ANSSWERE
Difficille hit ys to answsere thys demaunde; . . . . 243 Speke Parott 418
ANSWERE
But answere that I may, /For myselfe alway . . . . 266 Collyn Clout 785
I wyll answere lyke a clerke: . . . . 309 Why Come Ye 1208
Wherin this answere for hym we have comprisid, ... 314 Garlande 80
Yet shall I answere your grace as in this, ... 316 Garlande 144
When he is callid to answere to his name.' . . . . 325 Garlande 452
Wherof the answere restyth in my handis, ... 332 Garlande 724
Where ye must brevely answere to your name.' . . . . 343 Garlande 1092
To answere unto this noble audyence, ... 344 Garlande 1122
Ye coude nat corde tenus, /Nor answere verbo tenus, ... 377 Replycacion 105
A confutacion responsyve, or an inevytably prepensed answere . 382 Replycacion R
To answere or reply /Agaynst suche heresy. . . . . 383 Replycacion 312
ANSWERED
And I than softly answered to that clause, ... 48 Bowge 74
ANSWERYD
Wherto she answeryd, and brevely me tolde . . . . 328 Garlande 576
ANSWERYTH
Poeta Skelton answeryth . . . . 324 Garlande R
Poeta Skelton answeryth . . . . 324 Garlande R
Skelton Poeta answeryth . . . . 327 Garlande R
Poeta Skelton answeryth . . . . 332 Garlande R
Poeta Skelton answeryth . . . . 332 Garlande R
Poeta Skelton answeryth . . . . 335 Garlande R
ANT
Whan he saw an ant; . . . . 75 Phy Sparrow 133
ANTEOCUS
And of Anteocus, /And of Josephus . . . . 90 Phy Sparrow 736
ANTETYME
Without an antetyme or a stole; . . . . 150 Magnyfycence 359
ANTIOCHE
Whan he was creat pope /First in Antioche. . . . . 307 Why Come Ye 1143
ANTIOCHUS
And yet this proude Antiochus, ... 308 Why Come Ye 1175
ANTYQUYTE
As of antyquyte /It was ratyfyed, ... 264 Collyn Clout 713
  As] 'And' †Godfray 1531, Kele 1545.1, Marshe 1568
ANWYKE
Not from Anwyke unto Aungey. . . . . 171 Magnyfycence 1121
APACE
Had she not hyed apace, ... 229 El Rummynge 572
And ryn your way apace. 367 Albany 354
Go, lytell quayre, apace, ... 372 Albany 523
A PACE
Than sholde ye see there pressynge in a pace . . . . 47 Bowge 56
With that, Occupacioun presid in a pace; . . . . 344 Garlande 1144
APAYD
And you knew all ye would be ill apayd'. . . . . 139 Ven Tongues 72
With hym so wele apayd . . . . 297 Why Come Ye 731
APAYED
I have grete scorne and am ryghte evyll apayed.' . . . . . . 54 Bowge 298
Now, surely, Magnyfycence, I am ryght well apayed . . . . . 208 Magnyfycence 2402
APAYERE
For alle your proude prankyng, yor pride may apayere. . . . 122 Garnesche1 19
APART
For he setteth God apart. . . . . 308 Why Come Ye 1180
APARTE
As I know aparte . . . . 264 Collyn Clout 729
APASE
For passe-a-Pase apase ys gone to cache a molle, ... 243 Speke Parott 413
APELLES
And if Apelles your countenaunce had sene, ... 337 Garlande 894
APERE
And so doth it apere, ... 216 El Rummynge 59
  doth it] 'it dothe' Day 1560, Marshe 1568
as more at large it doth apere in the proces folowynge. . . 312 Garlande I
APES
Wherin he had apes and owles, ... 78 Phy Sparrow 258
Ye, for all thy mynde is on owles and apes. . . . . 171 Magnyfycence 1134
APHRIKE
Of Cartage in Aphrike; . . . . 364 Albany 196
APOYNTED
Mary, Welthe and I was apoynted to mete, ... 141 Magnyfycence 24
APOLLO
If Apollo wyll promyse . . . . 93 Phy Sparrow 863
Item Apollo that whirllid up his chare, ... 353 Garlande 1471
Owt of her bokis Apollo to rase. . . . . 353 Garlande 1480
Apollo to rase out of her ragman rollis. . . . . 354 Garlande 1490
APON
I am a mynyon to wayte apon a quene; . . . . 231 Speke Parott 19
  a (2)] 'the' Lant 1545, Kynge & Marche 1554, Day 1560,
  Marshe 1568
Suche statutes apon diettes, suche pyllyng and pollyng — . . 245 Speke Parott 495

APOSTATA —AQUAYNTE   Page   Title   Line

APOSTATA
Apostata Julianus /Nor yet Nestorianus, ...   70   Hauke   297
APOSTATAAS
And to synge from place to place, /Lyke apostataas. 256   Collyn Clout   386
APOSTELS
But of her apostels lyfe. 253   Collyn Clout   254
   her] 'theyr' Kele 1545.1, 'ther' MS Harley 2252
APOSTYLL
The apostyll Peter /Had but on pore myter 307   Why Come Ye   1139
   apostyll] 'wholly apostle' MS Rawlinson C. 813
APOSTROFACYON
By way of apostrofacyon   62   Hauke   30
APPAYRE
Tryvyals and quatryvyals so sore now they appayre, ...   235   Speke Parott   166
APPALL
And his honour appall.   279   Why Come Ye   23
APPALLE
Men say howe ye appalle   262   Collyn Clout   611
APPARAYLE
Her takelynge ryche and of hye apparayle;   47   Bowge   38
APPARE
Men say, ye can nat appare;   251   Collyn Clout   191
APPARELL
There apparell farre passynge beyonde that I can tell;   323   Garlande   394
APPARENTLY
Your mynde that can maynteyne so apparently;   317   Garlande   170
APPELS
And the appels of gold /Of Hesperides withhold, ...   104   Phy Sparrow   1301
APPERE
The story doth appere, ...   79   Phy Sparrow   300
That the lodesterre appere.   278   Collyn Clout   1258
As playnly it dothe appere, ...   307   Why Come Ye   1117
And ye wolde appere wyse   378   Replycacion   129
APPERETH
As appereth by theyr werkes, ...   250   Collyn Clout   151
APPERYTH
The whyte apperyth the better for the black, ...   347   Garlande   1237
APPETITE
'How say ye? Is this after your appetite?   331   Garlande   707
For to envyve Pandarus appetite;   336   Garlande   872
APPETYTE
I can not myne appetyte accomplysshe and fulfyll   160   Magnyfycence   733
Syr, ye shall folowe myne appetyte and intent.   180   Magnyfycence   1420
To do you servyce after your appetyte.   190   Magnyfycence   1793
APPETYTES
And quyckely your appetytes to sharpe and adresse;   183   Magnyfycence   1549
APPLES
Some apples, some peres, ...   225   El Rummynge   438
And the apples of golde /Of Hesperides withholde, ...   349   Garlande   1294
APPLE TRE
Suche apple tre, suche frute.   378   Replycacion   157
APPLY
That if I wolde apply /To wryte ornatly, ...   91   Phy Sparrow   780
   ornatly] 'ordinately' Kitson 1560.6, Marshe 1568
Whiche madly he dothe apply /Unto an extravagancy, ...   306   Why Come Ye   1104
APPLYE
I wyll my selfe applye, ...   339   Garlande   961
APPLYED
But our Grekis theyr Greke so well have applyed, ...   234   Speke Parott   145
APPOSE
What! Can ye agree thus and appose?   180   Magnyfycence   1425
Theyr shall no clergye appose   254   Collyn Clout   291
APPOSED
For that they are nat apposed   253   Collyn Clout   265
APPOSELLE
'Madame, your apposelle is wele inferrid, ...   316   Garlande   141
APPROCHE
He dyd never approche   307   Why Come Ye   1144
APRELL
Refresshyng myndys the Aprell shoure of rayne;   44   Balettys3   11
APRILL
After the Aprill showre;   340   Garlande   987
APROCHE
Avaunce your selfe to aproche and come nere.   48   Bowge   88
Hys presens to aproche;   126   Garnesche3   84
So shamfully to me, theyr mayster, to aproche, ...   205   Magnyfycence   2279
APTE
Ye be an apte man, as ony can be founde   50   Bowge   155
APTLYE
To lerne all langage and hyt to speke aptlye.   232   Speke Parott   45
AQUAYNTANCE
Knolege, aquayntance, resort, favour, with grace;   43   Balettys3   1
AQUAYNTAUNCE
What the devyll! Are ye two of aquayntaunce?   154   Magnyfycence   496
And to fall in aquayntaunce with every newe facyon, ...   183   Magnyfycence   1548
AQUAYNTE
Wynde you from wanhope and aquaynte you with me.   206   Magnyfycence   2340

AQUAYNTYD —ARAYE   Page   Title   Line

AQUAYNTYD
Yf noblenesse were aquayntyd with sober dyreccyon.   141   Magnyfycence   18
All delectacyons aquayntyd is with me;   146   Magnyfycence   209
AQUEINTED
Furdrers of love, with baudry aqueinted, ...   329   Garlande   609
AQUEINTYNG
Aqueintyng hym with the Musys nyne.   132   Garnesche5   100
AQUEYNTE
And to aqueynte you with carnall delectacyon;   183   Magnyfycence   1547
AQUENTAUNCE
Than there coude I none aquentaunce fynde;   47   Bowge   45
'Maystres,' quod I, 'I have none aquentaunce   48   Bowge   92
AQUENTYD
If thow war aquentyd with alle   133   Garnesche5   138
AQUENTYTH
As he that aquentyth hym with ydilnes.   318   Garlande   228
AQUYNO
Saynt Thomas de Aquyno, ...   381   Replycacion   279
AQUYTE
Wryght what thow wylte, I xall the aquyte.   134   Garnesche5   180
Be well assurid I shall aquyte your hyre, ...   327   Garlande   550
But if I sholde aquyte your kyndnes, ...   342   Garlande   1062
AR
By thy report ar wonte to be extolde   29   Dol Dethe   17
For I have dyscust /We ar but dust, ...   39   Coystrowne3   5
Though ye suppose all jeperdys ar paste, ...   45   Balettys4   1
Wherfore, as I be savyd, /Ye ar therfore beknavyd.   70   Hauke   310
They ar to diffuse for me: 90   Phy Sparrow   768
Whan other ar glad, ...   95   Phy Sparrow   938
And welthe ar com agayne, ...   111   Lawde   41
For your untruth now ar ye shent.   118   Ag Scottes   124
Thus for your guerdon quyt ar ye, ...   119   Ag Scottes   139
Ye were to hye, ye ar cast downe.   120   Ag Scottes   177
The tokens ar not good /To be true Englysh blood;   121   Ag Scottes2   22
As ye ar brystlyd on the bake for alle your gay gere.   122   Garnesche1   26
Ye countyre umwhyle to capcyously, and ar ye be dysiryd;   123   Garnesche2   11
To turney or to tante with me ye ar to fare to seke.   123   Garnesche2   37
Ye ar an eldyr steke;   126   Garnesche3   79
Yower termys ar to grose, ...   126   Garnesche3   96
Ye ar a comly crakar, ...   127   Garnesche3   110
Ye ar a fole owtelauyd;   128   Garnesche3   183
Ye ar dysposyd for to ly.   131   Garnesche5   64
To cal me lorell ye ar to lewde;   131   Garnesche5   85
Thow thou be pyllyd, thow ar nat sade.   132   Garnesche5   117
Thow ar frantyke and lakkyst wyt, ...   132   Garnesche5   118
Mole ruit sua, whose dictes ar pregnaunte -   232   Speke Parott   41
Now Neptune and Eolus ar agreed of lyclyhod, ...   239   Speke Parott   283
But lewdlye ar they lettyrd that your lernyng lackys, ...   239   Speke Parott   294
Ar mete for a swyne herde to hunte after hogges.   240   Speke Parott   321
Yet your problemes ar preignaunte and with loyalte acquayntyd.   240   Speke Parott   344
Wherfor your remorders ar madde or else starke blynde, ...   241   Speke Parott   369
  remorders] 'remordes' †MS Harley 2252
For reysons ar no resons but resons currant -   244   Speke Parott   443
He sayes we ar but crakers;   285   Why Come Ye   274
He sayth we ar to blame!   305   Why Come Ye   1049
wherein ar comprysyde many and dyvers   312   Garlande   I
'The sum of your purpose, as we ar advysid, ...   314   Garlande   78
Enforcid ar we you to recompence, ...   323   Garlande   416
That bounde ar we with all deu reverence, ...   324   Garlande   423
How ye ar welcome to this court of aray.   327   Garlande   539
'My frende, sith ye ar before us here present   344   Garlande   1121
Wherein many storis ar brevely contayned   347   Garlande   1224
What constellacions ar good or bad for men, ...   352   Garlande   1429
ARABE
There is no bawme ne gumme of Arabe   207   Magnyfycence   2347
ARABY
The byrde of Araby, ...   84   Phy Sparrow   513
Now with his gummys of Araby   309   Why Come Ye   1196
  gummys] 'gynnys' MS Rawlinson C. 813
Above, in the top, a byrde of Araby, ...   330   Garlande   667
ARACE
The chambres hangid with clothes of arace;   325   Garlande   475
ARAY
Your braggyng bost, your royall aray, ...   119   Ag Scottes   160
I advyse yow beware of thys war, rannge yow in aray.   123   Garnesche2   33
By crede, it wolde have fresshe aray, ...   153   Magnyfycence   460
For to excede /In suche aray.   165   Magnyfycence   896
Cockes harte! Tourne the; let me se thyne aray.   167   Magnyfycence   959
And where you had chaunges of ryche aray, ...   197   Magnyfycence   2010
Upon the holy daye, /Whan she doth her aray, ...   216   El Rummynge   67
That is a shreud aray!   218   El Rummynge   163
Arayse of ryche aray, ...   270   Collyn Clout   942
Occupacyon, is ryght goodly aray, ...   327   Garlande   528
How ye ar welcome to this court of aray.   327   Garlande   539
ARAYD
With Wofully Arayd and Shamefully Betrayd;   352   Garlande   1418
ARAYE
Came pressynge in one in a wonder araye.   60   Bowge   499

ARAYES — ARE	Page	Title	Line

ARAYES
Clenly to counterfet newe arayes; . . . . 152 Magnyfycence 426
ARAYSE
Araysa of ryche aray, ... 270 Collyn Clout 942
ARAM
Aram was fyred with Caldies fyer called Ur; . . . . 232 Speke Parott 64
ARCADY
Of Arcady the beares . . . . 79 Phy Sparrow 309
ARCET
As Palamon and Arcet, ... 87 Phy Sparrow 616
ARCHADY
Weth Amphion, and other musis of Archady . . . . 320 Garlande 273
ARDEN
In the forest of Arden. 88 Phy Sparrow 658
   of] not in Wyght 1553, Kitson 1560.6, Marshe 1568
ARE
Ye are to unhappy occasyons to fynde . . . . 38 Coystrownel 65
   occasyons] 'occasion' Marshe 1568
Saynge, 'Mayd, ye are in wyll . . . . 77 Phy Sparrow 222
His gummes rusty /Are full unlusty; . . . . 94 Phy Sparrow 915
That are so quyckely vayned, ... 99 Phy Sparrow 1121
How they are blynde /In theyr owne mynde, ... 115 Ag Scottes 7
They are so stowre, /So frantyke mad, ... 115 Ag Scottes 12
Are nat these Scottys /Folys and sottys, ... 116 Ag Scottes 29
Lost is your game, ye are checkmate. . . . . 118 Ag Scottes 128
Bolde bayarde, ye are to blynde, ... 126 Garnesche3 101
My scoles are not for unthriftes untaught, ... 138 Ven Tongues 26
But ye are so full of vertibilite, ... 138 Ven Tongues 42
Are sharper then swordes, sturdier then stones. . . . . 138 Ven Tongues 50
What shippis are sailing to Scalis Malis, ... 139 Ven Tongues 65
Welcome, frendys, ye are bothe unto me. . . . . 145 Magnyfycence 169
To se howe greable we are of one mynde; . . . . 146 Magnyfycence 199
What! I have aspyed ye are a carles page. . . . . 148 Magnyfycence 288
You are nothynge mete with us for to dwell, ... 149 Magnyfycence 304
And surely ye are to hym beholde, ... 149 Magnyfycence 333
Counterfet capytaynes by me are made; . . . . 152 Magnyfycence 436
What the devyll! Are ye two of aquayntaunce? . . . . 154 Magnyfycence 496
By the masse, for ye are able to dystroy an hole lande. . . . 154 Magnyfycence 513
Nowe therfore, whylest we are togyder — . . . . 155 Magnyfycence 546
I say, whylest we are togyder in same — . . . . 155 Magnyfycence 548
I say, come hyder. What are these twayne? . . . . 156 Magnyfycence 582
Knowe they not me? They are to blame. . . . . 157 Magnyfycence 593
But are ye not avysed to dwell where ye spake? . . . . 162 Magnyfycence 774
My wyttys be weke, my braynys are lyght; . . . . 169 Magnyfycence 1024
What? Wolde ye have mo folys, and are so many? . . . . 172 Magnyfycence 1170
Are not his wordys cursydly cowchyd? . . . . 175 Magnyfycence 1276
For by crafty conveyaunce wonderful thynges are wrought. . . 178 Magnyfycence 1371
What sholde ye do elles? Are not you a lorde? . . . . 185 Magnyfycence 1606
Stand up, syr. Ye are welcom to me. . . . . 186 Magnyfycence 1632
Largesse in wordes — for rewardes are but small. . . . . . . 189 Magnyfycence 1760
To make fayre promyse, what are ye the worse? . . . . 189 Magnyfycence 1761
Alasse, syr, ye are undone with stelyng and robbynge! . . . . 192 Magnyfycence 1852
In faythe, of his cofers the bottoms are bare. . . . . 201 Magnyfycence 2163
Me thynke ye are not gretly acomberyd wyth wyt. . . . . 203 Magnyfycence 2215
Nay, I know well inough ye are bothe well handyd . . . . . . 203 Magnyfycence 2230
Tushe! These maters that ye move are but soppys in ale; . . . 203 Magnyfycence 2233
Alasse, alasse, syrs, ye are to blame! . . . . 204 Magnyfycence 2245
Her eyen gowndy /Are full unsowndy, ... 215 El Rummynge 35
For they are blered; . . . . 215 El Rummynge 36
Her lyppes are so drye, ... 221 El Rummynge 272
They are shyre shakyng nought!' . . . . 226 El Rummynge 466
Yett dates now are deynte, and wax verye scante, ... 244 Speke Parott 440
For sothe, they are to lewde /To say so, all beshrewde! . . . 249 Collyn Clout 90
Howe they are able to make /With theyr golde and treasure . . 250 Collyn Clout 143
But they are lothe to mell, ... 250 Collyn Clout 162
They are fayne to play deuz decke. . . . . 250 Collyn Clout 166
Howebeit they are good men, ... 251 Collyn Clout 167
Some are insufficientes, ... 252 Collyn Clout 223
For that they are nat apposed . . . . 253 Collyn Clout 265
Myters are bought and solde; . . . . 254 Collyn Clout 290
What are they the worse? . . . . 254 Collyn Clout 295
Men say ye are tonge-tayde, ... 255 Collyn Clout 354
That good lawes are subverted . . . . 256 Collyn Clout 372
Relygyous men are fayne /For to tourne agayne . . . . 256 Collyn Clout 374
Your workes, they say, are straunge — . . . . 257 Collyn Clout 420
Theyr dyriges are forgotten, ... 257 Collyn Clout 425
   Theyr dyriges] 'The Diriges' Kele 1545.1, 'the dyrige'
   MS Harley 2252
Or elles they are madde . . . . 259 Collyn Clout 503
Howe they are to blame . . . . 259 Collyn Clout 509
Howe the people are glad . . . . 259 Collyn Clout 512
And some there are that rave, ... 259 Collyn Clout 514
And are somewhat suspecte /In Luthers secte. . . . . 260 Collyn Clout 544
Ye are so puffed with pryde, ... 261 Collyn Clout 593
Ye are the lesse to blame, ... 262 Collyn Clout 614
Lothe they are to lese . . . . 267 Collyn Clout 841
And say properly thei are sacerdotes . . . . 268 Collyn Clout 874
Theyr hertes are so fayntyd, ... 269 Collyn Clout 899

ARECTE — ARMES

	Page	Title	Line
Howe some of you are mellynge.	271	Collyn Clout	985
He sayes that we are recheles,	275	Collyn Clout	1176
Thynges that are amys,	278	Collyn Clout	1264
Our fagottes are all spent.	281	Why Come Ye	83
Our shepe are shrewdly shorn,	281	Why Come Ye	92
That they are but halfe men;	283	Why Come Ye	163
I drede we are bought and solde.	283	Why Come Ye	172
They are fel as any fyre!	285	Why Come Ye	249
Theyr wyttes, he saith, are dull;	286	Why Come Ye	309
He sayth, they are to seke	287	Why Come Ye	317
That they are so wo	294	Why Come Ye	613
For sylkes are wane.	302	Why Come Ye	920
Our nobles are gone	302	Why Come Ye	922
They are happy that wynnys,	302	Why Come Ye	927
Together are bended, /And so condyscended, bendyd] 'wendyd' MS Rawlinson C. 813	304	Why Come Ye	1022
False Scottes are ye.	359	Albany	26
Ye are a fals entrusar, /And a fals abusar,	364	Albany	227
Are ye nat frantyke madde, /And wretchedly bestadde,	368	Albany	363
Your braynes are ydell;	368	Albany	387
What losels than are ye	370	Albany	459
How that ye are lykely	371	Albany	510
Thus are they undone and utterly shamed.	374	Replycacion	17
Ye are brought to, 'Lo, Lo, Lo!'	376	Replycacion	72
Ye are unhappely ured.	377	Replycacion	95
Howe ye are this day,	379	Replycacion	177
That people are in great dout	380	Replycacion	224
Ye are but lydder logici, /But moche worse isagogici,	380	Replycacion	234
Wherfore ye are well checte,	380	Replycacion	238
To whom we are bounde echone	381	Replycacion	260
But mende your myndes that are mased;	382	Replycacion	293
We are kyndled in suche facyon	385	Replycacion	382

ARECTE

To you I arecte it, and cast /Therof the reformacyon.	143	Magnyfycence	94

ARECTYNG

Arectyng my syght toward the zodyake,	312	Garlande	1

ARERAGE

And rage in arerage	280	Why Come Ye	47

ARETHUSA

If Arethusa wyll send	93	Phy Sparrow	860

ARGYVA

Lyke to Argyva by just resemblaunce,	336	Garlande	843

ARGUE

Some argue secundum quid ad simpliciter,	235	Speke Parott	155

ARGUED

Well argued and surely on bothe sydes.	176	Magnyfycence	1304
Ye argued argumentes, /As it were upon the elenkes,	377	Replycacion	125

ARGUMENT

You to holde content /With myne argument;	143	Magnyfycence	109
Myne argument els koude not longe endure.	316	Garlande	147

ARGUMENTES

To maynteyne argumentes /Agaynst the sacramentes.	259	Collyn Clout	517
Ye argued argumentes, /As it were upon the elenkes,	377	Replycacion	125

ARGUS

Of Argus revengyd, recover when he may,	239	Speke Parott	288

ARION

Anacreon and Arion, /Sophocles and Philemon,	90	Phy Sparrow	763

ARISTIPPUS

Of auncyent Aristippus and such other mo,	233	Speke Parott	93

ARISTOTILLE

For men to loke on? Aristotille also,	315	Garlande	127

ARYNA

Lyke to Aryna, maydenly of porte,	336	Garlande	865

ARYSE

Me, passynge sore, myne herte than gan aryse;	58	Bowge	425

ARYSTOBELL

The story of Arystobell, /And of Constantynopell,	67	Hauke	212

ARYVYD

Ye fyrste aryvyd; whan broken was your mast Ye] 'The' †Fakes 1523	327	Garlande	542

ARKE

That made that great arke,	78	Phy Sparrow	257

ARMATYCKE

With armatycke gummes /That cost great sumes,	84	Phy Sparrow	520

ARME

Agayne rebellyonns arme the to make debate;	33	Dol Dethe	166
He set the arme proudly under the syde,	55	Bowge	321
To the increse of your honour then arme you with ryght,	211	Magnyfycence	2496
Agayne all remordes arme yow with paciens.	239	Speke Parott	298
Under her arme, me thought, she hade a boke.	327	Garlande	532
Your discharge here under myne arme is it.'	344	Garlande	1146

ARMED

Ye armed you with wille and left your wit behynd;	30	Dol Dethe	55

ARMELECHE

And ye be desolate as Armeleche.	114	Scot Kynge	24

ARMES

The armes of Calyce, I have no coyne nor crosse!	57	Bowge	398
Your harrold in armes not yet halfe expert.	118	Ag Scottes	98

ARMY —ART   Page   Title   Line

	Page	Title	Line
Cockes armes! What is he?	156	Magnyfycence	573
Cockes armes! Is that your name?	157	Magnyfycence	598
By the armes of Calys, well conceyved.	159	Magnyfycence	675
Nay, come at ones, for the armes of the dyce.	162	Magnyfycence	781
Cockes armes! It is not so, I trowe.	173	Magnyfycence	1202
Cockes armes! Thou shalte kepe the brewhouse boule.	176	Magnyfycence	1321
A, Cockes armes! Where myght suche one be founde?	184	Magnyfycence	1569
With, 'Cockes armes! Rest shall I none have	185	Magnyfycence	1615
Cockes armes, howe Pleasure plucked hym forth!	189	Magnyfycence	1735
Cockes armes, syrs, wyll ye not se	200	Magnyfycence	2109
Betwene his armes, he felt her body quake.	320	Garlande	301
Togeder in armes, as brethern, enbrasid;	323	Garlande	393

ARMY

What an army were ye?	364	Albany	216

ARMYD

Ye, syr, now am I armyd with good hope,	207	Magnyfycence	2378

ARMYE

Our armye waxeth dull,	282	Why Come Ye	150

ARMYS

As to enbrace you in myne armys twayne.	44	Balettys3	42
Cockys armys! He hath callyd for the twyce.	162	Magnyfycence	782
Cockys armys! This is a warke, I trowe.	170	Magnyfycence	1094
Cockys armys, a mete man for us!	172	Magnyfycence	1169
To exployte dedes of armys	370	Albany	467

ARMONY

To the hylles of Armony,	78	Phy Sparrow	247
With armony that synges	93	Phy Sparrow	866
To touche them with tauntes of your armony,	117	Ag Scottes	86
Whos hevenly armony was so passynge sure,	320	Garlande	274
Nor solempne Serenus, for all his armony	383	Replycacion	337

ARMORY

I have an hole armory of suche haburdashe in store;	175	Magnyfycence	1279

ARON

Lyke Aron and Ure,	250	Collyn Clout	152
And Aron sore he thret,	305	Why Come Ye	1068

ARONS

By Moyses and Arons rod,	63	Hauke	54
Vitulus in Oreb troubled Arons brayne;	232	Speke Parott	59

AROW

And with a venemous arow	104	Phy Sparrow	1292
And with a venemows arow	348	Garlande	1285

AROWE

With, 'Hey,' and with, 'Howe, /Syt we downe arowe	221	El Rummynge	290

ARRAY

So myche mokkyshe makyng of statutes of array -	245	Speke Parott	482

ARRE

Yet some folys say ye arre furnysshyd with knakkes,	239	Speke Parott	292
And howe your poemys arre barayne of polyshed eloquens,	240	Speke Parott	316

ARRECT

My supplycacyon to you I arrect,	313	Garlande	55

ARRECTINGE

Arrectinge unto your wyse examinacion	323	Garlande	410

ARRECTYD

Allectuary arrectyd to redres	44	Balettys3	8

ARRECTYNG

Devoutly arrectyng my prayer to Mynerve,	335	Garlande	824

ARRES

Yt bredth mothys in clothe of Arres.	131	Garnesche5	78

ARRYANS

And some be Arryans,	260	Collyn Clout	552

ARS

[Thy] myrrour may be the devyllys ars.	130	Garnesche5	18
Thy] 'They' †MS Harley 367			

ARSE

The devyll kysse his arse!	282	Why Come Ye	136
Of! by the harde arse!	288	Why Come Ye	386

ART

As thou art of mercy and pite the well,	34	Dol Dethe	198
Where thow art Lord and God omnipotent.	34	Dol Dethe	203
Thou slepyst to long, thou art begylde!	41	Balettys1	I
O Fortune unfrendly, Fortune unkynde thow art,	45	Balettys5	4
Loke on this tabull, /Whether thow art abull	68	Hauke	236
Thou art callyd of every man.	130	Garnesche5	24
Thow claimist the jentyll, thou art a curre;	131	Garnesche5	67
Me to beknave thow art to blame;	132	Garnesche5	107
I rayle to the soche as thow art.	133	Garnesche5	137
But whether art thou walkynge, in faythe unfaynyd?	161	Magnyfycence	762
By the masse, for the cowrte thou art a mete man;	161	Magnyfycence	764
Nay. Thou art a man good inough but for thy false hart.	162	Magnyfycence	769
Art thou so angry as thou semyst?	162	Magnyfycence	794
But what the devyll art thou	166	Magnyfycence	916
Thou art so feble-fantastycall,	170	Magnyfycence	1072
Nowe, in good faythe, thou art a fonde gest.	170	Magnyfycence	1096
By the masse, yet art thou more fole than I.	171	Magnyfycence	1111
Howe, where art thou? Come hether, Poverte.	195	Magnyfycence	1953
What begger art thou, that thus doth banne and wary?	203	Magnyfycence	2238
Thou art worth good and monny.'	220	El Rummynge	228
Thou art a graceles wyght	364	Albany	232

35

ARTE —AS   Page   Title   Line

ARTE
And shewed that in this arte I was not sure;   46   Bowge   19
   I] not in †Wynkyn de Worde 1499, 1510
'Than,' quod Hervy, 'why arte thou so dysmayde?'   54   Bowge   299
As thou arte, one that cam but yesterdaye,   55   Bowge   328
What arte thou? I sawe the nowe but late.'   56   Bowge   376
To us welcome thou arte, by Saynte Quyntyne!'   60   Bowge   511
But whoso understode /Of Medeas arte,   76   Phy Sparrow   202
So thou, foule cat that thou arte,   79   Phy Sparrow   302
I wote thou arte false ynoughe for one.   155   Magnyfycence   536
Tusshe! Fonnysshe Fansy, thou arte frantyke.   158   Magnyfycence   650
So thou arte personable to bere a pryncys baner.   161   Magnyfycence   767
What, Fansy! Arte thou here alone?   169   Magnyfycence 1044
What, horson! Arte thou suche a one?   174   Magnyfycence 1234
By Cockes woundes, a wonder felowe thou arte!   185   Magnyfycence 1619
By Cockes harte, thou arte a fyne mery knave.   191   Magnyfycence 1826
Torde! Thou arte good to be a man of warre.   202   Magnyfycence 2179
Ye, in faythe; or ellys thou arte to great a glotton.   204   Magnyfycence 2266
And so fer thou arte behynde of thy rent,   205   Magnyfycence 2294
That thou arte not worthy to loke God in the face.   205   Magnyfycence 2296
Thou arte not the fyrst hymselfe hath slayne.   206   Magnyfycence 2316
But of that supposicyon that callyd is arte,   236   Speke Parott   197
But the greatest parte /Is for they have but small arte   250   Collyn Clout   139
Of that heresy arte /Called Wytclyftista,   260   Collyn Clout   548
   Wytclyftista] 'Wicleuista' Marshe 1568
Some maysters of arte,   264   Collyn Clout   730
But a poore maister of arte!   292   Why Come Ye   512
Suche problemis to paynt it longyth to his arte.   347   Garlande   1246
ARTHUR
Arthur of Albyan, for all his brymme berde,   182   Magnyfycence 1502
ARTIKE
And of that pole artike whiche doth remayne   331   Garlande   695
ARTYCLES
Upon artycles judicyall, /To contende and to stryve   299   Why Come Ye   814
ARTYKE
Of our pole artyke, smylynge halfe in scorne   46   Bowge   5
ARTURIS
The Boke of the Rosiar; Prince Arturis Creacyoun;   345   Garlande   1178
ARTURYS
In Arturys auncyent actys nowhere ys provyd your pere;   123   Garnesche2   24
ARTURS
Or Arturs rounde table,   87   Phy Sparrow   634
AS
Fulfilled with honour, as all the world dothe ken,   30   Dol Dethe   30
   world] 'wold' Marshe 1568
He calde upon them, as menyall houshold men: 30   Dol Dethe   33
Demaundinge soche dutes as nedis most acord   31   Dol Dethe   66
Bluntly as bestis withe boste and with cry   31   Dol Dethe   83
As man that was innocent of trechery or trayne,   31   Dol Dethe   86
Valiant as Hector in every marciall nede,   33   Dol Dethe   138
As all his kuntrey kan testefy the same: 33   Dol Dethe   153
As perfightly as koude be thought or devysyd;   33   Dol Dethe   158
As perfightly as koude be thought or devysyd;   33   Dol Dethe   158
And as the lyonne whiche is of bestis kinge   33   Dol Dethe   167
In fee, as menyall men of his houshold,   34   Dol Dethe   185
Whom he as lorde worsheply manteynd,   34   Dol Dethe   186
As oft as thei call to ther remembrance   34   Dol Dethe   188
As oft as thei call to ther remembrance   34   Dol Dethe   188
To the pray we as Prince incomperable,   34   Dol Dethe   197
As thou art of mercy and pite the well,   34   Dol Dethe   198
As well it becomyth yow, a parysh towne clarke,   38   Coystrowne1   58
As well borne as ye full oft tyme beggys.   40   Coystrowne4   7
As well borne as ye full oft tyme beggys.   40   Coystrowne4   7
As proud a pohen as ye sprede,   41   Coystrowne4   13
As proud a pohen as ye sprede,   41   Coystrowne4   13
As to enbrace you in myne armys twayne.   44   Balettys3   42
As emperes the dyademe hath worne   46   Bowge   4
Under as coverte termes as coude be,   46   Bowge   10
Under as coverte termes as coude be,   46   Bowge   10
And to lye downe as soone as I m[e] dreste,   47   Bowge   33
   me] 'my' †Wynkyn de Worde 1499, 1510, Marshe 1568
And to lye downe as soone as I m[e] dreste,   47   Bowge   33
   me] 'my' †Wynkyn de Worde 1499, 1510, Marshe 1568
At Harwyche Porte, slumbrynge as I laye,   47   Bowge   34
But of eche thynge there as I toke hede,   47   Bowge   64
And as I stode redynge this verse myselfe allone,   48   Bowge   68
Levynge me stondynge as a mased man;   48   Bowge   83
Shyfte now therwith, let see, as ye can,   48   Bowge   99
For, as me thoughte, in our shyppe I dyde see   49   Bowge   132
As of your connynge, that is so excellent;   50   Bowge   149
Ye be an apte man, as ony can be founde   50   Bowge   155
And, as she wyll, so shall our grete shyppe sayle.   50   Bowge   172
But, as me thoughte, he ware on hym a cloke   51   Bowge   177
But as I stode musynge in my mynde,   52   Bowge   230
Harvy Ha[f]ter came lepynge, lyghte as lynde.   52   Bowge   231
   Hafter] 'Haster' †Wynkyn de Worde 1499, 1510, Marshe 1568
For and I studye sholde as ye doo nowe,   53   Bowge   242
For, as I trowe, I have sene you in dede   53   Bowge   248

	Page	Title	Line
As I be saved, it is a wonder case.	53	Bowge	273
For, as for me, I served here many a daye,	53	Bowge	274
Wyth that, as he departed soo fro me,	54	Bowge	281
Anone ther mette with him, as me thoughte,	54	Bowge	282
He frowned as he wolde swere by Cockes blode.	54	Bowge	287
His face was belymmed as byes had him stounge;	54	Bowge	289
That he loked pale as asshes to my syghte.	54	Bowge	293
'Now,' quod Dysdayne, 'as I shall saved be,	54	Bowge	297
As thou arte, one that cam but yesterdaye,	55	Bowge	328
'Quater treye dews' he clatered as he wente.	56	Bowge	347
To make the mery, as other felowes done?	57	Bowge	380
Had I as good an hors as she is a mare,	57	Bowge	407
Had I as good an hors as she is a mare,	57	Bowge	407
He ran as fast as ever that he myghte.	58	Bowge	415
He ran as fast as ever that he myghte.	58	Bowge	415
And as I stode and kyste asyde my syghte,	58	Bowge	418
kyste] 'caste' Marshe 1568			
That other loked as he wolde me have slayne.	58	Bowge	430
me have] 'have me' Wynkyn de Worde 1510			
And to mewarde as he gan for to coost,	58	Bowge	431
As I be saved at the dredefull daye,	58	Bowge	443
But as for that, connynge hath no foo	58	Bowge	447
I wolde eche man were as playne as I.	59	Bowge	463
I wolde eche man were as playne as I.	59	Bowge	463
Were I as you, I wolde ryde them full nere;	59	Bowge	472
Ye muste be ruled, as I shall tell you howe.	60	Bowge	493
Sodaynly, as he departed me fro,	60	Bowge	498
As I shall tell you, yf ye wyll harke agayne:	61	Bowge	520
And as he rounded thus in myne ere	61	Bowge	526
rounded] 'roynded' †Wynkyn de Worde 1499			
And as they came, the shypborde faste I hente,	61	Bowge	530
This worke devysed is /For suche as do amys,	61	Hauke	2
And specyally to controule /Such as have cure of soule,	62	Hauke	4
He shall be as now nameles,	62	Hauke	38
As preest unreverent,	63	Hauke	45
She loked as she had the frounce;	64	Hauke	85
frounce] 'fronnce' Kynge & Marche 1554, 'fronce' Day 1560			
Wherfore, as I be savyd, /Ye ar therfore beknavyd.	70	Hauke	309
As than befell to me.	72	Phy Sparrow	22
As though I had ben racked,	73	Phy Sparrow	47
Wanne, and blewe as lead:	73	Phy Sparrow	61
As famous poetes say;	74	Phy Sparrow	88
My sparow whyte as mylke,	77	Phy Sparrow	213
But as verely as ye be	78	Phy Sparrow	254
But as verely as ye be	78	Phy Sparrow	254
As prety and as prest	78	Phy Sparrow	264
As prety and as prest	78	Phy Sparrow	264
As my sparowe was.	78	Phy Sparrow	265
Had no such Phylyp as I,	78	Phy Sparrow	271
As well perceyve ye maye	81	Phy Sparrow	372
Horsly, as he had the mur;	82	Phy Sparrow	419
As patryarke or pope /In a blacke cope.	85	Phy Sparrow	528
As provost pryncypall, /To teach them theyr ordynall;	85	Phy Sparrow	554
As Palamon and Arcet,	87	Phy Sparrow	616
How she controlde /Her husbandes as she wolde,	87	Phy Sparrow	623
As Linus and Homerus, /Euphorion and Theocritus,	90	Phy Sparrow	761
For as I tofore have sayd,	90	Phy Sparrow	769
My style as yet direct	91	Phy Sparrow	772
So as it is enprowed,	91	Phy Sparrow	793
For as it is enployd,	91	Phy Sparrow	794
Yet as a woman may,	92	Phy Sparrow	820
As verely my hope is,	93	Phy Sparrow	874
And as that flode doth pas	93	Phy Sparrow	877
With vysage wan, /As swart as tan;	94	Phy Sparrow	911
swart] 'wart' †Kele 1545.2, Wyght 1553, Kitson 1560.6, 'swarte' Marshe 1568			
With vysage wan, /As swart as tan;	94	Phy Sparrow	911
swart] 'wart' †Kele 1545.2, Wyght 1553, Kitson 1560.6, 'swarte' Marshe 1568			
His bones crake, /Leane as a rake;	94	Phy Sparrow	913
His herte withall /Bytter as gall;	94	Phy Sparrow	917
And lede my fyst /As hym best lyst,	96	Phy Sparrow	973
As my maistres, /Of whom I thynk	96	Phy Sparrow	984
Fayre Lucres, as I wene,	97	Phy Sparrow	1018
As Nature cold devyse, /In most goodly wyse.	98	Phy Sparrow	1071
And handes soft as sylke,	99	Phy Sparrow	1119
So goodly as she dresses,	101	Phy Sparrow	1170
Than suche as have disdayned	106	Phy Sparrow	1374
That folowe as you may se.	106	Phy Sparrow	1379
you] 'ye' Wyght 1553, Kitson 1560.6, Marshe 1568			
As king moost sovereine	111	Lawde	52
Calliope, /As ye may se,	112	Calliope	2
As my soverayne /Moost of pleasure.	113	Calliope	23
And ye be desolate as Armeleche,	114	Scot Kynge	24
That is as trew /As blacke is blew /And grene is gray.	116	Ag Scottes	17
That is as trew /As blacke is blew /And grene is gray.	116	Ag Scottes	18
As it is enrolde, /Wrytten and tolde	116	Ag Scottes	39
Your beard so brym as bore at bay,	119	Ag Scottes	161

AS —AS

	Page	Title	Line
As it reprehendyng, /And venemously stingyng,	120	Ag Scottes2	9
Ye bere yow bolde as Barabas, or Syr Terry of Trac[e]. Trace] 'Tracy' †MS Harley 367	122	Garneschel	11
Ye fowle, fers and felle, as Syr Ferumbras the ffreke,	122	Garneschel	15
Thow ye be lusty as Syr Lybyus, launces to breke,	122	Garneschel	17
Nor blake Baltazar with hys basnet routh as a bere,	122	Garneschel	23
As ye ar brystlyd on the bake for alle your gay gere.	122	Garneschel	26
Crokyd as a camoke, and as a kowe calfles,	122	Garneschel	30
Crokyd as a camoke, and as a kowe calfles,	122	Garneschel	30
As a glede glowynge, your ien glyster as glasse,	122	Garneschel	37
As a glede glowynge, your ien glyster as glasse,	122	Garneschel	37
Howkyd as an hawkys beke, lyke Syr Topyas.	122	Garneschel	40
As wytles as a wylde goos, ye have but small remorrs	123	Garnesche2	18
As wytles as a wylde goos, ye have but small remorrs	123	Garnesche2	18
Cum Garnyche, cum Godfrey, with as many as ye may!	123	Garnesche2	32
Cum Garnyche, cum Godfrey, with as many as ye may!	123	Garnesche2	32
As hevery man wele seethe,	127	Garnesche3	125
As provithe well, in hys rethorikys olde,	130	Garnesche5	11
Lothsum as Lucifer lowest in helle.	130	Garnesche5	28
Me as hys master for to calle	132	Garnesche5	104
I rayle to the soche as thow art.	133	Garnesche5	137
As Persius and Juvynall,	133	Garnesche5	140
This Dundas, /This Scottishe as	135	Dundas	8
For, as I have rede in volumes olde,	137	Ven Tongues	5
To taunt theim like liddrons, lewde as thei bee.	138	Ven Tongues	29
A man may have welth, but not as he wolde,	141	Magnyfycence	14
Syr, as ye say. I have harde of your fame.	141	Magnyfycence	26
Your name is Lyberte, as I understande.	141	Magnyfycence	27
As at the fyrst oryggynall, by godly opynyon;	143	Magnyfycence	119
As I was wonte ever, at my fre wyll.	144	Magnyfycence	147
As your grace full nobly hath recountyd,	145	Magnyfycence	193
Of his rekenynge, as evydently we may	146	Magnyfycence	215
All that ye say is as trewe as the crede.	146	Magnyfycence	218
All that ye say is as trewe as the crede.	146	Magnyfycence	218
To shewe you playnly the trouth as I thynke.	147	Magnyfycence	253
As in that I wyll not be agaynst your pleasure.	148	Magnyfycence	276
But nowe, syr, as touchynge this letter –	149	Magnyfycence	331
At what place, nowe, as you gesse?	150	Magnyfycence	342
And made largesse, as I hyght,	150	Magnyfycence	364
By the way as I ryde and walke –	151	Magnyfycence	375
As men dare speke it hugger mugger:	151	Magnyfycence	387
And be as praty as she may,	153	Magnyfycence	464
And be as praty as she may,	153	Magnyfycence	464
And jet it joly as a jay.	153	Magnyfycence	465
As longe as I lyve, thou haste an heyre parent.	154	Magnyfycence	507
As longe as I lyve, thou haste an heyre parent.	154	Magnyfycence	507
For lyke as mustarde is sharpe of taste	155	Magnyfycence	552
As good to be occupyed as up and downe to trace	159	Magnyfycence	692
As good to be occupyed as up and downe to trace	159	Magnyfycence	692
And made as I had knowen nothynge of the case –	160	Magnyfycence	719
Amonge all suche persones as I well understonde	161	Magnyfycence	739
Art thou so angry as thou semyst?	162	Magnyfycence	794
As skante thou had no nede of me.	163	Magnyfycence	806
As well as me. I wolde, and I durste –	163	Magnyfycence	827
As well as me. I wolde, and I durste –	163	Magnyfycence	827
By Cryst, as mery as a Marche hare.	166	Magnyfycence	921
By Cryst, as mery as a Marche hare.	166	Magnyfycence	921
Tyll, as the devyll wolde, they fell a chydynge	166	Magnyfycence	940
As here after thou shalte knowe more.	167	Magnyfycence	953
So farly fayre as it lokys!	168	Magnyfycence	999
Her naylys sharpe as tenter-hokys!	168	Magnyfycence	1001
Somtyme I syt as I were solempe prowde;	168	Magnyfycence	1011
And as for me, I take but one folysshe way,	170	Magnyfycence	1076
In faythe, man, my brayne is as good as thyne.	170	Magnyfycence	1085
In faythe, man, my brayne is as good as thyne.	170	Magnyfycence	1085
Yes, yes! I am yet as full of game	172	Magnyfycence	1140
As ever I was, and as full of tryfyls –	172	Magnyfycence	1141
As ever I was, and as full of tryfyls –	172	Magnyfycence	1141
Mary, as for that, thou shalte sone here myne.	172	Magnyfycence	1153
Mary, as thou sayst, he gave me a blurre.	173	Magnyfycence	1179
Why, wenyst thou that I were as moche a fole as thou?	173	Magnyfycence	1188
Why, wenyst thou that I were as moche a fole as thou?	173	Magnyfycence	1188
As some be not ferre and yf it were well sought –	174	Magnyfycence	1241
For as sone as you come in Magnyfycence syght	176	Magnyfycence	1314
For as sone as you come in Magnyfycence syght	176	Magnyfycence	1314
'As oft as ye lyst, so honeste be savyd.	177	Magnyfycence	1348
'As oft as ye lyst, so honeste be savyd.	177	Magnyfycence	1348
As malypert tavernars that checke with theyr betters,	178	Magnyfycence	1362
Syr, as by my wyll, it shall be so no more.	178	Magnyfycence	1377
Nay. He shall be ruled even as I lyst.	179	Magnyfycence	1394
To rule as ye lyst, lo, here is Lyberte.	179	Magnyfycence	1413
Have welth at our gydynge to rule as we lyst?	179	Magnyfycence	1415
Syr, as I say, there was no faute in me.	180	Magnyfycence	1426
Syr, as me semeth, ye sholde be rulyd be me.	180	Magnyfycence	1433
And so as ye se it wyll be no better,	180	Magnyfycence	1438
Take it in worthe suche as ye fynde.	180	Magnyfycence	1439
For nowe, syrs, I am lyke as a prynce sholde be;	181	Magnyfycence	1457
Were never halfe so rychely as I am drest.	181	Magnyfycence	1483

	Page	Title	Line
I reyne in my robys, I rule as me lyst,	181	Magnyfycence	1485
Of all doughty I am doughtyest duke as I deme;	182	Magnyfycence	1499
I shall flappe hym as a fole to fall at my fete.	182	Magnyfycence	1507
As I be saved, with pleasure I am supprysyd	183	Magnyfycence	1529
As that I myght your noble grace content!	183	Magnyfycence	1534
Mary, your speche is as pleasant as though it were pend,	183	Magnyfycence	1538
Mary, your speche is as pleasant as though it were pend,	183	Magnyfycence	1538
So as ye be a prynce of great myght,	183	Magnyfycence	1545
The streynes of her vaynes as asure Inde blewe,	183	Magnyfycence	1553
As lyly whyte to loke upon her [l]eyre,	183	Magnyfycence	1555
leyre] 'heyre' †Rastell & Treveris C 1530, B			
Her eyen relucent as carbuncle so clere,	183	Magnyfycence	1556
Her lusty lyppes ruddy as the chery -	183	Magnyfycence	1558
And frowne it and face it, as thoughe ye wolde fyght;	185	Magnyfycence	1601
But do as ye lyst and take your owne way.	185	Magnyfycence	1604
As yf a man fortune to touche you on the quyke -	185	Magnyfycence	1611
I am forthwith as hole as a troute.	185	Magnyfycence	1624
I am forthwith as hole as a troute.	185	Magnyfycence	1624
My frende, as touchynge to this your mocyon,	186	Magnyfycence	1639
Do as moche as for myne owne father.	186	Magnyfycence	1642
Do as moche as for myne owne father.	186	Magnyfycence	1642
And surely, as I am nowe advysed,	186	Magnyfycence	1657
He telleth you trouth, syr, as I you ensure.	187	Magnyfycence	1679
Syr, God rewarde you as ye have deserved.	188	Magnyfycence	1701
But, and I were as ye, I wolde not set a gnat.	188	Magnyfycence	1704
Syr, as ye say. Nay, come on with me.	188	Magnyfycence	1707
Alas! My stomake fareth as it wolde cast.	188	Magnyfycence	1726
Not amonge noble men, as the worlde gothe.	189	Magnyfycence	1747
As in a tryfyll or in a thynge of nought,	189	Magnyfycence	1757
As gyvynge a thynge that ye never bought.	189	Magnyfycence	1758
Than is it done as it sholde be;	189	Magnyfycence	1764
To chose out ii., iii., of suche as you love best,	190	Magnyfycence	1769
And as for all other, let them trusse and packe;	190	Magnyfycence	1774
For as thou sayst, ryght so shall it be,	190	Magnyfycence	1783
For as thou wylte, so shall the game go;	190	Magnyfycence	1786
And suche as you wyll shall lacke no promocyon.	190	Magnyfycence	1789
And, syr as I was comynge to you hyder,	191	Magnyfycence	1813
Se, for God avowe, for colde as I chydder.	191	Magnyfycence	1817
Thy wordes hange togyder as fethers in the wynde.	191	Magnyfycence	1818
Nowe hath he ryght nought, naked as an asse.	193	Magnyfycence	1893
That hath deservyd it as well as he.	195	Magnyfycence	1952
That hath deservyd it as well as he.	195	Magnyfycence	1952
My colour is tawny, colouryd as a turffe;	195	Magnyfycence	1959
I am raggyd and rent, as ye may se;	195	Magnyfycence	1962
I lyve as me lyst, I lepe out at large;	199	Magnyfycence	2080
Thus totum in toto groweth up, as ye may se,	199	Magnyfycence	2099
For yf Measure had ruled Lyberte as he began,	200	Magnyfycence	2111
But nowe adayes as huksters they hucke and they stycke,	200	Magnyfycence	2121
As evydently in retchlesse youth ye may se	200	Magnyfycence	2133
Tyll, as ye se many tymes, they shame all theyr kynne.	201	Magnyfycence	2144
As for his plate of sylver and suche trasshe,	201	Magnyfycence	2164
As the worlde requyreth, but rather I am refused.	208	Magnyfycence	2412
Ye com hether as well as can be thought.	210	Magnyfycence	2459
Ye com hether as well as can be thought.	210	Magnyfycence	2459
Lyke as they were with buckels /Togyder made fast.	215	El Rummynge	46
With a payre of heles /As brode as two wheles.	216	El Rummynge	84
With a payre of heles /As brode as two wheles.	216	El Rummynge	84
She hobles as she gose /With her blanket hose	216	El Rummynge	85
she gose] 'a gose' Day 1560, Marshe 1568			
And, as men say, /She dwelt in Sothray,	216	El Rummynge	95
As wyse as an hare!	217	El Rummynge	112
As wyse as an hare!	217	El Rummynge	112
Some be flybytten, /Some skewed as a kytten;	218	El Rummynge	142
Clenly as yvell chevynge!	219	El Rummynge	186
For, as yll a patch as that,	219	El Rummynge	189
For, as yll a patch as that,	219	El Rummynge	189
Than swetely togither we ly, /As two pygges in a sty.'	220	El Rummynge	234
Than swetely] 'Thus swete' 1521 Fragment			
Be that as be maye;	221	El Rummynge	261
Anone cometh another, /As drye as the other,	221	El Rummynge	277
Anone cometh another, /As drye as the other,	221	El Rummynge	277
As cometh to her lot.	221	El Rummynge	282
But, Lorde, as she was testy, /Angry as a waspy!	222	El Rummynge	329
But, Lorde, as she was testy, /Angry as a waspy!	222	El Rummynge	330
I have as swete a breth	223	El Rummynge	345
As thou, wyth shamefull deth!'	223	El Rummynge	346
Snevelyng in her nose, /As though she had the pose.	223	El Rummynge	365
And, as she was drynkynge,	223	El Rummynge	370
As fayre and as whyte /As the fote of a kyte.	225	El Rummynge	424
As fayre and as whyte /As the fote of a kyte.	225	El Rummynge	424
As fayre and as whyte /As the fote of a kyte.	225	El Rummynge	425
And as she at her dyd pluck,	227	El Rummynge	504
And] not in Day 1560, Marshe 1568; pluck] 'pulck' †Lant 1545			
And began to paynty /As though she would faynty.	229	El Rummynge	585
She made it as koye /As a lege-de-moy;	229	El Rummynge	586
lege-de-moy] 'lege moy' †Lant 1545, Kynge & Marche 1554			
She made it as koye /As a lege-de-moy;	229	El Rummynge	587
lege-de-moy] 'lege moy' †Lant 1545, Kynge & Marche 1554			

AS —AS

	Page	Title	Line
As she was pevysshe nyse.	229	El Rummynge	589
My fethyrs fresshe as ys the emerawde grene,	231	Speke Parott	16
As [Per]cius, that poete, dothe reporte of me,	231	Speke Parott	27
Per]cius] 'precius' †MS Harley 2252			
Vis consilii expers, as techythe me Orace,	232	Speke Parott	40
'Peace, Parrot, ye prate as ye were ebrius!'	232	Speke Parott	68
As lyngua Latina, in scole matter occupyed;	234	Speke Parott	144
Confuse distrybutyve, as Parrot hath devysed,	236	Speke Parott	198
Shall lepe from this lyfe, as mery as we be.	236	Speke Parott	222
Shall lepe from this lyfe, as mery as we be.	236	Speke Parott	222
Alas, I am dysdayned, /And as a man halfe-maymed,	237	Speke Parott	253
That hang togedyr as fethyrs in the wynde;	239	Speke Parott	293
For Jerico and Jerssey shall mete togethyr as sone	239	Speke Parott	306
As he to exployte the man owte of the mone.	239	Speke Parott	307
As presydent and regente he rulythe every deall.	239	Speke Parott	312
Wherfor he may now come agayne as he wente,	240	Speke Parott	338
Non sine postica sanna, as I trowe,	240	Speke Parott	339
Or elles ye pynche curtesy, trulye as I trowe,	242	Speke Parott	395
Hys wolvys hede, wanne, bloo as lede, gapythe over the crowne:	244	Speke Parott	434
So manye bolde barons, there hertes as dull as lede;	245	Speke Parott	466
So manye bolde barons, there hertes as dull as lede;	245	Speke Parott	466
So royall a kyng, as reynythe uppon us all -	245	Speke Parott	468
To teche or to preche /As reason wyll reche?	247	Collyn Clout	14
For, as farre as I can se,	248	Collyn Clout	59
For, as farre as I can se,	248	Collyn Clout	59
As though they wolde flye /Aboute the sterry skye.	248	Collyn Clout	73
Aboute] 'Above' Kele 1545.1, Marshe 1568, MS Harley 2252			
And as for theyr connynge, /A glommynge and a mommynge,	248	Collyn Clout	82
And judge it as they wyll, /For other mens skyll,	249	Collyn Clout	98
Accomptynge them as fictyons.	249	Collyn Clout	114
As appereth by theyr werkes,	250	Collyn Clout	151
Take me as I entende,	251	Collyn Clout	185
I tell you as men say.	251	Collyn Clout	188
As at Sicientes,	252	Collyn Clout	222
As wyse as Jacke-a-Thrum,	253	Collyn Clout	282
Jacke] 'Tom' Kele 1545.1, Marshe 1568			
As wyse as Jacke-a-Thrum,	253	Collyn Clout	282
Jacke] 'Tom' Kele 1545.1, Marshe 1568			
As I go aboute,	253	Collyn Clout	286
And wandrynge as I walke,	254	Collyn Clout	287
Whyte as mares mylke;	254	Collyn Clout	315
mares] 'morowes' Kele 1545.1, Marshe 1568, 'marys' Harley 2252			
And say as untrewly /As the butterfly,	255	Collyn Clout	336
And say as untrewly /As the butterfly,	255	Collyn Clout	337
For elles, as I sayd before,	258	Collyn Clout	481
As ye may dayly se /Howe the lay fee	259	Collyn Clout	495
As cometh to theyr lottes,	260	Collyn Clout	565
As dayly men may se,	262	Collyn Clout	630
As of antyquyte /It was ratyfyed,	264	Collyn Clout	713
As] 'And' †Godfray 1531, Kele 1545.1, Marshe 1568			
As it is res certa	264	Collyn Clout	718
As I know aparte	264	Collyn Clout	729
Some lerned in other sawe, /As in divynyte,	265	Collyn Clout	733
So as they myght be /Compendyously conveyed,	265	Collyn Clout	767
Dronken as a mouse /At the ale house,	266	Collyn Clout	801
As wyse as Robyn Swyne,	266	Collyn Clout	806
As wyse as Robyn Swyne,	266	Collyn Clout	806
As wyse as Waltoms calfe,	266	Collyn Clout	809
As wyse as Waltoms calfe,	266	Collyn Clout	809
As limyters at large	267	Collyn Clout	834
As many a frere, God wote,	267	Collyn Clout	836
As now is made of late	269	Collyn Clout	914
As they were very sayntes.	269	Collyn Clout	921
And as farre as they dare set,	269	Collyn Clout	932
And as farre as they dare set,	269	Collyn Clout	932
Fresshe as flours in May;	270	Collyn Clout	943
As they suppose and gesse,	271	Collyn Clout	1010
As they may byde therby,	273	Collyn Clout	1062
To hynder no man /As nere as I can,	274	Collyn Clout	1110
To hynder no man /As nere as I can,	274	Collyn Clout	1110
Wherfore, as thynketh me,	274	Collyn Clout	1129
As noble [Isaias],	276	Collyn Clout	1206
Isaias] 'Ezechyes' †Godfray 1531, Kele 1545.1, Marshe 1568, 'I say was' MS Harley 2252			
As it is, it shall be styll,	277	Collyn Clout	1218
As they be sad sayne,	277	Collyn Clout	1230
sad] 'sayd' Kele 1545.1, Marshe 1568			
As well as other men.	277	Collyn Clout	1247
As well as other men.	277	Collyn Clout	1247
And beleve it as your crede.	278	Why Come Ye	2
And beleve it as your crede.	279	Why Come Ye	16
And beleve it as your crede.	279	Why Come Ye	28
As ryght as a rammes horne!	281	Why Come Ye	90
As ryght as a rammes horne!	281	Why Come Ye	90
As right as a cammocke croked!	281	Why Come Ye	117
As right as a cammocke croked!	281	Why Come Ye	117
Syt styll as they were dom.	283	Why Come Ye	199
They are fel as any fyre!	285	Why Come Ye	249

	Page	Title	Line
But as the worlde now gose,	286	Why Come Ye	285
But suche as he admyttes,	287	Why Come Ye	327
But, as some men sayne,	288	Why Come Ye	362
It shall be as he wyll.	289	Why Come Ye	419
As scrypture recordis /A cecitate cordis,	291	Why Come Ye	474
In writynge as we fynde	292	Why Come Ye	545
A kynge, as I have tolde,	293	Why Come Ye	563
And ruled as he wolde.	293	Why Come Ye	564
As herafter ben notyd:	293	Why Come Ye	573
For he wyll as sone smyght	293	Why Come Ye	582
His frende as his fo!	293	Why Come Ye	583
Counte himselfe as good as he;	294	Why Come Ye	590
Counte himselfe as good as he;	294	Why Come Ye	590
As ferce and as cruell	294	Why Come Ye	593
As ferce and as cruell	294	Why Come Ye	593
As the fynd of hell!	294	Why Come Ye	594
To speke with you as yet.'	295	Why Come Ye	632
As it were Jack Napis!	295	Why Come Ye	654
As wychecraft or charmyng;	295	Why Come Ye	665
As by myne auctor tried it was.	296	Why Come Ye	707
And to rule as hym lyst;	297	Why Come Ye	734
As myne auctor sayth.	297	Why Come Ye	745
As well calodemonyall /As to cacademonyall,	299	Why Come Ye	809
As well calodemonyall /As to cacademonyall,	299	Why Come Ye	810
Were gone as well as he!	300	Why Come Ye	836
Were gone as well as he!	300	Why Come Ye	836
And such as sell trotters, /Pytchars, potshordis. potshordis] 'pouchers' MS Rawlinson C. 813	302	Why Come Ye	911
And it be as I wene.	304	Why Come Ye	1007
But as touchynge dystrectyon, /With sober dyrectyon dystrectyon] 'dyscrecyon' Marshe 1568, MS Rawlinson C. 813	304	Why Come Ye	1008
For as for wytte,	304	Why Come Ye	1016
And as many as him lykys, him] 'he' MS Rawlinson C. 813	306	Why Come Ye	1080
And as many as him lykys, him] 'he' MS Rawlinson C. 813	306	Why Come Ye	1080
As playnly it dothe appere,	307	Why Come Ye	1117
As legatus a latere.'	308	Why Come Ye	1152
For as far as they can spy they] 'the' †Kele 1545.3	308	Why Come Ye	1172
For as far as they can spy they] 'the' †Kele 1545.3	308	Why Come Ye	1172
As Juvinall dothe recorde,	310	Why Come Ye2	11
as more at large it doth apere in the proces folowynge.	312	Garlande	I
How all thynge passyth as doth the somer flower,	312	Garlande	9
But sodeynly at ones, as I me advysed,	313	Garlande	36
As one in a trans or in an extasy,	313	Garlande	37
As goddesse inmortall she dyd represente;	313	Garlande	47
As I harde say, Dame Pallas was her name,	313	Garlande	48
And, as we dare, we fynde in hym grete lake: grete] 'a' Marshe 1568	314	Garlande	70
'The sum of your purpose, as we ar advysid,	314	Garlande	78
As sumtyme he must vyces remorde,	314	Garlande	86
And was Eschines rebukid as ye say?	316	Garlande	135
Yet shall I answere your grace as in this,	316	Garlande	144
As towchyng that Eschines is remembred,	316	Garlande	148
As Jerome, in his preamble Frater Ambrosius,	316	Garlande	162
Then he that doth worste is as good as the best.	317	Garlande	175
Then he that doth worste is as good as the best.	317	Garlande	175
As wele foly as wysdome oft ye do avaunce, ye do] 'tyme ye' MS Cotton Vitellius E.x	317	Garlande	180
As wele foly as wysdome oft ye do avaunce, ye do] 'tyme ye' MS Cotton Vitellius E.x	317	Garlande	180
And suche of my servauntes as I have promotyd,	318	Garlande	202
May be brought forth, such as can be founde,	318	Garlande	216
As he that aquentyth hym with ydilnes.	318	Garlande	228
As people halfe pevysshe, or men that were masyd.	319	Garlande	266
Anone all was whyste, as it were for the nonys,	319	Garlande	267
With heris encrisped yalowe as the golde, encrisped] 'enscrisped' †Fakes 1523	320	Garlande	289
He sange now, the tre as he did take	320	Garlande	300
And as I thus sadly amonge them avysid	323	Garlande	386
As I ymagenyd, repayrid unto me,	323	Garlande	392
Togeder in armes, as brethern, enbrasid;	323	Garlande	393
In maner and forme as ye shall after here.	323	Garlande	399
Under the forme as I sayd tofore, tofore] 'before' Marshe 1568	324	Garlande	443
Encrownyd as empresse of all this wordly fate, wordly] 'worldly' Marshe 1568	325	Garlande	486
With, 'I as good as thou, ifayth, and no better.'	326	Garlande	509
With, 'I as good as thou, ifayth, and no better.'	326	Garlande	509
'Lyke as the larke, upon the somers day,	327	Garlande	533
Welcome to me as hertely as herte can thynke!	327	Garlande	547
Welcome to me as hertely as herte can thynke!	327	Garlande	547
With suche communycacyon as came to our mynde;	328	Garlande	562
Some Romaine letters, as I understode;	328	Garlande	583
As quikly towchyd as it were flesshe and bones,	328	Garlande	592
As quikly towchyd as it were flesshe and bones,	328	Garlande	592

ASAYDE —ASCRY

	Page	Title	Line
As gastly that glaris, as grimly that gronis, ...	328	Garlande	593
As gastly that glaris, as grimly that gronis, ...	328	Garlande	593
As fersly frownynge as he had ben fyghtyng, ...	328	Garlande	594
As fersly frownynge as he had ben fyghtyng, ...	328	Garlande	594
Pope holy ypocrytis, as they were golde and hole, ...	329	Garlande	612
Masid as a Marche hare, he ran lyke a scut.	329	Garlande	632
Sometyme, as it semyth, when the mone light	330	Garlande	644
As dasid doterdis that dreme in their dumpis.'	332	Garlande	734
With fingers smale, and handis whyte as mylk;	334	Garlande	797
whyte] 'as white' Marshe 1568			
As a mariner that amasid is in a stormy rage, ...	335	Garlande	829
amasid] 'masid' MS Cotton Vitellius E.x			
In humble wyse as lowly as I may, ...	335	Garlande	837
In humble wyse as lowly as I may, ...	335	Garlande	837
As dame Thamarys, whiche toke the kyng of Perce, ...	336	Garlande	857
Cirus by name, as wrytith the story;	336	Garlande	858
Whome dame Nature, as wele I may reporte, ...	336	Garlande	867
But, as I sayd, your florisshinge tender age	337	Garlande	876
Ye be, as I devyne, ...	338	Garlande	911
As Machareus /Fayre Canace, ...	338	Garlande	933
Mirry Margaret, /As mydsomer flowre, ...	340	Garlande	1005
Jentill as fawcoun /Or hawke of the towre;	340	Garlande	1006
Of mirry Margarete, /As mydsomer flowre, ...	341	Garlande	1020
Jentyll as fawcoun /Or hawke of the towre, ...	341	Garlande	1021
As pacient and as styll, ...	341	Garlande	1023
As pacient and as styll, ...	341	Garlande	1023
And as full of good wyll, /As fayre Isaphill;	341	Garlande	1024
fayre] 'the fayre' MS Cotton Vitellius E.x			
And as full of good wyll, /As fayre Isaphill;	341	Garlande	1025
fayre] 'the fayre' MS Cotton Vitellius E.x			
As mirry Margarete, /This midsomer flowre, ...	341	Garlande	1034
This] 'The' MS Cotton Vitellius E.x			
Jentyll as fawcoun /Or hawke of the towre.	341	Garlande	1036
Was never halfe so fayre, as I wene, ...	342	Garlande	1077
Towarde the dore, as he were comyng oute, ...	343	Garlande	1095
Forthwith upon this, as it were in a thought, ...	343	Garlande	1100
And for as moche as, by the hy pretence	344	Garlande	1124
And for as moche as, by the hy pretence	344	Garlande	1124
in as moche as it were to longe a proces	345	Garlande	R
in as moche as it were to longe a proces	345	Garlande	R
Ladyes and gentylwomen suche as deservyd, ...	346	Garlande	1189
And suche as be counterfettis they be reservyd;	346	Garlande	1190
And after conveyauns as the world goos, ...	347	Garlande	1238
As so forthe per cetera;	349	Garlande	1314
That folowe as ye may se:	350	Garlande	1372
How her ble was bryght as blossom on the spray, ...	351	Garlande	1412
But yet for all that, be as be may, ...	352	Garlande	1415
As Skelton rehersith, with wordes few and playne, ...	353	Garlande	1466
Whiche redde on still, as it cam to her syght, ...	354	Garlande	1493
As hevy as the lede, ...	358	Garlande2	3
As hevy as the lede, ...	358	Garlande2	3
With mony, as men sayne, ...	358	Garlande2	14
Whiche be as trewe /As the gospell:	359	Albany	4
Whiche be as trewe /As the gospell:	359	Albany	5
As an hoost royall	360	Albany	61
Or els wyll I /Evydently /Shewe as it is:	361	Albany	86
To envade Englande, /As I understande.	361	Albany	106
Caried in a cage, /As it were a cotage, ...	365	Albany	256
As it were a gote /In a shepe cote, ...	365	Albany	265
And lurke there lyke an as	366	Albany	289
As though ye wolde parbrake /Your avauns to make, ...	367	Albany	322
So noble a prince as he /In all actyvite	368	Albany	395
Lyke cowardes as ye be	370	Albany	460
Of suche as be his foos	370	Albany	469
As all men can reporte.	370	Albany	474
as touchyng the tetrycall theologisacion of these demy divines,	374	Replycacion	I
As clerkes unassured, /With ignorance obscured:	377	Replycacion	93
Ye argued argumentes, /As it were upon the elenkes, ...	377	Replycacion	126
But, as the man sayes, ...	378	Replycacion	151
And be nowe as yll, ...	379	Replycacion	178
As ye were before.	379	Replycacion	180
As people halfe amased, ...	379	Replycacion	194
And in maner as abjecte, /For evermore suspecte, ...	380	Replycacion	240
In that faculte which shyned as Phebus bright;	383	Replycacion	333
As Grekes do it call, ...	384	Replycacion	369

ASAYDE

That never yet asayde /Of Elyconys well, ...	87	Phy Sparrow	609
And who can worke beste now shall be asayde;	334	Garlande	775

ASCENDENT

In Ariete /Ascendent a degre.	258	Collyn Clout	470
a degre] 'ad dextram' MS Lansdowne 762, 'a dextre' MS Harley 2252			

ASCENDYNGE

Scorpione ascendynge degrees twyse nyne;	312	Garlande	7

ASCRY

The Philistinis shuld hym ascry, ...	105	Phy Sparrow	1358
But now must I /Your Duke ascry /Of Albany	360	Albany	73

ASCRYBED — ASPYID

Entry	Page	Title	Line
ASCRYBED			
To whom be the laude ascrybed	93	Phy Sparrow	871
ASCRYE			
And shamfully you ascrye,	255	Collyn Clout	335
ASE			
With, 'trey duse ase', /And, 'ase in the face'.	301	Why Come Ye	879
ASHAMED			
I was ashamed so to here hym prate.	56	Bowge	373
Ye ought to be ashamed	274	Collyn Clout	1113
And yet he is ashamed	305	Why Come Ye	1052
ASHRIGE			
Of the Bonehoms of Ashrige besyde Barkamstede,	353	Garlande	1461
A pleasaunter place than Ashrige is, harde were to fynde,	353	Garlande	1465
were] 'where' †Fakes 1523			
ASYDE			
Gaspyng asyde, /Nakyd of hyde,	39	Coystrowne3	16
And as I stode and kyste asyde my syghte,	58	Bowge	418
kyste] 'caste' Marshe 1568			
Where lyberte is absent, set welthe asyde.	142	Magnyfycence	80
Convey it be crafte, lyft and lay asyde.	177	Magnyfycence	1357
Faythe and good hope I make asyde to stonde.	205	Magnyfycence	2288
Sodenly cherysshyd, and sodenly cast asyde;	212	Magnyfycence	2532
Set Sophia asyde, for every Jack Raker	235	Speke Parott	160
Sette asyde all sophysms, and speke now trew and playne.	244	Speke Parott	448
ASK			
To ask wher he fyndyth among hys monacordys	37	Coystrowne1	20
Ask all your neybours whether that I ly.	43	Balettys2	35
ASKE			
That vengeaunce I aske and crye,	78	Phy Sparrow	273
I can not tell you. Why aske you me?	157	Magnyfycence	628
Aske these two that there dothe dwell.	158	Magnyfycence	629
Though I aske mercy I must nedys be refusyd.	205	Magnyfycence	2299
I aske God mercy of my neglyge[sse],	207	Magnyfycence	2380
neglygesse] 'neglygence' †Rastell & Treveris C 1530, B			
Some men myght aske a question,	309	Why Come Ye	1202
aske] 'make' MS Rawlinson C. 813			
Graunt my petycyon, I aske you but ryght.'	318	Garlande	231
ASKED			
Of them demaunded and asked by the kynge;	31	Dol Dethe	79
She asked yf ever I dranke of saucys cuppe.	48	Bowge	73
Than asked she me, 'Syr, so God the spede,	48	Bowge	76
And we asked favoure, and favour she us gave.	49	Bowge	126
They asked never for mete	222	El Rummynge	304
ASKETH			
Of Bowge of Court she asketh what we wold have,	49	Bowge	125
To make suche trifels it asketh sum konnyng,	347	Garlande	1235
ASKYD			
And from whens come ye, and it myght be askyd?	141	Magnyfycence	29
ASKYNGE			
And graunte hym at his askynge	272	Collyn Clout	1027
ASKYTH			
It askyth lesure with good advert[ence].	141	Magnyfycence	42
advertence] 'advertysment' †Rastell & Treveris C 1530, B			
ASKRY			
But enforsed am I /Openly to askry	94	Phy Sparrow	903
In thys debate I the askry.	131	Garnesche5	66
The Phillistinis shulde hym askry,	350	Garlande	1351
ASKRYE			
Hath made askrye /And outcry	301	Why Come Ye	870
outcry] 'doute cry' MS Rawlinson C. 813			
ASLEPE			
Whan I was aslepe,	75	Phy Sparrow	162
ASMODEUS			
And Asmodeus of hell	284	Why Come Ye	209
ASONDER			
Thow kit asonder his perfight vitall threde.	32	Dol Dethe	126
Knowe ye not salte and suger asonder?	113	Scot Kynge	6
Know ye not suger and salt asonder?	118	Ag Scottes	96
That we thre galauntes sholde be longe asonder.	154	Magnyfycence	511
A hundred myle asonder	285	Why Come Ye	259
For he wyll tere it asonder!	296	Why Come Ye	671
The devyll of hell and he be seldome asonder.'	333	Garlande	765
ASONDRE			
Myght byte asondre thy throte!	79	Phy Sparrow	306
Byte asondre thy backe bone!	79	Phy Sparrow	312
ASPECTE			
Of Mercury undyr the trynall aspecte,	240	Speke Parott	325
ASPY			
A man kowd not aspy	111	Lawde	19
And where the two Trions a man shold aspy,	331	Garlande	699
Trions] 'Troons' †Fakes 1523			
ASPYED			
And your skrybe I have aspyed,	124	Garnesche3	3
What! I have aspyed ye are a carles page.	148	Magnyfycence	288
Without me be full ofte aspyed.	177	Magnyfycence	1355
It is sone aspyed where the thorne prikkith.	352	Garlande	1437
ASPYID			
That ever more after by it they were aspyid;	329	Garlande	627

ASSAY —ASTATE

	Page	Title	Line
ASSAY			
My wyt I shall assay	92	Phy Sparrow	821
To counterfet she wyll assay	153	Magnyfycence	462
And assay to crepe /Within the noble walles	249	Collyn Clout	125
ASSAYDE			
Yet at a brayde /He hath well assayde	84	Phy Sparrow	486
ASSAYE			
Or 'Shall I sayle wyth you' a felashyp assaye?	53	Bowge	254
Of thyne ale let us assaye,	224	El Rummynge	397
ASSAYES			
Thus am I occupyed at all assayes.	152	Magnyfycence	428
For there be horys there at all assayes.	204	Magnyfycence	2275
ASSAYLE			
And manly manyfolde, /Their enemyes to assayle	364	Albany	204
ASSAWTE			
Forthwith, he made on me a prowde assawte,	55	Bowge	316
ASSE			
Agayn Dundas, /That Scottishe asse.	135	Dundas	24
Dundas, /That dronke asse,	136	Dundas	55
A very fon, /A very asse /Wyll take upon /To compasse	164	Magnyfycence	864
They drove me to lernynge lyke a dull asse.	178	Magnyfycence	1386
Nowe hath he ryght nought, naked as an asse.	193	Magnyfycence	1893
ASSEMBLED			
Of a thousande poetes assembled togeder.	320	Garlande	286
ASSENCE			
And of the prescyence /Of divyne assence assence] 'essence' Marshe 1568	259	Collyn Clout	525
ASSENT			
Without the assent /Of your presydent;	272	Collyn Clout	1034
Of Fames court, by all our holl assent	324	Garlande	433
ASSENTE			
Of false collusyon confetryd by assente,	61	Bowge	527
ASSHES			
That he loked pale as asshes to my syghte.	54	Bowge	293
ASSIGNEMENT			
Theis people by me have none assignement,	317	Garlande	195
ASSIST			
Me to supporte, to helpe, and to assist,	335	Garlande	827
ASSYGNED			
Where as ye have, syr, to me them assygned,	145	Magnyfycence	177
Good Hope, your potecary, assygned am I,	207	Magnyfycence	2351
ASSYNGNED			
Nowe that ye have me chefe ruler assyngned,	146	Magnyfycence	202
ASSYNYD			
Tyburne thou me assynyd	128	Garnesche3	174
ASSYST			
Redy to assyst you in every tyme of nede;	30	Dol Dethe	58
God the assyst unto thyne heritage,	33	Dol Dethe	164
To assyst his noble grace,	371	Albany	491
ASSYSTE			
Cryst you assyste in your altrycacyon!	142	Magnyfycence	81
ASSYSTENCE			
Grace of assystence his measure to declare;	207	Magnyfycence	2373
ASSOYLE			
To shryve, assoyle, and to reles	268	Collyn Clout	875
ASSUERUS			
And of Mardocheus, /And of great Assuerus,	90	Phy Sparrow	740
ASSUR			
The lynage of Lot toke supporte of Assur;	232	Speke Parott	66
ASSURAUNCE			
And in your delynge so good assuraunce,	183	Magnyfycence	1523
Faythfull assuraunce with good peradvertaunce. Faythfull] 'Faythfully' †Rastell & Treveris C 1530, B	210	Magnyfycence	2472
Affyaunsynge her myne hole assuraunce	327	Garlande	555
ASSURDED			
Then he assurded into his exclamacyon his] 'this' Marshe 1568	320	Garlande	302
ASSURE			
You I assure, absens is my fo,	44	Balettys3	36
To assure you of my noble porte and fame,	145	Magnyfycence	163
No, that I assure you; loke who was the best:	181	Magnyfycence	1484
Howe it be, I wolde be ryght gladde, I you assure,	183	Magnyfycence	1527
Questyonlesse he doth me assure	208	Magnyfycence	2395
That can hymselfe assure	271	Collyn Clout	1002
For, but if your bounte did me assure,	316	Garlande	146
I you assure, /Ful wel I know	338	Garlande	926
ASSURED			
Than I assured hym my fydelyte,	52	Bowge	218
Ye may be assured /Your falshod discured	362	Albany	127
For be ye wele assured,	385	Replycacion	406
ASSURID			
Be well assurid I shall aqyute your hyre,	327	Garlande	550
That of your bounte so well have me assurid,	332	Garlande	729
ASSWAGE			
And pray to God your sorowes to asswage.	196	Magnyfycence	1989
ASTATE			
Of famous princis and lordis of astate,	29	Dol Dethe	16
Truly reportinge his right noble astate,	33	Dol Dethe	146

	Page	Title	Line
ASTATIS —AT			
Grow and encrese, remembre thyn astate!	33	Dol Dethe	163
Theyr astate to mayntayne;	286	Why Come Ye	311
Make him a great astate,	293	Why Come Ye	587
Made up a great astate	297	Why Come Ye	723
A lytell cryme in a great astate,	310	Why Come Ye2	13
To whos astate all noblenes most leven,	313	Garlande	54
leven] 'lene' †Fakes 1523, MS Cotton Vitellius E.x			
Under a gloryous cloth of astate,	325	Garlande	484
I her demaunded of them and ther astate.	329	Garlande	606
She brought me to a goodly chaumber of astate,	333	Garlande	768
to] 'into' MS Cotton Vitellius E.x			
The passynge bounte of your noble astate,	336	Garlande	841
Whos passynge bounte, and ryght noble astate,	336	Garlande	848
Whos passynge bounte, and ryght noble astate,	336	Garlande	855
Whos passyng bounte, and ryght noble astate,	336	Garlande	862
In her astate there sat the noble Quene	343	Garlande	1114
'Ryght high and myghty princes of astate,	344	Garlande	1128
In primis the Boke of Honorous Astate;	345	Garlande	1172
All the demenour of princely astate,	347	Garlande	1231
With ladyes of astate?	348	Garlande	1282
To rayle on his astate /With wordes inordinate?	370	Albany	461
ASTATIS			
To whome grete astatis obeyde and lowttede,	30	Dol Dethe	45
ASTONYED			
Thenne I, astonyed of that sodeyne fraye,	60	Bowge	501
ASTRAY			
For tunges untayde be renning astray.	138	Ven Tongues	37
Cyrcumspeccyon inhateth all rennynge astray,	209	Magnyfycence	2430
ASTREA			
Astrea, justice hight,	110	Lawde	15
ASTROLOBY			
In the volvell, in the quadrant and in the astroloby,	234	Speke Parott	135
ASTROLOGY			
By the astrology /That he hath naturally	84	Phy Sparrow	497
Som trete of theyr tirykis, som of astrology,	234	Speke Parott	137
Of Athlas astrology, and many noble thyngis,	331	Garlande	690
ASTROLOGYS			
It is good for astrologys,	258	Collyn Clout	466
ASTRONOMER			
By Albumazer /The astronomer,	84	Phy Sparrow	502
ASTRONOMY			
Nor by Ptholomy, /Prince of astronomy,	84	Phy Sparrow	504
Nor of good pollycy, /Nor of astronomy;	292	Why Come Ye	519
ASURE			
The streynes of her vaynes as asure Inde blewe,	183	Magnyfycence	1553
ASWAGE			
For to aswage your pride.	124	Garnesche3	23
For her vysage /It woldt aswage /A mannes courage.	214	El Rummynge	10
Dothe aswage and refrayne,	279	Why Come Ye	37
Of that the tempestous wynde wyll aswage	335	Garlande	831
tempestous] 'tempeous' †Fakes 1523, 'tempestuows' MS Cotton Vitellius E.x			
AT			
At his commaundement whiche had both day and night	30	Dol Dethe	31
Knyghtis and squyers, at every season when	30	Dol Dethe	32
Unkindly thei slew hym that help them oft at nede.	30	Dol Dethe	47
help] 'holp' Marshe 1568			
In a dysh dare he rush at the rypest;	37	Coystrowne1	46
To drynk at a draught a larg and a long.	38	Coystrowne1	49
For lordes and ladyes lerne at his scole;	38	Coystrowne1	52
At me, that medeled nothyng with youre wark.	38	Coystrowne1	61
Wryten at Croydon by Crowland in the Clay,	38	Coystrowne1	69
Ye rayll at ryot, recheles.	40	Coystrowne4	4
That wonnes at the Key in Temmys Strete.	41	Coystrowne4	30
Spur up at the hynder gyrth with, 'Gup, morell, gup!'	43	Balettys2	17
It can be no counsell that is cryed at the cros.	43	Balettys2	36
Skelton laureat, at the instance of a nobyll lady.	46	Balettys5	E
At our foly and our unstedfastnesse;	46	Bowge	6
Soo sore enwered that I was, at the laste,	47	Bowge	31
At Harwyche Porte, slumbrynge as I laye,	47	Bowge	34
She kyste an anker, and there she laye at rode,	47	Bowge	39
kyste] 'keste' Wynkyn de Worde 1510, 'kast' Marshe 1568			
Suspycyon, me thoughte, mette hym a brayde,	51	Bowge	181
He loked hawte; he sette eche man at noughte;	54	Bowge	284
hawte] 'hawtie' Marshe 1568			
Let us, therfore, shortely at a worde	54	Bowge	307
Wyth that came Ryotte, russhynge all at ones,	56	Bowge	344
'Nowe have at all, by Saynte Thomas of Kente!'	56	Bowge	348
Yet at the knee they were broken, I wene.	56	Bowge	357
How ofte he knocked at her klycked gate.	56	Bowge	371
And lete us laugh a placke or tweyne at nale.	57	Bowge	387
placke] 'plucke' Marshe 1568			
Now have at all that lyeth upon the burde.	57	Bowge	391
Have at the hasarde or at the dosen browne,	57	Bowge	393
Have at the hasarde or at the dosen browne,	57	Bowge	393
Whan that he was even at me almoost,	58	Bowge	432
As I be saved at the dredefull daye,	58	Bowge	443
Sterte all at ones, I lyked no thynge his playe,	60	Bowge	502

AT — AT

	Page	Title	Line
Into my chalys at mas,	66	Hauke	184
That was late slayn at Carowe	72	Phy Sparrow	8
And lerne to wepe at me!	73	Phy Sparrow	57
A fly, or a gnat, /He wolde flye at that;	75	Phy Sparrow	131
Alas, I was evyll at ease!	75	Phy Sparrow	144
Dame Sulpicia at Rome,	75	Phy Sparrow	148
That I brought up at Carowe.	78	Phy Sparrow	281
And go in at my spayre, go in] 'often' Kitson 1560.6	80	Phy Sparrow	345
And crepe in at my gore crepe] 'gape' Kitson 1560.6	80	Phy Sparrow	346
Shall rede the gospell at masse;	82	Phy Sparrow	423
Shall watche at this wake;	82	Phy Sparrow	437
To poore folke at large,	83	Phy Sparrow	456
At this Placebo	83	Phy Sparrow	466
Yet at a brayde /He hath well assayde	84	Phy Sparrow	485
Their husbandes to set at nought:	87	Phy Sparrow	627
At those dayes moch commended:	91	Phy Sparrow	796
To prayse her at the full;	102	Phy Sparrow	1222
By marcyall strength /He wan at length;	104	Phy Sparrow	1306
To lettred men at large:	105	Phy Sparrow	1361
And pray shall, /At this trentall	108	Epitaphe1	70
By your wanton wyll, syr, at a worde,	114	Scot Kynge	48
At hym example ye wolde none take;	115	Scot Kynge	60
And wyll not know /Theyr overthrow /At Branxton More?	115	Ag Scottes	11
At Floddon hyllys, /Our bowys, our byllys	116	Ag Scottes	25
At Branxton More and Floddon hylles,	119	Ag Scottes	131
Ye wantyd wyt, sir, at a worde,	119	Ag Scottes	147
Your beard so brym as bore at bay,	119	Ag Scottes	161
At Englysh bowes have fetched their banes.	120	Ag Scottes	173
He skantly loveth our kyng, /That grudgeth at this thing:	121	Ag Scottes2	36
At Orwelle hyr havyn your anggre was laules.	122	Garnesche1	33
Baile, baile at yow bothe, frantyke folys! Follow on the chase!	123	Garnesche2	31
At Gynys when ye ware /But a slendyr spere,	125	Garnesche3	40
At bothe endes ye stynke;	126	Garnesche3	81
At Oxforth, the universyte,	131	Garnesche5	81
For thou beggest at every mannes dur.	135	Dundas	26
What tidings at Tot[nam], what newis in Wales, Totnam] 'Totman' Marshe 1568	139	Ven Tongues	64
A fole is he with welth that fallyth at debate.	140	Magnyfycence	5
For lyberte at large is lothe to be stoppyd,	141	Magnyfycence	46
Lyberte at large wyll oft wax reklesse.	142	Magnyfycence	54
Wherfore at lyberte	142	Magnyfycence	65
To sporte at your pleasure, to ryn, and to ryde?	142	Magnyfycence	79
As at the fyrst orygynall, by godly opynyon;	143	Magnyfycence	119
As I was wonte ever, at my fre wyll.	144	Magnyfycence	147
Me semeth Magnyfycence is comynge here at hande.	145	Magnyfycence	162
S[e] at our eye the worlde day by day. Se] 'so' †Rastell & Treveris C 1530, B	146	Magnyfycence	216
That all men laugh at lyberte to scorne.	146	Magnyfycence	222
A, ye make me laughe at your inconstaunce.	147	Magnyfycence	236
It shalbe done at your commaundement.	147	Magnyfycence	239
Have ye not welthe here at your wyll?	148	Magnyfycence	284
Ye wante but a wylde flyeng bolte to shote at the buttes.	148	Magnyfycence	294
I shall loke in it at leasure better;	149	Magnyfycence	332
At what place, nowe, as you gesse?	150	Magnyfycence	342
By my trouthe, syr, at Pountesse.	150	Magnyfycence	343
Howe so? By God, at the see syde,	150	Magnyfycence	346
What! Sholde yu pynche at a pecke of [gr]otes grotes] 'otes' †Rastell & Treveris C 1530, B	151	Magnyfycence	384
Ye wolde sone pynche at a pecke of otes. otes] 'grotes' †Rastell & Treveris C 1530, B	151	Magnyfycence	385
Thus at the laste I brynge hym ryght	152	Magnyfycence	422
Thus am I occupyed at all assayes.	152	Magnyfycence	428
Ryches rydeth out, at home is poverte.	153	Magnyfycence	474
At his cloked counterfetynge dogges dothe barke.	153	Magnyfycence	482
Hem! That lyke I nothynge at all.	158	Magnyfycence	664
I laughe at all shrewdenes, and lye at lyberte.	160	Magnyfycence	735
I laughe at all shrewdenes, and lye at lyberte.	160	Magnyfycence	735
Nay, come at ones, for the armes of the dyce.	162	Magnyfycence	781
Yes, yes. He fell with me also at debate.	166	Magnyfycence	944
Somtyme I laughe at waggynge of a straw,	168	Magnyfycence	1014
Ye. But he wyll in at every mannes dore.	171	Magnyfycence	1130
Can he play well at the hoddypeke?	172	Magnyfycence	1161
That I laugh at for my dysporte.	174	Magnyfycence	1239
That every man lawghyth at his foly.	175	Magnyfycence	1251
So helpe me God, man, ever at the length	175	Magnyfycence	1258
Ryot at lyberte russheth it out styll.	176	Magnyfycence	1317
Trymme at her tayle or a man can turne a socke.	177	Magnyfycence	1346
Ye shall be occupyed, Welthe, at my wyll.	178	Magnyfycence	1380
At ones, and let hym not tary all day.	179	Magnyfycence	1400
Ye have eten sauce I trowe, at the Taylers Hall.	179	Magnyfycence	1404
Syr, I am here at your pleasure.	179	Magnyfycence	1409
Have welth at our gydynge to rule as we lyst?	179	Magnyfycence	1415
I have welth at wyll, largesse and lyberte.	181	Magnyfycence	1458
I shall flappe hym as a fole to fall at my fete.	182	Magnyfycence	1507
At your commaundement, syr, wyth all dew reverence.	182	Magnyfycence	1515
But yf it lyke your grace more at large	185	Magnyfycence	1589

	Page	Title	Line
Suche lustes at large may not be lefte behynde.	186	Magnyfycence	1628
Please it your grace at the contemplacyon	186	Magnyfycence	1633
Of our blessyd Lorde, syr, at the reverence –	186	Magnyfycence	1636
Howe be it, at your instaunce I wyll the rather	186	Magnyfycence	1641
Those thre wyll be redy even at your bekenynge;	190	Magnyfycence	1778
For the[m] shall you have at lyberte to lowte.	190	Magnyfycence	1779
them] 'then' †Rastell & Treveris C 1530, B			
To reche at a rat – I coude not her warne.	191	Magnyfycence	1809
I coude, and I lyst, garre you laughe at a game:	192	Magnyfycence	1835
The snyte snyveled in the snowte and smyled at the game.	192	Magnyfycence	1840
I rushe at them rughly and make them ly full lowe;	193	Magnyfycence	1884
Thys losyll was a lorde and lyvyd at his lust;	193	Magnyfycence	1886
I am baytyd with doggys at every mannys gate;	195	Magnyfycence	1961
Nowe must you lerne to begge at every mannes gate.	196	Magnyfycence	1981
At my devyse I with her met;	199	Magnyfycence	2075
I lyve as me lyst, I lepe out at large;	199	Magnyfycence	2080
At lyberte a man may be bolde for to brake;	199	Magnyfycence	2085
And pynche at the payment of a poddynge prycke;	200	Magnyfycence	2122
And some fall prechynge at the Toure Hyll;	200	Magnyfycence	2140
At lyberte to wander and walke over all,	201	Magnyfycence	2149
For there be horys there at all assayes.	204	Magnyfycence	2275
In tyme of dystresse I am redy at hande;	205	Magnyfycence	2285
And I, Myschefe, am comyn at nede,	205	Magnyfycence	2309
Ye, have done at ones without delay.	206	Magnyfycence	2319
Redresse sholde be at the rekenynge in every accompte,	208	Magnyfycence	2413
Syr, this letter ye sent to me at Pountes was enclosed.	209	Magnyfycence	2439
Commensynge this processe at mayster Redresse.	211	Magnyfycence	2481
Nowe pleasure at large, nowe in captyvyte;	212	Magnyfycence	2519
At home in her wonnynge;	216	El Rummynge	94
We wyll no farther ryme /Of it at this tyme.	220	El Rummynge	241
Some start in at the backe syde,	221	El Rummynge	263
But supped it up at ones,	224	El Rummynge	380
At the threshold comyng in,	227	El Rummynge	495
And as she at her dyd pluck,	227	El Rummynge	504
And] not in Day 1560, Marshe 1568; pluck] 'pulck' †Lant 1545			
She swynged up a quarte /At ones for her parte.	228	El Rummynge	569
swynged] 'swinge' Marshe 1568			
And silogisari was drowned at Sturbrydge Fayre;	235	Speke Parott	165
For Tytus at Dover abydythe in the rode;	239	Speke Parott	284
Of on and hothyr at me that have dysdayne.	242	Speke Parott	385
He facithe owte at a flusshe with, 'Shewe, take all!'	243	Speke Parott	430
For grocers were grugyd at and groynyd at but late;	244	Speke Parott	441
For grocers were grugyd at and groynyd at but late;	244	Speke Parott	441
So myche provision, and so lytell wytte at nede –	244	Speke Parott	454
As at Sicientes,	252	Collyn Clout	222
Howe some synge letabundus /At every ale stake,	253	Collyn Clout	249
At home full softe doth sytte.	255	Collyn Clout	328
No matyns at mydnyght,	256	Collyn Clout	406
Almoost nothynge at all.	261	Collyn Clout	610
And breke theyr hose at the kne,	262	Collyn Clout	629
And com forthe at large,	264	Collyn Clout	693
com forthe] 'conforte' †Godfray 1531, Kele 1545.1, Marshe 1568			
At the Brode gatus,	266	Collyn Clout	798
Dronken as a mouse /At the ale house,	266	Collyn Clout	802
At the good ale tappe,	266	Collyn Clout	804
As lymyters at large	267	Collyn Clout	834
For to shote a crowe /At her tyrly tyrlowe;	270	Collyn Clout	949
For ye play so at the chesse,	271	Collyn Clout	1009
But at the pleasure of one	272	Collyn Clout	1018
And graunte hym at his askynge	272	Collyn Clout	1027
At my style rude and playne,	273	Collyn Clout	1088
At Poules Crosse, or elswhere,	276	Collyn Clout	1182
Openly at Westmynstere	276	Collyn Clout	1183
And at the Austen Fryars	276	Collyn Clout	1186
And at Saynt Thomas of Akers	276	Collyn Clout	1188
Howe we wyll rule all at wyll	276	Collyn Clout	1190
And howe at a pronge	276	Collyn Clout	1194
At our pleasure and wyll.	276	Collyn Clout	1216
our] 'your' Kele 1545.1, Marshe 1568, 'owur' MS Harley 2252			
At dredfull Domesday.	277	Collyn Clout	1233
Shote anker, and lye at rode,	277	Collyn Clout	1255
The countrynge at Cales	280	Why Come Ye	77
The] 'They' †Kele 1545.3, Toy 1553, Kitson 1560.7, Marshe 1568			
We may blowe at the cole!	281	Why Come Ye	84
They shote all at one marke:	283	Why Come Ye	174
At the Cardynals hat.	283	Why Come Ye	175
They shote all at that!	283	Why Come Ye	176
They] 'Thy' †Kele 1545.3			
They shote at him with crownes.	283	Why Come Ye	178
But at the naked stewes	284	Why Come Ye	236
At the streme of Banockesburne	285	Why Come Ye	268
Dare nat loke out at dur	286	Why Come Ye	296
at] 'a' Kitson 1560.7, Marshe 1568			
To holde up their hande at the bar.	286	Why Come Ye	302
At the Commune Place,	287	Why Come Ye	319
Or at the Kynges Benche.	287	Why Come Ye	320
Stop at lawe tancrete,	289	Why Come Ye	420
He ruleth all at wyll	291	Why Come Ye	487

ATAME —ATTAMED

	Page	Title	Line
At them that be well borne;	294	Why Come Ye	600
'My lorde is nat at layser.	294	Why Come Ye	625
Tyll he cheked at the fyst,	297	Why Come Ye	735
He is at suche takynge,	302	Why Come Ye	936
At his owne desyer.	303	Why Come Ye	986
To dryve them at divisyon,	306	Why Come Ye	1094
At the cardys and haserdynge.	309	Why Come Ye	1193
I am forcebly constrayned /At Juvynals request	309	Why Come Ye	1211
At every solempne feest,	309	Why Come Ye	1215
And at more convenyent tyme	310	Why Come Ye2	21
studyously dyvysed at Sheryfhotten Castell,	312	Garlande	I
as more at large it doth apere in the proces folowynge.	312	Garlande	I
But sodeynly at ones, as I me advysed,	313	Garlande	36
And at your avauntage quikly it is	316	Garlande	142
Or elles he can nought bot whan he is at scole;	318	Garlande	205
'Prove his wytt', sayth he, 'at cardes or dyce,	318	Garlande	206
For that I wolde not with you fall at discorde.	318	Garlande	214
What poetis we have at our retenewe.	319	Garlande	238
With that there come in wonderly at ones	319	Garlande	269
Sterte all at ones an hundrethe fote backe.	320	Garlande	282
Enyus that wrate of mercyall kyng at lengthe;	321	Garlande	347
Tyll at the last they forcyd me sore,	324	Garlande	446
sore] 'so sore' Marshe 1568			
Tyll at the last theis noble poetis thre	326	Garlande	517
Of studyous doctryne when at the port salu	327	Garlande	541
Brainles blenkardis that blow at the cole,	329	Garlande	610
Powle hatchettis, that prate wyll at every ale pole,	329	Garlande	613
wyll] 'well' Marshe 1568			
With that I herd gunnis russhe out at ones,	329	Garlande	623
In derkenes thus dwelt we, tyll at the last	330	Garlande	650
And of your wyll the plainnes shew at large.'	332	Garlande	727
An hole reame he is able to set at devysion:	333	Garlande	758
And smerke, lyke a smythy kur, at sperkes of steile;	333	Garlande	762
Thus talkyng we went forth in at a postern gate.	333	Garlande	766
forth] not in MS Cotton Vitellius E.x			
She wonderyd, me thought, at my laurell grene;	343	Garlande	1116
Of my ladys grace at the contemplacyoun,	347	Garlande	1219
By merciall strength /He wan at length;	349	Garlande	1299
To letterd men at large.	350	Garlande	1354
How a do cam tryppyng in at the rerewarde,	351	Garlande	1385
With a sawte of solace at the longe last;	351	Garlande	1398
The millar durst not leve his wyfe at home.	352	Garlande	1417
At the castell of Warke,	359	Albany	30
At the castell of Warke.	362	Albany	148
Of brede at ylke mannes hecke.	363	Albany	155
At all houres to be redy	371	Albany	485
At the Thre Cranes,	374	Replycacion	9
With baudrie at her ye brayed;	376	Replycacion	48
For ye were worldly shamed, /At Poules Crosse openly,	376	Replycacion	63
At the feest of her concepcion	376	Replycacion	67
Therwith for to be founde /At the unyversyte,	378	Replycacion	148
And be brent at a stake,	382	Replycacion	295
Why fall ye at debate /With Skelton laureate,	382	Replycacion	300
That at his resurrection he harped out of hell	383	Replycacion	341
Why have ye than disdayne /At poetes, and complayne	384	Replycacion	352

ATAME
Men said they could not their tunges atame;	139	Ven Tongues	60

ATHLAS
Of Athlas astrology, and many noble thyngis,	331	Garlande	690

ATHRUST
An huswyfe of trust /Whan she is athrust,	220	El Rummynge	254

ATYRE
This theyr desyre, /This newe atyre.	165	Magnyfycence	888

ATROPOS
O Atropos, of the fatall systers iij,	32	Dol Dethe	120

ATT
Som sey I rayle att ryott recheles;	242	Speke Parott	387

ATTAYNE
Bot by them to knoulege ye may attayne	32	Dol Dethe	129
Cowde not rech nor attayne	68	Hauke	226
Your power coude no lenger attayne	114	Scot Kynge	54
Youre poverte cowde not attayne	119	Ag Scottes	151

ATTAYNTED
And they be so attaynted	269	Collyn Clout	900
And mad theyr hertes attaynted.	282	Why Come Ye	158
And so attaynted, /Lyke cowardes starke,	359	Albany	28
Moost false attaynted traytour,	371	Albany	493

ATTAYNTYD
Thow ye be tauntyd, Parotte, with tonges attayntyd,	240	Speke Parott	343
Whose tong ys attayntyd with slaundrys obliqui.	241	Speke Parott	363

ATTALUS
Or of A[t]talus the olde,	76	Phy Sparrow	191
Attalus] 'Artalus' †Kele 1545.2, Wyght 1553, Kitson 1560.6, Marshe 1568			

ATTAMED
Your madnesse she attamed;	376	Replycacion	61

	Page	Title	Line
ATTEINTID			
Fals forgers of mony, for kownnage atteintid,	329	Garlande	611
kownnage] 'coynnage' Marshe 1568			
ATTEYNE			
And not to wrythe, for he so wyll atteyne,	46	Bowge	22
wrythe] 'wryte' Wynkyn de Worde 1510, Marshe 1568			
And may not atteyne it by no medyacyon,	321	Garlande	319
ATTEMPERAUNCE			
In whose attemperaunce I have suche delyght,	145	Magnyfycence	189
ATTENDAUNCE			
And syr, ye must daunce attendaunce,	294	Why Come Ye	628
AUCTOR			
As by myne auctor tried it was.	296	Why Come Ye	707
(Myne auctor writeth the same);	297	Why Come Ye	727
As myne auctor sayth.	297	Why Come Ye	745
AUCTORITE			
That be set in auctorite.	174	Magnyfycence	1243
AUCTORYTE			
I, callynge to mynde the great auctoryte	46	Bowge	8
Make the churche to be /In smale auctoryte;	65	Hauke	140
But sey me yet, Syr Satropas, what auctoryte ye have	122	Garnesche1	13
But sey me yet, Syr Satrapas, wat auctoryte ye have	122	Garnesche1	20
But sey me yet, Syr Satrapas, what auctoryte ye have	122	Garnesche1	27
But sey me yet, Syr Satrapas, what auctoryte ye have	122	Garnesche1	34
But loke that ye occupye the auctoryte that I you gave.	180	Magnyfycence	1456
But men say your auctoryte	265	Collyn Clout	758
But men say] 'Men say but' †Godfray 1531, Kele 1545.1, Marshe 1568			
And set hym nobly /In great auctoryte	291	Why Come Ye	505
AUDELBY			
........mastres Audelby,	125	Garnesche3	55
AUDYENCE			
To answere unto this noble audyence,	344	Garlande	1122
And knowledge your offence /Before open audyence,	380	Replycacion	208
AUGMENT			
Her beautye to augment	97	Phy Sparrow	1041
AUGUSTINUS			
Or frere Augustinus,	265	Collyn Clout	740
AULTER			
From the aulter to the funt.	67	Hauke	189
AULUS			
Aulus Gelius, that noble historiar;	322	Garlande	351
AUNCETRY			
Dysparage ye myn auncetry?	131	Garnesche5	63
AUNCIENT			
The auncient acquaintance, madam, betwen us twayn,	42	Balettys2	1
Of auncient poetis, ye wote full wele, hath bene	314	Garlande	65
The poemis and storis auncient inbryngis	331	Garlande	689
After the auncient manner	360	Albany	62
AUNCYENT			
In Arturys auncyent actys nowhere ys provyd your pere;	123	Garnesche2	24
Of auncyent Aristippus and such other mo,	233	Speke Parott	93
For it is an auncyent brute,	378	Replycacion	156
AUNCYENTE			
These poetes of auncyente,	90	Phy Sparrow	767
AUNCYENTLY			
Of noble actis auncyently enrolde	29	Dol Dethe	15
AUNGEY			
Not from Anwyke unto Aungey.	171	Magnyfycence	1121
AUNGELL			
And of Castell Aungell the fenestrall,	351	Garlande	1387
AUNSWERE			
Skelton Laureate, Orator Regius, maketh this aunswere &c.	112	Calliope	I
AUQUARDE			
Of auquarde facyon,	259	Collyn Clout	523
AUREAT			
Of aureat poems they want ellumynynge;	32	Dol Dethe	128
With the aureat droppes,	93	Phy Sparrow	873
AUSTEN			
And at the Austen Fryars	276	Collyn Clout	1186
Saynt Jerome and saynt Austen,	381	Replycacion	277
AUTENTYKE			
In pulpyttes autentyke,	264	Collyn Clout	696
autentyke] 'attentyke' Kele 1545.1, 'antentike' Marshe 1568			
AUTER			
To hawke, or els to hunt /From the auter to the funt,	62	Hauke	10
The hy auter he strypte naked;	63	Hauke	49
AUTER STONE			
The blode ran downe raw /Upon the auter stone.	63	Hauke	59
AUTOMEDON			
Item A[u]tomedon of Loves Meditacyoun;	346	Garlande	1181
Automedon] 'Antomedon' †Fakes 1523, Marshe 1568 MS Cotton Vitellius E.x			
AUTORYTE			
But sey me now, Syr Satrapas, what autoryte ye have	121	Garnesche1	6
AUTUMPNE			
In autumpne, whan the sonne in Vyrgyne	46	Bowge	1

AVAYLE —AWAY   Page   Title   Line

AVAYLE
All those by whom ye have avayle.   41   Coystrowne4   18
Ye, for thy langage can not the avayle.   204   Magnyfycence   2249
What can it avayle /To dryve forth a snayle,   246   Collyn Clout   1
AVAYLED
But nothynge it avayled /To call Phylyp agayne   72   Phy Sparrow   25
AVAYLETH
What avayleth lordshype, yourselfe for to kyll   148   Magnyfycence   286
AVAYLYNGE
That nothynge is avaylynge;   275   Collyn Clout   1148
AVALE
Whan she lyst to avale,   99   Phy Sparrow   1117
AVAUNCE
Avaunce your selfe to aproche and come nere.   48   Bowge   88
And oftentymes I wolde myselfe avaunce   50   Bowge   143
Syr, hardely remembre what may your name avaunce.   148   Magnyfycence   277
Largesse is he that all prynces doth avaunce;   148   Magnyfycence   279
To shewe you my mynde myselfe I wyll avaunce,   182   Magnyfycence   1520
Howe connynge myght them avaunce,   262   Collyn Clout   617
Whereto made ye me hym to avaunce   315   Garlande   115
As wele foly as wysdome oft ye do avaunce,   317   Garlande   180
  ye do] 'tyme ye' MS Cotton Vitellius E.x
The huge myghty okes them selfe dyd avaunce,   320   Garlande   279
There Titus Lyvius hymselfe dyd avaunce   321   Garlande   344
And Iopas his instrument did avaunce,   331   Garlande   688
My pen I will avaunce   369   Albany   406
With sobre cyrcumstance, /Our myndes to avaunce   385   Replycacion   395
AVAUNCED
Avaunced by Pallas to laurell preferment.'   324   Garlande   434
AVAUNS
As though ye wolde parbrake /Your avauns to make,   367   Albany   323
AVAUNSID
Avaunsid I was to that degre;   131   Garnesche5   82
AVAUNSYD
Sodenly avaunsyd, and sodenly subdude;   212   Magnyfycence   2526
AVAUNSYNGE
Avaunsynge my selfe sum thanke to deserve,   335   Garlande   822
AVAUNT
Avaunt, rybawde, thi tung reclame!   132   Garnesche5   106
Avaunt, avaunt, thow slogysh......   132   Garnesche5   112
Avaunt, avaunt, thow slogysh......   132   Garnesche5   112
Avaunt, Syr Gye of Gaunt!   275   Collyn Clout   1155
Avaunt, lewde preest, avaunt!   275   Collyn Clout   1156
Avaunt, lewde preest, avaunt!   275   Collyn Clout   1156
Avaunt, syr doctour Deuyas!   275   Collyn Clout   1157
  Deuyas] 'Denyas' †Godfray 1531, 'dyvers' Marshe 1568,
  'Devias' MS Harley 2252
Avaunt to the devyll of hell!   275   Collyn Clout   1164
Avaunt, cowarde recrayed! /Thy pride shalbe alayd,   371   Albany   495
AVAUNTAGE
And at your avauntage quikly it is   316   Garlande   142
AVE
Your Pater noster, your Ave, nor your Crede.   137   Ven Tongues   19
AVENT
Avent, avent, my popagay!   35   Man Margery   3
Avent, avent, my popagay!   35   Man Margery   3
AVENTURE
Whatsomever aventure therof fall.   55   Bowge   336
I durse aventure to journey thorugh Fraunce;   57   Bowge   408
AVENTURIS
Of that aventuris, whiche made me sore agast.   330   Garlande   649
AVYCEN
With Ipocras and mayster Avycen,   352   Garlande   1426
AVYSE
Yet I avyse you to speke, for ony drede: 48   Bowge   90
By myne avyse use not with him to walke.   52   Bowge   210
AVYSED
But are ye not avysed to dwell where ye spake?   162   Magnyfycence   774
AVYSID
And as I thus sadly amonge them avysid   323   Garlande   386
AVYSYNGE
Avysynge me my penne awaye to pulle   46   Bowge   21
AVOYDYNGE
Of confuse tantum avoydynge the chekmate.   236   Speke Parott   196
AVOWE
Beware of him, for, I make God avowe,   51   Bowge   199
My wytte wolde waste, I make God avowe.   53   Bowge   243
'Welcome,' quod Ryote, 'I make God avowe.'   56   Bowge   378
Yes, syr, I gyve God avowe,   155   Magnyfycence   529
So is all the remenaunt, I make God avowe;   175   Magnyfycence   1283
Se, for God avowe, for colde as I chydder.   191   Magnyfycence   1817
I make God avowe ye wyll none other men have.   191   Magnyfycence   1827
AVOWED
What fault find ye herein but may be avowed.   138   Ven Tongues   41
AWAY
Fled away from hym, let hym ly in the dust,   30   Dol Dethe   39
She left hym slepyng and stale away,   42   Balettys1   14
My speche was taken away.   77   Phy Sparrow   229

AWAYE —BABI   Page   Title   Line

	Page	Title	Line
I threwe away for drede.	77	Phy Sparrow	236
Might plucke away thyne eares!	79	Phy Sparrow	310
From me was taken away	81	Phy Sparrow	374
Chaseth away Phebus bryght,	86	Phy Sparrow	572
All have ye lost and cast away.	119	Ag Scottes	163
Ye wolde have trysyd hys trowle away.	130	Garnesche5	36
Do away, I say, the devylles torde!	151	Magnyfycence	397
Howe coulde ye do that, and [I] was away?	154	Magnyfycence	504
I] not in †Rastell & Treveris C 1530, B			
Nay, come away, man! Thou playst the cayser,	162	Magnyfycence	787
I waraunt you I wyll not go away.	163	Magnyfycence	820
Nowe then goo we hens. Away the mare!	177	Magnyfycence	1325
It shall be done. Ye, but byd hym come away	179	Magnyfycence	1399
I say it is folly to gyve all welth away.	180	Magnyfycence	1430
Be wrastynge and wrythynge, and away drawe.	185	Magnyfycence	1608
And that ye wyll not cast hym away so sone.	186	Magnyfycence	1638
Here goth FOLY away.	192	Magnyfycence	SD
Ye be the thevys, I say, away my goodys dyd cary.	203	Magnyfycence	2239
How wysdom thorowe wantonnesse vanysshyth away;	213	Magnyfycence	2556
Wyddered lyke hay, /The woll worne away.	216	El Rummynge	63
With, 'Now away the mare,	217	El Rummynge	110
With, 'Hey, dogge, hay, /Have these hogges away!'	218	El Rummynge	169
hogges] 'dogges' Day 1560, Marshe 1568			
Ich am not cast away, /That can my husband say,	220	El Rummynge	219
But plucke away and pull /Theyr fleces of wull.	248	Collyn Clout	78
Plucke away the leedes /Over theyr heedes,	257	Collyn Clout	408
And sell away theyr belles	257	Collyn Clout	410
And bere it well away.	258	Collyn Clout	464
That hartes wyll ronne away,	280	Why Come Ye	54
There went the hare away;	281	Why Come Ye	120
Rynne away and crepe;	286	Why Come Ye	294
For prosperyte /Away than wyll fle.	300	Why Come Ye	863
To dryve away grace.	301	Why Come Ye	873
Wherfore then rasid ye not away	316	Garlande	137
With syngular pleasurs to dryve away the tyme,	326	Garlande	524
The blaste of the brynston blew away his brayne;	329	Garlande	631
I saw dyvers that were cariid away thens in cribbis,	330	Garlande	640
Wherof in substaunce I brought this away.	344	Garlande	1120
Go she never so gingirly, her honesty is gone away.	346	Garlande	1204
Twyt, Scot, thou ran away.'	363	Albany	160
Yet we bear away the bell,	363	Albany	183
But lepe away lyke frogges	364	Albany	212
But ran away quyte?	366	Albany	310
He ran away by nyght	366	Albany	311
Ye wolde ryn away rounde	367	Albany	348

AWAYE

	Page	Title	Line
Avysynge me my penne awaye to pulle	46	Bowge	21
She cherysshe[th] him, and hym she casseth awaye.'	49	Bowge	117
'cherysshed' †Wynkyn de Worde 1499, 1510, Marshe 1568;			
casseth] 'casteth' Wynkyn de Worde 1510, 'chasseth' Marshe 1568			
Here goth CLOKED COLUSYON awaye,	190	Magnyfycence	SD
Ye shall not bere awaye /Myne ale for nought,	218	El Rummynge	165
myne] 'my' Kynge & Marche 1554, Day 1560, Marshe 1568			
The hennes donge awaye,	219	El Rummynge	197
lyke a cowarde knyght, ran awaye shamfully	359	Albany	1
For in that fraye /Ye ranne awaye	360	Albany	36
He ran awaye by night.	360	Albany	71

AWAYTE

	Page	Title	Line
I dare not speke, we be so layde awayte,	59	Bowge	468
Ye, but how longe shall I here awayte?	151	Magnyfycence	398
And let the other another [time] awayte.	180	Magnyfycence	1454
time] not in †Rastell & Treveris C 1530, B			

AWE

	Page	Title	Line
To se you thus ruled and stande in suche awe.	178	Magnyfycence	1376

AWNE

	Page	Title	Line
That were aboute hym, his awne servauntis of trust,	30	Dol Dethe	37
For whos causis ye slew hym with your awne hande.	31	Dol Dethe	68
Hole ys that your brow that ye brake with Deu[ra]ndall your awne sworde; Deurandall] 'Deundall' †MS Harley 367	123	Garnesche2	8
Your awne lewdnes to amende.	124	Garnesche3	18
That nothynge had /There of their awne,	229	El Rummynge	609

AWNNER

	Page	Title	Line
The awnner therof is lady of estate,	47	Bowge	50

AWRYE

	Page	Title	Line
That standeth yet awrye;	308	Why Come Ye	1187

AXES

	Page	Title	Line
The fervent axes of love can not represse!	321	Garlande	315

AXYS

	Page	Title	Line
These feverous axys, the dedely wo and payne	44	Balettys3	9

BA

	Page	Title	Line
With 'Ba, ba, ba', and 'bas, bas, bas',	42	Balettys1	8
With 'Ba, ba, ba', and 'bas, bas, bas',	42	Balettys1	8
With 'Ba, ba, ba', and 'bas, bas, bas',	42	Balettys1	8

BABELL

	Page	Title	Line
A clatterynge and a babell	224	El Rummynge	387
babell] 'batell' 1521 Fragment			

BABI

	Page	Title	Line
Brought forth a godely babi!	339	Garlande	975

BABILL —BAGGE	Page	Title	Line

BABILL
Frome Babill towre to the hillis Caspian.' . . . . 327 Garlande 553
    Caspian] 'Gaspian' †Fakes 1523

BABILON
From Brytons Albion /To the towre of Babilon. . . . . 94 Phy Sparrow 888
    To] 'Bo' †Kele 1545.2

BABY
A, that were a baby to brace and to basse! . . . . 183 Magnyfycence 1560
I bassed that baby with harte so free; . . . . 198 Magnyfycence 2069
And her most blessed baby, ... 375 Replycacion 19

BABYLLES
He maketh them to bere babylles, and to bere a lowe sayle; . . 243 Speke Parott 428

BABYLON
Syrus, that soleme syar of Babylon, ... 181 Magnyfycence 1473
Ydolles of Babylon, /De terra Zabulon, ... 262 Collyn Clout 638

BABYLS
To beare fagottes for babyls. . . . . 379 Replycacion 175

BABYONE
Thou tode, thow scorpyon, /Thow bawdy babyone, ... 128 Garnesche3 163

BABLE
And heynously on her to bable . . . . 375 Replycacion 27

BABVELL
Or of Babvell besyde Bery . . . . 265 Collyn Clout 752

BACCHUS
But blessed Bacchus, the pleasant god of wyne, ... 321 Garlande 334
But blessed Bacchus, the pleasant god of wyne, ... 321 Garlande 341

BACE
He braggyth of hys byrth, that borne was full bace; . . . . . 37 Coystrownel 24
That shall bring you full bace . . . . 368 Albany 366

BACHELER
Doctour Daupatus, /And bacheler Bacheleratus, ... 266 Collyn Clout 800

BACHELERS
Nor bachelers of that faculte . . . . 266 Collyn Clout 791

BACHUS
But blessyd Bachus, potenciall god of strengthe, ... 322 Garlande 348
But blessyd Bachus was in there company, ... 322 Garlande 355
But blessyd Bachus most reverent and holy, ... 322 Garlande 362
But blessyd Bachus that never man forgate, ... 322 Garlande 369
But blessyd Bachus, that bote is of all bale, ... 322 Garlande 376
But blissed Bachus, that mastris oft didth frame, ... 322 Garlande 383

BACK
For before on your brest, and behind on your back . . . . . . 137 Ven Tongues 16
And say yll behynde his back, ... 310 Why Come Ye2 26

BACKE
Yet on my backe I bere suche lewde delynge. . . . . 59 Bowge 457
And tolde all the myschyef I coude behynde theyr backe, . . . 160 Magnyfycence 718
Sodenly promotyd, and sodenly put backe; . . . . 212 Magnyfycence 2531
With a croked backe. . . . . 215 El Rummynge 33
Some start in at the backe syde, ... 221 El Rummynge 263
He plucked hym backe, and he went afore. . . . . 319 Garlande 254
Sterte all at ones an hundrethe fote backe. . . . . 320 Garlande 282
With, 'Sir, I pray you, a lytyll tyme stande backe, ... 326 Garlande 505
There he putte backe . . . . 360 Albany 44
He reculed backe, /To his great lacke, ... 360 Albany 52

BACKE BONE
Byte asondre thy backe bone! . . . . 79 Phy Sparrow 312

BACKES
And cowardly tourne your backes . . . . 367 Albany 349

BACKIS
Turnd ther backis and let ther master fall, ... 31 Dol Dethe 94
    backis] 'backe' Marshe 1568

BACON FLYCKE
Another brought a spycke /Of a bacon flycke; . . . . 223 El Rummynge 336
Somtyme a bacon flycke /That is thre fyngers thycke . . . . . 267 Collyn Clout 844

BACUS
Nother crokyd Cacus, /Nor yet dronken Bacus; . . . . 67 Hauke 195
    Nother] 'Nor yet' Kynge & Marche 1554, Day 1560, Marshe 1568

BAD
He [b]ad the Phitonesse . . . . 105 Phy Sparrow 1345
    bad] 'had' †Kele 1545.2, Wyght 1553, Kitson 1560.6, Marshe 1568
And bad Elynour go bet, ... 222 El Rummynge 332
She went before, and bad me take good holde; . . . . 328 Garlande 573
Primo Regum expres, /He bad the Phitones . . . . 350 Garlande 1338
What constellacions ar good or bad for men, ... 352 Garlande 1429

BADDE
And eyther ye be to badde, ... 259 Collyn Clout 502

BADE
And another bade put out myne eye; . . . . 150 Magnyfycence 353
Another bade shave halfe my berde; . . . . 150 Magnyfycence 355
And some bade, 'Sere hym with a marke.' . . . . 150 Magnyfycence 360
Ye. But I bade hym pyke out of the gate; . . . . 166 Magnyfycence 946

BADNES
All good and no badnes, ... 341 Garlande 1010

BAGGE
I purpose to shake oute /All my connynge bagge, ... 248 Collyn Clout 51

BAGPYPE — BANDIS

BAGPYPE
A bagpype without blowynge standeth in no sted:	232	Speke Parott	75

bagpype] 'bagbyte' †Lant 1545, Kynge & Marche 1554

BAILE
They buskt them on a bushment them selfe in baile to bringe	31	Dol Dethe	81
Baile, baile at yow bothe, frantyke folys! Follow on the chase!	123	Garnesche2	31
Baile, baile at yow bothe, frantyke folys! Follow on the chase!	123	Garnesche2	31

BAILLYVE
HE WAS SOMTIME THE HOLY BAILLYVE OF DIS.	109	Epitaphe2	1

BAY
Your beard so brym as bore at bay,	119	Ag Scottes	161

BAYARDE
On Bayarde Mountalbon;	88	Phy Sparrow	656
Bolde bayarde, ye are to blynde,	126	Garnesche3	101

BAYARDYS BUN
A swete suger lofe and sowre bayardys bun	36	Coystrowne1	8

BAYNED
moche better bayned than brayned,	374	Replycacion	1

BAYTE
Counterfetynge is a proper bayte.	152	Magnyfycence	442
That weryed I wolde be on suche a bayte.	184	Magnyfycence	1568

BAYTETH
He bayteth them lyke a bere,	286	Why Come Ye	307

BAYTYD
I am baytyd with doggys at every mannys gate;	195	Magnyfycence	1961

BAK
Go watch a bole, your bak is brode.	35	Man Margery	12
When Mars retrogradant reversed his bak,	312	Garlande	3
I made it straunge, and drew bak ones or twyse,	324	Garlande	444

BAKE
As ye ar brystlyd on the bake for alle your gay gere.	122	Garnesche1	26
I wold sum manys bake ink-horne	133	Garnesche5	133
A wanton wenche and wele coude bake a cake;	351	Garlande	1413

BAKON
And brought a gambone /Of bakon that was resty;	222	El Rummynge	328

BALADE
The Balade also of the Mustarde Tarte.	347	Garlande	1245

BALADE BOKE
A balade boke before me for to laye,	53	Bowge	257

BALADIS
sum parte of Skeltons bokes and baladis with ditis of plesure,	345	Garlande	R

BALAK
With Balak and Balam,	301	Why Come Ye	896

BALAM
With Balak and Balam,	301	Why Come Ye	896

BALAS
Diamounde, or rubye, or balas of the beste,	241	Speke Parott	367

BALASSIS
With balassis and charbuncles the borders did shyne;	345	Garlande	1166

BALAUNCE
Ye counterway not evynly your balaunce;	317	Garlande	179

BALDE
With a balde face to toote;	82	Phy Sparrow	411

BALDOCK
The Jebet of Baldock was made for Jack Leg;	232	Speke Parott	73
To the gybbet of Baldock.	303	Why Come Ye	956

BALE
To the dyne dale /Of boteles bale,	40	Coystrowne3	46

boteles] 'botemles' Marshe 1568

What, loo, man, see here of a bale;	57	Bowge	389
And so, by these meanes, I brewe moche bale.	161	Magnyfycence	744
She is the bote of all my bale.	199	Magnyfycence	2070
But blessyd Bachus, that bote is of all bale,	322	Garlande	376

BALES
That bales begynne to brew.	280	Why Come Ye	63

BALETTYS
Here folowythe Dyvers Balettys and Dyties Solacyous	41	Balettys	1

BALKE
Were fayne with a chalke /To score on the balke,	230	El Rummynge	615

BALL
Fortune so tourneth the ball	262	Collyn Clout	632

BALLADE
A Ballade of the Scottysshe Kynge	113	Scot Kynge	1

BALLYVIS
The burgeis and the ballyvis of the v portis,	326	Garlande	514

BALTAZAR
Nor blake Baltazar with hys basnet routh as a bere,	122	Garnesche1	23

BALTHASOR
In Balthasor, whiche heled	308	Why Come Ye	1184
Balthasor, that helyd Domingos nose	309	Why Come Ye	1194

nose] 'pose' Marshe 1568

BALUA
Johannes Balua was his name	297	Why Come Ye	726

BAN
And beggers they ban,	301	Why Come Ye	891

BANDIS
It shall be losyd ful sone out of the bandis	332	Garlande	725

BANDYD —BARELLES   Page   Title   Line

BANDYD
To grope a gardevyaunce, though it be well bandyd. . . . . . . 203 Magnyfycence 2231
BANE
Your last deedly bane . . . . 366 Albany 284
BANER
So thou arte personable to bere a pryncess baner. . . . . . . 161 Magnyfycence 767
BANES
Of our Englysshe bowes ye have fette your banes. . . . . . . 115 Scot Kynge 65
At Englysh bowes have fetched their banes. . . . . 120 Ag Scottes 173
BANISSHED
That banisshed was he by his proposicyoun, ... 316 Garlande 132
    by] 'through' Marshe 1568
BANYSHED
And have you banyshed from you all dyspare? . . . . 208 Magnyfycence 2393
BANYSSHE
To banysshe pyte out of a maydens harte? . . . . 320 Garlande 308
BANYSSHED
Reson is banysshed thence, ... 279 Why Come Ye 12
And banysshed in effect . . . . 380 Replycacion 242
BANKE
Upon every banke /Of his herbers grene, ... 304 Why Come Ye 1002
Of Huntley banke, /Of Lowdyan, /Of Locryan, ... 359 Albany 19
BANKES
Ye had be better to have buskyd to Huntley Bankes, ... 114 Scot Kynge 50
    be] 'bet' †Fakes 1513
On Huntley bankes, /Take this our thankes; . . . . 136 Dundas 58
They play their olde pranckes /After Huntley Bankes. . . . . 285 Why Come Ye 267
Of the Scottysshe Bankes. . . . . 288 Why Come Ye 369
BANKETYNG
So myche bely-joye, and so wastefull banketyng; . . . . . . 245 Speke Parott 492
BANKETYNGE
With banketynge braynlesse, ... 280 Why Come Ye 71
BANKIS
The bankis enturfid with singular solas, ... 330 Garlande 655
BANKYS
Ye myght have buskyd you to Huntley Bankys; . . . . 119 Ag Scottes 149
BANNE
What begger art thou, that thus doth banne and wary? . . . . 203 Magnyfycence 2238
BANNER
Cros, staffe, lectryne and banner, ... 64 Hauke 114
Under the banner /Of all good manner, ... 356 Garlande 1572
With Sainct Cutberdes banner . . . . 360 Albany 63
BANNESHT
Treytory and treson he bannesht ought of sight. . . . . . . 33 Dol Dethe 151
BANNISSHED
Ovyde was bannisshed for suche a skyll, ... 314 Garlande 93
BANNYSSHE
But I most bannysshe hym frome my jurydiccyon, ... 318 Garlande 227
BANOCKESBURNE
At the streme of Banockesburne . . . . 285 Why Come Ye 268
BAR
Betwene Temple Bar /And the Crosse in Chepe, ... 223 El Rummynge 359
To holde up their hande at the bar. . . . . 286 Why Come Ye 302
BARABAS
Ye bere yow bolde as Barabas, or Syr Terry of Trac[e]. . . . 122 Garneschel 11
    Trace] 'Tracy' †MS Harley 367
BARAYNE
And howe your poemys arre barayne of polysshed eloquens, . . 240 Speke Parott 316
BARARAG
That bararag blowyth in every mercyall warre, ... 319 Garlande 236
To blowe bararag tyll bothe his eyne stare.' . . . . 319 Garlande 245
    bararag] 'bararag brag' MS Cotton Vitellius E.x
BARATOWS
Ageynst all baratows broisiours of olde, ... 331 Garlande 673
BARBELLIS
Enswymmyng with rochis, barbellis and bremis, ... 330 Garlande 661
BARBICAN
How than lyke a man he wan the barbican . . . . 351 Garlande 1397
BARBYD
Barbyd lyke a nonne . . . . 168 Magnyfycence 987
BARE
'Have in sergeaunt ferrour, myne horse behynde is bare.' . . 43 Balettys2 20
Upon his breste he bare a versynge boxe; . . . . 52 Bowge 232
His elbowe bare, he ware his gere so nye, ... 56 Bowge 361
Pandaer bare the bylles . . . . 88 Phy Sparrow 682
Ye bare yourselfe somwhat to bold; . . . . 118 Ag Scottes 125
They bare me in hande that I was a spye; . . . . 150 Magnyfycence 352
Nor Vespasyan, that bare in his nose a waspe, ... 182 Magnyfycence 1510
In faythe, of his cofers the bottoms are bare. . . . . 201 Magnyfycence 2163
Today in delyte, tomorowe bare of blysse; . . . . 213 Magnyfycence 2542
For the grene bare threde . . . . 216 El Rummynge 60
    For] 'And' Day 1560, Marshe 1568
And brynge them selfe bare, ... 217 El Rummynge 109
Cysly and Sare, /With theyr legges bare, ... 217 El Rummynge 120
That she thyder bare /To pay for her share. . . . . 228 El Rummynge 545
That our Savyour bare, /Whiche us redemed from care. . . . . 375 Replycacion 33
BARELLES
The lay men call them barelles . . . . 269 Collyn Clout 917

	Page	Title	Line
BARGE			
But yf reason be regent and ruler of your barge.	141	Magnyfycence	38
No stormy tempeste your barge shall overthrow.	327	Garlande	546
BARK			
Yet bere ye not to bold to braule ne to bark	38	Coystrownel	60
Bo-ho doth bark wel, Hough-ho he rulyth the ring;	234	Speke Parott	130
BARKAMSTEDE			
Of the Bonehoms of Ashrige besyde Barkamstede,	353	Garlande	1461
BARKE			
Wher Cerberus doth barke,	73	Phy Sparrow	85
His Englyssh whereat they barke	91	Phy Sparrow	798
At his cloked counterfetynge dogges dothe barke.	153	Magnyfycence	482
And some of them barke, /Clatter and carpe	260	Collyn Clout	546
That blaber, barke, and blother,	266	Collyn Clout	777
Thus boldly for to barke?	309	Why Come Ye	1205
All his delight was to braule and to barke	347	Garlande	1252
Thou dyd nothyng but barke	362	Albany	147
BARKYNG			
Barkyng and whynyng lyke churlysshe currys of kynde,	239	Speke Parott	295
BARLYHOOD			
She fyll in a wynkynge /With a barlyhood;	223	El Rummynge	372
BARNACLE			
The barnacle, the bussarde,	83	Phy Sparrow	450
BARNE			
An olde barne wolde be underset.	153	Magnyfycence	454
Flewe, I sholde say - in to an olde barne	191	Magnyfycence	1808
Some brought from the barne /Both benes and pease;	222	El Rummynge	312
BARNET			
Esebon, Marybon, Wheston next Barnet;	234	Speke Parott	127
BARON			
Duke, erle, baron, nor lorde,	287	Why Come Ye	342
BARONAGE			
His noble baronage /He putteth them in corage	370	Albany	465
BARONES			
For of all barones bolde I bere the bell;	182	Magnyfycence	1498
BARONS			
Barons, knightis, squyers, one and alle,	31	Dol Dethe	92
More specially barons, and thos knightis bold,	34	Dol Dethe	183
So manye bolde barons, there hertes as dull as lede;	245	Speke Parott	466
Our barons be so bolde,	286	Why Come Ye	292
BARRE			
Nor how farre Temple Barre is	267	Collyn Clout	826
BARREYNE			
Barreyne of eloquence,	372	Albany	517
BARRES			
And by the barres of her tayle	268	Collyn Clout	868
of] 'if' Marshe 1568, 'of' MS Harley 2252			
With glasse wyndowes and barres;	270	Collyn Clout	939
BARRID			
Towchid, and hard for to be barrid.	316	Garlande	143
barrid] 'debarrid' MS Cotton Vitellius E.x			
BARRYD			
Fast boltyd and barryd,	64	Hauke	92
So myche sayntuary brekyng, and prevylegidde barryd -	246	Speke Parott	503
BAS			
With 'Ba, ba, ba', and 'bas, bas, bas',	42	Balettys1	8
With 'Ba, ba, ba', and 'bas, bas, bas',	42	Balettys1	8
With 'Ba, ba, ba', and 'bas, bas, bas',	42	Balettys1	8
With, 'Bas me, buttyng, praty Cys',	130	Garnesche5	43
With, 'Bas, my pretty bonny,	220	El Rummynge	227
With, 'Bas me, swete Parrot, bas me, swete swete;'	233	Speke Parott	104
With, 'Bas me, swete Parrot, bas me, swete swete;'	233	Speke Parott	104
Nowe into the castell of Bas,	366	Albany	288
BASAN			
And Og, that fat hog of Basan, doth retayne	234	Speke Parott	122
of] 'or' Kynge & Marche 1554, Day 1560, Marshe 1568			
BASE			
Therfore ye kepe them base,	262	Collyn Clout	624
And his base progeny,	291	Why Come Ye	491
Thus he, borne so base,	294	Why Come Ye	622
Some haute and some base.	301	Why Come Ye	880
With Englyshe somwhat base,	367	Albany	356
BASELYE			
So bold and so braggyng, and was so baselye borne;	246	Speke Parott	507
BASYAN			
Nor Basyan the bolde, for all his brybaunce,	182	Magnyfycence	1503
BASYN			
A bolle or a basyn, I say, for Goddes brede!	189	Magnyfycence	1728
BASKED			
basked and baththed in their wylde burblyng and boylyng blode,	374	Replycacion	1
BASNET			
Nor blake Baltazar with hys basnet routh as a bere,	122	Garnesche1	23
BASSE			
A, that were a baby to brace and to basse!	183	Magnyfycence	1560
Nor basse her swete swete.	279	Why Come Ye	35
BASSED			
I bassed that baby with harte so free;	198	Magnyfycence	2069

BASSYD —BE	Page	Title	Line

BASSYD
Ye wolde have bassyd hyr bumme, ... 125 Garnesche3 62
BASTARDE
In bastarde ryme, after the dogrell gyse, ... 151 Magnyfycence 408
BASTYNG
The f[r]esche bastyng of hys cote 129 Garnesche3 200
    fresche] 'flesche' †MS Harley 367
BATAYLE
And some I vysyte [with] batayle, warre, and murther, ... 194 Magnyfycence 1912
    with] 'to' †Rastell & Treveris C 1530, B
Nor to derayne /Batayle agayne /Scornfull disdayne, ... 356 Garlande 1564
Nor no batayle mayntayne, ... 365 Albany 244
BATE
Suche temporall warre and bate . . . . 269 Collyn Clout 913
Faire fall that forster that so well can bate his hownde! . . . 313 Garlande 27
    well] not in MS Cotton Vitellius E.x
BATELL
Boldly bend you to batell, and buske your selfe to save. 122 Garnesche1 41
Ye. But thryfte and we have made a batell. . . . . 171 Magnyfycence 1136
BATH
And of the Wyfe of Bath, ... 87 Phy Sparrow 618
BATHED
His swerde hath bathed in the Scottes blode. . . . . 115 Scot Kynge 71
BATHYD
Bathyd with blysse, embracyd with comforte. . . . . 181 Magnyfycence 1472
BATHTHED
basked and baththed in their wylde burblyng and boyling blode, 374 Replycacion 1
BATOWE
What is this, a betell or a batowe or a buskyn lacyd? . . . . . 161 Magnyfycence 755
BATTAYLE
That late were discomfect with battayle marcyall. . . . . 117 Ag Scottes 84
In playn felde and battayle. . . . . 364 Albany 205
BAUD
He is named Troylus baud; . . . . 89 Phy Sparrow 721
BAUDETH
Gresed upon dyrt /That baudeth her skyrt. . . . . 216 El Rummynge 90
BAUDY
With baudy wordes unmete . . . . 376 Replycacion 49
BAUDRIE
With baudrie at her ye brayed; . . . . 376 Replycacion 48
BAUDRY
Furdrers of love, with baudry aqueinted, ... 329 Garlande 609
BAUMBEROW
From Baumberow to Bothombar . . . . 282 Why Come Ye 139
    Bothombar] 'Bothambar' Toy 1553, Kitson 1560.7, Marshe 1568
BAWDE
Ye bere out brothells lyke a bawde; 131 Garnesche5 73
BAWDIAS
Foo, foisty bawdias, sum smellid of the smoke. . . . . 330 Garlande 639
BAWDY
A bawdy dyscheclowte, /That bryngyth the worlde abowte 125 Garnesche3 36
Thou tode, thow scorpyon, /Thow bawdy babyone, ... 128 Garnesche3 163
It ys for no bawdy knave 132 Garnesche5 114
BAWDYAS
Fusty bawdyas, I sey nat alle. 131 Garnesche5 76
BAWDRY
Crimsin velvet for your bawdry. 130 Garnesche5 40
BAWME
There is no bawme ne gumme of Arabe . . . . 207 Magnyfycence 2347
BAWMYS
It passid all bawmys that ever were namyd, ... 331 Garlande 674
BE
By thy report ar wonte to be extolde . . . . 29 Dol Dethe 17
It may be regesterde of shamefull recorde. . . . . 30 Dol Dethe 28
Well may ye be cald commons most unkynd. . . . . 30 Dol Dethe 56
    ye] 'you' Marshe 1568
To the right of his prince which shold not be withstand; . . . 31 Dol Dethe 67
This noble man doutles had not be slayne. . . . . 31 Dol Dethe 74
    be] 'bene' Marshe 1568
O grounde ungracious, unhappy be thy fame, ... 32 Dol Dethe 116
Mi wordis unpullysht be nakide and playne, ... 32 Dol Dethe 127
As perflytely as koude be thought or devysyd; . . . . 33 Dol Dethe 158
And geve the grace to be more fortunate! . . . . 33 Dol Dethe 165
Unto thy subjectis be kurteis and beningne. . . . . 33 Dol Dethe 168
Stabille thy mynde constant to be and fast, ... 34 Dol Dethe 170
And be not light of credence in no case. . . . . 34 Dol Dethe 175
To soroufull weping thei ought to be constreynd, ... 34 Dol Dethe 187
Ay, beshrewe yow! Be my fay . . . . 35 Man Margery 1
This wanton clarkis be nyse allway. . . . . 35 Man Margery 2
Tully, valy, strawe, let be I say! . . . . 35 Man Margery 5
'Be Gad, ye be a praty pode, ... 35 Man Margery 8
'Be Gad, ye be a praty pode, ... 35 Man Margery 8
'What, and ye shal be my piggesnye?' . . . . 36 Man Margery 17
Be Crist, ye shall not! No, no, hardely! . . . . 36 Man Margery 18
I will not be japed bodely. . . . . 36 Man Margery 19
Be sumdele lyke in forme and shap, ... 36 Coystrowne1 9
Lo, Jak wold be a jentyl man! 37 Coystrowne1 14
He wold be made moch of and he wyst how; 37 Coystrowne1 33

	Page	Title	Line
For Jak wold be a jentylman, that late was a grome.	37	Coystrowne1	42
Correct fyrst thy self; walk, and be nought!	38	Coystrowne1	62
A proverbe of old, 'Say well or be styll':	38	Coystrowne1	64
It is generall /To be mortall:	39	Coystrowne3	8
Oure days be datyd /To be chekmatyd,	39	Coystrowne3	29
Oure days be datyd /To be chekmatyd,	39	Coystrowne3	30
O goodly chyld /Of Mary mylde, /Then be oure shylde!	40	Coystrowne3	43
That we be not exylyd	40	Coystrowne3	44
Though angelyk be youre smylyng,	41	Coystrowne4	15
But one thyng is: that ye be lewde!	41	Coystrowne4	27
Ye may be countyd comfort of all corage.	42	Balettys2	7
It can be no counsell that is cryed at the cros.	43	Balettys2	36
To be so cruell and so overthwart,	45	Balettys5	5
I am content so all partys be pleasyd:	45	Balettys5	11
Under as coverte termes as coude be,	46	Bowge	10
His hede maye be harde, but feble is his brayne!	46	Bowge	24
his] not in Marshe 1568			
Of golde of tessew the fynest that myghte be,	47	Bowge	59
To be so proude to prese so proudly uppe.	48	Bowge	71
Sayenge to me, 'Broder, be of good chere,	48	Bowge	86
Abasshe you not, but hardely be bolde,	48	Bowge	87
What though our chaffer be never so dere,	48	Bowge	89
That wyll for me be medyatoure and mene;	48	Bowge	93
Suwed to Fortune that she wold be theyre frynde.	49	Bowge	121
She promysed to us all she wolde be kynde;	49	Bowge	124
Ye be an apte man, as ony can be founde	50	Bowge	155
Ye be an apte man, as ony can be founde	50	Bowge	155
Ye be to her, yea, worth a thousande pounde.	50	Bowge	157
For here be dyverse to you that be unkynde.	50	Bowge	161
For here be dyverse to you that be unkynde.	50	Bowge	161
But this one thynge ye maye be sure of me,	50	Bowge	162
I can not flater, I muste be playne to the.	50	Bowge	164
And, yf nede be, a bolde worde I dare cracke.	50	Bowge	168
Nay, naye, be sure, whyles I am on your syde	50	Bowge	169
Ageynste you hardely; therefore be not afrayde	51	Bowge	174
I have a favoure to you, wherof it be	52	Bowge	206
I wolde noo thynge so playne be.	52	Bowge	214
To shewe you thynges that may not be disclosed.'	52	Bowge	217
To kepe it hymselfe; for than he myghte be sure	52	Bowge	222
Soo he departed. There he wolde be come,	52	Bowge	228
I dare not speke; I promysed to be dome.	52	Bowge	229
I wolde be mery that wynde that ever blowe,	53	Bowge	251
To be with you thus perte and thus bolde;	53	Bowge	265
But ye be welcome to our housholde.	53	Bowge	266
But wolde be glad of your company.	53	Bowge	268
As I be saved, it is a wonder case.	53	Bowge	273
And ye be welcome, syr, so God me save,	54	Bowge	279
'Now,' quod Dysdayne, 'as I shall saved be,	54	Bowge	297
There muste for hym be layde some prety beyte.	55	Bowge	312
We tweyne, I trowe, be not withoute dysceyte:	55	Bowge	313
I loked on hym, I wende he had be woode.	55	Bowge	320
Of my querell soone wolde I venged be.	55	Bowge	333
Well, ones thou shalte be chermed, iwus:	55	Bowge	340
We be thy betters, and so thou shalte us take,	55	Bowge	342
And wake all nyghte and slepe tyll it be none.	57	Bowge	382
Fye on this dyce, they be not worth a turde!	57	Bowge	392
Unthryftynes in hym may well be shewed,	58	Bowge	416
Unthryftynes] 'Unthryftnes' †Wynkyn de Worde 1499, 1510			
As I be saved at the dredefull daye,	58	Bowge	443
Ye be malygned sore, I you ensure,	59	Bowge	451
I dare not speke, we be so layde awayte,	59	Bowge	468
For some shall wene be hanged by the throte.	59	Bowge	476
Yf ye coude be otherwyse agrede,	59	Bowge	480
It wyll not be, his purse is not on-flote.	60	Bowge	488
Ye muste be ruled, as I shall tell you howe.	60	Bowge	493
Amendis maye be of that is now amys;	60	Bowge	494
In every poynte to be indyfferente,	61	Bowge	535
But yet oftyme suche dremes be founde trewe.	61	Bowge	538
That be so far abusyd /They cannot be excusyd	62	Hauke	5
That be so far abusyd /They cannot be excusyd	62	Hauke	6
In hope that no man shall /Be myscontent withall.	62	Hauke	28
Be] 'By' Kynge & Marche 1554			
He shall be as now nameles,	62	Hauke	38
But he shall not be blameles,	62	Hauke	39
Nor he shall not be shameles;	62	Hauke	40
He then, to be sure, /Callyd her with a lure.	63	Hauke	75
'These be my gospellers,	65	Hauke	120
These be my pystyllers,	65	Hauke	121
These be my querysters /To helpe me to synge,	65	Hauke	122
Make the churche to be /In smale auctoryte;	65	Hauke	139
How be it, mayden Meed /Made theym to be agreed;	65	Hauke	150
To be polutyd this;	66	Hauke	181
In them he no scolys /For braynsycke frantycke folys:	68	Hauke	248
Wherfore, as I be savyd, /Ye ar therfore beknavyd.	70	Hauke	309
The more shal be your mede.	72	Phy Sparrow	16
It can not be exprest /My sorowfull hevynesse,	72	Phy Sparrow	31
Of what estate ye be, /Of hye or lowe degre,	73	Phy Sparrow	54
That Phyllyp preserved may be!	74	Phy Sparrow	93

BE —BE

	Page	Title	Line
Phillip myght be bolde	76	Phy Sparrow	177
If any such might be found!	76	Phy Sparrow	188
And he shold be bought /For golde and fee,	76	Phy Sparrow	195
My sparowe than shuld be quycke	77	Phy Sparrow	205
But as verely as ye be	78	Phy Sparrow	254
No man can be sure	81	Phy Sparrow	370
So none be left behynde.	81	Phy Sparrow	389
He shall be the preest,	81	Phy Sparrow	400
That shall be theyr charge;	83	Phy Sparrow	457
He shall be th[e] sedeane,	85	Phy Sparrow	552
the] 'thye' †Kele 1545.2, 'thy' Wyght 1553, Kitson 1560.6, Marshe 1568			
shall be holy wather clarke.	86	Phy Sparrow	570
And hard to be enneude	91	Phy Sparrow	775
And worthy to be enrold.	91	Phy Sparrow	787
Though it be refused,	92	Phy Sparrow	816
To whom be the laude ascrybed	93	Phy Sparrow	871
That causeth me /Studious to be	95	Phy Sparrow	960
But yet certayne /I wyll be playne,	96	Phy Sparrow	967
Be] 'me' †Kele 1545.2			
Ever to be /Their true bedell	96	Phy Sparrow	979
It cannot be denayd /But it was well convayd,	98	Phy Sparrow	1065
I pray you it may be amendyd	102	Phy Sparrow	1246
If it be sadly dyscust.	102	Phy Sparrow	1250
Wherefore shulde I be blamed	103	Phy Sparrow	1255
She is worthy to be enrolde	103	Phy Sparrow	1258
His Dirige, her commendacyon /Can be no derogacyon,	103	Phy Sparrow	1277
Why shuld she be afrayde?	103	Phy Sparrow	1283
Sholde be set and sorted,	103	Phy Sparrow	1287
To be matriculate /With ladyes of estate?	104	Phy Sparrow	1288
What the cause may be /Of this perplexite!	106	Phy Sparrow	1369
I pray God they be payned	106	Phy Sparrow	1376
Though this knaves be deade,	106	Epitaphe	I
Laureat to be /Of fame royall;	112	Calliope	7
I dare be bolde /Thus for to were.	112	Calliope	11
To be so scornefull to your alye	113	Scot Kynge	13
And ye be desolate as Armeleche,	114	Scot Kynge	24
A kynge anoynted, and ye be non.	114	Scot Kynge	26
Parde ye be his homager	114	Scot Kynge	30
Ye be bounde tenauntes to his estate;	114	Scot Kynge	36
For a prysoner there now ye be	114	Scot Kynge	40
Thanked be saynte Gorge, our ladyes knythe,	114	Scot Kynge	42
Ye had be better to have busked to Huntley Bankes,	114	Scot Kynge	50
be] 'bet' †Fakes 1513			
Therfore ye be layde now full lowe.	114	Scot Kynge	53
A solempne sumner for to be?	116	Ag Scottes	51
Ye may be lorde of Locryan -	117	Ag Scottes	61
Thankyd be God in trinyte,	119	Ag Scottes	140
The tokens ar not good /To be true Englysh blood;	121	Ag Scottes2	23
Thow ye be lusty as Syr Lybyus, launces to breke,	122	Garneschel	17
Be the kynges most noble commandement.	122	Garneschel	E
Ye countyr umwhyle to capcyously, and ar ye be dysiryd;	123	Garnesche2	11
Yor moth etyn mokkysh maneres, they be all to-myryd.	123	Garnesche2	12
Your harte ys to hawte, iwys, yt wyll nat be alowde.	123	Garnesche2	26
Welle Be Seyn Crysteovyr Chalannger, et cetera	124	Garnesche3	I
I caste me nat to be od	124	Garnesche3	6
Ye wolde be callyd a maker,	127	Garnesche3	108
The nexte halter ther xall be	128	Garnesche3	176
That ther thou xuldyst be rachchyd	128	Garnesche3	180
Ye may wele be bedawyd,	128	Garnesche3	182
Well Be Seen Crystofer Chalangar, et cetera	129	Garnesche5	I
Of naturys workys, how they be	130	Garnesche5	9
[Thy] myrrour may be the devyllys ars.	130	Garnesche5	18
Thy] 'They' †MS Harley 367			
Thow thou be a jantyll man borne,	131	Garnesche5	69
Withowte thou leve thou shalt be chekt,	132	Garnesche5	109
Thow thou be pyllyd, thow ar nat sade.	132	Garnesche5	117
Thowth it be now ful tyde with the,	132	Garnesche5	120
Lerne or be lewde, I shrow thy face.	132	Garnesche5	127
Stop a tyd, and be welle ware	133	Garnesche5	162
Ye be nat cawte in an hempen snare.	133	Garnesche5	163
Of thi lewdenes that may be tolde.	134	Garnesche5	175
My study myght be better spynt;	134	Garnesche5	176
Al maters wel pondred and wel to be regarded,	137	Ven Tongues	1
How shuld a fals lying tung then be rewarded?	137	Ven Tongues	2
Such tunges shuld be torne out by the harde rootes,	137	Ven Tongues	3
Worketh more mischiefe than can be tolde;	137	Ven Tongues	8
That, if I wist not to be controlde,	137	Ven Tongues	9
Yet somwhat to say I dare well be bolde,	137	Ven Tongues	10
If there be none other mater but that,	137	Ven Tongues	14
Than to be founde in any such faute.	137	Ven Tongues	25
For though some be lidder, and list for to rayle,	138	Ven Tongues	30
Any such foly to rest or to be.	138	Ven Tongues	35
For tunges untayde be renning astray,	138	Ven Tongues	37
What fault find ye herein but may be avowed.	138	Ven Tongues	41
For men be now tratlers and tellers of tales;	139	Ven Tongues	63
And you knew all ye would be ill apayd'.	139	Ven Tongues	72
He might be sure to have shame ynough.	139	Ven Tongues	78

	Page	Title	Line
Be it erly or late, welth hath a season.	140	Magnyfycence	3
But men nowe a dayes so unhappely be uryd,	140	Magnyfycence	6
That nothynge than welth may worse be enduryd.	140	Magnyfycence	7
But yf prudence be proved with sad cyrcumspeccyon,	141	Magnyfycence	16
Welthe myght be wonne and made to the lure,	141	Magnyfycence	17
And eyther I am dysseyved, or ye be the same.	141	Magnyfycence	25
And from whens come ye, and it myght be askyd?	141	Magnyfycence	29
To tell you, syr, I dare not, leest I sholde be maskyd	141	Magnyfycence	30
How be it, lyberte may somtyme be to large,	141	Magnyfycence	37
But yf reason be regent and ruler of your barge.	141	Magnyfycence	38
That lyberte be lynkyd with the chayne of countenaunce,	141	Magnyfycence	44
For lyberte at large is lothe to be stoppyd,	141	Magnyfycence	46
But with countenaunce your corage must be croppyd.	141	Magnyfycence	47
God forbyd ye sholde be let	142	Magnyfycence	63
Mayster Measure, you be come in good season.	143	Magnyfycence	84
Can be content with Measure presence.	143	Magnyfycence	86
A, ye be wonders men!	143	Magnyfycence	89
So it in measure be.	143	Magnyfycence	101
With every condycyon measure must be sought.	143	Magnyfycence	115
So that lyberte be not lefte behynde.	144	Magnyfycence	129
All trebyllys and tenours be rulyd by a meyne.	144	Magnyfycence	137
So wolde I, but I wolde be lothe,	144	Magnyfycence	143
That wonte was to be formyst, now to come behynde.	144	Magnyfycence	144
Surely I am joyous that ye be myndyd thus;	144	Magnyfycence	156
So in his harte he may be glad of us.	145	Magnyfycence	158
Syr, though ye be a noble prynce of myght,	145	Magnyfycence	166
That Measure be mayster us semeth it is syttynge.	145	Magnyfycence	176
Then may I say that ye be servauntys myne.	145	Magnyfycence	183
For by measure I warne you we thynke to be gydyd;	145	Magnyfycence	184
Measure and I wyll never be devydyd,	145	Magnyfycence	186
Laudable your consayte is to be acountyd,	145	Magnyfycence	191
Measure with noblenesse sholde be alyde.	145	Magnyfycence	194
But plenarly all thought from you must be dyschargyd,	146	Magnyfycence	207
Bycause course of measure - yf I be in the way:	146	Magnyfycence	213
And from felycyte may not be forborne,	146	Magnyfycence	220
Welth and wyt, I say, be so threde bare worne,	146	Magnyfycence	223
But yf therof the soner amendys be made;	146	Magnyfycence	226
I wolde be rulyd and I myght for shame.	147	Magnyfycence	235
God forbede that it other wyse sholde be!	147	Magnyfycence	246
Sholde be your dwellynge, in my consyderacyon.	148	Magnyfycence	274
As in that I wyll not be agaynst your pleasure.	148	Magnyfycence	276
Largesse is laudable so it be in measure.	148	Magnyfycence	278
'in measure be' †Rastell & Treveris C 1530, B			
Syr, thanked be God, he hath his hele.	149	Magnyfycence	315
Your pleasure, syr shortely shall be done.	149	Magnyfycence	321
I pray you, syr, I may so be;	151	Magnyfycence	391
For, in fayth, ye be well met.	151	Magnyfycence	402
But nowe wyll I, that they be gone,	151	Magnyfycence	407
Counterfet maydenhode may well be borne,	152	Magnyfycence	445
Whan the noppe is rughe, it wolde be shorne.	153	Magnyfycence	448
An olde barne wolde be underset.	153	Magnyfycence	454
It wolde be masked in my net!	153	Magnyfycence	458
It wolde be nyce, thoughe I say nay;	153	Magnyfycence	459
And be as praty as she may,	153	Magnyfycence	464
Coll wolde go clenly, and it wyll not be,	153	Magnyfycence	476
And Annot wolde be nyce, and laughes, 'tehe wehe.'	153	Magnyfycence	477
This nonnes nowe and then, and it myght be,	154	Magnyfycence	488
That we thre galauntes sholde be longe asonder.	154	Magnyfycence	511
Ryght so a sharp fansy must be founde	155	Magnyfycence	553
Nay, and you be angry and overwharte,	156	Magnyfycence	562
Ye, and se howe it may be compast	156	Magnyfycence	567
Thy wordes be but wynde, never they have no wayght.	156	Magnyfycence	578
Cappe, syr. I say you be to bolde.	157	Magnyfycence	602
Syr, and yf ye wolde not be wrothe -	157	Magnyfycence	606
But I wyll be ruled after your counsell.	157	Magnyfycence	615
What the devyll! Howe may that be?	157	Magnyfycence	627
As good to be occupyed as up and downe to trace	159	Magnyfycence	692
Double delynge and I be all one;	159	Magnyfycence	696
And though I be so odyous a geste,	160	Magnyfycence	703
And yet, I trowe, some of you be better sped than I	160	Magnyfycence	722
Be lyght of byleve and hasty of credence;	161	Magnyfycence	740
Cankard Jacke Hare, loke thou be not rusty;	161	Magnyfycence	758
Dusty! Nay, syr, ye be all of the lusty;	161	Magnyfycence	760
Mary, with Magnyfycence I wolde be retaynyd.	161	Magnyfycence	763
Well, and I be a coward, there is mo than I.	162	Magnyfycence	770
Cannyst thou helpe in faver that I myght be brought?	162	Magnyfycence	777
And desyre me thy good mayster to be?	162	Magnyfycence	798
No; for or we stryke, we wyll be advysed twyse.	163	Magnyfycence	810
Why, shall he be of your bende?	163	Magnyfycence	818
Ye, but of my name let us be wyse.	167	Magnyfycence	963
There is many evyll faveryd, and thou be foule!	167	Magnyfycence	969
My wyttys be weke, my braynys are lyght;	169	Magnyfycence	1024
Ye. But trowest thou that he be not maungey?	171	Magnyfycence	1122
Grimbaldus gredy snatche a puddyng tyl the rost be redy.	172	Magnyfycence	1155
For be he cayser or be he kynge,	174	Magnyfycence	1214
For be he cayser or be he kynge,	174	Magnyfycence	1214
That rubbed she must be on the gall	174	Magnyfycence	1232
And those be they that come up of nought -	174	Magnyfycence	1240

BE —BE   Page   Title   Line

As some be not ferre and yf it were well sought —	174	Magnyfycence	1241
Suche dawys, what soever they be, ...	174	Magnyfycence	1242
That be set in auctorite.	174	Magnyfycence	1243
All that he dothe muste be alowde;	175	Magnyfycence	1247
There be two lyther, rude and ranke, ...	175	Magnyfycence	1266
And, be the mater yll more or lesse, ...	175	Magnyfycence	1272
By God, there be some that be shroudly towchyd.	175	Magnyfycence	1277
By God, there be some that be shroudly towchyd.	175	Magnyfycence	1277
For there be other that foly dothe use	175	Magnyfycence	1280
Nay, but fansy must be eyther fyrst or last.	176	Magnyfycence	1288
For drede, that we dare not ofte, lest we be spyed.	177	Magnyfycence	1339
'What howe! Be ye mery! Was it not well conveyed?'	177	Magnyfycence	1347
'As oft as ye lyst, so honeste be savyd.	177	Magnyfycence	1348
Alas, dere harte, loke that we be not perseyvyd!'	177	Magnyfycence	1349
Without me be full ofte aspyed.	177	Magnyfycence	1355
Convey it be crafte, lyft and lay asyde.	177	Magnyfycence	1357
Syr, as by my wyll, it shall be so no more.	178	Magnyfycence	1377
Ye shall be occupyed, Welthe, at my wyll.	178	Magnyfycence	1380
It is good yet that lyberte be ruled by reason.	178	Magnyfycence	1387
Yourselfe shall be ruled by lyberte and largesse.	179	Magnyfycence	1389
I am content so it in measure be.	179	Magnyfycence	1390
Not and your grace wolde be ruled by me.	179	Magnyfycence	1393
Nay. He shall be ruled even as I lyst.	179	Magnyfycence	1394
Be governed and gyded; wote ye what I say?	179	Magnyfycence	1397
It shall be done. Ye, but byd hym come away	179	Magnyfycence	1399
Be not to bolde my frende; I counsell you, bere a brayne. . . .	179	Magnyfycence	1405
Syr, yet without sapyence your substaunce may be smal;	179	Magnyfycence	1407
I truste your grace wyll be agreabyll	179	Magnyfycence	1417
So it be by mesure I am ryght well content.	180	Magnyfycence	1421
Whether sholde welth be rulyd by lyberte, ...	180	Magnyfycence	1431
Syr, as me semeth, ye sholde be rulyd be me.	180	Magnyfycence	1433
Syr, as me semeth, ye sholde be rulyd be me.	180	Magnyfycence	1433
Mayster Felycyte, let be your chydynge;	180	Magnyfycence	1437
And so as ye se it wyll be no better, ...	180	Magnyfycence	1438
And welth is nought worthe yf lyberte be behynde.	180	Magnyfycence	1442
Than waste must be welcome, and fare well thryfte.	180	Magnyfycence	1444
For nowe, syrs, I am lyke as a prynce sholde be;	181	Magnyfycence	1457
He may not be comparyd unto me.	181	Magnyfycence	1476
Howe be it, I wolde be ryght gladde, I you assure, ...	183	Magnyfycence	1527
Any thynge to do that myght be to your pleasure.	183	Magnyfycence	1528
As I be saved, with pleasure I am supprysyd	183	Magnyfycence	1529
So as ye be a prynce of great myght, ...	183	Magnyfycence	1545
These wordes in myne eyre, they be so lustely spoken, ...	184	Magnyfycence	1565
That on suche a female my flesshe wolde be wroken.	184	Magnyfycence	1566
That weryed I wolde be on suche a bayte.	184	Magnyfycence	1568
A, Cockes armes! Where myght suche one be founde?	184	Magnyfycence	1569
Nay, nay; for lesse I waraunt you to be sped, ...	184	Magnyfycence	1571
Why, wyl a maystres be wonne for money and for golde?	184	Magnyfycence	1575
But one thynge I warne you, prece forth and be bolde.	184	Magnyfycence	1582
Ye, but some be full koy and passynge harde harted.	184	Magnyfycence	1583
But, blessyd be our Lorde, they wyll be sone converted.	184	Magnyfycence	1584
But, blessyd be our Lorde, they wyll be sone converted.	184	Magnyfycence	1584
Why, wyll they then be intreted, the most and the lest?	184	Magnyfycence	1585
Wysely let these wordes in your mynde be wayed:	185	Magnyfycence	1593
By waywarde wylfulnes let eche thynge be convayed;	185	Magnyfycence	1594
Be it reason or none, it shall not gretely skyll;	185	Magnyfycence	1596
Be it ryght or wronge, by the advyse of me, ...	185	Magnyfycence	1597
Be wrastynge and wrythynge, and away drawe.	185	Magnyfycence	1608
And ye se a man that with hym ye be not pleased, ...	185	Magnyfycence	1609
And that your mynde can not well be eased —	185	Magnyfycence	1610
Tyll I be revenged on that horson knave.	185	Magnyfycence	1616
Suche lustes at large may not be lefte behynde.	186	Magnyfycence	1628
Syr, Sober Sadnesse cometh. Wherfore it be?	186	Magnyfycence	1631
Nay, syr. That affeccyon ought to be reserved, ...	186	Magnyfycence	1643
Notwithstandynge to you be it sayde	186	Magnyfycence	1651
Mesure, ye knowe wel, with hym I can not be content;	186	Magnyfycence	1656
What force ye, so that [y]e be payde?	187	Magnyfycence	1672
ye be] 'he be' †Rastell & Treveris C 1530, B			
I care not howe sone he be refused, ...	187	Magnyfycence	1683
So that I may craftely be excused.	187	Magnyfycence	1684
And we wyll be comonynge in the mene season.	187	Magnyfycence	1688
And made instance for me be lykelyhod.	188	Magnyfycence	1697
But thynke you with Magnyfycence I shal be reserved?	188	Magnyfycence	1702
The Holy Goost be with your grace.	188	Magnyfycence	1711
Wherfore I wyll that ye be resydent	188	Magnyfycence	1718
For your selfe. Syr, yf I myght permytted be, ...	188	Magnyfycence	1720
That day I se hym I shall be worse all nyght.	188	Magnyfycence	1724
So to be ruled by measure, it is a payne.	189	Magnyfycence	1739
Mary, I wene he wolde not be glad to come agayne.	189	Magnyfycence	1740
It is no wonder, therfore, thoughe ye be wrothe	189	Magnyfycence	1748
Than is it done as it sholde be;	189	Magnyfycence	1764
Say on; me thynke your reasons be profounde.	190	Magnyfycence	1767
Syr, of my counsayle this shall be the grounde:	190	Magnyfycence	1768
Those thre wyll be redy even at your bekenynge;	190	Magnyfycence	1778
For as thou sayst, ryght so shall it be, ...	190	Magnyfycence	1783
To be supervysour, and on Largesse also;	190	Magnyfycence	1785
A, syr, thy jarfawcon and thou be hanged togyder!	191	Magnyfycence	1812
I trowe it be a frost, for the way is slydder;	191	Magnyfycence	1816

	Page	Title	Line
When ye knowe that I knowe, ye wyll not be glad.	192	Magnyfycence	1844
Ye, let be thy japes, and tell me howe	192	Magnyfycence	1846
I pray the, Largesse, let be thy sobbynge.	192	Magnyfycence	1851
Man or woman, of what estate they be,	194	Magnyfycence	1898
Faders and moders that be neclygent,	194	Magnyfycence	1920
That rule not be mesure that they have in theyr handys,	195	Magnyfycence	1939
A, my bonys ake! My lymmys be sore!	195	Magnyfycence	1955
Fy, fy, that ever I sholde be brought in this snare!	196	Magnyfycence	1972
Nowe, syth it wyll no nother be,	196	Magnyfycence	1978
Alasse that ever I sholde be so shamed!	196	Magnyfycence	1982
In mysery and wretchydnesse thus to be lapped!	196	Magnyfycence	1985
And whan it pleaseth God, better may be.	196	Magnyfycence	1993
Alasse! With colde my lymmes shall be marde.	197	Magnyfycence	2004
With curteyns of sylke, ye were wonte to be drawe;	197	Magnyfycence	2014
curteyns of sylke] 'courtely sylkes' †Rastell & Treveris 1530B			
Nowe must be storm ybeten with showres and raynes.	197	Magnyfycence	2017
Your hede that was wonte to be happed moost drowpy and drowsy,	197	Magnyfycence	2018
Now shal ye be scabbed, scurvy, and lowsy.	197	Magnyfycence	2019
Ye, syr, yesterday wyll not be callyd agayne.	197	Magnyfycence	2031
A, howe my lymmys be lyther and lame!	198	Magnyfycence	2038
Better it is to begge than to be hangyd with shame.	198	Magnyfycence	2039
Yet many had lever hangyd to be	198	Magnyfycence	2040
With ye, mary, syrs, thus sholde it be:	198	Magnyfycence	2064
At lyberte a man may be bolde for to brake;	199	Magnyfycence	2085
For I am a vertue yf I be well used,	199	Magnyfycence	2101
And so shall a noble man nobly be servyd.	200	Magnyfycence	2120
In youth to be wanton, and let them have theyr wyll -	200	Magnyfycence	2137
Of worldly welthe, alasse, who can be sure?	201	Magnyfycence	2155
For to be wyse all men may lerne of me,	201	Magnyfycence	2158
Torde! Thou arte good to be a man of warre.	202	Magnyfycence	2179
By Cockes bones, I shall blysse the and thou be to bolde.	202	Magnyfycence	2182
Nay. Then thou wylte dynge the devyll and thou be not holde.	202	Magnyfycence	2183
But wottest thou, horson? I rede the to be wyse.	202	Magnyfycence	2184
Peas, or I shall wrynge thy be in a brake.	202	Magnyfycence	2187
Now let us be all one, and let us lyve in rest;	202	Magnyfycence	2202
For we be, syrs, but a fewe of the best.	202	Magnyfycence	2203
In faythe, and I wyll be to reason agreable.	203	Magnyfycence	2205
And thus to be facyd, I thynke it great skorne.	203	Magnyfycence	2217
And ye be a gentylman, ye have knavys condycyons.	203	Magnyfycence	2219
By God, I tell you, I wyll not be out facyd.	203	Magnyfycence	2220
By the masse, I warant the, I wyll not be bracyd.	203	Magnyfycence	2221
To grope a gardevyaunce, though it be well bandyd,	203	Magnyfycence	2231
Your trymynge and tramynge by me must be tangyd,	203	Magnyfycence	2234
Ye be the thevys, I say, away my goodys dyd cary.	203	Magnyfycence	2239
In fay, man, some rybbys of the motton be so ranke	204	Magnyfycence	2269
Ye shall be clappyd with a coloppe	204	Magnyfycence	2272
Som be wrestyd there that they thynke on it forty dayes,	204	Magnyfycence	2274
For there be horys there at all assayes.	204	Magnyfycence	2275
Though I aske mercy I must nedys be refusyd.	205	Magnyfycence	2299
No, no; for thy synnys be so excedynge farre,	205	Magnyfycence	2300
And loke that it be not longe	206	Magnyfycence	2311
A, blessyd may ye be, syr! What shall you I call?	206	Magnyfycence	2327
Your wordes be more sweter than ony precyous narde,	207	Magnyfycence	2345
With drammes of devocyon your dyet must be drest,	207	Magnyfycence	2358
Then shall you be sone delyvered from dystresse,	208	Magnyfycence	2383
Cryst be amonge you, and the Holy Goste!	208	Magnyfycence	2385
He be your conducte, the Lorde of myghtys moste!	208	Magnyfycence	2386
Syr, your requeste shall not be delayed.	208	Magnyfycence	2401
Nowe shall ye be renewyd with solace.	208	Magnyfycence	2404
To your requeste I shall be confyrmable.	208	Magnyfycence	2407
And be ruled by me, whiche am called Redresse.	208	Magnyfycence	2410
Redresse sholde be at the rekenynge in every accompte,	208	Magnyfycence	2413
Full many thynges there be that lacketh redresse,	209	Magnyfycence	2415
And made also mesure to be put fro me.	209	Magnyfycence	2446
It wolde be founde so yf it were well tryde.	210	Magnyfycence	2449
Ye com hether as well as can be thought.	210	Magnyfycence	2459
Accordynge to treuth they be well devysyd.	210	Magnyfycence	2470
Yf you be so myndyd, we be ryght glad.	210	Magnyfycence	2473
Yf you be so myndyd, we be ryght glad.	210	Magnyfycence	2473
Fyrst, from your magnyfycence syn must be abjectyd;	211	Magnyfycence	2484
Be gentyll, then, of corage, and lerne to be kynde;	211	Magnyfycence	2486
Be gentyll, then, of corage, and lerne to be kynde;	211	Magnyfycence	2486
For of noblenesse the chefe poynt is to be lyberall,	211	Magnyfycence	2487
So that your largesse be not to prodygall.	211	Magnyfycence	2488
That nothynge be gyven without consyderacyon.	211	Magnyfycence	2495
And ever let the drede of God be in your syght,	211	Magnyfycence	2498
Who lyst to consyder shall never be begylyd,	212	Magnyfycence	2512
Yf it be regystryd well in memory;	212	Magnyfycence	2513
How none estate lyvynge of hymselfe can be sure,	213	Magnyfycence	2557
Without our shyppe be sure, it is lykely to brast,	213	Magnyfycence	2562
Thus none estate lyvynge of hym[selfe] can be sure,	214	Magnyfycence	2564
hymselfe] 'hym' †Rastell & Treveris C 1530, B			
I am content, my frendys, that it so be.	214	Magnyfycence	2570
If that ye wyll /A whyle be styll,	214	El Rummynge	3
The devyll and she be syb.	217	El Rummynge	100
Some be flybytten, /Some skewed as a kytten;	218	El Rummynge	141
Abyde, abyde, /And to you shall be tolde	218	El Rummynge	157
For, be there never so moche prese,	218	El Rummynge	174

BE —BE		Page	Title	Line

	Page	Title	Line
This ale shal be thycker,	219	El Rummynge	205
It shall make you loke /Yonger than ye be	219	El Rummynge	214
Some go streyght thyder, /Be it slaty or slyder;	221	El Rummynge	258
Be that as be maye;	221	El Rummynge	261
Be that as be maye;	221	El Rummynge	261
Some lothe to be espyde,	221	El Rummynge	262
She semed to be a wytch.	226	El Rummynge	458
'They be wretchockes thou hast brought,	226	El Rummynge	465
They] 'The' Day 1560			
The devyll thereon be wroken!	227	El Rummynge	498
What nede all this be spoken?	227	El Rummynge	499
Properly payntyd to be my coverture;	231	Speke Parott	9
Some be to churlysshe, and some be to kynde.	233	Speke Parott	77
Some be to churlysshe, and some be to kynde.	233	Speke Parott	77
Parrot pretendith to be a bybyll clarke!'	234	Speke Parott	119
Yf fortune be frendly, and grace be the guyde,	234	Speke Parott	139
Yf fortune be frendly, and grace be the guyde,	234	Speke Parott	139
For aurea lyngua Greca ought to be magnyfyed,	234	Speke Parott	142
And yet he wolde be rekenyd pro Ariopagita;	235	Speke Parott	156
And every mad medler must now be a maker.	235	Speke Parott	161
And Donatus be dryven out of scole;	235	Speke Parott	170
'Cristecrosse and Saynt Nycholas, Parrot, be your good spede!'	236	Speke Parott	189
shall be his protectyon, his pavys and his wall.	236	Speke Parott	203
Shall lepe from this lyfe, as mery as we be.	236	Speke Parott	222
I wyl be ferme and stabyll, /And to yow servyceabyll,	237	Speke Parott	246
And also prophytabyll, /Yf ye be agreabyll,	237	Speke Parott	249
Be love I am constreyned /To be with yow retayned,	238	Speke Parott	257
Be love I am constreyned /To be with yow retayned,	238	Speke Parott	258
Hyt wyll not be refrayned:	238	Speke Parott	259
I pray yow be reclaymed,	238	Speke Parott	260
In there remembraunce ye may be inrolde.	239	Speke Parott	291
Now pas furthe, good Parott, Owur Lorde be your s[t]ede,	239	Speke Parott	313
stede] 'spede' †MS Harley 2252			
Thow ye be tauntyd, Parotte, with tonges attayntyd,	240	Speke Parott	343
Grete reysons with resons be now reprobitante,	244	Speke Parott	442
So myche crossyng and blyssyng and hym all be shrewde;	246	Speke Parott	516
It may well so be,	247	Collyn Clout	38
For though my ryme be ragged, /Tattered and jagged,	248	Collyn Clout	53
That the premenyre /Is lyke to be set afyre	249	Collyn Clout	109
Howebeit, some there be,	250	Collyn Clout	147
Than to be combred with care.	251	Collyn Clout	177
But ye loke to be let lose	252	Collyn Clout	213
And you wyll be stylla,	253	Collyn Clout	260
Without his vertue be greatter,	253	Collyn Clout	271
There may no cost be spared;	254	Collyn Clout	318
Wherfore men be supposynge	255	Collyn Clout	357
Shulde be lanternes of lyght.	257	Collyn Clout	440
The sonne somtyme to be	258	Collyn Clout	468
Agaynst the churche to be,	259	Collyn Clout	499
And eyther ye be to badde,	259	Collyn Clout	502
And some be Hussians,	260	Collyn Clout	551
And some be Arryans,	260	Collyn Clout	552
And some be Pollegyans,	260	Collyn Clout	553
They mought be better advysed	261	Collyn Clout	579
Then to be so dysgysed.	261	Collyn Clout	580
And where the prelates be /Come of lowe degre	261	Collyn Clout	585
For then ye wyll be wroken	261	Collyn Clout	598
And your tonsors be croppyd,	263	Collyn Clout	677
tonsors be croppyd] 'coursers betrapped' †Godfray 1531, Kele 1545.1, Marshe 1568			
Your eeres they be stopped!	263	Collyn Clout	678
The whiche shulde be /Bothe franke and free,	264	Collyn Clout	710
That wolde it shulde be noted	265	Collyn Clout	754
How scrypture shulde be coted,	265	Collyn Clout	755
Shulde be imprynted better	265	Collyn Clout	761
So as they myght be /Compendyously conveyed,	265	Collyn Clout	767
These words shuld be more weyed,	265	Collyn Clout	769
These words] 'Those words' Marshe 1568, 'This' MS Harley 2252			
Doctours that lerned be	266	Collyn Clout	790
Shall nat be objected by me.	266	Collyn Clout	794
by] 'for' Kele 1545.1, Marshe 1568, 'at by' MS Harley 2252			
This can nat be brought about	267	Collyn Clout	849
And they be so attaynted	269	Collyn Clout	900
That they be deefe and dum,	269	Collyn Clout	903
Without his presydent be by,	272	Collyn Clout	1042
Whether it be wronge or ryght	272	Collyn Clout	1055
And let be all your motynge,	273	Collyn Clout	1073
Of you that clerkes be,	273	Collyn Clout	1083
For those that vertuous be	273	Collyn Clout	1092
Wherfore shulde I be blamed?	274	Collyn Clout	1112
be] not in Marshe 1568			
Ye ought to be ashamed	274	Collyn Clout	1113
Agaynst me to be gr[am]ed,	274	Collyn Clout	1114
gramed] 'greved' †Godfray 1531, Kele 1545.1, Marshe 1568, MS Harley 2252			
Then yf any there be	274	Collyn Clout	1117
That his conscyence be nat clene,	274	Collyn Clout	1122
Great ydeottes they be,	274	Collyn Clout	1130

	Page	Title	Line
That be theyr prymates?	275	Collyn Clout	1151
And say howe that we be /Full of parcyallyte;	276	Collyn Clout	1192
They say many matters be borne	276	Collyn Clout	1198
To be tered thus and torne?	276	Collyn Clout	1201
Ye prechers shall be yawde:	276	Collyn Clout	1204
Some shall be sawde,	276	Collyn Clout	1205
For, be it good, be it yll,	276	Collyn Clout	1217
For, be it good, be it yll,	276	Collyn Clout	1217
As it is, it shall be styll,	277	Collyn Clout	1218
Lest they be Seduces,	277	Collyn Clout	1229
Seduces] 'Saducies' Marshe 1568, 'Adusayes' MS Harley 2252			
As they be sad sayne,	277	Collyn Clout	1230
sad] 'sayd' Kele 1545.1, Marshe 1568			
Whiche hate to be corrected	277	Collyn Clout	1235
Whan they be infected,	277	Collyn Clout	1236
Prynted for to be,	277	Collyn Clout	1239
Tyll the coost be clere	277	Collyn Clout	1257
This tale will be to trew:	280	Why Come Ye	65
Be it blacke or whight	281	Why Come Ye	115
It can not be moche worse.	282	Why Come Ye	138
Our lorde be his soccoure!	282	Why Come Ye	160
That be worth ii kues.	284	Why Come Ye	235
Their hertes be in thyr hose!	286	Why Come Ye	289
Our barons be so bolde,	286	Why Come Ye	292
Whether he be knyght or squyre,	287	Why Come Ye	344
He shulde be hyder brought;	287	Why Come Ye	351
I trow all wyll be nought,	287	Why Come Ye	353
Subtelly wrought shall be	288	Why Come Ye	364
I pray God be his gyde.	289	Why Come Ye	395
It shall be as he wyll.	289	Why Come Ye	419
Be it soure, be it swete!	289	Why Come Ye	422
Be it soure, be it swete!	289	Why Come Ye	422
Now yet all this myght be	290	Why Come Ye	446
Had nat our prynce be	292	Why Come Ye	539
And made to him be brought	293	Why Come Ye	552
That shall be a spectacle	293	Why Come Ye	568
At them that be well borne;	294	Why Come Ye	600
Thus dayly they be decked, /Taunted and checked,	294	Why Come Ye	611
Of what estate he be /Of spirituall dygnyte;	294	Why Come Ye	617
Tyll better layser be founde;	294	Why Come Ye	627
Such a casuelte shulde be sene	297	Why Come Ye	747
Be faythfull, trew and just	298	Why Come Ye	753
And soone may be perceyvid	298	Why Come Ye	782
Any man shulde be /In perplexyte /Of dyspleasure;	300	Why Come Ye	843
This shrewdly accordis /To be a cupborde for lordys!	302	Why Come Ye	914
For Folam peason /With him be nat geson;	304	Why Come Ye	1000
And it be as I wene.	304	Why Come Ye	1007
But all must be tryde,	304	Why Come Ye	1013
To be shamfully named!	305	Why Come Ye	1053
named] 'name' Marshe 1568			
And ofte prechours be blamed	305	Why Come Ye	1054
ofte] 'the' MS Rawlinson C. 813			
All thynges sholde be amended,	307	Why Come Ye	1111
To be under his subjectyon.	307	Why Come Ye	1126
Whether God be pleased or wroth.	307	Why Come Ye	1132
And so cruell hertyd, /That he wyll nat be convertyd;	308	Why Come Ye	1179
That] not in MS Rawlinson C. 813			
His fame to be encrest	309	Why Come Ye	1214
Whatsoever your name be?	309	Why Come Ye2	2
What though ye be namelesse,	309	Why Come Ye2	3
A daucock ye be, and so shal be styll!	310	Why Come Ye2	34
A daucock ye be, and so shal be styll!	310	Why Come Ye2	34
So that there workis myght famously be sene,	314	Garlande	67
How ryvers rin not tyll the spryng be full;	314	Garlande	81
Yet dyverse ther be, industryous of reason,	315	Garlande	106
ther] 'that' MS Cotton Vitellius E.x			
Yet harde is to make but sum fawt be founde.'	315	Garlande	112
For how shulde Cato els be callyd wyse,	315	Garlande	123
Towchid, and hard for to be barrid.	316	Garlande	143
barrid] 'debarrid' MS Cotton Vitellius E.x			
That he so sholde be, me semith it sittyng,	316	Garlande	149
it] 'it is' MS Cotton Vitellius E.x			
All be it grete parte he hath surrendred	316	Garlande	150
Be he never so lytell of substaunce,	317	Garlande	177
Sume be moche spokyn of for makynge of frays;	317	Garlande	182
Some be called crafty that can pyke a purse;	317	Garlande	184
pyke] 'kit' MS Cotton Vitellius E.x			
Some men be made of for the mokery;	317	Garlande	185
the] 'their' Marshe 1568			
Some famous wetewoldis, and they be moche wurs;	317	Garlande	187
Ryot and Revell be in your courte rowlis;	317	Garlande	192
Maintenaunce and Mischefe, theis be men of myght;	317	Garlande	193
For wysdome and sadnesse be out a sunnyng;	318	Garlande	201
be out] 'be set out' Marshe 1568, MS Cotton Vitellius E.x			
May be brought forth, such as can be founde,	318	Garlande	216
May be brought forth, such as can be founde,	318	Garlande	216
With laureat tryumphe why Skelton sholde be crownde.	318	Garlande	217
I am content that he be not exylide	318	Garlande	224

BE —BE

	Page	Title	Line
What he hath done, let it be brought to syght.	318	Garlande	230
'To your request we be well condiscendid;	318	Garlande	232
Alas, what ayle you to be so overthwhart,	320	Garlande	307
How that our Englysshe myght fresshely be ennewed;	323	Garlande	389
ennewed] 'a meude' †Fakes 1523			
But that I poynt you to be prothonatory	324	Garlande	432
That but if my warkes therto be agreable,	324	Garlande	439
Whiche shall be to you a sufferayne accessary,	326	Garlande	523
And we shall se you ageyne or it be pryme.'	326	Garlande	525
Be well assurid I shall aquyte your hyre,	327	Garlande	550
Wordes be swordes, and hard to call ageine.'	328	Garlande	567
'Go softly,' she sayd, 'the stones be full glint.'	328	Garlande	572
Be issuis and portis from all maner of nacyons';	328	Garlande	580
'Forsothe,' quod she, 'theys be haskardis and rebawdis,	329	Garlande	607
haskardis] 'hastardis' †Fakes 1523			
With other condycyons that well myght be left.	329	Garlande	615
Sume fayne themselfe folys, and wolde be callyd wyse,	329	Garlande	616
But hailid they be homwarde with sorow and shame.	329	Garlande	622
Or gummis of Saby so derely that be solde.	331	Garlande	675
Wherewith your spiritis may be revyvid.'	332	Garlande	713
O wele were hym that herof myght be sure,	332	Garlande	718
And if there be in it any thyng ment,	332	Garlande	723
It shall be losyd ful sone out of the bandis	332	Garlande	725
That I ne force what though it be discurid.	332	Garlande	731
I am not woundid but that I may be cured.	332	Garlande	732
The devyll of hell and he be seldome asonder.'	333	Garlande	765
And who can worke beste now shall be asayde;	334	Garlande	775
That for them some goodly conseyt be devysid,	335	Garlande	814
So I beseke Jhesu now to be my gyde.	335	Garlande	835
To be your remembrauncer, madame, I am bounde,	336	Garlande	864
Ye be, as I devyne,	338	Garlande	911
Be vertus well comprysid.	338	Garlande	921
Yowr name to se /It be enrolde, /Writtin with golde.	338	Garlande	938
Yet shall there be no restraynt	339	Garlande	956
Far may be sought	341	Garlande	1031
I wyll that ye shall be /In all benyngnyte	341	Garlande	1046
I for to be so myndles,	342	Garlande	1065
I dare wele saye that ye and I be sought.	343	Garlande	1089
Make no delay, for now ye must be brought	343	Garlande	1090
Of that shalbe resonde you ye must be content;	344	Garlande	1123
you] not in Marshe 1568			
Whiche in your recordes, I know well, be enrolde,	344	Garlande	1140
'Be mirry,' she sayd, 'be not afferde a whit,	344	Garlande	1145
'Be mirry,' she sayd, 'be not afferde a whit,	344	Garlande	1145
If ony recordis in noumbyr can be founde,	345	Garlande	1150
It wolde have made a man hole that had be ryght sekely,	345	Garlande	1162
Item the Boke to Speke Well or be Styll;	345	Garlande	1175
And suche as be counterfettis they be reservyd;	346	Garlande	1190
And suche as be counterfettis they be reservyd;	346	Garlande	1190
To be our kyng, of God preordinate.	347	Garlande	1232
To fayre maistres Anne that shuld have be sent,	347	Garlande	1241
Yet sum there be therewith that take grevaunce	348	Garlande	1257
His dirige, her commendacioun /Can be no derogacyoun;	348	Garlande	1270
Why shulde she be afrayd?	348	Garlande	1276
Shulde be set and sortyd, /To be matriculate	348	Garlande	1280
Shulde be set and sortyd, /To be matriculate	348	Garlande	1281
What the cause may be /Of this perplexyte.	350	Garlande	1362
I pray God they be paynyd	350	Garlande	1369
No man lyvyng, he sayth, can be sure;	351	Garlande	1403
The myllar was loth to be out of the way,	351	Garlande	1414
But yet for all that, be as he may,	352	Garlande	1415
But yet for all that, be as he may,	352	Garlande	1415
Vexilla regis he devysid to be displayd;	352	Garlande	1420
Whiche, if they be happy, have cause to beware	353	Garlande	1474
And when that I sawe it wolde no better be,	353	Garlande	1485
But that my peticyon wolde not be had,	353	Garlande	1486
Welcome shall ye /To sum men be;	355	Garlande	1541
For Latin warkis /Be good for clerkis,	355	Garlande	1543
Any worde defacid /That myght be rasid,	356	Garlande	1582
Both worde and dede /Should be agrede /In noblenes:	357	Garlande	1600
And the twayne last /Be withholde so fast	358	Garlande2	13
Whiche be as trewe /As the gospell:	359	Albany	4
That knowen ye shall be	361	Albany	114
To be knytte up with knottes	362	Albany	122
Ye may be assured /Your falshod discured	362	Albany	127
It is, and shal be	362	Albany	129
For ye be false echone,	362	Albany	132
Ye shall never be hable,	363	Albany	178
Yet somwhat ye be lyke	364	Albany	197
For feare thou shoulde be slayne	365	Albany	247
Be well ware what ye say.	367	Albany	331
What, wold Fraunces, our friar, /Be suche a false lyar,	368	Albany	374
What though my stile be rude?	369	Albany	419
Trouth ought to be rescude;	369	Albany	421
Trouthe should nat be subdude.	369	Albany	422
And what vertues be resydent	369	Albany	426
Lyke cowardes as ye be	370	Albany	460
Of suche as be his foos	370	Albany	469

BEAME — BECOMYTH

	Page	Title	Line
Than ye be a knappishe sorte	370	Albany	475
At all houres to be redy	371	Albany	485
Though your Englishe be rude,	372	Albany	516
shall evermore be, with all obsequious redynesse,	373	Replycacion	1
That they juge them selfe able to be	374	Replycacion	7
To beare a fagot, or to be enflamed.	374	Replycacion	16
to be farther delated and contynued,	374	Replycacion	1
and of every true Christen man laudably to be enployed,	374	Replycacion	1
Helas, ye wreches, ye may be wo!	376	Replycacion	77
Thus to be laughed to skorne,	376	Replycacion	82
To be blowen with the flye /Of horryble heresy.	376	Replycacion	85
Or be brende by and by,	377	Replycacion	89
Yet be meanes of that vyse	378	Replycacion	131
Can nat be unrewarded.	378	Replycacion	139
Therwith for to be founde /At the unyversyte,	378	Replycacion	147
Employed whiche myght have be	378	Replycacion	149
What may be ment hereby,	378	Replycacion	153
And be nowe as yll,	379	Replycacion	178
And so ye wyll be styll,	379	Replycacion	179
And feare leest they be out	380	Replycacion	225
And be brent at a stake,	382	Replycacion	295
that can or may be made or objected	382	Replycacion	R
Th[i]s may nat be remorded	383	Replycacion	323
This] 'Thus' †Pynson 1528			
For be ye wele assured,	385	Replycacion	406
BEAME			
Whose radiant beame /And relucent light	136	Dundas	45
BEAMES			
Lyke Phebus beames shyne.	101	Phy Sparrow	1174
BEANES			
Ye wyll neyther beanes ne peason.	252	Collyn Clout	212
Fede hym with beanes and pease!	275	Collyn Clout	1170
BEAR			
Yet we bear away the bell,	363	Albany	183
BEARD			
Your beard so brym as bore at bay,	119	Ag Scottes	161
Parrot hath a blacke beard and a fayre grene tayle.	233	Speke Parott	84
For Peter of Westminster hath shaven thy beard.	358	Couplet	2
BEARE			
To beare a fagot, or to be enflamed.	374	Replycacion	16
Ye were fayne to beare fagottes;	376	Replycacion	66
To beare fagottes for babyls.	379	Replycacion	175
BEARES			
Of Arcady the beares	79	Phy Sparrow	309
BEATEN			
Some beaten to the brayne;	276	Collyn Clout	1211
BEAUTE			
Whoos beaute, honoure, goodly porte,	47	Bowge	62
In beaute and vertew:	96	Phy Sparrow	993
In beaute and vertew:	98	Phy Sparrow	1058
In beaute and vertew:	98	Phy Sparrow	1087
In beaute and vertew:	100	Phy Sparrow	1140
In beaute and vertew:	100	Phy Sparrow	1165
In beaute and vertew:	102	Phy Sparrow	1212
In beaute and vertew:	102	Phy Sparrow	1235
BEAUTY			
In beauty and vertew:	99	Phy Sparrow	1111
BEAUTYE			
Her beautye to commende,	93	Phy Sparrow	859
In beautye and vertew:	97	Phy Sparrow	1026
Her beautye to augment	97	Phy Sparrow	1041
In beautye and vertew:	101	Phy Sparrow	1189
Enbudded with beautye and colour fresshe of hewe,	183	Magnyfycence	1554
BECAME			
But what became of the letter	155	Magnyfycence	531
Must counte what became	302	Why Come Ye	934
Whiche maner of abasshement became her not yll;	337	Garlande	889
Where it became, and whether it went,	347	Garlande	1243
BECAUSE			
Because that she dyd pas	75	Phy Sparrow	151
that] not in Marshe 1568			
Because I have wrytten and sayd	103	Phy Sparrow	1253
I speke the softlyer because he sholde not wete.	186	Magnyfycence	1654
Because of theyr neglygence and of theyr wanton vagys,	195	Magnyfycence	1942
BECHREWDE			
Lythe and lystyn, all bechrewde!	131	Garnesche5	86
BECKE			
And her becke so comely crokys!	168	Magnyfycence	1000
BECKED			
Methynke she is well becked to catche a rat.	166	Magnyfycence	927
BECOME			
A man can not wote where to become.	59	Bowge	466
It wolde not become them with me for to mell;	182	Magnyfycence	1497
BECOMETH			
But largesse becometh a state ryall.	151	Magnyfycence	383
BECOMYTH			
As well it becomyth yow, a parysh towne clarke,	38	Coystrownel	58
Lyberte in some cause becomyth a gentyll mynde -	146	Magnyfycence	212

BED —BEFORE Page Title Line

BED
'My lefe', she sayd, 'rowtyth in hys bed;	42	Balettys1	20
And brought home and layde in your bed.	184	Magnyfycence	1572
To walke on this walle she bed I sholde not stint;	328	Garlande	571
With litell besynes standith moche rest; in bed	351	Garlande	1410

BEDAWYD
Ye may wele be bedawyd,	128	Garnesche3	182

BEDDE ROULES
Have lost theyr bedde roules;	257	Collyn Clout	422
bedde] 'beade' Kele 1545.1, 'bede' MS Harley 2252			

BEDDES
Somtyme in lousy beddes.	263	Collyn Clout	659

BEDDES SYDE
Than Elynour dyd them hyde /Within her beddes syde.	229	El Rummynge	606

BEDELL
Ever to be /Their true bedell	96	Phy Sparrow	980

BEDE ROLLE
Set in our bede rolle,	81	Phy Sparrow	383

BEDE ROLLES
Set in our bede rolles,	72	Phy Sparrow	12

BEDE ROULE
Wryten in my bede roule!	77	Phy Sparrow	242

BEDES
Another brought her bedes /Of jet or of cole,	227	El Rummynge	523
But my bedes of amber.	229	El Rummynge	603

BEDFELLAW
Such a bedfellaw /Wold make one cast his craw.	226	El Rummynge	488

BEDLEME
Suche a madde bedleme	295	Why Come Ye	655

BEE
To taunt theim like liddrons, lewde as thei bee.	138	Ven Tongues	29

BEEN
I had not been here with you this nyght.	150	Magnyfycence	365
Full many a strong cyte and towne hath been wonne	184	Magnyfycence	1577
To have been a chapleyne,	295	Why Come Ye	643

BEERD
Caron with his beerd hore,	105	Phy Sparrow	1338

BEEST
Ther is no beest savage,	100	Phy Sparrow	1156
Fledde lyke a beest.	359	Albany	12

BEESTES
Beestes, byrdes, and foules,	78	Phy Sparrow	259
Upon these beestes rydynge,	270	Collyn Clout	966
I saye, ye braynlesse beestes,	381	Replycacion	263

BEFALL
Yet shamfully thei slew hym; that sham most them befall.	30	Dol Dethe	49
For your sake, what so ever befall;	188	Magnyfycence	1709

BEFELL
As than befell to me.	72	Phy Sparrow	22

BEFOLE
What, fonnysshe Foly! I befole thy face.	169	Magnyfycence	1045
What tydynges with you, syr? I befole thy brayne pan.	191	Magnyfycence	1805

BEFORE
And all is done ye lokyd for before,	45	Balettys4	2
A balade boke before me for to laye,	53	Bowge	257
Wyth cry unreverent, /Before the sacrament,	62	Hauke	12
And sware horryble othes /Before the face of God,	63	Hauke	53
Of my gowne before,	80	Phy Sparrow	347
Your wyll renne before your wytte.	113	Scot Kynge	12
Before the Frensshe kynge, Danes and other	114	Scot Kynge	15
Your wyll than ran before your wyt.	118	Ag Scottes	102
Ye hobble very homly before the kynges borde;	123	Garnesche2	10
Pride gothe before and schame commyth after.	133	Garnesche5	165
For before on your brest, and behind on your back	137	Ven Tongues	16
And flatered them with fables fayre before theyr face,	160	Magnyfycence	717
That never was /Abusyd before.	164	Magnyfycence	868
But I must tary here; go thou before.	167	Magnyfycence	954
Before or behynde;	168	Magnyfycence	986
That was before I set behynde;	168	Magnyfycence	1007
Fyrst I lay before them my bybyll	174	Magnyfycence	1220
The houndes ranne before, and the hare behynde.	191	Magnyfycence	1823
Syr, all this wolde have bene thought on before.	196	Magnyfycence	1970
Some run to far before, some run to far behynde,	233	Speke Parott	76
Whether ita were before non, or non before ita,	235	Speke Parott	158
Whether ita were before non, or non before ita,	235	Speke Parott	158
So myche spente before, and so myche unpayd behynde -	244	Speke Parott	461
For elles, as I sayd before,	258	Collyn Clout	481
And maketh them to bow theyr kne /Before his majeste.	286	Why Come Ye	313
maketh them] 'make' Toy 1553, Kitson 1560.7, Marshe 1568			
To seke before our grace.'	287	Why Come Ye	332
Before that he was made	293	Why Come Ye	562
Before some prothonotory, /Imperyall or papall.	299	Why Come Ye	819
And yet he payde before	302	Why Come Ye	946
Of noble Fame before the Quenes grace,	324	Garlande	419
All orators and poetis shulde thider go before,	325	Garlande	454
She went before, and bad me take good holde;	328	Garlande	573
That speke fayre before the and shrewdly behynde.	329	Garlande	620
Before my ladys grace, the Quene of Fame,	343	Garlande	1091

BEFOULE — BEGYN

	Page	Title	Line
Before remembred, me curteisly brought	343	Garlande	1102
me curteisly] 'kurteisly me' MS Cotton Vitellius E.x			
'My frende, sith ye ar before us here present	344	Garlande	1121
And plantid it there where never before was none, unshred	351	Garlande	1405
it there where] 'yet wher' Marshe 1568			
Before his noble grace	372	Albany	525
As ye were before.	379	Replycacion	180
And knowledge your offence /Before open audyence,	380	Replycacion	208

BEFOULE

I befoule his pate.	164	Magnyfycence	876

BEGAN

Tyll fykkill Fortune began on hym to frowne.	33	Dol Dethe	133
And thus to talke with me he began.	51	Bowge	196
For then began our myrth and game.	117	Ag Scottes	68
Comberaunce and trouble in Englande fyrst I began.	160	Magnyfycence	715
Than Rowlande the reve ran, and I began to rave,	192	Magnyfycence	1831
For yf Measure had ruled Lyberte as he began,	200	Magnyfycence	2111
Tell me brefly where upon ye began.	203	Magnyfycence	2224
But, syr, by me to rule fyrst ye began.	209	Magnyfycence	2431
Whan I began to brewe,	219	El Rummynge	209
She began to yane and gaspy,	222	El Rummynge	331
began] 'gan' 1521 Fragment			
Than began she to wepe,	223	El Rummynge	374
And there began a fabell,	224	El Rummynge	386
And began to preche	225	El Rummynge	448
Elynor began to chyde,	226	El Rummynge	464
Than began the sporte /Amonge that dronken sorte.	229	El Rummynge	574
And began to paynty /As though she would faynty.	229	El Rummynge	584
Wherof moche care began.	297	Why Come Ye	725
That this warke began	301	Why Come Ye	894
The hertis of the herd began for to grone, and fled	351	Garlande	1408
The howndes began to yerne and to quest; and dred	351	Garlande	1409

BEGANNE

I was your good lorde tyll that ye beganne	188	Magnyfycence	1714
Or that we beganne in the supplement,	323	Garlande	415
Pers Prater, the secund, that quarillis beganne;	330	Garlande	636

BEGARED

Theyr styrops of myxt golde begared,	254	Collyn Clout	317
begared] 'begarded' Marshe 1568, 'be gloryd' MS Harley 2252			

BEGGARY

In wretched beggary /And maungy misery,	362	Albany	137

BEGGARS

Or what actyvyte /Is in you, beggars braules,	364	Albany	218

BEGGE

Nowe must you lerne to begge at every mannes gate.	196	Magnyfycence	1981
For nowe go I wyll begge for you some mete.	197	Magnyfycence	2034
Better it is to begge than to be hangyd with shame.	198	Magnyfycence	2039
Then for to begge theyr mete for charyte.	198	Magnyfycence	2041
Yet were they better to begge, a great dele;	198	Magnyfycence	2043
Walke, Scot, go begge a byt	362	Albany	154

BEGGER

What begger art thou, that thus doth banne and wary?	203	Magnyfycence	2238
Cockys bonys! Thou begger, what is thy name?	203	Magnyfycence	2240

BEGGERS

So many vacabondes, so many beggers bolde,	245	Speke Parott	498
Ye raynbetyn beggers rejagged,	294	Why Come Ye	605
And beggers they ban,	301	Why Come Ye	891

BEGGERS BAGGYS

I wyll walke nowe with my beggers baggys,	197	Magnyfycence	2036

BEGGEST

For thou beggest at every mannes dur.	135	Dundas	26

BEGGYNGE

But beggynge is better medecyne for the necke.	198	Magnyfycence	2045

BEGGYS

As well borne as ye full oft tyme beggys.	40	Coystrowne4	7

BEGIN

God geve them good spede there warke to begin!	334	Garlande	793

BEGYLDE

Bot ther was fals packinge or els I am begylde,	31	Dol Dethe	71
Thou slepyst to long, thou art begylde!	41	Balettys1	I

BEGYLE

'Ye, soo,' quod Suspecte, 'he maye us bothe begyle.'	51	Bowge	189
He wyll begyle you and speke fayre to your face.	51	Bowge	200

BEGYLED

By Cloked Colusyon thus many one is begyled.	160	Magnyfycence	728
What! Hath Sadnesse begyled me so?	192	Magnyfycence	1855
Nay. Madnesse hath begyled you and many mo;	192	Magnyfycence	1856
Item Bowche of Courte, where Drede was begyled;	346	Garlande	1183

BEGYLYD

Who lyst to consyder shall never be begylyd,	212	Magnyfycence	2512

BEGYN

For now I wyll begyn	99	Phy Sparrow	1093
And now to begyn I wyll me adres,	117	Ag Scottes	89
I wolde begyn all myschyef, but I wolde bere no lacke.	160	Magnyfycence	720
And the sandes of Cefas begyn to waste and fade,	239	Speke Parott	281
Cefas] 'Tefas' †MS Harley 2252			
And the cokkes begyn to crowe agayne the day;	239	Speke Parott	286

	Page	Title	Line

BEGYNNE
Shall I begynne or ye?	143	Magnyfycence	103
Nay, ye shall begynne, by my wyll.	143	Magnyfycence	104
By God, yet it muste begynne moche of the.	154	Magnyfycence	514
That bales begynne to brew.	280	Why Come Ye	63
Of Englande, his workis here they begynne:	345	Garlande	1171

BEGYNNES
And wyth that she begynnes	228	El Rummynge	565

BEGYNNETH
Here begynneth a lytell treatyse named The Bowge of Courte	46	Bowge	I
and begynneth the Bowge of Courte brevely compyled.	49	Bowge	R
Magnyfycence to us begynneth to enclyne,	158	Magnyfycence	644
By Cockys body, here begynneth the game!	159	Magnyfycence	682
And thus begynneth the game.	217	El Rummynge	132

BEGYNNYTH
Yet so it is that a rumer begynnyth for to ryse	42	Balettys2	12

BEGON
Begon, and now with shame,	256	Collyn Clout	388

BEGONE
Of men and of bestis, and whereof they begone,	331	Garlande	692

BEHAVYD
Without crafte nothynge is well behavyd.	177	Magnyfycence	1350

BEHAVYNGE
Behavynge her so sure,	99	Phy Sparrow	1098

BEHAVOURE
Of youre behavoure curtes and benynge,	44	Balettys3	30

BEHELDE
Thenne I behelde how he dysgysed was:	56	Bowge	351

BEHIND
For before on your brest, and behind on your back	137	Ven Tongues	16

BEHINDE
Mi litell lady I may not leve behinde,	337	Garlande	878

BEHYND
Ye armed you with wille and left your wit behynd;	30	Dol Dethe	55
But behynd in our hose /We bere there a rose	136	Dundas	34

BEHYNDE
Take thys in worth, the best is behynde.	38	Coystrowne1	68
'Have in sergeaunt ferrour, myne horse behynde is bare.'	43	Balettys2	20
She goyth wyde behynde and hewyth never a dele:	43	Balettys2	24
But than I thoughte I wolde not dwell behynde:	47	Bowge	43
Whiche sat behynde a tra[v]es of sylke fyne,	47	Bowge	58
traves] 'tranes' †Wynken de Worde 1499, 1510, Marshe 1568			
Er I was ware, behynde me he sayde 'Bo!'	60	Bowge	500
So none be left behynde.	81	Phy Sparrow	389
Yet one thynge is behynde,	86	Phy Sparrow	603
Of thy lewdenes more ys behynde;	134	Garnesche5	173
So that lyberte be not lefte behynde.	144	Magnyfycence	129
That wonte was to be formyst, now to come behynde.	144	Magnyfycence	144
Who county[th] without me is caste to fer behynde	146	Magnyfycence	214
countyth] 'countyd' †Rastell & Treveris C 1530, B			
Me thought he called Fansy me behynde.	149	Magnyfycence	329
And tolde all the myschyef I coude behynde theyr backe,	160	Magnyfycence	718
Before or behynde;	168	Magnyfycence	986
That was before I set behynde;	168	Magnyfycence	1007
Somtyme, I say, behynde the dore for nede;	177	Magnyfycence	1341
And welth is nought worthe yf lyberte be behynde.	180	Magnyfycence	1442
Speke, I beseche the. Leve nothynge behynde.	183	Magnyfycence	1544
Suche lustes at large may not be lefte behynde.	186	Magnyfycence	1628
The houndes ranne before, and the hare behynde.	191	Magnyfycence	1823
And so fer thou arte behynde of thy rent,	205	Magnyfycence	2294
How fortuned you, Magnyfycence, so far to fal behynde?	209	Magnyfycence	2423
I shall it never forget nor leve it behynde,	212	Magnyfycence	2506
Some run to far before, some run to far behynde,	233	Speke Parott	76
So myche spente before, and so myche unpayd behynde –	244	Speke Parott	461
And say yll behynde his back,	310	Why Come Ye2	26
Plato, but for that he left wrytynge behynde,	315	Garlande	126
that] not in MS Cotton Vitellius E.x			
That speke fayre before the and shrewdly behynde.	329	Garlande	620
Behynde the taile of Ursa so clere;	331	Garlande	696
Of welth and solace no thynge left behynde;	332	Garlande	711
It is not my custome nor my gyse /To leve behynde	342	Garlande	1069
The Nacyoun of Folys he left not behynde.	353	Garlande	1470

BEHOLD
Behold, thou lyeste, luggard, alone!	42	Balettys1	25
Whych to behold makyth hevy hartys glad;	44	Balettys3	28
Thys rebell to behold,	64	Hauke	95
To behold and se /What hevynesse dyd me pange:	72	Phy Sparrow	43
Her to behold and se,	97	Phy Sparrow	1007
'Behold,' she sayd, 'and se	220	El Rummynge	217
That lordes and ladies thys pamflett may behold,	241	Speke Parott	358

BEHOLDE
Eternally /To beholde and se /The Trynyte!	40	Coystrowne3	58
Open myne hart, beholde my mynde expres.	44	Balettys3	39
Than to beholde youre bewteouse countenaunce:	44	Balettys3	44
But whan I dyd beholde	72	Phy Sparrow	39
Who so lyst beholde,	98	Phy Sparrow	1073
Beholde thy selfe, and thou mayst se.	130	Garnesche5	16
Thow xalte beholde no wher a warse;	130	Garnesche5	17

	Page	Title	Line
BEYGHT —BELLYS			
And surely ye are to hym beholde,	149	Magnyfycence	333
My buskyn wyde, /Ryche to beholde	164	Magnyfycence	854
Beholde howe Fortune o[n] hym hath frounde. on] 'of' †Rastell & Treveris C 1530, B	195	Magnyfycence	1947
This lyfe inconstant for to beholde and se:	212	Magnyfycence	2525
That Parrot the popagay hath pytye to beholde the] 'that' Day 1560, Marshe 1568	235	Speke Parott	167
Goe, lytyll quayre, pray them that yow beholde,	239	Speke Parott	290
And more horyble to beholde horyble] 'dyshonorable' MS Rawlinson C. 813	310	Why Come Ye2	15
The sygnes xii for to beholde a farre,	312	Garlande	2
That passynge goodly it was to beholde:	313	Garlande	42
'Theis yatis,' she sayd, 'which that ye beholde,	328	Garlande	579
Englisterd, that joyous it was to beholde.	330	Garlande	663
'Beholde and se in your advertysement	335	Garlande	808
To beholde how it was garnysshyd and bounde,	345	Garlande	1163
His countenaunce to beholde.	367	Albany	339
BEYGHT			
Shall cast a beyght,	361	Albany	110
BEYNG			
His grace beyng out of the way;	119	Ag Scottes	144
BEYNGE			
Our kynge than beynge out of the waye;	114	Scot Kynge	45
BEYOND			
And ferre beyond my merytys ye me commende and prayse.	183	Magnyfycence	1526
BEYONDE			
That all is without measure and fer beyonde the mone.	146	Magnyfycence	224
By God, syr, beyonde the se.	150	Magnyfycence	341
My persone prest /Beyonde all syse	164	Magnyfycence	845
Beyonde measure /My sleve is wyde;	164	Magnyfycence	849
Nay, beyonde all other set hym alone.	174	Magnyfycence	1235
There apparell farre passynge beyonde that I can tell;	323	Garlande	394
My name, I know well, beyonde that I am able,	324	Garlande	438
Your name recountynge beyonde the lande of Tyre,	327	Garlande	551
BEYTE			
There muste for hym be layde some prety beyte.	55	Bowge	312
BEK			
The shovelar with his brode bek;	82	Phy Sparrow	408
BEKE			
But whan I was sowing his beke,	77	Phy Sparrow	219
Howkyd as an hawkys beke, lyke Syr Topyas.	122	Garneschel	40
Wythe my beke bente, and my lytell wanton iye, and] not in Lant 1545, Kynge and Marche 1554, Day 1560, Marshe 1568	231	Speke Parott	15
With my beke I can pyke my lyttel praty too;	233	Speke Parott	107
Melpomene, that fayre mayde, she burneshed his beke:	236	Speke Parott	209
BEKENYNGE			
Those thre wyll be redy even at your bekenynge;	190	Magnyfycence	1778
BEKNAVE			
So curryshly to beknave me in the kynges place?	121	Garneschel	9
Me to beknave thow art to blame;	132	Garnesche5	107
BEKNAVYD			
Wherfore, as I be savyd, /Ye ar therfore beknavyd.	70	Hauke	310
BEKS			
In the Ster Chambre he noddis and beks,	287	Why Come Ye	339
BELAPPED			
In purple and paule belapped;	254	Collyn Clout	310
BELDYNGE			
The beldynge therof was passynge commendable;	328	Garlande	589
BELE			
Of Bele Isold his wyfe,	87	Phy Sparrow	643
'A strawe,' sayde Bele, 'stande utter,	228	El Rummynge	535
BELEVE			
And beleve it as your crede.	278	Why Come Ye	2
And beleve it as your crede.	279	Why Come Ye	16
And beleve it as your crede.	279	Why Come Ye	28
BELY			
For her mouth fomyd /And her bely groned:	223	El Rummynge	342
BELYES			
Where mennes belyes is mesured, there is no chere;	189	Magnyfycence	1742
BELY-JOYE			
So myche bely-joye, and so wastefull banketyng;	245	Speke Parott	492
BELYMMED			
His face was belymmed as byes had him stounge;	54	Bowge	289
BELL			
Boke, bell and candyll, /All that he myght handyll;	64	Hauke	112
For of all barones bolde I bere the bell;	182	Magnyfycence	1498
And lothe to hange the bell	250	Collyn Clout	163
Yet we bear away the bell,	363	Albany	183
BELLE			
Of all prowde knavys thow beryst the belle,	130	Garnesche5	27
BELLES			
And sell away theyr belles	257	Collyn Clout	410
BELLYALL			
A prelate potencyall /To rule under Bellyall,	294	Why Come Ye	592
To Pluto and Syr Bellyall,	299	Why Come Ye	806
BELLYS			
And let hym ryng the bellys;	84	Phy Sparrow	493

BELLUYNG —BENINGNE   Page   Title   Line

BELLUYNG
	Page	Title	Line
Where hartis belluyng, embosyd with distres,	312	Garlande	24

BELMAN
To make hym our belman,	84	Phy Sparrow	492

BELONGYNG
Belongyng to the Deite.	381	Replycacion	283

BELONGYTH
Lyberte to a lorde belongyth of ryght,	211	Magnyfycence	2489

BELS
Thus to ryng a peale /Wyth his hawkys bels?	65	Hauke	137

BELSABUB
Belsabub his soule save,	109	Epitaphe2	25

BEME
Ic dien is the language of the land of Beme;	233	Speke Parott	79

BEMIS
Whan Titan radiant burnisshith his bemis bryght,	327	Garlande	534

BEMOLE
Softly bemole /For my sparowes soule.	85	Phy Sparrow	534

BEN
Ye had not ben hable to have saide hym nay.	31	Dol Dethe	70
Alumbek sodyldym syllorym ben!	37	Coystrownel	16
Where hathe your dwellynge ben, er ye cam here?	53	Bowge	247
As though I had ben racked,	73	Phy Sparrow	47
I wold thou haddest ben blynde!	79	Phy Sparrow	285
Yet lyberte hath ben lockyd up and kept in the mew.	141	Magnyfycence	35
Yet measure hath ben so longe from us absent,	146	Magnyfycence	221
I trowe, by our lady, I had ben slayne,	150	Magnyfycence	348
Yet Fansy had ben dysc[r]yved.	155	Magnyfycence	535
dyscryved] 'dysceyved' †Rastell & Treveris C 1530, B			
By my trouthe, we had ben gone.	155	Magnyfycence	537
What! He hathe ben hurte with a stabbe?	171	Magnyfycence	1124
Mayster Survayour, where have ye ben so longe?	178	Magnyfycence	1382
By our lakyn, syr, I have ben a hawkyng for the wylde swan.	191	Magnyfycence	1806
This lurden that here lyeth had ben a noble man.	200	Magnyfycence	2112
For had ye not the soner ben my refuge,	206	Magnyfycence	2333
Of dampnacyon I had ben drawen in the luge.	206	Magnyfycence	2334
It had ben hers, I wene, /More then fourty yere;	215	El Rummynge	57
There hath ben greate war	223	El Rummynge	358
The prelates ben so haute /They say, and loke so hye	248	Collyn Clout	71
Howe in matters they ben rawe,	249	Collyn Clout	94
There hath ben moche excesse:	280	Why Come Ye	70
As herafter ben notyd:	293	Why Come Ye	573
He wolde have ben ryght fayne	295	Why Come Ye	642
With reasons that ben rawe.	306	Why Come Ye	1107
As fersly frownynge as he had ben fyghtyng,	328	Garlande	594
It had ben moche better	380	Replycacion	229

BENCHE
His rumpe also he frygges /Agaynst the hye benche.	219	El Rummynge	179
The Kynges Benche or Marshalsy,	275	Collyn Clout	1171
Or at the Kynges Benche.	287	Why Come Ye	320
Or to the Kynges Benche!'	290	Why Come Ye	433

BEND
Boldly bend you to batell, and buske your selfe to save.	122	Garnesche1	41

BENDE
Why, shall he be of your bende?	163	Magnyfycence	818

BENDED
Together are bended, /And so condyscended,	304	Why Come Ye	1022
bendyd] 'wendyd' MS Rawlinson C. 813			

BENE
'Pece,' quod Desyre, 'ye speke not worth a bene!	48	Bowge	95
Wher thou xulddst have bene shrynyd;	128	Garnesche3	175
Ye, syr, a blaunched almonde is no bene.	151	Magnyfycence	381
We have bene togyder bothe erly and late.	154	Magnyfycence	499
But Fansy, my frende, where have ye bene so longe?	154	Magnyfycence	500
By God, I have bene a praty pronge -	154	Magnyfycence	501
Syr, all this wolde have bene thought on before.	196	Magnyfycence	1970
Never had I bene brought in this case.	196	Magnyfycence	1977
For had I not bene, ye bothe had bene hangyd,	203	Magnyfycence	2235
For had I not bene, ye bothe had bene hangyd,	203	Magnyfycence	2235
Thou hast bene so waywarde, so wranglyng, and so wrothsome,	205	Magnyfycence	2293
Ye, syr, with adversyte I have bene vexyd;	210	Magnyfycence	2461
Of auncient poetis, ye wote full wele, hath bene	314	Garlande	65
Hath bene full often and yet is entendyng	344	Garlande	1131

BENEFYCE
His benefyce worth ten pounde,	264	Collyn Clout	725

BENES
Some brought from the barne /Both benes and pease;	222	El Rummynge	313

BENET
And sware by Saynt Benet,	224	El Rummynge	393

BENEVOLENCE
With proper captacyons of benevolence,	335	Garlande	815

BENIGNITE
His benignite /His royall dignyte,	370	Albany	455
He rules his cominalte /With all benignite.	370	Albany	464

BENINGE
Beninge, curteyse, of jentyll harte and mynde,	337	Garlande	880

BENINGNE
Unto thy subjectis be kurteis and beningne.	33	Dol Dethe	168

BENYFYCED —BERYST	Page	Title	Line

BENYFYCED
A parson benyfyced /But nothynge well advysed. . . . . 62 Hauke 36
BENYGNE
Lyke to Eneas benygne in worde and dede, ... 33 Dol Dethe 137
BENYGNYTE
Farewell benygnyte, /Farewell symplycyte, ... 261 Collyn Clout 589
BENYNGE
Of youre behavoure curtes and benynge, ... 44 Balettys3 30
Syr, then, with the favour of your benynge sufferaunce, ... 182 Magnyfycence 1519
'Madame, with favour of your benynge sufferaunce, ... 315 Garlande 113
But your benynge sufferaunce for my discharge I laid, ... 318 Garlande 213
'I thanke you, goodly maystres, to me most benynge, ... 332 Garlande 728
Benynge, corteise, and meke, /With wordes well devysid; . . . . 338 Garlande 918
BENYNGNYTE
I wyll that ye shall be /In all benyngnyte . . . . 341 Garlande 1047
BENT
With her browes bent . . . . 97 Phy Sparrow 1016
Her browys bent, /Her eyen glent; . . . . 167 Magnyfycence 979
And howe Cupyde shaked /His dart, and bent his bowe . . . . . . 270 Collyn Clout 947
And truly of theyr bownte thus were they bent . . . . 334 Garlande 806
BENTE
With browes bente, and gan on me to stare . . . . 48 Bowge 81
Wythe my beke bente, and my lytell wanton iye, ... 231 Speke Parott 15
and] not in Lant 1545, Kynge and Marche 1554, Day 1560,
Marshe 1568
BEQUETH
I bequeth yt hole to the. 128 Garnesche3 177
BEQUETHE
In faythe, and I bequethe hym the tothe ake. . . . . 204 Magnyfycence 2253
And I bequethe hym the bone ake. . . . . 204 Magnyfycence 2254
And I bequethe hym the gowte and the gyn. . . . . 204 Magnyfycence 2255
And I bequethe hym sorowe for his syn. . . . . 204 Magnyfycence 2256
BERDE
He gased on me with his gotyshe berde; . . . . 52 Bowge 237
By Goddis syde, my sworde thy berde shall shave! . . . . 55 Bowge 339
Another bade shave halfe my berde; . . . . 150 Magnyfycence 355
Arthur of Albyan, for all his brymme berde, ... 182 Magnyfycence 1502
And wyth a brystell of a bore his berde dyd I shave. . . . . . 192 Magnyfycence 1832
That his berde is so longe. . . . . 288 Why Come Ye 391
Caron with his berde hore, ... 349 Garlande 1331
And wele wotith the cat whos berde she likkith. . . . . 352 Garlande 1438
BERDED
And from the berded gotes /With theyr heery cotes; . . . . . . 250 Collyn Clout 158
BERE
Yet bere ye not to bold to braule ne to bark . . . . 38 Coystrownel 60
Yet on my backe I bere suche lewde delynge. . . . . 59 Bowge 457
Ye bere yourselfe somwhat to bolde, ... 114 Scot Kynge 34
Ye bere yow bolde as Barabas, or Syr Terry of Trac[e]. . . . . 122 Garneschel 11
Trace] 'Tracy' †MS Harley 367
Nor blake Baltazar with hys basnet routh as a bere, ... 122 Garneschel 23
Thow a Sarsens hed ye bere, ... 127 Garnesche3 123
Thow bere, thow brystlyd bore, /Thou Moryshe mantycore, ... 128 Garnesche3 164
Ye bere yow bold and brag 129 Garnesche3 187
Ye bere out brothells lyke a bawde; 131 Garnesche5 73
Take thys for that, bere thys in mynde, ... 134 Garnesche5 172
But behynd in our hose /We bere there a rose . . . . 136 Dundas 35
Welthe without measure wolde bere hymselfe to bolde; . . . . . 143 Magnyfycence 116
Two faces in a hode covertly I bere; . . . . 160 Magnyfycence 710
I wolde begyn all myschyef, but I wolde bere no lacke. . . . . 160 Magnyfycence 720
Thus can I lerne you, syrs, to bere the devyls sacke; . . . . . 160 Magnyfycence 721
So thou arte personable to bere a pryncces baner. . . . . 161 Magnyfycence 767
Ye, bere me this strawe to a dawys nest. . . . . 170 Magnyfycence 1097
Be not to bolde my frende; I counsell you, bere a brayne. . . . 179 Magnyfycence 1405
For of all barones bolde I bere the bell; . . . . 182 Magnyfycence 1498
Ye shall not bere awaye /Myne ale for nought, ... 218 El Rummynge 165
myne] 'my' Kynge & Marche 1554, Day 1560, Marshe 1568
Take up dyrt and all, /And bere out of the hall.' . . . . 219 El Rummynge 184
dyrt] 'drit' Kynge & Marche 1554, Day 1560, Marshe 1568
Bere them to your chamber.' . . . . 229 El Rummynge 604
Hyt ys no lytyll bordon to bere a grete mylle stone. . . . . . 240 Speke Parott 330
He maketh them to bere babylles, and to bere a lowe sayle; . . 243 Speke Parott 428
He maketh them to bere babylles, and to bere a lowe sayle; . . 243 Speke Parott 428
And bere it well away. . . . . 258 Collyn Clout 464
Men say, they bere no faces . . . . 269 Collyn Clout 896
Wyll ye bere no coles?' . . . . 285 Why Come Ye 243
He bayteth them lyke a bere, ... 286 Why Come Ye 307
Callid Speculum Principis, to bere in his honde, ... 347 Garlande 1229
BERES
Howe ye wyll beres bynde . . . . 364 Albany 209
BERETH
And bereth him there so stowte . . . . 287 Why Come Ye 340
He bereth the kyng on hand . . . . 290 Why Come Ye 452
BERIS
The wolvis, the beris also, ... 111 Lawde 23
BERY
Or of Babvell besyde Bery . . . . 265 Collyn Clout 752
BERYST
Of all prowde knavys thow beryst the belle, ... 130 Garnesche5 27

BERYTH—BEST

	Page	Title	Line
Beryst thou any rome? Or cannyst thou do ought?	162	Magnyfycence	776
BERYTH			
Of bewte that beryth the flower,	128	Garnesche3	149
BERYTHE			
Lyacon lawghyth thereatt and berythe hym more bolde;	242	Speke Parott	400
BESECHE			
Nowe, I beseche the, tell me what is thy name?	148	Magnyfycence	269
Speke, I beseche the. Leve nothynge behynde.	183	Magnyfycence	1544
Syr, I beseche you let pety have some place	188	Magnyfycence	1712
Se, syr, I beseche you, Largesse my brother.	192	Magnyfycence	1842
Your myndys I beseche you here in to expresse,	211	Magnyfycence	2480
Whereof I beseche you to tender the effecte.	313	Garlande	56
But yet I beseche your grace that good recorde	318	Garlande	215
good] not in MS Cotton Vitellius E.x			
BESECHYNGE			
Besechynge you that shall it see or rede,	61	Bowge	534
BESEKE			
So I beseke Jhesu now to be my gyde.	335	Garlande	835
BESEME			
To me all pryncces to lowte man bese[m]e.	182	Magnyfycence	1500
beseme] 'be sene' †Rastell & Treveris C 1530, B			
BESENE			
A man, but wonderly besene was he.	54	Bowge	283
All other transcendynge, the most rychely besene,	325	Garlande	483
Galathea, the made well besene,	342	Garlande	1076
BESHREW			
'I beshrew the for thy cummyng!'	227	El Rummynge	503
BESHREWDE			
Holde youre tong, now, all beshrewde!	41	Coystrowne4	28
For sothe, they are to lewde /To say so, all beshrewde!	249	Collyn Clout	91
BESHREWE			
Ay, beshrewe yow! Be my fay	35	Man Margery	1
BESHROWE			
A man may beshrowe your angry harte.	156	Magnyfycence	563
And I beshrowe hym that hath the worse.	171	Magnyfycence	1105
BESIDE			
beside the water of Twede, etc	359	Albany	I
Beside the water of Twede	371	Albany	514
BESINES			
Of this high courte the dayly besines;	326	Garlande	519
BESY			
Hys dyscant is besy, it is withoute a mene;	37	Coystrowne1	27
Els, I prayed hym with all my besy cure,	52	Bowge	221
Besy, braynles, to bralle and brage,	133	Garnesche5	148
And maketh hym besy where is no nede.	175	Magnyfycence	1249
Besy, besy, besy, and besynes agayne!	232	Speke Parott	57
Besy, besy, besy, and besynes agayne!	232	Speke Parott	57
Besy, besy, besy, and besynes agayne!	232	Speke Parott	57
It is a besy thynge	271	Collyn Clout	988
'Counterwayng your besy delygence	323	Garlande	414
My besy cure /To yow I owe;	338	Garlande	928
BESYDE			
I can do nothynge but he stonde besyde.	180	Magnyfycence	1449
Whylest I came to you, a lytell here besyde.	187	Magnyfycence	1686
Or of Babvell besyde Bery	265	Collyn Clout	752
All other besyde were counterfete they thought	343	Garlande	1106
All ... counterfete] 'that they ware were counterfettis' MS Cotton Vitellius E.x			
Of the Bonehoms of Ashrige besyde Barkamstede,	353	Garlande	1461
BESYNES			
Besy, besy, besy, and besynes agayne!	232	Speke Parott	57
'Que pensez-voz, Parrot? What meneth this besynes?'	232	Speke Parott	58
With litell besynes standith moche rest; in bed	351	Garlande	1410
BESYNESSE			
Helthe of body his besynesse to acheve;	207	Magnyfycence	2369
BESOUGHT			
Suppleyng to Fame, I besought her grace,	353	Garlande	1478
BESSE			
My propir Besse, /My praty Besse,	237	Speke Parott	235
My propir Besse, /My praty Besse,	237	Speke Parott	236
For slepyste thou, Besse,	237	Speke Parott	238
Or wakeste thow, Besse,	237	Speke Parott	239
My propyr Besse, /To turne agayne to me.	237	Speke Parott	250
I pray the, Besse, unfayned, /Yet com agayne to me!	238	Speke Parott	255
My propyr Besse, /And rorne agayne to me!	238	Speke Parott	261
Dame Dorothe and Lady Besse,	256	Collyn Clout	392
BEST			
The best chepe flessh that evyr I bought.'	36	Man Margery	24
He counteth in his countenaunce to checke with the best:	37	Coystrowne1	44
Take thys in worth, the best is behynde.	38	Coystrowne1	68
Of my trew hart, to love her best of all!	45	Balettys3	49
That wher I love best I dare not dyscure!	45	Balettys5	7
That where I love best I dare not dyscure.	46	Balettys5	14
Worrowyd her on that /Which I loved best.	72	Phy Sparrow	30
The best now that I maye	77	Phy Sparrow	237
The best that we can,	84	Phy Sparrow	491
And lede my fyst /As hym best lyst,	96	Phy Sparrow	973
Et iacet hic, like a best!	109	Epitaphe2	28

BESTAD — BETTER   Page   Title   Line

	Page	Title	Line
In faythe, yet am I occupied with the best;	160	Magnyfycence	705
It is best I fede my hawke now.	167	Magnyfycence	968
Fyrst to tell you what were best:	168	Magnyfycence	1022
No, that I assure you; loke who was the best:	181	Magnyfycence	1484
Howe say ye, syrs? Herein what is best?	186	Magnyfycence	1659
To chose out ii., iii., of suche as you love best,	190	Magnyfycence	1769
And from that they love best some I devorse;	194	Magnyfycence	1905
Mary, I defye thy best and thy worst.	202	Magnyfycence	2197
For we be, syrs, but a fewe of the best.	202	Magnyfycence	2203
But, Perseveraunce, me semyth your probleme was best;	212	Magnyfycence	2505
To cease me semeth best,	220	El Rummynge	235
To byrle them of the best.	221	El Rummynge	269
Renne who may renne best,	277	Collyn Clout	1223
Me semeth it for the best.	277	Collyn Clout	1250
For who can best lye,	300	Why Come Ye	858
best] not in MS Rawlinson C. 813			
He is best set by!	300	Why Come Ye	859
best] 'most' MS Rawlinson C. 813			
Of this vayne gloryous best,	309	Why Come Ye	1213
Then he that doth worste is as good as the best.	317	Garlande	175
Withoute deservynge shulde have the best game.	318	Garlande	221
That ever they saw, and wrought it was the best.	343	Garlande	1113
BESTAD			
Hardly bestad and driven is to hope	335	Garlande	830
and] not in MS Cotton Vitellius E.x			
BESTADDE			
Are ye nat frantyke madde, /And wretchedly bestadde,	368	Albany	364
BESTE			
That I ne wyste what to do was beste;	47	Bowge	30
Your beste gowne festyvalle.	125	Garnesche3	51
Lyberte without measure is acountyd for a beste;	144	Magnyfycence	138
In Salve festa dyes, toto ys the beste.	232	Speke Parott	49
ys the] 'theyr doth' Lant 1545, Kynge & Marche 1554, Day 1560, Marshe 1568			
Diamounde, or rubye, or balas of the beste,	241	Speke Parott	367
And who can worke beste now shall be asayde;	334	Garlande	775
BESTIS			
Bluntly as bestis withe boste and with cry	31	Dol Dethe	83
And as the lyonne whiche is of bestis kinge	33	Dol Dethe	167
Of men and of bestis, and whereof they begone,	331	Garlande	692
BESTYALL			
Some bestyall and untaught.	252	Collyn Clout	228
BESTOWDE			
Upon suche a sort was ille bestowde and spent.	32	Dol Dethe	98
BET			
And bad Elynour go bet,	222	El Rummynge	332
The grounde engrosyd and bet with bourne golde,	313	Garlande	41
She bet up a fyre with the sparkis full kene	330	Garlande	669
BETAKE			
Nowe to the devyll I the betake,	151	Magnyfycence	401
BETE			
That myne hert dyd bete,	73	Phy Sparrow	59
He bete downe to the grounde:	88	Phy Sparrow	671
He is so bete /With malyce, and frete	95	Phy Sparrow	930
Is there no horson that knave that wyll bete?'	185	Magnyfycence	1618
By the good Lorde, yet your temples bete.	189	Magnyfycence	1732
Bete a dum mouthe than a brainles scull;	314	Garlande	82
Bete] 'Better' Marshe 1568, MS Cotton Vitellius E.x			
BETELL			
What is this, a betell or a batowe or a buskyn lacyd?	161	Magnyfycence	755
BETEN			
Ye were beten weth your owne rod.	114	Scot Kynge	47
For myrth I have hym coryed, beten, and blyst,	185	Magnyfycence	1622
Here MAGNYFYCENCE is beten downe	193	Magnyfycence	SD
Beten with stormys of many a frowarde blast,	213	Magnyfycence	2560
BE TYME			
Hay, chysshe, come hyder! Nay, torde! Take hym be tyme.	171	Magnyfycence	1117
BETOKENETH			
Than ye know what betokeneth dulia:	382	Replycacion	288
BETRAY			
With trechery ye them betray.	130	Garnesche5	38
BETRAYD			
With Wofully Arayd and Shamefully Betrayd;	352	Garlande	1418
BETRAPPED			
With golde all betrapped,	254	Collyn Clout	309
BETTER			
He rydyth well the horse, but he rydyth better the mare.	43	Balettys2	21
The *better with his bumpe,	82	Phy Sparrow	432
*better] 'bitter' Wyght 1553, Kitson 1560.6, Marshe 1568			
Ye had be better to have busked to Huntley Bankes,	114	Scot Kynge	50
be] 'bet' †Fakes 1513			
With better frese lynyd;	125	Garnesche3	47
Ye myght no better a way;	125	Garnesche3	49
And occupyed no better your tole,	127	Garnesche3	118
It cumys the better for to dryve	132	Garnesche5	92
My study myght be better spynt;	134	Garnesche5	176
Set in better /Thy pentameter.	135	Dundas	5
I shall loke in it at leasure better;	149	Magnyfycence	332

BETTERS —BEWARE   Page   Title   Line

	Page	Title	Line
Myselfe coude not counterfet it better.	155	Magnyfycence	530
What! Is your conveyaunce no better.	155	Magnyfycence	542
That we can no better than so.	155	Magnyfycence	550
Let se, fynde you a better way.	156	Magnyfycence	560
Abyde. Lette me se. Take better hede.	157	Magnyfycence	595
In faythe, he were better to dwell in hell.	157	Magnyfycence	623
Mary, the better and Mesure were out.	158	Magnyfycence	656
And yet, I trowe, some of you be better sped than I	160	Magnyfycence	722
What the devyll! Can ye agre no better?	162	Magnyfycence	795
Whiche of you is the better man,	162	Magnyfycence	802
I wyll not gyve a halfepeny for to chose the better.	170	Magnyfycence	1067
In faythe, there is not a better dogge for hogges,	171	Magnyfycence	1120
Why, thynkys thou he can no better skyll?	172	Magnyfycence	1172
Not a better name under the sonne;	176	Magnyfycence	1310
And so as ye se it wyll be no better,	180	Magnyfycence	1438
Syr, I am the better of your noble reporte;	183	Magnyfycence	1541
Yet, syr, reserved your better advysement,	187	Magnyfycence	1661
It were better he spake with you or he wente,	187	Magnyfycence	1662
Well, for thy sake the better I may endure	187	Magnyfycence	1680
Ye, walke he must; it was no better worth.	189	Magnyfycence	1736
Nowe Measure is gone, I am the better pleased.	189	Magnyfycence	1738
Better to make iii. ryche than for to make many.	190	Magnyfycence	1772
Why, coulde not your wyt serve you no better?	193	Magnyfycence	1868
Alasse that I coude not myselfe no better gyde!	196	Magnyfycence	1986
And whan it pleaseth God, better may be.	196	Magnyfycence	1993
Remembre you better, syr. Beware what ye say,	196	Magnyfycence	1995
Better it is to begge than to be hangyd with shame.	198	Magnyfycence	2039
Yet were they better to begge, a great dele;	198	Magnyfycence	2043
But beggynge is better medecyne for the necke.	198	Magnyfycence	2045
I am the better yet in a bowget. And I the better in a male.	203	Magnyfycence	2232
I am the better yet in a bowget. And I the better in a male.	203	Magnyfycence	2232
But nowe I se well there is no better rede,	205	Magnyfycence	2305
And for to leve this letter, /Bicause it is no better;	220	El Rummynge	238
Doutlesse were moche better	253	Collyn Clout	272
were] 'where' Kele 1545.1			
They mought be better advysed	261	Collyn Clout	579
Shulde be imprynted better	265	Collyn Clout	761
And better perceyved, /And thankefullyer receyved,	265	Collyn Clout	770
And better shulde remayne /Amonge the people playne,	265	Collyn Clout	772
Ye knowe better than I.	273	Collyn Clout	1064
God sende us better luck!	282	Why Come Ye	123
God sende us better lucke, etc.	282	Why Come Ye	124
No better they agre!	288	Why Come Ye	375
Tyll better layser be founde;	294	Why Come Ye	627
For what is a man the better	295	Why Come Ye	669
Moche better can devyse	298	Why Come Ye	767
God of his miseracyon /Send better reformacyon!	305	Why Come Ye	1045
Also, to furnisshe better his excuse,	314	Garlande	92
With, 'I as good as thou, ifayth, and no better.'	326	Garlande	509
The whyte apperyth the better for the black,	347	Garlande	1237
And when that I sawe it wolde no better be,	353	Garlande	1485
So moche the better	355	Garlande	1539
moche better bayned than brayned,	374	Replycacion	1
Moche better other wayes.	378	Replycacion	150
It had ben moche better	380	Replycacion	229

BETTERS

	Page	Title	Line
We be thy betters, and so thou shalte us take,	55	Bowge	342
As malypert tavernars that checke with theyr betters,	178	Magnyfycence	1362

BETWEYN

	Page	Title	Line
Betweyn the tappett and the walle;	131	Garnesche5	75

BETWEN

	Page	Title	Line
The auncient acquaintance, madam, betwen us twayn,	42	Balettys2	1

BETWENE

	Page	Title	Line
Betwene the persone ye wote of, you -	59	Bowge	461
Was betwene you twayne, /Pyramus and Thesbe,	72	Phy Sparrow	20
Betwene my brestes softe	74	Phy Sparrow	125
With his byll betwene my lippes,	80	Phy Sparrow	359
And of the love betwene /Paris and Vyene;	88	Phy Sparrow	663
Pand[aer], that went betwene,	89	Phy Sparrow	717
Pandaer] 'pandara' †Kele 1545.2, Wyght 1553, Kitson 1560.6, Marshe 1568			
Betwene Temple Bar /And the Crosse in Chepe,	223	El Rummynge	359
Betwene the cup and the wall,	226	El Rummynge	473
Betwene his armes, he felt her body quake.	320	Garlande	301
Fortune to stande betwene you and the lyght.	344	Garlande	1134

BEVE

	Page	Title	Line
Of ladys a beve with all dew reverence:	334	Garlande	771
a beve] 'aboue' †Fakes 1523			

BEWAYLE

	Page	Title	Line
Bewayle thy fortune, with vaynys wan and blo.	45	Balettys5	3

BEWARE

	Page	Title	Line
Beware of him, for, I make God avowe,	51	Bowge	199
Thow ye prate lyke prowde Pylate, beware yet of chek mate.	123	Garnesche2	7
Thow ye prate lyke prowde Pylate, beware of cheke mate.	123	Garnesche2	14
Tho ye prate lyke prowde Pylate, beware of cheke mate.	123	Garnesche2	21
Thow ye prate lyke prowde Pylate, beware of cheke mate.	123	Garnesche2	28
I advyse yow beware of thys war, rannge yow in aray.	123	Garnesche2	33
Thow ye prate lyke prowde Pylate, beware of cheke mate.	123	Garnesche2	35

BE WARE —BY

	Page	Title	Line
Thow ye prate lyke prowde Pylate, beware of cheke mate.	124	Garnesche2	42
Er thow beware, that in a throw	132	Garnesche5	122
Wherfore, in welthe beware of woo,	132	Garnesche5	124
Hem, syr, yet beware of 'Had I wyste!'	146	Magnyfycence	211
All men beware of suche folys!	175	Magnyfycence	1265
Yet it is good to beware of 'had I wyst'.	179	Magnyfycence	1395
I counsayle them beware of adversyte.	194	Magnyfycence	1899
And beware of adversyte by my counsell,	195	Magnyfycence	1945
In welth to beware; and that is wyt.	196	Magnyfycence	1975
In welth to beware yf I had had grace,	196	Magnyfycence	1976
Remembre you better, syr. Beware what ye say,	196	Magnyfycence	1995
I warne you beware of to moche lyberte,	199	Magnyfycence	2088
In welthe beware of herde adversyte.	201	Magnyfycence	2159
Nowe I rede the beware. I have warned the twyse.	202	Magnyfycence	2185
Somtyme to fall, another tyme to beware:	207	Magnyfycence	2374
To lerne you hereafter for to beware withall.	207	Magnyfycence	2376
Ye, and beware of unhappy abusyon.	210	Magnyfycence	2452
Let hym well beware	263	Collyn Clout	665
Beware of a quenes yellynge!	271	Collyn Clout	987
But yet beware the rod	307	Why Come Ye	1137
Beware, for wrytyng remayneth of recorde!	314	Garlande	89
Beware of hym, I warne you; for and ye wist and] 'if' Marshe 1568	333	Garlande	754
Whiche, if they be happy, have cause to beware	353	Garlande	1474

BE WARE

Wherfore, of adversyte loke ye be ware;	195	Magnyfycence	1936

BEWRAPPED

Some hatted and some capped, /Rychly bewrapped,	254	Collyn Clout	312

BEWREYE

That noo man erthly coude hym bewreye, man] 'wan' †Wynkyn de Worde 1499	52	Bowge	223

BEWTE

In bewte and vertew.	94	Phy Sparrow	897
Of bewte that beryth the flower,	128	Garnesche3	149
Whose bewte blastyd was with the boystors wynde,	312	Garlande	20
Of all your bewte I suffyce not to wryght:	336	Garlande	875
With lillis whyte your bewte doth renewe. With lillis] 'The lylly' MS Cotton Vitellius E.x	337	Garlande	884
With lillys whyte your bewte dothe renewe.	337	Garlande	891
Fayre Diianira surmowntynge in bewte;	337	Garlande	901

BEWTEOUS

Your goodly port, your bewteous visage,	42	Balettys2	6

BEWTEOUSE

Than to beholde youre bewteouse countenaunce:	44	Balettys3	44

BICAUSE

And for to leve this letter, /Bicause it is no better;	220	El Rummynge	238
And bicause it is no swetter,	220	El Rummynge	239

BIL

With, 'He wrate suche a bil withouten dout',	139	Ven Tongues	70

BIRDBOLT

Strake one with a birdbolt to the hart rote;	351	Garlande	1380

BIRDE

Than a chyldis birde and a knavis wyfe?	352	Garlande	1452

BIRDIS

There birdis on the brere sange on every syde,	330	Garlande	653

BIRRALL

Of birrall enbosid wer the pyllers rownde;	325	Garlande	467

BIRTH

Lorde, how she made moche of her gentyll birth!	346	Garlande	1202

BITTER

From bitter wepinge hym self kan restrayne?	32	Dol Dethe	112
He payed a bitter pencyon /For mans redempcyon,	258	Collyn Clout	452

BY

Of hevenly poems, O Clyo, calde by name	29	Dol Dethe	8
By thy report ar wonte to be extolde	29	Dol Dethe	17
Of formar writinge by any presidente	30	Dol Dethe	23
Of them demaunded and asked by the kynge;	31	Dol Dethe	79
The myghty lyoun doutted by se and sande, sande] 'lande' Marshe 1568	32	Dol Dethe	109
Bot by them to knoulege ye may attayne	32	Dol Dethe	129
He to vouchesaf, by thy mediacioun,	35	Dol Dethe	209
Wryten at Croydon by Crowland in the Clay,	38	Coystrowne1	69
Then by my councell,	39	Coystrowne3	19
By Crede, I trust to se the day,	41	Coystrowne4	12
All those by whom ye have avayle.	41	Coystrowne4	18
devysyd by Master Skelton Laureat	41	Balettys	I
Hys jentyll curtoy[1], and set nowght by small naggys! curtoyl] 'curtoyt' †Rastell 1527.1	43	Balettys2	16
By theyr conusaunce knowing how they serve a wily py:	43	Balettys2	34
Though thou withdraw me from her by long dystaunce,	45	Balettys3	46
By radyante hete enryped hath our corne;	46	Bowge	2
Her chyef gentyllwoman, Daunger by her name,	48	Bowge	69
'In fayth,' quod she, 'by Bone aventure.'	49	Bowge	119
For by that Lorde that bought dere all mankynde,	50	Bowge	163
Whyles I have ought, by God, thou shalt not lacke,	50	Bowge	167
'By Cryste,' quod Favell, 'Drede is soleyne freke!	51	Bowge	187
By myne avyse use not with him to walke.	52	Bowge	210
'By God,' quod he, 'this and thus it is';	52	Bowge	225

BY —BY

	Page	Title	Line
'Prynces of youghte', can ye synge by rote?	53	Bowge	253
By Goddis soule, I wonder how ye gete	53	Bowge	262
He frowned as he wolde swere by Cockes blode.	54	Bowge	287
Hatred by the herte so had hym wrounge	54	Bowge	292
'By Cryste,' quod he, 'for it is shame to saye,	54	Bowge	300
By Goddis bones, but yf we have som sleyte,	54	Bowde	304
'By God,' quod Hervy, 'and it so happen myghte!	54	Bowge	306
'By him that me boughte,' than quod Dysdayne,	54	Bowge	309
Wylt thou abyde by the wordes agayne?	55	Bowge	324
By God, I have of the now grete dyspyte;	55	Bowge	325
By Goddis woundes, but for dysplesaunce,	55	Bowge	332
By Goddis syde, my sworde thy berde shall shave!	55	Bowge	339
'Nowe have at all, by Saynte Thomas of Kente!'	56	Bowge	348
And by his syde his whynarde and his pouche,	56	Bowge	363
By Goddis sydes, syns I her thyder broughte,	57	Bowge	404
By that lytel connynge that I have.	59	Bowge	450
By God, I saye, there is a grete herte-brennynge	59	Bowge	460
Now, by Saynte Fraunceys, that holy man and frere,	59	Bowge	470
And by my trouthe, but yf an ende they make,	59	Bowge	473
For some shall wene be hanged by the throte.	59	Bowge	476
To us welcome thou arte, by Saynte Quyntyne!'	60	Bowge	511
'But by that Lorde that is one, two and thre,	60	Bowge	512
He tolde me so, by God, ye maye truste me.	60	Bowge	514
To holde myne honde, by God, I had grete payne;	61	Bowge	522
Of false collusyon confetryd by assente,	61	Bowge	527
By reason nor by law;	62	Hauke	7
By reason nor by law;	62	Hauke	7
By way of apostrofacyon	62	Hauke	30
By Moyses and Arons rod,	63	Hauke	54
To hunte there by lyberte	64	Hauke	108
With Regum by and by;	66	Hauke	166
With Regum by and by;	66	Hauke	166
By wey of expyacyon /For reconcylyacyon.	66	Hauke	176
for reconcylyacyon] not in Day 1560, Marshe 1568			
Then moch more, by the rode,	66	Hauke	178
I have red theym poll by poll;	67	Hauke	211
compylyd by Mayster Skelton, poete laureate	71	Phy Sparrow	I
And take me by the lyp.	75	Phy Sparrow	140
That by representacyon /Of his image and facyon,	77	Phy Sparrow	214
By way of exclamacyon,	78	Phy Sparrow	274
By Gyb, our cat savage,	81	Phy Sparrow	375
Caught Phyllyp by the head,	81	Phy Sparrow	377
By the astrology /That he hath naturally	84	Phy Sparrow	497
By Albumazer /The astronomer,	84	Phy Sparrow	501
Nor by Ptholomy, /Prince of astronomy,	84	Phy Sparrow	503
Nor yet by Haly;	84	Phy Sparrow	505
Whom now and then /He plucketh by the hede	84	Phy Sparrow	511
/The storyes by name	88	Phy Sparrow	660
Which by his mercyfull rage	88	Phy Sparrow	670
mercyfull] 'unmercifull' Wyght 1553, Kitson 1560.6, Marshe 1568			
Whereof the elegy /Foloweth by and by.	92	Phy Sparrow	825
Whereof the elegy /Foloweth by and by.	92	Phy Sparrow	825
Whose fame by me shall sprede	93	Phy Sparrow	885
By discrete consyderacyon	102	Phy Sparrow	1247
and her foloweth an addicyon made by Maister Skelton.	103	Phy Sparrow	R
Made by protestacyon,	103	Phy Sparrow	1279
By Hercules that hell dyd harow,	104	Phy Sparrow	1291
By whose myght and mayne	104	Phy Sparrow	1297
By marcyall strength /He wan at length;	104	Phy Sparrow	1305
He plucked the bull /By the horned skull,	104	Phy Sparrow	1319
Also by Ecates bower	104	Phy Sparrow	1322
By the ugly Eumenides,	104	Phy Sparrow	1324
By the venemous serpent,	104	Phy Sparrow	1326
By Chemeras flames, /And all the dedly names	105	Phy Sparrow	1330
By the Stygyall flood,	105	Phy Sparrow	1334
By the feryman of hell,	105	Phy Sparrow	1337
And by her abusyons,	105	Phy Sparrow	1347
And by her supersticyons,	105	Phy Sparrow	1350
Now by these names thre,	105	Phy Sparrow	1363
By the holy rode,	108	Epitaphel	66
By extort trechery.	111	Lawde	28
But by the power and myght of God	114	Scot Kynge	46
By your wanton wyll, syr, at a worde,	114	Scot Kynge	48
But, by the power and myght of God,	119	Ag Scottes	145
By the kynges most noble commaundment.	124	Garnesche2	E
By the kynges most noble commaundment.	129	Garnesche3	E
By hole consent of theyr senate,	131	Garnesche5	83
Liing, spying by sutteltie and slyght,	133	Garnesche5	151
By the kyngys most noble commandemennt.	134	Garnesche5	E
By Jesu Christ, /Fals Scot, thou lyest:	135	Dundas	32
Such tunges shuld be torne out by the harde rootes,	137	Ven Tongues	3
Either by language or with my pen.	137	Ven Tongues	23
In realmes, in cities, by suche fals abusion.	139	Ven Tongues	56
l thyngys contryvyd by mannys reason,	140	Magnyfycence	1
For, when men by welth, they have lytell drede	140	Magnyfycence	10
By lyberte is done many a great excesse;	142	Magnyfycence	53
Howe be it, by protestacyon	143	Magnyfycence	97

	Page	Title	Line
Nay, ye shall begynne, by my wyll.	143	Magnyfycence	104
I[n] ponder, by number, by measure all thynge is wrought,	143	Magnyfycence	118
In] 'I' †Rastell & Treveris C 1530, B			
I[n] ponder, by number, by measure all thynge is wrought,	143	Magnyfycence	118
In] 'I' †Rastell & Treveris C 1530, B			
As at the fyrst orygynall, by godly opynyon;	143	Magnyfycence	119
All trebyllys and tenours be rulyd by a meyne.	144	Magnyfycence	137
For by measure I warne you we thynke to be gydyd;	145	Magnyfycence	184
Then, Lyberte, se that Measure by your gyde,	146	Magnyfycence	195
For I wyll use you by his advertysment.	146	Magnyfycence	196
By me all persons worke what they lyste.	146	Magnyfycence	210
S[e] at our eye the worlde day by day.	146	Magnyfycence	216
Se] 'so' †Rastell & Treveris C 1530, B			
By measure eche thynge duly is tryde.	147	Magnyfycence	244
But yf I were orderyd by just measure,	147	Magnyfycence	249
By God, syr, ye se but fewe wyse men of myne age.	148	Magnyfycence	289
That colyca passyo hath gropyd you by the guttys.	148	Magnyfycence	291
In fayth, I set not by the worlde two Dauncaster cuttys.	148	Magnyfycence	293
Gete you hens, I say, by my counsell.	149	Magnyfycence	306
By lakyn, syr, it hathe cost me pence	150	Magnyfycence	338
By God, syr, beyonde the se.	150	Magnyfycence	341
By my trouthe, syr, at Pountesse.	150	Magnyfycence	343
Howe so? By God, at the see syde,	150	Magnyfycence	346
I trowe, by our lady, I had ben slayne,	150	Magnyfycence	348
By your soth? Ye, and there is suche a wache,	150	Magnyfycence	350
By my trouthe, had I not payde and prayde,	150	Magnyfycence	363
By the way as I ryde and walke –	151	Magnyfycence	375
By Goddys body, I come streyte.	151	Magnyfycence	399
I set not by hym a fly	152	Magnyfycence	412
To counterfet I can by praty wayes:	152	Magnyfycence	424
Counterfet eyrnest by way of playes.	152	Magnyfycence	427
Counterfet capytaynes by me are mande;	152	Magnyfycence	436
Counterfet letters by the way of sleyght;	152	Magnyfycence	439
By crede, it wolde have fresshe aray,	153	Magnyfycence	460
Counterfet pleasure is borne out by me;	153	Magnyfycence	475
By God, I have bene about a praty pronge –	154	Magnyfycence	501
By God, we have made Magnyfycence to ete a flye.	154	Magnyfycence	503
By God, man, bothe his pagent and thyne he can play.	154	Magnyfycence	505
Say trouth? Yes, yes, by lakyn, I shall the warent,	154	Magnyfycence	506
By the masse, for ye are able to dystroy an hole lande.	154	Magnyfycence	513
By God, yet it muste begynne moche of the.	154	Magnyfycence	514
Who that is ruled by us, it shalbe longe or he thee.	154	Magnyfycence	515
By the masse, odly well alowde.	155	Magnyfycence	533
By God, had not I it convayed	155	Magnyfycence	534
By my trouthe, we had ben gone.	155	Magnyfycence	537
By Mesure mastered yet is he.	155	Magnyfycence	541
By Cockes harte, he loketh hye.	156	Magnyfycence	574
Nowe, by Cockes harte, well abyden!	156	Magnyfycence	576
By God, syr, this is Fansy Small-Brayne;	156	Magnyfycence	583
Knowe hym, syr, quod he. Yes, by Saynt Sym!	156	Magnyfycence	585
Ye, by the masse, this is even the same,	157	Magnyfycence	599
By God, we wolde gete us all thyder,	157	Magnyfycence	618
By the armes of Calys, well conceyved.	159	Magnyfycence	675
By Cockys body, here begynneth the game!	159	Magnyfycence	682
Craftynge and haftynge contryved is by me;	159	Magnyfycence	697
By the menys of myschyef to bryng all thynges to nought.	159	Magnyfycence	702
I can fede forth a fole and lede hym by the eyre;	160	Magnyfycence	712
By cloked colusyon, I say, and none other,	160	Magnyfycence	714
By Cloked Colusyon thus many one is begyled.	160	Magnyfycence	728
And so, by these meanes, I brewe moche bale.	161	Magnyfycence	744
By God, syr, what nede all this waste?	161	Magnyfycence	754
By the masse, for the cowrte thou art a mete man;	161	Magnyfycence	764
By Goddes fote, and I dare well fyght, for I wyll not start.	161	Magnyfycence	768
By Cockys harte, and call shall agayne!	162	Magnyfycence	783
By the masse, thou shalt byde my leyser.	162	Magnyfycence	788
No, by my trouthe, but crake grete wordes.	163	Magnyfycence	812
By Saynt Mary, he is a tawle man.	163	Magnyfycence	821
For pryde hath plucked the by the nose	163	Magnyfycence	826
By day or by nyght	164	Magnyfycence	860
By day or by nyght	164	Magnyfycence	860
Nowe welcom, by the God holy!	166	Magnyfycence	919
By Cryst, as mery as a Marche hare.	166	Magnyfycence	921
No, by the masse. What! Sholde I swere?	166	Magnyfycence	936
Ye, by Goddes sacrament; and with other mo.	166	Magnyfycence	942
By Goddes body, so dyd I.	166	Magnyfycence	947
By the masse, well done and boldely.	166	Magnyfycence	948
Howe so? By God, by a praty slyght,	167	Magnyfycence	952
Howe so? By God, by a praty slyght,	167	Magnyfycence	952
Mary, Lusty Pleasure, by myne advyse,	167	Magnyfycence	964
It is, by Jesse,	167	Magnyfycence	974
By my trouthe, she hathe a grete hede.	169	Magnyfycence	1048
By my trouthe, I trowe well;	169	Magnyfycence	1051
By my faythe, syr, the frubyssher hath my sworde.	170	Magnyfycence	1063
By God, I can tell the; and I wyll.	170	Magnyfycence	1071
In faythe, trouth thou sayst nowe, by God of heven!	170	Magnyfycence	1079
Nowe, of good felowshyp, let me by thy [d]ogge.	170	Magnyfycence	1082
dogge] 'hogge' †Rastell & Treveris C 1530, B			
By my syers soule, I fele no rayne.	170	Magnyfycence	1087

	Page	Title	Line
By the masse, I holde the madde.	170	Magnyfycence	1088
By my trouth, there is myne.	171	Magnyfycence	1103
Nowe, by my trouth, man, take, there is my purse; my] 'myne' †Rastell & Treveris C 1530, B	171	Magnyfycence	1104
By the masse, yet art thou more fole than I.	171	Magnyfycence	1111
No, by my trouthe. It is but the scurfe and the scabbe.	171	Magnyfycence	1123
By God, for snatchynge of puddynges and wortes.	171	Magnyfycence	1128
Ye, by the rode, even the same.	172	Magnyfycence	1139
By Cockes harte, I wene thou hast no more.	172	Magnyfycence	1146
By the harte of God, well done!	172	Magnyfycence	1156
By God, syr, Foly, myne owne sworne brother.	172	Magnyfycence	1159
Tell by thy trouth what sport can thou make.	172	Magnyfycence	1162
Nay, by Cockys harte, he ne reckys;	172	Magnyfycence	1167
Howe rode he by you? Howe put he to you?	173	Magnyfycence	1178
Yes, by my faythe, good Syr Johnn.	173	Magnyfycence	1186
Yes, yes, by my trouth. I holde the a grote	173	Magnyfycence	1193
Nowe, by the rode, and he wyll go nere.	173	Magnyfycence	1196
What hast thou founde there? By God, a lowse.	173	Magnyfycence	1198
By Cockes harte, I trowe thou lyste.	173	Magnyfycence	1199
By the masse, a Spaynysshe moght with a gray lyste!	173	Magnyfycence	1200
With, yes, by the rode of Wodstocke Parke.	174	Magnyfycence	1209
Ye, by God, syr. For a nede,	174	Magnyfycence	1237
By the good Lorde, truthe he sayth.	175	Magnyfycence	1252
Thynkyst thou not so, by thy fayth?	175	Magnyfycence	1253
By God, there be some that be shroudly towchyd.	175	Magnyfycence	1277
By the masse, I am glad I came hyder	176	Magnyfycence	1286
A, syr, a, a! Howe by that?	176	Magnyfycence	1296
By the masse, he shall hyght Consayte.	176	Magnyfycence	1309
By me conveyed is wanton insolence;	177	Magnyfycence	1335
By me is conveyed mykyll praty ware -	177	Magnyfycence	1340
And by crafty conveyaunce I wyll, and I can,	178	Magnyfycence	1359
Theyr conveyaunce weltyth the worke all by wyll;	178	Magnyfycence	1363
And some wyll convey by the pretence of sadnesse	178	Magnyfycence	1366
By crafty conveyaunce many one is brought up of nought;	178	Magnyfycence	1369
For by crafty conveyaunce wonderful thynges are wrought.	178	Magnyfycence	1371
By convayaunce crafty I have brought	178	Magnyfycence	1372
Syr, as by my wyll, it shall be so no more.	178	Magnyfycence	1377
Remembre ye not how my lyberte by mesure ruled was?	178	Magnyfycence	1383
It is good yet that lyberte be ruled by reason.	178	Magnyfycence	1387
Yourselfe shall be ruled by lyberte and largesse.	179	Magnyfycence	1389
Not and your grace wolde be ruled by me.	179	Magnyfycence	1393
Syr, by lyberte and largesse I wyll that ye shall	179	Magnyfycence	1396
Yet it is good wysdome to worke wysely by welth.	179	Magnyfycence	1401
Then fare well thryfte, by hym that crosse kyst!	179	Magnyfycence	1416
By theyr demenaunce, nor loss repryvable.	179	Magnyfycence	1419
So it be by mesure I am ryght well content.	180	Magnyfycence	1421
What! All by mesure, good syr, and none excesse?	180	Magnyfycence	1422
That was by the menys of to moche lyberte.	180	Magnyfycence	1424
Whether sholde welth be rulyd by lyberte,	180	Magnyfycence	1431
Or lyberte by welth? Let se, tell me that.	180	Magnyfycence	1432
I set not by the prowdest of them a prane,	181	Magnyfycence	1489
Ne by non other that any man can rehersse.	181	Magnyfycence	1490
Nor Alerycus, that rulyd the Gothyaunce by swerd,	182	Magnyfycence	1504
Nor Nero, that nother set by God nor man,	182	Magnyfycence	1509
I wolde I had, by hym that hell dyd harowe,	184	Magnyfycence	1561
By the meanes of money without ony gonne.	184	Magnyfycence	1578
By waywarde wylfulnes let eche thynge be convayed;	185	Magnyfycence	1594
Be it ryght or wronge, by the advyse of me,	185	Magnyfycence	1597
By Cockes woundes, a wonder felowe thou arte!	185	Magnyfycence	1619
Syr, so it is: this man is here by,	186	Magnyfycence	1649
By myne advyse, with you in fayth he shall not rest.	186	Magnyfycence	1660
Nowe, by your trouthe, gave he you not a brybe?	187	Magnyfycence	1665
Ye, by my trouthe, I shall waraunt you for me,	187	Magnyfycence	1669
What care I? By the masse, well sayd.	187	Magnyfycence	1671
By the masse, I have done that I can,	187	Magnyfycence	1693
By my trouth, I can not tell you that.	188	Magnyfycence	1703
By Magnyfycence nor none of his;	188	Magnyfycence	1705
By the good Lorde, yet your temples bete.	189	Magnyfycence	1732
So to be ruled by measure, it is a payne.	189	Magnyfycence	1739
But use your largesse by the advyse of me,	189	Magnyfycence	1765
Thou sayst truthe, by the harte that God me gave!	190	Magnyfycence	1782
By our lakyn, syr, I have ben a hawkyng for the wylde swan.	191	Magnyfycence	1806
She pynched her pynyon, by God, and catched harme.	191	Magnyfycence	1810
By Cockes harte, thou arte a fyne mery knave.	191	Magnyfycence	1826
What? Yes, by the rode, syr. It was I all this whyle	193	Magnyfycence	1870
Nowe is there no man that wyll set by hym a flye.	193	Magnyfycence	1889
Lydderyns so lytell set by Goddes lawes.	194	Magnyfycence	1919
And where the fader by wysdom worshyp hath wonne,	195	Magnyfycence	1934
And beware of adversyte by my counsell,	195	Magnyfycence	1945
For by robbynge they rynne to in manus tuas quecke;	198	Magnyfycence	2044
A, Lord God, how the gowte wryngeth me by the too.	198	Magnyfycence	2047
I plucked her by the patlet;	199	Magnyfycence	2074
By meanes of madnesse and to moche lyberte.	199	Magnyfycence	2100
Howe he is undone by the meanes of me?	200	Magnyfycence	2110
But by the way of fansy insolence;	200	Magnyfycence	2116
That nother they set by father and mother;	200	Magnyfycence	2142
With ye, syr, by Jesu, that slayne was with Jewes!	201	Magnyfycence	2167
By my trouthe, we have ryfled hym metely well.	201	Magnyfycence	2170

	Page	Title	Line
By the messe, I shall cleve thy heed to the waste.	201	Magnyfycence	2175
By Cockes bones, I shall blysse the and thou be to bolde.	202	Magnyfycence	2182
Go together by the heddys, and gyve me your swordys.	202	Magnyfycence	2199
By the masse, man, thou shall fynde me resonable.	202	Magnyfycence	2204
By our lakyn, syr, not by my wyll.	203	Magnyfycence	2208
By our lakyn, syr, not by my wyll.	203	Magnyfycence	2208
By the fayth that I owe to God, and I wyll syt styll.	203	Magnyfycence	2209
Nay, by Saynt Mary, it was ye called me knave.	203	Magnyfycence	2212
By God, I tell you, I wyll not be out facyd.	203	Magnyfycence	2220
By the masse, I warant the, I wyll not be bracyd.	203	Magnyfycence	2221
Your trymynge and tramynge by me must be tangyd,	203	Magnyfycence	2234
By Cockys bonys, it is the same.	204	Magnyfycence	2244
By myschefe to brevyate and shorten his dayes.	206	Magnyfycence	2338
Prosperyte [by] hym is gyven solacyously to man;	207	Magnyfycence	2367
by] 'to' †Rastell & Treveris C 1530, B			
And be ruled by me, whiche am called Redresse.	208	Magnyfycence	2410
But, syr, by me to rule fyrst ye began.	209	Magnyfycence	2431
Largesse, syr, by his credence was his name.	209	Magnyfycence	2441
And syt there by styll, /Erly and late.	217	El Rummynge	116
By hym that me bought!'	218	El Rummynge	167
For ye may prove it by me.'	219	El Rummynge	216
She swered by the Rode of Rest,	221	El Rummynge	271
Therefore, 'Fyll it by and by	221	El Rummynge	274
Therefore, 'Fyll it by and by	221	El Rummynge	274
I swere by all hallowe	222	El Rummynge	323
'By Chryst,' sayde she, 'thou lyest.	223	El Rummynge	344
And sware by Saynt Benet.	224	El Rummynge	393
And called for our dame, /Elynour by name.	229	El Rummynge	593
By Nature devysed of a wonderowus kynde,	231	Speke Parott	2
Where men of that contre by fortune me fynde,	231	Speke Parott	5
Thus dyvers of language by lernyng I grow:	233	Speke Parott	103
That they cannot say in Greke, rydynge by the way,	234	Speke Parott	146
He made you of nothynge by his magistye;	236	Speke Parott	219
Makyng hys pylgrimage by Nostre Dame de Crome:	239	Speke Parott	305
To rule ix realmes by one mannes wytte,	240	Speke Parott	333
As appereth by theyr werkes,	250	Collyn Clout	151
Set nought by golde ne grotes, /Theyr names yf I durst tell.	250	Collyn Clout	160
Dominus vobiscum by the hede,	252	Collyn Clout	230
By the breed that God brake,	253	Collyn Clout	251
By juste examynacyon /In connynge and conversacyon.	253	Collyn Clout	266
By pollynge and pyllage /In cytes and vyllage;	255	Collyn Clout	360
By taxynge and tollage,	255	Collyn Clout	362
Chryst by cruelte /Was nayled upon a tre;	258	Collyn Clout	450
Of preestly dygnytes /By theyr malygnytes.	260	Collyn Clout	539
By] 'But' Kele 1545.1, Marshe 1568			
And lewdely sayes by Chryst	261	Collyn Clout	575
Set nothynge by polytykes.	262	Collyn Clout	623
And also gratyfyed /By holy synodalles	264	Collyn Clout	716
Shall nat be objected by me.	266	Collyn Clout	794
by] 'for' Kele 1545.1, Marshe 1568, 'at by' MS Harley 2252			
For, by saynt Hyllary,	266	Collyn Clout	813
Though some of them by lyres.	267	Collyn Clout	833
lyres] 'lyers' Kele 1545.1, Marshe 1568, 'lyars' MS Harley 2252			
That they ought by the lawe	268	Collyn Clout	857
And by the barres of her tayle	268	Collyn Clout	868
of] 'if' Marshe 1568, 'of' MS Harley 2252			
And by Dudum, theyr Clementyne,	268	Collyn Clout	872
But by the helpe of Christen Clout.	268	Collyn Clout	879
By them to gette a name.	270	Collyn Clout	959
Conveyde by olyfauntes	270	Collyn Clout	962
And by unycornes /With theyr semely hornes;	270	Collyn Clout	964
By one mannes wytte.	271	Collyn Clout	993
Without his presydent be by,	272	Collyn Clout	1042
Permytted? By saynt Luke,	272	Collyn Clout	1046
Permytted] 'Permed' †Godfray 1531, 'Now' MS Harley 2252			
And by swete saynt Marke,	272	Collyn Clout	1047
Set hym fast by the fete!	275	Collyn Clout	1166
Have hym thyder by and by!	275	Collyn Clout	1172
Have hym thyder by and by!	275	Collyn Clout	1172
They set nat by us a shyttell;	276	Collyn Clout	1185
shytel] 'whystell' Kele 1545.1, Marshe 1568, 'shetyll' MS Harley 2252			
By the ryght of a rambes horne.	276	Collyn Clout	1199
By hoke ne by croke	277	Collyn Clout	1238
By hoke ne by croke	277	Collyn Clout	1238
compylyed by Mayster Skelton, Poete Laureate	278	Why Come Ye	I
Through suche abusyon, /And by suche illusyon,	279	Why Come Ye	20
/Is nothynge set by,	280	Why Come Ye	46
I drede, by swete Jesu,	280	Why Come Ye	64
And vexeth them day by day	282	Why Come Ye	155
He pluckes them by the hode,	286	Why Come Ye	304
And shakes them by the eare,	286	Why Come Ye	305
Of! by the harde arse!	288	Why Come Ye	386
Set hym fast by the fete!'	289	Why Come Ye	426
Have hym forthe by and by /To the Marshalsy,	289	Why Come Ye	431
Have hym forthe by and by /To the Marshalsy,	289	Why Come Ye	431
By him is subverted;	290	Why Come Ye	440

BY —BY

	Page	Title	Line
By God that me dere bought!	290	Why Come Ye	451
By] 'But' Marshe 1568			
By the dayes and by the wekes.	293	Why Come Ye	556
By the dayes and by the wekes.	293	Why Come Ye	556
I dought, lest by sorsery	295	Why Come Ye	663
And is governed by this mad kote!	295	Why Come Ye	668
And] not in Marshe 1568			
And settys nat by it a myte!	296	Why Come Ye	677
It was by nycromansy,	296	Why Come Ye	696
By carectes and conjuracyon	296	Why Come Ye	697
As by myne auctor tried it was.	296	Why Come Ye	707
By Lewes the kyng aforesayd,	297	Why Come Ye	730
By theyr cyrcumspection,	298	Why Come Ye	768
By way of commissyon	299	Why Come Ye	799
Farre by yonde Portyngale,	299	Why Come Ye	802
He is best set by!	300	Why Come Ye	859
best] 'most' MS Rawlinson C. 813			
Myght stande now by potters,	301	Why Come Ye	910
Myght] 'most' MS Rawlinson C. 813			
By nature of a newe writ.	302	Why Come Ye	939
For els by and by	303	Why Come Ye	964
For els by and by	303	Why Come Ye	964
I speke by protestacion:	305	Why Come Ye	1043
His madnesse by writynge,	305	Why Come Ye	1056
And by his legacy,	306	Why Come Ye	1103
By his former othe,	307	Why Come Ye	1131
By the craft of surgery,	308	Why Come Ye	1173
By whose suggestyon /I toke on hand this warke,	309	Why Come Ye	1203
suggestyon] 'subjectyon' MS Rawlinson C. 813			
by Mayster Skelton, Poete Laureat,	312	Garlande	I
Into the brayne by drynkyng over depe,	313	Garlande	33
That banisshed was he by his proposicyoun,	316	Garlande	132
by] 'through' Marshe 1568			
By Eschines rehersed to the grete glory	317	Garlande	166
Theis people by me have none assignement,	317	Garlande	195
Of them that have vertue by reason of cunnyng,	317	Garlande	198
Frome the laureat senate by force of proscripcyon.	318	Garlande	225
And may not atteyne it by no medyacyon,	321	Garlande	319
This sayd, a great nowmber folowyd by and by	321	Garlande	323
This sayd, a great nowmber folowyd by and by	321	Garlande	323
Lucilius and Valerius Maximus by name;	322	Garlande	380
Of all our hooll collage by the agreament,	324	Garlande	417
Of Fames court, by all our holl assent	324	Garlande	433
Avaunced by Pallas to laurell preferment.'	324	Garlande	434
This gentilwoman, that callyd was by name	327	Garlande	527
And with that worde she toke me by the honde.	328	Garlande	560
Sum medelynge spyes, by craft to grope thy mynde,	329	Garlande	617
That ever more after by it they were aspyid;	329	Garlande	627
That all the dayes of ther lyfe shall styck by ther rybbis.	330	Garlande	638
By meanys of a grosely endarkyd clowde	330	Garlande	645
With the nyne Muses, Pierides by name;	331	Garlande	680
with] 'wit' †Fakes 1523			
Now, by your faith, is not this theffect	333	Garlande	737
by] 'be' †Fakes 1523			
For by his devellysshe drift and graceles provision	333	Garlande	757
Turnyng on the ryght hande, by a windyng stayre,	333	Garlande	767
a] not in †Fakes 1523			
To worke me this chapelet by goode advysemente.	334	Garlande	807
Sith ye must nedis afforce it by pretence	335	Garlande	817
Lyke to Argyva by just resemblaunce,	336	Garlande	843
Cirus by name, as wrytith the story;	336	Garlande	858
By saynt Mary, my Lady,	339	Garlande	973
Partly by your councell,	342	Garlande	1054
By Maro, the Mantuan prudent,	342	Garlande	1080
Dyvysynge in pycture, by his industrious wit,	343	Garlande	1098
And for as moche as, by the hy pretence	344	Garlande	1124
That ye have now by the preemynence	344	Garlande	1125
by the] 'thorow' MS Cotton Vitellius E.x			
But if hastyve credence by mayntenance of myght	344	Garlande	1133
Rehersyng by ordre, and what is the grownde,	345	Garlande	1152
to reherse all by name that he hath compylyd, &c.	345	Garlande	R
His commedy, Achademios callyd by name;	346	Garlande	1184
Dyvysed by Skelton after the funerall rate;	348	Garlande	1256
But myrth and consolacyoun, /Made by protestacyoun,	348	Garlande	1272
By Hercules that hell did harow,	348	Garlande	1284
By whos myght and maine	348	Garlande	1290
By merciall strength /He wan at length;	349	Garlande	1298
He pluckid the bull /By the hornid scull,	349	Garlande	1312
Also by Hecates powre	349	Garlande	1315
powre] 'bowre' Marshe 1568			
By the ugly Eumenides,	349	Garlande	1317
By the venemows serpent	349	Garlande	1319
By Chemeras flamys, /And all the dedely namys	349	Garlande	1323
By the Stigiall flode,	349	Garlande	1327
By the feryman of hell,	349	Garlande	1330
And by her abusiouns, /And damnable illusiouns	350	Garlande	1340
Of mervelous conclusiouns, /And by her supersticiouns	350	Garlande	1343
Now by theys names thre,	350	Garlande	1356

BYBILLE — BYLL | Page | Title | Line

	Page	Title	Line
An hynde unhurt hit by casuelte, not bled	351	Garlande	1406
By there phesik doth many a man ease,	352	Garlande	1427
By Candelmes day what wedder shuld holde;	352	Garlande	1442
By Mary Gipcy, /Quod scripsi, scripsi;	353	Garlande	1455
For, by Juppiter and his high mageste,	353	Garlande	1488
To harnnes bryght, /By force of myght,	355	Garlande	1557
dyvysed by Mayster Skelton, Poete Laureat.	358	Garlande2	R
By the water of Twede,	359	Albany	31
That valiaunt knyght, /Putte you to flyght /By his valyaunce.	360	Albany	42
He ran awaye by night.	360	Albany	71
By your Duke of Albany.	363	Albany	162
By suche a dronken drane.	363	Albany	164
By suche a cowarde knyght,	363	Albany	166
He ran away by nyght	366	Albany	311
Than forthwith by and by	374	Replycacion	4
Than forthwith by and by	374	Replycacion	4
Thus by demeryttes of their abusyon,	374	Replycacion	14
Or be brende by and by,	377	Replycacion	89
Or be brende by and by,	377	Replycacion	89
By way of their devocion	378	Replycacion	136
And by Holy Churche correcte,	380	Replycacion	239
Wherefore by and by /Nowe consequently	383	Replycacion	314
Wherefore by and by /Nowe consequently	383	Replycacion	314
By whose inflammacion /Of spyrituall instygacion	384	Replycacion	379

BYBILLE

	Page	Title	Line
To syt hym upon, and rede Jacke a thrummis bybille,	318	Garlande	209
hym] not in MS Cotton Vitellius E.x			

BYBYLL

	Page	Title	Line
(The Bybyll wyll not ly)	66	Hauke	167
Fyrst I lay before them my bybyll	174	Magnyfycence	1220
Ye, of Jacke a Thrommys bybyll can ye make a glose.	180	Magnyfycence	1427
'And let me with you bybyll.'	228	El Rummynge	550

BYBYLL CLARKE

	Page	Title	Line
Parrot pretendith to be a bybyll clarke!'	234	Speke Parott	119

BYBLE

	Page	Title	Line
The Byble makith; with whos chast lyvynge	336	Garlande	846

BYCAUSE

	Page	Title	Line
Bycause his voyce is lowde,	82	Phy Sparrow	439
Bycause course of measure — yf I be in the way:	146	Magnyfycence	213
Ye wene that I am dronken bycause I loke pale.	147	Magnyfycence	259
Bycause I wolde prove men of theyr pacyence.	194	Magnyfycence	1917
Theyr chyldren, bycause that they have no mekenesse,	194	Magnyfycence	1924
Bycause the ale is good;	221	El Rummynge	284
Bycause they have proclamed	305	Why Come Ye	1055
Bycause that he his tyme studyously hath spent	314	Garlande	60
he his tyme] 'his tyme he' MS Cotton Vitellius E.x			
Bycause that ye encrese and amplyfy	323	Garlande	404
ye] not in †Fakes 1523			
Bycause ye her mysnamed,	376	Replycacion	59
Bycause ye have eaten a flye,	380	Replycacion	244

BYD

	Page	Title	Line
Byd hym take good hede of you, my synguler tresure.	149	Magnyfycence	317
It shall be done. Ye, but byd hym come away	179	Magnyfycence	1399

BYDE

	Page	Title	Line
In endles blis with the to byde and dwell	34	Dol Dethe	201
Swere and stare, and byde therby,	152	Magnyfycence	414
By the masse, thou shalt byde my leyser.	162	Magnyfycence	788
And get [y]ou home togyther; for Lyberte shall byde	180	Magnyfycence	1446
you] 'thou' †Rastell & Treveris C 1530, B			
As they may byde therby,	273	Collyn Clout	1062
That ye can nat byde thereby.	310	Why Come Ye2	28
Sume were to hasty and wold no man byde;	319	Garlande	249
That durst nat byde the sight	364	Albany	236
Ye durst byde on the grounde.	367	Albany	347

BYDENE

	Page	Title	Line
With suche storyes bydene	270	Collyn Clout	954

BYDYNG

	Page	Title	Line
In fayth, and without lyberte there is no bydyng.	158	Magnyfycence	662

BYE

	Page	Title	Line
'Forsoth,' quod I, 'to bye some of youre ware.'	48	Bowge	79

BYES

	Page	Title	Line
His face was belymmed as byes had him stounge;	54	Bowge	289

BYGGE

	Page	Title	Line
So bygge a bulke of brow-auntleres cabagyd that yere;	245	Speke Parott	488

BYYONDE

	Page	Title	Line
It was excedyng byyonde the commowne rate.	326	Garlande	488

BYL

	Page	Title	Line
This is the tenor of my byl,	310	Why Come Ye2	33

BYLDE

	Page	Title	Line
That can bylde his dwellinge house	298	Why Come Ye	757

BYLDYNG

	Page	Title	Line
So many howgye howsys byldyng, and so small howse-holdyng;	245	Speke Parott	494

BYLEVE

	Page	Title	Line
Counterfet prechynge, and byleve the contrary;	153	Magnyfycence	466
Be lyght of byleve and hasty of credence;	161	Magnyfycence	740

BYLL

	Page	Title	Line
And opened his prety byll,	77	Phy Sparrow	221
opened] 'open' Marshe 1568			

BYLLES —BYTYNG

	Page	Title	Line
With his byll betwene my lippes,	80	Phy Sparrow	359
A byll of recorde for an annuall rent.	187	Magnyfycence	1667
To herken Jacke and Gyll /Whan they put up a byll;	249	Collyn Clout	97
This byll well over loked,	281	Why Come Ye	118
That of Aconcyus whan she founde the byll	337	Garlande	886
Thynke what ye wyll /Of this wanton byll;	353	Garlande	1454

BYLLES
| Pandaer bare the bylles | 88 | Phy Sparrow | 682 |
| Our Englysh bowes, our Englysh bylles, | 119 | Ag Scottes | 132 |

BYLLYS
| At Floddon hyllys, /Our bowys, our byllys | 116 | Ag Scottes | 26 |

BYND
| Trouth doth me bynd /And loyalte | 96 | Phy Sparrow | 977 |

BYNDE
Agenst ye now I bynde;	128	Garnesche3	160
What, lyberte to measure then wolde ye bynde?	144	Magnyfycence	131
But hooly to perseveraunce my selfe I wyll bynde,	212	Magnyfycence	2507
Some with a sho clout /Bynde theyr heddes about;	218	El Rummynge	144
And bynde them to a stake,	303	Why Come Ye	984
Howe ye wyll beres bynde	364	Albany	209
Wherwith he dothe them bynde	371	Albany	484

BYRD
| That byrd ys nat honest | 129 | Garnesche3 | 197 |
| Parrot is a fayre byrd for a lady; | 236 | Speke Parott | 211 |

BYRDE
Whan thou my byrde untwynde!	79	Phy Sparrow	284
So trayterously my byrde to kyll	79	Phy Sparrow	322
Was never byrde in cage /More gentle of corage	80	Phy Sparrow	324
How my byrde so fayre,	80	Phy Sparrow	343
Every byrde in his laye:	81	Phy Sparrow	394
The byrde of Araby,	84	Phy Sparrow	513
Stowe, byrde, stowe, stowe!	167	Magnyfycence	967
A byrde full swete,	167	Magnyfycence	975
My name ys Parott, a byrde of Paradyse,	231	Speke Parott	1
'Parott ys a goodlye byrde and a pratye popagay.'	231	Speke Parott	14
and] not in Lant 1545, Kynge and Marche 1554, Day 1560, Marshe 1568			
Speke, Parotte, my swete byrde, and ye shall have a date,	243	Speke Parott	416
Nowe, Parott, my swete byrde, speke owte yet ons agayn,	244	Speke Parott	447
Above, in the top, a byrde of Araby,	330	Garlande	667

BYRDES
Beestes, byrdes, and foules,	78	Phy Sparrow	259
And not for byrdes smale.	80	Phy Sparrow	340
All maner of byrdes in your kynd;	81	Phy Sparrow	388
Amonge the byrdes smale,	340	Garlande	998

BYRDIS
Above all other byrdis, set Parrot alone.	233	Speke Parott	112
In nedill wark raysyng byrdis in bowris,	334	Garlande	804
byrdis in bowris] 'bothe birddis and bowres' MS Cotton Vitellius E.x			

BYRLE
| To byrle them of the best. | 221 | El Rummynge | 269 |

BYRNE
| And byrne you all to colles, | 362 | Albany | 152 |

BYRTH
| He braggyth of hys byrth, that borne was full bace; | 37 | Coystrownel | 24 |
| His byrth and rowme togeder, | 291 | Why Come Ye | 498 |

BYSE
| And byse, enpicturid with gressoppes and waspis, | 345 | Garlande | 1158 |

BYSELY
| For they that wyll so bysely smater | 175 | Magnyfycence | 1257 |

BYSY
Bysy, bysy, and ever bysy,	169	Magnyfycence	1039
Bysy, bysy, and ever bysy,	169	Magnyfycence	1039
Bysy, bysy, and ever bysy,	169	Magnyfycence	1039

BYSYDE
| In a certayne stede /Bysyde Lederhede. | 217 | El Rummynge | 98 |

BYSSHOP
And hym a bysshop make,	254	Collyn Clout	305
The bysshop on his carpet	255	Collyn Clout	327
Of no good bysshop speke I,	273	Collyn Clout	1095

BYSSHOPPES
What trowe ye they say more /Of the bysshoppes lore?	249	Collyn Clout	93
'Bysshoppes, yf they may,	249	Collyn Clout	122
Howe bysshoppes dysdayne /Sermons for to make,	250	Collyn Clout	133
And the dygnyte /Of the bysshoppes [s]ee.	259	Collyn Clout	501
see] 'fee' †Godfray 1531, Kele 1545.1, Marshe 1568			
Of bysshoppes they chat,	263	Collyn Clout	672
Ye bysshoppes of estates	263	Collyn Clout	690
For bysshoppes have protections,	268	Collyn Clout	891

BYT
| Hop Lobyn of Lowdeon wald have e byt of bred; | 232 | Speke Parott | 72 |
| Walke, Scot, go begge a byt | 362 | Albany | 154 |

BYTE
| Myght byte asondre thy throte! | 79 | Phy Sparrow | 306 |
| Byte asondre thy backe bone! | 79 | Phy Sparrow | 312 |

BYTYNG
| Wrythyng and wringyng, /Bytyng and styngyng; | 95 | Phy Sparrow | 944 |

BYTYNGE —BLAST   Page   Title   Line

BYTYNGE
His symplenesse resytynge, /Remordynge and bytynge,	305	Why Come Ye	1058

BYTTER
But under hony ofte tyme lyeth bytter gall,	49	Bowge	131
His herte withall /Bytter as gall;	94	Phy Sparrow	917
That with myxture of aloes and bytter gall	117	Ag Scottes	81
The bytter sayd boldly that they were to blame;	192	Magnyfycence	1837
Myxed with bytter alowes of herde adversyte.	207	Magnyfycence	2354

BYTTERNESSE
But fallyble flatery enmyxyd with bytternesse.	212	Magnyfycence	2516
But fallyble flatery enmyxyd with bytternesse.	212	Magnyfycence	2523

BYTWENE
Bytwene the tap[pet] and the wall.	174	Magnyfycence	1233
tappet] 'tap' †Rastell & Treveris C 1530, B			
Bytwene the clergye /And the temporaltye:	260	Collyn Clout	555
Bytwene some and some	288	Why Come Ye	388
Bytwene him and me;	308	Why Come Ye	1150
Men call a phenix; her wynges bytwene	330	Garlande	668
That bytwene you twayne	368	Albany	368

BLABER
That blaber, barke, and blother,	266	Collyn Clout	777

BLACK
The whyte apperyth the better for the black,	347	Garlande	1237

BLACKE
With vysage blacke and blo;	73	Phy Sparrow	75
As patryarke or pope /In a blacke cope.	85	Phy Sparrow	529
That is as trew /As blacke is blew /And grene is gray.	116	Ag Scottes	18
Parrot hath a blacke beard and a fayre grene tayle.	233	Speke Parott	84
Aut blacke monacorum,	256	Collyn Clout	381
Must cast up theyr blacke vayles	256	Collyn Clout	396
Be it blacke or whight	281	Why Come Ye	115
He morneth in blacke clothynge.	288	Why Come Ye	392

BLAYNES
I vysyte them somtyme with blaynes and with sores;	194	Magnyfycence	1901

BLAK
With, 'Fill the blak bowle /For Jayberdes sowle.'	108	Epitaphe1	73

BLAKE
Nor to the lake /Of fendys blake.	40	Coystrowne3	48
Among the Nones Blake.	72	Phy Sparrow	9
All the flees blake	76	Phy Sparrow	180
Nor blake Baltazar with hys basnet routh as a bere,	122	Garnesche1	23
I sey, ye solem Sarson, alle blake ys yor ble;	122	Garnesche1	36
Of the fendys blake;	303	Why Come Ye	975

BLAME
And were not thei to blame, I say also,	30	Dol Dethe	36
Gave me a taunte, and sayde I was to blame	48	Bowge	70
She was moch to blame;	89	Phy Sparrow	710
And no man wyll me blame,	94	Phy Sparrow	890
Me to beknave thow art to blame;	132	Garnesche5	107
Somtime women were put in great blame,	139	Ven Tongues	59
Knowe they not me? They are to blame.	157	Magnyfycence	593
The bytter sayd boldly that they were to blame;	192	Magnyfycence	1837
Alasse, alasse, syrs, ye are to blame!	204	Magnyfycence	2245
To gyve so hasty credence ye were moche to blame.	209	Magnyfycence	2443
Howe they are to blame	259	Collyn Clout	509
Ye are the lesse to blame,	262	Collyn Clout	614
But they wolde no man shuld them blame.	275	Collyn Clout	1142
He sayth we ar to blame!	305	Why Come Ye	1049
Blame Juvinall, and blame nat me.	309	Why Come Ye2	8
Blame Juvinall, and blame nat me.	309	Why Come Ye2	8
Ye put to blame ye wot nere whom.	310	Why Come Ye2	17
nere] 'nott' MS Rawlinson C. 813			
Item Good Advysement, that brainles doth blame;	346	Garlande	1186

BLAMED
Wherefore shulde I be blamed	103	Phy Sparrow	1255
Wherfore shulde I be blamed?	274	Collyn Clout	1112
be] not in Marshe 1568			
And ofte prechours be blamed	305	Why Come Ye	1054
ofte] 'the' MS Rawlinson C. 813			

BLAMELES
But he shall not be blameles,	62	Hauke	39

BLAMELESSE
Ye shall nat escape blamelesse,	309	Why Come Ye2	4
escape] 'be' MS Rawlinson C. 813			

BLANKET
She hobles as she gose /With her blanket hose	216	El Rummynge	86
she gose] 'a gose' Day 1560, Marshe 1568			

BLASE
Set in thy tayle a blase	79	Phy Sparrow	315

BLASED
Or els doutlesse ye shalbe blased,	382	Replycacion	294

BLASY
Moche of thy maneres I ca[n] blasy.	130	Garnesche5	32
can] 'cam' †MS Harley 367			

BLAST
Enbrethed with the blast of influence dyvyne,	33	Dol Dethe	157
Of foule detraccion God kepe the from the blast.	34	Dol Dethe	173
Beten with stormys of many a frowarde blast,	213	Magnyfycence	2560

BLASTE—BLYNDE

	Page	Title	Line
with the flyblowen blast	373	Replycacion	I
BLASTE			
To blowe a blaste with his long breth extendid;	319	Garlande	234
That longe tyme blewe a full timorous blaste,	319	Garlande	260
The blaste of the brynston blew away his brayne;	329	Garlande	631
Here you not Eolus for you blowyth a blaste?	343	Garlande	1088
you (1st)] 'ye' MS Cotton Vitellius E.x			
BLASTYD			
Whose bewte blastyd was with the boystors wynde,	312	Garlande	20
BLAUNCHED			
Ye, syr, a blaunched almonde is no bene.	151	Magnyfycence	381
BLE			
I sey, ye solem Sarson, alle blake ys yor ble;	122	Garneschel	36
How bright I am of ble!	220	El Rummynge	218
How her ble was bryght as blossom on the spray,	351	Garlande	1412
BLED			
Me semeth that ye have dronken more than ye have bled.	147	Magnyfycence	260
An hynde unhurt hit by casuelte, not bled	351	Garlande	1406
BLEDE			
A maynny of rude villayns made hym for to blede.	30	Dol Dethe	46
BLEDING			
Persyd with payn, bleding with wondes smart,	45	Balettys5	2
BLEMYSSHED			
And blemysshed is her name,	89	Phy Sparrow	712
BLENKARDIS			
Brainles blenkardis that blow at the cole,	329	Garlande	610
BLENNER-HAISET			
To maystres Jane Blenner-Haiset	339	Garlande	R
BLENNES			
And somtyme she blennes	219	El Rummynge	201
BLERDE			
Another wolde myne eye were blerde;	150	Magnyfycence	354
BLERE			
And so they blere your eye	263	Collyn Clout	684
BLERED			
For they are blered;	215	El Rummynge	36
BLEREED			
His eyen blereed, his face shone lyke a glas;	56	Bowge	353
BLERYD			
I wys, powle hachet, she bleryd thyne I!	42	Balettys1	28
BLESSE			
For whether he blesse or curse,	282	Why Come Ye	137
BLESSED			
And blessed her with a cup /Of newe ale in cornes.	224	El Rummynge	377
But blessed Bacchus, the pleasant god of wyne,	321	Garlande	334
But blessed Bacchus, the pleasant god of wyne,	321	Garlande	341
howe it was idolatry to offre to ymages of our blessed lady,	375	Replycacion	I
In the honour of our blessed lady,	375	Replycacion	18
And her most blessed baby,	375	Replycacion	19
BLESSYD			
When consecratyd was /The blessyd sacrament.	67	Hauke	186
But, blessyd be our Lorde, they wyll be sone converted.	184	Magnyfycence	1584
Of our blessyd Lorde, syr, at the reverence -	186	Magnyfycence	1636
A, blessyd may ye be, syr! What shall you I call?	206	Magnyfycence	2327
But blessyd Bachus, potenciall god of strengthe,	322	Garlande	348
But blessyd Bachus was in there company,	322	Garlande	355
But blessyd Bachus most reverent and holy,	322	Garlande	362
But blessyd Bachus that never man forgate,	322	Garlande	369
But blessyd Bachus, that bote is of all bale,	322	Garlande	376
BLEW			
The Indy saphyre blew /Her vaynes doth ennew;	97	Phy Sparrow	1031
That is as trew /As blacke is blew /And grene is gray.	116	Ag Scottes	18
The blaste of the brynston blew away his brayne;	329	Garlande	631
There blew in that gardynge a soft piplyng colde	331	Garlande	676
Grene, rede, tawny, whyte, purpill, and blew.	334	Garlande	800
whyte] 'whyght blak' MS Cotton Vitellius E.x			
BLEWE			
His cote was checked with patches rede and blewe;	56	Bowge	358
checked] 'checkered' Marshe 1568			
Wanne, and blewe as lead:	73	Phy Sparrow	61
That longe tyme blewe a full timorous blaste,	319	Garlande	260
BLIS			
In endles blis with the to byde and dwell	34	Dol Dethe	201
BLISSED			
But blissed Bachus, that mastris oft doth frame,	322	Garlande	383
BLISSYNG			
Goddes blissyng lyght on thy lytell swete musse!	238	Speke Parott	266
BLYNDE			
Woo is hym that is blynde and maye not see!	60	Bowge	518
I wold thou haddest ben blynde!	79	Phy Sparrow	285
How they are blynde /In theyr owne mynde,	115	Ag Scottes	7
Bolde bayarde, ye are to blynde,	126	Garnesche3	101
Howe be it, lyberte makyth many a man blynde;	142	Magnyfycence	52
I sawe a losell lede a lurden, and they were bothe blynde.	191	Magnyfycence	1824
Wherfor your remorders ar madde or else starke blynde,	241	Speke Parott	369
remorders] 'remordes' †MS Harley 2252			
And make the commons blynde.	263	Collyn Clout	663
Well-syghted when /He is amonge blynde men?	292	Why Come Ye	535

BLYNDED — BLOTHER

	Page	Title	Line
The blynde eteth many a flye.	378	Replycacion	152
BLYNDED			
And so farre blynded,	295	Why Come Ye	660
BLYNDNES			
That in me were grete blyndnes,	342	Garlande	1064
BLYNDNESSE			
Or wylfull blyndnesse,	290	Why Come Ye	469
BLYNKERD			
Thou blynkerd blowboll, thou wakyst to late;	42	Balettys1	24
BLYS			
There may no fraunchys /Nor worldly blys	39	Coystrowne3	27
And I am your, syr, so have I blys,	60	Bowge	495
A phenex it is /This herse that must blys	84	Phy Sparrow	519
BLYSSE			
It were an hevenly blysse	97	Phy Sparrow	1039
Where drede ledyth the daunce, there is no joy nor blysse.	142	Magnyfycence	76
Nowe Cryst it blysse!	167	Magnyfycence	973
Bathyd with blysse, embracyd with comforte.	181	Magnyfycence	1472
By Cockes bones, I shall blysse the and thou be to bolde.	202	Magnyfycence	2182
Today in delyte, tomorowe bare of blysse;	213	Magnyfycence	2542
BLYSSYNG			
So myche crossyng and blyssyng and hym all be shrewde;	246	Speke Parott	516
BLYST			
For myrth I have hym coryed, beten, and blyst,	185	Magnyfycence	1622
BLO			
Bewayle thy fortune, with vaynys wan and blo.	45	Balettys5	3
With vysage blacke and blo;	73	Phy Sparrow	75
The colour dedely, swarte, blo and wan	351	Garlande	1399
BLODE			
Of the blode royall descendinge nobelly;	29	Dol Dethe	4
Whiche wert endiyd with rede blode of the same	32	Dol Dethe	117
His noble blode never desteynyd was,	33	Dol Dethe	148
With thi blode precious our fenaunce thou dyd pay	34	Dol Dethe	195
He frowned as he wolde swere by Cockes blode.	54	Bowge	287
The blode ran downe raw /Upon the auter stone.	63	Hauke	58
Where Crystis precyous blode /Dayly offryd is,	66	Hauke	179
Or any of the blode.	76	Phy Sparrow	200
Me thought, of Phyllyps blode.	77	Phy Sparrow	226
His swerde hath bathed in the Scottes blode.	115	Scot Kynge	71
It was a ronner; nay, fole, I warant her blode warme.	191	Magnyfycence	1811
Here shalbe not great sheddynge of blode.	203	Magnyfycence	2207
For all their noble blode,	286	Why Come Ye	303
Where the sank royall is, Crystes blode so rede,	353	Garlande	1463
His blode with fonde dotage.	369	Albany	415
basked and baththed in their wylde burblyng and boyling blode,	374	Replycacion	I
BLOMMER			
Amonge all the blommer,	224	El Rummynge	407
BLOO			
For worldly shame I wax bothe wanne and bloo.	198	Magnyfycence	2054
Hys wolvys hede, wanne, bloo as lede, gapythe over the crowne:	244	Speke Parott	434
BLOOD			
The tokens ar not good /To be true Englysh blood;	121	Ag Scottes2	23
Where is nowe my kynne, my frendys, and my noble blood?	198	Magnyfycence	2060
BLOODE			
His corage manly, yet ther he shed his bloode.	32	Dol Dethe	103
The noble bloode royall	262	Collyn Clout	612
For lordes of noble bloode,	262	Collyn Clout	615
BLOSSOM			
This blossom of fressh colour,	98	Phy Sparrow	1055
This blossom of fressh coloure,	98	Phy Sparrow	1084
This blossom of fressh colour,	99	Phy Sparrow	1108
This] 'The' Wyght 1553, Kitson 1560.6, Marshe 1568			
Th[is] blossom of fressh coloure,	100	Phy Sparrow	1137
This] 'The' editions			
This blossom of fressh coloure,	101	Phy Sparrow	1186
The blossom on the spray,	340	Garlande	989
How her ble was bryght as blossom on the spray,	351	Garlande	1412
BLOSSOME			
This blossome of fresshe coulour,	94	Phy Sparrow	894
This blossome of fresh coloure,	96	Phy Sparrow	990
This blossome of fresshe coloure,	97	Phy Sparrow	1023
This blossome of fressh coloure,	100	Phy Sparrow	1162
This blossome of fressh coloure,	101	Phy Sparrow	1209
This] 'Thus' †Kele 1545.2			
This blossome of fresshe colour,	102	Phy Sparrow	1232
BLOSSOMS			
The enbuddid blossoms of roses rede of hew	337	Garlande	883
The enbuddid blossoms of] 'Enbuddid blossome with' MS Cotton Vitellius E.x			
BLOT			
Gup Scot, /Ye blot:	135	Dundas	2
A tolman to blot, /A rough foted Scot!	136	Dundas	40
And more paper I thinke to blot	299	Why Come Ye	826
BLOTHER			
I blunder, I bluster, I blowe, and I blother;	169	Magnyfycence	1037
Thus eche of other blother /The tone against the tother.	248	Collyn Clout	66
That blaber, barke, and blother,	266	Collyn Clout	777

BLOW —BOYCE   Page   Title   Line

BLOW
	Page	Title	Line
Thereof the fame dothe blow,	110	Lawde	4
Then ren they with lesinges, and blow them about,	139	Ven Tongues	69
Brainles blenkardis that blow at the cole,	329	Garlande	610

BLOWBOLL
Thou blynkerd blowboll, thou wakyst to late;	42	Balettys1	24

BLOWE
'Forsothe,' quod she, 'how ever blowe the wynde,	49	Bowge	110
I wolde be mery that wynde that ever blowe,	53	Bowge	251
I blunder, I bluster, I blowe, and I blother;	169	Magnyfycence	1037
And drynke tyll we blowe, /And pype tyrly-tyrlowe!'	221	El Rummynge	291
But hunte and blowe an horne,	262	Collyn Clout	621
We may blowe at the cole!	281	Why Come Ye	84
To blowe a blaste with his long breth extendid;	319	Garlande	234
Let hym blowe now, that we may take a vewe	319	Garlande	237
a] 'the' MS Cotton Vitellius E.x			
To blowe bararag tyll bothe his eyne stare.'	319	Garlande	245
bararag] 'bararag brag' MS Cotton Vitellius E.x			
Lyke to the boryall wyndes whan they blowe,	319	Garlande	261
So well entakeled, what wynde that ever blowe,	327	Garlande	545
that] 'so' Marshe 1568			

BLOWEN
But covetyse hath blowen you so full of wynde	148	Magnyfycence	290
To be blowen with the flye /Of horryble heresy.	376	Replycacion	85

BLOWYNG
With blowyng out your hornes,	380	Replycacion	215

BLOWYNGE
A bagpype without blowynge standeth in no sted:	232	Speke Parott	75
bagpype] 'bagbyte' †Lant 1545, Kynge & Marche 1554			

BLOWYTH
That bararag blowyth in every mercyall warre,	319	Garlande	236
Here you not Eolus for you blowyth a blaste?	343	Garlande	1088
you (1st)] 'ye' MS Cotton Vitellius E.x			

BLUNDER
I blunder, I bluster, I blowe, and I blother;	169	Magnyfycence	1037

BLUNDERAR
And what blunderar is yonder that playth didil diddil?	333	Garlande	740

BLUNDERYNG
I hate this blunderyng that thou doste make.	151	Magnyfycence	400

BLUNTLY
Bluntly as bestis withe boste and with cry	31	Dol Dethe	83

BLURRE
Mary, as thou sayst, he gave me a blurre.	173	Magnyfycence	1179

BLUSTER
I blunder, I bluster, I blowe, and I blother;	169	Magnyfycence	1037

BO
Er I was ware, behynde me he sayde 'Bo!'	60	Bowge	500

BOBBE
And whan I fayle, bobbe me on the noll!	53	Bowge	259

BOCHAS
There came John Bochas with his volumys grete;	322	Garlande	365

BOCHER
So bolde a braggyng bocher, and flesshe sold so dere;	245	Speke Parott	485

BOCHERS
For drede of the bochers dogge	286	Why Come Ye	298
That was cast out of a bochers stall!	291	Why Come Ye	494

BOCKYLL
Here is nothynge but the bockyll of a sho,	171	Magnyfycence	1107

BODE
They bode not till the rekenyng were discust.	30	Dol Dethe	40

BODELY
I will not be japed bodely.	36	Man Margery	19
For any bodely lust,	90	Phy Sparrow	731

BODY
I fele my body quake,	74	Phy Sparrow	105
By Goddys body, I come streyte.	151	Magnyfycence	399
By Cockys body, here begynneth the game!	159	Magnyfycence	682
By Goddes body, so dyd I.	166	Magnyfycence	947
Helthe of body his besynesse to acheve;	207	Magnyfycence	2369
For to love a certayne body	296	Why Come Ye	703
Betwene his armes, he felt her body quake.	320	Garlande	301

BODYES
And slew Gerion /With thre bodyes in one;	104	Phy Sparrow	1308
So many nobyll bodyes, undyr on dawys hedd;	245	Speke Parott	467
To fatte theyr bodyes full,	250	Collyn Clout	128
Their bodyes and their gode,	371	Albany	488

BODYS
Oure eyen synkyng, /Oure bodys stynkyng,	39	Coystrowne3	34
And slew Gerione /With thre bodys in one;	349	Garlande	1301

BOGHT
All mankynd, whom thou ful dere hast boght,	34	Dol Dethe	194

BO-HO
Bo-ho doth bark wel, Hough-ho he rulyth the ring;	234	Speke Parott	130

BO HO
With, 'Te he, ta ha, bo ho, bo ho!'	376	Replycacion	75
With, 'Te he, ta ha, bo ho, bo ho!'	376	Replycacion	75

BOYCE
Boyce recounfortyd with his philosophy;	322	Garlande	359

	Page	Title	Line
BOYES			
And boyes to the pylery gan me plucke,	150	Magnyfycence	356
That thou cannyst not growe out of thy boyes gere;	170	Magnyfycence	1075
What, that we used whan we were boyes?	172	Magnyfycence	1138
Naked boyes strydynge,	270	Collyn Clout	967
BOYLING			
basked and baththed in their wylde burblyng and boyling blode,	374	Replycacion	1
BOYLYD			
Ye rostyd and ye boylyd,	125	Garnesche3	29
BOYSTORS			
Whose bewte blastyd was with the boystors wynde,	312	Garlande	20
BOKE			
Caughte penne and ynke, and wroth this lytell boke.	61	Bowge	532
wroth] 'wrote' Wynkyn de Worde 1510, Marshe 1568			
Here after foloweth the boke entytuled Ware the Hauke	61	Hauke	1
Thys boke we have devysed, /Compendyously comprysed,	62	Hauke	23
Boke, bell and candyll, /All that he myght handyll;	64	Hauke	112
In the resydew of thys boke.	68	Hauke	234
Here after foloweth the boke of Phyllyp Sparowe	71	Phy Sparrow	1
Thus endeth the boke of Philip Sparow,	103	Phy Sparrow	E
Mary, syr, ye may swere it on a boke.	176	Magnyfycence	1292
Oreb et Zeb, of Judicum rede the boke.	234	Speke Parott	117
Boke and chalys gone quyte;	257	Collyn Clout	407
In devysynge of this boke,	266	Collyn Clout	784
Nor wyll suffre this boke	277	Collyn Clout	1237
Here after foloweth a lytell boke,	278	Why Come Ye	1
Under her arme, me thought, she hade a boke.	327	Garlande	532
To shew her boke; and she sayd, 'Here it is.'	344	Garlande	1148
'Yowre boke of remembrauns we will now that ye rede;	345	Garlande	1149
boke] 'bokes' †Fakes 1523			
With that, of the boke losende were the claspis.	345	Garlande	1156
In primis the Boke of Honorous Astate;	345	Garlande	1172
Item the Boke how Men Shulde Fle Synne;	345	Garlande	1173
Item the Boke to Speke Well or be Styll;	345	Garlande	1175
The Boke of the Rosiar; Prince Arturis Creacyoun;	345	Garlande	1178
The Quene of Fame commaundid shett fast the boke,	354	Garlande	1510
May happely loke /Upon your boke,	355	Garlande	1547
And wesely rede the Boke	384	Replycacion	360
BOKES			
With bokes that I have red,	90	Phy Sparrow	753
Or bokes to compyle /Of dyvers maner style,	247	Collyn Clout	9
Ye caste up then your bokes	261	Collyn Clout	596
sum parte of Skeltons bokes and baladis with ditis of plesure,	345	Garlande	R
BOKIS			
Out of my bokis full sone I shulde hym rase;	314	Garlande	72
But that his bokis, whiche he did devyse,	315	Garlande	124
For of my bokis parte ye shall se,	344	Garlande	1139
Owt of her bokis Apollo to rase.	353	Garlande	1480
BOKYS			
But who so that lokys /In the offycyallys bokys,	65	Hauke	146
BOLD			
More specially barons, and thos knightis bold,	34	Dol Dethe	183
Yet bere ye not to bold to braule ne to bark	38	Coystrowne1	60
Ye bare yourselfe somwhat to bold;	118	Ag Scottes	125
Ye bere yow bold and brag	129	Garnesche3	187
So bold and so braggyng, and was so baselye borne;	246	Speke Parott	507
BOLDE			
Abasshe you not, but hardely be bolde,	48	Bowge	87
And, yf nede be, a bolde worde I dare cracke.	50	Bowge	168
To be with you thus perte and thus bolde;	53	Bowge	265
Phillip myght be bolde	76	Phy Sparrow	177
Amonge huswyves bolde,	87	Phy Sparrow	621
It makethe lovers bolde	98	Phy Sparrow	1074
I dare be bolde /Thus for to were.	112	Calliope	11
Ye bere yourselfe somwhat to bolde,	114	Scot Kynge	34
Ye bere yow bolde as Barabas, or Syr Terry of Trac[e].	122	Garnesche1	11
Trace] 'Tracy' †MS Harley 367			
Bolde bayarde, ye are to blynde,	126	Garnesche3	101
Yet somwhat to say I dare well be bolde,	137	Ven Tongues	10
Welthe without measure wolde bere hymselfe to bolde;	143	Magnyfycence	116
Or who made you so bolde to interrupe my tale?	147	Magnyfycence	256
Cappe, syr. I say you be to bolde.	157	Magnyfycence	602
Ye, in faythe, a bolde man and a hardy,	162	Magnyfycence	771
A bolde man in a bole of newe ale in cornys.	162	Magnyfycence	772
Be not to bolde my frende; I counsell you, bere a brayne.	179	Magnyfycence	1405
For of all barones bolde I bere the bell;	182	Magnyfycence	1498
Nor Basyan the bolde, for all his brybaunce,	182	Magnyfycence	1503
But one thynge I warne you, prece forth and be bolde.	184	Magnyfycence	1582
At lyberte a man may be bolde for to brake;	199	Magnyfycence	2085
By Cockes bones, I shall blysse the and thou be to bolde.	202	Magnyfycence	2182
Lyacon lawghyth thereatt and berythe hym more bolde;	242	Speke Parott	400
So manye bolde barons, there hertes as dull as lede;	245	Speke Parott	466
So bolde a braggyng bocher, and flesshe sold so dere;	245	Speke Parott	485
So many vacabondes, so many beggers bolde,	245	Speke Parott	498
Our barons be so bolde,	286	Why Come Ye	292
But yet they were bolde	364	Albany	202
Of suche an bolde captayne	366	Albany	305
So hardy nor so bolde	367	Albany	338

BOLDELY
By the masse, well done and boldely.	166	Magnyfycence	948
So boldely dare controule	296	Why Come Ye	674

BOLDENES
Boldenes is to seke /The churche for to defende;	251	Collyn Clout	183

BOLDLY
Presed forthe boldly to witstand the myght, ...	31	Dol Dethe	87
Boldly bend you to batell, and buske your selfe to save. . . .	122	Garneschel	41
The bytter sayd boldly that they were to blame;	192	Magnyfycence	1837
Spare not thy selfe, but boldly the murder.	206	Magnyfycence	2318
Thus boldly for to barke?	309	Why Come Ye	1205

BOLDLYE
Whyche of yow fyrste dare boldlye plucke the crowe.	242	Speke Parott	396

BOLE
Go watch a bole, your bak is brode.	35	Man Margery	12
A bolde man in a bole of newe ale in cornys.	162	Magnyfycence	772

BOLLE
A bolle or a basyn, I say, for Goddes brede!	189	Magnyfycence	1728

BOLTE
Ye wante but a wylde flyeng bolte to shote at the buttes. . . .	148	Magnyfycence	294

BOLTYD
Fast boltyd and barryd, ...	64	Hauke	92

BONAM
Lo, Johnn a Bonam, where is thy brayne?	173	Magnyfycence	1204

BONDE TENENT
Ye were bonde tenent to his estate;	118	Ag Scottes	127

BONE
Your teth whett on this bone	258	Collyn Clout	476
whett on] 'whetten' †Godfray 1531, 'whette on' MS Harley 2252			

BONE AKE
And some to cry out of the bone ake;	194	Magnyfycence	1907
And I bequethe hym the bone ake.	204	Magnyfycence	2254

BONEHOMS
Of the Bonehoms of Ashrige besyde Barkamstede, ...	353	Garlande	1461

BONES
By Goddis bones, but yf we have som sleyte, ...	54	Bowge	304
And on the borde he whyrled a payre of bones, ...	56	Bowge	346
His bones crake, /Leane as a rake;	94	Phy Sparrow	912
Malicious tunges, though they have no bones, ...	138	Ven Tongues	49
Cockes bones! I ne tell can	162	Magnyfycence	801
Cockes bones! This is all of Johnn de Gay.	167	Magnyfycence	960
Cockes bones! Harde ye ever suche another?	192	Magnyfycence	1841
By Cockes bones, I shall blysse the and thou be to bolde. . . .	202	Magnyfycence	2182
The bones [of] her huckels	215	El Rummynge	45
of] not in †Lant 1545, Kynge & Marche 1554, Day 1560, Marshe 1568; huckels] 'buckels' Day, Marshe			
She founde therein no bones.	224	El Rummynge	381
bones] 'bornes' Day 1560			
As quikly towchyd as it were flesshe and bones, ...	328	Garlande	592
It made sum lympe-legged and broisid there bones;	329	Garlande	625
We shall breke thy bones	362	Albany	150

BONET
Then let them vale a bonet of their proud sayle, ...	138	Ven Tongues	32

BONYS
With synnews wyderyd, /With bonys shyderyd, ...	39	Coystrowne3	13
Cockys bonys! Herde ye ever syke another?	170	Magnyfycence	1090
Cockys bonys! It is a farle freke.	172	Magnyfycence	1160
A, my bonys ake! My lymmys be sore!	195	Magnyfycence	1955
Cockys bonys! Thou begger, what is thy name?	203	Magnyfycence	2240
By Cockys bonys, it is the same.	204	Magnyfycence	2244
And shryne your rotten bonys	255	Collyn Clout	346

BONNE
The hawke tyryd on a *bonne, ...	63	Hauke	60
*bonne] 'bone' Scattergood			
Her fethers donne; /Well faveryd bonne!	168	Magnyfycence	990

BONNY
With, 'Bas, my prety bonny, ...	220	El Rummynge	227

BOOKE
For on the booke I can not synge a note, ...	53	Bowge	255
I] not in †Wynkyn de Worde 1499			

BOOST
Thus they make theyr boost /Through every coost, ...	251	Collyn Clout	202
Ye boost, ye face, ye crake, ...	261	Collyn Clout	602
For all theyr boost, ...	359	Albany	11
Full of bragge and boost, ...	364	Albany	207

BORDE
Fynde some mene to caste him over the borde.'	54	Bowge	308
And on the borde he whyrled a payre of bones, ...	56	Bowge	346
Ye hobble very homly before the kynges borde;	123	Garnesche2	10
But rose from the borde	229	El Rummynge	591
Clappyng his rod on the borde.	283	Why Come Ye	190
In ernest or in borde:	298	Why Come Ye	785
In ernest or in borde.	367	Albany	319

BORDED
Marchauntes her borded to see what she had lode.	47	Bowge	40
lode] not in Marshe 1568			

BORDER
Upon Grenewytche border /Called Observaunce, ...	265	Collyn Clout	746

BORDERS —BOTE	Page	Title	Line

Thorowe out every border. . . . . 380 Replycacion 228
BORDERS
In your provyncyall borders, ... 252 Collyn Clout 221
With balassis and charbuncles the borders did shyne; . . . . . 345 Garlande 1166
BORDES
 Wherfore the bordes yet cry . . . . 78 Phy Sparrow 248
  bordes] 'byrdes' Wyght 1553, Kitson 1560.6, Marshe 1568
BORDEWS
 Than hath some shyppe that into Bordews sayle. . . . . 57 Bowge 406
BORDON
 Hyt ys no lytyll bordon to bere a grete mylle stone. . . . . 240 Speke Parott 330
BORE
 Your beard so brym as bore at bay, ... 119 Ag Scottes 161
 Nor no bore so brymly brystlyd ys with here, ... 122 Garneschel 25
 Thow bere, thow brystlyd bore, /Thou Moryshe mantycore, . . . 128 Garnesche3 164
 And wyth a brystell of a bore his berde dyd I shave. . . . . 192 Magnyfycence 1832
 The bore his tayle wrygges, ... 219 El Rummynge 177
BORE PYGGE
 And she brought a bore pygge. . . . . 228 El Rummynge 539
BORYALL
 Lyke to the boryall wyndes whan they blowe, ... 319 Garlande 261
BORNE
 He braggyth of hys byrth, that borne was full bace; . . . . . 37 Coystrownel 24
 As well borne as ye full oft tyme beggys. 40 Coystrowne4 7
 Thow thou be a jantyll man borne, ... 131 Garnesche5 69
 Counterfet maydenhode may well be borne, ... 152 Magnyfycence 445
 Counterfet pleasure is borne out by me; . . . . 153 Magnyfycence 475
 So he is the worste brawler that ever was borne. . . . . . . 202 Magnyfycence 2200
 Goddys fote! I warant you I am a gentylman borne; . . . . . . 203 Magnyfycence 2216
 So bold and so braggyng, and was so baselye borne; . . . . . 246 Speke Parott 507
 But noble men borne, /To lerne they have scorne, ... 262 Collyn Clout 619
 They say many matters be borne . . . . 276 Collyn Clout 1198
 Javell is nobly borne; . . . . 281 Why Come Ye 96
 Borne up on every syde . . . . 284 Why Come Ye 203
 But, however he was borne, ... 291 Why Come Ye 495
 At them that be well borne; . . . . 294 Why Come Ye 600
 Thus he, borne so base, ... 294 Why Come Ye 622
 And falsest forsworne /That ever were borne. . . . . 362 Albany 118
 Whan ye were bredde and borne, ... 376 Replycacion 80
BOROWE
 And thus, Sainct George to borowe, ... 371 Albany 506
BOROWED
 All that he wereth, it is borowed ware; . . . . 60 Bowge 489
BOROWGH
 Borowgh, cyte, and towne!' . . . . 302 Why Come Ye 932
BOROWYNGE
 With borowynge and cravynge, ... 281 Why Come Ye 101
  cravynge] 'cravyne' †Kele 1545.3
BOSKAGE
 And with suche forage /Hunte the boskage, ... 280 Why Come Ye 53
BOSOME
 In her bosome, lorde, how she was afrayd! . . . . 337 Garlande 887
  how] not in MS Cotton Vitellius E.x
BOST
 Your braggyng bost, your royall aray, ... 119 Ag Scottes 160
 With braggynge and with bost, ... 284 Why Come Ye 202
 For all theyr crack and bost, ... 285 Why Come Ye 256
  crack] 'crake' †Kele 1545.3, Toy 1553, Marshe 1568
 So braggynge all with bost . . . . 306 Why Come Ye 1074
 For all his crake and bost, ... 360 Albany 68
BOSTE
 Bluntly as bestis withe boste and with cry . . . . 31 Dol Dethe 83
 Such boste to make, /To prate and crake, ... 116 Ag Scottes 31
 He was wonte to boste, brage, and to brace; . . . . 193 Magnyfycence 1890
BOT
 Bot ther was fals packinge or els I am begylde, ... 31 Dol Dethe 71
 Bot men say thei wer lynked with a double chayn . . . . . . 31 Dol Dethe 75
 Bot all they fled from hym for falshode or fere. . . . . . . 31 Dol Dethe 91
 Bot by them to knoulege ye may attayne . . . . 32 Dol Dethe 129
 O yonge lyon, bot tender yet of age, ... 33 Dol Dethe 162
 Or elles he can nought bot whan he is at scole; . . . . . . 318 Garlande 205
BOTCHES
 With botches and carbuckyls in care I them knyt; . . . . . . 194 Magnyfycence 1902
BOTCHMENT
 And thou shalte have my hauke to a botchment. . . . . 171 Magnyfycence 1113
BOTE
 'Heve and how, rombelow, row the bote, Norman, rowe.' . . . . 53 Bowge 252
 He bote the lyppe; he loked passynge coye; . . . . 54 Bowge 288
  the] 'his' Wynkyn de Worde 1510
 Of your fathers bote, ... 78 Phy Sparrow 249
 That his owne lorde bote . . . . 79 Phy Sparrow 305
 Gydeth his bote with a prope; . . . . 105 Phy Sparrow 1341
 Your lothesum lere to loke on, lyke a gresyd bote dothe schyne. 123 Garnesche2 5
 She is the bote of all my bale. . . . . 199 Magnyfycence 2070
 But blessyd Bachus, that bote is of all bale, ... 322 Garlande 376
 Gydith his bote with a prop. . . . . 349 Garlande 1334

BOTELES —BOTTUMLES	Page	Title	Line

BOTELES
To the dyne dale /Of boteles bale, ... 40 Coystrowne3 46
    boteles] 'botemles' Marshe 1568
BOTELL
'How, hosteler, fetche my hors a botell of hay!' . . . . 234 Speke Parott 147
The umblis of venyson, the botell of wyne, ... 347 Garlande 1240
BOTES
Alasse! Where is my botes and my spores? . . . . 156 Magnyfycence 569
BOTH
At his commaundement whiche had both day and night . . . . . . 30 Dol Dethe 31
Of whom both Flaunders and Scotland stode in drede, ... 30 Dol Dethe 44
Curyowsly he can both counter and knak 37 Coystrowne1 17
She cheryshed hym both cheke and chyn 42 Balettys1 9
For whome Tyborne groneth both daye and nyghte. . . . . 58 Bowge 417
    whome] 'home' †Wynkyn de Worde 1499
The rose both white and rede . . . . 110 Lawde 1
Both lorde and knight to face; . . . . 111 Lawde 39
Xall kyt both wyght and grene: 127 Garnesche3 139
Some brought from the barne /Both benes and pease; . . . . . . 222 El Rummynge 313
My lyfe endurynge I shall both wryte and say, ... 335 Garlande 839
Thus passyth he the tyme both nyght and day, ... 352 Garlande 1423
Both worde and dede /Should be agrede /In noblenes: . . . . . 357 Garlande 1599
BOTHE
Adres the to me, whiche am bothe halt and lame, ... 29 Dol Dethe 10
Bothe temporall and spirituall for to complayne . . . . 34 Dol Dethe 181
'Ye, soo,' quod Suspecte, 'he maye us bothe begyle.' . . . . . 51 Bowge 189
You mantyca[re], ye maltaperte, ye can bothe wins and whyne; . 123 Garnesche2 4
    mantycare] 'mantyca' †MS Harley 367
Baile, baile at yow bothe, frantyke folys! Follow on the chase! 123 Garnesche2 31
At bothe endes ye stynke; 126 Garnesche3 81
Then ye must bothe consent . . . . 143 Magnyfycence 107
Welcome, frendys, ye are bothe unto me. . . . . 145 Magnyfycence 169
Welthe with Lyberte, with me bothe dwell ye shall, ... 145 Magnyfycence 174
To the gydynge of my measure you bothe commyttynge; . . . . . 145 Magnyfycence 175
We have bene togyder bothe erly and late. . . . . 154 Magnyfycence 499
By God, man, bothe his pagent and thyne he can play. . . . . . 154 Magnyfycence 505
I can dyssemble; I can bothe laughe and grone; . . . . 159 Magnyfycence 698
Do and undo, bothe togyder; . . . . 169 Magnyfycence 1034
In fayth, I can make you bothe folys, and I wyll. . . . . . . 172 Magnyfycence 1173
For you bothe it were inough. . . . . 173 Magnyfycence 1187
Well argued and surely on bothe sydes. . . . . 176 Magnyfycence 1304
Why, was not for money Troy bothe bought and solde? . . . . . 184 Magnyfycence 1576
With a good wyll, syr, God spede you bothe togyder. . . . . . 186 Magnyfycence 1648
And with a lyme rodde I toke them bothe togyder. . . . . 191 Magnyfycence 1815
I sawe a losell lede a lurden, and they were bothe blynde. . . 191 Magnyfycence 1824
The gander and the gose bothe grasynge on one grave. . . . . . 191 Magnyfycence 1830
Unto your maker that made bothe you and me; . . . . 196 Magnyfycence 1992
Nowe must ye suffre bothe hunger and colde. . . . . 197 Magnyfycence 2013
For worldly shame I wax bothe wanne and bloo. . . . . 198 Magnyfycence 2054
Nay, I know well inough ye are bothe well handyd . . . . 203 Magnyfycence 2230
For had I not bene, ye bothe had bene hangyd, ... 203 Magnyfycence 2235
Sodenly thus Fortune can bothe smyle and frowne, ... 212 Magnyfycence 2529
Sodenly thus Fortune can bothe smyle and frowne, ... 213 Magnyfycence 2536
My lytell legges, my fete bothe fete and clene, ... 231 Speke Parott 18
In Greke tong Parott can bothe speke and sey, ... 231 Speke Parott 26
Of the clergye all, /Bothe great and small. . . . . 249 Collyn Clout 118
I shall bothe wryte and say, ... 259 Collyn Clout 507
Bothe women and men, ... 260 Collyn Clout 532
The whiche shulde be /Bothe franke and free, ... 264 Collyn Clout 711
Bothe Gyll and Jacke at Noke . . . . 268 Collyn Clout 855
Bothe hartes and hyndes . . . . 280 Why Come Ye 55
To blowe bararag tyll bothe his eyne stare.' . . . . 319 Garlande 245
    bararag] 'bararag brag' MS Cotton Vitellius E.x
Her that is bothe womanly and wyse, ... 342 Garlande 1070
    womanly] 'maydenly' MS Cotton Vitellius E.x
Bothe Kyng Fraunces and the, ... 361 Albany 113
God sende them bothe myschauns! . . . . 363 Albany 176
And curse bothe nyght and day, ... 376 Replycacion 79
Dothe bothe write and call . . . . 383 Replycacion 320
BOTHOMBAR
From Baumberow to Bothombar . . . . 282 Why Come Ye 139
    Bothombar] 'Bothambar' Toy 1553, Kitson 1560.7, Marshe 1568
BOTOWME
And, 'Wynde me that botowme of such an hew', ... 334 Garlande 799
    an] 'a' MS Cotton Vitellius E.x
BOTTELL
A tonnell and a bottell, ... 224 El Rummynge 403
Of a lether bottell /With a knavysshe stoppell, ... 262 Collyn Clout 650
BOTTES
We have well eased you of the bottes. . . . . 115 Scot Kynge 63
We have well eased them of the bottes. . . . . 120 Ag Scottes 171
BOTTOMS
In faythe, of his cofers the bottoms are bare. . . . . 201 Magnyfycence 2163
BOTTONS
With burris rowth and bottons surffillyng, ... 334 Garlande 803
    rowth] 'rowgh' Marshe 1568
BOTTUMLES
Of Cochitos bottumles well; . . . . 349 Garlande 1329

BOTUMLES —BOWGET   Page   Title   Line

BOTUMLES
Of Cocitus botumles well; 105   Phy Sparrow   1336
BOUGETS
To fyll bougets and males 90   Phy Sparrow   752
BOUGHT
The best chepe flessh that evyr I bought.' 36   Man Margery   24
For by that Lorde that bought dere all mankynde, ... 50   Bowge   163
And he shold be bought /For golde and fee, ... 76   Phy Sparrow   195
Why, was not for money Troy bothe bought and solde? 184   Magnyfycence   1576
As gyvynge a thynge that ye never bought. 189   Magnyfycence   1758
Today in surety, tomorowe bought and solde; 213   Magnyfycence   2548
By hym that me bought!' 218   El Rummynge   167
Except mannes soule, that Chryst so dere bought; 236   Speke Parott   215
Myters are bought and solde; 254   Collyn Clout   290
How prelacye is solde and bought 261   Collyn Clout   583
I drede we are bought and solde. 283   Why Come Ye   172
By God that me dere bought! 290   Why Come Ye   451
    By] 'But' Marshe 1568
BOUGHTE
'By him that me boughte,' than quod Dysdayne, ... 54   Bowge   309
It were more thryft he boughte him a newe cote; 60   Bowge   487
BOULE
Cockes armes! Thou shalte kepe the brewhouse boule. 176   Magnyfycence   1321
BOUNCE
Wyth that he gave her a bounce 64   Hauke   86
BOUND
Wyth bound and rebound, bounsyngly take up 43   Balettys2   15
BOUNDE
That lyeth in cheynes bounde, ... 74   Phy Sparrow   90
And counterfet fredome that is bounde; 152   Magnyfycence   434
What brothell, I say, is yonder bounde in a mat? 199   Magnyfycence   2106
That bounde ar we with all deu reverence, ... 324   Garlande   423
To be your remembrauncer, madame, I am bounde, ... 336   Garlande   864
To beholde how it was garnysshyd and bounde, ... 345   Garlande   1163
To whom we are bounde echone 381   Replycacion   260
BOUNDE TENAUNTES
Ye be bounde tenauntes to his estate; 114   Scot Kynge   36
BOUNSES
With leapes and bounses; 104   Phy Sparrow   1315
BOUNSIS
With lepes and bounsis; 349   Garlande   1308
    with] 'wit' †Fakes 1523
BOUNSYNGLY
Wyth bound and rebound, bounsyngly take up 43   Balettys2   15
BOUNTE
Of thy bounte after the usuall rate 29   Dol Dethe   19
Thorow bounte of hym that formed all solace, ... 35   Dol Dethe   214
For, but if your bounte did me assure, ... 316   Garlande   146
And of there bounte they made me godely chere 323   Garlande   398
That of your bounte so well have me assurid; 332   Garlande   729
The passynge bounte of your noble astate, ... 336   Garlande   841
Whos passynge bounte, and ryght noble astate, ... 336   Garlande   848
Whos passynge bounte, and ryght noble astate, ... 336   Garlande   855
Whos passyng bounte, and ryght noble astate, ... 336   Garlande   862
Of your bounte the accustomable rate 344   Garlande   1130
BOURES
With halles and with boures, ... 270   Collyn Clout   937
BOURNE
The grounde engrosyd and bet with bourne golde, ... 313   Garlande   41
BOW
But she wold not bow. 63   Hauke   74
Ye lost your [h]olde, onbende your bow, ... 131   Garnesche5   49
    holde] 'bolde' †MS Harley 367
And maketh them to bow theyr kne /Before his majeste. 286   Why Come Ye   312
    maketh them] 'make' Toy 1553, Kitson 1560.7, Marshe 1568
BOWCHE
Item Bowche of Courte, where Drede was begyled; 346   Garlande   1183
BOWE
To make reconyng in the resseyte how Robyn loste hys bowe, . . 240   Speke Parott   341
And howe Cupyde shaked /His dart, and bent his bowe 270   Collyn Clout   947
BOWER
Also by Ecates bower 104   Phy Sparrow   1322
BOWES
Of our Englysshe bowes ye have fette your banes. 115   Scot Kynge   65
Our Englysh bowes, our Englysh bylles, ... 119   Ag Scottes   132
At Englysh bowes have fetched their banes. 120   Ag Scottes   173
BOWGE
Here begynneth a lytell treatyse named The Bowge of Courte . . 46   Bowge   I
The Bowge of Courte it hyghte for certeynte. 47   Bowge   49
    certeynte] 'certeynet' †Wynkyn de Worde 1499, 'certayne'
    Wynkyn de Worde 1510, 'certeynte' Marshe 1568
In Bowge of Courte chevysaunce to make; 48   Bowge   100
Of Bowge of Court she asketh what we wold have, ... 49   Bowge   125
and begynneth the Bowge of Courte brevely compyled. 49   Bowge   R
Thus endeth the Bowge of Courte. 61   Bowge   E
BOWGET
I am the better yet in a bowget. And I the better in a male. . 203   Magnyfycence   2232

	Page	Title	Line
BOWGHIS			
With braunches and bowghis of the swete olyve,	330	Garlande	670
BOWGY			
Also nat fare from Bowgy Row,	130	Garnesche5	47
BOWYS			
At Floddon hyllys, /Our bowys, our byllys	116	Ag Scottes	26
BOWLE			
With, 'Fill the blak bowle /For Jayberdes sowle.'	108	Epitaphe1	73
BOWNDIS			
Wythin the holy church bowndis,	62	Hauke	13
BOWNS			
Bowns, bowns, bowns! that all they out cryde.	329	Garlande	624
Bowns, bowns, bowns! that all they out cryde.	329	Garlande	624
Bowns, bowns, bowns! that all they out cryde.	329	Garlande	624
BOWNTE			
Of your bownte and of youre womanhod,	44	Balettys3	31
Bownte, and so gloryously ye have enrollyd	324	Garlande	437
That of our bownte we wyll hym rewarde:	334	Garlande	779
And truly of theyr bownte thus were they bent	334	Garlande	806
Humbly and low /Commendynge me /To yowre bownte.	338	Garlande	932
BOWRE			
And from the smokes sowre /Of Proserpinas bowre;	73	Phy Sparrow	83
The Repete of the Recule of Rosamundis bowre,	351	Garlande	1390
BOWRIS			
Engolerid goodly with hallis and bowris,	325	Garlande	460
Engolerid] 'Engalared' Marshe 1568			
In nedill wark raysyng byrdis in bowris,	334	Garlande	804
byrdis in bowris] 'bothe birddis and bowres' MS Cotton Vitellius E.x			
BOWSY			
Her face all bowsy,	215	El Rummynge	17
BOWUR			
Fresshely they dresse and make swete my bowur,	231	Speke Parott	12
BRABLYNG			
The starlyng with her brablyng;	83	Phy Sparrow	461
BRACE			
To face, to brace, /All voyde of grace,	116	Ag Scottes	33
Foly and fansy all where every man dothe face and brace.	177	Magnyfycence	1330
A, that were a baby to brace and to basse!	183	Magnyfycence	1560
He was wonte to boste, brage, and to brace;	193	Magnyfycence	1890
BRACELET			
Or a bracelet of her here,	89	Phy Sparrow	689
BRACERS			
Some facers, some bracers, some make great crackis;	317	Garlande	189
some] 'and sum' MS Cotton Vitellius E.x			
BRACYD			
By the masse, I warant the, I wyll not be bracyd.	203	Magnyfycence	2221
BRAG			
Ye bere yow bold and brag	129	Garnesche3	187
For I undertake /He wolde so brag and crake	303	Why Come Ye	977
For thou can not but brag	366	Albany	294
BRAGE			
Besy, braynles, to bralle and brage,	133	Garnesche5	148
He was wonte to boste, brage, and to brace;	193	Magnyfycence	1890
BRAGGE			
Full of bragge and boost,	364	Albany	207
BRAGGYNG			
Your braggyng bost, your royall aray,	119	Ag Scottes	160
So bolde a braggyng bocher, and flesshe sold so dere;	245	Speke Parott	485
So bold and so braggyng, and was so baselye borne;	246	Speke Parott	507
BRAGGYNGE			
With braggynge and with bost,	284	Why Come Ye	202
So braggynge all with bost	306	Why Come Ye	1074
BRAGGYTH			
He braggyth of hys byrth, that borne was full bace;	37	Coystrowne1	24
BRAINE			
For ydle jangelers have but lytill braine;	328	Garlande	566
BRAINLES			
Bete a dum mouthe than a brainles scull;	314	Garlande	82
Bete] 'Better' Marshe 1568, MS Cotton Vitellius E.x			
Brainles blenkardis that blow at the cole,	329	Garlande	610
Item Good Advysement, that brainles doth blame;	346	Garlande	1186
BRAYDE			
Suspycyon, me thoughte, mette hym at a brayde,	51	Bowge	181
Yet at a brayde /He hath well assayde	84	Phy Sparrow	485
BRAYED			
With baudrie at her ye brayed;	376	Replycacion	48
BRAYNE			
What frantyk frensy fyll in youre brayne?	30	Dol Dethe	51
His hede maye be harde, but feble is his brayne!	46	Bowge	24
his] not in Marshe 1568			
The pekysh parsons brayne	68	Hauke	225
A, Fansy, Fansy, God sende the brayne!	157	Magnyfycence	608
In faythe, man, my brayne is as good as thyne.	170	Magnyfycence	1085
The devyls torde for thy brayne!	170	Magnyfycence	1086
Lo, Johnn a Bonam, where is thy brayne?	173	Magnyfycence	1204
Be not to bolde my frende; I counsell you, bere a brayne.	179	Magnyfycence	1405
And some in the worlde, theyr brayne is so ydyll	200	Magnyfycence	2135

BRAYNED —BRAULE   Page   Title   Line

Vitulus in Oreb troubled Arons brayne;	232	Speke Parott	59
For Parrot to pyke upon, his brayne for to stable,	235	Speke Parott	184
Helas! I lamente the dull abusyd brayne,	242	Speke Parott	383
Or yf he speke playne, /Than he lacketh brayne:	247	Collyn Clout	27
Some beaten to the brayne;	276	Collyn Clout	1211
He sayth they have no brayne	286	Why Come Ye	310
Into the brayne by drynkyng over depe,	313	Garlande	33
Then sum wyll say he hath but lyttil brayne,	314	Garlande	87
The blaste of the brynston blew away his brayne;	329	Garlande	631
Your chefe cheftayne, /Voyde of all brayne,	360	Albany	49
To bring with hym more brayne	363	Albany	174

BRAYNED

Was moch more febler brayned.	64	Hauke	82
moche better bayned than brayned,	374	Replycacion	1

BRAYNE-PAN

Upon her brayne-pan, /Lyke an Egypcyan /Lapped about.	216	El Rummynge	77
Lapped] 'Capped' Kynge & Marche 1554, Day 1560, Marshe 1568			

BRAYNE PAN

What tydynges with you, syr? I befole thy brayne pan.	191	Magnyfycence	1805

BRAYNES

But lyke a March harum /His braynes were so parum.	64	Hauke	105
Myght fede them on thy braynes!	79	Phy Sparrow	295
That he wolde breke the braynes	304	Why Come Ye	990
Your braynes are ydell;	368	Albany	387

BRAYNE SEKE

With qui fuit brayne seke I have them brought;	176	Magnyfycence	1302

BRAYNYS

My wyttys be weke, my braynys are lyght;	169	Magnyfycence	1024

BRAYNLES

Besy, braynles, to bralle and brage,	133	Garnesche5	148
Wylfulnes and Braynles no[w] rule all the raye.	243	Speke Parott	421
now] 'no' †MS Harley 2252			
For Frantiknes and Wylfulnes and Braynles ensembyll,	243	Speke Parott	423
So braynles calvys hedes, so many shepis taylys;	245	Speke Parott	484

BRAYNLESSE

Why, welth hath made many a man braynlesse.	180	Magnyfycence	1423
With banketynge braynlesse,	280	Why Come Ye	71
But braynsyk and braynlesse, /Wytles and rechelesse,	304	Why Come Ye	1018
I saye, ye braynlesse beestes,	381	Replycacion	263

BRAYNPANNYS

He bresyth theyr braynpannys and makyth them to swell,	43	Balettys2	31

BRAYNSYCKE

In them be no scolys /For braynsycke frantycke folys:	68	Hauke	249
From Wynchelsee to Walys, /Non est braynsycke talys,	70	Hauke	324

BRAYNSYK

But braynsyk and braynlesse, /Wytles and rechelesse,	304	Why Come Ye	1018

BRAYNSYKE

And so braynsyke therwithall,	170	Magnyfycence	1073
What, brother braynsyke, how farest thou?	192	Magnyfycence	1845

BRAKE

Many a spere brake /For his ladyes sake;	87	Phy Sparrow	639
Experyence hath brought you in the same brake.	115	Scot Kynge	61
Experiens hath brought you in such a brake.	119	Ag Scottes	158
Hole ys your brow that ye brake with Deu[ra]ndall your awne sworde; Deurandall]'Deundall' †MS Harley 367	123	Garnesche2	8
At lyberte a man may be bolde for to brake;	199	Magnyfycence	2085
Peas, or I shall wrynge thy be in a brake.	202	Magnyfycence	2187
It was a stale to take /The devyll in a brake.	222	El Rummynge	325
stale] 'stale' 1521 Fragment, 'stare' †Lant 1545, Kynge & Marche 1554, Day 1560, Marshe 1568			
By the breed that God brake,	253	Collyn Clout	251
Brose them on a brake,	303	Why Come Ye	983
Brose] 'bruse' Toy 1553, Kitson 1560.7, Marshe 1568			
And brake up all his hoost.	360	Albany	67

BRALL

He doth revyle and brall	294	Why Come Ye	596
That list of there lewdnesse with hym for to brall.'	334	Garlande	786

BRALLE

Besy, braynles, to bralle and brage,	133	Garnesche5	148

BRANDE

Of all lewdnesse I kyndell the brande.	152	Magnyfycence	437

BRANXTON

And wyll not know /Theyr overthrow /At Branxton More?	115	Ag Scottes	11
At Branxton More and Flodden hylles,	119	Ag Scottes	131

BRAS

Forever in tables of bras,	75	Phy Sparrow	150

BRASED

And under that is brased	101	Phy Sparrow	1195

BRASY

Thou thynkyst thy selfe Syr Pers de Brasy,	130	Garnesche5	30

BRASSE

Another there was that ran /With a good brasse pan -	222	El Rummynge	317
From sylver to brasse,	301	Why Come Ye	903

BRAST

Ha, ha, ha! For laughter I am lyke to brast.	201	Magnyfycence	2160
Without our shyppe be sure, it is lykely to brast,	213	Magnyfycence	2562

BRAULE

Yet bere ye not to bold to braule ne to bark	38	Coystrownel	60

BRAULES — BRESTE

	Page	Title	Line
All his delight was to braule and to barke	347	Garlande	1252
BRAULES			
Or what actyvyte /Is in you, beggars braules,	364	Albany	218
BRAUNCHES			
With braunches and bowghis of the swete olyve,	330	Garlande	670
BRAWLE			
What! Woldest thou, lurden, with me brawle agayne?	188	Magnyfycence	1722
BRAWLER			
A bungler, a brawler, a pyker of quarellys!	37	Coystrownel	35
So he is the worste brawler that ever was borne.	202	Magnyfycence	2200
BRAWLYNG			
Vouchesafe to defend yow agayne the brawlyng scolde	241	Speke Parott	361
BREATH			
Well nye had stopped my breath.	73	Phy Sparrow	63
had] not in Wyght 1553, Kitson 1560.6, Marshe 1568			
BRECHE			
Of this gentell Jack Breche,	294	Why Come Ye	616
BRED			
Yet amonge noble men I was brought up and bred.	147	Magnyfycence	261
Hop Lobyn of Lowdeon wald have e byt of bred;	232	Speke Parott	72
Collustrum now for Parot, whyte bred and swete creme!	233	Speke Parott	82
So fatte a magott, bred of a flesshe-flye;	246	Speke Parott	509
That he shall never ete more bred.	299	Why Come Ye	796
BRED CROMMES			
And somtyme white bred crommes;	74	Phy Sparrow	123
BREDDE			
Whan ye were bredde and borne,	376	Replycacion	80
BREDE			
For this may brede to a confusyon,	59	Bowge	482
A bolle or a basyn, I say, for Goddes brede!	189	Magnyfycence	1728
Nowe must you monche mamockes and lumpes of brede;	197	Magnyfycence	2009
With moulde brede to eate -	263	Collyn Clout	653
To loke on God in fourme of brede,	272	Collyn Clout	1024
In length and brede.	355	Garlande	1552
Of brede at ylke mannes hecke.	363	Albany	155
BREDTH			
Yt bredth mothys in clothe of Arres.	131	Garnesche5	78
BREED			
By the breed that God brake,	253	Collyn Clout	251
BREFLY			
Brefly to touche of my purpose the effecte:	142	Magnyfycence	67
Tell me brefly where upon ye began.	203	Magnyfycence	2224
Unto this processe brefly compylyd,	212	Magnyfycence	2510
BREKE			
For she is trussed for to breke a launce.	57	Bowge	410
The law they shall not breke;	111	Lawde	30
Thow ye be lusty as Syr Lybyus, launces to breke,	122	Garneschel	17
A Tyborne checke /Shall breke his necke.	165	Magnyfycence	911
I shall breke your palettes, /Wythout ye now cease!'	223	El Rummynge	348
[And] of her husbandes breke.	225	El Rummynge	452
And] not in editions			
Sacro vatum, whereof to you I breke;	233	Speke Parott	97
Howe ye breke the dedes wylles,	257	Collyn Clout	417
And breke theyr hose at the kne,	262	Collyn Clout	629
That he wolde breke the braynes	304	Why Come Ye	990
For Margery wynshed, and breke her hinder girth;	346	Garlande	1201
We shall breke thy bones	362	Albany	150
The fynde, Scot, breke thy necke.	363	Albany	156
BREKES			
He brekes and defaces,	306	Why Come Ye	1090
BREMELY			
And bremely with your bristels	380	Replycacion	221
BREMIS			
Enswymmyng with rochis, barbellis and bremis,	330	Garlande	661
BRENDE			
Or be brende by and by,	377	Replycacion	89
BRENNETH			
That day and night brenneth styl,	79	Phy Sparrow	314
BRENNYNGE			
Of Ethna the brennynge hyll	79	Phy Sparrow	313
And some I vysyte with brennynge of fyre;	194	Magnyfycence	1908
And a brennynge sparke /Of Luthers warke,	260	Collyn Clout	542
BRENT			
That in hell is never brent,	104	Phy Sparrow	1327
Our talwod is all brent,	281	Why Come Ye	82
And be brent at a stake,	382	Replycacion	295
BRENTE			
That in hell is never brente,	349	Garlande	1320
BRERE			
There birdis on the brere sange on every syde,	330	Garlande	653
BRESYTH			
He bresyth theyr braynpannys and makyth them to swell,	43	Balettys2	31
BREST			
For before on your brest, and behind on your back	137	Ven Tongues	16
In your brest towardes this gentylman.	188	Magnyfycence	1713
BRESTE			
Upon his breste he bare a versynge boxe:	52	Bowge	232

BRESTES —BRYGHT   Page   Title   Line

BRESTES
	Page	Title	Line
Betwene my brestes softe	74	Phy Sparrow	125

BRETH
Gup, Cristian Clowte, your breth is stale,	36	Man Margery	27
With drawttys of deth /Stoppyng oure breth;	39	Coystrowne3	32
I have as swete a breth	223	El Rummynge	345
Her breth was soure and stale	226	El Rummynge	486
To blowe a blaste with his long breth extendid;	319	Garlande	234

BRETHE
Your brethe ys stronge and quike;	126	Garnesche3	78
Your brethe yt ys so felle	127	Garnesche3	142
With hys brethe so stronge,	128	Garnesche3	151
Sche seyd your brethe stanke lyke a broke;	131	Garnesche5	55
And her brethe strongely stanke,	228	El Rummynge	541

BRETHERN
Togeder in armes, as brethern, enbrasid;	323	Garlande	393
'So am I preventid of my brethern tweyne	324	Garlande	428

BREVELY
and begynneth the Bowge of Courte brevely compyled.	49	Bowge	R
Prepayre yow, Parrot, brevely your passage to take,	240	Speke Parott	324
Wherto she answeryd, and brevely me tolde	328	Garlande	576
Where ye must brevely answere to your name.'	343	Garlande	1092
Wherein many storis ar brevely contayned	347	Garlande	1224
Brevely and rounde /To me expounde.	361	Albany	82
Yet, brevely to conclude,	372	Albany	518

BREVYATE
By myschefe to brevyate and shorten his dayes.	206	Magnyfycence	2338

BREW
That bales begynne to brew.	280	Why Come Ye	63

BREWE
And so, by these meanes, I brewe moche bale.	161	Magnyfycence	744
Whan I began to brewe,	219	El Rummynge	209

BREWETH
She breweth noppy ale,	217	El Rummynge	102

BREWHOUSE
Cockes armes! Thou shalte kepe the brewhouse boule.	176	Magnyfycence	1321

BREWSYS
In my lady Brewsys howse.	125	Garnesche3	33

BRIGHT
How bright I am of ble!	220	El Rummynge	218
In that faculte which shyned as Phebus bright;	383	Replycacion	333

BRING
To bring with hym more brayne	363	Albany	174
Shulde bring about that thing.	367	Albany	335
That shall bring you full bace	368	Albany	366
For you to bring about	368	Albany	391

BRINGE
They buskt them on a bushment them selfe in baile to bringe	31	Dol Dethe	81
Thow bringe unto thy joye etermynable	34	Dol Dethe	199
Thow] 'how' †MS Royal 18 D.ii			
To bringe them to confusyon –	306	Why Come Ye	1096

BRINGES
That bringes you out of the way	379	Replycacion	170

BRINGETH
But all he bringeth to nought,	290	Why Come Ye	450

BRISTELS
And bremely with your bristels	380	Replycacion	221

BRITONS
The brutid Britons of Brutus Albion,	323	Garlande	405

BRYBAUNCE
Nor Basyan the bolde, for all his brybaunce,	182	Magnyfycence	1503

BRYBE
Nowe, by your trouthe, gave he you not a brybe?	187	Magnyfycence	1665

BRYBERY
Thefte also and pety brybery	177	Magnyfycence	1354
Fals trechery, /Fals brybery,	300	Why Come Ye	855
Some have a name for thefte and brybery;	317	Garlande	183
Ryot, reveler, railer, brybery, theft,	329	Garlande	614

BRYBOURY
To thefte and bryboury I make some fall,	174	Magnyfycence	1226

BRYDELYNGE CASTE
A brydelynge caste for that is in thy male!	57	Bowge	390

BRYDELL
Sche seyd how ye ded brydell,	126	Garnesche3	73
It is time for you to brydell	368	Albany	388

BRYDYLL
That they set theyr chyldren to rynne on the brydyll,	200	Magnyfycence	2136

BRYGE
Of Mantryble the Bryge, Malchus the Murryon,	122	Garnesche1	22

BRYGHT
Encleryd myrroure and perspectyve most bryght,	44	Balettys3	22
Chaseth away Phebus bryght,	86	Phy Sparrow	572
The bryght golden tresses	101	Phy Sparrow	1172
Luna that so bryght doth shyne,	105	Phy Sparrow	1365
Of ladies of bryght colour,	128	Garnesche3	148
A tappyster lyke a lady bryght:	152	Magnyfycence	420
With, 'my lady bryght and shene'.	304	Why Come Ye	1004

	Page	Title	Line
BRYM —BROISID			
Whan Titan radiant burnisshith his bemis bryght,	327	Garlande	534
Sume praysed the perle, some the stones bryght.	343	Garlande	1108
Luna that so bryght doth shene,	350	Garlande	1358
How her ble was bryght as blossom on the spray,	351	Garlande	1412
To harnnes bryght, /By force of myght,	355	Garlande	1556
BRYM			
Your beard so brym as bore at bay,	119	Ag Scottes	161
BRYMLY			
Nor no bore so brymly brystlyd ys with here,	122	Garneschel	25
He frownyth fyersly, brymly browde.	174	Magnyfycence	1245
BRYMME			
Arthur of Albyan, for all his brymme berde,	182	Magnyfycence	1502
BRYNG			
By the menys of myschyef to bryng all thynges to nought.	159	Magnyfycence	702
To bryng all the see into a cheryston pytte,	240	Speke Parott	331
And ye coude bryng /The matter about	361	Albany	92
BRYNGE			
To pardon thi servant and brynge to savacioun.	35	Dol Dethe	210
Bone aventure may brynge you in suche case	49	Bowge	104
To wete if he coulde brynge	76	Phy Sparrow	198
Brynge other wyves in thought	87	Phy Sparrow	626
Thus at the laste I brynge hym ryght	152	Magnyfycence	422
We had hym founde, we sholde hym brynge,	158	Magnyfycence	653
All this ye may easely brynge aboute.	158	Magnyfycence	655
To felowshyp with foly I can hym brynge.	174	Magnyfycence	1215
He can full craftely this matter brynge aboute.	187	Magnyfycence	1691
And brynge you agayne out of adversyte.	196	Magnyfycence	1999
And brynge them selfe bare,	217	El Rummynge	109
Brynge dysshes and platters,	217	El Rummynge	127
In stede of coyne and monny /Some brynge her a conny,	220	El Rummynge	245
Brynge wyth them malte or whete,	221	El Rummynge	267
And with her doth brynge	221	El Rummynge	278
And brynge the churche to the grounde.	259	Collyn Clout	494
And brynge in materyalytes	260	Collyn Clout	559
in materyalytes] 'him in maierialites' Marshe 1568			
Ye wyll brynge all to nought,	261	Collyn Clout	606
My lordis grace wyll brynge	302	Why Come Ye	949
And brynge it so lowe	303	Why Come Ye	951
That we shall brynge you personally present	324	Garlande	418
With all our strength that we can brynge about,	324	Garlande	424
That with them I went where they wolde me brynge,	324	Garlande	447
Our mayster shall you brynge,	368	Albany	384
BRYNGES			
And brynge[s] them in suche feare.	286	Why Come Ye	306
brynges] 'brynge' †Kele 1545.3, Toy 1553, Kitson 1560.7, Marshe 1568			
BRYNGETH			
And I Foly bryngeth them to qui fuit gadde;	176	Magnyfycence	1301
Some bryngeth her husbandis hood,	221	El Rummynge	283
Bryngeth all thynges under cure.	286	Why Come Ye	284
BRYNGGES			
Bryngges yow out of favyr with alle femall teggys:	122	Garneschel	31
BRYNGYTH			
A bawdy dyscheclowte, /That bryngyth the worlde abowte	125	Garnesche3	37
BRYNNYNG			
Oure gummys grynnyng, /Oure soulys brynnyng!	40	Coystrowne3	36
BRYNSTON			
The blaste of the brynston blew away his brayne;	329	Garlande	631
BRYSTELL			
And wyth a brystell of a bore his berde dyd I shave.	192	Magnyfycence	1832
BRYSTLED			
Brystled with here.	215	El Rummynge	21
BRYSTLYD			
Nor no bore so brymly brystlyd ys with here,	122	Garneschel	25
As ye ar brystlyd on the bake for alle your gay gere.	122	Garneschel	26
Thow bere, thow brystlyd bore, /Thou Moryshe mantycore,	128	Garnesche3	164
BRYSTOWE RED			
Her kyrtell Brystowe red,	216	El Rummynge	70
BRYTONS			
From Brytons Albion /To the towre of Babilon.	94	Phy Sparrow	887
To] 'Bo' †Kele 1545.2			
BRODE			
Go watch a bole, your bak is brode.	35	Man Margery	12
The shovelar with his brode bek;	82	Phy Sparrow	408
With a payre of heles /As brode as two wheles.	216	El Rummynge	84
Shulde open the brode gates	263	Collyn Clout	691
At the Brode gatus,	266	Collyn Clout	798
Under the kynges brode seale;	287	Why Come Ye	337
BRODE CLOTHE			
Without I myght cut it out of the brode clothe,	144	Magnyfycence	146
BRODER			
Sayenge to me, 'Broder, be of good chere,	48	Bowge	86
'God spede, broder,' to me quod he than,	51	Bowge	195
In fayth, broder Largesse, you have a mery mynde.	148	Magnyfycence	292
But, broder Foly, I wonder moche of one thynge,	170	Magnyfycence	1068
And Foly, my broder, that made you moche game.	193	Magnyfycence	1872
BROISID			
It made sum lympe-legged and broisid there bones;	329	Garlande	625

	Page	Title	Line
BROISIOURS			
Ageynst all baratows broisiours of olde,	331	Garlande	673
BROYLYD			
Ye fryed and ye broylyd,	125	Garnesche3	28
BROKE			
Sche seyd your brethe stanke lyke a broke;	131	Garnesche5	55
And ye may it broke,	219	El Rummynge	212
Farther in this broke,	266	Collyn Clout	782
BROKEN			
Yet at the knee they were broken, I wene.	56	Bowge	357
No broken galles /May there abyde	83	Phy Sparrow	473
No] 'Nor' Kitson 1560.6			
I knyt togyther many a broken threde.	177	Magnyfycence	1343
A, I have spyed ye can moche broken sorowe.	184	Magnyfycence	1587
And had broken her shyn	227	El Rummynge	494
Prisians hed broken now, handy-dandy,	235	Speke Parott	171
Ye fyrste aryvyd; whan broken was your mast	327	Garlande	542
Ye] 'The' †Fakes 1523			
Of broken warkis wrought many a goodly thyng,	334	Garlande	801
BROKYN			
Youre ugly tokyn /My mynd hath brokyn /From worldly lust;	39	Coystrowne3	2
BRONDE			
I make them to startyll and sparkyll lyke a bronde;	161	Magnyfycence	741
Of farvent charyte I quenche out the bronde;	205	Magnyfycence	2287
BROOD			
Come saylynge forth into that haven brood,	47	Bowge	37
BROSE			
Brose them on a brake,	303	Why Come Ye	983
Brose] 'bruse' Toy 1553, Kitson 1560.7, Marshe 1568			
BROTHELL			
What brothell, I say, is yonder bounde in a mat?	199	Magnyfycence	2106
BROTHELLS			
Ye bere out brothells lyke a bawde;	131	Garnesche5	73
BROTHER			
Ye ought to honour your lorde and brother.	114	Scot Kynge	16
Regardyd ye shuld your lord, your brother.	118	Ag Scottes	106
ye] 'you' Day 1560, Marshe 1568			
Your lorde, your brother, and your regent.	118	Ag Scottes	114
Cause have they none other /But for that he was brother,	120	Ag Scottes2	14
have they] 'they have' Day 1560, Marshe 1568			
brother] 'hys brother' Day 1560, Marshe 1568			
Brother unnaturall /Unto our kyng royall,	120	Ag Scottes2	15
Falshode in felowshyp is my sworne brother.	160	Magnyfycence	713
By God, syr, Foly, myne owne sworne brother.	172	Magnyfycence	1159
Se, syr, I beseche you, Largesse my brother.	192	Magnyfycence	1842
What, brother braynsyke, how farest thou?	192	Magnyfycence	1845
What, brother Perceveraunce, surely well met!	210	Magnyfycence	2458
'Brother Skelton, your endevorment	323	Garlande	400
BROUGHT			
So urgently I am brought /Into carefull thought.	74	Phy Sparrow	106
That I brought up at Carowe.	78	Phy Sparrow	281
She brought him in abusyon;	89	Phy Sparrow	708
Of Dyomedes stable /He brought out a rable	104	Phy Sparrow	1313
Experyence hath brought you in the same brake.	115	Scot Kynge	61
Experiens hath brought you in such a brake.	119	Ag Scottes	158
Hath brought nobil princes to extreme confusion.	139	Ven Tongues	58
Yet amonge noble men I was brought up and bred.	147	Magnyfycence	261
I trow I have brought you suche wrytynge of recorde,	149	Magnyfycence	309
Cannyst thou helpe in faver that I myght be brought?	162	Magnyfycence	777
A carlys sonne /Brought up of nought	165	Magnyfycence	899
With qui fuit brayne seke I have them brought;	176	Magnyfycence	1302
By crafty conveyaunce many one is brought up of nought;	178	Magnyfycence	1369
By convayaunce crafty I have brought	178	Magnyfycence	1372
Though al his conquestys were brought to rekenynge,	181	Magnyfycence	1468
And brought home and layde in your bed.	184	Magnyfycence	1572
Or ever we were ware, brought us in adversyte,	193	Magnyfycence	1863
Alasse, I say, where to am I brought?	196	Magnyfycence	1968
Fy, fy, that ever I sholde be brought in this snare!	196	Magnyfycence	1972
Never had I bene brought in this case.	196	Magnyfycence	1977
Ye, for nowe it hath brought the to confusyon;	200	Magnyfycence	2130
Magnyfycence I was, whom ye have brought to shame.	204	Magnyfycence	2241
Who brought you that letter? Wote ye what he hyght?	209	Magnyfycence	2440
Another brought her his cap	221	El Rummynge	285
And some brought sowre dowe;	221	El Rummynge	288
Some brought from the barne /Both benes and pease;	222	El Rummynge	312
And brought a gambone /Of bakon that was resty;	222	El Rummynge	327
Another brought a spycke /Of a bacon flycke;	223	El Rummynge	335
And brought a pottell-pycher,	224	El Rummynge	402
Another brought a skommer,	224	El Rummynge	408
And brought a peny cheke /To Dame Elynour	225	El Rummynge	415
brought] 'brought up' Day 1560, Marshe 1568			
And yet she brought her fees,	225	El Rummynge	428
Some brought walnuttes,	225	El Rummynge	437
Some brought theyr clyppyng sheres,	225	El Rummynge	439
Some brought this and that,	225	El Rummynge	440
Some brought I wote nere what,	225	El Rummynge	441
Some brought theyr husbands hat,	225	El Rummynge	442
Another brought two goslynges	226	El Rummynge	459

BROUGHTE—BULKE   Page   Title   Line

Entry	Page	Title	Line
She brought them in a wallet;	226	El Rummynge	461
She] 'Some' Day 1568, Marshe 1568			
'They be wretchockes thou hast brought,	226	El Rummynge	465
They] 'The' Day 1560			
Another brought her garlyke heddes;	227	El Rummynge	522
Another brought her bedes /Of jet or of cole,	227	El Rummynge	523
Some brought a wymble,	227	El Rummynge	526
Some brought a thymble,	227	El Rummynge	527
Some brought a sylke lace,	227	El Rummynge	528
Some brought a pyncase,	227	El Rummynge	529
And she brought a bore pygge.	228	El Rummynge	539
Jobab was brought up in the lande of Hus;	232	Speke Parott	65
Jobab] 'Iob' Day 1560, Marshe 1568			
And yf ye stande in doute /Who brought this ryme aboute,	248	Collyn Clout	48
Brought up of poore estate, /With pryde inordynate,	262	Collyn Clout	642
This can nat be brought about	267	Collyn Clout	849
He shulde be hyder brought;	287	Why Come Ye	351
And brought in quycke or dede,	288	Why Come Ye	359
To any good ende were brought.	290	Why Come Ye	449
The Gommoryans also /Were brought to deedly wo,	291	Why Come Ye	473
And made to him be brought	293	Why Come Ye	552
In Acon it was brought to pas,	296	Why Come Ye	706
Hath brought in dystresse,	305	Why Come Ye	1034
in] 'muche' MS Rawlinson C. 813			
May be brought forth, such as can be founde,	318	Garlande	216
What he hath done, let it be brought to syght.	318	Garlande	230
I can nat tell you, but that I was brought	325	Garlande	458
Into a felde she brought me wyde and large,	328	Garlande	568
In an herber I saw, brought where I was,	330	Garlande	652
She brought me to a goodly chaumber of astate,	333	Garlande	768
to] 'into' MS Cotton Vitellius E.x			
Brought forth a godely babi!	339	Garlande	975
Make no delay, for now ye must be brought	343	Garlande	1090
Before remembred, me curteisly brought	343	Garlande	1102
me curteisly] 'kurteisly me' MS Cotton Vitellius E.x			
Wherof in substaunce I brought this away.	344	Garlande	1120
And Cloked Collucyoun is brought in to clater	346	Garlande	1195
Of Diomedis stabyll /He brought out a rabyll	349	Garlande	1306
And to shame your selfe have brought.	376	Replycacion	58
Ye are brought to, 'Lo, Lo, Lo!'	376	Replycacion	72
BROUGHTE			
By Goddis sydes, syns I her thyder broughte,	57	Bowge	404
BROW			
Hole ys your brow that ye brake with Deu[ra]ndall your awne sworde; Deurandall] Deundall †MS Harley 367	123	Garnesche2	8
BROW-AUNTLERES			
So bygge a bulke of brow-auntleres cabagyd that yere;	245	Speke Parott	488
BROWDE			
He frownyth fyersly, brymly browde.	174	Magnyfycence	1245
BROWES			
With browes bente, and gan on me to stare	48	Bowge	81
With her browes bent	97	Phy Sparrow	1016
BROWGHT			
And browght Englond in wo;	111	Lawde	25
They browght them in soche paine.	111	Lawde	35
And of their shorte nyghtes; he browght in his songe	331	Garlande	703
The frame was browght forth with his wevyng pin.	334	Garlande	792
A tratyse he devysid and browght it to pas,	347	Garlande	1228
BROWYS			
Theyre browys all to-brokyn, such clappys they cach;	43	Balettys2	32
Her browys bent, /Her eyen glent;	167	Magnyfycence	979
BROWNE			
Have at the hasarde or at the dosen browne,	57	Bowge	393
BRUTE			
For it is an auncyent brute,	378	Replycacion	156
BRUTED			
Holy churche is bruted /And shamfully confuted.	258	Collyn Clout	487
BRUTID			
The cause why Demostenes so famously is brutid	316	Garlande	155
The brutid Britons of Brutus Albion,	323	Garlande	405
BRUTUS			
The brutid Britons of Brutus Albion,	323	Garlande	405
BUCK			
The harte, the hynde, the buck.	282	Why Come Ye	122
BUCKELL			
Ay, in my pouche a buckell I have founde;	57	Bowge	397
BUCKELS			
Lyke as they were with buckels /Togyder made fast.	215	El Rummynge	46
BUCOLYCALL			
Theocritus with his bucolycall relacyons;	321	Garlande	327
BUDGE FURRE			
In the stede of a budge furre.	169	Magnyfycence	1057
BUYLDYNGE			
Buyldynge royally /Theyr mancyons curyously,	269	Collyn Clout	934
BUKRAM			
Ye must weare bukram,	302	Why Come Ye	918
BULKE			
So bygge a bulke of brow-auntleres cabagyd that yere;	245	Speke Parott	488

BULL — BUT

	Page	Title	Line
BULL			
He plucked the bull /By the horned skull,	104	Phy Sparrow	1318
Lyke an oxe or a bull;	286	Why Come Ye	308
With a bull under lead,	299	Why Come Ye	798
For he hath suche a bull,	306	Why Come Ye	1078
He pluckid the bull /By the hornid scull,	349	Garlande	1311
BULLES			
And bulles papalles,	264	Collyn Clout	717
BULLY			
He lumbryth on a lewde lewte, 'Roty bully joyse',	37	Coystrownel	29
Rutty bully, joly rutterkyn, heyda!	161	Magnyfycence	747
BULLYFANT			
It was a bullyfant, /A gredy cormerant.	227	El Rummynge	520
BULLYONS			
The claspis and bullyons were worth a thousande pounde;	345	Garlande	1165
BULLYS			
So many bullys of pardon publysshed and shewyd;	246	Speke Parott	515
BULWARKE			
He was ther bulwarke, ther paves and ther wall,	30	Dol Dethe	48
BUMME			
Ye wolde have bassyd hyr bumme,	125	Garnesche3	62
BUMPE			
The *better with his bumpe,	82	Phy Sparrow	432
*better] 'bitter' Wyght 1553, Kitson 1560.6, Marshe 1568			
BUNGLER			
A bungler, a brawler, a pyker of quarellys!	37	Coystrownel	35
BURBLYNG			
basked and baththed in their wylde burblyng and boyling blode,	374	Replycacion	I
BURDE			
Now have at all that lyeth upon the burde.	57	Bowge	391
BURDEOU			
She could to Burdeo[u] sayle;	226	El Rummynge	454
Burdeou] 'burde on' †Lant 1545, Kynge & Marche 1554, Day 1560, Marshe 1568			
BURGEIS			
The burgeis and the ballyvis of the v portis,	326	Garlande	514
BURGONYONS			
What here ye of Burgonyons	288	Why Come Ye	370
Amonge the Burgonyons	302	Why Come Ye	923
BURY			
The monke of Bury then after them ensuyd,	323	Garlande	390
BURNESHED			
Melpomene, that fayre mayde, she burneshed his beke:	236	Speke Parott	209
BURNETH			
Out harowe! Hyll burneth! Where shall I me hyde?	206	Magnyfycence	2324
BURNISSHITH			
Whan Titan radiant burnisshith his bemis bryght,	327	Garlande	534
BURNYNGE			
For burnynge of his wynges;	73	Phy Sparrow	81
For burnynge of the sonne;	168	Magnyfycence	988
BURRIS			
With burris rowth and bottons surffillyng,	334	Garlande	803
rowth] 'rowgh' Marshe 1568			
BUSHMENT			
They buskt them on a bushment them selfe in baile to bringe	31	Dol Dethe	81
BUSY			
And your busy pratyng.	380	Replycacion	218
BUSYNESSE			
If further busynesse that ye make.	382	Replycacion	296
BUSKE			
Boldly bend you to batell, and buske your selfe to save.	122	Garneschel	41
BUSKED			
Ye had be better to have busked to Huntley Bankes,	114	Scot Kynge	50
be] 'bet' †Fakes 1513			
BUSKYD			
Ye myght have buskyd you to Huntley Bankys;	119	Ag Scottes	149
BUSKYN			
What is this, a betell or a batowe or a buskyn lacyd?	161	Magnyfycence	755
My buskyn wyde, /Ryche to beholde	164	Magnyfycence	853
BUSKT			
They buskt them on a bushment them selfe in baile to bringe	31	Dol Dethe	81
BUSSARDE			
The barnacle, the bussarde,	83	Phy Sparrow	450
BUSSHETH			
My heyre bussheth /So plesauntly;	163	Magnyfycence	835
BUT			
But had his nobillmen donn wel that day	31	Dol Dethe	69
'What, will ye do nothyng but play?'	35	Man Margery	4
But for in his gamut carp that he can,	37	Coystrownel	13
A red angry man, but easy to intrete.	37	Coystrownel	39
For I have dyscust /We ar but dust,	39	Coystrowne3	5
But to swete Jesu /On us then for to rew?	40	Coystrowne3	39
But graunt us grace /To se thy face,	40	Coystrowne3	49
But one thyng is: that ye be lewde!	41	Coystrowne4	27
But that I must wryte for my plesaunt pastaunce	42	Balettys2	4
He rydyth well the horse, but he rydyth better the mare.	43	Balettys2	21
But absens, alas, wyth tremelyng fere and drede,	44	Balettys3	34
But hatefull absens, to me so envyous,	45	Balettys3	45

BUT —BUT

	Page	Title	Line
But Fortune enforsyth me so carefully to endure,	46	Balettys5	13
But Ignorance full soone dyde me dyscure	46	Bowge	18
dyscure] 'dysture' †Wynkyn de Worde 1499, 1510			
His hede maye be harde, but feble is his brayne!	46	Bowge	24
his] not in Marshe 1568			
But of reproche surely he maye not mys	46	Bowge	26
But than I thoughte I wolde not dwell behynde;	47	Bowge	43
But who wyll have it muste paye therfore dere.	47	Bowge	53
But of eche thynge there as I toke hede,	47	Bowge	64
Abasshe you not, but hardely be bolde,	48	Bowge	87
And this an other, I have but smale substaunce.'	48	Bowge	94
And] 'But' Marshe 1568			
But, an he can Bone aventure take,	48	Bowge	102
an] 'and' Wynkyn de Worde 1510, Marshe 1568			
But of one thynge I werne you er I goo:	49	Bowge	106
werne] 'warne' Marshe 1568; 'or' Wynkyn de Worde 1510			
But under hony ofte tyme lyeth bytter gall,	49	Bowge	131
But my dysporte they could not well endure:	50	Bowge	145
But this one thynge ye maye be sure of me,	50	Bowge	162
Farewell tyll soone. But no word that I sayde!'	51	Bowge	175
But, as me thoughte, he ware on hym a cloke	51	Bowge	177
But I wolde telle you a thynge, and I durste.	51	Bowge	203
But I wonder what the devyll of helle	52	Bowge	208
For, but I trusted you, so God me save,	52	Bowge	213
But as I stode musynge in my mynde,	52	Bowge	230
But to the poynte shortely to procede,	53	Bowge	246
But ye be welcome to our housholde.	53	Bowge	266
But wolde be glad of your company.	53	Bowge	268
But I requyre you no worde that I saye!	54	Bowge	276
A man, but wonderly besene was he.	54	Bowge	283
To see Johan Dawes, that came but yesterdaye,	54	Bowge	301
By Goddis bones, but yf we have som sleyte,	54	Bowge	304
As thou arte, one that cam but yesterdaye,	55	Bowge	328
By Goddis woundes, but for dysplesaunce,	55	Bowge	332
But, no force, I shall ones mete with the;	55	Bowge	334
He had no pleasure but in harlotrye.	56	Bowge	374
What arte thou? I sawe the nowe but late.'	56	Bowge	376
This worlde is nothynge but ete, drynke and slepe,	57	Bowge	384
But there was poyntynge and noddynge with the hede,	58	Bowge	421
In no place well, but foles with hym fraye!	58	Bowge	446
hym] not in †Wynkyn de Worde 1499, Marshe 1568			
But as for that, connynge hath no foo	58	Bowge	447
But ye have crafte your selfe alwaye to save.	59	Bowge	452
But, what, a strawe! I maye not tell all thynge.	59	Bowge	459
Iwys I coude tell - but humlery, home,	59	Bowge	467
tell] 'not tell' Wynkyn de Worde 1510			
And by my trouthe, but yf an ende they make,	59	Bowge	473
But I am lothe for to reyse a smoke,	59	Bowge	479
More coude I saye, but what this is ynowe.	60	Bowge	491
'But by that Lorde that is one, two and thre,	60	Bowge	512
But to here the subtylte and the crafte,	61	Bowge	519
But that I drede mordre wolde come oute.	61	Bowge	524
But yet oftyme suche dremes be founde trewe.	61	Bowge	538
But that they playe the daw	62	Hauke	8
But suche dawes to amend,	62	Hauke	26
A parson benyfyced /But nothynge well advysed.	62	Hauke	37
But he shall not be blameles,	62	Hauke	39
But she wold not bow.	63	Hauke	74
But the fawconer unfayned	64	Hauke	81
But he sayde that he wolde	64	Hauke	97
But lyke a March harum /His braynes were so parum.	64	Hauke	104
But who so that lokys /In the offycyallys bokys,	65	Hauke	145
But let the matter slyp,	66	Hauke	154
And of the spyrytuall law /They made but a gewgaw,	66	Hauke	157
But nothynge it avayled /To call Phylyp agayne	72	Phy Sparrow	25
But all without redresse;	72	Phy Sparrow	33
But whan I dyd beholde	72	Phy Sparrow	39
No creature but that wolde /Have rewed upon me,	72	Phy Sparrow	41
Of God nothynge els crave I /But Phyllypes soule to kepe	73	Phy Sparrow	68
He dyd nothynge, perde, /But syt upon my kne.	76	Phy Sparrow	172
But whoso understode /Of Medeas arte,	76	Phy Sparrow	201
But all this is in vayne	77	Phy Sparrow	208
But whan I was sowing his beke,	77	Phy Sparrow	219
But as verely as ye be	78	Phy Sparrow	254
But my sparowe dyd pas	78	Phy Sparrow	266
But with a large and a longe	82	Phy Sparrow	426
And yet there is none /But one alone;	84	Phy Sparrow	517
But for the egle doth flye	85	Phy Sparrow	550
But whereto shuld I /Lenger morne or crye?	86	Phy Sparrow	594
But for I am a mayde, /Tymerous, halfe afrayde,	87	Phy Sparrow	607
For she dyd but fayne;	89	Phy Sparrow	695
But lyght for somer grene;	89	Phy Sparrow	719
And can but lytell skyll	90	Phy Sparrow	755
I am but a yong mayd,	91	Phy Sparrow	770
But plesaunt, easy and playne;	91	Phy Sparrow	802
But for my sparowes sake,	92	Phy Sparrow	819
But enforsed am I /Openly to askry	94	Phy Sparrow	902
Even nor morow; /But other mennes sorow	94	Phy Sparrow	925

	Page	Title	Line
But ever doth watch,	95	Phy Sparrow	929
But yet certayne /I wyll be playne,	95	Phy Sparrow	966
Be] 'me' †Kele 1545.2			
It cannot be denayd /But it was well convayd,	98	Phy Sparrow	1066
But ryght convenyently, /And full congruently,	98	Phy Sparrow	1069
Nor yet no vyllany, /But only fantasy;	100	Phy Sparrow	1135
But whereto shulde I note	100	Phy Sparrow	1145
But she wolde chaunge his mood,	100	Phy Sparrow	1158
But myrth and consolacyon	103	Phy Sparrow	1278
But whether it were so,	105	Phy Sparrow	1354
But Phylyp, I conjure the	105	Phy Sparrow	1362
But not worth thre skyppes of a pye.	113	Scot Kynge	10
But by the power and myght of God	114	Scot Kynge	46
But ye had some wyl[d] sede to sowe,	114	Scot Kynge	52
wyld] 'wyle' †Fakes 1513			
In comparyson but kynge Koppynge	117	Ag Scottes	57
But for the specyall consolacyon	117	Ag Scottes	75
But, by the power and myght of God,	119	Ag Scottes	145
Cause have they none other /But for that he was brother,	120	Ag Scottes2	14
have they] 'they have' Day 1560, Marshe 1568			
brother] 'hys brother' Day 1560, Marshe 1568			
But yf yt war Syr Tyrmagant that tyrnyd without nall;	121	Garnesche1	4
But sey me now, Syr Satrapas, what autoryte ye have	121	Garnesche1	6
But sey me yet, Syr Satropas, what auctoryte ye have	122	Garnesche1	13
But sey me yet, Syr Satrapas, wat auctoryte ye have	122	Garnesche1	20
But sey me yet, Syr Satrapas, what auctoryte ye have	122	Garnesche1	27
But sey me yet, Syr Satrapas, what auctoryte ye have	122	Garnesche1	34
As wytles as a wylde goos, ye have but small remorrs	123	Garnesche2	18
At Gynys when ye ware /But a slendyr spere,	125	Garnesche3	41
But sche of all men	125	Garnesche3	65
But now, gawdy, gresy Garnesche,	127	Garnesche3	120
Ye wan nothyng there but a mow:	131	Garnesche5	50
Ye wan nothyng there but a skorne;	131	Garnesche5	51
My tyme, I trow, I xulde but lese	133	Garnesche5	154
But now, my proces for to save,	133	Garnesche5	157
But for to serve the kynges entent,	134	Garnesche5	177
But behynd in our hose /We bere there a rose	136	Dundas	34
But thou lakest might,	136	Dundas	49
If there be none other mater but that,	137	Ven Tongues	14
But my learning is of an other degree	138	Ven Tongues	28
But yet I may say safely, so many wel lettred,	138	Ven Tongues	38
What fault find ye herein but may be avowed.	138	Ven Tongues	41
But ye are so full of vertibilite,	138	Ven Tongues	42
Nothing to write, but hay the gy of thre,	138	Ven Tongues	46
But men take upon theim nowe all the shame	139	Ven Tongues	61
But lering and lurking here and there like spies,	139	Ven Tongues	67
But if that I knewe what his name hight,	139	Ven Tongues	73
But men nowe a dayes so unhappely be uryd,	140	Magnyfycence	6
A man may have welth, but not as he wolde,	141	Magnyfycence	14
But yf prudence be proved with sad cyrcumspeccyon,	141	Magnyfycence	16
But wyll hath reason so under subjeccyon,	141	Magnyfycence	19
But where wonnys welthe, and a man wolde wyt?	141	Magnyfycence	22
But yf reason be regent and ruler of your barge.	141	Magnyfycence	38
But with countenaunce your corage must be croppyd,	141	Magnyfycence	47
But and you wolde me permyt	142	Magnyfycence	57
Softe, my frende. Herein your reason is but rawe.	142	Magnyfycence	70
So wolde I, but I wolde be lothe,	144	Magnyfycence	143
But have ye not herde say that wyll is no skyll?	144	Magnyfycence	148
There is no prynce but he hath nede of us thre -	145	Magnyfycence	159
But Measure, my frende, what hyght this mannys name?	145	Magnyfycence	165
But nowe let me knowe of your conversacyon.	145	Magnyfycence	170
But plenarly all thought from you must be dyschargyd,	146	Magnyfycence	207
But yf therof the soner amendys be made;	146	Magnyfycence	226
But yf I were orderyd by just measure,	147	Magnyfycence	249
But hyght you, Largesse, encreace of noble fame?	148	Magnyfycence	271
It is but a maddynge, these wayes that ye use.	148	Magnyfycence	285
By God, syr, ye se but fewe wyse men of myne age.	148	Magnyfycence	289
But covetyse hath blowen you so full of wynde	148	Magnyfycence	290
Ye wante but a wylde flyeng bolte to shote at the buttes.	148	Magnyfycence	294
But yf I coulde knowe a gose from a swanne.	148	Magnyfycence	299
But ofte tymes have I sene wyse men do mad dedys.	148	Magnyfycence	302
Nothynge but fare you well tyll sone -	149	Magnyfycence	319
Nay, syr, it was nothynge but your mynde.	149	Magnyfycence	330
But nowe, syr, as touchynge this letter -	149	Magnyfycence	331
But never was I in gretter fere.	150	Magnyfycence	345
That no man can scape but they hym cache.	150	Magnyfycence	351
But surely largesse saved my lyfe;	150	Magnyfycence	366
But largesse is not mete for every man.	150	Magnyfycence	369
No. But for you grete estates	150	Magnyfycence	370
But largesse becometh a state ryall.	151	Magnyfycence	383
But largesse may amende your name.	151	Magnyfycence	389
Ye, but how longe shall I here awayte?	151	Magnyfycence	398
But nowe wyll I, that they be gone,	151	Magnyfycence	407
I counterfet suger that is but *[s]ounde;	152	Magnyfycence	435
*sounde] 'founde' †Rastell & Treveris C 1530, B,			
'sande' Scattergood			
But counterfet coynes is laughynge to scorne;	152	Magnyfycence	446
Yet counterfet chafer is but evyll corne.	153	Magnyfycence	450

	Page	Title	Line
He wolde trotte gentylly, but he is to starke.	153	Magnyfycence	481
Chanons can not counterfet but upon thre.	154	Magnyfycence	492
But Fansy, my frende, where have ye bene so longe?	154	Magnyfycence	500
But I say, kepest thou the olde name styll that thou had?	155	Magnyfycence	516
But, syr, howe counterfetyd ye?	155	Magnyfycence	524
But is it not well? Howe thynkest thou?	155	Magnyfycence	528
But what became of the letter	155	Magnyfycence	531
Thy wordes be but wynde, never they have no wayght.	156	Magnyfycence	578
But I wyll be ruled after your counsell.	157	Magnyfycence	615
But tell me where aboute ye go.	157	Magnyfycence	617
Ye. But he spendeth it all in mesure.	157	Magnyfycence	621
Ye. But he is a captyvyte.	157	Magnyfycence	626
But shall I have myne olde name styll?	158	Magnyfycence	647
Nor no man in courte, but he,	158	Magnyfycence	660
In fayth, and Lybertyes rome is there but small.	158	Magnyfycence	663
But, Counterfet Countenaunce, go we togyder,	158	Magnyfycence	665
But then, syr, what shall I hyght?	159	Magnyfycence	669
But dyvysyon, dyssencyon, dyrysyon - these thre	159	Magnyfycence	700
I wolde begyn all myschyef, but I wolde bere no lacke.	160	Magnyfycence	720
My speche is all pleasure, but I stynge lyke a waspe.	160	Magnyfycence	730
I am never glad but whan I may do yll,	160	Magnyfycence	731
And never am I sory but whan that I se	160	Magnyfycence	732
That they wyll here no man but the fyrst tale.	161	Magnyfycence	743
But whether art thou walkynge, in faythe unfaynyd?	161	Magnyfycence	762
Nay. Thou art a man good inough but for thy false hart.	162	Magnyfycence	769
But are ye not avysed to dwell where ye spake?	162	Magnyfycence	774
Nay, in good faythe. It is but the gyse.	163	Magnyfycence	809
No, by my trouthe, but crake grete wordes.	163	Magnyfycence	812
But, syr, I wyll have this man with me.	163	Magnyfycence	815
But that the horson is prowde and hawte.	163	Magnyfycence	824
But nowe I wyll not say the worste.	163	Magnyfycence	828
But what the devyll art thou	166	Magnyfycence	916
But nowe what tydynges can you tell? Let se.	166	Magnyfycence	928
Ye. But I bade hym pyke out of the gate;	166	Magnyfycence	946
But I must tary here; go thou before.	167	Magnyfycence	954
Ye, but what shall I call my name?	167	Magnyfycence	958
Ye, but of my name let us be wyse.	167	Magnyfycence	963
But, in faythe, I am so occupyed	168	Magnyfycence	1019
But she is lesse a grete dele	169	Magnyfycence	1052
Ye, but I can somwhat more of the letter.	170	Magnyfycence	1066
But, broder Foly, I wonder moche of one thynge,	170	Magnyfycence	1068
And as for me, I take but one folysshe way,	170	Magnyfycence	1076
Nay, but wotest thou what I do say?	170	Magnyfycence	1092
Here is nothynge but the bockyll of a sho,	171	Magnyfycence	1107
Ye. But trowest thou that he be not maungey?	171	Magnyfycence	1122
No, by my trouthe. It is but the scurfe and the scabbe.	171	Magnyfycence	1123
Nay, in faythe, it was but a strype	171	Magnyfycence	1125
Ye. But he wyll in at every mannes dore.	171	Magnyfycence	1130
But I have thy pultre, and thou hast my catell.	171	Magnyfycence	1135
Ye. But thryfte and we have made a batell.	171	Magnyfycence	1136
But wylte thou make another on Gryme?	172	Magnyfycence	1151
Ye, but thou can play the fole without a vyser.	173	Magnyfycence	1177
But where gatte thou that mangey curre?	173	Magnyfycence	1180
But yet thou shalt holde me a fole styll.	173	Magnyfycence	1184
What canest thou do but play cocke wat?	173	Magnyfycence	1191
But nowe, forsothe, man, it maketh no mater;	175	Magnyfycence	1256
But all he dothe, and yf he reken well	175	Magnyfycence	1274
It is but foly every dell.	175	Magnyfycence	1275
But, I say, let se and yf thou have any more.	175	Magnyfycence	1278
Nay, but fansy must be eyther fyrst or last.	176	Magnyfycence	1288
But all is foly that I can se.	176	Magnyfycence	1291
But, for the, Fansy, Magnyfycence abydes.	176	Magnyfycence	1305
Ye. But tell me one thynge. What is that?	176	Magnyfycence	1318
But may I drynke therof whylest that I stare?	176	Magnyfycence	1322
So that there knowe no man but I and she.	177	Magnyfycence	1353
But some man wolde convey, and can not skyll,	178	Magnyfycence	1361
It shall be done. Ye, but byd hym come away	179	Magnyfycence	1399
I can do nothynge but he stonde besyde.	180	Magnyfycence	1449
But loke that ye occupye the auctoryte that I you gave.	180	Magnyfycence	1456
But I shall of Fortune rule the reyne.	181	Magnyfycence	1460
But I shall frounce them on the foretop and gar them to quake.	182	Magnyfycence	1514
But of your pacyence under the supporte,	183	Magnyfycence	1542
A maystres, I tell you, is but a small thynge.	184	Magnyfycence	1579
But one thynge I warne you, prece forth and be bolde.	184	Magnyfycence	1582
Ye, but some be full koy and passynge harde harted.	184	Magnyfycence	1583
But, blessyd be our Lorde, they wyll be sone converted.	184	Magnyfycence	1584
But yf it lyke your grace more at large	185	Magnyfycence	1589
But do as ye lyst and take your owne way.	185	Magnyfycence	1604
Yet I am not harte seke, but that me lyst.	185	Magnyfycence	1621
I may say to you I have but small devocyon.	186	Magnyfycence	1640
But yf it lyke you that I myght rowne in your eyre,	186	Magnyfycence	1645
To trust in me he is but dyssayved;	186	Magnyfycence	1652
That he knowe not but that I have supplyed	187	Magnyfycence	1663
But for all that he is lyke to have a glent.	187	Magnyfycence	1668
But yet, lo, I wolde, or that he wente,	187	Magnyfycence	1673
Nay, indede, but I sawe howe ye prayed,	188	Magnyfycence	1696
But thynke you with Magnyfycence I shal be reserved?	188	Magnyfycence	1702
But, and I were as ye, I wolde not set a gnat.	188	Magnyfycence	1704

BUT —BUT   Page   Title   Line

Entry	Page	Title	Line
A, my hede! But is the horson gone?	189	Magnyfycence	1729
For I here but fewe men that gyve ony prayse	189	Magnyfycence	1743
Largesse in wordes - for rewardes are but small.	189	Magnyfycence	1760
But use your largesse by the advyse of me,	189	Magnyfycence	1765
But nowe a dayes to stryke I have grete cause,	194	Magnyfycence	1918
Of correccyon, but let them have theyr wyll.	194	Magnyfycence	1930
Full fewe but they have envy of me.	195	Magnyfycence	1963
But yet, syr, nowe in this case	197	Magnyfycence	2032
But beggynge is better medecyne for the necke.	198	Magnyfycence	2045
But yet, syrs, hardely one thynge lerne of me:	199	Magnyfycence	2087
But he abused so his free lyberte,	200	Magnyfycence	2113
But by the way of fansy insolence.	200	Magnyfycence	2116
But nowe adayes as huksters they hucke and they stycke,	200	Magnyfycence	2121
But so longe they rekyn with theyr reasons amysse	200	Magnyfycence	2127
they] 'theyr' †Rastell & Treveris C 1530, B			
Ye, but thanke me therof every dele.	201	Magnyfycence	2171
Nay, to wrangle, I warant the, it is but a stone-caste.	201	Magnyfycence	2174
But wottest thou, horson? I rede the to be wyse.	202	Magnyfycence	2184
And yf there were none to dysplease but thou and I,	202	Magnyfycence	2194
Thou sholde not scape, horson, but thou sholde dye.	202	Magnyfycence	2195
In fayth, so to suffer the, it is but a skorne.	202	Magnyfycence	2201
For we be, syrs, but a fewe of the best.	202	Magnyfycence	2203
Well sayd. But, in fayth, what was your quarell?	203	Magnyfycence	2210
Thou sawe never yet but I dyd my parte,	203	Magnyfycence	2228
Tushe! These maters that ye move are but soppys in ale;	203	Magnyfycence	2233
Ye, but trowe you, syrs, that this is he?	204	Magnyfycence	2242
But nowe let us make mery and good chere.	204	Magnyfycence	2261
But they say it is a queysy mete;	204	Magnyfycence	2267
In Goddys mercy, I tell them, is but foly to truste;	205	Magnyfycence	2289
But nowe I se well there is no better rede,	205	Magnyfycence	2305
But sygh, and sorowe, and wysshe my selfe dede.	205	Magnyfycence	2306
Spare not thy selfe, but boldly the murder.	206	Magnyfycence	2318
But, my good sonne, lerne from dyspaire to flee;	206	Magnyfycence	2339
But thrughe good hope there may come remedy.	207	Magnyfycence	2344
For who loveth God can ayle nothynge but good.	207	Magnyfycence	2365
Ye, but have ye repentyd you with harte contryte?	208	Magnyfycence	2391
As the worlde requyreth, but rather I am refused.	208	Magnyfycence	2412
But redresse is redlesse and may do no correccyon.	209	Magnyfycence	2417
But, syr, by me to rule fyrst ye began.	209	Magnyfycence	2431
But good hope and redresse hath mendyd myne estate,	210	Magnyfycence	2462
But frendly I wyll refrayne you ferther, or we flyt:	211	Magnyfycence	2478
But wyfull waywardnesse muste walke out of the way;	211	Magnyfycence	2490
Remember this lyfe lastyth but a whyle.	211	Magnyfycence	2502
But, Perseveraunce, me semyth your probleme was best;	212	Magnyfycence	2505
But hooly to perseveraunce my selfe I wyll bynde,	212	Magnyfycence	2507
But fallyble flatery enmyxyd with bytternesse.	212	Magnyfycence	2516
But fallyble flatery enmyxyd with bytternesse.	212	Magnyfycence	2523
But she is not gryll,	214	El Rummynge	6
But ugly of chere,	214	El Rummynge	14
Never stoppynge /But ever droppynge;	215	El Rummynge	30
But to make up my tale,	217	El Rummynge	101
But drynke tyll they stare	217	El Rummynge	108
But let us turne playne, /There we lefte agayne.	219	El Rummynge	187
But we wyll turne playne /Where we left agayne.	220	El Rummynge	242
But, 'Drynke,' styll, 'Drynke, /And let the cat wynke!	222	El Rummynge	305
But, Lorde, as she was testy, /Angry as a waspy!	222	El Rummynge	329
But she spake somwhat thycke,	223	El Rummynge	338
But she was a foule slut,	223	El Rummynge	340
But supped it up at ones,	224	El Rummynge	380
But she had lost the stoppell,	224	El Rummynge	404
But they were sturdy and stubbed,	225	El Rummynge	422
stubbed] 'stubbled' Kynge & Marche 1554, Day 1560, Marshe 1568			
But of all this thronge /One came them amonge,	225	El Rummynge	445
But yet, for all that,	226	El Rummynge	490
But, syr, amonge all /That sate in that hall,	229	El Rummynge	580
But rose from the borde	229	El Rummynge	591
But the very grounde /Was for to compound	229	El Rummynge	596
But my bedes of amber.	229	El Rummynge	603
But some than sate ryght sad	229	El Rummynge	607
But, whan they shoulde walke,	230	El Rummynge	613
Moderata juvant but toto dothe exede;	232	Speke Parott	50
But reason and wytte wantythe theyr provynciall,	232	Speke Parott	53
In flattryng fables men fynde but lyttyl fayth;	233	Speke Parott	87
But moveatur terra, let the world wag,	233	Speke Parott	88
'But ware the cat, Parot, ware the fals cat!'	233	Speke Parott	99
But Parrot hath no favour to Esebon;	233	Speke Parott	111
But our Grekis theyr Greke so well have applyed,	234	Speke Parott	145
Nether wise nor wel lernid, but like hermaphradita:	235	Speke Parott	159
But of that supposicyon that callyd is arte,	236	Speke Parott	197
But that metaphora, alegoria withall,	236	Speke Parott	202
But Parot is my owne dere harte, and my dere derling.	236	Speke Parott	208
dere] (2nd) not in Day 1560, Marshe 1568			
But lewdlye ar they lettyrd that your lernyng lackys,	239	Speke Parott	294
Muche frutefull mater. But now for your defence,	239	Speke Parott	297
Some was but lityll and thynke more in there thowghte,	242	Speke Parott	388
For grocers were grugyd at and groynyd at but late;	244	Speke Parott	441
For reysons ar no resons but resons currant -	244	Speke Parott	443
'He is but a foole; /Let hym go to scole!'	247	Collyn Clout	28

	Page	Title	Line
But plucke away and pull /Theyr fleces of wull.	248	Collyn Clout	78
In theyr pryncypall cure /They make but lytell sure,	249	Collyn Clout	103
But ire and venyre,	249	Collyn Clout	106
But thus the people carke,	249	Collyn Clout	120
But slombre forth and slepe,	249	Collyn Clout	124
But the greatest parte /Is for they have but small arte	250	Collyn Clout	138
But the greatest parte /Is for they have but small arte	250	Collyn Clout	139
But this reason they take:	250	Collyn Clout	142
But they are lothe to mell,	250	Collyn Clout	162
But nowe every spirytuall father,	251	Collyn Clout	174
Spende? Nay, but spare!	251	Collyn Clout	178
But it is not worth a leke.	251	Collyn Clout	182
But ye loke to be let lose	252	Collyn Clout	213
But whan they have ones caught	252	Collyn Clout	229
But the moost parte in generall.	252	Collyn Clout	245
But of her apostels lyfe.	253	Collyn Clout	254
her] 'theyr' Kele 1545.1, 'ther' MS Harley 2252			
But a full purse.	254	Collyn Clout	293
For a symoniake /Is but a hermoniake;	254	Collyn Clout	297
But a chyldes play.	254	Collyn Clout	300
But howe the commons gronys, /And the people monys,	255	Collyn Clout	348
But from daye to daye delayde,	255	Collyn Clout	352
But dyssymulynge and glosynge,	255	Collyn Clout	356
But where theyr soules dwell,	257	Collyn Clout	427
But swete ypocras ye drynke,	258	Collyn Clout	456
But trouth can never lye.	258	Collyn Clout	485
But under your supporte,	259	Collyn Clout	505
But they have enterprysed /And shamfully surmysed	261	Collyn Clout	581
But noble men borne, /To lerne they have scorne,	262	Collyn Clout	619
But hunte and blowe an horne,	262	Collyn Clout	621
But the communalte ye call	262	Collyn Clout	637
But qui se existimat stare,	263	Collyn Clout	664
But mayster Damyan, /Or some other man	264	Collyn Clout	720
But the poore degre /Of the universyte;	265	Collyn Clout	735
But men say your auctoryte	265	Collyn Clout	758
But men say] 'Men say but' †Godfray 1531, Kele 1545.1, Marshe 1568			
But yf ye wolde take payne	265	Collyn Clout	763
But answere that I may, /For myselfe alway	266	Collyn Clout	785
But doctour Bullatus /Parum litteratus,	266	Collyn Clout	795
But they theyr tonges fyle,	267	Collyn Clout	850
But it is an olde sayd sawe	268	Collyn Clout	862
it] not in Kele 1545.1			
But whan the frere fell in the well	268	Collyn Clout	877
But by the helpe of Christen Clout.	268	Collyn Clout	879
But now my mynde ye understande,	268	Collyn Clout	887
But they have no affections	268	Collyn Clout	893
affections] 'afflictions' Kele 1545.1, 'affeccions' Harley 2252			
Can say nothynge but 'mum'.	269	Collyn Clout	905
That some of you but late	271	Collyn Clout	1011
But at the pleasure of one	272	Collyn Clout	1018
But that the parysshe clerke	272	Collyn Clout	1025
But they wyl talke of suche uncouthes,	272	Collyn Clout	1052
But nowe debetis scire /And groundly audire	273	Collyn Clout	1065
But olde servauntes ye chase	273	Collyn Clout	1077
But my recountynge is /Of them that do amys	274	Collyn Clout	1101
But that I wryte trewly.	274	Collyn Clout	1116
But lyve styll out of facyon,	275	Collyn Clout	1139
But they wolde no man shuld them blame.	275	Collyn Clout	1142
But yet they wyll occupye the same.	275	Collyn Clout	1144
But whan age seeth that rage	279	Why Come Ye	36
But /Helas! sage overage /So madly decayes,	279	Why Come Ye	40
So] 'To' Toy 1553, Kitson 1560.7, Marshe 1568			
There is no man but one	281	Why Come Ye	113
That they are but halfe men;	283	Why Come Ye	163
But yet they over-shote us	283	Why Come Ye	169
He loveth nothyng but golde;	284	Why Come Ye	208
But now upon this story	284	Why Come Ye	229
But at the naked stewes	284	Why Come Ye	236
He sayes we ar but crakers;	285	Why Come Ye	274
But as the worlde now gose,	286	Why Come Ye	285
But suche as he admyttes,	287	Why Come Ye	327
But to his sentence must accorde.	287	Why Come Ye	343
He is but an yonglyng,	287	Why Come Ye	348
But and it were well sought,	287	Why Come Ye	352
But, as some men sayne,	288	Why Come Ye	362
But within monethes thre	288	Why Come Ye	366
But speke ye no more of that,	288	Why Come Ye	382
But there is some travarse	288	Why Come Ye	387
But Hampton Court /Hath the preemynence!	289	Why Come Ye	408
That all is but nutshales	290	Why Come Ye	443
But all he bringeth to nought,	290	Why Come Ye	450
But he laythe all in the dyche,	290	Why Come Ye	455
But this madde Amalecke,	291	Why Come Ye	478
But, however he was borne,	291	Why Come Ye	495
But a poore maister of arte!	292	Why Come Ye	512
He doth but cloute and cobbill	292	Why Come Ye	527

	Page	Title	Line
But have ye nat harde this,	292	Why Come Ye	532
But what his grace doth thinke,	296	Why Come Ye	683
But wele I can tell	296	Why Come Ye	686
But was ravysht with a rage	296	Why Come Ye	691
But how that came aboute,	296	Why Come Ye	693
But let mi masters mathematical	296	Why Come Ye	708
But I wyll make further relacion	297	Why Come Ye	716
But the wyttys of many wyse	298	Why Come Ye	766
But harke, my frende, one worde	298	Why Come Ye	784
But he was so payned in the hede	299	Why Come Ye	795
I have told you part, but nat all.	299	Why Come Ye	822
He rod, but we ran.	301	Why Come Ye	887
'He rode not but he ran' MS Rawlinson C. 813			
But howe comme to pas	301	Why Come Ye	900
But the chefe of your fayre	301	Why Come Ye	909
But Englande may well say	302	Why Come Ye	928
Now nothynge but 'pay, pay!'	302	Why Come Ye	930
That ruleth but he alone,	304	Why Come Ye	996
But as touchynge dystrectyon, /With sober dyrectyon	304	Why Come Ye	1008
dystrectyon] 'dyscrecyon' Marshe 1568, MS Rawlinson C. 813			
But all must be tryde,	304	Why Come Ye	1013
But braynsyk and braynlesse, /Wytles and rechelesse,	304	Why Come Ye	1018
But tatterd and tuggyd, /Raggyd and ruggyd,	304	Why Come Ye	1026
tatterd] 'taxed' MS Rawlinson C. 813			
But to wryte of his shame	305	Why Come Ye	1048
But now he maketh objectyon,	307	Why Come Ye	1127
But] 'And', objectyon] 'dyrectyon' MS Rawlinson C. 813			
But yet beware the rod	307	Why Come Ye	1137
The apostyll Peter /Had but on pore myter	307	Why Come Ye	1140
apostyll] 'wholly apostle' MS Rawlinson C. 813			
But de absentibus nil nisi bonum.	310	Why Come Ye2	30
But now in welthe, now in adversyte.	312	Garlande	14
But of my purpose now turne we to the grownde.	313	Garlande	28
purpose] 'proces' MS Cotton Vitellius E.x			
But sodeynly at ones, as I me advysed,	313	Garlande	36
But to recounte her ryche abylyment,	313	Garlande	44
But, good madame, the accustome and usage	314	Garlande	64
But, how it is, Skelton is wonder slake,	314	Garlande	69
But sith he hath tastid of the sugred pocioun	314	Garlande	73
Then men wyll say how he doth but flatter.	314	Garlande	84
Then sum wyll say he hath but lyttil brayne,	314	Garlande	87
Yet harde is to make but sum fawt be founde.'	315	Garlande	112
But if he had made sum memoryall,	315	Garlande	118
But to do sumwhat iche man doth hym dres	315	Garlande	122
But that his bokis, whiche he did devyse,	315	Garlande	124
Plato, but for that he left wrytynge behynde,	315	Garlande	126
that] not in MS Cotton Vitellius E.x			
For, but if your bounte did me assure,	316	Garlande	146
But of that famous oratour, I say,	316	Garlande	158
But a grete parte yet ye have reservyd	317	Garlande	171
But...parte] 'Bot yit a grete parte' MS Cotton Vitellius E.x			
But whome that ye favoure, I se well, hath a name,	317	Garlande	176
But lytell or nothynge ye shall here tell	317	Garlande	197
ye shall] 'shall ye' MS Cotton Vitellius E.x			
Men of suche maters make but mummynge,	318	Garlande	200
but] 'but a' MS Cotton Vitellius E.x			
But your benynge sufferaunce for my discharge I laid,	318	Garlande	213
But yet I beseche your grace that good recorde	318	Garlande	215
good] not in MS Cotton Vitellius E.x			
But I most bannysshe hym frome my juryiccyon,	318	Garlande	227
But if that he purpose to make a redresse,	318	Garlande	229
Graunt my petycyon, I aske you but ryght.'	318	Garlande	231
But that he daunced for joye of that gle.	320	Garlande	278
But Phebus was formest of all that cam theder;	320	Garlande	287
But, for to preserve her maidenhode clene,	320	Garlande	293
maidenhode] 'maydenheed' Marshe 1568			
But now to helpe myselfe I am not able.	321	Garlande	312
But sith I have lost now that I entended,	321	Garlande	318
But blessed Bacchus, the pleasant god of wyne,	321	Garlande	334
But Bacchus, the pleasant god of wyne,	321	Garlande	341
But blessyd Bachus, potenciall god of strengthe,	322	Garlande	348
But blessyd Bachus was in there company,	322	Garlande	355
But blessyd Bachus most reverent and holy,	322	Garlande	362
But blessyd Bachus that never man forgate,	322	Garlande	369
But blessyd Bachus, that bote is of all bale,	322	Garlande	376
But blissed Bachus, that mastris oft doth frame,	322	Garlande	383
Thei wantid nothynge but the laurell;	323	Garlande	397
But what sholde I say? Ye wote what I entende,	324	Garlande	426
But that I poynt you to be prothonotary	324	Garlande	432
That but if my warkes therto be agreable,	324	Garlande	439
I can nat tell you, but that I was brought	325	Garlande	458
From you most we, but not longe to tary.	326	Garlande	520
To pas the tyme with, but let us wast no wynde.	328	Garlande	565
For ydle jangelers have but lytill braine,	328	Garlande	566
But one gate specyally, where as I stode,	328	Garlande	586
But hailid they be homwarde with sorow and shame.	329	Garlande	622
But wele may ye thynk I was no thyng prowde	330	Garlande	648
But, goodly maystres, one thynge ye me tell.'	332	Garlande	720

BUTE —BUTTYNG   Page   Title   Line

	Page	Title	Line
But my request is not so great a thynge,	332	Garlande	730
I am not woundid but that I may be cured.	332	Garlande	732
But if they were counterfettes that women them call,	334	Garlande	785
But, as I sayd, your florisshinge tender age	337	Garlande	876
But to do you servyce nedis now I must;	337	Garlande	879
to do you] 'do her' MS Cotton Vitellius E.x			
But if I sholde aquyte your kyndnes,	342	Garlande	1062
But, and I had leyser competent,	342	Garlande	1082
But when they sawe my lawrell rychely wrought,	343	Garlande	1105
There was amonge them no worde then but mum,	344	Garlande	1118
amonge them no worde] 'not a worde amonge them' MS Cotton Vitellius E.x			
But if hastyve credence by mayntenance of myght	344	Garlande	1133
But suche evydence I thynke for to enduce,	344	Garlande	1135
for to] 'for me to' MS Cotton Vitellius E.x			
But if he wryte oftenner than ones or twyse.'	345	Garlande	1155
It may wele ryme, but shroudly it doth accorde,	346	Garlande	1210
But what of that? Hard it is to please all men;	348	Garlande	1259
But myrth and consolacyoun, /Made by protestacyoun,	348	Garlande	1271
But whether it were so,	350	Garlande	1347
But, Phillip, I conjure the	350	Garlande	1355
But, lorde, how the parker was wroth with all.	351	Garlande	1386
But how it was, sum were to recheles,	351	Garlande	1393
The cheke and the nek but a shorte cast;	351	Garlande	1401
But yet for all that, be as be may,	352	Garlande	1415
But Marione Clarione was caught with a colde colde,	352	Garlande	1443
a colde colde] 'a colde' Marshe 1568			
But who may have a more ungracyous lyfe	352	Garlande	1451
a] not in Marshe 1568			
But that my peticyon wolde not be had,	353	Garlande	1486
What shuld I do but take it in gre?	353	Garlande	1487
But when of the laurell she made rehersall,	354	Garlande	1503
But then I drede	355	Garlande	1553
then] 'that' Marshe 1568			
But curteisly /That I have pende /For to deffend,	356	Garlande	1569
But of my spede /Small sekernes;	356	Garlande	1596
But now must I /Your Duke ascry /Of Albany	360	Albany	72
But ye meane a thyng	361	Albany	91
But our kyng royall	361	Albany	107
But flery, flatter and fayne;	362	Albany	135
Thou dyd nothyng but barke	362	Albany	147
But yet they were bolde	364	Albany	202
But ye and your hoost,	364	Albany	206
But lepe away lyke frogges	364	Albany	212
Ye make nought but ye marre.	364	Albany	226
But thou ran home agayne	365	Albany	246
But in a mountayne gay,	365	Albany	260
But hyde the, Sir Topias,	366	Albany	287
For thou can not but brag	366	Albany	294
Thy mellyng is but mockyng.	366	Albany	298
But ran away quyte?	366	Albany	310
If he on you but frounde	367	Albany	345
But nowe will I expounde	369	Albany	423
But madly it frames,	374	Replycacion	11
and yet they were but febly enformed	374	Replycacion	I
and have waded but weakly in his thre maner of clerkly workes,	374	Replycacion	I
But ye were confuse tantum,	377	Replycacion	111
But ye were folysshe nyse,	378	Replycacion	130
But under pacient tuicyon,	378	Replycacion	141
But, as the man sayes,	378	Replycacion	151
But with scornefull affection	379	Replycacion	190
Ye are but lydder logici, /But moche worse isagogici,	380	Replycacion	234
Ye are but lydder logici, /But moche worse isagogici,	380	Replycacion	235
But that princesse alone,	381	Replycacion	259
But, I trowe, your selfe ye overse	381	Replycacion	285
But mende your myndes that are mased;	382	Replycacion	293
Howe poetes do but fayne?	384	Replycacion	353

BUTE

Maye never dye, bute evermore endure.	46	Bowge	16

BUTTER

For we have egges and butter,	228	El Rummynge	536

BUTTERFLY

Lord, how he wolde pry /After the butterfly!	75	Phy Sparrow	135
Make a verse of my butterfly;	172	Magnyfycence	1149
Parrot is no woodecocke, nor no butterfly,	236	Speke Parott	206
And say as untrewly /As the butterfly,	255	Collyn Clout	337

BUTTERFLYE

He hawketh, me thynke, for a butterflye.	156	Magnyfycence	575
It is a Frenche butterflye.	169	Magnyfycence	1050
Than a butterflye of our lande.	169	Magnyfycence	1053

BUTTERFLLYIS

With butterfllyis and fresshe pecoke taylis,	345	Garlande	1159

BUTTES

Ye wante but a wylde flyeng bolte to shote at the buttes.	148	Magnyfycence	294

BUTTYNG

With, 'Bas me, buttyng, praty Cys',	130	Garnesche5	43

CABAGYD —CALIOPE   Page   Title   Line

CABAGYD
So bygge a bulke of brow-auntleres cabagyd that yere; 245   Speke Parott   488
CACADEMONYALL
As well calodemonyall /As to cacademonyall, ... 299   Why Come Ye   810
CACH
Theyre browys all to-brokyn, such clappys they cach; 43   Balettys2   32
CACHE
That no man can scape but they hym cache. 150   Magnyfycence   351
That made Cerberus to cache, the cur dogge of hell, ... 182   Magnyfycence   1495
They cast up theyr obedyence to cache me agayne; 201   Magnyfycence   2148
Racell, rulye ragged, she is like to cache colde; 242   Speke Parott   401
For passe-a-Pase apase ys gone to cache a molle, ... 243   Speke Parott   413
CACHYD
Fansy hath cachyd in a flye net 151   Magnyfycence   403
CACUS
Nother crokyd Cacus, /Nor yet dronken Bacus; 67   Hauke   194
     Nother] 'Nor yet' Kynge & Marche 1554, Day 1560, Marshe 1568
CADMUS
Cadmus, that his syster sought, ... 76   Phy Sparrow   194
CAGE
His hode all pounsed and garded lyke a cage. 60   Bowge   508
     hode] 'body' Marshe 1568
Was never byrde in cage /More gentle of corage 80   Phy Sparrow   324
A cage curyowsly carven, with sylver pynne, ... 231   Speke Parott   8
Caried in a cage, /As it were a cotage, ... 365   Albany   255
CAYFACE
Ye cappyd Cayface copious, your paltoke on your pate, ... 123   Garnesche2   6
Ye cappyd Cayface copyous, your paltoke on your pate, ... 123   Garnesche2   13
CAYFAS
Ye capyd Cayfas copyous, your paltoke on your pate, ... 123   Garnesche2   20
Ye cappyd Cayfas copyus, your paltoke on your pate, ... 123   Garnesche2   27
Ye cappyd Cayfas copyous, your paltoke on your pate, ... 123   Garnesche2   34
Ye cappyd Cayfas copyous, your paltoke on your pate, ... 124   Garnesche2   41
CAYRE
Syr capten of Catywade, catacumbas of Cayre, ... 122   Garnesche1   16
CAYSER
Nay, come away, man! Thou playst the cayser. 162   Magnyfycence   787
For be he cayser or be he kynge, ... 174   Magnyfycence   1214
CAYTYFE
For nowe wyll I from this caytyfe go, ... 195   Magnyfycence   1950
Take this caytyfe to thy lore. 195   Magnyfycence   1954
CAYTYVYS
Thy caytyvys carkes, cours and crasy; 130   Garnesche5   31
CAYUS
Syr Gy, Syr Gawen, Syr Cayus, for and Syr Olyvere, ... 123   Garnesche2   22
CAKE
Lyke a cake of tallowe; 222   El Rummynge   322
A wanton wenche and wele coude bake a cake; 351   Garlande   1413
CAL
In yor chalenge, Syr Chesten, to cal me a knave? 122   Garnesche1   21
To cal me knave thou takyst gret payne. 130   Garnesche5   20
To cal me lorell ye ar to lewde; 131   Garnesche5   85
Shet were the gatis; thei might wel knock and cal, ... 329   Garlande   604
CALCYDONY
Had gravin in it of calcydony a capytall A. 328   Garlande   587
CALD
Well may ye be cald commons most unkynd. 30   Dol Dethe   56
     ye] 'you' Marshe 1568
CALDE
Of hevenly poems, O Clyo, calde by name 29   Dol Dethe   8
He calde upon them, as menyall houshold men: 30   Dol Dethe   33
CALDEE
Yn Latyn, in Ebrue, and in Caldee, ... 231   Speke Parott   25
     and] 'Araby and' Lant 1545, Kynge and Marche 1554, Day 1560,
     Marshe 1568
CALDIES
Aram was fyred with Caldies fyer called Ur; 232   Speke Parott   64
CALDY
Some carectis of Caldy, sum Frensshe was full good; 328   Garlande   585
CALE
In your chalenge, Syr Chystyn, to cale me knave? 121   Garnesche1   7
CALED
Mary, syr, this gentylman caled me javell. 203   Magnyfycence   2211
CALES
The countrynge at Cales 280   Why Come Ye   77
     The] 'They' †Kele 1545.3, Toy 1553, Kitson 1560.7, Marshe 1568
CALETTES
Than Elynour sayde, 'Ye calettes, ... 223   El Rummynge   347
CALFE
And ye war herey, lyke a calfe; 131   Garnesche5   59
She yelled lyke a calfe! 227   El Rummynge   500
As wyse as Waltoms calfe, ... 266   Collyn Clout   809
CALFLES
Crokyd as a camoke, and as a kowe calfles, ... 122   Garnesche1   30
CALIOPE
Or els Caliope, /Or els Penolope; 97   Phy Sparrow   1020
Caliope poynted me where I shulde sit. 344   Garlande   1143

CALYCE —CALLETH   Page   Title   Line

CALYCE
Entry	Page	Title	Line
The armes of Calyce, I have no coyne nor crosse!	57	Bowge	398

CALYS
Entry	Page	Title	Line
By the armes of Calys, well conceyved.	159	Magnyfycence	675
From Calys to Dovyr, to Caunterbury in Kente,	240	Speke Parott	340

CALL
Entry	Page	Title	Line
As oft as thei call to ther remembrance	34	Dol Dethe	188
Which men the viii dedly syn call.	36	Coystrowne1	5
syn] 'sins' Marshe 1568			
But nothynge it avayled /To call Phylyp agayne	72	Phy Sparrow	26
To Jupyter I call, /Of heven emperyall,	86	Phy Sparrow	596
That cuckoldes men call;	88	Phy Sparrow	648
I conjure, Phylyp, and call	105	Phy Sparrow	1342
Unto your grace for grace now I call,	117	Ag Scottes	78
Thalya, my muse, for you also call I,	117	Ag Scottes	85
Chalenge yor selfe for a fole, call me no more knave.	122	Garnesche1	42
The amense therof is far to call agayne;	140	Magnyfycence	9
Pleasyth, your grace, Felycyte they me call.	145	Magnyfycence	171
What call ye him, this?	156	Magnyfycence	588
Cockys harte! Who is yonde that for the dothe call?	162	Magnyfycence	780
By Cockys harte, and call shall agayne!	162	Magnyfycence	783
Ye, but what shall I call my name?	167	Magnyfycence	958
Mayster Survayour, Largesse to me call.	179	Magnyfycence	1398
Wolde money, trowest thou, make suche one to the call?	184	Magnyfycence	1573
Call for a ca[u]dell and cast up your gorge,	185	Magnyfycence	1614
caudell] 'candell' †Rastell & Treveris C 1530, B			
Well, call hym, and let us here hym reason;	187	Magnyfycence	1687
A, blessyd may ye be, syr! What shall you I call?	206	Magnyfycence	2327
Parrot is no pendugum, that men call a carlyng,	236	Speke Parott	205
Parrot is no stameryng stare, that men call a starlyng;	236	Speke Parott	207
Men call you therfore prophanes.	252	Collyn Clout	207
An holy anker call	254	Collyn Clout	303
An] 'a' †Godfray 1531, Kele 1545.1, Marshe 1568			
And call a lorde a javell.	261	Collyn Clout	600
And to remembraunce call;	262	Collyn Clout	631
But the communalte ye call	262	Collyn Clout	637
The lay men call them barelles	269	Collyn Clout	917
And call to his mynde	291	Why Come Ye	499
Call forthe, let se where is your clarionar,	318	Garlande	233
With a frere of Fraunce men call Sir Gagwyne,	322	Garlande	374
Wordes be swordes, and hard to call ageine.'	328	Garlande	567
'What yate call ye this?' And she sayd, 'Anglea'.	328	Garlande	588
yate] 'gate' Marshe 1568			
Men call a phenix; her wynges bytwene	330	Garlande	668
But if they were counterfettes that women them call,	334	Garlande	785
To your remembraunce wherfore we must call	335	Garlande	812
Madame regent /I may you call /Of vertuows all.	339	Garlande	952
I conjure, Phillippe and call,	350	Garlande	1335
Men call it a toyle.	365	Albany	269
If ye to remembrance call	377	Replycacion	98
I call to this rekenyng	383	Replycacion	316
Dothe bothe write and call	383	Replycacion	320
As Grekes do it call,	384	Replycacion	369

CALLE
Entry	Page	Title	Line
In yor chalenge, Syr Chesten, to calle me a knave?	122	Garnesche1	14
In yor chalenge, Syr Chesten, to calle me a knave?	122	Garnesche1	28
In yor chalenge, Syr Chesten, to calle me a knave?	122	Garnesche1	35
For thes twayne whypslovens calle for a coke stole.	124	Garnesche2	38
The insyde ye ded calle	125	Garnesche3	50
Me as hys master for to calle	132	Garnesche5	104

CALLED
Entry	Page	Title	Line
In myne hostes house called Powers Keye,	47	Bowge	35
Is called Favore to stonde in her good grace.'	47	Bowge	55
The ravyn called Rolfe,	82	Phy Sparrow	414
Me thought he called Fan[s]y.	149	Magnyfycence	327
fansy] 'fanfy' †Rastell & Treveris C 1530, B			
Me thought he called Fansy me behynde.	149	Magnyfycence	329
Counterfet holynes is called ypocrysy;	153	Magnyfycence	469
Nay, by Saynt Mary, it was he called me knave.	203	Magnyfycence	2212
And be ruled by me, whiche am called Redresse.	208	Magnyfycence	2410
And called for our dame, /Elynour by name.	229	El Rummynge	592
Aram was fyred with Caldies fyer called Ur;	232	Speke Parott	64
Of that heresy arte /Called Wytclyftista,	260	Collyn Clout	549
Wytclyftista] 'Wicleuista' Marshe 1568			
Upon Grenewytche border /Called Observaunce,	265	Collyn Clout	747
In Tullis faculte /Called humanyte.	292	Why Come Ye	529
To a straunge jurisdictyon /Called Dymingis Dale,	299	Why Come Ye	801
Some be called crafty that can pyke a purse;	317	Garlande	184
pyke] 'kit' MS Cotton Vitellius E.x			
that this lytell pamphilet, called the Replicacion	373	Replycacion	1

CALLEST
Entry	Page	Title	Line
What callest thou thy dogge? Tusshe! His name is Gryme.	171	Magnyfycence	1118

CALLET
Entry	Page	Title	Line
She was a cumly callet.	226	El Rummynge	462

CALLETH
Entry	Page	Title	Line
There dwelleth a mayster men calleth Mesure -	158	Magnyfycence	631

CALLID —CAME

	Page	Title	Line
He calleth me his whytyng, /His mullyng and his [m]ytyng,	220	El Rummynge	223
mytyng] 'nytyng' †Lant 1545, Kynge & Marche 1554, 'nittinge' Day 1560, 'nittine' Marshe 1568			
He calleth us England men	285	Why Come Ye	275
He calleth them doddy patis;	295	Why Come Ye	652
He calleth the prechours dawis.	305	Why Come Ye	1061

CALLID
Of phylosophers callid the princypall,	315	Garlande	128
When he is callid to answere to his name.'	325	Garlande	452
Callid Speculum Principis, to bere in his honde,	347	Garlande	1229
Of the Mayden of Kent callid Counforte,	354	Garlande	1495

CALLIOPE
Why were ye Calliope, embrawdred with letters of golde?	112	Calliope	I
Calliope, /As ye may se,	112	Calliope	1
Of the Musys nyne, Calliope	131	Garnesche5	87

CALLYD
He then, to be sure, /Callyd her with a lure.	63	Hauke	76
She callyd yow Syr Gy of Gaunt,	126	Garnesche3	70
Ye wolde be callyd a maker,	127	Garnesche3	108
Thou art callyd of every man.	130	Garnesche5	24
Thow seyst I callyd the a pecok;	133	Garnesche5	128
Thow liist, I callyd the a wodcoke;	133	Garnesche5	129
Cockys armys! He hath callyd for the twyce.	162	Magnyfycence	782
Here is no man that callyd the hogge nor swyne.	170	Magnyfycence	1084
Ye, syr, yesterday wyll not be callyd agayne.	197	Magnyfycence	2031
But of that supposicyon that callyd is arte,	236	Speke Parott	197
Callyd Detraxion, encankryd with envye,	241	Speke Parott	362
For how shulde Cato els be callyd wyse,	315	Garlande	123
This gentilwoman, that callyd was by name	327	Garlande	527
Sume fayne themselfe folys, and wolde be callyd wyse,	329	Garlande	616
His commedy, Achademios callyd by name;	346	Garlande	1184

CALLYDST
Thow callyst me scallyd, thou callydst me mad;	132	Garnesche5	116

CALLYING
So myche callying on, and so smalle takyng hede;	245	Speke Parott	471

CALLYNGE
I, callynge to mynde the great auctoryte	46	Bowge	8

CALLYST
Thow callyst me scallyd, thou callydst me mad;	132	Garnesche5	116
What! Callyst thou me a donnyshe crowe?	170	Magnyfycence	1095

CALODEMONYALL
As well calodemonyall /As to cacademonyall,	299	Why Come Ye	809

CALS
And cals them cankerd knaves.	287	Why Come Ye	335

CALSTOCKE
Nor worth a sowre calstocke.	287	Why Come Ye	355

CALVYS HEDES
So braynles calvys hedes, so many shepis taylys;	245	Speke Parott	484

CAM
Where hathe your dwellynge ben, er ye cam here?	53	Bowge	247
As thou arte, one that cam but yesterdaye,	55	Bowge	328
Japhet, Cam, and Sem,	77	Phy Sparrow	244
To heven he shall, from heven he cam.	86	Phy Sparrow	582
I understonde to soone ye cam,	114	Scot Kynge	39
From whens that mastyfe cam.	298	Why Come Ye	777
To the court why I cam not,	299	Why Come Ye	827
Sem, Japheth, or Cam.	301	Why Come Ye	899
But Phebus was formest of all that cam theder;	320	Garlande	287
And turne home ageyne, for they cam al to late.	329	Garlande	605
How a do cam trippyng in at the rerewarde,	351	Garlande	1385
Whiche redde on still, as it cam to her syght,	354	Garlande	1493

CAMAMELL
Reflaring rosabell, /The flagrant camamell;	340	Garlande	978

CAME
To whome there came another gentylwoman.	48	Bowge	84
And whan he came walkynge soberly,	51	Bowge	190
Harvy Ha[f]ter came lepynge, lyghte as lynde.	52	Bowge	231
Hafter] 'Haster' †Wynkyn de Worde 1499, 1510, Marshe 1568			
To see Johan Dawes, that came but yesterdaye,	54	Bowge	301
Wyth that came Ryotte, russhynge all at ones,	56	Bowge	344
Anone Dyscymular came where I stode.	58	Bowge	427
Came pressynge in one in a wonder araye.	60	Bowge	499
Came for to slee me of mortall entente.	61	Bowge	529
And as they came, the shypborde faste I hente,	61	Bowge	530
Came runnynge with a dow,	63	Hauke	72
And came of a gentyll stocke,	86	Phy Sparrow	589
I understand, to sone ye came.	118	Ag Scottes	130
And grotes many one or I came to your presence.	150	Magnyfycence	339
And he that came fro to this place	150	Magnyfycence	372
By the masse, I am glad I came hyder	176	Magnyfycence	1286
Whylest I came to you, a lytell here besyde.	187	Magnyfycence	1686
And than came haltyng Jone	222	El Rummynge	326
Than thydder came dronken Ales	223	El Rummynge	351
And thyder came an hepe /Of mylstones in a route.'	223	El Rummynge	361
thyder] 'there' †Lant 1545, Kynge & Marche 1554, Day 1560, Marshe 1568			
Then came in a genet,	224	El Rummynge	392
But of all this thronge /One came them amonge,	225	El Rummynge	446

109

CAMMOCKE — CAN

	Page	Title	Line
There came an old rybybe;	227	El Rummynge	492
In came another dant, /With a gose and a gant.	227	El Rummynge	515
From whens that he came,	290	Why Come Ye	465
He came of the sank royall	291	Why Come Ye	493
But how that came aboute,	296	Why Come Ye	693
The lesarde came lepyng, and sayd that he must,	315	Garlande	104
There came John Bochas with his volumys grete;	322	Garlande	365
Some came to tell treuth, some came to lye,	326	Garlande	510
Some came to tell treuth, some came to lye,	326	Garlande	510
Some came to flater, some came to spye.	326	Garlande	511
Some came to flater, some came to spye.	326	Garlande	511
Came towarde me, and smylid halfe in game;	327	Garlande	529
With suche communycacyon as came to our mynde;	328	Garlande	562

CAMMOCKE
As right as a cammocke croked!	281	Why Come Ye	117

CAMOKE
Crokyd as a camoke, and as a kowe calfles,	122	Garnesche1	30

CAMOUSLY
Her nose somdele hoked /And camously croked,	215	El Rummynge	28

CAN
	Page	Title	Line
When he is well, yet can he not rest.	36	Coystrowne1	7
But for in his gamut carp that he can,	37	Coystrowne1	13
Curyowsly he can both counter and knak	37	Coystrowne1	17
What though ye can cownter Custodi nos?	38	Coystrowne1	57
It can be no counsell that is cryed at the cros.	43	Balettys2	36
Can touche a troughte and cloke it subtylly	46	Bowge	11
troughte] 'trouth' Wynkyn de Worde 1510, Marshe 1568; it] not in Marshe 1568			
Shyfte now therwith, let see, as ye can,	48	Bowge	99
But, an he can Bone aventure take,	48	Bowge	102
an] 'and' Wynkyn de Worde 1510, Marshe 1568			
There can no favour nor frendshyp hym forsake.	48	Bowge	103
Ye be an apte man, as ony can be founde	50	Bowge	155
'Pryncys of youghte', can ye synge by rote?	53	Bowge	253
And yet unneth I can have my lyvynge;	53	Bowge	275
It is a curtel that well can wynche and praunce;	57	Bowge	411
curtel] 'curtet' †Wynkyn de Worde 1499, 1510			
Save hym that nought can: scrypture sayth soo.	58	Bowge	448
The drevyll stondeth to herken, and he can.	59	Bowge	486
In every poynte that I can do or saye;	60	Bowge	496
In] 'To' Marshe 1568			
That if ye can fynde	78	Phy Sparrow	260
No man can be sure	81	Phy Sparrow	370
The best that we can,	84	Phy Sparrow	491
He can do nothyng ellys.	84	Phy Sparrow	494
Though I can rede and spell,	87	Phy Sparrow	612
And tell can a great pece	87	Phy Sparrow	630
What though I can fram	88	Phy Sparrow	659
though] 'thought' †Kele 1545.2			
And though I can expounde	88	Phy Sparrow	672
And can but lytell skyll	90	Phy Sparrow	755
No man that can amend	91	Phy Sparrow	809
No slepe can him catch,	95	Phy Sparrow	928
How that she can were /Gorgiously her gere;	101	Phy Sparrow	1178
No man can let me thynke,	101	Phy Sparrow	1199
His Dirige, her commendacyon /Can be no derogacyon,	103	Phy Sparrow	1277
Ye shew ryght well what good ye can;	117	Ag Scottes	60
You mantyca[re], ye maltaperte, ye can bothe wins and whyne;	123	Garnesche2	4
mantycare] 'mantyca' †MS Harley 367			
For reson can I non fynde	126	Garnesche3	104
Moche of thy maneres I ca[n] blasy.	130	Garnesche5	32
can] 'cam' †MS Harley 367			
To rayle with me that the can hyt.	132	Garnesche5	119
Thy fonde face can me nat fray.	134	Garnesche5	171
Worketh more mischiefe than can be tolde;	137	Ven Tongues	8
With, 'I can tel you what such a man said,	139	Ven Tongues	71
To that ye say I can well condyssende.	141	Magnyfycence	39
Or howe can you prove that there is felycyte,	142	Magnyfycence	77
Can be content with Measure presence.	143	Magnyfycence	86
For no dyscorde that any man can sawe;	145	Magnyfycence	187
This lynkyd chayne of love that can unbynde.	146	Magnyfycence	201
That with your lorde and mayster so pertly can prate!	149	Magnyfycence	305
That no man can scape but they hym cache.	150	Magnyfycence	351
To counterfet I can by praty wayes:	152	Magnyfycence	424
By God, man, bothe his pagent and thyne he can play.	154	Magnyfycence	505
That we can no better than so.	155	Magnyfycence	550
Can you remedy for a tysyke	156	Magnyfycence	555
What the devyll ayleth you? Can you not agree?	158	Magnyfycence	636
Why, can ye not put out that foule freke?	158	Magnyfycence	657
I can dyssemble; I can bothe laughe and grone;	159	Magnyfycence	698
I can dyssemble; I can bothe laughe and grone;	159	Magnyfycence	698
Playne delynge and I can never agre.	159	Magnyfycence	699
Full fewe that can themselfe of me excuse.	160	Magnyfycence	706
Devysynge the meanes and wayes that I can,	160	Magnyfycence	708
I can fede forth a fole and lede hym by the eyre;	160	Magnyfycence	712
Thus can I lerne you, syrs, to bere the devyls sacke;	160	Magnyfycence	721
Paynte to a purpose good countenaunce I can,	160	Magnyfycence	724
And craftely can I grope howe every man is mynded.	160	Magnyfycence	725

	Page	Title	Line
Ye, so I can devyse my gere after the cowrtly maner.	161	Magnyfycence	766
What the devyll! Can ye agre no better?	162	Magnyfycence	795
Cockes bones! I ne tell can	162	Magnyfycence	801
Or whiche of you can do most.	162	Magnyfycence	803
Ye, and do ryght good servyce he can.	163	Magnyfycence	822
That I can were /Courtly my gere!	163	Magnyfycence	833
But nowe what tydynges can you tell? Let se.	166	Magnyfycence	928
Yf I can fynde out	168	Magnyfycence	993
I can fynde fantasyes where none is;	169	Magnyfycence	1041
Ye, but I can somwhat more of the letter.	170	Magnyfycence	1066
By God, I can tell the; and I wyll.	170	Magnyfycence	1071
Than thou can in yerys seven.	170	Magnyfycence	1078
No? Yes, in faythe; I can versyfy.	172	Magnyfycence	1147
Can he play well at the hoddypeke?	172	Magnyfycence	1161
Tell by thy trouth what sport can thou make.	172	Magnyfycence	1162
Why, thynkys thou he can no better skyll?	172	Magnyfycence	1172
In fayth, I can make you bothe folys, and I wyll.	172	Magnyfycence	1173
In a cote thou can play well the dyser.	173	Magnyfycence	1176
Ye, but thou can play the fole without a vyser.	173	Magnyfycence	1177
In faythe, I can do mastryes, so I can.	173	Magnyfycence	1190
In faythe, I can do mastryes, so I can.	173	Magnyfycence	1190
Nay, it is I that foles can make;	174	Magnyfycence	1213
To felowshyp with foly I can hym brynge.	174	Magnyfycence	1215
But all is foly that I can se.	176	Magnyfycence	1291
I have an hoby can make larkys to dare;	177	Magnyfycence	1342
Trymme at her tayle or a man can turne a socke.	177	Magnyfycence	1346
My inwyt delynge there can no man dyscry.	177	Magnyfycence	1356
And by crafty conveyaunce I wyll, and I can,	178	Magnyfycence	1359
Crafty Conveyaunce can cloke hymselfe frome shame,	178	Magnyfycence	1370
Why, wene you that I can kepe hym longe styll?	179	Magnyfycence	1412
What! Can ye agree thus and appose?	180	Magnyfycence	1425
Ye, of Jacke a Thrommys bybyll can ye make a glose.	180	Magnyfycence	1427
I can do nothynge but he stonde besyde.	180	Magnyfycence	1449
Syr, we can do nothynge the one without the other.	180	Magnyfycence	1450
No stormy rage agaynst me can pervayle.	181	Magnyfycence	1465
Ne by non other that any man can rehersse.	181	Magnyfycence	1490
Nor no man on molde can make me aferd.	182	Magnyfycence	1505
He is not lyvynge your maners can amend;	183	Magnyfycence	1537
A, I have spyed ye can moche broken sorowe.	184	Magnyfycence	1587
All that I can his matter for to spede.	187	Magnyfycence	1664
He can full craftely this matter brynge aboute.	187	Magnyfycence	1691
By the masse, I have done that I can,	187	Magnyfycence	1693
That wantonly can wynke and wynche with her hele.	197	Magnyfycence	2023
Of worldly welthe, alasse, who can be sure?	201	Magnyfycence	2155
For who loveth God can ayle nothynge but good.	207	Magnyfycence	2365
Howe say you, syr? Can ye these wordys grope?	207	Magnyfycence	2377
Syr, the repentaunce I have no man can wryte.	208	Magnyfycence	2392
My wylfulnesse, syr, excuse I ne can.	209	Magnyfycence	2432
Ye com hether as well as can be thought.	210	Magnyfycence	2459
Sodenly thus Fortune can bothe smyle and frowne,	212	Magnyfycence	2529
Sodenly thus Fortune can bothe smyle and frowne,	213	Magnyfycence	2536
Shewyth wysdome to them that wysdome can take:	213	Magnyfycence	2554
How none estate lyvynge of hymselfe can be sure,	213	Magnyfycence	2557
Thus none estate lyvynge of hym[selfe] can be sure, hymselfe] 'hym' †Rastell & Treveris C 1530, B	214	Magnyfycence	2564
Ich am not cast away, /That can my husband say,	220	El Rummynge	220
Suche a webbe can spyn,	221	El Rummynge	255
'Heghe, ha, ha, Parott, ye can lawghe pratylye!'	231	Speke Parott	22
'Lyke owur pus catt Parott can mewte and crye.' owur] 'your' Lant 1545, Kynge & Marche 1554, Day 1560, Marshe 1568	231	Speke Parott	24
In Greke tong Parott can bothe speke and sey,	231	Speke Parott	26
Dowche Frenshe of Paris Parot can lerne,	231	Speke Parott	29
With Dowche, with Spaynyshe, my tonge can agree;	231	Speke Parott	32
In Englysshe to God Parott can supple: supple] 'shewe propyrlye' †MS Harley 2252	231	Speke Parott	33
With my beke I can pyke my lyttel praty too;	233	Speke Parott	107
Parot can say, 'Cesar, ave,' also;	233	Speke Parott	110
For though ye can tell in Greke what is phormio,	235	Speke Parott	151
That Pety Caton can scantly construe a verse,	235	Speke Parott	178
Can skantly the tensis of his conjugacyons;	235	Speke Parott	180
Syns Dewcalyons flodde there can no clerkes rede.	244	Speke Parott	455
Syns Dewcalyons flodde there can no clerkes fynde.	244	Speke Parott	462
Syns Dewcalyons flodde, I trow, no man can tell.	245	Speke Parott	490
What can it avayle /To dryve forth a snayle,	246	Collyn Clout	1
For, as farre as I can se,	248	Collyn Clout	59
But trouth can never lye.	258	Collyn Clout	485
That clerkely is, and can /Well scrypture expounde	264	Collyn Clout	722
That goostly can heale us;	265	Collyn Clout	742
He can nothynge smatter	267	Collyn Clout	814
Can say nothynge but 'mum'.	269	Collyn Clout	905
That can hymselfe assure	271	Collyn Clout	1002
To hynder no man /As nere as I can,	274	Collyn Clout	1110
That ryght no man can fonge.	276	Collyn Clout	1197
That he ne se can	283	Why Come Ye	182
How no man can him amende!	292	Why Come Ye	531
How can he do ryght?	293	Why Come Ye	581
That therwith can mell.	296	Why Come Ye	685

CANACE—CAN NAT

	Page	Title	Line
But wele I can tell	296	Why Come Ye	686
That can bylde his dwellinge house	298	Why Come Ye	757
Moche better can devyse	298	Why Come Ye	767
For who can best lye, ...	300	Why Come Ye	858
best] not in MS Rawlinson C. 813			
We can lacke no grace, ...	301	Why Come Ye	875
Non can have protectyon	304	Why Come Ye	1011
Non can have] 'They can have no' †Kele 1545.3, Toy 1553, Kitson 1560.7, Marshe 1568			
That he can onywhere gete, ...	306	Why Come Ye	1085
For as far as they can spy	308	Why Come Ye	1172
they] 'the' †Kele 1545.3			
Holde ye your tong, ye can no goode.	310	Why Come Ye2	20
ye] (1st) not in MS Rawlinson C. 813			
Few men can tell where the hynde calfe gose.	313	Garlande	26
tell] 'telle now' MS Cotton Vitellius E.x			
Faire fall that forster that so well can bate his hownde! . . .	313	Garlande	27
well] not in MS Cotton Vitellius E.x			
Your mynde that can maynteyne so apparently;	317	Garlande	170
Some be called crafty that can pyke a purse;	317	Garlande	184
pyke] 'kit' MS Cotton Vitellius E.x			
Or elles he can nought bot whan he is at scole;	318	Garlande	205
May be brought forth, such as can be founde, ...	318	Garlande	216
Can lay any werkis that he hath compylyd, ...	318	Garlande	223
Or elles, ye know well, I can do no lesse	318	Garlande	226
There apparell farre passynge beyonde that I can tell; . . .	323	Garlande	394
With all our strength that we can brynge about, ...	324	Garlande	424
Welcome to me as hertely as herte can thynke!	327	Garlande	547
Full gloryously can he glose, thy mynde for to fele;	333	Garlande	760
He can never leve warke whylis it is wele.	333	Garlande	763
And who can worke beste now shall be asayde;	334	Garlande	775
Far, far passynge /That I can endyght, ...	341	Garlande	1017
Erst that ye can fynde	341	Garlande	1032
that] 'than' MS Cotton Vitellius E.x			
If ony recordis in noumbyr can be founde, ...	345	Garlande	1150
Let se now for hym how ye can expounde;	345	Garlande	1153
His dirige, her commendacioun /Can be no derogacyoun; . . .	348	Garlande	1270
No man lyvyng, he sayth, can be sure;	351	Garlande	1403
And though Albumasar can the enforme and ken	352	Garlande	1428
If they can spy /Circumspectly	356	Garlande	1579
they] 'thy' †Fakes 1523			
No man can tell whether.	358	Garlande2	9
If ye wele can regarde	368	Albany	360
As all men can reporte.	370	Albany	474
All men can testifye.	376	Replycacion	64
that can or may be made or objected	382	Replycacion	R
Thus can harpe and syng	384	Replycacion	344

CANACE

As Machareus /Fayre Canace, ...	338	Garlande	934

CANCOUR

Ageynst all infeccyons with cancour enflamyd, ...	331	Garlande	672
cancour] 'rancour' Marshe 1568			

CANDELMAS

On Candelmas evyn, the kalendas of May.	38	Coystrowne1	70

CANDELMES

By Candelmes day what wedder shuld holde;	352	Garlande	1442

CANDYLL

Boke, bell and candyll, /All that he myght handyll; . . .	64	Hauke	112

CANE

Of Cato the counte, acountyd the cane, ...	181	Magnyfycence	1487
Or canves of Cane, ...	302	Why Come Ye	919

CANEST

What! Canest thou all this Latyn yet, ...	172	Magnyfycence	1143
What canest thou do but play cocke wat?	173	Magnyfycence	1191

CANKARD

And wenyst thow that I know not the, cankard Abusyon? . . .	161	Magnyfycence	757
Cankard Jacke Hare, loke thou be not rusty;	161	Magnyfycence	758

CANKARDE

Your cankarde cowardnesse /And your shamfull doublenesse. . . .	368	Albany	361

CANKERD

Lyke cankerd cowardes all, ...	283	Why Come Ye	165
And cals them cankerd knaves.	287	Why Come Ye	335
Lyke cankerd curres /Ye loste your spurres;	360	Albany	33
Whan ye cankerd knaves	363	Albany	184

CANKERED

So cankered and so full	91	Phy Sparrow	778

CANNAT

I cannat let the the knave to play, ...	134	Garnesche5	169

CAN NAT

Men say, ye can nat appare;	251	Collyn Clout	191
Some can nat declyne theyr name!	253	Collyn Clout	276
Some can nat scarsly rede, ...	253	Collyn Clout	277
'They can nat kepe theyr wyves	261	Collyn Clout	572
That ye can nat espye	263	Collyn Clout	685
This can nat be brought about	267	Collyn Clout	849
The devyll can nat stop their mouthes	272	Collyn Clout	1051
And can nat tell no cause why	274	Collyn Clout	1115
can nat] 'can' Marshe 1568, MS Harley 2252			

	Page	Title	Line
For age can nat rage,	279	Why Come Ye	34
Whiche he can nat se.	291	Why Come Ye	507
They can nat well tell	295	Why Come Ye	648
That he can nat parceyve	295	Why Come Ye	661
That ye can nat byde thereby.	310	Why Come Ye2	28
I can nat tell you, but that I was brought	325	Garlande	458
Can nat be unrewarded.	378	Replycacion	139

CANNE

Let se this checke yf ye voyde canne.	148	Magnyfycence	297

CANNEST

Well cannest thou helpe a preest to synge a songe.	187	Magnyfycence	1676

CANNYST

Beryst thou any rome? Or cannyst thou do ought?	162	Magnyfycence	776
Cannyst thou helpe in faver that I myght be brought?	162	Magnyfycence	777
That thou cannyst not growe out of thy boyes gere;	170	Magnyfycence	1075

CANNOT

That be so far abusyd /They cannot be excusyd	62	Hauke	6
I cannot me refrayne	97	Phy Sparrow	1009
It cannot be denayd /But it was well convayd,	98	Phy Sparrow	1065
Is to discommende /That they cannot amend,	103	Phy Sparrow	1271
Why, wenyst thou that I cannot make the play the fon?	173	Magnyfycence	1185
That they cannot say in Greke, rydynge by the way,	234	Speke Parott	146
To suche thynges ympossybyll, reason cannot consente;	240	Speke Parott	334
Som sey they cannot my parables expresse;	242	Speke Parott	386

CAN NOT

He can not fynd it in rule nor in space:	37	Coystrownel	22
Causyth me that I can not myself refrayne,	42	Balettys2	3
I can not flater, I muste be playne to the.	50	Bowge	164
He sayth he can not well accorde with the.'	51	Bowge	185
For on the booke I can not synge a note,	53	Bowge	255
I] not in †Wynkyn de Worde 1499			
A man can not wote where to become.	59	Bowge	466
It can not be exprest /My sorowfull hevynesse,	72	Phy Sparrow	31
He can not well fly, /Nor synge tunably;	83	Phy Sparrow	483
And can not in effect	91	Phy Sparrow	771
Yet to lie upon me they can not prevayle.	138	Ven Tongues	31
I trowe ye can not say nay moche to this:	142	Magnyfycence	74
That without largesse noblenesse can not rayne.	147	Magnyfycence	265
That can not counterfet a lye,	152	Magnyfycence	413
Chanons can not counterfet but upon thre.	154	Magnyfycence	492
I can not tell you. Why aske you me?	157	Magnyfycence	628
I can not myne appetyte accomplysshe and fulfyll	160	Magnyfycence	733
That useth me. /He can not thee.	164	Magnyfycence	862
And can not set herselfe to warke,	174	Magnyfycence	1230
But some man wolde convey, and can not skyll,	178	Magnyfycence	1361
Fortune to her lawys can not abandune me;	181	Magnyfycence	1459
And that your mynde can not well be eased -	185	Magnyfycence	1610
Mesure, ye knowe wel, with hym I can not be content;	186	Magnyfycence	1656
By my truth, I can not tell you that.	188	Magnyfycence	1703
It can not contynew long prosperyously;	200	Magnyfycence	2132
I can not tell of thy dysposycyons;	203	Magnyfycence	2218
Ye, for thy langage can not the avayle.	204	Magnyfycence	2249
For the welthe of this worlde can not indure.	213	Magnyfycence	2558
For the welthe of this worlde can not indure.	214	Magnyfycence	2565
It can not be moche worse.	282	Why Come Ye	138
I can not tell you what was the occasyon.	313	Garlande	35
not tell] 'not wele tell' MS Cotton Vitellius E.x			
The fervent axes of love can not represse!	321	Garlande	315
Plainly, I can not glose,	338	Garlande	910
For in owr courte, ye wote wele, his name can not ryse	345	Garlande	1154
Is to discommende /That they can not amende,	348	Garlande	1264
They can not come agayne.	358	Garlande2	15
For thou can not but brag	366	Albany	294

CANON

Good nonne, nor good canon,	274	Collyn Clout	1098
Strawe for lawe canon,	289	Why Come Ye	416

CANONICALL

Nor no lawe canonicall	308	Why Come Ye	1159

CANONICALLY

Protestacion alway canonically prepensed, professed,	373	Replycacion	I

CANST

That thou canst not have never mercy in his syght.	205	Magnyfycence	2303

CANTELL

A cantell of Essex chese	225	El Rummynge	429

CANTERBURY

That Saynt Thomas of Canterbury gave.	251	Collyn Clout	170
'That becket them gave' Kele 1545.1, Marshe 1568			

CANTORBURY

In the regstry /Of my lorde of Cantorbury,	307	Why Come Ye	1120

CANVES

Or canves of Cane,	302	Why Come Ye	919

CAP

It had a velvet cap,	74	Phy Sparrow	120
Why holde ye on yer cap, syr, then? Yor pardone ys expyryd.	123	Garnesche2	9
Another brought her his cap	221	El Rummynge	285
For a gun stone, I say, had all to-jaggid his cap,	329	Garlande	629
to-jaggid] 'to lagged' Marshe 1568			

CAPCYOUSLY — CARE

	Page	Title	Line

CAPCYOUSLY
Ye countyr umwhyle to capcyously, and ar ye be dysiryd; 123 Garnesche2 11
CAPITAYNE
Your capitayne ranne to go, ... 360 Albany 65
CAPITALL
I compas the conveyaunce unto the capitall .... 243 Speke Parott 411
CAPYD
Ye capyd Cayfas copyous, your paltoke on your pate, ... 123 Garnesche2 20
Ye capyd Cayfas copyus, your paltoke on your pate, ... 123 Garnesche2 27
CAPYTAYNES
Counterfet capytaynes by me are mande; .... 152 Magnyfycence 436
CAPYTALL
Had gravin in it of calcydony a capytall A. .... 328 Garlande 587
CAPON
Your gorge nat endued /Without a capon stued, ... 252 Collyn Clout 216
CAPONS
An eestryche fedder of a capons tayle .... 56 Bowge 366
  An] 'And' Marshe 1568
He eateth c[a]pons stewed, ... 284 Why Come Ye 221
  capons] 'copons' †Kele 1545.3
CAPPE
Cappe, syr. I say you be to bolde. .... 157 Magnyfycence 602
Where is my cappe? I have lost my hat! .... 169 Magnyfycence 1030
With money, yf it wyll happe /To catche the forked cappe. ... 249 Collyn Clout 89
Taketh his pyllyon and his cappe .... 266 Collyn Clout 803
CAPPED
Some hatted and some capped, /Rychly bewrapped, ... 254 Collyn Clout 311
CAPPYD
Ye cappyd Cayface copious, your paltoke on your pate, ... 123 Garnesche2 6
Ye cappyd Cayface copyous, your paltoke on your pate, ... 123 Garnesche2 13
Ye cappyd Cayfas copyous, your paltoke on your pate, ... 123 Garnesche2 34
Ye cappyd Cayfas copyous, your paltoke on your pate, ... 124 Garnesche2 41
CAPTACYONS
With proper captacyons of benevolence, ... 335 Garlande 815
CAPTAINE
Against our st[r]onge captaine; .... 365 Albany 245
  stronge] 'stonge' †Marshe 1568
CAPTAYNE
Suche a captayne of [h]ors .... 366 Albany 281
  hors] 'fors' †Marshe 1568
Of suche an bolde captayne .... 366 Albany 305
CAPTEN
Syr capten of Catywade, catacumbas of Cayre, ... 122 Garnesche1 16
CAPTYFE
Take hede of this captyfe that lyeth here on grounde. .... 195 Magnyfycence 1946
CAPTYVYTE
To lyve under lawe, it is captyvyte. .... 142 Magnyfycence 75
Ye. But he is a captyvyte. .... 157 Magnyfycence 626
That Israell relesyd of theyr captyvyte, ... 181 Magnyfycence 1474
Nowe pleasure at large, nowe in captyvyte; .... 212 Magnyfycence 2519
CARBUCKYLS
With botches and carbuckyls in care I them knyt; .... 194 Magnyfycence 1902
CARBUNCLE
Her eyen relucent as carbuncle so clere, ... 183 Magnyfycence 1556
CARCASSE
Nowe must I this carcasse lyft up. .... 195 Magnyfycence 1964
CARDE
And soo outface hym with a carde of ten.' .... 55 Bowge 315
CARDERS
Dysers, carders, tumblars with gambawdis, ... 329 Garlande 608
CARDES
'Prove his wytt', sayth he, 'at cardes or dyce, ... 318 Garlande 206
CARDINALS
Hath promised to hele our cardinals eye. .... 309 Why Come Ye 1197
CARDYNALL
Of Pope Julius cardys, he ys chefe Cardynall. .... 243 Speke Parott 431
In lykewyse now the same /Cardynall is promoted, ... 293 Why Come Ye 571
Or suche chaunce shulde fall /Unto our cardynall! ...... 297 Why Come Ye 749
To purvey for our cardynall /A palace pontifycall ...... 299 Why Come Ye 811
Of my Lorde Cardynall, ... 360 Albany 60
CARDYNALLES
Promoted was he /To a cardynalles dygnyte .... 297 Why Come Ye 729
CARDYNALL HAT
The Sygne of the Cardynall Hat, ... 284 Why Come Ye 238
CARDYNALS
To my Lorde Cardynals right noble grace etc .... 372 Albany E
CARDYNALS HAT
At the Cardynals hat. .... 283 Why Come Ye 175
He ware a cardynals hat; .... 297 Why Come Ye 743
CARDYS
Of Pope Julius cardys, he ys chefe Cardynall. .... 243 Speke Parott 431
At the cardys and haserdynge. .... 309 Why Come Ye 1193
CARE
Dyamand poyntyd to rase oute hartly care 44 Balettys3 19
Who rydeth on her, he nedeth not to care, ... 57 Bowge 409
That wrowght have moche care, ... 111 Lawde 24
I care nat what thow wryght or sey; 134 Garnesche5 168
I care muche the lesse what ever they say, ... 138 Ven Tongues 36

CARECTES — CAROWE

	Page	Title	Line
With care and with thought howe Jacke shall have Gyl?	148	Magnyfycence	287
I care not, I. Tell on for me.	158	Magnyfycence	634
Whan Mesure is gone, we may slee care.	176	Magnyfycence	1324
What care I? By the masse, well sayd.	187	Magnyfycence	1671
I care not howe sone he be refused,	187	Magnyfycence	1683
With botches and carbuckyls in care I them knyt;	194	Magnyfycence	1902
For when I come, comyth sorowe and care;	195	Magnyfycence	1937
I wenyd ones never to have knowen of care.	196	Magnyfycence	1973
Of erthely thynge I have no care nor charge.	199	Magnyfycence	2081
And let us sley care!'	217	El Rummynge	111
They care not what men saye!	221	El Rummynge	260
So lytell care for the comynweall, and so myche nede;	245	Speke Parott	473
And have full lytell care	250	Collyn Clout	130
Than to be combred with care.	251	Collyn Clout	177
What care they thoughe Gyll swete,	254	Collyn Clout	321
Wherof moche care began.	297	Why Come Ye	725
That shall cast you in care,	361	Albany	112
God sende you sorow and care!	363	Albany	181
That our Savyour bare, /Whiche us redemed from care.	375	Replycacion	34

CARECTES
By carectes and conjuracyon .... 296 Why Come Ye 697

CARECTIS
Some carectis of Caldy, sum Frensshe was full good; .... 328 Garlande 585

CAREDE
They saide they forsede not nor carede not to dy. .... 31 Dol Dethe 84

CAREFULL

To suffer me so carefull to endure,	45	Balettys5	6
So urgently I am brought /Into carefull thought.	74	Phy Sparrow	107
O hatefull happe, O carefull cruelte!	198	Magnyfycence	2049
This mysery, this carefull wrechydnesse?	201	Magnyfycence	2154
Some carefull cokwoldes, some have theyr wyves curs;	317	Garlande	186
The dolefull desteny, and the carefull chaunce,	348	Garlande	1255
Finally they fall to carefull confusyon,	374	Replycacion	15

CAREFULLY
But Fortune enforsyth me so carefully to endure, ... 46 Balettys5 13

CARELES
Careles and shamlesse, /Thriftles and gracelesse .... 304 Why Come Ye 1020
   Careles] 'Marcyles' MS Rawlinson C. 813

CARIED
Caried in a cage, /As it were a cotage, ... 365 Albany 255

CARIID
I saw dyvers that were cariid away thens in cribbis, ... 330 Garlande 640

CARY

For then shall we so craftely cary	159	Magnyfycence	683
Ye be the thevys, I say, away my goodys dyd cary.	203	Magnyfycence	2239
Cary sackes to the myll,	281	Why Come Ye	110

CARYED
Or of suche a mawment /Caryed in a tent. .... 365 Albany 258

CARYETH
He caryeth a kyng in hys sleve, yf all the worlde fayle; ... 243 Speke Parott 429

CARKAS
Youre carkas to kepe, /Lyke a sely shepe, ... 365 Albany 273

CARKE
But thus the people carke, ... 249 Collyn Clout 120

CARKES
Dysdayne, I wene, [t]his comerous car[k]es hyghte. ...... 54 Bowge 294
   this] 'his' editions; carkes] 'carbes' †Wynkyn de Worde 1499, 1510, 'crabes' Marshe 1568
Thy caytyvys carkes, cours and crasy; 130 Garnesche5 31

CARLE
A knave and a carle and all of one kynde? .... 191 Magnyfycence 1820

CARLES
What! I have aspyed ye are a carles page. .... 148 Magnyfycence 288

CARLESSE
Chefe counselour was carlesse, ... 280 Why Come Ye 79

CARLYLL
Yet they ryde and rinne from Carlyll to Kent. .... 317 Garlande 196
   they ryde and rinne] 'ryde they and ryn they' MS Cotton Vitellius E.x

CARLYNG
Parrot is no pendugum, that men call a carlyng, ... 236 Speke Parott 205

CARLYS
A carlys sonne /Brought up of nought .... 165 Magnyfycence 898

CARLYSHE
O cat of carlyshe kynde, ... 78 Phy Sparrow 282
   carlyshe] 'churlyshe' Kitson 1560.6, Marshe 1568

CARMELLUS
Or frere Carmellus, ... 265 Collyn Clout 741

CARNALL
And to aqueynte you with carnall delectacyon; .... 183 Magnyfycence 1547

CAROLLIS
There was counteryng of carollis in meter and verse ..... 331 Garlande 705
   and] 'and in' Marshe 1568

CARON
Caron with his beerd hore, ... 105 Phy Sparrow 1338
Caron with his berde hore, ... 349 Garlande 1331

CAROWE
That was late slayn at Carowe .... 72 Phy Sparrow 8

CARP — CAST   Page   Title   Line

That I brought up at Carowe.   78   Phy Sparrow   281
CARP
But for in his gamut carp that he can, ...   37   Coystrownel   13
CARPE
And some of them barke, /Clatter and carpe   260   Collyn Clout   547
They carpe of us lyke crakers;   276   Collyn Clout   1189
CARPET
For alle your carpet cousshons   124   Garnesche3   11
The bysshop on his carpet   255   Collyn Clout   327
CARPETTIS
The carpettis within and tappettis of pall;   325   Garlande   474
With that the tappettis and carpettis were layd, ...   334   Garlande   787
CART
Thys Doctor Deuyas commensyd in a cart;   38   Coystrownel   55
   Deuyas] 'dellias' Marshe 1568
CARTAGE
The cytye of Cartage, ...   88   Phy Sparrow   669
Nor yet [C]ypyo, that noble Cartage wanne, ...   182   Magnyfycence   1512
   Cypyo] 'Typyo' †Rastell & Treveris C 1530, B
Of Cartage in Aphrike;   364   Albany   196
CARTER
A carter a courtyer, it is a worthy warke, ...   153   Magnyfycence   483
CART LODE
And I love you an hole cart lode.'   35   Man Margery   9
CARVEN
A cage curyowsly carven, with sylver pynne, ...   231   Speke Parott   8
CASE
And be not light of credence in no case.   34   Dol Dethe   175
Bone aventure may brynge you in suche case   49   Bowge   104
As I be saved, it is a wonder case.   53   Bowge   273
And made as I had knowen nothynge of the case -   160   Magnyfycence   719
What, frantyke Fansy, in a foles case?   169   Magnyfycence   1046
The case requyreth. Alasse, alasse, an hevy metynge!   192   Magnyfycence   1847
Never had I bene brought in this case.   196   Magnyfycence   1977
But yet, syr, nowe in this case   197   Magnyfycence   2032
This is a pyteous case: 262   Collyn Clout   626
For the wele publyke /Of preesthode in this case;   264   Collyn Clout   698
In pletynge of theyr case   287   Why Come Ye   318
It is a wonders case: 295   Why Come Ye   657
   wonders] 'wonderous' Kitson 1560.7, Marshe 1568
Ever in one case.   301   Why Come Ye   882
And set you in suche case   368   Albany   367
Some juged in this case   379   Replycacion   197
CASES
In suche maner of cases, ...   269   Collyn Clout   895
CASKET
For he coude well upon a casket wayte, ...   60   Bowge   507
The locke of a casket to make to starte.   203   Magnyfycence   2229
CASPIAN
Frome Babill towre to the hillis Caspian.'   327   Garlande   553
   Caspian] 'Gaspian' †Fakes 1523
CASSAUNDER
Colyaunder, /Swete pomaunder, /Good Cassaunder;   341   Garlande   1028
CASSETH
She cherysshe[th] him, and hym she casseth awaye.'   49   Bowge   117
   'cherysshed' †Wynkyn de Worde 1499, 1510, Marshe 1568;
   casseth] 'casteth' Wynkyn de Worde 1510, 'chasseth' Marshe 1568
CAST
Ye cast all your corage uppon such courtly haggys!   43   Balettys2   19
Ware yet, I rede you, of Fortunes double cast, ...   45   Balettys4   3
Thus up and down my mynde was drawen and cast   47   Bowge   29
Adieu, syr sumner, cast of your crowne!   117   Ag Scottes   64
All have ye lost and cast away.   119   Ag Scottes   163
Ye were to hye, ye ar cast downe.   120   Ag Scottes   177
Cast of your crowne, cast up your crowne!   120   Ag Scottes   179
Cast of your crowne, cast up your crowne!   120   Ag Scottes   179
That cast such overthwartes /Percase have hollow hartes. . .   121   Ag Scottes2   37
To you I arecte it, and cast /Therof the reformacyon. . . .   143   Magnyfycence   94
Nay. Let us our heddes togyder cast.   156   Magnyfycence   566
That Mesure were cast out of the dores.   156   Magnyfycence   568
A peryllous thynge, to cast a cat   176   Magnyfycence   1297
Call for a ca[u]dell and cast up your gorge, ...   185   Magnyfycence   1614
   caudell] 'candell' †Rastell & Treveris C 1530, B
And that ye wyll not cast hym away so sone.   186   Magnyfycence   1638
Alas! My stomake fareth as it wolde cast.   188   Magnyfycence   1726
They cast up theyr obedyence to cache me agayne;   201   Magnyfycence   2148
Ha, ha, ha! For sporte I am lyke to spewe and cast.   201   Magnyfycence   2161
Sodenly set up, and sodenly cast downe.   212   Magnyfycence   2530
Sodenly cherysshyd, and sodenly cast asyde;   212   Magnyfycence   2532
Sodenly set up, and sodenly cast downe.   213   Magnyfycence   2537
Ich am not cast away, /That can my husband say, ...   220   El Rummynge   219
Such a bedfellaw /Wold make one cast his craw.   226   El Rummynge   489
With, 'Da causales,' is cast out of the gate, ...   235   Speke Parott   174
Must cast up theyr blacke vayles   256   Collyn Clout   396
They say they wyll you cast.   273   Collyn Clout   1070
Our mare hath cast her fole, ...   281   Why Come Ye   85
We have cast up our war, ...   282   Why Come Ye   140
That was cast out of a bochers stall!   291   Why Come Ye   494

CASTE —CATO

	Page	Title	Line
In the middis a coundight, that coryously was cast,	330	Garlande	658
The cheke and the nek but a shorte cast;	351	Garlande	1401
Suche trechery /And traytory /Is all your cast.	361	Albany	101
Shall cast a beyght,	361	Albany	110
That shall cast you in care,	361	Albany	112

CASTE
	Page	Title	Line
Fynde some mene to caste him over the borde.'	54	Bowge	308
Lorde, how that I wolde caste it full rounde!	57	Bowge	396
I caste me nat to be od	124	Garnesche3	6
Caste up your curyows wrytyng,	127	Garnesche3	112
He wyl cause yow caste your crawes,	128	Garnesche3	155
Who county[th] without me is caste to fer behynde	146	Magnyfycence	214
countyth] 'countyd' †Rastell & Treveris C 1530, B			
Ye caste up then your bokes	261	Collyn Clout	596
That towres and townes and trees downe caste,	319	Garlande	262

CASTELL
	Page	Title	Line
For to the castell of Norham	114	Scot Kynge	38
Unto the castell of Norram,	118	Ag Scottes	129
studyously dyvysed at Sheryfhotten Castell,	312	Garlande	1
And of Castell Aungell the fenestrall,	351	Garlande	1387
At the castell of Warke,	359	Albany	30
At the castell of Warke.	362	Albany	148
Thus in your cowardly castell	366	Albany	279
Nowe into the castell of Bas,	366	Albany	288

CASTETH
	Page	Title	Line
Whome she hateth, she casteth in the dyche,	49	Bowge	115
hateth] 'hatch' †Wynkyn de Worde 1499, 'hateth' Wynkyn de Worde 1510, Marshe 1568			

CASTYNG
	Page	Title	Line
In castyng, in turnynge, in florisshyng of flowris,	334	Garlande	802
Castyng my syght the chambre aboute,	343	Garlande	1093

CASTRIMERGIA
	Page	Title	Line
Welcome dame Simonia, /With dame Castrimergia,	284	Why Come Ye	216

CASUALL
	Page	Title	Line
Comprehendynge the worlde casuall and transytory,	212	Magnyfycence	2511

CASUELTE
	Page	Title	Line
Such a casuelte shulde be sene	297	Why Come Ye	747
An hynde unhurt hit by casuelte, not bled	351	Garlande	1406

CASWELTE
	Page	Title	Line
Yet ther may falle soche caswelte	132	Garnesche5	121

CAT
	Page	Title	Line
Whom Gyb our cat hath slayne.	72	Phy Sparrow	27
Gyb, I saye, our cat,	72	Phy Sparrow	28
That cat specyally,	78	Phy Sparrow	278
O cat of carlyshe kynde,	78	Phy Sparrow	282
carlyshe] 'churlyshe' Kitson 1560.6, Marshe 1568			
So thou, foule cat that thou arte,	79	Phy Sparrow	302
The false cat hath the slayne!	80	Phy Sparrow	330
By Gyb, our cat savage,	81	Phy Sparrow	375
A peryllous thynge, to cast a cat	176	Magnyfycence	1297
But, 'Drynke,' styll, 'Drynke, /And let the cat wynke!	222	El Rummynge	306
'But ware the cat, Parot, ware the fals cat!'	233	Speke Parott	99
'But ware the cat, Parot, ware the fals cat!'	233	Speke Parott	99
And wele wotith the cat whos berde she likkith.	352	Garlande	1438

CATACUMBAS
	Page	Title	Line
Syr capten of Catywade, catacumbas of Cayre,	122	Garnesche1	16

CATCH
	Page	Title	Line
No slepe can him catch,	95	Phy Sparrow	928

CATCHE
	Page	Title	Line
Myght catche the in theyr pawes,	79	Phy Sparrow	288
Methynke she is well becked to catche a rat.	166	Magnyfycence	927
They catche that catche may, kepe and holde fast,	189	Magnyfycence	1750
They catche that catche may, kepe and holde fast,	189	Magnyfycence	1750
Mary, Cryst graunt ye catche no colde on your fete!	191	Magnyfycence	1803
With money, yf it wyll happe /To catche the forked cappe.	249	Collyn Clout	89
To catche wynde with theyr ventayles.	256	Collyn Clout	398
For to catche more and more:	260	Collyn Clout	569
To catche that catche may,	280	Why Come Ye	51
To catche that catche may,	280	Why Come Ye	51
Whan the flye net was set for to catche a cote,	351	Garlande	1379

CATCHED
	Page	Title	Line
She pynched her pynyon, by God, and catched harme.	191	Magnyfycence	1810

CATE
	Page	Title	Line
Of Felyce fetewse and lytell prety Cate,	56	Bowge	370
Gyll swetis and Cate spynnys!	302	Why Come Ye	926
Cate] not in MS Rawlinson C. 813			

CATELYNE
	Page	Title	Line
With Salusty ageinst Lucius Catelyne,	321	Garlande	331

CATELL
	Page	Title	Line
But I have thy pultre, and thou hast my catell.	171	Magnyfycence	1135

CATHEDRALL
	Page	Title	Line
Theyr churches cathedrall.	271	Collyn Clout	979

CATYWADE
	Page	Title	Line
Syr capten of Catywade, catacumbas of Cayre,	122	Garnesche1	16

CATO
	Page	Title	Line
Of Cato the counte, acountyd the cane,	181	Magnyfycence	1487
For how shulde Cato els be callyd wyse,	315	Garlande	123

CATTE —CAWTE

	Page	Title	Line
CATTE			
With, 'Let the catte wynke!	258	Collyn Clout	457
CATTES			
Of cattes wylde and tame;	78	Phy Sparrow	276
These vylanous false cattes	80	Phy Sparrow	338
Aboute the cattes necke,	250	Collyn Clout	164
Within the cattes eare	298	Why Come Ye	758
CATULLUS			
Flaccus nor Catullus with hym may nat compare,	383	Replycacion	336
CAUDELL			
Call for a ca[u]dell and cast up your gorge,	185	Magnyfycence	1614
caudell] 'candell' †Rastell & Treveris C 1530, B			
CAUGHT			
Caught Phyllyp by the head,	81	Phy Sparrow	377
But whan they have ones caught	252	Collyn Clout	229
But Marione Clarione was caught with a colde colde,	352	Garlande	1443
a colde colde] 'a colde' Marshe 1568			
and whan they have ones superciliusly caught	374	Replycacion	1
CAUGHTE			
Caughte penne and ynke, and wroth this lytell boke.	61	Bowge	532
wroth] 'wrote' Wynkyn de Worde 1510, Marshe 1568			
CAUNTERBURY			
Of the Tales of Caunterbury	87	Phy Sparrow	614
From Calys to Dovyr, to Caunterbury in Kente,	240	Speke Parott	340
CAUSE			
And if ye lyst to know the cause why so,	44	Balettys3	38
That, so to saye, I had gyven her no cause.	48	Bowge	75
And this the cause doth shrynke.	66	Hauke	159
And now the cause is thus,	80	Phy Sparrow	363
What the cause may be /Of this perplexite!	106	Phy Sparrow	1369
Cause have they none other /But for that he was brother,	120	Ag Scottes2	13
have they] 'they have' Day 1560, Marshe 1568			
brother] 'hys brother' Day 1560, Marshe 1568			
He wyl cause yow caste your crawes,	128	Garnesche3	155
To tell you the cause me semeth it no nede.	140	Magnyfycence	8
Lyberte in some cause becomyth a gentyll mynde -	146	Magnyfycence	212
But nowe a dayes to stryke I have grete cause,	194	Magnyfycence	1918
Sothely to repent me I have grete cause;	209	Magnyfycence	2434
Jereboseth is Ebrue, who lyst the cause dyscus.	232	Speke Parott	67
cause] 'law' Day 1560, Marshe 1568			
Maner of cause to mone.	258	Collyn Clout	479
Have no cause to say	273	Collyn Clout	1093
have] 'hath' †Godfray 1531, 'have' MS Harley 2252			
And can nat tell no cause why	274	Collyn Clout	1115
can nat] 'can' Marshe 1568, MS Harley 2252			
Perceyve the cause why:	290	Why Come Ye	459
To cause the commune weale	298	Why Come Ye	770
The cause why Demostenes so famously is brutid	316	Garlande	155
Cause me to cese, /Amonge this prese,	339	Garlande	957
Yet nowe doutles ye geve me cause	341	Garlande	1041
For nowe dowtles ye geve me cause	342	Garlande	1049
Wherfore doutles ye geve me cause	342	Garlande	1057
What the cause may be /Of this perplexyte.	350	Garlande	1362
Whiche, if they be happy, have cause to beware	353	Garlande	1474
For the cause is this,	361	Albany	87
CAUSED			
Caused me of adversyte to fall in subjeccyon.	209	Magnyfycence	2425
And caused me also to use to moche lyberte,	209	Magnyfycence	2445
That caused you to devise	372	Albany	526
CAUSELES			
That mastres Punt put yow of, yt was nat alle causeles;	122	Garnesche1	32
O causeles cowardes, O hartles hardynes,	242	Speke Parott	390
CAUSES			
Expoundynge out theyr clauses, /And leve theyr owne causes.	249	Collyn Clout	101
Delay causes so longe	276	Collyn Clout	1196
CAUSETH			
Causeth him to gryn /And rejoyce therin;	94	Phy Sparrow	926
That causeth me /Studious to be	95	Phy Sparrow	959
Causeth myne hert to lepe;	97	Phy Sparrow	1015
That causeth I loke so donny.'	224	El Rummynge	400
CAUSIS			
For whos causis ye slew hym with your awne hande.	31	Dol Dethe	68
CAUSYTH			
Causyth me that I can not myself refrayne,	42	Balettys2	3
CAVELL			
Ye, wylte thou, hangman? I say, thou cavell!	202	Magnyfycence	2190
CAVES			
Must crepe in to your caves	363	Albany	185
CAWDELS			
Where you were wonte to have cawdels for your hede,	197	Magnyfycence	2008
CAWGHTE			
Lyacon of Libyk and Lydy hathe cawghte hys pray:	239	Speke Parott	289
CAWRY-MAWRY			
Some loke strawry, /Some cawry-mawry;	218	El Rummynge	150
CAWSYTHE			
Whyche cawsythe pore suters have many a hongry mele;	239	Speke Parott	311
CAWTE			
Ye be nat cawte in an hempen snare.	133	Garnesche5	163

CEASE —CHALYNGYR   Page   Title   Line

CEASE
To cease me semeth best, ... 220   El Rummynge   235
I shall breke your palettes, /Wythout ye now cease!' 223   El Rummynge   349
CEFAS
And the sandes of Cefas begyn to waste and fade, ... 239   Speke Parott   281
     Cefas] 'Tefas' †MS Harley 2252
CELESTYNE
Than Phebus in his spere celestyne, ... 47   Bowge   61
CENTAURES
One of the Centaures, /Or Onocentaures, /Or Hipocentaures; . . 104   Phy Sparrow   1294
CENTAWRIS
One of the Centawris, /Or Onocentauris, /Or Hippocentauris; . . 348   Garlande   1287
CERBERUS
Wher Cerberus doth barke, ... 73   Phy Sparrow   85
Then Cerberus the cur couching in the kenel of hel; 140   Ven Tongues   80
That made Cerberus to cache, the cur dogge of hell, ... 182   Magnyfycence   1495
CERCULETT
Abowte my necke a cerculett lyke the ryche rubye, ... 231   Speke Parott   17
CEREMONIALLYS
After ceremoniallys; 66   Hauke   173
CERTAYNE
But yet certayne /I wyll be playne, ... 95   Phy Sparrow   966
     Be] 'me' †Kele 1545.2
With her certayne /I wyll remayne 112   Calliope   21
In a certayne stede /Bysyde Lederhede. 217   El Rummynge   97
Under a certayne constellacion, ... 296   Why Come Ye   698
And a certayne fumygacion 296   Why Come Ye   699
For to love a certayne body 296   Why Come Ye   703
For certayne envectyfys, yet wrote he none ill, ... 315   Garlande   96
     certayne envectyfys] 'that he enveiyd' MS Cotton Vit.E.x
A Replycacion Agaynst Certayne Yong Scolers Abjured of Late, . 373   Replycacion   I
of certayne sophystycate scolers 373   Replycacion   I
CERTEYNTE
The Bowge of Courte it hyghte for certeynte. 47   Bowge   49
     certeynte] 'certeynet' †Wynkyn de Worde 1499, 'certayne'
     Wynkyn de Worde 1510, 'certeynte' Marshe 1568
CESAR
Of Judas Machabeus, /And of Cesar Julious; 88   Phy Sparrow   662
Nor Cesar July, that no man myght withstande, ... 181   Magnyfycence   1482
With tryumphes of Cesar 270   Collyn Clout   956
CESE
There was moche noyse, anone one cryed, 'Cese!' 47   Bowge   46
Cause me to cese, /Amonge this prese, ... 339   Garlande   957
CHACE
To put where he lyst, foly hath fre chace; 177   Magnyfycence   1329
We will so folowe in the chace 371   Albany   503
CHAFER
Yet counterfet chafer is but evyll corne. 153   Magnyfycence   450
CHAFFER
What though our chaffer be never so dere, ... 48   Bowge   89
Small chaffer doth ease /Sometyme, now and than. 222   El Rummynge   314
Deyntes for dammoysels, chaffer far-fet; 234   Speke Parott   129
CHAFFRE
This royall chaffre that is shypped here 47   Bowge   54
CHAYN
Bot men say thei wer lynked with a double chayn 31   Dol Dethe   75
Somtyme a prety chayn, ... 88   Phy Sparrow   688
CHAYNE
That lyberte be lynkyd with the chayne of countenaunce, ... 141   Magnyfycence   44
This lynkyd chayne of love that can unbynde. 146   Magnyfycence   201
CHAYNES
Of Lucyfer in his chaynes, ... 304   Why Come Ye   991
     Lucyfer] 'Lucyfers' †Kele 1545.3
CHAYRE
For Greci fari so occupyeth the chayre, ... 235   Speke Parott   163
Where the noble Cowntes of Surrey in a chayre 333   Garlande   769
Doctours of the chayre in the Vyntre 374   Replycacion   8
CHALANGAR
Skelton Lauryate Defender Agenst Master Garnesche Chalangar, . 122   Garnesche2   I
CHALANNGER
Welle Be Seyn Crysteovyr Chalannger, et cetera 124   Garnesche3   I
CHALENGE
In your chalenge, Syr Chystyn, to cale me knave? 121   Garnesche1   7
In yor chalenge, Syr Chesten, to calle me a knave? 122   Garnesche1   14
In yor chalenge, Syr Chesten, to cal me a knave? 122   Garnesche1   21
In yor chalenge, Syr Chesten, to calle me a knave? 122   Garnesche1   28
In yor chalenge, Syr Chesten, to calle me a knave? 122   Garnesche1   35
Chalenge yor selfe for a fole, call me no more knave. 122   Garnesche1   42
Me for to chalenge that of your chalennge makyth so lytyll fors. 123   Garnesche2   19
CHALENGER
Skelton Lauriate Defender Agenst Master Garnesche Chalenger, . 121   Garnesche1   I
CHALENNGE
Me for to chalenge that of your chalennge makyth so lytyll fors. 123   Garnesche2   19
CHALYNGYD
Sithe ye have me chalyngyd, Master Garnesche, ... 121   Garnesche1   1
CHALYNGYR
Soche an odyr chalyngyr cowde me no man wysch, ... 121   Garnesche1   3

CHALYS — CHASE

	Page	Title	Line
CHALYS			
Into my chalys at mas,	66	Hauke	184
Nec magis bestialis /That synggys with a chalys;	70	Hauke	327
Boke and chalys gone quyte;	257	Collyn Clout	407
CHALKE			
Why? Is he crossed than with a chalke?	166	Magnyfycence	950
Were fayne with a chalke /To score on the balke,	230	El Rummynge	614
CHAMBER			
Bere them to your chamber.'	229	El Rummynge	604
CHAMBRE			
Theyr chambre thus to dresse	270	Collyn Clout	975
That in the Chambre of Sterres	283	Why Come Ye	188
Castyng my syght the chambre aboute,	343	Garlande	1093
CHAMBRES			
Theyr chambres well sene,	270	Collyn Clout	955
The chambres hangid with clothes of arace;	325	Garlande	475
CHAMPYON			
He is our noble champyon,	114	Scot Kynge	25
CHANON			
Good frere, nor good chanon,	273	Collyn Clout	1097
CHANONS			
Chanons can not counterfet but upon thre.	154	Magnyfycence	492
CHAPELET			
upon a goodly Garlande or Chapelet of Laurell	312	Garlande	I
To worke me this chapelet by goode advysemente.	334	Garlande	807
In my goodly chapelet,	339	Garlande	970
upon a goodly Garlonde or Chapelet of Laurell,	358	Garlande2	R
CHAPELLETTES			
They made, with chapellettes and garlandes grene;	331	Garlande	684
CHAPITER			
Of suche an endarkid chapiter sum season.	315	Garlande	108
CHAPLAYNE			
A chaplayne of trust, /Layth all in the dust.	253	Collyn Clout	283
CHAPLEYNE			
To have been a chapleyne,	295	Why Come Ye	643
CHARBUNCLES			
With balassis and charbuncles the borders did shyne;	345	Garlande	1166
CHARE			
Right shall the foxis chare,	111	Lawde	22
Twyse! set hym a chare, or reche hym a stol	318	Garlande	208
Twyse] 'Twyshe' Marshe 1568, MS Cotton Vitellius E.x			
Item Apollo that whirllid up his chare,	353	Garlande	1471
CHARES			
Howe they ryde in goodly chares,	270	Collyn Clout	961
CHARGE			
That shall be theyr charge;	83	Phy Sparrow	457
With othyr menys charge;	129	Garnesche3	188
For whiche ende goth forwarde ye take lytell charge.	148	Magnyfycence	296
Of erthely thynge I have no care nor charge.	199	Magnyfycence	2081
For your spiryutall charge,	264	Collyn Clout	692
Wyll charge and dyscharge,	267	Collyn Clout	835
Strongly enbateld, moche costious of charge.	328	Garlande	570
Of what charge so ever ye lay ageinst me;	344	Garlande	1138
CHARITE			
Whose charite wele regarded	378	Replycacion	138
CHARYTE			
Amen, for saynt charyte	115	Scot Kynge	E
Wolde take, in the way of counterfet charyte,	154	Magnyfycence	489
Then for to begge theyr mete for charyte.	198	Magnyfycence	2041
Of farvent charyte I quenche out the bronde;	205	Magnyfycence	2287
Farewell humylyte, /Farewell good charyte!	261	Collyn Clout	592
Of your inward charyte;	300	Why Come Ye	838
Amen, /Of your inward charyte.	300	Why Come Ye	840
CHARLEMAYN			
Wryteth how Charlemayn	296	Why Come Ye	689
Wrought to Charlemayn the king,	296	Why Come Ye	701
CHARLEMAYNE			
To Rome, to Charlemayne,	88	Phy Sparrow	653
CHARME			
With a charme or twayne,	77	Phy Sparrow	206
And with good ale barme /She could make a charme	226	El Rummynge	456
CHARMYNG			
As wychecraft or charmyng;	295	Why Come Ye	665
CHARTER			
In the charter of dottage	255	Collyn Clout	366
Some shewid his salfe cundight, some shewid his charter,	326	Garlande	503
salfe cundight] 'safeconduct' Marshe 1568;			
charter] 'chart' Marshe 1568			
CHASE			
And in the holy place /She mutyd there a chase	63	Hauke	62
Baile, baile at yow bothe, frantyke folys! Follow on the chase!	123	Garnesche2	31
And all wayes to chase	264	Collyn Clout	699
But olde servauntes ye chase	273	Collyn Clout	1077
Folowynge the chase	301	Why Come Ye	872
Marke me that chase	301	Why Come Ye	883
me] 'well' MS Rawlinson C. 813			
And chase them thorowe the muse	380	Replycacion	212

CHASETH —CHECTE   Page   Title   Line

CHASETH
Chaseth away Phebus bryght, ...   86   Phy Sparrow   572
CHAST
To kepe his flesshe chast   284   Why Come Ye   219
The Byble makith; with whos chast lyvynge   336   Garlande   846
CHAT
What nede you with hym thus prate and chat?   180   Magnyfycence   1434
Of bysshoppes they chat, ...   263   Collyn Clout   672
CHATERYNGE
To claterynge, to chaterynge, to shorte, and to farre, ...   199   Magnyfycence   2096
CHATYNG
With chatyng and rechatyng, ...   380   Replycacion   217
CHATTER
The fleckyd pye to chatter   81   Phy Sparrow   397
CHATTERS
He chydeth and he chatters, /He prayeth and he patters; . . .   247   Collyn Clout   21
    prayeth] 'prates' Kele 1545.1, Marshe 1568, 'pratythe'
    MS Harley 2252
CHATTRYNGE
And the chattrynge swallow, ...   82   Phy Sparrow   404
CHAUCER
Chaucer, that famus clerke, ...   91   Phy Sparrow   800
And maister Chaucer, that nobly enterprysyd   323   Garlande   388
Mayster Chaucer to Skelton   323   Garlande   R
'O noble Chaucer, whos pullisshyd eloquence   324   Garlande   421
CHAUMBER
She brought me to a goodly chaumber of astate, ...   333   Garlande   768
    to] 'into' MS Cotton Vitellius E.x
CHAUNCE
and Muche Lamentable Chaunce   29   Dol Dethe   I
O dolorous chaunce of Fortuns fraward hande!   32   Dol Dethe   110
Till the chaunce ran ageyne hym of Fortuns double dyse. . . .   33   Dol Dethe   140
Of ther good lord the fate and dedely chaunce.   34   Dol Dethe   189
Of fortune this the chaunce /Standeth on varyaunce: 81   Phy Sparrow   366
To pronostycate truly the chaunce of fortunys dyse;   234   Speke Parott   136
Fortune may chaunce to flytte, ...   271   Collyn Clout   994
Or suche chaunce shulde fall /Unto our cardynall!   297   Why Come Ye   748
The dolefull desteny, and the carefull chaunce, ...   348   Garlande   1255
CHAUNCELAR
That he made him his chauncelar   297   Why Come Ye   732
CHAUNCERY
In the Chauncery where he syttes, ...   287   Why Come Ye   326
CHAUNGE
But she wolde chaunge his mood, ...   100   Phy Sparrow   1158
CHAUNGED
Chaunged to a dere, ...   79   Phy Sparrow   299
Was chaunged to an harte: 79   Phy Sparrow   301
Nay, nay. He hath chaunged his, and I have chaunged myne. . .   155   Magnyfycence   518
Nay, nay. He hath chaunged his, and I have chaunged myne. . .   155   Magnyfycence   518
CHAUNGES
And where you had chaunges of ryche aray, ...   197   Magnyfycence   2010
CHAUNTECLERE
Chaunteclere, our coke, ...   84   Phy Sparrow   495
CHAUNTERS
Our chaunters shalbe the cuckoue, ...   82   Phy Sparrow   428
CHAUNTYNG
The lusty chauntyng nyghtyngale;   82   Phy Sparrow   420
Your chorlyshe chauntyng ys all o lay.   129   Garnesche5   6
CHAUSER
In Chauser I am sped, ...   91   Phy Sparrow   788
CHAWCER
Gower, Chawcer, Lydgate, theis thre   343   Garlande   1101
CHAWNTYD
that curyowsly chawntyd, and curryshly cowntred, ...   36   Coystrowne   I
CHECKE
He counteth in his countenaunce to checke with the best: . .   37   Coystrowne1   44
Let se this checke yf ye voyde canne.   148   Magnyfycence   297
A Tyborne checke /Shall breke his necke.   165   Magnyfycence   910
As malypert tavernars that checke with theyr betters, ...   178   Magnyfycence   1362
For drede to have a checke.   250   Collyn Clout   165
CHECKED
His cote was checked with patches rede and blewe;   56   Bowge   358
    checked] 'checkered' Marshe 1568
Crossed? Ye, checked out of consayte.   166   Magnyfycence   951
Thus dayly they be decked, /Taunted and checked, ...   294   Why Come Ye   612
CHECKE MATE
I wyll not use you to play with me checke mate.   149   Magnyfycence   307
And he wyll play checke mate /With ryall majeste   293   Why Come Ye   588
CHECKER
And in the Checker he them cheks, ...   287   Why Come Ye   338
CHECKYNGES
Hennes, checkynges, and pygges.   284   Why Come Ye   223
CHECKMATE
Lost is your game, ye are checkmate.   118   Ag Scottes   128
Hath played so checkmate   271   Collyn Clout   1012
CHECTE
Wherfore ye are well checte, ...   380   Replycacion   238

121

CHEF —CHERLEMAYNE

CHEF
	Page	Title	Line
He was your chyfteyne, your shelde, your chef defens,	30	Dol Dethe	57
Of knightis, of squyers, chef lord of toure and toune,	33	Dol Dethe	132
To sorowfull harttis chef comfort and solace,	34	Dol Dethe	206

CHEFE
Nowe that ye have me chefe ruler assyngned,	146	Magnyfycence	202
For of noblenesse the chefe poynt is to be lyberall,	211	Magnyfycence	2487
Of Pope Julius cardys, he ys chefe Cardynall.	243	Speke Parott	431
Chefe counselour was carlesse,	280	Why Come Ye	79
The chefe of his owne counsell,	295	Why Come Ye	647
Chefe rote of his makynge.	298	Why Come Ye	755
But the chefe of your fayre	301	Why Come Ye	909
Whos flagraunt flower was chefe preservatyve	330	Garlande	671
Your chefe cheftayne, /Voyde of all brayne,	360	Albany	48
Of poetes chefe poete, saint Jerome dothe wright,	383	Replycacion	330

CHEFTAYN
Daryus, the doughty cheftayn of Perse -	181	Magnyfycence	1488

CHEFTAYNE
Your chefe cheftayne, /Voyde of all brayne,	360	Albany	48

CHEYNES
That lyeth in cheynes bounde,	74	Phy Sparrow	90

CHEKE
She cheryshed hym both cheke and chyn	42	Balettys1	9
A warte upon her cheke,	97	Phy Sparrow	1043
He coude not devyse the lest poynt of your cheke;	337	Garlande	896
The cheke and the nek but a shorte cast;	351	Garlande	1401

CHEKED
Tyll he cheked at the fyst,	297	Why Come Ye	735

CHEKE MATE
Thow ye prate lyke prowde Pylate, beware of cheke mate.	123	Garnesche2	14
Tho ye prate lyke prowde Pylate, beware of cheke mate.	123	Garnesche2	21
Thow ye prate lyke prowde Pylate, beware of cheke mate.	123	Garnesche2	28
Thow ye prate lyke prowde Pylate, beware of cheke mate.	123	Garnesche2	35
Thow ye prate lyke prowde Pylate, beware of cheke mate.	124	Garnesche2	42

CHEKES
With his ledder ey, /And chekes dry;	94	Phy Sparrow	909

CHEKMATE
Of confuse tantum avoydynge the chekmate.	236	Speke Parott	196

CHEK MATE
Gyve up your game, ye playe chek mate;	114	Scot Kynge	37
Thow ye prate lyke prowde Pylate, beware yet of chek mate.	123	Garnesche2	7
And mate you with chek mate.	368	Albany	386

CHEKMATYD
Oure days be datyd /To be chekmatyd,	39	Coystrowne3	30

CHEKS
And in the Checker he them cheks,	287	Why Come Ye	338

CHEKT
Withowte thou leve thou shalt be chekt,	132	Garnesche5	109

CHEMERAS
By Chemeras flames, /And all the dedly names	105	Phy Sparrow	1330
By Chemeras flamys, /And all the dedely namys	349	Garlande	1323

CHEPE
The best chepe flessh that evyr I bought.'	36	Man Margery	24
Betwene Temple Bar /And the Crosse in Chepe,	223	El Rummynge	360

CHERE
Wythe hevy chere, with dolorous hart and mynd,	34	Dol Dethe	176
Sayenge to me, 'Broder, be of good chere,	48	Bowge	86
Er this, whan that ye made me royall chere.	53	Bowge	249
Yes, syr, with ryght good chere.	143	Magnyfycence	112
Where mennes belyes is mesured, there is no chere;	189	Magnyfycence	1742
But nowe let us make mery and good chere.	204	Magnyfycence	2261
But ugly of chere,	214	El Rummynge	14
Jupyter for Saturne darre make no royall chere;	242	Speke Parott	399
Out of theyr cloyster and quere /With an hevy chere,	256	Collyn Clout	395
And of there bounte they made me godely chere	323	Garlande	398
Of Pliades he prechid with ther drowsy chere,	331	Garlande	697
Where I saw Janus, with his double chere,	354	Garlande	1515

CHERY
Emblomed lyke the chery,	97	Phy Sparrow	1038
Her lusty lyppes ruddy as the chery -	183	Magnyfycence	1558

CHERYSHED
She cheryshed hym both cheke and chyn	42	Balettys1	9

CHERYSSHED
That I have deynte to see the cherysshed thus?	55	Bowge	338
And cherysshed full dayntely,	86	Phy Sparrow	591

CHERYSSHETH
She cherysshe[th] him, and hym she casseth awaye.'	49	Bowge	117

'cherysshed] †Wynkyn de Worde 1499, 1510, Marshe 1568;
casseth] 'casteth' Wynkyn de Worde 1510, 'chasseth' Marshe 1568

CHERYSSHYD
Sodenly cherysshyd, and sodenly cast asyde;	212	Magnyfycence	2532

CHERYSTON PYTTE
To bryng all the see into a cheryston pytte,	240	Speke Parott	331

CHERYTE
So hote hatered agaynste the Chyrche, and cheryte so colde;	245	Speke Parott	500

CHERLEMAYNE
Cherlemayne, that mantenyd the nobles of Fraunce,	182	Magnyfycence	1501

CHERMED —CHOPPED   Page   Title   Line

CHERMED
Well, ones thou shalte be chermed, iwus: . . . . 55 Bowge 340
CHESE
A cantell of Essex chese . . . . 225 El Rummynge 429
Some to gather chese . . . . 267 Collyn Clout 840
CHESSE
For ye play so at the chesse, ... 271 Collyn Clout 1009
CHESSHYRE
What here ye of Chesshyre? . . . . 285 Why Come Ye 250
CHESTEN
In yor chalenge, Syr Chesten, to calle me a knave? . . . . . . 122 Garneschel 14
In yor chalenge, Syr Chesten, to cal me a knave? . . . . 122 Garneschel 21
In yor chalenge, Syr Chesten, to calle me a knave? . . . . . . 122 Garneschel 28
In yor chalenge, Syr Chesten, to calle me a knave? . . . . . . 122 Garneschel 35
CHEVALRY
Of chevalry he is the floure; . . . . 282 Why Come Ye 159
CHEVYNGE
Clenly as yvell chevynge! . . . . 219 El Rummynge 186
CHEVYSAUNCE
In Bowge of Courte chevysaunce to make; 48   Bowge 100
When we with Magnyfycence goodys made chevysaunce. . . . . . . 203 Magnyfycence 2236
CHEWE
To chewe and to gnawe . . . . 263 Collyn Clout 655
   gnawe] 'grawe' †Godfray 1531, 'gnawe' MS Harley 2252
CHIVALRY
Of chivalry the well, ... 365 Albany 238
CHYDDER
Se, for God avowe, for colde as I chydder. . . . . 191 Magnyfycence 1817
CHYDE
And in this wyse he gan with me to chyde. 55   Bowge 322
Elynor began to chyde, ... 226 El Rummynge 464
Nor for to chyde, /Nor for to hyde /You cowardly; . . . . . . 356 Garlande 1566
CHYDETH
He chydeth and he chatters, /He prayeth and he patters; . . . 247 Collyn Clout 21
   prayeth] 'prates' Kele 1545.1, Marshe 1568, 'pratythe'
   MS Harley 2252
CHYDYNG
With chydyng and with flytynge, ... 305 Why Come Ye 1059
   flytynge] 'fiting' †Kele 1545.3, Marshe 1568
CHYDYNGE
Tyll, as the devyll wolde, they fell a chydynge . . . . 166 Magnyfycence 940
Mayster Felycyte, let be your chydynge; . . . . 180 Magnyfycence 1437
CHYEF
Her chyef gentylwoman, Daunger by her name, ... 48   Bowge 69
CHYFE
Our soverayne lord, chyfe grounde . . . . 291 Why Come Ye 502
CHYFTEYNE
He was your chyfteyne, your shelde, your chef defens, ... 30   Dol Dethe 57
CHYLD
O goodly chyld /Of Mary mylde, /Then be oure shylde! 40   Coystrowne3 41
Plaut[us] in his comedies a chyld shall now reherse, ... 235 Speke Parott 176
CHYLDE
With 'Lullay, lullay', lyke a chylde, ... 41   Balettys1 I
CHYLDES
But a chyldes play. . . . . 254 Collyn Clout 300
CHYLDIS
Than a chyldis birde and a knavis wyfe? . . . . 352 Garlande 1452
CHYLDYS
Crafty conveyaunce is no chyldys game; . . . . 178 Magnyfycence 1368
CHYLDREN
And suffre theyr chyldren to have theyr entent, ... 194 Magnyfycence 1921
Them or theyr chyldren ofte tymes I dysmembre; . . . . 194 Magnyfycence 1923
Theyr chyldren, bycause that they have no mekenesse, ... 194 Magnyfycence 1924
Than from theyr chyldren to spare the rod . . . . 194 Magnyfycence 1929
Of some of theyr chyldren I stryke out the eye; . . . . 194 Magnyfycence 1933
That they set theyr chyldren to rynne on the brydyll, ... 200 Magnyfycence 2136
CHYLL
Tell you I chyll, ... 214 El Rummynge 1
CHYMNEYES
That maketh his nest /In chymneyes to rest; 83   Phy Sparow 471
CHYN
She cheryshed hym both cheke and chyn 42   Balettys1 9
The sker upon her chyn 98   Phy Sparow 1077
CHYNCHERDE
And not all the nygarde nor the chyncherde to play. . . . . . 211 Magnyfycence 2492
CHYPPES
Lyke sawdust or drye chyppes. . . . . 252 Collyn Clout 243
CHYRCHE
So hote hatered agaynste the Chyrche, and cheryte so colde; . 245 Speke Parott 500
Ageynst Holy Chyrche, the preste, and the clarke. . . . . . . 347 Garlande 1253
CHYSSHE
Hay, chysshe, come hyder! Nay, torde! Take hym be tyme. . . . 171 Magnyfycence 1117
CHYSTYN
In your chalenge, Syr Chystyn, to cale me knave? . . . . 121 Garneschel 7
CHOPPE
Suche logyke men woll choppe, ... 259 Collyn Clout 528
CHOPPED
And your tonges cropped, /Whan ye logyke chopped, ... 377 Replycacion 118

CHORLYSHE —CICERO | | Page | Title | Line

CHORLYSHE
Thou fowle, chorlyshe parote, ... 128 Garnesche3 167
Your chorlyshe chauntyng ys all o lay. 129 Garnesche5 6
CHOSE
I wyll not gyve a halfepeny for to chose the better. . . . . . 170 Magnyfycence 1067
To chose out ii., iii., of suche as you love best, ... 190 Magnyfycence 1769
Nay; rather wyll I chose to ryd me of this lyve . . . . 206 Magnyfycence 2321
CHOWGH
And the churlysshe chowgh; . . . . 83 Phy Sparrow 448
For Parot is no churlish chowgh, nor no flekyd pye, ... 236 Speke Parott 204
CHRIST
By Jesu Christ, /Fals Scot, thou lyest: . . . . 135 Dundas 32
Christ kepe King Henry the Eyght . . . . 298 Why Come Ye 772
Of our savyour Christ in his decacorde psautry, ... 383 Replycacion 340
CHRISTALL
Which is the most clere christall . . . . 375 Replycacion 31
CHRIST CROSSE
In your crosse rowe nor Christ crosse you spede, ... 137 Ven Tongues 18
CHRISTEN
But by the helpe of Christen Clout. . . . . 268 Collyn Clout 879
and of every true Christen man laudably to be enployed, . . . 374 Replycacion I
Of all good Christen order. . . . . 380 Replycacion 226
CHRISTES
What longeth to Christes humanyte. . . . . 381 Replycacion 286
CHRYST
Chryst sence you with a fryinge pan! - . . . . 117 Ag Scottes 62
  sence] 'fence' †Lant 1545
'By Chryst,' sayde she, 'thou lyest. . . . . 223 El Rummynge 344
Except mannes soule, that Chryst so dere bought; . . . . . . 236 Speke Parott 215
Chryst by cruelte /Was nayled upon a tre; . . . . 258 Collyn Clout 450
And lewdely sayes by Chryst . . . . 261 Collyn Clout 575
CHRYSTEN
And slew many a Chrysten man; . . . . 67 Hauke 215
CHRYSTES
And what ipostacis /Of Chrystes manhode is. . . . . 259 Collyn Clout 527
CHUK
With chuk, chuk, chuk, chuk. . . . . 340 Garlande 1003
With chuk, chuk, chuk, chuk. . . . . 340 Garlande 1003
With chuk, chuk, chuk, chuk. . . . . 340 Garlande 1003
With chuk, chuk, chuk, chuk. . . . . 340 Garlande 1003
CHUR
The woodhacke, that syngeth 'chur', ... 82 Phy Sparrow 418
CHURCH
Wythin the holy church bowndis, ... 62 Hauke 13
To hawke in my church of Dys. . . . . 62 Hauke 42
In my church hawke styll. . . . . 64 Hauke 99
Thus within the wals /Of holy church to deale, ... 65 Hauke 135
The church is thus abusyd, /Reproched and pollutyd; . . . . . 66 Hauke 160
In the church of Saynt Sophy; . . . . 67 Hauke 219
Dys church ye thus depravyd; . . . . 70 Hauke 308
CHURCH DORES
The church dores were sparred, ... 64 Hauke 91
CHURCHE
They rangyd Hankyn Bovy /My churche all abowte. . . . . 65 Hauke 118
Make the churche to be /In smale auctoryte; . . . . 65 Hauke 139
For in hoder-moder /The churche is put in faute. . . . . . . 248 Collyn Clout 70
Boldenes is to seke /The churche for to defende; . . . . . . 251 Collyn Clout 184
Holy churche is bruted /And shamfully confuted. . . . . 258 Collyn Clout 487
And brynge the churche to the grounde. . . . . 259 Collyn Clout 494
Agaynst the churche to be, ... 259 Collyn Clout 499
The churche to deprave. 259 Collyn Clout 513
How the churche hath to mykell . . . . 260 Collyn Clout 557
The churche hygh estates, ... 264 Collyn Clout 708
Agaynst holy churche estate, ... 269 Collyn Clout 915
Thus the churche remorde, ... 271 Collyn Clout 981
Holy churche our mother, ... 274 Collyn Clout 1105
Against the churche doth ryse. . . . . 306 Why Come Ye 1071
of our mother Holy Churche, etc. . . . . 373 Replycacion I
And by Holy Churche correcte, ... 380 Replycacion 239
CHURCHES
And meddels very lyght /In the churches ryght. . . . . 249 Collyn Clout 105
Aboute churches and market. . . . . 255 Collyn Clout 326
Theyr churches cathedrall. . . . . 271 Collyn Clout 979
in churches or elsewhere. . . . . 375 Replycacion I
Of Holy Churches lay. . . . . 379 Replycacion 171
CHURLES
Ye knaves, ye churles sonnys, ... 294 Why Come Ye 603
CHURLISH
For Parot is no churlish chowgh, nor no flekyd pye, ... 236 Speke Parott 204
CHURLYSSHE
And the churlysshe chowgh; . . . . 83 Phy Sparrow 448
Some be to churlysshe, and some be to kynde. . . . . 233 Speke Parott 77
Barkyng and whyning lyke churlysshe currys of kynde, ... 239 Speke Parott 295
CHUSE
Chuse them syt or flyt, ... 295 Why Come Ye 634
CICERO
Cicero with hys tong of golde. 130 Garnesche5 12
Prynce of eloquence, Tullius Cicero, ... 321 Garlande 330

	Page	Title	Line
CICEROS			
Were pullysshed with the fyle /Of Ciceros eloquence,	101	Phy Sparrow	1206
pullysshed] 'publysshed' †Kele 1545.2			
CIDIPPES			
Compare you I may to Cidippes, the mayd,	337	Garlande	885
CINTHEUS			
There Cintheus sat twynklyng upon his harpe stringis;	331	Garlande	687
CIRCUMSPECT			
Provydent, discrete, circumspect and wyse,	33	Dol Dethe	139
Provydent] 'Prudent' Marshe 1568			
CIRCUMSPECTLY			
If they can spy /Circumspectly	356	Garlande	1580
they] 'thy' †Fakes 1523			
CIROMANCY			
Som pseudo-propheta with ciromancy:	234	Speke Parott	138
CIRUS			
Cirus by name, as wrytith the story;	336	Garlande	858
CITACYONS			
With sommons and citacyons /And excommunycacyons	254	Collyn Clout	324
CITIES			
In realmes, in cities, by suche fals abusion.	139	Ven Tongues	56
CY-AND-SLIDDYR			
Over Scarpary mala vy, Monsyre Cy-and-sliddyr.	243	Speke Parott	414
CYATYCA			
Alasse, I have the cyatyca full evyll in my hyppe!	195	Magnyfycence	1956
CYPYO			
Nor yet [C]ypyo, that noble Cartage wanne,	182	Magnyfycence	1512
Cyppo] 'Typyo' †Rastell & Treveris C 1530, B			
CYRCUMSPECCYON			
But yf prudence be proved with sad cyrcumspeccyon,	141	Magnyfycence	16
To you recommendeth Sad Cyrcumspeccyon.	149	Magnyfycence	311
To sende over to me Sad Cyrcumspeccyon.	208	Magnyfycence	2400
Nowe welcome, forsoth, Sad Cyrcumspeccyon.	209	Magnyfycence	2418
Here cometh in SAD CYRCUMSPECCYON sayenge.	209	Magnyfycence	SD
Syr, the longe absence of you, Sad Cyrcumspeccyon,	209	Magnyfycence	2424
For where sad cyrcumspeccyon is longe out of the way,	209	Magnyfycence	2427
Cyrcumspeccyon inhateth all rennynge astray,	209	Magnyfycence	2430
And sad cyrcumspeccyon to me they have annexyd.	210	Magnyfycence	2463
And Sad Cyrcumspeccyon I marke in my mynde;	212	Magnyfycence	2504
And with sad cyrcumspeccyon correcte my vantonnesse.	212	Magnyfycence	2509
CYRCUMSPECTION			
By theyr cyrcumspection,	298	Why Come Ye	768
CYRCUMSTANCE			
With sobre cyrcumstance, /Our myndes to avaunce	385	Replycacion	394
CYRCUMSTAUNCE			
I wyll passe over the cyrcumstaunce	158	Magnyfycence	637
CYS			
With, 'Bas me, buttyng, praty Cys',	130	Garnesche5	43
CYSLY			
Cysly and Sare, /With theyr legges bare,	217	El Rummynge	119
CYTACYON			
Ye for to sende suche a cytacyon,	117	Ag Scottes	55
CYTE			
Full many a strong cyte and towne hath been wonne	184	Magnyfycence	1577
Borowgh, cyte, and towne!'	302	Why Come Ye	932
CYTES			
By pollynge and pyllage /In cytes and vyllage;	255	Collyn Clout	361
CYTIE			
Whych cytie myscreantys wan,	67	Hauke	214
CYTYE			
The cytye of Cartage,	88	Phy Sparrow	669
CYTRACE			
Wyth, 'Troll, cytrace and trovy,'	65	Hauke	116
CYVYLL			
For all maister Doctour of Cyvyll	277	Collyn Clout	1219
Or for lawe cyvyll;	289	Why Come Ye	418
CLAD			
Theyr sayll of solace most comfortably clad,	44	Balettys3	27
CLAIMIST			
Thow claimist the jentyll, thou art a curre;	131	Garnesche5	67
CLAY			
Wryten at Croydon by Crowland in the Clay,	38	Coystrowne1	69
Now from a kyng to a clot of clay.	119	Ag Scottes	165
CLAP			
The hawke with that clap /Fell downe with evyll hap.	64	Hauke	89
The Popes cur[se] gave you that clap.	119	Ag Scottes	169
curse] 'cures' †Lant 1545, Kynge & Marche 1554, Day 1560, Marshe 1568			
Theyr tonges thus do clap;	273	Collyn Clout	1058
CLAPPYD			
Ye shall be clappyd with a coloppe	204	Magnyfycence	2272
CLAPPYNG			
Clappyng his rod on the borde.	283	Why Come Ye	190
CLAPPYS			
Theyre browys all to-brokyn, such clappys they cach;	43	Balettys2	32
CLAPPYTH			
Comely he clappyth a payre of clavycordys;	37	Coystrowne1	36

CLARIONAR—CLEPE

	Page	Title	Line
CLARIONAR			
Call forthe, let se where is your clarionar,	318	Garlande	233
CLARIONE			
With Marione Clarione, sol, lucerne,	352	Garlande	1439
But Marione Clarione was caught with a colde colde,	352	Garlande	1443
a colde colde] 'a colde' Marshe 1568			
CLARIOUNS			
Of trumpettis and clariouns the noyse went to Rome;	354	Garlande	1507
CLARKE			
An holy water clarke a ruler of lordys.	37	Coystrownel	21
shall be holy wather clarke.	86	Phy Sparrow	570
A DEVOUTE TRENTALE FOR OLD JOHN CLARKE,	106	Epitaphel	1
A knokylbonyarde wyll counterfet a clarke;	153	Magnyfycence	480
Ageynst Holy Chyrche, the preste, and the clarke.	347	Garlande	1253
CLARKIS			
This wanton clarkis be nyse allway.	35	Man Margery	2
Plutarke and Petrarke, two famous clarkis;	322	Garlande	379
CLASPIS			
With that, of the boke losende were the claspis.	345	Garlande	1156
The claspis and bullyons were worth a thousande pounde;	345	Garlande	1165
CLATER			
Uppon me to clater or else to say yll.	38	Coystrownel	66
And Cloked Collucyoun is brought in to clater	346	Garlande	1195
CLATERARS			
Make noyse enoughe; for claterars love no peas.	319	Garlande	241
CLATERED			
'Quater treye dews' he clatered as he wente.	56	Bowge	347
CLATERING			
For clatering of me I would him sone quight;	139	Ven Tongues	74
CLATERYNGE			
Agaynst the prowde Scottys clateryngge,	115	Ag Scottes	1
To claterynge, to chaterynge, to shorte, and to farre,	199	Magnyfycence	2096
CLATYR			
So for a knave to clatyr;	126	Garnesche3	107
CLATTER			
Nay, lette us not clatter thus styll.	157	Magnyfycence	610
And some of them barke, /Clatter and carpe	260	Collyn Clout	547
Or more of this to clatter?	378	Replycacion	159
CLATTERYNGE			
A clatterynge and a babell	224	El Rummynge	387
babell] 'batell' 1521 Fragment			
CLATTERS			
He clyttreth and he clatters, /He medleth and he smatters,	247	Collyn Clout	23
CLAUSE			
And I than softly answered to that clause,	48	Bowge	74
Whiche conteyned in it a specyall clause	209	Magnyfycence	2436
Remembre you wele, poynt wele that clause,	316	Garlande	136
To wryte of you this goodli clause,	341	Garlande	1042
To wryte of yow this goodly clause,	342	Garlande	1050
To wryte of you this goodly clause,	342	Garlande	1058
CLAUSES			
Expoundynge out theyr clauses, /And leve theyr owne causes.	249	Collyn Clout	100
With clauses two or thre,	265	Collyn Clout	766
CLAVYCORDYS			
Comely he clappyth a payre of clavycordys;	37	Coystrownel	36
CLAWDYUS			
Nor Nero the worst, /Nor Clawdyus the curst;	67	Hauke	203
CLAWES			
To preche in any clawes,	375	Replycacion	38
CLEANE			
To make all thynge cleane;	229	El Rummynge	578
CLEMENCY			
The kynge his clemency	296	Why Come Ye	681
CLEMENTYNE			
And by Dudum, theyr Clementyne,	268	Collyn Clout	872
Another Clementyne also:	268	Collyn Clout	880
CLENCH			
She kykyth with her kalkyns and keylyth with a clench;	43	Balettys2	23
CLENE			
Play fayre-play, madame, and loke ye play clene,	43	Balettys2	41
She was not clene ensaymed,	63	Hauke	79
My lytell legges, my fete bothe fete and clene,	231	Speke Parott	18
That his conscyence be nat clene,	274	Collyn Clout	1122
They play nat all clene,	304	Why Come Ye	1006
Lest he wyll put it clene out,	309	Why Come Ye	1199
But, for to preserve her maidenhode clene,	320	Garlande	293
maidenhode] 'maydenheed' Marshe 1568			
CLENLY			
And countenaunce it clenly,	152	Magnyfycence	415
Clenly to counterfet newe arayes;	152	Magnyfycence	426
Coll wolde go clenly, and it wyll not be,	153	Magnyfycence	476
Ye, wylte thou clenly cle[v]e me in the clyfte with thy nose?	202	Magnyfycence	2176
cleve] 'clene' †Rastell & Treveris C 1530, B			
Clenly as yvell chevynge!	219	El Rummynge	186
CLENNESSE			
Of all pure clennesse virgynall,	375	Replycacion	32
CLEPE			
So I wolde clepe her! So I wolde kys her swete!	190	Magnyfycence	1802

CLERE — CLOKE

	Page	Title	Line
CLERE			
Pray to thy son above the starris clere,	35	Dol Dethe	208
His throte was clere and lusteły coude fayne.	52	Bowge	233
All the goodly sort /Of her fetures clere,	96	Phy Sparrow	1000
The orient perle so clere,	97	Phy Sparrow	1033
Her eyen relucent as carbuncle so clere,	183	Magnyfycence	1556
Her lothely lere /Is nothynge clere,	214	El Rummynge	13
The skye is clowdy, the coste is nothyng clere;	242	Speke Parott	397
Tyll the coost be clere	277	Collyn Clout	1257
Now clere wether, forthwith a stormy showre;	312	Garlande	12
The clowdis gan to clere, the myst was rarifiid;	330	Garlande	651
Behynde the taile of Ursa so clere;	331	Garlande	696
This columbyne clere and fresshest of coloure,	352	Garlande	1448
I wypid myne eyne for to make them clere.	354	Garlande	1513
Which is the most clere christall	375	Replycacion	31
CLERELY			
Clerely perceyve we may	281	Why Come Ye	119
CLERENES			
Of cristall the clerenes theis waters far past,	330	Garlande	660
CLERER			
In a trone whiche fer clerer dyde shyne	47	Bowge	60
clerer] 'clere' Marshe 1568			
CLERE STORY			
Englasid glittering with many a clere story;	325	Garlande	479
CLERGYE			
O connyng clergye, where ys your redynes	242	Speke Parott	392
Of the clergye all, /Bothe great and small.	249	Collyn Clout	117
Theyr shall no clergye appose	254	Collyn Clout	291
Bytwene the clergye /And the temporaltye:	260	Collyn Clout	555
CLERKE			
With a clerke that connynge is to prate.	59	Bowge	454
Chaucer, that famus clerke,	91	Phy Sparrow	800
Of owur clerke Cleros. Whythyr, thydyr and why not hethyr?	243	Speke Parott	412
And yet a noble clerke -	264	Collyn Clout	727
Good monke, nor good clerke,	274	Collyn Clout	1099
How Frauncis Petrarke, /That moche noble clerke,	296	Why Come Ye	688
I wyll answere lyke a clerke:	309	Why Come Ye	1208
I have devysyd for Skelton, my clerke;	334	Garlande	777
CLERKELY			
Lyke a clerkely hagge.	248	Collyn Clout	52
That clerkely is, and can /Well scrypture expounde	264	Collyn Clout	722
And so clerkely promoted,	265	Collyn Clout	756
CLERKES			
With notable clerkes; supply to them, I pray,	241	Speke Parott	359
Syns Dewcalyons flodde there can no clerkes rede.	244	Speke Parott	455
Syns Dewcalyons flodde there can no clerkes fynde.	244	Speke Parott	462
Clerkes out of measure,	250	Collyn Clout	145
Full worshypfull clerkes,	250	Collyn Clout	150
Of you that clerkes be,	273	Collyn Clout	1083
countyng them selfe clerkes exellently enformed	373	Replycacion	I
As clerkes unassured, /With ignorance obscured:	377	Replycacion	93
Count ye your selfe good clerkes,	381	Replycacion	273
CLERKIS			
For Latin warkis /Be good for clerkis,	355	Garlande	1543
CLERKLY			
and have waded but weakly in his thre maner of clerkly workes,	374	Replycacion	I
CLEROS			
Of owur clerke Cleros. Whythyr, thydyr and why not hethyr?	243	Speke Parott	412
CLEVE			
By the messe, I shall cleve thy heed to the waste.	201	Magnyfycence	2175
Ye, wylte thou clenly cle[v]e me in the clyfte with thy nose?	202	Magnyfycence	2176
cleve] 'clene' †Rastell & Treveris C 1530, B			
CLIFFES			
For the cliffes of Scaloppe they rore wellaway,	238	Speke Parott	280
CLYFTE			
Ye, wylte thou clenly cle[v]e me in the clyfte with thy nose?	202	Magnyfycence	2176
cleve] 'clene' †Rastell & Treveris C 1530, B			
CLYME			
And pyke a locke and clyme a wall.	174	Magnyfycence	1227
CLYMMETH			
That clymmeth hyer than he may fotynge have;	46	Bowge	27
CLYO			
Of hevenly poems, O Clyo, calde by name	29	Dol Dethe	8
CLYPPYNG SHERES			
Some brought theyr clyppyng sheres,	225	El Rummynge	439
CLYTTRETH			
He clyttreth and he clatters, /He medleth and he smatters,	247	Collyn Clout	23
CLOBBYD			
Hercules the herdy, with his stobburne clobbyd mase,	182	Magnyfycence	1494
CLOCKE			
Must tell what is of the clocke	84	Phy Sparrow	496
CLOYSTER			
That lustely they lepe somtyme theyr cloyster wall.	201	Magnyfycence	2150
Out of theyr cloyster and quere /With an hevy chere,	256	Collyn Clout	394
So close to kepe your cloyster virgynall,	320	Garlande	305
CLOKE			
And held with the commonns under a cloke,	31	Dol Dethe	76

CLOKED —CLOWTE

	Page	Title	Line
Can touche a troughte and cloke it subtylly	46	Bowge	11
troughte] 'trouth' Wynkyn de Worde 1510, Marshe 1568; it] not in Marshe 1568			
But, as me thoughte, he ware on hym a cloke	51	Bowge	177
Crafty Conveyaunce can cloke hymselfe frome shame, ...	178	Magnyfycence	1370
CLOKED			
Of fals fickil tunges suche cloked collusion	139	Ven Tongues	57
At his cloked counterfetynge dogges dothe barke.	153	Magnyfycence	482
Cockes harte! It is Cloked Colusyon!	157	Magnyfycence	596
Ye, for your wyt is cloked for the rayne.	157	Magnyfycence	609
By cloked colusyon, I say, and none other, ...	160	Magnyfycence	714
By Cloked Colusyon thus many one is begyled.	160	Magnyfycence	728
Here cometh in CLOKED COLUSYON with MESURE	186	Magnyfycence	SD
Here goth CLOKED COLUSYON awaye, ...	190	Magnyfycence	SD
And Cloked Collucyoun is brought in to clater	346	Garlande	1195
CLOKES			
Howe be it of scape thryfte your clokes smelleth musty.	161	Magnyfycence	761
CLOKYD			
For clokyd colusyon is a perylous thynge.	159	Magnyfycence	695
What! Wenyst thou that I knowe the not, Clokyd Colusyon? . . .	161	Magnyfycence	756
Nay. He that ye sent us, Clokyd Colusyon, ...	192	Magnyfycence	1859
Here cometh in CRAFTY CONVEYAUNCE [and] CLOKYD COLUSYON	201	Magnyfycence	SD
And kepe you from counterfaytynge of clokyd colusyon.	210	Magnyfycence	2453
CLOKYS			
Adewe, for I wyll not come in his clokys.	193	Magnyfycence	1874
CLOSE			
I gader togyther and close in my crop, ...	233	Speke Parott	94
So close to kepe your cloyster virgynall, ...	320	Garlande	305
CLOSED			
And sendeth you this wrytynge closed under sele.	149	Magnyfycence	312
CLOSYD			
What ever they say, /Jemmy is ded /And closyd in led, ...	116	Ag Scottes	22
CLOSTERS			
Of closters engrosyd with his ruddy flotis	321	Garlande	335
flotis] 'droppes' †Fakes, 'flotis' Marshe 1568			
CLOT			
Now from a kyng to a clot of clay.	119	Ag Scottes	165
CLOTH			
Under a gloryous cloth of astate, ...	325	Garlande	484
CLOTHE			
Ye kyt your clothe to large, ...	129	Garnesche3	189
Yt bredth mothys in clothe of Arres.	131	Garnesche5	78
What sayst? Here was to lytell clothe.	157	Magnyfycence	607
To clothe the nakyd where is lackynge a smocke –	177	Magnyfycence	1345
CLOTHE MAKYNGE			
Of his clothe makynge.	302	Why Come Ye	935
CLOTHES			
Or we shall the oute of thy clothes shake!'	55	Bowge	343
With clothes upon her hed /That wey a sowe of led, ...	216	El Rummynge	71
That wey] 'That they wey' Kynge & Marche 1554, Day 1560, Marshe 1568			
Clothes of golde and paules, ...	270	Collyn Clout	941
The chambres hangid with clothes of arace;	325	Garlande	475
CLOTHYNGE			
He morneth in blacke clothynge.	288	Why Come Ye	392
CLOTHYS			
He shoke downe all the clothys, ...	63	Hauke	51
CLOUDIS			
And all overcast with cloudis unkynde, ...	352	Garlande	1444
CLOUDY			
Towarde the cloudy skyes;	72	Phy Sparrow	38
And now the darke cloudy nyght	86	Phy Sparrow	571
CLOUT			
'Have here is for me, /A clout of London pynnes.'	228	El Rummynge	564
And let Collyn Clout have none	258	Collyn Clout	478
have none] 'alone' MS Lansdowne 762, 'alon' MS Harley 2252			
But by the helpe of Christen Clout.	268	Collyn Clout	879
Though I, Collyn Clout, ...	273	Collyn Clout	1081
Ye cobble and ye clout /Holy scripture so about, ...	380	Replycacion	222
CLOUTE			
My name is Collyn Cloute.	248	Collyn Clout	49
Thus I, Collyn Cloute, ...	253	Collyn Clout	285
He doth but cloute and cobbill	292	Why Come Ye	527
CLOWDE			
The facyoun of your fysnamy the devyl in a clowde;	123	Garnesche2	25
By meanys of a grosely endarkyd clowde	330	Garlande	645
CLOWDES			
Drove clowdes together lyke dryftis of snowe.	319	Garlande	263
CLOWDIS			
The clowdis gan to clere, the myst was rarifiid;	330	Garlande	651
CLOWDY			
Radyent Esperus, star of the clowdy nyght, ...	44	Balettys3	24
The skye is clowdy, the coste is nothyng clere;	242	Speke Parott	397
CLOWT			
With Colyn Clowt, Johnn Ive, with Joforth Jack;	347	Garlande	1234
CLOWTE			
Gup, Cristian Clowte, gup, Jak of the Vale, ...	35	Man Margery	6
Gup, Cristian Clowte, gup, Jak of the Vale, ...	36	Man Margery	13

	Page	Title	Line
CLOWTES —COCKYS			
Gup, Cristian Clowte, gup, Jak of the Vale,	36	Man Margery	20
Gup, Cristian Clowte, your breth is stale,	36	Man Margery	27
Gup, Cristian Clowte, gup, Jak of the Vale,	36	Man Margery	29
CLOWTES			
To tourne a fole out of his clowtes.	174	Magnyfycence	1211
CLUBBE			
Stryke the hogges with a clubbe,	218	El Rummynge	172
CLUBBED			
Myghty pestels and clubbed,	225	El Rummynge	423
CLUSTERS			
Of clusters engrosed with his ruddy flotes	321	Garlande	342
Of clusters engrosid with his ruddy [flotis]	322	Garlande	349
flotis] 'droppes' †Fakes 1523, 'dropes' Marshe 1568			
Of clusters engrosyd with his ruddy [flotis]	322	Garlande	356
flotis] 'dropis' †Fakes 1523, 'dropes' Marshe 1568			
Of clusters engrosid with his ruddy [flotis]	322	Garlande	363
flotis] 'dropis' †Fakes 1523, 'dropes' Marshe 1568			
Of clusters engrosed with his ruddy [flotis]	322	Garlande	370
flotis] 'dropis' †Fakes 1523, 'dropes' Marshe 1568			
Of clusters engrosyd with his ruddy [flotis]	322	Garlande	377
flotis] 'dropis' †Fakes 1523, 'dropes' Marshe 1568			
Of clusters engrosed with his ruddy [flotis]	322	Garlande	384
flotis] 'dropis' †Fakes 1523, 'dropes' Marshe 1568			
COARTE			
That ye would coarte and enforce me	138	Ven Tongues	45
COARTED			
And so streatly coarted	290	Why Come Ye	441
COBBILL			
He doth but cloute and cobbill	292	Why Come Ye	527
COBBLE			
Ye cobble and ye clout /Holy scripture so about,	380	Replycacion	222
COCHITOS			
Of Cochitos bottumles well;	349	Garlande	1329
COCITUS			
Of Cocitus botumles well;	105	Phy Sparrow	1336
COCKE			
For he was a prety cocke,	86	Phy Sparrow	588
'Lende here a cocke of hey,	229	El Rummynge	577
Or a stewed cocke	252	Collyn Clout	217
COCKES			
He frowned as he wolde swere by Cockes blode.	54	Bowge	287
Cockes woundes! Se, syrs, se, se!	156	Magnyfycence	572
Cockes armes! What is he?	156	Magnyfycence	573
By Cockes harte, he loketh hye.	156	Magnyfycence	574
Nowe, by Cockes harte, well abyden!	156	Magnyfycence	576
Cockes harte! It is Cloked Colusyon!	157	Magnyfycence	596
Cockes armes! Is that your name?	157	Magnyfycence	598
Cockes bones! I ne tell can	162	Magnyfycence	801
Cockes ha[r]te! I trowe thou wylte make a fray.	163	Magnyfycence	808
harte] 'hate' †Rastell & Treveris C 1530, B			
Cockes harte! Tourne the; let me se thyne aray.	167	Magnyfycence	959
Cockes bones! This is all of Johnn de Gay.	167	Magnyfycence	960
Cockes harte! I love suche japes.	171	Magnyfycence	1133
By Cockes harte, I wene thou hast no more.	172	Magnyfycence	1146
By Cockes harte, I trowe thou lyste.	173	Magnyfycence	1199
Cockes armes! It is not so, I trowe.	173	Magnyfycence	1202
Cockes armes! Thou shalte kepe the brewhouse boule.	176	Magnyfycence	1321
A, Cockes armes! Where myght suche one be founde?	184	Magnyfycence	1569
With, 'Cockes armes! Rest shall I none have	185	Magnyfycence	1615
By Cockes woundes, a wonder felowe thou arte!	185	Magnyfycence	1619
Cockes armes, howe Pleasure plucked hym forth!	189	Magnyfycence	1735
By Cockes harte, thou arte a fyne mery knave.	191	Magnyfycence	1826
Cockes bones! Harde ye ever suche another?	192	Magnyfycence	1841
Cockes armes, syrs, wyll ye not se	200	Magnyfycence	2109
By Cockes bones, I shall blysse the and thou be to bolde.	202	Magnyfycence	2182
COCKES COME			
Ye may weare a cockes come,	310	Why Come Ye2	18
COCKE WAT			
What canest thou do but play cocke wat?	173	Magnyfycence	1191
COCKING			
Thou mayst give up thy cocking.	366	Albany	299
COCKYS			
For Cockys harte, gyve me thy hande.	154	Magnyfycence	512
By Cockys body, here begynneth the game!	159	Magnyfycence	682
For Cockys harte, tary whylyst that I come agayne.	159	Magnyfycence	685
Cockys harte! Who is yonde that for the dothe call?	162	Magnyfycence	780
Cockys armys! He hath callyd for the twyce.	162	Magnyfycence	782
By Cockys harte, and call shall agayne!	162	Magnyfycence	783
Cockys harte! Thou lyest; I am no [h]ogge.	170	Magnyfycence	1083
hogge] 'dogge' †Rastell & Treveris C 1530, B			
Cockys bonys! Herde ye ever syke another?	170	Magnyfycence	1090
Cockys armys! This is a warke, I trowe.	170	Magnyfycence	1094
Cockys bonys! It is a farle freke.	172	Magnyfycence	1160
Nay, by Cockys harte, he ne reckys;	172	Magnyfycence	1167
Cockys armys, a mete man for us!	172	Magnyfycence	1169
Cockys bonys! Thou begger, what is thy name?	203	Magnyfycence	2240
By Cockys bonys, it is the same.	204	Magnyfycence	2244

	Page	Title	Line
COCKLY			
Nat worth a cockly fose!	286	Why Come Ye	288
COCK SURE			
He maketh himselfe cock sure.	286	Why Come Ye	282
COE			
We may not well forgo /The countrynge of the coe;	83	Phy Sparrow	468
COFER KAY			
Thryfte hathe lost her cofer kay.	155	Magnyfycence	527
COFERS			
In faythe, of his cofers the bottoms are bare.	201	Magnyfycence	2163
To make his cofers ryche;	290	Why Come Ye	454
COGNISAUNCE			
Controlle the cognisaunce of noble men	137	Ven Tongues	22
COYE			
He bote the lyppe; he loked passynge coye; the] 'his' Wynkyn de Worde 1510	54	Bowge	288
COYFE			
Sergyantes of the Coyfe eke,	287	Why Come Ye	316
COYNE			
The armes of Calyce, I have no coyne nor crosse!	57	Bowge	398
In stede of coyne and monny /Some brynge her a conny,	220	El Rummynge	244
COYNES			
But counterfet coynes is laughynge to scorne;	152	Magnyfycence	446
COYSTROWNE			
Skelton Laureat Agaynste a Comely Coystrowne	36	Coystrowne	I
Suche a foule coystrowne,	363	Albany	171
COKE			
Chaunteclere, our coke,	84	Phy Sparrow	495
COKERMOWTH			
What! Of Cokermowth spake I no worde.	170	Magnyfycence	1062
COKERMOWTHE			
Mary, syr, Cokermowthe is a good way hens.	170	Magnyfycence	1061
COKE STOLE			
For thes twayne whypslovens calle for a coke stole.	124	Garnesche2	38
COKKES			
And the cokkes begyn to crowe agayne the day;	239	Speke Parott	286
COKOLDES			
Lyke hen-herted cokoldes.	283	Why Come Ye	168
COKOLDRY			
Of cokoldry syde,	83	Phy Sparrow	475
COK WAT			
Than ye may commaunde me to gentil cok wat.	137	Ven Tongues	15
COK WATTES			
Thyse lewde cok wattes shall nevermore prevayle wattes] 'witts' Marshe 1568	51	Bowge	173
COKWOLDES			
Some carefull cokwoldes, some have theyr wyves curs;	317	Garlande	186
COLATION			
Of this isagogicall colation,	297	Why Come Ye	717
COLD			
Thus after her cold she cought a hete.	42	Balettys1	19
As Nature cold devyse, /In most goodly wyse.	98	Phy Sparrow	1071
So myche prevye wachyng in cold wynters nyghtes;	246	Speke Parott	512
COLDE			
My sparow dead and colde,	72	Phy Sparrow	40
My fyngers, dead and colde,	77	Phy Sparrow	233
And after a hete oft cometh a stormy colde.	141	Magnyfycence	13
Se howe he is wrapped for the colde.	157	Magnyfycence	603
Mary, Cryst graunt ye catche no colde on your fete!	191	Magnyfycence	1803
Se, for God avowe, for colde as I chydder.	191	Magnyfycence	1817
And now without measure he shal have hunger and colde.	193	Magnyfycence	1895
Alasse! With colde my lymmes shall be marde.	197	Magnyfycence	2004
Nowe must ye suffre bothe hunger and colde.	197	Magnyfycence	2013
Today hote, tomorowe outragyous colde;	213	Magnyfycence	2546
Racell, rulye ragged, she is like to cache colde;	242	Speke Parott	401
So hote hatered agaynste the Chyrche, and cheryte so colde;	245	Speke Parott	500
And from the sowth unto the north so colde,	328	Garlande	578
There blew in that gardynge a soft piplyng colde	331	Garlande	676
But Marione Clarione was caught with a colde colde, a colde colde] 'a colde' Marshe 1568	352	Garlande	1443
But Marione Clarione was caught with a colde colde, a colde colde] 'a colde' Marshe 1568	352	Garlande	1443
From rayne and from colde,	365	Albany	276
COLE			
Another brought her bedes /Of jet or of cole,	227	El Rummynge	524
We may blowe at the cole!	281	Why Come Ye	84
Jack Travell and Cole Crafter,	281	Why Come Ye	98
Brainles blenkardis that blow at the cole,	329	Garlande	610
COLE DUST			
Sche seyd ye war coluryd with cole dust;	131	Garnesche5	53
COLERAGE			
Ye make monkes to have the colerage make] 'haue' Kele 1545.1, Marshe 1568, 'make' MS Harley 2252; colerage] 'culerage' Kele 1545.1, 'colerage' Harley 2252	255	Collyn Clout	363
COLE RAKE			
And with a cole rake	303	Why Come Ye	982
COLES			
Wyll ye bere no coles?'	285	Why Come Ye	243

COLETH — COM

	Page	Title	Line
COLETH			
For so mote I hoppy, /It coleth well my croppy.'	228	El Rummynge	561
croppy] 'coppy' Day 1560, Marshe 1568			
COLYAUNDER			
Colyaunder, /Swete pomaunder, /Good Cassaunder;	341	Garlande	1026
COLYN			
What! Thou Colyn Cowarde, knowen and tryde!	202	Magnyfycence	2192
With Colyn Clowt, Johnn Ive, with Joforth Jack;	347	Garlande	1234
COLL			
Coll wolde go clenly, and it wyll not be,	153	Magnyfycence	476
COLLAGE			
That commytted is a collage	255	Collyn Clout	365
In our collage above the sterry sky,	323	Garlande	403
Of all our hooll collage by the agreament,	324	Garlande	417
COLLEGE			
In the college of musis goddes hystoriall,	29	Dol Dethe	9
And to his college conventuall,	299	Why Come Ye	808
COLLES			
And byrne you all to colles,	362	Albany	152
COLLYN			
My name is Collyn Cloute.	248	Collyn Clout	49
Thus I, Collyn Cloute,	253	Collyn Clout	285
What, Collyn, there thou shayles!	256	Collyn Clout	399
And let Collyn Clout have none	258	Collyn Clout	478
have none] 'alone' MS Lansdowne 762, 'alon' MS Harley 2252			
Though I, Collyn Clout,	273	Collyn Clout	1081
COLLUCYOUN			
And Cloked Collucyoun is brought in to clater	346	Garlande	1195
COLLUSION			
Of fals fickil tunges suche cloked collusion	139	Ven Tongues	57
COLLUSYON			
Of false collusyon confetryd by assente,	61	Bowge	527
Than, without collusyon,	279	Why Come Ye	17
COLOPPE			
Ye shall be clappyd with a coloppe	204	Magnyfycence	2272
COLOUR			
This blossom of fressh colour,	98	Phy Sparrow	1055
This blossom of fressh colour,	99	Phy Sparrow	1108
This] 'The' Wyght 1553, Kitson 1560.6, Marshe 1568			
This blossome of fresshe colour,	102	Phy Sparrow	1232
Adonis of freshe colour,	111	Lawde	43
Of ladies of bryght colour,	128	Garnesche3	148
Enbudded with beautye and colour fresshe of hewe,	183	Magnyfycence	1554
My colour is tawny, colouryd as a turffe;	195	Magnyfycence	1959
Her colour was full wan -	222	El Rummynge	318
The colour dedely, swarte, blo and wan	351	Garlande	1399
COLOURE			
This blossome of fresh coloure,	96	Phy Sparrow	990
This blossome of fresshe coloure,	97	Phy Sparrow	1023
This blossome of fressh coloure,	98	Phy Sparrow	1084
Th[is] blossom of fressh coloure,	100	Phy Sparrow	1137
This] 'The' editions			
This blossome of fressh coloure,	100	Phy Sparrow	1162
This blossome of fressh coloure,	101	Phy Sparrow	1186
This blossome of fressh coloure,	101	Phy Sparrow	1209
This] 'Thus' †Kele 1545.2			
This columbyne clere and fresshest of coloure,	352	Garlande	1448
COLOURYD			
My colour is tawny, colouryd as a turffe;	195	Magnyfycence	1959
COLOURS			
The kynges colours to threte.	127	Garnesche3	141
COLOWRE			
Enuwyd your colowre /Is lyke the dasy flowre	340	Garlande	985
your] 'her' MS Cotton Vitellius E.x			
COLOWUR			
So myche pelory pajauntes undyr colowur of good lawe;	245	Speke Parott	480
COLUMBYN			
The columbyn commendable	98	Phy Sparrow	1052
COLUMBYNE			
The praty primrose, /The goodly columbyne.	338	Garlande	913
The columbyne, the nepte,	340	Garlande	982
This columbyne clere and fresshest of coloure,	352	Garlande	1448
COLURYD			
Sche seyd ye war coluryd with cole dust;	131	Garnesche5	53
COLUSYON			
Cockes harte! It is Cloked Colusyon!	157	Magnyfycence	596
For clokyd colusyon is a perylous thynge.	159	Magnyfycence	695
By cloked colusyon, I say, and none other,	160	Magnyfycence	714
By Cloked Colusyon thus many one is begyled.	160	Magnyfycence	728
What! Wenyst thou that I knowe the not, Clokyd Colusyon?	161	Magnyfycence	756
Hem, Colusyon!	162	Magnyfycence	779
Here cometh in CLOKED COLUSYON with MESURE	186	Magnyfycence	SD
Here goth CLOKED COLUSYON awaye,	190	Magnyfycence	SD
Nay. He that ye sent us, Clokyd Colusyon,	192	Magnyfycence	1859
Here cometh in CRAFTY CONVEYAUNCE [and] CLOKYD COLUSYON	201	Magnyfycence	SD
And kepe you from counterfaytynge of clokyd colusyon.	210	Magnyfycence	2453
COM			
Shall now com and do right,	110	Lawde	17

COMBERAUNCE — COME | Page | Title | Line

	Page	Title	Line
They shall com to rekening,	111	Lawde	31
And welthe ar com agayne,	111	Lawde	41
Ye com hether as well as can be thought.	210	Magnyfycence	2459
I pray the, Besse, unfayned, /Yet com agayne to me!	238	Speke Parott	256
How the maters he mellis in com to small effecte;	240	Speke Parott	328
And com forthe at large,	264	Collyn Clout	693
com forthe] 'conforte' †Godfray 1531, Kele 1545.1, Marshe 1568			

COMBERAUNCE

	Page	Title	Line
Comberaunce and trouble in Englande fyrst I began.	160	Magnyfycence	715

COMBERYD

	Page	Title	Line
Shewyth nowe adayes howe the worlde comberyd is,	213	Magnyfycence	2539

COMBRED

	Page	Title	Line
Alas, dere sone, sore combred is thy mynde,	206	Magnyfycence	2325
Than to be combred with care.	251	Collyn Clout	177

COME

	Page	Title	Line
Come saylynge forth into that haven brood,	47	Bowge	37
'What movyd the,' quod she, 'hydder to come?'	48	Bowge	78
Avaunce your selfe to aproche and come nere.	48	Bowge	88
Soo he departed. There he wolde be come,	52	Bowge	228
Come whan it wyll, oppose the I shall,	55	Bowge	335
And tyll I come, have, here is myne hat to plege.'	57	Bowge	413
is] not in Marshe 1568			
Truste me, and yf it come to a nede;	59	Bowge	478
But that I drede mordre wolde come oute.	61	Bowge	524
The hawke had no lyst /To come to his fyst;	64	Hauke	84
Yet wyth a pretty gyn /I fortuned to come in,	64	Hauke	94
For it wold come and go,	75	Phy Sparrow	159
To wepe with me loke that ye come,	81	Phy Sparrow	387
Is it come unto your lot	116	Ag Scottes	50
Of that may come after; experyence trewe and playne,	141	Magnyfycence	11
And from whens come ye, and it myght be askyd?	141	Magnyfycence	29
Mayster Measure, you be come in good season.	143	Magnyfycence	84
Come of therfore, let se;	143	Magnyfycence	102
That wonte was to be formyst, now to come behynde.	144	Magnyfycence	144
From whens come you, syr, that no man lokyd after?	147	Magnyfycence	255
I shall come to you myselfe, I trowe, this afternone.	149	Magnyfycence	322
By Goddys body, I come streyte.	151	Magnyfycence	399
Counterfet Countenaunce, nay, come hyder –	155	Magnyfycence	547
For had you not come I had ryden.	156	Magnyfycence	577
I say, come hyder. What are these twayne?	156	Magnyfycence	582
For Cockys harte, tary whylyst that I come agayne.	159	Magnyfycence	685
Nay, come at ones, for the armes of the dyce.	162	Magnyfycence	781
To come to me I trowe he shalbe fayne.	162	Magnyfycence	784
Nay, come away, man! Thou playst the cayser.	162	Magnyfycence	787
He wyll come, man, when he may tende to.	162	Magnyfycence	790
Mary, I am come for the. For me?	166	Magnyfycence	929
To name thyselfe. Come of, it were done.	167	Magnyfycence	965
Hay, chysshe, come hyder! Nay, torde! Take hym be tyme.	171	Magnyfycence	1117
Come, Gryme! Come, Gryme! It is my praty dogges.	171	Magnyfycence	1119
Come, Gryme! Come, Gryme! It is my praty dogges.	171	Magnyfycence	1119
And those be they that come up of nought –	174	Magnyfycence	1240
For as sone as you come in Magnyfycence syght	176	Magnyfycence	1314
And next come I after, Crafty Conveyaunce.	177	Magnyfycence	1332
It shall be done. Ye, but byd hym come away	179	Magnyfycence	1399
Come hyther Largesse; take here Felycyte.	179	Magnyfycence	1411
Stande a lytell abacke, syr, and let hym come hyder.	186	Magnyfycence	1647
Come hyder, Pleasure; you shall here myne entent.	186	Magnyfycence	1655
That he come hyder, and to gyve hym a loke	187	Magnyfycence	1681
Syr, as ye say. Nay, come on with me.	188	Magnyfycence	1707
Mary, I wene he wolde not be glad to come agayne.	189	Magnyfycence	1740
Adewe, for I wyll not come in his clokys.	193	Magnyfycence	1874
For when I come, comyth sorowe and care;	195	Magnyfycence	1937
Howe, where art thou? Come hether, Poverte.	195	Magnyfycence	1953
What! Is the worlde thus come to passe?	200	Magnyfycence	2108
Howe many come to myschefe for to moche lyberte;	200	Magnyfycence	2134
Adewe, syrs, for I thynke leyst that I come to late.	201	Magnyfycence	2152
Ye, and when ye come out of the shoppe,	204	Magnyfycence	2271
But thrughe good hope there may come remedy.	207	Magnyfycence	2344
Come who so wyll /To Elynoure on the hyll,	217	El Rummynge	113
Some wenches come unlased, /Some huswyves come unbrased,	217	El Rummynge	133
unlased] 'unbrased' Day 1560, Marshe 1568			
Some wenches come unlased, /Some huswyves come unbrased,	217	El Rummynge	134
unlased] 'unbrased' Day 1560, Marshe 1568			
And sayth, 'Gossyp, come hyder,	219	El Rummynge	204
Wherfor he may now come agayne as he wente,	240	Speke Parott	338
After gloria, laus, /May come a soure sauce.	258	Collyn Clout	483
And come up of nought;	261	Collyn Clout	584
And where the prelates be /Come of lowe degre	261	Collyn Clout	586
'Come downe, on the devyll way.'	263	Collyn Clout	670
deuyll] 'deuils' Marshe 1568, 'devyll' MS Harley 2252			
It must come to his lot	265	Collyn Clout	750
When thei agayn thyder shal come,	268	Collyn Clout	883
Howe may this come to pas,	272	Collyn Clout	1021
which hath to name Why Come Ye Nat to Courte?	278	Why Come Ye	I
Why come ye nat to court?	279	Why Come Ye	31
To come to court agayne.	279	Why Come Ye	39
Why come ye nat to court?	289	Why Come Ye	401
No man dare come to the speche	294	Why Come Ye	615

COMEDIES —COMYNG

	Page	Title	Line
With that there come in wonderly at ones	319	Garlande	269
Where I sawe come after, I wote, full lytell lake	320	Garlande	285
And lette me come to delyver my lettre.'	326	Garlande	506
With, 'Now let me come', and 'Now let me go.'	326	Garlande	515
'Come on with me,' she sayd, 'let us not stonde';	328	Garlande	559
Hither they come crowdyng to get them a name,	329	Garlande	621
Come forth, jentylwomen, I pray you,' she sayd,	334	Garlande	773
They can not come agayne.	358	Garlande2	15
Come forthe, ye pope holy, /Full of melancoly!	381	Replycacion	247

COMEDIES

Plaut[us] in his comedies a chyld shall now reherse,	235	Speke Parott	176

COMELY

Skelton Laureat Agaynste a Comely Coystrowne	36	Coystrowne	I
Comely he clappyth a payre of clavycordys;	37	Coystrowne1	36
And her becke so comely crokys!	168	Magnyfycence	1000
Of a comely gyll /That dwelt on a hyll;	214	El Rummynge	4
Comely crynklyd, /Woundersly wrynklyd,	215	El Rummynge	18
And this comely dame,	216	El Rummynge	91

COMENDABLE

Convenable in sentence, Comendable, Lamentable,	39	Coystrowne3	I
Geyne surfetous suspecte the emeraud comendable;	44	Balettys3	20

COMEROUS

Dysdayne, I wene, [t]his comerous car[k]es hyghte. this] 'his' editions; carkes] 'carbes' †Wynkyn de Worde 1499, 1510, 'crabes' Marshe 1568	54	Bowge	294

COMETH

A false abstracte cometh from a fals concrete.	58	Bowge	439
And after a hete oft cometh a stormy colde.	141	Magnyfycence	13
And nowe it cometh to my remembraunce.	159	Magnyfycence	673
There cometh and groweth of my comynge;	159	Magnyfycence	694
Here cometh in CRAFTY CONVEYAUNCE	162	Magnyfycence	SD
Here cometh in FANSY craynge 'Stow, stow!'	165	Magnyfycence	SD
Here cometh in CRAFTY CONVEYAUNCE.	172	Magnyfycence	SD
And whan foly cometh, all is past.	176	Magnyfycence	1289
I wote not whether it cometh of the or of me,	176	Magnyfycence	1290
Here cometh in MAGNYFYCENCE with LYBERTE and FELYCYTE.	178	Magnyfycence	SD
Here cometh in FANSY.	179	Magnyfycence	SD
Here cometh in COURTLY ABUSYON, doynge reverence and courtesy.	182	Magnyfycence	SD
Here cometh in CLOKED COLUSYON with MESURE	186	Magnyfycence	SD
Syr, Sober Sadnesse cometh. Wherfore it be?	186	Magnyfycence	1631
Here cometh in FOLY.	191	Magnyfycence	SD
Here FANSY cometh in.	192	Magnyfycence	SD
Here cometh in ADVERSYTE.	193	Magnyfycence	SD
Here cometh in POVERTE.	195	Magnyfycence	SD
Here cometh in CRAFTY CONVEYAUNCE [and] CLOKYD COLUSYON	201	Magnyfycence	SD
Here cometh in SAD CYRCUMSPECCYON sayenge.	209	Magnyfycence	SD
Thyther cometh Kate,	217	El Rummynge	118
Than cometh an other gest;	221	El Rummynge	270
Anone cometh another, /As drye as the other,	221	El Rummynge	276
As cometh to her lot.	221	El Rummynge	282
Nowe in cometh another rabell;	224	El Rummynge	382
As cometh to theyr lottes,	260	Collyn Clout	565
That cometh to theyr handes;	269	Collyn Clout	931
All is fysshe that cometh to the net: to the net] 'to net' Marshe 1568, 'to nett' MS Harley 2252	269	Collyn Clout	933

COMFORT

To sorowfull harttis chef comfort and solace,	34	Dol Dethe	206
Ye may be countyd comfort of all corage.	42	Balettys2	7
Comfort had he none	89	Phy Sparrow	705
The hertes of England to comfort with gladnes.	117	Ag Scottes	88
Sodenly comfort, and sodenly adversyte;	212	Magnyfycence	2528
It was a new comfort of sorowis escapid.	330	Garlande	657
Contynuall comfort here ye may fynde,	332	Garlande	710

COMFORTABLE

Your comfortable advyse and wyt excedyth all gladnesse;	210	Magnyfycence	2477

COMFORTABLY

Theyr sayll of solace most comfortably clad,	44	Balettys3	27

COMFORTE

Condute of comforte and well most soverayne;	44	Balettys3	12
Some pleasure and comforte	77	Phy Sparrow	217
Bathyd with blysse, embracyd with comforte.	181	Magnyfycence	1472
To here your comon, it is my hygh comforte.	183	Magnyfycence	1539
To thanke God of his sonde; and comforte ye shal fynde.	207	Magnyfycence	2360
In trust wherof comforte his hart doth grope,	335	Garlande	832
Vertu, conyng, solace, pleasure, comforte.	337	Garlande	898
Vertu, connyng, solace, pleasure, comforte.	337	Garlande	905
Maintayne them with comforte	370	Albany	472

COMICAR

Mayster Terence, the famous comicar, comicar] 'conucar' †Fakes 1523	322	Garlande	353

COMINALTE

He rules his cominalte /With all benignite.	370	Albany	463

COMYN

And I, Myschefe, am comyn at nede,	205	Magnyfycence	2309

COMYNE HALL

And made her husband knyght /Of the comyne hall,	87	Phy Sparrow	647

COMYNG

At the threshold comyng in,	227	El Rummynge	495

COMYNGE —COMMENDYNGE

	Page	Title	Line
Towarde the dore, as he were comyng oute,	343	Garlande	1095
Was comyng downe /To make hym frowne	360	Albany	56
COMYNGE			
Me semeth Magnyfycence is comynge here at hande.	145	Magnyfycence	162
There cometh and groweth of my comynge;	159	Magnyfycence	694
And, syr as I was comynge to you hyder,	191	Magnyfycence	1813
For nowe I se comynge to youwarde Redresse.	208	Magnyfycence	2384
COMYNWEALL			
So lytell care for the comynweall, and so myche nede;	245	Speke Parott	473
COMYTH			
For when I come, comyth sorowe and care;	195	Magnyfycence	1937
COMLY			
Huf, a galante, Garnesche, loke on your comly cors!	123	Garnesche2	16
Ye ar a comly crakar,	127	Garnesche3	110
For all your comly crackes.	367	Albany	350
COMMANDEMENNT			
Hys noble pleasure and commandemennt,	134	Garnesche5	178
By the kyngys most noble commandemennt.	134	Garnesche5	E
COMMANDEMENT			
Be the kynges most noble commandement.	122	Garnesche1	E
COMMAUNDE			
That commaunde with you, me thought, a p[ra]ty space?	51	Bowge	198
commaunde] 'commened' Wynkyn de Worde 1510; 'party spake' †Wynkyn de Worde 1499, Marshe 1568, 'party space' WdeW 1510			
Than ye may commaunde me to gentil cok wat.	137	Ven Tongues	15
Welthe, gete you home and commaunde me to Mesure.	149	Magnyfycence	316
Is there ony thynge elles your grace wyll commaunde me?	149	Magnyfycence	318
Frantiknes dothe rule and all thyng commaunde;	243	Speke Parott	420
COMMAUNDEMENT			
At his commaundemente whiche had both day and night	30	Dol Dethe	31
It shalbe done at your commaundemente.	147	Magnyfycence	239
At your commaundement, syr, wyth all dew reverence.	182	Magnyfycence	1515
Nor to execute /His commaundement,	272	Collyn Clout	1033
How you gave me a ryall commaundement	313	Garlande	58
you] 'ye' Marshe 1568, MS Cotton Vitellius E.x			
a] 'in' MS Cot. Vit. E.x			
COMMAUNDID			
Dame Pallas commaundid that they shold me convay	325	Garlande	449
Forthwith she commaundid I shulde take my place.	344	Garlande	1142
So then commaundid she was upon this	344	Garlande	1147
The Quene of Fame commaundid shett fast the boke,	354	Garlande	1510
COMMAUNDYNGE			
Sharpely commaundynge eche man holde hys pece.	47	Bowge	47
COMMAUNDMENT			
By the kynges most noble commaundmnt.	124	Garnesche2	E
By the kynges most noble commaundmnt.	129	Garnesche3	E
COMME			
But howe comme to pas	301	Why Come Ye	900
COMMEDY			
His commedy, Achademios callyd by name;	346	Garlande	1184
COMMEMORACION			
In olde commemoracion /Most royall Englyssh nacion.	305	Why Come Ye	1039
COMMEN			
Youre key is commen and hangyth owte;	41	Coystrowne4	23
COMMENDABYLL			
My deysy delectabyll, /My prymerose commendabyll,	237	Speke Parott	242
COMMENDABLE			
With his knightes commendable,	87	Phy Sparrow	635
His mater is delectable, /Solacious and commendable;	91	Phy Sparrow	791
The columbyn commendable	98	Phy Sparrow	1052
The beldynge therof was passynge commendable;	328	Garlande	589
To iche of them rendryng thankis commendable,	335	Garlande	820
COMMENDACION			
To have so laudabyle a commendacion:	323	Garlande	408
Of poetes commendacion,	384	Replycacion	374
COMMENDACIONS			
THE COMMENDACIONS	92	Phy Sparrow	R
COMMENDACIOUN			
His dirige, her commendacioun /Can be no derogacyoun;	348	Garlande	1269
COMMENDACYON			
Is to take this commendacyon	93	Phy Sparrow	849
His Dirige, her commendacyon /Can be no derogacyon,	103	Phy Sparrow	1276
COMMENDACYOUN			
Item the Popingay, that hath in commendacyoun	346	Garlande	1188
COMMENDATION			
To make a relation /Of her commendation;	95	Phy Sparrow	962
To] 'Bo' †Kele 1545.2			
COMMENDE			
My sparowe to commende,	75	Phy Sparrow	155
Her beautye to commende,	93	Phy Sparrow	859
And ferre beyond my merytys ye me commende and prayse.	183	Magnyfycence	1526
COMMENDED			
At those dayes moch commended;	91	Phy Sparrow	796
COMMENDYD			
Sodenly commendyd, and sodenly fynde a lacke;	213	Magnyfycence	2533
COMMENDYNGE			
Humbly and low /Commendynge me /To yowre bownte.	338	Garlande	931

	Page	Title	Line

COMMENSYD — COMPANY

COMMENSYD
Thys Doctor Deuyas commensyd in a cart; . . . . 38 Coystrownel 55
  Deuyas] 'dellias' Marshe 1568
COMMENSYNG
Commensyng your proces after there degre, ... 335 Garlande 819
COMMENSYNGE
Commensynge this processe at mayster Redresse. . . . . 211 Magnyfycence 2481
COMMES
And donge, whan it commes, /In the ale tunnes. . . . . 219 El Rummynge 193
COMMETH
How commeth this to pas?' . . . . 77 Phy Sparrow 232
That now commeth to mynde: . . . . 86 Phy Sparrow 604
  to mynde] 'to mi mynde' Wyght 1553, Kitson 1560.6
All commeth to confusyon. . . . . 290 Why Come Ye 458
COMMISSYON
By way of commissyon . . . . 299 Why Come Ye 799
COMMITTYTH
Committyth all to God, and lettyth his shyp ryde; . . . . . . 335 Garlande 834
COMMY
Some have no mony /That thyder commy, ... 218 El Rummynge 161
COMMYNGE
That he to your courte is goyng and commynge, ... 316 Garlande 139
COMMYTED
And agayne all reason /Commyted open trayson . . . . 297 Why Come Ye 737
COMMYTH
Yt commyth the wele me to remorde, ... 132 Garnesche5 101
Pride gothe before and schame commyth after. 133 Garnesche5 165
Lo, hither commyth a goodly maystres, ... 326 Garlande 521
COMMYTTED
That commytted is a collage . . . . 255 Collyn Clout 365
COMMYTTYNGE
To the gydynge of my measure you bothe commyttynge; . . . . . 145 Magnyfycence 175
Commyttynge to me and to my felowes twayne . . . . 190 Magnyfycence 1791
Me humbly commyttynge unto Goddys wyll. . . . . 208 Magnyfycence 2382
COMMODITIS
Recountyng commoditis of many a straunge nacyon; . . . . . . 354 Garlande 1500
COMMON
Or for lawe common, ... 289 Why Come Ye 417
COMMONERS
I say, ye commoners, why wer ye so stark mad? . . . . 30 Dol Dethe 50
COMMONES
Were not thes commones uncurteis karlis of kynd . . . . 30 Dol Dethe 34
  not] 'no' †MS Royal 18 D.ii, 'not' Marshe 1568
COMMONNS
And held with the commonns under a cloke, ... 31 Dol Dethe 76
The commonns renyyd ther taxes to pay . . . . 31 Dol Dethe 78
COMMONS
Well may ye be cald commons most unkynd. . . . . 30 Dol Dethe 56
  ye] 'you' Marshe 1568
But howe the commons gronys, /And the people monys, ... 255 Collyn Clout 348
And make the commons blynde. . . . . 263 Collyn Clout 663
COMMOUN
Confeterd togeder of commoun concente . . . . 30 Dol Dethe 26
  commoun] 'cominion' Marshe 1568
COMMOUNS
The commouns overbace, ... 111 Lawde 37
COMMOWNE
It was excedyng byyonde the commowne rate. . . . . 326 Garlande 488
COMMUNALTE
But the communalte ye call . . . . 262 Collyn Clout 637
For the communalte reporte . . . . 271 Collyn Clout 1005
  reporte] not in Kele 1545.1, Marshe 1568, 'dothe reporte'
  MS Harley 2252
COMMUNE
They commune lyke sottes, ... 260 Collyn Clout 564
  sottes] 'scottes' Marshe 1568, 'sottes' MS Harley 2252
At the Commune Place, ... 287 Why Come Ye 319
To cause the commune weale . . . . 298 Why Come Ye 770
COMMUNEWELL
Agaynst the communewell, ... 255 Collyn Clout 359
COMMUNEWELTH
The communewelth decayde. . . . . 255 Collyn Clout 353
COMMUNE WELTH
That the commune welth . . . . 304 Why Come Ye 1024
COMMUNICACION
Standynge in sadde communicacion. . . . . 58 Bowge 420
COMMUNYCACYON
With suche communycacyon as came to our mynde; . . . . 328 Garlande 562
COMODY
With Plautus, that wrote full many a comody; . . . . 322 Garlande 354
  full] not in Marshe 1568
COMON
To here my comon, it is my hygh comforte. . . . . 183 Magnyfycence 1539
COMONYNGE
And we wyll be comonynge in the mene season. . . . . 187 Magnyfycence 1688
COMPANY
His soule mot receyve in to ther company, ... 35 Dol Dethe 213
But wolde be glad of your company. . . . . 53 Bowge 268

COMPARE —COMPRYSED

	Page	Title	Line
And thus with us good company to kepe.	57	Bowge	385
And every man gladly my company wolde refuse,	160	Magnyfycence	704
But blessyd Bachus was in there company,	322	Garlande	355
From all honest company,	380	Replycacion	243

COMPARE

	Page	Title	Line
Paregall to dukis, withe kingis he myght compare,	33	Dol Dethe	134
Your ruddys wyth ruddy rubys may compare;	44	Balettys3	16
Compare you I may to Cidippes, the mayd,	337	Garlande	885
With us for to compare.	363	Albany	179
Flaccus nor Catullus with hym may nat compare,	383	Replycacion	336

COMPARYD

	Page	Title	Line
He may not be comparyd unto me.	181	Magnyfycence	1476

COMPARYSON

	Page	Title	Line
In comparyson but kynge Koppynge	117	Ag Scottes	57
In comparyson of that whiche I ware.	343	Garlande	1107

COMPAS

	Page	Title	Line
Doublenes hatinge fals maters to compas,	33	Dol Dethe	150
I compas the conveyaunce unto the capitall	243	Speke Parott	411
With alys ensandid about in compas,	330	Garlande	654
I sawe maister Newton sit with his compas,	343	Garlande	1096

COMPASSE

	Page	Title	Line
A very fon, /A very asse /Wyll take upon /To compasse	164	Magnyfycence	866

COMPASSYD

	Page	Title	Line
Thorow treson, ageyn hym compassyd and wrought,	29	Dol Dethe	6
All thynge compassydd, no perpetuyte,	312	Garlande	13

COMPASSYON

	Page	Title	Line
Yet have compassyon upon my paynes stronge.'	320	Garlande	299

COMPAST

	Page	Title	Line
Ye, and se howe it may be compast	156	Magnyfycence	567
Thus ye have compast	361	Albany	102

COMPENDYOUSLY

	Page	Title	Line
Thys boke we have devysed, /Compendyously comprysed,	62	Hauke	24
So as they myght be /Compendyously conveyed,	265	Collyn Clout	768

COMPETENT

	Page	Title	Line
But, and I had leyser competent,	342	Garlande	1082

COMPILID

	Page	Title	Line
What Skelton hath compilid and wryton in dede,	345	Garlande	1151

COMPYLE

	Page	Title	Line
With pen and ynk /For to compyle /Some goodly style; goodly] 'godly' †Kele 1545.2	96	Phy Sparrow	987
Or bokes to compyle /Of dyvers maner style,	247	Collyn Clout	9

COMPYLED

	Page	Title	Line
and begynneth the Bowge of Courte brevely compyled.	49	Bowge	R
compyled by Mayster Skelton, poete laureate	71	Phy Sparrow	I
compyled by Mayster Skelton, Poete Laureate	278	Why Come Ye	I

COMPYLYD

	Page	Title	Line
Unto this processe brefly compylyd,	212	Magnyfycence	2510
Can lay any werkis that he hath compylyd,	318	Garlande	223
to reherse all by name that he hath compylyd, &c.	345	Garlande	R
Item New Gramer in Englysshe compylyd;	346	Garlande	1182

COMPLAINE

	Page	Title	Line
Theire grevis to complaine;	111	Lawde	34

COMPLAYNE

	Page	Title	Line
Bothe temporall and spirituall for to complayne	34	Dol Dethe	181
Thus for to complayne.	77	Phy Sparrow	209
And there agayne /Envy doth complayne, /And hath disdayne;	95	Phy Sparrow	964
Alas! Of Fortune I may well complayne.	197	Magnyfycence	2030
Dothe grudge and complayne /Upon the temporall men.	248	Collyn Clout	64
Complayne or do what ye wyll,	310	Why Come Ye2	31
Why have ye than disdayne /At poetes, and complayne	384	Replycacion	352

COMPLAYNED

	Page	Title	Line
And of this worke complayned,	106	Phy Sparrow	1375

COMPLAYNYD

	Page	Title	Line
And of this worke complaynyd,	350	Garlande	1368

COMPLAYNT

	Page	Title	Line
Of your complaynt it shal nat skyl.	310	Why Come Ye2	32

COMPLAYNTE

	Page	Title	Line
Therefore to make complaynte	62	Hauke	20

COMPLAYNTES

	Page	Title	Line
So many complayntes, and so smalle redresse;	245	Speke Parott	470

COMPOUND

	Page	Title	Line
But the very grounde /Was for to compound	229	El Rummynge	597

COMPOUNDE

	Page	Title	Line
I may compounde confectures for a cordyall,	117	Ag Scottes	82

COMPREHENDYNGE

	Page	Title	Line
Comprehendynge the worlde casuall and transytory,	212	Magnyfycence	2511

COMPRISE

	Page	Title	Line
In his mynde to comprise,	372	Albany	529

COMPRISED

	Page	Title	Line
And in my mynde I have comprised,	117	Ag Scottes	70

COMPRISID

	Page	Title	Line
Wherin this answere for hym we have comprisid,	314	Garlande	80
That in them comprisid consyderacyons;	352	Garlande	1422

COMPRISYDE

	Page	Title	Line
In me all onely wer sett and comprisyde,	33	Dol Dethe	156

COMPRYSED

	Page	Title	Line
Thys boke we have devysed, /Compendyously comprysed,	62	Hauke	24

COMPRYSID —CONFESSYNG   Page   Title   Line

COMPRYSID
	Page	Title	Line
In goodly wordes plesauntly comprysid,	335	Garlande	813
Be vertus well comprysid.	338	Garlande	921

COMPRYSYDE
wherein ar comprysyde many and dyvers	312	Garlande	1

COMSTE
'And, syr, in fayth, why comste not us amonge	57	Bowge	379

CONBYNED
So that welthe with measure shalbe conbyned,	145	Magnyfycence	179

CONCEYGHT
Take him in suche conceyght	292	Why Come Ye	541

CONCEYTE
How he is now taken in conceyte,	54	Bowge	302
'I wonder sore he is in such conceyte.'	54	Bowge	310
To tell you what conceyte	100	Phy Sparrow	1130
Encraumpysshed so sore was my conceyte,	312	Garlande	16

CONCEYVED
Conceyved and cought, /And was never tought	84	Phy Sparrow	499
And whan I perceyved /Her wart and conceyved,	98	Phy Sparrow	1064
By the armes of Calys, well conceyved.	159	Magnyfycence	675

CONCENTE
Confeterd togeder of commoun concente	30	Dol Dethe	26
commoun] 'cominion' Marshe 1568			
Concente to Phebus to have his herte in holde,	320	Garlande	292

CONCEPCION
At the feest of her concepcion	376	Replycacion	67

CONCERNYNG
The welle concernyng of all the hole lande,	31	Dol Dethe	65

CONCLUDE
What wote ye where upon I wyll conclude?	142	Magnyfycence	72
Thus wyll I conclude my style,	289	Why Come Ye	396
Yet, brevely to conclude,	372	Albany	518

CONCLUSIOUNS
Of mervelous conclusiouns, /And by her supersticiouns	350	Garlande	1342

CONCLUSYON
Withoute God make a good conclusyon.	59	Bowge	483
Thus in conclusyon,	89	Phy Sparrow	707
Marke well this conclusyon:	279	Why Come Ye	18
And fynally, in conclusyon,	306	Why Come Ye	1095

CONCLUSYONS
Of marveylus conclusyons,	105	Phy Sparrow	1349

CONCLUSYOUN
That in the conclusyoun	290	Why Come Ye	457

CONCRETE
A false abstracte cometh from a fals concrete.	58	Bowge	439
An abstract or a concrete,	289	Why Come Ye	421
abstract] 'obstract' †Kele 1545.3			

COND
Yf it were cond perfytely, and after the rate,	234	Speke Parott	143

CONDICIONS
In some of their condicions,	364	Albany	198

CONDICIOUNS
Of wonderfull condiciouns	350	Garlande	1344
Of] 'And' Marshe 1568			

CONDICYONS
Yet with lewde condicyons cotyd	293	Why Come Ye	572
cotyd] 'noted' Kitson 1560.7, Marshe 1568			

CONDISCENDID
'To your request we be well condiscendid;	318	Garlande	232

CONDISCENDYNG
To all that to reason is condiscendyng,	344	Garlande	1132
To all that to] 'to all tho that' †Fakes 1523			

CONDITYONS
And wonderfull condityons,	105	Phy Sparrow	1351

CONDYCYON
With every condycyon measure must be sought.	143	Magnyfycence	115

CONDYCYONNS
Ye have knavyche condycyonns.	124	Garnesche3	12

CONDYCYONS
And ye be a gentylman, ye have knavys condycyons.	203	Magnyfycence	2219
With other condycyons that well myght be left.	329	Garlande	615

CONDYSCENDED
Together are bended, /And so condyscended,	304	Why Come Ye	1023
bendyd] 'wendyd' MS Rawlinson C. 813			

CONDYSSENDE
To that ye say I can well condyssende.	141	Magnyfycence	39

CONDUCTE
He be your conducte, the Lorde of myghtys moste!	208	Magnyfycence	2386

CONDUTE
Condute of comforte and well most soverayne;	44	Balettys3	12

CONFECTIOUN
Withowte ye have a confectioun	128	Garnesche3	152

CONFECTURE
Sophisticatid craftely is many a confecture;	315	Garlande	110

CONFECTURES
I may compounde confectures for a cordyall,	117	Ag Scottes	82

CONFESSYNG
Confessyng howe ye dyde lye /In prechyng shamefully.	377	Replycacion	90

CONFETERD — CONNYNGLY   Page   Title   Line

CONFETERD
Confeterd togeder of commoun concente 30   Dol Dethe   26
   commoun] 'cominion' Marshe 1568
CONFETRYD
Of false collusyon confetryd by assente, ... 61   Bowge   527
CONFETTRED
Lyke heretykes confettred, ... 376   Replycacion   54
CONFYRMABLE
To your requeste I shall be confyrmable. 208   Magnyfycence   2407
CONFLEWENCE
To whose magnifycence /Is all the conflewence, ... 289   Why Come Ye   413
CONFORT
Confort, pleasure, and solace, ... 96   Phy Sparrow   1004
CONFOUNDE
The selfe same hounde /Myght the confounde, ... 79   Phy Sparrow   304
Wherwith Mesure to confounde. 155   Magnyfycence   554
That laboure to confounde 259   Collyn Clout   493
Let him never confounde 298   Why Come Ye   778
CONFUSED
So myche translacion into Englyshe confused; 244   Speke Parott   451
CONFUSION
Hath brought nobil princes to extreme confusion. 139   Ven Tongues   58
CONFUSYON
For this may brede to a confusyon, ... 59   Bowge   482
A, syr, I pray God gyve you confusyon! 157   Magnyfycence   597
Confusyon /Shall on hym lyght 164   Magnyfycence   858
Ye, for nowe it hath brought the to confusyon; 200   Magnyfycence   2130
Unto great confusyon 279   Why Come Ye   21
All commeth to confusyon. 290   Why Come Ye   458
To bringe them to confusyon - 306   Why Come Ye   1096
Finally they fall to carefull confusyon, ... 374   Replycacion   15
CONFUTACION
A confutacion responsyve, or an inevytably prepensed answere . 382   Replycacion   R
CONFUTED
Holy churche is bruted /And shamfully confuted. 258   Collyn Clout   488
CONFUTID
Eschines, whiche was not shamefully confutid 316   Garlande   157
CONGRUENCE
All other transcendyng, of very congruence 313   Garlande   52
CONGRUENTLY
But ryght convenyently, /And full congruently, ... 98   Phy Sparrow   1070
CONYNG
Vertu, conyng, solace, pleasure, comforte. 337   Garlande   898
CONJECT
'Now what ye mene, I trow I conject. 332   Garlande   735
CONJECTE
And shewe hym that all the world dothe conjecte, ... 240   Speke Parott   327
CONJECTURE
Sum what wolde gadder in there conjecture 315   Garlande   107
   conjecture] 'convecture' †Fakes 1523
CONJUGACYONS
Can skantly the tensis of his conjugacyons; 235   Speke Parott   180
CONJURACIONS
So myche conjuracions for elvysshe myday sprettes; 246   Speke Parott   514
CONJURACYON
By carectes and conjuracyon 296   Why Come Ye   697
CONJURE
I conjure the, Phillip Sparow, ... 104   Phy Sparrow   1290
I conjure, Phylyp, and call 105   Phy Sparrow   1342
But Phylyp, I conjure the 105   Phy Sparrow   1362
I conjure the, Phillip Sparow, ... 348   Garlande   1283
I conjure, Phillippe and call, ... 350   Garlande   1335
But, Phillip, I conjure the 350   Garlande   1355
CONNY
His nobbes and his conny, /His swetyng and his honny, ... 220   El Rummynge   225
In stede of coyne and monny /Some brynge her a conny, ... 220   El Rummynge   245
I were skynnes of conny, ... 224   El Rummynge   399
CONNYNG
O connyng clergye, where ys your redynes 242   Speke Parott   392
Vertu, connyng, solace, pleasure, comforte. 337   Garlande   905
and transcendingly sped in moche high connyng, ... 374   Replycacion   I
CONNYNGE
Excedynge ferther than his connynge is, ... 46   Bowge   23
I have to lytyll connynge to reporte. 47   Bowge   63
As of your connynge, that is so excellent; 50   Bowge   149
Loo, what it is a man to have connynge! 50   Bowge   153
To have that connynge and wayes that ye have! 53   Bowge   261
Alas, a connynge man ne dwelle maye 58   Bowge   445
But as for that, connynge hath no foo 58   Bowge   447
By that lytel connynge that I have. 59   Bowge   450
With a clerke that connynge is to prate. 59   Bowge   454
I purpose to shake oute /All my connynge bagge, ... 248   Collyn Clout   51
And as for theyr connynge, /A glommynge and a mommynge, . . . 248   Collyn Clout   82
And ryght slender connynge /Within theyr heedes wonnynge. . . 250   Collyn Clout   140
By juste examynacyon /In connynge and conversacyon. 253   Collyn Clout   267
Howe connynge myght them avaunce, ... 262   Collyn Clout   617
CONNYNGLY
So curiously, so craftely, so connyngly wroght, ... 325   Garlande   461

CONQUESTYS — CONSTREYND   Page   Title   Line

CONQUESTYS
Though al his conquestys were brought to rekenynge, ... 181   Magnyfycence   1468
CONQUINATE
That wolde intoxicate, /That wolde conquinate, ... 264   Collyn Clout   703
   intoxicate] 'intoxicall' †Godfray 1531, 'intrixicate'
   MS Harley 2252
CONSAYTE
Your consayte to debarre, ... 142   Magnyfycence   60
Laudable your consayte is to be acountyd, ... 145   Magnyfycence   191
To counterfet well is a good consayte. 152   Magnyfycence   444
That Fansy with his fonde consayte 159   Magnyfycence   678
Crossed? Ye, checked out of consayte. 166   Magnyfycence   951
So I am poynted after my consayte. 167   Magnyfycence   961
By the masse, he shall hyght Consayte. 176   Magnyfycence   1309
Whom? Lusty Pleasure or mery Consayte? 180   Magnyfycence   1452
They towche me so thorowly and tykyll my consayte, ... 184   Magnyfycence   1567
I wolde yet shewe you further of my consayte. 185   Magnyfycence   1591
Who is this? Consayte, syr, your owne man. 191   Magnyfycence   1804
Syr, to accompte you, the contynewe of my consayte 209   Magnyfycence   2421
CONSCIENS
In there absolute consciens 297   Why Come Ye   712
CONSCYENCE
Counterfet conscyence, pevysshe pope holy; 153   Magnyfycence   467
Dyseaso and sekenesse his conscyence to dyscryve; 207   Magnyfycence   2370
That his conscyence be nat clene, ... 274   Collyn Clout   1122
CONSECRATYD
When consecratyd was /The blessyd sacrament. 67   Hauke   185
CONSEYT
Of my wanton conseyt, unde depromo 233   Speke Parott   95
That for them some goodly conseyt be devysid, ... 335   Garlande   814
CONSENT
By hole consent of theyr senate, ... 131   Garnesche5   83
Then ye must bothe consent 143   Magnyfycence   107
Of one affynyte /Consent and agre 259   Collyn Clout   498
With me ye must consent 384   Replycacion   362
CONSENTE
To suche thynges ympossybyll, reason cannot consente; 240   Speke Parott   334
CONSEQUENTLY
Of that most folow then consequently, ... 317   Garlande   172
Wherefore by and by /Nowe consequently 383   Replycacion   315
CONSERNYNGE
Your noblenesse and honour consernynge. 146   Magnyfycence   204
CONSYDER
Tenderly to consyder in your advertence – 186   Magnyfycence   1635
Who lyst to consyder shall never be begylyd, ... 212   Magnyfycence   2512
If he coulde consyder 291   Why Come Ye   497
CONSYDERACION
In this consyderacion; 93   Phy Sparrow   850
CONSYDERACYON
By discrete consyderacyon 102   Phy Sparrow   1247
For no maner consyderacyon 117   Ag Scottes   73
Fyrst, I say, we owght to have in consyderacyon 141   Magnyfycence   43
Sholde be your dwellynge, in my consyderacyon. 148   Magnyfycence   274
That nothynge be gyven without consyderacyon. 211   Magnyfycence   2495
CONSYDERACYONS
That in them comprisid consyderacyons; 352   Garlande   1422
CONSYDRYNGE
A mad rekenynge, /Consydrynge all thynge, ... 116   Ag Scottes   46
CONSYSTORY
For his prerogatyve, /Within that consystory 299   Why Come Ye   817
CONSOLACYON
But myrth and consolacyon 103   Phy Sparrow   1278
But for the specyall consolacyon 117   Ag Scottes   75
CONSOLACYOUN
But myrth and consolacyoun, /Made by protestacyoun, ... 348   Garlande   1271
CONSOLATORY
Wordes that were moch consolatory 317   Garlande   165
CONSTANT
Stabille thy mynde constant to be and fast, ... 34   Dol Dethe   170
CONSTANTYNOPELL
The story of Arystobell, /And of Constantynopell, ... 67   Hauke   213
CONSTANTLY
justifyed, and constantly mainteyned; 374   Replycacion   I
CONSTELLACION
Under a certayne constellacion, ... 296   Why Come Ye   698
CONSTELLACIONS
What constellacions ar good or bad for men, ... 352   Garlande   1429
CONSTELLACYON
'O mercyles madame, hard is your constellacyon, ... 320   Garlande   304
CONSTYTUCYON
Decre and decretall, /Constytucyon provincyall, ... 308   Why Come Ye   1158
CONSTRAYNED
I am now constrayned, /With wordes nothing fayned, ... 120   Ag Scottes2   1
Whiche constrayned him forcebly 296   Why Come Ye   702
I am forcebly constrayned /At Juvynals request 309   Why Come Ye   1210
CONSTREYND
To sorowfull weping thei ought to be constreynd, ... 34   Dol Dethe   187

CONSTREYNED —CONTRADICTYONS   Page   Title   Line

CONSTREYNED
Be love I am constreyned /To be with yow retayned, ... 238 Speke Parott 257
CONSTREWE
Now construewe ye what is the resydewe. . . . . 61 Bowge 539
CONSTRUCTION
Ye may soone make construction . . . . 378 Replycacion 154
CONSTRUCTYON
To make a trewe constructyon. . . . . 253 Collyn Clout 269
CONSTRUE
That Pety Caton can scantly construe a verse, ... 235 Speke Parott 178
Construe nat worth a whystell . . . . 252 Collyn Clout 236
How be it, it were harde to construe this lecture; . . . . . . 315 Garlande 109
CONSULTACION
So myche consultacion, almoste to none entente; . . . . 244 Speke Parott 453
CONSUMETH
And thus this elf /Consumeth himself, ... 95 Phy Sparow 946
CONTAINE
Sex volumis engrosid together it doth containe. . . . . 354 Garlande 1502
CONTAYNE
Whylest I knowe that this letter dothe contayne. . . . . 149 Magnyfycence 324
CONTAYNED
No worse than is contayned . . . . 106 Phy Sparow 1377
Wherein many storis ar brevely contayned . . . . 347 Garlande 1224
CONTAYNYD
No wors than is contaynyd . . . . 350 Garlande 1370
    than] 'and' †Fakes 1523
CONTAMINATE
To contaminate /And to violate /The dygnyte lauryate. 126 Garnesche3 98
CONTEYNED
Whiche conteyned in it a specyall clause . . . . 209 Magnyfycence 2436
Conteyned in Magna Carta. 264 Collyn Clout 719
CONTEMMINATE
That wolde contemminate, /And that wolde vyolate, ... 264 Collyn Clout 704
    contemminate] 'contaminate' Marshe 1568, MS Harley 2252
CONTEMPLACYON
Please it your grace at the contemplacyon . . . . 186 Magnyfycence 1633
CONTEMPLACYONS
With Sacris Solempniis, and other contemplacyons, ... 352 Garlande 1421
CONTEMPLACYOUN
Of my ladys grace at the contemplacyoun, ... 347 Garlande 1219
CONTENDE
Upon artycles judicyall, /To contende and to stryve . . . . . . 299 Why Come Ye 815
CONTENONS
Yet your contenons oncomly, yor face ys nat fayer. 122 Garnesche1 18
CONTENT
I am content so all partys be pleasyd: 45 Balettys5 11
And peradventure I shall content your mynde. . . . . 142 Magnyfycence 49
Can be content with Measure presence. . . . . 143 Magnyfycence 86
You to holde content /With myne argument; . . . . 143 Magnyfycence 108
Well, I am content your wayes to take. . . . . 144 Magnyfycence 155
Yet gyve me thy dogge, and I am content; . . . . 171 Magnyfycence 1112
I am content so it in measure be. . . . . 179 Magnyfycence 1390
And what so we say, holde you content withall. . . . . 179 Magnyfycence 1406
So it be by mesure I am ryght well content. . . . . 180 Magnyfycence 1421
Nowe holde ye content, for there is none other shyfte. . . . . 180 Magnyfycence 1443
As that I myght your noble grace content! . . . . 183 Magnyfycence 1534
Mesure, ye knowe wel, with hym I can not be content; . . . . . 186 Magnyfycence 1656
I am content, my frendys, that it so be. . . . . 214 Magnyfycence 2570
Theyr curates to content . . . . 268 Collyn Clout 858
I am content that he be not exylide . . . . 318 Garlande 224
'Of your demawnd shew me the content, ... 332 Garlande 721
Of that shalbe resonde you ye must be content; . . . . 344 Garlande 1123
    you] not in Marshe 1568
CONTENTE
May this contente you and your mirry mynde? . . . . 332 Garlande 708
CONTERFET
And some wyll take upon them to conterfet letters, ... 178 Magnyfycence 1364
CONTYNEW
It can not contynew long prosperyously; . . . . 200 Magnyfycence 2132
Contynew still /With there good wyll. . . . . 356 Garlande 1585
CONTYNEWE
Ay to contynewe and styll to endure. . . . . 141 Magnyfycence 15
Syr, to accompte you, the contynewe of my consayte . . . . . . 209 Magnyfycence 2421
CONTYNUALL
Herber enverduryd, contynuall fressh and grene; 44 Balettys3 13
Contynuall comfort here ye may fynde, ... 332 Garlande 710
CONTYNUALLY
Contynually I shall remember . . . . 117 Ag Scottes 65
Enverdurid with levis contynually grene; . . . . 330 Garlande 666
CONTYNUED
to be farther delated and contynued, ... 374 Replycacion I
CONTYNWYTH
Measure contynwyth prosperyte and welthe. . . . . 144 Magnyfycence 141
CONTRADICCYOUN
Ageyne whom he cowde make no contradiccyoun?' . . . . 316 Garlande 133
CONTRADICTYONS
Agaynst the spiritual contradictyons, ... 249 Collyn Clout 113

CONTRADYCCYON — CONVEYDE

	Page	Title	Line
CONTRADYCCYON			
Contradyccyon to prove his sapyence;	207	Magnyfycence	2372
CONTRARY			
Counterfet prechynge, and byleve the contrary;	153	Magnyfycence	466
CONTRE			
The corte, the contre, wylage, and towne,	130	Garnesche5	25
Where men of that contre by fortune me fynde,	231	Speke Parott	5
CONTRYCION			
Howe ye have small contrycion	379	Replycacion	183
CONTRYTE			
With harte contryte make your supplycacyon	196	Magnyfycence	1991
Ye, but have ye repentyd you with harte contryte?	208	Magnyfycence	2391
CONTRYVED			
That your mad mynde contryved.	124	Garnesche3	4
Craftynge and haftynge contryved is by me;	159	Magnyfycence	697
CONTRYVYD			
1 thyngys contryvyd by mannys reason,	140	Magnyfycence	1
Sith I contryvyd first princyples medycynable?	321	Garlande	310
All thynge convenable here is contryvyd	332	Garlande	712
convenable] 'convenably' Marshe 1568			
'I have contryvyd for you a goodly warke,	334	Garlande	774
CONTROLD			
Wherof I hym controld;	64	Hauke	96
I hym] 'him I' Kynge & Marche 1554, Day 1560, Marshe 1568			
CONTROLDE			
How she controlde /Her husbandes as she wolde,	87	Phy Sparrow	622
That, if I wist not to be controlde,	137	Ven Tongues	9
CONTROLL			
The queresters to controll;	85	Phy Sparrow	564
CONTROLLE			
A pryste for to controlle.	126	Garnesche3	89
Controlle the cognisaunce of noble men	137	Ven Tongues	22
CONTROLLEYNGE			
With lyenge and controlleynge.	125	Garnesche3	39
CONTROULE			
And specyally to controule /Such as have cure of soule,	62	Hauke	3
So boldely dare controule	296	Why Come Ye	674
CONUSAUNCE			
By theyr conusaunce knowing how they serve a wily py:	43	Balettys2	34
CONVAY			
Dame Pallas commaundid that they shold me convay	325	Garlande	449
CONVAYAUNCE			
With Crafty Convayaunce. Ye, dyd they so?	166	Magnyfycence	941
By convayaunce crafty I have brought	178	Magnyfycence	1372
Here goth out CRAFTY CONVAYAUNCE.	179	Magnyfycence	SD
CONVAYD			
It cannot be denayd /But it was well convayd,	98	Phy Sparrow	1066
CONVAYED			
By God, had not I it conveyed	155	Magnyfycence	534
When we have hym thyder conveyed,	159	Magnyfycence	676
By waywarde wylfulnes let eche thynge be conveyed;	185	Magnyfycence	1594
CONVEY			
Convey yourselfe fyrst, let se.	163	Magnyfycence	816
Yet convey it craftely, and hardely spare not for me' —	177	Magnyfycence	1352
Convey it be crafte, lyft and lay asyde.	177	Magnyfycence	1357
But some man wolde convey, and can not skyll,	178	Magnyfycence	1361
And therwithall convey hymselfe into a payre of fetters;	178	Magnyfycence	1365
And some wyll convey by the pretence of sadnesse	178	Magnyfycence	1366
Require hym to convey yow ovyr the salte fome;	239	Speke Parott	302
CONVEYAUNCE			
What! Crafty Conveyaunce.	154	Magnyfycence	495
Crafty Conveyaunce, I sholde say, and I.	154	Magnyfycence	502
What! Is your conveyaunce no better.	155	Magnyfycence	542
And Crafty Conveyaunce, knowe you not hym?	156	Magnyfycence	584
Here cometh in CRAFTY CONVEYAUNCE	162	Magnyfycence	SD
Crafty Conveyaunce standeth in the strete	167	Magnyfycence	956
Here cometh in CRAFTY CONVEYAUNCE.	172	Magnyfycence	SD
from CRAFTY CONVEYAUNCE showlder.	173	Magnyfycence	SD
Here CRAFTY CONVEYAUNCE putteth of his gowne.	173	Magnyfycence	SD
to take money of CRAFTY CONVEYAUNCE, saynge to hym,	174	Magnyfycence	SD
CRAFTY CONVEYAUNCE alone in the place.	177	Magnyfycence	SD
And next come I after, Crafty Conveyaunce.	177	Magnyfycence	1332
And by crafty conveyaunce I wyll, and I can,	178	Magnyfycence	1359
Theyr conveyaunce weltyth the worke all by wyll;	178	Magnyfycence	1363
Tyll all theyr conveyaunce is turnyd into madnesse.	178	Magnyfycence	1367
Crafty conveyaunce is no chyldys game;	178	Magnyfycence	1368
By crafty conveyaunce many one is brought up of nought;	178	Magnyfycence	1369
Crafty Conveyaunce can cloke hymselfe frome shame,	178	Magnyfycence	1370
For by crafty conveyaunce wonderful thynges are wrought.	178	Magnyfycence	1371
And your Su[rvay]our, Crafty Conveyaunce,	192	Magnyfycence	1862
Survayour] 'supervysour' †Rastell & Treveris C 1530, B			
Here cometh in CRAFTY CONVEYAUNCE [and] CLOKYD COLUSYON	201	Magnyfycence	SD
I compas the conveyaunce unto the capitall	243	Speke Parott	411
With Crafty Conveyaunce dothe smater and flater,	346	Garlande	1194
CONVEYAUNS			
And after conveyauns as the world goos,	347	Garlande	1238
CONVEYDE			
Conveyde by olyfauntes	270	Collyn Clout	962

CONVEYED

	Page	Title	Line
By me conveyed is wanton insolence;	177	Magnyfycence	1335
Pryvy poyntmentys conveyed so properly;	177	Magnyfycence	1337
By me is conveyed mykyll praty ware –	177	Magnyfycence	1340
'What howe! Be ye mery! Was it not well conveyed?'	177	Magnyfycence	1347
So as they myght be /Compendyously conveyed,	265	Collyn Clout	768
How the warlde is conveyed.	298	Why Come Ye	783

CONVENABLE

Convenable in sentence, Comendable, Lamentable,	39	Coystrowne3	I
All thynge convenable here is contryvyd	332	Garlande	712
convenable] 'convenably' Marshe 1568			
With sentence fructuous and termes convenable.'	335	Garlande	821

CONVENIENT

Corage wyth lust, convenient tyme and space;	43	Balettys3	3

CONVENYENT

Convenyent persons for any prynce ryall.	145	Magnyfycence	173
For howe be it lyberte to welthe is convenyent,	146	Magnyfycence	219
For lyberalyte is most convenyent	200	Magnyfycence	2117
And at more convenyent tyme	310	Why Come Ye2	21

CONVENYENTLY

But ryght convenyently, /And full congruently,	98	Phy Sparrow	1069

CONVENT

Whom I nowe sommon and con[v]ent,	375	Replycacion	23
convent] 'content' †Pynson 1528			

CONVENTUALL

And to his college conventuall,	299	Why Come Ye	808

CONVERSACYON

But nowe let me knowe of your conversacyon.	145	Magnyfycence	170
By juste examynacyon /In connynge and conversacyon.	253	Collyn Clout	267

CONVERT

And any man convert	99	Phy Sparrow	1101

CONVERTED

But, blessyd be our Lorde, they wyll be sone converted.	184	Magnyfycence	1584

CONVERTYD

And so cruell hertyd, /That he wyll nat be convertyd;	308	Why Come Ye	1179
That] not in MS Rawlinson C. 813			

COOKE-STOLE

So myche towrnyng on the cooke-stole for every guy-gaw;	245	Speke Parott	481

COOST

And to mewarde as he gan for to coost,	58	Bowge	431
Thus they make theyr boost /Through every coost,	251	Collyn Clout	203
Tyll the coost be clere	277	Collyn Clout	1257
Of the Scottyshe coost,	359	Albany	10

COOTE

And also the mad coote,	82	Phy Sparrow	410

COPE

His hode was syde, his cope was roset graye;	58	Bowge	440
As patryarke or pope /In a blacke cope.	85	Phy Sparrow	529
What is this he wereth? A cope?	157	Magnyfycence	601
For, Goddes cope, thou wyll spende!	171	Magnyfycence	1115
And a poore cope	307	Why Come Ye	1141

COPIOUS

Ye cappyd Cayface copious, your paltoke on your pate,	123	Garnesche2	6

COPYEHOLD

Therfore ye lost your copyehold.	118	Ag Scottes	126

COPYHOLDE

Therfore ye have lost your copyholde.	114	Scot Kynge	35

COPYOUS

Ye cappyd Cayface copyous, your paltoke on your pate,	123	Garnesche2	13
Ye capyd Cayfas copyous, your paltoke on your pate,	123	Garnesche2	20
Ye cappyd Cayfas copyous, your paltoke on your pate,	123	Garnesche2	34
Ye cappyd Cayfas copyous, your paltoke on your pate,	124	Garnesche2	41

COPYOUSLY

Take upon me /Thus copyously to wryte,	273	Collyn Clout	1085
Take upon me] 'Take now upon' Kele 1545.1, 'I take now uppon' MS Harley 2252			

COPYUS

Ye capyd Cayfas copyus, your paltoke on your pate,	123	Garnesche2	27

COPPER

To copper, to tyn, /To lede, or alcumyn?	301	Why Come Ye	906

CORAGE

His corage manly, yet ther he shed his bloode.	32	Dol Dethe	103
Ye may be countyd comfort of all corage.	42	Balettys2	7
Ye cast all your corage uppon such courtly haggys!	43	Balettys2	19
Corage wyth lust, convenient tyme and space;	43	Balettys3	3
Was never byrde in cage /More gentle of corage	80	Phy Sparrow	325
Is turned into corage	85	Phy Sparrow	545
Emporturted with corage,	100	Phy Sparrow	1154
With myghty corage /A[d]aunted the rage /Of a lyon savage;	104	Phy Sparrow	1309
Adaunted] 'Auaunted' editions			
But with countenaunce your corage must be croppyd.	141	Magnyfycence	47
Ye, syr. From hym my corage shall never flyt.	210	Magnyfycence	2466
Whereto were most metely my corage to knyt?	211	Magnyfycence	2479
Be gentyll, then, of corage, and lerne to be kynde;	211	Magnyfycence	2486
Than wyll age have a corage	279	Why Come Ye	38
Them selfe to embesy with all there holl corage,	314	Garlande	66
To corage Demostenes was moche excitynge,	316	Garlande	152

CORAGIUS —COST

	Page	Title	Line
Of jentyll corage the perfight memory;	336	Garlande	860
perfight] 'profight' †Fakes 1523			
Devoyde of good corage,	369	Albany	411
His noble baronage /He putteth them in corage	370	Albany	466
CORAGIUS			
Wherein he reporteth of the coragius	317	Garlande	164
Wherein] 'Where' MS Cotton Vitellius E.x			
CORDYALL			
I may compounde confectures for a cordyall,	117	Ag Scottes	82
That gave Eschines suche a cordyall,	316	Garlande	131
That] 'Whiche' MS Cotton Vitellius E.x			
CORDYLAR			
So madde a cordylar, /So madde a murmurar?	368	Albany	375
CORYED			
For myrth I have hym coryed, beten, and blyst,	185	Magnyfycence	1622
CORYOUSLY			
In the middis a coundight, that coryously was cast,	330	Garlande	658
CORMERANT			
It was a bullyfant, /A gredy cormerant.	227	El Rummynge	521
CORMORAUNCE			
And the cormoraunce, /With the fesaunte,	83	Phy Sparrow	445
cormoraunce] 'cormoraunte' Wyght 1553, Kitson 1560.6, Marshe 1568			
CORNE			
By radyante hete enryped hath our corne;	46	Bowge	2
Yet counterfet chafer is but evyll corne.	153	Magnyfycence	450
To sowe corne in the see-sande, ther wyll no crope growe.	240	Speke Parott	342
Eyther corne or malte,	267	Collyn Clout	842
CORNER			
And with the corner of a Crede,	72	Phy Sparrow	15
No. In every corner he wyll peke,	158	Magnyfycence	658
CORNES			
And blessed her with a cup /Of newe ale in cornes.	224	El Rummynge	378
CORNYS			
A bolde man in a bole of newe ale in cornys.	162	Magnyfycence	772
CORNUCOPIA			
And offred to Cornucopia	104	Phy Sparrow	1320
And offred to Cornucopia;	349	Garlande	1313
CORONELL			
Was my fresshe coronell;	342	Garlande	1056
CORPORAS			
Upon my corporas face.	63	Hauke	63
CORRAGE			
With myghty corrage /Adauntid the rage /Of a lyon savage;	349	Garlande	1302
CORRECCYON			
Of correccyon, but let them have theyr wyll.	194	Magnyfycence	1930
But redresse is redlesse and may do no correccyon.	209	Magnyfycence	2417
Under proteccyon /Of sad correccyon,	356	Garlande	1575
CORRECT			
Correct fyrst thy self; walk, and be nought!	38	Coystrownel	62
It is sittynge that ye must hym correct.'	314	Garlande	77
CORRECTE			
Judycyall rygoure shall not me correcte -	142	Magnyfycence	69
And with sad cyrcumspeccyon correcte my vantonnesse.	212	Magnyfycence	2509
And by Holy Churche correcte,	380	Replycacion	239
CORRECTED			
Whiche hate to be corrected	277	Collyn Clout	1235
CORRECTION			
Ye suffred suche correction.	376	Replycacion	68
He counted it for no correction,	379	Replycacion	189
Sometyme for correction,	385	Replycacion	391
CORRECTIONS			
They say, to do corrections,	268	Collyn Clout	892
CORRECTYON			
Correctyon hath no place,	66	Hauke	162
And abyde the correctyon	304	Why Come Ye	1014
CORS			
Huf, a galante, Garnesche, loke on your comly cors!	123	Garnesche2	16
For harlottes hawnte thyn hatefull cors;	131	Garnesche5	72
CORSE			
This corse for to sence /With greate reverence,	85	Phy Sparrow	526
CORTE			
The corte, the contre, wylage, and towne,	130	Garnesche5	25
CORTEISE			
Benynge, corteise, and meke, /With wordes well devysid;	338	Garlande	918
So corteise, so kynde	341	Garlande	1033
COSMOGRAPHY			
Cosmography, and the stremys	93	Phy Sparrow	881
COST			
'Walke forth your way, ye cost me nought;	36	Man Margery	22
With armatycke gummes /That cost great sumes,	84	Phy Sparrow	521
On her moch love and cost,	89	Phy Sparrow	715
It cost me lytell nor nought.	101	Phy Sparrow	1203
nor] 'or' Wyght 1553, Kitson 1560.6, Marshe 1568			
By lakyn, syr, it hathe cost me pence	150	Magnyfycence	338
Shyt thy purse, dawe, and do no cost.	174	Magnyfycence	1207
Spare for no cost to gyve them pounde and peny;	190	Magnyfycence	1771
There may no cost be spared;	254	Collyn Clout	318

COSTE —COUDE

	Page	Title	Line
COSTE			
Spare for no coste;	165	Magnyfycence	891
It is coste loste	165	Magnyfycence	893
The skye is clowdy, the coste is nothyng clere;	242	Speke Parott	397
COSTERMONGER			
'Moryshe myne owne shelfe,' the costermonger sayth;	233	Speke Parott	85
COSTIOUS			
Strongly enbateld, moche costious of charge.	328	Garlande	570
COTAGE			
Caried in a cage, /As it were a cotage,	365	Albany	256
COTE			
His cote was checked with patches rede and blewe;	56	Bowge	358
checked] 'checkered' Marshe 1568			
It were more thryft he boughte him a newe cote;	60	Bowge	487
Ye had a knavysche cote	125	Garnesche3	44
The f[r]esche bastyng of hys cote	129	Garnesche3	200
fresche] 'flesche' †MS Harley 367			
In a cote thou can play well the dyser.	173	Magnyfycence	1176
That I shall laughe the out of thy cote.	173	Magnyfycence	1194
Nowe put on, fole, thy cote agayne.	173	Magnyfycence	1205
Flatterynge for a newe cote	267	Collyn Clout	838
Whan the flye net was set for to catche a cote,	351	Garlande	1379
COTE-ARMUR			
Haroldis they know thy cote-armur;	131	Garnesche5	68
COTE ARMURE			
Ye have loste spores, cote armure and sworde.	114	Scot Kynge	49
COTED			
How scrypture shulde be coted,	265	Collyn Clout	755
COTES			
And from the berded gotes /With theyr heery cotes;	250	Collyn Clout	159
In gray russet and heery cotes;	268	Collyn Clout	865
COTYD			
Yet with lewde condicyons cotyd	293	Why Come Ye	572
cotyd] 'noted' Kitson 1560.7, Marshe 1568			
COTTAGE			
For coverynge of an olde cottage	255	Collyn Clout	364
COTTYSWOLDE			
A shepe of Cottyswolde,	365	Albany	275
COUCHE			
For a wyndmil /Therin to couche styll	365	Albany	263
COUCHING			
Then Cerberus the cur couching in the kenel of hel;	140	Ven Tongues	80
COUCHYNGE			
Couchynge your drousy heddes	263	Collyn Clout	658
COUD			
I wold you coud! Then shuld ye se, mastres,	44	Balettys3	40
COUDE			
Under as coverte termes as coude be,	46	Bowge	10
Fraghted with plesure to what ye coude devyse.	47	Bowge	42
Than there coude I none aquentaunce fynde;	47	Bowge	45
Wyth fables false, that well coude fayne a tale;	49	Bowge	135
And Harvy Ha[f]ter that well coude picke a male;	50	Bowge	138
Hafter] 'Haster' †Wynkyn de Worde 1499, 1510, Marshe 1568			
They coude not faile, thei thought, they were so sure.	50	Bowge	142
Yf he coude fynde in herte to truste me.	52	Bowge	220
That noo man erthly coude hym bewreye,	52	Bowge	223
man] 'wan' †Wynkyn de Worde 1499			
His throte was clere and lustely coude fayne.	52	Bowge	233
I coude it skan and ye wolde it reherse.	53	Bowge	245
skan] 'stan' †Wynkyn de Worde 1499, 1510; it] (2nd) not in Marshe 1568			
I wyste never man that so soone coude wynne	53	Bowge	269
Counter he coude O lux upon a potte.	56	Bowge	365
Alas, I coude not dele so with a [J]ew.	59	Bowge	462
a Jew] 'on yew' †Wynkyn de Worde 1499, 'a yew' Wynkyn de Worde 1510, Marshe 1568			
Iwys I coude tell – but humlery, home, tell	59	Bowge	467
tell] 'not tell' Wynkyn de Worde 1510			
Yf ye coude be otherwyse agrede;	59	Bowge	480
More coude I saye, but what this is ynowe.	60	Bowge	491
For he coude well upon a casket wayte,	60	Bowge	507
I trowe she coude not amende	75	Phy Sparrow	156
Coude not my sampler holde;	77	Phy Sparrow	234
Your power coude no lenger attayne	114	Scot Kynge	54
Do what I coude to do you good.	150	Magnyfycence	335
Myselfe coude not counterfet it better.	155	Magnyfycence	530
And tolde all the myschyef I coude behynde theyr backe,	160	Magnyfycence	718
I coude holde you with suche talke hens tyll to morowe.	184	Magnyfycence	1588
To reche at a rat – I coude not her warne.	191	Magnyfycence	1809
I coude, and I lyst, garre you laughe at a game;	192	Magnyfycence	1835
Alasse that I coude not myselfe no better gyde!	196	Magnyfycence	1986
What coude the Turke do more	257	Collyn Clout	429
Ye coude none other gette	263	Collyn Clout	654
coude] 'wolde' Kele 1545.1, Marshe 1568, 'cowde' MS Harley 2252			
He coude nat synge hymselfe therout	268	Collyn Clout	878
Coude nat himselfe refrayne,	296	Why Come Ye	690
Suche an other there coude no man fynde;	325	Garlande	463

144

COUGH —COUNTED	Page	Title	Line

He coude not devyse the lest poynt of your cheke; . . . . 337 Garlande 896
I coude shew you suche a presedent . . . . 342 Garlande 1083
    you] not in MS Cotton Vitellius E.x
A wanton wenche and wele coude bake a cake; . . . . 351 Garlande 1413
And ye coude bryng /The matter about . . . . 361 Albany 92
Ye coude nat corde tenus, /Nor answere verbo tenus, ... 377 Replycacion 104

COUGH
Let him cough, rough or snevyll! . . . . 277 Collyn Clout 1221

COUGHE
What! Thou wylte coughe me a dawe for forty pens? . . . . . . 170 Magnyfycence 1060
A, I trowe ye shall coughe me a fole. . . . . 170 Magnyfycence 1064

COUGHT
Thus after her cold she cought a hete. 42 Balettys1 19
Conceyved and cought, /And was never tought . . . . 84 Phy Sparrow 499

COULD
But my dysporte they could not well endure: . . . . 50 Bowge 145
Of Marcus Marcellus /A proces I could tell us; . . . . 90 Phy Sparrow 735
Men said they could not their tunges atame; . . . . 139 Ven Tongues 60
I could make him shortly repent him for ever; . . . . 139 Ven Tongues 76
She could to Burdeo[u] sayle; . . . . 226 El Rummynge 454
    Burdeou] 'burde on' †Lant 1545, Kynge & Marche 1554,
    Day 1560, Marshe 1568
And with good ale barme /She could make a charme . . . . . . 226 El Rummynge 456
And skantly could go /For payne and for wo. . . . . 227 El Rummynge 513

COULDE
That he coulde there espye . . . . 76 Phy Sparrow 181
To wete if he coulde brynge . . . . 76 Phy Sparrow 198
He coulde not optayne . . . . 89 Phy Sparrow 697
Somwhat I coulde enferre . . . . 142 Magnyfycence 59
Ye coulde not ellys, I wote, with me endure. . . . . 147 Magnyfycence 247
But yf I coulde knowe a gose from a swanne. . . . . 148 Magnyfycence 299
Howe coulde ye do that, and [I] was away? . . . . 154 Magnyfycence 504
    I] not in †Rastell & Treveris C 1530, B
Why, coulde not your wyt serve you no better? . . . . 193 Magnyfycence 1868
She coulde not lye styly!' . . . . 224 El Rummynge 391
I coulde say some what, ... 288 Why Come Ye 381
If he coulde consyder . . . . 291 Why Come Ye 497

COULOUR
This blossome of fresshe coulour, ... 94 Phy Sparrow 894

COUNCELL
Then by my councell, ... 39 Coystrowne3 19
So lytell secretnese, and so myche grete councell; . . . . . 245 Speke Parott 465
Partly by your councell, ... 342 Garlande 1054

COUNDIGHT
In the middis a coundight, that coryously was cast, ... 330 Garlande 658

COUNFORTE
Of the Mayden of Kent callid Counforte, ... 354 Garlande 1495

COUNSAYLE
Syr, of my counsayle this shall be the grounde: . . . . 190 Magnyfycence 1768
I counsayle them beware of adversyte. . . . . 194 Magnyfycence 1899

COUNSEYLE
His counseyle secrete never to dyscure, ... 52 Bowge 219
    dyscure] 'dysture' †Wynkyn de Worde 1499, 1510
Your counseyle was not worth a flye. . . . . 113 Scot Kynge 14
Thrugh your counseyle your fader was slayne; . . . . 114 Scot Kynge 27

COUNSEL
Of our maisters counsel in everithing. . . . . 299 Why Come Ye 792

COUNSELL
It can be no counsell that is cryed at the cros. 43 Balettys2 36
Gete you hens, I say, by my counsell. . . . . 149 Magnyfycence 306
To counterfet thyr counsell they gyve me a fee. . . . . 154 Magnyfycence 491
But I wyll be ruled after your counsell. . . . . 157 Magnyfycence 615
Be not to bolde my frende; I counsell you, bere a brayne. . . 179 Magnyfycence 1405
And beware of adversyte by my counsell, ... 195 Magnyfycence 1945
Well, syr, after your counsell my mynde I wyll set. . . . . . 210 Magnyfycence 2457
Gravyte of counsell, provydence, and wyt; . . . . 210 Magnyfycence 2476
That ye gyve shrewed counsell . . . . 255 Collyn Clout 358
Agaynst us of the counsell? . . . . 275 Collyn Clout 1163
Of our graunde counsell? . . . . 288 Why Come Ye 380
The chefe of his owne counsell, ... 295 Why Come Ye 647
Of your noughty counsell, ... 380 Replycacion 213

COUNSELLE
That I must shewe you moche of my counselle – . . . . 52 Bowge 207

COUNSELOUR
Chefe counselour was carlesse, ... 280 Why Come Ye 79

COUNT
Ye count your selfe wele lettred: . . . . 376 Replycacion 55
Count ye your selfe good clerkes, ... 381 Replycacion 273

COUNTE
A counte to counterfet in a resayte – . . . . 152 Magnyfycence 443
Of Cato the counte, acountyd the cane, ... 181 Magnyfycence 1487
They counte it for a raylynge . . . . 275 Collyn Clout 1147
They counte us for lyars; . . . . 276 Collyn Clout 1187
Counte himselfe as good as he; . . . . 294 Why Come Ye 590
Must counte what became . . . . 302 Why Come Ye 934

COUNTED
Is counted for no rod; . . . . 275 Collyn Clout 1146
Extorcyon is counted with you for a knyght; . . . . 317 Garlande 194

COUNTEDE —COUNTERFET   Page   Title   Line

	Page	Title	Line
He counted it for no correction,	379	Replycacion	189
COUNTEDE			
Of whos [life] they countede not a fly.	31	Dol Dethe	95
life] not in †MS Royal 18 D.ii or Marshe 1568			
COUNTENAUNCE			
He counteth in his countenaunce to checke with the best:	37	Coystrownel	44
Remembryng your passyng goodly countenaunce,	42	Balettys2	5
Than to beholde youre bewteouse countenaunce:	44	Balettys3	44
I tell the, I am of countenaunce.	55	Bowge	330
That lyberte be lynkyd with the chayne of countenaunce,	141	Magnyfycence	44
But with countenaunce your corage must be croppyd.	141	Magnyfycence	47
For Counterfet Countenaunce knowen am I.	152	Magnyfycence	410
And countenaunce it clenly,	152	Magnyfycence	415
Counterfet Countenaunce every man dothe occupy.	153	Magnyfycence	472
Your counterfet countenaunce is all of nysyte,	153	Magnyfycence	478
What! Counterfet Countenaunce!	154	Magnyfycence	494
Counterfet Countenaunce, nay, come hyder –	155	Magnyfycence	547
Counterfet Countenaunce to have also,	158	Magnyfycence	645
But, Counterfet Countenaunce, go we togyder,	158	Magnyfycence	665
Paynte to a purpose good countenaunce I can,	160	Magnyfycence	724
And your demenour with Counterfet Countenaunce,	192	Magnyfycence	1861
Use not then your countenaunce for to counterfet.	210	Magnyfycence	2455
Terrible of countenaunce and passynge formydable,	328	Garlande	591
And if Apelles your countenaunce had sene,	337	Garlande	894
And grudge therat with frownyng countenaunce;	348	Garlande	1258
His countenaunce to beholde.	367	Albany	339
COUNTER			
Curyowsly he can both counter and knak	37	Coystrownel	17
He trymmyth in hys tenor to counter pyrdewy;	37	Coystrownel	26
Counter he coude O lux upon a potte.	56	Bowge	365
Nay, offer hym a counter in stede of a peny.	172	Magnyfycence	1171
COUNTERFAYTYNGE			
And kepe you from counterfaytynge of clokyd colusyon.	210	Magnyfycence	2453
COUNTERFEYTED			
That I counterfeyted you underneth a shrowde?	155	Magnyfycence	532
COUNTERFEYTES			
That counterfeytes and payntes	269	Collyn Clout	920
COUNTERFET			
For Counterfet Countenaunce knowen am I.	152	Magnyfycence	410
That can not counterfet a lye,	152	Magnyfycence	413
A knave wyll counterfet nowe a knyght,	152	Magnyfycence	417
To counterfet I can by praty wayes:	152	Magnyfycence	424
Of nyghtys to occupy counterfet kayes;	152	Magnyfycence	425
Clenly to counterfet newe arayes.	152	Magnyfycence	426
Counterfet eyrnest by way of playes.	152	Magnyfycence	427
Counterfet maters in the lawe of the lande –	152	Magnyfycence	431
And counterfet fredome that is bounde;	152	Magnyfycence	434
I counterfet suger that is but *[s]ounde;	152	Magnyfycence	435
*sounde] 'founde' †Rastell & Treveris C 1530, B, 'sande' Scattergood			
Counterfet capytaynes by me are mande;	152	Magnyfycence	436
Counterfet kyndnesse, and thynke dyscayte;	152	Magnyfycence	438
Counterfet letters by the way of sleyght;	152	Magnyfycence	439
Subtelly usynge counterfet weyght;	152	Magnyfycence	440
Counterfet langage, fayty bone geyte.	152	Magnyfycence	441
A counte to counterfet in a resayte –	152	Magnyfycence	443
To counterfet well is a good consayte.	152	Magnyfycence	444
Counterfet maydenhode may well be borne,	152	Magnyfycence	445
But counterfet coynes is laughynge to scorne;	152	Magnyfycence	446
Counterfet haltynge without a thorne;	153	Magnyfycence	449
Yet counterfet chafer is but evyll corne.	153	Magnyfycence	450
What! Wolde ye wyves counterfet	153	Magnyfycence	452
To counterfet she wyll assay	153	Magnyfycence	462
Counterfet prechynge, and byleve the contrary;	153	Magnyfycence	466
Counterfet conscyence, pevysshe pope holy;	153	Magnyfycence	467
Counterfet sadnesse, with delynge full madly;	153	Magnyfycence	468
Counterfet holynes is called ypocrysy;	153	Magnyfycence	469
Counterfet reason is not worth a flye;	153	Magnyfycence	470
Counterfet wysdome, and workes of foly;	153	Magnyfycence	471
Counterfet Countenaunce every man dothe occupy.	153	Magnyfycence	472
Counterfet worshyp outwarde men may se;	153	Magnyfycence	473
Counterfet pleasure is borne out by me;	153	Magnyfycence	475
Your counterfet countenaunce is all of nysyte,	153	Magnyfycence	478
A knowlybonyarde wyll counterfet a clarke;	153	Magnyfycence	480
A counterfet courtyer with a knaves marke.	154	Magnyfycence	486
To counterfet this freers have lerned me.	154	Magnyfycence	487
Wolde take, in the way of counterfet charyte,	154	Magnyfycence	489
To counterfet thyr counsell they gyve me a fee.	154	Magnyfycence	491
Chanons can not counterfet but upon thre.	154	Magnyfycence	492
What! Counterfet Countenaunce!	154	Magnyfycence	494
Myselfe coude not counterfet it better.	155	Magnyfycence	530
Counterfet Countenaunce, nay, come hyder –	155	Magnyfycence	547
Counterfet Countenaunce to have also,	158	Magnyfycence	645
But, Counterfet Countenaunce, go we togyder,	158	Magnyfycence	665
And I, am counterfet of one mynde and thought,	159	Magnyfycence	701
And your demenour with Counterfet Countenaunce,	192	Magnyfycence	1861
Use not then your countenaunce for to counterfet.	210	Magnyfycence	2455

	Page	Title	Line

COUNTERFETE — COURTE

COUNTERFETE
All other besyde were counterfete they thought . . . . 343 Garlande 1106
    All ... counterfete] 'that they ware were counterfettis' MS
    Cotton Vitellius E.x
COUNTERFETED
And counterfeted our names we have . . . . 158 Magnyfycence 641
COUNTERFETYD
But, syr, howe counterfetyd ye? . . . . 155 Magnyfycence 524
COUNTERFETYNGE
Counterfetynge is a proper bayte. . . . . 152 Magnyfycence 442
At his cloked counterfetynge dogges dothe barke. . . . . . . 153 Magnyfycence 482
COUNTERFETTES
But if they were counterfettes that women them call, ... 334 Garlande 785
COUNTERFETTIS
And suche as be counterfettis they be reservyd; . . . . 346 Garlande 1190
COUNTERYNG
There was counteryng of carollis in meter and verse . . . . . 331 Garlande 705
    and] 'and in' Marshe 1568
COUNTERWAY
Ye counterway not evynly your balaunce; . . . . 317 Garlande 179
COUNTERWAYNG
'Counterwayng your besy delygence . . . . 323 Garlande 414
Your noble demenour is counterwayng, ... 336 Garlande 847
COUNTES
To the ryght noble Countes of Surrey . . . . 335 Garlande R
COUNTETH
He counteth in his countenaunce to checke with the best: . . 37 Coystrowne1 44
He counteth them for gygawis; . . . . 305 Why Come Ye 1063
COUNTYD
Ye may be countyd comfort of all corage. 42 Balettys2 7
COUNTYNAUNCE
His countynaunce lyke a kayser. . . . . 294 Why Come Ye 624
COUNTYNG
countyng them selfe clerkes exellently enformed . . . . 373 Replycacion I
COUNTYR
Ye countyr umwhyle to capcyously, and ar ye be dysiryd; . . . 123 Garnesche2 11
COUNTYS
He countys them foles and dawes; . . . . 286 Why Come Ye 315
COUNTYTH
Who county[th] without me is caste to fer behynde . . . . . . 146 Magnyfycence 214
    countyth] 'countyd' †Rastell & Treveris C 1530, B
COUNTRYNGE
We may not well forgo /The countrynge of the coe; . . . . . . 83 Phy Sparrow 468
The countrynge at Cales . . . . 280 Why Come Ye 77
    The] 'They' †Kele 1545.3, Toy 1553, Kitson 1560.7, Marshe 1568
COUPLE
And all is not worth a couple of nut shalis. . . . . 139 Ven Tongues 66
COURAGE
For her vysage /It woldt aswage /A mannes courage. . . . . . 214 El Rummynge 11
Theyr courage to abate . . . . 270 Collyn Clout 973
And theyr courage abated, ... 283 Why Come Ye 162
COURS
Thy caytyvys carkes, cours and crasy; 130 Garnesche5 31
COURSE
Taking his course toward the west; . . . . 86 Phy Sparrow 573
Bycause course of measure – yf I be in the way: . . . . 146 Magnyfycence 213
Of wandryng of the mone, the course of the sun, ... 331 Garlande 691
COURSERS
Of coursers and rounses . . . . 104 Phy Sparrow 1314
Of coursers and rounsis . . . . 349 Garlande 1307
COURT
Of Bowge of Court she asketh what we wold have, ... 49 Bowge 125
Why come ye nat to court? . . . . 279 Why Come Ye 31
To come to court agayne. . . . . 279 Why Come Ye 39
Why come ye nat to court? . . . . 289 Why Come Ye 401
To whyche court? /To the kynges courte? . . . . 289 Why Come Ye 402
Or to Hampton Court? . . . . 289 Why Come Ye 404
Nay, to the kynges court! . . . . 289 Why Come Ye 405
But Hampton Court /Hath the preemynence! . . . . 289 Why Come Ye 408
Of the court royall . . . . 290 Why Come Ye 435
To kepe his court provyncyall . . . . 299 Why Come Ye 813
To the court why I cam not, ... 299 Why Come Ye 827
In whose court poynted is your place.' . . . . 324 Garlande 420
Of Fames court, by all our holl assent . . . . 324 Garlande 433
How ye ar welcome to this court of aray. . . . . 327 Garlande 539
Ther names recountyng in the court of Fame; . . . . 334 Garlande 781
In Fames court reportyng the same; . . . . 334 Garlande 783
COURTE
Here begynneth a lytell treatyse named The Bowge of Courte . . 46 Bowge I
The Bowge of Courte it hyghte for certeynte. . . . . 47 Bowge 49
    certeynte] 'certeynet' †Wynkyn de Worde 1499, 'certayne'
    Wynkyn de Worde 1510, 'certeynte' Marshe 1568
In Bowge of Courte chevysaunce to make; . . . . 48 Bowge 100
and begynneth the Bowge of Courte brevely compyled. . . . . . 49 Bowge R
'Forsothe,' quod I, 'in this courte I dwell nowe.' . . . . . 56 Bowge 377
For all our courte is full of dysceyte. . . . . 59 Bowge 469
Thus endeth the Bowge of Courte. . . . . 61 Bowge E
In the courte of Fame; . . . . 94 Phy Sparrow 892

147

COURTELY —COWARDLY   Page   Title   Line

Entry	Page	Title	Line
Nor no man in courte, but he,	158	Magnyfycence	660
which hath to name Why Come Ye Nat to Courte?	278	Why Come Ye	1
For the courte full unmete;	279	Why Come Ye	33
To whyche court? /To the kynges courte?	289	Why Come Ye	403
The kynges courte /Shulde have the excellence;	289	Why Come Ye	406
That in my courte Skelton shulde have a place,	313	Garlande	59
With laureate tryumphe in the courte of Fame,	314	Garlande	63
That he to your courte is goyng and commynge,	316	Garlande	139
Unto your palas, our noble courte of Fame,	318	Garlande	219
Of this high courte the dayly besines;	326	Garlande	519
For in owr courte, ye wote wele, his name can not ryse	345	Garlande	1154
Item Bowche of Courte, where Drede was begyled;	346	Garlande	1183
Of our noble courte is ones spoken owte,	353	Garlande	1482

COURTELY
With Courtely Abusyoun; who pryntith it wele in mynde	346	Garlande	1196

COURTE ROWLIS
Ryot and Revell be in your courte rowlis;	317	Garlande	192

COURTESY
Here cometh in COURTLY ABUSYON, doynge reverence and courtesy.	182	Magnyfycence	SD

COURTYER
A carter a courtyer, it is a worthy warke,	153	Magnyfycence	483
A counterfet courtyer with a knaves marke.	154	Magnyfycence	486

COURTLY
Ye cast all your corage uppon such courtly haggys!	43	Balettys2	19
The courtly gyse of the newe jet?	153	Magnyfycence	453
COURTLY ABUSYON alone in the place.	163	Magnyfycence	SD
That I can were /Courtly my gere!	163	Magnyfycence	834
Here cometh in COURTLY ABUSYON, doynge reverence and courtesy.	182	Magnyfycence	SD
And your payntyd Pleasure, Courtly Abusyon,	192	Magnyfycence	1860

COUSSHONS
For alle your carpet cousshons	124	Garnesche3	11

COVENT
Theyr covent to encrease.	267	Collyn Clout	847

COVER
His gowne so shorte that it ne cover myghte	56	Bowge	354
A spectacle case /To cover thy face, /With, tray deux ase.	136	Dundas	38
Decke your hofte and cover a lowce.	161	Magnyfycence	749
With, 'Fy, cover thy shap	227	El Rummynge	507
thy] 'the' Kynge & Marche 1554, Day 1560, Marshe 1568			

COVERYNGE
For coverynge of an olde cottage	255	Collyn Clout	364

COVERLET
Nowe lap you in a coverlet, full fayne that you may;	197	Magnyfycence	2011
How the grene coverlet sufferd grete pine;	351	Garlande	1378

COVERTE
Under as coverte termes as coude be,	46	Bowge	10

COVERTLY
Two faces in a hode covertly I bere;	160	Magnyfycence	710

COVERTURE
Properly payntyd to be my coverture;	231	Speke Parott	9

COVET
How there nys thynge that I covet so fayne	44	Balettys3	41

COVETYS
Envy, wrath, and lechery, /Covetys and glotony;	293	Why Come Ye	576

COVETYSE
But covetyse hath blowen you so full of wynde	148	Magnyfycence	290

COVYTOUS
With covytous ambycyon /And other superstycyon,	269	Collyn Clout	901
ambycyon] 'and ambycyon' Kele 1545.1, Marshe 1568, 'ambyssyon' MS Harley 2252			

COVYTOUSNESSE
And foule covytousnesse /And other wretchednesse,	247	Collyn Clout	42

COWARD
Well, and I be a coward, there is mo than I.	162	Magnyfycence	770

COWARDE
What! Thou Colyn Cowarde, knowen and tryde!	202	Magnyfycence	2192
lyke a cowarde knyght, ran awaye shamfully	359	Albany	1
Of this cowarde knyght,	359	Albany	15
Lyke a cowarde knyght	360	Albany	69
By suche a cowarde knyght,	363	Albany	166
Suche a starke cowarde,	363	Albany	169
No man hath harde /Of suche a cowarde,	365	Albany	253
Lyke a cowarde knyght.	366	Albany	313
Adue, cowarde, adue! /Fals knight and mooste untrue,	366	Albany	314
Avaunt, cowarde recrayed! /Thy pride shalbe alayd,	371	Albany	495

COWARDES
O causeles cowardes, O hartles hardynes,	242	Speke Parott	390
Lyke cankerd cowardes all,	283	Why Come Ye	165
And so attaynted, /Lyke cowardes starke,	359	Albany	29
For the moost recrayd /Cowardes afrayd,	362	Albany	116
In spyght of thy cowardes face,	369	Albany	408
Lyke cowardes as ye be	370	Albany	460
In spyght of thy cowardes face,	371	Albany	492

COWARDLY
To dele wyth her so cowardly;	42	Balettys1	27
Nor for to chyde, /Nor for to hyde /You cowardly;	356	Garlande	1568
This Duke so fell /Of Albany, /So cowardly	359	Albany	8
Thus in your cowardly castell	366	Albany	279

COWARDNESSE — CRAFTY

	Page	Title	Line
And cowardly tourne your backes	367	Albany	349
They fledde full cowardly.	371	Albany	515

COWARDNESSE

	Page	Title	Line
Your cankarde cowardnesse /And your shamfull doublenesse.	368	Albany	361

COWCHE-QUALE

	Page	Title	Line
To lowre, to droupe, to knele, to stowpe and to play cowche-quale;	243	Speke Parott	426

COWCHYD

	Page	Title	Line
Are not his wordys cursydly cowchyd?	175	Magnyfycence	1276

COWDE

	Page	Title	Line
Cowde not rech nor attayne	68	Hauke	226
Youre poverte cowde not attayne	119	Ag Scottes	151
Soche an odyr chalyngyr cowde me no man wysch,	121	Garneschel	3
Cowde hocupy ther no stede.	126	Garnesche3	69
The knave wolde make it koy, and he cowde;	175	Magnyfycence	1246
Put up his sworde, for he cowde make no warre,	312	Garlande	5
And many mo whome I cowde enduce;	314	Garlande	94
Ageyne whom he cowde make no contradiccyoun?'	316	Garlande	133
And cowde not wryght /Of Isabell Knyght.	342	Garlande	1066
I did what I cowde to scrape out the scrollis, scrape] 'scarpe' Marshe 1568	354	Garlande	1489

COWGHE

	Page	Title	Line
And I gyve hym the cowghe, the murre, and the pose.	204	Magnyfycence	2259

COWNTENAUNCE

	Page	Title	Line
How Cownterfet Cowntenaunce of the new get	346	Garlande	1193

COWNTER

	Page	Title	Line
What though ye can cownter Custodi nos?	38	Coystrownel	57

COWNTERFET

	Page	Title	Line
How Cownterfet Cowntenaunce of the new get	346	Garlande	1193

COWNTES

	Page	Title	Line
Where the noble Cowntes of Surrey in a chayre	333	Garlande	769

COWNTRED

	Page	Title	Line
that curyowsly chawntyd, and curryshly cowntred,	36	Coystrowne	I

COWRTE

	Page	Title	Line
By the masse, for the cowrte thou art a mete man;	161	Magnyfycence	764

COWRTLY

	Page	Title	Line
Ye, so I can devyse my gere after the cowrtly maner.	161	Magnyfycence	766

CRACK

	Page	Title	Line
For all theyr crack and bost, crack] 'crake' †Kele 1545.3, Toy 1553, Marshe 1568	285	Why Come Ye	256

CRACKE

	Page	Title	Line
And, yf nede be, a bolde worde I dare cracke.	50	Bowge	168

CRACKED

	Page	Title	Line
Wherewith my handes I wrange /That my senaws cracked	73	Phy Sparrow	46

CRACKES

	Page	Title	Line
For all your comly crackes.	367	Albany	350

CRACKIS

	Page	Title	Line
Some facers, some bracers, some make great crackis; some] 'and sum' MS Cotton Vitellius E.x	317	Garlande	189

CRADELL

	Page	Title	Line
Alasse in my cradell that I had not dyde!	196	Magnyfycence	1987
Another with a cradell,	224	El Rummynge	384

CRADELS

	Page	Title	Line
Marked in your cradels	379	Replycacion	174

CRAFT

	Page	Title	Line
By the craft of surgery,	308	Why Come Ye	1173
Sum medelynge spyes, by craft to grope thy mynde,	329	Garlande	617

CRAFTE

	Page	Title	Line
But ye have crafte your selfe alwaye to save.	59	Bowge	452
But to here the subtylte and the crafte,	61	Bowge	519
Without crafte nothynge is well behavyd.	177	Magnyfycence	1350
Convey it be crafte, lyft and lay asyde.	177	Magnyfycence	1357
You to devyse his crafte were to seke;	337	Garlande	893

CRAFTELY

	Page	Title	Line
Of poetes olde, whyche, full craftely,	46	Bowge	9
Craftely all thynges upryght to save:	158	Magnyfycence	642
For then shall we so craftely cary	159	Magnyfycence	683
And craftely can I grope howe every man is mynded.	160	Magnyfycence	725
Shall se many thyngys donne craftely.	177	Magnyfycence	1334
Yet convey it craftely, and hardely spare not for me' -	177	Magnyfycence	1352
So that I may craftely be excused.	187	Magnyfycence	1684
He can full craftely this matter brynge aboute.	187	Magnyfycence	1691
Sophisticatid craftely is many a confecture;	315	Garlande	110
Quintus Cursius, full craftely that wrate Cursius] 'Cursus' †Fakes 1523	322	Garlande	366
So curiously, so craftely, so connyngly wrowght,	325	Garlande	461

CRAFTER

	Page	Title	Line
Jack Travell and Cole Crafter,	281	Why Come Ye	98

CRAFTERS

	Page	Title	Line
And from crafters and hafters I you forfende.	210	Magnyfycence	2456

CRAFTY

	Page	Title	Line
I wolde I had a parte /Of her crafty magyke!	77	Phy Sparrow	204
What! Crafty Conveyaunce.	154	Magnyfycence	495
Crafty Conveyaunce, I sholde say, and I.	154	Magnyfycence	502
And Crafty Conveyaunce, knowe you not hym?	156	Magnyfycence	584
Here cometh in CRAFTY CONVEYAUNCE	162	Magnyfycence	SD
With Crafty Convayaunce. Ye, dyd they so?	166	Magnyfycence	941
Crafty Conveyaunce standeth in the strete	167	Magnyfycence	956

CRAFTYNGE — CREACYOUN   Page   Title   Line

	Page	Title	Line
Here cometh in CRAFTY CONVEYAUNCE.	172	Magnyfycence	SD
from CRAFTY CONVEYAUNCE showlder.	173	Magnyfycence	SD
Here CRAFTY CONVEYAUNCE putteth of his gowne.	173	Magnyfycence	SD
to take money of CRAFTY CONVEYAUNCE, saynge to hym,	174	Magnyfycence	SD
CRAFTY CONVEYAUNCE alone in the place.	177	Magnyfycence	SD
And next come I after, Crafty Conveyaunce.	177	Magnyfycence	1332
And by crafty conveyaunce I wyll, and I can,	178	Magnyfycence	1359
Crafty conveyaunce is no chyldys game;	178	Magnyfycence	1368
By crafty conveyaunce many one is brought up of nought;	178	Magnyfycence	1369
Crafty Conveyaunce can cloke hymselfe frome shame,	178	Magnyfycence	1370
For by crafty conveyaunce wonderful thynges are wrought.	178	Magnyfycence	1371
By convayaunce crafty I have brought	178	Magnyfycence	1372
Here goth out CRAFTY CONVAYAUNCE.	179	Magnyfycence	SD
A, I wolde to God that I were halfe so crafty	183	Magnyfycence	1532
For to use suche haftynge and crafty wayes.	187	Magnyfycence	1678
And your Su[rvay]our, Crafty Conveyaunce,	192	Magnyfycence	1862
Survayour] 'supervysour' †Rastell & Treveris C 1530, B			
Here cometh in CRAFTY CONVEYAUNCE [and] CLOKYD COLUSYON	201	Magnyfycence	SD
The crafty coistronus Cananeorum;	234	Speke Parott	123
In settyng out fresshely his crafty persuacyon,	316	Garlande	153
Some be called crafty that can pyke a purse;	317	Garlande	184
pyke] 'kit' MS Cotton Vitellius E.x			
With Crafty Conveyaunce dothe smater and flater,	346	Garlande	1194

CRAFTYNGE

Craftynge and haftynge contryved is by me;	159	Magnyfycence	697

CRAG

Thy munpynnys, and thy crag,	366	Albany	293

CRAYNGE

Here cometh in FANSY craynge 'Stow, stow!'	165	Magnyfycence	SD

CRAK

Nor durst nat crak a worde,	366	Albany	307

CRAKAR

Ye ar a comly crakar,	127	Garnesche3	110

CRAKE

His bones crake, /Leane as a rake;	94	Phy Sparrow	912
Such boste to make, /To prate and crake,	116	Ag Scottes	32
I am of fewe wordys. I love not to [crake].	162	Magnyfycence	775
crake] 'barke' †Rastell & Treveris C 1530, B			
No, by my trouthe, but crake grete wordes.	163	Magnyfycence	812
To crake and prate.	164	Magnyfycence	875
Nor none so hardy of them with me that durste crake,	182	Magnyfycence	1513
Ye boost, ye face, ye crake,	261	Collyn Clout	602
For I undertake /He wolde so brag and crake	303	Why Come Ye	977
For all his crake and bost,	360	Albany	68

CRAKED

There on he stode, and craked;	63	Hauke	50

CRAKERS

They carpe of us lyke crakers;	276	Collyn Clout	1189
He sayes we ar but crakers;	285	Why Come Ye	274

CRAKYNGE

With crakynge in suche wyse,	306	Why Come Ye	1073

CRANE

The crane with his trumpe,	82	Phy Sparrow	433
The crane and the curlewe therat gan to grame;	192	Magnyfycence	1839
Foted lyke a plane, /Legge[d] lyke a crane;	215	El Rummynge	50
Legged] 'Legges' †Lant 1545, Kynge & Marche 1554, Day 1560, Marshe 1568			

CRANES

Fesauntes, partryche and cranes;	252	Collyn Clout	206
At the Thre Cranes,	374	Replycacion	9

CRANYS

And for stalkynge cranys;	102	Phy Sparrow	1244
stalkynge] 'stalke' †Kele 1545.2			

CRASE

With pitche she patchid her pitcher shuld not crase;	346	Garlande	1209

CRASED

Me thought min hert was crased,	99	Phy Sparrow	1105

CRASY

Thy caytyvys carkes, cours and crasy;	130	Garnesche5	31

CRAVE

Of God nothynge els crave I /But Phyllypes soule to kepe	73	Phy Sparrow	67
Nowe gyve me somwhat, for God sake, I crave.	204	Magnyfycence	2251

CRAVED

'Though I shewe you curtesy, say not that I crave[d];	177	Magnyfycence	1351
craved] 'crave' †Rastell & Treveris C 1530, B			

CRAVYNGE

With borowynge and cravynge,	281	Why Come Ye	101
cravynge] 'cravyne' †Kele 1545.3			

CRAW

Such a bedfellaw /Wold make one cast his craw.	226	El Rummynge	489

CRAWES

He wyl cause yow caste your crawes,	128	Garnesche3	155

CREACYON

Of whose incyneracyon /There ryseth a new creacyon	85	Phy Sparrow	541
Of hevenly inspyracion /In laureate creacyon,	384	Replycacion	373

CREACYOUN

The Boke of the Rosiar; Prince Arturis Creacyoun;	345	Garlande	1178

CREAT —CRYDE

CREAT
	Page	Title	Line
Whan he was creat pope /First in Antioche.	307	Why Come Ye	1142

CREATE
For that pereles prynce that Parrot dyd create,	236	Speke Parott	218

CREATURE
No creature but that wolde /Have rewed upon me,	72	Phy Sparrow	41

CREAUNCER
The Duke of Yorkis creauncer whan Skelton was,	347	Garlande	1226

CREAUNSER
That creaunser was to thy sofre[yne] lorde;	132	Garnesche5	102
sofreyne] 'sofre' †MS Harley 367			

CREDE
By Crede, I trust to se the day,	41	Coystrowne4	12
And with the corner of a Crede,	72	Phy Sparrow	15
Your Pater noster, your Ave, nor your Crede.	137	Ven Tongues	19
All that ye say is as trewe as the crede.	146	Magnyfycence	218
By crede, it wolde have fresshe aray,	153	Magnyfycence	460
And wotteth never what thei rede, /Paternoster nor crede;	252	Collyn Clout	235
And beleve it as your crede.	278	Why Come Ye	2
And beleve it as your crede.	279	Why Come Ye	16
And beleve it as your crede.	279	Why Come Ye	28

CREDENCE
And be not light of credence in no case.	34	Dol Dethe	175
Be lyght of byleve and hasty of credence;	161	Magnyfycence	740
And is this the credence that I gave to the letter?	193	Magnyfycence	1867
Largesse, syr, by his credence was his name.	209	Magnyfycence	2441
To gyve so hasty credence ye were moche to blame.	209	Magnyfycence	2443
And to lyght in credence;	279	Why Come Ye	10
But if hastyve credence by mayntenance of myght	344	Garlande	1133
This mater to credence	372	Albany	522

CREDENSYNGE
In credensynge his tales,	290	Why Come Ye	442

CREISSEID
Goodly Creisseid, fayrer than Polexene,	336	Garlande	871

CREKE
The pepil durst not creke	111	Lawde	33
Gyve it up, and cry, 'creke', /Lyke an huddy peke.	366	Albany	300

CREKETH
'He cryeth and he creketh /He pryeth and he preketh,	247	Collyn Clout	19
preketh] 'peketh' Kele 1545.1, 'prekythe' MS Harley 2252			

CREME
Collustrum now for Parot, whyte bred and swete creme!	233	Speke Parott	82

CREPE
And crepe in at my gore	80	Phy Sparrow	346
crepe] 'gape' Kitson 1560.6			
In his hed to crepe;	95	Phy Sparrow	935
Wyll crepe upon us, and us to myschefe lede;	144	Magnyfycence	153
And assay to crepe /Within the noble walles	249	Collyn Clout	125
Rynne away and crepe;	286	Why Come Ye	294
Or of humors superflue, that often wyll crepe	313	Garlande	32
Must crepe in to your caves	363	Albany	185

CREPT
What though he crept so lowe?	76	Phy Sparrow	169
though] 'thought' †Kele 1545.2			

CRESSYDE
Upon fayre Cressyde,	88	Phy Sparrow	679

CRESUS
Of Kynge Cresus golde,	76	Phy Sparrow	190

CREWE
And ay he sange, 'In fayth, Decon, thou crewe.'	56	Bowge	360

CRIBBIS
I saw dyvers that were cariid away thens in cribbis,	330	Garlande	640

CRIMSIN
Crimsin velvet for your bawdry.	130	Garnesche5	40

CRIST
Be Crist, ye shall not! No, no, hardely!	36	Man Margery	18

CRISTALL
Of cristall the clerenes theis waters far past,	330	Garlande	660

CRISTECROSSE
'Cristecrosse and Saynt Nycholas, Parrot, be your good spede!'	236	Speke Parott	189

CRISTIAN
Gup, Cristian Clowte, gup, Jak of the Vale,	35	Man Margery	6
Gup, Cristian Clowte, gup, Jak of the Vale,	36	Man Margery	13
Gup, Cristian Clowte, gup, Jak of the Vale,	36	Man Margery	20
Gup, Cristian Clowte, your breth is stale,	36	Man Margery	27
Gup, Cristian Clowte, gup, Jak of the Vale,	36	Man Margery	29

CRY
Bluntly as bestis withe boste and with cry	31	Dol Dethe	83
Wyth cry unreverent, /Before the sacrament,	62	Hauke	11
With hogeous showte and cry.	63	Hauke	48
Wherfore the bordes yet cry	78	Phy Sparrow	248
bordes] 'byrdes' Wyght 1553, Kitson 1560.6, Marshe 1568			
Who is that that thus dyd cry?	149	Magnyfycence	326
And some to cry out of the bone ake;	194	Magnyfycence	1907
A cry anone forthwith she made proclame,	325	Garlande	453
Gyve it up, and cry, 'creke', /Lyke an huddy peke.	366	Albany	300

CRYDE
Some whispred, some rownyd, some spake, and some cryde,	319	Garlande	250

151

CRYE —CROPPED   Page   Title   Line

Bowns, bowns, bowns! that all they out cryde. 329   Garlande   624
CRYE
That vengeaunce I aske and crye, ... 78   Phy Sparrow   273
But whereto shuld I /Lenger morne or crye? 86   Phy Sparrow   595
'Lyke owur pus catt Parott can mewte and crye.' 231   Speke Parott   24
  owur] 'your' Lant 1545, Kynge & Marche 1554, Day 1560,
  Marshe 1568
Lyke houndes of hell, /They crye and they yell 251   Collyn Clout   199
And mercy for to crye, ... 377   Replycacion   88
And crye God mercy, lyke frantyke foles. 382   Replycacion   299
CRYED
It can be no counsell that is cryed at the cros. 43   Balettys2   36
There was moche noyse, anone one cryed, 'Cese!' 47   Bowge   46
And cryed, 'Stow, stow, stow!' 63   Hauke   73
CRYEST
That cryest 'Stow, stow'? 166   Magnyfycence   917
CRYETH
'He cryeth and he creketh /He pryeth and he preketh, ... 247   Collyn Clout   19
  preketh] 'peketh' Kele 1545.1, 'prekythe' MS Harley 2252
CRYID
'Triumpha, triumpha!' they cryid all aboute. 354   Garlande   1506
CRYME
To snappar and to fall /Into this opyn cryme; 65   Hauke   143
A lytell cryme in a great astate, ... 310   Why Come Ye2   13
CRYNKLYD
Comely crynklyd, /Woundersly wrynklyd, ... 215   El Rummynge   18
CRYST
Cryst you assyste in your altrycacyon! 142   Magnyfycence   81
By Cryst, as mery as a Marche hare. 166   Magnyfycence   921
Nowe Cryst it blysse! 167   Magnyfycence   973
Maysters, Cryst save everychone! 169   Magnyfycence   1043
Mary, Cryst graunt ye catche no colde on your fete! 191   Magnyfycence   1803
Cryst be amonge you, and the Holy Goste! 208   Magnyfycence   2385
CRYSTALLYNE
Of Eliconys waters crystallyne, ... 132   Garnesche5   99
CRYSTE
'By Cryste,' quod Favell, 'Drede is soleyne freke! 51   Bowge   187
'By Cryste,' quod he, 'for it is shame to saye, ... 54   Bowge   300
'Cryste save Kyng Herry the viiith, owur royall kyng, ... 231   Speke Parott   34
That pereles pomegarnat, Cryste save hyr nobyll grace!' . . . 231   Speke Parott   37
CRYSTEOVYR
Welle Be Seyn Crysteovyr Chalannger, et cetera 124   Garnesche3   I
CRYSTES
Was nevyr suche a senatour syn Crystes Incarnacion. 240   Speke Parott   337
Where the sank royall is, Crystes blode so rede, ... 353   Garlande   1463
CRYSTIS
Where Crystis precyous blode /Dayly offryd is, ... 66   Hauke   179
CRYSTYS
And I gyve hym Crystys curse 204   Magnyfycence   2257
CRYSTOFER
Well Be Seen Crystofer Chalangar, et cetera 129   Garnesche5   I
CROYDON
Wryten at Croydon by Crowland in the Clay, ... 38   Coystrownel   69
From Croydon into Kent 282   Why Come Ye   145
  into] 'to' Toy 1553, Kitson 1560.7, Marshe 1568
CROKE
By hoke ne by croke 277   Collyn Clout   1238
CROKED
Wyth 'Whom' and 'Ha' and with a croked loke, ... 51   Bowge   191
Her nose somdele hoked /And camously croked, ... 215   El Rummynge   28
With a croked backe. 215   El Rummynge   33
As right as a cammocke croked! 281   Why Come Ye   117
CROKENEBBED
She was somwhat foule, /Crokenebbed lyke an oule; 225   El Rummynge   427
  Crokenebbed] 'Croke necked' †Lant 1545, Kynge &
  Marche 1554, Day 1560, Marshe 1568
CROKYD
Nother crokyd Cacus, /Nor yet dronken Bacus; 67   Hauke   194
  Nother] 'Nor yet' Kynge & Marche 1554, Day 1560, Marshe 1568
He sayde, for a crokyd intent, ... 68   Hauke   228
Crokyd as a camoke, and as a kowe calfles, ... 122   Garneschel   30
CROKYS
And her becke so comely crokys! 168   Magnyfycence   1000
CROMMES
Let us wasshe our gommes /From the drye crommes!' 222   El Rummynge   308
CRONELL
Of laurell levis a cronell on his hede, ... 320   Garlande   288
A cronell of lawrell with verduris light and darke 334   Garlande   776
CRONYCLE
Sens Dewcalyons flodde, in no cronycle ys told. 246   Speke Parott   518
CROP
I gader togyther and close in my crop, ... 233   Speke Parott   94
CROPE
To sowe corne in the see-sande, ther wyll no crope growe. . . 240   Speke Parott   342
CROPPED
And your tonges cropped, /Whan ye logyke chopped, ... 377   Replycacion   117

CROPPY — CRUELL

CROPPY
For so mote I hoppy, /It coleth well my croppy.' . . . . 228 El Rummynge 561
   croppy] 'coppy' Day 1560, Marshe 1568
CROPPYD
But with countenaunce your corage must be croppyd. . . . . . . 141 Magnyfycence 47
And your tonsors be croppyd, ... 263 Collyn Clout 677
   tonsors be croppyd] 'coursers betrapped' †Godfray 1531,
   Kele 1545.1, Marshe 1568
CROS
It can be no counsell that is cryed at the cros. 43 Balettys2 36
Cros, staffe, lectryne and banner, ... 64 Hauke 114
CROSE
A myter nor a crose, ... 254 Collyn Clout 292
CROSSE
The armes of Calyce, I have no coyne nor crosse! . . . . 57 Bowge 398
The sensers and the crosse shall fet; . . . . 86 Phy Sparrow 568
Then fare well thryfte, by hym that crosse kyst! . . . . 179 Magnyfycence 1416
Betwene Temple Bar /And the Crosse in Chepe, ... 223 El Rummynge 360
Of a peny nor of a crosse . . . . 269 Collyn Clout 929
At Poules Crosse, or elswhere, ... 276 Collyn Clout 1182
For ye were worldly shamed, /At Poules Crosse openly, ... 376 Replycacion 63
CROSSED
Why? Is he crossed than with a chalke? . . . . 166 Magnyfycence 950
Crossed? Ye, checked out of consayte. . . . . 166 Magnyfycence 951
CROSSE ROWE
In your crosse rowe nor Christ crosse you spede, ... 137 Ven Tongues 18
CROSSYNG
So myche crossyng and blyssyng and hym all be shrewde; . . . . 246 Speke Parott 516
CROUCHE
Lordes must crouche and knele, ... 262 Collyn Clout 628
   crouche] 'couch' Marshe 1568, 'cruche' MS Harley 2252
CROUNE
Sayth, from thy to unto thi croune, ... 130 Garnesche5 26
CROW
Ye pressyd pertely to pluk a crow: 130 Garnesche5 48
The faucon from the crow, ... 298 Why Come Ye 775
CROWCHE
The devyll myghte daunce therin for ony crowche. . . . . 56 Bowge 364
CROWDYNG
Hither they come crowdyng to get them a name, ... 329 Garlande 621
CROWE
The crowe and the kyte; . . . . 82 Phy Sparrow 413
What! Callyst thou me a donnyshe crowe? . . . . 170 Magnyfycence 1095
And the cokkes begyn to crowe agayne the day; . . . . 239 Speke Parott 286
Whyche of yow fyrste dare boldlye plucke the crowe. . . . . . 242 Speke Parott 396
For to shote a crowe /At her tyrly tyrlowe; . . . . 270 Collyn Clout 948
CROWETH
And yet he croweth dayly . . . . 84 Phy Sparrow 506
CROWLAND
Wryten at Croydon by Crowland in the Clay, ... 38 Coystrowne1 69
CROWNDE
With laureat tryumphe why Skelton sholde be crownde. . . . . . 318 Garlande 217
CROWNE
A somner to were a kynges crowne. . . . . 115 Scot Kynge 67
Adieu, syr sumner, cast of your crowne! . . . . 117 Ag Scottes 64
A sumner to were a kynges crowne. . . . . 120 Ag Scottes 175
Syr sumner, now where is your crowne? . . . . 120 Ag Scottes 178
Cast of your crowne, cast up your crowne! . . . . 120 Ag Scottes 179
Cast of your crowne, cast up your crowne! . . . . 120 Ag Scottes 179
Syr sumner, now ye have lost your crowne. . . . . 120 Ag Scottes 180
Nowe must your fete lye hyer than your crowne. . . . . 197 Magnyfycence 2007
Wounded from the fote to the crowne of the hede: . . . . 207 Magnyfycence 2364
Hys wolvys hede, wanne, bloo as lede, gapythe over the crowne; 244 Speke Parott 434
And set hys crowne /On your owne heed . . . . 361 Albany 96
CROWNES
Wyth crownes and wyth scutus; . . . . 283 Why Come Ye 170
Wyth scutis and crownes of golde . . . . 283 Why Come Ye 171
They shote at him with crownes. . . . . 283 Why Come Ye 178
With crownes of golde enblased . . . . 283 Why Come Ye 179
CROWNYCLER
How maister Gaguine, the crownycler . . . . 297 Why Come Ye 718
CROWNYD
Wheron stode a lybbard, crownyd with golde and stones, ... 328 Garlande 590
CRUDE
Her mete was very crude, ... 63 Hauke 77
   mete] 'mere' Kynge & Marche 1554
CRUE
Adieu, Jayberd, adue. /I faith, dikkon, thou crue! 108 Epitaphe1 63
CRUELL
O cruell Mars, thou dedly god of war! . . . . 32 Dol Dethe 113
Goddes mooste cruell unto the lyfe of man, ... 32 Dol Dethe 121
To be so cruell and so overthwart, ... 45 Balettys5 5
Nother Zorobabell, /Nor cruell Jesabell; . . . . 67 Hauke 207
Tyll cruell fate made him to dy: . . . . 86 Phy Sparrow 592
So myche pride of prelattes, so cruell and so kene — . . . . . 245 Speke Parott 475
As ferce and as cruell . . . . 294 Why Come Ye 593

CRUELL HERTYD —CURIOUSLY   Page   Title   Line

CRUELL HERTYD
And so cruell hertyd, /That he wyll nat be convertyd;   308   Why Come Ye   1178
    That] not in MS Rawlinson C. 813
CRUELLY
For cruell[y] amonge them ther he was slayne.   32   Dol Dethe   105
    cruelly] 'cruell' †MS Royal 18 D.ii, Marshe 1568
This noble man that cruelly was slayne.   34   Dol Dethe   182
That slew so cruelly   78   Phy Sparrow   279
CRUELTE
Dysdayns, dystres, exylyd cruelte;   43   Balettys3   4
O hatefull happe, O carefull cruelte!   198   Magnyfycence   2049
Chryst by cruelte /Was nayled upon a tre;   258   Collyn Clout   450
Why have the goddes shewyd me this cruelte, ...   321   Garlande   309
CRUYSE
What! Then he may drynke out of a stone cruyse.   201   Magnyfycence   2166
CUCKOLDES
That cuckoldes men call;   88   Phy Sparrow   648
CUCKOUE
Our chaunters shalbe the cuckoue, ...   82   Phy Sparrow   428
CUE
In dede, syr, that lyberte was not worthe a cue.   141   Magnyfycence   36
CULE
The devyll kysse his cule!   282   Why Come Ye   133
    his] 'hes' †Kele 1545.3
CULVER
The culver, the stockedowve, ...   82   Phy Sparrow   429
CUM
Ye made your hawke to cum /Desuper candelabrum   69   Hauke   288
Cum Garnyche, cum Godfrey, with as many as ye may!   123   Garnesche2   32
Cum Garnyche, cum Godfrey, with as many as ye may!   123   Garnesche2   32
Tyll more matyr may cum.   129   Garnesche3   205
O Esebon, Esebon, to the is cum agayne   234   Speke Parott   120
To owur soleyne Seigneour Sadoke, desire hym to cum home, . . .   239   Speke Parott   304
Of Fame. Perceyvynge how that I was cum, ...   343   Garlande   1115
CUMYS
It cumys the better for to dryve   132   Garnesche5   92
CUMLY
She was a cumly callet.   226   El Rummynge   462
CUMMYNG
'I beshrew the for thy cummyng!'   227   El Rummynge   503
CUMMYTH
When Garnyche cummyth yow amonge   128   Garnesche3   150
CUNNYNG
Tholomye and Haly were cunnyng and wyse   234   Speke Parott   134
Of them that have vertue by reason of cunnyng, ...   317   Garlande   198
CUNNYNGLY
Raggid, and daggid, and cunnyngly cut;   329   Garlande   630
CUNTREIS
To all cuntreis aboute hym reporte me I dare: 33   Dol Dethe   136
CUP
With, 'Fyll the cup, fyll!'   217   El Rummynge   115
And blessed her with a cup /Of newe ale in cornes.   224   El Rummynge   377
Betwene the cup and the wall, ...   226   El Rummynge   473
CUPBORD
Your cupbord that was   301   Why Come Ye   901
CUPBORDE
This shrewdly accordis /To be a cupborde for lordys!   302   Why Come Ye   914
CUPYDE
And howe Cupyde shaked /His dart, and bent his bowe   270   Collyn Clout   946
Cupyde hath stryken so that she ne wolde   320   Garlande   291
CUPPE
She asked yf ever I dranke of saucys cuppe.   48   Bowge   73
CUR
Shake thy tayle, Scot, lyke a cur, ...   135   Dundas   25
Then Cerberus the cur couching in the kenel of hel;   140   Ven Tongues   80
That made Cerberus to cache, the cur dogge of hell, ...   182   Magnyfycence   1495
For drede of the mastyve cur, ...   286   Why Come Ye   297
CURATE
Devysed and also wrate /Uppon a lewde curate, ...   62   Hauke   35
A curate in specyall   65   Hauke   141
CURATES
Theyr curates to content   268   Collyn Clout   858
Agaynst curates, they repyne, ...   268   Collyn Clout   873
    They] not in Kele 1545.1, Marshe 1568, 'They' MS Harley 2252
CURE
Els, I prayed hym with all my besy cure, ...   52   Bowge   221
And specyally to controule /Such as have cure of soule, . . .   62   Hauke   4
In theyr pryncypall cure /They make but lytell sure, ...   249   Collyn Clout   102
Yet take they cure of soules, ...   252   Collyn Clout   233
    cure] 'cures' Kele 1545.1, Marshe 1568
For to kepe a cure, ...   253   Collyn Clout   279
Bryngeth all thynges under cure.   286   Why Come Ye   284
My besy cure /To yow I owe;   338   Garlande   928
CURED
I am not woundid but that I may be cured.   332   Garlande   732
CURIOUSLY
So curiously, so craftely, so connyngly wrowght, ...   325   Garlande   461

CURYOUSLY — CUT

	Page	Title	Line
CURYOUSLY			
Buyldynge royally /Theyr mancyons curyously,	269	Collyn Clout	935
Many divisis passynge curyously;	336	Garlande	853
CURYOWS			
Caste up your curyows wrytyng,	127	Garnesche3	112
CURYOWSLY			
that curyowsly chawntyd, and curryshly cowntred,	36	Coystrowne	1
Curyowsly he can both counter and knak	37	Coystrowne1	17
A cage curyowsly carven, with sylver pynne,	231	Speke Parott	8
CURLEWE			
And the denty curlewe,	83	Phy Sparrow	464
The crane and the curlewe therat gan to grame;	192	Magnyfycence	1839
CURRANT			
For reysons ar no resons but resons currant –	244	Speke Parott	443
CURRE			
Thow claimist the jentyll, thou art a curre;	131	Garnesche5	67
What pylde curre ledest thou in thy hande?	169	Magnyfycence	1054
A pylde curre? Ye, so I tell the, a pylde curre.	169	Magnyfycence	1055
A pylde curre? Ye, so I tell the, a pylde curre.	169	Magnyfycence	1055
What! Then he is some good poore mannes curre?	171	Magnyfycence	1129
But where gatte thou that mangey curre?	173	Magnyfycence	1180
Suche malyncoly mastyvys and mangye curre dogges	240	Speke Parott	320
So mangye a mastyfe curre, the grete greyhoundes pere;	245	Speke Parott	487
For and this curre do gnar,	286	Why Come Ye	300
CURRES			
Lyke cankerd curres /Ye loste your spurres;	360	Albany	33
CURRYS			
Barkyng and whynyng lyke churlysshe currys of kynde,	239	Speke Parott	295
CURRYSHLY			
that curyowsly chawntyd, and curryshly cowntred,	36	Coystrowne	1
So curryshly to beknave me in the kynges place?	121	Garnesche1	9
CURS			
Some carefull cokwoldes, some have theyr wyves curs;	317	Garlande	186
CURSE			
The Popes cur[se] gave you that clap.	119	Ag Scottes	169
curse] 'cures' †Lant 1545, Kynge & Marche 1554, Day 1560, Marshe 1568			
And I gyve hym Crystys curse	204	Magnyfycence	2257
A strawe for Goddes curse!	254	Collyn Clout	294
For whether he blesse or curse,	282	Why Come Ye	137
And curse bothe nyght and day,	376	Replycacion	79
CURSED			
And they cursed Datan	301	Why Come Ye	892
they cursed] 'the course' MS Rawlinson C. 813			
CURSEDLY			
That evermore wil ly /And say cursedly;	94	Phy Sparrow	907
CURSIUS			
Quintus Cursius, full craftely that wrate	322	Garlande	366
Cursius] 'Cursus' †Fakes 1523			
CURSYDLY			
Are not his wordys cursydly cowchyd?	175	Magnyfycence	1276
CURST			
Nor Nero the worst, /Nor Clawdyus the curst;	67	Hauke	203
CURTEISLY			
Before remembred, me curteisly brought	343	Garlande	1102
me curteisly] 'kurteisly me' MS Cotton Vitellius E.x			
But curteisly /That I have pende /For to deffend,	356	Garlande	1569
CURTEYNS			
With curteyns of sylke, ye were wonte to be drawe;	197	Magnyfycence	2014
curteyns of sylke] 'courtely sylkes' †Rastell & Treveris 1530B			
CURTEYS			
Nowe to curteys, forthwith unkynde;	168	Magnyfycence	1008
CURTEYSE			
Beninge, curteyse, of jentyll harte and mynde,	337	Garlande	880
CURTEL			
It is a curtel that well can wynche and praunce;	57	Bowge	411
curtel] 'curtet' †Wynkyn de Worde 1499, 1510			
CURTES			
Of youre behavoure curtes and benynge,	44	Balettys3	30
CURTESY			
'Though I shewe you curtesy, say not that I crave[d];	177	Magnyfycence	1351
craved] 'crave' †Rastell & Treveris C 1530, B			
Or elles ye pynche curtesy, trulye as I trowe,	242	Speke Parott	395
CURTESLYE			
With, 'Speke, Parott, I pray yow,' full curteslye they sey,	231	Speke Parott	13
CURTOYL			
Hys jentyll curtoy[l], and set nowght by small naggys!	43	Balettys2	16
curtoyl] 'curtoyt' †Rastell 1527.1			
CUSTOME			
It is not my custome nor my gyse /To leve behynde	342	Garlande	1068
CUSTRELL			
A custrell to dryve the devyll out of the derke,	154	Magnyfycence	485
CUT			
For to kepe his cut,	74	Phy Sparrow	118
With, 'Phyllyp, kepe your cut!'	74	Phy Sparrow	119
Sharper then raysors, that shave and cut throtes,	138	Ven Tongues	51
Without I myght cut it out of the brode clothe,	144	Magnyfycence	146
Or ellys with this knyfe cut out a tonge	206	Magnyfycence	2314

	Page	Title	Line
CUTBERDES —DAYLY			
She cut of her sho-sole,	224	El Rummynge	405
Raggid, and daggid, and cunnyngly cut;	329	Garlande	630
CUTBERDES			
With Sainct Cutberdes banner	360	Albany	63
CUTTYS			
In fayth, I set not by the worlde two Dauncaster cuttys.	148	Magnyfycence	293
D			
And sette to a D, /And then hyt ys 'Amend',	238	Speke Parott	275
to] not in †MS Harley 2252			
DADY			
Your mammy and your dady	339	Garlande	974
DAGGED			
Wyth theyr heles dagged, /Theyr kyrtelles all to-jagged,	217	El Rummynge	123
DAGGER			
I shall thrust in the my dagger – Thorowe the legge in to the hose.	202	Magnyfycence	2177
Holde thy hande, dawe, of thy dagger, and stynt of thy dyn;	202	Magnyfycence	2188
DAGGESWANE			
In faythe, he may dreme on a daggeswane for ony fether bed.	201	Magnyfycence	2169
DAGGID			
Raggid, and daggid, and cunnyngly cut;	329	Garlande	630
DAGMATISTA			
The devylyshe dagmatista.	260	Collyn Clout	550
DAGSWAYNE			
Suche a doutty dagswayne.	363	Albany	172
DAY			
At his commaundement whiche had both day and night	30	Dol Dethe	31
But had his nobillmen donn wel that day	31	Dol Dethe	69
By Crede, I trust to se the day,	41	Coystrowne4	12
That day and night brenneth styl,	79	Phy Sparrow	314
Musyng nyght and day,	89	Phy Sparrow	703
And the next day he shuld dye,	105	Phy Sparrow	1359
With the ix day of the same,	117	Ag Scottes	67
The outesyde every day,	125	Garnesche3	48
If they wer lyveyng thys day,	133	Garnesche5	142
S[e] at our eye the worlde day by day.	146	Magnyfycence	216
Se] 'so' †Rastell & Treveris C 1530, B			
S[e] at our eye the worlde day by day.	146	Magnyfycence	216
Se] 'so' †Rastell & Treveris C 1530, B			
What! Shall we jangle thus all the day styll?	156	Magnyfycence	565
By day or by nyght	164	Magnyfycence	860
That fell amonge us this same day?	166	Magnyfycence	933
I make on the one day, and I marre on the other.	169	Magnyfycence	1038
And therfore I growe more on one day	170	Magnyfycence	1077
To pyke theyr fyngers all the day longe;	174	Magnyfycence	1222
That wyll syt ydyll all the day	174	Magnyfycence	1229
At ones, and let hym not tary all day.	179	Magnyfycence	1400
That day I se hym I shall be worse all nyght.	188	Magnyfycence	1724
Yet it proveth eyrnest, ye may se, every day.	195	Magnyfycence	1949
'Parott hathe not dyned of all this long day;'	231	Speke Parott	23
And the cokkes begyn to crowe agayne the day;	239	Speke Parott	286
Tyll my dyenge day	259	Collyn Clout	506
Farewell, than, have good day!	280	Why Come Ye	57
And vexeth them day by day	282	Why Come Ye	155
And vexeth them day by day	282	Why Come Ye	155
Some sluggysh slovyns, that slepe day and nyght;	317	Garlande	191
'Lyke as the larke, upon the somers day,	327	Garlande	533
And the next day he shulde dye,	350	Garlande	1352
Thus passyth the tyme both nyght and day,	352	Garlande	1423
By Candelmes day what wedder shuld holde;	352	Garlande	1442
And curse bothe nyght and day,	376	Replycacion	79
Howe ye are this day,	379	Replycacion	177
DAYE			
Wolde to God it wolde please you some daye	53	Bowge	256
For, as for me, I served here many a daye,	53	Bowge	274
For whome Tyborne groneth both daye and nyghte.	58	Bowge	417
whome] 'home' †Wynkyn de Worde 1499			
As I be saved at the dredefull daye,	58	Bowge	443
Gyve me your honde, fare well and have good daye.'	60	Bowge	497
But from daye to daye delayde,	255	Collyn Clout	352
But from daye to daye delayde,	255	Collyn Clout	352
Than have good daye. Adewe!	280	Why Come Ye	58
DAYES			
So vertuously that hath his dayes spente;	50	Bowge	151
At those dayes moch commended;	91	Phy Sparrow	796
Som be wrestyd there that they thynke on it forty dayes,	204	Magnyfycence	2274
And so ungracyously thy dayes thou hast spent,	205	Magnyfycence	2295
By myschefe to brevyate and shorten his dayes.	206	Magnyfycence	2338
By the dayes and by the wekes.	293	Why Come Ye	556
That all the dayes of ther lyfe shall styck by ther rybbis.	330	Garlande	638
DAYLY			
The seconde was Suspecte, whiche that dayly	49	Bowge	136
Where Crystis precyous blode /Dayly offryd is,	66	Hauke	180
And yet he croweth dayly	84	Phy Sparrow	506
As ye may dayly se /Howe the lay fee	259	Collyn Clout	495
As dayly men may se,	262	Collyn Clout	630
Thus dayly they be decked, /Taunted and checked,	294	Why Come Ye	611
Of this high courte the dayly besines;	326	Garlande	519

DAYNNOUSLY — DAME

	Page	Title	Line
The False Fayth that Now Goth, which dayly is renude;	346	Garlande	1179
DAYNNOUSLY			
Full daynnously, and fro me she dyde fare,	48	Bowge	82
DAYNTELY			
And cherysshed full dayntely,	86	Phy Sparrow	591
DAYS			
Oure days be datyd /To be chekmatyd,	39	Coystrowne3	29
And of the winter days that hy them so fast,	331	Garlande	700
And of the somer days so longe that doth last,	331	Garlande	702
DAYSY			
The daysy delectable,	98	Phy Sparrow	1051
DAYSY FLOURE			
'My darlyng dere, my daysy floure,	41	Balettys1	1
DAY-WACH			
That he dryvyth them doune with dyntys on ther day-wach.	43	Balettys2	30
DAKERS			
What here ye of the lorde Dakers?	285	Why Come Ye	272
To my Lady Anne Dakers of the Sowth	337	Garlande	R
DALE			
To the dyne dale /Of boteles bale,	40	Coystrowne3	45
boteles] 'botemles' Marshe 1568			
To a straunge jurisdictyon /Called Dymingis Dale,	299	Why Come Ye	801
DALY			
To daly with yow she had no lust.	131	Garnesche5	54
DALYAUNCE			
The famylyaryte, the formar dalyaunce,	42	Balettys2	2
Her goodly dalyaunce,	99	Phy Sparrow	1095
That we delyte gretly in your dalyaunce.	183	Magnyfycence	1524
DALYDA			
With Dalyda to mell, /That wanton damosell.	284	Why Come Ye	211
that] 'the' Kitson 1560.7, Marshe 1568			
DALYRAG			
I say, Syr Dalyrag,	129	Garnesche3	186
Adue, nowe, Sir Wrig-wrag! /Adue, Sir Dalyrag!	366	Albany	297
DAM			
The golden ram /Of flemmynge dam,	301	Why Come Ye	898
DAME			
That Dame Menolope was never half so wyse;	42	Balettys2	11
Whoos name to tell is Dame Saunce-Pere.	47	Bowge	51
Di le xi, /Dame Margery, /Fa, re, my, my.	71	Phy Sparrow	4
Dame Sulpicia at Rome,	75	Phy Sparrow	148
And Dame Gaynour, his quene	87	Phy Sparrow	636
Dame Nature hath her lent	97	Phy Sparrow	1042
Lyke dame Flora, quene	101	Phy Sparrow	1183
Dame Venus of all pleasure,	102	Phy Sparrow	1227
She doth excede and pas /In prudence dame Pallas;	102	Phy Sparrow	1230
His dame and his syre	165	Magnyfycence	905
Sym Sadylgose was my syer, and Dawcocke my dame.	192	Magnyfycence	1834
And this comely dame,	216	El Rummynge	91
And Dame Elynour entrete	221	El Rummynge	268
And brought a peny cheke /To Dame Elynour	225	El Rummynge	416
brought] 'brought up' Day 1560, Marshe 1568			
Lyke an honest dame.	227	El Rummynge	511
'Dame Elynour,' sayde she,	228	El Rummynge	562
'Dame Elynour,' sayde they,	229	El Rummynge	576
And called for our dame, /Elynour by name.	229	El Rummynge	592
My lady mastres, Dame Phylology,	232	Speke Parott	43
mastres] 'maysters' Lant 1545, Kynge & Marche 1554, Day 1560, Marshe 1568			
Dame Sybly our abbesse,	256	Collyn Clout	391
Dame Dorothe and Lady Besse,	256	Collyn Clout	392
Dame Sare our pryoresse,	256	Collyn Clout	393
Dame Margeres soule out of hell.	268	Collyn Clout	876
With Dame Dyana naked;	270	Collyn Clout	944
With Dame Helyn the quene.	270	Collyn Clout	953
And also dame Prudence, /With sober Sapyence.	279	Why Come Ye	13
For Dame Philargerya /Hathe so his herte in holde,	284	Why Come Ye	206
Welcome dame Simonia, /With dame Castrimergia,	284	Why Come Ye	215
Welcome dame Simonia, /With dame Castrimergia,	284	Why Come Ye	216
As I harde say, Dame Pallas was her name,	313	Garlande	48
The Quene of Fame to Dame Pallas	313	Garlande	R
Dame Pallas to the Quene of Fame	314	Garlande	R
The Quene of Fame to Dame Pallas	315	Garlande	R
Dame Pallas to the Quene of Fame	316	Garlande	R
The Quene of Fame to Dame Pallas	316	Garlande	R
Dame Pallas to the Quene of Fame	317	Garlande	R
The Quene of Fame to Dame Pallas	318	Garlande	R
Dame Pallas to the Quene of Fame	318	Garlande	R
Of noble Dame Pallas, wherof I spake;	320	Garlande	284
Dame Pallas commaundid that they shold me convay	325	Garlande	449
And formest of all dame Flora, the quene	331	Garlande	685
As was Thamarys, whiche toke the kyng of Perce,	336	Garlande	857
Dame Agrippina also I may reherse	336	Garlande	859
Whome dame Nature, as wele I may reporte,	336	Garlande	867
Lyke to Dame Pasiphe;	342	Garlande	1048
How Dame Minerva first found the Olyve Tre, she red	351	Garlande	1404
Dun is in the myre, dame, reche me my spur.	352	Garlande	1433

	Page	Title	Line
DAMYAN			
But mayster Damyan, /Or some other man	264	Collyn Clout	720
DAMMOYSELS			
Deyntes for dammoysels, chaffer far-fet;	234	Speke Parott	129
DAMNABLE			
And by her abusiouns, /And damnable illusiouns	350	Garlande	1341
DAMOSELL			
With Dalyda to mell, /That wanton damosell. that] 'the' Kitson 1560.7, Marshe 1568	284	Why Come Ye	212
DAMPNABLE			
And dampnable illusyons	105	Phy Sparrow	1348
DAMPNACYON			
Of dampnacyon I had ben drawen in the luge.	206	Magnyfycence	2334
To theyr owne dampnacyon.	275	Collyn Clout	1140
DANE			
Dane Johnn Lydgate. Theis Englysshe poetis thre,	323	Garlande	391
DANES			
Before the Frensshe kynge, Danes and other	114	Scot Kynge	15
Ye rowe ranke Scottes and dronken Danes	115	Scot Kynge	64
DANGEROUS			
Gayne dangerous stormys theyr anker of supporte,	44	Balettys3	26
DANT			
In came another dant, /With a gose and a gant.	227	El Rummynge	515
DAPHNES			
Lamentyng Daphnes, whome with the darte of lede	320	Garlande	290
'Daphnes, my derlynge, why do you me refuse?	320	Garlande	297
Yet, in remembraunce of Daphnes transformacyon,	321	Garlande	320
DAR			
Agayne Frentike Frenesy there dar no man sey nay,	243	Speke Parott	422
Syns Dewcalyons flodde was nevyr, I dar sey.	245	Speke Parott	483
DARE			
To all cuntreis aboute hym reporte me I dare:	33	Dol Dethe	136
In a dysh here he rush at the rypest;	37	Coystrownel	46
For thus dare I say, without tradiccyon,	42	Balettys2	10
That wher I love best I dare not dyscure!	45	Balettys5	7
That where I love best I dare not dyscure,	46	Balettys5	14
For I dare saye that there nys erthly man	48	Bowge	101
And, yf nede be, a bolde worde I dare cracke.	50	Bowge	168
For here is none that dare well other truste;	51	Bowge	202
I dare not speke; I promysed to be dome.	52	Bowge	229
And I dare saye there is no man hereinne	53	Bowge	267
I dare not speke, we be so layde awayte,	59	Bowge	468
I dare be bolde /Thus for to were.	112	Calliope	11
Thus fortune hath tourned you, I dare well say,	119	Ag Scottes	164
Yet somwhat to say I dare well be bolde,	137	Ven Tongues	10
To tell yow, syr, I dare not, leest I sholde be maskyd	141	Magnyfycence	30
As men dare speke it hugger mugger:	151	Magnyfycence	387
By Goddes fote, and I dare well fyght, for I wyll not start.	161	Magnyfycence	768
For drede, that we dare not ofte, lest we be spyed.	177	Magnyfycence	1339
I have an hoby can make larkys to dare;	177	Magnyfycence	1342
What man is so maysyd with me that dare mete,	182	Magnyfycence	1506
Them that dare put theyr truste in me;	188	Magnyfycence	1699
Nowe dare he not for shame loke one in the face.	193	Magnyfycence	1891
Nay, horson, here is my glove. Take it up and thou dare.	202	Magnyfycence	2178
What! Wylte thou skelpe me? Thou dare not loke on a gnat.	202	Magnyfycence	2181
Nay, thou false harted dastarde! Thou dare not abyde.	202	Magnyfycence	2193
And yet I dare saye /She thynketh her selfe gaye	216	El Rummynge	64
In Achademia Parrot dare no probleme kepe,	235	Speke Parott	162
And 'Da racionales' dare not shew his pate.	235	Speke Parott	175
Let se who dare make up the reste.	242	Speke Parott	382
Whyche of yow fyrste dare boldlye plucke the crowe.	242	Speke Parott	396
For let se who that dare	251	Collyn Clout	179
Yf he on hym dare take	254	Collyn Clout	306
And he dare nat well neven	267	Collyn Clout	824
And as farre as they dare set,	269	Collyn Clout	932
Who dare say there agayne,	276	Collyn Clout	1214
Or who dare dysdayne,	276	Collyn Clout	1215
No man dare speke a worde,	283	Why Come Ye	191
Dare take nothynge on hande.	286	Why Come Ye	291
Dare nat loke out at dur at] 'a' Kitson 1560.7, Marshe 1568	286	Why Come Ye	296
Dare nat set theyr penne	287	Why Come Ye	323
That no man dare rowte;	287	Why Come Ye	341
Therewith I dare nat mell.	288	Why Come Ye	378
Yet proudly he dare pretende	292	Why Come Ye	530
No man dare him withsay.	294	Why Come Ye	598
No man dare come to the speche	294	Why Come Ye	615
So boldely dare controule	296	Why Come Ye	674
And dare use the experyens	297	Why Come Ye	711
Dare speke for his lyfe	306	Why Come Ye	1076
And, as we dare, we fynde in hym grete lake: grete] 'a' Marshe 1568	314	Garlande	70
I dare wele saye that ye and I be sought.	343	Garlande	1089
For ye dare nat abyde.	363	Albany	187
Yet ye dare do nothynge	364	Albany	211
That dare nat turne agayne,	366	Albany	306
I wondre howe ye dare	375	Replycacion	36

DARED —DAUNCE	Page	Title	Line

DARED
Sir Dunkan, ye dared.   365   Albany   271
DAREST
How darest thou, daucocke, mell?   275   Collyn Clout   1160
Howe darest thou, losell, ...   275   Collyn Clout   1161
DARYUS
Daryus, the doughty cheftayn of Perse -   181   Magnyfycence   1488
DARKE
And from the dennes darke   73   Phy Sparrow   84
And now the darke cloudy nyght   86   Phy Sparrow   571
His termes were not darke, ...   91   Phy Sparrow   801
A cronell of lawrell with verduris light and darke   334   Garlande   776
DARKES
And other wanton warkes /Whan the nyght darkes. 251   Collyn Clout   195
DARLYNG
'My darlyng dere, my daysy floure, ...   41   Balettys1   1
DARLYNGE
I daunsed the darlynge on my kne;   198   Magnyfycence   2066
DARRE
For drede ye darre not medyll with suche gere, ...   242   Speke Parott   394
Jupyter for Saturne darre make no royall chere;   242   Speke Parott   399
Moloc, that mawmett, there darre no man withsay;   243   Speke Parott   402
DART
And howe Cupyde shaked /His dart, and bent his bowe 270   Collyn Clout   947
DARTE
Lamentyng Daphnes, whome with the darte of lede   320   Garlande   290
DASED
My eyne were so dased;   99   Phy Sparrow   1106
And his eyen so dased, ...   283   Why Come Ye   181
DASID
As dasid doterdis that dreme in their dumpis.'   332   Garlande   734
It made sum mens eye dasild and dasid;   351   Garlande   1389
DASILD
It made sum mens eye dasild and dasid;   351   Garlande   1389
DASY
Enuwyd your colowre /Is lyke the dasy flowre   340   Garlande   986
  your] 'her' MS Cotton Vitellius E.x
This delycate dasy, this strawbery pretely set, ...   352   Garlande   1449
DASYNG
Dasyng after dotrellis, lyke drunkardis that dribbis; . . . 330   Garlande   641
DASSHED
His descant is dasshed full of dyscordes;   37   Coystrowne1   38
DASTARDE
Nay, thou false harted dastarde! Thou dare not abyde. . . . 202   Magnyfycence   2193
DASTARDIS
Some dronken dastardis with their dry soules;   317   Garlande   190
DASTARDYS
I dryve downe these dastardys with a dynt of my fyste. . .   181   Magnyfycence   1486
DATAN
And they cursed Datan   301   Why Come Ye   892
  they cursed] 'the course' MS Rawlinson C. 813
DATE
Regestringe trewly every formare date;   29   Dol Dethe   18
'Ay,' quod he, 'in the devylles date, ...   56   Bowge   375
Lete theym go lowse theym, in the devylles date.   59   Bowge   455
What neded that, in the dyvyls date?   166   Magnyfycence   943
Thanke the therof, in the devyls date!   201   Magnyfycence   2172
Then Parot moste have an almon or a date.   231   Speke Parott   7
Speke, Parotte, my swete byrde, and ye shall have a date,   243   Speke Parott   416
Now, Galathea, lett Parrot, I pray yow, have hys date - .   244   Speke Parott   439
Ryn God, rynne Devyll! Yet the date of Owur Lord   244   Speke Parott   444
And the date of the Devyll dothe shurewlye accord.   244   Speke Parott   445
Of honour and worshyp which hath the formar date: 336   Garlande   842
Of honour and worship it hath the formar date.   336   Garlande   849
Of honour and worship it hath the formar date.   336   Garlande   856
Of honour and worship it hath the formar date.   336   Garlande   863
DATES
Yett dates now are deynte, and wax verye scante, ...   244   Speke Parott   440
DATYD
Oure days be datyd /To be chekmatyd, ...   39   Coystrowne3   29
DAUCOCK
Construas hoc, /Domine Daucock!   68   Hauke   251
A daucock ye be, and so shal be styll!   310   Why Come Ye2   34
DAUCOCKE
How darest thou, daucocke, mell?   275   Collyn Clout   1160
DAUCOCKES
Wene ye, daucockes, to drive   368   Albany   380
DAUNCASTER
In fayth, I set not by the worlde two Dauncaster cuttys. .   148   Magnyfycence   293
DAUNCE
Fortune theyr frende, with whome oft she dyde daunce: . .   50   Bowge   141
The devyll myghte daunce therin for ony crowche.   56   Bowge   364
Where drede ledyth the daunce, there is no joy nor blysse.   142   Magnyfycence   76
I am so lyght /To daunce delyght;   164   Magnyfycence   841
I daunce up and downe tyll I am dyssy.   169   Magnyfycence   1040
With daunce on the le, the le!   198   Magnyfycence   2068
Whan the good ale soppe /Dothe daunce in theyr foretoppe; . 260   Collyn Clout   531
They wolde pype you another daunce.   262   Collyn Clout   618

159

DAUNCED —DAWNSYTH　　　　　　　　　　　　　　　　Page　　Title　　　　Line

And syr, ye must daunce attendaunce,	294	Why Come Ye	628
Some daunce the trace	301	Why Come Ye	881
And lepe frome the hylles to lerne for to daunce;	320	Garlande	280
Of somer, so formally she fotid the daunce.	331	Garlande	686
We shall pype you a daunce	371	Albany	498

DAUNCED

And howe Parys of Troy /Daunced a lege moy,	270	Collyn Clout	951
lege moy] 'lege de moy' Kele 1545.1, Marshe 1568			
But that he daunced for joye of that gle.	320	Garlande	278

DAUNGER

The sowle of this lorde from all daunger of hell,	34	Dol Dethe	200
That when ye thynke all daunger for to pas,	45	Balettys4	6
Her chyef gentylwoman, Daunger by her name,	48	Bowge	69
Gret daunger for the kynge,	126	Garnesche3	82
I drede no daunger; I dawnce all in delyte:	182	Magnyfycence	1492
So myche dowghtfull daunger, and so lytell drede;	245	Speke Parott	474

DAUNGEROUS

This daungerous dowsypere /Lyke a kynges pere!	295	Why Come Ye	639
How daungerous it were to stande in his lyght,	333	Garlande	755
were to stande in his lyght] 'is to stop up his sight' MS Cotton Vitellius E.x			

DAUNS

To dauns the hay or rune the ray;	134	Garnesche5	170

DAUNSED

I daunsed the darlynge on my kne;	198	Magnyfycence	2066

DAUNSID

Dryades there daunsid upon that goodly soile,	331	Garlande	679

DAUPATUS

Doctour Daupatus, /And bacheler Bacheleratus,	266	Collyn Clout	799

DAVID

Kyng David the prophete, of prophetes principall,	383	Replycacion	329

DAVYD

Davyd, that royall kyng,	383	Replycacion	317
For Davyd, our poete, harped so meloudiously	383	Replycacion	339

DAW

But that they playe the daw	62	Hauke	8
Delt he not lyke a daw?	65	Hauke	129
For though ye lyve a c. yere, ye shal dy a daw.	71	Hauke	334

DAWCOCK

Doctor Dawcock! /Ware the hawke!	70	Hauke	305

DAWCOCKE

This Doctour Dawcocke, Drede, I wene he hyghte.	54	Bowge	303
Doctor Dawcocke? /Ware the hawke!	69	Hauke	265
Domine Dawcocke? /Ware the hawke!	69	Hauke	275
Sym Sadylgose was my syer, and Dawcocke my dame.	192	Magnyfycence	1834

DAWCOKE

Domine Dawcoke? /Ware the hawke!	70	Hauke	295
Doctor Dawcoke! /Ware the hawke!	70	Hauke	329

DAWCOKKIS

Sum dysdanous dawcokkis that all men dispyse,	329	Garlande	618

DAWE

To fede a fole, and for to preye a dawe.	58	Bowge	437
preye] 'preue' Wynkyn de Worde 1510			
What! Thou wylte coughe me a dawe for forty pens?	170	Magnyfycence	1060
Shyt thy purse, dawe, and do no cost.	174	Magnyfycence	1207
Tushe! Holde your peas; ye speke lyke a dawe.	178	Magnyfycence	1379
To hardy, or to moche, to free of the dawe,	199	Magnyfycence	2090
Holde thy hande, dawe, of thy dagger, and stynt thy dyn;	202	Magnyfycence	2188

DAWES

To see Johan Dawes, that came but yesterdaye,	54	Bowge	301
But suche dawes to amend,	62	Hauke	26
Poppynge folysshe dawes.	285	Why Come Ye	264
He countys them foles and dawes;	286	Why Come Ye	315
To rayle on hym lyke dawes.	371	Albany	478
Lyke pratynge poppyng dawes,	375	Replycacion	39
And shewed your selfe dawes!	377	Replycacion	124

DAWIS

He calleth the prechours dawis.	305	Why Come Ye	1061

DAWYS

Ye, bere me this strawe to a dawys nest.	170	Magnyfycence	1097
Suche dawys, what soever they be,	174	Magnyfycence	1242
So many nobyll bodyes, undyr on dawys hedd;	245	Speke Parott	467

DAWKOCK

Domine Dawkock? /Ware the hawke!	70	Hauke	318
Ware] 'Whare' †Lant 1545			

DAWKOCKE

Doctor Dawkocke? /Ware the hawke!	69	Hauke	284
Ware] 'Whare' †Lant 1545			

DAWNCE

Foly fotyth it properly, fansy ledyth the dawnce,	177	Magnyfycence	1331
I drede no daunger; I dawnce all in delyte:	182	Magnyfycence	1492

DAWNS

That ye dawns all in a sute	379	Replycacion	168

DAWNSYS

He dawnsys so long, 'hey, troly, loly',	175	Magnyfycence	1250

DAWNSYTH

She dawnsyth varyaunce with mutabylyte,	197	Magnyfycence	2026

DAWPATE
Lyke a doctor dawpate, ... 126 Garnesche3 94
DE
How Syr Launcelote de Lake . . . . 87 Phy Sparrow 638
For Syr Frollo de Franko was never halfe so talle. 121 Garnesche1 5
Thou thynkyst thy selfe Syr Pers de Brasy, ... 130 Garnesche5 30
Cockes bones! This is all of Johnn de Gay. . . . . 167 Magnyfycence 960
Saynt Thomas de Aquyno, ... 381 Replycacion 279
DEAD
My sparow dead and colde, ... 72 Phy Sparrow 40
My vysage pale and dead, ... 73 Phy Sparrow 60
My fyngers, dead and colde, ... 77 Phy Sparrow 233
And slew him there starke dead. . . . . 81 Phy Sparrow 378
DEADE
Though this knaves be deade, ... 106 Epitaphe I
DEADLY
To forget deadly syn . . . . 98 Phy Sparrow 1081
DEALE
Thus within the wals /Of holy church to deale, ... 65 Hauke 135
Thus royally he dothe deale . . . . 287 Why Come Ye 336
All this he dothe deale . . . . 306 Why Come Ye 1101
  'Thys now he dothe meale' MS Rawlinson C. 813
That he setteth never a deale . . . . 307 Why Come Ye 1130
DEALYNG
And their dealyng double, ... 364 Albany 200
DEALL
As presydent and regente he rulythe every deall. . . . . . 239 Speke Parott 312
DEANES
Of prebendaries and deanes, ... 260 Collyn Clout 566
DEATH
The panges of hatefull death . . . . 73 Phy Sparrow 62
DEBARRE
Your consayte to debarre, ... 142 Magnyfycence 60
DEBATE
Agayne rebellyonns arme the to make debate; . . . . 33 Dol Dethe 166
In thys debate I the askry. 131 Garnesche5 66
A fole is he with welth that fallyth at debate. . . . . . 140 Magnyfycence 5
Yes, yes. He fell with me also at debate. . . . . 166 Magnyfycence 944
Why fall ye at debate /With Skelton laureate, ... 382 Replycacion 300
DEBATES
Largesse stynteth grete debates; . . . . 150 Magnyfycence 371
I sowe sedycyous sedes of dyscorde and debates. . . . . . 160 Magnyfycence 737
DECACORDE
Of our savyour Christ in his decacorde psautry, ... 383 Replycacion 340
DECADIS
With decadis historious, whiche that he mengith . . . . . 321 Garlande 345
DECAY
Now is your pryde fall to decay. . . . . 118 Ag Scottes 110
So myche decay of monesteries and relygious places; . . . 245 Speke Parott 499
And fall in suche decay, ... 263 Collyn Clout 668
  fall] 'false' Kele 1545.1, 'fall' MS Harley 2252
DECAYDE
The communewelth decayde. . . . . 255 Collyn Clout 353
DECAYES
But /Helas! sage overage /So madly decayes, ... 279 Why Come Ye 42
  So] 'To' Toy 1553, Kitson 1560.7, Marshe 1568
DECKE
Decke your hofte and cover a lowce. . . . . 161 Magnyfycence 749
They are fayne to play deuz decke. . . . . 250 Collyn Clout 166
DECKED
Thus dayly they be decked, /Taunted and checked, ... 294 Why Come Ye 611
DECLAMACYONS
Fyrst, olde Quintiliane with his Declamacyons; . . . . . 321 Garlande 326
  Declamacyons] 'declynacyons' †Fakes 1523
DECLARE
The pullyshed perle youre whytenes doth declare; 44 Balettys3 18
Grace of assystence his measure to declare; . . . . 207 Magnyfycence 2373
DECLARETH
And declareth our vyllany; . . . . 275 Collyn Clout 1174
DECLYNE
Some can nat declyne theyr name! . . . . 253 Collyn Clout 276
DECOLLACYON
On Saynt Johnn decollacyon . . . . 64 Hauke 100
DECON
And ay he sange, 'In fayth, Decon, thou crewe.' . . . . . 56 Bowge 360
DECRE
Irrevocable ys her decre; 130 Garnesche5 14
Decre and decretall, /Constytucyon provincyall, ... 308 Why Come Ye 1157
DECREES
Decrees or decretals, ... 65 Hauke 131
DECRETALL
Decre and decretall, /Constytucyon provincyall, ... 308 Why Come Ye 1157
DECRETALS
Decrees or decretals, ... 65 Hauke 131
DECTE
Ye decte you to dwell; . . . . 366 Albany 280
DED
Whether he were onlyve or ded; . . . . 89 Phy Sparrow 728

DEDDE —DEFEND	Page	Title	Line
What ever they say, /Jemmy is ded /And closyd in led,	116	Ag Scottes	21
The White there slew the Red starke ded.	119	Ag Scottes	138
The insyde ye ded calle	125	Garnesche3	50
Your drapry ye ded wante	125	Garnesche3	52
Sche seyd how ye ded brydell,	126	Garnesche3	73
Thus with yow sche ded wary,	126	Garnesche3	75
Ulula, Esebon, for Jepte is starke ded!	234	Speke Parott	126
When Parrot is ded, he dothe not putrefy;	236	Speke Parott	213
he] 'she' †Lant 1545, Kynge & Marche 1554, Day 1560, Marshe 1568			

DEDDE

In the pott your nose dedde snevyll;	124	Garnesche3	27

DEDE

Trew to his prince in word, in dede, and thought.	29	Dol Dethe	7
Lyke to Eneas benygne in worde and dede,	33	Dol Dethe	137
That they dyd such a dede,	70	Hauke	300
Samuell that was dede;	105	Phy Sparrow	1353
And say they so in very dede?	151	Magnyfycence	378
But sygh, and sorowe, and wysshe my selfe dede.	205	Magnyfycence	2306
And love that Lorde that for your love was dede,	207	Magnyfycence	2363
So many swannes dede, and so small revell -	245	Speke Parott	489
'The devyll,' they say, 'is dede, /The devyll is dede.'	247	Collyn Clout	36
'The devyll,' they say, 'is dede, /The devyll is dede.'	247	Collyn Clout	37
And brought in quycke or dede,	288	Why Come Ye	359
Is maister Mewtas dede,	298	Why Come Ye	787
Nay, nay, he is nat dede.	299	Why Come Ye	794
In very dede /How ye excede.	343	Garlande	1084
Of one Adame all a knave, late dede and gone -	347	Garlande	1247
Samuell that was dede.	350	Garlande	1346
Of Exione, his limbis dede and past,	351	Garlande	1400
his limbis] 'her lambis' †Fakes 1523, 'her lambe is' Marshe 1568			
Both worde and dede /Should be agrede /In noblenes:	357	Garlande	1599
Justyce now is dede;	358	Garlande2	1

DEDELY

The dedely fate, the dolefulle destenny	29	Dol Dethe	2
Wheron he gat his fynall dedely wounde.	32	Dol Dethe	119
Of ther good lord the fate and dedely chaunce.	34	Dol Dethe	189
He had forgoten all dedely syn.	42	Balettys1	11
These feverous axys, the dedely wo and payne	44	Balettys3	9
My dedely wo, my paynfull hevynes.	44	Balettys3	37
By Chemeras flamys, /And all the dedely namys	349	Garlande	1324
The colour dedely, swarte, blo and wan	351	Garlande	1399

DEDES

Howe ye breke the dedes wylles,	257	Collyn Clout	417
To exployte dedes of armys	370	Albany	467

DEDICATE

O dolorous Teusday, dedicate to thi name,	32	Dol Dethe	114

DEDYS

But ofte tymes have I sene wyse men do mad dedys.	148	Magnyfycence	302

DEDLY

O cruell Mars, thou dedly god of war!	32	Dol Dethe	113
Which men the viii dedly syn call.	36	Coystrowne1	5
syn] 'sins' Marshe 1568			
Go, pytyous hart, rasyd with dedly wo,	45	Balettys5	1
Encreaseth my dedly wo, /For my sparowe is go.	74	Phy Sparrow	113
By Chemeras flames, /And all the dedly names	105	Phy Sparrow	1331
O odyous dystresse, O dedly payne and woo!	198	Magnyfycence	2053

DEED

Iam iacet hic starke deed,	108	Epitaphe1	60
Whan he were deed.	361	Albany	98

DEEDLY

Mysdempte eche man, with face deedly and pale;	50	Bowge	137
The Gommoryans also /Were brought to deedly wo,	291	Why Come Ye	473
Your last deedly bane	366	Albany	284

DEEDMANS

Skelton Laureat, uppon a deedmans hed,	39	Coystrowne3	I

DEEFE

That they be deefe and dum,	269	Collyn Clout	903

DEFACES

He brekes and defaces,	306	Why Come Ye	1090

DEFACID

Any worde defacid /That myght be rasid,	356	Garlande	1581

DEFAMED

And wolde have her defamed,	376	Replycacion	60

DEFAUT

Sith he is slaundred for defaut of konnyng?'	316	Garlande	140

DEFAUTE

For defaute of measure all thynge dothe excede.	146	Magnyfycence	217
I knowe in hym no defaute	163	Magnyfycence	823
Tushe, tushe! It is a great defaute;	203	Magnyfycence	2222
For defaute of rescew,	280	Why Come Ye	59
A small defaute in a great lorde,	310	Why Come Ye2	12

DEFENCE

Muche frutefull mater. But now for your defence,	239	Speke Parott	297
On trouthe under defence	372	Albany	520

DEFEND

Vouchesafe to defend yow agayne the brawlyng scolde	241	Speke Parott	361

DEFENDAR —DELE   Page   Title   Line

DEFENDAR
Skelton Laureate Defendar Ageinst Lusty Garnyshe   129   Garnesche5   1
DEFENDE
Trew to his prince for to defende his right, ...   33   Dol Dethe   149
Thy selfe therfore defende.   128   Garnesche3   161
And defende it manerly.   152   Magnyfycence   416
Boldenes is to seke /The churche for to defende;   251   Collyn Clout   184
Howe ye pretende /For to defende   361   Albany   89
DEFENDER
Skelton Lauriate Defender Agenst Master Garnesche Chalenger, . .   121   Garnesche1   1
Skelton Lauryate Defender Agenst Master Garnesche Chalangar, . .   122   Garnesche2   1
DEFENDETH
Defendeth with his pen /All Englysh men   135   Dundas   21
DEFENS
He was your chyfteyne, your shelde, your chef defens, ...   30   Dol Dethe   57
DEFFEND
But curteisly /That I have pende /For to deffend, ...   356   Garlande   1571
DEFYE
Mary, I defye thy best and thy worst.   202   Magnyfycence   2197
DEFOYLE
Ye wolde defoyle the place   367   Albany   353
DEFOYLED
She had defoyled the place.   229   El Rummynge   573
DEFORMITE
Ye, syr, rayle all in deformite: 129   Garnesche5   7
DEGRE
Of what estate ye be, /Of hye or lowe degre, ...   73   Phy Sparrow   55
Whiche gave to me /The high degre   112   Calliope   6
It greyth nought for your degre   116   Ag Scottes   52
Avaunsid I was to that degre;   131   Garnesche5   82
If it lyke your grace to take it in degre.   182   Magnyfycence   1521
I am desyred with hyghest and lowest degre.   199   Magnyfycence   2079
Nowe well, nowe wo, nowe hy, nowe lawe degre;   212   Magnyfycence   2517
It is wronge with eche degre;   248   Collyn Clout   60
In Ariete /Ascendent a degre.   258   Collyn Clout   470
   a degre] 'ad dextram' MS Lansdowne 762, 'a dextre' MS Harley
   2252
And where the prelates be /Come of lowe degre   261   Collyn Clout   586
But the poore degre /Of the universyte;   265   Collyn Clout   735
That hath taken degre /In the unyversyte   266   Collyn Clout   792
Of hygh or lowe degre   274   Collyn Clout   1118
Out from a low degre, ...   291   Why Come Ye   506
To reche to suche degre, ...   292   Why Come Ye   538
Nor duke of hye degre, ...   294   Why Come Ye   619
We passe hym in degre   308   Why Come Ye   1151
Mayster doctor, in your degre, ...   309   Why Come Ye2   6
Commensyng your proces after there degre, ...   335   Garlande   819
Where all the sayd poetis sat in there degre.   343   Garlande   1104
DEGREE
But my learning is of an other degree   138   Ven Tongues   28
DEGREES
Scorpione ascendynge degrees twyse nyne;   312   Garlande   7
DEITE
Belongyng to the Deite.   381   Replycacion   283
DEYNTE
Deynte to have with us suche one in store, ...   50   Bowge   150
That I have deynte to see the cherysshed thus?   55   Bowge   338
Yett dates now are deynte, and wax verye scante, ...   244   Speke Parott   440
DEYNTELY
Deyntely dyetyd with dyvers delycate spyce, ...   231   Speke Parott   3
DEYNTES
Deyntes for dammoysels, chaffer far-fet;   234   Speke Parott   129
DEYSY
My deysy delectabyll, /My prymerose commendabyll, ...   237   Speke Parott   241
DEYTE
For drede ye dysplease the hygh deyte.   196   Magnyfycence   1996
DEKAY
Howe sodenly worldly welth dothe dekay;   213   Magnyfycence   2555
DEKKYD
Dekkyd lewdly in your gere, ...   125   Garnesche3   42
DELAY
Ye, have done at ones without delay.   206   Magnyfycence   2319
Delay causes so longe   276   Collyn Clout   1196
Recount, reporte, reherse without delay   336   Garlande   840
Make no delay, for now ye must be brought   343   Garlande   1090
DELAYDE
But from daye to daye delayde, ...   255   Collyn Clout   352
DELAYED
Syr, your requeste shall not be delayed.   208   Magnyfycence   2401
DELARAG
Let Syr Wrig-wrag wrastell with Syr Delarag: 233   Speke Parott   89
DELATED
to be farther delated and contynued, ...   374   Replycacion   1
DELE
Iwiss, ye dele uncurtesly;   36   Man Margery   15
To dele wyth her so cowardly;   42   Balettys1   27
She goyth wyde behynde and hewyth never a dele: 43   Balettys2   24
They sayde they hated for to dele with Drede.   50   Bowge   146

DELECTABYLL —DEMAUNDE   Page   Title   Line

Alas, I coude not dele so with a [J]ew.	59	Bowge	462
a Jew] 'on yew' †Wynkyn de Worde 1499, 'a yew' Wynkyn de Worde 1510, Marshe 1568			
Money they shall dele	83	Phy Sparrow	455
Sche sware with hyr ye xulde nat dele,	131	Garnesche5	57
But she is lesse a grete dele	169	Magnyfycence	1052
Yet were they better to begge, a great dele;	198	Magnyfycence	2043
Ye, but thanke me therof every dele.	201	Magnyfycence	2171
Ye wolde not dele with hym, thowgh that ye myght,	333	Garlande	756
though] 'thought' Marshe 1568, 'thowth' MS Cotton Vit.E.x			

DELECTABYLL

My deysy delectabyll, /My prymerose commendabyll,	237	Speke Parott	241

DELECTABLE

His mater is delectable, /Solacious and commendable;	91	Phy Sparrow	790
The daysy delectable,	98	Phy Sparrow	1051
More delectable than your langage to me.	207	Magnyfycence	2348
A ryght delectable tratyse	312	Garlande	I
Here endith a ryght delectable tratyse	358	Garlande2	E

DELECTABLY

whan they have delectably lycked a lytell	373	Replycacion	I

DELECTACYON

And to aqueynte you with carnall delectacyon;	183	Magnyfycence	1547

DELECTACYONS

All delectacyons aquayntyd is with me;	146	Magnyfycence	209

DELETH

Who deleth with shrewes hath nede to loke aboute!'	61	Bowge	525

DELIGHT

With trowth to medelle was all his hole delight,	33	Dol Dethe	152
In you he wolde have set his hole delight.	336	Garlande	874
All his delight was to braule and to barke	347	Garlande	1252

DELITE

How some delite for to lye, thycke and threfolde.	137	Ven Tongues	11

DELYAUNCE

Syr, without any longer delyaunce,	147	Magnyfycence	237

DELYBERACION

and with good delyberacion made,	373	Replycacion	I

DELYBERACYON

Yet we wyll therin take good delyberacyon.	148	Magnyfycence	275

DELYCATE

Deyntely dyetyd with dyvers delycate spyce,	231	Speke Parott	3
This delycate dasy, this strawbery pretely set,	352	Garlande	1449

DELYCATELYE

An almon now for Parott, delycatelye dreste;	232	Speke Parott	48

DELYGENCE

'Counterwayng your besy delygence	323	Garlande	414

DELYGHT

How in good horsmen ye set your hole delyght,	42	Balettys2	13
Of lust and of delyght,	93	Phy Sparrow	869
The lode stare of delyght,	102	Phy Sparrow	1226
Yet in this man you must set your delyght.	145	Magnyfycence	167
In whose attemperaunce I have suche delyght,	145	Magnyfycence	189
I am so lyght /To daunce delyght;	164	Magnyfycence	841
Alasse! To lyve longer I have no delyght;	205	Magnyfycence	2281
My delyght is solas, pleasure, dysporte and pley;	233	Speke Parott	108
So am I supprysyd with pleasure and delyght	327	Garlande	537
Longe to enjoy plesure, delyght, and lust:	337	Garlande	882
Wherfore delyght /I have to whryght.	339	Garlande	945
Of this warke they had so great delyght,	343	Garlande	1110
Wherfore to jeste /Is my delyght	359	Albany	14

DELYNGE

Yet on my backe I bere suche lewde delynge.	59	Bowge	457
Counterfet sadnesse, with delynge full madly;	153	Magnyfycence	468
And in your delynge so good assuraunce,	183	Magnyfycence	1523

DELYTE

Delyte, desyre, respyte, wyth lyberte;	43	Balettys3	2
I drede no daunger; I dawnce all in delyte:	182	Magnyfycence	1492
That we delyte gretly in your dalyaunce.	183	Magnyfycence	1524
It is semynge your pleasure ye delyte,	183	Magnyfycence	1546
He dynyd with delyte, with poverte he must sup.	195	Magnyfycence	1965
All her delyte is set in doublenesse.	197	Magnyfycence	2029
Today in delyte, tomorowe bare of blysse;	213	Magnyfycence	2542
Other for delyte /Or elles *to desyte?	247	Collyn Clout	7
Other] 'Eyther' Kele 1545.1; 'to desyte' MS Harley 2252, 'despyte' Kele 1545.1, Marshe 1568			
Ye lyve, they say, in delyte, /Drowned in deliciis,	257	Collyn Clout	441
Here dwellith pleasure, with lust and delyte;	332	Garlande	709

DELYVER

And lette me come to delyver my lettre.'	326	Garlande	506

DELYVERED

Where was it delyvered you? Shewe unto me.	150	Magnyfycence	340
Then shall you be sone delyvered from dystresse,	208	Magnyfycence	2383

DELL

It is but foly every dell.	175	Magnyfycence	1275

DELT

Delt he not lyke a fon?	65	Hauke	128
Delt he not lyke a daw?	65	Hauke	129

DEMAUNDE

Difficille hit ys to anssvere thys demaunde;	243	Speke Parott	418

DEMAUNDED — DEPRAVE	Page	Title	Line
DEMAUNDED			
Of them demaunded and asked by the kynge;	31	Dol Dethe	79
I her demaunded of them and ther astate.	329	Garlande	606
DEMAUNDINGE			
Demaundinge soche dutes as nedis most acord	31	Dol Dethe	66
DEMAWND			
'Of your demawnd shew me the content,	332	Garlande	721
DEME			
Deme what thou lyst, thou knowyst not my thought.	38	Coystrownel	63
Of all doughty I am doughtyest duke as I deme;	182	Magnyfycence	1499
DEMEANE			
The quere to demeane,	85	Phy Sparrow	553
Or els ye demeane you inordinatly;	317	Garlande	173
DEMEYNAUNCE			
Syr, ye shall hyght Good Demeynaunce.	159	Magnyfycence	674
DEMENAUNCE			
Demure demenaunce, womanly of porte;	43	Balettys3	6
By theyr demenaunce, nor loss repryvable.	179	Magnyfycence	1419
Item Royall Demenaunce Worshyp to Wynne;	345	Garlande	1174
DEMENE			
Go, litill quaire, /Demene you faire.	355	Garlande	1534
DEMENYNG			
Her demenyng /In every thynge,	341	Garlande	1014
DEMENOUR			
And your demenour with Counterfet Countenaunce,	192	Magnyfycence	1861
Your noble demenour is counterwayng,	336	Garlande	847
All the demenour of princely astate,	347	Garlande	1231
DEMENSY			
Despensyth with his demensy.	296	Why Come Ye	682
DEMERYTTES			
Thus by demeryttes of their abusyon,	374	Replycacion	14
DEMY DIVINES			
as touchyng the tetrycall theologisacion of these demy divines,	374	Replycacion	1
DEMYE			
Of Kyrkeby Kendall was his shorte demye;	56	Bowge	359
DEMYST			
Thow demyst my raylyng ovyrthwarthe;	133	Garnesche5	136
DEMONSTRACYON			
Of that I intende to make demonstracyon	141	Magnyfycence	41
DEMOSTENES			
To corage Demostenes was moche excitynge,	316	Garlande	152
The cause why Demostenes so famously is brutid	316	Garlande	155
Of Demostenes, that was his utter foo.	317	Garlande	167
DEMPTE			
I dempte and drede theyr talkynge was not good.	58	Bowge	426
DEMURE			
Demure demenaunce, womanly of porte;	43	Balettys3	6
So sad and so demure,	99	Phy Sparrow	1097
Goodly maystres Jane, /Sobre, demure Dyane;	102	Phy Sparrow	1224
Demure, sober and sad,	111	Lawde	54
Is lusty to loke on, plesaunte, demure, and sage:	336	Garlande	870
Is lusty to loke on, plesaunt, demure, and sage.	337	Garlande	877
Demure Diana womanly and sad,	337	Garlande	902
Maydenly demure, /Of womanhode the lure;	340	Garlande	991
DEN			
On to your lowsy den;	125	Garnesche3	64
Twyt, Scot, go kepe thy den.	362	Albany	145
DENAYD			
It cannot be denayd /But it was well convayd,	98	Phy Sparrow	1065
DENYED			
For many tymes moche kyndnesse is denyed	177	Magnyfycence	1338
Sodenly grauntyd, and sodenly denyed;	213	Magnyfycence	2534
DENNE			
Lyke foxes in theyr denne,	283	Why Come Ye	164
DENNES			
And from the dennes darke	73	Phy Sparrow	84
DENOMINACYONS			
And seryously she shewyd me ther denominacyons.	328	Garlande	581
DENTY			
And the denty curlewe,	83	Phy Sparrow	464
DEPARTE			
For welthe wyll sone departe the froo.	132	Garnesche5	125
That measure shall nevere departe from my syght.	145	Magnyfycence	190
Let us departe from hens home to my place.	151	Magnyfycence	394
DEPARTED			
Soo he departed. There he wolde be come,	52	Bowge	228
Wyth that, as he departed soo fro me,	54	Bowge	281
Sodaynly, as he departed me fro,	60	Bowge	498
Deth hath departed us twayne;	80	Phy Sparrow	329
DEPE			
From the marees depe /Of Acherontes well,	73	Phy Sparrow	69
Into the brayne by drynkyng over depe,	313	Garlande	33
DEPELY			
So depely drownyd I was in this dumpe,	312	Garlande	15
DEPENDED			
Your worship depended of his excellence.	31	Dol Dethe	59
DEPRAVE			
What ayle them to deprave /Phillip Sparowes grave?	103	Phy Sparrow	1274

DEPRAVYD — DESYER   Page   Title   Line

	Page	Title	Line
Why doste thow deprave /This royall reame,	136	Dundas	43
The churche to deprave.	259	Collyn Clout	513
This treatyse to deprave;	274	Collyn Clout	1132
What ayle them to deprave /Phillippe Sparows grave?	348	Garlande	1267
Ye rage and ye rave, /And your worshyp deprave:	363	Albany	191

DEPRAVYD

Dys church ye thus depravyd;	70	Hauke	308

DEPUTE

Whome he wyll depute?	272	Collyn Clout	1044

DEPUTYD

Have deputyd Measure hym to gyde?	147	Magnyfycence	243

DERAYNE

Nor to derayne /Batayle agayne /Scornfull disdayne,	356	Garlande	1563
Thou durst no felde derayne,	365	Albany	243

DERE

All mankynd, whom thou ful dere hast boght,	34	Dol Dethe	194
Maiden moste pure, and Goddis moder dere,	34	Dol Dethe	205
'My darlyng dere, my daysy floure,	41	Balettys1	1
But who wyll have it muste paye therfore dere.	47	Bowge	53
What though our chaffer be never so dere,	48	Bowge	89
For by that Lorde that bought dere all mankynde,	50	Bowge	163
Chaunged to a dere,	79	Phy Sparrow	299
Alas, dere harte, loke that we be not perseyvyd!'	177	Magnyfycence	1349
Alas, dere sone, sore combred is thy mynde,	206	Magnyfycence	2325
It was dere that was far fet!	223	El Rummynge	334
But Parot is my owne dere harte, and my dere derling.	236	Speke Parott	208
dere] (2nd) not in Day 1560, Marshe 1568			
But Parot is my owne dere harte, and my dere derling.	236	Speke Parott	208
dere] (2nd) not in Day 1560, Marshe 1568			
Except mannes soule, that Chryst so dere bought;	236	Speke Parott	215
So bolde a braggyng bocher, and flesshe sold so dere;	245	Speke Parott	485
By God that me dere bought!	290	Why Come Ye	451
By] 'But' Marshe 1568			

DERELY

Or gummis of Saby so derely that be solde.	331	Garlande	675

DERISYON

He hathe them in derisyon,	306	Why Come Ye	1092

DERKE

A custrell to dryve the devyll out of the derke,	154	Magnyfycence	485

DERKENES

In derkenes thus dwelt we, tyll at the last	330	Garlande	650

DERLING

But Parot is my owne dere harte, and my dere derling.	236	Speke Parott	208
dere] (2nd) not in Day 1560, Marshe 1568			

DERLYNG

For he is the kynges derlyng	295	Why Come Ye	666

DERLYNGE

'Daphnes, my derlynge, why do you me refuse?	320	Garlande	297

DEROGACYON

His Dirige, her commendacyon /Can be no derogacyon,	103	Phy Sparrow	1277
For elles it were to great a derogacyon	318	Garlande	218

DEROGACYOUN

His dirige, her commendacioun /Can be no derogacyoun;	348	Garlande	1270

DEROGATE

And that wolde derogate,	264	Collyn Clout	706

DERTMOUTH

Of Dertmouth, of Plummouth, of Portismouth also;	326	Garlande	513

DESCANT

His descant is dasshed full of dyscordes;	37	Coystrownel	38

DESCENDINGE

Of the blode royall descendinge nobelly;	29	Dol Dethe	4

DESCENDYNGE

Whan Scorpyon descendynge, /Was so then pretendynge	258	Collyn Clout	471

DESE

These swyne go to the hye dese,	218	El Rummynge	175

DESERVE

Avaunsynge my selfe sum thanke to deserve,	335	Garlande	822
For to deserve /Inmortall fame.	339	Garlande	966
Inmortall] 'The courte of' MS Cotton Vitellius E.x			

DESERVED

For of your grace I have it nought deserved.	186	Magnyfycence	1644
Syr, God rewarde you as ye have deserved.	188	Magnyfycence	1701
And ye have deserved this punysshment.	196	Magnyfycence	2003
'Maister Gower, I have nothyng deserved	323	Garlande	407

DESERVYD

That hath deservyd it as well as he.	195	Magnyfycence	1952
Largely rewardynge them that have deservyd;	200	Magnyfycence	2119
'A thanke to have, ye have well deservyd,	317	Garlande	169
Ye have deservyd to have an enplement	323	Garlande	402
We wyll understande how ye have it deservyd.'	344	Garlande	1127
Ladyes and gentylwomen suche as deservyd,	346	Garlande	1189

DESERVYNGE

Withoute deservynge shulde have the best game.	318	Garlande	221

DESIRE

To owur soleyne Seigneour Sadoke, desire hym to cum home,	239	Speke Parott	304

DESYER

At his owne desyer.	303	Why Come Ye	986

DESYRE — DETRACTYON   Page   Title   Line

DESYRE
Delyte, desyre, respyte, wyth lyberte; 43   Balettys3   2
Desyre her name was, and so she me tolde, ... 48   Bowge   85
'Pece,' quod Desyre, 'ye speke not worth a bene! 48   Bowge   95
His foule desyre /Wyll suffre no slepe 95   Phy Sparrow   933
And desyre me thy good mayster to be? 162   Magnyfycence   798
This theyr desyre, /This newe atyre. 165   Magnyfycence   887
Nay, fyrst Lusty Pleasure is my desyre to have; 180   Magnyfycence   1453
All men must folow his desyre. 287   Why Come Ye   345
   must] not in Marshe 1568
Welcome to me with all my hole desyre! 327   Garlande   548

DESYRED
I am desyred with hyghest and lowest degre. 199   Magnyfycence   2079

DESYRING
Desyring you above all thynge 299   Why Come Ye   828

DESYRIS
They folowe your desyris, ... 263   Collyn Clout   683

DESYROUS
Nothynge yerthly to me more desyrous 44   Balettys3   43

DESYTE
Other for delyte /Or elles *to desyte? 247   Collyn Clout   8
   Other] 'Eyther' Kele 1545.1; 'to desyte' MS Harley 2252,
   'despyte' Kele 1545.1, Marshe 1568

DESOLATE
And ye be desolate as Armeleche. 114   Scot Kynge   24

DESOLATION
Now all is out of facion, /Almost in desolation. 305   Why Come Ye   1042

DESPENSYTH
Despensyth with his demensy. 296   Why Come Ye   682

DESPITE
Thou hast in despite, /Thou donghyll knyght? 136   Dundas   47

DESPYGHT
Had yow most in despyght; 125   Garnesche3   66
Or elles for despyght, ... 272   Collyn Clout   1056

DESPYGHTYNG
And your spyghtfull despyghtyng, ... 127   Garnesche3   114

DESPYSE
And them to despyse 87   Phy Sparrow   624
This treatyse to despyse 103   Phy Sparrow   1252

DESPYTE
Howe the lay fee despyte 257   Collyn Clout   438
I do it nat for no despyte. 273   Collyn Clout   1086
   it for] 'it not for' Kele 1545.1, Marshe 1568

DESPYTYNGE
To use suche despytynge 274   Collyn Clout   1107
   despytynge] 'despysyng' Kele 1545.1, Marshe 1568, 'dysputyng'
   MS Harley 2252

DESTEYNYD
His noble blode never desteynyd was, ... 33   Dol Dethe   148

DESTENY
Alas, for dolefull desteny! 86   Phy Sparrow   593
I drede no dyntes of fatall desteny. 190   Magnyfycence   1798
The dolefull desteny, and the carefull chaunce, ... 348   Garlande   1255

DESTENNY
The dedely fate, the dolefulle destenny 29   Dol Dethe   2

DESTYNY
O feble fortune, O doulfull destyny! 198   Magnyfycence   2048

DET
Thou mokkyshe marmoset, /I will nat dy in [thy] det. 128   Garnesche3   173
   thy] 'they' †MS Harley 367

DETERMYNE
Determyne to amende all your wanton excesse; 208   Magnyfycence   2409
Whiche determyne playne 277   Collyn Clout   1231

DETERMYNED
Ye have determyned to make a fraye, ... 114   Scot Kynge   44

DETERMYNYD
I me determynyd for to sharpe my pen, ... 335   Garlande   823

DETESTABLE
With langage detestable; 375   Replycacion   28
Opinyons detestable /Of heresy execrable? 382   Replycacion   304

DETH
No man may hym hyde /From deth holow-eyed, ... 39   Coystrowne3   11
Deth wyll us quell /And with us mell. 39   Coystrowne3   23
With drawttys of deth /Stoppyng oure breth; 39   Coystrowne3   31
Deth hath departed us twayne; 80   Phy Sparrow   329
My Phyllyppes dolefull deth! 80   Phy Sparrow   352
As thou, wyth shamefull deth!' 223   El Rummynge   346

DETHE
Skelton Laureat Upon the Dolorus Dethe 29   Dol Dethe   I
Of this lordis dethe and of his murdrynge; 32   Dol Dethe   130
This lordis dethe, whos pere is hard to fynd, ... 34   Dol Dethe   178
For to lyve in mysery, it is herder than dethe. 205   Magnyfycence   2282

DETRACCION
Of foule detraccion God kepe the from the blast. 34   Dol Dethe   173

DETRACTIONS
enpoysoned with sclaunder and false detractions &c. 136   Ven Tongues   I

DETRACTYON
And through suche detractyon 273   Collyn Clout   1059

DETRAXION —DEVYLL   Page   Title   Line

DETRAXION
Callyd Detraxion, encankryd with envye, ...   241   Speke Parott   362
DEU
That bounde ar we with all deu reverence, ...   324   Garlande   423
DEUCALYONS
Deucalyons flode it hyght.   78   Phy Sparrow   253
DEUYAS
Thys Doctor Deuyas commensyd in a cart;   38   Coystrowne1   55
  Deuyas] 'dellias' Marshe 1568
Avaunt, syr doctour Deuyas!   275   Collyn Clout   1157
  Deuyas] 'Denyas' †Godfray 1531, 'dyvers' Marshe 1568,
  'Devias' MS Harley 2252
DEURANDALL
Hole ys your brow that ye brake with Deu[ra]ndall your awne . . 123   Garnesche2   8
  sworde; Deurandall] 'Deundall' †MS Harley 367
DEUZ
They are fayne to play deuz decke.   250   Collyn Clout   166
DEVELYSH
[Y]e develysh dogmatista, /Your hawke on your fista, ...   69   Hauke   255
  Ye] 'The' †Lant 1545, Kynge & Marche 1554, Day 1560,
  Marshe 1568
DEVELLYSSHE
For by his devellysshe drift and graceles provision   333   Garlande   757
DEVERSE
For reporte ryseth many deverse wayes.   317   Garlande   181
  For] not MS Cotton Vitellius E.x
DEVILL
The devill kis his culum!   108   Epitaphe1   79
The devill tere their tunges and pike out their ies!   139   Ven Tongues   68
And the devill downe dynge, ...   364   Albany   210
Sir Dunkan, in the devill waye, ...   367   Albany   330
DEVINYTE
No doctor of devinyte, ...   291   Why Come Ye   509
DEVISE
That caused you to devise   372   Albany   526
DEVISIS
Rendrynge my devisis I made in disporte   354   Garlande   1494
DEVYDYD
Measure and I wyll never be devydyd, ...   145   Magnyfycence   186
DEVYL
The facyoun of your fysnamy the devyl in a clowde;   123   Garnesche2   25
Of a dysour, a devyl way, grew a jentilman, ...   330   Garlande   635
DEVYLYSHE
The devylyshe dagmatista.   260   Collyn Clout   550
DEVYLL
But I wonder what the devyll of helle   52   Bowge   208
The devyll myghte daunce therin for ony crowche.   56   Bowge   364
What the devyll, man, myrthe was never one!   57   Bowge   388
  was never one] 'is here within' Marshe 1568
Eyther to the devyll or the trinite.   114   Scot Kynge   41
Nowe to the devyll I the betake, ...   151   Magnyfycence   401
A custrell to dryve the devyll out of the derke, ...   154   Magnyfycence   485
What the devyll! Are ye two of aquayntaunce?   154   Magnyfycence   496
What the devyll! Howe may that be?   157   Magnyfycence   627
What the devyll ayleth you? Can you not agree?   158   Magnyfycence   636
What the devyll! Who sent for the?   162   Magnyfycence   791
What the devyll, man, what thou menyst?   162   Magnyfycence   793
What the devyll! Can ye agre no better?   162   Magnyfycence   795
What the devyll! Where had we this joly jetter?   162   Magnyfycence   796
What the devyll! Use ye not to drawe no swordes?   163   Magnyfycence   811
But what the devyll art thou   166   Magnyfycence   916
What the devyll hast thou on thy fyste? An owle?   166   Magnyfycence   922
What the devyll! Never a why?   166   Magnyfycence   935
Tyll, as the devyll wolde, they fell a chydynge   166   Magnyfycence   940
The devyll spede whyt!   168   Magnyfycence   1006
Where the devyll gate he all these hurtes?   171   Magnyfycence   1127
What the devyll, man, your name shalbe the greter;   180   Magnyfycence   1440
And he go to the devyll, so that I may have my fee, ...   187   Magnyfycence   1670
Measure? Tut, what the devyll of hell!   189   Magnyfycence   1745
Nay. Then thou wylte dynge the devyll and thou be not holde. . 202   Magnyfycence   2183
The devyll and she be syb.   217   El Rummynge   100
It was a stale to take /The devyll in a brake.   222   El Rummynge   325
  stale] 'stale' 1521 Fragment, 'stare' †Lant 1545,
  Kynge & Marche 1554, Day 1560, Marshe 1568
For the devyll to eate;   225   El Rummynge   434
The devyll thereon be wroken!   227   El Rummynge   498
Ryn God, rynne Devyll! Yet the date of Owur Lord   244   Speke Parott   444
And the date of the Devyll dothe shurewlye accord.   244   Speke Parott   445
'The devyll,' they say, 'is dede, /The devyll is dede.' . . .   247   Collyn Clout   36
'The devyll,' they say, 'is dede, /The devyll is dede.' . . .   247   Collyn Clout   37
'Come downe, on the devyll way.'   263   Collyn Clout   670
  devyll] 'deuils' Marshe 1568, 'devyll' MS Harley 2252
The devyll can nat stop their mouthes   272   Collyn Clout   1051
Avaunt to the devyll of hell!   275   Collyn Clout   1164
Renne god, renne devyll, ...   277   Collyn Clout   1222
Than the devyll take all!   279   Why Come Ye   26
The devyll kysse his cule!   282   Why Come Ye   133
  his] 'hes' †Kele 1545.3

DEVYLLES —DEVORS

	Page	Title	Line
The devyll kysse his arse!	282	Why Come Ye	136
To the devyll Syr Sathanas,	299	Why Come Ye	805
Endlesse to dwell /With the devyll of hell!	303	Why Come Ye	972
The devyll spede whitte!	304	Why Come Ye	1017
It wolde make the devyll to swete!	306	Why Come Ye	1088
'The devyll wold swete' MS Rawlinson C. 813			
The devyll of hell and he be seldome asonder.'	333	Garlande	765
Nedes must he rin that the devyll dryvith.	352	Garlande	1434
DEVYLLES			
'Ay,' quod he, 'in the devylles date,	56	Bowge	375
Lete theym go lowse theym, in the devylles date.	59	Bowge	455
Do away, I say, the devylles torde!	151	Magnyfycence	397
DEVYLLYS			
[Thy] myrrour may be the devyllys ars.	130	Garnesche5	18
Thy] 'They' †MS Harley 367			
DEVYLLYSSHE			
Of one so devyllysshe a matter.	297	Why Come Ye	715
I saye, ye devyllysshe pages	381	Replycacion	271
Of heresy the devyllysshe scoles	382	Replycacion	298
DEVYLLYSSHELY			
And devyllysshely devysed /[The] people to seduce,	380	Replycacion	210
The] 'to' †Pynson 1528			
DEVYLS			
Thus can I lerne you, syrs, to bere the devyls sacke;	160	Magnyfycence	721
The devyls torde for thy brayne!	170	Magnyfycence	1086
Thanke the therof, in the devyls date!	201	Magnyfycence	2172
The devyls vycare generall,	299	Why Come Ye	807
That he wolde than make /The devyls to quake,	303	Why Come Ye	979
DEVYNE			
Ye be, as I devyne,	338	Garlande	911
DEVYSE			
Fraghted with plesure to what ye coude devyse.	47	Bowge	42
Me thoughte alwaye Dyscymular dyde devyse;	58	Bowge	424
To shew me their devyse	74	Phy Sparrow	100
Melodyously it to devyse	93	Phy Sparrow	864
As Nature cold devyse, /In most goodly wyse.	98	Phy Sparrow	1071
Ye, so I can devyse my gere after the cowrtly maner.	161	Magnyfycence	766
At my devyse I with her met;	199	Magnyfycence	2075
Moche better can devyse	298	Why Come Ye	767
But that his bokis, whiche he did devyse,	315	Garlande	124
So finally, when they had shewyd there devyse,	324	Garlande	442
You to devyse his crafte were to seke;	337	Garlande	893
He coude not devyse the lest poynt of your cheke;	337	Garlande	896
And specyally which glad was to devyse	342	Garlande	1071
DEVYSED			
This worke devysed is /For suche as do amys,	61	Hauke	1
Thys boke we have devysed, /Compendyously comprysed,	62	Hauke	23
Devysed and also wrate /Uppon a lewde curate,	62	Hauke	34
This tretise devysed it is	106	Epitaphe	I
So that now I have devysed,	117	Ag Scottes	69
Of your langage, it is so well devysed;	183	Magnyfycence	1530
By Nature devysed of a wonderowus kynde,	231	Speke Parott	2
Confuse distrybutyve, as Parrot hath devysed,	236	Speke Parott	198
And devyllysshely devysed /[The] people to seduce,	380	Replycacion	210
The] 'to' †Pynson 1528			
DEVYSER			
agaynst Skelton laureate, devyser of this Replycacyon, etc.	382	Replycacion	R
DEVYSID			
That for them some goodly conseyt be devysid,	335	Garlande	814
Benynge, corteise, and meke, /With wordes well devysid;	338	Garlande	919
A tratyse he devysid and browght it to pas,	347	Garlande	1228
Vexilla regis he devysid to be displayd;	352	Garlande	1420
DEVYSION			
An hole reame he is able to set at devysion:	333	Garlande	758
DEVYSYD			
As perfightly as koude be thought or devysyd;	33	Dol Dethe	158
Devysyd this gostly medytacyon in Englysh:	39	Coystrowne3	I
devysyd by Master Skelton Laureat	41	Balettys	I
Accordynge to treuth they be well devysyd.	210	Magnyfycence	2470
This treatyse, devysyd to make you dysporte,	213	Magnyfycence	2538
I have devysyd for Skelton, my clerke;	334	Garlande	777
DEVYSYNGE			
Devysynge the meanes and wayes that I can,	160	Magnyfycence	708
In devysynge of this boke	266	Collyn Clout	784
DEVOCION			
By way of their devocion	378	Replycacion	136
DEVOCYON			
I may say to you I have but small devocyon.	186	Magnyfycence	1640
Syr, syth that in me ye have suche devocyon,	190	Magnyfycence	1790
With drammes of devocyon your dyet must be drest,	207	Magnyfycence	2358
There is theyr hole devocyon,	248	Collyn Clout	87
DEVOYDE			
Devoyde of all nobles,	369	Albany	410
Devoyde of good corage,	369	Albany	411
Devoyde of wysdome sage,	369	Albany	412
DEVORS			
Haroldes from honor may the devors,	131	Garnesche5	71

DEVORSE —DIFFICILLE   Page   Title   Line

DEVORSE
And from that they love best some I devorse; 194   Magnyfycence   1905
DEVOUTE
A DEVOUTE TRENTALE FOR OLD JOHN CLARKE, ... 106   Epitaphe1   I
With wordes devoute and sentence agerdows, ... 347   Garlande   1250
Also a Devoute Prayer to Moyses Hornis, ... 351   Garlande   1381
Of his makyng devoute medytacyons; 352   Garlande   1419
DEVOUTLY
HIS EPITAPH FOLOWETH DEVOUTLY; 109   Epitaphe2   I
Theyr matyns madly sayde, /Nothynge devoutly prayde, ... 252   Collyn Clout   239
Devoutly arrectyng my prayer to Mynerve, ... 335   Garlande   824
DEW
At your commaundement, syr, wyth all dew reverence. 182   Magnyfycence   1515
Of ladys a beve with all dew reverence: 334   Garlande   771
    a beve] 'aboue' †Fakes 1523
DEWCALIONS
Syns Dewcalions flodde, was nevyr sene nor shall. 245   Speke Parott   469
DEWCALYONS
Syns Dewcalyons flodde there can no clerkes rede. 244   Speke Parott   455
Syns Dewcalyons flodde there can no clerkes fynde. 244   Speke Parott   462
Syns Dewcalyons flodde, I trowe, was nevyr sene. 245   Speke Parott   476
Syns Dewcalyons flodde was nevyr, I dar sey. 245   Speke Parott   483
Syns Dewcalyons flodde, I trow, no man can tell. 245   Speke Parott   490
Syns Dewcalyons flodde the world was never so yll. 245   Speke Parott   497
    the world] 'the world the world' †MS Harley 2252
Syns Dewcalyons flodde was nevyr sene nor lyerd. 246   Speke Parott   504
Syn Dewcalyons flodde, I make the faste and sure. 246   Speke Parott   511
Sens Dewcalyons flodde, in no cronycle ys told. 246   Speke Parott   518
DEWE
She dryveth downe the dewe 216   El Rummynge   82
DEWTY
Ye dyde not your dewty therin, ... 114   Scot Kynge   32
DEWTYES
Theyr dewtyes to withdrawe, ... 268   Collyn Clout   856
DIALETICALL
In your dialeticall /And principles silogisticall, ... 377   Replycacion   96
DIAMAUNTIS
With diamauntis and rubis there tabers were trasid, ... 323   Garlande   395
    tabers] 'taberdes' Marshe 1568
DIAMOUNDE
Diamounde, or rubye, or balas of the beste, ... 241   Speke Parott   367
DIANA
Diana in the woodes grene, ... 105   Phy Sparrow   1364
Unto Diana, the goddes inmortall, ... 320   Garlande   303
Demure Diana womanly and sad, ... 337   Garlande   902
Diana in the woddis grene, ... 350   Garlande   1357
DIASCORIDES
Though Galiene and Diascorides, ... 352   Garlande   1425
DICKEN
In fayth, Dicken, thou krew, etc.' 280   Why Come Ye   67
Dicken, thou krew doutlesse! 280   Why Come Ye   68
DICTES
Mole ruit sua, whose dictes ar pregnaunte - 232   Speke Parott   41
DID
Alas, ye madmen, to far ye did excede. 31   Dol Dethe   60
Sourmountinge in honour all erlis he did excede; 33   Dol Dethe   135
Me thought my sparow did spek, ... 77   Phy Sparrow   220
Grace the sede did sow. 110   Lawde   5
And whan Lucina plenarly did shyne, ... 312   Garlande   6
    plenarly] 'plenary' †Fakes 1523, Marshe 1568
And what estates to her did resorte, ... 313   Garlande   45
But that his bokis, whiche he did devyse, ... 315   Garlande   124
For, but if your bounte did me assure, ... 316   Garlande   146
Onely procedid for that he did outray 316   Garlande   156
So truely proporsionyd, and so well did gree, ... 320   Garlande   275
He sange also how, the tre as he did take 320   Garlande   300
Of Alexander; and Macrobius that did trete 322   Garlande   367
Unto this place all poetis there did sue, ... 325   Garlande   481
I sawe hir smyle, and I then did the same. 327   Garlande   530
    I then] 'than I' Marshe 1568
Of worldly trust, then did I you rescu; 327   Garlande   543
In lyke maner of wyse a myst did us shrowde; 330   Garlande   647
And Iopas his instrument did avaunce, ... 331   Garlande   688
Sat honorably, to whome did repaire 334   Garlande   770
With balassis and charbuncles the borders did shyne; 345   Garlande   1166
Was wrytin; and so she did her spede, ... 345   Garlande   1168
He did translate, enterprete, and disclose; 347   Garlande   1222
By Hercules that hell did harow, ... 348   Garlande   1284
How be it to Saull he did tell 350   Garlande   1350
I did what I cowde to scrape out the scrollis, ... 354   Garlande   1489
    scrape] 'scarpe' Marshe 1568
DIDIL DIDDIL
And what blunderar is yonder that playth didil diddil? . . . 333   Garlande   740
DIETTES
Suche statutes apon diettes, suche pyllyng and pollyng - . . 245   Speke Parott   495
DIFFICILLE
Difficille hit ys to answere thys demaunde; 243   Speke Parott   418

DIFFUSE —DISGYSEDE   Page   Title   Line

DIFFUSE
	Page	Title	Line
They ar to diffuse for me:	90	Phy Sparrow	768
Another manes mynde diffuse is to expounde;	315	Garlande	111
Percius presed forth with problemes diffuse;	321	Garlande	338

DIGNITE
The dignite lawreat for to have.	132	Garnesche5	115

DIGNYTE
His benignite /His royall dignyte,	370	Albany	456

DIIANIRA
Fayre Diianira surmowntynge in bewte;	337	Garlande	901

DIKKON
Adieu, Jayberd, adue. /I faith, dikkon, thou crue!	108	Epitaphe1	63

DILIGENCE
'Syt downe, fayre ladys, and do your diligence!	334	Garlande	772

DIN
My mynde of the grete din was somdele amasid.	354	Garlande	1512

DINNE
The dredefull dinne drove all the rowte on a rowe;	319	Garlande	264

DIODORUS
Diodorus Siculus of my translacyon	354	Garlande	1498

DIOGENES
Olde Diogenes, with other many mo,	315	Garlande	129

DIOLOGGIS
Item his Diologgis of Ymagynacyoun;	346	Garlande	1180

DIOMEDIS
Of Diomedis stabyll /He brought out a rabyll	349	Garlande	1305

DIRECT
My style as yet direct	91	Phy Sparrow	772

DIS
Of two knaves somtyme of Dis.	106	Epitaphe	I
SOMETYME THE HOLY PATRIARKE OF DIS.	106	Epitaphe1	I
HE WAS SOMTIME THE HOLY BAILLYVE OF DIS.	109	Epitaphe2	I
Of Dis Adam degebat:	109	Epitaphe2	1

DISABLE
Our glorious lady to disable,	375	Replycacion	26

DISCEYVE
How he doth hym disceyve.	295	Why Come Ye	662

DISCERNE
How men were wonte for to discerne	352	Garlande	1441

DISCHARGE
But your benynge sufferaunce for my discharge I laid,	318	Garlande	213
Of scrupulus dout. Wherfore, your mynde discharge,	332	Garlande	726
Your discharge here under myne arme is it.'	344	Garlande	1146
I wyll myselfe discharge	350	Garlande	1353

DISCLOSE
Wherto shuld I disclose	101	Phy Sparrow	1175
He did translate, enterprete, and disclose;	347	Garlande	1222

DISCLOSED
To shewe you thynges that may not be disclosed.'	52	Bowge	217

DISCOMFECT
That late were discomfect with battayle marcyall.	117	Ag Scottes	84

DISCOMMENDE
Is to discommende /That they cannot amend,	103	Phy Sparrow	1270
Is to discommende /That they can not amende,	348	Garlande	1263

DISCORAGE
For to disparage /And to discorage	384	Replycacion	356

DISCORDE
For that I wolde not with you fall at discorde.	318	Garlande	214

DISCRETE
Provydent, discrete, circumspect and wyse,	33	Dol Dethe	139
Provydent] 'Prudent' Marshe 1568			
By discrete consyderacyon	102	Phy Sparrow	1247
humbly submytted unto the ryght discrete reformacyon	373	Replycacion	I
Ye were nothyng discrete;	376	Replycacion	52

DISCRIPCION
Of all your feturs favorable to make tru discripcion,	42	Balettys2	8

DISCURED
Ye may be assured /Your falshod discured	362	Albany	128
Your selfe thus ye discured	377	Replycacion	92

DISCURID
That I ne force what though it be discurid.	332	Garlande	731

DISCUST
They bode not till the rekenyng were discust.	30	Dol Dethe	40
Whom fortune and fate playnly have discust	337	Garlande	881

DISDAYN
Yet is she fayne, /Voyde of disdayn,	112	Calliope	18

DISDAYNE
And there agayne /Envy doth complayne, /And hath disdayne;	95	Phy Sparrow	965
Odious Disdayne, why raist thou me on this facyon?	321	Garlande	317
Nor to derayne /Batayle agayne /Scornfull disdayne,	356	Garlande	1565
Why have ye than disdayne /At poetes, and complayne	384	Replycacion	351

DISDAYNED
Than suche as have disdayned	106	Phy Sparrow	1374

DISDAYNYD
Then such that have disdaynyd	350	Garlande	1367
that] 'as' †Fakes 1523			

DISGYSEDE
I sawe a pavylyon wondersly disgysede,	313	Garlande	38

	Page	Title	Line
DISLOYALL			
And ye were disloyall Amalec.	118	Ag Scottes	116
DISORDER			
Thus all thyng ye disorder	380	Replycacion	227
DISPARAGE			
Thus he dothe disparage	369	Albany	414
For to disparage /And to discorage	384	Replycacion	355
DISPARAGED			
Disparaged is her fame	89	Phy Sparrow	711
DISPARE			
Take no dispare,	355	Garlande	1535
DISPIGHT			
A vengeaunce and dispight /On the must nedes lyght	364	Albany	234
DISPITE			
Of fals double tunges in the dispite.	140	Ven Tongues	82
DISPYGHT			
For, if they understood /His traytourly dispyght,	121	Ag Scottes2	25
He hath dispyght and scorne	294	Why Come Ye	599
Not for to fyght /Ageyne dispyght,	356	Garlande	1562
And for to wright /In the dispyght	359	Albany	17
DISPYSE			
Sum dysdanous dawcokkis that all men dispyse,	329	Garlande	618
DISPLAYD			
Vexilla regis he devysid to be displayd;	352	Garlande	1420
DISPLEASE			
Displease not an hundreth for one mannes pleasure.	314	Garlande	90
DISPLESAUNT			
His foule semblaunt /All displesaunt; foule] 'feule' †Kele 1545.2, Wyght 1553	95	Phy Sparrow	937
Therby I shall purchace /No displesaunt rewarde,	368	Albany	359
DISPORTE			
Rendrynge my devisis I made in disporte	354	Garlande	1494
DISPUTED			
Agaynst her grace disputed	375	Replycacion	30
DISSUASYVE			
Of his onour, whos dissuasyve in wrytyng	316	Garlande	151
DISTICHON			
In his distichon made on verses twaine. distichon] 'distincyon' †Fakes 1523	353	Garlande	1467
DISTINCTIONS			
And some make distinctions multipliciter,	235	Speke Parott	157
DISTRES			
Where hartis belluyng, embosyd with distres,	312	Garlande	24
Of his pleasaunt paine there and his glad distres	351	Garlande	1391
DITIIS			
And Maxymyane, with his madde ditiis,	322	Garlande	360
DITIS			
Thes sorowfulle ditis that I may shew expres.	29	Dol Dethe	21
sum parte of Skeltons bokes and baladis with ditis of plesure,	345	Garlande	R
DIVERS			
Langagys divers; yet undyr that dothe reste	241	Speke Parott	365
DIVINITE			
Drowned in dregges of divinite,	374	Replycacion	6
DIVISION			
Such tunges unhappy hath made great division	139	Ven Tongues	55
DIVISIS			
Many divisis passynge curyously;	336	Garlande	853
DIVISYON			
To dryve them at divisyon,	306	Why Come Ye	1094
DIVYNE			
And of the prescyence /Of divyne assence assence] 'essence' Marshe 1568	259	Collyn Clout	525
Was made a divyne;	266	Collyn Clout	808
That of divyne myseracion	384	Replycacion	375
And divyne inspyracion	384	Replycacion	381
DIVYNITE			
In your divynite /Of Luthers affynite,	381	Replycacion	265
DIVYNYTE			
Some lerned in other sawe, /As in divynyte,	265	Collyn Clout	733
So that in divynyte	266	Collyn Clout	789
Or of Divynyte, or Doctour Dryvyll, Divynyte] 'Divine' Marshe 1568, 'deuynite' MS Harley 2252; Dryvyll] 'oryll' MS Harley 2252	277	Collyn Clout	1220
DY			
They saide they forsede not nor carede not to dy.	31	Dol Dethe	84
And dy we must.	39	Coystrowne3	6
I truste to quyte you or I dy!	41	Coystrowne4	21
I praye to God that it maye never dy.	53	Bowge	271
For though ye lyve a c. yere, ye shal dy a daw.	71	Hauke	334
Tyll cruell fate made him to dy:	86	Phy Sparrow	592
Thou mokkyshe marmoset, /I will nat dy in [thy] det. thy] 'they' †MS Harley 367	128	Garnesche3	173
DYADEME			
As emperes the dyademe hath worne	46	Bowge	4
DYAMAND			
Dyamand poyntyd to rase oute hartly care	44	Balettys3	19

DYAMAUNTIS —DYDE   Page   Title   Line

DYAMAUNTIS
Of dyamauntis pointed was the wall;   325   Garlande   473
    the] 'the rokky' Marshe 1568
DYAMOUNDE
I am the dyamounde dowtlesse of dygnyte.   181   Magnyfycence 1477
DYANA
With Dame Dyana naked;   270   Collyn Clout   944
DYANE
Goodly maystres Jane, /Sobre, demure Dyane;   102   Phy Sparrow   1224
DYCE
What, loo, man, see here of dyce a bale;   57   Bowge   389
Fye on this dyce, they be not worth a turde!   57   Bowge   392
Nay, come at ones, for the armes of the dyce.   162   Magnyfycence   781
'Prove his wytt', sayth he, 'at cardes or dyce, ...   318   Garlande   206
DYCHE
Whome she hateth, she casteth in the dyche, ...   49   Bowge   115
    hateth] 'hatch' †Wynkyn de Worde 1499, 'hateth' Wynkyn
    de Worde 1510, Marshe 1568
No force what thoughe his neyghbour dye in a dyche.   189   Magnyfycence 1752
But he laythe all in the dyche, ...   290   Why Come Ye   455
DYCKEN
'In faythe, Dycken, thou krew, ...   280   Why Come Ye   66
DYD
With thi blode precious our fenaunce thou dyd pay   34   Dol Dethe   195
The tyme whan Mars to werre hym dyd dres;   46   Bowge   7
That so far dyd excede;   67   Hauke   191
That they dyd such a dede, ...   70   Hauke   300
But whan I dyd beholde   72   Phy Sparrow   39
To behold and se /What hevynesse dyd me pange: 72   Phy Sparrow   44
Such paynes dyd me frete   73   Phy Sparrow   58
That myne hert dyd bete, ...   73   Phy Sparrow   59
Whom Theseus dyd afraye, ...   74   Phy Sparrow   86
Whom Hercules dyd outraye, ...   74   Phy Sparrow   87
Because that she dyd pas   75   Phy Sparrow   151
    that] not in Marshe 1568
He dyd nothynge, perde, /But syt upon my kne.   76   Phy Sparrow   171
But my sparowe dyd pas   78   Phy Sparrow   266
How Scipion dyd wake   88   Phy Sparrow   668
Wherfore all Troy dyd rew;   88   Phy Sparrow   676
How hartely he dyd it take   89   Phy Sparrow   692
And moche therof dyd make;   89   Phy Sparrow   693
For she dyd but fayne;   89   Phy Sparrow   695
How often dyd I tote   100   Phy Sparrow   1146
By Hercules that hell dyd harow, ...   104   Phy Sparrow   1291
How be it to Saull dyd he tell   105   Phy Sparrow   1357
Dyd never man good.   108   Epitaphel   67
Ye summond our kyng, why dyd ye so?   118   Ag Scottes   92
    ye] not in Kynge & Marche 1554, Day 1560, Marshe 1568
To you nothing it dyd accorde   118   Ag Scottes   93
Ye thought ye dyd yet valyauntly;   118   Ag Scottes   99
In double delyng so he dyd playe, ...   119   Ag Scottes   155
    In] 'An' Day 1560, Marshe 1568
Fortune on you therfore dyd frowne;   120   Ag Scottes   176
Agaynst whom he dyd fyght /Falsly agaynst all right, . . .   120   Ag Scottes2   17
Who is that that thus dyd cry?   149   Magnyfycence   326
Fyrst I dyd set;   165   Magnyfycence   879
With Crafty Convayaunce. Ye, dyd they so?   166   Magnyfycence   941
By Goddes body, so dyd I.   166   Magnyfycence   947
Mary, syr, so dyd he excede and passe, ...   178   Magnyfycence 1385
I wolde I had, by hym that hell dyd harowe, ...   184   Magnyfycence 1561
I wolde hauke whylest my hede dyd warke, ...   184   Magnyfycence 1563
And more than ever I dyd for ony man.   187   Magnyfycence 1694
A, syr, tolde I not you howe I dyd fynde   191   Magnyfycence 1819
And wyth a brystell of a bore his berde dyd I shave. . . .   192   Magnyfycence 1832
Thou sawe never yet but I dyd my parte, ...   203   Magnyfycence 2228
Ye be the thevys, I say, away my goodys dyd cary.   203   Magnyfycence 2239
This letter ye speke of never dyd I wryte.   209   Magnyfycence 2442
Her felowe dyd stammer and stut, ...   223   El Rummynge   339
An other than dyd hyche her, ...   224   El Rummynge   401
    hyche] 'hye' 1521 Fragment
Than Margery Mylkeducke /Her kyrtell she dyd uptucke . . .   225   El Rummynge   419
And as she at her dyd pluck, ...   227   El Rummynge   504
    And] not in Day 1560, Marshe 1568; pluck] 'pulck' †Lant 1545
Than Elynour dyd them hyde /Within her beddes syde.   229   El Rummynge   605
For that pereles prynce that Parrot dyd create, ...   236   Speke Parott   218
They dyd us a shrewde turne, ...   285   Why Come Ye   269
Dyd Moyses sore manase   305   Why Come Ye   1067
    sore] not in MS Rawlinson C. 813
He dyd never approche   307   Why Come Ye   1144
As goddesse inmortall she dyd represente;   313   Garlande   47
The huge myghty okes them selfe dyd avaunce, ...   320   Garlande   279
There Titus Lyvius hymselfe dyd avaunce   321   Garlande   344
Thou dyd nothyng but barke   362   Albany   147
Those wordes his grace dyd saye /Of an ammas gray.   372   Albany   530
That laughed whan he dyd pas   379   Replycacion   187
DYDE
Some of moralyte nobly dyde endyte;   46   Bowge   14
    moralyte] 'mortalyte' †Wynkyn de Worde 1499, Marshe 1568

DYE — DYMINGIS

	Page	Title	Line
But Ignorance full soone dyde me dyscure	46	Bowge	18
dyscure] 'dysture' †Wynkyn de Worde 1499, 1510			
In a trone whiche fer clerer dyde shyne	47	Bowge	60
clerer] 'clere' Marshe 1568			
In golde letters, this worde, whiche I dyde rede:	48	Bowge	66
Full daynnously, and fro me she dyde fare,	48	Bowge	82
For, as me thoughte, in our shyppe I dyde see	49	Bowge	132
Fortune theyr frende, with whome oft she dyde daunce:	50	Bowge	141
Whan there were dyverse that sore dyde you manace.	50	Bowge	159
His stomak stuffed ofte tymes dyde reboke.	51	Bowge	180
I wote, and he dyde, ye wolde me telle.	51	Bowge	205
He sayde of me, whan he with you dyde talke –	52	Bowge	209
Me thoughte alwaye Dyscymular dyde devyse;	58	Bowge	424
Thyse were the wordes he to me dyde saye.	58	Bowge	441
he] 'that he' Marshe 1568			
Ye summoned our kynge. Why dyde ye so?	113	Scot Kynge	2
To you no thyng it dyde accorde	113	Scot Kynge	3
Ye thought ye dyde it full valyauntolye,	113	Scot Kynge	9
Ye dyde not your dewty therin,	114	Scot Kynge	32
Alasse in my cradell that I had not dyde!	196	Magnyfycence	1987
That never dyde offence.	375	Replycacion	44
Confessyng howe ye dyde lye /In prechyng shamefully.	377	Replycacion	90
Ye dyde provoke and tyse,	378	Replycacion	132

DYE

	Page	Title	Line
Wed me or els I dye for thought!	36	Man Margery	26
Maye never dye, bute evermore endure.	46	Bowge	16
Whan I sawe my sparowe dye!	75	Phy Sparrow	146
That potencyally /May never dye	84	Phy Sparrow	515
And the next day he shuld dye,	105	Phy Sparrow	1359
Theyr names shall never dye.	106	Epitaphe	I
No force what thoughe his neyghbour dye in a dyche.	189	Magnyfycence	1752
Alasse, alasse, alasse! I dye for thought.	196	Magnyfycence	1969
Thou sholde not scape, horson, but thou sholde dye.	202	Magnyfycence	2195
Without drynke she must dye;	221	El Rummynge	273
That never may dye, nor never dye shall:	236	Speke Parott	216
That never may dye, nor never dye shall:	236	Speke Parott	216
Theyr neyghbours dye for meate.	254	Collyn Clout	320
And some of you shall dye /Lyke holy Jeremy;	276	Collyn Clout	1208
Item to Lerne You to Dye When ye Wyll;	345	Garlande	1176
to] 'do' †Fakes 1523			
And the next day he shulde dye,	350	Garlande	1352
With hym to lyve and dye,	371	Albany	486
That never more may dye.	380	Replycacion	246
Nor heresy wyll never dye.	385	Replycacion	408

DYED

	Page	Title	Line
Of grace out of the state /And dyed excomunycate.	121	Ag Scottes2	30
For, syth he dyed, largesse was lytell used.	148	Magnyfycence	282
And dyed stynkyngly marterd.	297	Why Come Ye	741

DYENGE

	Page	Title	Line
Tyll my dyenge day	259	Collyn Clout	506

DYET

	Page	Title	Line
With drammes of devocyon your dyet must be drest,	207	Magnyfycence	2358

DYETYD

	Page	Title	Line
Deyntely dyetyd with dyvers delycate spyce,	231	Speke Parott	3

DYFFAME

	Page	Title	Line
You thus to dyffame.	259	Collyn Clout	510

DYFFUSE

	Page	Title	Line
It is dyffuse to fynde	91	Phy Sparrow	806

DYG

	Page	Title	Line
It is perlous for a horseman to dyg in the trenche.	43	Balettys2	26

DYGGETH

	Page	Title	Line
He dyggeth so in the trenche	290	Why Come Ye	434

DYGNYTE

	Page	Title	Line
To contaminate /And to violate /The dygnyte lauryate.	126	Garnesche3	100
In dygnyte roiall that doth excelle.	132	Garnesche5	96
I am the dyamounde dowtlesse of dygnyte.	181	Magnyfycence	1477
And knowe your selfe mortal for all your dygnyte;	211	Magnyfycence	2499
Almoost two or three, /Of that dygnyte,	250	Collyn Clout	149
And the dygnyte /Of the bysshoppes [s]ee.	259	Collyn Clout	500
see] 'fee' †Godfray 1531, Kele 1545.1, Marshe 1568			
And set in majeste /And spirytuall dygnyte,	261	Collyn Clout	588
That hath no dygnyte	265	Collyn Clout	734
And your noble se /And your dygnyte	265	Collyn Clout	760
se] 'fee' Marshe 1568, 'see' MS Harley 2252			
Of what estate he be /Of spirituall dygnyte,	294	Why Come Ye	618
Promoted was he /To a cardynalles dygnyte	297	Why Come Ye	729
Of Rome to the see /Weth suche dygnyte.	307	Why Come Ye	1146

DYGNYTES

	Page	Title	Line
Of preestly dygnytes /By theyr malygnytes.	260	Collyn Clout	538
By] 'But' Kele 1545.1, Marshe 1568			

DYKES

	Page	Title	Line
Lepe over lakes and dykes,	262	Collyn Clout	622

DYLECTABLE

	Page	Title	Line
Her mouthe enbawmed, dylectable and mery,	183	Magnyfycence	1557

DYLYGENT

	Page	Title	Line
Intentyfe ay /And dylygent, /No tyme myspent;	339	Garlande	943

DYMINGIS

	Page	Title	Line
To a straunge jurisdictyon /Called Dymingis Dale,	299	Why Come Ye	801

DYMOSTENES —DYSCORDE   Page   Title   Line

DYMOSTENES
Dymostenes, that oratour royall, ... 316   Garlande   130
DYN
Soft, and make no dyn, ... 99   Phy Sparrow   1092
Holde thy hande, dawe, of thy dagger, and stynt of thy dyn; . . 202   Magnyfycence   2188
DYNDE
I sawe a sowter go to supper, or ever he had dynde. 191   Magnyfycence   1825
DYNE
To the dyne dale /Of boteles bale, ... 40   Coystrowne3   45
    boteles] 'botemles' Marshe 1568
DYNED
'Parott hathe not dyned of all this long day;' 231   Speke Parott   23
DYNGE
Nay. Then thou wylte dynge the devyll and thou be not holde. . 202   Magnyfycence   2183
And the devill downe dynge, ... 364   Albany   210
DYNYD
He dynyd with delyte, with poverte he must sup. 195   Magnyfycence   1965
DYNT
I dryve downe these dastardys with a dynt of my fyste. 181   Magnyfycence   1486
Vyle velyarde, thou must not nowe my dynt withstande; 193   Magnyfycence   1878
Thou must not abyde the dynt of my hande. 193   Magnyfycence   1879
DYNTES
I drede no dyntes of fatall desteny. 190   Magnyfycence   1798
DYNTYS
That he dryvyth them doune with dyntys on ther day-wach. . . . 43   Balettys2   30
DYOCLESYAN
Neither yet Dyoclesyan, /Nor yet Domysyan; 67   Hauke   192
DYOMEDES
Of Dyomedes stable /He brought out a rable 104   Phy Sparrow   1312
DYONYSYUS
Nother Olybryus, /Nor Dyonysyus; 67   Hauke   197
DYRECCYON
Yf noblenesse were aquayntyd with sober dyreccyon. 141   Magnyfycence   18
Take sad dyreccyon, and leve this wantonnesse. 144   Magnyfycence   149
DYRECTE
My style for to dyrecte, ... 257   Collyn Clout   435
DYRECTION
And theyr sad dyrection, ... 298   Why Come Ye   769
Sometyme for sadde dyrection, ... 385   Replycacion   390
DYRECTIONS
To take sadde dyrections. 268   Collyn Clout   894
    sadde] 'the sayd' Kele 1545.1, Marshe 1568
DYRECTYON
But as touchynge dystrectyon, /With sober dyrectyon 304   Why Come Ye   1009
    dystrectyon] 'dyscrecyon' Marshe 1568, MS Rawlinson C. 813
DYRIGES
Theyr dyriges are forgotten, ... 257   Collyn Clout   425
    Theyr dyriges] 'The Diriges' Kele 1545.1, 'the dyrige'
    MS Harley 2252
DYRYSYON
But dyvysyon, dyssencyon, dyrysyon – these thre 159   Magnyfycence   700
DYRT
Gresed upon dyrt /That baudeth her skyrt. 216   El Rummynge   89
Take up dyrt and all, /And bere out of the hall.' 219   El Rummynge   183
    dyrt] 'drit' Kynge & Marche 1554, Day 1560, Marshe 1568
DYRTY
And your dyrty endytyng, ... 127   Garnesche3   113
DYS
To hawke in my church of Dys. 62   Hauke   42
Dys church ye thus depravyd; 70   Hauke   308
And sey poetis no dys.... 132   Garnesche5   113
DYSAVAYLYNGE
In hyndrynge and dysavaylynge 274   Collyn Clout   1104
DYSCAYTE
Counterfet kyndnesse, and thynke dyscayte; 152   Magnyfycence   438
DYSCANT
Hys dyscant is besy, it is withoute a mene; 37   Coystrownel   27
DYSCEYGHT
From trechery and dysceyght, ... 298   Why Come Ye   773
DYSCEYTE
We tweyne, I trowe, be not withoute dysceyte: 55   Bowge   313
For all our courte is full of dysceyte. 59   Bowge   469
DYSCHARGE
I wyll my selfe dyscharge 105   Phy Sparrow   1360
Me to permyt my mynde to dyscharge, ... 185   Magnyfycence   1590
Wyll charge and dyscharge, ... 267   Collyn Clout   835
DYSCHARGYD
But plenarly all thought from you must be dyschargyd, ... 146   Magnyfycence   207
DYSCHECLOWTE
A bawdy dyscheclowte, /That bryngyth the worlde abowte 125   Garnesche3   36
DYSCYMULAR
Me thoughte alwaye Dyscymular dyde devyse; 58   Bowge   424
Anone Dyscymular came where I stode. 58   Bowge   427
DYSCONIUS
And of Syr Lybius /Named Dysconius; 88   Phy Sparrow   650
DYSCORDE
For no dyscorde that any man can sawe; 145   Magnyfycence   187
I sowe sedycyous sedes of dyscorde and debates. 160   Magnyfycence   737

	Page	Title	Line
DYSCORDES			
His descant is dasshed full of dyscordes;	37	Coystrowne1	38
DYSCREASE			
Now ebbe, now flowe, nowe increase, now dyscrease;	212	Magnyfycence	2521
DYSCRECION			
Dyscrecion ys modyr of nobyll vertues all;	232	Speke Parott	51
DYSCRESSYON			
So lytyll dyscressyon, and so myche reasonyng;	244	Speke Parott	456
DYSCRETE			
His wysdome is so dyscrete	289	Why Come Ye	423
DYSCRY			
My inwyt delynge there can no man dyscry.	177	Magnyfycence	1356
DYSCRYVE			
Dysease and sekenesse his conscyence to dyscryve;	207	Magnyfycence	2370
DYSCRYVED			
Yet Fansy had ben dysc[r]yved.	155	Magnyfycence	535
dyscryved] 'dysceyved' †Rastell & Treveris C 1530, B			
DYSCURE			
That wher I love best I dare not dyscure!	45	Balettys5	7
That where I love best I dare not dyscure.	46	Balettys5	14
But Ignorance full soone dyde me dyscure	46	Bowge	18
dyscure] 'dysture' †Wynkyn de Worde 1499, 1510			
His counseyle secrete never to dyscure,	52	Bowge	219
dyscure] 'dysture' †Wynkyn de Worde 1499, 1510			
DYSCUS			
Jereboseth is Ebrue, who lyst the cause dyscus.	232	Speke Parott	67
cause] 'law' Day 1560, Marshe 1568			
DYSCUST			
For I have dyscust /We ar but dust,	39	Coystrowne3	4
If it be sadly dyscust.	102	Phy Sparrow	1250
Hath for him dyscust	298	Why Come Ye	751
DYSDAYNE			
Dysdayne, Ryotte, Dyssymuler, Subtylte.	50	Bowge	140
Dysdayne, I wene, [t]his comerous car[k]es hyghte.	54	Bowge	294
this] 'his' editions; carkes] 'carbes' †Wynkyn de Worde 1499, 1510, 'crabes' Marshe 1568			
'Now,' quod Dysdayne, 'as I shall saved be,	54	Bowge	297
'By him that me boughte,' than quod Dysdayne,	54	Bowge	309
Dysdayne I sawe with Dyssymulacyon,	58	Bowge	419
Whereat he made dysdayne.	68	Hauke	224
Please it your grace to take no dysdayne,	147	Magnyfycence	252
And I tell you, I dysdayne moche of his mockys.	203	Magnyfycence	2227
And thowe sum dysdayne yow and sey how ye prate,	240	Speke Parott	315
Of on and hothyr at me that have dysdayne.	242	Speke Parott	385
Howe bysshoppes dysdayne /Sermons for to make,	250	Collyn Clout	133
Wherfore, take no dysdayne	273	Collyn Clout	1087
Or who dare dysdayne,	276	Collyn Clout	1215
DYSDAYNED			
Alas, I am dysdayned, /And as a man halfe-maymed,	237	Speke Parott	252
DYSDAYNESLYE			
So lordlye of hys lokes, and so dysdayneslye;	246	Speke Parott	508
DYSDAYNOUS			
Dysdaynous, dowble, ful of dyseyte,	133	Garnesche5	150
DYSDAYNOUSLY			
Raylynge haynously /And dysdaynously	260	Collyn Clout	537
DYSDAYNS			
Dysdayns, dystres, exylyd cruelte;	43	Balettys3	4
DYSDANOUS			
Sum dysdanous dawcokkis that all men dispyse,	329	Garlande	618
DYSE			
Till the chaunce ran ageyne hym of Fortuns double dyse.	33	Dol Dethe	140
To pronostycate truly the chaunce of fortunys dyse;	234	Speke Parott	136
DYSEASE			
For whose love, welcom dysease to me!	45	Balettys5	10
Thyselfe myschevynge to thyne endlesse dysease!	206	Magnyfycence	2342
Dysease and sekenesse his conscyence to dyscryve;	207	Magnyfycence	2370
Nowe ryche, nowe pore, nowe hole, now in dysease;	212	Magnyfycence	2518
DYSEASED			
Then feyne yourselfe dyseased, and make yourselfe seke.	185	Magnyfycence	1612
DYSEASYD			
For whose sake my hart is sore dyseasyd;	45	Balettys5	9
DYSEYTE			
Dysdaynous, dowble, ful of dyseyte,	133	Garnesche5	150
DYSER			
In a cote thou can play well the dyser.	173	Magnyfycence	1176
DYSERS			
Dysers, carders, tumblars with gambawdis,	329	Garlande	608
DYSGYSED			
Thenne I behelde how he dysgysed was:	56	Bowge	351
Of such mysadvysed /Parsons and dysgysed,	62	Hauke	22
Then to be so dysgysed.	261	Collyn Clout	580
DYSGORGED			
What have ye, villayn, forged, /And virulently dysgorged	367	Albany	321
DYSH			
In a dysh dare he rush at the rypest;	37	Coystrowne1	46
DYSHWASHER			
Ye war a kechyn page, /A dyshwasher, a dryvyll,	124	Garnesche3	26

DYSIRYD

Ye countyr umwhyle to capcyously, and ar ye be dysiryd; 123 Garnesche2 11

DYSMAYDE

'Than,' quod Hervy, 'why arte thou so dysmayde?' . . . . 54 Bowge 299

DYSMEMBRE

Them or theyr chyldren ofte tymes I dysmembre; . . . . 194 Magnyfycence 1923

DYSORDERETH

And so dysordereth this worlde over all, ... 141 Magnyfycence 20

DYSORDERYD

Where measure lackyth, all thynge dysorderyd is; . . . . 144 Magnyfycence 122

DYSOUR

Of a dysour, a devyl way, grew a jentilman, ... 330 Garlande 635

DYSPAIRE

But, my good sonne, lerne from dyspaire to flee; . . . . 206 Magnyfycence 2339

DYSPAYRE

That dyspayre well nyghe had myscheved me; . . . . 206 Magnyfycence 2332

DYSPARAGE

Dysparage ye myn auncetry? 131 Garnesche5 63

DYSPARE

Dyspare is my name, that adversyte dothe f[o]lowe; . . . . . . 205 Magnyfycence 2284
  folowe] 'felowe' †Rastell & Treveris C 1530, B,
  Douce Fragment d.7
And have you banyshed from you all dyspare? . . . . 208 Magnyfycence 2393

DYSPYGHT

Thus to rebuke me and have me in dyspyght! . . . . 205 Magnyfycence 2278

DYSPYSE

The prechour he dothe dyspyse . . . . 306 Why Come Ye 1072

DYSPYSED

I wyll have hym rehayted and dyspysed. . . . . 186 Magnyfycence 1658

DYSPYTE

By God, I have of the now grete dyspyte; . . . . 55 Bowge 325
In the dyspyte of me, ... 64 Hauke 109
Frete yourselfe for anger and for dyspyte; . . . . 185 Magnyfycence 1602
So innumerable, and so full of dyspyte, ... 205 Magnyfycence 2301

DYSPLEASE

For drede ye dysplease the hygh deyte. . . . . 196 Magnyfycence 1996
And yf there were none to dysplease but thou and I, ... 202 Magnyfycence 2194
A grete mysadventure, thy maker to dysplease, ... 206 Magnyfycence 2341
Nowe leve, nowe lothe, nowe please, nowe dysplease; . . . . . 212 Magnyfycence 2520

DYSPLEASETH

For there is nothynge that more dyspleaseth God . . . . 194 Magnyfycence 1928

DYSPLEASURE

Dyspleasure that you none take . . . . 143 Magnyfycence 98
Take no dyspleasure of that we say. . . . . 156 Magnyfycence 561
Any man shulde be /In perplexyte /Of dyspleasure; . . . . . . 300 Why Come Ye 845

DYSPLESAUNCE

By Goddis woundes, but for dysplesaunce, ... 55 Bowge 332

DYSPORT

How my dysport and play . . . . 81 Phy Sparrow 373

DYSPORTE

Transendyng plesure, surmountyng all dysporte; 43 Balettys3 7
But my dysporte they could not well endure: . . . . 50 Bowge 145
That I laugh at for my dysporte; . . . . 174 Magnyfycence 1239
This treatyse, devysyd to make you dysporte, ... 213 Magnyfycence 2538
And ye that have harde thys dysporte and game, ... 214 Magnyfycence 2571
My delyght is solas, pleasure, dysporte and pley; . . . . . . 233 Speke Parott 108

DYSPOSED

For now am I plenarely dysposed . . . . 52 Bowge 216

DYSPOSYCYONS

I can not well tell of your dysposycyons; . . . . 203 Magnyfycence 2218

DYSPOSYD

Ye ar dysposyd for to ly. 131 Garnesche5 64

DYSPUTACYON

Why, have you harde of our dysputacyon? . . . . 142 Magnyfycence 82

DYSPUTE

To here you two rutters dyspute togyder. . . . . 176 Magnyfycence 1287

DYSSAYVED

To trust in me he is but dyssayved; . . . . 186 Magnyfycence 1652

DYSSAYVYD

She hath dyssayvyd me with her doublenesse. . . . . 201 Magnyfycence 2157

DYSSEYVED

And eyther I am dysseyved, or ye be the same. . . . . 141 Magnyfycence 25

DYSSEMBLE

I can dyssemble; I can bothe laughe and grone; . . . . 159 Magnyfycence 698

DYSSENCYON

But dyvysyon, dyssencyon, dyrysyon - these thre . . . . 159 Magnyfycence 700

DYSSHES

Brynge dysshes and platters, ... 217 El Rummynge 127

DYSSY

I daunce up and downe tyll I am dyssy. . . . . 169 Magnyfycence 1040

DYSSYMULACYON

Dysdayne I sawe with Dyssymulacyon, ... 58 Bowge 419

DYSSYMULER

Dysdayne, Ryotte, Dyssymuler, Subtylte. . . . . 50 Bowge 140

DYSSYMULYNGE

But dyssymulynge and glosynge, ... 255 Collyn Clout 356

DYSTAUNCE

Though thou withdraw me from her by long dystaunce, ... 45 Balettys3 46

DYSTRECTYON—DO   Page   Title   Line

DYSTRECTYON
But as touchynge dystrectyon, /With sober dyrectyon   304   Why Come Ye   1008
 dystrectyon] 'dyscrecyon' Marshe 1568, MS Rawlinson C. 813
DYSTRES
Dysdayns, dystres, exylyd cruelte;   43   Balettys3   4
Of thoughtfull hertys plungyd in dystres;   44   Balettys3   10
DYSTRESSE
O odyous dystresse, O dedly payne and woo!   198   Magnyfycence   2053
In tyme of dystresse I am redy at hande;   205   Magnyfycence   2285
Then shall you be sone delyvered from dystresse, ...   208   Magnyfycence   2383
Hath brought in dystresse, ...   305   Why Come Ye   1034
 in] 'muche' MS Rawlinson C. 813
With hym in all dystresse, /Alway in redynesse   371   Albany   489
DYSTROY
By the masse, for ye are able to dystroy an hole lande. . . .   154   Magnyfycence   513
DYTIES
Here folowythe Dyvers Balettys and Dyties Solacyous   41   Balettys   I
DYVENDOP
The dyvendop to slepe;   83   Phy Sparrow   452
DYVERS
Here folowythe Dyvers Balettys and Dyties Solacyous   41   Balettys   I
UNTO DYVERS PEOPLE THAT REMORD THIS RYMYNG   120   Ag Scottes   R
Deyntely dyetyd with dyvers delycate spyce, ...   231   Speke Parott   3
These maydens full meryly with many a dyvers flowur   231   Speke Parott   11
 a] not in †MS Harley 2252
Thus dyvers of language by lernyng I grow: 233   Speke Parott   103
Or bokes to compyle /Of dyvers maner style, ...   247   Collyn Clout   10
Of dyvers great estates, ...   277   Collyn Clout   1246
wherein ar comprysyde many and dyvers   312   Garlande   I
I saw dyvers that were cariid away thens in cribbis, ...   330   Garlande   640
remordyng dyvers recrayed and moche unresonable errours . . .   373   Replycacion   I
DYVERSE
Dyverse in style, some spared not vyce to wrythe, ...   46   Bowge   13
 wrythe] 'wryte' Wynkyn de Worde 1510, Marshe 1568
Whan there were dyverse that sore dyde you manace.   50   Bowge   159
For here be dyverse to you that be unkynde.   50   Bowge   161
For I knowe dyverse that useth the same.   175   Magnyfycence   1255
Of dyverse mo that hauntyth my scolys.   175   Magnyfycence   1264
Yet dyverse ther be, industryous of reason, ...   315   Garlande   106
 ther] 'that' MS Cotton Vitellius E.x
Of poetis laureat of many dyverse nacyons;   321   Garlande   324
Of pursevantis ther presid in with many a dyverse tale: . . .   326   Garlande   492
 a] not in Marshe 1568
DYVERSYTE
There is a dyversyte   307   Why Come Ye   1149
DYVYLS
What neded that, in the dyvyls date?   166   Magnyfycence   943
DYVYNE
Enbrethed with the blast of influence dyvyne, ...   33   Dol Dethe   157
Thorow the grace dyvyne   93   Phy Sparrow   857
DYVYSED
studyously dyvysed at Sheryfhotten Castell, ...   312   Garlande   I
Dyvysed by Skelton after the funerall rate;   348   Garlande   1256
dyvysed by Mayster Skelton, Poete Laureat.   358   Garlande2   R
DYVYSYNGE
Dyvysynge in pycture, by his industrious wit, ...   343   Garlande   1098
DYVYSYON
But dyvysyon, dyssencyon, dyrysyon - these thre   159   Magnyfycence   700
DO
'What, will ye do nothyng but play?'   35   Man Margery   4
Good mastres Anne, there ye do shayle!   41   Coystrowne4   19
That I ne wyste what to do was beste;   47   Bowge   30
What thynge is that I maye do for you?   53   Bowge   240
'How do ye, mayster? Ye loke so soberly!   58   Bowge   442
In every poynte that I can do or saye.   60   Bowge   496
 In] 'To' Marshe 1568
This worke devysed is /For suche as do amys, ...   61   Hauke   2
And do what he wolde;   76   Phy Sparrow   178
He can do nothyng ellys.   84   Phy Sparrow   494
Shall now com and do right, ...   110   Lawde   17
O Gabionyte of Gabyone, why do ye gane and gaspe?   123   Garnesche2   15
But ofte tymes have I sene wyse men do mad dedys.   148   Magnyfycence   302
Do what I coude to do you good.   150   Magnyfycence   335
Do what I coude to do you good.   150   Magnyfycence   335
Do away, I say, the devylles torde!   151   Magnyfycence   397
What so ever I do, all men me prayse, ...   152   Magnyfycence   429
Howe coulde ye do that, and [I] was away?   154   Magnyfycence   504
 I] not in †Rastell & Treveris C 1530, B
With Magnyfycence in housholde do remayne;   157   Magnyfycence   613
Spell the remenaunt, and do togyder.   157   Magnyfycence   619
With Magnyfycence in housholde do remayne;   158   Magnyfycence   640
And do nothynge. How be it, full lytell grace   159   Magnyfycence   693
I am never glad but whan I may do yll, ...   160   Magnyfycence   731
Beryst thou any rome? Or cannyst thou do ought?   162   Magnyfycence   776
I may do somwhat, and more I thynke shall.   162   Magnyfycence   778
Abyde, syr, quod he! Mary, so I do.   162   Magnyfycence   789
Or whiche of you can do most.   162   Magnyfycence   803
Ye, and do ryght good servyce he can.   163   Magnyfycence   822

DOCTOR —DOCTOR

	Page	Title	Line
A very pore /That so wyll do,	164	Magnyfycence	870
Do and undo, bothe togyder;	169	Magnyfycence	1034
Nay, but wotest thou what I do say?	170	Magnyfycence	1092
Torde, I say! What have I do?	171	Magnyfycence	1106
In faythe, I can do mastryes, so I can.	173	Magnyfycence	1190
What canest thou do but play cocke wat?	173	Magnyfycence	1191
Shyt thy purse, dawe, and do no cost.	174	Magnyfycence	1207
For with foly so do I them lede	175	Magnyfycence	1260
And shall we have lyberte to do what we wyll?	176	Magnyfycence	1316
What sholde a man do with you? Loke you under [k]ay?	180	Magnyfycence	1429
kay] 'bay' †Rastell & Treveris C 1530, B			
Shewe us your mynde then, howe to do and what.	180	Magnyfycence	1435
I can do nothynge but he stonde besyde.	180	Magnyfycence	1449
Syr, we can do nothynge the one without the other.	180	Magnyfycence	1450
Plesyth it your grace to shewe what I do shall?	182	Magnyfycence	1517
Any thynge to do that myght be to your pleasure.	183	Magnyfycence	1528
What so ever ye do, folowe your owne wyll,	185	Magnyfycence	1595
But do as ye lyst and take your owne way.	185	Magnyfycence	1604
What sholde ye do elles? Are not you a lorde?	185	Magnyfycence	1606
Do as moche as for myne owne father.	186	Magnyfycence	1642
So I wote not what he sholde do here.	189	Magnyfycence	1741
To do you servyce after your appetyte.	190	Magnyfycence	1793
Some I make lame, and some I do kyll,	194	Magnyfycence	1931
But redresse is redlesse and may do no correccyon.	209	Magnyfycence	2417
And whyles the heedes do this, /The remenaunt is amys	249	Collyn Clout	115
What have laye men to do	251	Collyn Clout	196
Alas, why do ye nat handle	255	Collyn Clout	332
Ye do them wronge and no ryght	256	Collyn Clout	404
them] not in Marshe 1568			
What coude the Turke do more	257	Collyn Clout	429
Iche wotte what yche do thynke!'	258	Collyn Clout	458
yche do] 'eche other' Kele 1545.1, Marshe 1568			
And ye shall do the same,	259	Collyn Clout	508
He must do this werke;	264	Collyn Clout	728
What they do in hell.	267	Collyn Clout	823
What they do in heven;	267	Collyn Clout	825
They say, to do corrections,	268	Collyn Clout	892
Theyr tonges thus do clap;	273	Collyn Clout	1058
Or elles that they do lye,	273	Collyn Clout	1063
I do it nat for no despyte.	273	Collyn Clout	1086
it for] 'it not for' Kele 1545.1, Marshe 1568			
But my recountynge is /Of them that do amys	274	Collyn Clout	1102
To do shame, they have no shame;	275	Collyn Clout	1141
What may she do therto?'	281	Why Come Ye	87
'Do ryght and do no wronge.'	281	Why Come Ye	89
do no] 'no' Kitson 1560.7, Marshe 1568			
'Do ryght and do no wronge.'	281	Why Come Ye	89
do no] 'no' Kitson 1560.7, Marshe 1568			
To well they do agre,	286	Why Come Ye	278
With, 'Do thou for me,	286	Why Come Ye	279
And I shall do for the.'	286	Why Come Ye	280
For and this curre do gnar,	286	Why Come Ye	300
Thought to do a thynge	292	Why Come Ye	549
Slouthfull to do good,	293	Why Come Ye	577
How can he do ryght?	293	Why Come Ye	581
Lo, for to do shamfully	305	Why Come Ye	1046
Lo] 'Soo' MS Rawlinson C. 813			
No shame to do amys;	305	Why Come Ye	1051
The fyrst, to do him reverence,	307	Why Come Ye	1123
Complayne or do what ye wyll,	310	Why Come Ye2	31
But to do sumwhat iche man doth hym dres	315	Garlande	122
Few shall ye fynde or none that wyll do so.'	317	Garlande	168
As wele foly as wysdome oft ye do avaunce,	317	Garlande	180
ye do] 'tyme ye' MS Cotton Vitellius E.x			
Or elles, ye know well, I can do no lesse	318	Garlande	226
'Daphnes, my derlynge, why do you me refuse?	320	Garlande	297
How all that I do is under refformation,	323	Garlande	411
'Syt downe, fayre ladys, and do your diligence!	334	Garlande	772
For your pleasure do there endevourment,	335	Garlande	810
But to do you servyce nedis now I must;	337	Garlande	879
to do you] 'do her' MS Cotton Vitellius E.x			
How a do cam trippyng in at the rerewarde,	351	Garlande	1385
What myght she say? What myght he do therto?	351	Garlande	1395
What shuld I do but take it in gre?	353	Garlande	1487
Yet ye dare do nothynge	364	Albany	211
To worshyppe none ymages, /Nor do pylgrymages?	381	Replycacion	270
Whiche de latria do trete.	381	Replycacion	281
Howe poetes do fayne?	384	Replycacion	353
Ye do moche great outrage,	384	Replycacion	354
As Grekes do it call,	384	Replycacion	369
In this that I do make	385	Replycacion	399

DOCTOR

	Page	Title	Line
Thys Doctor Deuyas commensyd in a cart;	38	Coystrownel	55
Deuyas] 'dellias' Marshe 1568			
Doctor Dawcocke? /Ware the hawke!	69	Hauke	265
Doctor Dialetica? /Where fynde you in Ypotetica,	69	Hauke	267
Doctor Dawkocke? /Ware the hawke!	69	Hauke	284
Ware] 'Whare' †Lant 1545			

DOCTOUR — DOLOWRE

	Page	Title	Line
Doctor Dawcock! /Ware the hawke!	70	Hauke	305
Doctor Dawcoke! /Ware the hawke!	70	Hauke	329
Lyke a doctor dawpate,	126	Garnesche3	94
No doctor of devinyte,	291	Why Come Ye	509
Nor doctor of the law,	292	Why Come Ye	510
Now mayster doctor, howe say ye,	309	Why Come Ye2	1
Mayster doctor, in your degre,	309	Why Come Ye2	6
Maister doctor decretorum,	309	Why Come Ye2	9

DOCTOUR

	Page	Title	Line
This Doctour Dawcocke, Drede, I wene he hyghte.	54	Bowge	303
For Mayster Adulator, /And Doctour Assentator,	263	Collyn Clout	680
But doctour Bullatus /Parum litteratus,	266	Collyn Clout	795
Doctour Daupatus, /And bacheler Bacheleratus,	266	Collyn Clout	799
Avaunt, syr doctour Deuyas!	275	Collyn Clout	1157
Deuyas] 'Denyas' †Godfray 1531, 'dyvers' Marshe 1568, 'Devias' MS Harley 2252			
For all maister Doctour of Cyvyll	277	Collyn Clout	1219
Or of Divynyte, or Doctour Dryvyll,	277	Collyn Clout	1220
Divynyte] 'Divine' Marshe 1568, 'deuynite' MS Harley 2252; Dryvyll] 'oryll' MS Harley 2252			
Whom Hieronymus, /That doctour glorious,	383	Replycacion	319

DOCTOURS

	Page	Title	Line
Some doctours of lawe,	264	Collyn Clout	731
Doctours that lerned be	266	Collyn Clout	790
of the reverende prelates and moche noble doctours	373	Replycacion	I
Doctours of the chayre in the Vyntre	374	Replycacion	8
With other doctours many mo,	381	Replycacion	280

DOCTRYNE

	Page	Title	Line
Of studyous doctryne when at the port salu	327	Garlande	541

DODDY PATIS

	Page	Title	Line
He calleth them doddy patis;	295	Why Come Ye	652

DOG

	Page	Title	Line
Ye rayle, ye ryme, with, 'Hay, dog, hay!'	129	Garnesche5	5
Tut, Scot, I sey, /Go shake th[e], dog, hey!	135	Dundas	28
the] 'thy' Marshe 1568			

DOGGE

	Page	Title	Line
Go shake the, dogge, hay, syth ye wyll nedys!	148	Magnyfycence	303
Nowe, of good felowshyp, let me by thy [d]ogge.	170	Magnyfycence	1082
dogge] 'hogge' †Rastell & Treveris C 1530, B			
Let me have thy dogge, what soever I pay.	171	Magnyfycence	1101
Yet gyve me thy dogge, and I am content;	171	Magnyfycence	1112
Nowe take thou my dogge and gyve me thy fowle.	171	Magnyfycence	1116
What callest thou thy dogge? Tusshe! His name is Gryme.	171	Magnyfycence	1118
In faythe, there is not a better dogge for hogges,	171	Magnyfycence	1120
That made Cerberus to cache, the cur dogge of hell,	182	Magnyfycence	1495
With, 'Hey, dogge, hay, /Have these hogges away!'	218	El Rummynge	168
hogges] 'dogges' Day 1560, Marshe 1568			
For drede of the bochers dogge	286	Why Come Ye	298
With, 'hey, dogge, hay.'	360	Albany	37
Twyt, Scot, shake th[e] dogge, hay.	363	Albany	159
the] 'thy' †Marshe 1568			

DOGGES

	Page	Title	Line
At his cloked counterfetynge dogges dothe barke.	153	Magnyfycence	482
Come, Gryme! Come, Gryme! It is my praty dogges.	171	Magnyfycence	1119
Suche malyncoly mastyvys and mangye curre dogges	240	Speke Parott	320
And lyke maungy dogges.	364	Albany	215

DOGGYS

	Page	Title	Line
I am baytyd with doggys at every mannys gate;	195	Magnyfycence	1961

DOGMATISTA

	Page	Title	Line
[Y]e develysh dogmatista, /Your hawke on your fista,	69	Hauke	255
Ye] 'The' †Lant 1545, Kynge & Marche 1554, Day 1560, Marshe 1568			

DOGRELL

	Page	Title	Line
In bastarde ryme, after the dogrell gyse,	151	Magnyfycence	408

DOYNGE

	Page	Title	Line
In doynge his homage /Unto his soverayne.	80	Phy Sparrow	326
Here cometh in COURTLY ABUSYON, doynge reverence and courtesy.	182	Magnyfycence	SD

DOLEFULL

	Page	Title	Line
My Phyllyppes dolefull deth!	80	Phy Sparrow	352
Alas, for dolefull desteny!	86	Phy Sparrow	593
The dolefull desteny, and the carefull chaunce,	348	Garlande	1255

DOLEFULLE

	Page	Title	Line
The dedely fate, the dolefulle destenny	29	Dol Dethe	2

DOLOROUS

	Page	Title	Line
O dolorous chaunce of Fortuns fraward hande!	32	Dol Dethe	110
O dolorous Teusday, dedicate to thi name,	32	Dol Dethe	114
Wythe hevy chere, with dolorous hart and mynd,	34	Dol Dethe	176
With dolorous songes funerall,	81	Phy Sparrow	391
Of this dolorous mater.	81	Phy Sparrow	398
O dolorous herte, O harde adversyte!	198	Magnyfycence	2052

DOLOROUSLY

	Page	Title	Line
Here MAGNYFYCENCE dolorously maketh his mone.	198	Magnyfycence	SD

DOLORUS

	Page	Title	Line
Skelton Laureat Upon the Dolorus Dethe	29	Dol Dethe	I

DOLOWRE

	Page	Title	Line
And moche hevynesse, /And great dolowre	305	Why Come Ye	1036
dolowre] 'dullness' MS Rawlinson C. 813			

DOLOWRS — DOROTHE   Page   Title   Line

DOLOWRS
Exclude now all dolowrs. 110   Lawde   7
DOM
Syt styll as they were dom. 283   Why Come Ye   199
DOMAGE
To the domage and harmys 370   Albany   468
DOME
I dare not speke; I promysed to be dome. 52   Bowge   229
Nowe, after my dome, ... 75   Phy Sparrow   147
A thowsande, thowsande, I trow, to my dome, ... 354   Garlande   1505
DOMESDAY
At dredfull Domesday. 277   Collyn Clout   1233
DOMINGOS
Domingos nose that was wheled. 308   Why Come Ye   1185
   was] not in MS Rawlinson C. 813
Balthasor, that helyd Domingos nose 309   Why Come Ye   1194
   nose] 'pose' Marshe 1568
DOMINYK
Or elles frere Dominyk, ... 265   Collyn Clout   738
DOMYNGO
I meane Domyngo Lomelyn /That was wont to wyn 308   Why Come Ye   1190
DOMYNYON
Whych provyth well that measure shold have domynyon. 143   Magnyfycence   120
Measure is worthy to have domynyon. 144   Magnyfycence   127
DOMYSYAN
Neither yet Dyoclesyan, /Nor yet Domysyan; 67   Hauke   193
DONATUS
And Donatus be dryven out of scole; 235   Speke Parott   170
DONE
And all is done ye lokyd for before, ... 45   Balettys4   2
To make the mery, as other felowes done? 57   Bowge   380
By lyberte is done many a great excesse; 142   Magnyfycence   53
It shalbe done at your commaundement. 147   Magnyfycence   239
Your pleasure, syr shortely shall be done. 149   Magnyfycence   321
By the masse, well done and boldely. 166   Magnyfycence   948
To name thyselfe. Come of, it were done. 167   Magnyfycence   965
Nowe thou hast done me a pleasure grete. 171   Magnyfycence   1131
By the harte of God, well done! 172   Magnyfycence   1156
And, 'This is not well done, syr; take hede'; 175   Magnyfycence   1248
It shall be done. Ye, but byd hym come away 179   Magnyfycence   1399
Remembre the good servyce that Mesure hath you done, . . . 186   Magnyfycence   1637
By the masse, I have done that I can, ... 187   Magnyfycence   1693
Than is it done as it sholde be; 189   Magnyfycence   1764
Ye, have done at ones without delay. 206   Magnyfycence   2319
That were done in Fraunce, ... 297   Why Come Ye   720
What he hath done, let it be brought to syght. 318   Garlande   230
So have ye done, that meretoryously 323   Garlande   401
DONG CART
A dong cart or a tumrell 132   Garnesche5   93
DONGE
That the dowves donge downe mygth fall 66   Hauke   183
And donge, whan it commes, /In the ale tunnes. 219   El Rummynge   193
The hennes donge awaye, ... 219   El Rummynge   197
The donge of her hennes /And the ale togyder, ... 219   El Rummynge   202
DONGE CARTE
Sodaynly upstarte /From the donge carte, ... 262   Collyn Clout   645
DONGHYLL
Thou hast in despite, /Thou donghyll knyght? 136   Dundas   48
Of the donghyll, for small lucke 364   Albany   224
DONN
But had his nobillmen donn wel that day 31   Dol Dethe   69
DONNE
Her fethers donne; /Well faveryd bonne! 168   Magnyfycence   989
Shall se many thyngys donne craftely. 177   Magnyfycence   1334
DONNY
That causeth I loke so donny.' 224   El Rummynge   400
DONNYSHE
What! Callyst thou me a donnyshe crowe? 170   Magnyfycence   1095
DOO
For and I studye sholde as ye doo nowe, ... 53   Bowge   242
DOOTH
In double w[a]lles now he dooth dreme. 115   Scot Kynge   58
   walles] 'welles' †Fakes 1513
DORE
Ye. But he wyll in at every mannes dore. 171   Magnyfycence   1130
Somtyme, I say, behynde the dore for nede; 177   Magnyfycence   1341
The wolfe from the dore 250   Collyn Clout   153
Towarde the dore, as he were comyng oute, ... 343   Garlande   1095
DOREGATE
Of youre doregate ye have no doute. 41   Coystrowne4   26
DORES
That Mesure were cast out of the dores. 156   Magnyfycence   568
Hens, thou haynyarde, out of dores fast! 188   Magnyfycence   1725
DORMOWS
Dormiat in pace, lyke a dormows – 347   Garlande   1248
DOROTHE
Dame Dorothe and Lady Besse, ... 256   Collyn Clout   392

DOSEN —DOTH   Page   Title   Line

DOSEN
Have at the hasarde or at the dosen browne, ...   57   Bowge   393
DOST
On that syde, on thys syde thou dost gasy, ...   130   Garnesche5   29
What sayst thou, man? Why dost thou not supplye, ...   162   Magnyfycence   797
What! Fansy, my frende! Howe dost thou fare?   166   Magnyfycence   920
DOSTE
Why doste thow deprave /This royall reame, ...   136   Dundas   43
I hate this blunderyng that thou doste make.   151   Magnyfycence   400
DOTAGE
Of a lyke dotage.   296   Why Come Ye   692
His blode with fonde dotage.   369   Albany   415
DOTE
That made Troylus to dote   88   Phy Sparrow   678
DOTED
And yet the frere doted!   265   Collyn Clout   757
DOTERDIS
As dasid doterdis that dreme in their dumpis.'   332   Garlande   734
DOTERELL
The doterell, that folyshe pek;   82   Phy Sparrow   409
DOTERYLL
Nay, iwys, fole. It is a doteryll.   173   Magnyfycence   1175
DOTH
And so with your servantys he fersly doth fyght.   43   Balettys2   28
The pullyshed perle youre whytenes doth declare;   44   Balettys3   18
Syth all in substaunce of slumbrynge doth procede.   61   Bowge   536
And this the cause doth shrynke.   66   Hauke   159
Whom Tytus Lyvyus /In wrytynge doth enroll;   67   Hauke   210
That lyke a fende doth stare;   73   Phy Sparrow   77
Wher Cerberus doth barke, ...   73   Phy Sparrow   85
The story doth appere, ...   79   Phy Sparrow   300
Such fervent heat /His stomake doth freat;   83   Phy Sparrow   482
    doth freat] 'so great' †Kele 1545.2, Wyght 1553, Kitson 1560.6
Whan he doth her trede.   84   Phy Sparrow   512
What he doth fynde   85   Phy Sparrow   538
But for the egle doth flye   85   Phy Sparrow   550
And as that flode doth pas   93   Phy Sparrow   877
Ryght so she doth excede   93   Phy Sparrow   883
But ever doth watch, ...   95   Phy Sparrow   929
Himself doth slo /With payne and wo.   95   Phy Sparrow   947
And there agayne /Envy doth complayne, /And hath disdayne; . .   95   Phy Sparrow   964
Trouth doth me bynd /And loyalte   96   Phy Sparrow   977
Myne hert doth so enbrace, ...   96   Phy Sparrow   1005
The Indy saphyre blew /Her vaynes doth ennew;   97   Phy Sparrow   1032
She doth excede and pas /In prudence dame Pallas;   102   Phy Sparrow   1229
Luna that so bryght doth shyne, ...   105   Phy Sparrow   1365
Upon us he doth reigne   111   Lawde   50
How unfortunately he doth now spede;   115   Scot Kynge   57
Ungraciously howe he doth spede.   119   Ag Scottes   154
Your tethe teintyd with tawny; your semely snowte doth passe, .   122   Garnesche1   39
And so haynnously doth stynke, ...   127   Garnesche3   144
In dygnyte roiall that doth excelle.   132   Garnesche5   96
I parceyve well howe eche of you doth reason.   142   Magnyfycence   83
Largesse is he that all prynces doth avaunce;   148   Magnyfycence   279
He doth abuse /Hym selfe to to;   164   Magnyfycence   871
And howe styll she doth syt!   168   Magnyfycence   1003
That thou so hye fro me doth sprynge, ...   170   Magnyfycence   1069
I am Poverte that all men doth hate.   195   Magnyfycence   1960
Yonder is a horson for me doth rechate;   201   Magnyfycence   2151
What begger art thou, that thus doth banne and wary?   203   Magnyfycence   2238
Questyonlesse he doth me assure   208   Magnyfycence   2395
And so doth it apere, ...   216   El Rummynge   59
    doth it] 'it dothe' Day 1560, Marshe 1568
Upon the holy daye, /Whan she doth her aray, ...   216   El Rummynge   67
And with her doth brynge   221   El Rummynge   278
Small chaffer doth ease /Sometyme, now and than.   222   El Rummynge   314
Whan the mare doth keke;   225   El Rummynge   450
Our Thomasen she doth trip, our Jenet she doth shayle;   233   Speke Parott   83
Our Thomasen she doth trip, our Jenet she doth shayle;   233   Speke Parott   83
Ulula, Esebon, for Jeromy doth wepe!   234   Speke Parott   113
Sion is in sadness, Rachell ruly doth loke;   234   Speke Parott   114
And Og, that fat hog of Basan, doth retayne   234   Speke Parott   122
    of] 'or' Kynge & Marche 1554, Day 1560, Marshe 1568
Bo-ho doth bark wel, Hough-ho he rulyth the ring;   234   Speke Parott   130
From Scarpary to Tartary renoun therein doth spryng, ...   234   Speke Parott   131
Poynt well this probleme that Parrot doth prate, ...   236   Speke Parott   220
At home full softe doth sytte.   255   Collyn Clout   328
That doth thynke or wene   274   Collyn Clout   1121
For whyles he doth rule, ...   282   Why Come Ye   134
The Frenche men he doth fray, ...   282   Why Come Ye   154
Whyles the red hat doth endure, ...   286   Why Come Ye   281
He doth but cloute and cobbill   292   Why Come Ye   527
He doth revyle and brall   294   Why Come Ye   596
Whiche shrewdly doth accorde!   294   Why Come Ye   621
How he doth hym disceyve.   295   Why Come Ye   662
He sayth the kynge doth wryte, ...   296   Why Come Ye   678
But what his grace doth thinke, ...   296   Why Come Ye   683
Against the churche doth ryse.   306   Why Come Ye   1071

DOTHE —DOTHE   Page   Title   Line

	Page	Title	Line
as more at large it doth apere in the proces folowynge.	312	Garlande	1
How all thynge passyth as doth the somer flower,	312	Garlande	9
Then men wyll say how he doth but flatter.	314	Garlande	84
But to do sumwhat iche man doth hym dres	315	Garlande	122
Frome that I have sayde in no poynt doth vary,	316	Garlande	163
Then he that doth worste is as good as the best.	317	Garlande	175
But blissed Bachus, that mastris oft doth frame,	322	Garlande	383
That welny nothynge there doth remayne	324	Garlande	430
welny] 'welnere' Marshe 1568			
With, 'How doth the north?' 'What tydingis in the sowth?'	326	Garlande	498
And of that pole artike whiche doth remayne	331	Garlande	695
And of the somer days so longe that doth last,	331	Garlande	702
In trust wherof comforte his hart doth grope,	335	Garlande	832
With lillis whyte your bewte doth renewe.	337	Garlande	884
With lillis] 'The lylly' MS Cotton Vitellius E.x			
Item Good Advysement, that brainles doth blame;	346	Garlande	1186
It may wele ryme, but shroudly it doth accorde,	346	Garlande	1210
Luna that so bryght doth shene,	350	Garlande	1358
By there phesik doth many a man ease,	352	Garlande	1427
Sex volumis engrosid together it doth containe.	354	Garlande	1502

DOTHE

	Page	Title	Line
Fulfilled with honour, as all the world dothe ken,	30	Dol Dethe	30
world] 'wold' Marshe 1568			
In one rose now dothe grow;	110	Lawde	2
Thereof the fame dothe blow,	110	Lawde	4
His titille dothe recorde;	110	Lawde	11
In whome dothe wele acorde	110	Lawde	12
Your lothesum lere to loke on, lyke a gresyd bote dothe schyne.	123	Garnesche2	5
And so puauntely dothe smelle	127	Garnesche3	143
Dothe savyr halfe so souer	127	Garnesche3	146
Where measure is mayster, plenty dothe none offence;	144	Magnyfycence	121
For defaute of measure all thynge dothe excede.	146	Magnyfycence	217
Why kepte you it thus longe? Howe dothe he? Wele?	149	Magnyfycence	314
Whylest I knowe that this letter dothe contayne.	149	Magnyfycence	324
It dothe so sure nowe and than.	150	Magnyfycence	368
Tell you where of my name dothe ryse.	151	Magnyfycence	409
Counterfet Countenaunce every man dothe occupy.	153	Magnyfycence	472
At his cloked counterfetynge dogges dothe barke.	153	Magnyfycence	482
Aske these two that there dothe dwell.	158	Magnyfycence	629
Cockys harte! Who is yonde that for the dothe call?	162	Magnyfycence	780
He dothe mysse use /Eche man to [akuse],	164	Magnyfycence	873
akuse] 'take a fe' †Rastell & Treveris C 1530, B			
For so with fantasyes my wyt dothe flete	170	Magnyfycence	1080
All that he dothe muste be alowde;	175	Magnyfycence	1247
But all that he dothe, and yf he reken well	175	Magnyfycence	1274
For there be other that foly dothe use	175	Magnyfycence	1280
Foly and fansy all where every man dothe face and brace.	177	Magnyfycence	1330
A, syr, your grace me dothe extole and rayse;	183	Magnyfycence	1525
Dyspare is my name, that adversyte dothe f[o]lowe;	205	Magnyfycence	2284
folowe] 'felowe' †Rastell & Treveris C 1530, B, Douce Fragment d.7			
All that he sayth of trouthe dothe procede;	209	Magnyfycence	2426
Howe sodenly worldly welth dothe dekay;	213	Magnyfycence	2555
As [Per]cius, that poete, dothe reporte of me,	231	Speke Parott	27
Percius) 'precius' †MS Harley 2252			
Moderata juvant but toto dothe exede;	232	Speke Parott	50
When Parrot be ded, he dothe not putrefy;	236	Speke Parott	213
he] 'she' †Lant 1545, Kynge & Marche 1554, Day 1560, Marshe 1568			
Thus Parott dothe pray yow,	237	Speke Parott	225
And shewe hym that all the world dothe conjecte,	240	Speke Parott	327
Langagys divers; yet undyr that dothe reste	241	Speke Parott	365
Frantiknes dothe rule and all thyng commaunde;	243	Speke Parott	420
And the date of the Devyll dothe shurewlye accord.	244	Speke Parott	445
Dothe grudge and complayne /Upon the temporall men.	248	Collyn Clout	64
Howe some of you dothe eate /In lenton season flesshe meate,	251	Collyn Clout	204
Theyr moyles golde dothe eate,	254	Collyn Clout	319
Whan the good ale soppe /Dothe daunce in theyr foretoppe;	260	Collyn Clout	531
Howe the male dothe wrye.	263	Collyn Clout	686
wrye] 'wryte' Kele 1545.1, Marshe 1568, 'wrye' MS Harley 2252			
Agaynst us dothe prate.	276	Collyn Clout	1181
Dothe aswage and refrayne,	279	Why Come Ye	37
Dothe rynne lamentably.	280	Why Come Ye	48
The tyme dothe fast ensew	280	Why Come Ye	62
For Wyll dothe rule all thynge,	281	Why Come Ye	105
All that he dothe is ryght.	281	Why Come Ye	116
Thus royally he dothe deale	287	Why Come Ye	336
So he dothe undermynde,	290	Why Come Ye	437
And suche sleyghtes dothe fynde,	290	Why Come Ye	438
His Latyne tonge dothe hobbyll,	292	Why Come Ye	526
In whose place, /Dothe occupy,	300	Why Come Ye	851
The prechour he dothe dyspyse	306	Why Come Ye	1072
All this he dothe deale	306	Why Come Ye	1101
'Thys now he dothe meale' MS Rawlinson C. 813			
Whiche madly he dothe apply /Unto an extravagancy,	306	Why Come Ye	1104
As playnly it dothe appere,	307	Why Come Ye	1117
As Juvinall dothe recorde,	310	Why Come Ye2	11
With lillys whyte your bewte dothe renewe.	337	Garlande	891

183

DOTYNGE — DOUTLESSE

Entry	Page	Title	Line
With Crafty Conveyaunce dothe smater and flater,	346	Garlande	1194
Thus he dothe disparage	369	Albany	414
What noblenesse dothe abounde,	369	Albany	424
His subjectes he dothe supporte,	370	Albany	471
Wherwith he dothe them bynde	371	Albany	484
Who so dothe magnifye	381	Replycacion	255
Dothe bothe write and call	383	Replycacion	320
Rede what Jerome there dothe say/	383	Replycacion	328
Of poetes chefe poete, saint Jerome dothe wright,	383	Replycacion	330
Lyke unto Alcheus, he dothe hym magnify.	383	Replycacion	335
That he our penne dothe lede,	385	Replycacion	385

DOTYNGE

Entry	Page	Title	Line
How dotynge age wolde jape with yonge foly;	322	Garlande	361

DOTRELLIS

Entry	Page	Title	Line
Dasyng after dotrellis, lyke drunkardis that dribbis;	330	Garlande	641

DOTTAGE

Entry	Page	Title	Line
In the charter of dottage	255	Collyn Clout	366
That age for dottage /Is reconed nowadayes.	279	Why Come Ye	43
reconed] 'recovered' Toy 1553, Kitson 1560.7, Marshe 1568			

DOTTAGES

Entry	Page	Title	Line
Full of suche dottages,	381	Replycacion	272

DOUBLE

Entry	Page	Title	Line
Bot men say thei wer lynked with a double chayn	31	Dol Dethe	75
Till the chaunce ran ageyne hym of Fortuns double dyse.	33	Dol Dethe	140
Ware yet, I rede you, of Fortunes double cast,	45	Balettys4	3
In double w[a]lles now he dooth dreme.	115	Scot Kynge	58
walles] 'welles' †Fakes 1513			
Where I saw Janus, with his double chere,	354	Garlande	1515
And their dealyng double,	364	Albany	200

DOUBLE-COPE

Entry	Page	Title	Line
Tushe! It is Syr Johnn Double-[Cope].	157	Magnyfycence	605
Cope] 'cloke' †Rastell & Treveris C 1530, B			

DOUBLE DELINGE

Entry	Page	Title	Line
Let double delinge in the have no place,	34	Dol Dethe	174

DOUBLE DELYNG

Entry	Page	Title	Line
In double delyng so he dyd dreme,	119	Ag Scottes	155
In] 'An' Day 1560, Marshe 1568			

DOUBLE DELYNGE

Entry	Page	Title	Line
Double delynge and I be all one;	159	Magnyfycence	696

DOUBLENES

Entry	Page	Title	Line
Doublenes hatinge fals maters to compas,	33	Dol Dethe	150
That lyned was with doubtfull doublenes.	51	Bowge	178

DOUBLENESSE

Entry	Page	Title	Line
All her delyte is set in doublenesse.	197	Magnyfycence	2029
She hath dyssayvyd me with her doublenesse.	201	Magnyfycence	2157
Your cankarde cowardnesse /And your shamfull doublenesse.	368	Albany	362

DOUBLE TUNGE

Entry	Page	Title	Line
A fals double tunge is more fiers and fell	140	Ven Tongues	79

DOUBLE TUNGES

Entry	Page	Title	Line
Of fals double tunges in the dispite.	140	Ven Tongues	82

DOUBTFULL

Entry	Page	Title	Line
That lyned was with doubtfull doublenes.	51	Bowge	178

DOUGHT

Entry	Page	Title	Line
I dought, lest by sorsery	295	Why Come Ye	663

DOUGHTY

Entry	Page	Title	Line
Daryus, the doughty cheftayn of Perse –	181	Magnyfycence	1488
Of all doughty I am doughtyest duke as I deme;	182	Magnyfycence	1499

DOUGHTYEST

Entry	Page	Title	Line
Of all doughty I am doughtyest duke as I deme;	182	Magnyfycence	1499

DOULFULL

Entry	Page	Title	Line
O feble fortune, O doulfull destyny!	198	Magnyfycence	2048

DOUNE

Entry	Page	Title	Line
That he dryvyth them doune with dyntys on ther day-wach.	43	Balettys2	30
Gentle Paule lie doune thy sweard,	358	Couplet	1

DOUT

Entry	Page	Title	Line
With, 'He wrate suche a bil withouten dout',	139	Ven Tongues	70
I put you out of dout,	267	Collyn Clout	848
Yet sum surgions put a dout	309	Why Come Ye	1198
Of scrupulus dout. Wherfore, your mynde discharge,	332	Garlande	726
That people are in great dout	380	Replycacion	224

DOUTE

Entry	Page	Title	Line
Of youre doregate ye have no doute.	41	Coystrowne4	26
Whylest I have hym, I nede nothynge doute.	187	Magnyfycence	1692
And yf ye stande in doute /Who brought this ryme aboute,	248	Collyn Clout	47

DOUTY

Entry	Page	Title	Line
Howe the Douty Duke of Albany	359	Albany	I

DOUTLES

Entry	Page	Title	Line
Whos lordshepe doutles was slayne lamentably	29	Dol Dethe	5
This noble man doutles had not be slayne.	31	Dol Dethe	74
be] 'bene' Marshe 1568			
Yet nowe doutles ye geve me cause	341	Garlande	1041
Wherfore doutles ye geve me cause	342	Garlande	1057

DOUTLESSE

Entry	Page	Title	Line
Doutlesse were moche better	253	Collyn Clout	272
were] 'where' Kele 1545.1			
Dicken, thou krew doutlesse!	280	Why Come Ye	68
Or els doutlesse ye shalbe blased,	382	Replycacion	294

DOUTTED — DOWTLES   Page   Title   Line

DOUTTED
The myghty lyoun doutted by se and sande. 32   Dol Dethe   109
    sande] 'lande' Marshe 1568
DOUTTY
Ye Duke so doutty, /So sterne, so stoutty, ... 361   Albany   77
Suche a doutty dagswayne. 363   Albany   172
DOVER
For Tytus at Dover abydythe in the rode; 239   Speke Parott   284
DOVYR
From Calys to Dovyr, to Caunterbury in Kente, ... 240   Speke Parott   340
DOW
Came runnynge with a dow, ... 63   Hauke   72
DOWBYLL
So many holow hartes, and so dowbyll faces; 245   Speke Parott   502
DOWBLE
Dysdaynous, dowble, ful of dyseyte, ... 133   Garnesche5   150
DOWBLENES
Moche dowblenes of the worlde therin he may fynde. 346   Garlande   1197
DOWCHE
Dowche Frenshe of Paris Parot can lerne, ... 231   Speke Parott   29
With Dowche, with Spaynyshe, my tonge can agree; 231   Speke Parott   32
DOWE
And some brought sowre dowe: 221   El Rummynge   288
DOWGHTFULL
So myche dowghtfull daunger, and so lytell drede; 245   Speke Parott   474
DOWN
Thus up and down my mynde was drawen and cast 47   Bowge   29
Plucke down lede and theke with tyle; 169   Magnyfycence   1026
To jumbyll, to stombyll, to tumbyll down lyke folys; 243   Speke Parott   425
Is layd down to slepe, ... 358   Garlande2   4
DOWNE
'Rumbyll downe, tumbyll downe, hey, go, now, now!' 37   Coystrowne1   30
'Rumbyll downe, tumbyll downe, hey, go, now, now!' 37   Coystrowne1   30
What and he slyde downe, who shall hym save? 46   Bowge   28
And to lye downe as soone as I m[e] dreste, ... 47   Bowge   33
    me] 'my' †Wynkyn de Worde 1499, 1510, Marshe 1568
Now wolde to God thou wolde leye money downe! 57   Bowge   395
He shoke downe all the clothys, ... 63   Hauke   51
The blode ran downe raw /Upon the auter stone. 63   Hauke   58
The hawke with that clap /Fell downe with evyll hap. 64   Hauke   90
Downe went my offerynge box, ... 64   Hauke   111
Fell downe on thys manner. 64   Hauke   115
That the dowves donge downe myght fall 66   Hauke   183
The tearys downe hayled; 72   Phy Sparrow   24
I fell downe to the grounde. 72   Phy Sparrow   36
I kest downe that there was, ... 77   Phy Sparrow   230
He bete downe to the grounde: 88   Phy Sparrow   671
Your pompe and pryde hath layde a downe. 115   Scot Kynge   69
Ye were to hye, ye ar cast downe. 120   Ag Scottes   177
Thow mayst fale downe and ebbe full lowe. 132   Garnesche5   123
As good to be occupyed as up and downe to trace 159   Magnyfycence   692
Plucke downe an house and set up a rafter, ... 169   Magnyfycence   1032
I daunce up and downe tyll I am dyssy. 169   Magnyfycence   1040
I dryve downe these dastardys with a dynt of my fyste. 181   Magnyfycence   1486
Here MAGNYFYCENCE is beten downe 193   Magnyfycence   SD
I plucke downe kynge, prynce, lorde, and knyght; 193   Magnyfycence   1883
That was wonte to lye on fetherbeddes of downe; 197   Magnyfycence   2006
Sodenly set up and sodenly pluckyd downe. 197   Magnyfycence   2025
Sodenly set up, and sodenly cast downe. 212   Magnyfycence   2530
Sodenly set up, and sodenly cast downe. 213   Magnyfycence   2537
She dryveth downe the dewe 216   El Rummynge   82
With, 'Hey,' and with, 'Howe, /Syt we downe arowe 221   El Rummynge   290
Some for very nede /Layde downe a skeyne of threde, ... 222   El Rummynge   310
Some a pyllowe of downe, ... 227   El Rummynge   531
She sat downe in the place, ... 228   El Rummynge   551
He tryhumfythe, he trumpythe, he turnythe all up and downe, . . 244   Speke Parott   432
A thre-foted stole /That he may downe sytte, ... 247   Collyn Clout   31
'Come downe, on the devyll way.' 263   Collyn Clout   670
    devyll] 'deuils' Marshe 1568, 'devyll' MS Harley 2252
Howebeit they let downe fall 271   Collyn Clout   978
With, 'laughe and lay downe, ... 302   Why Come Ye   931
Downe this hye sprynge; 302   Why Come Ye   950
That towres and townes and trees downe caste, ... 319   Garlande   262
'Syt downe, fayre ladys, and do your diligence! 334   Garlande   772
Was comyng downe /To make hym frowne 360   Albany   56
And put hym downe, ... 361   Albany   95
And the devill downe dynge, ... 364   Albany   210
DOWSYPERE
This daungerous dowsypere /Lyke a kynges pere! 295   Why Come Ye   639
DOWTE
'Questionles no dowte of that ye say; 332   Garlande   714
DOWTES
Nay, I tell the, he maketh no dowtes 174   Magnyfycence   1210
DOWTY
What, have ye kythyd yow a knyght, Syr Dugles the dowty, . . . 121   Garnesche1   8
DOWTLES
Dowtles such losels 65   Hauke   138
For nowe dowtles ye geve me cause 342   Garlande   1049

	Page	Title	Line
DOWTLESS			
This dowtless ye ravyd,	70	Hauke	307
DOWTLESSE			
For dowtlesse I parceyve my magnyfycence	146	Magnyfycence	227
I am the dyamounde dowtlesse of dygnyte.	181	Magnyfycence	1477
DOWVES			
That the dowves donge downe myght fall	66	Hauke	183
DRABBES			
A sorte of foule drabbes /All scurvy with scabbes.	218	El Rummynge	139
DRAFFE			
For all your 'Draffe' yet and your 'Dreggys',	40	Coystrowne4	6
With, 'Get me a staffe, /The swyne eate my draffe!	218	El Rummynge	171
DRAGON			
And with a dragon kept	104	Phy Sparrow	1303
And with a dragon kepte	349	Garlande	1296
DRAGONES			
The dragones with their tonges	79	Phy Sparrow	292
DRAKE			
The ducke and the drake,	82	Phy Sparrow	436
the] not in †Kele 1545.2, Wyght 1553			
Syr drake of the lake, sir ducke	364	Albany	223
DRAMMES			
With drammes of devocyon your dyet must be drest,	207	Magnyfycence	2358
DRANE			
By suche a dronken drane.	363	Albany	164
DRANES			
The rude ranke Scottes, lyke dronken dranes,	120	Ag Scottes	172
DRANKE			
She asked yf ever I dranke of saucys cuppe.	48	Bowge	73
'I dranke not this sennet /A draught to my pay.	224	El Rummynge	394
She dranke so of the dregges,	226	El Rummynge	480
dregges] 'dragges' †Lant 1545, Kynge & Marche 1554, Day 1560			
She dranke on the mash fat.	226	El Rummynge	491
Yet, or she went, she dranke,	228	El Rummynge	542
And dranke a good lucke.	228	El Rummynge	567
He dranke eysell and gall	258	Collyn Clout	454
DRAPRY			
Your drapry ye ded wante	125	Garnesche3	52
DRAUGHT			
To drynk at a draught a larg and a long.	38	Coystrowne1	49
'I dranke not this sennet /A draught to my pay.	224	El Rummynge	395
For a draught of her lycour.	225	El Rummynge	417
her] not in †Lant 1545, Kynge & Marche 1554, Day 1560, Marshe 1568			
DRAW			
Wel, wyse men may ete the fysshe when ye shal draw the pole.	148	Magnyfycence	300
DRAWE			
What the devyll! Use ye not to drawe no swordes?	163	Magnyfycence	811
Be wrastynge and wrythynge, and away drawe.	185	Magnyfycence	1608
With curteyns of sylke, ye were wonte to be drawe;	197	Magnyfycence	2014
curteyns of sylke] 'courtely sylkes' †Rastell & Treveris 1530B			
And to the taverne let us drawe nere.	204	Magnyfycence	2262
To fysshe afore the nette and to drawe polys.	243	Speke Parott	427
Nor durst nat drawe his swerde	366	Albany	308
DRAWEN			
Thus up and down my mynde was drawen and cast	47	Bowge	29
Of dampnacyon I had ben drawen in the luge.	206	Magnyfycence	2334
Was hedyd, drawen, and quarterd,	297	Why Come Ye	740
There shalbe drawen a trayne	368	Albany	369
DRAWTTYS			
With drawttys of deth /Stoppyng oure breth;	39	Coystrowne3	31
DRED			
The howndes began to yerne and to quest; and dred	351	Garlande	1409
The fals Scottes for dred,	371	Albany	512
DREDE			
Of whom both Flaunders and Scotland stode in drede,	30	Dol Dethe	44
That with thy sworde enharpid of mortall drede	32	Dol Dethe	125
But absens, alas, wyth tremelyng fere and drede,	44	Balettys3	34
What is thy name?' and I sayde it was Drede.	48	Bowge	77
Yet I avyse you to speke, for ony drede:	48	Bowge	90
They sayde they hated for to dele with Drede.	50	Bowge	146
'In fayth,' quod Suspecte, 'spake Drede no worde of me?'	51	Bowge	183
'By Cryste,' quod Favell, 'Drede is soleyne freke!	51	Bowge	187
This Doctour Dawcocke, Drede, I wene he hyghte.	54	Bowge	303
I dempte and drede theyr talkynge was not good.	58	Bowge	426
But that I drede mordre wolde come oute.	61	Bowge	524
I threwe away for drede.	77	Phy Sparrow	236
For, when men by welth, they have lytell drede	140	Magnyfycence	10
Where drede ledyth the daunce, there is no joy nor blysse.	142	Magnyfycence	76
Ye, lyberte with measure nede never drede.	144	Magnyfycence	130
Monkys may not for drede that men sholde them se.	154	Magnyfycence	493
For drede, that we dare not ofte, lest we be spyed.	177	Magnyfycence	1339
I drede no daunger; I dawnce all in delyte:	182	Magnyfycence	1492
I drede no dyntes of fatall desteny.	190	Magnyfycence	1798
Lorde, so my flesshe trymblyth nowe for drede!	193	Magnyfycence	1875
For drede ye dysplease the hygh deyte.	196	Magnyfycence	1996
Of adversyte it is to stande in drede.	209	Magnyfycence	2428
And ever let the drede of God be in your syght,	211	Magnyfycence	2498

DREDEFULL —DRINKE   Page   Title   Line

For drede ye darre not medyll with suche gere,	242	Speke Parott	394
So myche dowghtfull daunger, and so lytell drede;	245	Speke Parott	474
For drede to have a checke.	250	Collyn Clout	165
And yet he wyll nat drede	253	Collyn Clout	278
It is to drede, men sayes,	277	Collyn Clout	1228
I drede, by swete Jesu,	280	Why Come Ye	64
I drede we are bought and solde.	283	Why Come Ye	172
For drede of the mastyve cur,	286	Why Come Ye	297
For drede of the bochers dogge	286	Why Come Ye	298
I drede of some false trayne	288	Why Come Ye	363
For drede of the red hat	288	Why Come Ye	383
Withouten drede or feare!	298	Why Come Ye	759
Item Bowche of Courte, where Drede was begyled;	346	Garlande	1183
For drede and he lerne them there A B C to spell.'	353	Garlande	1476
But then I drede	355	Garlande	1553
then] 'that' Marshe 1568			
Twene hope and drede /My lyfe I lede,	356	Garlande	1594

DREDEFULL

As I be saved at the dredefull daye,	58	Bowge	443
The dredefull dinne drove all the rowte on a rowe;	319	Garlande	264

DREDFULL

At dredfull Domesday.	277	Collyn Clout	1233
To gyde and to governe my dredfull tremlyng fist.	335	Garlande	828

DREGGES

She dranke so of the dregges,	226	El Rummynge	480
dregges] 'dragges' †Lant 1545, Kynge & Marche 1554, Day 1560			
Drowned in dregges of divinite,	374	Replycacion	6

DREGGYS

For all your 'Draffe' yet and your 'Dreggys',	40	Coystrowne4	6

DREME

In double w[a]lles now he dooth dreme.	115	Scot Kynge	58
walles] 'welles' †Fakes 1513			
In double delyng so he dyd dreme,	119	Ag Scottes	155
In] 'An' Day 1560, Marshe 1568			
In faythe, he may dreme on a daggeswane for ony fether bed.	201	Magnyfycence	2169
Tyll that he dreme and dronny;	220	El Rummynge	230
Of Scipions dreme what was the treu probate;	322	Garlande	368
As dasid doterdis that dreme in their dumpis.'	332	Garlande	734
And therwith, sodenly, out of my dreme I woke.	354	Garlande	1511
dreme] 'slepe' Marshe 1568			

DREMES

But yet oftyme suche dremes be founde trewe.	61	Bowge	538

DREMYNG

Dremyng in dumpys to wrangyll and to wrest,	37	Coystrowne1	47
All drowsy, dremyng, dround in slepe,	41	Balettys1	6

DREMYST

What dremyst thou, drunchard, drousy pate?	42	Balettys1	22

DRES

The tyme whan Mars to werre hym dyd dres;	46	Bowge	7
And my style dres /To this prosses.	96	Phy Sparrow	968
But to do sumwhat iche man doth hym dres	315	Garlande	122
To witchecraft her to dres,	350	Garlande	1339

DRESSE

To wytchcraft her to dresse,	105	Phy Sparrow	1346
Must mesure, in the mares name, you furnysshe and dresse?	179	Magnyfycence	1391
Fresshely they dresse and make swete my bowur,	231	Speke Parott	12
Theyr chambre thus to dresse	270	Collyn Clout	975
And nowe I wyll me dresse	369	Albany	399

DRESSES

So goodly as she dresses,	101	Phy Sparrow	1170

DREST

Properly drest /All poynte devyse,	164	Magnyfycence	842
Were never halfe so rychely as I am drest.	181	Magnyfycence	1483
With drammes of devocyon your dyet must be drest,	207	Magnyfycence	2358
With slaiis, with tavellis, with hedellis well drest;	334	Garlande	791

DRESTE

And to lye downe as soone as I m[e] dreste,	47	Bowge	33
me] 'my' †Wynkyn de Worde 1499, 1510, Marshe 1568			
An almon now for Parott, delycatelye dreste;	232	Speke Parott	48
Or eyndye sapher with oryente perlys dreste:	241	Speke Parott	368
perlys] 'prelys' †MS Harley 2252			

DREVYLL

Trowest thou, drevyll, I saye, thou gawdy knave,	55	Bowge	337
The drevyll stondeth to herken, and he can.	59	Bowge	486

DREW

I made it straunge, and drew bak ones or twyse,	324	Garlande	444

DREWE

And I drewe nere to herke what they two sayde.	51	Bowge	182
And I drewe nere to harke what they two sayde.	54	Bowge	296

DRIBBIS

Dasyng after dotrellis, lyke drunkardis that dribbis;	330	Garlande	641

DRIFT

For by his devellysshe drift and graceles provision	333	Garlande	757

DRIGHNES

Myne homely rudnes and drighnes to expelle	29	Dol Dethe	13

DRINKE

Drinke now whyle it is new;	219	El Rummynge	211

DRIVE —DRONKEN	Page	Title	Line

DRIVE
Wene ye, daucockes, to drive	368	Albany	380

DRIVEN
Hardly bestad and driven is to hope	335	Garlande	830
and] not in MS Cotton Vitellius E.x			
For you shalbe driven out	371	Albany	501

DRY
With his ledder ey, /And chekes dry;	94	Phy Sparrow	909
He wolde dry up the stremys	303	Why Come Ye	957
Some dronken dastardis with their dry soules;	317	Garlande	190
Immoysturid with mislyng and ay droppyng dry,	331	Garlande	698

DRYADES
Dryades there daunsid upon that goodly soile,	331	Garlande	679

DRYE
His nose a-droppynge, his lyppes were full drye;	56	Bowge	362
a-droppynge] 'droppynge' Marshe 1568			
Ye, for he hathe a full drye soule.	176	Magnyfycence	1320
Her lyppes are so drye,	221	El Rummynge	272
Anone cometh another, /As drye as the other,	221	El Rummynge	277
Let us wasshe our gommes /From the drye crommes!'	222	El Rummynge	308
Lyke sawdust or drye chyppes.	252	Collyn Clout	243
He wyll drynke us so drye,	303	Why Come Ye	965
so] not in MS Rawlinson C. 813			

DRYFTE
A good dryfte, syr, a praty fete!	189	Magnyfycence	1731

DRYFTIS
Drove clowdes together lyke dryftis of snowe.	319	Garlande	263

DRYNK
To drynk at a draught a larg and a long.	38	Coystrownel	49

DRYNKE
This worlde is nothynge but ete, drynke and slepe,	57	Bowge	384
And toke it oute in drynke,	66	Hauke	158
Nor sowtters to drynke wyne,	126	Garnesche3	87
I yave hym drynke of the sugryd welle	132	Garnesche5	98
But may I drynke therof whylest that I stare?	176	Magnyfycence	1322
What! Then he may drynke out of a stone cruyse.	201	Magnyfycence	2166
But drynke tyll they stare	217	El Rummynge	108
Without drynke she must dye;	221	El Rummynge	273
And drynke tyll we blowe, /And pype tyrly-tyrlowe!'	221	El Rummynge	291
But, 'Drynke,' styll, 'Drynke, /And let the cat wynke!	222	El Rummynge	305
But, 'Drynke,' styll, 'Drynke, /And let the cat wynke!	222	El Rummynge	305
But swete ypocras ye drynke,	258	Collyn Clout	456
Howe [ye] were wonte to drynke	262	Collyn Clout	649
ye] 'thy' †Godfray 1531, 'they' Kele 1545.1, Marshe 1568, MS Harley 2252			
To drynke and for to eate	284	Why Come Ye	217
He wyll drynke us so drye,	303	Why Come Ye	965
so] not in MS Rawlinson C. 813			

DRYNKYNG
Into the brayne by drynkyng over depe,	313	Garlande	33

DRYNKYNGE
And, as she was drynkynge,	223	El Rummynge	370
This is a solempne drynkynge.	228	El Rummynge	548

DRYVE
It cumys the better for to dryve	132	Garnesche5	92
A custrell to dryve the devyll out of the derke,	154	Magnyfycence	485
I dryve downe these dastardys with a dynt of my fyste.	181	Magnyfycence	1486
What can it avayle /To dryve forth a snayle,	246	Collyn Clout	2
To dryve away grace.	301	Why Come Ye	873
To dryve them at divisyon,	306	Why Come Ye	1094
With syngular pleasurs to dryve away the tyme,	326	Garlande	524
Our kyng for to dryve out	368	Albany	392

DRYVEN
And Donatus be dryven out of scole;	235	Speke Parott	170

DRYVETH
She dryveth downe the dewe	216	El Rummynge	82

DRYVITH
Nedes must he rin that the devyll dryvith.	352	Garlande	1434

DRYVYLL
Ye war a kechyn page, /A dyshwasher, a dryvyll,	124	Garnesche3	26
Or of Divynyte, or Doctour Dryvyll,	277	Collyn Clout	1220
Divynyte] 'Divine' Marshe 1568, 'deuynite' MS Harley 2252; Dryvyll] 'oryll' MS Harley 2252			

DRYVYTH
That he dryvyth them doune with dyntys on ther day-wach.	43	Balettys2	30

DRYVYTHE
Tyll Eufrates, that flodde, dryvythe me into Ynde,	231	Speke Parott	4

DROMADARY
Moche lyke a dromadary;	126	Garnesche3	74

DRONKE
Dundas, /That dronke asse,	136	Dundas	55
They have dronke up my swyllyng tubbe!'	218	El Rummynge	173

DRONKEN
Nother crokyd Cacus, /Nor yet dronken Bacus;	67	Hauke	195
Nother] 'Nor yet' Kynge & Marche 1554, Day 1560, Marshe 1568			
Ye rowe ranke Scottes and dronken Danes,	115	Scot Kynge	64
The rude ranke Scottes, lyke dronken dranes,	120	Ag Scottes	172
For ij dronken sowllys.	129	Garnesche3	194

	Page	Title	Line
Dundas, dronken and drowsy, /Skabed, scurvy and lowsy,	136	Dundas	50
Ye wene that I am dronken bycause I loke pale.	147	Magnyfycence	259
Me semeth that ye have dronken more than ye have bled.	147	Magnyfycence	260
Than thydder came dronken Ales	223	El Rummynge	351
Than began the sporte /Amonge that dronken sorte.	229	El Rummynge	575
God wote, with dronken nolles.	252	Collyn Clout	232
Dronken as a mouse /At the ale house,	266	Collyn Clout	801
Of theyr dronken nolles,	277	Collyn Clout	1242
Some dronken dastardis with their dry soules;	317	Garlande	190
By suche a dronken drane.	363	Albany	164
Ye were in a dronken hete.	376	Replycacion	53

DRONNY
| Tyll that he dreme and dronny; | 220 | El Rummynge | 230 |

DROPPES
| With the aureat droppes, | 93 | Phy Sparrow | 873 |

DROPPY
| Let us syppe and soppy, /And not spyll a droppy, | 228 | El Rummynge | 559 |

DROPPYNG
| Immoysturid with mislyng and ay droppyng dry, | 331 | Garlande | 698 |

DROPPYNGE
| Never stoppynge /But ever droppynge; | 215 | El Rummynge | 30 |

DROPSY
| The dropsy was in her legges; | 226 | El Rummynge | 481 |

DROUGHT
| Howe after a drought there fallyth a showre of rayne | 141 | Magnyfycence | 12 |

DROUND
| All drowsy, dremyng, dround in slepe, | 41 | Balettys1 | 6 |

DROUPE
| To lowre, to droupe, to knele, to stowpe and to play cowche-quale; | 243 | Speke Parott | 426 |

DROUPY
| Droupy and drowsy, /Scurvy and lowsy; | 214 | El Rummynge | 15 |

DROUSY
| Couchynge your drousy heddes | 263 | Collyn Clout | 658 |

DROUSY PATE
| What dremyst thou, drunchard, drousy pate? | 42 | Balettys1 | 22 |

DROVE
They drove me to lernynge lyke a dull asse.	178	Magnyfycence	1386
Drove clowdes together lyke dryftis of snowe.	319	Garlande	263
The dredefull dinne drove all the rowte on a rowe;	319	Garlande	264

DROWNE
| To drowne or to sle themselfe with a knyfe - | 194 | Magnyfycence | 1914 |

DROWNED
And silogisari was drowned at Sturbrydge Fayre;	235	Speke Parott	165
Ye lyve, they say, in delyte, /Drowned in deliciis,	257	Collyn Clout	442
Drowned in dregges of divinite,	374	Replycacion	6

DROWNYD
| So depely drownyd I was in this dumpe, | 312 | Garlande | 15 |

DROWPY
| Men sey ye wyll wax lowsy, /Drunkyn, drowpy, drowsy. | 127 | Garnesche3 | 136 |
| Your hede that was wonte to be happed moost drowpy and drowsy, | 197 | Magnyfycence | 2018 |

DROWSY
All drowsy, dremyng, dround in slepe,	41	Balettys1	6
Men sey ye wyll wax lowsy, /Drunkyn, drowpy, drowsy.	127	Garnesche3	136
Dundas, dronken and drowsy, /Skabed, scurvy and lowsy,	136	Dundas	50
Your hede that was wonte to be happed moost drowpy and drowsy,	197	Magnyfycence	2018
Droupy and drowsy, /Scurvy and lowsy;	214	El Rummynge	15
Of Pliades he prechid with ther drowsy chere,	331	Garlande	697
Trowth with a drowsy hede;	358	Garlande2	2

DRUNCHARD
| What dremyst thou, drunchard, drousy pate? | 42 | Balettys1 | 22 |

DRUNKARDIS
| Dasyng after dotrellis, lyke drunkardis that dribbis; | 330 | Garlande | 641 |

DRUNKYN
| Men sey ye wyll wax lowsy, /Drunkyn, drowpy, drowsy. | 127 | Garnesche3 | 136 |

DUCK
| 'Quake, quake,' sayd the duck /In that lampatrams lap.' | 227 | El Rummynge | 505 |

DUCKE
The ducke and the drake,	82	Phy Sparrow	436
the] not in †Kele 1545.2, Wyght 1553			
What! Margery Mylke Ducke, mermoset!	153	Magnyfycence	457
Syr Duke, nay, syr ducke,	364	Albany	222
Syr drake of the lake, sir ducke	364	Albany	223

DUD
| In dud frese ye war schrynyd, | 125 | Garnesche3 | 46 |

DUG
| Dug, dug, /Jug, jug, /Good yere and good luk, | 340 | Garlande | 1000 |
| Dug, dug, /Jug, jug, /Good yere and good luk, | 340 | Garlande | 1000 |

DUGGES
With dugges, dugges, dugges. /I shrewe thy Scottishe lugges,	366	Albany	291
With dugges, dugges, dugges. /I shrewe thy Scottishe lugges,	366	Albany	291
With dugges, dugges, dugges. /I shrewe thy Scottishe lugges,	366	Albany	291

DUGLES
| What, have ye kythyd yow a knyght, Syr Dugles the dowty, | 121 | Garnesche1 | 8 |

DUKE
| The one for a duke, the other for dun, | 37 | Coystrownel | 10 |
| Duke Theseus, and Partelet; | 87 | Phy Sparrow | 617 |

DUKIS —DURST   Page   Title   Line

Entry	Page	Title	Line
And of the Duke Hannyball,	88	Phy Sparrow	665
Hannyball] 'of Hannyball' Wyght 1553, Kitson 1560.6, Marshe 1568			
Of all doughty I am doughtyest duke as I deme;	182	Magnyfycence	1499
Neyther erle ne duke	272	Collyn Clout	1045
Duke, erle, baron, nor lorde,	287	Why Come Ye	342
Of the Duke of Albany,	288	Why Come Ye	357
Nor duke of hye degre,	294	Why Come Ye	619
The Duke of Yorkis creauncer whan Skelton was,	347	Garlande	1226
Howe the Douty Duke of Albany	359	Albany	1
This Duke so fell /Of Albany, /So cowardly	359	Albany	6
Duke of Albany, /Than shamefuly	360	Albany	50
But now must I /Your Duke ascry /Of Albany	360	Albany	73
Ye Duke so doutty, /So sterne, so stoutty,	361	Albany	77
By your Duke of Albany.	363	Albany	162
Sir Duke of Albany, /Right inconvenyently	363	Albany	188
Nat lyke Duke Hamylcar	363	Albany	192
Nor lyke Duke Hasdruball	363	Albany	195
Syr Duke, nay, syr ducke,	364	Albany	222
Harke yet, Sir Duke, a worde	367	Albany	318
Lyke to Duke Josue /And the valiaunt Machube,	370	Albany	442
With the Duke of Albany,	371	Albany	513

DUKIS

Entry	Page	Title	Line
Paregall to dukis, withe kingis he myght compare,	33	Dol Dethe	134
All kingis, all princis, all dukis, well thei ought	34	Dol Dethe	180

DULY

Entry	Page	Title	Line
By measure eche thynge duly is tryde.	147	Magnyfycence	244
So duly entunyd with every mesure,	320	Garlande	276
After all duly ordred obeisaunce,	335	Garlande	836
To se how duly ich thyng in ordre was,	343	Garlande	1094

DULL

Entry	Page	Title	Line
Of frowardes, and so dull,	91	Phy Sparrow	779
My reson rude and dull	102	Phy Sparrow	1221
They drove me to lernynge lyke a dull asse.	178	Magnyfycence	1386
Helas! I lamente the dull abusyd brayne,	242	Speke Parott	383
So manye bolde barons, there hertes as dull as lede;	245	Speke Parott	466
Theyr soules lame and dull;	250	Collyn Clout	129
Our armye waxeth dull,	282	Why Come Ye	150
Theyr wyttes, he saith, are dull;	286	Why Come Ye	309
Though his purs wax dull,	302	Why Come Ye	937
Is that our servaunt is sum what to dull;	314	Garlande	79
that] 'for that' MS Cotton Vitellius E.x			

DULLE

Entry	Page	Title	Line
For to illumyne, she sayde, I was to dulle,	46	Bowge	20

DUM

Entry	Page	Title	Line
That they be deefe and dum,	269	Collyn Clout	903
Bete a dum mouthe than a brainles scull;	314	Garlande	82
Bete] 'Better' Marshe 1568, MS Cotton Vitellius E.x			

DUMPE

Entry	Page	Title	Line
So depely drownyd I was in this dumpe,	312	Garlande	15

DUMPIS

Entry	Page	Title	Line
As dasid doterdis that dreme in their dumpis.'	332	Garlande	734

DUMPYS

Entry	Page	Title	Line
Dremyng in dumpys to wrangyll and to wrest,	37	Coystrownel	47

DUN

Entry	Page	Title	Line
The one for a duke, the other for dun,	37	Coystrownel	10
Dun is in the myre, dame, reche me my spur.	352	Garlande	1433

DUNBAR

Entry	Page	Title	Line
And ye proude Scottes of Dunbar,	114	Scot Kynge	29
And ye, proud Scot, Dunde, Dunbar	118	Ag Scottes	121
Dunde, Dunbar, /Walke, Scot, /Walke, sot,	136	Dundas	60
Dunbar, Dunde, /Ye shall trowe me,	359	Albany	24

DUNDAS

Entry	Page	Title	Line
This Dundas, /This Scottishe as	135	Dundas	7
Agayn Dundas, /That Scottishe asse.	135	Dundas	23
Dundas of Galaway	135	Dundas	29
Dundas, sir knave,	136	Dundas	42
Dundas, dronken and drowsy, /Skabed, scurvy and lowsy,	136	Dundas	50
Dundas, /That dronke asse,	136	Dundas	54

DUNDE

Entry	Page	Title	Line
And ye, proud Scot, Dunde, Dunbar	118	Ag Scottes	121
Dunde, Dunbar, /Walke, Scot, /Walke, sot,	136	Dundas	60
Dunbar, Dunde, /Ye shall trowe me,	359	Albany	24

DUNKAN

Entry	Page	Title	Line
Sir Dunkan, ye dared.	365	Albany	271
Sir Dunkan, in the devill waye,	367	Albany	330

DUNSTANE

Entry	Page	Title	Line
Saynt Dunstane, what was he?	307	Why Come Ye	1147

DUR

Entry	Page	Title	Line
For thou beggest at every mannes dur.	135	Dundas	26
Dare nat loke out at dur	286	Why Come Ye	296
at] 'a' Kitson 1560.7, Marshe 1568			

DURE

Entry	Page	Title	Line
Whyles the world shall dure:	89	Phy Sparrow	723

DURSE

Entry	Page	Title	Line
I durse aventure to journey thorugh Fraunce;	57	Bowge	408

DURST

Entry	Page	Title	Line
And the Pharasay /Then durst nothynge say,	66	Hauke	153

DURSTE —DWTE

	Page	Title	Line
The pepil durst not creke	111	Lawde	33
Set nought by golde ne grotes, /Theyr names yf I durst tell. . .	250	Collyn Clout	161
The millar durst not leve his wyfe at home.	352	Garlande	1417
He fledde and durst nat fyght;	360	Albany	70
That durst nat byde the sight	364	Albany	236
Thou durst no felde derayne, ...	365	Albany	243
That durst abyde no reknyng;	365	Albany	249
Nor durst nat crak a worde, ...	366	Albany	307
Nor durst nat drawe his swerde	366	Albany	308
For ye durst nat tarry	367	Albany	343
Ye durst byde on the grounde.	367	Albany	347

DURSTE

	Page	Title	Line
But I wolde telle you a thynge, and I durste.	51	Bowge	203
To you oonly, me thynke, I durste shryve me;	52	Bowge	215
As well as me. I wolde, and I durste -	163	Magnyfycence	827
Nor none so hardy of them with me that durste crake, ...	182	Magnyfycence	1513

DURTY

	Page	Title	Line
For thou shalt well knowe I am nother durty nor dusty.	161	Magnyfycence	759

DUST

	Page	Title	Line
Fled away from hym, let hym ly in the dust, ...	30	Dol Dethe	39
For I have dyscust /We ar but dust, ...	39	Coystrowne3	5
And nowe lyke a lurden he lyeth in the dust.	193	Magnyfycence	1887
Parrot sayth playnly, shall tourne all to dust.	236	Speke Parott	224
A chaplayne of trust, /Layth all in the dust.	253	Collyn Clout	284
With helpe of the ram, ley all in the dust.	315	Garlande	105

DUSTE

	Page	Title	Line
All grace and pyte I lay in the duste.	205	Magnyfycence	2290
Today a lorde, tomorowe ly in the duste:	213	Magnyfycence	2543
Today a man, tomorowe he lyeth in the duste:	213	Magnyfycence	2550

DUSTY

	Page	Title	Line
For thou shalt well knowe I am nother durty nor dusty.	161	Magnyfycence	759
Dusty! Nay, syr, ye be all of the lusty;	161	Magnyfycence	760

DUTES

	Page	Title	Line
Demaundinge soche dutes as nedis most acord	31	Dol Dethe	66

DWELL

	Page	Title	Line
In endles blis with the to byde and dwell	34	Dol Dethe	201
For wherso we dwell, ...	39	Coystrowne3	22
But than I thoughte I wolde not dwell behynde;	47	Bowge	43
To dwell with us and serve my ladyes grace.	50	Bowge	156
'Forsothe,' quod I, 'in this courte I dwell nowe.'	56	Bowge	377
Where the muses dwell:	87	Phy Sparrow	611
Welthe with Lyberte, with me bothe dwell ye shall, ...	145	Magnyfycence	174
You are nothynge mete with us for to dwell, ...	149	Magnyfycence	304
Why, shall we dwell togyder all thre?	154	Magnyfycence	509
And there they wolde ha[v]e me to dwell.	157	Magnyfycence	614
have] 'hane' †Rastell & Treveris C 1530, B			
Why, dwelleth Mesure where ye two dwell?	157	Magnyfycence	622
In faythe, he were better to dwell in hell.	157	Magnyfycence	623
Aske these two that there dothe dwell.	158	Magnyfycence	629
But are ye not avysed to dwell where ye spake?	162	Magnyfycence	774
Scantly one with measure that wyll dwell.	189	Magnyfycence	1746
To dwell amonge ladyes, Parrot, is mete.	233	Speke Parott	105
But where theyr soules dwell, ...	257	Collyn Clout	427
Endlesse to dwell /With the devyll of hell!	303	Why Come Ye	971
And here to inhabite and ay for to dwell!	332	Garlande	719
Ye decte you to dwell;	366	Albany	280
Olde patriarkes and prophetes in heven with him to dwell. . .	383	Replycacion	342

DWELLE

	Page	Title	Line
Alas, a connynge man ne dwelle maye	58	Bowge	445

DWELLES

	Page	Title	Line
And sojourns with them and dwelles.	384	Replycacion	378

DWELLETH

	Page	Title	Line
Why, dwelleth Mesure where ye two dwell?	157	Magnyfycence	622
There dwelleth a mayster men calleth Mesure -	158	Magnyfycence	631

DWELLINGE HOUSE

	Page	Title	Line
That can bylde his dwellinge house	298	Why Come Ye	757

DWELLITH

	Page	Title	Line
Here dwellith pleasure, with lust and delyte;	332	Garlande	709

DWELLYNGE

	Page	Title	Line
Where hathe your dwellynge ben, er ye cam here?	53	Bowge	247
Sholde be your dwellynge, in my consyderacyon.	148	Magnyfycence	274

DWELLYS

	Page	Title	Line
That within Englande dwellys.	303	Why Come Ye	962

DWELLYTH

	Page	Title	Line
To understande who dwellyth in yone pile, ...	333	Garlande	739
yone] 'yonder' MS Cotton Vitellius E.x			

DWELT

	Page	Title	Line
That right dwelt us among, ...	111	Lawde	20
For when ye dwelt there, ...	125	Garnesche3	43
Of a comely gyll /That dwelt on a hyll;	214	El Rummynge	5
And, as men say, /She dwelt in Sothray, ...	217	El Rummynge	96
In derkenes thus dwelt we, tyll at the last	330	Garlande	650

DWELTE

	Page	Title	Line
Ye never dwelte in suche an other place, ...	51	Bowge	201

DWTE

	Page	Title	Line
Of very dwte it may not well accorde, ...	318	Garlande	212

E —ECHONE

Entry	Page	Title	Line
E			
Hop Lobyn of Lowdeon wald have e byt of bred;	232	Speke Parott	72
EARE			
And shakes them by the eare,	286	Why Come Ye	305
Within the cattes eare	298	Why Come Ye	758
EARES			
Might plucke away thyne eares!	79	Phy Sparrow	310
EASE			
Alas, I was evyll at ease!	75	Phy Sparrow	144
That never have rest nor ease;	104	Phy Sparrow	1325
Small chaffer doth ease /Sometyme, now and than.	222	El Rummynge	314
And take theyr worldly ease	269	Collyn Clout	910
Lodge hym in Lytell Ease,	275	Collyn Clout	1169
That never have rest nor ease;	349	Garlande	1318
By there phesik doth many a man ease,	352	Garlande	1427
Wolde God, for your owne ease,	377	Replycacion	114
EASED			
We have well eased you of the bottes.	115	Scot Kynge	63
We have well eased them of the bottes.	120	Ag Scottes	171
And that your mynde can not well be eased –	185	Magnyfycence	1610
Syr, nowe me thynke your harte is well eased.	189	Magnyfycence	1737
EASELY			
All this ye may easely brynge aboute.	158	Magnyfycence	655
They molefy so easely my harte that was so harde.	207	Magnyfycence	2346
EASY			
A red angry man, but easy to intrete.	37	Coystrownel	39
Her har[n]es easy ferre and nere is soughte.	57	Bowge	403
harnes] 'harmes' †Wynkyn de Worde 1499, 1510, 'armes' Marshe 1568			
But plesaunt, easy and playne;	91	Phy Sparrow	802
Is easy to expounde,	298	Why Come Ye	781
EASYD			
Yet, and God wold, I wold my payne were easyd!	45	Balettys5	12
EATE			
The estryge, that wyll eate	83	Phy Sparrow	478
With, 'Get me a staffe, /The swyne eate my draffe!	218	El Rummynge	171
For the devyll to eate;	225	El Rummynge	434
Howe some of you dothe eate /In lenton season flesshe meate,	251	Collyn Clout	204
Theyr moyles golde dothe eate,	254	Collyn Clout	319
With moulde brede to eate –	263	Collyn Clout	653
To drynke and for to eate	284	Why Come Ye	217
Have made you eate the fly,	381	Replycacion	252
EATEN			
Bycause ye have eaten a flye,	380	Replycacion	244
EATETH			
He eateth c[a]pons stewed,	284	Why Come Ye	221
capons] 'copons' †Kele 1545.3			
EBBE			
Thow mayst fale downe and ebbe full lowe.	132	Garnesche5	123
Now ebbe, now flowe, nowe increase, now dyscrease;	212	Magnyfycence	2521
EBREW			
They had wrytyng, sum Greke, sum Ebrew,	328	Garlande	582
EBRON			
Nowe in valle Ebron Parrot is fayne to fede:	236	Speke Parott	188
EBRUE			
Yn Latyn, in Ebrue, and in Caldee,	231	Speke Parott	25
and] 'Araby and' Lant 1545, Kynge and Marche 1554, Day 1560, Marshe 1568			
Jereboseth is Ebrue, who lyst the cause dyscus.	232	Speke Parott	67
cause] 'law' Day 1560, Marshe 1568			
ECATES			
Also by Ecates bower	104	Phy Sparrow	1322
ECHE			
Eche man may sorow in his inward thought	34	Dol Dethe	177
Sharpely commaundynge eche man holde hys pece.	47	Bowge	47
But of eche thynge there as I toke hede,	47	Bowge	64
Mysdempte eche man, with face deedly and pale;	50	Bowge	137
He loked hawte; he sette eche man at noughte;	54	Bowge	284
hawte] 'hawtie' Marshe 1568			
I wolde eche man were as playne as I.	59	Bowge	463
And how they rode eche one	88	Phy Sparrow	655
I parceyve well howe eche of you doth reason.	142	Magnyfycence	83
By measure eche thynge duly is tryde,	147	Magnyfycence	244
Eche man to hynder I gape and I gaspe;	160	Magnyfycence	729
He dothe mysse use /Eche man to [akuse],	164	Magnyfycence	874
akuse] 'take a fe' †Rastell & Treveris C 1530, B			
Eche thynge is fayre when it is yonge; all hayle, owle!	167	Magnyfycence	970
By waywarde wylfulnes let eche thynge be convayed;	185	Magnyfycence	1594
And make eche man to sle other;	194	Magnyfycence	1913
Elynour made the pryce /For god ale eche whyt.	224	El Rummynge	411
It is wronge with eche degre;	248	Collyn Clout	60
Thus eche of other blother /The tone against the tother.	248	Collyn Clout	66
For eche man herkynde what she wolde to me say;	344	Garlande	1119
wolde to me] 'to me wold' MS Cotton Vitellius E.x			
ECHONE			
And rule them echone /In Lucyfers trone.	304	Why Come Ye	992
For ye be false echone,	362	Albany	132
To whom we are bounde echone	381	Replycacion	260

ECLIPSID —EYNE   Page   Title   Line

ECLIPSID
Sodenly is eclipsid in the wynter night, ... 330   Garlande   646
ECTOR
In loyalte and foy /Lyke to Ector of Troy, ... 369   Albany   437
EDDERS
And from Megeras edders, ... 73   Phy Sparrow   78
EDYNGEBORROW
Of Edyngeborrow and Saynt Jonys towne. 117   Ag Scottes   63
EDWARDE
Whan Edwarde of Karnarvan 285   Why Come Ye   270
EERE
An ynche above your eere, ... 263   Collyn Clout   674
EERES
Your eeres they be stopped! 263   Collyn Clout   678
EESTRYCHE FEDDER
An eestryche fedder of a capons tayle 56   Bowge   366
    An] 'And' Marshe 1568
EFFECT
And can not in effect 91   Phy Sparrow   771
And banysshed in effect 380   Replycacion   242
And a mysteriall, /And a mysticall, /Effect energiall, ... 384   Replycacion   368
EFFECTE
Brefly to touche of my purpose the effecte: 142   Magnyfycence   67
How the maters he mellis in com to small effecte; 240   Speke Parott   328
It may take some effecte! 257   Collyn Clout   436
Whereof I beseche you to tender the effecte. 313   Garlande   56
EG
In Popering grew peres, whan Parrot was an eg. 232   Speke Parott   70
EGEAS
Nor yet Egeas, /Nor yet Syr Pherumbras; 67   Hauke   204
EGERIA
Egeria, the goddesse, ... 100   Phy Sparrow   1152
EGGES
Full untydy tegges, /Lyke rotten egges. 218   El Rummynge   152
For we have egges and butter, ... 228   El Rummynge   536
EGYPCYAN
Upon her brayne-pan, /Lyke an Egypcyan /Lapped about. 216   El Rummynge   78
    Lapped] 'Capped' Kynge & Marche 1554, Day 1560, Marshe 1568
EGLE
But for the egle doth flye 85   Phy Sparrow   550
EIGHT
Noble Henry the eight, ... 110   Lawde   8
EITHER
Either by language or with my pen. 137   Ven Tongues   23
EY
With his ledder ey, /And chekes dry; 94   Phy Sparrow   908
EYE
With his wanton eye. 76   Phy Sparrow   182
Youre eye is out; adew, good nyght! 119   Ag Scottes   142
S[e] at our eye the worlde day by day. 146   Magnyfycence   216
    Se] 'so' †Rastell & Treveris C 1530, B
And another bade put out myne eye; 150   Magnyfycence   353
Another wolde myne eye were blerde; 150   Magnyfycence   354
Tusshe! Thy lyppes hange in thyne eye; 169   Magnyfycence   1049
    eye] 'eyen' †Rastell & Treveris C 1530, B
Of some of theyr chyldren I stryke out the eye; 194   Magnyfycence   1933
And so they blere your eye 263   Collyn Clout   684
With a flap afore his eye, ... 308   Why Come Ye   1169
    afore] 'before' Kitson 1560.7, Marshe 1568, MS Rawl. C. 813
Hath promised to hele our cardinals eye. 309   Why Come Ye   1197
It made sum mens eye dasild and dasid; 351   Garlande   1389
EYEN
Oure eyen synkyng, /Oure bodys stynkyng, ... 39   Coystrowne3   33
His eyen rollynge, his hondes faste they quoke; 51   Bowge   193
His eyen blereed, his face shone lyke a glas; 56   Bowge   353
Her eyen gray and stepe 97   Phy Sparrow   1014
Her browys bent, /Her eyen glent; 167   Magnyfycence   980
Her eyen relucent as carbuncle so clere, ... 183   Magnyfycence   1556
I make hevy hertys, with eyen full holowe. 205   Magnyfycence   2286
Her eyen gowndy /Are full unsowndy, ... 215   El Rummynge   34
And his eyen so dased, ... 283   Why Come Ye   181
EYES
Unneth I kest myne eyes 72   Phy Sparrow   37
To putte his eyes out 361   Albany   94
EYGHT
Royall Henry the eyght, ... 292   Why Come Ye   540
Christ kepe King Henry the Eyght 298   Why Come Ye   772
Noble Henry the Eyght 361   Albany   109
EYLES
Alas, and wellaway, /What eyles them thus to say? 261   Collyn Clout   578
EYLYTHE
What eylythe the, rebawde, on me to rave? 131   Garnesche5   79
EYNDYE
Or eyndye sapher with oryente perlys dreste: 241   Speke Parott   368
    perlys] 'prelys' †MS Harley 2252
EYNE
My eyne were so dased; 99   Phy Sparrow   1106

EYRE —ELYNOUR   Page   Title   Line

To blowe bararag tyll bothe his eyne stare.'   319   Garlande   245
    bararag] 'bararag brag' MS Cotton Vitellius E.x
I wypid myne eyne for to make them clere.   354   Garlande   1513
EYRE
    /And redolent of eyre, ...   84   Phy Sparrow   525
    I can fede forth a fole and lede hym by the eyre;   160   Magnyfycence   712
    So in theyr eyre I synge them a songe   174   Magnyfycence   1223
    These wordes in myne eyre, they be so lustely spoken, . . .   184   Magnyfycence   1565
    But yf it lyke you that I myght rowne in your eyre, ...   186   Magnyfycence   1645
EYRNEST
    Counterfet eyrnest by way of playes. 152   Magnyfycence   427
    Yet it proveth eyrnest, ye may se, every day.   195   Magnyfycence   1949
EYSELL
    He dranke eysell and gall   258   Collyn Clout   454
EYTHER
    Eyther to the devyll or the trinite. 114   Scot Kynge   41
    And eyther I am dysseyved, or ye be the same.   141   Magnyfycence   25
    Nay; eyther let me tell, or elles tell ye. 158   Magnyfycence   633
    Nay, but fansy must be eyther fyrst or last. 176   Magnyfycence   1288
    And eyther ye be to badde, ... 259   Collyn Clout   502
    Eyther analogice, /Or elles cathagorice, ... 266   Collyn Clout   787
    Eyther corne or malte, ... 267   Collyn Clout   842
    Eyther they wyll say he is to wyse, ...   318   Garlande   204
        wyll] 'shall' MS Cotton Vitellius E.x
EKE
    Sergyantes of the Coyfe eke, ... 287   Why Come Ye   316
E-LA
    To solfe above E-la - /Fa, lorell, fa, fa - 84   Phy Sparrow   487
        Fa] 'Ga' †Kele 1545.2, Wyght 1553, Kitson 1560.6
ELACYON
    He is in suche elacyon /Of his exaltacyon, ... 291   Why Come Ye   482
    of vaynglorious pompe and surcudant elacyon, ... 375   Replycacion   I
ELATE
    He is so ambicious, /So elate and so vicious, ...   308   Why Come Ye   1177
ELBOWE
    His elbowe bare, he ware his gere so nye, ...   56   Bowge   361
    Your fansy maketh myne elbowe to ake.   156   Magnyfycence   559
ELDYR STEKE
    Ye ar an eldyr steke;   126   Garnesche3   79
ELE
    'A slipper holde the taile is of an ele' 326   Garlande   501
ELECT
    In elect uteraunce to make memoryall!   29   Dol Dethe   11
    With Englysh wordes elect;   91   Phy Sparrow   773
        elect] 'clere' †Kele 1545.2, 'elect' Wyght 1553,
        Kitson 1560.6, Marshe 1568
ELECTE
    Or in electe utteraunce halfe so eloquent, ... 183   Magnyfycence   1533
    The favour of ladys with wordis electe, ...   314   Garlande   76
ELECTUARY
    of the lycorous electuary of lusty lernyng, ...   373   Replycacion   I
ELEGY
    Whereof the elegy /Foloweth by and by.   92   Phy Sparrow   824
ELEMENTAR
    Of fyre elementar in his supreme spere, ...   331   Garlande   694
ELENE
    Zeuxes, that enpicturid fare Elene the quene, ...   337   Garlande   892
ELENKES
    Nor knoweth not his elenkes, ... 267   Collyn Clout   818
        elenkes] 'eloquens' †Godfray 1531, Kele 1545.1, Marshe 1568
    Ye argued argumentes, /As it were upon the elenkes, ...   377   Replycacion   126
ELEPHANTIS
    Of elephantis tethe were the palace gatis, ... 325   Garlande   468
ELF
    And thus this elf /Consumeth himself, ...   95   Phy Sparrow   945
ELFE
    And yet, this gracelesse elfe, ... 307   Why Come Ye   1115
        gracelesse] 'ungratyous' MS Rawlinson C. 813
ELICONYS
    Of Eliconys waters crystallyne, ...   132   Garnesche5   99
ELINOUR
    Also the Tunnynge of Elinour Rummyng, ...   347   Garlande   1233
ELISABETH
    To my Lady Elisabeth Howarde 336   Garlande   R
ELYCONIS
    Of Elyconis well, refresshid with your grace, ...   314   Garlande   74
        Elyconis] 'Elycoms' †Fakes 1523, 'Heliconis' Marshe 1568
ELYCONYS
    With the freshe waters of Elyconys welle.   29   Dol Dethe   14
    That never yet asayde /Of Elyconys well, ...   87   Phy Sparrow   610
ELYNOR
    Elynor began to chyde, ... 226   El Rummynge   464
ELYNOUR
    The Tunnyng of Elynour Rummyng per Skelton Laureat.   214   El Rummynge   I
    I understande, her name /Is Elynour Rummynge, ...   216   El Rummynge   93
    With all theyr myght runnynge /To Elynour Rummynge, ...   217   El Rummynge   129
    Suche a lewde sorte /To Elynour resorte   218   El Rummynge   154
    Elynour swered, 'Nay, ...   218   El Rummynge   164

194

ELYNOURE — ELS   Page   Title   Line

	Page	Title	Line
Than Elynour taketh	219	El Rummynge	195
And Dame Elynour entrete	221	El Rummynge	268
And bad Elynour go bet,	222	El Rummynge	332
Than Elynour sayde, 'Ye calettes,	223	El Rummynge	347
Elynour toke her up	224	El Rummynge	376
Elynour, I the pray,	224	El Rummynge	396
Elynour made the pryce /For god ale eche whyt.	224	El Rummynge	410
And brought a peny cheke /To Dame Elynour	225	El Rummynge	416
brought] 'brought up' Day 1560, Marshe 1568			
Sayd Elynour Rummyng,	227	El Rummynge	502
Sayd Elynour, 'For shame!'	227	El Rummynge	510
Of Elynour for her ware,	228	El Rummynge	544
'Dame Elynour,' sayde she,	228	El Rummynge	562
'Dame Elynour,' sayde they,	229	El Rummynge	576
And called for our dame, /Elynour by name.	229	El Rummynge	593
With Elynour in the spence,	229	El Rummynge	598
Than Elynour dyd them hyde /Within her beddes syde.	229	El Rummynge	605
Of this mad mummynge /Of Elynour Rummynge.	230	El Rummynge	621

ELYNOURE

Come who so wyll /To Elynoure on the hyll,	217	El Rummynge	114

ELLES

Is there ony thynge elles your grace wyll commaunde me?	149	Magnyfycence	318
Or elles I had lost myne eres twayne.	150	Magnyfycence	349
Nay; eyther let me tell, or elles tell ye.	158	Magnyfycence	633
What sholde ye do elles? Are not you a lorde?	185	Magnyfycence	1606
Or elles ye pynche curtesy, trulye as I trowe,	242	Speke Parott	395
Other for delyte /Or elles *to desyte?	247	Collyn Clout	8
Other] 'Eyther' Kele 1545.1; 'to desyte' MS Harley 2252, 'despyte' Kele 1545.1, Marshe 1568			
Or elles they wolde se /Otherwyse,	247	Collyn Clout	39
And all that they have elles.	257	Collyn Clout	411
For elles, as I sayd before,	258	Collyn Clout	481
Or elles they are madde	259	Collyn Clout	503
Or elles frere Frederyk,	265	Collyn Clout	737
Or elles frere Dominyk,	265	Collyn Clout	738
Or elles yf we may	265	Collyn Clout	743
Or elles of the order	265	Collyn Clout	745
Or elles the poore Scot,	265	Collyn Clout	749
Eyther analogice, /Or elles cathagorice,	266	Collyn Clout	788
Or elles his substytute	272	Collyn Clout	1043
Or elles for despyght,	272	Collyn Clout	1056
Or elles that they do lye,	273	Collyn Clout	1063
Or elles in the myre	273	Collyn Clout	1069
Or elles go rost a stone!	281	Why Come Ye	112
Or elles he can nought bot whan he is at scole;	318	Garlande	205
For elles it were to great a derogacyon	318	Garlande	218
Or elles, ye know well, I can do no lesse	318	Garlande	226
I am elles rebukyd of that I intende,	324	Garlande	440

ELLIS

How far it was, or ellis within what howris,	325	Garlande	457
far] not in †Fakes 1523			

ELLYS

He can do nothyng ellys.	84	Phy Sparrow	494
What ellys? For otherwyse it were agaynst kynde;	144	Magnyfycence	132
Ye coulde not ellys, I wote, with me endure.	147	Magnyfycence	247
Or ellys some jangelynge Jacke of the Vale.	147	Magnyfycence	258
In faythe, ellys is there none in all Englonde.	170	Magnyfycence	1099
Thynke I not so, quod he. Ellys have I shame,	175	Magnyfycence	1254
Ye, in faythe; or ellys thou arte to great a glotton.	204	Magnyfycence	2266
Or ellys with this knyfe cut out a tonge	206	Magnyfycence	2314
I wolde he were somwhere ellys;	303	Why Come Ye	963

ELLS

Or ells with gret shame your game wylbe sene.	43	Balettys2	42
Elencticum, or ells enthimematicum,	236	Speke Parott	192

ELLUMYNYNGE

Of aureat poems they want ellumynynge;	32	Dol Dethe	128

ELME

Favoure we have toughther than ony elme,	49	Bowge	129
toughther] 'tougher' Wynkyn de Worde 1510, Marshe 1568			

ELOQUENCE

Of laureat Phebus holy the eloquence	33	Dol Dethe	160
Were pullysshed with the fyle /Of Ciceros eloquence,	101	Phy Sparrow	1206
pullysshed] 'publysshed' †Kele 1545.2			
Prynce of eloquence, Tullius Cicero,	321	Garlande	330
'O noble Chaucer, whos pullisshyd eloquence	324	Garlande	421
Barreyne of eloquence,	372	Albany	517

ELOQUENS

Settyng theyr myndys so moche of eloquens,	235	Speke Parott	181
And howe your poemys arre barayne of polyshed eloquens,	240	Speke Parott	316

ELOQUENT

Or in electe utteraunce halfe so eloquent,	183	Magnyfycence	1533

ELOQUENTLY

In poesy to endyte /And eloquently to wryte,	75	Phy Sparrow	153

ELS

Bot ther was fals packinge or els I am begylde,	31	Dol Dethe	71
Wed me or els I dye for thought!	36	Man Margery	26
Els, I prayed hym with all my besy cure,	52	Bowge	221

ELSE —ENBYBID

	Page	Title	Line
Or els I pas a peny to a pounde!	57	Bowge	394
I] not in Wynkyn de Worde 1510			
To hawke, or els to hunt /From the auter to the funt,	62	Hauke	9
He semeth a sysmatyke /Or els an heretike,	62	Hauke	18
Or els is thys Goddis law,	65	Hauke	130
Or holy sinodals, /Or els provincyals,	65	Hauke	133
Of God nothynge els crave I /But Phyllypes soule to kepe	73	Phy Sparrow	67
*Or els phylosophy /Maketh a great lye.	83	Phy Sparrow	476
*Or] 'Of' Scattergood			
An ouche or els a ryng,	88	Phy Sparrow	686
Or els fayre Polexene,	97	Phy Sparrow	1019
Or els Caliope, /Or els Penolope;	97	Phy Sparrow	1020
Or els Caliope, /Or els Penolope;	97	Phy Sparrow	1021
Els with hys stynkyng jawys	128	Garnesche3	154
In faythe, els had I gone to longe to scole,	148	Magnyfycence	298
Leve thy pratynge or els I shall lay the on the pate.	201	Magnyfycence	2173
Fyxt or els mobyll.	292	Why Come Ye	525
From golde to pewter /Or els to a newter,	301	Why Come Ye	905
For els by and by	303	Why Come Ye	964
Or els his surgions they lye;	308	Why Come Ye	1171
For how shulde Cato els be callyd wyse,	315	Garlande	123
Myne argument els koude not longe endure.	316	Garlande	147
Or els ye demeane you inordinatly;	317	Garlande	173
Els saye ye myght	342	Garlande	1063
Els ye shall pray /Them that ye may	356	Garlande	1583
Or els &c	357	Garlande	1602
Or els wyll I /Evydently /Shewe as it is:	361	Albany	84
Or els doutlesse ye shalbe blased,	382	Replycacion	294

ELSE

Uppon me to clater or else to say yll.	38	Coystrowne1	66
Wherfor your remorders ar madde or else starke blynde,	241	Speke Parott	369
remordes] 'remordes' †MS Harley 2252			

ELSEWHERE

in churches or elsewhere.	375	Replycacion	1

ELSWHERE

At Poules Crosse, or elswhere,	276	Collyn Clout	1182

ELVYSHE

So myche conjuracions for elvyshe myday sprettes;	246	Speke Parott	514

EMBASSADES

Embassades of all nacyons.	289	Why Come Ye	415

EMBESY

Them selfe to embesy with all there holl corage,	314	Garlande	66

EMBLOMED

Emblomed lyke the chery,	97	Phy Sparrow	1038

EMBOSYD

Where hartis belluyng, embosyd with distres,	312	Garlande	24

EMBRACYD

And not embracyd with pusyllanymyte.	146	Magnyfycence	206
Bathyd with blysse, embracyd with comforte.	181	Magnyfycence	1472

EMBRAUDRED

Embraudred, enlasid together, and fettred,	138	Ven Tongues	39

EMBRAWDRED

Why were ye Calliope, embrawdred with letters of golde?	112	Calliope	1

EMERAUD

Geyne surfetous suspecte the emeraud comendable;	44	Balettys3	20

EMERAWDE

My fethyrs fresshe as ys the emerawde grene,	231	Speke Parott	16

EMPERES

As emperes the dyademe hath worne	46	Bowge	4

EMPERYALL

To Jupyter I call, /Of heven emperyall,	86	Phy Sparrow	597

EMPERYALLE

O pereles Prince of hevyn emperyalle	34	Dol Dethe	190
O] not in Marshe 1568			

EMPEROUR

Our king, our emperour,	111	Lawde	47

EMPLOYED

Employed whiche myght have be	378	Replycacion	149

EMPORTURED

Emportured with corage,	100	Phy Sparrow	1154

EMPRESSE

Encrownyd as empresse of all this wordly fate,	325	Garlande	486
wordly] 'worldly' Marshe 1568			

ENBATELD

Strongly enbateld, moche costious of charge.	328	Garlande	570

ENBAWMED

Her mouthe enbawmed, dylectable and mery,	183	Magnyfycence	1557

ENBESID

With vertu enbesid all tymes and howris;	334	Garlande	805

ENBEWTID

Hath fresshely enbewtid with many a goodly sorte	336	Garlande	868

ENBYBE

To guyde my pen and my pen to enbybe!	117	Ag Scottes	79

ENBYBED

That my pen hath enbybed	93	Phy Sparrow	872

ENBYBID

Were newly enbybid; and rownd about the same	331	Garlande	682

	Page	Title	Line
ENBLASED			
With crownes of golde enblased	283	Why Come Ye	179
ENBOLNED			
Howe yong scolers nowe a dayes enbol[n]ed	373	Replycacion	1
enbolned] 'enbolmed' †Pynson 1528			
ENBOSED			
With wordes enbosed, /Ungraciously engrosed,	367	Albany	324
With your enbosed jawes	370	Albany	477
ENBOSID			
Of birrall enbosid wer the pyllers rownde;	325	Garlande	467
ENBRACE			
As to enbrace you in myne armys twayne.	44	Balettys3	42
Myne hert doth so enbrace,	96	Phy Sparrow	1005
Me to enbrace and love moost specyally.	190	Magnyfycence	1800
ENBRAID			
The saumpler to sow on, the lacis to enbraid;	334	Garlande	789
ENBRASED			
enbrased and enterlased with a moche fantasticall frenesy	374	Replycacion	1
ENBRASID			
Togeder in armes, as brethern, enbrasid;	323	Garlande	393
ENBRASYNGE			
Enbrasynge therewithall	99	Phy Sparrow	1127
ENBRAWDERID			
Enbrawderid the mantill /Is of yowr maydenhede.	338	Garlande	924
ENBRAWDERYD			
Enbrawderyd the mantyll /Is of yowre maydenhede.	338	Garlande	916
ENBRETHED			
Enbrethed with the blast of influence dyvyne,	33	Dol Dethe	157
ENBRETHYNG			
Enbrethyng of Zepherus with his pleasant wynde;	331	Garlande	677
ENBROWDER			
Sume to enbrowder put them in prese,	334	Garlande	794
ENBROWDRED			
Enbrowdred the mantill /Is of your maydenhede.	338	Garlande	908
maydenhede] 'maydenhode' †Fakes 1523			
ENBUDDED			
Enbudded with beautye and colour fresshe of hewe,	183	Magnyfycence	1554
ENBUDDID			
The enbuddid blossoms of roses rede of hew	337	Garlande	883
The enbuddid blossoms of] 'Enbuddid blossome with' MS Cotton Vitellius E.x			
ENBULYONED			
Where the postis wer enbulyoned with saphiris indy blew,	325	Garlande	478
ENCANKRYD			
Callyd Detraxion, encankryd with envye,	241	Speke Parott	362
ENCLERYD			
Encleryd myrroure and perspectyve most bryght,	44	Balettys3	22
ENCLYNE			
Magnyfycence to us begynneth to enclyne,	158	Magnyfycence	644
ENCLOSED			
Syr, this letter ye sent to me at Pountes was enclosed.	209	Magnyfycence	2439
ENCOVERDE			
Encoverde over with golde of tissew fyne;	345	Garlande	1164
ENCRAUMPYSSHED			
Encraumpysshed so sore was my conceyte,	312	Garlande	16
ENCREACE			
But hyght you, Largesse, encreace of noble fame?	148	Magnyfycence	271
ENCREASE			
Theyr covent to encrease.	267	Collyn Clout	847
If he to the ample encrease of his name	318	Garlande	222
ENCREASETH			
Encreaseth my dedly wo, /For my sparowe is go.	74	Phy Sparrow	113
ENCRESE			
Grow and encrese, remembre thyn astate!	33	Dol Dethe	163
Bycause that ye encrese and amplyfy	323	Garlande	404
ye] not in †Fakes 1523			
Sum pirlyng of goldde theyr worke to encrese	334	Garlande	796
For to encrese /Yowre goodly name.	339	Garlande	959
ENCREST			
His fame to be encrest	309	Why Come Ye	1214
ENCRISPED			
With heris encrisped yalowe as the golde,	320	Garlande	289
encrisped] 'enscrisped' †Fakes 1523			
ENCROWNYD			
Encrownyd as empresse of all this wordly fate,	325	Garlande	486
wordly] 'worldly' Marshe 1568			
ENDARKID			
Of suche an endarkid chapiter sum season.	315	Garlande	108
ENDARKYD			
By meanys of a grosely endarkyd clowde	330	Garlande	645
ENDE			
And by my trouthe, but yf an ende they make,	59	Bowge	473
For whiche ende goth forwarde ye take lytell charge.	148	Magnyfycence	296
An ende of an olde song:	281	Why Come Ye	88
To any good ende were brought.	290	Why Come Ye	449
ENDELES			
It were an endeles welth,	340	Garlande	995

	Page	Title	Line
ENDES			
At bothe endes ye stynke;	126	Garnesche3	81
ENDETH			
Thus endeth the prologue,	49	Bowge	R
Thus endeth the Bowge of Courte.	61	Bowge	E
Thus endeth the boke of Philip Sparow	103	Phy Sparow	E
Thus endeth the gest /Of this worthy fest.	230	El Rummynge	622
Thus endeth the Replicacyon of Skelton Laureate, etc.	386	Replycacion	E
ENDEVORMENT			
'Brother Skelton, your endevorment	323	Garlande	400
ENDEVOUR			
I wyll endevour me to order every thynge	146	Magnyfycence	203
And wyll not endevour hymselfe to purchase	314	Garlande	75
ENDEVOURE			
So I, iwus, /Endevoure me	338	Garlande	936
ENDEVOURMENT			
For your pleasure do there endevourment,	335	Garlande	810
ENDIYD			
Whiche wert endiyd with rede blode of the same	32	Dol Dethe	117
ENDITH			
Here endith a ryght delectable tratyse	358	Garlande2	E
ENDYGHT			
Far, far passynge /That I can endyght,	341	Garlande	1017
ENDYTE			
Some of moralyte nobly dyde endyte;	46	Bowge	14
moralyte] 'mortalyte' †Wynkyn de Worde 1499, Marshe 1568			
In poesy to endyte /And eloquently to wryte,	75	Phy Sparow	152
Me enfluence to endyte,	93	Phy Sparow	861
For to endyte, /And for to wryte,	95	Phy Sparow	952
ENDYTYNG			
And your dyrty endytyng,	127	Garnesche3	113
ENDLES			
In endles blis with the to byde and dwell	34	Dol Dethe	201
The prynce of endles wo;	73	Phy Sparow	73
ENDLESSE			
Thyselfe myschevynge to thyne endlesse dysease!	206	Magnyfycence	2342
Jhesus preserve you frome endlesse wo and shame.	214	Magnyfycence	2572
Endlesse to dwell /With the devyll of hell!	303	Why Come Ye	971
ENDUCE			
And many mo whome I cowde enduce;	314	Garlande	94
But suche evydence I thynke for to enduce,	344	Garlande	1135
for to] 'for me to' MS Cotton Vitellius E.x			
ENDUCED			
For ye have enduced a secte	380	Replycacion	236
ENDUDE			
She had not wel endude;	63	Hauke	78
Maistres Geretrude, /With womanhode endude,	341	Garlande	1044
Maistres Geretrude, /With womanhode endude,	342	Garlande	1052
Maistres Geretrude /With womanhode endude,	342	Garlande	1060
ENDUED			
Your gorge nat endued /Without a capon stued,	252	Collyn Clout	215
ENDURE			
To suffer me so carefull to endure,	45	Balettys5	6
But Fortune enforsyth me so carefully to endure,	46	Balettys5	13
Maye never dye, bute evermore endure.	46	Bowge	16
But my dysporte they could not well endure:	50	Bowge	145
Ay to contynewe and styll to endure.	141	Magnyfycence	15
Ye coulde not ellys, I wote, with me endure.	147	Magnyfycence	247
Endure? No, God wote, it were great payne.	147	Magnyfycence	248
For where is no mesure, howe may worshyp endure?	179	Magnyfycence	1408
Well, for thy sake the better I may endure	187	Magnyfycence	1680
How fortune wyll endure.	271	Collyn Clout	1003
Howe may we thus endure?	276	Collyn Clout	1202
Whyles the red hat doth endure,	286	Why Come Ye	281
Longe to endure in heale.	298	Why Come Ye	771
Myne argument els koude not longe endure.	316	Garlande	147
Jupiter hymselfe this lyfe myght endure;	332	Garlande	715
So shall your name endure perpetually,	336	Garlande	861
In fortunis favour ever to endure,	351	Garlande	1402
ENDURYD			
That nothynge than welth may worse be enduryd.	140	Magnyfycence	7
ENDURYNGE			
Under good hope endurynge ever styll,	208	Magnyfycence	2381
My lyfe endurynge I shall both wryte and say,	335	Garlande	839
ENEAS			
Lyke to Eneas benygne in worde and dede,	33	Dol Dethe	137
ENEIDOS			
Virgill the Mantuan, with his Eneidos;	321	Garlande	339
ENEMYES			
And manly manyfolde, /Their enemyes to assayle	364	Albany	204
ENERGIALL			
And a mysteriall, /And a mysticall, /Effect energiall,	384	Replycacion	368
ENFAYNTYD			
O manles manhod, enfayntyd all with fere,	242	Speke Parott	391
ENFATUATE			
The enfatuate fantasies, the wytles wylfulnes	242	Speke Parott	384
ENFERRE			
Somwhat I coulde enferre	142	Magnyfycence	59

ENFLAMED — ENGLYSSHE Page Title Line

ENFLAMED
To beare a fagot, or to be enflamed. . . . . 374 Replycacion 16
ENFLAMYD
Ageynst all infeccyons with cancour enflamyd, ... 331 Garlande 672
   cancour] 'rancour' Marshe 1568
ENFLORID
Enflorid with flowris and slymy snaylis, ... 345 Garlande 1160
ENFLUENCE
Me enfluence to endyte, ... 93 Phy Sparrow 861
ENFORCE
That ye would coarte and enforce me . . . . 138 Ven Tongues 45
ENFORCID
Enforcid ar we you to recompence, ... 323 Garlande 416
ENFORME
And though Albumasar can the enforme and ken . . . . 352 Garlande 1428
ENFORMED
countyng them selfe clerkes exellently enformed . . . . 374 Replycacion I
and yet they were but febly enformed . . . . 374 Replycacion I
ENFORSED
Enforsed to slepe and for to take some reste, ... 47 Bowge 32
But enforsed am I /Openly to askry . . . . 94 Phy Sparrow 902
ENFORSYTH
But Fortune enforsyth me so carefully to endure, ... 46 Balettys5 13
ENGENDRED
That was engendred then; . . . . 105 Phy Sparrow 1329
That was engendred then; . . . . 349 Garlande 1322
ENGLADID
Of the soneshyne engladid with the lyght, ... 327 Garlande 536
ENGLAND
England, now gaddir flowris, ... 110 Lawde 6
That maketh England faine. . . . . 111 Lawde 42
Our kynge of England for to syght, ... 117 Ag Scottes 53
   syght] 'fight' Day 1560, Marshe 1568
The hertes of England to comfort with gladnes. . . . . 117 Ag Scottes 88
He calleth us England men . . . . 285 Why Come Ye 275
ENGLANDE
In Englande and Fraunce which gretly was redouted, ... 30 Dol Dethe 43
Comberaunce and trouble in Englande fyrst I began. . . . . . 160 Magnyfycence 715
But Englande may well say . . . . 302 Why Come Ye 928
That within Englande dwellys. . . . . 303 Why Come Ye 962
Englande the flowr /Of relucent honowre, ... 305 Why Come Ye 1037
   Englande] 'To Englande' MS Rawlinson C. 813
Of Englande, his workis here they begynne: . . . . 345 Garlande 1171
Rejoyse, Englande, /And understande . . . . 359 Albany 1
To envade Englande, /As I understande. . . . . 361 Albany 105
Agaynst Englande to fyght. . . . . 364 Albany 231
ENGLASID
Englasid glittering with many a clere story; . . . . 325 Garlande 479
ENGLISHE
Though your Englishe be rude, ... 372 Albany 516
ENGLISHMEN
He rymes and railes /That Englishmen have tailes. . . . . . . 135 Dundas 10
ENGLISSHMEN
They have slain our Englisshmen . . . . 288 Why Come Ye 372
ENGLISTERD
Englisterd, that joyous it was to beholde. . . . . 330 Garlande 663
ENGLYSCHE
Your Englysche lew[d]ly ye sorte, ... 124 Garnesche3 19
   lewdly] 'lewly' †MS Harley 367
ENGLYSH
Devysyd this gostly medytacyon in Englysh: . . . . 39 Coystrowne3 I
With Englysh wordes elect; . . . . 91 Phy Sparrow 773
   elect] 'clere' †Kele 1545.2, 'elect' Wyght 1553,
   Kitson 1560.6, Marshe 1568
Gowers Englysh is olde /And of no value told; . . . . 91 Phy Sparrow 784
   told] 'is tolde' Wyght 1553, Kitson 1560.6, Marshe 1568
His Englysh well alowed, ... 91 Phy Sparrow 792
There is no Englysh voyd, ... 91 Phy Sparrow 795
Of all our royall Englysh nacyon. . . . . 117 Ag Scottes 76
Our Englysh bowes, our Englysh bylles, ... 119 Ag Scottes 132
Our Englysh bowes, our Englysh bylles, ... 119 Ag Scottes 132
At Englysh bowes have fetched their banes. . . . . 120 Ag Scottes 173
The tokens ar not good /To be true Englysh blood; . . . . . . 121 Ag Scottes2 23
Defendeth with his pen /All Englysh men . . . . 135 Dundas 22
ENGLYSHE
So myche translacion into Englyshe confused; . . . . 244 Speke Parott 451
Out of fresshe Latine into owre Englyshe playne, ... 354 Garlande 1499
With Englyshe somwhat base, ... 367 Albany 356
ENGLYSHEMEN
Of all trewe Englyshemen, ... 372 Albany 521
ENGLYSHE MEN
Mell nat wyth Englyshe men. . . . . 362 Albany 146
ENGLYSSH
His Englyssh whereat they barke . . . . 91 Phy Sparrow 798
Myne Englyssh halfe-abused; . . . . 92 Phy Sparrow 815
In olde commemoracion /Most royall Englyssh nacion. . . . . . 305 Why Come Ye 1040
ENGLYSSHE
Of our Englysshe bowes ye have fette your banes. . . . . . . 115 Scot Kynge 65

199

ENGLOND —ENPAVYD	Page	Title	Line
In Englysshe to God Parott can supple:	231	Speke Parott	33
supple] 'shewe propyrlye' †MS Harley 2252			
I saw Gower, that first garnisshed our Englysshe rude,	323	Garlande	387
How that our Englysshe myght fresshely be ennewed;	323	Garlande	389
ennewed] 'a meude' †Fakes 1523			
Dane John Lydgate. Theis Englysshe poetis thre,	323	Garlande	391
Oure Englysshe rude so fresshely hath set out,	324	Garlande	422
Item New Gramer in Englysshe compylyd;	346	Garlande	1182
Owt of Frensshe into Englysshe prose.	347	Garlande	1220
In Englysshe letter.	355	Garlande	1538
The Englysshe	383	Replycacion	R
ENGLOND			
All gyf Englond and Fraunce wer thorow sought.	34	Dol Dethe	179
And browght Englond in wo;	111	Lawde	25
That ever Englond had;	111	Lawde	53
The honor of Englond I lernyd to spelle,	132	Garnesche5	95
ENGLONDE			
Than in Englonde to playe ony suche prankes;	114	Scot Kynge	51
That all men it founde /Through out Englonde.	165	Magnyfycence	883
In faythe, ellys is there none in all Englonde.	170	Magnyfycence	1099
Now Henry the viij, Kyng of Englonde,	347	Garlande	1227
ENGOLERID			
Engolerid goodly with hallis and bowris,	325	Garlande	460
Engolerid] 'Engalared' Marshe 1568			
ENGRAPID			
Enrailid with rosers, and vinis engrapid;	330	Garlande	656
ENGROSED			
Of clusters engrosed with his ruddy flotes	321	Garlande	342
Of clusters engrosed with his ruddy [flotis]	322	Garlande	370
flotis] 'dropis' †Fakes 1523, 'dropes' Marshe 1568			
Of clusters engrosed with his ruddy [flotis]	322	Garlande	384
flotis] 'dropis' †Fakes 1523, 'dropes' Marshe 1568			
With wordes enbosed, /Ungraciously engrosed,	367	Albany	325
ENGROSID			
Of clusters engrosid with his ruddy [flotis]	322	Garlande	349
flotis] 'droppes' †Fakes 1523, 'dropes' Marshe 1568			
Of clusters engrosid with his ruddy [flotis]	322	Garlande	363
flotis] 'dropis' †Fakes 1523, 'dropes' Marshe 1568			
Sex volumis engrosid together it doth containe.	354	Garlande	1502
ENGROSYD			
The grounde engrosyd and bet with bourne golde,	313	Garlande	41
Of closters engrosyd with his ruddy flotis	321	Garlande	335
flotis] 'droppes' †Fakes, 'flotis' Marshe 1568			
Of clusters engrosyd with his ruddy [flotis]	322	Garlande	356
flotis] 'dropis' †Fakes 1523, 'dropes' Marshe 1568			
Of clusters engrosyd with his ruddy [flotis]	322	Garlande	377
flotis] 'dropis' †Fakes 1523, 'dropes' Marshe 1568			
ENGUSSHING			
With pypes of golde engusshing out stremes;	330	Garlande	659
ENHACHED			
Enhached on her fayre skyn,	98	Phy Sparrow	1078
ENHACHYDE			
Enhachyde with perle and stones preciously,	313	Garlande	40
ENHARDID			
Enhardid adyment the sement of your wall!	320	Garlande	306
ENHARPID			
That with thy sworde enharpid of mortall drede	32	Dol Dethe	125
ENYUS			
Enyus that wrate of mercyall war at lengthe;	321	Garlande	347
ENJOY			
Longe to enjoy plesure, delyght, and lust:	337	Garlande	882
ENKANKERD			
With my rude pen enkankerd all with rust,	33	Dol Dethe	142
ENLASID			
Embraudred, enlasid together, and fettred,	138	Ven Tongues	39
ENLOSENGED			
Enlosenged with many goodly platis	325	Garlande	469
ENMYS			
Withe his enmys that were stark mad and wode;	32	Dol Dethe	100
ENMYXYD			
But fallyble flatery enmyxyd with bytternesse.	212	Magnyfycence	2516
But fallyble flatery enmyxyd with bytternesse.	212	Magnyfycence	2523
ENNEUDE			
And hard to be enneude	91	Phy Sparrow	775
ENNEW			
The Indy saphyre blew /Her vaynes doth ennew;	97	Phy Sparrow	1032
ENNEWDE			
With trouthe it is ennewde.	369	Albany	420
ENNEWED			
Ennewed all with grace,	96	Phy Sparrow	1003
all with] 'with al' Wyght 1553, Kitson 1560.6, Marshe 1568			
How that our Englysshe myght fresshely be ennewed;	323	Garlande	389
ennewed] 'a meude' †Fakes 1523			
ENOUGHE			
Make noyse enoughe; for claterars love no peas.	319	Garlande	241
ENPAVYD			
With turkis and grossolitis enpavyd was the grounde;	325	Garlande	466

	Page	Title	Line

ENPICTURID
Zeuxes, that enpicturid fare Elene the quene, ... 337 Garlande 892
And byse, enpicturid with gressoppes and waspis, ... 345 Garlande 1158
ENPLEMENT
Ye have deservyd to have an enplement . . . . 323 Garlande 402
ENPLOYD
For as it is enployd, ... 91 Phy Sparrow 794
ENPLOYED
and of every true Christen man laudably to be enployed, ... 374 Replycacion 1
ENPOYSONED
enpoysoned with sclaunder and false detractions &c. . . . . . . 136 Ven Tongues 1
ENPRYNTYNG
Enpryntyng her wordes in my remembraunce, ... 327 Garlande 557
ENPROWED
So as it is enprowed, ... 91 Phy Sparrow 793
ENQUERE
Who lyst to enquere, ... 307 Why Come Ye 1118
ENRAILID
Enrailid with rosers, and vinis engrapid; . . . . 330 Garlande 656
ENRYCHE
Out of all measure themselfe to enryche; . . . . 189 Magnyfycence 1751
ENRYPED
By radyante hete enryped hath our corne; . . . . 46 Bowge 2
ENROLD
Though I have enrold . . . . 90 Phy Sparrow 749
And worthy to be enrold. 91 Phy Sparrow 787
ENROLDE
Of noble actis auncyently enrolde . . . . 29 Dol Dethe 15
She is worthy to be enrolde . . . . 103 Phy Sparrow 1258
Whose name enrolde /With silke and golde . . . . 112 Calliope 9
As it is enrolde, /Wrytten and tolde . . . . 116 Ag Scottes 39
Yowr name to se /It be enrolde, /Writtin with golde. . . . . . 338 Garlande 938
Whiche in your recordes, I know well, be enrolde, ... 344 Garlande 1140
ENROLL
Whom Tytus Lyvyus /In wrytynge doth enroll; . . . . 67 Hauke 210
ENROLLYD
Bownte, and so gloryously ye have enrollyd . . . . 324 Garlande 437
ENSAYMED
She was not clene ensaymed, ... 63 Hauke 79
ENSANDID
With alys ensandid about in compas, ... 330 Garlande 654
ENSEMBYLL
For Frantiknes and Wylfulnes and Braynles ensembyll, ... 243 Speke Parott 423
ENSEW
The tyme dothe fast ensew . . . . 280 Why Come Ye 62
ENSHRYNED
Ovyde, enshryned with the musis nyne; . . . . 321 Garlande 333
ENSILVRED
Whose skales ensilvred again the son beames . . . . 330 Garlande 662
ENSORBYD
Ensor[b]yd with the wawys savage and wode; . . . . 213 Magnyfycence 2561
  ensorbyd] 'ensordyd' †Rastell & Treveris C 1530, B
ENSOWKID
Ensowkid with sylt of the myry [w]ose, ... 312 Garlande 23
  sylt] 'fylt' †Fakes 1523; wose] 'mose' †Fakes 1523
ENSUYD
The monke of Bury then after them ensuyd, ... 323 Garlande 390
ENSUYNGE
All famous poetis ensuynge after me . . . . 321 Garlande 321
ENSURE
Ye be malygned sore, I you ensure, ... 59 Bowge 451
He telleth you trouth, syr, as I you ensure. . . . . 187 Magnyfycence 1679
ENSWYMMYNG
Enswymmyng with rochis, barbellis and bremis, ... 330 Garlande 661
ENTACHID
Of golde, entachid with many a precyous stone; . . . . 325 Garlande 470
ENTAKELED
So well entakeled, what wynde that ever blowe, ... 327 Garlande 545
  that] 'so' Marshe 1568
ENTEND
For only the substance of that I entend, ... 323 Garlande 412
ENTENDE
Take me as I entende, ... 251 Collyn Clout 185
But what sholde I say? Ye wote what I entende, ... 324 Garlande 426
ENTENDED
But sith I have lost now that I entended, ... 321 Garlande 318
ENTENDYNG
Hath bene full often and yet is entendyng . . . . 344 Garlande 1131
ENTENT
Male uryd was your fals entent . . . . 118 Ag Scottes 111
But for to serve the kynges entent, ... 134 Garnesche5 177
Take Lyberte to rule, and folowe myne entent. . . . . 147 Magnyfycence 238
Come hyder, Pleasure; you shall here myne entent. . . . . . . 186 Magnyfycence 1655
And suffre theyr chyldren to have theyr entent, ... 194 Magnyfycence 1921
ENTENTE
Fulfyld with malice of froward entente, ... 30 Dol Dethe 25
Came for to slee me of mortall entente. . . . . 61 Bowge 529
So myche consultacion, almoste to none entente; . . . . 244 Speke Parott 453

ENTENTES — ENWALLYD

	Page	Title	Line
And to none entente,	280	Why Come Ye	81
ENTENTES			
To serve for all ententes,	101	Phy Sparrow	1182
ENTENTIFLY			
Trust me, ententifly,	339	Garlande	962
ENTEREMENT			
With Phillyppes enterement.	103	Phy Sparrow	1281
No man to myscontent /With Phillippis enterement.	348	Garlande	1274
ENTERLASED			
enbrased and enterlased with a moche fantasticall frenesy	374	Replycacion	1
ENTERLUDE			
Of Vertu also the soverayne enterlude;	345	Garlande	1177
ENTERPRETACYON			
And of resyde[v]acyon /They make enterpretacyon resydevacyon] 'resdenacyon' †Godfray 1531, Kele 1545.1, Marshe 1568	259	Collyn Clout	522
ENTERPRETE			
He did translate, enterprete, and disclose;	347	Garlande	1222
ENTERPRISE			
This lytel enterprise;	372	Albany	527
ENTERPRYSE			
I am insuffycyent to make such enterpryse;	42	Balettys2	9
Now wyll I enterpryse,	93	Phy Sparrow	856
ENTERPRYSED			
No matter pretendyd, nor nothyng enterprysed,	236	Speke Parott	201
But they have enterprysed /And shamfully surmysed	261	Collyn Clout	581
ENTERPRYSYD			
And maister Chaucer, that nobly enterprysyd	323	Garlande	388
ENTERTEYND			
And all other gentelmen with hym enterteynd	34	Dol Dethe	184
ENTYTULED			
Here after foloweth the boke entytuled Ware the Hauke	61	Hauke	1
ENTRETE			
And Dame Elynour entrete	221	El Rummynge	268
ENTRUSAR			
Ye are a fals entrusar, /And a fals abusar,	364	Albany	227
ENTUNYD			
So duly entunyd with every mesure,	320	Garlande	276
ENTURFID			
The bankis enturfid with singular solas,	330	Garlande	655
ENUWYD			
Enuwyd your colowre /Is lyke the dasy flowre your] 'her' MS Cotton Vitellius E.x	340	Garlande	985
ENVADE			
To envade Englande, /As I understande.	361	Albany	105
ENVAYNED			
Saphyre of sadnes, envayned wyth Indy blew;	44	Balettys3	17
ENVAWTYD			
Envawtyd with rubies the vawte was of this place.	325	Garlande	476
ENVECTYFYS			
For certayne envectyfys, yet wrote he none ill, certayne envectyfys] 'that he enveiyd' MS Cotton Vit.E.x	315	Garlande	96
ENVERDURID			
Enverdurid with levis contynually grene;	330	Garlande	666
ENVERDURYD			
Herber enverduryd, contynuall fressh and grene;	44	Balettys3	13
ENVI			
Against odyous Envi,	94	Phy Sparrow	905
ENVY			
It is a perylous vyce, this envy.	58	Bowge	444
This fals Envy /Sayth that I /Use great folly	95	Phy Sparrow	949
And there agayne /Envy doth complayne, /And hath disdayne;	95	Phy Sparrow	964
Full fewe but they have envy of me.	195	Magnyfycence	1963
Envy, wrath, and lechery, /Coveteys and glotony;	293	Why Come Ye	575
Ageyne envy, /And obloquy. /And wote ye why?	355	Garlande	1558
ENVYE			
Envye hathe wasted hys lyver and his lounge;	54	Bowge	291
Callyd Detraxion, encankryd with envye,	241	Speke Parott	362
ENVYOUS			
But hatefull absens, to me so envyous,	45	Balettys3	45
Envyous Rancour truely he hight.	333	Garlande	753
ENVYRONDE			
He was envyronde aboute on every syde	32	Dol Dethe	99
ENVYRONN			
The world [envyronn], of hygh and low estate. envyronn] 'envyronnyd' †Rastell & Treveris C 1530, B	140	Magnyfycence	2
ENVYRONNED			
Thus, I say, I am envyronned with solace.	190	Magnyfycence	1797
ENVYROWNE			
This hous envyrowne was a myle about;	326	Garlande	489
ENVYVE			
For to envyve Pandarus appetite;	336	Garlande	872
ENVYVED			
That quyckly is envyved with rudyes of the rose,	183	Magnyfycence	1551
ENVYVID			
Envyvid picturis well towchid and quikly.	345	Garlande	1161
ENWALLYD			
Enwallyd aboute with the stony flint,	328	Garlande	569

	Page	Title	Line
ENWERED			
Soo sore enwered that I was, at the laste,	47	Bowge	31
EOLUS			
Now Neptune and Eolus ar agreed of lyclyhod,	239	Speke Parott	283
Eolus, your trumpet, that knowne is so farre,	319	Garlande	235
that] 'whiche' MS Cotton Vitellius E.x			
Here you not Eolus for you blowyth a blaste?	343	Garlande	1088
you (1st)] 'ye' MS Cotton Vitellius E.x			
EPIDAURES			
Slew of the Epidaures	104	Phy Sparrow	1293
EPIDAWRIS			
Slew of the Epidawris	348	Garlande	1286
EPITAPH			
HIS EPITAPH FOLOWETH DEVOUTLY;	109	Epitaphe2	1
He wrate an Epitaph for his grave stone,	347	Garlande	1249
EPITOMIS			
His Epitomis of the Myller and his joly Make;	351	Garlande	1411
EPYCURE			
Was nevyr suche a fylty gorgon, nor suche an epycure,	246	Speke Parott	510
EPYLOGACYON			
Some make epylogacyon /Of hygh predestynacyon;	259	Collyn Clout	519
EPYTAPHE			
An epytaphe I wold have /For Phyllyppes grave.	86	Phy Sparrow	605
An epytaphe to wryght	92	Phy Sparrow	822
EQUIPOLENS			
That in his equipolens	307	Why Come Ye	1134
EQUIVALENT			
He jugyth him equivalent /With God omnipotent.	307	Why Come Ye	1135
him] 'hymselfe' MS Rawlinson C. 813;			
equivalent] 'equypolent' Rawlinson C. 813			
EQUIVALENTLY			
And laude equivalently.	369	Albany	403
ER			
Yet have I knowen suche er this;	46	Bowge	25
But of one thynge I werne you er I goo:	49	Bowge	106
werne] 'warne' Marshe 1568; er] 'or' Wynkyn de Worde 1510			
Where hathe your dwellynge ben, er ye cam here?	53	Bowge	247
Er this, whan that ye made me royall chere.	53	Bowge	249
Er I was ware, behynde me he sayde 'Bo!'	60	Bowge	500
Er thow beware, that in a throw	132	Garnesche5	122
ERE			
I have an errande to rounde in your ere.	60	Bowge	513
And as he rounded thus in myne ere	61	Bowge	526
rounded] 'royndede' †Wynkyn de Worde 1499			
What he sayth and she sayth to lay good ere,	175	Magnyfycence	1269
ERECTYD			
Syth unto me formest this processe is erectyd,	211	Magnyfycence	2482
ERES			
Or elles I had lost myne eres twayne.	150	Magnyfycence	349
ERKITH			
Now hereof it erkith me lenger to wryte,	354	Garlande	1491
ERLE			
of the Mooste Honorable Erle of Northumberlande	29	Dol Dethe	1
The famous Erle of Northumberlande;	32	Dol Dethe	107
Mooste noble Erle! O fowle mysuryd grounde,	32	Dol Dethe	118
So forcibly upon this Erle thow ran,	32	Dol Dethe	124
That noble erle, the Whyte Lyon,	115	Scot Kynge	68
Neyther erle ne duke	272	Collyn Clout	1045
Yet the good Erle of Surray,	282	Why Come Ye	153
The Erle of Northumberlande	286	Why Come Ye	290
Duke, erle, baron, nor lorde,	287	Why Come Ye	342
Nor marques, erle, nor lorde;	294	Why Come Ye	620
The noble Erle of Surrey,	365	Albany	241
ERLIS			
Sourmountinge in honour all erlis he did excede;	33	Dol Dethe	135
ERLY			
Be it erly or late, welth hath a season.	140	Magnyfycence	3
We have bene togyder bothe erly and late.	154	Magnyfycence	499
And syt there by styll, /Erly and late.	217	El Rummynge	117
ERNEST			
In ernest and in game	89	Phy Sparrow	709
In ernest and in sport.	121	Ag Scottes2	34
In ernest and in game.	262	Collyn Clout	613
In ernest or in borde:	298	Why Come Ye	785
In ernest or in borde.	367	Albany	319
ERNYST			
Ye, to knackynge ernyst what and it preve?	141	Magnyfycence	33
ERRANDE			
I have an errande to rounde in your ere.	60	Bowge	513
ERRONYOUS			
Agaynst whiche erronyous errours,	375	Replycacion	1
ERROURS			
remordyng dyvers recrayed and moche unresonable errours	373	Replycacion	1
Agaynst whiche erronyous errours,	375	Replycacion	1
ERST			
Erst that ye can fynde	341	Garlande	1032
that] 'than' MS Cotton Vitellius E.x			

| ERSTE —ESTATES | Page | Title | Line |

ERSTE
Yow to remorde erste or they know your mynde.	241	Speke Parott	370

ERTH
Hevyn, hell and erth obey unto thi kall;	34	Dol Dethe	192

ERTHELY
'Noo thynge erthely that I wonder so sore	50	Bowge	148
All erthely tresoure it is surmountynge.	50	Bowge	154
Of erthely thynge I have no care nor charge.	199	Magnyfycence	2081

ERTHLY
For I dare saye that there nys erthly man	48	Bowge	101
That noo man erthly coude hym bewreye, ...	52	Bowge	223
man] 'wan' †Wynkyn de Worde 1499			
For, and I knowe ony erthly thynge	54	Bowge	277
That passeth all erthly good;	93	Phy Sparrow	876
all] 'all the' Wyght 1553, Kitson 1560.6, Marshe 1568			
That hath non erthly pere?	96	Phy Sparrow	1001
Thus in this worlde there is no erthly truste.	213	Magnyfycence	2544
Thus in this worlde there is no erthly truste.	213	Magnyfycence	2551

ESCAPE
Ye shall nat escape blamelesse, ...	309	Why Come Ye2	4
escape] 'be' MS Rawlinson C. 813			

ESCAPID
It was a new comfort of sorowis escapid.	330	Garlande	657

ESCHINES
That gave Eschines suche a cordyall, ...	316	Garlande	131
That] 'Whiche' MS Cotton Vitellius E.x			
And was Eschines rebukid as ye say?	316	Garlande	135
As towchyng that Eschines is remembred, ...	316	Garlande	148
From whiche Eschines had none evacyon.	316	Garlande	154
Eschines, whiche was not shamefully confutid	316	Garlande	157
By Eschines rehersed to the grete glory	317	Garlande	166

ESCRYE
Nor good preest I escrye, ...	273	Collyn Clout	1096
I escrye] 'of the clargy' Marshe 1568, 'askrye' Harley 2252			

ESEBON
But Parrot hath no favour to Esebon;	233	Speke Parott	111
Ulula, Esebon, for Jeromy doth wepe!	234	Speke Parott	113
O Esebon, Esebon, to the is cum agayne	234	Speke Parott	120
O Esebon, Esebon, to the is cum agayne	234	Speke Parott	120
Ulula, Esebon, for Jepte is starke ded!	234	Speke Parott	126
Esebon, Marybon, Wheston next Barnet;	234	Speke Parott	127

ESIODUS
Esiodus, the iconomicar, ...	321	Garlande	328
iconomicar] 'icononucar' †Fakes 1523, Marshe 1568			

ESPERUS
Radyent Esperus, star of the clowdy nyght, ...	44	Balettys3	24

ESPYDE
I have well espyde	39	Coystrowne3	9
Some lothe to be espyde, ...	221	El Rummynge	262

ESPYE
That he coulde there espye	76	Phy Sparrow	181
That ye can nat espye	263	Collyn Clout	685

ESSEX
A cantell of Essex chese	225	El Rummynge	429

EST
'The west is wyndy.' 'The est is metely wele.'	326	Garlande	499
How from the est unto the occident, ...	328	Garlande	577

ESTATE
The awnner therof is lady of estate, ...	47	Bowge	50
Of what estate ye be, /Of hye or lowe degre, ...	73	Phy Sparrow	54
To be matriculate /With ladyes of estate?	104	Phy Sparrow	1289
Ye be bounde tenauntes to his estate;	114	Scot Kynge	36
Ye were bonde tenent to his estate;	118	Ag Scottes	127
oratour to the kynges most royall estate.	120	Ag Scottes	E
The world [envyronn], of hygh and low estate.	140	Magnyfycence	2
envyronn] 'envyronnyd' †Rastell & Treveris C 1530, B			
Syr, yf I have offended your noble estate, ...	149	Magnyfycence	308
Man or woman, of what estate they be, ...	194	Magnyfycence	1898
For thoughe you were somtyme a noble estate, ...	196	Magnyfycence	1980
Where is nowe my welth and my noble estate?	198	Magnyfycence	2055
But good hope and redresse hath mendyd myne estate, ...	210	Magnyfycence	2462
How none estate lyvynge of hymselfe can be sure, ...	213	Magnyfycence	2557
Thus none estate lyvynge of hym[selfe] can be sure, ...	214	Magnyfycence	2564
hymselfe] 'hym' †Rastell & Treveris C 1530, B			
And send me to greate ladyes of estate;	231	Speke Parott	6
to greate ladyes] 'to grece to lordys' †MS Harley 2252			
Paregall with all prynces, farre passyng hys estate;	244	Speke Parott	436
Brought up of poore estate, /With pryde inordynate, ...	262	Collyn Clout	642
Agaynst holy churche estate, ...	269	Collyn Clout	915
For prelates of estate, ...	270	Collyn Clout	972
With lordes of great estate	271	Collyn Clout	1013
Of what estate he be /Of spirituall dygnyte;	294	Why Come Ye	617
I trust, to lowe estate	368	Albany	385

ESTATES
No. But for you grete estates	150	Magnyfycence	370
I muster, I medle amonge these grete estates;	160	Magnyfycence	736
Ye bysshoppes of estates	263	Collyn Clout	690
The churche hygh estates, ...	264	Collyn Clout	708

ESTRYCH —EVER	Page	Title	Line

Of dyvers great estates,	277	Collyn Clout	1246
And what estates to her did resorte,	313	Garlande	45
ESTRYCH			
Ic dien serveth for the estrych fether,	233	Speke Parott	78
the] not in †Kynge & Marche 1554, Day 1560, Marshe 1568			
ESTRYGE			
The estryge, that wyll eate	83	Phy Sparrow	478
ETE			
This worlde is nothynge but ete, drynke and slepe,	57	Bowge	384
Wel, wyse men may ete the fysshe when ye shal draw the pole.	148	Magnyfycence	300
By God, we have made Magnyfycence to ete a flye.	154	Magnyfycence	503
Yes, yet he wyll make the ete a gnat.	173	Magnyfycence	1192
Yes, yet] 'Yet yes' †Rastell & Treveris C 1530, B			
That he shall never ete more bred.	299	Why Come Ye	796
May ete pigges in lent for pikys	306	Why Come Ye	1081
For in lent he wyll ete	306	Why Come Ye	1083
wyll] 'doeth' MS Rawlinson C. 813			
ETEN			
She sayde she trowed that I had eten sause;	48	Bowge	72
had] not in †Wynkyn de Worde 1499, 1510			
Ye have eten sauce I trowe, at the Taylers Hall.	179	Magnyfycence	1404
Jone sayde she had eten a fyest.	223	El Rummynge	343
ETERMYNABLE			
Thow bringe unto thy joye etermynable	34	Dol Dethe	199
Thow] 'how' †MS Royal 18 D.ii			
ETERNALLY			
Eternally /To beholde and se /The Trynyte!	40	Coystrowne3	57
Undoubted ye had lost yourselfe eternally.	206	Magnyfycence	2335
ETETH			
The blynde eteth many a flye.	378	Replycacion	152
ETHNA			
Of Ethna the brennynge hyll	79	Phy Sparrow	313
ETYNGE			
That the horson had for etynge of a trype.	171	Magnyfycence	1126
EUFRATES			
Tyll Eufrates, that flodde, dryvythe me into Ynde,	231	Speke Parott	4
EUMENIDES			
By the ugly Eumenides,	104	Phy Sparrow	1324
By the ugly Eumenides,	349	Garlande	1317
EUPHORION			
As Linus and Homerus, /Euphorion and Theocritus,	90	Phy Sparrow	762
EVACYON			
From whiche Eschines had none evacyon.	316	Garlande	154
EVANDER			
Of Kyng Alexander; /And of Kyng Evander	90	Phy Sparrow	746
EVEN			
Whan that he was even at me almoost,	58	Bowge	432
And thoughte to lepe; and even with that woke,	61	Bowge	531
Even nor morow; /But other mennes sorow	94	Phy Sparrow	924
I folow even after your noble grace.	151	Magnyfycence	395
Ye, by the masse, this is even the same,	157	Magnyfycence	599
Even of purpose for the same.	167	Magnyfycence	957
Among this prese - /Even a hole mese -	168	Magnyfycence	996
Ye, by the rode, even the same.	172	Magnyfycence	1139
Nay. He shall be ruled even as I lyst.	179	Magnyfycence	1394
Those thre wyll be redy even at your bekenynge;	190	Magnyfycence	1778
EVER			
One ther is, and ever one shalbe,	45	Balettys5	8
She asked yf ever I dranke of saucys cuppe.	48	Bowge	73
'Forsothe,' quod she, 'how ever blowe the wynde,	49	Bowge	110
And ever he sange, 'Sythe I am no thynge playne'.	52	Bowge	235
I wolde be mery that wynde that ever blowe,	53	Bowge	251
And ever he threwe, and kyst I wote nere what;	56	Bowge	349
He ran as fast as ever that he myghte.	58	Bowge	415
Al floodes that ever was	93	Phy Sparrow	878
He frowneth ever; /He laugheth never,	94	Phy Sparrow	922
But ever doth watch,	95	Phy Sparrow	929
Ever to be /Their true bedell	96	Phy Sparrow	979
That ever Englond had;	111	Lawde	53
I could make him shortly repent him for ever;	139	Ven Tongues	76
As I was wonte ever, at my fre wyll.	144	Magnyfycence	147
Bysy, bysy, and ever bysy,	169	Magnyfycence	1039
Cockys bonys! Herde ye ever syke another?	170	Magnyfycence	1090
That ever thou thryve, God it forfende!	171	Magnyfycence	1114
As ever I was, and as full of tryfyls -	172	Magnyfycence	1141
So helpe me God, man, ever at the length	175	Magnyfycence	1258
And more than ever I dyd for ony man.	187	Magnyfycence	1694
I sawe a sowter go to supper, or ever he had dynde.	191	Magnyfycence	1825
If ever I herde syke another, God gyve me shame.	192	Magnyfycence	1833
Cockes bones! Harde ye ever suche another?	192	Magnyfycence	1841
Or ever we were ware, brought us in adversyte,	193	Magnyfycence	1863
Fy, fy, that ever I sholde be brought in this snare!	196	Magnyfycence	1972
Alasse that ever I sholde be so shamed!	196	Magnyfycence	1982
Alasse that ever I Magnyfycence was named!	196	Magnyfycence	1983

EVERITHING — EVERY	Page	Title	Line
Under good hope endurynge ever styll,	208	Magnyfycence	2381
And ye shall have more worshyp then ever ye had.	210	Magnyfycence	2474
And ever let the drede of God be in your syght,	211	Magnyfycence	2498
Never stoppynge /But ever droppynge;	215	El Rummynge	30
All that ever they ken	272	Collyn Clout	1053
Ever in one case.	301	Why Come Ye	882
It shall nat ever flowe.	303	Why Come Ye	952
nat ever flowe] 'neuer ouer flowe' MS Rawlinson C. 813			
And ever they pressed on me more and more,	324	Garlande	445
So well entakeled, what wynde that ever blowe,	327	Garlande	545
that] 'so' Marshe 1568			
That ever more after by it they were aspyid;	329	Garlande	627
It passid all bawmys that ever were namyd,	331	Garlande	674
That ever they saw, and wrought it was the best.	343	Garlande	1113
Of what charge so ever ye lay ageinst me;	344	Garlande	1138
For he was ever ageynst Goddis hows;	347	Garlande	1251
In fortunis favour ever to endure,	351	Garlande	1402
And falsest forsworne /That ever were borne.	362	Albany	118
And ever to remayne	362	Albany	136
With us, whan ever ye mell	363	Albany	182
EVERITHING			
Of our maisters counsel in everithing.	299	Why Come Ye	792
EVERY			
Regestringe trewly every formare date;	29	Dol Dethe	18
Knyghtis and squyers, at every season when	30	Dol Dethe	32
Redy to assyst you in every tyme of nede;	30	Dol Dethe	58
He was envyronde aboute on every syde	32	Dol Dethe	99
Valiant as Hector in every marciall nede,	33	Dol Dethe	138
Youre key is mete for every lok,	41	Coystrowne4	22
I shall the angre ones in every vayne!	55	Bowge	326
In every poynte that I can do or saye.	60	Bowge	496
In] 'To' Marshe 1568			
In every poynte to be indyfferente,	61	Bowge	535
Every byrde in his laye:	81	Phy Sparrow	394
Thus thorow every stede	110	Lawde	3
The outesyde every day,	125	Garnesche3	48
Thou art callyd of every man.	130	Garnesche5	24
For thou beggest at every mannes dur.	135	Dundas	26
With every condycyon measure must be sought.	143	Magnyfycence	115
And I am Lyberte, made of in every nacyon.	145	Magnyfycence	172
But largesse is not mete for every man.	150	Magnyfycence	369
Counterfet Countenaunce every man dothe occupy.	153	Magnyfycence	472
No. In every corner he wyll peke,	158	Magnyfycence	658
And every man gladly my company wolde refuse,	160	Magnyfycence	704
Howe I may hurte and hynder every man.	160	Magnyfycence	709
And craftely can I grope howe every man is mynded.	160	Magnyfycence	725
My purpose is to spy and to poynte every man;	160	Magnyfycence	726
To russhe it oute /In every route.	164	Magnyfycence	848
Ay warre and warre /In every place.	166	Magnyfycence	915
On this halfe and on every syde	168	Magnyfycence	1020
What! Fleyest thou his skynne every yere?	169	Magnyfycence	1058
Ye. But he wyll in at every mannes dore.	171	Magnyfycence	1130
That every man lawghyth at his foly.	175	Magnyfycence	1251
And tell to his sufferayne every whyt;	175	Magnyfycence	1270
It is but foly every dell.	175	Magnyfycence	1275
That every man almost groweth out of kynde.	175	Magnyfycence	1285
To se what foly is used in every place;	177	Magnyfycence	1327
Foly hath a rome, I say, in every route;	177	Magnyfycence	1328
Foly and fansy all where every man dothe face and brace.	177	Magnyfycence	1330
And to fall in aquayntaunce with every newe facyon.	183	Magnyfycence	1548
Yet it proveth eyrnest, ye may se, every day.	195	Magnyfycence	1949
I am baytyd with doggys at every mannys gate;	195	Magnyfycence	1961
Nowe must you lerne to begge at every mannes gate.	196	Magnyfycence	1981
Ye, but thanke me therof every dele.	201	Magnyfycence	2171
Redresse sholde be at the rekenynge in every accompte,	208	Magnyfycence	2413
Every man after his maner of wayes,	233	Speke Parott	90
Set Sophia asyde, for every Jack Raker	235	Speke Parott	160
And every mad medler must now be a maker.	235	Speke Parott	161
Let every man after his merit take his parte;	236	Speke Parott	199
As presydent and regente he rulythe every deall.	239	Speke Parott	312
So myche towrnyng on the cooke-stole for every guy-gaw;	245	Speke Parott	481
But nowe every spirytuall father,	251	Collyn Clout	174
Thus they make theyr boost /Through every coost,	251	Collyn Clout	203
Then renne they in every stede,	252	Collyn Clout	231
Howe some synge letabundus /At every ale stake,	253	Collyn Clout	249
Of every lyght quarell,	261	Collyn Clout	599
Borne up on every syde	284	Why Come Ye	203
Upon every banke /Of his herbers grene,	304	Why Come Ye	1002
At every solempne feest,	309	Why Come Ye	1215
On every halfe my reasons forthe I sought,	312	Garlande	10
On] 'One' †Fakes 1523			
That bararag blowyth in every mercyall warre,	319	Garlande	236
A wonderfull noyse, and on every syde	319	Garlande	247
So duly entunyd with every mesure,	320	Garlande	276
It is harde to tell of every mannes mouthe:	326	Garlande	500
Innumerable people pressed to every gate.	329	Garlande	603
Powle hatchettis, that prate wyll at every ale pole,	329	Garlande	613
wyll] 'well' Marshe 1568			

EVERYCHONE — EXCEDYNG

	Page	Title	Line
There birdis on the brere sange on every syde,	330	Garlande	653
Of my laurell the proces every whitte.	343	Garlande	1099
With aurum musicum every other lyne	345	Garlande	1167
In every marciall shoure,	365	Albany	240
and of every true Christen man laudably to be enployed,	374	Replycacion	1
Thorowe out every border.	380	Replycacion	228
To reverence in every place.	381	Replycacion	262

EVERYCHONE

Maysters, Cryst save everychone!	169	Magnyfycence	1043
Amongest you everychone	258	Collyn Clout	477
That wolde God everychone /Of his affynyte	300	Why Come Ye	834

EVERY THING

Whiche whils he lyvyd had fuyson of every thing,	32	Dol Dethe	131

EVERY THYNG

Where every thyng is ordenyd after your noble porte.	214	Magnyfycence	2568

EVERY THYNGE

I wyll endevour me to order every thynge	146	Magnyfycence	203
Her demenyng /In every thynge,	341	Garlande	1015

EVERMORE

Maye never dye, bute evermore endure.	46	Bowge	16
Farewell for evermore!	80	Phy Sparrow	334
That evermore wil ly /And say cursedly;	94	Phy Sparrow	906
'O thoughtfull herte,' was evermore his songe!	320	Garlande	296
shall evermore be, with all obsequious redynesse,	373	Replycacion	1
And in maner as abjecte, /For evermore suspecte,	380	Replycacion	241

EVIDENT

Howbeit the mater was evident and playne;	31	Dol Dethe	72

EVILL

Ye had evill spede.	359	Albany	32

EVYDENCE

But suche evydence I thynke for to enduce, for to] 'for me to' MS Cotton Vitellius E.x	344	Garlande	1135

EVYDENTLY

Of his rekenynge, as evydently we may	146	Magnyfycence	215
As evydently in retchlesse youth ye may se	200	Magnyfycence	2133
Or els wyll I /Evydently /Shewe as it is:	361	Albany	85

EVYLL

I have grete scorne and am ryghte evyll apayed.'	54	Bowge	298
The hawke with that clap /Fell downe with evyll hap.	64	Hauke	90
Alas, I was evyll at ease!	75	Phy Sparrow	144
That never ought the evyll wyll!	79	Phy Sparrow	323
It is evyll patchynge of that is torne.	153	Magnyfycence	447
Yet counterfet chafer is but evyll corne.	153	Magnyfycence	450
Lest that he thought that his money were evyll spente,	187	Magnyfycence	1674
Alasse, I have the cyatyca full evyll in my hyppe!	195	Magnyfycence	1956
Howe evyll theyr shepe fare.'	250	Collyn Clout	131
They have an evyll name,	275	Collyn Clout	1143
The prechers with evyll haylynge:	275	Collyn Clout	1149

EVYLL FAVERYD

There is many evyll faveryd, and thou be foule!	167	Magnyfycence	969

EVYN

On Candelmas evyn, the kalendas of May.	38	Coystrownel	70
Good evyn, good Robyn Hode!	283	Why Come Ye	197
Good evyn and good nyght!	302	Why Come Ye	916

EVYNLY

Ye counterway not evynly your balaunce;	317	Garlande	179

EVYR

The best chepe flessh that evyr I bought.'	36	Man Margery	24

EXALTACYON

He is in suche elacyon /Of his exaltacyon,	291	Why Come Ye	483

EXAMINACION

Arrectinge unto your wyse examinacion	323	Garlande	410

EXAMYNACYON

By juste examynacyon /In connynge and conversacyon.	253	Collyn Clout	266

EXAMPLE

At hym example ye wolde none take;	115	Scot Kynge	60
And, for example [y]e wold none take, ye] 'he' tLant 1545, Kynge & Marche 1554, Day 1560, Marshe 1568	119	Ag Scottes	157
To take, syrs, example of that I you tell,	195	Magnyfycence	1944
A playne example of worldly vaynglory,	212	Magnyfycence	2514

EXCEDE

Alas, ye madmen, to far ye did excede.	31	Dol Dethe	60
Sourmountinge in honour all erlis he did excede;	33	Dol Dethe	135
That so far dyd excede;	67	Hauke	191
Ryght so she doth excede	93	Phy Sparrow	883
She doth excede and pas /In prudence dame Pallas;	102	Phy Sparrow	1229
For defaute of measure all thynge dothe excede.	146	Magnyfycence	217
Say howe you excede in noblenesse,	151	Magnyfycence	376
For to excede /In suche aray.	165	Magnyfycence	895
Mary, syr, so dyd he excede and passe,	178	Magnyfycence	1385
In very dede /How ye excede.	343	Garlande	1085

EXCEDITH

This joy excedith all wordly sport and play, wordly] 'worldly' Marshe 1568	332	Garlande	716

EXCEDYNG

It was excedyng byyonde the commowne rate.	326	Garlande	488

EXCEDYNGE

	Page	Title	Line
Excedynge ferther than his connynge is,	46	Bowge	23
No, no; for thy synnys be so excedynge farre,	205	Magnyfycence	2300

EXCEDYTH
Your comfortable advyse and wyt excedyth all gladnesse;	210	Magnyfycence	2477

EXCELL
To wryte and tell /How women excell /In noblenes;	96	Phy Sparrow	982
Whiche soverenly in honoure shulde excell;	317	Garlande	199

EXCELLE
In dygnyte roiall that doth excelle.	132	Garnesche5	96

EXCELLENCE
Your worship depended of his excellence.	31	Dol Dethe	59
To prase her excellence!	101	Phy Sparrow	1207
To haute in excellence, /To lyght intellegence, lyght] 'lyght of' MS Rawlinson C. 813	279	Why Come Ye	8
The kynges courte /Shulde have the excellence;	289	Why Come Ye	407
Agaynst her excellence, /Agaynst her reverence,	375	Replycacion	40

EXCELLENT
As of your connynge, that is so excellent;	50	Bowge	149
Our kyng most excellent.	369	Albany	429

EXCELLENTE
Within that, a pryncos excellente of porte; that] 'it' MS Cotton Vitellius E.x	313	Garlande	43

EXCELLES
In poetes whiche excelles,	384	Replycacion	377

EXCEPT
Except mannes soule, that Chryst so dere bought;	236	Speke Parott	215

EXCESSE
By lyberte is done many a great excesse;	142	Magnyfycence	53
There is no excesse where measure hath his helthe.	144	Magnyfycence	140
What! All by mesure, good syr, and none excesse?	180	Magnyfycence	1422
Determyne to amende all your wanton excesse;	208	Magnyfycence	2409
There hath ben moche excesse:	280	Why Come Ye	70

EXCITYNGE
To corage Demostenes was moche excitynge,	316	Garlande	152

EXCLAMACYON
By way of exclamacyon,	78	Phy Sparrow	274
Then he assurded into his exclamacyon his] 'this' Marshe 1568	320	Garlande	302

EXCLUDE
Exclude now all dolowrs.	110	Lawde	7

EXCOMMUNYCACYONS
With sommons and citacyons /And excommunycacyons	254	Collyn Clout	325

EXCOMUNYCATE
Of grace out of the state /And dyed excomunycate.	121	Ag Scottes2	30

EXCUSE
Full fewe that can themselfe of me excuse.	160	Magnyfycence	706
My wylfulnesse, syr, excuse I ne can.	209	Magnyfycence	2432
Also, to furnisshe better his excuse,	314	Garlande	92
That I trust to make myne excuse	344	Garlande	1137

EXCUSED
Wherfore hold me excused	92	Phy Sparrow	813
I am sure ye wolde have me excused.	156	Magnyfycence	581
So that I may craftely be excused.	187	Magnyfycence	1684

EXCUSYD
That be so far abusyd /They cannot be excusyd	62	Hauke	6

EXECRABLE
Opinyons detestable /Of heresy execrable?	382	Replycacion	305

EXECUTE
Nor to execute /His commaundement,	272	Collyn Clout	1032

EXECUTYD
Sentence was executyd,	66	Hauke	175

EXEDE
Moderata juvant but toto dothe exede;	232	Speke Parott	50

EXELLENTLY
countyng them selfe clerkes exellently enformed	374	Replycacion	I

EXEMPLIFY
Whome ye represent and exemplify,	336	Garlande	854

EXEMPLYFYENGE
In exemplyfyenge /Great Alexander the kynge,	292	Why Come Ye	543

EXESSE
So myche papers weryng for ryghte a smalle exesse;	245	Speke Parott	479

EXHIBYCION
To gyve you exhibycion	378	Replycacion	143

EXIONE
Of Exione, his limbis dede and past, his limbis] 'her lambis' †Fakes 1523, 'her lambe is' Marshe 1568	351	Garlande	1400

EXYLE
Vyce to revyle /And synne to exyle?	247	Collyn Clout	12

EXYLIDE
I am content that he be not exylide	318	Garlande	224

EXYLYD
That we be not exylyd	40	Coystrowne3	44
Dysdayns, dystres, exylyd cruelte;	43	Balettys3	4

EXPELLE
Myne homely rudnes and drighnes to expelle	29	Dol Dethe	13

	Page	Title	Line
EXPENCE			
Not thorowe largesse of lyberall expence,	200	Magnyfycence	2115
To paye for her expence.	229	El Rummynge	599
So prodigall expence, and so shamfull reconyng;	244	Speke Parott	458
To scarce of your expence,	278	Why Come Ye	5
EXPERIENS			
Experiens hath brought you in such a brake.	119	Ag Scottes	158
EXPERYENCE			
Experyence hath brought you in the same brake.	115	Scot Kynge	61
Of that may come after; experyence trewe and playne,	141	Magnyfycence	11
EXPERYENS			
And dare use the experyens	297	Why Come Ye	711
EXPERT			
Your harrold in armes not yet halfe expert.	118	Ag Scottes	98
EXPERTE			
And your harolde no thynge experte;	113	Scot Kynge	8
EXPYACYON			
By wey of expyacyon /For reconcylyacyon. [for reconcylyacyon] not in Day 1560, Marshe 1568	66	Hauke	176
EXPYRYD			
Why holde ye on yer cap, syr, then? Yor pardone ys expyryd.	123	Garnesche2	9
EXPLOYTE			
As he to exployte the man owte of the mone.	239	Speke Parott	307
To exployte dedes of armys	370	Albany	467
EXPOUNDE			
And though I can expounde	88	Phy Sparrow	672
Now leve this jangelynge and to us expounde	147	Magnyfycence	262
That clerkely is, and can /Well scrypture expounde	264	Collyn Clout	723
Is easy to expounde,	298	Why Come Ye	781
Another manes mynde diffuse is to expounde;	315	Garlande	111
Wherof partely I purpose to expounde,	325	Garlande	464
Let se now for hym how ye can expounde;	345	Garlande	1153
Brevely and rounde /To me expounde.	361	Albany	83
But nowe will I expounde	369	Albany	423
EXPOUNDYNGE			
Expoundynge out theyr clauses, /And leve theyr owne causes.	249	Collyn Clout	100
EXPOUNDYTH			
Occupacyoun redith and expoundyth	345	Garlande	R
EXPRES			
Thes sorowfulle ditis that I may shew expres.	29	Dol Dethe	21
Open myne hart, beholde my mynde expres.	44	Balettys3	39
Of the whych proces /Ye may know more expres,	68	Hauke	232
For to expres /The noblenes /Of my maistres,	95	Phy Sparrow	956
Primo Regum expres, /He bad the Phitones	350	Garlande	1337
EXPRESSE			
She is playnly expresse	100	Phy Sparrow	1151
Primo Regum expresse,	105	Phy Sparrow	1344
The whiche were to longe nowe to expresse;	209	Magnyfycence	2416
Your myndys I besechе you here in to expresse,	211	Magnyfycence	2480
Som sey they cannot my parables expresse;	242	Speke Parott	386
Nor to expresse to his parson,	272	Collyn Clout	1036
For trewly to expresse,	280	Why Come Ye	69
Whiche, truly to expresse, /Is a forgetfulnesse,	290	Why Come Ye	467
His valiaunce to expresse,	369	Albany	400
EXPRESSED			
In thre poyntes expressed:	307	Why Come Ye	1122
EXPREST			
It can not be exprest /My sorowfull hevynesse,	72	Phy Sparrow	31
EXPRESTE			
Thus myche Parott hathe opynlye expreste;	242	Speke Parott	381
EXTASY			
As one in a trans or in an extasy,	313	Garlande	37
EXTENDID			
To blowe a blaste with his long breth extendid;	319	Garlande	234
EXTOLDE			
By thy report ar wonte to be extolde	29	Dol Dethe	17
Whiche was extolde /A thowsande folde	342	Garlande	1078
EXTOLE			
A, syr, your grace me dothe extole and rayse;	183	Magnyfycence	1525
EXTOLL			
What nedethe me for to extoll his fame	33	Dol Dethe	141
To extoll his noble grace	369	Albany	407
EXTOLLYD			
'So have ye me far passynge my meretis extollyd,	324	Garlande	435
EXTORCYON			
Extorcyon is counted with you for a knyght;	317	Garlande	194
EXTORT			
By extort trechery.	111	Lawde	28
EXTRAVAGANCY			
Whiche madly he dothe apply /Unto an extravagancy,	306	Why Come Ye	1105
EXTREME			
Hath brought nobil princes to extreme confusion.	139	Ven Tongues	58
FA			
And lerne me to synge Re my fa sol!	53	Bowge	258
FABELL			
And there began a fabell,	224	El Rummynge	386
FABIAN			
Howe frere Fabian with other mo	268	Collyn Clout	881

	Page	Title	Line
FABLE			
Though I remembre the fable	89	Phy Sparrow	724
Your frantyck fable not worth a fly, ...	118	Ag Scottes	104
This is no fable nor no lye;	296	Why Come Ye	705
FABLES			
Wyth fables false, that well coude fayne a tale;	49	Bowge	135
And flatered them with fables fayre before theyr face, ...	160	Magnyfycence	717
In flattryng fables men fynde but lyttyl fayth;	233	Speke Parott	87
FACE			
But graunt us grace /To se thy face, ...	40	Coystrowne3	50
Mysdempte eche man, with face deedly and pale;	50	Bowge	137
He wyll begyle you and speke fayre to your face.	51	Bowge	200
His face was belymmed as byes had him stounge;	54	Bowge	289
His eyen blereed, his face shone lyke a glas;	56	Bowge	353
And sware horryble othes /Before the face of God, ...	63	Hauke	53
Upon my corporas face.	63	Hauke	63
Alas, my face waxeth pale, ...	80	Phy Sparrow	341
With a balde face to toote;	82	Phy Sparrow	411
Her favour of her face	96	Phy Sparrow	1002
Such relucent grace /Is formed in her face;	100	Phy Sparrow	1160
Both lorde and knight to face, ...	111	Lawde	39
For you and your Scottes wolde tourne his face?	114	Scot Kynge	18
To face, to brace, /All voyde of grace, ...	116	Ag Scottes	33
From you, Syr Scot, wolde turne his face?	118	Ag Scottes	108
Ye gyrne grymly with your gomys and with yor grysly face. . .	122	Garnesche1	12
Yet your contenons oncomly, yor face ys nat fayer.	122	Garnesche1	18
Ye grounde yow upon Godfrey, that grysly gargons face, ...	123	Garnesche2	29
How the favyr of your face	124	Garnesche3	9
Your face I wyse to varnyshe	127	Garnesche3	121
Lerne or be lewde, I shrow thy face.	132	Garnesche5	127
Yt wold garnyche wyll thy face.	133	Garnesche5	135
Thy fonde face can me nat fray.	134	Garnesche5	171
A spectacle case /To cover thy face, /With, tray deux ase. . .	136	Dundas	38
That overgroweth a mannes face, ...	155	Magnyfycence	544
And flatered them with fables fayre before theyr face, ...	160	Magnyfycence	717
What, fonnysshe Foly! I befole thy face.	169	Magnyfycence	1045
Est [suavis vago] with a shrewde face vilis imago.	172	Magnyfycence	1154
suavis vago] 'snaui snago' †Rastell & Treveris C 1530, B			
Foly and fansy all where every man dothe face and brace. . . .	177	Magnyfycence	1330
And Thesius, th[at] prowde was Pluto to face -	182	Magnyfycence	1496
that] 'the' †Rastell & Treveris C 1530, B			
And frowne it and face it, as thoughe ye wolde fyght;	185	Magnyfycence	1601
Nowe dare he not for shame loke one in the face.	193	Magnyfycence	1891
That thou arte not worthy to loke God in the face.	205	Magnyfycence	2296
Her face all bowsy, ...	215	El Rummynge	17
Theyr lockes aboute theyr face, ...	218	El Rummynge	146
Her face glystryng lyke glas, ...	226	El Rummynge	482
With a sory face /Whey-wormed about;	228	El Rummynge	552
Ye boost, ye face, ye crake, ...	261	Collyn Clout	602
And mocke them to theyr face.	262	Collyn Clout	625
With, 'trey duse ase', /And, 'ase in the face'.	301	Why Come Ye	879
To face out his foly with a midsomer mase;	346	Garlande	1208
To loke hym in the face	367	Albany	352
In spyght of thy cowardes face, ...	369	Albany	408
In spyght of thy cowardes face, ...	371	Albany	492
For to tourne your face;	371	Albany	505
His foly so to face.	379	Replycacion	196
FACERS			
Some facers, some bracers, some make great crackis;	317	Garlande	189
some] 'and sum' MS Cotton Vitellius E.x			
FACES			
Than, in his hode, I sawe there faces tweyne:	58	Bowge	428
Two faces in a hode covertly I bere;	160	Magnyfycence	710
So many holow hartes, and so dowbyll faces;	245	Speke Parott	502
Men say, they bere no faces	269	Collyn Clout	896
FACION			
Now all is out of facion, /Almost in desolation.	305	Why Come Ye	1041
FACITHE			
He facithe owte at a flusshe with, 'Shewe, take all!'	243	Speke Parott	430
FACYD			
And thus to be facyd, I thynke it great skorne.	203	Magnyfycence	2217
FACYON			
He hawked on thys facyon, ...	64	Hauke	101
That by representacyon /Of his image and facyon, ...	77	Phy Sparrow	215
Of the same facyon /Without alteracyon, ...	85	Phy Sparrow	542
And I of the same facyon;	143	Magnyfycence	96
All this nacyon /I set on fyre; /In my facyon	165	Magnyfycence	886
And to fall in aquayntaunce with every newe facyon, ...	183	Magnyfycence	1548
For I am panged ofte tymes in this same facyon.	189	Magnyfycence	1734
Of auquarde facyon, ...	259	Collyn Clout	523
Though I wryte after this facyon;	273	Collyn Clout	1080
But lyve styll out of facyon, ...	275	Collyn Clout	1139
Odious Disdayne, why raist thou me on this facyon?	321	Garlande	317
We are kyndled in suche facyon	385	Replycacion	382
FACYOUN			
The facyoun of your fysnamy the devyl in a clowde;	123	Garnesche2	25
FACULTE			
Nor bachelers of that faculte	266	Collyn Clout	791

FADE —FAYNTE   Page   Title   Line

FADE
In Tullis faculte /Called humanyte.   292   Why Come Ye   528
Ornatly pullysshid after your faculte, ...   335   Garlande   816
In that faculte which shyned as Phebus bright;   383   Replycacion   333
FADE
Without measure lyghtly may fade, ...   146   Magnyfycence   228
And the sandes of Cefas begyn to waste and fade, ...   239   Speke Parott   281
  Cefas] 'Tefas' †MS Harley 2252
FADER
Thrugh your counseyle your fader was slayne;   114   Scot Kynge   27
And where the fader by wysdom worshyp hath wonne, ...   195   Magnyfycence   1934
FADERS
Faders and moders that be neclygent, ...   194   Magnyfycence   1920
I vysyte theyr faders and moders with sekenesse;   194   Magnyfycence   1925
FAGOT
To beare a fagot, or to be enflamed.   374   Replycacion   16
With his fagot in processyon.   379   Replycacion   188
FAGOTTES
Our fagottes are all spent.   281   Why Come Ye   83
Ye were fayne to beare fagottes;   376   Replycacion   66
To beare fagottes for babyls.   379   Replycacion   175
FAILE
They coude not faile, thei thought, they were so sure.   50   Bowge   142
FAINE
That maketh England faine.   111   Lawde   42
FAINT HARTED
and faint harted Frenchemen: 359   Albany   I
FAIRE
Faire fall that forster that so well can bate his hownde! . . . 313   Garlande   27
  well] not in MS Cotton Vitellius E.x
Go, litill quaire, /Demene you faire.   355   Garlande   1534
FAITH
Adieu, Jayberd, adue. /I faith, dikkon, thou crue!   108   Epitaphel   63
Now, by your faith, is not this theffect   333   Garlande   737
  by] 'be' †Fakes 1523
FAITHE
And to our faithe moche agreable, ...   382   Replycacion   290
FAITOURS
For frantick faitours half mad and half straught;   138   Ven Tongues   27
FAY
Ay, beshrewe yow! Be my fay   35   Man Margery   1
In fay, man, some rybbys of the motton be so ranke   204   Magnyfycence   2269
FAYER
Yet your contenons oncomly, yor face ys nat fayer.   122   Garneschel   18
FAYLE
Ye maye not fall; truste me, ye maye not fayle.   50   Bowge   170
And whan I fayle, bobbe me on the noll!   53   Bowge   259
Without fayle, syr, that is no nay: 209   Magnyfycence   2429
He caryeth a kyng in hys sleve, yf all the worlde fayle; . . .   243   Speke Parott   429
FAYLED
And that we fayled not for nothynge.   158   Magnyfycence   654
FAYN
An ussher of the hall fayn wold I get   37   Coystrownel   40
FAYNE
Your naturall lord? Alas, I kan not fayne.   30   Dol Dethe   54
He techyth them so wysely to solf and to fayne   38   Coystrownel   53
How there nys thynge that I covet so fayne   44   Balettys3   41
Wyth fables false, that well coude fayne a tale;   49   Bowge   135
His throte was clere and lustely coude fayne.   52   Bowge   233
I wyll not fayne nor forge;   64   Hauke   88
For she dyd but fayne;   89   Phy Sparrow   695
Alas, what shuld I fayne?   97   Phy Sparrow   1011
Yet is she fayne, /Voyde of disdayn, ...   112   Calliope   17
Frendshyp to fayne and thynke full lytherly.   160   Magnyfycence   723
To come to me I trowe he shalbe fayne.   162   Magnyfycence   784
Nowe lap you in a coverlet, full fayne that you may;   197   Magnyfycence   2011
Freers, with foly I make them so fayne   201   Magnyfycence   2147
Were fayne with a chalke /To score on the balke, ...   230   El Rummynge   614
Nowe in valle Ebron Parrot is fayne to fede: 236   Speke Parott   188
They are fayne to play deuz decke.   250   Collyn Clout   166
Relygyous men are fayne /For to tourne agayne   256   Collyn Clout   374
To flatter and to fayne, ...   268   Collyn Clout   861
He wolde have ben ryght fayne   295   Why Come Ye   642
Sume fayne themselfe folys, and wolde be callyd wyse, ...   329   Garlande   616
But flery, flatter and fayne;   362   Albany   135
To flye ye shalbe fayne   368   Albany   371
Ye were fayne to beare fagottes;   376   Replycacion   66
Fayne ye were to reny   377   Replycacion   87
Howe poetes do but fayne?   384   Replycacion   353
FAYNED
I am now constrayned, /With wordes nothing fayned, ...   120   Ag Scottes2   2
Under a fayned treatee.   288   Why Come Ye   365
FAYNYNGE
I hate this faynynge, fye upon it, fye!   59   Bowge   465
FAYNT
Fy, fy, for shame, ther hartis wer to faynt.   30   Dol Dethe   42
What though my penne wax faynt, ...   339   Garlande   954
FAYNTE
For fayth in hym is faynte.   62   Hauke   19

211

FAYNTED —FAYTHE   Page   Title   Line

FAYNTED
	Page	Title	Line
Theyr hertes are so faynted,	269	Collyn Clout	899
The French men he hath faynted,	282	Why Come Ye	157
Your hartes sore faynted,	359	Albany	27

FAYNTY
	Page	Title	Line
And began to paynty /As though she would faynty.	229	El Rummynge	585

FAYRE
	Page	Title	Line
Than Favell gan wyth fayre speche me to fede.	50	Bowge	147
He wyll begyle you and speke fayre to your face.	51	Bowge	200
How my byrde so fayre,	80	Phy Sparrow	343
Upon fayre Cressyde,	88	Phy Sparrow	679
Fayre Lucres, as I wene,	97	Phy Sparrow	1018
Or els fayre Polexene,	97	Phy Sparrow	1019
Enhached on her fayre skyn,	98	Phy Sparrow	1078
Honour to this fayre mayd;	103	Phy Sparrow	1254
And flatered them with fables fayre before theyr face,	160	Magnyfycence	717
Eche thynge is fayre when it is yonge; all hayle, owle!	167	Magnyfycence	970
So farly fayre as it lokys!	168	Magnyfycence	999
To fasten your fansy upon a fayre maystresse	183	Magnyfycence	1550
To make fayre promyse, what are ye the worse?	189	Magnyfycence	1761
In styckynge my selfe with this fayre knyfe.	206	Magnyfycence	2322
Today fayre wether, tomorowe a stormy rage;	213	Magnyfycence	2545
She is ugly fayre:	215	El Rummynge	26
As fayre and as whyte /As the fote of a kyte.	225	El Rummynge	424
Parrot hath a blacke beard and a fayre grene tayle.	233	Speke Parott	84
And silogisari was drowned at Sturbrydge Fayre;	235	Speke Parott	165
The progeny of Parrottis were fayre and favorable;	236	Speke Parott	187
Melpomene, that fayre mayde, she burneshed his beke:	236	Speke Parott	209
Parrot is a fayre byrd for a lady;	236	Speke Parott	211
Yet softe and fayre for swellynge,	271	Collyn Clout	986
But the chefe of your fayre	301	Why Come Ye	909
That speke fayre before the and shrewdly behynde.	329	Garlande	620
'Syt downe, fayre ladys, and do your diligence!	334	Garlande	772
Fayre Diianira surmowntynge in bewte;	337	Garlande	901
As Machareus /Fayre Canace,	338	Garlande	934
And as full of good wyll, /As fayre Isaphill;	341	Garlande	1025
fayre] 'the fayre' MS Cotton Vitellius E.x			
Was never halfe so fayre, as I wene,	342	Garlande	1077
To fayre maistres Anne that shuld have be sent,	347	Garlande	1241

FAYRE-PLAY
	Page	Title	Line
Play fayre-play, madame, and loke ye play clene,	43	Balettys2	41

FAYRER
	Page	Title	Line
Goodly Creisseid, fayrer than Polexene,	336	Garlande	871

FAYREST
	Page	Title	Line
For when he spekyth fayrest, then thynketh he moost yll;	333	Garlande	759

FAYRLY
	Page	Title	Line
My fansy fayrly on her I set;	199	Magnyfycence	2076

FAYTES
	Page	Title	Line
Fortunate in all his *faytes.	368	Albany	398
*faytes] 'fayctes' Scattergood			

FAYTH
	Page	Title	Line
Who spareth to speke, in fayth, he spareth to spede.'	48	Bowge	91
Yf ye have not, in fayth, I wyll you lene	48	Bowge	96
'In fayth,' quod she, 'by Bone aventure.'	49	Bowge	119
'In fayth,' quod Suspecte, 'spake Drede no worde of me?'	51	Bowge	183
Spake he, a fayth, no worde to you of me?	51	Bowge	204
And ay he sange, 'In fayth, Decon, thou crewe.'	56	Bowge	360
'And, syr, in fayth, why comste not us amonge	57	Bowge	379
That of our fayth the grownd is.	62	Hauke	14
For fayth in hym is faynte.	62	Hauke	19
In fayth, broder Largesse, you have a mery mynde.	148	Magnyfycence	292
In fayth, I set not by the worlde two Dauncaster cuttys.	148	Magnyfycence	293
In fayth, I wyll not say that ye shall prove a fole,	148	Magnyfycence	301
For, in fayth, ye be well met.	151	Magnyfycence	402
And yet, in fayth, man, we lacked the	155	Magnyfycence	538
In fayth, and without lyberte there is no bydyng.	158	Magnyfycence	662
In fayth, and Lybertyes rome is there but small.	158	Magnyfycence	663
Nay, in fayth, fyrst let me here thyne.	172	Magnyfycence	1152
In fayth, I can make you bothe folys, and I wyll.	172	Magnyfycence	1173
Thynkyst thou not so, by thy fayth?	175	Magnyfycence	1253
By myne advyse, with you in fayth he shall not rest.	186	Magnyfycence	1660
In fayth, so to suffer he, it is but a skorne.	202	Magnyfycence	2201
By the fayth that I owe to God, and I wyll syt styll.	203	Magnyfycence	2209
Well sayd. But, in fayth, what was your quarell?	203	Magnyfycence	2210
In flattryng fables men fynde but lyttyl fayth;	233	Speke Parott	87
In fayth, Dicken, thou krew, etc.'	280	Why Come Ye	67
He hath in him suche fayth.	290	Why Come Ye	445
In hym small fayth,	297	Why Come Ye	744
The False Fayth that Now Goth, which dayly is renude;	346	Garlande	1179

FAYTHE
	Page	Title	Line
In faythe, els had I gone to longe to scole,	148	Magnyfycence	298
In faythe, Largesse, welcome to me.	151	Magnyfycence	390
In faythe, Largesse I hyght;	155	Magnyfycence	520
In faythe, Mesure is lyke a tetter	155	Magnyfycence	543
In faythe, he were better to dwell in hell.	157	Magnyfycence	623
In faythe, yet am I occupyed with the best;	160	Magnyfycence	705
But whether art thou walkynge, in faythe unfaynyd?	161	Magnyfycence	762
Ye, in faythe, a bolde man and a hardy.	162	Magnyfycence	771

FAYTHFULL —FALL	Page	Title	Line

In faythe, I rule moche of the rost.	163	Magnyfycence	804
Nay, in good faythe. It is but the gyse.	163	Magnyfycence	809
In faythe, Lyberte is nowe a lusty spere.	166	Magnyfycence	937
But, in faythe, I am so occupyed	168	Magnyfycence	1019
Yes, in faythe, I thanke God I may here.	169	Magnyfycence	1059
By my faythe, syr, the frubyssher hath my sworde.	170	Magnyfycence	1063
In faythe, trouthe ye say, we wente togyder to scole.	170	Magnyfycence	1065
In faythe, trouth thou sayst nowe, by God of heven!	170	Magnyfycence	1079
In faythe, man, my brayne is as good as thyne.	170	Magnyfycence	1085
Nowe, in good faythe, thou art a fonde gest.	170	Magnyfycence	1096
In faythe, ellys is there none in all Englonde.	170	Magnyfycence	1099
In faythe, there is not a better dogge for hogges,	171	Magnyfycence	1120
Nay, in faythe, it was but a strype	171	Magnyfycence	1125
In faythe, I wolde thou had a marmosete.	171	Magnyfycence	1132
No? Yes, in faythe; I can versyfy.	172	Magnyfycence	1147
Yes, by my faythe, good Syr Johnn.	173	Magnyfycence	1186
In faythe, I can do mastryes, so I can.	173	Magnyfycence	1190
In good faythe, syr, me semeth he had the more wronge.	178	Magnyfycence	1384
In faythe, and your servyce ryght well shall I acquyte;	190	Magnyfycence	1794
What hast thou gotted, in faythe, to thy share?	201	Magnyfycence	2162
In faythe, of his cofers the bottoms are bare.	201	Magnyfycence	2163
In faythe, he may dreme on a daggeswane for ony fether bed.	201	Magnyfycence	2169
In faythe, and I wyll be to reason agreable.	203	Magnyfycence	2205
In faythe, I gyve the four quarters of a knave.	204	Magnyfycence	2252
In faythe, and I bequethe hym the tothe ake.	204	Magnyfycence	2253
Ye, in faythe; or ellys thou arte to great a glotton.	204	Magnyfycence	2266
Faythe and good hope I make asyde to stonde.	205	Magnyfycence	2288
'In faythe, Dycken, thou krew,	280	Why Come Ye	66
To whom we must gyve faythe,	384	Replycacion	348

FAYTHFULL

For ye have me whome faythfull ye shall fynde;	50	Bowge	166
Faythfull assuraunce with good peradvertaunce.	210	Magnyfycence	2472
Faythfull] 'Faythfully' †Rastell & Treveris C 1530, B			
Be faythfull, trew and just	298	Why Come Ye	753

FAYTORS

All flatringe faytors abhor and from the kast.	34	Dol Dethe	172

FAYTOUR

And false forsworne faytour.	371	Albany	494

FAL

How fortuned you, Magnyfycence, so far to fal behynde?	209	Magnyfycence	2423

FALE

Thow mayst fale downe and ebbe full lowe.	132	Garnesche5	123

FALYRE

This make I my falyre fonny,	220	El Rummynge	229

FALL

Turnd ther backis and let ther master fall,	31	Dol Dethe	94
backis] 'backe' Marshe 1568			
In pevyshnes yet they snapper and fall,	36	Coystrownel	4
they] 'the' †Rastell 1527			
That wyll abyde and never frome us fall.	49	Bowge	130
Ye maye not fall; truste me, ye maye not fayle.	50	Bowge	170
Fyrste pycke a quarell and fall oute with hym then,	55	Bowge	314
Whatsomever aventure therof fall.	55	Bowge	336
To snappar and to fall /Into this opyn cryme;	65	Hauke	142
That the dowves donge downe myght fall	66	Hauke	183
To mornynge loke that ye fall	81	Phy Sparrow	390
On knees to fall /To the foteball;	108	Epitaphel	71
And sende the Frensshe kynge suche another fall.	115	Scot Kynge	73
Now is your pryde fall to decay.	118	Ag Scottes	110
To thefte and bryboury I make some fall,	174	Magnyfycence	1226
Maketh man and woman in foly to fall.	176	Magnyfycence	1295
I shall flappe hym as a fole to fall at my fete.	182	Magnyfycence	1507
And to fall in aquayntaunce with every newe facyon,	183	Magnyfycence	1548
That for your sake I wyll fall on my kne.	186	Magnyfycence	1630
Yet ones agayne I shall fall on my kne	188	Magnyfycence	1708
And where soever you wyll fall to a rekenynge,	190	Magnyfycence	1777
That folowe theyr fansyes in foly to fall.	194	Magnyfycence	1897
Some fall to foly, them selfe for to spyll,	200	Magnyfycence	2139
And some fall prechynge at the Toure Hyll;	200	Magnyfycence	2140
Somtyme to fall, another tyme to beware:	207	Magnyfycence	2374
And nowe ye have had, syr, a wonderous fall,	207	Magnyfycence	2375
Caused me of adversyte to fall in subjeccyon.	209	Magnyfycence	2425
Of the terestre [t]rechery we fall in the flode,	213	Magnyfycence	2559
trechery] 'rechery' †Rastell & Treveris C 1530, B			
Seest thou not what is fall?	219	El Rummynge	182
That she was therewithall /Into a palsey fall;	226	El Rummynge	475
That Latinum fari may fall to rest and slepe,	235	Speke Parott	164
Theyr prymes and houres fall	252	Collyn Clout	241
A fatall fall for one	258	Collyn Clout	473
A fatal] 'All' Kele 1545.1, Marshe 1568, 'Affatuall' MS Lansdowne 762			
That honoure hath a great fall.	262	Collyn Clout	634
And fall in suche decay,	263	Collyn Clout	668
fall] 'false' Kele 1545.1, 'fall' MS Harley 2252			
Howebeit they let downe fall	271	Collyn Clout	978
A noble man may fall,	279	Why Come Ye	22
And fall to rest a whyle;	289	Why Come Ye	397
Or suche chaunce shulde fall /Unto our cardynall!	297	Why Come Ye	748

FALLE —FALSEHODE

	Page	Title	Line
Whan ye fall to redynge	300	Why Come Ye	830
Faire fall that forster that so well can bate his hownde! . . .	313	Garlande	27
well] not in MS Cotton Vitellius E.x			
For that I wolde not with you fall at discorde.	318	Garlande	214
And for your sake how fast to warke they fall:	335	Garlande	811
Finally they fall to carefull confusyon, ...	374	Replycacion	15
Why fall ye at debate /With Skelton laureate, ...	382	Replycacion	300

FALLE

	Page	Title	Line
Yet ther may falle soche caswelte	132	Garnesche5	121
Inordynate pride wyll have a falle.	133	Garnesche5	159

FALLETH

	Page	Title	Line
That he falleth into Acidiam, ...	290	Why Come Ye	466
into] 'in' Marshe 1568; Acidiam] 'Acisiam' †Kele 1545.3, Kitson 1560.7, Marshe 1568			

FALLYBLE

	Page	Title	Line
But fallyble flatery enmyxyd with bytternesse.	212	Magnyfycence	2516
But fallyble flatery enmyxyd with bytternesse.	212	Magnyfycence	2523

FALLYTH

	Page	Title	Line
Yt fallyth for no swyne	126	Garnesche3	86
A fole is he with welth that fallyth at debate.	140	Magnyfycence	5
Howe after a drought there fallyth a showre of rayne	141	Magnyfycence	12

FALLOWS

	Page	Title	Line
And Ryght is over the fallows	358	Garlande2	6
over the] 'ever' Marshe 1568			

FALOWE

	Page	Title	Line
Over the falowe, ...	216	El Rummynge	87

FALS

	Page	Title	Line
Bot ther was fals packinge or els I am begylde, ...	31	Dol Dethe	71
Doublenes hatinge fals maters to compas, ...	33	Dol Dethe	150
For one fals poynt she is wont to kepe in store, ...	45	Balettys4	4
A false abstracte cometh from a fals concrete.	58	Bowge	439
This fals Envy /Sayth that I /Use great folly	95	Phy Sparrow	949
Male uryd was your fals entent	118	Ag Scottes	111
Lyke that untrue rebell /Fals Kayn agaynst Abell.	121	Ag Scottes2	20
Thou fals, stynkyng serpent, ...	128	Garnesche3	171
Fleriing, flatyryng, fals and fykkelle, ...	133	Garnesche5	152
By Jesu Christ, /Fals Scot, thou lyest:	135	Dundas	33
How shuld a fals lying tung then be rewarded?	137	Ven Tongues	2
A fals lying tunge is harde to withholde;	137	Ven Tongues	6
In realmes, in cities, by suche fals abusion.	139	Ven Tongues	56
Of fals fickil tunges suche cloked collusion	139	Ven Tongues	57
A fals double tunge is more fiers and fell	140	Ven Tongues	79
Of fals double tunges in the dispite.	140	Ven Tongues	82
'But ware the cat, Parot, ware the fals cat!'	233	Speke Parott	99
Full ungracyously, /Fals flatery, ...	300	Why Come Ye	853
flatery] 'flatteryng' MS Rawlinson C. 813			
Fals trechery, /Fals brybery, ...	300	Why Come Ye	854
Fals trechery, /Fals brybery, ...	300	Why Come Ye	855
Fals forgers of mony, for kownnage atteintid, ...	329	Garlande	611
kownnage] 'coynnage' Marshe 1568			
Fals flaterers that fawne the, and kurris of kynde	329	Garlande	619
He fyndith fals mesuris out of his fonde fiddill.'	333	Garlande	741
fals mesuris out] 'owght fals mesuris' MS Cotton Vit.E.x			
A fals rekenyng	361	Albany	104
Ye are a fals entrusar, /And a fals abusar, ...	364	Albany	227
Ye are a fals entrusar, /And a fals abusar, ...	364	Albany	228
Adue, adue! /Fals knight and mooste untrue, ...	366	Albany	315
I render the fals rebelle	366	Albany	316
The fals Scottes for dred, ...	371	Albany	512

FALSE

	Page	Title	Line
Wyth fables false, that well coude fayne a tale;	49	Bowge	135
A false abstracte cometh from a fals concrete.	58	Bowge	439
A flaterynge knave and false he is, God wote.	59	Bowge	485
Of false collusyon confetryd by assente, ...	61	Bowge	527
The false cat hath the slayne!	80	Phy Sparrow	330
These vylanous false cattes	80	Phy Sparrow	338
enpoysoned with sclaunder and false detractions &c.	136	Ven Tongues	1
For his false lying, of that I spake never, ...	139	Ven Tongues	75
I wote thou arte false ynoughe for one.	155	Magnyfycence	536
Nay. Thou art a man good inough but for thy false hart. . .	162	Magnyfycence	769
With all his false lore -	257	Collyn Clout	430
Favell is false forsworne, ...	281	Why Come Ye	95
I drede of some false trayne	288	Why Come Ye	363
The False Fayth that Now Goth, which dayly is renude; . . .	346	Garlande	1179
False Scottes are ye.	359	Albany	26
For ye be false echone, ...	362	Albany	132
False and false agayne, ...	362	Albany	133
False and false agayne, ...	362	Albany	133
And their false sedycions, ...	364	Albany	199
What, wold Fraunces, our friar, /Be suche a false lyar, . .	368	Albany	374
Moost false attaynted traytour, ...	371	Albany	493
And false forsworne faytour.	371	Albany	494

FALSE HARTED

	Page	Title	Line
Nay, thou false harted dastarde! Thou dare not abyde. . . .	202	Magnyfycence	2193

FALSEHODE

	Page	Title	Line
Full moche flatery and falsehode I hyde;	177	Magnyfycence	1358

FALSELY —FAMOUS   Page   Title   Line

FALSELY
Full falsely on you they lye,	255	Collyn Clout	334
Howe falsely ye had surmysed,	380	Replycacion	209

FALSENESSE
Fyckell falsenesse, /Varyablenesse, /With unstablenesse.	247	Collyn Clout	44

FALSEST
And falsest forsworne /That ever were borne.	362	Albany	117

FALSHOD
Ye may be assured /Your falshod discured	362	Albany	128

FALSHODE
Bot all they fled from hym for falshode or fere.	31	Dol Dethe	91
Falshode in felowshyp is my sworne brother.	160	Magnyfycence	713

FALSLY
Falsly to slo ther moste singlar goode lorde?	30	Dol Dethe	27
slo] 'slee' Marshe 1568			
Agaynst whom he dyd fyght /Falsly agaynst all right,	120	Ag Scottes2	18
And falsly ye me reporte.	124	Garnesche3	20

FALS QUARTER
Some lokyd full smothely, and had a fals quarter,	326	Garlande	504
quarter] 'quart' Marshe 1568			

FAME
O grounde ungracious, unhappy be thy fame,	32	Dol Dethe	116
What nedethe me for to extoll his fame	33	Dol Dethe	141
Wherby I rede theyr renome and theyr fame	46	Bowge	15
Disparaged is her fame	89	Phy Sparrow	711
Whose fame by me shall sprede	93	Phy Sparrow	885
In the courte of Fame;	94	Phy Sparrow	892
Thereof the fame dothe blow,	110	Lawde	4
Laureat to be /Of fame royall;	112	Calliope	8
Syr, as ye say. I have harde of your fame.	141	Magnyfycence	26
To assure you of my noble porte and fame,	145	Magnyfycence	163
But hyght you, Largesse, encreace of noble fame?	148	Magnyfycence	271
And I truste to ratyfye and amende your fame.	208	Magnyfycence	2398
Of renowne and of fame	270	Collyn Clout	958
Of renowme and worldly fame	293	Why Come Ye	569
His fame to be encrest	309	Why Come Ye	1214
To whome supplyed the royall Quene of Fame.	313	Garlande	49
The Quene of Fame to Dame Pallas	313	Garlande	R
With laureate tryumphe in the courte of Fame.	314	Garlande	63
Dame Pallas to the Quene of Fame	314	Garlande	R
The Quene of Fame to Dame Pallas	315	Garlande	R
Dame Pallas to the Quene of Fame	316	Garlande	R
The Quene of Fame to Dame Pallas	316	Garlande	R
Dame Pallas to the Quene of Fame	317	Garlande	R
The Quene of Fame to Dame Pallas	318	Garlande	R
Unto your palas, our noble courte of Fame,	318	Garlande	219
Dame Pallas to the Quene of Fame	318	Garlande	R
There was suyng to the Quene of Fame;	319	Garlande	253
Propercius and Pisandros, poetis of noble fame;	322	Garlande	382
Of noble Fame before the Quenes grace,	324	Garlande	419
Into the ryche palace of the Quene of Fame:	325	Garlande	450
Wherin was set of Fame the noble Quene,	325	Garlande	482
Ther names recountyng in the court of Fame;	334	Garlande	781
For to deserve /Inmortall fame.	339	Garlande	967
Inmortall] 'The courte of' MS Cotton Vitellius E.x			
Before my ladys grace, the Quene of Fame,	343	Garlande	1091
Of Fame. Perceyvynge how that I was cum,	343	Garlande	1115
The Quene of Fame to Skelton	344	Garlande	R
Skelton Poeta to the Quene of Fame	344	Garlande	R
The Quene of Fame to Occupacioun	345	Garlande	R
Suppleyng to Fame, I besought her grace,	353	Garlande	1478
The Quene of Fame commaundid shett fast the boke,	354	Garlande	1510
That so indede /Your fame may sprede	355	Garlande	1551
The fame matryculate /Of poetes laureate.	384	Replycacion	357

FAMES
Of Fames court, by all our holl assent	324	Garlande	433
In Fames court reportyng the same;	334	Garlande	783

FAMILIARS
Of Tullis Familiars the translacyoun;	346	Garlande	1185

FAMYLYARYTE
The famylyaryte, the formar dalyaunce,	42	Balettys2	2

FAMYS
Occupacyon, Famys regestary,	326	Garlande	522

FAMOUS
Of famous princis and lordis of astate,	29	Dol Dethe	16
The famous Erle of Northumberlande;	32	Dol Dethe	107
As famous poetes say;	74	Phy Sparrow	88
The famous poettes saturicall,	133	Garnesche5	139
But of that famous oratour, I say,	316	Garlande	158
Some famous wetewoldis, and they be moche wurs;	317	Garlande	187
All famous poetis ensuynge after me	321	Garlande	321
Mayster Terence, the famous comicar,	322	Garlande	353
comicar] 'conucar' †Fakes 1523			
Poggeus also, that famous Florentine,	322	Garlande	372
Plutarke and Petrarke, two famous clarkis;	322	Garlande	379
Of porturature which was the famous Greke,	337	Garlande	895
In famous glory all other transcendyng,	344	Garlande	1129

FAMOUSLY

	Page	Title	Line
And famously proclamed?	103	Phy Sparrow	1257
So that there workis myght famously be sene,	314	Garlande	67
The cause why Demostenes so famously is brutid	316	Garlande	155

FAMULY
Togeder with servauntis of his famuly,	31	Dol Dethe	93

FAMUS
Chaucer, that famus clerke,	91	Phy Sparrow	800

FANCHYRCHE
Ye have a fantasy to Fanchyrche strete,	130	Garnesche5	41

FANGE
And he may fange us.	308	Why Come Ye	1156
And] 'That' Kitson 1560.7, Marshe 1568			

FANSY
What, Fansy! Fansy!	149	Magnyfycence	325
What, Fansy! Fansy!	149	Magnyfycence	325
Me thought he called Fan[s]y.	149	Magnyfycence	327
fansy] 'fanfy' †Rastell & Treveris C 1530, B			
Me thought he called Fansy me behynde.	149	Magnyfycence	329
Fansy hath cachyd in a flye net	151	Magnyfycence	403
But Fansy, my frende, where have ye bene so longe?	154	Magnyfycence	500
Yet Fansy had ben dysc[r]yved.	155	Magnyfycence	535
dyscryved] 'dysceyved' †Rastell & Treveris C 1530, B			
Ryght so a sharp fansy must be founde	155	Magnyfycence	553
Your fansy maketh myne elbowe to ake.	156	Magnyfycence	559
By God, syr, this is Fansy Small-Brayne;	156	Magnyfycence	583
A, Fansy, Fansy, God sende the brayne!	157	Magnyfycence	608
A, Fansy, Fansy, God sende the brayne!	157	Magnyfycence	608
Fansy and I, we twayne,	158	Magnyfycence	639
Tusshe! Fonnysshe Fansy, thou arte frantyke.	158	Magnyfycence	650
Ye. My fansy was out of owle flyght,	159	Magnyfycence	671
That Fansy with his fonde consayte	159	Magnyfycence	678
Here cometh in FANSY craynge 'Stow, stow!'	165	Magnyfycence	SD
What! Fansy, my frende! Howe dost thou fare?	166	Magnyfycence	920
Lo, this is /My fansy, iwys;	167	Magnyfycence	972
What, Fansy! Arte thou here alone?	169	Magnyfycence	1044
What, frantyke Fansy, in a foles case?	169	Magnyfycence	1046
Yet for my fansy sake, I say,	171	Magnyfycence	1100
What, Fansy! Let me se who is the tother.	172	Magnyfycence	1158
Thou must have thy fansy and thy wyll,	173	Magnyfycence	1183
Hem, Fansy! Regardes, voyes [vous].	173	Magnyfycence	1197
Nay, but fansy must be eyther fyrst or last.	176	Magnyfycence	1288
Howe frantyke fansy fyrst of all	176	Magnyfycence	1294
For, frantyke Fansy, thou makyst men madde;	176	Magnyfycence	1300
But, for the, Fansy, Magnyfycence abydes.	176	Magnyfycence	1305
Foly and fansy all where every man dothe face and brace.	177	Magnyfycence	1330
Foly fotyth it properly, fansy ledyth the dawnce,	177	Magnyfycence	1331
Here cometh in FANSY.	179	Magnyfycence	SD
Here goeth out FELYCYTE, LYBERTE and FANSY.	180	Magnyfycence	SD
To fasten your fansy upon a fayre maystresse	183	Magnyfycence	1550
Here FANSY cometh in.	192	Magnyfycence	SD
That you trustyd, and Fansy is my name;	193	Magnyfycence	1871
My fansy fayrly on her I set;	199	Magnyfycence	2076
But by the way of fansy insolence,	200	Magnyfycence	2116
A ha, fansy and foly met with you, I trowe.	210	Magnyfycence	2448

FANSYES
And let all your fansyes upon them rest.	190	Magnyfycence	1770
That folowe theyr fansyes in foly to fall.	194	Magnyfycence	1897
To full of fansyes, to lordly, to prowde,	199	Magnyfycence	2093

FANSY-SERVYCE
Frantyke Fansy-Servyce I hyght;	169	Magnyfycence	1023

FANTASIES
The enfatuate fantasies, the wytles wylfulnes	242	Speke Parott	384

FANTASY
Nor yet no vyllany, /But only fantasy;	100	Phy Sparrow	1135
Ye have a fantasy to Fanchyrche strete,	130	Garnesche5	41
Of frantycke frenesy /And folysshe fantasy,	283	Why Come Ye	187
Garnysshed fresshe after my fantasy,	313	Garlande	39

FANTASYES
I can fynde fantasyes where none is;	169	Magnyfycence	1041
For so with fantasyes my wyt dothe flete	170	Magnyfycence	1080
That folowe fonde fantasyes and vertu refuse.	175	Magnyfycence	1281
For thou fourmest suche fantasyes in theyr mynde	175	Magnyfycence	1284

FANTASTICALL
enbrased and enterlased with a moche fantasticall frenesy	374	Replycacion	1

FANTSY
To fat is hys fantsy, hys wyt is to lene.	37	Coystrownel	28

FAR
Alas, ye madmen, to far ye did excede.	31	Dol Dethe	60
Transcending f[a]r myne homely Muse that must	33	Dol Dethe	144
far] 'for' †MS Royal 18 D.ii, Marshe 1568			
Illumynyd wyth feturys far passyng my reporte;	44	Balettys3	23
That be so far abusyd /They cannot be excusyd	62	Hauke	5
All grace is far hym fro.	62	Hauke	16
That so far dyd excede;	67	Hauke	191
To far from the porpose,	126	Garnesche3	97
Rayle not so far.	136	Dundas	63
The amense therof is far to call agayne;	140	Magnyfycence	9

FARDER —FARVENT	Page	Title	Line

FARDER

How fortuned you, Magnyfycence, so far to fal behynde?	209	Magnyfycence	2423
It was dere that was far fet!	223	El Rummynge	334
Some run to far before, some run to far behynde,	233	Speke Parott	76
Some run to far before, some run to far behynde,	233	Speke Parott	76
For as far as they can spy	308	Why Come Ye	1172
they] 'the' †Kele 1545.3			
'So have ye me far passynge my meretis extollyd,	324	Garlande	435
How far it was, or ellis within what howris,	325	Garlande	457
far] not in †Fakes 1523			
Of cristall the clerenes theis waters far past,	330	Garlande	660
Far, far passynge /That I can endyght,	341	Garlande	1016
Far, far passynge /That I can endyght,	341	Garlande	1016
Far may be sought	341	Garlande	1031
Ye muse somwhat to far;	368	Albany	377

FARDER

They wyll no farder go.	269	Collyn Clout	908

FARE

Full daynnously, and fro me she dyde fare,	48	Bowge	82
To turney or to tante with me ye ar to fare to seke.	123	Garnesche2	37
Also nat fare from Bowgy Row,	130	Garnesche5	47
Nothynge but fare you well tyll sone -	149	Magnyfycence	319
What! Fansy, my frende! Howe dost thou fare?	166	Magnyfycence	920
Howe evyll theyr shepe fare.'	250	Collyn Clout	131
Zeuxes, that enpicturid fare Elene the quene,	337	Garlande	892
Unto the legend of fare Laodomi.	339	Garlande	972

FAREST

What, brother braynsyke, how farest thou?	192	Magnyfycence	1845

FARETH

Alas! My stomake fareth as it wolde cast.	188	Magnyfycence	1726

FAREWELL

Farewell tyll soone. But no word that I sayde!'	51	Bowge	175
Farewell Phyllyp, adew;	80	Phy Sparrow	331
Farewell without restore,	80	Phy Sparrow	333
Farewell for evermore!	80	Phy Sparrow	334
Farewell, my frende. Adue tyll sone.	167	Magnyfycence	966
Farewell benygnyte, /Farewell symplycyte,	261	Collyn Clout	589
Farewell benygnyte, /Farewell symplycyte,	261	Collyn Clout	590
Farewell humylyte, /Farewell good charyte!	261	Collyn Clout	591
Farewell humylyte, /Farewell good charyte!	261	Collyn Clout	592
Farewell, than, have good day!	280	Why Come Ye	57
Than farewell to the, /Welthfull Felycite;	300	Why Come Ye	860
Welthfull] 'Welthe full of felycyte' MS Rawlinson C. 813			

FARE WELL

'Fare well,' quod he, 'we wyll talke more of this.'	52	Bowge	227
Gyve me your honde, fare well and have good daye.'	60	Bowge	497
Then fare well thryfte, by hym that crosse kyst!	179	Magnyfycence	1416
Than waste must be welcome, and fare well thryfte.	180	Magnyfycence	1444
Fare well tyll sone; adue tyll to morowe.	192	Magnyfycence	1850

FAR-FET

Deyntes for dammoysels, chaffer far-fet;	234	Speke Parott	129

FARLE

Cockys bonys! It is a farle freke.	172	Magnyfycence	1160

FARLY

To mastres Anne, that farly swete,	41	Coystrowne4	29
Nay. It is a farly fowle.	166	Magnyfycence	923
So farly fayre as it lokys!	168	Magnyfycence	999
This is a farly fytte	255	Collyn Clout	329
farly] 'fearfull' †Godfray 1531, Kele 1545.1, Marshe 1568,			
'ffarly' MS Harley 2252			
Of suche a farly freke,	366	Albany	303

FARRE

To claterynge, to chaterynge, to shorte, and to farre,	199	Magnyfycence	2096
No, no; for thy synnys be so excedynge farre,	205	Magnyfycence	2300
Her youth is farre past;	215	El Rummynge	48
Paregall with all prynces, farre passyng hys estate;	244	Speke Parott	436
So myche forcastyng, and so farre an after-dele;	244	Speke Parott	463
For, as farre as I can see,	248	Collyn Clout	59
Nor how farre Temple Barre is	267	Collyn Clout	826
And as farre as they dare set,	269	Collyn Clout	932
And sayle nat farre abrode,	277	Collyn Clout	1256
And so farre blynded,	295	Why Come Ye	660
Farre by yonde Portyngale,	299	Why Come Ye	802
The sygnes xii for to beholde a farre,	312	Garlande	2
Eolus, your trumpet, that knowne is so farre,	319	Garlande	235
that] 'whiche' MS Cotton Vitellius E.x			
There apparell farre passynge beyonde that I can tell;	323	Garlande	394

FARRE FET

A, so! That syghe was farre fet!	199	Magnyfycence	2071

FARTE

A master, a mynstrell, a fydler, a farte.	38	Coystrownel	56

FARTHER

We wyll no farther ryme /Of it at this tyme.	220	El Rummynge	240
Farther in this broke,	266	Collyn Clout	782
Nor farther for to loke	266	Collyn Clout	783
Is farther than their wytte wyll reche.	374	Replycacion	13
to be farther delated and contynued,	374	Replycacion	1

FARVENT

Of farvent charyte I quenche out the bronde;	205	Magnyfycence	2287

FAST —FAUTE

FAST
	Page	Title	Line
Stabille thy mynde constant to be and fast,	34	Dol Dethe	170
They thronge in fast and flocked her aboute,	49	Bowge	122
He ran as fast as ever that he myghte.	58	Bowge	415
Fast boltyd and barryd,	64	Hauke	92
Of hym that wryteth to fast.	143	Magnyfycence	91
Hens, thou haynyarde, out of dores fast!	188	Magnyfycence	1725
They catche that catche may, kepe and holde fast,	189	Magnyfycence	1750
Lyke as they were with buckels /Togyder made fast.	215	El Rummynge	47
Therfore stande sure and fast.	273	Collyn Clout	1071
Set hym fast by the fete!	275	Collyn Clout	1166
The tyme dothe fast ensew	280	Why Come Ye	62
Set hym fast by the fete!'	289	Why Come Ye	426
And of the winter days that hy them so fast,	331	Garlande	700
And for your sake how fast to warke they fall:	335	Garlande	811
'Withdrawe your hande, the tyme passis fast.	343	Garlande	1086
The Quene of Fame commaundid shett fast the boke,	354	Garlande	1510
He turnyd his tirikkis, his volvell ran fast,	354	Garlande	1517
And the twayne last /Be withholde so fast	358	Garlande2	13
I make you fast and sure,	380	Replycacion	232

FASTE
His eyen rollynge, his hondes faste they quoke;	51	Bowge	193
And as they came, the shypborde faste I hente,	61	Bowge	530
Syn Dewcalyons flodde, I make the faste and sure.	246	Speke Parott	511
They presid in faste; some thought they were to longe;	319	Garlande	248

FASTEN
To fasten your fansy upon a fayre maystresse	183	Magnyfycence	1550

FASTYNGE
Whan hys grace ys fastynge,	126	Garnesche3	83

FAT
To fat is hys fantsy, hys wyt is to lene.	37	Coystrowne1	28
She is made for the malarde fat.	166	Magnyfycence	926
All foggy fat she was;	226	El Rummynge	483
And Og, that fat hog of Basan, doth retayne	234	Speke Parott	122
of] 'or' Kynge & Marche 1554, Day 1560, Marshe 1568			
'His heed is so fat	247	Collyn Clout	16

FATALL
O Atropos, of the fatall systers iij,	32	Dol Dethe	120
I drede no dyntes of fatall desteny.	190	Magnyfycence	1798
A fatall fall for one	258	Collyn Clout	473
A fatal] 'All' Kele 1545.1, Marshe 1568, 'Affatuall' MS Lansdowne 762			
Or it procedyd of fatall persuacyon,	313	Garlande	34
O fatall Fortune, what have I offendid?	321	Garlande	316

FATE
The dedely fate, the dolefulle destenny	29	Dol Dethe	2
Of ther good lord the fate and dedely chaunce.	34	Dol Dethe	189
Tyll cruell fate made him to dy:	86	Phy Sparow	592
'Fate, fate, fate, ye Irysh water-lag.'	233	Speke Parott	86
'Fate, fate, fate, ye Irysh water-lag.'	233	Speke Parott	86
'Fate, fate, fate, ye Irysh water-lag.'	233	Speke Parott	86
Encrownyd as empresse of all this wordly fate,	325	Garlande	486
wordly] 'worldly' Marshe 1568			
Whom fortune and fate playnly have discust	337	Garlande	881
Of Phillip Sparow the lamentable fate,	348	Garlande	1254

FATHER
The Father, the Son, the Holy Goste,	35	Dol Dethe	216
Though his father were a kyng;	89	Phy Sparow	698
Though ye untruly your father have slayne,	118	Ag Scottes	119
Do as moche as for myne owne father.	186	Magnyfycence	1642
That nother they set by father and mother;	200	Magnyfycence	2142
But nowe every spirytuall father,	251	Collyn Clout	174
Lost all his father wan.	285	Why Come Ye	271
all his] 'al that his' Toy 1553, Kitson 1560.7, Marshe 1568			

FATHERS
Of your fathers bote,	78	Phy Sparow	249

FATTE
With porpose and graundepose he may fede hym fatte,	239	Speke Parott	308
So many plucte partryches, and so fatte quaylles;	245	Speke Parott	486
So fatte a magott, bred of a flesshe-flye;	246	Speke Parott	509
To fatte theyr bodyes full,	250	Collyn Clout	128

FAUCON
The faucon from the crow,	298	Why Come Ye	775

FAUCONER
The fauconer then was prest,	63	Hauke	71
prest] 'priest' Kynge & Marche 1554, Day 1560			

FAUGHT
And lyke marciall Hector he faught them agayne	31	Dol Dethe	88

FAULT
What fault find ye herein but may be avowed.	138	Ven Tongues	41

FAUTE
Yet some men fynde a faute,	92	Phy Sparow	811
Than to be founde in any such faute.	137	Ven Tongues	25
Syr, as I say, there was no faute in me.	180	Magnyfycence	1426
For in hoder-moder /The churche is put in faute.	248	Collyn Clout	70
In you the faute is supposed	253	Collyn Clout	264
And all the faute they lay	256	Collyn Clout	402
the faute] not in Kele 1545.1, Marshe 1568			

FAVELL —FEDE   Page   Title   Line

  One faute or other in them shalbe notyd.   318   Garlande   203
FAVELL
  The fyrste was Favell, full of flatery, ...   49   Bowge   134
  Than Favell gan wyth fayre speche me to fede.   50   Bowge   147
  'By Cryste,' quod Favell, 'Drede is soleyne freke!   51   Bowge   187
  My tonge is with favell forked and tyned.   160   Magnyfycence   727
  Favell is false forsworne, ...   281   Why Come Ye   95
FAVER
  Cannyst thou helpe in faver that I myght be brought?   162   Magnyfycence   777
FAVERYD
  Her fethers donne; /Well faveryd bonne!   168   Magnyfycence   990
FAVYR
  Brynges yow out of favyr with alle femall teggys: 122   Garneschel   31
  How the favyr of your face   124   Garnesche3   9
  Ye loste hyr favyr quyt!   125   Garnesche3   67
FAVORABLE
  Of all your feturs favorable to make tru discripcion, ...   42   Balettys2   8
  The progeny of Parrottis were fayre and favorable;   236   Speke Parott   187
FAVORE
  Is called Favore to stonde in her good grace.'   47   Bowge   55
FAVOUR
  Knolege, aquayntance, resort, favour, with grace;   43   Balettys3   1
  There can no favour nor frendshyp hym forsake.   48   Bowge   103
  And we asked favoure, and favour she us gave.   49   Bowge   126
  Her favour of her face   96   Phy Sparrow   1002
  All with favour fret, ...   98   Phy Sparrow   1048
  Her favour to wyn;   98   Phy Sparrow   1082
  Syr, then, with the favour of your benynge sufferaunce, . . .   182   Magnyfycence   1519
  For in my favour I have you feffyd and seasyd.   183   Magnyfycence   1536
  But Parrot hath no favour to Esebon;   233   Speke Parott   111
  The favour of ladys with wordis electe, ...   314   Garlande   76
  'Madame, with favour of your benynge sufferaunce, ...   315   Garlande   113
  In fortunis favour ever to endure, ...   351   Garlande   1402
FAVOURE
  That ye shall stonde in favoure and in grace.   49   Bowge   105
  And we asked favoure, and favour she us gave.   49   Bowge   126
  Favoure we have toughther than ony elme, ...   49   Bowge   129
    toughther] 'tougher' Wynkyn de Worde 1510, Marshe 1568
  Ye stonde in favoure and Fortune is your gyde, ...   50   Bowge   171
  I have a favoure to you, wherof it be   52   Bowge   206
  The favoure that ye have with my lady.   53   Bowge   270
  Her favoure to purchase.   98   Phy Sparrow   1076
  But whome that ye favoure, I se well, hath a name, ...   317   Garlande   176
FAWCHYN
  Or I shal fawchyn thy flesshe and scrape the on the skyn. . . .   202   Magnyfycence   2189
FAWCON
  Also the noble fawcon, /With the gerfawcon, ...   85   Phy Sparrow   556
FAWCONER
  But the fawconer unfayned   64   Hauke   81
  Thys fawconer then gan showte, ...   65   Hauke   119
    then] not in Day 1560, Marshe 1568
FAWCOUN
  Jentill as fawcoun /Or hawke of the towre;   340   Garlande   1006
  Jentyll as fawcoun /Or hawke of the towre, ...   341   Garlande   1021
  Jentyll as fawcoun /Or hawke of the towre.   341   Garlande   1036
FAWNE
  Fals flaterers that fawne the, and kurris of kynde   329   Garlande   619
FAWT
  Yet harde is to make but sum fawt be founde.'   315   Garlande   112
FAWTE
  All left alone, alas, he fawte in vayne!   32   Dol Dethe   104
  He wente aboute to take me in a fawte: 55   Bowge   318
FE
  Alasse! Where is nowe my golde and fe?   196   Magnyfycence   1967
FEARE
  And brynge[s] them in suche feare.   286   Why Come Ye   306
    brynges] 'brynge' †Kele 1545.3, Toy 1553, Kitson 1560.7,
    Marshe 1568
  Withouten drede or feare!   298   Why Come Ye   759
  For feare thou shoulde be slayne   365   Albany   247
  And for feare par case   367   Albany   351
  And feare leest they be out   380   Replycacion   225
FEATES
  Ye have in feates of warre.   364   Albany   225
FEBLE
  His hede maye be harde, but feble is his brayne!   46   Bowge   24
    his] not in Marshe 1568
  O feble fortune, O doulfull destyny!   198   Magnyfycence   2048
FEBLE-FANTASTYCALL
  Thou art so feble-fantastycall, ...   170   Magnyfycence   1072
FEBLER
  Was moch more febler brayned.   64   Hauke   82
FEBLY
  and yet they were but febly enformed   374   Replycacion   I
FED
  And fed him with my spattyl, ...   80   Phy Sparrow   358
FEDE
  Than Favell gan wyth fayre speche me to fede.   50   Bowge   147

FEDERIS —FELYCYTE   Page   Title   Line

Entry	Page	Title	Line
To fede a fole, and for to preye a dawe.	58	Bowge	437
preye] 'preue' Wynkyn de Worde 1510			
His hawke shulde pray and fede /Upon a pigeons maw.	63	Hauke	56
Christi crucifixi /To fede uppon your fisty;	69	Hauke	291
Myght fede them on thy braynes!	79	Phy Sparrow	295
I can fede forth a fole and lede hym by the eyre;	160	Magnyfycence	712
It is best I fede my hawke now.	167	Magnyfycence	968
It is great almesse the hung[re] to fede,	177	Magnyfycence	1344
hungre] 'hunger' †Rastell & Treveris C 1530, B			
Nowe in valle Ebron Parrot is fayne to fede:	236	Speke Parott	188
With porpose and graundepose he may fede hym fatte,	239	Speke Parott	308
Howe they take no hede /Theyr sely shepe to fede,	248	Collyn Clout	77
Fede hym with beanes and pease!	275	Collyn Clout	1170
FEDERIS			
To shake my pygyons federis	69	Hauke	281
FEDERS			
With the feders of a quale	226	El Rummynge	453
FEE			
Alas his golde, his fee, his annuall rente,	32	Dol Dethe	97
In fee, as menyall men of his housholb,	34	Dol Dethe	185
And he shold be bought /For golde and fee,	76	Phy Sparrow	196
To counterfet thyr counsell they gyve me a fee.	154	Magnyfycence	491
And he go to the devyll, so that I may have my fee,	187	Magnyfycence	1670
Let neyther patent scape them nor fee;	190	Magnyfycence	1776
FEED			
And so the Scrybe was feed,	65	Hauke	151
FEERE			
We nede never feere	303	Why Come Ye	974
'We nedyd never to feyre' MS Rawlinson C. 813			
FEES			
And yet she brought her fees,	225	El Rummynge	428
And for to have his fees,	267	Collyn Clout	839
FEE SYMPLENES			
And of our fee symplenes	275	Collyn Clout	1175
fee] 'fre' Kele 1545.1, Marshe 1568, not in MS Harley 2252			
FEEST			
At every solempne feest,	309	Why Come Ye	1215
At the feest of her concepcion	376	Replycacion	67
FEFFYD			
For in my favour I have you feffyd and seasyd.	183	Magnyfycence	1536
FEIGHTYNGE			
He wyll set men a feightynge and syt hymselfe styll,	333	Garlande	761
set] 'stir' MS Cotton Vitellius E.x; a feightynge]			
'to brawlyng' MS Cotton Vitellius E.x			
FEYNE			
Then feyne yourselfe dyseased, and make yourselfe seke.	185	Magnyfycence	1612
FEYTIS			
Of the feytis of war	297	Why Come Ye	719
FEL			
They are fel as any fyre!	285	Why Come Ye	249
FELASHYP			
Or 'Shall I sayle wyth you' a felashyp assaye?	53	Bowge	254
FELAWES			
Me thoughte I see lewde felawes here and there	61	Bowge	528
FELDE			
Wan they the felde and lost theyr kynge?	115	Ag Scottes	3
They say they had /And wan the felde /With spere and shelde!	116	Ag Scottes	15
In a felde of grene peson	127	Garnesche3	127
Into a felde she brought me wyde and large,	328	Garlande	568
In playn felde and battayle.	364	Albany	205
Thou durst no felde derayne,	365	Albany	243
FELDEFARE			
The feldefare and the snyte;	82	Phy Sparrow	412
FELDFARE			
The feldfare wolde have fydled, and it wolde not frame;	192	Magnyfycence	1838
FELE			
I fele my body quake,	74	Phy Sparrow	105
By my syers soule, I fele no rayne.	170	Magnyfycence	1087
How fele you your selfe, my frend? How is your mynde?	208	Magnyfycence	2389
Full gloryously can he glose, thy mynde for to fele;	333	Garlande	760
FELETH			
And feleth hymselfe sycke,	274	Collyn Clout	1123
FELICITE			
That welthe and felicite is passynge small.	141	Magnyfycence	21
For Welthfull Felicite truly is my name.	141	Magnyfycence	23
FELYCE			
Of Felyce fetewse and lytell prety Cate,	56	Bowge	370
FELYCITE			
Than farewell to the, /Welthfull Felycite;	300	Why Come Ye	861
Welthfull] 'Welthe full of felycyte' MS Rawlinson C. 813			
FELYCYTE			
Or howe can you prove that there is felycyte,	142	Magnyfycence	77
Pleasyth, your grace, Felycyte they me call.	145	Magnyfycence	171
And from felycyte may not be forborne,	146	Magnyfycence	220
Thynke you that mynne frende Felycyte?	147	Magnyfycence	245
Here cometh in MAGNYFYCENCE with LYBERTE and FELYCYTE.	178	Magnyfycence	SD
Nay, nay; not so, my frende Felycyte.	179	Magnyfycence	1392
Come hyther Largesse; take here Felycyte.	179	Magnyfycence	1411

FELL —FERE

	Page	Title	Line
Mayster Felycyte, let be your chydynge;	180	Magnyfycence	1437
Here goeth out FELYCYTE, LYBERTE and FANSY.	180	Magnyfycence	SD
I folowe in felycyte without reversse;	181	Magnyfycence	1491
I have set my hole felycyte,	190	Magnyfycence	1788
Your welthe and felycyte, I trust we shall optayne	190	Magnyfycence	1792
For Lyberte is gone, and also Felycyte.	192	Magnyfycence	1857
And had robbyd you quyte from all felycyte.	193	Magnyfycence	1864
That may restore you agayne to felycyte,	196	Magnyfycence	1998
That nowe he hath loste all his felycyte;	200	Magnyfycence	2114
There to indeuer with all felycyte.	214	Magnyfycence	2569

FELL

	Page	Title	Line
Neyther flesh nor fell.	39	Coystrowne3	18
nor] 'not' Marshe 1568			
So fersly he fytyth, hys mynde is so fell,	43	Balettys2	29
And under the fell oft festerd is the sore:	45	Balettys4	5
The hawke with that clap /Fell downe with evyll hap.	64	Hauke	90
Fell downe on thys manner.	64	Hauke	115
I fell downe to the grounde.	72	Phy Sparrow	36
A fals double tunge is more fiers and fell	140	Ven Tongues	79
That fell amonge us this same day?	166	Magnyfycence	933
Tyll, as the devyll wolde, they fell a chydynge	166	Magnyfycence	940
Yes, yes. He fell with me also at debate.	166	Magnyfycence	944
And forthwith fell on slepe.	224	El Rummynge	375
And fell so wyde open	227	El Rummynge	496
But whan the frere fell in the well	268	Collyn Clout	877
He is so fyers and fell.	295	Why Come Ye	650
This Naman Sirus, /So fell and so irous,	308	Why Come Ye	1167
Sirus] 'tyrus' MS Rawlinson C. 813			
In slumbrynge I fell and halfe in a slepe;	313	Garlande	30
This Duke so fell /Of Albany, /So cowardly	359	Albany	6

FELLE

	Page	Title	Line
Ye fowle, fers and felle, as Syr Ferumbras the ffreke,	122	Garnesche1	15
Your brethe yt ys so felle	127	Garnesche3	142
I sey, thow felle and fowle flessh fly,	131	Garnesche5	65

FELOWE

	Page	Title	Line
Howe be it, that fonde felowe is a mery knave.	180	Magnyfycence	1455
By Cockes woundes, a wonder felowe thou arte!	185	Magnyfycence	1619
Her felowe dyd stammer and stut,	223	El Rummynge	339

FELOWES

	Page	Title	Line
To make the mery, as other felowes done?	57	Bowge	380
Commyttynge to me and to my felowes twayne	190	Magnyfycence	1791

FELOWSHYP

	Page	Title	Line
Falshode in felowshyp is my sworne brother.	160	Magnyfycence	713
Nowe, of good felowshyp, let me by thy [d]ogge.	170	Magnyfycence	1082
dogge] 'hogge' †Rastell & Treveris C 1530, B			
To felowshyp with foly I can hym brynge.	174	Magnyfycence	1215

FELT

	Page	Title	Line
Betwene his armes, he felt her body quake.	320	Garlande	301

FEMALE

	Page	Title	Line
That on suche a female my flesshe wolde be wroken.	184	Magnyfycence	1566

FEMALL

	Page	Title	Line
Bryngges yow out of favyr with alle femall teggys:	122	Garnesche1	31

FEN

	Page	Title	Line
In Lerna the Grekes fen,	105	Phy Sparrow	1328
In Lerna the Grekis fen	349	Garlande	1321

FENAUNCE

	Page	Title	Line
With thi blode precious our fenaunce thou dyd pay	34	Dol Dethe	195

FENDE

	Page	Title	Line
That lyke a fende doth stare;	73	Phy Sparrow	77
To the flingande fende of helle.	366	Albany	317
The fende scrache out your mawes!	371	Albany	479

FENDYS

	Page	Title	Line
And us redemede from the fendys pray.	34	Dol Dethe	196
Nor to the lake /Of fendys blake.	40	Coystrowne3	48
Of the fendys blake;	303	Why Come Ye	975

FENESTRALL

	Page	Title	Line
And of Castell Aungell the fenestrall,	351	Garlande	1387

FER

	Page	Title	Line
In a trone whiche fer clerer dyde shyne	47	Bowge	60
clerer] 'clere' Marshe 1568			
Who county[th] without me is caste to fer behynde	146	Magnyfycence	214
countyth] 'countyd' †Rastell & Treveris C 1530, B			
That all is without measure and fer beyonde the mone.	146	Magnyfycence	224
And so fer thou arte behynde of thy rent,	205	Magnyfycence	2294

FERCE

	Page	Title	Line
To ferce for none offence,	278	Why Come Ye	4
As ferce and as cruell	294	Why Come Ye	593

FERE

	Page	Title	Line
Bot all they fled from hym for falshode or fere.	31	Dol Dethe	91
But absens, alas, wyth tremelyng fere and drede,	44	Balettys3	34
Wherfore I fere ye wyll suffre payne.	114	Scot Kynge	28
But never was I in gretter fere.	150	Magnyfycence	345
I fere nothynge Fortunes perplexyte.	181	Magnyfycence	1461
To shewe you my mynde I wolde have the lesse fere.	186	Magnyfycence	1646
Some have so moche lyberte that they fere no synne,	200	Magnyfycence	2143
O manles manhod, enfayntyd all with fere,	242	Speke Parott	391
Hyt ys to fere leste he wolde were the garland on hys pate,	244	Speke Parott	435

FERY —FETHERBEDDES   Page   Title   Line

FERY
From Tyllbery fery /To the playne of Salysbery!	79	Phy Sparrow	320

FERYMAN
By the feryman of hell,	105	Phy Sparrow	1337
By the feryman of hell,	349	Garlande	1330

FERME
I wyl be ferme and stabyll, /And to yow servyceabyll,	237	Speke Parott	246

FERRE
Her har[n]es easy ferre and nere is soughte. harnes] 'harmes' †Wynkyn de Worde 1499, 1510, 'armes' Marshe 1568	57	Bowge	403
This letter was wryten ferre hence.	150	Magnyfycence	337
It is moche worthe that is ferre fet.	153	Magnyfycence	455
As some be not ferre and yf it were well sought -	174	Magnyfycence	1241
And ferre beyond my merytys ye me commende and prayse.	183	Magnyfycence	1526

FERS
Ye fowle, fers and felle, as Syr Ferumbras the ffreke,	122	Garnesche1	15

FERSLY
And so with your servantys he fersly doth fyght.	43	Balettys2	28
So fersly he fytyth, hys mynde is so fell,	43	Balettys2	29
As fersly frownynge as he had ben fyghtyng,	328	Garlande	594

FERTHER
Excedynge ferther than his connynge is,	46	Bowge	23
Then thus to you - Nay, suffer me yet ferther to say,	142	Magnyfycence	48
Lo, here is thy knyfe and a halter, and or we go ferther,	206	Magnyfycence	2317
But frendly I wyll refrayne you ferther, or we flyt:	211	Magnyfycence	2478

FERUMBRAS
Ye fowle, fers and felle, as Syr Ferumbras the ffreke,	122	Garnesche1	15

FERVENT
Such fervent heat /His stomake doth freat; doth freat] 'so great' †Kele 1545.2, Wyght 1553, Kitson 1560.6	83	Phy Sparrow	481
The fervent axes of love can not represse!	321	Garlande	315

FERVENTLY
So fervently I shake,	74	Phy Sparrow	104
fervently reboyled with the infatuate flames	374	Replycacion	1

FESAUNT
Fesaunt and partriche mewed,	284	Why Come Ye	222
Went with the pecok ageyne the fesaunt;	315	Garlande	103

FESAUNTE
And the cormoraunce, /With the fesaunte, cormoraunce] 'cormoraunte' Wyght 1553, Kitson 1560.6, Marshe 1568	83	Phy Sparrow	446

FESAUNTES
Fesauntes, partryche and cranes;	252	Collyn Clout	206

FESYCYAN
Syr, your fesycyan is the grace of God,	207	Magnyfycence	2349

FEST
Thus endeth the gest /Of this worthy fest.	230	El Rummynge	623

FESTE
There is no surfet where measure rulyth the feste;	144	Magnyfycence	139

FESTERD
And under the fell oft festerd is the sore:	45	Balettys4	5

FESTYVALLE
Your beste gowne festyvalle.	125	Garnesche3	51

FET
He sayde he wold not let /His houndys for to fet,	64	Hauke	107
The sensers and the crosse shall fet;	86	Phy Sparrow	568
Your reasons forth to fet.	142	Magnyfycence	64
It is moche worthe that is ferre fet.	153	Magnyfycence	455
And yet she wyll jet, /Lyke a joyly fet	215	El Rummynge	52
It was dere that was far fet!	223	El Rummynge	334

FETCHE
'How, hosteler, fetche my hors a botell of hay!'	234	Speke Parott	147

FETCHED
At Englysh bowes have fetched their banes.	120	Ag Scottes	173

FETE
She sparyd not to wete her fete.	42	Balettys1	16
A gose with the fete upon;	125	Garnesche3	31
She is furred for the hete /All to the fete;	167	Magnyfycence	978
I shall flappe hym as a fole to fall at my fete.	182	Magnyfycence	1507
A good dryfte, syr, a praty fete!	189	Magnyfycence	1731
Mary, Cryst graunt ye catche no colde on your fete!	191	Magnyfycence	1803
Nowe must your fete lye hyer than your crowne.	197	Magnyfycence	2007
And also theyr fete /Hardely full unswete;	217	El Rummynge	121
My lytell legges, my fete bothe fete and clene,	231	Speke Parott	18
My lytell legges, my fete bothe fete and clene,	231	Speke Parott	18
Set hym fast by the fete!	275	Collyn Clout	1166
Set hym fast by the fete!'	289	Why Come Ye	426

FETEWSE
Of Felyce fetewse and lytell prety Cate,	56	Bowge	370

FETHER
Ic dien serveth for the estrych fether, the] not in Kynge & Marche 1554, Day 1560, Marshe 1568	233	Speke Parott	78

FETHER BED
In faythe, he may dreme on a daggeswane for ony fether bed.	201	Magnyfycence	2169

FETHERBEDDES
That was wonte to lye on fetherbeddes of downe;	197	Magnyfycence	2006

		Page	Title	Line
FETHERS				
	For rufflynge of Phillips fethers,	73	Phy Sparrow	79
	For] 'From' Wyght 1553, Kitson 1560.6, Marshe 1568			
	And his fethers shake,	75	Phy Sparrow	163
	fethers] 'fether' †Kele 1545.2			
	Her fethers donne; /Well faveryd bonne!	168	Magnyfycence	989
	Thy wordes hange togyder as fethers in the wynde.	191	Magnyfycence	1818
FETHYRS				
	My fethyrs fresshe as ys the emerawde grene,	231	Speke Parott	16
	That hang togedyr as fethyrs in the wynde;	239	Speke Parott	293
FETTE				
	Of our Englysshe bowes ye have fette your banes.	115	Scot Kynge	65
FETTERS				
	In a payre of fetters or a payre of stockys.	141	Magnyfycence	31
	And therwithall convey hymselfe into a payre of fetters;	178	Magnyfycence	1365
FETTRED				
	Embraudred, enlasid together, and fettred,	138	Ven Tongues	39
FETURES				
	All the goodly sort /Of her fetures clere,	96	Phy Sparrow	1000
	Inpurtured with fetures after your purpose,	183	Magnyfycence	1552
FETURIS				
	Of womanly feturis, whos florysshyng tender age	336	Garlande	869
FETURYS				
	Illumynyd wyth feturys far passyng my reporte;	44	Balettys3	23
FETURS				
	Of all your feturs favorable to make tru discripcion,	42	Balettys2	8
FEVEROUS				
	These feverous axys, the dedely wo and payne	44	Balettys3	9
FEW				
	Few men can tell where the hynde calfe gose.	313	Garlande	26
	tell] 'telle now' MS Cotton Vitellius E.x			
	Few shall ye fynde or none that wyll do so.'	317	Garlande	168
	As Skelton rehersith, with wordes few and playne,	353	Garlande	1466
FEWE				
	By God, syr, ye se but fewe wyse men of myne age.	148	Magnyfycence	289
	Full fewe that can themselfe of me excuse.	160	Magnyfycence	706
	I am of fewe wordys. I love not to [crake].	162	Magnyfycence	775
	crake] 'barke' †Rastell & Treveris C 1530, B			
	For I here but fewe men that gyve ony prayse	189	Magnyfycence	1743
	Full fewe but they have envy of me.	195	Magnyfycence	1963
	For we be, syrs, but a fewe of the best.	202	Magnyfycence	2203
FEWER				
	And fewer wordes make.	92	Phy Sparrow	818
FFREKE				
	Ye fowle, fers and felle, as Syr Ferumbras the ffreke,	122	Garneschel	15
FICKIL				
	Of fals fickil tunges suche cloked collusion	139	Ven Tongues	57
FICTYONS				
	Accomptynge them as fictyons.	249	Collyn Clout	114
FIDDILL				
	He fyndith fals mesuris out of his fonde fiddill.'	333	Garlande	741
	fals mesuris out] 'owght fals mesuris' MS Cotton Vit.E.x			
FIERS				
	A fals double tunge is more fiers and fell	140	Ven Tongues	79
FIGHT				
	What movyd you agayn hym to war or to fight?	31	Dol Dethe	62
FIGURE				
	In figure wherof they were the laurell grene.	314	Garlande	68
	they were the] 'the were they' †Fakes 1523			
FIGURED				
	In hym is figured Melchisedeche,	114	Scot Kynge	23
FILL				
	With, 'Fill the blak bowle /For Jayberdes sowle.'	108	Epitaphe1	73
FINALLY				
	So finally, when they had shewyd there devyse,	324	Garlande	442
	Finally they fall to carefull confusyon,	374	Replycacion	15
FIND				
	What fault find ye herein but may be avowed.	138	Ven Tongues	41
FINGERS				
	With fingers smale, and handis whyte as mylk;	334	Garlande	797
	whyte] 'as white' Marshe 1568			
FIRST				
	First one wyth a ladell,	224	El Rummynge	383
	Yet whan he toke first his hat,	306	Why Come Ye	1108
	first] not in MS Rawlinson C. 813			
	Whan he was creat pope /First in Antioche.	307	Why Come Ye	1143
	Sith I contryvyd first princyples medycynable?	321	Garlande	310
	I saw Gower, that first garnisshed our Englysshe rude,	323	Garlande	387
	How Dame Minerva first found the Olyve Tre, she red	351	Garlande	1404
	The first twayne to wake;	358	Garlande2	11
FIST				
	To gyde and to governe my dredfull tremlyng fist.	335	Garlande	828
FISTA				
	[Y]e develysh dogmatista, /Your hawke on your fista,	69	Hauke	256
	Ye] 'The' †Lant 1545, Kynge & Marche 1554, Day 1560, Marshe 1568			
FISTY				
	Christi crucifixi /To fede uppon your fisty;	69	Hauke	291

	Page	Title	Line
FY			
Fy, fy, for shame, ther hartis wer to faynt.	30	Dol Dethe	42
Fy, fy, for shame, ther hartis wer to faynt.	30	Dol Dethe	42
What, wolde ye frompill me now? Fy, fy!	36	Man Margery	16
What, wolde ye frompill me now? Fy, fy!	36	Man Margery	16
That was theyr owne kynge. /Fy on that wynnyng!	116	Ag Scottes	24
That the Scottys may synge, /'Fy on the wynnynge!' synge] 'sin' Marshe 1568	116	Ag Scottes	48
Fy, fy, that ever I sholde be brought in this snare!	196	Magnyfycence	1972
Fy, fy, that ever I sholde be brought in this snare!	196	Magnyfycence	1972
With, 'Fy, cover thy shap thy] 'the' Kynge & Marche 1554, Day 1560, Marshe 1568	227	El Rummynge	507
FYCKELL			
Fyckell falsenesse, /Varyablenesse, /With unstablenesse.	247	Collyn Clout	44
FYDELYTE			
Than I assured hym my fydelyte,	52	Bowge	218
FYDLED			
The feldfare wolde have fydled, and it wolde not frame;	192	Magnyfycence	1838
FYDLER			
A master, a mynstrell, a fydler, a farte.	38	Coystrownel	56
FYE			
Fye on this dyce, they be not worth a turde!	57	Bowge	392
I hate this faynynge, fye upon it, fye!	59	Bowge	465
I hate this faynynge, fye upon it, fye!	59	Bowge	465
They may well say, fye on that wynnynge!	115	Ag Scottes	4
Fye on this worlde, full of trechery,	197	Magnyfycence	2020
Fye on this wynnyng allway! this] not in MS Rawlinson C. 813	302	Why Come Ye	929
FYER			
Aram was fyred with Caldies fyer called Ur;	232	Speke Parott	64
And set hell on fyer hell] 'all' Toy 1553, Kitson 1560.7, Marshe 1568	303	Why Come Ye	985
FYER DRAKE			
Lyke a fyer drake, fyer] 'fyrye' MS Rawlinson C. 813	303	Why Come Ye	981
FYERS			
He is so fyers and fell.	295	Why Come Ye	650
FYERSLY			
He frownyth fyersly, brymly browde.	174	Magnyfycence	1245
FYEST			
Jone sayde she had eten a fyest.	223	El Rummynge	343
FYGHT			
And so with your servantys he fersly doth fyght.	43	Balettys2	28
Agaynst whom he dyd fyght /Falsly agaynst all right,	120	Ag Scottes2	17
Thus make I them wyth thryft to fyght.	152	Magnyfycence	421
By Goddes fote, and I dare well fyght, for I wyll not start.	161	Magnyfycence	768
And frowne it and face it, as thoughe ye wolde fyght;	185	Magnyfycence	1601
Not for to fyght /Ageyne dispyght,	355	Garlande	1561
He fledde and durst nat fyght;	360	Albany	70
Agaynst Englande to fyght.	364	Albany	231
FYGHTYNG			
As fersly frownynge as he had ben fyghtyng,	328	Garlande	594
FYGURED			
In him is fygured Melchisedec,	118	Ag Scottes	115
FYKKELLE			
Fleriing, flatyryng, fals and fykkelle,	133	Garnesche5	152
FYKKILL			
Tyll fykkill Fortune began on hym to frowne.	33	Dol Dethe	133
FYLE			
Were pullysshed with the fyle /Of Ciceros eloquence, pullysshed] 'publysshed' †Kele 1545.2	101	Phy Sparrow	1205
But they theyr tonges fyle,	267	Collyn Clout	850
FYLYTHE			
That fylythe hys owne nest.	129	Garnesche3	198
FYLL			
What frantyk frensy fyll in youre brayne?	30	Dol Dethe	51
To fyll bougets and males	90	Phy Sparrow	752
I may no more speke tyll I have wept my fyll.	198	Magnyfycence	2063
With, 'Fyll the cup, fyll!'	217	El Rummynge	115
With, 'Fyll the cup, fyll!'	217	El Rummynge	115
Some fyll theyr pot full /Of good Lemster woll.	220	El Rummynge	251
Therefore, 'Fyll it by and by	221	El Rummynge	274
And fyll in good met; met] 'meate' Day 1560, Marshe 1568	222	El Rummynge	333
She fyll in a wynkynge /With a barlyhood;	223	El Rummynge	371
To fyll therwith your mawe -	263	Collyn Clout	656
The ruddy shamefastnes in her vysage fyll,	337	Garlande	888
FYLLY			
Of [a] foles fylly /That had a fole with Wylly, a] not in †Lant 1545, Kynge & Marche 1554, Day 1560, Marshe 1568; fylly] 'silly' Marshe 1568	224	El Rummynge	388
FYLTY			
Was nevyr suche a fylty gorgon, nor suche an epycure,	246	Speke Parott	510
FYNALL			
Wheron he gat his fynall dedely wounde.	32	Dol Dethe	119
FYNALLY			
And fynally, in conclusyon,	306	Why Come Ye	1095

FYND —FYNGERYNG   Page   Title   Line

FYND
This lordis dethe, whos pere is hard to fynd, ...   34   Dol Dethe   178
He can not fynd it in rule nor in space: 37   Coystrownel   22
I wot not where to fynd /Termes to serve my mynde.   91   Phy Sparrow   782
As the fynd of hell!   294   Why Come Ye   594
FYNDE
Ye are to unhappy occasyons to fynde   38   Coystrownel   65
  occasyons] 'occasion' Marshe 1568
Than there coude I none aquentaunce fynde;   47   Bowge   45
And how I maye that waye and meanes fynde.'   49   Bowge   109
For ye have me whome faythfull ye shall fynde;   50   Bowge   166
Yf he coude fynde in herte to truste me.   52   Bowge   220
Fynde some mene to caste him over the borde.'   54   Bowge   308
Doctor Dialetica, /Where fynde you in Ypotetica, ...   69   Hauke   268
That if ye can fynde   78   Phy Sparrow   260
The fynde was in thy mynde   78   Phy Sparrow   283
What he doth fynde   85   Phy Sparrow   538
It is dyffuse to fynde   91   Phy Sparrow   806
Yet some men fynde a faute, ...   92   Phy Sparrow   811
And therein reed /Shall fynde indeed   116   Ag Scottes   44
For reson can I non fynde   126   Garnesche3   104
Let se, fynde you a better way.   156   Magnyfycence   560
A man shall fynde /Many of her kynde, ...   167   Magnyfycence   983
Yf I can fynde out   168   Magnyfycence   993
I can fynde fantasyes where none is;   169   Magnyfycence   1041
Nay, nay. Thou shalt fynde hym another maner of man.   173   Magnyfycence   1189
Yet for his name we must fynde a [slyght].   176   Magnyfycence   1308
  slyght] shyfte †Rastell & Treveris C 1530, B
Take it in worthe suche as ye fynde.   180   Magnyfycence   1439
Then some occacyon or quarell ye must fynde, ...   185   Magnyfycence   1600
A, syr, tolde I not you howe I dyd fynde   191   Magnyfycence   1819
Lo, suche is this worlde! I fynde it wryt, ...   196   Magnyfycence   1974
By the masse, man, thou shall fynde me resonable.   202   Magnyfycence   2204
To thanke God of his sonde; and comforte ye shal fynde. . . .   207   Magnyfycence   2360
In all your warkys more grace shall ye fynde;   211   Magnyfycence   2485
Sodenly commendyd, and sodenly fynde a lacke;   213   Magnyfycence   2533
Where men of that contre by fortune me fynde, ...   231   Speke Parott   5
In flattryng fables men fynde but lyttyl fayth;   233   Speke Parott   87
For whoo lokythe wyselye in your warkys may fynde   239   Speke Parott   296
Syns Dewcalyons flodde there can no clerkes fynde.   244   Speke Parott   462
And suche sleyghtes dothe fynde, ...   290   Why Come Ye   438
In writynge as we fynde   292   Why Come Ye   545
And ye shall fynde surely   296   Why Come Ye   695
And, as we dare, we fynde in hym grete lake: 314   Garlande   70
  grete] 'a' Marshe 1568
Few shall ye fynde or none that wyll do so.'   317   Garlande   168
And ye shall well fynde he is a very fole;   318   Garlande   207
  well fynde] 'fynde wele' MS Cotton Vitellius E.x
Suche an other there coude no man fynde;   325   Garlande   463
To walke where we lyst, let us somwhat fynde   328   Garlande   564
Contynuall comfort here ye may fynde, ...   332   Garlande   710
Erst that ye can fynde   341   Garlande   1032
  that] 'than' MS Cotton Vitellius E.x
The menes to fynde /To please my mynde, ...   342   Garlande   1072
Moche dowblenes of the worlde therin he may fynde.   346   Garlande   1197
Fynde no mo suche fro Wanflete to Walis.   347   Garlande   1218
A pleasaunter place than Ashrige is, harde were to fynde, . . .   353   Garlande   1465
  were] 'where' †Fakes 1523
The fynde, Scot, breke thy necke.   363   Albany   156
The fynde of hell mot sterve the!   365   Albany   251
They fynde his grace so kynde;   371   Albany   483
Than shall ye fynde it fyrme and stable, ...   382   Replycacion   289
FYNDETH
He fyndeth a proporcyon in his prycke songe   38   Coystrownel   48
FYNDITH
He fyndith fals mesuris out of his fonde fiddill.'   333   Garlande   741
  fals mesuris out] 'owght fals mesuris' MS Cotton Vit.E.x
FYNDYTH
To ask wher he fyndyth among hys monacordys   37   Coystrownel   20
FYNE
Whiche sat behynde a tra[v]es of sylke fyne, ...   47   Bowge   58
  traves] 'tranes' †Wynkyn de Worde 1499, 1510, Marshe 1568
Of her heer so fyne, ...   101   Phy Sparrow   1173
By Cockes harte, thou arte a fyne mery knave.   191   Magnyfycence   1826
Tytan hathe truste up hys tressys of fyne golde;   242   Speke Parott   398
In rotchettes of fyne raynes, ...   254   Collyn Clout   314
Theyr tabertes of fyne sylke;   254   Collyn Clout   316
And take a fyne meritorum, /Contra regulam morum, ...   256   Collyn Clout   379
Encoverde over with golde of tissew fyne;   345   Garlande   1164
FYNEST
Of golde of tessew the fynest that myghte be, ...   47   Bowge   59
FYNGER
Upon my fynger aloft!   80   Phy Sparrow   356
poyntyng with his fynger, and sayth, ...   162   Magnyfycence   SD
FYNGERED
To se howe she is gumbed, /Fyngered and thumbed, ...   215   El Rummynge   41
FYNGERYNG
He fumblyth in hys fyngeryng an ugly good noyse;   37   Coystrownel   31

FYNGERS —FYXT   Page   Title   Line

FYNGERS
	Page	Title	Line
My fyngers, dead and colde,	77	Phy Sparrow	233
And with her fyngers smale,	99	Phy Sparrow	1118
To pyke theyr fyngers all the day longe;	174	Magnyfycence	1222
For my fyngers ytche.	230	El Rummynge	618
fyngers] 'fynger' Kynge & Marche 1554			
Somtyme a bacon flycke /That is thre fyngers thycke	267	Collyn Clout	845

FYRE
Whiche kyndelde the wyld fyre that made all this smoke.	31	Dol Dethe	77
Water in the one hande and fyre in the other.	160	Magnyfycence	711
All this nacyon /I set on fyre; /In my facyon	165	Magnyfycence	885
And some I vysyte with brennynge of fyre;	194	Magnyfycence	1908
That they wyll fyre one ungracyously in the flanke.	204	Magnyfycence	2270
They are fel as any fyre!	285	Why Come Ye	249
Wylde fyre and thonder;	285	Why Come Ye	257
She bet up a fyre with the sparkis full kene	330	Garlande	669
Of fyre elementar in his supreme spere,	331	Garlande	694

FYRED
Aram was fyred with Caldies fyer called Ur;	232	Speke Parott	64

FYRY
And from her fyry sparklynges,	73	Phy Sparrow	80

FYRMAMENT
To nombyr all the sterrys in the fyrmament,	240	Speke Parott	332

FYRME
Fyrst, I saye, with mynde fyrme and stable	208	Magnyfycence	2408
Than shall ye fynde it fyrme and stable,	382	Replycacion	289

FYRST
Correct fyrst thy self; walk, and be nought!	38	Coystrownel	62
Fyrst, I say, we owght to have in consyderacyon	141	Magnyfycence	43
Me, other fyrst or last,	143	Magnyfycence	93
As at the fyrst orygynall, by godly opynyon;	143	Magnyfycence	119
Comberaunce and trouble in Englande fyrst I began.	160	Magnyfycence	715
That they wyll here no man but the fyrst tale.	161	Magnyfycence	743
Convey yourselfe fyrst, let se.	163	Magnyfycence	816
Fyrst I dyd set;	165	Magnyfycence	879
Fyrst to tell you what were best:	168	Magnyfycence	1022
Nay, in fayth, fyrst let me here thyne.	172	Magnyfycence	1152
Fyrst I lay before them my bybyll	174	Magnyfycence	1220
Nay, but fansy must be eyther fyrst or last.	176	Magnyfycence	1288
Howe frantyke fansy fyrst of all	176	Magnyfycence	1294
Nay, fyrst Lusty Pleasure is my desyre to have;	180	Magnyfycence	1453
Thou arte not the fyrst hymselfe hath slayne.	206	Magnyfycence	2316
Fyrst, I saye, with mynde fyrme and stable	208	Magnyfycence	2408
But, syr, by me to rule fyrst ye began.	209	Magnyfycence	2431
Fyrst, from your magnyfycence syn must be abjectyd;	211	Magnyfycence	2484
The fyrst, to do him reverence,	307	Why Come Ye	1123
Fyrst, olde Quintiliane with his Declamacyons;	321	Garlande	326
Declamacyons] 'declynacyons' †Fakes 1523			

FYRSTE
The fyrste was Favell, full of flatery,	49	Bowge	134
Fyrste pycke a quarell and fall oute with hym then,	55	Bowge	314
Whyche of yow fyrste dare boldlye plucke the crowe.	242	Speke Parott	396
Ye fyrste aryvyd; whan broken was your mast	327	Garlande	542
Ye] 'The' †Fakes 1523			

FYSGYGGE
Than sterte forth a fysgygge	228	El Rummynge	538

FYSNAMY
The facyoun of your fysnamy the devyl in a clowde;	123	Garnesche2	25

FYSSHE
Wel, wyse men may ete the fysshe when ye shal draw the pole.	148	Magnyfycence	300
To fysshe afore the nette and to drawe polys.	243	Speke Parott	427
All is fysshe that cometh to the net:	269	Collyn Clout	933
to the net] 'to net' Marshe 1568, 'to nett' MS Harley 2252			

FYSSHES
That putteth fysshes to a fraye;	83	Phy Sparrow	463

FYST
The hawke had no lyst /To come to his fyst;	64	Hauke	84
And lede my fyst /As hym best lyst,	96	Phy Sparrow	972
What hast thou on thy fyst? A [k]esteryll?	173	Magnyfycence	1174
kesteryll] 'besteryll' †Rastell & Treveris C 1530, B			
Tyll he cheked at the fyst,	297	Why Come Ye	735

FYSTE
What the devyll hast thou on thy fyste? An owle?	166	Magnyfycence	922
I dryve downe these dastardys with a dynt of my fyste.	181	Magnyfycence	1486

FYSTIS
With her maungy fystis.	219	El Rummynge	200

FYSTY
Domine concupisti, /With thy hawke on thy fysty?	69	Hauke	260

FYTYTH
So fersly he fytyth, hys mynde is so fell,	43	Balettys2	29

FYTTE
This is a farly fytte	255	Collyn Clout	329
farly] 'fearfull' †Godfray 1531, Kele 1545.1, Marshe 1568, 'ffarly' MS Harley 2252			

FYVE
Pay Stokys hys fyve pownd.	128	Garnesche3	185

FYXT
Fyxt or els mobyll.	292	Why Come Ye	525

	Page	Title	Line
FLACCUS			
Flaccus nor Catullus with hym may nat compare,	383	Replycacion	336
FLAGRANT			
Reflaring rosabell, /The flagrant camamell;	340	Garlande	978
FLAGRAUNT			
Whos flagraunt flower was chefe preservatyve	330	Garlande	671
FLAYLE			
The flayle, the scourge of Almighty God.	308	Why Come Ye	1165
The flayle] not in MS Rawlinson C. 813			
FLAMES			
By Chemeras flames, /And all the dedly names	105	Phy Sparrow	1330
fervently reboyled with the infatuate flames	374	Replycacion	I
FLAMYS			
By Chemeras flamys, /And all the dedly namys	349	Garlande	1323
FLANDERKYNS			
And the Flanderkyns.	302	Why Come Ye	925
FLANKE			
That they wyll fyre one ungracyously in the flanke.	204	Magnyfycence	2270
FLAP			
With a flap afore his eye,	308	Why Come Ye	1169
afore] 'before' Kitson 1560.7, Marshe 1568, MS Rawl. C. 813			
FLAPPE			
I shall flappe hym as a fole to fall at my fete.	182	Magnyfycence	1507
FLAPPES			
Wyth theyr naked pappes, /That flyppes and flappes,	217	El Rummynge	136
FLATER			
I can not flater, I muste be playne to the.	50	Bowge	164
To flater and to flery is all my pretence	161	Magnyfycence	738
Some came to flater, some came to spye.	326	Garlande	511
With Crafty Conveyaunce dothe smater and flater,	346	Garlande	1194
FLATERED			
And flatered them with fables fayre before theyr face,	160	Magnyfycence	717
FLATERER			
There is no flaterer nor losyll so lyther,	146	Magnyfycence	200
FLATERERS			
Fals flaterers that fawne the, and kurris of kynde	329	Garlande	619
FLATERY			
The fyrste was Favell, full of flatery,	49	Bowge	134
Full moche flatery and falsehode I hyde;	177	Magnyfycence	1358
But fallyble flatery enmyxyd with bytternesse.	212	Magnyfycence	2516
But fallyble flatery enmyxyd with bytternesse.	212	Magnyfycence	2523
Full ungracyously, /Fals flatery,	300	Why Come Ye	853
FLATERYNGE			
A flaterynge knave and false he is, God wote.	59	Bowge	485
FLATYRYNG			
Fleriing, flatyryng, fals and fykkelle,	133	Garnesche5	152
FLATRINGE			
All flatringe faytors abhor and from the kast.	34	Dol Dethe	172
FLATTER			
What, shuld I flatter? What, shulde I glose or paynt?	30	Dol Dethe	41
To flatter and to fayne,	268	Collyn Clout	861
Then men wyll say how he doth but flatter.	314	Garlande	84
But flery, flatter and fayne;	362	Albany	135
FLATTERYNGE			
To flatterynge, to smatterynge, to to out of harre,	199	Magnyfycence	2095
Flatterynge for a newe cote	267	Collyn Clout	838
FLATTERS			
He gloseth and he flatters.'	247	Collyn Clout	25
FLATTRYNG			
In flattryng fables men fynde but lyttyl fayth;	233	Speke Parott	87
FLAUNDERS			
Of whom both Flaunders and Scotland stode in drede,	30	Dol Dethe	44
Some from Flaunders, sum from the se coste,	326	Garlande	496
FLAXE			
With flaxe and with towe;	221	El Rummynge	287
FLE			
and fle /From worldly vanyte	247	Collyn Clout	40
worldly] 'wordly' Kele 1545.1			
For prosperyte /Away than wyll fle.	300	Why Come Ye	863
Item the Boke how Men Shulde Fle Synne;	345	Garlande	1173
FLECE			
Of the Golden Flece,	87	Phy Sparrow	631
FLECES			
But plucke away and pull /Theyr fleces of wull.	248	Collyn Clout	79
FLECKYD			
The fleckyd pye to chatter	81	Phy Sparrow	397
FLED			
Fled away from hym, let hym ly in the dust,	30	Dol Dethe	39
Bot all they fled from hym for falshode or fere.	31	Dol Dethe	91
The hertis of the herd began for to grone, and fled	351	Garlande	1408
FLEDDE			
For yf I had not quyckely fledde the touche,	60	Bowge	503
Fledde lyke a beest.	359	Albany	12
He fledde and durst nat fyght;	360	Albany	70
They fledde full cowardly.	371	Albany	515
FLEE			
But, my good sonne, lerne from dyspaire to flee;	206	Magnyfycence	2339

	Page	Title	Line
FLEES			
All the flees blake	76	Phy Sparrow	180
FLEYEST			
What! Fleyest thou his skynne every yere?	169	Magnyfycence	1058
FLEKYD			
For Parot is no churlish chowgh, nor no flekyd pye,	236	Speke Parott	204
FLEMYNGE			
It was a Flemynge hyght Hansy.	149	Magnyfycence	328
FLEMMYNGE			
The golden ram /Of flemmynge dam,	301	Why Come Ye	898
FLERIING			
Fleriing, flatyryng, fals and fykkelle,	133	Garnesche5	152
FLERY			
To flater and to flery is all my pretence	161	Magnyfycence	738
But flery, flatter and fayne;	362	Albany	135
FLESH			
Neyther flesh nor fell.	39	Coystrowne3	18
nor] 'not' Marshe 1568			
FLESHE			
The fleshe thereof was ranke,	228	El Rummynge	540
FLESSH			
The best chepe flessh that evyr I bought.'	36	Man Margery	24
FLESSHE			
That on suche a female my flesshe wolde be wroken.	184	Magnyfycence	1566
Lorde, so my flesshe trymblyth nowe for drede!	193	Magnyfycence	1875
Or I shal fawchyn thy flesshe and scrape the on the skyn.	202	Magnyfycence	2189
So bolde a braggyng bocher, and flesshe sold so dere;	245	Speke Parott	485
To kepe his flesshe chast	284	Why Come Ye	219
As quikly towchyd as it were flesshe and bones,	328	Garlande	592
FLESSHE-FLYE			
So fatte a magott, bred of a flesshe-flye;	246	Speke Parott	509
FLESSHE FLYES			
Among the scabbed skyes /Of Wycliffes flesshe flyes.	378	Replycacion	166
FLESSHE MEATE			
Howe some of you dothe eate /In lenton season flesshe meate,	251	Collyn Clout	205
FLESSHE METE			
All maner of flesshe mete	306	Why Come Ye	1084
FLESSH FLY			
I sey, thow felle and fowle flessh fly,	131	Garnesche5	65
FLETE			
Here is none forsyth whether you flete or synke.	147	Magnyfycence	254
For so with fantasyes my wyt dothe flete	170	Magnyfycence	1080
Take him, wardeyn of the Flete,	275	Collyn Clout	1165
'Wardeyn of the Flete,	289	Why Come Ye	425
Your tonges were to flete;	376	Replycacion	50
FLEW			
His hawke then flew uppon /The rode, with Mary and Johnn.	65	Hauke	126
FLEWE			
Flewe, I sholde say – in to an olde barne	191	Magnyfycence	1808
FLINGANDE			
To the flingande fende of helle.	366	Albany	317
FLINT			
Enwallyd aboute with the stony flint,	328	Garlande	569
FLY			
Of whos [life] they counteed not a fly.	31	Dol Dethe	95
life] not in †MS Royal 18 D.ii or Marshe 1568			
He made his hawke to fly,	63	Hauke	47
For to let their hawkys fly	67	Hauke	218
To let theyr hawkys fly	70	Hauke	301
A fly, or a gnat, /He wolde flye at that;	75	Phy Sparrow	130
And fly so to and fro;	75	Phy Sparrow	160
fly] 'fle' Wyght 1553, Kitson 1560.6, Marshe 1568			
He can not well fly, /Nor synge tunably;	83	Phy Sparrow	483
I pray God, Phillip to heven may fly.	86	Phy Sparrow	580
That Phyllyp may fly /Above the starry sky,	86	Phy Sparrow	598
Your frantyck fable not worth a fly,	118	Ag Scottes	104
I set not by hym a fly	152	Magnyfycence	412
Not acquaynted worth a fly /With honorable Haly,	292	Why Come Ye	520
Have made you eate the fly,	381	Replycacion	252
FLYBYTTEN			
Some be flybytten, /Some skewed as a kytten;	218	El Rummynge	141
FLYBLOWEN			
with the flyblowen blast	373	Replycacion	I
odyous, orgulyous and flyblowen opynions etc.,	375	Replycacion	I
FLYCKERYNGE			
Flyckerynge with his wynges.	80	Phy Sparrow	348
FLYE			
A fly, or a gnat, /He wolde flye at that;	75	Phy Sparrow	131
But for the egle doth flye	85	Phy Sparrow	550
Your counseyle was not worth a flye.	113	Scot Kynge	14
Counterfet reason is not worth a flye;	153	Magnyfycence	470
A plummed partrydge all redy to flye.	153	Magnyfycence	479
By God, we have made Magnyfycence to ete a flye.	154	Magnyfycence	503
Me seme I flye,	163	Magnyfycence	839
I set not a flye and all go to all.	188	Magnyfycence	1710
Nowe is there no man that wyll set by hym a flye.	193	Magnyfycence	1889
As though they wolde flye /Aboute the sterry skye.	248	Collyn Clout	73
Aboute] 'Above' Kele 1545.1, Marshe 1568, MS Harley 2252			

FLYE NET —FLORYSSHETH   Page   Title   Line

```
And all nat worth a flye, . . . . . . . . . . . . . . . . . . . .   282   Why Come Ye    148
We set nat a flye . . . . . . . . . . . . . . . . . . . . . . .    363   Albany         161
To flye ye shalbe fayne . . . . . . . . . . . . . . . . . . . .    368   Albany         371
To be blowen with the flye /Of horryble heresy. . . . . . . . .    376   Replycacion     85
The blynde eteth many a flye. . . . . . . . . . . . . . . . . .    378   Replycacion    152
Bycause ye have eaten a flye, . . . . . . . . . . . . . . . . .    380   Replycacion    244
Ye saye that poetry /Maye nat flye so hye . . . . . . . . . . .    382   Replycacion    307
```
FLYE NET
```
Fansy hath cachyd in a flye net . . . . . . . . . . . . . . . .    151   Magnyfycence   403
Whan the flye net was set for to catche a cote, . . . . . . . .    351   Garlande      1379
```
FLYENG
```
Ye wante but a wylde flyeng bolte to shote at the buttes. . . .    148   Magnyfycence   294
```
FLYENGE
```
And was with flyenge wery. . . . . . . . . . . . . . . . . . .      63   Hauke           67
```
FLYGHT
```
To put them thus to flyght; . . . . . . . . . . . . . . . . . .    256   Collyn Clout   405
That valiaunt knyght, /Putte you to flyght /By his valyaunce. .    360   Albany          41
To put thy selfe to flyght. . . . . . . . . . . . . . . . . . .    364   Albany         233
```
FLYP-FLAP
```
With sum flyp-flap, . . . . . . . . . . . . . . . . . . . . . .    227   El Rummynge    508
```
FLYPPES
```
Wyth theyr naked pappes, /That flyppes and flappes, . . . . . .    217   El Rummynge    136
```
FLYT
```
Ye, syr. From hym my corage shall never flyt. . . . . . . . . .    210   Magnyfycence  2466
But frendly I wyll refrayne you ferther, or we flyt: . . . . .     211   Magnyfycence  2478
Chuse them syt or flyt, . . . . . . . . . . . . . . . . . . . .    295   Why Come Ye    634
```
FLYTYNGE
```
With chydyng and with flytynge, . . . . . . . . . . . . . . . .    305   Why Come Ye   1059
    flytynge] 'fiting' †Kele 1545.3, Marshe 1568
```
FLYTTE
```
Fortune may chaunce to flytte, . . . . . . . . . . . . . . . .     271   Collyn Clout   994
```
FLOCKE
```
Unneth they leve a locke /Of wolle amongest theyr flocke. . . .    248   Collyn Clout    81
```
FLOCKED
```
They thronge in fast and flocked her aboute, . . . . . . . . .      49   Bowge          122
```
FLOCKET
```
In her furred flocket, /And graye russet rocket, . . . . . . .     215   El Rummynge     53
```
FLOD
```
Of Thagus, that golden flod, . . . . . . . . . . . . . . . . .      93   Phy Sparrow    875
```
FLODDE
```
Tyll Eufrates, that flodde, dryvythe me into Ynde, . . . . . .     231   Speke Parott     4
Syns Dewcalyons flodde there can no clerkes rede. . . . . . . .    244   Speke Parott   455
Syns Dewcalyons flodde there can no clerkes fynde. . . . . . .     244   Speke Parott   462
Syns Dewcalions flodde, was nevyr sene nor shall. . . . . . . .    245   Speke Parott   469
Syns Dewcalions flodde, I trowe, was nevyr sene. . . . . . . .     245   Speke Parott   476
Syns Dewcalyons flodde was nevyr, I dar sey. . . . . . . . . .     245   Speke Parott   483
Syns Dewcalyons flodde, I trow, no man can tell. . . . . . . .     245   Speke Parott   490
Syns Dewcalyons flodde the world was never so yll. . . . . . .     245   Speke Parott   497
    the world] 'the world the world' †MS Harley 2252
Syns Dewcalyons flodde was nevyr sene nor lyerd. . . . . . . .     246   Speke Parott   504
Syn Dewcalyons flodde, I make the faste and sure. . . . . . . .    246   Speke Parott   511
Sens Dewcalyons flodde, in no cronycle ys told. . . . . . . . .    246   Speke Parott   518
Of the stormy flodde, . . . . . . . . . . . . . . . . . . . . .    277   Collyn Clout  1254
```
FLODDEN
```
At Branxton More and Flodden hylles, . . . . . . . . . . . . .     119   Ag Scottes     131
```
FLODDES
```
Lucina she wadythe among the watry floddes, . . . . . . . . . .    239   Speke Parott   285
```
FLODDON
```
At Floddon hyllys, /Our bowys, our byllys . . . . . . . . . . .    116   Ag Scottes      25
```
FLODE
```
That is a flode of hell; . . . . . . . . . . . . . . . . . . .      73   Phy Sparrow     71
Deucalyons flode it hyght. . . . . . . . . . . . . . . . . . .      78   Phy Sparrow    253
That were syns Noes flode; . . . . . . . . . . . . . . . . . .      78   Phy Sparrow    268
And as that flode doth pas . . . . . . . . . . . . . . . . . .      93   Phy Sparrow    877
Of the terestre [t]rechery we fall in the flode, . . . . . . .     213   Magnyfycence  2559
    trechery] 'rechery' †Rastell & Treveris C 1530, B
By the Stigiall flode, . . . . . . . . . . . . . . . . . . . .     349   Garlande      1327
```
FLOOD
```
By the Stygyall flood, . . . . . . . . . . . . . . . . . . . .     105   Phy Sparrow   1334
```
FLOODES
```
Al floodes that ever was . . . . . . . . . . . . . . . . . . .      93   Phy Sparrow    878
And the floodes in straunge remes, . . . . . . . . . . . . . .      93   Phy Sparrow    882
```
FLORA
```
Lyke dame Flora, quene . . . . . . . . . . . . . . . . . . . .     101   Phy Sparrow   1183
And formest of all dame Flora, the quene . . . . . . . . . . .     331   Garlande       685
```
FLORENTINE
```
Poggeus also, that famous Florentine, . . . . . . . . . . . . .    322   Garlande       372
```
FLORISHETH
```
She florisheth new and new . . . . . . . . . . . . . . . . . .      97   Phy Sparrow   1025
She florisheth new and new . . . . . . . . . . . . . . . . . .     101   Phy Sparrow   1188
```
FLORISSHINGE
```
But, as I sayd, your florisshinge tender age . . . . . . . . .     337   Garlande       876
```
FLORISSHYNG
```
In castyng, in turnynge, in florisshyng of flowris, . . . . . .    334   Garlande       802
```
FLORYSHETH
```
She florysheth new and new . . . . . . . . . . . . . . . . . .      98   Phy Sparrow   1057
```
FLORYSSHETH
```
She floryssheth new and new . . . . . . . . . . . . . . . . .       94   Phy Sparrow    896
```

FLORYSSHYNG —FLOWRES	Page	Title	Line

```
                                                              Page      Title         Line

    She floryssheth new and new  . . . . . . . . . . . . . .    100   Phy Sparrow    1139
    She florysseth new and new  . . . . . . . . . . . . . . .   102   Phy Sparrow    1234
FLORYSSHYNG
    Of womanly feturis, whos florysshyng tender age . . . . .   336   Garlande        869
FLORTHE
    Jacinctis and smaragdis out of the florthe they grew. . .   325   Garlande        480
FLOTES
    Of clusters engrosed with his ruddy flotes  . . . . . . .   321   Garlande        342
FLOTIS
    Of closters engrosyd with his ruddy flotis  . . . . . . .   321   Garlande        335
        flotis] 'droppes' †Fakes, 'flotis' Marshe 1568
    Of clusters engrosid with his ruddy [flotis]  . . . . . .   322   Garlande        349
        flotis] 'droppes' †Fakes 1523, 'dropes' Marshe 1568
    Of clusters engrosyd with his ruddy [flotis]  . . . . . .   322   Garlande        356
        flotis] 'dropis' †Fakes 1523, 'dropes' Marshe 1568
    Of clusters engrosid with his ruddy [flotis]  . . . . . .   322   Garlande        363
        flotis] 'dropis' †Fakes 1523, 'dropes' Marshe 1568
    Of clusters engrosed with his ruddy [flotis]  . . . . . .   322   Garlande        370
        flotis] 'dropis' †Fakes 1523, 'dropes' Marshe 1568
    Of clusters engrosyd with his ruddy [flotis]  . . . . . .   322   Garlande        377
        flotis] 'dropis' †Fakes 1523, 'dropes' Marshe 1568
    Of clusters engrosed with his ruddy [flotis]  . . . . . .   322   Garlande        384
        flotis] 'dropis' †Fakes 1523, 'dropes' Marshe 1568
FLOUR
    For this most goodly flour,  . . . . . . . . . . . . . .    99   Phy Sparrow    1107
    Of yowthe the godely flour,  . . . . . . . . . . . . . .   111   Lawde            44
FLOURE
    Of all women O floure withouten pere, . . . . . . . . . .    35   Dol Dethe       207
    For this most goodly floure,  . . . . . . . . . . . . . .    94   Phy Sparrow     893
    For this most goodly floure,  . . . . . . . . . . . . . .    96   Phy Sparrow     989
    For this most goodly floure,  . . . . . . . . . . . . . .    97   Phy Sparrow    1022
    [For] this most goodly floure,  . . . . . . . . . . . . .    98   Phy Sparrow    1054
        For] not in †Kele 1545.2, Wyght 1553, Kitson 1560.6, Marshe 1568
    For this most goodly floure,  . . . . . . . . . . . . . .    98   Phy Sparrow    1083
        goodly ] 'godly' †Kele 1545.2
    For this most goodly floure,  . . . . . . . . . . . . . .   100   Phy Sparrow    1136
    For this most goodly floure,  . . . . . . . . . . . . . .   100   Phy Sparrow    1161
    For this most goodly floure,  . . . . . . . . . . . . . .   101   Phy Sparrow    1185
        For] not in Kitson 1560.6, Marshe 1568
    For this most goodly floure,  . . . . . . . . . . . . . .   101   Phy Sparrow    1208
        For this] 'The' †Kele 1545.2, Marshe 1568
    [For] this most goodly floure,  . . . . . . . . . . . . .   102   Phy Sparrow    1231
        For] not in †Kele 1545.2, Wyght 1553, Kitson 1560.6,
        Marshe 1568; this] 'the' Wyght, Kitson, Marshe
    Slew all the floure /Of theyr honoure.  . . . . . . . . .   116   Ag Scottes       27
    And floure the more quycker;  . . . . . . . . . . . . . .   219   El Rummynge     206
    Of chevalry he is the floure; . . . . . . . . . . . . . .   282   Why Come Ye     159
    Of knighthode the floure  . . . . . . . . . . . . . . . .   365   Albany          239
FLOURISSHETH
    She flourissheth new and new  . . . . . . . . . . . . . .    96   Phy Sparrow     992
FLOURYSSHETH
    She flouryssheth new and new  . . . . . . . . . . . . . .    98   Phy Sparrow    1086
    She flouryssheth new and new  . . . . . . . . . . . . . .    99   Phy Sparrow    1110
    She flouryssheth new and new  . . . . . . . . . . . . . .   100   Phy Sparrow    1164
    She flouryssheth new and new  . . . . . . . . . . . . . .   102   Phy Sparrow    1211
FLOURS
    Fresshe as flours in May; . . . . . . . . . . . . . . . .   270   Collyn Clout    943
FLOWE
    Now ebbe, now flowe, nowe increase, now dyscrease;  . . .   212   Magnyfycence   2521
    It shall nat ever flowe.  . . . . . . . . . . . . . . . .   303   Why Come Ye     952
        nat ever flowe] 'neuer ouer flowe' MS Rawlinson C. 813
FLOWER
    That of Scotland ye lost the flower.  . . . . . . . . . .   119   Ag Scottes      134
    Of bewte that beryth the flower,  . . . . . . . . . . . .   128   Garnesche3      149
    How all thynge passyth as doth the somer flower,  . . . .   312   Garlande          9
    Whos flagraunt flower was chefe preservatyve  . . . . . .   330   Garlande        671
FLOWYN
    She had flowyn so oft,  . . . . . . . . . . . . . . . . .    63   Hauke            68
FLOWR
    Englande the flowr /Of relucent honowre,  . . . . . . . .   305   Why Come Ye    1037
        Englande] 'To Englande' MS Rawlinson C. 813
FLOWRE
    Princes of youth, and flowre of goodly porte, . . . . . .   337   Garlande        897
    Princes of youth, and flowre of goodly porte, . . . . . .   337   Garlande        904
    With margerain jentyll, /The flowre of goodlyhede,  . . .   337   Garlande        907
    With margerain jantill, /The flowre of goodlyhede,  . . .   338   Garlande        915
    With margerain jantill, /The flowre of goodlyhede,  . . .   338   Garlande        923
    Enuwyd your colowre /Is lyke the dasy flowre  . . . . . .   340   Garlande        986
        your] 'her' MS Cotton Vitellius E.x
    The fresshest flowre of May;  . . . . . . . . . . . . . .   340   Garlande        990
    Mirry Margaret, /As mydsomer flowre,  . . . . . . . . . .   340   Garlande       1005
    Of mirry Margarete, /As mydsomer flowre,  . . . . . . . .   341   Garlande       1020
    As mirry Margarete, /This midsomer flowre,  . . . . . . .   341   Garlande       1035
        This] 'The' MS Cotton Vitellius E.x
    This goodly flowre with stormis was untwynde. . . . . . .   352   Garlande       1445
FLOWRES
    Smale flowres helpt to sett . . . . . . . . . . . . . . .   339   Garlande        969
```

FLOWRIS —FOLY

FLOWRIS

	Page	Title	Line
England, now gaddir flowris,	110	Lawde	6
All frutis and flowris grew there in there kynde.	331	Garlande	678
and] not in †Fakes 1523			
In castyng, in turnynge, in florisshyng of flowris,	334	Garlande	802
The silke, the golde, the flowris fresshe to syght,	343	Garlande	1111
Enflorid with flowris and slymy snaylis,	345	Garlande	1160

FLOWRYSSHE

The red rose in honour to flowrysshe and sprynge!'	231	Speke Parott	35

FLOWUR

These maydens full meryly with many a dyvers flowur	231	Speke Parott	11
a] not in †MS Harley 2252			

FLUSSHE

He facithe owte at a flusshe with, 'Shewe, take all!'	243	Speke Parott	430

FO

To suffre hym slayn of his mortall fo?	30	Dol Dethe	38
You I assure, absens is my fo,	44	Balettys3	36
With, 'Fo, ther is a stenche!	219	El Rummynge	180
His frende as his fo!	293	Why Come Ye	583

FODE

Strawe, Jamys foder, ye play the fode;	35	Man Margery	10
Nay, I tell you, I am not wonte to fode	188	Magnyfycence	1698

FOGGY

All foggy fat she was;	226	El Rummynge	483

FOISTY

Foo, foisty bawdias, sum smellid of the smoke.	330	Garlande	639

FOY

In loyalte and foy /Lyke to Ector of Troy,	369	Albany	436

FOYNES

He foynes and he frygges;	284	Why Come Ye	224

FOLABILITE

And of frenetyke folabilite,	138	Ven Tongues	43

FOLAM

For Folam peason /With him be nat geson;	304	Why Come Ye	999

FOLE

Nay, jape not with hym, he is no small fole;	38	Coystrowne1	50
To fede a fole, and for to preye a dawe.	58	Bowge	437
preye] 'preue' Wynkyn de Worde 1510			
It was so prety a fole,	74	Phy Sparrow	115
Chalenge yor selfe for a fole, call me no more knave.	122	Garnesche1	42
Gup, gorbellyd Godfrey, gup, Garnysche, gaudy fole!	123	Garnesche2	36
Ye xulde have kowththyd me a fole.	127	Garnesche3	119
Ye ar a fole owtelauyd;	128	Garnesche3	183
A fole is he with welth that fallyth at debate.	140	Magnyfycence	5
What, syr, wolde ye make me a poppynge fole?	146	Magnyfycence	232
In fayth, I wyll not say that ye shall prove a fole,	148	Magnyfycence	301
I can fede forth a fole and fede hym by the eyre;	160	Magnyfycence	712
A, I trowe ye shall coughe me a fole.	170	Magnyfycence	1064
Ye, a fole the tone, and a fole the tother.	170	Magnyfycence	1091
Ye, a fole the tone, and a fole the tother.	170	Magnyfycence	1091
By the masse, yet art thou more fole than I.	171	Magnyfycence	1111
Nay, iwys, fole. It is a doteryll.	173	Magnyfycence	1175
Ye, but thou can play the fole without a vyser.	173	Magnyfycence	1177
But yet thou shalt holde me a fole styll.	173	Magnyfycence	1184
Why, wenyst thou that I were as moche a fole as thou?	173	Magnyfycence	1188
Nowe put on, fole, thy cote agayne.	173	Magnyfycence	1205
To tourne a fole out of his clowtes.	174	Magnyfycence	1211
And for a fole a man wolde hym take.	174	Magnyfycence	1212
I shall flappe hym as a fole to fall at my fete.	182	Magnyfycence	1507
It was a ronner; nay, fole, I warant her blode warme.	191	Magnyfycence	1811
I sende ofte tymes a fole to his sonne.	195	Magnyfycence	1935
Of [a] foles fylly /That had a fole with Wylly,	224	El Rummynge	389
a] not in †Lant 1545, Kynge & Marche 1554, Day 1560, Marshe 1568; fylly] 'silly' Marshe 1568			
'My propyr Parott, my lytell pratye fole.'	231	Speke Parott	20
And Inter didascolos is rekened for a fole;	235	Speke Parott	172
Our mare hath cast her fole,	281	Why Come Ye	85
And ye shall well fynde he is a very fole;	318	Garlande	207
well fynde] 'fynde wele' MS Cotton Vitellius E.x			

FOLES

In no place well, but foles with hym fraye!	58	Bowge	446
hym] not in †Wynkyn de Worde 1499, Marshe 1568			
What, frantyke Fansy, in a foles case?	169	Magnyfycence	1046
Nay, it is I that foles can make;	174	Magnyfycence	1213
And what maner of people he maketh foles?	174	Magnyfycence	1217
Of [a] foles fylly /That had a fole with Wylly,	224	El Rummynge	388
a] not in †Lant 1545, Kynge & Marche 1554, Day 1560, Marshe 1568; fylly] 'silly' Marshe 1568			
He countys them foles and dawes;	286	Why Come Ye	315
And to prove your selfe suche foles.	378	Replycacion	145
And crye God mercy, lyke frantyke foles.	382	Replycacion	299

FOLY

What willfull foly made you to ryse agayn	30	Dol Dethe	53
At our foly and our unstedfastnesse;	46	Bowge	6
Your foly ys to grett	127	Garnesche3	140
Any such foly to rest or to be.	138	Ven Tongues	35
This worlde is full of my foly.	152	Magnyfycence	411
Counterfet wysdome, and workes of foly;	153	Magnyfycence	471

	Page	Title	Line
FOLYS —FOLOWE			
What, fonnysshe Foly! I befole thy face.	169	Magnyfycence	1045
But, broder Foly, I wonder moche of one thynge,	170	Magnyfycence	1068
For all that my name hyght Foly,	171	Magnyfycence	1110
By God, syr, Foly, myne owne sworne brother.	172	Magnyfycence	1159
Here FOLY maketh semblaunt to take a lowse	173	Magnyfycence	SD
Here FOLY maketh semblaunt	173	Magnyfycence	SD
To felowshyp with foly I can hym brynge.	174	Magnyfycence	1215
That every man lawghyth at his foly.	175	Magnyfycence	1251
For with foly so do I them lede	175	Magnyfycence	1260
It is but foly every dell.	175	Magnyfycence	1275
For there be other that foly dothe use	175	Magnyfycence	1280
And whan foly cometh, all is past.	176	Magnyfycence	1289
But all is foly that I can se.	176	Magnyfycence	1291
Maketh man and woman in foly to fall.	176	Magnyfycence	1295
And I Foly bryngeth them to qui fuit gadde;	176	Magnyfycence	1301
Why, shall I not have Foly with me also?	176	Magnyfycence	1306
To se what foly is used in every place;	177	Magnyfycence	1327
Foly hath a rome, I say, in every route;	177	Magnyfycence	1328
To put where he lyst, foly hath fre chace;	177	Magnyfycence	1329
Foly and fansy all where every man dothe face and brace.	177	Magnyfycence	1330
Foly fotyth it properly, fansy ledyth the dawnce,	177	Magnyfycence	1331
I say it is foly to gyve all welth away.	180	Magnyfycence	1430
Here cometh in FOLY.	191	Magnyfycence	SD
Here goth FOLY away.	192	Magnyfycence	SD
And Foly, my broder, that made you moche game.	193	Magnyfycence	1872
That folowe theyr fansyes in foly to fall.	194	Magnyfycence	1897
It is foly to grudge agaynst his vysytacyon.	196	Magnyfycence	1990
It is foly agaynst God for to plete.	197	Magnyfycence	2035
Alasse my foly! Alasse my wanton wyll!	198	Magnyfycence	2062
Some fall to foly, them selfe for to spyll,	200	Magnyfycence	2139
Freers, with foly I make them so fayne	201	Magnyfycence	2147
In Goddys mercy, I tell them, is but foly to truste;	205	Magnyfycence	2289
Then ye of foly in tymes past you repent?	209	Magnyfycence	2433
'Then ye repent you of foly in tymes past' †Rastell & Treveris C 1530, B			
A ha, fansy and foly met with you, I trowe.	210	Magnyfycence	2448
Subtyle Sym Sly /With madde foly.	300	Why Come Ye	857
Sym Sly] 'Symonye' †Kele 1545.3			
He jugeth it no foly;	305	Why Come Ye	1047
As wele foly as wysdome oft ye do avaunce,	317	Garlande	180
ye do] 'tyme ye' MS Cotton Vitellius E.x			
How dotynge age wolde jape with yonge foly	322	Garlande	361
To face out her foly with a midsomer mase;	346	Garlande	1208
It is no foly to use the Walshemannys hoos.	347	Garlande	1239
Thorowe your owne foly,	376	Replycacion	84
His foly so to face.	379	Replycacion	196
FOLYS			
In them be no scolys /For braynsycke frantycke folys:	68	Hauke	249
Are nat these Scottys /Folys and sottys,	116	Ag Scottes	30
Baile, baile at yow bothe, frantyke folys! Follow on the chase!	123	Garnesche2	31
What? Wolde ye have mo folys, and are so many?	172	Magnyfycence	1170
In fayth, I can make you bothe folys, and I wyll.	172	Magnyfycence	1173
All men beware of suche folys!	175	Magnyfycence	1265
Yet some folys say ye arre furnysshyd with knakkes,	239	Speke Parott	292
To jumbyll, to stombyll, to tumbyll down lyke folys;	243	Speke Parott	425
Sume fayne themselfe folys, and wolde be callyd wyse,	329	Garlande	616
The Nacyoun of Folys he left not behynde.	353	Garlande	1470
FOLYSHE			
The doterell, that folyshe pek;	82	Phy Sparrow	409
FOLYSSHE			
And as for me, I take but one folysshe way,	170	Magnyfycence	1076
What! Wenyst thou that I were so folysshe and so fonde?	170	Magnyfycence	1098
Of frantycke frenesy /And folysshe fantasy,	283	Why Come Ye	187
Poppynge folysshe dawes.	285	Why Come Ye	264
But ye were folysshe nyse.	378	Replycacion	130
FOLYSSHLY			
And folysshly there fopped	377	Replycacion	120
FOLYSSHNES			
Of frantycknes and folysshnes whyche ys the grett state?	243	Speke Parott	417
FOLKE			
To poore folke at large,	83	Phy Sparrow	456
FOLLEST			
The follest sloven ondyr heven,	133	Garnesche5	145
FOLLY			
This fals Envy /Sayth that I /Use great folly	95	Phy Sparrow	951
FOLLOW			
Baile, baile at yow bothe, frantyke folys! Follow on the chase!	123	Garnesche2	31
FOLOW			
I folow even after your noble grace.	151	Magnyfycence	395
Whate sequele shall folow when pendugims mete togethyr?	243	Speke Parott	415
All men must folow his desyre.	287	Why Come Ye	345
must] not in Marshe 1568			
Of that most folow then consequently,	317	Garlande	172
FOLOWE			
That folowe as you may se.	106	Phy Sparrow	1379
you] 'ye' Wyght 1553, Kitson 1560.6, Marshe 1568			
Take Lyberte to rule, and folowe myne entent.	147	Magnyfycence	238
That folowe fonde fantasyes and vertu refuse.	175	Magnyfycence	1281

FOLOWETH—FORBYD

	Page	Title	Line
Syr, ye shall folowe myne appetyte and intent.	180	Magnyfycence	1420
I folowe in felycyte without reversse;	181	Magnyfycence	1491
What so ever ye do, folowe your owne wyll,	185	Magnyfycence	1595
That folowe theyr fansyes in foly to fall.	194	Magnyfycence	1897
Dyspare is my name, that adversyte dothe f[o]lowe;	205	Magnyfycence	2284
folowe] 'felowe' †Rastell & Treveris C 1530, B, Douce Fragment d.7			
They folowe your desyris,	263	Collyn Clout	683
That folowe as ye may se:	350	Garlande	1372
We will so folowe in the chace	371	Albany	503

FOLOWETH
Here after foloweth the boke entytuled Ware the Hauke	61	Hauke	1
Here after foloweth the boke of Phyllyp Sparowe	71	Phy Sparrow	1
Whereof the elegy /Foloweth by and by.	92	Phy Sparrow	825
and her foloweth an addicyon made by Maister Skelton.	103	Phy Sparrow	R
HIS EPITAPH FOLOWETH DEVOUTLY;	109	Epitaphe2	1
Here after foloweth a lytell boke,	278	Why Come Ye	1

FOLOWYD
This sayd, a great nowmber folowyd by and by	321	Garlande	323

FOLOWYNGE
Folowynge the chase	301	Why Come Ye	872
as more at large it doth apere in the proces folowynge.	312	Garlande	1

FOLOWYTHE
Here folowythe Dyvers Balettys and Dyties Solacyous	41	Balettys	1

FOME
Require hym to convey yow ovyr the salte fome;	239	Speke Parott	302

FOMYD
For her mouth fomyd /And her bely groned:	223	El Rummynge	341

FON
Delt he not lyke a fon?	65	Hauke	128
A very fon, /A very asse /Wyll take upon /To compasse	164	Magnyfycence	863
Why, wenyst thou that I cannot make the play the fon?	173	Magnyfycence	1185

FOND
Lo, these fond sottes /And tratlyng Skottys,	115	Ag Scottes	5

FONDE
This fonde frantyke fouconer,	63	Hauke	43
That scrybblyd your fonde scrolle,	126	Garnesche3	91
Thy fonde face can me nat fray.	134	Garnesche5	171
That Fansy with his fonde consayte	159	Magnyfycence	678
I move them, I mase them, I make them so fonde,	161	Magnyfycence	742
Nowe, in good faythe, thou art a fonde gest.	170	Magnyfycence	1096
What! Wenyst thou that I were so folysshe and so fonde?	170	Magnyfycence	1098
That folowe fonde fantasyes and vertu refuse.	175	Magnyfycence	1281
Howe be it, that fonde felowe is a mery knave.	180	Magnyfycence	1455
Your fonde hed in your furred hode!	310	Why Come Ye2	19
your] (2nd) 'a' MS Rawlinson C. 813			
He fyndith fals mesuris out of his fonde fiddill.'	333	Garlande	741
fals mesuris out] 'owght fals mesuris' MS Cotton Vit.E.x			
With fonde Fraunces, French kyng.	368	Albany	383
His blode with fonde dotage.	369	Albany	415

FONDNESSE
Nay. It was your fondnesse that ye have usyd.	193	Magnyfycence	1866

FONGE
That ryght no man can fonge.	276	Collyn Clout	1197

FONNE
Ye rostyd, lyke a fonne,	125	Garnesche3	30
This newe fonne jet	165	Magnyfycence	877

FONNY
This make I my falyre fonny,	220	El Rummynge	229

FONNYSSHE
Tusshe! Fonnysshe Fansy, thou arte frantyke.	158	Magnyfycence	650
What, fonnysshe Foly! I befole thy face.	169	Magnyfycence	1045

FOO
But as for that, connynge hath no foo	58	Bowge	447
Agaynst all [s]autes of your goostly foo.	206	Magnyfycence	2329
sautes] 'fautes' †Rastell & Treveris C 1530, B, Douce Fragment d.7			
Of Demostenes, that was his utter foo.	317	Garlande	167
Foo, foisty bawdias, sum smellid of the smoke.	330	Garlande	639

FOOLE
'He is but a foole; /Let hym go to scole!	247	Collyn Clout	28

FOOLYS
These frantyke foolys I hate most of all;	36	Coystrowne1	2

FOOS
Of suche as be his foos	370	Albany	469

FOOTE
And with his forme foote he shoke forthe this wrytyng:	328	Garlande	595

FOPPED
And folysshly there fopped	377	Replycacion	120

FORAGE
And with suche forage /Hunte the boskage,	280	Why Come Ye	52

FORBEDE
God forbede that it other wyse sholde be!	147	Magnyfycence	246

FORBERE
Lyberte, I wote well, forbere no man there may;	142	Magnyfycence	50
Why, wenest thou that I forbere the for thyne owne sake?	202	Magnyfycence	2186

FORBYD
God forbyd ye sholde be let	142	Magnyfycence	63

	Page	Title	Line
FORBORNE			
And from felycyte may not be forborne,	146	Magnyfycence	220
FORCASTYNG			
So myche forcastyng, and so farre an after-dele;	244	Speke Parott	463
FORCE			
But, no force, I shall ones mete with the;	55	Bowge	334
What force ye, so that [y]e be payde?	187	Magnyfycence	1672
ye be] 'he be' †Rastell & Treveris C 1530, B			
No force what thoughe his neyghbour dye in a dyche.	189	Magnyfycence	1752
That of force he must	298	Why Come Ye	752
Frome the laureat senate by force of proscripcyon.	318	Garlande	225
That I ne force what though it be discurid.	332	Garlande	731
To harnnes bryght, /By force of myght,	355	Garlande	1557
FORCEBLY			
Whiche constrayned him forcebly	296	Why Come Ye	702
I am forcebly constrayned /At Juvynals request	309	Why Come Ye	1210
FORCIBLY			
So forcibly upon this Erle thow ran,	32	Dol Dethe	124
FORCYD			
Tyll at the last they forcyd me sore,	324	Garlande	446
sore] 'so sore' Marshe 1568			
FOR-DREDE			
That made the Romaynes all /For-drede and to quake;	88	Phy Sparrow	667
That] 'What' †Kele 1545.2, Wyght 1553			
FORECASTELL			
The forecastell of my shyppe	277	Collyn Clout	1251
FORESAYD			
Over this, the foresayd lay	254	Collyn Clout	301
FOREST			
In the forest of Arden.	88	Phy Sparrow	658
of] not in Wyght 1553, Kitson 1560.6, Marshe 1568			
Thus stode I in the frytthy forest of Galtres,	312	Garlande	22
That in the forest was none so great a tre	320	Garlande	277
FORESTE			
in the foreste of Galtres,	312	Garlande	1
FORETOP			
But I shall frounce them on the foretop and gar them to quake.	182	Magnyfycence	1514
FORE TOP			
And with his [frownsid] fore top	105	Phy Sparrow	1340
frownsid] not in †Kele 1545.2, Wyght 1553, Kitson 1560.6, Marshe 1568			
FORETOPPE			
Whan the good ale soppe /Dothe daunce in theyr foretoppe;	260	Collyn Clout	531
FOREVER			
Forever in tables of bras,	75	Phy Sparrow	150
FORFENDE			
That ever thou thryve, God it forfende!	171	Magnyfycence	1114
And from crafters and hafters I you forfende.	210	Magnyfycence	2456
FORGATE			
But blessyd Bachus that never man forgate,	322	Garlande	369
FORGE			
I wyll not fayne nor forge;	64	Hauke	88
To styre up your stomake you must you forge,	185	Magnyfycence	1613
FORGED			
What have ye, villayn, forged, /And virulently dysgorged	367	Albany	320
FORGERS			
Fals forgers of mony, for kownnage atteintid,	329	Garlande	611
kownnage] 'coynnage' Marshe 1568			
FORGET			
To forget deadly syn	98	Phy Sparrow	1081
I shall it never forget nor leve it behynde,	212	Magnyfycence	2506
FORGETFULNESSE			
Whiche, truly to expresse, /Is a forgetfulnesse,	290	Why Come Ye	468
FORGEVE			
God forgeve hym his mysdedes.	107	Epitaphe1	19
FORGO			
We may not well forgo /The countrynge of the coe;	83	Phy Sparrow	467
FORGOTEN			
He had forgoten all dedely syn.	42	Balettys1	11
And have forgoten your old, trew, lovyng knyght.	42	Balettys2	14
Theyr lessons forgoten they have	251	Collyn Clout	169
FORGOTTEN			
Theyr dyriges are forgotten,	257	Collyn Clout	425
Theyr dyriges] 'The Diriges' Kele 1545.1, 'the dyrige' MS Harley 2252			
And vertue is forgotten,	261	Collyn Clout	597
FORKED			
My tonge is with favell forked and tyned.	160	Magnyfycence	727
With money, yf it wyll happe /To catche the forked cappe.	249	Collyn Clout	89
FORMALLY			
Of somer, so formally she fotid the daunce.	331	Garlande	686
FORMAR			
Of formar writinge by any presidente	30	Dol Dethe	23
The famylyaryte, the formar dalyaunce,	42	Balettys2	2
Of honour and worshyp which hath the formar date:	336	Garlande	842
Of honour and worship it hath the formar date.	336	Garlande	849
Of honour and worship it hath the formar date.	336	Garlande	856
Of honour and worship it hath the formar date.	336	Garlande	863

	Page	Title	Line
FORMARE			
Regestringe trewly every formare date;	29	Dol Dethe	18
FORMD			
That with one worde formd all thing of nought;	34	Dol Dethe	191
FORME			
Be sumdele lyke in forme and shap,	36	Coystrownel	9
In maner and forme as ye shall after here.	323	Garlande	399
Under the forme as I sayd tofore,	324	Garlande	443
tofore] 'before' Marshe 1568			
And with his forme foote he shoke forthe this wrytyng:	328	Garlande	595
FORMED			
Thorow bounte of hym that formed all solace,	35	Dol Dethe	214
Such relucent grace /Is formed in her face;	100	Phy Sparrow	1160
FORMER			
By his former othe,	307	Why Come Ye	1131
Returne we to our former processe.	384	Replycacion	R
FORMEST			
Syth unto me formest this processe is erectyd,	211	Magnyfycence	2482
But Phebus was formest of all that cam theder;	320	Garlande	287
And formest of all dame Flora, the quene	331	Garlande	685
FORMYDABLE			
Terrible of countenaunce and passynge formydable,	328	Garlande	591
FORMYST			
That wonte was to be formyst, now to come behynde.	144	Magnyfycence	144
FORS			
Me for to chalenge that of your chalennge makyth so lytyll fors.	123	Garnesche2	19
It made no great fors	366	Albany	282
FORSAYD			
So passyd we forthe into the forsayd place,	328	Garlande	561
FORSAKE			
There can no favour nor frendshyp hym forsake.	48	Bowge	103
And never wold him forsake.	90	Phy Sparrow	733
That wyll not I forsake,	143	Magnyfycence	100
For myschefe wyll mayster us yf measure us forsake.	144	Magnyfycence	154
Your ordenaunce, syr, I wyll not forsake.	145	Magnyfycence	181
And to forsake theyr corum	256	Collyn Clout	377
His owne realme to forsake?	367	Albany	328
Therfore I vyse you to forsake	382	Replycacion	297
FORSEDE			
They saide they forsede not nor carede not to dy.	31	Dol Dethe	84
FORSETH			
It forseth not of reason, so it kepe ryme.	172	Magnyfycence	1150
FORSYTH			
Here is none forsyth whether you flete or synke.	147	Magnyfycence	254
FORSOKE			
Whom he forsoke with teene,	90	Phy Sparrow	742
FORSOTH			
'Forsoth,' quod I, 'to bye some of youre ware.'	48	Bowge	79
Nowe welcome, forsoth, Sad Cyrcumspeccyon.	209	Magnyfycence	2418
FORSOTHE			
'Forsothe,' quod she, 'how ever blowe the wynde,	49	Bowge	110
'Forsothe,' quod I, 'in this courte I dwell nowe.'	56	Bowge	377
Abusyon /Forsothe I hyght;	164	Magnyfycence	857
But nowe, forsothe, man, it maketh no mater;	175	Magnyfycence	1256
Forsothe, tell on. Hast thou any mo?	175	Magnyfycence	1262
mo] 'more' †Rastell & Treveris C 1530, B			
'Forsothe,' quod she, 'theys be haskardis and rebawdis,	329	Garlande	607
haskardis] 'hastardis' †Fakes 1523			
FORSTER			
Faire fall that forster that so well can bate his hownde!	313	Garlande	27
well] not in MS Cotton Vitellius E.x			
Recoverd whan the forster was gone, and sped	351	Garlande	1407
FORSWORNE			
Favell is false forsworne,	281	Why Come Ye	95
And falsest forsworne /That ever were borne.	362	Albany	117
And false forsworne faytour.	371	Albany	494
FORTH			
'Walke forth your way, ye cost me nought;	36	Man Margery	22
Come saylynge forth into that haven brood,	47	Bowge	37
And so forth per cetera;	104	Phy Sparrow	1321
Shewe forth, I pray you, here in what you intende.	141	Magnyfycence	40
Your reasons forth to fet.	142	Magnyfycence	64
I can fede forth a fole and lede hym by the eyre;	160	Magnyfycence	712
But one thynge I warne you, prece forth and be bolde.	184	Magnyfycence	1582
Cockes armes, howe Pleasure plucked hym forth!	189	Magnyfycence	1735
Ye, for requiem eternam groweth forth of his nose.	204	Magnyfycence	2260
Than sterte forth a fysgygge	228	El Rummynge	538
What can it avayle /To dryve forth a snayle,	246	Collyn Clout	2
They lumber forth the lawe	249	Collyn Clout	95
But slombre forth and slepe,	249	Collyn Clout	124
May be brought forth, such as can be founde,	318	Garlande	216
Percius pressed forth with problemes diffuse;	321	Garlande	338
Thus passid we forth walkynge unto the pretory	325	Garlande	477
When they were past and wente forth on there way,	327	Garlande	526
Thus talkyng we went forth in at a postern gate,	333	Garlande	766
forth] not in MS Cotton Vitellius E.x			
Come forth, jentylwomen, I pray you,' she sayd,	334	Garlande	773
The frame was browght forth with his wevyng pin.	334	Garlande	792

FORTHE —FORTUNED | | Page | Title | Line

	Page	Title	Line
Brought forth a godely babi!	339	Garlande	975
FORTHE			
Pressed forthe boldly to witstand the myght,	31	Dol Dethe	87
Passe forthe, Parotte, towardes some passengere;	239	Speke Parott	301
And com forthe at large,	264	Collyn Clout	693
com forthe] 'conforte' †Godfray 1531, Kele 1545.1, Marshe 1568			
To shote forthe his shot;	265	Collyn Clout	751
Have hym forthe by and by /To the Marshalsy,	289	Why Come Ye	431
On every halfe my reasons forthe I sought,	312	Garlande	10
On] 'One' †Fakes 1523			
Call forthe, let se where is your clarionar,	318	Garlande	233
So passyd we forthe into the forsayd place,	328	Garlande	561
And with his forme foote he shoke forthe this wrytyng:	328	Garlande	595
As so forthe per cetera;	349	Garlande	1314
And porisshly forthe popped	377	Replycacion	121
Come forthe, ye pope holy, /Full of melancoly!	381	Replycacion	247
FORTHWITH			
Forthwith, he made on me a prowde assawte,	55	Bowge	316
Nowe to curteys, forthwith unkynde,	168	Magnyfycence	1008
All that I make forthwith I marre;	169	Magnyfycence	1036
I am forthwith as hole as a troute.	185	Magnyfycence	1624
Nowe she wyll laughe, forthwith she wyll frowne;	197	Magnyfycence	2024
Nowe all in welth, forthwith in poverte;	197	Magnyfycence	2027
And forthwith fell on slepe.	224	El Rummynge	375
Now clere wether, forthwith a stormy showre;	312	Garlande	12
Forthwith there rose amonge the thronge	319	Garlande	246
A cry anone forthwith she made proclame,	325	Garlande	453
Forthwith, I say, thus wandrynge in my thought,	325	Garlande	456
Forthwith upon this, as it were in a thought,	343	Garlande	1100
Forthwith she commaundid I shulde take my place.	344	Garlande	1142
Than forthwith by and by	374	Replycacion	4
That forthwith we must nede	385	Replycacion	387
FORTHWYTH			
For forthwyth there I had him slayne,	61	Bowge	523
FORTY			
What! Thou wylte coughe me a dawe for forty pens?	170	Magnyfycence	1060
Som be wrestyd there that they thynke on it forty dayes,	204	Magnyfycence	2274
FORTOP			
And with his frownsid fortop	349	Garlande	1333
FORTRESSE			
May wynne with a sawte the fortresse of the holde.	184	Magnyfycence	1581
FORTUNATE			
And geve the grace to be more fortunate!	33	Dol Dethe	165
Her marchaundyse is pure and fortunate,	47	Bowge	52
Her] 'Here' †Wynkyn de Worde 1499			
Fortunate in all his *faytes.	368	Albany	398
*faytes] 'fayctes' Scattergood			
FORTUNE			
Tyll fykkill Fortune began on hym to frowne.	33	Dol Dethe	133
Bewayle thy fortune, with vaynys wan and blo.	45	Balettys5	3
O Fortune unfrendly, Fortune unkynde thow art,	45	Balettys5	4
O Fortune unfrendly, Fortune unkynde thow art,	45	Balettys5	4
But Fortune enforsyth me so carefully to endure,	46	Balettys5	13
Fortune gydeth and ruleth all our shyppe.	49	Bowge	111
Suwed to Fortune that she wold be theyre frynde.	49	Bowge	121
The sayle is up, Fortune ruleth our helme,	49	Bowge	127
Fortune theyr frende, with whome oft she dyde daunce:	50	Bowge	141
Fortune to you gyftes of grace hath lente:	50	Bowge	152
Ye stonde in favoure and Fortune is your gyde,	50	Bowge	171
It is your fortune for to have that grace;	53	Bowge	272
Of fortune this the chaunce /Standeth on varyaunce:	81	Phy Sparrow	366
Thus fortune hath tourned you, I dare well say,	119	Ag Scottes	164
Fortune on you therfore dyd frowne.	120	Ag Scottes	176
I trowe good fortune hath annexyd us together,	146	Magnyfycence	198
Fortune to her lawys can not abandune me;	181	Magnyfycence	1459
But I shall of Fortune rule the reyne.	181	Magnyfycence	1460
As yf a man fortune to touche you on the quyke -	185	Magnyfycence	1611
Beholde howe Fortune o[n] hym hath frounde.	195	Magnyfycence	1947
on] 'of' †Rastell & Treveris C 1530, B			
Alas! Of Fortune I may well complayne.	197	Magnyfycence	2030
O feble fortune, O doulfull destyny!	198	Magnyfycence	2048
Set not all your affyaunce in Fortune full of gyle;	211	Magnyfycence	2501
Sodenly thus Fortune can bothe smyle and frowne,	212	Magnyfycence	2529
Sodenly thus Fortune can bothe smyle and frowne,	213	Magnyfycence	2536
Where men of that contre by fortune me fynde,	231	Speke Parott	5
Yf fortune be frendly, and grace be the guyde,	234	Speke Parott	139
Fortune so tourneth the ball	262	Collyn Clout	632
Fortune may chaunce to flytte,	271	Collyn Clout	994
How fortune wyll endure.	271	Collyn Clout	1003
I may fortune for to ryme	310	Why Come Ye2	22
How oftyn fortune varyeth in an howre,	312	Garlande	11
And if so hym fortune to wryte true and plaine,	314	Garlande	85
so] not in MS Cotton Vitellius E.x			
O fatall Fortune, what have I offendid?	321	Garlande	316
Whom fortune and fate playnly have discust	337	Garlande	881
Fortune to stande betwene you and the lyght.	344	Garlande	1134
FORTUNED			
Yet wyth a pretty gyn /I fortuned to come in,	64	Hauke	94

FORTUNES — FOUNDE

	Page	Title	Line
How fortuned you, Magnyfycence, so far to fal behynde?	209	Magnyfycence	2423
FORTUNES			
Ware yet, I rede you, of Fortunes double cast,	45	Balettys4	3
I fere nothynge Fortunes perplexyte.	181	Magnyfycence	1461
Syr, remembre the tourne of Fortunes whele,	197	Magnyfycence	2022
FORTUNIS			
In fortunis favour ever to endure,	351	Garlande	1402
FORTUNYS			
In Fortunys frendshyppe there is no stedfastnesse;	201	Magnyfycence	2156
To pronostycate truly the chaunce of fortunys dyse;	234	Speke Parott	136
FORTUNS			
O dolorous chaunce of Fortuns fraward hande!	32	Dol Dethe	110
Till the chaunce ran ageyne hym of Fortuns double dyse.	33	Dol Dethe	140
FORWARDE			
For whiche ende goth forwarde ye take lytell charge.	148	Magnyfycence	296
FOSE			
Nat worth a cockly fose!	286	Why Come Ye	288
FOTE			
Upon her prety fote?	100	Phy Sparrow	1147
By Goddes fote, and I dare well fyght, for I wyll not start.	161	Magnyfycence	768
Goddys fote! I warant you I am a gentylman borne;	203	Magnyfycence	2216
Wounded from the fote to the crowne of the hede:	207	Magnyfycence	2364
As fayre and as whyte /As the fote of a kyte.	225	El Rummynge	425
Was well a fote thycke,	225	El Rummynge	430
Leste that his fote slyppe,	263	Collyn Clout	666
Sterte all at ones an hundrethe fote backe.	320	Garlande	282
FOTEBALL			
On knees to fall /To the foteball;	108	Epitaphe1	72
FOTED			
Foted lyke a plane, /Legge[d] lyke a crane;	215	El Rummynge	49
Legged] 'Legges' †Lant 1545, Kynge & Marche 1554, Day 1560, Marshe 1568			
FOTID			
Of somer, so formally she fotid the daunce.	331	Garlande	686
FOTYNG			
Stande sure and take good fotyng,	273	Collyn Clout	1072
FOTYNGE			
That clymmeth hyer than he may fotynge have;	46	Bowge	27
FOTYS			
Thy slyppers they swap it, yet thou fotys it lyke a swanne.	161	Magnyfycence	765
FOTYTH			
Foly fotyth it properly, fansy ledyth the dawnce,	177	Magnyfycence	1331
FOUCONER			
This fonde frantyke fouconer,	63	Hauke	43
FOUGHT			
I herde say that adversyte with Magnyfycence had fought.	210	Magnyfycence	2460
FOULE			
Of foule detraccion God kepe the from the blast.	34	Dol Dethe	173
Gone is this knave, this rybaude foule and leude.	58	Bowge	414
And from foule Alecto,	73	Phy Sparrow	74
So thou, foule cat that thou arte,	79	Phy Sparrow	302
The owle, that is so foule,	82	Phy Sparrow	442
is] not in Kitson 1560.6, Marshe 1568			
His foule desyre /Wyll suffre no slepe	95	Phy Sparrow	933
His foule semblaunt /All displesaunt;	95	Phy Sparrow	936
foule] 'feule' †Kele 1545.2, Wyght 1553			
Why, can ye not put out that foule freke?	158	Magnyfycence	657
There is many evyll faveryd, and thou be foule!	167	Magnyfycence	969
A sorte of foule drabbes /All scurvy with scabbes.	218	El Rummynge	139
But she was a foule slut,	223	El Rummynge	340
She was somwhat foule, /Crokenebbed lyke an oule;	225	El Rummynge	426
Crokenebbed] 'Croke necked' †Lant 1545, Kynge & Marche 1554, Day 1560, Marshe 1568			
And foule covytousnesse /And other wretchednesse,	247	Collyn Clout	42
Suche a foule coystrowne,	363	Albany	171
FOULES			
Beestes, byrdes, and foules,	78	Phy Sparrow	259
FOUND			
She wadyd over, she found a man	42	Balettys1	17
If any such might be found!	76	Phy Sparrow	188
And I have found it trew.	219	El Rummynge	210
How Dame Minerva first found the Olyve Tre, she red	351	Garlande	1404
FOUNDACYONS			
And with foundacyons melles,	257	Collyn Clout	415
FOUNDE			
Therein they founde royall marchaundyse,	47	Bowge	41
Ye be an apte man, as ony can be founde	50	Bowge	155
Ay, in my pouche a buckell I have founde;	57	Bowge	397
But yet oftyme suche dremes be founde trewe.	61	Bowge	538
In Romaine letters I never founde lack	137	Ven Tongues	17
Than to be founde in any such faute.	137	Ven Tongues	25
Ryght so a sharp fansy must be founde	155	Magnyfycence	553
We had hym founde, we sholde hym brynge,	158	Magnyfycence	653
That all men it founde /Through out Englonde.	165	Magnyfycence	882
What hast thou founde there? By God, a lowse.	173	Magnyfycence	1198
A, Cockes armes! Where myght suche one be founde?	184	Magnyfycence	1569
It wolde be founde so yf it were well tryde.	210	Magnyfycence	2449
Ales founde therin no thornes,	224	El Rummynge	379

FOUNDERS — FRAME

	Page	Title	Line
She founde therein no bones.	224	El Rummynge	381
bones] 'bornes' Day 1560			
To him he hathe founde	291	Why Come Ye	501
Tyll better layser be founde;	294	Why Come Ye	627
Yet harde is to make but sum fawt be founde.'	315	Garlande	112
May be brought forth, such as can be founde,	318	Garlande	216
Anone, I sey, this trumpet were founde out,	319	Garlande	243
Habillimentis royall founde out industriously;	336	Garlande	851
That of Aconcyus whan she founde the byll	337	Garlande	886
If ony recordis in noumbyr can be founde,	345	Garlande	1150
And what honour is founde	369	Albany	425
Therwith for to be founde /At the unyversyte,	378	Replycacion	147

FOUNDERS

So that theyr founders soules	257	Collyn Clout	421
Theyr founders lye there rotten;	257	Collyn Clout	426

FOUR

Ye, thou haste the four quarters of a knave.	172	Magnyfycence	1165
In faythe, I gyve the four quarters of a knave.	204	Magnyfycence	2252

FOURE

Full subtyll persones in nombre foure and thre.	49	Bowge	133
With other foure of theyr affynyte:	50	Bowge	139
The foure ordres of freres.	267	Collyn Clout	832

FOURME

To loke on God in fourme of brede,	272	Collyn Clout	1024

FOURMEST

For thou fourmest suche fantasyes in theyr mynde	175	Magnyfycence	1284

FOURTY

It had ben hers, I wene, /More then fourty yere;	216	El Rummynge	58

FOWLE

Mooste noble Erle! O fowle mysuryd grounde,	32	Dol Dethe	118
Ye fowle, fers and felle, as Syr Ferumbras the ffreke,	122	Garnesche1	15
Thou fowle, chorlyshe parote,	128	Garnesche3	167
I sey, thow felle and fowle flessh fly,	131	Garnesche5	65
Nay. It is a farly fowle.	166	Magnyfycence	923
Nowe take thou my dogge and gyve me thy fowle.	171	Magnyfycence	1116
The reste of suche reconyng may make a fowle fraye.	243	Speke Parott	403

FOWND

Now have I fownd that I have sought,	36	Man Margery	23

FOX

And to halow there the fox.	64	Hauke	110
The hare, the fox, the gray,	281	Why Come Ye	121
Spekyng in paroblis, how the fox, the grey,	315	Garlande	101

FOXE

Me thoughte his gowne was all furred wyth foxe.	52	Bowge	234
Me] 'My' †Wynkyn de Worde 1499			
I saw a foxe sucke on a kowes ydder;	191	Magnyfycence	1814

FOXES

Lyke foxes in theyr denne,	283	Why Come Ye	164

FOXIS

Right shall the foxis chare,	111	Lawde	22

FRAGHTED

Fraghted with plesure to what ye coude devyse.	47	Bowge	42

FRAY

For whan she *fronneth she thynketh to make a fray.	49	Bowge	116
*fronneth] 'frouneth' Wynkyn de Worde 1510, Marshe 1568			
And was in suche a fray	77	Phy Sparrow	228
Ye were starke mad to make a fray,	119	Ag Scottes	143
Thy fonde face can me nat fray.	134	Garnesche5	171
Cockes ha[r]te! I trowe thou wylte make a fray.	163	Magnyfycence	808
harte] 'hate' †Rastell & Treveris C 1530, B			
Why, harde thou not of the fray,	166	Magnyfycence	932
The Frenche men he doth fray,	282	Why Come Ye	154
That put the in suche fray.	365	Albany	242

FRAYE

In no place well, but foles with hym fraye!	58	Bowge	446
hym] not in †Wynkyn de Worde 1499, Marshe 1568			
Thenne I, astonyed of that sodeyne fraye,	60	Bowge	501
That putteth fysshes to a fraye;	83	Phy Sparrow	463
Ye have determyned to make a fraye,	114	Scot Kynge	44
The reste of suche reconyng may make a fowle fraye.	243	Speke Parott	403
For in that fraye /Ye ranne awaye	360	Albany	35

FRAYES

Ye, for surety. Ofte peas is taken for frayes.	163	Magnyfycence	814

FRAYNE

Ones yet agayne /Of you I wolde frayne	289	Why Come Ye	400

FRAYS

Sume be moche spokyn of for makynge of frays;	317	Garlande	182

FRAM

What though I can fram	88	Phy Sparrow	659
though] 'thought' †Kele 1545.2			

FRAME

So out of frame, /So voyde of shame,	116	Ag Scottes	37
And takyn up in such a frame,	132	Garnesche5	110
What and I frame suche a slyght	159	Magnyfycence	677
The feldfare wolde have fydled, and it wolde not frame;	192	Magnyfycence	1838
Neyther frame a silogisme in phrisesomorum	235	Speke Parott	148
But blissed Bachus, that mastris oft doth frame,	322	Garlande	383
The frame was browght forth with his wevyng pin.	334	Garlande	792

FRAMED —FRE	Page	Title	Line

FRAMED
God of his goodnes him framed and wrought; .... 236 Speke Parott 212
FRAMES
But madly it frames, ... 374 Replycacion 11
FRANESY
And some I stryke with a franesy; .... 194 Magnyfycence 1932
FRANKE
Thought is franke and fre; .... 101 Phy Sparrow 1201
The whiche shulde be /Bothe franke and free, ... 264 Collyn Clout 711
FRANKO
For Syr Frollo de Franko was never halfe so talle. .... 121 Garneschel 5
FRANTICK
For frantick faitours half mad and half straught; .... 138 Ven Tongues 27
Now frantick, now starke wode! .... 293 Why Come Ye 578
FRANTIKNES
Frantiknes dothe rule and all thyng commaunde; .... 243 Speke Parott 420
For Frantiknes and Wylfulnes and Braynles ensembyll, ... 243 Speke Parott 423
FRANTYCK
Your frantyck fable not worth a fly, ... 118 Ag Scottes 104
FRANTYCKE
In them be no scolys /For braynsycke frantycke folys: ..... 68 Hauke 249
Now pandes mory, wax frantycke som men sey; .... 232 Speke Parott 46
  mory] 'mery' †MS Harley 2252; men] 'mad' †MS Harley 2252
Of frantycke frenesy /And folysshe fantasy, ... 283 Why Come Ye 186
FRANTYCKNES
Of frantycknes and folysshnes whyche ys the grett state? ... 243 Speke Parott 417
FRANTYK
What frantyk frensy fyll in youre brayne? .... 30 Dol Dethe 51
FRANTYKE
These frantyke foolys I hate most of all; .... 36 Coystrownel 2
This fonde frantyke fouconer, ... 63 Hauke 43
Than is he sad, /Frantyke and mad; .... 95 Phy Sparrow 940
They are so stowre, /So frantyke mad, ... 115 Ag Scottes 13
Baile, baile at yow bothe, frantyke folys! Follow on the chase! 123 Garnesche2 31
Thow ar frantyke and lakkyst wyt, ... 132 Garnesche5 118
Tusshe! Fonnysshe Fansy, thou arte frantyke. .... 158 Magnyfycence 650
Frantyke Fansy-Servyce I hyght; .... 169 Magnyfycence 1023
What, frantyke Fansy, in a foles case? .... 169 Magnyfycence 1046
Howe frantyke fansy fyrst of all .... 176 Magnyfycence 1294
For, frantyke Fansy, thou makyst men madde; .... 176 Magnyfycence 1300
Are ye nat frantyke madde, /And wretchedly bestadde, ... 368 Albany 363
Mad, frantyke and savage. .... 369 Albany 413
And crye God mercy, lyke frantyke foles. .... 382 Replycacion 299
FRAUDE
Howe they have no fraude. .... 267 Collyn Clout 853
  fraude] 'faude' †Godfray 1531, 'fawte' MS Harley 2252
FRAUNCE
In Englande and Fraunce which gretly was redouted, ... 30 Dol Dethe 43
All gyf Englond and Fraunce wer thorow sought. .... 34 Dol Dethe 179
I durse aventure to journey thorugh Fraunce; .... 57 Bowge 408
His tytle is true in Fraunce to raygne; .... 118 Ag Scottes 120
I reporte me herein to Kynge Lewes of Fraunce. .... 148 Magnyfycence 280
From out of Fraunce .... 165 Magnyfycence 878
Cherlemayne, that mantenyd the nobles of Fraunce, ... 182 Magnyfycence 1501
And a frere of Fraunce, ... 265 Collyn Clout 748
That were done in Fraunce, ... 297 Why Come Ye 720
With a frere of Fraunce men call Sir Gagwyne, ... 322 Garlande 374
Two thousande of Fraunce .... 360 Albany 43
Sende him to F[r]aunce agayne .... 363 Albany 173
  Fraunce] 'Faunce' †Marshe 1568
With Sir Fraunces of Fraunce .... 371 Albany 497
FRAUNCEYS
Now, by Saynte Fraunceys, that holy man and frere, ... 59 Bowge 470
FRAUNCES
To Fraunces the French kyng .... 299 Why Come Ye 791
Bothe Kyng Fraunces and the, ... 361 Albany 113
From Kynge Fraunces of Frauns. .... 363 Albany 175
Ye meane Fraunces, French kyng, ... 367 Albany 334
What, wold Fraunces, our friar, /Be suche a false lyar, ... 368 Albany 373
With fonde Fraunces, French kyng. .... 368 Albany 383
In spyght of kyng Fraunces, ... 369 Albany 409
With Sir Fraunces of Fraunce .... 371 Albany 497
FRAUNCHYS
There may no fraunchys /Nor worldly blys 39 Coystrowne3 26
FRAUNCIS
How Frauncis Petrarke, /That moche noble clerke, ... 296 Why Come Ye 687
FRAUNCYS
Or Frauncys Petrarke, /Alcheus or Sapho, ... 90 Phy Sparrow 758
  Or] 'Or of' Kitson 1560.6, Marshe 1568
FRAUNS
From Kynge Fraunces of Frauns. .... 363 Albany 175
FRAWARD
O dolorous chaunce of Fortuns fraward hande! .... 32 Dol Dethe 110
FRE
Thought is franke and fre; .... 101 Phy Sparrow 1201
And you have not your owne fre lyberte .... 142 Magnyfycence 78
As I was wonte ever, at my fre wyll. .... 144 Magnyfycence 147
If ye lyst to lyve after your fre lyberte. .... 146 Magnyfycence 208

FREAT —FRENSHE   Page   Title   Line

```
                                                             Page   Title          Line

To put where he lyst, foly hath fre chace; . . . . . . . . .  177   Magnyfycence   1329
I am so lusty to loke on, so freshe, and so fre, . . . . . .  201   Magnyfycence   2145
FREAT
Such fervent heat /His stomake doth freat; . . . . . . . . .   83   Phy Sparrow     482
    doth freat] 'so great' †Kele 1545.2, Wyght 1553, Kitson 1560.6
FREDERYK
Or elles frere Frederyk, . . . . . . . . . . . . . . . . . .  265   Collyn Clout    737
FREDOME
And counterfet fredome that is bounde; . . . . . . . . . . .  152   Magnyfycence    434
FREE
Take your pleasure and use free lyberte; . . . . . . . . . .  185   Magnyfycence   1598
I bassed that baby with harte so free; . . . . . . . . . . .  198   Magnyfycence   2069
To hardy, or to moche, to free of the dawe, . . . . . . . . . 199   Magnyfycence   2090
But he abused so his free lyberte, . . . . . . . . . . . . .  200   Magnyfycence   2113
The whiche shulde be /Bothe franke and free, . . . . . . . .  264   Collyn Clout    711
FREER
And wolde have made me Freer Tucke, . . . . . . . . . . . .   150   Magnyfycence    357
FREERS
To counterfet this freers have lerned me. . . . . . . . . .   154   Magnyfycence    487
Freers, with foly I make them so fayne . . . . . . . . . . .  201   Magnyfycence   2147
FREKE
'By Cryste,' quod Favell, 'Drede is soleyne freke! . . . . .   51   Bowge           187
Why, can ye not put out that foule freke? . . . . . . . . .   158   Magnyfycence    657
Cockys bonys! It is a farle freke. . . . . . . . . . . . . .  172   Magnyfycence   1160
Of suche a farly freke, . . . . . . . . . . . . . . . . . .  366   Albany          303
FRENCH
To Fraunces the French kyng . . . . . . . . . . . . . . . .  299   Why Come Ye     791
Ye meane Fraunces, French kyng, . . . . . . . . . . . . . .  367   Albany          334
With fonde Fraunces, French kyng. . . . . . . . . . . . . .  368   Albany          383
FRENCHE
Frenche kyng, or one or other; . . . . . . . . . . . . . .   118   Ag Scottes      105
It is a Frenche butterflye. . . . . . . . . . . . . . . . .  169   Magnyfycence   1050
With the Frenche kyng . . . . . . . . . . . . . . . . . . .  361   Albany          103
FRENCHEMEN
and faint harted Frenchemen: . . . . . . . . . . . . . . .   359   Albany            I
FRENCHE MEN
The Frenche men he doth fray, . . . . . . . . . . . . . . .  282   Why Come Ye     154
FRENCH MEN
The French men he hath faynted, . . . . . . . . . . . . . .  282   Why Come Ye     157
The French men he hathe so mated, . . . . . . . . . . . . .  282   Why Come Ye     161
FREND
How fele you your selfe, my frend? How is your mynde? . . .  208   Magnyfycence   2389
FRENDE
She that styreth the shyp, make her your frende.' . . . . .   49   Bowge           107
Fortune theyr frende, with whome oft she dyde daunce: . . .   50   Bowge           141
And, though I say it, I was myselfe your frende, . . . . .    50   Bowge           160
I hope here after a frende of you to have.' . . . . . . . .   54   Bowge           280
Softe, my frende. Herein your reason is but rawe. . . . . .  142   Magnyfycence     70
But Measure, my frende, what hyght this mannys name? . . .   145   Magnyfycence    165
Thynke you not thus my frende Felycyte? . . . . . . . . . .  147   Magnyfycence    245
But Fansy, my frende, where have ye bene so longe? . . . .   154   Magnyfycence    500
What! Fansy, my frende! Howe dost thou fare? . . . . . . .   166   Magnyfycence    920
Farewell, my frende. Adue tyll sone. . . . . . . . . . . .   167   Magnyfycence    966
Nay, nay; not so, my frende Felycyte. . . . . . . . . . . .  179   Magnyfycence   1392
Be not to bolde my frende; I counsell you, bere a brayne. .  179   Magnyfycence   1405
My frende, as touchynge to this your mocyon, . . . . . . .   186   Magnyfycence   1639
His frende as his fo! . . . . . . . . . . . . . . . . . . .  293   Why Come Ye     583
But harke, my frende, one worde . . . . . . . . . . . . . .  298   Why Come Ye     784
'My frende, sith ye ar before us here present . . . . . . .  344   Garlande       1121
FRENDYS
Welcome, frendys, ye are bothe unto me. . . . . . . . . . .  145   Magnyfycence    169
Where is nowe my kynne, my frendys, and my noble blood? . .  198   Magnyfycence   2060
I am content, my frendys, that it so be. . . . . . . . . .   214   Magnyfycence   2570
FRENDLY
But frendly I wyll refrayne you ferther, or we flyt: . . .   211   Magnyfycence   2478
Yf fortune be frendly, and grace be the guyde, . . . . . .   234   Speke Parott    139
FRENDSHYP
There can no favour nor frendshyp hym forsake. . . . . . .    48   Bowge           103
Frendshyp to fayne and thynke full lytherly. . . . . . . .   160   Magnyfycence    723
FRENDSHYPPE
In Fortunys frendshyppe there is no stedfastnesse; . . . .   201   Magnyfycence   2156
FRENESY
Agayne Frentike Frenesy there dar no man sey nay, . . . . .  243   Speke Parott    422
Of frantycke frenesy /And folysshe fantasy, . . . . . . . .  283   Why Come Ye     186
enbrased and enterlased with a moche fantasticall frenesy .  374   Replycacion       I
FRENESSYS
Phronessys for frenessys may not hold her way. . . . . . .   232   Speke Parott     47
FRENETYKE
And of frenetyke folabilite, . . . . . . . . . . . . . . .   138   Ven Tongues      43
FRENETYKES
Agaynst these frenetykes, /Agaynst these lunatykes, . . . .  385   Replycacion     400
FRENSCHE
Some from the mayne lande, some fro the Frensche hoste; . .  326   Garlande        497
FRENSHE
Dowche Frenshe of Paris Parot can lerne, . . . . . . . . .   231   Speke Parott     29
The kynges Frenshe secretary . . . . . . . . . . . . . . .   298   Why Come Ye     788
The Recule ageinst Gaguyne of the Frenshe nacyoun; . . . .   346   Garlande       1187
Owt of Frenshe into Englysshe prose. . . . . . . . . . . .   347   Garlande       1220
```

FRENSY — FRESSHEST

	Page	Title	Line
Graund juir, of this Frenshe proverbe olde,	352	Garlande	1440
FRENSY			
What frantyk frensy fyll in youre brayne?	30	Dol Dethe	51
What a frensy is this,	305	Why Come Ye	1050
That frensy nor jelousy	385	Replycacion	407
FRENSSHE			
Before the Frensshe kynge, Danes and other	114	Scot Kynge	15
And sende the Frensshe kynge suche another fall.	115	Scot Kynge	73
Some carectis of Caldy, sum Frensshe was full good;	328	Garlande	585
FRENTIKE			
Agayne Frentike Frenesy there dar no man sey nay,	243	Speke Parott	422
FRERE			
Now, by Saynte Frauncys, that holy man and frere,	59	Bowge	470
Or elles frere Frederyk,	265	Collyn Clout	737
Or elles frere Dominyk,	265	Collyn Clout	738
Or frere Hugulinus,	265	Collyn Clout	739
Or frere Augustinus,	265	Collyn Clout	740
Or frere Carmellus,	265	Collyn Clout	741
Gette a frere gray,	265	Collyn Clout	744
And a frere of Fraunce,	265	Collyn Clout	748
And yet the frere doted!	265	Collyn Clout	757
As many a frere, God wote,	267	Collyn Clout	836
But whan the frere fell in the well	268	Collyn Clout	877
Howe frere Fabian with other mo	268	Collyn Clout	881
Good frere, nor good chanon,	273	Collyn Clout	1097
With a frere of Fraunce men call Sir Gagwyne,	322	Garlande	374
FRERES			
Then all the freres letter.	265	Collyn Clout	762
The foure ordres of freres,	267	Collyn Clout	832
FRESCHE			
To poynt yow fresche and gay,	129	Garnesche3	191
The f[r]esche bastyng of hys cote	129	Garnesche3	200
fresche] 'flesche' †MS Harley 367			
FRESE			
In dud frese ye war schrynyd,	125	Garnesche3	46
With better frese lynyd;	125	Garnesche3	47
FRESH			
This blossome of fresh coloure,	96	Phy Sparrow	990
FRESHE			
With the freshe waters of Elyconys welle.	29	Dol Dethe	14
Adonis of freshe colour,	111	Lawde	43
I am so lusty to loke on, so freshe, and so fre,	201	Magnyfycence	2145
To get us there some freshe mete.	204	Magnyfycence	2264
Retoricyons and oratours in freshe humanyte,	236	Speke Parott	194
FRESSH			
Herber enverduryd, contynuall fressh and grene;	44	Balettys3	13
This blossom of fressh colour,	98	Phy Sparrow	1055
This blossom of fressh coloure,	98	Phy Sparrow	1084
This blossom of fressh colour,	99	Phy Sparrow	1108
This] 'The' Wyght 1553, Kitson 1560.6, Marshe 1568			
Th[is] blossom of fressh coloure,	100	Phy Sparrow	1137
This] 'The' editions			
This blossome of fressh coloure,	100	Phy Sparrow	1162
This blossom of fressh coloure,	101	Phy Sparrow	1186
This blossome of fressh coloure,	101	Phy Sparrow	1209
This] 'Thus' †Kele 1545.2			
FRESSHE			
Wyth fresshe utteraunce full sentencyously;	46	Bowge	12
Of fresshe youth agayne;	85	Phy Sparrow	546
This blossome of fresshe coulour,	94	Phy Sparrow	894
This blossome of fresshe coloure,	97	Phy Sparrow	1023
Her fresshe habylementes /With other implementes	101	Phy Sparrow	1180
This blossome of fresshe colour,	102	Phy Sparrow	1232
By crede, it wolde have fresshe aray,	153	Magnyfycence	460
All the newe gyse, fresshe and gaye,	153	Magnyfycence	463
Pullyshyd and fresshe is your ornacy.	183	Magnyfycence	1531
Enbudded with beautye and colour fresshe of hewe,	183	Magnyfycence	1554
My fethyrs fresshe as ys the emerawde grene,	231	Speke Parott	16
Fresshe as flours in May;	270	Collyn Clout	943
Garnysshed fresshe after my fantasy,	313	Garlande	39
And Homerus, the fresshe historiar;	321	Garlande	329
Whyles it remanyth fresshe in my mynde.	325	Garlande	465
Was my fresshe coronell;	342	Garlande	1056
The silke, the golde, the flowris fresshe to syght,	343	Garlande	1111
With butterfllyis and fresshe pecoke taylis,	345	Garlande	1159
Out of fresshe Latine into owre Englyshe playne,	354	Garlande	1499
FRESSHELY			
He set up fresshely upon his hat alofte.	56	Bowge	367
Fresshely they dresse and make swete my bowur,	231	Speke Parott	12
In settyng out fresshely his crafty persuacyon,	316	Garlande	153
How that our Englysshe myght fresshely be ennewed;	323	Garlande	389
ennewed] 'a meude' †Fakes 1523			
Oure Englysshe rude so fresshely hath set out,	324	Garlande	422
Hath fresshely enbewtid with many a goodly sorte	336	Garlande	868
FRESSHEST			
The fresshest flowre of May;	340	Garlande	990
This columbyne clere and fresshest of coloure,	352	Garlande	1448

FRET —FROM   Page   Title   Line

FRET
All with favour fret, ...   98   Phy Sparrow   1048
Fret all with orient perlys of garnate, ...   325   Garlande   485
FRETE
Such paynes dyd me frete   73   Phy Sparrow   58
He is so bete /With malyce, and frete   95   Phy Sparrow   931
Frete yourselfe` for anger and for dyspyte;   185   Magnyfycence   1602
FRIAR
What, wold Fraunces, our friar, /Be suche a false lyar, ...   368   Albany   373
FRISCAJOLY
and stoicall studiantes, and friscajoly yonkerkyns, ...   374   Replycacion   I
FRY
Of infernall posty, /Where soulis fry and rosty;   349   Garlande   1326
FRYARS
And at the Austen Fryars   276   Collyn Clout   1186
FRYE
Of infernall posty /Where soules frye and rousty;   105   Phy Sparrow   1333
  rousty] 'rosty' Marshe 1568
FRYED
Ye fryed and ye broylyd, ...   125   Garnesche3   28
FRYENGE
A fryenge pan, and a slyce.   224   El Rummynge   409
FRYGGES
His rumpe also he frygges /Agaynst the hye benche.   219   El Rummynge   178
He foynes and he frygges;   284   Why Come Ye   224
FRYINGE PAN
Chryst sence you with a fryinge pan! -   117   Ag Scottes   62
  sence] 'fence' †Lant 1545
FRYNDE
Suwed to Fortune that she wold be theyre frynde.   49   Bowge   121
FRYNDES
Soche pajantes with your fryndes ye play, ...   130   Garnesche5   37
FRYTTHY
Thus stode I in the frytthy forest of Galtres, ...   312   Garlande   22
FRO
Full daynnously, and fro me she dyde fare, ...   48   Bowge   82
Wyth that, as he departed soo fro me, ...   54   Bowge   281
Sodaynly, as he departed me fro, ...   60   Bowge   498
All grace is far hym fro.   62   Hauke   16
That Phillyp is gone me fro!   75   Phy Sparrow   142
And fly so to and fro;   75   Phy Sparrow   160
  fly] 'fle' Wyght 1553, Kitson 1560.6, Marshe 1568
That he is slayne me fro, ...   81   Phy Sparrow   364
To gete me fro them I had moche warke.   150   Magnyfycence   361
And he that I came fro to this place   150   Magnyfycence   372
That thou so hye fro me doth sprynge, ...   170   Magnyfycence   1069
Put fro you presumpcyon and admyt humylyte, ...   207   Magnyfycence   2361
And made also mesure to be put fro me.   209   Magnyfycence   2446
Some from the mayne lande, some fro the Frensche hoste;   326   Garlande   497
And all tyme wandred I thus to and fro, ...   326   Garlande   516
Fynde no mo suche fro Wanflete to Walis.   347   Garlande   1218
Wytlesse wandring to and fro!'   376   Replycacion   74
FROGGES
But lepe away lyke frogges   364   Albany   212
FROLLO
For Syr Frollo de Franko was never halfe so talle.   121   Garnesche1   5
FROM
Fled away from hym, let hym ly in the dust, ...   30   Dol Dethe   39
Bot all they fled from hym for falshode or fere.   31   Dol Dethe   91
From bitter wepinge hym self kan restrayne?   32   Dol Dethe   112
All flatringe faytors abhor and from the kast.   34   Dol Dethe   172
Of foule detraccion God kepe me from the blast.   34   Dol Dethe   173
And us redemede from the fendys pray.   34   Dol Dethe   196
The sowle of this lorde from all daunger of hell, ...   34   Dol Dethe   200
from an honorable Jentyllwoman for a token, ...   39   Coystrowne3   I
Youre ugly tokyn /My mynd hath brokyn /From worldly lust; . . .   39   Coystrowne3   3
No man may hym hyde /From deth holow-eyed, ...   39   Coystrowne3   11
Redeme us from this.   39   Coystrowne3   28
Thy lust and lykyng is from the gone;   42   Balettys1   23
Though thou withdraw me from her by long dystaunce, ...   45   Balettys3   46
A false abstracte cometh from a fals concrete.   58   Bowge   439
To hawke, or els to hunt /From the auter to the funt, ...   62   Hauke   10
From the aulter to the funt.   67   Hauke   189
From Granado to Galys, ...   70   Hauke   322
From Wynchelsee to Walys, /Non est braynsycke talys, ...   70   Hauke   323
From the marees depe /Of Acherontes well, ...   73   Phy Sparrow   69
And from the great Pluto, ...   73   Phy Sparrow   72
And from foule Alecto, ...   73   Phy Sparrow   74
And from Medusa, that mare, ...   73   Phy Sparrow   76
And from Megeras edders, ...   73   Phy Sparrow   78
And from her fyry sparklynges, ...   73   Phy Sparrow   80
And from the smokes sowre /Of Proserpinas bowre;   73   Phy Sparrow   82
And from the dennes darke   73   Phy Sparrow   84
F[rom] that hell-hounde   74   Phy Sparrow   89
  From] 'For' †Kele 1545.2, Wyght 1553, Kitson 1560.6,
  Marshe 1568
From Occyan the great se   79   Phy Sparrow   318
From Tyllbery fery /To the playne of Salysbery!   79   Phy Sparrow   320

FROM —FROM | Page | Title | Line

Text	Page	Title	Line
From me was taken away	81	Phy Sparrow	374
To heven he shall, from heven he cam.	86	Phy Sparrow	582
From one to the other,	88	Phy Sparrow	683
From her to hym agayn;	88	Phy Sparrow	687
From Brytons Albion /To the towre of Babilon.	94	Phy Sparrow	887
To] 'Bo' †Kele 1545.2			
That semyth from afar	97	Phy Sparrow	1046
That from the starry sky	110	Lawde	16
From you, Syr Scot, wolde turne his face?	118	Ag Scottes	108
Now from a kyng to a clot of clay.	119	Ag Scottes	165
To far from the porpose,	126	Garnesche3	97
Sayth, from thy to unto thi croune,	130	Garnesche5	26
Also nat fare from Bowgy Row,	130	Garnesche5	47
Haroldes from honor may the devors,	131	Garnesche5	71
God garde the, Garnyche, from the rope!	133	Garnesche5	161
And from whens come ye, and it myght be askyd?	141	Magnyfycence	29
Lyberte to let from all maner offence;	141	Magnyfycence	45
Lyberte is laudable and pryvylegyd from lawe.	142	Magnyfycence	68
That measure shall nevere departe from my syght.	145	Magnyfycence	190
But plenarly all thought from you must be dyschargyd,	146	Magnyfycence	207
And from felycyte may not be forborne,	146	Magnyfycence	220
Yet measure hath ben so longe from us absent,	146	Magnyfycence	221
And now wolde ye swarve from your owne ordynaunce?	147	Magnyfycence	234
From whens come you, syr, that no man lokyd after?	147	Magnyfycence	255
But yf I coulde knowe a gose from a swanne.	148	Magnyfycence	299
Let us departe from hens home to my place.	151	Magnyfycence	394
From that lorde to that lorde I rode and I ran.	160	Magnyfycence	716
From out of Fraunce	165	Magnyfycence	878
From Tyne to Trent,	167	Magnyfycence	981
From Stroude to Kent,	167	Magnyfycence	982
Not from Anwyke unto Aungey.	171	Magnyfycence	1121
from CRAFTY CONVEYAUNCE showlder.	173	Magnyfycence	SD
From qui fuit aliquid to shyre shakynge nought.	176	Magnyfycence	1303
Plucke from an hundred, and gyve it to thre;	190	Magnyfycence	1775
And had robbyd you quyte from all felycyte.	193	Magnyfycence	1864
and spoylyd from all his goodys and rayment.	193	Magnyfycence	SD
From God am sente to quyte the thy mede.	193	Magnyfycence	1877
And from that they love best some I devorse;	194	Magnyfycence	1905
Than from theyr chyldren to spare the rod	194	Magnyfycence	1929
For nowe wyll I from this caytyfe go,	195	Magnyfycence	1950
And from thens to the halfe strete,	204	Magnyfycence	2263
But, my good sonne, lerne from dyspaire to flee;	206	Magnyfycence	2339
Wynde you from wanhope and aquaynte you with me.	206	Magnyfycence	2340
Wounded from the fote to the crowne of the hede:	207	Magnyfycence	2364
Then shall you be sone delyvered from dystresse,	208	Magnyfycence	2383
And have you banyshed from you all dyspare?	208	Magnyfycence	2393
Is from adversyte Magnyfycence to unbynde.	209	Magnyfycence	2422
Howe be it, from you I receyved a letter [sent],	209	Magnyfycence	2435
sent] not in †Rastell & Treveris C 1530, B			
And kepe you from counterfaytynge of clokyd colusyon.	210	Magnyfycence	2453
And from crafters and hafters I you forfende.	210	Magnyfycence	2456
Ye, syr. From hym my corage shall never flyt.	210	Magnyfycence	2466
Fyrst, from your magnyfycence syn must be abjectyd;	211	Magnyfycence	2484
From tyde to tyde.	218	El Rummynge	155
Let us wasshe our gommes /From the drye crommes!'	222	El Rummynge	308
Some brought from the barne /Both benes and pease;	222	El Rummynge	312
But rose from the borde	229	El Rummynge	591
From Scarpary to Tartary renoun therein doth spryng,	234	Speke Parott	131
Shall lepe from this lyfe, as mery as we be.	236	Speke Parott	222
From Calys to Dovyr, to Caunterbury in Kente,	240	Speke Parott	340
and fle /From worldly vanyte	247	Collyn Clout	41
worldly] 'wordly' Kele 1545.1			
The wolfe from the dore	250	Collyn Clout	153
To wary and to kepe /From theyr goostly shepe,	250	Collyn Clout	155
And theyr spyrytuall lambes /Sequestred from rambes	250	Collyn Clout	157
And from the berded gotes /With theyr heery cotes;	250	Collyn Clout	158
But from daye to daye delayde,	255	Collyn Clout	352
And to synge from place to place, /Lyke apostataas.	256	Collyn Clout	385
From them for theyr lyves!'	261	Collyn Clout	573
Sodaynly upstarte /From the donge carte,	262	Collyn Clout	645
From the seven sterrys!	267	Collyn Clout	827
Wyll knowe a raven from a rayle,	268	Collyn Clout	869
From worldly wantones,	270	Collyn Clout	974
From the Pope of Rome	282	Why Come Ye	129
From Baumberow to Bothombar	282	Why Come Ye	139
Bothombar] 'Bothambar' Toy 1553, Kitson 1560.7, Marshe 1568			
From Croydon into Kent	282	Why Come Ye	145
into] 'to' Toy 1553, Kitson 1560.7, Marshe 1568			
From Wynchelsey to Rye	282	Why Come Ye	147
From Wentbridge to Hull,	282	Why Come Ye	149
From whens that he came,	290	Why Come Ye	465
Out from a low degre,	291	Why Come Ye	506
From trechery and dysceyght,	298	Why Come Ye	773
The faucon from the crow,	298	Why Come Ye	775
The wolfe from the lam;	298	Why Come Ye	776
From whens that mastyfe cam.	298	Why Come Ye	777
To kepe you from laughynge	299	Why Come Ye	829
From sylver to brasse,	301	Why Come Ye	903

FROME —FROWNYNG   Page   Title   Line

	Page	Title	Line
From golde to pewter /Or els to a newter,	301	Why Come Ye	904
From the puskylde pocky pose,	309	Why Come Ye	1195
puskylde] 'pusky' MS Rawlinson C. 813; pose] 'nose' Kitson 1560.7			
From whiche Eschines had none evacyon.	316	Garlande	154
Yet they ryde and rinne from Carlyll to Kent.	317	Garlande	196
they ryde and rinne] 'ryde they and ryn they' MS Cotton Vitellius E.x			
Frome Napuls, from Navern, and from Rouncevall,	326	Garlande	495
Frome Napuls, from Navern, and from Rouncevall,	326	Garlande	495
Some from Flaunders, sum from the se coste,	326	Garlande	496
Some from Flaunders, sum from the se coste,	326	Garlande	496
Some from the mayne lande, some fro the Frensche hoste;	326	Garlande	497
From you most we, but not longe to tary.	326	Garlande	520
From Sydony to the mount Olympyan,	327	Garlande	552
How from the est unto the occident,	328	Garlande	577
And from the sowth unto the north so colde,	328	Garlande	578
Be issuis and portis from all maner of nacyons';	328	Garlande	580
From the anker he kuttyth the gabyll rope,	335	Garlande	833
From the Scottish se /Unto Gabione.	362	Albany	130
From Kynge Fraunces of Frauns.	363	Albany	175
From rayne and from colde,	365	Albany	276
From rayne and from colde,	365	Albany	276
And from raynning of rappes,	366	Albany	277
That our Savyour bare, /Whiche us redemed from care.	375	Replycacion	34
From all honest company,	380	Replycacion	243

FROME

	Page	Title	Line
That wyll abyde and never frome us fall.	49	Bowge	130
To kepe him frome pykynge, it was a grete payne.	52	Bowge	236
Holde thy pease! Measure shall frome us walke.	166	Magnyfycence	949
Crafty Conveyaunce can cloke hymselfe frome shame,	178	Magnyfycence	1370
Jhesus preserve you frome endlesse wo and shame.	214	Magnyfycence	2572
His levis loste, the sappe was frome the rynde.	312	Garlande	21
Frome that I have sayde in no poynt doth vary,	316	Garlande	163
Frome the laureat senate by force of proscripcyon.	318	Garlande	225
But I most bannysshe hym frome my jurydiccyon,	318	Garlande	227
And lepe frome the hylles to lerne for to daunce;	320	Garlande	280
Frome Napuls, from Navern, and from Rouncevall,	326	Garlande	495
Frome Babill towre to the hillis Caspian.'	327	Garlande	553
Caspian] 'Gaspian' †Fakes 1523			

FROMPILL

	Page	Title	Line
What, wolde ye frompill me now? Fy, fy!	36	Man Margery	16

FRONNETH

	Page	Title	Line
For whan she *fronneth she thynketh to make a fray.	49	Bowge	116
*fronneth] 'frouneth' Wynkyn de Worde 1510, Marshe 1568			

FROO

	Page	Title	Line
For welthe wyll sone departe the froo.	132	Garnesche5	125
Lyke a wanton, whan I wyll, I rele to and froo.	233	Speke Parott	109

FROSLYNGES

	Page	Title	Line
That were noughty froslynges;	226	El Rummynge	460

FROST

	Page	Title	Line
I trowe it be a frost, for the way is slydder;	191	Magnyfycence	1816

FROSTIS

	Page	Title	Line
With frowarde frostis, alas, was all to-fret!	352	Garlande	1450

FROUNCE

	Page	Title	Line
She loked as she had the frounce;	64	Hauke	85
frounce] 'fronnce' Kynge & Marche 1554, 'fronce' Day 1560			
But I shall frounce them on the foretop and gar them to quake.	182	Magnyfycence	1514

FROUNDE

	Page	Title	Line
He frounde, he stared, he stampped where he stoode.	55	Bowge	319
Beholde howe Fortune o[n] hym hath frounde.	195	Magnyfycence	1947
on] 'of' †Rastell & Treveris C 1530, B			
If he on you but frounde	367	Albany	345

FROWARD

	Page	Title	Line
Fulfyld with malice of froward entente,	30	Dol Dethe	25

FROWARDE

	Page	Title	Line
Beten with stormys of many a frowarde blast,	213	Magnyfycence	2560
With frowarde frostis, alas, was all to-fret!	352	Garlande	1450
to all waywarde or frowarde altercacyons	382	Replycacion	R

FROWARDES

	Page	Title	Line
Of frowardes, and so dull,	91	Phy Sparrow	779

FROWNE

	Page	Title	Line
Tyll fykkill Fortune began on hym to frowne.	33	Dol Dethe	133
Fortune on you therfore dyd frowne;	120	Ag Scottes	176
And frowne it and face it, as thoughe ye wolde fyght;	185	Magnyfycence	1601
Nowe she wyll laughe, forthwith she wyll frowne;	197	Magnyfycence	2024
Sodenly thus Fortune can bothe smyle and frowne,	212	Magnyfycence	2529
Sodenly thus Fortune can bothe smyle and frowne,	213	Magnyfycence	2536
Was comyng downe /To make hym frowne	360	Albany	57

FROWNED

	Page	Title	Line
He frowned as he wolde swere by Cockes blode.	54	Bowge	287

FROWNETH

	Page	Title	Line
He frowneth ever; /He laugheth never,	94	Phy Sparrow	922
Me thynke she frowneth and lokys sowre.	166	Magnyfycence	924

FROWNYD

	Page	Title	Line
That frownyd on me full angerly and pale;	322	Garlande	375

FROWNYNG

	Page	Title	Line
And grudge therat with frownyng countenaunce;	348	Garlande	1258

	Page	Title	Line

FROWNYNGE
As fersly frownynge as he had ben fyghtyng, ... 328 Garlande 594
FROWNYTH
He frownyth fyersly, brymly browde. . . . . 174 Magnyfycence 1245
FROWNSID
And with his [frownsid] fore top . . . . 105 Phy Sparrow 1340
    frownsid] not in †Kele 1545.2, Wyght 1553, Kitson 1560.6,
    Marshe 1568
And with his frownsid fortop . . . . 349 Garlande 1333
FRUBYSSHER
By my faythe, syr, the frubyssher hath my sworde. . . . . . . 170 Magnyfycence 1063
FRUCTUOUS
With sentence fructuous and termes convenable.' . . . . 335 Garlande 821
FRUGALITE
His fr[u]galite, /His lyberalite, ... 370 Albany 449
    frugalite] 'fragalite' †Marshe 1568
FRUTE
Suche apple tre, suche frute. . . . . 378 Replycacion 157
FRUTEFULL
Muche frutefull mater. But now for your defence, ... 239 Speke Parott 297
FRUTIS
All frutis and flowris grew there in there kynde. . . . . . . 331 Garlande 678
    and] not in †Fakes 1523
FUCKE SAYLES
And set up theyr fucke sayles . . . . 256 Collyn Clout 397
    fucke sayles] 'flucke sayles' †Godfray 1531, 'fulke saylys'
    MS Harley 2252
FUYSON
Whiche whils he lyvyd had fuyson of every thing, ... 32 Dol Dethe 131
FUL
I wayle, I wepe, I sobbe, I sigh ful sore . . . . 29 Dol Dethe 1
All mankynd, whom thou ful dere hast boght, ... 34 Dol Dethe 194
Ful of greet knavys tethe, ... 127 Garnesche3 126
Thowth it be now ful tyde with the, ... 132 Garnesche5 120
Dysdaynous, dowble, ful of dyseyte, ... 133 Garnesche5 150
It shall be losyd ful sone out of the bandis . . . . 332 Garlande 725
I you assure, /Ful wel I know . . . . 338 Garlande 927
FULFILLED
Fulfilled with honour, as all the world dothe ken, ... 30 Dol Dethe 30
    world] 'wold' Marshe 1568
FULFYLD
Fulfyld with malice of froward entente, ... 30 Dol Dethe 25
FULFYLL
We your pleasure fulfyll. . . . . 143 Magnyfycence 106
I can not myne appetyte accomplysshe and fulfyll . . . . . . 160 Magnyfycence 733
FULL
O Quene of mercy, O lady full of grace, ... 34 Dol Dethe 204
He braggyth of hys byrth, that borne was full bace; 37 Coystrowne1 24
His descant is dasshed full of dyscordes; 37 Coystrowne1 38
And thy palace, /Full of solace, ... 40 Coystrowne3 54
As well borne as ye full oft tyme beggys. 40 Coystrowne4 7
Why so koy and full of skorne? 40 Coystrowne4 8
Full lyke a scorpyon styngyng 41 Coystrowne4 17
Whan Luna, full of mutabylyte, ... 46 Bowge 3
Of poetes olde, whyche, full craftely, ... 46 Bowge 9
Wyth fresshe utteraunce full sentencyously; . . . . 46 Bowge 12
But Ignorance full soone dyde me dyscure . . . . 46 Bowge 18
    dyscure] 'dysture' †Wynkyn de Worde 1499, 1510
Full daynnously, and fro me dyde fare. . . . . 48 Bowge 82
Full subtyll persones in nombre foure and thre. . . . . 49 Bowge 133
The fyrste was Favell, full of flatery, ... 49 Bowge 134
Me thoughte, of wordes that he had full a poke; . . . . 51 Bowge 179
Me thoughte his hede was full of gelousy, ... 51 Bowge 192
His nose a-droppynge, his lyppes were full drye; . . . . . . 56 Bowge 362
    a-droppynge] 'droppynge' Marshe 1568
Lorde, how that I wolde caste it full rounde! . . . . 57 Bowge 396
A spone of golde, full of hony swete, ... 58 Bowge 436
For all our courte is full of dysceyte. . . . . 59 Bowge 469
Were I as you, I wolde ryde them full nere; . . . . 59 Bowge 472
Full upon the gorge. . . . . 64 Hauke 87
And cherysshed full dayntely, ... 86 Phy Sparrow 591
So cankered and so full . . . . 91 Phy Sparrow 778
His gummes rusty /Are full unlusty; . . . . 94 Phy Sparrow 915
But ryght convenyently, /And full congruently, ... 98 Phy Sparrow 1070
To prayse her at the full; . . . . 102 Phy Sparrow 1222
Full of myschiefe and queed, ... 106 Epitaphe 1
Ye thought ye dyde it full valyauntolye, ... 113 Scot Kynge 9
Therfore ye be layde now full lowe. . . . . 114 Scot Kynge 53
His sone the lorde admyrall is full good, ... 115 Scot Kynge 70
Lusty Garnysche, lyke a lowse, ye jet full lyke a jaspe; . . . 123 Garnesche2 17
Row and full of lowsy here, ... 127 Garnesche3 124
Thow mayst fale downe and ebbe full lowe. 132 Garnesche5 123
But ye are so full of vertibilite, ... 138 Ven Tongues 42
Of me with your language full of vilany. . . . . 138 Ven Tongues 48
As your grace full nobly hath recountyd, ... 145 Magnyfycence 193
But covetyse hath blowen you so full of wynde . . . . 148 Magnyfycence 290
This worlde is full of my foly. . . . . 152 Magnyfycence 411
Counterfet sadnesse, with delynge full madly; . . . . 153 Magnyfycence 468

FULL —FULL	Page	Title	Line

	Page	Title	Line
And do nothynge. How be it, full lytell grace	159	Magnyfycence	693
Full fewe that can themselfe of me excuse.	160	Magnyfycence	706
Frendshyp to fayne and thynke full lytherly.	160	Magnyfycence	723
A byrde full swete,	167	Magnyfycence	975
For me full mete.	167	Magnyfycence	976
Yes, yes! I am yet as full of game	172	Magnyfycence	1140
As ever I was, and as full of tryfyls –	172	Magnyfycence	1141
Ye, for he hathe a full drye soule.	176	Magnyfycence	1320
Without me be full ofte aspyed.	177	Magnyfycence	1355
Full moche flatery and falsehode I hyde;	177	Magnyfycence	1358
Unto Magnyfycence a full ungracyous sorte,	178	Magnyfycence	1373
Full many a strong cyte and towne hath been wonne	184	Magnyfycence	1577
Ye, but some be full koy and passynge harde harted.	184	Magnyfycence	1583
He can full craftely this matter brynge aboute.	187	Magnyfycence	1691
I rushe at them rughly and make them ly full lowe;	193	Magnyfycence	1884
Some I make lyppers and lazars full horse;	194	Magnyfycence	1904
Alasse, I have the cyatyca full evyll in my hyppe!	195	Magnyfycence	1956
I am lowsy and unlykynge and full of scurffe;	195	Magnyfycence	1958
Full fewe but they have envy of me.	195	Magnyfycence	1963
Nowe lap you in a coverlet, full fayne that you may;	197	Magnyfycence	2011
Fye on this worlde, full of trechery,	197	Magnyfycence	2020
To full of fansyes, to lordly, to prowde,	199	Magnyfycence	2093
To jettynge, to jaggynge, and to full of japes,	199	Magnyfycence	2097
A, woo worthe the, Lyberte, nowe thou sayst full trewe;	199	Magnyfycence	2103
I make hevy hertys, with eyen full holowe.	205	Magnyfycence	2286
So innumerable, and so full of dyspyte,	205	Magnyfycence	2301
Full many thynges there be that lacketh redresse,	209	Magnyfycence	2415
Set not all your affyaunce in Fortune full of gyle;	211	Magnyfycence	2501
Her eyen gowndy /Are full unsowndy,	215	El Rummynge	35
And also theyr fete /Hardely full unswete;	217	El Rummynge	122
Theyr tresses untrust, /All full of unlust;	218	El Rummynge	148
Full untydy tegges, /Lyke rotten egges.	218	El Rummynge	151
Some fyll theyr pot full /Of good Lemster woll.	220	El Rummynge	251
Her thryfte is full thyn.	221	El Rummynge	256
Her colour was full wan –	222	El Rummynge	318
And she was full of tales,	223	El Rummynge	352
Full of magottes quycke;	225	El Rummynge	431
These maydens full meryly with many a dyvers flowur	231	Speke Parott	11
a] not in †MS Harley 2252			
With, 'Speke, Parott, I pray yow,' full curteslye they sey,	231	Speke Parott	13
To fatte theyr bodyes full,	250	Collyn Clout	128
And have full lytell care	250	Collyn Clout	130
Full worshypfull clerkes,	250	Collyn Clout	150
But a full purse.	254	Collyn Clout	293
At home full softe doth sytte.	255	Collyn Clout	328
Full falsely on you they lye,	255	Collyn Clout	334
Full of glotony /And of ypocrysy,	269	Collyn Clout	918
And full of wylfulnes,	276	Collyn Clout	1177
And say howe that we be /Full of parcyallyte;	276	Collyn Clout	1193
For the courte full unmete;	279	Why Come Ye	33
Full of pocky molys.	285	Why Come Ye	246
This man was full unable	292	Why Come Ye	537
They have the full intellygence,	297	Why Come Ye	710
Full ungracyously, /Fals flatery,	300	Why Come Ye	852
So full of malencoly,	308	Why Come Ye	1168
Of an oke, that somtyme grew full streyghte,	312	Garlande	18
Therto am I full insuffycyent;	313	Garlande	46
Of auncient poetis, ye wote full wele, hath bene	314	Garlande	65
Out of my bokis full sone I shulde hym rase;	314	Garlande	72
How ryvers rin not tyll the spryng be full;	314	Garlande	81
That longe tyme blewe a full timorous blaste,	319	Garlande	260
Where I sawe come after, I wote, full lytell lake	320	Garlande	285
With Plautus, that wrote full many a comody;	322	Garlande	354
full] not in Marshe 1568			
Senek full soberly with his tragediis;	322	Garlande	358
with] 'wit' †Fakes 1523			
Quintus Cursius, full craftely that wrate	322	Garlande	366
Cursius] 'Cursus' †Fakes 1523			
That frownyd on me full angerly and pale;	322	Garlande	375
Some lokyd full smothely, and had a fals quarter,	326	Garlande	504
quarter] 'quart' Marshe 1568			
'Go softly,' she sayd, 'the stones be full glint.'	328	Garlande	572
Some carectis of Caldy, sum Frensshe was full good;	328	Garlande	585
She bet up a fyre with the sparkis full kene	330	Garlande	669
Full gloryously can he glose, thy mynde for to fele;	333	Garlande	760
To weve in the stoule sume were full preste,	334	Garlande	790
And as full of good wyll, /As fayre Isaphill;	341	Garlande	1024
fayre] 'the fayre' MS Cotton Vitellius E.x			
Hath bene full often and yet is entendyng	344	Garlande	1131
And that it wolde please her, full tenderly I prayd,	353	Garlande	1479
God wote, theis wordes made me full sad;	353	Garlande	1484
Full of bragge and boost,	364	Albany	207
And full of waste wynde,	364	Albany	208
Full of scabbes and scaules,	364	Albany	219
Full soone ye should miscarry,	367	Albany	342
That shall bring you full bace	368	Albany	366
They fledde full cowardly.	371	Albany	515
howbeit they were puffed so full	375	Replycacion	I

FUMBLYTH —GAGUINE

	Page	Title	Line
Full of mockysshe scornes,	380	Replycacion	216
Come forthe, ye pope holy, /Full of melancoly!	381	Replycacion	248
Pufte full of heresy,	381	Replycacion	253
Full of suche dottages,	381	Replycacion	272

FUMBLYTH
He fumblyth in hys fyngeryng an ugly good noyse;	37	Coystrowne1	31

FUME
That in a fume or an hete,	289	Why Come Ye	424

FUMIGATION
To make a fumigation	84	Phy Sparrow	523
a] not in Wyght 1553, Kitson 1560.6, Marshe 1568			

FUMYGACION
And a certayne fumygacion	296	Why Come Ye	699

FUMOUSLY
And fumously adresse you with magnanymyte;	211	Magnyfycence	2497

FUNERALL
With dolorous songes funerall,	81	Phy Sparrow	391
Dyvysed by Skelton after the funerall rate;	348	Garlande	1256

FUNT
To hawke, or els to hunt /From the auter to the funt,	62	Hauke	10
From the aulter to the funt.	67	Hauke	189

FURDRERS
Furdrers of love, with baudry aqueinted,	329	Garlande	609

FURIOUS
That vilane hastarddis in ther furious tene,	30	Dol Dethe	24

FURY
And in theyr fury hoppe,	259	Collyn Clout	529

FURYOUS
That in a furyous rage	81	Phy Sparrow	376
a] not in Marshe 1568			

FURNISSHE
Also, to furnisshe better his excuse,	314	Garlande	92

FURNYSSHE
Must mesure, in the mares name, you furnysshe and dresse?	179	Magnyfycence	1391

FURNYSSHYD
Yet some folys say ye arre furnysshyd with knakkes,	239	Speke Parott	292

FURRED
Me thoughte his gowne was all furred wyth foxe.	52	Bowge	234
Me] 'My' †Wynkyn de Worde 1499			
She is furred for the hete /All to the fete;	167	Magnyfycence	977
In her furred flocket, /And graye russet rocket,	215	El Rummynge	53
Your fonde hed in your furred hode!	310	Why Come Ye2	19
your] (2nd) 'a' MS Rawlinson C. 813			

FURRYD
'My new furryd gowne, when it is worne –	40	Coystrowne4	10

FURST
Howbei[t], he is not furst hath had a los.	43	Balettys2	38
Howbeit] 'Howbeis' †Rastell 1527.1			

FURTHE
Now pas furthe, good Parott, Owur Lorde be your s[t]ede,	239	Speke Parott	313
stede] 'spede' †MS Harley 2252			

FURTHER
His maisters love to further,	88	Phy Sparrow	684
I wolde yet shewe you further of my consayte.	185	Magnyfycence	1591
I wyll no further ryme /Tyll another tyme;	284	Why Come Ye	230
But I wyll make further relacion	297	Why Come Ye	716
And a further rehersall	299	Why Come Ye	825
Ye shulde take further payne /To resorte agayne	379	Replycacion	201
If further busynesse that ye make.	382	Replycacion	296

FURTHERMORE
Then furthermore aboute me my syght I revolde,	330	Garlande	664

FUSTIANE
This fustiane maistres and this giggisse gase	346	Garlande	1206

FUSTY
Fusty bawdyas, I sey nat alle.	131	Garnesche5	76

GABIONE
From the Scottish se /Unto Gabione.	362	Albany	131

GABIONYTE
O Gabionyte of Gabyone, why do ye gane and gaspe?	123	Garnesche2	15

GABYLL ROPE
From the anker he kuttyth the gabyll rope,	335	Garlande	833

GABYONE
O Gabionyte of Gabyone, why do ye gane and gaspe?	123	Garnesche2	15

GAD
'Be Gad, ye be a praty pode,	35	Man Margery	8

GADDE
And I Foly bryngeth them to qui fuit gadde;	176	Magnyfycence	1301

GADDER
Sum what wolde gadder in there conjecture	315	Garlande	107
conjecture] 'convecture' †Fakes 1523			

GADDIR
England, now gaddir flowris,	110	Lawde	6

GADER
I gader togyther and close in my crop,	233	Speke Parott	94

GAGLYNGE
And the gaglynge gaunte,	83	Phy Sparrow	447

GAGUINE
How maister Gaguine, the crownycler	297	Why Come Ye	718

GAGUYNE —GAME	Page	Title	Line

GAGUYNE
The Recule ageinst Gaguyne of the Frenshe nacyoun; . . . . . . 346 Garlande 1187
GAGWYNE
With a frere of Fraunce men call Sir Gagwyne, ... 322 Garlande 374
GAINSAY
Reputyng hym unable /To gainsay replycable . . . . 382 Replycacion 303
GAY
Your Seven Systers, that gun so gay, ... 119 Ag Scottes 162
As ye ar brystlyd on the bake for alle your gay gere. . . . . . 122 Garneschel 26
To poynt yow fresche and gay. 129 Garnesche3 191
Go pley the, Garnyshe, garnysshed gay! 134 Garnesche5 167
Howe gay and howe stout . . . . 163 Magnyfycence 832
Cockes bones! This is all of Johnn de Gay. . . . . 167 Magnyfycence 960
And where I spy a nysot gay . . . . 174 Magnyfycence 1228
But in a mountayne gay, ... 365 Albany 260
GAYE
All the newe gyse, fresshe and gaye, ... 153 Magnyfycence 463
And yet I dare saye /She thynketh her selfe gaye . . . . 216 El Rummynge 65
GAYNE
Gayne dangerous stormys theyr anker of supporte, ... 44 Balettys3 26
GAYNOUR
And Dame Gaynour, his quene . . . . 87 Phy Sparrow 636
GALANTE
Huf, a galante, Garnesche, loke on your comly cors! 123 Garnesche2 16
GALANTYS
Galba, whom his galantys garde for agaspe, ... 182 Magnyfycence 1508
GALATHEA
Now, Galathea, lett Parrot, I pray yow, have hys date - . . . . 244 Speke Parott 439
Galathea, the made well besene, ... 342 Garlande 1076
GALAUNTES
That we thre galauntes sholde be longe asonder. . . . . 154 Magnyfycence 511
GALAWAY
With, 'Gup, Syr Scot of Galaway!' . . . . 118 Ag Scottes 109
Dundas of Galaway . . . . 135 Dundas 29
And the ragged ray /Of Galaway. . . . . 359 Albany 23
'Twyt, Scot, of Galaway. 363 Albany 158
GALBA
Galba, whom his galantys garde for agaspe, ... 182 Magnyfycence 1508
GALES
And of Saynte James in Gales, ... 223 El Rummynge 354
GALIENE
Though Galiene and Diascorides, ... 352 Garlande 1425
GALYS
From Granado to Galys, ... 70 Hauke 322
GALL
But under hony ofte tyme lyeth bytter gall, ... 49 Bowge 131
His herte withall /Bytter as gall; . . . . 94 Phy Sparrow 917
That with myxture of aloes and bytter gall . . . . 117 Ag Scottes 81
That rubbed she must be on the gall . . . . 174 Magnyfycence 1232
For [ye] scrape out good scrypture, and set in a gall: . . . . 235 Speke Parott 153
  ye] 'they' †Lant 1545, Kynge & Marche 1554, Day 1560,
  Marshe 1568
He dranke eysell and gall . . . . 258 Collyn Clout 454
Not rubbe you on the gall, ... 279 Why Come Ye 25
  you] 'hym' MS Rawlinson C. 813
Savynge he rubbid sum on the gall. . . . . 315 Garlande 97
  on] 'upon' Marshe 1568
GALLANDE
A rusty gallande, to-ragged and to-rente; . . . . 56 Bowge 345
GALLES
No broken galles /May there abyde . . . . 83 Phy Sparrow 473
  No] 'Nor' Kitson 1560.6
GALLYNG
Ware gallyng in the widders, ware of that wrenche! 43 Balettys2 25
GALTRES
in the foreste of Galtres, ... 312 Garlande I
Thus stode I in the frytthy forest of Galtres, ... 312 Garlande 22
GAMBAUDYNGE
With gambaudynge thryftlesse, ... 280 Why Come Ye 73
GAMBAWDIS
Such sacrificium laudis /He made with suche gambawdis. . . . . 63 Hauke 65
Dysers, carders, tumblars with gambawdis, ... 329 Garlande 608
GAMBONE
And brought a gambone /Of bakon that was resty; . . . . 222 El Rummynge 327
GAME
Or ells with gret shame your game wylbe sene. 43 Balettys2 42
In ernest and in game . . . . 89 Phy Sparrow 709
Gyve up your game, ye playe chek mate; . . . . 114 Scot Kynge 37
For then began our myrth and game. . . . . 117 Ag Scottes 68
Lost is your game, ye are checkmate. . . . . 118 Ag Scottes 128
By Cockys body, here begynneth the game! . . . . 159 Magnyfycence 682
Yes, yes! I am yet as full of game . . . . 172 Magnyfycence 1140
Crafty conveyaunce is no chyldys game; . . . . 178 Magnyfycence 1368
For as thou wylte, so shall the game go; . . . . 190 Magnyfycence 1786
I coude, and I lyst, garre you laughe at a game: . . . . 192 Magnyfycence 1835
The snyte snyveled in the snowte and smyled at the game. . . . 192 Magnyfycence 1840
And Foly, my broder, that made you moche game. . . . . 193 Magnyfycence 1872
For though we shewe you this in game and play, ... 195 Magnyfycence 1948

GAMUT — GARMENTES

	Page	Title	Line
And ye that have harde thys dysporte and game,	214	Magnyfycence	2571
And thus begynneth the game.	217	El Rummynge	132
And the selfe same game	256	Collyn Clout	387
In ernest and in game.	262	Collyn Clout	613
Of theyr game it is sene	304	Why Come Ye	1005
Withoute deservynge shulde have the best game.	318	Garlande	221
Came towarde me, and smylid halfe in game;	327	Garlande	529
Grene tre of laurell moche solacyous game	331	Garlande	683

GAMUT
But for in his gamut carp that he can,	37	Coystrowne1	13

GAN
With browes bente, and gan on me to stare	48	Bowge	81
Than Favell gan wyth fayre speche me to fede.	50	Bowge	147
And in this wyse he gan with me to chyde.	55	Bowge	322
'What, revell route!' quod he, and gan to rayle	56	Bowge	368
Me, passynge sore, myne herte than gan aryse;	58	Bowge	425
And to mewarde as he gan for to coost,	58	Bowge	431
Thys fawconer then gan showte,	65	Hauke	119
then] not in Day 1560, Marshe 1568			
And boyes to the pylery gan me plucke,	150	Magnyfycence	356
With my servauntys, and suche maystryes gan make,	188	Magnyfycence	1716
The crane and the curlewe therat gan to grame;	192	Magnyfycence	1839
Hay the gye and the gan!	301	Why Come Ye	888
The clowdis gan to clere, the myst was rarifiid;	330	Garlande	651

GANDER
The gose and the gander,	82	Phy Sparrow	435
The gander and the gose bothe grasynge on one grave.	191	Magnyfycence	1830
Alexander, a gander of Menanders pole,	235	Speke Parott	173
The gander, the gose, and the hudge oliphaunt,	315	Garlande	102

GANE
O Gabionyte of Gabyone, why do ye gane and gaspe?	123	Garnesche2	15

GANT
In came another dant, /With a gose and a gant.	227	El Rummynge	516

GAPE
Garnyche, ye gape to wyde:	124	Garnesche3	21
Eche man to hynder I gape and I gaspe;	160	Magnyfycence	729
They gaspe and they gape /All to have promocyon:	248	Collyn Clout	85

GAPIS
He grynnes and he gapis	295	Why Come Ye	653

GAPYTHE
Hys wolvys hede, wanne, bloo as lede, gapythe over the crowne:	244	Speke Parott	434

GAR
But I shall frounce them on the foretop and gar them to quake.	182	Magnyfycence	1514

GARDE
Now Garnyche, garde thy gummys;	128	Garnesche3	158
God garde the, Garnyche, from the rope!	133	Garnesche5	161
Galba, whom his galantys garde for agaspe,	182	Magnyfycence	1508
I garde her gaspe, I garde her gle,	198	Magnyfycence	2067
I garde her gaspe, I garde her gle,	198	Magnyfycence	2067
Of Pajauntis that were played in Joyows Garde;	351	Garlande	1383

GARDED
His hose was garded with a lyste of grene,	56	Bowge	356
His hode all pounsed and garded lyke a cage.	60	Bowge	508
hode] 'body' Marshe 1568			

GARDEVYAUNCE
To grope a gardevyaunce, though it be well bandyd.	203	Magnyfycence	2231

GARDYNGE
There blew in that gardynge a soft piplyng colde	331	Garlande	676

GARGONE
Thou gresly gargone glaymy,	128	Garnesche3	168
Garnyshe, gargone, gastly, gryme,	129	Garnesche5	1

GARGONS
Ye grounde yow upon Godfrey, that grysly gargons face,	123	Garnesche2	29

GARLAND
Hyt ys to fere leste he wolde were the garland on hys pate,	244	Speke Parott	435

GARLANDE
upon a goodly Garlande or Chapelet of Laurell	312	Garlande	1
Shall were a garlande of the laurell tre.'	321	Garlande	322

GARLANDES
They made, with chapellettes and garlandes grene;	331	Garlande	684

GARLANTES
With lauryat garlantes,	270	Collyn Clout	963

GARLEKE HED
Your pyllyd garleke hed	125	Garnesche3	68

GARLYCKE
They may garlycke pyll,	281	Why Come Ye	109

GARLYKE HEDDES
Another brought her garlyke heddes;	227	El Rummynge	522

GARLONDE
upon a goodly Garlonde or Chapelet of Laurell,	358	Garlande2	R

GARMENT
His gawdy garment with Scornnys was all wrought;	54	Bowge	285
Scornnys] 'storunys' †Wynkyn de Worde 1499, 1510, 'scornes' Marshe 1568			

GARMENTE
He was trussed in a garmente strayte –	60	Bowge	505

GARMENTES
So gorgyous garmentes, and so myche wrechydnese,	244	Speke Parott	459

GARNATE —GATE | | Page | Title | Line

GARNATE
Fret all with orient perlys of garnate, ... 325 Garlande 485
GARNESCHE
Skelton Lauriate Defender Agenst Master Garnesche Chalenger, . . 121 Garneschel I
Sithe ye have me chalyngyd, Master Garnesche, ... 121 Garneschel 1
Skelton Lauryate Defender Agenst Master Garnesche Chalangar, . . 122 Garnesche2 I
GARNISSHED
I saw Gower, that first garnisshed our Englysshe rude, ... 323 Garlande 387
Garnisshed with lawrell . . . . 342 Garlande 1055
GARNYCHE
Cum Garnyche, cum Godfrey, with as many as ye may! 123 Garnesche2 32
Skelton Lawryate Defender Agenyst Lusty Garnyche . . . . 124 Garnesche3 I
Garnyche, ye gape to wyde: 124 Garnesche3 21
When Garnyche cummyth yow amonge 128 Garnesche3 150
Now Garnyche, garde thy gummys; 128 Garnesche3 158
Yt wold garnyche wyll thy face. 133 Garnesche5 135
God garde the, Garnyche, from the rope! 133 Garnesche5 161
GARNYSCHE
Lusty Garnysche, lyke a lowse, ye jet full lyke a jaspe; . . . 123 Garnesche2 17
Gup, gorbellyd Godfrey, gup, Garnysche, gaudy fole! 123 Garnesche2 36
GARNYSHE
Skelton Laureate Defendar Ageinst Lusty Garnyshe . . . . 129 Garnesche5 I
Garnyshe, gargone, gastly, gryme, ... 129 Garnesche5 1
Garnyshe, ye gate of Gorge with gaudry 130 Garnesche5 39
Go pley the, Garnyshe, garnysshed gay! 134 Garnesche5 167
GARNYSHTE
Thow mantycore, ye marmset, garnyshte lyke a Greke, ... 124 Garnesche2 39
GARNYSSHED
Go pley the, Garnyshe, garnysshed gay! 134 Garnesche5 167
Garnysshed was her snout . . . . 228 El Rummynge 554
Garnysshed fresshe after my fantasy, ... 313 Garlande 39
GARNYSSHYD
To beholde how it was garnysshyd and bounde, ... 345 Garlande 1163
GARRE
I coude, and I lyst, garre you laughe at a game: . . . . 192 Magnyfycence 1835
GARTERYNGE
The garterynge of her hose? . . . . 101 Phy Sparrow 1176
GASE
That all the world may gase . . . . 79 Phy Sparrow 316
This fustiane maistres and this giggisse gase . . . . 346 Garlande 1206
GASED
He gased on me with his gotyshe berde; . . . . 52 Bowge 237
Upon her whan I gased, ... 99 Phy Sparrow 1104
Whereat a thousande gased, ... 379 Replycacion 193
GASID
Some tremblid, some girned, some gaspid, some gasid, ... 319 Garlande 265
Then to the hevyn sperycall upwarde I gasid, ... 354 Garlande 1514
GASY
On that syde, on thys syde thou dost gasy, ... 130 Garnesche5 29
GASYNG
And iche man stode gasyng and staryng upon other. . . . . . . 319 Garlande 268
GASYNGE
Your gasynge and your totynge . . . . 273 Collyn Clout 1074
GASPE
Somtyme he wolde gaspe . . . . 75 Phy Sparrow 128
O Gabionyte of Gabyone, why do ye gane and gaspe? 123 Garnesche2 15
Eche man to hynder I gape and I gaspe; . . . . 160 Magnyfycence 729
I garde her gaspe, I garde her gle, ... 198 Magnyfycence 2067
They gaspe and they gape /All to have promocyon: . . . . 248 Collyn Clout 85
GASPID
Some tremblid, some girned, some gaspid, some gasid, ... 319 Garlande 265
GASPY
She began to yane and gaspy, ... 222 El Rummynge 331
began] 'gan' 1521 Fragment
GASPYNG
Gaspyng asyde, /Nakyd of hyde, ... 39 Coystrowne3 16
GASTLY
With hys worme-etyn maw /And hys gastly jaw 39 Coystrowne3 15
With gastly hedes thre; . . . . 74 Phy Sparrow 91
In Plut[o]s gastly tower; . . . . 104 Phy Sparrow 1323
Plutos] 'Plutus' editions
Garnyshe, gargone, gastly, gryme, ... 129 Garnesche5 1
As gastly that glaris, as grimly that gronis, ... 328 Garlande 593
In Plutos gastly towre; . . . . 349 Garlande 1316
GAT
Wheron he gat his fynall dedely wounde. . . . . 32 Dol Dethe 119
And gat her great thanke . . . . 228 El Rummynge 543
GATE
Garnyshe, ye gate of Gorge with gaudry 130 Garnesche5 39
With, 'Gup, Syr Gy', ye gate a moke. 131 Garnesche5 56
Ye. But I bade hym pyke out of the gate; . . . . 166 Magnyfycence 946
Where the devyll gate he all these hurtes? . . . . 171 Magnyfycence 1127
I am baytyd with doggys at every mannys gate; . . . . 195 Magnyfycence 1961
Nowe must you lerne to begge at every mannes gate. . . . . . . 196 Magnyfycence 1981
With, 'Da causales,' is cast out of the gate, ... 235 Speke Parott 174
But one gate specyally, where as I stode, ... 328 Garlande 586
Innumerable people pressed to every gate. . . . . 329 Garlande 603

GATES —GELAWAYE   Page   Title   Line

GATES
  Nor Hanyball, agayne Rome gates that ranne, ...   182   Magnyfycence   1511
  Shulde open the brode gates   263   Collyn Clout   691
GATHER
  Gather up, thou wenche.   219   El Rummynge   181
  Some to gather chese   267   Collyn Clout   840
GATHERETH
  And gathereth up in store   260   Collyn Clout   568
    gathereth] 'gathered' Marshe 1568
GATIS
  Of elephantis tethe were the palace gatis, ...   325   Garlande   468
  Shet were the gatis; thei might wel knock and cal, ...   329   Garlande   604
GATTE
  But where gatte thou that mangey curre?   173   Magnyfycence   1180
GAUDE
  I shall gyve you a gaude of a goslynge that I gave, ...   191   Magnyfycence   1829
GAUDY
  Gup, gorbellyd Godfrey, gup, Garnysche, gaudy fole!   123   Garnesche2   36
GAUDRY
  Garnyshe, ye gate of Gorge with gaudry   130   Garnesche5   39
GAUNCE
  The heron so gaunce, ...   83   Phy Sparrow   444
    gaunce] 'gaunte' Wyght 1553, Kitson 1560.6, Marshe 1568
GAUNT
  She callyd yow Syr Gy of Gaunt, ...   126   Garnesche3   70
  Avaunt, Syr Gye of Gaunt!   275   Collyn Clout   1155
GAUNTE
  And the gaglynge gaunte, ...   83   Phy Sparrow   447
GAURE
  And nowe on me ye gaure and sporne.   204   Magnyfycence   2247
GAVE
  Yet whils he stode he gave them woundes wyde.   32   Dol Dethe   101
    Yet] 'Ye' Marshe 1568
  Gave me a taunte, and sayde I was to blame   48   Bowge   70
  And with that worde on me she gave a glome   48   Bowge   80
  And we asked favoure, and favour she us gave.   49   Bowge   126
  Soo greate pleasyre, or who to you it gave.   53   Bowge   263
  Wyth that he gave her a bounce   64   Hauke   86
  Gave hym his mortall wounde, ...   79   Phy Sparrow   298
  Whiche gave to me /The high degre   112   Calliope   5
  Agaynst you gave so sharpe a shower, ...   119   Ag Scottes   133
  The Popes cur[se] gave you that clap.   119   Ag Scottes   169
    curse] 'cures' †Lant 1545, Kynge & Marche 1554, Day 1560,
    Marshe 1568
  A kynge to me myn habyte gave   131   Garnesche5   80
  This ladyes have, /I it them gave.   165   Magnyfycence   890
  Mary, as thou sayst, he gave me a blurre.   173   Magnyfycence   1179
  But loke that ye occupye the auctoryte that I you gave.   180   Magnyfycence   1456
  Nowe, by your trouthe, gave he you not a brybe?   187   Magnyfycence   1665
  Thou sayst truthe, by the harte that God me gave!   190   Magnyfycence   1782
  I shall gyve you a gaude of a goslynge that I gave, ...   191   Magnyfycence   1829
  And is this the credence that I gave to the letter?   193   Magnyfycence   1867
  Mary, so ungoodly langage you me gave.   203   Magnyfycence   2213
  Gave me a gyfte in my neste when I lay, ...   232   Speke Parott   44
    I] 'he' †MS Harley 2252
  That Saynt Thomas of Canterbury gave.   251   Collyn Clout   170
    'That becket them gave' Kele 1545.1, Marshe 1568
  And gave him a realme to rule   293   Why Come Ye   559
  How you gave me a ryall commaundement   313   Garlande   58
    you] 'ye' Marshe 1568, MS Cotton Vitellius E.x;
    a] 'in' MS Cot. Vit. E.x
  That gave Eschines suche a cordyall, ...   316   Garlande   131
    That] 'Whiche' MS Cotton Vitellius E.x
  She loked hawtly, and gave on me a glum.   344   Garlande   1117
GAW
  Somtyme I wepe for a gew gaw;   168   Magnyfycence   1013
GAWDY
  His gawdy garment with Scornnys was all wrought;   54   Bowge   285
    Scornnys] 'storunys' †Wynkyn de Worde 1499, 1510,
    'scornes' Marshe 1568
  Trowest thou, drevyll, I saye, thou gawdy knave, ...   55   Bowge   337
  But now, gawdy, gresy Garnesche, ...   127   Garnesche3   120
GAWEN
  Of Gawen, and Syr Guy, ...   87   Phy Sparrow   629
  Syr Gy, Syr Gawen, Syr Cayus, for and Syr Olyvere, ...   123   Garnesche2   22
GE
  Ge heme! ge scour thy pot, ...   282   Why Come Ye   126
  Ge heme! ge scour thy pot, ...   282   Why Come Ye   126
  Go heme, ranke Scot, ge heme, ...   368   Albany   382
GEBALL
  Now Geball, Amon and Amaloch - 'Harke, harke, ...   234   Speke Parott   118
GEDEON
  Gedeon is gon, that Zalmane undertoke, ...   234   Speke Parott   116
GEYNE
  Geyne surfetous suspecte the emeraud comendable;   44   Balettys3   20
GELAWAYE
  Now ye proude Scottes of Gelawaye   114   Scot Kynge   19

GELIUS — GERY

	Page	Title	Line

GELIUS
Aulus Gelius, that noble historiar; . . . . 322 Garlande 351
GELOUSY
Me thoughte his hede was full of gelousy, ... 51 Bowge 192
GELT
Neyther gelt nor pawne. . . . . 229 El Rummynge 610
GENEALOGY
And his gresy genealogy, ... 291 Why Come Ye 492
GENERACION
Of unhappy generacion /And most ungracious nacion. . . . . . . 136 Dundas 52
GENERALL
It is generall /To be mortall: 39 Coystrowne3 7
But the moost parte in generall. . . . . 252 Collyn Clout 245
GENERRALL
In generrall wordes, I say not gretely nay, ... 315 Garlande 99
GENET
Then came in a genet, ... 224 El Rummynge 392
GENTELL
Of this gentell Jack Breche, ... 294 Why Come Ye 616
GENTELMEN
And all other gentelmen with hym enterteynd . . . . 34 Dol Dethe 184
GENTIL
Than ye may commaunde me to gentil cok wat. . . . . 137 Ven Tongues 15
GENTILWOMAN
This gentilwoman, that callyd was by name . . . . 327 Garlande 527
GENTYLL
And came of a gentyll stocke, ... 86 Phy Sparrow 589
Lyberte in some cause becomyth a gentyll mynde – . . . . . . 146 Magnyfycence 212
It is a gentyll reason of a rake. . . . . 156 Magnyfycence 557
Be gentyll, then, of corage, and lerne to be kynde; . . . . . 211 Magnyfycence 2486
The gentyll greyhownde. 298 Why Come Ye 779
Lorde, how she made moche of her gentyll birth! . . . . 346 Garlande 1202
GENTYLLY
He wolde trotte gentylly, but he is to starke. . . . . 153 Magnyfycence 481
GENTYLMAN
'Ye remembre the gentylman ryghte nowe . . . . 51 Bowge 197
Here you not howe this gentylman mockys? . . . . 141 Magnyfycence 32
Gyve this gentylman rome, syrs. Stonde utter! . . . . 161 Magnyfycence 753
Wyll ye se this gentylman is all in his skornys? . . . . . . 162 Magnyfycence 773
In your brest towardes this gentylman. . . . . 188 Magnyfycence 1713
Mary, syr, this gentylman caled me javell. . . . . 203 Magnyfycence 2211
Goddys fote! I warant you I am a gentylman borne; . . . . . . 203 Magnyfycence 2216
And ye be a gentylman, ye have knavys condycyons. . . . . . . 203 Magnyfycence 2219
GENTYLNES
Than thanked I hym for his grete gentylnes. . . . . 51 Bowge 176
GENTYLWOMAN
Her chyef gentylwoman, Daunger by her name, ... 48 Bowge 69
To whome there came another gentylwoman. . . . . 48 Bowge 84
GENTYLWOMEN
Of all gentylwomen he hath the scruteny, ... 334 Garlande 782
How theis ladys and gentylwomen all . . . . 335 Garlande 809
Ladyes and gentylwomen suche as deservyd, ... 346 Garlande 1189
GENTLE
Was never byrde in cage /More gentle of corage . . . . 80 Phy Sparrow 325
It were no gentle gyse . . . . 103 Phy Sparrow 1251
Gentle Paule lie doune thy sweard, ... 358 Couplet 1
GENTLY
Gently joynted, /Gresed and anoynted /Up to the knuckles: . . 215 El Rummynge 42
GEORGE
And swete Saynt George, our ladyes knyght! . . . . 119 Ag Scottes 141
And thus, Sainct George to borowe, ... 371 Albany 506
GERARCHY
In joy triumphaunt the hevenly *gerarchy, ... 35 Dol Dethe 211
   *gerarchy] 'gerarchy' †MS Royal 18 D.ii, Marshe 1568,
   'yerarchy' Scattergood
GERE
His elbowe bare, he ware his gere so nye, ... 56 Bowge 361
How that she can were /Gorgiously her gere, ... 101 Phy Sparrow 1179
As ye ar brystlyd on the bake for alle your gay gere. 122 Garnesche1 26
Dekkyd lewdly in your gere, ... 125 Garnesche3 42
Ye, so I can devyse my gere after the cowrtly maner. . . . . 161 Magnyfycence 766
That I can were /Courtly my gere! . . . . 163 Magnyfycence 834
That thou cannyst not growe out of thy boyes gere; . . . . . 170 Magnyfycence 1075
For drede ye darre not medyll with suche gere, ... 242 Speke Parott 394
GERETRUDE
To mastres Geretrude Statham . . . . 341 Garlande R
Maistres Geretrude, /With womanhode endude, ... 341 Garlande 1043
Maistres Geretrude, /With womanhode endude, ... 342 Garlande 1051
Maistres Geretrude /With womanhode endude, ... 342 Garlande 1059
GERFAWCON
Also the noble fawcon, /With the gerfawcon, ... 85 Phy Sparrow 557
GERION
And slew Gerion /With thre bodyes in one; . . . . 104 Phy Sparrow 1307
GERIONE
And slew Gerione /With thre bodys in one; . . . . 349 Garlande 1300
GERY
His seconde hawke wexyd gery . . . . 63 Hauke 66

GESON —GYDE   Page   Title   Line

GESON
Your wyt ys so geson, ...   127   Garnesche3   129
For Folam peason /With him be nat geson;   304   Why Come Ye   1000
GESSE
At what place, nowe, as you gesse?   150   Magnyfycence   342
As they suppose and gesse, ...   271   Collyn Clout 1010
GEST
Nowe, in good faythe, thou art a fonde gest.   170   Magnyfycence 1096
Than cometh an other gest;   221   El Rummynge   270
Thus endeth the gest /Of this worthy fest.   230   El Rummynge   622
To wryght of this glorious gest, ...   309   Why Come Ye   1212
  glorious] 'gromys' MS Rawlinson C. 813
GESTE
And though I be so odyous a geste, ...   160   Magnyfycence   703
GET
An ussher of the hall fayn wold I get   37   Coystrowne1   40
Get ye anothyr where ye may.   131   Garnesche5   62
Ye get therby a slendyr laude   131   Garnesche5   74
And get [y]ou home togyther; for Lyberte shall byde 180   Magnyfycence 1446
  you] 'thou' †Rastell & Treveris C 1530, B
Well, get you hens than and sende me some other.   180   Magnyfycence 1451
To get us there some freshe mete.   204   Magnyfycence 2264
With, 'Get me a staffe, /The swyne eate my draffe!   218   El Rummynge   170
Hither they come crowdyng to get them a name, ...   329   Garlande   621
How Cownterfet Cowntenaunce of the new get   346   Garlande   1193
GETE
By Goddis soule, I wonder how ye gete   53   Bowge   262
To wete yf Malkyn, my lemman, have gete oughte.   57   Bowge   401
Gete you hens, I say, by my counsell.   149   Magnyfycence   306
Welthe, gete you home and commaunde me to Mesure.   149   Magnyfycence   316
To gete me fro them I had moche warke.   150   Magnyfycence   361
By God, we wolde gete us all thyder, ...   157   Magnyfycence   618
That he can onywhere gete, ...   306   Why Come Ye   1085
GETEST
Sume sayd, 'Holde thy peas, thou getest here no more.' . . .   319   Garlande   257
GETTE
Ye coude none other gette   263   Collyn Clout   654
  coude] 'wolde' Kele 1545.1, Marshe 1568, 'cowde'
  MS Harley 2252
Gette a frere gray, ...   265   Collyn Clout   744
By them to gette a name.   270   Collyn Clout   959
GEVE
And geve the grace to be more fortunate!   33   Dol Dethe   165
Wherwith to geve you my regraciatory, ...   324   Garlande   431
God geve them good spede there warke to begin!   334   Garlande   793
Yet nowe dowtles ye geve me cause   341   Garlande   1041
For nowe dowtles ye geve me cause   342   Garlande   1049
Wherfore dowtles ye geve me cause   342   Garlande   1057
GEW
Somtyme I wepe for a gew gaw;   168   Magnyfycence 1013
GEWGAW
And of the spyrytuall law /They made but a gewgaw, ...   66   Hauke   157
GIGGISSE
This fustiane maistres and this giggisse gase   346   Garlande   1206
GINGERLY
With, 'Gingirly, go gingerly!' Her tayle was made of hay; . . 346   Garlande   1203
GINGIRLY
With, 'Gingirly, go gingerly!' Her tayle was made of hay; . . 346   Garlande   1203
Go she never so gingirly, her honesty is gone away.   346   Garlande   1204
GIPCY
By Mary Gipcy, /Quod scripsi, scripsi;   353   Garlande   1455
GIRNED
Some tremblid, some girned, some gaspid, some gasid, ...   319   Garlande   265
GIRTH
For Margery wynshed, and breke her hinder girth;   346   Garlande   1201
GIVE
Thou mayst give up thy cocking.   366   Albany   299
GY
Syr Gy, Syr Gawen, Syr Cayus, for and Syr Olyvere, ...   123   Garnesche2   22
She callyd yow Syr Gy of Gaunt, ...   126   Garnesche3   70
With, 'Gup, Syr Gy', ye gate a moke.   131   Garnesche5   56
GYB
Whom Gyb our cat hath slayne.   72   Phy Sparrow   27
Gyb, I saye, our cat, ...   72   Phy Sparrow   28
By Gyb, our cat savage, ...   81   Phy Sparrow   375
She is a tonnysh gyb;   217   El Rummynge   99
GYBBET
To the gybbet of Baldock.   303   Why Come Ye   956
GYDE
Ye stonde in favoure and Fortune is your gyde, ...   50   Bowge   171
Then, Lyberte, se that Measure by your gyde, ...   146   Magnyfycence   195
Have deputyd Measure hym to gyde?   147   Magnyfycence   243
Make indentures how ye and I shal gyde.   180   Magnyfycence 1448
To gyde them vertuously that wyll not remembre, ...   194   Magnyfycence 1922
Alasse that I coude not myselfe no better gyde!   196   Magnyfycence 1986
I pray God be his gyde.   289   Why Come Ye   395
To gyde and to governe my dredfull tremlyng fist.   335   Garlande   828
So I beseke Jhesu now to be my gyde.   335   Garlande   835

	Page	Title	Line
GYDED			
Be governed and gyded; wote ye what I say?	179	Magnyfycence	1397
GYDETH			
Fortune gydeth and ruleth all our shyppe.	49	Bowge	111
Gydeth his bote with a prope;	105	Phy Sparrow	1341
GYDITH			
Gydith his bote with a prop.	349	Garlande	1334
GYDYD			
For by measure I warne you we thynke to be gydyd;	145	Magnyfycence	184
GYDYNG			
For Lyberte he hath in gydyng.	158	Magnyfycence	661
Well gydyng ther glowtonn to kepe streit theyr sylk,	334	Garlande	795
ther] 'the' MS Cotton Vitellius E.x			
GYDYNGE			
In thys preestly gydynge	65	Hauke	125
In] 'Is' †Lant 1545			
To the gydynge of my measure you bothe commyttynge;	145	Magnyfycence	175
Mary, Mesure had hym a whyle in gydynge,	166	Magnyfycence	939
Have welth at our gydynge to rule as we lyst?	179	Magnyfycence	1415
I say that I wyll ye have hym in gydynge.	180	Magnyfycence	1436
GYE			
Avaunt, Syr Gye of Gaunt!	275	Collyn Clout	1155
GYF			
All gyf Englond and Fraunce wer thorow sought.	34	Dol Dethe	179
GYFTE			
Gave me a gyfte in my neste when I lay,	232	Speke Parott	44
I] 'he' †MS Harley 2252			
GYFTES			
Fortune to you gyftes of grace hath lente:	50	Bowge	152
GYGAWIS			
He counteth them for gygawis;	305	Why Come Ye	1063
GYGLYNGE			
To mery, to mad, to gyglynge, to nyse,	199	Magnyfycence	2092
GYL			
With care and with thought howe Jacke shall have Gyl?	148	Magnyfycence	287
GYLE			
Why, who wolde have thought in you suche gyle?	193	Magnyfycence	1869
Set not all your affyaunce in Fortune full of gyle;	211	Magnyfycence	2501
GYLL			
Of a comely gyll /That dwelt on a hyll;	214	El Rummynge	4
To herken Jacke and Gyll /Whan they put up a byll;	249	Collyn Clout	96
What care they thoughe Gyll swete,	254	Collyn Clout	321
Bothe Gyll and Jacke at Noke	268	Collyn Clout	855
Gyll swetis and Cate spynnys!	302	Why Come Ye	926
Cate] not in MS Rawlinson C. 813			
GYLLA			
'Welcom Jacke and Gylla!'	253	Collyn Clout	258
GYLLY			
With, 'Jast you, and gup, gylly,	224	El Rummynge	390
GYN			
Yet wyth a prety gyn /I fortuned to come in,	64	Hauke	93
And I bequethe hym the gowte and the gyn.	204	Magnyfycence	2255
GYNYS			
At Gynys when ye ware /But a slendyr spere,	125	Garnesche3	40
........gynys upon a gonge,	125	Garnesche3	56
GYRDETH			
And gyrdeth in her gytes /Stytched and pranked with pletes;	216	El Rummynge	68
GYRDLE			
Her hernest gyrdle, her weddynge rynge,	221	El Rummynge	280
hernest] 'haruest' Day 1560, 1521 Fragment			
GYRNE			
Ye gyrne grymly with your gomys and with yor grysly face.	122	Garnesche1	12
GYRTH			
Spur up at the hynder gyrth with, 'Gup, morell, gup!'	43	Balettys2	17
GYSE			
It were no gentle gyse	103	Phy Sparrow	1251
The gyse now a dayes /Of some janglynge jayes	103	Phy Sparrow	1268
In bastarde ryme, after the dogrell gyse,	151	Magnyfycence	408
The courtly gyse of the newe jet?	153	Magnyfycence	453
All the newe gyse, fresshe and gaye,	153	Magnyfycence	463
Nay, in good faythe. It is but the gyse.	163	Magnyfycence	809
Why, is this the gyse nowe adays?	163	Magnyfycence	813
Of the newe gyse,	164	Magnyfycence	846
It is the gyse nowe, I say, over all –	189	Magnyfycence	1759
Wrythen in wonder wyse /After the Sarasyns gyse,	216	El Rummynge	74
in] 'in a' Day 1560, Marshe 1568			
Lo, this is the gyse noweadays!	277	Collyn Clout	1227
Of your royall palace it is not the gyse,	315	Garlande	121
It is not my custome nor my gyse /To leve behynde	342	Garlande	1068
For the gyse nowadays	348	Garlande	1261
GYTES			
And gyrdeth in her gytes /Stytched and pranked with pletes;	216	El Rummynge	68
GYVE			
Gyve me your honde, fare well and have good daye.'	60	Bowge	497
To gyve her his hole hert.	99	Phy Sparrow	1102
Gyve up your game, ye playe chek mate;	114	Scot Kynge	37
Trewe you say, syr. Gyve me your hande.	141	Magnyfycence	28
To counterfet thyr counsell they gyve me a fee.	154	Magnyfycence	491

GYVEN —GLASID   Page   Title   Line

	Page	Title	Line
God gyve you a very myschaunce!	154	Magnyfycence	497
For Cockys harte, gyve me thy hande.	154	Magnyfycence	512
Yes, syr, I gyve God avowe,	155	Magnyfycence	529
A, syr, I pray God gyve you confusyon!	157	Magnyfycence	597
Gyve this gentylman rome, syrs. Stonde utter!	161	Magnyfycence	753
That men hym gyve.	165	Magnyfycence	908
I wyll not gyve a halfepeny for to chose the better.	170	Magnyfycence	1067
Yet gyve me thy dogge, and I am content;	171	Magnyfycence	1112
Nowe take thou my dogge and gyve me thy fowle.	171	Magnyfycence	1116
Gyve me my grote, for thou hast lost.	173	Magnyfycence	1206
I say it is foly to gyve all welth away.	180	Magnyfycence	1430
That he come hyder, and to gyve hym a loke	187	Magnyfycence	1681
God gyve hym a myscheffe! Nay, nowe let me alone.	189	Magnyfycence	1730
For I here but fewe men that gyve ony prayse	189	Magnyfycence	1743
Spare for no cost to gyve them pounde and peny;	190	Magnyfycence	1771
Gyve them more than ynoughe, and let them not lacke;	190	Magnyfycence	1773
Plucke from an hundred, and gyve it to thre;	190	Magnyfycence	1775
I shall gyve you a gaude of a goslynge that I gave,	191	Magnyfycence	1829
If ever I herde syke another, God gyve me shame.	192	Magnyfycence	1833
Go together by the heddys, and gyve me your swordys.	202	Magnyfycence	2199
Nowe gyve me somwhat, for God sake, I crave.	204	Magnyfycence	2251
In faythe, I gyve the four quarters of a knave.	204	Magnyfycence	2252
And I gyve hym Crystys curse	204	Magnyfycence	2257
And I gyve hym the cowghe, the murre, and the pose.	204	Magnyfycence	2259
And to that I say gyve good advysement.	208	Magnyfycence	2406
To gyve so hasty credence ye were moche to blame.	209	Magnyfycence	2443
God gyve it yll prevynge,	219	El Rummynge	185
And ye wyll gyve me a syppet /Of your stale ale,	223	El Rummynge	367
God gyve it yll hap!'	227	El Rummynge	509
God gyve it yll hayle,	230	El Rummynge	617
And howe whan ye gyve orders	252	Collyn Clout	220
That ye gyve shrewed counsell	255	Collyn Clout	358
Gog gyve you good yere, ye make me to smyle.	332	Garlande	736
Gyve it up, and cry, 'creke', /Lyke an huddy peke.	366	Albany	300
To gyve you exhibycion	378	Replycacion	143
To whom we must gyve faythe,	384	Replycacion	348

GYVEN

That, so to saye, I had gyven her no cause.	48	Bowge	75
I waraunt you I have gyven it a lasshe.	201	Magnyfycence	2165
Prosperyte [by] hym is gyven solacyusly to man; by] 'to' †Rastell & Treveris C 1530, B	207	Magnyfycence	2367
That nothynge be gyven without consyderacyon.	211	Magnyfycence	2495

GYVETH

Who so to me gyveth good advertence	177	Magnyfycence	1333

GYVYNGE

As gyvynge a thynge that ye never bought.	189	Magnyfycence	1758

GLAD

Whych to behold makyth hevy hartys glad;	44	Balettys3	28
But wolde be glad of your company.	53	Bowge	268
Whan other ar glad,	95	Phy Sparrow	938
That makith our hartis glad,	111	Lawde	51
So in his harte he may be glad of us.	145	Magnyfycence	158
I am never glad but whan I may do yll,	160	Magnyfycence	731
By the masse, I am glad I came hyder	176	Magnyfycence	1286
Mary, I wene he wolde not be glad to come agayne.	189	Magnyfycence	1740
When ye knowe that I knowe, ye wyll not be glad.	192	Magnyfycence	1844
With gommes goostly of glad herte and mynde,	207	Magnyfycence	2359
Yf you be so myndyd, we be ryght glad.	210	Magnyfycence	2473
Howe the people are glad	259	Collyn Clout	512
Is glad to please, and loth to offend.'	323	Garlande	413
Whiche glad am to please, and loth to offende'	324	Garlande	427
Which glad am to please, and lothe to offende.'	324	Garlande	441
Whos lusty lokis make hevy hartis glad;	337	Garlande	903
And specyally which glad was to devyse	342	Garlande	1071
Of his pleasaunt paine there and his glad distres	351	Garlande	1391

GLADDE

Howe be it, I wolde be ryght gladde, I you assure,	183	Magnyfycence	1527

GLADLY

And for his sake ryght gladly I wolde	149	Magnyfycence	334
And every man gladly my company wolde refuse,	160	Magnyfycence	704

GLADNES

The hertes of England to comfort with gladnes.	117	Ag Scottes	88
With solace and gladnes,	340	Garlande	1008

GLADNESSE

Your comfortable advyse and wyt excedyth all gladnesse;	210	Magnyfycence	2477

GLAYMY

Thou gresly gargone glaymy,	128	Garnesche3	168

GLAYRE

Lyke a ropy rayne, /A gummy glayre.	215	El Rummynge	25

GLARIS

As gastly that glaris, as grimly that gronis,	328	Garlande	593

GLAS

His eyen blereed, his face shone lyke a glas;	56	Bowge	353
Her face glystryng lyke glas,	226	El Rummynge	482
His plummet, his pensell, his spectacles of glas, of] 'with' †Fakes 1523	343	Garlande	1097

GLASID

Glittryng and glistryng and gloryously glasid,	351	Garlande	1388

GLASSE —GLUM   Page   Title   Line

GLASSE
That toteth oft in a glasse, ...   82   Phy Sparrow   422
As a glede glowynge, your ien glyster as glasse, ...   122   Garneschel   37
A myrrour of glasse, that I may tote therin;   231   Speke Parott   10
With glasse wyndowes and barres;   270   Collyn Clout   939
Is tourned to glasse, ...   301   Why Come Ye   902
GLE
I garde her gaspe, I garde her gle, ...   198   Magnyfycence   2067
But that he daunced for joye of that gle.   320   Garlande   278
GLEDE
As a glede glowynge, your ien glyster as glasse, ...   122   Garneschel   37
What is this, an owle or a glede?   169   Magnyfycence   1047
GLENES
Howe some of them glenes   260   Collyn Clout   567
GLENT
Her browys bent, /Her eyen glent;   167   Magnyfycence   980
But for all that he is lyke to have a glent.   187   Magnyfycence   1668
GLETTERYNGE
Gletterynge in golde.   164   Magnyfycence   855
GLINT
'Go softly,' she sayd, 'the stones be full glint.'   328   Garlande   572
GLISTRYNG
Glittryng and glistryng and gloryously glasid, ...   351   Garlande   1388
GLITTERING
Englasid glittering with many a clere story;   325   Garlande   479
GLITTERYNG
With hornnis twayne /Of glitteryng golde;   348   Garlande   1293
GLITTRYNG
Glittryng and glistryng and gloryously glasid, ...   351   Garlande   1388
GLYDE
Shall glyde and smothely slyppe   277   Collyn Clout   1252
GLYSTER
As a glede glowynge, your ien glyster as glasse, ...   122   Garneschel   37
GLYSTRYNG
Her face glystryng lyke glas, ...   226   El Rummynge   482
GLYTTERYNG
Of glytteryng gold;   104   Phy Sparrow   1300
GLOME
And with that worde on me she gave a glome   48   Bowge   80
GLOMMYNGE
And as for theyr connynge, /A glommynge and a mommynge, ...   248   Collyn Clout   83
GLORIOUS
With all the hole sorte of that glorious place, ...   35   Dol Dethe   212
And hath a glorious tayle, ...   82   Phy Sparrow   440
To wryght of this glorious gest, ...   309   Why Come Ye   1212
  glorious] 'gromys' MS Rawlinson C. 813
Our glorious lady to disable, ...   375   Replycacion   ˙ 26
That glorious mayde Mary;   381   Replycacion   256
That glorious mayde and mother, ...   381   Replycacion   257
Whom Hieronymus, /That doctour glorious, ...   383   Replycacion   319
Lyke to Pyndarus in glorious poetry, ...   383   Replycacion   334
GLORY
By Eschines rehersed to the grete glory   317   Garlande   166
In famous glory all other transcendyng, ...   344   Garlande   1129
And his glory to incres /Lyke to Scipiades, ...   369   Albany   438
GLORYOUS
Under a gloryous cloth of astate.   325   Garlande   484
GLORYOUSLY
For if he gloryously publisshe his matter, ...   314   Garlande   83
Bownte, and so gloryously ye have enrollyd   324   Garlande   437
Full gloryously can he glose, thy mynde for to fele;   333   Garlande   760
Glittryng and glistryng and gloryously glasid, ...   351   Garlande   1388
GLOSE
What, shuld I flatter? What, shulde I glose or paynt?   30   Dol Dethe   41
Ye, of Jacke a Thrommys bybyll can ye make a glose.   180   Magnyfycence   1427
Of the texte and the glose.   266   Collyn Clout   779
Full gloryously can he glose, thy mynde for to fele;   333   Garlande   760
Plainly, I can not glose, ...   338   Garlande   910
GLOSETH
He gloseth and he flatters.'   247   Collyn Clout   25
GLOSYNGE
But dyssymulynge and glosynge, ...   255   Collyn Clout   356
GLOTONY
Full of glotony /And of ypocrysy, ...   269   Collyn Clout   918
Envy, wrath, and lechery, /Covetys and glotony;   293   Why Come Ye   576
GLOTTON
Ye, in faythe; or ellys thou arte to great a glotton.   204   Magnyfycence   2266
GLOVE
Nay, horson, here is my glove. Take it up and thou dare. . . .   202   Magnyfycence   2178
GLOWYNGE
As a glede glowynge, your ien glyster as glasse, ...   122   Garneschel   37
GLOWTONN
Well gydyng ther glowtonn to kepe streit theyr sylk, ...   334   Garlande   795
  ther] 'the' MS Cotton Vitellius E.x
GLUM
And play scylence and glum, ...   269   Collyn Clout   904
That makys our syre to glum.   288   Why Come Ye   389
She loked hawtly, and gave on me a glum.   344   Garlande   1117

256

GNAR —GO | Page | Title | Line

GNAR
For and this curre do gnar, ... 286 Why Come Ye 300
GNAT
A fly, or a gnat, /He wolde flye at that; .... 75 Phy Sparrow 130
Yes, yet he wyll make the ete a gnat. .... 173 Magnyfycence 1192
   Yes, yet] 'Yet yes' †Rastell & Treveris C 1530, B
But, and I were as ye, I wolde not set a gnat. .... 188 Magnyfycence 1704
What! Wylte thou skelpe me? Thou dare not loke on a gnat. ... 202 Magnyfycence 2181
GNAWE
And gnawe the in theyr jawes! .... 79 Phy Sparrow 289
To chewe and to gnawe .... 263 Collyn Clout 655
   gnawe] 'grawe' †Godfray 1531, 'gnawe' MS Harley 2252
GO
Go watch a bole, your bak is brode. .... 35 Man Margery 12
'Rumbyll downe, tumbyll downe, hey, go, now, now!' .... 37 Coystrownel 30
Go, pytyous hart, rasyd with dedly wo, ... 45 Balettys5 1
Lete theym go lowse theym, in the devylles date. .... 59 Bowge 455
Encreaseth my dedly wo, /For my sparowe is go. .... 74 Phy Sparrow 114
For it wold come and go, ... 75 Phy Sparrow 159
Phyllyp had leve to go .... 76 Phy Sparrow 175
Alas, I wolde ryde and go .... 76 Phy Sparrow 186
And go in at my spayre, ... 80 Phy Sparrow 345
   go in] 'often' Kitson 1560.6
Kynge Jamy, Jomy your joye is all go. .... 113 Scot Kynge 1
Thow wrythtyst I xulde let the go pley; 134 Garnesche5 166
Go pley the, Garnyshe, garnysshed gay! 134 Garnesche5 167
Tut, Scot, I sey, /Go shake th[e], dog, hey! .... 135 Dundas 28
   the] 'thy' Marshe 1568
Go shake the, dogge, hay, syth ye wyll nedys! .... 148 Magnyfycence 303
Coll wolde go clenly, and it wyll not be, ... 153 Magnyfycence 476
We wyll remedy it, man, or we go; .... 155 Magnyfycence 551
But tell me where aboute ye go. .... 157 Magnyfycence 617
And wolde that we sholde for hym go - .... 158 Magnyfycence 646
But, Counterfet Countenaunce, go we togyder, ... 158 Magnyfycence 665
All thre, I say. Shall I go? Whyder? .... 158 Magnyfycence 666
Now let us go, and we shall, then. .... 159 Magnyfycence 687
I waraunt you I wyll not go away. .... 163 Magnyfycence 820
And so they go out of the place. .... 163 Magnyfycence SD
But I must tary here; go thou before. .... 167 Magnyfycence 954
Nowe, by the rode, and he wyll go nere. .... 173 Magnyfycence 1196
Yes. I shall tell you or I go .... 175 Magnyfycence 1263
Yes, perde, man, whether ye ryde or go. .... 176 Magnyfycence 1307
And he go to the devyll, so that I may have my fee, ... 187 Magnyfycence 1670
For go when ye shall, of you shall he mysse. .... 188 Magnyfycence 1706
I set not a flye and all go to all. .... 188 Magnyfycence 1710
Let them have all, and the other go without; .... 190 Magnyfycence 1780
For as thou wylte, so shall the game go; .... 190 Magnyfycence 1786
I sawe a sowter go to supper, or ever he had dynde. ..... 191 Magnyfycence 1825
For nowe wyll I from this caytyfe go, ... 195 Magnyfycence 1950
For nowe go I wyll begge for you some mete. .... 197 Magnyfycence 2034
Go together by the heddys, and gyve me your swordys. .... 202 Magnyfycence 2199
Go we nere and let us se. .... 204 Magnyfycence 2243
For the passyon of God, let us go thyther. .... 204 Magnyfycence 2276
Or that thy selfe thou go honge .... 206 Magnyfycence 2312
Lo, here is thy knyfe and a halter, and or we go ferther, ... 206 Magnyfycence 2317
These swyne go to the hye dese, ... 218 El Rummynge 175
For they go to roust, /Streyght over the ale-joust, ... 219 El Rummynge 191
Some go streyght thyder, /Be it slaty or slyder; .... 221 El Rummynge 257
And bad Elynour go bet, ... 222 El Rummynge 332
And skantly could go /For payne and for wo. .... 227 El Rummynge 513
Ye go about to amende, and ye mare all. .... 235 Speke Parott 154
Go, litelle quayre, namyd the Popagay, ... 238 Speke Parott 278
Go, propyr Parotte, my popagay, ... 241 Speke Parott 357
'He is but a foole; /Let hym go to scole!' .... 247 Collyn Clout 29
As I go aboute, ... 253 Collyn Clout 286
For you love to go trym, ... 262 Collyn Clout 641
Nowe wyll I go .... 267 Collyn Clout 828
And through all the worlde thei go .... 268 Collyn Clout 885
They wyll no farder go. .... 269 Collyn Clout 908
Or elles go rost a stone! .... 281 Why Come Ye 112
That of shulde go his hede, ... 288 Why Come Ye 358
Where ever he go or ryde .... 289 Why Come Ye 394
They wot not whether to go. .... 294 Why Come Ye 614
Let se, my syster, now spede you, go aboute. .... 319 Garlande 242
   you] not in MS Cotton Vitellius E.x
All orators and poetis shulde thider go before, ... 325 Garlande 454
With, 'Now let me come', and 'Now let me go.' .... 326 Garlande 515
'Go softly,' she sayd, 'the stones be full glint.' ...... 328 Garlande 572
With, 'Gingirly, go gingirly!' Her tayle was made of hay; ... 346 Garlande 1203
Go she never so gingirly, her honesty is gone away. ..... 346 Garlande 1204
Go, litill quaire, /Demene you faire. .... 355 Garlande 1533
Your capitayne ranne to go, ... 360 Albany 65
To go, to go, to go, ... 360 Albany 66
To go, to go, to go, ... 360 Albany 66
To go, to go, to go, ... 360 Albany 66
Twyt, Scot, go kepe thy den. .... 362 Albany 145
Walke, Scot, go begge a byt .... 362 Albany 154
Go heme, ranke Scot, ge heme, ... 368 Albany 382

GOD —GOD　　　　　　　　　　　　　　　　　　　　Page　Title　Line

	Page	Title	Line
Go, lytell quayre, quickly.	371	Albany	508
Go, lytell quayre, apace,	372	Albany	523
or to pray and go on pylgrimages,	375	Replycacion	1
Se where the heretykes go,	376	Replycacion	73

GOD

	Page	Title	Line
To slo ther owne lorde? God was not in ther mynde!	30	Dol Dethe	35
O cruell Mars, thou dedly god of war!	32	Dol Dethe	113
God the assyst unto thyne heritage,	33	Dol Dethe	164
I pray God sende the prosperous lyf and long,	34	Dol Dethe	169
Of foule detraccion God kepe the from the blast.	34	Dol Dethe	173
Where thow art Lord and God omnipotent.	34	Dol Dethe	203
In Trinitate one God of myghtis moste.	35	Dol Dethe	217
Yet, and God wold, I wold my payne were easyd!	45	Balettys5	12
Than asked she me, 'Syr, so God the spede,	48	Bowge	76
Whyles I have ought, by God, thou shalt not lacke,	50	Bowge	167
'God spede, broder,' to me quod he than,	51	Bowge	195
Beware of him, for, I make God avowe,	51	Bowge	199
For, but I trusted you, so God me save,	52	Bowge	213
'By God,' quod he, 'this and thus it is';	52	Bowge	225
'Syr, God you save, why loke you so sadde?	53	Bowge	239
My wytte wolde waste, I make God avowe.	53	Bowge	243
Holde up the helme, loke up and lete God stere:	53	Bowge	250
Wolde to God it wolde please you some daye	53	Bowge	256
I praye to God that it maye never dy.	53	Bowge	271
And ye be welcome, syr, so God me save,	54	Bowge	279
'By God,' quod Hervy, 'and it so happen myghte!	54	Bowge	306
By God, I have of the now grete dyspyte;	55	Bowge	325
'Welcome,' quod Ryote, 'I make God avowe.'	56	Bowge	378
Now wolde to God thou wolde leye money downe!	57	Bowge	395
By God, I saye, there is a grete herte-brennynge	59	Bowge	460
And so I wolde it were, so God me spede,	59	Bowge	481
Withoute God make a good conclusyon.	59	Bowge	483
A flaterynge knave and false he is, God wote.	59	Bowge	485
He tolde me so, by God, ye maye truste me.	60	Bowge	514
To holde myne honde, by God, I had grete payne;	61	Bowge	522
And sware horryble othes /Before the face of God,	63	Hauke	53
Of God nothynge els crave I /But Phyllypes soule to kepe	73	Phy Sparrow	67
Wolde God I had Zenophontes,	74	Phy Sparrow	98
God wot, we thought no syn -	76	Phy Sparrow	168
(God send the soule good rest!)	78	Phy Sparrow	262
God send them sorowe and shame!	78	Phy Sparrow	277
God sende my sparoes sole good rest!	86	Phy Sparrow	574
I pray God, Phillip to heven may fly.	86	Phy Sparrow	580
Of al good praiers God send him sum!	86	Phy Sparrow	584
Wolde God myne homely style	101	Phy Sparrow	1204
I pray God they be payned	106	Phy Sparrow	1376
God forgeve hym his mysdedes.	107	Epitaphe1	19
God save him in his right! /Amen	112	Lawde	56
But by the power and myght of God	114	Scot Kynge	46
God save kynge Henry and his lordes all	115	Scot Kynge	72
and God save noble Kynge Henry the viij.	115	Scot Kynge	E
Thankyd be God in trinyte,	119	Ag Scottes	140
But, by the power and myght of God,	119	Ag Scottes	145
God sende you wele good spede,	129	Garnesche3	202
God Latyn for Jake a Thrum,	129	Garnesche3	204
God garde the, Garnyche, from the rope!	133	Garnesche5	161
God forbyd ye sholde be let	142	Magnyfycence	63
It were a shame, to God I make an othe,	144	Magnyfycence	145
God forbede that it other wyse sholde be!	147	Magnyfycence	246
Endure? No, God wote, it were great payne.	147	Magnyfycence	248
By God, syr, ye se but fewe wyse men of myne age.	148	Magnyfycence	289
Syr, thanked be God, he hath his hele.	149	Magnyfycence	315
I pray God kepe you in that mood!	150	Magnyfycence	336
By God, syr, beyonde the se.	150	Magnyfycence	341
Howe so? By God, at the syde,	150	Magnyfycence	346
With ye, syr, so God me spede.	151	Magnyfycence	379
The grace of God under benedicite.	154	Magnyfycence	490
God gyve you a very myschaunce!	154	Magnyfycence	497
By God, I have bene about a praty pronge -	154	Magnyfycence	501
By God, we have made Magnyfycence to ete a flye.	154	Magnyfycence	503
By God, man, bothe his pagent and thyne he can play.	154	Magnyfycence	505
By God, yet it muste begynne moche of the.	154	Magnyfycence	514
Yes, syr, I gyve God avowe,	155	Magnyfycence	529
By God, had not I it convayed	155	Magnyfycence	534
By God, syr, this is Fansy Small-Brayne;	156	Magnyfycence	583
A, syr, I pray God gyve you confusyon!	157	Magnyfycence	597
A, Fansy, Fansy, God sende the brayne!	157	Magnyfycence	608
By God, we wolde gete us all thyder,	157	Magnyfycence	618
I pray God let you never to thee!	158	Magnyfycence	635
By God, syr, what nede all this waste?	161	Magnyfycence	754
Nowe welcom, by the God holy!	166	Magnyfycence	919
Howe so? By God, by a praty slyght,	167	Magnyfycence	952
Yes, in faythe, I thanke God I may here.	169	Magnyfycence	1059
By God, I can tell the; and I wyll.	170	Magnyfycence	1071
In faythe, truth thou sayst nowe, by God of heven!	170	Magnyfycence	1079
That ever thou thryve, God it forfende!	171	Magnyfycence	1114
By God, for snatchynge of puddynges and wortes.	171	Magnyfycence	1128
By the harte of God, well done!	172	Magnyfycence	1156

GOD—GOD | Page | Title | Line

	Page	Title	Line
By God, syr, Foly, myne owne sworne brother.	172	Magnyfycence	1159
What hast thou founde there? By God, a lowse.	173	Magnyfycence	1198
Ye, by God, syr. For a nede,	174	Magnyfycence	1237
So helpe me God, man, ever at the length	175	Magnyfycence	1258
By God, there be some that be shroudly towchyd.	175	Magnyfycence	1277
So is all the remenaunt, I make God avowe;	175	Magnyfycence	1283
God have mercy, good godfather.	176	Magnyfycence	1312
Nor Nero, that nother set by God nor man,	182	Magnyfycence	1509
A, I wolde to God that I were halfe so crafty	183	Magnyfycence	1532
With a good wyll, syr, God spede you bothe togyder.	186	Magnyfycence	1648
For, so helpe me God, for you he is not mete.	186	Magnyfycence	1653
Syr, God rewarde you as ye have deserved.	188	Magnyfycence	1701
God gyve hym a myscheffe! Nay, nowe let me alone.	189	Magnyfycence	1730
Nay, so God me helpe, it was no grete vexacyon;	189	Magnyfycence	1733
Thou sayst truthe, by the harte that God me gave!	190	Magnyfycence	1782
She pynched her pynyon, by God, and catched harme.	191	Magnyfycence	1810
Se, for God avowe, for colde as I chydder.	191	Magnyfycence	1817
I make God avowe ye wyll none other men have.	191	Magnyfycence	1827
What sayst thou? Mary, I pray God your mastershyp to save.	191	Magnyfycence	1828
If ever I herde syke another, God gyve me shame.	192	Magnyfycence	1833
From God am sente to quyte the thy mede.	193	Magnyfycence	1877
The stroke of God, Adversyte, I hyght.	193	Magnyfycence	1882
For there is nothynge that more dyspleaseth God	194	Magnyfycence	1928
All that God sendeth, take it in gre;	196	Magnyfycence	1979
And pray to God your sorowes to asswage.	196	Magnyfycence	1989
And whan it pleaseth God, better may be.	196	Magnyfycence	1993
Take it mekely, and thanke God of his grace;	197	Magnyfycence	2033
It is foly agaynst God for to plete.	197	Magnyfycence	2035
A, Lord God, how the gowte wryngeth me by the too.	198	Magnyfycence	2047
Then trust I to God and the holy rode,	203	Magnyfycence	2206
By the fayth that I owe to God, and I wyll syt styll.	203	Magnyfycence	2209
By God, I tell you, I wyll not be out facyd.	203	Magnyfycence	2220
Nowe gyve me somwhat, for God sake, I crave.	204	Magnyfycence	2251
For the passyon of God, let us go thyther.	204	Magnyfycence	2276
That thou arte not worthy to loke God in the face.	205	Magnyfycence	2296
Syr, your fesycyan is the grace of God,	207	Magnyfycence	2349
To thanke God of his sonde; and comforte ye shal fynde.	207	Magnyfycence	2360
And hartely thanke God of your adversyte;	207	Magnyfycence	2362
For who loveth God can ayle nothynge but good.	207	Magnyfycence	2365
I aske God mercy of my neglyge[sse],	207	Magnyfycence	2380
neglygesse] 'neglygence' †Rastell & Treveris C 1530, B			
And ever let the drede of God be in your syght,	211	Magnyfycence	2498
God gyve it yll prevynge,	219	El Rummynge	185
God sende you good sale!'	223	El Rummynge	369
Elynour made the pryce /For god ale eche whyt.	224	El Rummynge	411
God gyve it yll hap!'	227	El Rummynge	509
To paye,' sayde she, 'God wote,	229	El Rummynge	601
God gyve it yll hayle,	230	El Rummynge	617
In Englysshe to God Parott can supple:	231	Speke Parott	33
supple] 'shewe propyrlye' †MS Harley 2252			
God of his goodnes him framed and wrought;	236	Speke Parott	212
God amend all, /That all amend may!	241	Speke Parott	353
Ryn God, rynne Devyll! Yet the date of Owur Lord	244	Speke Parott	444
God wote, with dronken nolles.	252	Collyn Clout	232
By the breed that God brake,	253	Collyn Clout	251
God wotte, to theyr great paynes,	254	Collyn Clout	313
As many a frere, God wote,	267	Collyn Clout	836
God wotte, they take great payne	268	Collyn Clout	860
To loke on God in fourme of brede,	272	Collyn Clout	1024
Suche grace God them sende	274	Collyn Clout	1125
With them the worde of God	275	Collyn Clout	1145
Renne god, renne devyll,	277	Collyn Clout	1222
God sende us better luck!	282	Why Come Ye	123
God sende us better lucke, etc.	282	Why Come Ye	124
To know God nor man.	283	Why Come Ye	183
God save my Lorde Admyrell!	288	Why Come Ye	376
I pray God save the kynge.	289	Why Come Ye	393
I pray God be his gyde.	289	Why Come Ye	395
By God that me dere bought!	290	Why Come Ye	451
By] 'But' Marshe 1568			
That, God to recorde,	291	Why Come Ye	486
God wot, had lytell parte	292	Why Come Ye	513
Allmyghty God, I trust,	298	Why Come Ye	750
That wolde God everychone /Of his affynyte	300	Why Come Ye	834
God save his noble grace,	303	Why Come Ye	969
God of his miseracyon /Send better reformacyon!	305	Why Come Ye	1044
The worde of God to let.	305	Why Come Ye	1069
worde] 'wordis', to] 'he' MS Rawlinson C. 813			
Against their wylles, God wot.	306	Why Come Ye	1100
Whether God be pleased or wroth.	307	Why Come Ye	1132
He jugyth him equivalent /With God omnipotent.	307	Why Come Ye	1136
him] 'hymselfe' MS Rawlinson C. 813;			
equivalent] 'equypolent' Rawlinson C. 813			
And the stroke of God!	307	Why Come Ye	1138
Nowe God amende that is amys,	308	Why Come Ye	1162
The flayle, the scourge of Almighty God.	308	Why Come Ye	1165
The flayle] not in MS Rawlinson C. 813			
For he setteth God apart.	308	Why Come Ye	1180

GODDES —GOLD		Page	Title	Line
God sende him sorowe for his sinnes!		309	Why Come Ye	1201
But blessed Bacchus, the pleasant god of wyne,		321	Garlande	334
But blessed Bacchus, the pleasant god of wyne,		321	Garlande	341
But blessyd Bachus, potenciall god of strengthe,		322	Garlande	348
God geve them good spede there warke to begin!		334	Garlande	793
Committyth all to God, and lettyth his shyp ryde;		335	Garlande	834
A lyfe for God hymselfe		340	Garlande	996
To be our kyng, of God preordinate.		347	Garlande	1232
I pray God they be paynyd		350	Garlande	1369
God wote, theis wordes made me full sad;		353	Garlande	1484
God sende them bothe myschauns!		363	Albany	176
God sende you sorow and care!		363	Albany	181
God let you never thrive!		368	Albany	379
Wolde God, for your owne ease,		377	Replycacion	114
And crye God mercy, lyke frantyke foles.		382	Replycacion	299
God maketh his habytacion		384	Replycacion	376
Which is God of myghtes most,		385	Replycacion	384
GODDES				
In the college of musis goddes hystoriall,		29	Dol Dethe	9
Goddes mooste cruell unto the lyfe of man,		32	Dol Dethe	121
Sche praiid yow walke, on Goddes halfe!		131	Garnesche5	60
By Goddes fote, and I dare well fyght, for I wyll not start.		161	Magnyfycence	768
Ye, by Goddes sacrament; and with other mo.		166	Magnyfycence	942
By Goddes body, so dyd I.		166	Magnyfycence	947
For, Goddes cope, thou wyll spende!		171	Magnyfycence	1115
A bolle or a basyn, I say, for Goddes brede!		189	Magnyfycence	1728
Lydderyns so lytell set by Goddes lawes.		194	Magnyfycence	1919
That Goddes grace hath vexed you sharply		207	Magnyfycence	2352
Goddes blissyng lyght on thy lytell swete musse!		238	Speke Parott	266
A strawe for Goddes curse!		254	Collyn Clout	294
Alas, for Goddes wyll,		263	Collyn Clout	687
Must preche a Goddes halfe		266	Collyn Clout	810
Unto Diana, the goddes inmortall,		320	Garlande	303
Why have the goddes shewyd me this cruelte,		321	Garlande	309
Your sysmaticate sawes /Agaynst Goddes lawes,		377	Replycacion	123
GODDESSE				
Egeria, the goddesse,		100	Phy Sparrow	1152
As goddesse inmortall she dyd represente;		313	Garlande	47
GODDIS				
Maiden moste pure, and Goddis moder dere,		34	Dol Dethe	205
By Goddis soule, I wonder how ye gete		53	Bowge	262
By Goddis bones, but yf we have som sleyte,		54	Bowge	304
By Goddis woundes, but for dysplesaunce,		55	Bowge	332
By Goddis syde, my sworde thy berde shall shave!		55	Bowge	339
By Goddis sydes, syns I her thyder broughte,		57	Bowge	404
Or els is thys Goddis law,		65	Hauke	130
Shewynge him Goddis lawis.		305	Why Come Ye	1060
For he was ever ageynst Goddis hows;		347	Garlande	1251
GODDYS				
By Goddys body, I come streyte.		151	Magnyfycence	399
I am Goddys preposytour; I prynt them with a pen;		195	Magnyfycence	1941
Goddys fote! I warant you I am a gentylman borne!		203	Magnyfycence	2216
In Goddys mercy, I tell them, is but foly to truste;		205	Magnyfycence	2289
Me humbly commyttynge unto Goddys wyll.		208	Magnyfycence	2382
Than stande up, syr, in Goddys name!		208	Magnyfycence	2397
GODE				
Their bodyes and their gode,		371	Albany	488
GODELY				
Of yowthe the godely flour,		111	Lawde	44
And of there bounte they made me godely chere		323	Garlande	398
Brought forth a godely babi!		339	Garlande	975
GODFATHER				
God have mercy, good godfather.		176	Magnyfycence	1312
GODFREY				
with Gresy, Gorbelyd Godfrey et cetera		122	Garnesche2	1
Ye grounde yow upon Godfrey, that grysly gargons face,		123	Garnesche2	29
Cum Garnyche, cum Godfrey, with as many as ye may!		123	Garnesche2	32
Gup, gorbellyd Godfrey, gup, Garnysche, gaudy fole!		123	Garnesche2	36
GODLY				
Thorow his godly myght;		93	Phy Sparrow	870
As at the fyrst orygynall, by godly opynyon;		143	Magnyfycence	119
GODS				
'Ryse up, on Gods halfe,'		227	El Rummynge	501
GOE				
With ladyes I lerne and goe with them to scole.		231	Speke Parott	21
Goe, lytyll quayre, pray them that yow beholde,		239	Speke Parott	290
GOETH				
Here goeth out FELYCITE, LYBERTE and FANSY.		180	Magnyfycence	SD
Whan she goeth out /Her selfe for to shewe,		216	El Rummynge	80
GOG				
Gog gyve you good yere, ye make me to smyle.		332	Garlande	736
GOYNG				
That he to your courte is goyng and commynge,		316	Garlande	139
GOYTH				
She goyth wyde behynde and hewyth never a dele:		43	Balettys2	24
GOLD				
His mater is worth gold,		91	Phy Sparrow	786
Of glytteryng gold;		104	Phy Sparrow	1300

GOLDDE —GONE

	Page	Title	Line
And the appels of gold /Of Hesperides withhold,	104	Phy Sparrow	1301
Suche pollaxis and pyllers, suche mulys trapte with gold -	246	Speke Parott	517

GOLDDE

Sum pirlyng of goldde theyr worke to encrese	334	Garlande	796

GOLDE

Alas his golde, his fee, his annuall rente,	32	Dol Dethe	97
Of golde of tessew the fynest that myghte be,	47	Bowge	59
In golde letters, this worde, whiche I dyde rede:	48	Bowge	66
A spone of golde, full of hony swete,	58	Bowge	436
Of Kynge Cresus golde,	76	Phy Sparrow	190
And he shold be bought /For golde and fee,	76	Phy Sparrow	196
With letters of golde.	103	Phy Sparrow	1259
Why were ye Calliope, embrawdred with letters of golde?	112	Calliope	I
Whose name enrolde /With silke and golde	112	Calliope	10
Cicero with hys tong of golde.	130	Garnesche5	12
Wyth golde and grotes they grese my hande,	152	Magnyfycence	432
Gletterynge in golde.	164	Magnyfycence	855
Why, wyl a maystres be wonne for money and for golde?	184	Magnyfycence	1575
A goodly rybon, or a golde rynge,	184	Magnyfycence	1580
Somtyme without measure he trusted in golde;	193	Magnyfycence	1894
Alasse! Where is nowe my golde and fe?	196	Magnyfycence	1967
Where is nowe my golde upon them that I spent?	198	Magnyfycence	2058
Tytan hathe truste up hys tressys of fyne golde;	242	Speke Parott	398
Howe they are able to make /With theyr golde and treasure	250	Collyn Clout	144
Set nought by golde ne grotes, /Theyr names yf I durst tell.	250	Collyn Clout	160
Men say, for sylver and golde,	254	Collyn Clout	289
With golde all betrapped,	254	Collyn Clout	309
Theyr styrops of myxt golde begared,	254	Collyn Clout	317
begared] 'begarded' Marshe 1568, 'be glory̆d' MS Harley 2252			
Theyr moyles golde dothe eate,	254	Collyn Clout	319
Some wyl neyther golde ne grotes;	268	Collyn Clout	866
Clothes of golde and paules,	270	Collyn Clout	941
Wyth scutis and crownes of golde	283	Why Come Ye	171
With crownes of golde enblased	283	Why Come Ye	179
He loveth nothyng but golde;	284	Why Come Ye	208
Under a stone on a golde ryng	296	Why Come Ye	700
From golde to pewter /Or els to a newter,	301	Why Come Ye	904
Of his golde in store.	302	Why Come Ye	945
The grounde engrosyd and bet with bourne golde,	313	Garlande	41
With heris encrisped yalowe as the golde,	320	Garlande	289
encrisped] 'enscrisped' †Fakes 1523			
Of golde, entachid with many a precyous stone;	325	Garlande	470
Wheron stode a lybbard, crownyd with golde and stones,	328	Garlande	590
Pope holy ypocrytis, as they were golde and hole,	329	Garlande	612
With pypes of golde engusshing out stremes;	330	Garlande	659
Yowr name to se /It be enrolde, /Writtin with golde.	338	Garlande	939
With sylke and golde.	342	Garlande	1075
The silke, the golde, the flowris fresshe to syght,	343	Garlande	1111
Encoverde over with golde of tissew fyne;	345	Garlande	1164
With hornnis twayne /Of glitteryng golde;	348	Garlande	1293
And the apples of golde /Of Hesperides withholde,	349	Garlande	1294

GOLDEN

Of the Golden Flece,	87	Phy Sparrow	631
Of Thagus, that golden flod,	93	Phy Sparrow	875
With his golden sandes,	93	Phy Sparrow	879
The bryght golden tresses	101	Phy Sparrow	1172
The golden ram /Of flemmynge dam,	301	Why Come Ye	897
The margent was illumynid all with golden railles	345	Garlande	1157

GOLDFYNCHE

The goldfynche, the wagtayle;	81	Phy Sparrow	395

GOLDSMYTH

A goldsmyth youre mayre:	301	Why Come Ye	908

GOMYS

Ye gyrne grymly with your gomys and with yor grysly face.	122	Garnesche1	12

GOMMES

With gommes goostly of glad herte and mynde,	207	Magnyfycence	2359
Let us wasshe our gommes /From the drye crommes!'	222	El Rummynge	307

GOMMORYANS

The Gommoryans also /Were brought to deedly wo,	291	Why Come Ye	472

GON

Gedeon is gon, that Zalmane undertoke,	234	Speke Parott	116

GONE

Of hym that is gone, alas, withoute restore,	29	Dol Dethe	3
Thy lust and lykyng is from the gone;	42	Balettys1	23
Gone is this knave, this rybaude foule and leude.	58	Bowge	414
That Phillyp is gone me fro!	75	Phy Sparrow	142
For she was quyte gone;	89	Phy Sparrow	706
In faythe, els had I gone to longe to scole,	148	Magnyfycence	298
But nowe wyll I, that they be gone,	151	Magnyfycence	407
By my trouthe, we had ben gone,	155	Magnyfycence	537
Yet I wolde that ye had gone rather;	176	Magnyfycence	1313
All mesure and good rule is gone quyte.	176	Magnyfycence	1315
When Mesure is gone, what nedest thou spare?	176	Magnyfycence	1323
Whan Mesure is gone, we may slee care.	176	Magnyfycence	1324
A, my hede! But is the horson gone?	189	Magnyfycence	1729
Nowe Measure is gone, I am the better pleased.	189	Magnyfycence	1738
For Lyberte is gone, and also Felycyte.	192	Magnyfycence	1857
Gone? Alasse, ye have undone me!	192	Magnyfycence	1858

GONGE —GOOD   Page   Title   Line

For passe-a-Pase apase ys gone to cache a molle,	243	Speke Parott	413
Boke and chalys gone quyte;	257	Collyn Clout	407
Now he is gone to another stede	299	Why Come Ye	797
For he is well past and gone.	300	Why Come Ye	833
Were gone as well as he!	300	Why Come Ye	836
Our nobles are gone	302	Why Come Ye	922
I wolde he were gone;	304	Why Come Ye	994
That welny was loste when that we were gone.'	323	Garlande	406
welny] 'welnere' Marshe 1568			
Go she never so gingirly, her honesty is gone away.	346	Garlande	1204
Of one Adame all a knave, late dede and gone –	347	Garlande	1247
Recoverd whan the forster was gone, and sped	351	Garlande	1407
Gone to seke hallows, /With Reason together,	358	Garlande2	7

GONGE

........gynys upon a gonge,	125	Garnesche3	56

GONNE

Had ye gonne with me to scole,	127	Garnesche3	117
By the meanes of money without ony gonne.	184	Magnyfycence	1578

GON STONE

With a gon stone, /To make you to grone.	366	Albany	285

GOO

But of one thynge I werne you er I goo:	49	Bowge	106
werne] 'warne' Marshe 1568; er] 'or' Wynkyn de Worde 1510			
'Twyst,' quod Suspecte, 'goo playe; hym I ne reke!'	51	Bowge	186
Twyst] 'Whist' Wynkyn de Worde 1510, 'Twysshe' Marshe 1568			
Nowe then goo we hens. Away the mare!	177	Magnyfycence	1325
Ye, mary, is it. Ye, so mote I goo.	198	Magnyfycence	2046

GOOD

Of ther good lord the fate and dedely chaunce.	34	Dol Dethe	189
He fumblyth in hys fyngeryng an ugly good noyse;	37	Coystrowne1	31
Good mastres Anne, there ye do shayle!	41	Coystrowne4	19
How in good horsmen ye set your hole delyght,	42	Balettys2	13
Wordys well set with good habylyte;	43	Balettys3	5
Is called Favore to stonde in her good grace.'	47	Bowge	55
Sayenge to me, 'Broder, be of good chere,	48	Bowge	86
And thus with us good company to kepe.	57	Bowge	385
Had I as good an hors as she is a mare,	57	Bowge	407
I dempte and drede theyr talkynge was not good.	58	Bowge	426
Withoute God make a good conclusyon.	59	Bowge	483
Gyve me your honde, fare well and have good daye.'	60	Bowge	497
No good preest to offend,	62	Hauke	25
A porta inferi, /Good Lorde, have mercy	77	Phy Sparrow	240
(God send the soule good rest!)	78	Phy Sparrow	262
Was never none so good;	78	Phy Sparrow	269
God sende my sparoes sole good rest!	86	Phy Sparrow	574
Of al good praiers God send him sum!	86	Phy Sparrow	584
That passeth all erthly good;	93	Phy Sparrow	876
all] 'all the' Wyght 1553, Kitson 1560.6, Marshe 1568			
Dyd never man good.	108	Epitaphe1	67
Your pryd is paste, adwe, good nycht.	114	Scot Kynge	43
His sone the lorde admyrall is full good,	115	Scot Kynge	70
Ye shew ryght well what good ye can;	117	Ag Scottes	60
Youre eye is out; adew, good nyght!	119	Ag Scottes	142
The tokens ar not good /To be true Englysh blood;	121	Ag Scottes2	22
Is voyd of all good grace;	124	Garnesche3	10
Nor good ryme in yower mater.	126	Garnesche3	105
God sende you wele good spede,	129	Garnesche3	202
The starkest knave, and lest good kan,	130	Garnesche5	23
It askyth lesure with good advert[ence].	141	Magnyfycence	42
advertence] 'advertysment' †Rastell & Treveris C 1530, B			
Mayster Measure, you be come in good season.	143	Magnyfycence	84
Yes, syr, with ryght good chere.	143	Magnyfycence	112
I trowe good fortune hath annexyd us together,	146	Magnyfycence	198
Yet we wyll therin take good delyberacyon.	148	Magnyfycence	275
That I shall have you agayne my good lorde.	149	Magnyfycence	310
Byd hym take good hede of you, my synguler tresure.	149	Magnyfycence	317
And that he take good kepe to Lyberte.	149	Magnyfycence	320
Do what I coude to do you good.	150	Magnyfycence	335
To counterfet well is a good consayte.	152	Magnyfycence	444
Syr, ye shall hyght Good Demeynaunce.	159	Magnyfycence	674
As good to be occupyed as up and downe to trace	159	Magnyfycence	692
Paynte to a purpose good countenaunce I can,	160	Magnyfycence	724
Nay. Thou art a man good inough but for thy false hart.	162	Magnyfycence	769
And desyre me thy good mayster to be?	162	Magnyfycence	798
Nay, in good faythe. It is but the gyse.	163	Magnyfycence	809
Ye, and do ryght good servyce he can.	163	Magnyfycence	822
Mary, syr, Cokermowthe is a good way hens.	170	Magnyfycence	1061
Nowe, of good felowshyp, let me by thy [d]ogge.	170	Magnyfycence	1082
dogge] 'hogge' †Rastell & Treveris C 1530, B			
In faythe, man, my brayne is as good as thyne.	170	Magnyfycence	1085
Nowe, in good faythe, thou art a fonde gest.	170	Magnyfycence	1096
What! Then he is some poore mannes curre?	171	Magnyfycence	1129
Yes, by my faythe, good Syr Johnn.	173	Magnyfycence	1186
By the good Lorde, truthe he sayth.	175	Magnyfycence	1252
What he sayth and she sayth to lay good ere,	175	Magnyfycence	1269
God have mercy, good godfather.	176	Magnyfycence	1312
All mesure and good rule is gone quyte.	176	Magnyfycence	1315
Who so to me gyveth good advertence	177	Magnyfycence	1333

GOOD — GOOD

	Page	Title	Line
In good faythe, syr, me semeth he had the more wronge.	178	Magnyfycence	1384
It is good yet that lyberte be ruled by reason.	178	Magnyfycence	1387
Yet it is good to beware of 'had I wyst'.	179	Magnyfycence	1395
Yet it is good wysdome to worke wysely by welth.	179	Magnyfycence	1401
What! All by mesure, good syr, and none excesse?	180	Magnyfycence	1422
Yes, syr, so good man in you I se,	182	Magnyfycence	1522
And in your delynge so good assuraunce,	183	Magnyfycence	1523
Remembre the good servyce that Mesure hath you done,	186	Magnyfycence	1637
With a good wyll, syr, God spede you bothe togyder.	186	Magnyfycence	1648
I was your good lorde tyll that ye beganne	188	Magnyfycence	1714
A good dryfte, syr, a praty fete!	189	Magnyfycence	1731
By the good Lorde, yet your temples bete.	189	Magnyfycence	1732
Where is nowe all my pleasure and my worldly good?	198	Magnyfycence	2061
O good Lorde, howe longe shall I indure	201	Magnyfycence	2153
Torde! Thou arte good to be a man of warre.	202	Magnyfycence	2179
But nowe let us make mery and good chere.	204	Magnyfycence	2261
Faythe and good hope I make asyde to stonde.	205	Magnyfycence	2288
With this halter good and stronge;	206	Magnyfycence	2313
Good Hope, syr, my name is; remedy pryncypall	206	Magnyfycence	2328
But, my good sonne, lerne from dyspaire to flee;	206	Magnyfycence	2339
But thrughe good hope there may come remedy.	207	Magnyfycence	2344
Good Hope, your potecary, assygned am I,	207	Magnyfycence	2351
For who loveth God can ayle nothynge but good.	207	Magnyfycence	2365
Ye, syr, now am I armyd with good hope,	207	Magnyfycence	2378
Under good hope endurynge ever styll,	208	Magnyfycence	2381
Ye, holly to good hope I have made my repare.	208	Magnyfycence	2394
In good hope alway for to indure.	208	Magnyfycence	2396
Good Hope, I pray you with harty affeccyon	208	Magnyfycence	2399
And to that I say gyve good advysement.	208	Magnyfycence	2406
Syr, in good hope I am to amende.	210	Magnyfycence	2454
But good hope and redresse hath mendyd myne estate,	210	Magnyfycence	2462
Faythfull assuraunce with good peradvertaunce.	210	Magnyfycence	2472
Faythfull] 'Faythfully' †Rastell & Treveris C 1530, B			
And all good ale drynkers,	217	El Rummynge	106
Thou art worth good and monny.'	220	El Rummynge	228
Some ranne a good trot /With a skellet or a pot;	220	El Rummynge	249
Some fyll theyr pot full /Of good Lemster woll.	220	El Rummynge	252
And all for the good ale,	221	El Rummynge	265
ale] 'all' †Lant 1545			
Bycause the ale is good;	221	El Rummynge	284
Another there was that ran /With a good brasse pan —	222	El Rummynge	317
And fyll in good met;	222	El Rummynge	333
met] 'meate' Day 1560, Marshe 1568			
God sende you good sale!'	223	El Rummynge	369
And with good ale barme /She could make a charme	226	El Rummynge	455
For the good ale sake.	228	El Rummynge	534
And dranke a good lucke.	228	El Rummynge	567
For [ye] scrape out good scrypture, and set in a gall:	235	Speke Parott	153
ye] 'they' †Lant 1545, Kynge & Marche 1554, Day 1560, Marshe 1568			
How the rest of good lernyng is roufled up and trold.	235	Speke Parott	168
roufled] 'roulled' Day 1560, Marshe 1568			
'Cristecrosse and Saynt Nycholas, Parrot, be your good spede!'	236	Speke Parott	189
Now pas furthe, good Parott, Owur Lorde be your s[t]ede,	239	Speke Parott	313
stede] 'spede' †MS Harley 2252			
So myche pelory pajauntes undyr colowur of good lawe;	245	Speke Parott	480
Howebeit they are good men,	251	Collyn Clout	167
I speke nat of the good wyfe,	253	Collyn Clout	253
That good lawes are subverted	256	Collyn Clout	372
And good reason perverted.	256	Collyn Clout	373
It is good for astrologys,	258	Collyn Clout	466
Whan the good ale soppe /Dothe daunce in theyr foretoppe;	260	Collyn Clout	530
Farewell humylyte, /Farewell good charyte!	261	Collyn Clout	592
At the good ale tappe,	266	Collyn Clout	804
For lacke of good wyne;	266	Collyn Clout	805
Or to maynteyne good quarelles.	269	Collyn Clout	916
Wherfore he hath good ure	271	Collyn Clout	1001
Stande sure and take good fotyng,	273	Collyn Clout	1072
Of no good bysshop speke I,	273	Collyn Clout	1095
Nor good preest I escrye,	273	Collyn Clout	1096
I escrye] 'of the clargy' Marshe 1568, 'askrye' Harley 2252			
Good frere, nor good chanon,	273	Collyn Clout	1097
Good frere, nor good chanon,	273	Collyn Clout	1097
Good nonne, nor good canon,	274	Collyn Clout	1098
Good nonne, nor good canon,	274	Collyn Clout	1098
Good monke, nor good clerke,	274	Collyn Clout	1099
Good monke, nor good clerke,	274	Collyn Clout	1099
Nor of no good werke;	274	Collyn Clout	1100
Without good reason or skyll;	276	Collyn Clout	1191
For, be it good, be it yll,	276	Collyn Clout	1217
With all good myndes.	280	Why Come Ye	56
Farewell, than, have good day!	280	Why Come Ye	57
Than have good daye. Adewe!	280	Why Come Ye	58
Good Reason and good Skyll,	281	Why Come Ye	108
Good Reason and good Skyll,	281	Why Come Ye	108
Yet the good Erle of Surray,	282	Why Come Ye	153
Is nat my reason good?'	283	Why Come Ye	196
Good evyn, good Robyn Hode!	283	Why Come Ye	197

GOODE —GOODLY — Page — Title — Line

	Page	Title	Line
Good evyn, good Robyn Hode!	283	Why Come Ye	197
To any good ende were brought.	290	Why Come Ye	449
Nor of good pollycy, /Nor of astronomy;	292	Why Come Ye	518
Slouthfull to do good,	293	Why Come Ye	577
Counte himselfe as good as he;	294	Why Come Ye	590
Good evyn and good nyght!	302	Why Come Ye	916
Good evyn and good nyght!	302	Why Come Ye	916
Good Sprynge of Lanam	302	Why Come Ye	933
Without all good reason.	304	Why Come Ye	997
Shall never have good helth;	304	Why Come Ye	1025
Pyked out of all good lawe,	306	Why Come Ye	1106
of] not in Marshe 1568			
But, good madame, the accustome and usage	314	Garlande	64
'Soft, my good syster, and make there a pawse.	316	Garlande	134
my good syster] 'goode my sister' MS Cotton Vitellius E.x			
Then he that doth worste is as good as the best.	317	Garlande	175
But yet I beseche your grace that good recorde	318	Garlande	215
good] not in MS Cotton Vitellius E.x			
With, 'I as good as thou, ifayth, and no better.'	326	Garlande	509
She went before, and bad me take good holde;	328	Garlande	573
Some carectis of Caldy, sum Frensshe was full good;	328	Garlande	585
Gog gyve you good yere, ye make me to smyle.	332	Garlande	736
God geve them good spede there warke to begin!	334	Garlande	793
Dug, dug, /Jug, jug, /Good yere and good luk,	340	Garlande	1002
Dug, dug, /Jug, jug, /Good yere and good luk,	340	Garlande	1002
All good and no badnes,	341	Garlande	1010
And as full of good wyll, /As fayre Isaphill;	341	Garlande	1024
fayre] 'the fayre' MS Cotton Vitellius E.x			
Colyaunder, /Swete pomaunder, /Good Cassaunder;	341	Garlande	1028
Item Good Advysement, that brainles doth blame;	346	Garlande	1186
A good herynge of thes olde talis;	347	Garlande	1217
What constellacions ar good or bad for men,	352	Garlande	1429
Good luk this new yere, the olde yere is past.	354	Garlande	1518
For Latin warkis /Be good for clerkis,	355	Garlande	1543
Under the banner /Of all good manner,	356	Garlande	1573
Contynew still /With there good wyll.	356	Garlande	1586
Devoyde of good corage,	369	Albany	411
and with good delyberacion made,	373	Replycacion	1
Many a good man /And many a good woman,	378	Replycacion	134
Many a good man /And many a good woman,	378	Replycacion	135
Of all good Christen order.	380	Replycacion	226
Count ye your selfe good clerkes,	381	Replycacion	273
Of Good Advertysement,	384	Replycacion	361

GOODE

Falsly to slo ther moste singlar goode lorde?	30	Dol Dethe	27
slo] 'slee' Marshe 1568			
Alas for routhe, what thouthe his mynde wer goode,	32	Dol Dethe	102
Holde ye your tong, ye can no goode.	310	Why Come Ye2	20
ye] (1st) not in MS Rawlinson C. 813			
To worke me this chapelet by goode advysemente.	334	Garlande	807

GOODYS

and spoylyd from all his goodys and rayment.	193	Magnyfycence	SD
When we with Magnyfycence goodys made chevysaunce.	203	Magnyfycence	2236
Ye be the thevys, I say, away my goodys dyd cary.	203	Magnyfycence	2239

GOODLI

To wryte of you this goodli clause,	341	Garlande	1042

GOODLY

O goodly chyld /Of Mary mylde, /Then be oure shylde!	40	Coystrowne3	41
Remembryng your passyng goodly countenaunce,	42	Balettys2	5
Your goodly port, your bewteous visage,	42	Balettys2	6
Of lusty somer the passyng goodly quene;	44	Balettys3	14
Me thoughte I sawe a shyppe, goodly of sayle,	47	Bowge	36
Whoos beaute, honoure, goodly porte,	47	Bowge	62
Of that most goodly mayd	93	Phy Sparrow	852
goodly] 'godly' Wyght 1553, Kitson 1560.6, Marshe 1568			
For this most goodly floure,	94	Phy Sparrow	893
With pen and ynk /For to compyle /Some goodly style;	96	Phy Sparrow	988
goodly] 'godly' †Kele 1545.2			
For this most goodly floure,	96	Phy Sparrow	989
All the goodly sort /Of her fetures clere,	96	Phy Sparrow	999
For this most goodly floure,	97	Phy Sparrow	1022
[For] this most goodly floure,	98	Phy Sparrow	1054
For] not in †Kele 1545.2, Wyght 1553, Kitson 1560.6, Marshe 1568			
As Nature cold devyse, /In most goodly wyse.	98	Phy Sparrow	1072
For this most goodly floure,	98	Phy Sparrow	1083
goodly] 'godly' †Kele 1545.2			
Her goodly dalyaunce,	99	Phy Sparrow	1095
And her goodly pastaunce:	99	Phy Sparrow	1096
For this most goodly flour,	99	Phy Sparrow	1107
Her goodly myddell small	99	Phy Sparrow	1128
goodly] 'godly' †Kele 1545.2			
For this most goodly floure,	100	Phy Sparrow	1136
For this most goodly floure,	100	Phy Sparrow	1161
So goodly as she dresses,	101	Phy Sparrow	1170
For this most goodly floure,	101	Phy Sparrow	1185
For] not in Kitson 1560.6, Marshe 1568			
Her kyrtell so goodly lased,	101	Phy Sparrow	1194

GOODLYE —GORGE

	Page	Title	Line
For this most goodly floure,	101	Phy Sparrow	1208
For this] 'The' †Kele 1545.2, Marshe 1568			
Goodly maystres Jane, /Sobre, demure Dyane;	102	Phy Sparrow	1223
[For] this most goodly floure,	102	Phy Sparrow	1231
For] not in †Kele 1545.2, Wyght 1553, Kitson 1560.6, Marshe 1568; this] 'the' Wyght, Kitson, Marshe			
Alas, that goodly mayd,	103	Phy Sparrow	1282
That her goodly name, /Honorably reported,	103	Phy Sparrow	1285
A goodly rybon, or a golde rynge,	184	Magnyfycence	1580
Howe they ryde in goodly chares,	270	Collyn Clout	961
upon a goodly Garlande or Chapelet of Laurell	312	Garlande	I
That passynge goodly it was to beholde:	313	Garlande	42
Engolerid goodly with hallis and bowris,	325	Garlande	460
Engolerid] 'Engalared' Marshe 1568			
Enlosenged with many goodly platis	325	Garlande	469
Lo, hither commyth a goodly maystres,	326	Garlande	521
Occupacyon, is ryght goodly aray,	327	Garlande	528
With that on me she kest her goodly loke.	327	Garlande	531
Where I saw growyng a goodly laurell tre,	330	Garlande	665
Dryades there daunsid upon that goodly soile,	331	Garlande	679
But, goodly maystres, one thynge ye me tell.'	332	Garlande	720
'I thanke you, goodly maystres, to me most benynge,	332	Garlande	728
She brought me to a goodly chaumber of astate,	333	Garlande	768
to] 'into' MS Cotton Vitellius E.x			
'I have contryvyd for you a goodly warke,	334	Garlande	774
Of broken warkis wrought many a goodly thyng,	334	Garlande	801
In goodly wordes plesauntly comprysid,	335	Garlande	813
That for them some goodly conseyt be devysid,	335	Garlande	814
Thamar also wrought with her goodly honde	336	Garlande	852
Hath fresshely enbewtid with many a goodly sorte	336	Garlande	868
Goodly Creisseid, fayrer than Polexene,	336	Garlande	871
Princes of yowth, and flowre of goodly porte,	337	Garlande	897
Princes of youth, and flowre of goodly porte,	337	Garlande	904
The praty primrose, /The goodly columbyne.	338	Garlande	913
For to encrese /Yowre goodly name.	339	Garlande	960
In my goodly chapelet,	339	Garlande	970
To wryte of yow this goodly clause,	342	Garlande	1050
To wryte of you this goodly clause,	342	Garlande	1058
Alas, that goodly mayd,	348	Garlande	1275
That her goodly name, /Honorably reportid,	348	Garlande	1278
This goodly flowre with stormis was untwynde.	352	Garlande	1445
That goodly place to Skelton moost kynde,	353	Garlande	1462
And how Iollas lovyd goodly Phillis;	354	Garlande	1497
upon a goodly Garlonde or Chapelet of Laurell,	358	Garlande2	R
In his goodly person /Lyke unto Absolon,	369	Albany	434

GOODLYE

'Parott ys a goodlye byrde and a pratye popagay.'	231	Speke Parott	14
and] not in Lant 1545, Kynge and Marche 1554, Day 1560, Marshe 1568			

GOODLYEST

They seyd my lawrell was the goodlyest	343	Garlande	1112

GOODLYHEDE

With margerain jentyll, /The flowre of goodlyhede,	337	Garlande	907
With margerain jantill, /The flowre of goodlyhede,	338	Garlande	915
With margerain jantill, /The flowre of goodlyhede,	338	Garlande	923

GOODLYHOD

Remorse have I of youre most goodlyhod,	44	Balettys3	29

GOODNES

Plente of yll, of goodnes skant,	40	Coystrowne4	3
God of his goodnes him framed and wrought;	236	Speke Parott	212

GOOS

As wytles as a wylde goos, ye have but small remorrs	123	Garnesche2	18
The gray goos for to sho?	251	Collyn Clout	197
And after conveyauns as the world goos,	347	Garlande	1238
Where ever he rydes or goos.	370	Albany	470

GOOSE

To a pygge or to a goose,	252	Collyn Clout	214

GOOST

That one was lene and lyke a pyned goost,	58	Bowge	429
The Holy Goost be with your grace.	188	Magnyfycence	1711
Howe that ye sell /The grace of the Holy Goost.	251	Collyn Clout	201

GOOSTLY

Agaynst all [s]autes of your goostly foo.	206	Magnyfycence	2329
sautes] 'fautes' †Rastell & Treveris C 1530, B, Douce Fragment d.7			
With gommes goostly of glad herte and mynde,	207	Magnyfycence	2359
To wary and to kepe /From theyr goostly shepe,	250	Collyn Clout	155
That goostly can heale us;	265	Collyn Clout	742

GORBELYD

with Gresy, Gorbelyd Godfrey et cetera	122	Garnesche2	I

GORBELLYD

Gup, gorbellyd Godfrey, gup, Garnysche, gaudy fole!	123	Garnesche2	36

GORE

And crepe in at my gore	80	Phy Sparrow	346
crepe] 'gape' Kitson 1560.6			

GORGE

Full upon the gorge.	64	Hauke	87
Thanked be saynte Gorge, our ladyes knythe,	114	Scot Kynge	42

GORGIOUSLY—GOVERNE   Page   Title   Line

	Page	Title	Line
Of Lumbardy Gorge Hardyson,	130	Garnesche5	33
Garnyshe, ye gate of Gorge with gaudry	130	Garnesche5	39
Call for a ca[u]dell and cast up your gorge, caudell] 'candell' †Rastell & Treveris C 1530, B	185	Magnyfycence	1614
Your gorge nat endued /Without a capon stued,	252	Collyn Clout	215

GORGIOUSLY

How that she can were /Gorgiously her gere;	101	Phy Sparrow	1179

GORGYOUS

So gorgyous garmentes, and so myche wrechydnese,	244	Speke Parott	459

GORGON

Was nevyr suche a fylty gorgon, nor suche an epycure,	246	Speke Parott	510

GOSE

The gose and the gander,	82	Phy Sparrow	435
A gose with the fete upon;	125	Garnesche3	31
But yf I coulde knowe a gose from a swanne.	148	Magnyfycence	299
The gander and the gose bothe grasynge on one grave.	191	Magnyfycence	1830
She hobles as she gose /With her blanket hose she gose] 'a gose' Day 1560, Marshe 1568	216	El Rummynge	85
In came another dant, /With a gose and a gant.	227	El Rummynge	516
But as the worlde now gose,	286	Why Come Ye	285
For than thyne heed of gose.	288	Why Come Ye	385
The gray gose is no swan; no] 'a' MS Rawlinson C. 813	301	Why Come Ye	889
Few men can tell where the hynde calfe gose. tell] 'telle now' MS Cotton Vitellius E.x	313	Garlande	26
The gander, the gose, and the hudge oliphaunt,	315	Garlande	102
Yet whan the rayne rayneth and the gose wynkith	352	Garlande	1430
Lytill wotith the goslyng what the gose thynkith.	352	Garlande	1431

GOSHAUKE

The goshauke shall have a role	85	Phy Sparrow	563

GOSLENGES

The goslenges were untyde;	226	El Rummynge	463

GOSLYNG

Lytill wotith the goslyng what the gose thynkith.	352	Garlande	1431

GOSLYNGE

I shall gyve you a gaude of a goslynge that I gave,	191	Magnyfycence	1829

GOSLYNGES

Another brought two goslynges	226	El Rummynge	459

GOSPELL

Loke that ye spell /Well thys gospell;	39	Coystrowne3	21
Shall rede the gospell at masse;	82	Phy Sparrow	423
Neyther gospell nor pystell,	252	Collyn Clout	237
To amende the gospell,	267	Collyn Clout	821
Allygate the gospell	275	Collyn Clout	1162
Whiche be as trewe /As the gospell:	359	Albany	5
Of the gospell and the pystels	380	Replycacion	219

GOSPELLERS

'These be my gospellers,	65	Hauke	120

GOSSYP

And sayth, 'Gossyp, come hyder,	219	El Rummynge	204
Wyth, 'Lo, gossyp, iwys,	223	El Rummynge	356

GOST

With hete of the Holy Gost,	385	Replycacion	383

GOSTE

The Father, the Son, the Holy Goste,	35	Dol Dethe	216
Cryst be amonge you, and the Holy Goste!	208	Magnyfycence	2385

GOSTLY

Devysyd this gostly medytacyon in Englysh:	39	Coystrowne3	I

GOTE

She hath gote me more money with her tayle	57	Bowge	405
Thou rammysche, stynkyng gote,	128	Garnesche3	166
As it were a gote /In a shepe cote,	365	Albany	265

GOTES

And from the berded gotes /With theyr heery cotes;	250	Collyn Clout	158

GOTH

For whiche ende goth forwarde ye take lytell charge.	148	Magnyfycence	296
Here goth out CRAFTY CONVAYAUNCE.	179	Magnyfycence	SD
For ofte tymes suche a wamblynge goth over my harte;	185	Magnyfycence	1620
Here MESURE goth out of the place.	188	Magnyfycence	SD
Here goth CLOKED COLUSYON awaye,	190	Magnyfycence	SD
Here goth FOLY away.	192	Magnyfycence	SD
There goth many a lye	288	Why Come Ye	356
The False Fayth that Now Goth, which dayly is renude;	346	Garlande	1179

GOTHE

Pride gothe before and schame commyth after.	133	Garnesche5	165
Not amonge noble men, as the worlde gothe.	189	Magnyfycence	1747
Welthe without lyberte gothe all to wrake.	199	Magnyfycence	2086

GOTHYAUNCE

Nor Alerycus, that rulyd the Gothyaunce by swerd,	182	Magnyfycence	1504

GOTYSHE

He gased on me with his gotyshe berde;	52	Bowge	237

GOTTED

What hast thou gotted, in faythe, to thy share?	201	Magnyfycence	2162

GOUT

She had also the gout	226	El Rummynge	484

GOVERNE

To governe over all	271	Collyn Clout	991
To gyde and to governe my dredfull tremlyng fist.	335	Garlande	828

GOVERNED —GRACE   Page   Title   Line

GOVERNED

	Page	Title	Line
Be governed and gyded; wote ye what I say?	179	Magnyfycence	1397
And is governed by this mad kote!	295	Why Come Ye	668
And] not in Marshe 1568			

GOVERNYNGE

	Page	Title	Line
To put all the governynge,	298	Why Come Ye	761

GOWER

	Page	Title	Line
I saw Gower, that first garnisshed our Englysshe rude,	323	Garlande	387
Mayster Gower to Skelton	323	Garlande	R
Poeta Skelton to Maister Gower	323	Garlande	R
'Maister Gower, I have nothyng deserved	323	Garlande	407
Gower, Chawcer, Lydgate, theis thre	343	Garlande	1101

GOWERS

	Page	Title	Line
Gowers Englysh is olde /And of no value told;	91	Phy Sparrow	784
told] 'is tolde' Wyght 1553, Kitson 1560.6, Marshe 1568			

GOWNDY

	Page	Title	Line
Her eyen gowndy /Are full unsowndy,	215	El Rummynge	34

GOWNE

	Page	Title	Line
'My new furryd gowne, when it is worne –	40	Coystrowne4	10
Me thoughte his gowne was all furred wyth foxe.	52	Bowge	234
Me] 'My' †Wynkyn de Worde 1499			
His gowne so shorte that it ne cover myghte	56	Bowge	354
Of my gowne before,	80	Phy Sparrow	347
Your beste gowne festyvalle.	125	Garnesche3	51
His gowne so wyde	165	Magnyfycence	903
Here CRAFTY CONVEYAUNCE putteth of his gowne.	173	Magnyfycence	SD
Put on thy gowne agayne, for thou hast lost nowe.	173	Magnyfycence	1203
thou ... nowe] 'nowe thou hast lost' †Rastell & Treveris C 1530, B			
Some her husbandes gowne,	227	El Rummynge	530

GOWTE

	Page	Title	Line
With the gowte I make them to grone where they syt;	194	Magnyfycence	1903
A, Lord God, how the gowte wryngeth me by the too.	198	Magnyfycence	2047
And I bequethe hym the gowte and the gyn.	204	Magnyfycence	2255

GRACE

	Page	Title	Line
And geve the grace to be more fortunate!	33	Dol Dethe	165
O Quene of mercy, O lady full of grace,	34	Dol Dethe	204
Well of pite, of mercy, and of grace,	35	Dol Dethe	215
But graunt us grace /To se thy face,	40	Coystrowne3	49
Knolege, aquayntance, resort, favour, with grace;	43	Balettys3	1
Is called Favore to stonde in her good grace.'	47	Bowge	55
That ye shall stonde in favoure and in grace.	49	Bowge	105
Fortune to you gyftes of grace hath lente:	50	Bowge	152
To dwell with us and serve my ladyes grace.	50	Bowge	156
It is your fortune for to have that grace;	53	Bowge	272
All grace is far hym fro.	62	Hauke	16
And all for lacke of grace.	66	Hauke	163
Thorow the grace dyvyne	93	Phy Sparrow	857
Ennewed all with grace,	96	Phy Sparrow	1003
all with] 'with al' Wyght 1553, Kitson 1560.6, Marshe 1568			
To her to sewe for grace,	98	Phy Sparrow	1075
Such relucent grace /Is formed in her face;	100	Phy Sparrow	1159
Grace the sede did sow.	110	Lawde	5
For now the yeris of grace	111	Lawde	40
Trowe ye, Syr James, his noble grace	114	Scot Kynge	17
To face, to brace, /All voyde of grace,	116	Ag Scottes	34
Unto your grace for grace now I call,	117	Ag Scottes	78
Unto your grace for grace now I call,	117	Ag Scottes	78
Trowyd ye, Syr Jemy, his nobull grace	118	Ag Scottes	107
His grace beyng out of the way;	119	Ag Scottes	144
For lacke of grace hard was your hap;	119	Ag Scottes	168
Of grace out of the state /And dyed excomunycate.	121	Ag Scottes2	29
Is voyd of all good grace;	124	Garnesche3	10
Whan hys grace ys fastynge,	126	Garnesche3	83
To know thy selfe yf thow lake grace,	132	Garnesche5	126
Pleasyth, your grace, Felycyte they me call.	145	Magnyfycence	171
As your grace full nobly hath recountyd,	145	Magnyfycence	193
Please it your grace to take no dysdayne,	147	Magnyfycence	252
For largesse is a purchaser of pardon and of grace.	148	Magnyfycence	268
Is there ony thynge elles your grace wyll commaunde me?	149	Magnyfycence	318
Sayd I was mete for your grace.	150	Magnyfycence	373
I folow even after your noble grace.	151	Magnyfycence	395
The grace of God under benedicite.	154	Magnyfycence	490
And do nothynge. How be it, full lytell grace	159	Magnyfycence	693
Not and your grace wolde be ruled by me.	179	Magnyfycence	1393
Your grace sent for me, I wene. What is your wyll?	179	Magnyfycence	1410
I truste your grace wyll be agreabyll	179	Magnyfycence	1417
Plesyth it your grace to shewe what I do shall?	182	Magnyfycence	1517
If it lyke your grace to take it in degre.	182	Magnyfycence	1521
A, syr, your grace me dothe extole and rayse;	183	Magnyfycence	1525
As that I myght your noble grace content!	183	Magnyfycence	1534
But yf it lyke your grace more at large	185	Magnyfycence	1589
Please it your grace at the contemplacyon	186	Magnyfycence	1633
For of your grace I have it nought deserved.	186	Magnyfycence	1644
The Holy Goost be with your grace.	188	Magnyfycence	1711
Well were that lady myght stande in my grace,	190	Magnyfycence	1799
In welth to beware yf I had had grace,	196	Magnyfycence	1976
Take it mekely, and thanke God of his grace;	197	Magnyfycence	2033

GRACELES — GRAY-HERED

	Page	Title	Line
All grace and pyte I lay in the duste.	205	Magnyfycence	2290
Nay, nay, man. I loke never to have parte of his grace;	205	Magnyfycence	2297
Syr, your fesycyan is the grace of God,	207	Magnyfycence	2349
That Goddes grace hath vexed you sharply	207	Magnyfycence	2352
Grace of assystence his measure to declare;	207	Magnyfycence	2373
Of that I se you nowe in the state of grace.	208	Magnyfycence	2403
In all your warkys more grace shall ye fynde;	211	Magnyfycence	2485
That pereles pomegarnat, Cryste save hyr nobyll grace!'	231	Speke Parott	37
Yf fortune be frendly, and grace be the guyde,	234	Speke Parott	139
So myche of my lordes grace, and in hym no grace ys;	245	Speke Parott	501
So myche of my lordes grace, and in hym no grace ys;	245	Speke Parott	501
Howe that ye sell /The grace of the Holy Goost.	251	Collyn Clout	201
And have no grace to thynke	262	Collyn Clout	648
Of those that stande in your grace.	273	Collyn Clout	1076
Suche grace God them sende	274	Collyn Clout	1125
And lytell grace they have	274	Collyn Clout	1131
Suche grace that he us sende	278	Collyn Clout	1262
To seke before our grace.'	287	Why Come Ye	332
And Yorkes Place, /With, 'My lordes grace',	289	Why Come Ye	411
For my lordes grace	294	Why Come Ye	630
That the kynges grace	295	Why Come Ye	658
But what his grace doth thinke,	296	Why Come Ye	683
And graunt him grace to know	298	Why Come Ye	774
That there wantys grace	300	Why Come Ye	849
To dryve away grace.	301	Why Come Ye	873
We can lacke no grace,	301	Why Come Ye	875
For, 'my Lordes grace',	301	Why Come Ye	876
And, 'my ladies grace',	301	Why Come Ye	877
My lordys grace nameth it	302	Why Come Ye	940
My lordis grace wyll brynge	302	Why Come Ye	949
God save his noble grace,	303	Why Come Ye	969
Lyke Pharao, voyde of grace,	305	Why Come Ye	1066
Of my lordis grace nor his wyfe!	306	Why Come Ye	1077
Not unremembered it is unto your grace,	313	Garlande	57
Of Elyconis well, refresshid with your grace,	314	Garlande	74
Elyconis] 'Elycoms' †Fakes 1523, 'Heliconis' Marshe 1568			
Unto your grace then make I this motyve:	315	Garlande	114
Yet shall I answere your grace as in this,	316	Garlande	144
But yet I beseche your grace that good recorde	318	Garlande	215
good] not in MS Cotton Vitellius E.x			
Of noble Fame before the Quenes grace,	324	Garlande	419
Before my ladys grace, the Quene of Fame,	343	Garlande	1091
Of my ladys grace at the contemplacyoun,	347	Garlande	1219
Suppleyng to Fame, I besoughte her grace,	353	Garlande	1478
To rayle agaynst his grace	368	Albany	365
His grace to magnify	369	Albany	402
To extoll his noble grace	369	Albany	407
They fynde his grace so kynde;	371	Albany	483
To assyst his noble grace,	371	Albany	491
That ye shall have no grace	371	Albany	504
To my Lorde Cardynals right noble grace etc	372	Albany	E
Before his noble grace	372	Albany	525
Those wordes his grace dyd saye /Of an ammas gray.	372	Albany	530
Agaynst her grace disputed	375	Replycacion	30
And thought in hym smale grace	379	Replycacion	195
The ymage of her grace	381	Replycacion	261

GRACELES

	Page	Title	Line
For by his devellysshe drift and graceles provision	333	Garlande	757
Thou art a graceles wyght	364	Albany	232

GRACELESSE

	Page	Title	Line
Gronynge, grouchyng, gracelesse,	280	Why Come Ye	80
Careles and shamlesse, /Thriftles and gracelesse	304	Why Come Ye	1021
Careles] 'Marcyles' MS Rawlinson C. 813			
And yet, this gracelesse elfe,	307	Why Come Ye	1115
gracelesse] 'ungratyous' MS Rawlinson C. 813			

GRACES

	Page	Title	Line
To sowe the sede of graces.	269	Collyn Clout	898
sowe] 'save' †Godfray 1531, 'sowe' MS Harley 2252			

GRAY

	Page	Title	Line
In theyr amysse of gray;	85	Phy Sparrow	560
Her eyen gray and stepe	97	Phy Sparrow	1014
That is as trew /As blacke is blew /And grene is gray.	116	Ag Scottes	19
By the masse, a Spaynysshe moght with a gray lyste!	173	Magnyfycence	1200
The gray goos for to sho?	251	Collyn Clout	197
Gette a frere gray,	265	Collyn Clout	744
In gray russet and heery cotes;	268	Collyn Clout	865
The hare, the fox, the gray,	281	Why Come Ye	121
The gray gose is no swan;	301	Why Come Ye	889
no] 'a' MS Rawlinson C. 813			
Sterre of the morow gray,	340	Garlande	988
Those wordes his grace dyd saye /Of an ammas gray.	372	Albany	531

GRAYE

	Page	Title	Line
His hode was syde, his cope was roset graye;	58	Bowge	440
In her furred flocket, /And graye russet rocket,	215	El Rummynge	54
And have here a pylche of graye;	224	El Rummynge	398

GRAY-HERED

	Page	Title	Line
And she gray-hered;	215	El Rummynge	37

GRAYLE —GREAT   Page   Title   Line

GRAYLE
He shall syng the grayle;   82   Phy Sparrow   441
GRAMATOLYS
Then nodypollys and gramatolys of smalle intellygens: 240   Speke Parott   318
GRAME
The crane and the curlewe therat gan to grame;   192   Magnyfycence   1839
GRAMED
Agaynst me to be gr[am]ed, ...   274   Collyn Clout   1114
  gramed] 'greved' †Godfray 1531, Kele 1545.1, Marshe 1568,
  MS Harley 2252
GRAMER
Item New Gramer in Englysshe compylyd;   346   Garlande   1182
GRANADO
From Granado to Galys, ...   70   Hauke   322
GRAS
Ware of the lesard lyeth lurkyng in the gras.   45   Balettys4   7
GRASYNGE
The gander and the gose bothe grasynge on one grave.   191   Magnyfycence   1830
GRATYFYED
And also gratyfyed /By holy synodalles   264   Collyn Clout   715
GRAUNDE
Of our graunde counsell?   288   Why Come Ye   380
GRAUNDEPOSE
With porpose and graundepose he may fede hym fatte, ...   239   Speke Parott   308
GRAUNGE
Of an abbey ye make a graunge -   257   Collyn Clout   419
  ye] 'they' Kele 1545.1, 'to' MS Harley 2252
GRAUNT
But graunt us grace /To se thy face, ...   40   Coystrowne3   49
Mary, Cryst graunt ye catche no colde on your fete!   191   Magnyfycence   1803
And graunt him grace to know   298   Why Come Ye   774
And graunt him a place   303   Why Come Ye   970
Graunt my petycyon, I aske you but ryght.'   318   Garlande   231
GRAUNTE
And graunte hym at his askynge   272   Collyn Clout   1027
Graunte hym his lycence   272   Collyn Clout   1038
GRAUNTYD
Sodenly grauntyd, and sodenly denyed;   213   Magnyfycence   2534
GRAVE
An epytaphe I wold have /For Phyllyppes grave.   86   Phy Sparrow   606
What ayle them to deprave /Phillip Sparowes grave?   103   Phy Sparrow   1275
The gander and the gose bothe grasynge on one grave.   191   Magnyfycence   1830
What ayle them to deprave /Phillippe Sparows grave?   348   Garlande   1268
GRAVE STONE
He wrate an Epitaph for his grave stone, ...   347   Garlande   1249
GRAVIN
Had gravin in it of calcydony a capytall A.   328   Garlande   587
GRAVYD
For I have gravyd her wythin the secret wall   45   Balettys3   48
GRAVYTE
Gravyte of counsell, provydence, and wyt;   210   Magnyfycence   2476
Pretendynge gravyte /And seygnyoryte, ...   269   Collyn Clout   924
GRE
All that God sendeth, take it in gre;   196   Magnyfycence   1979
What shuld I do but take it in gre?   353   Garlande   1487
GREABLE
To se howe greable we are of one mynde;   146   Magnyfycence   199
GREAT
I, callynge to mynde the great auctoryte   46   Bowge   8
Great sorowe than ye myght se, ...   73   Phy Sparrow   56
And from the great Pluto, ...   73   Phy Sparrow   72
That made that great arke, ...   78   Phy Sparrow   257
From Occyan the great se   79   Phy Sparrow   318
To my great payne and wo.   81   Phy Sparrow   365
*Or els phylosophy /Maketh a great lye.   83   Phy Sparrow   477
  *Or] 'Of' Scattergood
An horshowe so great, ...   83   Phy Sparrow   479
With armatycke gummes /That cost great sumes, ...   84   Phy Sparrow   521
And tell can a great pece   87   Phy Sparrow   630
Upon a great payne, ...   88   Phy Sparrow   654
And of Mardocheus, /And of great Assuerus, ...   90   Phy Sparrow   740
And of Porcena the Great, ...   90   Phy Sparrow   747
This fals Envy /Sayth that I /Use great folly   95   Phy Sparrow   951
A kyng, a sumner! It was great wonder: 118   Ag Scottes   95
Such tunges unhappy hath made great division   139   Ven Tongues   55
Somtime women were put in great blame, ...   139   Ven Tongues   59
By lyberte is done many a great excesse;   142   Magnyfycence   53
Endure? No, God wote, it were great payne.   147   Magnyfycence   248
Why, man, it were to great a wonder   154   Magnyfycence   510
It is great almesse the hung[re] to fede, ...   177   Magnyfycence   1344
  hungre] 'hunger' †Rastell & Treveris C 1530, B
So as ye be a prynce of great myght, ...   183   Magnyfycence   1545
Yet were they better to begge, a great dele;   198   Magnyfycence   2043
Here shalbe not great sheddynge of blode.   203   Magnyfycence   2207
And thus to be facyd, I thynke it great skorne.   203   Magnyfycence   2217
Tushe, tushe! It is a great defaute;   203   Magnyfycence   2222
Ye, in faythe; or ellys thou arte to great a glotton.   204   Magnyfycence   2266
Theyr thrust was so great, ...   222   El Rummynge   303

	Page	Title	Line
GREATE —GREKIS			
And gat her great thanke	228	El Rummynge	543
Of the clergye all, /Bothe great and small.	249	Collyn Clout	118
And, for to say trouth, /A great parte is for slouth; for] 'full' †Godfray 1531, 'for' MS Harley 2252	250	Collyn Clout	137
God wotte, to theyr great paynes,	254	Collyn Clout	313
Alas, it is great ruthe!	255	Collyn Clout	343
That honoure hath a great fall.	262	Collyn Clout	634
God wotte, they take great payne	268	Collyn Clout	860
That they have great wonder	271	Collyn Clout	1006
With lordes of great estate	271	Collyn Clout	1013
Great ydeottes they be,	274	Collyn Clout	1130
Of dyvers great estates,	277	Collyn Clout	1246
Unto great confusyon	279	Why Come Ye	21
And set hym nobly /In great auctoryte	291	Why Come Ye	505
In exemplyfyenge /Great Alexander the kynge,	292	Why Come Ye	544
Make him a great astate,	293	Why Come Ye	587
Made up a great astate	297	Why Come Ye	723
It were great rewth	300	Why Come Ye	841
And moche hevynesse, /And great dolowre dolowre] 'dullness' MS Rawlinson C. 813	305	Why Come Ye	1036
Under strength of the great seale,	306	Why Come Ye	1102
Under the protectyon /Of the kynges great seale, great] 'brode' MS Rawlinson C. 813	307	Why Come Ye	1129
A small defaute in a great lorde,	310	Why Come Ye2	12
A lytell cryme in a great astate,	310	Why Come Ye2	13
Some facers, some bracers, some make great crackis; some] 'and sum' MS Cotton Vitellius E.x	317	Garlande	189
For elles it were to put a derogacyon	318	Garlande	218
That in the forest was none so great a tre	320	Garlande	277
This sayd, a great nowmber folowyd by and by	321	Garlande	323
But my request is not so great a thynge,	332	Garlande	730
Of this warke they had so great delyght,	343	Garlande	1110
To your great lacke /And utter shame	360	Albany	45
He reculed backe, /To his great lacke,	360	Albany	53
Lyke a great hill,	365	Albany	261
It made no great fors	366	Albany	282
That people are in great dout	380	Replycacion	224
To your great vyllony,	380	Replycacion	245
Ye do moche great outrage,	384	Replycacion	354
GREATE			
Soo greate pleasyre, or who to you it gave.	53	Bowge	263
It is greate scorne to see suche a hayne	55	Bowge	327
This corse for to sence /With greate reverence,	85	Phy Sparrow	527
There hath ben greate war	223	El Rummynge	358
It was huge and greate,	225	El Rummynge	432
And send me to greate ladyes of estate; to greate ladyes] 'to grece to lordys' †MS Harley 2252	231	Speke Parott	6
GREATEST			
But the greatest parte /Is for they have but small arte	250	Collyn Clout	138
GREATTER			
Without his vertue be greatter,	253	Collyn Clout	271
GRECE			
Of larde and of grece,	267	Collyn Clout	846
GREDY			
Of Inde the gredy grypes	79	Phy Sparrow	307
Grimbaldus gredy snatche a puddyng tyl the rost be redy.	172	Magnyfycence	1155
It was a bullyfant, /A gredy cormerant.	227	El Rummynge	521
GREDYNESSE			
Suche gredynesse, /Suche nedynesse,	305	Why Come Ye	1030
GREE			
So truely proporsionyd, and so well did gree,	320	Garlande	275
GREET			
Ful of greet knavys tethe,	127	Garnesche3	126
GREGORIE			
Saynt Gregorie and saynt Ambrose,	381	Replycacion	275
GREY			
Spekyng in paroblis, how the fox, the grey,	315	Garlande	101
GREYHOUNDES			
So mangye a mastyfe curre, the grete greyhoundes pere;	245	Speke Parott	487
GREYHOWNDE			
The gentyll greyhownde.	298	Why Come Ye	779
GREYTH			
It greyth nought for your degre	116	Ag Scottes	52
GREKE			
Thow mantycore, ye marmset, garnyshte lyke a Greke,	124	Garnesche2	39
In Greke tong Parott can bothe speke and sey,	231	Speke Parott	26
But our Grekis theyr Greke so well have applyed,	234	Speke Parott	145
That they cannot say in Greke, rydynge by the way,	234	Speke Parott	146
For though ye can tell in Greke what is phormio,	235	Speke Parott	151
Yet ye seke out your Greke in Capricornio;	235	Speke Parott	152
They had wrytyng, sum Greke, sum Ebrew,	328	Garlande	582
Of porturature which was the famous Greke,	337	Garlande	895
GREKES			
In Lerna the Grekes fen,	105	Phy Sparrow	1328
Among the Grekes most relucent of lyght,	383	Replycacion	332
As Grekes do it call,	384	Replycacion	369
GREKIS			
But our Grekis theyr Greke so well have applyed,	234	Speke Parott	145

GREKYS — GRETE

	Page	Title	Line
The noble Pamphila, quene of the Grekis londe,	336	Garlande	850
In Lerna the Grekis fen	349	Garlande	1321

GREKYS

	Page	Title	Line
Myden agan in Grekys tonge we rede,	232	Speke Parott	52
Our Grekys ye walow in the washbol Argolycorum;	235	Speke Parott	150

GRENE

	Page	Title	Line
Herber enverduryd, contynuall fressh and grene;	44	Balettys3	13
His hose was garded with a lyste of grene,	56	Bowge	356
But lyght for somer grene;	89	Phy Sparrow	719
Of lusty somer grene;	101	Phy Sparrow	1184
Diana in the woodes grene,	105	Phy Sparrow	1364
That is as trew /As blacke is blew /And grene is gray.	116	Ag Scottes	19
In a felde of grene peson	127	Garnesche3	127
Xall kyt both wyght and grene:	127	Garnesche3	139
For the grene bare threde	216	El Rummynge	60
For] 'And' Day 1560, Marshe 1568			
My fethyrs fresshe as ys the emerawde grene,	231	Speke Parott	16
Parrot hath a blacke beard and a fayre grene tayle.	233	Speke Parott	84
Upon every banke /Of his herbers grene,	304	Why Come Ye	1003
In figure wherof they were the laurell grene.	314	Garlande	68
they were the] 'the were they' †Fakes 1523			
Transformyd was she into the laurell grene.	320	Garlande	294
Enverdurid with levis contynually grene;	330	Garlande	666
Grene tre of laurell moche solacyous game	331	Garlande	683
They made, with chapellettes and garlandes grene;	331	Garlande	684
Grene, rede, tawny, whyte, purpill, and blew.	334	Garlande	800
whyte] 'whyght blak' MS Cotton Vitellius E.x			
In helpyng to warke my laurell grene	342	Garlande	1074
She wonderyd, me thought, at my laurell grene;	343	Garlande	1116
Diana in the woddis grene,	350	Garlande	1357
How the grene coverlet sufferd grete pine;	351	Garlande	1378

GRENEWYTCHE

	Page	Title	Line
Upon Grenewytche border /Called Observaunce,	265	Collyn Clout	746

GRESE

	Page	Title	Line
Wyth golde and grotes they grese my hande,	152	Magnyfycence	432

GRESED

	Page	Title	Line
Gently joynted, /Gresed and anoynted /Up to the knockles:	215	El Rummynge	43
Gresed upon dyrt /That baudeth her skyrt.	216	El Rummynge	89

GRESY

	Page	Title	Line
with Gresy, Gorbelyd Godfrey et cetera	122	Garnesche2	I
Of soche a gresy knyght?	125	Garnesche3	35
But now, gawdy, gresy Garnesche,	127	Garnesche3	120
And his gresy genealogy,	291	Why Come Ye	492

GRESYD

	Page	Title	Line
Your lothesum lere to loke on, lyke a gresyd bote dothe schyne.	123	Garnesche2	5

GRESLY

	Page	Title	Line
Thou gresly gargone glaymy,	128	Garnesche3	168

GRESSE

	Page	Title	Line
Unto me; alas, that herbe nor gresse	321	Garlande	314
gresse] 'gras' †Fakes 1523			

GRESSOP

	Page	Title	Line
Lorde, how he wolde hop /After the gressop!	75	Phy Sparrow	137

GRESSOPPES

	Page	Title	Line
And byse, enpicturid with gressoppes and waspis,	345	Garlande	1158

GRET

	Page	Title	Line
Or ells with gret shame your game wylbe sene.	43	Balettys2	42
Gret daunger for the kynge,	126	Garnesche3	82
To cal me knave thou takyst gret payne.	130	Garnesche5	20
And have taken ryght gret payne	295	Why Come Ye	644

GRETE

	Page	Title	Line
To whome grete astatis obeyde and lowttede,	30	Dol Dethe	45
To slo suche a lord, alas, it was grete shame.	33	Dol Dethe	154
slo] 'sle' Marshe 1568			
Thus, in a rowe, of martchauntes a grete route	49	Bowge	120
And, as she wyll, so shall our grete shyppe sayle.	50	Bowge	172
Than thanked I hym for his grete gentylnes.	51	Bowge	176
To kepe him frome pykynge, it was a grete payne.	52	Bowge	236
Loo, what is to you a pleasure grete	53	Bowge	260
I have grete scorne and am ryghte evyll apayed.'	54	Bowge	298
By God, I have of the now grete dyspyte;	55	Bowge	325
It is grete scorne to se a mysproude knave	59	Bowge	453
By God, I saye, there is a grete herte-brennynge	59	Bowge	460
To holde myne honde, by God, I had grete payne;	61	Bowge	522
No. But for you grete estates	150	Magnyfycence	370
Largesse stynteth grete debates;	150	Magnyfycence	371
I muster, I medle amonge these grete estates;	160	Magnyfycence	736
No, by my trouthe, but crake grete wordes.	163	Magnyfycence	812
By my trouthe, she hathe a grete hede.	169	Magnyfycence	1048
But she is lesse a grete dele	169	Magnyfycence	1052
Nowe thou hast done me a pleasure grete.	171	Magnyfycence	1131
Nay, so God me helpe, it was no grete vexacyon;	189	Magnyfycence	1733
Grete mervayle I had, and mused in my mynde.	191	Magnyfycence	1822
But nowe a dayes to stryke I have grete cause.	194	Magnyfycence	1918
A grete mysadventure, thy maker to dysplease,	206	Magnyfycence	2341
Sothely to repent me I have grete cause;	209	Magnyfycence	2434
Thowghe he pampyr not hys paunche with the grete seall;	239	Speke Parott	309
Hyt ys no lytyll bordon to bere a grete mylle stone.	240	Speke Parott	330
Grete reysons with resons be now reprobitante,	244	Speke Parott	442

GRETELY —GROINYNGE   Page   Title   Line

So lytell secretnese, and so myche grete councell;   245   Speke Parott   465
So mangye a mastyfe curre, the grete greyhoundes pere;   245   Speke Parott   487
With other abusyons grete;   306   Why Come Ye   1086
And, as we dare, we fynde in hym grete lake: 314   Garlande   70
   grete] 'a' Marshe 1568
Who wryteth wysely hath a grete treasure.   314   Garlande   91
All be it grete parte he hath surrendred   316   Garlande   150
By Eschines rehersed to the grete glory   317   Garlande   166
But a grete parte yet ye have reservyd   317   Garlande   171
   But...yet] 'Bot yit a grete parte' MS Cotton Vitellius E.x
There came John Bochas with his volumys grete;   322   Garlande   365
To tell all his towchis it were to grete wonder;   333   Garlande   764
That in me were grete blyndnes, ...   342   Garlande   1064
How the grene coverlet sufferd grete pine;   351   Garlande   1378
All orators and poetis, with other grete and smale, ...   354   Garlande   1504
My mynde of the grete din was somdele amasid.   354   Garlande   1512
They saye howe latria is an honour grete, ...   381   Replycacion   282
GRETELY
Be it reason or none, it shall not gretely skyll;   185   Magnyfycence   1596
In genenrall wordes, I say not gretely nay, ...   315   Garlande   99
GRETER
What the devyll, man, your name shalbe the greter;   180   Magnyfycence   1440
GRETLY
In Englande and Fraunce which gretly was redouted, ...   30   Dol Dethe   43
That we delyte gretly in your dalyaunce.   183   Magnyfycence   1524
And they never thryve in theyr age, it shall not gretly skyll.   200   Magnyfycence   2138
Me thynke ye are not gretly acomberyd wyth wyt.   203   Magnyfycence   2215
GRETT
Your foly ys to grett   127   Garnesche3   140
Of frantycknes and folysshnes whyche ys the grett state? . . .   243   Speke Parott   417
GRETTER
But never was I in gretter fere.   150   Magnyfycence   345
There were many wordes smaller and gretter, ...   326   Garlande   508
For your ignorance is gretter, ...   380   Replycacion   231
GREUYNED
Her skynne lose and slacke, /Greuyned lyke a sacke;   215   El Rummynge   32
   Greuyned] 'Grained' Day 1560, Marshe 1568
GREVANCE
Therefore no grevance, /I pray you, for to take, ...   385   Replycacion   397
GREVAUNCE
/Trouble and grevaunce.   81   Phy Sparrow   369
Yet sum there be therewith that take grevaunce   348   Garlande   1257
GREVETH
Trust me, Lyberte, it greveth me ryght sore   178   Magnyfycence   1375
GREVIS
Theire grevis to complaine;   111   Lawde   34
GREVYTH
Thys grevyth your husband, that ryght jentyll knyght, ...   43   Balettys2   27
GREW
In Popering grew peres, whan Parrot was an eg.   232   Speke Parott   70
Of an oke, that somtyme grew full streyghte, ...   312   Garlande   18
Jacinctis and smaragdis out of the florthe they grew.   325   Garlande   480
Of a dysour, a devyl way, grew a jentilman, ...   330   Garlande   635
All frutis and flowris grew there in there kynde.   331   Garlande   678
   and] not in †Fakes 1523
GRIMBALDUS
Grimbaldus gredy snatche a puddyng tyl the rost be redy.   . . .   172   Magnyfycence   1155
GRIMLY
As gastly that glaris, as grimly that gronis, ...   328   Garlande   593
GRYLL
But she is not gryll, ...   214   El Rummynge   6
GRYM
He is suche a grym syer, ...   303   Why Come Ye   987
GRYME
Garnyshe, gargone, gastly, gryme, ...   129   Garnesche5   1
What callest thou thy dogge? Tusshe! His name is Gryme. . . .   171   Magnyfycence   1118
Come, Gryme! Come, Gryme! It is my praty dogges.   171   Magnyfycence   1119
Come, Gryme! Come, Gryme! It is my praty dogges.   171   Magnyfycence   1119
But wylte thou make another on Gryme?   172   Magnyfycence   1151
GRYMLY
Ye gyrne grymly with your gomys and with yor grysly face. . . .   122   Garnesche1   12
Alas, wh[o] is yonder that grymly lokys?   193   Magnyfycence   1873
   who] 'why' †Rastell & Treveris C 1530, B
GRYN
Causeth him to gryn /And rejoyce therin;   94   Phy Sparrow   926
GRYNNES
He grynnes and he gapis   295   Why Come Ye   653
GRYNNYNG
Oure gummys grynnyng, /Oure soulys brynnyng!   40   Coystrowne3   35
GRYPES
Of Inde the gredy grypes   79   Phy Sparrow   307
GRYSLY
Ye gyrne grymly with your gomys and with yor grysly face. . . .   122   Garnesche1   12
Ye grounde yow upon Godfrey, that grysly gargons face, ...   123   Garnesche2   29
GROCERS
For grocers were grugyd at and groynyd at but late;   244   Speke Parott   441
GROINYNGE
[Your] gronynge, yor grontynge, yor groinynge lyke a swyne? . .   123   Garnesche2   2

272

GROYNIS —GROUNDE   Page   Title   Line

GROYNIS
Hoyning like hogges that groynis and wrotes.   137   Ven Tongues   4
GROYNYD
For grocers were grugyd at and groynyd at but late; 244   Speke Parott   441
GROYNNINGE
The Gruntyng and the Groynninge of the Gronnyng Swyne; . . .   351   Garlande   1376
   and the] 'a' †Fakes 1523; of the] not in †Fakes 1523
GROME
For Jak wold be a jentylman, that late was a grome.   37   Coystrownel   42
GRONDE
And for to telle the gronde, ...   128   Garnesche3   184
GRONE
Well may thou sygh, well may thou grone, ...   42   Balettys1   26
I can dyssemble; I can bothe laughe and grone;   159   Magnyfycence   698
With the gowte I make them to grone where they syt; 194   Magnyfycence   1903
The hertis of the herd began for to grone, and fled 351   Garlande   1408
With a gon stone, /To make you to grone.   366   Albany   286
GRONED
For her mouth fomyd /And her bely groned: 223   El Rummynge   342
GRONETH
For whome Tyborne groneth both daye and nyghte.   58   Bowge   417
   whome] 'home' †Wynkyn de Worde 1499
GRONID
The grownde gronid and tremblid, the noyse was so stowte. . . 354   Garlande   1509
GRONIS
As gastly that glaris, as grimly that gronis, ...   328   Garlande   593
GRONYNGE
[Your] gronynge, yor grontynge, yor groinynge lyke a swyne? . 123   Garnesche2   2
Gronynge, grouchyng, gracelesse, ...   280   Why Come Ye   80
GRONYS
But howe the commons gronys, /And the people monys, ...   255   Collyn Clout   348
GRONNYNG
The Gruntyng and the Groynninge of the Gronnyng Swyne; . . .   351   Garlande   1376
   and the] 'a' †Fakes 1523; of the] not in †Fakes 1523
GRONTYNGE
[Your] gronynge, yor grontynge, yor groinynge lyke a swyne? . 123   Garnesche2   2
GROPE
That all this matter must under grope.   157   Magnyfycence   600
And craftely can I grope howe every man is mynded.   160   Magnyfycence   725
To grope a gardevyaunce, though it be well bandyd.   203   Magnyfycence   2231
Howe say you, syr? Can ye these wordys grope?   207   Magnyfycence   2377
Sum medelynge spyes, by craft to grope thy mynde, ...   329   Garlande   617
In trust wherof comforte his hart doth grope, ...   335   Garlande   832
GROPYD
That colyca passyo hath gropyd you by the guttys.   148   Magnyfycence   291
GROSE
Yower termys ar to grose, ...   126   Garnesche3   96
GROSELY
By meanys of a grosely endarkyd clowde   330   Garlande   645
GROSSOLITIS
With turkis and grossolitis enpavyd was the grounde;   325   Garlande   466
GROTE
That shall them angre, I holde thereon a grote, ...   59   Bowge   475
Was skantly worthe a grote;   125   Garnesche3   45
Yes, yes, by my trouth. I holde the a grote   173   Magnyfycence   1193
Gyve me my grote, for thou hast lost.   173   Magnyfycence   1206
'I have no penny nor grote   229   El Rummynge   600
Preches for his grote, ...   267   Collyn Clout   837
GROTES
And grotes many one or I came to your presence.   150   Magnyfycence   339
What! Sholde you pynche at a pecke of [gr]otes   151   Magnyfycence   384
   grotes] 'otes' †Rastell & Treveris C 1530, B
Wyth golde and grotes they grese my hande, ...   152   Magnyfycence   432
Set nought by golde ne grotes, /Theyr names yf I durst tell.   250   Collyn Clout   160
Some wyl neyther golde ne grotes;   268   Collyn Clout   866
GROUCHYNG
Gronynge, grouchyng, gracelesse, ...   280   Why Come Ye   80
GROUNDE
The grounde of his quarell was for his sovereyn lord, . . .   31   Dol Dethe   64
O grounde ungracious, unhappy be thy fame, ...   32   Dol Dethe   116
Mooste noble Erle! O fowle mysuryd grounde, ...   32   Dol Dethe   118
I fell downe to the grounde.   72   Phy Sparrow   36
A thousand myle of grounde, ...   76   Phy Sparrow   187
That plucked Acteon to the grounde, ...   79   Phy Sparrow   297
He bete downe to the grounde: 88   Phy Sparrow   671
To se her treade the grounde   100   Phy Sparrow   1149
Ye grounde yow upon Godfrey, that grysly gargons face, . .   123   Garnesche2   29
Mary, upon trouth my reason I grounde, ...   147   Magnyfycence   264
Syr, of my counsayle this shall be the grounde: 190   Magnyfycence   1768
Take hede of this captyfe that lyeth here on grounde. . . .   195   Magnyfycence   1946
But the very grounde /Was for to compound   229   El Rummynge   596
And brynge the churche to the grounde.   259   Collyn Clout   494
And hys textes grounde -   264   Collyn Clout   724
   hys] not in Kele 1545.1, Marshe 1568
Our soverayne lord, chyfe grounde   291   Why Come Ye   502
The grounde engrosyd and bet with bourne golde, ...   313   Garlande   41
With turkis and grossolitis enpavyd was the grounde; . . .   325   Garlande   466

273

GROUNDED — GUN STONE

	Page	Title	Line
Of vertu and konnyng the well and perfight grounde;	336	Garlande	866
and] (1st) not in MS Cotton Vitellius E.x			
In shorte sentens, /Of your pretens /What is the grounde	361	Albany	81
Ye durst byde on the grounde.	367	Albany	347

GROUNDED

	Page	Title	Line
Grounded is your sentence	372	Albany	519

GROUNDLY

But nowe debetis scire /And groundly audire	273	Collyn Clout	1066

GROW

Grow and encrese, remembre thyn astate!	33	Dol Dethe	163
In one rose now dothe grow;	110	Lawde	2
And grow all oute of kynde,	126	Garnesche3	102
Thus dyvers of language by lernyng I grow:	233	Speke Parott	103

GROWE

That thou cannyst not growe out of thy boyes gere;	170	Magnyfycence	1075
And therfore I growe more on one day	170	Magnyfycence	1077
To sowe corne in the see-sande, ther wyll no crope growe.	240	Speke Parott	342
Ye growe nowe out of kynde.	263	Collyn Clout	661

GROWEN

His here was growen thorowe oute his hat.	56	Bowge	350

GROWETH

There cometh and groweth of my comynge;	159	Magnyfycence	694
That every man almost groweth out of kynde.	175	Magnyfycence	1285
Thus totum in toto groweth up, as ye may se,	199	Magnyfycence	2099
Ye, for requiem eternam groweth forth of his nose.	204	Magnyfycence	2260

GROWYNG

Where I saw growyng a goodly laurell tre,	330	Garlande	665

GROWND

That of our fayth the grownd is.	62	Hauke	14

GROWNDE

Of this matter the grownde	298	Why Come Ye	780
But of my purpose now turne we to the grownde.	313	Garlande	28
purpose] 'proces' MS Cotton Vitellius E.x			
Rehersyng by ordre, and what is the grownde,	345	Garlande	1152
The grownde gronid and tremblid, the noyse was so stowte.	354	Garlande	1509

GROWWE

They growwe very ranke	304	Why Come Ye	1001

GRUDGE

It is foly to grudge agaynst his vysytacyon.	196	Magnyfycence	1990
Dothe grudge and complayne /Upon the temporall men.	248	Collyn Clout	64
And grudge therat with frownyng countenaunce;	348	Garlande	1258

GRUDGETH

He skantly loveth our kyng, /That grudgeth at this thing:	121	Ag Scottes2	36

GRUGYD

For grocers were grugyd at and groynyd at but late;	244	Speke Parott	441
They grugyd and sayde	285	Why Come Ye	252

GRUNTYNG

The Gruntyng and the Groynninge of the Gronnyng Swyne;	351	Garlande	1376
and the] 'a' †Fakes 1523; of the] not in †Fakes 1523			

GUERDON

Thus for your guerdon quyt ar ye,	119	Ag Scottes	139

GUILLIAM

Gup, Guilliam Travillian!'	285	Why Come Ye	241

GUY

Of Gawen, and Syr Guy,	87	Phy Sparrow	629

GUYDE

To guyde my pen and my pen to enbybe!	117	Ag Scottes	79
Yf fortune be frendly, and grace be the guyde,	234	Speke Parott	139
To rule nor to guyde,	304	Why Come Ye	1012

GUYDED

She had her so guyded	226	El Rummynge	472

GUY-GAW

So myche towrnyng on the cooke-stole for every guy-gaw;	245	Speke Parott	481

GUMBED

To se howe she is gumbed, /Fyngered and thumbed,	215	El Rummynge	40

GUMME

There is no bawme ne gumme of Arabe	207	Magnyfycence	2347

GUMMES

With armatycke gummes /That cost great sumes,	84	Phy Sparrow	520
His gummes rusty /Are full unlusty;	94	Phy Sparrow	914

GUMMIS

Or gummis of Saby so derely that be solde.	331	Garlande	675

GUMMY

Lyke a ropy rayne, /A gummy glayre.	215	El Rummynge	25

GUMMYS

Oure gummys grynnyng, /Oure soulys brynnyng!	40	Coystrowne3	35
Now Garnyche, garde thy gummys;	128	Garnesche3	158
Now with his gummys of Araby	309	Why Come Ye	1196
gummys] 'gynnys' MS Rawlinson C. 813			

GUN

Your Seven Systers, that gun so gay,	119	Ag Scottes	162

GUNNIS

With that I herd gunnis russhe out at ones,	329	Garlande	623

GUNNYS

My serpentins and my gunnys	128	Garnesche3	159

GUN STONE

For a gun stone, I say, had all to-jaggid his cap,	329	Garlande	629
to-jaggid] 'to lagged' Marshe 1568			

GUP —HAD   Page   Title   Line

GUP
Gup, Cristian Clowte, gup, Jak of the Vale,	35	Man Margery	6
Gup, Cristian Clowte, gup, Jak of the Vale,	35	Man Margery	6
Gup, Cristian Clowte, gup, Jak of the Vale,	36	Man Margery	13
Gup, Cristian Clowte, gup, Jak of the Vale,	36	Man Margery	13
Gup, Cristian Clowte, gup, Jak of the Vale,	36	Man Margery	20
Gup, Cristian Clowte, gup, Jak of the Vale,	36	Man Margery	20
Gup, Cristian Clowte, your breth is stale,	36	Man Margery	27
Gup, Cristian Clowte, gup, Jak of the Vale,	36	Man Margery	29
Gup, Cristian Clowte, gup, Jak of the Vale,	36	Man Margery	29
Spur up at the hynder gyrth with, 'Gup, morell, gup!'	43	Balettys2	17
Spur up at the hynder gyrth with, 'Gup, morell, gup!'	43	Balettys2	17
With, 'Gup, Syr Scot of Galaway!'	118	Ag Scottes	109
Gup, gorbellyd Godfrey, gup, Garnysche, gaudy fole!	123	Garnesche2	36
Gup, gorbellyd Godfrey, gup, Garnysche, gaudy fole!	123	Garnesche2	36
Gup, marmeset, jast ye morelle!	124	Garnesche3	13
With, 'Gup, Syr Gy', ye gate a moke.	131	Garnesche5	56
Gup Scot, /Ye blot:	135	Dundas	1
With, 'Jast you, and gup, gylly,	224	El Rummynge	390
With, 'Gup, levell suse!'	282	Why Come Ye	142
With, 'Gup, hore, gup! Now gup,	284	Why Come Ye	240
With, 'Gup, hore, gup! Now gup,	284	Why Come Ye	240
With, 'Gup, hore, gup! Now gup,	284	Why Come Ye	240
Gup, Guilliam Travillian!'	285	Why Come Ye	241

GUTTYS
That colyca passyo hath gropyd you by the guttys.	148	Magnyfycence	291

HA
Wyth 'Whom' and 'Ha' and with a croked loke,	51	Bowge	191
Ha, ha, ha! Herke, syrs, harke!	171	Magnyfycence	1109
Ha, ha, ha! Herke, syrs, harke!	171	Magnyfycence	1109
Ha, ha, ha! Herke, syrs, harke!	171	Magnyfycence	1109
Ha, ha, ha,	173	Magnyfycence	1201
Ha, ha, ha,	173	Magnyfycence	1201
Ha, ha, ha,	173	Magnyfycence	1201
Ha, ha, ha! For laughter I am lyke to brast.	201	Magnyfycence	2160
Ha, ha, ha! For laughter I am lyke to brast.	201	Magnyfycence	2160
Ha, ha, ha! For laughter I am lyke to brast.	201	Magnyfycence	2160
Ha, ha, ha! For sporte I am lyke to spewe and cast.	201	Magnyfycence	2161
Ha, ha, ha! For sporte I am lyke to spewe and cast.	201	Magnyfycence	2161
Ha, ha, ha! For sporte I am lyke to spewe and cast.	201	Magnyfycence	2161
A ha, fansy and foly met with you, I trowe.	210	Magnyfycence	2448
'Heghe, ha, ha, Parott, ye can lawghe pratylye!'	231	Speke Parott	22
'Heghe, ha, ha, Parott, ye can lawghe pratylye!'	231	Speke Parott	22

HABARION
Thow wolde have scoryd hys habarion;	130	Garnesche5	34

HABILLIMENTIS
Habillimentis royall founde out industriously;	336	Garlande	851

HABYLEMENTES
Her fresshe habylementes /With other implementes	101	Phy Sparrow	1180

HABYLYTE
Wordys well set with good habylyte;	43	Balettys3	5

HABYTACION
God maketh his habytacion	384	Replycacion	376

HABYTE
A kynge to me myn habyte gave	131	Garnesche5	80

HABLE
Ye had not ben hable to have saide hym nay.	31	Dol Dethe	70
Ye shall never be hable,	363	Albany	178

HABURDASHE
I have an hole armory of suche haburdashe in store;	175	Magnyfycence	1279

HACH
Whose jalawsy malycyous makyth them to lepe the hach!	43	Balettys2	33

HAD
At his commaundement whiche had both day and night	30	Dol Dethe	31
Where was your wit and reson ye shuld have had?	30	Dol Dethe	52
your] 'ys' †MS Royal 18 D.ii			
But had his nobillmen donn wel that day	31	Dol Dethe	69
Ye had not ben hable to have saide hym nay.	31	Dol Dethe	70
For yf they had occupied ther spere and ther shelde	31	Dol Dethe	73
This noble man doutles had not be slayne.	31	Dol Dethe	74
be] 'bene' Marshe 1568			
Whiche whils he lyvyd had fuyson of every thing,	32	Dol Dethe	131
He had forgoten all dedely syn.	42	Balettys1	11
Howbei[t], he is not furst hath had a los.	43	Balettys2	38
Howbeit] 'Howbeis' †Rastell 1527.1			
Marchauntes her borded to see what she had lode.	47	Bowge	40
lode] not in Marshe 1568			
She sayde she trowed that I had eten sause;	48	Bowge	72
had] not in †Wynkyn de Worde 1499, 1510			
That, so to saye, I had gyven her no cause.	48	Bowge	75
Me thoughte, of wordes that he had full a poke;	51	Bowge	179
His face was belymmed as byes had him stounge;	54	Bowge	289
Hatred by the herte so had hym wrounge	54	Bowge	292
I loked on hym, I wende he had be woode.	55	Bowge	320
He had no pleasure but in harlotrye.	56	Bowge	374
Had I as good an hors as she is a mare,	57	Bowge	407
For yf I had not quyckely fledde the touche,	60	Bowge	503
He had plucte oute the nobles of my pouche.	60	Bowge	504

HAD — HAD | Page | Title | Line

Text	Page	Title	Line
To holde myne honde, by God, I had grete payne;	61	Bowge	522
For forthwyth there I had him slayne,	61	Bowge	523
She had flowyn so oft,	63	Hauke	68
She had not wel endude;	63	Hauke	78
The hawke had no lyst /To come to his fyst;	64	Hauke	83
She loked as she had the frounce;	64	Hauke	85
frounce] 'fronnce' Kynge & Marche 1554, 'fronce' Day 1560			
As though I had ben racked,	73	Phy Sparrow	47
Well nye had stopped my breath.	73	Phy Sparrow	63
had] not in Wyght 1553, Kitson 1560.6, Marshe 1568			
Wolde God I had Zenophontes,	74	Phy Sparrow	98
Whan she had lost her joye,	74	Phy Sparrow	110
It had a velvet cap,	74	Phy Sparrow	120
Phyllyp had leve to go	76	Phy Sparrow	175
I wolde I had a parte /Of her crafty magyke!	76	Phy Sparrow	203
Wherin he had apes and owles,	78	Phy Sparrow	258
Had no such Phylyp as I,	78	Phy Sparrow	271
Had I of his swete musse;	80	Phy Sparrow	362
his] 'this' †Kele 1545.2, Wyght 1553			
Horsly, as he had the mur;	82	Phy Sparrow	419
Comfort had he none	89	Phy Sparrow	705
How she me had reclaymed,	99	Phy Sparrow	1125
I had than in a tryce,	100	Phy Sparrow	1131
That ever Englond had;	111	Lawde	53
Ye had be better to have busked to Huntley Bankes,	114	Scot Kynge	50
be] 'bet' †Fakes 1513			
But ye had some wyl[d] sede to sowe,	114	Scot Kynge	52
wyld] 'wyle' †Fakes 1513			
They say they had /And wan the felde /With spere and shelde!	116	Ag Scottes	14
Ye had a knavysche cote	125	Garnesche3	44
Had yow most in despyght;	125	Garnesche3	66
Had ye gonne with me to scole,	127	Garnesche3	117
I wolde ye had kyst hyr on the tayle!	130	Garnesche5	46
Sche wolde nat of yt thow had sworne.	131	Garnesche5	52
To daly with yow she had no lust.	131	Garnesche5	54
Hem, syr, yet beware of 'Had I wyste!'	146	Magnyfycence	211
In faythe, els had I gone to longe to scole,	148	Magnyfycence	298
Had I not opened my purse wyde,	150	Magnyfycence	347
I trowe, by our lady, I had ben slayne,	150	Magnyfycence	348
Or elles I had lost myne eres twayne.	150	Magnyfycence	349
To gete me fro them I had moche warke.	150	Magnyfycence	361
By my trouthe, had I not payde and prayde,	150	Magnyfycence	363
I had not been here with you this nyght.	150	Magnyfycence	365
If you had with you largesse.	151	Magnyfycence	377
But I say, kepest thou the olde name styll that thou had?	155	Magnyfycence	516
By God, had not I it convayed	155	Magnyfycence	534
Yet Fansy had ben dysc[r]yved.	155	Magnyfycence	535
dyscryved] 'dysceyved' †Rastell & Treveris C 1530, B			
By my trouthe, we had ben gone.	155	Magnyfycence	537
For had you not come I had ryden.	156	Magnyfycence	577
For had you not come I had ryden.	156	Magnyfycence	577
We had hym founde, we sholde hym brynge,	158	Magnyfycence	653
And made as I had knowen nothynge of the case —	160	Magnyfycence	719
What the devyll! Where had we this joly jetter?	162	Magnyfycence	796
As skante thou had no nede of me.	163	Magnyfycence	806
Mary, Mesure had hym a whyle in gydynge,	166	Magnyfycence	939
That the horson had for etynge of a trype,	171	Magnyfycence	1126
In faythe, I wolde thou had a marmosete.	171	Magnyfycence	1132
Yet I wolde that ye had gone rather;	176	Magnyfycence	1313
In good faythe, syr, me semeth he had the more wronge.	178	Magnyfycence	1384
Yet it is good to beware of 'had I wyst'.	179	Magnyfycence	1395
That all the oryent had in subjeccyon,	181	Magnyfycence	1467
I wolde I had, by hym that hell dyd harowe,	184	Magnyfycence	1561
This is a wyse man, syr, where so ever ye hym had.	187	Magnyfycence	1689
Grete mervayle I had, and mused in my mynde.	191	Magnyfycence	1822
I sawe a sowter go to supper, or ever he had dynde.	191	Magnyfycence	1825
And had robbyd you quyte from all felycyte.	193	Magnyfycence	1864
In welth beware yf I had had grace,	196	Magnyfycence	1976
In welth beware yf I had had grace,	196	Magnyfycence	1976
Never had I bene brought in this case.	196	Magnyfycence	1977
Alasse in my cradell that I had not dyde!	196	Magnyfycence	1987
And where you had chaunges of ryche aray,	197	Magnyfycence	2010
Yet many had lever hangyd to be	198	Magnyfycence	2040
Where is nowe all my servauntys that I had here a late?	198	Magnyfycence	2057
For yf Measure had ruled Lyberte as he began,	200	Magnyfycence	2111
This lurden that here lyeth had ben a noble man.	200	Magnyfycence	2112
For had I not bene, ye bothe had bene hangyd,	203	Magnyfycence	2235
For had I not bene, ye bothe had bene hangyd,	203	Magnyfycence	2235
That dyspayre well nyghe had myscheved me;	206	Magnyfycence	2332
For had ye not the soner ben my refuge,	206	Magnyfycence	2333
Of dampnacyon I had ben drawen in the luge.	206	Magnyfycence	2334
Undoubted ye had lost yourselfe eternally.	206	Magnyfycence	2335
And nowe ye have had, syr, a wonderous fall,	207	Magnyfycence	2375
I herde say that adversyte with Magnyfycence had fought.	210	Magnyfycence	2460
And ye shall have more worshyp then ever ye had.	210	Magnyfycence	2474
It had ben hers, I wene, /More then fourty yere;	215	El Rummynge	57
Jone sayde she had eten a fyest.	223	El Rummynge	343
Snevelyng in her nose, /As though she had the pose.	223	El Rummynge	365

HADDE —HAISET

	Page	Title	Line
Of [a] foles fylly /That had a fole with Wylly,	224	El Rummynge	389
a] not in †Lant 1545, Kynge & Marche 1554, Day 1560, Marshe 1568; fylly] 'silly' Marshe 1568			
But she had lost the stoppell.	224	El Rummynge	404
Than sterte in made Kyt, /That had lytell wyt;	225	El Rummynge	413
She had her so guyded	226	El Rummynge	472
She had also the gout	226	El Rummynge	484
And had broken her shyn	227	El Rummynge	494
She had a wyde wesant;	227	El Rummynge	517
wyde] 'wyse' Kynge & Marche 1554			
Had she not hyed apace,	229	El Rummynge	572
She had defoyled the place.	229	El Rummynge	573
That nothynge had /There of their awne,	229	El Rummynge	608
That had not a penny,	230	El Rummynge	612
Men say, they had rather	251	Collyn Clout	175
They had lever to please	269	Collyn Clout	909
God wot, had lytell parte	292	Why Come Ye	513
Had nat our prynce be	292	Why Come Ye	539
The apostyll Peter /Had but on pore myter	307	Why Come Ye	1140
apostyll] 'wholly apostle' MS Rawlinson C. 813			
But if he had made sum memoryall,	315	Garlande	118
Recorde the same? Or why is had in mynde	315	Garlande	125
From whiche Eschines had none evacyon.	316	Garlande	154
Had I never sene, some softer, some lowder;	320	Garlande	271
So finally, when they had shewyd there devyse,	324	Garlande	442
Some lokyd full smothely, and had a fals quarter,	326	Garlande	504
quarter] 'quart' Marshe 1568			
They had wrytyng, sum Greke, sum Ebrew,	328	Garlande	582
Had gravin in it of calcydony a capytall A.	328	Garlande	587
As fersly frownynge as he had ben fyghtyng,	328	Garlande	594
For a gun stone, I say, had all to-jaggid his cap,	329	Garlande	629
to-jaggid] 'to lagged' Marshe 1568			
With a pellit of pevisshenes they had suche a stroke,	330	Garlande	637
Troilus, I trowe, if that he had you sene,	336	Garlande	873
And if Apelles your countenaunce had sene,	337	Garlande	894
That for her trowth is in remembraunce had;	337	Garlande	900
But, and I had leyser competent,	342	Garlande	1082
Of this warke they had so great delyght,	343	Garlande	1110
It wolde have made a man hole that had be ryght sekely,	345	Garlande	1162
But that my peticyon wolde not be had,	353	Garlande	1486
Ye had evill spede.	359	Albany	32
If that ye had tane	366	Albany	283
That wyse Harpocrates /Had your mouthes stopped,	377	Replycacion	116
Some of you had ten pounde,	378	Replycacion	146
And thought, if ye had right,	379	Replycacion	200
Howe falsely ye had surmysed,	380	Replycacion	209
It had ben moche better	380	Replycacion	229
Ye had never lerned letter,	380	Replycacion	230

HADDE

	Page	Title	Line
How ofte he hadde hit Jenet on the tayle,	56	Bowge	369
hadde] 'not' Marshe 1568			

HADDEST

	Page	Title	Line
I wold thou haddest ben blynde!	79	Phy Sparrow	285

HADE

	Page	Title	Line
Under her arme, me thought, she hade a boke.	327	Garlande	532

HAFTAR

	Page	Title	Line
Harkyn herto, ye Harvy Ha[f]tar,	133	Garnesche5	164
Haftar] 'Hastar' †MS Harley 367			

HAFTE

	Page	Title	Line
And whan I sawe the horsons wolde you hafte,	61	Bowge	521

HAFTER

	Page	Title	Line
And Harvy Ha[f]ter that well coude picke a male;	50	Bowge	138
Hafter] 'Haster' †Wynkyn de Worde 1499, 1510, Marshe 1568			
Harvy Ha[f]ter came lepynge, lyghte as lynde.	52	Bowge	231
Hafter] 'Haster' †Wynkyn de Worde 1499, 1510, Marshe 1568			
To Hervy Ha[f]ter than he spake of me,	54	Bowge	295
Hafter] 'Haster' †Wynkyn de Worde 1499, 1510, Marshe 1568			
'Turde,' quod Ha[f]ter, 'I wyll the nothynge layne,	55	Bowge	311
layne] 'sayne' †Wynkyn de Worde 1499, Marshe 1568			
Nowe, benedicite, ye wene I were some hafter,	147	Magnyfycence	257
Havell and Harvy Hafter,	281	Why Come Ye	97

HAFTERS

	Page	Title	Line
And from crafters and hafters I you forfende.	210	Magnyfycence	2456

HAFTYNGE

	Page	Title	Line
With haftynge and with polleynge,	125	Garnesche3	38
Craftynge and haftynge contryved is by me;	159	Magnyfycence	697
For to use suche haftynge and crafty wayes.	187	Magnyfycence	1678

HAG

	Page	Title	Line
Lyke a Scottyshe hag.	366	Albany	295

HAGGE

	Page	Title	Line
Lyke a clerkely hagge.	248	Collyn Clout	52

HAGGYS

	Page	Title	Line
Ye cast all your corage uppon such courtly haggys!	43	Balettys2	19

HAILID

	Page	Title	Line
But hailid they be homwarde with sorow and shame.	329	Garlande	622

HAISET

	Page	Title	Line
Sith mistres Jane Haiset	339	Garlande	968

HAY —HALFEPENY					Page	Title		Line

HAY
	Page	Title	Line
Ye rayle, ye ryme, with, 'Hay, dog, hay!'	129	Garnesche5	5
Ye rayle, ye ryme, with, 'Hay, dog, hay!'	129	Garnesche5	5
To dauns the hay or rune the ray;	134	Garnesche5	170
Go shake the, dogge, hay, syth ye wyll nedys!	148	Magnyfycence	303
Hay, chysshe, come hyder! Nay, torde! Take hym be tyme.	171	Magnyfycence	1117
Wyddered lyke hay, /The woll worne away.	216	El Rummynge	62
With, 'Hey, dogge, hay, /Have these hogges away!'	218	El Rummynge	168
hogges] 'dogges' Day 1560, Marshe 1568			
'How, hosteler, fetche my hors a botell of hay!'	234	Speke Parott	147
With, 'Gingirly, go gingerly!' Her tayle was made of hay;	346	Garlande	1203
With, 'hey, dogge, hay.'	360	Albany	37
Twyt, Scot, shake th[e] dogge, hay.	363	Albany	159
the] 'thy' †Marshe 1568			

HAYLE
And of their taunting toies rest with il hayle.	138	Ven Tongues	33
Eche thynge is fayre when it is yonge; all hayle, owle!	167	Magnyfycence	970
Ly styll, ly styll nowe, with yll hayle!	204	Magnyfycence	2248
God gyve it yll hayle,	230	El Rummynge	617

HAYLED
The tearys downe hayled;	72	Phy Sparrow	24

HAYLES
Yet thus with yll hayles	256	Collyn Clout	400

HAYLYNGE
The prechers with evyll haylynge:	275	Collyn Clout	1149

HAYNE
It is greate scorne to see suche a hayne	55	Bowge	327

HAYNYARDE
Hens, thou haynyarde, out of dores fast!	188	Magnyfycence	1725

HAYNNOUSLY
And so haynnously doth stynke,	127	Garnesche3	144

HAYNOUSLY
Raylynge haynously /And dysdaynously	260	Collyn Clout	536

HAY THE GY
Nothing to write, but hay the gy of thre,	138	Ven Tongues	46

HAY THE GYE
Hay the gye and the gan!	301	Why Come Ye	888

HAKE
With, 'Welcome, hake and make!'	253	Collyn Clout	250

HAKNEY
I am no hakney for your rode;	35	Man Margery	11

HALF
That Dame Menolope was never half so wyse;	42	Balettys2	11
Whan I loked on hym, my purse was half aferde.	52	Bowge	238
In maner half with shame;	89	Phy Sparrow	713
For frantick faitours half mad and half straught;	138	Ven Tongues	27
For frantick faitours half mad and half straught;	138	Ven Tongues	27

HALFE
Of our pole artyke, smylynge halfe in scorne	46	Bowge	5
Never halfe the payne	72	Phy Sparrow	19
Halfe slumbrynge, in a sounde	72	Phy Sparrow	35
But for I am a mayde, /Tymerous, halfe afrayde,	87	Phy Sparrow	608
Your harrold in armes not yet halfe expert.	118	Ag Scottes	98
For Syr Frollo of Franko was never halfe so talle.	121	Garnesche1	5
Dothe savyr halfe so souer	127	Garnesche3	146
Sche praiid yow walke, on Goddes halfe!	131	Garnesche5	60
Another bade shave halfe my berde;	150	Magnyfycence	355
On this halfe and on every syde	168	Magnyfycence	1020
Were never halfe so rychely as I am drest.	181	Magnyfycence	1483
A, I wolde to God that I were halfe so crafty	183	Magnyfycence	1532
Or in electe utteraunce halfe so eloquent,	183	Magnyfycence	1533
And from thens to the halfe strete,	204	Magnyfycence	2263
She semed halfe a leche,	225	El Rummynge	447
'Ryse up, on Gods halfe,'	227	El Rummynge	501
Up she stert, halfe lame,	227	El Rummynge	512
She was not halfe so wyse	229	El Rummynge	588
Must preche a Goddes halfe	266	Collyn Clout	810
Parchaunce halfe a yere;	295	Why Come Ye	637
On every halfe my reasons forthe I sought,	312	Garlande	10
On] 'One' †Fakes 1523			
In slumbrynge I fell and halfe in a slepe;	313	Garlande	30
As people halfe pevysshe, or men that were masyd.	319	Garlande	266
Came towarde me, and smylid halfe in game;	327	Garlande	529
Was never halfe so fayre, as I wene,	342	Garlande	1077
With that I stode up, halfe sodenly afrayd,	353	Garlande	1477
It is halfe a supersticyon	378	Replycacion	142
As people halfe amased,	379	Replycacion	194

HALFE-ABUSED
Myne Englyssh halfe-abused;	92	Phy Sparrow	815

HALFE HERETYKES
Suche maner of sysmatykes /And halfe heretykes,	264	Collyn Clout	701

HALFE-MAYMED
Alas, I am dysdayned, /And as a man halfe-maymed,	237	Speke Parott	253

HALFE MEN
That they are but halfe men;	283	Why Come Ye	163

HALFEPENY
I wyll not gyve a halfepeny for to chose the better.	170	Magnyfycence	1067

HALY —HANDE   Page   Title   Line

HALY
Nor yet by Haly;   84   Phy Sparrow   505
Tholomye and Haly were cunnyng and wyse 234   Speke Parott   134
Not acquaynted worth a fly /With honorable Haly, ... 292   Why Come Ye   521
HALL
An ussher of the hall fayn wold I get   37   Coystrowne1   40
Rudely revilyng me in the kynges noble hall, ...   121   Garnesche1   2
Measure is mete for a marchauntes hall   151   Magnyfycence   382
Ye have eten sauce I trowe, at the Taylers Hall.   179   Magnyfycence   1404
Take up dyrt and all, /And bere out of the hall.'   219   El Rummynge   184
   dyrt] 'drit' Kynge & Marche 1554, Day 1560, Marshe 1568
But, syr, amonge all /That sate in that hall, ...   229   El Rummynge   581
Within Westmynster Hall.   287   Why Come Ye   325
HALLE
An hundred steppis mountyng to the halle, ...   325   Garlande   471
HALLES
Of the kynges halles, ...   249   Collyn Clout   127
With halles and with boures, ...   270   Collyn Clout   937
HALLIS
Engolerid goodly with hallis and bowris, ...   325   Garlande   460
   Engolerid] 'Engalared' Marshe 1568
HALLOWS
Gone to seke hallows, /With Reason together, ...   358   Garlande2   7
HALOW
And to halow there the fox.   64   Hauke   110
This herse for to halow.   82   Phy Sparrow   405
HALPENY
That men shall scantly /Have peny or halpeny.   303   Why Come Ye   968
HALSE
A, Lorde, so I wolde halse her hartely!   190   Magnyfycence   1801
HALSYD
That halsyd her hartely and kyst her swete.   42   Balettys1   18
HALT
Adres the to me, whiche am bothe halt and lame, ...   29   Dol Dethe   10
That wyll make you to halt and to hoppe.   204   Magnyfycence   2273
HALTE
Some with the marmoll to halte I them make;   194   Magnyfycence   1906
HALTED
She halted of a kybe, ...   227   El Rummynge   493
HALTER
The nexte halter ther xall be   128   Garnesche3   176
And some for to hange themselfe in an halter;   194   Magnyfycence   1911
With this halter good and stronge;   206   Magnyfycence   2313
Lo, here is thy knyfe and a halter, and or we go ferther, . .   206   Magnyfycence   2317
Shall I myselfe hange with an halter? Nay, ...   206   Magnyfycence   2320
HALTERS
Of halters and ropes   362   Albany   123
HALTITH
And 'He haltith often that hath a kyby hele.'   326   Garlande   502
HALTYNG
And than came haltyng Jone   222   El Rummynge   326
HALTYNGE
Counterfet haltynge without a thorne;   153   Magnyfycence   449
HAMYLCAR
Nat lyke Duke Hamylcar   363   Albany   192
HAMMER
Hampar with your hammer upon thy styth, ...   71   Hauke   332
HAMPAR
Hampar with your hammer upon thy styth, ...   71   Hauke   332
HAMPTON
Or to Hampton Court?   289   Why Come Ye   404
But Hampton Court /Hath the preemynence!   289   Why Come Ye   408
HAND
Wherwyth my hand she strayned, ...   99   Phy Sparrow   1122
My hand it is unstable, ...   102   Phy Sparrow   1220
He bereth the kyng on hand   290   Why Come Ye   452
By whose suggestyon /I toke on hand this warke, ...   309   Why Come Ye   1204
   suggestyon] 'subjectyon' MS Rawlinson C. 813
HANDE
For whos causis ye slew hym with your awne hande.   31   Dol Dethe   68
O dolorous chaunce of Fortuns fraward hande!   32   Dol Dethe   110
Trewe you say, syr. Gyve me your hande.   141   Magnyfycence   28
Me semeth Magnyfycence is comynge here at hande.   145   Magnyfycence   162
They bare me in hande that I was a spye;   150   Magnyfycence   352
Wyth golde and grotes they grese my hande, ...   152   Magnyfycence   432
For Cockys harte, gyve me thy hande.   154   Magnyfycence   512
Water in the one hande and fyre in the other.   160   Magnyfycence   711
What pylde curre ledest thou in thy hande?   169   Magnyfycence   1054
Yes. With his hande I made hym to subscrybe   187   Magnyfycence   1666
Thou must not abyde the dynt of my hande.   193   Magnyfycence   1879
Holde thy hande, dawe, of thy dagger, and stynt of thy dyn; .   202   Magnyfycence   2188
In tyme of dystresse I am redy at hande;   205   Magnyfycence   2285
For they must take in hande   268   Collyn Clout   888
Than to take on hande   269   Collyn Clout   911
Dare take nothynge on hande.   286   Why Come Ye   291
To holde up their hande at the bar.   286   Why Come Ye   302
The kynges owne hande, ...   296   Why Come Ye   676
Into one mannys hande;   298   Why Come Ye   763

HANDELL —HAPPELY | Page | Title | Line

HANDE
Turnyng on the ryght hande, by a windyng stayre, a] not in †Fakes 1523	333	Garlande	767
'Withdrawe your hande, the tyme passis fast.	343	Garlande	1086

HANDELL
Lo, syrs, thus I handell them all	194	Magnyfycence	1896

HANDES
Wherewith my handes I wrange /That my senaws cracked	72	Phy Sparrow	45
And handes soft as sylke,	99	Phy Sparrow	1119
With that her hed shaked /And her handes quaked.	226	El Rummynge	477
That cometh to theyr handes;	269	Collyn Clout	931

HANDIS
Wherof the answere restyth in my handis,	332	Garlande	724
With fingers smale, and handis whyte as mylk; whyte] 'as white' Marshe 1568	334	Garlande	797

HANDYD
Nay, I know well inough ye are bothe well handyd	203	Magnyfycence	2230

HANDY-DANDY
Prisians hed broken now, handy-dandy,	235	Speke Parott	171

HANDYLL
Boke, bell and candyll, /All that he myght handyll;	64	Hauke	113

HANDYS
That rule not be mesure that they have in theyr handys,	195	Magnyfycence	1939

HANDLE
Alas, why do ye nat handle	255	Collyn Clout	332

HANG
That hang togedyr as fethyrs in the wynde;	239	Speke Parott	293
And hang you upon polles	362	Albany	151

HANGE
To Tyburne, where they hange on hyght.	152	Magnyfycence	423
Tusshe! Thy lyppes hange in thyne eye; eye] 'eyen' †Rastell & Treveris C 1530, B	169	Magnyfycence	1049
Save a stronge thefe and hange a trew man.	178	Magnyfycence	1360
Thy wordes hange togyder as fethers in the wynde.	191	Magnyfycence	1818
And some for to hange themselfe in an halter;	194	Magnyfycence	1911
Shall I myselfe hange with an halter? Nay,	206	Magnyfycence	2320
And lothe to hange the bell	250	Collyn Clout	163
That wyll hed us and hange us,	308	Why Come Ye	1154

HANGED
For some shall wene be hanged by the throte.	59	Bowge	476
A, syr, thy jarfawcon and thou be hanged togyder!	191	Magnyfycence	1812
Some hanged, some slayne,	276	Collyn Clout	1210

HANGID
The chambres hangid with clothes of arace;	325	Garlande	475

HANGIS
That all his trust hangis trust] 'harte' MS Rawlinson C. 813	308	Why Come Ye	1183

HANGYD
Better it is to begge than to be hangyd with shame.	198	Magnyfycence	2039
Yet many had lever hangyd to be	198	Magnyfycence	2040
For had I not bene, ye bothe had bene hangyd,	203	Magnyfycence	2235
So many thevys hangyd, and thevys neverthelesse;	245	Speke Parott	477

HANGYNGE
Hangynge about the walles	270	Collyn Clout	940

HANGYTH
Youre key is commen and hangyth owte;	41	Coystrowne4	23

HANGMAN
Ye, wylte thou, hangman? I say, thou cavell!	202	Magnyfycence	2190

HANYBALL
Nor Hanyball, agayne Rome gates that ranne,	182	Magnyfycence	1511
Nor lyke his sonne Hanyball,	363	Albany	194

HANKYN BOVY
They rangyd Hankyn Bovy /My churche all abowte.	65	Hauke	117

HANNYBALL
And of the Duke Hannyball, Hannyball] 'of Hannyball' Wyght 1553, Kitson 1560.6, Marshe 1568	88	Phy Sparrow	665

HANSY
It was a Flemynge hyght Hansy.	149	Magnyfycence	328

HAP
Your hap was unhappy, to ill was your spede.	31	Dol Dethe	61
Hys hart is to hy to have any hap;	37	Coystrowne1	12
Hys hed was hevy, such was his hap,	41	Balettys1	5
The hawke with that clap /Fell downe with evyll hap.	64	Hauke	90
For lacke of grace hard was your hap;	119	Ag Scottes	168
God gyve it yll hap!'	227	El Rummynge	509
Or howeever it hap,	273	Collyn Clout	1057
And one ther was there, I wondred of his hap,	329	Garlande	628

HAPPE
And happe you the whyles with these homly raggys.	197	Magnyfycence	2037
O hatefull happe, O carefull cruelte!	198	Magnyfycence	2049
With money, yf it wyll happe /To catche the forked cappe.	249	Collyn Clout	88

HAPPED
My hawke is rammysshe, and it happed that she ran —	191	Magnyfycence	1807
Alasse that ever I was so harde happed	196	Magnyfycence	1984
Your hede that was wonte to be happed moost drowpy and drowsy,	197	Magnyfycence	2018

HAPPELY
Some men may happely rew,	280	Why Come Ye	60
Men may happely se	288	Why Come Ye	367

	Page	Title	Line
HAPPEN —HARE			
May happely loke /Upon your boke,	355	Garlande	1546
HAPPEN			
'By God,' quod Hervy, 'and it so happen myghte!	54	Bowge	306
HAPPID			
Moche mischefe, I hyght you, amonge theem ther happid.	330	Garlande	643
HAPPY			
I am not happy, I renne ay on the losse!	57	Bowge	399
They are happy that wynnys,	302	Why Come Ye	927
Whiche, if they be happy, have cause to beware	353	Garlande	1474
HARD			
This lordis dethe, whos pere is hard to fynd,	34	Dol Dethe	178
And hard to be enneude	91	Phy Sparrow	775
For lacke of grace hard was your hap;	119	Ag Scottes	168
Towchid, and hard for to be barrid.	316	Garlande	143
barrid] 'debarrid' MS Cotton Vitellius E.x			
'O mercyles madame, hard is your constellacyon,	320	Garlande	304
Wordes be swordes, and hard to call ageine.'	328	Garlande	567
But what of that? Hard it is to please all men;	348	Garlande	1259
HARDE			
In sesons past who hathe harde or sene	30	Dol Dethe	22
His hede maye be harde, but feble is his brayne!	46	Bowge	24
his] not in Marshe 1568			
Such tunges shuld be torne out by the harde rootes,	137	Ven Tongues	3
A fals lying tunge is harde to withholde;	137	Ven Tongues	6
Syr, as ye say. I have harde of your fame.	141	Magnyfycence	26
Why, have you harde of our dysputacyon?	142	Magnyfycence	82
Why, harde thou not of the fray	166	Magnyfycence	932
Cockes bones! Harde ye ever suche another?	192	Magnyfycence	1841
Alasse that ever I was so harde happed	196	Magnyfycence	1984
Ye, syr, nowe must ye lerne to lye harde,	197	Magnyfycence	2005
O dolorous herte, O harde adversyte!	198	Magnyfycence	2052
There was never so harde a storme of mysery,	207	Magnyfycence	2343
They molefy so easely my harte that was so harde.	207	Magnyfycence	2346
And ye that have harde thys dysporte and game,	214	Magnyfycence	2571
To kepe so harde a rule,	254	Collyn Clout	307
Of! by the harde arse!	288	Why Come Ye	386
But have ye nat harde this,	292	Why Come Ye	532
As I harde say, Dame Pallas was her name,	313	Garlande	48
How be it, it were harde to construe this lecture;	315	Garlande	109
Yet harde is to make but sum fawt be founde.'	315	Garlande	112
With that I harde the noyse of a trumpe,	319	Garlande	259
It is harde to tell of every mannes mouthe:	326	Garlande	500
Harde to make ought of that is nakid nought;	346	Garlande	1205
A pleasaunter place than Ashrige is, harde were to fynde,	353	Garlande	1465
were] 'where' †Fakes 1523			
No man hath harde /Of suche a cowarde,	365	Albany	252
HARDE HARTED			
Ye, but some be full koy and passynge harde harted.	184	Magnyfycence	1583
HARDELY			
Be Crist, ye shall not! No, no, hardely!	36	Man Margery	18
Ly styll hardely, and take a nap.'	41	Balettys1	4
Abasshe you not, but hardely be bolde,	48	Bowge	87
Ageynste you hardely; therefore be not afrayde.	51	Bowge	174
No, no, syr, hardely!	78	Phy Sparrow	272
Syr, hardely remembre what may your name avaunce.	148	Magnyfycence	277
Yet convey it craftely, and hardely spare not for me' -	177	Magnyfycence	1352
But yet, syrs, hardely one thynge lerne of me:	199	Magnyfycence	2087
And also theyr fete /Hardely full unswete;	217	El Rummynge	122
And for no man hardely let hym spare	319	Garlande	244
HARD HERTYD			
Though ye wer hard hertyd,	341	Garlande	1038
HARDY			
Ye, in faythe, a bolde man and a hardy.	162	Magnyfycence	771
No man so hardy to worke agaynst my wyll.	181	Magnyfycence	1479
Nor none so hardy of them with me that durste crake,	182	Magnyfycence	1513
To hardy, or to moche, to free of the dawe,	199	Magnyfycence	2090
And nat so hardy on his hede	272	Collyn Clout	1023
nat] 'not' Marshe 1568, MS Harley 2252			
So hardy to make suete,	272	Collyn Clout	1031
Nat so hardy on theyr pates!	275	Collyn Clout	1152
None so hardy to speke.	287	Why Come Ye	328
So hardy nor so bolde	367	Albany	338
Of hardy merciall actes,	368	Albany	397
HARDY-DARDY			
So myche hardy-dardy, and so lytell manlynes;	244	Speke Parott	457
HARDYNES			
O causeles cowardes, O hartles hardynes,	242	Speke Parott	390
HARDYSON			
Of Lumbardy Gorge Hardyson,	130	Garnesche5	33
HARDLY			
Hardly bestad and driven is to hope	335	Garlande	830
and] not in MS Cotton Vitellius E.x			
HARE			
Here is a leysshe of ratches to renne an hare!	156	Magnyfycence	586
Cankard Jacke Hare, loke thou be not rusty;	161	Magnyfycence	758
So how, I say, the hare is squat!	176	Magnyfycence	1299
The houndes ranne before, and the hare behynde.	191	Magnyfycence	1823
As wyse as an hare!	217	El Rummynge	112

	Page	Title	Line
There went the hare away;	281	Why Come Ye	120
The hare, the fox, the gray,	281	Why Come Ye	121

HARYS

	Page	Title	Line
Say to me, Jacke Harys, /Quare accuparis	69	Hauke	277

HARKE

	Page	Title	Line
And I drewe nere to harke what they two sayde.	54	Bowge	296
As I shall tell you, yf ye wyll harke agayne:	61	Bowge	520
Ha, ha, ha! Herke, syrs, harke!	171	Magnyfycence	1109
Now Geball, Amon and Amaloch - 'Harke, harke,	234	Speke Parott	118
Now Geball, Amon and Amaloch - 'Harke, harke,	234	Speke Parott	118
Harke, howe the losell prates /With a wyde wesaunt!	275	Collyn Clout	1153
But harke, my frende, one worde	298	Why Come Ye	784
And men lyst to harke,	309	Why Come Ye	1206
Harke yet, Sir Duke, a worde	367	Albany	318

HARKEN

	Page	Title	Line
'Harken,' quod he, 'loo here myne honde in thyne;	60	Bowge	510

HARKYN

	Page	Title	Line
Harkyn herto, ye Harvy Ha[f]tar, Haftar] 'Hastar' †MS Harley 367	133	Garnesche5	164

HARLOTRYE

	Page	Title	Line
He had no pleasure but in harlotrye.	56	Bowge	374

HARLOTTES

	Page	Title	Line
For harlottes hawnte thyn hatefull cors;	131	Garnesche5	72
Of harlottes to use soche an harres,	131	Garnesche5	77

HARME

	Page	Title	Line
She pynched her pynyon, by God, and catched harme.	191	Magnyfycence	1810

HARMYS

	Page	Title	Line
To the domage and harmys	370	Albany	468

HARNES

	Page	Title	Line
Her har[n]es easy ferre and nere is soughte. harnes] 'harmes' †Wynkyn de Worde 1499, 1510, 'armes' Marshe 1568	57	Bowge	403

HARNNES

	Page	Title	Line
To harnnes bryght, /By force of myght,	355	Garlande	1556

HAROLDE

	Page	Title	Line
And your harolde no thynge experte;	113	Scot Kynge	8

HAROLDES

	Page	Title	Line
Haroldes from honor may the devors,	131	Garnesche5	71

HAROLDIS

	Page	Title	Line
Haroldis they know thy cote-armur;	131	Garnesche5	68

HAROW

	Page	Title	Line
By Hercules that hell dyd harow,	104	Phy Sparrow	1291
By Hercules that hell did harow,	348	Garlande	1284

HAROWE

	Page	Title	Line
I wolde I had, by hym that hell dyd harowe,	184	Magnyfycence	1561
Out harowe! Hyll burneth! Where shall I me hyde?	206	Magnyfycence	2324

HARPE

	Page	Title	Line
And wrest up my harpe	259	Collyn Clout	490
Thus can harpe and syng	384	Replycacion	344
With his harpe of prophesy /And spyrituall poetry,	384	Replycacion	345

HARPED

	Page	Title	Line
For Davyd, our poete, harped so meloudiously	383	Replycacion	339
That at his resurrection he harped out of hell	383	Replycacion	341

HARPE STRINGIS

	Page	Title	Line
There Cintheus sat twynklyng upon his harpe stringis;	331	Garlande	687

HARPE STRYNGGES

	Page	Title	Line
His tunable harpe stryngges	93	Phy Sparrow	865

HARPYNG

	Page	Title	Line
In metricall muses, his harpyng we may spare;	383	Replycacion	338

HARPOCRATES

	Page	Title	Line
That wyse Harpocrates /Had your mouthes stopped,	377	Replycacion	115

HARRE

	Page	Title	Line
All is out of harre	165	Magnyfycence	912
To flatterynge, to smatterynge, to to out of harre,	199	Magnyfycence	2095

HARRES

	Page	Title	Line
Of harlottes to use soche an harres,	131	Garnesche5	77

HARRY

	Page	Title	Line
If our moost royall Harry	367	Albany	340

HARROLD

	Page	Title	Line
Your harrold in armes not yet halfe expert.	118	Ag Scottes	98

HART

	Page	Title	Line
Wythe hevy chere, with dolorous hart and mynd,	34	Dol Dethe	176
Hys hart is to hy to have any hap;	37	Coystrowne1	12
Which makyth my hart oft to lepe and sprynge	44	Balettys3	32
Open myne hart, beholde my mynde expres.	44	Balettys3	39
Of my trew hart, to love her best of all!	45	Balettys3	49
Go, pytyous hart, rasyd with dedly wo,	45	Balettys5	1
For whose sake my hart is sore dyseasyd;	45	Balettys5	9
An hart was slayne /With hornes twayne	104	Phy Sparrow	1298
So prowde of hart, /So overthwart,	116	Ag Scottes	35
Nay. Thou art a man good inough but for thy false hart.	162	Magnyfycence	769
In trust wherof comforte his hart doth grope,	335	Garlande	832
An hart was slayne	348	Garlande	1291
With hole hart and true mynde,	371	Albany	482

HART BLODE

	Page	Title	Line
And to spende their hart blode,	371	Albany	487

HART BLOODE

	Page	Title	Line
He ragyd and rent out your hart bloode;	119	Ag Scottes	136

HARTE —HAS   Page   Title   Line

HARTE
Was chaunged to an harte:	79	Phy Sparrow	301
Your harte ys to hawte, iwys, yt wyll nat be alowde.	123	Garnesche2	26
So in his harte he may be glad of us.	145	Magnyfycence	158
For Cockys harte, gyve me thy hande.	154	Magnyfycence	512
A man may beshrowe your angry harte.	156	Magnyfycence	563
By Cockes harte, he loketh hye.	156	Magnyfycence	574
Nowe, by Cockes harte, well abyden!	156	Magnyfycence	576
Cockes harte! It is Cloked Colusyon!	157	Magnyfycence	596
For Cockys harte, tary whylyst that I come agayne.	159	Magnyfycence	685
Cockys harte! Who is yonde that for the dothe call?	162	Magnyfycence	780
By Cockys harte, and call shall agayne!	162	Magnyfycence	783
What! Is thy harte pryckyd with such a prowde pynne?	162	Magnyfycence	785
Cockes ha[r]te! I trowe thou wylte make a fray.	163	Magnyfycence	808
harte] 'hate' †Rastell & Treveris C 1530, B			
Cockes harte! Tourne the; let me se thyne aray.	167	Magnyfycence	959
Cockys harte! Thou lyest; I am no [h]ogge.	170	Magnyfycence	1083
hogge] 'dogge' †Rastell & Treveris C 1530, B			
Cockes harte! I love suche japes.	171	Magnyfycence	1133
By Cockes harte, I wene thou hast no more.	172	Magnyfycence	1146
By the harte of God, well done!	172	Magnyfycence	1156
Nay, by Cockys harte, he ne reckys;	172	Magnyfycence	1167
By Cockes harte, I trowe thou lyste.	173	Magnyfycence	1199
Alas, dere harte, loke that we be not perseyvyd!'	177	Magnyfycence	1349
For ofte tymes suche a wamblynge goth over my harte;	185	Magnyfycence	1620
Syr, nowe me thynke your harte is well eased.	189	Magnyfycence	1737
Thou sayst truthe, by the harte that God me gave!	190	Magnyfycence	1782
By Cockes harte, thou arte a fyne mery knave.	191	Magnyfycence	1826
He knewe not hymselfe, his harte was so hye;	193	Magnyfycence	1888
With harte contryte make your supplycacyon	196	Magnyfycence	1991
I bassed that baby with harte so free;	198	Magnyfycence	2069
My harte is holly on her set;	199	Magnyfycence	2073
They molefy so easely my harte that was so harde.	207	Magnyfycence	2346
Ye, but have ye repentyd you with harte contryte?	208	Magnyfycence	2391
But Parot is my owne dere harte, and my dere derling.	236	Speke Parott	208
dere] (2nd) not in Day 1560, Marshe 1568			
My harte is so sore payned,	237	Speke Parott	254
The harte, the hynde, the buck.	282	Why Come Ye	122
To banysshe pyte out of a maydens harte?	320	Garlande	308
Beninge, curteyse, of jentyll harte and mynde,	337	Garlande	880

HARTELY
That halsyd her hartely and kyst her swete.	42	Balettys1	18
How hartely he dyd it take	89	Phy Sparrow	692
Then I pray the hartely,	172	Magnyfycence	1148
That for hym to laboure he hath prayde me hartely;	186	Magnyfycence	1650
A, Lorde, so I wolde halse her hartely!	190	Magnyfycence	1801
And hartely thanke God of your adversyte;	207	Magnyfycence	2362

HARTES
That cast such overthwartes /Percase have hollow hartes.	121	Ag Scottes2	38
So many holow hartes, and so dowbyll faces;	245	Speke Parott	502
That hartes wyll ronne away,	280	Why Come Ye	54
Bothe hartes and hyndes	280	Why Come Ye	55
Your hartes sore fayntd,	359	Albany	27

HARTE SEKE
Yet I am not harte seke, but that me lyst.	185	Magnyfycence	1621

HARTIS
Fy, fy, for shame, ther hartis wer to faynt.	30	Dol Dethe	42
That makith our hartis glad,	111	Lawde	51
Where hartis belluyng, embosyd with distres,	312	Garlande	24
Whos lusty lokis make hevy hartis glad;	337	Garlande	903

HARTY
This wrytynge is welcome with harty affeccyon!	149	Magnyfycence	313
Good Hope, I pray you with harty affeccyon	208	Magnyfycence	2399

HARTYS
Whych to behold makyth hevy hartys glad;	44	Balettys3	28

HARTLES
O causeles cowardes, O hartles hardynes,	242	Speke Parott	390

HARTLY
Yet sumwhat wright supprisid with hartly lust,	33	Dol Dethe	145
hartly] 'herty' Marshe 1568			
Dyamand poyntyd to rase oute hartly care	44	Balettys3	19

HART ROTE
And his swete hart rote,	295	Why Come Ye	667
Strake one with a birdbolt to the hart rote;	351	Garlande	1380

HARTTIS
To sorowfull harttis chef comfort and solace,	34	Dol Dethe	206

HARVY
And Harvy Ha[f]ter that well coude picke a male;	50	Bowge	138
Hafter] 'Haster' †Wynkyn de Worde 1499, 1510, Marshe 1568			
Harvy Ha[f]ter came lepynge, lyghte as lynde.	52	Bowge	231
Hafter] 'Haster' †Wynkyn de Worde 1499, 1510, Marshe 1568			
Harkyn herto, ye Harvy Ha[f]tar,	133	Garnesche5	164
Haftar] 'Hastar' †MS Harley 367			
Havell and Harvy Hafter,	281	Why Come Ye	97

HARWYCHE
At Harwyche Porte, slumbrynge as I laye,	47	Bowge	34

HAS
Which to thi resemblance wonderusly has wrought	34	Dol Dethe	193

HASARDE — HATETH	Page	Title	Line

HASARDE
Have at the hasarde or at the dosen browne, ... 57 Bowge 393
HASDRUBALL
Nor lyke Duke Hasdruball .... 363 Albany 195
HASERDYNGE
At the cardys and haserdynge. .... 309 Why Come Ye 1193
HASKARDIS
'Forsothe,' quod she, 'theys be haskardis and rebawdis, ... 329 Garlande 607
   haskardis] 'hastardis' †Fakes 1523
HAST
All mankynd, whom thou ful dere hast boght, ... 34 Dol Dethe 194
Soche pelfry thou hast pachchyd, ... 128 Garnesche3 178
For thow hast a long snowte, ... 133 Garnesche5 130
Thou hast in despite, /Thou donghyll knyght? .... 136 Dundas 47
In all this hast whether wyll ye ryde? .... 156 Magnyfycence 570
Thou hast made me play the jeu dehayte. .... 156 Magnyfycence 579
What the devyll hast thou on thy fyste? An owle? ...... 166 Magnyfycence 922
Nowe thou hast done me a pleasure grete. .... 171 Magnyfycence 1131
But I have thy pultre, and thou hast my catell. ...... 171 Magnyfycence 1135
By Cockes harte, I wene thou hast no more. .... 172 Magnyfycence 1146
What hast thou on thy fyst? A [k]esteryll? .... 173 Magnyfycence 1174
   kesteryll] 'besteryll' †Rastell & Treveris C 1530, B
Than wyll I say that thou hast no pere. .... 173 Magnyfycence 1195
What hast thou founde there? By God, a lowse. .... 173 Magnyfycence 1198
Put on thy gowne agayne, for thou hast lost nowe. ...... 173 Magnyfycence 1203
   thou ... nowe] 'nowe thou hast lost' †Rastell & Treveris C 1530, B
Gyve me my grote, for thou hast lost. .... 173 Magnyfycence 1206
Nowe hast thou not a prowde mocke and a starke? .... 174 Magnyfycence 1208
Hast thou ony more? Let se, procede. .... 174 Magnyfycence 1236
Forsothe, tell on. Hast thou any mo? .... 175 Magnyfycence 1262
   mo] 'more' †Rastell & Treveris C 1530, B
What hast thou gotted, in faythe, to thy share? .... 201 Magnyfycence 2162
Thou hast bene so waywarde, so wranglyng, and so wrothsome, .. 205 Magnyfycence 2293
And so ungracyously thy dayes thou hast spent, ... 205 Magnyfycence 2295
And agayne thy maker thou hast made suche warre, ... 205 Magnyfycence 2302
She ran in all the hast /Unbrased and unlast, ... 222 El Rummynge 319
'They be wretchockes thou hast brought, ... 226 El Rummynge 465
   They] 'The' Day 1560
Thou hast to lytell myght .... 364 Albany 230
HASTARDDIS
That vilane hastarddis in ther furious tene, ... 30 Dol Dethe 24
HASTE
As longe as I lyve, thou haste an heyre parent. .... 154 Magnyfycence 507
Ye, thou haste the four quarters of a knave. .... 172 Magnyfycence 1165
HASTY
Be lyght of byleve and hasty of credence; .... 161 Magnyfycence 740
To gyve so hasty credence ye were moche to blame. .... 209 Magnyfycence 2443
To hasty of sentence, ... 278 Why Come Ye 3
Sume were to hasty and wold no man byde; .... 319 Garlande 249
HASTYVE
But if hastyve credence by mayntenance of myght .... 344 Garlande 1133
HAT
His here was growen thorowe oute his hat. .... 56 Bowge 350
He set up fresshely upon his hat alofte. .... 56 Bowge 367
And tyll I come, have, here is myne hat to plege.' .... 57 Bowge 413
   is] not in Marshe 1568
Where is my cappe? I have lost my hat! .... 169 Magnyfycence 1030
Some brought theyr husbands hat, ... 225 El Rummynge 442
Whyles the red hat doth endure, ... 286 Why Come Ye 281
The red hat with his lure .... 286 Why Come Ye 283
For drede of the red hat .... 288 Why Come Ye 383
Yet whan he toke first his hat, ... 306 Why Come Ye 1108
   first] not in MS Rawlinson C. 813
HATCHET
Some layde to pledge /Theyr hatchet and theyr wedge, ... 221 El Rummynge 294
HATE
These frantyke foolys I hate most of all; 36 Coystrowne1 2
I hate this faynynge, fye upon it, fye! .... 59 Bowge 465
I hate this wayes agayne you that they take! .... 59 Bowge 471
   this] 'these' Wynkyn de Worde 1510
I hate this blunderyng that thou doste make. .... 151 Magnyfycence 400
I am Poverte that all men doth hate. .... 195 Magnyfycence 1960
Whiche hate to be corrected .... 277 Collyn Clout 1235
Nacion moost in hate, /Proude and poore of state. ...... 362 Albany 143
HATED
They sayde they hated for to dele with Drede. .... 50 Bowge 146
HATEFULL
But hatefull absens, to me so envyous, ... 45 Balettys3 45
The panges of hatefull death .... 73 Phy Sparrow 62
For harlottes hawnte thyn hatefull cors; 131 Garnesche5 72
O hatefull happe, O carefull cruelte! .... 198 Magnyfycence 2049
HATERED
So hote hatered agaynste the Chyrche, and cheryte so colde; .. 245 Speke Parott 500
HATETH
Whome she hateth shall over the see-boorde skyp. .... 49 Bowge 112
   see-boorde] 'shyp borde' Marshe 1568

HATH —HATH | Page | Title | Line

	Page	Title	Line
Whome she hateth, she casteth in the dyche,	49	Bowge	115
hateth] 'hatch' †Wynkyn de Worde 1499, 'hateth' Wynkyn de Worde 1510, Marshe 1568			

HATH

	Page	Title	Line
Yet, for his love that all hath wrought,	36	Man Margery	25
Youre ugly tokyn /My mynd hath brokyn /From worldly lust;	39	Coystrowne3	2
I wys he hath an hevy hed,'	42	Balettys1	21
Howbei[t], he is not furst hath had a los.	43	Balettys2	38
Howbeit] 'Howbeis' †Rastell 1527.1			
By radyante hete enryped hath our corne;	46	Bowge	2
As emperes the dyademe hath worne	46	Bowge	4
Whyles she laugheth and hath luste for to playe.	49	Bowge	114
laugheth] 'laughed' †Wynkyn de Worde 1499			
So vertuously that hath his dayes spente;	50	Bowge	151
Fortune to you gyftes of grace hath lente:	50	Bowge	152
She hath gote me more money with her tayle	57	Bowge	405
Than hath some shyppe that into Bordews sayle.	57	Bowge	406
But as for that, connynge hath no foo	58	Bowge	447
Who deleth with shrewes hath nede to loke aboute!'	61	Bowge	525
Correctyon hath no place,	66	Hauke	162
Whom Gyb our cat hath slayne.	72	Phy Sparrow	27
Deth hath departed us twayne;	80	Phy Sparrow	329
The false cat hath the slayne!	80	Phy Sparrow	330
And hath a glorious tayle,	82	Phy Sparrow	440
Yet at a brayde /He hath well assayde	84	Phy Sparrow	486
By the astrology /That he hath naturally	84	Phy Sparrow	498
Troylus also hath lost	89	Phy Sparrow	714
Hath won nothing, I wene,	89	Phy Sparrow	718
Those maters that he hath pende;	92	Phy Sparrow	810
That Placebo hath sayd	93	Phy Sparrow	853
That my pen hath enbybed	93	Phy Sparrow	872
His serpentes tonge /That many one hath stonge;	94	Phy Sparrow	921
And there agayne /Envy doth complayne, /And hath disdayne;	95	Phy Sparrow	965
That hath non erthly pere?	96	Phy Sparrow	1001
And so hath ravyshed me	96	Phy Sparrow	1006
Dame Nature hath her lent	97	Phy Sparrow	1042
For thought hath lyberte,	101	Phy Sparrow	1200
And where my pen hath offendyd,	102	Phy Sparrow	1245
Experyence hath brought you in the same brake.	115	Scot Kynge	61
Your pompe and pryde hath layde a downe.	115	Scot Kynge	69
His swerde hath bathed in the Scottes blode.	115	Scot Kynge	71
Experiens hath brought you in such a brake.	119	Ag Scottes	158
Thus fortune hath tourned you, I dare well say,	119	Ag Scottes	164
Waywardly wrowght she hath in the,	130	Garnesche5	15
Hath pointyd me to rayle on the.	131	Garnesche5	88
Such tunges unhappy hath made great division	139	Ven Tongues	55
Hath brought nobil princes to extreme confusion.	139	Ven Tongues	58
Be it erly or late, welth hath a season.	140	Magnyfycence	3
But wyll hath reason so under subjeccyon,	141	Magnyfycence	19
Why, to say what he wyll, Lyberte hath leve.	141	Magnyfycence	34
Yet lyberte hath ben lockyd up and kept in the mew.	141	Magnyfycence	35
There is no excesse where measure hath his helthe.	144	Magnyfycence	140
There is no prynce but he hath nede of us thre –	145	Magnyfycence	159
As your grace full nobly hath recountyd,	145	Magnyfycence	193
I trowe good fortune hath annexyd us together,	146	Magnyfycence	198
Yet measure hath ben so longe from us absent,	146	Magnyfycence	221
I say, without largesse worshyp hath no place,	148	Magnyfycence	267
But covetyse hath blowen you so full of wynde	148	Magnyfycence	290
That colyca passyo hath gropyd you by the guttys.	148	Magnyfycence	291
Syr, thanked be God, he hath his hele.	149	Magnyfycence	315
Fansy hath cachyd in a flye net	151	Magnyfycence	403
Nay, nay. He hath chaunged his, and I have chaunged myne.	155	Magnyfycence	518
Hath Magnyfycence ony tresure?	157	Magnyfycence	620
Ye. And he hath rule of all his tresure.	158	Magnyfycence	632
For Lyberte he hath in gydyng.	158	Magnyfycence	661
Cockys armys! He hath callyd for the twyce.	162	Magnyfycence	782
For pryde hath plucked the by the nose	163	Magnyfycence	826
Whylyst he hath ought.	165	Magnyfycence	901
By my faythe, syr, the frubyssher hath my sworde.	170	Magnyfycence	1063
And I beshrowe hym that hath the worse.	171	Magnyfycence	1105
And hath so mased a wandrynge wyt?	172	Magnyfycence	1144
That wyt he wantyth when he hath moste nede.	175	Magnyfycence	1261
Foly hath a rome, I say, in every route;	177	Magnyfycence	1328
To put where he lyst, foly hath fre chace;	177	Magnyfycence	1329
Why, welth hath made many a man braynlesse.	180	Magnyfycence	1423
Full many a strong cyte and towne hath been wonne	184	Magnyfycence	1577
Remembre the good servyce that Mesure hath you done,	186	Magnyfycence	1637
That for hym to laboure he hath prayde me hartely;	186	Magnyfycence	1650
What! Hath Sadnesse begyled me so?	192	Magnyfycence	1855
Nay. Madnesse hath begyled you and many mo;	192	Magnyfycence	1856
Nowe hath he ryght nought, naked as an asse.	193	Magnyfycence	1893
And where the fader by wysdom worshyp hath wonne,	195	Magnyfycence	1934
Beholde howe Fortune o[n] hym hath frounde.	195	Magnyfycence	1947
on] 'of' †Rastell & Treveris C 1530, B			
That hath deservyd it as well as he.	195	Magnyfycence	1952
That nowe he hath loste all his felycyte;	200	Magnyfycence	2114
Ye, for nowe it hath brought the to confusyon;	200	Magnyfycence	2130
Some hath so moche lyberte of one thynge and other,	200	Magnyfycence	2141

	Page	Title	Line
She hath dyssayvyd me with her doublenesse.	201	Magnyfycence	2157
Thou arte not the fyrst hymselfe hath slayne.	206	Magnyfycence	2316
That you hath punysshed with his sharpe rod.	207	Magnyfycence	2350
That Goddes grace hath vexed you sharply	207	Magnyfycence	2352
Ye, syr, he is sory for that he hath offendyd.	208	Magnyfycence	2388
But good hope and redresse hath mendyd myne estate,	210	Magnyfycence	2462
What this man hath sayd, perceyve ye his sentence?	210	Magnyfycence	2465
Today maysterfest, tomorowe he hath no holde;	213	Magnyfycence	2549
There hath ben greate war	223	El Rummynge	358
Parrot hath a blacke beard and a fayre grene tayle.	233	Speke Parott	84
But Parrot hath no favour to Esebon;	233	Speke Parott	111
That Parrot the popagay hath pytye to beholde	235	Speke Parott	167
the] 'that' Day 1560, Marshe 1568			
Confuse distrybutyve, as Parrot hath devysed,	236	Speke Parott	198
For in this processe, Parrot nothing hath surmysed,	236	Speke Parott	200
Yf ye take well therwith /It hath in it some pyth.	248	Collyn Clout	58
take] 'talke' Kele 1545.1, Marshe 1568			
Yet swete meate hath soure sauce,	258	Collyn Clout	448
How the churche hath to mykell	260	Collyn Clout	557
That honoure hath a great fall.	262	Collyn Clout	634
That hath no dygnyte	265	Collyn Clout	734
That hath taken degre /In the unyversyte	266	Collyn Clout	792
That nede hath no lawe.	268	Collyn Clout	863
Wherfore he hath good ure	271	Collyn Clout	1001
Hath played so checkmate	271	Collyn Clout	1012
which hath to name Why Come Ye Nat to Courte?	278	Why Come Ye	I
There hath ben moche excesse:	280	Why Come Ye	70
Our mare hath cast her fole,	281	Why Come Ye	85
And, 'Mocke hath lost her sho;	281	Why Come Ye	86
The French men he hath faynted,	282	Why Come Ye	157
But Hampton Court /Hath the preemynence!	289	Why Come Ye	409
He hath in him suche fayth.	290	Why Come Ye	445
He hath dispyght and scorne	294	Why Come Ye	599
Hath nowe no tyme nor space	295	Why Come Ye	631
Hath for him dyscust	298	Why Come Ye	751
Hath made askrye /And outcry	301	Why Come Ye	870
outcry] 'doute cry' MS Rawlinson C. 813			
Hath brought in dystresse,	305	Why Come Ye	1034
in] 'muche' MS Rawlinson C. 813			
For he hath suche a bull,	306	Why Come Ye	1078
Hath promised to hele our cardinals eye.	309	Why Come Ye	1197
Bycause that he his tyme studyously hath spent	314	Garlande	60
he his tyme] 'his tyme he' MS Cotton Vitellius E.x			
Of auncient poetis, ye wote full wele, hath bene	314	Garlande	65
For, ne were onely he hath your promocyon,	314	Garlande	71
But sith he hath tastid of the sugred pocioun	314	Garlande	73
Then sum wyll say he hath but lyttil brayne,	314	Garlande	87
Who wryteth wysely hath a grete treasure.	314	Garlande	91
All be it grete parte he hath surrendred	316	Garlande	150
For if ye laude hym whome honour hath opprest,	317	Garlande	174
But whome that ye favoure, I se well, hath a name,	317	Garlande	176
Can lay any werkis that he hath compylyd,	318	Garlande	223
What he hath done, let it be brought to syght.	318	Garlande	230
Cupyde hath stryken so that she ne wolde	320	Garlande	291
Oure Englysshe rude so fresshely hath set out,	324	Garlande	422
And 'He haltith often that hath a kyby hele.'	326	Garlande	502
For of all ladyes he hath the library,	334	Garlande	780
Of all gentylwomen he hath the scruteny,	334	Garlande	782
Of honour and worshyp which hath the formar date:	336	Garlande	842
Of honour and worship it hath the formar date.	336	Garlande	849
Of honour and worship it hath the formar date.	336	Garlande	856
Of honour and worship it hath the formar date.	336	Garlande	863
Hath fresshely enbewtid with many a goodly sorte	336	Garlande	868
And hath smale lust to paint?	339	Garlande	955
Hath bene full often and yet is entendyng	344	Garlande	1131
What Skelton hath compilid and wryton in dede,	345	Garlande	1151
to reherse all by name that he hath compylyd, &c.	345	Garlande	R
Item the Popingay, that hath in commendacyoun	346	Garlande	1188
For Peter of Westminster hath shaven thy beard.	358	Couplet	2
No man hath harde /Of suche a cowarde,	365	Albany	252

HATHE

	Page	Title	Line
In sesons past who hathe harde or sene	30	Dol Dethe	22
Where hathe your dwellynge ben, er ye cam here?	53	Bowge	247
Envye hathe wasted hys lyver and his lounge;	54	Bowge	291
By lakyn, syr, it hathe cost me pence	150	Magnyfycence	338
Thryfte hathe lost her cofer kay.	155	Magnyfycence	527
Tushe! He that hathe nede, man, let hym rynne.	162	Magnyfycence	786
By my trouthe, she hathe a grete hede.	169	Magnyfycence	1048
What! He hathe ben hurte with a stabbe?	171	Magnyfycence	1124
Ye, for he hathe a full drye soule.	176	Magnyfycence	1320
'Parott hathe not dyned of all this long day;'	231	Speke Parott	23
Lyacon of Libyk and Lydy hathe cawghte hys pray;	239	Speke Parott	289
Muche money, men sey, there madly he hathe spente;	240	Speke Parott	335
Thus myche Parott hathe opynlye expreste;	242	Speke Parott	381
Tytan hathe truste up hys tressys of fyne golde;	242	Speke Parott	398
For of owur regente the regiment he hathe, ex qua vi,	244	Speke Parott	437
That hathe the strokes alone;	281	Why Come Ye	114
The French men he hathe so mated,	282	Why Come Ye	161

	Page	Title	Line
HATINGE —HAVE			
For he hathe all the sayenge /Without any renayenge.	283	Why Come Ye	192
For Dame Philargerya /Hathe so his herte in holde,	284	Why Come Ye	207
To him he hathe founde	291	Why Come Ye	501
And hathe his pasport to pas	299	Why Come Ye	803
He hathe them in derisyon,	306	Why Come Ye	1092
Hathe made himselfe abbot	306	Why Come Ye	1099
HATINGE			
Doublenes hatinge fals maters to compas,	33	Dol Dethe	150
HATRED			
Hatred by the herte so had hym wrounge	54	Bowge	292
HATTED			
Some hatted and some capped, /Rychly bewrapped,	254	Collyn Clout	311
HAUKE			
Here after foloweth the boke entytuled Ware the Hauke	61	Hauke	I
Ware the hauke!	68	Hauke	252
And thou shalte have my hauke to a botchment.	171	Magnyfycence	1113
I wolde hauke whylest my hede dyd warke,	184	Magnyfycence	1563
And hauke on hobby larkes	251	Collyn Clout	193
HAUNTYTH			
Of dyverse mo that hauntyth my scolys.	175	Magnyfycence	1264
HAUTE			
He solfyth to haute, hys trybyll is to hy;	37	Coystrownel	23
And say he wryteth to haute.	92	Phy Sparrow	812
My scole is more solem and somwhat more haute	137	Ven Tongues	24
The one of you is to proude, the other is to haute.	203	Magnyfycence	2223
The prelates ben so haute /They say, and loke so hye	248	Collyn Clout	71
To haute in excellence, /To lyght intellegence,	279	Why Come Ye	8
lyght] 'lyght of' MS Rawlinson C. 813			
Some haute and some base.	301	Why Come Ye	880
HAVE			
Where was your wit and reson ye shuld have had?	30	Dol Dethe	52
your] 'ys' †MS Royal 18 D.ii			
Ye had not ben hable to have saide hym nay.	31	Dol Dethe	70
Let double delinge in the have no place,	34	Dol Dethe	174
Now have I fownd that I have sought,	36	Man Margery	23
Now have I fownd that I have sought,	36	Man Margery	23
Hys hart is to hy to have any hap;	37	Coystrownel	12
Now have I shewyd you part of your proud mynde;	38	Coystrownel	67
For I have dyscust /We ar but dust,	39	Coystrowne3	4
I have well espyde	39	Coystrowne3	9
To whom then shall we sew /For to have rescew,	40	Coystrowne3	38
Of me and other ye may have nede.	41	Coystrowne4	14
All those by whom ye have avayle.	41	Coystrowne4	18
Of youre doregate ye have no doute.	41	Coystrowne4	26
And have forgoten your old, trew, lovyng knyght.	42	Balettys2	14
'Have in sergeaunt ferrour, myne horse behynde is bare.'	43	Balettys2	20
Remorse have I of youre most goodlyhod,	44	Balettys3	29
Abashyth me, albeit I have no nede.	44	Balettys3	35
For I have gravyd her wythin the secret wall	45	Balettys3	48
Yet have I knowen suche er this;	46	Bowge	25
That clymmeth hyer than he may fotynge have;	46	Bowge	27
But wyll have it muste paye therfore dere.	47	Bowge	53
I have to lytyll connynge to reporte.	47	Bowge	63
'Maystres,' quod I, 'I have none aquentaunce	48	Bowge	92
And this an other, I have but smale substaunce.'	48	Bowge	94
And] 'But' Marshe 1568			
Yf ye have not, in fayth, I wyll you lene	48	Bowge	96
Bone aventure have here now in your honde.	48	Bowge	98
'Alas,' quod I, 'how myghte I have her sure?'	49	Bowge	118
And I with them prayed her to have in mynde.	49	Bowge	123
Of Bowge of Court she asketh what we wold have,	49	Bowge	125
Favoure we have toughter than ony elme,	49	Bowge	129
toughter] 'tougher' Wynkyn de Worde 1510, Marshe 1568			
Deynte to have with us suche one in store,	50	Bowge	150
Loo, what it is a man to have connynge!	50	Bowge	153
For ye have me whome faythfull ye shall fynde;	50	Bowge	166
Whyles I have ought, by God, thou shalt not lacke,	50	Bowge	167
I have a favoure to you, wherof it be	52	Bowge	206
The soveraynst thynge that ony man maye have	52	Bowge	211
For, as I trowe, I have sene you in dede	53	Bowge	248
To have that connynge and wayes that ye have!	53	Bowge	261
To have that connynge and wayes that ye have!	53	Bowge	261
The favoure that ye have with my lady.	53	Bowge	270
It is your fortune for to have that grace;	53	Bowge	272
And yet unneth I can have my lyvynge;	53	Bowge	275
That is agayne you, you shall have wetynge;	54	Bowge	278
I hope here after a frende of you to have.'	54	Bowge	280
I have grete scorne and am ryghte evyll apayed.'	54	Bowge	298
By Goddis bones, but yf we have som sleyte,	54	Bowge	304
By God, I have of the now grete dyspyte;	55	Bowge	325
That I have deynte to see the cherysshed thus?	55	Bowge	338
'Nowe have at all, by Saynte Thomas of Kente!'	56	Bowge	348
Now have at all that lyeth upon the burde.	57	Bowge	391
Have at the hasarde or at the dosen browne,	57	Bowge	393
Ay, in my pouche a buckell I have founde;	57	Bowge	397
The armes of Calyce, I have no coyne nor crosse!	57	Bowge	398
To wete yf Malkyn, my lemman, have gete oughte.	57	Bowge	401

	Page	Title	Line
And tyll I come, have, here is myne hat to plege.'	57	Bowge	413
is] not in Marshe 1568			
That other loked as he wolde me have slayne.	58	Bowge	430
me have] 'have me' Wynkyn de Worde 1510			
By that lytel connynge that I have.	59	Bowge	450
But ye have crafte your selfe alwaye to save.	59	Bowge	452
I have a stoppynge oyster in my poke,	59	Bowge	477
And I am your, syr, so have I blys,	60	Bowge	495
Gyve me your honde, fare well and have good daye.'	60	Bowge	497
I have not sene suche anothers page -	60	Bowge	506
I have an errande to rounde in your ere.	60	Bowge	513
And specyally to controule /Such as have cure of soule,	62	Hauke	4
Thys boke we have devysed, /Compendyously comprysed,	62	Hauke	23
I have red theym poll by poll;	67	Hauke	211
No creature but that wolde /Have rewed upon me,	72	Phy Sparrow	42
A porta inferi, /Good Lorde, have mercy	77	Phy Sparrow	240
I wolde have yet a nest	78	Phy Sparrow	263
have] 'yet have' Wyght 1553, Kitson 1560.6, Marshe 1568			
All way to have pleasure.	81	Phy Sparrow	371
The goshauke shall have a role	85	Phy Sparrow	563
On Phillips soule have pyte!	86	Phy Sparrow	587
An epytaphe I wold have /For Phyllyppes grave.	86	Phy Sparrow	605
And though that rede have I	87	Phy Sparrow	628
Though I have enrold	90	Phy Sparrow	749
With bokes that I have red,	90	Phy Sparrow	753
For as I tofore have sayd,	90	Phy Sparrow	769
His tales I have red;	91	Phy Sparrow	789
And now men wold have amended	91	Phy Sparrow	797
If I have not well perused	92	Phy Sparrow	814
To have in remembraunce	99	Phy Sparrow	1094
have] 'heue' †Kele 1545.2			
I have not offended, I trust,	102	Phy Sparrow	1249
Because I have wrytten and sayd	103	Phy Sparrow	1253
That I Jane have named,	103	Phy Sparrow	1256
have] not in Marshe 1568			
All the wyttes they have.	103	Phy Sparrow	1273
That never have rest nor ease;	104	Phy Sparrow	1325
Than suche as have disdayned	106	Phy Sparrow	1374
That wrowght have moche care,	111	Lawde	24
Therfore ye have lost your copyholde.	114	Scot Kynge	35
Ye have determyned to make a fraye,	114	Scot Kynge	44
Ye have loste spores, cote armure and sworde.	114	Scot Kynge	49
Ye had be better to have busked to Huntley Bankes,	114	Scot Kynge	50
be] 'bet' †Fakes 1513			
We have well eased you of the bottes.	115	Scot Kynge	63
Of our Englysshe bowes ye have fette your banes.	115	Scot Kynge	65
So that now I have devysed,	117	Ag Scottes	69
And in my mynde I have comprised,	117	Ag Scottes	70
Though ye untruly your father have slayne,	118	Ag Scottes	119
Ye myght have buskyd you to Huntley Bankys;	119	Ag Scottes	149
All have ye lost and cast away.	119	Ag Scottes	163
We have well eased them of the bottes.	120	Ag Scottes	171
At Englysh bowes have fetched their banes.	120	Ag Scottes	173
Syr sumner, now ye have lost your crowne.	120	Ag Scottes	180
Cause have they none other /But for that he was brother,	120	Ag Scottes2	13
have they] 'they have' Day 1560, Marshe 1568			
brother] 'hys brother' Day 1560, Marshe 1568			
That cast such overthwartes /Percase have hollow hartes.	121	Ag Scottes2	38
Sithe ye have me chalyngyd, Master Garnesche,	121	Garnesche1	1
But sey me now, Syr Satrapas, what autoryte ye have	121	Garnesche1	6
What, have ye kythyd yow a knyght, Syr Dugles the dowty,	121	Garnesche1	8
But sey me yet, Syr Satropas, what auctoryte ye have	122	Garnesche1	13
But sey me yet, Syr Satrapas, wat auctoryte ye have	122	Garnesche1	20
But sey me yet, Syr Satrapas, what auctoryte ye have	122	Garnesche1	27
But sey me yet, Syr Satrapas, what auctoryte ye have	122	Garnesche1	34
As wytles as a wylde goos, ye have but small remorrs	123	Garnesche2	18
I have your lewde letter receyvyd,	124	Garnesche3	1
And well I have yt perseyved,	124	Garnesche3	2
And your skrybe I have aspyed,	124	Garnesche3	3
Ye have knavyche condycyonns.	124	Garnesche3	12
Ye wolde have bassyd hyr bumme,	125	Garnesche3	62
So that sche wolde have kum	125	Garnesche3	63
Ye xulde have kowththyd me a fole.	127	Garnesche3	119
Withowte ye have a confectioun	128	Garnesche3	152
Wher thou xulddst have bene shrynyd;	128	Garnesche3	175
I have receyvyd your secunde ryme.	129	Garnesche5	2
Ye have nat red the properte	129	Garnesche5	8
Thow wolde have scoryd hys habarion;	130	Garnesche5	34
Ye wolde have trysyd hys trowle away.	130	Garnesche5	36
Ye have a fantasy to Fanchyrche strete,	130	Garnesche5	41
The dignite lawreat for to have.	132	Garnesche5	115
I have red, and rede I xall,	133	Garnesche5	158
Inordynate pride wyll have a falle.	133	Garnesche5	159
He rymes and railes /That Englishmen have tailes.	135	Dundas	10
With thy versyfyeng rayles /How they have tayles.	135	Dundas	31
For, as I have rede in volumes olde,	137	Ven Tongues	5
Malicious tunges, though they have no bones,	138	Ven Tongues	49
He might be sure to have shame ynough.	139	Ven Tongues	78

	Page	Title	Line
HAVE —HAVE			
For, when men by welth, they have lytell drede	140	Magnyfycence	10
A man may have welth, but not as he wolde, ...	141	Magnyfycence	14
Syr, as ye say. I have harde of your fame.	141	Magnyfycence	26
Fyrst, I say, we owght to have in consyderacyon	141	Magnyfycence	43
And you have not your owne fre lyberte	142	Magnyfycence	78
Why, have you harde of our dysputacyon?	142	Magnyfycence	82
Syr, yf any worde have past	143	Magnyfycence	92
Whych provyth well that measure shold have domynyon.	143	Magnyfycence	120
Measure is worthy to have domynyon.	144	Magnyfycence	127
But have ye not herde say that wyll is no skyll?	144	Magnyfycence	148
Where as ye have, syr, to me them assygned, ...	145	Magnyfycence	177
In whose attemperaunce I have suche delyght, ...	145	Magnyfycence	189
Then shall you have with you prosperyte resydent.	146	Magnyfycence	197
Nowe that ye have me chefe ruler assyngned, ...	146	Magnyfycence	202
Have deputyd Measure hym to gyde?	147	Magnyfycence	243
Me semeth that ye have dronken more than ye have bled.	147	Magnyfycence	260
Me semeth that ye have dronken more than ye have bled.	147	Magnyfycence	260
Why have ye hym named and all other refused?	148	Magnyfycence	281
Have ye not welthe here at your wyll?	148	Magnyfycence	284
With care and with thought howe Jacke shall have Gyl?	148	Magnyfycence	287
What! I have aspyed ye are a carles page.	148	Magnyfycence	288
In fayth, broder Largesse, you have a mery mynde.	148	Magnyfycence	292
But ofte tymes have I sene wyse men do mad dedys.	148	Magnyfycence	302
Syr, yf I have offended your noble estate, ...	149	Magnyfycence	308
I trow I have brought you suche wrytynge of recorde, ...	149	Magnyfycence	309
That I shall have you agayne my good lorde.	149	Magnyfycence	310
And wolde have made me Freer Tucke, ...	150	Magnyfycence	357
They have made me here to put the stone;	151	Magnyfycence	406
By crede, it wolde have fresshe aray, ...	153	Magnyfycence	460
To counterfet this freers have lerned me.	154	Magnyfycence	487
Yes, yes, syr. He and I have met.	154	Magnyfycence	498
We have bene togyder bothe erly and late.	154	Magnyfycence	499
But Fansy, my frende, where have ye bene so longe?	154	Magnyfycence	500
By God, I have bene about a praty pronge -	154	Magnyfycence	501
By God, we have made Magnyfycence to ete a flye.	154	Magnyfycence	503
Yet have we pycked out a rome for the.	154	Magnyfycence	508
Nay, nay. He hath chaunged his, and I have chaunged myne. . . .	155	Magnyfycence	518
Thy wordes be but wynde, never they have no wayght.	156	Magnyfycence	578
And yf ye knewe howe I have mused, ...	156	Magnyfycence	580
I am sure ye wolde have me excused.	156	Magnyfycence	581
And there they wolde ha[v]e me to dwell.	157	Magnyfycence	614
have] 'hane' †Rastell & Treveris C 1530, B			
And have you not amonge you Lyberte?	157	Magnyfycence	625
And counterfeted our names we have	158	Magnyfycence	641
Counterfet Countenaunce to have also, ...	158	Magnyfycence	645
But shall I have myne olde name styll?	158	Magnyfycence	647
Pease! I have not yet sayd what I wyll.	158	Magnyfycence	648
So that we have no lyberte;	158	Magnyfycence	659
When we have hym thyder convayed, ...	159	Magnyfycence	676
That he shall have you in the stede of sadnesse, ...	159	Magnyfycence	680
But, syr, I wyll have this man with me.	163	Magnyfycence	815
This ladyes have, /I it them gave.	165	Magnyfycence	889
He wyll have wrought	165	Magnyfycence	902
What! Whom have we here, Jenkyn Joly?	166	Magnyfycence	918
I have not kept her yet thre wokys, ...	168	Magnyfycence	1002
I have a thynge for to say, ...	168	Magnyfycence	1017
Where is my cappe? I have lost my hat!	169	Magnyfycence	1030
I wyll not have it so, I wyll have it this.	169	Magnyfycence	1042
I wyll not have it so, I wyll have it this.	169	Magnyfycence	1042
Let me have thy dogge, what soever I pay.	171	Magnyfycence	1101
Thou shalte have my purse, and I wyll have thyne.	171	Magnyfycence	1102
Thou shalte have my purse, and I wyll have thyne.	171	Magnyfycence	1102
Torde, I say! What have I do?	171	Magnyfycence	1106
And thou shalte have my hauke to a botchment.	171	Magnyfycence	1113
But I have thy pultre, and thou hast my catell.	171	Magnyfycence	1135
Ye. But thryfte and we have made a batell.	171	Magnyfycence	1136
A, holde thy peas! I have the tothe ake.	172	Magnyfycence	1163
The tothe ake! Lo, a torde ye have.	172	Magnyfycence	1164
What? Wolde ye have mo folys, and are so many?	172	Magnyfycence	1170
Thou must have thy fansy and thy wyll, ...	173	Magnyfycence	1183
I have another maner of sorte	174	Magnyfycence	1238
Thynke I not so, quod he. Ellys have I shame, ...	175	Magnyfycence	1254
But, I say, let se and yf thou have any more.	175	Magnyfycence	1278
I have an hole armory of suche haburdashe in store;	175	Magnyfycence	1279
With qui fuit brayne seke I have them brought;	176	Magnyfycence	1302
Why, shall I not have Foly with me also?	176	Magnyfycence	1306
God have mercy, good godfather.	176	Magnyfycence	1312
And shall we have lyberte to do what we wyll?	176	Magnyfycence	1316
I have an hoby can make larkys to dare;	177	Magnyfycence	1342
By convayaunce crafty I have brought	178	Magnyfycence	1372
For all hokes unhappy to me have resorte.	178	Magnyfycence	1374
Mayster Survayour, where have ye ben so longe?	178	Magnyfycence	1382
Ye have eten sauce I trowe, at the Taylers Hall.	179	Magnyfycence	1404
Have welth at our gydynge to rule as we lyst?	179	Magnyfycence	1415
I say that I wyll ye have hym in gydynge.	180	Magnyfycence	1436
Nay, fyrst Lusty Pleasure is my desyre to have;	180	Magnyfycence	1453
I have welth at wyll, largesse and lyberte.	181	Magnyfycence	1458
I have wynde and wether over all to sayle;	181	Magnyfycence	1464

HAVE —HAVE	Page	Title	Line
For in my favour I have you feffyd and seasyd.	183	Magnyfycence	1536
A, I have spyed ye can moche broken sorowe.	184	Magnyfycence	1587
With, 'Cockes armes! Rest shal I none have	185	Magnyfycence	1615
For myrth I have hym coryed, beten, and blyst,	185	Magnyfycence	1622
I may say to you I have but small devocyon.	186	Magnyfycence	1640
For of your grace I have it nought deserved.	186	Magnyfycence	1644
To shewe you my mynde I wolde have the lesse fere.	186	Magnyfycence	1646
I wyll have hym rehayted and dyspysed.	186	Magnyfycence	1658
That he knowe not but that I have supplyed	187	Magnyfycence	1663
But for all that he is lyke to have a glent.	187	Magnyfycence	1668
And he go to the devyll, so that I may have my fee,	187	Magnyfycence	1670
Whylest I have hym, I nede nothynge doute.	187	Magnyfycence	1692
By the masse, I have done that I can,	187	Magnyfycence	1693
Syr, God rewarde you as ye have deserved.	188	Magnyfycence	1701
Syr, I beseche you let pety have some place	188	Magnyfycence	1712
Have hym hens, I say, out of my syght!	188	Magnyfycence	1723
With Mesure. Where as all noblenes is, there I have past:	189	Magnyfycence	1749
Let me have the rule of your purse.	189	Magnyfycence	1762
I have taken it to Largesse and Lyberte.	189	Magnyfycence	1763
For the[m] shall you have at lyberte to lowte.	190	Magnyfycence	1779
them] 'then' †Rastell & Treveris C 1530, B			
Let them have all, and the other go without;	190	Magnyfycence	1780
Thus joy without mesure you shall have.	190	Magnyfycence	1781
I have set my hole felycyte,	190	Magnyfycence	1788
Syr, syth that in me ye have suche devocyon,	190	Magnyfycence	1790
By our lakyn, syr, I have ben a hawkyng for the wylde swan.	191	Magnyfycence	1806
I make God avowe ye wyll none other men have.	191	Magnyfycence	1827
The feldfare wolde have fydled, and it wolde not frame;	192	Magnyfycence	1838
Take hede of your selfe, for nowe ye have nede.	192	Magnyfycence	1854
Gone? Alasse, ye have undone me!	192	Magnyfycence	1858
Why, is this the largesse that I have usyd?	193	Magnyfycence	1865
Nay. It was your fondnesse that ye have usyd.	193	Magnyfycence	1866
Why, who wolde have thought in you suche gyle?	193	Magnyfycence	1869
And now without measure he shal have hunger and colde.	193	Magnyfycence	1895
Of sorowfull servauntes I have many scores:	194	Magnyfycence	1900
But nowe a dayes to stryke I have grete cause,	194	Magnyfycence	1918
And suffre theyr chyldren to have theyr entent,	194	Magnyfycence	1921
Theyr chyldren, bycause that they have no mekenesse,	194	Magnyfycence	1924
Of correccyon, but let them have theyr wyll.	194	Magnyfycence	1930
That rule not be mesure that they have in theyr handys,	195	Magnyfycence	1939
Alasse, I have the cyatyca full evyll in my hyppe!	195	Magnyfycence	1956
Full fewe but they have envy of me.	195	Magnyfycence	1963
Syr, all this wolde have bene thought on before.	196	Magnyfycence	1970
I wenyd ones never to have knowen of care.	196	Magnyfycence	1973
And ye have deserved this punysshment.	196	Magnyfycence	2003
Where you were wonte to have cawdels for your hede,	197	Magnyfycence	2008
I may no more speke tyll I have wept my fyll.	198	Magnyfycence	2063
Of erthely thynge I have no care nor charge.	199	Magnyfycence	2081
Largely rewardynge them that have deservyd;	200	Magnyfycence	2119
In youth to be wanton, and let them have theyr wyll -	200	Magnyfycence	2137
Some have so moche lyberte that they fere no synne,	200	Magnyfycence	2143
I waraunt you I have gyven it a lasshe.	201	Magnyfycence	2165
By my trouthe, we have ryfled hym metely well.	201	Magnyfycence	2170
Nowe I rede the beware. I have warned the twyse.	202	Magnyfycence	2185
A, shall we have more of this maters yet?	203	Magnyfycence	2214
And ye be a gentylman, ye have knavys condycyons.	203	Magnyfycence	2219
Magnyfycence I was, whom ye have brought to shame.	204	Magnyfycence	2241
Thus to rebuke me and have me in dyspyght!	205	Magnyfycence	2278
Alasse! To lyve longer I have no delyght;	205	Magnyfycence	2281
Nay, nay, man. I loke never to have parte of his grace;	205	Magnyfycence	2297
For I have so ungracyously my lyfe mysusyd,	205	Magnyfycence	2298
That thou canst not have never mercy in his syght.	205	Magnyfycence	2303
Ye, have done at ones without delay.	206	Magnyfycence	2319
And nowe ye have had, syr, a wonderous fall,	207	Magnyfycence	2375
Ye, but have ye repentyd you with harte contryte?	208	Magnyfycence	2391
Syr, the repentaunce I have no man can wryte.	208	Magnyfycence	2392
And have you banyshed from you all dyspare?	208	Magnyfycence	2393
Ye, holly to good hope I have made my repare.	208	Magnyfycence	2394
Sothely to repent me I have grete cause;	209	Magnyfycence	2434
Ye, syr, with adversyte I have bene vexyd;	210	Magnyfycence	2461
And sad cyrcumspeccyon to me they have annexyd.	210	Magnyfycence	2463
And ye shall have more worshyp then ever ye had.	210	Magnyfycence	2474
Measure of your lustys must have the oversyght,	211	Magnyfycence	2491
Of that I have mysdone to make a redresse,	212	Magnyfycence	2508
This mater we have movyd, you myrthys to make,	213	Magnyfycence	2552
And ye that have harde thys dysporte and game,	214	Magnyfycence	2571
A man wolde have pytty	215	El Rummynge	39
To have of her tunnynge.	217	El Rummynge	130
Some have no herelace,	218	El Rummynge	145
Some have no mony /That thyder commy,	218	El Rummynge	160
With, 'Hey, dogge, hay, /Have these hogges away!'	218	El Rummynge	169
hogges] 'dogges' Day 1560, Marshe 1568			
They have dronke up my swyllyng tubbe!'	218	El Rummynge	173
And I have found it trew.	219	El Rummynge	210
And have here a pecke of ry.'	221	El Rummynge	275
I have as swete a breth	223	El Rummynge	345
And have here a pylche of graye;	224	El Rummynge	398
Ones hed wold have aked /To se her naked.	226	El Rummynge	478

HAVE — HAVE

Entry	Page	Title	Line
For we have egges and butter,	228	El Rummynge	536
'Have here is for me, /A clout of London pynnes.'	228	El Rummynge	563
'I have no penny nor grote	229	El Rummynge	600
I have wrytten so mytche	230	El Rummynge	619
Then Parot moste have an almon or a date.	231	Speke Parott	7
Hop Lobyn of Lowdeon wald have e byt of bred;	232	Speke Parott	72
I pray you, let Parot have lyberte to speke.	233	Speke Parott	98
Let Parrot, I pray you, have lyberte to prate,	234	Speke Parott	141
But our Grekis theyr Greke so well have applyed,	234	Speke Parott	145
I pray you, lett Parrot have lyberte to speke.	236	Speke Parott	210
We have longyd and lokyd long tyme for that,	239	Speke Parott	310
Whyche cawsythe pore suters have many a hongry mele;	239	Speke Parott	311
Of on and hothyr at me that have dysdayne.	242	Speke Parott	385
Speke, Parotte, my swete byrde, and ye shall have a date,	243	Speke Parott	416
Now, Galathea, lett Parrot, I pray you, have hys date –	244	Speke Parott	439
They gaspe and they gape /All to have promocyon:	248	Collyn Clout	86
Men say they have prescrypcyons	249	Collyn Clout	112
And have full lytell care	250	Collyn Clout	130
But the greatest parte /Is for they have but small arte	250	Collyn Clout	139
For drede to have a checke.	250	Collyn Clout	165
Theyr lessons forgoten they have	251	Collyn Clout	169
In this that I have pende.	251	Collyn Clout	187
What have laye men to do	251	Collyn Clout	196
But whan they have ones caught	252	Collyn Clout	229
You shall have your wylla!'	253	Collyn Clout	261
They have none instructyon	253	Collyn Clout	268
Ye make monkes to have the colerage	255	Collyn Clout	363
make] 'haue' Kele 1545.1, Marshe 1568, 'make' MS Harley 2252; colerage] 'culerage' Kele 1545.1, 'colerage' Harley 2252			
Ye have so overthwarted,	256	Collyn Clout	371
And all that they have elles.	257	Collyn Clout	411
Have lost theyr bedde roules;	257	Collyn Clout	422
bedde] 'beade' Kele 1545.1, 'bede' MS Harley 2252			
Shall have penalte /For your iniquite.	258	Collyn Clout	461
And let Collyn Clout have none	258	Collyn Clout	478
have none] 'alone' MS Lansdowne 762, 'alon' MS Harley 2252			
And some have a smacke /Of Luthers sacke,	260	Collyn Clout	540
And they have to lytell,	260	Collyn Clout	558
But they have enterprysed /And shamfully surmysed	261	Collyn Clout	581
And yf ye may have layser,	261	Collyn Clout	605
ye] 'you' Kele 1545.1, Marshe 1568, 'ye' MS Harley 2252			
But noble men borne, /To lerne they have scorne,	262	Collyn Clout	620
And have no grace to thynke	262	Collyn Clout	648
Many one ye have untwynde	263	Collyn Clout	662
ye have untwynde] 'have but wynde' †Godfray 1531, Kele 1545.1, Marshe 1568			
And have suche a tryppe,	263	Collyn Clout	667
And have aures patentes	263	Collyn Clout	675
And have theyr lyberte,	264	Collyn Clout	712
And for to have his fees,	267	Collyn Clout	839
Howe they have no fraude.	267	Collyn Clout	853
fraude] 'faude' †Godfray 1531, 'fawte' MS Harley 2252			
For bysshoppes have protections,	268	Collyn Clout	891
But they have no affections	268	Collyn Clout	893
affections] 'afflictions' Kele 1545.1, 'affeccions' Harley 2252			
For they wyll have no losse	269	Collyn Clout	928
That they have great wonder	271	Collyn Clout	1006
Have no cause to say	273	Collyn Clout	1093
have] 'hath' †Godfray 1531, 'have' MS Harley 2252			
For no man have I named.	274	Collyn Clout	1111
And lytell grace they have	274	Collyn Clout	1131
Nor wyll have no resytynge	274	Collyn Clout	1135
To do shame, they have no shame;	275	Collyn Clout	1141
They have an evyll name,	275	Collyn Clout	1143
Have hym thyder by and by!	275	Collyn Clout	1172
Than wyll age have a corage	279	Why Come Ye	38
Farewell, than, have good day!	280	Why Come Ye	57
Than have good daye. Adewe!	280	Why Come Ye	58
For we have spente our shot!	282	Why Come Ye	127
We shall have a tot quot	282	Why Come Ye	128
We have cast up our war,	282	Why Come Ye	140
They have layde all in the myre.	285	Why Come Ye	251
He sayth they have no brayne	286	Why Come Ye	310
They have slain our Englisshmen	288	Why Come Ye	372
The kynges courte /Shulde have the excellence;	289	Why Come Ye	407
Than, 'Have him to the Towre /Saunz aulter remedy!	289	Why Come Ye	429
Have hym forthe by and by /To the Marshalsy,	289	Why Come Ye	431
Men wolde have the lesse scorne	291	Why Come Ye	496
But have ye nat harde this,	292	Why Come Ye	532
A kynge, as I have tolde,	293	Why Come Ye	563
He wolde have ben ryght fayne	295	Why Come Ye	642
To have been a chapleyne,	295	Why Come Ye	643
And have taken ryght gret payne	295	Why Come Ye	644
I have no pen nor inke	296	Why Come Ye	684
They have the full intellygence,	297	Why Come Ye	710
I have told you part, but nat all.	299	Why Come Ye	822
That men shall scantly /Have peny or halpeny.	303	Why Come Ye	968

HAVELL —HAVELL						Page		Title		Line

	Page	Title	Line
Non can have protectyon	304	Why Come Ye	1011
Non can have] 'They can have no' †Kele 1545.3, Toy 1553, Kitson 1560.7, Marshe 1568			
Shall never have good helth;	304	Why Come Ye	1025
Bycause they have proclamed	305	Why Come Ye	1055
That in my courte Skelton shulde have a place,	313	Garlande	59
Wherin this answere for hym we have comprisid,	314	Garlande	80
Or wherto shulde he have the prerogatyve,	315	Garlande	117
the] 'that' MS Cotton Vitellius E.x			
Wherby he myght have a name inmortall?	315	Garlande	119
Frome that I have sayde in no poynt doth vary,	316	Garlande	163
'A thanke to have, ye have well deservyd,	317	Garlande	169
'A thanke to have, ye have well deservyd,	317	Garlande	169
But a grete parte yet ye have reservyd	317	Garlande	171
But...yet] 'Bot yit a grete parte' MS Cotton Vitellius E.x			
Some have a name for thefte and brybery;	317	Garlande	183
Some carefull cokwoldes, some have theyr wyves curs;	317	Garlande	186
Theis people by me have none assignement,	317	Garlande	195
Of them that have vertue by reason of cunnyng,	317	Garlande	198
And suche of my servauntes as I have promotyd,	318	Garlande	202
'To make repugnaunce agayne that ye have sayde,	318	Garlande	211
Withoute deservynge shulde have the best game.	318	Garlande	221
What poetis we have at our retenewe.	319	Garlande	238
With hevynge and shovynge, 'have in' and 'have oute';	319	Garlande	251
With hevynge and shovynge, 'have in' and 'have oute';	319	Garlande	251
'Nay, holde thy tunge,' quod another, 'let me have the name.'	319	Garlande	255
Concente to Phebus to have his herte in holde,	320	Garlande	292
Yet loke on me, that lovyd you have so longe,	320	Garlande	298
Yet have compassyon upon my paynes stronge.'	320	Garlande	299
Why have the goddes shewyd me this cruelte,	321	Garlande	309
O fatall Fortune, what have I offendid?	321	Garlande	316
But sith I have lost now that I entended,	321	Garlande	318
So have ye done, that meretoryously	323	Garlande	401
Ye have deservyd to have an enplement	323	Garlande	402
Ye have deservyd to have an enplement	323	Garlande	402
'Maister Gower, I have nothyng deserved	323	Garlande	407
To have so laudabyle a commendacion:	323	Garlande	408
'So have ye me far passynge my meretis extollyd,	324	Garlande	435
Bownte, and so gloryously ye have enrollyd	324	Garlande	437
And then she sayd, 'Whylis we have tyme and space	328	Garlande	563
For ydle jangelers have but lytill braine;	328	Garlande	566
That of your bounte so well have me assurid;	332	Garlande	729
'I have contryvyd for you a goodly warke,	334	Garlande	774
I have devysyd for Skelton, my clerke;	334	Garlande	777
For to his servyce I have suche regarde,	334	Garlande	778
In you he wolde have set his hole delight.	336	Garlande	874
Whom fortune and fate playnly have discust	337	Garlande	881
Wherfore delyght /I have to whryght.	339	Garlande	946
That ye have now by the preemynence	344	Garlande	1125
by the] 'thorow' MS Cotton Vitellius E.x			
We wyll understande how ye have it deservyd.'	344	Garlande	1127
It wolde have made a man hole that had be ryght sekely,	345	Garlande	1162
To fayre maistres Anne that shuld have be sent,	347	Garlande	1241
All the wittis they have.	348	Garlande	1266
That never have rest nor ease;	349	Garlande	1318
Then such that have disdaynyd	350	Garlande	1367
that] 'as' †Fakes 1523			
But who may have a more ungracyous lyfe	352	Garlande	1451
a] not in Marshe 1568			
Whiche, if they be happy, have cause to beware	353	Garlande	1474
Ye shall have nede /You for to spede	355	Garlande	1554
Ye] 'You' Marshe 1568			
But curteisly /That I have pende /For to deffend,	356	Garlande	1570
Thus ye have compast	361	Albany	102
Ye have in feates of warre.	364	Albany	225
What have ye, villayn, forged, /And virulently dysgorged	367	Albany	320
That ye shall have no grace	371	Albany	504
Ye shall have shame and sorowe.	371	Albany	507
whan they have delectably lycked a lytell	373	Replycacion	I
and whan they have ones superciliusly caught	374	Replycacion	I
and have waded but weakly in his thre maner of clerkly workes,	374	Replycacion	I
That leudly have their tyme spent,	375	Replycacion	24
For shamefully ye have wrought,	376	Replycacion	57
And to shame your selfe have brought.	376	Replycacion	58
And wolde have her defamed,	376	Replycacion	60
Employed whiche myght have be	378	Replycacion	149
Men have you in suspicion	379	Replycacion	182
Howe ye have small contrycion	379	Replycacion	183
Of that ye have myswrought;	379	Replycacion	184
To places where ye have preched,	379	Replycacion	203
For ye have enduced a secte	380	Replycacion	236
Bycause ye have eaten a flye,	380	Replycacion	244
Have made you eate the fly,	381	Replycacion	252
Ye have reed them, I suppose,	381	Replycacion	276
If ye have reed de hyperdulia,	382	Replycacion	287
Why have ye than disdayne /At poetes, and complayne	384	Replycacion	351

HAVELL

	Page	Title	Line
Havell and Harvy Hafter,	281	Why Come Ye	97

	Page	Title	Line
With, 'Stowpe, thou havell! /Rynne thou javell!	294	Why Come Ye	607

HAVEN

	Page	Title	Line
Come saylynge forth into that haven brood,	47	Bowge	37

HAVYN

	Page	Title	Line
At Orwelle hyr havyn your anggre was laules.	122	Garnesche1	33

HAWE

	Page	Title	Line
For totum in toto is not worth an hawe –	199	Magnyfycence	2089
So myche presonment, for matyrs not worth a hawe;	245	Speke Parott	478

HAWKE

	Page	Title	Line
PROLOGUS SKELTONIDIS LAUREATI SUPER WARE THE HAWKE	61	Hauke	R
To hawke, or els to hunt /From the auter to the funt,	62	Hauke	9
To hawke in my church of Dys.	62	Hauke	42
He made his hawke to fly,	63	Hauke	47
His hawke shulde pray and fede /Upon a pigeons maw.	63	Hauke	56
The hawke tyryd on a *bonne,	63	Hauke	60
*bonne] 'bone' Scattergood			
His seconde hawke wexyd gery	63	Hauke	66
The hawke had no lyst /To come to his fyst;	64	Hauke	83
The hawke with that clap /Fell downe with evyll hap.	64	Hauke	89
In my church hawke styll.	64	Hauke	99
His hawke then flew uppon /The rode, with Mary and Johnn.	65	Hauke	126
[Y]e develysh dogmatista, /Your hawke on your fista,	69	Hauke	256
Ye] 'The' †Lant 1545, Kynge & Marche 1554, Day 1560, Marshe 1568			
To hawke when [you] lista	69	Hauke	257
you] 'your' editions			
Domine concupisti, /With thy hawke on thy fysty?	69	Hauke	260
Doctor Dawcocke? /Ware the hawke!	69	Hauke	266
Domine Dawcocke? /Ware the hawke!	69	Hauke	276
Doctor Dawcocke? /Ware the hawke!	69	Hauke	285
Ware] 'Whare' †Lant 1545			
Ye made your hawke to cum /Desuper candelabrum	69	Hauke	288
Domine Dawcoke? /Ware the hawke!	70	Hauke	296
Doctor Dawcock! /Ware the hawke!	70	Hauke	306
Domine Dawkock? /Ware the hawke!	70	Hauke	319
Ware] 'Whare' †Lant 1545			
Doctor Dawcocke? /Ware the hawke!	70	Hauke	330
Torde! Man, it is an hawke of the towre.	166	Magnyfycence	925
It is best I fede my hawke now.	167	Magnyfycence	968
My hawke is rammysshe, and it happed that she ran –	191	Magnyfycence	1807
Jentill as fawcoun /Or hawke of the towre;	340	Garlande	1007
Jentyll as fawcoun /Or hawke of the towre.	341	Garlande	1022
Jentyll as fawcoun /Or hawke of the towre.	341	Garlande	1037

HAWKED

	Page	Title	Line
He hawked on thys facyon,	64	Hauke	101

HAWKES

	Page	Title	Line
My hawkes to mattens rynge!'	65	Hauke	124

HAWKETH

	Page	Title	Line
He hawketh, me thynke, for a butterflye.	156	Magnyfycence	575

HAWKYNG

	Page	Title	Line
By our lakyn, syr, I have ben a hawkyng for the wylde swan.	191	Magnyfycence	1806

HAWKYS

	Page	Title	Line
That preest that hawkys so,	62	Hauke	15
Thus to ryng a peale /Wyth his hawkys bels?	65	Hauke	137
For to let their hawkys fly	67	Hauke	218
To use youre hawkys forica /In propitiatorio,	69	Hauke	271
To let theyr hawkys fly	70	Hauke	301
Howkyd as an hawkys beke, lyke Syr Topyas.	122	Garnesche1	40

HAWNTE

	Page	Title	Line
For harlottes hawnte thyn hatefull cors;	131	Garnesche5	72

HAWTE

	Page	Title	Line
He loked hawte; he sette eche man at noughte;	54	Bowge	284
hawte] 'hawtie' Marshe 1568			
Your harte ys to hawte, iwys, yt wyll nat be alowde.	123	Garnesche2	26
But that the horson is prowde and hawte.	163	Magnyfycence	824

HAWTLY

	Page	Title	Line
She loked hawtly, and gave on me a glum.	344	Garlande	1117

HE

	Page	Title	Line
He calde upon them, as menyall houshold men:	30	Dol Dethe	33
He was ther bulwarke, ther paves and ther wall,	30	Dol Dethe	48
He was your chyfteyne, your shelde, your chef defens,	30	Dol Dethe	57
And lyke marciall Hector he faught them agayne	31	Dol Dethe	88
He was envyronde aboute on every syde	32	Dol Dethe	99
Yet whils he stode he gave them woundes wyde.	32	Dol Dethe	101
Yet] 'Ye' Marshe 1568			
Yet whils he stode he gave them woundes wyde.	32	Dol Dethe	101
Yet] 'Ye' Marshe 1568			
His corage manly, yet ther he shed his bloode.	32	Dol Dethe	103
All left alone, alas, he fawte in vayne!	32	Dol Dethe	104
For cruell[y] amonge them ther he was slayne.	32	Dol Dethe	105
cruelly] 'cruell' †MS Royal 18 D.ii, Marshe 1568			
What man, remembring how shamfully he was slayn,	32	Dol Dethe	111
Wheron he gat his fynall dedely wounde.	32	Dol Dethe	119
Whiche whils he lyvyd had fuyson of every thing,	32	Dol Dethe	131
Paregall to dukis, withe kingis he myght compare,	33	Dol Dethe	134
Sourmountinge in honour all erlis he did excede;	33	Dol Dethe	135
Treytory and treson he bannesht ought of sight.	33	Dol Dethe	151
Whom he as lorde worsheply manteynd,	34	Dol Dethe	186

HE —HE

	Page	Title	Line
He to vouchesaf, by thy mediacioun,	35	Dol Dethe	209
When he is well, yet can he not rest.	36	Coystrowne1	7
When he is well, yet can he not rest.	36	Coystrowne1	7
But for in his gamut carp that he can,	37	Coystrowne1	13
Curyowsly he can both counter and knak	37	Coystrowne1	17
To ask wher he fyndyth among hys monacordys	37	Coystrowne1	20
He can not fynd it in rule nor in space:	37	Coystrowne1	22
He solfyth to haute, hys trybyll is to hy;	37	Coystrowne1	23
He braggyth of hys byrth, that borne was full bace;	37	Coystrowne1	24
He trymmyth in hys tenor to counter pyrdewy;	37	Coystrowne1	26
He lumbryth on a lewde lewte, 'Roty bully joyse',	37	Coystrowne1	29
He fumblyth in hys fyngeryng an ugly good noyse;	37	Coystrowne1	31
He wold be made moch of and he wyst how;	37	Coystrowne1	33
He wold be made moch of and he wyst how;	37	Coystrowne1	33
Comely he clappyth a payre of clavycordys;	37	Coystrowne1	36
He whystelyth so swetely he makyth me to swete;	37	Coystrowne1	37
He whystelyth so swetely he makyth me to swete;	37	Coystrowne1	37
He counteth in his countenaunce to checke with the best:	37	Coystrowne1	44
In a dysh dare he rush at the rypest;	37	Coystrowne1	46
He fyndeth a proporcyon in his prycke songe	38	Coystrowne1	48
Nay, jape not with hym, he is no small fole;	38	Coystrowne1	50
He techyth them so wysely to solf and to fayne	38	Coystrowne1	53
Let me', quod he, 'ly in your lap.'	41	Balettys1	2
That of hys love he toke no kepe,	41	Balettys1	7
That he wyst never where he was;	42	Balettys1	10
That he wyst never where he was;	42	Balettys1	10
He had forgoten all dedely syn.	42	Balettys1	11
He wantyd wyt her love to wyn:	42	Balettys1	12
He trusted her payment and lost all hys pray.	42	Balettys1	13
I wys he hath an hevy hed,'	42	Balettys1	21
He rydyth well the horse, but he rydyth better the mare.	43	Balettys2	21
He rydyth well the horse, but he rydyth better the mare.	43	Balettys2	21
And so with your servantys he fersly doth fyght.	43	Balettys2	28
So fersly he fytyth, hys mynde is so fell,	43	Balettys2	29
That he dryvyth them doune with dyntys on ther day-wach.	43	Balettys2	30
He bresyth theyr braynpannys and makyth them to swell,	43	Balettys2	31
Howbei[t], he is not furst hath had a los.	43	Balettys2	38
Howbeit] 'Howbeis' †Rastell 1527.1			
And not to wrythe, for he so wyll atteyne,	46	Bowge	22
wrythe] 'wryte' Wynkyn de Worde 1510, Marshe 1568			
But of reproche surely he maye not mys	46	Bowge	26
That clymmeth hyer than he may fotynge have;	46	Bowge	27
What and he slyde downe, who shall hym save?	46	Bowge	28
'Maysters', he sayde, 'the shyp that ye here see,	47	Bowge	48
Who spareth to speke, in fayth, he spareth to spede.'	48	Bowge	91
But, an he can Bone aventure take,	48	Bowge	102
an] 'and' Wynkyn de Worde 1510, Marshe 1568			
But, as me thoughte, he ware on hym a cloke	51	Bowge	177
Me thoughte, of wordes that he had full a poke;	51	Bowge	179
He sayth he can not well accorde with the.'	51	Bowge	185
He sayth he can not well accorde with the.'	51	Bowge	185
'Ye, soo,' quod Suspecte, 'he maye us bothe begyle.'	51	Bowge	189
And whan he came walkynge soberly,	51	Bowge	190
And to mewarde the strayte waye he toke.	51	Bowge	194
'God spede, broder,' to me quod he than,	51	Bowge	195
And thus to talke with me he began.	51	Bowge	196
He wyll begyle you and speke fayre to your face.	51	Bowge	200
Spake he, a fayth, no worde to you of me?	51	Bowge	204
I wote, and he dyde, ye wolde me telle.	51	Bowge	205
He sayde of me, whan he with you dyde talke –	52	Bowge	209
He sayde of me, whan he with you dyde talke –	52	Bowge	209
Yf he coude fynde in herte to truste me.	52	Bowge	220
To kepe it hymselfe; for than he myghte be sure	52	Bowge	222
'By God,' quod he, 'this and thus it is';	52	Bowge	225
And of his mynde he shewed me all and some.	52	Bowge	226
'Fare well,' quod he, 'we wyll talke more of this.'	52	Bowge	227
Soo he departed. There he wolde be come,	52	Bowge	228
Soo he departed. There he wolde be come,	52	Bowge	228
Upon his breste he bare a versynge boxe;	52	Bowge	232
And ever he sange, 'Sythe I am no thynge playne'.	52	Bowge	235
He gased on me with his gotyshe berde;	52	Bowge	237
Wyth that, as he departed soo fro me,	54	Bowge	281
A man, but wonderly besene was he.	54	Bowge	283
He loked hawte; he sette eche man at noughte;	54	Bowge	284
hawte] 'hawtie' Marshe 1568			
He loked hawte; he sette eche man at noughte;	54	Bowge	284
hawte] 'hawtie' Marshe 1568			
He frowned as he wolde swere by Cockes blode.	54	Bowge	287
He frowned as he wolde swere by Cockes blode.	54	Bowge	287
He bote the lyppe; he loked passynge coye;	54	Bowge	288
the] 'his' Wynkyn de Worde 1510			
He bote the lyppe; he loked passynge coye;	54	Bowge	288
the] 'his' Wynkyn de Worde 1510			
That he loked pale as asshes to my syghte.	54	Bowge	293
To Hervy Ha[f]ter than he spake of me,	54	Bowge	295
Hafter] 'Haster' †Wynkyn de Worde 1499, 1510, Marshe 1568			
'By Cryste,' quod he, 'for it is shame to saye,	54	Bowge	300
How he is now taken in conceyte,	54	Bowge	302

	Page	Title	Line
This Doctour Dawcocke, Drede, I wene he hyghte.	54	Bowge	303
It is lyke he wyll stonde in our lyghte!'	54	Bowge	305
our] 'your' Marshe 1568			
'I wonder sore he is in such conceyte.'	54	Bowge	310
Forthwith, he made on me a prowde assawte,	55	Bowge	316
He wente aboute to take me in a fawte:	55	Bowge	318
He frounde, he stared, he stampped where he stoode.	55	Bowge	319
He frounde, he stared, he stampped where he stoode.	55	Bowge	319
He frounde, he stared, he stampped where he stoode.	55	Bowge	319
He frounde, he stared, he stampped where he stoode.	55	Bowge	319
I loked on hym, I wende he had be woode.	55	Bowge	320
He set the arme proudly under the syde,	55	Bowge	321
And in this wyse he gan with me to chyde.	55	Bowge	322
And on the borde he whyrled a payre of bones,	56	Bowge	346
'Quater treye dews' he clatered as he wente.	56	Bowge	347
'Quater treye dews' he clatered as he wente.	56	Bowge	347
And ever he threwe, and kyst I wote nere what;	56	Bowge	349
Thenne I behelde how he dysgysed was:	56	Bowge	351
His rumpe, he wente so all for somer lyghte;	56	Bowge	355
And ay he sange, 'In fayth, Decon, thou crewe.'	56	Bowge	360
His elbowe bare, he ware his gere so nye,	56	Bowge	361
Counter he coude O lux upon a potte.	56	Bowge	365
He set up fresshely upon his hat alofte.	56	Bowge	367
'What, revell route!' quod he, and gan to rayle	56	Bowge	368
How ofte he hadde hit Jenet on the tayle,	56	Bowge	369
hadde] 'not' Marshe 1568			
How ofte he knocked at her klycked gate.	56	Bowge	371
He had no pleasure but in harlotrye.	56	Bowge	374
'Ay,' quod he, 'in the devylles date,	56	Bowge	375
Who rydeth on her, he nedeth not to care,	57	Bowge	409
He ran as fast as ever that he myghte.	58	Bowge	415
He ran as fast as ever that he myghte.	58	Bowge	415
That other loked as he wolde me have slayne.	58	Bowge	430
me have] 'have me' Wynkyn de Worde 1510			
And to mewarde as he gan for to coost,	58	Bowge	431
Whan that he was even at me almoost,	58	Bowge	432
Thyse were the wordes he to me dyde saye.	58	Bowge	441
he] 'that he' Marshe 1568			
A flaterynge knave and false he is, God wote.	59	Bowge	485
The drevyll stondeth to herken, and he can.	59	Bowge	486
It were more thryft he boughte him a newe cote;	60	Bowge	487
All that he wereth, it is borowed ware;	60	Bowge	489
Sodaynly, as he departed me fro,	60	Bowge	498
Er I was ware, behynde me he sayde 'Bo!'	60	Bowge	500
He had plucte oute the nobles of my pouche.	60	Bowge	504
He was trussed in a garmente strayte –	60	Bowge	505
For he coude well upon a casket wayte,	60	Bowge	507
Lyghte lyme-fynger, he toke none other wage.	60	Bowge	509
'Harken,' quod he, 'loo here myne honde in thyne;	60	Bowge	510
He tolde me so, by God, ye maye truste me.	60	Bowge	514
And as he rounded thus in myne ere	61	Bowge	526
rounded] 'roynded' †Wynkyn de Worde 1499			
He semeth a sysmatyke /Or els an heretike,	62	Hauke	17
He shall be as now nameles,	62	Hauke	38
But he shall not be blameles,	62	Hauke	39
Nor he shall not be shameles;	62	Hauke	40
For sure he wrought amys	62	Hauke	41
He made his hawke to fly,	63	Hauke	47
The hy auter he strypte naked;	63	Hauke	49
There on he stode, and craked;	63	Hauke	50
He shoke downe all the clothys,	63	Hauke	51
Or that he thens yede,	63	Hauke	55
Such sacrificium laudis /He made with suche gambawdis.	63	Hauke	65
He then, to be sure, /Callyd her with a lure.	63	Hauke	75
Wyth that he gave her a bounce	64	Hauke	86
But he sayde that he wolde	64	Hauke	97
But he sayde that he wolde	64	Hauke	97
He hawked on thys facyon,	64	Hauke	101
He sayde he wold not let /His houndys for to fet,	64	Hauke	106
He sayde he wold not let /His houndys for to fet,	64	Hauke	106
Boke, bell and candyll, /All that he myght handyll;	64	Hauke	113
Delt he not lyke a fon?	65	Hauke	128
Delt he not lyke a daw?	65	Hauke	129
There he may se and reed	65	Hauke	147
he] 'her' Marshe 1568			
And that he wysshed withall	66	Hauke	182
He sayd that he wold hunt	67	Hauke	188
He sayd that he wold hunt	67	Hauke	188
Whereat he made dysdayne.	68	Hauke	224
He sayde, for a crokyd intent,	68	Hauke	228
And this he overthwartyd.	68	Hauke	230
Somtyme he wolde gaspe	75	Phy Sparrow	128
Whan he sawe a waspe;	75	Phy Sparrow	129
A fly, or a gnat, /He wolde flye at that;	75	Phy Sparrow	131
And prytely he wolde pant	75	Phy Sparrow	132
Whan he saw an ant;	75	Phy Sparrow	133
Lord, how he wolde pry /After the butterfly!	75	Phy Sparrow	134
Lorde, how he wolde hop /After the gressop!	75	Phy Sparrow	136

HE — HE

	Page	Title	Line
Than he wold lepe and skyp,	75	Phy Sparrow	139
Wherewith he wolde make	76	Phy Sparrow	164
What though he crept so lowe?	76	Phy Sparrow	169
though] 'thought' †Kele 1545.2			
He dyd nothynge, perde, /But syt upon my kne.	76	Phy Sparrow	171
Phyllyp, though he were nyse,	76	Phy Sparrow	173
And do what he wolde;	76	Phy Sparrow	178
That he coulde there espye	76	Phy Sparrow	181
And he shold be bought /For golde and fee,	76	Phy Sparrow	195
He shuld over the see	76	Phy Sparrow	197
To wete if he coulde brynge	76	Phy Sparrow	198
Wherin he had apes and owles,	78	Phy Sparrow	258
That he is slayne me fro,	81	Phy Sparrow	364
He shall be the preest,	81	Phy Sparrow	400
Horsly, as he had the mur;	82	Phy Sparrow	419
He shall syng the grayle;	82	Phy Sparrow	441
He can not well fly, /Nor synge tunably;	83	Phy Sparrow	483
Yet at a brayde /He hath well assayde	84	Phy Sparrow	486
He can do nothyng ellys.	84	Phy Sparrow	494
By the astrology /That he hath naturally	84	Phy Sparrow	498
And yet he croweth dayly	84	Phy Sparrow	506
Whom now and then /He plucketh by the hede	84	Phy Sparrow	511
Whan he doth her trede.	84	Phy Sparrow	512
Whyles he senseth [the herse],	85	Phy Sparrow	530
the herse] not in †Kele 1545.2, Wyght 1553, Kitson 1560.6, Marshe 1568			
He shall synge the verse	85	Phy Sparrow	531
What he doth fynde	85	Phy Sparrow	538
He shall be th[e] sedeane,	85	Phy Sparrow	552
the] 'thye' †Kele 1545.2, 'thy' Wyght 1553, Kitson 1560.6, Marshe 1568			
To heven he shall, from heven he cam.	86	Phy Sparrow	582
To heven he shall, from heven he cam.	86	Phy Sparrow	582
For he was a prety cocke,	86	Phy Sparrow	588
He bete downe to the grounde:	88	Phy Sparrow	671
How hartely he dyd it take	89	Phy Sparrow	692
He coulde not optayne	89	Phy Sparrow	697
Comfort had he none	89	Phy Sparrow	705
He is named Troylus baud;	89	Phy Sparrow	721
Of that name he is sure	89	Phy Sparrow	722
Whether he were onlyve or ded;	89	Phy Sparrow	728
Whom he forsoke with teene,	90	Phy Sparrow	742
With whom he ledd a plesaunt life;	90	Phy Sparrow	744
Ne worde he wrote in vayne.	91	Phy Sparrow	803
Yet wryteth he in his kynd,	91	Phy Sparrow	808
Those maters that he hath pende;	92	Phy Sparrow	810
And say he wryteth to haute.	92	Phy Sparrow	812
He frowneth ever; /He laugheth never,	94	Phy Sparrow	922
He frowneth ever; /He laugheth never,	94	Phy Sparrow	923
He is so bete /With malyce, and frete	95	Phy Sparrow	930
Than is he sad, /Frantyke and mad;	95	Phy Sparrow	939
By marcyall strength /He wan at length;	104	Phy Sparrow	1306
Of Dyomedes stable /He brought out a rable	104	Phy Sparrow	1313
He plucked the bull /By the horned skull,	104	Phy Sparrow	1318
He [b]ad the Phitonesse	105	Phy Sparrow	1345
bad] 'had' †Kele 1545.2, Wyght 1553, Kitson 1560.6, Marshe 1568			
He were idem in numero,	105	Phy Sparrow	1355
How be it to Saull dyd he tell	105	Phy Sparrow	1357
And the next day he shuld dye,	105	Phy Sparrow	1359
HE WAS SOMTIME THE HOLY BAILLYVE OF DIS.	109	Epitaphe2	1
Upon us he doth reigne	111	Lawde	50
He is our noble champyon,	114	Scot Kynge	25
How unfortunately he doth now spede;	115	Scot Kynge	57
In double w[a]lles now he dooth dreme.	115	Scot Kynge	58
walles] 'welles' †Fakes 1513			
He is our noble Scipione;	118	Ag Scottes	117
He ragyd and rent out your hart bloode;	119	Ag Scottes	136
He the White, and ye the Red,	119	Ag Scottes	137
ye] 'you' Day 1560, Marshe 1568			
Ungraciously how he doth speed.	119	Ag Scottes	154
In double delyng so he dyd dreame,	119	Ag Scottes	155
In] 'An' Day 1560, Marshe 1568			
That he is kyng without a reme;	119	Ag Scottes	156
Cause have they none other /But for that he was brother,	120	Ag Scottes2	14
have they] 'they have' Day 1560, Marshe 1568			
brother] 'hys brother' Day 1560, Marshe 1568			
Agaynst whom he dyd fyght /Falsly agaynst all right,	120	Ag Scottes2	17
He was a recrayed knyght,	121	Ag Scottes2	26
And for he was a kyng, /The more shamefull rekenyng	121	Ag Scottes2	31
He skantly loveth our kyng, /That grudgeth at this thing:	121	Ag Scottes2	35
He wyl cause yow caste your crawes,	128	Garnesche3	155
And he that scryblyd your scrolles,	129	Garnesche3	192
Yf he wyst what sum wotte,	129	Garnesche3	199
Within thy skyn he xall remayne.	130	Garnesche5	22
He rymes and railes /That Englishmen have tailes.	135	Dundas	9
For ye said, that he said, that I said, wote ye what?	137	Ven Tongues	12
I made, he said, a windmil of an olde mat.	137	Ven Tongues	13

HE — HE

	Page	Title	Line
He saith untruly, to say that I would	137	Ven Tongues	21
With, 'He wrate suche a bil withouten dout',	139	Ven Tongues	70
Although he made it never so tough,	139	Ven Tongues	77
He might be sure to have shame ynough.	139	Ven Tongues	78
A fole is he with welth that fallyth at debate.	140	Magnyfycence	5
A man may have welth, but not as he wolde,	141	Magnyfycence	14
Why, to say what he wyll, Lyberte hath leve.	141	Magnyfycence	34
If lyberte sholde lepe and renne where he lyst	144	Magnyfycence	133
So in his harte he may be glad of us.	145	Magnyfycence	158
There is no prynce but he hath nede of us thre —	145	Magnyfycence	159
Perceyve you not howe lothe he was to abyde	147	Magnyfycence	241
Largesse is he that all pryncces doth avaunce;	148	Magnyfycence	279
For, syth he dyed, largesse was lytell used.	148	Magnyfycence	282
Why kepte you it thus longe? Howe dothe he? Wele?	149	Magnyfycence	314
Syr, thanked be God, he hath his hele.	149	Magnyfycence	315
And that he take good kepe to Lyberte.	149	Magnyfycence	320
Me thought he called Fan[s]y.	149	Magnyfycence	327
fansy] 'fanfy' †Rastell & Treveris C 1530, B			
Me thought he called Fansy me behynde.	149	Magnyfycence	329
And he that I came fro to this place	150	Magnyfycence	372
He wolde trotte gentylly, but he is to starke.	153	Magnyfycence	481
He wolde trotte gentylly, but he is to starke.	153	Magnyfycence	481
Yes, yes, syr. He and I have met.	154	Magnyfycence	498
By God, man, bothe his pagent and thyne he can play.	154	Magnyfycence	505
Who that is ruled by us, it shalbe longe or he thee.	154	Magnyfycence	515
Nay, nay. He hath chaunged his, and I have chaunged myne.	155	Magnyfycence	518
By Mesure mastered yet is he.	155	Magnyfycence	541
So he ruleth over all our place.	155	Magnyfycence	545
Cockes armes! What is he?	156	Magnyfycence	573
By Cockes harte, he loketh hye.	156	Magnyfycence	574
He hawketh, me thynke, for a butterflye.	156	Magnyfycence	575
Knowe hym, syr, quod he. Yes, by Saynt Sym!	156	Magnyfycence	585
I trowe that he is —	156	Magnyfycence	589
What is this he wereth? A cope?	157	Magnyfycence	601
Se howe he is wrapped for the colde.	157	Magnyfycence	603
Ye. But he spendeth it all in mesure.	157	Magnyfycence	621
In faythe, he were better to dwell in hell.	157	Magnyfycence	623
Yet where we wonne, nowe there wonneth he.	157	Magnyfycence	624
Ye. But he is a captyvyte.	157	Magnyfycence	626
Ye. And he hath rule of all his tresure.	158	Magnyfycence	632
Mary, syr, he told us, when	158	Magnyfycence	652
No. In every corner he wyll peke,	158	Magnyfycence	658
Nor no man in courte, but he,	158	Magnyfycence	660
For Lyberte he hath in gydyng.	158	Magnyfycence	661
That he shall have you in the stede of sadnesse,	159	Magnyfycence	680
Cockys armys! He hath callyd for the twyce.	162	Magnyfycence	782
To come to me I trowe he shalbe fayne.	162	Magnyfycence	784
Tushe! He that hathe nede, man, let hym rynne.	162	Magnyfycence	786
Abyde, syr, quod he! Mary, so I do.	162	Magnyfycence	789
He wyll come, man, when he may tende to.	162	Magnyfycence	790
He wyll come, man, when he may tende to.	162	Magnyfycence	790
Here he is nowe, man. Mayst thou not se?	162	Magnyfycence	792
Why, shall he be of your bende?	163	Magnyfycence	818
By Saynt Mary, he is a tawle man.	163	Magnyfycence	821
Ye, and do ryght good servyce he can.	163	Magnyfycence	822
That useth me. /He can not thee.	164	Magnyfycence	862
He doth abuse /Hym selfe to to;	164	Magnyfycence	871
He dothe mysse use /Eche man to [akuse],	164	Magnyfycence	873
akuse] 'take a fe' †Rastell & Treveris C 1530, B			
Whylyst he hath ought.	165	Magnyfycence	901
He wyll have wrought	165	Magnyfycence	902
That he may hyde	165	Magnyfycence	904
Why, under whom was he abydynge?	166	Magnyfycence	938
Yes, yes. He fell with me also at debate.	166	Magnyfycence	944
With the also? What! He playeth the state?	166	Magnyfycence	945
Why? Is he crossed than with a chalke?	166	Magnyfycence	950
Ye. But trowest thou that he be not maungey?	171	Magnyfycence	1122
What! He hathe ben hurte with a stabbe?	171	Magnyfycence	1124
Where the devyll gate he all these hurtes?	171	Magnyfycence	1127
What! Then he is some good poore mannes curre?	171	Magnyfycence	1129
Ye. But he wyll in at every mannes dore.	171	Magnyfycence	1130
Can he play well at the hoddypeke?	172	Magnyfycence	1161
Nay, by Cockys harte, he ne reckys;	172	Magnyfycence	1167
For he wyll speke to Magnyfycence thus.	172	Magnyfycence	1168
Why, thynkys thou he can no better skyll?	172	Magnyfycence	1172
Howe rode he by you? Howe put he to you?	173	Magnyfycence	1178
Howe rode he by you? Howe put he to you?	173	Magnyfycence	1178
Mary, as thou sayst, he gave me a blurre.	173	Magnyfycence	1179
Yes, yet he wyll make the ete a gnat.	173	Magnyfycence	1192
Yes, yet] 'Yet yes' †Rastell & Treveris C 1530, B			
Nowe, by the rode, and he wyll go nere.	173	Magnyfycence	1196
Nay, I tell the, he maketh no dowtes	174	Magnyfycence	1210
For be he cayser or be he kynge,	174	Magnyfycence	1214
For be he cayser or be he kynge,	174	Magnyfycence	1214
And what maner of people he maketh foles?	174	Magnyfycence	1217
Anone he waxyth so hy and prowde,	174	Magnyfycence	1244
He frownyth fyersly, brymly browde.	174	Magnyfycence	1245
The knave wolde make it koy, and he cowde;	175	Magnyfycence	1246

	Page	Title	Line
All that he dothe muste be alowde;	175	Magnyfycence	1247
He dawnsys so long, 'hey, troly, loly',	175	Magnyfycence	1250
By the good Lorde, truthe he sayth.	175	Magnyfycence	1252
Thynke I not so, quod he. Ellys have I shame,	175	Magnyfycence	1254
That wyt he wantyth when he hath moste nede.	175	Magnyfycence	1261
That wyt he wantyth when he hath moste nede.	175	Magnyfycence	1261
What he sayth and she sayth to lay good ere,	175	Magnyfycence	1269
And then he is moche made of for his [wyt]; wyt] 'whyt' †Rastell & Treveris C 1530, B	175	Magnyfycence	1271
He wyll make it mykyll worse than it is;	175	Magnyfycence	1273
But all that he dothe, and yf he reken well	175	Magnyfycence	1274
But all that he dothe, and yf he reken well	175	Magnyfycence	1274
By the masse, he shall hyght Consayte.	176	Magnyfycence	1309
Ye, for he hathe a full drye soule.	176	Magnyfycence	1320
To put where he lyst, foly hath fre chace;	177	Magnyfycence	1329
In good faythe, syr, me semeth he had the more wronge.	178	Magnyfycence	1384
Mary, syr, so dyd he excede and passe,	178	Magnyfycence	1385
Nay. He shall be ruled even as I lyst.	179	Magnyfycence	1394
I can do nothynge but he stonde besyde.	180	Magnyfycence	1449
He may not be comparyd unto me.	181	Magnyfycence	1476
He is not lyvynge your maners can amend;	183	Magnyfycence	1537
That for hym to laboure he hath prayde me hartely;	186	Magnyfycence	1650
To trust in me he is but dyssayved;	186	Magnyfycence	1652
For, so helpe me God, for you he is not mete.	186	Magnyfycence	1653
I speke the softlyer because he sholde not wete.	186	Magnyfycence	1654
By myne advyse, with you in fayth he shall not rest.	186	Magnyfycence	1660
It were better he spake with you or he wente,	187	Magnyfycence	1662
It were better he spake with you or he wente,	187	Magnyfycence	1662
That he knowe not but that I have supplyed	187	Magnyfycence	1663
Nowe, by your trouthe, gave he you not a brybe?	187	Magnyfycence	1665
But for all that he is lyke to have a glent.	187	Magnyfycence	1668
And he go to the devyll, so that I may have my fee,	187	Magnyfycence	1670
But yet, lo, I wolde, or that he wente,	187	Magnyfycence	1673
Lest that he thought that his money were evyll spente,	187	Magnyfycence	1674
That he wolde loke on hym, thoughe it were not longe.	187	Magnyfycence	1675
He telleth you trouth, syr, as I you ensure.	187	Magnyfycence	1679
That he come hyder, and to gyve hym a loke	187	Magnyfycence	1681
That he shall lyke the worse all this woke.	187	Magnyfycence	1682
I care not howe sone he be refused,	187	Magnyfycence	1683
Where is he? Mary, I made hym abyde	187	Magnyfycence	1685
He can full craftely this matter brynge aboute.	187	Magnyfycence	1691
For go when ye shall, of you shall he mysse.	188	Magnyfycence	1706
Ye, walke he must; it was no better worth.	189	Magnyfycence	1736
Mary, I wene he wolde not be glad to come agayne.	189	Magnyfycence	1740
So I wote not what he sholde do here.	189	Magnyfycence	1741
I sawe a sowter go to supper, or ever he had dynde.	191	Magnyfycence	1825
Nay. He that ye sent us, Clokyd Colusyon,	192	Magnyfycence	1859
And nowe lyke a lurden he lyeth in the dust.	193	Magnyfycence	1887
He knewe not hymselfe, his harte was so hye;	193	Magnyfycence	1888
He was wonte to boste, brage, and to brace;	193	Magnyfycence	1890
Nowe dare he not for shame loke one in the face.	193	Magnyfycence	1891
Nowe hath he ryght nought, naked as an asse.	193	Magnyfycence	1893
Somtyme without measure he trusted in golde;	193	Magnyfycence	1894
And now without measure he shal have hunger and colde.	193	Magnyfycence	1895
That hath deservyd it as well as he.	195	Magnyfycence	1952
He dynyd with delyte, with poverte he must sup.	195	Magnyfycence	1965
He dynyd with delyte, with poverte he must sup.	195	Magnyfycence	1965
He woteth not what welth is that never was sore.	196	Magnyfycence	1971
Put your wyll to his wyll, for surely it is he	196	Magnyfycence	1997
And remembre he suffered moche more for your sake;	196	Magnyfycence	2001
Howe be it of all synne he was innocent,	196	Magnyfycence	2002
What is he lyvynge that lyberte wolde lacke?	199	Magnyfycence	2083
Howe he is undone by the meanes of me?	200	Magnyfycence	2110
For yf Measure had ruled Lyberte as he began,	200	Magnyfycence	2111
But he abused so his free lyberte,	200	Magnyfycence	2113
That nowe he hath loste all his felycyte;	200	Magnyfycence	2114
What! Then he may drynke out of a stone cruyse.	201	Magnyfycence	2166
He may rynse a pycher, for his plate is to wed.	201	Magnyfycence	2168
In faythe, he may dreme on a daggeswane for ony fether bed.	201	Magnyfycence	2169
So he is the worste brawler that ever was borne.	202	Magnyfycence	2200
Mary, syr, he sayd that he was the pratyer man	203	Magnyfycence	2225
Mary, syr, he sayd that he was the pratyer man	203	Magnyfycence	2225
Ye, but trowe you, syrs, that this is he?	204	Magnyfycence	2242
He may helpe you. He may mende your mode.	207	Magnyfycence	2366
He may helpe you. He may mende your mode.	207	Magnyfycence	2366
He be your conducte, the Lorde of myghtys moste!	208	Magnyfycence	2386
Ye, syr, he is sory for that he hath offendyd.	208	Magnyfycence	2388
Ye, syr, he is sory for that he hath offendyd.	208	Magnyfycence	2388
Questyonlesse he doth me assure	208	Magnyfycence	2395
All that he sayth of trouthe dothe procede;	209	Magnyfycence	2426
Who brought you that letter? Wote ye what he hyght?	209	Magnyfycence	2440
Truth it is, syr; for after he wrought me moch shame,	209	Magnyfycence	2444
Today maysterfest, tomorowe he hath no holde;	213	Magnyfycence	2549
Today a man, tomorowe he lyeth in the duste;	213	Magnyfycence	2550
His rumpe also he frygges /Agaynst the hye benche.	219	El Rummynge	178
He calleth me his whytyng, /His mullyng and his [m]ytyng, mytyng] 'nytyng' †Lant 1545, Kynge & Marche 1554, 'nittinge' Day 1560, 'nittine' Marshe 1568	220	El Rummynge	223

HE —HE	Page	Title	Line
Tyll that he dreme and dronny;	220	El Rummynge	230
Than wyll he rout and snort;	220	El Rummynge	232
Bo-ho doth bark wel, Hough-ho he rulyth the ring;	234	Speke Parott	130
With, 'He sayd,' and 'We said.' Ich wot now what ich wot,	234	Speke Parott	132
And yet he wolde be rekenyd pro Ariopagita;	235	Speke Parott	156
When Parrot is ded, he dothe not putrefy; he] 'she' †Lant 1545, Kynge & Marche 1554, Day 1560, Marshe 1568	236	Speke Parott	213
He made you of nothynge by his magistye;	236	Speke Parott	219
Whate mone he made when Pamphylus loste hys make.	237	Speke Parott	234
For replicacion restles that he of late ther made;	239	Speke Parott	282
Of Argus revengyd, recover when he may,	239	Speke Parott	288
As he to exployte the man owte of the mone.	239	Speke Parott	307
With porpose and graundepose he may fede hym fatte,	239	Speke Parott	308
Thowghe he pampyr not hys paunche with the grete seall;	239	Speke Parott	309
As presydent and regente he rulythe every deall.	239	Speke Parott	312
How the maters he mellis in com to small effecte;	240	Speke Parott	328
For he wantythe of hys wyttes that all wold rule alone;	240	Speke Parott	329
Muche money, men sey, there madly he hathe spente;	240	Speke Parott	335
Wherfor he may now come agayne as he wente,	240	Speke Parott	338
Wherfor he may now come agayne as he wente,	240	Speke Parott	338
He maketh them to bere babylles, and to bere a lowe sayle;	243	Speke Parott	428
He caryeth a kyng in hys sleve, yf all the worlde fayle;	243	Speke Parott	429
He facithe owte at a flusshe with, 'Shewe, take all!'	243	Speke Parott	430
Of Pope Julius cardys, he ys chefe Cardynall.	243	Speke Parott	431
He tryhumfythe, he trumpythe, he turnythe all up and downe,	244	Speke Parott	432
He tryhumfythe, he trumpythe, he turnythe all up and downe,	244	Speke Parott	432
He tryhumfythe, he trumpythe, he turnythe all up and downe,	244	Speke Parott	432
Hyt ys to fere leste he wolde were the garland on hys pate,	244	Speke Parott	435
For of owur regente the regiment he hathe, ex qua vi,	244	Speke Parott	437
He wottyth never what /Ne whereof he speketh.'	247	Collyn Clout	17
He wottyth never what /Ne whereof he speketh.'	247	Collyn Clout	18
'He cryeth and he creketh /He pryeth and he preketh, preketh] 'peketh' Kele 1545.1, 'prekythe' MS Harley 2252	247	Collyn Clout	19
'He cryeth and he creketh /He pryeth and he preketh, preketh] 'peketh' Kele 1545.1, 'prekythe' MS Harley 2252	247	Collyn Clout	19
'He cryeth and he creketh /He pryeth and he preketh, preketh] 'peketh' Kele 1545.1, 'prekythe' MS Harley 2252	247	Collyn Clout	20
'He cryeth and he creketh /He pryeth and he preketh, preketh] 'peketh' Kele 1545.1, 'prekythe' MS Harley 2252	247	Collyn Clout	20
He chydeth and he chatters, /He prayeth and he patters; prayeth] 'prates' Kele 1545.1, Marshe 1568, 'pratythe' MS Harley 2252	247	Collyn Clout	21
He chydeth and he chatters, /He prayeth and he patters; prayeth] 'prates' Kele 1545.1, Marshe 1568, 'pratythe' MS Harley 2252	247	Collyn Clout	21
He chydeth and he chatters, /He prayeth and he patters; prayeth] 'prates' Kele 1545.1, Marshe 1568, 'pratythe' MS Harley 2252	247	Collyn Clout	22
He chydeth and he chatters, /He prayeth and he patters; prayeth] 'prates' Kele 1545.1, Marshe 1568, 'pratythe' MS Harley 2252	247	Collyn Clout	22
He clyttreth and he clatters, /He medleth and he smatters,	247	Collyn Clout	23
He clyttreth and he clatters, /He medleth and he smatters,	247	Collyn Clout	23
He clyttreth and he clatters, /He medleth and he smatters,	247	Collyn Clout	24
He clyttreth and he clatters, /He medleth and he smatters,	247	Collyn Clout	24
He gloseth and he flatters.'	247	Collyn Clout	25
He gloseth and he flatters.'	247	Collyn Clout	25
Or yf he speke playne, /Than he lacketh brayne:	247	Collyn Clout	26
Or yf he speke playne, /Than he lacketh brayne:	247	Collyn Clout	27
'He is but a foole; /Let hym go to scole!	247	Collyn Clout	28
A thre-foted stole /That he may downe sytte,	247	Collyn Clout	31
For he lacketh wytte.'	247	Collyn Clout	32
And yf that he hytte /The nayle on the hede	247	Collyn Clout	33
And yet he wyll nat drede	253	Collyn Clout	278
Yf he on hym dare take	254	Collyn Clout	306
He payed a bitter pencyon /For mans redempcyon,	258	Collyn Clout	452
He dranke eysell and gall	258	Collyn Clout	454
He must do this werke;	264	Collyn Clout	728
He can nothynge smatter	267	Collyn Clout	814
And yet he wyll melle	267	Collyn Clout	820
And he dare nat well neven	267	Collyn Clout	824
He coude nat synge hymselfe therout	268	Collyn Clout	878
And whan he weneth to sytte	271	Collyn Clout	995
Yet may he mysse the quysshon!	271	Collyn Clout	996
Wherfore he hath good ure	271	Collyn Clout	1001
Whome he wyll depute?	272	Collyn Clout	1044
He sayes that we are recheles,	275	Collyn Clout	1176
Suche grace that he us sende	278	Collyn Clout	1262
He ruleth alway styll.	281	Why Come Ye	107
All that he dothe is ryght.	281	Why Come Ye	116
For whyles he doth rule,	282	Why Come Ye	134
For whether he blesse or curse,	282	Why Come Ye	137
The Frenche men he doth fray,	282	Why Come Ye	154
With all the power he may.	282	Why Come Ye	156
The French men he hath fayntned,	282	Why Come Ye	157
Of chevalry he is the floure;	282	Why Come Ye	159
The French men he hathe so mated,	282	Why Come Ye	161

HE —HE   Page   Title   Line

	Page	Title	Line
That he ne se can	283	Why Come Ye	182
He is set so hye /In his ierarchy	283	Why Come Ye	184
All maters there he marres,	283	Why Come Ye	189
For he hathe all the sayenge /Without any renayenge.	283	Why Come Ye	192
He rolleth in his recordes,	283	Why Come Ye	194
He sayth, 'How saye ye, my lordes?	283	Why Come Ye	195
He ruleth all the roste	283	Why Come Ye	201
He loveth nothyng but golde;	284	Why Come Ye	208
He eateth c[a]pons stewed,	284	Why Come Ye	221
capons] 'copons' †Kele 1545.3			
He foynes and he frygges;	284	Why Come Ye	224
He foynes and he frygges;	284	Why Come Ye	224
He maketh us Jack Rakers;	285	Why Come Ye	273
He sayes we ar but crakers;	285	Why Come Ye	274
He calleth us England men	285	Why Come Ye	275
For the Scottes and he,	286	Why Come Ye	277
He maketh himselfe cock sure.	286	Why Come Ye	282
He pluckes them by the hode,	286	Why Come Ye	304
He bayteth them lyke a bere,	286	Why Come Ye	307
Theyr wyttes, he saith, are dull;	286	Why Come Ye	309
He sayth they have no brayne	286	Why Come Ye	310
He countys them foles and dawes;	286	Why Come Ye	315
He sayth, they are to seke	287	Why Come Ye	317
He wryngeth them suche a wrenche,	287	Why Come Ye	321
In the Chauncery where he syttes,	287	Why Come Ye	326
But suche as he admyttes,	287	Why Come Ye	327
He sayth, 'Thou huddy peke!	287	Why Come Ye	329
He rages and he raves,	287	Why Come Ye	334
He rages and he raves,	287	Why Come Ye	334
Thus royally he dothe deale	287	Why Come Ye	336
And in the Checker he them cheks,	287	Why Come Ye	338
In the Ster Chambre he noddis and beks,	287	Why Come Ye	339
Whether he be knyght or squyre,	287	Why Come Ye	344
He is but an yonglyng,	287	Why Come Ye	348
He shulde be hyder brought;	287	Why Come Ye	351
He morneth in blacke clothynge.	288	Why Come Ye	392
Where ever he go or ryde	289	Why Come Ye	394
It shall be as he wyll.	289	Why Come Ye	419
He dyggeth so in the trenche	290	Why Come Ye	434
That he ruleth them all.	290	Why Come Ye	436
So he dothe undermynde,	290	Why Come Ye	437
He hath in him suche fayth.	290	Why Come Ye	445
If that that he wrought	290	Why Come Ye	448
But all he bringeth to nought,	290	Why Come Ye	450
He bereth the kyng on hand	290	Why Come Ye	452
That he must pyll his lande	290	Why Come Ye	453
But he laythe all in the dyche,	290	Why Come Ye	455
He is so ambicyous,	290	Why Come Ye	461
From whens that he came,	290	Why Come Ye	465
That he falleth into Acidiam,	290	Why Come Ye	466
into] 'in' Marshe 1568; Acidiam] 'Acisiam' †Kele 1545.3,			
Kitson 1560.7, Marshe 1568			
He regardeth lordes /No more than potshordes.	291	Why Come Ye	480
He is in suche elacyon /Of his exaltacyon,	291	Why Come Ye	482
He ruleth all at wyll	291	Why Come Ye	487
He came of the sank royall	291	Why Come Ye	493
But, however he was borne,	291	Why Come Ye	495
If he coulde consyder	291	Why Come Ye	497
To him he hathe founde	291	Why Come Ye	501
Whiche he can nat se.	291	Why Come Ye	507
For he was, parde,	291	Why Come Ye	508
He doth but cloute and cobbill	292	Why Come Ye	527
Yet proudly he dare pretende	292	Why Come Ye	530
Well-syghted when /He is amonge blynde men?	292	Why Come Ye	535
That he set him on heyght,	292	Why Come Ye	542
He made a kynge royall,	293	Why Come Ye	558
Before that he was made	293	Why Come Ye	562
And ruled as he wolde.	293	Why Come Ye	564
How can he do ryght?	293	Why Come Ye	581
For he wyll as sone smyght	293	Why Come Ye	582
And he wyll play checke mate /With ryall majeste	293	Why Come Ye	588
Counte himselfe as good as he;	294	Why Come Ye	590
He doth revyle and brall	294	Why Come Ye	596
He hath dispyght and scorne	294	Why Come Ye	599
He rebukes them and rayles,	294	Why Come Ye	601
Of what estate he be /Of spirituall dygnyte;	294	Why Come Ye	617
Thus he, borne so base,	294	Why Come Ye	622
He wolde have ben ryght fayne	295	Why Come Ye	642
With a poore knyght, /Whatsoever he hyght!	295	Why Come Ye	646
He is so fyers and fell.	295	Why Come Ye	650
He rayles and he ratis,	295	Why Come Ye	651
He rayles and he ratis,	295	Why Come Ye	651
He calleth them doddy patis;	295	Why Come Ye	652
He grynnes and he gapis	295	Why Come Ye	653
He grynnes and he gapis	295	Why Come Ye	653
That he can nat parceyve	295	Why Come Ye	661
How he doth hym disceyve.	295	Why Come Ye	662
For he is the kynges derlyng	295	Why Come Ye	666

HE —HE

	Page	Title	Line
For he wyll tere it asonder!	296	Why Come Ye	671
He sayth the kynge doth wryte,	296	Why Come Ye	678
And writeth he wottith nat what.	296	Why Come Ye	679
wottith] 'wot' Toy 1553, Kitson 1560.7, Marshe 1568			
Promoted was he /To a cardynalles dygnyte	297	Why Come Ye	728
That he made him his chauncelar	297	Why Come Ye	732
Tyll he cheked at the fyst,	297	Why Come Ye	735
Wherfore he suffred payn,	297	Why Come Ye	739
He ware a cardynals hat;	297	Why Come Ye	743
That of force he must	298	Why Come Ye	752
For he sent in writynge	299	Why Come Ye	790
Nay, nay, he is nat dede.	299	Why Come Ye	794
But he was so payned in the hede	299	Why Come Ye	795
That he shall never ete more bred.	299	Why Come Ye	796
Now he is gone to another stede	299	Why Come Ye	797
For he is well past and gone.	300	Why Come Ye	833
Were gone as well as he!	300	Why Come Ye	836
He is best set by!	300	Why Come Ye	859
best] 'most' MS Rawlinson C. 813			
He rod, but we ran.	301	Why Come Ye	887
'He rode not but he ran' MS Rawlinson C. 813			
He is at suche takynge,	302	Why Come Ye	936
He must tax for his wull	302	Why Come Ye	938
He must pay agayn	302	Why Come Ye	943
And yet he payde before	302	Why Come Ye	946
He wolde dry up the stremys	303	Why Come Ye	957
For with us he so mellys	303	Why Come Ye	961
I wolde he were somwhere ellys;	303	Why Come Ye	963
He wyll drynke us so drye,	303	Why Come Ye	965
so] not in MS Rawlinson C. 813			
For and he were there,	303	Why Come Ye	973
For I undertake /He wolde so brag and crake	303	Why Come Ye	977
That he wolde than make /The devyls to quake,	303	Why Come Ye	978
He is suche a grym syer,	303	Why Come Ye	987
That he wolde breke the braynes	304	Why Come Ye	990
I wolde he were gone;	304	Why Come Ye	994
That ruleth but he alone,	304	Why Come Ye	996
He kepeth them in subjectyon.	304	Why Come Ye	1010
He jugeth it no foly;	305	Why Come Ye	1047
He sayth we ar to blame!	305	Why Come Ye	1049
And yet he is ashamed	305	Why Come Ye	1052
He calleth the prechours dawis.	305	Why Come Ye	1061
He counteth them for gygawis;	305	Why Come Ye	1063
And Aron sore he thret,	305	Why Come Ye	1068
The prechour he dothe dyspyse	306	Why Come Ye	1072
For he hath suche a bull,	306	Why Come Ye	1078
He may take whom he wull,	306	Why Come Ye	1079
He may take whom he wull,	306	Why Come Ye	1079
For in lent he wyll ete	306	Why Come Ye	1083
wyll] 'doeth' MS Rawlinson C. 813			
That he can onywhere gete,	306	Why Come Ye	1085
He brekes and defaces,	306	Why Come Ye	1090
He hathe them in derisyon,	306	Why Come Ye	1092
All this he dothe deale	306	Why Come Ye	1101
'Thys now he dothe meale' MS Rawlinson C. 813			
Whiche madly he dothe apply /Unto an extravagancy,	306	Why Come Ye	1104
Yet whan he toke first his hat,	306	Why Come Ye	1108
first] not in MS Rawlinson C. 813			
He said he knew what was what.	306	Why Come Ye	1109
He said he knew what was what.	306	Why Come Ye	1109
All justyce he pretended:	307	Why Come Ye	1110
All wronges he wolde redresse,	307	Why Come Ye	1112
All injuris he wolde represse,	307	Why Come Ye	1113
All perjuris he wolde oppresse.	307	Why Come Ye	1114
He is perjured himselfe.	307	Why Come Ye	1116
To whom he was professed	307	Why Come Ye	1121
But now he maketh objectyon,	307	Why Come Ye	1127
But] 'And', objectyon] 'dyrectyon' MS Rawlinson C. 813			
That he setteth never a deale	307	Why Come Ye	1130
He makith so proude pretens,	307	Why Come Ye	1133
He jugyth him equivalent /With God omnipotent.	307	Why Come Ye	1135
him] 'hymselfe' MS Rawlinson C. 813;			
equivalent] 'equypolent' Rawlinson C. 813			
Whan he was creat pope /First in Antioche.	307	Why Come Ye	1142
He dyd never approche	307	Why Come Ye	1144
'Saynt Dunstane, what was he?	307	Why Come Ye	1147
'Nothynge,' he sayth, 'lyke to We.	307	Why Come Ye	1148
to we] 'to mee' Toy 1553, Kitson 1560.7, Marshe 1568,			
'we' MS Rawlinson C. 813			
And he may fange us.	308	Why Come Ye	1156
And] 'That' Kitson 1560.7, Marshe 1568			
For I suppose that he is	308	Why Come Ye	1163
Men wene that he is pocky,	308	Why Come Ye	1170
wene that] 'say' MS Rawlinson C. 813			
He is so ambicious, /So elate and so vicious,	308	Why Come Ye	1176
And so cruell hertyd, /That he wyll nat be convertyd;	308	Why Come Ye	1179
That] not in MS Rawlinson C. 813			
For he setteth God apart.	308	Why Come Ye	1180

HE —HE   Page   Title   Line

He is nowe so overthwart, ...	308	Why Come Ye	1181
nowe] not in MS Rawlinson C. 813			
Lest he wyll put it clene out, ...	309	Why Come Ye	1199
Put up his sworde, for he cowde make no warre, ...	312	Garlande	5
Bycause that he his tyme studyously hath spent	314	Garlande	60
he his tyme] 'his tyme he' MS Cotton Vitellius E.x			
For, ne were onely he hath your promocyon, ...	314	Garlande	71
But sith he hath tastid of the sugred pocioun	314	Garlande	73
For if he gloryously publisshe his matter, ...	314	Garlande	83
Then men wyll say how he doth but flatter.	314	Garlande	84
As sumtyme he must vyces remorde, ...	314	Garlande	86
Then sum wyll say he hath but lyttil brayne, ...	314	Garlande	87
For certayne envectyfys, yet wrote he none ill, ...	315	Garlande	96
certayne envectyfys] 'that he enveiyd' MS Cotton Vit.E.x			
Savynge he rubbid sum on the gall.	315	Garlande	97
on] 'upon' Marshe 1568			
The lesarde came lepyng, and sayd that he must, ...	315	Garlande	104
Or wherto shulde he have the prerogatyve, ...	315	Garlande	117
the] 'that' MS Cotton Vitellius E.x			
But if he had made sum memoryall, ...	315	Garlande	118
Wherby he myght have a name inmortall?	315	Garlande	119
But that his bokis, whiche he did devyse, ...	315	Garlande	124
Plato, but for that he left wrytynge behynde, ...	315	Garlande	126
that] not in MS Cotton Vitellius E.x			
That banisshed was he by his proposicyoun, ...	316	Garlande	132
by] 'through' Marshe 1568			
Ageyne whom he cowde make no contradiccyoun?'	316	Garlande	133
That he to your courte is goyng and commynge, ...	316	Garlande	139
Sith he is slaundred for defaut of konnyng?'	316	Garlande	140
That he so sholde be, me semith it sittyng, ...	316	Garlande	149
it] 'it is' MS Cotton Vitellius E.x			
All be it grete parte he hath surrendred	316	Garlande	150
Onely procedid for that he did outray	316	Garlande	156
For though he were venquesshid, yet was he not shamyd:	316	Garlande	161
For] 'Sithe' MS Cotton Vitellius E.x			
For though he were venquesshid, yet was he not shamyd:	316	Garlande	161
For] 'Sithe' MS Cotton Vitellius E.x			
Wherein he reporteth of the coragius	317	Garlande	164
Wherein] 'Where' MS Cotton Vitellius E.x			
Then he that doth worste is as good as the best.	317	Garlande	175
Be he never so lytell of substaunce, ...	317	Garlande	177
Eyther they wyll say he is to wyse, ...	318	Garlande	204
wyll] 'shall' MS Cotton Vitellius E.x			
Or elles he can nought bot whan he is at scole;	318	Garlande	205
Or elles he can nought bot whan he is at scole;	318	Garlande	205
'Prove his wytt', sayth he, 'at cardes or dyce, ...	318	Garlande	206
And ye shall well fynde he is a very fole;	318	Garlande	207
well fynde] 'fynde wele' MS Cotton Vitellius E.x			
For truly it were a pyte that he sat ydle'.	318	Garlande	210
If he to the ample encrease of his name	318	Garlande	222
Can lay any werkis that he hath compylyd, ...	318	Garlande	223
I am content that he be not exylide	318	Garlande	224
As he that aquentyth hym with ydilnes.	318	Garlande	228
But if that he purpose to make a redresse, ...	318	Garlande	229
What he hath done, let it be brought to syght.	318	Garlande	230
He plucked hym backe, and he went afore.	319	Garlande	254
He plucked hym backe, and he went afore.	319	Garlande	254
But that he daunced for joye of that gle.	320	Garlande	278
He sange also how, the tre as he did take	320	Garlande	300
He sange also how, the tre as he did take	320	Garlande	300
Betwene his armes, he felt her body quake.	320	Garlande	301
Then he assurded into his exclamacyon	320	Garlande	302
his] 'this' Marshe 1568			
With decadis historious, whiche that he mengith	321	Garlande	345
'There shal he here what she wyl to hym say	325	Garlande	451
wyl to hym] 'to hym will' Marshe 1568			
When he is callid to answere to his name.'	325	Garlande	452
And 'He haltith often that hath a kyby hele.'	326	Garlande	502
As fersly frownynge as he had ben fyghtyng, ...	328	Garlande	594
And with his forme foote he shoke forthe this wrytyng:	328	Garlande	595
Masid as a Marche hare, he ran lyke a scut.	329	Garlande	632
Of Pliades he prechid with ther drowsy chere, ...	331	Garlande	697
And of their shorte nyghtes; he browght in his songe	331	Garlande	703
He fyndith fals mesuris out of his fonde fiddill.'	333	Garlande	741
fals mesuris out] 'owght fals mesuris' MS Cotton Vit.E.x			
Envyous Rancour truely he hight.	333	Garlande	753
An hole reame he is able to set at devysion:	333	Garlande	758
For when he spekyth fayrest, then thynketh he moost yll; . . .	333	Garlande	759
For when he spekyth fayrest, then thynketh he moost yll; . . .	333	Garlande	759
Full gloryously can he glose, thy mynde for to fele;	333	Garlande	760
He wyll set men a feightynge and syt hymselfe styll, ...	333	Garlande	761
set] 'stir' MS Cotton Vitellius E.x; a feightynge]			
'to brawlyng' MS Cotton Vitellius E.x			
He can never leve warke whylis it is wele.	333	Garlande	763
The devyll of hell and he be seldome asonder.'	333	Garlande	765
For of all ladyes he hath the library, ...	334	Garlande	780
Of all gentylwomen he hath the scruteny, ...	334	Garlande	782
For yet of women he never sayd shame, ...	334	Garlande	784

HEAD — HED

	Page	Title	Line
From the anker he kuttyth the gabyll rope,	335	Garlande	833
Troilus, I trowe, if that he had you sene,	336	Garlande	873
In you he wolde have set his hole delight.	336	Garlande	874
He coude not devyse the lest poynt of your cheke;	337	Garlande	896
Towarde the dore, as he were comyng oute,	343	Garlande	1095
But if he wryte oftenner than ones or twyse.'	345	Garlande	1155
to reherse all by name that he hath compylyd, &c.	345	Garlande	R
Moche dowblenes of the worlde therin he may fynde.	346	Garlande	1197
To her he wrote many maters of myrthe;	346	Garlande	1199
He did translate, enterprete, and disclose;	347	Garlande	1222
A tratyse he devysid and browght it to pas,	347	Garlande	1228
He wrate therof many a praty lyne,	347	Garlande	1242
He wrate an Epitaph for his grave stone,	347	Garlande	1249
For he was ever ageynst Goddis hows;	347	Garlande	1251
By merciall strength /He wan at length;	349	Garlande	1299
Of Diomedis stabyll /He brought out a rabyll	349	Garlande	1306
He pluckid the bull /By the hornid scull,	349	Garlande	1311
Primo Regum expres, /He bad the Phitones	350	Garlande	1338
He were idem in numero,	350	Garlande	1348
How be it to Saull he did tell	350	Garlande	1350
And the next day he shulde dye,	350	Garlande	1352
He wrate of a muse throw a mud wall;	351	Garlande	1384
What myght she say? What myght he do therto?	351	Garlande	1395
How than lyke a man he wan the barbican	351	Garlande	1397
No man lyvyng, he sayth, can be sure;	351	Garlande	1403
Whether he rode to Swaffhamm or to Some,	352	Garlande	1416
Swaffhamm] 'Swasshamm' †Fakes 1523, Marshe 1568			
Vexilla regis he devysid to be displayd;	352	Garlande	1420
Thus passyth he the tyme both nyght and day,	352	Garlande	1423
He is not wyse ageyne the streme that stryvith.	352	Garlande	1432
Nedes must he rin that the devyll dryvith.	352	Garlande	1434
Whereupon he metrefyde after his mynde;	353	Garlande	1464
The Nacyoun of Folys he left not behynde.	353	Garlande	1470
For drede and he lerne them there A B C to spell.'	353	Garlande	1476
He turnyd his tirikkis, his volvell ran fast,	354	Garlande	1517
There he putte backe	360	Albany	44
He reculed backe, /To his great lacke,	360	Albany	52
Whan he herde tell /That my Lorde Amrell	360	Albany	54
He fledde and durst nat fyght;	360	Albany	70
He ran awaye by night.	360	Albany	71
Whan he were deed.	361	Albany	98
He ran away by nyght	366	Albany	311
Ye saye that he and ye —	367	Albany	332
Whyche he and ye? Let se;	367	Albany	333
If he on you but frounde	367	Albany	345
So noble a prince as he /In all actyvite	368	Albany	395
Thus he dothe disparage	369	Albany	414
He rules his cominalte /With all benignite.	370	Albany	463
His noble baronage /He putteth them in corage	370	Albany	466
Where ever he rydes or goos.	370	Albany	470
His subjectes he dothe supporte,	370	Albany	471
All his subjectes and he /Moost lovyngly agre	371	Albany	480
Wherwith he dothe them bynde	371	Albany	484
That laughed whan he dyd pas	379	Replycacion	187
He counted it for no correction,	379	Replycacion	189
Lyke unto Alcheus, he dothe hym magnify.	383	Replycacion	335
That at his resurrection he harped out of hell	383	Replycacion	341
That he our penne dothe lede,	385	Replycacion	385

HEAD

	Page	Title	Line
Ye prycke me in the head!'	77	Phy Sparrow	224
Caught Phyllyp by the head,	81	Phy Sparrow	377

HEALE

	Page	Title	Line
That goostly can heale us;	265	Collyn Clout	742
Longe to endure in heale.	298	Why Come Ye	771

HEAR

	Page	Title	Line
Myne hear ryght upstode,	77	Phy Sparrow	227

HEAT

	Page	Title	Line
Such fervent heat /His stomake doth freat;	83	Phy Sparrow	481
doth freat] 'so great' †Kele 1545.2, Wyght 1553, Kitson 1560.6			

HECATES

	Page	Title	Line
Also by Hecates powre	349	Garlande	1315
powre] 'bowre' Marshe 1568			

HECKE

	Page	Title	Line
Of brede at ylke mannes hecke.	363	Albany	155

HECTOR

	Page	Title	Line
And lyke marciall Hector he faught them agayne	31	Dol Dethe	88
Valiant as Hector in every marciall nede,	33	Dol Dethe	138
Noble Hector of Troye,	74	Phy Sparrow	111
Of Hector of Troye	88	Phy Sparrow	673

HECTORS

	Page	Title	Line
Like Andromach, Hectors wyfe,	74	Phy Sparrow	108

HED

	Page	Title	Line
Skelton Laureat, uppon a deedmans hed,	39	Coystrowne3	I
Hys hed was hevy, such was his hap,	41	Balettys1	5
I wys he hath an hevy hed,'	42	Balettys1	21
In his hed to crepe;	95	Phy Sparrow	935
........hyr husbandes hed,	125	Garnesche3	58
Thow a Sarsens hed ye bere,	127	Garnesche3	123

HEDD — HEERY

	Page	Title	Line
With clothes upon her hed /That wey a sowe of led,	216	El Rummynge	71
That wey] 'That they wey' Kynge & Marche 1554, Day 1560, Marshe 1568			
With that her hed shaked /And her handes quaked.	226	El Rummynge	476
Ones hed wold have aked /To se her naked.	226	El Rummynge	478
A narrow unfethered and without an hed,	232	Speke Parott	74
Prisians hed broken now, handy-dandy,	235	Speke Parott	171
That wyll hed us and hange us,	308	Why Come Ye	1154
Your fonde hed in your furred hode!	310	Why Come Ye2	19
your] (2nd) 'a' MS Rawlinson C. 813			

HEDD
So many nobyll bodyes, undyr on dawys hedd;	245	Speke Parott	467

HEDDES
Nay. Let us our heddes togyder cast.	156	Magnyfycence	566
Some with a sho clout /Bynde theyr heddes about;	218	El Rummynge	144
Couchynge your drousy heddes	263	Collyn Clout	658

HEDDYS
Go together by the heddys, and gyve me your swordys.	202	Magnyfycence	2199

HEDE
His hede maye be harde, but feble is his brayne!	46	Bowge	24
his] not in Marshe 1568			
But of eche thynge there as I toke hede,	47	Bowge	64
Me thoughte his hede was full of gelousy,	51	Bowge	192
His hede was hevy for watchynge overnyghte,	56	Bowge	352
But there was poyntynge and noddynge with the hede,	58	Bowge	421
Whom now and then /He pluckyth by the hede	84	Phy Sparrow	511
Of the kynge of Naverne ye may take hede	115	Scot Kynge	56
Rowlynge in yower holow hede, ugly to see;	122	Garneschel	38
Byd hym take good hede of you, my syngulér tresure.	149	Magnyfycence	317
Abyde. Lette me se. Take better hede.	157	Magnyfycence	595
By my trouthe, she hathe a grete hede.	169	Magnyfycence	1048
And, 'This is not well done, syr; take hede';	175	Magnyfycence	1248
I wolde hauke whylest my hede dyd warke,	184	Magnyfycence	1563
Abyde, syr, abyde. Let me holde your hede.	189	Magnyfycence	1727
A, my hede! But is the horson gone?	189	Magnyfycence	1729
Ye sent us a supervysour for to take hede;	192	Magnyfycence	1853
Take hede of your selfe, for nowe ye have nede.	192	Magnyfycence	1854
Take hede of this captyfe that lyeth here on grounde.	195	Magnyfycence	1946
Where you were wonte to have cawdels for your hede,	197	Magnyfycence	2008
Your hede that was wonte to be happed moost drowpy and drowsy,	197	Magnyfycence	2018
Wounded from the fote to the crowne of the hede:	207	Magnyfycence	2364
Hys wolvys hede, wanne, bloo as lede, gapythe over the crowne:	244	Speke Parott	434
So myche callyng on, and so smalle takyng hede;	245	Speke Parott	471
And yf that he hytte /The nayle on the hede	247	Collyn Clout	34
Howe they take no hede /Theyr sely shepe to fede,	248	Collyn Clout	76
Dominus vobiscum by the hede,	252	Collyn Clout	230
And nat so hardy on his hede	272	Collyn Clout	1023
nat] 'not' Marshe 1568, MS Harley 2252			
All noble men of this take hede,	278	Why Come Ye	1
of this] not in MS Rawlinson C. 813			
All noble men of this take hede,	279	Why Come Ye	15
All noble men of this take hede,	279	Why Come Ye	27
That of shulde go his hede,	288	Why Come Ye	358
One wyse mannys hede	298	Why Come Ye	764
But he was so payned in the hede	299	Why Come Ye	795
Of laurell levis a cronell on his hede,	320	Garlande	288
Set on your hede this laurell whiche is wrought.	343	Garlande	1087
Trowth with a drowsy hede;	358	Garlande2	2

HEDELLIS
With slaiis, with tavellis, with hedellis well drest;	334	Garlande	791

HEDES
With gastly hedes thre;	74	Phy Sparrow	91
And some theyr hedes mew.	280	Why Come Ye	61
some] not in Toy 1553, Kitson 1560.7, Marshe 1568			

HEDGE
Over the hedge and pale,	221	El Rummynge	264

HEDYD
Was hedyd, drawen, and quarterd,	297	Why Come Ye	740

HEED
Never a toth in his heed.	108	Epitaphe1	61
Of the kynge of Naverne ye might take heed,	119	Ag Scottes	153
By the messe, I shall cleve thy heed to the waste.	201	Magnyfycence	2175
'His heed is so fat	247	Collyn Clout	16
For than thyne heed of gose.	288	Why Come Ye	385
And set hys crowne /On your owne heed	361	Albany	97

HEEDES
And whyles the heedes do this, /The remenaunt is amys	249	Collyn Clout	115
And ryght slender connynge /Within theyr heedes wonnynge.	250	Collyn Clout	141
Plucke away the leedes /Over theyr heedes,	257	Collyn Clout	409
Your heedes for to hyde	363	Albany	186

HEER
Of her heer so fyne,	101	Phy Sparrow	1173

HEERE
That though ye rounde your heere	263	Collyn Clout	673

HEERY
And from the berded gotes /With theyr heery cotes;	250	Collyn Clout	159
In gray russet and heery cotes;	268	Collyn Clout	865

| HEGHE —HELL | Page | Title | Line |

HEGHE
'Heghe, ha, ha, Parott, ye can lawghe pratylye!' . . . . 231 Speke Parott 22
HEY
Wyth, 'Hey, troly-loly-lo, whip here, Jak', ... 37 Coystrownel 15
'Rumbyll downe, tumbyll downe, hey, go, now, now!' . . . . . . 37 Coystrownel 30
With hey, lullay, &c. . . . . 41 Balettysl R
With hey, lullay, &c. . . . . 42 Balettysl Rub
Wyth hey, lullay, &c. . . . . 42 Balettysl Rub
Wit[h], 'Hey, howe, rumbelowe,' /Rumpopulorum, ... 108 Epitaphel 80
  With] 'Wit' Marshe 1568
Tut, Scot, I sey, /Go shake th[e], dog, hey! . . . . 135 Dundas 28
  the] 'thy' Marshe 1568
He dawnsys so long, 'hey, troly, loly', ... 175 Magnyfycence 1250
With, 'Hey, dogge, hay, /Have these hogges away!' . . . . . . 218 El Rummynge 168
  hogges] 'dogges' Day 1560, Marshe 1568
With, 'Hey,' and with, 'Howe, /Syt we downe arowe . . . . . . 221 El Rummynge 289
'Lende here a cocke of hey, ... 229 El Rummynge 577
With, 'hey, dogge, hay.' . . . . 360 Albany 37
HEYDA
Rutty bully, joly rutterkyn, heyda! . . . . 161 Magnyfycence 747
HEYGHT
That he set him on heyght, ... 292 Why Come Ye 542
A myghty tre and of a noble heyght, ... 312 Garlande 19
HEYNOUSLY
And heynously on her to bable . . . . 375 Replycacion 27
HEYRE
My heyre bussheth /So plesauntly; . . . . 163 Magnyfycence 835
HEYRE PARENT
As longe as I lyve, thou haste an heyre parent. . . . . 154 Magnyfycence 507
HEKELL
Theyr hekell and theyr rele, ... 222 El Rummynge 295
HEL
Then Cerberus the cur couching in the kenel of hel; . . . . . 140 Ven Tongues 80
HELAS
Helas! I lamente the dull abusyd brayne, ... 242 Speke Parott 383
Helas, I say, helas! . . . . 272 Collyn Clout 1020
Helas, I say, helas! . . . . 272 Collyn Clout 1020
But /Helas! sage overage /So madly decayes, ... 279 Why Come Ye 41
  So] 'To' Toy 1553, Kitson 1560.7, Marshe 1568
Helas, my herte is sory . . . . 284 Why Come Ye 227
Helas, ye wreches, ye may be wo! . . . . 376 Replycacion 77
HELD
And held with the commonns under a cloke, ... 31 Dol Dethe 76
HELE
Ware, ware, the mare wynsyth wyth her wanton hele! 43 Balettys2 22
Syr, thanked be God, he hath his hele. . . . . 149 Magnyfycence 315
That wantonly can wynke and wynche with her hele. . . . . . . 197 Magnyfycence 2023
Hath promised to hele our cardinals eye. . . . . 309 Why Come Ye 1197
And 'He haltith often that hath a kyby hele.' . . . . 326 Garlande 502
HELED
In Balthasor, whiche heled . . . . 308 Why Come Ye 1184
It was nat heled alderbest, ... 308 Why Come Ye 1188
HELES
With heles short and rounde. . . . . 100 Phy Sparrow 1150
With a payre of heles /As brode as two wheles. . . . . 216 El Rummynge 83
Wyth theyr heles dagged, /Theyr kyrtelles all to-jagged, . . 217 El Rummynge 123
HELYD
Balthasor, that helyd Domingos nose . . . . 309 Why Come Ye 1194
  nose] 'pose' Marshe 1568
HELYN
With Dame Helyn the quene. . . . . 270 Collyn Clout 953
HELL
Hevyn, hell and erth obey unto thi kall; . . . . 34 Dol Dethe 192
The sowle of this lorde from all daunger of hell, ... 34 Dol Dethe 200
That is a flode of hell; . . . . 73 Phy Sparrow 71
By Hercules that hell dyd harow, ... 104 Phy Sparrow 1291
That in hell is never brent, ... 104 Phy Sparrow 1327
By the feryman of hell, ... 105 Phy Sparrow 1337
Procerpina in hell, ... 105 Phy Sparrow 1366
In faythe, he were better to dwell in hell. . . . . 157 Magnyfycence 623
That made Cerberus to cache, the cur dogge of hell, ... 182 Magnyfycence 1495
I wolde I had, by hym that hell dyd harowe, ... 184 Magnyfycence 1561
Measure? Tut, what the devyll of hell! . . . . 189 Magnyfycence 1745
Lyke houndes of hell, /They crye and they yell . . . . 251 Collyn Clout 198
What they do in hell. . . . . 267 Collyn Clout 823
Dame Margeres soule out of hell. . . . . 268 Collyn Clout 876
Avaunt to the devyll of hell! . . . . 275 Collyn Clout 1164
The way to heven or to hell!' . . . . 277 Collyn Clout 1226
And Asmodeus of hell . . . . 284 Why Come Ye 209
As the fynd of hell! . . . . 294 Why Come Ye 594
Endlesse to dwell /With the devyll of hell! . . . . 303 Why Come Ye 972
And set hell on fyer . . . . 303 Why Come Ye 985
  hell] 'all' Toy 1553, Kitson 1560.7, Marshe 1568
The devyll of hell and he be seldome asonder.' . . . . 333 Garlande 765
By Hercules that hell did harow, ... 348 Garlande 1284
That in hell is never brente, ... 349 Garlande 1320
By the feryman of hell, ... 349 Garlande 1330
Proserpina in hell, ... 350 Garlande 1359

	Page	Title	Line
The fynde of hell mot sterve the!	365	Albany	251
To hunt them into hell,	380	Replycacion	214
That at his resurrection he harped out of hell	383	Replycacion	341

HELLE

But I wonder what the devyll of helle	52	Bowge	208
Lothsum as Lucifer lowest in helle.	130	Garnesche5	28
To the flingande fende of helle.	366	Albany	317

HELL-HOUNDE

F[rom] that hell-hounde	74	Phy Sparrow	89
From] 'For' †Kele 1545.2, Wyght 1553, Kitson 1560.6, Marshe 1568			

HELME

The sayle is up, Fortune ruleth our helme,	49	Bowge	127
Holde up the helme, loke up and lete God stere:	53	Bowge	250

HELP

Unkindly thei slew hym that help them oft at nede.	30	Dol Dethe	47
help] 'holp' Marshe 1568			

HELPE

To the for succour, to the for helpe I kall,	29	Dol Dethe	12
These be my querysters /To helpe me to synge,	65	Hauke	123
Do mi nus, /Helpe nowe swete Jesus!	74	Phy Sparrow	96
With helpe of the red sparow	82	Phy Sparrow	403
Must helpe us to houle;	82	Phy Sparrow	443
Cannyst thou helpe in faver that I myght be brought?	162	Magnyfycence	777
So helpe me God, man, ever at the length	175	Magnyfycence	1258
For, so helpe me God, for you he is not mete.	186	Magnyfycence	1653
Well cannest thou helpe a preest to synge a songe.	187	Magnyfycence	1676
Nay, so God me helpe, it was no grete vexacyon;	189	Magnyfycence	1733
He may helpe you. He may mende your mode.	207	Magnyfycence	2366
To helpe withall a stytch;	226	El Rummynge	457
But be the helpe of Christen Clout.	268	Collyn Clout	879
With helpe of the ram, ley all in the dust.	315	Garlande	105
I helpe all other of there infirmite,	321	Garlande	311
But now to helpe myselfe I am not able.	321	Garlande	312
Me to supporte, to helpe, and to assist,	335	Garlande	827
To helpe you to promocion,	378	Replycacion	137

HELPYNG

In helpyng to warke my laurell grene	342	Garlande	1074

HELPT

Smale flowres helpt to sett	339	Garlande	969

HELTH

Holde thy tonge, and thou love thy helth.	179	Magnyfycence	1402
Shall never have good helth;	304	Why Come Ye	1025
It were an hevenly helth,	340	Garlande	994

HELTHE

There is no excesse where measure hath his helthe.	144	Magnyfycence	140
Helthe of body his besynesse to acheve;	207	Magnyfycence	2369

HEM

Hem, syr, yet beware of 'Had I wyste!'	146	Magnyfycence	211
Hem! That lyke I nothynge at all.	158	Magnyfycence	664
Hem, Colusyon!	162	Magnyfycence	779
Hem, Fansy! Regardes, voyes [vous].	173	Magnyfycence	1197

HEME

Ge heme! ge scour thy pot,	282	Why Come Ye	126
Go heme, ranke Scot, ge heme,	368	Albany	382
Go heme, ranke Scot, ge heme,	368	Albany	382

HEMPEN

Ye be nat cawte in an hempen snare.	133	Garnesche5	163

HEN

With Partlot his hen,	84	Phy Sparrow	509
To treade the prety wren /That is our Ladyes hen.	86	Phy Sparrow	601
Moche herted lyke an hen.	251	Collyn Clout	168
Stronge-herted lyke an hen.	285	Why Come Ye	276

HENCE

Wherfore, Measure, take Lyberte with you hence,	146	Magnyfycence	230
This letter was wryten ferre hence.	150	Magnyfycence	337

HEN-HERTED

Lyke hen-herted cokoldes.	283	Why Come Ye	168

HENNES

The hennes ron in the mashfat;	219	El Rummynge	190
The hennes donge awaye,	219	El Rummynge	197
The donge of her hennes /And the ale togyder,	219	El Rummynge	202
Hennes, checkynges, and pygges.	284	Why Come Ye	223

HENRY

Noble Henry the eight,	110	Lawde	8
God save kynge Henry and his lordes all	115	Scot Kynge	72
and God save noble Kynge Henry the viij.	115	Scot Kynge	E
Royall Henry the eyght,	292	Why Come Ye	540
Christ kepe King Henry the Eyght	298	Why Come Ye	772
Now Henry the viij, Kyng of Englonde,	347	Garlande	1227
Noble Henry the Eyght	361	Albany	109

HENS

Gete you hens, I say, by my counsell.	149	Magnyfycence	306
Let us departe from hens home to my place.	151	Magnyfycence	394
Mary, syr, Cokermowthe is a good way hens.	170	Magnyfycence	1061
Nowe then goo we hens. Away the mare!	177	Magnyfycence	1325
Well, get you hens than and sende me some other.	180	Magnyfycence	1451
I coude holde you with suche talke hens tyll to morowe.	184	Magnyfycence	1588

HENTE —HER | Page | Title | Line

Text	Page	Title	Line
Have hym hens, I say, out of my syght!	188	Magnyfycence	1723
Hens, thou haynyarde, out of dores fast!	188	Magnyfycence	1725
And therfore hye you hens, and take this oversyght.	190	Magnyfycence	1795

HENTE

Text	Page	Title	Line
And as they came, the shypborde faste I hente,	61	Bowge	530

HEPE

Text	Page	Title	Line
And thyder came an hepe /Of mylstones in a route.'	223	El Rummynge	361
thyder] 'there' †Lant 1545, Kynge & Marche 1554, Day 1560, Marshe 1568			

HER

Text	Page	Title	Line
He wantyd wyt her love to wyn:	42	Balettys1	12
He trusted her payment and lost all hys pray.	42	Balettys1	13
She sparyd not to wete her fete.	42	Balettys1	16
That halsyd her hartely and kyst her swete.	42	Balettys1	18
That halsyd her hartely and kyst her swete.	42	Balettys1	18
Thus after her cold she cought a hete.	42	Balettys1	19
To dele wyth her so cowardly;	42	Balettys1	27
Ware, ware, the mare wynsyth wyth her wanton hele!	43	Balettys2	22
She kykyth with her kalkyns and keylyth with a clench;	43	Balettys2	23
Though thou withdraw me from her by long dystaunce,	45	Balettys3	46
For I have gravyd her wythin the secret wall	45	Balettys3	48
Of my trew hart, to love her best of all!	45	Balettys3	49
Her takelynge ryche and of hye apparayle;	47	Bowge	38
Marchauntes her borded to see what she had lode.	47	Bowge	40
lode] not in Marshe 1568			
Her marchaundyse is ryche and fortunate,	47	Bowge	52
Her] 'Here' †Wynkyn de Worde 1499			
Is called Favore to stonde in her good grace.'	47	Bowge	55
Amonge all other was wrytten in her trone,	47	Bowge	65
Her chyef gentylwoman, Daunger by her name,	48	Bowge	69
Her chyef gentylwoman, Daunger by her name,	48	Bowge	69
That, so to saye, I had gyven her no cause.	48	Bowge	75
Desyre her name was, and so she me tolde,	48	Bowge	85
She that styreth the shyp, make her your frende.'	49	Bowge	107
'Alas,' quod I, 'how myghte I have her sure?'	49	Bowge	118
They thronge in fast and flocked her aboute,	49	Bowge	122
And I with them prayed her to have in mynde.	49	Bowge	123
Ye be to her, yea, worth a thousande pounde.	50	Bowge	157
I herde her speke of you within shorte space,	50	Bowge	158
shorte] 'a shorte' Wynkyn de Worde 1510			
How ofte he knocked at her klycked gate.	56	Bowge	371
I lete her to hyre that men maye on her ryde;	57	Bowge	402
I lete her to hyre that men maye on her ryde;	57	Bowge	402
Her har[n]es easy ferre and more is soughte.	57	Bowge	403
harnes] 'harmes' †Wynkyn de Worde 1499, 1510, 'armes' Marshe 1568			
By Goddis sydes, syns I her thyder broughte,	57	Bowge	404
She hath gote me more money with her tayle	57	Bowge	405
Who rydeth on her, he nedeth not to care,	57	Bowge	409
To her wyll I nowe all my poverte lege.	57	Bowge	412
That on the rode loft /She perkyd her to rest.	63	Hauke	70
He then, to be sure, /Callyd her with a lure.	63	Hauke	76
Her mete was very crude,	63	Hauke	77
mete] 'mere' Kynge & Marche 1554			
Wyth that he gave her a bounce	64	Hauke	86
Worrowyd her on that /Which I loved best.	72	Phy Sparrow	29
And from her fyry sparklynges,	73	Phy Sparrow	80
Was wery of her lyfe,	74	Phy Sparrow	109
Whan she had lost her joye,	74	Phy Sparrow	110
I wolde I had a parte /Of her crafty magyke!	77	Phy Sparrow	204
The popyngay to tell her tale,	82	Phy Sparrow	421
The mavys with her whystell	82	Phy Sparrow	424
The threstyl with her warblyng;	83	Phy Sparrow	460
The starlyng with her brablyng;	83	Phy Sparrow	461
Whan he doth her trede,	84	Phy Sparrow	512
Whan her tale is tolde	87	Phy Sparrow	620
How she controlde /Her husbandes as she wolde,	87	Phy Sparrow	623
And made her husband knyght /Of the comyne hall,	87	Phy Sparrow	646
From her to hym agayn;	88	Phy Sparrow	687
Or a bracelet of her here,	89	Phy Sparrow	689
That token for her sake;	89	Phy Sparrow	691
Disparaged is her fame	89	Phy Sparrow	711
And blemysshed is her name,	89	Phy Sparrow	712
On her moch love and cost,	89	Phy Sparrow	715
To her husband most trew,	89	Phy Sparrow	726
Her wyt stood her in sted	89	Phy Sparrow	729
Her wyt stood her in sted	89	Phy Sparrow	729
To Ulixes her make,	90	Phy Sparrow	732
And for her sparow prayd /In lamentable wyse.	93	Phy Sparrow	854
Her beautye to commende,	93	Phy Sparrow	859
Though I regester her name	94	Phy Sparrow	891
To make a relation /Of her commendation;	95	Phy Sparrow	962
To] 'Bo' †Kele 1545.2			
All the goodly sort /Of her fetures clere,	96	Phy Sparrow	1000
Her favour of her face	96	Phy Sparrow	1002
Her favour of her face	96	Phy Sparrow	1002
Her to behold and se,	97	Phy Sparrow	1007

	Page	Title	Line
To loke on her agayne.	97	Phy Sparrow	1010
on] 'to' Marshe 1568			
With her aye to remayne.	97	Phy Sparrow	1013
Her eyen gray and stepe	97	Phy Sparrow	1014
With her browes bent	97	Phy Sparrow	1016
The Indy saphyre blew /Her vaynes doth ennew;	97	Phy Sparrow	1032
The whytnesse of her lere;	97	Phy Sparrow	1034
Her lyppes soft and mery	97	Phy Sparrow	1037
Her sugred mouth to kysse.	97	Phy Sparrow	1040
Her beautye to augment	97	Phy Sparrow	1041
Dame Nature hath her lent	97	Phy Sparrow	1042
A warte upon her cheke,	97	Phy Sparrow	1043
In her vysage a skar	97	Phy Sparrow	1045
And whan I perceyved /Her wart and conceyved,	98	Phy Sparrow	1064
To her to sewe for grace,	98	Phy Sparrow	1075
Her favoure to purchase.	98	Phy Sparrow	1076
The sker upon her chyn	98	Phy Sparrow	1077
Enhached on her fayre skyn,	98	Phy Sparrow	1078
Her favour to wyn;	98	Phy Sparrow	1082
Her goodly dalyaunce,	99	Phy Sparrow	1095
And her goodly pastaunce:	99	Phy Sparrow	1096
Behavynge her so sure,	99	Phy Sparrow	1098
To gyve her his hole hert.	99	Phy Sparrow	1102
Upon her whan I gased,	99	Phy Sparrow	1104
And to amende her tale,	99	Phy Sparrow	1116
And with her fyngers smale,	99	Phy Sparrow	1118
And me to her retayned,	99	Phy Sparrow	1126
Her goodly myddell small	99	Phy Sparrow	1128
goodly] 'godly' †Kele 1545.2			
Upon her prety fote?	100	Phy Sparrow	1147
To se her treade the grounde	100	Phy Sparrow	1149
And lyke to her image,	100	Phy Sparrow	1153
Such relucent grace /Is formed in her face;	100	Phy Sparrow	1160
Of her heer so fyne,	101	Phy Sparrow	1173
The garterynge of her hose?	101	Phy Sparrow	1176
How that she can were /Gorgiously her gere;	101	Phy Sparrow	1179
Her fresshe habylementes /With other implementes	101	Phy Sparrow	1180
Her kyrtell so goodly lased,	101	Phy Sparrow	1194
To prase her excellence!	101	Phy Sparrow	1207
To prayse her at the full;	102	Phy Sparrow	1222
and her foloweth an addicyon made by Maister Skelton.	103	Phy Sparrow	R
His Dirige, her commendacyon /Can be no derogacyon,	103	Phy Sparrow	1276
That her goodly name, /Honorably reported,	103	Phy Sparrow	1285
To wytchcraft her to dresse,	105	Phy Sparrow	1346
And by her abusyons,	105	Phy Sparrow	1347
And by her supersticyons,	105	Phy Sparrow	1350
Of her I holde /And her housholde;	112	Calliope	13
Of her I holde /And her housholde;	112	Calliope	14
Me to retayne /Her serviture.	112	Calliope	20
With her certayne /I wyll remayne	112	Calliope	21
Irrevocable ys her decre;	130	Garnesche5	14
Thryfte hathe lost her cofer kay.	155	Magnyfycence	527
Her browys bent, /Her eyen glent;	167	Magnyfycence	979
Her browys bent, /Her eyen glent;	167	Magnyfycence	980
A man shall fynde /Many of her kynde,	167	Magnyfycence	984
Her fethers donne; /Well faveryd bonne!	168	Magnyfycence	989
And her becke so comely crokys!	168	Magnyfycence	1000
Her naylys sharpe as tenter-hokys!	168	Magnyfycence	1001
I have not kept her yet thre wokys,	168	Magnyfycence	1002
I kyndell in her suche a lyther sparke	174	Magnyfycence	1231
Trymme at her tayle or a man can turne a socke.	177	Magnyfycence	1346
Fortune to her lawys can not abandune me;	181	Magnyfycence	1459
The streynes of her vaynes as asure Inde blewe,	183	Magnyfycence	1553
As lyly whyte to loke upon her [l]eyre,	183	Magnyfycence	1555
leyre] 'heyre' †Rastell & Treveris C 1530, B			
Her eyen relucent as carbuncle so clere,	183	Magnyfycence	1556
Her mouthe enbawmed, dylectable and mery,	183	Magnyfycence	1557
Her lusty lyppes ruddy as the chery -	183	Magnyfycence	1558
A, Lorde, so I wolde halse her hartely!	190	Magnyfycence	1801
So I wolde clepe her! So I wolde kys her swete!	190	Magnyfycence	1802
So I wolde clepe her! So I wolde kys her swete!	190	Magnyfycence	1802
To reche a rat - I coude not her warne.	191	Magnyfycence	1809
She pynched her pynyon, by God, and catched harme.	191	Magnyfycence	1810
It was a ronner; nay, fole, I warant her blode warme.	191	Magnyfycence	1811
That wantonly can wynke and wynche with her hele.	197	Magnyfycence	2023
In her promyse there is no sykernesse,	197	Magnyfycence	2028
All her delyte is set in doublenesse.	197	Magnyfycence	2029
I kyst her swete, and she kyssyd me;	198	Magnyfycence	2065
I garde her gaspe, I garde her gle,	198	Magnyfycence	2067
I garde her gaspe, I garde her gle,	198	Magnyfycence	2067
My harte is holly on her set;	199	Magnyfycence	2073
I plucked her by the patlet;	199	Magnyfycence	2074
At my devyse I with her met;	199	Magnyfycence	2075
My fansy fayrly on her I set;	199	Magnyfycence	2076
She hath dyssayvyd me with her doublenesse.	201	Magnyfycence	2157
For her vysage /It woldt aswage /A mannes courage.	214	El Rummynge	9
Her lothely lere /Is nothynge clere,	214	El Rummynge	12
Her face all bowsy,	215	El Rummynge	17

	Page	Title	Line
Her lewde lyppes twayne, /They slaver, men sayne,	215	El Rummynge	22
Her nose somdele hoked /And camously croked,	215	El Rummynge	27
Her skynne lose and slacke, /Greuyned lyke a sacke;	215	El Rummynge	31
Greuyned] 'Grained' Day 1560, Marshe 1568			
Her eyen gowndy /Are full unsowndy,	215	El Rummynge	34
The bones [of] her huckels	215	El Rummynge	45
of] not in †Lant 1545, Kynge & Marche 1554, Day 1560, Marshe 1568; huckels] 'buckels' Day, Marshe			
Her youth is farre past;	215	El Rummynge	48
In her furred flocket, /And graye russet rocket,	215	El Rummynge	53
Her huke of Lyncole grene,	215	El Rummynge	56
Upon the holy daye, /Whan she doth her aray,	216	El Rummynge	67
And gyrdeth in her gytes /Stytched and pranked with pletes;	216	El Rummynge	68
Her kyrtell Brystowe red,	216	El Rummynge	70
With clothes upon her hed /That wey a sowe of led,	216	El Rummynge	71
That wey] 'That they wey' Kynge & Marche 1554, Day 1560, Marshe 1568			
Upon her brayne-pan, /Lyke an Egypcyan /Lapped about.	216	El Rummynge	77
Lapped] 'Capped' Kynge & Marche 1554, Day 1560, Marshe 1568			
She hobles as she gose /With her blanket hose	216	El Rummynge	86
she gose] 'a gose' Day 1560, Marshe 1568			
Her shone smered wyth talowe,	216	El Rummynge	88
Gresed upon dyrt /That baudeth her skyrt.	216	El Rummynge	90
I understande, her name /Is Elynour Rummynge,	216	El Rummynge	92
At home in her wonnynge;	216	El Rummynge	94
To have of her tunnynge.	217	El Rummynge	130
The sowe with her pygges;	219	El Rummynge	176
With her maungy fystis.	219	El Rummynge	200
The donge of her hennes /And the ale togyder,	219	El Rummynge	202
In stede of coyne and monny /Some brynge her a conny,	220	El Rummynge	245
Her thryfte is full thyn.	221	El Rummynge	256
Her lyppes are so drye,	221	El Rummynge	272
And with her doth brynge	221	El Rummynge	278
Her hernest gyrdle, her weddynge rynge,	221	El Rummynge	280
hernest] 'haruest' Day 1560, 1521 Fragment			
Her hernest gyrdle, her weddynge rynge,	221	El Rummynge	280
hernest] 'haruest' Day 1560, 1521 Fragment			
To pay for her scot	221	El Rummynge	281
As cometh to her lot.	221	El Rummynge	282
Some bryngeth her husbandis hood,	221	El Rummynge	283
Another brought her his cap	221	El Rummynge	285
Her colour was full wan –	222	El Rummynge	318
Her tonge was very quycke	223	El Rummynge	337
Her felowe dyd stammer and stut,	223	El Rummynge	339
For her mouth fomyd /And her bely groned:	223	El Rummynge	341
For her mouth fomyd /And her bely groned:	223	El Rummynge	342
She spake thus in her snout,	223	El Rummynge	363
spake thus] 'speketh this' †Lant 1545, Kynge & Marche 1554, Day 1560, Marshe 1568			
Snevelyng in her nose, /As though she had the pose.	223	El Rummynge	364
Elynour toke her up	224	El Rummynge	376
And blessed her with a cup /Of newe ale in cornes.	224	El Rummynge	377
An other than dyd hyche her,	224	El Rummynge	401
hyche] 'hye' 1521 Fragment			
She cut of her sho-sole,	224	El Rummynge	405
For a draught of her lycour.	225	El Rummynge	417
her] not in †Lant 1545, Kynge & Marche 1554, Day 1560, Marshe 1568			
Than Margery Mylkeducke /Her kyrtell she dyd uptucke	225	El Rummynge	419
An ynche above her kne,	225	El Rummynge	420
Her legges that ye myght se;	225	El Rummynge	421
ye] 'he' 1521 Fragment			
And yet she brought her fees,	225	El Rummynge	428
[And] of her husbandes breke.	225	El Rummynge	452
And] not in editions			
She had her so guyded	226	El Rummynge	472
With that her hed shaked /And her handes quaked.	226	El Rummynge	476
With that her hed shaked /And her handes quaked.	226	El Rummynge	477
Ones hed wold have aked /To se her naked.	226	El Rummynge	479
The dropsy was in her legges;	226	El Rummynge	481
Her face glystryng lyke glas,	226	El Rummynge	482
In all her joyntes about;	226	El Rummynge	485
Her breth was soure and stale	226	El Rummynge	486
And had broken her shyn	227	El Rummynge	494
That one might se her token.	227	El Rummynge	497
And as she at her dyd pluck,	227	El Rummynge	504
And] not in Day 1560, Marshe 1568; pluck] 'pulck' †Lant 1545			
Another brought her garlyke heddes;	227	El Rummynge	522
Another brought her bedes /Of jet or of cole,	227	El Rummynge	523
Some her husbandes gowne,	227	El Rummynge	530
And her brethe strongely stanke,	228	El Rummynge	541
And gat her great thanke	228	El Rummynge	543
Of Elynour for her ware,	228	El Rummynge	544
That she thyder bare /To pay for her share.	228	El Rummynge	546
Garnysshed was her snout	228	El Rummynge	554
The pot to her plucke,	228	El Rummynge	566
She swynged up a quarte /At ones for her parte.	228	El Rummynge	569
swynged] 'swinge' Marshe 1568			

	Page	Title	Line
Her paunche was so puffed	228	El Rummynge	570
To paye for her expence.	229	El Rummynge	599
Than Elynour dyd them hyde /Within her beddes syde.	229	El Rummynge	606
Phronessys for frenessys may not hold her way.	232	Speke Parott	47
They make her wynche and kycke,	251	Collyn Clout	181
Under her surfled smocke	252	Collyn Clout	218
And her wanton wodicocke.	252	Collyn Clout	219
But of her apostels lyfe.	253	Collyn Clout	254
her] 'theyr' Kele 1545.1, 'ther' MS Harley 2252			
And by the barres of her tayle	268	Collyn Clout	868
of] 'if' Marshe 1568, 'of' MS Harley 2252			
For to shote a crowe /At her tyrly tyrlowe;	270	Collyn Clout	949
Nor basse her swete swete.	279	Why Come Ye	35
Our mare hath cast her fole,	281	Why Come Ye	85
And, 'Mocke hath lost her sho;	281	Why Come Ye	86
But to recounte her ryche abylyment,	313	Garlande	44
And what estates to her did resorte,	313	Garlande	45
As I harde say, Dame Pallas was her name,	313	Garlande	48
But, for to preserve her maidenhode clene,	320	Garlande	293
maidenhode] 'maydenheed' Marshe 1568			
Betwene his armes, he felt her body quake.	320	Garlande	301
With that on me she kest her goodly loke.	327	Garlande	531
Under her arme, me thought, she hade a boke.	327	Garlande	532
Mountith on hy with her melodious lay,	327	Garlande	535
I thanked her moche of her most noble offer,	327	Garlande	554
I thanked her moche of her most noble offer,	327	Garlande	554
Affyaunsynge her myne hole assuraunce	327	Garlande	555
For her pleasure to make a large profer,	327	Garlande	556
Enpryntyng her wordes in my remembraunce,	327	Garlande	557
To owe her my servyce with true perseveraunce.	327	Garlande	558
Then questionyd I her what thos yatis ment;	328	Garlande	575
thos] 'these' Marshe 1568			
I her demaunded of them and ther astate.	329	Garlande	606
Men call a phenix; her wynges bytwene	330	Garlande	668
Thamar also wrought with her goodly honde	336	Garlande	852
In her bosome, lorde, how she was afrayd!	337	Garlande	887
how] not in MS Cotton Vitellius E.x			
The ruddy shamefastnes in her vysage fyll,	337	Garlande	888
Whiche maner of abasshement became her not yll;	337	Garlande	889
That for her trowth is in remembraunce had;	337	Garlande	900
Therfore I render of her the memory	339	Garlande	971
Her demenyng /In every thynge,	341	Garlande	1014
Her that is bothe womanly and wyse,	342	Garlande	1070
womanly] 'maydenly' MS Cotton Vitellius E.x			
In her astate there sat the noble Quene	343	Garlande	1114
To shew her boke; and she sayd, 'Here it is.'	344	Garlande	1148
Was wrytin; and so she did her spede,	345	Garlande	1168
To her he wrote many maters of myrthe;	346	Garlande	1199
For Margery wynshed, and breke her hinder girth;	346	Garlande	1201
Lorde, how she made moche of her gentyll birth!	346	Garlande	1202
With, 'Gingirly, go gingerly!' Her tayle was made of hay;	346	Garlande	1203
Go she never so gingirly, her honesty is gone away.	346	Garlande	1204
To face out her foly with a midsomer mase;	346	Garlande	1208
With pitche she patchid her pitcher shuld not crase;	346	Garlande	1209
His dirige, her commendacioun /Can be no derogacyoun;	348	Garlande	1269
That her goodly name, /Honorably reportid,	348	Garlande	1278
To witchecraft her to dres,	350	Garlande	1339
And by her abusiouns, /And damnable illusiouns	350	Garlande	1340
Of mervelous conclusiouns, /And by her supersticiouns	350	Garlande	1343
Though Jak sayd nay, yet Mok there loste her sho;	351	Garlande	1396
How her ble was bryght as blossom on the spray,	351	Garlande	1412
Suppleyng to Fame, I beseych her grace,	353	Garlande	1478
And that it wolde please her, full tenderly I prayd,	353	Garlande	1479
Owt of her bokis Apollo to rase.	353	Garlande	1480
Apollo to rase out of her ragman rollis.	354	Garlande	1490
Whiche redde on still, as it cam to her syght,	354	Garlande	1493
And her most blessed baby,	375	Replycacion	19
And heynously on her to bable	375	Replycacion	27
Agaynst her grace disputed	375	Replycacion	30
Agaynst her excellence, /Agaynst her reverence,	375	Replycacion	40
Agaynst her excellence, /Agaynst her reverence,	375	Replycacion	41
Agaynst her preemynence, /Agaynst her magnifycence,	375	Replycacion	42
Agaynst her preemynence, /Agaynst her magnifycence,	375	Replycacion	43
With baudrie at her ye brayed;	376	Replycacion	48
Bycause ye her mysnamed,	376	Replycacion	59
And wolde have her defamed,	376	Replycacion	60
At the feest of her concepcion	376	Replycacion	67
The ymage of her grace	381	Replycacion	261
HERAFTER			
We shall here more herafter!	281	Why Come Ye	99
As herafter ben notyd:	293	Why Come Ye	573
Herafter perchaunce I shall	299	Why Come Ye	823
HERBE			
Unto me; alas, that herbe nor gresse	321	Garlande	314
gresse] 'gras' †Fakes 1523			
HERBER			
Herber enverduryd, contynuall fressh and grene;	44	Balettys3	13
In an herber I saw, brought where I was,	330	Garlande	652

HERBERS —HERE   Page   Title   Line

HERBERS
Upon every banke /Of his herbers grene, ...   304   Why Come Ye   1003
HERCULES
Whom Hercules dyd outraye, ...   74   Phy Sparrow   87
By Hercules that hell dyd harow, ...   104   Phy Sparrow   1291
Hercules the herdy, with his stobburne clobbyd mase, ...   182   Magnyfycence   1494
By Hercules that hell did harow, ...   348   Garlande   1284
In merciall prowes /Lyke unto Hercules, ...   369   Albany   431
HERD
With that I herd gunnis russhe out at ones, ...   329   Garlande   623
The hertis of the herd began for to grone, and fled   351   Garlande   1408
HERDE
I herde her speke of you within shorte space, ...   50   Bowge   158
    shorte] 'a shorte' Wynkyn de Worde 1510
But have ye not herde say that wyll is no skyll?   144   Magnyfycence   148
Cockys bonys! Herde ye ever syke another?   170   Magnyfycence   1090
I trowe ye herde yourselfe what I sayd.   188   Magnyfycence   1695
If ever I herde syke another, God gyve me shame.   192   Magnyfycence   1833
In welthe to beware of herde adversyte.   201   Magnyfycence   2159
Myxed with bytter alowes of herde adversyte.   207   Magnyfycence   2354
I herde say that adversyte with Magnyfycence had fought. . . .   210   Magnyfycence   2460
Whan he herde tell /That my Lorde Amrell   360   Albany   54
HERDELY
And after his mynde herdely your selfe adresse, ...   144   Magnyfycence   151
HERDER
For to lyve in mysery, it is herder than dethe.   205   Magnyfycence   2282
HERDY
Hercules the herdy, with his stobburne clobbyd mase, ...   182   Magnyfycence   1494
HERE
Wyth, 'Hey, troly-loly-lo, whip here, Jak', ...   37   Coystrownel   15
Here folowythe Dyvers Balettys and Dyties Solacyous   41   Balettys   I
Here begynneth a lytell treatyse named The Bowge of Courte . .   46   Bowge   I
'Maysters', he sayde, 'the shyp that ye here see, ...   47   Bowge   48
This royall chaffre that is shypped here   47   Bowge   54
Bone aventure have here now in your honde.   48   Bowge   98
For here be dyverse to you that be unkynde.   50   Bowge   161
For here is none that dare well other truste;   51   Bowge   202
Is lytyll to saye, and moche to here and see;   52   Bowge   212
Where hathe your dwellynge ben, er ye cam here?   53   Bowge   247
For, as for me, I served here many a daye, ...   53   Bowge   274
His here was growen thorowe oute his hat.   56   Bowge   350
I was ashamed so to here hym prate.   56   Bowge   373
What, loo, man, see here of dyce a bale;   57   Bowge   389
And tyll I come, have, here is myne hat to plege.'   57   Bowge   413
    is] not in Marshe 1568
It is a worlde, I saye, to here of some -   59   Bowge   464
    to] 'te' †Wynkyn de Worde 1499, 'to' Wynkyn de Worde 1510,
    Marshe 1568
'Harken,' quod he, 'loo here myne honde in thyne;   60   Bowge   510
But to here the subtylte and the crafte, ...   61   Bowge   519
Me thoughte I see lewde felawes here and there   61   Bowge   528
Or a bracelet of her here, ...   89   Phy Sparrow   689
Nor no bore so brymly brystlyd ys with here, ...   122   Garneschel   25
Row and full of lowsy here, ...   127   Garnesche3   124
But lering and lurking here and there like spies, ...   139   Ven Tongues   67
Here you not howe this gentylman mockys?   141   Magnyfycence   32
Me pacyently to here.   143   Magnyfycence   111
Me semeth Magnyfycence is comynge here at hande.   145   Magnyfycence   162
Here is none forsyth whether you flete or synke.   147   Magnyfycence   254
Have ye not welthe here at your wyll?   148   Magnyfycence   284
I pray you, Larges, here to remayne, ...   149   Magnyfycence   323
I had not been here with you this nyght.   150   Magnyfycence   365
And in dede, syr, I here men talke -   151   Magnyfycence   374
Ye, but how longe shall I here awayte?   151   Magnyfycence   398
They have made me here to put the stone;   151   Magnyfycence   406
Here is a leysshe of ratches to renne an hare!   156   Magnyfycence   586
What sayst? Here was to lytell clothe.   157   Magnyfycence   607
Here is a pystell of a postyke!   158   Magnyfycence   649
By Cockys body, here begynneth the game!   159   Magnyfycence   682
Then for the season that I here shall walke, ...   159   Magnyfycence   691
That they wyll here no man but the fyrst tale.   161   Magnyfycence   743
Here cometh in CRAFTY CONVEYAUNCE.   162   Magnyfycence   SD
Here he is nowe, man. Mayst thou not se?   162   Magnyfycence   792
Well, tary here tyll I for you sende.   163   Magnyfycence   817
Tary here. Wote ye what I say?   163   Magnyfycence   819
Here cometh in FANSY craynge 'Stow, stow!'   165   Magnyfycence   SD
What! Whom have we here, Jenkyn Joly?   166   Magnyfycence   918
But I must tary here; go thou before.   167   Magnyfycence   954
What, Fansy! Arte thou here alone?   169   Magnyfycence   1044
Yes, in faythe, I thanke God I may here.   169   Magnyfycence   1059
And thy wyt wanderynge here and there, ...   170   Magnyfycence   1074
Here is no man that callyd the hogge nor swyne.   170   Magnyfycence   1084
Why, sayst thou that I was here yesterday?   170   Magnyfycence   1093
Here is nothynge but the bockyll of a sho, ...   171   Magnyfycence   1107
Nay, in fayth, fyrst let me here thyne.   172   Magnyfycence   1152
Mary, as for that, thou shalte sone here myne.   172   Magnyfycence   1153
Here cometh in CRAFTY CONVEYAUNCE.   172   Magnyfycence   SD
Here FOLY maketh semblaunt to take a lowse   173   Magnyfycence   SD

HERE — HERE

	Page	Title	Line
Here CRAFTY CONVEYAUNCE putteth of his gowne.	173	Magnyfycence	SD
Here FOLY maketh semblaunt	173	Magnyfycence	SD
Nay, wylte thou here nowe of his scoles,	174	Magnyfycence	1216
Ye. Let us here a worde or twayne.	174	Magnyfycence	1218
To here you two rutters dyspute togyder.	176	Magnyfycence	1287
Here cometh in MAGNYFYCENCE with LYBERTE and FELYCYTE.	178	Magnyfycence	SD
Here goth out CRAFTY CONVAYAUNCE.	179	Magnyfycence	SD
Here cometh in FANSY.	179	Magnyfycence	SD
Syr, I am here at your pleasure.	179	Magnyfycence	1409
Come hyther Largesse; take here Felycyte.	179	Magnyfycence	1411
To rule as ye lyst, lo, here is Lyberte.	179	Magnyfycence	1413
I am here redy. What! Shall we	179	Magnyfycence	1414
Here goeth out FELYCYTE, LYBERTE and FANSY.	180	Magnyfycence	SD
Here cometh in COURTLY ABUSYON, doynge reverence and courtesy.	182	Magnyfycence	SD
Let us here of your pleasure, to passe the tyme withall.	182	Magnyfycence	1518
To here your comon, it is my hygh comforte.	183	Magnyfycence	1539
If it wolde lyke you to here my pore mynde –	183	Magnyfycence	1543
Here no man what so ever they say	185	Magnyfycence	1603
Here cometh in CLOKED COLUSYON with MESURE	186	Magnyfycence	SD
Stande styll here, and ye shall se	186	Magnyfycence	1629
Syr, so it is: this man is here by,	186	Magnyfycence	1649
Come hyder, Pleasure; you shall here myne entent.	186	Magnyfycence	1655
Whylest I came to you, a lytell here besyde.	187	Magnyfycence	1686
Well, call hym, and let us here hym reason;	187	Magnyfycence	1687
Here MESURE goth out of the place.	188	Magnyfycence	SD
So I wote not what he sholde do here.	189	Magnyfycence	1741
For I here but fewe men that gyve ony prayse	189	Magnyfycence	1743
And here I make the upon Lyberte	190	Magnyfycence	1784
Here goth CLOKED COLUSYON awaye,	190	Magnyfycence	SD
Here cometh in FOLY.	191	Magnyfycence	SD
Here FANSY cometh in.	192	Magnyfycence	SD
Here goth FOLY away.	192	Magnyfycence	SD
Here cometh in ADVERSYTE.	193	Magnyfycence	SD
Here MAGNYFYCENCE is beten downe	193	Magnyfycence	SD
Take hede of this captyfe that lyeth here on grounde.	195	Magnyfycence	1946
Here cometh in POVERTE.	195	Magnyfycence	SD
Here MAGNYFYCENCE dolorously maketh his mone.	198	Magnyfycence	SD
Where is nowe all my servauntys that I had here a late?	198	Magnyfycence	2057
This lurden that here lyeth had ben a noble man.	200	Magnyfycence	2112
Here cometh in CRAFTY CONVEYAUNCE [and] CLOKYD COLUSYON	201	Magnyfycence	SD
Nay, horson, here is my glove. Take it up and thou dare.	202	Magnyfycence	2178
Here shalbe not great sheddynge of blode.	203	Magnyfycence	2207
Lo, here is thy knyfe and a halter, and or we go ferther,	206	Magnyfycence	2317
Here MAGNYFYCENCE wolde slee hymselfe with a knyfe.	206	Magnyfycence	SD
Here cometh in SAD CYRCUMSPECCYON sayenge.	209	Magnyfycence	SD
Brystled with here.	215	El Rummynge	21
And have here a pecke of ry.'	221	El Rummynge	275
Here was scant thryft /Whan they made suche shyft.	222	El Rummynge	301
'Lo, here is an olde typpet,	223	El Rummynge	366
And have here a pylche of graye;	224	El Rummynge	398
With here and there a puscull,	228	El Rummynge	555
'Have here is for me, /A clout of London pynnes.'	228	El Rummynge	563
'Lende here a cocke of hey,	229	El Rummynge	577
To practise or postyll thys prosses here and there?	242	Speke Parott	393
I here the people talke.	254	Collyn Clout	288
To here the people jangle.	255	Collyn Clout	330
That a man shall here a masse,	272	Collyn Clout	1022
Nor wyll here no prechynge,	274	Collyn Clout	1133
We shall here more herafter!	281	Why Come Ye	99
What here ye of Lancashyre?	285	Why Come Ye	247
What here ye of Chesshyre?	285	Why Come Ye	250
What here ye of the Scottes?	285	Why Come Ye	262
What here ye of the lorde Dakers?	285	Why Come Ye	272
What here ye of the lord Rose?	286	Why Come Ye	286
What here ye of Burgonyons	288	Why Come Ye	370
What here ye of Mutrell?	288	Why Come Ye	377
Yet what here ye tell	288	Why Come Ye	379
But lytell or nothynge ye shall here tell ye shall] 'shall ye' MS Cotton Vitellius E.x	317	Garlande	197
Sume sayd, 'Holde thy peas, thou getest here no more.'	319	Garlande	257
In maner and forme as ye shall after here.	323	Garlande	399
'There shal he here what she wyl to hym say wyl to hym] 'to hym will' Marshe 1568	325	Garlande	451
Here dwellith pleasure, with lust and delyte;	332	Garlande	709
Contynuall comfort here ye may fynde,	332	Garlande	710
All thynge convenable here is contryvyd convenable] 'convenably' Marshe 1568	332	Garlande	712
And here to inhabite and ay for to dwell!	332	Garlande	719
To here this nightingale,	340	Garlande	997
Here you not Eolus for you blowyth a blaste? you (1st)] 'ye' MS Cotton Vitellius E.x	343	Garlande	1088
'My frende, sith ye ar before us here present	344	Garlande	1121
Of laureat triumphe, your place is here reservyd, triumphe] 'promocioun' MS Cotton Vitellius E.x	344	Garlande	1126
Your discharge here under myne arme is it.'	344	Garlande	1146
To shew her boke; and she sayd, 'Here it is.'	344	Garlande	1148
Of Englande, his workis here they begynne:	345	Garlande	1171
Here endith a ryght delectable tratyse	358	Garlande2	E

	Page	Title	Line
HEREAFTER			
Wherof hereafter, I thinke for to write,	140	Ven Tongues	81
To lerne you hereafter for to beware withall.	207	Magnyfycence	2376
HERE AFTER			
I hope here after a frende of you to have.'	54	Bowge	280
Here after foloweth the boke entytuled Ware the Hauke	61	Hauke	I
Here after foloweth the boke of Phyllyp Sparowe	71	Phy Sparrow	I
As here after thou shalte knowe more.	167	Magnyfycence	953
Here after foloweth a lytell boke,	278	Why Come Ye	I
HEREBY			
What may be ment hereby,	378	Replycacion	153
HEREIN			
What fault find ye herein but may be avowed.	138	Ven Tongues	41
Softe, my frende. Herein your reason is but rawe.	142	Magnyfycence	70
I reporte me herein to Kynge Lewes of Fraunce.	148	Magnyfycence	280
Howe say ye, syrs? Herein what is best?	186	Magnyfycence	1659
Herein I wyll aforse me to shewe you my mynde:	211	Magnyfycence	2483
HERE IN			
Shewe forth, I pray you, here in what you intende.	141	Magnyfycence	40
Your myndys I beseche you here in to expresse,	211	Magnyfycence	2480
HEREINNE			
And I dare saye there is no man hereinne	53	Bowge	267
HEREY			
And ye war herey, lyke a calfe;	131	Garnesche5	59
HERELACE			
Some have no herelace,	218	El Rummynge	145
HEREOF			
And make hereof a syckyll or a saw,	71	Hauke	333
Now hereof it erkith me lenger to wryte,	354	Garlande	1491
HERESY			
Of that heresy arte /Called Wytclyftista, Wytclyftista] 'Wicleuista' Marshe 1568	260	Collyn Clout	548
Agaynst this horryble heresy	375	Replycacion	21
To be blowen with the flye /Of horryble heresy.	376	Replycacion	86
Ye soored over hye /In the ierarchy /Of Jovenyans heresy,	378	Replycacion	163
His heresy to supporte;	379	Replycacion	192
With heresy all infecte.	380	Replycacion	237
Pufte full of heresy,	381	Replycacion	253
Of heresy the devyllysshe scoles	382	Replycacion	298
Opinyons detestable /Of heresy execrable?	382	Replycacion	305
To answere or reply /Agaynst suche heresy.	383	Replycacion	313
Nor heresy wyll never dye.	385	Replycacion	408
HERETIKE			
He semeth a sysmatyke /Or els an heretike,	62	Hauke	18
HERETIKES			
Of these yong heretikes, that stynke unbrent,	375	Replycacion	22
HERETYKE			
A subtyll sysmatyke, /Ryght nere an heretyke,	121	Ag Scottes2	28
HERETYKES			
and rechelesse yonge heretykes lately abjured, etc.	373	Replycacion	I
Ye heretykes recrayed, /Wotte ye what ye sayed	375	Replycacion	45
Lyke heretykes confettred,	376	Replycacion	54
Se where the heretykes go,	376	Replycacion	73
Agaynst these sysmatykes, /Agaynst these heretykes,	385	Replycacion	403
HERETYKIS			
After the sectes of heretykis!	306	Why Come Ye	1082
HERIS			
With heris encrisped yalowe as the golde, encrisped] 'enscrisped' †Fakes 1523	320	Garlande	289
HERITAGE			
God the assyst unto thyne heritage,	33	Dol Dethe	164
HERITYKES			
The heritykes ragged ray,	379	Replycacion	169
HERYNGE			
Saltfysshe, stockfyssh nor herynge,	252	Collyn Clout	209
A good herynge of thes olde talis;	347	Garlande	1217
HERYNGES			
Or to make a sayle /Of a herynges tayle?	246	Collyn Clout	4
HERKE			
And I drewe nere to herke what they two sayde.	51	Bowge	182
What! I say, herke a worde.	151	Magnyfycence	396
Ha, ha, ha! Herke, syrs, harke!	171	Magnyfycence	1109
Therupon must herke,	272	Collyn Clout	1026
HERKEN			
The drevyll stondeth to herken, and he can.	59	Bowge	486
To herken Jacke and Gyll /Whan they put up a byll;	249	Collyn Clout	96
HERKYNDE			
For eche man herkynde what she wolde to me say; wolde to me] 'to me wold' MS Cotton Vitellius E.x	344	Garlande	1119
HERMONIAKE			
For a symoniake /Is but a hermoniake;	254	Collyn Clout	297
HERNEST			
Her hernest gyrdle, her weddynge rynge, hernest] 'haruest' Day 1560, 1521 Fragment	221	El Rummynge	280
HEROF			
O wele were hym that herof myght be sure,	332	Garlande	718

	Page	Title	Line

HERON — HETE

HERON
The heron so gaunce, ... 83 Phy Sparrow 444
    gaunce] 'gaunte' Wyght 1553, Kitson 1560.6, Marshe 1568
HERPED
Orpheus, the Traciane, herped meledyously . . . . 320 Garlande 272
HERRY
'Cryste save Kyng Herry the viiith, owur royall kyng, ... 231 Speke Parott 34
HERS
It had ben hers, I wene, /More then fourty yere; . . . . 215 El Rummynge 57
HERSE
This herse for to halow. . . . . 82 Phy Sparrow 405
A phenex it is /This herse that must blys . . . . 84 Phy Sparrow 519
Whyles he senseth [the herse], ... 85 Phy Sparrow 530
    the herse] not in †Kele 1545.2, Wyght 1553, Kitson 1560.6, Marshe 1568
HERSELFE
And can not set herselfe to warke, ... 174 Magnyfycence 1230
HER SELFE
And yet I dare saye /She thynketh her selfe gaye . . . . . . 216 El Rummynge 65
Whan she goeth out /Her selfe for to shewe, ... 216 El Rummynge 81
HERT
That myne hert dyd bete, ... 73 Phy Sparrow 59
Alas, my hert it stynges, ... 80 Phy Sparrow 349
Alas, myne hert it sleth . . . . 80 Phy Sparrow 351
Myne hert doth so enbrace, ... 96 Phy Sparrow 1005
Causeth myne hert to lepe; . . . . 97 Phy Sparrow 1015
To gyve her his hole hert. 99 Phy Sparrow 1102
Me thought min hert was crased, ... 99 Phy Sparrow 1105
HERTE
Yf he coude fynde in herte to truste me. . . . . 52 Bowge 220
Hatred by the herte so had hym wrounge . . . . 54 Bowge 292
Plucke up thyne herte upon a mery pyne, ... 57 Bowge 386
Me, passynge sore, myne herte than gan aryse; . . . . 58 Bowge 425
His herte withall /Bytter as gall; . . . . 94 Phy Sparrow 916
With all my herte intere. 143 Magnyfycence 113
O dolorous herte, O harde adversyte! . . . . 198 Magnyfycence 2052
With gommes goostly of glad herte and mynde, ... 207 Magnyfycence 2359
With herte moste tendyr, ... 237 Speke Parott 226
Myne herte hyt ys with the. . . . . 237 Speke Parott 240
For Dame Philargerya /Hathe so his herte in holde, ... 284 Why Come Ye 207
Helas, my herte is sory . . . . 284 Why Come Ye 227
Concente to Phebus to have his herte in holde, ... 320 Garlande 292
'O thoughtfull herte,' was evermore his songe! . . . . 320 Garlande 296
Welcome to me as hertely as herte can thynke! . . . . 327 Garlande 547
Thy herte wolde nat serve the. . . . . 365 Albany 250
HERTE-BRENNYNGE
By God, I saye, there is a grete herte-brennynge . . . . . . 59 Bowge 460
HERTED
Moche herted lyke an hen. 251 Collyn Clout 168
HERTELY
Welcome to me as hertely as herte can thynke! . . . . 327 Garlande 547
To Mercury also hertely prayed I then, ... 335 Garlande 826
HERTES
The hertes of England to comfort with gladnes. . . . . 117 Ag Scottes 88
So manye bolde barons, there hertes as dull as lede; . . . . 245 Speke Parott 466
Theyr hertes are so faynted, ... 269 Collyn Clout 899
And mad theyr hertes attaynted. . . . . 282 Why Come Ye 158
Their hertes be in thyr hose! . . . . 286 Why Come Ye 289
Your hertes than were hosed, /Your relacions reposed; . . . 377 Replycacion 107
HERTIS
The hertis of the herd began for to grone, and fled . . . . 351 Garlande 1408
HERTYS
Of thoughtfull hertys plungyd in dystres; 44 Balettys3 10
I make hevy hertys, with eyen full holowe. . . . . 205 Magnyfycence 2286
HERTO
Harkyn herto, ye Harvy Ha[f]tar, ... 133 Garnesche5 164
    Haftar] 'Hastar' †MS Harley 367
HERT ROTE
It raysed myne hert rote . . . . 100 Phy Sparrow 1148
HERVY
To Hervy Ha[f]ter than he spake of me, ... 54 Bowge 295
    Hafter] 'Haster' †Wynkyn de Worde 1499, 1510, Marshe 1568
'Than,' quod Hervy, 'why arte thou so dysmayde?' . . . . . . 54 Bowge 299
'By God,' quod Hervy, 'and it so happen myghte! . . . . 54 Bowge 306
HESPERIDES
And the appels of gold /Of Hesperides withhold, ... 104 Phy Sparrow 1302
And the apples of golde /Of Hesperides withholde, ... 349 Garlande 1295
HESTER
And of Hester his other wyfe, ... 90 Phy Sparrow 743
HETE
Thus after her cold she cought a hete. 42 Balettys1 19
By radyante hete enryped hath our corne; . . . . 46 Bowge 2
Now upon thys hete /Rankely whan ye swete, ... 127 Garnesche3 133
And after a hete oft cometh a stormy colde. . . . . 141 Magnyfycence 13
She is furred for the hete /All to the fete; . . . . 167 Magnyfycence 977
It wyll stryke a man myschevously in a hete. . . . . 204 Magnyfycence 2268
That in a fume or an hete, ... 289 Why Come Ye 424
Ye were in a dronken hete. 376 Replycacion 53

HETHER —HILLIS

	Page	Title	Line
With hete of the Holy Gost,	385	Replycacion	383

HETHER

	Page	Title	Line
Howe, where art thou? Come hether, Poverte.	195	Magnyfycence	1953
Ye com hether as well as can be thought.	210	Magnyfycence	2459

HETHYR

	Page	Title	Line
Of owur clerke Cleros. Whythyr, thydyr and why not hethyr?	243	Speke Parott	412

HEVE

	Page	Title	Line
'Heve and how, rombelow, row the bote, Norman, rowe.'	53	Bowge	252

HEVEN

	Page	Title	Line
I pray God, Phillip to heven may fly.	86	Phy Sparrow	580
To heven he shall, from heven he cam.	86	Phy Sparrow	582
To heven he shall, from heven he cam.	86	Phy Sparrow	582
To Jupyter I call, /Of heven emperyall,	86	Phy Sparrow	597
The follest sloven ondyr heven,	133	Garnesche5	145
In faythe, trouth thou sayst nowe, by God of heven!	170	Magnyfycence	1079
What they do in heven;	267	Collyn Clout	825
The way to heven or to hell!'	277	Collyn Clout	1226
Olde patriarkes and prophetes in heven with him to dwell.	383	Replycacion	342

HEVENLY

	Page	Title	Line
Of hevenly poems, O Clyo, calde by name	29	Dol Dethe	8
In joy triumphaunt the hevenly *gerarchy,	35	Dol Dethe	211
*gerarchy] 'gerarchy' †MS Royal 18 D.ii, Marshe 1568, 'yerarchy' Scattergood			
And to purchace /Thyne hevenly place	40	Coystrowne3	52
It were an hevenly blysse	97	Phy Sparrow	1039
Whos hevenly armony was so passynge sure,	320	Garlande	274
It were an hevenly helth,	340	Garlande	994
Of hevenly inspyracion /In laureate creacyon,	384	Replycacion	372

HEVERY

	Page	Title	Line
As hevery man wele seethe,	127	Garnesche3	125

HEVY

	Page	Title	Line
Wythe hevy chere, with dolorous hart and mynd,	34	Dol Dethe	176
Hys hed was hevy, such was his hap,	41	Balettys1	5
I wys he hath an hevy hed,'	42	Balettys1	21
Whych to behold makyth hevy hartys glad;	44	Balettys3	28
His hede was hevy for watchynge overnyghte,	56	Bowge	352
The case requyreth. Alasse, alasse, an hevy metynge!	192	Magnyfycence	1847
I make hevy hertys, with eyen full holowe.	205	Magnyfycence	2286
Out of theyr cloyster and quere /With an hevy chere,	256	Collyn Clout	395
Whos lusty lokis make hevy hartis glad;	337	Garlande	903
As hevy as the lede,	358	Garlande2	3

HEVYN

	Page	Title	Line
O pereles Prince of hevyn emperyalle	34	Dol Dethe	190
O] not in Marshe 1568			
Hevyn, hell and erth obey unto thi kall;	34	Dol Dethe	192
Of all nacyons under the hevyn,	36	Coystrowne1	1
Renownyd lady above the sterry hevyn,	313	Garlande	51
The starry hevyn, me thought, shoke with the showte;	354	Garlande	1508
Then to the hevyn sperycall upwarde I gasid,	354	Garlande	1514

HEVYNES

	Page	Title	Line
My dedely wo, my paynfull hevynes.	44	Balettys3	37

HEVYNESSE

	Page	Title	Line
It can not be exprest /My sorowfull hevynesse,	72	Phy Sparrow	32
To behold and se /What hevynesse dyd me pange:	72	Phy Sparrow	44
And moche hevynesse, /And great dolowre	305	Why Come Ye	1035
dolowre] 'dullness' MS Rawlinson C. 813			

HEVYNGE

	Page	Title	Line
With hevynge and shovynge, 'have in' and 'have oute';	319	Garlande	251

HEW

	Page	Title	Line
And, 'Wynde me that botowme of such an hew',	334	Garlande	799
an] 'a' MS Cotton Vitellius E.x			
The enbuddid blossoms of roses rede of hew	337	Garlande	883
The enbuddid blossoms of] 'Enbuddid blossome with' MS Cotton Vitellius E.x			
Right so, madame, the roses redde of hew	337	Garlande	890

HEWE

	Page	Title	Line
Enbudded with beautye and colour fresshe of hewe,	183	Magnyfycence	1554

HEWYTH

	Page	Title	Line
She goyth wyde behynde and hewyth never a dele:	43	Balettys2	24

HIERONYMUS

	Page	Title	Line
Whom Hieronymus, /That doctour glorious,	383	Replycacion	318

HIGH

	Page	Title	Line
Whiche gave to me /The high degre	112	Calliope	6
Of this high courte the dayly besines;	326	Garlande	519
'Ryght high and myghty princes of astate,	344	Garlande	1128
For, by Juppiter and his high mageste,	353	Garlande	1488
and transcendingly sped in moche high connyng,	374	Replycacion	I

HIGHT

	Page	Title	Line
Astrea, justice hight,	110	Lawde	15
But if that I knewe what his name hight,	139	Ven Tongues	73
Envyous Rancour truely he hight.	333	Garlande	753

HIH

	Page	Title	Line
Our prince of hih honour,	111	Lawde	45

HILL

	Page	Title	Line
Lyke a great hill,	365	Albany	261

HILLIS

	Page	Title	Line
Frome Babill towre to the hillis Caspian.'	327	Garlande	553
Caspian] 'Gaspian' †Fakes 1523			

	Page	Title	Line

HILT
Of knightly prowes the sworde, pomel, and hilt,	32	Dol Dethe	108

HIM
She cherysshe[th] him, and hym she casseth awaye.'	49	Bowge	117
'cherysshed' †Wynkyn de Worde 1499, 1510, Marshe 1568; casseth] 'casseth' Wynkyn de Worde 1510, 'chasseth' Marshe 1568			
What, lete us holde him up, man, for a whyle.'	51	Bowge	188
Beware of him, for, I make God avowe,	51	Bowge	199
By myne avyse use not with him to walke.	52	Bowge	210
To kepe him frome pykynge, it was a grete payne.	52	Bowge	236
Anone ther mette with him, as me thoughte,	54	Bowge	282
His face was belymmed as byes had him stounge;	54	Bowge	289
It was no tyme with him to jape nor toye.	54	Bowge	290
Fynde some mene to caste him over the borde.'	54	Bowge	308
'By him that me boughte,' than quod Dysdayne,	54	Bowge	309
It were more thryft he boughte him a newe cote;	60	Bowge	487
For forthwyth there I had him slayne,	61	Bowge	523
And for to take him in	76	Phy Sparrow	166
In him it was no vyse;	76	Phy Sparrow	174
I played with him tytell-tattyll,	80	Phy Sparrow	357
And fed him with my spattyl,	80	Phy Sparrow	358
And slew him there starke dead.	81	Phy Sparrow	378
Of al good praiers God send him sum!	86	Phy Sparrow	584
Tyll cruell fate made him to dy:	86	Phy Sparrow	592
She brought him in abusyon;	89	Phy Sparrow	708
And never wold him forsake.	90	Phy Sparrow	733
Causeth him to gryn /And rejoyce therin;	94	Phy Sparrow	926
No slepe can him catch,	95	Phy Sparrow	928
God save him in his right! /Amen	112	Lawde	56
In him is fygured Melchisedec,	118	Ag Scottes	115
Of him shuld men report,	121	Ag Scottes2	33
For clatering of me I would him sone quight;	139	Ven Tongues	74
I could make him shortly repent him for ever;	139	Ven Tongues	76
I could make him shortly repent him for ever;	139	Ven Tongues	76
What call ye him, this?	156	Magnyfycence	588
God of his goodnes him framed and wrought;	236	Speke Parott	212
Take him, wardeyn of the Flete,	275	Collyn Clout	1165
Let him cough, rough or snevyll!	277	Collyn Clout	1221
They shote at him with crownes.	283	Why Come Ye	178
They make him so amased,	283	Why Come Ye	180
And bereth him there so stowte	287	Why Come Ye	340
Whan him lyst to lowre,	289	Why Come Ye	428
Than, 'Have him to the Towre /Saunz aulter remedy!	289	Why Come Ye	429
By him is subverted;	290	Why Come Ye	440
He hath in him suche fayth.	290	Why Come Ye	445
To him he hathe founde	291	Why Come Ye	501
How no man can him amende!	292	Why Come Ye	531
Take him in suche conceyght	292	Why Come Ye	541
That he set him on heyght,	292	Why Come Ye	542
And made to him be brought	293	Why Come Ye	552
And gave him a realme to rule	293	Why Come Ye	559
Make him a great astate,	293	Why Come Ye	587
No man dare him withsay.	294	Why Come Ye	598
Whiche constrayned him forcebly	296	Why Come Ye	702
That he made him his chauncelar	297	Why Come Ye	732
Hath for him dyscust	298	Why Come Ye	751
And graunt him grace to know	298	Why Come Ye	774
Let him never confounde	298	Why Come Ye	778
Whiche pyncheth him sore!	302	Why Come Ye	948
And graunt him a place	303	Why Come Ye	970
For Folam peason /With him be nat geson;	304	Why Come Ye	1000
Shewynge him Goddis lawis.	305	Why Come Ye	1060
And as many as him lykys,	306	Why Come Ye	1080
him] 'he' MS Rawlinson C. 813			
The fyrst, to do him reverence,	307	Why Come Ye	1123
He jugyth him equivalent /With God omnipotent.	307	Why Come Ye	1135
him] 'hymselfe' MS Rawlinson C. 813; equivalent] 'equypolent' Rawlinson C. 813			
Bytwene him and me;	308	Why Come Ye	1150
And make him lame of his neder limmes.	309	Why Come Ye	1200
God sende him sorowe for his sinnes!	309	Why Come Ye	1201
Sende him to F[r]aunce agayne	363	Albany	173
Fraunce] 'Faunce' †Marshe 1568			
Olde patriarkes and prophetes in heven with him to dwell.	383	Replycacion	342

HIMSELF
And thus this elf /Consumeth himself,	95	Phy Sparrow	946
Himselfe doth slo /With payne and wo.	95	Phy Sparrow	947

HIMSELFE
He maketh himselfe cock sure.	286	Why Come Ye	282
Counte himselfe as good as he;	294	Why Come Ye	590
Coude nat himselfe refrayne	296	Why Come Ye	690
Hathe made himselfe abbot	306	Why Come Ye	1099
He is perjured himselfe.	307	Why Come Ye	1116

HINDER
For Margery wynshed, and breke her hinder girth;	346	Garlande	1201

HIPOCENTAURES
One of the Centaures, /Or Onocentaures, /Or Hipocentaures;	104	Phy Sparrow	1296

HIPPOCENTAURIS —HIS	Page	Title	Line

HIPPOCENTAURIS

	Page	Title	Line
One of the Centawris, /Or Onocentauris, /Or Hippocentauris;	348	Garlande	1289

HIR

	Page	Title	Line
I sawe hir smyle, and I then did the same.	327	Garlande	530
I then] 'than I' Marshe 1568			

HIS

	Page	Title	Line
Trew to his prince in word, in dede, and thought.	29	Dol Dethe	7
At his commaundement whiche had both day and night	30	Dol Dethe	31
That were aboute hym, his awne servauntis of trust,	30	Dol Dethe	37
To suffre hym slayn of his mortall fo?	30	Dol Dethe	38
Your worship depended of his excellence.	31	Dol Dethe	59
The grounde of his quarell was for his sovereyn lord,	31	Dol Dethe	64
The grounde of his quarell was for his sovereyn lord,	31	Dol Dethe	64
To the right of his prince which shold not be withstand;	31	Dol Dethe	67
But had his nobillmen donn wel that day	31	Dol Dethe	69
Togeder with servauntis of his famuly,	31	Dol Dethe	93
Alas his golde, his fee, his annuall rente,	32	Dol Dethe	97
Alas his golde, his fee, his annuall rente,	32	Dol Dethe	97
Alas his golde, his fee, his annuall rente,	32	Dol Dethe	97
Withe his enmys that were stark mad and wode;	32	Dol Dethe	100
Alas for routhe, what thouthe his mynde wer goode,	32	Dol Dethe	102
His corage manly, yet ther he shed his bloode.	32	Dol Dethe	103
His corage manly, yet ther he shed his bloode.	32	Dol Dethe	103
Wheron he gat his fynall dedely wounde.	32	Dol Dethe	119
Thow kit asonder his perfight vitall threde.	32	Dol Dethe	126
Of this lordis dethe and of his murdrynge;	32	Dol Dethe	130
What nedethe me for to extoll his fame	33	Dol Dethe	141
Whos noble actis shew worsheply his name,	33	Dol Dethe	143
Truly reportinge his right noble astate,	33	Dol Dethe	146
His noble blode never desteynyd was,	33	Dol Dethe	148
Trew to his prince for to defende his right,	33	Dol Dethe	149
Trew to his prince for to defende his right,	33	Dol Dethe	149
With trowth to medelle was all his hole delight,	33	Dol Dethe	152
As all his kuntrey kan testefy the same:	33	Dol Dethe	153
All were to litill for his magnyficence.	33	Dol Dethe	161
Eche man inward sorow in his inward thought	34	Dol Dethe	177
In fee, as menyall men of his houshold,	34	Dol Dethe	185
His soule mot receyve in to ther company,	35	Dol Dethe	213
Yet, for his love that all hath wrought,	36	Man Margery	25
But for in his gamut carp that he can,	37	Coystrownel	13
His descant is dasshed full of dyscordes;	37	Coystrownel	38
He counteth in his countenaunce to checke with the best:	37	Coystrownel	44
A malaperte medler that pryeth for his pray,	37	Coystrownel	45
He fyndeth a proporcyon in his prycke songe	38	Coystrownel	48
For lordes and ladyes lerne at his scole;	38	Coystrownel	52
Hys hed was hevy, such was his hap,	41	Balettys1	5
Excedynge ferther than his connynge is,	46	Bowge	23
His hede maye be harde, but feble is his brayne!	46	Bowge	24
his] not in Marshe 1568			
His hede maye be harde, but feble is his brayne!	46	Bowge	24
his] not in Marshe 1568			
Of one and other that wolde his lady see,	47	Bowge	57
Than Phebus in his spere celestyne,	47	Bowge	61
So vertuously that hath his dayes spente;	50	Bowge	151
Than thanked I hym for his grete gentylnes.	51	Bowge	176
His stomak stuffed ofte tymes dyde reboke.	51	Bowge	180
Me thoughte his hede was full of gelousy,	51	Bowge	192
His eyen rollynge, his hondes faste they quoke;	51	Bowge	193
His eyen rollynge, his hondes faste they quoke;	51	Bowge	193
His counseyle secrete never to dyscure,	52	Bowge	219
dyscure] 'dysture' †Wynkyn de Worde 1499, 1510			
Whyles of his mynde it were lockte with the keye.	52	Bowge	224
And of his mynde he shewed me all and some.	52	Bowge	226
Upon his breste he bare a versynge boxe;	52	Bowge	232
His throte was clere and lustely coude fayne.	52	Bowge	233
Me thoughte his gowne was all furred wyth foxe.	52	Bowge	234
Me] 'My' †Wynkyn de Worde 1499			
He gased on me with his gotyshe berde;	52	Bowge	237
His gawdy garment with Scornnys was all wrought;	54	Bowge	285
Scornnys] 'storunys' †Wynkyn de Worde 1499, 1510, 'scornes' Marshe 1568			
With Indygnacyon lyned was his hode;	54	Bowge	286
His face was belymmed as byes had him stounge;	54	Bowge	289
Envye hathe wasted hys lyver and his lounge;	54	Bowge	291
His here was growen thorowe oute his hat.	56	Bowge	350
His here was growen thorowe oute his hat.	56	Bowge	350
His hede was hevy for watchynge overnyghte,	56	Bowge	352
His eyen blereed, his face shone lyke a glas;	56	Bowge	353
His eyen blereed, his face shone lyke a glas;	56	Bowge	353
His gowne so shorte that it ne cover myghte	56	Bowge	354
His rumpe, he wente so all for somer lyghte;	56	Bowge	355
His hose was garded with a lyste of grene,	56	Bowge	356
His cote was checked with patches rede and blewe;	56	Bowge	358
checked] 'checkered' Marshe 1568			
Of Kyrkeby Kendall was his shorte demye;	56	Bowge	359
His elbowe bare, he ware his gere so nye,	56	Bowge	361
His elbowe bare, he ware his gere so nye,	56	Bowge	361

	Page	Title	Line
His nose a-droppynge, his lyppes were full drye;	56	Bowge	362
a-droppynge] 'droppynge' Marshe 1568			
His nose a-droppynge, his lyppes were full drye;	56	Bowge	362
a-droppynge] 'droppynge' Marshe 1568			
And by his syde his whynarde and his pouche,	56	Bowge	363
And by his syde his whynarde and his pouche,	56	Bowge	363
And by his syde his whynarde and his pouche,	56	Bowge	363
He set up fresshely upon his hat alofte.	56	Bowge	367
What sholde I tell more of his rebaudrye?	56	Bowge	372
Than, in his hode, I sawe there faces tweyne:	58	Bowge	428
I saw a knyfe hyd in his one sleve,	58	Bowge	433
And in his other sleve, me thought I sawe	58	Bowge	435
His hode was syde, his cope was roset graye;	58	Bowge	440
His hode was syde, his cope was roset graye;	58	Bowge	440
It wyll not be, his purse is not on-flote.	60	Bowge	488
His wytte is thynne, his hode is threde-bare.	60	Bowge	490
His wytte is thynne, his hode is threde-bare.	60	Bowge	490
Sterte all at ones, I lyked no thynge his playe,	60	Bowge	502
His hode all pounsed and garded lyke a cage.	60	Bowge	508
hode] 'body' Marshe 1568			
Wyth his polutyd pawtenar,	63	Hauke	44
He made his hawke to fly,	63	Hauke	47
His hawke shulde pray and fede /Upon a pigeons maw.	63	Hauke	56
His seconde hawke wexyd gery	63	Hauke	66
The hawke had no lyst /To come to his fyst;	64	Hauke	84
But lyke a March harum /His braynes were so parum.	64	Hauke	105
He sayde he wold not let /His houndys for to fet,	64	Hauke	107
His hawke then flew uppon /The rode, with Mary and Johnn.	65	Hauke	126
Thus to ryng a peale /Wyth his hawkys bels?	65	Hauke	137
For burnynge of his wynges;	73	Phy Sparrow	81
For to kepe his cut,	74	Phy Sparrow	118
And his fethers shake,	75	Phy Sparrow	163
fethers] 'fether' †Kele 1545.2			
With his wanton eye.	76	Phy Sparrow	182
Cadmus, that his syster sought,	76	Phy Sparrow	194
That by representacyon /Of his image and facyon,	77	Phy Sparrow	215
But whan I was sowing his beke,	77	Phy Sparrow	219
And opened his prety byll,	77	Phy Sparrow	221
opened] 'open' Marshe 1568			
Is for his soule to pray:	77	Phy Sparrow	238
Gave hym his mortall wounde,	79	Phy Sparrow	298
That his owne lorde bote	79	Phy Sparrow	305
In doynge his homage /Unto his soverayne.	80	Phy Sparrow	326
In doynge his homage /Unto his soverayne.	80	Phy Sparrow	327
Flyckerynge with his wynges.	80	Phy Sparrow	348
With his byll betwene my lippes,	80	Phy Sparrow	359
Had I of his swete musse?	80	Phy Sparrow	362
his] 'this' †Kele 1545.2, Wyght 1553			
Every byrde in his laye:	81	Phy Sparrow	394
The larke with his longe to;	82	Phy Sparrow	406
The shovelar with his brode bek;	82	Phy Sparrow	408
His playne songe to solfe;	82	Phy Sparrow	415
The *better with his bumpe,	82	Phy Sparrow	432
*better] 'bitter' Wyght 1553, Kitson 1560.6, Marshe 1568			
The crane with his trumpe,	82	Phy Sparrow	433
Bycause his voyce is lowde,	82	Phy Sparrow	439
That maketh his nest /In chymneyes to rest;	83	Phy Sparrow	470
Such fervent heat /His stomake doth freat;	83	Phy Sparrow	482
doth freat] 'so great' †Kele 1545.2, Wyght 1553, Kitson 1560.6			
With Partlot his hen,	84	Phy Sparrow	509
Plinni sheweth all /In his Story Naturall,	85	Phy Sparrow	537
Taking his course toward the west;	86	Phy Sparrow	573
With his knightes commendable,	87	Phy Sparrow	635
And Dame Gaynour, his quene	87	Phy Sparrow	636
Many a spere brake /For his ladyes sake;	87	Phy Sparrow	640
Of Bele Isold his wyfe,	87	Phy Sparrow	643
Which by his mercyfull rage	88	Phy Sparrow	670
mercyfull] 'unmercifull' Wyght 1553, Kitson 1560.6, Marshe 1568			
His maisters love to further,	88	Phy Sparrow	684
Though his father were a kyng;	89	Phy Sparrow	698
And of Vesca his queene,	90	Phy Sparrow	741
And of Hester his other wyfe,	90	Phy Sparrow	743
His mater is worth gold,	91	Phy Sparrow	786
His tales I have red;	91	Phy Sparrow	789
His mater is delectable, /Solacious and commendable;	91	Phy Sparrow	790
His Englysh well alowed,	91	Phy Sparrow	792
His Englyssh whereat they barke	91	Phy Sparrow	798
His termes were not darke,	91	Phy Sparrow	801
The sentence of his mynde,	91	Phy Sparrow	807
Yet wryteth he in his kynd,	91	Phy Sparrow	808
His tunable harpe stryngges	93	Phy Sparrow	865
Thorow his godly myght;	93	Phy Sparrow	870
With his golden sandes,	93	Phy Sparrow	879
With his ledder ey, /And chekes dry;	94	Phy Sparrow	908
His bones crake, /Leane as a rake;	94	Phy Sparrow	912
His gummes rusty /Are full unlusty;	94	Phy Sparrow	914
His herte withall /Bytter as gall;	94	Phy Sparrow	916

	Page	Title	Line
HIS —HIS			
His lyver, his longe /With anger is wronge;	94	Phy Sparrow	918
longe] 'longes' Wyght 1553, Kitson 1560.6, Marshe 1568			
His lyver, his longe /With anger is wronge;	94	Phy Sparrow	918
longe] 'longes' Wyght 1553, Kitson 1560.6, Marshe 1568			
His serpentes tonge /That many one hath stonge;	94	Phy Sparrow	920
His foule desyre /Wyll suffre no slepe	95	Phy Sparrow	933
In his hed to crepe;	95	Phy Sparrow	935
His foule semblaunt /All displesaunt;	95	Phy Sparrow	936
foule] 'feule' †Kele 1545.2, Wyght 1553			
His tong never styll /For to say yll,	95	Phy Sparrow	941
To gyve her his hole hert.	99	Phy Sparrow	1102
But she wolde chaunge his mood,	100	Phy Sparrow	1158
His Dirige, her commendacyon /Can be no derogacyon,	103	Phy Sparrow	1276
Caron with his beerd hore,	105	Phy Sparrow	1338
And with his [frownsid] fore top	105	Phy Sparrow	1340
frownsid] not in †Kele 1545.2, Wyght 1553, Kitson 1560.6, Marshe 1568			
Gydeth his bote with a prope;	105	Phy Sparrow	1341
God forgeve hym his mysdedes.	107	Epitaphe1	19
Never a toth in his heed.	108	Epitaphe1	61
The devill kis his culum!	108	Epitaphe1	79
HIS EPITAPH FOLOWETH DEVOUTLY;	109	Epitaphe2	I
Belsabub his soule save,	109	Epitaphe2	25
His titille dothe recorde;	110	Lawde	11
God save him in his right! /Amen	112	Lawde	56
Trowe ye, Syr James, his noble grace	114	Scot Kynge	17
For you and your Scottes wolde tourne his face?	114	Scot Kynge	18
Parde ye be his homager	114	Scot Kynge	30
And suters to his parlyment.	114	Scot Kynge	31
Ye be bounde tenauntes to his estate;	114	Scot Kynge	36
His sone the lorde admyrall is full good,	115	Scot Kynge	70
His swerde hath bathed in the Scottes blode.	115	Scot Kynge	71
God save kynge Henry and his lordes all	115	Scot Kynge	72
Trowyd ye, Syr Jemy, his nobull grace	118	Ag Scottes	107
From you, Syr Scot, wolde turne his face?	118	Ag Scottes	108
His tytle is true in Fraunce to raygne;	118	Ag Scottes	120
Pardy, ye were his homager,	118	Ag Scottes	122
And suter to his parlyament.	118	Ag Scottes	123
Ye were bonde tenent to his estate;	118	Ag Scottes	127
His grace beyng out of the way;	119	Ag Scottes	144
For, if they understode /His traytourly dispyght,	121	Ag Scottes2	25
Defendeth with his pen /All Englysh men	135	Dundas	21
But if that I knewe what his name hight,	139	Ven Tongues	73
For his false lying, of that I spake never,	139	Ven Tongues	75
Oracius to recorde in his volumys olde,	143	Magnyfycence	114
There is no excesse where measure hath his helthe.	144	Magnyfycence	140
And after his mynde herdely your selfe adresse,	144	Magnyfycence	151
So in his harte he may be glad of us.	145	Magnyfycence	158
And lyberte his large with measure shall make.	145	Magnyfycence	180
For I wyll use you by his advertysment.	146	Magnyfycence	196
Of his rekenynge, as evydently we may	146	Magnyfycence	215
Syr, thanked be God, he hath his hele.	149	Magnyfycence	315
And for his sake ryght gladly I wolde	149	Magnyfycence	334
At his cloked counterfetynge dogges dothe barke.	153	Magnyfycence	482
That with his whyp his mares was wonte to yarke;	153	Magnyfycence	484
That with his whyp his mares was wonte to yarke;	153	Magnyfycence	484
By God, man, bothe his pagent and thyne he can play.	154	Magnyfycence	505
Nay, nay. He hath chaunged his, and I have chaunged myne.	155	Magnyfycence	518
Nowe what is his name? And what is thyne?	155	Magnyfycence	519
Ye. And he hath rule of all his tresure.	158	Magnyfycence	632
His name Largesse, Surveyaunce myne.	158	Magnyfycence	643
And in his servyce the to retayne,	159	Magnyfycence	668
That Fansy with his fonde consayte	159	Magnyfycence	678
Wyll ye se this gentylman is all in his skornys?	162	Magnyfycence	773
poyntyng with his fynger, and sayth,	162	Magnyfycence	SD
I befoule his pate.	164	Magnyfycence	876
His gowne so wyde	165	Magnyfycence	903
His dame and his syre	165	Magnyfycence	905
His dame and his syre	165	Magnyfycence	905
Within his slyve;	165	Magnyfycence	906
Spende all his hyre	165	Magnyfycence	907
A Tyborne checke /Shall breke his necke.	165	Magnyfycence	911
Yet I solde his skynne to Mackemurre,	169	Magnyfycence	1056
What! Fleyest thou his skynne every yere?	169	Magnyfycence	1058
What callest thou thy dogge? Tusshe! His name is Gryme.	171	Magnyfycence	1118
Mary, it was his, and nowe it is myne.	173	Magnyfycence	1181
And was it his, and nowe it is thyne?	173	Magnyfycence	1182
Here CRAFTY CONVEYAUNCE putteth of his gowne.	173	Magnyfycence	SD
To tourne a fole out of his clowtes.	174	Magnyfycence	1211
Nay, wylte thou here nowe of his scoles,	174	Magnyfycence	1216
That every man lawghyth at his foly.	175	Magnyfycence	1251
And tell to his sufferayne every whyt;	175	Magnyfycence	1270
And then he is moche made of for his [wyt];	175	Magnyfycence	1271
wyt] 'whyt' †Rastell & Treveris C 1530, B			
Are not his wordys cursydly cowchyd?	175	Magnyfycence	1276
Yet for his name we must fynde a [slyght].	176	Magnyfycence	1308
slyght] shyfte †Rastell & Treveris C 1530, B			
Take of his substaunce a sure inventory,	180	Magnyfycence	1445

HIS —HIS   Page   Title   Line

Though al his conquestys were brought to rekenynge,	181	Magnyfycence	1468
To rayne, for all his marcyall affeccyon;	181	Magnyfycence	1470
For al his pompe, for all his ryall trone,	181	Magnyfycence	1475
For al his pompe, for all his ryall trone,	181	Magnyfycence	1475
Hercules the herdy, with his stobburne clobbyd mase,	182	Magnyfycence	1494
Arthur of Albyan, for all his brymme berde,	182	Magnyfycence	1502
Nor Basyan the bolde, for all his brybaunce,	182	Magnyfycence	1503
Galba, whom his galantys garde for agaspe,	182	Magnyfycence	1508
Nor Vespasyan, that bare in his nose a waspe,	182	Magnyfycence	1510
All that I can his matter for to spede.	187	Magnyfycence	1664
Yes. With his hande I made hym to subscrybe	187	Magnyfycence	1666
Lest that he thought that his money were evyll spente,	187	Magnyfycence	1674
By Magnyfycence nor yet none of his;	188	Magnyfycence	1705
No force what thoughe his neyghbour dye in a dyche.	189	Magnyfycence	1752
And wyth a brystell of a bore his berde dyd I shave.	192	Magnyfycence	1832
Adewe, for I wyll not come in his clokys.	193	Magnyfycence	1874
and spoylyd from all his goodys and rayment.	193	Magnyfycence	SD
Thys losyll was a lorde and lyvyd at his lust;	193	Magnyfycence	1886
He knewe not hymselfe, his harte was so hye;	193	Magnyfycence	1888
I sende ofte tymes a fole to his sonne.	195	Magnyfycence	1935
It is foly to grudge agaynst his vysytacyon.	196	Magnyfycence	1990
Put your wyll to his wyll, for surely it is he	196	Magnyfycence	1997
Take it mekely, and thanke God of his grace;	197	Magnyfycence	2033
Here MAGNYFYCENCE dolorously maketh his mone.	198	Magnyfycence	SD
But he abused so his free lyberte,	200	Magnyfycence	2113
That nowe he hath loste all his felycyte;	200	Magnyfycence	2114
A prynce to use with all his hole intent,	200	Magnyfycence	2118
Spare for the spence of a noble that his honour myght save,	200	Magnyfycence	2125
In faythe, of his cofers the bottoms are bare.	201	Magnyfycence	2163
As for his plate of sylver and suche trasshe,	201	Magnyfycence	2164
He may rynse a pycher, for his plate is to wed.	201	Magnyfycence	2168
And I tell you, I dysdayne moche of his mockys.	203	Magnyfycence	2227
And I bequethe hym sorowe for his syn.	204	Magnyfycence	2256
With never a peny in his purse.	204	Magnyfycence	2258
Ye, for requiem eternam groweth forth of his nose.	204	Magnyfycence	2260
Nay, nay, man. I loke never to have parte of his grace;	205	Magnyfycence	2297
That thou canst not have never mercy in his syght.	205	Magnyfycence	2303
By myschefe to brevyate and shorten his dayes.	206	Magnyfycence	2338
That you hath punysshed with his sharpe rod.	207	Magnyfycence	2350
To thanke God of his sonde; and comforte ye shal fynde.	207	Magnyfycence	2360
Helthe of body his besynesse to acheve;	207	Magnyfycence	2369
Dysease and sekenesse his conscyence to dyscryve;	207	Magnyfycence	2370
Afflyccyon and trouble to prove his pacyence;	207	Magnyfycence	2371
Contradyccyon to prove his sapyence;	207	Magnyfycence	2372
Grace of assystence his measure to declare;	207	Magnyfycence	2373
Largesse, syr, by his credence was his name.	209	Magnyfycence	2441
Largesse, syr, by his credence was his name.	209	Magnyfycence	2441
What this man hath sayd, perceyve ye his sentence?	210	Magnyfycence	2465
The bore his tayle wrygges,	219	El Rummynge	177
His rumpe also he frygges /Agaynst the hye benche.	219	El Rummynge	178
He calleth me his whytyng, /His mullyng and his [m]ytyng, mytyng] 'nytyng' †Lant 1545, Kynge & Marche 1554, 'nittinge' Day 1560, 'nittine' Marshe 1568	220	El Rummynge	223
He calleth me his whytyng, /His mullyng and his [m]ytyng, mytyng] 'nytyng' †Lant 1545, Kynge & Marche 1554, 'nittinge' Day 1560, 'nittine' Marshe 1568	220	El Rummynge	224
He calleth me his whytyng, /His mullyng and his [m]ytyng, mytyng] 'nytyng' †Lant 1545, Kynge & Marche 1554, 'nittinge' Day 1560, 'nittine' Marshe 1568	220	El Rummynge	224
His nobbes and his conny, /His swetyng and his honny,	220	El Rummynge	225
His nobbes and his conny, /His swetyng and his honny,	220	El Rummynge	225
His nobbes and his conny, /His swetyng and his honny,	220	El Rummynge	226
His nobbes and his conny, /His swetyng and his honny,	220	El Rummynge	226
Another brought her his cap	221	El Rummynge	285
Such a bedfellaw /Wold make one cast his craw.	226	El Rummynge	489
Every man after his maner of wayes,	233	Speke Parott	90
Madionita Jetro, our Moyses kepyth his shepe;	234	Speke Parott	115
And 'Da racionales' dare not shew his pate.	235	Speke Parott	175
Plaut[us] in his comedies a chyld shall now reherse,	235	Speke Parott	176
And medyll with Quintylyan in his Decla[m]acyons, Declamacyons] 'Declaracyons' †Lant 1545, Kynge & Marche 1554, Day 1560, Marshe 1568	235	Speke Parott	177
Can skantly the tensis of his conjugacyons;	235	Speke Parott	180
For Parrot to pyke upon, his brayne for to stable,	235	Speke Parott	184
Let every man after his merit take his parte;	236	Speke Parott	199
Let every man after his merit take his parte;	236	Speke Parott	199
shall be his protectyon, his pavys and his wall.	236	Speke Parott	203
shall be his protectyon, his pavys and his wall.	236	Speke Parott	203
shall be his protectyon, his pavys and his wall.	236	Speke Parott	203
Melpomene, that fayre mayde, she burneshed his beke:	236	Speke Parott	209
God of his goodnes him framed and wrought;	236	Speke Parott	212
He made you of nothynge by his magistye;	236	Speke Parott	219
'His heed is so fat	247	Collyn Clout	16
Without his vertue be greatter,	253	Collyn Clout	271
The bysshop on his carpet	255	Collyn Clout	327
With all his false lore -	257	Collyn Clout	430
Leste that his fote slyppe,	263	Collyn Clout	666
His benefyce worth ten pounde,	264	Collyn Clout	725

HIS—HIS

	Page	Title	Line
It must come to his lot	265	Collyn Clout	750
To shote forthe his shot;	265	Collyn Clout	751
Taketh his pyllyon and his cappe	266	Collyn Clout	803
Taketh his pyllyon and his cappe	266	Collyn Clout	803
Nor knoweth not his elenkes,	267	Collyn Clout	818
elenkes] 'eloquens' †Godfray 1531, Kele 1545.1, Marshe 1568			
Nor his predicamentes;	267	Collyn Clout	819
Preches for his grote,	267	Collyn Clout	837
And for to have his fees,	267	Collyn Clout	839
And howe Cupyde shaked /His dart, and bent his bowe	270	Collyn Clout	947
And howe Cupyde shaked /His dart, and bent his bowe	270	Collyn Clout	947
And of his Pompeyus warre,	270	Collyn Clout	957
And nat so hardy on his hede	272	Collyn Clout	1023
nat] 'not' Marshe 1568, MS Harley 2252			
And graunte hym at his askynge	272	Collyn Clout	1027
Nor to execute /His commaundement,	272	Collyn Clout	1033
Nor to expresse to his parson,	272	Collyn Clout	1036
Graunte hym his lycence	272	Collyn Clout	1038
To prease to his presence;	272	Collyn Clout	1039
Without his presydent be by,	272	Collyn Clout	1042
Or elles his substytute	272	Collyn Clout	1043
That his conscyence be nat clene,	274	Collyn Clout	1122
Whan that his pleasure is.	278	Collyn Clout	1265
And his honour appall.	279	Why Come Ye	23
The devyll kysse his cule!	282	Why Come Ye	133
his] 'hes' †Kele 1545.3			
The devyll kysse his arse!	282	Why Come Ye	136
Our lorde be his soccoure!	282	Why Come Ye	160
And his eyen so dased,	283	Why Come Ye	181
He is set so hye /In his ierarchy	283	Why Come Ye	185
Clappyng his rod on the borde.	283	Why Come Ye	190
He rolleth in his recordes,	283	Why Come Ye	194
For Dame Philargerya /Hathe so his herte in holde,	284	Why Come Ye	207
Maketh his membres swell	284	Why Come Ye	210
To kepe his flesshe chast	284	Why Come Ye	219
Lost all his father wan.	285	Why Come Ye	271
all his] 'al that his' Toy 1553, Kitson 1560.7, Marshe 1568			
The red hat with his lure	286	Why Come Ye	283
And maketh them to bow theyr kne /Before his majeste.	286	Why Come Ye	313
maketh them] 'make' Toy 1553, Kitson 1560.7, Marshe 1568			
But to his sentence must accorde.	287	Why Come Ye	343
All men must folow his desyre.	287	Why Come Ye	345
must] not in Marshe 1568			
That of shulde go his hede,	288	Why Come Ye	358
That his berde is so longe.	288	Why Come Ye	391
I pray God be his gyde.	289	Why Come Ye	395
His wysdome is so dyscrete	289	Why Come Ye	423
And of his royall powre	289	Why Come Ye	427
In credensynge his tales,	290	Why Come Ye	442
That he must pyll his lande	290	Why Come Ye	453
To make his cofers ryche;	290	Why Come Ye	454
He is in suche elacyon /Of his exaltacyon,	291	Why Come Ye	483
Of his wretched originall,	291	Why Come Ye	490
And his base progeny,	291	Why Come Ye	491
And his gresy genealogy,	291	Why Come Ye	492
His byrth and rowme togeder,	291	Why Come Ye	498
And call to his mynde	291	Why Come Ye	499
His Latyne tonge dothe hobbyll,	292	Why Come Ye	526
Whiche, of his royall mynde	292	Why Come Ye	546
And of his noble pleasure	292	Why Come Ye	547
Whiche his lyvenge wan	293	Why Come Ye	554
His frende as his fo!	293	Why Come Ye	583
His frende as his fo!	293	Why Come Ye	583
His servauntes menyall	294	Why Come Ye	595
His countynaunce lyke a kayser.	294	Why Come Ye	624
And his layser abyde,	295	Why Come Ye	636
The chefe of his owne counsell,	295	Why Come Ye	647
And his swete hart rote,	295	Why Come Ye	667
The kynge his clemency	296	Why Come Ye	681
Despensyth with his demensy.	296	Why Come Ye	682
But what his grace doth thinke,	296	Why Come Ye	683
Johannes Balua was his name	297	Why Come Ye	726
That he made him his chauncelar	297	Why Come Ye	732
And against his lorde soverayn!	297	Why Come Ye	738
Chefe rote of his makynge.	298	Why Come Ye	755
That can bylde his dwellinge house	298	Why Come Ye	757
And his untrew adversary?	298	Why Come Ye	789
And hathe his pasport to pas	299	Why Come Ye	803
And to his college conventuall,	299	Why Come Ye	808
To kepe his court provyncyall	299	Why Come Ye	813
For his prerogatyve, /Within that consystory	299	Why Come Ye	816
That wolde God everychone /Of his affynyte	300	Why Come Ye	835
Of his clothe makynge.	302	Why Come Ye	935
Though his purs wax dull,	302	Why Come Ye	937
He must tax for his wull	302	Why Come Ye	938
In the spyght of his tethe	302	Why Come Ye	942
Of his golde in store.	302	Why Come Ye	945
God save his noble grace,	303	Why Come Ye	969

	Page	Title	Line
At his owne desyer.	303	Why Come Ye	986
Of Lucyfer in his chaynes,	304	Why Come Ye	991
Lucyfer] 'Lucyfers' †Kele 1545.3			
Upon every banke /Of his herbers grene,	304	Why Come Ye	1003
Of his wylfull affectyon.	304	Why Come Ye	1015
his] 'him' Toy 1553, Kitson 1560.7, Marshe 1568			
God of his miseracyon /Send better reformacyon!	305	Why Come Ye	1044
But to wryte of his shame	305	Why Come Ye	1048
His madnesse by writynge,	305	Why Come Ye	1056
His symplenesse resytynge, /Remordynge and bytynge,	305	Why Come Ye	1057
Dare speke for his lyfe	306	Why Come Ye	1076
Of my lordis grace nor his wyfe!	306	Why Come Ye	1077
And by his legacy,	306	Why Come Ye	1103
Yet whan he toke first his hat,	306	Why Come Ye	1108
first] not in MS Rawlinson C. 813			
To be under his subjectyon.	307	Why Come Ye	1126
By his former othe,	307	Why Come Ye	1131
That in his equipolens	307	Why Come Ye	1134
With a flap afore his eye,	308	Why Come Ye	1169
afore] 'before' Kitson 1560.7, Marshe 1568, MS Rawl. C. 813			
Or els his surgions they lye;	308	Why Come Ye	1171
That all his trust hangis	308	Why Come Ye	1183
trust] 'harte' MS Rawlinson C. 813			
Now with his gummys of Araby	309	Why Come Ye	1196
gummys] 'gynnys' MS Rawlinson C. 813			
And make him lame of his neder limmes.	309	Why Come Ye	1200
God sende him sorowe for his sinnes!	309	Why Come Ye	1201
His fame to be encrest	309	Why Come Ye	1214
And say yll behynde his back,	310	Why Come Ye2	26
When Mars retrogradant reversed his bak,	312	Garlande	3
Lorde of the yere in his orbicular,	312	Garlande	4
Put up his sworde, for he cowde make no warre,	312	Garlande	5
His levis loste, the sappe was frome the rynde.	312	Garlande	21
Faire fall that forster that so well can bate his hownde!	313	Garlande	27
well] not in MS Cotton Vitellius E.x			
Bycause that he his tyme studyously hath spent	314	Garlande	60
he his tyme] 'his tyme he' MS Cotton Vitellius E.x			
Of your request, regestred is his name	314	Garlande	62
For if he gloryously publisshe his matter,	314	Garlande	83
And how his wordes with reason wyll not accorde.	314	Garlande	88
Also, to furnisshe better his excuse,	314	Garlande	92
A poete somtyme may for his pleasure taunt,	315	Garlande	100
But that his bokis, whiche he did devyse,	315	Garlande	124
That banisshed was he by his proposicyoun,	316	Garlande	132
by] 'through' Marshe 1568			
His name? Or why is it, I you praye,	316	Garlande	138
Of his onoure, whos dissuasyve in wrytyng	316	Garlande	151
In settyng out fresshely his crafty persuacyon,	316	Garlande	153
As Jerome, in his preamble Frater Ambrosius,	316	Garlande	162
Of Demostenes, that was his utter foo.	317	Garlande	167
'Prove his wytt', sayth he, 'at cardes or dyce,	318	Garlande	206
If he to the ample encrease of his name	318	Garlande	222
To blowe a blaste with his long breth extendid;	319	Garlande	234
To blowe bararag tyll bothe his eyne stare.'	319	Garlande	245
bararag] 'bararag brag' MS Cotton Vitellius E.x			
Of laurell levis a cronell on his hede,	320	Garlande	288
Concente to Phebus to have his herte in holde,	320	Garlande	292
Meddelyd with murnynge the moost parte of his muse,	320	Garlande	295
murnynge] 'murmynge' †Fakes 1523			
'O thoughtfull herte,' was evermore his songe!	320	Garlande	296
Betwene his armes, he felt her body quake.	320	Garlande	301
Then he assurded into his exclamacyon	320	Garlande	302
his] 'this' Marshe 1568			
Fyrst, olde Quintiliane with his Declamacyons;	321	Garlande	326
Declamacyons] 'declynacyons' †Fakes 1523			
Theocritus with his bucolycall relacyons;	321	Garlande	327
Of closters engrosyd with his ruddy flotis	321	Garlande	335
flotis] 'droppes' †Fakes 1523, 'flotis' Marshe 1568			
Virgill the Mantuan, with his Eneidos;	321	Garlande	339
Of clusters engrosed with his ruddy flotes	321	Garlande	342
Of clusters engrosid with his ruddy [flotis]	322	Garlande	349
flotis] 'droppes' †Fakes 1523, 'dropes' Marshe 1568			
Orace also with his new poetry;	322	Garlande	352
Of clusters engrosyd with his ruddy [flotis]	322	Garlande	356
flotis] 'dropis' †Fakes 1523, 'dropes' Marshe 1568			
Senek full soberly with his tragediis;	322	Garlande	358
with] 'wit' †Fakes 1523			
Boyce recounfortyd with his philosophy;	322	Garlande	359
And Maxymyane, with his madde ditiis,	322	Garlande	360
Of clusters engrosid with his ruddy [flotis]	322	Garlande	363
flotis] 'dropis' †Fakes 1523, 'dropes' Marshe 1568			
There came Johnn Bochas with his volumys grete;	322	Garlande	365
Of clusters engrosed with his ruddy [flotis]	322	Garlande	370
flotis] 'dropis' †Fakes 1523, 'dropes' Marshe 1568			
Of clusters engrosyd with his ruddy [flotis]	322	Garlande	377
flotis] 'dropis' †Fakes 1523, 'dropes' Marshe 1568			
Of clusters engrosed with his ruddy [flotis]	322	Garlande	384
flotis] 'dropis' †Fakes 1523, 'dropes' Marshe 1568			

HIS — HIS	Page	Title	Line
When he is callid to answere to his name.'	325	Garlande	452
Some shewid his salfe cundight, some shewid his charter,	326	Garlande	503
salfe cundight] 'safeconduct' Marshe 1568; charter] 'chart' Marshe 1568			
Some shewid his salfe cundight, some shewid his charter,	326	Garlande	503
salfe cundight] 'safeconduct' Marshe 1568; charter] 'chart' Marshe 1568			
Whan Titan radiant burnisshith his bemis bryght,	327	Garlande	534
And with his forme foote he shoke forthe this wrytyng:	328	Garlande	595
And one ther was there, I wondred of his hap,	329	Garlande	628
For a gun stone, I say, had all to-jaggid his cap,	329	Garlande	629
to-jaggid] 'to lagged' Marshe 1568			
The blaste of the brynston blew away his brayne;	329	Garlande	631
Enbrethyng of Zepherus with his pleasant wynde;	331	Garlande	677
There Cintheus sat twynklyng upon his harpe stringis;	331	Garlande	687
And Iopas his instrument did avaunce,	331	Garlande	688
Of fyre elementar in his supreme spere,	331	Garlande	694
And of their shorte nyghtes; he browght in his songe	331	Garlande	703
He fyndith fals mesuris out of his fonde fiddill.'	333	Garlande	741
fals mesuris out] 'owght fals mesuris' MS Cotton Vit.E.x			
His name for to know if that ye lyst,	333	Garlande	752
How daungerous it were to stande in his lyght,	333	Garlande	755
were to stande in his lyght] 'is to stop up his sight' MS Cotton Vitellius E.x			
For by his devellysshe drift and graceles provision	333	Garlande	757
To tell all his towchis it were to grete wonder;	333	Garlande	764
For to his servyce I have suche regarde,	334	Garlande	778
The frame was browght forth with his wevyng pin.	334	Garlande	792
In trust wherof comforte his hart doth grope,	335	Garlande	832
Committyth all to God, and lettyth his shyp ryde;	335	Garlande	834
In you he wolde have set his hole delight.	336	Garlande	874
You to devyse his crafte were to seke;	337	Garlande	893
I sawe maister Newton sit with his compas,	343	Garlande	1096
His plummet, his pensell, his spectacles of glas,	343	Garlande	1097
of] 'with' †Fakes 1523			
His plummet, his pensell, his spectacles of glas,	343	Garlande	1097
of] 'with' †Fakes 1523			
His plummet, his pensell, his spectacles of glas,	343	Garlande	1097
of] 'with' †Fakes 1523			
Dyvysynge in pycture, by his industrious wit,	343	Garlande	1098
For in owr courte, ye wote wele, his name can not ryse	345	Garlande	1154
Of Englande, his workis here they begynne:	345	Garlande	1171
Item his Diologgis of Ymagynacyoun;	346	Garlande	1180
His commedy, Achademios callyd by name;	346	Garlande	1184
Callid Speculum Principis, to bere in his honde,	347	Garlande	1229
Suche problemis to paynt it longyth to his arte.	347	Garlande	1246
He wrate an Epitaph for his grave stone,	347	Garlande	1249
All his delight was to braule and to barke	347	Garlande	1252
Who list amende it, let hym set to his penne.	348	Garlande	1260
His dirige, her commendacioun /Can be no derogacyoun;	348	Garlande	1269
Caron with his berde hore,	349	Garlande	1331
And with his frownsid fortop	349	Garlande	1333
Gydith his bote with a prop.	349	Garlande	1334
Of his pleasaunt paine there and his glad distres	351	Garlande	1391
Of his pleasaunt paine there and his glad distres	351	Garlande	1391
Of Exione, his limbis dede and past,	351	Garlande	1400
his limbis] 'her lambis' †Fakes 1523, 'her lambe is' Marshe 1568			
His Epitomis of the Myller and his joly Make;	351	Garlande	1411
His Epitomis of the Myller and his joly Make;	351	Garlande	1411
The millar durst not leve his wyfe at home.	352	Garlande	1417
Of his makyng devoute medytacyons;	352	Garlande	1419
Whereupon he metrefyde after his mynde;	353	Garlande	1464
In his distichon made on verses twaine.	353	Garlande	1467
distichon] 'distincyon' †Fakes 1523			
Item Apollo that whirllid up his chare,	353	Garlande	1471
For, by Juppiter and his high mageste,	353	Garlande	1488
Where I saw Janus, with his double chere,	354	Garlande	1515
Makynge his almanak for the new yere;	354	Garlande	1516
He turnyd his tirikkis, his volvell ran fast,	354	Garlande	1517
He turnyd his tirikkis, his volvell ran fast,	354	Garlande	1517
With all his hoost	359	Albany	9
That valiaunt knyght, /Putte you to flyght /By his valyaunce.	360	Albany	42
He reculed backe, /To his great lacke,	360	Albany	53
And brake up all his hoost.	360	Albany	67
For all his crake and bost,	360	Albany	68
To putte his eyes out	361	Albany	94
Nor lyke his sonne Hanyball,	363	Albany	194
Nor durst nat drawe his swerde	366	Albany	308
His owne realme to forsake?	367	Albany	328
His countenaunce to beholde.	367	Albany	339
To rayle agaynst his grace	368	Albany	365
Our kyng out of his reme?	368	Albany	381
Of this, his realme royall /And lande imperiall,	368	Albany	393
Fortunate in all his *faytes.	368	Albany	398
*faytes] 'fayctes' Scattergood			
His valiaunce to expresse,	369	Albany	400
His grace to magnify	369	Albany	402

	Page	Title	Line
To extoll his noble grace	369	Albany	407
His blode with fonde dotage.	369	Albany	415
In his goodly person /Lyke unto Absolon,	369	Albany	434
And his glory to incres /Lyke to Scipiades,	369	Albany	438
All the roiall sorte /Of his nobilyte,	370	Albany	446
His magnanymyte, /His animosite,	370	Albany	447
His magnanymyte, /His animosite,	370	Albany	448
His fr[u]galite, /His lyberalite, frugalite] 'fragalite' †Marshe 1568	370	Albany	449
His fr[u]galite, /His lyberalite, frugalite] 'fragalite' †Marshe 1568	370	Albany	450
His affabilite, /His humanyte,	370	Albany	451
His affabilite, /His humanyte,	370	Albany	452
His stabilite, /His humilite,	370	Albany	453
His stabilite, /His humilite,	370	Albany	454
His benignite /His royall dignyte,	370	Albany	455
His benignite /His royall dignyte,	370	Albany	456
To rayle on his astate /With wordes inordinate?	370	Albany	461
He rules his cominalte /With all benignite.	370	Albany	463
His noble baronage /He putteth them in corage	370	Albany	465
Of suche as be his foos	370	Albany	469
His subjectes he dothe supporte,	370	Albany	471
Of his moste princely porte,	370	Albany	473
All his subjectes and he /Moost lovyngly agre	371	Albany	480
They fynde his grace so kynde;	371	Albany	483
To assyst his noble grace,	371	Albany	491
Before his noble grace	372	Albany	525
In his mynde to comprise,	372	Albany	529
Those wordes his grace dyd saye /Of an ammas gray.	372	Albany	530
and have waded but weakly in his thre maner of clerkly workes,	374	Replycacion	1
With his fagot in processyon.	379	Replycacion	188
His heresy to supporte;	379	Replycacion	192
His foly so to face.	379	Replycacion	196
In his pystell ad Paulinum,	383	Replycacion	325
Nor solempne Serenus, for all his armony	383	Replycacion	337
In metricall muses, his harpyng we may spare;	383	Replycacion	338
Of our savyour Christ in his decacorde psautry,	383	Replycacion	340
That at his resurrection he harped out of hell	383	Replycacion	341
With his harpe of prophesy /And spyrituall poetry,	384	Replycacion	345
Warblynge with his strynges	384	Replycacion	349
God maketh his habytacion	384	Replycacion	376

HISTORIAR

	Page	Title	Line
And Homerus, the fresshe historiar;	321	Garlande	329
Aulus Gelius, that noble historiar;	322	Garlande	351

HISTORIOUS

	Page	Title	Line
Of these historious tales,	90	Phy Sparrow	751
With decadis historious, whiche that he mengith	321	Garlande	345

HISTORY

	Page	Title	Line
That wrote the history of Jugurta also;	321	Garlande	332

HIT

	Page	Title	Line
How ofte he hadde hit Jenet on the tayle, hadde] 'not' Marshe 1568	56	Bowge	369
Difficille hit ys to answsere thys demaunde;	243	Speke Parott	418
An hynde unhurt hit by casuelte, not bled	351	Garlande	1406

HITHER

	Page	Title	Line
Lo, hither commyth a goodly maystres,	326	Garlande	521
Hither they come crowdyng to get them a name,	329	Garlande	621

HY

	Page	Title	Line
Hys hart is to hy to have any hap;	37	Coystrowne1	12
He solfyth to haute, hys trybyll is to hy;	37	Coystrowne1	23
Above the sky /That is so hy,	40	Coystrowne3	56
The hy auter he strypte naked;	63	Hauke	49
Mirres vous y, /Loke nat to hy.	124	Garnesche2	E
For measure is a meane, nother to hy nor to lawe,	145	Magnyfycence	188
Anone he waxyth so hy and prowde,	174	Magnyfycence	1244
Nowe well, nowe wo, nowe hy, nowe lawe degre;	212	Magnyfycence	2517
Mountith on hy with her melodious lay,	327	Garlande	535
And of the winter days that hy them so fast,	331	Garlande	700
And for as moche as, by the hy pretence	344	Garlande	1124

HYCHE

	Page	Title	Line
An other than dyd hyche her, hyche] 'hye' 1521 Fragment	224	El Rummynge	401

HYD

	Page	Title	Line
I saw a knyfe hyd in his one sleve,	58	Bowge	433
Sodenly hyd, and sodenly spyed;	213	Magnyfycence	2535

HYDDER

	Page	Title	Line
'What movyd the,' quod she, 'hydder to come?'	48	Bowge	78

HYDE

	Page	Title	Line
No man may hym hyde /From deth holow-eyed,	39	Coystrowne3	10
Gaspyng asyde, /Nakyd of hyde,	39	Coystrowne3	17
Yower knavery I wyll nat hyde,	124	Garnesche3	22
That he may hyde	165	Magnyfycence	904
Full moche flatery and falsehode I hyde;	177	Magnyfycence	1358
Out harowe! Hyll burneth! Where shall I me hyde?	206	Magnyfycence	2324
Than Elynour dyd them hyde /Within her beddes syde.	229	El Rummynge	605
Nor for to chyde, /Nor for to hyde /You cowardly;	356	Garlande	1567
Your heedes for to hyde	363	Albany	186
And hyde you under logges,	364	Albany	213

HYDED —HYGHTE	Page	Title	Line
But hyde the, Sir Topias,	366	Albany	287
HYDED			
Like an onyon syded, /Lyke tan ledder hyded.	226	El Rummynge	471
HYDER			
Counterfet Countenaunce, nay, come hyder –	155	Magnyfycence	547
I say, come hyder. What are these twayne?	156	Magnyfycence	582
Hyder and thyder, I wote not whyder;	169	Magnyfycence	1033
Hay, chysshe, come hyder! Nay, torde! Take hym be tyme.	171	Magnyfycence	1117
By the masse, I am glad I came hyder	176	Magnyfycence	1286
Stande a lytell abacke, syr, and let hym come hyder.	186	Magnyfycence	1647
Come hyder, Pleasure; you shall here myne entent.	186	Magnyfycence	1655
That he come hyder, and to gyve hym a loke	187	Magnyfycence	1681
And, syr as I was comynge to you hyder,	191	Magnyfycence	1813
Syr, after your message I hyed me hyder streyght,	209	Magnyfycence	2419
And sayth, 'Gossyp, come hyder,	219	El Rummynge	204
He shulde be hyder brought;	287	Why Come Ye	351
HYE			
Her takelynge ryche and of hye apparayle;	47	Bowge	38
Of what estate ye be, /Of hye or lowe degre,	73	Phy Sparrow	55
Ye were to hye, ye ar cast downe.	120	Ag Scottes	177
By Cockes harte, he loketh hye.	156	Magnyfycence	574
That thou so hye fro me doth sprynge,	170	Magnyfycence	1069
And therfore hye you hens, and take this oversyght.	190	Magnyfycence	1795
He knewe not hymselfe, his harte was so hye;	193	Magnyfycence	1888
These swyne go to the hye dese,	218	El Rummynge	175
His rumpe also he frygges /Agaynst the hye benche.	219	El Rummynge	179
The prelates ben so haute /They say, and loke so hye	248	Collyn Clout	72
He is set so hye /In his ierarchy	283	Why Come Ye	184
Set up a wretche on hye,	293	Why Come Ye	585
Nor duke of hye degre,	294	Why Come Ye	619
Downe this hye sprynge;	302	Why Come Ye	950
Ye soored over hye /In the ierarchy /Of Jovenyans heresy,	378	Replycacion	161
Ye saye that poetry /Maye nat flye so hye	382	Replycacion	307
HYED			
Syr, after your message I hyed me hyder streyght,	209	Magnyfycence	2419
Had she not hyed apace,	229	El Rummynge	572
HYER			
That clymmeth hyer than he may fotynge have;	46	Bowge	27
Wryteth after an hyer rate;	91	Phy Sparrow	805
Nowe must your fete lye hyer than your crowne.	197	Magnyfycence	2007
HYEST			
Hyest in the skye,	85	Phy Sparrow	551
HYE WAYE			
They holde the hye waye,	221	El Rummynge	259
HYGH			
The world [envyronn], of hygh and low estate.	140	Magnyfycence	2
envyronn] 'envyronnyd' †Rastell & Treveris C 1530, B			
To here your comon, it is my hygh comforte.	183	Magnyfycence	1539
For drede my dysplease the hygh deyte.	196	Magnyfycence	1996
Some make epylogacyon /Of hygh predestynacyon;	259	Collyn Clout	520
Your hygh and lordely lokes.	261	Collyn Clout	595
The churche hygh estates,	264	Collyn Clout	708
Of hygh or lowe degre	274	Collyn Clout	1118
'Prynces moost pusant, of hygh preemynence,	313	Garlande	50
HYGHEST			
I am desyred with hyghest and lowest degre.	199	Magnyfycence	2079
HYGHLY			
Truste me, with you I am hyghly pleasyd;	183	Magnyfycence	1535
HYGHT			
Deucalyons flode it hyght.	78	Phy Sparrow	253
Jane this maystres hyght,	102	Phy Sparrow	1225
Who lyst to knowe, Magnyfycence I hyght.	145	Magnyfycence	164
But Measure, my frende, what hyght this mannys name?	145	Magnyfycence	165
Largesse, that all lordes sholde love, syr, I hyght.	148	Magnyfycence	270
But hyght you, Largesse, encreace of noble fame?	148	Magnyfycence	271
Though Largesse ye hyght your langage is to large;	148	Magnyfycence	295
It was a Flemynge hyght Hansy.	149	Magnyfycence	328
And made largesse, as I hyght,	150	Magnyfycence	364
To Tyburne, where they hange on hyght.	152	Magnyfycence	423
In faythe, Largesse I hyght;	155	Magnyfycence	520
But then, syr, what shall I hyght?	159	Magnyfycence	669
Syr, ye shall hyght Good Demeynaunce.	159	Magnyfycence	674
Abusyon /Forsothe I hyght;	164	Magnyfycence	857
Mary, thou jettes it of hyght.	167	Magnyfycence	962
Frantyke Fansy-Servyce I hyght.	169	Magnyfycence	1023
For all that my name hyght Foly,	171	Magnyfycence	1110
By the masse, he shall hyght Consayte.	176	Magnyfycence	1309
The stroke of God, Adversyte, I hyght.	193	Magnyfycence	1882
Who brought you that letter? Wote ye what he hyght?	209	Magnyfycence	2440
'Soft,' quod one hyght Sybbyll,	228	El Rummynge	549
hyght] 'high' Day 1560, Marshe 1568			
With a poore knyght, /Whatsoever he hyght!	295	Why Come Ye	646
Moche mischefe, I hyght you, amonge theem ther happid.	330	Garlande	643
HYGHTE			
The Bowge of Courte it hyghte for certeynte.	47	Bowge	49
certeynte] 'certeynet' †Wynkyn de Worde 1499, 'certayne'			
Wynkyn de Worde 1510, 'certeynte' Marshe 1568			

HYLL —HYM	Page	Title	Line
Dysdayne, I wene, [t]his comerous car[k]es hyghte.	54	Bowge	294
this] 'his' editions; carkes] 'carbes' †Wynkyn de Worde 1499, 1510, 'crabes' Marshe 1568			
This Doctour Dawcocke, Drede, I wene he hyghte.	54	Bowge	303
HYLL			
Of Ethna the brennynge hyll	79	Phy Sparrow	313
And some fall prechynge at the Toure Hyll;	200	Magnyfycence	2140
Out harowe! Hyll burneth! Where shall I me hyde?	206	Magnyfycence	2324
Of a comely gyll /That dwelt on a hyll;	214	El Rummynge	5
Come who so wyll /To Elynoure on the hyll, ...	217	El Rummynge	114
HYLLARY			
For, by saynt Hyllary, ...	266	Collyn Clout	813
HYLLES			
To the hylles of Armony, ...	78	Phy Sparrow	247
At Branxton More and Flodden hylles, ...	119	Ag Scottes	131
And lepe frome the hylles to lerne for to daunce;	320	Garlande	280
HYLLYS			
At Floddon hyllys, /Our bowys, our byllys	116	Ag Scottes	25
HYM			
Of hym that is gone, alas, withoute restore, ...	29	Dol Dethe	3
Thorow treson, ageyn hym compassyd and wrought, ...	29	Dol Dethe	6
That were aboute hym, his awne servauntis of trust, ...	30	Dol Dethe	37
To suffre hym slayn of his mortall fo?	30	Dol Dethe	38
Fled away from hym, let hym ly in the dust, ...	30	Dol Dethe	39
Fled away from hym, let hym ly in the dust, ...	30	Dol Dethe	39
A maynny of rude villayns made hym for to blede.	30	Dol Dethe	46
Unkindly thei slew hym that help them oft at nede.	30	Dol Dethe	47
help] 'holp' Marshe 1568			
Yet shamfully thei slew hym; that sham most them befall. . . .	30	Dol Dethe	49
What movyd you agayn hym to war or to fight?	31	Dol Dethe	62
For whos causis ye slew hym with your awne hande.	31	Dol Dethe	68
Ye had not ben hable to have saide hym nay.	31	Dol Dethe	70
Trustinge in noble men that wer with hym there;	31	Dol Dethe	90
Bot all they fled from hym for falshode or fere.	31	Dol Dethe	91
Take up whos wolde, for ther they let hym ly.	32	Dol Dethe	96
Tyll fykkill Fortune began on hym to frowne.	33	Dol Dethe	133
To all cuntreis aboute hym reporte me I dare:	33	Dol Dethe	136
Till the chaunce ran ageyne hym of Fortuns double dyse.	33	Dol Dethe	140
And all other gentelmen with hym enterteynd	34	Dol Dethe	184
Thorow bounte of hym that formed all solace, ...	35	Dol Dethe	214
Nay, jape not with hym, he is no small fole;	38	Coystrowne1	50
that was sent to hym	39	Coystrowne3	I
No man may hym hyde /From deth holow-eyed, ...	39	Coystrowne3	10
She cheryshed hym both cheke and chyn	42	Balettys1	9
She left hym slepyng and stale away, ...	42	Balettys1	14
The tyme whan Mars to werre hym dyd dres;	46	Bowge	7
What and he slyde downe, who shall hym save?	46	Bowge	28
There can no favour nor frendshyp hym forsake.	48	Bowge	103
She cherysshe[th] him, and hym she casseth awaye.'	49	Bowge	117
'cherysshed' †Wynkyn de Worde 1499, 1510, Marshe 1568; casseth] 'casteth' Wynkyn de Worde 1510, 'chasseth' Marshe 1568			
Than thanked I hym for his grete gentylnes.	51	Bowge	176
But, as me thoughte, he ware on hym a cloke	51	Bowge	177
Suspycyon, me thoughte, mette hym at a brayde, ...	51	Bowge	181
'Twyst,' quod Suspecte, 'goo playe; hym I ne reke!'	51	Bowge	186
Twyst] 'Whist' Wynkyn de Worde 1510, 'Twysshe' Marshe 1568			
Than I assured hym my fydelyte, ...	52	Bowge	218
Els, I prayed hym with all my besy cure, ...	52	Bowge	221
That noo man erthly coude hym bewreye, ...	52	Bowge	223
man] 'wan' †Wynkyn de Worde 1499			
Whan I loked on hym, my purse was half aferde.	52	Bowge	238
Hatred by the herte so had hym wrounge	54	Bowge	292
There muste for hym be layde some prety beyte.	55	Bowge	312
Fyrste pycke a quarell and fall oute with hym then, ...	55	Bowge	314
And soo outface hym with a carde of ten.'	55	Bowge	315
I loked on hym, I wende he had be woode.	55	Bowge	320
I was ashamed so to here hym prate.	56	Bowge	373
Unthryftynes in hym may well be shewed, ...	58	Bowge	416
Unthryftynes] 'Unthryftenes' †Wynkyn de Worde 1499, 1510			
In no place well, but foles with hym fraye!	58	Bowge	446
hym] not in †Wynkyn de Worde 1499, Marshe 1568			
Save hym that nought can: scrypture sayth soo.	58	Bowge	448
Woo is hym that is blynde and maye not see!	60	Bowge	518
All grace is far hym fro.	62	Hauke	16
For fayth in hym is faynte.	62	Hauke	19
Wherof I hym controld;	64	Hauke	96
I hym] 'him I' Kynge & Marche 1554, Day 1560, Marshe 1568			
Gave hym his mortall wounde.	79	Phy Sparrow	298
To make hym our belman, ...	84	Phy Sparrow	492
And let hym ryng the bellys;	84	Phy Sparrow	493
Men se hym now and than	88	Phy Sparrow	657
than] 'then' Marshe 1568			
From her to hym agayn;	88	Phy Sparrow	687
She made hym to syng	89	Phy Sparrow	701
And lede my fyst /As hym best lyst, ...	96	Phy Sparrow	973
The Philistinis shuld hym ascry, ...	105	Phy Sparrow	1358
God forgeve hym his mysdedes.	107	Epitaphe1	19
In hym is figured Melchisedeche, ...	114	Scot Kynge	23

	Page	Title	Line
At hym example ye wolde none take;	115	Scot Kynge	60
Upon hym for to take	126	Garnesche3	92
I yave hym drynke of the sugryd welle	132	Garnesche5	98
Aqueintyng hym with the Musys nyne.	132	Garnesche5	100
Of hym that wryteth to fast.	143	Magnyfycence	91
Where with to rule hym with the wrythyng of a rest.	144	Magnyfycence	136
And rule hym after the rule of your scole.	146	Magnyfycence	231
Have deputyd Measure hym to gyde?	147	Magnyfycence	243
Why have ye hym named and all other refused?	148	Magnyfycence	281
Byd hym take good hede of you, my synguler tresure.	149	Magnyfycence	317
And surely ye are to hym beholde,	149	Magnyfycence	333
That no man can scape but they hym cache.	150	Magnyfycence	351
And some bade, 'Sere hym with a marke.'	150	Magnyfycence	360
I set not by hym a fly	152	Magnyfycence	412
Thus at the laste I brynge hym ryght	152	Magnyfycence	422
And Crafty Conveyaunce, knowe you not hym?	156	Magnyfycence	584
Knowe hym, syr, quod he. Yes, by Saynt Sym!	156	Magnyfycence	585
And wolde that we sholde for hym go -	158	Magnyfycence	646
We had hym founde, we sholde hym brynge,	158	Magnyfycence	653
We had hym founde, we sholde hym brynge,	158	Magnyfycence	653
When we have hym thyder convayed,	159	Magnyfycence	676
I can fede forth a fole and lede hym by the eyre;	160	Magnyfycence	712
Tushe! He that hathe nede, man, let hym rynne.	162	Magnyfycence	786
I knowe in hym no defaute	163	Magnyfycence	823
Confusyon /Shall on hym lyght	164	Magnyfycence	859
That men hym gyve.	165	Magnyfycence	908
Mary, Mesure had hym a whyle in gydynge,	166	Magnyfycence	939
Ye. But I bade hym pyke out of the gate;	166	Magnyfycence	946
And I beshrowe hym that hath the worse.	171	Magnyfycence	1105
Hay, chysshe, come hyder! Nay, torde! Take hym be tyme.	171	Magnyfycence	1117
Nay, offer hym a counter in stede of a peny.	172	Magnyfycence	1171
Nay, nay. Thou shalt fynde hym another maner of man.	173	Magnyfycence	1189
to take money of CRAFTY CONVEYAUNCE, saynge to hym,	174	Magnyfycence	SD
And for a fole a man wolde hym take.	174	Magnyfycence	1212
To felowshyp with foly I can hym brynge.	174	Magnyfycence	1215
Nay, beyonde all other set hym alone.	174	Magnyfycence	1235
And maketh hym besy where is no nede.	175	Magnyfycence	1249
I make hym lese moche of theyr strength;	175	Magnyfycence	1259
It shall be done. Ye, but byd hym come away	179	Magnyfycence	1399
At ones, and let hym not tary all day.	179	Magnyfycence	1400
Why, wene you that I can kepe hym longe styll?	179	Magnyfycence	1412
Then fare well thryfte, by hym that crosse kyst!	179	Magnyfycence	1416
What nede you with hym thus prate and chat?	180	Magnyfycence	1434
I say that I wyll ye have hym in gydynge.	180	Magnyfycence	1436
I shall flappe hym as a fole to fall at my fete.	182	Magnyfycence	1507
I wolde I had, by hym that hell dyd harowe,	184	Magnyfycence	1561
And ye se a man that with hym ye be not pleased,	185	Magnyfycence	1609
For myrth I have hym coryed, beten, and blyst,	185	Magnyfycence	1622
Hym that I loved not, and made hym to loute;	185	Magnyfycence	1623
Hym that I loved not, and made hym to loute;	185	Magnyfycence	1623
And that ye wyll not cast hym away so sone.	186	Magnyfycence	1638
Stande a lytell abacke, syr, and let hym come hyder.	186	Magnyfycence	1647
That for hym to laboure he hath prayde me hartely;	186	Magnyfycence	1650
Mesure, ye knowe wel, with hym I can not be content;	186	Magnyfycence	1656
I wyll have hym rehayted and dyspysed.	186	Magnyfycence	1658
Yes. With his hande I made hym to subscrybe	187	Magnyfycence	1666
That he wolde loke on hym, thoughe it were not longe.	187	Magnyfycence	1675
That he come hyder, and to gyve hym a loke	187	Magnyfycence	1681
Where is he? Mary, I made hym abyde	187	Magnyfycence	1685
Well, call hym, and let us here hym reason;	187	Magnyfycence	1687
Well, call hym, and let us here hym reason;	187	Magnyfycence	1687
This is a wyse man, syr, where so ever ye hym had.	187	Magnyfycence	1689
Whylest I have hym, I nede nothynge doute.	187	Magnyfycence	1692
Have hym hens, I say, out of my syght!	188	Magnyfycence	1723
That day I se hym I shall be worse all nyght.	188	Magnyfycence	1724
God gyve hym a myscheffe! Nay, nowe let me alone.	189	Magnyfycence	1730
Cockes armes, howe Pleasure plucked hym forth!	189	Magnyfycence	1735
Nowe is there no man that wyll set by hym a flye.	193	Magnyfycence	1889
All worldly welth for hym to lytell was;	193	Magnyfycence	1892
Beholde howe Fortune o[n] hym hath frounde.	195	Magnyfycence	1947
on] 'of' †Rastell & Treveris C 1530, B			
By my trouthe, we have ryfled hym metely well.	201	Magnyfycence	2170
Abyde, syr, abyde; I shall make hym to pysse.	204	Magnyfycence	2250
In faythe, and I bequethe hym the tothe ake.	204	Magnyfycence	2253
And I bequethe hym the bone ake.	204	Magnyfycence	2254
And I bequethe hym the gowte and the gyn.	204	Magnyfycence	2255
And I bequethe hym sorowe for his syn.	204	Magnyfycence	2256
And I gyve hym Crystys curse	204	Magnyfycence	2257
And I gyve hym the cowghe, the murre, and the pose.	204	Magnyfycence	2259
Prosperyte [by] hym is gyven solacyusly to man;	207	Magnyfycence	2367
by] 'to' †Rastell & Treveris C 1530, B			
Adversyte to hym therwith nowe and than;	207	Magnyfycence	2368
Ye, syr. From hym my corage shall never flyt.	210	Magnyfycence	2466
By hym that me bought!'	218	El Rummynge	167
Require hym to convey yow ovyr the salte fome;	239	Speke Parott	302
To owur soleyne Seigneour Sadoke, desire hym to cum home,	239	Speke Parott	304
With porpose and graundepose he may fede hym fatte,	239	Speke Parott	308
And shewe hym that all the world dothe conjecte,	240	Speke Parott	327

HYM SELF —HYMSELFE   Page   Title   Line

Text	Page	Title	Line
Lyacon lawghyth thereatt and berythe hym more bolde;	242	Speke Parott	400
So myche of my lordes grace, and in hym no grace ys;	245	Speke Parott	501
So myche crossyng and blyssyng and hym all be shrewde;	246	Speke Parott	516
'He is but a foole; /Let hym go to scole!	247	Collyn Clout	29
Uppon hym for to take /A mattocke or a rake.	253	Collyn Clout	273
And hym a bysshop make,	254	Collyn Clout	305
Yf he on hym dare take	254	Collyn Clout	306
Let hym well beware	263	Collyn Clout	665
And graunte hym at his askynge	272	Collyn Clout	1027
Graunte hym his lycence	272	Collyn Clout	1038
Nor to speke to hym secretly, /Openly nor prevyly,	272	Collyn Clout	1040
Set hym fast by the fete!	275	Collyn Clout	1166
Lodge hym in Lytell Ease,	275	Collyn Clout	1169
Fede hym with beanes and pease!	275	Collyn Clout	1170
Have hym thyder by and by!	275	Collyn Clout	1172
Set hym fast by the fete!'	289	Why Come Ye	426
Have hym forthe by and by /To the Marshalsy,	289	Why Come Ye	431
And set hym nobly /In great auctoryte	291	Why Come Ye	504
Whan they with hym shulde mell,	295	Why Come Ye	649
Is toward hym so mynded,	295	Why Come Ye	659
How he doth hym disceyve.	295	Why Come Ye	662
With hym so wele apayd	297	Why Come Ye	731
And to rule as hym lyst;	297	Why Come Ye	734
In hym was small fayth,	297	Why Come Ye	744
The seconde, to owe hym obedyence,	307	Why Come Ye	1124
We passe hym in degre	308	Why Come Ye	1151
And, as we dare, we fynde in hym grete lake: grete] 'a' Marshe 1568	314	Garlande	70
Out of my bokis full sone I shulde hym rase;	314	Garlande	72
It is sittynge that ye must hym correct.'	314	Garlande	77
Wherin this answere for hym we have comprisid,	314	Garlande	80
And if so hym fortune to wryte true and plaine, so] not in MS Cotton Vitellius E.x	314	Garlande	85
It was not for hym to abyde the tryall. abyde] 'byde' MS Cotton Vitellius E.x	315	Garlande	98
Whereto made ye me hym to avaunce	315	Garlande	115
But to do sumwhat iche man doth hym dres	315	Garlande	122
Among my recordes suffer hym namyd,	316	Garlande	160
For if ye laude hym whome honour hath opprest,	317	Garlande	174
Twyse! set hym a chare, or reche hym a stol Twyse] 'Twyshe' Marshe 1568, MS Cotton Vitellius E.x	318	Garlande	208
Twyse! set hym a chare, or reche hym a stol Twyse] 'Twyshe' Marshe 1568, MS Cotton Vitellius E.x	318	Garlande	208
To syt hym upon, and rede Jacke a thrummis bybille, hym] not in MS Cotton Vitellius E.x	318	Garlande	209
But I most bannysshe hym frome my jurydiccyon,	318	Garlande	227
As he that aquentyth hym with ydilnes.	318	Garlande	228
Let hym blowe now, that we may take a vewe a] 'the' MS Cotton Vitellius E.x	319	Garlande	237
And for no man hardely let hym spare	319	Garlande	244
He plucked hym backe, and he went afore.	319	Garlande	254
'There shal he here what she wyl to hym say wyl to hym] 'to hym will' Marshe 1568	325	Garlande	451
O wele were hym that herof myght be sure,	332	Garlande	718
Beware of hym, I warne you; for and ye wist and] 'if' Marshe 1568	333	Garlande	754
Ye wolde not dele with hym, thowgh that ye myght, though] 'thought' Marshe 1568, 'thowth' MS Cotton Vit.E.x	333	Garlande	756
That of our bownte we wyll hym rewarde:	334	Garlande	779
That list of there lewdnes suffer with hym for to brall.'	334	Garlande	786
Wele was hym that thereupon myght stare.	343	Garlande	1109
Let se now for hym how ye can expounde;	345	Garlande	1153
Who list amende it, let hym set to his penne.	348	Garlande	1260
The Phillistinis shulde hym askry,	350	Garlande	1351
In ryming and raylyng with hym for to mell,	353	Garlande	1475
Was comyng downe /To make hym frowne	360	Albany	57
And to make hym lowre,	360	Albany	58
And put hym downe,	361	Albany	95
To bring with hym more brayne	363	Albany	174
That no man hym kyll;	365	Albany	264
About hym a parke /Of a madde warke,	365	Albany	267
With hym to stryve a stownde.	367	Albany	344
To loke hym in the face	367	Albany	352
To rayle on hym lyke dawes.	371	Albany	478
With hym to lyve and dye,	371	Albany	486
With hym in all dystresse, /Alway in redynesse	371	Albany	489
And hym moost lowly pray,	372	Albany	528
And thought in hym smale grace	379	Replycacion	195
Reputyng hym unable /To gainsay replycable	382	Replycacion	302
Lyke unto Alcheus, he dothe hym magnify.	383	Replycacion	335
Flaccus nor Catullus with hym may nat compare,	383	Replycacion	336

HYM SELF

Text	Page	Title	Line
From bitter wepinge hym self kan restrayne?	32	Dol Dethe	112

HYMSELFE

Text	Page	Title	Line
To kepe it hymselfe; for than he myghte be sure	52	Bowge	222
Welthe without measure wolde bere hymselfe to bolde;	143	Magnyfycence	116
And therwithall convey hymselfe into a payre of fetters;	178	Magnyfycence	1365
Crafty Conveyaunce can cloke hymselfe frome shame,	178	Magnyfycence	1370

HYM SELFE —HYS

	Page	Title	Line
He knewe not hymselfe, his harte was so hye;	193	Magnyfycence	1888
Thou arte not the fyrst hymselfe hath slayne.	206	Magnyfycence	2316
Here MAGNYFYCENCE wolde slee hymselfe with a knyfe.	206	Magnyfycence	SD
Who knoweth me, hymselfe may never sloo.	206	Magnyfycence	2330
How none estate lyvynge of hymselfe can be sure,	213	Magnyfycence	2557
Thus none estate lyvynge of hym[selfe] can be sure, hymselfe] 'hym' †Rastell & Treveris C 1530, B	214	Magnyfycence	2564
He coude nat synge hymselfe therout	268	Collyn Clout	878
That can hymselfe assure	271	Collyn Clout	1002
And feleth hymselfe sycke,	274	Collyn Clout	1123
And wyll not endevour hymselfe to purchase	314	Garlande	75
To se if Skelton wyll put hymselfe in prease wyll] 'dare' MS Cotton Vitellius E.x	319	Garlande	239
There Titus Lyvius hymselfe dyd avaunce	321	Garlande	344
Jupiter hymselfe this lyfe myght endure;	332	Garlande	715
He wyll set men a feightynge and syt hymselfe styll, set] 'stir' MS Cotton Vitellius E.x; a feightynge] 'to brawlyng' MS Cotton Vitellius E.x	333	Garlande	761
A lyfe for God hymselfe	340	Garlande	996

HYM SELFE

	Page	Title	Line
He doth abuse /Hym selfe to to;	164	Magnyfycence	872
So myche serchyng of loselles, and ys hym selfe so lewde;	246	Speke Parott	513

HYNDE

	Page	Title	Line
The harte, the hynde, the buck.	282	Why Come Ye	122
An hynde unhurt hit by casuelte, not bled	351	Garlande	1406

HYNDE CALFE

	Page	Title	Line
Few men can tell where the hynde calfe gose. tell] 'telle now' MS Cotton Vitellius E.x	313	Garlande	26

HYNDER

	Page	Title	Line
Spur up at the hynder gyrth with, 'Gup, morell, gup!'	43	Balettys2	17
Howe I may hurte and hynder every man.	160	Magnyfycence	709
Eche man to hynder I gape and I gaspe;	160	Magnyfycence	729
To hynder no man /As nere as I can,	274	Collyn Clout	1109

HYNDERAUNCE

	Page	Title	Line
In hynderaunce of welthe and prosperyte.	160	Magnyfycence	734

HYNDES

	Page	Title	Line
Bothe hartes and hyndes	280	Why Come Ye	55

HYNDRYNGE

	Page	Title	Line
In hyndrynge and dysavaylynge	274	Collyn Clout	1104

HYPPE

	Page	Title	Line
Alasse, I have the cyatyca full evyll in my hyppe!	195	Magnyfycence	1956

HYR

	Page	Title	Line
At Orwelle hyr havyn your anggre was laules.	122	Garneschel	33
........hyr husbandes hed,	125	Garnesche3	58
To hyr love ye nowte rechyd.	125	Garnesche3	61
Ye wolde have bassyd hyr bumme,	125	Garnesche3	62
Ye loste hyr favyr quyt!	125	Garnesche3	67
I wolde ye had kyst hyr on the tayle!	130	Garnesche5	46
Sche sware with hyr ye xulde nat dele,	131	Garnesche5	57
Howe hyr ale is solde /To mawte and to molde.	218	El Rummynge	158
That pereles pomegarnat, Cryste save hyr nobyll grace!'	231	Speke Parott	37

HYRE

	Page	Title	Line
I lete her to hyre that men maye on her ryde;	57	Bowge	402
Spende all his hyre	165	Magnyfycence	907
They were nat payde their hyre.	285	Why Come Ye	248
Be well assurid I shall aquyte your hyre,	327	Garlande	550

HYS

	Page	Title	Line
and madly in hys musykkys mokkyshly made agaynste	36	Coystrowne	1
Hys hart is to hy to have any hap;	37	Coystrowne1	12
Of Martyn Swart and all hys mery men.	37	Coystrowne1	18
Lord, how Perkyn is proud of hys Pohen!	37	Coystrowne1	19
To ask wher he fyndyth among hys monacordys	37	Coystrowne1	20
He solfyth to haute, hys trybyll is to hy;	37	Coystrowne1	23
He braggyth of hys byrth, that borne was full bace;	37	Coystrowne1	24
Hys musyk withoute mesure, to sharp is hys my;	37	Coystrowne1	25
Hys musyk withoute mesure, to sharp is hys my;	37	Coystrowne1	25
He trymmyth in hys tenor to counter pyrdewy;	37	Coystrowne1	26
Hys dyscant is besy, it is withoute a mene;	37	Coystrowne1	27
To fat is hys fantsy, hys wyt is to lene.	37	Coystrowne1	28
To fat is hys fantsy, hys wyt is to lene.	37	Coystrowne1	28
He fumblyth in hys fyngeryng an ugly good noyse;	37	Coystrowne1	31
With hys worme-etyn maw /And hys gastly jaw	39	Coystrowne3	14
With hys worme-etyn maw /And hys gastly jaw	39	Coystrowne3	15
Hys hed was hevy, such was his hap,	41	Balettys1	5
That of hys love he toke no kepe,	41	Balettys1	7
He trusted her payment and lost all hys pray.	42	Balettys1	13
'My lefe', she sayd, 'rowtyth in hys bed;	42	Balettys1	20
Hys jentyll curtoyl[1], and set nowght by small naggys! curtoyl] 'curtoyt' †Rastell 1527.1	43	Balettys2	16
So fersly he fytyth, hys mynde is so fell,	43	Balettys2	29
Sharpely commaundynge eche man holde hys pece.	47	Bowge	47
Envye hathe wasted hys lyver and his lounge;	54	Bowge	291
Nor blake Baltazar with hys basnet routh as a bere,	122	Garneschel	23
Whan hys grace ys fastynge,	126	Garnesche3	83
Hys presens to aproche,	126	Garnesche3	84
With hys brethe so stronge,	128	Garnesche3	151
Agenst hys poysond infeccioun,	128	Garnesche3	153
Els with hys stynkyng jawys	128	Garnesche3	154

HYSTORIALL — HOGGE

	Page	Title	Line
Pay Stokys hys fyve pownd.	128	Garnesche3	185
That fylythe hys owne nest.	129	Garnesche3	198
The f[r]esche bastyng of hys cote	129	Garnesche3	200
fresche] 'flesche' †MS Harley 367			
As provithe well, in hys rethorikys olde,	130	Garnesche5	11
Cicero with hys tong of golde.	130	Garnesche5	12
Thow wolde have scoryd hys habarion;	130	Garnesche5	34
Ye wolde have trysyd hys trowle away.	130	Garnesche5	36
Me as hys master for to calle	132	Garnesche5	104
In hys lernyng primordiall.	132	Garnesche5	105
Hys noble pleasure and commandemennt,	134	Garnesche5	178
Whate mone he made when Pamphylus loste hys make.	237	Speke Parott	234
Lyacon of Libyk and Lydy hathe cawghte hys pray:	239	Speke Parott	289
Makyng hys pylgrimage by Nostre Dame de Crome:	239	Speke Parott	305
Thowghe he pampyr not hys paunche with the grete seall;	239	Speke Parott	309
For he wantythe of hys wyttes that all wold rule alone;	240	Speke Parott	329
To make reconyng in the resseyte how Robyn loste hys bowe,	240	Speke Parott	341
Tytan hathe truste up hys tressys of fyne golde;	242	Speke Parott	398
He caryeth a kyng in hys sleve, yf all the worlde fayle;	243	Speke Parott	429
Hys wolvys hede, wanne, bloo as lede, gapythe over the crowne:	244	Speke Parott	434
Hyt ys to fere leste he wolde were the garland on hys pate,	244	Speke Parott	435
Paregall with all prynces, farre passyng hys estate;	244	Speke Parott	436
Now, Galathea, lett Parrot, I pray yow, have hys date -	244	Speke Parott	439
So lordlye of hys lokes, and so dysdayneslye;	246	Speke Parott	508
And hys textes grounde -	264	Collyn Clout	724
hys] not in Kele 1545.1, Marshe 1568			
And set hys crowne /On your owne heed	361	Albany	96

HYSTORIALL

In the college of musis goddes hystoriall,	29	Dol Dethe	9

HYT

To rayle with me that the can hyt.	132	Garnesche5	119
To lerne all langage and hyt to speke aptlye.	232	Speke Parott	45
And hyt to remembyr.	237	Speke Parott	228
Myne herte hyt ys with the.	237	Speke Parott	240
Hyt wyll not be refrayned:	238	Speke Parott	259
And sette to a D, /And then hyt ys 'Amend',	238	Speke Parott	276
to] not in †MS Harley 2252			
Hyt ys no lytyll bordon to bere a grete mylle stone.	240	Speke Parott	330
How thys prosses I prate of, ys not all for nowghte.	242	Speke Parott	389
Hyt ys to fere leste he wolde were the garland on hys pate,	244	Speke Parott	435

HYTHER

Come hyther Largesse; take here Felycyte.	179	Magnyfycence	1411

HYTTE

And yf that he hytte /The nayle on the hede	247	Collyn Clout	33

HOBBY

The hobby and the muskette	86	Phy Sparrow	567
So I myght hobby for suche a lusty larke.	184	Magnyfycence	1564

HOBBY LARKES

And hauke on hobby larkes	251	Collyn Clout	193

HOBBYLL

His Latyne tonge dothe hobbyll,	292	Why Come Ye	526

HOBBLE

Ye hobble very homly before the kynges borde;	123	Garnesche2	10

HOBY

I have an hoby can make larkys to dare;	177	Magnyfycence	1342

HOBLES

She hobles as she gose /With her blanket hose	216	El Rummynge	85
she gose] 'a gose' Day 1560, Marshe 1568			

HOCUPY

Cowde hocupy ther no stede.	126	Garnesche3	69

HODDYPEKE

Can he play well at the hoddypeke?	172	Magnyfycence	1161

HODDY POULE

Now suche a hoddy poule	296	Why Come Ye	673

HODE

With Indygnacyon lyned was his hode;	54	Bowge	286
Than, in his hode, I sawe there faces tweyne:	58	Bowge	428
His hode was syde, his cope was roset graye;	58	Bowge	440
His wytte is thynne, his hode is threde-bare.	60	Bowge	490
His hode all pounsed and garded lyke a cage.	60	Bowge	508
hode] 'body' Marshe 1568			
Two faces in a hode covertly I bere;	160	Magnyfycence	710
Good evyn, good Robyn Hode!	283	Why Come Ye	197
He pluckes them by the hode,	286	Why Come Ye	304
Your fonde hed in your furred hode!	310	Why Come Ye2	19
your] (2nd) 'a' MS Rawlinson C. 813			

HODER-MODER

For in hoder-moder /The churche is put in faute.	248	Collyn Clout	69

HOFTE

Decke your hofte and cover a lowce.	161	Magnyfycence	749

HOG

And Og, that fat hog of Basan, doth retayne	234	Speke Parott	122
of] 'or' Kynge & Marche 1554, Day 1560, Marshe 1568			

HOGEOUS

With hogeous showte and cry.	63	Hauke	48

HOGGE

Cockys harte! Thou lyest; I am no [h]ogge.	170	Magnyfycence	1083
hogge] 'dogge' †Rastell & Treveris C 1530, B			

HOGGES —HOLE   Page   Title   Line

Entry	Page	Title	Line
Here is no man that callyd the hogge nor swyne.	170	Magnyfycence	1084
Wold wyrry them lyke an hogge.	286	Why Come Ye	299

HOGGES

Entry	Page	Title	Line
Hoyning like hogges that groynis and wrotes.	137	Ven Tongues	4
In faythe, there is not a better dogge for hogges,	171	Magnyfycence	1120
With, 'Hey, dogge, hay, /Have these hogges away!' hogges] 'dogges' Day 1560, Marshe 1568	218	El Rummynge	169
Stryke the hogges with a clubbe,	218	El Rummynge	172
Ar mete for a swyne herde to hunte after hogges.	240	Speke Parott	321
Lyke pygges and lyke hogges	364	Albany	214

HOYNING

Entry	Page	Title	Line
Hoyning like hogges that groynis and wrotes.	137	Ven Tongues	4

HOKE

Entry	Page	Title	Line
By hoke ne by croke	277	Collyn Clout	1238

HOKED

Entry	Page	Title	Line
Her nose somdele hoked /And camously croked,	215	El Rummynge	27

HOKES

Entry	Page	Title	Line
For all hokes unhappy to me have resorte.	178	Magnyfycence	1374

HOLD

Entry	Page	Title	Line
Wherfore hold me excused	92	Phy Sparrow	813
Phronessys for frenessys may not hold her way.	232	Speke Parott	47

HOLDE

Entry	Page	Title	Line
Holde youre tong, now, all beshrewde!	41	Coystrowne4	28
Sharpely commaundynge eche man holde hys pece.	47	Bowge	47
What, lete us holde him up, man, for a whyle.'	51	Bowge	188
Holde up the helme, loke up and lete God stere:	53	Bowge	250
That shall them angre, I holde thereon a grote,	59	Bowge	475
To holde myne honde, by God, I had grete payne;	61	Bowge	522
Coude not my sampler holde;	77	Phy Sparrow	234
Of her I holde /And her housholde;	112	Calliope	13
Why holde ye on yer cap, syr, then? Yor pardone ys expyryd.	123	Garnesche2	9
Ye lost your [h]olde, onbende your bow, holde] 'bolde' †MS Harley 367	131	Garnesche5	49
A reme of papyr wyll nat holde	134	Garnesche5	174
You to holde content /With myne argument;	143	Magnyfycence	108
Tusche, holde your pece! Your langage is vayne.	147	Magnyfycence	251
Tushe! Holde your pece.	156	Magnyfycence	590
Holde thy pease! Measure shall frome us walke.	166	Magnyfycence	949
By the masse, I holde the madde.	170	Magnyfycence	1088
A, holde thy peas! I have the tothe ake.	172	Magnyfycence	1163
But yet thou shalt holde me a fole styll.	173	Magnyfycence	1184
Yes, yes, by my trouth. I holde the a grote	173	Magnyfycence	1193
Tushe! Holde your peas; ye speke lyke a dawe.	178	Magnyfycence	1379
Tushe! Holde your peas; ye speke out of season.	178	Magnyfycence	1388
Holde thy tonge, and thou love thy helth.	179	Magnyfycence	1402
And what so we say, holde you content withall.	179	Magnyfycence	1406
Nowe holde ye content, for there is none other shyfte.	180	Magnyfycence	1443
May wynne with a sawte the fortresse of the holde.	184	Magnyfycence	1581
I coude holde you with suche talke hens tyll to morowe.	184	Magnyfycence	1588
Abyde, syr, abyde. Let me holde your hede.	189	Magnyfycence	1727
They catche that catche may, kepe and holde fast,	189	Magnyfycence	1750
A thousande pounde with lyberte may holde no tacke.	199	Magnyfycence	2084
Nay. Then thou wylte dynge the devyll and thou be not holde.	202	Magnyfycence	2183
Holde thy hande, dawe, of thy dagger, and stynt of thy dyn;	202	Magnyfycence	2188
Today maysterfest, tomorowe he hath no holde;	213	Magnyfycence	2549
They holde the hye waye,	221	El Rummynge	259
For Dame Philargerya /Hathe so his herte in holde,	284	Why Come Ye	207
To holde up their hande at the bar.	286	Why Come Ye	302
Holde ye your tong, ye can no goode. ye] (1st) not in MS Rawlinson C. 813	310	Why Come Ye2	20
'Nay, holde thy tunge,' quod another, 'let me have the name.'	319	Garlande	255
Sume sayd, 'Holde thy peas, thou getest here no more.'	319	Garlande	257
Concente to Phebus to have his herte in holde,	320	Garlande	292
'A slipper holde the taile is of an ele'	326	Garlande	501
She went before, and bad me take good holde;'	328	Garlande	573
By Candelmes day what wedder shuld holde;	352	Garlande	1442

HOLDES

Entry	Page	Title	Line
They kepe them in theyr holdes	283	Why Come Ye	167

HOLE

Entry	Page	Title	Line
The welle concernyng of all the hole lande,	31	Dol Dethe	65
With trowth to medelle was all his hole delight,	33	Dol Dethe	152
If the hole quere of the Musis nyne	33	Dol Dethe	155
With all the hole sorte of that glorious place,	35	Dol Dethe	212
And I love you an hole cart lode.'	35	Man Margery	9
How in good horsmen ye set your hole delyght,	42	Balettys2	13
On all the hole nacyon	78	Phy Sparrow	275
And all the hole warke	87	Phy Sparrow	642
Now myne hole imaginacion	93	Phy Sparrow	847
To gyve her his hole hert.	99	Phy Sparrow	1102
Hole ys your brow that ye brake with Deu[ra]ndall your awne sworde; Deurandall] 'Deundall' †MS Harley 367	123	Garnesche2	8
I bequeth yt hole to the.	128	Garnesche3	177
By hole consent of theyr senate,	131	Garnesche5	83
To preche out of the pylery hole	150	Magnyfycence	358
By the masse, for ye are able to dystroy an hole lande.	154	Magnyfycence	513
And shortly shewe you the hole substaunce.	158	Magnyfycence	638
Among this prese - /Even a hole mese -	168	Magnyfycence	996
I have an hole armory of suche haburdashe in store;	175	Magnyfycence	1279

HOLY—HOMAGE	Page	Title	Line
I am forthwith as hole as a troute.	185	Magnyfycence	1624
I have set my hole felycyte,	190	Magnyfycence	1788
A prynce to use with all his hole intent,	200	Magnyfycence	2118
Nowe ryche, nowe pore, nowe hole, now in dysease;	212	Magnyfycence	2518
And stopped therewith the hole.	224	El Rummynge	406
That of theyr scole maters lost is the hole sentens.	235	Speke Parott	182
There is theyr hole devocyon,	248	Collyn Clout	87
Amongest the hole rout	273	Collyn Clout	1082
Is all my hole wrytynge;	274	Collyn Clout	1108
The thirde, with hole affectyon	307	Why Come Ye	1125
Amonge the thickeste of all the hole rowte,	319	Garlande	240
Welcome to me with all my hole desyre!	327	Garlande	548
Affyaunsynge her myne hole assuraunce	327	Garlande	555
Pope holy ypocrytis, as they were golde and hole,	329	Garlande	612
An hole reame he is able to set at devysion:	333	Garlande	758
In you he wolde have set his hole delight.	336	Garlande	874
It wolde have made a man hole that had be ryght sekely,	345	Garlande	1162
With hole hart and true mynde,	371	Albany	482

HOLY

Of laureat Phebus holy the eloquence	33	Dol Dethe	160
The Father, the Son, the Holy Goste,	35	Dol Dethe	216
Now, by Saynte Fraunceys, that holy man and frere,	59	Bowge	470
Wythin the holy church bowndis,	62	Hauke	13
And in the holy place /She mutyd there a chase	63	Hauke	61
Or holy sinodals, /Or els provincyals,	65	Hauke	132
Thus within the wals /Of holy church to deale,	65	Hauke	135
SOMETYME THE HOLY PATRIARKE OF DIS.	106	Epitaphe1	I
By the holy rode,	108	Epitaphe1	66
HE WAS SOMTIME THE HOLY BAILLYVE OF DIS.	109	Epitaphe2	I
Nowe welcom, by the God holy!	166	Magnyfycence	919
The Holy Goost be with your grace.	188	Magnyfycence	1711
To homly, to holy, to lewde, or to lowde,	199	Magnyfycence	2094
Then trust I to God and the holy rode,	203	Magnyfycence	2206
Cryst be amonge you, and the Holy Goste!	208	Magnyfycence	2385
Howe that ye sell /The grace of the Holy Goost.	251	Collyn Clout	201
Nor in holy lenton season	252	Collyn Clout	211
An holy anker call	254	Collyn Clout	303
An] 'a' †Godfray 1531, Kele 1545.1, Marshe 1568			
Holy churche is bruted /And shamfully confuted.	258	Collyn Clout	487
And also gratyfyed /By holy synodalles	264	Collyn Clout	716
Agaynst holy churche estate,	269	Collyn Clout	915
Holy churche our mother,	274	Collyn Clout	1105
The holy prophet, was;	276	Collyn Clout	1207
was] 'Ozeas' MS Harley 2252			
And some of you shall dye /Lyke holy Jeremy;	276	Collyn Clout	1209
And of holy scriptures sawis,	305	Why Come Ye	1062
But blessyd Bachus most reverent and holy,	322	Garlande	362
Pope holy ypocrytis, as they were golde and hole,	329	Garlande	612
Ageynst Holy Chyrche, the preste, and the clarke.	347	Garlande	1253
of our mother Holy Churche, etc.	373	Replycacion	I
Of Holy Churches lay.	379	Replycacion	171
Ye cobble and ye clout /Holy scripture so about,	380	Replycacion	223
And by Holy Churche correcte,	380	Replycacion	239
Come forthe, ye pope holy, /Full of melancoly!	381	Replycacion	247
With other many holy men,	381	Replycacion	278
With hete of the Holy Gost,	385	Replycacion	383

HOLY DAYE

Upon the holy daye, /Whan she doth her aray,	216	El Rummynge	66

HOLYNES

Counterfet holynes is called ypocrysy;	153	Magnyfycence	469
That nonnes wyl leve theyr holynes and ryn after me;	201	Magnyfycence	2146

HOLYNESSE

And all suche holynesse.	271	Collyn Clout	977

HOLYS

That occupy theyr holys;	285	Why Come Ye	245

HOLY WATER

An holy water clarke a ruler of lordys.	37	Coystrowne1	21

HOLY WATHER

shall be holy wather clarke.	86	Phy Sparrow	570

HOLL

Them selfe to embesy with all there holl corage,	314	Garlande	66
Of Fames court, by all our holl assent	324	Garlande	433

HOLLY

That holly my mynde with you is myscontente;	188	Magnyfycence	1717
My harte is holly on her set;	199	Magnyfycence	2073
Ye, holly to good hope I have made my repare.	208	Magnyfycence	2394

HOLLOW

That cast such overthwartes /Percase have hollow hartes.	121	Ag Scottes2	38

HOLOW

Rowlynge in yower holow hede, ugly to see;	122	Garneschel	38
So many holow hartes, and so dowbyll faces;	245	Speke Parott	502

HOLOWE

I make hevy hertys, with eyen full holowe.	205	Magnyfycence	2286

HOLOW-EYED

No man may hym hyde /From deth holow-eyed,	39	Coystrowne3	11

HOMAGE

In doynge his homage /Unto his soverayne.	80	Phy Sparrow	326

HOMAGER — HONOUR

	Page	Title	Line
HOMAGER			
Parde ye be his homager	114	Scot Kynge	30
Pardy, ye were his homager, ...	118	Ag Scottes	122
HOME			
Iwys I coude tell - but humlery, home, ...	59	Bowge	467
tell] 'not tell' Wynkyn de Worde 1510			
Welthe, gete you home and commaunde me to Mesure.	149	Magnyfycence	316
Let us departe from hens home to my place.	151	Magnyfycence	394
Ryches rydeth out, at home is poverte.	153	Magnyfycence	474
And get [y]ou home togyther; for Lyberte shall byde	180	Magnyfycence	1446
you] 'thou' †Rastell & Treveris C 1530, B			
And brought home and layde in your bed.	184	Magnyfycence	1572
Home to your paleys with joy and ryalte.	214	Magnyfycence	2567
At home in her wonnynge;	216	El Rummynge	94
Home to resorte Jerobesethe perswade;	238	Speke Parott	279
To owur soleyne Seigneour Sadoke, desire hym to cum home, . . .	239	Speke Parott	304
At home full softe doth sytte.	255	Collyn Clout	328
With, 'Tourne all home agayne!'	282	Why Come Ye	151
And turne home ageyne, for they cam al to late.	329	Garlande	605
The millar durst not leve his wyfe at home.	352	Garlande	1417
But thou ran home agayne	365	Albany	246
HOMELY			
Myne homely rudnes and drighnes to expelle	29	Dol Dethe	13
Transcending f[a]r myne homely Muse that must	33	Dol Dethe	144
far] 'for' †MS Royal 18 D.ii, Marshe 1568			
Syr, pardone me, I am an homely knave	53	Bowge	264
Wolde God myne homely style	101	Phy Sparrow	1204
HOMERUS			
As Linus and Homerus, /Euphorion and Theocritus, ...	90	Phy Sparrow	761
And Homerus, the fresshe historiar;	321	Garlande	329
HOMYCIDE			
O homycide, whiche sleest all that thou kan, ...	32	Dol Dethe	123
HOMYLYEST			
In the homylyest wyse, ...	87	Phy Sparrow	625
HOMLY			
Ye hobble very homly before the kynges borde;	123	Garnesche2	10
And happe you the whyles with these homly raggys.	197	Magnyfycence	2037
To homly, to holy, to lewde, or to lowde, ...	199	Magnyfycence	2094
HOMWARDE			
But hailid they be homwarde with sorow and shame.	329	Garlande	622
HONDE			
Bone aventure have here now in your honde.	48	Bowge	98
Gyve me your honde, fare well and have good daye.'	60	Bowge	497
'Harken,' quod he, 'loo here myne honde in thyne;	60	Bowge	510
To holde myne honde, by God, I had grete payne;	61	Bowge	522
And with that worde she toke me by the honde.	328	Garlande	560
Thamar also wrought with her goodly honde	336	Garlande	852
Callid Speculum Principis, to bere in his honde, ...	347	Garlande	1229
HONDES			
His eyen rollynge, his hondes faste they quoke;	51	Bowge	193
HONEST			
That byrd ys nat honest	129	Garnesche3	197
An honest person, I tell you, and a sad.	187	Magnyfycence	1690
Lyke an honest dame.	227	El Rummynge	511
In honest myrth, parde, requyreth no lack;	347	Garlande	1236
From all honest company, ...	380	Replycacion	243
HONESTE			
'As oft as ye lyst, so honeste be savyd.	177	Magnyfycence	1348
HONESTY			
Go she never so gingirly, her honesty is gone away.	346	Garlande	1204
To pyke out honesty of suche a potshorde.	346	Garlande	1211
HONGE			
Or that thy selfe thou go honge	206	Magnyfycence	2312
HONGRY			
Whyche cawsythe pore suters have many a hongry mele;	239	Speke Parott	311
HONY			
But under hony ofte tyme lyeth bytter gall, ...	49	Bowge	131
A spone of golde, full of hony swete, ...	58	Bowge	436
HONNY			
His nobbes and his conny, /His swetyng and his honny, ...	220	El Rummynge	226
And some a pot with honny, ...	220	El Rummynge	246
HONOR			
Haroldes from honor may the devors, ...	131	Garnesche5	71
The honor of Englond I lernyd to spelle, ...	132	Garnesche5	95
To yow thre this honor shalbe reserved	323	Garlande	409
HONORABLE			
of the Mooste Honorable Erle of Northumberlande	29	Dol Dethe	I
from an honorable Jentyllwoman for a token, ...	39	Coystrowne3	I
Not acquaynted worth a fly /With honorable Haly, ...	292	Why Come Ye	521
HONORABLY			
That her goodly name, /Honorably reported, ...	103	Phy Sparrow	1286
Sat honorably, to whome did repaire	334	Garlande	770
That her goodly name, /Honorably reportid, ...	348	Garlande	1279
HONOROUS			
In primis the Boke of Honorous Astate;	345	Garlande	1172
HONOUR			
Fulfilled with honour, as all the world dothe ken, ...	30	Dol Dethe	30
world] 'wold' Marshe 1568			

HONOURE —HORE

	Page	Title	Line
Sourmountinge in honour all erlis he did excede;	33	Dol Dethe	135
That I may say /Honour alway /Of womankynd!	96	Phy Sparrow	975
Honour to this fayre mayd;	103	Phy Sparrow	1254
Our prince of hih honour,	111	Lawde	45
Ye ought to honour your lorde and brother.	114	Scot Kynge	16
Your noblenesse and honour consernynge.	146	Magnyfycence	204
All honour to me must nedys stowpe and lene.	181	Magnyfycence	1462
Spare for the spence of a noble that his honour myght save,	200	Magnyfycence	2125
To the increse of your honour then arme you with ryght,	211	Magnyfycence	2496
The red rose in honour to flowrysshe and sprynge!'	231	Speke Parott	35
Pompe, pryde, honour, ryches and worldly lust,	236	Speke Parott	223
And his honour appall.	279	Why Come Ye	23
For if ye laude hym whome honour hath opprest,	317	Garlande	174
Of honour and worshyp which hath the formar date:	336	Garlande	842
Of honour and worship it hath the formar date.	336	Garlande	849
Of honour and worship it hath the formar date.	336	Garlande	856
Of honour and worship it hath the formar date.	336	Garlande	863
Paregall in honour unto Penolepe,	337	Garlande	899
And what honour is founde	369	Albany	425
In the honour of our blessed lady,	375	Replycacion	18
They saye howe latria is an honour grete,	381	Replycacion	282

HONOURE

	Page	Title	Line
Whoos beaute, honoure, goodly porte,	47	Bowge	62
Slew all the floure /Of theyr honoure.	116	Ag Scottes	28
That honoure hath a great fall.	262	Collyn Clout	634
Whiche soverenly in honoure shulde excell;	317	Garlande	199

HONOWRE

	Page	Title	Line
Honowre with renowne wyll ren on that syde. on] 'of' Kynge & Marche 1554, Day 1560, Marshe 1568	234	Speke Parott	140
Englande the flowr /Of relucent honowre, Englande] 'To Englande' MS Rawlinson C. 813	305	Why Come Ye	1038

HOOD

	Page	Title	Line
Some bryngeth her husbandis hood,	221	El Rummynge	283

HOOLY

	Page	Title	Line
And I my selfe hooly to you wyll inclyne.	145	Magnyfycence	182
But hooly to perseveraunce my selfe I wyll bynde,	212	Magnyfycence	2507

HOOLL

	Page	Title	Line
Of all our hooll collage by the agreament,	324	Garlande	417

HOOS

	Page	Title	Line
It is no foly to use the Walshemannys hoos.	347	Garlande	1239

HOOST

	Page	Title	Line
Of the Scottysshe hoost.	285	Why Come Ye	255
With all his hoost	359	Albany	9
As an hoost royall	360	Albany	61
And brake up all his hoost.	360	Albany	67
But ye and your hoost,	364	Albany	206

HOP

	Page	Title	Line
Lorde, how he wolde hop /After the gressop!	75	Phy Sparrow	136

HOPE

	Page	Title	Line
I hope here after a frende of you to have.'	54	Bowge	280
In hope that no man shall /Be myscontent withall. Be] 'By' Kynge & Marche 1554	62	Hauke	27
As verely my hope is,	93	Phy Sparrow	874
Presumptuous pride ys all thyn hope;	133	Garnesche5	160
Faythe and good hope I make asyde to stonde.	205	Magnyfycence	2288
Good Hope, syr, my name is; remedy pryncypall	206	Magnyfycence	2328
But thrughe good hope there may come remedy.	207	Magnyfycence	2344
Good Hope, your potecary, assygned am I,	207	Magnyfycence	2351
Ye, syr, now am I armyd with good hope,	207	Magnyfycence	2378
Under good hope endurynge ever styll,	208	Magnyfycence	2381
Ye, holly to good hope I have made my repare.	208	Magnyfycence	2394
In good hope alway for to indure.	208	Magnyfycence	2396
Good Hope, I pray you with harty affeccyon	208	Magnyfycence	2399
Syr, in good hope I am to amende.	210	Magnyfycence	2454
But good hope and redresse hath mendyd myne estate,	210	Magnyfycence	2462
Hardly bestad and driven is to hope and] not in MS Cotton Vitellius E.x	335	Garlande	830
Twene hope and drede /My lyfe I lede,	356	Garlande	1594

HOP LOBBYN

	Page	Title	Line
Ye play Hop Lobbyn of Lowdean;	117	Ag Scottes	59

HOP LOBYN

	Page	Title	Line
Hop Lobyn of Lowdeon wald have e byt of bred;	232	Speke Parott	72

HOPPE

	Page	Title	Line
That wyll make you to halt and to hoppe.	204	Magnyfycence	2273
And in theyr fury hoppe,	259	Collyn Clout	529

HOPPED

	Page	Title	Line
And in the pulpete hopped,	377	Replycacion	119

HOPPY

	Page	Title	Line
For so mote I hoppy, /It coleth well my croppy.' croppy] 'coppy' Day 1560, Marshe 1568	228	El Rummynge	560

HORACE

	Page	Title	Line
Horace and noble Marciall,	133	Garnesche5	141

HORE

	Page	Title	Line
Caron with his beerd hore,	105	Phy Sparrow	1338
With, 'Gup, hore, gup! Now gup,	284	Why Come Ye	240
Caron with his berde hore,	349	Garlande	1331

	Page	Title	Line

HORYBLE
And more horyble to beholde . . . . horyble] 'dyshonorable' MS Rawlinson C. 813	310	Why Come Ye2	15

HORYS
For there be horys there at all assayes.	204	Magnyfycence	2275

HORNE
But hunte and blowe an horne, ...	262	Collyn Clout	621

HORNED
He plucked the bull /By the horned skull, ...	104	Phy Sparrow	1319

HORNE KEKE
Of suche an horne keke	366	Albany	304

HORNES
An hart was slayne /With hornes twayne	104	Phy Sparrow	1299
And by unycornes /With theyr semely hornes;	270	Collyn Clout	965
With blowyng out your hornes, ...	380	Replycacion	215

HORNID
He pluckid the bull /By the hornid scull, ...	349	Garlande	1312

HORNIS
Also a Devoute Prayer to Moyses Hornis, ...	351	Garlande	1381

HORNNIS
With hornnis twayne /Of glitteryng golde;	348	Garlande	1292

HORRYBLE
And sware horryble othes /Before the face of God, ...	63	Hauke	52
Agaynst this horryble heresy	375	Replycacion	21
To be blowen with the flye /Of horryble heresy.	376	Replycacion	86

HORS
Had I as good an hors as she is a mare, ...	57	Bowge	407
'How, hosteler, fetche my hors a botell of hay!'	234	Speke Parott	147
Suche a captayne of [h]ors . . . . hors] 'fors' †Marshe 1568	366	Albany	281

HORSE
'Myne horse is sold, I wene', you say;	40	Coystrowne4	9
'Have in sergeaunt ferrour, myne horse behynde is bare.' . . .	43	Balettys2	20
He rydyth well the horse, but he rydyth better the mare. . . .	43	Balettys2	21
Some I make lyppers and lazars full horse;	194	Magnyfycence	1904

HORSEMAN
It is perlous for a horseman to dyg in the trenche.	43	Balettys2	26

HORSE-MYLL
A trym-tram for an horse-myll it were a nyse thyng, ...	234	Speke Parott	128

HORSHOWE
An horshowe so great, ...	83	Phy Sparrow	479

HORSLY
Horsly, as he had the mur;	82	Phy Sparrow	419

HORSMEN
How in good horsmen ye set your hole delyght, ...	42	Balettys2	13

HORSON
Why, wenyst thou, horson, that I were so mad?	155	Magnyfycence	517
But that the horson is prowde and hawte.	163	Magnyfycence	824
That the horson had for etynge of a trype.	171	Magnyfycence	1126
What, horson! Arte thou suche a one?	174	Magnyfycence	1234
Tyll I be revenged on that horson knave.	185	Magnyfycence	1616
Is there no horson that knave that wyll bete?'	185	Magnyfycence	1618
A, my hede! But is the horson gone?	189	Magnyfycence	1729
Yonder is a horson for me doth rechate;	201	Magnyfycence	2151
Nay, horson, here is my glove. Take it up and thou dare. . . .	202	Magnyfycence	2178
But wottest thou, horson? I rede the to be wyse.	202	Magnyfycence	2184
Thou sholde not scape, horson, but thou sholde dye.	202	Magnyfycence	2195
Nay, iche shall wrynge the, horson, on the wryst.	202	Magnyfycence	2196

HORSONS
And whan I sawe the horsons wolde you hafte, ...	61	Bowge	521
'Ye horsons, ye vassayles, ...	294	Why Come Ye	602

HOSE
His hose was garded with a lyste of grene, ...	56	Bowge	356
The garterynge of her hose?	101	Phy Sparrow	1176
But behynd in our hose /We bere there a rose	136	Dundas	34
Al of pleasure /My hose strayte tyde;	164	Magnyfycence	852
I shall thrust in the my dagger - Thorowe the legge in to the hose.	202	Magnyfycence	2177
She hobles as she gose /With her blanket hose . . . . she gose] 'a gose' Day 1560, Marshe 1568	216	El Rummynge	86
Some their hose, some their shone;	220	El Rummynge	248
And breke theyr hose at the kne, ...	262	Collyn Clout	629
And make a Welchmans hose	266	Collyn Clout	778
Their hertes be in thyr hose!	286	Why Come Ye	289

HOSED
Your hertes than were hosed, /Your relacions reposed;	377	Replycacion	107

HOSTE
Some from the mayne lande, some fro the Frensche hoste; . . .	326	Garlande	497

HOSTELER
'How, hosteler, fetche my hors a botell of hay!'	234	Speke Parott	147

HOSTES
In myne hostes house called Powers Keye, ...	47	Bowge	35

HOTE
And of the love so hote	88	Phy Sparrow	677
Today hote, tomorowe outragyous colde;	213	Magnyfycence	2546
So hote hatered agaynste the Chyrche, and cheryte so colde; . .	245	Speke Parott	500

HOTHYR
Of on and hothyr at me that have dysdayne.	242	Speke Parott	385

HOUGH-HO —HOW	Page	Title	Line

HOUGH-HO
Bo-ho doth bark wel, Hough-ho he rulyth the ring;   234   Speke Parott   130
HOULE
Must helpe us to houle;   82   Phy Sparrow   443
HOUNDE
Melanchates, that hounde   79   Phy Sparrow   296
The selfe same hounde /Mygth the confounde,   79   Phy Sparrow   303
HOUNDES
The houndes ranne before, and the hare behynde.   191   Magnyfycence   1823
Lyke houndes of hell, /They crye and they yell   251   Collyn Clout   198
HOUNDYS
He sayde he wold not let /His houndys for to fet,   64   Hauke   107
HOURE
And within an houre after,   169   Magnyfycence   1031
HOURES
Theyr prymes and houres fall   252   Collyn Clout   241
The mountenaunce of two houres.   288   Why Come Ye   361
At all houres to be redy   371   Albany   485
HOUS
This hous envyrowne was a myle about;   326   Garlande   489
HOUSE
In myne hostes house called Powers Keye,   47   Bowge   35
Plucke downe an house and set up a rafter,   169   Magnyfycence   1032
HOUSHOLD
He calde upon them, as menyall houshold men: 30   Dol Dethe   33
In fee, as menyall men of his houshold,   34   Dol Dethe   185
HOUSHOLDE
But ye be welcome to our housholde.   53   Bowge   266
Of her I holde /And her housholde;   112   Calliope   14
With Magnyfycence in housholde do remayne;   157   Magnyfycence   613
With Magnyfycence in housholde do remayne;   158   Magnyfycence   640
HOUSHOLDES
Small housholdes woll kepe,   249   Collyn Clout   123
HOVYR-WACHYD
And so thy selfe hovyr-wachyd   128   Garnesche3   179
HOW
What man, remembring how shamfully he was slayn,   32   Dol Dethe   111
Lord, how Perkyn is proud of hys Pohen!   37   Coystrownel   19
He wold be made moch of and he wyst how;   37   Coystrownel   33
How in good horsmen ye set your hole delyght,   42   Balettys2   13
By theyr conusaunce knowing how they serve a wily py: 43   Balettys2   34
How there nys thynge that I covet so fayne   44   Balettys3   41
And how I maye that waye and meanes fynde.'   49   Bowge   109
'Forsothe,' quod she, 'how ever blowe the wynde,   49   Bowge   110
'Alas,' quod I, 'how myghte I have her sure?'   49   Bowge   118
'Heve and how, rombelow, row the bote, Norman, rowe.' 53   Bowge   252
By Goddis soule, I wonder how ye gete   53   Bowge   262
How he is now taken in conceyte,   54   Bowge   302
Thenne I behelde how he dysgysed was: 56   Bowge   351
How ofte he hadde hit Jenet on the tayle,   56   Bowge   369
  hadde] 'not' Marshe 1568
How ofte he knocked at her klycked gate.   56   Bowge   371
Lorde, how that I wolde caste it full rounde!   57   Bowge   396
'How do ye, mayster? Ye loke so soberly!   58   Bowge   442
How I, Skelton laureat,   62   Hauke   33
How the Temple was kept,   66   Hauke   168
How the Temple was swept,   66   Hauke   169
Whan I remembre agayn /How mi Philyp was slayn,   72   Phy Sparrow   18
Lord, how he wolde pry /After the butterfly!   75   Phy Sparrow   134
Lorde, how he wolde hop /After the gressop!   75   Phy Sparrow   136
How commeth this to pas?'   77   Phy Sparrow   232
How my byrde so fayre,   80   Phy Sparrow   343
How pretely it wolde syt   80   Phy Sparrow   354
How my dysport and play   81   Phy Sparrow   373
How she controlde /Her husbandes as she wolde,   87   Phy Sparrow   622
How Jason it wan,   87   Phy Sparrow   632
How Syr Launcelote de Lake   87   Phy Sparrow   638
And how they were sommonde   88   Phy Sparrow   652
And how they rode eche one   88   Phy Sparrow   655
How Scipion dyd wake   88   Phy Sparrow   668
How hartely he dyd it take   89   Phy Sparrow   692
To wryte and tell /How women excell /In noblenes;   96   Phy Sparrow   982
How shall I report   96   Phy Sparrow   998
Lorde, how I was payned!   99   Phy Sparrow   1123
How she me had reclaymed,   99   Phy Sparrow   1125
How often dyd I tote   100   Phy Sparrow   1146
How that she can were /Gorgiously her gere;   101   Phy Sparrow   1178
How unfortunately he doth now spede;   115   Scot Kynge   57
How they are blynde /In theyr owne mynde,   115   Ag Scottes   7
Ungraciously how he doth speed.   119   Ag Scottes   154
How may I your mokery mekely tollerate,   123   Garnesche2   1
How the favyr of your face   124   Garnesche3   9
Sche seyd how ye ded brydell,   126   Garnesche3   73
How olde proverbys say,   129   Garnesche3   196
Of naturys workys, how they be   130   Garnesche5   9
With thy versyfyeng rayles /How they have tayles.   135   Dundas   31
How shuld a fals lying tung then be rewarded?   137   Ven Tongues   2
How some delite for to lye, thycke and threfolde.   137   Ven Tongues   11

Entry	Page	Title	Line
Ye, but how longe shall I here awayte?	151	Magnyfycence	398
So how, I say, the hare is squat!	176	Magnyfycence	1299
Remembre ye not how my lyberte by mesure ruled was?	178	Magnyfycence	1383
Make indentures how ye and I shal gyde.	180	Magnyfycence	1448
What, brother braynsyke, how farest thou?	192	Magnyfycence	1845
A, Lord God, how the gowte wryngeth me by the too.	198	Magnyfycence	2047
How fele you your selfe, my frend? How is your mynde?	208	Magnyfycence	2389
How fele you your selfe, my frend? How is your mynde?	208	Magnyfycence	2389
How fortuned you, Magnyfycence, so far to fal behynde?	209	Magnyfycence	2423
How wysdom thorowe wantonnesse vanysshyth away;	213	Magnyfycence	2556
How none estate lyvynge of hymselfe can be sure,	213	Magnyfycence	2557
How bright I am of ble!	220	El Rummynge	218
'Mete, mete, for Parrot, mete I say, how!'	233	Speke Parott	102
'How, hosteler, fetche my hors a botell of hay!'	234	Speke Parott	147
How the rest of good lernyng is roufled up and trold.	235	Speke Parott	168
roufled] 'roulled' Day 1560, Marshe 1568			
And remembre amonge how Parrot and ye	236	Speke Parott	221
And thowe sum dysdayne yow and sey how ye prate,	240	Speke Parott	315
How the maters he mellis in com to small effecte;	240	Speke Parott	328
To make reconyng in the resseyte how Robyn loste hys bowe,	240	Speke Parott	341
How thys prosses I prate of, hyt ys not all for nowghte.	242	Speke Parott	389
How the churche hath to mykell	260	Collyn Clout	557
How prelacye is solde and bought	261	Collyn Clout	583
How scrypture shulde be coted,	265	Collyn Clout	755
Nor how farre Temple Barre is	267	Collyn Clout	826
How fortune wyll endure.	271	Collyn Clout	1003
How darest thou, daucocke, mell?	275	Collyn Clout	1160
He sayth, 'How saye ye, my lordes?	283	Why Come Ye	195
I understande how that	284	Why Come Ye	237
How noble and how kynde	291	Why Come Ye	500
How noble and how kynde	291	Why Come Ye	500
How no man can him amende!	292	Why Come Ye	531
How an one-eyed man is	292	Why Come Ye	533
How can he do ryght?	293	Why Come Ye	581
How he doth hym disceyve.	295	Why Come Ye	662
How Frauncis Petrarke, /That moche noble clerke,	296	Why Come Ye	687
Wryteth how Charlemayn	296	Why Come Ye	689
But how that came aboute,	296	Why Come Ye	693
How maister Gaguine, the crownycler	297	Why Come Ye	718
Maketh remembraunce /How Kynge Lewes of late	297	Why Come Ye	722
How the warlde is conveyed.	298	Why Come Ye	783
How all thynge passyth as doth the somer flower,	312	Garlande	9
How oftyn fortune varyeth in an howre,	312	Garlande	11
How you gave me a ryall commaundement	313	Garlande	58
you] 'ye' Marshe 1568, MS Cotton Vitellius E.x; a] 'in' MS Cot. Vit. E.x			
But, how it is, Skelton is wonder slake,	314	Garlande	69
How ryvers rin not tyll the spryng be full;	314	Garlande	81
Then men wyll say how he doth but flatter.	314	Garlande	84
And how his wordes with reason wyll not accorde.	314	Garlande	88
Spekyng in paroblis, how the fox, the grey,	315	Garlande	101
For how shulde Cato els be callyd wyse,	315	Garlande	123
He sange also how, the tre as he did take	320	Garlande	300
How dotynge age wolde jape with yonge foly;	322	Garlande	361
How that our Englysshe myght fresshely be ennewed;	323	Garlande	389
ennewed] 'a meude' †Fakes 1523			
How all that I do is under refformation,	323	Garlande	411
How far it was, or ellis within what howris,	325	Garlande	457
far] not in †Fakes 1523			
With, 'How doth the north?' 'What tydingis in the sowth?'	326	Garlande	498
Another tolde how shyppes wente to wrak.	326	Garlande	507
How ye ar welcome to this court of aray.	327	Garlande	539
How from the est unto the occident,	328	Garlande	577
How wronge was no ryght, and ryght was no wronge;	331	Garlande	704
'How say ye? Is this after your appetite?	331	Garlande	707
How daungerous it were to stande in his lyght,	333	Garlande	755
were to stande in his lyght] 'is to stop up his sight' MS Cotton Vitellius E.x			
How theis ladys and gentylwomen all	335	Garlande	809
And for your sake how fast to warke they fall:	335	Garlande	811
In her bosome, lorde, how she was afrayd!	337	Garlande	887
how] not in MS Cotton Vitellius E.x			
In very dede /How ye excede.	343	Garlande	1085
To se how duly ich thyng in ordre was,	343	Garlande	1094
Of Fame. Perceyvynge how that I was cum,	343	Garlande	1115
We wyll understande how ye have it deservyd.'	344	Garlande	1127
Let se now for hym how ye can expounde;	345	Garlande	1153
To beholde how it was garnysshyd and bounde,	345	Garlande	1163
Item the Boke how Men Shulde Fle Synne;	345	Garlande	1173
How Cowntertet Cowntenaunce of the new get	346	Garlande	1193
Lorde, how she made moche of her gentyll birth!	346	Garlande	1202
And how that it was wantonly spent;	347	Garlande	1244
How the grene coverlet sufferd grete pine;	351	Garlande	1378
How a do cam trippyng in at the rerewarde,	351	Garlande	1385
But, lorde, how the parker was wroth with all.	351	Garlande	1386
But how it was, sum were to recheles,	351	Garlande	1393
How than lyke a man he wan the barbican	351	Garlande	1397
How Dame Minerva first found the Olyve Tre, she red	351	Garlande	1404

HOWARDE — HOWE

	Page	Title	Line
How her ble was bryght as blossom on the spray,	351	Garlande	1412
How men were wonte for to discerne	352	Garlande	1441
And how Iollas lovyd goodly Phillis;	354	Garlande	1497
How that ye are lykely	371	Albany	510

HOWARDE

	Page	Title	Line
To my Lady Elisabeth Howarde	336	Garlande	R
To my Lady Mirriell Howarde	337	Garlande	R

HOWBEIT

	Page	Title	Line
Howbeit the mater was evident and playne;	31	Dol Dethe	72
Howbei[t], he is not furst hath had a los.	43	Balettys2	38
Howbeit] 'Howbeis' †Rastell 1527.1			
howbeit they were puffed so full	375	Replycacion	1

HOW BE IT

	Page	Title	Line
How be it, mayden Meed /Made theym to be agreed;	65	Hauke	149
How be it to Saull dyd he tell	105	Phy Sparrow	1357
How be it, lyberte may somtyme be to large,	141	Magnyfycence	37
And do nothynge. How be it, full lytell grace	159	Magnyfycence	693
How be it the primordyall	291	Why Come Ye	489
the] 'they be' Kitson 1560.7, Marshe 1568			
How be it, it were harde to construe this lecture;	315	Garlande	109
How be it to Saull he did tell	350	Garlande	1350

HOWE

	Page	Title	Line
Ye muste be ruled, as I shall tell you howe.	60	Bowge	493
Wit[h], 'Hey, howe, rumbelowe,' /Rumpopulorum,	108	Epitaphel	80
With] 'Wit' Marshe 1568			
Howe after a drought there fallyth a showre of rayne	141	Magnyfycence	12
Here you not howe this gentylman mockys?	141	Magnyfycence	32
Or howe can you prove that there is felycyte,	142	Magnyfycence	77
I parceyve well howe eche of you doth reason.	142	Magnyfycence	83
Measure is treasure. Howe say ye, is it not this?	144	Magnyfycence	125
To se howe greable we are of one mynde;	146	Magnyfycence	199
Perceyve you not howe lothe he was to abyde	147	Magnyfycence	241
With care and with thought howe Jacke shall have Gyl?	148	Magnyfycence	287
Why kepte you it thus longe? Howe dothe he? Wele?	149	Magnyfycence	314
Howe so? By God, at the see syde,	150	Magnyfycence	346
Say howe you excede in noblenesse,	151	Magnyfycence	376
Howe coulde ye do that, and [I] was away?	154	Magnyfycence	504
I] not in †Rastell & Treveris C 1530, B			
But, syr, howe counterfetyd ye?	155	Magnyfycence	524
But is it not well? Howe thynkest thou?	155	Magnyfycence	528
Ye, and se howe it may be compast	156	Magnyfycence	567
And yf ye knewe howe I have mused,	156	Magnyfycence	580
Se you not howe they prece	156	Magnyfycence	591
Se howe he is wrapped for the colde.	157	Magnyfycence	603
What the devyll! Howe may that be?	157	Magnyfycence	627
Tell on, syr. Howe then?	158	Magnyfycence	651
Howe I may hurte and hynder every man.	160	Magnyfycence	709
And craftely can I grope howe every man is mynded.	160	Magnyfycence	725
Howe sayst thou, man? Am not I a joly rutter?	161	Magnyfycence	752
Howe gay and howe stout	163	Magnyfycence	832
Howe gay and howe stout	163	Magnyfycence	832
What! Fansy, my frende! Howe dost thou fare?	166	Magnyfycence	920
Howe so? Tell me, I the pray.	166	Magnyfycence	931
Howe so? By God, by a praty slyght,	167	Magnyfycence	952
Howe standeth the wynde	168	Magnyfycence	985
And howe styll she doth syt!	168	Magnyfycence	1003
Howe rode he by you? Howe put he to you?	173	Magnyfycence	1178
Howe rode he by you? Howe put he to you?	173	Magnyfycence	1178
And teche them howe they sholde syt ydyll	174	Magnyfycence	1221
Howe frantyke fansy fyrst of all	176	Magnyfycence	1294
A, syr, a, a! Howe by that?	176	Magnyfycence	1296
'What howe! Be ye mery! Was it not well conveyed?'	177	Magnyfycence	1347
For where is no mesure, howe may worshyp endure?	179	Magnyfycence	1408
Shewe us your mynde then, howe to do and what.	180	Magnyfycence	1435
Howe lyke you? Ye lacke, syr, suche a lusty lasse.	183	Magnyfycence	1559
A, howe my stomake wambleth! I am all in a swete.	185	Magnyfycence	1617
Howe say ye, syrs? Herein what is best?	186	Magnyfycence	1659
I care not howe sone he be refused,	187	Magnyfycence	1683
Nay, indede, but I sawe howe ye prayed,	188	Magnyfycence	1696
Cockes armes, howe Pleasure plucked hym forth!	189	Magnyfycence	1735
A, syr, tolde I not you howe I dyd fynde	191	Magnyfycence	1819
Howe a wodcocke wrastled with a larke that was lame;	192	Magnyfycence	1836
Ye, let be thy japes, and tell me howe	192	Magnyfycence	1846
Beholde howe Fortune o[n] hym hath frounde.	195	Magnyfycence	1947
on] 'of' †Rastell & Treveris C 1530, B			
Howe, where art thou? Come hether, Poverte.	195	Magnyfycence	1953
A, howe my lymmys be lyther and lame!	198	Magnyfycence	2038
Howe he is undone by the meanes of me?	200	Magnyfycence	2110
Howe many come to myschefe for to moche lyberte;	200	Magnyfycence	2134
O good Lorde, howe longe shall I indure	201	Magnyfycence	2153
Howe say you, syr? Can ye these wordys grope?	207	Magnyfycence	2377
Remembre you, therfore, howe late ye were low.	210	Magnyfycence	2451
Howe in this worlde there is no seke[r]nesse,	212	Magnyfycence	2515
sekernesse] 'sekenesse' †Rastell & Treveris C 1530, B			
Shewyng nowe adayes howe the worlde comberyd is,	213	Magnyfycence	2539
Howe sodenly worldly welth dothe dekay;	213	Magnyfycence	2555
To se howe she is gumbed, /Fyngered and thumbed,	215	El Rummynge	40
Howe hyr ale is solde /To mawte and to molde.	218	El Rummynge	158

HOWEBEIT —HOWER

	Page	Title	Line
With, 'Hey,' and with, 'Howe, /Syt we downe arowe	221	El Rummynge	289
And howe your poemys arre barayne of polyshed eloquens,	240	Speke Parott	316
Howe they take no hede /Theyr sely shepe to fede,	248	Collyn Clout	76
Howe in matters they ben rawe,	249	Collyn Clout	94
I wote never howe they warke,	249	Collyn Clout	119
Howe evyll theyr shepe fare.'	250	Collyn Clout	131
Howe bysshoppes dysdayne /Sermons for to make,	250	Collyn Clout	133
Howe they are able to make /With theyr golde and treasure	250	Collyn Clout	143
Howe that ye sell /The grace of the Holy Goost.	251	Collyn Clout	200
Howe some of you dothe eate /In lenton season flesshe meate,	251	Collyn Clout	204
And howe whan ye gyve orders	252	Collyn Clout	220
Howe some synge letabundus /At every ale stake,	253	Collyn Clout	248
Reporte howe the pope may	254	Collyn Clout	302
Howe warely they wrangle!	255	Collyn Clout	331
But howe the commons gronys, /And the people monys,	255	Collyn Clout	348
Howe ye breke the dedes wylles,	257	Collyn Clout	417
Howe the lay fee despyte	257	Collyn Clout	438
As ye may dayly se /Howe the lay fee	259	Collyn Clout	496
Howe they are to blame	259	Collyn Clout	509
Howe the people are glad	259	Collyn Clout	512
Howe some of them glenes	260	Collyn Clout	567
Men say howe ye appalle	262	Collyn Clout	611
Howe connynge myght them avaunce,	262	Collyn Clout	617
Howe [ye] were wonte to drynke	262	Collyn Clout	649
ye] 'thy' †Godfray 1531, 'they' Kele 1545.1, Marshe 1568, MS Harley 2252			
Howe the male dothe wrye.	263	Collyn Clout	686
wrye] 'wryte' Kele 1545.1, Marshe 1568, 'wrye' MS Harley 2252			
Howe they have no fraude.	267	Collyn Clout	853
fraude] 'faude' †Godfray 1531, 'fawte' MS Harley 2252			
Howe frere Fabian with other mo	268	Collyn Clout	881
Howe lusty Venus quaked,	270	Collyn Clout	945
And howe Cupyde shaked /His dart, and bent his bowe	270	Collyn Clout	946
And howe Parys of Troy /Daunced a lege moy,	270	Collyn Clout	950
lege moy] 'lege de moy' Kele 1545.1, Marshe 1568			
Howe all the worlde stares	270	Collyn Clout	960
Howe they ryde in goodly chares,	270	Collyn Clout	961
Howe some of you are mellynge.	271	Collyn Clout	985
Howe may this come to pas,	272	Collyn Clout	1021
And howe may this accorde,	272	Collyn Clout	1029
Harke, howe the losell prates /With a wyde wesaunt!	275	Collyn Clout	1153
Howe darest thou, losell,	275	Collyn Clout	1161
Howe we wyll rule all at wyll	276	Collyn Clout	1190
And say howe that we be /Full of parcyallyte;	276	Collyn Clout	1192
And howe at a pronge	276	Collyn Clout	1194
Howe may we thus endure?	276	Collyn Clout	1202
But howe comme to pas	301	Why Come Ye	900
Now mayster doctor, howe say ye,	309	Why Come Ye2	1
Howe the Douty Duke of Albany	359	Albany	1
Howe ye pretende /For to defende	361	Albany	88
Howe ye wyll beres bynde	364	Albany	209
Howe ye wyll undertake	367	Albany	326
Howe yong scolers nowe a dayes enbol[n]ed	373	Replycacion	1
enbolned] 'enbolmed' †Pynson 1528			
howe it was idolatry to offre to ymages of our blessed lady,	375	Replycacion	1
I wondre howe ye dare	375	Replycacion	36
Confessyng howe ye dyde lye /In prechyng shamefully.	377	Replycacion	90
Howe syllogisari /Non est ex particulari,	377	Replycacion	99
Howe ye are this day,	379	Replycacion	177
Howe ye have small contrycion	379	Replycacion	183
Howe falsely ye had surmysed,	380	Replycacion	209
They saye howe latria is an honour grete,	381	Replycacion	282
Howe poetes do but fayne?	384	Replycacion	353
Howe there is a spyrituall,	384	Replycacion	365

HOWEBEIT

	Page	Title	Line
Howebeit, some there be,	250	Collyn Clout	147
Howebeit they are good men,	251	Collyn Clout	167
Howebeit, per assimile, /Some men thynke that ye	258	Collyn Clout	459
Howebeit they let downe fall	271	Collyn Clout	978

HOWE BE IT

	Page	Title	Line
Howe be it, lyberte makyth many a man blynde;	142	Magnyfycence	52
Howe be it, by protestacyon	143	Magnyfycence	97
For howe be it lyberte to welthe is convenyent,	146	Magnyfycence	219
Howe be it of scape thryfte your clokes smelleth musty.	161	Magnyfycence	761
Howe be it, I say,	165	Magnyfycence	897
Howe be it, that fonde felowe is a mery knave.	180	Magnyfycence	1455
Howe be it, I wolde be ryght gladde, I you assure,	183	Magnyfycence	1527
Howe be it, at your instaunce I wyll the rather	186	Magnyfycence	1641
Howe be it of all synne he was innocent,	196	Magnyfycence	2002
Howe be it, from you I receyved a letter [sent],	209	Magnyfycence	2435
sent] not in †Rastell & Treveris C 1530, B			
Howe be it I rede	357	Garlande	1598
Howe be it, loyally	369	Albany	404

HOWEEVER

	Page	Title	Line
Or howeever it hap,	273	Collyn Clout	1057

HOWER

	Page	Title	Line
To make within an hower,	293	Why Come Ye	566

	Page	Title	Line
HOWEVER			
But, however he was borne,	291	Why Come Ye	495
HOWGYE			
So many howgye howsys byldyng, and so small howse-holdyng;	245	Speke Parott	494
HOWKYD			
Howkyd as an hawkys beke, lyke Syr Topyas.	122	Garneschel	40
HOWNDE			
Faire fall that forster that so well can bate his hownde! well] not in MS Cotton Vitellius E.x	313	Garlande	27
A jentyll hownde shulde never play the kur.	352	Garlande	1436
HOWNDES			
The howndes began to yerne and to quest; and dred	351	Garlande	1409
HOWRE			
How oftyn fortune varyeth in an howre,	312	Garlande	11
To se this howre now, that I may say,	327	Garlande	538
HOWRIS			
How far it was, or ellis within what howris, far] not in †Fakes 1523	325	Garlande	457
With vertu enbesid all tymes and howris;	334	Garlande	805
HOWS			
For he was ever ageynst Goddis hows;	347	Garlande	1251
HOWSE			
In my lady Brewsys howse.	125	Garnesche3	33
HOWSE-HOLDYNG			
So many howgye howsys byldyng, and so small howse-holdyng;	245	Speke Parott	494
HOWSHOLDE			
That sadly rule not theyr howsholde men.	195	Magnyfycence	1940
HOWSYS			
So many howgye howsys byldyng, and so small howse-holdyng;	245	Speke Parott	494
HOWST			
Howst the, lyuer god van hemrik, ic seg;	232	Speke Parott	69
HUCKE			
But nowe adayes as huksters they hucke and they stycke,	200	Magnyfycence	2121
HUCKELS			
The bones [of] her huckels of] not in †Lant 1545, Kynge & Marche 1554, Day 1560, Marshe 1568; huckels] 'buckels' Day, Marshe	215	El Rummynge	45
HUDDY PEKE			
He sayth, 'Thou huddy peke!	287	Why Come Ye	329
Gyve it up, and cry, 'creke', /Lyke an huddy peke.	366	Albany	301
HUDGE			
The gander, the gose, and the hudge oliphaunt,	315	Garlande	102
HUF			
Huf, a galante, Garnesche, loke on your comly cors!	123	Garnesche2	16
HUFFA			
Huffa, huffa, taunderum, taunderum, tayne, huffa, huffa!	161	Magnyfycence	745
Huffa, huffa, taunderum, taunderum, tayne, huffa, huffa!	161	Magnyfycence	745
Huffa, huffa, taunderum, taunderum, tayne, huffa, huffa!	161	Magnyfycence	745
Huffa, huffa, taunderum, taunderum, tayne, huffa, huffa!	161	Magnyfycence	745
HUGE			
It was huge and greate,	225	El Rummynge	432
The huge myghty okes them selfe dyd avaunce,	320	Garlande	279
HUGGER MUGGER			
As men dare speke it hugger mugger:	151	Magnyfycence	387
HUGULINUS			
Or frere Hugulinus,	265	Collyn Clout	739
HUKE			
Her huke of Lyncole grene,	215	El Rummynge	56
HUKSTERS			
But nowe adayes as huksters they hucke and they stycke,	200	Magnyfycence	2121
HULL			
From Wentbridge to Hull,	282	Why Come Ye	149
HUMANYTE			
Retoricyons and oratours in freshe humanyte,	236	Speke Parott	194
In Tullis faculte /Called humanyte.	292	Why Come Ye	529
His affabilite, /His humanyte,	370	Albany	452
What longeth to Christes humanyte.	381	Replycacion	286
HUMBLE			
In humble wyse as lowly as I may,	335	Garlande	837
In moost humble wyse,	372	Albany	524
HUMBLY			
Me humbly commyttynge unto Goddys wyll.	208	Magnyfycence	2382
Humbly and low /Commendynge me /To yowre bownte.	338	Garlande	930
humbly submytted unto the ryght discrete reformacyon	373	Replycacion	1
HUMILITE			
His stabilite, /His humilite,	370	Albany	454
HUMYLYTE			
Put fro you presumpcyon and admyt humylyte,	207	Magnyfycence	2361
Farewell humylyte, /Farewell good charyte!	261	Collyn Clout	591
HUMLERY			
Iwys I coude tell – but humlery, home, tell] 'not tell' Wynkyn de Worde 1510	59	Bowge	467
HUMORS			
Or of humors superflue, that often wyll crepe	313	Garlande	32
HUNDERD			
This hunderd yere scantly	111	Lawde	18
An hunderd pounde and more, An] 'And' †Kele 1545.3	302	Why Come Ye	947

HUNDRED —ICHE   Page   Title   Line

HUNDRED
	Page	Title	Line
Plucke from an hundred, and gyve it to thre;	190	Magnyfycence	1775
A hundred myle asonder	285	Why Come Ye	259
An hundred steppis mountyng to the halle,	325	Garlande	471
with an hundred thousande tratlande Scottes	359	Albany	1

HUNDRETH
	Page	Title	Line
It were worth an hundreth pound	76	Phy Sparrow	189
Displease not an hundreth for one mannes pleasure.	314	Garlande	90
If xii were let in, xii hundreth stode without.	326	Garlande	490

HUNDRETHE
	Page	Title	Line
Sterte all at ones an hundrethe fote backe.	320	Garlande	282

HUNGER
	Page	Title	Line
And now without measure he shal have hunger and colde.	193	Magnyfycence	1895
Nowe must ye suffre bothe hunger and colde.	197	Magnyfycence	2013

HUNGRE
	Page	Title	Line
It is great almesse the hung[re] to fede,	177	Magnyfycence	1344
hungre] 'hunger' †Rastell & Treveris C 1530, B			

HUNT
	Page	Title	Line
To hawke, or els to hunt /From the auter to the funt,	62	Hauke	9
He sayd that he wold hunt	67	Hauke	188
To hunt them into hell,	380	Replycacion	214

HUNTE
	Page	Title	Line
To hunte there by lyberte	64	Hauke	108
Ar mete for a swyne herde to hunte after hogges.	240	Speke Parott	321
For some say ye hunte in parkes	251	Collyn Clout	192
ye] 'they' †Godfray 1531, 'ye' MS Harley 2252; in parkes] 'partrykes' †Godfray 1531			
But hunte and blowe an horne,	262	Collyn Clout	621
And with suche forage /Hunte the boskage,	280	Why Come Ye	53

HUNTLEY
	Page	Title	Line
Ye had be better to have buskyd to Huntley Bankes,	114	Scot Kynge	50
be] 'bet' †Fakes 1513			
Ye myght have buskyd you to Huntley Bankys;	119	Ag Scottes	149
On Huntley bankes, /Take this our thankes;	136	Dundas	58
They play their olde pranckes /After Huntley Bankes.	285	Why Come Ye	267
Of Huntley banke, /Of Lowdyan, /Of Locryan,	359	Albany	19

HURT
	Page	Title	Line
It was no hurt, I trowe.	76	Phy Sparrow	170

HURTE
	Page	Title	Line
Howe I may hurte and hynder every man.	160	Magnyfycence	709
What! He hathe ben hurte with a stabbe?	171	Magnyfycence	1124
And thus they hurte theyr soules,	255	Collyn Clout	341

HURTES
	Page	Title	Line
Where the devyll gate he all these hurtes?	171	Magnyfycence	1127

HUS
	Page	Title	Line
Jobab was brought up in the lande of Hus;	232	Speke Parott	65
Jobab] 'Iob' Day 1560, Marshe 1568			

HUSBAND
	Page	Title	Line
Thys grevyth your husband, that ryght jentyll knyght,	43	Balettys2	27
For your jentyll husband sorowfull am I;	43	Balettys2	37
And made her husband knyght /Of the comyne hall,	87	Phy Sparrow	646
To her husband most trew,	89	Phy Sparrow	726
Ich am not cast away, /That can my husband say,	220	El Rummynge	220

HUSBANDE
	Page	Title	Line
'And therfore shall my husbande pay'.	153	Magnyfycence	461

HUSBANDES
	Page	Title	Line
How she controlde /Her husbandes as she wolde,	87	Phy Sparrow	623
Their husbandes to set at nought:	87	Phy Sparrow	627
........hyr husbandes hed,	125	Garnesche3	58
[And] of her husbandes breke.	225	El Rummynge	452
And] not in editions			
Some her husbandes gowne,	227	El Rummynge	530

HUSBANDIS
	Page	Title	Line
Some bryngeth her husbandis hood,	221	El Rummynge	283

HUSBANDS
	Page	Title	Line
Some brought theyr husbands hat,	225	El Rummynge	442

HUSSEY
	Page	Title	Line
To maystres Margaret Hussey	340	Garlande	R

HUSSIANS
	Page	Title	Line
And some be Hussians,	260	Collyn Clout	551

HUSWYFE
	Page	Title	Line
An huswyfe of trust /Whan she is athrust,	220	El Rummynge	253

HUSWYVES
	Page	Title	Line
Amonge huswyves bolde,	87	Phy Sparrow	621
Some wenches come unlased, /Some huswyves come unbrased,	217	El Rummynge	134
unlased] 'unbrased' Day 1560, Marshe 1568			

ICH
	Page	Title	Line
Ich am not cast away, /That can my husband say,	220	El Rummynge	219
With, 'He sayd,' and 'We said.' Ich wot now what ich wot,	234	Speke Parott	132
With, 'He sayd,' and 'We said.' Ich wot now what ich wot,	234	Speke Parott	132
To se how duly ich thyng in ordre was,	343	Garlande	1094

ICHE
	Page	Title	Line
Nay, iche shall wrynge the, horson, on the wryst.	202	Magnyfycence	2196
Iche wotte what yche do thynke!'	258	Collyn Clout	458
yche do] 'eche other' Kele 1545.1, Marshe 1568			
But to do sumwhat iche man doth hym dres	315	Garlande	122
And iche man stode gasyng and staryng upon other.	319	Garlande	268
To iche of them rendryng thankis commendable,	335	Garlande	820

ICONOMICAR —IGNORANCE   Page   Title   Line

ICONOMICAR
  Esiodus, the iconomicar, ...   321   Garlande   328
    iconomicar] 'icononucar' †Fakes 1523, Marshe 1568
IDIOSY
  Your madde ipocrisy, /And your idiosy, ...   381   Replycacion   250
IDOLATRY
  howe it was idolatry to offre to ymages of our blessed lady, . 375   Replycacion   1
  To preche it idolatry, ...   381   Replycacion   254
IEN
  As a glede glowynge, your ien glyster as glasse, ...   122   Garneschel   37
IERARCHY
  He is set so hye /In his ierarchy   283   Why Come Ye   185
  Ye soored over hye /In the ierarchy /Of Jovenyans heresy, . .   378   Replycacion   162
IES
  The devill tere their tunges and pike out their ies! 139   Ven Tongues   68
IF
  If the hole quere of the Musis nyne   33   Dol Dethe   155
  And if ye lyst to know the cause why so, ...   44   Balettys3   38
  If it please you to loke   68   Hauke   233
  If any such might be found!   76   Phy Sparrow   188
  To wete if he coulde brynge   76   Phy Sparrow   198
  That if ye can fynde   78   Phy Sparrow   260
  That if I wolde apply /To wryte ornatly, ...   91   Phy Sparrow   780
    ornatly] 'ordinately' Kitson 1560.6, Marshe 1568
  If I have not well perused   92   Phy Sparrow   814
  If Arethusa wyll send   93   Phy Sparrow   860
  If Apollo wyll promyse   93   Phy Sparrow   863
  If it be sadly dyscust.   102   Phy Sparrow   1250
  For, if they understood /His traytourly dispyght, ...   121   Ag Scottes2   24
  If thow war metely machchyd.   128   Garnesche3   181
  If thow war aquentyd with alle   133   Garnesche5   138
  If they wer lyveyng thys day, ...   133   Garnesche5   142
  That, if I wist not to be controlde, ...   137   Ven Tongues   9
  If there be none other mater but that, ...   137   Ven Tongues   14
  But if that I knewe what his name hight, ...   139   Ven Tongues   73
  If lyberte sholde lepe and renne where he lyst   144   Magnyfycence   133
  If ye lyst to lyve after your fre lyberte.   146   Magnyfycence   208
  If you had with you largesse, ...   151   Magnyfycence   377
  If it lyke your grace to take it in degre.   182   Magnyfycence   1521
  If it wolde lyke you to here my pore mynde -   183   Magnyfycence   1543
  If ever I herde syke another, God gyve me shame.   192   Magnyfycence   1833
  If that ye wyll /A whyle be styll, ...   214   El Rummynge   2
  If that that he wrought   290   Why Come Ye   448
  If he coulde consyder   291   Why Come Ye   497
  For if he gloryously publisshe his matter, ...   314   Garlande   83
  And if so hym fortune to wryte true and plaine, ...   314   Garlande   85
    so] not in MS Cotton Vitellius E.x
  But if he had made sum memoryall, ...   315   Garlande   118
  With your reformacion, if I say amis, ...   316   Garlande   145
  For, but if your bounte did me assure, ...   316   Garlande   146
  For if ye laude hym whome honour hath opprest, ...   317   Garlande   174
  If he to the ample encrease of his name   318   Garlande   222
  But if that he purpose to make a redresse, ...   318   Garlande   229
  To se if Skelton wyll put hymselfe in prease   319   Garlande   239
    wyll] 'dare' MS Cotton Vitellius E.x
  To owe to yow our servyce, and more if we mowte!   324   Garlande   425
  That but if my warkes therto be agreable, ...   324   Garlande   439
  If xii were let in, xii hundreth stode without.   326   Garlande   490
  And if be in it any thyng ment, ...   332   Garlande   723
  His name for to know if that ye lyst, ...   333   Garlande   752
  But if they were counterfettes that women them call, ...   334   Garlande   785
  Troilus, I trowe, if that he had you sene, ...   336   Garlande   873
  And if Apelles your countenaunce had sene, ...   337   Garlande   894
  But if I sholde aquyte your kyndnes, ...   342   Garlande   1062
  But if hastyve credence by mayntenance of myght   344   Garlande   1133
  If ony recordis in noumbyr can be founde, ...   345   Garlande   1150
  But if he wryte oftenner than ones or twyse.'   345   Garlande   1155
  Whiche, if they be happy, have cause to beware   353   Garlande   1474
  If they can spy /Circumspectly   356   Garlande   1579
    they] 'thy' †Fakes 1523
  If that ye had tane   366   Albany   283
  If our moost royall Harry   367   Albany   340
  If he on you but frounde   367   Albany   345
  If ye wele can regarde   368   Albany   360
  That if I wolde reporte   370   Albany   444
  If ye to remembrance call   377   Replycacion   98
  For, if it were well sought, ...   379   Replycacion   185
  And thought, if ye had right, ...   379   Replycacion   200
  If ye have reed of hyperdulia, ...   382   Replycacion   287
  If further busynesse that ye make.   382   Replycacion   296
  Than, if this noble kyng, ...   384   Replycacion   343
  For if ye sadly loke, ...   384   Replycacion   359
IFAYTH
  With, 'I as good as thou, ifayth, and no better.'   326   Garlande   509
IGNORANCE
  But Ignorance full soone dyde me dyscure   46   Bowge   18
    dyscure] 'dysture' †Wynkyn de Worde 1499, 1510
  As clerkes unassured, /With ignorance obscured: 377   Replycacion   94

IYE —INCORRIGIBLE   Page   Title   Line

For your ignorance is gretter,	380	Replycacion	231
IYE			
Wythe my beke bente, and my lytell wanton iye, and] not in Lant 1545, Kynge and Marche 1554, Day 1560, Marshe 1568	231	Speke Parott	15
IL			
And of their taunting toies rest with il hayle.	138	Ven Tongues	33
ILES			
Unto the Iles of Orchady,	79	Phy Sparrow	319
Of the out iles the rough-foted Scottes,	120	Ag Scottes	170
ILL			
Your hap was unhappy, to ill was your spede.	31	Dol Dethe	61
And you knew all ye would be ill apayd'.	139	Ven Tongues	72
For certayne envectyfys, yet wrote he none ill, certayne envectyfys] 'that he enveiyd' MS Cotton Vit.E.x	315	Garlande	96
ILLE			
Upon suche a sort was ille bestowde and spent.	32	Dol Dethe	98
ILLUMYN			
Illumyn me, your poete and your scrybe,	117	Ag Scottes	80
ILLUMYNE			
For to illumyne, she sayde, I was to dulle,	46	Bowge	20
ILLUMYNID			
The margent was illumynid all with golden railles	345	Garlande	1157
ILLUMYNYD			
Illumynyd wyth feturys far passyng my reporte;	44	Balettys3	23
ILLUSIOUNS			
And by her abusiouns, /And damnable illusiouns	350	Garlande	1341
ILLUSYON			
Through suche abusyon, /And by suche illusyon,	279	Why Come Ye	20
ILLUSYONS			
And dampnable illusyons	105	Phy Sparrow	1348
IMAGE			
That by representacyon /Of his image and facyon,	77	Phy Sparrow	215
And lyke to her image,	100	Phy Sparrow	1153
IMAGINACION			
Now myne hole imaginacion	93	Phy Sparrow	847
IMCOMPERABLE			
Relucent smaragd, objecte imcomperable;	44	Balettys3	21
IMMEDIATLY			
Occupacyon, immediatly to rede.	345	Garlande	1169
IMMOYSTURID			
Immoysturid with mislyng and ay droppyng dry,	331	Garlande	698
IMMORTALLY			
Immortally whiche is inmaculate?	33	Dol Dethe	147
IMPECHMENT			
That I shall suffer none impechment	179	Magnyfycence	1418
IMPERIALL			
Of this, his realme royall /And lande imperiall,	368	Albany	394
IMPERYALL			
Before some prothonotory, /Imperyall or papall.	299	Why Come Ye	820
IMPLEMENTES			
Her fresshe habylementes /With other implementes	101	Phy Sparrow	1181
IMPORTE			
To me it myght importe	77	Phy Sparrow	216
IMPORTUNATE			
[Your] pride ys alle to peviche, your porte importunate;	123	Garnesche2	3
IMPORTUNE			
With one vice importune thei playnly said nay.	31	Dol Dethe	80
IMPOSSIBLE			
For it is impossible	368	Albany	390
IMPRYNTED			
Shulde be imprynted better	265	Collyn Clout	761
IMPRUDENT			
and to preche to people imprudent perilously,	375	Replycacion	1
INBRYNGIS			
The poemis and storis auncient inbryngis	331	Garlande	689
INCARNACION			
Was nevyr suche a senatour syn Crystes Incarnacion.	240	Speke Parott	337
INCYNERACYON			
Of whose incyneracyon /There ryseth a new creacyon	85	Phy Sparrow	540
INCLERYD			
A myrrour incleryd is this interlude,	212	Magnyfycence	2524
INCLYNE			
And I my selfe hooly to you wyll inclyne.	145	Magnyfycence	182
INCOMMODITE			
Myxte with sum incommodite,	130	Garnesche5	10
INCOMPERABLE			
To the pray we as Prince incomperable,	34	Dol Dethe	197
INCOMPORABYLL			
'With Kateryne incomporabyll, owur royall quene also,	231	Speke Parott	36
INCONSTANT			
This lyfe inconstant for to beholde and se:	212	Magnyfycence	2525
INCONSTAUNCE			
A, ye make me laughe at your inconstaunce.	147	Magnyfycence	236
INCONVENYENTLY			
Sir Duke of Albany, /Right inconvenyently	363	Albany	189
INCORRIGIBLE			
Shameles, and mercyles, /Incorrigible and insaciate;	276	Collyn Clout	1179

INCREASE —INFLAMMACION   Page   Title   Line

INCREASE
   Now ebbe, now flowe, nowe increase, now dyscrease;   212   Magnyfycence   2521
INCRES
   And his glory to incres /Lyke to Scipiades, ...   369   Albany   438
INCRESE
   To the incresse of your honour then arme you with ryght, ...   211   Magnyfycence   2496
INDE
   Of Inde the gredy grypes   79   Phy Sparrow   307
INDE BLEWE
   The streynes of her vaynes as asure Inde blewe, ...   183   Magnyfycence   1553
INDEDE
   Playne matter indede, /Whoso lyst to rede   85   Phy Sparrow   548
   Nay, indede, but I sawe howe ye prayed, ...   188   Magnyfycence   1696
   That so indede /Your fame may sprede   355   Garlande   1550
IN DEDE
   For, as I trowe, I have sene you in dede   53   Bowge   248
   I wyll not saye it is mater in dede, ...   61   Bowge   537
   In dede, syr, that lyberte was not worthe a cue.   141   Magnyfycence   36
   And in dede, syr, I here men talke -   151   Magnyfycence   374
   Knowe you not me, syrs? No, in dede.   157   Magnyfycence   594
   And yet in dede   165   Magnyfycence   892
   Laye men say, in dede, ...   248   Collyn Clout   75
   What Skelton hath compilid and wryton in dede, ...   345   Garlande   1151
INDEED
   That thys is matter indeed.   65   Hauke   148
   And therein reed /Shall fynde indeed   116   Ag Scottes   44
INDEMPNITE
   And so largely to lay for myne indempnite, ...   344   Garlande   1136
INDEMPNYTE
   With all solempnyte, /For theyr indempnyte;   269   Collyn Clout   927
INDENTURES
   Make indentures how ye and I shal gyde.   180   Magnyfycence   1448
INDEUER
   There to indeuer with all felycyte.   214   Magnyfycence   2569
INDY
   The Indy saphyre blew /Her vaynes doth ennew;   97   Phy Sparrow   1031
INDY BLEW
   Saphyre of sadnes, envayned wyth Indy blew;   44   Balettys3   17
   Where the postis wer enbulyoned with saphiris indy blew, . . .   325   Garlande   478
INDYFFERENTE
   In every poynte to be indyfferente, ...   61   Bowge   535
INDYGNACYON
   With Indygnacyon lyned was his hode;   54   Bowge   286
INDYTE
   To ryme or to rayle, /To wryte or to indyte, ...   247   Collyn Clout   6
INDURE
   O good Lorde, howe longe shall I indure   201   Magnyfycence   2153
   In good hope alway for to indure.   208   Magnyfycence   2396
   For the welthe of this worlde can not indure.   213   Magnyfycence   2558
   For the welthe of this worlde can not indure.   214   Magnyfycence   2565
INDUSTRIOUS
   Dyvysynge in pycture, by his industrious wit, ...   343   Garlande   1098
INDUSTRIOUSLY
   Habillimentis royall founde out industriously;   336   Garlande   851
INDUSTRY
   Of suche an industry /And suche a pregnacy, ...   384   Replycacion   370
INDUSTRYOUS
   Yet dyverse ther be, industryous of reason, ...   315   Garlande   106
   ther] 'that' MS Cotton Vitellius E.x
INEVYTABLY
   A confutacion responsyve, or an inevytably prepensed answere .   382   Replycacion   R
INEXPLICABILL
   My vyolet amyabyll, /My joye inexplicabill, ...   237   Speke Parott   244
INFALLIBLY
   And infallibly agre /Of necessyte, ...   384   Replycacion   363
INFATUATE
   fervently reboyled with the infatuate flames   374   Replycacion   I
INFECCIOUN
   Agenst hys poysond infeccioun, ...   128   Garnesche3   153
INFECCYONS
   Ageynst all infeccyons with cancour enflamyd, ...   331   Garlande   672
   cancour] 'rancour' Marshe 1568
INFECTE
   Thy tong untawte, with poyson infecte, ...   132   Garnesche5   108
   With heresy all infecte.   380   Replycacion   237
INFECTED
   Whan they be infected, ...   277   Collyn Clout   1236
INFERNALL
   Of infernall posty /Where soules frye and rousty;   105   Phy Sparrow   1332
   rousty] 'rosty' Marshe 1568
   Of infernall posty, /Where soulis fry and rosty;   349   Garlande   1325
INFERRID
   'Madame, your apposelle is wele inferrid, ...   316   Garlande   141
INFIRMITE
   I helpe all other of there infirmite, ...   321   Garlande   311
INFLAMMACION
   By whose inflammacion /Of spyrituall instygacion   384   Replycacion   379

INFLUENCE —INSUFFYCYENT   Page   Title   Line

INFLUENCE
Enbrethed with the blast of influence dyvyne, ... 33   Dol Dethe   157
INFORME
Us to informe and ken - 143   Magnyfycence   88
She to vowchesafe me to informe and ken; 335   Garlande   825
INGROSED
Yet let us se this matter thorowly ingrosed. 209   Magnyfycence   2438
INHABITE
And here to inhabite and ay for to dwell! 332   Garlande   719
INHATETH
Cyrcumspeccyon inhateth all rennynge astray, ... 209   Magnyfycence   2430
INIQUITE
Shall have penalte /For your iniquite. 258   Collyn Clout   462
INJURIS
All injuris he wolde represse, ... 307   Why Come Ye   1113
INKE
I have no pen nor inke 296   Why Come Ye   684
INK-HORNE
I wold sum manys bake ink-horne 133   Garnesche5   133
INLARGYD
In joy and myrthe your mynde shalbe inlargyd 146   Magnyfycence   205
INMACULATE
Immortally whiche is inmaculate? 33   Dol Dethe   147
INMORTALL
As goddesse inmortall she dyd represente; 313   Garlande   47
Wherby he myght have a name inmortall? 315   Garlande   119
Unto Diana, the goddes inmortall, ... 320   Garlande   303
For to deserve /Inmortall fame. 339   Garlande   967
    Inmortall] 'The courte of' MS Cotton Vitellius E.x
INNE
That inne, is now shyt up, ... 284   Why Come Ye   239
INNOCENT
As man that was innocent of trechery or trayne, ... 31   Dol Dethe   86
Howe be it of all synne he was innocent, ... 196   Magnyfycence   2002
INNUMERABLE
So innumerable, and so full of dyspyte, ... 205   Magnyfycence   2301
Innumerable people presed to every gate. 329   Garlande   603
INORDINATE
Is moche more inordinate, ... 310   Why Come Ye2   14
To rayle on his astate /With wordes inordinate? 370   Albany   462
INORDINATLY
Above all other inordinatly. 296   Why Come Ye   704
Or els ye demeane you inordinatly; 317   Garlande   173
INORDYNATE
Inordynate pride wyll have a falle. 133   Garnesche5   159
Brought up of poore estate, /With pryde inordynate, ... 262   Collyn Clout   643
INOUGH
Nay. Thou art a man good inough but for thy false hart. . . . 162   Magnyfycence   769
For you bothe it were inough. 173   Magnyfycence   1187
Nay, I know well inough ye are bothe well handyd 203   Magnyfycence   2230
INPURTURED
Inpurtured with fetures after your purpose, ... 183   Magnyfycence   1552
INROLDE
In there remembraunce ye may be inrolde. 239   Speke Parott   291
INSACIATE
Shameles, and mercyles, /Incorrigible and insaciate; 276   Collyn Clout   1179
INSENSATE
of their insensate sensualyte, ... 374   Replycacion   I
INSYDE
The insyde ye ded calle 125   Garnesche3   50
INSOLENCE
And it is wonder that your wylde insolence 143   Magnyfycence   85
By me conveyed is wanton insolence; 177   Magnyfycence   1335
But by the way of fansy insolence. 200   Magnyfycence   2116
INSPYRACION
Of hevenly inspyracion /In laureate creacyon, ... 384   Replycacion   372
And divyne inspyracion 384   Replycacion   381
INSTANCE
Skelton laureat, at the instance of a nobyll lady. 46   Balettys5   E
Of my pore instance and supplycacyon, ... 186   Magnyfycence   1634
And made instance for me be lykelyhod. 188   Magnyfycence   1697
INSTAUNCE
Howe be it, at your instaunce I wyll the rather 186   Magnyfycence   1641
INSTYGACION
By whose inflammacion /Of spyrytuall instygacion 384   Replycacion   380
INSTRUCTION
With right lytell instruction; 378   Replycacion   155
INSTRUCTYON
They have none instructyon 253   Collyn Clout   268
INSTRUMENT
And Iopas his instrument did avaunce, ... 331   Garlande   688
INSUFFICIENT
Though insufficient am I 369   Albany   401
INSUFFYCYENT
I am insuffycyent to make such enterpryse; 42   Balettys2   9
Therto am I full insuffycyent; 313   Garlande   46

INTELLEGENCE

To haute in excellence, /To lyght intellegence, ... 279 Why Come Ye 9
  lyght] 'lyght of' MS Rawlinson C. 813

INTELLYGENCE

Wyll knowe none intellygence .... 275 Collyn Clout 1137
They have the full intellygence, ... 297 Why Come Ye 710

INTELLYGENS

Then nodypollys and gramatolys of smalle intellygens: ..... 240 Speke Parott 318

INTENDE

And wyll never intende 124 Garnesche3 17
Shewe forth, I pray you, here in what you intende. ...... 141 Magnyfycence 40
Of that I intende to make demonstracyon .... 141 Magnyfycence 41
I am elles rebukyd of that I intende, ... 324 Garlande 440

INTENT

He sayde, for a crokyd intent, ... 68 Hauke 228
Syr, ye shall folowe myne appetyte and intent. .... 180 Magnyfycence 1420
A prynce to use with all his hole intent, ... 200 Magnyfycence 2118

INTENTYFE

Intentyfe ay /And dylygent, /No tyme myspent; .... 338 Garlande 942

INTERE

With all my herte intere. .... 143 Magnyfycence 113

INTERLUDE

A myrrour incleryd is this interlude, ... 212 Magnyfycence 2524

INTERRUPE

Or who made you so bolde to interrupe my tale? .... 147 Magnyfycence 256

INTO

Come saylynge forth into that haven brood, ... 47 Bowge 37
Than hath some shyppe that into Bordews sayle. .... 57 Bowge 406
To snappar and to fall /Into this opyn cryme; .... 65 Hauke 143
Into my chalys at mas, ... 66 Hauke 184
So urgently I am brought /Into carefull thought. .... 74 Phy Sparrow 107
Is turned into corage .... 85 Phy Sparrow 545
Into Perce and Mede, ... 93 Phy Sparrow 886
And therwithall convey hymselfe into a payre of fetters; ... 178 Magnyfycence 1365
Tyll all theyr conveyaunce is turnyd into madnesse. ..... 178 Magnyfycence 1367
And skommeth it into a tray .... 219 El Rummynge 198
  into] 'in' Day 1560, Marshe 1568
That she was therewithall /Into a palsey fall; .... 226 El Rummynge 475
Tyll Eufrates, that flodde, dryvythe me into Ynde, ... 231 Speke Parott 4
To bryng all the see into a cheryston pytte, ... 240 Speke Parott 331
So myche translacion into Englyshe confused; .... 244 Speke Parott 451
Turne monasteries into water mylles, ... 257 Collyn Clout 418
We tourne ryght into wronge, ... 276 Collyn Clout 1195
From Croydon into Kent .... 282 Why Come Ye 145
  into] 'to' Toy 1553, Kitson 1560.7, Marshe 1568
Into a mouse hole they wolde .... 286 Why Come Ye 293
That he falleth into Acidiam, ... 290 Why Come Ye 466
  into] 'in' Marshe 1568; Acidiam] 'Acisiam' †Kele 1545.3,
  Kitson 1560.7, Marshe 1568
Into one mannys hande; .... 298 Why Come Ye 763
Into the brayne by drynkyng over depe, ... 313 Garlande 33
Transformyd was she into the laurell grene. .... 320 Garlande 294
Then he assurded into his exclamacyon .... 320 Garlande 302
  his] 'this' Marshe 1568
Into the ryche palace of the Quene of Fame: .... 325 Garlande 450
Into a palace with turrettis and towris, ... 325 Garlande 459
So passyd we forthe into the forsayd place, ... 328 Garlande 561
Into a felde she brought me wyde and large, ... 328 Garlande 568
Into that place where as they left me, ... 343 Garlande 1103
Owt of Frenshe into Englysshe prose. .... 347 Garlande 1220
Out of fresshe Latine into owre Englyshe playne, ... 354 Garlande 1499
Nowe into the castell of Bas, ... 366 Albany 288
To hunt them into hell, ... 380 Replycacion 214

IN TO

His soule mot receyve in to ther company, ... 35 Dol Dethe 213
Flewe, I sholde say – in to an olde barne .... 191 Magnyfycence 1808
I shall thrust in the my dagger – Thorowe the legge in to the 202 Magnyfycence 2177
  hose.
Must crepe in to your caves .... 363 Albany 185

INTOXICATE

That wolde intoxicate, /That wolde conquinate, ... 264 Collyn Clout 702
  intoxicate] 'intoxicall' †Godfray 1531, 'intrixicate'
  MS Harley 2252

INTRETE

A red angry man, but easy to intrete. 37 Coystrowne1 39

INTRETED

Why, wyll they then be intreted, the most and the lest? .... 184 Magnyfycence 1585

INVECTYVE

This invectyve to make /For some peoples sake .... 120 Ag Scottes2 3

INVENTORY

Take of his substaunce a sure inventory, ... 180 Magnyfycence 1445

INWARD

Eche man may sorow in his inward thought .... 34 Dol Dethe 177
Wherwith the Sodomites /Lost theyr inward syghtes. ..... 291 Why Come Ye 471
Of your inward charyte; .... 300 Why Come Ye 838
Amen, /Of your inward charyte. .... 300 Why Come Ye 840

INWYT DELYNGE

My inwyt delynge there can no man dyscry. .... 177 Magnyfycence 1356

IOLLAS —IS

	Page	Title	Line
IOLLAS			
And how Iollas lovyd goodly Phillis;	354	Garlande	1497
IOPAS			
And Iopas his instrument did avaunce,	331	Garlande	688
IPOCRAS			
With Ipocras and mayster Avycen,	352	Garlande	1426
IPOCRISY			
Your madde ipocrisy, /And your idiosy,	381	Replycacion	249
IPOSTACIS			
And what ipostacis /Of Chrystes manhode is.	259	Collyn Clout	526
IRYSH			
To angre the Scottes and Irysh keterynges withall,	117	Ag Scottes	83
'Fate, fate, fate, ye Irysh water-lag.'	233	Speke Parott	86
IROUS			
This Naman Sirus, /So fell and so irous,	308	Why Come Ye	1167
Sirus] 'tyrus' MS Rawlinson C. 813			
IRREVOCABLE			
Irrevocable ys her decre;	130	Garnesche5	14
IS			
Of hym that is gone, alas, withoute restore,	29	Dol Dethe	3
Immortally whiche is inmaculate?	33	Dol Dethe	147
And as the lyonne whiche is of bestis kinge	33	Dol Dethe	167
This lordis dethe, whos pere is hard to fynd,	34	Dol Dethe	178
Go watch a bole, your bak is brode.	35	Man Margery	12
Gup, Cristian Clowte, your breth is stale,	36	Man Margery	27
When he is well, yet can he not rest.	36	Coystrowne1	7
Hys hart is to hy to have any hap;	37	Coystrowne1	12
Lord, how Perkyn is proud of hys Pohen!	37	Coystrowne1	19
He solfyth to haute, hys trybyll is to hy;	37	Coystrowne1	23
Hys musyk withoute mesure, to sharp is hys my;	37	Coystrowne1	25
Hys dyscant is besy, it is withoute a mene;	37	Coystrowne1	27
Hys dyscant is besy, it is withoute a mene;	37	Coystrowne1	27
To fat is hys fantsy, hys wyt is to lene.	37	Coystrowne1	28
To fat is hys fantsy, hys wyt is to lene.	37	Coystrowne1	28
His descant is dasshed full of dyscordes;	37	Coystrowne1	38
Nay, jape not with hym, he is no small fole;	38	Coystrowne1	50
It is a solempne syre and a solayne,	38	Coystrowne1	51
Take thys in worth, the best is behynde.	38	Coystrowne1	68
It is generall /To be mortall:	39	Coystrowne3	7
Above the sky /That is so hy,	40	Coystrowne3	56
Youre medelyng, mastres, is manerles;	40	Coystrowne4	2
To prayse youre porte it is nedeles;	40	Coystrowne4	5
'Myne horse is sold, I wene', you say;	40	Coystrowne4	9
'My new furryd gowne, when it is worne –	40	Coystrowne4	10
Yet is youre tong an adders tayle,	41	Coystrowne4	16
Youre key is mete for every lok,	41	Coystrowne4	22
Youre key is commen and hangyth owte;	41	Coystrowne4	23
Youre key is redy, we nede not knok	41	Coystrowne4	24
But one thyng is: that ye be lewde!	41	Coystrowne4	27
Thy lust and lykyng is from the gone;	42	Balettys1	23
Yet so it is that a rumer begynnyth for to ryse	42	Balettys2	12
'Have in sergeaunt ferrour, myne horse behynde is bare.'	43	Balettys2	20
It is perlous for a horseman to dyg in the trenche.	43	Balettys2	26
So fersly he fytyth, hys mynde is so fell,	43	Balettys2	29
It can be no counsell that is cryed at the cros.	43	Balettys2	36
Howbei[t], he is not furst hath had a los.	43	Balettys2	38
Howbeit] 'Howbeis' †Rastell 1527.1			
You I assure, absens is my fo,	44	Balettys3	36
And all is done ye lokyd for before,	45	Balettys4	2
For one fals poynt she is wont to kepe in store,	45	Balettys4	4
And under the fell oft festerd is the sore:	45	Balettys4	5
One ther is, and ever one shalbe,	45	Balettys5	8
For whose sake my hart is sore dyseasyd;	45	Balettys5	9
Excedynge ferther than his connynge is,	46	Bowge	23
His hede maye be harde, but feble is his brayne!	46	Bowge	24
his] not in Marshe 1568			
The awnner therof is lady of estate,	47	Bowge	50
Whoos name to tell is Dame Saunce-Pere.	47	Bowge	51
Her marchaundyse is ryche and fortunate,	47	Bowge	52
Her] 'Here' †Wynkyn de Worde 1499			
This royall chaffre that is shypped here	47	Bowge	54
Is called Favore to stonde in her good grace.'	47	Bowge	55
What is thy name?' and I sayde it was Drede.	48	Bowge	77
Whome she loveth, of all plesyre is ryche	49	Bowge	113
The sayle is up, Fortune ruleth our helme,	49	Bowge	127
As of your connynge, that is so excellent;	50	Bowge	149
Loo, what it is a man to have connynge!	50	Bowge	153
All erthely tresoure it is surmountynge.	50	Bowge	154
Ye stonde in favoure and Fortune is your gyde,	50	Bowge	171
'By Cryste,' quod Favell, 'Drede is soleyne freke!	51	Bowge	187
For here is none that dare well other truste;	51	Bowge	202
Is lytyll to saye, and moche to here and see;	52	Bowge	212
'By God,' quod he, 'this and thus it is';	52	Bowge	225
What thynge is that I maye do for you?	53	Bowge	240
Loo, what is to you a pleasure grete	53	Bowge	260
And I dare saye there is no man hereinne	53	Bowge	267
It is your fortune for to have that grace;	53	Bowge	272
As I be saved, it is a wonder case.	53	Bowge	273

IS—IS   Page   Title   Line

Entry	Page	Title	Line
That is agayne you, you shall have wetynge;	54	Bowge	278
'By Cryste,' quod he, 'for it is shame to saye,	54	Bowge	300
How he is now taken in conceyte,	54	Bowge	302
It is lyke he wyll stonde in our lyghte!'	54	Bowge	305
our] 'your' Marshe 1568			
'I wonder sore he is in such conceyte.'	54	Bowge	310
It is greate scorne to see suche a hayne	55	Bowge	327
This worlde is nothynge but ete, drynke and slepe,	57	Bowge	384
A brydelynge caste for that is in thy male!	57	Bowge	390
Her har[n]es easy ferre and nere is soughte.	57	Bowge	403
harnes] 'harmes' †Wynkyn de Worde 1499, 1510, 'armes' Marshe 1568			
Had I as good an hors as she is a mare,	57	Bowge	407
For she is trussed for to breke a launce.	57	Bowge	410
It is a curtel that well can wynche and praunce;	57	Bowge	411
curtel] 'curtet' †Wynkyn de Worde 1499, 1510			
And tyll I come, have, here is myne hat to plege.'	57	Bowge	413
is] not in Marshe 1568			
Gone is this knave, this rybaude foule and leude.	58	Bowge	414
It is a perylous vyce, this envy.	58	Bowge	444
It is grete scorne to se a mysproude knave	59	Bowge	453
With a clerke that connynge is to prate.	59	Bowge	454
By God, I saye, there is a grete herte-brennynge	59	Bowge	460
It is a worlde, I saye, to here of some –	59	Bowge	464
to] 'te' †Wynkyn de Worde 1499, 'to' Wynkyn de Worde 1510, Marshe 1568			
For all our courte is full of dysceyte.	59	Bowge	469
A flaterynge knave and false he is, God wote.	59	Bowge	485
It wyll not be, his purse is not on-flote.	60	Bowge	488
All that he wereth, it is borowed ware;	60	Bowge	489
His wytte is thynne, his hode is threde-bare.	60	Bowge	490
His wytte is thynne, his hode is threde-bare.	60	Bowge	490
More coude I saye, but what this is ynowe.	60	Bowge	491
Amendis maye be of that is now amys;	60	Bowge	494
'But by that Lorde that is one, two and thre,	60	Bowge	512
Woo is hym that is blynde and maye not see!	60	Bowge	518
Woo is hym that is blynde and maye not see!	60	Bowge	518
I wyll not saye it is mater in dede,	61	Bowge	537
Now constrewe ye what is the resydewe.	61	Bowge	539
This worke devysed is /For suche as do amys,	61	Hauke	1
That of our fayth the grownd is.	62	Hauke	14
All grace is far hym fro.	62	Hauke	16
For fayth in hym is faynte.	62	Hauke	19
Or els is thys Goddis law,	65	Hauke	130
That thys is matter indeed.	65	Hauke	148
The church is thus abusyd, /Reproched and pollutyd;	66	Hauke	160
Where Crystis precyous blode /Dayly offryd is,	66	Hauke	180
Pla ce bo, /Who is there, who?	71	Phy Sparrow	2
That is a flode of hell;	73	Phy Sparrow	71
Encreaseth my dedly wo, /For my sparowe is go.	74	Phy Sparrow	114
That Phillyp is gone me fro!	75	Phy Sparrow	142
But all this is in vayne	77	Phy Sparrow	208
Is for his soule to pray:	77	Phy Sparrow	238
And now the cause is thus,	80	Phy Sparrow	363
That he is slayne me fro,	81	Phy Sparrow	364
Bycause his voyce is lowde,	82	Phy Sparrow	439
The owle, that is so lewde,	82	Phy Sparrow	442
is] not in Kitson 1560.6, Marshe 1568			
Must tell what is of the clocke	84	Phy Sparrow	496
And yet there is none /But one alone;	84	Phy Sparrow	516
A phenex it is /This herse that must blys	84	Phy Sparrow	518
Is turned into corage	85	Phy Sparrow	545
To treade the pretty wren /That is our Ladyes hen.	86	Phy Sparrow	601
Yet one thynge is behynde,	86	Phy Sparrow	603
Whan her tale is tolde	87	Phy Sparrow	620
Disparaged is her fame	89	Phy Sparrow	711
And blemysshed is her name,	89	Phy Sparrow	712
He is named Troylus baud;	89	Phy Sparrow	721
Of that name he is sure	89	Phy Sparrow	722
Our naturall tong is rude,	91	Phy Sparrow	774
Our language is so rusty,	91	Phy Sparrow	777
Gowers Englysh is olde /And of no value told;	91	Phy Sparrow	784
told] 'is tolde' Wyght 1553, Kitson 1560.6, Marshe 1568			
His mater is worth gold,	91	Phy Sparrow	786
His mater is delectable, /Solacious and commendable;	91	Phy Sparrow	790
So as it is enprowed,	91	Phy Sparrow	793
For as it is enployd,	91	Phy Sparrow	794
There is no Englysh voyd,	91	Phy Sparrow	795
It is dyffuse to fynde	91	Phy Sparrow	806
Is to take this commendacyon	93	Phy Sparrow	849
As verely my hope is,	93	Phy Sparrow	874
I trust it is no shame,	94	Phy Sparrow	889
His lyver, his longe /With anger is wronge;	94	Phy Sparrow	919
longe] 'longes' Wyght 1553, Kitson 1560.6, Marshe 1568			
He is so bete /With malyce, and frete	95	Phy Sparrow	930
Than is he sad, /Frantyke and mad;	95	Phy Sparrow	939
So properly it is set:	98	Phy Sparrow	1049
She is the vyolet,	98	Phy Sparrow	1050

	Page	Title	Line
She is playnly expresse	100	Phy Sparrow	1151
Ther is no beest savage, ...	100	Phy Sparrow	1156
Such relucent grace /Is formed in her face;	100	Phy Sparrow	1160
It is for to suppose	101	Phy Sparrow	1177
And under that is brased	101	Phy Sparrow	1195
Thought is franke and fre;	101	Phy Sparrow	1201
My pen it is unable, ...	102	Phy Sparrow	1219
My hand it is unstable, ...	102	Phy Sparrow	1220
She is worthy to be enrolde	103	Phy Sparrow	1258
Is to discommende /That they cannot amend, ...	103	Phy Sparrow	1270
That in hell is never brent, ...	104	Phy Sparrow	1327
No worse than is contayned	106	Phy Sparrow	1377
This tretise devysed it is	106	Epitaphe	I
Regent is she, /Of poetes al, ...	112	Calliope	3
Yet is she fayne, /Voyde of disdayn, ...	112	Calliope	17
Kynge Jamy, Jomy your joye is all go.	113	Scot Kynge	1
A kynge a somner it is wonder;	113	Scot Kynge	5
In hym is figured Melchisedeche, ...	114	Scot Kynge	23
He is our noble champyon, ...	114	Scot Kynge	25
Your pryd is paste, adwe, good nycht.	114	Scot Kynge	43
That is a kynge without a realme.	115	Scot Kynge	59
It is not syttynge in tour nor towne	115	Scot Kynge	66
His sone the lorde admyrall is full good, ...	115	Scot Kynge	70
That is as trew /As blacke is blew /And grene is gray.	116	Ag Scottes	17
That is as trew /As blacke is blew /And grene is gray.	116	Ag Scottes	18
That is as trew /As blacke is blew /And grene is gray.	116	Ag Scottes	19
What ever they say, /Jemmy is ded /And closyd in led, ...	116	Ag Scottes	21
As it is enrolde, /Wrytten and tolde	116	Ag Scottes	39
Is it come unto your lot	116	Ag Scottes	50
Now is your pryde fall to decay.	118	Ag Scottes	110
In him is fygured Melchisedec, ...	118	Ag Scottes	115
He is our noble Scipione;	118	Ag Scottes	117
His tytle is true in Fraunce to raygne;	118	Ag Scottes	120
Lost is your game, ye are checkmate.	118	Ag Scottes	128
Youre eye is out; adew, good nyght!	119	Ag Scottes	142
That he is kyng without a reme;	119	Ag Scottes	156
It is not syttyng in tower and towne	120	Ag Scottes	174
syttyng] 'fytting' Kynge & Marche 1554			
Syr sumner, now where is your crowne?	120	Ag Scottes	178
Is voyd of all good grace;	124	Garnesche3	10
A fals lying tunge is harde to withholde;	137	Ven Tongues	6
My scole is more solem and somwhat more haute	137	Ven Tongues	24
But my learning is of an other degree	138	Ven Tongues	28
There is no noble man wil judge in me	138	Ven Tongues	34
And all is not worth a couple of nut shalis.	139	Ven Tongues	66
A fals double tunge is more fiers and fell	140	Ven Tongues	79
Welth is of wysdome the very trewe probate.	140	Magnyfycence	4
A fole is he with welth that fallyth at debate.	140	Magnyfycence	5
The amense therof is far to call agayne;	140	Magnyfycence	9
That welthe and felicite is passynge small.	141	Magnyfycence	21
For Welthfull Felicite truly is my name.	141	Magnyfycence	23
Your name is Lyberte, as I understande.	141	Magnyfycence	27
For lyberte at large is lothe to be stoppyd, ...	141	Magnyfycence	46
It is so swete in all maner of kynde.	142	Magnyfycence	51
By lyberte is done many a great excesse;	142	Magnyfycence	53
Lyberte is laudable and pryvylegyd from lawe.	142	Magnyfycence	68
Softe, my frende. Herein your reason is but rawe.	142	Magnyfycence	70
I say there is no welthe where as lyberte is subdude.	142	Magnyfycence	73
I say there is no welthe where as lyberte is subdude.	142	Magnyfycence	73
To lyve under lawe, it is captyvyte.	142	Magnyfycence	75
Where drede ledyth the daunce, there is no joy nor blysse. . .	142	Magnyfycence	76
Or howe can you prove that there is felycyte, ...	142	Magnyfycence	77
Where lyberte is absent, set welthe asyde.	142	Magnyfycence	80
And it is wonder that your wylde insolence	143	Magnyfycence	85
Your langage is lyke the penne	143	Magnyfycence	90
It is reason and skyll	143	Magnyfycence	105
I[n] ponder, by nomber, by measure all thynge is wrought, . .	143	Magnyfycence	118
In] 'I' †Rastell & Treveris C 1530, B			
Where measure is mayster, plenty dothe none offence;	144	Magnyfycence	121
Where measure lackyth, all thynge dysorderyd is;	144	Magnyfycence	122
Where measure is absent, ryot kepeth resydence;	144	Magnyfycence	123
Where measure is ruler, there is nothynge amysse.	144	Magnyfycence	124
Where measure is ruler, there is nothynge amysse.	144	Magnyfycence	124
Measure is treasure. Howe say ye, is it not this?	144	Magnyfycence	125
Measure is treasure. Howe say ye, is it not this?	144	Magnyfycence	125
Measure is worthy to have domynyon.	144	Magnyfycence	127
Lyberte without measure is acountyd for a beste;	144	Magnyfycence	138
There is no surfet where measure rulyth the feste;	144	Magnyfycence	139
There is no excesse where measure hath his helthe.	144	Magnyfycence	140
But have ye not herde say that wyll is no skyll?	144	Magnyfycence	148
It i[s] no maystery. Tushe, let Measure procede, ...	144	Magnyfycence	150
is] 'it' †Rastell & Treveris C 1530, B			
There is no prynce but he hath nede of us thre -	145	Magnyfycence	159
Me semeth Magnyfycence is comynge here at hande.	145	Magnyfycence	162
And, syr, this other mannys name is Lyberte.	145	Magnyfycence	168
That Measure be mayster us semeth it is syttynge.	145	Magnyfycence	176
Wherin it is necessary my pleasure you knowe:	145	Magnyfycence	185
For measure is a meane, nother to hy nor to lawe, ...	145	Magnyfycence	188

	Page	Title	Line
Laudable your consayte is to be acountyd,	145	Magnyfycence	191
There is no flaterer nor losyll so lyther,	146	Magnyfycence	200
All delectacyons aquayntyd is with me;	146	Magnyfycence	209
Who county[th] without me is caste to fer behynde	146	Magnyfycence	214
countyth] 'countyd' †Rastell & Treveris C 1530, B			
All that ye say is as trewe as the crede.	146	Magnyfycence	218
For howe be it lyberte to welthe is convenyent,	146	Magnyfycence	219
That all is without measure and fer beyonde the mone.	146	Magnyfycence	224
Then noblenesse, I se well, is almoste undone,	146	Magnyfycence	225
It is a wanton thynge, this Lyberte.	147	Magnyfycence	240
By measure eche thynge duly is tryde.	147	Magnyfycence	244
Tusche, holde your pece! Your langage is vayne.	147	Magnyfycence	251
Here is none forsyth whether you flete or synke.	147	Magnyfycence	254
For largesse is a purchaser of pardon and of grace.	148	Magnyfycence	268
Nowe, I beseche the, tell me what is thy name?	148	Magnyfycence	269
Largesse is laudable so it be in measure.	148	Magnyfycence	278
'in measure be' †Rastell & Treveris C 1530, B			
Largesse is he that all prynces doth avaunce;	148	Magnyfycence	279
It is but a maddynge, these wayes that ye use.	148	Magnyfycence	285
Though Largesse ye hyght your langage is to large;	148	Magnyfycence	295
This wrytynge is welcome with harty affeccyon!	149	Magnyfycence	313
Is there ony thynge elles your grace wyll commaunde me?	149	Magnyfycence	318
Who is that that thus dyd cry?	149	Magnyfycence	326
By your soth? Ye, and there is suche a wache,	150	Magnyfycence	350
But largesse is not mete for every man.	150	Magnyfycence	369
Yet mesure is a mery mene.	151	Magnyfycence	380
Ye, syr, a blaunched almonde is no bene.	151	Magnyfycence	381
Measure is mete for a marchauntes hall	151	Magnyfycence	382
Thus is the talkynge of one and of oder,	151	Magnyfycence	386
'A lorde a negarde, it is a shame.'	151	Magnyfycence	388
This worlde is full of my foly.	152	Magnyfycence	411
And counterfet fredome that is bounde;	152	Magnyfycence	434
I counterfet suger that is but *[s]ounde;	152	Magnyfycence	435
*sounde] 'founde' †Rastell & Treveris C 1530, B, 'sande' Scattergood			
Counterfetynge is a proper bayte.	152	Magnyfycence	442
To counterfet well is a good consayte.	152	Magnyfycence	444
But counterfet coynes is laughynge to scorne;	152	Magnyfycence	446
It is evyll patchynge of that is torne.	153	Magnyfycence	447
It is evyll patchynge of that is torne.	153	Magnyfycence	447
Whan the noppe is rughe, it wolde be shorne.	153	Magnyfycence	448
Yet counterfet chafer is but evyll corne.	153	Magnyfycence	450
All thynge is worse whan it is worne.	153	Magnyfycence	451
All thynge is worse whan it is worne.	153	Magnyfycence	451
It is moche worthe that is ferre fet.	153	Magnyfycence	455
It is moche worthe that is ferre fet.	153	Magnyfycence	455
Counterfet holynes is called ypocrysy;	153	Magnyfycence	469
Counterfet reason is not worth a flye;	153	Magnyfycence	470
Ryches rydeth out, at home is poverte.	153	Magnyfycence	474
Counterfet pleasure is borne out by me;	153	Magnyfycence	475
Your counterfet countenaunce is all of nysyte,	153	Magnyfycence	478
He wolde trotte gentylly, but he is to starke.	153	Magnyfycence	481
A carter a courtyer, it is a worthy warke,	153	Magnyfycence	483
Who that is ruled by us, it shalbe longe or he thee.	154	Magnyfycence	515
Nowe what is his name? And what is thyne?	155	Magnyfycence	519
Nowe what is his name? And what is thyne?	155	Magnyfycence	519
But is it not well? Howe thynkest thou?	155	Magnyfycence	528
What! Is Largesse without lyberte?	155	Magnyfycence	540
By Mesure mastered yet is he.	155	Magnyfycence	541
What! Is your conveyaunce no better.	155	Magnyfycence	542
In faythe, Mesure is lyke a tetter	155	Magnyfycence	543
Tushe, a strawe! It is a shame	155	Magnyfycence	549
For lyke as mustarde is sharpe of taste	155	Magnyfycence	552
It is a gentyll reason of a rake.	156	Magnyfycence	557
Alasse! Where is my botes and my spores?	156	Magnyfycence	569
Cockes armes! What is he?	156	Magnyfycence	573
By God, syr, this is Fansy Small-Brayne;	156	Magnyfycence	583
Here is a leysshe of ratches to renne an hare!	156	Magnyfycence	586
Woo is that purse that ye shall share!	156	Magnyfycence	587
I trowe that he is -	156	Magnyfycence	589
Cockes harte! It is Cloked Colusyon!	157	Magnyfycence	596
Cockes armes! Is that your name?	157	Magnyfycence	598
Ye, by the masse, this is even the same,	157	Magnyfycence	599
What is this he wereth? A cope?	157	Magnyfycence	601
Se howe he is wrapped for the colde.	157	Magnyfycence	603
Is it not a vestment? A, ye wante a rope.	157	Magnyfycence	604
Tushe! It is Syr Johnn Double-[Cope].	157	Magnyfycence	605
Cope] 'cloke' †Rastell & Treveris C 1530, B			
Ye, for your wyt is cloked for the rayne.	157	Magnyfycence	609
Tell me, syrs, what is your wyll?	157	Magnyfycence	611
Syr, it is so that these twayne	157	Magnyfycence	612
Ye. But he is a captyvyte.	157	Magnyfycence	626
Here is a pystell of a postyke!	158	Magnyfycence	649
In fayth, and without lyberte there is no bydyng.	158	Magnyfycence	662
In fayth, and Lybertyes rome is there but small.	158	Magnyfycence	663
For it is out of my mynde quyght.	159	Magnyfycence	672
For clokyd colusyon is a perylous thynge.	159	Magnyfycence	695
Craftynge and haftynge contryved is by me;	159	Magnyfycence	697

	Page	Title	Line
Falshode in felowshyp is my sworne brother.	160	Magnyfycence	713
And craftely can I grope howe every man is mynded.	160	Magnyfycence	725
My purpose is to spy and to poynte every man;	160	Magnyfycence	726
My tonge is with favell forked and tyned.	160	Magnyfycence	727
By Cloked Colusyon thus many one is begyled.	160	Magnyfycence	728
My speche is all pleasure, but I stynge lyke a waspe.	160	Magnyfycence	730
To flater and to flery is all my pretence	161	Magnyfycence	738
What is this, a betell or a batowe or a buskyn lacyd?	161	Magnyfycence	755
Well, and I be a coward, there is mo than I.	162	Magnyfycence	770
Wyll ye se this gentylman is all in his skornys?	162	Magnyfycence	773
Cockys harte! Who is yonde that for the dothe call?	162	Magnyfycence	780
What! Is thy harte pryckyd with such a prowde pynne?	162	Magnyfycence	785
Here he is nowe, man. Mayst thou not se?	162	Magnyfycence	792
Whiche of you is the better man,	162	Magnyfycence	802
Nay, in good faythe. It is but the gyse.	163	Magnyfycence	809
Why, is this the gyse nowe adays?	163	Magnyfycence	813
Ye, for surety. Ofte peas is taken for frayes.	163	Magnyfycence	814
By Saynt Mary, he is a tawle man.	163	Magnyfycence	821
But that the horson is prowde and hawte.	163	Magnyfycence	824
Beyonde measure /My sleve is wyde;	164	Magnyfycence	850
It is coste loste	165	Magnyfycence	893
All is out of harre	165	Magnyfycence	912
Nay. It is a farly fowle.	166	Magnyfycence	923
Torde! Man, it is an hawke of the towre.	166	Magnyfycence	925
She is made for the malarde fat.	166	Magnyfycence	926
Methynke she is well becked to catche a rat.	166	Magnyfycence	927
In faythe, Lyberte is nowe a lusty spere.	166	Magnyfycence	937
Why? Is he crossed than with a chalke?	166	Magnyfycence	950
Cockes bones! This is all of Johnn de Gay.	167	Magnyfycence	960
It is best I fede my hawke now.	167	Magnyfycence	968
There is many evyll faveryd, and thou be foule!	167	Magnyfycence	969
Eche thynge is fayre when it is yonge; all hayle, owle!	167	Magnyfycence	970
Eche thynge is fayre when it is yonge; all hayle, owle!	167	Magnyfycence	970
Lo, this is /My fansy, iwys;	167	Magnyfycence	971
It is, by Jesse,	167	Magnyfycence	974
She is furred for the hete /All to the fete;	167	Magnyfycence	977
Teuyt, teuyt! /Where is my wyt?	168	Magnyfycence	1005
For it is I that other whyle	169	Magnyfycence	1025
Where is my cappe? I have lost my hat!	169	Magnyfycence	1030
I can fynde fantasyes where none is;	169	Magnyfycence	1041
What is this, an owle or a glede?	169	Magnyfycence	1047
It is a Frenche butterflye.	169	Magnyfycence	1050
But she is lesse a grete dele	169	Magnyfycence	1052
Mary, syr, Cokermowthe is a good way hens.	170	Magnyfycence	1061
Here is no man that callyd the hogge nor swyne.	170	Magnyfycence	1084
In faythe, man, my brayne is as good as thyne.	170	Magnyfycence	1085
Cockys armys! This is a warke, I trowe.	170	Magnyfycence	1094
In faythe, ellys is there none in all Englonde.	170	Magnyfycence	1099
By my trouth, there is myne.	171	Magnyfycence	1103
Nowe, by my trouth, man, take, there is my purse; my] 'myne' †Rastell & Treveris C 1530, B	171	Magnyfycence	1104
Here is nothynge but the bockyll of a sho,	171	Magnyfycence	1107
What callest thou thy dogge? Tusshe! His name is Gryme.	171	Magnyfycence	1118
Come, Gryme! Come, Gryme! It is my praty dogges.	171	Magnyfycence	1119
In faythe, there is not a better dogge for hogges,	171	Magnyfycence	1120
No, by my trouthe. It is but the scurfe and the scabbe.	171	Magnyfycence	1123
What! Then he is some good poore mannes curre?	171	Magnyfycence	1129
Ye, for all thy mynde is on owles and apes.	171	Magnyfycence	1134
What, Fansy! Let me se who is the tother.	172	Magnyfycence	1158
Cockys bonys! It is a farle freke.	172	Magnyfycence	1160
Nay, iwys, fole. It is a doteryll.	173	Magnyfycence	1175
Mary, it was his, and nowe it is myne.	173	Magnyfycence	1181
And was it his, and nowe it is thyne?	173	Magnyfycence	1182
Cockes armes! It is not so, I trowe.	173	Magnyfycence	1202
Lo, Johnn a Bonam, where is thy brayne?	173	Magnyfycence	1204
Nay, it is I that foles can make;	174	Magnyfycence	1213
And, 'This is not well done, syr; take hede';	175	Magnyfycence	1248
And maketh hym besy where is no nede.	175	Magnyfycence	1249
And then he is moche made of for his [wyt]; wyt] 'whyt' †Rastell & Treveris C 1530, B	175	Magnyfycence	1271
He wyll make it mykyll worse than it is;	175	Magnyfycence	1273
It is but foly every dell.	175	Magnyfycence	1275
Nay, that is my parte that thou spekest of nowe.	175	Magnyfycence	1282
So is all the remenaunt, I make God avowe;	175	Magnyfycence	1283
And whan foly cometh, all is past.	176	Magnyfycence	1289
But all is foly that I can se.	176	Magnyfycence	1291
So how, I say, the hare is squat!	176	Magnyfycence	1299
All mesure and good rule is gone quyte.	176	Magnyfycence	1315
Ye. But tell me one thynge. What is that?	176	Magnyfycence	1318
Who is mayster of the masshe fat?	176	Magnyfycence	1319
When Mesure is gone, what nedest thou spare?	176	Magnyfycence	1323
Whan Mesure is gone, we may slee care.	176	Magnyfycence	1324
It is wonder to se the worlde aboute,	177	Magnyfycence	1326
To se what foly is used in every place;	177	Magnyfycence	1327
By me conveyed is wanton insolence;	177	Magnyfycence	1335
For many tymes moche kyndnesse is denyed	177	Magnyfycence	1338
By me is conveyed mykyll praty ware –	177	Magnyfycence	1340

IS — IS | Page | Title | Line

Text	Page	Title	Line
It is great almesse the hung[re] to fede,	177	Magnyfycence	1344
hungre] 'hunger' †Rastell & Treveris C 1530, B			
To clothe the nakyd where is lackynge a smocke -	177	Magnyfycence	1345
Without crafte nothynge is well behavyd.	177	Magnyfycence	1350
Tyll all theyr conveyaunce is turnyd into madnesse.	178	Magnyfycence	1367
Crafty conveyaunce is no chyldys game;	178	Magnyfycence	1368
By crafty conveyaunce many one is brought up of nought;	178	Magnyfycence	1369
Yet Lyberte without rule is not worth a strawe.	178	Magnyfycence	1378
All that ye say, syr, is reason and skyll.	178	Magnyfycence	1381
It is good yet that lyberte be ruled by reason.	178	Magnyfycence	1387
Yet it is good to beware of 'had I wyst'.	179	Magnyfycence	1395
Yet it is good wysdome to worke wysely by welth.	179	Magnyfycence	1401
For where is no mesure, howe may worshyp endure?	179	Magnyfycence	1408
Your grace sent for me, I wene. What is your wyll?	179	Magnyfycence	1410
To rule as ye lyst, lo, here is Lyberte.	179	Magnyfycence	1413
I say it is foly to gyve all welth away.	180	Magnyfycence	1430
For welth without largesse is all out of kynde.	180	Magnyfycence	1441
And welth is nought worthe yf lyberte be behynde.	180	Magnyfycence	1442
Nowe holde ye content, for there is none other shyfte.	180	Magnyfycence	1443
Nay, fyrst Lusty Pleasure is my desyre to have;	180	Magnyfycence	1453
Howe be it, that fonde felowe is a mery knave.	180	Magnyfycence	1455
Surely it is I that all may save and spyll,	181	Magnyfycence	1478
My name is Magnyfycence, man most of myght.	182	Magnyfycence	1493
What man is so maysyd with me that dare mete,	182	Magnyfycence	1506
Of your langage, it is so well devysed;	183	Magnyfycence	1530
Pullyshyd and fresshe is your ornacy.	183	Magnyfycence	1531
He is not lyvynge your maners can amend;	183	Magnyfycence	1537
Mary, your speche is as pleasant as though it were pend,	183	Magnyfycence	1538
To here your comon, it is my hygh comforte.	183	Magnyfycence	1539
Poynt devyse, all pleasure is your porte.	183	Magnyfycence	1540
It is semynge your pleasure ye delyte,	183	Magnyfycence	1546
That quyckly is envyved with rudyes of the rose,	183	Magnyfycence	1551
A maystres, I tell you, is but a small thynge.'	184	Magnyfycence	1579
Is there no horson that knave that wyll bete?'	185	Magnyfycence	1618
It is none abusyon, syr, in a noble man.	185	Magnyfycence	1626
It is a pryncely pleasure and a lordly mynde.	186	Magnyfycence	1627
Syr, so it is: this man is here by,	186	Magnyfycence	1649
Syr, so it is: this man is here by,	186	Magnyfycence	1649
To trust in me he is but dyssayved;	186	Magnyfycence	1652
For, so helpe me God, for you he is not mete.	186	Magnyfycence	1653
Howe say ye, syrs? Herein what is best?	186	Magnyfycence	1659
But for all that he is lyke to have a glent.	187	Magnyfycence	1668
So it is all the maner nowe a dayes	187	Magnyfycence	1677
Where is he? Mary, I made hym abyde	187	Magnyfycence	1685
This is a wyse man, syr, where so ever ye hym had.	187	Magnyfycence	1689
That holly my mynde with you is myscontente;	188	Magnyfycence	1717
A, my hede! But is the horson gone?	189	Magnyfycence	1729
Syr, nowe me thynke your harte is well eased.	189	Magnyfycence	1737
Nowe Measure is gone, I am the better pleased.	189	Magnyfycence	1738
So to be ruled by measure, it is a payne.	189	Magnyfycence	1739
Where mennes belyes is mesured, there is no chere;	189	Magnyfycence	1742
Where mennes belyes is mesured, there is no chere;	189	Magnyfycence	1742
It is no wonder, therfore, thoughe ye be wrothe	189	Magnyfycence	1748
With Mesure. Where as all noblenes is, there I have past:	189	Magnyfycence	1749
It is the gyse nowe, I say, over all -	189	Magnyfycence	1759
Than is it done as it sholde be;	189	Magnyfycence	1764
Who is this? Consayte, syr, your owne man.	191	Magnyfycence	1804
My hawke is rammysshe, and it happed that she ran -	191	Magnyfycence	1807
I trowe it be a frost, for the way is slydder;	191	Magnyfycence	1816
What! Is all your myrthe nowe tourned to sorowe?	192	Magnyfycence	1849
For Lyberte is gone, and also Felycyte.	192	Magnyfycence	1857
Why, is this the largesse that I have usyd?	193	Magnyfycence	1865
And is this the credence that I gave to the letter?	193	Magnyfycence	1867
That you trustyd, and Fansy is my name;	193	Magnyfycence	1871
Alas, wh[o] is yonder that grymly lokys?	193	Magnyfycence	1873
who] 'why' †Rastell & Treveris C 1530, B			
Here MAGNYFYCENCE is beten downe	193	Magnyfycence	SD
Nowe is there no man that wyll set by hym a flye.	193	Magnyfycence	1889
An all is for theyr ungracyous lyfe.	194	Magnyfycence	1915
Yet sometyme I stryke where is none offence,	194	Magnyfycence	1916
For there is nothynge that more dyspleaseth God	194	Magnyfycence	1928
Alasse, where is youth that was wont for to skyppe?	195	Magnyfycence	1957
My colour is tawny, colouryd as a turffe;	195	Magnyfycence	1959
Alasse! Where is nowe my golde and fe?	196	Magnyfycence	1967
He woteth not what welth is that never was sore.	196	Magnyfycence	1971
Lo, suche is this worlde! I fynde it wryt,	196	Magnyfycence	1974
In welth to beware; and that is wyt.	196	Magnyfycence	1975
It is foly to grudge agaynst his vysytacyon.	196	Magnyfycence	1990
Put your wyll to his wyll, for surely it is he	196	Magnyfycence	1997
In her promyse there is no sykernesse,	197	Magnyfycence	2028
All her delyte is set in doublenesse.	197	Magnyfycence	2029
It is foly agaynst God for to plete.	197	Magnyfycence	2035
Better it is to begge than to be hangyd with shame.	198	Magnyfycence	2039
But beggynge is better medecyne for the necke.	198	Magnyfycence	2045
Ye, mary, is it. Ye, so mote I goo.	198	Magnyfycence	2046
Where is nowe my welth and my noble estate?	198	Magnyfycence	2055
Where is nowe my treasure, my landes, and my rent?	198	Magnyfycence	2056
Where is nowe all my servauntys that I had here a late?	198	Magnyfycence	2057

Text	Page	Title	Line
Where is nowe my golde upon them that I spent?	198	Magnyfycence	2058
Where is nowe all my ryche abylement?	198	Magnyfycence	2059
Where is nowe my kynne, my frendys, and my noble blood?	198	Magnyfycence	2060
Where is nowe all my pleasure and my worldly good?	198	Magnyfycence	2061
She is the bote of all my bale.	199	Magnyfycence	2070
My harte is holly on her set;	199	Magnyfycence	2073
In lust and lykynge my name is Lyberte.	199	Magnyfycence	2078
What is he lyvynge that lyberte wolde lacke?	199	Magnyfycence	2083
For totum in toto is not worth an hawe -	199	Magnyfycence	2089
What, a very vengeaunce, I say! Who is that?	199	Magnyfycence	2105
What brothell, I say, is yonder bounde in a mat?	199	Magnyfycence	2106
What! Is the worlde thus come to passe?	200	Magnyfycence	2108
Howe he is undone by the meanes of me?	200	Magnyfycence	2110
For lyberalyte is most convenyent	200	Magnyfycence	2117
That they lose theyr lyberte and all that there is.	200	Magnyfycence	2128
And some in the worlde, theyr brayne is so ydyll	200	Magnyfycence	2135
Yonder is a horson for me doth rechate;	201	Magnyfycence	2151
In Fortunys frendshyppe there is no stedfastnesse;	201	Magnyfycence	2156
He may rynse a pycher, for his plate is to wed.	201	Magnyfycence	2168
Nay, to wrangle, I warant the, it is but a stone-caste.	201	Magnyfycence	2174
Nay, horson, here is my glove. Take it up and thou dare.	202	Magnyfycence	2178
So he is the worste brawler that ever was borne.	202	Magnyfycence	2200
In fayth, so to suffer he, it is but a skorne.	202	Magnyfycence	2201
Tushe, tushe! It is a great defaute;	203	Magnyfycence	2222
The one of you is to proude, the other is to haute.	203	Magnyfycence	2223
The one of you is to proude, the other is to haute.	203	Magnyfycence	2223
Cockys bonys! Thou begger, what is thy name?	203	Magnyfycence	2240
Ye, but trowe you, syrs, that this is he?	204	Magnyfycence	2242
By Cockys bonys, it is the same.	204	Magnyfycence	2244
Why, is there any store of rawe motton?	204	Magnyfycence	2265
But they say it is a queysy mete;	204	Magnyfycence	2267
For to lyve in mysery, it is herder than dethe.	205	Magnyfycence	2282
Dyspare is my name, that adversyte dothe f[o]lowe; folowe] 'felowe' †Rastell & Treveris C 1530, B, Douce Fragment d.7	205	Magnyfycence	2284
In Goddys mercy, I tell them, is but foly to truste;	205	Magnyfycence	2289
It is to late nowe thy synnys to repent.	205	Magnyfycence	2292
But nowe I se well there is no better rede,	205	Magnyfycence	2305
Lo, here is thy knyfe and a halter, and or we go ferther,	206	Magnyfycence	2317
Alas, dere sone, sore combred is thy mynde,	206	Magnyfycence	2325
Good Hope, syr, my name is; remedy pryncypall	206	Magnyfycence	2328
There is no man may synne more mortally	206	Magnyfycence	2336
There is no bawme ne gumme of Arabe	207	Magnyfycence	2347
Syr, your fesycyan is the grace of God,	207	Magnyfycence	2349
Prosperyte [by] hym is gyven solacyusly to man; by] 'to' †Rastell & Treveris C 1530, B	207	Magnyfycence	2367
Syr, is your pacyent any thynge amendyd?	208	Magnyfycence	2387
Ye, syr, he is sory for that he hath offendyd.	208	Magnyfycence	2388
How fele you your selfe, my frend? How is your mynde?	208	Magnyfycence	2389
Redresse my name is, that lytell am I used	208	Magnyfycence	2411
But redresse is redlesse and may do no correccyon.	209	Magnyfycence	2417
Is from adversyte Magnyfycence to unbynde.	209	Magnyfycence	2422
For where sad cyrcumspeccyon is longe out of the way,	209	Magnyfycence	2427
Of adversyte it is to stande in drede.	209	Magnyfycence	2428
Without fayle, syr, that is no nay:	209	Magnyfycence	2429
Truth it is, syr; for after he wrought me moch shame,	209	Magnyfycence	2444
Well, I perceyve in you there is moche sadnesse,	210	Magnyfycence	2475
Syth unto me formest this processe is erectyd,	211	Magnyfycence	2482
For of noblenesse the chefe poynt is to be lyberall,	211	Magnyfycence	2487
Howe in this worlde there is no seke[r]nesse, sekernesse] 'sekenesse' †Rastell & Treveris C 1530, B	212	Magnyfycence	2515
So in this worlde there is no sykernesse,	212	Magnyfycence	2522
A myrrour incleryd is this interlude,	212	Magnyfycence	2524
Shewyth nowe adayes howe the worlde comberyd is,	213	Magnyfycence	2539
Today it is well, tomorowe it is all amysse;	213	Magnyfycence	2541
Today it is well, tomorowe it is all amysse;	213	Magnyfycence	2541
Thus in this worlde there is no erthly truste.	213	Magnyfycence	2544
Thus in this worlde there is no erthly truste.	213	Magnyfycence	2551
Without our shyppe be sure, it is lykely to brast,	213	Magnyfycence	2562
Yet of magnyfycence oft made is the mast:	213	Magnyfycence	2563
Where every thyng is ordenyd after your noble porte.	214	Magnyfycence	2568
But she is not gryll,	214	El Rummynge	6
For she is somwhat sage	214	El Rummynge	7
Her lothely lere /Is nothynge clere,	214	El Rummynge	13
She is ugly fayre:	215	El Rummynge	26
To se howe she is gumbed, /Fyngered and thumbed,	215	El Rummynge	40
Her youth is farre past;	215	El Rummynge	48
I understande, her name /Is Elynour Rummynge,	216	El Rummynge	93
She is a tonnysh gyb;	217	El Rummynge	99
Howe hyr ale is solde /To mawte and to molde,	218	El Rummynge	158
That is a shreud aray!	218	El Rummynge	163
With, 'Fo, ther is a stenche!	219	El Rummynge	180
Seest thou not what is fall?	219	El Rummynge	182
Where as the yeest is,	219	El Rummynge	199
Drinke now whyle it is new;	219	El Rummynge	211
And for to leve this letter, /Bicause it is no better;	220	El Rummynge	238
And bicause it is no swetter,	220	El Rummynge	239
An huswyfe of trust /Whan she is athrust,	220	El Rummynge	254

IS —IS   Page   Title   Line

	Page	Title	Line
Her thryfte is full thyn.	221	El Rummynge	256
Bycause the ale is good;	221	El Rummynge	284
Thus and thus it is,	223	El Rummynge	357
'Lo, here is an olde typpet,	223	El Rummynge	366
This is a solempne drynkynge.	228	El Rummynge	548
'This ale,' sayd she, 'is noppy;	228	El Rummynge	557
'Have here is for me, /A clout of London pynnes.'	228	El Rummynge	563
To wyse is no vertue, to medlyng, to restles;	232	Speke Parott	61
In mesure is tresure, cum sensu maturato;	232	Speke Parott	62
Jereboseth is Ebrue, who lyst the cause dyscus.	232	Speke Parott	67
cause] 'law' Day 1560, Marshe 1568			
'What is this to purpose?' Over in a whynnymeg!	232	Speke Parott	71
Ic dien is the language of the land of Beme;	233	Speke Parott	79
In Affryc tongue byrsa is a thonge of lether;	233	Speke Parott	80
In Palestina there is Jerusalem.	233	Speke Parott	81
With, 'Who is there? A mayd?' Nay, nay, I trow!	233	Speke Parott	100
To dwell amonge ladyes, Parrot, is mete.	233	Speke Parott	105
My delyght is solas, pleasure, dysporte and pley;	233	Speke Parott	108
Sion is in sadness, Rachell ruly doth loke;	234	Speke Parott	114
Gedeon is gon, that Zalmane undertoke,	234	Speke Parott	116
O Esebon, Esebon, to the is cum agayne	234	Speke Parott	120
Ulula, Esebon, for Jepte is starke ded!	234	Speke Parott	126
For though ye can tell in Greke what is phormio,	235	Speke Parott	151
How the rest of good lernyng is roufled up and trold.	235	Speke Parott	168
roufled] 'roulled' Day 1560, Marshe 1568			
And Inter didascolos is rekened for a fole;	235	Speke Parott	172
With, 'Da causales,' is cast out of the gate,	235	Speke Parott	174
That of theyr scole maters lost is the hole sentens.	235	Speke Parott	182
Nowe in valle Ebron Parrot is fayne to fede;	236	Speke Parott	188
But of that supposicyon that callyd is arte,	236	Speke Parott	197
For Parot is no churlish chowgh, nor no flekyd pye,	236	Speke Parott	204
Parrot is no pendugum, that men call a carlyng,	236	Speke Parott	205
Parrot is no woodecocke, nor no butterfly,	236	Speke Parott	206
Parrot is no stameryng stare, that men call a starlyng;	236	Speke Parott	207
But Parot is my owne dere harte, and my dere derling.	236	Speke Parott	208
dere] (2nd) not in Day 1560, Marshe 1568			
Parrot is a fayre byrd for a lady	236	Speke Parott	211
When Parrot is ded, he dothe not putrefy;	236	Speke Parott	213
he] 'she' †Lant 1545, Kynge & Marche 1554, Day 1560, Marshe 1568			
My harte is so sore payned,	237	Speke Parott	254
Le tonsan de Jason is lodgid among the shrowdes;	239	Speke Parott	287
There is none that your name woll abbrogate	240	Speke Parott	317
The skye is clowdy, the coste is nothyng clere;	242	Speke Parott	397
The skye is clowdy, the coste is nothyng clere;	242	Speke Parott	397
Racell, rulye ragged, she is like to cache colde;	242	Speke Parott	401
'His heed is so fat	247	Collyn Clout	16
'He is but a foole; /Let hym go to scole!	247	Collyn Clout	28
'The devyll,' they say, 'is dede, /The devyll is dede.'	247	Collyn Clout	36
'The devyll,' they say, 'is dede, /The devyll is dede.'	247	Collyn Clout	37
My name is Collyn Cloute.	248	Collyn Clout	49
It is wronge with eche degre;	248	Collyn Clout	60
For in hoder-moder /The churche is put in faute.	248	Collyn Clout	70
There is theyr hole devocyon,	248	Collyn Clout	87
That the premenyre /Is lyke to be set afyre	249	Collyn Clout	109
And whyles the heedes do this, /The remenaunt is amys	249	Collyn Clout	116
And, for to say trouth, /A great parte is for slouth;	250	Collyn Clout	137
for] 'full' †Godfray 1531, 'for' MS Harley 2252			
But the greatest parte /Is for they have but small arte	250	Collyn Clout	139
And yet that is a pleasure.	250	Collyn Clout	146
But it is not worth a leke.	251	Collyn Clout	182
Boldenes is to seke /The churche for to defende;	251	Collyn Clout	183
It is nat for your werynge,	252	Collyn Clout	210
Theyr lernynge is so small,	252	Collyn Clout	240
In you the faute is supposed	253	Collyn Clout	264
And in nothynge is sure.	253	Collyn Clout	280
For a symoniake /Is but a hermoniake;	254	Collyn Clout	297
This is a farly fytte	255	Collyn Clout	329
farly] 'fearfull' †Godfray 1531, Kele 1545.1, Marshe 1568, 'ffarly' MS Harley 2252			
Alas, it is great ruthe!	255	Collyn Clout	343
That commytted is a collage	255	Collyn Clout	365
It is good for astrologys,	258	Collyn Clout	466
Holy churche is bruted /And shamfully confuted.	258	Collyn Clout	487
Whan there is never a whytte,	259	Collyn Clout	516
And what ipostacis /Of Chrystes manhode is.	259	Collyn Clout	527
How prelacye is solde and bought	261	Collyn Clout	583
And vertue is forgotten,	261	Collyn Clout	597
And that is all your thought.	261	Collyn Clout	607
Theyr rule is very small,	261	Collyn Clout	609
This is a pyteous case:	262	Collyn Clout	626
All this is out of mynde.	263	Collyn Clout	660
All] 'Alas' Kele 1545.1, Marshe 1568, 'All' MS Harley 2252			
As it is res certa	264	Collyn Clout	718
That clerkely is, and can /Well scrypture expounde	264	Collyn Clout	722
Nor how farre Temple Barre is	267	Collyn Clout	826
Somtyme a bacon flycke /That is thre fyngers thycke	267	Collyn Clout	845

	Page	Title	Line
But it is an olde sayd sawe	268	Collyn Clout	862
it] not in Kele 1545.1			
As now is made of late	269	Collyn Clout	914
All is fysshe that cometh to the net:	269	Collyn Clout	933
to the net] 'to net' Marshe 1568, 'to nett' MS Harley 2252			
That is a speculacyon	270	Collyn Clout	970
It is a besy thynge	271	Collyn Clout	988
This is a wonderous warke!	272	Collyn Clout	1048
Somwhat there is amysse!	272	Collyn Clout	1050
For I rebuke no man /That vertuous is.	273	Collyn Clout	1090
But my recountynge is /Of them that do amys	274	Collyn Clout	1101
Is all my hole wrytynge;	274	Collyn Clout	1108
Is counted for no rod;	275	Collyn Clout	1146
That nothynge is avaylynge;	275	Collyn Clout	1148
Is nat this a shamfull scorne	276	Collyn Clout	1200
As it is, it shall be styll, ...	277	Collyn Clout	1218
Lo, this is the gyse noweadayes!	277	Collyn Clout	1227
It is to drede, men sayes, ...	277	Collyn Clout	1228
Whan that his pleasure is.	278	Collyn Clout	1265
Reson is banysshed thence, ...	279	Why Come Ye	12
For age is a page	279	Why Come Ye	32
That age for dottage /Is reconed nowadayes.	280	Why Come Ye	44
reconed] 'recovered' Toy 1553, Kitson 1560.7, Marshe 1568			
/Is nothynge set by, ...	280	Why Come Ye	46
Our talwod is all brent, ...	281	Why Come Ye	82
For thrifte is threde bare worn, ...	281	Why Come Ye	91
And trouthe is all to-torne;	281	Why Come Ye	93
Wysdom is laught to skorne, ...	281	Why Come Ye	94
Favell is false forsworne, ...	281	Why Come Ye	95
Javell is nobly borne;	281	Why Come Ye	96
There is no man but one	281	Why Come Ye	113
All that he dothe is ryght.	281	Why Come Ye	116
All is warse and warse.	282	Why Come Ye	135
Of chevalry he is the floure;	282	Why Come Ye	159
It is a wonders warke.	283	Why Come Ye	173
He is set so hye /In his ierarchy	283	Why Come Ye	184
Is nat my reason good?'	283	Why Come Ye	196
This is a postels lyfe.	284	Why Come Ye	226
Helas, my herte is sory	284	Why Come Ye	227
Small newes that true is	284	Why Come Ye	234
That inne, is now shyt up, ...	284	Why Come Ye	239
This is a trew text!	285	Why Come Ye	261
Thy lernynge is to lewde, ...	287	Why Come Ye	330
Thy tonge is nat well thewde, ...	287	Why Come Ye	331
That is another thyng.	287	Why Come Ye	347
He is but an yonglyng, ...	287	Why Come Ye	348
There is a whyspring and a whipling	287	Why Come Ye	350
There] 'Her' Kitson 1560.7, Marshe 1568			
But there is some travarse	288	Why Come Ye	387
It is somewhat wronge	288	Why Come Ye	390
That his berde is so longe.	288	Why Come Ye	391
To whose magnifycence /Is all the conflewence, ...	289	Why Come Ye	413
His wysdome is so dyscrete	289	Why Come Ye	423
By him is subverted;	290	Why Come Ye	440
That all is but nutshales	290	Why Come Ye	443
He is so ambicyous, ...	290	Why Come Ye	461
Whiche, truly to expresse, /Is a forgetfulnesse, ...	290	Why Come Ye	468
He is in suche elacyon /Of his exaltacyon, ...	291	Why Come Ye	482
How an one-eyed man is	292	Why Come Ye	533
Well-syghted when /He is amonge blynde men?	292	Why Come Ye	535
Suche is a kynges power	293	Why Come Ye	565
In lykewyse now the same /Cardynall is promoted, ...	293	Why Come Ye	571
'My lorde is nat at layser.	294	Why Come Ye	625
He is so fyers and fell.	295	Why Come Ye	650
It is a wonders case:	295	Why Come Ye	657
wonders] 'wonderous' Kitson 1560.7, Marshe 1568			
Is toward hym so mynded, ...	295	Why Come Ye	659
For he is the kynges derlyng	295	Why Come Ye	666
And is governed by this mad kote!	295	Why Come Ye	668
And] not in Marshe 1568			
For what is a man the better	295	Why Come Ye	669
This is no fable nor no lye;	296	Why Come Ye	705
Yet it is a wyly mouse	298	Why Come Ye	756
It is a nyce reconynge	298	Why Come Ye	760
Is easy to expounde, ...	298	Why Come Ye	781
How the warlde is conveyed.	298	Why Come Ye	783
Is maister Mewtas dede, ...	298	Why Come Ye	787
Nay, nay, he is nat dede.	299	Why Come Ye	794
Now he is gone to another stede	299	Why Come Ye	797
For he is well past and gone.	300	Why Come Ye	833
Where trouth is abhorde, ...	300	Why Come Ye	847
It is a playne recorde	300	Why Come Ye	848
He is best set by!	300	Why Come Ye	859
best] 'most' MS Rawlinson C. 813			
For, 'Synke quater trey' /Is a tall man.	301	Why Come Ye	886
tall] 'toll' MS Rawlinson C. 813			
The gray gose is no swan;	301	Why Come Ye	889
no] 'a' MS Rawlinson C. 813			

	Page	Title	Line
Is tourned to glasse,	301	Why Come Ye	902
He is at suche takynge,	302	Why Come Ye	936
He is suche a grym syer,	303	Why Come Ye	987
For amonge us is none	304	Why Come Ye	995
Of theyr game it is sene	304	Why Come Ye	1005
Now all is out of facion, /Almost in desolation.	305	Why Come Ye	1041
What a frensy is this,	305	Why Come Ye	1050
And yet he is ashamed	305	Why Come Ye	1052
He is perjured himselfe.	307	Why Come Ye	1116
There is a dyversyte	307	Why Come Ye	1149
Nowe God amende that is amys;	308	Why Come Ye	1162
For I suppose that he is	308	Why Come Ye	1163
Men wene that he is pocky,	308	Why Come Ye	1170
wene that] 'say' MS Rawlinson C. 813			
It is manus Domini.	308	Why Come Ye	1174
He is so ambicious, /So elate and so vicious,	308	Why Come Ye	1176
He is nowe so overthwart,	308	Why Come Ye	1181
nowe] not in MS Rawlinson C. 813			
Is moche more inordinate,	310	Why Come Ye2	14
For small is your sadnesse	310	Why Come Ye2	24
This is the tenor of my byl,	310	Why Come Ye2	33
Not unremembered it is unto your grace,	313	Garlande	57
Of your request, regestred is his name	314	Garlande	62
But, how it is, Skelton is wonder slake,	314	Garlande	69
But, how it is, Skelton is wonder slake,	314	Garlande	69
It is sittynge that ye must hym correct.	314	Garlande	77
Is that our servaunt is sum what to dull;	314	Garlande	79
that] 'for that' MS Cotton Vitellius E.x			
Is that our servaunt is sum what to dull;	314	Garlande	79
that] 'for that' MS Cotton Vitellius E.x			
Sophisticatid craftely is many a confecture;	315	Garlande	110
Another manes mynde diffuse is to expounde;	315	Garlande	111
Yet harde is to make but sum fawt be founde.'	315	Garlande	112
Of your royall palace it is not the gyse,	315	Garlande	121
Recorde the same? Or why is had in mynde	315	Garlande	125
His name? Or why is it, I you praye,	316	Garlande	138
That he to your courte is goyng and commynge,	316	Garlande	139
Sith he is slaundred for defaut of konnyng?'	316	Garlande	140
'Madame, your apposelle is wele inferrid,	316	Garlande	141
And at your avauntage quikly it is	316	Garlande	142
As towchyng that Eschines is remembred,	316	Garlande	148
The cause why Demostenes so famously is brutid	316	Garlande	155
Then he that doth worste is as good as the best.	317	Garlande	175
Extorcyon is counted with you for a knyght;	317	Garlande	194
Eyther they wyll say he is to wyse,	318	Garlande	204
wyll] 'shall' MS Cotton Vitellius E.x			
Or elles he can nought bot whan he is at scole;	318	Garlande	205
And ye shall well fynde he is a very fole;	318	Garlande	207
well fynde] 'fynde wele' MS Cotton Vitellius E.x			
Call forthe, let se where is your clarionar,	318	Garlande	233
Eolus, your trumpet, that knowne is so farre,	319	Garlande	235
that] 'whiche' MS Cotton Vitellius E.x			
'O mercyles madame, hard is your constellacyon,	320	Garlande	304
That profyteth all other is nothynge profytable	321	Garlande	313
But blessyd Bachus, that bote is of all bale,	322	Garlande	376
How all that I do is under refformation,	323	Garlande	411
Is glad to please, and loth to offend.'	323	Garlande	413
In whose court poynted is your place.'	324	Garlande	420
When he is callid to answere to his name.'	325	Garlande	452
'The west is wyndy.' 'The est is metely wele.'	326	Garlande	499
'The west is wyndy.' 'The est is metely wele.'	326	Garlande	499
It is harde to tell of every mannes mouthe:	326	Garlande	500
'A slipper holde the taile is of an ele'	326	Garlande	501
Occupacyon, is ryght goodly aray,	327	Garlande	528
Sodenly is eclipsid in the wynter night,	330	Garlande	646
'How say ye? Is this after your appetite?	331	Garlande	707
All thynge convenable here is contryvyd	332	Garlande	712
convenable] 'convenably' Marshe 1568			
Paradyce this place is of syngular pleasure.	332	Garlande	717
What it is, and where upon it standis;	332	Garlande	722
But my request is not so great a thynge,	332	Garlande	730
Now, by your faith, is not this theffect	333	Garlande	737
by] 'be' †Fakes 1523			
And what blunderar is yonder that playth didil diddil?	333	Garlande	740
An hole reame he is able to set at devysion:	333	Garlande	758
He can never leve warke whylis it is wele.	333	Garlande	763
As a mariner that amasid is in a stormy rage,	335	Garlande	829
amasid] 'masid' MS Cotton Vitellius E.x			
Hardly bestad and driven is to hope	335	Garlande	830
and] not in MS Cotton Vitellius E.x			
Your noble demenour is counterwayng,	336	Garlande	847
Is lusty to loke on, pleasaunte, demure, and sage:	336	Garlande	870
Is lusty to loke on, plesaunt, demure, and sage.	337	Garlande	877
That for her trowth is in remembraunce had;	337	Garlande	900
Enbrowdred the mantill /Is of your maydenhede.	338	Garlande	909
maydenhede] 'maydenhode' †Fakes 1523			
Enbrawderyd the mantyll /Is of yowre maydenhede.	338	Garlande	917
Enbrawderid the mantill /Is of yowr maydenhede.	338	Garlande	925

ISABELL —IT

	Page	Title	Line
Enuwyd your colowre /Is lyke the dasy flowre	340	Garlande	986
your] 'her' MS Cotton Vitellius E.x			
It is not my custome nor my gyse /To leve behynde	342	Garlande	1068
Her that is bothe womanly and wyse,	342	Garlande	1070
womanly] 'maydenly' MS Cotton Vitellius E.x			
Set on your hede this laurell whiche is wrought.	343	Garlande	1087
Of laureat triumphe, your place is here reservyd,	344	Garlande	1126
triumphe] 'promocioun' MS Cotton Vitellius E.x			
Hath bene full often and yet is entendyng	344	Garlande	1131
To all that to reason is condiscendyng,	344	Garlande	1132
To all that to] 'to all tho that' †Fakes 1523			
Your discharge here under myne arme is it.'	344	Garlande	1146
To shew her boke; and she sayd, 'Here it is.'	344	Garlande	1148
Rehersyng by ordre, and what is the grownde,	345	Garlande	1152
The False Fayth that Now Goth, which dayly is renude;	346	Garlande	1179
And Cloked Collucyoun is brought in to clater	346	Garlande	1195
Go she never so gingirly, her honesty is gone away.	346	Garlande	1204
Harde to make ought of that is nakid nought;	346	Garlande	1205
Wonder is to wryte what wrenchis she wrowght,	346	Garlande	1207
It is no foly to use the Walshemannys hoos.	347	Garlande	1239
But what of that? Hard it is to please all men;	348	Garlande	1259
Is to discommende /That they can not amende,	348	Garlande	1263
That in hell is never brente,	349	Garlande	1320
No wors than is contaynyd	350	Garlande	1370
than] 'and' †Fakes 1523			
Notwithstandynge it is remedeles;	351	Garlande	1394
He is not wyse ageyne the streme that stryvith.	352	Garlande	1432
Dun is in the myre, dame, reche me my spur.	352	Garlande	1433
When the stede is stolyn, spar the stable dur.	352	Garlande	1435
It is sone aspyed where the thorne prikkith.	352	Garlande	1437
Where the sank royall is, Crystes blode so rede,	353	Garlande	1463
A pleasaunter place than Ashrige is, harde were to fynde,	353	Garlande	1465
were] 'where' †Fakes 1523			
Of our noble courte is ones spoken owte,	353	Garlande	1482
Good luk this new yere, the olde yere is past.	354	Garlande	1518
Justyce now is dede;	358	Garlande2	1
Is layd down to slepe,	358	Garlande2	4
And Ryght is over the fallows	358	Garlande2	6
over the] 'ever' Marshe 1568			
Wherfore to jeste /Is my delyght	359	Albany	14
In shorte sentens, /Of your pretens /What is the grounde	361	Albany	81
Or els wyll I /Evydently /Shewe as it is:	361	Albany	86
For the cause is this,	361	Albany	87
Suche trechery /And traytory /Is all your cast.	361	Albany	101
It is, and shal be	362	Albany	129
Or what actyvyte /Is in you, beggars braules,	364	Albany	218
Thy mellyng is but mockyng.	366	Albany	298
It is time for you to brydell	368	Albany	388
For it is impossible	368	Albany	390
It is a rechelesse rage,	369	Albany	417
With trouthe it is ennewde.	369	Albany	420
And what honour is founde	369	Albany	425
My lernyng is to small	370	Albany	457
Grounded is your sentence	372	Albany	519
Is farther than their wytte wyll reche.	374	Replycacion	13
Which is the most clere christall	375	Replycacion	31
Your lernyng is starke nought,	376	Replycacion	56
It is halfe a supersticyon	378	Replycacion	142
For it is an auncyent brute,	378	Replycacion	156
For your ignorance is gretter,	380	Replycacion	231
They saye howe latria is an honour grete,	381	Replycacion	282
For it is wele recorded	383	Replycacion	324
Howe there is a spyrituall,	384	Replycacion	365
Which is God of myghtes most,	385	Replycacion	384

ISABELL

	Page	Title	Line
To maystres Isabell Pennell	339	Garlande	R
My mayden Isabell,	340	Garlande	976
To maystres Isabell Knyght	342	Garlande	R
And cowde not wryght /Of Isabell Knyght.	342	Garlande	1067

ISAGOGICALL

	Page	Title	Line
Of this isagogicall colation,	297	Why Come Ye	717

ISAIAS

	Page	Title	Line
As noble [Isaias],	276	Collyn Clout	1206
Isaias] 'Ezechyes' †Godfray 1531, Kele 1545.1, Marshe 1568, 'I say was' MS Harley 2252			

ISAPHILL

	Page	Title	Line
And as full of good wyll, /As fayre Isaphill;	341	Garlande	1025
fayre] 'the fayre' MS Cotton Vitellius E.x			

ISOLD

	Page	Title	Line
Of Bele Isold his wyfe,	87	Phy Sparrow	643

ISRAELL

	Page	Title	Line
That Israell releysyd of theyr captyvyte,	181	Magnyfycence	1474

ISSUIS

	Page	Title	Line
Be issuis and portis from all maner of nacyons';	328	Garlande	580

IT

	Page	Title	Line
It may be regesterde of shamefull recorde.	30	Dol Dethe	28
To slo suche a lord, alas, it was grete shame.	33	Dol Dethe	154
slo] 'sle' Marshe 1568			

IT — IT

	Page	Title	Line
He can not fynd it in rule nor in space:	37	Coystrowne1	22
Hys dyscant is besy, it is withoute a mene;	37	Coystrowne1	27
It semyth the sobbyng of an old sow!	37	Coystrowne1	32
It is a solempne syre and a solayne,	38	Coystrowne1	51
As well it becomyth yow, a parysh towne clarke,	38	Coystrowne1	58
It is generall /To be mortall:	39	Coystrowne3	7
To prayse your porte it is nedeles;	40	Coystrowne4	5
'My new furryd gowne, when it is worne –	40	Coystrowne4	10
Yet so it is that a rumer begynnyth for to ryse	42	Balettys2	12
It is perlous for a horseman to dyg in the trenche.	43	Balettys2	26
It can be no counsell that is cryed at the cros.	43	Balettys2	36
Can touche a troughte and cloke it subtylly	46	Bowge	11
troughte] 'trouth' Wynkyn de Worde 1510, Marshe 1568; it] not in Marshe 1568			
The Bowge of Courte it hyghte for certeynte.	47	Bowge	49
certeynte] 'certeynet' †Wynkyn de Worde 1499, 'certayne' Wynkyn de Worde 1510, 'certeynte' Marshe 1568			
But who wyll have it muste paye therfore dere.	47	Bowge	53
What is thy name?' and I sayde it was Drede.	48	Bowge	77
Loo, what it is a man to have connynge!	50	Bowge	153
All erthely tresoure it is surmountynge.	50	Bowge	154
And, though I say it, I was myselfe your frende,	50	Bowge	160
I have a favoure to you, wherof it be	52	Bowge	206
To kepe it hymselfe; for than he myghte be sure	52	Bowge	222
Whyles of his mynde it were lockte with the keye.	52	Bowge	224
'By God,' quod he, 'this and thus it is';	52	Bowge	225
To kepe him frome pykynge, it was a grete payne.	52	Bowge	236
I coude it skan and ye wolde it reherse.	53	Bowge	245
skan] 'stan' †Wynkyn de Worde 1499, 1510; it] (2nd) not in Marshe 1568			
I coude it skan and ye wolde it reherse.	53	Bowge	245
skan] 'stan' †Wynkyn de Worde 1499, 1510; it] (2nd) not in Marshe 1568			
Wolde to God it wolde please you some daye	53	Bowge	256
Soo greate pleasyre, or who to you it gave.	53	Bowge	263
I praye to God that it maye never dy.	53	Bowge	271
It is your fortune for to have that grace;	53	Bowge	272
As I be saved, it is a wonder case.	53	Bowge	273
It was no tyme with him to jape nor toye.	54	Bowge	290
'By Cryste,' quod he, 'for it is shame to saye,	54	Bowge	300
It is lyke he wyll stonde in our lyghte!'	54	Bowge	305
our] 'your' Marshe 1568			
'By God,' quod Hervy, 'and it so happen myghte!'	54	Bowge	306
It is greate scorne to see suche a hayne	55	Bowge	327
Come whan it wyll, oppose the I shall,	55	Bowge	335
His gowne so shorte that it ne cover myghte	56	Bowge	354
And wake all nyghte and slepe tyll it be none.	57	Bowge	382
Lorde, how that I wolde caste it full rounde!	57	Bowge	396
It is a curtel that well can wynche and praunce;	57	Bowge	411
curtel] 'curtet' †Wynkyn de Worde 1499, 1510			
It is a perylous vyce, this envy.	58	Bowge	444
It is grete scorne to se a mysproude knave	59	Bowge	453
It is a worlde, I saye, to here of some –	59	Bowge	464
to] 'te' †Wynkyn de Worde 1499, 'to' Wynkyn de Worde 1510, Marshe 1568			
I hate this faynynge, fye upon it, fye!	59	Bowge	465
Truste me, and yf it come to a nede;	59	Bowge	478
And so I wolde it were, so God me spede,	59	Bowge	481
It were more thryft he boughte him a newe cote;	60	Bowge	487
It wyll not be, his purse is not on-flote.	60	Bowge	488
All that he wereth, it is borowed ware;	60	Bowge	489
Besechynge you that shall it see or rede,	61	Bowge	534
I wyll not saye it is mater in dede,	61	Bowge	537
And toke it oute in drynke,	66	Hauke	158
When it was polutyd	66	Hauke	174
If it please you to loke	68	Hauke	233
But nothynge it avayled /To call Phylyp agayne	72	Phy Sparrow	25
It can not be exprest /My sorowfull hevynesse,	72	Phy Sparrow	31
It was so prety a fole,	74	Phy Sparrow	115
It wold set on a stole,	74	Phy Sparrow	116
set] 'sit' Wyght 1553, Kitson 1560.6, Marshe 1568			
It had a velvet cap,	74	Phy Sparrow	120
It wolde lye and rest –	75	Phy Sparrow	126
It was propre and prest.	75	Phy Sparrow	127
Alas, it wyll me slo,	75	Phy Sparrow	141
For it wold come and go,	75	Phy Sparrow	159
And on me it wolde lepe	75	Phy Sparrow	161
It was no hurt, I trowe.	76	Phy Sparrow	170
In him it was no vyse;	76	Phy Sparrow	174
It were worth an hundreth pound	76	Phy Sparrow	189
To me it myght importe	77	Phy Sparrow	216
Deucalyons flode it hyght.	78	Phy Sparrow	253
And it were a Jewe,	80	Phy Sparrow	335
were] 'where' †Kele 1545.2			
It wolde make one rew	80	Phy Sparrow	336
Alas, my hert it stynges,	80	Phy Sparrow	349
Alas, myne hert it sleth	80	Phy Sparrow	351
Whan I remembre it,	80	Phy Sparrow	353

	Page	Title	Line
How pretely it wolde syt	80	Phy Sparrow	354
It was my prety Phyppes!	80	Phy Sparrow	360
A phenex it is /This herse that must blys	84	Phy Sparrow	518
How Jason it wan,	87	Phy Sparrow	632
How hartely he dyd it take	89	Phy Sparrow	692
So as it is enprowed,	91	Phy Sparrow	793
For as it is enployd,	91	Phy Sparrow	794
It is dyffuse to fynde	91	Phy Sparrow	806
Though it be refused,	92	Phy Sparrow	816
In worth I shall it take,	92	Phy Sparrow	817
Melodyously it to devyse	93	Phy Sparrow	864
I trust it is no shame,	94	Phy Sparrow	889
It wer a plesaunt payne	97	Phy Sparrow	1012
It were an hevenly blysse	97	Phy Sparrow	1039
So properly it is set:	98	Phy Sparrow	1049
It cannot be denayd /But it was well convayd,	98	Phy Sparrow	1065
It cannot be denayd /But it was well convayd,	98	Phy Sparrow	1066
It makethe lovers bolde	98	Phy Sparrow	1074
It wold make any man	98	Phy Sparrow	1080
It raysed myne hert rote	100	Phy Sparrow	1148
It is for to suppose	101	Phy Sparrow	1177
It cost me lytell nor nought.	101	Phy Sparrow	1203
nor] 'or' Wyght 1553, Kitson 1560.6, Marshe 1568			
My pen it is unable,	102	Phy Sparrow	1219
My hand it is unstable,	102	Phy Sparrow	1220
I pray you it may be amendyd	102	Phy Sparrow	1246
If it be sadly dyscust.	102	Phy Sparrow	1250
It were no gentle gyse	103	Phy Sparrow	1251
But whether it were so,	105	Phy Sparrow	1354
This tretise devysed it is	106	Epitaphe	1
To you no thyng it dyde accorde	113	Scot Kynge	3
A kynge a somner it is wonder;	113	Scot Kynge	5
Ye thought ye dyde it full valyauntolye,	113	Scot Kynge	9
Wyerfore ye may it now repent.	114	Scot Kynge	33
It is not syttynge in tour nor towne	115	Scot Kynge	66
As it is enrolde, /Wrytten and tolde	116	Ag Scottes	39
Is it come unto your lot	116	Ag Scottes	50
It greyth nought for your degre	116	Ag Scottes	52
It shameth all your noughty nacyon,	117	Ag Scottes	56
To you nothing it dyd accorde	118	Ag Scottes	93
A kyng, a sumner! It was great wonder:	118	Ag Scottes	95
It is not syttyng in tower and towne	120	Ag Scottes	174
syttyng] 'fytting' Kynge & Marche 1554			
As it reprehendyng, /And venemously stingyng,	120	Ag Scottes2	9
It semyth nat thy pyllyd pate	132	Garnesche5	89
It cumys the better for to dryve	132	Garnesche5	92
It plesyth that noble prince roiall	132	Garnesche5	103
It ys for no bawdy knave	132	Garnesche5	114
Thowth it be now ful tyde with the,	132	Garnesche5	120
It ys nat mete for soche a knave.	133	Garnesche5	156
Although he made it never so tough,	139	Ven Tongues	77
Be it erly or late, welth hath a season.	140	Magnyfycence	3
To tell you the cause me semeth it no nede.	140	Magnyfycence	8
And from whens come ye, and it myght be askyd?	141	Magnyfycence	29
Ye, to knackynge ernyst what and it preve?	141	Magnyfycence	33
It askyth lesure with good advert[ence].	141	Magnyfycence	42
advertence] 'advertysment' †Rastell & Treveris C 1530, B			
It is so swete in all maner of kynde.	142	Magnyfycence	51
To lyve under lawe, it is captyvyte.	142	Magnyfycence	75
And it is wonder that your wylde insolence	143	Magnyfycence	85
Wolde it please you then -	143	Magnyfycence	87
To you I arecte it, and cast /Therof the reformacyon.	143	Magnyfycence	94
So it in measure be.	143	Magnyfycence	101
It is reason and skyll	143	Magnyfycence	105
Measure is treasure. Howe say ye, is it not this?	144	Magnyfycence	125
What ellys? For otherwyse it were agaynst kynde;	144	Magnyfycence	132
It were no vertue, it were a thynge unblyst.	144	Magnyfycence	134
It were no vertue, it were a thynge unblyst.	144	Magnyfycence	134
It were a myschefe, yf lyberte lacked a reyne	144	Magnyfycence	135
It were a shame, to God I make an othe,	144	Magnyfycence	145
Without I myght cut it out of the brode clothe,	144	Magnyfycence	146
It i[s] no maystery. Tushe, let Measure procede,	144	Magnyfycence	150
is] 'it' †Rastell & Treveris C 1530, B			
That Measure be mayster us semeth it is syttynge.	145	Magnyfycence	176
Wherin it is necessary my pleasure you knowe:	145	Magnyfycence	185
It shalbe done at your commaundement.	147	Magnyfycence	239
It is a wanton thynge, this Lyberte.	147	Magnyfycence	240
God forbede that it other wyse sholde be!	147	Magnyfycence	246
Endure? No, God wote, it were great payne.	147	Magnyfycence	248
It were not possyble me longe to retayne.	147	Magnyfycence	250
Please it your grace to take no dysdayne,	147	Magnyfycence	252
Largesse is laudable so it be in measure.	148	Magnyfycence	278
'in measure be' †Rastell & Treveris C 1530, B			
It is but a maddynge, these wayes that ye use.	148	Magnyfycence	285
Why kepte yt it thus longe? Howe dothe he? Wele?	149	Magnyfycence	314
It was a Flemynge hyght Hansy.	149	Magnyfycence	328
Nay, syr, it was nothynge but your mynde.	149	Magnyfycence	330
I shall loke in it at leasure better;	149	Magnyfycence	332

	Page	Title	Line
By lakyn, syr, it hathe cost me pence	150	Magnyfycence	338
Where was it delyvered you? Shewe unto me.	150	Magnyfycence	340
It dothe so sure nowe and than.	150	Magnyfycence	368
As men dare speke it hugger mugger;	151	Magnyfycence	387
'A lorde a negarde, it is a shame.'	151	Magnyfycence	388
And countenaunce it clenly,	152	Magnyfycence	415
And defende it manerly.	152	Magnyfycence	416
It is evyll patchynge of that is torne.	153	Magnyfycence	447
Whan the noppe is rughe, it wolde be shorne.	153	Magnyfycence	448
All thynge is worse whan it is worne.	153	Magnyfycence	451
It is moche worthe that is ferre fet.	153	Magnyfycence	455
It wolde be masked in my net!	153	Magnyfycence	458
It wolde be nyce, thoughe I say nay;	153	Magnyfycence	459
By crede, it wolde have fresshe aray,	153	Magnyfycence	460
And jet it joly as a jay.	153	Magnyfycence	465
Coll wolde go clenly, and it wyll not be,	153	Magnyfycence	476
A carter a courtyer, it is a worthy warke,	153	Magnyfycence	483
This nonnes nowe and then, and it myght be,	154	Magnyfycence	488
Why, man, it were to great a wonder	154	Magnyfycence	510
By God, yet it muste begynne moche of the.	154	Magnyfycence	514
Who that is ruled by us, it shalbe longe or he thee.	154	Magnyfycence	515
But is it not well? Howe thynkest thou?	155	Magnyfycence	528
Myselfe coude not counterfet it better.	155	Magnyfycence	530
By God, had not I it convayed	155	Magnyfycence	534
Tushe, a strawe! It is a shame	155	Magnyfycence	549
We wyll remedy it, man, or we go;	155	Magnyfycence	551
It is a gentyll reason of a rake.	156	Magnyfycence	557
Ye, and se howe it may be compast	156	Magnyfycence	567
I trowe it shall not nede to abyde.	156	Magnyfycence	571
Cockes harte! It is Cloked Colusyon!	157	Magnyfycence	596
Is it not a vestment? A, ye wante a rope.	157	Magnyfycence	604
Tushe! It is Syr John Double-[Cope].	157	Magnyfycence	605
Cope] 'cloke' †Rastell & Treveris C 1530, B			
Syr, it is so that these twayne	157	Magnyfycence	612
Ye. But he spendeth it all in mesure.	157	Magnyfycence	621
For it is out of my mynde quyght.	159	Magnyfycence	672
And nowe it cometh to my remembraunce.	159	Magnyfycence	673
Thy slyppers they swap it, yet thou fotys it lyke a swanne.	161	Magnyfycence	765
Thy slyppers they swap it, yet thou fotys it lyke a swanne.	161	Magnyfycence	765
Nay, in good faythe. It is but the gyse.	163	Magnyfycence	809
To russhe it oute /In every route.	164	Magnyfycence	847
That all men it founde /Through out Englonde.	165	Magnyfycence	882
This ladyes have, /I it them gave.	165	Magnyfycence	890
It is coste loste	165	Magnyfycence	893
Nay. It is a farly fowle.	166	Magnyfycence	923
Torde! Man, it is an hawke of the towre.	166	Magnyfycence	925
Mary, thou jettes it of hyght.	167	Magnyfycence	962
To name thyselfe. Come of, it were done.	167	Magnyfycence	965
It is best I fede my hawke now.	167	Magnyfycence	968
Eche thynge is fayre when it is yonge; all hayle, owle!	167	Magnyfycence	970
Nowe Cryst it blysse!	167	Magnyfycence	973
It is, by Jesse,	167	Magnyfycence	974
So farly fayre as it lokys!	168	Magnyfycence	999
And ye may lese it for a pynne.	168	Magnyfycence	1016
For it is I that other whyle	169	Magnyfycence	1025
I wyll not have it so, I wyll have it this.	169	Magnyfycence	1042
I wyll not have it so, I wyll have it this.	169	Magnyfycence	1042
It is a Frenche butterflye.	169	Magnyfycence	1050
That ever thou thryve, God it forfende!	171	Magnyfycence	1114
Come, Gryme! Come, Gryme! It is my praty dogges.	171	Magnyfycence	1119
No, by my trouthe. It is but the scurfe and the scabbe.	171	Magnyfycence	1123
Nay, in faythe, it was but a strype	171	Magnyfycence	1125
It forseth not of reason, so it kepe ryme.	172	Magnyfycence	1150
It forseth not of reason, so it kepe ryme.	172	Magnyfycence	1150
Cockys bonys! It is a farle freke.	172	Magnyfycence	1160
Nay, iwys, fole. It is a doteryll.	173	Magnyfycence	1175
Mary, it was his, and nowe it is myne.	173	Magnyfycence	1181
Mary, it was his, and nowe it is myne.	173	Magnyfycence	1181
And was it his, and nowe it is thyne?	173	Magnyfycence	1182
And was it his, and nowe it is thyne?	173	Magnyfycence	1182
For you bothe it were inough.	173	Magnyfycence	1187
Cockes armes! It is not so, I trowe.	173	Magnyfycence	1202
Nay, it is I that foles can make;	174	Magnyfycence	1213
As some be not ferre and yf it were well sought –	174	Magnyfycence	1241
The knave wolde make it koy, and he cowde;	175	Magnyfycence	1246
But nowe, forsothe, man, it maketh no mater;	175	Magnyfycence	1256
He wyll make it mykyll worse than it is;	175	Magnyfycence	1273
He wyll make it mykyll worse than it is;	175	Magnyfycence	1273
It is but foly every dell.	175	Magnyfycence	1275
I wote not whether it cometh of the or of me,	176	Magnyfycence	1290
Mary, syr, ye may swere it on a boke.	176	Magnyfycence	1292
Ryot at lyberte russheth it out styll.	176	Magnyfycence	1317
It is wonder to se the worlde aboute,	177	Magnyfycence	1326
Foly fotyth it properly, fansy ledyth the dawnce,	177	Magnyfycence	1331
It is great almesse the hung[re] to fede,	177	Magnyfycence	1344
hungre] 'hunger' †Rastell & Treveris C 1530, B			
'What howe! Be ye mery! Was it not well conveyed?'	177	Magnyfycence	1347
Yet convey it craftely, and hardely spare not for me' –	177	Magnyfycence	1352

	Page	Title	Line
Convey it be crafte, lyft and lay asyde.	177	Magnyfycence	1357
Trust me, Lyberte, it greveth me ryght sore	178	Magnyfycence	1375
Syr, as by my wyll, it shall be so no more.	178	Magnyfycence	1377
It is good yet that lyberte be ruled by reason.	178	Magnyfycence	1387
I am content so it in measure be.	179	Magnyfycence	1390
Yet it is good to beware of 'had I wyst'.	179	Magnyfycence	1395
It shall be done. Ye, but byd hym come away	179	Magnyfycence	1399
Yet it is good wysdome to worke wysely by welth.	179	Magnyfycence	1401
So it be by mesure I am ryght well content.	180	Magnyfycence	1421
I say it is foly to gyve all welth away.	180	Magnyfycence	1430
And so as ye se it wyll be no better,	180	Magnyfycence	1438
Take it in worthe suche as ye fynde.	180	Magnyfycence	1439
Surely it is I that all may save and spyll,	181	Magnyfycence	1478
It wolde not become them with me for to mell;	182	Magnyfycence	1497
Plesyth it your grace to shewe what I do shall?	182	Magnyfycence	1517
If it lyke your grace to take it in degre.	182	Magnyfycence	1521
If it lyke your grace to take it in degre.	182	Magnyfycence	1521
Of your langage, it is so well devysed;	183	Magnyfycence	1530
Mary, your speche is as pleasant as though it were pend,	183	Magnyfycence	1538
To here your comon, it is my hygh comforte.	183	Magnyfycence	1539
If it wolde lyke you to here my pore mynde -	183	Magnyfycence	1543
It is semynge your pleasure ye delyte,	183	Magnyfycence	1546
But yf it lyke your grace more at large	185	Magnyfycence	1589
Let se what ye say. Shewe it strayte.	185	Magnyfycence	1592
Be it reason or none, it shall not gretely skyll;	185	Magnyfycence	1596
Be it reason or none, it shall not gretely skyll;	185	Magnyfycence	1596
Be it ryght or wronge, by the advyse of me,	185	Magnyfycence	1597
And frowne it and face it, as thoughe ye wolde fyght;	185	Magnyfycence	1601
And frowne it and face it, as thoughe ye wolde fyght;	185	Magnyfycence	1601
It is none abusyon, syr, in a noble man.	185	Magnyfycence	1626
It is a pryncely pleasure and a lordly mynde.	186	Magnyfycence	1627
Syr, Sober Sadnesse cometh. Wherfore it be?	186	Magnyfycence	1631
Please it your grace at the contemplacyon	186	Magnyfycence	1633
For of your grace I have it nought deserved.	186	Magnyfycence	1644
But yf it lyke you that I myght rowne in your eyre,	186	Magnyfycence	1645
Syr, so it is: this man is here by,	186	Magnyfycence	1649
Notwithstandynge to you be it sayde	186	Magnyfycence	1651
It were better he spake with you or he wente,	187	Magnyfycence	1662
That he wolde loke on hym, thoughe it were not longe.	187	Magnyfycence	1675
So it is all the maner nowe a dayes	187	Magnyfycence	1677
Alas! My stomake fareth as it wolde cast.	188	Magnyfycence	1726
Nay, so God me helpe, it was no grete vexacyon;	189	Magnyfycence	1733
Ye, walke he must; it was no better worth.	189	Magnyfycence	1736
So to be ruled by measure, it is a payne.	189	Magnyfycence	1739
It is no wonder, therfore, thoughe ye be wrothe	189	Magnyfycence	1748
It is the gyse nowe, I say, over all -	189	Magnyfycence	1759
I have taken it to Largesse and Lyberte.	189	Magnyfycence	1763
Than is it done as it sholde be;	189	Magnyfycence	1764
Than is it done as it sholde be;	189	Magnyfycence	1764
Plucke from an hundred, and gyve it to thre;	190	Magnyfycence	1775
For as thou sayst, ryght so shall it be,	190	Magnyfycence	1783
My hawke is rammysshe, and it happed that she ran -	191	Magnyfycence	1807
It was a ronner; nay, fole, I warant her blode warme.	191	Magnyfycence	1811
I trowe it be a frost, for the way is slydder;	191	Magnyfycence	1816
The feldfare wolde have fydled, and it wolde not frame;	192	Magnyfycence	1838
Nay. It was your fondnesse that ye have usyd.	193	Magnyfycence	1866
What? Yes, by the rode, syr. It was I all this whyle	193	Magnyfycence	1870
Yet it proveth eyrnest, ye may se, every day.	195	Magnyfycence	1949
That hath deservyd it as well as he.	195	Magnyfycence	1952
Lo, suche is this worlde! I fynde it wryt,	196	Magnyfycence	1974
Nowe, syth it wyll no nother be,	196	Magnyfycence	1978
All that God sendeth, take it in gre;	196	Magnyfycence	1979
It is foly to grudge agaynst his vysytacyon.	196	Magnyfycence	1990
And whan it pleaseth God, better may be.	196	Magnyfycence	1993
Put your wyll to his wyll, for surely it is he	196	Magnyfycence	1997
Take it mekely, and thanke God of his grace;	197	Magnyfycence	2033
It is foly agaynst God for to plete.	197	Magnyfycence	2035
Better it is to begge than to be hangyd with shame.	198	Magnyfycence	2039
They thynke it no shame to robbe and stele;	198	Magnyfycence	2042
Ye, mary, is it. Ye, so mote I goo.	198	Magnyfycence	2046
With ye, mary, syrs, thus sholde it be;	198	Magnyfycence	2064
Ye, for nowe it hath brought the to confusyon;	200	Magnyfycence	2130
It can not contynew long prosperyously;	200	Magnyfycence	2132
And they never thryve in theyr age, it shall not gretly skyll.	200	Magnyfycence	2138
I waraunt you I have gyven it a lasshe.	201	Magnyfycence	2165
Nay, to wrangle, I warant the, it is but a stone-caste.	201	Magnyfycence	2174
Nay, horson, here is my glove. Take it up and thou dare.	202	Magnyfycence	2178
In fayth, so to suffer the, it is but a skorne.	202	Magnyfycence	2201
Nay, by Saynt Mary, it was ye called me knave.	203	Magnyfycence	2212
And thus to be facyd, I thynke it great skorne.	203	Magnyfycence	2217
Tushe, tushe! It is a great defaute;	203	Magnyfycence	2222
To grope a gardevyaunce, though it be well bandyd.	203	Magnyfycence	2231
By Cockys bonys, it is the same.	204	Magnyfycence	2244
I was your mayster, though ye thynke it skorne;	204	Magnyfycence	2246
But they say it is a queysy mete;	204	Magnyfycence	2267
It wyll stryke a man myschevously in a hete.	204	Magnyfycence	2268
Som be wrestyd there that they thynke on it forty dayes,	204	Magnyfycence	2274
For to lyve in mysery, it is herder than dethe.	205	Magnyfycence	2282

IT — IT

	Page	Title	Line
It is to late nowe thy synnys to repent.	205	Magnyfycence	2292
And loke that it be not longe	206	Magnyfycence	2311
I to mynyster it, you to receyve it ofte -	207	Magnyfycence	2356
I to mynyster it, you to receyve it ofte -	207	Magnyfycence	2356
Of adversyte it is to stande in drede.	209	Magnyfycence	2428
Whiche conteyned in it a specyall clause	209	Magnyfycence	2436
Truth it is, syr; for after he wrought me moch shame,	209	Magnyfycence	2444
It wolde be founde so yf it were well tryde.	210	Magnyfycence	2449
It wolde be founde so yf it were well tryde.	210	Magnyfycence	2449
I shall it never forget nor leve it behynde,	212	Magnyfycence	2506
I shall it never forget nor leve it behynde,	212	Magnyfycence	2506
Yf it be regystryd well in memory;	212	Magnyfycence	2513
Today it is well, tomorowe it is all amysse;	213	Magnyfycence	2541
Today it is well, tomorowe it is all amysse;	213	Magnyfycence	2541
Without our shyppe be sure, it is lykely to brast,	213	Magnyfycence	2562
I am content, my frendys, that it so be.	214	Magnyfycence	2570
For her vysage /It woldt aswage /A mannes courage.	214	El Rummynge	10
It had ben hers, I wene, /More then fourty yere;	215	El Rummynge	57
And so doth it apere,	216	El Rummynge	59
doth it] 'it dothe' Day 1560, Marshe 1568			
It wygges and it wagges /Lyke tawny saffron bagges;	218	El Rummynge	137
It wygges and it wagges /Lyke tawny saffron bagges;	218	El Rummynge	137
God gyve it yll prevynge,	219	El Rummynge	185
And donge, whan it commes, /In the ale tunnes.	219	El Rummynge	193
And skommeth it into a tray	219	El Rummynge	198
into] 'in' Day 1560, Marshe 1568			
For I may tell you, /I lerned it of a Jewe,	219	El Rummynge	208
And I have found it trew.	219	El Rummynge	210
Drinke now whyle it is new;	219	El Rummynge	211
And ye may it broke,	219	El Rummynge	212
It shall make you loke /Yonger than ye be	219	El Rummynge	213
For ye may prove it by me.'	219	El Rummynge	216
And for to leve this letter, /Bicause it is no better;	220	El Rummynge	238
And bicause it is no swetter,	220	El Rummynge	239
We wyll no farther ryme /Of it at this tyme.	220	El Rummynge	241
Some go streyght thyder, /Be it slaty or slyder;	221	El Rummynge	258
Therefore, 'Fyll it by and by	221	El Rummynge	274
It was a stale to take /The devyll in a brake.	222	El Rummynge	324
stale] 'stale' 1521 Fragment, 'stare' †Lant 1545,			
Kynge & Marche 1554, Day 1560, Marshe 1568			
It was dere that was far fet!	223	El Rummynge	334
Thus and thus it is,	223	El Rummynge	357
But supped it up at ones,	224	El Rummynge	380
It was huge and greate,	225	El Rummynge	432
It was tart and punyete.	225	El Rummynge	435
God gyve it yll hap!'	227	El Rummynge	509
It was a bullyfant, /A gredy cormerant.	227	El Rummynge	520
For so mote I hoppy, /It coleth well my croppy.'	228	El Rummynge	561
croppy] 'coppy' Day 1560, Marshe 1568			
She made it as koye /As a lege-de-moy;	229	El Rummynge	586
lege-de-moy] 'lege moy' †Lant 1545, Kynge & Marche 1554			
God gyve it yll hayle,	230	El Rummynge	617
A trym-tram for an horse-myll it were a nyse thyng,	234	Speke Parott	128
Yf it were cond perfytely, and after the rate,	234	Speke Parott	143
What can it avayle /To dryve forth a snayle,	246	Collyn Clout	1
It standeth in no stede:	247	Collyn Clout	35
It may well so be,	247	Collyn Clout	38
Yf ye take well therwith /It hath in it some pyth.	248	Collyn Clout	58
take] 'talke' Kele 1545.1, Marshe 1568			
Yf ye take well therwith /It hath in it some pyth.	248	Collyn Clout	58
take] 'talke' Kele 1545.1, Marshe 1568			
It is wronge with eche degre;	248	Collyn Clout	60
With money, yf it wyll happe /To catche the forked cappe.	249	Collyn Clout	88
And judge as they wyll, /For other mens skyll,	249	Collyn Clout	98
But it is not worth a leke.	251	Collyn Clout	182
It is nat for your werynge,	252	Collyn Clout	210
Alas, it is great ruthe!	255	Collyn Clout	343
It may take some effecte!	257	Collyn Clout	436
And bere it well away.	258	Collyn Clout	464
Yf it please nat theologys	258	Collyn Clout	465
nat theologys] 'the not onely' MS Lansdowne 762 'not			
theologi' MS Harley 2252			
It is good for astrologys,	258	Collyn Clout	466
For it maketh me sad	259	Collyn Clout	511
As of antyquyte /It was ratyfyed,	264	Collyn Clout	714
As] 'And' †Godfray 1531, Kele 1545.1, Marshe 1568			
As it is res certa	264	Collyn Clout	718
It must come to his lot	265	Collyn Clout	750
That wolde it shulde be noted	265	Collyn Clout	754
Though it were never so playne,	265	Collyn Clout	765
But it is an olde sayd sawe	268	Collyn Clout	862
it] not in Kele 1545.1			
It is a besy thynge	271	Collyn Clout	988
Whether it be wronge or ryght	272	Collyn Clout	1055
Or howeever it hap,	273	Collyn Clout	1057
I do it nat for no despyte.	273	Collyn Clout	1086
it for] 'it not for' Kele 1545.1, Marshe 1568			
They counte it for a raylynge	275	Collyn Clout	1147

	Page	Title	Line
For, be it good, be it yll,	276	Collyn Clout	1217
For, be it good, be it yll,	276	Collyn Clout	1217
As it is, it shall be styll,	277	Collyn Clout	1218
As it is, it shall be styll,	277	Collyn Clout	1218
It is to drede, men sayes,	277	Collyn Clout	1228
And so it semeth they play,	277	Collyn Clout	1234
Me semeth it for the best.	277	Collyn Clout	1250
And beleve it as your crede.	278	Why Come Ye	2
And beleve it as your crede.	279	Why Come Ye	16
And beleve it as your crede.	279	Why Come Ye	28
Be it blacke or whight	281	Why Come Ye	115
It can not be moche worse.	282	Why Come Ye	138
It is a wonders warke.	283	Why Come Ye	173
But and it were well sought,	287	Why Come Ye	352
It is somewhat wronge	288	Why Come Ye	390
It shall be as he wyll.	289	Why Come Ye	419
Be it soure, be it swete!	289	Why Come Ye	422
Be it soure, be it swete!	289	Why Come Ye	422
As it were Jack Napis!	295	Why Come Ye	654
It is a wonders case:	295	Why Come Ye	657
wonders] 'wonderous' Kitson 1560.7, Marshe 1568			
For he wyll tere it asonder!	296	Why Come Ye	671
And settys nat by it a myte!	296	Why Come Ye	677
It was by nycromansy,	296	Why Come Ye	696
In Acon it was brought to pas,	296	Why Come Ye	706
As by myne auctor tried it was.	296	Why Come Ye	707
Yet it is a wyly mouse	298	Why Come Ye	756
It is a nyce reconynge	298	Why Come Ye	760
It were great rewth	300	Why Come Ye	841
It is a playne recorde	300	Why Come Ye	848
My lordys grace nameth it	302	Why Come Ye	940
And brynge it so lowe	303	Why Come Ye	951
It shall nat ever flowe.	303	Why Come Ye	952
nat ever flowe] 'neuer ouer flowe' MS Rawlinson C. 813			
Of theyr game it is sene	304	Why Come Ye	1005
And it be as I wene.	304	Why Come Ye	1007
He jugeth it no foly;	305	Why Come Ye	1047
It wolde make the devyll to swete!	306	Why Come Ye	1088
'The devyll wold swete' MS Rawlinson C. 813			
As playnly it dothe appere,	307	Why Come Ye	1117
It is manus Domini.	308	Why Come Ye	1174
It was nat heled alderbest,	308	Why Come Ye	1188
It standeth somwhat on the west;	308	Why Come Ye	1189
Lest he wyll put it clene out,	309	Why Come Ye	1199
Of your complaynt it shal nat skyl.	310	Why Come Ye2	32
as more at large it doth apere in the proces folowynge.	312	Garlande	1
And whether it were of ymagynacyon,	313	Garlande	31
Or it procedyd of fatall persuacyon,	313	Garlande	34
That passynge goodly it was to beholde:	313	Garlande	42
Not unremembered it is unto your grace,	313	Garlande	57
But, how it is, Skelton is wonder slake,	314	Garlande	69
It is sittynge that ye must hym correct.'	314	Garlande	77
It was not for hym to abyde the tryall.	315	Garlande	98
abyde] 'byde' MS Cotton Vitellius E.x			
How be it, it were harde to construe this lecture;	315	Garlande	109
Of your royall palace it is not the gyse,	315	Garlande	121
His name? Or why is it, I you praye,	316	Garlande	138
And at your avauntage quikly it is	316	Garlande	142
That he so sholde be, me semith it sittyng,	316	Garlande	149
it] 'it is' MS Cotton Vitellius E.x			
All be it grete parte he hath surrendred	316	Garlande	150
For truly it were a pyte that he sat ydle'.	318	Garlande	210
Of very dwte it may not well accorde,	318	Garlande	212
For elles it were to great a derogacyon	318	Garlande	218
What he hath done, let it be brought to syght.	318	Garlande	230
Anone all was whyste, as it were for the nonys,	319	Garlande	267
And may not atteyne it by no medyacyon,	321	Garlande	319
I made it straunge, and drew bak ones or twyse,	324	Garlande	444
How far it was, or ellis within what howris,	325	Garlande	457
far] not in †Fakes 1523			
That all the worde, I trowe, and it were sought,	325	Garlande	462
worde] 'worlde' Marshe 1568			
Whyles it remanyth fresshe in my mynde.	325	Garlande	465
It was excedyng byyonde the commowne rate.	326	Garlande	488
It is harde to tell of every mannes mouthe:	326	Garlande	500
And we shall se you ageyne or it be pryme.'	326	Garlande	525
Had gravin in it of calcydony a capytall A.	328	Garlande	587
As quikly towchyd as it were flesshe and bones,	328	Garlande	592
It made sum lympe-legged and broisid there bones;	329	Garlande	625
That ever more after by it they were aspyid;	329	Garlande	627
Sometyme, as it semyth, when the mone light	330	Garlande	644
It was a new comfort of sorowis escapid.	330	Garlande	657
Englisterd, that joyous it was to beholde.	330	Garlande	663
It passid all bawmys that ever were namyd,	331	Garlande	674
So many, that longe it were to reherse.	331	Garlande	706
it] 'in' Marshe 1568			
What it is, and where upon it standis;	332	Garlande	722
What it is, and where upon it standis;	332	Garlande	722

363

ITEM—ITEM

	Page	Title	Line
And if there be in it any thyng ment,	332	Garlande	723
It shall be losyd ful sone out of the bandis	332	Garlande	725
That I ne force what though it be discurid.	332	Garlande	731
How daungerous it were to stande in his lyght,	333	Garlande	755
were to stande in his lyght] 'is to stop up his sight' MS Cotton Vitellius E.x			
He can never leve warke whylis it is wele.	333	Garlande	763
To tell all his towchis it were to grete wonder;	333	Garlande	764
Sith ye must nedis afforce it by pretence	335	Garlande	817
Of honour and worship it hath the formar date.	336	Garlande	849
Of honour and worship it hath the formar date.	336	Garlande	856
Of honour and worship it hath the formar date.	336	Garlande	863
Yowr name to se /It be enrolde, /Writtin with golde.	338	Garlande	938
It were an hevenly helth,	340	Garlande	994
It were an endeles welth,	340	Garlande	995
It is not my custome nor my gyse /To leve behynde	342	Garlande	1068
Forthwith upon this, as it were in a thought,	343	Garlande	1100
That ever they saw, and wrought it was the best.	343	Garlande	1113
We wyll understande how ye have it deservyd.'	344	Garlande	1127
Your discharge here under myne arme is it.'	344	Garlande	1146
To shew her boke; and she sayd, 'Here it is.'	344	Garlande	1148
It wolde have made a man hole that had be ryght sekely,	345	Garlande	1162
To beholde how it was garnysshyd and bounde,	345	Garlande	1163
in as moche as it were to longe a proces	345	Garlande	R
With Courtely Abusyoun; who pryntith it wele in mynde	346	Garlande	1196
Yet, thoughe I say it, therby lyith a tale,	346	Garlande	1200
I] 'ye' †Fakes 1523			
It may wele ryme, but shroudly it doth accorde,	346	Garlande	1210
It may wele ryme, but shroudly it doth accorde,	346	Garlande	1210
A tratyse he devysid and browght it to pas,	347	Garlande	1228
To make suche trifels it asketh sum konnyng,	347	Garlande	1235
It is no foly to use the Walshemannys hoos.	347	Garlande	1239
Where it became, and whether it went,	347	Garlande	1243
Where it became, and whether it went,	347	Garlande	1243
And how that it was wantonly spent;	347	Garlande	1244
Suche problemis to paynt it longyth to his arte.	347	Garlande	1246
But what of that? Hard it is to please all men;	348	Garlande	1259
Who list amende it, let hym set to his penne.	348	Garlande	1260
But whether it were so,	350	Garlande	1347
It made sum mens eye dasild and dasid;	351	Garlande	1389
But how it was, sum were to recheles,	351	Garlande	1393
Notwithstandynge it is remedeles;	351	Garlande	1394
And plantid it there where never before was none, unshred	351	Garlande	1405
it there where] 'yet wher' Marshe 1568			
It is sone aspyed where the thorne prikkith.	352	Garlande	1437
It made them to skip, to stampe, and to stare,	353	Garlande	1473
And that it wolde please her, full tenderly I prayd,	353	Garlande	1479
It must nedes after rin all the worlde aboute.'	353	Garlande	1483
And when that I sawe it wolde no better be,	353	Garlande	1485
What shuld I do but take it in gre?	353	Garlande	1487
Now hereof it erkith me lenger to wryte,	354	Garlande	1491
Whiche redde on still, as it cam to her syght,	354	Garlande	1493
Who redyth it ones wolde rede it agayne;	354	Garlande	1501
Who redyth it ones wolde rede it agayne;	354	Garlande	1501
Sex volumis engrosid together it doth containe.	354	Garlande	1502
Or els wyll I /Evydently /Shewe as it is:	361	Albany	86
It shalbe your lottes	362	Albany	121
It is, and shal be	362	Albany	129
Caried in a cage, /As it were a cotage,	365	Albany	256
As it were a gote /In a shepe cote,	365	Albany	265
Men call it a toyle.	365	Albany	269
It made no great fors	366	Albany	282
Gyve it up, and cry, 'creke', /Lyke an huddy peke.	366	Albany	300
It is time for you to brydell	368	Albany	388
For it is impossible	368	Albany	390
It is a rechelesse rage,	369	Albany	417
With trouthe it is ennewde.	369	Albany	420
But madly it frames,	374	Replycacion	11
howe it idolatry to offre to ymages of our blessed lady,	375	Replycacion	I
Ye argued argumentes, /As it were upon the elenkes,	377	Replycacion	126
I saye it for no sedicion,	378	Replycacion	140
It is halfe a supersticyon	378	Replycacion	142
For it is an auncyent brute,	378	Replycacion	156
For, if it were well sought,	379	Replycacion	185
He counted it for no correction,	379	Replycacion	189
Toke it for a sporte,	379	Replycacion	191
It had ben moche better	380	Replycacion	229
To preche it idolatry,	381	Replycacion	254
Than shall ye fynde it fyrme and stable,	382	Replycacion	289
For it is wele recorded	383	Replycacion	324
As Grekes do it call,	384	Replycacion	369

ITEM

	Page	Title	Line
Item the Boke how Men Shulde Fle Synne;	345	Garlande	1173
Item Royall Demenaunce Worshyp to Wynne;	345	Garlande	1174
Item the Boke to Speke Well or be Styll;	345	Garlande	1175
Item to Lerne You to Dye When ye Wyll;	345	Garlande	1176
to] 'do' †Fakes 1523			
Item his Diologgis of Ymagynacyoun;	346	Garlande	1180

IVE — JAK

	Page	Title	Line
Item A[u]tomedon of Loves Meditacyoun;	346	Garlande	1181
Automedon] 'Antomedon' †Fakes 1523, Marshe 1568 MS Cotton Vitellius E.x			
Item New Gramer in Englysshe compylyd;	346	Garlande	1182
Item Bowche of Courte, where Drede was begyled;	346	Garlande	1183
Item Good Advysement, that brainles doth blame;	346	Garlande	1186
Item the Popingay, that hath in commendacyoun	346	Garlande	1188
Item Apollo that whirllid up his chare,	353	Garlande	1471

IVE

	Page	Title	Line
With Colyn Clowt, Johnn Ive, with Joforth Jack;	347	Garlande	1234

IWISS

	Page	Title	Line
Iwiss, ye dele uncurtesly;	36	Man Margery	15

IWYS

	Page	Title	Line
Iwys I coude tell — but humlery, home,	59	Bowge	467
tell] 'not tell' Wynkyn de Worde 1510			
Your harte ys to hawte, iwys, yt wyll nat be alowde.	123	Garnesche2	26
Lo, this is /My fansy, iwys;	167	Magnyfycence	972
Nay, iwys, fole. It is a doteryll.	173	Magnyfycence	1175
Wyth, 'Lo, gossyp, iwys,	223	El Rummynge	356
We supposed, iwys, /That she rose to pys;	229	El Rummynge	594

I WYS

	Page	Title	Line
I wys he hath an hevy hed,'	42	Balettys1	21
I wys, powle hachet, she bleryd thyne I!	42	Balettys1	28

IWUS

	Page	Title	Line
Well, ones thou shalte be chermed, iwus:	55	Bowge	340
So I, iwus, /Endevoure me	338	Garlande	935

JACINCTIS

	Page	Title	Line
Jacinctis and smaragdis out of the florthe they grew.	325	Garlande	480

JACK

	Page	Title	Line
The Jebet of Baldock was made for Jack Leg;	232	Speke Parott	73
Jack Travell and Cole Crafter,	281	Why Come Ye	98
Of this gentell Jack Breche,	294	Why Come Ye	616
With Colyn Clowt, Johnn Ive, with Joforth Jack;	347	Garlande	1234

JACKE

	Page	Title	Line
Say to me, Jacke Harys, /Quare accuparis	69	Hauke	277
With care and with thought howe Jacke shall have Gyl?	148	Magnyfycence	287
Cankard Jacke Hare, loke thou be not rusty;	161	Magnyfycence	758
To herken Jacke and Gyll /Whan they put up a byll;	249	Collyn Clout	96
'Welcom Jacke and Gylla!'	253	Collyn Clout	258

JACKE A THROMMYS

	Page	Title	Line
Ye, of Jacke a Thrommys bybyll can ye make a glose.	180	Magnyfycence	1427

JACKE-A-THRUM

	Page	Title	Line
As wyse as Jacke-a-Thrum,	253	Collyn Clout	282
Jacke] 'Tom' Kele 1545.1, Marshe 1568			

JACKE A THRUMMIS

	Page	Title	Line
To syt hym upon, and rede Jacke a thrummis bybille,	318	Garlande	209
hym] not in MS Cotton Vitellius E.x			

JACKE AT NOKE

	Page	Title	Line
Bothe Gyll and Jacke at Noke	268	Collyn Clout	855

JACKENAPES

	Page	Title	Line
To mockynge, to mowynge, to lyke a jackenapes —	199	Magnyfycence	2098

JACKE OF THE NOCKE

	Page	Title	Line
Or Jacke of the Nocke?	254	Collyn Clout	322

JACKE OF THE VALE

	Page	Title	Line
Or ellys some jangelynge Jacke of the Vale.	147	Magnyfycence	258

JACK NAPIS

	Page	Title	Line
As it were Jack Napis!	295	Why Come Ye	654

JACK RAKER

	Page	Title	Line
Set Sophia asyde, for every Jack Raker	235	Speke Parott	160

JACK RAKERS

	Page	Title	Line
He maketh us Jack Rakers;	285	Why Come Ye	273

JACOUNCE

	Page	Title	Line
Maters more precious than the ryche jacounce,	241	Speke Parott	366

JAGGED

	Page	Title	Line
For though my ryme be ragged, /Tattered and jagged,	248	Collyn Clout	54

JAGGYNGE

	Page	Title	Line
To jettynge, to jaggynge, and to full of japes,	199	Magnyfycence	2097

JAY

	Page	Title	Line
The janglynge jay to rayle,	81	Phy Sparrow	396
And jet it joly as a jay.	153	Magnyfycence	465

JAYBERD

	Page	Title	Line
John Jayberd et Adam all a knave,	106	Epitaphe	I
Ioannes Jayberd qui vocatur,	107	Epitaphe1	7
John Jayberd, incola de Dis;	108	Epitaphe1	57
Adieu, Jayberd, adue. /I faith, dikkon, thou crue!	108	Epitaphe1	62
Vale, Jayberd, valde male!	109	Epitaphe1	89

JAYBERDE

	Page	Title	Line
Jayberde nomenquae dedere;	107	Epitaphe1	23

JAYBERDES

	Page	Title	Line
With, 'Fill the blak bowle /For Jayberdes sowle.'	108	Epitaphe1	74

JAYES

	Page	Title	Line
The gyse now a dayes /Of some janglynge jayes	103	Phy Sparrow	1269

JAYS

	Page	Title	Line
Of sum jangelyng jays	348	Garlande	1262

JAYST

	Page	Title	Line
With, 'Jayst ye, Jenet of Spayne, for your tayll waggys,'	43	Balettys2	18

JAK

	Page	Title	Line
Lo, Jak wold be a jentyl man!	37	Coystrowne1	14

JAKE A THRUM — JASPE

	Page	Title	Line
Wyth, 'Hey, troly-loly-lo, whip here, Jak',	37	Coystrowne1	15
For Jak wold be a jentylman, that late was a grome.	37	Coystrowne1	42
Jak wold jet and yet Jyll sayd nay;	37	Coystrowne1	43
Though Jak sayd nay, yet Mok there loste her sho;	351	Garlande	1396

JAKE A THRUM

	Page	Title	Line
God Latyn for Jake a Thrum,	129	Garnesche3	204

JAKE RAKAR

	Page	Title	Line
And make moche lyke Jake Rakar;	127	Garnesche3	109

JAK OF THE VALE

	Page	Title	Line
Gup, Cristian Clowte, gup, Jak of the Vale,	35	Man Margery	6
Gup, Cristian Clowte, gup, Jak of the Vale,	36	Man Margery	13
Gup, Cristian Clowte, gup, Jak of the Vale,	36	Man Margery	20
Gup, Cristian Clowte, gup, Jak of the Vale,	36	Man Margery	29

JALAWSY

	Page	Title	Line
Whose jalawsy malycyous makyth them to lepe the hach!	43	Balettys2	33

JAMES

	Page	Title	Line
Trowe ye, Syr James, his noble grace	114	Scot Kynge	17
And of Saynte James in Gales,	223	El Rummynge	354

JAMY

	Page	Title	Line
Kynge Jamy, Jomy your joye is all go.	113	Scot Kynge	1
King Jamy, Jemmy, Jocky my jo,	118	Ag Scottes	91
jo] 'joye' Kynge & Marche 1554, Day 1560, Marshe 1568			

JAMYS

	Page	Title	Line
On pylgrimage to Saynt Jamys,	102	Phy Sparrow	1242
pylgrimage] 'pilgrimages' Marshe 1568			

JAMYS FODER

	Page	Title	Line
Strawe, Jamys foder, ye play the fode;	35	Man Margery	10

JANE

	Page	Title	Line
Goodly maystres Jane, /Sobre, demure Dyane;	102	Phy Sparrow	1223
Jane this maystres hyght,	102	Phy Sparrow	1225
That I Jane have named,	103	Phy Sparrow	1256
have] not in Marshe 1568			
To maystres Jane Blenner-Haiset	339	Garlande	R
Sith mistres Jane Haiset	339	Garlande	968

JANGELERS

	Page	Title	Line
For ydle jangelers have but lytill braine;	328	Garlande	566

JANGELYNG

	Page	Title	Line
Of sum jangelyng jays	348	Garlande	1262

JANGELYNGE

	Page	Title	Line
Or ellys some jangelynge Jacke of the Vale.	147	Magnyfycence	258
Now leve this jangelynge and to us expounde	147	Magnyfycence	262

JANGYLL

	Page	Title	Line
That lyst for to jangyll /And waywardly to wrangyll	120	Ag Scottes2	5

JANGLE

	Page	Title	Line
What! Shall we jangle thus all the day styll?	156	Magnyfycence	565
To here the people jangle.	255	Collyn Clout	330
Why jangle you suche jestes,	381	Replycacion	264

JANGLYNG

	Page	Title	Line
Open your janglyng jawes,	375	Replycacion	37

JANGLYNGE

	Page	Title	Line
The janglynge jay to rayle,	81	Phy Sparrow	396
The gyse now a dayes /Of some janglynge jayes	103	Phy Sparrow	1269

JANTILL

	Page	Title	Line
With margerain jantill, /The flowre of goodlyhede,	338	Garlande	914
With margerain jantill, /The flowre of goodlyhede,	338	Garlande	922

JANTYLL

	Page	Title	Line
Thow thou be a jantyll man borne,	131	Garnesche5	69

JANUAY

	Page	Title	Line
That jentyll Jorge the Januay,	130	Garnesche5	35

JANUS

	Page	Title	Line
Where I saw Janus, with his double chere,	354	Garlande	1515

JAPE

	Page	Title	Line
Nay, jape not with hym, he is no small fole;	38	Coystrowne1	50
It was no tyme with him to jape nor toye.	54	Bowge	290
And make therof a jape!	248	Collyn Clout	84
How dotynge age wolde jape with yonge foly;	322	Garlande	361

JAPED

	Page	Title	Line
I will not be japed bodely.	36	Man Margery	19

JAPES

	Page	Title	Line
For all these japes yet that [y]e make –	156	Magnyfycence	558
ye] 'we' †Rastell & Treveris C 1530, B			
Cockes harte! I love suche japes.	171	Magnyfycence	1133
Remembrest thou not the japes and the toyes –	171	Magnyfycence	1137
Ye, let be thy japes, and tell me howe	192	Magnyfycence	1846
To jettynge, to jaggynge, and to full of japes,	199	Magnyfycence	2097

JAPHET

	Page	Title	Line
Japhet, Cam, and Sem,	77	Phy Sparrow	244

JAPHETH

	Page	Title	Line
Sem, Japheth, or Cam.	301	Why Come Ye	899

JAR

	Page	Title	Line
All out of joynt ye jar.	368	Albany	378

JARFAWCON

	Page	Title	Line
A, syr, thy jarfawcon and thou be hanged togyder!	191	Magnyfycence	1812

JASON

	Page	Title	Line
How Jason it wan,	87	Phy Sparrow	632

JASPE

	Page	Title	Line
Lusty Garnysche, lyke a lowse, ye jet full lyke a jaspe;	123	Garnesche2	17

JASPER —JEREMY   Page   Title   Line

JASPER
One of jasper, another of whalis bone;   325   Garlande   472
JAST
Gup, marmeset, jast ye morelle!   124   Garnesche3   13
With, 'Jast you, and gup, gylly, ...   224   El Rummynge   390
With, 'Jast you, I say, Jullian!   285   Why Come Ye   242
JAVELL
Nay, thou rude ravener, rayne beten javell!   202   Magnyfycence   2191
Mary, syr, this gentylman caled me javell.   203   Magnyfycence   2211
And call a lorde a javell.   261   Collyn Clout   600
Javell is nobly borne;   281   Why Come Ye   96
With, 'Stowpe, thou havell! /Rynne thou javell!   294   Why Come Ye   608
JAW
With hys worme-etyn maw /And hys gastly jaw   39   Coystrowne3   15
JAWED
Jawed lyke a jetty;   215   El Rummynge   38
JAWES
And gnawe the in theyr jawes!   79   Phy Sparrow   289
With your enbosed jawes   370   Albany   477
Open your janglyng jawes, ...   375   Replycacion   37
JAWYS
Els with hys stynkyng jawys   128   Garnesche3   154
JEBET
The Jebet of Baldock was made for Jack Leg;   232   Speke Parott   73
JELOFER
This jelofer amyable;   98   Phy Sparrow   1053
JELOFFER
The jeloffer well set, /The propre vyolet;   340   Garlande   983
This jeloffer jentyll, this rose, this lylly flowre, ...   352   Garlande   1446
JELOFFER FLOWRE
In plantynge and pluckynge a propre jeloffer flowre;   351   Garlande   1392
JELOUSY
That frensy nor jelousy   385   Replycacion   407
JEMY
Trowyd ye, Syr Jemy, his nobull grace   118   Ag Scottes   107
JEMMY
What ever they say, /Jemmy is ded /And closyd in led, ...   116   Ag Scottes   21
Joly Jemmy, ye scornefull Scot, ...   116   Ag Scottes   49
Of the prowde Scot, kynge Jemmy, ...   117   Ag Scottes   71
King Jamy, Jemmy, Jocky my jo, ...   118   Ag Scottes   91
   jo] 'joye' Kynge & Marche 1554, Day 1560, Marshe 1568
AGAYNST THE SCOT JEMMY   120   Ag Scottes   R
JENET
With, 'Jayst ye, Jenet of Spayne, for your tayll waggys,' . .   43   Balettys2   18
How ofte he hadde hit Jenet on the tayle, ...   56   Bowge   369
   hadde] 'not' Marshe 1568
Our Thomasen she doth trip, our Jenet she doth shayle; . . .   233   Speke Parott   83
JENKYN
What! Whom have we here, Jenkyn Joly?   166   Magnyfycence   918
JENTILL
Jentill as fawcoun /Or hawke of the towre;   340   Garlande   1006
JENTILMAN
Of a dysour, a devyl way, grew a jentilman, ...   330   Garlande   635
JENTYLL
Hys jentyll curtoy[l], and set nowght by small naggys! . . .   43   Balettys2   16
   curtoyl] 'curtoyt' †Rastell 1527.1
Thys grevyth your husband, that ryght jentyll knyght, ...   43   Balettys2   27
For your jentyll husband sorowfull am I;   43   Balettys2   37
That jentyll Jorge the Januay, ...   130   Garnesche5   35
Thow claimist the jentyll, thou art a curre;   131   Garnesche5   67
Of jentyll corage the perfight memory;   336   Garlande   860
   perfight] 'profight' †Fakes 1523
Beninge, curteyse, of jentyll harte and mynde, ...   337   Garlande   880
With margerain jentyll, /The flowre of goodlyhede, ...   337   Garlande   906
Jentyll as fawcoun /Or hawke of the towre, ...   341   Garlande   1021
Jentyll as fawcoun /Or hawke of the towre.   341   Garlande   1036
A jentyll hownde shulde never play the kur.   352   Garlande   1436
This jeloffer jentyll, this rose, this lylly flowre, ...   352   Garlande   1446
JENTYLLWOMAN
from an honorable Jentyllwoman for a token, ...   39   Coystrowne3   I
JENTYLMAN
For Jak wold be a jentylman, that late was a grome.   37   Coystrowne1   42
JENTYL MAN
Lo, Jak wold be a jentyl man!   37   Coystrowne1   14
JENTYLNES
Yet jentylnes in the ys thred-bare worne.   131   Garnesche5   70
JENTYLWOMEN
Come forth, jentylwomen, I pray you,' she sayd, ...   334   Garlande   773
JEPERDYS
Though ye suppose all jeperdys ar paste, ...   45   Balettys4   1
JEPTE
Ulula, Esebon, for Jepte is starke ded!   234   Speke Parott   126
JEREBOSETH
Jereboseth is Ebrue, who lyst the cause dyscus.   232   Speke Parott   67
   cause] 'law' Day 1560, Marshe 1568
JEREMY
And some of you shall dye /Lyke holy Jeremy;   276   Collyn Clout   1209
Of Jeremy the whyskynge rod, ...   308   Why Come Ye   1164

JERICO —JOHN   Page   Title   Line

JERICO
For Jerico and Jerssey shall mete togethyr as sone   239   Speke Parott   306
JEROBESETHE
Home to resorte Jerobesethe perswade;   238   Speke Parott   279
JEROME
As Jerome, in his preamble Frater Ambrosius, ...   316   Garlande   162
Saynt Jerome and saynt Austen, ...   381   Replycacion   277
Rede what Jerome there dothe say/   383   Replycacion   328
Of poetes chefe poete, saint Jerome dothe wright, ...   383   Replycacion   330
And saynt Jerome saythe, ...   384   Replycacion   347
JEROMY
Ulula, Esebon, for Jeromy doth wepe!   234   Speke Parott   113
JERSSEY
For Jerico and Jerssey shall mete togethyr as sone   239   Speke Parott   306
JERUSALEM
In Palestina there is Jerusalem.   233   Speke Parott   81
JESABELL
Nother Zorobabell, /Nor cruell Jesabell;   67   Hauke   207
JESSE
It is, by Jesse, ...   167   Magnyfycence   974
JESTE
Wherfore to jeste /Is my delyght   359   Albany   13
JESTES
Why jangle you suche jestes, ...   381   Replycacion   264
JESU
But to swete Jesu /On us then for to rew?   40   Coystrowne3   39
By Jesu Christ, /Fals Scot, thou lyest: 135   Dundas   32
Nowe Jesu preserve you, syr, prynce most of myght.   190   Magnyfycence   1796
With ye, syr, by Jesu, that slayne was with Jewes!   201   Magnyfycence   2167
O mercyfull Jesu, ...   257   Collyn Clout   433
Towarde the porte salue /Of our Savyoure Jesu, ...   278   Collyn Clout   1261
I drede, by swete Jesu, ...   280   Why Come Ye   64
JESUS
Do mi nus, /Helpe nowe swete Jesus!   74   Phy Sparrow   96
JET
Jak wold jet and yet Jyll sayd nay;   37   Coystrowne1   43
Lusty Garnysche, lyke a lowse, ye jet full lyke a jaspe; . . .   123   Garnesche2   17
The courtly gyse of the newe jet?   153   Magnyfycence   453
And jet it joly as a jay.   153   Magnyfycence   465
This newe fonne jet   165   Magnyfycence   877
And yet she wyll jet, /Lyke a joyly fet   215   El Rummynge   51
Another brought her bedes /Of jet or of cole, ...   227   El Rummynge   524
JETRO
Madionita Jetro, our Moyses kepyth his shepe;   234   Speke Parott   115
JETTER
What the devyll! Where had we this joly jetter?   162   Magnyfycence   796
JETTES
Mary, thou jettes it of hyght.   167   Magnyfycence   962
JETTY
Jawed lyke a jetty;   215   El Rummynge   38
JETTYNGE
To jettynge, to jaggynge, and to full of japes, ...   199   Magnyfycence   2097
JEW
Alas, I coude not dele so with a [J]ew.   59   Bowge   462
 a Jew] 'on yew' †Wynkyn de Worde 1499, 'a yew' Wynkyn
 de Worde 1510, Marshe 1568
JEWE
And it were a Jewe, ...   80   Phy Sparrow   335
 were] 'where' †Kele 1545.2
For I may tell you, /I lerned it of a Jewe, ...   219   El Rummynge   208
Turke, Sarazyn or Jewe?   257   Collyn Clout   431
JEWELL
A precyous jewell, no rycher in this londe: 48   Bowge   97
JEWES
With ye, syr, by Jesu, that slayne was with Jewes!   201   Magnyfycence   2167
JHESU
So I beseke Jhesu now to be my gyde.   335   Garlande   835
JHESUS
Jhesus preserve you frome endlesse wo and shame.   214   Magnyfycence   2572
JYLL
Jak wold jet and yet Jyll sayd nay;   37   Coystrowne1   43
JO
King Jamy, Jemmy, Jocky my jo, ...   118   Ag Scottes   91
 jo] 'joye' Kynge & Marche 1554, Day 1560, Marshe 1568
JOBAB
Jobab was brought up in the lande of Hus;   232   Speke Parott   65
 Jobab] 'Iob' Day 1560, Marshe 1568
JOCKY
King Jamy, Jemmy, Jocky my jo, ...   118   Ag Scottes   91
 jo] 'joye' Kynge & Marche 1554, Day 1560, Marshe 1568
JOFORTH
With Colyn Clowt, Johnn Ive, with Joforth Jack;   347   Garlande   1234
JOHAN
To see Johan Dawes, that came but yesterdaye, ...   54   Bowge   301
JOHANNES
Johannes Balua was his name   297   Why Come Ye   726
JOHN
John Jayberd et Adam all a knave, ...   106   Epitaphe   1

JOHNN —JUDICYALL

Entry	Page	Title	Line
A DEVOUTE TRENTALE FOR OLD JOHN CLARKE,	106	Epitaphel	1
John Jayberd, incola de Dis;	108	Epitaphel	57

JOHNN

On Saynt Johnn decollacyon	64	Hauke	100
His hawke then flew uppon /The rode, with Mary and Johnn.	65	Hauke	127
Also Johnn Lydgate	91	Phy Sparrow	804
Tushe! It is Syr Johnn Double-[Cope].	157	Magnyfycence	605
Cope] 'cloke' †Rastell & Treveris C 1530, B			
Cockes bones! This is all of Johnn de Gay.	167	Magnyfycence	960
Yes, by my faythe, good Syr Johnn.	173	Magnyfycence	1186
Lo, Johnn a Bonam, where is thy brayne?	173	Magnyfycence	1204
There came Johnn Bochas with his volumys grete;	322	Garlande	365
Dane Johnn Lydgate. Theis Englysshe poetis thre,	323	Garlande	391
With Colyn Clowt, Johnn Ive, with Joforth Jack;	347	Garlande	1234

JOY

In joy triumphaunt the hevenly *gerarchy,	35	Dol Dethe	211
*gerarchy] 'gerarchy' †MS Royal 18 D.ii, Marshe 1568,			
'yerarchy' Scattergood			
Our welth, our worldly joy,	111	Lawde	49
Your welth, your joy, your sport, your play,	119	Ag Scottes	159
Where drede ledyth the daunce, there is no joy nor blysse.	142	Magnyfycence	76
In joy and myrthe your mynde shalbe inlargyd	146	Magnyfycence	205
Thus joy without mesure you shall have.	190	Magnyfycence	1781
Home to your paleys with joy and ryalte.	214	Magnyfycence	2567
Made lusty sporte and joy	270	Collyn Clout	952
This joy excedith all wordly sport and play,	332	Garlande	716
wordly] 'worldly' Marshe 1568			

JOYE

Thow bringe unto thy joye etermynable	34	Dol Dethe	199
Thow] 'how' †MS Royal 18 D.ii			
Whan she had lost her joye,	74	Phy Sparrow	110
That was all theyr joye,	88	Phy Sparrow	674
Kynge Jamy, Jomy your joye is all go.	113	Scot Kynge	1
My vyolet amyabyll, /My joye inexplicabill,	237	Speke Parott	244
But that he daunced for joye of that gle.	320	Garlande	278

JOYLY

And yet she wyll jet, /Lyke a joyly fet	215	El Rummynge	52

JOYNT

All out of joynt ye jar.	368	Albany	378

JOYNTE

And specyally to redresse that were out of joynte.	208	Magnyfycence	2414

JOYNTED

Gently joynted, /Gresed and anoynted /Up to the knockles:	215	El Rummynge	42

JOYNTES

In all her joyntes about;	226	El Rummynge	485

JOYOUS

Surely I am joyous that ye be myndyd thus;	144	Magnyfycence	156
Englisterd, that joyous it was to beholde.	330	Garlande	663

JOYOUSLY

So joyously, /So maydenly, /So womanly	341	Garlande	1011

JOYOWS

Of Pajauntis that were played in Joyows Garde;	351	Garlande	1383

JOYSE

He lumbryth on a lewde lewte, 'Roty bully joyse',	37	Coystrownel	29

JOLY

Joly Jemmy, ye scornefull Scot,	116	Ag Scottes	49
And jet it joly as a jay.	153	Magnyfycence	465
Rutty bully, joly rutterkyn, heyda!	161	Magnyfycence	747
Howe sayst thou, man? Am not I a joly rutter?	161	Magnyfycence	752
What the devyll! Where had we this joly jetter?	162	Magnyfycence	796
What! Whom have we here, Jenkyn Joly?	166	Magnyfycence	918
His Epitomis of the Myller and his joly Make;	351	Garlande	1411

JOMY

Kynge Jamy, Jomy your joye is all go.	113	Scot Kynge	1

JONE

And than came haltyng Jone	222	El Rummynge	326
Jone sayde she had eten a fyest.	223	El Rummynge	343

JONYS

Of Edyngeborrow and Saynt Jonys towne.	117	Ag Scottes	63

JORGE

That jentyll Jorge the Januay,	130	Garnesche5	35

JOSEPHUS

And of Anteocus, /And of Josephus	90	Phy Sparrow	737

JOSUE

Lyke to Duke Josue /And the valiaunt Machube,	370	Albany	442

JOURNEY

I durse aventure to journey thorugh Fraunce;	57	Bowge	408
In this your journey to prospere and spede.	239	Speke Parott	314

JOVENYANS

Ye soored over hye /In the ierarchy /Of Jovenyans heresy,	378	Replycacion	163

JUDAS

Of Judas Machabeus, /And of Cesar Julious;	88	Phy Sparrow	661
Quod magnus est dominus Judas Scarioth.	234	Speke Parott	133

JUDGE

There is no noble man wil judge in me	138	Ven Tongues	34
And judge it as they wyll, /For other mens skyll,	249	Collyn Clout	98

JUDICYALL

Upon artycles judicyall, /To contende and to stryve	299	Why Come Ye	814

	Page	Title	Line

JUDICUM
Oreb et Zeb, of Judicum rede the boke. . . . . 234 Speke Parott 117

JUDYCYALL
Judycyall rygoure shall not me correcte - . . . . 142 Magnyfycence 69

JUG
Dug, dug, /Jug, jug, /Good yere and good luk, ... 340 Garlande 1001
Dug, dug, /Jug, jug, /Good yere and good luk, ... 340 Garlande 1001

JUGE
That they juge them selfe able to be . . . . 374 Replycacion 7

JUGED
Some juged in this case . . . . 379 Replycacion 197

JUGES
Juges of the kynges lawes, ... 286 Why Come Ye 314

JUGETH
He jugeth it no foly; . . . . 305 Why Come Ye 1047

JUGYTH
He jugyth him equivalent /With God omnipotent. . . . . 307 Why Come Ye 1135
  him] 'hymselfe' MS Rawlinson C. 813;
  equivalent] 'equypolent' Rawlinson C. 813

JUGURTA
That wrote the history of Jugurta also; . . . . 321 Garlande 332

JULIANUS
Apostata Julianus /Nor yet Nestorianus, ... 70 Hauke 297

JULIOUS
Of Judas Machabeus, /And of Cesar Julious; . . . . 88 Phy Sparrow 662

JULIUS
Of Pope Julius cardys, he ys chefe Cardynall. . . . . 243 Speke Parott 431

JULY
Nor Cesar July, that no man myght withstande, ... 181 Magnyfycence 1482

JULLIAN
With, 'Jast you, I say, Jullian! . . . . 285 Why Come Ye 242

JUMBYLL
To jumbyll, to stombyll, to tumbyll down lyke folys; . . . . 243 Speke Parott 425

JUPITER
So Jupiter me socour, ... 94 Phy Sparrow 895
So Jupiter me socoure, ... 97 Phy Sparrow 1024
So Jupiter me succour, ... 98 Phy Sparrow 1056
So Jupiter me socoure, ... 98 Phy Sparrow 1085
So Jupiter me succoure, ... 100 Phy Sparrow 1138
So Jupiter me succour, ... 100 Phy Sparrow 1163
So Jupiter me socoure, ... 101 Phy Sparrow 1187
So Jupiter me succoure, ... 101 Phy Sparrow 1210
So Jupiter me socoure, ... 102 Phy Sparrow 1233
Jupiter hymselfe this lyfe myght endure; . . . . 332 Garlande 715

JUPYTER
To Jupyter pray we . . . . 74 Phy Sparrow 92
To Jupyter I call, /Of heven emperyall, ... 86 Phy Sparrow 596
So Jupyter me socoure, ... 96 Phy Sparrow 991
So Jupyter me socour, ... 99 Phy Sparrow 1109
Jupyter for Saturne darre make no royall chere; . . . . . . 242 Speke Parott 399

JUPPITER
For, by Juppiter and his high mageste, ... 353 Garlande 1488

JURISDICTYON
To a straunge jurisdictyon /Called Dymingis Dale, ... 299 Why Come Ye 800

JURYDICCYON
But I most bannysshe hym frome my jurydiccyon, ... 318 Garlande 227

JURYSDICTYONS
In theyr jurysdictyons, ... 249 Collyn Clout 110

JUST
To kepe just playne songe . . . . 82 Phy Sparrow 427
That she was true and just, ... 90 Phy Sparrow 730
But yf I were orderyd by just measure, ... 147 Magnyfycence 249
Be faythfull, trew and just . . . . 298 Why Come Ye 753
Lyke to Argyva by just resemblaunce, ... 336 Garlande 843

JUSTE
By juste examynacyon /In connynge and conversacyon. . . . . 253 Collyn Clout 266

JUSTICE
Astrea, justice hight, ... 110 Lawde 15

JUSTIFYED
justifyed, and constantly mainteyned; . . . . 374 Replycacion 1

JUSTYCE
All justyce he pretended: . . . . 307 Why Come Ye 1110
Justyce now is dede; 358 Garlande2 1

JUVENALL
Juvenall was thret, parde, for to kyll . . . . 315 Garlande 95
Juvenall satirray, that men makythe to muse; . . . . 321 Garlande 340

JUVINALL
Blame Juvinall, and blame nat me. . . . . 309 Why Come Ye2 8
As Juvinall dothe recorde, ... 310 Why Come Ye2 11

JUVYNALL
As Persius and Juvynall, ... 133 Garnesche5 140

JUVYNALS
I am forcebly constrayned /At Juvynals request . . . . 309 Why Come Ye 1211

KAY
What sholde a man do with you? Loke you under [k]ay? . . . . 180 Magnyfycence 1429
  kay] 'bay' †Rastell & Treveris C 1530, B

KAYES
Of nyghtys to occupy counterfet kayes; . . . . 152 Magnyfycence 425

KAYN —KEPE   Page   Title   Line

KAYN
Lyke that untrue rebell /Fals Kayn agaynst Abell.   121   Ag Scottes2   20
KAYSER
To rule kynge and kayser.   261   Collyn Clout   604
For kynge nor kayser sake, ...   272   Collyn Clout   1017
His countynaunce lyke a kayser.   294   Why Come Ye   624
KALENDAS
On Candelmas evyn, the kalendas of May.   38   Coystrowne1   70
KALKYNS
She kykyth with her kalkyns and keylyth with a clench;   . . .   43   Balettys2   23
KALL
To the for succour, to the for helpe I kall, ...   29   Dol Dethe   12
Hevyn, hell and erth obey unto thi kall;   34   Dol Dethe   192
KAN
Your naturall lord? Alas, I kan not fayne.   30   Dol Dethe   54
From bitter wepinge hym self kan restrayne?   32   Dol Dethe   112
O homycide, whiche sleest all that thou kan, ...   32   Dol Dethe   123
As all his kuntrey kan testefy the same: 33   Dol Dethe   153
Thowthe ye kan skylle of large and longe, ...   129   Garnesche5   3
The starkest knave, and lest good kan, ...   130   Garnesche5   23
KARLIS
Were not thes commones uncurteis karlis of kynd   30   Dol Dethe   34
    not] 'no' †MS Royal 18 D.ii, 'not' Marshe 1568
KARNARVAN
Whan Edwarde of Karnarvan   285   Why Come Ye   270
KAST
All flatringe faytors abhor and from the kast.   34   Dol Dethe   172
KATE
Thyther cometh Kate, ...   217   El Rummynge   118
KATERYNE
'With Kateryne incomporabyll, owur royall quene also, ...   231   Speke Parott   36
KECHYN PAGE
Ye war a kechyn page, /A dyshwasher, a dryvyll, ...   124   Garnesche3   25
KEY
Youre key is mete for every lok, ...   41   Coystrowne4   22
Youre key is commen and hangyth owte;   41   Coystrowne4   23
Youre key is redy, we nede not knok   41   Coystrowne4   24
That wonnes at the Key in Temmys Strete.   41   Coystrowne4   30
KEYE
In myne hostes house called Powers Keye, ...   47   Bowge   35
Whyles of his mynde it were lockte with the keye.   52   Bowge   224
KEYLYTH
She kykyth with her kalkyns and keylyth with a clench;   . . .   43   Balettys2   23
KEKE
Whan the mare doth keke;   225   El Rummynge   450
KEN
Fulfilled with honour, as all the world dothe ken, ...   30   Dol Dethe   30
    world] 'wold' Marshe 1568
Now Phebus me ken /To sharpe my pen, ...   96   Phy Sparrow   970
Us to informe and ken -   143   Magnyfycence   88
Suche ye may well knowe and ken   260   Collyn Clout   533
All that ever they ken   272   Collyn Clout 1053
She to vowchesafe me to informe and ken;   335   Garlande   825
And though Albumasar can the enforme and ken   352   Garlande   1428
KENDALL
Of Kyrkeby Kendall was his shorte demye;   56   Bowge   359
KENE
So tranchaunt and so kene, ...   127   Garnesche3   138
So myche pride of prelattes, so cruell and so kene -   245   Speke Parott   475
She bet up a fyre with the sparkis full kene   330   Garlande   669
KENEL
Then Cerberus the cur couching in the kenel of hel;   140   Ven Tongues   80
KENT
From Stroude to Kent, ...   167   Magnyfycence   982
From Croydon into Kent   282   Why Come Ye   145
    into] 'to' Toy 1553, Kitson 1560.7, Marshe 1568
Yet they ryde and rinne from Carlyll to Kent.   317   Garlande   196
    they ryde and rinne] 'ryde they and ryn they' MS Cotton
    Vitellius E.x
Of the Mayden of Kent callid Counforte, ...   354   Garlande   1495
KENTE
'Nowe have at all, by Saynte Thomas of Kente!'   56   Bowge   348
From Calys to Dovyr, to Caunterbury in Kente, ...   240   Speke Parott   340
KEPE
Of foule detraccion God kepe the from the blast.   34   Dol Dethe   173
That of hys love he toke no kepe, ...   41   Balettys1   7
For oure fals poynt she is wont to kepe in store, ...   45   Balettys4   4
To kepe it hymselfe; for than he myghte be sure   52   Bowge   222
To kepe him frome pykynge, it was a grete payne.   52   Bowge   236
And thus with us good company to kepe.   57   Bowge   385
With moch matter more, /That I kepe in store.   67   Hauke   221
Of God nothynge els crave I /But Phyllypes soule to kepe . . .   73   Phy Sparrow   68
For to kepe his cut, ...   74   Phy Sparrow   118
With, 'Phyllyp, kepe your cut!'   74   Phy Sparrow   119
To kepe just playne songe   82   Phy Sparrow   427
That I kepe in store.   126   Garnesche3   77
And that he take good kepe to Lyberte.   149   Magnyfycence   320
I pray God kepe you in that mood!   150   Magnyfycence   336

KEPEST —KYKYTH   Page   Title   Line

	Page	Title	Line
Tushe, man! I kepe some Latyn in store.	172	Magnyfycence	1145
It forseth not of reason, so it kepe ryme,	172	Magnyfycence	1150
Cockes armes! Thou shalte kepe the brewhouse boule.	176	Magnyfycence	1321
Why, wene you that I can kepe hym longe styll?	179	Magnyfycence	1412
They catche that catche may, kepe and holde fast,	189	Magnyfycence	1750
And kepe you from counterfaytynge of clokyd colusyon.	210	Magnyfycence	2453
In Achademia Parrot dare no probleme kepe,	235	Speke Parott	162
Small housholdes woll kepe,	249	Collyn Clout	123
To wary and to kepe /From theyr goostly shepe,	250	Collyn Clout	154
For to kepe a cure,	253	Collyn Clout	279
To kepe so harde a rule,	254	Collyn Clout	307
'They can nat kepe theyr wyves	261	Collyn Clout	572
Therfore ye kepe them base,	262	Collyn Clout	624
That ye kepe them so under;	271	Collyn Clout	1007
ye] 'we' Kele 1545.1, 'ye' MS Harley 2252			
Where these kepe residence,	279	Why Come Ye	11
They kepe them in theyr holdes	283	Why Come Ye	167
To kepe his flesshe chast	284	Why Come Ye	219
Christ kepe King Henry the Eyght	298	Why Come Ye	772
To kepe his court provyncyall	299	Why Come Ye	813
To kepe you from laughynge	299	Why Come Ye	829
So close to kepe your cloyster virgynall,	320	Garlande	305
Well gydyng ther glowtonn to kepe streit theyr sylk,	334	Garlande	795
ther] 'the' MS Cotton Vitellius E.x			
And takith no kepe;	358	Garlande2	5
takith] 'bidythe' Marshe 1568			
Twyt, Scot, go kepe thy den.	362	Albany	145
Youre carkas to kepe, /Lyke a sely shepe,	365	Albany	273
KEPEST			
But I say, kepest thou the olde name styll that thou had?	155	Magnyfycence	516
KEPETH			
Where measure is absent, ryot kepeth resydence;	144	Magnyfycence	123
He kepeth them in subjectyon.	304	Why Come Ye	1010
KEPYNGE			
With me in kepynge suche a Phylyp Sparowe.	184	Magnyfycence	1562
KEPYTH			
Madionita Jetro, our Moyses kepyth his shepe;	234	Speke Parott	115
KEPT			
How the Temple was kept,	66	Hauke	168
And with a dragon kept	104	Phy Sparrow	1303
Yet lyberte hath ben lockyd up and kept in the mew.	141	Magnyfycence	35
I have not kept her yet thre wokys,	168	Magnyfycence	1002
KEPTE			
Why kepte you it thus longe? Howe dothe he? Wele?	149	Magnyfycence	314
And with a dragon kepte	349	Garlande	1296
KEST			
Unneth I kest myne eyes	72	Phy Sparrow	37
I kest downe that there was,	77	Phy Sparrow	230
With that on me she kest her goodly loke.	327	Garlande	531
KESTERYLL			
What hast thou on thy fyst? A [k]esteryll?	173	Magnyfycence	1174
kesteryll] 'besteryll' †Rastell & Treveris C 1530, B			
KESTRELL			
The kestrell in all this warke	86	Phy Sparrow	569
KETERYNG			
Lyke a Scottyshe keteryng	365	Albany	248
KETERYNGES			
To angre the Scottes and Irysh keterynges withall,	117	Ag Scottes	83
KING			
Of this our noble king	111	Lawde	29
Our king, our emperour,	111	Lawde	47
As king moost sovereine	111	Lawde	52
King Jamy, Jemmy, Jocky my jo,	118	Ag Scottes	91
jo] 'joye' Kynge & Marche 1554, Day 1560, Marshe 1568			
Wrought to Charlemayn the king,	296	Why Come Ye	701
Christ kepe King Henry the Eyght	298	Why Come Ye	772
KINGE			
And as the lyonne whiche is of bestis kinge	33	Dol Dethe	167
KINGES			
Of ix kinges realmys,	303	Why Come Ye	958
realmys] 'realme' Marshe 1568			
KINGIS			
Agayne the kingis plesure to wrastel or to wringe.	31	Dol Dethe	82
Paregall to dukis, withe kingis he myght compare,	33	Dol Dethe	134
All kingis, all princis, all dukis, well thei ought	34	Dol Dethe	180
Of kingis line moost streight,	110	Lawde	10
KIS			
The devill kis his culum!	108	Epitaphel	79
KIT			
Thow kit asonder his perfight vitall threde.	32	Dol Dethe	126
KYBE			
She halted of a kybe,	227	El Rummynge	493
KYBY			
And 'He haltith often that hath a kyby hele.'	326	Garlande	502
KYCKE			
They make her wynche and kycke,	251	Collyn Clout	181
KYKYTH			
She kykyth with her kalkyns and keylyth with a clench;	43	Balettys2	23

KYLL —KYNG   Page   Title   Line

KYLL
Agayne me for to kyll!   77   Phy Sparrow   223
So trayterously my byrde to kyll   79   Phy Sparrow   322
What avayleth lordshype, yourselfe for to kyll   148   Magnyfycence   286
Some I make lame, and some I do kyll, ...   194   Magnyfycence   1931
Juvenall was thret, parde, for to kyll   315   Garlande   95
That no man hym kyll;   365   Albany   264
KYND
Were not thes commones uncurteis karlis of kynd   30   Dol Dethe   34
  not] 'no' †MS Royal 18 D.ii, 'not' Marshe 1568
All maner of byrdes in your kynd;   81   Phy Sparrow   388
Yet wryteth he in his kynd, ...   91   Phy Sparrow   808
KYNDE
She promysed to us all she wolde be kynde;   49   Bowge   124
Any of my sparowes kynde, ...   78   Phy Sparrow   261
O cat of carlyshe kynde, ...   78   Phy Sparrow   282
  carlyshe] 'churlyshe' Kitson 1560.6, Marshe 1568
Of this phenyx kynde;   85   Phy Sparrow   539
And grow all oute of kynde, ...   126   Garnesche3   102
It is so swete in all maner of kynde.   142   Magnyfycence   51
What ellys? For otherwyse it were agaynst kynde;   144   Magnyfycence   132
A man shall fynde /Many of her kynde, ...   167   Magnyfycence   984
That every man almost groweth out of kynde.   175   Magnyfycence   1285
For welth without largesse is all out of kynde.   180   Magnyfycence   1441
A knave and a carle and all of one kynde?   191   Magnyfycence   1820
Thyselfe that thou wolde sloo agaynst nature and kynde. . .   206   Magnyfycence   2326
Be gentyll, then, of corage, and lerne to be kynde;   211   Magnyfycence   2486
By Nature devysed of a wonderowus kynde, ...   231   Speke Parott   2
Some be to churlysshe, and some be to kynde.   233   Speke Parott   77
Barkyng and whyning lyke churlysshe currys of kynde, . . .   239   Speke Parott   295
Ye growe nowe out of kynde.   263   Collyn Clout   661
How noble and how kynde   291   Why Come Ye   500
Fals flaterers that fawne the, and kurris of kynde   329   Garlande   619
All frutis and flowris grew there in there kynde.   331   Garlande   678
  and] not in †Fakes 1523
So corteise, so kynde   341   Garlande   1033
That goodly place to Skelton moost kynde, ...   353   Garlande   1462
They fynde his grace so kynde;   371   Albany   483
KYNDELDE
Whiche kyndelde the wyld fyre that made all this smoke. . . .   31   Dol Dethe   77
KYNDELL
Of all lewdnesse I kyndell the brande.   152   Magnyfycence   437
I kyndell in her suche a lyther sparke   174   Magnyfycence   1231
KYNDLE
Kyndle in me suche plente of thy nobles, ...   29   Dol Dethe   20
KYNDLED
We are kyndled in suche facyon   385   Replycacion   382
KYNDNES
But if I sholde aquyte your kyndnes, ...   342   Garlande   1062
KYNDNESSE
Counterfet kyndnesse, and thynke dyscayte;   152   Magnyfycence   438
For many tymes moche kyndnesse is denyed   177   Magnyfycence   1338
KYNG
Though his father were a kyng;   89   Phy Sparrow   698
Of Kyng Alexander; /And of Kyng Evander   90   Phy Sparrow   745
Of Kyng Alexander; /And of Kyng Evander   90   Phy Sparrow   746
In the name of Kyng Saul;   105   Phy Sparrow   1343
A Lawde And Prayse Made for Our Sovereigne Lord the Kyng . .   110   Lawde   I
Unto our prince, anoynted kyng.   117   Ag Scottes   58
Ye summond our kyng, why dyd ye so?   118   Ag Scottes   92
  ye] not in Kynge & Marche 1554, Day 1560, Marshe 1568
To summon our kyng, your soveraygne lorde.   118   Ag Scottes   94
A kyng, a sumner! It was great wonder: 118   Ag Scottes   95
Frenche kyng, or one or other;   118   Ag Scottes   105
Anoynted kyng, and ye were none.   118   Ag Scottes   118
With our kyng royall war to mayntayne.   119   Ag Scottes   152
That he is kyng without a reme;   119   Ag Scottes   156
Now from a kyng to a clot of clay.   119   Ag Scottes   165
Brother unnaturall /Unto our kyng royall, ...   120   Ag Scottes2   16
And for he was a kyng, /The more shamefull rekenyng . . .   121   Ag Scottes2   31
He skantly loveth our kyng, /That grudgeth at this thing: 121   Ag Scottes2   35
'Cryste save Herry the viiith, owur royall kyng, ...   231   Speke Parott   34
'Cryste save Kyng Herry the viiith, owur royall kyng, . . .   231   Speke Parott   34
He caryeth a kyng in hys sleve, yf all the worlde fayle;   243   Speke Parott   429
So royall a kyng, as reynythe uppon us all --   245   Speke Parott   468
He bereth the kyng on hand   290   Why Come Ye   452
By Lewes the kyng aforesayd, ...   297   Why Come Ye   730
To Fraunces the French kyng   299   Why Come Ye   791
As dame Thamarys, whiche toke the kyng of Perce, ...   336   Garlande   857
Now Henry the viij, Kyng of Englonde, ...   347   Garlande   1227
To be our kyng, of God preordinate.   347   Garlande   1232
In the name of Kyng Saull;   350   Garlande   1336
The yonge Scottyshe kyng, ...   361   Albany   90
With the Frenche kyng   361   Albany   103
But our royall kyng   361   Albany   107
Bothe Kyng Fraunces and the, ...   361   Albany   113
Our royall kyng to make   367   Albany   327
Ye meane Fraunces, French kyng, ...   367   Albany   334

KYNGE —KYNGES

	Page	Title	Line
Our kyng out of his reme?	368	Albany	381
With fonde Fraunces, French kyng.	368	Albany	383
Our kyng for to dryve out	368	Albany	392
In spyght of kyng Fraunces,	369	Albany	409
Our kyng most excellent.	369	Albany	429
Davyd, that royall kyng,	383	Replycacion	317
Kyng David the prophete, of prophetes principall,	383	Replycacion	329
Than, if this noble kyng,	384	Replycacion	343

KYNGE

	Page	Title	Line
Of them demaunded and asked by the kynge;	31	Dol Dethe	79
Of Kynge Cresus golde,	76	Phy Sparrow	190
Kynge Phylyp of Macedony	78	Phy Sparrow	270
Of Trystram, and Kynge Marke,	87	Phy Sparrow	641
A Ballade of the Scottysshe Kynge	113	Scot Kynge	I
Kynge Jamy, Jomy your joye is all go.	113	Scot Kynge	1
Ye summoned our kynge. Why dyde ye so?	113	Scot Kynge	2
To sommon our kynge your soverayne lorde.	113	Scot Kynge	4
A kynge a somner it is wonder;	113	Scot Kynge	5
Before the Frensshe kynge, Danes and other	114	Scot Kynge	15
For your kynge may synge welawaye.	114	Scot Kynge	20
Now must ye knowe our kynge for your regent,	114	Scot Kynge	21
A kynge anoynted, and ye be non.	114	Scot Kynge	26
Our kynge than beynge out of the waye;	114	Scot Kynge	45
Warre with our kynge to meyntayne.	114	Scot Kynge	55
Of the kynge of Naverne ye may take hede	115	Scot Kynge	56
That is a kynge without a realme.	115	Scot Kynge	59
God save kynge Henry and his lordes all	115	Scot Kynge	72
And sende the Frensshe kynge suche another fall.	115	Scot Kynge	73
and God save noble Kynge Henry the viij.	115	Scot Kynge	E
Wan they the felde and lost theyr kynge?	115	Ag Scottes	3
That was theyr owne kynge. /Fy on that wynnyng!	116	Ag Scottes	23
Our kynge of England for to syght,	117	Ag Scottes	53
syght] 'fight' Day 1560, Marshe 1568			
In comparyson but kynge Koppynge	117	Ag Scottes	57
Of the prowde Scot, kynge Jemmy,	117	Ag Scottes	71
Of the kynge of Naverne ye might take heed,	119	Ag Scottes	153
Gret daunger for the kynge,	126	Garnesche3	82
A kynge to me myn habyte gave	131	Garnesche5	80
I reporte me herein to Kynge Lewes of Fraunce.	148	Magnyfycence	280
For be he cayser or be he kynge,	174	Magnyfycence	1214
Alexander, of Macedony kynge,	181	Magnyfycence	1466
I plucke downe kynge, prynce, lorde, and knyght;	193	Magnyfycence	1883
To rule kynge and kayser	261	Collyn Clout	604
For one man to rule a kynge]	271	Collyn Clout	989
kynge] 'gyng' Kele 1545.1, 'kyng' MS Harley 2252			
For kynge nor kayser sake,	272	Collyn Clout	1017
What say ye of the Scottysh kynge?	287	Why Come Ye	346
I pray God save the kynge.	289	Why Come Ye	393
In exemplyfyenge /Great Alexander the kynge,	292	Why Come Ye	544
That perteyneth to a kynge,	293	Why Come Ye	550
He made a kynge royall,	293	Why Come Ye	558
A kynge, as I have tolde,	293	Why Come Ye	563
He sayth the kynge doth wryte,	296	Why Come Ye	678
The kynge his clemency	296	Why Come Ye	681
Maketh remembraunce /How Kynge Lewes of late	297	Why Come Ye	722
To our most royall kynge,	298	Why Come Ye	754
Moche money of the kynge	309	Why Come Ye	1192
The noble wyfe of Polimites kynge;	336	Garlande	844
From Kynge Fraunces of Frauns.	363	Albany	175

KYNGES

	Page	Title	Line
Of princes and of kynges	93	Phy Sparrow	867
A somner to were a kynges crowne.	115	Scot Kynge	67
A sumner to were a kynges crowne.	120	Ag Scottes	175
oratour to the kynges most royall estate.	120	Ag Scottes	E
Rudely revilyng me in the kynges noble hall,	121	Garnesche1	2
So curryshly to beknave me in the kynges place?	121	Garnesche1	9
Be the kynges most noble commandement.	122	Garnesche1	E
Ye hobble very homly before the kynges borde;	123	Garnesche2	10
By the kynges most noble commaundment.	124	Garnesche2	E
The kynges colours to threte.	127	Garnesche3	141
By the kynges most noble commaundment.	129	Garnesche3	E
But for to serve the kynges entent,	134	Garnesche5	177
Of the kynges halles,	249	Collyn Clout	127
The Kynges Benche or Marshalsy,	275	Collyn Clout	1171
Juges of the kynges lawes,	286	Why Come Ye	314
Or at the Kynges Benche.	287	Why Come Ye	320
Under the kynges brode seale;	287	Why Come Ye	337
To whyche court? /To the kynges courte?	289	Why Come Ye	403
Nay, to the kynges court!	289	Why Come Ye	405
The kynges courte /Shulde have the excellence;	289	Why Come Ye	406
Or to the Kynges Benche!'	290	Why Come Ye	433
That the kynges mynde	290	Why Come Ye	439
Suche is a kynges power	293	Why Come Ye	565
This daungerous dowsypere /Lyke a kynges pere!	295	Why Come Ye	640
That the kynges grace	295	Why Come Ye	658
For he is the kynges derlyng	295	Why Come Ye	666
For the kynges letter?	295	Why Come Ye	670
The kynges owne hande,	296	Why Come Ye	676

KYNGYS —KNAVE

	Page	Title	Line
The kynges Frenshe secretary	298	Why Come Ye	788
Under the protectyon /Of the kynges great seale,	307	Why Come Ye	1129
great] 'brode' MS Rawlinson C. 813			

KYNGYS
By the kyngys most noble commandemennt.	134	Garnesche5	E

KYNNE
Where is nowe my kynne, my frendys, and my noble blood?	198	Magnyfycence	2060
Tyll, as ye se many tymes, they shame all theyr kynne.	201	Magnyfycence	2144

KYRY
To postell upon a kyry,	265	Collyn Clout	753

KYRKEBY
Of Kyrkeby Kendall was his shorte demye;	56	Bowge	359

KYRTELL
Her kyrtell so goodly lased,	101	Phy Sparrow	1194
Her kyrtell Brystowe red,	216	El Rummynge	70
Than Margery Mylkeducke /Her kyrtell she dyd uptucke	225	El Rummynge	419

KYRTELLES
Wyth theyr heles dagged, /Theyr kyrtelles all to-jagged,	217	El Rummynge	124

KYS
And now must kys the post;	89	Phy Sparrow	716
So I wolde clepe her! So I wolde kys her swete!	190	Magnyfycence	1802
Whan we kys and play /In lust and in lykyng.	220	El Rummynge	221

KYSE
Yower lothesum lypps love well to kyse,	130	Garnesche5	44

KYSSE
Her sugred mouth to kysse.	97	Phy Sparrow	1040
The devyll kysse his cule!	282	Why Come Ye	133
his] 'hes' †Kele 1545.3			
The devyll kysse his arse!	282	Why Come Ye	136

KYSSYD
I kyst her swete, and she kyssyd me;	198	Magnyfycence	2065

KYST
That halsyd her hartely and kyst her swete.	42	Balettys1	18
And ever he threwe, and kyst I wote nere what;	56	Bowge	349
When ye kyst a shepys ie,	125	Garnesche3	54
I wolde ye had kyst hyr on the tayle!	130	Garnesche5	46
Then fare well thryfte, by hym that crosse kyst!	179	Magnyfycence	1416
I kyst her swete, and she kyssyd me;	198	Magnyfycence	2065

KYSTE
She kyste an anker, and there she laye at rode,	47	Bowge	39
kyste] 'keste' Wynkyn de Worde 1510, 'kast' Marshe 1568			
And as I stode and kyste asyde my syghte,	58	Bowge	418
kyste] 'caste' Marshe 1568			

KYT
Xall kyt both wyght and grene:	127	Garnesche3	139
Ye kyt your clothe to large,	129	Garnesche3	189
Than sterte in made Kyt, /That had lytell wyt?	224	El Rummynge	412

KYTE
The crowe and the kyte;	82	Phy Sparrow	413
As fayre and as whyte /As the fote of a kyte.	225	El Rummynge	425

KYTHYD
What, have ye kythyd yow a knyght, Syr Dugles the dowty,	121	Garnesche1	8

KYTTEN
Some be flybytten, /Some skewed as a kytten;	218	El Rummynge	142

KLYCKED GATE
How ofte he knocked at her klycked gate.	56	Bowge	371

KNACKYNGE
Ye, to knackynge ernyst what and it preve?	141	Magnyfycence	33

KNAK
Curyowsly he can both counter and knak	37	Coystrowne1	17

KNAKKES
Yet some folys say ye arre furnysshyd with knakkes,	239	Speke Parott	292

KNAPPISHE
Than ye be a knappishe sorte	370	Albany	475

KNAVATE
Fratres, orate, /For this knavate,	108	Epitaphe1	65

KNAVE
Syr, pardone me, I am an homely knave	53	Bowge	264
Trowest thou, drevyll, I saye, thou gawdy knave,	55	Bowge	337
Gone is this knave, this rybaude foule and leude.	58	Bowge	414
It is grete scorne to se a mysproude knave	59	Bowge	453
A flaterynge knave and false he is, God wote.	59	Bowge	485
Qui iacet hic, like a knave!	109	Epitaphe2	26
In your chalenge, Syr Chystyn, to cale me knave?	121	Garnesche1	7
In yor chalenge, Syr Chesten, to calle me a knave?	122	Garnesche1	14
In yor chalenge, Syr Chesten, to cal me a knave?	122	Garnesche1	21
In yor chalenge, Syr Chesten, to calle me a knave?	122	Garnesche1	28
In yor chalenge, Syr Chesten, to calle me a knave?	122	Garnesche1	35
Chalenge yor selfe for a fole, call me no more knave.	122	Garnesche1	42
So for a knave to clatyr;	126	Garnesche3	107
Wyth, 'Knave, syr, knave, and knave agenne',	130	Garnesche5	19
Wyth, 'Knave, syr, knave, and knave agenne',	130	Garnesche5	19
Wyth, 'Knave, syr, knave, and knave agenne',	130	Garnesche5	19
To cal me knave thou takyst gret payne.	130	Garnesche5	20
The prowdyst knave yet of us tewyne	130	Garnesche5	21
The starkest knave, and lest good kan,	130	Garnesche5	23
It ys for no bawdy knave	132	Garnesche5	114
It ys nat mete for soche a knave.	133	Garnesche5	156

	Page	Title	Line
KNAVERY —KNYGHT			
I cannat let the the knave to play,	134	Garnesche5	169
Dundas, sir knave,	136	Dundas	42
A knave wyll counterfet nowe a knyght,	152	Magnyfycence	417
Ye, thou haste the four quarters of a knave.	172	Magnyfycence	1165
The knave wolde make it koy, and he cowde;	175	Magnyfycence	1246
Howe be it, that fonde felowe is a mery knave.	180	Magnyfycence	1455
Tyll I be revenged on that horson knave.	185	Magnyfycence	1616
Is there no horson that knave that wyll bete?'	185	Magnyfycence	1618
A knave and a carle and all of one kynde?	191	Magnyfycence	1820
By Cockes harte, thou arte a fyne mery knave.	191	Magnyfycence	1826
And spende C s. for the pleasure of a knave.	200	Magnyfycence	2126
Nay, by Saynt Mary, it was ye called me knave.	203	Magnyfycence	2212
In faythe, I gyve the four quarters of a knave.	204	Magnyfycence	2252
A knyght a knave ye make.	261	Collyn Clout	601
ye] 'to' Kele 1545.1, Marshe 1568, 'ye' MS Harley 2252			
Of one Adame all a knave, late dede and gone -	347	Garlande	1247
KNAVERY			
Yower knavery I wyll nat hyde,	124	Garnesche3	22
KNAVES			
Of two knaves somtyme of Dis.	106	Epitaphe	I
Though this knaves be deade,	106	Epitaphe	I
A counterfet courtyer with a knaves marke.	154	Magnyfycence	486
And cals them cankerd knaves.	287	Why Come Ye	335
Ye knaves, ye churles sonnys,	294	Why Come Ye	603
Whan ye cankerd knaves	363	Albany	184
KNAVIS			
Than a chyldis birde and a knavis wyfe?	352	Garlande	1452
KNAVYCHE			
Ye have knavyche condycyonns.	124	Garnesche3	12
KNAVYS			
Ful of greet knavys tethe,	127	Garnesche3	126
Of all prowde knavys thow beryst the belle,	130	Garnesche5	27
And ye be a gentylman, ye have knavys condycyons.	203	Magnyfycence	2219
KNAVYSCHE			
Ye had a knavysche cote	125	Garnesche3	44
KNAVYSSHE			
Of a lether bottell /With a knavysshe stoppell,	262	Collyn Clout	651
KNE			
He dyd nothynge, perde, /But syt upon my kne.	76	Phy Sparrow	172
That for your sake I wyll fall on my kne.	186	Magnyfycence	1630
Yet ones agayne I shall fall on my kne	188	Magnyfycence	1708
I daunsed the darlynge on my kne;	198	Magnyfycence	2066
An ynche above her kne,	225	El Rummynge	420
And breke theyr hose at the kne,	262	Collyn Clout	629
And maketh them to bow theyr kne /Before his majeste.	286	Why Come Ye	312
maketh them] 'make' Toy 1553, Kitson 1560.7, Marshe 1568			
KNEE			
Yet at the knee they were broken, I wene.	56	Bowge	357
KNEES			
On knees to fall /To the foteball;	108	Epitaphe1	71
KNELE			
To lowre, to droupe, to knele, to stowpe and to play cowche-quale;	243	Speke Parott	426
Lordes must crouche and knele,	262	Collyn Clout	628
crouche] 'couch' Marshe 1568, 'cruche' MS Harley 2252			
KNEW			
Yet long tyme she ne knew	89	Phy Sparrow	727
And you knew all ye would be ill apayd'.	139	Ven Tongues	72
He said he knew what was what.	306	Why Come Ye	1109
KNEWE			
But if that I knewe what his name hight,	139	Ven Tongues	73
And yf ye knewe howe I have mused,	156	Magnyfycence	580
Mary, I knewe the when thou waste a ladde.	170	Magnyfycence	1089
He knewe not hymselfe, his harte was so hye;	193	Magnyfycence	1888
KNIGHT			
Both lorde and knight to face;	111	Lawde	39
And Martis lusty knight;	112	Lawde	55
Adue, cowarde, adue! /Fals knight and mooste untrue,	366	Albany	315
KNIGHTES			
With his knightes commendable,	87	Phy Sparrow	635
KNIGHTHODE			
Of knighthode the floure	365	Albany	239
KNIGHTIS			
Barons, knightis, squyers, one and alle,	31	Dol Dethe	92
Of knightis, of squyers, chef lord of toure and toune,	33	Dol Dethe	132
More specially barons, and thos knightis bold,	34	Dol Dethe	183
KNIGHTLY			
Of knightly prowes the sworde, pomel, and hilt,	32	Dol Dethe	108
KNYFE			
I saw a knyfe hyd in his one sleve,	58	Bowge	433
To drowne or to sle themselfe with a knyfe -	194	Magnyfycence	1914
Or ellys with this knyfe cut out a tonge	206	Magnyfycence	2314
Lo, here is thy knyfe and a halter, and or we go ferther,	206	Magnyfycence	2317
In styckynge my selfe with this fayre knyfe.	206	Magnyfycence	2322
Here MAGNYFYCENCE wolde slee hymselfe with a knyfe.	206	Magnyfycence	SD
KNYGHT			
So noble a man, so valiaunt lorde and knyght	30	Dol Dethe	29
The nobelnes of the northe, this valyant lorde and knyght,	31	Dol Dethe	85

KNYGHTIS —KNOWE

	Page	Title	Line
And have forgoten your old, trew, lovyng knyght.	42	Balettys2	14
Thys grevyth your husband, that ryght jentyll knyght,	43	Balettys2	27
And made her husband knyght /Of the comyne hall,	87	Phy Sparrow	646
And swete Saynt George, our ladyes knyght!	119	Ag Scottes	141
He was a recrayed knyght,	121	Ag Scottes2	26
What, have ye kythyd yow a knyght, Syr Dugles the dowty,	121	Garnesche1	8
Of soche a gresy knyght?	125	Garnesche3	35
Thou hast in despite, /Thou donghyll knyght?	136	Dundas	48
A knave wyll counterfet nowe a knyght,	152	Magnyfycence	417
And I am made a knyght.	155	Magnyfycence	521
I plucke downe kynge, prynce, lorde, and knyght;	193	Magnyfycence	1883
A knyght a knave ye make.	261	Collyn Clout	601
ye] 'to' Kele 1545.1, Marshe 1568, 'ye' MS Harley 2252			
Squyre, knyght and lorde	271	Collyn Clout	980
Whether he be knyght or squyre,	287	Why Come Ye	344
With a poore knyght, /Whatsoever he hyght!	295	Why Come Ye	645
My lorde now and syr knyght,	302	Why Come Ye	915
now] not in MS Rawlinson C. 813			
Extorcyon is counted with you for a knyght;	317	Garlande	194
To maystres Isabell Knyght	342	Garlande	R
And cowde not wryght /Of Isabell Knyght.	342	Garlande	1067
lyke a cowarde knyght, ran awaye shamfully	359	Albany	I
Of this cowarde knyght,	359	Albany	15
That valiaunt knyght, /Putte you to flyght /By his valyaunce.	360	Albany	40
Lyke a cowarde knyght	360	Albany	69
By suche a cowarde knyght,	363	Albany	166
And an untrewe knyght.	364	Albany	229
Lyke a cowarde knyght.	366	Albany	313

KNYGHTIS

	Page	Title	Line
Knyghtis and squyers, at every season when	30	Dol Dethe	32

KNYT

	Page	Title	Line
I knyt togyther many a broken threde.	177	Magnyfycence	1343
With botches and carbuckyls in care I them knyt;	194	Magnyfycence	1902
Whereto were most metely my corage to knyt?	211	Magnyfycence	2479
With a whym-wham /Knyt with a trym-tram	216	El Rummynge	76

KNYTHE

	Page	Title	Line
Thanked be saynte Gorge, our ladyes knythe,	114	Scot Kynge	42

KNYTTE

	Page	Title	Line
To be knytte up with knottes	362	Albany	122

KNOCK

	Page	Title	Line
Shet were the gatis; thei might wel knock and cal,	329	Garlande	604

KNOCKED

	Page	Title	Line
How ofte he knocked at her klycked gate.	56	Bowge	371

KNOCKLES

	Page	Title	Line
Gently joynted, /Gresed and anoynted /Up to the knockles:	215	El Rummynge	44

KNOK

	Page	Title	Line
Youre key is redy, we nede not knok	41	Coystrowne4	24

KNOKYLBONYARDE

	Page	Title	Line
A knokylbonyarde wyll counterfet a clarke;	153	Magnyfycence	480

KNOLEGE

	Page	Title	Line
Knolege, aquayntance, resort, favour, with grace;	43	Balettys3	1

KNOTTES

	Page	Title	Line
To be knytte up with knottes	362	Albany	122

KNOULEGE

	Page	Title	Line
Bot by them to knoulege ye may attayne	32	Dol Dethe	129

KNOUTE

	Page	Title	Line
The [kn]oute and the [r]owgh;	83	Phy Sparrow	449
knout] 'route' †Kele 1545.2, Wyght 1553, Kitson 1560.6, Marshe 1568; rowgh] 'kowgh' †Kele, Wyght, Kitson, Marshe			

KNOW

	Page	Title	Line
And if ye lyst to know the cause why so,	44	Balettys3	38
Of the whych proces /Ye may know more expres,	68	Hauke	232
And wyll not know /Theyr overthrow /At Branxton More?	115	Ag Scottes	9
Know ye not suger and salt asonder?	118	Ag Scottes	96
Haroldis they know thy cote-armur;	131	Garnesche5	68
To know thy selfe yf thow lake grace,	132	Garnesche5	126
And wenyst thow that I know not the, cankard Abusyon?	161	Magnyfycence	757
Nay, I know well inough ye are bothe well handyd	203	Magnyfycence	2230
Yow to remorde erste or they know your mynde.	241	Speke Parott	370
As I know aparte	264	Collyn Clout	729
To know God nor man.	283	Why Come Ye	183
And graunt him grace to know	298	Why Come Ye	774
Or elles, ye know well, I can do no lesse	318	Garlande	226
My name, I know well, beyonde that I am able,	324	Garlande	438
His name for to know if that ye lyst,	333	Garlande	752
I you assure, /Ful wel I know	338	Garlande	927
Whiche in your recordes, I know well, be enrolde,	344	Garlande	1140
Than ye know what betokeneth dulia:	382	Replycacion	288

KNOWE

	Page	Title	Line
For, and I knowe ony erthly thynge	54	Bowge	277
What weneste I were? I trowe thou knowe not me.	55	Bowge	331
I knowe your vertu and your lytterkture	59	Bowge	449
lytterkture] 'lytterature' Wynkyn de Worde 1510			
Knowe ye not salte and suger asonder?	113	Scot Kynge	6
Now must ye knowe our kynge for your regent,	114	Scot Kynge	21
Who lyst to knowe, Magnyfycence I hyght.	145	Magnyfycence	164
But nowe let me knowe of your conversacyon.	145	Magnyfycence	170
Wherin it is necessary my pleasure you knowe:	145	Magnyfycence	185

	Page	Title	Line

KNOWEN —KUR

```
But yf I coulde knowe a gose from a swanne. . . . . . . . . . .   148   Magnyfycence    299
Whylest I knowe that this letter dothe contayne. . . . . . .     149   Magnyfycence    324
And Crafty Conveyaunce, knowe you not hym? . . . . . . . . .     156   Magnyfycence    584
Knowe hym, syr, quod he. Yes, by Saynt Sym! . . . . . . . . .    156   Magnyfycence    585
For to knowe your name? . . . . . . . . . . . . . . . . . . .    157   Magnyfycence    592
Knowe they not me? They are to blame. . . . . . . . . . . . .    157   Magnyfycence    593
Knowe you not me, syrs? No, in dede. . . . . . . . . . . . .     157   Magnyfycence    594
What! Wenyst thou that I knowe the not, Clokyd Colusyon? . . .   161   Magnyfycence    756
For thou shalt well knowe I am nother durty nor dusty. . . . .   161   Magnyfycence    759
I knowe in hym no defaute . . . . . . . . . . . . . . . . . .    163   Magnyfycence    823
As here after thou shalte knowe more. . . . . . . . . . . . .    167   Magnyfycence    953
For I knowe dyverse that useth the same. . . . . . . . . . .     175   Magnyfycence   1255
So that there knowe no man but I and she. . . . . . . . . . .    177   Magnyfycence   1353
Mesure, ye knowe wel, with hym I can not be content; . . . .     186   Magnyfycence   1656
That he knowe not but that I have supplyed . . . . . . . . .     187   Magnyfycence   1663
When ye knowe that I knowe, ye wyll not be glad. . . . . . .     192   Magnyfycence   1844
When ye knowe that I knowe, ye wyll not be glad. . . . . . .     192   Magnyfycence   1844
And knowe your selfe mortal for all your dygnyte; . . . . . .    211   Magnyfycence   2499
Suche ye may well knowe and ken . . . . . . . . . . . . . . .    260   Collyn Clout    533
Wyll knowe a raven from a rayle, . . . . . . . . . . . . . .     268   Collyn Clout    869
Ye knowe better than I. . . . . . . . . . . . . . . . . . . .    273   Collyn Clout   1064
Wyll knowe none intellygence . . . . . . . . . . . . . . . .     275   Collyn Clout   1137
```
KNOWEN
```
Yet have I knowen suche er this; . . . . . . . . . . . . . .      46   Bowge            25
For Counterfet Countenaunce knowen am I. . . . . . . . . . .     152   Magnyfycence    410
And made as I had knowen nothynge of the case - . . . . . . .    160   Magnyfycence    719
I wenyd ones never to have knowen of care. . . . . . . . . .     196   Magnyfycence   1973
What! Thou Colyn Cowarde, knowen and tryde! . . . . . . . . .    202   Magnyfycence   2192
That knowen ye shall be . . . . . . . . . . . . . . . . . . .    361   Albany          114
```
KNOWETH
```
Who knoweth me, hymselfe may never sloo. . . . . . . . . . .     206   Magnyfycence   2330
Nor knoweth not his elenkes, . . . . . . . . . . . . . . . .     267   Collyn Clout    818
   elenkes] 'eloquens' †Godfray 1531, Kele 1545.1, Marshe 1568
```
KNOWING
```
By theyr conusaunce knowing how they serve a wily py: . . . .     43   Balettys2        34
```
KNOWYST
```
Deme what thou lyst, thou knowyst not my thought. . . . . . .     38   Coystrowne1      63
```
KNOWLEDGE
```
And knowledge your offence /Before open audyence, . . . . . .    380   Replycacion     207
```
KNOWNE
```
Eolus, your trumpet, that knowne is so farre, . . . . . . . .    319   Garlande        235
   that] 'whiche' MS Cotton Vitellius E.x
```
KOY
```
Why so koy and full of skorne? . . . . . . . . . . . . . . .      40   Coystrowne4       8
The knave wolde make it koy, and he cowde; . . . . . . . . .     175   Magnyfycence   1246
Ye, but some be full koy and passynge harde harted. . . . . .    184   Magnyfycence   1583
```
KOYE
```
She made it as koye /As a lege-de-moy; . . . . . . . . . . .     229   El Rummynge     586
   lege-de-moy] 'lege moy' †Lant 1545, Kynge & Marche 1554
```
KONNYNG
```
Sith he is slaundred for defaut of konnyng?' . . . . . . . .     316   Garlande        140
Of vertu and konnyng the well and perfight grounde; . . . . .    336   Garlande        866
   and] (1st) not in MS Cotton Vitellius E.x
To make suche trifels it asketh sum konnyng, . . . . . . . .     347   Garlande       1235
```
KOPPYNGE
```
In comparyson but kynge Koppynge . . . . . . . . . . . . . .     117   Ag Scottes       57
```
KOTE
```
And is governed by this mad kote! . . . . . . . . . . . . . .    295   Why Come Ye     668
   And] not in Marshe 1568
```
KOUDE
```
As perfightly as koude be thought or devysyd; . . . . . . . .     33   Dol Dethe       158
Myne argument els koude not longe endure. . . . . . . . . . .    316   Garlande        147
```
KOWD
```
A man kowd not aspy . . . . . . . . . . . . . . . . . . . . .    111   Lawde            19
```
KOWE
```
Crokyd as a camoke, and as a kowe calfles, . . . . . . . . .     122   Garnesche1       30
```
KOWES
```
I saw a foxe sucke on a kowes ydder; . . . . . . . . . . . .     191   Magnyfycence   1814
```
KOWNNAGE
```
Fals forgers of mony, for kownnage atteintid, . . . . . . . .    329   Garlande        611
   kownnage] 'coynnage' Marshe 1568
```
KOWTHTHYD
```
Ye xulde have kowththyd me a fole. . . . . . . . . . . . . .     127   Garnesche3      119
```
KREW
```
'In faythe, Dycken, thou krew, . . . . . . . . . . . . . . .     280   Why Come Ye      66
In fayth, Dicken, thou krew, etc.' . . . . . . . . . . . . .     280   Why Come Ye      67
Dicken, thou krew doutlesse! . . . . . . . . . . . . . . . .     280   Why Come Ye      68
```
KUES
```
That be worth ii kues. . . . . . . . . . . . . . . . . . . .     284   Why Come Ye     235
```
KUKKOWE
```
Ye syng allway the kukkowe songe. . . . . . . . . . . . . . .    129   Garnesche5        4
```
KUM
```
So that sche wolde have kum . . . . . . . . . . . . . . . . .    125   Garnesche3       63
```
KUNTREY
```
As all his kuntrey kan testefy the same: . . . . . . . . . .      33   Dol Dethe       153
```
KUR
```
A jentyll hownde shulde never play the kur. . . . . . . . . .    352   Garlande       1436
```

	Page	Title	Line
KURRIS			
Fals flaterers that fawne the, and kurris of kynde	329	Garlande	619
KURTEIS			
Unto thy subjectis be kurteis and beningne.	33	Dol Dethe	168
KUS			
Now kusse me, Parot, kus me, kus, kus;	238	Speke Parott	265
Now kusse me, Parot, kus me, kus, kus;	238	Speke Parott	265
Now kusse me, Parot, kus me, kus, kus;	238	Speke Parott	265
KUSSE			
Many a prety kusse	80	Phy Sparrow	361
Now kusse me, Parot, kus me, kus, kus;	238	Speke Parott	265
KUTTYTH			
From the anker he kuttyth the gabyll rope,	335	Garlande	833
LABOURE			
That for hym to laboure he hath prayde me hartely;	186	Magnyfycence	1650
Or suche laboure to take.	250	Collyn Clout	135
That laboure to confounde	259	Collyn Clout	493
LACE			
Some brought a sylke lace,	227	El Rummynge	528
LACIS			
The saumpler to sow on, the lacis to enbraid;	334	Garlande	789
LACYD			
What is this, a betell or a batowe or a buskyn lacyd?	161	Magnyfycence	755
LACK			
In Romaine letters I never founde lack	137	Ven Tongues	17
To put any man in lack	310	Why Come Ye2	25
In honest myrth, parde, requyreth no lack;	347	Garlande	1236
LACKE			
Whyles I have ought, by God, thou shalt not lacke,	50	Bowge	167
And all for lacke of grace.	66	Hauke	163
For lacke of grace hard was your hap;	119	Ag Scottes	168
I wolde begyn all myschyef, but I wolde bere no lacke.	160	Magnyfycence	720
Howe lyke you? Ye lacke, syr, suche a lusty lasse.	183	Magnyfycence	1559
Gyve them more than ynoughe, and let them not lacke;	190	Magnyfycence	1773
And suche as you wyll shall lacke no promocyon.	190	Magnyfycence	1789
What is he lyvynge that lyberte wolde lacke?	199	Magnyfycence	2083
Sodenly commendyd, and sodenly fynde a lacke;	213	Magnyfycence	2533
For lacke of good wyne;	266	Collyn Clout	805
We can lacke no grace,	301	Why Come Ye	875
To your great lacke /And utter shame	360	Albany	45
He reculed backe, /To his great lacke,	360	Albany	53
LACKED			
It were a myschefe, yf lyberte lacked a reyne	144	Magnyfycence	135
And yet, in fayth, man, we lacked the	155	Magnyfycence	538
LACKETH			
Full many thynges there be that lacketh redresse,	209	Magnyfycence	2415
Or yf he speke playne, /Than he lacketh brayne:	247	Collyn Clout	27
For he lacketh wytte.'	247	Collyn Clout	32
LACKYNGE			
To clothe the nakyd where is lackynge a smocke –	177	Magnyfycence	1345
LACKYS			
But lewdlye ar they lettyrd that your lernyng lackys,	239	Speke Parott	294
LACKYTH			
Where measure lackyth, all thynge dysorderyd is;	144	Magnyfycence	122
LACRYMABLE			
Lacrymable, Profytable for the soule.	39	Coystrowne3	I
LADDE			
Mary, I knewe the when thou waste a ladde.	170	Magnyfycence	1089
LADELL			
First one wyth a ladell,	224	El Rummynge	383
LADIES			
Of ladies of bryght colour,	128	Garnesche3	148
That lordes and ladies thys pamflett may behold,	241	Speke Parott	358
And, 'my ladies grace',	301	Why Come Ye	877
LADY			
O Quene of mercy, O lady full of grace,	34	Dol Dethe	204
Skelton laureat, at the instance of a nobyll lady.	46	Balettys5	E
The awnner therof is lady of estate,	47	Bowge	50
Of one and other that wolde his lady see,	47	Bowge	57
The favoure that ye have with my lady.	53	Bowge	270
In my lady Brewsys howse.	125	Garnesche3	33
I trowe, by our lady, I had ben slayne,	150	Magnyfycence	348
A tappyster lyke a lady bryght:	152	Magnyfycence	420
Well were that lady myght stande in my grace,	190	Magnyfycence	1799
My lady mastres, Dame Phylology,	232	Speke Parott	43
mastres] 'maysters' Lant 1545, Kynge & Marche 1554, Day 1560, Marshe 1568			
Parrot is a fayre byrd for a lady;	236	Speke Parott	211
My lady nowe she ronnes,	256	Collyn Clout	390
Dame Dorothe and Lady Besse,	256	Collyn Clout	392
With, 'my lady bryght and shene'.	304	Why Come Ye	1004
Renownyd lady above the sterry hevyn,	313	Garlande	51
Then to this lady and soverayne of this palace	326	Garlande	491
To my Lady Elisabeth Howarde	336	Garlande	R
To my Lady Mirriell Howarde	337	Garlande	R
Mi litell lady I may not leve behinde,	337	Garlande	878
To my Lady Anne Dakers of the Sowth	337	Garlande	R
By saynt Mary, my Lady,	339	Garlande	973

	Page	Title	Line
howe it was idolatry to offre to ymages of our blessed lady,	375	Replycacion	1
In the honour of our blessed lady,	375	Replycacion	18
Our glorious lady to disable,	375	Replycacion	26

LADYES

	Page	Title	Line
For lordes and ladyes lerne at his scole;	38	Coystrownel	52
To dwell with us and serve my ladyes grace.	50	Bowge	156
To treade the pretty wren /That is our Ladyes hen.	86	Phy Sparrow	601
Many a spere brake /For his ladyes sake;	87	Phy Sparrow	640
To be matriculate /With ladyes of estate?	104	Phy Sparrow	1289
Thanked be saynte Gorge, our ladyes knythe,	114	Scot Kynge	42
And swete Saynt George, our ladyes knyght!	119	Ag Scottes	141
This ladyes have, /I it them gave.	165	Magnyfycence	889
And send me to greate ladyes of estate;	231	Speke Parott	6
to greate ladyes] 'to grece to lordys' †MS Harley 2252			
With ladyes I lerne and goe with them to scole.	231	Speke Parott	21
To dwell amonge ladyes, Parrot, is mete.	233	Speke Parott	105
For of all ladyes he hath the library,	334	Garlande	780
Ladyes and gentylwomen suche as deservyd,	346	Garlande	1189
With ladyes of astate?	348	Garlande	1282

LADYN

	Page	Title	Line
I am not ladyn of liddyrnes with lumpis,	332	Garlande	733

LADYS

	Page	Title	Line
The favour of ladys with wordis electe,	314	Garlande	76
Of ladys a beve with all dew reverence:	334	Garlande	771
a beve] 'aboue' †Fakes 1523			
'Syt downe, fayre ladys, and do your diligence!'	334	Garlande	772
Whereon theis ladys softly myght rest,	334	Garlande	788
How theis ladys and gentylwomen all	335	Garlande	809
Before my ladys grace, the Quene of Fame,	343	Garlande	1091
Of my ladys grace at the contemplacyoun,	347	Garlande	1219

LAID

	Page	Title	Line
But your benynge sufferaunce for my discharge I laid,	318	Garlande	213

LAY

	Page	Title	Line
The song of lovers lay;	89	Phy Sparrow	702
And wretchedly ye lay starke naked.	119	Ag Scottes	167
starke naked] 'starke your naked' Kynge & Marche 1554, Day 1560, 'starke all naked' Marshe 1568			
Your chorlyshe chauntyng ys all o lay.	129	Garnesche5	6
Fyrst I lay before them my bybyll	174	Magnyfycence	1220
What he sayth and she sayth to lay good ere,	175	Magnyfycence	1269
Convey it be crafte, lyft and asyde.	177	Magnyfycence	1357
Leve thy pratynge or els I shall lay the on the pate.	201	Magnyfycence	2173
All grace and pyte I lay in the duste.	205	Magnyfycence	2290
Gave me a gyfte in my neste when I lay,	232	Speke Parott	44
I] 'he' †MS Harley 2252			
Over this, the foresayd lay	254	Collyn Clout	301
And all the faute they lay	256	Collyn Clout	402
the faute] not in Kele 1545.1, Marshe 1568			
Lay salve to your owne sore,	258	Collyn Clout	480
With, 'laughe and lay downe,'	302	Why Come Ye	931
Can lay any werkis that he hath compylyd,	318	Garlande	223
Mountith on hy with her melodious lay,	327	Garlande	535
And so largely to lay for myne indempnite,	344	Garlande	1136
Of what charge so ever ye lay ageinst me;	344	Garlande	1138
Of Holy Churches lay.	379	Replycacion	171

LAYD

	Page	Title	Line
Your lege ye layd and your aly,	118	Ag Scottes	103
With that the tappettis and carpettis were layd,	334	Garlande	787
Is layd down to slepe,	358	Garlande2	4

LAYDE

	Page	Title	Line
There muste for hym be layde some prety beyte.	55	Bowge	312
I dare not speke, we be so layde awayte,	59	Bowge	468
Therfore ye be layde now full lowe.	114	Scot Kynge	53
Your pompe and pryde hath layde a downe.	115	Scot Kynge	69
And brought home and layde in your bed.	184	Magnyfycence	1572
Some layde to pledge /Theyr hatchet and theyr wedge,	221	El Rummynge	293
They layde to pledge theyr wharrowe,	222	El Rummynge	298
Some for very nede /Layde downe a skeyne of threde,	222	El Rummynge	310
They have layde all in the myre.	285	Why Come Ye	251

LAYE

	Page	Title	Line
At Harwyche Porte, slumbrynge as I laye,	47	Bowge	34
She kyste an anker, and there she laye at rode,	47	Bowge	39
kyste] 'keste' Wynkyn de Worde 1510, 'kast' Marshe 1568			
A balade boke before me for to laye,	53	Bowge	257
Every byrde in his laye:	81	Phy Sparrow	394

LAYE MEN

	Page	Title	Line
Laye men say, in dede,	248	Collyn Clout	75
What have laye men to do	251	Collyn Clout	196

LAY FEE

	Page	Title	Line
The lay fee people rayles.	256	Collyn Clout	401
Howe the lay fee despyte	257	Collyn Clout	438
As ye may dayly se /Howe the lay fee	259	Collyn Clout	496
To the people of lay fee,	381	Replycacion	267

LAY MEN

	Page	Title	Line
The lay men call them barelles	269	Collyn Clout	917

LAYNE

	Page	Title	Line
'Turde,' quod Ha[f]ter, 'I wyll the nothynge layne,	55	Bowge	311
layne] 'sayne' †Wynkyn de Worde 1499, Marshe 1568			

	Page	Title	Line
LAYSER			
And yf ye may have layser,	261	Collyn Clout	605
ye] 'you' Kele 1545.1, Marshe 1568, 'ye' MS Harley 2252			
'My lorde is nat at layser.	294	Why Come Ye	625
Tyll better layser be founde;	294	Why Come Ye	627
And his layser abyde,	295	Why Come Ye	636
LAYTH			
A chaplayne of trust, /Layth all in the dust.	253	Collyn Clout	284
LAYTHE			
But he laythe all in the dyche,	290	Why Come Ye	455
LAKE			
Nor to the lake /Of fendys blake.	40	Coystrowne3	47
How Syr Launcelote de Lake	87	Phy Sparrow	638
To know thy selfe yf thow lake grace,	132	Garnesche5	126
And, as we dare, we fynde in hym grete lake:	314	Garlande	70
grete] 'a' Marshe 1568			
Where I sawe come after, I wote, full lytell lake	320	Garlande	285
Syr drake of the lake, sir ducke	364	Albany	223
LAKES			
Lepe over lakes and dykes,	262	Collyn Clout	622
LAKEST			
But thou lakest might,	136	Dundas	49
LAKYN			
By lakyn, syr, it hathe cost me pence	150	Magnyfycence	338
Say trouth? Yes, yes, by lakyn, I shall the warent,	154	Magnyfycence	506
By our lakyn, syr, I have ben a hawkyng for the wylde swan.	191	Magnyfycence	1806
By our lakyn, syr, not by my wyll.	203	Magnyfycence	2208
LAKKYST			
Thow ar frantyke and lakkyst wyt,	132	Garnesche5	118
LAM			
The wolfe from the lam;	298	Why Come Ye	776
LAMBES			
And theyr spyrytuall lambes /Sequestred from rambes	250	Collyn Clout	156
LAME			
Adres the to me, whiche am bothe halt and lame,	29	Dol Dethe	10
With skolding and sklaundering make their tungs lame.	139	Ven Tongues	62
Howe a wodcocke wrastled with a larke that was lame;	192	Magnyfycence	1836
Some I make lame, and some I do kyll,	194	Magnyfycence	1931
A, howe my lymmys be lyther and lame!	198	Magnyfycence	2038
Up she stert, halfe lame,	227	El Rummynge	512
Theyr soules lame and dull;	250	Collyn Clout	129
And make him lame of his neder limmes.	309	Why Come Ye	1200
LAMENTABLE			
and Muche Lamentable Chaunce	29	Dol Dethe	I
Convenable in sentence, Comendable, Lamentable,	39	Coystrowne3	I
And for her sparow prayd /In lamentable wyse.	93	Phy Sparrow	855
Of Phillip Sparow the lamentable fate,	348	Garlande	1254
LAMENTABLY			
Whos lordshepe doutles was slayne lamentably	29	Dol Dethe	5
Dothe rynne lamentably.	280	Why Come Ye	48
LAMENTACYON			
Of any sorowfull lamentacyon,	117	Ag Scottes	74
LAMENTE			
Helas! I lamente the dull abusyd brayne,	242	Speke Parott	383
LAMENTYNG			
Lamentyng Daphnes, whome with the darte of lede	320	Garlande	290
LAMPATRAMS			
'Quake, quake,' sayd the duck /In that lampatrams lap.	227	El Rummynge	506
LANAM			
Good Sprynge of Lanam	302	Why Come Ye	933
LANCASHYRE			
What here ye of Lancashyre?	285	Why Come Ye	247
LAND			
Ic dien is the language of the land of Beme;	233	Speke Parott	79
LANDE			
The welle concernyng of all the hole lande,	31	Dol Dethe	65
Counterfet maters in the lawe of the lande -	152	Magnyfycence	431
By the masse, for ye are able to dystroy an hole lande.	154	Magnyfycence	513
Than a butterflye of our lande.	169	Magnyfycence	1053
Pocenya, the prowde provoste of Turky lande,	181	Magnyfycence	1480
Jobab was brought up in the lande of Hus;	232	Speke Parott	65
Jobab] 'Iob' Day 1560, Marshe 1568			
That he must pyll his lande	290	Why Come Ye	453
All the rule of this lande,	298	Why Come Ye	762
Your name recountynge beyonde the lande of Tyre,	327	Garlande	551
Of this, his realme royall /And lande imperiall,	368	Albany	394
Of your lande in shorte space.	371	Albany	502
LANDES			
Where is nowe my treasure, my landes, and my rent?	198	Magnyfycence	2056
Of theyr predyall landes,	269	Collyn Clout	930
LANDYS			
For I stryke lordys of realmes and landys	195	Magnyfycence	1938
LANGAGE			
Your langage is lyke the penne	143	Magnyfycence	90
Tusche, holde your pece! Your langage is vayne.	147	Magnyfycence	251
Why that ye sayd our langage was in vayne.	147	Magnyfycence	263
Though Largesse ye hyght your langage is to large;	148	Magnyfycence	295
Counterfet langage, fayty bone geyte.	152	Magnyfycence	441

LANGAGYS —LARGESSE   Page   Title   Line

	Page	Title	Line
Of your langage, it is so well devysed;	183	Magnyfycence	1530
Mary, so ungoodly langage you me gave.	203	Magnyfycence	2213
Ye, for thy langage can not the avayle.	204	Magnyfycence	2249
More delectable than your langage to me.	207	Magnyfycence	2348
To lerne all langage and hyt to speke aptlye.	232	Speke Parott	45
Suche lewde langage ye spake.	367	Albany	329
With langage detestable;	375	Replycacion	28

LANGAGYS

Langagys divers; yet undyr that dothe reste	241	Speke Parott	365

LANGUAGE

Our language is so rusty,	91	Phy Sparrow	777
Either by language or with my pen.	137	Ven Tongues	23
Of me with your language full of vilany.	138	Ven Tongues	48
Ic dien is the language of the land of Beme;	233	Speke Parott	79
Thus dyvers of language by lernyng I grow:	233	Speke Parott	103
With language thus poluted	258	Collyn Clout	486

LANNERS

The lanners and the marlyons	85	Phy Sparrow	565
the] not in Wyght 1553, Kitson 1560.6, Marshe 1568			

LANTERNES

Shulde be lanternes of lyght.	257	Collyn Clout	440
Lyke lanternes of lyght,	264	Collyn Clout	694

LAODOMI

Unto the legend of fare Laodomi.	339	Garlande	972

LAP

Let me', quod he, 'ly in your lap.'	41	Balettys1	2
And wold syt upon my lap,	74	Phy Sparrow	121
Nowe lap you in a coverlet, full fayne that you may;	197	Magnyfycence	2011
'Quake, quake,' sayd the duck /In that lampatrams lap.	227	El Rummynge	506

LAPPED

In mysery and wretchydnesse thus to be lapped!	196	Magnyfycence	1985
Alas, syr! So I am lapped in adversyte	206	Magnyfycence	2331
Upon her brayne-pan, /Lyke an Egypcyan /Lapped about.	216	El Rummynge	79
Lapped] 'Capped' Kynge & Marche 1554, Day 1560, Marshe 1568			

LAPWYNG

With Puwyt the lapwyng,	82	Phy Sparrow	430

LARDE

Of larde and of grece,	267	Collyn Clout	846

LARG

To drynk at a draught a larg and a long.	38	Coystrownel	49

LARGE

But with a large and a longe	82	Phy Sparrow	426
To poore folke at large,	83	Phy Sparrow	456
To lettred men at large:	105	Phy Sparrow	1361
Ye kyt your clothe to large,	129	Garnesche3	189
Thowthe ye kan skylle of large and longe,	129	Garnesche5	3
How be it, lyberte may somtyme be to large,	141	Magnyfycence	37
For lyberte at large is lothe to be stoppyd,	141	Magnyfycence	46
Lyberte at large wyll oft wax reklesse.	142	Magnyfycence	54
And lyberte his large with measure shall make.	145	Magnyfycence	180
Though Largesse ye hyght your langage is to large;	148	Magnyfycence	295
So large a man, and so lytell of stature!	155	Magnyfycence	523
But yf it lyke your grace more at large	185	Magnyfycence	1589
Suche lustes at large may not be lefte behynde.	186	Magnyfycence	1628
I lyve as me lyst, I lepe out at large;	199	Magnyfycence	2080
Nowe pleasure at large, nowe in captyvyte;	212	Magnyfycence	2519
And com forthe at large,	264	Collyn Clout	693
com forthe] 'conforte' †Godfray 1531, Kele 1545.1, Marshe 1568			
As limyters at large	267	Collyn Clout	834
To large in neglygence,	278	Why Come Ye	6
as more at large it doth apere in the proces folowynge.	312	Garlande	I
For her pleasure to make a large profer,	327	Garlande	556
Into a felde she brought me wyde and large,	328	Garlande	568
And of your wyll the plainnes shew at large.'	332	Garlande	727
To letterd men at large.	350	Garlande	1354

LARGELY

Largely rewardynge them that have deservyd;	200	Magnyfycence	2119
And so largely to lay for myne indempnite,	344	Garlande	1136

LARGER

And therof ye shall a larger profe se.	188	Magnyfycence	1700
Make a larger memoryall	299	Why Come Ye	824
larger] 'large' Marshe 1568			

LARGES

I pray you, Larges, here to remayne,	149	Magnyfycence	323

LARGESSE

That without largesse noblenesse can not rayne.	147	Magnyfycence	265
I say, without largesse worshyp hath no place,	148	Magnyfycence	267
For largesse is a purchaser of pardon and of grace.	148	Magnyfycence	268
Largesse, that all lordes sholde love, syr, I hyght.	148	Magnyfycence	270
But hyght you, Largesse, encreace of noble fame?	148	Magnyfycence	271
Largesse is laudable so it be in measure.	148	Magnyfycence	278
'in measure be' †Rastell & Treveris C 1530, B			
Largesse is he that all prynces doth avaunce;	148	Magnyfycence	279
For, syth he dyed, largesse was lytell used.	148	Magnyfycence	282
In fayth, broder Largesse, you have a mery mynde.	148	Magnyfycence	292
Though Largesse ye hyght your langage is to large;	148	Magnyfycence	295
And made largesse, as I hyght,	150	Magnyfycence	364
But surely largesse saved my lyfe;	150	Magnyfycence	366

LARKE—LATELY

	Page	Title	Line
For largesse stynteth all maner of stryfe.	150	Magnyfycence	367
But largesse is not mete for every man.	150	Magnyfycence	369
Largesse stynteth grete debates;	150	Magnyfycence	371
If you had with you largesse.	151	Magnyfycence	377
But largesse becometh a state ryall.	151	Magnyfycence	383
But largesse may amende your name.	151	Magnyfycence	389
In faythe, Largesse, welcome to me.	151	Magnyfycence	390
Of Largesse under the pretence.	151	Magnyfycence	405
In faythe, Largesse I hyght;	155	Magnyfycence	520
What! Is Largesse without lyberte?	155	Magnyfycence	540
His name Largesse, Surveyaunce myne.	158	Magnyfycence	643
Yourselfe shall be ruled by lyberte and largesse.	179	Magnyfycence	1389
Syr, by lyberte and largesse I wyll that ye shall	179	Magnyfycence	1396
Mayster Survayour, Largesse to me call.	179	Magnyfycence	1398
Come hyther Largesse; take here Felycyte.	179	Magnyfycence	1411
For welth without largesse is all out of kynde.	180	Magnyfycence	1441
I have welth at wyll, largesse and lyberte.	181	Magnyfycence	1458
Yet somtyme, parde, I must use largesse.	189	Magnyfycence	1755
Largesse in wordes - for rewardes are but small.	189	Magnyfycence	1760
I have taken it to Largesse and Lyberte.	189	Magnyfycence	1763
But use your largesse by the advyse of me,	189	Magnyfycence	1765
To be supervysour, and on Largesse also;	190	Magnyfycence	1785
Se, syr, I beseche you, Largesse my brother.	192	Magnyfycence	1842
I pray the, Largesse, let be thy sobbynge.	192	Magnyfycence	1851
Why, is this the largesse that I have usyd?	193	Magnyfycence	1865
Not thorowe largesse of lyberall expence,	200	Magnyfycence	2115
A laudable largesse, I tell you, for a lorde,	200	Magnyfycence	2123
That I sholde use largesse. Nay, syr, there a pause.	209	Magnyfycence	2437
Largesse, syr, by his credence was his name.	209	Magnyfycence	2441
So that your largesse be not to prodygall.	211	Magnyfycence	2488

LARKE

	Page	Title	Line
The larke with his longe to;	82	Phy Sparrow	406
So I myght hobby for suche a lusty larke.	184	Magnyfycence	1564
Howe a wodcocke wrastled with a larke that was lame;	192	Magnyfycence	1836
'Lyke as the larke, upon the somers day,	327	Garlande	533

LARKYS

	Page	Title	Line
I have an hoby can make larkys to dare;	177	Magnyfycence	1342

LAS

	Page	Title	Line
With some Scotyshe [l]as, las] 'as' †Marshe 1568	366	Albany	290

LASED

	Page	Title	Line
Her kyrtell so goodly lased,	101	Phy Sparrow	1194

LASSE

	Page	Title	Line
Howe lyke you? Ye lacke, syr, suche a lusty lasse.	183	Magnyfycence	1559

LASSES

	Page	Title	Line
Spent among wanton lasses;	257	Collyn Clout	424

LASSHE

	Page	Title	Line
I waraunt you I have gyven it a lasshe.	201	Magnyfycence	2165

LAST

	Page	Title	Line
Me, other fyrst or last,	143	Magnyfycence	93
Nay, but fansy must be eyther fyrst or last.	176	Magnyfycence	1288
Tyll at the last they forcyd me sore, sore] 'so sore' Marshe 1568	324	Garlande	446
Tyll at the last theis noble poetis thre	326	Garlande	517
In derkenes thus dwelt we, tyll at the last	330	Garlande	650
And of the somer days so longe that doth last,	331	Garlande	702
With a sawte of solace at the longe last;	351	Garlande	1398
And the twayne last /Be withholde so fast	358	Garlande2	12
Your last deedly bane	366	Albany	284

LASTE

	Page	Title	Line
Soo sore enwered that I was, at the laste,	47	Bowge	31
Thus at the laste I brynge hym ryght	152	Magnyfycence	422

LASTYTH

	Page	Title	Line
Remember this lyfe lastyth but a whyle.	211	Magnyfycence	2502

LATE

	Page	Title	Line
For Jak wold be a jentylman, that late was a grome.	37	Coystrownel	42
Thou blynkerd blowboll, thou wakyst to late;	42	Balettys1	24
What arte thou? I sawe the nowe but late.'	56	Bowge	376
That was late slayn at Carowe	72	Phy Sparrow	8
That late were discomfect with battayle marcyall.	117	Ag Scottes	84
Be it erly or late, welth hath a season.	140	Magnyfycence	3
We have bene togyder bothe erly and late.	154	Magnyfycence	499
Where is nowe all my servauntys that I had here a late?	198	Magnyfycence	2057
Adewe, syrs, for I thynke leyst that I come to late.	201	Magnyfycence	2152
It is to late nowe thy synnys to repent.	205	Magnyfycence	2292
Remembre you, therfore, howe late ye were low.	210	Magnyfycence	2451
And syt there by styll, /Erly and late.	217	El Rummynge	117
For replicacion restles that he of late ther made;	239	Speke Parott	282
For grocers were grugyd at and groynyd at but late;	244	Speke Parott	441
As now is made of late	269	Collyn Clout	914
That some of you but late	271	Collyn Clout	1011
Maketh remembraunce /How Kynge Lewes of late	297	Why Come Ye	722
And turne home ageyne, for they cam al to late.	329	Garlande	605
Of one Adame all a knave, late dede and gone -	347	Garlande	1247
A Replycacion Agaynst Certayne Yong Scolers Abjured of Late,	373	Replycacion	I
Now of late abjured, /Most unhappely ured;	385	Replycacion	404

LATELY

	Page	Title	Line
and rechelesse yonge heretykes lately abjured, etc.	373	Replycacion	I

	Page	Title	Line
LATIN			
For Latin warkis /Be good for clerkis,	355	Garlande	1542
Yet now and then /Sum Latin men	355	Garlande	1545
LATINE			
Out of fresshe Latine into owre Englyshe playne,	354	Garlande	1499
LATYN			
God Latyn for Jake a Thrum,	129	Garnesche3	204
What! Canest thou all this Latyn yet,	172	Magnyfycence	1143
Tushe, man! I kepe some Latyn in store.	172	Magnyfycence	1145
Yn Latyn, in Ebrue, and in Caldee,	231	Speke Parott	25
and] 'Araby and' Lant 1545, Kynge and Marche 1554, Day 1560, Marshe 1568			
LATYNE			
In Latyne playne and lyght,	92	Phy Sparrow	823
In the Latyne synge we,	291	Why Come Ye	476
His Latyne tonge dothe hobbyll,	292	Why Come Ye	526
LAUD			
Yet for a speciall laud	89	Phy Sparrow	720
LAUDABYLE			
To have so laudabyle a commendacion:	323	Garlande	408
LAUDABLE			
Lyberte is laudable and pryvylegyd from lawe.	142	Magnyfycence	68
Laudable your consayte is to be acountyd,	145	Magnyfycence	191
Largesse is laudable so it be in measure.	148	Magnyfycence	278
'in measure be' †Rastell & Treveris C 1530, B			
A laudable largesse, I tell you, for a lorde,	200	Magnyfycence	2123
LAUDABLY			
and of every true Christen man laudably to be enployed,	374	Replycacion	I
LAUDE			
To whom be the laude ascrybed	93	Phy Sparrow	871
Ye get therby a slendyr laude	131	Garnesche5	74
For if ye laude hym whome honour hath opprest,	317	Garlande	174
And laude equivalently.	369	Albany	403
LAUGH			
And lete us laugh a placke or tweyne at nale.	57	Bowge	387
placke] 'plucke' Marshe 1568			
That all men laugh at lyberte to scorne.	146	Magnyfycence	222
That I laugh at for my dysporte;	174	Magnyfycence	1239
LAUGHE			
A, ye make me laughe at your inconstaunce.	147	Magnyfycence	236
I can dyssemble; I can bothe laughe and grone;	159	Magnyfycence	698
Whan other men laughe, than study I and muse,	160	Magnyfycence	707
I laughe at all shrewdenes, and lye at lyberte.	160	Magnyfycence	735
Somtyme I laughe over lowde;	168	Magnyfycence	1012
Somtyme I laughe at waggynge of a straw,	168	Magnyfycence	1014
That I shall laughe the out of thy cote.	173	Magnyfycence	1194
I coude, and I lyst, garre you laughe at a game:	192	Magnyfycence	1835
Nowe she wyll laughe, forthwith she wyll frowne;	197	Magnyfycence	2024
With, 'laughe and lay downe,	302	Why Come Ye	931
LAUGHED			
Thus to be laughed to skorne,	376	Replycacion	82
That laughed whan he dyd pas	379	Replycacion	187
LAUGHES			
And Annot wolde be nyce, and laughes, 'tehe wehe.'	153	Magnyfycence	477
LAUGHETH			
Whyles she laugheth and hath luste for to playe.	49	Bowge	114
laugheth] 'laughed' †Wynkyn de Worde 1499			
He frowneth ever; /He laugheth never,	94	Phy Sparrow	923
LAUGHYNGE			
But counterfet coynes is laughynge to scorne;	152	Magnyfycence	446
To kepe you from laughynge	299	Why Come Ye	829
LAUGHT			
Wysdom is laught to skorne,	281	Why Come Ye	94
LAUGHTER			
with a lusty laughter.	201	Magnyfycence	SD
Ha, ha, ha! For laughter I am lyke to brast.	201	Magnyfycence	2160
LAULES			
At Orwelle hyr havyn your anggre was laules.	122	Garnesche1	33
LAUNCE			
For she is trussed for to breke a launce.	57	Bowge	410
LAUNCELOTE			
How Syr Launcelote de Lake	87	Phy Sparrow	638
LAUNCES			
Thow ye be lusty as Syr Lybyus, launces to breke,	122	Garnesche1	17
LAUREAT			
Skelton Laureat Upon the Dolorus Dethe	29	Dol Dethe	I
Of laureat Phebus holy the eloquence	33	Dol Dethe	160
Skelton Laureat Agaynste a Comely Coystrowne	36	Coystrowne	I
Quod Skelton, laureat.	38	Coystrowne2	E
Skelton Laureat, uppon a deedmans hed,	39	Coystrowne3	I
devysyd by Master Skelton Laureat	41	Balettys	I
Quod Skelton laureat.	43	Balettys2	E
Quod Skelton laureat.	45	Balettys3	E
Quod Skelton laureat.	45	Balettys4	E
Skelton laureat, at the instance of a nobyll lady.	46	Balettys5	E
per Skelton laureat	61	Hauke	I
How I, Skelton laureat,	62	Hauke	33
Quod Skelton laureat.	71	Hauke	E

LAUREATE—LAWE   Page   Title   Line

	Page	Title	Line
Laureat to be /Of fame royall;	112	Calliope	7
I am laureat, I am no lorell.	124	Garnesche3	14
Skelton laureat /After this rate	135	Dundas	19
The Tunnyng of Elynour Rummyng per Skelton Laureat.	214	El Rummynge	I
Quod Skelton Laureat.	230	El Rummynge	E
Quod Skelton Laureat	230	El Rummynge	E
by Mayster Skelton, Poete Laureat,	312	Garlande	I
Unto the rowme of laureat promotyve?	315	Garlande	116
With laureat tryumphe why Skelton sholde be crownde.	318	Garlande	217
Frome the laureat senate by force of proscripcyon.	318	Garlande	225
Of poetis laureat of many dyverse nacyons;	321	Garlande	324
Of laureat triumphe, your place is here reservyd,	344	Garlande	1126
triumphe] 'promocioun' MS Cotton Vitellius E.x			
dyvysed by Mayster Skelton, Poete Laureat.	358	Garlande2	R
Skelton Laureat: obsequious et loyall.	372	Albany	E

LAUREATE

	Page	Title	Line
Quod Skelton laureate.	42	Balettys1	E
compyled by Mayster Skelton, poete laureate	71	Phy Sparrow	I
Skelton Laureate, Orator Regius, maketh this aunswere &c.	112	Calliope	I
Skelton laureate Agaynst The Scottes	115	Ag Scottes	I
Quod Skelton laureate,	120	Ag Scottes	E
Skelton Laureate Defendar Ageinst Lusty Garnyshe	129	Garnesche5	I
Skelton laureate Oratoris Regis tertio	136	Ven Tongues	I
compyled by Mayster Skelton, Poete Laureate	278	Why Come Ye	I
With laureate tryumphe in the courte of Fame.	314	Garlande	63
'Of your oratour and poete laureate	345	Garlande	1170
Skelton Laureate etc	359	Albany	I
of Skelton laureate, orator regius,	373	Replycacion	I
agaynst Skelton laureate, devyser of this Replycacyon, etc.	382	Replycacion	R
Why fall ye at debate /With Skelton laureate,	382	Replycacion	301
The fame matryculate /Of poetes laureate.	384	Replycacion	358
Of hevenly inspyracion /In laureate creacyon,	384	Replycacion	373
Thus endeth the Replicacyon of Skelton Laureate, etc.	386	Replycacion	E

LAURELL

	Page	Title	Line
upon a goodly Garlande or Chapelet of Laurell	312	Garlande	I
In figure wherof they were the laurell grene.	314	Garlande	68
they were the] 'the were they' †Fakes 1523			
Transformyd was she into the laurell grene.	320	Garlande	294
Shall were a garlande of the laurell tre.'	321	Garlande	322
Thei wantid nothynge but the laurell;	323	Garlande	397
Avaunced by Pallas to laurell preferment.'	324	Garlande	434
Grene tre of laurell moche solacyous game	331	Garlande	683
In helpyng to warke my laurell grene	342	Garlande	1074
Set on your hede this laurell whiche is wrought.	343	Garlande	1087
Of my laurell the proces every whitte.	343	Garlande	1099
She wonderyd, me thought, at my laurell grene;	343	Garlande	1116
But when of the laurell she made rehersall,	354	Garlande	1503
upon a goodly Garlonde or Chapelet of Laurell,	358	Garlande2	R

LAURELLE

	Page	Title	Line
Prennees en gre The Laurelle.	357	Garlande	14

LAURELL LEVIS

	Page	Title	Line
Of laurell levis a cronell on his hede,	320	Garlande	288

LAURELL TRE

	Page	Title	Line
Where I saw growyng a goodly laurell tre,	330	Garlande	665

LAURIATE

	Page	Title	Line
Skelton Lauriate Defender Agenst Master Garnesche Chalenger,	121	Garnesche1	I

LAURYAT

	Page	Title	Line
With lauryat garlantes,	270	Collyn Clout	963

LAURYATE

	Page	Title	Line
Skelton Lauryate Defender Agenst Master Garnesche Chalangar,	122	Garnesche2	I

LAW

	Page	Title	Line
By reason nor by law;	62	Hauke	7
Or els is thys Goddis law,	65	Hauke	130
And of the spyrytuall law /They made but a gewgaw,	66	Hauke	156
The law they shall not breke;	111	Lawde	30
Nor doctor of the law,	292	Why Come Ye	510

LAWDE

	Page	Title	Line
A Lawde And Prayse Made for Our Sovereigne Lord the Kyng	110	Lawde	I

LAWE

	Page	Title	Line
Lyberte is laudable and pryvylegyd from lawe.	142	Magnyfycence	68
To lyve under lawe, it is captyvyte.	142	Magnyfycence	75
For measure is a meane, nother to hy nor to lawe,	145	Magnyfycence	188
Counterfet maters in the lawe of the lande -	152	Magnyfycence	431
Let your lust and lykynge stande for a lawe.	185	Magnyfycence	1607
Nowe well, nowe wo, nowe hy, nowe lawe degre;	212	Magnyfycence	2517
So myche pelory pajauntes undyr colowur of good lawe;	245	Speke Parott	480
They lumber forth the lawe	249	Collyn Clout	95
Some doctours of lawe,	264	Collyn Clout	731
That they ought by the lawe	268	Collyn Clout	857
That nede hath no lawe.	268	Collyn Clout	863
Strawe for lawe canon,	289	Why Come Ye	416
Or for lawe common,	289	Why Come Ye	417
Or for lawe cyvyll;	289	Why Come Ye	418
Stop at lawe tancrete,	289	Why Come Ye	420
Pyked out of all good lawe,	306	Why Come Ye	1106
of] not in Marshe 1568			
Nor no lawe canonicall	308	Why Come Ye	1159

LAWES —LEEDES Page Title Line

LAWES
Lydderyns so lytell set by Goddes lawes. . . . . 194 Magnyfycence 1919
That good lawes are subverted . . . . 256 Collyn Clout 372
Juges of the kynges lawes, ... 286 Why Come Ye 314
Your sysmaticate sawes /Agaynst Goddes lawes, ... 377 Replycacion 123

LAWGHE
'Heghe, ha, ha, Parott, ye can lawghe pratylye!' . . . . 231 Speke Parott 22

LAWGHYTH
That every man lawghyth at his foly. . . . . 175 Magnyfycence 1251
Lyacon lawghyth thereatt and berythe hym more bolde; . . . . . 242 Speke Parott 400

LAWIS
Shewynge him Goddis lawis. . . . . 305 Why Come Ye 1060

LAWYS
Fortune to her lawys can not abandune me; . . . . 181 Magnyfycence 1459

LAWREAT
The dignite lawreat for to have. 132 Garnesche5 115

LAWRELL
A cronell of lawrell with verduris light and darke . . . . . . 334 Garlande 776
Garnisshed with lawrell . . . . 342 Garlande 1055
But when they sawe my lawrell rychely wrought, ... 343 Garlande 1105
They seyd my lawrell was the goodlyest . . . . 343 Garlande 1112

LAWRYAT
Quod Skelton Lawryat . . . . 246 Speke Parott 3

LAWRYATE
Skelton Lawryate Defender Agenyst Lusty Garnyche . . . . 124 Garnesche3 I

LAZARS
Some I make lyppers and lazars full horse; . . . . 194 Magnyfycence 1904

LE
With daunce on the le, the le! . . . . 198 Magnyfycence 2068
With daunce on the le, the le! . . . . 198 Magnyfycence 2068

LEAD
Wanne, and blewe as lead: . . . . 73 Phy Sparrow 61
With a bull under lead, ... 299 Why Come Ye 798

LEANE
His bones crake, /Leane as a rake; . . . . 94 Phy Sparrow 913

LEAPES
With leapes and bounses; . . . . 104 Phy Sparrow 1315

LEARNING
But my learning is of an other degree . . . . 138 Ven Tongues 28
And so little learning, so lewdly alowed, ... 138 Ven Tongues 40

LEASURE
I shall loke in it at leasure better; . . . . 149 Magnyfycence 332

LECHE
She semed halfe a leche, ... 225 El Rummynge 447

LECHERY
Envy, wrath, and lechery, /Covetys and glotony; . . . . 293 Why Come Ye 575

LECTRYNE
Cros, staffe, lectryne and banner, ... 64 Hauke 114

LECTUARY
Nowe must I make you a lectuary softe - . . . . 207 Magnyfycence 2355

LECTURE
How be it, it were harde to construe this lecture; . . . . . . 315 Garlande 109

LED
What ever they say, /Jemmy is ded /And closyd in led, ... 116 Ag Scottes 22
With clothes upon her hed /That wey a sowe of led, ... 216 El Rummynge 72
   That wey] 'That they wey' Kynge & Marche 1554, Day 1560,
   Marshe 1568

LEDD
With whom he ledd a plesaunt life; . . . . 90 Phy Sparrow 744

LEDDER
With his ledder ey, /And chekes dry; . . . . 94 Phy Sparrow 908
Like an onyon syded, /Lyke tan ledder hyded. . . . . 226 El Rummynge 471

LEDE
And lede my fyst /As hym best lyst, ... 96 Phy Sparrow 972
. . . . .malle of lede, ... 125 Garnesche3 59
Wyll crepe upon us, and us to myschefe lede; . . . . 144 Magnyfycence 153
I can fede forth a fole and lede hym by the eyre; . . . . . . 160 Magnyfycence 712
Plucke down lede and theke with tyle; . . . . 169 Magnyfycence 1026
For with foly so do I them lede . . . . 175 Magnyfycence 1260
I sawe a losell lede a lurden, and they were bothe blynde. . . 191 Magnyfycence 1824
Ye, ryd thy selfe rather than this lyfe for to lede. . . . . . 205 Magnyfycence 2307
Out of thy lyfe the for to lede. . . . . 205 Magnyfycence 2310
Hys wolvys hede, wanne, bloo as lede, gapythe over the crowne: 244 Speke Parott 434
So manye bolde barons, there hertes as dull as lede; . . . . . 245 Speke Parott 466
To copper, to tyn, /To lede, or alcumyn? . . . . 301 Why Come Ye 907
Lamentyng Daphnes, whome with the darte of lede . . . . 320 Garlande 290
Twene hope and drede /My lyfe I lede, ... 356 Garlande 1595
As hevy as the lede, ... 358 Garlande2 3
That he our penne dothe lede, ... 385 Replycacion 385

LEDERHEDE
In a certayne stede /Bysyde Lederhede. . . . . 217 El Rummynge 98

LEDEST
What pylde curre ledest thou in thy hande? . . . . 169 Magnyfycence 1054

LEDYTH
Where drede ledyth the daunce, there is no joy nor blysse. . . 142 Magnyfycence 76
Foly fotyth it properly, fansy ledyth the dawnce, ... 177 Magnyfycence 1331

LEEDES
Plucke away the leedes /Over theyr heedes, ... 257 Collyn Clout 408

	Page	Title	Line
LEEST			
To tell you, syr, I dare not, leest I sholde be maskyd	141	Magnyfycence	30
And feare leest they be out	380	Replycacion	225
LEFE			
'My lefe', she sayd, 'rowtyth in hys bed;	42	Balettys1	20
Ye, tourne over the lefe, rede there, and loke	176	Magnyfycence	1293
LEFT			
Ye armed you with wille and left your wit behynd;	30	Dol Dethe	55
All left alone, alas, he fawte in vayne!	32	Dol Dethe	104
She left hym slepyng and stale away,	42	Balettys1	14
So none be left behynde.	81	Phy Sparrow	389
But we wyll turne playne /Where we left agayne.	220	El Rummynge	243
Plato, but for that he left wrytynge behynde,	315	Garlande	126
that] not in MS Cotton Vitellius E.x			
With other condycyons that well myght be left.	329	Garlande	615
Of welth and solace no thynge left behynde;	332	Garlande	711
Into that place where as they left me,	343	Garlande	1103
The Nacyoun of Folys he left not behynde.	353	Garlande	1470
LEFTE			
So that lyberte be not lefte behynde.	144	Magnyfycence	129
Suche lustes at large may not be lefte behynde.	186	Magnyfycence	1628
But let us turne playne, /There we lefte agayne.	219	El Rummynge	188
LEG			
The Jebet of Baldock was made for Jack Leg;	232	Speke Parott	73
LEGACY			
And by his legacy,	306	Why Come Ye	1103
LEGE			
To her wyll I nowe all my poverte lege.	57	Bowge	412
Your lege ye layd and your aly,	118	Ag Scottes	103
LEGE-DE-MOY			
She made it as koye /As a lege-de-moy;	229	El Rummynge	587
lege-de-moy] 'lege moy' †Lant 1545, Kynge & Marche 1554			
LEGE MOY			
And howe Parys of Troy /Daunced a lege moy,	270	Collyn Clout	951
lege moy] 'lege de moy' Kele 1545.1, Marshe 1568			
LEGEND			
Unto the legend of fare Laodomi.	339	Garlande	972
LEGGE			
I shall thrust in the my dagger - Thorowe the legge in to the hose.	202	Magnyfycence	2177
LEGGED			
Foted lyke a plane, /Legge[d] lyke a crane;	215	El Rummynge	50
Legged] 'Legges' †Lant 1545, Kynge & Marche 1554, Day 1560, Marshe 1568			
LEGGES			
Yor wynde-schakyn shankkes, yor longe *lothy legges,	122	Garneschel	29
*lothy] 'lothly' Scattergood			
Cysly and Sare, /With theyr legges bare,	217	El Rummynge	120
Her legges that ye myght se;	225	El Rummynge	421
ye] 'he' 1521 Fragment			
The dropsy was in her legges;	226	El Rummynge	481
My lytell legges, my fete bothe fete and clene,	231	Speke Parott	18
LEY			
With helpe of the ram, ley all in the dust.	315	Garlande	105
LEYE			
Now wolde to God thou wolde leye money downe!	57	Bowge	395
LEYRE			
As lyly whyte to loke upon her [l]eyre,	183	Magnyfycence	1555
leyre] 'heyre' †Rastell & Treveris C 1530, B			
LEYSER			
By the masse, thou shalt byde my leyser.	162	Magnyfycence	788
But, and I had leyser competent,	342	Garlande	1082
LEYSSHE			
Here is a leysshe of ratches to renne an hare!	156	Magnyfycence	586
LEYST			
Adewe, syrs, for I thynke leyst that I come to late.	201	Magnyfycence	2152
LEKE			
Of the vertue of an unset leke;	225	El Rummynge	451
But it is not worth a leke.	251	Collyn Clout	182
LEKES			
With plantyng of lekes	293	Why Come Ye	555
LEMMAN			
To wete yf Malkyn, my lemman, have gete oughte.	57	Bowge	401
LEMMANNS			
With Lumbardes lemmanns for to mete,	130	Garnesche5	42
LEMSTER			
Some fyll theyr pot full /Of good Lemster woll.	220	El Rummynge	252
LENDE			
'Lende here a cocke of hey,	229	El Rummynge	577
LENE			
To fat is hys fantsy, hys wyt is to lene.	37	Coystrownel	28
Yf ye have not, in fayth, I wyll you lene	48	Bowge	96
That one was lene and lyke a pyned goost,	58	Bowge	429
All honour to me must nedys stowpe and lene.	181	Magnyfycence	1462
LENETH			
She leneth them on the same,	217	El Rummynge	131
on] 'of' Day 1560, Marshe 1568			

LENGER —LERNE   Page   Title   Line

LENGER
	Page	Title	Line
But whereto shuld I /Lenger morne or crye?	86	Phy Sparrow	595
Your power coude no lenger attayne	114	Scot Kynge	54
Now hereof it erkith me lenger to wryte,	354	Garlande	1491

LENGTH
By marcyall strength /He wan at length;	104	Phy Sparrow	1306
So helpe me God, man, ever at the length	175	Magnyfycence	1258
By merciall strength /He wan at length;	349	Garlande	1299
In length and brede.	355	Garlande	1552

LENGTHE
Enyus that wrate of mercyall war at lengthe;	321	Garlande	347

LENT
Dame Nature hath her lent	97	Phy Sparrow	1042
For prestes and for lonys /Lent and never payde,	255	Collyn Clout	351
In open tyde and in lent.	268	Collyn Clout	859
open tyde] 'open tyme' Kele 1545.1, Marshe 1568, 'Ester tyde' MS Harley 2252			
Our mony madly lent,	282	Why Come Ye	143
lent] 'sent' Marshe 1568			
In lent, for a repast,	284	Why Come Ye	220
May ete pigges in lent for pikys	306	Why Come Ye	1081
For in lent he wyll ete	306	Why Come Ye	1083
wyll] 'doeth' MS Rawlinson C. 813			
That, me to rest, I lent me to a stumpe	312	Garlande	17
Then I me lent, and loked over the wall:	329	Garlande	602

LENTE
Fortune to you gyftes of grace hath lente:	50	Bowge	152
In so moche the stumpe, whereto I me lente	320	Garlande	281

LENTON
Howe some of you dothe eate /In lenton season flesshe meate,	251	Collyn Clout	205
Nor in holy lenton season	252	Collyn Clout	211

LEOPARDES
The leopardes savage, /The lyons in theyr rage,	79	Phy Sparrow	286

LEPE
Whose jalawsy malycyous makyth them to lepe the hach!	43	Balettys2	33
Which makyth my hart oft to lepe and sprynge	44	Balettys3	32
And thoughte to lepe; and even with that woke,	61	Bowge	531
Than he wold lepe and skyp,	75	Phy Sparrow	139
And on me it wolde lepe	75	Phy Sparrow	161
Causeth myne hert to lepe;	97	Phy Sparrow	1015
If lyberte sholde lepe and renne where he lyst	144	Magnyfycence	133
I lyve as me lyst, I lepe out at large;	199	Magnyfycence	2080
That lustely they lepe somtyme theyr cloyster wall.	201	Magnyfycence	2150
Shall lepe from this lyfe, as mery as we be.	236	Speke Parott	222
And lepe out of theyr lyppes	252	Collyn Clout	242
Lepe over lakes and dykes,	262	Collyn Clout	622
And lepe frome the hylles to lerne for to daunce;	320	Garlande	280
But lepe away lyke frogges	364	Albany	212

LEPES
With lepes and bounsis;	349	Garlande	1308
with] 'wit' †Fakes 1523			

LEPYNG
The lesarde came lepyng, and sayd that he must,	315	Garlande	104

LEPYNGE
Harvy Ha[f]ter came lepynge, lyghte as lynde.	52	Bowge	231
Hafter] 'Haster' †Wynkyn de Worde 1499, 1510, Marshe 1568			

LERE
The whytnesse of her lere;	97	Phy Sparrow	1034
Your lothesum lere to loke on, lyke a gresyd bote dothe schyne.	123	Garnesche2	5
Theys lythers I lerne them for to lere,	175	Magnyfycence	1268
Her lothely lere /Is nothynge clere,	214	El Rummynge	12

LERING
But lering and lurking here and there like spies,	139	Ven Tongues	67

LERNA
In Lerna the Grekes fen,	105	Phy Sparrow	1328
In Lerna the Grekis fen	349	Garlande	1321

LERNE
For lordes and ladyes lerne at his scole;	38	Coystrowne1	52
And lerne me to synge Re my fa sol!	53	Bowge	258
And lerne to wepe at me!	73	Phy Sparrow	73
Rede and lerne ye may,	129	Garnesche3	195
Lerne or be lewde, I shrow thy face.	132	Garnesche5	127
Thus can I lerne you, syrs, to bere the devyls sacke;	160	Magnyfycence	721
Theys lythers I lerne them for to lere,	175	Magnyfycence	1268
Nowe must you lerne to begge at every mannes gate.	196	Magnyfycence	1981
Ye, syr, nowe must ye lerne to lye harde,	197	Magnyfycence	2005
Nowe must ye lerne to lye on the strawe.	197	Magnyfycence	2015
But yet, syrs, hardely one thynge lerne of me:	199	Magnyfycence	2087
For to be wyse all men may lerne of me,	201	Magnyfycence	2158
But, my good sonne, lerne from dyspaire to flee;	206	Magnyfycence	2339
To lerne you hereafter for to beware withall.	207	Magnyfycence	2376
Be gentyll, then, of corage, and lerne to be kynde;	211	Magnyfycence	2486
With ladyes I lerne and goe with them to scole.	231	Speke Parott	21
Dowche Frensche of Paris Parot can lerne,	231	Speke Parott	29
To lerne all langage and hyt to speke aptlye.	232	Speke Parott	45
But noble men borne, /To lerne they have scorne,	262	Collyn Clout	620
And lepe frome the hylles to lerne for to daunce;	320	Garlande	280

LERNED — LET

	Page	Title	Line
Item to Lerne You to Dye When ye Wyll;	345	Garlande	1176
to] 'do' †Fakes 1523			
For drede and he lerne them there A B C to spell.'	353	Garlande	1476

LERNED

	Page	Title	Line
And lerned after my scole	74	Phy Sparrow	117
To counterfet this freers have lerned me.	154	Magnyfycence	487
For I may tell you, /I lerned it of a Jewe,	219	El Rummynge	208
Some lerned in other sawe, /As in divynyte,	264	Collyn Clout	732
Doctours that lerned be	266	Collyn Clout	790
That all our lerned men	287	Why Come Ye	322
Ye had never lerned letter,	380	Replycacion	230

LERNID

	Page	Title	Line
Nether wise nor wel lernid, but like hermaphradita:	235	Speke Parott	159

LERNYD

	Page	Title	Line
Ye lernyd of sum py-bakar.	127	Garnesche3	111
The honor of Englond I lernyd to spelle,	132	Garnesche5	95

LERNYNG

	Page	Title	Line
In hys lernyng primordiall.	132	Garnesche5	105
Thus dyvers of language by lernyng I grow:	233	Speke Parott	103
How the rest of good lernyng is roufled up and trold.	235	Speke Parott	168
roufled] 'roulled' Day 1560, Marshe 1568			
But lewdlye ar they lettyrd that your lernyng lackys,	239	Speke Parott	294
My lernyng is to small	370	Albany	457
of the lycorous electuary of lusty lernyng,	373	Replycacion	1
Your lernyng is starke nought,	376	Replycacion	56
And your lollardy lernyng teched,	379	Replycacion	204

LERNYNGE

	Page	Title	Line
They drove me to lernynge lyke a dull asse.	178	Magnyfycence	1386
Theyr lernynge is so small,	252	Collyn Clout	240
After olde seygnours, /And the lernynge of Lytelton Tenours	256	Collyn Clout	370
Thy lernynge is to lewde,	287	Why Come Ye	330

LESARD

	Page	Title	Line
Ware of the lesard lyeth lurkyng in the gras.	45	Balettys4	7

LESARDE

	Page	Title	Line
The lesarde came lepyng, and sayd that he must,	315	Garlande	104

LESE

	Page	Title	Line
My tyme, I trow, I xulde but lese	133	Garnesche5	154
And ye may lese it for a pynne.	168	Magnyfycence	1016
I make hym lese moche of theyr strength;	175	Magnyfycence	1259
Lothe they are to lese	267	Collyn Clout	841

LESINGES

	Page	Title	Line
Then ren they with lesinges, and blow them about,	139	Ven Tongues	69

LESSE

	Page	Title	Line
I care muche the lesse what ever they say,	138	Ven Tongues	36
But she is lesse a grete dele	169	Magnyfycence	1052
And, be the mater yll more or lesse,	175	Magnyfycence	1272
Nay, nay; for lesse I waraunt you to be sped,	184	Magnyfycence	1571
To shewe you my mynde I wolde have the lesse fere.	186	Magnyfycence	1646
Ye are the lesse to blame,	262	Collyn Clout	614
Yet they mervayle so moche lesse,	271	Collyn Clout	1008
Men wolde have the lesse scorne	291	Why Come Ye	496
Or elles, ye know well, I can do no lesse	318	Garlande	226
With all the prese that there was lesse and more.	325	Garlande	455
A lesse lumpe of logyke,	374	Replycacion	2

LESSON

	Page	Title	Line
Redresse, in my remembraunce your lesson shall rest;	211	Magnyfycence	2503

LESSONS

	Page	Title	Line
Theyr lessons forgoten they have	251	Collyn Clout	169

LEST

	Page	Title	Line
The starkest knave, and lest good kan,	130	Garnesche5	23
For drede, that we dare not ofte, lest we be spyed.	177	Magnyfycence	1339
Why, wyll they then be intreted, the most and the lest?	184	Magnyfycence	1585
Lest that he thought that his money were evyll spente,	187	Magnyfycence	1674
Lest they be Seduces,	277	Collyn Clout	1229
Seduces] 'Saducies' Marshe 1568, 'Adusayes' MS Harley 2252			
I dought, lest by sorsery	295	Why Come Ye	663
Lest he wyll put it clene out,	309	Why Come Ye	1199
He coude not devyse the lest poynt of your cheke;	337	Garlande	896

LESTE

	Page	Title	Line
Hyt ys to fere leste he wolde were the garland on hys pate,	244	Speke Parott	435
Leste that his fote slyppe,	263	Collyn Clout	666

LESURE

	Page	Title	Line
It askyth lesure with good advert[ence].	141	Magnyfycence	42
advertence] 'advertysment' †Rastell & Treveris C 1530, B			

LET

	Page	Title	Line
Fled away from hym, let hym ly in the dust,	30	Dol Dethe	39
Turnd ther backis and let ther master fall,	31	Dol Dethe	94
backis] 'backe' Marshe 1568			
Take up whos wolde, for ther they let hym ly.	32	Dol Dethe	96
Let double delinge in the have no place,	34	Dol Dethe	174
Tully, valy, strawe, let be I say!	35	Man Margery	5
Let me', quod he, 'ly in your lap.'	41	Balettys1	2
Let not all the world make an owtcry;	43	Balettys2	40
Shyfte now therwith, let see, as ye can,	48	Bowge	99
Let us, therfore, shortely at a worde	54	Bowge	307
He sayde he wold not let /His houndys for to fet,	64	Hauke	106
But let the matter slyp,	66	Hauke	154
For to let their hawkys fly	67	Hauke	218

LET —LET | Page | Title | Line

Entry	Page	Title	Line
To let theyr hawkys fly	70	Hauke	301
Let some poetes wryte	78	Phy Sparrow	252
Let us now whysper /A Pater noster.	81	Phy Sparrow	384
And let hym ryng the bellys;	84	Phy Sparrow	493
No man can let me thynke,	101	Phy Sparrow	1199
Thow wrythtyst I xulde let the go pley;	134	Garnesche5	166
I cannat let the the knave to play,	134	Garnesche5	169
Then let them vale a bonet of their proud sayle,	138	Ven Tongues	32
Lyberte to let from all maner offence;	141	Magnyfycence	45
God forbyd ye sholde be let	142	Magnyfycence	63
Come of therfore, let se;	143	Magnyfycence	102
It i[s] no maystery. Tushe, let Measure procede, is] 'it' †Rastell & Treveris C 1530, B	144	Magnyfycence	150
But nowe let me knowe of your conversacyon.	145	Magnyfycence	170
Let se this checke yf ye voyde canne.	148	Magnyfycence	297
Let us departe from hens home to my place.	151	Magnyfycence	394
Let se, fynde you a better way.	156	Magnyfycence	560
Nay. Let us our heddes togyder cast.	156	Magnyfycence	566
Nay; eyther let me tell, or elles tell ye.	158	Magnyfycence	633
I pray God let you never to thee!	158	Magnyfycence	635
Now let us go, and we shall, then.	159	Magnyfycence	687
Nowe let se. Quyte you lyke praty men!	159	Magnyfycence	688
Tushe! He that hathe nede, man, let hym rynne.	162	Magnyfycence	786
Convey yourselfe fyrst, let se.	163	Magnyfycence	816
What nowe? Let se /Who loketh on me	163	Magnyfycence	829
But nowe what tydynges can you tell? Let se.	166	Magnyfycence	928
Cockes harte! Tourne the; let me se thyne aray.	167	Magnyfycence	959
Ye, but of my name let us be wyse.	167	Magnyfycence	963
Nowe let me se about	168	Magnyfycence	991
Nowe, of good felowshyp, let me by thy [d]ogge. dogge] 'hogge' †Rastell & Treveris C 1530, B	170	Magnyfycence	1082
Let me have thy dogge, what soever I pay.	171	Magnyfycence	1101
Nay, in fayth, fyrst let me here thyne.	172	Magnyfycence	1152
What, Fansy! Let me se who is the tother.	172	Magnyfycence	1158
Ye. Let us here a worde or twayne.	174	Magnyfycence	1218
Hast thou ony more? Let se, procede.	174	Magnyfycence	1236
But, I say, let se and yf thou have any more.	175	Magnyfycence	1278
At ones, and let hym not tary all day.	179	Magnyfycence	1400
Or lyberte by welth? Let se, tell me that.	180	Magnyfycence	1432
Mayster Felycyte, let be your chydynge;	180	Magnyfycence	1437
And let the other another [time] awayte. time] not in †Rastell & Treveris C 1530, B	180	Magnyfycence	1454
Let us here of your pleasure, to passe the tyme withall.	182	Magnyfycence	1518
Let se what ye say. Shewe it strayte.	185	Magnyfycence	1592
Wysely let these wordes in your mynde be wayed:	185	Magnyfycence	1593
By waywarde wylfulnes let eche thynge be convayed;	185	Magnyfycence	1594
Let your lust and lykynge stande for a lawe.	185	Magnyfycence	1607
Stande a lytell abacke, syr, and let hym come hyder.	186	Magnyfycence	1647
Well, call hym, and let us here hym reason;	187	Magnyfycence	1687
Syr, I beseche you let pety have some place	188	Magnyfycence	1712
With me no longer. Say somwhat nowe, let se,	188	Magnyfycence	1719
Abyde, syr, abyde. Let me holde your hede.	189	Magnyfycence	1727
God gyve hym a myscheffe! Nay, nowe let me alone.	189	Magnyfycence	1730
Let me have the rule of your purse.	189	Magnyfycence	1762
And let all your fansyes upon them rest.	190	Magnyfycence	1770
Gyve them more than ynoughe, and let them not lacke;	190	Magnyfycence	1773
And as for all other, let them trusse and packe;	190	Magnyfycence	1774
Let neyther patent scape them nor fee;	190	Magnyfycence	1776
Let them have all, and the other go without;	190	Magnyfycence	1780
Ye, let be thy japes, and tell me howe	192	Magnyfycence	1846
I pray the, Largesse, let be thy sobbynge.	192	Magnyfycence	1851
Of correccyon, but let them have theyr wyll.	194	Magnyfycence	1930
To love that lovesome I wyll not let;	199	Magnyfycence	2072
In youth to be wanton, and let them have theyr wyll —	200	Magnyfycence	2137
Now let us be all one, and let us lyve in rest;	202	Magnyfycence	2202
Now let us be all one, and let us lyve in rest;	202	Magnyfycence	2202
Go we nere and let us se.	204	Magnyfycence	2243
But nowe let us make mery and good chere.	204	Magnyfycence	2261
And to the taverne let us drawe nere.	204	Magnyfycence	2262
For the passyon of God, let us go thyther.	204	Magnyfycence	2276
Yet let us se this matter thorowly ingrosed.	209	Magnyfycence	2438
Let never negarshyp your noblenesse affray;	211	Magnyfycence	2493
And ever let the drede of God be in your syght,	211	Magnyfycence	2498
And let us sley care!'	217	El Rummynge	111
But let us turne playne, /There we lefte agayne.	219	El Rummynge	187
But, 'Drynke,' styll, 'Drynke, /And let the cat wynke!	222	El Rummynge	306
Let us wasshe our gommes /From the drye crommes!'	222	El Rummynge	307
Of thyne ale let us assaye.	224	El Rummynge	397
'And let me with you bybyll.'	228	El Rummynge	550
Let us syppe and soppy, /And not spyll a droppy,	228	El Rummynge	558
But moveatur terra, let the world wag,	233	Speke Parott	88
Let Syr Wrig-wrag wrastell with Syr Delarag:	233	Speke Parott	89
I pray you, let Parot have lyberte to speake.	233	Speke Parott	98
Let Parrot, I pray you, have lyberte to prate,	234	Speke Parott	141
Let every man after his merit take his parte;	236	Speke Parott	199
I pray you, let Parrot have lyberte to speke.	236	Speke Parott	210
Let se who dare make up the reste.	242	Speke Parott	382
'He is but a foole; /Let hym go to scole!'	247	Collyn Clout	29

	Page	Title	Line
LETE —LETTYTH			
For let se who that dare	251	Collyn Clout	179
But ye loke to be let lose	252	Collyn Clout	213
With, 'Let the catte wynke!	258	Collyn Clout	457
And let Collyn Clout have none	258	Collyn Clout	478
have none] 'alone' MS Lansdowne 762, 'alon' MS Harley 2252			
Let hym well beware	263	Collyn Clout	665
Howebeit they let downe fall	271	Collyn Clout	978
And let be all your motynge,	273	Collyn Clout	1073
And let our matters pas!	275	Collyn Clout	1159
matters] 'matter' Kele 1545.1, 'maters' Marshe 1568, 'medlyng' MS Harley 2252			
Let him cough, rough or snevyll!	277	Collyn Clout	1221
And let take all the rest!	277	Collyn Clout	1224
But let mi masters mathematical	296	Why Come Ye	708
Let him never confounde	298	Why Come Ye	778
The worde of God to let.	305	Why Come Ye	1069
worde] 'wordis', to] 'he' MS Rawlinson C. 813			
Shall let the preest pontyficall	308	Why Come Ye	1160
What he hath done, let it be brought to syght.	318	Garlande	230
Call forthe, let se where is your clarionar,	318	Garlande	233
Let hym blowe now, that we may take a vewe	319	Garlande	237
a] 'the' MS Cotton Vitellius E.x			
Let se, my syster, now spede you, go aboute.	319	Garlande	242
you] not in MS Cotton Vitellius E.x			
And for no man hardely let hym spare	319	Garlande	244
'Nay, holde thy tunge,' quod another, 'let me have the name.'	319	Garlande	255
If xii were let in, xii hundreth stode without.	326	Garlande	490
With, 'Now let me come', and 'Now let me go.'	326	Garlande	515
With, 'Now let me come', and 'Now let me go.'	326	Garlande	515
'Come on with me,' she sayd, 'let us not stonde';	328	Garlande	559
To walke where we lyst, let us somwhat fynde	328	Garlande	564
To pas the tyme with, but let us wast no wynde.	328	Garlande	565
Let se now for hym how ye can expounde;	345	Garlande	1153
Who list amende it, let hym set to his penne.	348	Garlande	1260
Whyche he and ye? Let se;	367	Albany	333
God let you never thrive!	368	Albany	379
LETE			
'Why? What than? Wylte thou lete men to speke?	51	Bowge	184
What, lete us holde him up, man, for a whyle.'	51	Bowge	188
Holde up the helme, loke up and lete God stere:	53	Bowge	250
And lete us laugh a placke or tweyne at nale.	57	Bowge	387
placke] 'plucke' Marshe 1568			
I lete her to hyre that men maye on her ryde;	57	Bowge	402
Lete theym go lowse theym, in the devylles date.	59	Bowge	455
LETHER			
In Affryc tongue byrsa is a thonge of lether;	233	Speke Parott	80
Of a lether bottell /With a knavysshe stoppell,	262	Collyn Clout	650
LETT			
Now, Galathea, lett Parrot, I pray yow, have hys date –	244	Speke Parott	439
LETTE			
Abyde. Lette me se. Take better hede.	157	Magnyfycence	595
Nay, lette us not clatter thus styll.	157	Magnyfycence	610
Than lette reason you supporte,	271	Collyn Clout	1004
And lette me come to delyver my lettre.'	326	Garlande	506
LETTER			
I have your lewde letter receyvyd,	124	Garnesche3	1
Whylest I knowe that this letter dothe contayne.	149	Magnyfycence	324
But nowe, syr, as touchynge this letter -	149	Magnyfycence	331
This letter was wryten ferre hence.	150	Magnyfycence	337
But what became of the letter	155	Magnyfycence	531
Ye, but I can somwhat more of the letter.	170	Magnyfycence	1066
And is this the credence that I gave to the letter?	193	Magnyfycence	1867
Howe be it, from you I receyved a letter [sent],	209	Magnyfycence	2435
sent] not in †Rastell & Treveris C 1530, B			
Syr, this letter ye sent to me at Pountes was enclosed.	209	Magnyfycence	2439
Who brought you that letter? Wote ye what he hyght?	209	Magnyfycence	2440
This letter ye speke of never dyd I wryte.	209	Magnyfycence	2442
And for to leve this letter, /Bicause it is no better;	220	El Rummynge	237
A preest without a letter,	253	Collyn Clout	270
Then all the freres letter.	265	Collyn Clout	762
For the kynges letter?	295	Why Come Ye	670
In Englysshe letter.	355	Garlande	1538
Ye had never lerned letter,	380	Replycacion	230
LETTERD			
To letterd men at large.	350	Garlande	1354
LETTERS			
In golde letters, this worde, whiche I dyde rede:	48	Bowge	66
With letters of golde.	103	Phy Sparrow	1259
Why were ye Calliope, embrawdred with letters of golde?	112	Calliope	I
In Romaine letters I never founde lack	137	Ven Tongues	17
Counterfet letters by the way of sleyght;	152	Magnyfycence	439
And some wyll take upon them to conterfet letters,	178	Magnyfycence	1364
Some Romaine letters, as I understode;	328	Garlande	583
LETTYRD			
But lewdlye ar they lettyrd that your lernyng lackys,	239	Speke Parott	294
LETTYTH			
Committyth all to God, and lettyth his shyp ryde;	335	Garlande	834

LETTRE —LEWDNES   Page   Title   Line

LETTRE
	Page	Title	Line
And lette me come to delyver my lettre.'	326	Garlande	506

LETTRED
	Page	Title	Line
To lettred men at large:	105	Phy Sparrow	1361
But yet I may say safely, so many wel lettred,	138	Ven Tongues	38
Ye count your selfe wele lettred:	376	Replycacion	55

LEUDE
	Page	Title	Line
Gone is this knave, this rybaude foule and leude.	58	Bowge	414

LEUDLY
	Page	Title	Line
to prate and to preche proudly and leudly, and loudly to lye;	374	Replycacion	1
That leudly have their tyme spent,	375	Replycacion	24

LEVE
	Page	Title	Line
Phyllyp had leve to go	76	Phy Sparrow	175
That never wyll leve theyr tratlynge:	115	Ag Scottes	2
Withowte thou leve thou shalt be chekt,	132	Garnesche5	109
Why, to say what he wyll, Lyberte hath leve.	141	Magnyfycence	34
Take sad dyreccyon, and leve this wantonnesse.	144	Magnyfycence	149
Now leve this jangelynge and to us expounde	147	Magnyfycence	262
Speke, I beseche the. Leve nothynge behynde.	183	Magnyfycence	1544
Ye, syr, ye; leve all this rage,	196	Magnyfycence	1988
That nonnes wyl leve theyr holynes and ryn after me;	201	Magnyfycence	2146
Leve thy pratynge or els I shall lay the on the pate.	201	Magnyfycence	2173
I shall it never forget nor leve it behynde,	212	Magnyfycence	2506
Nowe leve, nowe lothe, nowe please, nowe dysplease;	212	Magnyfycence	2520
And for to leve this letter, /Bicause it is no better;	220	El Rummynge	237
Unneth they leve a locke /Of wolle amongest theyr flocke.	248	Collyn Clout	80
Expoundynge out theyr clauses, /And leve theyr owne causes.	249	Collyn Clout	101
He can never leve warke whylis it is wele.	333	Garlande	763
Mi litell lady I may not leve behinde,	337	Garlande	878
It is not my custome nor my gyse /To leve behynde	342	Garlande	1069
The millar durst not leve his wyfe at home.	352	Garlande	1417

LEVELL SUSE
	Page	Title	Line
With, 'Gup, levell suse!'	282	Why Come Ye	142

LEVEN
	Page	Title	Line
To whos astate all noblenes most leven,	313	Garlande	54
leven] 'lene' †Fakes 1523, MS Cotton Vitellius E.x			

LEVER
	Page	Title	Line
Yet many had lever hangyd to be	198	Magnyfycence	2040
They had lever to please	269	Collyn Clout	909

LEVETH
	Page	Title	Line
and leveth MAGNYFYCENCE alone in the place.	190	Magnyfycence	SD

LEVIS
	Page	Title	Line
His levis loste, the sappe was frome the rynde.	312	Garlande	21
Enverdurid with levis contynually grene;	330	Garlande	666

LEVYNGE
	Page	Title	Line
Levynge me stondynge as a mased man;	48	Bowge	83

LEWDE
	Page	Title	Line
He lumbryth on a lewde lewte, 'Roty bully joyse',	37	Coystrowne1	29
But one thyng is: that ye be lewde!	41	Coystrowne4	27
Thyse lewde cok wattes shall nevermore prevayle	51	Bowge	173
wattes] 'witts' Marshe 1568			
Yet on my backe I bere suche lewde delynge.	59	Bowge	457
Me thoughte I see lewde felawes here and there	61	Bowge	528
Devysed and also wrate /Uppon a lewde curate,	62	Hauke	35
I have your lewde letter receyvyd,	124	Garnesche3	1
To cal me lorell ye ar to lewde;	131	Garnesche5	85
Lerne or be lewde, I shrow thy face.	132	Garnesche5	127
Prowde, peviche, lyddyr and lewde,	133	Garnesche5	146
To taunt theim like liddrons, lewde as thei bee.	138	Ven Tongues	29
To homly, to holy, to lewde, or to lowde,	199	Magnyfycence	2094
Her lewde lyppes twayne, /They slaver, men sayne,	215	El Rummynge	22
Suche a lewde sorte /To Elynour resorte	218	El Rummynge	153
So myche serchyng of loselles, and ys hym selfe so lewde;	246	Speke Parott	513
For sothe, they are to lewde /To say so, all beshrewde!	249	Collyn Clout	90
Avaunt, lewde preest, avaunt!	275	Collyn Clout	1156
Thy lernynge is to lewde,	287	Why Come Ye	330
Yet with lewde condicyons cotyd	293	Why Come Ye	572
cotyd] 'noted' Kitson 1560.7, Marshe 1568			
Suche lewde langage ye spake.	367	Albany	329
I say, thou lewde lurdayne,	367	Albany	336

LEWDELY
	Page	Title	Line
Lewdely your tyme ye spende,	124	Garnesche3	15
And lewdely sayes by Chryst	261	Collyn Clout	575

LEWDENES
	Page	Title	Line
Of thy lewdenes more ys behynde;	134	Garnesche5	173
Of thi lewdenes that may be tolde.	134	Garnesche5	175

LEWDLY
	Page	Title	Line
Your Englysche lew[d]ly ye sorte,	124	Garnesche3	19
lewdly] 'lewly' †MS Harley 367			
Dekkyd lewdly in your gere,	125	Garnesche3	42
And so little learning, so lewdly alowed,	138	Ven Tongues	40
And I to suffre you lewdly to ly	138	Ven Tongues	47
What! Lyest thou there lyngrynge, lewdly and lothsome?	205	Magnyfycence	2291

LEWDLYE
	Page	Title	Line
But lewdlye ar they lettyrd that your lernyng lackys,	239	Speke Parott	294

LEWDNES
	Page	Title	Line
Your awne lewdnes to amende.	124	Garnesche3	18

	Page	Title	Line
LEWDNESSE			
Of all lewdnesse I kyndell the brande.	152	Magnyfycence	437
That list of there lewdnesse with hym for to brall.'	334	Garlande	786
LEWES			
I reporte me herein to Kynge Lewes of Fraunce.	148	Magnyfycence	280
Maketh remembraunce /How Kynge Lewes of late	297	Why Come Ye	722
By Lewes the kyng aforesayd, ...	297	Why Come Ye	730
LEWTE			
He lumbryth on a lewde lewte, 'Roty bully joyse', ...	37	Coystrownel	29
LIBYK			
Lyacon of Libyk and Lydy hathe cawghte hys pray:	239	Speke Parott	289
LIBRARY			
For of all ladyes he hath the library, ...	334	Garlande	780
LIDDER			
For though some be lidder, and list for to rayle, ...	138	Ven Tongues	30
LIDDERONS			
Some lidderons, some losels, some noughty packis;	317	Garlande	188
LIDDYRNES			
I am not ladyn of liddyrnes with lumpis, ...	332	Garlande	733
LIDDRONS			
To taunt theim like liddrons, lewde as thei bee.	138	Ven Tongues	29
LIDGATE			
Mayster Lidgate, of your accustomable	324	Garlande	436
LIE			
Yet to lie upon me they can not prevayle.	138	Ven Tongues	31
Gentle Paule lie doune thy sweard, ...	358	Couplet	1
LIEUTENAUNT			
I say, lieutenaunt of the Toure, ...	275	Collyn Clout	1167
LIFE			
Of whos [life] they countede not a fly.	31	Dol Dethe	95
life] not in †MS Royal 18 D.ii or Marshe 1568			
With whom he ledd a plesaunt life;	90	Phy Sparrow	744
LIGHT			
And be not light of credence in no case.	34	Dol Dethe	175
Whose radiant beame /And relucent light	136	Dundas	46
A cronell of lawrell with verduris light and darke	334	Garlande	776
LIING			
Liing, spying by suttelte and slyght, ...	133	Garnesche5	151
LIIST			
Thow liist, I callyd the a wodcoke;	133	Garnesche5	129
LIKE			
Like Andromach, Hectors wyfe, ...	74	Phy Sparrow	108
Qui iacet hic, like a knave!	109	Epitaphe2	26
Et iacet hic, like a best!	109	Epitaphe2	28
Hoyning like hogges that groynis and wrotes.	137	Ven Tongues	4
To taunt theim like liddrons, lewde as thei bee.	138	Ven Tongues	29
But lering and lurking here and there like spies, ...	139	Ven Tongues	67
Like an onyon syded, /Lyke tan ledder hyded.	226	El Rummynge	470
Nether wise nor wel lernid, but like hermaphradita:	235	Speke Parott	159
Racell, rulye ragged, she is like to cache colde;	242	Speke Parott	401
Therin, like a royle, ...	365	Albany	270
LIKKITH			
And wele wotith the cat whos berde she likkith.	352	Garlande	1438
LILLIS			
With lillis whyte your bewte doth renewe.	337	Garlande	884
With lillis] 'The lylly' MS Cotton Vitellius E.x			
LILLYS			
With lillys whyte your bewte dothe renewe.	337	Garlande	891
LIMBIS			
Of Exione, his limbis dede and past, ...	351	Garlande	1400
his limbis] 'her lambis' †Fakes 1523, 'her lambe is' Marshe 1568			
LIMYTERS			
As limyters at large	267	Collyn Clout	834
LIMMES			
And make him lame of his neder limmes.	309	Why Come Ye	1200
LINE			
Of kingis line moost streight, ...	110	Lawde	10
LINUS			
As Linus and Homerus, /Euphorion and Theocritus, ...	90	Phy Sparrow	761
LIPPES			
With his byll betwene my lippes, ...	80	Phy Sparrow	359
LIST			
For though some be lidder, and list for to rayle, ...	138	Ven Tongues	30
That list of there lewdnesse with hym for to brall.'	334	Garlande	786
In you, who list to seke, ...	338	Garlande	920
Who list to rede.	342	Garlande	1081
Who list amende it, let hym set to his penne.	348	Garlande	1260
LISTA			
To hawke when [you] lista	69	Hauke	257
you] 'your' editions			
LITELL			
Mi litell lady I may not leve behinde, ...	337	Garlande	878
With litell besynes standith moche rest; in bed	351	Garlande	1410
LITELLE			
Go, litelle quayre, namyd the Popagay, ...	238	Speke Parott	278
LITILL			
All were to litill for his magnyficence.	33	Dol Dethe	161

LITYLL —LYBERTE	Page	Title	Line

LITYLL

Go, litill quaire, /Demene you faire.	355	Garlande	1533

LITYLL

Some say but lityll and thynke more in there thowghte, ...	242	Speke Parott	388

LITTLE

And so little learning, so lewdly alowed, ...	138	Ven Tongues	40

LY

Fled away from hym, let hym ly in the dust, ...	30	Dol Dethe	39
Take up whos wolde, for ther they let hym ly.	32	Dol Dethe	96
Let me', quod he, 'ly in your lap.'	41	Balettys1	2
'Ly styll', quod she, 'my paramoure, ...	41	Balettys1	3
Ly styll hardely, and take a nap.'	41	Balettys1	4
Ask all your neybours whether that I ly.	43	Balettys2	35
(The Bybyll wyll not ly)	66	Hauke	167
That evermore wil ly /And say cursedly;	94	Phy Sparrow	906
Yet, where so ever they ly	106	Epitaphe	I
Ye ar dysposyd for to ly.	131	Garnesche5	64
And I to suffre you lewdly to ly	138	Ven Tongues	47
Ly there, losell, for all thy pompe and pryde;	193	Magnyfycence	1880
I rushe at them rughly and make them ly full lowe;	193	Magnyfycence	1884
Ly styll, ly styll nowe, with yll hayle!	204	Magnyfycence	2248
Ly styll, ly styll nowe, with yll hayle!	204	Magnyfycence	2248
Today a lorde, tomorowe ly in the duste:	213	Magnyfycence	2543
Than swetely togither we ly, /As two pygges in a sty.'	220	El Rummynge	233
Than swetely] 'Thus swete' 1521 Fragment			

LYACON

Lyacon of Libyk and Lydy hathe cawghte hys pray:	239	Speke Parott	289
Lyacon lawghyth thereatt and berythe hym more bolde;	242	Speke Parott	400

LYAR

What, wold Fraunces, our friar, /Be suche a false lyar, ...	368	Albany	374

LYARS

They counte us for lyars;	276	Collyn Clout	1187

LYBANY

[The] *serpens of Lybany	79	Phy Sparrow	290
The] 'These' †Kele 1545.2, Wyght 1553, Kitson 1560.6, Marshe 1568; *serpens] 'serpentes' Wyght, Kitson, Marshe			

LYBBARD

Wheron stode a lybbard, crownyd with golde and stones, ...	328	Garlande	590

LYBERALITE

His fr[u]galite, /His lyberalite, ...	370	Albany	450
frugalite] 'fragalite' †Marshe 1568			

LYBERALYTE

For lyberalyte is most convenyent	200	Magnyfycence	2117

LYBERALL

Not thorowe largesse of lyberall expence, ...	200	Magnyfycence	2115
For of noblenesse the chefe poynt is to be lyberall, ...	211	Magnyfycence	2487

LYBERTE

Delyte, desyre, respyte, wyth lyberte;	43	Balettys3	2
To hunte there by lyberte	64	Hauke	108
For thought hath lyberte, ...	101	Phy Sparrow	1200
Your name is Lyberte, as I understande.	141	Magnyfycence	27
Why, to say what he wyll, Lyberte hath leve.	141	Magnyfycence	34
Yet lyberte hath ben lockyd up and kept in the mew.	141	Magnyfycence	35
In dede, syr, that lyberte was not worthe a cue.	141	Magnyfycence	36
How be it, lyberte may somtyme be to large, ...	141	Magnyfycence	37
That lyberte be lynkyd with the chayne of countenaunce, . . .	141	Magnyfycence	44
Lyberte to let from all maner offence;	141	Magnyfycence	45
For lyberte at large is lothe to be stoppyd, ...	141	Magnyfycence	46
Lyberte, I wote well, forbere no man there may;	142	Magnyfycence	50
Howe be it, lyberte makyth many a man blynde;	142	Magnyfycence	52
By lyberte is done many a great excesse;	142	Magnyfycence	53
Lyberte at large wyll oft wax reklesse.	142	Magnyfycence	54
Wherfore at lyberte	142	Magnyfycence	65
Lyberte is laudable and pryvylegyd from lawe.	142	Magnyfycence	68
I say there is no welthe where as lyberte is subdude.	142	Magnyfycence	73
And you have not your owne fre lyberte	142	Magnyfycence	78
Where lyberte is absent, set welthe asyde.	142	Magnyfycence	80
Lyberte without measure prove a thynge of nought.	143	Magnyfycence	117
So that lyberte be not lefte behynde.	144	Magnyfycence	129
Ye, lyberte with measure nede never drede.	144	Magnyfycence	130
What, lyberte to measure then wolde ye bynde?	144	Magnyfycence	131
If lyberte sholde lepe and renne where he lyst	144	Magnyfycence	133
It were a myschefe, yf lyberte lacked a reyne	144	Magnyfycence	135
Lyberte without measure is acountyd for a beste;	144	Magnyfycence	138
Welthe, with Measure and plesaunt Lyberte.	145	Magnyfycence	160
And, syr, this other mannys name is Lyberte.	145	Magnyfycence	168
And I am Lyberte, made of in every nacyon.	145	Magnyfycence	172
Welthe with Lyberte, with me bothe dwell ye shall, ...	145	Magnyfycence	174
And lyberte his large with measure shall make.	145	Magnyfycence	180
Then, Lyberte, se that Measure by your gyde, ...	146	Magnyfycence	195
If ye lyst to lyve after your fre lyberte.	146	Magnyfycence	208
Lyberte in some cause becomyth a gentyll mynde -	146	Magnyfycence	212
For howe be it lyberte to welthe is convenyent, ...	146	Magnyfycence	219
That all men laugh at lyberte to scorne.	146	Magnyfycence	222
Of to moche lyberte under the offence;	146	Magnyfycence	229
Wherfore, Measure, take Lyberte with you hence, ...	146	Magnyfycence	230
Take Lyberte to rule, and folowe myne entent.	147	Magnyfycence	238
It is a wanton thynge, this Lyberte.	147	Magnyfycence	240
And that he take good kepe to Lyberte.	149	Magnyfycence	320

LYBERTYES — LYDGATE

	Page	Title	Line
For to speke with Lyberte.	155	Magnyfycence	539
What! Is Largesse without lyberte?	155	Magnyfycence	540
And have you not amonge you Lyberte?	157	Magnyfycence	625
So that we have no lyberte;	158	Magnyfycence	659
For Lyberte he hath in gydyng.	158	Magnyfycence	661
In fayth, and without lyberte there is no bydyng.	158	Magnyfycence	662
I laughe at all shrewdenes, and lye at lyberte.	160	Magnyfycence	735
In faythe, Lyberte is nowe a lusty spere.	166	Magnyfycence	937
And shall we have lyberte to do what we wyll?	176	Magnyfycence	1316
Ryot at lyberte russheth it out styll.	176	Magnyfycence	1317
Here cometh in MAGNYFYCENCE with LYBERTE and FELYCYTE.	178	Magnyfycence	SD
Trust me, Lyberte, it greveth me ryght sore	178	Magnyfycence	1375
Yet Lyberte without rule is not worth a strawe.	178	Magnyfycence	1378
Remembre ye not how my lyberte by mesure ruled was?	178	Magnyfycence	1383
It is good yet that lyberte be ruled by reason.	178	Magnyfycence	1387
Yourselfe shall be ruled by lyberte and largesse.	179	Magnyfycence	1389
Syr, by lyberte and largesse I wyll that ye shall	179	Magnyfycence	1396
To rule as ye lyst, lo, here is Lyberte.	179	Magnyfycence	1413
That was by the menys of to moche lyberte.	180	Magnyfycence	1424
Whether sholde welth be rulyd by lyberte,	180	Magnyfycence	1431
Or lyberte by welth? Let se, tell me that.	180	Magnyfycence	1432
And welth is nought worthe yf lyberte be behynde.	180	Magnyfycence	1442
And get [y]ou home togyther; for Lyberte shall byde you] 'thou' †Rastell & Treveris C 1530, B	180	Magnyfycence	1446
Here goeth out FELYCYTE, LYBERTE and FANSY.	180	Magnyfycence	SD
I have welth at wyll, largesse and lyberte.	181	Magnyfycence	1458
Take your pleasure and use free lyberte;	185	Magnyfycence	1598
I have taken it to Largesse and Lyberte.	189	Magnyfycence	1763
And I shall waraunt you welth and lyberte.	190	Magnyfycence	1766
For the[m] shall you have at lyberte to lowte. them] 'then' †Rastell & Treveris C 1530, B	190	Magnyfycence	1779
And here I make the upon Lyberte	190	Magnyfycence	1784
For Lyberte is gone, and also Felycyte.	192	Magnyfycence	1857
In lust and lykynge my name is Lyberte.	199	Magnyfycence	2078
What is he lyvynge that lyberte wolde lacke?	199	Magnyfycence	2083
A thousande pounde with lyberte may holde no tacke.	199	Magnyfycence	2084
At lyberte a man may be bolde for to brake;	199	Magnyfycence	2085
Welthe without lyberte gothe all to wrake.	199	Magnyfycence	2086
I warne you beware of to moche lyberte,	199	Magnyfycence	2088
By meanes of madnesse and to moche lyberte.	199	Magnyfycence	2100
A, woo worthe the, Lyberte, nowe thou sayst full trewe;	199	Magnyfycence	2103
For yf Measure had ruled Lyberte as he began,	200	Magnyfycence	2111
But he abused so his free lyberte,	200	Magnyfycence	2113
That they lose theyr lyberte and all that there is.	200	Magnyfycence	2128
Howe many come to myschefe for to moche lyberte;	200	Magnyfycence	2134
Some hath so moche lyberte of one thynge and other,	200	Magnyfycence	2141
Some have so moche lyberte that they fere no synne,	200	Magnyfycence	2143
At lyberte to wander and walke over all,	201	Magnyfycence	2149
And caused me also to use to moche lyberte,	209	Magnyfycence	2445
Lyberte to a lorde belongyth of ryght,	211	Magnyfycence	2489
I pray you, let Parot have lyberte to speke.	233	Speke Parott	98
Let Parrot, I pray you, have lyberte to prate,	234	Speke Parott	141
I pray you, let Parrot have lyberte to speke.	236	Speke Parott	210
And have theyr lyberte,	264	Collyn Clout	712

LYBERTYES
In fayth, and Lybertyes rome is there but small.	158	Magnyfycence	663

LYBIUS
And of Syr Lybius /Named Dysconius;	88	Phy Sparrow	649

LYBYUS
Thow ye be lusty as Syr Lybyus, launces to breke,	122	Garneschel	17

LYCAON
The wylde wolfe Lycaon	79	Phy Sparrow	311

LYCE
Of vermyne and of lyce	364	Albany	220

LYCENCE
Graunte hym his lycence	272	Collyn Clout	1038

LYCKED
whan they have delectably lycked a lytell	373	Replycacion	I

LYCLYHOD
Now Neptune and Eolus ar agreed of lyclyhod,	239	Speke Parott	283

LYCON
Nor Lycon, that lothly luske, in myn opynyon,	122	Garneschel	24

LYCOROUS
of the lycorous electuary of lusty lernyng,	373	Replycacion	I

LYCOUR
For a draught of her lycour. her] not in †Lant 1545, Kynge & Marche 1554, Day 1560, Marshe 1568	225	El Rummynge	417

LYDDER
Ye are but lydder logici, /But moche worse isagogici,	380	Replycacion	234

LYDDERYNS
Lydderyns so lytell set by Goddes lawes.	194	Magnyfycence	1919

LYDDYR
Prowde, peviche, lyddyr and lewde,	133	Garnesche5	146

LYDGATE
Also John Lydgate	91	Phy Sparrow	804
Dane Johnn Lydgate. Theis Englysshe poetis thre,	323	Garlande	391
Mayster Lydgate to Skelton	324	Garlande	R

LYDY —LYGHT Page Title Line

Gower, Chawcer, Lydgate, theis thre	343	Garlande	1101

LYDY

Lyacon of Libyk and Lydy hathe cawghte hys pray:	239	Speke Parott	289

LYE

And to lye downe as soone as I m[e] dreste, me] 'my' †Wynkyn de Worde 1499, 1510, Marshe 1568	47	Bowge	33
It wolde lye and rest -	75	Phy Sparrow	126
And nowe they lye and rote;	78	Phy Sparrow	251
*Or els phylosophy /Maketh a great lye. *Or] 'Of' Scattergood	83	Phy Sparrow	477
How some delite for to lye, thycke and threfolde.	137	Ven Tongues	11
That can not counterfet a lye,	152	Magnyfycence	413
I laughe at all shrewdenes, and lye at lyberte.	160	Magnyfycence	735
Ye, syr, nowe must ye lerne to lye harde,	197	Magnyfycence	2005
That was wonte to lye on fetherbeddes of downe;	197	Magnyfycence	2006
Nowe must your fete lye hyer than your crowne.	197	Magnyfycence	2007
Nowe must ye lerne to lye on the strawe.	197	Magnyfycence	2015
She coulde not lye styllyl'	224	El Rummynge	391
Full falsely on you they lye,	255	Collyn Clout	334
Theyr founders lye there rotten;	257	Collyn Clout	426
But trouth can never lye.	258	Collyn Clout	485
Or elles that they do lye,	273	Collyn Clout	1063
Shote anker, and lye at rode,	277	Collyn Clout	1255
There goth many a lye	288	Why Come Ye	356
This is no fable nor no lye;	296	Why Come Ye	705
For who can best lye, best] not in MS Rawlinson C. 813	300	Why Come Ye	858
Or els his surgions they lye;	308	Why Come Ye	1171
Some came to tell treuth, some came to lye,	326	Garlande	510
to prate and to preche proudly and leudly, and loudly to lye;	374	Replycacion	I
Confessyng howe ye dyde lye /In prechyng shamefully.	377	Replycacion	90

LYENGE

With lyenge and controlleynge.	125	Garnesche3	39

LYERD

Syns Dewcalyons flodde was nevyr sene nor lyerd.	246	Speke Parott	504

LYEST

By Jesu Christ, /Fals Scot, thou lyest:	135	Dundas	33
Cockys harte! Thou lyest; I am no [h]ogge. hogge] 'dogge' †Rastell & Treveris C 1530, B	170	Magnyfycence	1083
What! Lyest thou there lyngrynge, lewdly and lothsome?	205	Magnyfycence	2291
'By Chryst,' sayde she, 'thou lyest.	223	El Rummynge	344

LYESTE

Behold, thou lyeste, luggard, alone!	42	Balettys1	25

LYETH

Ware of the lesard lyeth lurkyng in the gras.	45	Balettys4	7
But under hony ofte tyme lyeth bytter gall,	49	Bowge	131
Now have at all that lyeth upon the burde.	57	Bowge	391
That lyeth in cheynes bounde,	74	Phy Sparrow	90
And nowe lyke a lurden he lyeth in the dust.	193	Magnyfycence	1887
Take hede of this captyfe that lyeth here on grounde.	195	Magnyfycence	1946
This lurden that here lyeth had ben a noble man.	200	Magnyfycence	2112
Today a man, tomorowe he lyeth in the duste:	213	Magnyfycence	2550

LYF

I pray God sende the prosperous lyf and long,	34	Dol Dethe	169

LYFE

Goddes mooste cruell unto the lyfe of man,	32	Dol Dethe	121
That no lyfe well nye remayned.	73	Phy Sparrow	49
For that I was robbed /Of my sparowes lyfe.	73	Phy Sparrow	52
Was wery of her lyfe,	74	Phy Sparrow	109
But surely largesse saved my lyfe;	150	Magnyfycence	366
An all is for theyr ungracyous lyfe.	194	Magnyfycence	1915
For I have so ungracyously my lyfe mysusyd,	205	Magnyfycence	2298
Ye, ryd thy selfe rather than this lyfe for to lede.	205	Magnyfycence	2307
Out of thy lyfe the for to lede.	205	Magnyfycence	2310
Remember this lyfe lastyth but a whyle.	211	Magnyfycence	2502
This lyfe inconstant for to beholde and se:	212	Magnyfycence	2525
Shall lepe from this lyfe, as mery as we be.	236	Speke Parott	222
But of her apostels lyfe. her] 'theyr' Kele 1545.1, 'ther' MS Harley 2252	253	Collyn Clout	254
This is a postels lyfe.	284	Why Come Ye	226
Dare speke for his lyfe	306	Why Come Ye	1076
That all the dayes of ther lyfe shall styck by ther rybbis.	330	Garlande	638
Jupiter hymselfe this lyfe myght endure;	332	Garlande	715
My lyfe endurynge I shall both wryte and say,	335	Garlande	839
A lyfe for God hymselfe	340	Garlande	996
Of Mannes Lyfe the Peregrynacioun,	347	Garlande	1221
But who may have a more ungracyous lyfe a] not in Marshe 1568	352	Garlande	1451
Twene hope and drede /My lyfe I lede,	356	Garlande	1595

LYFT

Convey it be crafte, lyft and lay asyde.	177	Magnyfycence	1357
Nowe must I this carcasse lyft up.	195	Magnyfycence	1964

LYGHT

Lodestar to lyght these lovers to theyr porte,	44	Balettys3	25
Some say she was lyght,	87	Phy Sparrow	645
But lyght for somer grene;	89	Phy Sparrow	719
In Latyne playne and lyght,	92	Phy Sparrow	823
Be lyght of byleve and hasty of credence;	161	Magnyfycence	740

LYGHTE — LYKE

	Page	Title	Line
I am so lyght /To daunce delyght;	164	Magnyfycence	840
Confusyon /Shall on hym lyght	164	Magnyfycence	859
My wyttys be weke, my braynys are lyght;	169	Magnyfycence	1024
Goddes blissyng lyght on thy lytell swete musse!	238	Speke Parott	266
And meddels very lyght /In the churches ryght.	249	Collyn Clout	104
Shulde be lanternes of lyght.	257	Collyn Clout	440
Of every lyght quarell,	261	Collyn Clout	599
Lyke lanternes of lyght,	264	Collyn Clout	694
To haute in excellence, /To lyght intellegence,	279	Why Come Ye	9
lyght] 'lyght of' MS Rawlinson C. 813			
And to lyght in credence.	279	Why Come Ye	10
Of the soneshyne engladid with the lyght,	327	Garlande	536
How daungerous it were to stande in his lyght,	333	Garlande	755
were to stande in his lyght] 'is to stop up his sight' MS Cotton Vitellius E.x			
Lodesterre of lyght, /Moche relucent;	339	Garlande	949
Lodesterre] 'Lede sterre' †Fakes 1523			
Fortune to stande betwene you and the lyght.	344	Garlande	1134
A vengeaunce and dispight /On the must nedes lyght	364	Albany	235
Your penaunce was to lyght;	379	Replycacion	199
Among the Grekes most relucent of lyght,	383	Replycacion	332

LYGHTE

Harvy Ha[f]ter came lepynge, lyghte as lynde.	52	Bowge	231
Hafter] 'Haster' †Wynkyn de Worde 1499, 1510, Marshe 1568			
It is lyke he wyll stonde in our lyghte!'	54	Bowge	305
our] 'your' Marshe 1568			
His rumpe, he wente so all for somer lyghte;	56	Bowge	355
Lyghte lyme-fynger, he toke none other wage.	60	Bowge	509

LYGHTLY

Without measure lyghtly may fade,	146	Magnyfycence	228

LYING

How shuld a fals lying tung then be rewarded?	137	Ven Tongues	2
A fals lying tunge is harde to withholde;	137	Ven Tongues	6
For his false lying, of that I spake never,	139	Ven Tongues	75

LYITH

Yet, thoughe I say it, therby lyith a tale,	346	Garlande	1200
I] 'ye' †Fakes 1523			

LYKE

And lyke marciall Hector he faught them agayne	31	Dol Dethe	88
Lyke to Eneas benygne in worde and dede,	33	Dol Dethe	137
Be sumdele lyke in forme and shap,	36	Coystrownel	9
Full lyke a scorpyon styngyng	41	Coystrowne4	17
With 'Lullay, lullay', lyke a chylde,	41	Balettys1	I
It is lyke he wyll stonde in our lyghte!'	54	Bowge	305
our] 'your' Marshe 1568			
His eyen bleered, his face shone lyke a glas;	56	Bowge	353
That one was lene and lyke a pyned goost,	58	Bowge	429
His hode all pounsed and garded lyke a cage.	60	Bowge	508
hode] 'body' Marshe 1568			
But lyke a March harum /His braynes were so parum.	64	Hauke	104
Delt he not lyke a fon?	65	Hauke	128
Delt he not lyke a daw?	65	Hauke	129
That lyke a fende doth stare;	73	Phy Sparrow	77
In lyke maner also	74	Phy Sparrow	112
Lyke a valyaunt man;	87	Phy Sparrow	633
Emblomed lyke the chery,	97	Phy Sparrow	1038
Lyke to the radyant star,	98	Phy Sparrow	1047
And lyke to her image,	100	Phy Sparrow	1153
Lyke Phebus beames shyne.	101	Phy Sparrow	1174
Lyke dame Flora, quene	101	Phy Sparrow	1183
The rude ranke Scottes, lyke dronken dranes,	120	Ag Scottes	172
Lyke that untrue rebell /Fals Kayn agaynst Abell.	121	Ag Scottes2	19
Howkyd as an hawkys beke, lyke Syr Topyas.	122	Garneschel	40
[Your] gronynge, yor grontynge, yor groinynge lyke a swyne?	123	Garnesche2	2
Your lothesum lere to loke on, lyke a gresyd bote dothe schyne.	123	Garnesche2	5
Thow ye prate lyke prowde Pylate, beware yet of chek mate.	123	Garnesche2	7
Thow ye prate lyke prowde Pylate, beware of cheke mate.	123	Garnesche2	14
Lusty Garnysche, lyke a lowse, ye jet full lyke a jaspe;	123	Garnesche2	17
Lusty Garnysche, lyke a lowse, ye jet full lyke a jaspe;	123	Garnesche2	17
Tho ye prate lyke prowde Pylate, beware of cheke mate.	123	Garnesche2	21
Thow ye prate lyke prowde Pylate, beware of cheke mate.	123	Garnesche2	28
Thow ye prate lyke prowde Pylate, beware of cheke mate.	123	Garnesche2	35
Thow mantycore, ye marmset, garnyshte lyke a Greke,	124	Garnesche2	39
Thow ye prate lyke prowde Pylate, beware of cheke mate.	124	Garnesche2	42
Ye rostyd, lyke a fonne,	125	Garnesche3	30
Nosyd lyke an olyfaunt,	126	Garnesche3	71
Moche lyke a dromadary;	126	Garnesche3	74
Lyke a doctor dawpate,	126	Garnesche3	94
And make moche lyke Jake Rakar;	127	Garnesche3	109
Slaveryng lyke a slymy snayle.	130	Garnesche5	45
Sche seyd your brethe stanke lyke a broke;	131	Garnesche5	55
For ye war smery, lyke a sele,	131	Garnesche5	58
And ye war herey, lyke a calfe;	131	Garnesche5	59
Ye bere out brothells lyke a bawde;	131	Garnesche5	73
Prickyd lyke an unicorne.	133	Garnesche5	132
Shake thy tayle, Scot, lyke a cur,	135	Dundas	25
Your langage is lyke the penne	143	Magnyfycence	90

LYKE —LYKE   Page   Title   Line

Text	Page	Title	Line
A lurdayne lyke a lorde to [s]yght,	152	Magnyfycence	418
syght] 'fyght' †Rastell & Treveris C 1530, B			
A mynstrell lyke a man of myght,	152	Magnyfycence	419
A tappyster lyke a lady bryght:	152	Magnyfycence	420
In faythe, Mesure is lyke a tetter	155	Magnyfycence	543
For lyke as mustarde is sharpe of taste	155	Magnyfycence	552
Hem! That lyke I nothynge at all.	158	Magnyfycence	664
Nowe let se. Quyte you lyke praty men!	159	Magnyfycence	688
My speche is all pleasure, but I stynge lyke a waspe.	160	Magnyfycence	730
I make them to startyll and sparkyll lyke a bronde;	161	Magnyfycence	741
Thy slyppers they swap it, yet thou fotys it lyke a swanne.	161	Magnyfycence	765
Barbyd lyke a nonne	168	Magnyfycence	987
Tushe! Holde your peas; ye speke lyke a dawe.	178	Magnyfycence	1379
They drove me to lernynge lyke a dull asse.	178	Magnyfycence	1386
For nowe, syrs, I am lyke as a prynce sholde be;	181	Magnyfycence	1457
If it lyke your grace to take it in degre.	182	Magnyfycence	1521
If it wolde lyke you to here my pore mynde –	183	Magnyfycence	1543
Howe lyke you? Ye lacke, syr, suche a lusty lasse.	183	Magnyfycence	1559
But yf it lyke your grace more at large	185	Magnyfycence	1589
But yf it lyke you that I myght rowne in your eyre,	186	Magnyfycence	1645
But for all that he is lyke to have a glent.	187	Magnyfycence	1668
That he shall lyke the worse all this woke.	187	Magnyfycence	1682
And nowe lyke a lurden he lyeth in the dust.	193	Magnyfycence	1887
Of some I wrynge of the necke lyke a wyre;	194	Magnyfycence	1909
To mockynge, to mowynge, to lyke a jackenapes –	199	Magnyfycence	2098
Ha, ha, ha! For laughter I am lyke to brast.	201	Magnyfycence	2160
Ha, ha, ha! For sporte I am lyke to spewe and cast.	201	Magnyfycence	2161
Lyke a rost pygges eare,	215	El Rummynge	20
Lyke a ropy rayne, /A gummy glayre.	215	El Rummynge	24
Her skynne lose and slacke, /Greuyned lyke a sacke;	215	El Rummynge	32
Greuyned] 'Grained' Day 1560, Marshe 1568			
Jawed lyke a jetty;	215	El Rummynge	38
Lyke as they were with buckels /Togyder made fast.	215	El Rummynge	46
Foted lyke a plane, /Legge[d] lyke a crane;	215	El Rummynge	49
Legged] 'Legges' †Lant 1545, Kynge & Marche 1554, Day 1560, Marshe 1568			
Foted lyke a plane, /Legge[d] lyke a crane;	215	El Rummynge	50
Legged] 'Legges' †Lant 1545, Kynge & Marche 1554, Day 1560, Marshe 1568			
And yet she wyll jet, /Lyke a joyly fet	215	El Rummynge	52
/Loke lyke sere wedes,	216	El Rummynge	61
Wyddered lyke hay, /The woll worne away.	216	El Rummynge	62
Upon her brayne-pan, /Lyke an Egypcyan /Lapped about.	216	El Rummynge	78
Lapped] 'Capped' Kynge & Marche 1554, Day 1560, Marshe 1568			
It wygges and it wagges /Lyke tawny saffron bagges;	218	El Rummynge	138
Full untydy tegges, /Lyke rotten egges.	218	El Rummynge	152
Lyke a cake of tallowe;	222	El Rummynge	322
She was somwhat foule, /Crokenebbed lyke an oule;	225	El Rummynge	427
Crokenebbed] 'Croke necked' †Lant 1545, Kynge & Marche 1554, Day 1560, Marshe 1568			
Like an onyon syded, /Lyke tan ledder hyded.	226	El Rummynge	471
Her face glystryng lyke glas,	226	El Rummynge	482
She yelled lyke a calfe!	227	El Rummynge	500
Lyke an honest dame.	227	El Rummynge	511
Necked lyke an olyfant;	227	El Rummynge	519
Lyke a scabbyd muscull.	228	El Rummynge	556
There was a prycke-me-denty, /Sat lyke a seynty,	229	El Rummynge	583
Abowte my necke a cerculett lyke the ryche rubye,	231	Speke Parott	17
'Lyke owur pus catt Parott can mewte and crye.'	231	Speke Parott	24
owur] 'your' Lant 1545, Kynge & Marche 1554, Day 1560, Marshe 1568			
Lyke a wanton, whan I wyll, I rele to and froo.	233	Speke Parott	109
Barkyng and whynyng lyke churlysshe currys of kynde,	239	Speke Parott	295
Addressyng your selfe, lyke a sadde messengere,	239	Speke Parott	303
To jumbyll, to stombyll, to tumbyll down lyke folys;	243	Speke Parott	425
Lyke a clerkely hagge.	248	Collyn Clout	52
That the premenyre /Is lyke to be set afyre	249	Collyn Clout	109
Lyke Aron and Ure,	250	Collyn Clout	152
Moche herted lyke an hen.	251	Collyn Clout	168
Lyke houndes of hell, /They crye and they yell	251	Collyn Clout	198
Lyke sawdust or drye chyppes.	252	Collyn Clout	243
Lyke princeps aquilonis,	255	Collyn Clout	345
princeps] 'prynces' Kele 1545.1, Marshe 1568, 'prinopes' MS Harley 2252			
And to synge from place to place, /Lyke apostataas.	256	Collyn Clout	386
Thus the people telles, /Rayles lyke rebelles,	257	Collyn Clout	413
And talkes lyke tytyvylles	257	Collyn Clout	416
talkes] 'talke' †Godfray 1531, Kele 1545.1, Marshe 1568			
They commune lyke sottes,	260	Collyn Clout	564
sottes] 'scottes' Marshe 1568, 'sottes' MS Harley 2252			
Lyke lanternes of lyght,	264	Collyn Clout	694
In matters that them lyke	269	Collyn Clout	922
They carpe of us lyke crakers;	276	Collyn Clout	1189
And some of you shall dye /Lyke holy Jeremy;	276	Collyn Clout	1209
Lyke foxes in theyr denne,	283	Why Come Ye	164
Lyke cankerd cowardes all,	283	Why Come Ye	165
Lyke urcheons in a stone wall,	283	Why Come Ye	166
urcheons] 'heons' †Kele 1545.3, Marshe 1568			

LYKED —LYKYS

	Page	Title	Line
Lyke hen-herted cokoldes.	283	Why Come Ye	168
Stronge-herted lyke an hen.	285	Why Come Ye	276
Lyke a mayny of shepe	286	Why Come Ye	295
Wold wyrry them lyke an hogge.	286	Why Come Ye	299
He bayteth them lyke a bere,	286	Why Come Ye	307
Lyke an oxe or a bull;	286	Why Come Ye	308
Lyke to a Mamelek,	291	Why Come Ye	479
a Mamelek] 'Amamelek' †Kele 1545.3, Toy 1553, Kitson 1560.7, Marshe 1568			
Lyke Mahounde in a play.	294	Why Come Ye	597
His countynaunce lyke a kayser.	294	Why Come Ye	624
This daungerous dowsypere /Lyke a kynges pere!	295	Why Come Ye	640
Of a lyke dotage.	296	Why Come Ye	692
Lyke a fyer drake,	303	Why Come Ye	981
fyer] 'fyrye' MS Rawlinson C. 813			
Lyke Pharao, voyde of grace,	305	Why Come Ye	1066
This maumet in lyke wyse	306	Why Come Ye	1070
'Nothynge,' he sayth, 'lyke to We.	307	Why Come Ye	1148
to we] 'to mee' Toy 1553, Kitson 1560.7, Marshe 1568, 'we' MS Rawlinson C. 813			
I wyll answere lyke a clerke:	309	Why Come Ye	1208
Lyke to the boryall wyndes whan they blowe,	319	Garlande	261
Drove clowdes together lyke dryftis of snowe.	319	Garlande	263
'Lyke as the larke, upon the somers day,	327	Garlande	533
Masid as a Marche hare, he ran lyke a scut.	329	Garlande	632
Dasyng after dotrellis, lyke drunkardis that dribbis;	330	Garlande	641
In lyke maner of wyse a myst did us shrowde;	330	Garlande	647
And smerke, lyke a smythy kur, at sperkes of steile;	333	Garlande	762
Lyke to Argyva by just resemblaunce,	336	Garlande	843
Lyke to Aryna, maydenly of porte,	336	Garlande	865
Enuwyd your colowre /Is lyke the dasy flowre your] 'her' MS Cotton Vitellius E.x	340	Garlande	986
Lyke to Dame Pasiphe;	342	Garlande	1048
Dormiat in pace, lyke a dormows -	347	Garlande	1248
How than lyke a man he wan the barbican	351	Garlande	1397
lyke a cowarde knyght, ran awaye shamfully	359	Albany	1
Fledde lyke a beest.	359	Albany	12
And so attaynted, /Lyke cowardes starke,	359	Albany	29
Lyke cankerd curres /Ye loste your spurres;	360	Albany	33
Lyke a cowarde knyght	360	Albany	69
Nat lyke Duke Hamylcar	363	Albany	192
Nor lyke his sonne Hanyball,	363	Albany	194
Nor lyke Duke Hasdruball	363	Albany	195
Yet somwhat ye be lyke	364	Albany	197
But lepe away lyke frogges	364	Albany	212
Lyke pygges and lyke hogges	364	Albany	214
Lyke pygges and lyke hogges	364	Albany	214
And lyke maungy dogges.	364	Albany	215
Lyke a Scottyshe keteryng	365	Albany	248
Lyke a great hill,	365	Albany	261
Youre carkas to kepe, /Lyke a sely shepe,	365	Albany	274
And lurke there lyke an as	366	Albany	289
Lyke a Scottyshe hag.	366	Albany	295
Gyve it up, and cry, 'creke', /Lyke an huddy peke.	366	Albany	301
Lyke a cowarde knyght.	366	Albany	313
In merciall prowes /Lyke unto Hercules,	369	Albany	431
In prudence and wysdom /Lyke unto Salamon,	369	Albany	433
In his goodly person /Lyke unto Absolon,	369	Albany	435
In loyalte and foy /Lyke to Ector of Troy,	369	Albany	437
And his glory to incres /Lyke to Scipiades,	370	Albany	439
In royal mageste /Lyke unto Ptholome,	370	Albany	441
Lyke to Duke Josue /And the valiaunt Machube,	370	Albany	442
Lyke cowardes as ye be	370	Albany	460
To rayle on hym lyke dawes.	371	Albany	478
Lyke pratynge poppyng dawes,	375	Replycacion	39
Lyke heretykes confettred,	376	Replycacion	54
There, lyke a sorte of sottes,	376	Replycacion	65
And crye God mercy, lyke frantyke foles.	382	Replycacion	299
Lyke to Pyndarus in glorious poetry,	383	Replycacion	334
Lyke unto Alcheus, he dothe hym magnify.	383	Replycacion	335

LYKED

Sterte all at ones, I lyked no thynge his playe,	60	Bowge	502

LYKELY

Without our shyppe be sure, it is lykely to brast,	213	Magnyfycence	2562
How that ye are lykely	371	Albany	510

LYKELYHOD

And made instance for me be lykelyhod.	188	Magnyfycence	1697

LYKEWYSE

In lykewyse now the same /Cardynall is promoted,	293	Why Come Ye	570

LYKYNG

Thy lust and lykyng is from the gone;	42	Balettys1	23
Whan we kys and play /In lust and in lykyng.	220	El Rummynge	222

LYKYNGE

Let your lust and lykynge stande for a lawe.	185	Magnyfycence	1607
In lust and lykynge my name is Lyberte.	199	Magnyfycence	2078

LYKYS

And as many as him lykys,	306	Why Come Ye	1080
him] 'he' MS Rawlinson C. 813			

LYLE — LYRES   Page   Title   Line

LYLE
    For Sir William Lyle /Within shorte whyle, ... 360   Albany   38
LYLY
    As lyly whyte to loke upon her [l]eyre, ... 183   Magnyfycence   1555
        leyre] 'heyre' †Rastell & Treveris C 1530, B
LYLLY FLOWRE
    This jeloffer jentyll, this rose, this lylly flowre, ... 352   Garlande   1446
LYLSE WULSE
    A webbe of lylse wulse, ... 282   Why Come Ye   131
LYME-FYNGER
    Lyghte lyme-fynger, he toke none other wage. 60   Bowge   509
LYMERIK
    Of Lymerik, of Loreine, of Spayne, of Portyngale, ... 326   Garlande   494
LYME RODDE
    And with a lyme rodde I toke them bothe togyder. 191   Magnyfycence   1815
LYMMES
    Alasse! With colde my lymmes shall be marde. 197   Magnyfycence   2004
LYMMYS
    A, my bonys ake! My lymmys be sore! 195   Magnyfycence   1955
    A, howe my lymmys be lyther and lame! 198   Magnyfycence   2038
LYMPE-LEGGED
    It made sum lympe-legged and broisid there bones; 329   Garlande   625
LYNAGE
    The lynage of Lot toke supporte of Assur; 232   Speke Parott   66
LYNCOLE GRENE
    Her huke of Lyncole grene, ... 215   El Rummynge   56
LYNDE
    Harvy Ha[f]ter came lepynge, lyghte as lynde. 52   Bowge   231
        Hafter] 'Haster' †Wynkyn de Worde 1499, 1510, Marshe 1568
LYNE
    With aurum musicum every other lyne 345   Garlande   1167
    He wrate therof many a praty lyne, ... 347   Garlande   1242
LYNED
    That lyned was with doubtfull doublenes. 51   Bowge   178
    With Indygnacyon lyned was his hode; 54   Bowge   286
LYNGRYNGE
    What! Lyest thou there lyngrynge, lewdly and lothsome? . . . 205   Magnyfycence   2291
LYNYD
    With better frese lynyd; 125   Garnesche3   47
LYNKED
    Bot men say thei wer lynked with a double chayn 31   Dol Dethe   75
LYNKES
    Some podynges and lynkes, ... 225   El Rummynge   443
LYNKYD
    That lyberte be lynkyd with the chayne of countenaunce, . . . 141   Magnyfycence   44
    This lynkyd chayne of love that can unbynde. 146   Magnyfycence   201
LYON
    O yonge lyon, bot tender yet of age, ... 33   Dol Dethe   162
    With myghty corage /A[d]aunted the rage /Of a lyon savage; . . 104   Phy Sparrow   1311
        Adaunted] 'Auaunted' editions
    That noble erle, the Whyte Lyon, ... 115   Scot Kynge   68
    The White Lyon, there rampaunt of moode, ... 119   Ag Scottes   135
    The nebbis of a lyon they make to trete and trembyll, ... 243   Speke Parott   424
    With myghty corrage /Adauntid the rage /Of a lyon savage; . . . 349   Garlande   1304
    Agaynst the lyon white, ... 366   Albany   309
LYONNE
    And as the lyonne whiche is of bestis kinge 33   Dol Dethe   167
LYONS
    The leopardes savage, /The lyons in theyr rage, ... 79   Phy Sparrow   287
LYOUN
    The myghty lyoun doutted by se and sande. 32   Dol Dethe   109
        sande] 'lande' Marshe 1568
LYP
    And take me by the lyp. 75   Phy Sparrow   140
LYPPE
    He bote the lyppe; he loked passynge coye; 54   Bowge   288
        the] 'his' Wynkyn de Worde 1510
LYPPERS
    Some I make lyppers and lazars full horse; 194   Magnyfycence   1904
LYPPES
    His nose a-droppynge, his lyppes were full drye; 56   Bowge   362
        a-droppynge] 'droppynge' Marshe 1568
    Her lyppes soft and mery 97   Phy Sparrow   1037
    Tusshe! Thy lyppes hange in thyne eye; 169   Magnyfycence   1049
        eye] 'eyen' †Rastell & Treveris C 1530, B
    Her lusty lyppes ruddy as the chery - 183   Magnyfycence   1558
    Her lewde lyppes twayne, /They slaver, men sayne 215   El Rummynge   22
    Her lyppes are so drye, ... 221   El Rummynge   272
    And lepe out of theyr lyppes 252   Collyn Clout   242
    With your lyppes polluted 375   Replycacion   29
LYPPS
    Yower lothesum lypps love well to kyse, ... 130   Garnesche5   44
LYRES
    Though some of them by lyres. 267   Collyn Clout   833
        lyres] 'lyers' Kele 1545.1, Marshe 1568, 'lyars'
        MS Harley 2252

LYRICALL —LYTELL

	Page	Title	Line
LYRICALL			
Resembled to Symonides, that poete lyricall	383	Replycacion	331
Symonides] 'Symphonides' †Pynson 1528			
LYST			
Deme what thou lyst, thou knowyst not my thought.	38	Coystrownel	63
And if ye lyst to know the cause why so,	44	Balettys3	38
The hawke had no lyst /To come to his fyst;	64	Hauke	83
Whoso lyst the story to se.	76	Phy Sparrow	193
Playne matter indede, /Whoso lyst to rede	85	Phy Sparrow	549
And lede my fyst /As hym best lyst,	96	Phy Sparrow	973
Who so lyst to seke	97	Phy Sparrow	1044
Who so lyst beholde,	98	Phy Sparrow	1073
Whan she lyst to avale,	99	Phy Sparrow	1117
Within this quaire? /Who lyst repayre	116	Ag Scottes	42
lyst] 'lyst to' Kynge & Marche 1554, Day 1560, Marshe 1568			
That lyst for to jangyll /And waywardly to wrangyll	120	Ag Scottes2	5
If lyberte sholde lepe and renne where he lyst	144	Magnyfycence	133
Who lyst to knowe, Magnyfycence I hyght.	145	Magnyfycence	164
If ye lyst to lyve after your fre lyberte.	146	Magnyfycence	208
To put where he lyst, foly hath fre chace;	177	Magnyfycence	1329
'As oft as ye lyst, so honeste be savyd.	177	Magnyfycence	1348
Nay. He shall be ruled even as I lyst.	179	Magnyfycence	1394
To rule as ye lyst, lo, here is Lyberte.	179	Magnyfycence	1413
Have welth at our gydynge to rule as we lyst?	179	Magnyfycence	1415
I reyne in my robys, I rule as me lyst,	181	Magnyfycence	1485
But do as ye lyst and take your owne way.	185	Magnyfycence	1604
Yet I am not harte seke, but that me lyst.	185	Magnyfycence	1621
I coude, and I lyst, garre you laughe at a game:	192	Magnyfycence	1835
I lyve as me lyst, I lepe out at large;	199	Magnyfycence	2080
Who lyst to consyder shall never be begylyd,	212	Magnyfycence	2512
To the pythe of the mater who lyst to resorte:	213	Magnyfycence	2540
Jereboseth is Ebrue, who lyst the cause dyscus.	232	Speke Parott	67
cause] 'law' Day 1560, Marshe 1568			
Whan him lyst to lowre,	289	Why Come Ye	428
And to rule as hym lyst;	297	Why Come Ye	734
Who lyst to enquere,	307	Why Come Ye	1118
And men lyst to harke,	309	Why Come Ye	1206
To walke where we lyst, let us somwhat fynde	328	Garlande	564
His name for to know if that ye lyst,	333	Garlande	752
Lyst with you to varry	367	Albany	341
LYSTE			
His hose was garded with a lyste of grene,	56	Bowge	356
By me all persons worke what they lyste.	146	Magnyfycence	210
By Cockes harte, I trowe thou lyste.	173	Magnyfycence	1199
By the masse, a Spaynysshe moght with a gray lyste!	173	Magnyfycence	1200
LYSTYN			
Lythe and lystyn, all bechrewde!	131	Garnesche5	86
LYTEL			
By that lytel connynge that I have.	59	Bowge	450
This lytel enterprise;	372	Albany	527
LYTELL			
Here begynneth a lytell treatyse named The Bowge of Courte	46	Bowge	1
Of Felyce fetewse and lytell prety Cate,	56	Bowge	370
Caughte penne and ynke, and wroth this lytell boke.	61	Bowge	532
wroth] 'wrote' Wynkyn de Worde 1510, Marshe 1568			
To pyke my lytell too,	76	Phy Sparrow	176
My lytell prety sparowe	78	Phy Sparrow	280
And can but lytell skyll	90	Phy Sparrow	755
It cost me lytell nor nought.	101	Phy Sparrow	1203
nor] 'or' Wyght 1553, Kitson 1560.6, Marshe 1568			
To write some lytell tragedy,	117	Ag Scottes	72
For, when men by welth, they have lytell drede	140	Magnyfycence	10
Nowe pleasyth you a lytell whyle to stande;	145	Magnyfycence	161
For, syth he dyed, largesse was lytell used.	148	Magnyfycence	282
For whiche ende goth forwarde ye take lytell charge.	148	Magnyfycence	296
So large a man, and so lytell of stature!	155	Magnyfycence	523
What sayst? Here was to lytell clothe.	157	Magnyfycence	607
And do nothynge. How be it, full lytell grace	159	Magnyfycence	693
And I so lytell alway styll.	170	Magnyfycence	1070
Stande a lytell abacke, syr, and let hym come hyder.	186	Magnyfycence	1647
Whylest I came to you, a lytell here besyde.	187	Magnyfycence	1686
All worldly welth for hym to lytell was;	193	Magnyfycence	1892
Lydderyns so lytell set by Goddes lawes.	194	Magnyfycence	1919
Redresse my name is, that lytell am I used	208	Magnyfycence	2411
Than sterte in made Kyt, /That had lytell wyt;	225	El Rummynge	413
Wythe my beke bente, and my lytell wanton iye,	231	Speke Parott	15
and] not in Lant 1545, Kynge and Marche 1554, Day 1560, Marshe 1568			
My lytell legges, my fete bothe fete and clene,	231	Speke Parott	18
'My propyr Parott, my lytell pratye fole.'	231	Speke Parott	20
Goddes blissyng lyght on thy lytell swete musse!	238	Speke Parott	266
So many morall maters, and so lytell usyd;	244	Speke Parott	449
many] 'many many' †MS Harley 2252			
So myche nobyll prechyng, and so lytell amendment;	244	Speke Parott	452
So myche provision, and so lytell wytte at nede -	244	Speke Parott	454
So myche hardy-dardy, and so lytell manlynes;	244	Speke Parott	457
So myche poletyke pratyng, and so lytell stondythe in stede;	244	Speke Parott	464
So lytell secretnese, and so myche grete councell;	245	Speke Parott	465

	Page	Title	Line
So lytell care for the comynweall, and so myche nede;	245	Speke Parott	473
So myche dowghtfull daunger, and so lytell drede;	245	Speke Parott	474
So pynchyng and sparyng, and so lytell profyte growth;	245	Speke Parott	493
In theyr pryncypall cure /They make but lytell sure,	249	Collyn Clout	103
And have full lytell care	250	Collyn Clout	130
And they have to lytell,	260	Collyn Clout	558
And lytell grace they have	274	Collyn Clout	1131
Lodge hym in Lytell Ease,	275	Collyn Clout	1169
Here after foloweth a lytell boke,	278	Why Come Ye	I
God wot, had lytell parte	292	Why Come Ye	513
A lytell cryme in a great astate,	310	Why Come Ye2	13
Be he never so lytell of substaunce,	317	Garlande	177
But lytell or nothynge ye shall here tell	317	Garlande	197
ye shall] 'shall ye' MS Cotton Vitellius E.x			
Where I sawe come after, I wote, full lytell lake	320	Garlande	285
Thou hast to lytell myght	364	Albany	230
Go, lytell quayre, quickly.	371	Albany	508
Go, lytell quayre, apace,	372	Albany	523
that this lytell pamphlet, called the Replicacion	373	Replycacion	I
whan they have delectably lycked a lytell	373	Replycacion	I
A lytell ragge of rethorike,	374	Replycacion	1
With right lytell instruction;	378	Replycacion	155

LYTELTON

After olde seygnours, /And the lernynge of Lytelton Tenours	256	Collyn Clout	370

LYTHE

Lythe and lystyn, all bechrewde!	131	Garnesche5	86

LYTHER

There is no flaterer nor losyll so lyther,	146	Magnyfycence	200
I kyndell in her suche a lyther sparke	174	Magnyfycence	1231
There be two lyther, rude and ranke,	175	Magnyfycence	1266
A, howe my lymmys be lyther and lame!	198	Magnyfycence	2038

LYTHERLY

Frendshyp to fayne and thynke full lytherly.	160	Magnyfycence	723

LYTHERS

Theys lythers I lerne them for to lere,	175	Magnyfycence	1268

LYTILL

For ydle jangelers have but lytill braine;	328	Garlande	566
Lytill wotith the goslyng what the gose thynkith.	352	Garlande	1431

LYTYLL

I have to lytyll connynge to reporte.	47	Bowge	63
Is lytyll to saye, and moche to here and see;	52	Bowge	212
Me for to chalenge that of your chalennge makyth so lytyll fors.	123	Garnesche2	19
Lytyll wyt in your scrybys nolle	126	Garnesche3	90
Non phanum, sed prophanum, standyth in lytyll sted:	234	Speke Parott	125
Goe, lytyll quayre, pray them that yow beholde,	239	Speke Parott	290
Hyt ys no lytyll bordon to bere a grete mylle stone.	240	Speke Parott	330
So lytyll dyscressyon, and so myche reasonyng;	244	Speke Parott	456
So many trusys takyn, and so lytyll perfyte trowthe;	245	Speke Parott	491
perfyte] 'profyte' tMS Harley 2252			
With, 'Sir, I pray you, a lytyll tyme stande backe,	326	Garlande	505

LYTTEL

With my beke I can pyke my lyttel praty too;	233	Speke Parott	107

LYTTERATURE

Than all your lytterature.	380	Replycacion	233

LYTTERKTURE

I knowe your vertu and your lytterkture	59	Bowge	449
lytterkture] 'lytterature' Wynkyn de Worde 1510			

LYTTIL

Then sum wyll say he hath but lyttil brayne,	314	Garlande	87

LYTTYL

In flattryng fables men fynde but lyttyl fayth;	233	Speke Parott	87

LYVE

For though ye lyve a c. yere, ye shal dy a daw.	71	Hauke	334
To lyve under lawe, it is captyvyte.	142	Magnyfycence	75
If ye lyst to lyve after your fre lyberte.	146	Magnyfycence	208
As longe as I lyve, thou haste an heyre parent.	154	Magnyfycence	507
That ever noblenesse sholde lyve thus wretchydly!	197	Magnyfycence	2021
I lyve as me lyst, I lepe out at large;	199	Magnyfycence	2080
Now let us be all one, and let us lyve in rest;	202	Magnyfycence	2202
Alasse! To lyve longer I have no delyght;	205	Magnyfycence	2281
For to lyve in mysery, it is herder than dethe.	205	Magnyfycence	2282
Nay; rather wyll I chose to ryd me of this lyve	206	Magnyfycence	2321
Ye lyve, they say, in delyte, /Drowned in deliciis,	257	Collyn Clout	441
But lyve styll out of facyon,	275	Collyn Clout	1139
With hym to lyve and dye,	371	Albany	486

LYVED

When the Scotte lyved	116	Ag Scottes	R

LYVEYNG

If they wer lyveyng thys day,	133	Garnesche5	142

LYVENGE

Whiche his lyvenge wan	293	Why Come Ye	554

LYVER

Envye hathe wasted hys lyver and his lounge;	54	Bowge	291
Might poyson thy lyver and longes!	79	Phy Sparrow	293
His lyver, his longe /With anger is wronge;	94	Phy Sparrow	918
longe] 'longes' Wyght 1553, Kitson 1560.6, Marshe 1568			

LYVES

From them for theyr lyves!'	261	Collyn Clout	573

LYVEST —LOYALLY   Page   Title   Line

LYVEST
The worlde waxyth wery of the; thou lyvest to longe. 205   Magnyfycence   2308
LYVIUS
There Titus Lyvius hymselfe dyd avaunce 321   Garlande   344
LYVYD
Whiche whils he lyvyd had fuyson of every thing, ... 32   Dol Dethe   131
Thys losyll was a lorde and lyvyd at his lust; 193   Magnyfycence   1886
LYVYNG
My lyvyng to reprehende; 124   Garnesche3   16
No man lyvyng, he sayth, can be sure; 351   Garlande   1403
LYVYNGE
And yet unneth I can have my lyvynge; 53   Bowge   275
He is not lyvynge your maners can amend; 183   Magnyfycence   1537
What is he lyvynge that lyberte wolde lacke? 199   Magnyfycence   2083
How none estate lyvynge of hymselfe can be sure, ... 213   Magnyfycence   2557
Thus none estate lyvynge of hym[selfe] can be sure, ... 214   Magnyfycence   2564
    hymselfe] 'hym' †Rastell & Treveris C 1530, B
The Byble makith; with whos chast lyvynge 336   Garlande   846
LYVYUS
Whom Tytus Lyvyus /In wrytynge doth enroll; 67   Hauke   209
LO
Lo, Jak wold be a jentyl man! 37   Coystrowne1   14
Lo, these fond sottes /And tratlyng Skottys, ... 115   Ag Scottes   5
Lo, this is /My fansy, iwys; 167   Magnyfycence   971
The tothe ake! Lo, a torde ye have. 172   Magnyfycence   1164
Lo, Johnn a Bonam, where is thy brayne? 173   Magnyfycence   1204
To rule as ye lyst, lo, here is Lyberte. 179   Magnyfycence   1413
But yet, lo, I wolde, or that he wente, ... 187   Magnyfycence   1673
Lo, syrs, thus I handell them all 194   Magnyfycence   1896
Lo, suche is this worlde! I fynde it wryt, ... 196   Magnyfycence   1974
I shall skelpe the on the skalpe; lo, seest thou that? 202   Magnyfycence   2180
Lo, here is thy knyfe and a halter, and or we go ferther, . . 206   Magnyfycence   2317
Wyth, 'Lo, gossyp, iwys, ... 223   El Rummynge   356
'Lo, here is an olde typpet, ... 223   El Rummynge   366
Lo, this is the gyse noweadayes! 277   Collyn Clout   1227
Lo, yet for all that 297   Why Come Ye   742
Lo, for to do shamfully 305   Why Come Ye   1046
    Lo] 'Soo' MS Rawlinson C. 813
Unto me sayd, 'Lo, syr, now ye may se 326   Garlande   518
Lo, hither commyth a goodly maystres, ... 326   Garlande   521
Ye are brought to, 'Lo, Lo, Lo! 376   Replycacion   72
Ye are brought to, 'Lo, Lo, Lo! 376   Replycacion   72
Ye are brought to, 'Lo, Lo, Lo! 376   Replycacion   72
LOCKE
And pyke a locke and clyme a wall. 174   Magnyfycence   1227
The locke of a casket to make to starte. 203   Magnyfycence   2229
Unneth they leve a locke /Of wolle amongest theyr flocke. . . 248   Collyn Clout   80
LOCKES
Theyr lockes aboute theyr face, ... 218   El Rummynge   146
LOCKYD
Yet lyberte hath ben lockyd up and kept in the mew. 141   Magnyfycence   35
LOCKYS
Then I was in opynynge of lockys; 203   Magnyfycence   2226
LOCKTE
Whyles of his mynde it were lockte with the keye. 52   Bowge   224
LOCRYAN
Ye may be lorde of Locryan - 117   Ag Scottes   61
Of Huntley banke, /Of Lowdyan, /Of Locryan, ... 359   Albany   21
LODE
Marchauntes her borded to see what she had lode. 47   Bowge   40
    lode] not in Marshe 1568
LODESTAR
Lodestar to lyght these lovers to theyr porte, ... 44   Balettys3   25
LODE STARE
The lode stare of delyght, ... 102   Phy Sparrow   1226
LODESTERRE
That the lodesterre appere. 278   Collyn Clout   1258
Lodesterre of lyght, /Moche relucent; 339   Garlande   949
    Lodesterre] 'Lede sterre' †Fakes 1523
LODGE
Lodge hym in Lytell Ease, ... 275   Collyn Clout   1169
LODGED
Lodged in the strawe, ... 263   Collyn Clout   657
LODGID
Le tonsan de Jason is lodgid among the shrowdes; 239   Speke Parott   287
LOGGES
And hyde you under logges, ... 364   Albany   213
LOGICIONS
For logicions to loke on, somwhat sophistice; 236   Speke Parott   193
LOGYCALL
analeticall, topicall, and logycall: 375   Replycacion   I
LOGYKE
Suche logyke men woll choppe, ... 259   Collyn Clout   528
Of logyke nor scole matter, ... 267   Collyn Clout   815
A lesse lumpe of logyke, ... 374   Replycacion   2
And your tonges cropped, /Whan ye logyke chopped, ... 377   Replycacion   118
LOYALLY
Howe be it, loyally 369   Albany   404

LOYALTE —LOKES   Page   Title   Line

LOYALTE
Trouth doth me bynd /And loyalte   96   Phy Sparrow   978
Yet your problemes ar preignaunte and with loyalte acquayntyd.   240   Speke Parott   344
In loyalte and foy /Lyke to Ector of Troy, ...   369   Albany   436
LOK
Youre key is mete for every lok, ...   41   Coystrowne4   22
LOKE
Loke that ye spell /Well thys gospell;   39   Coystrowne3   20
Play fayre-play, madame, and loke ye play clene, ...   43   Balettys2   41
Wyth 'Whom' and 'Ha' and with a croked loke, ...   51   Bowge   191
'Syr, God you save, why loke you so sadde?   53   Bowge   239
Holde up the helme, loke up and lete God stere: 53   Bowge   250
With scornfull loke mevyd all in moode.   55   Bowge   317
   scornfull] 'scorfull' Marshe 1568
'How do ye, mayster? Ye loke so soberly!   58   Bowge   442
Who deleth with shrewes hath nede to loke aboute!'   61   Bowge   525
To loke on this were tyme.   65   Hauke   144
Loke now in Exodi, ...   66   Hauke   164
If it please you to loke   68   Hauke   233
Loke on this tabull, /Whether thou art abull   68   Hauke   235
To wepe with me loke that ye come, ...   81   Phy Sparrow   387
To mornynge loke that ye fall   81   Phy Sparrow   390
To loke on her agayne.   97   Phy Sparrow   1010
   on] 'to' Marshe 1568
Your lothesum lere to loke on, lyke a gresyd bote dothe schyne.   123   Garnesche2   5
Huf, a galante, Garnesche, loke on your comly cors!   123   Garnesche2   16
Mirres vous y, /Loke nat to hy.   124   Garnesche2   E
Ye wene that I am dronken bycause I loke pale.   147   Magnyfycence   259
I shall loke in it at leasure better;   149   Magnyfycence   332
Cankard Jacke Hare, loke thou be not rusty;   161   Magnyfycence   758
Ye, tourne over the lefe, rede there, and loke   176   Magnyfycence   1293
Alas, dere harte, loke that we be not perseyvyd!'   177   Magnyfycence   1349
What sholde a man do with you? Loke you under [k]ay?   180   Magnyfycence   1429
   kay] 'bay' †Rastell & Treveris C 1530, B
But loke that ye occupye the auctoryte that I you gave. . . .   180   Magnyfycence   1456
No, that I assure you; loke who was the best: 181   Magnyfycence   1484
As lyly whyte to loke upon her [l]eyre   183   Magnyfycence   1555
   leyre] 'heyre' †Rastell & Treveris C 1530, B
That he wolde loke on hym, thoughe it were not longe.   187   Magnyfycence   1675
That he come hyder, and to gyve hym a loke   187   Magnyfycence   1681
What tydynges with you, syr, that you loke so sad?   192   Magnyfycence   1843
Nowe dare he not for shame loke one in the face.   193   Magnyfycence   1891
Wherfore, of adversyte loke ye be ware;   195   Magnyfycence   1936
Therefore poverte loke pacyently ye take, ...   196   Magnyfycence   2000
I am so lusty to loke on, so freshe, and so fre, ...   201   Magnyfycence   2145
What! Wylte thou skelpe me? Thou dare not loke on a gnat. . .   202   Magnyfycence   2181
That thou arte not worthy to loke God in the face.   205   Magnyfycence   2296
Nay, nay, man. I loke never to have parte of his grace; . . .   205   Magnyfycence   2297
And loke that it be not longe   206   Magnyfycence   2311
/Loke lyke sere wedes, ...   216   El Rummynge   61
Some loke strawry, /Some cawry-mawry;   218   El Rummynge   149
It shall make you loke /Yonger than ye be   219   El Rummynge   213
That causeth I loke so donny.'   224   El Rummynge   400
Sion is in sadness, Rachell ruly doth loke;   234   Speke Parott   114
For logicions to loke on, somwhat sophistice;   236   Speke Parott   193
The prelates ben so haute /They say, and loke so hye   248   Collyn Clout   72
But ye loke to be let lose   252   Collyn Clout   213
Nor farther for to loke   266   Collyn Clout   783
To loke on God in fourme of brede, ...   272   Collyn Clout   1024
Dare nat loke out at dur   286   Why Come Ye   296
   at] 'a' Kitson 1560.7, Marshe 1568
For men to loke on? Aristotille also, ...   315   Garlande   127
Yet loke on me, that lovyd you have so longe, ...   320   Garlande   298
With that on me she kest her goodly loke.   327   Garlande   531
Is lusty to loke on, plesaunte, demure, and sage: 336   Garlande   870
Is lusty to loke on, plesaunt, demure, and sage.   337   Garlande   877
May happely loke /Upon your boke, ...   355   Garlande   1546
To loke hym in the face   367   Albany   352
I rede you, loke about;   371   Albany   500
For if ye sadly loke, ...   384   Replycacion   359
LOKED
Whan I loked on hym, my purse was half aferde.   52   Bowge   238
He loked hawte; he sette eche man at noughte;   54   Bowge   284
   hawte] 'hawtie' Marshe 1568
He bote the lyppe; he loked passynge coye;   54   Bowge   288
   the] 'his' Wynkyn de Worde 1510
That he loked pale as asshes to my syghte.   54   Bowge   293
I loked on hym, I wende he had be woode.   55   Bowge   320
That other loked as he wolde me have slayne.   58   Bowge   430
   me have] 'have me' Wynkyn de Worde 1510
She loked as she had the frounce;   64   Hauke   85
   frounce] 'fronnce' Kynge & Marche 1554, 'fronce' Day 1560
This byll well over loked, ...   281   Why Come Ye   118
Then I me lent, and loked over the wall: 329   Garlande   602
She loked hawtly, and gave on me a glum.   344   Garlande   1117
LOKES
So lordlye of hys lokes, and so dysdayneslye;   246   Speke Parott   508
Your hygh and lordely lokes.   261   Collyn Clout   595

LOKETH—LONGE	Page	Title	Line
LOKETH			
By Cockes harte, he loketh hye.	156	Magnyfycence	574
What nowe? Let se /Who loketh on me	163	Magnyfycence	830
LOKIS			
Whos lusty lokis make hevy hartis glad;	337	Garlande	903
LOKYD			
And all is done ye lokyd for before,	45	Balettys4	2
From whens come you, syr, that no man lokyd after?	147	Magnyfycence	255
We have longyd and lokyd long tyme for that,	239	Speke Parott	310
Some lokyd full smothely, and had a fals quarter,	326	Garlande	504
quarter] 'quart' Marshe 1568			
LOKYS			
But who so that lokys /In the offycyallys bokys,	65	Hauke	145
Me thynke she frowneth and lokys sowre.	166	Magnyfycence	924
So farly fayre as it lokys!	168	Magnyfycence	999
Alas, wh[o] is yonder that grymly lokys?	193	Magnyfycence	1873
who] 'why' †Rastell & Treveris C 1530, B			
LOKYTHE			
For whoo lokythe wyselye in your warkys may fynde	239	Speke Parott	296
LOLY			
He dawnsys so long, 'hey, troly, loly',	175	Magnyfycence	1250
LOLLARDY			
And your lollardy lernyng teched,	379	Replycacion	204
LOME			
To weve all in one lome	282	Why Come Ye	130
LOMELYN			
I meane Domyngo Lomelyn /That was wont to wyn	308	Why Come Ye	1190
LONDE			
A precyous jewell, no rycher in this londe:	48	Bowge	97
The noble Pamphila, quene of the Grekis londe,	336	Garlande	850
LONDON			
'Have here is for me, /A clout of London pynnes.'	228	El Rummynge	564
LONG			
I pray God sende the prosperous lyf and long,	34	Dol Dethe	169
To drynk at a draught a larg and a long.	38	Coystrownel	49
Nor stand long wrestyng there aboute;	41	Coystrowne4	25
Thou slepyst to long, thou art begylde!	41	Balettys1	I
Though thou withdraw me from her by long dystaunce,	45	Balettys3	46
Yet long tyme she ne knew	89	Phy Sparrow	727
For thow hast a long snowte,	133	Garnesche5	130
He dawnsys so long, 'hey, troly, loly',	175	Magnyfycence	1250
It can not contynew long prosperyously;	200	Magnyfycence	2132
'Parott hathe not dyned of all this long day;'	231	Speke Parott	23
We have longyd and lokyd long tyme for that,	239	Speke Parott	310
To blowe a blaste with his long breth extendid;	319	Garlande	234
LONGE			
Thou muste swere and stare, man, aldaye longe,	57	Bowge	381
For allbeit that this longe not to me,	59	Bowge	456
The larke with his longe to;	82	Phy Sparrow	406
But with a large and a longe	82	Phy Sparrow	426
The wodcocke with the longe nose;	83	Phy Sparrow	459
His lyver, his longe /With anger is wronge;	94	Phy Sparrow	918
longe] 'longes' Wyght 1553, Kitson 1560.6, Marshe 1568			
With sydes longe and streyte;	100	Phy Sparrow	1129
Yor wynde-schakyn shankkes, yor longe *lothy legges,	122	Garnesche1	29
*lothy] 'lothly' Scattergood			
.... sat sumwhat to longe;	125	Garnesche3	57
Thowthe ye kan skylle of large and longe,	129	Garnesche5	3
Yet measure hath ben so longe from us absent,	146	Magnyfycence	221
It were not possyble me longe to retayne.	147	Magnyfycence	250
In faythe, els had I gone to longe to scole,	148	Magnyfycence	298
Why kepte you it thus longe? Howe dothe he? Wele?	149	Magnyfycence	314
Ye, but how longe shall I here awayte?	151	Magnyfycence	398
But Fansy, my frende, where have ye bene so longe?	154	Magnyfycence	500
As longe as I lyve, thou haste an heyre parent.	154	Magnyfycence	507
That we thre galauntes sholde be longe asonder.	154	Magnyfycence	511
Who that is ruled by us, it shalbe longe or he thee.	154	Magnyfycence	515
That Mesure shall not there longe tary.	159	Magnyfycence	684
To pyke theyr fyngers all the day longe;	174	Magnyfycence	1222
And make them so longe to muse	174	Magnyfycence	1224
Mayster Survayour, where have ye ben so longe?	178	Magnyfycence	1382
Why, wene you that I can kepe hym longe styll?	179	Magnyfycence	1412
That he wolde loke on hym, thoughe it were not longe.	187	Magnyfycence	1675
But so longe they rekyn with theyr reasons amysse	200	Magnyfycence	2127
they] 'theyr' †Rastell C 1530, B			
O good Lorde, howe longe shall I indure	201	Magnyfycence	2153
The worlde waxyth wery of the; thou lyvest to longe.	205	Magnyfycence	2308
And loke that it be not longe	206	Magnyfycence	2311
Alarum, alarum! To longe we abyde!	206	Magnyfycence	2323
The whiche were to longe nowe to expresse;	209	Magnyfycence	2416
Syr, the longe absence of you, Sad Cyrcumspeccyon,	209	Magnyfycence	2424
For where sad cyrcumspeccyon is longe out of the way,	209	Magnyfycence	2427
Delay causes so longe	276	Collyn Clout	1196
That his berde is so longe.	288	Why Come Ye	391
(A proverbe longe ago.)	293	Why Come Ye	584
Longe to endure in heale.	298	Why Come Ye	771
Ran on the raunge so longe, that I suppose	313	Garlande	25
Myne argument els koude not longe endure.	316	Garlande	147

LONGE NECKED — LORDE

	Page	Title	Line
They presid in faste; some thought they were to longe;	319	Garlande	248
That longe tyme blewe a full timorous blaste,	319	Garlande	260
Yet loke on me, that lovyd you have so longe,	320	Garlande	298
From you most we, but not longe to tary.	326	Garlande	520
And of the wynter nyghtes that tary so longe,	331	Garlande	701
And of the somer days so longe that doth last,	331	Garlande	702
So many, that longe it were to reherse.	331	Garlande	706
it] 'in' Marshe 1568			
Longe to enjoy plesure, delyght, and lust:	337	Garlande	882
in as moche as it were to place a proces	345	Garlande	R
That unremembred longe tyme remayned.	347	Garlande	1225
With a sawte of solace at the longe last;	351	Garlande	1398

LONGE NECKED
Thou losell longe necked!'	294	Why Come Ye	610

LONGER
Syr, without any longer delyaunce,	147	Magnyfycence	237
With me no longer. Say somwhat nowe, let se,	188	Magnyfycence	1719
Alasse! To lyve longer I have no delyght;	205	Magnyfycence	2281

LONGES
Might poyson thy lyver and longes!	79	Phy Sparrow	293

LONGETH
What longeth to Christes humanyte.	381	Replycacion	286

LONGYD
We have longyd and lokyd long tyme for that,	239	Speke Parott	310

LONGYTH
Suche problemis to paynt it longyth to his arte.	347	Garlande	1246

LONYS
For prestes and for lonys /Lent and never payde,	255	Collyn Clout	350

LOO
Loo, what it is a man to have connynge!	50	Bowge	153
Loo, what is to you a pleasure grete	53	Bowge	260
What, loo, man, see here of dyce a bale;	57	Bowge	389
'Harken,' quod he, 'loo here myne honde in thyne;	60	Bowge	510

LORD
Your naturall lord? Alas, I kan not fayne.	30	Dol Dethe	54
What aylde you to slo your lord ageyn all right?	31	Dol Dethe	63
slo] 'sle' Marshe 1568			
The grounde of his quarell was for his sovereyn lord,	31	Dol Dethe	64
Of knightis, of squyers, chef lord of toure and toune,	33	Dol Dethe	132
To slo suche a lord, alas, it was grete shame.	33	Dol Dethe	154
slo] 'sle' Marshe 1568			
Of ther good lord the fate and dedely chaunce.	34	Dol Dethe	189
Where thow art Lord and God omnipotent.	34	Dol Dethe	203
Lord, how Perkyn is proud of hys Pohen!	37	Coystrownel	19
Lord, how he wolde pry /After the butterfly!	75	Phy Sparrow	134
A Lawde And Prayse Made for Our Sovereigne Lord the Kyng	110	Lawde	I
Your soverayne lord, our prynce of myght.	117	Ag Scottes	54
Regardyd ye shuld your lord, your brother.	118	Ag Scottes	106
ye] 'you' Day 1560, Marshe 1568			
A, Lord God, how the gowte wryngeth me by the too.	198	Magnyfycence	2047
Ryn God, rynne Devyll! Yet the date of Owur Lord	244	Speke Parott	444
What here ye of the lord Rose?	286	Why Come Ye	286
Our soverayne lord, chyfe grounde	291	Why Come Ye	502

LORDE
Falsly to slo ther moste singlar goode lorde?	30	Dol Dethe	27
slo] 'slee' Marshe 1568			
So noble a man, so valiaunt lorde and knyght	30	Dol Dethe	29
To slo ther owne lorde? God was not in ther mynde!	30	Dol Dethe	35
The nobelnes of the northe, this valyant lorde and knyght,	31	Dol Dethe	85
Whom he as lorde worsheply manteynd,	34	Dol Dethe	186
The sowle of this lorde from all daunger of hell,	34	Dol Dethe	200
For by that Lorde that bought dere all mankynde,	50	Bowge	163
Lorde, how that I wolde caste it full rounde!	57	Bowge	396
'But by that Lorde that is one, two and thre,	60	Bowge	512
Lorde, how he wolde hop /After the gressop!	75	Phy Sparrow	136
A porta inferi, /Good Lorde, have mercy	77	Phy Sparrow	240
That his owne lorde bote	79	Phy Sparrow	305
Our Lorde thy soule reskew!	80	Phy Sparrow	332
Lorde, how I was payned!	99	Phy Sparrow	1123
Thy loving sovereine lorde,	110	Lawde	9
Both lorde and knight to face;	111	Lawde	39
To sommon your kynge your soverayne lorde.	113	Scot Kynge	4
Ye ought to honour your lorde and brother.	114	Scot Kynge	16
Your soverayne lorde and presedent.	114	Scot Kynge	22
His sone the lorde admyrall is full good,	115	Scot Kynge	70
Ye may be lorde of Locryan -	117	Ag Scottes	61
To summon your kyng, your soveraygne lorde.	118	Ag Scottes	94
Your soveraygne lorde most reverent,	118	Ag Scottes	113
Your lorde, your brother, and your regent.	118	Ag Scottes	114
That creaunser was to thy sofre[yne] lorde;	132	Garnesche5	102
sofreyne] 'sofre' †MS Harley 367			
That with your lorde and mayster so pertly can prate!	149	Magnyfycence	305
That I shall have you agayne my good lorde.	149	Magnyfycence	310
'A lorde a negarde, it is a shame.'	151	Magnyfycence	388
A lurdayne lyke a lorde to [s]yght,	152	Magnyfycence	418
syght] 'fyght' †Rastell & Treveris C 1530, B			
From that lorde to that lorde I rode and I ran.	160	Magnyfycence	716
From that lorde to that lorde I rode and I ran.	160	Magnyfycence	716

LORDELY —LORE Page Title Line

	Page	Title	Line
By the good Lorde, truthe he sayth.	175	Magnyfycence	1252
But, blessyd be our Lorde, they wyll be sone converted.	184	Magnyfycence	1584
What sholde ye do elles? Are not you a lorde?	185	Magnyfycence	1606
Of our blessyd Lorde, syr, at the reverence –	186	Magnyfycence	1636
I was your good lorde tyll that ye beganne	188	Magnyfycence	1714
By the good Lorde, yet your temples bete.	189	Magnyfycence	1732
A, Lorde, so I wolde halse her hartely!	190	Magnyfycence	1801
Lorde, so my flesshe trymblyth nowe for drede!	193	Magnyfycence	1875
I plucke downe kynge, prynce, lorde, and knyght;	193	Magnyfycence	1883
Thys losyll was a lorde and lyvyd at his lust;	193	Magnyfycence	1886
A laudable largesse, I tell you, for a lorde,	200	Magnyfycence	2123
O good Lorde, howe longe shall I indure	201	Magnyfycence	2153
And therfore our Lorde sende you a very wengaunce!	203	Magnyfycence	2237
And love that Lorde that for your love was dede,	207	Magnyfycence	2363
He be your conducte, the Lorde of myghtys moste!	208	Magnyfycence	2386
Lyberte to a lorde belongyth of ryght,	211	Magnyfycence	2489
Today a lorde, tomorowe ly in the duste:	213	Magnyfycence	2543
But, Lorde, as she was testy, /Angry as a waspy!	222	El Rummynge	329
Now pas furthe, good Parott, Owur Lorde be your s[t]ede, stede] 'spede' †MS Harley 2252	239	Speke Parott	313
And call a lorde a javell.	261	Collyn Clout	600
Squyre, knyght and lorde	271	Collyn Clout	980
No man to our sovereygne lorde	272	Collyn Clout	1030
Our lorde be his soccoure!	282	Why Come Ye	160
What here ye of the lorde Dakers?	285	Why Come Ye	272
Duke, erle, baron, nor lorde,	287	Why Come Ye	342
God save my Lorde Admyrell!	288	Why Come Ye	376
Of our soverayne lorde,	291	Why Come Ye	485
Nor marques, erle, nor lorde;	294	Why Come Ye	620
'My lorde is nat at layser.	294	Why Come Ye	625
And against his lorde soverayn!	297	Why Come Ye	738
My lorde now and syr knyght, now] not in MS Rawlinson C. 813	302	Why Come Ye	915
Wherof this ungracyous lorde	306	Why Come Ye	1098
In the regstry /Of my lorde of Cantorbury,	307	Why Come Ye	1120
A small defaute in a great lorde,	310	Why Come Ye2	12
Lorde of the yere in his orbicular,	312	Garlande	4
In her bosome, lorde, how she was afrayd! how] not in MS Cotton Vitellius E.x	337	Garlande	887
Lorde, how she made moche of her gentyll birth!	346	Garlande	1202
But, lorde, how the parker was wroth with all.	351	Garlande	1386
Whan he herde tell /That my Lorde Amrell	360	Albany	55
Of my Lorde Cardynall,	360	Albany	60
Of my Lorde Amrell,	365	Albany	237
To my Lorde Cardynals right noble grace etc	372	Albany	E

LORDELY

	Page	Title	Line
Your hygh and lordely lokes.	261	Collyn Clout	595

LORDES

	Page	Title	Line
For lordes and ladyes lerne at his scole;	38	Coystrownel	52
God save kynge Henry and his lordes all	115	Scot Kynge	72
Largesse, that all lordes sholde love, syr, I hyght.	148	Magnyfycence	270
That lordes and ladies thys pamflett may behold,	241	Speke Parott	358
So myche of my lordes grace, and in hym no grace ys;	245	Speke Parott	501
For the lordes temporall,	261	Collyn Clout	608
For lordes of noble bloode,	262	Collyn Clout	615
Lordes must crouche and knele, crouche] 'couch' Marshe 1568, 'cruche' MS Harley 2252	262	Collyn Clout	628
With lordes of great estate	271	Collyn Clout	1013
He sayth, 'How saye ye, my lordes?	283	Why Come Ye	195
And Yorkes Place, /With, 'My lordes grace',	289	Why Come Ye	411
He regardeth lordes /No more than potshordes.	291	Why Come Ye	480
For my lordes grace	294	Why Come Ye	630
For, 'my Lordes grace',	301	Why Come Ye	876

LORDIS

	Page	Title	Line
Of famous princis and lordis of astate,	29	Dol Dethe	16
Of this lordis dethe and of his murdrynge;	32	Dol Dethe	130
This lordis dethe, whose pere is hard to fynd,	34	Dol Dethe	178
My lordis grace wyll brynge	302	Why Come Ye	949
Of my lordis grace nor his wyfe!	306	Why Come Ye	1077

LORDYS

	Page	Title	Line
An holy water clarke a ruler of lordys.	37	Coystrownel	21
For I stryke lordys of realmes and landys	195	Magnyfycence	1938
This shrewdly accordis /To be a cupborde for lordys!	302	Why Come Ye	914
My lordys grace nameth it	302	Why Come Ye	940

LORDLY

	Page	Title	Line
It is a pryncely pleasure and a lordly mynde.	186	Magnyfycence	1627
To full of fansyes, to lordly, to prowde,	199	Magnyfycence	2093

LORDLYE

	Page	Title	Line
So lordlye of hys lokes, and so dysdayneslye;	246	Speke Parott	508

LORDSHEPE

	Page	Title	Line
Whos lordshepe doutles was slayne lamentably	29	Dol Dethe	5

LORDSHYPE

	Page	Title	Line
What avayleth lordshype, yourselfe for to kyll	148	Magnyfycence	286

LORE

	Page	Title	Line
Take this caytyfe to thy lore.	195	Magnyfycence	1954
What trowe ye they say more /Of the bysshoppes lore?	249	Collyn Clout	93
With all his false lore –	257	Collyn Clout	430

LOREINE
Of Lymerik, of Loreine, of Spayne, of Portyngale, ... 326 Garlande 494
LORELL
To solfe above E-la - /Fa, lorell, fa, fa - .... 84 Phy Sparrow 488
   Fa] 'Ga' †Kele 1545.2, Wyght 1553, Kitson 1560.6
I am laureat, I am no lorell. 124 Garnesche3 14
To cal me lorell ye ar to lewde; 131 Garnesche5 85
LOS
Howbei[t], he is not furst hath had a los. 43 Balettys2 38
   Howbeit] 'Howbeis' †Rastell 1527.1
LOSE
That they lose theyr lyberte and all that there is. .... 200 Magnyfycence 2128
Her skynne lose and slacke, /Greuyned lyke a sacke; ...... 215 El Rummynge 31
   Greuyned] 'Grained' Day 1560, Marshe 1568
But ye loke to be let lose .... 252 Collyn Clout 213
LOSELL
I sawe a losell lede a lurden, and they were bothe blynde. ... 191 Magnyfycence 1824
Ly there, losell, for all thy pompe and pryde; ...... 193 Magnyfycence 1880
Harke, howe the losell prates /With a wyde wesaunt! ...... 275 Collyn Clout 1153
Howe darest thou, losell, ... 275 Collyn Clout 1161
Thou losell longe necked!' .... 294 Why Come Ye 610
LOSELLES
So myche serchyng of loselles, and ys hym selfe so lewde; ... 246 Speke Parott 513
And thus the loselles stryves, ... 261 Collyn Clout 574
LOSELRY
Or suche other loselry .... 295 Why Come Ye 664
LOSELS
Dowtles such losels .... 65 Hauke 138
Some lidderons, some losels, some noughty packis; .... 317 Garlande 188
What losels than are ye .... 370 Albany 459
LOSENDE
With that, of the boke losende were the claspis. .... 345 Garlande 1156
LOSYD
It shall be losyd ful sone out of the bandis .... 332 Garlande 725
LOSYLL
There is no flaterer nor losyll so lyther, ... 146 Magnyfycence 200
Thys losyll was a lorde and lyvyd at his lust; .... 193 Magnyfycence 1886
LOSS
By theyr demenaunce, nor loss repryvable. .... 179 Magnyfycence 1419
LOSSE
I am not happy, I renne ay on the losse! .... 57 Bowge 399
So myche losse of merchaundyse, and so remedyles; .... 245 Speke Parott 472
For they wyll have no losse .... 269 Collyn Clout 928
LOST
He trusted her payment and lost all hys pray. 42 Balettys1 13
Whan she had lost her joye, ... 74 Phy Sparrow 110
Troylus also hath lost .... 89 Phy Sparrow 714
Therfore ye have lost your copyholde. .... 114 Scot Kynge 35
Wan they the felde and lost theyr kynge? .... 115 Ag Scottes 3
Therfore ye lost your copyhold. .... 118 Ag Scottes 126
Lost is your game, ye are checkmate. .... 118 Ag Scottes 128
That of Scotland ye lost the flower. .... 119 Ag Scottes 134
Ye lost your spurrys, ye lost you sworde. .... 119 Ag Scottes 148
Ye lost your spurrys, ye lost you sworde. .... 119 Ag Scottes 148
All have ye lost and cast away. .... 119 Ag Scottes 163
Syr sumner, now ye have lost your crowne. .... 120 Ag Scottes 180
Ye lost your [h]olde, onbende your bow, ... 131 Garnesche5 49
   holde] 'bolde' †MS Harley 367
And thus there ye lost yower pray; 131 Garnesche5 61
Or elles I had lost myne eres twayne. .... 150 Magnyfycence 349
Thryfte hathe lost her cofer kay. .... 155 Magnyfycence 527
Where is my cappe? I have lost my hat! .... 169 Magnyfycence 1030
Put on thy gowne agayne, for thou hast lost nowe. .... 173 Magnyfycence 1203
   thou ... nowe] 'nowe thou hast lost' †Rastell & Treveris C
   1530, B
Gyve me my grote, for thou hast lost. .... 173 Magnyfycence 1206
Undoubted ye had lost yourselfe eternally. .... 206 Magnyfycence 2335
But she had lost the stoppell. .... 224 El Rummynge 404
That of theyr scole maters lost is the hole sentens. ..... 235 Speke Parott 182
Have lost theyr bedde roules; .... 257 Collyn Clout 422
   bedde] 'beade' Kele 1545.1, 'bede' MS Harley 2252
And, 'Mocke hath lost her sho; .... 281 Why Come Ye 86
Lost all his father wan. .... 285 Why Come Ye 271
   all his] 'al that his' Toy 1553, Kitson 1560.7, Marshe 1568
Wherwith the Sodomites /Lost theyr inward syghtes. ...... 291 Why Come Ye 471
But sith I have lost now that I entended, ... 321 Garlande 318
LOSTE
Ye have loste spores, cote armure and sworde. .... 114 Scot Kynge 49
Ye loste hyr favyr quyt! 125 Garnesche3 67
It is coste loste .... 165 Magnyfycence 893
That nowe he hath loste all his felycyte; .... 200 Magnyfycence 2114
Whate mone he made when Pamphylus loste hys make. ...... 237 Speke Parott 234
To make reconyng in the resseyte how Robyn loste hys bowe, .. 240 Speke Parott 341
His levis loste, the sappe was frome the rynde. .... 312 Garlande 21
That welny was loste when that we were gone.' .... 323 Garlande 406
   welny] 'welnere' Marshe 1568
Though Jak sayd nay, yet Mok there loste her sho; .... 351 Garlande 1396
Lyke cankerd curres /Ye loste your spurres; .... 360 Albany 34

LOT —LOVE Page Title Line

LOT
Is it come unto your lot	116	Ag Scottes	50
As cometh to her lot.	221	El Rummynge	282
The lynage of Lot toke supporte of Assur;	232	Speke Parott	66
It must come to his lot	265	Collyn Clout	750

LOTH
Is glad to please, and loth to offend.'	323	Garlande	413
Whiche glad am to please, and loth to offende'	324	Garlande	427
The myllar was loth to be out of the way,	351	Garlande	1414

LOTHE
But I am lothe for to reyse a smoke,	59	Bowge	479
For lyberte at large is lothe to be stoppyd,	141	Magnyfycence	46
So wolde I, but I wolde be lothe,	144	Magnyfycence	143
Perceyve you not howe lothe he was to abyde	147	Magnyfycence	241
Nowe leve, nowe lothe, nowe please, nowe dysplease;	212	Magnyfycence	2520
Some lothe to be espyde,	221	El Rummynge	262
But they are lothe to mell,	250	Collyn Clout	162
And lothe to hange the bell	250	Collyn Clout	163
For lothe I am to offende	251	Collyn Clout	186
I am lothe to tell all;	262	Collyn Clout	636
Lothe they are to lese	267	Collyn Clout	841
Which glad am to please, and lothe to offende.'	324	Garlande	441

LOTHELY
Her lothely lere /Is nothynge clere,	214	El Rummynge	12

LOTHESUM
Your lothesum lere to loke on, lyke a gresyd bote dothe schyne.	123	Garnesche2	5
Yower lothesum lypps love well to kyse,	130	Garnesche5	44

LOTHY
Yor wynde-schakyn shankkes, yor longe *lothy legges, *lothy] 'lothly' Scattergood	122	Garnesche1	29

LOTHLY
Nor Lycon, that lothly luske, in myn opynyon,	122	Garnesche1	24

LOTHSOME
What! Lyest thou there lyngrynge, lewdly and lothsome?	205	Magnyfycence	2291

LOTHSUM
Lothsum as Lucifer lowest in helle.	130	Garnesche5	28

LOTHSUMNESSE
In lousy lothsumnesse, /And scabbed scorffynesse,	362	Albany	139

LOTTES
As cometh to theyr lottes,	260	Collyn Clout	565
It shalbe your lottes	362	Albany	121

LOUDLY
to prate and to preche proudly and leudly, and loudly to lye;	374	Replycacion	1

LOUNGE
Envye hathe wasted hys lyver and his lounge;	54	Bowge	291

LOURE
Make this lurdeyne for to loure;	275	Collyn Clout	1168

LOUSY
Somtyme in lousy beddes.	263	Collyn Clout	659
In lousy lothsumnesse, /And scabbed scorffynesse,	362	Albany	139

LOUTE
Hym that I loved not, and made hym to loute;	185	Magnyfycence	1623

LOVE
And I love you an hole cart lode.'	35	Man Margery	9
Yet, for his love that all hath wrought,	36	Man Margery	25
That of hys love he toke no kepe,	41	Balettys1	7
He wantyd wyt her love to wyn:	42	Balettys1	12
Of my trew hart, to love her best of all!	45	Balettys3	49
That wher I love best I dare not dyscure!	45	Balettys5	7
For whose love, welcom dysease to me!	45	Balettys5	10
That where I love best I dare not dyscure.	46	Balettys5	14
And of the love betwene /Paris and Vyene;	88	Phy Sparrow	663
And of the love so hote	88	Phy Sparrow	677
His maisters love to further,	88	Phy Sparrow	684
On her moch love and cost,	89	Phy Sparrow	715
To hyr love ye nowte rechyd.	125	Garnesche3	61
Yower lothesum lypps love well to kyse,	130	Garnesche5	44
This lynkyd chayne of love that can unbynde,	146	Magnyfycence	201
Largesse, that all lordes sholde love, syr, I hyght.	148	Magnyfycence	270
I am of fewe wordys. I love not to [crake]. crake] 'barke' †Rastell & Treveris C 1530, B	162	Magnyfycence	775
With a pere my love you may wynne,	168	Magnyfycence	1015
Cockes harte! I love suche japes.	171	Magnyfycence	1133
Holde thy tonge, and thou love thy helth.	179	Magnyfycence	1402
To chose out ii., iii., of suche as you love best,	190	Magnyfycence	1769
Me to enbrace and love moost specyally.	190	Magnyfycence	1800
And from that they love best some I devorse;	194	Magnyfycence	1905
To love that lovesome I wyll not let;	199	Magnyfycence	2072
And love that Lorde that for your love was dede,	207	Magnyfycence	2363
And love that Lorde that for your love was dede,	207	Magnyfycence	2363
Be love I am constreyned /To be with yow retayned,	238	Speke Parott	257
For you love to go trym,	262	Collyn Clout	641
For to love a certayne body	296	Why Come Ye	703
And whome ye love not ye wyll put to shame.	317	Garlande	178
Make noyse enoughe; for claterars love no peas.	319	Garlande	241
The fervent axes of love can not represse!	321	Garlande	315
Furdrers of love, with baudry aqueinted,	329	Garlande	609

LOVED —LOWTE	Page	Title	Line

LOVED
Worrowyd her on that /Which I loved best. . . . . 72 Phy Sparrow 30
Hym that I loved not, and made hym to loute; . . . . 185 Magnyfycence 1623
LOVERS
Lodestar to lyght these lovers to theyr porte, ... 44 Balettys3 25
The song of lovers lay; . . . . 89 Phy Sparrow 702
It makethe lovers bolde . . . . 98 Phy Sparrow 1074
A lovers pylgrimage. . . . . 100 Phy Sparrow 1155
Of Lovers Testamentis and of There Wanton Wyllis, ... 354 Garlande 1496
LOVES
Item A[u]tomedon of Loves Meditacyoun; . . . . 346 Garlande 1181
   Automedon] 'Antomedon' †Fakes 1523, Marshe 1568 MS Cotton
   Vitellius E.x
LOVESOME
To love that lovesome I wyll not let; . . . . 199 Magnyfycence 2072
LOVETH
Whome she loveth, of all plesyre is ryche . . . . 49 Bowge 113
He skantly loveth our kyng, /That grudgeth at this thing: . . . 121 Ag Scottes2 35
For who loveth God can ayle nothynge but good. . . . . 207 Magnyfycence 2365
He loveth nothyng but golde; . . . . 284 Why Come Ye 208
LOVING
Thy loving sovereine lorde, ... 110 Lawde 9
LOVYD
Yet loke on me, that lovyd you have so longe, ... 320 Garlande 298
And how Iollas lovyd goodly Phillis; . . . . 354 Garlande 1497
LOVYNG
And have forgoten your old, trew, lovyng knyght. 42 Balettys2 14
LOVYNGLY
All his subjectes and he /Moost lovyngly agre . . . . 371 Albany 481
LOW
The world [envyronn], of hygh and low estate. . . . . 140 Magnyfycence 2
   envyronn] 'envyronnyd' †Rastell & Treveris C 1530, B
Remembre you, therfore, howe late ye were low. . . . . 210 Magnyfycence 2451
Out from a low degre, ... 291 Why Come Ye 506
Humbly and low /Commendynge me /To yowre bownte. . . . . 338 Garlande 930
LOWCE
Decke your hofte and cover a lowce. . . . . 161 Magnyfycence 749
LOWDE
Bycause his voyce is lowde, ... 82 Phy Sparrow 439
Somtyme I laughe over lowde; . . . . 168 Magnyfycence 1012
To homly, to holy, to lewde, or to lowde, ... 199 Magnyfycence 2094
LOWDEAN
Ye play Hop Lobbyn of Lowdean; . . . . 117 Ag Scottes 59
LOWDEON
Hop Lobyn of Lowdeon wald have e byt of bred; . . . . 232 Speke Parott 72
LOWDER
Had I never sene, some softer, some lowder; . . . . 320 Garlande 271
LOWDYAN
Of Huntley banke, /Of Lowdyan, /Of Locryan, ... 359 Albany 20
LOWE
Of what estate ye be, /Of hye or lowe degre, ... 73 Phy Sparrow 55
What though he crept so lowe? . . . . 76 Phy Sparrow 169
   though] 'thought' †Kele 1545.2
Therfore ye be layde now full lowe. . . . . 114 Scot Kynge 53
Thow mayst fale downe and ebbe full lowe. 132 Garnesche5 123
I rushe at them rughly and make them ly full lowe; . . . . . . 193 Magnyfycence 1884
He maketh them to bere babylles, and to bere a lowe sayle; . . 243 Speke Parott 428
And where the prelates be /Come of lowe degre . . . . 261 Collyn Clout 586
Of hygh or lowe degre . . . . 274 Collyn Clout 1118
And brynge it so lowe . . . . 303 Why Come Ye 951
I trust, to lowe estate . . . . 368 Albany 385
LOWEST
Lothsum as Lucifer lowest in helle. 130 Garnesche5 28
I am desyred with hyghest and lowest degre. . . . . 199 Magnyfycence 2079
LOWLY
In humble wyse as lowly as I may, ... 335 Garlande 837
And hym moost lowly pray, ... 372 Albany 528
LOWRE
To lowre, to droupe, to knele, to stowpe and to play . . . . . 243 Speke Parott 426
   cowche-quale;
Whan him lyst to lowre, ... 289 Why Come Ye 428
And to make hym lowre, ... 360 Albany 58
LOWSE
Lete theym go lowse theym, in the devylles date. . . . . 59 Bowge 455
Lusty Garnysche, lyke a lowse, ye jet full lyke a jaspe; . . . 123 Garnesche2 17
Here FOLY maketh semblaunt to take a lowse . . . . 173 Magnyfycence SD
What hast thou founde there? By God, a lowse. . . . . 173 Magnyfycence 1198
LOWSY
On to your lowsy den; 125 Garnesche3 64
Row and full of lowsy here, ... 127 Garnesche3 124
Men sey ye wyll wax lowsy, /Drunkyn, drowpy, drowsy. 127 Garnesche3 135
Dundas, dronken and drowsy, /Skabed, scurvy and lowsy, ... 136 Dundas 51
I am lowsy and unlykynge and full of scurffe; . . . . 195 Magnyfycence 1958
Now shal ye be scabbed, scurvy, and lowsy. . . . . 197 Magnyfycence 2019
Droupy and drowsy, /Scurvy and lowsy; . . . . 214 El Rummynge 16
LOWTE
To me all prynces to lowte man bese[m]e. . . . . 182 Magnyfycence 1500
   beseme] 'be sene' †Rastell & Treveris C 1530, B

LOWTTEDE — LURE

	Page	Title	Line
For the[m] shall you have at lyberte to lowte.	190	Magnyfycence	1779
them] 'then' †Rastell & Treveris C 1530, B			
LOWTTEDE			
To whome grete astatis obeyde and lowttede,	30	Dol Dethe	45
LUCAN			
Lucan, with Stacius in Achilliedos;	321	Garlande	337
LUCIFER			
Lothsum as Lucifer lowest in helle.	130	Garnesche5	28
LUCILIUS			
Lucilius and Valerius Maximus by name;	322	Garlande	380
LUCINA			
Lucina she wadythe among the watry floddes,	239	Speke Parott	285
And whan Lucina plenarly did shyne,	312	Garlande	6
plenarly] 'plenary' †Fakes 1523, Marshe 1568			
LUCIUS			
With Salusty ageinst Lucius Catelyne,	321	Garlande	331
LUCYFER			
Of Lucyfer in his chaynes,	304	Why Come Ye	991
Lucyfer] 'Lucyfers' †Kele 1545.3			
LUCYFERS			
And rule them echone /In Lucyfers trone.	304	Why Come Ye	993
LUCK			
God sende us better luck!	282	Why Come Ye	123
LUCKE			
And dranke a good lucke.	228	El Rummynge	567
God sende us better lucke, etc.	282	Why Come Ye	124
Of the donghyll, for small lucke	364	Albany	224
LUCRES			
Fayre Lucres, as I wene,	97	Phy Sparrow	1018
LUGE			
Of dampnacyon I had ben drawen in the luge.	206	Magnyfycence	2334
LUGGARD			
Behold, thou lyeste, luggard, alone!	42	Balettys1	25
LUGGES			
With dugges, dugges, dugges. /I shrewe thy Scottishe lugges,	366	Albany	292
LUGGYNG			
And with myghty luggyng,	104	Phy Sparrow	1316
And with myghty luggyng, /Wrastelynge and tuggyng,	349	Garlande	1309
LUK			
Dug, dug, /Jug, jug, /Good yere and good luk,	340	Garlande	1002
Good luk this new yere, the olde yere is past.	354	Garlande	1518
LUKE			
Permytted? By saynt Luke,	272	Collyn Clout	1046
Permytted] 'Permed' †Godfray 1531, 'Now' MS Harley 2252			
LULLAY			
With 'Lullay, lullay', lyke a chylde,	41	Balettys1	I
With 'Lullay, lullay', lyke a chylde,	41	Balettys1	I
With hey, lullay, &c.	41	Balettys1	R
With hey, lullay, &c.	42	Balettys1	Rub
Wyth hey, lullay, &c.	42	Balettys1	Rub
LUMBARDES			
With Lumbardes lemmanns for to mete,	130	Garnesche5	42
LUMBARDY			
Of Lumbardy Gorge Hardyson,	130	Garnesche5	33
LUMBER			
They lumber forth the lawe	249	Collyn Clout	95
LUMBERDES			
That Lumberdes nose meane I	308	Why Come Ye	1186
LUMBRYTH			
He lumbryth on a lewde lewte, 'Roty bully joyse',	37	Coystrowne1	29
LUMPE			
A lesse lumpe of logyke,	374	Replycacion	2
LUMPES			
Nowe must you monche mamockes and lumpes of brede;	197	Magnyfycence	2009
LUMPIS			
I am not ladyn of liddyrnes with lumpis,	332	Garlande	733
LUNA			
Whan Luna, full of mutabylyte,	46	Bowge	3
Luna that so bryght doth shyne,	105	Phy Sparrow	1365
Luna that so bryght doth shene,	350	Garlande	1358
LUNATYKE			
And a lunatyke overage.	369	Albany	418
LUNATYKES			
Agaynst these frenetykes, /Agaynst these lunatykes,	385	Replycacion	401
LURDAYNE			
A lurdayne lyke a lorde to [s]yght,	152	Magnyfycence	418
syght] 'fyght' †Rastell & Treveris C 1530, B			
I say, thou lewde lurdayne,	367	Albany	336
LURDEYNE			
Make this lurdeyne for to loure;	275	Collyn Clout	1168
LURDEN			
What! Woldest thou, lurden, with me brawle agayne?	188	Magnyfycence	1722
I sawe a losell lede a lurden, and they were bothe blynde.	191	Magnyfycence	1824
And nowe lyke a lurden he lyeth in the dust.	193	Magnyfycence	1887
This lurden that here lyeth had ben a noble man.	200	Magnyfycence	2112
LURE			
He then, to be sure, /Callyd her with a lure.	63	Hauke	76
She wold make to the lure	99	Phy Sparrow	1100

LURKE — MACKEMURRE

	Page	Title	Line
Welthe myght be wonne and made to the lure,	141	Magnyfycence	17
The red hat with his lure	286	Why Come Ye	283
Maydenly demure, /Of womanhode the lure;	340	Garlande	992

LURKE

And lurke there lyke an as	366	Albany	289

LURKING

But lering and lurking here and there like spies,	139	Ven Tongues	67

LURKYNG

Ware of the lesard lyeth lurkyng in the gras.	45	Balettys4	7

LUSKE

Nor Lycon, that lothly luske, in myn opynyon,	122	Garnesche1	24

LUST

	Page	Title	Line
Yet sumwhat wright supprisid with hartly lust, hartly] 'herty' Marshe 1568	33	Dol Dethe	145
Youre ugly tokyn /My mynd hath brokyn /From worldly lust;	39	Coystrowne3	3
Thy lust and lykyng is from the gone;	42	Balettys1	23
Corage wyth lust, convenient tyme and space;	43	Balettys3	3
For any bodely lust,	90	Phy Sparrow	731
Of lust and of delyght,	93	Phy Sparrow	869
To daly with yow she had no lust.	131	Garnesche5	54
Let your lust and lykynge stande for a lawe.	185	Magnyfycence	1607
Thys losyll was a lorde and lyvyd at his lust;	193	Magnyfycence	1886
In lust and lykynge my name is Lyberte.	199	Magnyfycence	2078
Whan we kys and play /In lust and in lykyng.	220	El Rummynge	222
Pompe, pryde, honour, ryches and worldly lust,	236	Speke Parott	223
Here dwellith pleasure, with lust and delyte;	332	Garlande	709
Longe to enjoy plesure, delyght, and lust:	337	Garlande	882
And hath smale lust to paint?	339	Garlande	955

LUSTE

Whyles she laugheth and hath luste for to playe. laugheth] 'laughed' †Wynkyn de Worde 1499	49	Bowge	114

LUSTELY

His throte was clere and lustely coude fayne.	52	Bowge	233
These wordes in myne eyre, they be so lustely spoken,	184	Magnyfycence	1565
That lustely they lepe somtyme theyr cloyster wall.	201	Magnyfycence	2150

LUSTES

Suche lustes at large may not be lefte behynde.	186	Magnyfycence	1628

LUSTY

Of lusty somer the passyng goodly quene;	44	Balettys3	14
The lusty chauntyng nyghtyngale;	82	Phy Sparrow	420
With pullysshed termes lusty;	91	Phy Sparrow	776
The lusty ruby ruddes	97	Phy Sparrow	1035
Of lusty somer grene;	101	Phy Sparrow	1184
And Martis lusty knight;	112	Lawde	55
Thow ye be lusty as Syr Lybyus, launces to breke,	122	Garnesche1	17
Lusty Garnysche, lyke a lowse, ye jet full lyke a jaspe;	123	Garnesche2	17
Skelton Lawryate Defender Agenyst Lusty Garnyche	124	Garnesche3	I
Skelton Laureate Defendar Ageinst Lusty Garnyshe	129	Garnesche5	I
Dusty! Nay, syr, ye be all of the lusty;	161	Magnyfycence	760
In faythe, Lyberte is nowe a lusty spere.	166	Magnyfycence	937
Mary, Lusty Pleasure, by myne advyse,	167	Magnyfycence	964
Whom? Lusty Pleasure or mery Consayte?	180	Magnyfycence	1452
Nay, fyrst Lusty Pleasure is my desyre to have;	180	Magnyfycence	1453
Her lusty lyppes ruddy as the chery –	183	Magnyfycence	1558
Howe lyke you? Ye lacke, syr, suche a lusty lasse.	183	Magnyfycence	1559
So I myght hobby for suche a lusty larke.	184	Magnyfycence	1564
I am so lusty to loke on, so freshe, and so fre,	201	Magnyfycence	2145
with a lusty laughter.	201	Magnyfycence	SD
Howe lusty Venus quaked,	270	Collyn Clout	945
Made lusty sporte and joy	270	Collyn Clout	952
Is lusty to loke on, plesaunte, demure, and sage:	336	Garlande	870
Is lusty to loke on, plesaunt, demure, and sage.	337	Garlande	877
Whos lusty lokis make hevy hartis glad;	337	Garlande	903
of the lycorous electuary of lusty lernyng,	373	Replycacion	I

LUSTYS

Measure of your lustys must have the oversyght,	211	Magnyfycence	2491

LUTE

Ye strynged so Luthers lute	379	Replycacion	167

LUTHERS

And some have a smacke /Of Luthers sacke,	260	Collyn Clout	541
And a brennynge sparke /Of Luthers warke,	260	Collyn Clout	543
And are somewhat suspecte /In Luthers secte.	260	Collyn Clout	545
Ye strynged so Luthers lute	379	Replycacion	167
In your divynite /Of Luthers affynite,	381	Replycacion	266

MACEDONY

Kynge Phylyp of Macedony	78	Phy Sparrow	270
Alexander, of Macedony kynge,	181	Magnyfycence	1466

MACHABEUS

Of Judas Machabeus, /And of Cesar Julious;	88	Phy Sparrow	661

MACHAREUS

As Machareus /Fayre Canace,	338	Garlande	933

MACHCHYD

If thow war metely machchyd.	128	Garnesche3	181

MACHUBE

Lyke to Duke Josue /And the valiaunt Machube,	370	Albany	443

MACKEMURRE

Yet I solde his skynne to Mackemurre,	169	Magnyfycence	1056

	Page	Title	Line
MACROBIUS			
Of Alexander; and Macrobius that did trete	322	Garlande	367
MAD			
I say, ye commoners, why wer ye so stark mad?	30	Dol Dethe	50
Withe his enmys that were stark mad and wode;	32	Dol Dethe	100
And also the mad coote,	82	Phy Sparrow	410
Than is he sad, /Frantyke and mad;	95	Phy Sparrow	940
They are so stowre, /So frantyke mad,	115	Ag Scottes	13
A mad rekenynge, /Consydrynge all thynge,	116	Ag Scottes	45
Ye were starke mad to make a fray,	119	Ag Scottes	143
That your mad mynde contryved.	124	Garnesche3	4
Thow callyst me scallyd, thou callydst me mad;	132	Garnesche5	116
For frantick faitours half mad and half straught;	138	Ven Tongues	27
But ofte tymes have I sene wyse men do mad dedys.	148	Magnyfycence	302
Why, wenyst thou, horson, that I were so mad?	155	Magnyfycence	517
To mery, to mad, to gyglynge, to nyse,	199	Magnyfycence	2092
Of this mad mummynge /Of Elynour Rummynge.	230	El Rummynge	620
And every mad medler must now be a maker.	235	Speke Parott	161
And mad a worthy trewse.	282	Why Come Ye	141
mad] 'made' Toy 1553, Kitson 1560.7, Marshe 1568			
And mad theyr hertes attaynted.	282	Why Come Ye	158
And is governed by this mad kote!	295	Why Come Ye	668
And] not in Marshe 1568			
Mustred ther amonge them with many a mad tale;	322	Garlande	373
And such a mad ymage	365	Albany	254
Mad, frantyke and savage.	369	Albany	413
MADAM			
The auncient acquaintance, madam, betwen us twayn,	42	Balettys2	1
MADAME			
Advertysyng you, madame, to warke more secretly,	43	Balettys2	39
Play fayre-play, madame, and loke ye play clene,	43	Balettys2	41
Madame regent of the scyence sevyn	313	Garlande	53
scyence] 'sciences' Marshe 1568			
But, good madame, the accustome and usage	314	Garlande	64
'Madame, with favour of your benynge sufferaunce,	315	Garlande	113
'Madame, your apposelle is wele inferrid,	316	Garlande	141
'O mercyles madame, hard is your constellacyon,	320	Garlande	304
Unto you, madame, I make reconusaunce,	335	Garlande	838
To be your remembrauncer, madame, I am bounde,	336	Garlande	864
Right so, madame, the roses redde of hew	337	Garlande	890
Madame regent /I may you call /Of vertuows all.	339	Garlande	951
MADD			
So myche newe makyng, and so madd tyme spente;	244	Speke Parott	450
MADDE			
A wonder thynge that ye waxe not madde!	53	Bowge	241
Somtyme to mery, somtyme to madde;	168	Magnyfycence	1010
By the masse, I holde the madde.	170	Magnyfycence	1088
For, frantyke Fansy, thou makyst men madde;	176	Magnyfycence	1300
Wherfor your remorders ar madde or else starke blynde,	241	Speke Parott	369
remorders] 'remordes' †MS Harley 2252			
Or elles they are madde	259	Collyn Clout	503
But this madde Amalecke,	291	Why Come Ye	478
Suche a madde bedleme	295	Why Come Ye	655
Subtyle Sym Sly /With madde foly.	300	Why Come Ye	857
Sym Sly] 'Symonye' †Kele 1545.3			
And Maxymyane, with his madde ditiis,	322	Garlande	360
About hym a parke /Of a madde warke,	365	Albany	268
Are ye nat frantyke madde, /And wretchedly bestadde,	368	Albany	363
So madde a cordylar, /So madde a murmurar?	368	Albany	375
So madde a cordylar, /So madde a murmurar?	368	Albany	376
I saye, thou madde Marche hare,	375	Replycacion	35
Your madde ipocrisy, /And your idiosy,	381	Replycacion	249
MADDYNGE			
It is but a maddynge, these wayes that ye use.	148	Magnyfycence	285
MADE			
A maynny of rude villayns made hym for to blede.	30	Dol Dethe	46
What willfull foly made you to ryse agayn	30	Dol Dethe	53
Whiche kyndelde the wyld fyre that made all this smoke.	31	Dol Dethe	77
and madly in hys musykkys mokkyshly made agaynste	36	Coystrowne	1
He wold be made moch of and he wyst how;	37	Coystrownel	33
Er this, whan that ye made me royall chere.	53	Bowge	249
Forthwith, he made on me a prowde assawte,	55	Bowge	316
He made his hawke to fly,	63	Hauke	47
Such sacrificium laudis /He made with suche gambawdis.	63	Hauke	65
How be it, mayden Meed /Made theym to be agreed;	65	Hauke	150
And made truth to tryp;	66	Hauke	155
And of the spyrytuall law /They made but a gewgaw,	66	Hauke	157
Whereat he made dysdayne.	68	Hauke	224
Ye made your hawke to cum /Desuper candelabrum	69	Hauke	288
That made that great arke,	78	Phy Sparrow	257
Were made for myse and rattes,	80	Phy Sparrow	339
Tyll cruell fate made him to dy;	86	Phy Sparrow	592
And made her husband knyght /Of the comyne hall,	87	Phy Sparrow	646
That made the Romaynes all /For-drede and to quake;	88	Phy Sparrow	666
That] 'What' †Kele 1545.2, Wyght 1553			
That made Troylus to dote	88	Phy Sparrow	678
That made the male to wryng;	89	Phy Sparrow	700
the] 'tha' †Kele 1545.2			

MADE — MADE

	Page	Title	Line
She made hym to syng	89	Phy Sparrow	701
That made the Romayns to s[wea]t:	90	Phy Sparrow	748
sweat] 'smart' †Kele 1545.2, Wyght 1553, Kitson 1560.6, Marshe 1568			
She made me sore amased	99	Phy Sparrow	1103
and her foloweth an addicyon made by Maister Skelton.	103	Phy Sparrow	R
Made by protestacyon,	103	Phy Sparrow	1279
A Lawde And Prayse Made for Our Sovereigne Lord the Kyng	110	Lawde	I
For youre owne tayle ye made a rod.	119	Ag Scottes	146
owne] not in Day 1560, Marshe 1568			
I was made poete lawreate.	131	Garnesche5	84
I made, he said, a windmil of an olde mat.	137	Ven Tongues	13
Such tunges unhappy hath made great division	139	Ven Tongues	55
Although he made it never so tough,	139	Ven Tongues	77
Welthe myght be wonne and made to the lure,	141	Magnyfycence	17
And I am Lyberte, made of in every nacyon.	145	Magnyfycence	172
But yf therof the soner amendys be made;	146	Magnyfycence	226
Or who made you so bolde to interrupe my tale?	147	Magnyfycence	256
And wolde have made me Freer Tucke,	150	Magnyfycence	357
And made largesse, as I hyght,	150	Magnyfycence	364
They have made me here to put the stone;	151	Magnyfycence	406
And mekyll am I made of nowe adays.	152	Magnyfycence	430
By God, we have made Magnyfycence to ete a flye.	154	Magnyfycence	503
And I am made a knyght.	155	Magnyfycence	521
Thou hast made me play the jeu dehayte.	156	Magnyfycence	579
And made as I had knowen nothynge of the case –	160	Magnyfycence	719
Made purveaunce /And suche ordenaunce,	165	Magnyfycence	880
She is made for the malarde fat.	166	Magnyfycence	926
Ye. But thryfte and we have made a batell.	171	Magnyfycence	1136
And then he is moche made of for his [wyt];	175	Magnyfycence	1271
wyt] 'whyt' †Rastell & Treveris C 1530, B			
Why, welth hath made many a man braynlesse.	180	Magnyfycence	1423
That ratyd the Romaynes and made them yll rest,	181	Magnyfycence	1481
That made Cerberus to cache, the cur dogge of hell,	182	Magnyfycence	1495
Hym that I loved not, and made hym to loute;	185	Magnyfycence	1623
Yes. With his hande I made hym to subscrybe	187	Magnyfycence	1666
Where is he? Mary, I made hym abyde	187	Magnyfycence	1685
And made instance for me be lykelyhod.	188	Magnyfycence	1697
And Foly, my broder, that made you moche game.	193	Magnyfycence	1872
Unto your maker that made bothe you and me;	196	Magnyfycence	1992
When we with Magnyfycence goodys made chevysaunce.	203	Magnyfycence	2236
And agayne thy maker thou hast made suche warre,	205	Magnyfycence	2302
Ye, holly to good hope I have made my repare.	208	Magnyfycence	2394
And made also mesure to be put fro me.	209	Magnyfycence	2446
Today a yoman, tomorowe made of page;	213	Magnyfycence	2547
Yet of magnyfycence oft made is the mast:	213	Magnyfycence	2563
Lyke as they were with buckels /Togyder made fast.	215	El Rummynge	47
Here was scant thryft /Whan they made suche shyft.	222	El Rummynge	302
And so was made the peace.	223	El Rummynge	350
the peace] 'the drunken peace' †Lant 1545, Kynge & Marche 1554, Day 1560, Marshe 1568			
Elynour made the pryce /For god ale eche whyt.	224	El Rummynge	410
Than sterte in made Kyt, /That had lytell wyt;	224	El Rummynge	412
She made it as koye /As a lege-de-moy;	229	El Rummynge	586
lege-de-moy] 'lege moy' †Lant 1545, Kynge & Marche 1554			
Melchisedeck mercyfull made Moloc mercyles.	232	Speke Parott	60
The Jebet of Baldock was made for Jack Leg;	232	Speke Parott	73
He made you of nothynge by his magistye;	236	Speke Parott	219
Whate mone he made when Pamphylus loste hys make.	237	Speke Parott	234
For replicacion restles that he of late ther made;	239	Speke Parott	282
For protestacyon made	266	Collyn Clout	780
Was made a divyne;	266	Collyn Clout	808
As now is made of late	269	Collyn Clout	914
Made lusty sporte and joy	270	Collyn Clout	952
And made to him be brought	293	Why Come Ye	552
He made a kynge royall,	293	Why Come Ye	558
Before that he was made	293	Why Come Ye	562
Made up a great astate	297	Why Come Ye	723
That he made him his chauncelar	297	Why Come Ye	732
Hath made askrye /And outcry	301	Why Come Ye	870
outcry] 'doute cry' MS Rawlinson C. 813			
Hathe made himselfe abbot	306	Why Come Ye	1099
Whereto made ye me hym to avaunce	315	Garlande	115
But if he had made sum memoryall,	315	Garlande	118
Some men be made of for the mokery;	317	Garlande	185
the] 'their' Marshe 1568			
And of there bounte they made me godely chere	323	Garlande	398
I made it straunge, and drew bak ones or twyse,	324	Garlande	444
A cry anone forthwith she made proclame,	325	Garlande	453
It made sum lympe-legged and broisid there bones;	329	Garlande	625
Sum were made pevysshe, porisshly pynk iyde,	329	Garlande	626
Of that aventuris, whiche made me sore agast.	330	Garlande	649
They made, with chapellettes and garlandes grene;	331	Garlande	684
Stedfast of thought, /Wele made, wele wrought;	341	Garlande	1030
Galathea, the made well besene,	342	Garlande	1076
It wolde have made a man hole that had be ryght sekely,	345	Garlande	1162
Lorde, how she made moche of her gentyll birth!	346	Garlande	1202
With, 'Gingirly, go gingerly!' Her tayle was made of hay;	346	Garlande	1203

MADIONITA — MAGNYFYCENCE

	Page	Title	Line
But myrth and consolacyoun, /Made by protestacyoun,	348	Garlande	1272
It made sum mens eye dasild and dasid;	351	Garlande	1389
In his distichon made on verses twaine.	353	Garlande	1467
distichon] 'distincyon' †Fakes 1523			
That made sum to snurre and snuf in the wynde;	353	Garlande	1472
snurre] 'surt' †Fakes 1523			
It made them to skip, to stampe, and to stare,	353	Garlande	1473
God wote, theis wordes made me full sad;	353	Garlande	1484
Rendrynge my devisis I made in disporte	354	Garlande	1494
But when of the laurell she made rehersall,	354	Garlande	1503
With the Romayns that made war,	363	Albany	193
It made no great fors	366	Albany	282
and with good delyberacion made,	373	Replycacion	I
Have made you eate the fly,	381	Replycacion	252
that can or may be made or objected	382	Replycacion	R

MADIONITA

Madionita Jetro, our Moyses kepyth his shepe;	234	Speke Parott	115

MADLY

and madly in hys musykkys mokkyshly made agaynste	36	Coystrowne	I
Counterfet sadnesse, with delynge full madly;	153	Magnyfycence	468
Muche money, men sey, there madly he hathe spente;	240	Speke Parott	335
Theyr matyns madly sayde, /Nothynge devoutly prayde,	252	Collyn Clout	238
But /Helas! sage overage /So madly decayes,	279	Why Come Ye	42
So] 'To' Toy 1553, Kitson 1560.7, Marshe 1568			
Our mony madly lent,	282	Why Come Ye	143
lent] 'sent' Marshe 1568			
And mor madly spent.	282	Why Come Ye	144
Whiche madly he dothe apply /Unto an extravagancy,	306	Why Come Ye	1104
Yourselfe madly ye overse!	309	Why Come Ye2	7
But madly it frames,	374	Replycacion	11

MADMEN

Alas, ye madmen, to far ye did excede.	31	Dol Dethe	60

MADNES

Moche mirthe and no madnes,	340	Garlande	1009

MADNESSE

Put Magnyfycence in suche a madnesse	159	Magnyfycence	679
Tyll all theyr conveyaunce is turnyd into madnesse.	178	Magnyfycence	1367
Nay. Madnesse hath begyled you and many mo;	192	Magnyfycence	1856
By meanes of madnesse and to moche lyberte.	199	Magnyfycence	2100
His madnesse by writynge,	305	Why Come Ye	1056
Somwhat of your madnesse;	310	Why Come Ye2	23
Your madnesse she attamed;	376	Replycacion	61

MAGESTE

For, by Juppiter and his high mageste,	353	Garlande	1488
In royal mageste /Lyke unto Ptholome,	370	Albany	440

MAGISTYE

He made you of nothynge by his magistye;	236	Speke Parott	219

MAGYKE

I wolde I had a parte /Of her crafty magyke!	77	Phy Sparrow	204

MAGNANYMYTE

And fumously adresse you with magnanymyte;	211	Magnyfycence	2497
His magnanymyte, /His animosite,	370	Albany	447

MAGNIFY

His grace to magnify	369	Albany	402
Lyke unto Alcheus, he dothe hym magnify.	383	Replycacion	335

MAGNIFYCENCE

To whose magnificence /Is all the conflewence,	289	Why Come Ye	412
Agaynst her preemynence, /Agaynst her magnifycence,	375	Replycacion	43

MAGNIFYE

To magnifye their names.	374	Replycacion	10
Your names to magnifye,	378	Replycacion	164
Who so dothe magnifye	381	Replycacion	255

MAGNYFICENCE

All were to litill for his magnyficence.	33	Dol Dethe	161

MAGNYFYCENCE

Magnyfycence to mayntayne, your promosyon shalbe.	144	Magnyfycence	157
Me semeth Magnyfycence is comynge here at hande.	145	Magnyfycence	162
Who lyst to knowe, Magnyfycence I hyght.	145	Magnyfycence	164
For dowtlesse I parceyve my magnyfycence	146	Magnyfycence	227
With Magnyfycence, this noble prynce of myght,	148	Magnyfycence	273
This noble man Magnyfycence,	151	Magnyfycence	404
By God, we have made Magnyfycence to ete a flye.	154	Magnyfycence	503
With Magnyfycence in housholde do remayne;	157	Magnyfycence	613
Hath Magnyfycence ony tresure?	157	Magnyfycence	620
With Magnyfycence in housholde do remayne;	158	Magnyfycence	640
Magnyfycence to us begynneth to enclyne,	158	Magnyfycence	644
To Magnyfycence with us twayne.	158	Magnyfycence	667
Put Magnyfycence in suche a madnesse	159	Magnyfycence	679
Mary, with Magnyfycence I wolde be retaynyd.	161	Magnyfycence	763
For he wyll speke to Magnyfycence thus.	172	Magnyfycence	1168
But, for the, Fansy, Magnyfycence abydes.	176	Magnyfycence	1305
With Magnyfycence thou shalte wonne.	176	Magnyfycence	1311
For as sone as you come in Magnyfycence syght	176	Magnyfycence	1314
Unto Magnyfycence a full ungracyous sorte,	178	Magnyfycence	1373
Here cometh in MAGNYFYCENCE with LYBERTE and FELYCYTE.	178	Magnyfycence	SD
MAGNYFYCENCE alone in the place.	181	Magnyfycence	SD
My name is Magnyfycence, man most of myght.	182	Magnyfycence	1493
Welcom, Pleasure, to our magnyfycence.	182	Magnyfycence	1516

MAGNYFYED — MAY

	Page	Title	Line
But thynke you with Magnyfycence I shal be reserved?	188	Magnyfycence	1702
By Magnyfycence nor yet none of his;	188	Magnyfycence	1705
and leveth MAGNYFYCENCE alone in the place.	190	Magnyfycence	SD
Here MAGNYFYCENCE is beten downe	193	Magnyfycence	SD
Alasse that ever I Magnyfycence was named!	196	Magnyfycence	1983
Here MAGNYFYCENCE dolorously maketh his mone.	198	Magnyfycence	SD
I am Magnyfycence, that somtyme thy mayster was.	200	Magnyfycence	2107
When we with Magnyfycence goodys made chevysaunce.	203	Magnyfycence	2236
Magnyfycence I was, whom ye have brought to shame.	204	Magnyfycence	2241
Here MAGNYFYCENCE wolde slee hymselfe with a knyfe.	206	Magnyfycence	SD
Now, surely, Magnyfycence, I am ryght well apayed	208	Magnyfycence	2402
Is from adversyte Magnyfycence to unbynde.	209	Magnyfycence	2422
How fortuned you, Magnyfycence, so far to fal behynde?	209	Magnyfycence	2423
I herde say that adversyte with Magnyfycence had fought.	210	Magnyfycence	2460
Fyrst, from your magnyfycence syn must be abjectyd;	211	Magnyfycence	2484
Yet of magnyfycence oft made is the mast:	213	Magnyfycence	2563
And of Magnyfycence a notable mater,	346	Garlande	1192

MAGNYFYED

	Page	Title	Line
For aurea lyngua Greca ought to be magnyfyed,	234	Speke Parott	142

MAGOTT

	Page	Title	Line
So fatte a magott, bred of a flesshe-flye;	246	Speke Parott	509

MAGOTTES

	Page	Title	Line
Full of magottes quycke;	225	El Rummynge	431

MAHOUNDE

	Page	Title	Line
Lyke Mahounde in a play.	294	Why Come Ye	597

MAIDEN

	Page	Title	Line
Maiden moste pure, and Goddis moder dere,	34	Dol Dethe	205

MAIDENES

	Page	Title	Line
And wrapt in a maidenes smocke,	86	Phy Sparrow	590

MAIDENHODE

	Page	Title	Line
But, for to preserve her maidenhode clene,	320	Garlande	293
maidenhode] 'maydenheed' Marshe 1568			

MAINE

	Page	Title	Line
By whos myght and maine	348	Garlande	1290

MAINTAYNE

	Page	Title	Line
Maintayne them with comforte	370	Albany	472

MAINTEYNE

	Page	Title	Line
To mainteyne with your skoles,	378	Replycacion	144

MAINTEYNED

	Page	Title	Line
justifyed, and constantly mainteyned;	374	Replycacion	I

MAINTENAUNCE

	Page	Title	Line
Maintenaunce and Mischefe, theis be men of myght;	317	Garlande	193

MAISTER

	Page	Title	Line
Maister sophista, /Ye simplex silogista,	68	Hauke	253
and her foloweth an addicyon made by Maister Skelton.	103	Phy Sparrow	R
For all maister Doctour of Cyvyll	277	Collyn Clout	1219
But a poore maister of arte!	292	Why Come Ye	512
How maister Gaguine, the crownycler	297	Why Come Ye	718
Is maister Mewtas dede,	298	Why Come Ye	787
Maister doctor decretorum,	309	Why Come Ye2	9
And maister Chaucer, that nobly enterprysyd	323	Garlande	388
Poeta Skelton to Maister Gower	323	Garlande	R
'Maister Gower, I have nothyng deserved	323	Garlande	407
I sawe maister Newton sit with his compas,	343	Garlande	1096
in maister Porphiris problemes,	374	Replycacion	I

MAISTERS

	Page	Title	Line
His maisters love to further,	88	Phy Sparrow	684
Of our maisters counsel in everithing.	299	Why Come Ye	792

MAISTRES

	Page	Title	Line
For to expres /The noblenes /Of my maistres,	95	Phy Sparrow	958
As my maistres, /Of whom I thynk	96	Phy Sparrow	984
Maistres Geretrude, /With womanhode endude,	341	Garlande	1043
Maistres Geretrude, /With womanhode endude,	342	Garlande	1051
Maistres Geretrude /With womanhode endude,	342	Garlande	1059
This fustiane maistres and this giggisse gase	346	Garlande	1206
To fayre maistres Anne that shuld have be sent,	347	Garlande	1241

MAY

	Page	Title	Line
Thes sorowfulle ditis that I may shew expres.	29	Dol Dethe	21
It may be regesterde of shamefull recorde.	30	Dol Dethe	28
Well may ye be cald commons most unkynd.	30	Dol Dethe	56
ye] 'you' Marshe 1568			
Bot by them to knoulege ye may attayne	32	Dol Dethe	129
Eche man may sorow in his inward thought	34	Dol Dethe	177
On Candelmas evyn, the kalendas of May.	38	Coystrowne1	70
No man may hym hyde /From deth holow-eyed,	39	Coystrowne3	10
There may no fraunchys /Nor worldly blys	39	Coystrowne3	26
Of me and other ye may have nede.	41	Coystrowne4	14
Well may thou sygh, well may thou grone,	42	Balettys1	26
Well may thou sygh, well may thou grone,	42	Balettys1	26
Ye may be countyd comfort of all corage.	42	Balettys3	7
Your ruddys wyth ruddy rubys may compare;	44	Balettys3	16
That clymmeth hyer than he may fotynge have;	46	Bowge	27
Bone aventure may brynge you in suche case	49	Bowge	104
To shewe you thynges that may not be disclosed.'	52	Bowge	217
Unthryftynes in hym may well be shewed,	58	Bowge	416
Unthryftynes] 'Unthryftnes' †Wynkyn de Worde 1499, 1510			
For this may brede to a confusyon,	59	Bowge	482

	Page	Title	Line
There he may se and reed	65	Hauke	147
he] 'her' Marshe 1568			
Of the whych proces /Ye may know more expres,	68	Hauke	232
That Phyllyp preserved may be!	74	Phy Sparrow	93
That all the world may gase	79	Phy Sparrow	316
We may not well forgo /The countrynge of the coe;	83	Phy Sparrow	467
No broken galles /May there abyde	83	Phy Sparrow	474
No] 'Nor' Kitson 1560.6			
That potencyally /May never dye	84	Phy Sparrow	515
I pray God, Phillip to heven may fly.	86	Phy Sparrow	580
That Phyllyp may fly /Above the starry sky,	86	Phy Sparrow	598
Yet as a woman may,	92	Phy Sparrow	820
That I may say /Honour alway /Of womankynd!	96	Phy Sparrow	974
She may well represent	97	Phy Sparrow	1017
Such pleasures that I may	101	Phy Sparrow	1196
I pray you it may be amendyd	102	Phy Sparrow	1246
What the cause may be /Of this perplexite!	106	Phy Sparrow	1369
That folowe as you may se.	106	Phy Sparrow	1379
you] 'ye' Wyght 1553, Kitson 1560.6, Marshe 1568			
Calliope, /As ye may se,	112	Calliope	2
For your kynge may synge welawaye.	114	Scot Kynge	20
Wyerfore ye may it now repent.	114	Scot Kynge	33
Of the kynge of Naverne ye may take hede	115	Scot Kynge	56
They may well say, fye on that wynnynge!	115	Ag Scottes	4
That the Scottys may synge, /'Fy on the wynnynge!'	116	Ag Scottes	47
synge] 'sin' Marshe 1568			
Ye may be lorde of Locryan -	117	Ag Scottes	61
I may compounde confectures for a cordyall,	117	Ag Scottes	82
For alle your proude prankyng, yor pride may apayere.	122	Garnesche1	19
How may I your mokery mekely tollerate,	123	Garnesche2	1
Cum Garnyche, cum Godfrey, with as many as ye may!	123	Garnesche2	32
Ye may wele be bedawyd,	128	Garnesche3	182
Rede and lerne ye may,	129	Garnesche3	195
Tyll more matyr may cum.	129	Garnesche3	205
[Thy] myrrour may be the devyllys ars.	130	Garnesche5	18
Thy] 'They' †MS Harley 367			
Get ye anothyr where ye may.	131	Garnesche5	62
Haroldes from honor may the devors,	131	Garnesche5	71
Yet ther may falle soche caswelte	132	Garnesche5	121
Of thi lewdenes that may be tolde.	134	Garnesche5	175
Than ye may commaunde me to gentil cok wat.	137	Ven Tongues	15
But yet I may say safely, so many wel lettred,	138	Ven Tongues	38
What fault find ye herein but may be avowed.	138	Ven Tongues	41
That nothynge than welth may worse be enduryd,	140	Magnyfycence	7
Of that may come after; experyence trewe and playne,	141	Magnyfycence	11
A man may have welth, but not as he wolde,	141	Magnyfycence	14
How be it, lyberte may somtyme be to large,	141	Magnyfycence	37
Lyberte, I wote well, forbere no man there may;	142	Magnyfycence	50
So in his harte he may be glad of us.	145	Magnyfycence	158
Then may I say that ye be servauntys myne.	145	Magnyfycence	183
Of his rekenynge, as evydently we may	146	Magnyfycence	215
And from felycyte may not be forborne,	146	Magnyfycence	220
Without measure lyghtly may fade,	146	Magnyfycence	228
Syr, hardely remembre what may your name avaunce.	148	Magnyfycence	277
Wel, wyse men may ete the fysshe when ye shal draw the pole.	148	Magnyfycence	300
But largesse may amende your name.	151	Magnyfycence	389
I pray you, syr, I may so be;	151	Magnyfycence	391
In stede of ryght that wronge may stande;	152	Magnyfycence	433
Counterfet maydenhode may well be borne,	152	Magnyfycence	445
And be as praty as she may,	153	Magnyfycence	464
Counterfet worshyp outwarde men may se;	153	Magnyfycence	473
Monkys may not for drede that men sholde them se.	154	Magnyfycence	493
A man may beshrowe your angry harte.	156	Magnyfycence	563
Ye, and se howe it may be compast	156	Magnyfycence	567
What the devyll! Howe may that be?	157	Magnyfycence	627
All this ye may easely brynge aboute.	158	Magnyfycence	655
To passe the tyme and order whyle a man may talke	159	Magnyfycence	689
Howe I may hurte and hynder every man.	160	Magnyfycence	709
I am never glad but whan I may do yll,	160	Magnyfycence	731
I may do somwhat, and more I thynke shall.	162	Magnyfycence	778
He wyll come, man, when he may tende to.	162	Magnyfycence	790
That he may hyde	165	Magnyfycence	904
With a pere my love you may wynne,	168	Magnyfycence	1015
And ye may lese it for a pynne.	168	Magnyfycence	1016
And I may tende therto for play;	168	Magnyfycence	1018
That I wote not where I may rest.	168	Magnyfycence	1021
Yes, in faythe, I thanke God I may here.	169	Magnyfycence	1059
Mary, syr, ye may swere it on a boke.	176	Magnyfycence	1292
But may I drynke therof whylest that I stare?	176	Magnyfycence	1322
Whan Mesure is gone, we may slee care.	176	Magnyfycence	1324
Syr, yet without sapyence your substaunce may be smal;	179	Magnyfycence	1407
For where is no mesure, howe may worshyp endure?	179	Magnyfycence	1408
He may not be comparyd unto me.	181	Magnyfycence	1476
Surely it is I that all may save and spyll,	181	Magnyfycence	1478
May wynne with a sawte the fortresse of the holde.	184	Magnyfycence	1581
Suche lustes at large may not be lefte behynde.	186	Magnyfycence	1628
I may say to you I have but small devocyon.	186	Magnyfycence	1640
And he go to the devyll, so that I may have my fee,	187	Magnyfycence	1670

MAY —MAY   Page   Title   Line

Well, for thy sake the better I may endure	187	Magnyfycence	1680
So that I may craftely be excused.	187	Magnyfycence	1684
They catche that catche may, kepe and holde fast,	189	Magnyfycence	1750
Yet it proveth eyrnest, ye may se, every day.	195	Magnyfycence	1949
I am raggyd and rent, as ye may se;	195	Magnyfycence	1962
And whan it pleaseth God, better may be.	196	Magnyfycence	1993
That may restore you agayne to felycyte,	196	Magnyfycence	1998
Nowe lap you in a coverlet, full fayne that you may;	197	Magnyfycence	2011
Alas! Of Fortune I may well complayne.	197	Magnyfycence	2030
I may no more speke tyll I have wept my fyll.	198	Magnyfycence	2063
A thousande pounde with lyberte may holde no tacke.	199	Magnyfycence	2084
At lyberte a man may be bolde for to brake;	199	Magnyfycence	2085
Thus totum in toto groweth up, as ye may se,	199	Magnyfycence	2099
That I used the to moche sore may I rewe.	199	Magnyfycence	2104
As evydently in retchlesse youth ye may se	200	Magnyfycence	2133
For to be wyse all men may wene of me,	201	Magnyfycence	2158
What! Then he may drynke out of a stone cruyse.	201	Magnyfycence	2166
He may rynse a pycher, for his plate is to wed.	201	Magnyfycence	2168
In faythe, he may dreme on a daggeswane for ony fether bed.	201	Magnyfycence	2169
Alasse, my wyckydnesse, that may I wyte!	205	Magnyfycence	2304
A, blessyd may ye be, syr! What shall you I call?	206	Magnyfycence	2327
Who knoweth me, hymselfe may never sloo.	206	Magnyfycence	2330
There is no man may synne more mortally	206	Magnyfycence	2336
But thrughe good hope there may come remedy.	207	Magnyfycence	2344
He may helpe you. He may mende your mode.	207	Magnyfycence	2366
He may helpe you. He may mende your mode.	207	Magnyfycence	2366
But redresse is redlesse and may do no correccyon.	209	Magnyfycence	2417
For I may tell you, /I lerned it of a Jewe,	219	El Rummynge	207
And ye may it broke,	219	El Rummynge	212
For ye may prove it by me.'	219	El Rummynge	216
A myrrour of glasse, that I may tote therin;	231	Speke Parott	10
Phronessys for frenessys may not hold her way.	232	Speke Parott	47
That Latinum fari may fall to rest and slepe,	235	Speke Parott	164
That never may dye, nor never dye shall:	236	Speke Parott	216
Of Argus revengyd, recover when he may,	239	Speke Parott	288
In there remembraunce ye may be inrolde.	239	Speke Parott	291
For whoo lokythe wyselye in your warkys may fynde	239	Speke Parott	296
With porpose and graundepose he may fede hym fatte,	239	Speke Parott	308
Parott, ye may prate thys undyr protestacion,	240	Speke Parott	336
Wherfor he may now come agayne as he wente,	240	Speke Parott	338
God amend all, /That all amend may!	241	Speke Parott	354
That lordes and ladies thys pamflett may behold,	241	Speke Parott	358
The reste of suche reconyng may make a fowle fraye.	243	Speke Parott	403
A thre-foted stole /That he may downe sytte,	247	Collyn Clout	31
It may well so be,	247	Collyn Clout	38
'Bysshoppes, yf they may,	249	Collyn Clout	122
Amende whan ye may,	251	Collyn Clout	189
Reporte howe the pope may	254	Collyn Clout	302
There may no cost be spared;	254	Collyn Clout	318
It may take some effecte!	257	Collyn Clout	436
After gloria, laus, /May come a soure sauce.	258	Collyn Clout	483
As ye may dayly se /Howe the lay fee	259	Collyn Clout	495
Suche ye may well knowe and ken	260	Collyn Clout	533
That no man may abyde	261	Collyn Clout	594
And yf ye may have layser,	261	Collyn Clout	605
ye] 'you' Kele 1545.1, Marshe 1568, 'ye' MS Harley 2252			
As dayly men may se,	262	Collyn Clout	630
Or elles yf we may	265	Collyn Clout	743
But answere that I may, /For myselfe alway	266	Collyn Clout	785
Fresshe as flours in May;	270	Collyn Clout	943
Fortune may chaunce to flytte,	271	Collyn Clout	994
Yet may he mysse the quysshon!	271	Collyn Clout	996
Howe may this come to pas,	272	Collyn Clout	1021
And howe may this accorde,	272	Collyn Clout	1029
As they may byde therby,	273	Collyn Clout	1062
Howe may we thus endure?	276	Collyn Clout	1202
Renne who may renne best,	277	Collyn Clout	1223
A noble man may fall,	279	Why Come Ye	22
To catche that catche may,	280	Why Come Ye	51
Some men may happely rew,	280	Why Come Ye	60
We may blowe at the cole!	281	Why Come Ye	84
What may she do therto?'	281	Why Come Ye	87
They may garlycke pyll,	281	Why Come Ye	109
Or pescoddes they may shyll,	281	Why Come Ye	111
Clerely percevye we may	281	Why Come Ye	119
With all the power he may.	282	Why Come Ye	156
Men may happely se	288	Why Come Ye	367
May stande somwhat in stede.	298	Why Come Ye	765
And soone may be perceyvid	298	Why Come Ye	782
But Englande may well say	302	Why Come Ye	928
He may take whom he wull,	306	Why Come Ye	1079
May ete pigges in lent for pikys	306	Why Come Ye	1081
And he may fange us.	308	Why Come Ye	1156
And] 'That' Kitson 1560.7, Marshe 1568			
Ye may weare a cockes come,	310	Why Come Ye2	18
I may fortune for to ryme	310	Why Come Ye2	22
A poete somtyme may for his pleasure taunt,	315	Garlande	100
Whiche passid all other; wherfore I may	316	Garlande	159

MAYD —MAYE

	Page	Title	Line
Of very dwte it may not well accorde,	318	Garlande	212
May be brought forth, such as can be founde,	318	Garlande	216
Let hym blowe now, that we may take a vewe	319	Garlande	237
a] 'the' MS Cotton Vitellius E.x			
And may not atteyne it by no medyacyon,	321	Garlande	319
Unto me sayd, 'Lo, syr, now ye may se	326	Garlande	518
To se this howre now, that I may say,	327	Garlande	538
But wele may ye thynk I was no thyng prowde	330	Garlande	648
May this contente you and your mirry mynde?	332	Garlande	708
Contynuall comfort here ye may fynde,	332	Garlande	710
Wherewith your spiritis may be revyvid.'	332	Garlande	713
I am not woundid but that I may be cured.	332	Garlande	732
In humble wyse as lowly as I may,	335	Garlande	837
Dame Agrippina also I may reherse	336	Garlande	859
Whome dame Nature, as wele I may reporte,	336	Garlande	867
Mi litell lady I may not leve behinde,	337	Garlande	878
Compare you I may to Cidippes, the mayd,	337	Garlande	885
Phedra ye may /Wele represent;	338	Garlande	940
Madame regent /I may you call /Of vertuows all.	339	Garlande	952
The fresshest flowre of May;	340	Garlande	990
Far may be sought	341	Garlande	1031
Moche dowblenes of the worlde therin he may fynde.	346	Garlande	1197
It may wele ryme, but shroudly it doth accorde,	346	Garlande	1210
What the cause may be /Of this perplexyte.	350	Garlande	1362
That folowe as ye may se:	350	Garlande	1372
But yet for all that, be as be may,	352	Garlande	1415
But who may have a more ungracyous lyfe	352	Garlande	1451
a] not in Marshe 1568			
May happely loke /Upon your boke,	355	Garlande	1546
That so indede /Your fame may sprede	355	Garlande	1551
Els ye shall pray /Them that ye may	356	Garlande	1584
Ye may be assured /Your falshod discured	362	Albany	127
Helas, ye wreches, ye may be wo!	376	Replycacion	77
Ye may syng weleaway	376	Replycacion	78
What may be ment hereby,	378	Replycacion	153
Ye may soone make construction	378	Replycacion	154
That never more may dye.	380	Replycacion	246
that can or may be made or objected	382	Replycacion	R
Th[i]s may nat be remorded	383	Replycacion	323
This] 'Thus' †Pynson 1528			
Where worde for worde ye may	383	Replycacion	327
Flaccus nor Catullus with hym may nat compare,	383	Replycacion	336
In metricall muses, his harpyng we may spare;	383	Replycacion	338

MAYD

	Page	Title	Line
Saynge, 'Mayd, ye are in wyll	77	Phy Sparrow	222
I am but a yong mayd,	91	Phy Sparrow	770
Of that most goodly mayd	93	Phy Sparrow	852
goodly] 'godly' Wyght 1553, Kitson 1560.6, Marshe 1568			
Honour to this fayre mayd;	103	Phy Sparrow	1254
Alas, that goodly mayd,	103	Phy Sparrow	1282
With, 'Who is there? A mayd?' Nay, nay, I trow!	233	Speke Parott	100
Compare you I may to Cidippes, the mayd,	337	Garlande	885
Alas, that goodly mayd,	348	Garlande	1275

MAYDE

	Page	Title	Line
But for I am a mayde, /Tymerous, halfe afrayde,	87	Phy Sparrow	607
Melpomene, that fayre mayde, she burneshed his beke:	236	Speke Parott	209
Spareth neither mayde ne wyfe.	284	Why Come Ye	225
That glorious mayde Mary;	381	Replycacion	256
That glorious mayde and mother,	381	Replycacion	257

MAYDEN

	Page	Title	Line
How be it, mayden Meed /Made theym to be agreed;	65	Hauke	149
O mayden, wydow, and wyfe,	73	Phy Sparrow	53
My mayden Isabell,	340	Garlande	976
Of the Mayden of Kent callid Counforte,	354	Garlande	1495

MAYDENHEDE

	Page	Title	Line
Enbrowdred the mantill /Is of your maydenhede.	338	Garlande	909
maydenhede] 'maydenhode' †Fakes 1523			
Enbrawderyd the mantyll /Is of yowre maydenhede.	338	Garlande	917
Enbrawderid the mantill /Is of yowr maydenhede.	338	Garlande	925

MAYDENHODE

	Page	Title	Line
Counterfet maydenhode may well be borne,	152	Magnyfycence	445

MAYDENLY

	Page	Title	Line
Lyke to Aryna, maydenly of porte,	336	Garlande	865
Maydenly demure, /Of womanhode the lure;	340	Garlande	991
So joyously, /So maydenly, /So womanly	341	Garlande	1012

MAYDENS

	Page	Title	Line
These maydens full meryly with many a dyvers flowur	231	Speke Parott	11
a] not in †MS Harley 2252			
To banysshe pyte out of a maydens harte?	320	Garlande	308

MAYE

	Page	Title	Line
Maye never dye, bute evermore endure.	46	Bowge	16
His hede maye be harde, but feble is his brayne!	46	Bowge	24
his] not in Marshe 1568			
But of reproche surely he maye not mys	46	Bowge	26
And how I that waye and meanes fynde.'	49	Bowge	109
But this one thynge ye maye be sure of me,	50	Bowge	162
Ye maye not fall; truste me, ye maye not fayle.	50	Bowge	170
Ye maye not fall; truste me, ye maye not fayle.	50	Bowge	170

	Page	Title	Line
MAYED —MAYSTERFEST			
'Ye, soo,' quod Suspecte, 'he maye us bothe begyle.'	51	Bowge	189
The soveraynst thynge that ony man maye have	52	Bowge	211
What thynge is that I maye do for you?	53	Bowge	240
I praye to God that it maye never dy.	53	Bowge	271
I lete her to hyre that men maye on her ryde;	57	Bowge	402
Alas, a connynge man ne dwelle maye	58	Bowge	445
But, what, a strawe! I maye not tell all thynge.	59	Bowge	459
Amendis maye be of that is now amys;	60	Bowge	494
He tolde me so, by God, ye maye truste me.	60	Bowge	514
Woo is hym that is blynde and maye not see!	60	Bowge	518
The best now that I maye	77	Phy Sparrow	237
As well perceyve ye maye	81	Phy Sparrow	372
Be that as be maye;	221	El Rummynge	261
Ye saye that poetry /Maye nat flye so hye	382	Replycacion	307
MAYED			
Of Mary, mother and mayed?	376	Replycacion	47
MAYNE			
Vigorously upon them with myght and with mayne,	31	Dol Dethe	89
By whose myght and mayne	104	Phy Sparrow	1297
MAYNE LANDE			
Some from the mayne lande, some fro the Frensche hoste;	326	Garlande	497
MAYNY			
A mayny of marefoles	285	Why Come Ye	244
Lyke a mayny of shepe	286	Why Come Ye	295
MAYNNY			
A maynny of rude villayns made hym for to blede.	30	Dol Dethe	46
MAYNTAYNE			
With our kyng royall war to mayntayne.	119	Ag Scottes	152
Magnyfycence to mayntayne, your promosyon shalbe.	144	Magnyfycence	157
And our matters mayntayne,	276	Collyn Clout	1213
Theyr astate to mayntayne;	286	Why Come Ye	311
Nor no batayle mayntayne,	365	Albany	244
MAYNTEYNE			
To maynteyne argumentes /Agaynst the sacramentes.	259	Collyn Clout	517
Or to maynteyne good quarelles.	269	Collyn Clout	916
Your mynde that can maynteyne so apparently;	317	Garlande	170
MAYNTEN			
Right to maynten and to resist all wronge.	34	Dol Dethe	171
MAYNTENANCE			
But if hastyve credence by mayntenance of myght	344	Garlande	1133
MAYRE			
A goldsmyth youre mayre:	301	Why Come Ye	908
MAYSYD			
What man is so maysyd with me that dare mete,	182	Magnyfycence	1506
MAYST			
Beholde thy selfe, and thou mayst se.	130	Garnesche5	16
Thow mayst fale downe and ebbe full lowe.	132	Garnesche5	123
Here he is nowe, man. Mayst thou not se?	162	Magnyfycence	792
Thou mayst give up thy cocking.	366	Albany	299
MAYSTE			
Thou mayste not studye or muse on the mone.	57	Bowge	383
MAYSTER			
'How do ye, mayster? Ye loke so soberly!	58	Bowge	442
compyled by Mayster Skelton, poete laureate	71	Phy Sparrow	I
Mayster Measure, you be come in good season.	143	Magnyfycence	84
Where measure is mayster, plenty dothe none offence;	144	Magnyfycence	121
For myschefe wyll mayster us yf measure us forsake.	144	Magnyfycence	154
That Measure be mayster us semeth it is syttynge.	145	Magnyfycence	176
That with your lorde and mayster so pertly can prate!	149	Magnyfycence	305
There dwelleth a mayster men calleth Mesure -	158	Magnyfycence	631
And desyre me thy good mayster to be?	162	Magnyfycence	798
Who is mayster of the masshe fat?	176	Magnyfycence	1319
Mayster Survayour, where have ye ben so longe?	178	Magnyfycence	1382
Mayster Survayour, Largesse to me call.	179	Magnyfycence	1398
Mayster Felycyte, let be your chydynge;	180	Magnyfycence	1437
I am Magnyfycence, that somtyme thy mayster was.	200	Magnyfycence	2107
I was your mayster, though ye thynke it skorne;	204	Magnyfycence	2246
So shamfully to me, theyr mayster, to aproche,	205	Magnyfycence	2279
Commensynge this processe at mayster Redresse.	211	Magnyfycence	2481
For Mayster Adulator, /And Doctour Assentator,	263	Collyn Clout	679
But mayster Damyan, /Or some other man	264	Collyn Clout	720
compyled by Mayster Skelton, Poete Laureate	278	Why Come Ye	I
Now mayster doctor, howe say ye,	309	Why Come Ye2	1
Mayster doctor, in your degre,	309	Why Come Ye2	6
by Mayster Skelton, Poete Laureat,	312	Garlande	I
Mayster Terence, the famous comicar, comicar] 'conucar' †Fakes 1523	322	Garlande	353
Mayster Gower to Skelton	323	Garlande	R
Mayster Chaucer to Skelton	323	Garlande	R
Mayster Lydgate to Skelton	324	Garlande	R
Mayster Lidgate, of your accustomable	324	Garlande	436
With Ipocras and mayster Avycen,	352	Garlande	1426
dyvysed by Mayster Skelton, Poete Laureat.	358	Garlande2	R
Our mayster shall you brynge,	368	Albany	384
MAYSTERFEST			
Today maysterfest, tomorowe he hath no holde;	213	Magnyfycence	2549

| MAYSTERY —MAKE | Page | Title | Line |

MAYSTERY
It i[s] no maystery. Tushe, let Measure procede, is] 'it' †Rastell & Treveris C 1530, B	144	Magnyfycence	150

MAYSTERS
'Maysters,' he sayde, 'the shyp that ye here see,	47	Bowge	48
With us olde servauntes such maysters to playe.	55	Bowge	329
Maysters, Cryst save everychone!	169	Magnyfycence	1043
Some maysters of arte,	264	Collyn Clout	730

MAYSTRES
'Maystres,' quod I, 'I have none aquentaunce	48	Bowge	92
'Maystres,' quod I, 'I praye you tell me why soo,	49	Bowge	108
Goodly maystres Jane, /Sobre, demure Dyane;	102	Phy Sparrow	1223
Jane this maystres hyght,	102	Phy Sparrow	1225
Why, wyl a maystres be wonne for money and for golde?	184	Magnyfycence	1575
A maystres, I tell you, is but a small thynge.	184	Magnyfycence	1579
Lo, hither commyth a goodly maystres,	326	Garlande	521
But, goodly maystres, one thynge ye me tell.'	332	Garlande	720
'I thanke you, goodly maystres, to me most benynge,	332	Garlande	728
To maystres Jane Blenner-Haiset	339	Garlande	R
To maystres Isabell Pennell	339	Garlande	R
To maystres Margaret Hussey	340	Garlande	R
To maystres Isabell Knyght	342	Garlande	R
Of Manerly Margery Maystres Mylke and Ale; Margery Maystres] 'maistres Margery' Marshe 1568	346	Garlande	1198

MAYSTRESSE
To fasten your fansy upon a fayre maystresse	183	Magnyfycence	1550

MAYSTRYES
With my servauntys, and suche maystryes gan make,	188	Magnyfycence	1716

MAJESTE
And set in majeste /And spirytuall dygnyte,	261	Collyn Clout	587
And maketh them to bow theyr kne /Before his majeste. maketh them] 'make' Toy 1553, Kitson 1560.7, Marshe 1568	286	Why Come Ye	313
And he wyll play checke mate /With ryall majeste	293	Why Come Ye	589

MAKE
In elect uteraunce to make memoryall!	29	Dol Dethe	11
Agayne rebellyonns arme me to make debate;	33	Dol Dethe	166
Of all your feturs favorable to make tru discripcion,	42	Balettys2	8
I am insuffycyent to make such enterpryse;	42	Balettys2	9
Let not all the world make an owtcry;	43	Balettys2	40
In Bowge of Courte chevysaunce to make;	48	Bowge	100
She that styreth the shyp, make her your frende.'	49	Bowge	107
For whan she *fronneth she thynketh to make a fray, *fronneth] 'frouneth' Wynkyn de Worde 1510, Marshe 1568	49	Bowge	116
With them to make solace and pleasure;	50	Bowge	144
Beware of him, for, I make God avowe,	51	Bowge	199
My wytte wolde waste, I make God avowe.	53	Bowge	243
Tell me your mynde, me thynke ye make a verse,	53	Bowge	244
'Welcome,' quod Ryote, 'I make God avowe.'	56	Bowge	378
To make the mery, as other felowes done?	57	Bowge	380
And by my trouthe, but yf an ende they make,	59	Bowge	473
Withoute God make a good conclusyon.	59	Bowge	483
Therefore to make complaynte	62	Hauke	20
I shall you make relacyon	62	Hauke	29
Make the churche to be /In smale auctoryte;	65	Hauke	139
And make hereof a syckyll or a saw,	71	Hauke	333
Moderatly to take /This sorow that I make	74	Phy Sparrow	102
Wherewith he wolde make	76	Phy Sparrow	164
It wolde make one rew	80	Phy Sparrow	336
To make hym our belman,	84	Phy Sparrow	492
To make a fumigation a] not in Wyght 1553, Kitson 1560.6, Marshe 1568	84	Phy Sparrow	523
And moche therof dyd make;	89	Phy Sparrow	693
To Ulixes her make,	90	Phy Sparrow	732
And fewer wordes make.	92	Phy Sparrow	818
And to make an outcri an] 'a' †Kele 1545.2	94	Phy Sparrow	904
To make a relation /Of her commendation; To] 'Bo' †Kele 1545.2	95	Phy Sparrow	961
It wold make any man	98	Phy Sparrow	1080
Soft, and make no dyn,	99	Phy Sparrow	1092
She wold make to the lure	99	Phy Sparrow	1100
Ye have determyned to make a fraye,	114	Scot Kynge	44
Such boste to make, /To prate and crake,	116	Ag Scottes	31
A medley to make of myrth with sadnes,	117	Ag Scottes	87
Ye were starke mad to make a fray,	119	Ag Scottes	143
This invectyve to make /For some peoples sake	120	Ag Scottes2	3
Agennst me for to make,	126	Garnesche3	93
And make moche lyke Jake Rakar;	127	Garnesche3	109
And make youer stomake seke	128	Garnesche3	156
With skolding and sklaundering make their tungs lame.	139	Ven Tongues	62
I could make him shortly repent him for ever;	139	Ven Tongues	76
Of that I intende to make demonstracyon	141	Magnyfycence	41
Some reason we must make.	143	Magnyfycence	99
It were a shame, to God I make an othe,	144	Magnyfycence	145
And lyberte his large with measure shall make.	145	Magnyfycence	180
What, syr, wolde ye make me a poppynge fole?	146	Magnyfycence	232
A, ye make me laughe at your inconstaunce.	147	Magnyfycence	236
I hate this blunderyng that thou doste make.	151	Magnyfycence	400

MAKE —MAKE

	Page	Title	Line
Thus make I them wyth thryft to fyght.	152	Magnyfycence	421
For all these japes yet that [y]e make –	156	Magnyfycence	558
ye] 'we' †Rastell & Treveris C 1530, B			
I make them to startyll and sparkyll lyke a bronde;	161	Magnyfycence	741
I move them, I mase them, I make them so fonde,	161	Magnyfycence	742
Cockes ha[r]te! I trowe thou wylte make a fray.	163	Magnyfycence	808
harte] 'hate' †Rastell & Treveris C 1530, B			
Make a wyndmyll of a mat –	169	Magnyfycence	1028
Of a spyndell I wyll make a sparre;	169	Magnyfycence	1035
All that I make forthwith I marre;	169	Magnyfycence	1036
I make on the one day, and I marre on the other.	169	Magnyfycence	1038
Make a verse of my butterfly;	172	Magnyfycence	1149
But wylte thou make another on Gryme?	172	Magnyfycence	1151
Tell by thy trouth what sport can thou make.	172	Magnyfycence	1162
In fayth, I can make you bothe folys, and I wyll.	172	Magnyfycence	1173
Why, wenyst thou that I cannot make the play the fon?	173	Magnyfycence	1185
Yes, yet he wyll make the ete a gnat.	173	Magnyfycence	1192
Yes, yet] 'Yet yes' †Rastell & Treveris C 1530, B			
Nay, it is I that foles can make;	174	Magnyfycence	1213
And make them so longe to muse	174	Magnyfycence	1224
To thefte and bryboury I make some fall,	174	Magnyfycence	1226
The knave wolde make it koy, and he cowde;	175	Magnyfycence	1246
I make them lese moche of theyr strength;	175	Magnyfycence	1259
He wyll make it mykyll worse than it is;	175	Magnyfycence	1273
So is all the remenaunt, I make God avowe;	175	Magnyfycence	1283
I have an hoby can make larkys to dare;	177	Magnyfycence	1342
Ye, of Jacke a Thrommys bybyll can ye make a glose.	180	Magnyfycence	1427
Make indentures how ye and I shal gyde.	180	Magnyfycence	1448
Nor no man on molde can make me aferd.	182	Magnyfycence	1505
Wolde money, trowest thou, make suche one to the call?	184	Magnyfycence	1573
Then feyne yourselfe dyseased, and make yourselfe seke.	185	Magnyfycence	1612
With my servauntys, and suche maystryes gan make,	188	Magnyfycence	1716
To make fayre promyse, what are ye the worse?	189	Magnyfycence	1761
Better to make iii. ryche than for to make many.	190	Magnyfycence	1772
Better to make iii. ryche than for to make many.	190	Magnyfycence	1772
And here I make the upon Lyberte	190	Magnyfycence	1784
I make God avowe ye wyll none other men have.	191	Magnyfycence	1827
I rushe at them rughly and make them ly full lowe;	193	Magnyfycence	1884
And in theyr moste truste I make them overthrowe.	193	Magnyfycence	1885
With the gowte I make them to grone where they syt;	194	Magnyfycence	1903
Some I make lyppers and lazars full horse;	194	Magnyfycence	1904
Some with the marmoll to halte I them make;	194	Magnyfycence	1906
And some I make in a rope to totter and walter;	194	Magnyfycence	1910
And make eche man to sle other;	194	Magnyfycence	1913
Some I make lame, and some I do kyll,	194	Magnyfycence	1931
With harte contryte make your supplycacyon	196	Magnyfycence	1991
Freers, with foly I make them so fayne	201	Magnyfycence	2147
The locke of a casket to make to starte.	203	Magnyfycence	2229
Abyde, syr, abyde; I shall make hym to pysse.	204	Magnyfycence	2250
But nowe let us make mery and good chere.	204	Magnyfycence	2261
That wyll make you to halt and to hoppe.	204	Magnyfycence	2273
I make hevy hertys, with eyen full holowe.	205	Magnyfycence	2286
Faythe and good hope I make asyde to stonde.	205	Magnyfycence	2288
Nowe must I make you a lectuary softe –	207	Magnyfycence	2355
Of that I have mysdone to make a redresse,	212	Magnyfycence	2508
This treatyse, devysyd to make you dysporte,	213	Magnyfycence	2538
This mater we have movyd, you myrthys to make,	213	Magnyfycence	2552
But to make up my tale,	217	El Rummynge	101
It shall make you loke /Yonger than ye be	219	El Rummynge	213
This make I my falyre fonny,	220	El Rummynge	229
And with good ale barme /She could make a charme	226	El Rummynge	456
Such a bedfellaw /Wold make one cast his craw.	226	El Rummynge	489
And all this shyfte they make	228	El Rummynge	533
To make all thynge cleane;	229	El Rummynge	578
Fresshely they dresse and make swete my bowur,	231	Speke Parott	12
And some make distinctions multipliciter,	235	Speke Parott	157
Make moche of Parrot, the popegay ryall.	236	Speke Parott	217
the] 'that' Kynge & Marche 1554, Day 1560, Marshe 1568			
Whate mone he made when Pamphylus loste hys make.	237	Speke Parott	234
To make reconyng in the resseyte how Robyn loste hys bowe,	240	Speke Parott	341
Let se who dare make up the reste.	242	Speke Parott	382
Jupyter for Saturne darre make no royall chere;	242	Speke Parott	399
The reste of suche reconyng may make a fowle fraye.	243	Speke Parott	403
The nebbis of a lyon they make to trete and trembyll,	243	Speke Parott	424
Syn Dewcalyons flodde, I make the faste and sure.	246	Speke Parott	511
Or to make a sayle /Of a herynges tayle?	246	Collyn Clout	3
Alas, they make me shoder,	248	Collyn Clout	68
And make therof a jape!	248	Collyn Clout	84
In theyr pryncypall cure /They make but lytell sure,	249	Collyn Clout	103
Howe bysshoppes dysdayne /Sermons for to make,	250	Collyn Clout	134
Howe they are able to make /With theyr golde and treasure	250	Collyn Clout	143
They make her wynche and kycke,	251	Collyn Clout	181
Thus they make theyr boost /Through every coost,	251	Collyn Clout	202
With, 'Welcome, hake and make!'	253	Collyn Clout	250
To make a trewe constructyon.	253	Collyn Clout	269
And no more ye make	254	Collyn Clout	298
And hym a bysshop make,	254	Collyn Clout	305

MAKER —MAKER | Page | Title | Line

	Page	Title	Line
Ye make monkes to have the colerage	255	Collyn Clout	363
make] 'haue' Kele 1545.1, Marshe 1568, 'make' MS Harley 2252; colerage] 'culerage' Kele 1545.1, 'colerage' Harley 2252			
Of an abbey ye make a graunge -	257	Collyn Clout	419
ye] 'they' Kele 1545.1, 'to' MS Harley 2252			
Some make epylogacyon /Of hygh predestynacyon;	259	Collyn Clout	519
And of resyde[v]acyon /They make enterpretacyon	259	Collyn Clout	522
resydevacyon] 'resdenacyon' †Godfray 1531, Kele 1545.1, Marshe 1568			
And make moche varyans	260	Collyn Clout	554
Of parsons and vycaryes /They make many outcryes:	261	Collyn Clout	571
A knyght a knave ye make.	261	Collyn Clout	601
ye] 'to' Kele 1545.1, Marshe 1568, 'ye' MS Harley 2252			
And make the commons blynde.	263	Collyn Clout	663
And make a Welchmans hose	266	Collyn Clout	778
And make a pleasaunt style	267	Collyn Clout	851
Alone, and make rekenynge	271	Collyn Clout	990
That they shall mell nor make,	271	Collyn Clout	1015
So hardy to make suete,	272	Collyn Clout	1031
Make ye no murmuracyon	273	Collyn Clout	1079
Make this lurdeyne for to loure;	275	Collyn Clout	1168
Wherfore we make you sure,	276	Collyn Clout	1203
So /That rage must make pyllage	280	Why Come Ye	50
They make him so amased,	283	Why Come Ye	180
They make us all sottes,	285	Why Come Ye	263
They make us to pyll strawes;	285	Why Come Ye	265
To make his cofers ryche;	290	Why Come Ye	454
To make up one of nought,	293	Why Come Ye	551
To make within an hower,	293	Why Come Ye	566
Make him a great astate,	293	Why Come Ye	587
But I wyll make further relacion	297	Why Come Ye	716
To make all or to mar,	297	Why Come Ye	733
To make sommons peremtory	299	Why Come Ye	818
Make a larger memoryall	299	Why Come Ye	824
larger] 'large' Marshe 1568			
For I make you sure,	300	Why Come Ye	846
That he wolde than make /The devyls to quake,	303	Why Come Ye	978
It wolde make the devyll to swete!	306	Why Come Ye	1088
'The devyll wold swete' MS Rawlinson C. 813			
And make him lame of his neder limmes.	309	Why Come Ye	1200
Put up his sworde, for he cowde make no warre,	312	Garlande	5
Yet harde is to make but sum fawt be founde.'	315	Garlande	112
Unto your grace then make I this motyve:	315	Garlande	114
Ageyne whom he cowde make no contradiccyoun?	316	Garlande	133
'Soft, my good syster, and make there a pawse.	316	Garlande	134
my good syster] 'goode my sister' MS Cotton Vitellius E.x			
Some facers, some bracers, some make great crackis;	317	Garlande	189
some] 'and sum' MS Cotton Vitellius E.x			
Men of suche maters make but mummynge,	318	Garlande	200
but] 'but a' MS Cotton Vitellius E.x			
'To make repugnaunce agayne that ye have sayde,	318	Garlande	211
But if that he purpose to make a redresse,	318	Garlande	229
Make noyse enoughe; for claterars love no peas.	319	Garlande	241
'Make rowme,' sayd another, 'ye prese all to sore,'	319	Garlande	256
For her pleasure to make a large profer,	327	Garlande	556
Gog gyve you good yere, ye make me to smyle.	332	Garlande	736
Of your questyon ye make all this whyle	333	Garlande	738
Unto you, madame, I make reconusaunce,	335	Garlande	838
Whos lusty lokis make hevy hartis glad;	337	Garlande	903
Wherfore, I make you sure,	340	Garlande	993
I make you sure] 'I yow assure' MS Cotton Vitellius E.x			
Make no delay, for now ye must be brought	343	Garlande	1090
That I trust to make myne excuse	344	Garlande	1137
Harde to make ought of that is nakid nought;	346	Garlande	1205
To make suche trifels it asketh sum konnyng,	347	Garlande	1235
His Epitomis of the Myller and his joly Make;	351	Garlande	1411
I wypid myne eyne for to make them clere.	354	Garlande	1513
Was comyng downe /To make hym frowne	360	Albany	57
And to make hym lowre,	360	Albany	58
Ye make nought but ye marre.	364	Albany	226
With a gon stone, /To make you to grone.	366	Albany	286
As though ye wolde parbrake /Your avauns to make,	367	Albany	323
Our royall kyng to make	367	Albany	327
or to make oblacions to any ymages of sayntes,	375	Replycacion	1
Ye may soone make construction	378	Replycacion	154
And there to make relacion /In open predycacion,	379	Replycacion	205
I make you fast and sure,	380	Replycacion	232
Wherfore make ye no mo restrayntes,	382	Replycacion	292
If further busynesse that ye make.	382	Replycacion	296
In this that I do make	385	Replycacion	399

MAKER

	Page	Title	Line
Ye wolde be callyd a maker,	127	Garnesche3	108
Unto your maker that made bothe you and me;	196	Magnyfycence	1992
And agayne thy maker thou hast made suche warre,	205	Magnyfycence	2302
A grete mysadventure, thy maker to dysplease,	206	Magnyfycence	2341
A wrechyd man, syr, to my maker unkynde,	208	Magnyfycence	2390
And every mad medler must now be a maker.	235	Speke Parott	161

	Page	Title	Line
MAKERELL			
A makerell nor a wyteyng:	127	Garnesche3	116
MAKETH			
That maketh his nest /In chymneyes to rest;	83	Phy Sparrow	470
*Or els phylosophy /Maketh a great lye.	83	Phy Sparrow	477
*Or] 'Of' Scattergood			
That maketh England faine.	111	Lawde	42
Skelton Laureate, Orator Regius, maketh this aunswere &c.	112	Calliope	1
Your fansy maketh myne elbowe to ake.	156	Magnyfycence	559
Here FOLY maketh semblaunt to take a lowse	173	Magnyfycence	SD
Here FOLY maketh semblaunt	173	Magnyfycence	SD
Nay, I tell the, he maketh no dowtes	174	Magnyfycence	1210
And what maner of people he maketh foles?	174	Magnyfycence	1217
And maketh hym besy where is no nede.	175	Magnyfycence	1249
But nowe, forsothe, man, it maketh no mater;	175	Magnyfycence	1256
Maketh man and woman in foly to fall.	176	Magnyfycence	1295
Money maketh marchauntes, I tell you, over all.	184	Magnyfycence	1574
Here MAGNYFYCENCE dolorously maketh his mone.	198	Magnyfycence	SD
And maketh thereof port-sale	217	El Rummynge	103
port-sale] 'pore sale' Kynge & Marche 1554, Day 1560			
He maketh them to bere babylles, and to bere a lowe sayle;	243	Speke Parott	428
For it maketh me sad	259	Collyn Clout	511
Maketh his membres swell	284	Why Come Ye	210
He maketh us Jack Rakers;	285	Why Come Ye	273
He maketh himselfe cock sure.	286	Why Come Ye	282
And maketh them to bow theyr kne /Before his majeste.	286	Why Come Ye	312
maketh them] 'make' Toy 1553, Kitson 1560.7, Marshe 1568			
Maketh remembraunce /How Kynge Lewes of late	297	Why Come Ye	721
But now he maketh objectyon,	307	Why Come Ye	1127
But] 'And', objectyon] 'dyrectyon' MS Rawlinson C. 813			
God maketh his habytacion	384	Replycacion	376
And maketh in us suche spede	385	Replycacion	386
MAKETHE			
It makethe lovers bolde	98	Phy Sparrow	1074
MAKITH			
That makith our hartis glad,	111	Lawde	51
And makith suche provisyon	306	Why Come Ye	1093
He makith so proude pretens,	307	Why Come Ye	1133
The Byble makith; with whos chast lyvynge	336	Garlande	846
MAKYNG			
Agaynst this my makyng, /Their males therat shakyng,	120	Ag Scottes2	7
Makyng hys pylgrimage by Nostre Dame de Crome:	239	Speke Parott	305
So myche newe makyng, and so madd tyme spente;	244	Speke Parott	450
So myche mokkyshe makyng of statutes of array -	245	Speke Parott	482
Of his makyng devoute medytacyons;	352	Garlande	1419
MAKYNGE			
Chefe rote of his makynge.	298	Why Come Ye	755
Sume be moche spokyn of for makynge of frays;	317	Garlande	182
Makynge his almanak for the new yere;	354	Garlande	1516
MAKYS			
That makys our syre to glum.	288	Why Come Ye	389
MAKYST			
For, frantyke Fansy, thou makyst men madde;	176	Magnyfycence	1300
MAKYTH			
He whystelyth so swetely he makyth me to swete;	37	Coystrowne1	37
He bresyth theyr braynpannys and makyth them to swell,	43	Balettys2	31
Whose jalawsy malycyous makyth them to lepe the hach!	43	Balettys2	33
Whych to behold makyth hevy hartys glad;	44	Balettys3	28
Which makyth my hart oft to lepe and sprynge	44	Balettys3	32
Me for to chalenge that of your chalennge makyth so lytyll fors.	123	Garnesche2	19
Howe be it, lyberte makyth many a man blynde;	142	Magnyfycence	52
MAKYTHE			
Juvenall satirray, that men makythe to muse;	321	Garlande	340
MALAPERT			
Your sumner to saucy, to malapert;	118	Ag Scottes	97
Malapert, medyllar, nothyng well thewde,	133	Garnesche5	147
MALAPERTE			
A malaperte medler that pryeth for his pray,	37	Coystrowne1	45
In your somnynge ye were to malaperte,	113	Scot Kynge	7
MALAPERTLY			
And so malapertly withstande	296	Why Come Ye	675
MALARDE			
She is made for the malarde fat.	166	Magnyfycence	926
MALCHUS			
Of Mantryble the Bryge, Malchus the Murryon,	122	Garnesche1	22
MALE			
And Harvy Ha[f]ter that well coude picke a male;	50	Bowge	138
Hafter] 'Haster' †Wynkyn de Worde 1499, 1510, Marshe 1568			
A brydelynge caste for that is in thy male!	57	Bowge	390
That made the male to wryng;	89	Phy Sparrow	700
the] 'tha' †Kele 1545.2			
I am the better yet in a bowget. And I the better in a male.	203	Magnyfycence	2232
Howe the male dothe wrye.	263	Collyn Clout	686
wrye] 'wryte' Kele 1545.1, Marshe 1568, 'wrye' MS Harley 2252			
MALENCOLY			
So full of malencoly,	308	Why Come Ye	1168
MALES			
To fyll bougets and males	90	Phy Sparrow	752

MALE URYD —MAN   Page   Title   Line

Agaynst this my makyng, /Their males therat shakyng, ...   120   Ag Scottes2   8
Wrang us on the [m]ales!   280   Why Come Ye   78
   males] 'wales' †Kele 1545.3, Toy 1553, Kitson 1560.7,
   Marshe 1568
MALE URYD
Male uryd was your fals entent   118   Ag Scottes   111
MALICE
Fulfyld with malice of froward entente, ...   30   Dol Dethe   25
MALICIOUS
Malicious tunges, though they have no bones, ...   138   Ven Tongues   49
MALIS
What shippis are sailing to Scalis Malis, ...   139   Ven Tongues   65
MALYCE
He is so bete /With malyce, and frete   95   Phy Sparrow   931
That agaynst preesthode /Theyr malyce sprede abrode, ...   260   Collyn Clout 535
   agaynst] 'agayn' Marshe 1568
MALYCYOUS
Whose jalawsy malycyous makyth them to lepe the hach!   43   Balettys2   33
MALYGNED
Ye be malygned sore, I you ensure, ...   59   Bowge   451
MALYGNYTES
Of preestly dygnytes /By theyr malygnytes.   260   Collyn Clout 539
   By] 'But' Kele 1545.1, Marshe 1568
MALYNCOLY
Suche malyncoly mastyvys and mangye curre dogges   240   Speke Parott 320
MALYPERT
As malypert tavernars that checke with theyr betters, ...   178   Magnyfycence 1362
MALKYN
To wete yf Malkyn, my lemman, have gete oughte.   57   Bowge   401
MALLARDE
With the wylde mallarde;   83   Phy Sparrow   451
   wylde] 'wynde' †Kele 1545.2
MALLE
. . . . .malle of lede, ...   125   Garnesche3   59
MALTAPERTE
You mantyca[re], ye maltaperte, ye can bothe wins and whyne; .   123   Garnesche2   4
   mantycare] 'mantyca' †MS Harley 367
MALTE
Brynge wyth them malte or whete, ...   221   El Rummynge   267
Eyther corne or malte, ...   267   Collyn Clout 842
MAMELEK
Lyke to a Mamelek, ...   291   Why Come Ye   479
   a Mamelek] 'Amamelek' †Kele 1545.3, Toy 1553, Kitson 1560.7,
   Marshe 1568
MAMMY
Your mammy and your dady   339   Garlande   974
MAMMOCKES
Whan mammockes was your meate, ...   263   Collyn Clout 652
MAMOCKES
Nowe must you monche mamockes and lumpes of brede;   197   Magnyfycence 2009
MAN
So noble a man, so valiaunt lorde and knyght   30   Dol Dethe   29
This noble man doutles had not be slayne.   31   Dol Dethe   74
   be] 'bene' Marshe 1568
As man that was innocent of trechery or trayne, ...   31   Dol Dethe   86
What man, remembring how shamfully he was slayn, ...   32   Dol Dethe   111
When thou shoke thi sword so noble a man to mar!   32   Dol Dethe   115
Goddes mooste cruell unto the lyfe of man, ...   32   Dol Dethe   121
Eche man may sorow in his inward thought   34   Dol Dethe   177
This noble man that cruelly was slayne.   34   Dol Dethe   182
A red angry man, but easy to intrete.   37   Coystrowne1   39
No man may hym hyde /From deth holow-eyed, ...   39   Coystrowne3   10
She wadyd over, she found a man   42   Balettys1   17
Sharpely commaundynge eche man holde hys pece.   47   Bowge   47
Levynge me stondynge as a mased man;   48   Bowge   83
For I dare saye that there nys erthly man   48   Bowge   101
Mysdempte eche man, with face deedly and pale;   50   Bowge   137
Loo, what it is a man to have connynge!   50   Bowge   153
Ye be an apte man, as ony can be founde   50   Bowge   155
And ye nede ought, man, shewe to me your mynde, ...   50   Bowge   165
What, lete us holde him up, man, for a whyle.'   51   Bowge   188
The soveraynst thynge that ony man maye have   52   Bowge   211
That noo man erthly coude hym bewreye, ...   52   Bowge   223
   man] 'wan' †Wynkyn de Worde 1499
And I dare saye there is no man hereinne   53   Bowge   267
I wyste never man that so soone coude wynne   53   Bowge   269
A man, but wonderly besene was he.   54   Bowge   283
He loked hawte; he sette eche man at noughte;   54   Bowge   284
   hawte] 'hawtie' Marshe 1568
Thou muste swere and stare, man, aldaye longe, ...   57   Bowge   381
What the devyll, man, myrthe was never one!   57   Bowge   388
   was never one] 'is here within' Marshe 1568
What, loo, man, see here of dyce a bale;   57   Bowge   389
Alas, a connynge man ne dwelle maye   58   Bowge   445
I wolde eche man were as playne as I.   59   Bowge   463
A man can not wote where to become.   59   Bowge   466
Now, by Saynte Frauncys, that holy man and frere, ...   59   Bowge   470
Naye, see where yonder stondeth the teder man!   59   Bowge   484

MAN — MAN

	Page	Title	Line
I wolde therwith no man were myscontente;	61	Bowge	533
In hope that no man shall /Be myscontent withall.	62	Hauke	27
Be] 'By' Kynge & Marche 1554			
And slew many a Chrysten man;	67	Hauke	215
No man can be sure	81	Phy Sparrow	370
That no man abydes,	84	Phy Sparrow	508
Lyke a valyaunt man;	87	Phy Sparrow	633
No man that can amend	91	Phy Sparrow	809
And no man wyll me blame,	94	Phy Sparrow	890
It wold make any man	98	Phy Sparrow	1080
And any man convert	99	Phy Sparrow	1101
No man can let me thynke,	101	Phy Sparrow	1199
No man to myscontent	103	Phy Sparrow	1280
Dyd never man good.	108	Epitaphe1	67
A man kowd not aspy	111	Lawde	19
No man for them wil speke.	111	Lawde	32
Soche an odyr chalyngyr cowde me no man wysch,	121	Garnesche1	3
As hevery man wele seethe,	127	Garnesche3	125
Thou art callyd of every man.	130	Garnesche5	24
Thow thou be a jantyll man borne,	131	Garnesche5	69
There is no noble man wil judge in me	138	Ven Tongues	34
With, 'I can tel you what such a man said,	139	Ven Tongues	71
A man may have welth, but not as he wolde,	141	Magnyfycence	14
But where wonnys welthe, and a man wolde wyt?	141	Magnyfycence	22
Lyberte, I wote well, forbere no man there may;	142	Magnyfycence	50
Howe be it, lyberte makyth many a man blynde;	142	Magnyfycence	52
Yet in this man you must set your delyght.	145	Magnyfycence	167
For no dyscorde that any man can sawe;	145	Magnyfycence	187
From whens come you, syr, that no man lokyd after?	147	Magnyfycence	255
That no man can scape but they hym cache.	150	Magnyfycence	351
But largesse is not mete for every man.	150	Magnyfycence	369
This noble man Magnyfycence,	151	Magnyfycence	404
A mynstrell lyke a man of myght,	152	Magnyfycence	419
Counterfet Countenaunce every man dothe occupy.	153	Magnyfycence	472
By God, man, bothe his pagent and thyne he can play.	154	Magnyfycence	505
Why, man, it were to great a wonder	154	Magnyfycence	510
So large a man, and so lytell of stature!	155	Magnyfycence	523
And yet, in fayth, man, we lacked the	155	Magnyfycence	538
We wyll remedy it, man, or we go;	155	Magnyfycence	551
A man may beshrowe your angry harte.	156	Magnyfycence	563
Nor no man in courte, but he,	158	Magnyfycence	660
To passe the tyme and order whyle a man may talke	159	Magnyfycence	689
And every man gladly my company wolde refuse,	160	Magnyfycence	704
Howe I may hurte and hynder every man.	160	Magnyfycence	709
And craftely can I grope howe every man is mynded.	160	Magnyfycence	725
My purpose is to spy and to poynte every man;	160	Magnyfycence	726
Eche man to hynder I gape and I gaspe,	160	Magnyfycence	729
That they wyll here no man but the fyrst tale.	161	Magnyfycence	743
Howe sayst thou, man? Am not I a joly rutter?	161	Magnyfycence	752
By the masse, for the cowrte thou art a mete man;	161	Magnyfycence	764
Nay. Thou art a man good inough but for thy false hart.	162	Magnyfycence	769
Ye, in faythe, a bolde man and a hardy.	162	Magnyfycence	771
A bolde man in a bole of newe ale in cornys.	162	Magnyfycence	772
Tushe! He that hathe nede, man, let hym rynne.	162	Magnyfycence	786
Nay, come away, man! Thou playst the cayser.	162	Magnyfycence	787
He wyll come, man, when he may tende to.	162	Magnyfycence	790
Here he is nowe, man. Mayst thou not se?	162	Magnyfycence	792
What the devyll, man, what thou menyst?	162	Magnyfycence	793
What sayst thou, man? Why dost thou not supplye,	162	Magnyfycence	797
Whiche of you is the better man,	162	Magnyfycence	802
But, syr, I wyll have this man with me.	163	Magnyfycence	815
By Saynt Mary, he is a tawle man.	163	Magnyfycence	821
He dothe mysse use /Eche man to [akuse],	164	Magnyfycence	874
akuse] 'take a fe' †Rastell & Treveris C 1530, B			
Torde! Man, it is an hawke of the towre.	166	Magnyfycence	925
A man shall fynde /Many of her kynde,	167	Magnyfycence	983
Pease, man, pease! /I rede we sease.	168	Magnyfycence	997
Here is no man that callyd the hogge nor swyne.	170	Magnyfycence	1084
In faythe, man, my brayne is as good as thyne.	170	Magnyfycence	1085
Nowe, by my trouth, man, take, there is my purse;	171	Magnyfycence	1104
my] 'myne' †Rastell & Treveris C 1530, B			
Tushe, man! I kepe some Latyn in store.	172	Magnyfycence	1145
Cockys armys, a mete man for us!	172	Magnyfycence	1169
Nay, nay. Thou shalt fynde hym another maner of man.	173	Magnyfycence	1189
And for a fole a man wolde hym take.	174	Magnyfycence	1212
That every man lawghyth at his foly.	175	Magnyfycence	1251
But nowe, forsothe, man, it maketh no mater;	175	Magnyfycence	1256
So helpe me God, man, ever at the length	175	Magnyfycence	1258
That every man almost groweth out of kynde.	175	Magnyfycence	1285
Maketh man and woman in foly to fall.	176	Magnyfycence	1295
Upon a naked man and yf she scrat.	176	Magnyfycence	1298
Yes, perde, man, whether that ye ryde or go.	176	Magnyfycence	1307
Foly and fansy all where every man dothe face and brace.	177	Magnyfycence	1330
Trymme at her tayle or a man can turne a socke.	177	Magnyfycence	1346
So that there knowe no man but I and she.	177	Magnyfycence	1353
My inwyt delynge there can no man dyscry.	177	Magnyfycence	1356
Save a stronge thefe and hange a trew man.	178	Magnyfycence	1360
But some man wolde convey, and can not skyll,	178	Magnyfycence	1361

MAN —MAN   Page   Title   Line

Why, welth hath made many a man braynlesse.	180	Magnyfycence	1423
What sholde a man do with you? Loke you under [k]ay?	180	Magnyfycence	1429
kay] 'bay' †Rastell & Treveris C 1530, B			
What the devyll, man, your name shalbe the greter;	180	Magnyfycence	1440
No man so hardy to worke agaynst my wyll.	181	Magnyfycence	1479
Nor Cesar July, that no man myght withstande,	181	Magnyfycence	1482
Ne by non other that any man can rehersse.	181	Magnyfycence	1490
My name is Magnyfycence, man most of myght.	182	Magnyfycence	1493
To me all prynces to lowte man bese[m]e.	182	Magnyfycence	1500
beseme] 'be sene' †Rastell & Treveris C 1530, B			
Nor no man on molde can make me aferd.	182	Magnyfycence	1505
What man is so maysyd with me that dare mete,	182	Magnyfycence	1506
Nor Nero, that nother set by God nor man,	182	Magnyfycence	1509
Yes, syr, so good man in you I se,	182	Magnyfycence	1522
Here no man what so ever they say	185	Magnyfycence	1603
And ye se a man that with hym ye be not pleased,	185	Magnyfycence	1609
As yf a man fortune to touche you on the quyke -	185	Magnyfycence	1611
It is none abusyon, syr, in a noble man.	185	Magnyfycence	1626
Syr, so it is: this man is here by,	186	Magnyfycence	1649
This is a wyse man, syr, where so ever ye hym had.	187	Magnyfycence	1689
And more than ever I dyd for ony man.	187	Magnyfycence	1694
Who is this? Consayte, syr, your owne man.	191	Magnyfycence	1804
Nowe is there no man that wyll set by hym a flye.	193	Magnyfycence	1889
Man or woman, of what estate they be,	194	Magnyfycence	1898
And make eche man to sle other;	194	Magnyfycence	1913
At lyberte a man may be bolde for to brake;	199	Magnyfycence	2085
This lurden that here lyeth had ben a noble man.	200	Magnyfycence	2112
And so shall a noble man nobly be servyd.	200	Magnyfycence	2120
Torde! Thou arte good to be a man of warre.	202	Magnyfycence	2179
By the masse, man, thou shall fynde me resonable.	202	Magnyfycence	2204
Mary, syr, he sayd that he was the pratyer man	203	Magnyfycence	2225
It wyll stryke a man myschevously in a hete.	204	Magnyfycence	2268
In fay, man, some rybbys of the motton be so ranke	204	Magnyfycence	2269
Nay, nay, man. I loke never to have parte of his grace;	205	Magnyfycence	2297
There is no man may synne more mortally	206	Magnyfycence	2336
Prosperyte [by] hym is gyven solacyusly to man;	207	Magnyfycence	2367
by] 'to' †Rastell & Treveris C 1530, B			
A wrechyd man, syr, to my maker unkynde.	208	Magnyfycence	2390
Syr, the repentaunce I have no man can wryte.	208	Magnyfycence	2392
What this man hath sayd, perceyve ye his sentence?	210	Magnyfycence	2465
Today a man, tomorowe he lyeth in the duste:	213	Magnyfycence	2550
A man wolde have pytty	215	El Rummynge	39
Every man after his maner of wayes,	233	Speke Parott	90
Let every man after his merit take his parte;	236	Speke Parott	199
Alas, I am dysdayned, /And as a man halfe-maymed,	237	Speke Parott	253
As he to exployte the man owte of the mone.	239	Speke Parott	307
Moloc, that mawmett, there darre no man withsay;	243	Speke Parott	402
Agayne Frentike Frenesy there dar no man sey nay,	243	Speke Parott	422
Syns Dewcalyons flodde, I trow, no man can tell.	245	Speke Parott	490
A man myght say in mocke,	255	Collyn Clout	338
That no man may abyde	261	Collyn Clout	594
But mayster Damyan, /Or some other man	264	Collyn Clout	721
For one man to rule a kynge	271	Collyn Clout	989
kynge] 'gyng' Kele 1545.1, 'kyng' MS Harley 2252			
That a man shall here a masse,	272	Collyn Clout	1022
No man to our sovereygne lorde	272	Collyn Clout	1030
For I rebuke no man /That vertuous is.	273	Collyn Clout	1089
To hynder no man /As nere as I can,	274	Collyn Clout	1109
For no man have I named.	274	Collyn Clout	1111
Any man to offende.	274	Collyn Clout	1128
But they wolde no man shuld them blame.	275	Collyn Clout	1142
That ryght no man can fonge.	276	Collyn Clout	1197
For that no man shulde se	277	Collyn Clout	1240
A noble man may fall,	279	Why Come Ye	22
There is no man but one	281	Why Come Ye	113
To know God nor man.	283	Why Come Ye	183
No man dare speke a worde,	283	Why Come Ye	191
That no man dare rowte;	287	Why Come Ye	341
How no man can him amende!	292	Why Come Ye	531
How an one-eyed man is	292	Why Come Ye	533
This man was full unable	292	Why Come Ye	537
A wretched poore man	293	Why Come Ye	553
Shulde this man of suche mode	293	Why Come Ye	579
No man dare him withsay.	294	Why Come Ye	598
No man dare come to the speche	294	Why Come Ye	615
For what is a man the better	295	Why Come Ye	669
Of a poore wretchid man,	297	Why Come Ye	724
Any man shulde be /In perplexyte /Of dyspleasure;	300	Why Come Ye	843
For, 'Synke quater trey' /Is a tall man.	301	Why Come Ye	886
tall] 'toll' MS Rawlinson C. 813			
To put any man in lack	310	Why Come Ye2	25
But to do sumwhat iche man doth hym dres	315	Garlande	122
That any man under supportacyon	318	Garlande	220
And for no man hardely let hym spare	319	Garlande	244
Sume moche to hasty and wold no man byde;	319	Garlande	249
And iche man stode gasyng and staryng upon other.	319	Garlande	268
But blessyd Bachus that never man forgate,	322	Garlande	369
Suche an other there coude no man fynde;	325	Garlande	463

MANACE —MANY   Page   Title   Line

	Page	Title	Line
And where the two Trions a man shold aspy,	331	Garlande	699
Trions] 'Troons' †Fakes 1523			
For eche man herkynde what she wolde to me say;	344	Garlande	1119
wolde to me] 'to me wold' MS Cotton Vitellius E.x			
It wolde have made a man hole that had be ryght sekely,	345	Garlande	1162
No man to myscontent /With Phillippis enterement.	348	Garlande	1273
How than lyke a man he wan the barbican	351	Garlande	1397
No man lyvyng, he sayth, can be sure;	351	Garlande	1403
By there phesik doth many a man ease,	352	Garlande	1427
No man can tell whether.	358	Garlande2	9
No man wyll undertake	358	Garlande2	10
No man hath harde /Of suche a cowarde,	365	Albany	252
That no man hym kyll;	365	Albany	264
and of every true Christen man laudably to be enployed,	374	Replycacion	1
Many a good man /And many a good woman,	378	Replycacion	134
But, as the man sayes,	378	Replycacion	151

MANACE

	Page	Title	Line
Whan there were dyverse that sore dyde you manace.	50	Bowge	159

MANASE

	Page	Title	Line
Dyd Moyses sore manase	305	Why Come Ye	1067
sore] not in MS Rawlinson C. 813			

MANCYONS

	Page	Title	Line
Buyldynge royally /Theyr mancyons curyously,	269	Collyn Clout	935

MANDE

	Page	Title	Line
Counterfet capytaynes by me are mande;	152	Magnyfycence	436

MANER

	Page	Title	Line
In lyke maner also	74	Phy Sparrow	112
All maner of byrdes in your kynd;	81	Phy Sparrow	388
In maner half with shame;	89	Phy Sparrow	713
For no maner consyderacyon	117	Ag Scottes	73
Lyberte to let from all maner offence;	141	Magnyfycence	45
It is so swete in all maner of kynde.	142	Magnyfycence	51
For largesse stynteth all maner of stryfe.	150	Magnyfycence	367
Ye, so I can devyse my gere after the cowrtly maner.	161	Magnyfycence	766
Nay, nay. Thou shalt fynde hym another maner of man.	173	Magnyfycence	1189
And what maner of people he maketh foles?	174	Magnyfycence	1217
Syr, of my maner I shall tell you the playne:	174	Magnyfycence	1219
I have another maner of sorte	174	Magnyfycence	1238
So it is all the maner nowe a dayes	187	Magnyfycence	1677
Every man after his maner of wayes,	233	Speke Parott	90
Or bokes to compyle /Of dyvers maner style,	247	Collyn Clout	10
Maner of cause to mone.	258	Collyn Clout	479
Suche maner of sysmatykes /And halfe heretykes,	264	Collyn Clout	700
After this maner rates;	264	Collyn Clout	709
All maner of abjections;	268	Collyn Clout	890
In suche maner of cases,	269	Collyn Clout	895
All maner of flesshe mete	306	Why Come Ye	1084
In maner and forme as ye shall after here.	323	Garlande	399
There were, I say, of all maner of sortis,	326	Garlande	512
Be issuis and portis from all maner of nacyons';	328	Garlande	580
In lyke maner of wyse a myst did us shrowde;	330	Garlande	647
Whiche maner of abasshement became her not yll;	337	Garlande	889
And in abhominacion /Of all maner of nacion,	362	Albany	142
And of all maner vyce?	364	Albany	221
and have waded but weakly in his thre maner of clerkly workes,	374	Replycacion	1
And in maner as abjecte, /For evermore suspecte,	380	Replycacion	240

MANERES

	Page	Title	Line
Yor moth etyn mokkysh maneres, they be all to-myryd.	123	Garnesche2	12
Moche of thy maneres I ca[n] blasy.	130	Garnesche5	32
can] 'cam' †MS Harley 367			

MANERLES

	Page	Title	Line
Youre medelyng, mastres, is manerles;	40	Coystrowne4	2

MANERLY

	Page	Title	Line
With manerly Margery Mylk and Ale.	35	Man Margery	7
With manerly Margery Mylk and Ale.	36	Man Margery	14
With manerly Margery Mylk and Ale.	36	Man Margery	21
With manerly Margery Milk and Ale.	36	Man Margery	28
With manerly Margery Mylk and Ale.	36	Man Margery	30
And defende it manerly.	152	Magnyfycence	416
Of Manerly Margery Maystres Mylke and Ale;	346	Garlande	1198
Margery Maystres] 'maistres Margery' Marshe 1568			

MANERS

	Page	Title	Line
He is not lyvynge your maners can amend;	183	Magnyfycence	1537

MANES

	Page	Title	Line
Another manes mynde diffuse is to expounde;	315	Garlande	111

MANGEY

	Page	Title	Line
But where gatte thou that mangey curre?	173	Magnyfycence	1180

MANGYE

	Page	Title	Line
Suche malyncoly mastyvys and mangye curre dogges	240	Speke Parott	320
So mangye a mastyfe curre, the grete greyhoundes pere;	245	Speke Parott	487

MANHOD

	Page	Title	Line
O manles manhod, enfayntyd all with fere,	242	Speke Parott	391

MANHODE

	Page	Title	Line
And what ipostacis /Of Chrystes manhode is.	259	Collyn Clout	527

MANY

	Page	Title	Line
And to remember many a praty thynge;	44	Balettys3	33
For, as for me, I served here many a daye,	53	Bowge	274
And many wordes sayde in secrete wyse;	58	Bowge	422

Text	Page	Title	Line
And slew many a Chrysten man;	67	Hauke	215
And many tymes and ofte	74	Phy Sparrow	124
Many tymes and ofte,	80	Phy Sparrow	355
Many a prety kusse	80	Phy Sparrow	361
Many a spere brake /For his ladyes sake;	87	Phy Sparrow	639
His serpentes tonge /That many one hath stonge;	94	Phy Sparrow	921
Cum Garnyche, cum Godfrey, with as many as ye may!	123	Garnesche2	32
But yet I may say safely, so many wel lettred,	138	Ven Tongues	38
Howe be it, lyberte makyth many a man blynde;	142	Magnyfycence	52
By lyberte is done many a great excesse;	142	Magnyfycence	53
And grotes many one or I came to your presence.	150	Magnyfycence	339
By Cloked Colusyon thus many one is begyled.	160	Magnyfycence	728
There is many evyll faveryd, and thou be foule!	167	Magnyfycence	969
A man shall fynde /Many of her kynde,	167	Magnyfycence	984
What? Wolde ye have mo folys, and are so many?	172	Magnyfycence	1170
Shall se many thyngys donne craftely.	177	Magnyfycence	1334
For many tymes moche kyndnesse is denyed	177	Magnyfycence	1338
I knyt togyther many a broken threde.	177	Magnyfycence	1343
By crafty conveyaunce many one is brought up of nought;	178	Magnyfycence	1369
Why, welth hath made many a man braynlesse.	180	Magnyfycence	1423
Full many a strong cyte and towne hath been wonne	184	Magnyfycence	1577
Better to make iii. ryche than for to make many.	190	Magnyfycence	1772
Nay. Madnesse hath begyled you and many mo;	192	Magnyfycence	1856
Of sorowfull servauntes I have many scores;	194	Magnyfycence	1900
I vysyte them and stryke them with many sore plagys.	195	Magnyfycence	1943
Yet many had lever hangyd to be	198	Magnyfycence	2040
Howe many come to myschefe for to moche lyberte;	200	Magnyfycence	2134
Tyll, as ye se many tymes, they shame all theyr kynne.	201	Magnyfycence	2144
Full many thynges there be that lacketh redresse,	209	Magnyfycence	2415
Beten with stormys of many a frowarde blast,	213	Magnyfycence	2560
These maydens full meryly with many a dyvers flowur	231	Speke Parott	11
a] not in †MS Harley 2252			
Whyche cawsythe pore suters have many a hongry mele;	239	Speke Parott	311
So many morall maters, and so lytell usyd;	244	Speke Parott	449
many] 'many many' †MS Harley 2252			
So many nobyll bodyes, undyr on dawys hedd;	245	Speke Parott	467
So many complayntes, and so smalle redresse;	245	Speke Parott	470
So many thevys hangyd, and thevys nevertholesse;	245	Speke Parott	477
So braynles calvys hedes, so many shepis taylys;	245	Speke Parott	484
So many plucte partryches, and so fatte quaylles;	245	Speke Parott	486
So many swannes dede, and so small revell -	245	Speke Parott	489
So many trusys takyn, and so lytyll perfyte trowthe;	245	Speke Parott	491
perfyte] 'profyte' †MS Harley 2252			
So many howgye howsys byldyng, and so small howse-holdyng;	245	Speke Parott	494
So many vacabondes, so many beggers bolde,	245	Speke Parott	498
So many vacabondes, so many beggers bolde,	245	Speke Parott	498
So many holow hartes, and so dowbyll faces;	245	Speke Parott	502
So many bullys of pardon publysshed and shewyd;	246	Speke Parott	515
Of parsons and vycaryes /They make many outcryes:	261	Collyn Clout	571
Many one ye have untwynde	263	Collyn Clout	662
ye have untwynde] 'have but wynde' †Godfray 1531, Kele 1545.1, Marshe 1568			
As many a frere, God wote,	267	Collyn Clout	836
They say many matters be borne	276	Collyn Clout	1198
There goth many a lye	288	Why Come Ye	356
But the wyttys of many wyse	298	Why Come Ye	766
And as many as him lykys,	306	Why Come Ye	1080
him] 'he' MS Rawlinson C. 813			
wherein ar comprysyde many and dyvers	312	Garlande	1
And many mo whome I cowde enduce;	314	Garlande	94
Sophisticatid craftely is many a confecture;	315	Garlande	110
Olde Diogenes, with other many mo,	315	Garlande	129
For reporte ryseth many deverse wayes.	317	Garlande	181
For] not MS Cotton Vitellius E.x			
Of poetis laureat of many dyverse nacyons;	321	Garlande	324
With Plautus, that wrote full many a comody;	322	Garlande	354
full] not in Marshe 1568			
Mustred ther amonge them with many a mad tale;	322	Garlande	373
Enlosenged with many goodly platis	325	Garlande	469
Of golde, entachid with many a precyous stone;	325	Garlande	470
Englasid glittering with many a clere story;	325	Garlande	479
Of pursevantis ther presid in with many a dyverse tale:	326	Garlande	492
a] not in Marshe 1568			
There were many wordes smaller and gretter,	326	Garlande	508
Of Athlas astrology, and many noble thyngis,	331	Garlande	690
So many, that longe it were to reherse.	331	Garlande	706
it] 'in' Marshe 1568			
Of broken warkis wrought many a goodly thyng,	334	Garlande	801
Many divisis passynge curyously;	336	Garlande	853
Hath fresshely enbewtid with many a goodly sorte	336	Garlande	868
To her he wrote many maters of myrthe;	346	Garlande	1199
Wherein many storis ar brevely contayned	347	Garlande	1224
He wrate therof many a praty lyne,	347	Garlande	1242
By there phesik doth many a man ease,	352	Garlande	1427
Recountyng commoditis of many a straunge nacyon;	354	Garlande	1500
And suche wondringes many mo.	376	Replycacion	76
Many a good man /And many a good woman,	378	Replycacion	134
Many a good man /And many a good woman,	378	Replycacion	135

	Page	Title	Line
The blynde eteth many a flye.	378	Replycacion	152
Ye pyke out many thystels,	380	Replycacion	220
With other many holy men,	381	Replycacion	278
With other doctours many mo,	381	Replycacion	280

MANYE

	Page	Title	Line
So manye bolde barons, there hertes as dull as lede;	245	Speke Parott	466

MANYFOLDE

	Page	Title	Line
And manly manyfolde, /Their enemyes to assayle	364	Albany	203

MANYS

	Page	Title	Line
I wold sum manys bake ink-horne	133	Garnesche5	133

MANKYND

	Page	Title	Line
All mankynd, whom thou ful dere hast boght,	34	Dol Dethe	194

MANKYNDE

	Page	Title	Line
For by that Lorde that bought dere all mankynde,	50	Bowge	163

MANLES

	Page	Title	Line
O manles manhod, enfayntyd all with fere,	242	Speke Parott	391

MANLY

	Page	Title	Line
His corage manly, yet ther he shed his bloode.	32	Dol Dethe	103
And manly manyfolde, /Their enemyes to assaye	364	Albany	203

MANLYNES

	Page	Title	Line
So myche hardy-dardy, and so lytell manlynes;	244	Speke Parott	457

MANNER

	Page	Title	Line
Fell downe on thys manner.	64	Hauke	115
Under the banner /Of all good manner,	356	Garlande	1573
After the aunclent manner	360	Albany	62

MANNES

	Page	Title	Line
For thou beggest at every mannes dur.	135	Dundas	26
That overgroweth a mannes face,	155	Magnyfycence	544
What! Then he is some good poore mannes curre?	171	Magnyfycence	1129
Ye. But he wyll in at every mannes dore.	171	Magnyfycence	1130
Nowe must you lerne to begge at every mannes gate.	196	Magnyfycence	1981
For her vysage /It woldt aswage /A mannes courage.	214	El Rummynge	11
Except mannes soule, that Chryst so dere bought;	236	Speke Parott	215
To rule ix realmes by one mannes wytte,	240	Speke Parott	333
By one mannes wytte.	271	Collyn Clout	993
Displease not an hundreth for one mannes pleasure.	314	Garlande	90
It is harde to tell of every mannes mouthe:	326	Garlande	500
Of Mannes Lyfe the Peregrynacioun,	347	Garlande	1221
Of brede at ylke mannes hecke.	363	Albany	155
To no mannes anoyance.	385	Replycacion	396

MANNYS

	Page	Title	Line
1 thyngys contryvyd by mannys reason,	140	Magnyfycence	1
But Measure, my frende, what hyght this mannys name?	145	Magnyfycence	165
And, syr, this other mannys name is Lyberte.	145	Magnyfycence	168
I am baytyd with doggys at every mannys gate;	195	Magnyfycence	1961
Into one mannys hande;	298	Why Come Ye	763
One wyse mannys hede	298	Why Come Ye	764

MANS

	Page	Title	Line
He payed a bitter pencyon /For mans redempcyon,	258	Collyn Clout	453

MANTEYND

	Page	Title	Line
Whom he as lorde worsheply manteynd,	34	Dol Dethe	186

MANTENYD

	Page	Title	Line
Cherlemayne, that mantenyd the nobles of Fraunce,	182	Magnyfycence	1501

MANTILL

	Page	Title	Line
Enbrowdred the mantill /Is of your maydenhede.	338	Garlande	908
maydenhede] 'maydenhode' †Fakes 1523			
Enbrawderid the mantill /Is of yowr maydenhede.	338	Garlande	924

MANTYCARE

	Page	Title	Line
You mantyca[re], ye maltaperte, ye can bothe wins and whyne;	123	Garnesche2	4
mantyca] 'mantyca' †MS Harley 367			

MANTYCORE

	Page	Title	Line
Thow mantycore, ye marmset, garnyshte lyke a Greke,	124	Garnesche2	39
Thow bere, thow brystlyd bore, /Thou Moryshe mantycore,	128	Garnesche3	165

MANTYCORS

	Page	Title	Line
The mantycors of the montaynes	79	Phy Sparrow	294

MANTYLL

	Page	Title	Line
Enbrawderyd the mantyll /Is of yowre maydenhede.	338	Garlande	916

MANTRYBLE

	Page	Title	Line
Of Mantryble the Bryge, Malchus the Murryon,	122	Garnesche1	22

MANTUAN

	Page	Title	Line
Virgill the Mantuan, with his Eneidos;	321	Garlande	339
By Maro, the Mantuan prudent,	342	Garlande	1080

MAPELY ROTE

	Page	Title	Line
Also the Murnyng of the Mapely Rote;	351	Garlande	1377
Murnyng] 'murmyng' †Fakes 1523			

MAR

	Page	Title	Line
When thou shoke thi sword so noble a man to mar!	32	Dol Dethe	115
And mar all they warke;	91	Phy Sparrow	799
To make all or to mar,	297	Why Come Ye	733

MARCELLUS

	Page	Title	Line
Of Marcus Marcellus /A proces I could tell us;	90	Phy Sparrow	734

MARCHAUNDYSE

	Page	Title	Line
Therein they founde royall marchaundyse,	47	Bowge	41
Her marchaundyse is ryche and fortunate,	47	Bowge	52
Her] 'Here' †Wynkyn de Worde 1499			

MARCHAUNTES

	Page	Title	Line
Marchauntes her borded to see what she had lode.	47	Bowge	40
lode] not in Marshe 1568			

MARCHE HARE — MARY

	Page	Title	Line
Measure is mete for a marchauntes hall	151	Magnyfycence	382
Money maketh marchauntes, I tell you, over all.	184	Magnyfycence	1574
MARCHE HARE			
By Cryst, as mery as a Marche hare.	166	Magnyfycence	921
Masid as a Marche hare, he ran lyke a scut.	329	Garlande	632
I saye, thou madde Marche hare,	375	Replycacion	35
MARCH HARUM			
But lyke a March harum /His braynes were so parum.	64	Hauke	104
MARCIALL			
And lyke marciall Hector he faught them agayne	31	Dol Dethe	88
Valiant as Hector in every marciall nede,	33	Dol Dethe	138
Horace and noble Marciall,	133	Garnesche5	141
In every marciall shoure,	365	Albany	240
MARCYALL			
By marcyall strength /He wan at length;	104	Phy Sparrow	1305
That late were discomfect with battayle marcyall.	117	Ag Scottes	84
To rayne, for all his marcyall affeccyon;	181	Magnyfycence	1470
MARCUS			
Of Marcus Marcellus /A proces I could tell us;	90	Phy Sparrow	734
MARDE			
Alasse! With colde my lymmes shall be marde.	197	Magnyfycence	2004
MARDOCHEUS			
And of Mardocheus, /And of great Assuerus,	90	Phy Sparrow	739
MARE			
He rydyth well the horse, but he rydyth better the mare.	43	Balettys2	21
Ware, ware, the mare wynsyth wyth her wanton hele!	43	Balettys2	22
Had I as good an hors as she is a mare,	57	Bowge	407
And from Medusa, that mare,	73	Phy Sparrow	76
Nowe then goo we hens. Away the mare!	177	Magnyfycence	1325
With, 'Now away the mare,	217	El Rummynge	110
Whan the mare doth keke;	225	El Rummynge	450
Ye go about to amende, and ye mare all.	235	Speke Parott	154
Shoo the mockyssh mare;	251	Collyn Clout	180
Our mare hath cast her fole,	281	Why Come Ye	85
MAREES			
From the marees depe /Of Acherontes well,	73	Phy Sparrow	69
MAREFOLES			
A mayny of marefoles	285	Why Come Ye	244
MARES			
That with his whyp his mares was wonte to yarke;	153	Magnyfycence	484
Must mesure, in the mares name, you furnysshe and dresse?	179	Magnyfycence	1391
MARES MYLKE			
Whyte as mares mylke;	254	Collyn Clout	315
mares] 'morowes' Kele 1545.1, Marshe 1568, 'marys' Harley 2252			
MARGARET			
To mastres Margaret Tylney	338	Garlande	R
To maystres Margaret Hussey	340	Garlande	R
Mirry Margaret, /As mydsomer flowre,	340	Garlande	1004
MARGARETE			
Of mirry Margarete, /As mydsomer flowre,	341	Garlande	1019
As mirry Margarete, /This midsomer flowre,	341	Garlande	1034
This] 'The' MS Cotton Vitellius E.x			
MARGARITE			
Of Margarite, /Perle orient,	339	Garlande	947
MARGENT			
The margent was illumynid all with golden railles	345	Garlande	1157
MARGERAIN			
With margerain jentyll, /The flowre of goodlyhede,	337	Garlande	906
With margerain jantill, /The flowre of goodlyhede,	338	Garlande	914
With margerain jantill, /The flowre of goodlyhede,	338	Garlande	922
MARGERES			
Dame Margeres soule out of hell.	268	Collyn Clout	876
MARGERY			
With manerly Margery Mylk and Ale.	35	Man Margery	7
With manerly Margery Mylk and Ale.	36	Man Margery	14
With manerly Margery Mylk and Ale.	36	Man Margery	21
With manerly Margery Milk and Ale.	36	Man Margery	28
With manerly Margery Mylk and Ale.	36	Man Margery	30
Di le xi, /Dame Margery, /Fa, re, my, my.	71	Phy Sparrow	4
What! Margery Mylke Ducke, mermoset!	153	Magnyfycence	457
Than Margery Mylkeducke /Her kyrtell she dyd uptucke	225	El Rummynge	418
To Margery and to Maude	267	Collyn Clout	852
To mastres Margery Wentworthe	337	Garlande	R
Of Manerly Margery Maystres Mylke and Ale;	346	Garlande	1198
Margery Maystres] 'maistres Margery' Marshe 1568			
For Margery wynshed, and breke her hinder girth;	346	Garlande	1201
MARINER			
As a mariner that amasid is in a stormy rage,	335	Garlande	829
amasid] 'masid' MS Cotton Vitellius E.x			
MARIONE			
With Marione Clarione, sol, lucerne,	352	Garlande	1439
But Marione Clarione was caught with a colde colde,	352	Garlande	1443
a colde colde] 'a colde' Marshe 1568			
MARY			
O goodly chyld /Of Mary mylde, /Then be oure shylde!	40	Coystrowne3	42
His hawke then flew uppon /The rode, with Mary and Johnn.	65	Hauke	127
Mary, Welthe and I was apoynted to mete,	141	Magnyfycence	24
Mary, upon trouth my reason I grounde,	147	Magnyfycence	264

MARYBON—MARRE

	Page	Title	Line
Mary, syr, ye were afrayde.	150	Magnyfycence	362
Mary, so wyll we also.	157	Magnyfycence	616
Mary, syr, he told us, when	158	Magnyfycence	652
Mary, the better and Mesure were out.	158	Magnyfycence	656
Mary, with Magnyfycence I wolde be retaynyd.	161	Magnyfycence	763
Abyde, syr, quod he! Mary, so I do.	162	Magnyfycence	789
Nede? Yes, Mary. I say not nay.	163	Magnyfycence	807
By Saynt Mary, he is a tawle man.	163	Magnyfycence	821
Mary, I am come for the. For me?	166	Magnyfycence	929
No, Mary; not yet.	166	Magnyfycence	934
Mary, Mesure had hym a whyle in gydynge,	166	Magnyfycence	939
Mary, thou jettes it of hyght.	167	Magnyfycence	962
Mary, Lusty Pleasure, by myne advyse,	167	Magnyfycence	964
Mary, syr, Cokermowthe is a good way hens.	170	Magnyfycence	1061
Mary, I knewe the when thou waste a ladde.	170	Magnyfycence	1089
Mary, as for that, thou shalte sone here myne.	172	Magnyfycence	1153
Mary, as thou sayst, he gave me a blurre.	173	Magnyfycence	1179
Mary, it was his, and nowe it is myne.	173	Magnyfycence	1181
Mary, syr, ye may swere it on a boke.	176	Magnyfycence	1292
Mary, syr, so dyd he excede and passe,	178	Magnyfycence	1385
Mary, your speche is as pleasant as though it were pend,	183	Magnyfycence	1538
Where is he? Mary, I made hym abyde	187	Magnyfycence	1685
Mary, I wene he wolde not be glad to come agayne.	189	Magnyfycence	1740
Ye, Mary, somtyme - in a messe of vergesse,	189	Magnyfycence	1756
Mary, Cryst graunt ye catche no colde on your fete!	191	Magnyfycence	1803
What sayst thou? Mary, I pray God your mastershyp to save.	191	Magnyfycence	1828
Ye, mary, is it. Ye, so mote I goo.	198	Magnyfycence	2046
With ye, mary, syrs, thus sholde it be:	198	Magnyfycence	2064
Mary, I defye thy best and thy worst.	202	Magnyfycence	2197
Mary, syr, this gentylman caled me javell.	203	Magnyfycence	2211
Nay, by Saynt Mary, it was ye called me knave.	203	Magnyfycence	2212
Mary, so ungoodly langage you me gave.	203	Magnyfycence	2213
Mary, syr, he sayd that he was the pratyer man	203	Magnyfycence	2225
And Saynt Mary Spytell	276	Collyn Clout	1184
By saynt Mary, my Lady,	339	Garlande	973
By Mary Gipcy, /Quod scripsi, scripsi;	353	Garlande	1455
Of Mary, mother and mayed?	376	Replycacion	47
That glorious mayde Mary;	381	Replycacion	256

MARYBON

	Page	Title	Line
Esebon, Marybon, Wheston next Barnet;	234	Speke Parott	127

MARYES

	Page	Title	Line
Speke, Parotte, I pray yow, for Maryes saake,	237	Speke Parott	233

MARK

	Page	Title	Line
Note and mark wyl thys parcele;	132	Garnesche5	97

MARKE

	Page	Title	Line
Of Trystram, and Kynge Marke,	87	Phy Sparrow	641
And some bade, 'Sere hym with a marke.'	150	Magnyfycence	360
A counterfet courtyer with a knaves marke.	154	Magnyfycence	486
And in my purse was twenty marke.	171	Magnyfycence	1108
And Sad Cyrcumspeccyon I marke in my mynde;	212	Magnyfycence	2504
Or scante worth twenty marke,	264	Collyn Clout	726
And by swete saynt Marke,	272	Collyn Clout	1047
Marke well this conclusyon:	279	Why Come Ye	18
They shote all at one marke:	283	Why Come Ye	174
Marke me that chase	301	Why Come Ye	883
me] 'well' MS Rawlinson C. 813			
And my wordes marke,	309	Why Come Ye	1207
And, my wordes marke truly,	310	Why Come Ye2	27
'And espetyally to make a lye' MS Rawlinson C. 813			

MARKED

	Page	Title	Line
Marked in your cradels	379	Replycacion	174

MARKET

	Page	Title	Line
Aboute churches and market.	255	Collyn Clout	326

MARLYONS

	Page	Title	Line
The lanners and the marlyons	85	Phy Sparrow	565
the] not in Wyght 1553, Kitson 1560.6, Marshe 1568			

MARMESET

	Page	Title	Line
Gup, marmeset, jast ye morelle!	124	Garnesche3	13

MARMOLL

	Page	Title	Line
Some with the marmoll to halte I them make;	194	Magnyfycence	1906

MARMOSET

	Page	Title	Line
Thou mokkyshe marmoset, /I will nat dy in [thy] det.	128	Garnesche3	172
thy] 'they' †MS Harley 367			

MARMOSETE

	Page	Title	Line
In faythe, I wolde thou had a marmosete.	171	Magnyfycence	1132

MARMSET

	Page	Title	Line
Thow mantycore, ye marmset, garnyshte lyke a Greke,	124	Garnesche2	39

MARO

	Page	Title	Line
By Maro, the Mantuan prudent,	342	Garlande	1080

MAROCK

	Page	Title	Line
Thorow the streytes of Marock	303	Why Come Ye	955
of] not in Toy 1553, Kitson 1560.7, Marshe 1568			

MARQUES

	Page	Title	Line
Nor marques, erle, nor lorde;	294	Why Come Ye	620

MARRE

	Page	Title	Line
All that I make forthwith I marre;	169	Magnyfycence	1036
I make on the one day, and I marre on the other.	169	Magnyfycence	1038
Ye make nought but ye marre.	364	Albany	226

	Page	Title	Line
MARRES			
All maters there he marres,	283	Why Come Ye	189
MARS			
O cruell Mars, thou dedly god of war!	32	Dol Dethe	113
The tyme whan Mars to werre hym dyd dres;	46	Bowge	7
When Mars retrogradant reversed his bak,	312	Garlande	3
MARSHALSY			
The Kynges Benche or Marshalsy,	275	Collyn Clout	1171
Have hym forthe by and by /To the Marshalsy,	290	Why Come Ye	432
MARTCHAUNTES			
Thus, in a rowe, of martchauntes a grete route	49	Bowge	120
MARTERD			
And dyed stynkingly marterd.	297	Why Come Ye	741
MARTIS			
And Martis lusty knight;	112	Lawde	55
MARTYN			
Of Martyn Swart and all hys mery men.	37	Coystrownel	18
MARTYNET			
The spynke and the martynet also;	82	Phy Sparrow	407
MARVEYLUS			
Of marveylus conclusyons,	105	Phy Sparrow	1349
MAS			
Into my chalys at mas,	66	Hauke	184
Prate of thy matens and thy mas,	275	Collyn Clout	1158
MASE			
I move them, I mase them, I make them so fonde,	161	Magnyfycence	742
Hercules the herdy, with his stobburne clobbyd mase,	182	Magnyfycence	1494
To face out her foly with a midsomer mase;	346	Garlande	1208
MASED			
Levynge me stondynge as a mased man;	48	Bowge	83
And hath so mased a wandrynge wyt?	172	Magnyfycence	1144
But mende your myndes that are mased;	382	Replycacion	293
MASHE BOLLE			
The mashe bolle, and shaketh	219	El Rummynge	196
MASHFAT			
The hennes ron in the mashfat;	219	El Rummynge	190
MASH FAT			
She dranke on the mash fat.	226	El Rummynge	491
MASID			
Masid as a Marche hare, he ran lyke a scut.	329	Garlande	632
MASYD			
Masyd, wytles smery smyth,	71	Hauke	331
As people halfe pevysshe, or men that were masyd.	319	Garlande	266
MASKED			
It wolde be masked in my net!	153	Magnyfycence	458
MASKYD			
To tell you, syr, I dare not, leest I sholde be maskyd	141	Magnyfycence	30
MASSE			
The requiem masse to synge, /Softly warbelynge, Softly] 'Loftly' Marshe 1568	81	Phy Sparrow	401
Shall rede the gospell at masse;	82	Phy Sparrow	423
By the masse, for ye are able to dystroy an hole lande.	154	Magnyfycence	513
By the masse, odly well alowde.	155	Magnyfycence	533
Ye, by the masse, this is even the same,	157	Magnyfycence	599
By the masse, for the cowrte thou art a mete man;	161	Magnyfycence	764
By the masse, thou shalt byde my leyser.	162	Magnyfycence	788
No, by the masse. What! Sholde I swere?	166	Magnyfycence	936
By the masse, well done and boldely.	166	Magnyfycence	948
By the masse, I holde the madde.	170	Magnyfycence	1088
By the masse, yet art thou more fole than I.	171	Magnyfycence	1111
By the masse, a Spaynysshe moght with a gray lyste!	173	Magnyfycence	1200
By the masse, I am glad I came hyder	176	Magnyfycence	1286
By the masse, he shall hyght Consayte.	176	Magnyfycence	1309
What care I? By the masse, well sayd.	187	Magnyfycence	1671
By the masse, I have done that I can,	187	Magnyfycence	1693
By the masse, man, thou shall fynde me resonable.	202	Magnyfycence	2204
By the masse, I warant the, I wyll not be bracyd.	203	Magnyfycence	2221
That a man shall here a masse,	272	Collyn Clout	1022
MASSES			
The money for theyr masses	257	Collyn Clout	423
MASSHE FAT			
Who is mayster of the masshe fat?	176	Magnyfycence	1319
MAST			
Yet of magnyfycence oft made is the mast:	213	Magnyfycence	2563
Ye fyrste aryvyd; whan broken was your mast Ye] 'The' †Fakes 1523	327	Garlande	542
MASTER			
Turnd ther backis and let ther master fall, backis] 'backe' Marshe 1568	31	Dol Dethe	94
A master, a mynstrell, a fydler, a farte.	38	Coystrownel	56
devysyd by Master Skelton Laureat	41	Balettys	I
Skelton Lauriate Defender Agenst Master Garnesche Chalenger,	121	Garneschel	I
Sithe ye have me chalyngyd, Master Garnesche,	121	Garneschel	1
Skelton Lauryate Defender Agenst Master Garnesche Chalangar,	122	Garnesche2	I
MASTERED			
By Mesure mastered yet is he.	155	Magnyfycence	541
MASTERFULLY			
So masterfully upon you for to take	188	Magnyfycence	1715

	Page	Title	Line
MASTERS			
But let mi masters mathematical	296	Why Come Ye	708
MASTERSHYP			
What sayst thou? Mary, I pray God your mastershyp to save. . .	191	Magnyfycence	1828
MASTYFE			
So mangye a mastyfe curre, the grete greyhoundes pere;	245	Speke Parott	487
From whens that mastyfe cam.	298	Why Come Ye	777
MASTYVE			
For drede of the mastyve cur, ...	286	Why Come Ye	297
MASTYVYS			
Suche malyncoly mastyvys and mangye curre dogges	240	Speke Parott	320
MASTRES			
Youre medelyng, mastres, is manerles;	40	Coystrowne4	2
Good mastres Anne, there ye do shayle!	41	Coystrowne4	19
To mastres Anne, that farly swete, ...	41	Coystrowne4	29
I wold you coud! Then shuld ye se, mastres, ...	44	Balettys3	40
That mastres Punt put yow of, yt was nat alle causeles;	122	Garneschel	32
. . . . mastres Audelby, ...	125	Garnesche3	55
My lady mastres, Dame Phylology, ...	232	Speke Parott	43
mastres] 'maysters' Lant 1545, Kynge & Marche 1554, Day 1560, Marshe 1568			
To mastres Margery Wentworthe	337	Garlande	R
To mastres Margaret Tylney	338	Garlande	R
To mastres Geretrude Statham	341	Garlande	R
MASTRIS			
But blissed Bachus, that mastris oft doth frame, ...	322	Garlande	383
MASTRYES			
In faythe, I can do mastryes, so I can.	173	Magnyfycence	1190
MAT			
I made, he said, a windmil of an olde mat.	137	Ven Tongues	13
Make a wyndmyll of a mat -	169	Magnyfycence	1028
What brothell, I say, is yonder bounde in a mat?	199	Magnyfycence	2106
MATE			
And mate you with chek mate.	368	Albany	386
MATED			
The French men he hathe so mated, ...	282	Why Come Ye	161
MATENS			
Prate of thy matens and thy mas, ...	275	Collyn Clout	1158
MATER			
Howbeit the mater was evident and playne;	31	Dol Dethe	72
I wyll not saye it is mater in dede, ...	61	Bowge	537
Of this dolorous mater.	81	Phy Sparrow	398
His mater is worth gold, ...	91	Phy Sparrow	786
His mater is delectable, /Solacious and commendable;	91	Phy Sparrow	790
With moche mater more	126	Garnesche3	76
Nor good ryme in yower mater.	126	Garnesche3	105
If there be none other mater but that, ...	137	Ven Tongues	14
But nowe, forsothe, man, it maketh no mater;	175	Magnyfycence	1256
And, be the mater yll more or lesse, ...	175	Magnyfycence	1272
To the pythe of the mater who lyst to resorte:	213	Magnyfycence	2540
This mater have movyd, you myrthys to make, ...	213	Magnyfycence	2552
Muche frutefull mater. But now for your defence, ...	239	Speke Parott	297
And of Magnyfycence a notable mater, ...	346	Garlande	1192
This mater to credence	372	Albany	522
MATERYALYTES			
And brynge in materyalytes	260	Collyn Clout	559
in materyalytes] 'him in maierialites' Marshe 1568			
MATERS			
Doublenes hatinge fals maters to compas, ...	33	Dol Dethe	150
Those maters that he hath pende;	92	Phy Sparrow	810
Al maters wel pondred and wel to be regarded, ...	137	Ven Tongues	1
Counterfet maters in the lawe of the lande -	152	Magnyfycence	431
A, shall we have more of this maters yet?	203	Magnyfycence	2214
Tushe! These maters that ye move are but soppys in ale;	203	Magnyfycence	2233
How the maters he mellis in com to small effecte;	240	Speke Parott	328
Maters more precious than the ryche jacounce, ...	241	Speke Parott	366
So many morall maters, and so lytell usyd;	244	Speke Parott	449
many] 'many many' †MS Harley 2252			
All maters there he marres, ...	283	Why Come Ye	189
Men of suche maters make but mummynge, ...	318	Garlande	200
but] 'but a' MS Cotton Vitellius E.x			
With maters that amount the Romayns in substaunce;	321	Garlande	346
To her he wrote many maters of myrthe;	346	Garlande	1199
MATHEMATICAL			
But let mi masters mathematical	296	Why Come Ye	708
MATYNS			
Theyr matyns madly sayde, /Nothynge devoutly prayde, ...	252	Collyn Clout	238
No matyns at mydnyght, ...	256	Collyn Clout	406
MATYR			
Tyll more matyr may cum.	129	Garnesche3	205
MATYRS			
So myche presonment, for matyrs not worth a hawe;	245	Speke Parott	478
MATRICULATE			
To be matriculate /With ladyes of estate?	104	Phy Sparrow	1288
Shulde be set and sortyd, /To be matriculate	348	Garlande	1281
MATRYCULAT			
the ix Musys of polytyke poems and poettys matryculat.	36	Coystrowne	I

MATRYCULATE — ME | Page | Title | Line

MATRYCULATE
The fame matryculate /Of poetes laureate. . . . . 384 Replycacion 357
MATTENS
My hawkes to mattens rynge!' . . . . 65 Hauke 124
MATTER
That thys is matter indeed. . . . . 65 Hauke 148
But let the matter slyp, ... 66 Hauke 154
With moch matter more, /That I kepe in store. . . . . 67 Hauke 220
This matter trew and playne, ... 85 Phy Sparrow 547
Playne matter indede, /Whoso lyst to rede . . . . 85 Phy Sparrow 548
The matter were to nyse, ... 100 Phy Sparrow 1132
That all this matter must under grope. . . . . 157 Magnyfycence 600
All that I can his matter for to spede. . . . . 187 Magnyfycence 1664
He can full craftely this matter brynge aboute. . . . . 187 Magnyfycence 1691
Yet let us se this matter thorowly ingrosed. . . . . 209 Magnyfycence 2438
No matter pretendyd, nor nothyng enterprysed, ... 236 Speke Parott 201
Of one so devyllysshe a matter. . . . . 297 Why Come Ye 715
Of this matter the grownde . . . . 298 Why Come Ye 780
Upon this matter mistycall . . . . 299 Why Come Ye 821
For if he gloryously publisshe his matter, ... 314 Garlande 83
And ye coude bryng /The matter about . . . . 361 Albany 93
Retourne we to our matter. . . . . 378 Replycacion 160
MATTERS
Howe in matters they ben rawe, ... 249 Collyn Clout 94
In matters that them lyke . . . . 269 Collyn Clout 922
And let our matters pas! . . . . 275 Collyn Clout 1159
    matters] 'matter' Kele 1545.1, 'maters' Marshe 1568,
    'medlyng' MS Harley 2252
They say many matters be borne . . . . 276 Collyn Clout 1198
And our matters mayntayne, ... 276 Collyn Clout 1213
MATTOCKE
Uppon hym for to take /A mattocke or a rake. . . . . 253 Collyn Clout 274
The mattocke and the shovll . . . . 262 Collyn Clout 646
MATTOKE
A mattoke and a spade, ... 293 Why Come Ye 561
MAUDE
Maude Ruggy thyther skyppped: . . . . 226 El Rummynge 467
To Margery and to Maude . . . . 267 Collyn Clout 852
MAUMET
This maumet in lyke wyse . . . . 306 Why Come Ye 1070
MAUNCHET
A maunchet for morell thereon to snap. 37 Coystrowne1 11
MAUNGEY
Ye. But trowest thou that he be not maungey? . . . . 171 Magnyfycence 1122
MAUNGY
With her maungy fystis. . . . . 219 El Rummynge 200
In wretched beggary /And maungy misery, ... 362 Albany 138
And lyke maungy dogges. . . . . 364 Albany 215
MAVYS
The mavys with her whystell . . . . 82 Phy Sparrow 424
MAW
With hys worme-etyn maw /And hys gastly jaw 39 Coystrowne3 14
His hawke shulde pray and fede /Upon a pigeons maw. . . . . . . 63 Hauke 57
MAWE
To fyll therwith your mawe – . . . . 263 Collyn Clout 656
MAWES
The fende scrache out your mawes! . . . . 371 Albany 479
MAWMENT
Thou murrioun, thow mawment, ... 128 Garnesche3 170
Or of suche a mawment /Caryed in a tent. . . . . 365 Albany 257
MAWMETT
Moloc, that mawmett, there darre no man withsay; . . . . 243 Speke Parott 402
MAWTE
Howe hyr ale is solde /To mawte and to molde. . . . . 218 El Rummynge 159
MAXIMUS
Lucilius and Valerius Maximus by name; . . . . 322 Garlande 380
MAXYMYANE
And Maxymyane, with his madde ditiis, ... 322 Garlande 360
ME
Adres the to me, whiche am bothe halt and lame, ... 29 Dol Dethe 10
Kyndle in me suche plente of thy nobles, ... 29 Dol Dethe 20
To all cuntreis aboute hym reporte me I dare: . . . . 33 Dol Dethe 136
What nedethe me for to extoll his fame . . . . 33 Dol Dethe 141
In me all onely wer sett and comprisyde, ... 33 Dol Dethe 156
To me also all thouthe yt wer promysyde . . . . 33 Dol Dethe 159
What, wolde ye frompill me now? Fy, fy! . . . . 36 Man Margery 16
'Walke forth your way, ye cost me nought; . . . . 36 Man Margery 22
Wed me or els I dye for thought! . . . . 36 Man Margery 26
He whystelyth so swetely he makyth me to swete; 37 Coystrowne1 37
At me, that medeled nothyng with youre wark. 38 Coystrowne1 61
Uppon me to clater or else to say yll. 38 Coystrowne1 66
Of me and other ye may have nede. 41 Coystrowne4 14
Let me', quod he, 'ly in your lap.' 41 Balettys1 2
Causyth me that I can not myself refrayne, ... 42 Balettys2 3
Abashyth me, albeit I have no nede. 44 Balettys3 35
Nothynge yerthly to me more desyrous 44 Balettys3 43
But hatefull absens, to me so envyous, ... 45 Balettys3 45
Though thou withdraw me from her by long dystaunce, ... 45 Balettys3 46

ME — ME

	Page	Title	Line
To suffer me so carefull to endure,	45	Balettys5	6
For whose love, welcom dysease to me!	45	Balettys5	10
But Fortune enforsyth me so carefully to endure,	46	Balettys5	13
But Ignorance full soone dyde me dyscure	46	Bowge	18
dyscure] 'dysture' †Wynkyn de Worde 1499, 1510			
Avysynge me my penne awaye to pulle	46	Bowge	21
And to lye downe as soone as I m[e] dreste,	47	Bowge	33
me] 'my' †Wynkyn de Worde 1499, 1510, Marshe 1568			
Me thoughte I sawe a shyppe, goodly of sayle,	47	Bowge	36
Gave me a taunte, and sayde I was to blame	48	Bowge	70
Than asked me, 'Syr, so God the spede,	48	Bowge	76
And with that worde on me she gave a glome	48	Bowge	80
With browes bente, and gan on me to stare	48	Bowge	81
Full daynnously, and fro me she dyde fare,	48	Bowge	82
Levynge me stondynge as a mased man;	48	Bowge	83
Desyre her name was, and so she me tolde,	48	Bowge	85
Sayenge to me, 'Broder, be of good chere,	48	Bowge	86
That wyll for me be medyatoure and mene;	48	Bowge	93
'Maystres,' quod I, 'I praye you tell me why soo,	49	Bowge	108
For, as me thoughte, in our shyppe I dyde see	49	Bowge	132
Than Favell gan wyth fayre speche me to fede.	50	Bowge	147
But this one thynge ye maye be sure of me,	50	Bowge	162
And ye nede ought, man, shewe to me your mynde,	50	Bowge	165
For ye have me whome faythfull ye shall fynde;	50	Bowge	166
Ye maye not fall; truste me, ye maye not fayle.	50	Bowge	170
But, as me thoughte, he ware on hym a cloke	51	Bowge	177
Me thoughte, of wordes that he had full a poke;	51	Bowge	179
Suspycyon, me thoughte, mette hym at a brayde,	51	Bowge	181
'In fayth,' quod Suspecte, 'spake Drede no worde of me?'	51	Bowge	183
Me thoughte his hede was full of gelousy,	51	Bowge	192
'God spede, broder,' to me quod he than,	51	Bowge	195
And thus to talke with me he began.	51	Bowge	196
That commaunde with you, me thought, a p[ra]ty space?	51	Bowge	198
commaunde] 'commened' Wynkyn de Worde 1510; 'party spake'			
†Wynkyn de Worde 1499, Marshe 1568, 'party space' WdeW 1510			
Spake he, a fayth, no worde to you of me?	51	Bowge	204
I wote, and he dyde, ye wolde me telle.	51	Bowge	205
He sayde of me, whan he with you dyde talke -	52	Bowge	209
For, but I trusted you, so God me save,	52	Bowge	213
To you oonly, me thynke, I durste shryve me;	52	Bowge	215
To you oonly, me thynke, I durste shryve me;	52	Bowge	215
Yf he coude fynde in herte to truste me.	52	Bowge	220
And of his mynde he shewed me all and some.	52	Bowge	226
Me thoughte his gowne was all furred wyth foxe.	52	Bowge	234
Me] 'My' †Wynkyn de Worde 1499			
He gased on me with his gotyshe berde;	52	Bowge	237
Tell me your mynde, me thynke ye make a verse,	53	Bowge	244
Tell me your mynde, me thynke ye make a verse,	53	Bowge	244
Er this, whan that ye made me royall chere.	53	Bowge	249
A balade boke before me for to laye,	53	Bowge	257
And lerne me to synge Re my fa sol!	53	Bowge	258
And whan I fayle, bobbe me on the noll!	53	Bowge	259
Syr, pardone me, I am an homely knave	53	Bowge	264
For, as for me, I served here many a daye,	53	Bowge	274
And ye be welcome, syr, so God me save,	54	Bowge	279
Wyth that, as he departed soo fro me,	54	Bowge	281
Anone ther mette with him, as me thoughte,	54	Bowge	282
To Hervy Ha[f]ter than he spake of me,	54	Bowge	295
Hafter] 'Haster' †Wynkyn de Worde 1499, 1510, Marshe 1568			
'By him that me boughte,' than quod Dysdayne,	54	Bowge	309
Forthwith, he made on me a prowde assawte,	55	Bowge	316
He wente aboute to take me in a fawte:	55	Bowge	318
And in this wyse he gan with me to chyde.	55	Bowge	322
What weneste I were? I trowe thou knowe not me.	55	Bowge	331
She hath gote me more money with her tayle	57	Bowge	405
Me thoughte alwaye Dyscymular dyde devyse;	58	Bowge	424
Me, passynge sore, myne herte than gan aryse;	58	Bowge	425
That other loked as he wolde me have slayne.	58	Bowge	430
me have] 'have me' Wynkyn de Worde 1510			
Whan that he was even at me almoost,	58	Bowge	432
And in his other sleve, me thought I sawe	58	Bowge	435
Thyse were the wordes he to me dyde saye.	58	Bowge	441
he] 'that he' Marshe 1568			
For allbeit that this longe not to me,	59	Bowge	456
Truste me, and yf it come to a nede;	59	Bowge	478
And so I wolde it were, so God me spede,	59	Bowge	481
Gyve me your honde, fare well and have good daye.'	60	Bowge	497
Sodaynly, as he departed me fro,	60	Bowge	498
Er I was ware, behynde me he sayde 'Bo!'	60	Bowge	500
He tolde me so, by God, ye maye truste me.	60	Bowge	514
He tolde me so, by God, ye maye truste me.	60	Bowge	514
Me thoughte I see lewde felawes here and there	61	Bowge	528
Came for to slee me of mortall entente.	61	Bowge	529
In the dyspyte of me,	64	Hauke	109
These be my querysters /To helpe me to synge,	65	Hauke	123
Say to me, Jacke Harys, /Quare accuparis	69	Hauke	277
As than befell to me.	72	Phy Sparrow	22
No creature but that wolde /Have rewed upon me,	72	Phy Sparrow	42

	Page	Title	Line
ME —ME			
To behold and se /What hevynesse dyd me pange:	72	Phy Sparrow	44
And lerne to wepe at me!	73	Phy Sparrow	57
Such paynes dyd me frete	73	Phy Sparrow	58
Amen, say ye with me!	74	Phy Sparrow	94
To shew me their devyse	74	Phy Sparrow	100
And take me by the lyp.	75	Phy Sparrow	140
Alas, it wyll me slo,	75	Phy Sparrow	141
That Phillyp is gone me fro!	75	Phy Sparrow	142
And on me it wolde lepe	75	Phy Sparrow	161
Me often for to wake	76	Phy Sparrow	165
And playe with me agayne.	77	Phy Sparrow	207
To me it myght importe	77	Phy Sparrow	216
Me thought my sparow did spek,	77	Phy Sparrow	220
Agayne me for to kyll!	77	Phy Sparrow	223
Ye prycke me in the head!'	77	Phy Sparrow	224
Me thought, of Phyllyps blode.	77	Phy Sparrow	226
Shewe me the ryght path	78	Phy Sparrow	246
That he is slayne me fro,	81	Phy Sparrow	364
From me was taken away	81	Phy Sparrow	374
To wepe with me loke that ye come,	81	Phy Sparrow	387
They ar to diffuse for me:	90	Phy Sparrow	768
Wherfore hold me excused	92	Phy Sparrow	813
Me enfluence to endyte,	93	Phy Sparrow	861
Whose fame by me shall sprede	93	Phy Sparrow	885
And no man wyll me blame,	94	Phy Sparrow	890
So Jupiter me socour,	94	Phy Sparrow	895
That causeth me /Studious to be	95	Phy Sparrow	959
Now Phebus me ken /To sharpe my pen,	96	Phy Sparrow	970
Trouth doth me bynd /And loyalte	96	Phy Sparrow	977
So Jupyter me socoure,	96	Phy Sparrow	991
And so hath ravyshed me	96	Phy Sparrow	1006
I cannot me refrayne	97	Phy Sparrow	1009
So Jupiter me socoure,	97	Phy Sparrow	1024
So Jupiter me succour,	98	Phy Sparrow	1056
So Jupiter me socoure,	98	Phy Sparrow	1085
She made me sore amased	99	Phy Sparrow	1103
Me thought min hert was crased,	99	Phy Sparrow	1105
So Jupyter me socour,	99	Phy Sparrow	1109
Unneth I me refrayned,	99	Phy Sparrow	1124
How she me had reclaymed,	99	Phy Sparrow	1125
And me to her retayned,	99	Phy Sparrow	1126
So Jupiter me succoure,	100	Phy Sparrow	1138
So Jupiter me succour,	100	Phy Sparrow	1163
So Jupiter me socoure,	101	Phy Sparrow	1187
No man can let me thynke,	101	Phy Sparrow	1199
It cost me lytell nor nought.	101	Phy Sparrow	1203
nor] 'or' Wyght 1553, Kitson 1560.6, Marshe 1568			
So Jupiter me succoure,	101	Phy Sparrow	1210
So Jupiter me socoure,	102	Phy Sparrow	1233
And shew now unto me	106	Phy Sparrow	1368
Whiche gave to me /The high degre	112	Calliope	5
Me to retayne /Her serviture,	112	Calliope	19
Illumyn me, your poete and your scrybe,	117	Ag Scottes	80
And now to begyn I wyll me adres,	117	Ag Scottes	89
Sithe ye have me chalyngyd, Master Garnesche,	121	Garnesche1	1
Rudely revilyng me in the kynges noble hall,	121	Garnesche1	2
Soche an odyr chalyngyr cowde me no man wysch,	121	Garnesche1	3
But sey me now, Syr Satrapas, what autoryte ye have	121	Garnesche1	6
In your chalenge, Syr Chystyn, to cale me knave?	121	Garnesche1	7
So curryshly to beknave me in the kynges place?	121	Garnesche1	9
But sey me yet, Syr Satropas, what auctoryte ye have	122	Garnesche1	13
In yor chalenge, Syr Chesten, to calle me a knave?	122	Garnesche1	14
But sey me yet, Syr Satrapas, wat auctoryte ye have	122	Garnesche1	20
In yor chalenge, Syr Chesten, to cal me a knave?	122	Garnesche1	21
But sey me yet, Syr Satrapas, what auctoryte ye have	122	Garnesche1	27
In yor chalenge, Syr Chesten, to calle me a knave?	122	Garnesche1	28
But sey me yet, Syr Satrapas, what auctoryte ye have	122	Garnesche1	34
In yor chalenge, Syr Chesten, to calle me a knave?	122	Garnesche1	35
Chalenge yor selfe for a fole, call me no more knave.	122	Garnesche1	42
Me for to chalenge that of your chalennge makyth so lytyll fors.	123	Garnesche2	19
Your stondarde, Syr Olifranke, agenst me for to splay;	123	Garnesche2	30
To turney or to tante with me ye ar to fare to seke.	123	Garnesche2	37
I caste me nat to be od	124	Garnesche3	6
And falsly ye me reporte.	124	Garnesche3	20
Agennst me for to make,	126	Garnesche3	93
Had ye gonne with me to scole,	127	Garnesche3	117
Ye xulde have kowththyd me a fole.	127	Garnesche3	119
Tyburne thou me assynyd	128	Garnesche3	174
That nature wrowght in yow and me,	130	Garnesche5	13
To cal me knave thou takyst gret payne.	130	Garnesche5	20
With, 'Bas me, buttyng, praty Cys',	130	Garnesche5	43
What eylythe the, rebawde, on me to rave?	131	Garnesche5	79
A kynge to me myn habyte gave	131	Garnesche5	80
To cal me lorell ye ar to lewde;	131	Garnesche5	85
Hath pointyd me to rayle on the.	131	Garnesche5	88
Yt commyth the wele me to remorde,	132	Garnesche5	101
Me as hys master for to calle	132	Garnesche5	104
Me to beknave thow art to blame;	132	Garnesche5	107

ME —ME   Page   Title   Line

	Page	Title	Line
Thow callyst me scallyd, thou callydst me mad;	132	Garnesche5	116
Thow callyst me scallyd, thou callydst me mad;	132	Garnesche5	116
To rayle with me that the can hyt.	132	Garnesche5	119
Thy fonde face can me nat fray.	134	Garnesche5	171
Than ye may commaunde me to gentil cok wat.	137	Ven Tongues	15
Yet to lie upon me they can not prevayle.	138	Ven Tongues	31
There is no noble man wil judge in me	138	Ven Tongues	34
That ye would coarte and enforce me	138	Ven Tongues	45
Of me with your language full of vilany.	138	Ven Tongues	48
For clatering of me I would him sone quight;	139	Ven Tongues	74
To tell you the cause me semeth it no nede.	140	Magnyfycence	8
Trewe you say, syr. Gyve me your hande.	141	Magnyfycence	28
Then thus to you – Nay, suffer me yet ferther to say,	142	Magnyfycence	48
But and you wolde me permyt	142	Magnyfycence	57
Say what ye wyll to me.	142	Magnyfycence	66
Judycyall rygoure shall not me correcte –	142	Magnyfycence	69
Yet suffer me to say the surpluse of my sawe.	142	Magnyfycence	71
Me, other fyrst or last,	143	Magnyfycence	93
Me pacyently to here.	143	Magnyfycence	111
Me semeth Magnyfycence is comynge here at hande.	145	Magnyfycence	162
Welcome, frendys, ye are bothe unto me.	145	Magnyfycence	169
But nowe let me knowe of your conversacyon.	145	Magnyfycence	170
Pleasyth, your grace, Felycyte they me call.	145	Magnyfycence	171
Welthe with Lyberte, with me bothe dwell ye shall,	145	Magnyfycence	174
Where as ye have, syr, to me them assygned,	145	Magnyfycence	177
Nowe that ye have me chefe ruler assyngned,	146	Magnyfycence	202
I wyll endevour me to order every thynge	146	Magnyfycence	203
All delectacyons aquayntyd is with me;	146	Magnyfycence	209
By me all persons worke what they lyste.	146	Magnyfycence	210
Who county[th] without me is caste to fer behynde countyth] 'countyd' †Rastell & Treveris C 1530, B	146	Magnyfycence	214
What, syr, wolde ye make me a poppynge fole?	146	Magnyfycence	232
A, ye make me laughe at your inconstaunce.	147	Magnyfycence	236
Ye coulde not ellys, I wote, with me endure.	147	Magnyfycence	247
It were not possyble me longe to retayne.	147	Magnyfycence	250
Me semeth that ye have dronken more than ye have bled.	147	Magnyfycence	260
Nowe, I beseche the, tell me what is thy name?	148	Magnyfycence	269
I reporte me herein to Kynge Lewes of Fraunce.	148	Magnyfycence	280
I wyll not use you to play with me checke mate.	149	Magnyfycence	307
Welthe, gete you home and commaunde me to Mesure.	149	Magnyfycence	316
Is there ony thynge elles your grace wyll commaunde me?	149	Magnyfycence	318
Me thought he called Fan[s]y. fansy] 'fanfy' †Rastell & Treveris C 1530, B	149	Magnyfycence	327
Me thought he called Fansy me behynde.	149	Magnyfycence	329
Me thought he called Fansy me behynde.	149	Magnyfycence	329
By lakyn, syr, it hathe cost me pence	150	Magnyfycence	338
Where was it delyvered you? Shewe unto me.	150	Magnyfycence	340
This wrytynge was taken me there,	150	Magnyfycence	344
They bare me in hande that I was a spye;	150	Magnyfycence	352
And boyes to the pylery gan me plucke,	150	Magnyfycence	356
And wolde have made me Freer Tucke,	150	Magnyfycence	357
To gete me fro them I had moche warke.	150	Magnyfycence	361
With ye, syr, so God me spede.	151	Magnyfycence	379
In faythe, Largesse, welcome to me.	151	Magnyfycence	390
They have made me here to put the stone;	151	Magnyfycence	406
What so ever I do, all men me prayse,	152	Magnyfycence	429
Counterfet capytaynes by me are mande;	152	Magnyfycence	436
Counterfet pleasure is borne out by me;	153	Magnyfycence	475
To counterfet this freers have lerned me.	154	Magnyfycence	487
To counterfet thyr counsell they gyve me a fee.	154	Magnyfycence	491
For Cockys harte, gyve me thy hande.	154	Magnyfycence	512
Sure Surveyaunce I named me.	155	Magnyfycence	525
He hawketh, me thynke, for a butterflye.	156	Magnyfycence	575
Thou hast made me play the jeu dehayte.	156	Magnyfycence	579
I am sure ye wolde have me excused.	156	Magnyfycence	581
Knowe they not me? They are to blame.	157	Magnyfycence	593
Knowe you not me, syrs? No, in dede.	157	Magnyfycence	594
Abyde. Lette me se. Take better hede.	157	Magnyfycence	595
Tell me, syrs, what is your wyll?	157	Magnyfycence	611
And there they wolde ha[v]e me to dwell. have] 'hane' †Rastell & Treveris C 1530, B	157	Magnyfycence	614
But tell me where aboute ye go.	157	Magnyfycence	617
I can not tell you. Why aske you me?	157	Magnyfycence	628
Syr, the playnesse you me tell. you me tell] 'you tell me' †Rastell & Treveris C 1530, B	158	Magnyfycence	630
Nay; eyther let me tell, or elles tell ye.	158	Magnyfycence	633
I care not, I. Tell on for me.	158	Magnyfycence	634
Craftynge and haftynge contryved is by me;	159	Magnyfycence	697
Full fewe that can themselfe of me excuse.	160	Magnyfycence	706
To come to me I trowe he shalbe fayne.	162	Magnyfycence	784
And desyre me thy good mayster to be?	162	Magnyfycence	798
Spekest thou to me?	162	Magnyfycence	799
As skante thou had no nede of me.	163	Magnyfycence	806
But, syr, I wyll have this man with me.	163	Magnyfycence	815
As well as me. I wolde, and I durste –	163	Magnyfycence	827
What nowe? Let se /Who loketh on me	163	Magnyfycence	830
Me seme I flye,	163	Magnyfycence	839
That useth me. /He can not thee.	164	Magnyfycence	861

438

ME — ME   Page   Title   Line

Wyth me wyll wonne	165	Magnyfycence	900
Me thynke she frowneth and lokys sowre.	166	Magnyfycence	924
Mary, I am come for the. For me?	166	Magnyfycence	929
Howe so? Tell me, I the pray.	166	Magnyfycence	931
Yes, yes. He fell with me also at debate.	166	Magnyfycence	944
Cockes harte! Tourne the; let me se thyne aray.	167	Magnyfycence	959
For me full mete.	167	Magnyfycence	976
Nowe let me se about	168	Magnyfycence	991
What! Thou wylte coughe me a dawe for forty pens?	170	Magnyfycence	1060
A, I trowe ye shall coughe me a fole.	170	Magnyfycence	1064
That thou so hye fro me doth sprynge,	170	Magnyfycence	1069
And as for me, I take but one folysshe way,	170	Magnyfycence	1076
Nowe, of good felowshyp, let me by thy [d]ogge,	170	Magnyfycence	1082
dogge] 'hogge' †Rastell & Treveris C 1530, B			
What! Callyst thou me a donnyshe crowe?	170	Magnyfycence	1095
Ye, bere me this strawe to a dawys nest.	170	Magnyfycence	1097
Let me have thy dogge, what soever I pay.	171	Magnyfycence	1101
Yet gyve me thy dogge, and I am content;	171	Magnyfycence	1112
Nowe take thou my dogge and gyve me thy fowle.	171	Magnyfycence	1116
Nowe thou hast done me a pleasure grete.	171	Magnyfycence	1131
Nay, in fayth, fyrst let me here thyne.	172	Magnyfycence	1152
What, Fansy! Let me se who is the tother.	172	Magnyfycence	1158
Mary, as thou sayst, he gave me a blurre.	173	Magnyfycence	1179
But yet thou shalt holde me a fole styll.	173	Magnyfycence	1184
Gyve me my grote, for thou hast lost.	173	Magnyfycence	1206
So helpe me God, man, ever at the length	175	Magnyfycence	1258
I wote not whether it cometh of the or of me,	176	Magnyfycence	1290
Why, shall I not have Foly with me also?	176	Magnyfycence	1306
Ye. But tell me one thynge. What is that?	176	Magnyfycence	1318
Who so to me gyveth good advertence	177	Magnyfycence	1333
By me conveyed is wanton insolence;	177	Magnyfycence	1335
By me is conveyed mykyll praty ware –	177	Magnyfycence	1340
Yet convey it craftely, and hardely spare not for me' –	177	Magnyfycence	1352
Without me be full ofte aspyed.	177	Magnyfycence	1355
For all hokes unhappy to me have resorte.	178	Magnyfycence	1374
Trust me, Lyberte, it greveth me ryght sore	178	Magnyfycence	1375
Trust me, Lyberte, it greveth me ryght sore	178	Magnyfycence	1375
In good faythe, syr, me semeth he had the more wronge.	178	Magnyfycence	1384
They drove me to lernynge lyke a dull asse.	178	Magnyfycence	1386
Not and your grace wolde be ruled by me.	179	Magnyfycence	1393
Mayster Survayour, Largesse to me call.	179	Magnyfycence	1398
Your grace sent for me, I wene. What is your wyll?	179	Magnyfycence	1410
Syr, as I say, there was no faute in me.	180	Magnyfycence	1426
Or lyberte by welth? Let se, tell me that.	180	Magnyfycence	1432
Syr, as me semeth, ye sholde be rulyd be me.	180	Magnyfycence	1433
Syr, as me semeth, ye sholde be rulyd be me.	180	Magnyfycence	1433
And wayte upon me. And yet for a memory,	180	Magnyfycence	1447
Well, get you hens than and sende me some other.	180	Magnyfycence	1451
Fortune to her lawys can not abandune me;	181	Magnyfycence	1459
All honour to me must nedys stowpe and lene.	181	Magnyfycence	1462
No stormy rage agaynst me can pervayle.	181	Magnyfycence	1465
He may not be comparyd unto me.	181	Magnyfycence	1476
I reyne in my robys, I rule as me lyst,	181	Magnyfycence	1485
It wolde not become them with me for to mell;	182	Magnyfycence	1497
To me all prynces to lowte man bese[m]e.	182	Magnyfycence	1500
beseme] 'be sene' †Rastell & Treveris C 1530, B			
Nor no man on molde can make me aferd.	182	Magnyfycence	1505
What man is so maysyd with me that dare mete,	182	Magnyfycence	1506
Nor none so hardy of them with me that durste crake,	182	Magnyfycence	1513
A, syr, your grace me dothe extole and rayse;	183	Magnyfycence	1525
And ferre beyond my merytys ye me commende and prayse.	183	Magnyfycence	1526
Truste me, with you I am hyghly pleasyd;	183	Magnyfycence	1535
With me in kepynge suche a Phylyp Sparowe.	184	Magnyfycence	1562
They towche me so thorowly and tykyll my consayte,	184	Magnyfycence	1567
Me to permyt my mynde to dyscharge,	185	Magnyfycence	1590
Be it ryght or wronge, by the advyse of me,	185	Magnyfycence	1597
Yet I am not harte seke, but me lyst.	185	Magnyfycence	1621
Stand up, syr. Ye are welcom to me.	186	Magnyfycence	1632
That for hym to laboure he hath prayde me hartely;	186	Magnyfycence	1650
To trust in me he is but dyssayved;	186	Magnyfycence	1652
For, so helpe me God, for you he is not mete.	186	Magnyfycence	1653
Ye, by my trouthe, I shall waraunt you for me,	187	Magnyfycence	1669
And made instance for me be lykelyhod.	188	Magnyfycence	1697
Them that dare put theyr truste in me;	188	Magnyfycence	1699
Syr, as ye say. Nay, come on with me.	188	Magnyfycence	1707
With me no longer. Say somwhat nowe, let se,	188	Magnyfycence	1719
What! Woldest thou, lurden, with me brawle agayne?	188	Magnyfycence	1722
Abyde, syr, abyde. Let me holde your hede.	189	Magnyfycence	1727
God gyve hym a myscheffe! Nay, nowe let me alone.	189	Magnyfycence	1730
Nay, so God me helpe, it was no grete vexacyon;	189	Magnyfycence	1733
Syr, nowe me thynke your harte is well eased.	189	Magnyfycence	1737
Let me have the rule of your purse.	189	Magnyfycence	1762
But use your largesse by the advyse of me,	189	Magnyfycence	1765
Say on; me thynke your reasons be profounde.	190	Magnyfycence	1767
Thou sayst truthe, by the harte that God me gave!	190	Magnyfycence	1782
Syr, syth that in me ye have suche devocyon,	190	Magnyfycence	1790
Commyttynge to me and to my felowes twayne	190	Magnyfycence	1791
Me to enbrace and love moost specyally.	190	Magnyfycence	1800

ME — ME

	Page	Title	Line
If ever I herde syke another, God gyve me shame.	192	Magnyfycence	1833
Ye, let be thy japes, and tell me howe	192	Magnyfycence	1846
What! Hath Sadnesse begyled me so?	192	Magnyfycence	1855
Gone? Alasse, ye have undone me!	192	Magnyfycence	1858
Full fewe but they have envy of me.	195	Magnyfycence	1963
Ryse up, syr, and welcom unto me.	195	Magnyfycence	1966
Unto your maker that made bothe you and me;	196	Magnyfycence	1992
A, Lord God, how the gowte wryngeth me by the too.	198	Magnyfycence	2047
I kyst her swete, and she kyssyd me;	198	Magnyfycence	2065
I lyve as me lyst, I lepe out at large;	199	Magnyfycence	2080
But yet, syrs, hardely one thynge lerne of me:	199	Magnyfycence	2087
Howe he is undone by the meanes of me?	200	Magnyfycence	2110
That nonnes wyl leve theyr holynes and ryn after me;	201	Magnyfycence	2146
They cast up theyr obedyence to cache me agayne;	201	Magnyfycence	2148
Yonder is a horson for me doth rechate;	201	Magnyfycence	2151
She hath dyssayvyd me with her doublenesse.	201	Magnyfycence	2157
For to be wyse all men may lerne of me,	201	Magnyfycence	2158
Ye, but thanke me therof every dele.	201	Magnyfycence	2171
Ye, wylte thou clenly cle[v]e me in the clyfte with thy nose? cleve] 'clene' †Rastell & Treveris C 1530, B	202	Magnyfycence	2176
What! Wylte thou skelpe me? Thou dare not loke on a gnat.	202	Magnyfycence	2181
Go together by the heddys, and gyve me your swordys.	202	Magnyfycence	2199
By the masse, man, thou shall fynde me resonable.	202	Magnyfycence	2204
Mary, syr, this gentylman caled me javell.	203	Magnyfycence	2211
Nay, by Saynt Mary, it was ye called me knave.	203	Magnyfycence	2212
Mary, so ungoodly langage you me gave.	203	Magnyfycence	2213
Me thynke ye are not gretly acomberyd wyth wyt.	203	Magnyfycence	2215
Tell me brefly where upon ye began.	203	Magnyfycence	2224
Your trymynge and tramynge by me must be tangyd,	203	Magnyfycence	2234
And nowe on me ye gaure and sporne.	204	Magnyfycence	2247
Nowe gyve me somwhat, for God sake, I crave.	204	Magnyfycence	2251
Alas, myn owne servauntys to shew me such reproche!	205	Magnyfycence	2277
Thus to rebuke me and have me in dyspyght!	205	Magnyfycence	2278
Thus to rebuke me and have me in dyspyght!	205	Magnyfycence	2278
So shamfully to me, theyr mayster, to aproche,	205	Magnyfycence	2279
I am wery of the worlde, for unkyndnesse me sleeth.	205	Magnyfycence	2283
Nay; rather wyll I chose to ryd me of this lyve	206	Magnyfycence	2321
Out harowe! Hyll burneth! Where shall I me hyde?	206	Magnyfycence	2324
Who knoweth me, hymselfe may never sloo.	206	Magnyfycence	2330
That dyspayre well nyghe had myscheved me;	206	Magnyfycence	2332
Wynde you from wanhope and aquaynte you with me.	206	Magnyfycence	2340
More delectable than your langage to me.	207	Magnyfycence	2348
And sore I repent me of my wylfulnesse;	207	Magnyfycence	2379
Me humbly commyttynge unto Goddys wyll.	208	Magnyfycence	2382
Questyonlesse he doth me assure	208	Magnyfycence	2395
To sende over to me Sad Cyrcumspeccyon.	208	Magnyfycence	2400
And be ruled by me, whiche am called Redresse.	208	Magnyfycence	2410
Syr, after your message I hyed me hyder streyght,	209	Magnyfycence	2419
Caused me of adversyte to fall in subjeccyon.	209	Magnyfycence	2425
But, syr, by me to rule fyrst ye began.	209	Magnyfycence	2431
Sothely to repent me I have grete cause;	209	Magnyfycence	2434
Syr, this letter ye sent to me at Pountes was enclosed.	209	Magnyfycence	2439
Truth it is, syr; for after he wrought me moch shame,	209	Magnyfycence	2444
And caused me also to use to moche lyberte,	209	Magnyfycence	2445
And made also mesure to be put fro me.	209	Magnyfycence	2446
And sad cyrcumspeccyon to me they have annexyd.	210	Magnyfycence	2463
Syth unto me formest this processe is erectyd,	211	Magnyfycence	2482
Herein I wyll aforse me to shewe you my mynde:	211	Magnyfycence	2483
But, Perseveraunce, me semyth your probleme was best;	212	Magnyfycence	2505
By hym that me bought!'	218	El Rummynge	167
With, 'Get me a staffe, /The swyne eate my draffe!	218	El Rummynge	170
For ye may prove it by me.'	219	El Rummynge	216
He calleth me his whytyng, /His mullyng and his [m]ytyng, mytyng] 'nytyng' †Lant 1545, Kynge & Marche 1554, 'nittine' Day 1560, 'nittine' Marshe 1568	220	El Rummynge	223
To cease me semeth best,	220	El Rummynge	235
And ye wyll gyve me a syppet /Of your stale ale,	223	El Rummynge	367
'And let me with you bybyll.'	228	El Rummynge	550
'Have here is for me, /A clout of London pynnes.'	228	El Rummynge	563
Tyll Eufrates, that flodde, dryvythe me into Ynde,	231	Speke Parott	4
Where men of that contre by fortune me fynde,	231	Speke Parott	5
And send me to greate ladyes of estate; to greate ladyes] 'to grece to lordys' †MS Harley 2252	231	Speke Parott	6
As [Per]cius, that poete, dothe reporte of me, Percius] 'precius' †MS Harley 2252	231	Speke Parott	27
Vis consilii expers, as techythe me Orace,	232	Speke Parott	40
Gave me a gyfte in my neste when I lay, I] 'he' †MS Harley 2252	232	Speke Parott	44
With, 'Bas me, swete Parrot, bas me, swete swete;'	233	Speke Parott	104
With, 'Bas me, swete Parrot, bas me, swete swete;'	233	Speke Parott	104
Turne ons agayne to me;	237	Speke Parott	237
Nowe torne agayne to me.	237	Speke Parott	245
My propyr Besse, /To turne agayne to me.	237	Speke Parott	251
I pray the, Besse, unfayned, /Yet com agayne to me!	238	Speke Parott	256
My propyr Besse, /And torne agayne to me!	238	Speke Parott	262
Now kusse me, Parot, kus me, kus, kus;	238	Speke Parott	265
Now kusse me, Parot, kus me, kus, kus;	238	Speke Parott	265
Of on and hothyr at me that have dysdayne.	242	Speke Parott	385

ME—ME

	Page	Title	Line
Alas, they make me shoder,	248	Collyn Clout	68
Take me as I entende,	251	Collyn Clout	185
I reporte me to you.	257	Collyn Clout	432
For Tholome tolde me	258	Collyn Clout	467
For it maketh me sad	259	Collyn Clout	511
Shall nat be objected by me.	266	Collyn Clout	794
by] 'for' Kele 1545.1, Marshe 1568, 'at by' MS Harley 2252			
Take upon me /Thus copyously to wryte,	273	Collyn Clout	1084
Take upon me] 'Take now upon' Kele 1545.1, 'I take now uppon' MS Harley 2252			
Why than /Wreke ye your anger on me?	273	Collyn Clout	1091
Agaynst me to be gr[am]ed,	274	Collyn Clout	1114
gramed] 'greved' †Godfray 1531, Kele 1545.1, Marshe 1568, MS Harley 2252			
Wherfore, as thynketh me,	274	Collyn Clout	1129
Me semeth it for the best.	277	Collyn Clout	1250
With, 'Do thou for me,	286	Why Come Ye	279
By God that me dere bought!	290	Why Come Ye	451
By] 'But' Marshe 1568			
Tell you the rest; for me they shal.	296	Why Come Ye	709
Tell me nowe in this stede,	298	Why Come Ye	786
Marke me that chase	301	Why Come Ye	883
me] 'well' MS Rawlinson C. 813			
Bytwene him and me;	308	Why Come Ye	1150
Blame Juvinall, and blame nat me.	309	Why Come Ye2	8
That, me to rest, I lent me to a stumpe	312	Garlande	17
That, me to rest, I lent me to a stumpe	312	Garlande	17
But sodeynly at ones, as I me advysed,	313	Garlande	36
How you gave me a ryall commaundement	313	Garlande	58
you] 'ye' Marshe 1568, MS Cotton Vitellius E.x; a] 'in' MS Cot. Vit. E.x			
Whereto made ye me hym to avaunce	315	Garlande	115
For, but if your bounte did me assure,	316	Garlande	146
That he so sholde be, me semith it sittyng,	316	Garlande	149
it] 'it is' MS Cotton Vitellius E.x			
Theis people by me have none assignement,	317	Garlande	195
'Nay, holde thy tunge,' quod another, 'let me have the name.'	319	Garlande	255
In so moche the stumpe, whereto I me lente	320	Garlande	281
'Daphnes, my derlynge, why do you me refuse?	320	Garlande	297
Yet loke on me, that lovyd you have so longe,	320	Garlande	298
Why have the goddes shewyd me this cruelte,	321	Garlande	309
Unto me; alas, that herbe nor gresse	321	Garlande	314
gresse] 'gras' †Fakes 1523			
Odious Disdayne, why raist thou me on this facyon?	321	Garlande	317
All famous poetis ensuynge after me	321	Garlande	321
That frownyd on me full angerly and pale;	322	Garlande	375
As I ymagenyd, repayrid unto me,	323	Garlande	392
And of there bounte they made me godely chere	323	Garlande	398
'So have ye me far passynge my meretis extollyd,	324	Garlande	435
And ever they presed on me more and more,	324	Garlande	445
Tyll at the last they forcyd me sore,	324	Garlande	446
sore] 'so sore' Marshe 1568			
That with them I went where they wolde me brynge,	324	Garlande	447
Dame Pallas commaundid that they shold me convay	325	Garlande	449
And lette me come to delyver my lettre.'	326	Garlande	506
With, 'Now let me come', and 'Now let me go.'	326	Garlande	515
With, 'Now let me come', and 'Now let me go.'	326	Garlande	515
Unto me sayd, 'Lo, syr, now ye may se	326	Garlande	518
Came towarde me, and smylid halfe in game;	327	Garlande	529
With that on me she kest her goodly loke.	327	Garlande	531
Under her arme, me thought, she hade a boke.	327	Garlande	532
Welcome to me as hertely as herte can thynke!	327	Garlande	547
Welcome to me with all my hole desyre!	327	Garlande	548
'Come on with me,' she sayd, 'let us not stonde';	328	Garlande	559
And with that worde she toke me by the honde.	328	Garlande	560
Into a felde she brought me wyde and large,	328	Garlande	568
She went before, and bad me take good holde;	328	Garlande	573
Wherto she answeryd, and brevely me tolde	328	Garlande	576
And seryously she shewyd me ther denominacyons.	328	Garlande	581
Then I me lent, and loked over the wall:	329	Garlande	602
And, sir, amonge all me thought I saw twaine,	329	Garlande	633
Of that aventuris, whiche made me sore agast.	330	Garlande	649
Then furthermore aboute me my syght I revolde,	330	Garlande	664
But, goodly maystres, one thynge ye me tell.'	332	Garlande	720
'Of your demawnd shew me the content,	332	Garlande	721
'I thanke you, goodly maystres, to me most benynge,	332	Garlande	728
That of your bounte so well have me assurid;	332	Garlande	729
Gog gyve you good yere, ye make me to smyle.	332	Garlande	736
She brought me to a goodly chaumber of astate,	333	Garlande	768
to] 'into' MS Cotton Vitellius E.x			
With, 'Reche me that skane of tewly sylk';	334	Garlande	798
And, 'Wynde me that botowme of such an hew',	334	Garlande	799
an] 'a' MS Cotton Vitellius E.x			
To worke me this chapelet by goode advysemente.	334	Garlande	807
I me determynyd for to sharpe my pen,	335	Garlande	823
She to vowchesafe me to informe and ken;	335	Garlande	825
Me to supporte, to helpe, and to assist,	335	Garlande	827
Humbly and low /Commendynge me /To yowre bownte.	338	Garlande	931

MEALE —MEASURE	Page	Title	Line
So I, iwus, /Endevoure me	338	Garlande	936
Cause me to cese, /Amonge this prese,	339	Garlande	957
Trust me, ententifly,	339	Garlande	962
Yet nowe doutles ye geve me cause	341	Garlande	1041
For nowe dowtles ye geve me cause	342	Garlande	1049
Wherfore doutles ye geve me cause	342	Garlande	1057
That in me were grete blyndnes,	342	Garlande	1064
Before remembred, me curteisly brought	343	Garlande	1102
me curteisly] 'kurteisly me' MS Cotton Vitellius E.x			
Into that place where as they left me,	343	Garlande	1103
She wonderyd, me thought, at my laurell grene;	343	Garlande	1116
She loked hawtly, and gave on me a glum.	344	Garlande	1117
For eche man herkynde what she wolde to me say;	344	Garlande	1119
wolde to me] 'to me wold' MS Cotton Vitellius E.x			
Of what charge so ever ye lay ageinst me;	344	Garlande	1138
And so Occupacyon, your regester, me told.'	344	Garlande	1141
Caliope poynted me where I shulde sit.	344	Garlande	1143
And shew now unto me	350	Garlande	1361
Dun is in the myre, dame, reche me my spur.	352	Garlande	1433
God wote, theis wordes made me full sad;	353	Garlande	1484
Now hereof it erkith me lenger to wryte,	354	Garlande	1491
The starry hevyn, me thought, shoke with the showte;	354	Garlande	1508
Dunbar, Dunde, /Ye shall trowe me,	359	Albany	25
Brevely and rounde /To me expounde.	361	Albany	83
And nowe I wyll me dresse	369	Albany	399
With me ye must consent	384	Replycacion	362

MEALE

Somtyme meale and salte,	267	Collyn Clout	843

MEANE

For measure is a meane, nother to hy nor to lawe,	145	Magnyfycence	188
Ye wote well what we meane.'	229	El Rummynge	579
That Lumberdes nose meane I	308	Why Come Ye	1186
I meane Domyngo Lomelyn /That was wont to wyn	308	Why Come Ye	1190
But ye meane a thyng	361	Albany	91
Ye meane Fraunces, French kyng,	367	Albany	334

MEANES

And how I maye that waye and meanes fynde.'	49	Bowge	109
Devysynge the meanes and wayes that I can,	160	Magnyfycence	708
And so, by these meanes, I brewe moche bale.	161	Magnyfycence	744
By the meanes of money without ony gonne.	184	Magnyfycence	1578
By meanes of madnesse and to moche lyberte.	199	Magnyfycence	2100
Howe he is undone by the meanes of me?	200	Magnyfycence	2110
Yet be meanes of that vyse	378	Replycacion	131

MEANYS

By meanys of a grosely endarkyd clowde	330	Garlande	645

MEASURE

Mayster Measure, you be come in good season.	143	Magnyfycence	84
Can be content with Measure presence.	143	Magnyfycence	86
So it in measure be.	143	Magnyfycence	101
With every condycyon measure must be sought.	143	Magnyfycence	115
Welthe without measure wolde bere hymselfe to bolde;	143	Magnyfycence	116
Lyberte without measure prove a thynge of nought.	143	Magnyfycence	117
I[n] ponder, by nomber, by measure all thynge is wrought,	143	Magnyfycence	118
In] 'I' †Rastell & Treveris C 1530, B			
Whych provyth well that measure shold have domynyon.	143	Magnyfycence	120
Where measure is mayster, plenty dothe none offence;	144	Magnyfycence	121
Where measure lackyth, all thynge dysorderyd is;	144	Magnyfycence	122
Where measure is absent, ryot kepeth resydence;	144	Magnyfycence	123
Where measure is ruler, there is nothynge amysse.	144	Magnyfycence	124
Measure is treasure. Howe say ye, is it not this?	144	Magnyfycence	125
Measure is worthy to have domynyon.	144	Magnyfycence	127
Ye, lyberte with measure nede never drede.	144	Magnyfycence	130
What, lyberte to measure then wolde ye bynde?	144	Magnyfycence	131
Lyberte without measure is acountyd for a beste;	144	Magnyfycence	138
There is no surfet where measure rulyth the feste;	144	Magnyfycence	139
There is no excesse where measure hath his helthe.	144	Magnyfycence	140
Measure contynwyth prosperyte and welthe.	144	Magnyfycence	141
It i[s] no maystery. Tushe, let Measure procede,	144	Magnyfycence	150
is] 'it' †Rastell & Treveris C 1530, B			
For, without measure, poverte and nede	144	Magnyfycence	152
For myschefe wyll mayster us yf measure us forsake.	144	Magnyfycence	154
Welthe, with Measure and plesaunt Lyberte.	145	Magnyfycence	160
But Measure, my frende, what hyght this mannys name?	145	Magnyfycence	165
To the gydynge of my measure you bothe commyttynge;	145	Magnyfycence	175
That Measure be mayster us semeth it is syttynge.	145	Magnyfycence	176
So that welthe with measure shalbe conbyned,	145	Magnyfycence	179
And lyberte his large with measure shall make.	145	Magnyfycence	180
For by measure I warne you we thynke to be gydyd;	145	Magnyfycence	184
Measure and I wyll never be devydyd,	145	Magnyfycence	186
For measure is a meane, nother to hy nor to lawe,	145	Magnyfycence	188
That measure shall nevere departe from my syght.	145	Magnyfycence	190
For welthe without measure sodenly wyll slyde.	145	Magnyfycence	192
Measure with noblenesse sholde be alyde.	145	Magnyfycence	194
Then, Lyberte, se that Measure by your gyde,	146	Magnyfycence	195
Bycause course of measure - yf I be in the way:	146	Magnyfycence	213
For defaute of measure all thynge dothe excede.	146	Magnyfycence	217
Yet measure hath ben so longe from us absent,	146	Magnyfycence	221
That all is without measure and fer beyonde the mone.	146	Magnyfycence	224

MEATE —MEDLEY   Page   Title   Line

	Page	Title	Line
Without measure lyghtly may fade,	146	Magnyfycence	228
Wherfore, Measure, take Lyberte with you hence,	146	Magnyfycence	230
The rule of Measure, notwithstandynge we	147	Magnyfycence	242
Have deputyd Measure hym to gyde?	147	Magnyfycence	243
By measure eche thynge duly is tryde.	147	Magnyfycence	244
But yf I were orderyd by just measure,	147	Magnyfycence	249
Largesse is laudable so it be in measure.	148	Magnyfycence	278
'in measure be' †Rastell & Treveris C 1530, B			
Measure is mete for a marchauntes hall	151	Magnyfycence	382
Beyonde measure /My sleve is wyde;	164	Magnyfycence	849
Holde thy pease! Measure shall frome us walke.	166	Magnyfycence	949
I am content so it in measure be.	179	Magnyfycence	1390
Nowe Measure is gone, I am the better pleased.	189	Magnyfycence	1738
So to be ruled by measure, it is a payne.	189	Magnyfycence	1739
Unto measure, I say, nowe a days.	189	Magnyfycence	1744
Measure? Tut, what the devyll of hell!	189	Magnyfycence	1745
Scantly one with measure that wyll dwell.	189	Magnyfycence	1746
Out of all measure themselfe to enryche;	189	Magnyfycence	1751
With pollynge and pluckynge out of all measure,	189	Magnyfycence	1753
Somtyme without measure he trusted in golde;	193	Magnyfycence	1894
And now without measure he shal have hunger and colde.	193	Magnyfycence	1895
For yf Measure had ruled Lyberte as he began,	200	Magnyfycence	2111
Grace of assystence his measure to declare;	207	Magnyfycence	2373
Measure of your lustys must have the oversyght,	211	Magnyfycence	2491
Clerkes out of measure,	250	Collyn Clout	145
MEATE			
In the stede of meate	83	Phy Sparrow	480
And myghty stronge meate	225	El Rummynge	433
Theyr neyghbours dye for meate.	254	Collyn Clout	320
Whan mammockes was your meate,	263	Collyn Clout	652
MEDDELYD			
Meddelyd with murnynge the moost parte of his muse,	320	Garlande	295
murnynge] 'murmynge' †Fakes 1523			
MEDDELS			
And meddels very lyght /In the churches ryght.	249	Collyn Clout	104
MEDE			
The more shal be your mede.	72	Phy Sparrow	16
Into Perce and Mede,	93	Phy Sparrow	886
From God am sente to quyte the thy mede.	193	Magnyfycence	1877
MEDEAS			
But whoso understode /Of Medeas arte,	76	Phy Sparrow	202
MEDECYNE			
But beggynge is better medecyne for the necke.	198	Magnyfycence	2045
MEDELED			
At me, that medeled nothyng with youre wark.	38	Coystrowne1	61
MEDELYD			
Metrifyde merely, medelyd with scornis;	351	Garlande	1382
scornis] 'stormis' †Fakes 1523			
MEDELYNG			
Youre medelyng, mastres, is manerles;	40	Coystrowne4	2
MEDELYNGE			
Sum medelynge spyes, by craft to grope thy mynde,	329	Garlande	617
MEDELLE			
With trowth to medelle was all his hole delight,	33	Dol Dethe	152
MEDIACIOUN			
He to vouchesaf, by thy mediacioun,	35	Dol Dethe	209
MEDITACYON			
And a mete meditacyon	270	Collyn Clout	971
MEDITACYOUN			
Item A[u]tomedon of Loves Meditacyoun;	346	Garlande	1181
Automedon] 'Antomedon' †Fakes 1523, Marshe 1568 MS Cotton			
Vitellius E.x			
MEDYACYON			
And may not atteyne it by no medyacyon,	321	Garlande	319
MEDYATOURE			
That wyll for me be medyatoure and mene;	48	Bowge	93
MEDYCYNABLE			
Sith I contryvyd first princyples medycynable?	321	Garlande	310
MEDYLL			
And medyll with Quintylyan in his Decla[m]acyons,	235	Speke Parott	177
Declamacyons] 'Declaracyons' †Lant 1545, Kynge & Marche 1554,			
Day 1560, Marshe 1568			
For drede ye darre not medyll with suche gere,	242	Speke Parott	394
MEDYLLAR			
Malapert, medyllar, nothyng well thewde,	133	Garnesche5	147
MEDYTACION			
And studyous medytacion	93	Phy Sparrow	848
MEDYTACYON			
Devysyd this gostly medytacyon in Englysh:	39	Coystrowne3	I
MEDYTACYONS			
Of his makyng devoute medytacyons;	352	Garlande	1419
MEDYTATYON			
Whylis I stode musynge in this medytatyon,	313	Garlande	29
MEDLE			
I muster, I medle amonge these grete estates;	160	Magnyfycence	736
MEDLEY			
A medley to make of myrth with sadnes,	117	Ag Scottes	87

		Page	Title	Line
MEDLER				
A malaperte medler that pryeth for his pray,		37	Coystrowne1	45
And every mad medler must now be a maker.		235	Speke Parott	161
MEDLETH				
He clyttreth and he clatters, /He medleth and he smatters,		247	Collyn Clout	24
MEDLYNG				
To wyse is no vertue, to medlyng, to restles;		232	Speke Parott	61
MEDUSA				
And from Medusa, that mare,		73	Phy Sparrow	76
MEED				
How be it, mayden Meed /Made theym to be agreed;		65	Hauke	149
MEGERAS				
And from Megeras edders,		73	Phy Sparrow	78
MEYNE				
All trebyllys and tenours be rulyd by a meyne.		144	Magnyfycence	137
MEYNTAYNE				
Warre with our kynge to meyntayne.		114	Scot Kynge	55
MEKE				
Wranglynge, waywyrde, wytles, wraw, and nothyng meke.		124	Garnesche2	40
Benynge, corteise, and meke, /With wordes well devysid;		338	Garlande	918
MEKELY				
How may I your mokery mekely tollerate,		123	Garnesche2	1
Take it mekely, and thanke God of his grace;		197	Magnyfycence	2033
MEKENESSE				
Theyr chyldren, bycause that they have no mekenesse,		194	Magnyfycence	1924
MEKYLL				
And mekyll am I made of nowe adays.		152	Magnyfycence	430
MELANCHATES				
Melanchates, that hounde		79	Phy Sparrow	296
MELANCOLY				
And of melancoly mutabilite,		138	Ven Tongues	44
Come forthe, ye pope holy, /Full of melancoly!		381	Replycacion	248
MELCHISEDEC				
In him is fygured Melchisedec,		118	Ag Scottes	115
MELCHISEDECHE				
In hym is figured Melchisedeche,		114	Scot Kynge	23
MELCHISEDECK				
Melchisedeck mercyfull made Moloc mercyles.		232	Speke Parott	60
MELE				
Mele, salte or other thynge,		221	El Rummynge	279
Whyche cawsythe pore suters have many a hongry mele;		239	Speke Parott	311
MELEDYOUSLY				
Orpheus, the Traciane, herped meledyously		320	Garlande	272
MELL				
Deth wyll us quell /And with us mell.		39	Coystrowne3	24
It wolde not become them with me for to mell;		182	Magnyfycence	1497
But they are lothe to mell,		250	Collyn Clout	162
Therwith I wyll nat mell.		257	Collyn Clout	428
That they shall mell nor make,		271	Collyn Clout	1015
How darest thou, daucocke, mell?		275	Collyn Clout	1160
With Dalyda to mell, /That wanton damosell. that] 'the' Kitson 1560.7, Marshe 1568		284	Why Come Ye	211
Therewith I dare nat mell.		288	Why Come Ye	378
Whan they with hym shulde mell,		295	Why Come Ye	649
That therwith can mell.		296	Why Come Ye	685
In ryming and raylyng with hym for to mell,		353	Garlande	1475
Mell nat wyth Englyshe men.		362	Albany	146
With us, whan ever ye mell		363	Albany	182
MELLE				
Than with my poems for to melle.		132	Garnesche5	94
And yet he wyll melle		267	Collyn Clout	820
MELLES				
And with foundacyons melles,		257	Collyn Clout	415
MELLIS				
How the maters he mellis in com to small effecte;		240	Speke Parott	328
MELLYNG				
Thy mellyng is but mockyng.		366	Albany	298
MELLYNGE				
Howe some of you are mellynge.		271	Collyn Clout	985
MELLYS				
For with us he so mellys		303	Why Come Ye	961
MELODIOUS				
Mountith on hy with her melodious lay,		327	Garlande	535
MELODYOUSLY				
Melodyously it to devyse		93	Phy Sparrow	864
MELOTTES				
Some walke about in melottes,		268	Collyn Clout	864
MELOUDIOUSLY				
For Davyd, our poete, harped so meloudiously		383	Replycacion	339
MELPOMENE				
Melpomene, that fayre mayde, she burneshed his beke:		236	Speke Parott	209
MELPOMONE				
Melpomone, O muse tragedyall,		117	Ag Scottes	77
MEMBRES				
Maketh his membres swell		284	Why Come Ye	210
MEMORY				
And wayte upon me. And yet for a memory,		180	Magnyfycence	1447
Yf it be regystryd well in memory;		212	Magnyfycence	2513

	Page	Title	Line
MEMORYALL —MEN			
Of jentyll corage the perfight memory;	336	Garlande	860
perfight] 'profight' †Fakes 1523			
Therfore I render of her the memory	339	Garlande	971
MEMORYALL			
In elect uteraunce to make memoryall!	29	Dol Dethe	11
Make a larger memoryall	299	Why Come Ye	824
larger] 'large' Marshe 1568			
But if he had made sum memoryall,	315	Garlande	118
MEN			
He calde upon them, as menyall houshold men:	30	Dol Dethe	33
Bot men say thei wer lynked with a double chayn	31	Dol Dethe	75
Trustinge in noble men that wer with hym there;	31	Dol Dethe	90
In fee, as menyall men of his houshold,	34	Dol Dethe	185
Which men the viii dedly syn call.	36	Coystrowne1	5
syn] 'sins' Marshe 1568			
Of Martyn Swart and all hys mery men.	37	Coystrowne1	18
'Why? What than? Wylte thou lete men to speke?	51	Bowge	184
I lete her to hyre that men maye on her ryde;	57	Bowge	402
That cuckoldes men call;	88	Phy Sparrow	648
Men se hym now and than	88	Phy Sparrow	657
than] 'then' Marshe 1568			
And now men wold have amended	91	Phy Sparrow	797
Yet some men fynde a faute,	92	Phy Sparrow	811
To lettred men at large:	105	Phy Sparrow	1361
Of him shuld men report,	121	Ag Scottes2	33
But sche of all men	125	Garnesche3	65
Men sey ye wyll wax lowsy, /Drunkyn, drowpy, drowsy.	127	Garnesche3	135
Defendeth with his pen /All Englysh men	135	Dundas	22
Controlle the cognisaunce of noble men	137	Ven Tongues	22
Men said they could not their tunges atame;	139	Ven Tongues	60
But men take upon theim nowe all the shame	139	Ven Tongues	61
For men be now tratlers and tellers of tales;	139	Ven Tongues	63
But men nowe a dayes so unhappely be uryd,	140	Magnyfycence	6
For, when men by welth, they have lytell drede	140	Magnyfycence	10
A, ye be wonders men!	143	Magnyfycence	89
That all men laugh at lyberte to scorne.	146	Magnyfycence	222
Yet amonge noble men I was brought up and bred.	147	Magnyfycence	261
By God, syr, ye se but fewe wyse men of myne age.	148	Magnyfycence	289
Wel, wyse men may ete the fysshe when ye shal draw the pole.	148	Magnyfycence	300
But ofte tymes have I sene wyse men do mad dedys.	148	Magnyfycence	302
And in dede, syr, I here men talke -	151	Magnyfycence	374
As men dare speke it hugger mugger:	151	Magnyfycence	387
What so ever I do, all men me prayse,	152	Magnyfycence	429
Counterfet worshyp outwarde men may se;	153	Magnyfycence	473
Monkys may not for drede that men sholde them se.	154	Magnyfycence	493
There dwelleth a mayster men calleth Mesure -	158	Magnyfycence	631
Nowe let se. Quyte you lyke praty men!	159	Magnyfycence	688
Whan other men laughe, than study I and muse,	160	Magnyfycence	707
That all men it founde /Through out Englonde.	165	Magnyfycence	882
That men hym gyve.	165	Magnyfycence	908
All men beware of suche folys!	175	Magnyfycence	1265
For, frantyke Fansy, thou makyst men madde;	176	Magnyfycence	1300
For I here but fewe men that gyve ony prayse	189	Magnyfycence	1743
I make God avowe ye wyll none other men have.	191	Magnyfycence	1827
Bycause I wolde prove men of theyr pacyence.	194	Magnyfycence	1917
That sadly rule not theyr howsholde men.	195	Magnyfycence	1940
I am Poverte that all men doth hate.	195	Magnyfycence	1960
For to be wyse all men may lerne of me,	201	Magnyfycence	2158
Her lewde lyppes twayne, /They slaver, men sayne,	215	El Rummynge	23
And, as men say, /She dwelt in Sothray,	216	El Rummynge	95
They care not what men saye!	221	El Rummynge	260
Where men of that contre by fortune me fynde,	231	Speke Parott	5
Now pandes mory, wax frantycke som men sey;	232	Speke Parott	46
mory] 'mery' †MS Harley 2252; men] 'mad' †MS Harley 2252			
In flattryng fables men fynde but lyttyl fayth;	233	Speke Parott	87
Parrot is no pendugum, that men call a carlyng,	236	Speke Parott	205
Parrot is no stameryng stare, that men call a starlyng;	236	Speke Parott	207
Muche money, men sey, there madly he hathe spente;	240	Speke Parott	335
Dothe grudge and complayne /Upon the temporall men.	248	Collyn Clout	65
Men say they have prescrypcyons	249	Collyn Clout	112
Howebeit they are good men,	251	Collyn Clout	167
Men say, they had rather	251	Collyn Clout	175
I tell you as men say.	251	Collyn Clout	188
Men say, ye can nat appare;	251	Collyn Clout	191
Men call you therfore prophanes.	252	Collyn Clout	207
Men say, for sylver and golde,	254	Collyn Clout	289
Of symony, men say,	254	Collyn Clout	299
Men say ye are tonge-tayde,	255	Collyn Clout	354
Wherfore men be supposynge	255	Collyn Clout	357
Relygyous men are fayne /For to tourne agayne	256	Collyn Clout	374
Howebeit, per assimile, /Some men thynke that ye	258	Collyn Clout	460
Suche logyke men woll choppe,	259	Collyn Clout	528
Bothe women and men,	260	Collyn Clout	532
Men say howe ye appalle	262	Collyn Clout	611
As dayly men may se,	262	Collyn Clout	630
But men say your auctoryte	265	Collyn Clout	758
But men say] 'Men say but' †Godfray 1531, Kele 1545.1, Marshe 1568			

MENANDER — MENYS

Entry	Page	Title	Line
Men say, they bere no faces	269	Collyn Clout	896
Agaynst all spirytuall men.	272	Collyn Clout	1054
It is to drede, men sayes,	277	Collyn Clout	1228
As well as other men.	277	Collyn Clout	1247
All noble men of this take hede,	278	Why Come Ye	1
of this] not in MS Rawlinson C. 813			
All noble men of this take hede,	279	Why Come Ye	15
All noble men of this take hede,	279	Why Come Ye	27
Some men may happely rew,	280	Why Come Ye	60
He calleth us England men	285	Why Come Ye	275
That all our lerned men	287	Why Come Ye	322
All men must folow his desyre.	287	Why Come Ye	345
must] not in Marshe 1568			
But, as some men sayne,	288	Why Come Ye	362
Men may happely se	288	Why Come Ye	367
Men wolde have the lesse scorne	291	Why Come Ye	496
Well-syghted when /He is amonge blynde men?	292	Why Come Ye	535
All noble men shulde outface,	294	Why Come Ye	623
That men shall scantly /Have peny or halpeny.	303	Why Come Ye	967
Men wene that he is pocky,	308	Why Come Ye	1170
wene that] 'say' MS Rawlinson C. 813			
Some men myght aske a question,	309	Why Come Ye	1202
aske] 'make' MS Rawlinson C. 813			
And men lyst to harke,	309	Why Come Ye	1206
Few men can tell where the hynde calfe gose.	313	Garlande	26
tell] 'telle now' MS Cotton Vitellius E.x			
Then men wyll say how he doth but flatter.	314	Garlande	84
For men to loke on? Aristotille also,	315	Garlande	127
Some men be made of for the mokery;	317	Garlande	185
the] 'their' Marshe 1568			
Maintenaunce and Mischefe, theis be men of myght;	317	Garlande	193
Men of suche maters make but mummynge,	318	Garlande	200
but] 'but a' MS Cotton Vitellius E.x			
As people halfe pevysshe, or men that were masyd.	319	Garlande	266
Juvenall satirray, that men makythe to muse;	321	Garlande	340
With a frere of Fraunce men call Sir Gagwyne,	322	Garlande	374
Sum dysdanous dawcokkis that all men dispyse,	329	Garlande	618
Men call a phenix; her wynges bytwene	330	Garlande	668
Of men and of bestis, and whereof they begone,	331	Garlande	692
He wyll set men a feightynge and syt hymselfe styll,	333	Garlande	761
set] 'stir' MS Cotton Vitellius E.x; a feightynge]			
'to brawlyng' MS Cotton Vitellius E.x			
Item the Boke how Men Shulde Fle Synne;	345	Garlande	1173
But what of that? Hard it is to please all men;	348	Garlande	1259
To letterd men at large.	350	Garlande	1354
What constellacions ar good or bad for men,	352	Garlande	1429
How men were wonte for to discerne	352	Garlande	1441
Welcome shall ye /To sum men be;	355	Garlande	1541
Yet now and then /Sum Latin men	355	Garlande	1545
With mony, as men sayne,	358	Garlande2	14
Men call it a toyle.	365	Albany	269
As all men can reporte.	370	Albany	474
All men can testifye.	376	Replycacion	64
And yet some men say,	379	Replycacion	176
Men have you in suspicion	379	Replycacion	182
With other many holy men,	381	Replycacion	278

MENANDER

Entry	Page	Title	Line
The swan of Menander,	82	Phy Sparrow	434

MENANDERS

Entry	Page	Title	Line
Alexander, a gander of Menanders pole,	235	Speke Parott	173

MENDE

Entry	Page	Title	Line
He may helpe you. He may mende your mode.	207	Magnyfycence	2366
But mende your myndes that are mased;	382	Replycacion	293

MENDYD

Entry	Page	Title	Line
But good hope and redresse hath mendyd myne estate,	210	Magnyfycence	2462

MENE

Entry	Page	Title	Line
Hys dyscant is besy, it is withoute a mene;	37	Coystrownel	27
That wyll for me be medyatoure and mene;	48	Bowge	93
Fynde some mene to caste him over the borde.'	54	Bowge	308
In A loco, I mene juxta B:	60	Bowge	517
Yet mesure is a mery mene.	151	Magnyfycence	380
I synge of two partys without a mene.	181	Magnyfycence	1463
And we wyll be comonynge in the mene season.	187	Magnyfycence	1688
Nat for that I mene	297	Why Come Ye	746
'Now what ye mene, I trow I conject.	332	Garlande	735

MENES

Entry	Page	Title	Line
The menes to fynde /To please my mynde,	342	Garlande	1072

MENETH

Entry	Page	Title	Line
'Que pensez-voz, Parrot? What meneth this besynes?'	232	Speke Parott	58

MENGITH

Entry	Page	Title	Line
With decadis historious, whiche that he mengith	321	Garlande	345

MENYALL

Entry	Page	Title	Line
He calde upon them, as menyall houshold men:	30	Dol Dethe	33
In fee, as menyall men of his houshold,	34	Dol Dethe	185
His servauntes menyall	294	Why Come Ye	595

MENYS

Entry	Page	Title	Line
With othyr menys charge;	129	Garnesche3	188
By the menys of myschefe to bryng all thynges to nought.	159	Magnyfycence	702

	Page	Title	Line
MENYST —MERY			
That was by the menys of to moche lyberte.	180	Magnyfycence	1424
MENYST			
What the devyll, man, what thou menyst?	162	Magnyfycence	793
MENNES			
Even nor morow; /But other mennes sorow	94	Phy Sparrow	925
Where mennes belyes is mesured, there is no chere;	189	Magnyfycence	1742
MENNY			
Suche were there menny	230	El Rummynge	611
MENOLOPE			
That Dame Menolope was never half so wyse;	42	Balettys2	11
MENS			
And judge it as they wyll, /For other mens skyll,	249	Collyn Clout	99
It made sum mens eye dasild and dasid;	351	Garlande	1389
MENT			
What the sentence ment.	68	Hauke	227
Then questionyd I her what thos yatis ment;	328	Garlande	575
thos] 'these' Marshe 1568			
And if there be in it any thyng ment,	332	Garlande	723
What may be ment hereby,	378	Replycacion	153
MERCHAUNDYSE			
So myche losse of merchaundyse, and so remedyles;	245	Speke Parott	472
MERCIALL			
By merciall strength /He wan at length;	349	Garlande	1298
Of hardy merciall actes,	368	Albany	397
In merciall prowes /Lyke unto Hercules,	369	Albany	430
MERCILES			
All merciles in the ys no pite!	32	Dol Dethe	122
MERCY			
As thou art of mercy and pite the well,	34	Dol Dethe	198
O Quene of mercy, O lady full of grace,	34	Dol Dethe	204
Well of pite, of mercy, and of grace,	35	Dol Dethe	215
A porta inferi, /Good Lorde, have mercy	77	Phy Sparrow	240
God have mercy, good godfather.	176	Magnyfycence	1312
In Goddys mercy, I tell them, is but foly to truste;	205	Magnyfycence	2289
Though I aske mercy I must nedys be refusyd.	205	Magnyfycence	2299
That thou canst not have never mercy in his syght.	205	Magnyfycence	2303
I aske God mercy of my neglyge[sse],	207	Magnyfycence	2380
neglygesse] 'neglygence' †Rastell & Treveris C 1530, B			
And mercy for to crye,	377	Replycacion	88
And crye God mercy, lyke frantyke foles.	382	Replycacion	299
MERCYALL			
That bararag blowyth in every mercyall warre,	319	Garlande	236
Enyus that wrate of mercyall war at lengthe;	321	Garlande	347
MERCYFULL			
Which by his mercyfull rage	88	Phy Sparrow	670
mercyfull] 'unmercifull' Wyght 1553, Kitson 1560.6, Marshe 1568			
Melchisedeck mercyfull made Moloc mercyles.	232	Speke Parott	60
O mercyfull Jesu,	257	Collyn Clout	433
MERCYLES			
Melchisedeck mercyfull made Moloc mercyles.	232	Speke Parott	60
Shameles, and mercyles, /Incorrigible and insaciate;	276	Collyn Clout	1178
'O mercyles madame, hard is your constellacyon,	320	Garlande	304
MERCURY			
Of Mercury undyr the trynall aspecte,	240	Speke Parott	325
To Mercury also hertely prayed I then,	335	Garlande	826
MERELY			
So merely syngeth the nyghtyngale!	199	Magnyfycence	2077
Metrifyde merely, medelyd with scornis;	351	Garlande	1382
scornis] 'stormis' †Fakes 1523			
MERETIS			
'So have ye me far passynge my meretis extollyd,	324	Garlande	435
MERETORYOUSLY			
So have ye done, that meretoryously	323	Garlande	401
MERIT			
Let every man after his merit take his parte;	236	Speke Parott	199
MERITORY			
In rendrynge to you thankkis meritory,	324	Garlande	429
MERY			
Of Martyn Swart and all hys mery men.	37	Coystrownel	18
I wolde be mery that wynde that ever blowe,	53	Bowge	251
To make the mery, as other felowes done?	57	Bowge	380
Plucke up thyne herte upon a mery pyne,	57	Bowge	386
Some sad storyes, some mery,	87	Phy Sparrow	615
Her lyppes soft and mery	97	Phy Sparrow	1037
To thynke a mery thought	101	Phy Sparrow	1202
The mery moneth of September,	117	Ag Scottes	66
In fayth, broder Largesse, you have a mery mynde.	148	Magnyfycence	292
Yet mesure is a mery mene.	151	Magnyfycence	380
By Cryst, as mery as a Marche hare.	166	Magnyfycence	921
Somtyme to mery, somtyme to madde;	168	Magnyfycence	1010
'What howe! Be ye mery! Was it not well conveyed?'	177	Magnyfycence	1347
Whom? Lusty Pleasure or mery Consayte?	180	Magnyfycence	1452
Howe be it, that fonde felowe is a mery knave.	180	Magnyfycence	1455
Her mouthe enbawmed, dylectable and mery,	183	Magnyfycence	1557
By Cockes harte, thou arte a fyne mery knave.	191	Magnyfycence	1826
To mery, to mad, to gyglynge, to nyse,	199	Magnyfycence	2092
But nowe let us make mery and good chere.	204	Magnyfycence	2261

	Page	Title	Line
Shall lepe from this lyfe, as mery as we be.	236	Speke Parott	222
MERYLY			
These maydens full meryly with many a dyvers flowur	231	Speke Parott	11
a] not in †MS Harley 2252			
MERYTYS			
And ferre beyond my merytys ye me commende and prayse.	183	Magnyfycence	1526
MERMOSET			
What! Margery Mylke Ducke, mermoset!	153	Magnyfycence	457
MERVAYLE			
Grete mervayle I had, and mused in my mynde.	191	Magnyfycence	1822
Yet they mervayle so moche lesse,	271	Collyn Clout	1008
MERVELOUS			
Of mervelous conclusiouns, /And by her supersticiouns	350	Garlande	1342
MESE			
Among this prese - /Even a hole mese -	168	Magnyfycence	996
MESSAGE			
Syr, after your message I hyed me hyder streyght,	209	Magnyfycence	2419
MESSE			
Ye, Mary, somtyme - in a messe of vergesse,	189	Magnyfycence	1756
By the messe, I shall cleve thy heed to the waste.	201	Magnyfycence	2175
MESSENGERE			
Addressyng your selfe, lyke a sadde messengere,	239	Speke Parott	303
MESURE			
Hys musyk withoute mesure, to sharp is hys my;	37	Coystrowne1	25
Welthe, gete you home and commaunde me to Mesure.	149	Magnyfycence	316
Yet mesure is a mery mene.	151	Magnyfycence	380
By Mesure mastered yet is he.	155	Magnyfycence	541
In faythe, Mesure is lyke a tetter	155	Magnyfycence	543
Wherwith Mesure to confounde.	155	Magnyfycence	554
That Mesure were cast out of the dores.	156	Magnyfycence	568
Ye. But he spendeth it all in mesure.	157	Magnyfycence	621
Why, dwelleth Mesure where ye two dwell?	157	Magnyfycence	622
There dwelleth a mayster men calleth Mesure -	158	Magnyfycence	631
Mary, the better and Mesure were out.	158	Magnyfycence	656
That Mesure shall not there longe tary.	159	Magnyfycence	684
Mary, Mesure had hym a whyle in gydynge,	166	Magnyfycence	939
All mesure and good rule is gone quyte.	176	Magnyfycence	1315
When Mesure is gone, what nedest thou spare?	176	Magnyfycence	1323
Whan Mesure is gone, we may slee care.	176	Magnyfycence	1324
Remembre ye not how my lyberte by mesure ruled was?	178	Magnyfycence	1383
Must mesure, in the mares name, you furnysshe and dresse?	179	Magnyfycence	1391
For where is no mesure, howe may worshyp endure?	179	Magnyfycence	1408
So it be by mesure I am ryght well content.	180	Magnyfycence	1421
What! All by mesure, good syr, and none excesse?	180	Magnyfycence	1422
Here cometh in CLOKED COLUSYON with MESURE	186	Magnyfycence	SD
Remembre the good servyce that Mesure hath you done,	186	Magnyfycence	1637
Mesure, ye knowe wel, with hym I can not be content;	186	Magnyfycence	1656
Here MESURE goth out of the place.	188	Magnyfycence	SD
With Mesure. Where as all noblenes is, there I have past:	189	Magnyfycence	1749
Thus joy without mesure you shall have.	190	Magnyfycence	1781
That rule not be mesure that they have in theyr handys,	195	Magnyfycence	1939
And made also mesure to be put fro me.	209	Magnyfycence	2446
In mesure is tresure, cum sensu maturato:	232	Speke Parott	62
Transcendynge out of mesure,	292	Why Come Ye	548
So duly entunyd with every mesure,	320	Garlande	276
MESURED			
Where mennes belyes is mesured, there is no chere;	189	Magnyfycence	1742
MESURIS			
He fyndith fals mesuris out of his fonde fiddill.'	333	Garlande	742
fals mesuris out] 'owght fals mesuris' MS Cotton Vit.E.x			
MET			
For, in fayth, ye be well met.	151	Magnyfycence	402
Yes, yes, syr. He and I have met.	154	Magnyfycence	498
At my devyse I with her met;	199	Magnyfycence	2075
A ha, fansy and foly met with you, I trowe.	210	Magnyfycence	2448
What, brother Perceveraunce, surely well met!	210	Magnyfycence	2458
And fyll in good met;	222	El Rummynge	333
met] 'meate' Day 1560, Marshe 1568			
METE			
Youre key is mete for every lok,	41	Coystrowne4	22
But, no force, I shall ones mete with the;	55	Bowge	334
Her mete was very crude,	63	Hauke	77
mete] 'mere' Kynge & Marche 1554			
With Lumbardes lemmanns for to mete,	130	Garnesche5	42
It ys nat mete for soche a knave.	133	Garnesche5	156
Mary, Welthe and I was apoynted to mete,	141	Magnyfycence	24
You are nothynge mete with us for to dwell,	149	Magnyfycence	304
But largesse is not mete for every man.	150	Magnyfycence	369
Sayd I was mete for your grace.	150	Magnyfycence	373
Measure is mete for a marchauntes hall	151	Magnyfycence	382
By the masse, for the cowrte thou art a mete man;	161	Magnyfycence	764
With whom shall I there mete.	167	Magnyfycence	955
For me full mete.	167	Magnyfycence	976
That wysdome and I shall seldome mete.	170	Magnyfycence	1081
Cockys armys, a mete man for us!	172	Magnyfycence	1169
What man is so maysyd with me that dare mete,	182	Magnyfycence	1506
For, so helpe me God, for you he is not mete.	186	Magnyfycence	1653
For nowe go I wyll begge for you some mete.	197	Magnyfycence	2034

METELY — MIRRY

	Page	Title	Line
Then for to begge theyr mete for charyte.	198	Magnyfycence	2041
To get us there some freshe mete.	204	Magnyfycence	2264
But they say it is a queysy mete;	204	Magnyfycence	2267
They asked never for mete	222	El Rummynge	304
'Mete, mete, for Parrot, mete I say, how!'	233	Speke Parott	102
'Mete, mete, for Parrot, mete I say, how!'	233	Speke Parott	102
'Mete, mete, for Parrot, mete I say, how!'	233	Speke Parott	102
To dwell amonge ladyes, Parrot, is mete.	233	Speke Parott	105
For Jerico and Jerssey shall mete togethyr as sone	239	Speke Parott	306
Ar mete for a swyne herde to hunte after hogges.	240	Speke Parott	321
Whate sequele shall folow when pendugims mete togethyr?	243	Speke Parott	415
More mete in a pyllory -	266	Collyn Clout	812
And a mete meditacyon	270	Collyn Clout	971

METELY

	Page	Title	Line
If thow war metely machchyd.	128	Garnesche3	181
By my trouthe, we have ryfled hym metely well.	201	Magnyfycence	2170
Whereto were most metely my corage to knyt?	211	Magnyfycence	2479
'The west is wyndy.' 'The est is metely wele.'	326	Garlande	499

METER

	Page	Title	Line
There was counteryng of carollis in meter and verse	331	Garlande	705
and] 'and in' Marshe 1568			

METHYNKE

	Page	Title	Line
Methynke she is well becked to catche a rat.	166	Magnyfycence	927

METYNGE

	Page	Title	Line
The case requyreth. Alasse, alasse, an hevy metynge!	192	Magnyfycence	1847

METREFYDE

	Page	Title	Line
Whereupon he metrefyde after his mynde;	353	Garlande	1464

METRICALL

	Page	Title	Line
In metricall muses, his harpyng we may spare;	383	Replycacion	338

METRIFYDE

	Page	Title	Line
Metrifyde merely, medelyd with scornis;	351	Garlande	1382
scornis] 'stormis' †Fakes 1523			

METTE

	Page	Title	Line
Suspycyon, me thoughte, mette hym at a brayde,	51	Bowge	181
Anone ther mette with him, as me thoughte,	54	Bowge	282

MEVYD

	Page	Title	Line
With scornfull loke mevyd all in moode.	55	Bowge	317
scornfull] 'scorfull' Marshe 1568			

MEW

	Page	Title	Line
Yet lyberte hath ben lockyd up and kept in the mew.	141	Magnyfycence	35
And some theyr hedes mew.	280	Why Come Ye	61
some] not in Toy 1553, Kitson 1560.7, Marshe 1568			

MEWARDE

	Page	Title	Line
And to mewarde the strayte waye he toke.	51	Bowge	194
And to mewarde as he gan for to coost,	58	Bowge	431

MEWED

	Page	Title	Line
Fesaunt and partriche mewed,	284	Why Come Ye	222

MEWTAS

	Page	Title	Line
Is maister Mewtas dede,	298	Why Come Ye	787
And pray for Mewtas sowle;	300	Why Come Ye	832

MEWTE

	Page	Title	Line
'Lyke owur pus catt Parott can mewte and crye.'	231	Speke Parott	24
owur] 'your' Lant 1545, Kynge & Marche 1554, Day 1560, Marshe 1568			

MI

	Page	Title	Line
Mi wordis unpullysht be nakide and playne,	32	Dol Dethe	127
Whan I remembre agayn /How mi Philyp was slayn,	72	Phy Sparrow	18
But let mi masters mathematical	296	Why Come Ye	708
Mi litell lady I may not leve behinde,	337	Garlande	878

MIDDIS

	Page	Title	Line
In the middis a coundight, that coryously was cast,	330	Garlande	658

MIDSOMER

	Page	Title	Line
As mirry Margarete, /This midsomer flowre,	341	Garlande	1035
This] 'The' MS Cotton Vitellius E.x			
To face out her foly with a midsomer mase;	346	Garlande	1208

MIGHT

	Page	Title	Line
If any such might be found!	76	Phy Sparrow	188
Might poyson thy lyver and longes!	79	Phy Sparrow	293
Might plucke away thyne eares!	79	Phy Sparrow	310
Of the kynge of Naverne ye might take heed,	119	Ag Scottes	153
But thou lakest might,	136	Dundas	49
He might be sure to have shame ynough.	139	Ven Tongues	78
That one might se her token.	227	El Rummynge	497
Shet were the gatis; thei might wel knock and cal,	329	Garlande	604

MILK

	Page	Title	Line
With manerly Margery Milk and Ale.	36	Man Margery	28

MILLAR

	Page	Title	Line
The millar durst not leve his wyfe at home.	352	Garlande	1417

MIN

	Page	Title	Line
Me thought min hert was crased,	99	Phy Sparrow	1105

MINERVA

	Page	Title	Line
How Dame Minerva first found the Olyve Tre, she red	351	Garlande	1404

MIRRIELL

	Page	Title	Line
To my Lady Mirriell Howarde	337	Garlande	R

MIRRY

	Page	Title	Line
May this contente you and your mirry mynde?	332	Garlande	708
Mirry Margaret, /As mydsomer flowre,	340	Garlande	1004
Of mirry Margarete, /As mydsomer flowre,	341	Garlande	1019

	Page	Title	Line
As mirry Margarete, /This midsomer flowre,	341	Garlande	1034
This] 'The' MS Cotton Vitellius E.x			
'Be mirry,' she sayd, 'be not afferde a whit,	344	Garlande	1145
MIRTHE			
Moche mirthe and no madnes,	340	Garlande	1009
MISCARY			
Full soone ye should miscary,	367	Albany	342
MISCHEFE			
Maintenaunce and Mischefe, theis be men of myght;	317	Garlande	193
Moche mischefe, I hyght you, amonge theem ther happid.	330	Garlande	643
MISCHIEFE			
Worketh more mischiefe than can be tolde;	137	Ven Tongues	8
MISERACYON			
God of his miseracyon /Send better reformacyon!	305	Why Come Ye	1044
MISERY			
In wretched beggary /And maungy misery,	362	Albany	138
MISLYNG			
Immoysturid with mislyng and ay droppyng dry,	331	Garlande	698
MISTYCALL			
Upon this matter mistycall	299	Why Come Ye	821
MISTRES			
Sith mistres Jane Haiset	339	Garlande	968
MY			
With my rude pen enkankerd all with rust,	33	Dol Dethe	142
Ay, beshrewe yow! Be my fay	35	Man Margery	1
Avent, avent, my popagay!	35	Man Margery	3
'What, and ye shal be my piggesnye?'	36	Man Margery	17
Deme what thou lyst, thou knowyst not my thought.	38	Coystrownel	63
Youre ugly tokyn /My mynd hath brokyn /From worldly lust;	39	Coystrowne3	2
Then by my councell,	39	Coystrowne3	19
'My new furryd gowne, when it is worne –	40	Coystrowne4	10
'My darlyng dere, my daysy floure,	41	Balettys1	1
'My darlyng dere, my daysy floure,	41	Balettys1	1
'Ly styll', quod she, 'my paramoure,	41	Balettys1	3
'My lefe', she sayd, 'rowtyth in hys bed;	42	Balettys1	20
But that I must wryte for my plesaunt pastaunce	42	Balettys2	4
Illumynyd wyth feturys far passyng my reporte;	44	Balettys3	23
Which makyth my hart oft to lepe and sprynge	44	Balettys3	32
You I assure, absens is my fo,	44	Balettys3	36
My dedely wo, my paynfull hevynes.	44	Balettys3	37
My dedely wo, my paynfull hevynes.	44	Balettys3	37
Open myne hart, beholde my mynde expres.	44	Balettys3	39
Of my trew hart, to love her best of all!	45	Balettys3	49
For whose sake my hart is sore dyseasyd;	45	Balettys5	9
Yet, and God wold, I wold my payne were easyd!	45	Balettys5	12
Avysynge me my penne awaye to pulle	46	Bowge	21
Thus up and down my mynde was drawen and cast	47	Bowge	29
But my dysporte they could not well endure:	50	Bowge	145
To dwell with us and serve my ladyes grace.	50	Bowge	156
That I must shewe you moche of my counselle –	52	Bowge	207
Than I assured hym my fydelyte,	52	Bowge	218
Els, I prayed hym with all my besy cure,	52	Bowge	221
But as I stode musynge in my mynde,	52	Bowge	230
Whan I loked on hym, my purse was half aferde.	52	Bowge	238
My wytte wolde waste, I make God avowe.	53	Bowge	243
And lerne me to synge Re my fa sol!	53	Bowge	258
The favoure that ye have with my lady.	53	Bowge	270
And yet unneth I can have my lyvynge;	53	Bowge	275
That he loked pale as asshes to my syghte.	54	Bowge	293
Of my querell soone wolde I venged be.	55	Bowge	333
By Goddis syde, my sworde thy berde shall shave!	55	Bowge	339
Ay, in my pouche a buckell I have founde;	57	Bowge	397
To wete yf Malkyn, my lemman, have gete oughte.	57	Bowge	401
To her wyll I nowe all my poverte lege.	57	Bowge	412
And as I stode and kyste asyde my syghte,	58	Bowge	418
kyste] 'caste' Marshe 1568			
Yet on my backe I bere suche lewde delynge.	59	Bowge	457
And by my trouthe, but yf an ende they make,	59	Bowge	473
I have a stoppynge oyster in my poke,	59	Bowge	477
He had plucte oute the nobles of my pouche.	60	Bowge	504
To hawke in my church of Dys.	62	Hauke	42
Upon my corporas face.	63	Hauke	63
Agaynst my mynde and wyll	64	Hauke	98
In my church hawke styll.	64	Hauke	99
Downe went my offerynge box,	64	Hauke	111
They rangyd Hankyn Bovy /My churche all abowte.	65	Hauke	118
'These be my gospellers,	65	Hauke	120
These be my pystyllers,	65	Hauke	121
These be my querysters /To helpe me to synge,	65	Hauke	122
My hawkes to mattens rynge!'	65	Hauke	124
Into my chalys at mas,	66	Hauke	184
Wherto shuld I rehers /The sentens of my vers?	68	Hauke	247
To shake in my pygyons federis	69	Hauke	281
It can not be exprest /My sorowfull hevynesse,	72	Phy Sparrow	32
My sparow dead and colde,	72	Phy Sparrow	40
Wherewith my handes I wrange /That my senaws cracked	72	Phy Sparrow	45
Wherewith my handes I wrange /That my senaws cracked	73	Phy Sparrow	46
For that I was robbed /Of my sparowes lyfe.	73	Phy Sparrow	52

	Page	Title	Line
My vysage pale and dead,	73	Phy Sparrow	60
Well nye had stopped my breath.	73	Phy Sparrow	63
had] not in Wyght 1553, Kitson 1560.6, Marshe 1568			
I fele my body quake,	74	Phy Sparrow	105
Encreaseth my dedly wo, /For my sparowe is go.	74	Phy Sparrow	113
Encreaseth my dedly wo, /For my sparowe is go.	74	Phy Sparrow	114
And lerned after my scole	74	Phy Sparrow	117
And wold syt upon my lap,	74	Phy Sparrow	121
Betwene my brestes softe	74	Phy Sparrow	125
Whan I sawe my sparowe dye!	75	Phy Sparrow	146
Nowe, after my dome,	75	Phy Sparrow	147
My sparowe to commende,	75	Phy Sparrow	155
Of my sparowe royall.	75	Phy Sparrow	158
Upon my naked skyn.	76	Phy Sparrow	167
He dyd nothynge, perde, /But syt upon my kne.	76	Phy Sparrow	172
To pyke my lytell too,	76	Phy Sparrow	176
My sparowe than shuld be quycke	77	Phy Sparrow	205
I toke my sampler ones	77	Phy Sparrow	210
My sparow whyte as mylke,	77	Phy Sparrow	213
For my solas and sporte.	77	Phy Sparrow	218
Me thought my sparow did spek,	77	Phy Sparrow	220
With that my nedle waxed red,	77	Phy Sparrow	225
waxed] 'ware' Marshe 1568			
My speche was taken away.	77	Phy Sparrow	229
My fyngers, dead and colde,	77	Phy Sparrow	233
Coude not my sampler holde;	77	Phy Sparrow	234
My nedle and threde	77	Phy Sparrow	235
Upon my sparowes soule,	77	Phy Sparrow	241
Wryten in my bede roule!	77	Phy Sparrow	242
Any of my sparowes kynde.	78	Phy Sparrow	261
As my sparowe was.	78	Phy Sparrow	265
But my sparowe dyd pas	78	Phy Sparrow	266
My lytell prety sparowe	78	Phy Sparrow	280
Whan thou my byrde untwynde,	79	Phy Sparrow	284
So trayterously my byrde to kyll	79	Phy Sparrow	322
To se my sorow new.	80	Phy Sparrow	337
Alas, my face waxeth pale,	80	Phy Sparrow	341
How my byrde so fayre,	80	Phy Sparrow	343
And go in at my spayre,	80	Phy Sparrow	345
go in] 'often' Kitson 1560.6			
And crepe in at my gore	80	Phy Sparrow	346
crepe] 'gape' Kitson 1560.6			
Of my gowne before,	80	Phy Sparrow	347
Alas, my hert it stynges,	80	Phy Sparrow	349
My Phyllyppes dolefull deth!	80	Phy Sparrow	352
Upon my fynger aloft!	80	Phy Sparrow	356
And fed him with my spattyl,	80	Phy Sparrow	358
With his byll betwene my lippes,	80	Phy Sparrow	359
It was my prety Phyppes!	80	Phy Sparrow	360
To my great payne and wo.	81	Phy Sparrow	365
How my dysport and play	81	Phy Sparrow	373
Softly bemole /For my sparowes soule.	85	Phy Sparrow	535
God sende my sparoes sole good rest!	86	Phy Sparrow	574
My style as yet direct	91	Phy Sparrow	772
I wot not where to fynd /Termes to serve my mynde.	91	Phy Sparrow	783
But for my sparowes sake,	92	Phy Sparrow	819
My wyt I shall assay	92	Phy Sparrow	821
And with my pen to wryte;	93	Phy Sparrow	862
That my pen hath enbybed	93	Phy Sparrow	872
As verely my hope is,	93	Phy Sparrow	874
And spend my tyme /In prose and ryme,	95	Phy Sparrow	954
For to expres /The noblenes /Of my maistres,	95	Phy Sparrow	958
And my style dres /To this prosses.	96	Phy Sparrow	968
Now Phebus me ken /To sharpe my pen,	96	Phy Sparrow	971
And lede my fyst /As hym best lyst,	96	Phy Sparrow	972
As my maistres, /Of whom I thynk	96	Phy Sparrow	984
My eyne were so dased;	99	Phy Sparrow	1106
Wherwyth my hand she strayned,	99	Phy Sparrow	1122
My pen it is unable,	102	Phy Sparrow	1219
My hand it is unstable,	102	Phy Sparrow	1220
My reson rude and dull	102	Phy Sparrow	1221
And where my pen hath offendyd,	102	Phy Sparrow	1245
As my soverayne /Moost of pleasure.	113	Calliope	23
And in my mynde I have comprised,	117	Ag Scottes	70
To guyde my pen and my pen to enbybe!	117	Ag Scottes	79
To guyde my pen and my pen to enbybe!	117	Ag Scottes	79
Thalya, my muse, for you also call I,	117	Ag Scottes	85
To you rehersyng the somme of my proces.	117	Ag Scottes	90
King Jamy, Jemmy, Jocky my jo,	118	Ag Scottes	91
jo] 'joye' Kynge & Marche 1554, Day 1560, Marshe 1568			
Agaynst this my makyng, /Their males therat shakyng,	120	Ag Scottes2	7
My lyvyng to reprehende;	124	Garnesche3	16
In my lady Brewsys howse.	125	Garnesche3	33
My serpentins and my gunnys	128	Garnesche3	159
My serpentins and my gunnys	128	Garnesche3	159
I rekyn yow in my rowllys,	129	Garnesche3	193
Than with my poems for to melle.	132	Garnesche5	94
Thow demyst my raylyng ovyrthwarthe;	133	Garnesche5	136

MY — MY

	Page	Title	Line
My tyme, I trow, I xulde but lese	133	Garnesche5	154
But now, my proces for to save,	133	Garnesche5	157
My study myght be better spynt;	134	Garnesche5	176
Either by language or with my pen.	137	Ven Tongues	23
My scole is more solem and somwhat more haute	137	Ven Tongues	24
My scoles are not for unthriftes untaught,	138	Ven Tongues	26
But my learning is of an other degree	138	Ven Tongues	28
For Welthfull Felicite truly is my name.	141	Magnyfycence	23
To shewe parte of my wyt,	142	Magnyfycence	58
Brefly to touche of my purpose the effecte:	142	Magnyfycence	67
Softe, my frende. Herein your reason is but rawe.	142	Magnyfycence	70
Yet suffer me to say the surpluse of my sawe.	142	Magnyfycence	71
Nay, ye shall begynne, by my wyll.	143	Magnyfycence	104
With all my herte intere.	143	Magnyfycence	113
Unto your rule I wyll annex my mynde.	144	Magnyfycence	142
As I was wonte ever, at my fre wyll.	144	Magnyfycence	147
To assure you of my noble porte and fame,	145	Magnyfycence	163
But Measure, my frende, what hyght this mannys name?	145	Magnyfycence	165
To the gydynge of my measure you bothe commyttynge;	145	Magnyfycence	175
Wherin it is necessary my pleasure you knowe:	145	Magnyfycence	185
That measure shall nevere departe from my syght.	145	Magnyfycence	190
For dowtlesse I parceyve my magnyfycence	146	Magnyfycence	227
Thynke you not thus my frende Felycyte?	147	Magnyfycence	245
Or who made you so bolde to interrupe my tale?	147	Magnyfycence	256
Mary, upon trouth my reason I grounde,	147	Magnyfycence	264
Sholde be your dwellynge, in my consyderacyon.	148	Magnyfycence	274
Gete you hens, I say, by my counsell.	149	Magnyfycence	306
That I shall have you agayne my good lorde.	149	Magnyfycence	310
Byd hym take good hede of you, my synguler tresure.	149	Magnyfycence	317
By my trouthe, syr, at Pountesse.	150	Magnyfycence	343
Had I not opened my purse wyde,	150	Magnyfycence	347
Another bade shave halfe my berde;	150	Magnyfycence	355
By my trouthe, had I not payde and prayde,	150	Magnyfycence	363
But surely largesse saved my lyfe;	150	Magnyfycence	366
And of my servyce you shall not mysse.	151	Magnyfycence	392
Let us departe from hens home to my place.	151	Magnyfycence	394
Tell you where of my name dothe ryse.	151	Magnyfycence	409
This worlde is full of my foly.	152	Magnyfycence	411
Wyth golde and grotes they grese my hande,	152	Magnyfycence	432
It wolde be masked in my net!	153	Magnyfycence	458
'And therfore shall my husbande pay'.	153	Magnyfycence	461
But Fansy, my frende, where have ye bene so longe?	154	Magnyfycence	500
By my trouthe, we had ben gone.	155	Magnyfycence	537
Alasse! Where is my botes and my spores?	156	Magnyfycence	569
Alasse! Where is my botes and my spores?	156	Magnyfycence	569
Ye. My fansy was out of owle flyght,	159	Magnyfycence	671
For it is out of my mynde quyght.	159	Magnyfycence	672
And nowe it cometh to my remembraunce.	159	Magnyfycence	673
There cometh and groweth of my comynge;	159	Magnyfycence	694
And every man gladly my company wolde refuse,	160	Magnyfycence	704
Falshode in felowshyp is my sworne brother.	160	Magnyfycence	713
My purpose is to spy and to poynte every man;	160	Magnyfycence	726
My tonge is with favell forked and tyned.	160	Magnyfycence	727
My speche is all pleasure, but I stynge lyke a waspe.	160	Magnyfycence	730
To flater and to flery is all my pretence	161	Magnyfycence	738
Ye, so I can devyse my gere after the cowrtly maner.	161	Magnyfycence	766
By the masse, thou shalt byde my leyser.	162	Magnyfycence	788
No, by my trouthe, but crake grete wordes.	163	Magnyfycence	812
That I can were /Courtly my gere!	163	Magnyfycence	834
My heyre bussheth /So plesauntly;	163	Magnyfycence	835
My robe russheth /So ruttyngly;	163	Magnyfycence	837
My persone prest /Beyonde all syse	164	Magnyfycence	844
Beyonde measure /My sleve is wyde;	164	Magnyfycence	850
Al of fansy /My hose strayte tyde;	164	Magnyfycence	852
My buskyn wyde, /Ryche to beholde	164	Magnyfycence	853
All this nacyon /I set on fyre; /In my facyon	165	Magnyfycence	886
What! Fansy, my frende! Howe dost thou fare?	166	Magnyfycence	920
Ye, but what shall I call my name?	167	Magnyfycence	958
So I am poynted after my consayte.	167	Magnyfycence	961
Ye, but of my name let us be wyse.	167	Magnyfycence	963
Farewell, my frende. Adue tyll sone.	167	Magnyfycence	966
It is best I fede my hawke now.	167	Magnyfycence	968
Lo, this is /My fansy, iwys;	167	Magnyfycence	972
Teuyt, teuyt! /Where is my wyt?	168	Magnyfycence	1005
With a pere my love you may wynne,	168	Magnyfycence	1015
My wyttys be weke, my braynys are lyght;	169	Magnyfycence	1024
My wyttys be weke, my braynys are lyght;	169	Magnyfycence	1024
Where is my cappe? I have lost my hat!	169	Magnyfycence	1030
Where is my cappe? I have lost my hat!	169	Magnyfycence	1030
By my trouthe, she hathe a grete hede.	169	Magnyfycence	1048
By my trouthe, I trowe well;	169	Magnyfycence	1051
By my fayth, syr, the frubyssher hath my sworde.	170	Magnyfycence	1063
By my fayth, syr, the frubyssher hath my sworde.	170	Magnyfycence	1063
For so with fantasyes my wyt dothe flete	170	Magnyfycence	1080
In faythe, man, my brayne is as good as thyne.	170	Magnyfycence	1085
By my syers soule, I fele no rayne;	170	Magnyfycence	1087
Yet for my fansy sake, I say,	171	Magnyfycence	1100
Thou shalte have my purse, and I wyll have thyne.	171	Magnyfycence	1102

MY —MY	Page	Title	Line

Quote	Page	Title	Line
By my trouth, there is myne.	171	Magnyfycence	1103
Nowe, by my trouth, man, take, there is my purse; my] 'myne' †Rastell & Treveris C 1530, B	171	Magnyfycence	1104
Nowe, by my trouth, man, take, there is my purse; my] 'myne' †Rastell & Treveris C 1530, B	171	Magnyfycence	1104
And in my purse was twenty marke.	171	Magnyfycence	1108
For all that my name hyght Foly,	171	Magnyfycence	1110
And thou shalte have my hauke to a botchment.	171	Magnyfycence	1113
Nowe take thou my dogge and gyve me thy fowle.	171	Magnyfycence	1116
Come, Gryme! Come, Gryme! It is my praty dogges.	171	Magnyfycence	1119
No, by my trouthe. It is but the scurfe and the scabbe.	171	Magnyfycence	1123
But I have thy pultre, and thou hast my catell.	171	Magnyfycence	1135
Make a verse of my butterfly;	172	Magnyfycence	1149
Yes, by my faythe, good Syr Johnn.	173	Magnyfycence	1186
Yes, yes, by my trouth. I holde the a grote	173	Magnyfycence	1193
Gyve me my grote, for thou hast lost.	173	Magnyfycence	1206
Syr, of my maner I shall tell you the playne:	174	Magnyfycence	1219
Fyrst I lay before them my bybyll	174	Magnyfycence	1220
That I laugh at for my dysporte;	174	Magnyfycence	1239
Of dyverse mo that hauntyth my scolys.	175	Magnyfycence	1264
Nay, that is my parte that thou spekest of nowe.	175	Magnyfycence	1282
My inwyt delynge there can no man dyscry.	177	Magnyfycence	1356
Syr, as by my wyll, it shall be so no more.	178	Magnyfycence	1377
Ye shall be occupyed, Welthe, at my wyll.	178	Magnyfycence	1380
Remembre ye not how my lyberte by mesure ruled was?	178	Magnyfycence	1383
Nay, nay; not so, my frende Felycyte.	179	Magnyfycence	1392
Be not to bolde my frende; I counsell you, bere a brayne.	179	Magnyfycence	1405
Nay, fyrst Lusty Pleasure is my desyre to have;	180	Magnyfycence	1453
Myght seme ryght wel under my proteccyon	181	Magnyfycence	1469
No man so hardy to worke agaynst my wyll.	181	Magnyfycence	1479
I reyne in my robys, I rule as me lyst,	181	Magnyfycence	1485
I dryve downe these dastardys with a dynt of my fyste.	181	Magnyfycence	1486
My name is Magnyfycence, man most of myght.	182	Magnyfycence	1493
I shall flappe hym as a fole to fall at my fete.	182	Magnyfycence	1507
To shewe you my mynde myselfe I wyll avaunce,	182	Magnyfycence	1520
And ferre beyond my merytys ye me commende and prayse.	183	Magnyfycence	1526
For in my favour I have you feffyd and seasyd.	183	Magnyfycence	1536
To here your comon, it is my hygh comforte.	183	Magnyfycence	1539
If it wolde lyke you to here my pore mynde –	183	Magnyfycence	1543
I wolde hauke whylest my hede dyd warke,	184	Magnyfycence	1563
That on suche a female my flesshe wolde be wroken.	184	Magnyfycence	1566
They towche me so thorowly and tykyll my consayte,	184	Magnyfycence	1567
Me to permyt my mynde to dyscharge,	185	Magnyfycence	1590
I wolde yet shewe you further of my consayte.	185	Magnyfycence	1591
Thy wordes and my mynde odly well accorde.	185	Magnyfycence	1605
A, howe my stomake wambleth! I am all in a swete.	185	Magnyfycence	1617
For ofte tymes suche a wamblynge goth over my harte;	185	Magnyfycence	1620
That for your sake I wyll fall on my kne.	186	Magnyfycence	1630
Of my pore instance and supplycacyon,	186	Magnyfycence	1634
My frende, as touchynge to this your mocyon,	186	Magnyfycence	1639
To shewe you my mynde I wolde have the lesse fere.	186	Magnyfycence	1646
Ye, by my trouthe, I shall waraunt you for me,	187	Magnyfycence	1669
And he go to the devyll, so that I may have my fee,	187	Magnyfycence	1670
By my trouth, I can not tell you that.	188	Magnyfycence	1703
Yet ones agayne I shall fall on my kne	188	Magnyfycence	1708
With my servauntys, and suche maystryes gan make,	188	Magnyfycence	1716
That holly my mynde with you is myscontente;	188	Magnyfycence	1717
Have hym hens, I say, out of my syght!	188	Magnyfycence	1723
Alas! My stomake fareth as it wolde cast.	188	Magnyfycence	1726
A, my hede! But is the horson gone?	189	Magnyfycence	1729
Syr, of my counsayle this shall be the grounde:	190	Magnyfycence	1768
I have set my hole felycyte,	190	Magnyfycence	1788
Commyttynge to me and to my felowes twayne	190	Magnyfycence	1791
Well were that lady myght stande in my grace,	190	Magnyfycence	1799
My hawke is rammysshe, and it happed that she ran –	191	Magnyfycence	1807
Grete mervayle I had, and mused in my mynde.	191	Magnyfycence	1822
Sym Sadylgose was my syer, and Dawcocke my dame.	192	Magnyfycence	1834
Sym Sadylgose was my syer, and Dawcocke my dame.	192	Magnyfycence	1834
Se, syr, I beseche you, Largesse me knowe my brother.	192	Magnyfycence	1842
That you trustyd, and Fansy is my name;	193	Magnyfycence	1871
And Foly, my broder, that made you moche game.	193	Magnyfycence	1872
Lorde, so my flesshe trymblyth nowe for drede!	193	Magnyfycence	1875
Vyle velyarde, thou must not nowe my dynt withstande;	193	Magnyfycence	1878
Thou must not abyde the dynt of my hande.	193	Magnyfycence	1879
And beware of adversyte by my counsell,	195	Magnyfycence	1945
A, my bonys ake! My lymmys be sore!	195	Magnyfycence	1955
A, my bonys ake! My lymmys be sore!	195	Magnyfycence	1955
Alasse, I have the cyatyca full evyll in my hyppe!	195	Magnyfycence	1956
My colour is tawny, colouryd as a turffe;	195	Magnyfycence	1959
Alasse! Where is nowe my golde and fe?	196	Magnyfycence	1967
Alasse in my cradell that I had not dyde!	196	Magnyfycence	1987
Alasse! With colde my lymmes shall be marde.	197	Magnyfycence	2004
I wyll walke nowe with my beggers baggys,	197	Magnyfycence	2036
A, howe my lymmys be lyther and lame!	198	Magnyfycence	2038
Where is nowe my welth and my noble estate?	198	Magnyfycence	2055
Where is nowe my welth and my noble estate?	198	Magnyfycence	2055
Where is nowe my treasure, my landes, and my rent?	198	Magnyfycence	2056
Where is nowe my treasure, my landes, and my rent?	198	Magnyfycence	2056

MY—MY

	Page	Title	Line
Where is nowe my treasure, my landes, and my rent?	198	Magnyfycence	2056
Where is nowe all my servauntys that I had here a late?	198	Magnyfycence	2057
Where is nowe my golde upon them that I spent?	198	Magnyfycence	2058
Where is nowe all my ryche abylement?	198	Magnyfycence	2059
Where is nowe my kynne, my frendys, and my noble blood?	198	Magnyfycence	2060
Where is nowe my kynne, my frendys, and my noble blood?	198	Magnyfycence	2060
Where is nowe my kynne, my frendys, and my noble blood?	198	Magnyfycence	2060
Where is nowe all my pleasure and my worldly good?	198	Magnyfycence	2061
Where is nowe all my pleasure and my worldly good?	198	Magnyfycence	2061
Alasse my foly! Alasse my wanton wyll!	198	Magnyfycence	2062
Alasse my foly! Alasse my wanton wyll!	198	Magnyfycence	2062
I may no more speke tyll I have wept my fyll.	198	Magnyfycence	2063
I daunsed the darlynge on my kne;	198	Magnyfycence	2066
She is the bote of all my bale.	199	Magnyfycence	2070
My harte is holly on her set;	199	Magnyfycence	2073
At my devyse I with her met;	199	Magnyfycence	2075
My fansy fayrly on her I set;	199	Magnyfycence	2076
In lust and lykynge my name is Lyberte.	199	Magnyfycence	2078
By my trouthe, we have ryfled hym metely well.	201	Magnyfycence	2170
I shall thrust in the my dagger - Thorowe the legge in to the hose.	202	Magnyfycence	2177
Nay, horson, here is my glove. Take it up and thou dare.	202	Magnyfycence	2178
By our lakyn, syr, not by my wyll.	203	Magnyfycence	2208
Thou sawe never yet but I dyd my parte,	203	Magnyfycence	2228
Ye be the thevys, I say, away my goodys dyd cary.	203	Magnyfycence	2239
Dyspare is my name, that adversyte dothe f[o]lowe; folowe] 'felowe' †Rastell & Treveris C 1530, B, Douce Fragment d.7	205	Magnyfycence	2284
For I have so ungracyously my lyfe mysusyd,	205	Magnyfycence	2298
Alasse, my wyckydnesse, that may I wyte!	205	Magnyfycence	2304
Good Hope, syr, my name is; remedy pryncypall	206	Magnyfycence	2328
For had ye not the soner ben my refuge,	206	Magnyfycence	2333
But, my good sonne, lerne from dyspaire to flee;	206	Magnyfycence	2339
They molefy so easely my harte that was so harde.	207	Magnyfycence	2346
And sore I repent me of my wylfulnesse;	207	Magnyfycence	2379
I aske God mercy of my neglyge[sse], neglygesse] 'neglygence' †Rastell & Treveris C 1530, B	207	Magnyfycence	2380
How fele you your selfe, my frend? How is your mynde?	208	Magnyfycence	2389
A wrechyd man, syr, to my maker unkynde.	208	Magnyfycence	2390
Ye, holly to good hope I have made my repare.	208	Magnyfycence	2394
Redresse my name is, that lytell am I used	208	Magnyfycence	2411
Syr, to accompte you, the contynewe of my consayte	209	Magnyfycence	2421
My wylfulnesse, syr, excuse I ne can.	209	Magnyfycence	2432
Surely my welthe with them was overthrow.	210	Magnyfycence	2450
Well, syr, after your counsell my mynde I wyll set.	210	Magnyfycence	2457
Ye, syr. From hym my corage shall never flyt.	210	Magnyfycence	2466
Whereto were most metely my corage to knyt?	211	Magnyfycence	2479
Herein I wyll aforse me to shewe you my mynde:	211	Magnyfycence	2483
Redresse, in my remembraunce your lesson shall rest;	211	Magnyfycence	2503
And Sad Cyrcumspeccyon I marke in my mynde;	212	Magnyfycence	2504
And with sad cyrcumspeccyon correcte my vantonnesse.	212	Magnyfycence	2509
I am content, my frendys, that it so be.	214	Magnyfycence	2570
But to make up my tale,	217	El Rummynge	101
With, 'Get me a staffe, /The swyne eate my draffe!'	218	El Rummynge	171
They have dronke up my swyllyng tubbe!'	218	El Rummynge	173
Ich am not cast away, /That can my husband say,	220	El Rummynge	220
With, 'Bas, my prety bonny,	220	El Rummynge	227
This make I my falyre fonny,	220	El Rummynge	229
'I dranke not this sennet /A draught to my pay.	224	El Rummynge	395
Nowe truly, to my thynkynge,	228	El Rummynge	547
For so mote I hoppy, /It coleth well my croppy.' croppy] 'coppy' Day 1560, Marshe 1568	228	El Rummynge	561
For wasshyng of my throte;	229	El Rummynge	602
But my bedes of amber.	229	El Rummynge	603
For my fyngers ytche. fyngers] 'fynger' Kynge & Marche 1554	230	El Rummynge	618
My name ys Parott, a byrde of Paradyse,	231	Speke Parott	1
Properly payntyd to be my coverture;	231	Speke Parott	9
Fresshely they dresse and make swete my bowur,	231	Speke Parott	12
Wythe my beke bente, and my lytell wanton iye, and] not in Lant 1545, Kynge and Marche 1554, Day 1560, Marshe 1568	231	Speke Parott	15
Wythe my beke bente, and my lytell wanton iye, and] not in Lant 1545, Kynge and Marche 1554, Day 1560, Marshe 1568	231	Speke Parott	15
My fethyrs fresshe as ys the emerawde grene,	231	Speke Parott	16
Abowte my necke a cerculett lyke the ryche rubye,	231	Speke Parott	17
My lytell legges, my fete bothe fete and clene,	231	Speke Parott	18
My lytell legges, my fete bothe fete and clene,	231	Speke Parott	18
'My propyr Parott, my lytell pratye fole.'	231	Speke Parott	20
'My propyr Parott, my lytell pratye fole.'	231	Speke Parott	20
Pronownsyng my purpose after my properte,	231	Speke Parott	30
Pronownsyng my purpose after my properte,	231	Speke Parott	30
With Dowche, with Spaynyshe, my tonge can agree;	231	Speke Parott	32
My lady mastres, Dame Phylology, mastres] 'maysters' Lant 1545, Kynge & Marche 1554, Day 1560, Marshe 1568	232	Speke Parott	43

	Page	Title	Line
Gave me a gyfte in my neste when I lay,	232	Speke Parott	44
I] 'he' †MS Harley 2252			
I gader togyther and close in my crop,	233	Speke Parott	94
Of my wanton conseyt, unde depromo	233	Speke Parott	95
With my beke I can pyke my lyttel praty too;	233	Speke Parott	107
With my beke I can pyke my lyttel praty too;	233	Speke Parott	107
My delyght is solas, pleasure, dysporte and pley;	233	Speke Parott	108
'How, hosteler, fetche my hors a botell of hay!'	234	Speke Parott	147
But Parot is my owne dere harte, and my dere derling.	236	Speke Parott	208
dere] (2nd) not in Day 1560, Marshe 1568			
But Parot is my owne dere harte, and my dere derling.	236	Speke Parott	208
dere] (2nd) not in Day 1560, Marshe 1568			
My propir Besse, /My praty Besse,	237	Speke Parott	235
My propir Besse, /My praty Besse,	237	Speke Parott	236
My deysy delectabyll, /My prymerose commendabyll,	237	Speke Parott	241
My deysy delectabyll, /My prymerose commendabyll,	237	Speke Parott	242
My vyolet amyabyll, /My joye inexplicabill,	237	Speke Parott	243
My vyolet amyabyll, /My joye inexplicabill,	237	Speke Parott	244
My propyr Besse, /To turne agayne to me.	237	Speke Parott	250
My harte is so sore payned,	237	Speke Parott	254
My propyr Besse, /And torne agayne to me!	238	Speke Parott	261
Go, propyr Parotte, my popagay,	241	Speke Parott	357
O My Parrot, O unice dilecte, votorum meorum	242	Speke Parott	376
Som sey they cannot my parables expresse;	242	Speke Parott	386
Speke, Parotte, my swete byrde, and ye shall have a date,	243	Speke Parott	416
Nowe, Parott, my swete byrde, speke owte yet ons agayn,	244	Speke Parott	447
So myche of my lordes grace, and in hym no grace ys;	245	Speke Parott	501
My name is Collyn Cloute	248	Collyn Cloute	49
I purpose to shake oute /All my connynge bagge,	248	Collyn Cloute	51
For though my ryme be ragged, /Tattered and jagged,	248	Collyn Cloute	53
'My prety Petronylla,	253	Collyn Cloute	259
My lady nowe she ronnes,	256	Collyn Cloute	390
My style for to dyrecte,	257	Collyn Cloute	435
My penne nowe wyll I sharpe,	259	Collyn Cloute	489
And wrest up my harpe	259	Collyn Cloute	490
Tyll my dyenge day	259	Collyn Cloute	506
But now my mynde ye understande,	268	Collyn Cloute	887
Nowe trewely, to my thynkyng,	270	Collyn Cloute	969
At my style rude and playne,	273	Collyn Cloute	1088
But my recountynge is /Of them that do amys	274	Collyn Cloute	1101
Is all my hole wrytynge;	274	Collyn Cloute	1108
Nowe to withdrawe my pen,	277	Collyn Cloute	1248
The forecastell of my shyppe	277	Collyn Cloute	1251
My shyp nowe wyll I stere	278	Collyn Cloute	1259
stere] 'pere' Kele 1545.1, Marshe 1568, 'stere' MS Harley 2252			
He sayth, 'How saye ye, my lordes?	283	Why Come Ye	195
Is nat my reason good?'	283	Why Come Ye	196
Helas, my herte is sory	284	Why Come Ye	227
God save my Lorde Admyrell!	288	Why Come Ye	376
Thus wyll I conclude my style,	289	Why Come Ye	396
And Yorkes Place, /With, 'My lordes grace',	289	Why Come Ye	411
'My lorde is nat at layser.	294	Why Come Ye	625
For my lordes grace	294	Why Come Ye	630
But harke, my frende, one worde	298	Why Come Ye	784
For, 'my Lordes grace',	301	Why Come Ye	876
And, 'my ladies grace',	301	Why Come Ye	877
My lorde now and syr knyght,	302	Why Come Ye	915
now] not in MS Rawlinson C. 813			
My lordys grace nameth it	302	Why Come Ye	940
My lordis grace wyll brynge	302	Why Come Ye	949
With, 'my lady bryght and shene',	304	Why Come Ye	1004
Of my lordis grace nor his wyfe!	306	Why Come Ye	1077
In the regstry /Of my lorde of Cantorbury,	307	Why Come Ye	1120
And my wordes marke	309	Why Come Ye	1207
And, my wordes marke truly,	310	Why Come Ye2	27
'And espetyally to make a lye' MS Rawlinson C. 813			
This is the tenor of my byl,	310	Why Come Ye2	33
Arectyng my syght toward the zodyake,	312	Garlande	1
In place alone then musynge in my thought	312	Garlande	8
On every halfe my reasons forthe I sought,	312	Garlande	10
On] 'One' †Fakes 1523			
Encraumpysshed so sore was my conceyte,	312	Garlande	16
But of my purpose now turne we to the grownde.	313	Garlande	28
purpose] 'proces' MS Cotton Vitellius E.x			
Garnysshed fresshe after my fantasy,	313	Garlande	39
My supplycacyon to you I arrect,	313	Garlande	55
That in my courte Skelton shulde have a place,	313	Garlande	59
Out of my bokis full sone I shulde hym rase;	314	Garlande	72
'Soft, my good syster, and make there a pawse.	316	Garlande	134
my good syster] 'goode my sister' MS Cotton Vitellius E.x			
Among my recordes suffer hym namyd,	316	Garlande	160
And suche of my servauntes as I have promotyd,	318	Garlande	202
But your benynge sufferaunce for my discharge I laid,	318	Garlande	213
But I most bannysshe hym frome my juryediccyon,	318	Garlande	227
Graunt my petycyon, I aske you but ryght.'	318	Garlande	231
Let se, my syster, now spede you, go aboute.	319	Garlande	242
you] not in MS Cotton Vitellius E.x			

	Page	Title	Line
'Daphnes, my derlynge, why do you me refuse?	320	Garlande	297
Yet have compassyon upon my paynes stronge.'	320	Garlande	299
'So am I preventid of my brethern tweyne	324	Garlande	428
Wherwith to geve you my regraciatory,	324	Garlande	431
'So have ye me far passynge my meretis extollyd,	324	Garlande	435
My name, I know well, beyonde that I am able,	324	Garlande	438
That but if my warkes therto be agreable,	324	Garlande	439
Forthwith, I say, thus wandrynge in my thought,	325	Garlande	456
Whyles it remanyth fresshe in my mynde.	325	Garlande	465
And lette me come to delyver my lettre.'	326	Garlande	506
Welcome to me with all my hole desyre!	327	Garlande	548
And for my sake spare neyther pen nor ynke;	327	Garlande	549
Enpryntyng her wordes in my remembraunce,	327	Garlande	557
To owe her my servyce with true perseveraunce.	327	Garlande	558
Then furthermore aboute me my syght I revolde,	330	Garlande	664
Wherof the answere restyth in my handis,	332	Garlande	724
But my request is not so great a thynge,	332	Garlande	730
I have devysyd for Skelton, my clerke;	334	Garlande	777
I me determynyd for to sharpe my pen,	335	Garlande	823
Devoutly arrectyng my prayer to Mynerve,	335	Garlande	824
To gyde and to governe my dredfull tremlyng fist.	335	Garlande	828
So I beseke Jhesu now to be my gyde.	335	Garlande	835
My lyfe endurynge I shall both wryte and say,	335	Garlande	839
To my Lady Elisabeth Howarde	336	Garlande	R
To my Lady Mirriell Howarde	337	Garlande	R
To my Lady Anne Dakers of the Sowth	337	Garlande	R
My besy cure /To yow I owe;	338	Garlande	928
What though my penne wax faynt,	339	Garlande	954
In my goodly chapelet,	339	Garlande	970
By saynt Mary, my Lady,	339	Garlande	973
My mayden Isabell,	340	Garlande	976
Was my fresshe coronell;	342	Garlande	1056
It is not my custome nor my gyse /To leve behynde	342	Garlande	1068
It is not my custome nor my gyse /To leve behynde	342	Garlande	1068
The menes to fynde /To please my mynde,	342	Garlande	1073
In helpyng to warke my laurell grene	342	Garlande	1074
Before my ladys grace, the Quene of Fame,	343	Garlande	1091
Castyng my syght the chambre aboute,	343	Garlande	1093
Of my laurell the proces every whitte.	343	Garlande	1099
But when they sawe my lawrell rychely wrought,	343	Garlande	1105
They seyd my lawrell was the goodlyest	343	Garlande	1112
She wonderyd, me thought, at my laurell grene;	343	Garlande	1116
'My frende, sith ye ar before us here present	344	Garlande	1121
For of my bokis parte ye shall se,	344	Garlande	1139
Forthwith she commaundid I shulde take my place.	344	Garlande	1142
Of my ladys grace at the contemplacyoun,	347	Garlande	1219
Dun is in the myre, dame, reche me my spur.	352	Garlande	1433
But that my peticyon wolde not be had,	353	Garlande	1486
Rendrynge my devisis I made in disporte	354	Garlande	1494
Diodorus Siculus of my translacyon	354	Garlande	1498
A thowsande, thowsande, I trow, to my dome,	354	Garlande	1505
And therwith, sodenly, out of my dreme I woke.	354	Garlande	1511
dreme] 'slepe' Marshe 1568			
My mynde of the grete din was somdele amasid.	354	Garlande	1512
Twene hope and drede /My lyfe I lede,	356	Garlande	1595
But of my spede /Small sekernes;	356	Garlande	1596
Wherfore to jeste /Is my delyght	359	Albany	14
Whan he herde tell /That my Lorde Amrell	360	Albany	55
Of my Lorde Cardynall,	360	Albany	60
Of my Lorde Amrell,	365	Albany	237
My pen I will avaunce	369	Albany	406
What though my stile be rude?	369	Albany	419
My lernyng is to small	370	Albany	457
That I wrate with my pen.	372	Albany	523
To my Lorde Cardynals right noble grace etc	372	Albany	E
MYCHE			
Thus myche Parott hathe opynlye expreste;	242	Speke Parott	381
So myche newe makyng, and so madd tyme spente;	244	Speke Parott	450
So myche translacion into Englyshe confused;	244	Speke Parott	451
So myche nobyll prechyng, and so lytell amendment;	244	Speke Parott	452
So myche consultacion, almoste to none entente;	244	Speke Parott	453
So myche provision, and so lytell wytte at nede -	244	Speke Parott	454
So lytyll dyscressyon, and so myche reasonyng;	244	Speke Parott	456
So myche hardy-dardy, and so lytell manlynes;	244	Speke Parott	457
So gorgyous garmentes, and so myche wrechydnese,	244	Speke Parott	459
So myche portlye pride, with pursys penyles;	244	Speke Parott	460
So myche spente before, and so myche unpayd behynde -	244	Speke Parott	461
So myche spente before, and so myche unpayd behynde	244	Speke Parott	461
So myche forcastyng, and so farre an after-dele;	244	Speke Parott	463
So myche poletyke pratyng, and so lytell stondythe in stede;	244	Speke Parott	464
So lytell secretnese, and so myche grete councell;	245	Speke Parott	465
So myche callyng on, and so smalle takyng hede;	245	Speke Parott	471
So myche losse of merchaundyse, and so remedyles;	245	Speke Parott	472
So lytell care for the comynweall, and so myche nede;	245	Speke Parott	473
So myche dowghtfull daunger, and so lytell drede;	245	Speke Parott	474
So myche pride of prelattes, so cruell and so kene -	245	Speke Parott	475
So myche presonment, for matyrs not worth a hawe;	245	Speke Parott	478
So myche papers weryng for ryghte a smalle exesse;	245	Speke Parott	479

MYDAY SPRETTES —MYGHT

	Page	Title	Line
So myche pelory pajauntes undyr colowur of good lawe;	245	Speke Parott	480
So myche towrnyng on the cooke-stole for every guy-gaw;	245	Speke Parott	481
So myche mokkyshe makyng of statutes of array -	245	Speke Parott	482
So myche bely-joye, and so wastefull banketyng;	245	Speke Parott	492
So myche decay of monesteries and relygious places;	245	Speke Parott	499
So myche of my lordes grace, and in hym no grace ys;	245	Speke Parott	501
So myche sayntuary brekyng, and prevylegidde barryd -	246	Speke Parott	503
So myche raggyd ryghte of a rammes horne;	246	Speke Parott	505
So myche prevye wachyng in cold wynters nyghtes;	246	Speke Parott	512
So myche serchyng of loselles, and ys hym selfe so lewde;	246	Speke Parott	513
So myche conjuracions for elvyshe myday sprettes;	246	Speke Parott	514
So myche crossyng and blyssyng and hym all be shrewde;	246	Speke Parott	516

MYDAY SPRETTES

So myche conjuracions for elvyshe myday sprettes;	246	Speke Parott	514

MYDDELL

Her goodly myddell small	99	Phy Sparrow	1128
goodly] 'godly' †Kele 1545.2			

MYDNYGHT

No matyns at mydnyght,	256	Collyn Clout	406

MYDSOMER

Mirry Margaret, /As mydsomer flowre,	340	Garlande	1005
Of mirry Margarete, /As mydsomer flowre,	341	Garlande	1020

MYGHT

Pressed forthe boldly to witstand the myght,	31	Dol Dethe	87
Vigorously upon them with myght and with mayne,	31	Dol Dethe	89
Paregall to dukis, withe kingis he myght compare,	33	Dol Dethe	134
Boke, bell and candyll, /All that he myght handyll;	64	Hauke	113
That the dowves donge downe myght fall	66	Hauke	183
Great sorowe than ye myght se,	73	Phy Sparrow	56
Phillip myght be bolde	76	Phy Sparrow	177
To me it myght importe	77	Phy Sparrow	216
Myght catche the in theyr pawes,	79	Phy Sparrow	288
Myght stynge the venymously!	79	Phy Sparrow	291
Myght fede them on thy braynes!	79	Phy Sparrow	295
The selfe same hounde /Myght the confounde,	79	Phy Sparrow	304
Myght byte asondre thy throte!	79	Phy Sparrow	306
Myght tere out all thy trypes!	79	Phy Sparrow	308
Thorow his godly myght;	93	Phy Sparrow	870
By whose myght and mayne	104	Phy Sparrow	1297
But by the power and myght of God	114	Scot Kynge	46
Your soverayne lord, our prynce of myght.	117	Ag Scottes	54
But, by the power and myght of God,	119	Ag Scottes	145
Ye myght have buskyd you to Huntley Bankys;	119	Ag Scottes	149
Ye myght no better a way;	125	Garnesche3	49
My study myght be better spynt;	134	Garnesche5	176
Welthe myght be wonne and made to the lure,	141	Magnyfycence	17
And from whens come ye, and it myght be askyd?	141	Magnyfycence	29
Without I myght cut it out of the brode clothe,	144	Magnyfycence	146
Syr, though ye be a noble prynce of myght,	145	Magnyfycence	166
I wolde be rulyd and I myght for shame.	147	Magnyfycence	235
With Magnyfycence, this noble prynce of myght,	148	Magnyfycence	273
A mynstrell lyke a man of myght,	152	Magnyfycence	419
This nonnes nowe and then, and it myght be,	154	Magnyfycence	488
Cannyst thou helpe in faver that I myght be brought?	162	Magnyfycence	777
Myght seme ryght wel under my proteccyon	181	Magnyfycence	1469
Nor Cesar July, that no man myght withstande,	181	Magnyfycence	1482
My name is Magnyfycence, man most of myght.	182	Magnyfycence	1493
Any thynge to do that myght be to your pleasure.	183	Magnyfycence	1528
As that I myght your noble grace content!	183	Magnyfycence	1534
So as ye be a prynce of great myght,	183	Magnyfycence	1545
So I myght hobby for suche a lusty larke.	184	Magnyfycence	1564
A, Cockes armes! Where myght suche one be founde?	184	Magnyfycence	1569
But yf it lyke you that I myght rowne in your eyre,	186	Magnyfycence	1645
For your selfe. Syr, yf I myght permytted be,	188	Magnyfycence	1720
Nowe Jesu preserve you, syr, prynce most of myght.	190	Magnyfycence	1796
Well were that lady myght stande in my grace,	190	Magnyfycence	1799
I wolde tell you and yf I myght for wepynge.	192	Magnyfycence	1848
Spare for the spence of a noble that his honour myght save,	200	Magnyfycence	2125
That somtyme was a noble prynce of myght!	205	Magnyfycence	2280
Then welthe with you myght in no wyse abyde.	210	Magnyfycence	2447
With all theyr myght runnynge /To Elynour Rummynge,	217	El Rummynge	128
Her legges that ye myght se;	225	El Rummynge	421
ye] 'he' 1521 Fragment			
A man myght say in mocke,	255	Collyn Clout	338
Howe connynge myght them avaunce,	262	Collyn Clout	617
That all the worlde myght say,	263	Collyn Clout	669
So as they myght be /Compendyously conveyed,	265	Collyn Clout	767
Now yet all this myght be	290	Why Come Ye	446
Rule the swerde of myght?	293	Why Come Ye	580
Myght stande now by potters,	301	Why Come Ye	910
Myght] 'most' MS Rawlinson C. 813			
Some men myght aske a question,	309	Why Come Ye	1202
aske] 'make' MS Rawlinson C. 813			
So that there workis myght famously be sene,	314	Garlande	67
Wherby he myght have a name inmortall?	315	Garlande	119
Maintenaunce and Mischefe, theis be men of myght;	317	Garlande	193
How that our Englysshe myght fresshely be enewed;	323	Garlande	389
ennewed] 'a meude' †Fakes 1523			

MYGHTE — MYN

	Page	Title	Line
With other condycyons that well myght be left.	329	Garlande	615
Jupiter hymselfe this lyfe myght endure;	332	Garlande	715
O wele were hym that herof myght be sure,	332	Garlande	718
Ye wolde not dele with hym, thowgh that ye myght,	333	Garlande	756
though] 'thought' Marshe 1568, 'thowth' MS Cotton Vit.E.x			
Whereon theis ladys softly myght rest,	334	Garlande	788
Els saye ye myght	342	Garlande	1063
Wele was hym that thereupon myght stare.	343	Garlande	1109
But if hastyve credence by mayntenance of myght	344	Garlande	1133
By whos myght and maine	348	Garlande	1290
What myght she say? What myght he do therto?	351	Garlande	1395
What myght she say? What myght he do therto?	351	Garlande	1395
To harnnes bryght, /By force of myght,	355	Garlande	1557
Any worde defacid /That myght be rasid,	356	Garlande	1582
We set nat a myght	363	Albany	165
Thou hast to lytell myght	364	Albany	230
Employed whiche myght have be	378	Replycacion	149

MYGHTE

	Page	Title	Line
Of golde of tessew the fynest that myghte be,	47	Bowge	59
'Alas,' quod I, 'how myghte I have her sure?'	49	Bowge	118
To kepe it hymselfe; for than he myghte be sure	52	Bowge	222
'By God,' quod Hervy, 'and it so happen myghte!	54	Bowge	306
His gowne so shorte that it ne cover myghte	56	Bowge	354
The devyll myghte daunce therin for ony crowche.	56	Bowge	364
He ran as fast as ever that he myghte.	58	Bowge	415

MYGHTES

	Page	Title	Line
Which is God of myghtes most,	385	Replycacion	384

MYGHTIS

	Page	Title	Line
In Trinitate one God of myghtis moste.	35	Dol Dethe	217

MYGHTY

	Page	Title	Line
The myghty lyoun doutted by se and sande.	32	Dol Dethe	109
sande] 'lande' Marshe 1568			
With myghty corage /A[d]aunted the rage /Of a lyon savage;	104	Phy Sparrow	1309
Adaunted] 'Auaunted' editions			
And with myghty luggyng,	104	Phy Sparrow	1316
Myghty pestels and clubbed,	225	El Rummynge	423
And myghty stronge meate	225	El Rummynge	433
A myghty tre and of a noble heyght,	312	Garlande	19
The huge myghty okes them selfe dyd avaunce,	320	Garlande	279
'Ryght high and myghty princes of astate,	344	Garlande	1128
With myghty corrage /Adauntid the rage /Of a lyon savage;	349	Garlande	1302
And with myghty luggyng, /Wrastelynge and tuggyng,	349	Garlande	1309

MYGHTYS

	Page	Title	Line
He be your conducte, the Lorde of myghtys moste!	208	Magnyfycence	2386

MYKELL

	Page	Title	Line
How the churche hath to mykell	260	Collyn Clout	557

MYKYLL

	Page	Title	Line
He wyll make it mykyll worse than it is;	175	Magnyfycence	1273
By me is conveyed mykyll praty ware -	177	Magnyfycence	1340

MYKKYLLE

	Page	Title	Line
Scornefull and mokkyng over to mykkylle.	133	Garnesche5	153

MYLDE

	Page	Title	Line
O goodly chyld /Of Mary mylde, /Then be oure shylde!	40	Coystrowne3	42

MYLE

	Page	Title	Line
A thousand myle of grounde,	76	Phy Sparrow	187
A hundred myle asonder	285	Why Come Ye	259
This hous envyrowne was a myle about;	326	Garlande	489

MYLK

	Page	Title	Line
With manerly Margery Mylk and Ale.	35	Man Margery	7
With manerly Margery Mylk and Ale.	36	Man Margery	14
With manerly Margery Mylk and Ale.	36	Man Margery	21
With manerly Margery Mylk and Ale.	36	Man Margery	30
With fingers smale, and handis whyte as mylk;	334	Garlande	797
whyte] 'as white' Marshe 1568			

MYLKE

	Page	Title	Line
My sparow whyte as mylke,	77	Phy Sparrow	213
Whyter than the mylke,	99	Phy Sparrow	1120
the] not in Kitson 1560.6, Marshe 1568			
What! Margery Mylke Ducke, mermoset!	153	Magnyfycence	457
Of Manerly Margery Maystres Mylke and Ale;	346	Garlande	1198
Margery Maystres] 'maistres Margery' Marshe 1568			

MYLKEDUCKE

	Page	Title	Line
Than Margery Mylkeducke /Her kyrtell she dyd uptucke	225	El Rummynge	418

MYLL

	Page	Title	Line
Cary sackes to the myll,	281	Why Come Ye	110

MYLLAR

	Page	Title	Line
The myllar was loth to be out of the way,	351	Garlande	1414

MYLLER

	Page	Title	Line
His Epitomis of the Myller and his joly Make;	351	Garlande	1411

MYLLE STONE

	Page	Title	Line
Hyt ys no lytyll bordon to bere a grete mylle stone.	240	Speke Parott	330

MYLSTONES

	Page	Title	Line
And thyder came an hepe /Of mylstones in a route.'	223	El Rummynge	362
thyder] 'there' †Lant 1545, Kynge & Marche 1554, Day 1560, Marshe 1568			

MYN

	Page	Title	Line
Nor Lycon, that lothly luske, in myn opynyon,	122	Garnesche1	24
Dysparage ye myn auncetry?	131	Garnesche5	63

MYND —MYNDE

	Page	Title	Line
A kynge to me myn habyte gave	131	Garnesche5	80
Alas, myn owne servauntys to shew me such reproche!	205	Magnyfycence	2277

MYND

	Page	Title	Line
Wythe hevy chere, with dolorous hart and mynd,	34	Dol Dethe	176
Youre ugly tokyn /My mynd hath brokyn /From worldly lust;	39	Coystrowne3	2

MYNDE

	Page	Title	Line
To slo ther owne lorde? God was not in ther mynde!	30	Dol Dethe	35
Alas for routhe, what thouthe his mynde wer goode,	32	Dol Dethe	102
Stabille thy mynde constant to be and fast,	34	Dol Dethe	170
Now have I shewyd you part of your proud mynde;	38	Coystrowne1	67
So fersly he fytyth, hys mynde is so fell,	43	Balettys2	29
Open myne hart, beholde my mynde expres.	44	Balettys3	39
I, callynge to mynde the great auctoryte	46	Bowge	8
Thus up and down my mynde was drawen and cast	47	Bowge	29
And I with them prayed her to have in mynde.	49	Bowge	123
And ye nede ought, man, shewe to me your mynde,	50	Bowge	165
Whyles of his mynde it were lockte with the keye.	52	Bowge	224
And of his mynde he shewed me all and some.	52	Bowge	226
But as I stode musynge in my mynde,	52	Bowge	230
Tell me your mynde, me thynke ye make a verse,	53	Bowge	244
Agaynst my mynde and wyll	64	Hauke	98
The fynde was in thy mynde	78	Phy Sparrow	283
That now commeth to mynde:	86	Phy Sparrow	604
to mynde] 'to mi mynde' Wyght 1553, Kitson 1560.6			
I wot not where to fynd /Termes to serve my mynde.	91	Phy Sparrow	783
The sentence of his mynde,	91	Phy Sparrow	807
How they are blynde /In theyr owne mynde,	115	Ag Scottes	8
And in my mynde I have comprised,	117	Ag Scottes	70
That your mad mynde contryved.	124	Garnesche3	4
To occupy so your mynde;	126	Garnesche3	103
Take thys for that, bere thys in mynde,	134	Garnesche5	172
And peradventure I shall content your mynde.	142	Magnyfycence	49
Unto your rule I wyll annex my mynde.	144	Magnyfycence	142
And after his mynde herdely your selfe adresse,	144	Magnyfycence	151
To se howe greable we are of one mynde;	146	Magnyfycence	199
In joy and myrthe your mynde shalbe inlargyd	146	Magnyfycence	205
Lyberte in some cause becomyth a gentyll mynde -	146	Magnyfycence	212
Plucke up your mynde, syr, what ayle you to muse?	148	Magnyfycence	283
In fayth, broder Largesse, you have a mery mynde.	148	Magnyfycence	292
Nay, syr, it was nothynge but your mynde.	149	Magnyfycence	330
For it is out of my mynde quyght.	159	Magnyfycence	672
And I, am counterfet of one mynde and thought,	159	Magnyfycence	701
Ye, for all thy mynde is on owles and apes.	171	Magnyfycence	1134
For thou fourmest suche fantasyes in theyr mynde	175	Magnyfycence	1284
Shewe us your mynde then, howe to do and what.	180	Magnyfycence	1435
To shewe you my mynde myselfe I wyll avaunce,	182	Magnyfycence	1520
If it wolde lyke you to here my pore mynde -	183	Magnyfycence	1543
Me to permyt my mynde to dyscharge,	185	Magnyfycence	1590
Wysely let these wordes in your mynde be wayed:	185	Magnyfycence	1593
And yf you se ony thynge agaynst your mynde,	185	Magnyfycence	1599
Thy wordes and my mynde odly well accorde.	185	Magnyfycence	1605
And that your mynde can not well be eased -	185	Magnyfycence	1610
It is a pryncely pleasure and a lordly mynde.	186	Magnyfycence	1627
To shewe you my mynde I wolde have the lesse fere.	186	Magnyfycence	1646
That holly my mynde with you is myscontente;	188	Magnyfycence	1717
Grete mervayle I had, and mused in my mynde,	191	Magnyfycence	1822
Alas, dere sone, sore combred is thy mynde,	206	Magnyfycence	2325
With gommes goostly of glad herte and mynde,	207	Magnyfycence	2359
How fele you your selfe, my frend? How is your mynde?	208	Magnyfycence	2389
Fyrst, I saye, with mynde fyrme and stable	208	Magnyfycence	2408
For to understande your pleasure and also your mynde.	209	Magnyfycence	2420
Well, syr, after your counsell my mynde I wyll set.	210	Magnyfycence	2457
Herein I wyll aforse me to shewe you my mynde:	211	Magnyfycence	2483
And Sad Cyrcumspeccyon I marke in my mynde;	212	Magnyfycence	2504
Yow to remorde erste or they know your mynde.	241	Speke Parott	370
All this is out of mynde.	263	Collyn Clout	660
All] 'Alas' Kele 1545.1, Marshe 1568, 'All' MS Harley 2252			
But now my mynde ye understande,	268	Collyn Clout	887
That the kynges mynde	290	Why Come Ye	439
And call to his mynde	291	Why Come Ye	499
Whiche, of his royall mynde	292	Why Come Ye	546
Another manes mynde diffuse is to expounde;	315	Garlande	111
Recorde the same? Or why is had in mynde	315	Garlande	125
Your mynde that can maynteyne so apparently;	317	Garlande	170
Whyles it remanyth fresshe in my mynde.	325	Garlande	465
With suche communycacyon as came to our mynde;	328	Garlande	562
Sum medelynge spyes, by craft to grope thy mynde,	329	Garlande	617
May this contente you and your mirry mynde?	332	Garlande	708
Of scrupulus dout. Wherfore, your mynde discharge,	332	Garlande	726
Full gloryously can he glose, thy mynde for to fele;	333	Garlande	760
Beninge, curteyse, of jentyll harte and mynde,	337	Garlande	880
The menes to fynde /To please my mynde,	342	Garlande	1073
With Courtely Abusyoun; who pryntith it wele in mynde	346	Garlande	1196
Whereupon he metrefyde after his mynde;	353	Garlande	1464
My mynde of the grete din was somdele amasid.	354	Garlande	1512
With hole hart and true mynde,	371	Albany	482
In his mynde to comprise,	372	Albany	529

MYNDED —MYNYON	Page	Title	Line

MYNDED
And craftely can I grope howe every man is mynded.	160	Magnyfycence	725
Is toward hym so mynded,	295	Why Come Ye	659

MYNDES
With all good myndes.	280	Why Come Ye	56
But mende your myndes that are mased;	382	Replycacion	293
With sobre cyrcumstance, /Our myndes to avaunce	385	Replycacion	395

MYNDYD
Surely I am joyous that ye be myndyd thus;	144	Magnyfycence	156
Yf you be so myndyd, we be ryght glad.	210	Magnyfycence	2473

MYNDYS
Refresshyng myndys the Aprell shoure of rayne;	44	Balettys3	11
Your myndys I beseche you here in to expresse,	211	Magnyfycence	2480
Settyng theyr myndys so moche of eloquens,	235	Speke Parott	181

MYNDLES
I for to be so myndles,	342	Garlande	1065

MYNE
Myne homely rudnes and drighnes to expelle	29	Dol Dethe	13
Transcending f[a]r myne homely Muse that must far] 'for' †MS Royal 18 D.ii, Marshe 1568	33	Dol Dethe	144
'Myne horse is sold, I wene', you say;	40	Coystrowne4	9
'Have in sergeaunt ferrour, myne horse behynde is bare.'	43	Balettys2	20
Open myne hart, beholde my mynde expres.	44	Balettys3	39
As to enbrace you in myne armys twayne.	44	Balettys3	42
In myne hostes house called Powers Keye,	47	Bowge	35
By myne avyse use not with him to walke.	52	Bowge	210
And tyll I come, have, here is myne hat to plege.' is] not in Marshe 1568	57	Bowge	413
Me, passynge sore, myne herte than gan aryse;	58	Bowge	425
'Harken,' quod he, 'loo here myne honde in thyne;	60	Bowge	510
To holde myne honde, by God, I had grete payne;	61	Bowge	522
And as he rounded thus in myne ere rounded] 'roynded' †Wynkyn de Worde 1499	61	Bowge	526
Unneth I kest myne eyes	72	Phy Sparrow	37
That myne hert dyd bete,	73	Phy Sparrow	59
Myne hear ryght upstode,	77	Phy Sparrow	227
Alas, myne hert it sleth	80	Phy Sparrow	351
Myne Englyssh halfe-abused;	92	Phy Sparrow	815
Now myne hole imaginacion	93	Phy Sparrow	847
Myne hert doth so enbrace,	96	Phy Sparrow	1005
Causeth myne hert to lepe;	97	Phy Sparrow	1015
It raysed myne hert rote	100	Phy Sparrow	1148
Wolde God myne homely style	101	Phy Sparrow	1204
You to holde content /With myne argument;	143	Magnyfycence	109
Yes, questyonlesse, in myne opynyon;	144	Magnyfycence	126
Then may I say that ye be servauntys myne.	145	Magnyfycence	183
Take Lyberte to rule, and folowe myne entent.	147	Magnyfycence	238
By God, syr, ye se but fewe wyse men of myne age.	148	Magnyfycence	289
Or elles I had lost myne eres twayne.	150	Magnyfycence	349
And another bade put out myne eye;	150	Magnyfycence	353
Another wolde myne eye were blerde;	150	Magnyfycence	354
Nay, nay. He hath chaunged his, and I have chaunged myne.	155	Magnyfycence	518
Your fansy maketh myne elbowe to ake.	156	Magnyfycence	559
His name Largesse, Surveyaunce myne.	158	Magnyfycence	643
But shall I have myne olde name styll?	158	Magnyfycence	647
I can not myne appetyte accomplysshe and fulfyll	160	Magnyfycence	733
Mary, Lusty Pleasure, by myne advyse,	167	Magnyfycence	964
By my trouth, there is myne.	171	Magnyfycence	1103
Mary, as for that, thou shalte sone here myne.	172	Magnyfycence	1153
By God, syr, Foly, myne owne sworne brother.	172	Magnyfycence	1159
Mary, it was his, and nowe it is myne.	173	Magnyfycence	1181
Syr, ye shall folowe myne appetyte and intent.	180	Magnyfycence	1420
These wordes in myne eyre, they be so lustely spoken,	184	Magnyfycence	1565
Do as moche as for myne owne father.	186	Magnyfycence	1642
Come hyder, Pleasure; you shall here myne entent.	186	Magnyfycence	1655
By myne advyse, with you in fayth he shall not rest.	186	Magnyfycence	1660
But good hope and redresse hath mendyd myne estate,	210	Magnyfycence	2462
Ye shall not bere awaye /Myne ale for nought, myne] 'my' Kynge & Marche 1554, Day 1560, Marshe 1568	218	El Rummynge	166
'Moryshe myne owne shelfe,' the costermonger sayth;	233	Speke Parott	85
Myne herte hyt ys with the.	237	Speke Parott	240
As by myne auctor tried it was.	296	Why Come Ye	707
(Myne auctor writeth the same);	297	Why Come Ye	727
As myne auctor sayth.	297	Why Come Ye	745
Myne argument els koude not longe endure.	316	Garlande	147
Affyaunsynge her myne hole assuraunce	327	Garlande	555
And so largely to lay for myne indempnite,	344	Garlande	1136
That I trust to make myne excuse	344	Garlande	1137
Your discharge here under myne arme is it.'	344	Garlande	1146
I wypid myne eyne for to make them clere.	354	Garlande	1513
After myne allegyaunce	369	Albany	405

MYNERVE
Devoutly arrectyng my prayer to Mynerve,	335	Garlande	824

MYNYON
I am a mynyon to wayte apon a quene; a (2)] 'the' Lant 1545, Kynge & Marche 1554, Day 1560, Marshe 1568	231	Speke Parott	19

MYNYSTER
I to mynyster it, you to receyve it ofte - . . . . 207 Magnyfycence 2356
MYNSTRELL
A master, a mynstrell, a fydler, a farte. 38   Coystrowne1   56
A mynstrell lyke a man of myght, ... 152 Magnyfycence 419
MYNSTRELS
A murmer of mynstrels, that suche another . . . . 320 Garlande   270
MYRACLE
And worke suche a myracle, ... 293 Why Come Ye 567
MYRE
Or elles in the myre . . . . 273 Collyn Clout 1069
They have layde all in the myre. . . . . 285 Why Come Ye 251
Dun is in the myre, dame, reche me my spur. . . . . 352 Garlande   1433
MYRY
Ensowkid with sylt of the myry [w]ose,   312 Garlande   23
    sylt] 'fylt' †Fakes 1523; wose] 'mose' †Fakes 1523
MYRROUR
[Thy] myrrour may be the devyllys ars. 130 Garnesche5   18
    Thy] 'They' †MS Harley 367
A myrrour incleryd is this interlude, ... 212 Magnyfycence 2524
A myrrour of glasse, that I may tote therin; . . . . 231 Speke Parott 10
The myrrour that I tote in, quasi diaphonum, ... 236 Speke Parott 190
MYRROURE
Encleryd myrroure and perspectyve most bryght, ... 44   Balettys3   22
MYRTH
But myrth and consolacyon . . . . 103 Phy Sparrow 1278
For then began our myrth and game. . . . . 117 Ag Scottes   68
A medley to make of myrth with sadnes, ... 117 Ag Scottes   87
For myrth I have hym coryed, beten, and blyst, ... 185 Magnyfycence 1622
In honest myrth, parde, requyreth no lack; . . . . 347 Garlande   1236
But myrth and consolacyoun, /Made by protestacyoun, ... 348 Garlande   1271
MYRTHE
What the devyll, man, myrthe was never one! . . . . 57 Bowge   388
    was never one] 'is here within' Marshe 1568
In joy and myrthe your mynde shalbe inlargyd . . . . 146 Magnyfycence 205
What! Is all your myrthe nowe tourned to sorowe? . . . . 192 Magnyfycence 1849
To her he wrote many maters of myrthe; . . . . 346 Garlande   1199
MYRTHYS
This mater we have movyd, you myrthys to make, ... 213 Magnyfycence 2552
MYS
But of reproche surely he maye not mys 46   Bowge   26
MYSADVENTURE
A grete mysadventure, thy maker to dysplease, ... 206 Magnyfycence 2341
MYSADVYSED
Of such mysadvysed /Parsons and dysgysed, ... 62   Hauke   21
MYSCHAUNCE
God gyve you a very myschaunce! . . . . 154 Magnyfycence 497
MYSCHAUNS
God sende them bothe myschauns! . . . . 363 Albany   176
Shall tourne you to myschauns. . . . . 371 Albany   499
MYSCHEFE
It were a myschefe, yf lyberte lacked a reyne . . . . 144 Magnyfycence 135
Wyll crepe upon us, and us to myschefe lede; . . . . 144 Magnyfycence 153
For myschefe wyll mayster us yf measure us forsake. . . . . . . 144 Magnyfycence 154
Then myschefe sodaynly I them sende; . . . . 194 Magnyfycence 1927
Howe many come to myschefe for to moche lyberte; . . . . 200 Magnyfycence 2134
And I, Myschefe, am comyn at nede, ... 205 Magnyfycence 2309
By myschefe to brevyate and shorten his dayes. . . . . 206 Magnyfycence 2338
MYSCHEFFE
God gyve hym a myscheffe! Nay, nowe let me alone. . . . . 189 Magnyfycence 1730
And take myscheffe and vengeaunce of other mo . . . . 195 Magnyfycence 1951
MYSCHEVE
Wheron was wryten this worde, Myscheve. 58   Bowge   434
MYSCHEVED
That dyspayre well nyghe had myscheved me; . . . . 206 Magnyfycence 2332
MYSCHEVYNGE
Thyselfe myschevynge to thyne endlesse dysease! . . . . 206 Magnyfycence 2342
MYSCHEVOUSLY
It wyll stryke a man myschevously in a hete. . . . . 204 Magnyfycence 2268
MYSCHIEFE
Full of myschiefe and queed, ... 106 Epitaphe   I
MYSCHYEF
By the menys of myschyef to bryng all thynges to nought. . . . 159 Magnyfycence 702
And tolde all the myschyef I coude behynde theyr backe, ... 160 Magnyfycence 718
I wolde begyn all myschyef, but I wolde bere no lacke. . . . . 160 Magnyfycence 720
MYSCONTENT
In hope that no man shall /Be myscontent withall. 62   Hauke   28
    Be] 'By' Kynge & Marche 1554
No man to myscontent . . . . 103 Phy Sparrow 1280
No man to myscontent /With Phillippis enterement. . . . . 348 Garlande   1273
MYSCONTENTE
I wolde therwith no man were myscontente; 61   Bowge   533
That holly my mynde with you is myscontente; . . . . 188 Magnyfycence 1717
MYSCREANTYS
Whych cytie myscreantys wan, ... 67   Hauke   214
MYSDEDE
I am Adversyte, that for thy mysdede . . . . 193 Magnyfycence 1876

461

MYSDEDES —MYTERS

MYSDEDES
God forgeve hym his mysdedes. 107 Epitaphe1 19
MYSDEMPTE
Mysdempte eche man, with face deedly and pale; . . . . 50 Bowge 137
MYSDONE
Of that I have mysdone to make a redresse, ... 212 Magnyfycence 2508
MYSE
Were made for myse and rattes, ... 80 Phy Sparrow 339
MYSELF
Causyth me that I can not myself refrayne, ... 42 Balettys2 3
MYSELFE
Amonge all other I put myselfe in prece. . . . . 47 Bowge 44
And as I stode redynge this verse myselfe allone, ... 48 Bowge 68
And oftentymes I wolde myselfe avaunce . . . . 50 Bowge 143
And, though I say it, I was myselfe your frende, ... 50 Bowge 160
I shall come to you myselfe, I trowe, this afternone. . . . . . 149 Magnyfycence 322
Myselfe coude not counterfet it better. . . . . 155 Magnyfycence 530
To shewe you my mynde myselfe I wyll avaunce, ... 182 Magnyfycence 1520
Alasse that I coude not myselfe no better gyde! . . . . 196 Magnyfycence 1986
Shall I myselfe hange with an halter? Nay, ... 206 Magnyfycence 2320
But answere that I may, /For myselfe alway . . . . 266 Collyn Clout 786
But now to helpe myselfe I am not able. . . . . 321 Garlande 312
I wyll myselfe discharge . . . . 350 Garlande 1353
MY SELFE
I wyll my selfe dyscharge . . . . 105 Phy Sparrow 1360
And I my selfe hooly to you wyll inclyne. . . . . 145 Magnyfycence 182
But sygh, and sorowe, and wysshe my selfe dede. . . . . 205 Magnyfycence 2306
In styckynge my selfe with this fayre knyfe. . . . . 206 Magnyfycence 2322
But hooly to perseveraunce my selfe I wyll bynde, ... 212 Magnyfycence 2507
Avaunsynge my selfe sum thanke to deserve, ... 335 Garlande 822
I wyll my selfe applye, ... 339 Garlande 961
MYSERABLENESSE
Myserablenesse, /With wretchydnesse, ... 305 Why Come Ye 1032
MYSERABLY
For mysery /With penury /Myserably /And wretchydly . . . . . . 300 Why Come Ye 868
MYSERACION
That of divyne myseracion . . . . 384 Replycacion 375
MYSERE
O syghynge sorowe, O thoughtfull mysere! . . . . 198 Magnyfycence 2050
MYSERY
In mysery and wretchydnesse thus to be lapped! . . . . 196 Magnyfycence 1985
This mysery, this carefull wrechydnesse? . . . . 201 Magnyfycence 2154
For to lyve in mysery, it is herder than dethe. . . . . 205 Magnyfycence 2282
There was never so harde a storme of mysery, ... 207 Magnyfycence 2343
For mysery /With penury /Myserably /And wretchydly . . . . . . 300 Why Come Ye 866
MYSNAMED
Bycause ye her mysnamed, ... 376 Replycacion 59
MYSPENT
Intentyfe ay /And dylygent, /No tyme myspent; . . . . 339 Garlande 944
MYSPROUDE
It is grete scorne to se a mysproude knave . . . . 59 Bowge 453
MYSSE
And of my servyce you shall not mysse. . . . . 151 Magnyfycence 392
For go when ye shall, of you shall he mysse. . . . . 188 Magnyfycence 1706
Yet may he mysse the quysshon! . . . . 271 Collyn Clout 996
MYSSE USE
He dothe mysse use /Eche man to [akuse], ... 164 Magnyfycence 873
   akuse] 'take a fe' †Rastell & Treveris C 1530, B
MYST
In lyke maner of wyse a myst did us shrowde; . . . . 330 Garlande 647
The clowdis gan to clere, the myst was rarifiid; . . . . 330 Garlande 651
For there ye myst no[r] quosshons. . . . . 377 Replycacion 113
   your] 'you' †Pynson 1528
MYSTERIALL
And a mysteriall, /And a mysticall, /Effect energiall, ... 384 Replycacion 366
MYSTICALL
And a mysteriall, /And a mysticall, /Effect energiall, ... 384 Replycacion 367
MYSURYD
Mooste noble Erle! O fowle mysuryd grounde, ... 32 Dol Dethe 118
MYSUSYD
For I have so ungracyously my lyfe mysusyd, ... 205 Magnyfycence 2298
MYSWROUGHT
Of that ye have myswrought; . . . . 379 Replycacion 184
MYTCHE
I have wrytten so mytche . . . . 230 El Rummynge 619
MYTE
And settys nat by it a myte! . . . . 296 Why Come Ye 677
MYTEYNG
For alle ys nat worthe a myteyng, ... 127 Garnesche3 115
MYTER
A myter nor a crose, ... 254 Collyn Clout 292
The apostyll Peter /Had but on pore myter . . . . 307 Why Come Ye 1140
   apostyll] 'wholly apostle' MS Rawlinson C. 813
MYTERS
Myters are bought and solde; . . . . 254 Collyn Clout 290

	Page	Title	Line

MYTYNG
He calleth me his whytyng, /His mullyng and his [m]ytyng, . . . 220 El Rummynge 224
   mytyng] 'nytyng' †Lant 1545, Kynge & Marche 1554,
   'nittinge' Day 1560, 'nittine' Marshe 1568

MYXED
Myxed with bytter alowes of herde adversyte. . . . . 207 Magnyfycence 2354

MYXT
Theyr styrops of myxt golde begared, ... 254 Collyn Clout 317
   begared] 'begarded' Marshe 1568, 'be gloryd' MS Harley 2252

MYXTE
Myxte with sum incommodite, ... 130 Garnesche5 10

MYXTURE
That with myxture of aloes and bytter gall . . . . 117 Ag Scottes 81

MO
Or such other poetes mo, ... 90 Phy Sparrow 760
They shall wirry no mo, ... 111 Lawde 26
Well, and I be a coward, there is mo than I. . . . . 162 Magnyfycence 770
Ye, by Goddes sacrament; and with other mo. . . . . 166 Magnyfycence 942
What? Wolde ye have mo folys, and are so many? . . . . . . 172 Magnyfycence 1170
Forsothe, tell on. Hast thou any mo? . . . . 175 Magnyfycence 1262
   mo] 'more' †Rastell & Treveris C 1530, B
Of dyverse mo that hauntyth my scolys. . . . . 175 Magnyfycence 1264
Nay. Madnesse hath begyled you and many mo; . . . . 192 Magnyfycence 1856
And take myscheffe and vengeaunce of other mo . . . . 195 Magnyfycence 1951
Of auncyent Aristippus and such other mo, ... 233 Speke Parott 93
And tell of other mo, ... 267 Collyn Clout 829
Howe frere Fabian with other mo . . . . 268 Collyn Clout 881
And many mo whome I cowde enduce; . . . . 314 Garlande 94
Olde Diogenes, with other many mo, ... 315 Garlande 129
Fynde no mo suche fro Wanflete to Walis. . . . . 347 Garlande 1218
And suche wondringes many mo. . . . . 376 Replycacion 76
With other doctours many mo, ... 381 Replycacion 280
Wherfore make ye no mo restrayntes, ... 382 Replycacion 292

MOBYLL
Fyxt or els mobyll. . . . . 292 Why Come Ye 525

MOCH
He wold be made moch of and he wyst how; 37 Coystrowne1 33
Was moch more febler brayned. . . . . 64 Hauke 82
Then moch more, by the rode, ... 66 Hauke 178
With moch matter more, /That I kepe in store. . . . . 67 Hauke 220
That worketh moch scath . . . . 87 Phy Sparrow 619
   That] 'Thay' †Kele 1545.2, Wyght 1553, Kitson 1560.6
For whom was moch stryfe; . . . . 87 Phy Sparrow 644
She was moch to blame; . . . . 89 Phy Sparrow 710
On her moch love and cost, ... 89 Phy Sparrow 715
At those dayes moch commended; . . . . 91 Phy Sparrow 796
Truth it is, syr; for after he wrought me moch shame, . . . 209 Magnyfycence 2444
Wordes that were moch consolatory . . . . 317 Garlande 165

MOCHE
There was moche noyse, anone one cryed, 'Cese!' . . . . . . 47 Bowge 46
That I must shewe you moche of my counselle – . . . . 52 Bowge 207
Is lytyll to saye, and moche to here and see; . . . . 52 Bowge 212
And moche therof dyd make; . . . . 89 Phy Sparrow 693
That wrowght have moche care, ... 111 Lawde 24
Moche lyke a dromadary; 126 Garnesche3 74
With moche mater more 126 Garnesche3 76
And make moche lyke Jake Rakar; 127 Garnesche3 109
Moche of thy maneres I ca[n] blasy. 130 Garnesche5 32
   can] 'cam' †MS Harley 367
I trowe ye can not say nay moche to this: . . . . 142 Magnyfycence 74
Of to moche lyberte under the offence; . . . . 146 Magnyfycence 229
To gete me fro them I had moche warke. . . . . 150 Magnyfycence 361
It is moche worthe that is ferre fet. . . . . 153 Magnyfycence 455
By God, yet it muste begynne moche of the. . . . . 154 Magnyfycence 514
And so, by these meanes, I brewe moche bale. . . . . 161 Magnyfycence 744
In faythe, I rule moche of the rost. . . . . 163 Magnyfycence 804
Moche more than nede . . . . 165 Magnyfycence 894
But, broder Foly, I wonder moche of one thynge, ... 170 Magnyfycence 1068
Why, wenyst thou that I were as moche a fole as thou? . . . 173 Magnyfycence 1188
I make hym lese moche of theyr strength; . . . . 175 Magnyfycence 1259
And then he is moche made of for his [wyt]; . . . . 175 Magnyfycence 1271
   wyt] 'whyt' †Rastell & Treveris C 1530, B
For many tymes moche kyndnesse is denyed . . . . 177 Magnyfycence 1338
Full moche flatery and falsehode I hyde; . . . . 177 Magnyfycence 1358
That was by the menys of to moche lyberte. . . . . 180 Magnyfycence 1424
A, I have spyed ye can moche broken sorowe. . . . . 184 Magnyfycence 1587
Do as moche as for myne owne father. . . . . 186 Magnyfycence 1642
And Foly, my broder, that made you moche game. . . . . 193 Magnyfycence 1872
And remembre he suffered moche more for your sake; . . . . . 196 Magnyfycence 2001
I warne you beware of to moche lyberte, ... 199 Magnyfycence 2088
To hardy, or to moche, to free of the dawe, ... 199 Magnyfycence 2090
By meanes of madnesse and to moche lyberte. . . . . 199 Magnyfycence 2100
That I used the to moche sore may I rewe. . . . . 199 Magnyfycence 2104
Howe many come to myschefe for to moche lyberte; . . . . . . 200 Magnyfycence 2134
Some hath so moche lyberte of one thynge and other, ... 200 Magnyfycence 2141
Some have so moche lyberte that they fere no synne, ... 200 Magnyfycence 2143
And I tell you, I dysdayne moche of his mockys. . . . . . . 203 Magnyfycence 2227
To gyve so hasty credence ye were moche to blame. . . . . . 209 Magnyfycence 2443

MOCYON — MOYLES

	Page	Title	Line
And caused me also to use to moche lyberte,	209	Magnyfycence	2445
Well, I perceyve in you there is moche sadnesse,	210	Magnyfycence	2475
For, be there never so moche prese,	218	El Rummynge	174
Settyng theyr myndys so moche of eloquens,	235	Speke Parott	181
Make moche of Parrot, the popegay ryall.	236	Speke Parott	217
the] 'that' Kynge & Marche 1554, Day 1560, Marshe 1568			
Moche herted lyke an hen.	251	Collyn Clout	168
Spende moche of theyr share	251	Collyn Clout	176
Doutlesse were moche better	253	Collyn Clout	272
were] 'where' Kele 1545.1			
And make moche varyans	260	Collyn Clout	554
Yet they mervayle so moche lesse,	271	Collyn Clout	1008
There hath ben moche excesse:	280	Why Come Ye	70
It can not be moche worse.	282	Why Come Ye	138
And so moche oblivyous	290	Why Come Ye	464
Wherat moche I wonder	296	Why Come Ye	672
How Frauncis Petrarke, /That moche noble clerke,	296	Why Come Ye	688
Wherof moche care began.	297	Why Come Ye	725
Moche better can devyse	298	Why Come Ye	767
And moche hevynesse, /And great dolowre	305	Why Come Ye	1035
dolowre] 'dullness' MS Rawlinson C. 813			
Moche money of the kynge	309	Why Come Ye	1192
Is moche more inordinate,	310	Why Come Ye2	14
To corage Demostenes was moche excitynge,	316	Garlande	152
Sume be moche spokyn of for makynge of frays;	317	Garlande	182
Some famous wetewoldis, and they be moche wurs;	317	Garlande	187
In so moche the stumpe, whereto I me lente	320	Garlande	281
I thanked her moche of her most noble offer,	327	Garlande	554
Strongly enbateld, moche costious of charge.	328	Garlande	570
Moche mischefe, I hyght you, amonge theem ther happid.	330	Garlande	643
Grene tre of laurell moche solacyous game	331	Garlande	683
Lodesterre of lyght, /Moche relucent;	339	Garlande	950
Lodesterre] 'Lede sterre' †Fakes 1523			
Moche mirthe and no madnes,	340	Garlande	1009
And for as moche as, by the hy pretence	344	Garlande	1124
in as moche as it were to longe a proces	345	Garlande	R
Moche dowblenes of the worlde therin he may fynde.	346	Garlande	1197
Lorde, how she made moche of her gentyll birth!	346	Garlande	1202
With litell besynes standith moche rest; in bed	351	Garlande	1410
So moche the better	355	Garlande	1539
remordyng dyvers recrayed and moche unresonable errours	373	Replycacion	I
of the reverende prelates and moche noble doctours	373	Replycacion	I
of the moche vayne glorious pipplyng wynde,	373	Replycacion	I
in the moche studious scolehous of scrupulous philology,	373	Replycacion	I
and transcendingly sped in moche high connyng,	374	Replycacion	I
moche better bayned than brayned,	374	Replycacion	I
enbrased and enterlased with a moche fantasticall frenesy	374	Replycacion	I
Moche better other wayes.	378	Replycacion	150
It had ben moche better	380	Replycacion	229
Ye are but lydder logici, /But moche worse isagogici,	380	Replycacion	235
And to our faithe moche agreable,	382	Replycacion	290
Ye do moche great outrage,	384	Replycacion	354

MOCYON

	Page	Title	Line
My frende, as touchynge to this your mocyon,	186	Magnyfycence	1639

MOCKE

	Page	Title	Line
Nowe hast thou not a prowde mocke and a starke?	174	Magnyfycence	1208
A man myght say in mocke,	255	Collyn Clout	338
And mocke them to theyr face.	262	Collyn Clout	625
And, 'Mocke hath lost her sho;	281	Why Come Ye	86

MOCKYNG

	Page	Title	Line
Thy mellyng is but mockyng.	366	Albany	298

MOCKYNGE

	Page	Title	Line
To mockynge, to mowynge, to lyke a jackenapes -	199	Magnyfycence	2098

MOCKYS

	Page	Title	Line
Here you not howe this gentylman mockys?	141	Magnyfycence	32
And I tell you, I dysdayne moche of his mockys.	203	Magnyfycence	2227

MOCKYSSH

	Page	Title	Line
Shoo the mockyssh mare;	251	Collyn Clout	180

MOCKYSSHE

	Page	Title	Line
Full of mockysshe scornes,	380	Replycacion	216

MODE

	Page	Title	Line
He may helpe you. He may mende your mode.	207	Magnyfycence	2366
Shulde this man of suche mode	293	Why Come Ye	579

MODER

	Page	Title	Line
Maiden moste pure, and Goddis moder dere,	34	Dol Dethe	205

MODERACYON

	Page	Title	Line
In your rewardys use suche moderacyon	211	Magnyfycence	2494

MODERATLY

	Page	Title	Line
Moderatly to take /This sorow that I make	74	Phy Sparrow	101

MODERS

	Page	Title	Line
Faders and moders that be neclygent,	194	Magnyfycence	1920
I vysyte theyr faders and moders with sekenesse;	194	Magnyfycence	1925

MODYR

	Page	Title	Line
Dyscrecion ys modyr of nobyll vertues all;.	232	Speke Parott	51

MOGHT

	Page	Title	Line
By the masse, a Spaynysshe moght with a gray lyste!	173	Magnyfycence	1200

MOYLES

	Page	Title	Line
Theyr moyles golde dothe eate,	254	Collyn Clout	319

	Page	Title	Line
MOYSES			
By Moyses and Arons rod,	63	Hauke	54
Madionita Jetro, our Moyses kepyth his shepe;	234	Speke Parott	115
Dyd Moyses sore manase	305	Why Come Ye	1067
sore] not in MS Rawlinson C. 813			
Also a Devoute Prayer to Moyses Hornis,	351	Garlande	1381
MOK			
Though Jak sayd nay, yet Mok there loste her sho;	351	Garlande	1396
MOKE			
With, 'Gup, Syr Gy', ye gate a moke.	131	Garnesche5	56
MOKERY			
How may I your mokery mekely tollerate,	123	Garnesche2	1
Some men be made of for the mokery;	317	Garlande	185
the] 'their' Marshe 1568			
MOKKYNG			
Scornefull and mokkyng over to mykkylle.	133	Garnesche5	153
MOKKYSH			
Yor moth etyn mokkysh maneres, they be all to-myryd.	123	Garnesche2	12
MOKKYSHE			
Thou mokkyshe marmoset, /I will nat dy in [thy] det.	128	Garnesche3	172
thy] 'they' †MS Harley 367			
So myche mokkyshe makyng of statutes of array -	245	Speke Parott	482
MOKKYSHLY			
and madly in hys musykkys mokkyshly made agaynste	36	Coystrowne	I
MOLDE			
Nor no man on molde can make me aferd.	182	Magnyfycence	1505
Howe hyr ale is solde /To mawte and to molde.	218	El Rummynge	159
MOLEFY			
They molefy so easely my harte that was so harde.	207	Magnyfycence	2346
MOLYS			
Full of pocky molys.	285	Why Come Ye	246
MOLLE			
For passe-a-Pase apase ys gone to cache a molle,	243	Speke Parott	413
MOLOC			
Melchisedeck mercyfull made Moloc mercyles.	232	Speke Parott	60
Moloc, that mawmett, there darre no man withsay;	243	Speke Parott	402
MOMMYNGE			
And as for theyr connynge, /A glommynge and a mommynge,	248	Collyn Clout	83
MONACORDYS			
To ask wher he fyndyth among hys monacordys	37	Coystrowne1	20
MONASTERIES			
Turne monasteries into water mylles,	257	Collyn Clout	418
MONCHE			
Nowe must you monche mamockes and lumpes of brede;	197	Magnyfycence	2009
MONE			
Thou mayste not studye or muse on the mone.	57	Bowge	383
That all is without measure and fer beyonde the mone.	146	Magnyfycence	224
Here MAGNYFYCENCE dolorously maketh his mone.	198	Magnyfycence	SD
Whate mone he made when Pamphylus loste hys make.	237	Speke Parott	234
As he to exployte the man owte of the mone.	239	Speke Parott	307
Maner of cause to mone.	258	Collyn Clout	479
Of wandryng of the mone, the course of the sun,	331	Garlande	691
MONEY			
Now wolde to God thou wolde leye money downe!	57	Bowge	395
She hath gote me more money with her tayle	57	Bowge	405
Money they shall dele	83	Phy Sparrow	455
to take money of CRAFTY CONVEYAUNCE, saynge to hym,	173	Magnyfycence	SD
Wyll ye spende ony money? Ye, a thousande pounde.	184	Magnyfycence	1570
Wolde money, trowest thou, make suche one to the call?	184	Magnyfycence	1573
Money maketh marchauntes, I tell you, over all.	184	Magnyfycence	1574
Why, wyl a maystres be wonne for money and for golde?	184	Magnyfycence	1575
Why, was not for money Troy bothe bought and solde?	184	Magnyfycence	1576
By the meanes of money without ony gonne.	184	Magnyfycence	1578
Lest that he thought that his money were evyll spente,	187	Magnyfycence	1674
Muche money, men sey, there madly he hathe spente;	240	Speke Parott	335
With money, yf it wyll happe /To catche the forked cappe.	249	Collyn Clout	88
The money for theyr masses	257	Collyn Clout	423
Moche money of the kynge	309	Why Come Ye	1192
MONE LIGHT			
Sometyme, as it semyth, when the mone light	330	Garlande	644
MONESTERIES			
So myche decay of monesteries and relygious places;	245	Speke Parott	499
MONETH			
The mery moneth of September,	117	Ag Scottes	66
MONETHES			
But within monethes thre	288	Why Come Ye	366
MONY			
Some have no mony /That thyder commy,	218	El Rummynge	160
Our mony madly lent,	282	Why Come Ye	143
lent] 'sent' Marshe 1568			
Fals forgers of mony, for kownnage atteintid,	329	Garlande	611
kownnage] 'coynnage' Marshe 1568			
With mony, as men sayne,	358	Garlande2	14
MONYS			
But howe the commons gronys, /And the people monys,	255	Collyn Clout	349
MONKE			
Good monke, nor good clerke,	274	Collyn Clout	1099
The monke of Bury then after them ensuyd,	323	Garlande	390

MONKES —MORE   Page   Title   Line

MONKES
Ye make monkes to have the colerage 255   Collyn Clout   363
    make] 'haue' Kele 1545.1, Marshe 1568, 'make' MS Harley 2252;
    colerage] 'culerage' Kele 1545.1, 'colerage' Harley 2252
MONKYS
Monkys may not for drede that men sholde them se. 154   Magnyfycence   493
MONNY
Thou art worth good and monny.' 220   El Rummynge   228
In stede of coyne and monny /Some brynge her a conny, ... 220   El Rummynge   244
MONSYRE
Over Scarpary mala vy, Monsyre Cy-and-sliddyr. 243   Speke Parott   414
MONTAYNES
The mantycors of the montaynes 79   Phy Sparrow   294
MOOD
But she wolde chaunge his mood, ... 100   Phy Sparrow   1158
Who so therat pyketh mood, ... 121   Ag Scottes2   21
    whoso] 'but who so' Day 1560, Marshe 1568
I pray God kepe you in that mood! 150   Magnyfycence   336
MOODE
With scornfull loke mevyd all in moode. 55   Bowge   317
    scornfull] 'scorfull' Marshe 1568
The White Lyon, there rampaunt of moode, ... 119   Ag Scottes   135
MOOST
Of kingis line moost streight, ... 110   Lawde   10
As king moost sovereine 111   Lawde   52
As my soverayne /Moost of pleasure. 113   Calliope   24
Me to enbrace and love moost specyally. 190   Magnyfycence   1800
Your hede that was wonte to be happed moost drowpy and drowsy, 197   Magnyfycence   2018
But the moost parte in generall. 252   Collyn Clout   245
'Prynces moost pusant, of hygh preemynence, ... 313   Garlande   50
Meddelyd with murnynge the moost parte of his muse, ... 320   Garlande   295
    murnynge] 'murmynge' †Fakes 1523
For when he spekyth fayrest, then thynketh he moost yll; . . . 333   Garlande   759
That goodly place to Skelton moost kynde, ... 353   Garlande   1462
For the moost recrayd /Cowardes afrayd, ... 362   Albany   115
Nacion moost in hate, /Proude and poore of state. 362   Albany   143
If our moost royall Harry 367   Albany   340
All his subjectes and he /Moost lovyngly agre 371   Albany   481
Moost false attaynted traytour, ... 371   Albany   493
In moost humble wyse, ... 372   Albany   524
And hym moost lowly pray, ... 372   Albany   528
MOOSTE
of the Mooste Honorable Erle of Northumberlande 29   Dol Dethe   I
Mooste noble Erld! O fowle mysuryd grounde, ... 32   Dol Dethe   118
Goddes mooste cruell unto the lyfe of man, ... 32   Dol Dethe   121
Adue, cowarde, adue! /Fals knight and mooste untrue, ... 366   Albany   315
MOR
And mor madly spent. 282   Why Come Ye   144
MORALYTE
Some of moralyte nobly dyde endyte; 46   Bowge   14
    moralyte] 'mortalyte' †Wynkyn de Worde 1499, Marshe 1568
MORALL
So many morall maters, and so lytell usyd; 244   Speke Parott   449
    many] 'many many' †MS Harley 2252
MORDRE
But that I drede mordre wolde come oute. 61   Bowge   524
MORE
And geve the grace to be more fortunate! 33   Dol Dethe   165
More specially barons, and thos knightis bold, ... 34   Dol Dethe   183
Advertysyng you, madame, to warke more secretly, ... 43   Balettys2   39
Nothynge yerthly to me more desyrous 44   Balettys3   43
'Fare well,' quod he, 'we wyll talke more of this.' 52   Bowge   227
What sholde I tell more of his rebaudrye? 56   Bowge   372
She hath gote me more money with her tayle 57   Bowge   405
It were more thryft he boughte him a newe cote; 60   Bowge   487
More coude I saye, but what this is ynowe. 60   Bowge   491
Adewe tyll soone, we shall speke more of this. 60   Bowge   492
Was moch more febler brayned. 64   Hauke   82
Then moch more, by the rode, ... 66   Hauke   178
With moch matter more, /That I kepe in store. 67   Hauke   220
Of the whych proces /Ye may know more expres, ... 68   Hauke   232
The more shal be your mede. 72   Phy Sparrow   16
Was never byrde in cage /More gentle of corage 80   Phy Sparrow   325
That never more slept, ... 104   Phy Sparrow   1304
And that was the more wrong. 111   Lawde   21
Therfor no more they shall 111   Lawde   36
And wyll not know /Theyr overthrow /At Branxton More? 115   Ag Scottes   11
At Branxton More and Flodden hylles. 119   Ag Scottes   131
And for he was a kyng, /The more shamefull rekenyng 121   Ag Scottes2   32
Chalenge yor selfe for a fole, call me no more knave. 122   Garnesche1   42
With moche mater more 126   Garnesche3   76
Tyll more matyr may cum. 129   Garnesche3   205
Of thy lewdenes more ys behynde; 134   Garnesche5   173
Worketh more mischiefe than can be tolde; 137   Ven Tongues   8
My scole is more solem and somwhat more haute 137   Ven Tongues   24
My scole is more solem and somwhat more haute 137   Ven Tongues   24
More stinging then scorpions that stang Pharaotis. 138   Ven Tongues   52
More venemous and much more virulent 138   Ven Tongues   53

MORELL — MOROW

	Page	Title	Line
More venemous and much more virulent	138	Ven Tongues	53
A fals double tunge is more fiers and fell	140	Ven Tongues	79
Me semeth that ye have dronken more than ye have bled.	147	Magnyfycence	260
Togyder we wyll talke more of this.	151	Magnyfycence	393
I may do somwhat, and more I thynke shall.	162	Magnyfycence	778
Moche more than nede	165	Magnyfycence	894
As here after thou shalte knowe more.	167	Magnyfycence	953
Ye, but I can somwhat more of the letter.	170	Magnyfycence	1066
And therfore I growe more on one day	170	Magnyfycence	1077
By the masse, yet art thou more fole than I.	171	Magnyfycence	1111
By Cockes harte, I wene thou hast no more.	172	Magnyfycence	1146
Hast thou ony more? Let se, procede.	174	Magnyfycence	1236
And, be the mater yll more or lesse,	175	Magnyfycence	1272
But, I say, let se and yf thou have any more.	175	Magnyfycence	1278
Syr, as by my wyll, it shall be so no more.	178	Magnyfycence	1377
In good faythe, syr, me semeth he had the more wronge.	178	Magnyfycence	1384
But yf it lyke your grace more at large	185	Magnyfycence	1589
And more than ever I dyd for ony man.	187	Magnyfycence	1694
Gyve them more than ynoughe, and let them not lacke;	190	Magnyfycence	1773
For there is nothynge that more dyspleaseth God	194	Magnyfycence	1928
And remembre he suffered moche more for your sake;	196	Magnyfycence	2001
I may no more speke tyll I have wept my fyll.	198	Magnyfycence	2063
A, shall we have more of this maters yet?	203	Magnyfycence	2214
There is no man may synne more mortally	206	Magnyfycence	2336
Your wordes be more sweter than ony precyous narde,	207	Magnyfycence	2345
More delectable than your langage to me.	207	Magnyfycence	2348
And ye shall have more worshyp then ever ye had.	210	Magnyfycence	2474
In all your warkys more grace shall ye fynde;	211	Magnyfycence	2485
It had ben hers, I wene, /More then fourty yere;	216	El Rummynge	58
And floure the more quycker;	219	El Rummynge	206
Maters more precious than the ryche jacounce,	241	Speke Parott	366
Some say but lityll and thynke more in there thowghte,	242	Speke Parott	388
Lyacon lawghyth thereatt and berythe hym more bolde;	242	Speke Parott	400
What trowe ye they say more /Of the bysshoppes lore?	249	Collyn Clout	92
And no more ye make	254	Collyn Clout	298
What coude the Turke do more	257	Collyn Clout	429
For to catche more and more:	260	Collyn Clout	569
For to catche more and more:	260	Collyn Clout	569
Shall I tell you more? Ye, shall.	262	Collyn Clout	635
These words shuld be more weyed,	265	Collyn Clout	769
These words] 'Those words' Marshe 1568, 'This' MS Harley 2252			
More mete in a pyllory -	266	Collyn Clout	812
We shall here more herafter!	281	Why Come Ye	99
But speke ye no more of that,	288	Why Come Ye	382
He regardeth lordes /No more than potshordes.	291	Why Come Ye	481
That he shall never ete more bred.	299	Why Come Ye	796
And more paper I thinke to blot	299	Why Come Ye	826
An hunderd pounde and more,	302	Why Come Ye	947
An] 'And' †Kele 1545.3			
Is moche more inordinate,	310	Why Come Ye2	14
And more horyble to beholde	310	Why Come Ye2	15
horyble] 'dyshonorable' MS Rawlinson C. 813			
And at more convenyent tyme	310	Why Come Ye2	21
as more at large it doth apere in the proces folowynge.	312	Garlande	1
Sume sayd, 'Holde thy peas, thou getest here no more.'	319	Garlande	257
To owe to yow our servyce, and more if we mowte!	324	Garlande	425
And ever they pressed on me more and more,	324	Garlande	445
And ever they pressed on me more and more,	324	Garlande	445
With all the prese that there was lesse and more.	325	Garlande	455
That ever more after by it they were aspyid;	329	Garlande	627
That never more slepte	349	Garlande	1297
But who may have a more ungracyous lyfe	352	Garlande	1451
a] not in Marshe 1568			
To bring with hym more brayne	363	Albany	174
Wherto shuld I more speke	366	Albany	302
Over this, for a more ample processe	374	Replycacion	1
Or more of this to clatter?	378	Replycacion	159
What shulde I recken more?	379	Replycacion	181
That never more may dye.	380	Replycacion	246

MORELL

A maunchet for morell thereon to snap.	37	Coystrowne1	11
Spur up at the hynder gyrth with, 'Gup, morell, gup!'	43	Balettys2	17

MORELLE

Gup, marmeset, jast ye morelle!	124	Garnesche3	13

MORYSHE

Thow bere, thow brystlyd bore, /Thou Moryshe mantycore,	128	Garnesche3	165
'Moryshe myne owne shelfe,' the costermonger sayth;	233	Speke Parott	85

MORNE

The tarsell gentyll, /They shall morne soft and styll	85	Phy Sparrow	559
But whereto shuld I /Lenger morne or crye?	86	Phy Sparrow	595

MORNETH

He morneth in blacke clothynge.	288	Why Come Ye	392

MORNING GOUNES

Shall stand in their morning gounes;	85	Phy Sparrow	566

MORNYNGE

To mornynge loke that ye fall	81	Phy Sparrow	390

MOROW

Even nor morow; /But other mennes sorow	94	Phy Sparrow	924

	Page	Title	Line
Sterre of the morow gray, ...	340	Garlande	988
MORTAL			
And knowe your selfe mortal for all your dygnyte;	211	Magnyfycence	2499
MORTALL			
To suffre hym slayn of his mortall fo?	30	Dol Dethe	38
That with thy sworde enharpid of mortall drede	32	Dol Dethe	125
It is generall /To be mortall:	39	Coystrowne3	8
Came for to slee me of mortall entente.	61	Bowge	529
Gave hym his mortall wounde, ...	79	Phy Sparrow	298
Ye, all thyng mortall shall torne unto nought	236	Speke Parott	214
MORTALLY			
There is no man may synne more mortally	206	Magnyfycence	2336
MOST			
Yet shamfully thei slew hym; that sham most them befall. . . .	30	Dol Dethe	49
Well may ye be cald commons most unkynd.	30	Dol Dethe	56
ye] 'you' Marshe 1568			
Demaundinge soche dutes as nedis most acord	31	Dol Dethe	66
These frantyke foolys I hate most of all;	36	Coystrowne1	2
Condute of comforte and well most soverayne;	44	Balettys3	12
Encleryd myrroure and perspectyve most bryght, ...	44	Balettys3	22
Theyr sayll of solace most comfortably clad, ...	44	Balettys3	27
Remorse have I of youre most goodlyhod, ...	44	Balettys3	29
With the turtyll most trew.	83	Phy Sparrow	465
Of Penelope most stable, ...	89	Phy Sparrow	725
To her husband most trew, ...	89	Phy Sparrow	726
Of that most goodly mayd	93	Phy Sparrow	852
goodly] 'godly' Wyght 1553, Kitson 1560.6, Marshe 1568			
For this most goodly floure, ...	94	Phy Sparrow	893
For this most goodly floure, ...	96	Phy Sparrow	989
For this most goodly floure, ...	97	Phy Sparrow	1022
[For] this most goodly floure, ...	98	Phy Sparrow	1054
For] not in †Kele 1545.2, Wyght 1553, Kitson 1560.6, Marshe 1568			
As Nature cold devyse, /In most goodly wyse.	98	Phy Sparrow	1072
For this most goodly floure, ...	98	Phy Sparrow	1083
goodly] 'godly' †Kele 1545.2			
For this most goodly flour, ...	99	Phy Sparrow	1107
For this most goodly floure, ...	100	Phy Sparrow	1136
For this most goodly floure, ...	100	Phy Sparrow	1161
For this most goodly floure, ...	101	Phy Sparrow	1185
For] not in Kitson 1560.6, Marshe 1568			
For this most goodly floure, ...	101	Phy Sparrow	1208
For this] 'The' †Kele 1545.2, Marshe 1568			
[For] this most goodly floure, ...	102	Phy Sparrow	1231
For] not in †Kele 1545.2, Wyght 1553, Kitson 1560.6, Marshe 1568; this] 'the' Wyght, Kitson, Marshe			
Your soveraygne lorde most reverent, ...	118	Ag Scottes	113
oratour to the kynges most royall estate.	120	Ag Scottes	E
Be the kynges most noble commandement.	122	Garnesche1	E
By the kynges most noble commaundment.	124	Garnesche2	E
Had yow most in despyght;	125	Garnesche3	66
By the kynges most noble commaundment.	129	Garnesche3	E
By the kyngys most noble commademennt.	134	Garnesche5	E
Of unhappy generacion /And most ungracious nacion.	136	Dundas	53
Or whiche of you can do most.	162	Magnyfycence	803
My name is Magnyfycence, man most of myght.	182	Magnyfycence	1493
Why, wyll they then be intreted, the most and the lest?	184	Magnyfycence	1585
Nowe Jesu preserve you, syr, prynce most of myght.	190	Magnyfycence	1796
For lyberalyte is most convenyent	200	Magnyfycence	2117
Whereto were most metely my corage to knyt?	211	Magnyfycence	2479
To our most royall kynge, ...	298	Why Come Ye	754
In olde commemoracion /Most royall Englyssh nacion.	305	Why Come Ye	1040
To whos astate all noblenes most leven, ...	313	Garlande	54
leven] 'lene' †Fakes 1523, MS Cotton Vitellius E.x			
Of that moste folow then consequently, ...	317	Garlande	172
But I most bannysshe hym frome my jurydiccyon, ...	318	Garlande	227
But blessyd Bachus most reverent and holy, ...	322	Garlande	362
All other transcendynge, the most rychely besene, ...	325	Garlande	483
From you most we, but not longe to tary.	326	Garlande	520
I thanked her moche of her most noble offer, ...	327	Garlande	554
'I thanke you, goodly maystres, to me most benynge, ...	332	Garlande	728
Our kyng most excellent.	369	Albany	429
And her most blessed baby, ...	375	Replycacion	19
Which is the most clere christall	375	Replycacion	31
Among the Grekes most relucent of lyght, ...	383	Replycacion	332
Which is God of myghtes most, ...	385	Replycacion	384
Now of late abjured, /Most unhappely ured;	385	Replycacion	405
MOSTE			
Falsly to slo ther moste singlar goode lorde?	30	Dol Dethe	27
slo] 'slee' Marshe 1568			
Maiden moste pure, and Goddis moder dere, ...	34	Dol Dethe	205
In Trinitate one God of myghtis moste.	35	Dol Dethe	217
That wyt he wantyth when he hath moste nede.	175	Magnyfycence	1261
And in theyr moste truste I make them overthrowe.	193	Magnyfycence	1885
He be your conducte, the Lorde of myghtys moste!	208	Magnyfycence	2386
Then Parot moste have an almon or a date.	231	Speke Parott	7
With herte moste tendyr, ...	237	Speke Parott	226
Of his moste princely porte, ...	370	Albany	473

	Page	Title	Line

MOT
His soule mot receyve in to ther company, — 35, Dol Dethe, 213
The fynde of hell mot sterve the! — 365, Albany, 251

MOTE
Ye, mary, is it. Ye, so mote I goo. — 198, Magnyfycence, 2046
For so mote I hoppy, /It coleth well my croppy.' — 228, El Rummynge, 560
 croppy] 'coppy' Day 1560, Marshe 1568

MOTHE-EATEN
Rudely rayne-beaten, /Rusty and mothe-eaten, — 248, Collyn Clout, 56
 mothe] 'moche' †Godfray 1531, 'moughte' Kele 1545.1, 'mothe' MS Harley 2252

MOTHER
That nother they set by father and mother; — 200, Magnyfycence, 2142
Holy churche our mother, — 274, Collyn Clout, 1105
of our mother Holy Churche, etc. — 373, Replycacion, 1
Of Mary, mother and mayed? — 376, Replycacion, 47
That glorious mayde and mother, — 381, Replycacion, 257

MOTH ETYN
Yor moth etyn mokkysh maneres, they be all to-myryd. — 123, Garnesche2, 12

MOTHYS
Yt bredth mothys in clothe of Arres. — 131, Garnesche5, 78

MOTYNGE
And let be all your motynge, — 273, Collyn Clout, 1073

MOTYVE
Unto your grace then make I this motyve: — 315, Garlande, 114

MOTTON
Why, is there any store of rawe motton? — 204, Magnyfycence, 2265
In fay, man, some rybbys of the motton be so ranke — 204, Magnyfycence, 2269

MOUGHT
They mought be better advysed — 261, Collyn Clout, 579

MOULDE
With moulde brede to eate - — 263, Collyn Clout, 653

MOUNT
From Sydony to the mount Olympyan, — 327, Garlande, 552

MOUNTAYNE
But in a mountayne gay, — 365, Albany, 260

MOUNTALBON
On Bayarde Mountalbon; — 88, Phy Sparrow, 656

MOUNTENAUNCE
The mountenaunce of two houres. — 288, Why Come Ye, 361

MOUNTITH
Mountith on hy with her melodious lay, — 327, Garlande, 535

MOUNTYNG
An hundred steppis mountyng to the halle, — 325, Garlande, 471

MOURNYNG
Mournyng all alone, — 89, Phy Sparrow, 704

MOUSE
Dronken as a mouse /At the ale house, — 266, Collyn Clout, 801
Yet it is a wyly mouse — 298, Why Come Ye, 756

MOUSE HOLE
Into a mouse hole they wolde — 286, Why Come Ye, 293

MOUTH
Her sugred mouth to kysse. — 97, Phy Sparrow, 1040
For her mouth fomyd /And her bely groned: — 223, El Rummynge, 341

MOUTHE
Her mouthe enbawmed, dylectable and mery, — 183, Magnyfycence, 1557
Bete a dum mouthe than a brainles scull; — 314, Garlande, 82
 Bete] 'Better' Marshe 1568, MS Cotton Vitellius E.x
It is harde to tell of every mannes mouthe: — 326, Garlande, 500

MOUTHES
The devyll can nat stop their mouthes — 272, Collyn Clout, 1051
That wyse Harpocrates /Had your mouthes stopped, — 377, Replycacion, 116

MOVE
I move them, I mase them, I make them so fonde, — 161, Magnyfycence, 742
Tushe! These maters that ye move are but soppys in ale; — 203, Magnyfycence, 2233

MOVED
I was sore moved to aforce the same, — 46, Bowge, 17

MOVYD
What movyd you agayn hym to war or to fight? — 31, Dol Dethe, 62
'What movyd the,' quod she, 'hydder to come?' — 48, Bowge, 78
This mater we have movyd, you myrthys to make, — 213, Magnyfycence, 2552

MOW
Ye wan nothyng there but a mow: — 131, Garnesche5, 50

MOWYNGE
To mockynge, to mowynge, to lyke a jackenapes - — 199, Magnyfycence, 2098

MOWTE
To owe to yow our servyce, and more if we mowte! — 324, Garlande, 425

MUCH
More venemous and much more virulent — 138, Ven Tongues, 53

MUCHE
and Muche Lamentable Chaunce — 29, Dol Dethe, 1
I care muche the lesse what ever they say, — 138, Ven Tongues, 36
Muche frutefull mater. But now for your defence, — 239, Speke Parott, 297
Muche money, men sey, there madly he hathe spente; — 240, Speke Parott, 335

MUD
He wrate of a muse throw a mud wall; — 351, Garlande, 1384

MULE
To ryde upon a mule — 254, Collyn Clout, 308

MULYS —MUSYS   Page   Title   Line

MULYS
Suche pollaxis and pyllers, suche mulys trapte with gold - ..   246   Speke Parott   517
MULLYNG
He calleth me his whytyng, /His mullyng and his [m]ytyng, ...   220   El Rummynge   224
  mytyng] 'nytyng' †Lant 1545, Kynge & Marche 1554,
  'nittinge' Day 1560, 'nittine' Marshe 1568
MUM
Can say nothynge but 'mum'.   269   Collyn Clout   905
There was amonge them no worde then but mum, ...   344   Garlande   1118
  amonge them no worde] 'not a worde amonge them' MS Cotton
  Vitellius E.x
MUMMYNGE
Of this mad mummynge /Of Elynour Rummynge.   230   El Rummynge   620
Men of suche maters make but mummynge, ...   318   Garlande   200
  but] 'but a' MS Cotton Vitellius E.x
MUNPYNNYS
Thy munpynnys, and thy crag, ...   366   Albany   293
MUR
Horsly, as he had the mur;   82   Phy Sparrow   419
MURDER
Spare not thy selfe, but boldly the murder.   206   Magnyfycence   2318
MURDRYNGE
Of this lordis dethe and of his murdrynge;   32   Dol Dethe   130
MURMER
A murmer of mynstrels, that suche another   320   Garlande   270
MURMURACYON
Make ye no murmuracyon   273   Collyn Clout   1079
MURMURAR
So madde a cordylar, /So madde a murmurar?   368   Albany   376
MURNYNG
Also the Murnyng of the Mapely Rote;   351   Garlande   1377
  Murnyng] 'murmyng' †Fakes 1523
MURNYNGE
Meddelyd with murnynge the moost parte of his muse, ...   320   Garlande   295
  murnynge] 'murmynge' †Fakes 1523
MURRE
And I gyve hym the cowghe, the murre, and the pose.   204   Magnyfycence   2259
MURRIOUN
Thou murrioun, thow mawment, ...   128   Garnesche3   170
MURRYON
Of Mantryble the Bryge, Malchus the Murryon, ...   122   Garnesche1   22
MURTHER
And some I vysyte [with] batayle, warre, and murther, ...   194   Magnyfycence   1912
  with] 'to' †Rastell & Treveris C 1530, B
MUSCULL
Lyke a scabbyd muscull.   228   El Rummynge   556
MUSE
Transcending f[a]r myne homely Muse that must   33   Dol Dethe   144
  far] 'for' †MS Royal 18 D.ii, Marshe 1568
Thou mayste not studye or muse on the mone.   57   Bowge   383
Melpomone, O muse tragedyall, ...   117   Ag Scottes   77
Thalya, my muse, for you also call I, ...   117   Ag Scottes   85
Plucke up your mynde, syr, what ayle you to muse?   148   Magnyfycence   283
Whan other men laughe, than study I and muse, ...   160   Magnyfycence   707
And make them so longe to muse   174   Magnyfycence   1224
Meddelyd with murnynge the moost parte of his muse, ...   320   Garlande   295
  murnynge] 'murmynge' †Fakes 1523
Juvenall satirray, that men makythe to muse;   321   Garlande   340
He wrate of a muse throw a mud wall;   351   Garlande   1384
Ye muse somwhat to far;   368   Albany   377
And chase them thorowe the muse   380   Replycacion   212
MUSED
And yf ye knewe howe I have mused, ...   156   Magnyfycence   580
Grete mervayle I had, and mused in my mynde.   191   Magnyfycence   1822
MUSES
Where the muses dwell: 87   Phy Sparrow   611
Of the Muses nyne, ...   93   Phy Sparrow   858
With the nyne Muses, Pierides by name;   331   Garlande   680
  with] 'wit' †Fakes 1523
In metricall muses, his harpyng we may spare;   383   Replycacion   338
MUSIS
In the college of musis goddes hystoriall, ...   29   Dol Dethe   9
If the hole quere of the Musis nyne   33   Dol Dethe   155
Weth Amphion, and other musis of Archady   320   Garlande   273
Ovyde, enshryned with the musis nyne;   321   Garlande   333
MUSYK
Hys musyk withoute mesure, to sharp is hys my;   37   Coystrowne1   25
MUSYKKYS
and madly in hys musykkys mokkyshly made agaynste   36   Coystrowne   I
MUSYNG
Musyng nyght and day, ...   89   Phy Sparrow   703
MUSYNGE
But as I stode musynge in my mynde, ...   52   Bowge   230
In place alone then musynge in my thought   312   Garlande   8
Whylis I stode musynge in this medytatyon, ...   313   Garlande   29
MUSYS
the ix Musys of polytyke poems and poettys matryculat. . . .   36   Coystrowne   I
Of the Musys nyne, Calliope   131   Garnesche5   87

MUSKETTE —MUST   Page   Title   Line

Aqueintyng hym with the Musys nyne.   132   Garnesche5   100
MUSKETTE
The hobby and the muskette   86   Phy Sparrow   567
MUSSE
Had I of his swete musse;   80   Phy Sparrow   362
   his] 'this' †Kele 1545.2, Wyght 1553
Goddes blissyng lyght on thy lytell swete musse!   238   Speke Parott   266
MUST
Transcending f[a]r myne homely Muse that must   33   Dol Dethe   144
   far] 'for' †MS Royal 18 D.ii, Marshe 1568
And dy we must.   39   Coystrowne3   6
But that I must wryte for my plesaunt pastaunce   42   Balettys2   4
That I must shewe you moche of my counselle -   52   Bowge   207
Must helpe us to houle;   82   Phy Sparrow   443
Must tell what is of the clocke   84   Phy Sparrow   496
A phenex it is /This herse that must blys   84   Phy Sparrow   519
And now must kys the post;   89   Phy Sparrow   716
Now must ye knowe our kynge for your regent, ...   114   Scot Kynge   21
But with countenaunce your corage must be croppyd.   141   Magnyfycence   47
Some reason we must make.   143   Magnyfycence   99
Then ye must bothe consent   143   Magnyfycence   107
With every condycyon measure must be sought.   143   Magnyfycence   115
Yet in this man you must set your delyght.   145   Magnyfycence   167
But plenarly all thought from you must be dyschargyd, ...   146   Magnyfycence   207
Ryght so a sharp fansy must be founde   155   Magnyfycence   553
That all this matter must under grope.   157   Magnyfycence   600
But I must tary here; go thou before.   167   Magnyfycence   954
Thou must have thy fansy and thy wyll, ...   173   Magnyfycence   1183
That rubbed she must be on the gall   174   Magnyfycence   1232
Nay, but fansy must be eyther fyrst or last.   176   Magnyfycence   1288
Yet for his name we must fynde a [slyght].   176   Magnyfycence   1308
   slyght] shyfte †Rastell & Treveris C 1530, B
Must mesure, in the mares name, you furnysshe and dresse? . .   179   Magnyfycence   1391
Than waste must be welcome, and fare well thryfte.   180   Magnyfycence   1444
All honour to me must nedys stowpe and lene.   181   Magnyfycence   1462
Then some occacyon or quarell ye must fynde, ...   185   Magnyfycence   1600
To styre up your stomake you must you forge, ...   185   Magnyfycence   1613
Ye, walke he must; it was no better worth.   189   Magnyfycence   1736
Thus must ye stuffe and store your treasure.   189   Magnyfycence   1754
Yet somtyme, parde, I must use largesse.   189   Magnyfycence   1755
Vyle velyarde, thou must not nowe my dynt withstande;   193   Magnyfycence   1878
Thou must not abyde the dynt of my hande.   193   Magnyfycence   1879
Nowe must I this carcasse lyft up.   195   Magnyfycence   1964
He dynyd with delyte, with poverte he must sup.   195   Magnyfycence   1965
Nowe must you lerne to begge at every mannes gate.   196   Magnyfycence   1981
Ye, syr, nowe must ye lerne to lye harde, ...   197   Magnyfycence   2005
Nowe must your fete lye hyer than your crowne.   197   Magnyfycence   2007
Nowe must you monche mamockes and lumpes of brede;   197   Magnyfycence   2009
Nowe must ye suffre bothe hunger and colde.   197   Magnyfycence   2013
Nowe must ye lerne to lye on the strawe.   197   Magnyfycence   2015
Nowe must be storm ybeten with showres and raynes.   197   Magnyfycence   2017
Your trymynge and tramynge by me must be tangyd, ...   203   Magnyfycence   2234
Though I aske mercy I must nedys be refusyd.   205   Magnyfycence   2299
Nowe must I make you a lectuary softe -   207   Magnyfycence   2355
With drammes of devocyon your dyet must be drest, ...   207   Magnyfycence   2358
Fyrst, from your magnyfycence syn must be abjectyd;   211   Magnyfycence   2484
Measure of your lustys must have the oversyght, ...   211   Magnyfycence   2491
Without drynke she must dye;   221   El Rummynge   273
And every mad medler must now be a maker.   235   Speke Parott   161
Must cast up theyr blacke vayles   256   Collyn Clout   396
Lordes must crouche and knele, ...   262   Collyn Clout   628
   crouche] 'couch' Marshe 1568, 'cruche' MS Harley 2252
He must do this werke;   264   Collyn Clout   728
It must come to his lot   265   Collyn Clout   750
Must preche a Goddes halfe   266   Collyn Clout   810
For they must take in hande   268   Collyn Clout   888
Therupon must herke, ...   272   Collyn Clout   1026
So /That rage must make pyllage   280   Why Come Ye   50
They must stande all afar   286   Why Come Ye   301
But to his sentence must accorde.   287   Why Come Ye   343
All men must folow his desyre.   287   Why Come Ye   345
   must] not in Marshe 1568
That he must pyll his lande   290   Why Come Ye   453
Syr, ye must tary a stounde, ...   294   Why Come Ye   626
And syr, ye must daunce attendaunce, ...   294   Why Come Ye   628
That of force he must   298   Why Come Ye   752
Than must we agre /With poverte;   300   Why Come Ye   864
Ye must weare bukram, ...   302   Why Come Ye   918
Must counte what became   302   Why Come Ye   934
He must tax for his wull   302   Why Come Ye   938
He must pay agayn   302   Why Come Ye   943
But all must be tryde, ...   304   Why Come Ye   1013
It is sittynge that ye must hym correct.'   314   Garlande   77
As sumtyme he must vyces remorde, ...   314   Garlande   86
The lesarde came lepyng, and sayd that he must, ...   315   Garlande   104
To your remembraunce wherfore ye must call   335   Garlande   812
Sith ye must nedis afforce it by pretence   335   Garlande   817

MUSTARDE —NAY   Page   Title   Line

Text	Page	Title	Line
But to do you servyce nedis now I must;	337	Garlande	879
to do you] 'do her' MS Cotton Vitellius E.x			
Make no delay, for now ye must be brought	343	Garlande	1090
Where ye must brevely answere to your name.'	343	Garlande	1092
Of that shalbe resonde you ye must be content;	344	Garlande	1123
you] not in Marshe 1568			
Nedes must he rin that the devyll dryvith.	352	Garlande	1434
It must nedes after rin all the worlde aboute.'	353	Garlande	1483
But now must I /Your Duke ascry /Of Albany	360	Albany	72
Must crepe in to your caves	363	Albany	185
A vengeaunce and dispight /On the must nedes lyght	364	Albany	235
To this ye nedes must agre.	381	Replycacion	284
To whom we must gyve faythe,	384	Replycacion	348
With me ye must consent	384	Replycacion	362
That forthwith we must nede	385	Replycacion	387

MUSTARDE

For lyke as mustarde is sharpe of taste	155	Magnyfycence	552
The Balade also of the Mustarde Tarte.	347	Garlande	1245

MUSTE

But who wyll have it muste paye therfore dere.	47	Bowge	53
I can not flater, I muste be playne to the.	50	Bowge	164
There muste for hym be layde some prety beyte.	55	Bowge	312
Thou muste swere and stare, man, aldaye longe,	57	Bowge	381
Now renne muste I to the stewys syde	57	Bowge	400
Ye muste be ruled, as I shall tell you howe.	60	Bowge	493
And I muste you requyre	143	Magnyfycence	110
By God, yet it muste begynne moche of the.	154	Magnyfycence	514
All that he dothe muste be alowde;	175	Magnyfycence	1247
But wyfull waywardnesse muste walke out of the way;	211	Magnyfycence	2490

MUSTER

I muster, I medle amonge these grete estates;	160	Magnyfycence	736

MUSTY

Howe be it of scape thryfte your clokes smelleth musty.	161	Magnyfycence	761

MUSTRED

Mustred ther amonge them with many a mad tale;	322	Garlande	373

MUTABILITE

And of melancoly mutabilite,	138	Ven Tongues	44

MUTABYLYTE

Whan Luna, full of mutabylyte,	46	Bowge	3
She dawnsyth varyaunce with mutabylyte,	197	Magnyfycence	2026

MUTYD

And in the holy place /She mutyd there a chase	63	Hauke	62

MUTRELL

What here ye of Mutrell?	288	Why Come Ye	377

NACION

Of unhappy generacion /And most ungracious nacion.	136	Dundas	53
In olde commemoracion /Most royall Englyssh nacion.	305	Why Come Ye	1040
And in abhominacion /Of all maner of nacion,	362	Albany	142
Nacion moost in hate, /Proude and poore of state.	362	Albany	143

NACYON

On all the hole nacyon	78	Phy Sparrow	275
It shameth all your noughty nacyon,	117	Ag Scottes	56
Of all our royall Englysh nacyon.	117	Ag Scottes	76
And I am Lyberte, made of in every nacyon.	145	Magnyfycence	172
All this nacyon /I set on fyre /In my facyon	165	Magnyfycence	884
Recountyng commoditis of many a straunge nacyon;	354	Garlande	1500

NACYONS

Of all nacyons under the hevyn,	36	Coystrownel	1
Embassades of all nacyons.	289	Why Come Ye	415
Of poetis laureat of many dyverse nacyons;	321	Garlande	324
Be issuis and portis from all maner of nacyons';	328	Garlande	580

NACYOUN

The Recule ageinst Gaguyne of the Frenshe nacyoun;	346	Garlande	1187
The Nacyoun of Folys he left not behynde.	353	Garlande	1470

NAGGYS

Hys jentyll curtoy[l], and set nowght by small naggys!	43	Balettys2	16
curtoyl] 'curtoyt' †Rastell 1527.1			

NAY

Ye had not ben hable to have saide hym nay.	31	Dol Dethe	70
With one vice importune thei playnly said nay.	31	Dol Dethe	80
Jak wold jet and yet Jyll sayd nay;	37	Coystrownel	43
Nay, jape not with hym, he is no small fole;	38	Coystrownel	50
Nay, naye, be sure, whyles I am on your syde	50	Bowge	169
Then thus to you - Nay, suffer me yet ferther to say,	142	Magnyfycence	48
I trowe ye can not say nay moche to this:	142	Magnyfycence	74
Nay, ye shall begynne, by my wyll.	143	Magnyfycence	104
Nay, syr, it was nothynge but your mynde.	149	Magnyfycence	330
It wolde be nyce, thoughe I say nay;	153	Magnyfycence	459
Nay, nay. He hath chaunged his, and I have chaunged myne.	155	Magnyfycence	518
Nay, nay. He hath chaunged his, and I have chaunged myne.	155	Magnyfycence	518
Counterfet Countenaunce, nay, come hyder -	155	Magnyfycence	547
Nay, and you be angry and overwharte,	156	Magnyfycence	562
Nay. Let us our heddes togyder cast.	156	Magnyfycence	566
Nay, lette us not clatter thus styll.	157	Magnyfycence	610
Nay; eyther let me tell, or elles tell ye.	158	Magnyfycence	633
Dusty! Nay, syr, ye be all of the lusty;	161	Magnyfycence	760
Nay. Thou art a man good inough but for thy false hart.	162	Magnyfycence	769
Nay, come at ones, for the armes of the dyce.	162	Magnyfycence	781

NAYE — NAKED

	Page	Title	Line
Nay, come away, man! Thou playst the cayser.	162	Magnyfycence	787
Nede? Yes, Mary. I say not nay.	163	Magnyfycence	807
Nay, in good faythe. It is but the gyse.	163	Magnyfycence	809
Nay. Purchace ye a pardon for the pose,	163	Magnyfycence	825
Nay. It is a farly fowle.	166	Magnyfycence	923
Nay, but wotest thou what I do say?	170	Magnyfycence	1092
Hay, chysshe, come hyder! Nay, torde! Take hym be tyme.	171	Magnyfycence	1117
Nay, in faythe, it was but a strype	171	Magnyfycence	1125
Nay, in fayth, fyrst let me here thyne.	172	Magnyfycence	1152
Nay, by Cockys harte, he ne reckys;	172	Magnyfycence	1167
Nay, offer hym a counter in stede of a peny.	172	Magnyfycence	1171
Nay, iwys, fole. It is a doteryll.	173	Magnyfycence	1175
Nay, nay. Thou shalt fynde hym another maner of man.	173	Magnyfycence	1189
Nay, nay. Thou shalt fynde hym another maner of man.	173	Magnyfycence	1189
Nay, I tell the, he maketh no dowtes	174	Magnyfycence	1210
Nay, it is I that foles can make;	174	Magnyfycence	1213
Nay, wylte thou here nowe of his scoles,	174	Magnyfycence	1216
Nay, beyonde all other set hym alone.	174	Magnyfycence	1235
Nay, that is my parte that thou spekest of nowe.	175	Magnyfycence	1282
Nay, but fansy must be eyther fyrst or last.	176	Magnyfycence	1288
Nay, nay; not so, my frende Felycyte.	179	Magnyfycence	1392
Nay, nay; not so, my frende Felycyte.	179	Magnyfycence	1392
Nay. He shall be ruled even as I lyst.	179	Magnyfycence	1394
Nay, fyrst Lusty Pleasure is my desyre to have;	180	Magnyfycence	1453
Nay, nay; for lesse I waraunt you to be sped,	184	Magnyfycence	1571
Nay, nay; for lesse I waraunt you to be sped,	184	Magnyfycence	1571
Nay, syr. That affeccyon ought to be reserved,	186	Magnyfycence	1643
Nay, indede, but I sawe howe ye prayed,	188	Magnyfycence	1696
Nay, I tell you, I am not wonte to fode	188	Magnyfycence	1698
Syr, as ye say. Nay, come on with me.	188	Magnyfycence	1707
God gyve hym a myscheffe! Nay, nowe let me alone.	189	Magnyfycence	1730
Nay, so God me helpe, it was no grete vexacyon;	189	Magnyfycence	1733
It was a ronner; nay, fole, I warant her blode warme.	191	Magnyfycence	1811
Nay. Madnesse hath begyled you and many mo;	192	Magnyfycence	1856
Nay. He that ye sent us, Clokyd Colusyon,	192	Magnyfycence	1859
Nay. It was your fondnesse that ye have usyd.	193	Magnyfycence	1866
Nay, to wrangle, I warant the, it is but a stone-caste.	201	Magnyfycence	2174
Nay, horson, here is my glove. Take it up and thou dare.	202	Magnyfycence	2178
Nay. Then thou wylte dynge the devyll and thou be not holde.	202	Magnyfycence	2183
Nay, thou rude ravener, rayne beten javell!	202	Magnyfycence	2191
Nay, thou false harted dastarde! Thou dare not abyde.	202	Magnyfycence	2193
Nay, iche shall wrynge the, horson, on the wryst.	202	Magnyfycence	2196
Nay, by Saynt Mary, it was ye called me knave.	203	Magnyfycence	2212
Nay, I know well inough ye are bothe well handyd	203	Magnyfycence	2230
Nay, nay, man. I loke never to have parte of his grace;	205	Magnyfycence	2297
Nay, nay, man. I loke never to have parte of his grace;	205	Magnyfycence	2297
Shall I myselfe hange with an halter? Nay,	206	Magnyfycence	2320
Nay; rather wyll I chose to ryd me of this lyve	206	Magnyfycence	2321
Without fayle, syr, that is no nay:	209	Magnyfycence	2429
That I sholde use largesse. Nay, syr, there a pause.	209	Magnyfycence	2437
Elynour swered, 'Nay,	218	El Rummynge	164
With, 'Who is there? A mayd?' Nay, nay, I trow!	233	Speke Parott	100
With, 'Who is there? A mayd?' Nay, nay, I trow!	233	Speke Parott	100
Agayne Frentike Frenesy there dar no man sey nay,	243	Speke Parott	422
Spende? Nay, but spare!	251	Collyn Clout	178
Nay, to the kynges court!	289	Why Come Ye	405
Nay, nay, he is nat dede.	299	Why Come Ye	794
Nay, nay, he is nat dede.	299	Why Come Ye	794
In generrall wordes, I say not gretely nay,	315	Garlande	99
'Nay, holde thy tunge,' quod another, 'let me have the name.'	319	Garlande	255
Though Jak sayd nay, yet Mok there loste her sho;	351	Garlande	1396
'Nay, sir' she sayd, 'what so in this place	353	Garlande	1481
Syr Duke, nay, syr ducke,	364	Albany	222
In a tent? Nay. Nay.	365	Albany	259
In a tent? Nay. Nay.	365	Albany	259

NAYE

	Page	Title	Line
Nay, naye, be sure, whyles I am on your syde	50	Bowge	169
Naye, strawe for tales, thou shalte not rule us;	55	Bowge	341
Naye, see where yonder stondeth the teder man!	59	Bowge	484

NAYLE

	Page	Title	Line
And yf that he hytte /The nayle on the hede	247	Collyn Clout	34

NAYLED

	Page	Title	Line
Chryst by cruelte /Was nayled upon a tre;	258	Collyn Clout	451

NAYLYS

	Page	Title	Line
Her naylys sharpe as tenter-hokys!	168	Magnyfycence	1001

NAYTHYR

	Page	Title	Line
That naythyr pump nor synke	127	Garnesche3	145

NAKED

	Page	Title	Line
The hy auter he strypte naked;	63	Hauke	49
Upon my naked skyn.	76	Phy Sparrow	167
And wretchedly ye lay starke naked.	119	Ag Scottes	167
starke naked] 'starke your naked' Kynge & Marche 1554, Day 1560, 'starke all naked' Marshe 1568			
Upon a naked man and yf she scrat.	176	Magnyfycence	1298
Nowe hath he ryght nought, naked as an asse.	193	Magnyfycence	1893
Wyth theyr naked pappes, /That flyppes and flappes,	217	El Rummynge	135
Ones hed wold have aked /To se her naked.	226	El Rummynge	479
With Dame Dyana naked;	270	Collyn Clout	944

NAKID —NAME	Page	Title	Line
Naked boyes strydynge, ...	270	Collyn Clout	967
But at the naked stewes	284	Why Come Ye	236
NAKID			
Harde to make ought of that is nakid nought;	346	Garlande	1205
NAKIDE			
Mi wordis unpullysht be nakide and playne, ...	32	Dol Dethe	127
NAKYD			
Gaspyng asyde, /Nakyd of hyde, ...	39	Coystrowne3	17
To clothe the nakyd where is lackynge a smocke -	177	Magnyfycence	1345
NALE			
And lete us laugh a placke or tweyne at nale.	57	Bowge	387
placke] 'plucke' Marshe 1568			
NALL			
But yf yt war Syr Tyrmagant that tyrnyd without nall;	121	Garneschel	4
NAMAN			
This Naman Sirus, /So fell and so irous, ...	308	Why Come Ye	1166
Sirus] 'tyrus' MS Rawlinson C. 813			
NAME			
Of hevenly poems, O Clyo, calde by name	29	Dol Dethe	8
O dolorous Teusday, dedicate to thi name, ...	32	Dol Dethe	114
Whos noble actis shew worsheply his name, ...	33	Dol Dethe	143
Whoos name to tell is Dame Saunce-Pere.	47	Bowge	51
Her chyef gentylwoman, Daunger by her name, ...	48	Bowge	69
What is thy name?' and I sayde it was Drede.	48	Bowge	77
Desyre her name was, and so she me tolde, ...	48	Bowge	85
Whose name regystred was	75	Phy Sparrow	149
/The storyes by name	88	Phy Sparrow	660
And blemysshed is her name, ...	89	Phy Sparrow	712
Of that name he is sure	89	Phy Sparrow	722
Though I regester her name	94	Phy Sparrow	891
That her goodly name, /Honorably reported, ...	103	Phy Sparrow	1285
In the name of Kyng Saul;	105	Phy Sparrow	1343
Whose name enrolde /With silke and golde	112	Calliope	9
But if that I knewe what his name hight, ...	139	Ven Tongues	73
For Welthfull Felicite truly is my name.	141	Magnyfycence	23
Your name is Lyberte, as I understande.	141	Magnyfycence	27
But Measure, my frende, what hyght this mannys name?	145	Magnyfycence	165
And, syr, this other mannys name is Lyberte.	145	Magnyfycence	168
Nowe, I beseche the, tell me what is thy name?	148	Magnyfycence	269
Syr, hardely remembre what may your name avaunce.	148	Magnyfycence	277
But largesse may amende your name.	151	Magnyfycence	389
Tell you where of my name dothe ryse.	151	Magnyfycence	409
But I say, kepest thou the olde name styll that thou had? . .	155	Magnyfycence	516
Nowe what is his name? And what is thyne?	155	Magnyfycence	519
For to knowe your name?	157	Magnyfycence	592
Cockes armes! Is that your name?	157	Magnyfycence	598
His name Largesse, Surveyaunce myne.	158	Magnyfycence	643
But shall I have myne olde name styll?	158	Magnyfycence	647
And Sober Sadnesse shalbe your name?	159	Magnyfycence	681
Ye, but what shall I call my name?	167	Magnyfycence	958
Ye, but of my name let us be wyse.	167	Magnyfycence	963
To name thyselfe. Come of, it were done.	167	Magnyfycence	965
For all that my name hyght Foly, ...	171	Magnyfycence	1110
What callest thou thy dogge? Tusshe! His name is Gryme. . . .	171	Magnyfycence	1118
Yet for his name we must fynde a [slyght].	176	Magnyfycence	1308
slyght] shyfte †Rastell & Treveris C 1530, B			
Not a better name under the sonne;	176	Magnyfycence	1310
Must mesure, in the mares name, you furnysshe and dresse? . .	179	Magnyfycence	1391
What the devyll, man, your name shalbe the greter;	180	Magnyfycence	1440
My name is Magnyfycence, man most of myght.	182	Magnyfycence	1493
That you trustyd, and Fansy is my name;	193	Magnyfycence	1871
In lust and lykynge my name is Lyberte.	199	Magnyfycence	2078
Cockys bonys! Thou begger, what is thy name?	203	Magnyfycence	2240
Dyspare is my name, that adversyte dothe f[o]lowe;	205	Magnyfycence	2284
folowe] 'felowe' †Rastell & Treveris C 1530, B, Douce Fragment d.7			
Good Hope, syr, my name is; remedy pryncypall	206	Magnyfycence	2328
Than stande up, syr, in Goddys name!	208	Magnyfycence	2397
Redresse my name is, that lytell am I used	208	Magnyfycence	2411
Largesse, syr, by his credence was his name.	209	Magnyfycence	2441
I understande, her name /Is Elynour Rummynge, ...	216	El Rummynge	92
And called for our dame, /Elynour by name.	229	El Rummynge	593
My name ys Parott, a byrde of Paradyse, ...	231	Speke Parott	1
There is none that your name woll abbrogate	240	Speke Parott	317
My name is Collyn Cloute.	248	Collyn Clout	49
Some can nat declyne theyr name!	253	Collyn Clout	276
By them to gette a name.	270	Collyn Clout	959
They have an evyll name, ...	275	Collyn Clout	1143
which hath to name Why Come Ye Nat to Courte?	278	Why Come Ye	I
Johannes Balua was his name	297	Why Come Ye	726
Whatsoever your name be?	309	Why Come Ye2	2
As I harde say, Dame Pallas was her name, ...	313	Garlande	48
Of your request, regestred is his name	314	Garlande	62
Wherby he myght have a name inmortall?	315	Garlande	119
His name? Or why is it, I you praye, ...	316	Garlande	138
But whome that ye favoure, I se well, hath a name, ...	317	Garlande	176
Some have a name for thefte and brybery;	317	Garlande	183
If he to the ample encrease of his name	318	Garlande	222

	Page	Title	Line
NAMED —NAT			
'Nay, holde thy tunge,' quod another, 'let me have the name.'	319	Garlande	255
Lucilius and Valerius Maximus by name;	322	Garlande	380
My name, I know well, beyonde that I am able,	324	Garlande	438
When he is callid to answere to his name.'	325	Garlande	452
This gentilwoman, that callyd was by name	327	Garlande	527
Your name recountynge beyonde the lande of Tyre,	327	Garlande	551
Hither they come crowdyng to get them a name,	329	Garlande	621
With the nyne Muses, Pierides by name;	331	Garlande	680
with] 'wit' †Fakes 1523			
His name for to know if that ye lyst,	333	Garlande	752
Cirus by name, as wrytith the story;	336	Garlande	858
So shall your name endure perpetually,	336	Garlande	861
Yowr name to se /It be enrolde, /Writtin with golde.	338	Garlande	937
For to encrese /Yowre goodly name.	339	Garlande	960
Where ye must brevely answere to your name.'	343	Garlande	1092
For in owr courte, ye wote wele, his name can not ryse	345	Garlande	1154
to reherse all by name that he hath compylyd, &c.	345	Garlande	R
His commedy, Achademios callyd by name;	346	Garlande	1184
That her goodly name, /Honorably reportid,	348	Garlande	1278
In the name of Kyng Saull;	350	Garlande	1336
Of your Scottysshe name.	360	Albany	47
Whose name over all	361	Albany	108
NAMED			
Here begynneth a lytell treatyse named The Bowge of Courte	46	Bowge	I
And of Syr Lybius /Named Dysconius;	88	Phy Sparrow	650
He is named Troylus baud;	89	Phy Sparrow	721
That I Jane have named,	103	Phy Sparrow	1256
have] not in Marshe 1568			
Why have ye hym named and all other refused?	148	Magnyfycence	281
Sure Surveyaunce I named me.	155	Magnyfycence	525
Alasse that ever I Magnyfycence was named!	196	Magnyfycence	1983
For no man have I named.	274	Collyn Clout	1111
To be shamfully named!	305	Why Come Ye	1053
named] 'name' Marshe 1568			
NAMELES			
He shall be as now nameles,	62	Hauke	38
NAMELESSE			
What though ye be namelesse,	309	Why Come Ye2	3
NAMES			
By Chemeras flames, /And all the dedly names	105	Phy Sparrow	1331
Now by these names thre,	105	Phy Sparrow	1363
Theyr names shall never dye.	106	Epitaphe	I
And counterfeted our names we have	158	Magnyfycence	641
Set nought by golde ne grotes, /Theyr names yf I durst tell.	250	Collyn Clout	161
Parte of there names I thynke to specefye:	321	Garlande	325
Ther names recountyng in the court of Fame;	334	Garlande	781
Now by theys names thre,	350	Garlande	1356
To magnifye their names.	374	Replycacion	10
Your names to magnifye,	378	Replycacion	164
NAMETH			
My lordys grace nameth it	302	Why Come Ye	940
NAMYD			
Go, litelle quayre, namyd the Popagay,	238	Speke Parott	278
Among my recordes suffer hym namyd,	316	Garlande	160
It passid all bawmys that ever were namyd,	331	Garlande	674
NAMYS			
By Chemeras flamys, /And all the dedely namys	349	Garlande	1324
NAP			
Ly styll hardely, and take a nap.'	41	Balettys1	4
NAPERY			
Some of the napery;	227	El Rummynge	532
NAPULS			
Frome Napuls, from Navern, and from Rouncevall,	326	Garlande	495
NARDE			
Your wordes be more sweter than ony precyous narde,	207	Magnyfycence	2345
NARROW			
A narrow unfethered and without an hed,	232	Speke Parott	74
NARROWE			
And some went so narrowe	222	El Rummynge	297
NAT			
Are nat these Scottys /Folys and sottys,	116	Ag Scottes	29
Yet your contenons oncomly, yor face ys nat fayer.	122	Garneschel	18
That mastres Punt put yow of, yt was nat alle causeles;	122	Garneschel	32
Your harte ys to hawte, iwys, yt wyll nat be alowde.	123	Garnesche2	26
Mirres vous y, /Loke nat to hy.	124	Garnesche2	E
I caste me nat to be od	124	Garnesche3	6
Yower knavery I wyll nat hyde,	124	Garnesche3	22
For alle ys nat worthe a myteyng,	127	Garnesche3	115
So suerly yt xall nat tarnishe.	127	Garnesche3	122
Thou mokkyshe marmoset, /I will nat dy in [thy] det.	128	Garnesche3	173
thy] 'they' †MS Harley 367			
That byrd ys nat honest	129	Garnesche5	197
Ye have nat red the properte	129	Garnesche5	8
Also nat fare from Bowgy Row,	130	Garnesche5	47
Sche wolde nat of yt thow had sworne.	131	Garnesche5	52
Sche sware with hyr ye xulde nat dele,	131	Garnesche5	57
Fusty bawdyas, I sey nat alle.	131	Garnesche5	76
It semyth nat thy pyllyd pate	132	Garnesche5	89

	Page	Title	Line
Thow thou be pyllyd, thow ar nat sade.	132	Garnesche5	117
It ys nat mete for soche a knave.	133	Garnesche5	156
Ye be nat cawte in an hempen snare.	133	Garnesche5	163
I care nat what thow wryght or sey;	134	Garnesche5	168
Thy fonde face can me nat fray.	134	Garnesche5	171
A reme of papyr wyll nat holde	134	Garnesche5	174
It is nat for your werynge,	252	Collyn Clout	210
Your gorge nat endued /Without a capon stued,	252	Collyn Clout	215
Construe nat worth a whystell	252	Collyn Clout	236
I speke nat nowe of all,	252	Collyn Clout	244
I speke nat of the good wyfe,	253	Collyn Clout	253
For that they are nat apposed	253	Collyn Clout	265
And yet he wyll nat drede	253	Collyn Clout	278
Alas, why do ye nat handle	255	Collyn Clout	332
And nat par service de socage,	256	Collyn Clout	368
Therwith I wyll nat mell.	257	Collyn Clout	428
Yf it please nat theologys	258	Collyn Clout	465
nat theologys] 'the not onely' MS Lansdowne 762 'not theologi' MS Harley 2252			
That I wyll nat wade	266	Collyn Clout	781
Shall nat be objected by me.	266	Collyn Clout	794
by] 'for' Kele 1545.1, Marshe 1568, 'at by' MS Harley 2252			
And he dare nat well neven	267	Collyn Clout	824
He coude nat synge hymselfe therout	268	Collyn Clout	878
And nat so hardy on his hede	272	Collyn Clout	1023
nat] 'not' Marshe 1568, MS Harley 2252			
I do it nat for no despyte.	273	Collyn Clout	1086
it for] 'it not for' Kele 1545.1, Marshe 1568			
That his conscyence be nat clene,	274	Collyn Clout	1122
For I wyll nat pretende	274	Collyn Clout	1127
Nat so hardy on theyr pates!	275	Collyn Clout	1152
They set nat by us a shyttell;	276	Collyn Clout	1185
shytell] 'whystell' Kele 1545.1, Marshe 1568, 'shetyll' MS Harley 2252			
Is nat this a shamfull scorne	276	Collyn Clout	1200
We set nat a nutte shell	277	Collyn Clout	1225
We shulde nat ryse agayne	277	Collyn Clout	1232
And sayle nat farre abrode,	277	Collyn Clout	1256
which hath to name Why Come Ye Nat to Courte?	278	Why Come Ye	I
Why come ye nat to court?	279	Why Come Ye	31
And all nat worth a flye,	282	Why Come Ye	148
Is nat my reason good?'	283	Why Come Ye	196
They were nat payde their hyre.	285	Why Come Ye	248
Theyr wages were nat payde.	285	Why Come Ye	253
Nat worth a cockly fose!	286	Why Come Ye	288
Dare nat loke out at dur	286	Why Come Ye	296
at] 'a' Kitson 1560.7, Marshe 1568			
Dare nat set theyr penne	287	Why Come Ye	323
Thy tonge is nat well thewde,	287	Why Come Ye	331
Nat worth a shyttel-cocke,	287	Why Come Ye	354
Therewith I dare nat mell.	288	Why Come Ye	378
Why come ye nat to court?	289	Why Come Ye	401
But have ye nat harde this,	292	Why Come Ye	532
Had nat our prynce be	292	Why Come Ye	539
Ye rebads nat worth two plummis!	294	Why Come Ye	604
'My lorde is nat at layser,	294	Why Come Ye	625
And settys nat by it a myte!	296	Why Come Ye	677
And writeth he wottith nat what.	296	Why Come Ye	679
wottith] 'wot' Toy 1553, Kitson 1560.7, Marshe 1568			
Coude nat himselfe refrayne,	296	Why Come Ye	690
Nat for that I mene	297	Why Come Ye	746
Nay, nay, he is nat dede.	299	Why Come Ye	794
I have told you part, but nat all.	299	Why Come Ye	822
It shall nat ever flowe.	303	Why Come Ye	952
nat ever flowe] 'neuer ouer flowe' MS Rawlinson C. 813			
For Folam peason /With him be nat geson;	304	Why Come Ye	1000
They play nat all clene,	304	Why Come Ye	1006
And so cruell hertyd, /That he wyll nat be convertyd;	308	Why Come Ye	1179
That] not in MS Rawlinson C. 813			
It was nat heled alderbest,	308	Why Come Ye	1188
Ye shall nat escape blamelesse,	309	Why Come Ye2	4
escape] 'be' MS Rawlinson C. 813			
Blame Juvinall, and blame nat me.	309	Why Come Ye2	8
Of your complaynt it shal nat skyl.	310	Why Come Ye2	32
He fledde and durst nat fyght;	360	Albany	70
Mell nat wyth Englyshe men.	362	Albany	146
We set nat a flye	363	Albany	161
We set nat a prane	363	Albany	163
We set nat a myght	363	Albany	165
For ye dare nat abyde.	363	Albany	187
Nat lyke Duke Hamylcar	363	Albany	192
That durst nat byde the sight	364	Albany	236
Thy herte wolde nat serve the.	365	Albany	250
That dare nat turne agayne,	366	Albany	306
Nor durst nat crak a worde,	366	Albany	307
Nor durst nat drawe his swerde	366	Albany	308
For ye durst nat tarry	367	Albany	343

NATURALL — NEDE

	Page	Title	Line
Nat for a thousande poun[de]	367	Albany	346
pounde] 'pouned' †Marshe 1568			
Are ye nat frantyke madde, /And wretchedly bestadde, ...	368	Albany	363
Trouthe should nat be subdude.	369	Albany	422
Your sermon was nat swete;	376	Replycacion	51
Sive sic, sive nat so, ...	376	Replycacion	71
Ye coude nat corde tenus, /Nor answere verbo tenus, ...	377	Replycacion	104
Ye saye that poetry /Maye nat flye so hye	382	Replycacion	307
Th[i]s may nat be remorded	383	Replycacion	323
This] 'Thus' †Pynson 1528			
Flaccus nor Catullus with hym may nat compare, ...	383	Replycacion	336

NATURALL

Your naturall lord? Alas, I kan not fayne.	30	Dol Dethe	54
The naturall sonnes thre	78	Phy Sparrow	255
Plinni sheweth all /In his Story Naturall, ...	85	Phy Sparrow	537
Our naturall tong is rude, ...	91	Phy Sparrow	774

NATURALLY

By the astrology /That he hath naturally	84	Phy Sparrow	498

NATURE

Dame Nature hath her lent	97	Phy Sparrow	1042
As Nature cold devyse, /In most goodly wyse.	98	Phy Sparrow	1071
That nature wrowght in yow and me, ...	130	Garnesche5	13
A rebellyon agaynst nature -	155	Magnyfycence	522
Thyselfe that thou wolde sloo agaynst nature and kynde.	206	Magnyfycence	2326
By Nature devysed of a wonderowus kynde, ...	231	Speke Parott	2
By nature of a newe writ.	302	Why Come Ye	939
Whome dame Nature, as wele I may reporte, ...	336	Garlande	867

NATURYS

Of naturys workys, how they be	130	Garnesche5	9

NAVERN

Frome Napuls, from Navern, and from Rouncevall, ...	326	Garlande	495

NAVERNE

Of the kynge of Naverne ye may take hede	115	Scot Kynge	56
Of the kynge of Naverne ye might take heed, ...	119	Ag Scottes	153

NE

Yet bere ye not to bold to braule ne to bark	38	Coystrowne1	60
That I ne wyste what to do was beste;	47	Bowge	30
'Twyst,' quod Suspecte, 'goo playe; hym I ne reke!'	51	Bowge	186
Twyst] 'Whist' Wynkyn de Worde 1510, 'Twysshe' Marshe 1568			
His gowne so shorte that it ne cover myghte	56	Bowge	354
Alas, a connynge man ne dwelle maye	58	Bowge	445
Yet long tyme she ne knew	89	Phy Sparrow	727
Ne worde he wrote in vayne.	91	Phy Sparrow	803
Ne no tyger so wood, ...	100	Phy Sparrow	1157
Cockes bones! I ne tell can	162	Magnyfycence	801
Nay, by Cockys harte, he ne reckys;	172	Magnyfycence	1167
Ne by non other that any man can rehersse.	181	Magnyfycence	1490
There is no bawme ne gumme of Arabe	207	Magnyfycence	2347
My wylfulnesse, syr, excuse I ne can.	209	Magnyfycence	2432
He wottyth never what /Ne whereof he speketh.'	247	Collyn Clout	18
Set nought by golde ne grotes, /Theyr names yf I durst tell. .	250	Collyn Clout	160
Ye wyll neyther beanes ne peason.	252	Collyn Clout	212
Some wyl neyther golde ne grotes;	268	Collyn Clout	866
Neyther erle ne duke	272	Collyn Clout	1045
By hoke ne by croke	277	Collyn Clout	1238
That he ne se can	283	Why Come Ye	182
Spareth neither mayde ne wyfe.	284	Why Come Ye	225
For, ne were onely he hath your promocyon, ...	314	Garlande	71
Cupyde hath stryken so that she ne wolde	320	Garlande	291
That I ne force what though it be discurid.	332	Garlande	731
And so observe /That ye ne swarve	339	Garlande	965

NEBBIS

The nebbis of a lyon they make to trete and trembyll, ...	243	Speke Parott	424

NECESSARY

Wherin it is necessary my pleasure you knowe:	145	Magnyfycence	185

NECESSYTE

And infallibly agre /Of necessyte, ...	384	Replycacion	364

NECKE

A Tyborne checke /Shall breke his necke.	165	Magnyfycence	911
Of some I wrynge of the necke lyke a wyre;	194	Magnyfycence	1909
But beggynge is better medecyne for the necke.	198	Magnyfycence	2045
Abowte my necke a cerculett lyke the ryche rubye, ...	231	Speke Parott	17
Aboute the cattes necke, ...	250	Collyn Clout	164
The fynde, Scot, breke thy necke.	363	Albany	156

NECKED

Necked lyke an olyfant;	227	El Rummynge	519

NECLYGENT

Faders and moders that be neclygent, ...	194	Magnyfycence	1920

NEDE

Unkindly thei slew hym that help them oft at nede.	30	Dol Dethe	47
help] 'holp' Marshe 1568			
Redy to assyst you in every tyme of nede;	30	Dol Dethe	58
Valiant as Hector in every marciall nede, ...	33	Dol Dethe	138
Of me and other ye may have nede.	41	Coystrowne4	14
Youre key is redy, we nede not knok	41	Coystrowne4	24
Abashyth me, albeit I have no nede.	44	Balettys3	35
And ye nede ought, man, shewe to me your mynde, ...	50	Bowge	165
And, yf nede be, a bolde worde I dare cracke.	50	Bowge	168

	Page	Title	Line
Truste me, and yf it come to a nede;	59	Bowge	478
Who deleth with shrewes hath nede to loke aboute!'	61	Bowge	525
To tell you the cause me semeth it no nede.	140	Magnyfycence	8
Ye, lyberte with measure nede never drede.	144	Magnyfycence	130
For, without measure, poverte and nede	144	Magnyfycence	152
There is no prynce but he hath nede of us thre –	145	Magnyfycence	159
I trowe it shall not nede to abyde.	156	Magnyfycence	571
By God, syr, what nede all this waste?	161	Magnyfycence	754
Tushe! He that hathe nede, man, let hym rynne.	162	Magnyfycence	786
As skante thou had no nede of me.	163	Magnyfycence	806
Nede? Yes, Mary. I say not nay.	163	Magnyfycence	807
Moche more than nede	165	Magnyfycence	894
Ye, by God, syr. For a nede,	174	Magnyfycence	1237
And maketh hym besy where is no nede.	175	Magnyfycence	1249
That wyt he wantyth when he hath moste nede.	175	Magnyfycence	1261
Somtyme, I say, behynde the dore for nede;	177	Magnyfycence	1341
What nede you with hym thus prate and chat?	180	Magnyfycence	1434
Whylest I have hym, I nede nothynge doute.	187	Magnyfycence	1692
Take hede of your selfe, for nowe ye have nede.	192	Magnyfycence	1854
What a very vengeaunce nede all these wordys?	202	Magnyfycence	2198
And I, Myschefe, am comyn at nede,	205	Magnyfycence	2309
Some for very nede /Layde downe a skeyne of threde,	222	El Rummynge	309
What nede all this be spoken?	227	El Rummynge	499
So myche provision, and so lytell wytte at nede –	244	Speke Parott	454
So lytell care for the comynweall, and so myche nede;	245	Speke Parott	473
That nede hath no lawe.	268	Collyn Clout	863
We nede never feere	303	Why Come Ye	974
'We nedyd never to feyre' MS Rawlinson C. 813			
Ye shall have nede /You for to spede	355	Garlande	1554
Ye] 'You' Marshe 1568			
That forthwith we must nede	385	Replycacion	387

NEDED

	Page	Title	Line
What neded that, in the dyvyls date?	166	Magnyfycence	943

NEDELES

	Page	Title	Line
To prayse your porte it is nedeles;	40	Coystrowne4	5

NEDELL

	Page	Title	Line
Theyr nedell and theyr thymbell:	222	El Rummynge	300

NEDER

	Page	Title	Line
And make him lame of his neder limmes.	309	Why Come Ye	1200

NEDES

	Page	Title	Line
Nedes must he rin that the devyll dryvith.	352	Garlande	1434
It must nedes after rin all the worlde aboute.'	353	Garlande	1483
A vengeaunce and dispight /On the must nedes lyght	364	Albany	235
To this ye nedes must agre.	381	Replycacion	284

NEDEST

	Page	Title	Line
When Mesure is gone, what nedest thou spare?	176	Magnyfycence	1323

NEDETH

	Page	Title	Line
Who rydeth on her, he nedeth not to care,	57	Bowge	409

NEDETHE

	Page	Title	Line
What nedethe me for to extoll his fame	33	Dol Dethe	141

NEDILL WARK

	Page	Title	Line
In nedill wark raysyng byrdis in bowris,	334	Garlande	804
byrdis in bowris] 'bothe birddis and bowres' MS Cotton Vitellius E.x			

NEDIS

	Page	Title	Line
Demaundinge soche dutes as nedis most acord	31	Dol Dethe	66
Sith ye must nedis afforce it by pretence	335	Garlande	817
But to do you servyce nedis now I must;	337	Garlande	879
to do you] 'do her' MS Cotton Vitellius E.x			

NEDYNESSE

	Page	Title	Line
Suche gredynesse, /Suche nedynesse,	305	Why Come Ye	1031

NEDYS

	Page	Title	Line
Go shake the, dogge, hay, syth ye wyll nedys!	148	Magnyfycence	303
All honour to me must nedys stowpe and lene.	181	Magnyfycence	1462
Though I aske mercy I must nedys be refusyd.	205	Magnyfycence	2299

NEDLE

	Page	Title	Line
With that my nedle waxed red,	77	Phy Sparrow	225
waxed] 'ware' Marshe 1568			
My nedle and threde	77	Phy Sparrow	235

NEGARDE

	Page	Title	Line
'A lorde a negarde, it is a shame.'	151	Magnyfycence	388

NEGARSHYP

	Page	Title	Line
Let never negarshyp your noblenesse affray;	211	Magnyfycence	2493

NEGLYGENCE

	Page	Title	Line
Because of theyr neglygence and of theyr wanton vagys,	195	Magnyfycence	1942
To refourme theyr neglygence,	275	Collyn Clout	1138
To large in neglygence,	278	Why Come Ye	6

NEGLYGESSE

	Page	Title	Line
I aske God mercy of my neglyge[sse],	207	Magnyfycence	2380
neglygesse] 'neglygence' †Rastell & Treveris C 1530, B			

NEITHER

	Page	Title	Line
Neither yet Dyoclesyan, /Nor yet Domysyan;	67	Hauke	192
Spareth neither mayde ne wyfe.	284	Why Come Ye	225

NEYBOURS

	Page	Title	Line
Ask all your neybours whether that I ly.	43	Balettys2	35

NEYGHBOUR

	Page	Title	Line
No force what thoughe his neyghbour dye in a dyche.	189	Magnyfycence	1752

NEYGHBOURS —NEVER   Page   Title   Line

NEYGHBOURS
Theyr neyghbours dye for meate.   254   Collyn Clout   320
NEYTHER
That neyther they synge wel prycke song nor playne.   38   Coystrowne1   54
Neyther flesh nor fell.   39   Coystrowne3   18
  nor] 'not' Marshe 1568
Neyther wryte nor say;   101   Phy Sparrow   1197
Let neyther patent scape them nor fee;   190   Magnyfycence   1776
Neyther gelt nor pawne.   229   El Rummynge   610
Neyther frame a silogisme in phrisesomorum   235   Speke Parott   148
Ye wyll neyther beanes ne peason.   252   Collyn Clout   212
Neyther gospell nor pystell, ...   252   Collyn Clout   237
Neyther sylogysare, /Nor of [enthymemar]e;   267   Collyn Clout   816
  enthymemare] 'emptymeniare' †Godfray 1531, Kele 1545.1,
  Marshe 1568, 'entimemare' MS Harley 2252
Some wyl neyther golde ne grotes;   268   Collyn Clout   866
Neyther erle ne duke   272   Collyn Clout   1045
And for my sake spare neyther pen nor ynke;   327   Garlande   549
That neyther of you twayne   367   Albany   337
NEYTHYR
With neythyr of yow tewyne: 124   Garnesche3   7
NEK
The cheke and the nek but a shorte cast;   351   Garlande   1401
NEPTALYM
De terra Neptalym;   262   Collyn Clout   640
NEPTE
The columbyne, the nepte, ...   340   Garlande   982
NEPTUNE
Now Neptune and Eolus ar agreed of lyclyhod, ...   239   Speke Parott   283
NERE
Avaunce your selfe to aproche and come nere.   48   Bowge   88
And I drewe nere to herke what they two sayde.   51   Bowge   182
And I drewe nere to harke what they two sayde.   54   Bowge   296
And ever he threwe, and kyst I wote nere what;   56   Bowge   349
Her har[n]es easy ferre and nere is soughte.   57   Bowge   403
  harnes] 'harmes' †Wynkyn de Worde 1499, 1510, 'armes'
  Marshe 1568
Were I as you, I wolde ryde them full nere;   59   Bowge   472
A subtyll sysmatyke, /Ryght nere an heretyke, ...   121   Ag Scottes2   28
Nowe, by the rode, and he wyll go nere.   173   Magnyfycence   1196
Go we nere and let us se.   204   Magnyfycence   2243
And to the taverne let us drawe nere.   204   Magnyfycence   2262
Some brought I wote nere what, ...   225   El Rummynge   441
To hynder no man /As nere as I can, ...   274   Collyn Clout   1110
And yet never the nere!   295   Why Come Ye   638
Ye put to blame ye wot nere whom.   310   Why Come Ye2   17
  nere] 'nott' MS Rawlinson C. 813
NERO
Nor Nero the worst, /Nor Clawdyus the curst;   67   Hauke   202
Nor Nero, that nother set by God nor man, ...   182   Magnyfycence   1509
NEST
I wolde have yet a nest   78   Phy Sparrow   263
  have yet] 'yet have' Wyght 1553, Kitson 1560.6, Marshe 1568
That maketh his nest /In chymneyes to rest;   83   Phy Sparrow   470
That fylythe hys owne nest.   129   Garnesche3   198
Ye, bere me this strawe to a dawys nest.   170   Magnyfycence   1097
NESTE
Gave me a gyfte in my neste when I lay, ...   232   Speke Parott   44
  I] 'he' †MS Harley 2252
NESTORIANUS
Apostata Julianus /Nor yet Nestorianus, ...   70   Hauke   298
NET
It wolde be masked in my net!   153   Magnyfycence   458
All is fysshe that cometh to the net: 269   Collyn Clout   933
  to the net] 'to net' Marshe 1568, 'to nett' MS Harley 2252
NETHER
Nether wise nor wel lernid, but like hermaphradita: 235   Speke Parott   159
NETTE
To fysshe afore the nette and to drawe polys.   243   Speke Parott   427
NEVEN
And he dare nat well neven   267   Collyn Clout   824
NEVER
His noble blode never desteynyd was, ...   33   Dol Dethe   148
That he wyst never where he was;   42   Balettys1   10
That Dame Menolope was never half so wyse;   42   Balettys2   11
She goyth wyde behynde and hewyth never a dele: 43   Balettys2   24
Yet shall she never oute of remembraunce, ...   45   Balettys3   47
Maye never dye, bute evermore endure.   46   Bowge   16
What though our chaffer be never so dere, ...   48   Bowge   89
That wyll abyde and never frome us fall.   49   Bowge   130
Ye never dwelte in suche an other place, ...   51   Bowge   201
His counseyle secrete never to dyscure, ...   52   Bowge   219
  dyscure] 'dysture' †Wynkyn de Worde 1499, 1510
I wyste never man that so soone coude wynne   53   Bowge   269
I praye to God that it maye never dy.   53   Bowge   271
What the devyll, man, myrthe was never one!   57   Bowge   388
  was never one] 'is here within' Marshe 1568
Wrought never such a worke, ...   67   Hauke   217

479

NEVER —NEVER   Page   Title   Line

Phrase	Page	Title	Line
Never halfe the payne	72	Phy Sparrow	19
Was never none so good;	78	Phy Sparrow	269
That never ought the evyll wyll!	79	Phy Sparrow	323
Was never byrde in cage /More gentle of corage	80	Phy Sparrow	324
Conceyved and cought, /And was never tought	84	Phy Sparrow	500
That potencyally /May never dye	84	Phy Sparrow	515
That never yet asayde /Of Elyconys well,	87	Phy Sparrow	609
And never wold him forsake.	90	Phy Sparrow	733
He frowneth ever; /He laugheth never,	94	Phy Sparrow	923
His tong never styll /For to say yll,	95	Phy Sparrow	941
That never more slept,	104	Phy Sparrow	1304
That never have rest nor ease;	104	Phy Sparrow	1325
That in hell is never brent,	104	Phy Sparrow	1327
Theyr names shall never dye.	106	Epitaphe	1
Never a toth in his heed.	108	Epitaphe1	61
Dyd never man good.	108	Epitaphe1	67
That never wyll leve theyr tratlynge:	115	Ag Scottes	2
For Syr Frollo de Franko was never halfe so talle.	121	Garneschel	5
And wyll never intende	124	Garnesche3	17
In Romaine letters I never founde lack	137	Ven Tongues	17
For his false lying, of that I spake never,	139	Ven Tongues	75
Although he made it never so tough,	139	Ven Tongues	77
Ye, lyberte with measure nede never drede.	144	Magnyfycence	130
Measure and I wyll never be devydyd,	145	Magnyfycence	186
But never was I in gretter fere.	150	Magnyfycence	345
Thy wordes be but wynde, never they have no wayght.	156	Magnyfycence	578
I pray God let you never to thee!	158	Magnyfycence	635
Playne delynge and I can never agre.	159	Magnyfycence	699
I am never glad but whan I may do yll,	160	Magnyfycence	731
And never am I sory but whan that I se	160	Magnyfycence	732
That never was /Abusyd before.	164	Magnyfycence	867
What the devyll! Never a whyt?	166	Magnyfycence	935
Were never halfe so rychely as I am drest.	181	Magnyfycence	1483
As gyvynge a thynge that ye never bought.	189	Magnyfycence	1758
He woteth not what welth is that never was sore.	196	Magnyfycence	1971
I wenyd ones never to have knowen of care.	196	Magnyfycence	1973
Never had I bene brought in this case.	196	Magnyfycence	1977
And they never thryve in theyr age, it shall not gretly skyll.	200	Magnyfycence	2138
Thou sawe never yet but I dyd my parte,	203	Magnyfycence	2228
With never a peny in his purse.	204	Magnyfycence	2258
Nay, nay, man. I loke never to have parte of his grace;	205	Magnyfycence	2297
That thou canst not have never mercy in his syght.	205	Magnyfycence	2303
Who knoweth me, hymselfe may never sloo.	206	Magnyfycence	2330
There was never so harde a storme of mysery,	207	Magnyfycence	2343
This letter ye speke of never dyd I wryte.	209	Magnyfycence	2442
Ye, syr. From hym my corage shall never flyt.	210	Magnyfycence	2466
Let never negarshyp your noblenesse affray;	211	Magnyfycence	2493
I shall it never forget nor leve it behynde,	212	Magnyfycence	2506
Who lyst to consyder shall never be begylyd,	212	Magnyfycence	2512
Never stoppynge /But ever droppynge;	215	El Rummynge	29
For, be there never so moche prese,	218	El Rummynge	174
They asked never for mete	222	El Rummynge	304
She sayde never a worde,	229	El Rummynge	590
That never may dye, nor never dye shall:	236	Speke Parott	216
That never may dye, nor never dye shall:	236	Speke Parott	216
Syns Dewcalyons flodde the world was never so yll.	245	Speke Parott	497
the world] 'the world the world' †MS Harley 2252			
He wottyth never what /Ne whereof he speketh.'	247	Collyn Clout	17
I wote never howe they warke,	249	Collyn Clout	119
And wotteth never what thei rede, /Paternoster nor crede;	252	Collyn Clout	234
For prestes and for lonys /Lent and never payde,	255	Collyn Clout	351
But trouth can never lye.	258	Collyn Clout	485
Whan there is never a whytte,	259	Collyn Clout	516
Though it were never so playne,	265	Collyn Clout	765
And never a Scot slayne!	282	Why Come Ye	152
And yet never the nere!	295	Why Come Ye	638
Let him never confounde	298	Why Come Ye	778
That he shall never ete more bred.	299	Why Come Ye	796
We nede never feere	303	Why Come Ye	974
'We nedyd never to feyre' MS Rawlinson C. 813			
Shall never have good helth;	304	Why Come Ye	1025
That he setteth never a deale	307	Why Come Ye	1130
He dyd never approche	307	Why Come Ye	1144
Be he never so lytell of substaunce,	317	Garlande	177
Had I never sene, some softer, some lowder;	320	Garlande	271
But blessyd Bachus that never man forgate,	322	Garlande	369
He can never leve warke whylis it is wele.	333	Garlande	763
For yet of women he never sayd shame,	334	Garlande	784
Was never halfe so fayre, as I wene,	342	Garlande	1077
Go she never so gingirly, her honesty is gone away.	346	Garlande	1204
That never more slepte	349	Garlande	1297
That never have rest nor ease;	349	Garlande	1318
That in hell is never brente,	349	Garlande	1320
And plantid it there where never before was none, unshred	351	Garlande	1405
it there where] 'yet wher' Marshe 1568			
A jentyll hownde shulde never play the kur.	352	Garlande	1436
Never true nor playne,	362	Albany	134
Ye shall never be hable,	363	Albany	178

NEVERE — NEWTER

	Page	Title	Line
And never tourne agayne.	368	Albany	372
God let you never thrive!	368	Albany	379
That never dyde offence.	375	Replycacion	44
Ye had never lerned letter,	380	Replycacion	230
That never more may dye.	380	Replycacion	246
So was there never another,	381	Replycacion	258
Nor heresy wyll never dye.	385	Replycacion	408

NEVERE

That measure shall nevere departe from my syght.	145	Magnyfycence	190

NEVERMORE

Thyse lewde cok wattes shall nevermore prevayle wattes] 'witts' Marshe 1568	51	Bowge	173

NEVERTHELESSE

So many thevys hangyd, and thevys neverthelesse;	245	Speke Parott	477

NEVYR

Was nevyr suche a senatour syn Crystes Incarnacion.	240	Speke Parott	337
Syns Dewcalions flodde, was nevyr sene nor shall.	245	Speke Parott	469
Syns Dewcalyons flodde, I trowe, was nevyr sene.	245	Speke Parott	476
Syns Dewcalyons flodde was nevyr, I dar sey.	245	Speke Parott	483
Syns Dewcalyons flodde was nevyr sene nor lyerd.	246	Speke Parott	504
Was nevyr suche a fylty gorgon, nor suche an epycure,	246	Speke Parott	510

NEW

'My new furryd gowne, when it is worne –	40	Coystrowne4	10
To se my sorow new.	80	Phy Sparrow	337
Of whose incyneracyon /There ryseth a new creacyon	85	Phy Sparrow	541
A thousand new and old	90	Phy Sparrow	750
She floryssheth new and new	94	Phy Sparrow	896
She floryssheth new and new	94	Phy Sparrow	896
She flourissheth new and new	96	Phy Sparrow	992
She flourissheth new and new	96	Phy Sparrow	992
She florisheth new and new	97	Phy Sparrow	1025
She florisheth new and new	97	Phy Sparrow	1025
She florysheth new and new	98	Phy Sparrow	1057
She florysheth new and new	98	Phy Sparrow	1057
She flouryssheth new and new	98	Phy Sparrow	1086
She flouryssheth new and new	98	Phy Sparrow	1086
She flouryssheth new and new	99	Phy Sparrow	1110
She flouryssheth new and new	99	Phy Sparrow	1110
She floryssheth new and new	100	Phy Sparrow	1139
She floryssheth new and new	100	Phy Sparrow	1139
She flouryssheth new and new	100	Phy Sparrow	1164
She flouryssheth new and new	100	Phy Sparrow	1164
She florisheth new and new	101	Phy Sparrow	1188
She florisheth new and new	101	Phy Sparrow	1188
She flouryssheth new and new	102	Phy Sparrow	1211
She flouryssheth new and new	102	Phy Sparrow	1211
She floryssheth new and new	102	Phy Sparrow	1234
She floryssheth new and new	102	Phy Sparrow	1234
Drinke now whyle it is new;	219	El Rummynge	211
Orace also with his new poetry;	322	Garlande	352
Your storme dryven shyppe I repared new,	327	Garlande	544
I sawe a thowsande yatis new and olde.	328	Garlande	574
Some were olde wryten, sum were writen new,	328	Garlande	584
It was a new comfort of sorowis escapid.	330	Garlande	657
Item New Gramer in Englysshe compylyd;	346	Garlande	1182
How Cownterfet Cowntenaunce of the new get	346	Garlande	1193
Makynge his almanak for the new yere;	354	Garlande	1516
Good luk this new yere, the olde yere is past.	354	Garlande	1518

NEWE

It were more thryft he boughte him a newe cote;	60	Bowge	487
Clenly to counterfet newe arayes;	152	Magnyfycence	426
The courtly gyse of the newe jet?	153	Magnyfycence	453
All the newe gyse, fresshe and gaye,	153	Magnyfycence	463
A bolde man in a bole of newe ale in cornys.	162	Magnyfycence	772
Of the newe gyse,	164	Magnyfycence	846
This newe fonne jet	165	Magnyfycence	877
This theyr desyre, /This newe atyre.	165	Magnyfycence	888
And to fall in aquayntaunce with every newe facyon,	183	Magnyfycence	1548
And blessed her with a cup /Of newe ale in cornes.	224	El Rummynge	378
So myche newe makyng, and so madd tyme spente;	244	Speke Parott	450
Flatterynge for a newe cote	267	Collyn Clout	838
By nature of a newe writ.	302	Why Come Ye	939
These tidinges newe,	359	Albany	3

NEWES

What newes? What news?	284	Why Come Ye	233
Small newes that true is	284	Why Come Ye	234

NEW-FOUNDE

Owur new-founde A. B. C.	238	Speke Parott	277

NEWIS

What tidings at Tot[nam], what newis in Wales, Totnam] 'Totman' Marshe 1568	139	Ven Tongues	64

NEWLY

Were newly enbybid; and rownd about the same	331	Garlande	682

NEWS

What newes? What news?	284	Why Come Ye	233

NEWTER

From golde to pewter /Or els to a newter,	301	Why Come Ye	905

481

	Page	Title	Line
NEWTON			
I sawe maister Newton sit with his compas,	343	Garlande	1096
NEXT			
And the next day he shuld dye,	105	Phy Sparrow	1359
And next come I after, Crafty Conveyaunce.	177	Magnyfycence	1332
Esebon, Marybon, Wheston next Barnet;	234	Speke Parott	127
They were, whan they were next.	285	Why Come Ye	260
they] 'the' †Kele 1545.3			
And the next day he shulde dye,	350	Garlande	1352
NEXTE			
The nexte halter ther xall be	128	Garnesche3	176
Some ranne the nexte way, sume ranne abowte.	319	Garlande	252
NIGHT			
At his commaundement whiche had both day and night	30	Dol Dethe	31
That day and night brenneth styl,	79	Phy Sparrow	314
Sodenly is eclipsid in the wynter night,	330	Garlande	646
He ran awaye by night.	360	Albany	71
NIGHTINGALE			
To here this nightingale,	340	Garlande	997
NYCE			
It wolde be nyce, thoughe I say nay;	153	Magnyfycence	459
And Annot wolde be nyce, and laughes, 'tehe wehe.'	153	Magnyfycence	477
It is a nyce reconynge	298	Why Come Ye	760
NYCHOLAS			
'Cristecrosse and Saynt Nycholas, Parrot, be your good spede!'	236	Speke Parott	189
NYCHT			
Your pryd is paste, adwe, good nycht.	114	Scot Kynge	43
NYCROMANSY			
It was by nycromansy,	296	Why Come Ye	696
NYE			
His elbowe bare, he ware his gere so nye,	56	Bowge	361
That no lyfe well nye remayned.	73	Phy Sparrow	49
Well nye had stopped my breath.	73	Phy Sparrow	63
had] not in Wyght 1553, Kitson 1560.6, Marshe 1568			
And suck us so nye,	303	Why Come Ye	966
NYFYLS			
Nil, nichelum, nihil - anglice nyfyls.	172	Magnyfycence	1142
NYGARDE			
And not all the nygarde nor the chyncherde to play.	211	Magnyfycence	2492
NYGHE			
That dyspayre well nyghe had myscheved me;	206	Magnyfycence	2332
NYGHT			
Radyent Esperus, star of the clowdy nyght,	44	Balettys3	24
And now the darke cloudy nyght	86	Phy Sparrow	571
Musyng nyght and day,	89	Phy Sparrow	703
Youre eye is out; adew, good nyght!	119	Ag Scottes	142
I had not been here with you this nyght.	150	Magnyfycence	365
Ye and I talkyd therof to nyght.	159	Magnyfycence	670
By day or by nyght	164	Magnyfycence	860
That day I se hym I shall be worse all nyght.	188	Magnyfycence	1724
And other wanton warkes /Whan the nyght darkes.	251	Collyn Clout	195
Good evyn and good nyght!	302	Why Come Ye	916
Some sluggysh slovyns, that slepe day and nyght;	317	Garlande	191
Thus passyth he the tyme both nyght and day,	352	Garlande	1423
He ran away by nyght	366	Albany	311
And curse bothe nyght and day,	376	Replycacion	79
NYGHTE			
And wake all nyghte and slepe tyll it be none.	57	Bowge	382
For whome Tyborne groneth both daye and nyghte.	58	Bowge	417
whome] 'home' †Wynkyn de Worde 1499			
NYGHTES			
So myche prevye wachyng in cold wynters nyghtes;	246	Speke Parott	512
And of the wynter nyghtes that tary so longe,	331	Garlande	701
And of their shorte nyghtes; he browght in his songe	331	Garlande	703
NYGHTYNGALE			
The lusty chauntyng nyghtyngale;	82	Phy Sparrow	420
So merely syngeth the nyghtyngale!	199	Magnyfycence	2077
NYGHTYS			
Of nyghtys to occupy counterfet kayes;	152	Magnyfycence	425
NYGHTLY			
And nyghtly the tydes	84	Phy Sparrow	507
nyghtly] 'nyghly' †Kele 1545.2			
NYNE			
If the hole quere of the Musis nyne	33	Dol Dethe	155
Of the Muses nyne,	93	Phy Sparrow	858
Of the Musys nyne, Calliope	131	Garnesche5	87
Aqueintyng hym with the Musys nyne.	132	Garnesche5	100
Scorpione ascendynge degrees twyse nyne;	312	Garlande	7
Ovyde, enshryned with the musis nyne;	321	Garlande	333
With the nyne Muses, Pierides by name;	331	Garlande	680
with] 'wit' †Fakes 1523			
NYS			
How there nys thynge that I covet so fayne	44	Balettys3	41
For I dare saye that there nys erthly man	48	Bowge	101
NYSE			
This wanton clarkis be nyse allway.	35	Man Margery	2
Phyllyp, though he were nyse,	76	Phy Sparrow	173
The matter were to nyse,	100	Phy Sparrow	1132

NYSYTE —NO

	Page	Title	Line
To mery, to mad, to gyglynge, to nyse,	199	Magnyfycence	2092
As she was pevysshe nyse.	229	El Rummynge	589
A trym-tram for an horse-myll it were a nyse thyng,	234	Speke Parott	128
But ye were folysshe nyse.	378	Replycacion	130

NYSYTE

	Page	Title	Line
Your counterfet countenaunce is all of nysyte,	153	Magnyfycence	478

NYSOT

	Page	Title	Line
And where I spy a nysot gay	174	Magnyfycence	1228

NO

	Page	Title	Line
All mercilles in the ys no pite!	32	Dol Dethe	122
Let double delinge in the have no place,	34	Dol Dethe	174
And be not light of credence in no case.	34	Dol Dethe	175
I am no hakney for your rode;	35	Man Margery	11
Be Crist, ye shall not! No, no, hardely!	36	Man Margery	18
Be Crist, ye shall not! No, no, hardely!	36	Man Margery	18
Nay, jape not with hym, he is no small fole;	38	Coystrowne1	50
No man may hym hyde /From deth holow-eyed,	39	Coystrowne3	10
There may no fraunchys /Nor worldly blys	39	Coystrowne3	26
Of youre doregate ye have no doute.	41	Coystrowne4	26
That of hys love he toke no kepe,	41	Balettys1	7
It can be no counsell that is cryed at the cros.	43	Balettys2	36
Abashyth me, albeit I have no nede.	44	Balettys3	35
That, so to saye, I had gyven her no cause.	48	Bowge	75
A precyous jewell, no rycher in this londe:	48	Bowge	97
There can no favour nor frendshyp hym forsake.	48	Bowge	103
We wante no wynde to passe now over all;	49	Bowge	128
Farewell tyll soone. But no word that I sayde!'	51	Bowge	175
'In fayth,' quod Suspecte, 'spake Drede no worde of me?'	51	Bowge	183
Spake he, a fayth, no worde to you of me?	51	Bowge	204
And ever he sange, 'Sythe I am no thynge playne'.	52	Bowge	235
And I dare saye there is no man hereinne	53	Bowge	267
But I requyre you no worde that I saye!	54	Bowge	276
It was no tyme with him to jape nor toye.	54	Bowge	290
But, no force, I shall ones mete with the;	55	Bowge	334
He had no pleasure but in harlotrye.	56	Bowge	374
The armes of Calyce, I have no coyne nor crosse!	57	Bowge	398
They wandred ay and stode styll in no stede.	58	Bowge	423
In no place well, but foles with hym fraye!	58	Bowge	446
hym] not in †Wynkyn de Worde 1499, Marshe 1568			
But as for that, connynge hath no foo	58	Bowge	447
Sterte all at ones, I lyked no thynge his playe,	60	Bowge	502
I wolde therwith no man were myscontente;	61	Bowge	533
No good preest to offend,	62	Hauke	25
In hope that no man shall /Be myscontent withall.	62	Hauke	27
Be] 'By' Kynge & Marche 1554			
The hawke had no lyst /To come to his fyst;	64	Hauke	83
Correctyon hath no place,	66	Hauke	162
Of no tyrand I rede,	67	Hauke	190
In them be no scolys /For braynsycke frantycke folys:	68	Hauke	248
For no reverens thou sparys	69	Hauke	280
reverens] 'revens' Kynge & Marche 1554, Day 1560, Marshe 1568			
No creature but that wolde /Have rewed upon me,	72	Phy Sparrow	41
That no lyfe well nye remayned.	73	Phy Sparrow	49
God wot, we thought no syn -	76	Phy Sparrow	168
It was no hurt, I trowe.	76	Phy Sparrow	170
In him it was no vyse;	76	Phy Sparrow	174
Had no such Phylyp as I,	78	Phy Sparrow	271
No, no, syr, hardely!	78	Phy Sparrow	272
No, no, syr, hardely!	78	Phy Sparrow	272
No man can be sure	81	Phy Sparrow	370
No broken galles /May there abyde	83	Phy Sparrow	473
No] 'Nor' Kitson 1560.6			
That no man abydes,	84	Phy Sparrow	508
Gowers Englysh is olde /And of no value told;	91	Phy Sparrow	785
told] 'is tolde' Wyght 1553, Kitson 1560.6, Marshe 1568			
There is no Englysh voyd,	91	Phy Sparrow	795
No man that can amend	91	Phy Sparrow	809
I trust it is no shame,	94	Phy Sparrow	889
And no man wyll me blame,	94	Phy Sparrow	890
No slepe can him catch,	95	Phy Sparrow	928
His foule desyre /Wyll suffre no slepe	95	Phy Sparrow	934
Soft, and make no dyn,	99	Phy Sparrow	1092
And yet there was no vyce,	100	Phy Sparrow	1133
Nor yet no vyllany, /But only fantasy;	100	Phy Sparrow	1134
Ther is no beest savage,	100	Phy Sparrow	1156
Ne no tyger so wood,	100	Phy Sparrow	1157
No man can let me thynke,	101	Phy Sparrow	1199
It were no gentle gyse	103	Phy Sparrow	1251
His Dirige, her commendacyon /Can be no derogacyon,	103	Phy Sparrow	1277
No man to myscontent	103	Phy Sparrow	1280
No worse than is contayned	106	Phy Sparrow	1377
They shall wirry no mo,	111	Lawde	26
No man for them wil speke.	111	Lawde	32
Therfor no more they shall	111	Lawde	36
To you no thyng it dyde accorde	113	Scot Kynge	3
And your harolde no thynge experte;	113	Scot Kynge	8
Your power coude no lenger attayne	114	Scot Kynge	54

NO —NO

	Page	Title	Line
For no maner consyderacyon	117	Ag Scottes	73
Soche an odyr chalyngyr cowde me no man wysch,	121	Garneschel	3
Nor no bore so brymly brystlyd ys with here,	122	Garneschel	25
Chalenge yor selfe for a fole, call me no more knave.	122	Garneschel	42
I am laureat, I am no lorell.	124	Garnesche3	14
Ye myght no better a way;	125	Garnesche3	49
Cowde hocupy ther no stede.	126	Garnesche3	69
Yt fallyth for no swyne	126	Garnesche3	86
And occupyed no better your tole,	127	Garnesche3	118
To daly with yow she had no lust.	131	Garnesche5	54
And sey poetis no dys....	132	Garnesche5	113
It ys for no bawdy knave	132	Garnesche5	114
There is no noble man wil judge in me	138	Ven Tongues	34
Malicious tunges, though they have no bones,	138	Ven Tongues	49
To tell you the cause me semeth it no nede.	140	Magnyfycence	8
Lyberte, I wote well, forbere no man there may;	142	Magnyfycence	50
I say there is no welthe where as lyberte is subdude.	142	Magnyfycence	73
Where drede ledyth the daunce, there is no joy nor blysse.	142	Magnyfycence	76
It were no vertue, it were a thynge unblyst.	144	Magnyfycence	134
There is no surfet where measure rulyth the feste;	144	Magnyfycence	139
There is no excesse where measure hath his helthe.	144	Magnyfycence	140
But have ye not herde say that wyll is no skyll?	144	Magnyfycence	148
It i[s] no maystery. Tushe, let Measure procede, is] 'it' †Rastell & Treveris C 1530, B	144	Magnyfycence	150
There is no prynce but he hath nede of us thre -	145	Magnyfycence	159
For no dyscorde that any man can sawe;	145	Magnyfycence	187
There is no flaterer nor losyll so lyther,	146	Magnyfycence	200
Endure? No, God wote, it were great payne.	147	Magnyfycence	248
Please it your grace to take no dysdayne.	147	Magnyfycence	252
From whens come you, syr, that no man lokyd after?	147	Magnyfycence	255
I say, without largesse worshyp hath no place,	148	Magnyfycence	267
That no man can scape but they hym cache.	150	Magnyfycence	351
No. But for you grete estates	150	Magnyfycence	370
Ye, syr, a blaunched almonde is no bene.	151	Magnyfycence	381
What! Is your conveyaunce no better.	155	Magnyfycence	542
That we can no better than so.	155	Magnyfycence	550
Take no dyspleasure of that we say.	156	Magnyfycence	561
Thy wordes be but wynde, never they have no wayght.	156	Magnyfycence	578
Knowe you not me, syrs? No, in dede.	157	Magnyfycence	594
No. In every corner he wyll peke,	158	Magnyfycence	658
So that we have no lyberte;	158	Magnyfycence	659
Nor no man in courte, but he,	158	Magnyfycence	660
In fayth, and without lyberte there is no bydyng.	158	Magnyfycence	662
I wolde begyn all myschyef, but I wolde bere no lacke.	160	Magnyfycence	720
That they wyll here no man but the fyrst tale.	161	Magnyfycence	743
What the devyll! Can ye agre no better?	162	Magnyfycence	795
As skante thou had no nede of me.	163	Magnyfycence	806
No; for or we stryke, we wyll be advysed twyse.	163	Magnyfycence	810
What the devyll! Use ye not to drawe no swordes?	163	Magnyfycence	811
No, by my trouthe, but crake grete wordes.	163	Magnyfycence	812
I knowe in hym no defaute	163	Magnyfycence	823
Spare for no coste;	165	Magnyfycence	891
No, Mary; not yet.	166	Magnyfycence	934
No, by the masse. What! Sholde I swere?	166	Magnyfycence	936
What! Of Cokermowth spake I no worde.	170	Magnyfycence	1062
Cockys harte! Thou lyest; I am no [h]ogge. hogge] 'dogge' †Rastell & Treveris C 1530, B	170	Magnyfycence	1083
Here is no man that callyd the hogge nor swyne.	170	Magnyfycence	1084
By my syers soule, I fele no rayne.	170	Magnyfycence	1087
No, by my trouthe. It is but the scurfe and the scabbe.	171	Magnyfycence	1123
By Cockes harte, I wene thou hast no more.	172	Magnyfycence	1146
No? Yes, in faythe; I can versyfy.	172	Magnyfycence	1147
Why, thynkys thou he can no better skyll?	172	Magnyfycence	1172
Than wyll I say that thou hast no pere.	173	Magnyfycence	1195
Shyt thy purse, dawe, and do no cost.	174	Magnyfycence	1207
Nay, I tell the, he maketh no dowtes	174	Magnyfycence	1210
And maketh hym besy where is no nede.	175	Magnyfycence	1249
But nowe, forsothe, man, it maketh no mater;	175	Magnyfycence	1256
So that there knowe no man but I and she.	177	Magnyfycence	1353
My inwyt delynge there can no man dyscry.	177	Magnyfycence	1356
Crafty conveyaunce is no chyldys game;	178	Magnyfycence	1368
Syr, as by my wyll, it shall be so no more.	178	Magnyfycence	1377
For where is no mesure, howe may worshyp endure?	179	Magnyfycence	1408
Syr, as I say, there was no faute in me.	180	Magnyfycence	1426
And so as ye se it wyll be no better,	180	Magnyfycence	1438
No stormy rage agaynst me can pervayle.	181	Magnyfycence	1465
No man so hardy to worke agaynst my wyll.	181	Magnyfycence	1479
Nor Cesar July, that no man myght withstande,	181	Magnyfycence	1482
No, that I assure you; loke who was the best:	181	Magnyfycence	1484
I drede no daunger; I dawnce all in delyte:	182	Magnyfycence	1492
Nor no man on molde can make me aferd.	182	Magnyfycence	1505
Here no man what so ever they say	185	Magnyfycence	1603
Is there no horson that knave that wyll bete?'	185	Magnyfycence	1618
With me no longer. Say somwhat nowe, let se,	188	Magnyfycence	1719
Nay, so God me helpe, it was no grete vexacyon;	189	Magnyfycence	1733
Ye, walke he must; it was no better worth.	189	Magnyfycence	1736
Where mennes belyes is mesured, there is no chere;	189	Magnyfycence	1742
It is no wonder, therfore, thoughe ye be wrothe	189	Magnyfycence	1748

	Page	Title	Line
NO—NO			
No force what thoughe his neyghbour dye in a dyche.	189	Magnyfycence	1752
Spare for no cost to gyve them pounde and peny;	190	Magnyfycence	1771
And suche as you wyll shall lacke no promocyon.	190	Magnyfycence	1789
I drede no dyntes of fatall desteny.	190	Magnyfycence	1798
Mary, Cryst graunt ye catche no colde on your fete!	191	Magnyfycence	1803
Why, coulde not your wyt serve you no better?	193	Magnyfycence	1868
Nowe is there no man that wyll set by hym a flye.	193	Magnyfycence	1889
Theyr chyldren, bycause that they have no mekenesse,	194	Magnyfycence	1924
Nowe, syth it wyll no nother be,	196	Magnyfycence	1978
Alasse that I coude not myselfe no better gyde!	196	Magnyfycence	1986
In her promyse there is no sykernesse,	197	Magnyfycence	2028
They thynke it no shame to robbe and stele;	198	Magnyfycence	2042
I may no more speke tyll I have wept my fyll.	198	Magnyfycence	2063
Of erthely thynge I have no care nor charge.	199	Magnyfycence	2081
A thousande pounde with lyberte may holde no tacke.	199	Magnyfycence	2084
Some have so moche lyberte that they fere no synne,	200	Magnyfycence	2143
In Fortunys frendshyppe there is no stedfastnesse;	201	Magnyfycence	2156
Alasse! To lyve longer I have no delyght;	205	Magnyfycence	2281
No, no; for thy synnys be so excedynge farre,	205	Magnyfycence	2300
No, no; for thy synnys be so excedynge farre,	205	Magnyfycence	2300
But nowe I se well there is no better rede,	205	Magnyfycence	2305
There is no man may synne more mortally	206	Magnyfycence	2336
There is no bawme ne gumme of Arabe	207	Magnyfycence	2347
Syr, the repentaunce I have no man can wryte.	208	Magnyfycence	2392
But redresse is redlesse and may do no correccyon.	209	Magnyfycence	2417
Without fayle, syr, that is no nay:	209	Magnyfycence	2429
Then welthe with you myght in no wyse abyde.	210	Magnyfycence	2447
Howe in this worlde there is no seke[r]nesse,	212	Magnyfycence	2515
sekernesse] 'sekenesse' †Rastell & Treveris C 1530, B			
So in this worlde there is no sykernesse,	212	Magnyfycence	2522
Thus in this worlde there is no erthly truste.	213	Magnyfycence	2544
Today maysterfest, tomorowe he hath no holde;	213	Magnyfycence	2549
Thus in this worlde there is no erthly truste.	213	Magnyfycence	2551
Some have no herelace,	218	El Rummynge	145
Some have no mony /That thyder commy,	218	El Rummynge	160
And for to leve this letter, /Bicause it is no better;	220	El Rummynge	238
And bicause it is no swetter,	220	El Rummynge	239
We wyll no farther ryme /Of it at this tyme.	220	El Rummynge	240
Ales founde therin no thornes,	224	El Rummynge	379
She founde therein no bones.	224	El Rummynge	381
bones] 'bornes' Day 1560			
'I have no penny nor grote	229	El Rummynge	600
To wyse is no vertue, to medlyng, to restles;	232	Speke Parott	61
A bagpype without blowynge standeth in no sted:	232	Speke Parott	75
bagpype] 'bagbyte' †Lant 1545, Kynge & Marche 1554			
But Parrot hath no favour to Esebon;	233	Speke Parott	111
In Achademia Parrot dare no probleme kepe,	235	Speke Parott	162
No matter pretendyd, nor nothyng enterprysed,	236	Speke Parott	201
For Parot is no churlish chowgh, nor no flekyd pye,	236	Speke Parott	204
For Parot is no churlish chowgh, nor no flekyd pye,	236	Speke Parott	204
Parrot is no pendugum, that men call a carlyng,	236	Speke Parott	205
Parrot is no woodecocke, nor no butterfly,	236	Speke Parott	206
Parrot is no woodecocke, nor no butterfly,	236	Speke Parott	206
Parrot is no stameryng stare, that men call a starlyng;	236	Speke Parott	207
Hyt ys no lytyll bordon to bere a grete mylle stone.	240	Speke Parott	330
To sowe corne in the see-sande, ther wyll no crope growe.	240	Speke Parott	342
Jupyter for Saturne darre make no royall chere;	242	Speke Parott	399
Moloc, that mawmett, there darre no man withsay;	243	Speke Parott	402
Agayne Frentike Frenesy there darre no man sey nay,	243	Speke Parott	422
For reysons ar no resons but resons currant -	244	Speke Parott	443
Syns Dewcalyons flodde there can no clerkes rede.	244	Speke Parott	455
Syns Dewcalyons flodde there can no clerkes fynde.	244	Speke Parott	462
Syns Dewcalyons flodde, I trow, no man can tell.	245	Speke Parott	490
So myche of my lordes grace, and in hym no grace ys;	245	Speke Parott	501
Sens Dewcalyons flodde, in no cronycle ys told.	246	Speke Parott	518
It standeth in no stede:	247	Collyn Clout	35
Howe they take no hede /Theyr sely shepe to fede,	248	Collyn Clout	76
Ye pyke no shrympes nor pranes,	252	Collyn Clout	208
Theyr shall no clergye appose	254	Collyn Clout	291
And no more ye make	254	Collyn Clout	298
There may no cost be spared;	254	Collyn Clout	318
Ye do them wronge and no ryght	256	Collyn Clout	404
them] not in Marshe 1568			
No matyns at mydnyght,	256	Collyn Clout	406
That no man may abyde	261	Collyn Clout	594
And have no grace to thynke	262	Collyn Clout	648
That hath no dygnyte	265	Collyn Clout	734
Howe they have no fraude.	267	Collyn Clout	853
fraude] 'faude' †Godfray 1531, 'fawte' MS Harley 2252			
That nede hath no lawe.	268	Collyn Clout	863
But they have no affections	268	Collyn Clout	893
affections] 'afflictions' Kele 1545.1, 'affeccions' Harley 2252			
Men say, they bere no faces	269	Collyn Clout	896
They wyll no farder go.	269	Collyn Clout	908
For they wyll have no losse	269	Collyn Clout	928
No man to our sovereygne lorde	272	Collyn Clout	1030
Make ye no murmuracyon	273	Collyn Clout	1079

NO —NO

	Page	Title	Line
I do it nat for no despyte.	273	Collyn Clout	1086
it for] 'it not for' Kele 1545.1, Marshe 1568			
Wherfore, take no dysdayne	273	Collyn Clout	1087
For I rebuke no man /That vertuous is.	273	Collyn Clout	1089
Have no cause to say	273	Collyn Clout	1093
have] 'hath' †Godfray 1531, 'have' MS Harley 2252			
Of no good bysshop speke I,	273	Collyn Clout	1095
Nor of no good werke;	274	Collyn Clout	1100
To hynder no man /As nere as I can,	274	Collyn Clout	1109
For no man have I named.	274	Collyn Clout	1111
And can nat tell no cause why	274	Collyn Clout	1115
can nat] 'can' Marshe 1568, MS Harley 2252			
Nor wyll here no prechynge,	274	Collyn Clout	1133
Nor no vertuous techynge,	274	Collyn Clout	1134
Nor wyll have no resytynge	274	Collyn Clout	1135
To do shame, they have no shame;	275	Collyn Clout	1141
But they wolde no man shuld them blame.	275	Collyn Clout	1142
Is counted for no rod;	275	Collyn Clout	1146
That ryght no man can fonge.	276	Collyn Clout	1197
For that no man shulde se	277	Collyn Clout	1240
'Do ryght and do no wronge.'	281	Why Come Ye	89
do no] 'no' Kitson 1560.7, Marshe 1568			
There vayleth no resonynge;	281	Why Come Ye	104
There is no man but one	281	Why Come Ye	113
No man dare speke a worde,	283	Why Come Ye	191
I wyll no further ryme /Tyll another tyme;	284	Why Come Ye	230
Wyll ye bere no coles?'	285	Why Come Ye	243
He sayth they have no brayne	286	Why Come Ye	310
That no man dare rowte;	287	Why Come Ye	341
No better they agre!	288	Why Come Ye	375
But speke ye no more of that,	288	Why Come Ye	382
He regardeth lordes /No more than potshordes.	291	Why Come Ye	481
No doctor of devinyte,	291	Why Come Ye	509
How no man can him amende!	292	Why Come Ye	531
No man dare him withsay.	294	Why Come Ye	598
No man dare come to the speche	294	Why Come Ye	615
Hath nowe no tyme nor space	295	Why Come Ye	631
I have no pen nor inke	296	Why Come Ye	684
This is no fable nor no lye;	296	Why Come Ye	705
This is no fable nor no lye;	296	Why Come Ye	705
We can lacke no grace,	301	Why Come Ye	875
The gray gose is no swan;	301	Why Come Ye	889
no] 'a' MS Rawlinson C. 813			
He jugeth it no foly;	305	Why Come Ye	1047
No shame to do amys;	305	Why Come Ye	1051
That no prechour almost	306	Why Come Ye	1075
Nor no lawe canonicall	308	Why Come Ye	1159
Holde ye your tong, ye can no goode.	310	Why Come Ye2	20
ye] (1st) not in MS Rawlinson C. 813			
Put up his sworde, for he cowde make no warre,	312	Garlande	5
All thynge compassyd, no perpetuyte,	312	Garlande	13
Ageyne whom he cowde make no contradiccyoun?'	316	Garlande	133
Frome that I have sayde in no poynt doth vary,	316	Garlande	163
Or elles, ye know well, I can do no lesse	318	Garlande	226
Make noyse enoughe; for claterars love no peas.	319	Garlande	241
And for no man hardely let hym spare	319	Garlande	244
Sume were to hasty and wold no man byde;	319	Garlande	249
Sume sayd, 'Holde thy peas, thou getest here no more.'	319	Garlande	257
And may not atteyne it by no medyacyon,	321	Garlande	319
Suche an other there coude no man fynde;	325	Garlande	463
With, 'I as good as thou, ifayth, and no better.'	326	Garlande	509
No stormy tempeste your barge shall overthrow.	327	Garlande	546
To pas the tyme with, but let us wast no wynde.	328	Garlande	565
But wele may ye thynk I was no thyng prowde	330	Garlande	648
How wronge was no ryght, and ryght was no wronge;	331	Garlande	704
How wronge was no ryght, and ryght was no wronge;	331	Garlande	704
'Questionles no dowte of that ye say;	332	Garlande	714
Intentyfe ay /And dylygent, /No tyme myspent;	339	Garlande	944
Yet shall there be no restraynt	339	Garlande	956
Moche mirthe and no madnes,	340	Garlande	1009
All good and no badnes,	341	Garlande	1010
Make no delay, for now ye must be brought	343	Garlande	1090
There was amonge them no worde then but mum,	344	Garlande	1118
amonge them no worde] 'not a worde amonge them' MS Cotton Vitellius E.x			
Fynde no mo suche fro Wanflete to Walis.	347	Garlande	1218
In honest myrth, parde, requyreth no lack;	347	Garlande	1236
It is no foly to use the Walshemannys hoos.	347	Garlande	1239
His dirige, her commendacioun /Can be no derogacyoun;	348	Garlande	1270
No man to myscontent /With Phillippis enterement.	348	Garlande	1273
No wors than is contaynyd	350	Garlande	1370
than] 'and' †Fakes 1523			
No man lyvyng, he sayth, can be sure;	351	Garlande	1403
And when that I sawe it wolde no better be,	353	Garlande	1485
Take no dispare,	355	Garlande	1535
And takith no kepe;	358	Garlande2	5
takith] 'bidythe' Marshe 1568			
No man can tell whether.	358	Garlande2	9

NOBBES — NOBLE

	Page	Title	Line
No man wyll undertake	358	Garlande2	10
Thou durst no felde derayne,	365	Albany	243
Nor no batayle mayntayne,	365	Albany	244
That durst abyde no reknyng;	365	Albany	249
No man hath harde /Of suche a cowarde,	365	Albany	252
That no man hym kyll;	365	Albany	264
It made no great fors	366	Albany	282
Therby I shall purchase /No displesaunt rewarde,	368	Albany	359
That ye shall have no grace	371	Albany	504
I saye it for no sedicion,	378	Replycacion	140
He counted it for no correction,	379	Replycacion	189
Your penaunce toke no place,	379	Replycacion	198
Wherfore make ye no mo restrayntes,	382	Replycacion	292
To no mannes anoyance.	385	Replycacion	396
Therefore no grevance, /I pray you, for to take,	385	Replycacion	397

NOBBES

	Page	Title	Line
His nobbes and his conny, /His swetyng and his honny,	220	El Rummynge	225

NOBELLY

	Page	Title	Line
Of the blode royall descendinge nobelly;	29	Dol Dethe	4

NOBELNES

	Page	Title	Line
The nobelnes of the northe, this valyant lorde and knyght,	31	Dol Dethe	85

NOBIL

	Page	Title	Line
Hath brought nobil princes to extreme confusion.	139	Ven Tongues	58

NOBILYTE

	Page	Title	Line
All the roiall sorte /Of his nobilyte,	370	Albany	446

NOBILLMEN

	Page	Title	Line
But had his nobillmen donn wel that day	31	Dol Dethe	69

NOBYLL

	Page	Title	Line
Skelton laureat, at the instance of a nobyll lady.	46	Balettys5	E
That pereles pomegarnat, Cryste save hyr nobyll grace!'	231	Speke Parott	37
Dyscrecion ys modyr of nobyll vertues all;	232	Speke Parott	51
So myche nobyll prechyng, and so lytell amendment;	244	Speke Parott	452
So many nobyll bodyes, undyr on dawys hedd;	245	Speke Parott	467

NOBLE

	Page	Title	Line
Of noble actis auncyently enrolde	29	Dol Dethe	15
So noble a man, so valiaunt lorde and knyght	30	Dol Dethe	29
This noble man doutles had not be slayne.	31	Dol Dethe	74
be] 'bene' Marshe 1568			
Trustinge in noble men that wer with hym there;	31	Dol Dethe	90
When thou shoke thi sword so noble a man to mar!	32	Dol Dethe	115
Mooste noble Erle! O fowle mysuryd grounde,	32	Dol Dethe	118
Whos noble actis shew worsheply his name,	33	Dol Dethe	143
Truly reportinge his right noble astate,	33	Dol Dethe	146
His noble blode never desteynyd was,	33	Dol Dethe	148
This noble man that cruelly was slayne.	34	Dol Dethe	182
Noble Hector of Troye;	74	Phy Sparrow	111
Also the noble fawcon, /With the gerfawcon,	85	Phy Sparrow	556
Noble Henry the eight,	110	Lawde	8
Of this our noble king	111	Lawde	29
Trowe ye, Syr James, his noble grace	114	Scot Kynge	17
He is our noble champyon,	114	Scot Kynge	25
That noble erle, the Whyte Lyon,	115	Scot Kynge	68
and God save noble Kynge Henry the viij.	115	Scot Kynge	E
He is our noble Scipione;	118	Ag Scottes	117
Rudely revilyng me in the kynges noble hall,	121	Garneschel	2
Be the kynges most noble commandement.	122	Garneschel	E
By the kynges most noble commaundment.	124	Garnesche2	E
By the kynges most noble commaundment.	129	Garnesche3	E
It plesyth that noble prince roiall	132	Garnesche5	103
Horace and noble Marciall,	133	Garnesche5	141
Hys noble pleasure and commandemennt,	134	Garnesche5	178
By the kyngys most noble commaundement.	134	Garnesche5	E
Controlle the cognisaunce of noble men	137	Ven Tongues	22
There is no noble man wil judge in me	138	Ven Tongues	34
To assure you of my noble porte and fame,	145	Magnyfycence	163
Syr, though ye be a noble prynce of myght,	145	Magnyfycence	166
Yet amonge noble men I was brought up and bred.	147	Magnyfycence	261
But hyght you, Largesse, encrease of noble fame?	148	Magnyfycence	271
With Magnyfycence, this noble prynce of myght,	148	Magnyfycence	273
Syr, yf I have offended your noble estate,	149	Magnyfycence	308
I folow even after your noble grace.	151	Magnyfycence	395
This noble man Magnyfycence,	151	Magnyfycence	404
Nor yet [C]ypyo, that noble Cartage wanne,	182	Magnyfycence	1512
Cypyo] 'Typyo' †Rastell & Treveris C 1530, B			
As that I myght your noble grace content!	183	Magnyfycence	1534
Syr, I am the better of your noble reporte;	183	Magnyfycence	1541
It is none abusyon, syr, in a noble man.	185	Magnyfycence	1626
For thoughe you were somtyme a noble estate,	196	Magnyfycence	1980
Where is nowe my welth and my noble estate?	198	Magnyfycence	2055
Where is nowe my kynne, my frendys, and my noble blood?	198	Magnyfycence	2060
This lurden that here lyeth had ben a noble man.	200	Magnyfycence	2112
And so shall a noble man nobly be servyd.	200	Magnyfycence	2120
Spare for the spence of a noble that his honour myght save,	200	Magnyfycence	2125
That somtyme was a noble prynce of myght!	205	Magnyfycence	2280
Where every thyng is ordenyd after your noble porte.	214	Magnyfycence	2568
And assay to crepe /Within the noble walles	249	Collyn Clout	126
The noble bloode royall	262	Collyn Clout	612
For lordes of noble bloode,	262	Collyn Clout	615

NOBLE MEN — NOBLY

Entry	Page	Title	Line
And yet a noble clerke	264	Collyn Clout	727
And your noble se /And your dygnyte	265	Collyn Clout	759
se] 'fee' Marshe 1568, 'see' MS Harley 2252			
As noble [Isaias],	276	Collyn Clout	1206
Isaias] 'Ezechyes' †Godfray 1531, Kele 1545.1, Marshe 1568, 'I say was' MS Harley 2252			
All noble men of this take hede,	278	Why Come Ye	1
of this] not in MS Rawlinson C. 813			
All noble men of this take hede,	279	Why Come Ye	15
A noble man may fall,	279	Why Come Ye	22
All noble men of this take hede,	279	Why Come Ye	27
For all their noble blode,	286	Why Come Ye	303
How noble and how kynde	291	Why Come Ye	500
And of his noble pleasure	292	Why Come Ye	547
All noble men shulde outface,	294	Why Come Ye	623
How Frauncis Petrarke, /That moche noble clerke,	296	Why Come Ye	688
God save his noble grace,	303	Why Come Ye	969
A myghty tre and of a noble heyght,	312	Garlande	19
Unto your palas, our noble courte of Fame,	318	Garlande	219
Of noble Dame Pallas, wherof I spake;	320	Garlande	284
Aulus Gelius, that noble historiar;	322	Garlande	351
With Vincencius in Speculo, that wrote noble warkis;	322	Garlande	381
Propercius and Pisandros, poetis of noble fame;	322	Garlande	382
Of noble Fame before the Quenes grace,	324	Garlande	419
'O noble Chaucer, whos pullisshyd eloquence	324	Garlande	421
Wherin was set of Fame the noble Quene,	325	Garlande	482
Tyll at the last theis noble poetis thre	326	Garlande	517
I thanked her moche of her most noble offer,	327	Garlande	554
Of Athlas astrology, and many noble thyngis,	331	Garlande	690
Where the noble Cowntes of Surrey in a chayre	333	Garlande	769
To the ryght noble Countes of Surrey	335	Garlande	R
The passynge bounte of your noble astate,	336	Garlande	841
The noble wyfe of Polimites kynge;	336	Garlande	844
Your noble demenour is counterwayng,	336	Garlande	847
Whos passynge bounte, and ryght noble astate,	336	Garlande	848
The noble Pamphila, quene of the Grekis londe,	336	Garlande	850
Whos passynge bounte, and ryght noble astate,	336	Garlande	855
Whos passyng bounte, and ryght noble astate,	336	Garlande	862
In her astate there sat the noble Quene	343	Garlande	1114
To answere unto this noble audyence,	344	Garlande	1122
And of Soveraynte a noble pamphelet;	346	Garlande	1191
Of our noble courte is ones spoken owte,	353	Garlande	1482
With the noble powre	360	Albany	59
Noble Henry the Eyght	361	Albany	109
The noble Erle of Surrey,	365	Albany	241
So noble a prince as he /In all actyvite	368	Albany	395
To extoll his noble grace	369	Albany	407
His noble baronage /He putteth them in corage	370	Albany	465
To assyst his noble grace,	371	Albany	491
To my Lorde Cardynals right noble grace etc	372	Albany	E
Before his noble grace	372	Albany	525
of the reverende prelates and moche noble doctours	373	Replycacion	I
Than, if this noble kyng,	384	Replycacion	343

NOBLE MEN

Entry	Page	Title	Line
Not amonge noble men, as the worlde gothe.	189	Magnyfycence	1747
But noble men borne, /To lerne they have scorne,	262	Collyn Clout	619

NOBLENES

Entry	Page	Title	Line
For to expres /The noblenes /Of my maistres,	95	Phy Sparrow	957
To wryte and tell /How women excell /In noblenes;	96	Phy Sparrow	983
With Mesure. Where as all noblenes is, there I have past:	189	Magnyfycence	1749
To whos astate all noblenes most leven,	313	Garlande	54
leven] 'lene' †Fakes 1523, MS Cotton Vitellius E.x			
Both worde and dede /Should be agrede /In noblenes:	357	Garlande	1601

NOBLENESSE

Entry	Page	Title	Line
Yf noblenesse were aquayntyd with sober dyreccyon.	141	Magnyfycence	18
Measure with noblenesse sholde be alyde.	145	Magnyfycence	194
Your noblenesse and honour consernynge.	146	Magnyfycence	204
Then noblenesse, I se well, is almoste undone,	146	Magnyfycence	225
That without largesse noblenesse can not rayne.	147	Magnyfycence	265
Say howe you excede in noblenesse,	151	Magnyfycence	376
That ever noblenesse sholde lyve thus wretchydly!	197	Magnyfycence	2021
For of noblenesse the chefe poynt is to be lyberall,	211	Magnyfycence	2487
Let never negarshyp your noblenesse affray;	211	Magnyfycence	2493
What noblenesse dothe abounde,	369	Albany	424

NOBLES

Entry	Page	Title	Line
Kyndle in me suche plente of thy nobles,	29	Dol Dethe	20
He had plucte oute the nobles of my pouche.	60	Bowge	504
Cherlemayne, that mantenyd the nobles of Fraunce,	182	Magnyfycence	1501
Our nobles are gone	302	Why Come Ye	922
Devoyde of all nobles,	369	Albany	410

NOBLY

Entry	Page	Title	Line
Some of moralyte nobly dyde endyte;	46	Bowge	14
moralyte] 'mortalyte' †Wynkyn de Worde 1499, Marshe 1568			
As your grace full nobly hath recountyd,	145	Magnyfycence	193
And so shall a noble man nobly be servyd.	200	Magnyfycence	2120
Javell is nobly borne;	281	Why Come Ye	96
And set hym nobly /In great auctoryte	291	Why Come Ye	504
And maister Chaucer, that nobly enterprysyd	323	Garlande	388

NOBULL —NONE   Page   Title   Line

NOBULL
Trowyd ye, Syr Jemy, his nobull grace   118   Ag Scottes   107
NODDIS
In the Ster Chambre he noddis and beks, ...   287   Why Come Ye   339
NODDYNGE
But there was poyntynge and noddynge with the hede, ...   58   Bowge   421
NODDY POLLES
Nor of theyr noddy polles, ...   277   Collyn Clout 1243
NODY POLLE
Nor seche a nody polle   126   Garnesche3   88
NODYPOLLYS
Then nodypollys and gramatolys of smalle intellygens: 240   Speke Parott 318
NOE
Of Noe the patryarke, ...   78   Phy Sparrow   256
NOES
That were syns Noes flode;   78   Phy Sparrow   268
NOYSE
He fumblyth in hys fyngeryng an ugly good noyse;   37   Coystrowne1   31
There was moche noyse, anone one cryed, 'Cese!'   47   Bowge   46
Make noyse enoughe; for claterars love no peas.   319   Garlande   241
A wonderfull noyse, and on every syde   319   Garlande   247
With that I harde the noyse of a trumpe, ...   319   Garlande   259
Of trumpettis and clariouns the noyse went to Rome;   354   Garlande   1507
The grownde gronid and tremblid, the noyse was so stowte. . . .   354   Garlande   1509
NOLL
And whan I fayle, bobbe me on the noll!   53   Bowge   259
NOLLE
Lytyll wyt in your scrybys nolle   126   Garnesche3   90
NOLLES
God wote, with dronken nolles.   252   Collyn Clout 232
Of theyr dronken nolles, ...   277   Collyn Clout 1242
NOMBER
I[n] ponder, by nomber, by measure all thynge is wrought, . . .   143   Magnyfycence 118
    In] 'I' †Rastell & Treveris C 1530, B
NOMBYR
To nombyr all the sterrys in the fyrmament, ...   240   Speke Parott 332
NOMBRE
Full subtyll persones in nombre foure and thre.   49   Bowge   133
NON
Put up your purs, ye shall non pay!'   40   Coystrowne4   11
That hath non erthly pere?   96   Phy Sparrow   1001
A kynge anoynted, and ye be non.   114   Scot Kynge   26
For reson can I non fynde   126   Garnesche3   104
Ne by non other that any man can rehersse.   181   Magnyfycence 1490
Non can have protectyon   304   Why Come Ye   1011
    Non can have] 'They can have no' †Kele 1545.3, Toy 1553,
    Kitson 1560.7, Marshe 1568
NONE
Than there coude I none aquentaunce fynde;   47   Bowge   45
'Maystres,' quod I, 'I have none aquentaunce   48   Bowge   92
For here is none that dare well other truste;   51   Bowge   202
And wake all nyghte and slepe tyll it be none.   57   Bowge   382
Lyghte lyme-fynger, he toke none other wage.   60   Bowge   509
Was never none so good;   78   Phy Sparrow   269
So none be left behynde.   81   Phy Sparrow   389
And yet there is none /But one alone;   84   Phy Sparrow   516
Comfort had he none   89   Phy Sparrow   705
At hym example ye wolde none take;   115   Scot Kynge   60
Anoynted kyng, and ye were none.   118   Ag Scottes   118
And, for example [y]e wold none take, ...   119   Ag Scottes   157
    ye] 'he' †Lant 1545, Kynge & Marche 1554, Day 1560,
    Marshe 1568
Cause have they none other /But for that he was brother, . . .   120   Ag Scottes2   13
    have they] 'they have' Day 1560, Marshe 1568
    brother] 'hys brother' Day 1560, Marshe 1568
If there be none other mater but that, ...   137   Ven Tongues   14
Dyspleasure that you none cause   143   Magnyfycence   98
Where measure is mayster, plenty dothe none offence;   144   Magnyfycence 121
Here is none forsyth whether you flete or synke.   147   Magnyfycence 254
Tushe, a strawe! I thought none yll.   156   Magnyfycence 564
By cloked colusyon, I say, and none other, ...   160   Magnyfycence 714
I can fynde fantasyes where none is;   169   Magnyfycence 1041
In faythe, ellys is there none in all Englonde.   170   Magnyfycence 1099
That I shall suffer none impechment   179   Magnyfycence 1418
What! All by mesure, good syr, and none excesse?   180   Magnyfycence 1422
Nowe holde ye content, for there is none other shyfte.   180   Magnyfycence 1443
Nor none so hardy of them with me that durste crake, ...   182   Magnyfycence 1513
Be it reason or none, it shall not gretely skyll;   185   Magnyfycence 1596
With, 'Cockes armes! Rest shall I none have   185   Magnyfycence 1615
It is none abusyon, syr, in a noble man.   185   Magnyfycence 1626
By Magnyfycence nor yet none of his;   188   Magnyfycence 1705
I make God avowe ye wyll none other men have.   191   Magnyfycence 1827
Yet sometyme I stryke where is none offence.   194   Magnyfycence 1916
And yf there were none to dysplease but thou and I, ...   202   Magnyfycence 2194
How none estate lyvynge of hymselfe can be sure, ...   213   Magnyfycence 2557
Thus none estate lyvynge of hym[selfe] can be sure, ...   214   Magnyfycence 2564
    hymselfe] 'hym' †Rastell & Treveris C 1530, B
There is none that your name woll abbrogate   240   Speke Parott 317

NONES — NOR

	Page	Title	Line
So myche consultacion, almoste to none entente;	244	Speke Parott	453
They have none instructyon	253	Collyn Clout	268
And let Collyn Clout have none	258	Collyn Clout	478
have none] 'alone' MS Lansdowne 762, 'alon' MS Harley 2252			
Ye coude none other gette	263	Collyn Clout	654
coude] 'wolde' Kele 1545.1, Marshe 1568, 'cowde' MS Harley 2252			
Wyll knowe none intellygence	275	Collyn Clout	1137
To ferce for none offence,	278	Why Come Ye	4
And to none entente,	280	Why Come Ye	81
None so hardy to speke.	287	Why Come Ye	328
Nor of none other saw;	292	Why Come Ye	511
For amonge us is none	304	Why Come Ye	995
For certayne envectyfys, yet wrote he none ill,	315	Garlande	96
certayne envectyfys] 'that he enveiyd' MS Cotton Vit.E.x			
From whiche Eschines had none evacyon.	316	Garlande	154
Few shall ye fynde or none that wyll do so.'	317	Garlande	168
Theis people by me have none assignement,	317	Garlande	195
That in the forest was none so great a tre	320	Garlande	277
None so ryche stones in Turkey to sell;	323	Garlande	396
And plantid it there where never before was none, unshred	351	Garlande	1405
it there where] 'yet wher' Marshe 1568			
To worshyppe none ymages, /Nor do pylgrymages?	381	Replycacion	269

NONES

	Page	Title	Line
Among the Nones Blake.	72	Phy Sparrow	9
Of purpose, for the nones,	77	Phy Sparrow	211

NONYS

	Page	Title	Line
Anone all was whyste, as it were for the nonys,	319	Garlande	267

NONNE

	Page	Title	Line
Barbyd lyke a nonne	168	Magnyfycence	987
Good nonne, nor good canon,	274	Collyn Clout	1098

NONNES

	Page	Title	Line
This nonnes nowe and then, and it myght be,	154	Magnyfycence	488
That nonnes wyl leve theyr holynes and ryn after me;	201	Magnyfycence	2146
Amongest the sely nonnes.	256	Collyn Clout	389

NOO

	Page	Title	Line
I wolde noo thynge so playne be.	52	Bowge	214
That noo man erthly coude hym bewreye,	52	Bowge	223
man] 'wan' †Wynkyn de Worde 1499			

NOO THYNGE

	Page	Title	Line
'Noo thynge erthely that I wonder so sore	50	Bowge	148

NOPPE

	Page	Title	Line
Whan the noppe is rughe, it wolde be shorne.	153	Magnyfycence	448

NOPPY

	Page	Title	Line
She breweth noppy ale,	217	El Rummynge	102
'This ale,' sayd she, 'is noppy;	228	El Rummynge	557

NOR

	Page	Title	Line
They saide they forsede not nor carede not to dy.	31	Dol Dethe	84
He can not fynd it in rule nor in space:	37	Coystrownel	22
That neyther they synge wel prycke song nor playne.	38	Coystrownel	54
Neyther flesh nor fell.	39	Coystrowne3	18
nor] 'not' Marshe 1568			
There may no fraunchys /Nor worldly blys	39	Coystrowne3	27
Nor to the lake /Of fendys blake.	40	Coystrowne3	47
Nor stand long wrestyng there aboute;	41	Coystrowne4	25
There can no favour nor frendshyp hym forsake.	48	Bowge	103
It was no tyme with him to jape nor toye.	54	Bowge	290
The armes of Calyce, I have no coyne nor crosse!	57	Bowge	398
By reason nor by law;	62	Hauke	7
Nor he shall not be shameles;	62	Hauke	40
I wyll not fayne nor forge;	64	Hauke	88
Neither yet Dyoclesyan, /Nor yet Domysyan;	67	Hauke	193
Nother crokyd Cacus, /Nor yet dronken Bacus;	67	Hauke	195
Nother] 'Nor yet' Kynge & Marche 1554, Day 1560, Marshe 1568			
Nother Olybryus, /Nor Dyonysyus;	67	Hauke	197
Nor Sardanapall, /Unhappyest of all;	67	Hauke	200
Nor Nero the worst, /Nor Clawdyus the curst;	67	Hauke	202
Nor Nero the worst, /Nor Clawdyus the curst;	67	Hauke	203
Nor yet Egeas, /Nor yet Syr Pherumbras;	67	Hauke	204
Nor yet Egeas, /Nor yet Syr Pherumbras;	67	Hauke	205
Nother Zorobabell, /Nor cruell Jesabell;	67	Hauke	207
Nor yet Tarquinius,	67	Hauke	208
Yet the Sowden, nor the Turke,	67	Hauke	216
Cowde not rech nor attayne	68	Hauke	226
Apostata Julianus /Nor yet Nestorianus,	70	Hauke	298
He can not well fly, /Nor synge tunably;	83	Phy Sparrow	484
Nor by Ptholomy, /Prince of astronomy,	84	Phy Sparrow	503
Nor yet by Haly;	84	Phy Sparrow	505
Even nor morow; /But other mennes sorow	94	Phy Sparrow	924
Nor yet no vyllany, /But only fantasy;	100	Phy Sparrow	1134
Neyther wryte nor say;	101	Phy Sparrow	1197
It cost me lytell nor nought.	101	Phy Sparrow	1203
nor] 'or' Wyght 1553, Kitson 1560.6, Marshe 1568			
That never have rest nor ease;	104	Phy Sparrow	1325
Nor wrote the rosary	111	Lawde	27
It is not syttynge in tour nor towne	115	Scot Kynge	66
Nor blake Baltazar with hys basnet routh as a bere,	122	Garneschel	23
Nor Lycon, that lothly luske, in myn opynyon,	122	Garneschel	24

	Page	Title	Line
Nor no bore so brymly brystlyd ys with here,	122	Garnesche1	25
Pyramus, nor Priamus, nor Syr Pyrrus the prowde,	123	Garnesche2	23
Pyramus, nor Priamus, nor Syr Pyrrus the prowde,	123	Garnesche2	23
Nor sowtters to drynke wyne,	126	Garnesche3	87
Nor seche a nody polle	126	Garnesche3	88
Nor good ryme in yower mater.	126	Garnesche3	105
A makerell nor a wyteyng:	127	Garnesche3	116
That naythyr pump nor synke	127	Garnesche3	145
In your crosse rowe nor Christ crosse you spede,	137	Ven Tongues	18
Your Pater noster, your Ave, nor your Crede.	137	Ven Tongues	19
Where drede ledyth the daunce, there is no joy nor blysse.	142	Magnyfycence	76
For measure is a meane, nother to hy nor to lawe,	145	Magnyfycence	188
There is no flaterer nor losyll so lyther,	146	Magnyfycence	200
Nor no man in courte, but he,	158	Magnyfycence	660
For thou shalt well knowe I am nother durty nor dusty.	161	Magnyfycence	759
Here is no man that callyd the hogge nor swyne.	170	Magnyfycence	1084
By theyr demenaunce, nor loss repryvable.	179	Magnyfycence	1419
Nor Cesar July, that no man myght withstande,	181	Magnyfycence	1482
Nor Basyan the bolde, for all his brybaunce,	182	Magnyfycence	1503
Nor Alerycus, that rulyd the Gothyaunce by swerd,	182	Magnyfycence	1504
Nor no man on molde can make me aferd.	182	Magnyfycence	1505
Nor Nero, that nother set by God nor man,	182	Magnyfycence	1509
Nor Nero, that nother set by God nor man,	182	Magnyfycence	1509
Nor Vespasyan, that bare in his nose a waspe,	182	Magnyfycence	1510
Nor Hanyball, agayne Rome gates that ranne,	182	Magnyfycence	1511
Nor yet [C]ypyo, that noble Cartage wanne, Cypyo] 'Typyo' †Rastell & Treveris C 1530, B	182	Magnyfycence	1512
Nor none so hardy of them with me that durste crake,	182	Magnyfycence	1513
By Magnyfycence nor yet none of his;	188	Magnyfycence	1705
Let neyther patent scape them nor fee;	190	Magnyfycence	1776
Of erthely thynge I have no care nor charge.	199	Magnyfycence	2081
And not all the nygarde nor the chyncherde to play.	211	Magnyfycence	2492
I shall it never forget nor leve it behynde,	212	Magnyfycence	2506
'I have no penny nor grote	229	El Rummynge	600
Neyther gelt nor pawne.	229	El Rummynge	610
Nether wise nor wel lernid, but like hermaphradita:	235	Speke Parott	159
No matter pretendyd, nor nothyng enterprysed,	236	Speke Parott	201
For Parot is no churlish chowgh, nor no flekyd pye,	236	Speke Parott	204
Parrot is no woodecocke, nor no butterfly,	236	Speke Parott	206
That never may dye, nor never dye shall:	236	Speke Parott	216
Syns Dewcalions flodde, was nevyr sene nor shall.	245	Speke Parott	469
Syns Dewcalyons flodde was nevyr sene nor lyerd.	246	Speke Parott	504
Was nevyr suche a fylty gorgon, nor suche an epycure,	246	Speke Parott	510
Ye pyke no shrympes nor pranes,	252	Collyn Clout	208
Saltfysshe, stockfyssh nor herynge,	252	Collyn Clout	209
Nor in holy lenton season	252	Collyn Clout	211
And wotteth never what thei rede, /Paternoster nor crede;	252	Collyn Clout	235
Neyther gospell nor pystell,	252	Collyn Clout	237
A myter nor a crose,	254	Collyn Clout	292
Nor farther for to loke	266	Collyn Clout	783
Nor bachelers of that faculte	266	Collyn Clout	791
Of logyke nor scole matter,	267	Collyn Clout	815
Neyther sylogysare, /Nor of [enthymemar]e; enthymemare] 'emptymeniare' †Godfray 1531, Kele 1545.1, Marshe 1568, 'entimemare' MS Harley 2252	267	Collyn Clout	817
Nor knoweth not his elenkes, elenkes] 'eloquens' †Godfray 1531, Kele 1545.1, Marshe 1568	267	Collyn Clout	818
Nor his predicamentes;	267	Collyn Clout	819
Nor how farre Temple Barre is	267	Collyn Clout	826
Of a peny nor of a crosse	269	Collyn Clout	929
That they shall mell nor make,	271	Collyn Clout	1015
Nor upon them take,	272	Collyn Clout	1016
For kynge nor kayser sake,	272	Collyn Clout	1017
Nor to execute /His commaundement,	272	Collyn Clout	1032
Nor to expresse to his parson,	272	Collyn Clout	1036
Nor to speke to hym secretly, /Openly nor prevyly,	272	Collyn Clout	1040
Nor to speke to hym secretly, /Openly nor prevyly,	272	Collyn Clout	1041
Nor good preest I escrye, I escrye] 'of the clargy' Marshe 1568, 'askrye' Harley 2252	273	Collyn Clout	1096
Good frere, nor good chanon,	273	Collyn Clout	1097
Good nonne, nor good canon,	274	Collyn Clout	1098
Good monke, nor good clerke,	274	Collyn Clout	1099
Nor of no good werke;	274	Collyn Clout	1100
Nor wyll here no prechynge,	274	Collyn Clout	1133
Nor no vertuous techynge,	274	Collyn Clout	1134
Nor wyll have no resytynge	274	Collyn Clout	1135
Nor wyll suffre this boke	277	Collyn Clout	1237
Nor rede in any scrolles,	277	Collyn Clout	1241
Nor of theyr noddy polles,	277	Collyn Clout	1243
Nor of theyr sely soules,	277	Collyn Clout	1244
Nor of some wytles pates	277	Collyn Clout	1245
Nor basse her swete swete.	279	Why Come Ye	35
To know God nor man.	283	Why Come Ye	183
Duke, erle, baron, nor lorde,	287	Why Come Ye	342
Nor worth a sowre calstocke.	287	Why Come Ye	355
Nor doctor of the law,	292	Why Come Ye	510
Nor of none other saw;	292	Why Come Ye	511
Nor of philosophy, /Nor of philology,	292	Why Come Ye	516

	Page	Title	Line
Nor of philosophy, /Nor of philology,	292	Why Come Ye	517
Nor of good pollycy, /Nor of astronomy;	292	Why Come Ye	518
Nor of good pollycy, /Nor of astronomy;	292	Why Come Ye	519
Nor with royall Ptholomy, /Nor with Albumasar,	292	Why Come Ye	522
Nor with royall Ptholomy, /Nor with Albumasar,	292	Why Come Ye	523
Nor duke of hye degre,	294	Why Come Ye	619
Nor marques, erle, nor lorde;	294	Why Come Ye	620
Nor marques, erle, nor lorde;	294	Why Come Ye	620
Hath nowe no tyme nor space	295	Why Come Ye	631
I have no pen nor inke	296	Why Come Ye	684
This is no fable nor no lye;	296	Why Come Ye	705
To rule nor to guyde,	304	Why Come Ye	1012
Of my lordis grace nor his wyfe!	306	Why Come Ye	1077
Nor no lawe canonicall	308	Why Come Ye	1159
Nor yet shall scape shamlesse.	309	Why Come Ye2	5
shall] not in MS Rawlinson C. 813			
Unto me; alas, that herbe nor gresse	321	Garlande	314
gresse] 'gras' †Fakes 1523			
And for my sake spare neyther pen nor ynke;	327	Garlande	549
It is not my custome nor my gyse /To leve behynde	342	Garlande	1068
That never have rest nor ease;	349	Garlande	1318
Nor to derayne /Batayle agayne /Scornfull disdayne,	356	Garlande	1563
Nor for to chyde, /Nor for to hyde /You cowardly;	356	Garlande	1566
Nor for to chyde, /Nor for to hyde /You cowardly;	356	Garlande	1567
Never true nor playne,	362	Albany	134
Nor lyke his sonne Hanyball,	363	Albany	194
Nor lyke Duke Hasdruball	363	Albany	195
Nor no batayle mayntayne,	365	Albany	244
Nor durst nat crak a worde,	366	Albany	307
Nor durst nat drawe his swerde	366	Albany	308
So hardy nor so bolde	367	Albany	338
Ye coude nat corde tenus, /Nor answere verbo tenus,	377	Replycacion	105
To worshyppe none ymages, /Nor do pylgrymages?	381	Replycacion	270
In theology, /Nor analogy,	383	Replycacion	309
Nor philology, /Nor philosophy,	383	Replycacion	310
Nor philology, /Nor philosophy,	383	Replycacion	311
Flaccus nor Catullus with hym may nat compare,	383	Replycacion	336
Nor solempne Serenus, for all his armony	383	Replycacion	337
That frensy nor jelousy	385	Replycacion	407
Nor heresy wyll never dye.	385	Replycacion	408

NORHAM

	Page	Title	Line
For to the castell of Norham	114	Scot Kynge	38

NORMAN

	Page	Title	Line
'Heve and how, rombelow, row the bote, Norman, rowe.'	53	Bowge	252

NORRAM

	Page	Title	Line
Unto the castell of Norram,	118	Ag Scottes	129

NORTH

	Page	Title	Line
With, 'How doth the north?' 'What tydingis in the sowth?'	326	Garlande	498
And from the sowth unto the north so colde,	328	Garlande	578

NORTHE

	Page	Title	Line
The nobelnes of the northe, this valyant lorde and knyght,	31	Dol Dethe	85

NORTHUMBERLANDE

	Page	Title	Line
of the Mooste Honorable Erle of Northumberlande	29	Dol Dethe	I
The famous Erle of Northumberlande;	32	Dol Dethe	107
The Erle of Northumberlande	286	Why Come Ye	290

NOSE

	Page	Title	Line
His nose a-droppynge, his lyppes were full drye;	56	Bowge	362
a-droppynge] 'droppynge' Marshe 1568			
The wodcocke with the longe nose;	83	Phy Sparrow	459
In the pott your nose dedde snevyll;	124	Garnesche3	27
A semly nose and a stowte,	133	Garnesche5	131
Wer thi nose spectacle case;	133	Garnesche5	134
For thy Scottyshe nose,	136	Dundas	36
For pryde hath plucked the by the nose	163	Magnyfycence	826
Nor Vespasyan, that bare in his nose a waspe,	182	Magnyfycence	1510
Ye, wylte thou clenly cle[v]e me in the clyfte with thy nose?	202	Magnyfycence	2176
cleve] 'clene' †Rastell & Treveris C 1530, B			
Ye, for requiem eternam groweth forth of his nose.	204	Magnyfycence	2260
Her nose somdele hoked /And camously croked,	215	El Rummynge	27
Snevelyng in her nose, /As though she had the pose.	223	El Rummynge	364
Take peper in the nose;	288	Why Come Ye	384
Domingos nose that was wheled.	308	Why Come Ye	1185
was] not in MS Rawlinson C. 813			
That Lumberdes nose meane I	308	Why Come Ye	1186
Balthasor, that helyd Domingos nose	309	Why Come Ye	1194
nose] 'pose' Marshe 1568			

NOSYD

	Page	Title	Line
Nosyd lyke an olyfaunt,	126	Garnesche3	71

NOT

	Page	Title	Line
Were not thes commones uncurteis karlis of kynd	30	Dol Dethe	34
not] 'no' †MS Royal 18 D.ii, 'not' Marshe 1568			
To slo ther owne lorde? God was not in ther mynde!	30	Dol Dethe	35
And were not thei to blame, I say also,	30	Dol Dethe	36
They bode not till the rekenyng were discust.	30	Dol Dethe	40
Your naturall lord? Alas, I kan not fayne.	30	Dol Dethe	54
To the right of his prince which shold not be withstand;	31	Dol Dethe	67
Ye had not ben hable to have saide hym nay.	31	Dol Dethe	70

NOT — NOT

	Page	Title	Line
This noble man doutles had not be slayne.	31	Dol Dethe	74
be] 'bene' Marshe 1568			
They saide they forsede not nor carede not to dy.	31	Dol Dethe	84
They saide they forsede not nor carede not to dy.	31	Dol Dethe	84
Of whos [life] they countede not a fly.	31	Dol Dethe	95
life] not in †MS Royal 18 D.ii or Marshe 1568			
And be not light of credence in no case.	34	Dol Dethe	175
Be Crist, ye shall not! No, no, hardely!	36	Man Margery	18
I will not be japed bodely.	36	Man Margery	19
When he is well, yet can he not rest.	36	Coystrowne1	7
Nay, jape not with hym, he is no small fole;	38	Coystrowne1	50
Yet bere ye not to bold to braule ne to bark	38	Coystrowne1	60
Deme what thou lyst, thou knowyst not my thought.	38	Coystrowne1	63
That we be not exylyd	40	Coystrowne3	44
Youre key is redy, we nede not knok	41	Coystrowne4	24
She sparyd not to wete her fete.	42	Balettys1	16
Howbei[t], he is not furst hath had a los.	43	Balettys2	38
Howbeit] 'Howbeis' †Rastell 1527.1			
Let not all the world make an owtcry;	43	Balettys2	40
That wher I love best I dare not dyscure!	45	Balettys5	7
That where I love best I dare not dyscure.	46	Balettys5	14
Dyverse in style, some spared not vyce to wrythe,	46	Bowge	13
wrythe] 'wryte' Wynkyn de Worde 1510, Marshe 1568			
And shewed that in this arte I was not sure;	46	Bowge	19
I] not in †Wynkyn de Worde 1499, 1510			
And not to wrythe, for he so wyll atteyne,	46	Bowge	22
wrythe] 'wryte' Wynkyn de Worde 1510, Marshe 1568			
But of reproche surely he maye not mys	46	Bowge	26
But than I thoughte I wolde not dwell behynde;	47	Bowge	43
Abasshe you not, but hardely be bolde,	48	Bowge	87
'Pece,' quod Desyre, 'ye speke not worth a bene!	48	Bowge	95
Yf ye have not, in fayth, I wyll you lene	48	Bowge	96
They coude not faile, thei thought, they were so sure.	50	Bowge	142
But my dysporte they could not well endure:	50	Bowge	145
Whyles I have ought, by God, thou shalt not lacke,	50	Bowge	167
Ye maye not fall; truste me, ye maye not fayle.	50	Bowge	170
Ye maye not fall; truste me, ye maye not fayle.	50	Bowge	170
Ageynste you hardely; therefore be not afrayde.	51	Bowge	174
By myne avyse use not with him to walke.	52	Bowge	210
To shewe you thynges that may not be disclosed.'	52	Bowge	217
I dare not speke; I promysed to be dome.	52	Bowge	229
A wonder thynge that ye waxe not madde!	53	Bowge	241
We tweyne, I trowe, be not withoute dysceyte:	55	Bowge	313
What weneste I were? I trowe thou knowe not me.	55	Bowge	331
Naye, strawe for tales, thou shalte not rule us;	55	Bowge	341
'And, syr, in fayth, why comste not us amonge	57	Bowge	379
Thou mayste not studye or muse on the mone.	57	Bowge	383
Fye on this dyce, they be not worth a turde!	57	Bowge	392
I am not happy, I renne ay on the lossel	57	Bowge	399
Who rydeth on her, he nedeth not to care,	57	Bowge	409
I dempte and drede theyr talkynge was not good.	58	Bowge	426
For allbeit that this longe not to me,	59	Bowge	456
But, what, a strawe! I maye not tell all thynge.	59	Bowge	459
Alas, I coude not dele so with a [J]ew.	59	Bowge	462
a Jew] 'on yew' †Wynkyn de Worde 1499, 'a yew' Wynkyn de Worde 1510, Marshe 1568			
I dare not speke, we be so layde awayte,	59	Bowge	468
It wyll not be, his purse is not on-flote.	60	Bowge	488
It wyll not be, his purse is not on-flote.	60	Bowge	488
For yf I had not quyckely fledde the touche,	60	Bowge	503
I have not sene suche anothers page –	60	Bowge	506
There I wynked on you – wote ye not where?	60	Bowge	516
Woo is hym that is blynde and maye not see!	60	Bowge	518
I wyll not saye it is mater in dede,	61	Bowge	537
But he shall not be blameles,	62	Hauke	39
Nor he shall not be shameles;	62	Hauke	40
But she wold not bow.	63	Hauke	74
She had not wel endude;	63	Hauke	78
She was not clene ensaymd,	63	Hauke	79
She was not wel reclaymed,	63	Hauke	80
I wyll not fayne nor forge;	64	Hauke	88
He sayde he wold not let /His houndys for to fet,	64	Hauke	106
Delt he not lyke a fon?	65	Hauke	128
Delt he not lyke a daw?	65	Hauke	129
(The Bybyll wyll not ly)	66	Hauke	167
Cowde not rech nor attayne	68	Hauke	226
I trowe she coude not amende	75	Phy Sparrow	156
Coude not my sampler holde;	77	Phy Sparrow	234
And not for byrdes smale.	80	Phy Sparrow	340
We may not well forgo /The countrynge of the coe;	83	Phy Sparrow	467
He coulde not optayne	89	Phy Sparrow	697
I wot not where to fynd /Termes to serve my mynde.	91	Phy Sparrow	782
His termes were not darke,	91	Phy Sparrow	801
If I have not well perused	92	Phy Sparrow	814
Yet though I wryte not with ynke,	101	Phy Sparrow	1198
I have not offended, I trust,	102	Phy Sparrow	1249
A man kowd not aspy	111	Lawde	19
The law they shall not breke;	111	Lawde	30

NOT — NOT | | Page | Title | Line

	Page	Title	Line
The pepil durst not creke	111	Lawde	33
Knowe ye not salte and suger asonder?	113	Scot Kynge	6
But not worth thre skyppes of a pye.	113	Scot Kynge	10
Your counseyle was not worth a flye.	113	Scot Kynge	14
Ye dyde not your dewty therin,	114	Scot Kynge	32
It is not syttynge in tour nor towne	115	Scot Kynge	66
And wyll not know /Theyr overthrow /At Branxton More?	115	Ag Scottes	9
Know ye not suger and salt asonder?	118	Ag Scottes	96
Your harrold in armes not yet halfe expert.	118	Ag Scottes	98
Not worth thre skyppes of a pye.	118	Ag Scottes	100
Your frantyck fable not worth a fly,	118	Ag Scottes	104
Youre poverte cowde not attayne	119	Ag Scottes	151
It is not syttyng in tower and towne	120	Ag Scottes	174
syttyng] 'fytting' Kynge & Marche 1554			
The tokens ar not good /To be true Englysh blood;	121	Ag Scottes2	22
Rayle not so far.	136	Dundas	63
That, if I wist not to be controlde,	137	Ven Tongues	9
My scoles are not for unthriftes untaught,	138	Ven Tongues	26
Men said they could not their tunges atame;	139	Ven Tongues	60
And all is not worth a couple of nut shalis.	139	Ven Tongues	66
A man may have welth, but not as he wolde,	141	Magnyfycence	14
To tell you, syr, I dare not, leest I sholde be maskyd	141	Magnyfycence	30
Here ye not howe this gentylman mockys?	141	Magnyfycence	32
In dede, syr, that lyberte was not worthe a cue.	141	Magnyfycence	36
Judycyall rygoure shall not me correcte –	142	Magnyfycence	69
And you have not your owne fre lyberte	142	Magnyfycence	78
That wyll not I forsake,	143	Magnyfycence	100
Measure is treasure. Howe say ye, is it not this?	144	Magnyfycence	125
So that lyberte be not lefte behynde.	144	Magnyfycence	129
But have ye not herde say that wyll is no skyll?	144	Magnyfycence	148
Your ordenaunce, syr, I wyll not forsake.	145	Magnyfycence	181
And not embracyd with pusyllanymyte.	146	Magnyfycence	206
And from felycyte may not be forborne.	146	Magnyfycence	220
Why, were not your selfe agreed to the same,	147	Magnyfycence	233
Perceyve you not howe lothe he was to abyde	147	Magnyfycence	241
Thynke you not thus my frende Felycyte?	147	Magnyfycence	245
Ye coulde not ellys, I wote, with me endure.	147	Magnyfycence	247
It were not possyble me longe to retayne.	147	Magnyfycence	250
As in that I wyll not be agaynst your pleasure.	148	Magnyfycence	276
Have ye not welthe here at your wyll?	148	Magnyfycence	284
In fayth, I set not by the worlde two Dauncaster cuttys.	148	Magnyfycence	293
In fayth, I wyll not say that ye shall prove a fole,	148	Magnyfycence	301
I wyll not use you to play with me checke mate.	149	Magnyfycence	307
Had I not opened my purse wyde,	150	Magnyfycence	347
By my trouthe, had I not payde and prayde,	150	Magnyfycence	363
I had not been here with you this nyght.	150	Magnyfycence	365
But largesse is not mete for every man.	150	Magnyfycence	369
And of my servyce you shall not mysse.	151	Magnyfycence	392
I set not by hym a fly	152	Magnyfycence	412
Counterfet reason is not worth a flye;	153	Magnyfycence	470
Coll wolde go clenly, and it wyll not be,	153	Magnyfycence	476
Monkys may not for drede that men sholde them se.	154	Magnyfycence	493
But is it not well? Howe thynkest thou?	155	Magnyfycence	528
Myselfe coude not counterfet it better.	155	Magnyfycence	530
By God, had not I it convayed	155	Magnyfycence	534
I trowe it shall not nede to abyde.	156	Magnyfycence	571
For had you not come I had ryden.	156	Magnyfycence	577
And Crafty Conveyaunce, knowe you not hym?	156	Magnyfycence	584
Se you not howe they prece	156	Magnyfycence	591
Knowe they not me? They are to blame.	157	Magnyfycence	593
Knowe you not me, syrs? No, in dede.	157	Magnyfycence	594
Is it not a vestment? A, ye wante a rope.	157	Magnyfycence	604
Syr, and yf ye wolde not be wrothe –	157	Magnyfycence	606
Nay, lette us not clatter thus styll.	157	Magnyfycence	610
And have you not amonge you Lyberte?	157	Magnyfycence	625
I care not, I. Tell on for me.	158	Magnyfycence	634
What the devyll ayleth you? Can you not agree?	158	Magnyfycence	636
Pease! I have not yet sayd what I wyll.	158	Magnyfycence	648
And that we fayled not for nothynge.	158	Magnyfycence	654
Why, can ye not put out that foule freke?	158	Magnyfycence	657
That Mesure shall not there longe tary.	159	Magnyfycence	684
Howe sayst thou, man? Am not I a joly rutter?	161	Magnyfycence	752
What! Wenyst thou that I knowe the not, Clokyd Colusyon?	161	Magnyfycence	756
And wenyst thow that I know not the, cankard Abusyon?	161	Magnyfycence	757
Cankard Jacke Hare, loke thou be not rusty;	161	Magnyfycence	758
By Goddes fote, and I dare well fyght, for I wyll not start.	161	Magnyfycence	768
But are ye not avysed to dwell where ye spake?	162	Magnyfycence	774
I am of fewe wordys. I love not to [crake].	162	Magnyfycence	775
crake] 'barke' †Rastell & Treveris C 1530, B			
Here he is nowe, man. Mayst thou not se?	162	Magnyfycence	792
What sayst thou, man? Why dost thou not supplye,	162	Magnyfycence	797
Nede? Yes, Mary. I say not nay.	163	Magnyfycence	807
What the devyll! Use ye not to drawe no swordes?	163	Magnyfycence	811
I waraunt you I wyll not go away.	163	Magnyfycence	820
But nowe I wyll not say the worste.	163	Magnyfycence	828
Why, harde thou not of the fray	166	Magnyfycence	932
No, Mary; not yet.	166	Magnyfycence	934
I have not kept her yet thre wokys,	168	Magnyfycence	1002

NOT —NOT   Page   Title   Line

That I wote not where I may rest.   168   Magnyfycence   1021
Hyder and thyder, I wote not whyder;   169   Magnyfycence   1033
I wyll not have it so, I wyll have it this.   169   Magnyfycence   1042
I wyll not gyve a halfepeny for to chose the better.   170   Magnyfycence   1067
That thou cannyst not growe out of thy boyes gere;   170   Magnyfycence   1075
In faythe, there is not a better dogge for hogges, ...   171   Magnyfycence   1120
Not from Anwyke unto Aungey.   171   Magnyfycence   1121
Ye. But trowest thou that he be not maungey?   171   Magnyfycence   1122
Remembrest thou not the japes and the toyes -   171   Magnyfycence   1137
It forseth not of reason, so it kepe ryme.   172   Magnyfycence   1150
Cockes armes! It is not so, I trowe.   173   Magnyfycence   1202
Nowe hast thou not a prowde mocke and a starke?   174   Magnyfycence   1208
As some be not ferre and yf it were well sought -   174   Magnyfycence   1241
And, 'This is not well done, syr; take hede';   175   Magnyfycence   1248
Thynkyst thou not so, by thy fayth?   175   Magnyfycence   1253
Thynke I not so, quod he. Ellys have I shame, ...   175   Magnyfycence   1254
Are not his wordys cursydly cowchyd?   175   Magnyfycence   1276
I wote not whether it cometh of the or of me, ...   176   Magnyfycence   1290
Why, shall I not have Foly with me also?   176   Magnyfycence   1306
Not a better name under the sonne;   176   Magnyfycence   1310
For drede, that we dare not ofte, lest we be spyed.   177   Magnyfycence   1339
'What howe! Be ye mery! Was it not well conveyed?'   177   Magnyfycence   1347
Alas, dere harte, loke that we be not perseyvyd!'   177   Magnyfycence   1349
'Though I shewe you curtesy, say not that I crave[d]; . . .   177   Magnyfycence   1351
    craved] 'crave' †Rastell & Treveris C 1530, B
Yet convey it craftely, and hardely spare not for me' - . .   177   Magnyfycence   1352
Yet Lyberte without rule is not worth a strawe.   178   Magnyfycence   1378
Remembre ye not how my lyberte by mesure ruled was?   178   Magnyfycence   1383
Nay, nay; not so, my frende Felycyte.   179   Magnyfycence   1392
Not and your grace wolde be ruled by me.   179   Magnyfycence   1393
At ones, and let hym not tary all day.   179   Magnyfycence   1400
Be not to bolde my frende; I counsell you, bere a brayne. .   179   Magnyfycence   1405
He may not be comparyd unto me.   181   Magnyfycence   1476
I set not by the prowdest of them a prane, ...   181   Magnyfycence   1489
It wolde not become them with me for to mell;   182   Magnyfycence   1497
He is not lyvynge your maners can amend;   183   Magnyfycence   1537
Why, was not for money Troy bothe bought and solde?   184   Magnyfycence   1576
Be it reason or none, it shall not gretely skyll;   185   Magnyfycence   1596
What sholde ye do elles? Are not you a lorde?   185   Magnyfycence   1606
And ye se a man that with hym ye be not pleased, ...   185   Magnyfycence   1609
Yet I am not harte seke, but that me lyst.   185   Magnyfycence   1621
Hym that I loved not, and made hym to loute;   185   Magnyfycence   1623
Suche lustes at large may not be lefte behynde.   186   Magnyfycence   1628
And that ye wyll not cast hym away so sone.   186   Magnyfycence   1638
For, so helpe me God, for you he is not mete.   186   Magnyfycence   1653
I speke the softlyer because he sholde not wete.   186   Magnyfycence   1654
By myne advyse, with you in fayth he shall not rest.   186   Magnyfycence   1660
That he knowe not but that I have supplyed   187   Magnyfycence   1663
Nowe, by your trouthe, gave ye not a brybe?   187   Magnyfycence   1665
That he wolde loke on hym, thoughe it were not longe. . . .   187   Magnyfycence   1675
I care not howe sone he be refused, ...   187   Magnyfycence   1683
Nay, I tell you, I am not wonte to fode   188   Magnyfycence   1698
But, and I were as ye, I wolde not set a gnat.   188   Magnyfycence   1704
I set not a flye and all go to all.   188   Magnyfycence   1710
Mary, I wene he wolde not be glad to come agayne.   189   Magnyfycence   1740
So I wote not what he sholde do here.   189   Magnyfycence   1741
Not amonge noble men, as the worlde gothe.   189   Magnyfycence   1747
Gyve them more than ynoughe, and let them not lacke;   190   Magnyfycence   1773
To reche at a rat - I coude not her warne.   191   Magnyfycence   1809
A, syr, tolde I not you howe I dyd fynde   191   Magnyfycence   1819
The feldfare wolde have fydled, and it wolde not frame; . .   192   Magnyfycence   1838
When ye knowe that I knowe, ye wyll not be glad.   192   Magnyfycence   1844
Why, coulde not your wyt serve you no better?   193   Magnyfycence   1868
Adewe, for I wyll not come in his clokys.   193   Magnyfycence   1874
Vyle velyarde, thou must not nowe my dynt withstande; . . .   193   Magnyfycence   1878
Thou must not abyde the dynt of my hande.   193   Magnyfycence   1879
He knewe not hymselfe, his harte was so hye;   193   Magnyfycence   1888
Nowe dare he not for shame loke one in the face.   193   Magnyfycence   1891
To gyde them vertuously that wyll not remembre, ...   194   Magnyfycence   1922
And yf I se therby they wyll not amende, ...   194   Magnyfycence   1926
That rule not be mesure that they have in theyr handys, . .   195   Magnyfycence   1939
That sadly rule not theyr howsholde men.   195   Magnyfycence   1940
He woteth not what welth is that never was sore.   196   Magnyfycence   1971
Alasse that I coude not myselfe no better gyde!   196   Magnyfycence   1986
Alasse in my cradell that I had not dyde!   196   Magnyfycence   1987
Alasse! I wote not what I sholde pray.   196   Magnyfycence   1994
Ye, syr, yesterday wyll not be callyd agayne.   197   Magnyfycence   2031
To love that lovesome I wyll not let;   199   Magnyfycence   2072
For totum in toto is not worth an hawe -   199   Magnyfycence   2089
Cockes armes, syrs, wyll ye not se   200   Magnyfycence   2109
Not thorowe largesse of lyberall expence, ...   200   Magnyfycence   2115
And they never thryve in theyr age, it shall not gretly skyll.   200   Magnyfycence   2138
What! Wylte thou skelpe me? Thou dare not loke on a gnat. . .   202   Magnyfycence   2181
Nay. Then thou wylte dynge the devyll and thou be not holde. .   202   Magnyfycence   2183
Nay, thou false harted dastarde! Thou dare not abyde.   202   Magnyfycence   2193
Thou sholde not scape, horson, but thou sholde dye.   202   Magnyfycence   2195
Here shalbe not great sheddynge of blode.   203   Magnyfycence   2207
By our lakyn, syr, not by my wyll.   203   Magnyfycence   2208

495

Entry	Page	Title	Line
Me thynke ye are not gretly acomberyd wyth wyt.	203	Magnyfycence	2215
By God, I tell you, I wyll not be out facyd.	203	Magnyfycence	2220
By the masse, I warant the, I wyll not be bracyd.	203	Magnyfycence	2221
For had I not bene, ye bothe had bene hangyd,	203	Magnyfycence	2235
That thou arte not worthy to loke God in the face.	205	Magnyfycence	2296
That thou canst not have never mercy in his syght.	205	Magnyfycence	2303
And loke that it be not longe	206	Magnyfycence	2311
Thou arte not the fyrst hymselfe hath slayne.	206	Magnyfycence	2316
Spare not thy selfe, but boldly the murder.	206	Magnyfycence	2318
For had ye not the soner ben my refuge,	206	Magnyfycence	2333
Syr, your requeste shall not be delayed.	208	Magnyfycence	2401
Use not then your countenaunce for to counterfet.	210	Magnyfycence	2455
So that your largesse be not to prodygall.	211	Magnyfycence	2488
And not all the nygarde nor the chyncherde to play.	211	Magnyfycence	2492
Set not all your affyaunce in Fortune full of gyle;	211	Magnyfycence	2501
But she is not gryll,	214	El Rummynge	6
Ye shall not bere awaye /Myne ale for nought,	218	El Rummynge	165
myne] 'my' Kynge & Marche 1554, Day 1560, Marshe 1568			
Seest thou not what is fall?	219	El Rummynge	182
Ich am not cast away, /That can my husband say,	220	El Rummynge	219
They care not what men saye!	221	El Rummynge	260
She coulde not lye styllyl'	224	El Rummynge	391
'I dranke not this sennet /A draught to my pay.	224	El Rummynge	394
Let us syppe and soppy, /And not spyll a droppy,	228	El Rummynge	559
Had she not hyed apace,	229	El Rummynge	572
She was not halfe so wyse	229	El Rummynge	588
That had not a penny,	230	El Rummynge	612
'Parott hathe not dyned of all this long day;'	231	Speke Parott	23
Phronessys for frenessys may not hold her way.	232	Speke Parott	47
And 'Da racionales' dare not shew his pate.	235	Speke Parott	175
When Parrot is ded, he dothe not putrefy;	236	Speke Parott	213
he] 'she' †Lant 1545, Kynge & Marche 1554, Day 1560, Marshe 1568			
Hyt wyll not be refrayned:	238	Speke Parott	259
Thowghe he pampyr not hys paunche with the grete seall;	239	Speke Parott	309
How thys prosses I prate of, hyt ys not all for nowghte.	242	Speke Parott	389
For drede ye darre not medyll with suche gere,	242	Speke Parott	394
Of owur clerke Cleros. Whythyr, thydyr and why not hethyr?	243	Speke Parott	412
So myche presonment, for matyrs not worth a hawe;	245	Speke Parott	478
But it is not worth a leke.	251	Collyn Clout	182
Nor knoweth not his elenkes,	267	Collyn Clout	818
elenkes] 'eloquens' †Godfray 1531, Kele 1545.1, Marshe 1568			
Not rubbe you on the gall,	279	Why Come Ye	25
you] 'hym' MS Rawlinson C. 813			
Not acquaynted worth a fly /With honorable Haly,	292	Why Come Ye	520
They wot not whether to go.	294	Why Come Ye	614
To the court why I cam not,	299	Why Come Ye	827
Not unremembered it is unto your grace,	313	Garlande	57
And wyll not endevour hymselfe to purchase	314	Garlande	75
How ryvers rin not tyll the spryng be full;	314	Garlande	81
And how his wordes with reason wyll not accorde.	314	Garlande	88
Displease not an hundreth for one mannes pleasure.	314	Garlande	90
It was not for hym to abyde the tryall.	315	Garlande	98
abyde] 'byde' MS Cotton Vitellius E.x			
In generrall wordes, I say not gretely nay,	315	Garlande	99
Of your royall palace it is not the gyse,	315	Garlande	121
Wherfore then rasid ye not away	316	Garlande	137
Myne argument els koude not longe endure.	316	Garlande	147
Eschines, whiche was not shamefully confutid	316	Garlande	157
For though he were venquesshid, yet was he not shamyd:	316	Garlande	161
For] 'Sithe' MS Cotton Vitellius E.x			
And whome ye love not ye wyll put to shame.	317	Garlande	178
Ye counterway not evynly your balaunce;	317	Garlande	179
Of very dwte it may not well accorde,	318	Garlande	212
For that I wolde not with you fall at discorde.	318	Garlande	214
I am content that he be not exylide	318	Garlande	224
But now to helpe myselfe I am not able.	321	Garlande	312
And may not atteyne it by no medyacyon,	321	Garlande	319
From you most we, but not longe to tary.	326	Garlande	520
'Come on with me,' she sayd, 'let us not stonde';	328	Garlande	559
To walke on this walle she bed I sholde not stint;	328	Garlande	571
But my request is not so great a thynge,	332	Garlande	730
I am not woundid but that I may be cured.	332	Garlande	732
I am not ladyn of liddyrnes with lumpis,	332	Garlande	733
Now, by your faith, is not this theffect	333	Garlande	737
by] 'be' †Fakes 1523			
Ye wolde not dele with hym, thowgh that ye myght,	333	Garlande	756
thowgh] 'thought' Marshe 1568, 'thowth' MS Cotton Vit.E.x			
Of all your bewte I suffyce not to wryght:	336	Garlande	875
Mi litell lady I may not leve behinde,	337	Garlande	878
Whiche maner of abasshement became her not yll;	337	Garlande	889
He coude not devyse the lest poynt of your cheke;	337	Garlande	896
And cowde not wryght /Of Isabell Knyght.	342	Garlande	1066
It is not my custome nor my gyse /To leve behynde	342	Garlande	1068
Here you not Eolus for you blowyth a blaste?	343	Garlande	1088
you (1st)] 'ye' MS Cotton Vitellius E.x			
'Be mirry,' she sayd, 'be not afferde a whit,	344	Garlande	1145
With pitche she patchid her pitcher shuld not crase;	346	Garlande	1209

NOTABLE —NOTHYNGE   Page   Title   Line

	Page	Title	Line
An hynde unhurt hit by casuelte, not bled	351	Garlande	1406
The millar durst not leve his wyfe at home.	352	Garlande	1417
He is not wyse ageyne the streme that stryvith.	352	Garlande	1432
The Nacyoun of Folys he left not behynde.	353	Garlande	1470
But that my peticyon wolde not be had,	353	Garlande	1486
Not for to fyght /Ageyne dispyght,	355	Garlande	1561

NOTABLE

With notable clerkes; supply to them, I pray,	241	Speke Parott	359
Theis notable poetis refresshid there throtis.	322	Garlande	385
And of Magnyfycence a notable mater,	346	Garlande	1192

NOTARIES

Under a notaries sygne	266	Collyn Clout	807

a] 'an' Kele 1545.1, 'a' MS Harley 2252

NOTE

For on the booke I can not synge a note,	53	Bowge	255

I] not in †Wynkyn de Worde 1499

But whereto shulde I note	100	Phy Sparrow	1145
Note and mark wyl thys parcele;	132	Garnesche5	97

NOTED

That wolde it shulde be noted	265	Collyn Clout	754

NOTHER

Nother crokyd Cacus, /Nor yet dronken Bacus;	67	Hauke	194

Nother] 'Nor yet' Kynge & Marche 1554, Day 1560, Marshe 1568

Nother Olybryus, /Nor Dyonysyus;	67	Hauke	196
Nother Phalary, /Rehersyd in Valery,	67	Hauke	198
Nother Zorobabell, /Nor cruell Jesabell;	67	Hauke	206
For measure is a meane, nother to hy nor to lawe,	145	Magnyfycence	188
For thou shalt well knowe I am nother durty nor dusty.	161	Magnyfycence	759
Nor Nero, that nother set by God nor man,	182	Magnyfycence	1509
Nowe, syth it wyll no nother be,	196	Magnyfycence	1978
That nother they set by father and mother;	200	Magnyfycence	2142

NOTHING

Hath won nothing, I wene,	89	Phy Sparrow	718
To you nothing it dyd accorde	118	Ag Scottes	93
I am now constrayned, /With wordes nothing fayned,	120	Ag Scottes2	2
Rebukyng and remordyng, /And nothing accordyng.	120	Ag Scottes2	12
Nothing to write, but hay the gy of thre,	138	Ven Tongues	46
For in this processe, Parrot nothing hath surmysed,	236	Speke Parott	200

NOTHYNG

'What, will ye do nothyng but play?'	35	Man Margery	4
At me, that medeled nothyng with youre wark.	38	Coystrownel	61
He can do nothyng ellys.	84	Phy Sparrow	494
Yet I am nothyng sped,	90	Phy Sparrow	754
Wranglynge, waywyrde, wytles, wraw, and nothyng meke.	124	Garnesche2	40
Ye wan nothyng there but a mow:	131	Garnesche5	50
Ye wan nothyng there but a skorne;	131	Garnesche5	51
Malapert, medyllar, nothyng well thewde,	133	Garnesche5	147
No matter pretendyd, nor nothyng enterprysed,	236	Speke Parott	201
The skye is clowdy, the coste is nothyng clere;	242	Speke Parott	397
He loveth nothyng but golde;	284	Why Come Ye	208
'Maister Gower, I have nothyng deserved	323	Garlande	407
Thou dyd nothyng but barke	362	Albany	147
Ye were nothyng discrete;	376	Replycacion	52

NOTHYNGE

Nothynge yerthly to me more desyrous	44	Balettys3	43
'Turde,' quod Ha[f]ter, 'I wyll the nothynge layne,	55	Bowge	311

layne] 'sayne' †Wynkyn de Worde 1499, Marshe 1568

This worlde is nothynge but ete, drynke and slepe,	57	Bowge	384
A parson benyfyced /But nothynge well advysed.	62	Hauke	37
And the Pharasay /Then durst nothynge say,	66	Hauke	153
But nothynge it avayled /To call Phylyp agayne	72	Phy Sparrow	25
Of God nothynge els crave I /But Phyllypes soule to kepe	73	Phy Sparrow	67
He dyd nothynge, perde, /But syt upon my kne.	76	Phy Sparrow	171
And nothynge wantonly,	98	Phy Sparrow	1068
That nothynge than welth may worse be enduryd.	140	Magnyfycence	7
Where measure is ruler, there is nothynge amysse.	144	Magnyfycence	124
You are nothynge mete with us for to dwell,	149	Magnyfycence	304
Nothynge but fare you well tyll sone -	149	Magnyfycence	319
Nay, syr, it was nothynge but your mynde.	149	Magnyfycence	330
And that we fayled not for nothynge.	158	Magnyfycence	654
Hem! That lyke I nothynge at all.	158	Magnyfycence	664
And do nothynge. How be it, full lytell grace	159	Magnyfycence	693
And made as I had knowen nothynge of the case -	160	Magnyfycence	719
Here is nothynge but the bockyll of a sho,	171	Magnyfycence	1107
Without crafte nothynge is well behavyd.	177	Magnyfycence	1350
I can do nothynge but he stonde besyde.	180	Magnyfycence	1449
Syr, we can do nothynge the one without the other.	180	Magnyfycence	1450
I fere nothynge Fortunes perplexyte.	181	Magnyfycence	1461
Speke, I beseche the. Leve nothynge behynde.	183	Magnyfycence	1544
Whylest I have hym, I nede nothynge doute.	187	Magnyfycence	1692
For there is nothynge that more dyspleaseth God	194	Magnyfycence	1928
For who loveth God can ayle nothynge but good.	207	Magnyfycence	2365
That nothynge be gyven without consyderacyon.	211	Magnyfycence	2495
Her lothely lere /Is nothynge clere,	214	El Rummynge	13
That wyll nothynge spare,	217	El Rummynge	107
She was nothynge plesant;	227	El Rummynge	518
That nothynge had /There of their awne,	229	El Rummynge	608
He made you of nothynge by his magistye;	236	Speke Parott	219

497

NO THYNGE — NOW	Page	Title	Line
Theyr matyns madly sayde, /Nothynge devoutly prayde,	252	Collyn Clout	239
And in nothynge is sure.	253	Collyn Clout	280
And therof speke nothynge	255	Collyn Clout	355
Almoost nothynge at all.	261	Collyn Clout	610
Set nothynge by polytykes.	262	Collyn Clout	623
He can nothynge smatter	267	Collyn Clout	814
Can say nothynge but 'mum'.	269	Collyn Clout	905
That nothynge is avaylynge;	275	Collyn Clout	1148
/Is nothynge set by,	280	Why Come Ye	46
Nothynge to purpose	286	Why Come Ye	287
Dare take nothynge on hande.	286	Why Come Ye	291
Now nothynge but 'pay, pay!'	302	Why Come Ye	930
'Nothynge,' he sayth, 'lyke to We.	307	Why Come Ye	1148
to we] 'to mee' Toy 1553, Kitson 1560.7, Marshe 1568, 'we' MS Rawlinson C. 813			
But lytell or nothynge ye shall here tell	317	Garlande	197
ye shall] 'shall ye' MS Cotton Vitellius E.x			
That profyteth all other is nothynge profytable	321	Garlande	313
Thei wantid nothynge but the laurell;	323	Garlande	397
That welny nothynge there doth remayne	324	Garlande	430
welny] 'welnere' Marshe 1568			
Yet ye dare do nothynge	364	Albany	211
NO THYNGE			
Of welth and solace no thynge left behynde;	332	Garlande	711
NOTYD			
As herafter ben notyd:	293	Why Come Ye	573
One faute or other in them shalbe notyd.	318	Garlande	203
NOTWITHSTANDYNGE			
The rule of Measure, notwithstandynge we	147	Magnyfycence	242
Notwithstandynge to you be it sayde	186	Magnyfycence	1651
Notwithstandynge it is remedeles;	351	Garlande	1394
NOUGHT			
That with one worde formd all thing of nought;	34	Dol Dethe	191
'Walke forth your way, ye cost me nought;	36	Man Margery	22
Correct fyrst thy self; walk, and be nought!	38	Coystrownel	62
Save hym that nought can: scrypture sayth soo.	58	Bowge	448
Their husbandes to set at nought:	87	Phy Sparrow	627
It cost me lytell nor nought.	101	Phy Sparrow	1203
nor] 'or' Wyght 1553, Kitson 1560.6, Marshe 1568			
It greyth nought for your degre	116	Ag Scottes	52
Lyberte without measure prove a thynge of nought.	143	Magnyfycence	117
By the menys of myschyef to bryng all thynges to nought.	159	Magnyfycence	702
A carlys sonne /Brought up of nought	165	Magnyfycence	899
And those be they that come up of nought –	174	Magnyfycence	1240
From qui fuit aliquid to shyre shakynge nought.	176	Magnyfycence	1303
By crafty conveyaunce many one is brought up of nought;	178	Magnyfycence	1369
And welth is nought worthe yf lyberte be behynde.	180	Magnyfycence	1442
For of your grace I have it nought deserved.	186	Magnyfycence	1644
As in a tryfyll or in a thynge of nought.	189	Magnyfycence	1757
Nowe hath he ryght nought, naked as an asse.	193	Magnyfycence	1893
Ye shall not bere awaye /Myne ale for nought,	218	El Rummynge	166
myne] 'my' Kynge & Marche 1554, Day 1560, Marshe 1568			
They are shyre shakyng nought!'	226	El Rummynge	466
Ye, all thyng mortall shall torne unto nought	236	Speke Parott	214
Set nought by golde ne grotes, /Theyr names yf I durst tell.	250	Collyn Clout	160
And come up of nought;	261	Collyn Clout	584
Ye wyll brynge all to nought,	261	Collyn Clout	606
I trow all wyll be nought,	287	Why Come Ye	353
But all he bringeth to nought,	290	Why Come Ye	450
To make up one of nought,	293	Why Come Ye	551
Or elles he can nought bot whan he is at scole;	318	Garlande	205
Harde to make ought of that is nakid nought;	346	Garlande	1205
Ye make nought but ye marre.	364	Albany	226
Your lernyng is starke nought,	376	Replycacion	56
NOUGHTE			
He loked hawte; he sette eche man at noughte;	54	Bowge	284
hawte] 'hawtie' Marshe 1568			
NOUGHTY			
It shameth all your noughty nacyon,	117	Ag Scottes	56
That were noughty froslynges;	226	El Rummynge	460
Some lidderons, some losels, some noughty packis;	317	Garlande	188
Of your noughty counsell,	380	Replycacion	213
NOUMBYR			
If ony recordis in noumbyr can be founde,	345	Garlande	1150
NOW			
What, wolde ye frompill me now? Fy, fy!	36	Man Margery	16
Now have I fownd that I myne sought,	36	Man Margery	23
'Rumbyll downe, tumbyll downe, hey, go, now, now!'	37	Coystrownel	30
'Rumbyll downe, tumbyll downe, hey, go, now, now!'	37	Coystrownel	30
Now have I shewyd you part of your proud mynde;	38	Coystrownel	67
Holde youre tong, now, all beshrewde!	41	Coystrowne4	28
Bone aventure have here now in your honde.	48	Bowge	98
Shyfte now therwith, let see, as ye can,	48	Bowge	99
We wante no wynde to passe now over all;	49	Bowge	128
For now am I plenarely dysposed	52	Bowge	216
'Now,' quod Dysdayne, 'as I shall saved be,	54	Bowge	297
How he is now taken in conceyte,	54	Bowge	302
By God, I have of the now grete dyspyte;	55	Bowge	325

	Page	Title	Line
Now have at all that lyeth upon the burde.	57	Bowge	391
Now wolde to God thou wolde leye money downe!	57	Bowge	395
Now renne muste I to the stewys syde	57	Bowge	400
Ryghte now I spake with one, I trowe, I see -	59	Bowge	458
Now, by Saynte Fraunceys, that holy man and frere,	59	Bowge	470
Amendis maye be of that is now amys;	60	Bowge	494
Now construe ye what is the resydewe.	61	Bowge	539
He shall be as now nameles,	62	Hauke	38
Loke now in Exodi,	66	Hauke	164
The best now that I maye	77	Phy Sparrow	237
And now the cause is thus,	80	Phy Sparrow	363
Let us now whysper /A Pater noster.	81	Phy Sparrow	384
Whom now and then /He plucketh by the hede	84	Phy Sparrow	510
And now the darke cloudy nyght	86	Phy Sparrow	571
That now commeth to mynde:	86	Phy Sparrow	604
to mynde] 'to mi mynde' Wyght 1553, Kitson 1560.6			
Men se hym now and than	88	Phy Sparrow	657
than] 'then' Marshe 1568			
And now must kys the post;	89	Phy Sparrow	716
And now men wold have amended	91	Phy Sparrow	797
Now myne hole imaginacion	93	Phy Sparrow	847
Now wyll I enterpryse,	93	Phy Sparrow	856
Now Phebus me ken /To sharpe my pen,	96	Phy Sparrow	970
For now I wyll begyn	99	Phy Sparrow	1093
Now by these names thre,	105	Phy Sparrow	1363
And shew now unto me	106	Phy Sparrow	1368
In one rose now dothe grow;	110	Lawde	2
England, now gaddir flowris,	110	Lawde	6
Exclude now all dolowrs.	110	Lawde	7
Shall now com and do right,	110	Lawde	17
For now the yeris of grace	111	Lawde	40
Now ye proude Scottes of Gelawaye	114	Scot Kynge	19
Now must ye knowe our kynge for your regent,	114	Scot Kynge	21
Wyerfore ye may it now repent.	114	Scot Kynge	33
For a prysoner there now ye be	114	Scot Kynge	40
Therfore ye be layde now full lowe.	114	Scot Kynge	53
How unfortunately he doth now spede;	115	Scot Kynge	57
In double w[a]lles now he dooth dreme.	115	Scot Kynge	58
walles] 'welles' †Fakes 1513			
So that now I have devysed,	117	Ag Scottes	69
Unto your grace for grace now I call,	117	Ag Scottes	78
And now to begyn I wyll me adres,	117	Ag Scottes	89
Now is your pryde fall to decay.	118	Ag Scottes	110
For your untruth now ar ye shent.	118	Ag Scottes	124
Now from a kyng to a clot of clay.	119	Ag Scottes	165
Syr sumner, now where is your crowne?	120	Ag Scottes	178
Syr sumner, now ye have lost your crowne.	120	Ag Scottes	180
I am now constrayned, /With wordes nothing fayned,	120	Ag Scottes2	1
But sey me now, Syr Satrapas, what autoryte ye have	121	Garnesche1	6
But now, gawdy, gresy Garnesche,	127	Garnesche3	120
Now upon thys hete /Rankely whan ye swete,	127	Garnesche3	133
Now Garnyche, garde thy gummys;	128	Garnesche3	158
Agenst ye now I bynde;	128	Garnesche3	160
Thowth it be now ful tyde with the,	132	Garnesche5	120
But now, my proces for to save,	133	Garnesche5	157
For men be now tratlers and tellers of tales;	139	Ven Tongues	63
That wonte was to be formyst, now to come behynde.	144	Magnyfycence	144
And now wolde ye swarve from your owne ordynaunce?	147	Magnyfycence	234
Now leve this jangelynge and to us expounde	147	Magnyfycence	262
Now let us go, and we shall, then.	159	Magnyfycence	687
It is best I fede my hawke now.	167	Magnyfycence	968
Thy pleasure now with payne and trouble shalbe tryde.	193	Magnyfycence	1881
And now without measure he shal have hunger and colde.	193	Magnyfycence	1895
Now shal ye be scabbed, scurvy, and lowsy.	197	Magnyfycence	2019
Now let us be all one, and let us lyve in rest;	202	Magnyfycence	2202
Ye, syr, now am I armyd with good hope,	207	Magnyfycence	2378
Now, surely, Magnyfycence, I am ryght well apayed	208	Magnyfycence	2402
Nowe ryche, nowe pore, nowe hole, now in dysease;	212	Magnyfycence	2518
Now ebbe, now flowe, nowe increase, now dyscrease;	212	Magnyfycence	2521
Now ebbe, now flowe, nowe increase, now dyscrease;	212	Magnyfycence	2521
Now ebbe, now flowe, nowe increase, now dyscrease;	212	Magnyfycence	2521
With, 'Now away the mare,	217	El Rummynge	110
Drinke now whyle it is new;	219	El Rummynge	211
Small chaffer doth ease /Sometyme, now and than.	222	El Rummynge	315
I shall breke your palettes, /Wythout ye now cease!'	223	El Rummynge	349
Now pandes mory, wax frantycke som men sey;	232	Speke Parott	46
mory] 'mery' †MS Harley 2252; men] 'mad' †MS Harley 2252			
An almon now for Parott, delycatelye dreste;	232	Speke Parott	48
Collustrum now for Parot, whyte bred and swete creme!	233	Speke Parott	82
Now Geball, Amon and Amaloch - 'Harke, harke,	234	Speke Parott	118
With, 'He sayd,' and 'We said.' Ich wot now what ich wot,	234	Speke Parott	132
And every bache medler must now be a maker.	235	Speke Parott	161
Tryvyals and quatryvyals so sore now they appayre,	235	Speke Parott	166
Prisians hed broken now, handy-dandy,	235	Speke Parott	171
Plaut[us] in his comedies a chyld shall now reherse,	235	Speke Parott	176
Now a nutmeg, a nutmeg, cum gariopholo,	235	Speke Parott	183
To rekyn with thys recule now	237	Speke Parott	227

NOWADAYES — NOWE

	Page	Title	Line
NOWADAYES			
That age for dottage /Is reconed nowadayes.	280	Why Come Ye	44
reconed] 'recovered' Toy 1553, Kitson 1560.7, Marshe 1568			
NOW A DAYES			
The gyse now a dayes /Of some janglynge jayes	103	Phy Sparrow	1268
NOWADAYS			
For the gyse nowadays	348	Garlande	1261
NOWE			
'Ye remembre the gentylman ryghte nowe	51	Bowge	197
For and I studye sholde as ye doo nowe,	53	Bowge	242
'Nowe have at all, by Saynte Thomas of Kente!'	56	Bowge	348
What arte thou? I sawe the nowe but late.'	56	Bowge	376
'Forsothe,' quod I, 'in this courte I dwell nowe.'	56	Bowge	377
To her wyll I nowe all my poverte lege.	57	Bowge	412
Do mi nus, /Helpe nowe swete Jesus!	74	Phy Sparrow	96
Nowe, after my dome,	75	Phy Sparrow	147
And nowe they lye and rote;	78	Phy Sparrow	251
But men take upon theim nowe all the shame	139	Ven Tongues	61
Nowe pleasyth you a lytell whyle to stande;	145	Magnyfycence	161
But nowe let me knowe of your conversacyon.	145	Magnyfycence	170
Nowe that ye have me chefe ruler assyngned,	146	Magnyfycence	202
Nowe, benedicite, ye wene I were some hafter,	147	Magnyfycence	257
Nowe, I beseche the, tell me what is thy name?	148	Magnyfycence	269
But nowe, syr, as touchynge this letter –	149	Magnyfycence	331
At what place, nowe, as you gesse?	150	Magnyfycence	342
It dothe so sure nowe and than.	150	Magnyfycence	368
Nowe to the devyll I the betake,	151	Magnyfycence	401
But nowe wyll I, that they be gone,	151	Magnyfycence	407
A knave wyll counterfet nowe a knyght,	152	Magnyfycence	417
What! Wanton, wanton, nowe well ymet!	153	Magnyfycence	456
This nonnes nowe and then, and it myght be,	154	Magnyfycence	488
Nowe what is his name? And what is thyne?	155	Magnyfycence	519
Nowe therfore, whylest we are togyder –	155	Magnyfycence	546
Nowe, by Cockes harte, well abyden!	156	Magnyfycence	576
Yet where we wonne, nowe there wonneth he.	157	Magnyfycence	624
And nowe it cometh to my remembraunce.	159	Magnyfycence	673
Nowe let se. Quyte you lyke praty men!	159	Magnyfycence	688
Here he is nowe, man. Mayst thou not se?	162	Magnyfycence	792
But nowe I wyll not say the worste.	163	Magnyfycence	828
What nowe? Let se /Who loketh on me	163	Magnyfycence	829
Nowe welcom, by the God holy!	166	Magnyfycence	919
But nowe what tydynges can you tell? Let se.	166	Magnyfycence	928
In faythe, Lyberte is nowe a lusty spere.	166	Magnyfycence	937
Nowe Cryst it blysse!	167	Magnyfycence	973
Nowe let me se about	168	Magnyfycence	991
Nowe to curteys, forthwith unkynde;	168	Magnyfycence	1008
Nowe I wyll this, and nowe I wyll that –	169	Magnyfycence	1027
Nowe I wyll this, and nowe I wyll that –	169	Magnyfycence	1027
Nowe I wolde – and I wyst what –	169	Magnyfycence	1029
In faythe, trouth thou sayst nowe, by God of heven!	170	Magnyfycence	1079
Nowe, of good felowshyp, let me by thy [d]ogge.	170	Magnyfycence	1082
dogge] 'hogge' †Rastell & Treveris C 1530, B			
Nowe, in good faythe, thou art a fonde gest.	170	Magnyfycence	1096
Nowe, by my trouth, man, take, there is my purse;	171	Magnyfycence	1104
my] 'myne' †Rastell & Treveris C 1530, B			
Nowe take thou my dogge and gyve me thy fowle.	171	Magnyfycence	1116
Nowe thou hast done me a pleasure grete.	171	Magnyfycence	1131
Mary, it was his, and nowe it is myne.	173	Magnyfycence	1181
And was it his, and nowe it is thyne?	173	Magnyfycence	1182
Nowe, by the rode, and he wyll go nere.	173	Magnyfycence	1196
Put on thy gowne agayne, for thou hast lost nowe.	173	Magnyfycence	1203
thou ... nowe] 'nowe thou hast lost' †Rastell & Treveris C 1530, B			
Nowe put on, fole, thy cote agayne.	173	Magnyfycence	1205
Nowe hast thou not a prowde mocke and a starke?	174	Magnyfycence	1208
Nay, wylte thou here nowe of his scoles,	174	Magnyfycence	1216
But nowe, forsothe, man, it maketh no mater;	175	Magnyfycence	1256
Nay, that is my parte that thou spekest of nowe.	175	Magnyfycence	1282
Nowe then goo we hens. Away the mare!	177	Magnyfycence	1325
Nowe holde ye content, for there is none other shyfte.	180	Magnyfycence	1443
For nowe, syrs, I am lyke as a prynce sholde be;	181	Magnyfycence	1457
For suche abusyon I use nowe and than.	185	Magnyfycence	1625
And surely, as I am nowe advysed,	186	Magnyfycence	1657
Nowe, by your trouthe, gave he you not a brybe?	187	Magnyfycence	1665
With me no longer. Say somwhat nowe, let se,	188	Magnyfycence	1719
God gyve hym a myscheffe! Nay, nowe let me alone.	189	Magnyfycence	1730
Syr, nowe me thynke your harte is well eased.	189	Magnyfycence	1737
Nowe Measure is gone, I am the better pleased.	189	Magnyfycence	1738
It is the gyse nowe, I say, over all –	189	Magnyfycence	1759
Nowe Jesu preserve you, syr, prynce most of myght.	190	Magnyfycence	1796
What! Is all your myrthe nowe tourned to sorowe?	192	Magnyfycence	1849
Take hede of your selfe, for nowe ye have nede.	192	Magnyfycence	1854
Lorde, so my flesshe trymblyth nowe for drede!	193	Magnyfycence	1875
Vyle velyarde, thou must not nowe my dynt withstande;	193	Magnyfycence	1878
And nowe lyke a lurden he lyeth in the dust.	193	Magnyfycence	1887
Nowe is there no man that wyll set by hym a flye.	193	Magnyfycence	1889
Nowe dare he not for shame loke one in the face.	193	Magnyfycence	1891
Nowe hath he ryght nought, naked as an asse.	193	Magnyfycence	1893

NOWE—NOWE

	Page	Title	Line
For nowe wyll I from this caytyfe go,	195	Magnyfycence	1950
Nowe must I this carcasse lyft up.	195	Magnyfycence	1964
Alasse! Where is nowe my golde and fe?	196	Magnyfycence	1967
Nowe, syth it wyll no nother be,	196	Magnyfycence	1978
Nowe must you lerne to begge at every mannes gate.	196	Magnyfycence	1981
Ye, syr, nowe must ye lerne to lye harde,	197	Magnyfycence	2005
Nowe must your fete lye hyer than your crowne.	197	Magnyfycence	2007
Nowe must you monche mamockes and lumpes of brede;	197	Magnyfycence	2009
Nowe lap you in a coverlet, full fayne that you may;	197	Magnyfycence	2011
Nowe must ye suffre bothe hunger and colde.	197	Magnyfycence	2013
Nowe must ye lerne to lye on the strawe.	197	Magnyfycence	2015
Nowe must be storm ybeten with showres and raynes.	197	Magnyfycence	2017
Nowe she wyll laughe, forthwith she wyll frowne;	197	Magnyfycence	2024
Nowe all in welth, forthwith in poverte;	197	Magnyfycence	2027
But yet, syr, nowe in this case	197	Magnyfycence	2032
For nowe go I wyll begge for you some mete.	197	Magnyfycence	2034
I wyll walke nowe with my beggers baggys,	197	Magnyfycence	2036
Where is nowe my welth and my noble estate?	198	Magnyfycence	2055
Where is nowe my treasure, my landes, and my rent?	198	Magnyfycence	2056
Where is nowe all my servauntys that I had here a late?	198	Magnyfycence	2057
Where is nowe all my golde upon them that I spent?	198	Magnyfycence	2058
Where is nowe all my ryche abylement?	198	Magnyfycence	2059
Where is nowe my kynne, my frendys, and my noble blood?	198	Magnyfycence	2060
Where is nowe all my pleasure and my worldly good?	198	Magnyfycence	2061
A, woo worthe the, Lyberte, nowe thou sayst full trewe;	199	Magnyfycence	2103
That nowe he hath loste all his felycyte;	200	Magnyfycence	2114
Ye, for nowe it hath brought the to confusyon;	200	Magnyfycence	2130
Nowe I rede the beware. I have warned the twyse.	202	Magnyfycence	2185
And nowe on me ye gaure and sporne.	204	Magnyfycence	2247
Ly styll, ly styll nowe, with yll hayle!	204	Magnyfycence	2248
Nowe gyve me somwhat, for God sake, I crave.	204	Magnyfycence	2251
But nowe let us make mery and good chere.	204	Magnyfycence	2261
It is to late nowe thy synnys to repent.	205	Magnyfycence	2292
But nowe I se well there is no better rede,	205	Magnyfycence	2305
Nowe must I make you a lectuary softe –	207	Magnyfycence	2355
Adversyte to hym therwith nowe and than;	207	Magnyfycence	2368
And nowe ye have had, syr, a wonderous fall,	207	Magnyfycence	2375
For nowe I se comynge to youwarde Redresse.	208	Magnyfycence	2384
Of that I se you nowe in the state of grace.	208	Magnyfycence	2403
Nowe shall ye be renewyd with solace.	208	Magnyfycence	2404
Take nowe upon you this abylyment,	208	Magnyfycence	2405
The whiche were to longe nowe to expresse;	209	Magnyfycence	2416
Nowe welcome, forsoth, Sad Cyrcumspeccyon.	209	Magnyfycence	2418
Nowe well, nowe wo, nowe hy, nowe lawe degre;	212	Magnyfycence	2517
Nowe well, nowe wo, nowe hy, nowe lawe degre;	212	Magnyfycence	2517
Nowe well, nowe wo, nowe hy, nowe lawe degre;	212	Magnyfycence	2517
Nowe well, nowe wo, nowe hy, nowe lawe degre;	212	Magnyfycence	2517
Nowe ryche, nowe pore, nowe hole, now in dysease;	212	Magnyfycence	2518
Nowe ryche, nowe pore, nowe hole, now in dysease;	212	Magnyfycence	2518
Nowe ryche, nowe pore, nowe hole, now in dysease;	212	Magnyfycence	2518
Nowe pleasure at large, nowe in captyvyte;	212	Magnyfycence	2519
Nowe pleasure at large, nowe in captyvyte;	212	Magnyfycence	2519
Nowe leve, nowe lothe, nowe please, nowe dysplease;	212	Magnyfycence	2520
Nowe leve, nowe lothe, nowe please, nowe dysplease;	212	Magnyfycence	2520
Nowe leve, nowe lothe, nowe please, nowe dysplease;	212	Magnyfycence	2520
Now ebbe, now flowe, nowe increase, now dyscrease;	212	Magnyfycence	2521
Nowe semyth us syttynge that ye then resorte	214	Magnyfycence	2566
Nowe in cometh another rabell;	224	El Rummynge	382
Nowe truly, to my thynkynge,	228	El Rummynge	547
Nowe in valle Ebron Parrot is fayne to fede:	236	Speke Parott	188
Nowe torne agayne to me.	237	Speke Parott	245
Nowe, Parott, my swete byrde, speke owte yet ons agayn,	244	Speke Parott	447
But nowe every spyrytuall father,	251	Collyn Clout	174
I speke nat nowe of all,	252	Collyn Clout	244
My lady nowe she ronnes,	256	Collyn Clout	390
My penne nowe wyll I sharpe,	259	Collyn Clout	489
Ye growe nowe out of kynde.	263	Collyn Clout	661
Nowe wyll I go	267	Collyn Clout	828
Nowe trewely, to my thynkyng,	270	Collyn Clout	969
But nowe debetis scire /And groundly audire	273	Collyn Clout	1065
Nowe to withdrawe my pen,	277	Collyn Clout	1248
My shyp nowe wyll I stere	278	Collyn Clout	1259
stere] 'pere' Kele 1545.1, Marshe 1568, 'stere' MS Harley 2252			
Hath nowe no tyme nor space	295	Why Come Ye	631
Tell me nowe in this stede,	298	Why Come Ye	786
Nowe God amende that is amys;	308	Why Come Ye	1162
He is nowe so overthwart,	308	Why Come Ye	1181
nowe] not in MS Rawlinson C. 813			
Yet nowe doutles ye geve me cause	341	Garlande	1041
For nowe dowtles ye geve me cause	342	Garlande	1049
Nowe into the castell of Bas,	366	Albany	288
Adue, nowe, Sir Wrig-wrag! /Adue, Sir Dalyrag!	366	Albany	296
And nowe I wyll me dresse	369	Albany	399
But nowe will I expounde	369	Albany	423
Whom I nowe sommon and con[v]ent,	375	Replycacion	23
convent] 'content' †Pynson 1528			

NOWEADAYES —O

	Page	Title	Line
And be nowe as yll,	379	Replycacion	178
Wherefore by and by /Nowe consequently	383	Replycacion	315
NOWEADAYES			
Lo, this is the gyse noweadayes!	277	Collyn Clout	1227
NOWE ADAYES			
But nowe adayes as huksters they hucke and they stycke,	200	Magnyfycence	2121
Shewyth nowe adayes howe the worlde comberyd is,	213	Magnyfycence	2539
NOWE A DAYES			
But men nowe a dayes so unhappely be uryd,	140	Magnyfycence	6
So it is all the maner nowe a dayes	187	Magnyfycence	1677
But nowe a dayes to stryke I have grete cause,	194	Magnyfycence	1918
Howe yong scolers nowe a dayes enbol[n]ed	373	Replycacion	1
enbolned] 'enbolmed' †Pynson 1528			
NOWE ADAYS			
And mekyll am I made of nowe adays.	152	Magnyfycence	430
Why, is this the gyse nowe adays?	163	Magnyfycence	813
NOWE A DAYS			
Unto measure, I say, nowe a days.	189	Magnyfycence	1744
NOWGHT			
Hys jentyll curtoy[l], and set nowght by small naggys!	43	Balettys2	16
curtoyl] 'curtoyt' †Rastell 1527.1			
NOWGHTE			
How thys prosses I prate of, hyt ys not all for nowghte.	242	Speke Parott	389
NO WHER			
Thow xalte beholde no wher a warse;	130	Garnesche5	17
NOWHERE			
In Arturys auncyent actys nowhere ys provyd your pere;	123	Garnesche2	24
NO WHERE			
Thou shalt no where rede	70	Hauke	299
NOWMBER			
This sayd, a great nowmber folowyd by and by	321	Garlande	323
NOWTE			
To hyr love ye nowte rechyd.	125	Garnesche3	61
NUTMEG			
Now a nutmeg, a nutmeg, cum gariopholo,	235	Speke Parott	183
Now a nutmeg, a nutmeg, cum gariopholo,	235	Speke Parott	183
NUTSHALES			
That all is but nutshales	290	Why Come Ye	443
NUT SHALIS			
And all is not worth a couple of nut shalis.	139	Ven Tongues	66
NUTTE SHELL			
We set nat a nutte shell	277	Collyn Clout	1225
O			
Of hevenly poems, O Clyo, calde by name	29	Dol Dethe	8
O dolorous chaunce of Fortuns fraward hande!	32	Dol Dethe	110
O cruell Mars, thou dedly god of war!	32	Dol Dethe	113
O dolorous Teusday, dedicate to thi name,	32	Dol Dethe	114
O grounde ungracious, unhappy be thy fame,	32	Dol Dethe	116
Mooste noble Erle! O fowle mysuryd grounde,	32	Dol Dethe	118
O Atropos, of the fatall systers iij,	32	Dol Dethe	120
O homycide, whiche sleest all that thou kan,	32	Dol Dethe	123
O yonge lyon, bot tender yet of age,	33	Dol Dethe	162
O pereles Prince of hevyn emperyalle	34	Dol Dethe	190
O] not in Marshe 1568			
O Quene of mercy, O lady full of grace,	34	Dol Dethe	204
O Quene of mercy, O lady full of grace,	34	Dol Dethe	204
Of all women O floure withouten pere,	35	Dol Dethe	207
O goodly chyld /Of Mary mylde, /Then be oure shylde!	40	Coystrowne3	41
O Fortune unfrendly, Fortune unkynde thow art,	45	Balettys5	4
O pryeest unreverent.	67	Hauke	187
O mayden, wydow, and wyfe,	73	Phy Sparrow	53
O cat of carlyshe kynde,	78	Phy Sparrow	282
carlyshe] 'churlyshe' Kitson 1560.6, Marshe 1568			
Melpomone, O muse tragedyall,	117	Ag Scottes	77
O Gabionyte of Gabyone, why do ye gane and gaspe?	123	Garnesche2	15
Your chorlyshe chauntyng ys all o lay.	129	Garnesche5	6
O feble fortune, O doulfull destyny!	198	Magnyfycence	2048
O feble fortune, O doulfull destyny!	198	Magnyfycence	2048
O hatefull happe, O carefull cruelte!	198	Magnyfycence	2049
O hatefull happe, O carefull cruelte!	198	Magnyfycence	2049
O syghynge sorowe, O thoughtfull mysere!	198	Magnyfycence	2050
O syghynge sorowe, O thoughtfull mysere!	198	Magnyfycence	2050
O rydlesse rewthe, O paynfull poverte!	198	Magnyfycence	2051
O rydlesse rewthe, O paynfull poverte!	198	Magnyfycence	2051
O dolorous herte, O harde adversyte!	198	Magnyfycence	2052
O dolorous herte, O harde adversyte!	198	Magnyfycence	2052
O odyous dystresse, O dedly payne and woo!	198	Magnyfycence	2053
O odyous dystresse, O dedly payne and woo!	198	Magnyfycence	2053
O good Lorde, howe longe shall I indure	201	Magnyfycence	2153
O Esebon, Esebon, to the is cum agayne	234	Speke Parott	120
O My Parrot, O unice dilecte, votorum meorum	242	Speke Parott	376
O causeles cowardes, O hartles hardynes,	242	Speke Parott	390
O causeles cowardes, O hartles hardynes,	242	Speke Parott	390
O manles manhod, enfayntyd all with fere,	242	Speke Parott	391
O connyng clergye, where ys your redynes	242	Speke Parott	392
O mercyfull Jesu,	257	Collyn Clout	433
'O thoughtfull herte,' was evermore his songe!	320	Garlande	296
'O mercyles madame, hard is your constellacyon,	320	Garlande	304

OBEDYENCE —OCCUPYED	Page	Title	Line

	Page	Title	Line
O fatall Fortune, what have I offendid?	321	Garlande	316
'O noble Chaucer, whos pullisshyd eloquence	324	Garlande	421
O wele were hym that herof myght be sure, ...	332	Garlande	718
O ye wretched Scottes, /Ye puaunt pyspottes, ...	362	Albany	119
O Scottes parjured, /Unhaply ured, ...	362	Albany	125

OBEDYENCE

They cast up theyr obedyence to cache me agayne;	201	Magnyfycence	2148
The seconde, to owe hym obedyence, ...	307	Why Come Ye	1124

OBEISAUNCE

After all duly ordred obeisaunce, ...	335	Garlande	836

OBEY

Hevyn, hell and erth obey unto thi kall;	34	Dol Dethe	192

OBEYDE

To whome grete astatis obeyde and lowttede, ...	30	Dol Dethe	45

OBJECTE

Relucent smaragd, objecte imcomperable;	44	Balettys3	21

OBJECTED

Shall nat be objected by me.	266	Collyn Clout	794
by] 'for' Kele 1545.1, Marshe 1568, 'at by' MS Harley 2252			
that can or may be made or objected	382	Replycacion	R

OBJECTYON

But now he maketh objectyon, ...	307	Why Come Ye	1127
But] 'And', objectyon] 'dyrectyon' MS Rawlinson C. 813			

OBLACIONS

or to make oblacions to any ymages of sayntes, ...	375	Replycacion	I

OBLIQUI

Whose tong ys attayntyd with slaundrys obliqui.	241	Speke Parott	363

OBLIVYOUS

And so moche oblivyous	290	Why Come Ye	464

OBLOQUY

Ageyne envy, /And obloquy. /And wote ye why?	355	Garlande	1559

OBSCURED

As clerkes unassured, /With ignorance obscured:	377	Replycacion	94

OBSEQUIOUS

shall evermore be, with all obsequious redynesse, ...	373	Replycacion	I

OBSERVAUNCE

Upon Grenewytche border /Called Observaunce, ...	265	Collyn Clout	747

OBSERVE

And so observe /That ye ne swarve	339	Garlande	964

OCCACYON

Then some occacyon or quarell ye must fynde, ...	185	Magnyfycence	1600

OCCASIONYD

What thynge occasionyd the showris of rayne, ...	331	Garlande	693

OCCASYON

I can not tell you what was the occasyon.	313	Garlande	35
not tell] 'not wele tell' MS Cotton Vitellius E.x			

OCCASYONS

Ye are to unhappy occasyons to fynde	38	Coystrownel	65
occasyons] 'occasion' Marshe 1568			

OCCIDENT

How from the est unto the occident, ...	328	Garlande	577

OCCYAN

From Occyan the great se	79	Phy Sparrow	318

OCCUPACIOUN

With that, Occupacioun presid in a pace;	344	Garlande	1144
The Quene of Fame to Occupacioun	345	Garlande	R

OCCUPACYON

Occupacyon, Famys regestary, ...	326	Garlande	522
Occupacyon, is ryght goodly aray, ...	327	Garlande	528
Occupacyon to Skelton	331	Garlande	R
Occupacyon to Skelton	332	Garlande	R
Occupacyon to Skelton	332	Garlande	R
Occupacyon to Skelton	335	Garlande	R
Occupacyon to Skelton	343	Garlande	R
And so Occupacyon, your regester, me told.'	344	Garlande	1141
Occupacyon, immediatly to rede.	345	Garlande	1169
To Occupacyon I wyll agayne resorte, ...	354	Garlande	1492

OCCUPACYOUN

Occupacyoun to Skelton	327	Garlande	R
Occupacyoun redith and expoundyth	345	Garlande	R

OCCUPIED

For yf they had occupied ther spere and ther shelde	31	Dol Dethe	73

OCCUPY

To occupy so your mynde;	126	Garnesche3	103
Of nyghtys to occupy counterfet kayes;	152	Magnyfycence	425
Counterfet Countenaunce every man dothe occupy.	153	Magnyfycence	472
Of one thynge and other to occupy the place, ...	159	Magnyfycence	690
They occupy them so /With syngynge Placebo, ...	269	Collyn Clout	906
That occupy theyr holys;	285	Why Come Ye	245
In whose place, /Dothe occupy, ...	300	Why Come Ye	851

OCCUPYE

But loke that ye occupye the auctoryte that I you gave. . . .	180	Magnyfycence	1456
To occupye suche places, ...	269	Collyn Clout	897
But yet they wyll occupye the same.	275	Collyn Clout	1144

OCCUPYED

And occupyed no better your tole, ...	127	Garnesche3	118
Thus am I occupyed at all assayes.	152	Magnyfycence	428
As good to be occupyed as up and downe to trace	159	Magnyfycence	692

OCCUPYETH — OFT

	Page	Title	Line
In faythe, yet am I occupyed with the best;	160	Magnyfycence	705
But, in faythe, I am so occupyed	168	Magnyfycence	1019
Ye shall be occupyed, Welthe, at my wyll.	178	Magnyfycence	1380
Alasse, that ever I occupyed suche abusyon!	200	Magnyfycence	2129
For where I am occupyed and usyd wylfully,	200	Magnyfycence	2131
As lyngua Latina, in scole matter occupyed;	234	Speke Parott	144
That occupyed a showell,	293	Why Come Ye	560

OCCUPYETH
For Greci fari so occupyeth the chayre,	235	Speke Parott	163

OD
I caste me nat to be od	124	Garnesche3	6

ODER
Thus is the talkynge of one and of oder,	151	Magnyfycence	386

ODIOUS
Odious Disdayne, why raist thou me on this facyon?	321	Garlande	317

ODYOUS
Against odyous Envi,	94	Phy Sparrow	905
And though I be so odyous a geste,	160	Magnyfycence	703
O odyous dystresse, O dedly payne and woo!	198	Magnyfycence	2053
And payned you with a purgacyon of odyous poverte,	207	Magnyfycence	2353
odyous, orgulyous and flyblowen opynions etc.,	375	Replycacion	1

ODLY
By the masse, odly well alowde.	155	Magnyfycence	533
Thy wordes and my mynde odly well accorde.	185	Magnyfycence	1605

OFFENCE
Lyberte to let from all maner offence;	141	Magnyfycence	45
Where measure is mayster, plenty dothe none offence;	144	Magnyfycence	121
Of to moche lyberte under the offence;	146	Magnyfycence	229
Yet sometyme I stryke where is none offence,	194	Magnyfycence	1916
To ferce for none offence,	278	Why Come Ye	4
That never dyde offence.	375	Replycacion	44
And knowledge your offence /Before open audyence,	380	Replycacion	207

OFFEND
No good preest to offend,	62	Hauke	25
For to offend your presydent,	118	Ag Scottes	112
Is glad to please, and loth to offend.'	323	Garlande	413

OFFENDE
For lothe I am to offende	251	Collyn Clout	186
Any man to offende.	274	Collyn Clout	1128
Whiche glad am to please, and loth to offende'	324	Garlande	427
Which glad am to please, and lothe to offende.'	324	Garlande	441

OFFENDED
I have not offended, I trust,	102	Phy Sparrow	1249
Syr, yf I have offended your noble estate,	149	Magnyfycence	308

OFFENDID
O fatall Fortune, what have I offendid?	321	Garlande	316

OFFENDYD
And where my pen hath offendyd,	102	Phy Sparrow	1245
Ye, syr, he is sory for that he hath offendyd.	208	Magnyfycence	2388

OFFER
Nay, offer hym a counter in stede of a peny.	172	Magnyfycence	1171
To offer to the ale tap,	221	El Rummynge	286
To offer to the ale-pole.	227	El Rummynge	525
I thanked her moche of her most noble offer,	327	Garlande	554

OFFERYNGE BOX
Downe went my offerynge box,	64	Hauke	111

OFFYCYALLYS
But who so that lokys /In the offycyallys bokys,	65	Hauke	146

OFFRE
howe it was idolatry to offre to ymages of our blessed lady,	375	Replycacion	1

OFFRED
And offred to Cornucopia	104	Phy Sparrow	1320
And offred to Cornucopia;	349	Garlande	1313

OFFRYD
Aut sanguis vitulorum, /Was offryd within the wallys,	66	Hauke	172
Where Crystis precyous blode /Dayly offryd is,	66	Hauke	180

OFSPRYNGE
Any of the ofsprynge	76	Phy Sparrow	199
ofsprynge] 'sprynge' Kitson 1560.6, Marshe 1568			

OFT
Unkindly thei slew hym that help them oft at nede.	30	Dol Dethe	47
help] 'holp' Marshe 1568			
As oft as thei call to ther remembrance	34	Dol Dethe	188
Which makyth my hart oft to lepe and sprynge	44	Balettys3	32
And under the fell oft festerd is the sore:	45	Balettys4	5
Fortune theyr frende, with whome oft she dyde daunce:	50	Bowge	141
She had flowyn so oft,	63	Hauke	68
Oft tyme after pleasaunce,	81	Phy Sparrow	368
That toteth oft in a glasse,	82	Phy Sparrow	422
And after a hete oft cometh a stormy colde.	141	Magnyfycence	13
Lyberte at large wyll oft wax reklesse.	142	Magnyfycence	54
'As oft as ye lyst, so honeste be savyd.	177	Magnyfycence	1348
Yet of magnyfycence oft made is the mast:	213	Magnyfycence	2563
As wele foly as wysdome oft ye do avaunce,	317	Garlande	180
ye do] 'tyme ye' MS Cotton Vitellius E.x			
But blissed Bachus, that mastris oft doth frame,	322	Garlande	383

OFTE —OLDE   Page   Title   Line

OFTE
How ofte he hadde hit Jenet on the tayle, ...   56   Bowge   369
  hadde] 'not' Marshe 1568
How ofte he knocked at her klycked gate.   56   Bowge   371
And many tymes and ofte   74   Phy Sparrow   124
Many tymes and ofte, ...   80   Phy Sparrow   355
Ye, for surety. Ofte peas is taken for frayes.   163   Magnyfycence   814
For drede, that we dare not ofte, lest we be spyed.   177   Magnyfycence   1339
Without me be full ofte aspyed.   177   Magnyfycence   1355
I to mynyster it, you to receyve it ofte -   207   Magnyfycence   2356
And ofte prechours be blamed   305   Why Come Ye   1054
  ofte] 'the' MS Rawlinson C. 813
OFTEN
Me often for to wake   76   Phy Sparrow   165
How often dyd I tote   100   Phy Sparrow   1146
Or of humors superflue, that often wyll crepe   313   Garlande   32
And 'He haltith often that hath a kyby hele.'   326   Garlande   502
Hath bene full often and yet is entendyng   344   Garlande   1131
OFTENNER
But if he wryte oftenner than ones or twyse.'   345   Garlande   1155
OFTENTYMES
And oftentymes I wolde myselfe avaunce   50   Bowge   143
OFTE TYME
But under hony ofte tyme lyeth bytter gall, ...   49   Bowge   131
OFTE TYMES
His stomak stuffed ofte tymes dyde reboke.   51   Bowge   180
But ofte tymes have I sene wyse men do mad dedys.   148   Magnyfycence   302
For ofte tymes suche a wamblynge goth over my harte;   185   Magnyfycence   1620
For I am panged ofte tymes in this same facyon.   189   Magnyfycence   1734
Them or theyr chyldren ofte tymes I dysmembre;   194   Magnyfycence   1923
I sende ofte tymes a fole to his sonne.   195   Magnyfycence   1935
OFTYME
But yet oftyme suche dremes be founde trewe.   61   Bowge   538
OFTYN
How oftyn fortune varyeth in an howre, ...   312   Garlande   11
OFTNAR
Oftnar than ones or twyse, ...   378   Replycacion   133
OFT TYME
As well borne as ye full oft tyme beggys.   40   Coystrowne4   7
OG
And Og, that fat hog of Basan, doth retayne   234   Speke Parott   122
  of] 'or' Kynge & Marche 1554, Day 1560, Marshe 1568
OYLE
Phillis and Testalis, ther tressis with oyle   331   Garlande   681
OKE
Of an oke, that somtyme grew full streyghte, ...   312   Garlande   18
OKES
The huge myghty okes them selfe dyd avaunce, ...   320   Garlande   279
OLD
It semyth the sobbyng of an old sow!   37   Coystrowne1   32
A proverbe of old, 'Say well or be styll':   38   Coystrowne1   64
And have forgoten your old, trew, lovyng knyght.   42   Balettys2   14
A thousand new and old   90   Phy Sparrow   750
A DEVOUTE TRENTALE FOR OLD JOHN CLARKE, ...   106   Epitaphe1   I
There came an old rybybe;   227   El Rummynge   492
OLDE
Of poetes olde, whyche, full craftely, ...   46   Bowge   9
With us olde servauntes such maysters to playe.   55   Bowge   329
Or of A[t]talus the olde, ...   76   Phy Sparrow   191
  Attalus] 'Artalus' †Kele 1545.2, Wyght 1553, Kitson 1560.6,
  Marshe 1568
Savyng that olde age   85   Phy Sparrow   544
Gowers Englysh is olde /And of no value told;   91   Phy Sparrow   784
  told] 'is tolde' Wyght 1553, Kitson 1560.6, Marshe 1568
Though I waxe olde /And somdele sere, ...   112   Calliope   15
How olde proverbys say, ...   129   Garnesche3   196
As provithe well, in hys rethorikys olde, ...   130   Garnesche5   11
For, as I have rede in volumes olde, ...   137   Ven Tongues   5
I made, he said, a windmil of an olde mat.   137   Ven Tongues   13
Oracius to recorde in his volumys olde, ...   143   Magnyfycence   114
An olde barne wolde be underset.   153   Magnyfycence   454
But I say, kepest thou the olde name styll that thou had? . . .   155   Magnyfycence   516
But shall I have myne olde name styll?   158   Magnyfycence   647
Flewe, I sholde say - in to an olde barne   191   Magnyfycence   1808
'Lo, here is an olde typpet, ...   223   El Rummynge   366
For coverynge of an olde cottage   255   Collyn Clout   364
After olde seygnours, /And the lernynge of Lytelton Tenours . .   256   Collyn Clout   369
But it is an olde sayd sawe   268   Collyn Clout   862
  it] not in Kele 1545.1
A quayle, the rayle, the olde raven.   268   Collyn Clout   870
But olde servauntes ye chase   273   Collyn Clout   1077
An ende of an olde song: 281   Why Come Ye   88
They play their olde pranckes /After Huntley Bankes.   285   Why Come Ye   266
In olde commemoracion /Most royall Englyssh nacion.   305   Why Come Ye   1039
Olde Diogenes, with other many mo, ...   315   Garlande   129
Fyrst, olde Quintiliane with his Declamacyons;   321   Garlande   326
  Declamacyons] 'declynacyons' †Fakes 1523
I sawe a thowsande yatis new and olde.   328   Garlande   574

505

	Page	Title	Line
OLIFRANKE —ON			
Some were olde wryten, sum were writen new,	328	Garlande	584
Ageynst all baratows broisiours of olde,	331	Garlande	673
A good herynge of thes olde talis;	347	Garlande	1217
Graund juir, of this Frenshe proverbe olde,	352	Garlande	1440
Good luk this new yere, the olde yere is past.	354	Garlande	1518
Olde patriarkes and prophetes in heven with him to dwell.	383	Replycacion	342
OLIFRANKE			
Your stondarde, Syr Olifranke, agenst me for to splay;	123	Garnesche2	30
OLIPHAUNT			
The gander, the gose, and the hudge oliphaunt,	315	Garlande	102
OLYBRYUS			
Nother Olybryus, /Nor Dyonysyus;	67	Hauke	196
OLYFANT			
Necked lyke an olyfant;	227	El Rummynge	519
OLYFAUNT			
Nosyd lyke an olyfaunt,	126	Garnesche3	71
OLYFAUNTES			
Conveyde by olyfauntes	270	Collyn Clout	962
OLYMPYAN			
From Sydony to the mount Olympyan,	327	Garlande	552
OLYVE			
With braunches and bowghis of the swete olyve,	330	Garlande	670
How Dame Minerva first found the Olyve Tre, she red	351	Garlande	1404
OLYVERE			
Syr Gy, Syr Gawen, Syr Cayus, for and Syr Olyvere,	123	Garnesche2	22
OMNIPOTENT			
Where thow art Lord and God omnipotent.	34	Dol Dethe	203
He jugyth him equivalent /With God omnipotent.	307	Why Come Ye	1136
him] 'hymselfe' MS Rawlinson C. 813;			
equivalent] 'equypolent' Rawlinson C. 813			
ON			
They buskt them on a bushment them selfe in baile to bringe	31	Dol Dethe	81
He was envyronde aboute on every syde	32	Dol Dethe	99
Tyll fykkill Fortune began on hym to frowne.	33	Dol Dethe	133
He lumbryth on a lewde lewte, 'Roty bully joyse',	37	Coystrowne1	29
On Candelmas evyn, the kalendas of May.	38	Coystrowne1	70
But to swete Jesu /On us then for to rew?	40	Coystrowne3	40
That he dryvyth them doune with dyntys on ther day-wach.	43	Balettys2	30
And with that worde on me she gave a glome	48	Bowge	80
With browes bente, and gan on me to stare	48	Bowge	81
Nay, naye, be sure, whyles I am on your syde	50	Bowge	169
But, as me thoughte, he ware on hym a cloke	51	Bowge	177
He gased on me with his gotyshe berde;	52	Bowge	237
Whan I loked on hym, my purse was half aferde.	52	Bowge	238
For on the booke I can not synge a note,	53	Bowge	255
I] not in †Wynkyn de Worde 1499			
And whan I fayle, bobbe me on the noll!	53	Bowge	259
Forthwith, he made on me a prowde assawte,	55	Bowge	316
I loked on hym, I wende he had be woode.	55	Bowge	320
And on the borde he whyrled a payre of bones,	56	Bowge	346
How ofte he hadde hit Jenet on the tayle,	56	Bowge	369
hadde] 'not' Marshe 1568			
Thou mayste not studye or muse on the mone.	57	Bowge	383
Fye on this dyce, they be not worth a turde!	57	Bowge	392
I am not happy, I renne ay on the losse!	57	Bowge	399
I lete her to hyre that men maye on her ryde;	57	Bowge	402
Who rydeth on her, he nedeth not to care,	57	Bowge	409
And on that sleve these wordes were wrete:	58	Bowge	438
Yet on my backe I bere suche lewde delynge.	59	Bowge	457
There I wynked on you – wote ye not where?	60	Bowge	516
There on he stode, and craked;	63	Hauke	50
The hawke tyryd on a *bonne,	63	Hauke	60
*bonne] 'bone' Scattergood			
That on the rode loft /She perkyd her to rest.	63	Hauke	69
On Saynt Johnn decollacyon	64	Hauke	100
He hawked on thys facyon,	64	Hauke	101
Fell downe on thys manner.	64	Hauke	115
To loke on this were tyme.	65	Hauke	144
Loke on this tabull, /Whether thou art abull	68	Hauke	235
[Y]e develysh dogmatista, /Your hawke on your fista,	69	Hauke	256
Ye] 'The' †Lant 1545, Kynge & Marche 1554, Day 1560, Marshe 1568			
Domine concupisti, /With thy hawke on thy fysty?	69	Hauke	260
Worrowyd her on that /Which I loved best.	72	Phy Sparrow	29
It wold set on a stole,	74	Phy Sparrow	116
set] 'sit' Wyght 1553, Kitson 1560.6, Marshe 1568			
And on me it wolde lepe	75	Phy Sparrow	161
On all the hole nacyon	78	Phy Sparrow	275
Myght fede them on thy braynes!	79	Phy Sparrow	295
Of fortune this the chaunce /Standeth on varyaunce:	81	Phy Sparrow	367
On Phillips soule have pyte!	86	Phy Sparrow	587
On Bayarde Mountalbon;	88	Phy Sparrow	656
On her moch love and cost,	89	Phy Sparrow	715
To loke on her agayne.	97	Phy Sparrow	1010
on] 'to' Marshe 1568			
Enhached on her fayre skyn,	98	Phy Sparrow	1078
On pylgrimage to Saynt Jamys,	102	Phy Sparrow	1242
pylgrimage] 'pilgrimages' Marshe 1568			

ON —ON	Page	Title	Line
On knees to fall /To the foteball;	108	Epitaphe1	71
They may well say, fye on that wynnynge!	115	Ag Scottes	4
That was theyr owne kynge. /Fy on that wynnyng!	116	Ag Scottes	24
That the Scottys may synge, /'Fy on the wynnynge!'	116	Ag Scottes	48
synge] 'sin' Marshe 1568			
Fortune on you therfore dyd frowne;	120	Ag Scottes	176
As ye ar brystlyd on the bake for alle your gay gere.	122	Garnesche1	26
Your lothesum lere to loke on, lyke a gresyd bote dothe schyne.	123	Garnesche2	5
Ye cappyd Cayface copious, your paltoke on your pate,	123	Garnesche2	6
Why holde ye on yer cap, syr, then? Yor pardone ys expyryd.	123	Garnesche2	9
Ye cappyd Cayface copyous, your paltoke on your pate,	123	Garnesche2	13
Huf, a galante, Garnesche, loke on your comly cors!	123	Garnesche2	16
Ye capyd Cayfas copyous, your paltoke on your pate,	123	Garnesche2	20
Ye capyd Cayfas copyus, your paltoke on your pate,	123	Garnesche2	27
Baile, baile at yow bothe, frantyke folys! Follow on the chase!	123	Garnesche2	31
Ye cappyd Cayfas copyous, your paltoke on your pate,	123	Garnesche2	34
Ye cappyd Cayfas copyous, your paltoke on your pate,	124	Garnesche3	41
On to your lowsy den;	125	Garnesche3	64
On that syde, on thys syde thou dost gasy,	130	Garnesche5	29
On that syde, on thys syde thou dost gasy,	130	Garnesche5	29
I wolde ye had kyst hyr on the tayle!	130	Garnesche5	46
Sche praiid yow walke, on Goddes halfe!	131	Garnesche5	60
What eylythe the, rebawde, on me to rave?	131	Garnesche5	79
Hath pointyd me to rayle on the.	131	Garnesche5	88
On Huntley bankes, /Take this our thankes;	136	Dundas	58
For before on your brest, and behind on your back	137	Ven Tongues	16
For before on your brest, and behind on your back	137	Ven Tongues	16
To Tyburne, where they hange on hyght.	152	Magnyfycence	423
I care not, I. Tell on for me.	158	Magnyfycence	634
Tell on, syr. Howe then?	158	Magnyfycence	651
What nowe? Let se /Who loketh on me	163	Magnyfycence	830
Confusyon /Shall on hym lyght	164	Magnyfycence	859
All this nacyon /I set on fyre; /In my facyon	165	Magnyfycence	885
What the devyll hast thou on thy fyste? An owle?	166	Magnyfycence	922
On this halfe and on every syde	168	Magnyfycence	1020
On this halfe and on every syde	168	Magnyfycence	1020
I make on the one day, and I marre on the other.	169	Magnyfycence	1038
I make on the one day, and I marre on the other.	169	Magnyfycence	1038
And therfore I growe more on one day	170	Magnyfycence	1077
Ye, for all thy mynde is on owles and apes.	171	Magnyfycence	1134
But wylte thou make another on Gryme?	172	Magnyfycence	1151
What hast thou on thy fyst? A [k]esteryll?	173	Magnyfycence	1174
kesteryll] 'besteryll' †Rastell & Treveris C 1530, B			
Put on thy gowne agayne, for thou hast lost nowe.	173	Magnyfycence	1203
thou ... nowe] 'nowe thou hast lost' †Rastell & Treveris C 1530, B			
Nowe put on, fole, thy cote agayne.	173	Magnyfycence	1205
That rubbed she must be on the gall	174	Magnyfycence	1232
Forsothe, tell on. Hast thou any mo?	175	Magnyfycence	1262
mo] 'more' †Rastell & Treveris C 1530, B			
Mary, syr, ye may swere it on a boke.	176	Magnyfycence	1292
Well argued and surely on bothe sydes.	176	Magnyfycence	1304
Nor no man on molde can make me aferd.	182	Magnyfycence	1505
But I shall frounce them on the foretop and gar them to quake.	182	Magnyfycence	1514
That on suche a female my flesshe wolde be wroken.	184	Magnyfycence	1566
That weryed I wolde be on suche a bayte.	184	Magnyfycence	1568
As yf a man fortune to touche you on the quyke –	185	Magnyfycence	1611
Tyll I be revenged on that horson knave.	185	Magnyfycence	1616
That for your sake I wyll fall on my kne.	186	Magnyfycence	1630
That he wolde loke on hym, thoughe it were not longe.	187	Magnyfycence	1675
Syr, as ye say. Nay, come on with me.	188	Magnyfycence	1707
Yet ones agayne I shall fall on my kne	188	Magnyfycence	1708
Say on; me thynke your reasons be profounde.	190	Magnyfycence	1767
To be supervysour, and on Largesse also;	190	Magnyfycence	1785
Mary, Cryst graunt ye catche no colde on your fete!	191	Magnyfycence	1803
I saw a foxe sucke on a kowes ydder;	191	Magnyfycence	1814
The gander and the gose bothe grasynge on one grave.	191	Magnyfycence	1830
Take hede of this captyfe that lyeth here on grounde.	195	Magnyfycence	1946
Beholde howe Fortune o[n] by thym hath frounde.	195	Magnyfycence	1947
on] 'of' †Rastell & Treveris C 1530, B			
Syr, all this wolde have bene thought on before.	196	Magnyfycence	1970
That was wonte to lye on fetherbeddes of downe;	197	Magnyfycence	2006
Nowe must ye lerne to lye on the strawe.	197	Magnyfycence	2015
Fye on this worlde, full of trechery,	197	Magnyfycence	2020
I daunsed the darlynge on my kne;	198	Magnyfycence	2066
With daunce on the le, the le!	198	Magnyfycence	2068
My harte is holly on her set;	199	Magnyfycence	2073
My fansy fayrly on her I set;	199	Magnyfycence	2076
That they set theyr chyldren to rynne on the brydyll,	200	Magnyfycence	2136
I am so lusty to loke on, so freshe, and so fre,	201	Magnyfycence	2145
In faythe, he may dreme on a daggeswane for ony fether bed.	201	Magnyfycence	2169
Leve thy pratynge or els I shall lay the on the pate.	201	Magnyfycence	2173
I shall skelpe the on the skalpe; lo, seest thou that?	202	Magnyfycence	2180
What! Wylte thou skelpe me? Thou dare not loke on a gnat.	202	Magnyfycence	2181
Or I shall fawchyn thy flesshe and scrape the on the skyn.	202	Magnyfycence	2189
Nay, iche shall wrynge the, horson, on the wryst.	202	Magnyfycence	2196
And nowe on me ye gaure and sporne.	204	Magnyfycence	2247
Som be wrestyd there that they thynke on it forty dayes,	204	Magnyfycence	2274

	Page	Title	Line
Of a comely gyll /That dwelt on a hyll;	214	El Rummynge	5
Come who so wyll /To Elynoure on the hyll,	217	El Rummynge	114
She leneth them on the same,	217	El Rummynge	131
on] 'of' Day 1560, Marshe 1568			
And forthwith fell on slepe.	224	El Rummynge	375
She dranke on the mash fat.	226	El Rummynge	491
'Ryse up, on Gods halfe,'	227	El Rummynge	501
Were fayne with a chalke /To score on the balke,	230	El Rummynge	615
Or score on the tayle.	230	El Rummynge	616
Honowre with renowne wyll ren on that syde.	234	Speke Parott	140
on] 'of' Kynge & Marche 1554, Day 1560, Marshe 1568			
For logicions to loke on, somwhat sophistice;	236	Speke Parott	193
Goddes blissyng lyght on thy lytell swete musse!	238	Speke Parott	266
Of on and hothyr at me that have dysdayne.	242	Speke Parott	385
Hyt ys to fere leste he wolde were the garland on hys pate,	244	Speke Parott	435
So many nobyll bodyes, undyr on dawys hedd;	245	Speke Parott	467
So myche callying on, and so smalle takyng hede;	245	Speke Parott	471
So myche towrnyng on the cooke-stole for every guy-gaw;	245	Speke Parott	481
And yf that he hytte /The nayle on the hede	247	Collyn Clout	34
And hauke on hobby larkes	251	Collyn Clout	193
Yf he on hym dare take	254	Collyn Clout	306
The bysshop on his carpet	255	Collyn Clout	327
Full falsely on you they lye,	255	Collyn Clout	334
Your teth whett on this bone	258	Collyn Clout	476
whett on] 'whetten' †Godfray 1531, 'whette on' MS Harley 2252			
Presumyng on theyr owne wytte,	259	Collyn Clout	515
owne] not in Marshe 1568			
'Come downe, on the devyll way.'	263	Collyn Clout	670
devyll] 'deuils' Marshe 1568, 'devyll' MS Harley 2252			
Than to take on hande	269	Collyn Clout	911
And nat so hardy on his hede	272	Collyn Clout	1023
nat] 'not' Marshe 1568, MS Harley 2252			
To loke on God in fourme of brede,	272	Collyn Clout	1024
Why than /Wreke ye your anger on me?	273	Collyn Clout	1091
Or touched on the quycke,	274	Collyn Clout	1124
Nat so hardy on theyr pates!	275	Collyn Clout	1152
Not rubbe you on the gall,	279	Why Come Ye	25
you] 'hym' MS Rawlinson C. 813			
Wrang us on the [m]ales!	280	Why Come Ye	78
males] 'wales' †Kele 1545.3, Toy 1553, Kitson 1560.7, Marshe 1568			
Clappyng his rod on the borde.	283	Why Come Ye	190
Borne up on every syde	284	Why Come Ye	203
Dare take nothynge on hande.	286	Why Come Ye	291
He bereth the kyng on hand	290	Why Come Ye	452
That he set him on heyght,	292	Why Come Ye	542
Set up a wretche on hye,	293	Why Come Ye	585
Under a stone on a golde ryng	296	Why Come Ye	700
Fye on this wynnyng allway!	302	Why Come Ye	929
this] not in MS Rawlinson C. 813			
Brose them on a brake,	303	Why Come Ye	983
Brose] 'bruse' Toy 1553, Kitson 1560.7, Marshe 1568			
And set hell on fyer	303	Why Come Ye	985
hel] 'all' Toy 1553, Kitson 1560.7, Marshe 1568			
The apostyll Peter /Had but on pore myter	307	Why Come Ye	1140
apostyll] 'wholly apostle' MS Rawlinson C. 813			
It standeth somwhat on the west;	308	Why Come Ye	1189
By whose suggestyon /I toke on hand this warke,	309	Why Come Ye	1204
suggestyon] 'subjectyon' MS Rawlinson C. 813			
On every halfe my reasons forthe I sought,	312	Garlande	10
On] 'One' †Fakes 1523			
Ran on the raunge so longe, that I suppose	313	Garlande	25
Savynge he rubbid sum on the gall.	315	Garlande	97
on] 'upon' Marshe 1568			
For men to loke on? Aristotille also,	315	Garlande	127
A wonderfull noyse, and on every syde	319	Garlande	247
A thowsande thowsande I sawe on a plumpe.	319	Garlande	258
The dredefull dinne drove all the rowte on a rowe;	319	Garlande	264
Of laurell levis a cronell on his hede,	320	Garlande	288
Yet loke on me, that lovyd you have so longe,	320	Garlande	298
Odious Disdayne, why raist thou me on this facyon?	321	Garlande	317
That frownyd on me full angerly and pale;	322	Garlande	375
And ever they pressed on me more and more,	324	Garlande	445
When they were past and wente forth on there way,	327	Garlande	526
With that on me she kest her goodly loke.	327	Garlande	531
Mountith on hy with her melodious lay,	327	Garlande	535
'Come on with me,' she sayd, 'let us not stonde';	328	Garlande	559
To walke on this walle she bed I sholde not stint;	328	Garlande	571
There birdis on the brere sange on every syde,	330	Garlande	653
There birdis on the brere sange on every syde,	330	Garlande	653
Turnyng on the ryght hande, by a windyng stayre,	333	Garlande	767
a] not in †Fakes 1523			
The saumpler to sow on, the lacis to enbraid;	334	Garlande	789
Is lusty to loke on, plesaunte, demure, and sage:	336	Garlande	870
Is lusty to loke on, plesaunt, demure, and sage.	337	Garlande	877
The blossom on the spray,	340	Garlande	989
Set on your hede this laurell whiche is wrought.	343	Garlande	1087
She loked hawtly, and gave on me a glum.	344	Garlande	1117

ONBENDE — ONE

	Page	Title	Line
How her ble was bryght as blossom on the spray,	351	Garlande	1412
In his distichon made on verses twaine.	353	Garlande	1467
distichon] 'distincyon' †Fakes 1523			
Whiche redde on still, as it cam to her syght,	354	Garlande	1493
And set hys crowne /On your owne heed	361	Albany	97
A vengeaunce and dispight /On the must nedes lyght	364	Albany	235
If he on you but frounde	367	Albany	345
Ye durst byde on the grounde.	367	Albany	347
To rayle on his astate /With wordes inordinate?	370	Albany	461
To rayle on hym lyke dawes.	371	Albany	478
On trouthe under defence	372	Albany	520
or to pray and go on pylgrimages,	375	Replycacion	1
And heynously on her to bable	375	Replycacion	27

ONBENDE

Ye lost your [h]olde, onbende your bow,	131	Garnesche5	49
holde] 'bolde' †MS Harley 367			

ONCOMLY

Yet your contenons oncomly, yor face ys nat fayer.	122	Garnesche1	18

ONDYR

The follest sloven ondyr heven,	133	Garnesche5	145

ONE

	Page	Title	Line
With one vice importune thei playnly said nay.	31	Dol Dethe	80
Barons, knightis, squyers, one and alle,	31	Dol Dethe	92
That with one worde formd all thing of nought;	34	Dol Dethe	191
In Trinitate one God of myghtis moste.	35	Dol Dethe	217
The one for a duke, the other for dun,	37	Coystrowne1	10
But one thyng is: that ye be lewde!	41	Coystrowne4	27
For one fals poynt she is wont to kepe in store,	45	Balettys4	4
One ther is, and ever one shalbe,	45	Balettys5	8
One ther is, and ever one shalbe,	45	Balettys5	8
There was moche noyse, anone one cryed, 'Cese!'	47	Bowge	46
Of one and other that wolde his lady see,	47	Bowge	57
But of one thynge I werne you er I goo:	49	Bowge	106
werne] 'warne' Marshe 1568; er] 'or' Wynkyn de Worde 1510			
Deynte to have with us suche one in store,	50	Bowge	150
But this one thynge ye maye be sure of me,	50	Bowge	162
As thou arte, one that cam but yesterdaye,	55	Bowge	328
What the devyll, man, myrthe was never one!	57	Bowge	388
was never one] 'is here within' Marshe 1568			
That one was lene and lyke a pyned goost,	58	Bowge	429
I saw a knyfe hyd in his one sleve,	58	Bowge	433
Ryghte now I spake with one, I trowe, I see –	59	Bowge	458
Came pressynge in one in a wonder araye.	60	Bowge	499
'But by that Lorde that is one, two and thre,	60	Bowge	512
It wolde make one rew	80	Phy Sparrow	336
And yet there is none /But one alone;	84	Phy Sparrow	517
Yet one thynge is behynde,	86	Phy Sparrow	603
And how they rode eche one	88	Phy Sparrow	655
From one to the other,	88	Phy Sparrow	683
His serpentes tonge /That many one hath stonge;	94	Phy Sparrow	921
One of the Centaures, /Or Onocentaures, /Or Hipocentaures;	104	Phy Sparrow	1294
And slew Gerion /With thre bodyes in one;	104	Phy Sparrow	1308
In one rose now dothe grow;	110	Lawde	2
Frenche kyng, or one or other;	118	Ag Scottes	105
They wolde the wryght, all with one stevyn,	133	Garnesche5	144
To se howe greable we are of one mynde;	146	Magnyfycence	199
And grotes many one or I came to your presence.	150	Magnyfycence	339
Thus is the talkynge of one and of oder,	151	Magnyfycence	386
I wote thou arte false ynoughe for one.	155	Magnyfycence	536
We wyll se you shortly, one of us twayne.	159	Magnyfycence	686
Of one thynge and other to occupy the place,	159	Magnyfycence	690
Double delynge and I be all one;	159	Magnyfycence	696
And I, am counterfet of one mynde and thought,	159	Magnyfycence	701
Water in the one hande and fyre in the other.	160	Magnyfycence	711
By Cloked Colusyon thus many one is begyled.	160	Magnyfycence	728
I make on the one day, and I marre on the other.	169	Magnyfycence	1038
But, broder Foly, I wonder moche of one thynge,	170	Magnyfycence	1068
And as for me, I take but one folysshe way,	170	Magnyfycence	1076
And therfore I growe more on one day	170	Magnyfycence	1077
What, horson! Arte thou suche a one?	174	Magnyfycence	1234
Ye. But tell me one thynge. What is that?	176	Magnyfycence	1318
By crafty conveyaunce many one is brought up of nought;	178	Magnyfycence	1369
Syr, we can do nothynge the one without the other.	180	Magnyfycence	1450
A, Cockes armes! Where myght suche one be founde?	184	Magnyfycence	1569
Wolde money, trowest thou, make suche one to the call?	184	Magnyfycence	1573
But one thynge I warne you, prece forth and be bolde.	184	Magnyfycence	1582
Scantly one with measure that wyll dwell.	189	Magnyfycence	1746
A knave and a carle and all of one kynde?	191	Magnyfycence	1820
The gander and the gose bothe grasynge on one grave.	191	Magnyfycence	1830
Nowe dare he not for shame loke one in the face.	193	Magnyfycence	1891
But yet, syrs, hardely one thynge lerne of me:	199	Magnyfycence	2087
Some hath so moche lyberte of one thynge and other,	200	Magnyfycence	2141
Now let us be all one, and let us lyve in rest;	202	Magnyfycence	2202
The one of you is to proude, the other is to haute.	203	Magnyfycence	2223
That they wyll fyre one ungracyously in the flanke.	204	Magnyfycence	2270
First one wyth a ladell,	224	El Rummynge	383
But of all this thronge /One came them amonge,	225	El Rummynge	446
Such a bedfellaw /Wold make one cast his craw.	226	El Rummynge	489

ONE-EYED — ONY

	Page	Title	Line
That one might se her token.	227	El Rummynge	497
'Soft,' quod one hyght Sybbyll,	228	El Rummynge	549
hyght] 'high' Day 1560, Marshe 1568			
To rule ix realmes by one mannes wytte,	240	Speke Parott	333
A fatall fall for one	258	Collyn Clout	473
A fatal] 'All' Kele 1545.1, Marshe 1568, 'Affatuall' MS Lansdowne 762			
Of one affynyte /Consent and agre	259	Collyn Clout	497
Many one ye have untwynde	263	Collyn Clout	662
ye have untwynde] 'have but wynde' †Godfray 1531, Kele 1545.1, Marshe 1568			
For one man to rule a kynge	271	Collyn Clout	989
kynge] 'gyng' Kele 1545.1, 'kyng' MS Harley 2252			
By one mannes wytte.	271	Collyn Clout	993
But at the pleasure of one	272	Collyn Clout	1018
One agayne another.	274	Collyn Clout	1106
There is no man but one	281	Why Come Ye	113
To weve all in one lome	282	Why Come Ye	130
They shote all at one marke:	283	Why Come Ye	174
To make up one of nought,	293	Why Come Ye	551
Of one so devyllysshe a matter.	297	Why Come Ye	715
Into one mannys hande;	298	Why Come Ye	763
One wyse mannys hede	298	Why Come Ye	764
But harke, my frende, one worde	298	Why Come Ye	784
Ever in one case.	301	Why Come Ye	882
As one in a trans or in an extasy,	313	Garlande	37
Displease not an hundreth for one mannes pleasure.	314	Garlande	90
One faute or other in them shalbe notyd.	318	Garlande	203
One of jasper, another of whalis bone;	325	Garlande	472
But one gate specyally, where as I stode,	328	Garlande	586
And one ther was there, I wondred of his hap,	329	Garlande	628
The one was a tumblar, that afterwarde againe	330	Garlande	634
But, goodly maystres, one thynge ye me tell.'	332	Garlande	720
Of one Adame all a knave, late dede and gone -	347	Garlande	1247
One of the Centauris, /Or Onocentauris, /Or Hippocentauris;	348	Garlande	1287
And slew Gerione /With thre bodys in one;	349	Garlande	1301
Strake one with a birdbolt to the hart rote;	351	Garlande	1380
One of you there was	379	Replycacion	186

ONE-EYED

	Page	Title	Line
How an one-eyed man is	292	Why Come Ye	533

ONELY

	Page	Title	Line
In me all onely wer sett and comprisyde,	33	Dol Dethe	156
For, ne were onely he hath your promocyon,	314	Garlande	71
Onely procedid for that he did outray	316	Garlande	156

ONES

	Page	Title	Line
I shall the angre ones in every vayne!	55	Bowge	326
But, no force, I shall ones mete with the;	55	Bowge	334
Well, ones thou shalte be chermed, iwus:	55	Bowge	340
Wyth that came Ryotte, russhynge all at ones,	56	Bowge	344
Sterte all at ones, I lyked no thynge his playe,	60	Bowge	502
I toke my sampler ones	77	Phy Sparrow	210
And that I sayd ones yet I say agayne:	147	Magnyfycence	266
Nay, come at ones, for the armes of the dyce.	162	Magnyfycence	781
At ones, and let hym not tary all day.	179	Magnyfycence	1400
Yet ones agayne I shall fall on my kne	188	Magnyfycence	1708
I wenyd ones never to have knowen of care.	196	Magnyfycence	1973
Ye, have done at ones without delay.	206	Magnyfycence	2319
But supped it up at ones,	224	El Rummynge	380
Ones hed wold have aked /To se her naked.	226	El Rummynge	478
She swynged up a quarte /At ones for her parte.	228	El Rummynge	569
swynged] 'swinge' Marshe 1568			
But whan they have ones caught	252	Collyn Clout	229
Ones yet agayne /Of you I wolde frayne	289	Why Come Ye	399
But sodeynly at ones, as I me advysed,	313	Garlande	36
With that there come in wonderly at ones	319	Garlande	269
Sterte all at ones an hundrethe fote backe.	320	Garlande	282
I made it straunge, and drew bak ones or twyse,	324	Garlande	444
With that I herd gunnis russhe out at ones,	329	Garlande	623
But if he wryte oftenner than ones or twyse.'	345	Garlande	1155
Of our noble courte is ones spoken owte,	353	Garlande	1482
Who redyth it ones wolde rede it agayne;	354	Garlande	1501
Twyt, Scot, yet agayne ones,	362	Albany	149
and whan they have ones superciliusly caught	374	Replycacion	I
Oftnar than ones or twyse,	378	Replycacion	133

ON-FLOTE

	Page	Title	Line
It wyll not be, his purse is not on-flote.	60	Bowge	488

ONY

	Page	Title	Line
Yet I avyse you to speke, for ony drede:	48	Bowge	90
Favoure we have toughther than ony elme,	49	Bowge	129
toughther] 'tougher' Wynkyn de Worde 1510, Marshe 1568			
Ye be an apte man, as ony can be founde	50	Bowge	155
The soveraynst thynge that ony man maye have	52	Bowge	211
For, and I knowe ony erthly thynge	54	Bowge	277
The devyll myghte daunce therin for ony crowche.	56	Bowge	364
Than in Englonde to playe ony suche prankes;	114	Scot Kynge	51
Hath Magnyfycence ony tresure?	157	Magnyfycence	620
Hast thou ony more? Let se, procede.	174	Magnyfycence	1236
Wyll ye spende ony money? Ye, a thousande pounde.	184	Magnyfycence	1570

ONYON —OR

	Page	Title	Line
By the meanes of money without ony gonne.	184	Magnyfycence	1578
And more than ever I dyd for ony man.	187	Magnyfycence	1694
For I here but fewe men that gyve ony prayse	189	Magnyfycence	1743
In faythe, he may dreme on a daggeswane for ony fether bed.	201	Magnyfycence	2169
Your wordes be more sweter than ony precyous narde,	207	Magnyfycence	2345
If ony recordis in noumbyr can be founde,	345	Garlande	1150

ONYON

Like an onyon syded, /Lyke tan ledder hyded.	226	El Rummynge	470

ONYONS

And the Spainyardes onyons?	288	Why Come Ye	371
And Spanyardes onyons,	302	Why Come Ye	924

ONY THYNGE

Is there ony thynge elles your grace wyll commaunde me?	149	Magnyfycence	318
And yf you se ony thynge agaynst your mynde,	185	Magnyfycence	1599

ONYWHERE

That he can onywhere gete,	306	Why Come Ye	1085

ONLY

Nor yet no vyllany, /But only fantasy;	100	Phy Sparrow	1135
For only the substance of that I entend,	323	Garlande	412

ONLYVE

Whether he were onlyve or ded;	89	Phy Sparrow	728

ONOCENTAURES

One of the Centaures, /Or Onocentaures, /Or Hipocentaures;	104	Phy Sparrow	1295

ONOCENTAURIS

One of the Centawris, /Or Onocentauris, /Or Hippocentauris;	348	Garlande	1288

ONOUR

Of his onour, whos dissuasyve in wrytyng	316	Garlande	151

ONS

Turne ons agayne to me;	237	Speke Parott	237
Nowe, Parott, my swete byrde, speke owte yet ons agayn,	244	Speke Parott	447

OONLY

To you oonly, me thynke, I durste shryve me;	52	Bowge	215

OPEN

Open myne hart, beholde my mynde expres.	44	Balettys3	39
And fell so wyde open	227	El Rummynge	496
Shulde open the brode gates	263	Collyn Clout	691
In open tyde and in lent.	268	Collyn Clout	859
open tyde] 'open tyme' Kele 1545.1, Marshe 1568, 'Ester tyde' MS Harley 2252			
And agayne all reason /Commyted open trayson	297	Why Come Ye	737
Open your janglyng jawes,	375	Replycacion	37
And there to make relacion /In open predycacion,	379	Replycacion	206
And knowledge your offence /Before open audyence,	380	Replycacion	208

OPENED

And opened his pretty byll,	77	Phy Sparrow	221
opened] 'open' Marshe 1568			
Had I not opened my purse wyde,	150	Magnyfycence	347

OPENLY

But enforsed am I /Openly to askry	94	Phy Sparrow	903
Nor to speke to hym secretly, /Openly nor prevyly,	272	Collyn Clout	1041
The vyllayne precheth openly	275	Collyn Clout	1173
Openly at Westmynstere	276	Collyn Clout	1183
And openly in that place	287	Why Come Ye	333
For ye were worldly shamed, /At Poules Crosse openly,	376	Replycacion	63

OPINYONS

Opinyons detestable /Of heresy execrable?	382	Replycacion	304

OPYN

To snappar and to fall /Into this opyn cryme;	65	Hauke	143

OPYNIONS

odyous, orgulyous and flyblowen opynions etc.,	375	Replycacion	I

OPYNYNGE

Then I was in opynynge of lockys;	203	Magnyfycence	2226

OPYNYON

Nor Lycon, that lothly luske, in myn opynyon,	122	Garneschel	24
As at the fyrst orygynall, by godly opynyon;	143	Magnyfycence	119
Yes, questyonlesse, in myne opynyon;	144	Magnyfycence	126

OPYNLYE

Thus myche Parott hathe opynlye expreste;	242	Speke Parott	381

OPPOSE

Come whan it wyll, oppose the I shall,	55	Bowge	335

OPPOSED

Whan prelacy you opposed.	377	Replycacion	106

OPPRESSE

All perjuris he wolde oppresse.	307	Why Come Ye	1114

OPPREST

For if ye laude hym whome honour hath opprest,	317	Garlande	174

OPTAYNE

He coulde not optayne	89	Phy Sparrow	697
Your welthe and felycyte, I trust we shall optayne	190	Magnyfycence	1792

OR

In sesons past who hathe harde or sene	30	Dol Dethe	22
What, shuld I flatter? What, shulde I glose or paynt?	30	Dol Dethe	41
What movyd you agayn hym to war or to fight?	31	Dol Dethe	62
Bot ther was fals packinge or els I am begylde,	31	Dol Dethe	71
Agayne the kingis plesure to wrastel or to wringe.	31	Dol Dethe	82
As man that was innocent of trechery or trayne,	31	Dol Dethe	86
Bot all they fled from hym for falshode or fere.	31	Dol Dethe	91
As perfightly as koude be thought or devysyd;	33	Dol Dethe	158

OR —OR   Page   Title   Line

Entry	Page	Title	Line
Wed me or els I dye for thought!	36	Man Margery	26
A proverbe of old, 'Say well or be styll':	38	Coystrowne1	64
Uppon me to clater or else to say yll.	38	Coystrowne1	66
I truste to quyte you or I dy!	41	Coystrowne4	21
Or ells with gret shame your game wylbe sene.	43	Balettys2	42
Or 'Shall I sayle wyth you' a felashyp assaye?	53	Bowge	254
Soo greate pleasyre, or who to you it gave.	53	Bowge	263
Or we shall the oute of thy clothes shake!'	55	Bowge	343
Thou mayste not studye or muse on the mone.	57	Bowge	383
And lete us laugh a placke or tweyne at nale.	57	Bowge	387
placke] 'plucke' Marshe 1568			
Have at the hasarde or at the dosen browne,	57	Bowge	393
Or els I pas a peny to a pounde!	57	Bowge	394
I] not in Wynkyn de Worde 1510			
In every poynte that I can do or saye.	60	Bowge	496
In] 'To' Marshe 1568			
Besechynge you that shall it see or rede,	61	Bowge	534
To hawke, or els to hunt /From the auter to the funt,	62	Hauke	9
He semeth a sysmatyke /Or els an heretike,	62	Hauke	18
Or that he thens yede,	63	Hauke	55
Or els is thys Goddis law,	65	Hauke	130
Decrees or decretals,	65	Hauke	131
Or holy sinodals, /Or els provincyals,	65	Hauke	132
Or holy sinodals, /Or els provincyals,	65	Hauke	133
Then in a tabull playne /I wroute a verse or twayne,	68	Hauke	223
To rede or to spell /What these verses tell.	68	Hauke	237
Or in Cathagoria /Latina sive Dorica,	69	Hauke	269
And make hereof a syckyll or a saw,	71	Hauke	333
Of what estate ye be, /Of hye or lowe degre,	73	Phy Sparrow	55
Or Socrates the wyse,	74	Phy Sparrow	99
A fly, or a gnat, /He wolde flye at that;	75	Phy Sparrow	130
Or of A[t]talus the olde,	76	Phy Sparrow	191
Attalus] 'Artalus' †Kele 1545.2, Wyght 1553, Kitson 1560.6, Marshe 1568			
Or any of the blode.	76	Phy Sparrow	200
With a charme or twayne,	77	Phy Sparrow	206
*Or els phylosophy /Maketh a great lye.	83	Phy Sparrow	476
*Or] 'Of' Scattergood			
As patryarke or pope /In a blacke cope.	85	Phy Sparrow	528
But whereto shuld I /Lenger morne or crye?	86	Phy Sparrow	595
Or Arturs rounde table,	87	Phy Sparrow	634
An ouche or els a ryng,	88	Phy Sparrow	686
Or a bracelet of her here,	89	Phy Sparrow	689
Whether he were onlyve or ded;	89	Phy Sparrow	728
Of Ovyd or Virgyll, /Or of Plutharke,	90	Phy Sparrow	756
Of Ovyd or Virgyll, /Or of Plutharke,	90	Phy Sparrow	757
Or Frauncys Petrarke, /Alcheus or Sapho,	90	Phy Sparrow	758
Or] 'Or of' Kitson 1560.6, Marshe 1568			
Or Frauncys Petrarke, /Alcheus or Sapho,	90	Phy Sparrow	759
Or] 'Or of' Kitson 1560.6, Marshe 1568			
Or such other poetes mo,	90	Phy Sparrow	760
Or els fayre Polexene,	97	Phy Sparrow	1019
Or els Caliope, /Or els Penolope;	97	Phy Sparrow	1020
Or els Caliope, /Or els Penolope;	97	Phy Sparrow	1021
One of the Centaures, /Or Onocentaures, /Or Hipocentaures;	104	Phy Sparrow	1295
One of the Centaures, /Or Onocentaures, /Or Hipocentaures;	104	Phy Sparrow	1296
In verses two or thre	106	Phy Sparrow	1378
Eyther to the devyll or the trinite.	114	Scot Kynge	41
Frenche kyng, or one or other;	118	Ag Scottes	105
Frenche kyng, or one or other;	118	Ag Scottes	105
Ye bere yow bolde as Barabas, or Syr Terry of Trac[e].	122	Garnesche1	11
Trace] 'Tracy' †MS Harley 367			
To turney or to tante with me ye ar to fare to seke.	123	Garnesche2	37
A pykes or a twybyll;	126	Garnesche3	72
A dong cart or a tumrell	132	Garnesche5	93
Lerne or be lewde, I shrow thy face.	132	Garnesche5	127
I care nat what thow wryght or sey;	134	Garnesche5	168
To dauns the hay or rune the ray;	134	Garnesche5	170
Scrybbyl thow, scrybyll thow, rayle or wryght,	134	Garnesche5	179
Either by language or with my pen.	137	Ven Tongues	23
Any such foly to rest or to be,	138	Ven Tongues	35
Then any poysoned tode, or any serpent.	138	Ven Tongues	54
Be it erly or late, welth hath a season.	140	Magnyfycence	3
And eyther I am dysseyved, or ye be the same.	141	Magnyfycence	25
In a payre of fetters or a payre of stockys.	141	Magnyfycence	31
Or howe can you prove that there is felycyte,	142	Magnyfycence	77
Me, other fyrst or last,	143	Magnyfycence	93
Shall I begynne or ye?	143	Magnyfycence	103
Here is none forsyth whether you flete or synke.	147	Magnyfycence	254
Or who made you so bolde to interrupe my tale?	147	Magnyfycence	256
Or ellys some jangelynge Jacke of the Vale.	147	Magnyfycence	258
And grotes many one or I came to your presence.	150	Magnyfycence	339
Or elles I had lost myne eres twayne.	150	Magnyfycence	349
Without an antetyme or a stole;	150	Magnyfycence	359
Who that is ruled by us, it shalbe longe or he thee.	154	Magnyfycence	515
We wyll remedy it, man, or we go;	155	Magnyfycence	551
Nay; eyther let me tell, or elles tell ye.	158	Magnyfycence	633
What is this, a betell or a batowe or a buskyn lacyd?	161	Magnyfycence	755

OR—OR

	Page	Title	Line
What is this, a betell or a batowe or a buskyn lacyd?	161	Magnyfycence	755
Beryst thou any rome? Or cannyst thou do ought?	162	Magnyfycence	776
Or whiche of you can do most.	162	Magnyfycence	803
No; for or we stryke, we wyll be advysed twyse.	163	Magnyfycence	810
By day or by nyght	164	Magnyfycence	860
Before or behynde;	168	Magnyfycence	986
What is this, an owle or a glede?	169	Magnyfycence	1047
For be he cayser or be he kynge,	174	Magnyfycence	1214
Ye. Let us here a worde or twayne.	174	Magnyfycence	1218
Yes. I shall tell you or I go	175	Magnyfycence	1263
And, be the mater yll more or lesse,	175	Magnyfycence	1272
Nay, but fansy must be eyther fyrst or last.	176	Magnyfycence	1288
I wote not whether it cometh of the or of me,	176	Magnyfycence	1290
Yes, perde, man, whether that ye ryde or go.	176	Magnyfycence	1307
Trymme at her tayle or a man can turne a socke.	177	Magnyfycence	1346
Or lyberte by welth? Let se, tell me that.	180	Magnyfycence	1432
Whom? Lusty Pleasure or mery Consayte?	180	Magnyfycence	1452
Or in electe utteraunce halfe so eloquent,	183	Magnyfycence	1533
A goodly rybon, or a golde rynge,	184	Magnyfycence	1580
Be it reason or none, it shall not gretely skyll;	185	Magnyfycence	1596
Be it ryght or wronge, by the advyse of me,	185	Magnyfycence	1597
Then some occacyon or quarell ye must fynde,	185	Magnyfycence	1600
It were better he spake with you or he wente,	187	Magnyfycence	1662
But yet, lo, I wolde, or that he wente,	187	Magnyfycence	1673
I wolde to you say a worde or twayne.	188	Magnyfycence	1721
A bolle or a basyn, I say, for Goddes brede!	189	Magnyfycence	1728
As in a tryfyll or in a thynge of nought,	189	Magnyfycence	1757
I sawe a sowter go to supper, or ever he had dynde.	191	Magnyfycence	1825
Or ever we were ware, brought us in adversyte,	193	Magnyfycence	1863
Man or woman, of what estate they be,	194	Magnyfycence	1898
To drowne or to sle themselfe with a knyfe –	194	Magnyfycence	1914
Them or theyr chyldren ofte tymes I dysmembre;	194	Magnyfycence	1923
To hardy, to moche, to free of the dawe,	199	Magnyfycence	2090
To homly, to holy, to lewde, or to lowde,	199	Magnyfycence	2094
Leve thy pratynge or els I shall lay the on the pate.	201	Magnyfycence	2173
Peas, or I shall wrynge thy be in a brake.	202	Magnyfycence	2187
Or I shal fawchyn thy flesshe and scrape the on the skyn.	202	Magnyfycence	2189
Ye, in faythe; or ellys thou arte to great a glotton.	204	Magnyfycence	2266
Or that thy selfe thou go honge	206	Magnyfycence	2312
Or ellys with this knyfe cut out a tonge	206	Magnyfycence	2314
Lo, here is thy knyfe and a halter, and or we go ferther,	206	Magnyfycence	2317
But frendly I wyll refrayne you ferther, or we flyt:	211	Magnyfycence	2478
Yeres two or thre,	219	El Rummynge	215
Some ranne a good trot /With a skellet or a pot;	220	El Rummynge	250
Some go streyght thyder, /Be it slaty or slyder;	221	El Rummynge	258
Brynge wyth them malte or whete,	221	El Rummynge	267
Mele, salte or other thynge,	221	El Rummynge	279
Another brought her bedes /Of jet or of cole,	227	El Rummynge	524
Yet, or she went, she dranke,	228	El Rummynge	542
Or score on the tayle.	230	El Rummynge	616
Then Parot moste have an almon or a date.	231	Speke Parott	7
Whether ita were before non, or non before ita,	235	Speke Parott	158
Elencticum, or ells enthimematicum,	236	Speke Parott	192
Or wakeste thow, Besse,	237	Speke Parott	239
Diamounde, or rubye, or balas of the beste,	241	Speke Parott	367
Diamounde, or rubye, or balas of the beste,	241	Speke Parott	367
Or eyndye sapher with oryente perlys dreste: perlys] 'prelys' †MS Harley 2252	241	Speke Parott	368
Wherfor your remorders ar madde or else starke blynde, remorders] 'remordes' †MS Harley 2252	241	Speke Parott	369
Yow to remorde erste or they know your mynde.	241	Speke Parott	370
To practise or postyll thys prosses here and there?	242	Speke Parott	393
Or elles ye pynche curtesy, trulye as I trowe,	242	Speke Parott	395
Or to make a sayle /Of a herynges tayle?	246	Collyn Clout	3
To ryme or to rayle, /To wryte or to indyte,	246	Collyn Clout	5
To ryme or to rayle, /To wryte or to indyte,	247	Collyn Clout	6
Other for delyte /Or elles *to desyte? Other] 'Eyther' Kele 1545.1; 'to desyte' MS Harley 2252, 'despyte' Kele 1545.1, Marshe 1568	247	Collyn Clout	8
Or bokes to compyle /Of dyvers maner style,	247	Collyn Clout	9
To teche or to preche /As reason wyll reche?	247	Collyn Clout	13
Or yf he spake playne, /Than he lacketh brayne:	247	Collyn Clout	26
Or elles they wolde se /Otherwyse,	247	Collyn Clout	39
Or suche laboure to take.	250	Collyn Clout	135
Almoost two or three, /Of that dygnyte,	250	Collyn Clout	148
To a pygge or to a goose,	252	Collyn Clout	214
Or a stewed cocke	252	Collyn Clout	217
Lyke sawdust or drye chyppes.	252	Collyn Clout	243
Uppon hym for to take /A mattocke or a rake.	253	Collyn Clout	274
Or Jacke of the Nocke?	254	Collyn Clout	322
Turke, Sarazyn or Jewe?	257	Collyn Clout	431
Or elles they are madde	259	Collyn Clout	503
But mayster Damyan, /Or some other man	264	Collyn Clout	721
Or scante worth twenty marke,	264	Collyn Clout	726
Or elles frere Frederyk,	265	Collyn Clout	737
Or elles frere Domynyk,	265	Collyn Clout	738
Or frere Hugulinus,	265	Collyn Clout	739
Or frere Augustinus,	265	Collyn Clout	740

OR — OR

	Page	Title	Line
Or frere Carmellus,	265	Collyn Clout	741
Or elles yf we may	265	Collyn Clout	743
Or elles of the order	265	Collyn Clout	745
Or elles the poore Scot,	265	Collyn Clout	749
Or of Babvell besyde Bery	265	Collyn Clout	752
To preche a worde or twayne,	265	Collyn Clout	764
With clauses two or thre,	265	Collyn Clout	766
Eyther analogice, /Or elles cathagorice,	266	Collyn Clout	788
Eyther corne or malte,	267	Collyn Clout	842
Or to maynteyne good quarelles.	269	Collyn Clout	916
Or elles his substytute	272	Collyn Clout	1043
Whether it be wronge or ryght	272	Collyn Clout	1055
Or elles for despyght,	272	Collyn Clout	1056
Or howeever it hap,	273	Collyn Clout	1057
Or elles that they do lye,	273	Collyn Clout	1063
Or elles in the myre	273	Collyn Clout	1069
Of hygh or lowe degre	274	Collyn Clout	1118
Of the spirytualte /Or of the temporalte,	274	Collyn Clout	1120
That doth thynke or wene	274	Collyn Clout	1121
Or touched on the quycke,	274	Collyn Clout	1124
The Kynges Benche or Marshalsy,	275	Collyn Clout	1171
At Poules Crosse, or elswhere,	276	Collyn Clout	1182
Without good reason or skyll;	276	Collyn Clout	1191
Or who dare dysdayne,	276	Collyn Clout	1215
Or of Divynyte, or Doctour Dryvyll,	277	Collyn Clout	1220
Divynyte] 'Divine' Marshe 1568, 'deuynite' MS Harley 2252; Dryvyll] 'oryll' MS Harley 2252			
Or of Divynyte, or Doctour Dryvyll,	277	Collyn Clout	1220
Divynyte] 'Divine' Marshe 1568, 'deuynite' MS Harley 2252; Dryvyll] 'oryll' MS Harley 2252			
Let him cough, rough or snevyll!	277	Collyn Clout	1221
The way to heven or to hell!'	277	Collyn Clout	1226
Or pescoddes they may shyll,	281	Why Come Ye	111
Or elles go rost a stone!	281	Why Come Ye	112
Be it blacke or whight	281	Why Come Ye	115
For whether he blesse or curse,	282	Why Come Ye	137
Lyke an oxe or a bull;	286	Why Come Ye	308
Or at the Kynges Benche.	287	Why Come Ye	320
Whether he be knyght or squyre,	287	Why Come Ye	344
And brought in quycke or dede,	288	Why Come Ye	359
Where ever he go or ryde	289	Why Come Ye	394
Or to Hampton Court?	289	Why Come Ye	404
Or for lawe common,	289	Why Come Ye	417
Or for lawe cyvyll;	289	Why Come Ye	418
An abstract or a concrete,	289	Why Come Ye	421
abstract] 'obstract' †Kele 1545.3			
That in a fume or an hete,	289	Why Come Ye	424
Or to the Kynges Benche!'	290	Why Come Ye	433
Or wylfull blyndnesse,	290	Why Come Ye	469
Without reason or skyll.	291	Why Come Ye	488
Or yet of trivials;	292	Why Come Ye	515
Fyxt or els mobyll.	292	Why Come Ye	525
Chuse them syt or flyt,	295	Why Come Ye	634
Stande, walke, or ryde –	295	Why Come Ye	635
Or suche other loselry	295	Why Come Ye	664
As wychecraft or charmyng;	295	Why Come Ye	665
To make all or to mar,	297	Why Come Ye	733
Or suche chaunce shulde fall /Unto our cardynall!	297	Why Come Ye	748
Withouten drede or feare!	298	Why Come Ye	759
In ernest or in borde:	298	Why Come Ye	785
Before some prothonotory, /Imperyall or papall.	299	Why Come Ye	820
Sem, Japheth, or Cam.	301	Why Come Ye	899
From golde to pewter /Or els to a newter,	301	Why Come Ye	905
To copper, to tyn, /To lede, or alcumyn?	301	Why Come Ye	907
Or canves of Cane,	302	Why Come Ye	919
A thousande or twayne	302	Why Come Ye	944
That men shall scantly /Have peny or halpeny.	303	Why Come Ye	968
Whether God be pleased or wroth.	307	Why Come Ye	1132
Or els his surgions they lye;	308	Why Come Ye	1171
Complayne or do what ye wyll,	310	Why Come Ye2	31
upon a goodly Garlande or Chapelet of Laurell	312	Garlande	1
Or of humors superflue, that often wyll crepe	313	Garlande	32
Or it procedyd of fatall persuacyon,	313	Garlande	34
As one in a trans or in an extasy,	313	Garlande	37
Or wherto shulde he have the prerogatyve,	315	Garlande	117
the] 'that' MS Cotton Vitellius E.x			
Recorde the same? Or why is had in mynde	315	Garlande	125
His name? Or why is it, I you praye,	316	Garlande	138
Few shall ye fynde or none that wyll do so.'	317	Garlande	168
Or els ye demeane you inordinatly;	317	Garlande	173
But lytell or nothynge ye shall here tell	317	Garlande	197
ye shall] 'shall ye' MS Cotton Vitellius E.x			
One faute or other in them shalbe notyd.	318	Garlande	203
Or elles he can nought bot whan he is at scole;	318	Garlande	205
'Prove his wytt', sayth he, 'at cardes or dyce,	318	Garlande	206
Twyse! set hym a chare, or reche hym a stol	318	Garlande	208
Twyse] 'Twyshe' Marshe 1568, MS Cotton Vitellius E.x			
Or elles, ye know well, I can do no lesse	318	Garlande	226

ORACE — ORDYNAUNCE

	Page	Title	Line
As people halfe pevysshe, or men that were masyd.	319	Garlande	266
Or that we beganne in the supplement,	323	Garlande	415
I made it straunge, and drew bak ones or twyse,	324	Garlande	444
How far it was, or ellis within what howris, far] not in †Fakes 1523	325	Garlande	457
And we shall se you ageyne or it be pryme.'	326	Garlande	525
Or gummis of Saby so derely that be solde.	331	Garlande	675
Jentill as fawcoun /Or hawke of the towre;	340	Garlande	1007
Or suffice to wryght	341	Garlande	1018
Jentyll as fawcoun /Or hawke of the towre,	341	Garlande	1022
Jentyll as fawcoun /Or hawke of the towre.	341	Garlande	1037
But if he wryte oftenner than ones or twyse.'	345	Garlande	1155
Item the Boke to Speke Well or be Styll;	345	Garlande	1175
One of the Centawris, /Or Onocentauris, /Or Hippocentauris;	348	Garlande	1288
One of the Centawris, /Or Onocentauris, /Or Hippocentauris;	348	Garlande	1289
In verses two or thre	350	Garlande	1371
Whether he rode to Swaffhamm or to Some, Swaffhamm] 'Swasshamm' †Fakes 1523, Marshe 1568	352	Garlande	1416
What constellacions ar good or bad for men,	352	Garlande	1429
Or els &c	357	Garlande	1602
upon a goodly Garlonde or Chapelet of Laurell,	358	Garlande2	R
With a worde or twayne /In sentence playne.	361	Albany	75
Or els wyll I /Evydently /Shewe as it is:	361	Albany	84
Or what actyvyte /Is in you, beggars braules,	364	Albany	217
Or of suche a mawment /Caryed in a tent.	365	Albany	257
In ernest or in borde.	367	Albany	319
Where ever he rydes or goos.	370	Albany	470
A pece or a patche of philosophy,	374	Replycacion	3
To beare a fagot, or to be enflamed.	374	Replycacion	16
or to pray and go on pylgrimages,	375	Replycacion	I
or to make oblacions to any ymages of sayntes,	375	Replycacion	I
in churches or elsewhere.	375	Replycacion	I
Or be brende by and by,	377	Replycacion	89
Oftnar than ones or twyse,	378	Replycacion	133
Or more of this to clatter?	378	Replycacion	159
Or els doutlesse ye shalbe blased,	382	Replycacion	294
A confutacion responsyve, or an inevytably prepensed answere	382	Replycacion	R
to all waywarde or frowarde altercacyons	382	Replycacion	R
that can or may be made or objected	382	Replycacion	R
that can or may be made or objected	382	Replycacion	R
To answere or reply /Agaynst suche heresy.	383	Replycacion	312

ORACE

Vis consilii expers, as techythe me Orace,	232	Speke Parott	40
Orace also with his new poetry;	322	Garlande	352

ORACIUS

Oracius to recorde in his volumys olde,	143	Magnyfycence	114

ORATORS

These orators and poetes refresshed there throtis.	321	Garlande	336
These orators and poetes refreshed their throtes.	321	Garlande	343
Theis orators and poetis refreshed there throtis.	322	Garlande	350
Their orators and poetis refresshed there throtis.	322	Garlande	357
Theis orators and poetis refresshed there throtis.	322	Garlande	364
These orators and poetis refresshid ther throtis.	322	Garlande	371
Theis orators and poetis refresshid there throtis.	322	Garlande	378
All orators and poetis shulde thider go before,	325	Garlande	454
All orators and poetis, with other grete and smale,	354	Garlande	1504

ORATOUR

oratour to the kynges most royall estate.	120	Ag Scottes	E
Dymostenes, that oratour royall,	316	Garlande	130
But of that famous oratour, I say,	316	Garlande	158
'Of your oratour and poete laureate	345	Garlande	1170

ORATOURS

Retoricyons and oratours in freshe humanyte,	236	Speke Parott	194

ORBICULAR

Lorde of the yere in his orbicular,	312	Garlande	4

ORCHADY

Unto the Iles of Orchady,	79	Phy Sparrow	319

ORDENAUNCE

Your ordenaunce, syr, I wyll not forsake.	145	Magnyfycence	181
Made purveaunce /And suche ordenaunce,	165	Magnyfycence	881
Syrs, I am agreed to abyde your ordenaunce –	210	Magnyfycence	2471

ORDENYD

Where every thyng is ordenyd after your noble porte.	214	Magnyfycence	2568

ORDER

Suche order I trust with them for to take,	145	Magnyfycence	178
I wyll endevour me to order every thynge	146	Magnyfycence	203
To passe the tyme and order whyle a man may talke	159	Magnyfycence	689
Or elles of the order	265	Collyn Clout	745
Of all good Christen order.	380	Replycacion	226

ORDERYD

But yf I were orderyd by just measure,	147	Magnyfycence	249

ORDERS

And howe whan ye gyve orders	252	Collyn Clout	220

ORDYNALL

As provost pryncypall, /To teach them theyr ordynall;	85	Phy Sparrow	555

ORDYNAUNCE

And now wolde ye swarve from your owne ordynaunce?	147	Magnyfycence	234

515

ORDRE —OTHER   Page   Title   Line

ORDRE
	Page	Title	Line
To se how duly ich thyng in ordre was,	343	Garlande	1094
Rehersyng by ordre, and what is the grownde,	345	Garlande	1152

ORDRED
After all duly ordred obeisaunce,	335	Garlande	836

ORDRES
The foure ordres of freres,	267	Collyn Clout	832

ORE
That roweth with a rude ore	105	Phy Sparrow	1339
That rowyth with a rude ore,	349	Garlande	1332

OREB
Vitulus in Oreb troubled Arons brayne;	232	Speke Parott	59
Oreb et Zeb, of Judicum rede the boke.	234	Speke Parott	117

ORGULYOUS
odyous, orgulyous and flyblowen opynions etc.,	375	Replycacion	1

ORIENT
In thy palace above the orient,	34	Dol Dethe	202
The orient perle so clere,	97	Phy Sparrow	1033
Fret all with orient perlys of garnate,	325	Garlande	485
Of Margarite, /Perle orient,	339	Garlande	948

ORIGINALL
Of his wretched originall,	291	Why Come Ye	490

ORYENT
That all the oryent had in subjeccyon,	181	Magnyfycence	1467

ORYENTE
Or eyndye sapher with oryente perlys dreste: perlys] 'prelys' †MS Harley 2252	241	Speke Parott	368

ORYGYNALL
As at the fyrst orygynall, by godly opynyon;	143	Magnyfycence	119

ORNACY
Pullyshyd and fresshe is your ornacy.	183	Magnyfycence	1531

ORNATE
Support Parrot, I pray you, with your suffrage ornate,	236	Speke Parott	195
So ryally, so rychely, so passyngly ornate,	325	Garlande	487

ORNATLY
That if I wolde apply /To wryte ornatly, ornatly] 'ordinately' Kitson 1560.6, Marshe 1568	91	Phy Sparrow	781
Ornatly pullysshid after your faculte,	335	Garlande	816

ORPHEUS
Orpheus, the Traciane, herped meledyously	320	Garlande	272

ORWELLE
At Orwelle hyr havyn your anggre was laules.	122	Garneschel	33

OSPRAYE
The roke, with the ospraye	83	Phy Sparrow	462

OTES
Ye wolde sone pynche at a pecke of otes. otes] 'grotes' †Rastell & Treveris C 1530, B	151	Magnyfycence	385

OTHE
It were a shame, to God I make an othe,	144	Magnyfycence	145
By his former othe,	307	Why Come Ye	1131

OTHER
And all other gentelmen with hym enterteynd	34	Dol Dethe	184
The one for a duke, the other for dun,	37	Coystrowne1	10
Of me and other ye may have nede.	41	Coystrowne4	14
Amonge all other I put myselfe in prece.	47	Bowge	44
Of one and other that wolde his lady see,	47	Bowge	57
Amonge all other was wrytten in her trone,	47	Bowge	65
With other foure of theyr affynyte:	50	Bowge	139
For here is none that dare well other truste;	51	Bowge	202
To make the mery, as other felowes done?	57	Bowge	380
That other loked as he wolde me have slayne. me have] 'have me' Wynkyn de Worde 1510	58	Bowge	430
And in his other sleve, me thought I sawe	58	Bowge	435
Lyghte lyme-fynger, he toke none other wage.	60	Bowge	509
Brynge other wyves in thought	87	Phy Sparrow	626
From one to the other,	88	Phy Sparrow	683
And of Hester his other wyfe,	90	Phy Sparrow	743
Or such other poetes mo,	90	Phy Sparrow	760
All other of whom we rede,	93	Phy Sparrow	884
Even nor morow; /But other mennes sorow	94	Phy Sparrow	925
Whan other ar glad,	95	Phy Sparrow	938
Her fresshe habylementes /With other implementes	101	Phy Sparrow	1181
Before the Frensshe kynge, Danes and other	114	Scot Kynge	15
Frenche kyng, or one or other;	118	Ag Scottes	105
Cause have they none other /But for that he was brother, have they] 'they have' Day 1560, Marshe 1568 brother] 'hys brother' Day 1560, Marshe 1568	120	Ag Scottes2	13
If there be none other mater but that,	137	Ven Tongues	14
Me, other fyrst or last,	143	Magnyfycence	93
And, syr, this other mannys name is Lyberte.	145	Magnyfycence	168
God forbede that it other wyse sholde be!	147	Magnyfycence	246
Why have ye hym named and all other refused?	148	Magnyfycence	281
Of one thynge and other to occupy the place,	159	Magnyfycence	690
Whan other men laughe, than study I and muse,	160	Magnyfycence	707
Water in the one hande and fyre in the other.	160	Magnyfycence	711
By cloked colusyon, I say, and none other,	160	Magnyfycence	714
Ye, by Goddes sacrament; and with other mo.	166	Magnyfycence	942
For it is I that other whyle	169	Magnyfycence	1025

	Page	Title	Line
I make on the one day, and I marre on the other.	169	Magnyfycence	1038
Nay, beyonde all other set hym alone.	174	Magnyfycence	1235
For there be other that foly dothe use	175	Magnyfycence	1280
Nowe holde ye content, for there is none other shyfte.	180	Magnyfycence	1443
Syr, we can do nothynge the one without the other.	180	Magnyfycence	1450
Well, get you hens than and sende me some other.	180	Magnyfycence	1451
And let the other another [time] awayte.	180	Magnyfycence	1454
time] not in †Rastell & Treveris C 1530, B			
Ne by non other that any man can rehersse.	181	Magnyfycence	1490
And as for all other, let them trusse and packe;	190	Magnyfycence	1774
Let them have all, and the other go without;	190	Magnyfycence	1780
I make God avowe ye wyll none other men have.	191	Magnyfycence	1827
And make eche man to sle other;	194	Magnyfycence	1913
And take myscheffe and vengeaunce of other mo	195	Magnyfycence	1951
Some hath so moche lyberte of one thynge and other,	200	Magnyfycence	2141
The one of you is to proude, the other is to haute.	203	Magnyfycence	2223
Anone cometh another, /As drye as the other,	221	El Rummynge	277
Mele, salte or other thynge,	221	El Rummynge	279
Of auncyent Aristippus and such other mo,	233	Speke Parott	93
Above all other byrdis, set Parrot alone.	233	Speke Parott	112
Other for delyte /Or elles *to desyte?	247	Collyn Clout	7
Other] 'Eyther' Kele 1545.1; 'to desyte' MS Harley 2252, 'despyte' Kele 1545.1, Marshe 1568			
And foule covytousnesse /And other wretchednesse,	247	Collyn Clout	43
Thus eche of other blother /The tone against the tother.	248	Collyn Clout	66
And judge it as they wyll, /For other mens skyll,	249	Collyn Clout	99
And other wanton warkes /Whan the nyght darkes.	251	Collyn Clout	194
Ye coude none other gette	263	Collyn Clout	654
coude] 'wolde' Kele 1545.1, Marshe 1568, 'cowde' MS Harley 2252			
But mayster Damyan, /Or some other man	264	Collyn Clout	721
Some lerned in other sawe, /As in divynyte,	264	Collyn Clout	732
Than a thousande thousande other	266	Collyn Clout	776
And tell of other mo,	267	Collyn Clout	829
Howe frere Fabian with other mo	268	Collyn Clout	881
With covytous ambycyon /And other superstycyon,	269	Collyn Clout	902
ambycyon] 'and ambycyon' Kele 1545.1, Marshe 1568, 'ambyssyon' MS Harley 2252			
As well as other men.	277	Collyn Clout	1247
That any other sayth,	290	Why Come Ye	444
Nor of none other saw;	292	Why Come Ye	511
Or suche other loselry	295	Why Come Ye	664
Above all other inordinatly.	296	Why Come Ye	704
With other abusyons grete;	306	Why Come Ye	1086
Than any other a thousand folde.	310	Why Come Ye2	16
any] 'yn any' MS Rawlinson C. 813			
All other transcendyng, of very congruence	313	Garlande	52
Olde Diogenes, with other many mo,	315	Garlande	129
Whiche passid all other; wherfore I may	316	Garlande	159
One faute or other in them shalbe notyd.	318	Garlande	203
And iche man stode gasyng and staryng upon other,	319	Garlande	268
Weth Amphion, and other musis of Archady	320	Garlande	273
I helpe all other of there infirmite,	321	Garlande	311
That profyteth all other is nothynge profytable	321	Garlande	313
All other transcendynge, the most rychely besene,	325	Garlande	483
With other condycyons that well myght be left.	329	Garlande	615
All other besyde were counterfete they thought	343	Garlande	1106
All ... counterfete] 'that they ware were counterfettis' MS Cotton Vitellius E.x			
In famous glory all other transcendyng,	344	Garlande	1129
With aurum musicum every other lyne	345	Garlande	1167
With Sacris Solempniis, and other contemplacyons,	352	Garlande	1421
All orators and poetis, with other grete and smale,	354	Garlande	1504
Moche better other wayes.	378	Replycacion	150
With other many holy men,	381	Replycacion	278
With other doctours many mo,	381	Replycacion	280

OTHERWYSE

	Page	Title	Line
Yf ye coude be otherwyse agrede;	59	Bowge	480
What ellys? For otherwyse it were agaynst kynde;	144	Magnyfycence	132
Or elles they wolde se /Otherwyse,	247	Collyn Clout	40

OTHES

	Page	Title	Line
And sware horryble othes /Before the face of God,	63	Hauke	52

OTHYR

	Page	Title	Line
With othyr menys charge;	129	Garnesche3	188

OUCHE

	Page	Title	Line
An ouche or els a ryng,	88	Phy Sparrow	686

OUGHT

	Page	Title	Line
Treytory and treson he bannesht ought of sight.	33	Dol Dethe	151
All kingis, all princis, all dukis, well thei ought	34	Dol Dethe	180
To soroufull weping thei ought to be constreynd,	34	Dol Dethe	187
And ye nede ought, man, shewe to me your mynde,	50	Bowge	165
Whyles I have ought, by God, thou shalt not lacke,	50	Bowge	167
That never ought the evyll wyll!	79	Phy Sparrow	323
Ye ought to honour your lorde and brother.	114	Scot Kynge	16
Beryst thou any rome? Or cannyst thou do ought?	162	Magnyfycence	776
Whylyst he hath ought.	165	Magnyfycence	901
Nay, syr. That affeccyon ought to be reserved,	186	Magnyfycence	1643
For aurea lyngua Greca ought to be magnyfyed,	234	Speke Parott	142

OUGHTE —OUR	Page	Title	Line
That they ought by the lawe	268	Collyn Clout	857
Ye ought to be ashamed	274	Collyn Clout	1113
Harde to make ought of that is nakid nought;	346	Garlande	1205
Trouth ought to be rescude;	369	Albany	421

OUGHTE

To wete yf Malkyn, my lemman, have gete oughte.	57	Bowge	401

OULE

She was somwhat foule, /Crokenebbed lyke an oule; Crokenebbed] 'Croke necked' †Lant 1545, Kynge & Marche 1554, Day 1560, Marshe 1568	225	El Rummynge	427

OUR

With thi blode precious our fenaunce thou dyd pay	34	Dol Dethe	195
By radyante hete enryped hath our corne;	46	Bowge	2
Of our pole artyke, smylynge halfe in scorne	46	Bowge	5
At our foly and our unstedfastnesse;	46	Bowge	6
At our foly and our unstedfastnesse;	46	Bowge	6
What though our chaffer be never so dere,	48	Bowge	89
Fortune gydeth and ruleth all our shyppe.	49	Bowge	111
The sayle is up, Fortune ruleth our helme,	49	Bowge	127
For, as me thoughte, in our shyppe I dyde see	49	Bowge	132
And, as she wyll, so shall our grete shyppe sayle.	50	Bowge	172
But ye be welcome to our housholde.	53	Bowge	266
It is lyke he wyll stonde in our lyghte!' our] 'your' Marshe 1568	54	Bowge	305
For all our courte is full of dysceyte.	59	Bowge	469
That of our fayth the grownd is.	62	Hauke	14
Set in our bede rolles,	72	Phy Sparrow	12
Whom Gyb our cat hath slayne.	72	Phy Sparrow	27
Gyb, I saye, our cat,	72	Phy Sparrow	28
Our Lorde thy soule reskew!	80	Phy Sparrow	332
By Gyb, our cat savage,	81	Phy Sparrow	375
Set in our bede rolle,	81	Phy Sparrow	383
Our chaunters shalbe the cuckoue,	82	Phy Sparrow	428
To make hym our belman,	84	Phy Sparrow	492
Chaunteclere, our coke,	84	Phy Sparrow	495
To treade the prety wren /That is our Ladyes hen.	86	Phy Sparrow	601
Our naturall tong is rude,	91	Phy Sparrow	774
Our language is so rusty,	91	Phy Sparrow	777
A Lawde And Prayse Made for Our Sovereigne Lord the Kyng	110	Lawde	I
Of this our noble king	111	Lawde	29
Our prince of hih honour,	111	Lawde	45
Our paves, our succour,	111	Lawde	46
Our paves, our succour,	111	Lawde	46
Our king, our emperour,	111	Lawde	47
Our king, our emperour,	111	Lawde	47
Our Priamus of Troy,	111	Lawde	48
Our welth, our worldly joy,	111	Lawde	49
Our welth, our worldly joy,	111	Lawde	49
That makith our hartis glad,	111	Lawde	51
Ye summoned our kynge. Why dyde ye so?	113	Scot Kynge	2
To sommon our kynge your soverayne lorde.	113	Scot Kynge	4
Now must ye knowe our kynge for your regent,	114	Scot Kynge	21
He is our noble champyon,	114	Scot Kynge	25
Thanked be saynte Gorge, our ladyes knythe,	114	Scot Kynge	42
Our kynge than beynge out of the waye;	114	Scot Kynge	45
Warre with our kynge to meyntayne.	114	Scot Kynge	55
Of our Englysshe bowes ye have fette your banes.	115	Scot Kynge	65
At Floddon hyllys, /Our bowys, our byllys	116	Ag Scottes	26
At Floddon hyllys, /Our bowys, our byllys	116	Ag Scottes	26
Our kynge of England for to syght, syght] 'fight' Day 1560, Marshe 1568	117	Ag Scottes	53
Your soverayne lord, our prynce of myght.	117	Ag Scottes	54
Unto our prince, anoynted kyng.	117	Ag Scottes	58
For then began our myrth and game.	117	Ag Scottes	68
Of all our royall Englysh nacyon.	117	Ag Scottes	76
Ye summond our kyng, why dyd ye so? ye] not in Kynge & Marche 1554, Day 1560, Marshe 1568	118	Ag Scottes	92
To summon our kyng, your soveraygne lorde.	118	Ag Scottes	94
He is our noble Scipione;	118	Ag Scottes	117
Our Englysh bowes, our Englysh bylles,	119	Ag Scottes	132
Our Englysh bowes, our Englysh bylles,	119	Ag Scottes	132
And swete Saynt George, our ladyes knyght!	119	Ag Scottes	141
With our kyng royall war to mayntayne.	119	Ag Scottes	152
Brother unnaturall /Unto our kyng royall,	120	Ag Scottes2	16
He skantly loveth our kyng, /That grudgeth at this thing:	121	Ag Scottes2	35
But behynd in our hose /We bere there a rose	136	Dundas	34
On Huntley bankes, /Take this our thankes;	136	Dundas	59
Why, have you harde of our dysputacyon?	142	Magnyfycence	82
S[e] at our eye the worlde day by day. Se] 'so' †Rastell & Treveris C 1530, B	146	Magnyfycence	216
Why that ye sayd our langage was in vayne.	147	Magnyfycence	263
I trowe, by our lady, I had ben slayne,	150	Magnyfycence	348
So he ruleth over all our place.	155	Magnyfycence	545
Nay. Let us our heddes togyder cast.	156	Magnyfycence	566
And counterfeted our names we have	158	Magnyfycence	641
Than a butterflye of our lande.	169	Magnyfycence	1053
Have welth at our gydynge to rule as we lyst?	179	Magnyfycence	1415
Welcom, Pleasure, to our magnyfycence.	182	Magnyfycence	1516

518

	Page	Title	Line
But, blessyd be our Lorde, they wyll be sone converted.	184	Magnyfycence	1584
Of our blessyd Lorde, syr, at the reverence -	186	Magnyfycence	1636
By our lakyn, syr, I have ben a hawkyng for the wylde swan.	191	Magnyfycence	1806
By our lakyn, syr, not by my wyll.	203	Magnyfycence	2208
And therfore our Lorde sende you a very wengaunce!	203	Magnyfycence	2237
Without our shyppe be sure, it is lykely to brast,	213	Magnyfycence	2562
For, after all our sport,	220	El Rummynge	231
Let us wasshe our gommes /From the drye crommes!'	222	El Rummynge	307
And called for our dame, /Elynour by name.	229	El Rummynge	592
Our Thomasen she doth trip, our Jenet she doth shayle;	233	Speke Parott	83
Our Thomasen she doth trip, our Jenet she doth shayle;	233	Speke Parott	83
Madionita Jetro, our Moyses kepyth his shepe;	234	Speke Parott	115
But our Grekis theyr Greke so well have applyed,	234	Speke Parott	145
Our Grekys ye walow in the washbol Argolycorum;	235	Speke Parott	150
Dame Sybly our abbesse,	256	Collyn Clout	391
Dame Sare our pryoresse,	256	Collyn Clout	393
No man to our sovereygne lorde	272	Collyn Clout	1030
Holy churche our mother,	274	Collyn Clout	1105
And let our matters pas!	275	Collyn Clout	1159
matters] 'matter' Kele 1545.1, 'maters' Marshe 1568, 'medlyng' MS Harley 2252			
And declareth our vyllany;	275	Collyn Clout	1174
And of our fee symplenes	275	Collyn Clout	1175
fee] 'fre' Kele 1545.1, Marshe 1568, not in MS Harley 2252			
And our matters mayntayne,	276	Collyn Clout	1213
At our pleasure and wyll.	276	Collyn Clout	1216
our] 'your' Kele 1545.1, Marshe 1568, 'owur' MS Harley 2252			
Towarde the porte salue /Of our Savyoure Jesu,	278	Collyn Clout	1261
Our talwod is all brent,	281	Why Come Ye	82
Our fagottes are all spent.	281	Why Come Ye	83
Our mare hath cast her fole,	281	Why Come Ye	85
Our shepe are shrewdly shorn,	281	Why Come Ye	92
For we have spente our shot!	282	Why Come Ye	127
We have cast up our war,	282	Why Come Ye	140
Our mony madly lent,	282	Why Come Ye	143
lent] 'sent' Marshe 1568			
Our armye waxeth dull,	282	Why Come Ye	150
Our lorde be his soccoure!	282	Why Come Ye	160
Our barons be so bolde,	286	Why Come Ye	292
That all our lerned men	287	Why Come Ye	322
To seke before our grace.'	287	Why Come Ye	332
They have slain our Englisshmen	288	Why Come Ye	372
Of our graunde counsell?	288	Why Come Ye	380
That makys our syre to glum.	288	Why Come Ye	389
Of our soverayne lorde,	291	Why Come Ye	485
Our soverayne lord, chyfe grounde	291	Why Come Ye	502
Than, our processe for to stable,	292	Why Come Ye	536
Had nat our prynce be	292	Why Come Ye	539
Or suche chaunce shulde fall /Unto our cardynall!	297	Why Come Ye	749
To our most royall kynge,	298	Why Come Ye	754
Of our maisters counsel in everithing.	299	Why Come Ye	792
To purvey for our cardynall /A palace pontifycall	299	Why Come Ye	811
Our royals that shone,	302	Why Come Ye	921
Our nobles are gone	302	Why Come Ye	922
Hath promised to hele our cardinals eye.	309	Why Come Ye	1197
Is that our servaunt is sum what to dull;	314	Garlande	79
that] 'for that' MS Cotton Vitellius E.x			
Unto your palas, our noble courte of Fame,	318	Garlande	219
What poetis we have at our retenewe.	319	Garlande	238
I saw Gower, that first garnisshed our Englysshe rude,	323	Garlande	387
How that our Englysshe mygth fresshely be ennewed;	323	Garlande	389
ennewed] 'a meude' †Fakes 1523			
In our collage above the sterry sky,	323	Garlande	403
Of all our hooll collage by the agreament,	324	Garlande	417
With all our strength that we can brynge about,	324	Garlande	424
To owe to yow our servyce, and more if we mowte!	324	Garlande	425
Of Fames court, by all our holl assent	324	Garlande	433
With suche communycacyon as came to our mynde;	328	Garlande	562
That of our bownte we wyll hym rewarde:	334	Garlande	779
To be our kyng, of God preordinate.	347	Garlande	1232
Of our noble courte is ones spoken owte,	353	Garlande	1482
But our kyng royall	361	Albany	107
Against our st[r]onge captaine;	365	Albany	245
stronge] 'stonge' †Marshe 1568			
Our royall kyng to make	367	Albany	327
If our moost royall Harry	367	Albany	340
What, wold Fraunces, our friar, /Be suche a false lyar,	368	Albany	373
Our kyng out of his reme?	368	Albany	381
Our mayster shall you brynge,	368	Albany	384
Our kyng for to dryve out	368	Albany	392
In our royall regent,	369	Albany	427
Our perelesse president,	369	Albany	428
Our kyng most excellent.	369	Albany	429
of our mother Holy Churche, etc.	373	Replycacion	I
howe it was idolatry to offre to ymages of our blessed lady,	375	Replycacion	I
In the honour of our blessed lady,	375	Replycacion	18
Our glorious lady to disable,	375	Replycacion	26
That our Savyour bare, /Whiche us redemed from care.	375	Replycacion	33

OURE —OUT

	Page	Title	Line
Retourne we to our matter.	378	Replycacion	160
And to our faithe moche agreable,	382	Replycacion	290
For Davyd, our poete, harped so meloudiously	383	Replycacion	339
Of our savyour Christ in his decacorde psautry,	383	Replycacion	340
Returne we to our former processe.	384	Replycacion	R
That he our penne dothe lede,	385	Replycacion	385
With sobre cyrcumstance, /Our myndes to avaunce	385	Replycacion	395

OURE

	Page	Title	Line
For all oure pamperde paunchys,	39	Coystrowne3	25
Oure days be datyd /To be chekmatyd,	39	Coystrowne3	29
With drawttys of deth /Stoppyng oure breth;	39	Coystrowne3	32
Oure eyen synkyng, /Oure bodys stynkyng,	39	Coystrowne3	33
Oure eyen synkyng, /Oure bodys stynkyng,	39	Coystrowne3	34
Oure gummys grynnyng, /Oure soulys brynnyng!	40	Coystrowne3	35
Oure gummys grynnyng, /Oure soulys brynnyng!	40	Coystrowne3	36
O goodly chyld /Of Mary mylde, /Then be oure shylde!	40	Coystrowne3	43
Oure Englysshe rude so fresshely hath set out,	324	Garlande	422

OUT

	Page	Title	Line
Myght tere out all thy trypes!	79	Phy Sparrow	308
Of Dyomedes stable /He brought out a rable	104	Phy Sparrow	1313
Our kynge than beynge out of the waye;	114	Scot Kynge	45
So out of frame, /So voyde of shame,	116	Ag Scottes	37
He ragyd and rent out your hart bloode;	119	Ag Scottes	136
Youre eye is out; adew, good nyght!	119	Ag Scottes	142
His grace beyng out of the way;	119	Ag Scottes	144
Out of your robes ye were shaked,	119	Ag Scottes	166
your] not in Kynge & Marche 1554, Day 1560, Marshe 1568			
Of the out iles the rough-foted Scottes,	120	Ag Scottes	170
Of grace out of the state /And dyed excomunycate.	121	Ag Scottes2	29
Bryngges yow out of favyr with alle femall teggys:	122	Garnesche1	31
Ye rayle all out of seson.	127	Garnesche3	130
Ye bere out brothells lyke a bawde;	131	Garnesche5	73
Such tunges shuld be torne out by the harde rootes,	137	Ven Tongues	3
The devill tere their tunges and pike out their ies!	139	Ven Tongues	68
Without I myght cut it out of the brode clothe,	144	Magnyfycence	146
And another bade put out myne eye;	150	Magnyfycence	353
To preche out of the pylery hole	150	Magnyfycence	358
Ryches rydeth out, at home is poverte.	153	Magnyfycence	474
Counterfet pleasure is borne out by me;	153	Magnyfycence	475
A custrell to dryve the devyll out of the derke,	154	Magnyfycence	485
Yet have we pycked out a rome for the.	154	Magnyfycence	508
That Mesure were cast out of the dores.	156	Magnyfycence	568
Mary, the better and Mesure were out.	158	Magnyfycence	656
Why, can ye not put out that foule freke?	158	Magnyfycence	657
Ye. My fansy was out of owle flyght,	159	Magnyfycence	671
For it is out of my mynde quyght.	159	Magnyfycence	672
And so they go out of the place.	163	Magnyfycence	SD
From out of Fraunce	165	Magnyfycence	878
All is out of harre	165	Magnyfycence	912
And out of trace,	166	Magnyfycence	913
Ye. But I bade hym pyke out of the gate;	166	Magnyfycence	946
Crossed? Ye, checked out of consayte.	166	Magnyfycence	951
Yf I can fynde out	168	Magnyfycence	993
That thou cannyst not growe out of thy boyes gere;	170	Magnyfycence	1075
That I shall laughe the out of thy cote.	173	Magnyfycence	1194
To tourne a fole out of his clowtes.	174	Magnyfycence	1211
That every man almost groweth out of kynde.	175	Magnyfycence	1285
Ryot at lyberte russheth it out styll.	176	Magnyfycence	1317
Tushe! Holde your peas; ye speke out of season.	178	Magnyfycence	1388
Here goth out CRAFTY CONVAYAUNCE.	179	Magnyfycence	SD
For welth without largesse is all out of kynde.	180	Magnyfycence	1441
Here goeth out FELYCYTE, LYBERTE and FANSY.	180	Magnyfycence	SD
Have hym hens, I say, out of my syght!	188	Magnyfycence	1723
Here MESURE goth out of the place.	188	Magnyfycence	SD
Hens, thou haynyarde, out of dores fast!	188	Magnyfycence	1725
Out of all measure themselfe to enryche;	189	Magnyfycence	1751
With pollynge and pluckynge out of all measure,	189	Magnyfycence	1753
To chose out ii., iii., of suche as you love best,	190	Magnyfycence	1769
And some to cry out of the bone ake;	194	Magnyfycence	1907
Of some of theyr chyldren I stryke out the eye;	194	Magnyfycence	1933
And brynge you agayne out of adversyte.	196	Magnyfycence	1999
I lyve as me lyst, I lepe out at large;	199	Magnyfycence	2080
To flatterynge, to smatterynge, to out of harre,	199	Magnyfycence	2095
What! Then he may drynke out of a stone cruyse.	201	Magnyfycence	2166
Ye, and when ye come out of the shoppe,	204	Magnyfycence	2271
Of farvent charyte I quenche out the bronde;	205	Magnyfycence	2287
Out of thy lyfe the for to lede.	205	Magnyfycence	2310
Or ellys with this knyfe cut out a tonge	206	Magnyfycence	2314
Of thy throte bole, and ryd the out of payne.	206	Magnyfycence	2315
Out harowe! Hyll burneth! Where shall I me hyde?	206	Magnyfycence	2324
And specyally to redresse that were out of joynte.	208	Magnyfycence	2414
For where sad cyrcumspeccyon is longe out of the way,	209	Magnyfycence	2427
But wyfull waywardnesse muste walke out of the way;	211	Magnyfycence	2490
Whan she goeth out /Her selfe for to shewe,	216	El Rummynge	80
Take up dyrt and all, /And bere out of the hall.'	219	El Rummynge	184
dyrt] 'drit' Kynge & Marche 1554, Day 1560, Marshe 1568			
Yet ye seke out your Greke in Capricornio;	235	Speke Parott	152

OUTCRI —OUTE	Page	Title	Line
For [ye] scrape out good scrypture, and set in a gall:	235	Speke Parott	153
ye] 'they' †Lant 1545, Kynge & Marche 1554, Day 1560, Marshe 1568			
And Donatus be dryven out of scole;	235	Speke Parott	170
With, 'Da causales,' is cast out of the gate,	235	Speke Parott	174
Expoundynge out theyr clauses, /And leve theyr owne causes.	249	Collyn Clout	100
Clerkes out of measure,	250	Collyn Clout	145
And lepe out of theyr lyppes	252	Collyn Clout	242
Out of the stony wall,	254	Collyn Clout	304
Out of theyr cloyster and quere /With an hevy chere,	256	Collyn Clout	394
All this is out of mynde.	263	Collyn Clout	660
All] 'Alas' Kele 1545.1, Marshe 1568, 'All' MS Harley 2252			
Ye growe nowe out of kynde.	263	Collyn Clout	661
I put you out of dout,	267	Collyn Clout	848
Dame Margeres soule out of hell.	268	Collyn Clout	876
And put them out of theyr place.	273	Collyn Clout	1078
That I speke out of the way.	273	Collyn Clout	1094
But lyve styll out of facyon,	275	Collyn Clout	1139
Out of the wawes wodde	277	Collyn Clout	1253
Dare nat loke out at dur	286	Why Come Ye	296
at] 'a' Kitson 1560.7, Marshe 1568			
That was cast out of a bochers stall!	291	Why Come Ye	494
Out from a low degre,	291	Why Come Ye	506
Transcendynge out of mesure,	292	Why Come Ye	548
And all out of season!	304	Why Come Ye	998
Now all is out of facion, /Almost in desolation.	305	Why Come Ye	1041
Pyked out of all good lawe,	306	Why Come Ye	1106
of] not in Marshe 1568			
Lest he wyll put it clene out,	309	Why Come Ye	1199
Out of my bokis full sone I shulde hym rase;	314	Garlande	72
In settyng out fresshely his crafty persuacyon,	316	Garlande	153
For wysdome and sadnesse be out a sunnyng;	318	Garlande	201
be out] 'be set out' Marshe 1568, MS Cotton Vitellius E.x			
Anone, I sey, this trumpet were founde out,	319	Garlande	243
To banysshe pyte out of a maydens harte?	320	Garlande	308
Oure Englysshe rude so fresshely hath set out,	324	Garlande	422
Jacinctis and smaragdis out of the florthe they grew.	325	Garlande	480
With that I herd gunnis russhe out at ones,	329	Garlande	623
Bowns, bowns, bowns! that all they out cryde.	329	Garlande	624
With pypes of golde engusshing out stremes;	330	Garlande	659
It shall be losyd ful sone out of the bandis	332	Garlande	725
He fyndith fals mesuris out of his fonde fiddill.'	333	Garlande	741
fals mesuris out] 'owght fals mesuris' MS Cotton Vit.E.x			
Habillimentis royall founde out industriously;	336	Garlande	851
To face out her foly with a midsomer mase;	346	Garlande	1208
To pyke out honesty of suche a potshorde.	346	Garlande	1211
Of Diomedis stabyll /He brought out a rabyll	349	Garlande	1306
The myllar was loth to be out of the way,	351	Garlande	1414
I did what I cowde to scrape out the scrollis,	354	Garlande	1489
scrape] 'scarpe' Marshe 1568			
Apollo to rase out of her ragman rollis.	354	Garlande	1490
Out of fresshe Latine into owre Englyshe playne,	354	Garlande	1499
And therwith, sodenly, out of my dreme I woke.	354	Garlande	1511
dreme] 'slepe' Marshe 1568			
To putte his eyes out	361	Albany	94
All out of joynt ye jar.	368	Albany	378
Our kyng out of his reme?	368	Albany	381
Our kyng for to dryve out	368	Albany	392
The fende scrache out your mawes!	371	Albany	479
For you shalbe driven out	371	Albany	501
That bringes you out of the way	379	Replycacion	170
With blowyng out your hornes,	380	Replycacion	215
Ye pyke out many thystels,	380	Replycacion	220
And feare leest they be out	380	Replycacion	225
That at his resurrection he harped out of hell	383	Replycacion	341
OUTCRI			
And to make an outcri	94	Phy Sparrow	904
an] 'a' †Kele 1545.2			
OUTCRY			
Hath made askrye /And outcry	301	Why Come Ye	871
outcry] 'doute cry' MS Rawlinson C. 813			
OUTCRYES			
Of parsons and vycaryes /They make many outcryes:	261	Collyn Clout	571
OUTE			
Dyamand poyntyd to rase oute hartly care	44	Balettys3	19
Yet shall she never oute of remembraunce,	45	Balettys3	47
Fyrste pycke a quarell and fall oute with hym then,	55	Bowge	314
Or we shall the oute of thy clothes shake!'	55	Bowge	343
He had plucte oute the nobles of my pouche.	60	Bowge	504
But that I drede mordre wolde come oute.	61	Bowge	524
And toke it oute in drynke,	66	Hauke	158
And grow all oute of kynde,	126	Garnesche3	102
To russhe it oute /In every route.	164	Magnyfycence	847
I purpose to shake oute /All my connynge bagge,	248	Collyn Clout	50
Oute of theyr stronge townes	283	Why Come Ye	177
Rede ye the story oute,	296	Why Come Ye	694
With hevynge and shovynge, 'have in' and 'have oute';	319	Garlande	251
Towarde the dore, as he were comyng oute,	343	Garlande	1095

OUTESYDE —OVERTHROW   Page   Title   Line

OUTESYDE
The outesyde every day, ... 125   Garnesche3   48
OUTFACE
And soo outface hym with a carde of ten.' 55   Bowge   315
All noble men shulde outface, ... 294   Why Come Ye   623
OUT FACYD
By God, I tell you, I wyll not be out facyd. 203   Magnyfycence   2220
OUT YLES
Of the out yles ye rough foted Scottes 115   Scot Kynge   62
OUTRAGE
Ye do moche great outrage, ... 384   Replycacion   354
OUTRAGYOUS
Today hote, tomorowe outragyous colde; 213   Magnyfycence   2546
OUTRAY
Onely procedid for that he did outray 316   Garlande   156
OUTRAYE
Whom Hercules dyd outraye, ... 74   Phy Sparrow   87
OUTWARDE
Counterfet worshyp outwarde men may se; 153   Magnyfycence   473
OVER
She wadyd over, she found a man 42   Balettys1   17
Whome she hateth shall over the see-boorde skyp. 49   Bowge   112
  see-boorde] 'shyp borde' Marshe 1568
We wante no wynde to passe now over all; 49   Bowge   128
Fynde some mene to caste him over the borde.' 54   Bowge   308
He shuld over the see 76   Phy Sparrow   197
Shall sayle over the see, ... 102   Phy Sparrow   1240
That wont wer over all 111   Lawde   38
Scornefull and mokkyng over to mykkylle. 133   Garnesche5   153
And so dysordereth this worlde over all, ... 141   Magnyfycence   20
So he ruleth over all our place. 155   Magnyfycence   545
I wyll passe over the cyrcumstaunce 158   Magnyfycence   637
Somtyme I laughe over lowde; 168   Magnyfycence   1012
Ye, tourne over the lefe, rede there, and loke 176   Magnyfycence   1293
I have wynde and wether over all to sayle; 181   Magnyfycence   1464
Money maketh marchauntes, I tell you, over all. 184   Magnyfycence   1574
For ofte tymes suche a wamblynge goth over my harte; 185   Magnyfycence   1620
It is the gyse nowe, I say, over all - 189   Magnyfycence   1759
At lyberte to wander and walke over all, ... 201   Magnyfycence   2149
To sende over to me Sad Cyrcumspeccyon. 208   Magnyfycence   2400
Over the falowe, ... 216   El Rummynge   87
For they go to roust, /Streyght over the ale-joust, ... 219   El Rummynge   192
Over the hedge and pale, ... 221   El Rummynge   264
'What is this to purpose?' Over in a whynnymeg! 232   Speke Parott   71
Over Scarpary mala vy, Monsyre Cy-and-sliddyr. 243   Speke Parott   414
Hys wolvys hede, wanne, bloo as lede, gapythe over the crowne: 244   Speke Parott   434
Over this, the foresayd lay 254   Collyn Clout   301
Plucke away the leedes /Over theyr heedes, ... 257   Collyn Clout   409
Lepe over lakes and dykes, ... 262   Collyn Clout   622
To you that over the whele 262   Collyn Clout   627
And ruleth so over all 262   Collyn Clout   633
Yet over all that, ... 263   Collyn Clout   671
To governe over all 271   Collyn Clout   991
This byll well over loked, ... 281   Why Come Ye   118
Thus thwartyng over thom, ... 283   Why Come Ye   200
Into the brayne by drynkyng over depe, ... 313   Garlande   33
Then I me lent, and loked over the wall: 329   Garlande   602
Encoverde over with golde of tissew fyne; 345   Garlande   1164
And Ryght is over the fallows 358   Garlande2   6
  over the] 'ever' Marshe 1568
Whose name over all 361   Albany   108
Over all the world[e] to sprede. 371   Albany   511
  worlde] 'worlds' †Marshe 1568
Over this, for a more ample processe 374   Replycacion   I
Ye soored over hye /In the ierarchy /Of Jovenyans heresy, . . . 378   Replycacion   161
OVERAGE
But /Helas! sage overage /So madly decayes, ... 279   Why Come Ye   41
  So] 'To' Toy 1553, Kitson 1560.7, Marshe 1568
And a lunatyke overage. 369   Albany   418
OVERBACE
The commouns overbace, ... 111   Lawde   37
OVERCAST
And all overcast with cloudis unkynde, ... 352   Garlande   1444
OVERGROWETH
That overgroweth a mannes face, ... 155   Magnyfycence   544
OVERNYGHTE
His hede was hevy for watchynge overnyghte, ... 56   Bowge   352
OVERSE
Yourselfe madly ye overse! 309   Why Come Ye2   7
But, I trowe, your selfe ye overse 381   Replycacion   285
OVER-SHOTE
But yet they over-shote us 283   Why Come Ye   169
OVERSYGHT
And therfore hye you hens, and take this oversyght. 190   Magnyfycence   1795
Measure of your lustys must have the oversyght, ... 211   Magnyfycence   2491
OVERTHROW
And wyll not know /Theyr overthrow /At Branxton More? 115   Ag Scottes   10
Surely my welthe with them was overthrow. 210   Magnyfycence   2450

OVERTHROWE—OWRE   Page   Title   Line

	Page	Title	Line
No stormy tempeste your barge shall overthrow.	327	Garlande	546
OVERTHROWE			
And in theyr moste truste I make them overthrowe.	193	Magnyfycence	1885
OVERTHWART			
To be so cruell and so overthwart,	45	Balettys5	5
So prowde of hart, /So overthwart,	116	Ag Scottes	36
He is nowe so overthwart,	308	Why Come Ye	1181
nowe] not in MS Rawlinson C. 813			
OVERTHWARTED			
Ye have so overthwarted,	256	Collyn Clout	371
OVERTHWARTES			
That cast such overthwartes /Percase have hollow hartes.	121	Ag Scottes2	37
OVERTHWARTYD			
And this he overthwartyd.	68	Hauke	230
OVERTHWHART			
Alas, what ayle you to be so overthwhart,	320	Garlande	307
OVERWHARTE			
Nay, and you be angry and overwharte,	156	Magnyfycence	562
OVYD			
Of Ovyll or Virgyll, /Or of Plutharke,	90	Phy Sparrow	756
OVYDE			
Ovyde was bannisshed for suche a skyll,	314	Garlande	93
Ovyde, enshryned with the musis nyne;	321	Garlande	333
OVYR			
Ovyr the perke to pryk.	128	Garnesche3	157
Require hym to convey yow ovyr the salte fome;	239	Speke Parott	302
OVYRTHWARTHE			
Thow demyst my raylyng ovyrthwarthe;	133	Garnesche5	136
OWE			
By the fayth that I owe to God, and I wyll syt styll.	203	Magnyfycence	2209
The seconde, to owe hym obedyence,	307	Why Come Ye	1124
To owe to yow our servyce, and more if we mowte!	324	Garlande	425
To owe her my servyce with true perseveraunce.	327	Garlande	558
My besy cure /To yow I owe;	338	Garlande	929
OWERS			
And all Scotlande owers	288	Why Come Ye	360
OWGHT			
Fyrst, I say, we owght to have in consyderacyon	141	Magnyfycence	43
OWLE			
The owle, that is so foule,	82	Phy Sparrow	442
is] not in Kitson 1560.6, Marshe 1568			
What the devyll hast thou on thy fyste? An owle?	166	Magnyfycence	922
Eche thynge is fayre when it is yonge; all hayle, owle!	167	Magnyfycence	970
What is this, an owle or a glede?	169	Magnyfycence	1047
OWLE FLYGHT			
Ye. My fansy was out of owle flyght,	159	Magnyfycence	671
In the owle flyght	366	Albany	312
OWLES			
Wherin he had apes and owles,	78	Phy Sparrow	258
Ye, for all thy mynde is on owles and apes.	171	Magnyfycence	1134
OWNE			
To slo ther owne lorde? God was not in ther mynde!	30	Dol Dethe	35
That his owne lorde bote	79	Phy Sparrow	305
Ye were beten weth your owne rod.	114	Scot Kynge	47
How they are blynde /In theyr owne mynde,	115	Ag Scottes	8
That was theyr owne kynge. /Fy on that wynnyng!	116	Ag Scottes	23
For youre owne tayle ye made a rod.	119	Ag Scottes	146
owne] not in Day 1560, Marshe 1568			
That fylythe hys owne nest.	129	Garnesche3	198
And you have not your owne fre lyberte	142	Magnyfycence	78
And now wolde ye swarve from your owne ordynaunce?	147	Magnyfycence	234
By God, syr, Foly, myne owne sworne brother.	172	Magnyfycence	1159
What so ever ye do, folowe your owne wyll,	185	Magnyfycence	1595
But do as ye lyst and take your owne way.	185	Magnyfycence	1604
Do as moche as for myne owne father.	186	Magnyfycence	1642
Who is this? Consayte, syr, your owne man.	191	Magnyfycence	1804
Why, wenest thou that I forbere the for thyne owne sake?	202	Magnyfycence	2186
Alas, myn owne servauntys to shew me such reproche!	205	Magnyfycence	2277
'Moryshe myne owne shelfe,' the costermonger sayth;	233	Speke Parott	85
But Parot is my owne dere harte, and my dere derling.	236	Speke Parott	208
dere] (2nd) not in Day 1560, Marshe 1568			
Expoundynge out theyr clauses, /And leve theyr owne causes.	249	Collyn Clout	101
Lay salve to your owne sore,	258	Collyn Clout	480
Presumyng on theyr owne wytte,	259	Collyn Clout	515
owne] not in Marshe 1568			
To theyr owne dampnacyon.	275	Collyn Clout	1140
The chefe of his owne counsell,	295	Why Come Ye	647
The kynges owne hande,	296	Why Come Ye	676
At his owne desyer.	303	Why Come Ye	986
And set hys crowne /On your owne heed	361	Albany	97
His owne realme to forsake?	367	Albany	328
Thorowe your owne foly,	376	Replycacion	84
Wolde God, for your owne ease,	377	Replycacion	114
OWR			
For in owr courte, ye wote wele, his name can not ryse	345	Garlande	1154
OWRE			
Out of fresshe Latine into owre Englyshe playne,	354	Garlande	1499

OWT
	Page	Title	Line
Owt of Frenshe into Englysshe prose.	347	Garlande	1220
Owt of her bokis Apollo to rase.	353	Garlande	1480

OWTCRY
Let not all the world make an owtcry;	43	Balettys2	40

OWTE
Youre key is commen and hangyth owte;	41	Coystrowne4	23
Ye ryme yet owte of reson;	127	Garnesche3	128
As he to exployte the man owte of the mone.	239	Speke Parott	307
He facithe owte at a flusshe with, 'Shewe, take all!'	243	Speke Parott	430
Nowe, Parott, my swete byrde, speke owte yet ons agayn,	244	Speke Parott	447
Of our noble courte is ones spoken owte,	353	Garlande	1482

OWTELAUYD
Ye ar a fole owtelauyd;	128	Garnesche3	183

OWUR
'Lyke owur pus catt Parott can mewte and crye.' owur] 'your' Lant 1545, Kynge & Marche 1554, Day 1560, Marshe 1568	231	Speke Parott	24
'Cryste save Kyng Herry the viiith, owur royall kyng,	231	Speke Parott	34
'With Kateryne incomporabyll, owur royall quene also,	231	Speke Parott	36
Owur new-founde A. B. C.	238	Speke Parott	277
To owur soleyne Seigneour Sadoke, desire hym to cum home,	239	Speke Parott	304
Now pas furthe, good Parott, Owur Lorde be your s[t]ede, stede] 'spede' †MS Harley 2252	239	Speke Parott	313
And sadlye salute owur solen Syre Sydrake,	240	Speke Parott	326
Of owur clerke Cleros. Whythyr, thydyr and why not hethyr?	243	Speke Parott	412
For of owur regente the regiment he hathe, ex qua vi,	244	Speke Parott	437
Ryn God, rynne Devyll! Yet the date of Owur Lord	244	Speke Parott	444

OXE
Lyke an oxe or a bull;	286	Why Come Ye	308

OXFORTH
At Oxforth, the universyte,	131	Garnesche5	81

PACHCHYD
Soche pelfry thou hast pachchyd,	128	Garnesche3	178

PACIENS
Agayne all remordes arme yow with paciens.	239	Speke Parott	298

PACIENT
And take pacient sufferaunce,	294	Why Come Ye	629
As pacient and as styll,	341	Garlande	1023
But under pacient tuicyon,	378	Replycacion	141
Sometyme under protection /Of pacient sufferance,	385	Replycacion	393

PACYENCE
But of your pacyence under the supporte,	183	Magnyfycence	1542
Bycause I wolde prove men of theyr pacyence;	194	Magnyfycence	1917
Afflyccyon and trouble to prove his pacyence;	207	Magnyfycence	2371

PACYENT
Under supportacyon /Of your pacyent tolleracyon,	62	Hauke	32
And under pacyent tolleracyon	93	Phy Sparrow	851
Under supportacyon /Of pacyent tolleracyon.	142	Magnyfycence	62
Syr, is your pacyent any thynge amendyd?	208	Magnyfycence	2387

PACYENTLY
Me pacyently to here.	143	Magnyfycence	111
Therefore poverte loke pacyently ye take,	196	Magnyfycence	2000

PACKE
And as for all other, let them trusse and packe;	190	Magnyfycence	1774

PACKINGE
Bot ther was fals packinge or els I am begylde,	31	Dol Dethe	71

PACKIS
Some lidderons, some losels, some noughty packis;	317	Garlande	188

PAGE
To poynte this proude page a place and a rome,	37	Coystrowne1	41
I have not sene suche anothers page -	60	Bowge	506
What! I have aspyed ye are a carles page.	148	Magnyfycence	288
Today a yoman, tomorowe made of page;	213	Magnyfycence	2547
For age is a page	279	Why Come Ye	32
A prince to play the page	369	Albany	416

PAGENT
By God, man, bothe his pagent and thyne he can play.	154	Magnyfycence	505

PAGES
I saye, ye devyllysshe pages	381	Replycacion	271

PAINE
They browght them in soche paine.	111	Lawde	35
Of his pleasaunt paine there and his glad distres	351	Garlande	1391

PAINT
And hath smale lust to paint?	339	Garlande	955

PAY
The commonns renyyd ther taxes to pay	31	Dol Dethe	78
With thi blode precious our fenaunce thou dyd pay	34	Dol Dethe	195
Put up your purs, ye shall non pay!'	40	Coystrowne4	11
Pay Stokys hys fyve pownd.	128	Garnesche3	185
'And therfore shall my husbande pay'.	153	Magnyfycence	461
Let me have thy dogge, what soever I pay.	171	Magnyfycence	1101
For theyr ale to pay;	218	El Rummynge	162
To pay for her scot	221	El Rummynge	281
'I dranke not this sennet /A draught to my pay.	224	El Rummynge	395
That she thyder bare /To pay for her share.	228	El Rummynge	546
Now nothynge but 'pay, pay!'	302	Why Come Ye	930
Now nothynge but 'pay, pay!'	302	Why Come Ye	930

PAYDE—PALACE

	Page	Title	Line
He must pay agayn	302	Why Come Ye	943
PAYDE			
By my trouthe, had I not payde and prayde, ...	150	Magnyfycence	363
What force ye, so that [y]e be payde?	187	Magnyfycence	1672
ye be] 'he be' †Rastell & Treveris C 1530, B			
For prestes and for lonys /Lent and never payde, ...	255	Collyn Clout	351
They were nat payde their hyre.	285	Why Come Ye	248
Theyr wages were nat payde.	285	Why Come Ye	253
And yet he payde before	302	Why Come Ye	946
PAYE			
But who wyll have it muste paye therfore dere.	47	Bowge	53
To paye for her expence.	229	El Rummynge	599
To paye,' sayde she, 'God wote, ...	229	El Rummynge	601
PAYED			
He payed a bitter pencyon /For mans redempcyon, ...	258	Collyn Clout	452
PAYMENT			
He trusted her payment and lost all hys pray.	42	Balettys1	13
And pynche at the payment of a poddynge prycke;	200	Magnyfycence	2122
PAYN			
Persyd with payn, bleding with wondes smart, ...	45	Balettys5	2
Wherfore he suffred payn, ...	297	Why Come Ye	739
PAYNE			
These feverous axys, the dedely wo and payne	44	Balettys3	9
Yet, and God wold, I wold my payne were easyd!	45	Balettys5	12
To kepe him frome pykynge, it was a grete payne.	52	Bowge	236
To holde myne honde, by God, I had grete payne;	61	Bowge	522
Never halfe the payne	72	Phy Sparrow	19
To my great payne and wo.	81	Phy Sparrow	365
Upon a great payne, ...	88	Phy Sparrow	654
Himself doth slo /With payne and wo.	95	Phy Sparrow	948
It wer a plesaunt payne	97	Phy Sparrow	1012
Wherfore I fere ye wyll suffre payne.	114	Scot Kynge	28
To cal me knave thou takyst gret payne.	130	Garnesche5	20
Endure? No, God wote, it were great payne.	147	Magnyfycence	248
So to be ruled by measure, it is a payne.	189	Magnyfycence	1739
Thy pleasure now with payne and trouble shalbe tryde.	193	Magnyfycence	1881
O odyous dystresse, O dedly payne and woo!	198	Magnyfycence	2053
Of thy throte bole, and ryd the out of payne.	206	Magnyfycence	2315
And skantly could go /For payne and for wo.	227	El Rummynge	514
But yf ye wolde take payne	265	Collyn Clout	763
God wotte, they take great payne	268	Collyn Clout	860
And have taken ryght gret payne	295	Why Come Ye	644
That shalbe to your payne?	368	Albany	370
Ye shulde take further payne /To resorte agayne	379	Replycacion	201
PAYNED			
So payned and so strayned	73	Phy Sparrow	48
Lorde, how I was payned!	99	Phy Sparrow	1123
I pray God they be payned	106	Phy Sparrow	1376
And payned you with a purgacyon of odyous poverte, ...	207	Magnyfycence	2353
My harte is so sore payned, ...	237	Speke Parott	254
But he was so payned in the hede	299	Why Come Ye	795
And so payned with pangis, ...	308	Why Come Ye	1182
PAYNES			
Such paynes dyd me frete	73	Phy Sparrow	58
God wotte, to theyr great paynes, ...	254	Collyn Clout	313
Yet have compassyon upon my paynes stronge.'	320	Garlande	299
PAYNFULL			
My dedely wo, my paynfull hevynes.	44	Balettys3	37
O rydlesse rewthe, O paynfull poverte!	198	Magnyfycence	2051
PAYNYD			
I pray God they be paynyd	350	Garlande	1369
PAYNT			
What, shuld I flatter? What, shulde I glose or paynt?	30	Dol Dethe	41
Suche problemis to paynt it longyth to his arte.	347	Garlande	1246
PAYNTE			
Paynte to a purpose good countenaunce I can, ...	160	Magnyfycence	724
PAYNTES			
That counterfeytes and payntes	269	Collyn Clout	920
PAYNTY			
And began to paynty /As though she would faynty.	229	El Rummynge	584
PAYNTYD			
And your payntyd Pleasure, Courtly Abusyon, ...	192	Magnyfycence	1860
Properly payntyd to be my coverture;	231	Speke Parott	9
PAYRE			
Comely he clappyth a payre of clavycordys;	37	Coystrowne1	36
And on the borde he whyrled a payre of bones, ...	56	Bowge	346
In a payre of fetters or a payre of stockys.	141	Magnyfycence	31
In a payre of fetters or a payre of stockys.	141	Magnyfycence	31
And therwithall convey hymselfe into a payre of fetters; . . .	178	Magnyfycence	1365
With a payre of heles /As brode as two wheles.	216	El Rummynge	83
And of pygeons a payre.'	228	El Rummynge	537
PAJANTES			
Soche pajantes with your fryndes ye play, ...	130	Garnesche5	37
PAJAUNTIS			
Of Pajauntis that were played in Joyows Garde;	351	Garlande	1383
PALACE			
In thy palace above the orient, ...	34	Dol Dethe	202
And thy palace, /Full of solace, ...	40	Coystrowne3	53

	Page	Title	Line
To purvey for our cardynall /A palace pontifycall	299	Why Come Ye	812
Of your royall palace it is not the gyse,	315	Garlande	121
Into the ryche palace of the Quene of Fame:	325	Garlande	450
Into a palace with turrettis and towris,	325	Garlande	459
Of elephantis tethe were the palace gatis,	325	Garlande	468
Then to this lady and soverayne of this palace	326	Garlande	491

PALAMON
As Palamon and Arcet,	87	Phy Sparrow	616

PALAS
Unto your palas, our noble courte of Fame,	318	Garlande	219

PALE
Mysdempte eche man, with face deedly and pale;	50	Bowge	137
That he loked pale as asshes to my syghte.	54	Bowge	293
My vysage pale and dead,	73	Phy Sparrow	60
Alas, my face waxeth pale,	80	Phy Sparrow	341
Ye wene that I am dronken bycause I loke pale.	147	Magnyfycence	259
Over the hedge and pale,	221	El Rummynge	264
That frownyd on me full angerly and pale;	322	Garlande	375

PALEYS
Home to your paleys with joy and ryalte.	214	Magnyfycence	2567

PALESTINA
In Palestina there is Jerusalem.	233	Speke Parott	81

PALETTES
I shall breke your palettes, /Wythout ye now cease!'	223	El Rummynge	348

PALYARD
With, 'Skyre-galyard, prowde palyard, vaunte-parler, ye prate!'	244	Speke Parott	433

PALYARDE
Suche a proude palyarde, /Suche a skyrgaliarde,	363	Albany	167

PALL
The carpettis within and tappettis of pall;	325	Garlande	474

PALLAS
She doth excede and pas /In prudence dame Pallas;	102	Phy Sparrow	1230
As I harde say, Dame Pallas was her name,	313	Garlande	48
The Quene of Fame to Dame Pallas	313	Garlande	R
Dame Pallas to the Quene of Fame	314	Garlande	R
The Quene of Fame to Dame Pallas	315	Garlande	R
Dame Pallas to the Quene of Fame	316	Garlande	R
The Quene of Fame to Dame Pallas	316	Garlande	R
Dame Pallas to the Quene of Fame	317	Garlande	R
The Quene of Fame to Dame Pallas	318	Garlande	R
Dame Pallas to the Quene of Fame	318	Garlande	R
Of noble Dame Pallas, wherof I spake;	320	Garlande	284
Avaunced by Pallas to laurell preferment.'	324	Garlande	434
Unto the pavylyon where Pallas was syttyng.	324	Garlande	448
Dame Pallas commaundid that they shold me convay	325	Garlande	449

PALSEY
That she was therewithall /Into a palsey fall;	226	El Rummynge	475

PALTOKE
Ye cappyd Cayface copious, your paltoke on your pate,	123	Garnesche2	6
Ye cappyd Cayface copyous, your paltoke on your pate,	123	Garnesche2	13
Ye capyd Cayfas copyous, your paltoke on your pate,	123	Garnesche2	20
Ye capyd Cayfas copyus, your paltoke on your pate,	123	Garnesche2	27
Ye cappyd Cayfas copyous, your paltoke on your pate,	123	Garnesche2	34
Ye cappyd Cayfas copyous, your paltoke on your pate,	124	Garnesche2	41

PAMFLETT
That lordes and ladies thys pamflett may behold,	241	Speke Parott	358

PAMPERDE
For all oure pamperde paunchys,	39	Coystrowne3	25

PAMPHELET
And of Soveraynte a noble pamphelet;	346	Garlande	1191

PAMPHILA
The noble Pamphila, quene of the Grekis londe,	336	Garlande	850

PAMPHILET
that this lytell pamphilet, called the Replicacion	373	Replycacion	I

PAMPHYLUS
Whate mone he made when Pamphylus loste hys make.	237	Speke Parott	234

PAMPYR
Thowghe he pampyr not hys paunche with the grete seall;	239	Speke Parott	309

PAN
Another there was that ran /With a good brasse pan –	222	El Rummynge	317
A fryenge pan, and a slyce.	224	El Rummynge	409

PANDAER
Pandaer bare the bylles	88	Phy Sparrow	682
Pand[aer], that went betwene,	89	Phy Sparrow	717
Pandaer] 'pandara' †Kele 1545.2, Wyght 1553, Kitson 1560.6, Marshe 1568			

PANDARUS
For to envyve Pandarus appetite;	336	Garlande	872

PANGE
To behold and se /What hevynesse dyd me pange:	72	Phy Sparrow	44

PANGED
For I am panged ofte tymes in this same facyon.	189	Magnyfycence	1734

PANGES
The panges of hatefull death	73	Phy Sparrow	62

PANGIS
And so payned with pangis,	308	Why Come Ye	1182

PANT
And prytely he wolde pant	75	Phy Sparrow	132

PAPALL —PARLYAMENT	Page	Title	Line

PAPALL
Before some prothonotory, /Imperyall or papall. . . . . 299 Why Come Ye 820
PAPALLES
And bulles papalles, ... 264 Collyn Clout 717
PAPER
And more paper I thinke to blot . . . . 299 Why Come Ye 826
PAPERS
So myche papers weryng for ryghte a smalle exesse; . . . . . . 245 Speke Parott 479
PAPYR
A reme of papyr wyll nat holde 134 Garnesche5 174
PAPPES
Wyth theyr naked pappes, /That flyppes and flappes, ... 217 El Rummynge 135
PARABYLL
For trowthe in parabyll ye wantonlye pronounce, ... 241 Speke Parott 364
PARABLES
Som sey they cannot my parables expresse; . . . . 242 Speke Parott 386
PARADYCE
In Paradyce, that place of pleasure perdurable, ... 236 Speke Parott 186
Paradyce this place is of syngular pleasure. . . . . 332 Garlande 717
PARADYSE
My name ys Parott, a byrde of Paradyse, ... 231 Speke Parott 1
PARAMOURE
'Ly styll', quod she, 'my paramoure, ... 41 Balettys1 3
PARATO
Quod Parato . . . . 234 Speke Parott 140b
PARBRAKE
As though ye wolde parbrake /Your avauns to make, ... 367 Albany 322
PARCEYVE
I parceyve well howe eche of you doth reason. . . . . 142 Magnyfycence 83
For dowtlesse I parceyve my magnyfycence . . . . 146 Magnyfycence 227
That he can nat parceyve . . . . 295 Why Come Ye 661
PARCELE
Note and mark wyl thys parcele; 132 Garnesche5 97
PARCELL
Perceyve ye this parcell? . . . . 142 Magnyfycence 55
PARCHAUNCE
Parchaunce halfe a yere; . . . . 295 Why Come Ye 637
PARCYALL
And your parcyall promotynge . . . . 273 Collyn Clout 1075
PARCYALLYTE
And say howe that we be /Full of parcyallyte; . . . . 276 Collyn Clout 1193
PARDE
Par[d]e, remembre whan ye were there, ... 60 Bowge 515
  Parde] 'Parte' †Wynkyn de Worde 1499, 1510, Marshe 1568
Parde ye be his homager . . . . 114 Scot Kynge 30
For he was, parde, ... 291 Why Come Ye 508
Juvenall was thret, parde, for to kyll . . . . 315 Garlande 95
In honest myrth, parde, requyreth no lack; . . . . 347 Garlande 1236
PARDY
Pardy, ye were his homager, ... 118 Ag Scottes 122
PARDON
To pardon thi servant and brynge to savacioun. . . . . 35 Dol Dethe 210
For largesse is a purchaser of pardon and of grace. . . . . . . 148 Magnyfycence 268
Nay. Purchace ye a pardon for the pose, ... 163 Magnyfycence 825
Your rudeness to pardon and also that they wolde . . . . 241 Speke Parott 360
So many bullys of pardon publysshed and shewyd; . . . . 246 Speke Parott 515
PARDONE
Syr, pardone me, I am an homely knave . . . . 53 Bowge 264
Why holde ye on yer cap, syr, then? Yor pardone ys expyryd. . . 123 Garnesche2 9
PAREGALL
Paregall to dukis, withe kingis he myght compare, ... 33 Dol Dethe 134
Paregall with all prynces, farre passyng hys estate; . . . . . 244 Speke Parott 436
Paregall in honour unto Penolepe, ... 337 Garlande 899
PARGAME
The ryche prynce of Pargame, ... 76 Phy Sparrow 192
PARIS
And of the love betwene /Paris and Vyene; . . . . 88 Phy Sparrow 664
Dowche Frenshe of Paris Parot can lerne, ... 231 Speke Parott 29
PARYS
And howe Parys of Troy /Daunced a lege moy, ... 270 Collyn Clout 950
  lege moy] 'lege de moy' Kele 1545.1, Marshe 1568
PARYSH
As well it becomyth yow, a parysh towne clarke, ... 38 Coystrowne1 58
PARYSSHE CLERKE
But that the parysshe clerke . . . . 272 Collyn Clout 1025
PARJURED
O Scottes parjured, /Unhaply ured, ... 362 Albany 125
PARKE
With, yes, by the rode of Wodstocke Parke. . . . . 174 Magnyfycence 1209
About hym a parke /Of a madde warke, ... 365 Albany 267
PARKER
But, lorde, how the parker was wroth with all. . . . . 351 Garlande 1386
PARKES
For some say ye hunte in parkes . . . . 251 Collyn Clout 192
  ye] 'they' †Godfray 1531, 'ye' MS Harley 2252;
  in parkes] 'partrykes' †Godfray 1531
PARLYAMENT
And suter to his parlyament. . . . . 118 Ag Scottes 123

	Page	Title	Line

PARLYMENT — PARROT

PARLYMENT
	Page	Title	Line
And suters to his parlyment.	114	Scot Kynge	31

PAROBLIS
Spekyng in paroblis, how the fox, the grey,	315	Garlande	101

PAROT
Then Parot moste have an almon or a date.	231	Speke Parott	7
Dowche Frenshe of Paris Parot can lerne,	231	Speke Parott	29
'Souentez foyz, Parot, en sovenaunte.'	232	Speke Parott	42
Collustrum now for Parot, whyte bred and swete creme!	233	Speke Parott	82
I pray you, let Parot have lyberte to speke.	233	Speke Parott	98
'But ware the cat, Parot, ware the fals cat!'	233	Speke Parott	99
Parot can say, 'Cesar, ave,' also;	233	Speke Parott	110
For Parot is no churlish chowgh, nor no flekyd pye,	236	Speke Parott	204
But Parot is my owne dere harte, and my dere derling.	236	Speke Parott	208
dere] (2nd) not in Day 1560, Marshe 1568			
Quod Parot, thy popagay royall.	238	Speke Parott	262a
Quod] 'Quid' †MS Harley 2252			
Now kusse me, Parot, kus me, kus, kus;	238	Speke Parott	265

PAROTE
Thou fowle, chorlyshe parote,	128	Garnesche3	167

PAROTT
Speke Parott	230	El Rummynge	1
My name ys Parott, a byrde of Paradyse,	231	Speke Parott	1
With, 'Speke, Parott, I pray yow,' full curteslye they sey,	231	Speke Parott	13
'Parott ys a goodlye byrde and a pratye popagay.'	231	Speke Parott	14
and] not in Lant 1545, Kynge and Marche 1554, Day 1560, Marshe 1568			
'My propyr Parott, my lytell pratye fole.'	231	Speke Parott	20
'Heghe, ha, ha, Parott, ye can lawghe pratylye!'	231	Speke Parott	22
'Parott hathe not dyned of all this long day;'	231	Speke Parott	23
'Lyke owur pus catt Parott can mewte and crye.'	231	Speke Parott	24
owur] 'your' Lant 1545, Kynge & Marche 1554, Day 1560, Marshe 1568			
In Greke tong Parott can bothe speke and sey,	231	Speke Parott	26
With, 'Parlez byen, Parott, ow parles ryen.'	231	Speke Parott	31
In Englysshe to God Parott can supple:	231	Speke Parott	33
supple] 'shewe propyrlye' †MS Harley 2252			
Parott saves habeler Castyllano,	232	Speke Parott	38
An almon now for Parott, delycatelye dreste;	232	Speke Parott	48
Thus Parott dothe pray yow,	237	Speke Parott	225
Now pas furthe, good Parott, Owur Lorde be your s[t]ede,	239	Speke Parott	313
stede] 'spede' †MS Harley 2252			
Parott, ye may prate thys undyr protestacion,	240	Speke Parott	336
Amen, quod Parott, /The royall popagay.	241	Speke Parott	355
Thus myche Parott hathe opynlye expreste;	242	Speke Parott	381
Nowe, Parott, my swete byrde, speke owte yet ons agayn,	244	Speke Parott	447

PAROTTE
Speke, Parotte, I pray yow, for Maryes saake,	237	Speke Parott	233
Passe forthe, Parotte, towardes some passengere;	239	Speke Parott	301
Thow ye be tauntyd, Parotte, with tonges attayntyd,	240	Speke Parott	343
Go, propyr Parotte, my popagay,	241	Speke Parott	357
Speke, Parotte, my swete byrde, and ye shall have a date,	243	Speke Parott	416

PARROT
'Que pensez-voz, Parrot? What meneth this besynes?'	232	Speke Parott	58
'Peace, Parrot, ye prate as ye were ebrius!'	232	Speke Parott	68
In Popering grew peres, whan Parrot was an eg.	232	Speke Parott	70
Parrot hath a blacke beard and a fayre grene tayle.	233	Speke Parott	84
Ware, ryat, Parrot, ware ryot, ware that!	233	Speke Parott	101
'Mete, mete, for Parrot, mete I say, how!'	233	Speke Parott	102
With, 'Bas me, swete Parrot, bas me, swete swete;'	233	Speke Parott	104
To dwell amonge ladyes, Parrot, is mete.	233	Speke Parott	105
'Parrot, Parrot, Parrot, praty popigay!'	233	Speke Parott	106
'Parrot, Parrot, Parrot, praty popigay!'	233	Speke Parott	106
'Parrot, Parrot, Parrot, praty popigay!'	233	Speke Parott	106
But Parrot hath no favour to Esebon;	233	Speke Parott	111
Above all other byrdis, set Parrot alone.	233	Speke Parott	112
Parrot pretendith to be a bybyll clarke!'	234	Speke Parott	119
Let Parrot, I pray you, have lyberte to prate,	234	Speke Parott	141
In Achademia Parrot dare no probleme kepe,	235	Speke Parott	162
That Parrot the popagay hath pytye to beholde	235	Speke Parott	167
the] 'that' Day 1560, Marshe 1568			
For Parrot to pyke upon, his brayne for to stable,	235	Speke Parott	184
Nowe in valle Ebron Parrot is fayne to fede:	236	Speke Parott	188
'Cristecrosse and Saynt Nycholas, Parrot, be your good spede!'	236	Speke Parott	189
Support Parrot, I pray you, with your suffrage ornate,	236	Speke Parott	195
Confuse distrybutyve, as Parrot hath devysed,	236	Speke Parott	198
For in this processe, Parrot nothing hath surmysed,	236	Speke Parott	200
Parrot is no pendugum, that men call a carlyng,	236	Speke Parott	205
Parrot is no woodecocke, nor no butterfly,	236	Speke Parott	206
Parrot is no stameryng stare, that men call a starlyng;	236	Speke Parott	207
I pray you, let Parrot have lyberte to speke.	236	Speke Parott	210
Parrot is a fayre byrd for a lady:	236	Speke Parott	211
When Parrot is ded, he dothe not putrefy;	236	Speke Parott	213
he] 'she' †Lant 1545, Kynge & Marche 1554, Day 1560, Marshe 1568			
Make moche of Parrot, the popegay ryall.	236	Speke Parott	217
the] 'that' Kynge & Marche 1554, Day 1560, Marshe 1568			
For that pereles prynce that Parrot dyd create,	236	Speke Parott	218

PARROTT—PAS | Page | Title | Line

	Page	Title	Line
Poynt well this probleme that Parrot doth prate,	236	Speke Parott	220
And remembre amonge how Parrot and ye	236	Speke Parott	221
Parrot sayth playnly, shall tourne all to dust.	236	Speke Parott	224
Prepayre yow, Parrot, brevely your passage to take,	240	Speke Parott	324
O My Parrot, O unice dilecte, votorum meorum	242	Speke Parott	376
Now, Galathea, lett Parrot, I pray yow, have hys date -	244	Speke Parott	439
Dixit, quod Parrot	246	Speke Parott	E

PARROTT

'Hec res acu tangitur, Parrott, par ma foye - '	232	Speke Parott	55
'Tycez-vous, Parrott, tenes-vous coye.'	232	Speke Parott	56
Dixit, quod Parrott, the royall popagay.	243	Speke Parott	404
Dixit, quod Parrott, the popagay royall.	244	Speke Parott	446

PARROTTIS

The progeny of Parrottis were fayre and favorable;	236	Speke Parott	187

PARSON

A parson benyfyced /But nothynge well advysed.	62	Hauke	36
Nor to expresse to his parson,	272	Collyn Clout	1036

PARSONS

Of such mysadvysed /Parsons and dysgysed,	62	Hauke	22
The pekysh parsons brayne	68	Hauke	225
Of parsons and vycaryes /They make many outcryes:	261	Collyn Clout	570

PART

Now have I shewyd you part of your proud mynde;	38	Coystrownel	67
I have told you part, but nat all.	299	Why Come Ye	822

PARTE

I wolde I had a parte /Of her crafty magyke!	76	Phy Sparrow	203
To shewe parte of my wyt,	142	Magnyfycence	58
Nay, that is my parte that thou spekest of nowe.	175	Magnyfycence	1282
Thou sawe never yet but I dyd my parte,	203	Magnyfycence	2228
Nay, nay, man. I loke never to have parte of his grace;	205	Magnyfycence	2297
She swynged up a quarte /At ones for her parte.	228	El Rummynge	569
swynged] 'swinge' Marshe 1568			
Let every man after his merit take his parte;	236	Speke Parott	199
And, for to say trouth, /A great parte is for slouth;	250	Collyn Clout	137
for] 'full' †Godfray 1531, 'for' MS Harley 2252			
But the greatest parte /Is for they have but small arte	250	Collyn Clout	138
But the moost parte in generall.	252	Collyn Clout	245
God wot, had lytell parte	292	Why Come Ye	513
All be it grete parte he hath surrendred	316	Garlande	150
But a grete parte yet ye have reservyd	317	Garlande	171
But...yet] 'Bot yit a grete parte' MS Cotton Vitellius E.x			
Meddelyd with murnynge the moost parte of his muse,	320	Garlande	295
murnynge] 'murmynge' †Fakes 1523			
Parte of there names I thynke to specefye:	321	Garlande	325
For of my bokis parte ye shall se,	344	Garlande	1139
sum parte of Skeltons bokes and baladis with ditis of plesure,	345	Garlande	R

PARTELET

Duke Theseus, and Partelet;	87	Phy Sparrow	617

PARTELY

Wherof partely I purpose to expounde,	325	Garlande	464

PARTYS

I am content so all partys be pleasyd:	45	Balettys5	11
I synge of two partys without a mene.	181	Magnyfycence	1463

PARTLY

Partly by your councell,	342	Garlande	1054

PARTLOT

With Partlot his hen,	84	Phy Sparrow	509

PARTRICHE

Fesaunt and partriche mewed,	284	Why Come Ye	222

PARTRYCHE

The partryche, the quayle;	82	Phy Sparrow	416
Fesauntes, partryche and cranes;	252	Collyn Clout	206
Some plucke a partryche in remotes,	268	Collyn Clout	867

PARTRYCHES

So many plucte partryches, and so fatte quaylles;	245	Speke Parott	486

PARTRYDGE

A plummed partrydge all redy to flye.	153	Magnyfycence	479

PARVERTYD

The wordis were parvertyd;	68	Hauke	229

PAS

That when ye thynke all daunger for to pas,	45	Balettys4	6
Or els I pas a peny to a pounde!	57	Bowge	394
I] not in Wynkyn de Worde 1510			
Because that she dyd pas	75	Phy Sparrow	151
that] not in Marshe 1568			
How commeth this to pas?'	77	Phy Sparrow	232
But my sparowe dyd pas	78	Phy Sparrow	266
And as that flode doth pas	93	Phy Sparrow	877
She doth excede and pas /In prudence dame Pallas;	102	Phy Sparrow	1229
Now pas furthe, good Parott, Owur Lorde be your s[t]ede,	239	Speke Parott	313
stede] 'spede' †MS Harley 2252			
Howe may this come to pas,	272	Collyn Clout	1021
And let our matters pas!	275	Collyn Clout	1159
matters] 'matter' Kele 1545.1, 'maters' Marshe 1568, 'medlyng' MS Harley 2252			
In Acon it was brought to pas,	296	Why Come Ye	706
And hathe his pasport to pas	299	Why Come Ye	803
But howe comme to pas	301	Why Come Ye	900

PASIPHE —PASTE

	Page	Title	Line
To pas the tyme in slowthfull ydelnes,	315	Garlande	120
To pas the tyme with, but let us wast no wynde.	328	Garlande	565
A tratyse he devysid and browght it to pas,	347	Garlande	1228
That laughed whan he dyd pas	379	Replycacion	187

PASIPHE
Lyke to Dame Pasiphe;	342	Garlande	1048

PASPORT
And hathe his pasport to pas	299	Why Come Ye	803

PASSAGE
Prepayre yow, Parrot, brevely your passage to take,	240	Speke Parott	324

PASSE
We wante no wynde to passe now over all;	49	Bowge	128
Your tethe teintyd with tawny; your semely snowte doth passe,	122	Garneschel	39
I wyll passe over the cyrcumstaunce	158	Magnyfycence	637
To passe the tyme and order whyle a man may talke	159	Magnyfycence	689
Mary, syr, so dyd he excede and passe,	178	Magnyfycence	1385
Let us here of your pleasure, to passe the tyme withall.	182	Magnyfycence	1518
What! Is the worlde thus come to passe?	200	Magnyfycence	2108
Passe forthe, Parotte, towardes some passengere;	239	Speke Parott	301
We passe hym in degre	308	Why Come Ye	1151

PASSE-A-PASE
For passe-a-Pase apase ys gone to cache a molle,	243	Speke Parott	413

PASSENGERE
Passe forthe, Parotte, towardes some passengere;	239	Speke Parott	301

PASSETH
That passeth all erthly good;	93	Phy Sparrow	876
all] 'all the' Wyght 1553, Kitson 1560.6, Marshe 1568			

PASSID
Whiche passid all other; wherfore I may	316	Garlande	159
Thus passid we forth walkynge unto the pretory	325	Garlande	477
It passid all bawmys that ever were namyd,	331	Garlande	674

PASSIS
'Withdrawe your hande, the tyme passis fast.	343	Garlande	1086

PASSYD
So passyd we forthe into the forsayd place,	328	Garlande	561

PASSYNG
Remembryng your passyng goodly countenaunce,	42	Balettys2	5
Of lusty somer the passyng goodly quene;	44	Balettys3	14
Illumynyd wyth feturys far passyng my reporte;	44	Balettys3	23
Ye, syr, passyng well.	142	Magnyfycence	56
Paregall with all prynces, farre passyng hys estate;	244	Speke Parott	436
Whos passyng bounte, and ryght noble astate,	336	Garlande	862

PASSYNGE
He bote the lyppe; he loked passynge coye;	54	Bowge	288
the] 'his' Wynkyn de Worde 1510			
Me, passynge sore, myne herte than gan aryse;	58	Bowge	425
That welthe and felicite is passynge small.	141	Magnyfycence	21
Ye, but some be full koy and passynge harde harted.	184	Magnyfycence	1583
That passynge goodly it was to beholde:	313	Garlande	42
Whos hevenly armony was so passynge sure,	320	Garlande	274
There apparell farre passynge beyonde that I can tell;	323	Garlande	394
'So have ye me far passynge my meretis extollyd,	324	Garlande	435
The beldynge therof was passynge commendable;	328	Garlande	589
Terrible of countenaunce and passynge formydable,	328	Garlande	591
The passynge bounte of your noble astate,	336	Garlande	841
Whos passynge bounte, and ryght noble astate,	336	Garlande	848
Many divisis passynge curyously;	336	Garlande	853
Whos passynge bounte, and ryght noble astate,	336	Garlande	855
Far, far passynge /That I can endyght,	341	Garlande	1016

PASSYNGLY
So ryally, so rychely, so passyngly ornate,	325	Garlande	487

PASSYON
For the passyon of God, let us go thyther.	204	Magnyfycence	2276

PASSYTH
How all thynge passyth as doth the somer flower,	312	Garlande	9
Thus passyth he the tyme both nyght and day,	352	Garlande	1423

PAST
In sesons past who hathe harde or sene	30	Dol Dethe	22
Syr, yf any worde have past	143	Magnyfycence	92
And whan foly cometh, all is past.	176	Magnyfycence	1289
With Mesure. Where as all noblenes is, there I have past:	189	Magnyfycence	1749
Then ye of foly in tymes past you repent?	209	Magnyfycence	2433
'Then ye repent you of foly in tymes past' †Rastell & Treveris C 1530, B			
Her youth is farre past;	215	El Rummynge	48
For he is well past and gone.	300	Why Come Ye	833
When they were past and wente forth on there way,	327	Garlande	526
Of your acqueintaunce I was in tymes past,	327	Garlande	540
Of cristall the clerenes theis waters far past,	330	Garlande	660
Of Exione, his limbis dede and past,	351	Garlande	1400
his limbis] 'her lambis' †Fakes 1523, 'her lambe is' Marshe 1568			
Good luk this new yere, the olde yere is past.	354	Garlande	1518

PASTAUNCE
But that I must wryte for my plesaunt pastaunce	42	Balettys2	4
And her goodly pastaunce:	99	Phy Sparrow	1096

PASTE
Though ye suppose all jeperdys ar paste,	45	Balettys4	1

	Page	Title	Line
PATCH —PEACE			
Your pryd is paste, adwe, good nycht.	114	Scot Kynge	43
PATCH			
For, as yll a patch as that,	219	El Rummynge	189
PATCHE			
A pece or a patche of philosophy,	374	Replycacion	3
PATCHES			
His cote was checked with patches rede and blewe; checked] 'checkered' Marshe 1568	56	Bowge	358
PATCHID			
With pitche she patchid her pitcher shuld not crase;	346	Garlande	1209
PATCHYNGE			
It is evyll patchynge of that is torne.	153	Magnyfycence	447
To prate for the patchynge of a pot sharde!	200	Magnyfycence	2124
PATE			
Ye cappyd Cayface copious, your paltoke on your pate,	123	Garnesche2	6
Ye cappyd Cayface copyous, your paltoke on your pate,	123	Garnesche2	13
Ye capyd Cayfas copyous, your paltoke on your pate,	123	Garnesche2	20
Ye cappyd Cayfas copyus, your paltoke on your pate,	123	Garnesche2	27
Ye cappyd Cayfas copyous, your paltoke on your pate,	123	Garnesche2	34
Ye cappyd Cayfas copyous, your paltoke on your pate,	124	Garnesche2	41
It semyth nat thy pyllyd pate	132	Garnesche5	89
I befoule his pate.	164	Magnyfycence	876
Leve thy pratynge or els I shall lay the on the pate.	201	Magnyfycence	2173
And 'Da racionales' dare not shew his pate.	235	Speke Parott	175
Hyt ys to fere leste he wolde were the garland on hys pate,	244	Speke Parott	435
PATENT			
Let neyther patent scape them nor fee;	190	Magnyfycence	1776
PATERNOSTER			
And wotteth never what thei rede, /Paternoster nor crede;	252	Collyn Clout	235
PATER NOSTER			
Let us now whysper /A Pater noster.	81	Phy Sparrow	385
Your Pater noster, your Ave, nor your Crede.	137	Ven Tongues	19
PATERNOSTER PEKES			
Of suche paternoster pekes /All the worlde spekes.	253	Collyn Clout	262
PATES			
Nat so hardy on theyr pates!	275	Collyn Clout	1152
Nor of some wytles pates	277	Collyn Clout	1245
PATH			
Shewe me the ryght path	78	Phy Sparrow	246
PATLET			
I plucked her by the patlet;	199	Magnyfycence	2074
PATRIARKE			
SOMETYME THE HOLY PATRIARKE OF DIS.	106	Epitaphel	I
PATRIARKES			
Olde patriarkes and prophetes in heven with him to dwell.	383	Replycacion	342
PATRYARKE			
Of Noe the patryarke,	78	Phy Sparrow	256
As patryarke or pope /In a blacke cope.	85	Phy Sparrow	528
PATTERS			
He chydeth and he chatters, /He prayeth and he patters; prayeth] 'prates' Kele 1545.1, Marshe 1568, 'pratythe' MS Harley 2252	247	Collyn Clout	22
PAULE			
In purple and paule belapped;	254	Collyn Clout	310
Gentle Paule lie doune thy sweard,	358	Couplet	1
PAULES			
Clothes of golde and paules,	270	Collyn Clout	941
PAUNCHE			
Her paunche was so puffed	228	El Rummynge	570
Thowghe he pampyr not hys paunche with the grete seall;	239	Speke Parott	309
PAUNCHYS			
For all oure pamperde paunchys,	39	Coystrowne3	25
PAUSE			
That I sholde use largesse. Nay, syr, there a pause.	209	Magnyfycence	2437
PAVES			
He was ther bulwarke, ther paves and ther wall,	30	Dol Dethe	48
Our paves, our succour,	111	Lawde	46
PAVYLYON			
I sawe a pavylyon wondersly disgysede,	313	Garlande	38
Unto the pavylyon where Pallas was syttyng.	324	Garlande	448
PAVYS			
shall be his protectyon, his pavys and his wall.	236	Speke Parott	203
PAWES			
Myght catche the in theyr pawes,	79	Phy Sparrow	288
PAWNE			
Neyther gelt nor pawne.	229	El Rummynge	610
PAWSE			
'Soft, my good syster, and make there a pawse. my good syster] 'goode my sister' MS Cotton Vitellius E.x	316	Garlande	134
PAWTENAR			
Wyth his polutyd pawtenar,	63	Hauke	44
PEACE			
And so was made the peace. the peace] 'the drunken peace' †Lant 1545, Kynge & Marche 1554, Day 1560, Marshe 1568	223	El Rummynge	350
'Peace, Parrot, ye prate as ye were ebrius!'	232	Speke Parott	68
Pratynge for peace peaslesse.	280	Why Come Ye	76

PEALE —PEND

	Page	Title	Line

PEALE
Thus to ryng a peale /Wyth his hawkys bels? . . . . 65 Hauke 136
PEAS
Ye, for surety. Ofte peas is taken for frayes. . . . . 163 Magnyfycence 814
A, holde thy peas! I have the tothe ake. . . . . 172 Magnyfycence 1163
Tushe! Holde your peas; ye speke lyke a dawe. . . . . 178 Magnyfycence 1379
Tushe! Holde your peas; ye speke out of season. . . . . 178 Magnyfycence 1388
Peas, or I shall wrynge thy be in a brake. . . . . 202 Magnyfycence 2187
Make noyse enoughe; for claterars love no peas. . . . . 319 Garlande 241
Sume sayd, 'Holde thy peas, thou getest here no more.' . . . . 319 Garlande 257
PEASE
Pease! I have not yet sayd what I wyll. . . . . 158 Magnyfycence 648
Holde thy pease! Measure shall frome us walke. . . . . 166 Magnyfycence 949
Pease, man, pease! /I rede we sease. . . . . 168 Magnyfycence 997
Pease, man, pease! /I rede we sease. . . . . 168 Magnyfycence 997
Some brought from the barne /Both benes and pease; . . . . . . 222 El Rummynge 313
Fede hym with beanes and pease! . . . . 275 Collyn Clout 1170
PEASLESSE
Pratynge for peace peaslesse. . . . . 280 Why Come Ye 76
PEASON
Ye wyll neyther beanes ne peason. . . . . 252 Collyn Clout 212
For Folam peason /With him be nat geson; . . . . 304 Why Come Ye 999
PECE
Sharpely commaundynge eche man holde hys pece. . . . . 47 Bowge 47
'Pece,' quod Desyre, 'ye speke not worth a bene! . . . . 48 Bowge 95
And tell can a great pece . . . . 87 Phy Sparrow 630
Tusche, holde your pece! Your langage is vayne. . . . . 147 Magnyfycence 251
Tushe! Holde your pece. . . . . 156 Magnyfycence 590
A pece or a patche of philosophy, ... 374 Replycacion 3
PECKE
What! Sholde you pynche at a pecke of [gr]otes . . . . 151 Magnyfycence 384
   grotes] 'otes' †Rastell & Treveris C 1530, B
Ye wolde sone pynche at a pecke of otes. . . . . 151 Magnyfycence 385
   otes] 'grotes' †Rastell & Treveris C 1530, B
And have here a pecke of ry.' . . . . 221 El Rummynge 275
PECKED
Thou pevysshe pye pecked, ... 294 Why Come Ye 609
PECOCKE
The pecocke so prowde, ... 82 Phy Sparrow 438
PECOK
Thow seyst I callyd the a pecok; 133 Garnesche5 128
Went with the pecok ageyne the fesaunt; . . . . 315 Garlande 103
PECOKE
With butterfllyis and fresshe pecoke taylis, ... 345 Garlande 1159
PEK
The doterell, that folyshe pek; . . . . 82 Phy Sparrow 409
PEKE
No. In every corner he wyll peke, ... 158 Magnyfycence 658
PEKYSH
The pekysh parsons brayne . . . . 68 Hauke 225
PELFRY
Soche pelfry thou hast pachchyd, ... 128 Garnesche3 178
PELLIT
With a pellit of pevisshenes they had suche a stroke, ... 330 Garlande 637
PELORY PAJAUNTES
So myche pelory pajauntes undyr colowur of good lawe; . . . . 245 Speke Parott 480
PEN
With my rude pen enkankerd all with rust, ... 33 Dol Dethe 142
And with my pen to wryte; . . . . 93 Phy Sparrow 862
That my pen hath enbybed . . . . 93 Phy Sparrow 872
Now Phebus me ken /To sharpe my pen, ... 96 Phy Sparrow 971
With pen and ynk /For to compyle /Some goodly style; . . . . . 96 Phy Sparrow 986
   goodly] 'godly' †Kele 1545.2
My pen it is unable, ... 102 Phy Sparrow 1219
And where my pen hath offendyd, ... 102 Phy Sparrow 1245
To guyde my pen and my pen to enbybe! . . . . 117 Ag Scottes 79
To guyde my pen and my pen to enbybe! . . . . 117 Ag Scottes 79
Defendeth with his pen /All Englysh men . . . . 135 Dundas 21
Either by language or with my pen. . . . . 137 Ven Tongues 23
I am Goddys preposytour; I prynt them with a pen; . . . . . . 195 Magnyfycence 1941
Nowe to withdrawe my pen, ... 277 Collyn Clout 1248
I have no pen nor inke . . . . 296 Why Come Ye 684
And for my sake spare neyther pen nor ynke; . . . . 327 Garlande 549
I me determynyd for to sharpe my pen, ... 335 Garlande 823
My pen I will avaunce . . . . 369 Albany 406
That I wrate with my pen. 372 Albany 523
PENALTE
Shall have penalte /For your iniquite. . . . . 258 Collyn Clout 461
PENAUNCE
Your penaunce toke no place, ... 379 Replycacion 198
Your penaunce was to lyght; . . . . 379 Replycacion 199
PENCE
By lakyn, syr, it hathe cost me pence . . . . 150 Magnyfycence 338
PENCYON
He payed a bitter pencyon /For mans redempcyon, ... 258 Collyn Clout 452
PEND
Mary, your speche is as pleasant as though it were pend, . . . 183 Magnyfycence 1538

PENDE —PERADVERTAUNCE   Page   Title   Line

PENDE
- Those maters that he hath pende; 92   Phy Sparrow   810
- In this that I have pende. 251   Collyn Clout   187
- But curteisly /That I have pende /For to deffend, ... 356   Garlande   1570

PENDUGIMS
- Whate sequele shall folow when pendugims mete togethyr? . . . 243   Speke Parott   415

PENDUGUM
- Parrot is no pendugum, that men call a carlyng, ... 236   Speke Parott   205

PENELOPE
- Of Penelope most stable, ... 89   Phy Sparrow   725

PENY
- Or els I pas a peny to a pounde! 57   Bowge   394
  - I] not in Wynkyn de Worde 1510
- Nay, offer hym a counter in stede of a peny. 172   Magnyfycence   1171
- Spare for no cost to gyve them pounde and peny; 190   Magnyfycence   1771
- With never a peny in his purse. 204   Magnyfycence   2258
- Of a peny nor of a crosse 269   Collyn Clout   929
- That men shall scantly /Have peny or halpeny. 303   Why Come Ye   968

PENY CHEKE
- And brought a peny cheke /To Dame Elynour 225   El Rummynge   415
  - brought] 'brought up' Day 1560, Marshe 1568

PENYLES
- So myche portlye pride, with pursys penyles; 244   Speke Parott   460

PENNE
- Avysynge me my penne awaye to pulle 46   Bowge   21
- Caughte penne and ynke, and wroth this lytell boke. 61   Bowge   532
  - wroth] 'wrote' Wynkyn de Worde 1510, Marshe 1568
- Your langage is lyke the penne 143   Magnyfycence   90
- My penne nowe wyll I sharpe, ... 259   Collyn Clout   489
- Dare nat set theyr penne 287   Why Come Ye   323
- What though my penne wax faynt, ... 339   Garlande   954
- Who list amende it, let hym set to his penne. 348   Garlande   1260
- That he our penne dothe lede, ... 385   Replycacion   385
- With penne and ynke procede, ... 385   Replycacion   388

PENNELL
- To maystres Isabell Pennell 339   Garlande   R

PENNY
- 'I have no penny nor grote 229   El Rummynge   600
- That had not a penny, ... 230   El Rummynge   612

PENOLEPE
- Paregall in honour unto Penolepe, ... 337   Garlande   899

PENOLOPE
- Or els Caliope, /Or els Penolope; 97   Phy Sparrow   1021

PENS
- What! Thou wylte coughe me a dawe for forty pens? 170   Magnyfycence   1060

PENSELL
- His plummet, his pensell, his spectacles of glas, ... 343   Garlande   1097
  - of] 'with' †Fakes 1523

PENTAMETER
- Set in better /Thy pentameter. 135   Dundas   6

PENURY
- For mysery /With penury /Myserably /And wretchydly 300   Why Come Ye   867

PEOPLE
- UNTO DYVERS PEOPLE THAT REMORD THIS RYMYNG 120   Ag Scottes   R
- And what maner of people he maketh foles? 174   Magnyfycence   1217
- But thus the people carke, ... 249   Collyn Clout   120
- I here the people talke. 254   Collyn Clout   288
- The poore people they yoke 254   Collyn Clout   323
- To here the people jangle. 255   Collyn Clout   330
- But howe the commons gronys, /And the people monys, ... 255   Collyn Clout   349
- The lay fee people rayles. 256   Collyn Clout   401
- Thus the people telles, /Rayles lyke rebelles, ... 257   Collyn Clout   412
- Howe the people are glad 259   Collyn Clout   512
- And better shulde remayne /Amonge the people playne, ... 265   Collyn Clout   773
- With all temporall people 271   Collyn Clout   982
- That the people talke this, ... 272   Collyn Clout   1049
- Theis people by me have none assignement, ... 317   Garlande   195
- As people halfe pevysshe, or men that were masyd. 319   Garlande   266
- Innumerable people presed to every gate. 329   Garlande   603
- and to preche to people imprudent perilously, ... 375   Replycacion   I
- As people halfe amased, ... 379   Replycacion   194
- And devyllysshely devysed /[The] people to seduce, ... 380   Replycacion   211
  - The] 'to' †Pynson 1528
- That people are in great dout 380   Replycacion   224
- To the people of lay fee, ... 381   Replycacion   267

PEOPLES
- This invectyve to make /For some peoples sake 120   Ag Scottes2   4
- In the peoples syght, ... 264   Collyn Clout   695

PEPER
- Take peper in the nose; 288   Why Come Ye   384

PEPIL
- The pepil durst not creke 111   Lawde   33

PERADVENTURE
- And peradventure I shall content your mynde. 142   Magnyfycence   49

PERADVERTAUNCE
- Faythfull assuraunce with good peradvertaunce. 210   Magnyfycence   2472
  - Faythfull] 'Faythfully' †Rastell & Treveris C 1530, B

PERCASE —PERYLOUS   Page   Title   Line

PERCASE
That cast such overthwartes /Percase have hollow hartes. . . .   121   Ag Scottes2   38
PER CASE
Yet sayst thou, per case   301   Why Come Ye   874
PERCE
Into Perce and Mede, ...   93   Phy Sparrow   886
As dame Thamarys, whiche toke the kyng of Perce, ...   336   Garlande   857
PERCEYVE
As well perceyve ye maye   81   Phy Sparrow   372
Perceyve ye this parcell?   142   Magnyfycence   55
Perceyve you not howe lothe he was to abyde   147   Magnyfycence   241
What this man hath sayd, perceyve ye his sentence?   210   Magnyfycence   2465
Well, I perceyve in you there is moche sadnesse, ...   210   Magnyfycence   2475
Perceyve the cause why: 290   Why Come Ye   459
PERCEYVED
And whan I perceyved /Her wart and conceyved, ...   98   Phy Sparrow   1063
And better perceyved, /And thankefullyer receyved, ...   265   Collyn Clout   770
PERCEYVID
And soone may be perceyvid   298   Why Come Ye   782
PERCEYVYNGE
Of Fame. Perceyvynge how that I was cum, ...   343   Garlande   1115
PERCEVERAUNCE
What, brother Perceveraunce, surely well met!   210   Magnyfycence   2458
PERCEVYE
Clerely percevye we may   281   Why Come Ye   119
PERCHAUNCE
Herafter perchaunce I shall   299   Why Come Ye   823
PERCIUS
As [Per]cius, that poete, dothe reporte of me, ...   231   Speke Parott   27
   Percius] 'precius' †MS Harley 2252
Percius presed forth with problemes diffuse;   321   Garlande   338
PERCY
Alas for pite that Percy thus was spylt, ...   32   Dol Dethe   106
PERDE
He dyd nothynge, perde, /But syt upon my kne.   76   Phy Sparrow   171
Yes, perde, man, whether that ye ryde or go.   176   Magnyfycence   1307
PERDURABLE
In Paradyce, that place of pleasure perdurable, ...   236   Speke Parott   186
PERE
This lordis dethe, whos pere is hard to fynd, ...   34   Dol Dethe   178
Of all women O floure withouten pere, ...   35   Dol Dethe   207
That hath non erthly pere?   96   Phy Sparrow   1001
In Arturys auncyent actys nowhere ys provyd your pere;   123   Garnesche2   24
With a pere my love you may wynne, ...   168   Magnyfycence   1015
Than wyll I say that thou hast no pere.   173   Magnyfycence   1195
So mangye a mastyfe curre, the grete greyhoundes pere;   245   Speke Parott   487
This daungerous dowsypere /Lyke a kynges pere!   295   Why Come Ye   640
PEREGRYNACIOUN
Of Mannes Lyfe the Peregrynacioun, ...   347   Garlande   1221
PERELES
O pereles Prince of hevyn emperyalle   34   Dol Dethe   190
   O] not in Marshe 1568
That pereles pomegarnat, Cryste save hyr nobyll grace!'   231   Speke Parott   37
For that pereles prynce that Parrot dyd create, ...   236   Speke Parott   218
This primerose pereles, this propre vyolet, ...   352   Garlande   1447
PERELESSE
Our perelesse president, ...   369   Albany   428
PEREMTORY
To make sommons peremtory   299   Why Come Ye   818
PERES
Some apples, some peres, ...   225   El Rummynge   438
In Popering grew peres, whan Parrot was an eg.   232   Speke Parott   70
PERFIGHT
Thow kit asonder his perfight vitall threde.   32   Dol Dethe   126
Of jentyll corage the perfight memory;   336   Garlande   860
   perfight] 'profight' †Fakes 1523
Of vertu and konnyng the well and perfight grounde;   336   Garlande   866
   and] (1st) not in MS Cotton Vitellius E.x
PERFIGHTLY
As perfightly as koude be thought or devysyd;   33   Dol Dethe   158
PERFYTE
So many trusys takyn, and so lytyll perfyte trowthe;   245   Speke Parott   491
   perfyte] 'profyte' †MS Harley 2252
PERFYTELY
Yf it were cond perfytely, and after the rate, ...   234   Speke Parott   143
PERFYTENESSE
With suche perfytenesse   271   Collyn Clout   976
PERIHERMENIALL
surmysed unsurely in their perihermeniall principles, ...   374   Replycacion   I
PERILOUSLY
and to preche to people imprudent perilously, ...   375   Replycacion   I
PERYLLOUS
A peryllous thynge, to cast a cat   176   Magnyfycence   1297
That was a peryllous rekenyng!   299   Why Come Ye   793
PERYLOUS
It is a perylous vyce, this envy.   58   Bowge   444
For clokyd colusyon is a perylous thynge.   159   Magnyfycence   695

PERJURED — PERTE

PERJURED
	Page	Title	Line
He is perjured himselfe.	307	Why Come Ye	1116

PERJURIS
All perjuris he wolde oppresse.	307	Why Come Ye	1114

PERKE
Ovyr the perke to pryk.	128	Garnesche3	157

PERKYD
That on the rode loft /She perkyd her to rest.	63	Hauke	70

PERKYN
Lord, how Perkyn is proud of hys Pohen!	37	Coystrowne1	19

PERLE
The pullyshed perle youre whytenes doth declare;	44	Balettys3	18
The orient perle so clere,	97	Phy Sparrow	1033
Enhachyde with perle and stones preciously,	313	Garlande	40
Of Margarite, /Perle orient,	339	Garlande	948
Sume praysed the perle, some the stones bryght.	343	Garlande	1108

PERLES
With perles and precyous stonys.	255	Collyn Clout	347

PERLESSE
For I am prynce perlesse, provyd of porte,	181	Magnyfycence	1471

PERLYS
Or eyndye sapher with oryente perlys dreste:	241	Speke Parott	368
perlys] 'prelys' †MS Harley 2252			
Fret all with orient perlys of garnate,	325	Garlande	485

PERLOUS
It is perlous for a horseman to dyg in the trenche.	43	Balettys2	26

PERMYT
But and you wolde me permyt	142	Magnyfycence	57
Me to permyt my mynde to dyscharge,	185	Magnyfycence	1590

PERMYTTED
For your selfe. Syr, yf I myght permytted be,	188	Magnyfycence	1720
Permytted? By saynt Luke,	272	Collyn Clout	1046
Permytted] 'Permed' †Godfray 1531, 'Now' MS Harley 2252			

PERPETUALLY
So shall your name endure perpetually,	336	Garlande	861

PERPETUYTE
All thynge compassyd, no perpetuyte,	312	Garlande	13

PERPLEXITE
What the cause may be /Of this perplexite!	106	Phy Sparrow	1370

PERPLEXYTE
I fere nothynge Fortunes perplexyte.	181	Magnyfycence	1461
Any man shulde be /In perplexyte /Of dyspleasure;	300	Why Come Ye	844
What the cause may be /Of this perplexyte.	350	Garlande	1363

PERS
Thou thynkyst thy selfe Syr Pers de Brasy,	130	Garnesche5	30
Symkyn Tytyvell and Pers Pykthanke.	175	Magnyfycence	1267
Pers Prater, the secund, that quarillis beganne;	330	Garlande	636

PERSE
Daryus, the doughty cheftayn of Perse —	181	Magnyfycence	1488

PERSEYVED
And well I have yt perseyved,	124	Garnesche3	2

PERSEYVYD
Alas, dere harte, loke that we be not perseyvyd,'	177	Magnyfycence	1349

PERSEVERAUNCE
But, Perseveraunce, me semyth your probleme was best;	212	Magnyfycence	2505
But hooly to perseveraunce my selfe I wyll bynde,	212	Magnyfycence	2507
To owe her my servyce with true perseveraunce.	327	Garlande	558

PERSIUS
As Persius and Juvynall,	133	Garnesche5	140

PERSYD
Persyd with payn, bleding with wondes smart,	45	Balettys5	2

PERSON
An honest person, I tell you, and a sad.	187	Magnyfycence	1690
In his goodly person /Lyke unto Absolon,	369	Albany	434

PERSONABLE
So thou arte personable to bere a prynces baner.	161	Magnyfycence	767

PERSONALLY
That we shall brynge you personally present	324	Garlande	418

PERSONE
Betwene the persone ye wote of, you —	59	Bowge	461
My persone prest /Beyonde all syse	164	Magnyfycence	844

PERSONES
Full subtyll persones in nombre foure and thre.	49	Bowge	133
Amonge all suche persones as I well understonde	161	Magnyfycence	739

PERSONS
Convenyent persons for any prynce ryall.	145	Magnyfycence	173
By me all persons worke what they lyste.	146	Magnyfycence	210

PERSPECTYVE
Encleryd myrroure and perspectyve most bryght,	44	Balettys3	22

PERSUACYON
Or it procedyd of fatall persuacyon,	313	Garlande	34
In settyng out fresshely his crafty persuacyon,	316	Garlande	153

PERSWADE
Home to resorte Jerobesethe perswade;	238	Speke Parott	279

PERTE
To be so perte to prese so proudly uppe.	48	Bowge	71
To be with you thus perte and thus bolde;	53	Bowge	265

PERTEYNETH — PHILARGERYA   Page   Title   Line

PERTEYNETH
That perteyneth to a kynge, ... 293   Why Come Ye   550
PERTELY
Ye pressyd pertely to pluk a crow: 130   Garnesche5   48
PERTLY
That with your lorde and mayster so pertly can prate! 149   Magnyfycence   305
PERUSED
If I have not well perused 92   Phy Sparrow   814
PERVAYLE
No stormy rage agaynst me can pervayle. 181   Magnyfycence   1465
PERVERTED
And good reason perverted. 256   Collyn Clout   373
PESCODDES
Or pescoddes they may shyll, ... 281   Why Come Ye   111
PESON
In a felde of grene peson 127   Garnesche3   127
PESTELS
Myghty pestels and clubbed, ... 225   El Rummynge   423
PETER
The apostyll Peter /Had but on pore myter 307   Why Come Ye   1139
    apostyll] 'wholly apostle' MS Rawlinson C. 813
For Peter of Westminster hath shaven thy beard. 358   Couplet   2
PETICYON
But that my peticyon wolde not be had, ... 353   Garlande   1486
PETY
Thefte also and pety brybery 177   Magnyfycence   1354
Syr, I beseche you let pety have some place 188   Magnyfycence   1712
PETYCYON
Graunt my petycyon, I aske you but ryght.' 318   Garlande   231
PETRARKE
Or Frauncys Petrarke, /Alcheus or Sapho, ... 90   Phy Sparrow   758
    Or] 'Or of' Kitson 1560.6, Marshe 1568
How Frauncis Petrarke, /That moche noble clerke, ... 296   Why Come Ye   687
Plutarke and Petrarke, two famous clarkis; 322   Garlande   379
PETRONYLLA
'My prety Petronylla, ... 253   Collyn Clout   259
PEVICHE
[Your] pride ys alle to peviche, your porte importunate; . . . 123   Garnesche2   3
Prowde, peviche, lyddyr and lewde, ... 133   Garnesche5   146
PEVISSHENES
With a pellit of pevisshenes they had suche a stroke, ... 330   Garlande   637
PEVYSH
This pevysh proud, thys prendergest, ... 36   Coystrowne1   6
Your pryde was pevysh to play such prankys: 119   Ag Scottes   150
PEVYSHNES
In pevyshnes yet they snapper and fall, ... 36   Coystrowne1   4
    they] 'the' †Rastell 1527
PEVYSSHE
Counterfet conscyence, pevysshe pope holy; 153   Magnyfycence   467
As she was pevysshe nyse. 229   El Rummynge   589
Thou pevysshe pye pecked, ... 294   Why Come Ye   609
As people halfe pevysshe, or men that were masyd. 319   Garlande   266
Sum were made pevysshe, porisshly pynk iyde, ... 329   Garlande   626
that popoholy and pevysshe presumpcion provoked them to publysshe   375   Replycacion   1
PEWTER
From golde to pewter /Or els to a newter, ... 301   Why Come Ye   904
PHALARY
Nother Phalary, /Rehersyd in Valery, ... 67   Hauke   198
PHARAO
Lyke Pharao, voyde of grace, ... 305   Why Come Ye   1066
PHARAOTIS
More stinging then scorpions that stang Pharaotis. 138   Ven Tongues   52
PHARASAY
And the Pharasay /Then durst nothynge say, ... 66   Hauke   152
PHEBUS
Of laureat Phebus holy the eloquence 33   Dol Dethe   160
Than Phebus in his spere celestyne, ... 47   Bowge   61
Chaseth away Phebus bryght, ... 86   Phy Sparrow   572
Now Phebus me ken /To sharpe my pen, ... 96   Phy Sparrow   970
Lyke Phebus beames shyne. 101   Phy Sparrow   1174
But Phebus was formest of all that cam theder; 320   Garlande   287
Concente to Phebus to have his herte in holde, ... 320   Garlande   292
In that faculte which shyned as Phebus bright; 383   Replycacion   333
PHEDRA
Phedra ye may /Wele represent; 338   Garlande   940
PHENEX
A phenex it is /This herse that must blys 84   Phy Sparrow   518
PHENIX
Men call a phenix; her wynges bytwene 330   Garlande   668
PHENYX
Of this phenyx kynde; 85   Phy Sparrow   539
PHERUMBRAS
Nor yet Egeas, /Nor yet Syr Pherumbras; 67   Hauke   205
PHESIK
By there phesik doth many a man ease, ... 352   Garlande   1427
PHILARGERYA
For Dame Philargerya /Hathe so his herte in holde, ... 284   Why Come Ye   206

PHILEMON —PHYLOLOGY   Page   Title   Line

PHILEMON
Anacreon and Arion, /Sophocles and Philemon, ...   90   Phy Sparrow   764
PHILIP
For the sowle of Philip Sparowe, ...   72   Phy Sparrow   7
Thus endeth the boke of Philip Sparow, ...   103   Phy Sparrow   E
PHILISTINIS
The Philistinis shuld hym ascry, ...   105   Phy Sparrow   1358
PHILISTION
/Philistion and Phorocides;   90   Phy Sparrow   766
PHILYP
Whan I remembre agayn /How mi Philyp was slayn, ...   72   Phy Sparrow   18
PHILLIP
Phillip myght be bolde   76   Phy Sparrow   177
Phillip wolde seke and take   76   Phy Sparrow   179
I pray God, Phillip to heven may fly.   86   Phy Sparrow   580
What ayle them to deprave /Phillip Sparowes grave?   103   Phy Sparrow   1275
I conjure the, Phillip Sparow, ...   104   Phy Sparrow   1290
Of Phillip Sparow the lamentable fate, ...   348   Garlande   1254
I conjure the, Phillip Sparow, ...   348   Garlande   1283
But, Phillip, I conjure the   350   Garlande   1355
PHILLIPPE
What ayle them to deprave /Phillippe Sparows grave?   348   Garlande   1268
I conjure, Phillippe and call, ...   350   Garlande   1335
PHILLIPPIS
No man to myscontent /With Phillippis enterement.   348   Garlande   1274
PHILLIPS
For rufflynge of Phillips fethers, ...   73   Phy Sparrow   79
  For] 'From' Wyght 1553, Kitson 1560.6, Marshe 1568
On Phillips soule have pyte!   86   Phy Sparrow   587
PHILLIS
Phillis and Testalis, ther tressis with oyle   331   Garlande   681
And how Iollas lovyd goodly Phillis;   354   Garlande   1497
PHILLISTINIS
The Phillistinis shulde hym askry, ...   350   Garlande   1351
PHILLYP
That Phillyp is gone me fro!   75   Phy Sparrow   142
PHILLYPPES
With Phillyppes enterement.   103   Phy Sparrow   1281
PHILOLOGY
Nor of philosophy, /Nor of philology, ...   292   Why Come Ye   517
in the moche studious scolehous of scrupulous philology, . . .   373   Replycacion   I
Nor philology, /Nor philosophy, ...   383   Replycacion   310
PHILOSOPHIA
Adew Philosophia, /Adew Theologia.   284   Why Come Ye   213
PHILOSOPHY
Nor of philosophy, /Nor of philology, ...   292   Why Come Ye   516
Boyce recounfortyd with his philosophy;   322   Garlande   359
A pece or a patche of philosophy, ...   374   Replycacion   3
Nor philology, /Nor philosophy, ...   383   Replycacion   311
PHITONES
Primo Regum expres, /He bad the Phitones   350   Garlande   1338
PHITONESSE
He [b]ad the Phitonesse   105   Phy Sparrow   1345
  bad] 'had' †Kele 1545.2, Wyght 1553, Kitson 1560.6, Marshe 1568
PHYLYP
But nothynge it avayled /To call Phylyp agayne   72   Phy Sparrow   26
Kynge Phylyp of Macedony   78   Phy Sparrow   270
Had no such Phylyp as I, ...   78   Phy Sparrow   271
For Phylyp Sparowes soule   81   Phy Sparrow   382
  Phylyp] 'Phyyp' †Kele 1545.2
I conjure, Phylyp, and call   105   Phy Sparrow   1342
But Phylyp, I conjure the   105   Phy Sparrow   1362
With me in kepynge suche a Phylyp Sparowe.   184   Magnyfycence   1562
PHYLLIP
For Phyllip Sparowes sake!   74   Phy Sparrow   103
PHYLLYP
Here after foloweth the boke of Phyllyp Sparowe   71   Phy Sparrow   I
That Phyllyp preserved may be!   74   Phy Sparrow   93
With, 'Phyllyp, kepe your cut!'   74   Phy Sparrow   119
Phyllyp, though he were nyse, ...   76   Phy Sparrow   173
Phyllyp had leve to go   76   Phy Sparrow   175
Farewell Phyllyp, adew;   80   Phy Sparrow   331
Caught Phyllyp by the head, ...   81   Phy Sparrow   377
That Phyllyp may fly /Above the starry sky, ...   86   Phy Sparrow   598
PHYLLYPES
Of God nothynge els crave I /But Phyllypes soule to kepe . . .   73   Phy Sparrow   68
PHYLLYPPES
My Phyllyppes dolefull deth!   80   Phy Sparrow   352
Dirige for Phyllyppes soule;   85   Phy Sparrow   562
An epytaphe I wold have /For Phyllyppes grave.   86   Phy Sparrow   606
PHYLLYPS
Me thought, of Phyllyps blode.   77   Phy Sparrow   226
PHYLOLOGY
My lady mastres, Dame Phylology, ...   232   Speke Parott   43
  mastres] 'maysters' Lant 1545, Kynge & Marche 1554, Day 1560, Marshe 1568

	Page	Title	Line
PHYLOSOPHERS			
Of phylosophers callid the princypall,	315	Garlande	128
PHYLOSOPHY			
*Or els phylosophy /Maketh a great lye.	83	Phy Sparrow	476
*Or] 'Of' Scattergood			
PHYP			
And whan I sayd, 'Phyp, Phyp,'	75	Phy Sparrow	138
And whan I sayd, 'Phyp, Phyp,'	75	Phy Sparrow	138
PHYPPES			
It was my prety Phyppes!	80	Phy Sparrow	360
PHYSYKE			
That sheweth yourselfe thus spedde in physyke?	156	Magnyfycence	556
PHOROCIDES			
/Philistion and Phorocides;	90	Phy Sparrow	766
PHRONESSYS			
Phronessys for frenessys may not hold her way.	232	Speke Parott	47
PICKE			
And Harvy Ha[f]ter that well coude picke a male;	50	Bowge	138
Hafter] 'Haster' †Wynkyn de Worde 1499, 1510, Marshe 1568			
PICTURIS			
Envyvid picturis well towchid and quikly.	345	Garlande	1161
PIERIDES			
With the nyne Muses, Pierides by name;	331	Garlande	680
with] 'wit' †Fakes 1523			
PIGEONS			
His hawke shulde pray and fede /Upon a pigeons maw.	63	Hauke	57
PIGGES			
May ete pigges in lent for pikys	306	Why Come Ye	1081
PIGGESNYE			
'What, and ye shal be my piggesnye?'	36	Man Margery	17
PIKE			
The devill tere their tunges and pike out their ies!	139	Ven Tongues	68
PIKYS			
May ete pigges in lent for pikys	306	Why Come Ye	1081
PILE			
To understande who dwellyth in yone pile,	333	Garlande	739
yone] 'yonder' MS Cotton Vitellius E.x			
PINE			
How the grene coverlet sufferd grete pine;	351	Garlande	1378
PIPLYNG			
There blew in that gardynge a soft piplyng colde	331	Garlande	676
PIPPLYNG			
of the moche vayne glorious pipplyng wynde,	373	Replycacion	1
PIRLYNG			
Sum pirlyng of goldde theyr worke to encrese	334	Garlande	796
PISANDROS			
Propercius and Pisandros, poetis of noble fame;	322	Garlande	382
PITCHE			
With pitche she patchid her pitcher shuld not crase;	346	Garlande	1209
PITCHER			
With pitche she patchid her pitcher shuld not crase;	346	Garlande	1209
PITE			
Alas for pite that Percy thus was spylt,	32	Dol Dethe	106
All merciles in the ys no pite!	32	Dol Dethe	122
As thou art of mercy and pite the well,	34	Dol Dethe	198
Well of pite, of mercy, and of grace,	35	Dol Dethe	215
PY			
By theyr conusaunce knowing how they serve a wily py:	43	Balettys2	34
PY-BAKAR			
Ye lernyd of sum py-bakar.	127	Garnesche3	111
PYCHER			
He may rynse a pycher, for his plate is to wed.	201	Magnyfycence	2168
PYCKE			
Fyrste pycke a quarell and fall oute with hym then,	55	Bowge	314
PYCKED			
Yet have we pycked out a rome for the.	154	Magnyfycence	508
PYCTURE			
Dyvysynge in pycture, by his industrious wit,	343	Garlande	1098
PYE			
The fleckyd pye to chatter	81	Phy Sparrow	397
But not worth thre skyppes of a pye.	113	Scot Kynge	10
Not worth thre skyppes of a pye.	118	Ag Scottes	100
For Parot is no churlish chowgh, nor no flekyd pye,	236	Speke Parott	204
Thou pevysshe pye pecked,	294	Why Come Ye	609
PYGEONS			
And of pygeons a payre.'	228	El Rummynge	537
PYGGE			
To a pygge or to a goose,	252	Collyn Clout	214
PYGGES			
The sowe with her pygges;	219	El Rummynge	176
Than swetely togither we ly, /As two pygges in a sty.'	220	El Rummynge	234
Than swetely] 'Thus swete' 1521 Fragment			
Hennes, checkynges, and pygges.	284	Why Come Ye	223
Lyke pygges and lyke hogges	364	Albany	214
PYGGES EARE			
Lyke a rost pygges eare,	215	El Rummynge	20
PYGGYS-NY			
What prate ye, praty pyggys-ny?	41	Coystrowne4	20

PYGYONS —PYNCHETH   Page   Title   Line

PYGYONS
To shake my pygyons federis   69   Hauke   281
PYKE
To pyke my lytell too, ...   76   Phy Sparrow   176
Ye. But I bade hym pyke out of the gate;   166   Magnyfycence   946
To pyke theyr fyngers all the day longe;   174   Magnyfycence   1222
And pyke a locke and clyme a wall.   174   Magnyfycence   1227
With my beke I can pyke my lyttel praty too;   233   Speke Parott   107
For Parrot to pyke upon, his brayne for to stable, ...   235   Speke Parott   184
Ye pyke no shrympes nor pranes, ...   252   Collyn Clout   208
Some be called crafty that can pyke a purse;   317   Garlande   184
  pyke] 'kit' MS Cotton Vitellius E.x
To pyke out honesty of suche a potshorde.   346   Garlande   1211
Ye pyke out many thystels, ...   380   Replycacion   220
PYKED
Pyked out of all good lawe, ...   306   Why Come Ye   1106
  of] not in Marshe 1568
PYKER
A bungler, a brawler, a pyker of quarellys!   37   Coystrowne1   35
PYKES
A pykes or a twybyll;   126   Garnesche3   72
PYKETH
Who so therat pyketh mood, ...   121   Ag Scottes2   21
  whoso] 'but who so' Day 1560, Marshe 1568
PYKYNGE
To kepe him frome pykynge, it was a grete payne.   52   Bowge   236
PYKTHANKE
Symkyn Tytyvell and Pers Pykthanke.   175   Magnyfycence   1267
PYLATE
Thow ye prate lyke prowde Pylate, beware yet of chek mate. . .   123   Garnesche2   7
Thow ye prate lyke prowde Pylate, beware of cheke mate.   123   Garnesche2   14
Tho ye prate lyke prowde Pylate, beware of cheke mate.   123   Garnesche2   21
Thow ye prate lyke prowde Pylate, beware of cheke mate.   123   Garnesche2   28
Thow ye prate lyke prowde Pylate, beware of cheke mate.   123   Garnesche2   35
Thow ye prate lyke prowde Pylate, beware of cheke mate.   124   Garnesche2   42
PYLCHE
And have here a pylche of graye;   224   El Rummynge   398
PYLDE
What pylde curre ledest thou in thy hande?   169   Magnyfycence   1054
A pylde curre? Ye, so I tell the, a pylde curre.   169   Magnyfycence   1055
A pylde curre? Ye, so I tell the, a pylde curre.   169   Magnyfycence   1055
PYLERY
And boyes to the pylery gan me plucke, ...   150   Magnyfycence   356
To preche out of the pylery hole   150   Magnyfycence   358
PYLGRIMAGE
A lovers pylgrimage.   100   Phy Sparrow   1155
On pylgrimage to Saynt Jamys, ...   102   Phy Sparrow   1242
  pylgrimage] 'pilgrimages' Marshe 1568
Makyng hys pylgrimage by Nostre Dame de Crome: 239   Speke Parott   305
PYLGRIMAGES
or to pray and go on pylgrimages, ...   375   Replycacion   1
PYLGRYMAGES
To worshyppe none ymages, /Nor do pylgrymages?   381   Replycacion   270
PYLL
They may garlycke pyll, ...   281   Why Come Ye   109
They make us to pyll strawes;   285   Why Come Ye   265
That he must pyll his lande   290   Why Come Ye   453
PYLLAGE
By pollynge and pyllage /In cytes and vyllage;   255   Collyn Clout   360
So /That rage must make pyllage   280   Why Come Ye   50
PYLLERS
Suche pollaxis and pyllers, suche mulys trapte with gold - . .   246   Speke Parott   517
Of birrall enbosid wer the pyllers rownde;   325   Garlande   467
PYLLYD
Your pyllyd garleke hed   125   Garnesche3   68
It semyth nat thy pyllyd pate   132   Garnesche5   89
Thow thou be pyllyd, thow ar nat sade.   132   Garnesche5   117
PYLLYNG
Suche statutes apon diettes, suche pyllyng and pollyng - . . .   245   Speke Parott   495
PYLLYON
Taketh his pyllyon and his cappe   266   Collyn Clout   803
PYLLORY
More mete in a pyllory -   266   Collyn Clout   812
PYLLOWE
Some a pyllowe of downe, ...   227   El Rummynge   531
PYNCASE
Some brought a pyncase, ...   227   El Rummynge   529
PYNCHE
What! Sholde you pynche at a pecke of [gr]otes   151   Magnyfycence   384
  grotes] 'otes' †Rastell & Treveris C 1530, B
Ye wolde sone pynche at a pecke of otes.   151   Magnyfycence   385
  otes] 'grotes' †Rastell & Treveris C 1530, B
And pynche at the payment of a poddynge prycke;   200   Magnyfycence   2122
Or elles ye pynche curtesy, trulye as I trowe, ...   242   Speke Parott   395
PYNCHED
She pynched her pynyon, by God, and catched harme.   191   Magnyfycence   1810
PYNCHETH
Whiche pyncheth him sore!   302   Why Come Ye   948

	Page	Title	Line

PYNCHYNG
So pynchyng and sparyng, and so lytell profyte growth; .... 245 Speke Parott 493

PYNDARUS
Pyndarus and [S]ymonides . . . . 90 Phy Sparrow 765
  Symonides] 'Dymonides' †Kele 1545.2, Wyght 1553,
  Kitson 1560.6, Marshe 1568
Lyke to Pyndarus in glorious poetry, ... 383 Replycacion 334

PYNE
Plucke up thyne herte upon a mery pyne, ... 57 Bowge 386

PYNED
That one was lene and lyke a pyned goost, ... 58 Bowge 429

PYNYON
She pynched her pynyon, by God, and catched harme. . . . . . 191 Magnyfycence 1810

PYNK IYDE
Sum were made pevysshe, porisshly pynk iyde, ... 329 Garlande 626

PYNNE
What! Is thy harte pryckyd with such a prowde pynne? . . . . 162 Magnyfycence 785
And ye may lese it for a pynne. . . . . 168 Magnyfycence 1016
A cage curyowsly carven, with sylver pynne, ... 231 Speke Parott 8

PYNNES
'Have here is for me, /A clout of London pynnes.' . . . . . 228 El Rummynge 564

PYPE
And drynke tyll we blowe, /And pype tyrly-tyrlowe!' . . . . 221 El Rummynge 292
They wolde pype you another daunce. . . . . 262 Collyn Clout 618
And pype in a quibyble, ... 368 Albany 389
We shall pype you a daunce . . . . 371 Albany 498

PYPES
With pypes of golde engusshing out stremes; . . . . 330 Garlande 659

PYRAMUS
Was betwene you twayne, /Pyramus and Thesbe, ... 72 Phy Sparrow 21
Pyramus, nor Priamus, nor Syr Pyrrus the prowde, ... 123 Garnesche2 23

PYRDEWY
He trymmyth in hys tenor to counter pyrdewy; 37 Coystrowne1 26

PYRRUS
Pyramus, nor Priamus, nor Syr Pyrrus the prowde, ... 123 Garnesche2 23

PYS
We supposed, iwys, /That she rose to pys; . . . . 229 El Rummynge 595

PYSPOTTES
O ye wretched Scottes, /Ye puaunt pyspottes, ... 362 Albany 120

PYSSE
Abyde, syr, abyde; I shall make hym to pysse. . . . . 204 Magnyfycence 2250

PYST
She pyst where she stood. . . . . 223 El Rummynge 373

PYSTELL
Shall rede there the pystell. . . . . 82 Phy Sparrow 425
Here is a pystell of a postyke! . . . . 158 Magnyfycence 649
Neyther gospell nor pystell, ... 252 Collyn Clout 237
In his pystell ad Paulinum, ... 383 Replycacion 325

PYSTELS
Of the gospell and the pystels . . . . 380 Replycacion 219

PYSTYLLERS
These be my pystyllers, ... 65 Hauke 121

PYTCHARS
And such as sell trotters, /Pytchars, potshordis. . . . . . 302 Why Come Ye 912
  potshordis] 'pouchers' MS Rawlinson C. 813

PYTE
On Phillips soule have pyte! . . . . 86 Phy Sparrow 587
All grace and pyte I lay in the duste. . . . . 205 Magnyfycence 2290
For truly it were a pyte that he sat ydle'. . . . . 318 Garlande 210
To banysshe pyte out of a maydens harte? . . . . 320 Garlande 308

PYTEYUS
Tellynge this pyteyus tale, ... 80 Phy Sparrow 342

PYTEOUS
This is a pyteous case: . . . . 262 Collyn Clout 626

PYTH
Yf ye take well therwith /It hath in it some pyth. . . . . 248 Collyn Clout 58
  take] 'talke' Kele 1545.1, Marshe 1568

PYTHE
To the pythe of the mater who lyst to resorte: . . . . . . 213 Magnyfycence 2540

PYTYE
That Parrot the popagay hath pytye to beholde . . . . 235 Speke Parott 167
  the] 'that' Day 1560, Marshe 1568

PYTYOUS
Go, pytyous hart, rasyd with dedly wo, ... 45 Balettys5 1

PYTTY
A man wolde have pytty . . . . 215 El Rummynge 39

PLACE
Let double delinge in the have no place, ... 34 Dol Dethe 174
With all the hole sorte of that glorious place, ... 35 Dol Dethe 212
To poynte this proude page a place and a rome, ... 37 Coystrowne1 41
And to purchace /Thyne hevenly place 40 Coystrowne3 52
Ye never dwelte in suche an other place, ... 51 Bowge 201
In no place well, but foles with hym fraye! . . . . 58 Bowge 446
  hym] not in †Wynkyn de Worde 1499, Marshe 1568
And in the holy place /She mutyd there a chase . . . . . . 63 Hauke 61
Correctyon hath no place, ... 66 Hauke 162
So curryshly to beknave me in the kynges place? 121 Garnesche1 9
I say, without largesse worshyp hath no place, ... 148 Magnyfycence 267

PLACES —PLAY

	Page	Title	Line
At what place, nowe, as you gesse?	150	Magnyfycence	342
And he that I came fro to this place	150	Magnyfycence	372
Let us departe from hens home to my place.	151	Magnyfycence	394
So he ruleth over all our place.	155	Magnyfycence	545
Of one thynge and other to occupy the place,	159	Magnyfycence	690
And so they go out of the place.	163	Magnyfycence	SD
COURTLY ABUSYON alone in the place.	163	Magnyfycence	SD
Ay warre and warre /In every place.	166	Magnyfycence	915
CRAFTY CONVEYAUNCE alone in the place.	177	Magnyfycence	SD
To se what foly is used in every place;	177	Magnyfycence	1327
MAGNYFYCENCE alone in the place.	181	Magnyfycence	SD
Syr, I beseche you let pety have some place	188	Magnyfycence	1712
Here MESURE goth out of the place.	188	Magnyfycence	SD
and leveth MAGNYFYCENCE alone in the place.	190	Magnyfycence	SD
She sat downe in the place,	228	El Rummynge	551
She had defoyled the place.	229	El Rummynge	573
In Paradyce, that place of pleasure perdurable,	236	Speke Parott	186
And to synge from place to place, /Lyke apostataas.	256	Collyn Clout	385
And to synge from place to place, /Lyke apostataas.	256	Collyn Clout	385
And put them out of theyr place.	273	Collyn Clout	1078
At the Commune Place,	287	Why Come Ye	319
And openly in that place	287	Why Come Ye	333
And Yorkes Place, /With, 'My lordes grace',	289	Why Come Ye	410
In whose place, /Dothe occupy,	300	Why Come Ye	850
And graunt him a place	303	Why Come Ye	970
In place alone then musynge in my thought	312	Garlande	8
That in my courte Skelton shulde have a place,	313	Garlande	59
In whose court poynted is your place.'	324	Garlande	420
Envawtyd with rubies the vawte was of this place.	325	Garlande	476
Unto this place all poetis there did sue,	325	Garlande	481
So passyd we forthe into the forsayd place,	328	Garlande	561
Paradyce this place is of syngular pleasure.	332	Garlande	717
Into that place where as they left me,	343	Garlande	1103
Of laureat triumphe, your place is here reservyd,	344	Garlande	1126
triumphe] 'promocioun' MS Cotton Vitellius E.x			
Forthwith she commaundid I shulde take my place.	344	Garlande	1142
That goodly place to Skelton moost kynde,	353	Garlande	1462
A pleasaunter place than Ashrige is, harde were to fynde, were] 'where' †Fakes 1523	353	Garlande	1465
'Nay, sir' she sayd, 'what so in this place	353	Garlande	1481
Ye wolde defoyle the place	367	Albany	353
Your penaunce toke no place,	379	Replycacion	198
To reverence in every place.	381	Replycacion	262

PLACES

So myche decay of monesteries and relygious places;	245	Speke Parott	499
To occupye suche places,	269	Collyn Clout	897
For all privileged places	306	Why Come Ye	1089
To places where ye have preched,	379	Replycacion	203

PLACIS

| All placis of relygion | 306 | Why Come Ye | 1091 |

PLACKE

| And lete us laugh a placke or tweyne at nale. placke] 'plucke' Marshe 1568 | 57 | Bowge | 387 |

PLAGYS

| I vysyte them and stryke them with many sore plagys. | 195 | Magnyfycence | 1943 |

PLAINE

| And if so hym fortune to wryte true and plaine, so] not in MS Cotton Vitellius E.x | 314 | Garlande | 85 |

PLAINLY

| Plainly, I can not glose, | 338 | Garlande | 910 |

PLAINNES

| And of your wyll the plainnes shew at large.' | 332 | Garlande | 727 |

PLAY

'What, will ye do nothyng but play?'	35	Man Margery	4
Strawe, Jamys foder, ye play the fode;	35	Man Margery	10
Play fayre-play, madame, and loke ye play clene,	43	Balettys2	41
Play fayre-play, madame, and loke ye play clene,	43	Balettys2	41
How my dysport and play	81	Phy Sparrow	373
Ye play Hop Lobbyn of Lowdean;	117	Ag Scottes	59
Your pryde was pevysh to play such prankys:	119	Ag Scottes	150
Your welth, your joy, your sport, your play,	119	Ag Scottes	159
Soche pajantes with your fryndes ye play,	130	Garnesche5	37
I cannat let the the knave to play,	134	Garnesche5	169
I wyll not use you to play with me checke mate.	149	Magnyfycence	307
By God, man, bothe his pagent and thyne he can play.	154	Magnyfycence	505
Thou hast made me play the jeu dehayte.	156	Magnyfycence	579
And I may tende therto for play;	168	Magnyfycence	1018
Can he play well at the hoddypeke?	172	Magnyfycence	1161
In a cote thou can play well the dyser.	173	Magnyfycence	1176
Ye, but thou can play the fole without a vyser.	173	Magnyfycence	1177
Why, wenyst thou that I cannot make the play the fon?	173	Magnyfycence	1185
What canest thou do but play cocke wat?	173	Magnyfycence	1191
For though we shewe you this in game and play,	195	Magnyfycence	1948
And not all the nygarde nor the chyncherde to play.	211	Magnyfycence	2492
Precely purposyd under pretence of play,	213	Magnyfycence	2553
Whan we kys and play /In lust and in lykyng.	220	El Rummynge	221
To lowre, to droupe, to knele, to stowpe and to play cowche-quale;	243	Speke Parott	426

PLAYE —PLAYNLY

	Page	Title	Line
They are fayne to play deuz decke.	250	Collyn Clout	166
But a chyldes play.	254	Collyn Clout	300
And play scylence and glum,	269	Collyn Clout	904
For ye play so at the chesse,	271	Collyn Clout	1009
And so it semeth they play,	277	Collyn Clout	1234
They play their olde pranckes /After Huntley Bankes.	285	Why Come Ye	266
And he wyll play checke mate /With ryall majeste	293	Why Come Ye	588
Lyke Mahounde in a play.	294	Why Come Ye	597
In the tennys play,	301	Why Come Ye	884
They play nat all clene,	304	Why Come Ye	1006
This joy excedith all wordly sport and play,	332	Garlande	716
wordly] 'worldly' Marshe 1568			
Sumtyme with sadnes, sumtyme with play.	352	Garlande	1424
A jentyll hownde shulde never play the kur.	352	Garlande	1436
A prince to play the page	369	Albany	416

PLAYE

	Page	Title	Line
Whyles she laugheth and hath luste for to playe.	49	Bowge	114
laugheth] 'laughed' †Wynkyn de Worde 1499			
'Twyst,' quod Suspecte, 'goo playe; hym I ne reke!'	51	Bowge	186
Twyst] 'Whist' Wynkyn de Worde 1510, 'Twysshe' Marshe 1568			
With us olde servauntes such maysters to playe.	55	Bowge	329
Sterte all at ones, I lyked no thynge his playe,	60	Bowge	502
But that they playe the daw	62	Hauke	8
And playe with me agayne.	77	Phy Sparrow	207
Gyve up your game, ye playe chek mate;	114	Scot Kynge	37
Than in Englonde to playe ony suche prankes;	114	Scot Kynge	51

PLAYED

	Page	Title	Line
I played with him tytell-tattyll,	80	Phy Sparrow	357
Hath played so checkmate	271	Collyn Clout	1012
Of Pajauntis that were played in Joyows Garde;	351	Garlande	1383

PLAYES

	Page	Title	Line
Counterfet eyrnest by way of playes.	152	Magnyfycence	427

PLAYETH

	Page	Title	Line
With the also? What! He playeth the state?	166	Magnyfycence	945

PLAYN

	Page	Title	Line
In playn felde and battayle.	364	Albany	205

PLAYNE

	Page	Title	Line
Howbeit the mater was evident and playne;	31	Dol Dethe	72
Mi wordis unpullysht be nakide and playne,	32	Dol Dethe	127
That neyther they synge wel prycke song nor playne.	38	Coystrownel	54
I can not flater, I muste be playne to the.	50	Bowge	164
I wolde noo thynge so playne be.	52	Bowge	214
And ever he sange, 'Sythe I am no thynge playne'.	52	Bowge	235
I wolde eche man were as playne as I.	59	Bowge	463
Then in a tabull playne /I wroute a verse or twayne,	68	Hauke	222
From Tyllbery fery /To the playne of Salysbery!	79	Phy Sparrow	321
This matter trew and playne,	85	Phy Sparrow	547
Playne matter indede, /Whoso lyst to rede	85	Phy Sparrow	548
The story telleth playne,	89	Phy Sparrow	696
But plesaunt, easy and playne;	91	Phy Sparrow	802
In Latyne playne and lyght,	92	Phy Sparrow	823
But yet certayne /I wyll be playne,	96	Phy Sparrow	967
Be] 'me' †Kele 1545.2			
That in wordes playne	97	Phy Sparrow	1008
Of that may come after; experyence trewe and playne,	141	Magnyfycence	11
Syr, of my maner I shall tell you the playne:	174	Magnyfycence	1219
A playne example of worldly vaynglory,	212	Magnyfycence	2514
But let us turne playne, /There we lefte agayne.	219	El Rummynge	187
But we wyll turne playne /Where we left agayne.	220	El Rummynge	242
Sette asyde all sophysms, and speke now trew and playne.	244	Speke Parott	448
Or yf he speke playne, /Than he lacketh brayne:	247	Collyn Clout	26
The temporalte say playne	250	Collyn Clout	132
Though it were never so playne,	265	Collyn Clout	765
And better shulde remayne /Amonge the people playne,	265	Collyn Clout	773
At my style rude and playne,	273	Collyn Clout	1088
Whiche determyne playne	277	Collyn Clout	1231
It is a playne recorde	300	Why Come Ye	848
As Skelton rehersith, with wordes few and playne,	353	Garlande	1466
Out of fresshe Latine into owre Englyshe playne,	354	Garlande	1499
With a worde or twayne /In sentence playne.	361	Albany	76
Never true nor playne,	362	Albany	134

PLAYNE DELYNGE

	Page	Title	Line
Playne delynge and I can never agre.	159	Magnyfycence	699

PLAYNE SONGE

	Page	Title	Line
His playne songe to solfe;	82	Phy Sparrow	415
To kepe just playne songe	82	Phy Sparrow	427

PLAYNESSE

	Page	Title	Line
Syr, the playnesse you me tell.	158	Magnyfycence	630
you me tell] 'you tell me' †Rastell & Treveris C 1530, B			

PLAYNLY

	Page	Title	Line
With one vice importune thei playnly said nay.	31	Dol Dethe	80
She is playnly expresse	100	Phy Sparrow	1151
To shewe you playnly the trouth as I thynke.	147	Magnyfycence	253
Parrot sayth playnly, shall tourne all to dust.	236	Speke Parott	224
To tell the trouth playnly,	290	Why Come Ye	460
As playnly it dothe appere,	307	Why Come Ye	1117
Whom fortune and fate playnly have discust	337	Garlande	881

PLAYST —PLEASURE	Page	Title	Line

PLAYST
Nay, come away, man! Thou playst the cayser. . . . . 162 Magnyfycence 787
PLAYTH
And what blunderar is yonder that playth didil diddil? . . . . 333 Garlande 740
PLANE
Foted lyke a plane, /Legge[d] lyke a crane; . . . . 215 El Rummynge 49
    Legged] 'Legges' †Lant 1545, Kynge & Marche 1554, Day 1560,
    Marshe 1568
PLANTID
And plantid it there where never before was none, unshred . . . 351 Garlande 1405
    it there where] 'yet wher' Marshe 1568
PLANTYNG
With plantyng of lekes . . . . 293 Why Come Ye 555
PLANTYNGE
In plantynge and pluckynge a propre jeloffer flowre; . . . . . 351 Garlande 1392
PLATE
As for his plate of sylver and suche trasshe, ... 201 Magnyfycence 2164
He may rynse a pycher, for his plate is to wed. . . . . 201 Magnyfycence 2168
PLATIS
Enlosenged with many goodly platis . . . . 325 Garlande 469
PLATO
Plato, but for that he left wrytynge behynde, ... 315 Garlande 126
    that] not in MS Cotton Vitellius E.x
PLATTERS
Brynge dysshes and platters, ... 217 El Rummynge 127
PLAUTUS
Plaut[us] in his comedies a chyld shall now reherse, ... 235 Speke Parott 176
With Plautus, that wrote full many a comody; . . . . 322 Garlande 354
    full] not in Marshe 1568
PLEASANT
Mary, your speche is as pleasant as though it were pend, . . . 183 Magnyfycence 1538
But blessed Bacchus, the pleasant god of wyne, ... 321 Garlande 334
But blessed Bacchus, the pleasant god of wyne, ... 321 Garlande 341
Enbrethyng of Zepherus with his pleasant wynde; . . . . 331 Garlande 677
PLEASAUNCE
Oft tyme after pleasaunce, ... 81 Phy Sparrow 368
PLEASAUNT
And of all pleasaunt thynges, ... 93 Phy Sparrow 868
And make a pleasaunt style . . . . 267 Collyn Clout 851
Of his pleasaunt paine there and his glad distres . . . . . . 351 Garlande 1391
PLEASAUNTER
A pleasaunter place than Ashrige is, harde were to fynde, . . . 353 Garlande 1465
    were] 'where' †Fakes 1523
PLEASE
Wolde to God it wolde please you some daye . . . . 53 Bowge 256
If it please you to loke . . . . 68 Hauke 233
Wolde it please you then - . . . . 143 Magnyfycence 87
Please it your grace to take no dysdayne, ... 147 Magnyfycence 252
Please it your grace at the contemplacyon . . . . 186 Magnyfycence 1633
Nowe leve, nowe lothe, nowe please, nowe dysplease; . . . . . 212 Magnyfycence 2520
Yf it please nat theologys . . . . 258 Collyn Clout 465
    nat theologys] 'the not onely' MS Lansdowne 762 'not
    theologi' MS Harley 2252
They had lever to please . . . . 269 Collyn Clout 909
Is glad to please, and loth to offend.' . . . . 323 Garlande 413
Whiche glad am to please, and loth to offende' . . . . 324 Garlande 427
Which glad am to please, and lothe to offende.' . . . . 324 Garlande 441
The menes to fynde /To please my mynde, ... 342 Garlande 1073
But what of that? Hard it is to please all men; . . . . 348 Garlande 1259
And that it wolde please her, full tenderly I prayd, ... 353 Garlande 1479
PLEASED
And ye se a man that with hym ye be not pleased, ... 185 Magnyfycence 1609
Nowe Measure is gone, I am the better pleased. . . . . 189 Magnyfycence 1738
Whether God be pleased or wroth. . . . . 307 Why Come Ye 1132
PLEASETH
And whan it pleaseth God, better may be. . . . . 196 Magnyfycence 1993
PLEASYD
I am content so all partys be pleasyd: 45 Balettys5 11
Truste me, with you I am hyghly pleasyd; . . . . 183 Magnyfycence 1535
PLEASYRE
Soo greate pleasyre, or who to you it gave. . . . . 53 Bowge 263
PLEASYTH
Nowe pleasyth you a lytell whyle to stande; . . . . 145 Magnyfycence 161
Pleasyth, your grace, Felycyte they me call. . . . . 145 Magnyfycence 171
PLEASURE
With them to make solace and pleasure; . . . . 50 Bowge 144
Loo, what is to you a pleasure grete . . . . 53 Bowge 260
He had no pleasure but in harlotrye. . . . . 56 Bowge 374
Some pleasure and comforte . . . . 77 Phy Sparrow 217
All way to have pleasure. . . . . 81 Phy Sparrow 371
Confort, pleasure, and solace, ... 96 Phy Sparrow 1004
With wordes of pleasure . . . . 99 Phy Sparrow 1099
Dame Venus of all pleasure, ... 102 Phy Sparrow 1227
As my soverayne /Moost of pleasure. . . . . 113 Calliope 24
Hys noble pleasure and commandemennt, ... 134 Garnesche5 178
To sporte at your pleasure, to ryn, and to ryde? . . . . . . 142 Magnyfycence 79
We your pleasure fulfyll. . . . . 143 Magnyfycence 106
Wherin it is necessary my pleasure you knowe: . . . . 145 Magnyfycence 185

PLEASURES —PLESYRE

	Page	Title	Line
As in that I wyll not be agaynst your pleasure.	148	Magnyfycence	276
Your pleasure, syr shortely shall be done.	149	Magnyfycence	321
Counterfet pleasure is borne out by me;	153	Magnyfycence	475
My speche is all pleasure, but I stynge lyke a waspe.	160	Magnyfycence	730
Al of pleasure /My hose strayte tyde;	164	Magnyfycence	851
Mary, Lusty Pleasure, by myne advyse,	167	Magnyfycence	964
Nowe thou hast done me a pleasure grete.	171	Magnyfycence	1131
Syr, I am here at your pleasure.	179	Magnyfycence	1409
Whom? Lusty Pleasure or mery Consayte?	180	Magnyfycence	1452
Nay, fyrst Lusty Pleasure is my desyre to have;	180	Magnyfycence	1453
Welcom, Pleasure, to our magnyfycence.	182	Magnyfycence	1516
Let us here of your pleasure, to passe the tyme withall.	182	Magnyfycence	1518
Any thynge to do that myght be to your pleasure.	183	Magnyfycence	1528
As I be saved, with pleasure I am supprysyd	183	Magnyfycence	1529
Poynt devyse, all pleasure is your porte.	183	Magnyfycence	1540
It is semynge your pleasure ye delyte,	183	Magnyfycence	1546
Take your pleasure and use free lyberte;	185	Magnyfycence	1598
It is a pryncely pleasure and a lordly mynde.	186	Magnyfycence	1627
Come hyder, Pleasure; you shall here myne entent.	186	Magnyfycence	1655
Cockes armes, howe Pleasure plucked hym forth!	189	Magnyfycence	1735
For in Pleasure and Surveyaunce and also in the,	190	Magnyfycence	1787
And your payntyd Pleasure, Courtly Abusyon,	192	Magnyfycence	1860
Thy pleasure now with payne and trouble shalbe tryde.	193	Magnyfycence	1881
Where is nowe all my pleasure and my worldly good?	198	Magnyfycence	2061
And spende C s. for the pleasure of a knave.	200	Magnyfycence	2126
For to understande your pleasure and also your mynde.	209	Magnyfycence	2420
Nowe pleasure at large, nowe in captyvyte;	212	Magnyfycence	2519
My delyght is solas, pleasure, dysporte and pley;	233	Speke Parott	108
In Paradyce, that place of pleasure perdurable,	236	Speke Parott	186
And yet that is a pleasure.	250	Collyn Clout	146
But at the pleasure of one	272	Collyn Clout	1018
At our pleasure and wyll.	276	Collyn Clout	1216
our] 'your' Kele 1545.1, Marshe 1568, 'owur' MS Harley 2252			
Whan that his pleasure is.	278	Collyn Clout	1265
And of his noble pleasure	292	Why Come Ye	547
solacyous and ryght pregnant allectyues of syngular pleasure,	312	Garlande	1
Displease not an hundreth for one mannes pleasure.	314	Garlande	90
A poete somtyme may for his pleasure taunt,	315	Garlande	100
So am I supprysyd with pleasure and delyght	327	Garlande	537
For her pleasure to make a large profer,	327	Garlande	556
Here dwellith pleasure, with lust and delyte;	332	Garlande	709
Paradyce this place is of syngular pleasure.	332	Garlande	717
For your pleasure do there endevourment,	335	Garlande	810
Vertu, conyng, solace, pleasure, comforte.	337	Garlande	898
Vertu, connyng, solace, pleasure, comforte.	337	Garlande	905

PLEASURES
Such pleasures that I may	101	Phy Sparrow	1196

PLEASURS
With syngular pleasurs to dryve away the tyme,	326	Garlande	524

PLEDGE
Some layde to pledge /Theyr hatchet and theyr wedge,	221	El Rummynge	293
They layde to pledge theyr wharrowe,	222	El Rummynge	298

PLEGE
And tyll I come, have, here is myne hat to plege.'	57	Bowge	413
is] not in Marshe 1568			

PLEY
Soche pollyng pajaunttis ye pley,	129	Garnesche3	190
Thow wrythtyst I xulde let the go pley;	134	Garnesche5	166
Go pley the, Garnyshe, garnysshed gay!	134	Garnesche5	167
My delyght is solas, pleasure, dysporte and pley;	233	Speke Parott	108

PLENARELY
For now am I plenarely dysposed	52	Bowge	216

PLENARLY
But plenarly all thought from you must be dyschargyd,	146	Magnyfycence	207
And whan Lucina plenarly did shyne,	312	Garlande	6
plenarly] 'plenary' †Fakes 1523, Marshe 1568			

PLENTE
Kyndle in me suche plente of thy nobles,	29	Dol Dethe	20
Plente of yll, of goodnes skant,	40	Coystrowne4	3

PLENTY
Where measure is mayster, plenty dothe none offence;	144	Magnyfycence	121

PLESANT
She was nothynge plesant;	227	El Rummynge	518

PLESAUNT
But that I must wryte for my plesaunt pastaunce	42	Balettys2	4
With whom he ledd a plesaunt life;	90	Phy Sparrow	744
But plesaunt, easy and playne;	91	Phy Sparrow	802
It wer a plesaunt payne	97	Phy Sparrow	1012
Welthe, with Measure and plesaunt Lyberte.	145	Magnyfycence	160
Is lusty to loke on, plesaunt, demure, and sage.	337	Garlande	877

PLESAUNTE
Is lusty to loke on, plesaunte, demure, and sage:	336	Garlande	870

PLESAUNTLY
My heyre bussheth /So plesauntly;	163	Magnyfycence	836
In goodly wordes plesauntly comprysid,	335	Garlande	813

PLESYRE
Whome she loveth, of all plesyre is ryche	49	Bowge	113

PLESYTH—PLUTO   Page   Title   Line

PLESYTH
It plesyth that noble prince roiall 132   Garnesche5   103
Plesyth it your grace to shewe what I do shall? 182   Magnyfycence   1517

PLESURE
Agayne the kingis plesure to wrastel or to wringe. 31   Dol Dethe   82
Transendyng plesure, surmountyng all dysporte; 43   Balettys3   7
Fraghted with plesure to what ye coude devyse. 47   Bowge   42
Longe to enjoy plesure, delyght, and lust: 337   Garlande   882
sum parte of Skeltons bokes and baladis with ditis of plesure, 345   Garlande   R

PLETE
It is foly agaynst God for to plete. 197   Magnyfycence   2035
To plete a trew tryall 287   Why Come Ye   324

PLETES
And gyrdeth in her gytes /Stytched and pranked with pletes; . . 216   El Rummynge   69

PLETYNGE
In pletynge of theyr case 287   Why Come Ye   318

PLIADES
Of Pliades he prechid with ther drowsy chere, ... 331   Garlande   697

PLINNI
Plinni sheweth all /In his Story Naturall, ... 85   Phy Sparrow   536

PLOVER
The plover with us to wayle; 82   Phy Sparrow   417

PLUCK
And as she at her dyd pluck, ... 227   El Rummynge   504
    And] not in Day 1560, Marshe 1568; pluck] 'pulck' †Lant 1545

PLUCKE
Plucke up thyne herte upon a mery pyne, ... 57   Bowge   386
Might plucke away thyne eares! 79   Phy Sparrow   310
Plucke up your mynde, syr, what ayle you to muse? 148   Magnyfycence   283
And boyes to the pylery gan me plucke, ... 150   Magnyfycence   356
Plucke down lede and theke with tyle; 169   Magnyfycence   1026
Plucke downe an house and set up a rafter, ... 169   Magnyfycence   1032
Plucke from a hundred, and gyve it to thre; 190   Magnyfycence   1775
I plucke downe kynge, prynce, lorde, and knyght; 193   Magnyfycence   1883
The pot to her plucke, ... 228   El Rummynge   566
Whyche of yow fyrste dare boldlye plucke the crowe. 242   Speke Parott   396
But plucke away and pull /Theyr fleces of wull. 248   Collyn Clout   78
Plucke away the leedes /Over theyr heedes, ... 257   Collyn Clout   408
Some plucke a partryche in remotes, ... 268   Collyn Clout   867

PLUCKED
That plucked Acteon to the grounde, ... 79   Phy Sparrow   297
He plucked the bull /By the horned skull, ... 104   Phy Sparrow   1318
For pryde hath plucked the by the nose 163   Magnyfycence   826
Cockes armes, howe Pleasure plucked hym forth! 189   Magnyfycence   1735
I plucked her by the patlet; 199   Magnyfycence   2074
He plucked hym backe, and he went afore. 319   Garlande   254

PLUCKES
He pluckes them by the hode, ... 286   Why Come Ye   304

PLUCKETH
Whom now and then /He plucketh by the hede 84   Phy Sparrow   511

PLUCKID
He pluckid the bull /By the hornid scull, ... 349   Garlande   1311

PLUCKYD
Sodenly set up and sodenly pluckyd downe; 197   Magnyfycence   2025

PLUCKYNGE
With pollynge and pluckynge out of all measure, ... 189   Magnyfycence   1753
In plantynge and pluckynge a propre jeloffer flowre; 351   Garlande   1392

PLUCTE
He had plucte oute the nobles of my pouche. 60   Bowge   504
So many plucte partryches, and so fatte quaylles; 245   Speke Parott   486

PLUK
Ye pressyd pertely to pluk a crow: 130   Garnesche5   48

PLUMMED
A plummed partrydge all redy to flye. 153   Magnyfycence   479

PLUMMET
His plummet, his pensell, his spectacles of glas, ... 343   Garlande   1097
    of] 'with' †Fakes 1523

PLUMMIS
Ye rebads nat worth two plummis! 294   Why Come Ye   604

PLUMMOUTH
Of Dertmouth, of Plummouth, of Portismouth also; 326   Garlande   513

PLUMPE
A thowsande thowsande I sawe on a plumpe. 319   Garlande   258

PLUNGYD
Of thoughtfull hertys plungyd in dystres; 44   Balettys3   10

PLURALYTES
And qualyfyed qualytes /Of pluralytes, ... 260   Collyn Clout   561

PLUTARKE
Plutarke and Petrarke, two famous clarkis; 322   Garlande   379

PLUTHARKE
Of Ovyd or Virgyll, /Or of Plutharke, ... 90   Phy Sparrow   757

PLUTO
And from the great Pluto, ... 73   Phy Sparrow   72
And Thesius, th[at] prowde was Pluto to face - 182   Magnyfycence   1496
    that] 'the' †Rastell & Treveris C 1530, B
To Pluto and Syr Bellyall, ... 299   Why Come Ye   806

PLUTOS —POETIS   Page   Title   Line

PLUTOS
	Page	Title	Line
In Plut[o]s gastly tower;	104	Phy Sparrow	1323
Plutos] 'Plutus' editions			
In Plutos gastly towre;	349	Garlande	1316

POCENYA
Pocenya, the prowde provoste of Turky lande,	181	Magnyfycence	1480

POCIOUN
But sith he hath tastid of the sugred pocioun	314	Garlande	73

POCKY
Full of pocky molys.	285	Why Come Ye	246
Men wene that he is pocky,	308	Why Come Ye	1170
wene that] 'say' MS Rawlinson C. 813			
From the puskylde pocky pose,	309	Why Come Ye	1195
puskylde] 'pusky' MS Rawlinson C. 813; pose] 'nose' Kitson 1560.7			

PODDYNGE PRYCKE
And pynche at the payment of a poddynge prycke;	200	Magnyfycence	2122

PODE
'Be Gad, ye be a praty pode,	35	Man Margery	8

PODYNGES
Some podynges and lynkes,	225	El Rummynge	443

POEMIS
The poemis and storis auncient inbryngis	331	Garlande	689

POEMYS
And howe your poemys arre barayne of polyshed eloquens,	240	Speke Parott	316

POEMS
Of hevenly poems, O Clyo, calde by name	29	Dol Dethe	8
Of aureat poems they want ellumynynge;	32	Dol Dethe	128
the ix Musys of polytyke poems and poettys matryculat.	36	Coystrowne	I
Than with my poems for to melle.	132	Garnesche5	94

POESY
In poesy to endyte /And eloquently to wryte,	75	Phy Sparrow	152

POETA
Poeta Skelton to Maister Gower	323	Garlande	R
Poeta Skelton answeryth	324	Garlande	R
Poeta Skelton answeryth	324	Garlande	R
Poeta Skelton	353	Garlande	R

POETE
compyled by Mayster Skelton, poete laureate	71	Phy Sparrow	I
Illumyn me, your poete and your scrybe,	117	Ag Scottes	80
As [Per]cius, that poete, dothe reporte of me,	231	Speke Parott	27
Percius] 'precius' †MS Harley 2252			
compyled by Mayster Skelton, Poete Laureate	278	Why Come Ye	I
by Mayster Skelton, Poete Laureat,	312	Garlande	I
A poete somtyme may for his pleasure taunt,	315	Garlande	100
'Of your oratour and poete laureate	345	Garlande	1170
dyvysed by Mayster Skelton, Poete Laureat.	358	Garlande2	R
Poete of poetes all, /And prophete princypall.	383	Replycacion	321
Of poetes chefe poete, saint Jerome dothe wright,	383	Replycacion	330
Resembled to Symonides, that poete lyricall	383	Replycacion	331
Symonides] 'Symphonides' †Pynson 1528			
For Davyd, our poete, harped so meloudiously	383	Replycacion	339

POETE LAWREATE
I was made poete lawreate.	131	Garnesche5	84

POETES
Of poetes olde, whyche, full craftely,	46	Bowge	9
As famous poetes say;	74	Phy Sparrow	88
Let some poetes wryte	78	Phy Sparrow	252
Or such other poetes mo,	90	Phy Sparrow	760
These poetes of auncyente,	90	Phy Sparrow	767
Regent is she, /Of poetes al,	112	Calliope	4
Of a thousande poetes assembled togeder.	320	Garlande	286
These orators and poetes refresshed there throtis.	321	Garlande	336
These orators and poetes refreshed their throtes.	321	Garlande	343
Poete of poetes all, /And prophete princypall.	383	Replycacion	321
Of poetes chefe poete, saint Jerome dothe wright,	383	Replycacion	330
Why have ye than disdayne /At poetes, and complayne	384	Replycacion	352
Howe poetes do but fayne?	384	Replycacion	353
The fame matryculate /Of poetes laureate.	384	Replycacion	358
Of poetes commendacion,	384	Replycacion	374
In poetes whiche excelles,	384	Replycacion	377

POETIS
And sey poetis no dys.....	132	Garnesche5	113
Of auncient poetis, ye wote full wele, hath bene	314	Garlande	65
What poetis we have at our retenewe.	319	Garlande	238
All famous poetis ensuynge after me	321	Garlande	321
Of poetis laureat of many dyverse nacyons;	321	Garlande	324
Theis orators and poetis refresshed there throtis.	322	Garlande	350
Their orators and poetis refresshed there throtis.	322	Garlande	357
Theis orators and poetis refresshed there throtis.	322	Garlande	364
These orators and poetis refresshid ther throtis.	322	Garlande	371
Theis orators and poetis refresshid there throtis.	322	Garlande	378
Propercius and Pisandros, poetis of noble fame;	322	Garlande	382
Theis notable poetis refresshid there throtis.	322	Garlande	385
Dane Johnn Lydgate. Theis Englysshe poetis thre,	323	Garlande	391
All orators and poetis shulde thider go before,	325	Garlande	454
Unto this place all poetis there did sue,	325	Garlande	481
Tyll at the last theis noble poetis thre	326	Garlande	517

POETRY —POLYTYKE	Page	Title	Line
Where all the sayd poetis sat in there degre.	343	Garlande	1104
All orators and poetis, with other grete and smale, ...	354	Garlande	1504
POETRY			
Orace also with his new poetry;	322	Garlande	352
Ye saye that poetry /Maye nat flye so hye	382	Replycacion	306
Lyke to Pyndarus in glorious poetry, ...	383	Replycacion	334
With his harpe of prophesy /And spyrituall poetry, ...	384	Replycacion	346
POETTES			
The famous poettes saturicall, ...	133	Garnesche5	139
POETTYS			
the ix Musys of polytyke poems and poettys matryculat.	36	Coystrowne	I
POGGEUS			
Poggeus also, that famous Florentine, ...	322	Garlande	372
POHEN			
Lord, how Perkyn is proud of hys Pohen!	37	Coystrowne1	19
As proud a pohen as ye sprede, ...	41	Coystrowne4	13
POINTED			
Of dyamauntis pointed was the wall;	325	Garlande	473
the] 'the rokky' Marshe 1568			
POINTYD			
Hath pointyd me to rayle on the.	131	Garnesche5	88
POYETE			
A lauryate poyete for to rate.	126	Garnesche3	95
POYET LAWREAT			
Agenst a poyet lawreat	132	Garnesche5	90
POYLE			
Some were of Poyle, and sum were of Trace, ...	326	Garlande	493
POYNT			
For one fals poynt she is wont to kepe in store, ...	45	Balettys4	4
To poynt yow fresche and gay.	129	Garnesche3	191
For of noblenesse the chefe poynt is to be lyberall, ...	211	Magnyfycence	2487
Poynt well this probleme that Parrot doth prate, ...	236	Speke Parott	220
Remembre you wele, poynt wele that clause, ...	316	Garlande	136
Frome that I have sayde in no poynt doth vary, ...	316	Garlande	163
But that I poynt you to be prothonotary	324	Garlande	432
He coude not devyse the lest poynt of your cheke;	337	Garlande	896
POYNT DEVYSE			
Poynt devyse, all pleasure is your porte.	183	Magnyfycence	1540
POYNTE			
To poynte this proude page a place and a rome, ...	37	Coystrowne1	41
But to the poynte shortely to procede, ...	53	Bowge	246
In every poynte that I can do or saye.	60	Bowge	496
In] 'To' Marshe 1568			
In every poynte to be indyfferente, ...	61	Bowge	535
My purpose is to spy and to poynte every man;	160	Magnyfycence	726
POYNTED			
So I am poynted after my consayte.	167	Magnyfycence	961
In whose court poynted is your place.'	324	Garlande	420
Caliope poynted me where I shulde sit.	344	Garlande	1143
POYNTES			
In thre poyntes expressed:	307	Why Come Ye	1122
POYNTYD			
Dyamand poyntyd to rase oute hartly care	44	Balettys3	19
POYNTYNG			
poyntyng with his fynger, and sayth, ...	162	Magnyfycence	SD
POYNTYNGE			
But there was poyntynge and noddynge with the hede, ...	58	Bowge	421
POYNTMENTYS			
Pryvy poyntmentys conveyed so properly;	177	Magnyfycence	1337
POYSON			
Might poyson thy lyver and longes!	79	Phy Sparrow	293
Thy tong untawte, with poyson infecte, ...	132	Garnesche5	108
POYSOND			
Agenst hys poysond infeccioun, ...	128	Garnesche3	153
POYSONED			
Then any poysoned tode, or any serpent.	138	Ven Tongues	54
POKE			
Me thoughte, of wordes that he had full a poke;	51	Bowge	179
I have a stoppynge oyster in my poke, ...	59	Bowge	477
POLE			
Of our pole artyke, smylynge halfe in scorne	46	Bowge	5
Wel, wyse men may ete the fysshe when ye shal draw the pole. .	148	Magnyfycence	300
Alexander, a gander of Menanders pole, ...	235	Speke Parott	173
And of that pole artike whiche doth remayne	331	Garlande	695
POLETYKE			
So myche poletyke pratyng, and so lytell stondythe in stede; .	244	Speke Parott	464
POLEXENE			
Or els fayre Polexene, ...	97	Phy Sparrow	1019
Goodly Creisseid, fayrer than Polexene, ...	336	Garlande	871
POLIMITES			
The noble wyfe of Polimites kynge;	336	Garlande	844
POLYS			
To fysshe afore the nette and to drawe polys.	243	Speke Parott	427
POLYSHED			
And howe your poemys arre barayne of polyshed eloquens, . . .	240	Speke Parott	316
POLYTYKE			
the ix Musys of polytyke poems and poettys matryculat.	36	Coystrowne	I
They shewe them polytyke, ...	269	Collyn Clout	923

	Page	Title	Line
POLYTYKES			
Set nothynge by polytykes.	262	Collyn Clout	623
POLL			
I have red theym poll by poll;	67	Hauke	211
I have red theym poll by poll;	67	Hauke	211
POLLAXIS			
Suche pollaxis and pyllers, suche mulys trapte with gold –	246	Speke Parott	517
POLLEGYANS			
And some be Pollegyans,	260	Collyn Clout	553
POLLEYNGE			
With haftynge and with polleynge,	125	Garnesche3	38
POLLES			
And hang you upon polles	362	Albany	151
POLLYCY			
Nor of good pollycy, /Nor of astronomy;	292	Why Come Ye	518
POLLYNG			
Suche statutes apon diettes, suche pyllyng and pollyng –	245	Speke Parott	495
POLLYNGE			
With pollynge and pluckynge out of all measure,	189	Magnyfycence	1753
By pollynge and pyllage /In cytes and vyllage;	255	Collyn Clout	360
With pollynge and shavynge,	281	Why Come Ye	100
POLLYNG PAJAUNTTIS			
Soche pollyng pajaunttis ye pley,	129	Garnesche3	190
POLLUTED			
With your lyppes polluted	375	Replycacion	29
POLLUTYD			
The church is thus abusyd, /Reproched and pollutyd;	66	Hauke	161
POLUTED			
With language thus poluted	258	Collyn Clout	486
POLUTYD			
Wyth his polutyd pawtenar,	63	Hauke	44
When it was polutyd	66	Hauke	174
To be polutyd this;	66	Hauke	181
POMAUNDER			
Colyaunder, /Swete pomaunder, /Good Cassaunder;	341	Garlande	1027
POMEGARNAT			
That pereles pomegarnat, Cryste save hyr nobyll grace!'	231	Speke Parott	37
POMEL			
Of knightly prowes the sworde, pomel, and hilt,	32	Dol Dethe	108
POMPE			
Your pompe and pryde hath layde a downe.	115	Scot Kynge	69
For al his pompe, for all his ryall trone,	181	Magnyfycence	1475
Ly there, losell, for all thy pompe and pryde;	193	Magnyfycence	1880
Pompe, pryde, honour, ryches and worldly lust,	236	Speke Parott	223
With pompe and with pryde,	284	Why Come Ye	204
of vaynglorious pompe and surcudant elacyon,	375	Replycacion	1
POMPED			
And where that ye were pomped with what that ye wolde,	197	Magnyfycence	2012
POMPEYUS			
And of his Pompeyus warre,	270	Collyn Clout	957
PONDER			
I[n] ponder, by number, by measure all thynge is wrought,	143	Magnyfycence	118
In] 'I' †Rastell & Treveris C 1530, B			
PONDRED			
Al maters wel pondred and wel to be regarded,	137	Ven Tongues	1
PONTIFYCALL			
To purvey for our cardynall /A palace pontifycall	299	Why Come Ye	812
PONTYFICALL			
Shall let the preest pontyficall	308	Why Come Ye	1160
POORE			
To poore folke at large,	83	Phy Sparrow	456
What! Then he is some good poore mannes curre?	171	Magnyfycence	1129
The poore people they yoke	254	Collyn Clout	323
Brought up of poore estate, /With pryde inordynate,	262	Collyn Clout	642
But the poore degre /Of the universyte;	265	Collyn Clout	735
Or elles the poore Scot,	265	Collyn Clout	749
But a poore maister of arte!	292	Why Come Ye	512
A wretched poore man	293	Why Come Ye	553
And of this poore vassall	293	Why Come Ye	557
With a poore knyght, /Whatsoever he hyght!	295	Why Come Ye	645
Of a poore wretchid man,	297	Why Come Ye	724
And a poore cope	307	Why Come Ye	1141
Nacion moost in hate, /Proude and poore of state.	362	Albany	144
POPAGAY			
Avent, avent, my popagay!	35	Man Margery	3
'Parott ys a goodlye byrde and a pratye popagay.'	231	Speke Parott	14
and] not in Lant 1545, Kynge and Marche 1554, Day 1560, Marshe 1568			
That Parrot the popagay hath pytye to beholde	235	Speke Parott	167
the] 'that' Day 1560, Marshe 1568			
Quod Parot, thy popagay royall.	238	Speke Parott	262a
Quod] 'Quid' †MS Harley 2252			
Go, litelle quayre, namyd the Popagay,	238	Speke Parott	278
Amen, quod Parott, /The royall popagay.	241	Speke Parott	356
Go, propyr Parotte, my popagay.	241	Speke Parott	357
Dixit, quod Parrott, the royall popagay.	243	Speke Parott	404
Yet, aftyr the sagacite of a popagay,	243	Speke Parott	419
Dixit, quod Parrott, the popagay royall.	244	Speke Parott	446

POPE —PORT-SALE   Page   Title   Line

POPE
   As patryarke or pope /In a blacke cope.   85   Phy Sparrow   528
   Of Pope Julius cardys, he ys chefe Cardynall.   243   Speke Parott   431
   Reporte howe the pope may   254   Collyn Clout   302
   From the Pope of Rome   282   Why Come Ye   129
   Whan he was creat pope /First in Antioche.   307   Why Come Ye   1142
   Pope holy ypocrytis, as they were golde and hole, ...   329   Garlande   612
   Come forthe, ye pope holy, /Full of melancoly!   381   Replycacion   247
POPEGAY
   Make moche of Parrot, the popegay ryall.   236   Speke Parott   217
      the] 'that' Kynge & Marche 1554, Day 1560, Marshe 1568
POPE HOLY
   Counterfet conscyence, pevysshe pope holy;   153   Magnyfycence   467
POPERING
   In Popering grew peres, whan Parrot was an eg.   232   Speke Parott   70
POPES
   The Popes cur[se] gave you that clap.   119   Ag Scottes   169
      curse] 'cures' †Lant 1545, Kynge & Marche 1554, Day 1560,
      Marshe 1568
POPHOLY
   that popholy and pevysshe presumpcion provoked them to publysshe 375   Replycacion   I
POPIGAY
   'Parrot, Parrot, Parrot, praty popigay!'   233   Speke Parott   106
POPINGAY
   Item the Popingay, that hath in commendacyoun   346   Garlande   1188
POPYNGAY
   The popyngay to tell her tale, ...   82   Phy Sparrow   421
POPPED
   And porisshly forthe popped   377   Replycacion   121
POPPYNG
   Lyke pratynge poppyng dawes, ...   375   Replycacion   39
POPPYNGE
   What, syr, wolde ye make me a poppynge fole?   146   Magnyfycence   232
   Poppynge folysshe dawes.   285   Why Come Ye   264
PORCENA
   And of Porcena the Great, ...   90   Phy Sparrow   747
PORE
   A very pore /That so wyll do, ...   164   Magnyfycence   869
   If it wolde lyke you to here my pore mynde -   183   Magnyfycence   1543
   Of my pore instance and supplycacyon, ...   186   Magnyfycence   1634
   Nowe ryche, nowe pore, nowe hole, now in dysease;   212   Magnyfycence   2518
   Whyche cawsythe pore suters have many a hongry mele;   239   Speke Parott   311
   The apostyll Peter /Had but on pore myter   307   Why Come Ye   1140
      apostyll] 'wholly apostle' MS Rawlinson C. 813
PORISSHLY
   Sum were made pevysshe, porisshly pynk iyde, ...   329   Garlande   626
   And porisshly forthe popped   377   Replycacion   121
PORPHIRIS
   in maister Porphiris problemes, ...   374   Replycacion   I
PORPOSE
   To far from the porpose, ...   126   Garnesche3   97
   With porpose and graundepose he may fede hym fatte, ...   239   Speke Parott   308
PORT
   Your goodly port, your bewteous visage, ...   42   Balettys2   6
PORTE
   To prayse your porte it is nedeles;   40   Coystrowne4   5
   Demure demenaunce, womanly of porte;   43   Balettys3   6
   Lodestar to lyght these lovers to theyr porte, ...   44   Balettys3   25
   At Harwyche Porte, slumbrynge as I laye, ...   47   Bowge   34
   Whoos beaute, honoure, goodly porte, ...   47   Bowge   62
   [Your] pride ys alle to peviche, your porte importunate; . . .   123   Garnesche2   3
   To assure you of my noble porte and fame, ...   145   Magnyfycence   163
   For I am prynce perlesse, provyd of porte, ...   181   Magnyfycence   1471
   Poynt devyse, all pleasure is your porte.   183   Magnyfycence   1540
   Where every thyng is ordenyd after your noble porte.   214   Magnyfycence   2568
   Within that, a pryncces excellente of porte;   313   Garlande   43
      that] 'it' MS Cotton Vitellius E.x
   Lyke to Aryna, maydenly of porte, ...   336   Garlande   865
   Princes of yowth, and flowre of goodly porte, ...   337   Garlande   897
   Princes of youth, and flowre of goodly porte, ...   337   Garlande   904
   Of his moste princely porte, ...   370   Albany   473
PORTE SALUE
   Towarde the porte salue /Of our Savyoure Jesu, ...   278   Collyn Clout   1260
PORTIS
   The burgeis and the ballyvis of the v portis, ...   326   Garlande   514
   Be issuis and portis from all maner of nacyons';   328   Garlande   580
PORTISMOUTH
   Of Dertmouth, of Plummouth, of Portismouth also;   326   Garlande   513
PORTYNGALE
   Farre by yonde Portyngale, ...   299   Why Come Ye   802
   Of Lymerik, of Loreine, of Spayne, of Portyngale, ...   326   Garlande   494
PORTYNGALES
   And of the Portyngales;   223   El Rummynge   355
PORTLYE
   So myche portlye pride, with pursys penyles;   244   Speke Parott   460
PORT-SALE
   And maketh thereof port-sale   217   El Rummynge   103
      port-sale] 'pore sale' Kynge & Marche 1554, Day 1560

	Page	Title	Line
PORT SALU			
Of studyous doctryne when at the port salu	327	Garlande	541
PORTURATURE			
Of porturature which was the famous Greke,	337	Garlande	895
POSE			
Nay. Purchace ye a pardon for the pose,	163	Magnyfycence	825
And I gyve hym the cowghe, the murre, and the pose.	204	Magnyfycence	2259
Snevelyng in her nose, /As though she had the pose.	223	El Rummynge	365
From the puskylde pocky pose,	309	Why Come Ye	1195
puskylde] 'pusky' MS Rawlinson C. 813; pose] 'nose' Kitson 1560.7			
POSSYBLE			
It were not possyble me longe to retayne.	147	Magnyfycence	250
POST			
And now must kys the post;	89	Phy Sparrow	716
POSTELL			
To postell upon a kyry,	265	Collyn Clout	753
POSTELS			
This is a postels lyfe.	284	Why Come Ye	226
POSTERN GATE			
Thus talkyng we went forth in at a postern gate.	333	Garlande	766
forth] not in MS Cotton Vitellius E.x			
POSTIS			
Where the postis wer enbulyoned with saphiris indy blew,	325	Garlande	478
POSTY			
Of infernall posty /Where soules frye and rousty;	105	Phy Sparrow	1332
rousty] 'rosty' Marshe 1568			
Of infernall posty, /Where soulis fry and rosty;	349	Garlande	1325
POSTYKE			
Here is a pystell of a postyke!	158	Magnyfycence	649
POSTYLL			
To practise or postyll thys prosses here and there?	242	Speke Parott	393
POT			
And some a pot with honny,	220	El Rummynge	246
Some ranne a good trot /With a skellet or a pot;	220	El Rummynge	250
Some fyll theyr pot full /Of good Lemster woll.	220	El Rummynge	251
The pot to her plucke,	228	El Rummynge	566
Ge heme! ge scour thy pot,	282	Why Come Ye	126
POTECARY			
Good Hope, your potecary, assygned am I,	207	Magnyfycence	2351
POTENCIALL			
But blessyd Bachus, potenciall god of strengthe,	322	Garlande	348
POTENCYALL			
A prelate potencyall /To rule under Bellyall,	294	Why Come Ye	591
POTENCYALLY			
That potencyally /May never dye	84	Phy Sparrow	514
POTESTATE			
And suche a potestate,	303	Why Come Ye	989
POTESTOLATE			
And suche a potestolate,	303	Why Come Ye	988
And] 'And make' MS Rawlinson C. 813; potestate] 'prostrate' Toy 1553, Kitson 1560.7, Marshe 1568			
POT SHARDE			
To prate for the patchynge of a pot sharde!	200	Magnyfycence	2124
POTSHORDE			
To pyke out honesty of suche a potshorde.	346	Garlande	1211
POTSHORDES			
He regardeth lordes /No more than potshordes.	291	Why Come Ye	481
POTSHORDIS			
And such as sell trotters, /Pytchars, potshordis.	302	Why Come Ye	912
potshordis] 'pouchers' MS Rawlinson C. 813			
POTT			
In the pott your nose dedde snevyll;	124	Garnesche3	27
POTTE			
Counter he coude O lux upon a potte.	56	Bowge	365
POTTELL-PYCHER			
And brought a pottell-pycher,	224	El Rummynge	402
POTTERS			
Myght stande now by potters,	301	Why Come Ye	910
Myght] 'most' MS Rawlinson C. 813			
POUCHE			
And by his syde his whynarde and his pouche,	56	Bowge	363
Ay, in my pouche a buckell I have founde;	57	Bowge	397
He had plucte oute the nobles of my pouche.	60	Bowge	504
POULES			
Ware the wether cocke /Of the steple of Poules.	255	Collyn Clout	340
At Poules Crosse, or elswhere,	276	Collyn Clout	1182
For ye were worldly shamed, /At Poules Crosse openly,	376	Replycacion	63
POUND			
It were worth an hundreth pound	76	Phy Sparrow	189
POUNDE			
Ye be to her, yea, worth a thousande pounde.	50	Bowge	157
Or els I pas a peny to a pounde!	57	Bowge	394
I] not in Wynkyn de Worde 1510			
Wyll ye spende ony money? Ye, a thousande pounde.	184	Magnyfycence	1570
Spare for no cost to gyve them pounde and peny;	190	Magnyfycence	1771
A thousande pounde with lyberte may holde no tacke.	199	Magnyfycence	2084
His benefyce worth ten pounde,	264	Collyn Clout	725

POUNSED —PRAY

	Page	Title	Line
An hunderd pounde and more,	302	Why Come Ye	947
An] 'And' †Kele 1545.3			
The claspis and bullyons were worth a thousande pounde;	345	Garlande	1165
Nat for a thousande poun[de]	367	Albany	346
pounde] 'pouned' †Marshe 1568			
Some of you had ten pounde,	378	Replycacion	146

POUNSED
His hode all pounsed and garded lyke a cage.	60	Bowge	508
hode] 'body' Marshe 1568			

POUNTES
Syr, this letter ye sent to me at Pountes was enclosed.	209	Magnyfycence	2439

POUNTESSE
By my trouthe, syr, at Pountesse.	150	Magnyfycence	343

POVERTE
To her wyll I nowe all my poverte lege.	57	Bowge	412
Youre poverte cowde not attayne	119	Ag Scottes	151
For, without measure, poverte and nede	144	Magnyfycence	152
Ryches rydeth out, at home is poverte.	153	Magnyfycence	474
Howe, where art thou? Come hether, Poverte.	195	Magnyfycence	1953
Here cometh in POVERTE.	195	Magnyfycence	SD
I am Poverte that all men doth hate.	195	Magnyfycence	1960
He dynyd with delyte, with poverte he must sup.	195	Magnyfycence	1965
Therefore poverte loke pacyently ye take,	196	Magnyfycence	2000
Nowe all in welth, forthwith in poverte;	197	Magnyfycence	2027
O rydlesse rewthe, O paynfull poverte!	198	Magnyfycence	2051
And payned you with a purgacyon of odyous poverte,	207	Magnyfycence	2353
Sodenly ryches, and sodenly poverte;	212	Magnyfycence	2527
Than must we agre /With poverte;	300	Why Come Ye	865

POWER
But by the power and myght of God	114	Scot Kynge	46
Your power coude no lenger attayne	114	Scot Kynge	54
But, by the power and myght of God,	119	Ag Scottes	145
With all the power he may.	282	Why Come Ye	156
Suche is a kynges power	293	Why Come Ye	565

POWERS
In myne hostes house called Powers Keye,	47	Bowge	35

POWLE HACHET
I wys, powle hachet, she bleryd thyne I!	42	Balettys1	28

POWLE HATCHETTIS
Powle hatchettis, that prate wyll at every ale pole,	329	Garlande	613
wyll] 'well' Marshe 1568			

POWND
Pay Stokys hys fyve pownd.	128	Garnesche3	185

POWRE
And of his royall powre	289	Why Come Ye	427
Also by Hecates powre	349	Garlande	1315
powre] 'bowre' Marshe 1568			
With the noble powre	360	Albany	59

PRACTIQUE
To practique suche abolete sciens.	297	Why Come Ye	713
practique] 'practyve' †Kele 1545.3			

PRACTISE
To practise or postyll thys prosses here and there?	242	Speke Parott	393

PRAIERS
Of al good praiers God send him sum!	86	Phy Sparrow	584

PRAIID
Sche praiid yow walke, on Goddes halfe!	131	Garnesche5	60

PRAY
I pray God sende the prosperous lyf and long,	34	Dol Dethe	169
And us redemede from the fendys pray.	34	Dol Dethe	196
To the pray we as Prince incomperable,	34	Dol Dethe	197
Pray to thy son above the starris clere,	35	Dol Dethe	208
A malaperte medler that pryeth for his pray,	37	Coystrowne1	45
He trusted her payment and lost all hys pray.	42	Balettys1	13
His hawke shulde pray and fede /Upon a pigeons maw.	63	Hauke	56
To Jupyter pray we	74	Phy Sparrow	92
Is for his soule to pray:	77	Phy Sparrow	238
Some to wepe, and some to pray,	81	Phy Sparrow	393
I pray God, Phillip to heven may fly.	86	Phy Sparrow	580
I pray you it may be amendyd	102	Phy Sparrow	1246
I pray God they be payned	106	Phy Sparrow	1376
I pray you all,	108	Epitaphe1	68
And pray shall, /At this trentall	108	Epitaphe1	69
And thus there ye lost yower pray;	131	Garnesche5	61
Shewe forth, I pray you, here in what you intende.	141	Magnyfycence	40
I pray you, Larges, here to remayne,	149	Magnyfycence	323
I pray God kepe you in that mood!	150	Magnyfycence	336
I pray you, syr, I may so be;	151	Magnyfycence	391
A, syr, I pray God gyve you confusyon!	157	Magnyfycence	597
I pray God let you never to thee!	158	Magnyfycence	635
Howe so? Tell me, I the pray.	166	Magnyfycence	931
Then I pray the hartely,	172	Magnyfycence	1148
What sayst thou? Mary, I pray God your mastershyp to save.	191	Magnyfycence	1828
I pray the, Largesse, let be thy sobbynge.	192	Magnyfycence	1851
And pray to God your sorowes to asswage.	196	Magnyfycence	1989
Alasse! I wote not what I sholde pray.	196	Magnyfycence	1994
Good Hope, I pray you with harty affeccyon	208	Magnyfycence	2399
Elynour, I the pray,	224	El Rummynge	396

PRAYD —PRATE

	Page	Title	Line
With, 'Speke, Parott, I pray yow,' full curteslye they sey,	231	Speke Parott	13
I pray you, let Parot have lyberte to speke.	233	Speke Parott	98
Let Parrot, I pray you, have lyberte to prate,	234	Speke Parott	141
Support Parrot, I pray you, with your suffrage ornate,	236	Speke Parott	195
I pray you, let Parrot have lyberte to speke.	236	Speke Parott	210
Thus Parott dothe pray yow,	237	Speke Parott	225
Speke, Parotte, I pray yow, for Maryes saake,	237	Speke Parott	233
I pray the, Besse, unfayned, /Yet com agayne to me!	238	Speke Parott	255
I pray yow be reclaymed,	238	Speke Parott	260
Lyacon of Libyk and Lydy hathe cawghte hys pray:	239	Speke Parott	289
Goe, lytyll quayre, pray them that yow beholde,	239	Speke Parott	290
With notable clerkes; supply to them, I pray,	241	Speke Parott	359
Now, Galathea, lett Parrot, I pray yow, have hys date –	244	Speke Parott	439
I pray God save the kynge.	289	Why Come Ye	393
I pray God be his gyde.	289	Why Come Ye	395
And pray for Mewtas sowle;	300	Why Come Ye	832
With, 'Sir, I pray you, a lytyll tyme stande backe,	326	Garlande	505
Come forth, jentylwomen, I pray you,' she sayd,	334	Garlande	773
I pray God they be paynyd	350	Garlande	1369
Els ye shall pray /Them that ye may	356	Garlande	1583
And hym moost lowly pray,	372	Albany	528
or to pray and go on pylgrimages,	375	Replycacion	1
Therefore no grevance, /I pray you, for to take,	385	Replycacion	398

PRAYD

Prayd Troylus for to were	89	Phy Sparrow	690
And for her sparow prayd /In lamentable wyse.	93	Phy Sparrow	854
And that it wolde please her, full tenderly I prayd,	353	Garlande	1479

PRAYDE

By my trouthe, had I not payde and prayde,	150	Magnyfycence	363
That for hym to laboure he hath prayde me hartely;	186	Magnyfycence	1650
Theyr matyns madly sayde, /Nothynge devoutly prayde,	252	Collyn Clout	239

PRAYE

'Maystres,' quod I, 'I praye you tell me why soo,	49	Bowge	108
I praye to God that it maye never dy.	53	Bowge	271
His name? Or why is it, I you praye,	316	Garlande	138

PRAYED

And I with them prayed her to have in mynde.	49	Bowge	123
Els, I prayed hym with all my besy cure,	52	Bowge	221
Nay, indede, but I sawe howe ye prayed,	188	Magnyfycence	1696
To Mercury also hertely prayed I then,	335	Garlande	826

PRAYER

Devoutly arrectyng my prayer to Mynerve,	335	Garlande	824
Also a Devoute Prayer to Moyses Hornis,	351	Garlande	1381

PRAYETH

He chydeth and he chatters, /He prayeth and he patters; prayeth] 'prates' Kele 1545.1, Marshe 1568, 'pratythe' MS Harley 2252	247	Collyn Clout	22

PRAYSE

To prayse your porte it is nedeles;	40	Coystrowne4	5
To prayse her at the full;	102	Phy Sparrow	1222
A Lawde And Prayse Made for Our Sovereigne Lord the Kyng	110	Lawde	1
What so ever I do, all men me prayse,	152	Magnyfycence	429
And ferre beyond my merytys ye me commende and prayse.	183	Magnyfycence	1526
For I here but fewe men that gyve ony prayse	189	Magnyfycence	1743

PRAYSED

Sume praysed the perle, some the stones bryght.	343	Garlande	1108

PRANCKES

They play their olde pranckes /After Huntley Bankes.	285	Why Come Ye	266

PRANE

I set not by the prowdest of them a prane,	181	Magnyfycence	1489
We set nat a prane	363	Albany	163

PRANES

Ye pyke no shrympes nor pranes,	252	Collyn Clout	208

PRANYS

For shrympes, and for pranys,	102	Phy Sparrow	1243

PRANKED

And gyrdeth in her gytes /Stytched and pranked with pletes;	216	El Rummynge	69

PRANKES

Than in Englonde to playe ony suche prankes;	114	Scot Kynge	51
That ratis and rankis /That prates and prankes	136	Dundas	57
The trechery and the prankes	288	Why Come Ye	368

PRANKYNG

For alle your proude prankyng, yor pride may apayere.	122	Garneschel	19

PRANKYS

Your pryde was pevysh to play such prankys:	119	Ag Scottes	150

PRASE

To prase her excellence!	101	Phy Sparrow	1207

PRATE

What prate ye, praty pyggys-ny?	41	Coystrowne4	20
I was ashamed so to here hym prate.	56	Bowge	373
With a clerke that connynge is to prate.	59	Bowge	454
Such boste to make, /To prate and crake,	116	Ag Scottes	32
Thow ye prate lyke prowde Pylate, beware yet of chek mate.	123	Garnesche2	7
Thow ye prate lyke prowde Pylate, beware of cheke mate.	123	Garnesche2	14
Tho ye prate lyke prowde Pylate, beware of cheke mate.	123	Garnesche2	21
Thow ye prate lyke prowde Pylate, beware of cheke mate.	123	Garnesche2	28
Thow ye prate lyke prowde Pylate, beware of cheke mate.	123	Garnesche2	35
Thow ye prate lyke prowde Pylate, beware of cheke mate.	124	Garnesche2	42

PRATED — PRECHE

	Page	Title	Line
That with your lorde and mayster so pertly can prate!	149	Magnyfycence	305
To crake and prate.	164	Magnyfycence	875
What! Wyll ye waste wynde and prate thus in vayne?	179	Magnyfycence	1403
What nede you with hym thus prate and chat?	180	Magnyfycence	1434
To prate for the patchynge of a pot sharde!	200	Magnyfycence	2124
'Peace, Parott, ye prate as ye were ebrius!'	232	Speke Parott	68
Let Parrot, I pray you, have lyberte to prate,	234	Speke Parott	141
Poynt well this probleme that Parrot doth prate,	236	Speke Parott	220
And thowe sum dysdayne yow and sey how ye prate,	240	Speke Parott	315
Parott, ye may prate thys undyr protestacion,	240	Speke Parott	336
How thys prosses I prate of, hyt ys not all for nowghte.	242	Speke Parott	389
With, 'Skyre-galyard, prowde palyard, vaunte-parler, ye prate!'	244	Speke Parott	433
Prate of thy matens and thy mas,	275	Collyn Clout	1158
Agaynst us dothe prate.	276	Collyn Clout	1181
Powle hatchettis, that prate wyll at every ale pole,	329	Garlande	613
wyll] 'well' Marshe 1568			
to prate and to preche proudly and leudly, and loudly to lye;	374	Replycacion	1

PRATED

This was properly prated, syrs! What sayd a?	161	Magnyfycence	746

PRATER

Pers Prater, the secund, that quarillis beganne;	330	Garlande	636

PRATES

That ratis and rankis /That prates and prankes	136	Dundas	57
Harke, howe the losell prates /With a wyde wesaunt!	275	Collyn Clout	1153

PRATY

'Be Gad, ye be a praty pode,	35	Man Margery	8
What prate ye, praty pyggys-ny?	41	Coystrowne4	20
And to remember many a praty thynge;	44	Balettys3	33
That commaunde with you, me thought, a p[ra]ty space?	51	Bowge	198
commaunde] 'commened' Wynkyn de Worde 1510; 'party spake' †Wynkyn de Worde 1499, Marshe 1568, 'party space' WdeW 1510			
With, 'Bas me, buttyng, praty Cys",	130	Garnesche5	43
To counterfet I can by praty wayes:	152	Magnyfycence	424
And be as praty as she may,	153	Magnyfycence	464
By God, I have bene about a praty pronge -	154	Magnyfycence	501
Nowe let se. Quyte you lyke praty men!	159	Magnyfycence	688
Howe so? By God, by a praty slyght,	167	Magnyfycence	952
Come, Gryme! Come, Gryme! It is my praty dogges.	171	Magnyfycence	1119
By me is conveyed mykyll praty ware -	177	Magnyfycence	1340
A good dryfte, syr, a praty fete!	189	Magnyfycence	1731
'Parrot, Parrot, Parrot, praty popigay!'	233	Speke Parott	106
With my beke I can pyke my lyttel praty too;	233	Speke Parott	107
My propir Besse, /My praty Besse,	237	Speke Parott	236
The praty primrose, /The goodly columbyne.	338	Garlande	912
The praty strawberry;	340	Garlande	981
He wrate therof many a praty lyne,	347	Garlande	1242

PRATYE

'Parott ys a goodlye byrde and a pratye popagay.'	231	Speke Parott	14
and] not in Lant 1545, Kynge and Marche 1554, Day 1560, Marshe 1568			
'My propyr Parott, my lytell pratye fole.'	231	Speke Parott	20

PRATYER

Mary, syr, he sayd that he was the pratyer man	203	Magnyfycence	2225

PRATYLYE

'Heghe, ha, ha, Parott, ye can lawghe pratylye!'	231	Speke Parott	22

PRATYNG

So myche poletyke pratyng, and so lytell stondythe in stede;	244	Speke Parott	464
And your busy pratyng.	380	Replycacion	218

PRATYNGE

Leve thy pratynge or els I shall lay the on the pate.	201	Magnyfycence	2173
Pratynge for peace peaslesse.	280	Why Come Ye	76
Lyke pratynge poppyng dawes,	375	Replycacion	39

PRAUNCE

It is a curtel that well can wynche and praunce;	57	Bowge	411
curtel] 'curtet' †Wynkyn de Worde 1499, 1510			

PREAMBLE

As Jerome, in his preamble Frater Ambrosius,	316	Garlande	162

PREASE

To prease to his presence;	272	Collyn Clout	1039
To se if Skelton wyll put hymselfe in prease	319	Garlande	239
wyll] 'dare' MS Cotton Vitellius E.x			

PREBENDARIES

Of prebendaries and deanes,	260	Collyn Clout	566

PRECE

Amonge all other I put myselfe in prece.	47	Bowge	44
Se you not howe they prece	156	Magnyfycence	591
But one thynge I warne you, prece forth and be bolde.	184	Magnyfycence	1582

PRECELY

Precely purposyd under pretence of play,	213	Magnyfycence	2553

PRECHE

To preche out of the pylery hole	150	Magnyfycence	358
And began to preche	225	El Rummynge	448
To teche or to preche /As reason wyll reche?	247	Collyn Clout	13
To preche a worde or twayne,	265	Collyn Clout	764
Must preche a Goddes halfe	266	Collyn Clout	810
And wyll preche and tell	267	Collyn Clout	822
To preche, and withstande	268	Collyn Clout	889
For all that they preche and teche	374	Replycacion	12

PRECHED — PREGNANT

	Page	Title	Line
to prate and to preche proudly and leudly, and loudly to lye;	374	Replycacion	1
and to preche to people imprudent perilously,	375	Replycacion	1
To preche in any clawes,	375	Replycacion	38
To preche it idolatry,	381	Replycacion	254

PRECHED

To places where ye have preched,	379	Replycacion	203

PRECHERS

The prechers with evyll haylynge:	275	Collyn Clout	1149
Ye prechers shall be yawde:	276	Collyn Clout	1204

PRECHES

Preches for his grote,	267	Collyn Clout	837

PRECHETH

The vyllayne precheth openly	275	Collyn Clout	1173

PRECHID

Of Pliades he prechid with ther drowsy chere,	331	Garlande	697

PRECHYD

........that ye ther prechyd,	125	Garnesche3	60

PRECHYNG

So myche nobyll prechyng, and so lytell amendment;	244	Speke Parott	452
Confessyng howe ye dyde lye /In prechyng shamefully.	377	Replycacion	91

PRECHYNGE

Counterfet prechynge, and byleve the contrary;	153	Magnyfycence	466
And some fall prechynge at the Toure Hyll;	200	Magnyfycence	2140
Nor wyll here no prechynge,	274	Collyn Clout	1133

PRECHOUR

The prechour he dothe dyspyse	306	Why Come Ye	1072
That no prechour almost	306	Why Come Ye	1075

PRECHOURS

And ofte prechours be blamed	305	Why Come Ye	1054
ofte] 'the' MS Rawlinson C. 813			
He calleth the prechours dawis.	305	Why Come Ye	1061

PRECIOUS

With thi blode precious our fenaunce thou dyd pay	34	Dol Dethe	195
Maters more precious than the ryche jacounce,	241	Speke Parott	366

PRECIOUSLY

Enhachyde with perle and stones preciously,	313	Garlande	40

PRECYOUS

A precyous jewell, no rycher in this londe:	48	Bowge	97
Where Crystis precyous blode /Dayly offryd is,	66	Hauke	179
Your wordes be more sweter than ony precyous narde,	207	Magnyfycence	2345
With perles and precyous stonys.	255	Collyn Clout	347
Of golde, entachid with many a precyous stone;	325	Garlande	470

PRECYOUSE

The topas rych and precyouse in vertew;	44	Balettys3	15

PREDESTYNACYON

Some make epylogacyon /Of hygh predestynacyon;	259	Collyn Clout	520

PREDICAMENTES

Nor his predicamentes;	267	Collyn Clout	819

PREDYALL

Of theyr predyall landes,	269	Collyn Clout	930

PREDYCACION

And there to make relacion /In open predycacion,	379	Replycacion	206

PREEMYNENCE

But Hampton Court /Hath the preemynence!	289	Why Come Ye	409
'Prynces moost pusant, of hygh preemynence,	313	Garlande	50
That ye have now by the preemynence	344	Garlande	1125
by the] 'thorow' MS Cotton Vitellius E.x			
Agaynst her preemynence, /Agaynst her magnifycence,	375	Replycacion	42

PREEST

That preest that hawkys so,	62	Hauke	15
No good preest to offend,	62	Hauke	25
As preest unreverent,	63	Hauke	45
He shall be the preest,	81	Phy Sparrow	400
Well cannest thou helpe a preest to synge a songe.	187	Magnyfycence	1676
A preest without a letter,	253	Collyn Clout	270
Agaynst the sely preest.	261	Collyn Clout	576
Nor good preest I escrye,	273	Collyn Clout	1096
I escrye] 'of the clargy' Marshe 1568, 'askrye' Harley 2252			
Avaunt, lewde preest, avaunt!	275	Collyn Clout	1156
Shall let the preest pontyficall	308	Why Come Ye	1160

PREESTES

And whan ye were preestes shorne,	376	Replycacion	81

PREESTHODE

That agaynst preesthode /Theyr malyce sprede abrode,	260	Collyn Clout	534
agaynst] 'agayn' Marshe 1568			
For the wele publyke /Of preesthode in this case;	264	Collyn Clout	698

PREESTLY

In thys preestly gydynge	65	Hauke	125
In] 'Is' †Lant 1545			
Of preestly dygnytes /By theyr malygnytes.	260	Collyn Clout	538
By] 'But' Kele 1545.1, Marshe 1568			

PREFERMENT

Avaunced by Pallas to laurell preferment.'	324	Garlande	434

PREGNACY

Of suche an industry /And suche a pregnacy,	384	Replycacion	371

PREGNANT

solacyous and ryght pregnant allectyues of syngular pleasure,	312	Garlande	1

	Page	Title	Line

PREGNAUNTE
Mole ruit sua, whose dictes ar pregnaunte - . . . . 232 Speke Parott 41
PREIGNAUNTE
Yet your problemes ar preignaunte and with loyalte acquayntyd. 240 Speke Parott 344
PREYE
To fede a fole, and for to preye a dawe. . . . . 58 Bowge 437
 preye] 'preue' Wynkyn de Worde 1510
PREKETH
'He cryeth and he creketh /He pryeth and he preketh, ... 247 Collyn Clout 20
 preketh] 'peketh' Kele 1545.1, 'prekythe' MS Harley 2252
PRELACY
Of all this prelacy, ... 291 Why Come Ye 503
Whan prelacy you opposed. . . . . 377 Replycacion 106
PRELACYE
How prelacye is solde and bought . . . . 261 Collyn Clout 583
PRELATE
So rygorous revelyng, in a prelate specially; . . . . 246 Speke Parott 506
A prelate potencyall /To rule under Bellyall, ... 294 Why Come Ye 591
Suche a prelate, I trowe, /Were worthy to rowe . . . . 303 Why Come Ye 953
PRELATES
The prelates ben so haute /They say, and loke so hye . . . . . 248 Collyn Clout 71
In you prelates, and say . . . . 256 Collyn Clout 403
 In] 'On' Marshe 1568, 'In' MS Harley 2252
You prelates, that of ryght . . . . 257 Collyn Clout 439
And where the prelates be /Come of lowe degre . . . . 261 Collyn Clout 585
Why syt ye prelates styll . . . . 263 Collyn Clout 688
For prelates of estate, ... 270 Collyn Clout 972
'Shall they taunt us prelates, ... 275 Collyn Clout 1150
 taunt] 'daunt' Kele 1545.1, Marshe 1568, 'teche' MS
 Harley 2252
of the reverende prelates and moche noble doctours . . . . . 373 Replycacion I
PRELATTES
So myche pride of prelattes, so cruell and so kene - . . . . . 245 Speke Parott 475
PREMENYRE
That the premenyre /Is lyke to be set afyre . . . . 249 Collyn Clout 108
In your convenire /Of this premenyre, ... 273 Collyn Clout 1068
PRENDERGEST
This pevysh proud, thys prendergest, ... 36 Coystrownel 6
PREORDINATE
To be our kyng, of God preordinate. . . . . 347 Garlande 1232
PREPAYRE
Prepayre yow, Parrot, brevely your passage to take, ... 240 Speke Parott 324
PREPARED
And thus ye prepared . . . . 365 Albany 272
PREPENSED
Protestacion alway canonically prepensed, professed, ... 373 Replycacion I
A confutacion responsyve, or an inevytably prepensed answere . 382 Replycacion R
PREPOSYCYON
For I rede a preposycyon: . . . . 271 Collyn Clout 997
 rede a] 'reda' Marshe 1568, 'rede by' MS Harley 2252
PREPOSYTOUR
I am Goddys preposytour; I prynt them with a pen; . . . . . . 195 Magnyfycence 1941
PREROGATYVE
For his prerogatyve, /Within that consystory . . . . 299 Why Come Ye 816
Or wherto shulde he have the prerogatyve, ... 315 Garlande 117
 the] 'that' MS Cotton Vitellius E.x
PRESCYENCE
And of the prescyence /Of divyne assence . . . . 259 Collyn Clout 524
 assence] 'essence' Marshe 1568
PRESCRYPCYONS
Men say they have prescrypcyons . . . . 249 Collyn Clout 112
PRESE
To be so perte to prese so proudly uppe. . . . . 48 Bowge 71
Among this prese - /Even a hole mese - . . . . 168 Magnyfycence 995
For, be there never so moche prese, ... 218 El Rummynge 174
'Make rowme,' sayd another, 'ye prese all to sore,' . . . . . 319 Garlande 256
With all the prese that lesse and more. . . . . 325 Garlande 455
Sume to enbrowder put them in prese, ... 334 Garlande 794
Cause me to cese, /Amonge this prese, ... 339 Garlande 958
PRESED
Presed forthe boldly to witstand the myght, ... 31 Dol Dethe 87
Percius pressed forth with problemes diffuse; . . . . 321 Garlande 338
And ever they presed on me more and more, ... 324 Garlande 445
Innumerable people presed to every gate. . . . . 329 Garlande 603
PRESEDENT
Your soverayne lorde and presedent. . . . . 114 Scot Kynge 22
I coude shew you suche a presedent . . . . 342 Garlande 1083
 you] not in MS Cotton Vitellius E.x
PRESENCE
Can be content with Measure presence. . . . . 143 Magnyfycence 86
And grotes many one or I came to your presence. . . . . 150 Magnyfycence 339
To prease to his presence; . . . . 272 Collyn Clout 1039
PRESENS
Hys presens to aproche; 126 Garnesche3 84
PRESENT
That we shall brynge you personally present . . . . 324 Garlande 418
'My frende, sith ye ar before us here present . . . . 344 Garlande 1121

PRESERVATYVE—PRETY   Page   Title   Line

PRESERVATYVE
Whos flagraunt flower was chefe preservatyve   330   Garlande   671
PRESERVE
Nowe Jesu preserve you, syr, prynce most of myght.   190   Magnyfycence 1796
Jhesus preserve you frome endlesse wo and shame.   214   Magnyfycence 2572
But, for to preserve her maidenhode clene, ...   320   Garlande   293
  maidenhode] 'maydenheed' Marshe 1568
PRESERVED
That Phyllyp preserved may be!   74   Phy Sparrow   93
PRESID
They presid in faste; some thought they were to longe;   319   Garlande   248
Of pursevantis ther presid in with many a dyverse tale: 326   Garlande   492
  a] not in Marshe 1568
With that, Occupacioun presid in a pace;   344   Garlande   1144
PRESIDENT
Our perelesse president, ...   369   Albany   428
PRESIDENTE
Of formar writinge by any presidente   30   Dol Dethe   23
PRESYDENT
For to offend your presydent, ...   118   Ag Scottes   112
I am presydent of prynces; I prycke them with pryde.   199   Magnyfycence 2082
As presydent and regente he rulythe every deall.   239   Speke Parott   312
Without the assent /Of your presydent;   272   Collyn Clout 1035
Without his presydent be by, ...   272   Collyn Clout 1042
PRESYOUS
Somtyme a presyous thyng, ...   88   Phy Sparrow   685
PRESONMENT
So myche presonment, for matyrs not worth a hawe;   245   Speke Parott   478
PRESSES
So properly she presses   101   Phy Sparrow   1171
PRESSYD
Ye pressyd pertely to pluk a crow: 130   Garnesche5   48
PRESSYNGE
Than sholde ye see there pressynge in a pace   47   Bowge   56
Came pressynge in one in a wonder araye.   60   Bowge   499
PREST
The fauconer then was prest, ...   63   Hauke   71
  prest] 'priest' Kynge & Marche 1554, Day 1560
It was propre and prest.   75   Phy Sparrow   127
As prety and as prest   78   Phy Sparrow   264
My persone prest /Beyonde all syse   164   Magnyfycence   844
PRESTE
To weve in the stoule sume were full preste, ...   334   Garlande   790
Ageynst Holy Chyrche, the preste, and the clarke.   347   Garlande   1253
PRESTES
For prestes and for lonys /Lent and never payde, ...   255   Collyn Clout   350
PRESUMCYON
Presumcyon and vayne glory, ...   293   Why Come Ye   574
PRESUMYNG
Presumyng on theyr owne wytte, ...   259   Collyn Clout   515
  owne] not in Marshe 1568
PRESUMPCION
that popholy and pevysshe presumpcion provoked them to publysshe   375   Replycacion   I
PRESUMPCYON
Put fro you presumpcyon and admyt humylyte, ...   207   Magnyfycence 2361
PRESUMPTUOUS
Presumptuous pride ys all thyn hope;   133   Garnesche5   160
PRETELY
How pretely it wolde syt   80   Phy Sparrow   354
This delycate dasy, this strawbery pretely set, ...   352   Garlande   1449
PRETENCE
Of Largesse under the pretence.   151   Magnyfycence   405
To flater and to flery is all my pretence   161   Magnyfycence   738
And some wyll convey by the pretence of sadnesse   178   Magnyfycence 1366
Precely purposyd under pretence of play, ...   213   Magnyfycence 2553
Sith ye must nedis afforce it by pretence   335   Garlande   817
And for as moche as, by the hy pretence   344   Garlande   1124
PRETENDE
Though she wolde pretende   75   Phy Sparrow   154
For I wyll nat pretende   274   Collyn Clout 1127
Yet proudly he dare pretende   292   Why Come Ye   530
Howe ye pretende /For to defende   361   Albany   88
PRETENDED
All justyce he pretended: 307   Why Come Ye   1110
PRETENDITH
Parrot pretendith to be a bybyll clarke!'   234   Speke Parott   119
PRETENDYD
No matter pretendyd, nor nothyng enterprysed, ...   236   Speke Parott   201
PRETENDYNGE
Whan Scorpyon descendynge, /Was so then pretendynge   258   Collyn Clout   472
Pretendynge gravyte /And seygnyoryte, ...   269   Collyn Clout   924
PRETENS
He makith so proude pretens, ...   307   Why Come Ye   1133
In shorte sentens, /Of your pretens /What is the grounde . . .   361   Albany   80
PRETY
There muste for hym be layde some prety beyte.   55   Bowge   312
Of Felyce fetewse and lytell prety Cate, ...   56   Bowge   370
Yet wyth a prety gyn /I fortuned to come in, ...   64   Hauke   93

PRETORY —PRINCIPLES	Page	Title	Line
It was so prety a fole,	74	Phy Sparrow	115
And opened his prety byll,	77	Phy Sparrow	221
opened] 'open' Marshe 1568			
As prety and as prest	78	Phy Sparrow	264
My lytell portly sparowe	78	Phy Sparrow	280
Remembrynge prety thynges!	80	Phy Sparrow	350
It was my prety Phyppes!	80	Phy Sparrow	360
Many a prety kusse	80	Phy Sparrow	361
For he was a prety cocke,	86	Phy Sparrow	588
To treade the prety wren /That is our Ladyes hen.	86	Phy Sparrow	600
Somtyme a prety chayn,	88	Phy Sparrow	688
Upon her prety fote?	100	Phy Sparrow	1147
With, 'Bas, my prety bonny,	220	El Rummynge	227
'My prety Petronylla,	253	Collyn Clout	259
PRETORY			
Thus passid we forth walkynge unto the pretory	325	Garlande	477
PREVAYLE			
Thyse lewde cok wattes shall nevermore prevayle	51	Bowge	173
wattes] 'witts' Marshe 1568			
Yet to lie upon me they can not prevayle.	138	Ven Tongues	31
PREVE			
Ye, to knackynge ernyst what and it preve?	141	Magnyfycence	33
Wherfore I preve,	165	Magnyfycence	909
PREVENTID			
'So am I preventid of my brethern tweyne	324	Garlande	428
PREVYE			
So myche prevye wachyng in cold wynters nyghtes;	246	Speke Parott	512
PREVYLEGIDDE			
So myche sayntuary brekyng, and prevylegidde barryd -	246	Speke Parott	503
PREVYLY			
Nor to speke to hym secretly, /Openly nor prevyly,	272	Collyn Clout	1041
PREVYNGE			
God gyve it yll prevynge,	219	El Rummynge	185
PRIAMUS			
Our Priamus of Troy,	111	Lawde	48
Pyramus, nor Priamus, nor Syr Pyrrus the prowde,	123	Garnesche2	23
PRICKYD			
Prickyd lyke an unicorne.	133	Garnesche5	132
PRIDE			
For alle your proude prankyng, yor pride may apayere.	122	Garnesche1	19
[Your] pride ys alle to peviche, your porte importunate;	123	Garnesche2	3
For to aswage your pride.	124	Garnesche3	23
Inordynate pride wyll have a falle.	133	Garnesche5	159
Presumptuous pride ys all thyn hope;	133	Garnesche5	160
Pride gothe before and schame commyth after.	133	Garnesche5	165
So myche portlye pride, with pursys penyles;	244	Speke Parott	460
So myche pride of prelattes, so cruell and so kene -	245	Speke Parott	475
Avaunt, cowarde recrayed! /Thy pride shalbe alayd,	371	Albany	496
PRIKKITH			
It is sone aspyed where the thorne prikkith.	352	Garlande	1437
PRIMEROSE			
This primerose pereles, this propre vyolet,	352	Garlande	1447
PRIMORDIALL			
In hys lernyng primordiall.	132	Garnesche5	105
PRIMORDYALL			
How be it the primordyall	291	Why Come Ye	489
the] 'they be' Kitson 1560.7, Marshe 1568			
PRIMROSE			
The praty primrose, /The goodly columbyne.	338	Garlande	912
PRINCE			
Trew to his prince in word, in dede, and thought.	29	Dol Dethe	7
To the right of his prince which shold not be withstand;	31	Dol Dethe	67
Trew to his prince for to defende his right,	33	Dol Dethe	149
O pereles Prince of hevyn emperyalle	34	Dol Dethe	190
O] not in Marshe 1568			
To the pray we as Prince incomperable,	34	Dol Dethe	197
Nor by Ptholomy, /Prince of astronomy,	84	Phy Sparrow	504
Our prince of hih honour,	111	Lawde	45
Unto our prince, anoynted kyng.	117	Ag Scottes	58
It plesyth that noble prince roiall	132	Garnesche5	103
The Boke of the Rosiar; Prince Arturis Creacyoun;	345	Garlande	1178
So noble a prince as he /In all actyvite	368	Albany	395
A prince to play the page	369	Albany	416
PRINCELY			
All the demenour of princely astate,	347	Garlande	1231
Of his moste princely porte,	370	Albany	473
PRINCES			
Of princes and of kynges	93	Phy Sparrow	867
Hath brought nobil princes to extreme confusion.	139	Ven Tongues	58
Princes of youth, and flowre of goodly porte,	337	Garlande	897
Princes of youth, and flowre of goodly porte,	337	Garlande	904
'Ryght high and myghty princes of astate,	344	Garlande	1128
PRINCESSE			
But that princesse alone,	381	Replycacion	259
PRINCIPALL			
Kyng David the prophete, of prophetes principall,	383	Replycacion	329
PRINCIPLES			
surmysed unsurely in their perihermeniall principles,	374	Replycacion	I

PRINCIS —PRYNCES   Page   Title   Line

	Page	Title	Line
In your dialeticall /And principles silogisticall,	377	Replycacion	97
PRINCIS			
Of famous princis and lordis of astate,	29	Dol Dethe	16
All kingis, all princis, all dukis, well thei ought	34	Dol Dethe	180
PRINCYPALL			
Of phylosophers callid the princypall,	315	Garlande	128
Poete of poetes all, /And prophete princypall.	383	Replycacion	322
PRINCYPLES			
Sith I contryvyd first princyples medycynable?	321	Garlande	310
PRISIANS			
Prisians hed broken now, handy-dandy,	235	Speke Parott	171
PRIVILEGED			
For all privileged places	306	Why Come Ye	1089
PRY			
Lord, how he wolde pry /After the butterfly!	75	Phy Sparrow	134
PRYCE			
Elynour made the pryce /For god ale eche whyt.	224	El Rummynge	410
PRYCKE			
Ye prycke me in the head!'	77	Phy Sparrow	224
I am president of prynces; I prycke them with pryde.	199	Magnyfycence	2082
PRYCKE-ME-DENTY			
There was a prycke-me-denty, /Sat lyke a seynty,	229	El Rummynge	582
PRYCKE SONG			
That neyther they synge wel prycke song nor playne.	38	Coystrownel	54
PRYCKE SONGE			
He fyndeth a proporcyon in his prycke songe	38	Coystrownel	48
PRYCKYD			
What! Is thy harte pryckyd with such a prowde pynne?	162	Magnyfycence	785
PRYD			
Your pryd is paste, adwe, good nycht.	114	Scot Kynge	43
PRYDE			
Your pompe and pryde hath layde a downe.	115	Scot Kynge	69
Now is your pryde fall to decay.	118	Ag Scottes	110
Your pryde was pevysh to play such prankys:	119	Ag Scottes	150
For pryde hath plucked the by the nose	163	Magnyfycence	826
Ly there, losell, for all thy pompe and pryde;	193	Magnyfycence	1880
I am president of prynces; I prycke them with pryde.	199	Magnyfycence	2082
Pompe, pryde, honour, ryches and worldly lust,	236	Speke Parott	223
Ye are so puffed with pryde,	261	Collyn Clout	593
Brought up of poore estate, /With pryde inordynate,	262	Collyn Clout	643
With pompe and with pryde,	284	Why Come Ye	204
PRYEEST			
O pryeest unreverent.	67	Hauke	187
PRYETH			
A malaperte medler that pryeth for his pray,	37	Coystrownel	45
'He cryeth and he creketh /He pryeth and he preketh,	247	Collyn Clout	20
preketh] 'peketh' Kele 1545.1, 'prekythe' MS Harley 2252			
PRYK			
Ovyr the perke to pryk.	128	Garnesche3	157
PRYMATES			
That be theyr prymates?	275	Collyn Clout	1151
PRYME			
And we shall se you ageyne or it be pryme.'	326	Garlande	525
PRYMEROSE			
My deysy delectabyll, /My prymerose commendabyll,	237	Speke Parott	242
PRYMES			
Theyr prymes and houres fall	252	Collyn Clout	241
PRYNCE			
The prynce of endles wo;	73	Phy Sparrow	73
The ryche prynce of Pargame,	76	Phy Sparrow	192
Your soverayne lord, our prynce of myght.	117	Ag Scottes	54
There is no prynce but he hath nede of us thre –	145	Magnyfycence	159
Syr, though ye be a noble prynce of myght,	145	Magnyfycence	166
Convenyent persons for any prynce ryall.	145	Magnyfycence	173
With Magnyfycence, this noble prynce of myght,	148	Magnyfycence	273
For nowe, syrs, I am lyke as a prynce sholde be;	181	Magnyfycence	1457
For I am prynce perlesse, provyd of porte,	181	Magnyfycence	1471
So as ye be a prynce of great myght,	183	Magnyfycence	1545
Nowe Jesu preserve you, syr, prynce most of myght.	190	Magnyfycence	1796
I plucke downe kynge, prynce, lorde, and knyght;	193	Magnyfycence	1883
A prynce to use with all his hole intent,	200	Magnyfycence	2118
That somtyme was a noble prynce of myght!	205	Magnyfycence	2280
For that pereles prynce that Parrot dyd create,	236	Speke Parott	218
Had nat our prynce be	292	Why Come Ye	539
Prynce of eloquence, Tullius Cicero,	321	Garlande	330
PRYNCELY			
It is a pryncely pleasure and a lordly mynde.	186	Magnyfycence	1627
PRYNCES			
'Prynces of youghte', can ye synge by rote?	53	Bowge	253
Largesse is he that all prynces doth avaunce;	148	Magnyfycence	279
So thou arte personable to bere a pryncres baner.	161	Magnyfycence	767
To me all prynces to lowte man bese[m]e.	182	Magnyfycence	1500
beseme] 'be sene' †Rastell & Treveris C 1530, B			
I am president of prynces; I prycke them with pryde.	199	Magnyfycence	2082
Paregall with all prynces, farre passyng hys estate;	244	Speke Parott	436
Within that, a pryncres excellente of porte;	313	Garlande	43
that] 'it' MS Cotton Vitellius E.x			
'Pryncres moost pusant, of hygh preemynence,	313	Garlande	50

PRYNCYPALL — PROFESSYOUN   Page   Title   Line

PRYNCYPALL
As provost pryncypall, /To teach them theyr ordynall;   85   Phy Sparrow   554
Good Hope, syr, my name is; remedy pryncypall   206   Magnyfycence   2328
In theyr pryncypall cure /They make but lytell sure,   249   Collyn Clout   102
PRYNT
I am Goddys preposytour; I prynt them with a pen;   195   Magnyfycence   1941
PRYNTED
Prynted for to be,   277   Collyn Clout   1239
PRYNTITH
With Courtely Abusyoun; who pryntith it wele in mynde   346   Garlande   1196
PRYORESSE
Dame Sare our pryoresse,   256   Collyn Clout   393
PRYSONER
For a prysoner there now ye be   114   Scot Kynge   40
PRYSTE
A pryste for to controlle.   126   Garnesche3   89
PRYTELY
And prytely he wolde pant   75   Phy Sparrow   132
PRYVY
Pryvy poyntmentys conveyed so properly;   177   Magnyfycence   1337
PRYVYLEGYD
Lyberte is laudable and pryvylegyd from lawe.   142   Magnyfycence   68
PROBATE
Welth is of wysdome the very trewe probate.   140   Magnyfycence   4
Of Scipions dreme what was the treu probate;   322   Garlande   368
PROBLEME
But, Perseveraunce, me semyth your probleme was best;   212   Magnyfycence   2505
In Achademia Parrot dare no probleme kepe,   235   Speke Parott   162
Poynt well this probleme that Parrot doth prate,   236   Speke Parott   220
PROBLEMES
Yet your problemes ar preignaunte and with loyalte acquayntyd. 240   Speke Parott   344
Percius pressed forth with problemes diffuse;   321   Garlande   338
in maister Porphiris problemes,   374   Replycacion   I
PROBLEMIS
Suche problemis to paynt it longyth to his arte.   347   Garlande   1246
PROCEDE
But to the poynte shortely to procede,   53   Bowge   246
Syth all in substaunce of slumbrynge doth procede.   61   Bowge   536
It i[s] no maystery. Tushe, let Measure procede,   144   Magnyfycence   150
   is] 'it' †Rastell & Treveris C 1530, B
Hast thou ony more? Let se, procede.   174   Magnyfycence   1236
All that he sayth of trouthe dothe procede;   209   Magnyfycence   2426
And so procede /In you to rede,   355   Garlande   1548
With penne and ynke procede,   385   Replycacion   388
PROCEDID
Onely procedid for that he did outray   316   Garlande   156
PROCEDYD
Or it procedyd of fatall persuacyon,   313   Garlande   34
PROCERPINA
Procerpina in hell,   105   Phy Sparrow   1366
PROCES
Of the whych proces /Ye may know more expres,   68   Hauke   231
Of Marcus Marcellus /A proces I could tell us;   90   Phy Sparrow   735
To you rehersyng the somme of my proces.   117   Ag Scottes   90
But now, my proces for to save,   133   Garnesche5   157
as more at large it doth apere in the proces folowynge.   312   Garlande   I
Commensyng your proces after there degre,   335   Garlande   819
Of my laurell the proces every whitte.   343   Garlande   1099
in as moche as it were to longe a proces   345   Garlande   R
PROCESSE
Commensynge this processe at mayster Redresse.   211   Magnyfycence   2481
Syth unto me formest this processe is erectyd,   211   Magnyfycence   2482
Unto this processe brefly compylyd,   212   Magnyfycence   2510
For in this processe, Parrot nothing hath surmysed,   236   Speke Parott   200
Than, our processe for to stable,   292   Why Come Ye   536
Over this, for a more ample processe   374   Replycacion   I
Returne we to our former processe.   384   Replycacion   R
PROCESSYON
With his fagot in processyon.   379   Replycacion   188
PROCLAME
A cry anone forthwith she made proclame,   325   Garlande   453
PROCLAMED
And famously proclamed?   103   Phy Sparrow   1257
Bycause they have proclamed   305   Why Come Ye   1055
PRODIGALL
So prodigall expence, and so shamfull reconyng;   244   Speke Parott   458
PRODYGALL
So that your largesse be not to prodygall.   211   Magnyfycence   2488
PROFE
And therof ye shall a larger profe se.   188   Magnyfycence   1700
PROFER
For her pleasure to make a large profer,   327   Garlande   556
PROFESSED
To whom he was professed   307   Why Come Ye   1121
Protestacion alway canonically prepensed, professed,   373   Replycacion   I
PROFESSYOUN
Of your professyoun unto umanyte,   335   Garlande   818

PROFYTABLE — PROPHETES

	Page	Title	Line
PROFYTABLE			
Lacrymable, Profytable for the soule.	39	Coystrowne3	1
That profyteth all other is nothynge profytable	321	Garlande	313
PROFYTE GROWTH			
So pynchyng and sparyng, and so lytell profyte growth;	245	Speke Parott	493
PROFYTETH			
That profyteth all other is nothynge profytable	321	Garlande	313
PROFOUNDE			
Say on; me thynke your reasons be profounde.	190	Magnyfycence	1767
PROGENY			
The progeny of Parrottis were fayre and favorable;	236	Speke Parott	187
And his base progeny,	291	Why Come Ye	491
PROLOGUE			
Thus endeth the prologue,	49	Bowge	R
PROMISED			
Hath promised to hele our cardinals eye.	309	Why Come Ye	1197
PROMYSE			
If Apollo wyll promyse	93	Phy Sparrow	863
To make fayre promyse, what are ye the worse?	189	Magnyfycence	1761
In her promyse there is no sykernesse,	197	Magnyfycence	2028
PROMYSED			
She promysed to us all she wolde be kynde;	49	Bowge	124
I dare not speke; I promysed to be dome.	52	Bowge	229
PROMYSYDE			
To me also all thouthe yt wer promysyde	33	Dol Dethe	159
PROMOCION			
To helpe you to promocion,	378	Replycacion	137
PROMOCYON			
And suche as you wyll shall lacke no promocyon.	190	Magnyfycence	1789
They gaspe and they gape /All to have promocyon:	248	Collyn Clout	86
For, ne were onely he hath your promocyon,	314	Garlande	71
PROMOSYON			
Magnyfycence to mayntayne, your promosyon shalbe.	144	Magnyfycence	157
PROMOTED			
And so clerkely promoted,	265	Collyn Clout	756
In lykewyse now the same /Cardynall is promoted,	293	Why Come Ye	571
Promoted was he /To a cardynalles dygnyte	297	Why Come Ye	728
PROMOTYD			
Sodenly promotyd, and sodenly put backe;	212	Magnyfycence	2531
And suche of my servauntes as I have promotyd,	318	Garlande	202
PROMOTYNGE			
And your parcyall promotynge	273	Collyn Clout	1075
PROMOTYVE			
Unto the rowme of laureat promotyve?	315	Garlande	116
PRONGE			
By God, I have bene about a praty pronge -	154	Magnyfycence	501
And howe at a pronge	276	Collyn Clout	1194
PRONOSTYCATE			
To pronostycate truly the chaunce of fortunys dyse;	234	Speke Parott	136
PRONOUNCE			
For trowthe in parabyll ye wantonlye pronounce,	241	Speke Parott	364
PRONOWNSYNG			
Pronownsyng my purpose after my properte,	231	Speke Parott	30
PROP			
Gydith his bote with a prop.	349	Garlande	1334
PROPE			
Gydeth his bote with a prope;	105	Phy Sparrow	1341
PROPER			
Counterfetynge is a proper bayte.	152	Magnyfycence	442
With proper captacyons of benevolence,	335	Garlande	815
PROPERCIUS			
Propercius and Pisandros, poetis of noble fame;	322	Garlande	382
PROPERLY			
So properly it is set:	98	Phy Sparrow	1049
So properly she presses	101	Phy Sparrow	1171
This was properly prated, syrs! What sayd a?	161	Magnyfycence	746
Properly drest /All poynte devyse,	164	Magnyfycence	842
Foly fotyth it properly, fansy ledyth the dawnce,	177	Magnyfycence	1331
Pryvy poyntmentys conveyed so properly;	177	Magnyfycence	1337
Properly payntyd to be my coverture;	231	Speke Parott	9
And say properly thei are sacerdotes	268	Collyn Clout	874
PROPERTE			
Ye have nat red the properte	129	Garnesche5	8
Pronownsyng my purpose after my properte,	231	Speke Parott	30
PROPHANES			
Men call you therfore prophanes.	252	Collyn Clout	207
PROPHESY			
With his harpe of prophesy /And spyrituall poetry,	384	Replycacion	345
PROPHET			
The holy prophet, was;	276	Collyn Clout	1207
was] 'Ozeas' MS Harley 2252			
PROPHETE			
Poete of poetes all, /And prophete princypall.	383	Replycacion	322
Kyng David the prophete, of prophetes principall,	383	Replycacion	329
PROPHETES			
Kyng David the prophete, of prophetes principall,	383	Replycacion	329
Olde patriarkes and prophetes in heven with him to dwell.	383	Replycacion	342

PROPHYTABYLL —PROUDE	Page	Title	Line

PROPHYTABYLL
And also prophytabyll, /Yf ye be agreabyll, ... 237 Speke Parott 248
PROPIR
My propir Besse, /My praty Besse, ... 237 Speke Parott 235
PROPYR
'My propyr Parott, my lytell pratye fole.' . . . . 231 Speke Parott 20
My propyr Besse, /To turne agayne to me. . . . . 237 Speke Parott 250
My propyr Besse, /And torne agayne to me! . . . . 238 Speke Parott 261
Go, propyr Parotte, my popagay, ... 241 Speke Parott 357
PROPORCYON
He fyndeth a proporcyon in his prycke songe . . . . 38 Coystrownel 48
PROPORSIONYD
So truely proporsionyd, and so well did gree, ... 320 Garlande 275
PROPOSICYOUN
That banisshed was he by his proposicyoun, ... 316 Garlande 132
  by] 'through' Marshe 1568
PROPRE
It was propre and prest. 75 Phy Sparrow 127
The jeloffer well set, /The propre vyolet; . . . . 340 Garlande 984
In plantynge and pluckynge a propre jeloffer flowre; . . . . . 351 Garlande 1392
This primerose pereles, this propre vyolet, ... 352 Garlande 1447
PROSCRIPCYON
Frome the laureat senate by force of proscripcyon. . . . . . . 318 Garlande 225
PROSE
And spend my tyme /In prose and ryme, ... 95 Phy Sparrow 955
Owt of Frenshe into Englysshe prose. . . . . 347 Garlande 1220
PROSECUTE
What shulde I prosecute, ... 378 Replycacion 158
PROSERPINA
Proserpina in hell, ... 350 Garlande 1359
PROSERPINAS
And from the smokes sowre /Of Proserpinas bowre; . . . . 73 Phy Sparrow 83
PROSPERE
In this your journey to prospere and spede. . . . . 239 Speke Parott 314
PROSPERYOUSLY
It can not contynew long prosperyously; . . . . 200 Magnyfycence 2132
PROSPERYTE
Measure contynwyth prosperyte and welthe. . . . . 144 Magnyfycence 141
Then shall you have with you prosperyte resydent. . . . . . . 146 Magnyfycence 197
In hynderaunce of welthe and prosperyte. . . . . 160 Magnyfycence 734
Prosperyte [by] hym is gyven solacyusly to man; . . . . 207 Magnyfycence 2367
  by] 'to' †Rastell & Treveris C 1530, B
For prosperyte /Away than wyll fle. . . . . 300 Why Come Ye 862
PROSPEROUS
I pray God sende the prosperous lyf and long, ... 34 Dol Dethe 169
PROSSES
And my style dres /To this prosses. . . . . 96 Phy Sparrow 969
How thys prosses I prate of, hyt ys not all for nowghte. . . . 242 Speke Parott 389
To practise or postyll thys prosses here and there? . . . . . 242 Speke Parott 393
PROTECCYON
Myght seme ryght wel under my proteccyon . . . . 181 Magnyfycence 1469
Under proteccyon /Of sad correccyon, ... 356 Garlande 1574
PROTECTION
Sometyme under protection /Of pacient sufferance, ... 385 Replycacion 392
PROTECTIONS
For bysshoppes have protections, ... 268 Collyn Clout 891
PROTECTYON
shall be his protectyon, his pavys and his wall. . . . . 236 Speke Parott 203
Non can have protectyon . . . . 304 Why Come Ye 1011
  Non can have] 'They can have no' †Kele 1545.3, Toy 1553,
  Kitson 1560.7, Marshe 1568
Under the protectyon /Of the kynges great seale, ... 307 Why Come Ye 1128
  great] 'brode' MS Rawlinson C. 813
PROTESTACION
Parott, ye may prate thys undyr protestacion, ... 240 Speke Parott 336
I speke by protestacion: . . . . 305 Why Come Ye 1043
Protestacion alway canonically prepensed, professed, ... 373 Replycacion I
PROTESTACYON
Made by protestacyon, ... 103 Phy Sparrow 1279
Howe be it, by protestacyon . . . . 143 Magnyfycence 97
For protestacyon made . . . . 266 Collyn Clout 780
PROTESTACYOUN
But myrth and consolacyoun, /Made by protestacyoun, ... 348 Garlande 1272
PROTHONATORY
But that I poynt you to be prothonatory . . . . 324 Garlande 432
PROTHONOTORY
Before some prothonotory, /Imperyall or papall. . . . . 299 Why Come Ye 819
PROUD
This pevysh proud, thys prendergest, ... 36 Coystrownel 6
Lord, how Perkyn is proud of hys Pohen! . . . . 37 Coystrownel 19
Now have I shewyd you part of your proud mynde; . . . . 38 Coystrownel 67
As proud a pohen as ye sprede, ... 41 Coystrowne4 13
And ye, proud Scot, Dunde, Dunbar . . . . 118 Ag Scottes 121
Then let them vale a bonet of their proud sayle, ... 138 Ven Tongues 32
PROUDE
To poynte this proude page a place and a rome, ... 37 Coystrownel 41
Now ye proude Scottes of Gelawaye . . . . 114 Scot Kynge 19
And ye proude Scottes of Dunbar, ... 114 Scot Kynge 29

PROUDLY —PROWDE   Page   Title   Line

	Page	Title	Line
For alle your proude prankyng, yor pride may apayere.	122	Garneschel	19
The one of you is to proude, the other is to haute.	203	Magnyfycence	2223
He makith so proude pretens,	307	Why Come Ye	1133
And yet this proude Antiochus,	308	Why Come Ye	1175
Nacion moost in hate, /Proude and poore of state.	362	Albany	144
Suche a proude palyarde, /Suche a skyrgaliarde,	363	Albany	167
Suche a proude pultrowne,	363	Albany	170

PROUDLY

To be so perte to prese so proudly uppe.	48	Bowge	71
He set the arme proudly under the syde,	55	Bowge	321
Yet proudly he dare pretende	292	Why Come Ye	530
to prate and to preche proudly and leudly, and loudly to lye;	374	Replycacion	1

PROVE

Or howe can you prove that there is felycyte,	142	Magnyfycence	77
Lyberte without measure prove a thynge of nought.	143	Magnyfycence	117
In fayth, I wyll not say that ye shall prove a fole,	148	Magnyfycence	301
Bycause I wolde prove men of theyr pacyence.	194	Magnyfycence	1917
Afflyccyon and trouble to prove his pacyence;	207	Magnyfycence	2371
Contradyccyon to prove his sapyence;	207	Magnyfycence	2372
For ye may prove it by me.'	219	El Rummynge	216
'Prove his wytt', sayth he, 'at cardes or dyce,	318	Garlande	206
And to prove your selfe suche foles.	378	Replycacion	145

PROVED

But yf prudence be proved with sad cyrcumspeccyon,	141	Magnyfycence	16

PROVERBE

A proverbe of old, 'Say well or be styll':	38	Coystrowne1	64
(A proverbe longe ago.)	293	Why Come Ye	584
Graund juir, of this Frenshe proverbe olde,	352	Garlande	1440

PROVERBYS

How olde proverbys say,	129	Garnesche3	196

PROVETH

Yet it proveth eyrnest, ye may se, every day.	195	Magnyfycence	1949

PROVINCYALL

Decre and decretall, /Constytucyon provincyall,	308	Why Come Ye	1158

PROVINCYALS

Or holy sinodals, /Or els provincyals,	65	Hauke	133

PROVISION

So myche provision, and so lytell wytte at nede -	244	Speke Parott	454
For by his devellysshe drift and graceles provision	333	Garlande	757

PROVISYON

And makith suche provisyon	306	Why Come Ye	1093

PROVITHE

As provithe well, in hys rethorikys olde,	130	Garnesche5	11

PROVYD

In Arturys auncyent actys nowhere ys provyd your pere;	123	Garnesche2	24
For I am prynce perlesse, provyd of porte,	181	Magnyfycence	1471

PROVYDENCE

Gravyte of counsell, provydence, and wyt;	210	Magnyfycence	2476

PROVYDENT

Provydent, discrete, circumspect and wyse,	33	Dol Dethe	139
Provydent] 'Prudent' Marshe 1568			

PROVYNCIALL

But reason and wytte wantythe theyr provynciall,	232	Speke Parott	53

PROVYNCYALL

In your provyncyall borders,	252	Collyn Clout	221
To kepe his court provyncyall	299	Why Come Ye	813

PROVYTH

Whych provyth well that measure shold have domynyon.	143	Magnyfycence	120

PROVOKE

And somtyme they provoke	268	Collyn Clout	854
Ye dyde provoke and tyse,	378	Replycacion	132

PROVOKED

that popholy and pevysshe presumpcion provoked them to publysshe	375	Replycacion	1

PROVOST

As provost pryncypall, /To teach them theyr ordynall;	85	Phy Sparrow	554

PROVOSTE

Pocenya, the prowde provoste of Turky lande,	181	Magnyfycence	1480

PROWDE

Forthwith, he made on me a prowde assawte,	55	Bowge	316
The pecocke so prowde,	82	Phy Sparrow	438
Agaynst the prowde Scottys claterynge,	115	Ag Scottes	1
So prowde of hart, /So overthwart,	116	Ag Scottes	35
Of the prowde Scot, kynge Jemmy,	117	Ag Scottes	71
Thow ye prate lyke prowde Pylate, beware yet of chek mate.	123	Garnesche2	7
Thow ye prate lyke prowde Pylate, beware of cheke mate.	123	Garnesche2	14
Tho ye prate lyke prowde Pylate, beware of cheke mate.	123	Garnesche2	21
Pyramus, nor Priamus, nor Syr Pyrrus the prowde,	123	Garnesche2	23
Thow ye prate lyke prowde Pylate, beware of cheke mate.	123	Garnesche2	28
Thow ye prate lyke prowde Pylate, beware of cheke mate.	123	Garnesche2	35
Thow ye prate lyke prowde Pylate, beware of cheke mate.	124	Garnesche2	42
Of all prowde knavys thow beryst the belle,	130	Garnesche5	27
Prowde, peviche, lyddyr and lewde,	133	Garnesche5	146
What! Is thy harte pryckyd with such a prowde pynne?	16?	Magnyfycence	785
But that the horson is prowde and hawte.	163	Magnyfycence	824
Somtyme I syt as I were solempe prowde;	168	Magnyfycence	1011
Nowe hast thou not a prowde mocke and a starke?	174	Magnyfycence	1208
Anone he waxyth so hy and prowde,	174	Magnyfycence	1244
Pocenya, the prowde provoste of Turky lande,	181	Magnyfycence	1480

PROWDEST — PUNYSSHMENT

	Page	Title	Line
And Thesius, th[at] prowde was Pluto to face –	182	Magnyfycence	1496
that] 'the' †Rastell & Treveris C 1530, B			
To full of fansyes, to lordly, to prowde,	199	Magnyfycence	2093
With, 'Skyre-galyard, prowde palyard, vaunte-parler, ye prate!'	244	Speke Parott	433
But wele may ye thynk I was no thyng prowde	330	Garlande	648

PROWDEST
I set not by the prowdest of them a prane,	181	Magnyfycence	1489

PROWDYST
The prowdyst knave yet of us tewyne	130	Garnesche5	21

PROWES
Of knightly prowes the sworde, pomel, and hilt,	32	Dol Dethe	108
In merciall prowes /Lyke unto Hercules,	369	Albany	430

PRUDENCE
She doth excede and pas /In prudence dame Pallas;	102	Phy Sparrow	1230
But yf prudence be proved with sad cyrcumspeccyon,	141	Magnyfycence	16
And also dame Prudence, /With sober Sapyence.	279	Why Come Ye	13
In prudence and wysdom /Lyke unto Salamon,	369	Albany	432

PRUDENT
Prudent Rebecca, of whome remembraunce	336	Garlande	845
By Maro, the Mantuan prudent,	342	Garlande	1080

PSALME
With this psalme, Domine, probasti me,	102	Phy Sparrow	1239

PSAUTRY
Of our savyour Christ in his decacorde psautry,	383	Replycacion	340

PTHOLOME
In royal mageste /Lyke unto Ptholome,	370	Albany	441

PTHOLOMY
Nor by Ptholomy, /Prince of astronomy,	84	Phy Sparrow	503
Nor with royall Ptholomy, /Nor with Albumasar,	292	Why Come Ye	522

PUAUNT
O ye wretched Scottes, /Ye puaunt pyspottes,	362	Albany	120

PUAUNTELY
And so puauntely dothe smelle	127	Garnesche3	143

PUBLISSHE
For if he gloryously publisshe his matter,	314	Garlande	83

PUBLYSSHE
that popholy and pevysshe presumpcion provoked them to publysshe	375	Replycacion	I

PUBLYSSHED
So many bullys of pardon publysshed and shewyd;	246	Speke Parott	515

PUDDYNG
Grimbaldus gredy snatche a puddyng tyl the rost be redy.	172	Magnyfycence	1155

PUDDYNGES
By God, for snatchynge of puddynges and wortes.	171	Magnyfycence	1128

PUFFED
Her paunche was so puffed	228	El Rummynge	570
Ye are so puffed with pryde,	261	Collyn Clout	593
howbeit they were puffed so full	375	Replycacion	I

PUFFYN
The puffyn and the tele,	83	Phy Sparrow	454
puffyn] 'pussyn' †Kele 1545.2			

PUFTE
Pufte full of heresy,	381	Replycacion	253

PULL
But plucke away and pull /Theyr fleces of wull.	248	Collyn Clout	78

PULLE
Avysynge me my penne awaye to pulle	46	Bowge	21

PULLISSHYD
'O noble Chaucer, whos pullisshyd eloquence	324	Garlande	421

PULLYSHED
The pullyshed perle youre whytenes doth declare;	44	Balettys3	18

PULLYSHYD
Pullyshyd and fresshe is your ornacy.	183	Magnyfycence	1531

PULLYSSHED
With pullysshed termes lusty;	91	Phy Sparrow	776
Were pullysshed with the fyle /Of Ciceros eloquence,	101	Phy Sparrow	1205
pullysshed] 'publysshed' †Kele 1545.2			

PULLYSSHID
Ornatly pullysshid after your faculte,	335	Garlande	816

PULPETE
And in the pulpete hopped,	377	Replycacion	119

PULPYT
In the pulpyt solempnely –	266	Collyn Clout	811

PULPYTTES
In pulpyttes autentyke,	264	Collyn Clout	696
autentyke] 'attentyke' Kele 1545.1, 'antentike' Marshe 1568			

PULTRE
But I have thy pultre, and thou hast my catell.	171	Magnyfycence	1135

PULTROWNE
Suche a proude pultrowne,	363	Albany	170

PUMP
That naythyr pump nor synke	127	Garnesche3	145

PUNYETE
It was tart and punyete.	225	El Rummynge	435

PUNYSSHED
That you hath punysshed with his sharpe rod.	207	Magnyfycence	2350

PUNYSSHMENT
And ye have deserved this punysshment.	196	Magnyfycence	2003

	Page	Title	Line
PUNT			
That mastres Punt put yow of, yt was nat alle causeles;	122	Garneschel	32
PURCHACE			
And to purchace /Thyne hevenly place	40	Coystrowne3	51
Nay. Purchace ye a pardon for the pose,	163	Magnyfycence	825
Therby I shall purchace /No displesaunt rewarde,	367	Albany	358
PURCHASE			
Her favoure to purchase.	98	Phy Sparrow	1076
And wyll not endevour hymselfe to purchase	314	Garlande	75
PURCHASER			
For largesse is a purchaser of pardon and of grace.	148	Magnyfycence	268
PURE			
Maiden moste pure, and Goddis moder dere,	34	Dol Dethe	205
Of all pure clennesse virgynall,	375	Replycacion	32
PURGACYON			
And payned you with a purgacyon of odyous poverte,	207	Magnyfycence	2353
PURPILL			
Grene, rede, tawny, whyte, purpill, and blew.	334	Garlande	800
whyte] 'whyght blak' MS Cotton Vitellius E.x			
PURPLE			
In purple and paule belapped;	254	Collyn Clout	310
PURPOSE			
Of purpose, for the nones,	77	Phy Sparrow	211
Brefly to touche of my purpose the effecte:	142	Magnyfycence	67
Paynte to a purpose good countenaunce I can,	160	Magnyfycence	724
My purpose is to spy and to poynte every man;	160	Magnyfycence	726
Even of purpose for the same.	167	Magnyfycence	957
Sore sayde, I tell you, and well to the purpose.	180	Magnyfycence	1428
Inputured with fetures after your purpose,	183	Magnyfycence	1552
Pronownsyng my purpose after my properte,	231	Speke Parott	30
'What is this to purpose?' Over in a whynnymeg!	232	Speke Parott	71
I purpose to shake oute /All my connynge bagge,	248	Collyn Clout	50
Nothynge to purpose	286	Why Come Ye	287
But of my purpose now turne we to the grownde.	313	Garlande	28
purpose] 'proces' MS Cotton Vitellius E.x			
'The sum of your purpose, as we ar advysid,	314	Garlande	78
But if that he purpose to make a redresse,	318	Garlande	229
Wherof partely I purpose to expounde,	325	Garlande	464
I purpose for to reply	375	Replycacion	20
PURPOSYD			
Precely purposyd under pretence of play,	213	Magnyfycence	2553
PURS			
Put up your purs, ye shall non pay!'	40	Coystrowne4	11
Though his purs wax dull,	302	Why Come Ye	937
PURSE			
Whan I loked on hym, my purse was half aferde.	52	Bowge	238
It wyll not be, his purse is not on-flote.	60	Bowge	488
Had I not opened my purse wyde,	150	Magnyfycence	347
Woo is that purse that ye shall share!	156	Magnyfycence	587
Thou shalte have my purse, and I wyll have thyne.	171	Magnyfycence	1102
Nowe, by my trouth, man, take, there is my purse;	171	Magnyfycence	1104
my] 'myne' †Rastell & Treveris C 1530, B			
And in my purse was twenty marke.	171	Magnyfycence	1108
Shyt thy purse, dawe, and do no cost.	174	Magnyfycence	1207
Let me have the rule of your purse.	189	Magnyfycence	1762
With never a peny in his purse.	204	Magnyfycence	2258
But a full purse.	254	Collyn Clout	293
Some be called crafty that can pyke a purse;	317	Garlande	184
pyke] 'kit' MS Cotton Vitellius E.x			
PURSEVANTIS			
Of pursevantis ther presid in with many a dyverse tale:	326	Garlande	492
a] not in Marshe 1568			
PURSYS			
So myche portlye pride, with pursys penyles;	244	Speke Parott	460
PURVEAUNCE			
Made purveaunce /And suche ordenaunce,	165	Magnyfycence	880
PURVEY			
To purvey for our cardynall /A palace pontifycall	299	Why Come Ye	811
PUSANT			
'Prynces moost pusant, of hygh preemynence,	313	Garlande	50
PUS CATT			
'Lyke owur pus catt Parott can mewte and crye.'	231	Speke Parott	24
owur] 'your' Lant 1545, Kynge & Marche 1554, Day 1560, Marshe 1568			
PUSCULL			
With here and there a puscull,	228	El Rummynge	555
PUSYLLANYMYTE			
And not embracyd with pusyllanymyte.	146	Magnyfycence	206
PUSKYLDE			
From the puskylde pocky pose,	309	Why Come Ye	1195
puskylde] 'pusky' MS Rawlinson C. 813; pose] 'nose' Kitson 1560.7			
PUT			
Put up your purs, ye shall non pay!'	40	Coystrowne4	11
Amonge all other I put myselfe in prece.	47	Bowge	44
That mastres Punt put yow of, yt was nat alle causeles;	122	Garneschel	32
Somtime women were put in great blame,	139	Ven Tongues	59
And another bade put out myne eye;	150	Magnyfycence	353

PUTREFY — QUARELL

	Page	Title	Line
They have made me here to put the stone;	151	Magnyfycence	406
Why, can ye not put out that foule freke?	158	Magnyfycence	657
Put Magnyfycence in suche a madnesse	159	Magnyfycence	679
Howe rode he by you? Howe put he to you?	173	Magnyfycence	1178
Put on thy gowne agayne, for thou hast lost nowe.	173	Magnyfycence	1203
thou ... nowe] 'nowe thou hast lost' †Rastell & Treveris C 1530, B			
Nowe put on, fole, thy cote agayne.	173	Magnyfycence	1205
To put where he lyst, foly hath fre chace;	177	Magnyfycence	1329
Them that dare put theyr truste in me;	188	Magnyfycence	1699
Put your wyll to his wyll, for surely it is he	196	Magnyfycence	1997
Put fro you presumpcyon and admyt humylyte,	207	Magnyfycence	2361
And made also mesure to be put fro me.	209	Magnyfycence	2446
Sodenly promotyd, and sodenly put backe;	212	Magnyfycence	2531
For in hoder-moder /The churche is put in faute.	248	Collyn Clout	70
To herken Jacke and Gyll /Whan they put up a byll;	249	Collyn Clout	97
To put them thus to flyght;	256	Collyn Clout	405
I put you out of dout,	267	Collyn Clout	848
They put you to your actyon.	273	Collyn Clout	1060
And put them out of theyr place.	273	Collyn Clout	1078
To put all the governynge,	298	Why Come Ye	761
Yet sum surgions put a dout	309	Why Come Ye	1198
Lest he wyll put it clene out,	309	Why Come Ye	1199
Ye put to blame ye wot nere whom.	310	Why Come Ye2	17
nere] 'nott' MS Rawlinson C. 813			
To put any man in lack	310	Why Come Ye2	25
Put up his sworde, for he cowde make no warre,	312	Garlande	5
And whome ye love not ye wyll put to shame.	317	Garlande	178
To se if Skelton wyll put hymselfe in prease	319	Garlande	239
wyll] 'dare' MS Cotton Vitellius E.x			
Sume to enbrowder put them in prese,	334	Garlande	794
And put hym downe,	361	Albany	95
To put thy selfe to flyght.	364	Albany	233
That put the in suche fray.	365	Albany	242

PUTREFY

	Page	Title	Line
When Parrot is ded, he dothe not putrefy;	236	Speke Parott	213
he] 'she' †Lant 1545, Kynge & Marche 1554, Day 1560, Marshe 1568			

PUTTE

	Page	Title	Line
That valiaunt knyght, /Putte you to flyght /By his valyaunce.	360	Albany	41
There he putte backe	360	Albany	44
To putte his eyes out	361	Albany	94

PUTTETH

	Page	Title	Line
That putteth fysshes to a fraye;	83	Phy Sparrow	463
Here CRAFTY CONVEYAUNCE putteth of his gowne.	173	Magnyfycence	SD
And putteth them to sylence	305	Why Come Ye	1064
His noble baronage /He putteth them in corage	370	Albany	466

PUWYT

	Page	Title	Line
With Puwyt the lapwyng,	82	Phy Sparrow	430

QUADRANT

	Page	Title	Line
In the volvell, in the quadrant and in the astroloby,	234	Speke Parott	135

QUAIRE

	Page	Title	Line
Within this quaire? /Who lyst repayre	116	Ag Scottes	41
lyst] 'lyst to' Kynge & Marche 1554, Day 1560, Marshe 1568			
Go, litill quaire, /Demene you faire.	355	Garlande	1533

QUAYLE

	Page	Title	Line
The partryche, the quayle;	82	Phy Sparrow	416
A quayle, the rayle, the olde raven.	268	Collyn Clout	870

QUAYLLES

	Page	Title	Line
So many plucte partryches, and so fatte quaylles;	245	Speke Parott	486

QUAYRE

	Page	Title	Line
Go, litele quayre, namyd the Popagay,	238	Speke Parott	278
Goe, lytyll quayre, pray them that yow beholde,	239	Speke Parott	290
Go, lytell quayre, quickly.	371	Albany	508
Go, lytell quayre, apace,	372	Albany	523

QUAKE

	Page	Title	Line
I fele my body quake,	74	Phy Sparrow	105
That made the Romaynes all /For-drede and to quake;	88	Phy Sparrow	667
That] 'What' †Kele 1545.2, Wyght 1553			
But I shall frounce them on the foretop and gar them to quake.	182	Magnyfycence	1514
'Quake, quake,' sayd the duck /In that lampatrams lap.	227	El Rummynge	505
'Quake, quake,' sayd the duck /In that lampatrams lap.	227	El Rummynge	505
That he wolde than make /The devyls to quake,	303	Why Come Ye	979
Betwene his armes, he felt her body quake.	320	Garlande	301

QUAKED

	Page	Title	Line
With that her hed shaked /And her handes quaked.	226	El Rummynge	477
Howe lusty Venus quaked,	270	Collyn Clout	945

QUALE

	Page	Title	Line
With the feders of a quale	226	El Rummynge	453

QUALYFYED

	Page	Title	Line
And qualyfyed qualytes /Of pluralytes,	260	Collyn Clout	560

QUALYTES

	Page	Title	Line
And qualyfyed qualytes /Of pluralytes,	260	Collyn Clout	560

QUARELL

	Page	Title	Line
The grounde of his quarell was for his sovereyn lord,	31	Dol Dethe	64
Fyrste pycke a quarell and fall oute with hym then,	55	Bowge	314
Then some occacyon or quarell ye must fynde,	185	Magnyfycence	1600
Well sayd. But, in fayth, what was your quarell?	203	Magnyfycence	2210

QUARELLES —QUESTYON | Page | Title | Line

Entry	Page	Title	Line
Of every lyght quarell,	261	Collyn Clout	599
QUARELLES			
Or to maynteyne good quarelles.	269	Collyn Clout	916
QUARELLYS			
A bungler, a brawler, a pyker of quarellys!	37	Coystrownel	35
QUARILLIS			
Pers Prater, the secund, that quarillis begannne;	330	Garlande	636
QUARTE			
She swynged up a quarte /At ones for her parte.	228	El Rummynge	568
swynged] 'swinge' Marshe 1568			
QUARTERD			
Was hedyd, drawen, and quarterd,	297	Why Come Ye	740
QUARTERS			
Ye, thou haste the four quarters of a knave.	172	Magnyfycence	1165
In faythe, I gyve the four quarters of a knave.	204	Magnyfycence	2252
QUATRIVIALS			
Of the quatrivials,	292	Why Come Ye	514
QUATRYVYALS			
Tryvyals and quatryvyals so sore now they appayre,	235	Speke Parott	166
QUECKE			
For by robbynge they rynne to in manus tuas quecke;	198	Magnyfycence	2044
QUEED			
Full of myschiefe and queed,	106	Epitaphe	I
QUEENE			
And of Vesca his queene,	90	Phy Sparrow	741
QUEYSY			
But they say it is a queysy mete;	204	Magnyfycence	2267
QUELL			
Deth wyll us quell /And with us mell.	39	Coystrowne3	23
QUENCHE			
Of farvent charyte I quenche out the bronde;	205	Magnyfycence	2287
QUENE			
O Quene of mercy, O lady full of grace,	34	Dol Dethe	204
Of lusty somer the passyng goodly quene;	44	Balettys3	14
And Dame Gaynour, his quene	87	Phy Sparrow	636
Lyke dame Flora, quene	101	Phy Sparrow	1183
I am a mynyon to wayte apon a quene;	231	Speke Parott	19
a (2)] 'the' Lant 1545, Kynge & Marche 1554, Day 1560, Marshe 1568			
'With Kateryne incomporabyll, owur royall quene also,	231	Speke Parott	36
With Dame Helyn the quene.	270	Collyn Clout	953
To whome supplyed the royall Quene of Fame.	313	Garlande	49
The Quene of Fame to Dame Pallas	313	Garlande	R
Dame Pallas to the Quene of Fame	314	Garlande	R
The Quene of Fame to Dame Pallas	315	Garlande	R
Dame Pallas to the Quene of Fame	316	Garlande	R
The Quene of Fame to Dame Pallas	316	Garlande	R
Dame Pallas to the Quene of Fame	317	Garlande	R
The Quene of Fame to Dame Pallas	318	Garlande	R
Dame Pallas to the Quene of Fame	318	Garlande	R
There was suyng to the Quene of Fame;	319	Garlande	253
Into the ryche palace of the Quene of Fame:	325	Garlande	450
Wherin was set of Fame the noble Quene,	325	Garlande	482
And formest of all dame Flora, the quene	331	Garlande	685
The noble Pamphila, quene of the Grekis londe,	336	Garlande	850
Zeuxes, that enpicturid fare Elene the quene,	337	Garlande	892
Before my ladys grace, the Quene of Fame,	343	Garlande	1091
In her astate there sat the noble Quene	343	Garlande	1114
The Quene of Fame to Skelton	344	Garlande	R
Skelton Poeta to the Quene of Fame	344	Garlande	R
The Quene of Fame to Occupacioun	345	Garlande	R
The Quene of Fame commaundid shett fast the boke,	354	Garlande	1510
QUENES			
Beware of a quenes yellynge!	271	Collyn Clout	987
Of noble Fame before the Quenes grace,	324	Garlande	419
QUERE			
If the hole quere of the Musis nyne	33	Dol Dethe	155
The quere to demeane,	85	Phy Sparrow	553
Out of theyr cloyster and quere /With an hevy chere,	256	Collyn Clout	394
QUERELL			
Of my querell soone wolde I venged be.	55	Bowge	333
QUERESTERS			
The queresters to controll;	85	Phy Sparrow	564
QUERYSTERS			
These be my querysters /To helpe me to synge,	65	Hauke	122
QUEST			
The howndes began to yerne and to quest; and dred	351	Garlande	1409
QUESTION			
Some men myght aske a question,	309	Why Come Ye	1202
aske] 'make' MS Rawlinson C. 813			
QUESTIONYD			
Then questionyd I her what thos yatis ment;	328	Garlande	575
thos] 'these' Marshe 1568			
QUESTIONLES			
'Questionles no dowte of that ye say;	332	Garlande	714
QUESTYON			
Of your questyon ye make all this whyle	333	Garlande	738

QUESTYONLESSE —QUOD	Page	Title	Line

QUESTYONLESSE
Yes, questyonlesse, in myne opynyon;	144	Magnyfycence	126
Questyonlesse he doth me assure	208	Magnyfycence	2395

QUIBYBLE
And pype in a quibyble,	368	Albany	389

QUICKLY
Go, lytell quayre, quickly.	371	Albany	508

QUIGHT
For clatering of me I would him sone quight;	139	Ven Tongues	74

QUIKE
Your brethe ys stronge and quike;	126	Garnesche3	78

QUIKLY
And at your avauntage quikly it is	316	Garlande	142
As quikly towchyd as it were flesshe and bones,	328	Garlande	592
Envyvid picturis well towchid and quikly.	345	Garlande	1161

QUINTILIANE
Fyrst, olde Quintiliane with his Declamacyons; Declamacyons] 'declynacyons' †Fakes 1523	321	Garlande	326

QUINTYLYAN
And medyll with Quintylyan in his Decla[m]acyons, Declamacyons] 'Declaracyons' †Lant 1545, Kynge & Marche 1554, Day 1560, Marshe 1568	235	Speke Parott	177

QUINTUS
Quintus Cursius, full craftely that wrate Cursius] 'Cursus' †Fakes 1523	322	Garlande	366

QUYCKE
My sparowe than shuld be quycke	77	Phy Sparrow	205
Her tonge was very quycke	223	El Rummynge	337
Full of magottes quycke;	225	El Rummynge	431
Or touched on the quycke,	274	Collyn Clout	1124
And brought in quycke or dede,	288	Why Come Ye	359

QUYCKELY
For yf I had not quyckely fledde the touche,	60	Bowge	503
That are so quyckely vayned,	99	Phy Sparrow	1121
And quyckely your appetytes to sharpe and adresse;	183	Magnyfycence	1549

QUYCKER
And floure the more quycker;	219	El Rummynge	206

QUYCKLY
That quyckly is envyved with rudyes of the rose,	183	Magnyfycence	1551

QUYGHT
For it is out of my mynde quyght.	159	Magnyfycence	672

QUYKE
As yf a man fortune to touche you on the quyke -	185	Magnyfycence	1611

QUYNTYNE
To us welcome thou arte, by Saynte Quyntyne!'	60	Bowge	511

QUYSSHON
Yet may he mysse the quysshon!	271	Collyn Clout	996

QUYT
Thus for your guerdon quyt ar ye,	119	Ag Scottes	139
Ye loste hyr favyr quyt!	125	Garnesche3	67

QUYTE
I truste to quyte you or I-dy!	41	Coystrowne4	21
For she was quyte gone;	89	Phy Sparrow	706
Nowe let se. Quyte you lyke praty men!	159	Magnyfycence	688
All mesure and good rule is gone quyte.	176	Magnyfycence	1315
And had robbyd you quyte from all felycyte.	193	Magnyfycence	1864
From God am sente to quyte the thy mede.	193	Magnyfycence	1877
Boke and chalys gone quyte;	257	Collyn Clout	407
But ran away quyte?	366	Albany	310

QUOD
Quod Skelton, laureat.	38	Coystrowne2	E
Let me', quod he, 'ly in your lap.'	41	Balettys1	2
'Ly styll', quod she, 'my paramoure,	41	Balettys1	3
Quod Skelton laureate.	42	Balettys1	E
Quod Skelton laureat.	43	Balettys2	E
Quod Skelton laureat.	45	Balettys3	E
Quod Skelton laureat.	45	Balettys4	E
'What movyd the,' quod she, 'hydder to come?'	48	Bowge	78
'Forsoth,' quod I, 'to bye some of youre ware.'	48	Bowge	79
'Maystres,' quod I, 'I have none aquentaunce	48	Bowge	92
'Pece,' quod Desyre, 'ye speke not worth a bene!	48	Bowge	95
'Maystres,' quod I, 'I praye you tell me why soo,	49	Bowge	108
'Forsothe,' quod she, 'how ever blowe the wynde,	49	Bowge	110
'Alas,' quod I, 'how myghte I have her sure?'	49	Bowge	118
'In fayth,' quod she, 'by Bone aventure.'	49	Bowge	119
'In fayth,' quod Suspecte, 'spake Drede no worde of me?'	51	Bowge	183
'Twyst,' quod Suspecte, 'goo playe; hym I ne reke!' Twyst] 'Whist' Wynkyn de Worde 1510, 'Twysshe' Marshe 1568	51	Bowge	186
'By Cryste,' quod Favell, 'Drede is soleyne freke!	51	Bowge	187
'Ye, soo,' quod Suspecte, 'he maye us bothe begyle.'	51	Bowge	189
'God spede, broder,' to me quod he than,	51	Bowge	195
'By God,' quod he, 'this and thus it is';	52	Bowge	225
'Fare well,' quod he, 'we wyll talke more of this.'	52	Bowge	227
'Now,' quod Dysdayne, 'as I shall saved be,	54	Bowge	297
'Than,' quod Hervy, 'why arte thou so dysmayde?'	54	Bowge	299
'By Cryste,' quod he, 'for it is shame to saye,	54	Bowge	300
'By God,' quod Hervy, 'and it so happen myghte!	54	Bowge	306
'By him that me boughte,' than quod Dysdayne,	54	Bowge	309

QUOKE —RAGGED   Page   Title   Line

	Page	Title	Line
'Turde,' quod Ha[f]ter, 'I wyll the nothynge layne,	55	Bowge	311
layne] 'sayne' †Wynkyn de Worde 1499, Marshe 1568			
'What, revell route!' quod he, and gan to rayle	56	Bowge	368
'Ay,' quod he, 'in the devylles date,	56	Bowge	375
'Forsothe,' quod I, 'in this courte I dwell nowe.'	56	Bowge	377
'Welcome,' quod Ryote, 'I make God avowe.'	56	Bowge	378
'Harken,' quod he, 'loo here myne honde in thyne;	60	Bowge	510
Quod Skelton laureat.	71	Hauke	E
Quod Skelton laureate,	120	Ag Scottes	E
Knowe hym, syr, quod he. Yes, by Saynt Sym!	156	Magnyfycence	585
Abyde, syr, quod he! Mary, so I do.	162	Magnyfycence	789
Thynke I not so, quod he. Ellys have I shame,	175	Magnyfycence	1254
'Soft,' quod one hyght Sybbyll,	228	El Rummynge	549
hyght] 'high' Day 1560, Marshe 1568			
Quod Skelton Laureat.	230	El Rummynge	E
Quod Skelton Laureat	230	El Rummynge	E
Quod Parato	234	Speke Parott	140b
Quod Parot, thy popagay royall.	238	Speke Parott	262a
Quod] 'Quid' †MS Harley 2252			
Amen, quod Parott, /The royall popagay.	241	Speke Parott	355
Dixit, quod Parrott, the royall popagay.	243	Speke Parott	404
Dixit, quod Parrott, the popagay royall.	244	Speke Parott	446
Dixit, quod Parrot	246	Speke Parott	E
Quod Skelton Lawryat	246	Speke Parott	3
'Nay, holde thy tunge,' quod another, 'let me have the name.'	319	Garlande	255
'Forsothe,' quod she, 'theys be haskardis and rebawdis,	329	Garlande	607
haskardis] 'hastardis' †Fakes 1523			

QUOKE
His eyen rollynge, his hondes faste they quoke;	51	Bowge	193

QUOSSHONS
For there ye myst you[r] quosshons.	377	Replycacion	113
your] 'you' †Pynson 1528			

RABELL
Nowe in cometh another rabell;	224	El Rummynge	382

RABYLL
Of Diomedis stabyll /He brought out a rabyll	349	Garlande	1306

RABLE
Of Dyomedes stable /He brought out a rable	104	Phy Sparrow	1313
Ye Scottes all the rable,	363	Albany	177

RACELL
Racell, rulye ragged, she is like to cache colde;	242	Speke Parott	401

RACHCHYD
That ther thou xuldyst be rachchyd	128	Garnesche3	180

RACHELL
Sion is in sadness, Rachell ruly doth loke;	234	Speke Parott	114

RACKED
As though I had ben racked,	73	Phy Sparrow	47

RADIANT
Whose radiant beame /And relucent light	136	Dundas	45
Whan Titan radiant burnisshith his bemis bryght,	327	Garlande	534

RADYANT
Lyke to the radyant star,	98	Phy Sparrow	1047

RADYANTE
By radyante hete enryped hath our corne;	46	Bowge	2

RADYENT
Radyent Esperus, star of the clowdy nyght,	44	Balettys3	24

RAFTER
Plucke downe an house and set up a rafter,	169	Magnyfycence	1032

RAGE
The leopardes savage, /The lyons in theyr rage,	79	Phy Sparrow	287
That in a furyous rage	81	Phy Sparrow	376
Which by his mercyfull rage	88	Phy Sparrow	670
mercyfull] 'unmercifull' Wyght 1553, Kitson 1560.6, Marshe 1568			
With myghty corage /A[d]aunted the rage /Of a lyon savage;	104	Phy Sparrow	1310
Adaunted] 'Auaunted' editions			
No stormy rage agaynst me can pervayle.	181	Magnyfycence	1465
Ye, syr, ye; leve all this rage,	196	Magnyfycence	1988
Today fayre wether, tomorowe a stormy rage;	213	Magnyfycence	2545
For age can nat rage,	279	Why Come Ye	34
But whan age seeth that rage	279	Why Come Ye	36
And rage in arerage	280	Why Come Ye	47
So /That rage must make pyllage	280	Why Come Ye	50
But was ravysht with a rage	296	Why Come Ye	691
As a mariner that amasid is in a stormy rage,	335	Garlande	829
amasid] 'masid' MS Cotton Vitellius E.x			
With myghty corrage /Adauntid the rage /Of a lyon savage;	349	Garlande	1303
Ye rage and ye rave, /And your worshyp deprave:	363	Albany	190
It is a rechelesse rage,	369	Albany	417

RAGES
He rages and he raves,	287	Why Come Ye	334
Raylyng in your rages	381	Replycacion	268

RAGGE
A lytell ragge of rethorike,	374	Replycacion	1

RAGGED
Racell, rulye ragged, she is like to cache colde;	242	Speke Parott	401
For though my ryme be ragged, /Tattered and jagged,	248	Collyn Clout	53

RAGGID — RAYNE-BEATEN

	Page	Title	Line
Ye recrayed ruffyns all ragged!'	294	Why Come Ye	606
And the ragged ray /Of Galaway.	359	Albany	22
The heritykes ragged ray,	379	Replycacion	169

RAGGID
	Page	Title	Line
Raggid, and daggid, and cunnyngly cut;	329	Garlande	630

RAGGYD
	Page	Title	Line
I am raggyd and rent, as ye may se;	195	Magnyfycence	1962
So myche raggyd ryghte of a rammes horne;	246	Speke Parott	505
But tatterd and tuggyd, /Raggyd and ruggyd,	304	Why Come Ye	1027
tatterd] 'taxed' MS Rawlinson C. 813

RAGGYS
	Page	Title	Line
And happe you the whyles with these homly raggys.	197	Magnyfycence	2037

RAGYD
	Page	Title	Line
He ragyd and rent out your hart bloode;	119	Ag Scottes	136

RAGMAN ROLLIS
	Page	Title	Line
Apollo to rase out of her ragman rollis.	354	Garlande	1490

RAILER
	Page	Title	Line
Ryot, reveler, railer, brybery, theft,	329	Garlande	614

RAILES
	Page	Title	Line
He rymes and railes /That Englishmen have tailes.	135	Dundas	9

RAILLES
	Page	Title	Line
The margent was illumynid all with golden railles	345	Garlande	1157

RAIST
	Page	Title	Line
Odious Disdayne, why raist thou me on this facyon?	321	Garlande	317

RAY
	Page	Title	Line
To dauns the hay or rune the ray;	134	Garnesche5	170
And the ragged ray /Of Galaway.	359	Albany	22
The heritykes ragged ray,	379	Replycacion	169

RAYE
	Page	Title	Line
Wylfulnes and Braynles no[w] rule all the raye.	243	Speke Parott	421
now] 'no' †MS Harley 2252

RAYGNE
	Page	Title	Line
His tytle is true in Fraunce to raygne;	118	Ag Scottes	120

RAYLE
	Page	Title	Line
'What, revell route!' quod he, and gan to rayle	56	Bowge	368
The janglynge jay to rayle,	81	Phy Sparrow	396
Ye rayle all out of seson.	127	Garnesche3	130
Ye rayle, ye ryme, with, 'Hay, dog, hay!'	129	Garnesche5	5
Ye, syr, rayle all in deformite:	129	Garnesche5	7
Hath pointyd me to rayle on the.	131	Garnesche5	88
To rayle with me that the can hyt.	132	Garnesche5	119
I rayle to the soche as thow art.	133	Garnesche5	137
Scrybbyl thow, scrybyll thow, rayle or wryght,	134	Garnesche5	179
Rayle not so far.	136	Dundas	63
For though some be lidder, and list for to rayle,	138	Ven Tongues	30
Som sey I rayle att ryott recheles;	242	Speke Parott	387
To ryme or to rayle, /To wryte or to indyte,	246	Collyn Clout	5
Wyll knowe a raven from a rayle,	268	Collyn Clout	869
A quayle, the rayle, the olde raven.	268	Collyn Clout	870
To rayle agaynst his grace	368	Albany	365
To rayle on his astate /With wordes inordinate?	370	Albany	461
To rayle on hym lyke dawes.	371	Albany	478

RAYLES
	Page	Title	Line
With thy versyfeyng rayles /How they have tayles.	135	Dundas	30
The lay fee people rayles.	256	Collyn Clout	401
Thus the people telles, /Rayles lyke rebelles,	257	Collyn Clout	413
He rebukes them and rayles,	294	Why Come Ye	601
He rayles and he ratis,	295	Why Come Ye	651

RAYLYNG
	Page	Title	Line
Thow demyst my raylyng ovyrthwarthe;	133	Garnesche5	136
In ryming and raylyng with hym for to mell,	353	Garlande	1475
Raylyng in your rages	381	Replycacion	268

RAYLYNGE
	Page	Title	Line
Raylynge haynously /And dysdaynously	260	Collyn Clout	536
They counte it for a raylynge	275	Collyn Clout	1147

RAYLL
	Page	Title	Line
Ye rayll at ryot, recheles.	40	Coystrowne4	4

RAYMENT
	Page	Title	Line
and spoylyd from all his goodys and rayment.	193	Magnyfycence	SD

RAYNBETYN
	Page	Title	Line
Ye raynbetyn beggers rejagged,	294	Why Come Ye	605

RAYNE
	Page	Title	Line
Refresshyng myndys the Aprell shoure of rayne;	44	Balettys3	11
Howe after a drought there fallyth a showre of rayne	141	Magnyfycence	12
That without largesse noblenesse can not rayne.	147	Magnyfycence	265
Ye, for your wyt is cloked for the rayne.	157	Magnyfycence	609
By my syers soule, I fele no rayne.	170	Magnyfycence	1087
To rayne, for all his marcyall affeccyon;	181	Magnyfycence	1470
Lyke a ropy rayne, /A gummy glayre.	215	El Rummynge	24
And we wyll rule and rayne,	276	Collyn Clout	1212
What thynge occasionyd the showris of rayne,	331	Garlande	693
Yet whan the rayne rayneth and the gose wynkith	352	Garlande	1430
From rayne and from colde,	365	Albany	276

RAYNE-BEATEN
	Page	Title	Line
Rudely rayne-beaten, /Rusty and mothe-eaten,	248	Collyn Clout	55
mothe] 'moche' †Godfray 1531, 'moughte' Kele 1545.1, 'mothe' MS Harley 2252

RAYNE BETEN —RANNE   Page   Title   Line

RAYNE BETEN
Nay, thou rude ravener, rayne beten javell! 202   Magnyfycence   2191
RAYNES
Your skynne that was wrapped in shertes of Raynes, ... 197   Magnyfycence   2016
Nowe must be storm ybeten with showres and raynes. 197   Magnyfycence   2017
In rotchettes of fyne raynes, ... 254   Collyn Clout   314
RAYNETH
Yet whan the rayne rayneth and the gose wynkith 352   Garlande   1430
RAYNNING
And from raynning of rappes, ... 366   Albany   277
RAYSE
A, syr, your grace me dothe extole and rayse; 183   Magnyfycence   1525
RAYSED
It raysed myne hert rote 100   Phy Sparrow   1148
She raysed up in that stede 105   Phy Sparrow   1352
She raysed up in that stede 350   Garlande   1345
RAYSYNG
In nedill wark raysyng byrdis in bowris, ... 334   Garlande   804
   byrdis in bowris] 'bothe birddis and bowres' MS Cotton
   Vitellius E.x
RAYSORS
Sharper then raysors, that shave and cut throtes, ... 138   Ven Tongues   51
RAKE
His bones crake, /Leane as a rake; 94   Phy Sparrow   913
It is a gentyll reason of a rake. 156   Magnyfycence   557
Uppon hym for to take /A mattocke or a rake. 253   Collyn Clout   274
RAM
The golden ram /Of flemmynge dam, ... 301   Why Come Ye   897
With helpe of the ram, ley all in the dust. 315   Garlande   105
RAMBES
And theyr spyrytuall lambes /Sequestred from rambes 250   Collyn Clout   157
RAMBES HORNE
By the ryght of a rambes horne. 276   Collyn Clout   1199
RAMMES HORNE
So myche raggyd ryghte of a rammes horne; 246   Speke Parott   505
As ryght as a rammes horne! 281   Why Come Ye   90
RAMMYSCHE
Thou rammysche, stynkyng gote, ... 128   Garnesche3   166
RAMMYSSHE
My hawke is rammysshe, and it happed that she ran - 191   Magnyfycence   1807
RAMPAUNT
The White Lyon, there rampaunt of moode, ... 119   Ag Scottes   135
RAN
So forcibly upon this Erle thow ran, ... 32   Dol Dethe   124
Till the chaunce ran ageyne hym of Fortuns double dyse. . . . 33   Dol Dethe   140
He ran as fast as ever that he myghte. 58   Bowge   415
The blode ran downe raw /Upon the auter stone. 63   Hauke   58
Your wyll than ran before your wyt. 118   Ag Scottes   102
From that lorde to that lorde I rode and I ran. 160   Magnyfycence   716
My hawke is rammysshe, and it happed that she ran - 191   Magnyfycence   1807
Than Rowlande the reve ran, and I began to rave, ... 192   Magnyfycence   1831
Another there was that ran /With a good brasse pan - 222   El Rummynge   316
She ran in all the hast /Unbrased and unlast, ... 222   El Rummynge   319
He rod, but we ran. 301   Why Come Ye   887
   'He rode not but he ran' MS Rawlinson C. 813
Ran on the raunge so longe, that I suppose 313   Garlande   25
Masid as a Marche hare, he ran lyke a scut. 329   Garlande   632
He turnyd his tirikkis, his volvell ran fast, ... 354   Garlande   1517
lyke a cowarde knyght, ran awaye shamfully 359   Albany   I
He ran awaye by night. 360   Albany   71
Twyt, Scot, thou ran away.' 363   Albany   160
But thou ran home agayne 365   Albany   246
But ran away quyte? 366   Albany   310
He ran away by nyght 366   Albany   311
RANCOUR
Envyous Rancour truely he hight. 333   Garlande   753
RANGYD
They rangyd Hankyn Bovy /My churche all abowte. 65   Hauke   117
RANKE
Ye rowe ranke Scottes and dronken Danes 115   Scot Kynge   64
The rude ranke Scottes, lyke dronken dranes, ... 120   Ag Scottes   172
There be two lyther, rude and ranke, ... 175   Magnyfycence   1266
In fay, man, some rybbys of the motton be so ranke 204   Magnyfycence   2269
The fleshe thereof was ranke, ... 228   El Rummynge   540
They growwe very ranke 304   Why Come Ye   1001
Of the Scottes ranke 359   Albany   18
Go heme, ranke Scot, ge heme, ... 368   Albany   382
RANKELY
Now upon thys hete /Rankely whan ye swete, ... 127   Garnesche3   134
RANKIS
That ratis and rankis /That prates and prankes 136   Dundas   56
RANNE
Nor Hanyball, agayne Rome gates that ranne, ... 182   Magnyfycence   1511
The houndes ranne before, and the hare behynde. 191   Magnyfycence   1823
Some ranne a good trot /With a skellet or a pot; 220   El Rummynge   249
Some ranne the nexte way, sume ranne abowte. 319   Garlande   252
Some ranne the nexte way, sume ranne abowte. 319   Garlande   252
For in that fraye /Ye ranne awaye 360   Albany   36

RANNGE —RE   Page   Title   Line

	Page	Title	Line
Your capitayne ranne to go,	360	Albany	65
RANNGE			
I advyse yow beware of thys war, rannge yow in aray.	123	Garnesche2	33
RAPPES			
And from raynning of rappes,	366	Albany	277
RARIFIID			
The clowdis gan to clere, the myst was rarifiid;	330	Garlande	651
RASE			
Dyamand poyntyd to rase oute hartly care	44	Balettys3	19
Out of my bokis full sone I shulde hym rase;	314	Garlande	72
Owt of her bokis Apollo to rase.	353	Garlande	1480
Apollo to rase out of her ragman rollis.	354	Garlande	1490
RASID			
Wherfore then rasid ye not away	316	Garlande	137
Any worde defacid /That myght be rasid,	356	Garlande	1582
RASYD			
Go, pytyous hart, rasyd with dedly wo,	45	Balettys5	1
RAT			
Methynke she is well becked to catche a rat.	166	Magnyfycence	927
To reche at a rat - I coude not her warne.	191	Magnyfycence	1809
RATCHES			
Here is a leysshe of ratches to renne an hare!	156	Magnyfycence	586
RATE			
Of thy bounte after the usuall rate	29	Dol Dethe	19
Wryteth after an hyer rate;	91	Phy Sparrow	805
A lauryate poyete for to rate.	126	Garnesche3	95
Skelton laureat /After this rate	135	Dundas	20
Yf it were cond perfytely, and after the rate,	234	Speke Parott	143
After suche a rate,	271	Collyn Clout	1014
And after this rate	276	Collyn Clout	1180
It was excedyng byyonde the commowne rate.	326	Garlande	488
Of your bounte the accustomable rate	344	Garlande	1130
Dyvysed by Skelton after the funerall rate;	348	Garlande	1256
Though I you wrate /After this rate	355	Garlande	1537
RATES			
After this maner rates;	264	Collyn Clout	709
RATHER			
Yet I wolde that ye had gone rather;	176	Magnyfycence	1313
Howe be it, at your instaunce I wyll the rather	186	Magnyfycence	1641
Ye, ryd thy selfe rather than this lyfe for to lede.	205	Magnyfycence	2307
Nay; rather wyll I chose to ryd me of this lyve	206	Magnyfycence	2321
As the worlde requyreth, but rather I am refused.	208	Magnyfycence	2412
Men say, they had rather	251	Collyn Clout	175
RATIS			
That ratis and rankis /That prates and prankes	136	Dundas	56
He rayles and he ratis,	295	Why Come Ye	651
RATYD			
That ratyd the Romaynes and made them yll rest,	181	Magnyfycence	1481
RATYFYE			
And I truste to ratyfye and amende your fame.	208	Magnyfycence	2398
RATYFYED			
As of antyquyte /It was ratyfyed,	264	Collyn Clout	714
As] 'And' †Godfray 1531, Kele 1545.1, Marshe 1568			
RATTES			
Were made for myse and rattes,	80	Phy Sparrow	339
RAUNGE			
Ran on the raunge so longe, that I suppose	313	Garlande	25
RAVE			
What eylythe the, rebawde, on me to rave?	131	Garnesche5	79
Than Rowlande the reve ran, and I began to rave,	192	Magnyfycence	1831
And some there are that rave,	259	Collyn Clout	514
Ye rage and ye rave, /And your worshyp deprave:	363	Albany	190
RAVEN			
Wyll knowe a raven from a rayle,	268	Collyn Clout	869
A quayle, the rayle, the olde raven.	268	Collyn Clout	870
RAVENER			
Nay, thou rude ravener, rayne beten javell!	202	Magnyfycence	2191
RAVES			
He rages and he raves,	287	Why Come Ye	334
RAVYD			
This dowtless ye ravyd,	70	Hauke	307
RAVYN			
The ravyn called Rolfe,	82	Phy Sparrow	414
RAVYNGE			
With revynge and ravynge,	281	Why Come Ye	102
RAVYSHED			
And so hath ravyshed me	96	Phy Sparrow	1006
RAVYSHT			
But was ravysht with a rage	296	Why Come Ye	691
RAW			
The blode ran downe raw /Upon the auter stone.	63	Hauke	58
RAWE			
Softe, my frende. Herein your reason is but rawe.	142	Magnyfycence	70
Why, is there any store of rawe motton?	204	Magnyfycence	2265
Howe in matters they ben rawe,	249	Collyn Clout	94
With reasons that ben rawe.	306	Why Come Ye	1107
RE			
And lerne me to synge Re my fa sol!	53	Bowge	258

REALME —REBELLYON   Page   Title   Line

REALME
That is a kynge without a realme.   115   Scot Kynge   59
And rule a realme royall   271   Collyn Clout   992
And gave him a realme to rule   293   Why Come Ye   559
His owne realme to forsake?   367   Albany   328
Of this, his realme royall /And lande imperiall, ...   368   Albany   393
REALMES
In realmes, in cities, by suche fals abusion.   139   Ven Tongues   56
For I stryke lordys of realmes and landys   195   Magnyfycence   1938
To rule ix realmes by one mannes wytte, ...   240   Speke Parott   333
REALMYS
Of ix kinges realmys, ...   303   Why Come Ye   958
  realmys] 'realme' Marshe 1568
REAME
Why doste thow deprave /This royall reame, ...   136   Dundas   44
For to rewle this reame, ...   295   Why Come Ye   656
An hole reame he is able to set at devysion: 333   Garlande   758
REASON
By reason nor by law;   62   Hauke   7
1 thyngys contryvyd by mannys reason, ...   140   Magnyfycence   1
But wyll hath reason so under subjeccyon, ...   141   Magnyfycence   19
But yf reason be regent and ruler of your barge.   141   Magnyfycence   38
Softe, my frende. Herein your reason is but rawe.   142   Magnyfycence   70
I parceyve well howe eche of you doth reason.   142   Magnyfycence   83
Some reason we must make.   143   Magnyfycence   99
It is reason and skyll   143   Magnyfycence   105
Mary, upon trouth my reason I grounde, ...   147   Magnyfycence   264
Counterfet reason is not worth a flye;   153   Magnyfycence   470
It is a gentyll reason of a rake.   156   Magnyfycence   557
It forseth not of reason, so it kepe ryme.   172   Magnyfycence   1150
All that ye say, syr, is reason and skyll.   178   Magnyfycence   1381
It is good yet that lyberte be ruled by reason.   178   Magnyfycence   1387
Be it reason or none, it shall not gretely skyll;   185   Magnyfycence   1596
Well, call hym, and let us here hym reason;   187   Magnyfycence   1687
In faythe, and I wyll be to reason agreable.   203   Magnyfycence   2205
But reason and wytte wantynge theyr provynciall, ...   232   Speke Parott   53
To rude ys there reason to reche to your sentence;   240   Speke Parott   319
To suche thynges ympossybyll, reason cannot consente;   240   Speke Parott   334
To teche or to preche /As reason wyll reche?   247   Collyn Clout   14
But this reason they take: 250   Collyn Clout   142
And good reason perverted.   256   Collyn Clout   373
Than lette reason you supporte, ...   271   Collyn Clout   1004
Without good reason or skyll;   276   Collyn Clout   1191
Good Reason and good Skyll, ...   281   Why Come Ye   108
Is nat my reason good?'   283   Why Come Ye   196
Without reason or skyll.   291   Why Come Ye   488
And agayne all reason /Commyted open trayson   297   Why Come Ye   736
Without all good reason.   304   Why Come Ye   997
And how his wordes with reason wyll not accorde.   314   Garlande   88
Yet dyverse ther be, industryous of reason, ...   315   Garlande   106
  ther] 'that' MS Cotton Vitellius E.x
Of them that have vertue by reason of cunnyng, ...   317   Garlande   198
To all that to reason is condiscendyng, ...   344   Garlande   1132
  To all tho that] 'to all tho that' †Fakes 1523
Gone to seke hallows, /With Reason together, ...   358   Garlande2   8
REASONYNG
So lytyll dyscressyon, and so myche reasonyng;   244   Speke Parott   456
REASONS
Your reasons forth to fet.   142   Magnyfycence   64
Say on; me thynke your reasons be profounde.   190   Magnyfycence   1767
But so longe they rekyn with theyr reasons amysse   200   Magnyfycence   2127
  they] 'theyr' †Rastell & Treveris C 1530, B
With reasons that ben rawe.   306   Why Come Ye   1107
On every halfe my reasons forthe I sought, ...   312   Garlande   10
  On] 'One' †Fakes 1523
REBADS
Ye rebads nat worth two plummis!   294   Why Come Ye   604
REBAUDRYE
What sholde I tell more of his rebaudrye?   56   Bowge   372
REBAWDE
What eylythe the, rebawde, on me to rave?   131   Garnesche5   79
REBAWDIS
'Forsothe,' quod she, 'theys be haskardis and rebawdis, . . .   329   Garlande   607
  haskardis] 'hastardis' †Fakes 1523
REBECCA
Prudent Rebecca, of whome remembraunce   336   Garlande   845
REBELL
Thys rebell to behold, ...   64   Hauke   95
Lyke that untrue rebell /Fals Kayn agaynst Abell.   121   Ag Scottes2   19
REBELLE
I render the fals rebelle   366   Albany   316
REBELLES
Thus the people telles, /Rayles lyke rebelles, ...   257   Collyn Clout   413
Agayne all suche rebelles   259   Collyn Clout   492
REBELLYNGE
In spekynge and rebellynge   274   Collyn Clout   1103
REBELLYON
A rebellyon agaynst nature –   155   Magnyfycence   522

572

	Page	Title	Line
REBELLYONNS			
Agayne rebellyonns arme the to make debate;	33	Dol Dethe	166
REBOYLED			
fervently reboyled with the infatuate flames	374	Replycacion	1
REBOKE			
His stomak stuffed ofte tymes dyde reboke.	51	Bowge	180
REBOUND			
Wyth bound and rebound, bounsyngly take up	43	Balettys2	15
REBUKE			
Thus to rebuke me and have me in dyspyght!	205	Magnyfycence	2278
For I rebuke no man /That vertuous is.	273	Collyn Clout	1089
REBUKES			
He rebukes them and rayles,	294	Why Come Ye	601
REBUKID			
And was Eschines rebukid as ye say?	316	Garlande	135
REBUKYD			
I am elles rebukyd of that I intende,	324	Garlande	440
REBUKYNG			
Rebukyng and remordyng, /And nothing accordyng.	120	Ag Scottes2	11
RECEYVE			
His soule mot receyve in to ther company,	35	Dol Dethe	213
I to mynyster it, you to receyve it ofte -	207	Magnyfycence	2356
RECEYVED			
Howe be it, from you I receyved a letter [sent],	209	Magnyfycence	2435
sent] not in †Rastell & Treveris C 1530, B			
And better perceyved, /And thankefullyer receyved,	265	Collyn Clout	771
RECEYVYD			
I have your lewde letter receyvyd,	124	Garnesche3	1
I have receyvyd your secunde ryme.	129	Garnesche5	2
RECH			
Cowde not rech nor attayne	68	Hauke	226
RECHATE			
Yonder is a horson for me doth rechate;	201	Magnyfycence	2151
RECHATYNG			
With chatyng and rechatyng,	380	Replycacion	217
RECHE			
To reche at a rat - I coude not her warne.	191	Magnyfycence	1809
To rude ys there reason to reche to your sentence;	240	Speke Parott	319
To teche or to preche /As reason wyll reche?	247	Collyn Clout	14
To reche to suche degre,	292	Why Come Ye	538
Twyse! set hym a chare, or reche hym a stol	318	Garlande	208
Twyse] 'Twyshe' Marshe 1568, MS Cotton Vitellius E.x			
With, 'Reche me that skane of tewly sylk';	334	Garlande	798
Dun is in the myre, dame, reche me my spur.	352	Garlande	1433
Is farther than their wytte wyll reche.	374	Replycacion	13
RECHELES			
Ye rayll at ryot, recheles.	40	Coystrowne4	4
Som sey I rayle att ryott recheles;	242	Speke Parott	387
He sayes that we are recheles,	275	Collyn Clout	1176
But how it was, sum were to recheles,	351	Garlande	1393
RECHELESSE			
With ryotynge rechelesse,	280	Why Come Ye	72
But braynsyk and braynlesse, /Wytles and rechelesse,	304	Why Come Ye	1019
It is a rechelesse rage,	369	Albany	417
and rechelesse yonge heretykes lately abjured, etc.	373	Replycacion	1
of their rechelesse youthe and wytlesse wontonnesse,	374	Replycacion	1
RECHYD			
To hyr love ye nowte rechyd.	125	Garnesche3	61
RECKEN			
What shulde I recken more?	379	Replycacion	181
RECKYS			
Nay, by Cockys harte, he ne reckys;	172	Magnyfycence	1167
RECLAYMED			
She was not wel reclaymed;	63	Hauke	80
How she me had reclaymed,	99	Phy Sparrow	1125
I pray yow be reclaymed,	238	Speke Parott	260
RECLAME			
Avaunt, rybawde, thi tung reclame!	132	Garnesche5	106
RECOMMENDETH			
To you recommendeth Sad Cyrcumspeccyon,	149	Magnyfycence	311
RECOMPENCE			
To slacke in recompence,	279	Why Come Ye	7
Enforcid ar we you to recompence,	323	Garlande	416
RECONCYLYACYON			
By wey of expyacyon /For reconcylyacyon.	66	Hauke	177
for reconcylyacyon] not in Day 1560, Marshe 1568			
RECONED			
That age for dottage /Is reconed nowadayes.	280	Why Come Ye	44
reconed] 'recovered' Toy 1553, Kitson 1560.7, Marshe 1568			
RECONYNG			
To make reconyng in the resseyte how Robyn loste hys bowe,	240	Speke Parott	341
The reste of suche reconyng may make a fowle fraye.	243	Speke Parott	403
So prodigall expence, and so shamfull reconyng;	244	Speke Parott	458
RECONYNGE			
It is a nyce reconynge	298	Why Come Ye	760
RECONUSAUNCE			
Unto you, madame, I make reconusaunce,	335	Garlande	838

RECORDE —REDE   Page   Title   Line

RECORDE
It may be regesterde of shamefull recorde.   30   Dol Dethe   28
His titille dothe recorde;   110   Lawde   11
Oracius to recorde in his volumys olde, ...   143   Magnyfycence   114
I trow I have brought you suche wrytynge of recorde, ...   149   Magnyfycence   309
A byll of recorde for an annuall rent.   187   Magnyfycence   1667
That, God to recorde, ...   291   Why Come Ye   486
It is a playne recorde   300   Why Come Ye   848
Saint Albons, to recorde, ...   306   Why Come Ye   1097
As Juvinall dothe recorde, ...   310   Why Come Ye2   11
Beware, for wrytyng remayneth of recorde!   314   Garlande   89
Recorde the same? Or why is had in mynde   315   Garlande   125
But yet I beseche your grace that good recorde   318   Garlande   215
    good] not in MS Cotton Vitellius E.x
RECORDED
For it is wele recorded   383   Replycacion   324
RECORDES
He rolleth in his recordes, ...   283   Why Come Ye   194
Among my recordes suffer hym namyd, ...   316   Garlande   160
Whiche in your recordes, I know well, be enrolde, ...   344   Garlande   1140
RECORDIS
As scrypture recordis /A cecitate cordis, ...   291   Why Come Ye   474
If ony recordis in noumbyr can be founde, ...   345   Garlande   1150
RECOUNFORTYD
Boyce recounfortyd with his philosophy;   322   Garlande   359
RECOUNT
Recount, reporte, reherse without delay   336   Garlande   840
For to recount them all.   370   Albany   458
RECOUNTE
Recounte, reporte and tell   87   Phy Sparrow   613
But to recounte her ryche abylyment, ...   313   Garlande   44
RECOUNTYD
As your grace full nobly hath recountyd, ...   145   Magnyfycence   193
RECOUNTYNG
Ther names recountyng in the court of Fame;   334   Garlande   781
Recountyng commoditis of many a straunge nacyon;   354   Garlande   1500
RECOUNTYNGE
But my recountynge is /Of them that do amys   274   Collyn Clout   1101
Your name recountynge beyonde the lande of Tyre, ...   327   Garlande   551
RECOVER
Of Argus revengyd, recover when he may, ...   239   Speke Parott   288
RECOVERD
Recoverd whan the forster was gone, and sped   351   Garlande   1407
RECRAYD
For the moost recrayd /Cowardes afrayd, ...   362   Albany   115
RECRAYED
He was a recrayed knyght, ...   121   Ag Scottes2   26
Ye recrayed ruffyns all ragged!'   294   Why Come Ye   606
Avaunt, cowarde recrayed! /Thy pride shalbe alayd, ...   371   Albany   495
remordyng dyvers recrayed and moche unresonable errours . .   373   Replycacion   1
Ye heretykes recrayed, /Wotte ye what ye sayed   375   Replycacion   45
RECTYFYE
To rectyfye and amende   278   Collyn Clout   1263
RECULE
To rekyn with thys recule now   237   Speke Parott   227
RECULED
He reculed backe, /To his great lacke, ...   360   Albany   52
RED
A red angry man, but easy to intrete.   37   Coystrowne1   39
I have red theym poll by poll;   67   Hauke   211
With that my nedle waxed red, ...   77   Phy Sparrow   225
    waxed] 'ware' Marshe 1568
With helpe of the red sparow   82   Phy Sparrow   403
With bokes that I have red, ...   90   Phy Sparrow   753
His tales I have red;   91   Phy Sparrow   789
He the White, and ye the Red, ...   119   Ag Scottes   137
    ye] 'you' Day 1560, Marshe 1568
The White there slew the Red starke ded.   119   Ag Scottes   138
Ye have nat red the properte   129   Garnesche5   8
I have red, and rede I xall, ...   133   Garnesche5   158
The red rose in honour to flowrysshe and sprynge!'   231   Speke Parott   35
Whyles the red hat doth endure, ...   286   Why Come Ye   281
The red hat with his lure   286   Why Come Ye   283
For drede of the red hat   288   Why Come Ye   383
How Dame Minerva first found the Olyve Tre, she red   351   Garlande   1404
REDBREST
And Robyn Redbrest   81   Phy Sparrow   399
REDDE
Right so, madame, the roses redde of hew   337   Garlande   890
Whiche redde on still, as it cam to her syght, ...   354   Garlande   1493
REDE
Whiche wert endiyd with rede blode of the same   32   Dol Dethe   117
Ware yet, I rede you, of Fortunes double cast, ...   45   Balettys4   3
Wherby I rede theyr renome and theyr fame   46   Bowge   15
In golde letters, this worde, whiche I dyde rede: 48   Bowge   66
His cote was checked with patches rede and blewe;   56   Bowge   358
    checked] 'checkered' Marshe 1568
Besechynge you that shall it see or rede, ...   61   Bowge   534

REDELY — REDOLENT

	Page	Title	Line
Of no tyrand I rede,	67	Hauke	190
To rede or to spell /What these verses tell.	68	Hauke	237
Thou shalt no where rede	70	Hauke	299
Shall rede the gospell at masse;	82	Phy Sparrow	423
Shall rede there the pystell.	82	Phy Sparrow	425
Playne matter indede, /Whoso lyst to rede	85	Phy Sparrow	549
Though I can rede and spell,	87	Phy Sparrow	612
And though that rede have I	87	Phy Sparrow	628
All other of whom we rede,	93	Phy Sparrow	884
The rose both white and rede	110	Lawde	1
Rede and lerne ye may,	129	Garnesche3	195
I have red, and rede I xall,	133	Garnesche5	158
For, as I have rede in volumes olde,	137	Ven Tongues	5
Pease, man, pease! /I rede we sease.	168	Magnyfycence	998
Ye, tourne over the lefe, rede there, and loke	176	Magnyfycence	1293
But wottest thou, horson? I rede the to be wyse.	202	Magnyfycence	2184
Nowe I rede the beware. I have warned the twyse.	202	Magnyfycence	2185
But nowe I se well there is no better rede,	205	Magnyfycence	2305
Myden agan in Grekys tonge we rede,	232	Speke Parott	52
Oreb et Zeb, of Judicum rede the boke.	234	Speke Parott	117
Syns Dewcalyons flodde there can no clerkes rede.	244	Speke Parott	455
And wotteth never what thei rede, /Paternoster nor crede;	252	Collyn Clout	234
Some can nat scarsly rede,	253	Collyn Clout	277
For I rede a preposycyon:	271	Collyn Clout	997
rede a] 'reda' Marshe 1568, 'rede by' MS Harley 2252			
Nor rede in any scrolles,	277	Collyn Clout	1241
Rede ye the story oute,	296	Why Come Ye	694
To syt hym upon, and rede Jacke a thrummis bybille,	318	Garlande	209
hym] not in MS Cotton Vitellius E.x			
Grene, rede, tawny, whyte, purpill, and blew.	334	Garlande	800
whyte] 'whyght blak' MS Cotton Vitellius E.x			
The enbuddid blossoms of roses rede of hew	337	Garlande	883
The enbuddid blossoms of] 'Enbuddid blossome with' MS Cotton Vitellius E.x			
Who list to rede.	342	Garlande	1081
'Yowre boke of remembrauns we will now that ye rede;	345	Garlande	1149
boke] 'bokes' †Fakes 1523			
Occupacyon, immediatly to rede.	345	Garlande	1169
The Tratyse of the Triumphis of the Rede Rose,	347	Garlande	1223
Therin to rede, and to understande	347	Garlande	1230
Where the sank royall is, Crystes blode so rede,	353	Garlande	1463
Who redyth it ones wolde rede it agayne;	354	Garlande	1501
And so procede /In you to rede,	355	Garlande	1549
Howe be it I rede	357	Garlande	1598
I rede you, loke about;	371	Albany	500
Shew them that shall you rede	371	Albany	509
Rede what Jerome there dothe say/	383	Replycacion	328
And wesely rede the Boke	384	Replycacion	360

REDELY

Ye, so redely and so sone!	172	Magnyfycence	1157

REDEME

Redeme us from this.	39	Coystrowne3	28
To redeme us with all.	258	Collyn Clout	455

REDEMED

That our Savyour bare, /Whiche us redemed from care.	375	Replycacion	34

REDEMEDE

And us redemede from the fendys pray.	34	Dol Dethe	196

REDEMPCYON

He payed a bitter pencyon /For mans redempcyon,	258	Collyn Clout	453

REDES

Redes shrewdly and spelles,	257	Collyn Clout	414
redes] 'rede' †Godfray 1531, Kele 1545.1, Marshe 1568			

REDITH

Occupacyoun redith and expoundyth	345	Garlande	R

REDY

Redy to assyst you in every tyme of nede;	30	Dol Dethe	58
Youre key is redy, we nede not knok	41	Coystrowne4	24
A plummed partrydge all redy to flye.	153	Magnyfycence	479
Grimbaldus gredy snatche a puddyng tyl the rost be redy.	172	Magnyfycence	1155
I am here redy. What! Shall we	179	Magnyfycence	1414
Those thre wyll be redy even at your bekenynge;	190	Magnyfycence	1778
In tyme of dystresse I am redy at hande;	205	Magnyfycence	2285
At all houres to be redy	371	Albany	485

REDYNES

O connyng clergye, where ys your redynes	242	Speke Parott	392

REDYNESSE

With hym in all dystresse, /Alway in redynesse	371	Albany	490
shall evermore be, with all obsequious redynesse,	373	Replycacion	1

REDYNGE

And as I stode redynge this verse myselfe allone,	48	Bowge	68
Whan ye fall to redynge	300	Why Come Ye	830

REDYTH

Who redyth it ones wolde rede it agayne;	354	Garlande	1501

REDLESSE

But redresse is redlesse and may do no correccyon.	209	Magnyfycence	2417

REDOLENT

/And redolent of eyre,	84	Phy Sparrow	525

REDOUTED — REGARDED   Page   Title   Line

REDOUTED
In Englande and Fraunce which gretly was redouted, ...   30   Dol Dethe   43
REDRES
Allectuary arrectyd to redres   44   Balettys3   8
REDRESSE
But all without redresse;   72   Phy Sparrow   33
For nowe I se comynge to youwarde Redresse.   208   Magnyfycence   2384
And be ruled by me, whiche am called Redresse.   208   Magnyfycence   2410
Redresse my name is, that lytell am I used   208   Magnyfycence   2411
Redresse sholde be at the rekenynge in every accompte, . . .   208   Magnyfycence   2413
And specyally to redresse that were out of joynte.   208   Magnyfycence   2414
Full many thynges there be that lacketh redresse, ...   209   Magnyfycence   2415
But redresse is redlesse and may do no correccyon.   209   Magnyfycence   2417
But good hope and redresse hath mendyd myne estate, ...   210   Magnyfycence   2462
Commensynge this processe at mayster Redresse.   211   Magnyfycence   2481
Redresse, in my remembraunce your lesson shall rest;   211   Magnyfycence   2503
Of that I have mysdone to make a redresse, ...   212   Magnyfycence   2508
So many complayntes, and so smalle redresse;   245   Speke Parott   470
All wronges he wolde redresse, ...   307   Why Come Ye   1112
But if that he purpose to make a redresse, ...   318   Garlande   229
REED
There he may se and reed   65   Hauke   147
  he] 'her' Marshe 1568
And therein reed /Shall fynde indeed   116   Ag Scottes   43
Ye have reed them, I suppose, ...   381   Replycacion   276
If ye have reed de hyperdulia, ...   382   Replycacion   287
REFFORMATION
How all that I do is under refformation, ...   323   Garlande   411
REFLAYRE
Swete of refla[yre]   84   Phy Sparrow   524
  reflayre] 'reflary' †Kele 1545.2, Wyght 1553, Kitson 1560.6,
  Marshe 1568
REFLARING
Reflaring rosabell, /The flagrant camamell;   340   Garlande   977
REFORMACION
With your reformacion, if I say amis, ...   316   Garlande   145
REFORMACYON
Of your wyse reformacyon;   102   Phy Sparrow   1248
To you I arecte it, and cast /Therof the reformacyon.   143   Magnyfycence   95
God of his miseracyon /Send better reformacyon!   305   Why Come Ye   1045
With toleracyon /And supportacyon /Of reformacyon, ...   356   Garlande   1578
humbly submytted unto the ryght discrete reformacyon   373   Replycacion   1
REFOURME
To refourme theyr neglygence, ...   275   Collyn Clout   1138
REFRAYNE
Causyth me that I can not myself refrayne, ...   42   Balettys2   3
I cannot me refrayne   97   Phy Sparrow   1009
But frendly I wyll refrayne you ferther, or we flyt: 211   Magnyfycence   2478
Dothe aswage and refrayne, ...   279   Why Come Ye   37
Coude nat himselfe refrayne, ...   296   Why Come Ye   690
REFRAYNED
Unneth I me refrayned, ...   99   Phy Sparrow   1124
Hyt wyll not be refrayned: 238   Speke Parott   259
REFRESHED
These orators and poetes refreshed their throtes.   321   Garlande   343
REFRESSHED
These orators and poetes refresshed there throtis.   321   Garlande   336
Theis orators and poetis refresshed there throtis.   322   Garlande   350
Their orators and poetis refresshed there throtis.   322   Garlande   357
Theis orators and poetis refresshed there throtis.   322   Garlande   364
REFRESSHID
Of Elyconis well, refresshid with your grace, ...   314   Garlande   74
  Elyconis] 'Elycoms' †Fakes 1523, 'Heliconis' Marshe 1568
These orators and poetis refresshid ther throtis.   322   Garlande   371
Theis orators and poetis refresshid there throtis.   322   Garlande   378
Theis notable poetis refresshid there throtis.   322   Garlande   385
REFRESSHYNG
Refresshyng myndys the Aprell shoure of rayne;   44   Balettys3   11
REFUGE
For had ye not the soner ben my refuge, ...   206   Magnyfycence   2333
REFUSE
And every man gladly my company wolde refuse, ...   160   Magnyfycence   704
That folowe fonde fantasyes and vertu refuse.   175   Magnyfycence   1281
'Daphnes, my derlynge, why do you me refuse?   320   Garlande   297
REFUSED
Though it be refused, ...   92   Phy Sparrow   816
Why have ye hym named and all other refused?   148   Magnyfycence   281
I care not howe sone he be refused, ...   187   Magnyfycence   1683
As the worlde requyreth, but rather I am refused.   208   Magnyfycence   2412
REFUSYD
Though I aske mercy I must nedys be refusyd.   205   Magnyfycence   2299
REGARDE
For to his servyce I have suche regarde, ...   334   Garlande   778
If ye wele can regarde   368   Albany   360
REGARDED
Al maters wel pondred and wel to be regarded, ...   137   Ven Tongues   1
Whose charite wele regarded   378   Replycacion   138

REGARDETH —REJOYCE   Page   Title   Line

REGARDETH
He regardeth lordes /No more than potshordes.	291	Why Come Ye	480

REGARDYD
Regardyd ye shuld your lord, your brother.	118	Ag Scottes	106
ye] 'you' Day 1560, Marshe 1568			

REGENT
Regent is she, /Of poetes al,	112	Calliope	3
Now must ye knowe our kynge for your regent,	114	Scot Kynge	21
Your lorde, your brother, and your regent.	118	Ag Scottes	114
But yf reason be regent and ruler of your barge.	141	Magnyfycence	38
Seon, the regent Amorreorum,	234	Speke Parott	121
Madame regent of the scyence sevyn	313	Garlande	53
scyence] 'sciences' Marshe 1568			
Madame regent /I may you call /Of vertuows all.	339	Garlande	951
In our royall regent,	369	Albany	427

REGENTE
As presydent and regente he rulythe every deall.	239	Speke Parott	312
For of owur regente the regiment he hathe, ex qua vi,	244	Speke Parott	437

REGESTARY
Occupacyon, Famys regestary,	326	Garlande	522

REGESTER
Though I regester her name	94	Phy Sparrow	891
And so Occupacyon, your regester, me told.'	344	Garlande	1141

REGESTERDE
It may be regesterde of shamefull recorde.	30	Dol Dethe	28

REGESTRED
Of your request, regestred is his name	314	Garlande	62

REGESTRINGE
Regestringe trewly every formare date;	29	Dol Dethe	18

REGIMENT
For of owur regente the regiment he hathe, ex qua vi,	244	Speke Parott	437

REGYSTRED
Whose name regystred was	75	Phy Sparrow	149

REGYSTRYD
Yf it be regystryd well in memory;	212	Magnyfycence	2513

REGRACIATORY
Wherwith to geve you my regraciatory,	324	Garlande	431

REGSTRY
In the regstry /Of my lorde of Cantorbury,	307	Why Come Ye	1119

REHAYTED
I wyll have hym rehayted and dyspysed.	186	Magnyfycence	1658

REHERS
Wherto shuld I rehers /The sentens of my vers?	68	Hauke	246

REHERSALL
And a further rehersall	299	Why Come Ye	825
But when of the laurell she made rehersall,	354	Garlande	1503

REHERSE
I coude it skan and ye wolde it reherse.	53	Bowge	245
skan] 'stan' †Wynkyn de Worde 1499, 1510; it] (2nd) not in Marshe 1568			
Plaut[us] in his comedies a chyld shall now reherse,	235	Speke Parott	176
And reherse them agayne,	266	Collyn Clout	775
So many, that longe it were to reherse.	331	Garlande	706
it] 'in' Marshe 1568			
Recount, reporte, reherse without delay	336	Garlande	840
Dame Agrippina also I may reherse	336	Garlande	859
to reherse all by name that he hath compylyd, &c.	345	Garlande	R

REHERSED
By Eschines rehersed to the grete glory	317	Garlande	166

REHERSITH
As Skelton rehersith, with wordes few and playne,	353	Garlande	1466

REHERSYD
Nother Phalary, /Rehersyd in Valery,	67	Hauke	199

REHERSYNG
To you rehersyng the somme of my proces.	117	Ag Scottes	90
Rehersyng by ordre, and what is the grownde,	345	Garlande	1152

REHERSSE
Ne by non other that any man can rehersse.	181	Magnyfycence	1490

REIGNE
Upon us he doth reigne	111	Lawde	50

REYGNE
To reygne and to rule;	262	Collyn Clout	647

REYNE
It were a myschefe, yf lyberte lacked a reyne	144	Magnyfycence	135
But I shall of Fortune rule the reyne.	181	Magnyfycence	1460
I reyne in my robys, I rule as me lyst,	181	Magnyfycence	1485

REYNYTHE
So royall a kyng, as reynythe uppon us all -	245	Speke Parott	468

REYSE
But I am lothe for to reyse a smoke,	59	Bowge	479

REYSONS
Grete reysons with resons be now reprobitante,	244	Speke Parott	442
For reysons ar no resons but resons currant -	244	Speke Parott	443

REJAGGED
Ye raynbetyn beggers rejagged,	294	Why Come Ye	605

REJOYCE
Causeth him to gryn /And rejoyce therin;	95	Phy Sparrow	927

REJOYSE —REMAYNETH   Page   Title   Line

REJOYSE
Rejoyse, Englande, /And understande   359   Albany   1
REKE
'Twyst,' quod Suspecte, 'goo playe; hym I ne reke!'   51   Bowge   186
  Twyst] 'Whist' Wynkyn de Worde 1510, 'Twysshe' Marshe 1568
REKEN
But all that he dothe, and yf he reken well   175   Magnyfycence   1274
REKENED
And Inter didascolos is rekened for a fole;   235   Speke Parott   172
REKENING
They shall com to rekening, ...   111   Lawde   31
REKENYD
And yet he wolde be rekenyd pro Ariopagita;   235   Speke Parott   156
REKENYNG
They bode not till the rekenyng were discust.   30   Dol Dethe   40
And for he was a kyng, /The more shamefull rekenyng   121   Ag Scottes2   32
That was a peryllous rekenyng!   299   Why Come Ye   793
A fals rekenyng   361   Albany   104
I call to this rekenyng   383   Replycacion   316
REKENYNGE
A mad rekenynge, /Consydrynge all thynge, ...   116   Ag Scottes   45
Of his rekenynge, as evydently we may   146   Magnyfycence   215
Though al his conquestys were brought to rekenynge, ...   181   Magnyfycence   1468
And where soever you wyll fall to a rekenynge, ...   190   Magnyfycence   1777
Redresse sholde be at the rekenynge in every accompte, . . .   208   Magnyfycence   2413
Alone, and make rekenynge   271   Collyn Clout   990
REKYN
I rekyn yow in my rowllys, ...   129   Garnesche3   193
But so longe they rekyn with theyr reasons amysse   200   Magnyfycence   2127
  they] 'theyr' †Rastell & Treveris C 1530, B
To rekyn with thys recule now   237   Speke Parott   227
REKLESSE
Lyberte at large wyll oft wax reklesse.   142   Magnyfycence   54
REKNYNG
That durst abyde no reknyng;   365   Albany   249
RELACION
But I wyll make further relacion   297   Why Come Ye   716
And there to make relacion /In open predycacion, ...   379   Replycacion   205
RELACIONS
Your hertes than were hosed, /Your relacions reposed;   377   Replycacion   108
RELACYON
I shall you make relacyon   62   Hauke   29
RELACYONS
Theocritus with his bucolycall relacyons;   321   Garlande   327
RELATION
To make a relation /Of her commendation;   95   Phy Sparrow   961
  To] 'Bo' †Kele 1545.2
RELE
Theyr hekell and theyr rele, ...   222   El Rummynge   295
Lyke a wanton, whan I wyll, I rele to and froo.   233   Speke Parott   109
RELEYSYD
That Israell releysyd of theyr captyvyte, ...   181   Magnyfycence   1474
RELES
To shryve, assoyle, and to reles   268   Collyn Clout   875
RELYGION
All placis of relygion   306   Why Come Ye   1091
RELYGIOUS
So myche decay of monesteries and relygious places;   245   Speke Parott   499
RELYGYOUS
Relygyous men are fayne /For to tourne agayne   256   Collyn Clout   374
RELUCENT
Relucent smaragd, objecte imcomperable;   44   Balettys3   21
Such relucent grace /Is formed in her face;   100   Phy Sparrow   1159
Whose radiant beame /And relucent light   136   Dundas   46
Her eyen relucent as carbuncle so clere, ...   183   Magnyfycence   1556
Englande the flowr /Of relucent honowre, ...   305   Why Come Ye   1038
  Englande] 'To Englande' MS Rawlinson C. 813
Lodesterre of lyght, /Moche relucent;   339   Garlande   950
  Lodesterre] 'Lede sterre' †Fakes 1523
Among the Grekes most relucent of lyght, ...   383   Replycacion   332
REMAYNE
With her aye to remayne.   97   Phy Sparrow   1013
With her certayne /I wyll remayne   112   Calliope   22
Within thy skyn he xall remayne.   130   Garnesche5   22
I pray you, Larges, here to remayne, ...   149   Magnyfycence   323
With Magnyfycence in housholde do remayne;   157   Magnyfycence   613
With Magnyfycence in housholde do remayne;   158   Magnyfycence   640
And better shulde remayne /Amonge the people playne, ...   265   Collyn Clout   772
That welny nothynge there doth remayne   324   Garlande   430
  welny] 'welnere' Marshe 1568
And of that pole artike whiche doth remayne   331   Garlande   695
And ever to remayne   362   Albany   136
REMAYNED
That no lyfe well nye remayned.   73   Phy Sparrow   49
That unremembred longe tyme remayned.   347   Garlande   1225
REMAYNETH
Beware, for wrytyng remayneth of recorde!   314   Garlande   89

	Page	Title	Line
REMANYTH			
Whyles it remanyth fresshe in my mynde.	325	Garlande	465
REME			
That he is kyng without a reme;	119	Ag Scottes	156
A reme of papyr wyll nat holde	134	Garnesche5	174
Our kyng out of his reme?	368	Albany	381
REMEDELES			
Notwithstandynge it is remedeles;	351	Garlande	1394
REMEDY			
We wyll remedy it, man, or we go;	155	Magnyfycence	551
Can you remedy for a tysyke	156	Magnyfycence	555
Good Hope, syr, my name is; remedy pryncypall	206	Magnyfycence	2328
But thrughe good hope there may come remedy.	207	Magnyfycence	2344
Than, 'Have him to the Towre /Saunz aulter remedy!	289	Why Come Ye	430
REMEDYLES			
So myche losse of merchaundyse, and so remedyles;	245	Speke Parott	472
REMEMBER			
And to remember many a praty thynge;	44	Balettys3	33
Contynually I shall remember	117	Ag Scottes	65
Remember this lyfe lastyth but a whyle.	211	Magnyfycence	2502
REMEMBYR			
And hyt to remembyr.	237	Speke Parott	228
REMEMBRANCE			
As oft as thei call to ther remembrance	34	Dol Dethe	188
If ye to remembrance call	377	Replycacion	98
REMEMBRAUNCE			
Yet shall she never oute of remembraunce, ...	45	Balettys3	47
To have in remembraunce	99	Phy Sparrow	1094
have] 'heue' †Kele 1545.2			
And nowe it cometh to my remembraunce.	159	Magnyfycence	673
Redresse, in my remembraunce your lesson shall rest;	211	Magnyfycence	2503
In there remembraunce ye may be inrolde.	239	Speke Parott	291
And to remembraunce call;	262	Collyn Clout	631
Maketh remembraunce /How Kynge Lewes of late	297	Why Come Ye	721
Yet, in remembraunce of Daphnes transformacyon, ...	321	Garlande	320
Enpryntyng her wordes in my remembraunce, ...	327	Garlande	557
To your remembraunce wherfore ye must call	335	Garlande	812
Prudent Rebecca, of whome remembraunce	336	Garlande	845
That for her trowth is in remembraunce had;	337	Garlande	900
REMEMBRAUNCER			
To be your remembrauncer, madame, I am bounde, ...	336	Garlande	864
REMEMBRAUNS			
'Yowre boke of remembrauns we will now that ye rede;	345	Garlande	1149
boke] 'bokes' †Fakes 1523			
REMEMBRE			
Grow and encrese, remembre thyn astate!	33	Dol Dethe	163
'Ye remembre the gentylman ryghte nowe	51	Bowge	197
Par[d]e, remembre whan ye were there, ...	60	Bowge	515
Parde] 'Parte' †Wynkyn de Worde 1499, 1510, Marshe 1568			
Whan I remembre agayn /How mi Philyp was slayn, ...	72	Phy Sparrow	17
Whan I remembre it, ...	80	Phy Sparrow	353
Though I remembre the fable	89	Phy Sparrow	724
Syr, hardely remembre what may your name avaunce.	148	Magnyfycence	277
Remembre ye not how my lyberte by mesure ruled was?	178	Magnyfycence	1383
Remembre the good servyce that Mesure hath you done, ...	186	Magnyfycence	1637
To gyde them vertuously that wyll not remembre, ...	194	Magnyfycence	1922
Remembre you better, syr. Beware what ye say, ...	196	Magnyfycence	1995
And remembre he suffered moche more for your sake;	196	Magnyfycence	2001
Syr, remembre the tourne of Fortunes whele, ...	197	Magnyfycence	2022
Remembre you, therfore, howe late ye were low.	210	Magnyfycence	2451
And remembre amonge how Parrot and ye	236	Speke Parott	221
Remembre you wele, poynt wele that clause, ...	316	Garlande	136
REMEMBRED			
As towchyng that Eschines is remembred, ...	316	Garlande	148
Before remembred, me curteisly brought	343	Garlande	1102
me curteisly] 'kurteisly me' MS Cotton Vitellius E.x			
REMEMBREST			
'Remembrest thou what thou sayd yesternyght?	55	Bowge	323
Remembrest thou not the japes and the toyes -	171	Magnyfycence	1137
REMEMBRING			
What man, remembring how shamfully he was slayn, ...	32	Dol Dethe	111
REMEMBRYNG			
Remembryng your passyng goodly countenaunce, ...	42	Balettys2	5
REMEMBRYNGE			
Remembrynge prety thynges!	80	Phy Sparrow	350
REMENAUNT			
Spell the remenaunt, and do togyder.	157	Magnyfycence	619
So is all the remenaunt, I make God avowe;	175	Magnyfycence	1283
And whyles the heedes do this, /The remenaunt is amys	249	Collyn Clout	116
REMES			
And the floodes in straunge remes, ...	93	Phy Sparrow	882
REMORD			
UNTO DYVERS PEOPLE THAT REMORD THIS RYMYNG	120	Ag Scottes	R
REMORDE			
Yt commyth the wele me to remorde, ...	132	Garnesche5	101
Yow to remorde erste or they know your mynde.	241	Speke Parott	370
Thus the churche remorde.	271	Collyn Clout	981
As sumtyme he must vyces remorde, ...	314	Garlande	86

REMORDED — RENWDE   Page   Title   Line

REMORDED
Th[i]s may nat be remorded 383   Replycacion   323
   This] 'Thus' †Pynson 1528
REMORDERS
Wherfor your remorders ar madde or else starke blynde, ... 241   Speke Parott   369
   remorders] 'remordes' †MS Harley 2252
REMORDES
Agayne all remordes arme yow with paciens. 239   Speke Parott   298
REMORDYNG
Rebukyng and remordyng, /And nothing accordyng. 120   Ag Scottes2   11
remordyng dyvers recrayed and moche unresonable errours 373   Replycacion   1
REMORDYNGE
His symplenesse resytynge, /Remordynge and bytynge, ... 305   Why Come Ye   1058
REMORRS
As wytles as a wylde goos, ye have but small remorrs 123   Garnesche2   18
REMORSE
Remorse have I of youre most goodlyhod, ... 44   Balettys3   29
REMOTES
Some plucke a partryche in remotes, ... 268   Collyn Clout   867
REN
Then ren they with lesinges, and blow them about, ... 139   Ven Tonques   69
Honowre with renowne wyll ren on that syde. 234   Speke Parott   140
   on] 'of' Kynge & Marche 1554, Day 1560, Marshe 1568
RENAYENGE
For he hathe all the sayenge /Without any renayenge. 283   Why Come Ye   193
RENDER
Therfore I render of her the memory 339   Garlande   971
I render the fals rebelle 366   Albany   316
RENDRYNG
To iche of them rendryng thankis commendable, ... 335   Garlande   820
RENDRYNGE
In rendrynge to you thankkis meritory, ... 324   Garlande   429
Rendrynge my devisis I made in disporte 354   Garlande   1494
RENEWE
With lillis whyte your bewte doth renewe. 337   Garlande   884
   With lillis] 'The lylly' MS Cotton Vitellius E.x
With lillys whyte your bewte dothe renewe. 337   Garlande   891
RENEWYD
Nowe shall ye be renewyd with solace. 208   Magnyfycence   2404
RENY
Fayne ye were to reny 377   Replycacion   87
RENYYD
The commonns renyyd ther taxes to pay 31   Dol Dethe   78
RENNE
I am not happy, I renne ay on the losse! 57   Bowge   399
Now renne muste I to the stewys syde 57   Bowge   400
Your wyll renne before your wytte. 113   Scot Kynge   12
If lyberte sholde lepe and renne where he lyst 144   Magnyfycence   133
Here is a leysshe of ratches to renne an hare! 156   Magnyfycence   586
Some renne tyll they swete, ... 221   El Rummynge   266
Then renne they in every stede, ... 252   Collyn Clout   231
They renne agaynst the steple, ... 271   Collyn Clout   983
Renne god, renne devyll, ... 277   Collyn Clout   1222
Renne god, renne devyll, ... 277   Collyn Clout   1222
Renne who may renne best, ... 277   Collyn Clout   1223
Renne who may renne best, ... 277   Collyn Clout   1223
RENNETH
That some of them renneth strayght to the stuse. 174   Magnyfycence   1225
RENNING
For tunges untayde be renning astray. 138   Ven Tonques   37
RENNYNGE
Cyrcumspeccyon inhateth all rennynge astray, ... 209   Magnyfycence   2430
RENOME
Wherby I rede theyr renome and theyr fame 46   Bowge   15
RENOUN
From Scarpary to Tartary renoun therein doth spryng, ... 234   Speke Parott   131
RENOWME
Of renowme and worldly fame 293   Why Come Ye   569
RENOWNE
Honowre with renowne wyll ren on that syde. 234   Speke Parott   140
   on] 'of' Kynge & Marche 1554, Day 1560, Marshe 1568
Of renowne and of fame 270   Collyn Clout   958
RENOWNYD
Renownyd lady above the sterry hevyn, ... 313   Garlande   51
RENT
He ragyd and rent out your hart bloode; 119   Ag Scottes   136
A byll of recorde for an annuall rent. 187   Magnyfycence   1667
I am raggyd and rent, as ye may se; 195   Magnyfycence   1962
Where is nowe my treasure, my landes, and my rent? 198   Magnyfycence   2056
And so fer thou arte behynde of thy rent, ... 205   Magnyfycence   2294
RENTE
Alas his golde, his fee, his annuall rente, ... 32   Dol Dethe   97
RENUDE
With vertu well renude. 342   Garlande   1053
With vertu well renude. 342   Garlande   1061
The False Fayth that Now Goth, which dayly is renude; 346   Garlande   1179
RENWDE
With vertu well renwde. 341   Garlande   1045

REPAIRE
Sat honorably, to whome did repaire . . . . 334 Garlande 770
REPAYRE
That was wont to repayre, ... 80 Phy Sparrow 344
Within this quaire? /Who lyst repayre . . . . 116 Ag Scottes 42
    lyst] 'lyst to' Kynge & Marche 1554, Day 1560, Marshe 1568
REPAYRID
As I ymagenyd, repayrid unto me, ... 323 Garlande 392
REPARE
Ye, holly to good hope I have made my repare. . . . . 208 Magnyfycence 2394
REPARED
Your storme dryven shyppe I repared new, ... 327 Garlande 544
REPAST
In lent, for a repast, ... 284 Why Come Ye 220
REPENT
Wyerfore ye may it now repent. . . . . 114 Scot Kynge 33
I could make him shortly repent him for ever; . . . . 139 Ven Tongues 76
It is to late nowe thy synnys to repent. . . . . 205 Magnyfycence 2292
And sore I repent me of my wylfulnesse; . . . . 207 Magnyfycence 2379
Then ye of foly in tymes past you repent? . . . . 209 Magnyfycence 2433
    'Then ye repent you of foly in tymes past' †Rastell &
    Treveris C 1530, B
Sothely to repent me I have grete cause; . . . . 209 Magnyfycence 2434
REPENTAUNCE
With rubarbe of repentaunce in you for to rest; . . . . 207 Magnyfycence 2357
Syr, the repentaunce I have no man can wryte. . . . . 208 Magnyfycence 2392
REPENTYD
Ye, but have ye repentyd you with harte contryte? . . . . 208 Magnyfycence 2391
REPETE
The Repete of the Recule of Rosamundis bowre, ... 351 Garlande 1390
REPYNE
Agaynst curates, they repyne, ... 268 Collyn Clout 873
    They] not in Kele 1545.1, Marshe 1568, 'They' MS Harley 2252
REPLICACION
For replicacion restles that he of late ther made; . . . . . . 239 Speke Parott 282
that this lytell pamphilet, called the Replicacion . . . . . . 373 Replycacion I
REPLICACYON
Thus endeth the Replicacyon of Skelton Laureate, etc. . . . . . 386 Replycacion E
REPLY
I purpose for to reply . . . . 375 Replycacion 20
To answere or reply /Agaynst suche heresy. . . . . 383 Replycacion 312
REPLYCABLE
Reputyng hym unable /To gainsay replycable . . . . 382 Replycacion 303
REPLYCACION
A Replycacion Agaynst Certayne Yong Scolers Abjured of Late, . 373 Replycacion I
REPLYCACYON
agaynst Skelton laureate, devyser of this Replycacyon, etc. . . 382 Replycacion R
REPORT
By thy report ar wonte to be extolde . . . . 29 Dol Dethe 17
How shall I report . . . . 96 Phy Sparrow 998
Of him shuld men report, ... 121 Ag Scottes2 33
REPORTE
To all cuntreis aboute hym reporte me I dare: . . . . 33 Dol Dethe 136
Illumynyd wyth feturys far passyng my reporte; 44 Balettys3 23
I have to lytyll connynge to reporte. . . . . 47 Bowge 63
Recounte, reporte and tell . . . . 87 Phy Sparrow 613
And falsly ye me reporte. 124 Garnesche3 20
I reporte me herein to Kynge Lewes of Fraunce. . . . . 148 Magnyfycence 280
Syr, I am the better of your noble reporte; . . . . 183 Magnyfycence 1541
As [Per]cius, that poete, dothe reporte of me, ... 231 Speke Parott 27
    Percius] 'precius' †MS Harley 2252
Reporte howe the pope may . . . . 254 Collyn Clout 302
I reporte me to you. . . . . 257 Collyn Clout 432
Of this to reporte. . . . . 259 Collyn Clout 504
For the communalte reporte . . . . 271 Collyn Clout 1005
    reporte] not in Kele 1545.1, Marshe 1568, 'dothe reporte'
    MS Harley 2252
For reporte ryseth many deverse wayes. . . . . 317 Garlande 181
    For] not MS Cotton Vitellius E.x
Recount, reporte, reherse without delay . . . . 336 Garlande 840
Whome dame Nature, as wele I may reporte, ... 336 Garlande 867
That if I wolde reporte . . . . 370 Albany 444
As all men can reporte. . . . . 370 Albany 474
REPORTED
That her goodly name, /Honorably reported, ... 103 Phy Sparrow 1286
REPORTETH
Wherein he reporteth of the coragius . . . . 317 Garlande 164
    Wherein] 'Where' MS Cotton Vitellius E.x
REPORTID
That her goodly name, /Honorably reportid, ... 348 Garlande 1279
REPORTINGE
Truly reportinge his right noble astate, ... 33 Dol Dethe 146
REPORTYNG
In Fames court reportyng the same; . . . . 334 Garlande 783
REPORTYNGE
Reportynge the vertues all . . . . 75 Phy Sparrow 157
REPOSED
Your hertes than were hosed, /Your relacions reposed; . . . . . 377 Replycacion 108

REPREHENDE — RESYDENCE Page Title Line

REPREHENDE
My lyvyng to reprehende; 124 Garnesche3 16
REPREHENDYNG
As it reprehendyng, /And venemously stingyng, ... 120 Ag Scottes2 9
REPRESENT
She may well represent . . . . 97 Phy Sparrow 1017
Whome ye represent and exemplify, ... 336 Garlande 854
Phedra ye may /Wele represent; . . . . 338 Garlande 941
REPRESENTACYON
That by representacyon /Of his image and facyon, ... 77 Phy Sparrow 214
REPRESENTE
As goddesse inmortall she dyd represente; . . . . 313 Garlande 47
REPRESSE
All injuris he wolde represse, ... 307 Why Come Ye 1113
The fervent axes of love can not represse! . . . . 321 Garlande 315
REPRYVABLE
By theyr demenaunce, nor loss repryvable. . . . . 179 Magnyfycence 1419
REPROBITANTE
Grete reysons with resons be now reprobitante, ... 244 Speke Parott 442
REPROCHE
But of reproche surely he maye not mys . . . . 46 Bowge 26
Yt ys to your reproche. 126 Garnesche3 85
Alas, myn owne servauntys to shew me such reproche! . . . . . 205 Magnyfycence 2277
REPROCHED
The church is thus abusyd, /Reproched and pollutyd; . . . . . 66 Hauke 161
REPUGNAUNCE
'To make repugnaunce agayne that ye have sayde, ... 318 Garlande 211
REPUTYNG
Reputyng hym unable /To gainsay replycable . . . . 382 Replycacion 302
REQUEST
I am forcebly constrayned /At Juvynals request . . . . 309 Why Come Ye 1211
Of your request, regestred is his name . . . . 314 Garlande 62
'To your request we be well condiscendid; . . . . 318 Garlande 232
But my request is not so great a thynge, ... 332 Garlande 730
REQUESTE
Syr, your requeste shall not be delayed. . . . . 208 Magnyfycence 2401
To your requeste I shall be confyrmable. . . . . 208 Magnyfycence 2407
REQUIEM
The requiem masse to synge, /Softly warbelynge, ... 81 Phy Sparrow 401
    Softly] 'Loftly' Marshe 1568
REQUIRE
Require hym to convey yow ovyr the salte fome; . . . . 239 Speke Parott 302
REQUYRE
But I requyre you no worde that I saye! . . . . 54 Bowge 276
And I muste you requyre . . . . 143 Magnyfycence 110
REQUYRETH
The case requyreth. Alasse, alasse, an hevy metynge! . . . . 192 Magnyfycence 1847
As the worlde requyreth, but rather I am refused. . . . . . . 208 Magnyfycence 2412
In honest myrth, parde, requyreth no lack; . . . . 347 Garlande 1236
REREWARDE
How a do cam trippyng in at the rerewarde, ... 351 Garlande 1385
RESAYTE
A counte to counterfet in a resayte - . . . . 152 Magnyfycence 443
RESCEW
To whom then shall we sew /For to have rescew, ... 40 Coystrowne3 38
For defaute of rescew, ... 280 Why Come Ye 59
RESCU
Of worldly trust, then did I you rescu; . . . . 327 Garlande 543
RESCUDE
Trouth ought to be rescude; . . . . 369 Albany 421
RESCUE
You supporte and rescue, ... 257 Collyn Clout 434
    rescue] 'rescite' Marshe 1568
RESEMBLANCE
Which to thi resemblance wonderusly has wrought . . . . 34 Dol Dethe 193
RESEMBLAUNCE
Lyke to Argyva by just resemblaunce, ... 336 Garlande 843
RESEMBLE
Resemble the rose buddes; . . . . 97 Phy Sparrow 1036
RESEMBLED
Resembled to Symonides, that poete lyricall . . . . 383 Replycacion 331
    Symonides] 'Symphonides' †Pynson 1528
RESERVED
Nay, syr. That affeccyon ought to be reserved, ... 186 Magnyfycence 1643
Yet, syr, reserved your better advysement, ... 187 Magnyfycence 1661
But thynke you with Magnyfycence I shal be reserved? . . . . 188 Magnyfycence 1702
To yow thre this honor shalbe reserved . . . . 323 Garlande 409
RESERVYD
But a grete parte yet ye have reservyd . . . . 317 Garlande 171
    But...yet] 'Bot yit a grete parte' MS Cotton Vitellius E.x
Of laureat triumphe, your place is here reservyd, ... 344 Garlande 1126
    triumphe] 'promocioun' MS Cotton Vitellius E.x
And suche as be counterfettis they be reservyd; . . . . 346 Garlande 1190
RESIST
Right to maynten and to resist all wronge. . . . . 34 Dol Dethe 171
RESYDENCE
Where measure is absent, ryot kepeth resydence; . . . . 144 Magnyfycence 123
Where these kepe resydence, ... 279 Why Come Ye 11

RESYDENT — REST

	Page	Title	Line
RESYDENT			
Then shall you have with you prosperyte resydent.	146	Magnyfycence	197
Wherfore I wyll that ye be resydent	188	Magnyfycence	1718
And what vertues be resydent	369	Albany	426
RESYDEVACYON			
And of resyde[v]acyon /They make enterpretacyon resydevacyon] 'resdenacyon' †Godfray 1531, Kele 1545.1, Marshe 1568	259	Collyn Clout	521
RESYDEW			
In the resydew of thys boke.	68	Hauke	234
RESYDEWE			
Now constrewe ye what is the resydewe.	61	Bowge	539
RESYTYNGE			
Nor wyll have no resytynge	274	Collyn Clout	1135
His symplenesse resytynge, /Remordynge and bytynge,	305	Why Come Ye	1057
RESKEW			
Our Lorde thy soule reskew!	80	Phy Sparrow	332
RESON			
Where was your wit and reson ye shuld have had? your] 'ys' †MS Royal 18 D.ii	30	Dol Dethe	52
My reson rude and dull	102	Phy Sparrow	1221
For reson can I non fynde	126	Garnesche3	104
Ye ryme yet owte of reson;	127	Garnesche3	128
So ys all thyng wrowghte wylfully withowte reson and skylle.	245	Speke Parott	496
Reson is banysshed thence,	279	Why Come Ye	12
RESONABLE			
By the masse, man, thou shall fynde me resonable.	202	Magnyfycence	2204
RESONDE			
Of that shalbe resonde you ye must be content; you] not in Marshe 1568	344	Garlande	1123
RESONYNGE			
There vayleth no resonynge;	281	Why Come Ye	104
RESONS			
Grete reysons with resons be now reprobitante,	244	Speke Parott	442
For reysons ar no resons but resons currant –	244	Speke Parott	443
For reysons ar no resons but resons currant –	244	Speke Parott	443
RESORT			
Knolege, aquayntance, resort, favour, with grace;	43	Balettys3	1
RESORTE			
For all hokes unhappy to me have resorte.	178	Magnyfycence	1374
To the pythe of the mater who lyst to resorte:	213	Magnyfycence	2540
Nowe semyth us syttynge that ye then resorte	214	Magnyfycence	2566
Suche a lewde sorte /To Elynour resorte	218	El Rummynge	154
Home to resorte Jerobesethe perswade;	238	Speke Parott	279
And what estates to her did resorte,	313	Garlande	45
To Occupacyon I wyll agayne resorte,	354	Garlande	1492
Ye shulde take further payne /To resorte agayne	379	Replycacion	202
RESPYTE			
Delyte, desyre, respyte, wyth lyberte;	43	Balettys3	2
RESPONSYVE			
A confutacion responsyve, or an inevytably prepensed answere	382	Replycacion	R
RESSEYTE			
To make reconyng in the resseyte how Robyn loste hys bowe,	240	Speke Parott	341
REST			
When he is well, yet can he not rest.	36	Coystrownel	7
That on the rode loft /She perkyd her to rest.	63	Hauke	70
It wolde lye and rest –	75	Phy Sparrow	126
(God send the soule good rest!)	78	Phy Sparrow	262
That maketh his nest /In chymneyes to rest;	83	Phy Sparrow	471
God sende my sparoes sole good rest!	86	Phy Sparrow	574
That never have rest nor ease;	104	Phy Sparrow	1325
And of their taunting toies rest with il hayle.	138	Ven Tongues	33
Any such foly to rest or to be.	138	Ven Tongues	35
Where with to rule hym with the wrythyng of a rest.	144	Magnyfycence	136
That I wote not where I may rest.	168	Magnyfycence	1021
That ratyd the Romaynes and made them yll rest,	181	Magnyfycence	1481
With, 'Cockes armes! Rest shall I none have	185	Magnyfycence	1615
By myne advyse, with you in fayth he shall not rest.	186	Magnyfycence	1660
And let all your fansyes upon them rest,	190	Magnyfycence	1770
Now let us be all one, and let us lyve in rest;	202	Magnyfycence	2202
With rubarbe of repentaunce in you for to rest;	207	Magnyfycence	2357
Redresse, in my remembraunce your lesson shall rest;	211	Magnyfycence	2503
And of this tale to rest,	220	El Rummynge	236
She swered by the Rode of Rest,	221	El Rummynge	271
That Latinum fari may fall to rest and slepe,	235	Speke Parott	164
How the rest of good lernyng is roufled up and trold. roufled] 'roulled' Day 1560, Marshe 1568	235	Speke Parott	168
That ruleth the rest alone.	272	Collyn Clout	1019
And let take all the rest!	277	Collyn Clout	1224
And now a whyle to rest,	277	Collyn Clout	1249
And fall to rest a whyle;	289	Why Come Ye	397
And so to rest a whyle etc.	289	Why Come Ye	398
Tell you the rest; for me they shal.	296	Why Come Ye	709
That, me to rest, I lent me to a stumpe	312	Garlande	17
Whereon theis ladys softly myght rest,	334	Garlande	788
That never have rest nor ease;	349	Garlande	1318
With litell besynes standith moche rest; in bed	351	Garlande	1410

	Page	Title	Line
RESTE			
Enforsed to slepe and for to take some reste,	47	Bowge	32
Langagys divers; yet undyr that dothe reste	241	Speke Parott	365
Let se who dare make up the reste.	242	Speke Parott	382
The reste of suche reconyng may make a fowle fraye.	243	Speke Parott	403
RESTY			
And brought a gambone /Of bakon that was resty;	222	El Rummynge	328
RESTYTH			
Wherof the answere restyth in my handis,	332	Garlande	724
RESTLES			
To wyse is no vertue, to medlyng, to restles;	232	Speke Parott	61
For replicacion restles that he of late ther made;	239	Speke Parott	282
RESTLESSE			
Treatinge of trewse restlesse,	280	Why Come Ye	75
RESTORE			
Of hym that is gone, alas, withoute restore,	29	Dol Dethe	3
Farewell without restore,	80	Phy Sparrow	333
That may restore you agayne to felycyte,	196	Magnyfycence	1998
RESTRAYNE			
From bitter wepinge hym self kan restrayne?	32	Dol Dethe	112
RESTRAYNT			
Yet shall there be no restraynt	339	Garlande	956
RESTRAYNTES			
Wherfore make ye no mo restrayntes,	382	Replycacion	292
RESURRECTION			
That at his resurrection he harped out of hell	383	Replycacion	341
RETAYNE			
Me to retayne /Her serviture.	112	Calliope	19
It were not possyble me longe to retayne.	147	Magnyfycence	250
And in his servyce the to retayne.	159	Magnyfycence	668
And Og, that fat hog of Basan, doth retayne of] 'or' Kynge & Marche 1554, Day 1560, Marshe 1568	234	Speke Parott	122
That wolde your wordes retayne	266	Collyn Clout	774
RETAYNED			
And me to her retayned,	99	Phy Sparrow	1126
Be love I am constreyned /To be with yow retayned,	238	Speke Parott	258
RETAYNYD			
Mary, with Magnyfycence I wolde be retaynyd.	161	Magnyfycence	763
RETCHLESSE			
As evydently in retchlesse youth ye may se	200	Magnyfycence	2133
RETENEWE			
What poetis we have at our retenewe.	319	Garlande	238
RETHORIKE			
A lytell ragge of rethorike,	374	Replycacion	1
RETHORIKYS			
As provithe well, in hys rethorikys olde,	130	Garnesche5	11
RETORICYONS			
Retoricyons and oratours in freshe humanyte,	236	Speke Parott	194
RETOURNE			
Retourne we to our matter.	378	Replycacion	160
RETROGRADANT			
When Mars retrogradant reversed his bak,	312	Garlande	3
RETURNE			
Returne we to our former processe.	384	Replycacion	R
REVE			
Than Rowlande the reve ran, and I began to rave,	192	Magnyfycence	1831
REVELER			
Ryot, reveler, railer, brybery, theft,	329	Garlande	614
REVELYNG			
So rygorous revelyng, in a prelate specially;	246	Speke Parott	506
REVELL			
So many swannes dede, and so small revell -	245	Speke Parott	489
Ryot and Revell be in your courte rowlis;	317	Garlande	192
REVELL ROUTE			
'What, revell route!' quod he, and gan to rayle	56	Bowge	368
REVENGED			
Tyll I be revenged on that horson knave.	185	Magnyfycence	1616
REVENGYD			
Of Argus revengyd, recover when he may,	239	Speke Parott	288
REVERENCE			
This corse for to sence /With greate reverence,	85	Phy Sparrow	527
Here cometh in COURTLY ABUSYON, doynge reverence and courtesy.	182	Magnyfycence	SD
At your commaundement, syr, wyth all dew reverence.	182	Magnyfycence	1515
Of our blessyd Lorde, syr, at the reverence -	186	Magnyfycence	1636
The fyrst, to do him reverence,	307	Why Come Ye	1123
That bounde ar we with all deu reverence,	324	Garlande	423
Of ladys a beve with all dew reverence: a beve] 'aboue' †Fakes 1523	334	Garlande	771
Agaynst her excellence, /Agaynst her reverence,	375	Replycacion	41
To reverence in every place.	381	Replycacion	262
REVERENDE			
of the reverende prelates and moche noble doctours	373	Replycacion	I
REVERENS			
For no reverens thou sparys reverens] 'revens' Kynge & Marche 1554, Day 1560, Marshe 1568	69	Hauke	280
REVERENT			
Your soveraygne lorde most reverent,	118	Ag Scottes	113

REVERSED — RYALTE

	Page	Title	Line
But blessyd Bachus most reverent and holy,	322	Garlande	362

REVERSED
When Mars retrogradant reversed his bak,	312	Garlande	3

REVERSSE
I folowe in felycyte without reversse;	181	Magnyfycence	1491

REVILYNG
Rudely revilyng me in the kynges noble hall,	121	Garneschel	2

REVYLE
Vyce to revyle /And synne to exyle?	247	Collyn Clout	11
He doth revyle and brall	294	Why Come Ye	596

REVYNGE
With revynge and ravynge,	281	Why Come Ye	102

REVYVID
Wherewith your spiritis may be revyvid.'	332	Garlande	713

REVOLDE
Then furthermore aboute me my syght I revolde,	330	Garlande	664

REW
But to swete Jesu /On us then for to rew?	40	Coystrowne3	40
It wolde make one rew	80	Phy Sparrow	336
Wherfore all Troy dyd rew;	88	Phy Sparrow	676
Some men may happely rew,	280	Why Come Ye	60

REWARDE
Syr, God rewarde you as ye have deserved.	188	Magnyfycence	1701
That of our bownte we wyll hym rewarde:	334	Garlande	779
Therby I shall purchace /No displesaunt rewarde,	368	Albany	359

REWARDED
How shuld a fals lying tung then be rewarded?	137	Ven Tongues	2

REWARDES
Largesse in wordes – for rewardes are but small.	189	Magnyfycence	1760

REWARDYNGE
Largely rewardynge them that have deservyd;	200	Magnyfycence	2119

REWARDYS
In your rewardys use suche moderacyon	211	Magnyfycence	2494

REWE
That I used the to moche sore may I rewe.	199	Magnyfycence	2104

REWED
No creature but that wolde /Have rewed upon me,	72	Phy Sparrow	42

REWLE
For to rewle this reame,	295	Why Come Ye	656

REWTH
It were great rewth	300	Why Come Ye	841

REWTHE
O rydlesse rewthe, O paynfull poverte!	198	Magnyfycence	2051

RIGHT
What aylde you to slo your lord ageyn all right?	31	Dol Dethe	63
slo] 'sle' Marshe 1568			
To the right of his prince which shold not be withstand;	31	Dol Dethe	67
Truly reportinge his right noble astate,	33	Dol Dethe	146
Trew to his prince for to defende his right,	33	Dol Dethe	149
Right to maynten and to resist all wronge.	34	Dol Dethe	171
Shall now com and do right,	110	Lawde	17
That right dwelt us among,	111	Lawde	20
Right shall the foxis chare,	111	Lawde	22
God save him in his right! /Amen	112	Lawde	56
Agaynst whom he dyd fyght /Falsly agaynst all right,	120	Ag Scottes2	18
As right as a cammocke croked!	281	Why Come Ye	117
Right so, madame, the roses redde of hew	337	Garlande	890
Sir Duke of Albany, /Right inconvenyently	363	Albany	189
To my Lorde Cardynals right noble grace etc	372	Albany	E
With right lytell instruction;	378	Replycacion	155
And thought, if ye had right,	379	Replycacion	200

RIN
How ryvers rin not tyll the spryng be full;	314	Garlande	81
Nedes must he rin that the devyll dryvith.	352	Garlande	1434
It must nedes after rin all the worlde aboute.'	353	Garlande	1483

RING
Bo-ho doth bark wel, Hough-ho he rulyth the ring;	234	Speke Parott	130

RINNE
Yet they ryde and rinne from Carlyll to Kent.	317	Garlande	196
they ryde and rinne] 'ryde they and ryn they' MS Cotton Vitellius E.x			

RY
And have here a pecke of ry.'	221	El Rummynge	275

RYALL
Convenyent persons for any prynce ryall.	145	Magnyfycence	173
But largesse becometh a state ryall.	151	Magnyfycence	383
For al his pompe, for all his ryall trone,	181	Magnyfycence	1475
Make moche of Parrot, the popegay ryall.	236	Speke Parott	217
the] 'that' Kynge & Marche 1554, Day 1560, Marshe 1568			
And he wyll play checke mate /With ryall majeste	293	Why Come Ye	589
How you gave me a ryall commaundement	313	Garlande	58
you] 'ye' Marshe 1568, MS Cotton Vitellius E.x; a] 'in' MS Cot. Vit. E.x			

RYALLY
So ryally, so rychely, so passyngly ornate,	325	Garlande	487

RYALTE
Home to your paleys with joy and ryalte.	214	Magnyfycence	2567

RYAT —RYFLED | Page | Title | Line

RYAT
Ware, ryat, Parrot, ware ryot, ware that! . . . . 233 Speke Parott 101
RYBAUDE
Gone is this knave, this rybaude foùle and leude. . . . . 58 Bowge 414
RYBAWDE
Avaunt, rybawde, thi tung reclame! 132 Garnesche5 106
RYBBIS
That all the dayes of ther lyfe shall styck by ther rybbis. . . 330 Garlande 638
RYBBYS
In fay, man, some rybbys of the motton be so ranke . . . . . . 204 Magnyfycence 2269
RYBYBE
There came an old rybybe; . . . . 227 El Rummynge 492
RYBON
A goodly rybon, or a golde rynge, ... 184 Magnyfycence 1580
RYBSKYN
Theyr rybskyn and theyr spyndell, ... 222 El Rummynge 299
RYCH
The topas rych and precyouse in vertew; 44 Balettys3 15
RYCHE
Her takelynge ryche and of hye apparayle; . . . . 47 Bowge 38
Her marchaundyse is ryche and fortunate, ... 47 Bowge 52
  Her] 'Here' †Wynkyn de Worde 1499
Whome she loveth, of all plesyre is ryche . . . . 49 Bowge 113
The ryche prynce of Pargame, ... 76 Phy Sparrow 192
My buskyn wyde, /Ryche to beholde . . . . 164 Magnyfycence 854
Better to make iii. ryche than for to make many. . . . . 190 Magnyfycence 1772
And where you had chaunges of ryche aray, ... 197 Magnyfycence 2010
Where is nowe all my ryche abylement? . . . . 198 Magnyfycence 2059
Nowe ryche, nowe pore, nowe hole, now in dyseaee; . . . . . . 212 Magnyfycence 2518
Abowte my necke a cerculett lyke the ryche rubye, ... 231 Speke Parott 17
Maters more precious than the ryche jacounce, ... 241 Speke Parott 366
Arayse of ryche aray, ... 270 Collyn Clout 942
To make his cofers ryche; . . . . 290 Why Come Ye 454
But to recounte her ryche abylyment, ... 313 Garlande 44
None so ryche stones in Turkey to sell; . . . . 323 Garlande 396
Into the ryche palace of the Quene of Fame: . . . . 325 Garlande 450
RYCHELY
Were never halfe so rychely as I am drest. . . . . 181 Magnyfycence 1483
All other transcendynge, the most rychely besene, ... 325 Garlande 483
So ryally, so rychely, so passyngly ornate, ... 325 Garlande 487
But when they sawe my lawrell rychely wrought, ... 343 Garlande 1105
RYCHER
A precyous jewell, no rycher in this londe: . . . . 48 Bowge 97
RYCHES
Ryches rydeth out, at home is poverte. . . . . 153 Magnyfycence 474
Sodenly ryches, and sodenly poverte; . . . . 212 Magnyfycence 2527
Pompe, pryde, honour, ryches and worldly lust, ... 236 Speke Parott 223
RYCHLY
Some hatted and some capped, /Rychly bewrapped, ... 254 Collyn Clout 312
RYD
Ye, ryd thy selfe rather than this lyfe for to lede. . . . . 205 Magnyfycence 2307
Of thy throte bole, and ryd the out of payne. . . . . 206 Magnyfycence 2315
Nay; rather wyll I chose to ryd me of this lyve . . . . 206 Magnyfycence 2321
RYDE
I lete her to hyre that men maye on her ryde; . . . . 57 Bowge 402
Were I as you, I wolde ryde them full nere; . . . . 59 Bowge 472
Alas, I wolde ryde and go . . . . 76 Phy Sparrow 186
To sporte at your pleasure, to ryn, and to ryde? . . . . . . 142 Magnyfycence 79
By the way as I ryde and walke - . . . . 151 Magnyfycence 375
In all this hast whether wyll ye ryde? . . . . 156 Magnyfycence 570
Yes, perde, man, whether that ye ryde or go. . . . . 176 Magnyfycence 1307
To ryde upon a mule . . . . 254 Collyn Clout 308
Howe they ryde in goodly chares, ... 270 Collyn Clout 961
Where ever he go or ryde . . . . 289 Why Come Ye 394
Stande, walke, or ryde - . . . . 295 Why Come Ye 635
Yet they ryde and rinne from Carlyll to Kent. . . . . 317 Garlande 196
  they ryde and rinne] 'ryde they and ryn they' MS Cotton
    Vitellius E.x
Committyth all to God, and lettyth his shyp ryde; . . . . . . 335 Garlande 834
RYDEN
For had you not come I had ryden. . . . . 156 Magnyfycence 577
RYDES
Where ever he rydes or goos. . . . . 370 Albany 470
RYDETH
Who rydeth on her, he nedeth not to care, ... 57 Bowge 409
Ryches rydeth out, at home is poverte. . . . . 153 Magnyfycence 474
RYDYNGE
That they cannot say in Greke, rydynge by the way, ... 234 Speke Parott 146
Upon these beestes rydynge, ... 270 Collyn Clout 966
RYDYTH
He rydyth well the horse, but he rydyth better the mare. . . 43 Balettys2 21
He rydyth well the horse, but he rydyth better the mare. . . 43 Balettys2 21
RYDLESSE
O rydlesse rewthe, O paynfull poverte! . . . . 198 Magnyfycence 2051
RYE
From Wynchelsey to Rye . . . . 282 Why Come Ye 147
RYFLED
By my trouthe, we have ryfled hym metely well. . . . . 201 Magnyfycence 2170

	Page	Title	Line
RYGHT			
Thys grevyth your husband, that ryght jentyll knyght,	43	Balettys2	27
Myne hear ryght upstode,	77	Phy Sparrow	227
Shewe me the ryght path	78	Phy Sparrow	246
Ryght so she doth excede	93	Phy Sparrow	883
But ryght convenyently, /And full congruently,	98	Phy Sparrow	1069
Ye shew ryght well what good ye can;	117	Ag Scottes	60
A subtyll sysmatyke, /Ryght nere an heretyke,	121	Ag Scottes2	28
Yes, syr, with ryght good chere.	143	Magnyfycence	112
Unto that same I am ryght well agrede,	144	Magnyfycence	128
Ye, syr, undoubted. Then, of very ryght,	148	Magnyfycence	272
And for his sake ryght gladly I wolde	149	Magnyfycence	334
Thus at the laste I brynge hym ryght	152	Magnyfycence	422
In stede of ryght that wronge may stande;	152	Magnyfycence	433
Ryght so a sharp fansy must be founde	155	Magnyfycence	553
Ye, and do ryght good servyce he can.	163	Magnyfycence	822
Trust me, Lyberte, it greveth me ryght sore	178	Magnyfycence	1375
So it be by mesure I am ryght well content.	180	Magnyfycence	1421
Myght seme ryght wel under my proteccyon	181	Magnyfycence	1469
Howe be it, I wolde be ryght gladde, I you assure,	183	Magnyfycence	1527
Be it ryght or wronge, by the advyse of me,	185	Magnyfycence	1597
For as thou sayst, ryght so shall it be,	190	Magnyfycence	1783
In faythe, and your servyce ryght well shall I acquyte;	190	Magnyfycence	1794
Nowe hath he ryght nought, naked as an asse.	193	Magnyfycence	1893
Now, surely, Magnyfycence, I am ryght well apayed	208	Magnyfycence	2402
Yf you be so myndyd, we be ryght glad.	210	Magnyfycence	2473
Lyberte to a lorde belongyth of ryght,	211	Magnyfycence	2489
To the increse of your honour then arme you with ryght,	211	Magnyfycence	2496
But some than sate ryght sad	229	El Rummynge	607
And meddels very lyght /In the churches ryght.	249	Collyn Clout	105
And ryght slender connynge /Within theyr heedes wonnynge.	250	Collyn Clout	140
Ye do them wronge and no ryght	256	Collyn Clout	404
them] not in Marshe 1568			
You prelates, that of ryght	257	Collyn Clout	439
Whether it be wronge or ryght	272	Collyn Clout	1055
We tourne ryght into wronge,	276	Collyn Clout	1195
That ryght no man can fonge.	276	Collyn Clout	1197
By the ryght of a rambes horne.	276	Collyn Clout	1199
'Do ryght and do no wronge.'	281	Why Come Ye	89
do no] 'no' Kitson 1560.7, Marshe 1568			
As ryght as a rammes horne!	281	Why Come Ye	90
All that he dothe is ryght.	281	Why Come Ye	116
How can he do ryght?	293	Why Come Ye	581
He wolde have ben ryght fayne	295	Why Come Ye	642
And have taken ryght gret payne	295	Why Come Ye	644
A ryght delectable tratyse	312	Garlande	I
solacyous and ryght pregnant allectyues of syngular pleasure,	312	Garlande	I
Graunt my petycyon, I aske you but ryght.'	318	Garlande	231
Occupacyon, is ryght goodly aray,	327	Garlande	528
How wronge was no ryght, and ryght was no wronge;	331	Garlande	704
How wronge was no ryght, and ryght was no wronge;	331	Garlande	704
Turnyng on the ryght hande, by a windyng stayre,	333	Garlande	767
a] not in †Fakes 1523			
To the ryght noble Countes of Surrey	335	Garlande	R
Whos passynge bounte, and ryght noble astate,	336	Garlande	848
Whos passynge bounte, and ryght noble astate,	336	Garlande	855
Whos passyng bounte, and ryght noble astate,	336	Garlande	862
'Ryght high and myghty princes of astate,	344	Garlande	1128
It wolde have made a man hole that had be ryght sekely,	345	Garlande	1162
And Ryght is over the fallows	358	Garlande2	6
over the] 'ever' Marshe 1568			
Here endith a ryght delectable tratyse	358	Garlande2	E
humbly submytted unto the ryght discrete reformacyon	373	Replycacion	I
RYGHTE			
'Ye remembre the gentylman ryghte nowe	51	Bowge	197
I have grete scorne and am ryghte evyll apayed.'	54	Bowge	298
Ryghte now I spake with one, I trowe, I see -	59	Bowge	458
So myche papers weryng for ryghte a smalle exesse;	245	Speke Parott	479
So myche raggyd ryghte of a rammes horne;	246	Speke Parott	505
RYGOROUS			
So rygorous revelyng, in a prelate specially;	246	Speke Parott	506
RYGOURE			
Judycyall rygoure shall not me correcte -	142	Magnyfycence	69
RYME			
And spend my tyme /In prose and ryme,	95	Phy Sparrow	955
Nor good ryme in yower mater.	126	Garnesche3	105
Ye ryme yet owte of reson;	127	Garnesche3	128
I have receyvyd your secunde ryme.	129	Garnesche5	2
Ye rayle, ye ryme, with, 'Hay, dog, hay!'	129	Garnesche5	5
In bastarde ryme, after the dogrell gyse,	151	Magnyfycence	408
It forseth not of reason, so it kepe ryme.	172	Magnyfycence	1150
We wyll no farther ryme /Of it at this tyme.	220	El Rummynge	240
To ryme or to rayle, /To wryte or to indyte,	246	Collyn Clout	5
And yf ye stande in doute /Who brought this ryme aboute,	248	Collyn Clout	48
For though my ryme be ragged, /Tattered and jagged,	248	Collyn Clout	53
I wyll no further ryme /Tyll another tyme;	284	Why Come Ye	230
I may fortune for to ryme	310	Why Come Ye2	22
It may wele ryme, but shroudly it doth accorde,	346	Garlande	1210

RYMES —ROBYS   Page   Title   Line

RYMES
He rymes and railes /That Englishmen have tailes.   135   Dundas   9
RYMING
In ryming and raylyng with hym for to mell, ...   353   Garlande   1475
RYMYNG
UNTO DYVERS PEOPLE THAT REMORD THIS RYMYNG   120   Ag Scottes   R
RYN
To sporte at your pleasure, to ryn, and to ryde?   142   Magnyfycence   79
That nonnes wyl leve theyr holynes and ryn after me;   201   Magnyfycence   2146
Ryn God, rynne Devyll! Yet the date of Owur Lord   244   Speke Parott   444
Ye wolde ryn away rounde   367   Albany   348
And ryn your way apace.   367   Albany   354
RYNDE
His levis loste, the sappe was frome the rynde.   312   Garlande   21
RYNG
Thus to ryng a peale /Wyth his hawkys bels?   65   Hauke   136
And let hym ryng the bellys;   84   Phy Sparrow   493
An ouche or els a ryng, ...   88   Phy Sparrow   686
Under a stone on a golde ryng   296   Why Come Ye   700
RYNGE
My hawkes to mattens rynge!'   65   Hauke   124
A goodly rybon, or a golde rynge, ...   184   Magnyfycence   1580
RYNNE
Tushe! He that hathe nede, man, let hym rynne.   162   Magnyfycence   786
For by robbynge they rynne to in manus tuas quecke;   198   Magnyfycence   2044
That they set theyr chyldren to rynne on the brydyll, ...   200   Magnyfycence   2136
Ryn God, rynne Devyll! Yet the date of Owur Lord   244   Speke Parott   444
Dothe rynne lamentably.   280   Why Come Ye   48
Rynne away and crepe;   286   Why Come Ye   294
With, 'Stowpe, thou havell! /Rynne thou javell!   294   Why Come Ye   608
RYNSE
He may rynse a pycher, for his plate is to wed.   201   Magnyfycence   2168
RYOT
Ye rayll at ryot, recheles.   40   Coystrowne4   4
Where measure is absent, ryot kepeth resydence;   144   Magnyfycence   123
Ryot at lyberte russheth it out styll.   176   Magnyfycence   1317
Ware, ryat, Parrot, ware ryot, ware that!   233   Speke Parott   101
Ryot and Revell be in your courte rowlis;   317   Garlande   192
Ryot, reveler, railer, brybery, theft, ...   329   Garlande   614
RYOTE
'Welcome,' quod Ryote, 'I make God avowe.'   56   Bowge   378
RYOTYNGE
With ryotynge rechelesse, ...   280   Why Come Ye   72
RYOTT
Som sey I rayle att ryott recheles;   242   Speke Parott   387
RYOTTE
Dysdayne, Ryotte, Dyssymuler, Subtylte.   50   Bowge   140
Wyth that came Ryotte, russhynge all at ones, ...   56   Bowge   344
RYPEST
In a dysh dare he rush at the rypest;   37   Coystrowne1   46
RYSE
What willfull foly made you to ryse agayn   30   Dol Dethe   53
Yet so it is that a rumer begynnyth for to ryse   42   Balettys2   12
Tell you where of my name dothe ryse.   151   Magnyfycence   409
Ryse up, syr, and welcom unto me.   195   Magnyfycence   1966
'Ryse up, on Gods halfe,'   227   El Rummynge   501
We shulde nat ryse agayne   277   Collyn Clout   1232
Against the churche doth ryse.   306   Why Come Ye   1071
For in owr courte, ye wote wele, his name can not ryse . . .   345   Garlande   1154
RYSETH
Of whose incyneracyon /There ryseth a new creacyon   85   Phy Sparrow   541
For reporte ryseth many deverse wayes.   317   Garlande   181
   For] not MS Cotton Vitellius E.x
RYVERS
The ryvers rowth, the waters wan;   42   Balettys1   15
All ryvers and wellys, ...   303   Why Come Ye   959
How ryvers rin not tyll the spryng be full;   314   Garlande   81
ROBBE
They thynke it no shame to robbe and stele;   198   Magnyfycence   2042
ROBBED
For that I was robbed /Of my sparowes lyfe.   73   Phy Sparrow   51
ROBBYD
And had robbyd you quyte from all felycyte.   193   Magnyfycence   1864
ROBBYNGE
Alasse, syr, ye are undone with stelyng and robbynge!   192   Magnyfycence   1852
For by robbynge they rynne to in manus tuas quecke;   198   Magnyfycence   2044
ROBE
My robe russheth /So ruttyngly;   163   Magnyfycence   837
ROBES
Out of your robes ye were shaked, ...   119   Ag Scottes   166
   your] not in Kynge & Marche 1554, Day 1560, Marshe 1568
ROBYN
And Robyn Redbrest   81   Phy Sparrow   399
To make reconyng in the resseyte how Robyn loste hys bowe, . .   240   Speke Parott   341
As wyse as Robyn Swyne, ...   266   Collyn Clout   806
Good evyn, good Robyn Hode!   283   Why Come Ye   197
ROBYS
I reyne in my robys, I rule as me lyst, ...   181   Magnyfycence   1485

588

ROCHIS
Enswymmyng with rochis, barbellis and bremis, ... 330 Garlande 661
ROCKE
Theyr rocke, theyr spynnyng whele. .... 222 El Rummynge 296
ROCKET
In her furred flocket, /And graye russet rocket, ... 215 El Rummynge 54
ROD
By Moyses and Arons rod, ... 63 Hauke 54
Ye were beten weth your owne rod. .... 114 Scot Kynge 47
For youre owne tayle ye made a rod. .... 119 Ag Scottes 146
    owne] not in Day 1560, Marshe 1568
Savynge your usscheres rod, ... 124 Garnesche3 5
Than from theyr chyldren to spare the rod .... 194 Magnyfycence 1929
That you hath punysshed with his sharpe rod. .... 207 Magnyfycence 2350
Is counted for no rod; .... 275 Collyn Clout 1146
Clappyng his rod on the borde. .... 283 Why Come Ye 190
He rod, but we ran. .... 301 Why Come Ye 887
    'He rode not but he ran' MS Rawlinson C. 813
But yet beware the rod .... 307 Why Come Ye 1137
Of Jeremy the whyskynge rod, ... 308 Why Come Ye 1164
RODE
I am no hakney for your rode; .... 35 Man Margery 11
She kyste an anker, and there she laye at rode, ... 47 Bowge 39
    kyste] 'keste' Wynkyn de Worde 1510, 'kast' Marshe 1568
His hawke then flew uppon /The rode, with Mary and Johnn. ... 65 Hauke 127
Then moch more, by the rode, ... 66 Hauke 178
And how they rode eche one .... 88 Phy Sparrow 655
By the holy rode, ... 108 Epitaphel 66
From that lorde to that lorde I rode and I ran. .... 160 Magnyfycence 716
Ye, by the rode, even the same. .... 172 Magnyfycence 1139
Howe rode he by you? Howe put he to you? .... 173 Magnyfycence 1178
Nowe, by the rode, and he wyll go nere. .... 173 Magnyfycence 1196
With, yes, by the rode of Wodstocke Parke. .... 174 Magnyfycence 1209
What? Yes, by the rode, syr. It was I all this whyle ..... 193 Magnyfycence 1870
Then trust I to God and the holy rode, ... 203 Magnyfycence 2206
She swered by the Rode of Rest, ... 221 El Rummynge 271
For Tytus at Dover abydythe in the rode; .... 239 Speke Parott 284
Shote anker, and lye at rode, ... 277 Collyn Clout 1255
Whether he rode to Swaffhamm or to Some, ... 352 Garlande 1416
    Swaffhamm] 'Swasshamm' †Fakes 1523, Marshe 1568
RODE LOFT
That on the rode loft /She perkyd her to rest. .... 63 Hauke 69
ROIALL
In dygnyte roiall that doth excelle. 132 Garnesche5 96
It plesyth that noble prince roiall 132 Garnesche5 103
All the roiall sorte /Of his nobilyte, ... 370 Albany 445
ROYAL
In royal mageste /Lyke unto Ptholome, ... 370 Albany 440
ROYALL
Of the blode royall descendinge nobelly; .... 29 Dol Dethe 4
Therein they founde royall marchaundyse, ... 47 Bowge 41
This royall chaffre that is shypped here .... 47 Bowge 54
Er this, whan that ye made me royall chere. .... 53 Bowge 249
Of my sparowe royall. .... 75 Phy Sparrow 158
Laureat to be /Of fame royall; .... 112 Calliope 8
Of all our royall Englysh nacyon. .... 117 Ag Scottes 76
With our kyng royall war to mayntayne. .... 119 Ag Scottes 152
Your braggyng bost, your royall aray, ... 119 Ag Scottes 160
oratour to the kynges most royall estate. .... 120 Ag Scottes E
Brother unnaturall /Unto our kyng royall, ... 120 Ag Scottes2 16
Why doste thow deprave /This royall reame, ... 136 Dundas 44
'Cryste save Kyng Herry the viiith, owur royall kyng, ... 231 Speke Parott 34
'With Kateryne incomporabyll, owur royall quene also, ... 231 Speke Parott 36
Quod Parot, thy popagay royall. .... 238 Speke Parott 262a
    Quod] 'Quid' †MS Harley 2252
Amen, quod Parott, /The royall popagay. .... 241 Speke Parott 356
Jupyter for Saturne darre make no royall chere; .... 242 Speke Parott 399
Dixit, quod Parrott, the royall popagay. .... 243 Speke Parott 404
Dixit, quod Parrott, the popagay royall. .... 244 Speke Parott 446
So royall a kyng, as reynythe uppon us all - .... 245 Speke Parott 468
The noble bloode royall .... 262 Collyn Clout 612
And rule a realme royall .... 271 Collyn Clout 992
And of his royall powre .... 289 Why Come Ye 427
Of the court royall .... 290 Why Come Ye 435
Nor with royall Ptholomy, /Nor with Albumasar, ... 292 Why Come Ye 522
Royall Henry the eyght, ... 292 Why Come Ye 540
Whiche, of his royall mynde .... 292 Why Come Ye 546
He made a kynge royall, ... 293 Why Come Ye 558
To our most royall kynge, ... 298 Why Come Ye 754
In olde commemoracion /Most royall Englyssh nacion. ..... 305 Why Come Ye 1040
To whome supplyed the royall Quene of Fame. .... 313 Garlande 49
Of your royall palace it is not the gyse, ... 315 Garlande 121
Dymostenes, that oratour royall, ... 316 Garlande 130
Habillimentis royall founde out industriously; .... 336 Garlande 851
Item Royall Demenaunce Worshyp to Wynne; .... 345 Garlande 1174
As an hoost royall .... 360 Albany 61
But our kyng royall .... 361 Albany 107
Our royall kyng to make .... 367 Albany 327

ROYALLY —ROSE   Page   Title   Line

ROYALLY (cont.)
If our moost royall Harry	367	Albany	340
Of this, his realme royall /And lande imperiall,	368	Albany	393
In our royall regent,	369	Albany	427
His benignite /His royall dignyte,	370	Albany	456
Davyd, that royall kyng,	383	Replycacion	317

ROYALLY
Buyldynge royally /Theyr mancyons curyously,	269	Collyn Clout	934
Thus royally he dothe deale	287	Why Come Ye	336

ROYALS
Our royals that shone,	302	Why Come Ye	921

ROYLE
Therin, like a royle,	365	Albany	270

ROKE
The roke, with the ospraye	83	Phy Sparrow	462

ROLE
The goshauke shall have a role	85	Phy Sparrow	563

ROLFE
The ravyn called Rolfe,	82	Phy Sparrow	414

ROLLETH
He rolleth in his recordes,	283	Why Come Ye	194

ROLLYNGE
His eyen rollynge, his hondes faste they quoke;	51	Bowge	193

ROMAINE
In Romaine letters I never founde lack	137	Ven Tongues	17
Some Romaine letters, as I understode;	328	Garlande	583

ROMAYNES
That made the Romaynes all /For-drede and to quake; That] 'What' †Kele 1545.2, Wyght 1553	88	Phy Sparrow	666
That ratyd the Romaynes and made them yll rest,	181	Magnyfycence	1481

ROMAYNS
That made the Romayns to s[wea]t: sweat] 'smart' †Kele 1545.2, Wyght 1553, Kitson 1560.6, Marshe 1568	90	Phy Sparrow	748
With maters that amount the Romayns in substaunce;	321	Garlande	346
With the Romayns that made war,	363	Albany	193

ROMBELOW
'Heve and how, rombelow, row the bote, Norman, rowe.'	53	Bowge	252

ROME
To poynte this proude page a place and a rome,	37	Coystrownel	41
Dame Sulpicia at Rome,	75	Phy Sparrow	148
To Rome, to Charlemayne,	88	Phy Sparrow	653
Yet have we pycked out a rome for the.	154	Magnyfycence	508
In fayth, and Lybertyes rome is there but small.	158	Magnyfycence	663
Gyve this gentylman rome, syrs. Stonde utter!	161	Magnyfycence	753
Beryst thou any rome? Or cannyst thou do ought?	162	Magnyfycence	776
Foly hath a rome, I say, in every route;	177	Magnyfycence	1328
Nor Hanyball, agayne Rome gates that ranne,	182	Magnyfycence	1511
From the Pope of Rome	282	Why Come Ye	129
Of Rome to the see /Weth suche dygnyte.	307	Why Come Ye	1145
Of trumpettis and clariouns the noyse went to Rome;	354	Garlande	1507

RON
The hennes ron in the mashfat;	219	El Rummynge	190

RONNE
That hartes wyll ronne away,	280	Why Come Ye	54

RONNER
It was a ronner; nay, fole, I warant her blode warme.	191	Magnyfycence	1811

RONNES
My lady nowe she ronnes,	256	Collyn Clout	390

ROOTES
Such tunges shuld be torne out by the harde rootes,	137	Ven Tongues	3

ROPE
God garde the, Garnyche, from the rope!	133	Garnesche5	161
Is it not a vestment? A, ye wante a rope.	157	Magnyfycence	604
And some I make in a rope to totter and walter;	194	Magnyfycence	1910

ROPES
Of halters and ropes	362	Albany	123

ROPY
Lyke a ropy rayne, /A gummy glayre.	215	El Rummynge	24

RORE
For the cliffes of Scaloppe they rore wellaway,	238	Speke Parott	280

ROSABELL
Reflaring rosabell, /The flagrant camamell;	340	Garlande	977

ROSARY
Nor wrote the rosary	111	Lawde	27
The ruddy rosary, /The soverayne rosemary,	340	Garlande	979

ROSE
The rose both white and rede	110	Lawde	1
In one rose now dothe grow;	110	Lawde	2
But behynd in our hose /We bere there a rose	136	Dundas	35
That quyckly is envyved with rudyes of the rose,	183	Magnyfycence	1551
But rose from the borde	229	El Rummynge	591
We supposed, iwys, /That she rose to pys;	229	El Rummynge	595
The red rose in honour to flowrysshe and sprynge!'	231	Speke Parott	35
What here ye of the lord Rose?	286	Why Come Ye	286
Forthwith there rose amonge the thronge	319	Garlande	246
The Tratyse of the Triumphis of the Rede Rose,	347	Garlande	1223
This jeloffer jentyll, this rose, this lylly flowre,	352	Garlande	1446

ROSE BUDDES —ROUTH	Page	Title	Line

ROSE BUDDES
Resemble the rose buddes; .... 97 Phy Sparrow 1036
ROSEMARY
The ruddy rosary, /The soverayne rosemary, ... 340 Garlande 980
ROSERS
Enrailid with rosers, and vinis engrapid; .... 330 Garlande 656
ROSES
The enbuddid blossoms of roses rede of hew .... 337 Garlande 883
    The enbuddid blossoms of] 'Enbuddid blossome with' MS Cotton Vitellius E.x
Right so, madame, the roses redde of hew .... 337 Garlande 890
ROSET
His hode was syde, his cope was roset graye; .... 58 Bowge 440
ROSIAR
The Boke of the Rosiar; Prince Arturis Creacyoun; .... 345 Garlande 1178
ROST
In faythe, I rule moche of the rost. .... 163 Magnyfycence 804
Grimbaldus gredy snatche a puddyng tyl the rost be redy. ... 172 Magnyfycence 1155
Lyke a rost pygges eare, ... 215 El Rummynge 20
Or elles go rost a stone! .... 281 Why Come Ye 112
ROSTE
Rule the roste! Thou woldest, ye, ... 163 Magnyfycence 805
    Thou woldest, ye] 'ye thou woldest' †Rastell & Treveris C 1530, B
He ruleth all the roste .... 283 Why Come Ye 201
ROSTY
Of infernall posty, /Where soulis fry and rosty; .... 349 Garlande 1326
ROSTYD
Ye rostyd and ye boylyd, ... 125 Garnesche3 29
Ye rostyd, lyke a fonne, ... 125 Garnesche3 30
ROTCHETTES
In rotchettes of fyne raynes, ... 254 Collyn Clout 314
ROTE
'Prynces of youghte', can ye synge by rote? .... 53 Bowge 253
And nowe they lye and rote; .... 78 Phy Sparrow 251
Chefe rote of his makynge. .... 298 Why Come Ye 755
ROTY
He lumbryth on a lewde lewte, 'Roty bully joyse', ... 37 Coystrownel 29
ROTTEN
Full untydy tegges, /Lyke rotten egges. .... 218 El Rummynge 152
And shryne your rotten bonys .... 255 Collyn Clout 346
Theyr founders lye there rotten; .... 257 Collyn Clout 426
ROUFLED
How the rest of good lernyng is roufled up and trold. .... 235 Speke Parott 168
    roufled] 'roulled' Day 1560, Marshe 1568
ROUGH
Let him cough, rough or snevyll! .... 277 Collyn Clout 1221
ROUGH-FOTED
Of the out iles the rough-foted Scottes, ... 120 Ag Scottes 170
ROUGH FOTED
Of the out yles ye rough foted Scottes .... 115 Scot Kynge 62
A tolman to blot, /A rough foted Scot! .... 136 Dundas 41
ROUNCEVALL
Frome Napuls, from Navern, and from Rouncevall, ... 326 Garlande 495
ROUNDE
Lorde, how that I wolde caste it full rounde! .... 57 Bowge 396
I have an errande to rounde in your ere. .... 60 Bowge 513
Or Arturs rounde table, ... 87 Phy Sparrow 634
With heles short and rounde. .... 100 Phy Sparrow 1150
Well rounde aboute. .... 163 Magnyfycence 831
That though ye rounde your heere .... 263 Collyn Clout 673
Brevely and rounde /To me expounde. .... 361 Albany 82
Ye wolde ryn away rounde .... 367 Albany 348
ROUNDED
And as he rounded thus in myne ere .... 61 Bowge 526
    rounded] 'roynded' †Wynkyn de Worde 1499
ROUNSES
Of coursers and rounses .... 104 Phy Sparrow 1314
ROUNSIS
Of coursers and rounsis .... 349 Garlande 1307
ROUST
For they go to roust, /Streyght over the ale-joust, ... 219 El Rummynge 191
ROUSTY
Of infernall posty /Where soules frye and rousty; ...... 105 Phy Sparrow 1333
    rousty] 'rosty' Marshe 1568
ROUT
Than wyll he rout and snort; .... 220 El Rummynge 232
Amongest the hole rout .... 273 Collyn Clout 1082
ROUTE
Thus, in a rowe, of martchauntes a grete route .... 49 Bowge 120
To russhe it oute /In every route. .... 164 Magnyfycence 848
Foly hath a rome, I say, in every route; .... 177 Magnyfycence 1328
And thyder came an hepe /Of mylstones in a route.' ..... 223 El Rummynge 362
    thyder] 'there' †Lant 1545, Kynge & Marche 1554, Day 1560, Marshe 1568
ROUTH
Nor blake Baltazar with hys basnet routh as a bere, ... 122 Garneschel 23

	Page	Title	Line
ROUTHE			
Alas for routhe, what thouthe his mynde wer goode,	32	Dol Dethe	102
ROW			
'Heve and how, rombelow, row the bote, Norman, rowe.'	53	Bowge	252
Row and full of lowsy here,	127	Garnesche3	124
Also nat fare from Bowgy Row,	130	Garnesche5	47
ROWE			
Thus, in a rowe, of martchauntes a grete route	49	Bowge	120
'Heve and how, rombelow, row the bote, Norman, rowe.'	53	Bowge	252
Ye rowe ranke Scottes and dronken Danes	115	Scot Kynge	64
Suche a prelate, I trowe, /Were worthy to rowe	303	Why Come Ye	954
The dredefull dinne drove all the rowte on a rowe;	319	Garlande	264
ROWETH			
That roweth with a rude ore	105	Phy Sparrow	1339
ROWGH			
The [kn]oute and the [r]owgh;	83	Phy Sparrow	449
knout] 'route' †Kele 1545.2, Wyght 1553, Kitson 1560.6, Marshe 1568; rowgh] 'kowgh' †Kele, Wyght, Kitson, Marshe			
ROWYTH			
That rowyth with a rude ore,	349	Garlande	1332
ROWLANDE			
Than Rowlande the reve ran, and I began to rave,	192	Magnyfycence	1831
ROWLYNGE			
Rowlynge in yower holow hede, ugly to see;	122	Garnesche1	38
ROWLLYS			
I rekyn yow in my rowllys,	129	Garnesche3	193
ROWME			
His byrth and rowme togeder,	291	Why Come Ye	498
Unto the rowme of laureat promotyve?	315	Garlande	116
'Make rowme,' sayd another, 'ye prese all to sore,'	319	Garlande	256
ROWND			
Were newly enbybid; and rownd about the same	331	Garlande	682
ROWNDE			
Of birrall enbosid wer the pyllers rownde;	325	Garlande	467
ROWNE			
But yf it lyke you that I myght rowne in your eyre,	186	Magnyfycence	1645
ROWNYD			
Some whispred, some rownyd, some spake, and some cryde,	319	Garlande	250
ROWTE			
In all this rowte	168	Magnyfycence	992
That no man dare rowte;	287	Why Come Ye	341
Amonge the thickeste of all the hole rowte,	319	Garlande	240
The dredefull dinne drove all the rowte on a rowe;	319	Garlande	264
ROWTH			
The ryvers rowth, the waters wan;	42	Balettys1	15
With burris rowth and bottons surffillyng,	334	Garlande	803
rowth] 'rowgh' Marshe 1568			
ROWTYTH			
'My lefe', she sayd, 'rowtyth in hys bed;	42	Balettys1	20
RUBARBE			
With rubarbe of repentaunce in you for to rest;	207	Magnyfycence	2357
RUBBE			
Not rubbe you on the gall,	279	Why Come Ye	25
you] 'hym' MS Rawlinson C. 813			
RUBBED			
That rubbed she must be on the gall	174	Magnyfycence	1232
RUBBID			
Savynge he rubbid sum on the gall.	315	Garlande	97
on] 'upon' Marshe 1568			
RUBIES			
Envawtyd with rubies the vawte was of this place.	325	Garlande	476
RUBIS			
With diamauntis and rubis there tabers were trasid,	323	Garlande	395
tabers] 'taberdes' Marshe 1568			
RUBY			
The lusty ruby ruddes	97	Phy Sparrow	1035
RUBYE			
Abowte my necke a cercculett lyke the ryche rubye,	231	Speke Parott	17
Diamounde, or rubye, or balas of the beste,	241	Speke Parott	367
RUBYS			
Your ruddys wyth ruddy rubys may compare;	44	Balettys3	16
RUDDES			
The lusty ruby ruddes	97	Phy Sparrow	1035
RUDDY			
Your ruddys wyth ruddy rubys may compare;	44	Balettys3	16
Her lusty lyppes ruddy as the chery -	183	Magnyfycence	1558
Of closters engrosyd with his ruddy flotis	321	Garlande	335
flotis] 'droppes' †Fakes, 'flotis' Marshe 1568			
Of clusters engrosed with his ruddy flotes	321	Garlande	342
Of clusters engrosid with his ruddy [flotis]	322	Garlande	349
flotis] 'droppes' †Fakes 1523, 'dropes' Marshe 1568			
Of clusters engrosyd with his ruddy [flotis]	322	Garlande	356
flotis] 'dropis' †Fakes 1523, 'dropes' Marshe 1568			
Of clusters engrosid with his ruddy [flotis]	322	Garlande	363
flotis] 'dropis' †Fakes 1523, 'dropes' Marshe 1568			
Of clusters engrosed with his ruddy [flotis]	322	Garlande	370
flotis] 'dropis' †Fakes 1523, 'dropes' Marshe 1568			

RUDDYS —RULE   Page   Title   Line

	Page	Title	Line
Of clusters engrosyd with his ruddy [flotis]	322	Garlande	377
flotis] 'dropis' †Fakes 1523, 'dropes' Marshe 1568			
Of clusters engrosed with his ruddy [flotis]	322	Garlande	384
flotis] 'dropis' †Fakes 1523, 'dropes' Marshe 1568			
The ruddy shamefastnes in her vysage fyll,	337	Garlande	888
The ruddy rosary, /The soverayne rosemary,	340	Garlande	979
RUDDYS			
Your ruddys wyth ruddy rubys may compare;	44	Balettys3	16
RUDE			
A maynny of rude villayns made hym for to blede.	30	Dol Dethe	46
With my rude pen enkankerd all with rust,	33	Dol Dethe	142
Our naturall tong is rude,	91	Phy Sparrow	774
My reson rude and dull	102	Phy Sparrow	1221
That roweth with a rude ore	105	Phy Sparrow	1339
The rude ranke Scottes, lyke dronken dranes,	120	Ag Scottes	172
There be two lyther, rude and ranke,	175	Magnyfycence	1266
Nay, thou rude ravener, rayne beten javell!	202	Magnyfycence	2191
To rude ys there reason to reche to your sentence;	240	Speke Parott	319
At my style rude and playne,	273	Collyn Clout	1088
I saw Gower, that first garnisshed our Englysshe rude,	323	Garlande	387
Oure Englysshe rude so fresshely hath set out,	324	Garlande	422
That rowyth with a rude ore,	349	Garlande	1332
What though my stile be rude?	369	Albany	419
Though your Englishe be rude,	372	Albany	516
RUDELY			
Rudely revilyng me in the kynges noble hall,	121	Garneschel	2
Rudely rayne-beaten, /Rusty and mothe-eaten,	248	Collyn Clout	55
mothe] 'moche' †Godfray 1531, 'moughte' Kele 1545.1, 'mothe' MS Harley 2252			
RUDENESS			
Your rudeness to pardon and also that they wolde	241	Speke Parott	360
RUDYES			
That quyckly is envyved with rudyes of the rose,	183	Magnyfycence	1551
RUDNES			
Myne homely rudnes and drighnes to expelle	29	Dol Dethe	13
RUFFYNS			
Ye recrayed ruffyns all ragged!'	294	Why Come Ye	606
RUFFLYNGE			
For rufflynge of Phillips fethers,	73	Phy Sparrow	79
For] 'From' Wyght 1553, Kitson 1560.6, Marshe 1568			
RUGGY			
Maude Ruggy thyther skypped:	226	El Rummynge	467
RUGGYD			
But tatterd and tuggyd, /Raggyd and ruggyd,	304	Why Come Ye	1027
tatterd] 'taxed' MS Rawlinson C. 813			
RUGHE			
Whan the noppe is rughe, it wolde be shorne.	153	Magnyfycence	448
RUGHLY			
I rushe at them rughly and make them ly full lowe;	193	Magnyfycence	1884
RULE			
He can not fynd it in rule nor in space:	37	Coystrownel	22
Naye, strawe for tales, thou shalte not rule us;	55	Bowge	341
Where to rule hym with the wrythyng of a rest.	144	Magnyfycence	136
Unto your rule I wyll annex my mynde.	144	Magnyfycence	142
And rule hym after the rule of your scole.	146	Magnyfycence	231
And rule hym after the rule of your scole.	146	Magnyfycence	231
Take Lyberte to rule, and folowe myne entent.	147	Magnyfycence	238
The rule of Measure, notwithstandynge we	147	Magnyfycence	242
Ye. And he hath rule of all his tresure.	158	Magnyfycence	632
In faythe, I rule moche of the rost.	163	Magnyfycence	804
Rule the roste! Thou woldest, ye,	163	Magnyfycence	805
Thou woldest, ye] 'ye thou woldest' †Rastell & Treveris C 1530, B			
All mesure and good rule is gone quyte.	176	Magnyfycence	1315
Yet Lyberte without rule is not worth a strawe.	178	Magnyfycence	1378
To rule as ye lyst, lo, here is Lyberte.	179	Magnyfycence	1413
Have welth at our gydynge to rule as we lyst?	179	Magnyfycence	1415
But I shall of Fortune rule the reyne.	181	Magnyfycence	1460
I reyne in my robys, I rule as me lyst,	181	Magnyfycence	1485
Let me have the rule of your purse.	189	Magnyfycence	1762
That rule not be mesure that they have in theyr handys,	195	Magnyfycence	1939
That sadly rule not theyr howsholde men.	195	Magnyfycence	1940
But, syr, by me to rule fyrst ye began.	209	Magnyfycence	2431
For he wantythe of hys wyttes that all wold rule alone;	240	Speke Parott	329
To rule ix realmes by one mannes wytte,	240	Speke Parott	333
Frantiknes dothe rule and all thyng commaunde;	243	Speke Parott	420
Wylfulnes and Braynles no[w] rule all the raye.	243	Speke Parott	421
now] 'no' †MS Harley 2252			
To kepe so harde a rule,	254	Collyn Clout	307
And rule all thynges alone.	258	Collyn Clout	475
To rule kynge and kayser.	261	Collyn Clout	604
Theyr rule is very small,	261	Collyn Clout	609
To reygne and to rule;	262	Collyn Clout	647
For one man to rule a kynge	271	Collyn Clout	989
kynge] 'gyng' Kele 1545.1, 'kyng' MS Harley 2252			
And rule a realme royall	271	Collyn Clout	992
Howe we wyll rule all at wyll	276	Collyn Clout	1190
And we wyll rule and rayne,	276	Collyn Clout	1212

RULED —RUSH

	Page	Title	Line
For Wyll dothe rule all thynge,	281	Why Come Ye	105
For whyles he doth rule,	282	Why Come Ye	134
And gave him a realme to rule	293	Why Come Ye	559
Rule the swerde of myght?	293	Why Come Ye	580
A prelate potencyall /To rule under Bellyall,	294	Why Come Ye	592
And to rule as hym lyst;	297	Why Come Ye	734
All the rule of this lande,	298	Why Come Ye	762
And rule them echone /In Lucyfers trone.	304	Why Come Ye	992
To rule nor to guyde,	304	Why Come Ye	1012

RULED

	Page	Title	Line
Ye muste be ruled, as I shall tell you howe.	60	Bowge	493
Who that is ruled by us, it shalbe longe or he thee.	154	Magnyfycence	515
But I wyll be ruled after your counsell.	157	Magnyfycence	615
To se you thus ruled and stande in suche awe.	178	Magnyfycence	1376
Remembre ye not how my lyberte by mesure ruled was?	178	Magnyfycence	1383
It is good yet that lyberte be ruled by reason.	178	Magnyfycence	1387
Yourselfe shall be ruled by lyberte and largesse.	179	Magnyfycence	1389
Not and your grace wolde be ruled by me.	179	Magnyfycence	1393
Nay. He shall be ruled even as I lyst.	179	Magnyfycence	1394
So to be ruled by measure, it is a payne.	189	Magnyfycence	1739
For yf Measure had ruled Lyberte as he began,	200	Magnyfycence	2111
And be ruled by me, whiche am called Redresse.	208	Magnyfycence	2410
And ruled as he wolde.	293	Why Come Ye	564

RULER

	Page	Title	Line
An holy water clarke a ruler of lordys.	37	Coystrownel	21
But yf reason be regent and ruler of your barge.	141	Magnyfycence	38
Where measure is ruler, there is nothynge amysse.	144	Magnyfycence	124
Nowe that ye have me chefe ruler assyngned,	146	Magnyfycence	202

RULES

	Page	Title	Line
He rules his cominalte /With all benignite.	370	Albany	463

RULETH

	Page	Title	Line
Fortune gydeth and ruleth all our shyppe.	49	Bowge	111
The sayle is up, Fortune ruleth our helme,	49	Bowge	127
So he ruleth over all our place.	155	Magnyfycence	545
And ruleth so over all	262	Collyn Clout	633
That ruleth the rest alone.	272	Collyn Clout	1019
He ruleth alway styll.	281	Why Come Ye	107
He ruleth all the roste	283	Why Come Ye	201
That he ruleth them all.	290	Why Come Ye	436
He ruleth all at wyll	291	Why Come Ye	487
That ruleth but he alone,	304	Why Come Ye	996

RULY

	Page	Title	Line
Sion is in sadness, Rachell ruly doth loke;	234	Speke Parott	114

RULYD

	Page	Title	Line
All trebyllys and tenours be rulyd by a meyne.	144	Magnyfycence	137
I wolde be rulyd and I myght for shame.	147	Magnyfycence	235
Whether sholde welth be rulyd by lyberte,	180	Magnyfycence	1431
Syr, as me semeth, ye sholde be rulyd be me.	180	Magnyfycence	1433
Nor Alerycus, that rulyd the Gothyaunce by swerd,	182	Magnyfycence	1504

RULYE

	Page	Title	Line
Racell, rulye ragged, she is like to cache colde;	242	Speke Parott	401

RULYTH

	Page	Title	Line
There is no surfet where measure rulyth the feste;	144	Magnyfycence	139
Bo-ho doth bark wel, Hough-ho he rulyth the ring;	234	Speke Parott	130

RULYTHE

	Page	Title	Line
As presydent and regente he rulythe every deall.	239	Speke Parott	312

RUMBELOWE

	Page	Title	Line
Wit[h], 'Hey, howe, rumbelowe,' /Rumpopulorum, With] 'Wit' Marshe 1568	108	Epitaphe1	80

RUMBYLL

	Page	Title	Line
'Rumbyll downe, tumbyll downe, hey, go, now, now!'	37	Coystrownel	30

RUMER

	Page	Title	Line
Yet so it is that a rumer begynnyth for to ryse	42	Balettys2	12

RUMMYNG

	Page	Title	Line
The Tunnyng of Elynour Rummyng per Skelton Laureat.	214	El Rummynge	I
Sayd Elynour Rummyng,	227	El Rummynge	502
Also the Tunnynge of Elinour Rummyng,	347	Garlande	1233

RUMMYNGE

	Page	Title	Line
I understande, her name /Is Elynour Rummynge,	216	El Rummynge	93
With all theyr myght runnynge /To Elynour Rummynge,	217	El Rummynge	129
Of this mad mummynge /Of Elynour Rummynge.	230	El Rummynge	621

RUMPE

	Page	Title	Line
His rumpe, he wente so all for somer lyghte;	56	Bowge	355
His rumpe also he frygges /Agaynst the hye benche.	219	El Rummynge	178

RUMPOPULORUM

	Page	Title	Line
Wit[h], 'Hey, howe, rumbelowe,' /Rumpopulorum, With] 'Wit' Marshe 1568	108	Epitaphe1	81

RUN

	Page	Title	Line
Some run to far before, some run to far behynde,	233	Speke Parott	76
Some run to far before, some run to far behynde,	233	Speke Parott	76

RUNE

	Page	Title	Line
To dauns the hay or rune the ray;	134	Garnesche5	170

RUNNYNGE

	Page	Title	Line
Came runnynge with a dow,	63	Hauke	72
With all theyr myght runnynge /To Elynour Rummynge,	217	El Rummynge	128

RUSH

	Page	Title	Line
In a dysh dare he rush at the rypest;	37	Coystrownel	46

	Page	Title	Line
RUSHE			
I rushe at them rughly and make them ly full lowe;	193	Magnyfycence	1884
RUSSET			
In her furred flocket, /And graye russet rocket,	215	El Rummynge	54
In gray russet and heery cotes;	268	Collyn Clout	865
RUSSHE			
To russhe it oute /In every route.	164	Magnyfycence	847
With that I herd gunnis russhe out at ones,	329	Garlande	623
RUSSHETH			
My robe russheth /So ruttyngly;	163	Magnyfycence	837
Ryot at lyberte russheth it out styll.	176	Magnyfycence	1317
RUSSHYNGE			
Wyth that came Ryotte, russhynge all at ones,	56	Bowge	344
RUST			
With my rude pen enkankerd all with rust,	33	Dol Dethe	142
RUSTY			
A rusty gallande, to-ragged and to-rente;	56	Bowge	345
Our language is so rusty,	91	Phy Sparrow	777
His gummes rusty /Are full unlusty;	94	Phy Sparrow	914
Cankard Jacke Hare, loke thou be not rusty;	161	Magnyfycence	758
Rudely rayne-beaten, /Rusty and mothe-eaten,	248	Collyn Clout	56
mothe] 'moche' †Godfray 1531, 'moughte' Kele 1545.1, 'mothe' MS Harley 2252			
RUTHE			
Alas, it is great ruthe!	255	Collyn Clout	343
RUTTER			
Howe sayst thou, man? Am not I a joly rutter?	161	Magnyfycence	752
RUTTERKYN			
Rutty bully, joly rutterkyn, heyda!	161	Magnyfycence	747
RUTTERS			
To here you two rutters dyspute togyder.	176	Magnyfycence	1287
RUTTY			
Rutty bully, joly rutterkyn, heyda!	161	Magnyfycence	747
RUTTYNGLY			
My robe russheth /So ruttyngly;	163	Magnyfycence	838
SAAKE			
Speke, Parotte, I pray yow, for Maryes saake,	237	Speke Parott	233
SABY			
Or gummis of Saby so derely that be solde.	331	Garlande	675
SACERDOTES			
And say properly thei are sacerdotes	268	Collyn Clout	874
SACKE			
Thus can I lerne you, syrs, to bere the devyls sacke;	160	Magnyfycence	721
Her skynne lose and slacke, /Greuyned lyke a sacke;	215	El Rummynge	32
Greuyned] 'Grained' Day 1560, Marshe 1568			
And some have a smacke /Of Luthers sacke,	260	Collyn Clout	541
SACKES			
Cary sackes to the myll,	281	Why Come Ye	110
SACRAMENT			
Wyth cry unreverent, /Before the sacrament,	62	Hauke	12
Streyght to the sacrament	63	Hauke	46
When consecratyd was /The blessyd sacrament.	67	Hauke	186
Ye, by Goddes sacrament; and with other mo.	166	Magnyfycence	942
SACRAMENTES			
To mayntene argumentes /Agaynst the sacramentes.	259	Collyn Clout	518
SACRE			
The sacre with them shall say	85	Phy Sparrow	561
SACRYNGE			
For to se the sacrynge?	272	Collyn Clout	1028
SAD			
Some sad storyes, some mery,	87	Phy Sparrow	615
Than is he sad, /Frantyke and mad;	95	Phy Sparrow	939
So sad and so demure,	99	Phy Sparrow	1097
Demure, sober and sad,	111	Lawde	54
But yf prudence be proved with sad cyrcumspeccyon,	141	Magnyfycence	16
Take sad dyreccyon, and leve this wantonnesse.	144	Magnyfycence	149
To you recommendeth Sad Cyrcumspeccyon,	149	Magnyfycence	311
An honest person, I tell you, and a sad.	187	Magnyfycence	1690
What tydynges with you, syr, that you loke so sad?	192	Magnyfycence	1843
To sober, to sad, to subtell, to wyse,	199	Magnyfycence	2091
To sende over to me Sad Cyrcumspeccyon.	208	Magnyfycence	2400
Nowe welcome, forsoth, Sad Cyrcumspeccyon.	209	Magnyfycence	2418
Here cometh in SAD CYRCUMSPECCYON sayenge.	209	Magnyfycence	SD
Syr, the longe absence of you, Sad Cyrcumspeccyon,	209	Magnyfycence	2424
For where sad cyrcumspeccyon is longe out of the way,	209	Magnyfycence	2427
And sad cyrcumspeccyon to me they have annexyd.	210	Magnyfycence	2463
And Sad Cyrcumspeccyon I marke in my mynde;	212	Magnyfycence	2504
And with sad cyrcumspeccyon correcte my vantonnesse.	212	Magnyfycence	2509
But some than sate ryght sad	229	El Rummynge	607
For it maketh me sad	259	Collyn Clout	511
As they be sad sayne,	277	Collyn Clout	1230
sad] 'sayd' Kele 1545.1, Marshe 1568			
And theyr sad dyrection,	298	Why Come Ye	769
Demure Diana womanly and sad,	337	Garlande	902
God wote, theis wordes made me full sad;	353	Garlande	1484
Under proteccyon /Of sad correccyon,	356	Garlande	1575
SADDE			
'Syr, God you save, why loke you so sadde?	53	Bowge	239

SADE —SAY   Page   Title   Line

SADE
Standynge in sadde communicacion.   58   Bowge   420
Somtyme to sober, somtyme to sadde;   168   Magnyfycence   1009
Addressyng your selfe, lyke a sadde messengere, ...   239   Speke Parott   303
To take sadde dyrections.   268   Collyn Clout   894
   sadde] 'the sayd' Kele 1545.1, Marshe 1568
Sometyme for sadde dyrection.   385   Replycacion   390
SADE
Thow thou be pyllyd, thow ar nat sade.   132   Garnesche5   117
SADYLGOSE
Sym Sadylgose was my syer, and Dawcocke my dame.   192   Magnyfycence   1834
SADLY
If it be sadly dyscust.   102   Phy Sparrow   1250
That sadly rule not theyr howsholde men.   195   Magnyfycence   1940
And as I thus sadly amonge them avysid   323   Garlande   386
For if ye sadly loke, ...   384   Replycacion   359
SADLYE
And sadlye salute owur solen Syre Sydrake, ...   240   Speke Parott   326
SADNES
Saphyre of sadnes, envayned wyth Indy blew;   44   Balettys3   17
A medley to make of myrth with sadnes, ...   117   Ag Scottes   87
Sumtyme with sadnes, sumtyme with play.   352   Garlande   1424
SADNESS
Sion is in sadness, Rachell ruly doth loke;   234   Speke Parott   114
SADNESSE
Counterfet sadnesse, with delynge full madly;   153   Magnyfycence   468
That he shall have you in the stede of sadnesse, ...   159   Magnyfycence   680
And Sober Sadnesse shalbe your name?   159   Magnyfycence   681
And some wyll convey by the pretence of sadnesse   178   Magnyfycence   1366
Syr, Sober Sadnesse cometh. Wherfore it be?   186   Magnyfycence   1631
What! Hath Sadnesse begyled me so?   192   Magnyfycence   1855
Well, I perceyve in you there is moche sadnesse, ...   210   Magnyfycence   2475
For small is your sadnesse   310   Why Come Ye2   24
For wysdome and sadnesse be out a sunnyng;   318   Garlande   201
   be out] 'be set out' Marshe 1568, MS Cotton Vitellius E.x
SADOKE
To owur soleyne Seigneour Sadoke, desire hym to cum home, . . .   239   Speke Parott   304
SAFELY
But yet I may say safely, so many wel lettred, ...   138   Ven Tongues   38
SAFFRON BAGGES
It wygges and it wagges /Lyke tawny saffron bagges;   218   El Rummynge   138
SAGACITE
Yet, aftyr the sagacite of a popagay, ...   243   Speke Parott   419
SAGE
Adrastus wise and sage.   110   Lawde   14
For she is somwhat sage   214   El Rummynge   7
But /Helas! sage overage /So madly decayes, ...   279   Why Come Ye   41
   So] 'To' Toy 1553, Kitson 1560.7, Marshe 1568
Is lusty to loke on, plesaunte, demure, and sage: 336   Garlande   870
Is lusty to loke on, plesaunt, demure, and sage.   337   Garlande   877
Devoyde of wysdome sage, ...   369   Albany   412
SAID
With one vice importune thei playnly said nay.   31   Dol Dethe   80
For ye said, that he said, that I said, wote ye what?   137   Ven Tongues   12
For ye said, that he said, that I said, wote ye what?   137   Ven Tongues   12
For ye said, that he said, that I said, wote ye what?   137   Ven Tongues   12
I made, he said, a windmil of an olde mat.   137   Ven Tongues   13
Men said they could not their tunges atame;   139   Ven Tongues   60
With, 'I can tel you what such a man said, ...   139   Ven Tongues   71
With, 'He sayd,' and 'We said.' Ich wot now what ich wot, . . .   234   Speke Parott   132
He said he knew what was what.   306   Why Come Ye   1109
SAIDE
Ye had not ben hable to have saide hym nay.   31   Dol Dethe   70
They saide they forsede not nor carede not to dy.   31   Dol Dethe   84
SAILING
What shippis are sailing to Scalis Malis, ...   139   Ven Tongues   65
SAINCT
With Sainct Cutberdes banner   360   Albany   63
And Sainct Williams also.   360   Albany   64
And thus, Sainct George to borowe, ...   371   Albany   506
SAINT
Saint Albons, to recorde, ...   306   Why Come Ye   1097
Of poetes chefe poete, saint Jerome dothe wright, ...   383   Replycacion   330
SAITH
He saith untruly, to say that I would   137   Ven Tongues   21
Theyr wyttes, he saith, are dull;   286   Why Come Ye   309
SAY
And were not thei to blame, I say also, ...   30   Dol Dethe   36
I say, ye commoners, why wer ye so stark mad?   30   Dol Dethe   50
Bot men say thei wer lynked with a double chayn   31   Dol Dethe   75
Tully, valy, strawe, let be I say!   35   Man Margery   5
A proverbe of old, 'Say well or be styll':   38   Coystrowne1   64
Uppon me to clater or else to say yll.   38   Coystrowne1   66
'Myne horse is sold, I wene', you say;   40   Coystrowne4   9
For thus dare I say, without tradiccyon, ...   42   Balettys2   10
And, though I say it, I was myselfe your frende, ...   50   Bowge   160
And the Pharasay /Then durst nothynge say, ...   66   Hauke   153
Say to me, Jacke Harys, /Quare accuparis   69   Hauke   277
As famous poetes say;   74   Phy Sparrow   88

SAY —SAY | Page | Title | Line

	Page	Title	Line
Amen, say ye with me!	74	Phy Sparrow	94
Alas, I say agayne,	80	Phy Sparrow	328
Some to synge, and some to say,	81	Phy Sparrow	392
The sacre with them shall say	85	Phy Sparrow	561
Some say she was lyght,	87	Phy Sparrow	645
And say he wryteth to haute.	92	Phy Sparrow	812
That evermore wil ly /And say cursedly;	94	Phy Sparrow	907
His tong never styll /For to say yll,	95	Phy Sparrow	942
That I may say /Honour alway /Of womankynd!	96	Phy Sparrow	974
Neyther wryte nor say;	101	Phy Sparrow	1197
They may well say, fye on that wynnynge!	115	Ag Scottes	4
They say they had /And wan the felde /With spere and shelde!	116	Ag Scottes	14
What ever they say, /Jemmy is ded /And closyd in led,	116	Ag Scottes	20
Thus fortune hath tourned you, I dare well say,	119	Ag Scottes	164
I say, Syr Dalyrag,	129	Garnesche3	186
How olde proverbys say,	129	Garnesche3	196
Of the wote I what they wolde say;	133	Garnesche5	143
Yet somwhat to say I dare well be bolde,	137	Ven Tongues	10
He saith untruly, to say that I would	137	Ven Tongues	21
I care muche the lesse what ever they say,	138	Ven Tongues	36
But yet I may say safely, so many wel lettred,	138	Ven Tongues	38
Syr, as ye say. I have harde of your fame.	141	Magnyfycence	26
Trewe you say, syr. Gyve me your hande.	141	Magnyfycence	28
Why, to say what he wyll, Lyberte hath leve.	141	Magnyfycence	34
To that ye say I can well condyssende.	141	Magnyfycence	39
Fyrst, I say, we owght to have in consyderacyon	141	Magnyfycence	43
Then thus to you - Nay, suffer me yet ferther to say,	142	Magnyfycence	48
Say what ye wyll to me.	142	Magnyfycence	66
Yet suffer me to say the surpluse of my sawe.	142	Magnyfycence	71
I say there is no welthe where as lyberte is subdude.	142	Magnyfycence	73
I trowe ye can not say nay moche to this:	142	Magnyfycence	74
Measure is treasure. Howe say ye, is it not this?	144	Magnyfycence	125
But have ye not herde say that wyll is no skyll?	144	Magnyfycence	148
Then may I say that ye be servauntys myne.	145	Magnyfycence	183
All that ye say is as trewe as the crede.	146	Magnyfycence	218
Welth and wyt, I say, be so threde bare worne,	146	Magnyfycence	223
And that I sayd ones yet I say agayne:	147	Magnyfycence	266
I say, without largesse worshyp hath no place,	148	Magnyfycence	267
In fayth, I wyll not say that ye shall prove a fole,	148	Magnyfycence	301
Gete you hens, I say, by my counsell.	149	Magnyfycence	306
Say howe you excede in noblenesse,	151	Magnyfycence	376
And say they so in very dede?	151	Magnyfycence	378
What! I say, herke a worde.	151	Magnyfycence	396
Do away, I say, the devylles torde!	151	Magnyfycence	397
It wolde be nyce, thoughe I say nay;	153	Magnyfycence	459
Crafty Conveyaunce, I sholde say, and I.	154	Magnyfycence	502
Say trouth? Yes, yes, by lakyn, I shall the warent,	154	Magnyfycence	506
But I say, kepest thou the olde name styll that thou had?	155	Magnyfycence	516
I say, whylest we are togyder in same -	155	Magnyfycence	548
Take no dyspleasure of that we say.	156	Magnyfycence	561
I say, come hyder. What are these twayne?	156	Magnyfycence	582
Cappe, syr. I say you be to bolde.	157	Magnyfycence	602
All thre, I say. Shall I go? Whyder?	158	Magnyfycence	666
By cloked colusyon, I say, and none other,	160	Magnyfycence	714
Nede? Yes, Mary. I say not nay.	163	Magnyfycence	807
Tary here. Wote ye what I say?	163	Magnyfycence	819
But nowe I wyll not say the worste.	163	Magnyfycence	828
Howe be it, I say,	165	Magnyfycence	897
Ye, for the, so I say.	166	Magnyfycence	930
I have a thynge for to say,	168	Magnyfycence	1017
In faythe, trouthe ye say, we wente togyder to scole.	170	Magnyfycence	1065
Nay, but wotest thou what I do say?	170	Magnyfycence	1092
Yet for my fansy sake, I say,	171	Magnyfycence	1100
Torde, I say! What have I do?	171	Magnyfycence	1106
Wotyst thou, I say, to whom thou spekys?	172	Magnyfycence	1166
Than wyll I say that thou hast no pere.	173	Magnyfycence	1195
But, I say, let se and yf thou have any more.	175	Magnyfycence	1278
So how, I say, the hare is squat!	176	Magnyfycence	1299
Foly hath a rome, I say, in every route;	177	Magnyfycence	1328
Somtyme, I say, behynde the dore for nede;	177	Magnyfycence	1341
'Though I shewe you curtesy, say not that I crave[d];	177	Magnyfycence	1351
craved] 'crave' †Rastell & Treveris C 1530, B			
All that ye say, syr, is reason and skyll.	178	Magnyfycence	1381
Be governed and gyded; wote ye what I say?	179	Magnyfycence	1397
And what so we say, holde you content withall.	179	Magnyfycence	1406
Syr, as I say, there was no faute in me.	180	Magnyfycence	1426
I say it is foly to gyve all welth away.	180	Magnyfycence	1430
I say that I wyll ye have hym in gydynge.	180	Magnyfycence	1436
Let se what ye say. Shewe it strayte.	185	Magnyfycence	1592
Here no man what so ever they say	185	Magnyfycence	1603
I may say to you I have but small devocyon.	186	Magnyfycence	1640
Howe say ye, syrs? Herein what is best?	186	Magnyfycence	1659
Syr, as ye say. Nay, come on with me.	188	Magnyfycence	1707
With me no longer. Say somwhat nowe, let se,	188	Magnyfycence	1719
I wolde to you say a worde or twayne.	188	Magnyfycence	1721
Have hym hens, I say, out of my syght!	188	Magnyfycence	1723
A bolle or a basyn, I say, for Goddes brede!	189	Magnyfycence	1728
Unto measure, I say, nowe a days.	189	Magnyfycence	1744

SAY —SAY   Page   Title   Line

	Page	Title	Line
It is the gyse nowe, I say, over all -	189	Magnyfycence	1759
Say on; me thynke your reasons be profounde.	190	Magnyfycence	1767
Thus, I say, I am envyronned with solace.	190	Magnyfycence	1797
Flewe, I sholde say - in to an olde barne	191	Magnyfycence	1808
Alasse, I say, where to am I brought?	196	Magnyfycence	1968
Remembre you better, syr. Beware what ye say,	196	Magnyfycence	1995
What, a very vengeaunce, I say! Who is that?	199	Magnyfycence	2105
What brothell, I say, is yonder bounde in a mat?	199	Magnyfycence	2106
Ye, wylte thou, hangman? I say, thou cavell!	202	Magnyfycence	2190
Ye be the thevys, I say, away my goodys dyd cary.	203	Magnyfycence	2239
But they say it is a queysy mete;	204	Magnyfycence	2267
Howe say you, syr? Can ye these wordys grope?	207	Magnyfycence	2377
And to that I say gyve good advysement.	208	Magnyfycence	2406
I herde say that adversyte with Magnyfycence had fought.	210	Magnyfycence	2460
And, as men say, /She dwelt in Sothray,	216	El Rummynge	95
Ich am not cast away, /That can my husband say,	220	El Rummynge	220
'Mete, mete, for Parrot, mete I say, how!'	233	Speke Parott	102
Parot can say, 'Cesar, ave,' also;	233	Speke Parott	110
That they cannot say in Greke, rydynge by the way,	234	Speke Parott	146
Yet some folys say ye arre furnysshyd with knakkes,	239	Speke Parott	292
Some say but lityll and thynke more in there thowghte,	242	Speke Parott	388
'The devyll,' they say, 'is dede, /The devyll is dede.'	247	Collyn Clout	36
The prelates ben so haute /They say, and loke so hye	248	Collyn Clout	72
Laye men say, in dede,	248	Collyn Clout	75
For sothe, they are to lewde /To say so, all beshrewde!	249	Collyn Clout	91
What trowe ye they say more /Of the bysshoppes lore?	249	Collyn Clout	92
Men say they have prescrypcyons	249	Collyn Clout	112
The temporalte say playne	250	Collyn Clout	132
And, for to say trouth, /A great parte is for slouth;	250	Collyn Clout	136
for] 'full' †Godfray 1531, 'for' MS Harley 2252			
Men say, they had rather	251	Collyn Clout	175
I tell you as men say.	251	Collyn Clout	188
Men say, ye can nat appare;	251	Collyn Clout	191
For some say ye hunte in parkes	251	Collyn Clout	192
ye] 'they' †Godfray 1531, 'ye' MS Harley 2252; in parkes] 'partrykes' †Godfray 1531			
Men say, for sylver and golde,	254	Collyn Clout	289
Of symony, men say,	254	Collyn Clout	299
And say as untrewly /As the butterfly,	255	Collyn Clout	336
A man myght say in mocke,	255	Collyn Clout	338
Some say ye sytte in trones,	255	Collyn Clout	344
Men say ye are tonge-tayde,	255	Collyn Clout	354
In you prelates, and say	256	Collyn Clout	403
In] 'On' Marshe 1568, 'In' MS Harley 2252			
Your workes, they say, are straunge -	257	Collyn Clout	420
Ye lyve, they say, in delyte, /Drowned in deliciis,	257	Collyn Clout	441
Nota what I say	258	Collyn Clout	463
'Note well what to say' MS Lansdowne 762 'Note whayte I say' MS Harley 2252			
I shall bothe wryte and say,	259	Collyn Clout	507
Alas, and wellaway, /What eyles them thus to say?	261	Collyn Clout	578
Men say howe ye appalle	262	Collyn Clout	611
That all the worlde myght say,	263	Collyn Clout	669
But men say your auctoryte	265	Collyn Clout	758
But men say] 'Men say but' †Godfray 1531, Kele 1545.1, Marshe 1568			
And say properly thei are sacerdotes	268	Collyn Clout	874
They say, to do corrections,	268	Collyn Clout	892
Men say, they bere no faces	269	Collyn Clout	896
Can say nothynge but 'mum'.	269	Collyn Clout	905
Helas, I say, helas!	272	Collyn Clout	1020
And whether they say trewly	273	Collyn Clout	1061
They say they wyll you cast.	273	Collyn Clout	1070
Have no cause to say	273	Collyn Clout	1093
have] 'hath' †Godfray 1531, 'have' MS Harley 2252			
I say, lieutenaunt of the Toure,	275	Collyn Clout	1167
And say howe that we be /Full of parcyallyte;	276	Collyn Clout	1192
They say many matters be borne	276	Collyn Clout	1198
Who dare say there agayne,	276	Collyn Clout	1214
Some say 'yes', and some	283	Why Come Ye	198
With, 'Jast you, I say, Jullian!	285	Why Come Ye	242
What say ye of the Scottysh kynge?	287	Why Come Ye	346
I coulde say some what,	288	Why Come Ye	381
Amen, amen, say ye	300	Why Come Ye	837
But Englande may well say	302	Why Come Ye	928
Now mayster doctor, howe say ye,	309	Why Come Ye2	1
And say yll behynde his back,	310	Why Come Ye2	26
As I harde say, Dame Pallas was her name,	313	Garlande	48
Then men wyll say how he doth but flatter.	314	Garlande	84
Then sum wyll say he hath but lyttil brayne,	314	Garlande	87
In generrall wordes, I say not gretely nay,	315	Garlande	99
And was Eschines rebukid as ye say?	316	Garlande	135
With your reformacion, if I say amis,	316	Garlande	145
But of that famous oratour, I say,	316	Garlande	158
Eyther they wyll say he is to wyse,	318	Garlande	204
wyll] 'shall' MS Cotton Vitellius E.x			
But what sholde I say? Ye wote what I entende,	324	Garlande	426

SAYD —SAYDE	Page	Title	Line
'There shal he here what she wyl to hym say	325	Garlande	451
wyl to hym] 'to hym will' Marshe 1568			
Forthwith, I say, thus wandrynge in my thought, ...	325	Garlande	456
There were, I say, of all maner of sortis, ...	326	Garlande	512
To se this howre now, that I may say, ...	327	Garlande	538
For a gun stone, I say, had all to-jaggid his cap, ...	329	Garlande	629
to-jaggid] 'to lagged' Marshe 1568			
'How say ye? Is this after your appetite?	331	Garlande	707
'Questionles no dowte of that ye say;	332	Garlande	714
My lyfe endurynge I shall both wryte and say, ...	335	Garlande	839
For eche man herkynde what she wolde to me say;	344	Garlande	1119
wolde to me] 'to me wold' MS Cotton Vitellius E.x			
Yet, thoughe I say it, therby lyith a tale, ...	346	Garlande	1200
I] 'ye' †Fakes 1523			
What myght she say? What myght he do therto?	351	Garlande	1395
Be well ware what ye say.	367	Albany	331
I say, thou lewde lurdayne, ...	367	Albany	336
And yet some men say, ...	379	Replycacion	176
Rede what Jerome there dothe say/	383	Replycacion	328
SAYD			
Jak wold jet and yet Jyll sayd nay;	37	Coystrownel	43
'My lefe', she sayd, 'rowtyth in hys bed;	42	Balettys1	20
'Remembrest thou what thou sayd yesternyght?	55	Bowge	323
He sayd that he wold hunt	67	Hauke	188
And whan I sayd, 'Phyp, Phyp,'	75	Phy Sparrow	138
And sayd, 'Alas, alas, ...	77	Phy Sparrow	231
And what they wrote and sayd, ...	88	Phy Sparrow	680
For as I tofore have sayd, ...	90	Phy Sparrow	769
That Placebo hath sayd	93	Phy Sparrow	853
Because I have wrytten and sayd	103	Phy Sparrow	1253
Why that ye sayd our langage was in vayne.	147	Magnyfycence	263
And that I sayd ones yet I say agayne:	147	Magnyfycence	266
Sayd I was mete for your grace.	150	Magnyfycence	373
Pease! I have not yet sayd what I wyll.	158	Magnyfycence	648
This was properly prated, syrs! What sayd a?	161	Magnyfycence	746
What care I? By the masse, well sayd.	187	Magnyfycence	1671
I trowe ye herde yourselfe what I sayd.	188	Magnyfycence	1695
The bytter sayd boldly that they were to blame;	192	Magnyfycence	1837
Well sayd. But, in fayth, what was your quarell?	203	Magnyfycence	2210
Mary, syr, he sayd that he was the pratyer man	203	Magnyfycence	2225
What this man hath sayd, perceyve ye his sentence?	210	Magnyfycence	2465
'Behold,' she sayd, 'and se	220	El Rummynge	217
Sayd Elynour Rummyng, ...	227	El Rummynge	502
'Quake, quake,' sayd the duck /In that lampatrams lap.	227	El Rummynge	505
Sayd Elynour, 'For shame!'	227	El Rummynge	510
'This ale,' sayd she, 'is noppy;	228	El Rummynge	557
With, 'He sayd,' and 'We said.' Ich wot now what ich wot, . .	234	Speke Parott	132
For elles, as I sayd before, ...	258	Collyn Clout	481
But it is an olde sayd sawe	268	Collyn Clout	862
it] not in Kele 1545.1			
The lesarde came lepyng, and sayd that he must, ...	315	Garlande	104
'Make rowme,' sayd another, 'ye prese all to sore,'	319	Garlande	256
Sume sayd, 'Holde thy peas, thou getest here no more.'	319	Garlande	257
This sayd, a great nowmber folowyd by and by	321	Garlande	323
Under the forme as I sayd tofore, ...	324	Garlande	443
tofore] 'before' Marshe 1568			
Unto me sayd, 'Lo, syr, now ye may se	326	Garlande	518
'Come on with me,' she sayd, 'let us not stonde';	328	Garlande	559
And then she sayd, 'Whylis we have tyme and space	328	Garlande	563
'Go softly,' she sayd, 'the stones be full glint.'	328	Garlande	572
'Theis yatis,' she sayd, 'which that ye beholde, ...	328	Garlande	579
'What yate call ye this?' And she sayd, 'Anglea'.	328	Garlande	588
yate] 'gate' Marshe 1568			
Come forth, jentylwomen, I pray you,' she sayd, ...	334	Garlande	773
For yet of women he never sayd shame, ...	334	Garlande	784
But, as I sayd, your florisshinge tender age	337	Garlande	876
Where all the sayd poetis sat in there degre.	343	Garlande	1104
'Be mirry,' she sayd, 'be not afferde a whit, ...	344	Garlande	1145
To shew her boke; and she sayd, 'Here it is.'	344	Garlande	1148
Though Jak sayd nay, yet Mok there loste her sho;	351	Garlande	1396
'Nay, sir' she sayd, 'what so in this place	353	Garlande	1481
SAYDE			
For to illumyne, she sayde, I was to dulle, ...	46	Bowge	20
'Maysters', he sayde, 'the shyp that ye here see, ...	47	Bowge	48
Gave me a taunte, and sayde I was to blame	48	Bowge	70
She sayde she trowed that I had eten sause;	48	Bowge	72
had] not in †Wynkyn de Worde 1499, 1510			
What is thy name?' and I sayde it was Drede.	48	Bowge	77
They sayde they hated for to dele with Drede.	50	Bowge	146
Farewell tyll soone. But no word that I sayde!'	51	Bowge	175
And I drewe nere to herke what they two sayde.	51	Bowge	182
He sayde of me, whan he with you dyde talke –	52	Bowge	209
And I drewe nere to harke what they two sayde.	54	Bowge	296
And many wordes sayde in secrete wyse;	58	Bowge	422
Er I was ware, behynde me he sayde 'Bo!'	60	Bowge	500
But he sayde that he wolde	64	Hauke	97
He sayde he wold not let /His houndys for to fet, ...	64	Hauke	106
He sayde, for a crokyd intent, ...	68	Hauke	228

SAYE—SAYNE

	Page	Title	Line
Sore sayde, I tell you, and well to the purpose.	180	Magnyfycence	1428
Notwithstandynge to you be it sayde	186	Magnyfycence	1651
Jone sayde she had eten a fyest.	223	El Rummynge	343
'By Chryst,' sayde she, 'thou lyest.	223	El Rummynge	344
Than Elynour sayde, 'Ye calettes,	223	El Rummynge	347
'A strawe,' sayde Bele, 'stande utter,	228	El Rummynge	535
'Dame Elynour,' sayde she,	228	El Rummynge	562
'Dame Elynour,' sayde they,	229	El Rummynge	576
She sayde never a worde,	229	El Rummynge	590
To paye,' sayde she, 'God wote,	229	El Rummynge	601
Theyr matyns madly sayde, /Nothynge devoutly prayde,	252	Collyn Clout	238
They grugyd and sayde	285	Why Come Ye	252
Some sayde they were afrayde	285	Why Come Ye	254
Frome that I have sayde in no poynt doth vary,	316	Garlande	163
'To make repugnaunce agayne that ye have sayde,	318	Garlande	211

SAYE

That, so to saye, I had gyven her no cause.	48	Bowge	75
For I dare saye that there nys erthly man	48	Bowge	101
Is lytyll to saye, and moche to here and see;	52	Bowge	212
And I dare saye there is no man hereinne	53	Bowge	267
But I requyre you no worde that I saye!	54	Bowge	276
'By Cryste,' quod he, 'for it is shame to saye,	54	Bowge	300
Trowest thou, drevyll, I saye, thou gawdy knave,	55	Bowge	337
Thyse were the wordes he to me dyde saye.	58	Bowge	441
he] 'that he' Marshe 1568			
By God, I saye, there is a grete herte-brennynge	59	Bowge	460
It is a worlde, I saye, to here of some -	59	Bowge	464
to] 'te' †Wynkyn de Worde 1499, 'to' Wynkyn de Worde 1510, Marshe 1568			
Yet wyll I saye some wordes for your sake	59	Bowge	474
More coude I saye, but what this is ynowe.	60	Bowge	491
In every poynte that I can do or saye.	60	Bowge	496
In] 'To' Marshe 1568			
I wyll not saye it is mater in dede,	61	Bowge	537
Gyb, I saye, our cat,	72	Phy Sparrow	28
Fyrst, I saye, with mynde fyrme and stable	208	Magnyfycence	2408
And yet I dare saye /She thynketh her selfe gaye	216	El Rummynge	64
They care not what men saye!	221	El Rummynge	260
He sayth, 'How saye ye, my lordes?	283	Why Come Ye	195
Els saye ye myght	342	Garlande	1063
I dare wele saye that ye and I be sought.	343	Garlande	1089
'Twyt, Scot,' agayne I saye,	363	Albany	157
Ye saye that he and ye -	367	Albany	332
Those wordes his grace dyd saye /Of an ammas gray.	372	Albany	530
I saye, thou madde Marche hare,	375	Replycacion	35
I saye it for no sedicion,	378	Replycacion	140
I saye, ye braynlesse beestes,	381	Replycacion	263
I saye, ye devyllysshe pages	381	Replycacion	271
They saye howe latria is an honour grete,	381	Replycacion	282
Ye saye that poetry /Maye nat flye so hye	382	Replycacion	306

SAYED

Ye heretykes recrayed, /Wotte ye what ye sayed	375	Replycacion	46

SAYENGE

Sayenge to me, 'Broder, be of good chere,	48	Bowge	86
Here cometh in SAD CYRCUMSPECCYON sayenge.	209	Magnyfycence	SD
For he hathe all the sayenge /Without any renayenge.	283	Why Come Ye	192

SAYES

Pawbe une aruer, so the Welche man sayes.	233	Speke Parott	91
And lewdely sayes by Chryst	261	Collyn Clout	575
He sayes that we are recheles,	275	Collyn Clout	1176
It is to drede, men sayes,	277	Collyn Clout	1228
He sayes we ar but crakers;	285	Why Come Ye	274
But, as the man sayes,	378	Replycacion	151

SAYLE

Me thoughte I sawe a shyppe, goodly of sayle,	47	Bowge	36
The sayle is up, Fortune ruleth our helme,	49	Bowge	127
And, as she wyll, so shall our grete shyppe sayle.	50	Bowge	172
Or 'Shall I sayle wyth you' a felashyp assaye?	53	Bowge	254
Than hath some shyppe that into Bordews sayle.	57	Bowge	406
Shall sayle over the see,	102	Phy Sparrow	1240
Then let them vale a bonet of their proud sayle,	138	Ven Tongues	32
I have wynde and wether over all to sayle;	181	Magnyfycence	1464
She could to Burdeo[u] sayle;	226	El Rummynge	454
Burdeou] 'burde on' †Lant 1545, Kynge & Marche 1554, Day 1560, Marshe 1568			
He maketh them to bere babylles, and to bere a lowe sayle;	243	Speke Parott	428
Or to make a sayle /Of a herynges tayle?	246	Collyn Clout	3
And sayle nat farre abrode,	277	Collyn Clout	1256

SAYLYNGE

Come saylynge forth into that haven brood,	47	Bowge	37

SAYLL

Theyr sayll of solace most comfortably clad,	44	Balettys3	27

SAYNE

Her lewde lyppes twayne, /They slaver, men sayne,	215	El Rummynge	23
As they be sad sayne,	277	Collyn Clout	1230
sad] 'sayd' Kele 1545.1, Marshe 1568			
But, as some men sayne,	288	Why Come Ye	362
With mony, as men sayne,	358	Garlande2	14

SAYNGE —SAKE   Page   Title   Line

SAYNGE
	Page	Title	Line
Saynge, 'Mayd, ye are in wyll	77	Phy Sparrow	222
to take money of CRAFTY CONVEYAUNCE, saynge to hym,	174	Magnyfycence	SD

SAYNT
	Page	Title	Line
On Saynt Johnn decollacyon	64	Hauke	100
In the church of Saynt Sophy;	67	Hauke	219
On pylgrimage to Saynt Jamys,	102	Phy Sparrow	1242
pylgrimage] 'pilgrimages' Marshe 1568			
Amen, for saynt charyte	115	Scot Kynge	E
Of Edyngeborrow and Saynt Jonys towne.	117	Ag Scottes	63
And swete Saynt George, our ladyes knyght!	119	Ag Scottes	141
Knowe hym, syr, quod he. Yes, by Saynt Sym!	156	Magnyfycence	585
By Saynt Mary, he is a tawle man.	163	Magnyfycence	821
Nay, by Saynt Mary, it was ye called me knave.	203	Magnyfycence	2212
And sware by Saynt Benet,	224	El Rummynge	393
'Cristecrosse and Saynt Nycholas, Parrot, be your good spede!'	236	Speke Parott	189
That Saynt Thomas of Canterbury gave.	251	Collyn Clout	170
'That becket them gave' Kele 1545.1, Marshe 1568			
For, by saynt Hyllary,	266	Collyn Clout	813
Permytted? By saynt Luke,	272	Collyn Clout	1046
Permytted] 'Permed' †Godfray 1531, 'Now' MS Harley 2252			
And by swete saynt Marke,	272	Collyn Clout	1047
And Saynt Mary Spytell	276	Collyn Clout	1184
And at Saynt Thomas of Akers	276	Collyn Clout	1188
Saynt Dunstane, what was he?	307	Why Come Ye	1147
By saynt Mary, my Lady,	339	Garlande	973
Saynt Gregorie and saynt Ambrose,	381	Replycacion	275
Saynt Gregorie and saynt Ambrose,	381	Replycacion	275
Saynt Jerome and saynt Austen,	381	Replycacion	277
Saynt Jerome and saynt Austen,	381	Replycacion	277
Saynt Thomas de Aquyno,	381	Replycacion	279
And saynt Jerome saythe,	384	Replycacion	347

SAYNTE
	Page	Title	Line
'Nowe have at all, by Saynte Thomas of Kente!'	56	Bowge	348
Now, by Saynte Fraunceys, that holy man and frere,	59	Bowge	470
To us welcome thou arte, by Saynte Quyntyne!'	60	Bowge	511
Thanked be saynte Gorge, our ladyes knythe,	114	Scot Kynge	42
And of Saynte James in Gales,	223	El Rummynge	354

SAYNTES
	Page	Title	Line
As they were very sayntes.	269	Collyn Clout	921
or to make oblacions to any ymages of sayntes,	375	Replycacion	I
To worshyppe ymages of sayntes.	382	Replycacion	291

SAYNTUARY BREKYNG
	Page	Title	Line
So myche sayntuary brekyng, and prevylegidde barryd —	246	Speke Parott	503

SAYST
	Page	Title	Line
What sayst? Here was to lytell clothe.	157	Magnyfycence	607
Howe sayst thou, man? Am not I a joly rutter?	161	Magnyfycence	752
What sayst thou, man? Why dost thou not supplye,	162	Magnyfycence	797
In faythe, trouth thou sayst nowe, by God of heven!	170	Magnyfycence	1079
Why, sayst thou that I was here yesterday?	170	Magnyfycence	1093
Mary, as thou sayst, he gave me a blurre.	173	Magnyfycence	1179
Thou sayst truthe, by the harte that God me gave!	190	Magnyfycence	1782
For as thou sayst, ryght so shall it be,	190	Magnyfycence	1783
What sayst thou? Mary, I pray God your mastershyp to save.	191	Magnyfycence	1828
A, woo worthe the, Lyberte, nowe thou sayst full trewe;	199	Magnyfycence	2103
Yet sayst thou, per case	301	Why Come Ye	874

SAYTH
	Page	Title	Line
He sayth he can not well accorde with the.'	51	Bowge	185
Save hym that nought can: scrypture sayth soo.	58	Bowge	448
This fals Envy /Sayth that I /Use great folly	95	Phy Sparrow	950
Sayth, from thy to unto thi croune,	130	Garnesche5	26
poyntyng with his fynger, and sayth,	162	Magnyfycence	SD
By the good Lorde, truthe he sayth.	175	Magnyfycence	1252
What he sayth and she sayth to lay good ere,	175	Magnyfycence	1269
What he sayth and she sayth to lay good ere,	175	Magnyfycence	1269
All that he sayth of trouthe dothe procede;	209	Magnyfycence	2426
And sayth, 'Gossyp, come hyder,	219	El Rummynge	204
'Moryshe myne owne shelfe,' the costermonger sayth;	233	Speke Parott	85
Parrot sayth playnly, shall tourne all to dust.	236	Speke Parott	224
He sayth, 'How saye ye, my lordes?	283	Why Come Ye	195
He sayth they have no brayne	286	Why Come Ye	310
He sayth, they are to seke	287	Why Come Ye	317
He sayth, 'Thou huddy peke!	287	Why Come Ye	329
That any other sayth,	290	Why Come Ye	444
He sayth the kynge doth wryte,	296	Why Come Ye	678
As myne auctor sayth.	297	Why Come Ye	745
He sayth we ar to blame!	305	Why Come Ye	1049
'Nothynge,' he sayth, 'lyke to We.	307	Why Come Ye	1148
to we] 'to mee' Toy 1553, Kitson 1560.7, Marshe 1568,			
'we' MS Rawlinson C. 813			
'Prove his wytt', sayth he, 'at cardes or dyce,	318	Garlande	206
No man lyvyng, he sayth, can be sure;	351	Garlande	1403

SAYTHE
	Page	Title	Line
And saynt Jerome saythe,	384	Replycacion	347

SAKE
	Page	Title	Line
For whose sake my hart is sore dyseasyd;	45	Balettys5	9
Yet wyll I saye some wordes for your sake	59	Bowge	474
For that swete soules sake,	72	Phy Sparrow	10

	Page	Title	Line
For Phyllip Sparowes sake!	74	Phy Sparrow	103
Many a spere brake /For his ladyes sake;	87	Phy Sparrow	640
That token for her sake;	89	Phy Sparrow	691
But for my sparowes sake,	92	Phy Sparrow	819
This invectyve to make /For some peoples sake	120	Ag Scottes2	4
And for his sake ryght gladly I wolde	149	Magnyfycence	334
Yet for my fansy sake, I say,	171	Magnyfycence	1100
That for your sake I wyll fall on my kne.	186	Magnyfycence	1630
Well, for thy sake the better I may endure	187	Magnyfycence	1680
For your sake, what so ever befall;	188	Magnyfycence	1709
And remembre he suffered moche more for your sake;	196	Magnyfycence	2001
Why, wenest thou that I forbere for thyne owne sake?	202	Magnyfycence	2186
Nowe gyve me somwhat, for God sake, I crave.	204	Magnyfycence	2251
For the good ale sake.	228	El Rummynge	534
I am sory for your sake!	253	Collyn Clout	252
For kynge nor kayser sake,	272	Collyn Clout	1017
And for my sake spare neyther pen nor ynke;	327	Garlande	549
And for your sake how fast to warke they fall:	335	Garlande	811

SALAMON

	Page	Title	Line
In prudence and wysdom /Lyke unto Salamon,	369	Albany	433

SALE

	Page	Title	Line
God sende you good sale!'	223	El Rummynge	369

SALFE CUNDIGHT

	Page	Title	Line
Some shewid his salfe cundight, some shewid his charter,	326	Garlande	503
salfe cundight] 'safeconduct' Marshe 1568; charter] 'chart' Marshe 1568			

SALYSBERY

	Page	Title	Line
From Tyllbery fery /To the playne of Salysbery!	79	Phy Sparrow	321

SALLOWE

	Page	Title	Line
Tawny, swart and sallowe,	222	El Rummynge	321
sallowe] 'swallowe' Kynge & Marche 1554, Day 1560, Marshe 1568			

SALT

	Page	Title	Line
Know ye not suger and salt asonder?	118	Ag Scottes	96
Some a salt, and some a spone,	220	El Rummynge	247

SALTE

	Page	Title	Line
Knowe ye not salte and suger asonder?	113	Scot Kynge	6
Mele, salte or other thynge,	221	El Rummynge	279
Require hym to convey yow ovyr the salte fome;	239	Speke Parott	302
Somtyme meale and salte,	267	Collyn Clout	843

SALTFYSSHE

	Page	Title	Line
Saltfysshe, stockfyssh nor herynge,	252	Collyn Clout	209

SALUSTY

	Page	Title	Line
With Salusty ageinst Lucius Catelyne,	321	Garlande	331

SALUTACYONS

	Page	Title	Line
With, 'Aveto' in Greco, and such solempne salutacyons,	235	Speke Parott	179

SALUTE

	Page	Title	Line
And sadlye salute owur solen Syre Sydrake,	240	Speke Parott	326

SALVE

	Page	Title	Line
Lay salve to your owne sore,	258	Collyn Clout	480

SAME

	Page	Title	Line
Whiche wert endiyd with rede blode of the same	32	Dol Dethe	117
As all his kuntrey kan testefy the same:	33	Dol Dethe	153
I was sore moved to aforce the same,	46	Bowge	17
Of the same facyon /Without alteracyon,	85	Phy Sparrow	542
Experyence hath brought you in the same brake.	115	Scot Kynge	61
With the ix day of the same,	117	Ag Scottes	67
And eyther I am dysseyved, or ye be the same.	141	Magnyfycence	25
And I of the same facyon;	143	Magnyfycence	96
Unto that same I am ryght well agrede,	144	Magnyfycence	128
Why, were not your selfe agreed to the same,	147	Magnyfycence	233
I say, whylest we are togyder in same -	155	Magnyfycence	548
Ye, by the masse, this is even the same,	157	Magnyfycence	599
That fell amonge us this same day?	166	Magnyfycence	933
Even of purpose for the same.	167	Magnyfycence	957
Ye, by the rode, even the same.	172	Magnyfycence	1139
For I knowe dyverse that useth the same.	175	Magnyfycence	1255
For I am panged ofte tymes in this same facyon.	189	Magnyfycence	1734
By Cockys bonys, it is the same.	204	Magnyfycence	2244
She leneth them on the same,	217	El Rummynge	131
on] 'of' Day 1560, Marshe 1568			
And ye shall do the same,	259	Collyn Clout	508
But yet they wyll occupye the same.	275	Collyn Clout	1144
In lykewyse now the same /Cardynall is promoted,	293	Why Come Ye	570
(Myne auctor writeth the same);	297	Why Come Ye	727
Recorde the same? Or why is had in mynde	315	Garlande	125
I sawe hir smyle, and I then did the same.	327	Garlande	530
I then] 'than I' Marshe 1568			
Were newly enbybid; and rownd about the same	331	Garlande	682
In Fames court reportyng the same;	334	Garlande	783

SAMPLER

	Page	Title	Line
I toke my sampler ones	77	Phy Sparrow	210
Coude not my sampler holde;	77	Phy Sparrow	234

SAMUELL

	Page	Title	Line
Samuell that was dede;	105	Phy Sparrow	1353
The selfe same Samuell,	105	Phy Sparrow	1356
Samuell that was dede.	350	Garlande	1346
The selfe same Samuell,	350	Garlande	1349

	Page	Title	Line
SANDE			
The myghty lyoun doutted by se and sande.	32	Dol Dethe	109
sande] 'lande' Marshe 1568			
SANDES			
With his golden sandes, ...	93	Phy Sparrow	879
And the sandes of Cefas begyn to waste and fade, ...	239	Speke Parott	281
Cefas] 'Tefas' †MS Harley 2252			
SANGE			
And ever he sange, 'Sythe I am no thynge playne'.	52	Bowge	235
And ay he sange, 'In fayth, Decon, thou crewe.'	56	Bowge	360
He sange also how, the tre as he did take	320	Garlande	300
There birdis on the brere sange on every syde, ...	330	Garlande	653
SANK ROYALL			
He came of the sank royall	291	Why Come Ye	493
Where the sank royall is, Crystes blode so rede, ...	353	Garlande	1463
SAPHER			
Or eyndye sapher with oryente perlys dreste:	241	Speke Parott	368
perlys] 'prelys' †MS Harley 2252			
SAPHIRIS			
Where the postis wer enbulyoned with saphiris indy blew, . . .	325	Garlande	478
SAPHYRE			
Saphyre of sadnes, envayned wyth Indy blew;	44	Balettys3	17
The Indy saphyre blew /Her vaynes doth ennew;	97	Phy Sparrow	1031
SAPHO			
Or Frauncys Petrarke, /Alcheus or Sapho, ...	90	Phy Sparrow	759
Or] 'Or of' Kitson 1560.6, Marshe 1568			
SAPYENCE			
Syr, yet without sapyence your substaunce may be smal;	179	Magnyfycence	1407
Contradyccyon to prove his sapyence;	207	Magnyfycence	2372
And also dame Prudence, /With sober Sapyence.	279	Why Come Ye	14
SAPPE			
His levis loste, the sappe was frome the rynde.	312	Garlande	21
SARASYNS			
Wrythen in wonder wyse /After the Sarasyns gyse, ...	216	El Rummynge	74
in] 'in a' Day 1560, Marshe 1568			
SARAZYN			
Turke, Sarazyn or Jewe?	257	Collyn Clout	431
SARDANAPALL			
Nor Sardanapall, /Unhappyest of all;	67	Hauke	200
SARE			
Cysly and Sare, /With theyr legges bare, ...	217	El Rummynge	119
Dame Sare our pryoresse, ...	256	Collyn Clout	393
SARSENS			
Thow a Sarsens hed ye bere, ...	127	Garnesche3	123
SARSON			
I sey, ye solem Sarson, alle blake ys yor ble;	122	Garnesche1	36
SAT			
Whiche sat behynde a tra[v]es of sylke fyne, ...	47	Bowge	58
traves] 'tranes' †Wynkyn de Worde 1499, 1510, Marshe 1568			
. . . . sat sumwhat to longe;	125	Garnesche3	57
She sat downe in the place, ...	228	El Rummynge	551
There was a prycke-me-denty, /Sat lyke a seynty, ...	229	El Rummynge	583
For truly it were a pyte that he sat ydle'.	318	Garlande	210
There Cintheus sat twynklyng uppon his harpe stringis;	331	Garlande	687
Sat honorably, to whome did repaire	334	Garlande	770
Where all the sayd poetis sat in there degre.	343	Garlande	1104
In her astate there sat the noble Quene	343	Garlande	1114
SATE			
But, syr, amonge all /That sate in that hall, ...	229	El Rummynge	581
But some than sate ryght sad	229	El Rummynge	607
SATHANAS			
To the devyll Syr Sathanas, ...	299	Why Come Ye	805
SATIRRAY			
Juvenall satirray, that men makythe to muse;	321	Garlande	340
SATRAPAS			
But sey me now, Syr Satrapas, what autoryte ye have	121	Garnesche1	6
But sey me yet, Syr Satrapas, wat auctoryte ye have	122	Garnesche1	20
But sey me yet, Syr Satrapas, what auctoryte ye have	122	Garnesche1	27
But sey me yet, Syr Satrapas, what auctoryte ye have	122	Garnesche1	34
SATROPAS			
But sey me yet, Syr Satropas, what auctoryte ye have	122	Garnesche1	13
SATURICALL			
The famous poettes saturicall, ...	133	Garnesche5	139
SATURNE			
Jupyter for Saturne darre make no royall chere;	242	Speke Parott	399
SAUCE			
Ye have eten sauce I trowe, at the Taylers Hall.	179	Magnyfycence	1404
Yet swete meate hath soure sauce, ...	258	Collyn Clout	448
After gloria, laus, /May come a soure sauce.	258	Collyn Clout	483
SAUCY			
Your sumner to saucy, to malapert;	118	Ag Scottes	97
SAUCYS			
She asked yf ever I dranke of saucys cuppe.	48	Bowge	73
SAUL			
In the name of Kyng Saul;	105	Phy Sparrow	1343
SAULL			
How be it to Saull dyd he tell	105	Phy Sparrow	1357
In the name of Kyng Saull;	350	Garlande	1336

SAUMPLER —SAWDUST

	Page	Title	Line

SAUMPLER
How be it to Saull he did tell .... 350 Garlande 1350
The saumpler to sow on, the lacis to enbraid; .... 334 Garlande 789
SAUNCE-PERE
Whoos name to tell is Dame Saunce-Pere. .... 47 Bowge 51
SAUSE
She sayde she trowed that I had eten sause; .... 48 Bowge 72
  had] not in †Wynkyn de Worde 1499, 1510
SAUTES
Agaynst all [s]autes of your goostly foo. .... 206 Magnyfycence 2329
  sautes] 'fautes' †Rastell & Treveris C 1530, B,
  Douce Fragment d.7
SAVACIOUN
To pardon thi servant and brynge to savacioun. .... 35 Dol Dethe 210
SAVAGE
The leopardes savage, /The lyons in theyr rage, ... 79 Phy Sparrow 286
By Gyb, our cat savage, ... 81 Phy Sparrow 375
Ther is no beest savage, ... 100 Phy Sparrow 1156
With myghty corage /A[d]aunted the rage /Of a lyon savage, .. 104 Phy Sparrow 1311
  Adaunted] 'Auaunted' editions
Ensor[b]yd with the wawys savage and wode; .... 213 Magnyfycence 2561
  ensorbyd] 'ensordyd' †Rastell & Treveris C 1530, B
With myghty corrage /Adauntid the rage /Of a lyon savage; ... 349 Garlande 1304
Mad, frantyke and savage. .... 369 Albany 413
SAVE
What and he slyde downe, who shall hym save? .... 46 Bowge 28
For, but I trusted you, so God me save, ... 52 Bowge 213
'Syr, God you save, why loke you so sadde? .... 53 Bowge 239
And ye be welcome, syr, so God me save, ... 54 Bowge 279
Save hym that nought can: scrypture sayth soo. .... 58 Bowge 448
But ye have crafte your selfe alwaye to save. .... 59 Bowge 452
Belsabub his soule save, ... 109 Epitaphe2 25
God save him in his right! /Amen .... 112 Lawde 56
God save kynge Henry and his lordes all .... 115 Scot Kynge 72
and God save noble Kynge Henry the viij. .... 115 Scot Kynge E
Boldly bend you to batell, and buske your selfe to save. ... 122 Garnesche1 41
But now, my proces for to save, ... 133 Garnesche5 157
Craftely all thynges upryght to save: .... 158 Magnyfycence 642
Maysters, Cryst save everychone! .... 169 Magnyfycence 1043
Save a stronge thefe and hange a trew man. .... 178 Magnyfycence 1360
Surely it is I that all may save and spyll, ... 181 Magnyfycence 1478
What sayst thou? Mary, I pray God your mastershyp to save. . 191 Magnyfycence 1828
Spare for the spence of a noble that his honour myght save, .. 200 Magnyfycence 2125
'Cryste save Kyng Herry the viiith, owur royall kyng, ... 231 Speke Parott 34
That pereles pomegarnat, Cryste save hyr nobyll grace!' ... 231 Speke Parott 37
God save my Lorde Admyrell! .... 288 Why Come Ye 376
I pray God save the kynge. .... 289 Why Come Ye 393
God save his noble grace, ... 303 Why Come Ye 969
SAVED
As I be saved, it is a wonder case. .... 53 Bowge 273
'Now,' quod Dysdayne, 'as I shall saved be, ... 54 Bowge 297
As I be saved at the dredefull daye, ... 58 Bowge 443
But surely largesse saved my lyfe; .... 150 Magnyfycence 366
As I be saved, with pleasure I am supprysyd .... 183 Magnyfycence 1529
SAVYD
Wherfore, as I be savyd, /Ye ar therfore beknavyd. ...... 70 Hauke 309
'As oft as ye lyst, so honeste be savyd. .... 177 Magnyfycence 1348
SAVYNG
Savyng that olde age .... 85 Phy Sparrow 544
SAVYNGE
Savynge your usscheres rod, ... 124 Garnesche3 5
Savynge he rubbid sum on the gall. .... 315 Garlande 97
  on] 'upon' Marshe 1568
SAVYOUR
That our Savyour bare, /Whiche us redemed from care. .... 375 Replycacion 33
Of our savyour Christ in his decacorde psautry, ... 383 Replycacion 340
SAVYOURE
Towarde the porte salue /Of our Savyoure Jesu, ... 278 Collyn Clout 1261
SAVYR
Dothe savyr halfe so souer 127 Garnesche3 146
SAW
I saw a knyfe hyd in his one sleve, ... 58 Bowge 433
And make hereof a syckyll or a saw, ... 71 Hauke 333
Whan he saw an ant; .... 75 Phy Sparrow 133
I saw a foxe sucke on a kowes ydder; .... 191 Magnyfycence 1814
Nor of none other saw; .... 292 Why Come Ye 511
I saw Gower, that first garnisshed our Englysshe rude, ... 323 Garlande 387
And, sir, amonge all me thought I saw twaine, ... 329 Garlande 633
I saw dyvers that were cariid away thens in cribbis, ... 330 Garlande 640
In an herber I saw, brought where I was, ... 330 Garlande 652
Where I saw growyng a goodly laurell tre, ... 330 Garlande 665
That ever they saw, and wrought it was the best. .... 343 Garlande 1113
Where I saw Janus, with his double chere, ... 354 Garlande 1515
SAWDE
Some shall be sawde, ... 276 Collyn Clout 1205
SAWDUST
Lyke sawdust or drye chyppes. .... 252 Collyn Clout 243

SAWE —SCHAME   Page   Title   Line

SAWE
Me thoughte I sawe a shyppe, goodly of sayle, ...   47   Bowge   36
What arte thou? I sawe the nowe but late.'   56   Bowge   376
Dysdayne I sawe with Dyssymulacyon, ...   58   Bowge   419
Than, in his hode, I sawe there faces tweyne: 58   Bowge   428
And in his other sleve, me thought I sawe   58   Bowge   435
And whan I sawe the horsons wolde you hafte, ...   61   Bowge   521
Whan he sawe a waspe;   75   Phy Sparrow   129
Whan I sawe my sparowe dye!   75   Phy Sparrow   146
Yet suffer me to say the surplure of my sawe.   142   Magnyfycence   71
For no dyscorde that any man can sawe;   145   Magnyfycence   187
Nay, indede, but I sawe howe ye prayed, ...   188   Magnyfycence 1696
I sawe a wethercocke wagge with the wynde!   191   Magnyfycence 1821
I sawe a losell lede a lurden, and they were bothe blynde. . .   191   Magnyfycence 1824
I sawe a sowter go to supper, or ever he had dynde.   191   Magnyfycence 1825
Thou sawe never yet but I dyd my parte, ...   203   Magnyfycence 2228
Some lerned in other sawe, /As in divynyte, ...   264   Collyn Clout   732
But it is an olde sayd sawe   268   Collyn Clout   862
    it] not in Kele 1545.1
I sawe a pavylyon wonderly disgysede, ...   313   Garlande   38
A thowsande thowsande I sawe on a plumpe.   319   Garlande   258
Where I sawe come after, I wote, full lytell lake   320   Garlande   285
I sawe hir smyle, and I then did the same.   327   Garlande   530
    I then] 'than I' Marshe 1568
I sawe a thowsande yatis new and olde.   328   Garlande   574
I sawe maister Newton sit with his compas, ...   343   Garlande   1096
But when they sawe my lawrell rychely wrought, ...   343   Garlande   1105
And when that I sawe it wolde no better be, ...   353   Garlande   1485
SAWES
Your sysmaticate sawes /Agaynst Goddes lawes, ...   377   Replycacion   122
SAWIS
And of holy scriptures sawis, ...   305   Why Come Ye   1062
SAWTE
May wynne with a sawte the fortresse of the holde.   184   Magnyfycence 1581
With a sawte of solace at the longe last;   351   Garlande   1398
SCABBE
No, by my trouthe. It is but the scurfe and the scabbe. . . .   171   Magnyfycence 1123
SCABBED
Now shal ye be scabbed, scurvy, and lowsy.   197   Magnyfycence 2019
In lousy lothsumnesse, /And scabbed scorffynesse, ...   362   Albany   140
Among the scabbed skyes /Of Wycliffes flesshe flyes.   378   Replycacion   165
SCABBES
A sorte of foule drabbes /All scurvy with scabbes.   218   El Rummynge   140
Full of scabbes and scaules, ...   364   Albany   219
SCABBYD
Your skyn scabbyd and scurvy, ...   127   Garnesche3   131
Lyke a scabbyd muscull.   228   El Rummynge   556
SCALIS
What shippis are sailing to Scalis Malis, ...   139   Ven Tongues   65
SCALLYD
Thow callyst me scallyd, thou callydst me mad;   132   Garnesche5   116
SCALOPPE
For the cliffes of Scaloppe they rore wellaway, ...   238   Speke Parott   280
SCANT
Here was scant thryft /Whan they made suche shyft.   222   El Rummynge   301
SCANTE
Yett dates now are deynte, and wax verye scante, ...   244   Speke Parott   440
Or scante worth twenty marke, ...   264   Collyn Clout   726
SCANTLY
This hunderd yere scantly   111   Lawde   18
Scantly one with measure that wyll dwell.   189   Magnyfycence 1746
That Pety Caton can scantly construe a verse, ...   235   Speke Parott   178
That men shall scantly /Have peny or halpeny.   303   Why Come Ye   967
SCAPE
That no man can scape but they hym cache.   150   Magnyfycence   351
Let neyther patent scape them nor fee;   190   Magnyfycence 1776
Thou sholde not scape, horson, but thou sholde dye.   202   Magnyfycence 2195
Nor yet shall scape shamlesse.   309   Why Come Ye2   5
    shall] not in MS Rawlinson C. 813
SCAPE THRYFTE
Howe be it of scape thryfte your clokes smelleth musty.   161   Magnyfycence   761
SCARCE
To scarce of your expence, ...   278   Why Come Ye   5
SCARIOTH
Quod magnus est dominus Judas Scarioth.   234   Speke Parott   133
SCARPARY
From Scarpary to Tartary renoun therein doth spryng, ...   234   Speke Parott   131
Over Scarpary mala vy, Monsyre Cy-and-sliddyr.   243   Speke Parott   414
SCARSLY
Some can nat scarsly rede, ...   253   Collyn Clout   277
SCATH
That worketh moch scath   87   Phy Sparrow   619
    That] 'Thay' †Kele 1545.2, Wyght 1553, Kitson 1560.6
SCAULES
Full of scabbes and scaules, ...   364   Albany   219
SCHAME
Pride gothe before and schame commyth after.   133   Garnesche5   165

605

SCHE —SCORNE   Page   Title   Line

SCHE
	Page	Title	Line
So that sche wolde have kum	125	Garnesche3	63
But sche of all men	125	Garnesche3	65
Sche seyd how ye ded brydell,	126	Garnesche3	73
Thus with yow sche ded wary,	126	Garnesche3	75
Sche wolde nat of yt thow had sworne.	131	Garnesche5	52
Sche seyd ye war coluryd with cole dust;	131	Garnesche5	53
Sche seyd your brethe stanke lyke a broke;	131	Garnesche5	55
Sche sware with hyr ye xulde nat dele,	131	Garnesche5	57
Sche praiid yow walke, on Goddes halfe!	131	Garnesche5	60

SCHYNE
	Page	Title	Line
Your lothesum lere to loke on, lyke a gresyd bote dothe schyne.	123	Garnesche2	5

SCHRYNYD
	Page	Title	Line
In dud frese ye war schrynyd,	125	Garnesche3	46

SCIENS
	Page	Title	Line
To practique suche abolete sciens.	297	Why Come Ye	713
practique] 'practyve' †Kele 1545.3			

SCIPIADES
	Page	Title	Line
And his glory to incres /Lyke to Scipiades,	370	Albany	439

SCIPION
	Page	Title	Line
How Scipion dyd wake	88	Phy Sparrow	668

SCIPIONE
	Page	Title	Line
He is our noble Scipione;	118	Ag Scottes	117

SCIPIONS
	Page	Title	Line
Of Scipions dreme what was the treu probate;	322	Garlande	368

SCYENCE
	Page	Title	Line
Madame regent of the scyence sevyn	313	Garlande	53
scyence] 'sciences' Marshe 1568			

SCYLENCE
	Page	Title	Line
And play scylence and glum,	269	Collyn Clout	904

SCLAUNDER
	Page	Title	Line
enpoysoned with sclaunder and false detractions &c.	136	Ven Tongues	1

SCLAUNDEROUS
	Page	Title	Line
A sclaunderous tunge, a tunge of a skolde,	137	Ven Tongues	7

SCLAUNDRYNGE
	Page	Title	Line
In sclaundrynge you for truthe.	255	Collyn Clout	342

SCOLDE
	Page	Title	Line
Vouchesafe to defend yow agayne the brawlyng scolde	241	Speke Parott	361

SCOLE
	Page	Title	Line
For lordes and ladyes lerne at his scole;	38	Coystrownel	52
And lerned after my scole	74	Phy Sparrow	117
Had ye gonne with me to scole,	127	Garnesche3	117
My scole is more solem and somwhat more haute	137	Ven Tongues	24
And rule hym after the rule of your scole.	146	Magnyfycence	231
In faythe, els had I gone to longe to scole,	148	Magnyfycence	298
In faythe, trouthe ye say, we wente togyder to scole.	170	Magnyfycence	1065
With ladyes I lerne and goe with them to scole.	231	Speke Parott	21
And Donatus be dryven out of scole;	235	Speke Parott	170
'He is but a foole; /Let hym go to scole!	247	Collyn Clout	29
Or elles he can nought bot whan he is at scole;	318	Garlande	205

SCOLEHOUS
	Page	Title	Line
in the moche studious scolehous of scrupulous philology,	373	Replycacion	1

SCOLE MATERS
	Page	Title	Line
That of theyr scole maters lost is the hole sentens.	235	Speke Parott	182

SCOLE MATTER
	Page	Title	Line
As lyngua Latina, in scole matter occupyed;	234	Speke Parott	144
Of logyke nor scole matter,	267	Collyn Clout	815

SCOLERS
	Page	Title	Line
A Replycacion Agaynst Certayne Yong Scolers Abjured of Late,	373	Replycacion	1
of certayne sophystycate scolers	373	Replycacion	1
Howe yong scolers nowe a dayes enbol[n]ed	373	Replycacion	1
enbolned] 'enbolmed' †Pynson 1528			

SCOLES
	Page	Title	Line
My scoles are not for unthriftes untaught,	138	Ven Tongues	26
Nay, wylte thou here nowe of his scoles,	174	Magnyfycence	1216
Of heresy the devyllysshe scoles	382	Replycacion	298

SCOLYS
	Page	Title	Line
In them be no scolys /For braynsycke frantycke folys:	68	Hauke	248
Of dyverse mo that hauntyth my scolys.	175	Magnyfycence	1264

SCORE
	Page	Title	Line
Were fayne with a chalke /To score on the balke,	230	El Rummynge	615
Or score on the tayle.	230	El Rummynge	616

SCORES
	Page	Title	Line
Of sorowfull servauntes I have many scores:	194	Magnyfycence	1900

SCORFFYNESSE
	Page	Title	Line
In lousy lothsumnesse, /And scabbed scorffynesse,	362	Albany	140

SCORYD
	Page	Title	Line
Thow wolde have scoryd hys habarion;	130	Garnesche5	34

SCORNE
	Page	Title	Line
Of our pole artyke, smylynge halfe in scorne	46	Bowge	5
I have grete scorne and am ryghte evyll apayed.'	54	Bowge	298
It is greate scorne to see suche a hayne	55	Bowge	327
It is grete scorne to se a mysproude knave	59	Bowge	453
That all men laugh at lyberte to scorne.	146	Magnyfycence	222
But counterfet coynes is laughynge to scorne;	152	Magnyfycence	446
But noble men borne, /To lerne they have scorne,	262	Collyn Clout	620
Is nat this a shamfull scorne	276	Collyn Clout	1200
Men wolde have the lesse scorne	291	Why Come Ye	496

SCORNEFULL — SCOTTES

	Page	Title	Line
He hath dispyght and scorne	294	Why Come Ye	599
SCORNEFULL			
To be so scornefull to your alye	113	Scot Kynge	13
Joly Jemmy, ye scornefull Scot,	116	Ag Scottes	49
Scornefull and mokkyng over to mykkylle.	133	Garnesche5	153
But with scornefull affection	379	Replycacion	190
SCORNES			
Full of mockysshe scornes,	380	Replycacion	216
SCORNFULL			
With scornfull loke mevyd all in moode.	55	Bowge	317
scornfull] 'scorfull' Marshe 1568			
Nor to derayne /Batayle agayne /Scornfull disdayne,	356	Garlande	1565
SCORNIS			
Metrifyde merely, medelyd with scornis;	351	Garlande	1382
scornis] 'stormis' †Fakes 1523			
SCORNNYS			
His gawdy garment with Scornnys was all wrought;	54	Bowge	285
Scornnys] 'storunys' †Wynkyn de Worde 1499, 1510,			
'scornes' Marshe 1568			
SCORPIONE			
Scorpione ascendynge degrees twyse nyne;	312	Garlande	7
SCORPIONS			
More stinging then scorpions that stang Pharaotis.	138	Ven Tongues	52
SCORPYON			
Full lyke a scorpyon styngyng	41	Coystrowne4	17
Thou tode, thow scorpyon, /Thow bawdy babyone,	128	Garnesche3	162
Whan Scorpyon descendynge, /Was so then pretendynge	258	Collyn Clout	471
SCOT			
Joly Jemmy, ye scornefull Scot,	116	Ag Scottes	49
When the Scot was slayne	117	Ag Scottes	R
Of the prowde Scot, kynge Jemmy,	117	Ag Scottes	71
From you, Syr Scot, wolde turne his face?	118	Ag Scottes	108
With, 'Gup, Syr Scot of Galaway!'	118	Ag Scottes	109
And ye, proud Scot, Dunde, Dunbar	118	Ag Scottes	121
AGAYNST THE SCOT JEMMY	120	Ag Scottes	R
Gup Scot, /Ye blot:	135	Dundas	1
Shake thy tayle, Scot, lyke a cur,	135	Dundas	25
Tut, Scot, I sey, /Go shake th[e], dog, hey!	135	Dundas	27
the] 'thy' Marshe 1568			
By Jesu Christ, /Fals Scot, thou lyest:	135	Dundas	33
A tolman to blot, /A rough foted Scot!	136	Dundas	41
Dunde, Dunbar, /Walke, Scot, /Walke, sot,	136	Dundas	61
To pay for her scot	221	El Rummynge	281
Or elles the poore Scot,	265	Collyn Clout	749
Twit, Andrewe! Twit, Scot!	282	Why Come Ye	125
Scot] 'scote' †Kele 1545.3			
And never a Scot slayne!	282	Why Come Ye	152
Twyt, Scot, go kepe thy den.	362	Albany	145
Twyt, Scot, yet agayne ones,	362	Albany	149
With, 'twyt Scot, twyt Scot, twyt.'	362	Albany	153
With, 'twyt Scot, twyt Scot, twyt.'	362	Albany	153
Walke, Scot, go begge a byt	362	Albany	154
The fynde, Scot, breke thy necke.	363	Albany	156
'Twyt, Scot,' agayne I saye,	363	Albany	157
'Twyt, Scot, of Galaway.	363	Albany	158
Twyt, Scot, shake th[e] dogge, hay.	363	Albany	159
the] 'thy' †Marshe 1568			
Twyt, Scot, thou ran away.'	363	Albany	160
Go heme, ranke Scot, ge heme,	368	Albany	382
SCOTYSHE			
With some Scotyshe [l]as,	366	Albany	290
las] 'as' †Marshe 1568			
SCOTLAND			
Of whom both Flaunders and Scotland stode in drede,	30	Dol Dethe	44
That of Scotland ye lost the flower.	119	Ag Scottes	134
SCOTLANDE			
And all Scotlande owers	288	Why Come Ye	360
SCOTTE			
When the Scotte lyved	116	Ag Scottes	R
SCOTTES			
For you and your Scottes wolde tourne his face?	114	Scot Kynge	18
Now ye proude Scottes of Gelawaye	114	Scot Kynge	19
And ye proude Scottes of Dunbar,	114	Scot Kynge	29
Of the out yles ye rough foted Scottes	115	Scot Kynge	62
Ye rowe ranke Scottes and dronken Danes	115	Scot Kynge	64
His swerde hath bathed in the Scottes blode.	115	Scot Kynge	71
Skelton laureate Agaynst The Scottes	115	Ag Scottes	I
To angre the Scottes and Irysh keterynges withall,	117	Ag Scottes	83
Of the out iles the rough-foted Scottes,	120	Ag Scottes	170
The rude ranke Scottes, lyke dronken dranes,	120	Ag Scottes	172
What here ye of the Scottes?	285	Why Come Ye	262
For the Scottes and he,	286	Why Come Ye	277
with an hundred thousande tratlande Scottes	359	Albany	I
Of the Scottes ranke	359	Albany	18
False Scottes are ye.	359	Albany	26
O ye wretched Scottes, /Ye puaunt pyspottes,	362	Albany	119
O Scottes parjured, /Unhaply ured,	362	Albany	125
Ye Scottes all the rable,	363	Albany	177

	Page	Title	Line
SCOTTISH — SCULL			
The fals Scottes for dred,	371	Albany	512
SCOTTISH			
From the Scottish se /Unto Gabione.	362	Albany	130
SCOTTISHE			
This Dundas, /This Scottishe as	135	Dundas	8
Agayn Dundas, /That Scottishe asse.	135	Dundas	24
With dugges, dugges, dugges. /I shrewe thy Scottishe lugges,	366	Albany	292
SCOTTYS			
Agaynst the prowde Scottys claterynge,	115	Ag Scottes	1
Are nat these Scottys /Folys and sottys,	116	Ag Scottes	29
That the Scottys may synge, /'Fy on the wynnynge!'	116	Ag Scottes	47
synge] 'sin' Marshe 1568			
SCOTTYSH			
What say ye of the Scottysh kynge?	287	Why Come Ye	346
SCOTTYSHE			
For thy Scottyshe nose,	136	Dundas	36
Of the Scottyshe coost,	359	Albany	10
The yonge Scottyshe kyng,	361	Albany	90
Lyke a Scottyshe keteryng	365	Albany	248
Lyke a Scottyshe hag.	366	Albany	295
SCOTTYSSHE			
A Ballade of the Scottysshe Kynge	113	Scot Kynge	1
Of the Scottysshe hoost.	285	Why Come Ye	255
Of the Scottysshe Bankes.	288	Why Come Ye	369
Of your Scottysshe name.	360	Albany	47
SCOUR			
Ge heme! ge scour thy pot,	282	Why Come Ye	126
SCOURGE			
The flayle, the scourge of Almighty God.	308	Why Come Ye	1165
The flayle] not in MS Rawlinson C. 813			
SCRACHE			
The fende scrache out your mawes!	371	Albany	479
SCRAPE			
Or I shal fawchyn thy flesshe and scrape the on the skyn.	202	Magnyfycence	2189
For [ye] scrape out good scrypture, and set in a gall:	235	Speke Parott	153
ye] 'they' †Lant 1545, Kynge & Marche 1554, Day 1560, Marshe 1568			
I did what I cowde to scrape out the scrollis,	354	Garlande	1489
scrape] 'scarpe' Marshe 1568			
SCRAT			
Upon a naked man and yf she scrat.	176	Magnyfycence	1298
SCRIPTURE			
Ye cobble and ye clout /Holy scripture so about,	380	Replycacion	223
SCRIPTURES			
And of holy scriptures sawis,	305	Why Come Ye	1062
SCRYBBYL			
Scrybbyl thow, scrybyll thow, rayle or wryght,	134	Garnesche5	179
SCRYBBLYD			
That scrybblyd your fonde scrolle,	126	Garnesche3	91
SCRYBE			
And so the Scrybe was feed,	65	Hauke	151
Illumyn me, your poete and your scrybe,	117	Ag Scottes	80
SCRYBYLL			
Scrybbyl thow, scrybyll thow, rayle or wryght,	134	Garnesche5	179
SCRYBYS			
Lytyll wyt in your scrybys nolle	126	Garnesche3	90
SCRYBLYD			
And he that scryblyd your scrolles,	129	Garnesche3	192
SCRYPTURE			
Save hym that nought can: scrypture sayth soo.	58	Bowge	448
For [ye] scrape out good scrypture, and set in a gall:	235	Speke Parott	153
ye] 'they' †Lant 1545, Kynge & Marche 1554, Day 1560, Marshe 1568			
That clerkely is, and can /Well scrypture expounde	264	Collyn Clout	723
How scrypture shulde be coted,	265	Collyn Clout	755
As scrypture recordis /A cecitate cordis,	291	Why Come Ye	474
SCRYVE			
To take upon the for to scryve;	132	Garnesche5	91
SCROLLE			
That scrybblyd your fonde scrolle,	126	Garnesche3	91
SCROLLES			
And he that scryblyd your scrolles,	129	Garnesche3	192
Nor rede in any scrolles,	277	Collyn Clout	1241
SCROLLIS			
I did what I cowde to scrape out the scrollis,	354	Garlande	1489
scrape] 'scarpe' Marshe 1568			
SCROWLE			
Of this wanton scrowle.	300	Why Come Ye	831
SCRUPULOUS			
in the moche studious scolehous of scrupulous philology,	373	Replycacion	1
SCRUPULUS			
Of scrupulus dout. Wherfore, your mynde discharge,	332	Garlande	726
SCRUTENY			
Of all gentylwomen he hath the scruteny,	334	Garlande	782
SCULL			
Bete a dum mouthe than a brainles scull;	314	Garlande	82
Bete] 'Better' Marshe 1568, MS Cotton Vitellius E.x			
He pluckid the bull /By the hornid scull,	349	Garlande	1312

SCURFE —SE   Page   Title   Line

SCURFE
No, by my trouthe. It is but the scurfe and the scabbe. . . . . 171 Magnyfycence 1123
SCURFFE
I am lowsy and unlykynge and full of scurffe; . . . . 195 Magnyfycence 1958
SCURVY
Your skyn scabbyd and scurvy, ... 127 Garnesche3 131
Dundas, dronken and drowsy, /Skabed, scurvy and lowsy, ... 136 Dundas 51
Now shal ye be scabbed, scurvy, and lowsy. . . . . 197 Magnyfycence 2019
Droupy and drowsy, /Scurvy and lowsy; . . . . 214 El Rummynge 16
A sorte of foule drabbes /All scurvy with scabbes. . . . . . . 218 El Rummynge 140
SCUT
Masid as a Marche hare, he ran lyke a scut. . . . . 329 Garlande 632
SCUTIS
Wyth scutis and crownes of golde . . . . 283 Why Come Ye 171
SCUTUS
Wyth crownes and wyth scutus; . . . . 283 Why Come Ye 170
SE
The myghty lyoun doutted by se and sande. . . . . 32 Dol Dethe 109
   sande] 'lande' Marshe 1568
But graunt us grace /To se thy face, ... 40 Coystrowne3 50
Eternally /To beholde and se /The Trynyte! 40 Coystrowne3 58
By Crede, I trust to se the day, ... 41 Coystrowne4 12
I wold you coud! Then shuld ye se, mastres, ... 44 Balettys3 40
It is grete scorne to se a mysproude knave . . . . 59 Bowge 453
There he may se and reed . . . . 65 Hauke 147
   he] 'her' Marshe 1568
To behold and se /What hevynesse dyd me pange: . . . . 72 Phy Sparrow 43
Great sorowe than ye myght se, ... 73 Phy Sparrow 56
Whoso lyst the story to se. . . . . 76 Phy Sparrow 193
From Occyan the great se . . . . 79 Phy Sparrow 318
To se my sorow new. . . . . 80 Phy Sparrow 337
Men se hym now and than . . . . 88 Phy Sparrow 657
   than] 'then' Marshe 1568
Her to behold and se, ... 97 Phy Sparrow 1007
To se her treade the grounde . . . . 100 Phy Sparrow 1149
That folowe as you may se. . . . . 106 Phy Sparrow 1379
   you] 'ye' Wyght 1553, Kitson 1560.6, Marshe 1568
Calliope, /As ye may se, ... 112 Calliope 2
Beholde thy selfe, and thou mayst se. 130 Garnesche5 16
Come of therfore, let se; . . . . 143 Magnyfycence 102
Then, Lyberte, se that Measure by your gyde, ... 146 Magnyfycence 195
To se howe greable we are of one mynde; . . . . 146 Magnyfycence 199
S[e] at our eye the worlde day by day. . . . . 146 Magnyfycence 216
   Se] 'so' †Rastell & Treveris C 1530, B
Then noblenesse, I se well, is almoste undone, ... 146 Magnyfycence 225
By God, syr, ye se but fewe wyse men of myne age. . . . . 148 Magnyfycence 289
Let se this checke yf ye voyde canne. . . . . 148 Magnyfycence 297
By God, syr, beyonde the se. . . . . 150 Magnyfycence 341
Counterfet worshyp outwarde men may se; . . . . 153 Magnyfycence 473
Monkys may not for drede that men sholde them se. . . . . 154 Magnyfycence 493
Let se, fynde you a better way. . . . . 156 Magnyfycence 560
Ye, and se howe it may be compast . . . . 156 Magnyfycence 567
Cockes woundes! Se, syrs, se, se! . . . . 156 Magnyfycence 572
Cockes woundes! Se, syrs, se, se! . . . . 156 Magnyfycence 572
Cockes woundes! Se, syrs, se, se! . . . . 156 Magnyfycence 572
Se you not howe they prece . . . . 156 Magnyfycence 591
Abyde. Lette me se. Take better hede. . . . . 157 Magnyfycence 595
Se howe he is wrapped for the colde. . . . . 157 Magnyfycence 603
We wyll se you shortly, one of us twayne. . . . . 159 Magnyfycence 686
Nowe let se. Quyte you lyke praty men! . . . . 159 Magnyfycence 688
And never am I sory but whan that I se . . . . 160 Magnyfycence 732
Wyll ye se this gentylman is all in his skornys? . . . . 162 Magnyfycence 773
Here he is nowe, man. Mayst thou not se? . . . . 162 Magnyfycence 792
Convey yourselfe fyrst, let se. . . . . 163 Magnyfycence 816
What nowe? Let se /Who loketh on me . . . . 163 Magnyfycence 829
But nowe what tydynges can you tell? Let se. . . . . 166 Magnyfycence 928
Cockes harte! Tourne the; let me se thyne aray. . . . . 167 Magnyfycence 959
Nowe let me se about . . . . 168 Magnyfycence 991
What, Fansy! Let me se who is the tother. . . . . 172 Magnyfycence 1158
Hast thou ony more? Let se, procede. . . . . 174 Magnyfycence 1236
But, I say, let se and yf thou have any more. . . . . 175 Magnyfycence 1278
But all is foly that I can se. . . . . 176 Magnyfycence 1291
It is wonder to se the worlde aboute, ... 177 Magnyfycence 1326
To se what foly is used in every place; . . . . 177 Magnyfycence 1327
Shall se many thyngys donne craftely. . . . . 177 Magnyfycence 1334
To se you thus ruled and stande in suche awe. . . . . 178 Magnyfycence 1376
Or lyberte by welth? Let se, tell me that. . . . . 180 Magnyfycence 1432
And so as ye se it wyll be no better, ... 180 Magnyfycence 1438
Yes, syr, so good man in you I se, ... 182 Magnyfycence 1522
Let se what ye say. Shewe it strayte. . . . . 185 Magnyfycence 1592
And yf you se ony thynge agaynst your mynde, ... 185 Magnyfycence 1599
And se a man that with hym ye be not pleased, ... 185 Magnyfycence 1609
Stande styll here, and ye shall se . . . . 186 Magnyfycence 1629
And therof ye shall a larger profe se. . . . . 188 Magnyfycence 1700
With me no longer. Say somwhat nowe, let se, ... 188 Magnyfycence 1719
That day I se hym I shall be worse all nyght. . . . . 188 Magnyfycence 1724
Se, for God avowe, for colde as I chydder. . . . . 191 Magnyfycence 1817
Se, syr, I beseche you, Largesse my brother. . . . . 192 Magnyfycence 1842

SEALE —SECRETE   Page   Title   Line

Text	Page	Title	Line
And yf I se therby they wyll not amende,	194	Magnyfycence	1926
Yet it proveth eyrnest, ye may se, every day.	195	Magnyfycence	1949
I am raggyd and rent, as ye may se;	195	Magnyfycence	1962
Thus totum in toto groweth up, as ye may se,	199	Magnyfycence	2099
Cockes armes, syrs, wyll ye not se	200	Magnyfycence	2109
As evydently in retchlesse youth ye may se	200	Magnyfycence	2133
Tyll, as ye se many tymes, they shame all theyr kynne.	201	Magnyfycence	2144
Go we nere and let us se.	204	Magnyfycence	2243
But nowe I se well there is no better rede,	205	Magnyfycence	2305
For nowe I se comynge to youwarde Redresse.	208	Magnyfycence	2384
Of that I se you nowe in the state of grace.	208	Magnyfycence	2403
Yet let us se this matter thorowly ingrosed.	209	Magnyfycence	2438
This lyfe inconstant for to beholde and se:	212	Magnyfycence	2525
To se howe she is gumbed, /Fyngered and thumbed,	215	El Rummynge	40
'Behold,' she sayd, 'and se	220	El Rummynge	217
Her legges that ye myght se;	225	El Rummynge	421
ye] 'he' 1521 Fragment			
Ones hed wold have aked /To se her naked.	226	El Rummynge	479
That one might se her token.	227	El Rummynge	497
Let se who dare make up the reste.	242	Speke Parott	382
Or elles they wolde se /Otherwyse,	247	Collyn Clout	39
For, as farre as I can se,	248	Collyn Clout	59
For let se who that dare	251	Collyn Clout	179
As ye may dayly se /Howe the lay fee	259	Collyn Clout	495
As dayly men may se,	262	Collyn Clout	630
And your noble se /And your dygnyte	265	Collyn Clout	759
se] 'fee' Marshe 1568, 'see' MS Harley 2252			
For to se the sacrynge?	272	Collyn Clout	1028
For that no man shulde se	277	Collyn Clout	1240
That he ne se can	283	Why Come Ye	182
Men may happely se	288	Why Come Ye	367
Whiche he can nat se.	291	Why Come Ye	507
But whome that ye favoure, I se well, hath a name,	317	Garlande	176
Call forthe, let se where is your clarionar,	318	Garlande	233
To se if Skelton wyll put hymselfe in prease	319	Garlande	239
wyll] 'dare' MS Cotton Vitellius E.x			
Let se, my syster, now spede you, go aboute.	319	Garlande	242
you] not in MS Cotton Vitellius E.x			
Unto me sayd, 'Lo, syr, now ye may se	326	Garlande	518
And we shall se you ageyne or it be pryme.'	326	Garlande	525
To se this howre now, that I may. say,	327	Garlande	538
'Beholde and se in your advertysement	335	Garlande	808
Yowr name to se /It be enrolde, /Writtin with golde.	338	Garlande	937
To se how duly ich thyng in ordre was,	343	Garlande	1094
For of my bokis parte ye shall se,	344	Garlande	1139
Let se now for hym how ye can expounde;	345	Garlande	1153
That folowe as ye may se:	350	Garlande	1372
From the Scottish se /Unto Gabione.	362	Albany	130
Whyche he? Let se;	367	Albany	333
Se where the heretykes go,	376	Replycacion	73

SEALE

Text	Page	Title	Line
Under the kynges brode seale;	287	Why Come Ye	337
Under strength of the great seale,	306	Why Come Ye	1102
Under the protectyon /Of the kynges great seale,	307	Why Come Ye	1129
great] 'brode' MS Rawlinson C. 813			

SEALL

Text	Page	Title	Line
Thowghe he pampyr not hys paunche with the grete seall;	239	Speke Parott	309

SEASE

Text	Page	Title	Line
Pease, man, pease! /I rede we sease.	168	Magnyfycence	998

SEASYD

Text	Page	Title	Line
For in my favour I have you feffyd and seasyd.	183	Magnyfycence	1536

SEASON

Text	Page	Title	Line
Knyghtis and squyers, at every season when	30	Dol Dethe	32
Be it erly or late, welth hath a season.	140	Magnyfycence	3
Mayster Measure, you be come in good season.	143	Magnyfycence	84
Then for the season that I here shall walke,	159	Magnyfycence	691
Tushe! Holde your peas; ye speke out of season.	178	Magnyfycence	1388
And we wyll be comonynge in the mene season.	187	Magnyfycence	1688
Howe some of you dothe eate /In lenton season flesshe meate,	251	Collyn Clout	205
Nor in holy lenton season	252	Collyn Clout	211
And all out of season!	304	Why Come Ye	998
Of suche an endarkid chapiter sum season.	315	Garlande	108

SECHE

Text	Page	Title	Line
Nor seche a nody polle	126	Garnesche3	88

SECONDE

Text	Page	Title	Line
The seconde was Suspecte, whiche that dayly	49	Bowge	136
His seconde hawke wexyd gery	63	Hauke	66
The seconde, to owe hym obedyence,	307	Why Come Ye	1124

SE COSTE

Text	Page	Title	Line
Some from Flaunders, sum from the se coste,	326	Garlande	496

SECRET

Text	Page	Title	Line
For I have gravyd her wythin the secret wall	45	Balettys3	48

SECRETARY

Text	Page	Title	Line
The kynges Frenshe secretary	298	Why Come Ye	788

SECRETE

Text	Page	Title	Line
His counseyle secrete never to dyscure,	52	Bowge	219
dyscure] 'dysture' †Wynkyn de Worde 1499, 1510			
And many wordes sayde in secrete wyse;	58	Bowge	422

SECRETLY —SEY   Page   Title   Line

SECRETLY
Advertysyng you, madame, to warke more secretly, ...   43   Balettys2   39
Nor to speke to hym secretly, /Openly nor prevyly, ...   272   Collyn Clout   1040
SECRETNESE
So lytell secretnese, and so myche grete councell;   245   Speke Parott   465
SECTE
And are somewhat suspecte /In Luthers secte.   260   Collyn Clout   545
For ye have enduced a secte   380   Replycacion   236
SECTES
After the sectes of heretykis!   306   Why Come Ye   1082
SECUND
Pers Prater, the secund, that quarillis beganne;   330   Garlande   636
SECUNDE
I have receyvyd your secunde ryme.   129   Garnesche5   2
SEDE
Grace the sede did sow.   110   Lawde   5
But ye had some wyl[d] sede to sowe, ...   114   Scot Kynge   52
  wyld] 'wyle' †Fakes 1513
To sowe the sede of graces.   269   Collyn Clout   898
  sowe] 'save' †Godfray 1531, 'sowe' MS Harley 2252
SEDEANE
He shall be th[e] sedeane, ...   85   Phy Sparrow   552
  the] 'thye' †Kele 1545.2, 'thy' Wyght 1553, Kitson 1560.6,
  Marshe 1568
SEDES
I sowe sedycyous sedes of dyscorde and debates.   160   Magnyfycence   737
SEDICION
I saye it for no sedicion, ...   378   Replycacion   140
SEDYCIONS
And their false sedycions, ...   364   Albany   199
SEDYCYOUS
I sowe sedycyous sedes of dyscorde and debates.   160   Magnyfycence   737
SEDUCE
And devyllysshely devysed /[The] people to seduce, ...   380   Replycacion   211
  The] 'to' †Pynson 1528
SEDUCES
Lest they be Seduces, ...   277   Collyn Clout   1229
  Seduces] 'Saducies' Marshe 1568, 'Adusayes' MS Harley 2252
SEE
Marchauntes her borded to see what she had lode.   47   Bowge   40
  lode] not in Marshe 1568
'Maysters', he sayde, 'the shyp that ye here see, ...   47   Bowge   48
Than sholde ye see there pressynge in a pace   47   Bowge   56
Of one and other that wolde his lady see   47   Bowge   57
Shyfte now therwith, let see, as ye can, ...   48   Bowge   99
For, as me thoughte, in our shyppe I dyde see   49   Bowge   132
Is lytyll to saye, and moche to here and see;   52   Bowge   212
To see Johan Dawes, that came but yesterdaye, ...   54   Bowge   301
It is greate scorne to see suche a hayne   55   Bowge   327
That I have deynte to see the cherysshed thus?   55   Bowge   338
What, loo, man, see here of dyce a bale;   57   Bowge   389
Ryghte now I spake with one, I trowe, I see –   59   Bowge   458
Naye, see where yonder stondeth the teder man!   59   Bowge   484
Woo is hym that is blynde and maye not see!   60   Bowge   518
Me thoughte I see lewde felawes here and there   61   Bowge   528
Besechynge you that shall it see or rede, ...   61   Bowge   534
He shuld over the see   76   Phy Sparrow   197
Shall sayle over the see, ...   102   Phy Sparrow   1240
Rowlynge in yower holow hede, ugly to see;   122   Garnesche1   38
Howe so? By God, at the see syde, ...   150   Magnyfycence   346
To bryng all the see into a cheryston pytte, ...   240   Speke Parott   331
And the dygnyte /Of the bysshoppes [s]ee.   259   Collyn Clout   501
  see] 'fee' †Godfray 1531, Kele 1545.1, Marshe 1568
Of Rome to the see /Weth suche dygnyte.   307   Why Come Ye   1145
SEE-BOORDE
Whome she hateth shall over the see-boorde skyp.   49   Bowge   112
  see-boorde] 'shyp borde' Marshe 1568
SEEN
Well Be Seen Crystofer Chalangar, et cetera   129   Garnesche5   1
SEE-SANDE
To sowe corne in the see-sande, ther wyll no crope growe. . . .   240   Speke Parott   342
SEEST
I shall skelpe the on the skalpe; lo, seest thou that?   202   Magnyfycence   2180
Seest thou not what is fall?   219   El Rummynge   182
SEETH
But whan age seeth that rage   279   Why Come Ye   36
SEETHE
As hevery man wele seethe, ...   127   Garnesche3   125
SEIGNEOUR
To owur soleyne Seigneour Sadoke, desire hym to cum home, . . .   239   Speke Parott   304
SEY
But sey me now, Syr Satrapas, what autoryte ye have   121   Garnesche1   6
But sey me yet, Syr Satropas, what auctoryte ye have   122   Garnesche1   13
But sey me yet, Syr Satrapas, wat auctoryte ye have   122   Garnesche1   20
But sey me yet, Syr Satrapas, what auctoryte ye have   122   Garnesche1   27
But sey me yet, Syr Satrapas, what auctoryte ye have   122   Garnesche1   34
I sey, ye solem Sarson, alle blake ys yor ble;   122   Garnesche1   36
Men sey ye wyll wax lowsy, /Drunkyn, drowpy, drowsy.   127   Garnesche3   135

611

SEYD —SEM   Page   Title   Line

	Page	Title	Line
I sey, thow felle and fowle flessh fly,	131	Garnesche5	65
Fusty bawdyas, I sey nat alle.	131	Garnesche5	76
And sey poetis no dys.....	132	Garnesche5	113
I care nat what thow wryght or sey;	134	Garnesche5	168
Tut, Scot, I sey, /Go shake th[e], dog, hey!	135	Dundas	27
the] 'thy' Marshe 1568			
With, 'Speke, Parott, I pray yow,' full curteslye they sey,	231	Speke Parott	13
In Greke tong Parott can bothe speke and sey,	231	Speke Parott	26
Now pandes mory, wax frantycke som men sey;	232	Speke Parott	46
mory] 'mery' †MS Harley 2252; men] 'mad' †MS Harley 2252			
And thowe sum dysdayne yow and sey how ye prate,	240	Speke Parott	315
Muche money, men sey, there madly he hathe spente;	240	Speke Parott	335
Som sey they cannot my parables expresse;	242	Speke Parott	386
Som sey I rayle att ryott recheles;	242	Speke Parott	387
Agayne Frentike Frenesy there dar no man sey nay,	243	Speke Parott	422
Syns Dewcalyons flodde was nevyr, I dar sey.	245	Speke Parott	483
Sey this and sey that:	247	Collyn Clout	15
Sey this and sey that:	247	Collyn Clout	15
And surely thus they sey:	249	Collyn Clout	121
Anone, I sey, this trumpet were founde out,	319	Garlande	243

SEYD

	Page	Title	Line
Sche seyd how ye ded brydell,	126	Garnesche3	73
Sche seyd ye war coluryd with cole dust;	131	Garnesche5	53
Sche seyd your brethe stanke lyke a broke;	131	Garnesche5	55
They seyd my lawrell was the goodlyest	343	Garlande	1112

SEYGNYORYTE

	Page	Title	Line
Pretendynge gravyte /And seygnyoryte,	269	Collyn Clout	925

SEYGNOURS

	Page	Title	Line
After olde seygnours, /And the lernynge of Lytelton Tenours	256	Collyn Clout	369

SEYMY

	Page	Title	Line
Thou swety sloven seymy,	128	Garnesche3	169

SEYN

	Page	Title	Line
Welle Be Seyn Crysteovyr Chalannger, et cetera	124	Garnesche3	I

SEYNTY

	Page	Title	Line
There was a prycke-me-denty, /Sat lyke a seynty,	229	El Rummynge	583

SEYST

	Page	Title	Line
Thow seyst I callyd the a pecok;	133	Garnesche5	128

SEKE

	Page	Title	Line
And seke after small wormes,	74	Phy Sparrow	122
Phillip wolde seke and take	76	Phy Sparrow	179
Who so lyst to seke	97	Phy Sparrow	1044
To turney or to tante with me ye ar to fare to seke.	123	Garnesche2	37
And make youer stomake seke	128	Garnesche3	156
Then feyne yourselfe dyseased, and make yourselfe seke.	185	Magnyfycence	1612
She semed somdele seke,	225	El Rummynge	414
Yet ye seke out your Greke in Capricornio,	235	Speke Parott	152
Boldenes is to seke /The churche for to defende;	251	Collyn Clout	183
He sayth, they are to seke	287	Why Come Ye	317
To seke before our grace.'	287	Why Come Ye	332
You to devyse his crafte were to seke;	337	Garlande	893
In you, who list to seke,	338	Garlande	920
Gone to seke hallows, /With Reason together,	358	Garlande2	7

SEKELY

	Page	Title	Line
It wolde have made a man hole that had be ryght sekely,	345	Garlande	1162

SEKENESSE

	Page	Title	Line
I vysyte theyr faders and moders with sekenesse;	194	Magnyfycence	1925
Dysease and sekenesse his conscyence to dyscryve;	207	Magnyfycence	2370

SEKERNES

	Page	Title	Line
But of my spede /Small sekernes;	356	Garlande	1597

SEKERNESSE

	Page	Title	Line
Howe in this worlde there is no seke[r]nesse,	212	Magnyfycence	2515
sekernesse] 'sekenesse' †Rastell & Treveris C 1530, B			

SELDOME

	Page	Title	Line
That wysdome and I shall seldome mete.	170	Magnyfycence	1081
The devyll of hell and he be seldome asonder.'	333	Garlande	765

SELE

	Page	Title	Line
For ye war smery, lyke a sele,	131	Garnesche5	58
And sendeth you this wrytynge closed under sele.	149	Magnyfycence	312

SELFE SAME

	Page	Title	Line
The selfe same hounde /Myght the confounde,	79	Phy Sparrow	303
The selfe same Samuell,	105	Phy Sparrow	1356
And the selfe same game	256	Collyn Clout	387
The selfe same Samuell,	350	Garlande	1349

SELY

	Page	Title	Line
Howe they take no hede /Theyr sely shepe to fede,	248	Collyn Clout	77
Amongest the sely nonnes.	256	Collyn Clout	389
Agaynst the sely preest.	261	Collyn Clout	576
Nor of theyr sely soules,	277	Collyn Clout	1244
Youre carkas to kepe, /Lyke a sely shepe,	365	Albany	274

SELL

	Page	Title	Line
Howe that ye sell /The grace of the Holy Goost.	251	Collyn Clout	200
And sell away theyr belles	257	Collyn Clout	410
And such as sell trotters, /Pytchars, potshordis.	302	Why Come Ye	911
potshordis] 'pouchers' MS Rawlinson C. 813			
None so ryche stones in Turkey to sell;	323	Garlande	396

SEM

	Page	Title	Line
Japhet, Cam, and Sem,	77	Phy Sparrow	244
Sem, Japheth, or Cam.	301	Why Come Ye	899

SEMBLAUNT —SENDE

	Page	Title	Line
SEMBLAUNT			
His foule semblaunt /All displesaunt;	95	Phy Sparrow	936
foule] 'feule' †Kele 1545.2, Wyght 1553			
Here FOLY maketh semblaunt to take a lowse	173	Magnyfycence	SD
Here FOLY maketh semblaunt	173	Magnyfycence	SD
SEME			
Me seme I flye,	163	Magnyfycence	839
Myght seme ryght wel under my proteccyon	181	Magnyfycence	1469
SEMED			
She semed somdele seke,	225	El Rummynge	414
She semed halfe a leche,	225	El Rummynge	447
She semed to be a wytch.	226	El Rummynge	458
SEMELY			
Your tethe teintyd with tawny; your semely snowte doth passe,	122	Garnesche1	39
So semely a snowte	168	Magnyfycence	994
And by unycornes /With theyr semely hornes;	270	Collyn Clout	965
SEMENT			
Enhardid adyment the sement of your wall!	320	Garlande	306
SEMETH			
He semeth a sysmatyke /Or els an heretike,	62	Hauke	17
To tell you the cause me semeth it no nede.	140	Magnyfycence	8
Me semeth Magnyfycence is comynge here at hande.	145	Magnyfycence	162
That Measure be mayster us semeth it is syttynge.	145	Magnyfycence	176
Me semeth that ye have dronken more than ye have bled.	147	Magnyfycence	260
In good faythe, syr, me semeth he had the more wronge.	178	Magnyfycence	1384
Syr, as me semeth, ye sholde be rulyd be me.	180	Magnyfycence	1433
To cease me semeth best,	220	El Rummynge	235
And so it semeth they play,	277	Collyn Clout	1234
Me semeth it for the best.	277	Collyn Clout	1250
SEMEWE			
The semewe and the tytmose;	83	Phy Sparrow	458
SEMITH			
That he so sholde be, me semith it sittyng,	316	Garlande	149
it] 'it is' MS Cotton Vitellius E.x			
SEMYNGE			
It is semynge your pleasure ye delyte,	183	Magnyfycence	1546
SEMYST			
Art thou so angry as thou semyst?	162	Magnyfycence	794
SEMYTH			
It semyth the sobbyng of an old sow!	37	Coystrownel	32
That semyth from afar	97	Phy Sparrow	1046
It semyth nat thy pyllyd pate	132	Garnesche5	89
But, Perseveraunce, me semyth your probleme was best;	212	Magnyfycence	2505
Nowe semyth us syttynge that ye then resorte	214	Magnyfycence	2566
Sometyme, as it semyth, when the mone light	330	Garlande	644
SEMLY			
A semly nose and a stowte,	133	Garnesche5	131
SENATE			
By hole consent of theyr senate,	131	Garnesche5	83
Frome the laureat senate by force of proscripcyon.	318	Garlande	225
SENATOUR			
Was nevyr suche a senatour syn Crystes Incarnacion.	240	Speke Parott	337
SENAWS			
Wherewith my handes I wrange /That my senaws cracked	73	Phy Sparrow	46
SENCE			
This corse for to sence /With greate reverence,	85	Phy Sparrow	526
Chryst sence you with a fryinge pan! –	117	Ag Scottes	62
sence] 'fence' †Lant 1545			
SEND			
(God send the soule good rest!)	78	Phy Sparrow	262
God send them sorowe and shame!	78	Phy Sparrow	277
Of al good praiers God send him sum!	86	Phy Sparrow	584
If Arethusa wyll send	93	Phy Sparrow	860
And send me to greate ladyes of estate;	231	Speke Parott	6
to greate ladyes] 'to grece to lordys' †MS Harley 2252			
God of his miseracyon /Send better reformacyon!	305	Why Come Ye	1045
SENDE			
I pray God sende the prosperous lyf and long,	34	Dol Dethe	169
God sende my sparoes sole good rest!	86	Phy Sparrow	574
And sende the Frensshe kynge suche another fall.	115	Scot Kynge	73
Ye for to sende suche a cytacyon,	117	Ag Scottes	55
God sende you wele good spede,	129	Garnesche3	202
A, Fansy, Fansy, God sende the brayne!	157	Magnyfycence	608
Well, tary here tyll I for you sende.	163	Magnyfycence	817
Well, get you hens than and sende me some other.	180	Magnyfycence	1451
Then myschefe sodaynly I them sende;	194	Magnyfycence	1927
I sende ofte tymes a fole to his sonne.	195	Magnyfycence	1935
And therfore our Lorde sende you a very wengaunce!	203	Magnyfycence	2237
To sende over to me Sad Cyrcumspeccyon.	208	Magnyfycence	2400
God sende you good sale!'	223	El Rummynge	369
Suche grace God them sende	274	Collyn Clout	1125
Suche grace that he us sende	278	Collyn Clout	1262
God sende us better luck!	282	Why Come Ye	123
God sende us better lucke, etc.	282	Why Come Ye	124
God sende him sorowe for his sinnes!	309	Why Come Ye	1201
Sende him to F[r]aunce agayne	363	Albany	173
Fraunce] 'Faunce' †Marshe 1568			
God sende them bothe myschauns!	363	Albany	176

	Page	Title	Line
God sende you sorow and care!	363	Albany	181
SENDETH			
And sendeth you this wrytynge closed under sele.	149	Magnyfycence	312
All that God sendeth, take it in gre;	196	Magnyfycence	1979
SENE			
In sesons past who hathe harde or sene	30	Dol Dethe	22
Or ells with gret shame your game wylbe sene.	43	Balettys2	42
For, as I trowe, I have sene you in dede	53	Bowge	248
I have not sene suche anothers page –	60	Bowge	506
But ofte tymes have I sene wyse men do mad dedys.	148	Magnyfycence	302
Syns Dewcalyons flodde, was nevyr sene nor shall.	245	Speke Parott	469
Syns Dewcalyons flodde, I trowe, was nevyr sene.	245	Speke Parott	476
Syns Dewcalyons flodde was nevyr sene nor lyerd.	246	Speke Parott	504
Theyr chambres well sene,	270	Collyn Clout	955
Such a casuelte shulde be sene	297	Why Come Ye	747
Of theyr game it is sene	304	Why Come Ye	1005
So that there workis myght famously be sene,	314	Garlande	67
Had I never sene, some softer, some lowder;	320	Garlande	271
Troilus, I trowe, if that he had you sene,	336	Garlande	873
And if Apelles your countenaunce had sene,	337	Garlande	894
SENEK			
Senek full soberly with his tragediis;	322	Garlande	358
with] 'wit' †Fakes 1523			
SENNET			
'I dranke not this sennet /A draught to my pay.	224	El Rummynge	394
SENS			
Sens Dewcalyons flodde, in no cronycle ys told.	246	Speke Parott	518
SENSERS			
The sensers and the crosse shall fet;	86	Phy Sparrow	568
SENSETH			
Whyles he senseth [the herse],	85	Phy Sparrow	530
the herse] not in †Kele 1545.2, Wyght 1553, Kitson 1560.6, Marshe 1568			
SENSUALYTE			
of their insensate sensualyte,	374	Replycacion	I
SENT			
that was sent to hym	39	Coystrowne3	I
What the devyll! Who sent for the?	162	Magnyfycence	791
Your grace sent for me, I wene. What is your wyll?	179	Magnyfycence	1410
Ye sent us a supervysour for to take hede;	192	Magnyfycence	1853
Nay. He that ye sent us, Clokyd Colusyon,	192	Magnyfycence	1859
Howe be it, from you I receyved a letter [sent],	209	Magnyfycence	2435
sent] not in †Rastell & Treveris C 1530, B			
Syr, this letter ye sent to me at Pountes was enclosed.	209	Magnyfycence	2439
For he sent in writynge	299	Why Come Ye	790
To fayre maistres Anne that shuld have be sent,	347	Garlande	1241
SENTE			
From God am sente to quyte the thy mede.	193	Magnyfycence	1877
SENTENCE			
Convenable in sentence, Comendable, Lamentable,	39	Coystrowne3	I
Sentence was executyd,	66	Hauke	175
What the sentence ment.	68	Hauke	227
The sentence of his mynde,	91	Phy Sparrow	807
What this man hath sayd, perceyve ye his sentence?	210	Magnyfycence	2465
Suche shredis of sentence, strowed in the shop	233	Speke Parott	92
To rude ys there reason to reche to your sentence;	240	Speke Parott	319
To hasty of sentence,	278	Why Come Ye	3
But to his sentence must accorde.	287	Why Come Ye	343
With sentence fructuous and termes convenable.'	335	Garlande	821
With wordes devoute and sentence agerdows,	347	Garlande	1250
With a worde or twayne /In sentence playne.	361	Albany	76
Grounded is your sentence	372	Albany	519
SENTENCYOUSLY			
Wyth fresshe utteraunce full sentencyously;	46	Bowge	12
SENTENS			
Wherto shuld I rehers /The sentens of my vers?	68	Hauke	247
That of theyr scole maters lost is the hole sentens.	235	Speke Parott	182
In shorte sentens, /Of your pretens /What is the grounde	361	Albany	79
SEON			
Seon, the regent Amorreorum,	234	Speke Parott	121
SEPTEMBER			
The mery moneth of September,	117	Ag Scottes	66
SEQUELE			
Whate sequele shall folow when pendugims mete togethyr?	243	Speke Parott	415
SEQUESTRED			
And theyr spyrytuall lambes /Sequestred from rambes	250	Collyn Clout	157
SERCHYNG			
So myche serchyng of loselles, and ys hym selfe so lewde;	246	Speke Parott	513
SERE			
Though I waxe olde /And somdele sere,	112	Calliope	16
And some bade, 'Sere hym with a marke.'	150	Magnyfycence	360
/Loke lyke sere wedes,	216	El Rummynge	61
SERENUS			
Nor solempne Serenus, for all his armony	383	Replycacion	337
SERGEAUNT FERROUR			
'Have in sergeaunt ferrour, myne horse behynde is bare.'	43	Balettys2	20
SERGYANTES			
Sergyantes of the Coyfe eke,	287	Why Come Ye	316

	Page	Title	Line
SERYOUSLY			
And seryously she shewyd me ther denominacyons.	328	Garlande	581
SERMON			
Your sermon was nat swete;	376	Replycacion	51
SERMONS			
Howe bysshoppes dysdayne /Sermons for to make,	250	Collyn Clout	134
SERPENS			
[The] *serpens of Lybany	79	Phy Sparrow	290
The] 'These' †Kele 1545.2, Wyght 1553, Kitson 1560.6, Marshe 1568; *serpens] 'serpentes' Wyght, Kitson, Marshe			
SERPENT			
By the venemous serpent,	104	Phy Sparrow	1326
Thou fals, stynkyng serpent,	128	Garnesche3	171
Then any poysoned tode, or any serpent.	138	Ven Tongues	54
By the venemows serpent	349	Garlande	1319
SERPENTES			
His serpentes tonge /That many one hath stonge;	94	Phy Sparrow	920
SERPENTINS			
My serpentins and my gunnys	128	Garnesche3	159
SERVANT			
To pardon thi servant and brynge to savacioun.	35	Dol Dethe	210
SERVANTYS			
And so with your servantys he fersly doth fyght.	43	Balettys2	28
SERVAUNT			
Is that our servaunt is sum what to dull;	314	Garlande	79
that] 'for that' MS Cotton Vitellius E.x			
SERVAUNTES			
With us olde servauntes such maysters to playe.	55	Bowge	329
Of sorowfull servauntes I have many scores:	194	Magnyfycence	1900
But olde servauntes ye chase	273	Collyn Clout	1077
His servauntes menyall	294	Why Come Ye	595
And suche of my servauntes as I have promotyd,	318	Garlande	202
SERVAUNTIS			
That were aboute hym, his awne servauntis of trust,	30	Dol Dethe	37
Togeder with servauntis of his famuly,	31	Dol Dethe	93
SERVAUNTYS			
Then may I say that ye be servauntys myne.	145	Magnyfycence	183
With my servauntys, and suche maystryes gan make,	188	Magnyfycence	1716
Where is nowe all my servauntys that I had here a late?	198	Magnyfycence	2057
Alas, myn owne servauntys to shew me such reproche!	205	Magnyfycence	2277
SERVE			
By theyr conusaunce knowing how they serve a wily py:	43	Balettys2	34
To dwell with us and serve my ladyes grace.	50	Bowge	156
I wot not where to fynd /Termes to serve my mynde.	91	Phy Sparrow	783
To serve for all ententes,	101	Phy Sparrow	1182
But for to serve the kynges entent,	134	Garnesche5	177
Why, coulde not your wyt serve you no better?	193	Magnyfycence	1868
Thy herte wolde nat serve the.	365	Albany	250
SERVED			
For, as for me, I served here many a daye,	53	Bowge	274
SERVETH			
Ic dien serveth for the estrych fether,	233	Speke Parott	78
the] not in Kynge & Marche 1554, Day 1560, Marshe 1568			
SERVITURE			
Me to retayne /Her servituture.	112	Calliope	20
SERVYCE			
And of my servyce you shall not mysse.	151	Magnyfycence	392
And in his servyce the to retayne.	159	Magnyfycence	668
Ye, and do ryght good servyce he can.	163	Magnyfycence	822
Remembre the good servyce that Mesure hath you done,	186	Magnyfycence	1637
To do you servyce after your appetyte.	190	Magnyfycence	1793
In faythe, and your servyce ryght well shall I acquyte;	190	Magnyfycence	1794
In your servyce; and, to the accomplysshement	314	Garlande	61
To owe to yow our servyce, and more if we mowte!	324	Garlande	425
To owe her my servyce with true perseveraunce.	327	Garlande	558
For to his servyce I have suche regarde,	334	Garlande	778
But to do you servyce nedis now I must;	337	Garlande	879
to do you] 'do her' MS Cotton Vitellius E.x			
SERVYCEABYLL			
I wyl be ferme and stabyll, /And to yow servyceabyll,	237	Speke Parott	247
SERVYD			
And so shall a noble man nobly be servyd.	200	Magnyfycence	2120
SESON			
Ye rayle all out of seson.	127	Garnesche3	130
SESONS			
In sesons past who hathe harde or sene	30	Dol Dethe	22
SET			
How in good horsmen ye set your hole delyght,	42	Balettys2	13
Hys jentyll curtoy[1], and set nowght by small naggys!	43	Balettys2	16
curtoy] 'curtoyt' †Rastell 1527.1			
Wordys well set with good habylyte;	43	Balettys3	5
He set the arme proudly under the syde,	55	Bowge	321
He set up fresshely upon his hat aflofte.	56	Bowge	367
Set in our bede rolles,	72	Phy Sparrow	12
It wold set on a stole,	74	Phy Sparrow	116
set] 'sit' Wyght 1553, Kitson 1560.6, Marshe 1568			
Set in thy tayle a blase	79	Phy Sparrow	315
Set in our bede rolle,	81	Phy Sparrow	383

SETT —SETTE

	Page	Title	Line
Their husbandes to set at nought:	87	Phy Sparrow	627
So properly it is set:	98	Phy Sparrow	1049
And set so womanly,	98	Phy Sparrow	1067
Sholde be set and sorted,	103	Phy Sparrow	1287
Set in better /Thy pentameter.	135	Dundas	5
Where lyberte is absent, set welthe asyde.	142	Magnyfycence	80
Yet in this man you must set your delyght.	145	Magnyfycence	167
In fayth, I set not by the worlde two Dauncaster cuttys.	148	Magnyfycence	293
I set not by hym a fly	152	Magnyfycence	412
Fyrst I dyd set;	165	Magnyfycence	879
All this nacyon /I set on fyre; /In my facyon	165	Magnyfycence	885
That was before I set behynde;	168	Magnyfycence	1007
Plucke downe an house and set up a rafter,	169	Magnyfycence	1032
And can not set herselfe to warke,	174	Magnyfycence	1230
Nay, beyonde all other set hym alone.	174	Magnyfycence	1235
That be set in auctorite.	174	Magnyfycence	1243
I set not by the prowdest of them a prane,	181	Magnyfycence	1489
Nor Nero, that nother set by God nor man,	182	Magnyfycence	1509
But, and I were as ye, I wolde not set a gnat.	188	Magnyfycence	1704
I set not a flye and all go to all.	188	Magnyfycence	1710
I have set my hole felycyte,	190	Magnyfycence	1788
Nowe is there no man that wyll set by hym a flye.	193	Magnyfycence	1889
Lydderyns so lytell set by Goddes lawes.	194	Magnyfycence	1919
Sodenly set up and sodenly pluckyd downe;	197	Magnyfycence	2025
All her delyte is set in doublenesse.	197	Magnyfycence	2029
My harte is holly on her set;	199	Magnyfycence	2073
My fansy fayrly on her I set;	199	Magnyfycence	2076
That they set theyr chyldren to rynne on the brydyll,	200	Magnyfycence	2136
That nother they set by father and mother;	200	Magnyfycence	2142
Well, syr, after your counsell my mynde I wyll set.	210	Magnyfycence	2457
Set not all your affyaunce in Fortune full of gyle;	211	Magnyfycence	2501
Sodenly set up, and sodenly cast downe.	212	Magnyfycence	2530
Sodenly set up, and sodenly cast downe.	213	Magnyfycence	2537
Above all other byrdis, set Parrot alone.	233	Speke Parott	112
For [ye] scrape out good scrypture, and set in a gall:	235	Speke Parott	153
ye] 'they' †Lant 1545, Kynge & Marche 1554, Day 1560, Marshe 1568			
Set Sophia asyde, for every Jack Raker	235	Speke Parott	160
That the premenyre /Is lyke to be set afyre	249	Collyn Clout	109
Set nought by golde ne grotes, /Theyr names yf I durst tell.	250	Collyn Clout	160
And set up theyr fucke sayles	256	Collyn Clout	397
fucke sayles] 'flucke sayles' †Godfray 1531, 'fulke saylys' MS Harley 2252			
And set in majeste /And spirytuall dygnyte,	261	Collyn Clout	587
Set nothynge by polytykes.	262	Collyn Clout	623
And as farre as they dare set,	269	Collyn Clout	932
Set hym fast by the fete!	275	Collyn Clout	1166
They set nat by us a shyttell;	276	Collyn Clout	1185
shytell] 'whystell' Kele 1545.1, Marshe 1568, 'shetyll' MS Harley 2252			
We set nat a nutte shell	277	Collyn Clout	1225
/Is nothynge set by,	280	Why Come Ye	46
He is set so hye /In his ierarchy	283	Why Come Ye	184
Dare nat set theyr penne	287	Why Come Ye	323
Set hym fast by the fete!'	289	Why Come Ye	426
And set hym nobly /In great auctoryte	291	Why Come Ye	504
That he set him on heyght,	292	Why Come Ye	542
Set up a wretche on hye,	293	Why Come Ye	585
He is best set by!	300	Why Come Ye	859
best] 'most' MS Rawlinson C. 813			
And set hell on fyer	303	Why Come Ye	985
hell] 'all' Toy 1553, Kitson 1560.7, Marshe 1568			
Twyse! set hym a chare, or reche hym a stol	318	Garlande	208
Twyse] 'Twyshe' Marshe 1568, MS Cotton Vitellius E.x			
Oure Englysshe rude so fresshely hath set out,	324	Garlande	422
Wherin was set of Fame the noble Quene,	325	Garlande	482
An hole reame he is able to set at devysion:	333	Garlande	758
He wyll set men a feightynge and syt hymselfe styll,	333	Garlande	761
set] 'stir' MS Cotton Vitellius E.x; a feightynge] 'to brawlyng' MS Cotton Vitellius E.x			
In you he wolde have set his hole delight.	336	Garlande	874
The jeloffer well set, /The propre vyolet,	340	Garlande	983
Set on your hede this laurell whiche is wrought.	343	Garlande	1087
Who list amende it, let hym set to his penne.	348	Garlande	1260
Shulde be set and sortyd, /To be matriculate	348	Garlande	1280
Whan the flye net was set for to catche a cote,	351	Garlande	1379
This delycate dasy, this strawbery pretely set,	352	Garlande	1449
And set hys crowne /On your owne heed	361	Albany	96
We set nat a flye	363	Albany	161
We set nat a prane	363	Albany	163
We set nat a myght	363	Albany	165
And set you in suche case	368	Albany	367
SETT			
In me all onely wer sett and comprisyde,	33	Dol Dethe	156
Smale flowres helpt to sett	339	Garlande	969
SETTE			
He loked hawte; he sette eche man at noughte;	54	Bowge	284
hawte] 'hawtie' Marshe 1568			

SETTETH —SHALBE   Page   Title   Line

	Page	Title	Line
And sette to a D, /And then hyt ys 'Amend', ...	238	Speke Parott	275
to] not in †MS Harley 2252			
Sette asyde all sophysms, and speke now trew and playne. . . .	244	Speke Parott	448
And sette suche a snare	361	Albany	111
SETTETH			
That he setteth never a deale	307	Why Come Ye	1130
For he setteth God apart.	308	Why Come Ye	1180
SETTYNG			
Settyng theyr myndys so moche of eloquens, ...	235	Speke Parott	181
In settyng out fresshely his crafty persuacyon, ...	316	Garlande	153
SETTYS			
And settys nat by it a myte!	296	Why Come Ye	677
SEVEN			
Your Seven Systers, that gun so gay, ...	119	Ag Scottes	162
Than thou can in yerys seven.	170	Magnyfycence	1078
From the seven sterrys!	267	Collyn Clout	827
SEVYN			
For though they stumble in the synnys sevyn, ...	36	Coystrowne1	3
Madame regent of the scyence sevyn	313	Garlande	53
scyence] 'sciences' Marshe 1568			
SEW			
To whom then shall we sew /For to have rescew, ...	40	Coystrowne3	37
SEWE			
To her to sewe for grace, ...	98	Phy Sparrow	1075
SEX			
Sex volumis engrosid together it doth containe.	354	Garlande	1502
SHAYLE			
Good mastres Anne, there ye do shayle!	41	Coystrowne4	19
Our Thomasen she doth trip, our Jenet she doth shayle;	233	Speke Parott	83
Ye shayle inter enigmata	379	Replycacion	172
SHAYLES			
What, Collyn, there thou shayles!	256	Collyn Clout	399
SHAKE			
Or we shall the oute of thy clothes shake!'	55	Bowge	343
To shake my pygyons federis	69	Hauke	281
So fervently I shake, ...	74	Phy Sparrow	104
And his fethers shake, ...	75	Phy Sparrow	163
fethers] 'fether' †Kele 1545.2			
Shake thy tayle, Scot, lyke a cur, ...	135	Dundas	25
Tut, Scot, I sey, /Go shake th[e], dog, hey!	135	Dundas	28
the] 'thy' Marshe 1568			
Go shake the, dogge, hay, syth ye wyll nedys!	148	Magnyfycence	303
I purpose to shake oute /All my connynge bagge, ...	248	Collyn Clout	50
To shudder and to shake	303	Why Come Ye	980
Twyt, Scot, shake th[e] dogge, hay.	363	Albany	159
the] 'thy' †Marshe 1568			
SHAKED			
Out of your robes ye were shaked, ...	119	Ag Scottes	166
your] not in Kynge & Marche 1554, Day 1560, Marshe 1568			
With that her hed shaked /And her handes quaked.	226	El Rummynge	476
And howe Cupyde shaked /His dart, and bent his bowe	270	Collyn Clout	946
SHAKES			
And shakes them by the eare, ...	286	Why Come Ye	305
SHAKETH			
The mashe bolle, and shaketh	219	El Rummynge	196
SHAKYNG			
Agaynst this my makyng, /Their males therat shakyng, ...	120	Ag Scottes2	8
They are shyre shakyng nought!'	226	El Rummynge	466
SHAKYNGE			
From qui fuit aliquid to shyre shakynge nought.	176	Magnyfycence	1303
SHAL			
'What, and ye shal be my piggesnye?'	36	Man Margery	17
For though ye lyve a c. yere, ye shal dy a daw.	71	Hauke	334
The more shal be your mede.	72	Phy Sparrow	16
Wel, wyse men may ete the fysshe when ye shal draw the pole. .	148	Magnyfycence	300
Make indentures how ye and I shal gyde.	180	Magnyfycence	1448
But thynke ye with Magnyfycence I shal be reserved?	188	Magnyfycence	1702
And now without measure he shal have hunger and colde.	193	Magnyfycence	1895
Now shal ye be scabbed, scurvy, and lowsy.	197	Magnyfycence	2019
Or I shal fawchyn thy flesshe and scrape the on the skyn. . .	202	Magnyfycence	2189
To thanke God of his sonde; and comforte ye shal fynde. . . .	207	Magnyfycence	2360
This ale shal be thycker, ...	219	El Rummynge	205
When thei agayn thyder shal come, ...	268	Collyn Clout	883
Tell you the rest; for me they shal.	296	Why Come Ye	709
Of your complaynt it shal nat skyl.	310	Why Come Ye2	32
A daucock ye be, and so shal be styll!	310	Why Come Ye2	34
'There shal he here what she wyl to hym say	325	Garlande	451
wyl to hym] 'to hym will' Marshe 1568			
It is, and shal be	362	Albany	129
SHALBE			
One ther is, and ever one shalbe, ...	45	Balettys5	8
Our chaunters shalbe the cuckoue, ...	82	Phy Sparrow	428
Magnyfycence to mayntayne, your promosyon shalbe.	144	Magnyfycence	157
So that welthe with measure shalbe conbyned, ...	145	Magnyfycence	179
In joy and myrthe your mynde shalbe inlargyd	146	Magnyfycence	205
It shalbe done at your commaundement.	147	Magnyfycence	239
Who that is ruled by us, it shalbe longe or he thee.	154	Magnyfycence	515
And Sober Sadnesse shalbe your name?	159	Magnyfycence	681

SHALL —SHALL   Page   Title   Line

To come to me I trowe he shalbe fayne.	162	Magnyfycence	784
What the devyll, man, your name shalbe the greter;	180	Magnyfycence	1440
Thy pleasure now with payne and trouble shalbe tryde.	193	Magnyfycence	1881
Here shalbe not great sheddynge of blode.	203	Magnyfycence	2207
One faute or other in them shalbe notyd.	318	Garlande	203
To yow thre this honor shalbe reserved	323	Garlande	409
Of that shalbe resonde you ye must be content; you] not in Marshe 1568	344	Garlande	1123
It shalbe your lottes	362	Albany	121
There shalbe drawen a trayne	368	Albany	369
That shalbe to your payne?	368	Albany	370
To flye ye shalbe fayne	368	Albany	371
Avaunt, cowarde recrayed! /Thy pride shalbe alayd,	371	Albany	496
For you shalbe driven out	371	Albany	501
Or els doutlesse ye shalbe blased,	382	Replycacion	294

SHALL

Be Crist, ye shall not! No, no, hardely!	36	Man Margery	18
To whom then shall we sew /For to have rescew,	40	Coystrowne3	37
Put up your purs, ye shall non pay!'	40	Coystrowne4	11
Yet shall she never oute of remembraunce,	45	Balettys3	47
What and he slyde downe, who shall hym save?	46	Bowge	28
That ye shall stonde in favoure and in grace.	49	Bowge	105
Whome she hateth shall over the see-boorde skyp. see-boorde] 'shyp borde' Marshe 1568	49	Bowge	112
For ye have me whome faythfull ye shall fynde;	50	Bowge	166
And, as she wyll, so shall our grete shyppe sayle.	50	Bowge	172
Thyse lewde cok wattes shall nevermore prevayle wattes] 'witts' Marshe 1568	51	Bowge	173
Or 'Shall I sayle wyth you' a felashyp assaye?	53	Bowge	254
That is agayne you, you shall have wetynge;	54	Bowge	278
'Now,' quod Dysdayne, 'as I shall saved be,	54	Bowge	297
I shall the angre ones in every vayne!	55	Bowge	326
But, no force, I shall ones mete with the;	55	Bowge	334
Come whan it wyll, oppose the I shall,	55	Bowge	335
By Goddis syde, my sworde thy berde shall shave!	55	Bowge	339
Or we shall the oute of thy clothes shake!'	55	Bowge	343
That shall them angre, I holde thereon a grote,	59	Bowge	475
For some shall wene be hanged by the throte.	59	Bowge	476
Adewe tyll soone, we shall speke more of this.	60	Bowge	492
Ye muste be ruled, as I shall tell you howe.	60	Bowge	493
As I shall tell you, yf ye wyll harke agayne:	61	Bowge	520
Besechynge you that shall it see or rede,	61	Bowge	534
In hope that no man shall /Be myscontent withall. Be] 'By' Kynge & Marche 1554	62	Hauke	27
I shall you make relacyon	62	Hauke	29
He shall be as now nameles,	62	Hauke	38
But he shall not be blameles,	62	Hauke	39
Nor he shall not be shameles;	62	Hauke	40
He shall be the preest,	81	Phy Sparrow	400
Shall rede the gospell at masse;	82	Phy Sparrow	423
Shall rede there the pystell.	82	Phy Sparrow	425
The versycles shall syng.	82	Phy Sparrow	431
Shall watche at this wake;	82	Phy Sparrow	437
He shall syng the grayle;	82	Phy Sparrow	441
Money they shall dele	83	Phy Sparrow	455
That shall be theyr charge;	83	Phy Sparrow	457
He shall synge the verse	85	Phy Sparrow	531
He shall be th[e] sedeane, the] 'thye' †Kele 1545.2, 'thy' Wyght 1553, Kitson 1560.6, Marshe 1568	85	Phy Sparrow	552
The tarsell gentyll, /They shall morne soft and styll	85	Phy Sparrow	559
The sacre with them shall say	85	Phy Sparrow	561
The goshauke shall have a role	85	Phy Sparrow	563
Shall stand in their morning gounes;	85	Phy Sparrow	566
The sensers and the crosse shall fet;	86	Phy Sparrow	568
shall be holy wather clarke.	86	Phy Sparrow	570
To heven he shall, from heven he cam.	86	Phy Sparrow	582
Whyles the world shall dure:	89	Phy Sparrow	723
In worth I shall it take,	92	Phy Sparrow	817
My wyt I shall assay	92	Phy Sparrow	821
Whose fame by me shall sprede	93	Phy Sparrow	885
How shall I report	96	Phy Sparrow	998
Shall sayle over the see,	102	Phy Sparrow	1240
Theyr names shall never dye.	106	Epitaphe	1
And pray shall, /At this trentall	108	Epitaphe1	69
Shall now com and do right,	110	Lawde	17
Right shall the foxis chare,	111	Lawde	22
They shall wirry no mo,	111	Lawde	26
The law they shall not breke;	111	Lawde	30
They shall com to rekening,	111	Lawde	31
Therfor no more they shall	111	Lawde	36
And therein reed /Shall fynde indeed	116	Ag Scottes	44
Contynually I shall remember	117	Ag Scottes	65
And peradventure I shall content your mynde.	142	Magnyfycence	49
Judycyall rygoure shall not me correcte -	142	Magnyfycence	69
Shall I begynne or ye?	143	Magnyfycence	103
Nay, ye shall begynne, by my wyll.	143	Magnyfycence	104
Welthe with Lyberte, with me bothe dwell ye shall,	145	Magnyfycence	174

SHALL—SHALL

	Page	Title	Line
And lyberte his large with measure shall make.	145	Magnyfycence	180
That measure shall nevere departe from my syght.	145	Magnyfycence	190
Then shall you have with you prosperyte resydent.	146	Magnyfycence	197
With care and with thought howe Jacke shall have Gyl?	148	Magnyfycence	287
In fayth, I wyll not say that ye shall prove a fole,	148	Magnyfycence	301
That I shall have you agayne my good lorde.	149	Magnyfycence	310
Your pleasure, syr shortely shall be done.	149	Magnyfycence	321
I shall come to you myselfe, I trowe, this afternone.	149	Magnyfycence	322
I shall loke in it at leasure better;	149	Magnyfycence	332
And of my servyce you shall not mysse.	151	Magnyfycence	392
Ye, but how longe shall I here awayte?	151	Magnyfycence	398
'And therfore shall my husbande pay'.	153	Magnyfycence	461
Say trouth? Yes, yes, by lakyn, I shall the warent,	154	Magnyfycence	506
Why, shall we dwell togyder all thre?	154	Magnyfycence	509
What! Shall we jangle thus all the day styll?	156	Magnyfycence	565
I trowe it shall not nede to abyde.	156	Magnyfycence	571
Woo is that purse that ye shall share!	156	Magnyfycence	587
But shall I have myne olde name styll?	158	Magnyfycence	647
All thre, I say. Shall I go? Whyder?	158	Magnyfycence	666
But then, syr, what shall I hyght?	159	Magnyfycence	669
Syr, ye shall hyght Good Demeynaunce.	159	Magnyfycence	674
That he shall have you in the stede of sadnesse,	159	Magnyfycence	680
For then shall we so craftely cary	159	Magnyfycence	683
That Mesure shall not there longe tary.	159	Magnyfycence	684
Now let us go, and we shall, then.	159	Magnyfycence	687
Then for the season that I here shall walke,	159	Magnyfycence	691
I may do somwhat, and more I thynke shall.	162	Magnyfycence	778
By Cockys harte, and call shall agayne!	162	Magnyfycence	783
Why, shall he be of your bende?	163	Magnyfycence	818
Confusyon /Shall on hym lyght	164	Magnyfycence	859
A Tyborne checke /Shall breke his necke.	165	Magnyfycence	911
Holde thy pease! Measure shall frome us walke.	166	Magnyfycence	949
With whom shall I there mete.	167	Magnyfycence	955
Ye, but what shall I call my name?	167	Magnyfycence	958
A man shall fynde /Many of her kynde,	167	Magnyfycence	983
A, I trowe ye shall coughe me a fole.	170	Magnyfycence	1064
That wysdome and I shall seldome mete.	170	Magnyfycence	1081
That I shall laughe the out of thy cote.	173	Magnyfycence	1194
Syr, of my maner I shall tell you the playne:	174	Magnyfycence	1219
Yes. I shall tell you or I go	175	Magnyfycence	1263
Why, shall I not have Foly with me also?	176	Magnyfycence	1306
By the masse, he shall hyght Consayte.	176	Magnyfycence	1309
And shall we have lyberte to do what we wyll?	176	Magnyfycence	1316
Shall se many thyngys donne craftely.	177	Magnyfycence	1334
Syr, as by my wyll, it shall be so no more.	178	Magnyfycence	1377
Ye shall be occupyed, Welthe, at my wyll.	178	Magnyfycence	1380
Yourselfe shall be ruled by lyberte and largesse.	179	Magnyfycence	1389
Nay. He shall be ruled even as I lyst.	179	Magnyfycence	1394
Syr, by lyberte and largesse I wyll that ye shall	179	Magnyfycence	1396
It shall be done. Ye, but byd hym come away	179	Magnyfycence	1399
I am here redy. What! Shall we	179	Magnyfycence	1414
That I shall suffer none impechment	179	Magnyfycence	1418
Syr, ye shall folowe myne appetyte and intent.	180	Magnyfycence	1420
And get [y]ou home togyther; for Lyberte shall byde you] 'thou' †Rastell & Treveris C 1530, B	180	Magnyfycence	1446
But I shall of Fortune rule the reyne.	181	Magnyfycence	1460
I shall flappe hym as a fole to fall at my fete.	182	Magnyfycence	1507
But I shall frounce them on the foretop and gar them to quake.	182	Magnyfycence	1514
Plesyth it your grace to shewe what I do shall?	182	Magnyfycence	1517
Be it reason or none, it shall not gretely skyll;	185	Magnyfycence	1596
With, 'Cockes armes! Rest shall I none have	185	Magnyfycence	1615
Stande styll here, and ye shall se	186	Magnyfycence	1629
Come hyder, Pleasure; you shall here myne entent.	186	Magnyfycence	1655
By myne advyse, with you in fayth he shall not rest.	186	Magnyfycence	1660
Ye, by my trouthe, I shall waraunt you for me,	187	Magnyfycence	1669
That he shall lyke the worse all this woke.	187	Magnyfycence	1682
And therof ye shall a larger profe se.	188	Magnyfycence	1700
For go when ye shall, of you shall he mysse.	188	Magnyfycence	1706
For go when ye shall, of you shall he mysse.	188	Magnyfycence	1706
Yet ones agayne I shall fall on my kne	188	Magnyfycence	1708
That day I se hym I shall be worse all nyght.	188	Magnyfycence	1724
And I shall waraunt you welth and lyberte.	190	Magnyfycence	1766
Syr, of my counsayle this shall be the grounde:	190	Magnyfycence	1768
For the[m] you have at lyberte to lowte. them] 'then' †Rastell & Treveris C 1530, B	190	Magnyfycence	1779
Thus joy without mesure you shall have.	190	Magnyfycence	1781
For as thou sayst, ryght so shall it be,	190	Magnyfycence	1783
For as thou wylte, so shall the game go;	190	Magnyfycence	1786
And suche as you wyll shall lacke no promocyon.	190	Magnyfycence	1789
Your welthe and felycyte, I trust we shall optayne	190	Magnyfycence	1792
In faythe, and your servyce ryght well shall I acquyte;	190	Magnyfycence	1794
I shall gyve you a gaude of a goslynge that I gave,	191	Magnyfycence	1829
Alasse! With colde my lymmes shall be marde.	197	Magnyfycence	2004
And so shall a noble man nobly be servyd.	200	Magnyfycence	2120
And they never thryve in theyr age, it shall not gretly skyll.	200	Magnyfycence	2138
O good Lorde, howe longe shall I indure	201	Magnyfycence	2153
Leve thy pratynge or els I shall lay the on the pate.	201	Magnyfycence	2173
By the messe, I shall cleve thy heed to the waste.	201	Magnyfycence	2175

SHALL—SHALL | | Page | Title | Line

I shall thrust in the my dagger - Thorowe the legge in to the hose.	202	Magnyfycence	2177
I shall skelpe the on the skalpe; lo, seest thou that?	202	Magnyfycence	2180
By Cockes bones, I shall blysse the and thou be to bolde.	202	Magnyfycence	2182
Peas, or I shall wrynge thy be in a brake.	202	Magnyfycence	2187
Nay, iche shall wrynge the, horson, on the wryst.	202	Magnyfycence	2196
By the masse, man, thou shall fynde me resonable.	202	Magnyfycence	2204
A, shall we have more of this maters yet?	203	Magnyfycence	2214
Abyde, syr, abyde; I shall make hym to pysse.	204	Magnyfycence	2250
Ye shall be clappyd with a coloppe	204	Magnyfycence	2272
Shall I myselfe hange with an halter? Nay,	206	Magnyfycence	2320
Out harowe! Hyll burneth! Where shall I me hyde?	206	Magnyfycence	2324
A, blessyd may ye be, syr! What shall you I call?	206	Magnyfycence	2327
Then shall you be sone delyvered from dystresse,	208	Magnyfycence	2383
Syr, your requeste shall not be delayed.	208	Magnyfycence	2401
Nowe shall ye be renewyd with solace.	208	Magnyfycence	2404
To your requeste I shall be confyrmable.	208	Magnyfycence	2407
Ye, syr. From hym my corage shall never flyt.	210	Magnyfycence	2466
And ye shall have more worshyp then ever ye had.	210	Magnyfycence	2474
In all your warkys more grace shall ye fynde;	211	Magnyfycence	2485
Redresse, in my remembraunce your lesson shall rest;	211	Magnyfycence	2503
I shall it never forget nor leve it behynde,	212	Magnyfycence	2506
Who lyst to consyder shall never be begylyd,	212	Magnyfycence	2512
Abyde, abyde, /And to you shall be tolde	218	El Rummynge	157
Ye shall not bere awaye /Myne ale for nought,	218	El Rummynge	165
myne] 'my' Kynge & Marche 1554, Day 1560, Marshe 1568			
It shall make you loke /Yonger than ye be	219	El Rummynge	213
I shall breke your palettes, /Wythout ye now cease!'	223	El Rummynge	348
Plaut[us] in his comedies a chyld shall now reherse,	235	Speke Parott	176
shall be his protectyon, his pavys and his wall.	236	Speke Parott	203
Ye, all thyng mortall shall torne unto nought	236	Speke Parott	214
That never may dye, nor never dye shall:	236	Speke Parott	216
Shall lepe from this lyfe, as mery as we be.	236	Speke Parott	222
Parrot sayth playnly, shall tourne all to dust.	236	Speke Parott	224
For Jerico and Jerssey shall mete togethyr as sone	239	Speke Parott	306
Whate sequele shall folow when pendugims mete togethyr?	243	Speke Parott	415
Speke, Parotte, my swete byrde, and ye shall have a date,	243	Speke Parott	416
Syns Dewcalions flodde, was nevyr sene nor shall.	245	Speke Parott	469
You shall have your wylla!'	253	Collyn Clout	261
Theyr shall no clergye appose	254	Collyn Clout	291
Shall have penalte /For your iniquite.	258	Collyn Clout	461
That shall sytte in a trone	258	Collyn Clout	474
shall sytte] 'syttys nowe' MS Lansdowne 762 'shuld sytte' MS Harley 2252			
I shall bothe wryte and say,	259	Collyn Clout	507
And ye shall do the same,	259	Collyn Clout	508
Shall I tell you more? Ye, shall.	262	Collyn Clout	635
Shall I tell you more? Ye, shall.	262	Collyn Clout	635
Shall nat be objected by me.	266	Collyn Clout	794
by] 'for' Kele 1545.1, Marshe 1568, 'at by' MS Harley 2252			
That they shall mell nor make,	271	Collyn Clout	1015
That a man shall here a masse,	272	Collyn Clout	1022
'Shall they taunt us prelates,	275	Collyn Clout	1150
taunt] 'daunt' Kele 1545.1, Marshe 1568, 'teche' MS Harley 2252			
Ye prechers shall be yawde:	276	Collyn Clout	1204
Some shall be sawde,	276	Collyn Clout	1205
And some of you shall dye /Lyke holy Jeremy;	276	Collyn Clout	1208
As it is, it shall be styll,	277	Collyn Clout	1218
Shall glyde and smothely slyppe	277	Collyn Clout	1252
And yf ye thynke this shall	279	Why Come Ye	24
We shall here more herafter!	281	Why Come Ye	99
We shall have a tot quot	282	Why Come Ye	128
And I shall do for the.'	286	Why Come Ye	280
Subtelly wrought shall be	288	Why Come Ye	364
It shall be as he wyll.	289	Why Come Ye	419
That shall be a spectacle	293	Why Come Ye	568
And thus they shall syt -	295	Why Come Ye	633
And ye shall fynde surely	296	Why Come Ye	695
That he shall never ete more bred.	299	Why Come Ye	796
Herafter perchaunce I shall	299	Why Come Ye	823
It shall nat ever flowe.	303	Why Come Ye	952
nat ever flowe] 'neuer ouer flowe' MS Rawlinson C. 813			
That men shall scantly /Have peny or halpeny.	303	Why Come Ye	967
Shall never have good helth;	304	Why Come Ye	1025
Shall let the preest pontyficall	308	Why Come Ye	1160
Ye shall nat escape blamelesse,	309	Why Come Ye2	4
escape] 'be' MS Rawlinson C. 813			
Nor yet shall scape shamlesse.	309	Why Come Ye2	5
shall] not in MS Rawlinson C. 813			
Yet shall I answere your grace as in this,	316	Garlande	144
Few shall ye fynde or none that wyll do so.'	317	Garlande	168
But lytell or nothynge ye shall here tell	317	Garlande	197
ye shall] 'shall ye' MS Cotton Vitellius E.x			
And ye shall well fynde he is a very fole;	318	Garlande	207
well fynde] 'fynde wele' MS Cotton Vitellius E.x			
Shall were a garlande of the laurell tre.'	321	Garlande	322
In maner and forme as ye shall after here.	323	Garlande	399

SHALT —SHAME

	Page	Title	Line
That we shall brynge you personally present	324	Garlande	418
Whiche shall be to you a sufferayne accessary,	326	Garlande	523
And we shall se you ageyne or it be pryme.'	326	Garlande	525
No stormy tempeste your barge shall overthrow.	327	Garlande	546
Be well assurid I shall aqyute your hyre,	327	Garlande	550
That all the dayes of ther lyfe shall styck by ther rybbis.	330	Garlande	638
It shall be losyd ful sone out of the bandis	332	Garlande	725
And who can worke beste now shall be asayde;	334	Garlande	775
My lyfe endurynge I shall both wryte and say,	335	Garlande	839
So shall your name endure perpetually,	336	Garlande	861
Yet shall there be no restraynt	339	Garlande	956
I wyll ye shall be /In all benyngnyte	341	Garlande	1046
For of my bokis parte ye shall se,	344	Garlande	1139
Welcome shall ye /To sum men be;	355	Garlande	1540
Ye shall have nede /You for to spede	355	Garlande	1554
Ye] 'You' Marshe 1568			
Els ye shall pray /Them that ye may	356	Garlande	1583
Dunbar, Dunde, /Ye shall trowe me,	359	Albany	25
Shall cast a beyght,	361	Albany	110
That shall cast you in care,	361	Albany	112
That knowen ye shall be	361	Albany	114
We shall breke thy bones	362	Albany	150
Ye shall never be hable,	363	Albany	178
Therby I shall purchace /No displesaunt rewarde,	367	Albany	358
That shall bring you full bace	368	Albany	366
Our mayster shall you brynge,	368	Albany	384
We shall pype you a daunce	371	Albany	498
Shall tourne you to myschauns.	371	Albany	499
That ye shall have no grace	371	Albany	504
Ye shall have shame and sorowe.	371	Albany	507
Shew them that shall you rede	371	Albany	509
shall evermore be, with all obsequious redynesse,	373	Replycacion	1
Than shall ye fynde it fyrme and stable,	382	Replycacion	289

SHALT

	Page	Title	Line
Whyles I have ought, by God, thou shalt not lacke,	50	Bowge	167
Thou shalt no where rede	70	Hauke	299
Withowte thou leve thou shalt be chekt,	132	Garnesche5	109
For thou shalt well knowe I am nother durty nor dusty.	161	Magnyfycence	759
By the masse, thou shalt byde my leyser.	162	Magnyfycence	788
But yet thou shalt holde me a fole styll.	173	Magnyfycence	1184
Nay, nay. Thou shalt fynde hym another maner of man.	173	Magnyfycence	1189

SHALTE

	Page	Title	Line
Well, ones thou shalte be chermed, iwus:	55	Bowge	340
Naye, strawe for tales, thou shalte not rule us;	55	Bowge	341
We be thy betters, and so thou shalte us take,	55	Bowge	342
As here after thou shalte knowe more.	167	Magnyfycence	953
Thou shalte have my purse, and I wyll have thyne.	171	Magnyfycence	1102
And thou shalte have my hauke to a botchment.	171	Magnyfycence	1113
Mary, as for that, thou shalte sone here myne.	172	Magnyfycence	1153
With Magnyfycence thou shalte wonne.	176	Magnyfycence	1311
Cockes armes! Thou shalte kepe the brewhouse boule.	176	Magnyfycence	1321

SHAM

	Page	Title	Line
Yet shamfully thei slew hym; that sham most them befall.	30	Dol Dethe	49

SHAME

	Page	Title	Line
Fy, fy, for shame, ther hartis wer to faynt.	30	Dol Dethe	42
To slo suche a lord, alas, it was grete shame.	33	Dol Dethe	154
slo] 'sle' Marshe 1568			
Or ells with gret shame your game wylbe sene.	43	Balettys2	42
'By Cryste,' quod he, 'for it is shame to saye,	54	Bowge	300
God send them sorowe and shame!	78	Phy Sparrow	277
In maner half with shame;	89	Phy Sparrow	713
I trust it is no shame,	94	Phy Sparrow	889
Why shuld she take shame	103	Phy Sparrow	1284
So out of frame, /So voyde of shame,	116	Ag Scottes	38
That all the warlde wyll spye your shame.	132	Garnesche5	111
But men take upon theim nowe all the shame	139	Ven Tongues	61
He might be sure to have shame ynough.	139	Ven Tongues	78
It were a shame, to God I make an othe,	144	Magnyfycence	145
I wolde be rulyd and I myght for shame.	147	Magnyfycence	235
'A lorde a negarde, it is a shame.'	151	Magnyfycence	388
Tushe, a strawe! It is a shame	155	Magnyfycence	549
Thynke I not so, quod he. Ellys have I shame,	175	Magnyfycence	1254
Crafty Conveyaunce can cloke hymselfe frome shame,	178	Magnyfycence	1370
If ever I herde syke another, God gyve me shame.	192	Magnyfycence	1833
Nowe dare he not for shame loke one in the face.	193	Magnyfycence	1891
Better it is to begge than to be hangyd with shame.	198	Magnyfycence	2039
They thynke it no shame to robbe and stele;	198	Magnyfycence	2042
For worldly shame I wax bothe wanne and bloo.	198	Magnyfycence	2054
Tyll, as ye se many tymes, they shame all theyr kynne.	201	Magnyfycence	2144
Magnyfycence I was, whom ye have brought to shame.	204	Magnyfycence	2241
Truth it is, syr; for after he wrought me moch shame,	209	Magnyfycence	2444
Jhesus preserve you frome endlesse wo and shame.	214	Magnyfycence	2572
Sayd Elynour, 'For shame!'	227	El Rummynge	510
Alas, for very shame,	253	Collyn Clout	275
Begon, and now with shame,	256	Collyn Clout	388
To do shame, they have no shame;	275	Collyn Clout	1141
To do shame, they have no shame;	275	Collyn Clout	1141
But to wryte of his shame	305	Why Come Ye	1048

SHAMED — SHARPER

	Page	Title	Line
No shame to do amys;	305	Why Come Ye	1051
And whome ye love not ye wyll put to shame.	317	Garlande	178
But hailid they be homwarde with sorow and shame.	329	Garlande	622
For yet of women he never sayd shame,	334	Garlande	784
Why shulde she take shame	348	Garlande	1277
To your great lacke /And utter shame	360	Albany	46
Ye shall have shame and sorowe.	371	Albany	507
And to shame your selfe have brought.	376	Replycacion	58

SHAMED

Alasse that ever I sholde be so shamed!	196	Magnyfycence	1982
Thus are they undone and utterly shamed.	374	Replycacion	17
For ye were worldly shamed, /At Poules Crosse openly,	376	Replycacion	62

SHAMEFASTNES

The ruddy shamefastnes in her vysage fyll,	337	Garlande	888

SHAMEFULY

Duke of Albany, /Than shamefuly	360	Albany	51

SHAMEFULL

It may be regesterde of shamefull recorde.	30	Dol Dethe	28
And for he was a kyng, /The more shamefull rekenyng	121	Ag Scottes2	32
As thou, wyth shamefull deth!'	223	El Rummynge	346

SHAMEFULLY

Eschines, whiche was not shamefully confutid	316	Garlande	157
With Wofully Arayd and Shamefully Betrayd;	352	Garlande	1418
For shamefully ye have wrought,	376	Replycacion	57
Confessyng howe ye dyde lye /In prechyng shamefully.	377	Replycacion	91

SHAMELES

Nor he shall not be shameles;	62	Hauke	40
Shameles, and mercyles, /Incorrigible and insaciate;	276	Collyn Clout	1178

SHAMETH

It shameth all your noughty nacyon,	117	Ag Scottes	56

SHAMFULL

So prodigall expence, and so shamfull reconyng;	244	Speke Parott	458
Is nat this a shamfull scorne	276	Collyn Clout	1200
Your cankarde cowardnesse /And your shamfull doublenesse.	368	Albany	362

SHAMFULLY

Yet shamfully thei slew hym; that sham most them befall.	30	Dol Dethe	49
What man, remembring how shamfully he was slayn,	32	Dol Dethe	111
So shamfully to me, theyr mayster, to aproche,	205	Magnyfycence	2279
And shamfully you ascrye,	255	Collyn Clout	335
Holy churche is bruted /And shamfully confuted.	258	Collyn Clout	488
But they have enterprysed /And shamfully surmysed	261	Collyn Clout	582
Lo, for to do shamfully	305	Why Come Ye	1046
Lo] 'Soo' MS Rawlinson C. 813			
To be shamfully named!	305	Why Come Ye	1053
named] 'name' Marshe 1568			
lyke a cowarde knyght, ran awaye shamfully	359	Albany	1

SHAMYD

For though he were venquesshid, yet was he not shamyd:	316	Garlande	161
For] 'Sithe' MS Cotton Vitellius E.x			

SHAMLES

So shamles and so vicyous,	290	Why Come Ye	462
and] 'an' †Kele 1545.3			

SHAMLESSE

Careles and shamlesse, /Thriftles and gracelesse	304	Why Come Ye	1020
Careles] 'Marcyles' MS Rawlinson C. 813			
Nor yet shall scape shamlesse.	309	Why Come Ye2	5
shall] not in MS Rawlinson C. 813			

SHANKKES

Yor wynde-schakyn shankkes, yor longe *lothy legges,	122	Garneschel	29
*lothy] 'lothly' Scattergood			

SHAP

Be sumdele lyke in forme and shap,	36	Coystrownel	9
With, 'Fy, cover thy shap	227	El Rummynge	507
thy] 'the' Kynge & Marche 1554, Day 1560, Marshe 1568			

SHARE

Woo is that purse that ye shall share!	156	Magnyfycence	587
What hast thou gotted, in faythe, to thy share?	201	Magnyfycence	2162
That she thyder bare /To pay for her share.	228	El Rummynge	546
Spende moche of theyr share	251	Collyn Clout	176

SHARP

Hys musyk withoute mesure, to sharp is hys my;	37	Coystrownel	25
Ryght so a sharp fansy must be founde	155	Magnyfycence	553
With sharp twynkyng trebelles	259	Collyn Clout	491

SHARPE

Now Phebus me ken /To sharpe my pen,	96	Phy Sparrow	971
Agaynst you gave so sharpe a shower,	119	Ag Scottes	133
For lyke as mustarde is sharpe of taste	155	Magnyfycence	552
Her naylys sharpe as tenter-hokys!	168	Magnyfycence	1001
And quyckely your appetytes to sharpe and adresse;	183	Magnyfycence	1549
That you hath punysshed with his sharpe rod.	207	Magnyfycence	2350
My penne nowe wyll I sharpe,	259	Collyn Clout	489
I me determynyd for to sharpe my pen,	335	Garlande	823

SHARPELY

Sharpely commaundynge eche man holde hys pece.	47	Bowge	47

SHARPER

Are sharper then swordes, sturdier then stones.	138	Ven Tongues	50
Sharper then raysors, that shave and cut throtes,	138	Ven Tongues	51

SHARPLY —SHE   Page   Title   Line

SHARPLY
	Page	Title	Line
That Goddes grace hath vexed you sharply	207	Magnyfycence	2352

SHAVE
	Page	Title	Line
By Goddis syde, my sworde thy berde shall shave!	55	Bowge	339
Sharper then raysors, that shave and cut throtes,	138	Ven Tongues	51
Another bade shave halfe my berde;	150	Magnyfycence	355
And wyth a brystell of a bore his berde dyd I shave.	192	Magnyfycence	1832

SHAVEN
	Page	Title	Line
For Peter of Westminster hath shaven thy beard.	358	Couplet	2

SHAVYN
	Page	Title	Line
Shavyn and shorne, /And all threde bare worne!	304	Why Come Ye	1028

SHAVYNGE
	Page	Title	Line
With pollynge and shavynge,	281	Why Come Ye	100

SHE
	Page	Title	Line
'Ly styll', quod she, 'my paramoure,	41	Balettys1	3
She cheryshed hym both cheke and chyn	42	Balettys1	9
She left hym slepyng and stale away,	42	Balettys1	14
She sparyd not to wete her fete.	42	Balettys1	16
She wadyd over, she found a man	42	Balettys1	17
She wadyd over, she found a man	42	Balettys1	17
Thus after her cold she cought a hete.	42	Balettys1	19
'My lefe', she sayd, 'rowtyth in hys bed;	42	Balettys1	20
I wys, powle hachet, she bleryd thyne I!	42	Balettys1	28
She kykyth with her kalkyns and keylyth with a clench;	43	Balettys2	23
She goyth wyde behynde and hewyth never a dele:	43	Balettys2	24
Yet shall she never oute of remembraunce,	45	Balettys3	47
For one fals poynt she is wont to kepe in store,	45	Balettys4	4
For to illumyne, she sayde, I was to dulle,	46	Bowge	20
She kyste an anker, and there she laye at rode,	47	Bowge	39
kyste] 'keste' Wynkyn de Worde 1510, 'kast' Marshe 1568			
She kyste an anker, and there she laye at rode,	47	Bowge	39
kyste] 'keste' Wynkyn de Worde 1510, 'kast' Marshe 1568			
Marchauntes her borded to see what she had lode.	47	Bowge	40
lode] not in Marshe 1568			
She sayde she trowed that I had eten sause;	48	Bowge	72
had] not in †Wynkyn de Worde 1499, 1510			
She sayde she trowed that I had eten sause;	48	Bowge	72
had] not in †Wynkyn de Worde 1499, 1510			
She asked yf ever I dranke of saucys cuppe.	48	Bowge	73
Than asked she me, 'Syr, so God the spede,	48	Bowge	76
'What movyd she,' quod she, 'hydder to come?'	48	Bowge	78
And with that worde on me she gave a glome	48	Bowge	80
Full daynnously, and fro me she dyde fare,	48	Bowge	82
Desyre her name was, and so she me tolde,	48	Bowge	85
She that styreth the shyp, make her your frende.'	49	Bowge	107
'Forsothe,' quod she, 'how ever blowe the wynde,	49	Bowge	110
Whome she hateth shall over the see-boorde skyp.	49	Bowge	112
see-boorde] 'shyp borde' Marshe 1568			
Whome she loveth, of all plesyre is ryche	49	Bowge	113
Whyles she laugheth and hath luste for to playe.	49	Bowge	114
laugheth] 'laughed' †Wynkyn de Worde 1499			
Whome she hateth, she casteth in the dyche,	49	Bowge	115
hateth] 'hatch' †Wynkyn de Worde 1499, 'hateth' Wynkyn de Worde 1510, Marshe 1568			
Whome she hateth, she casteth in the dyche,	49	Bowge	115
hateth] 'hatch' †Wynkyn de Worde 1499, 'hateth' Wynkyn de Worde 1510, Marshe 1568			
For whan she *fronneth she thynketh to make a fray.	49	Bowge	116
*fronneth] 'frouneth' Wynkyn de Worde 1510, Marshe 1568			
For whan she *fronneth she thynketh to make a fray.	49	Bowge	116
*fronneth] 'frouneth' Wynkyn de Worde 1510, Marshe 1568			
She cherysshe[th] him, and hym she casseth awaye.'	49	Bowge	117
'cherysshed' †Wynkyn de Worde 1499, 1510, Marshe 1568; casseth] 'casteth' Wynkyn de Worde 1510, 'chasseth' Marshe 1568			
She cherysshe[th] him, and hym she casseth awaye.'	49	Bowge	117
'cherysshed' †Wynkyn de Worde 1499, 1510, Marshe 1568; casseth] 'casteth' Wynkyn de Worde 1510, 'chasseth' Marshe 1568			
'In fayth,' quod she, 'by Bone aventure.'	49	Bowge	119
Suwed to Fortune that she wold be theyre frynde.	49	Bowge	121
She promysed to us all she wolde be kynde;	49	Bowge	124
She promysed to us all she wolde be kynde;	49	Bowge	124
Of Bowge of Court she asketh what we wold have,	49	Bowge	125
And we asked favoure, and favour she us gave.	49	Bowge	126
Fortune theyr frende, with whome oft she dyde daunce:	50	Bowge	141
And, as she wyll, so shall our grete shyppe sayle.	50	Bowge	172
She hath gote me more money with her tayle	57	Bowge	405
Had I as good an hors as she is a mare,	57	Bowge	407
For she is trussed for to breke a launce.	57	Bowge	410
And in the holy place /She mutyd there a chase	63	Hauke	62
She had flowyn so oft,	63	Hauke	68
That on the rode loft /She perkyd her to rest.	63	Hauke	70
But she wold not bow.	63	Hauke	74
She had not wel endude;	63	Hauke	78
She was not clene ensaymed,	63	Hauke	79
She was not wel reclaymed,	63	Hauke	80
She loked as she had the frounce;	64	Hauke	85
frounce] 'fronnce' Kynge & Marche 1554, 'fronce' Day 1560			

SHE — SHE

	Page	Title	Line
She loked as she had the frounce;	64	Hauke	85
frounce] 'fronnce' Kynge & Marche 1554, 'fronce' Day 1560			
Whan she had lost her joye,	74	Phy Sparrow	110
Because that she dyd pas	75	Phy Sparrow	151
that] not in Marshe 1568			
Though she wolde pretende	75	Phy Sparrow	154
I trowe she coude not amende	75	Phy Sparrow	156
How she controlde /Her husbandes as she wolde,	87	Phy Sparrow	622
How she controlde /Her husbandes as she wolde,	87	Phy Sparrow	623
Some say she was lyght,	87	Phy Sparrow	645
For she dyd but fayne;	89	Phy Sparrow	695
She made hym to syng	89	Phy Sparrow	701
For she was quyte gone;	89	Phy Sparrow	706
She brought him in abusyon;	89	Phy Sparrow	708
She was moch to blame;	89	Phy Sparrow	710
Yet long tyme she ne knew	89	Phy Sparrow	727
That she was true and just,	90	Phy Sparrow	730
Ryght so she doth excede	93	Phy Sparrow	883
She floryssheth new and new	94	Phy Sparrow	896
She flourissheth new and new	96	Phy Sparrow	992
She may well represent	97	Phy Sparrow	1017
She florisheth new and new	97	Phy Sparrow	1025
She is the vyolet,	98	Phy Sparrow	1050
She floryssheth new and new	98	Phy Sparrow	1057
She flouryssheth new and new	98	Phy Sparrow	1086
She wold make to the lure	99	Phy Sparrow	1100
She made me sore amased	99	Phy Sparrow	1103
She flouryssheth new and new	99	Phy Sparrow	1110
Whan she lyst to avale,	99	Phy Sparrow	1117
Wherwyth my hand she strayned,	99	Phy Sparrow	1122
How she me had reclaymed,	99	Phy Sparrow	1125
She floryssheth new and new	100	Phy Sparrow	1139
She is playnly expresse	100	Phy Sparrow	1151
But she wolde chaunge his mood,	100	Phy Sparrow	1158
She flouryssheth new and new	100	Phy Sparrow	1164
So goodly as she dresses,	101	Phy Sparrow	1170
So properly she presses	101	Phy Sparrow	1171
How that she can were /Gorgiously her gere;	101	Phy Sparrow	1178
She florisheth new and new	101	Phy Sparrow	1188
She flouryssheth new and new	102	Phy Sparrow	1211
She doth excede and pas /In prudence dame Pallas;	102	Phy Sparrow	1229
She floryssheth new and new	102	Phy Sparrow	1234
She is worthy to be enrolde	103	Phy Sparrow	1258
Why shuld she be afrayde?	103	Phy Sparrow	1283
Why shuld she take shame	103	Phy Sparrow	1284
She raysed up in that stede	105	Phy Sparrow	1352
Regent is she, /Of poetes al,	112	Calliope	3
Yet is she fayne, /Voyde of disdayn,	112	Calliope	17
She callyd yow Syr Gy of Gaunt,	126	Garnesche3	70
Waywardly wrowght she hath in the,	130	Garnesche5	15
To daly with yow she had no lust,	131	Garnesche5	54
To counterfet she wyll assay	153	Magnyfycence	462
And be as praty as she may,	153	Magnyfycence	464
Me thynke she frowneth and lokys sowre.	166	Magnyfycence	924
She is made for the malarde fat.	166	Magnyfycence	926
Methynke she is well becked to catche a rat.	166	Magnyfycence	927
She is furred for the hete /All to the fete;	167	Magnyfycence	977
And howe styll she doth syt!	168	Magnyfycence	1003
By my trouthe, she hathe a grete hede.	169	Magnyfycence	1048
But she is lesse a grete dele	169	Magnyfycence	1052
That rubbed she must be on the gall	174	Magnyfycence	1232
What he sayth and she sayth to lay good ere,	175	Magnyfycence	1269
Upon a naked man and yf she scrat,	176	Magnyfycence	1298
So that there knowe no man but I and she.	177	Magnyfycence	1353
My hawke is rammysshe, and it happed that she ran —	191	Magnyfycence	1807
She pynched her pynyon, by God, and catched harme.	191	Magnyfycence	1810
Nowe she wyll laughe, forthwith she wyll frowne;	197	Magnyfycence	2024
Nowe she wyll laughe, forthwith she wyll frowne;	197	Magnyfycence	2024
She dawnsyth varyaunce with mutabylyte,	197	Magnyfycence	2026
I kyst her swete, and she kyssyd me;	198	Magnyfycence	2065
She is the bote of all my bale.	199	Magnyfycence	2070
She hath dyssayvyd me with her doublenesse.	201	Magnyfycence	2157
But she is not gryll,	214	El Rummynge	6
For she is somwhat sage	214	El Rummynge	7
She is ugly fayre:	215	El Rummynge	26
And she gray-hered;	215	El Rummynge	37
To se howe she is gumbed, /Fyngered and thumbed,	215	El Rummynge	40
And yet she wyll jet, /Lyke a joyly fet	215	El Rummynge	51
And yet I dare saye /She thynketh her selfe gaye	216	El Rummynge	65
Upon the holy daye, /Whan she doth her aray,	216	El Rummynge	67
Whan she goeth out /Her selfe for to shewe,	216	El Rummynge	80
She dryveth downe the dewe	216	El Rummynge	82
She hobles as she gose /With her blanket hose	216	El Rummynge	85
she gose] 'a gose' Day 1560, Marshe 1568			
She hobles as she gose /With her blanket hose	216	El Rummynge	85
she gose] 'a gose' Day 1560, Marshe 1568			
And, as men say, /She dwelt in Sothray,	217	El Rummynge	96
She is a tonnysh gyb;	217	El Rummynge	99

624

	Page	Title	Line
The devyll and she be syb.	217	El Rummynge	100
She breweth noppy ale,	217	El Rummynge	102
She leneth them on the same,	217	El Rummynge	131
on] 'of' Day 1560, Marshe 1568			
And somtyme she blennes	219	El Rummynge	201
'Behold,' she sayd, 'and se	220	El Rummynge	217
An huswyfe of trust /Whan she is athrust,	220	El Rummynge	254
She swered by the Rode of Rest,	221	El Rummynge	271
Without drynke she must dye;	221	El Rummynge	273
She ran in all the hast /Unbrased and unlast,	222	El Rummynge	319
But, Lorde, as she was testy, /Angry as a waspy!	222	El Rummynge	329
She began to yane and gaspy,	222	El Rummynge	331
began] 'gan' 1521 Fragment			
But she spake somwhat thycke,	223	El Rummynge	338
But she was a foule slut,	223	El Rummynge	340
Jone sayde she had eten a fyest.	223	El Rummynge	343
'By Chryst,' sayde she, 'thou lyest.	223	El Rummynge	344
And she was full of tales,	223	El Rummynge	352
She spake thus in her snout,	223	El Rummynge	363
spake thus] 'speketh this' †Lant 1545, Kynge & Marche 1554, Day 1560, Marshe 1568			
Snevelyng in her nose, /As though she had the pose.	223	El Rummynge	365
And, as she was drynkynge,	223	El Rummynge	370
She fyll in a wynkynge /With a barlyhood;	223	El Rummynge	371
She pyst where she stood.	223	El Rummynge	373
She pyst where she stood.	223	El Rummynge	373
Than began she to wepe,	223	El Rummynge	374
She founde therein no bones.	224	El Rummynge	381
bones] 'bornes' Day 1560			
She coulde not lye styllyl'	224	El Rummynge	391
But she had lost the stoppell.	224	El Rummynge	404
She cut of her sho-sole,	224	El Rummynge	405
She semed somdele seke,	225	El Rummynge	414
Than Margery Mylkeducke /Her kyrtell she dyd uptucke	225	El Rummynge	419
She was somwhat foule, /Crokenebbed lyke an oule;	225	El Rummynge	426
Crokenebbed] 'Croke necked' †Lant 1545, Kynge & Marche 1554, Day 1560, Marshe 1568			
And yet she brought her fees,	225	El Rummynge	428
She semed halfe a leche,	225	El Rummynge	447
She could to Burdeo[u] sayle;	226	El Rummynge	454
Burdeou] 'burde on' †Lant 1545, Kynge & Marche 1554, Day 1560, Marshe 1568			
And with good ale barme /She could make a charme	226	El Rummynge	456
She semed to be a wytch.	226	El Rummynge	458
She brought them in a wallet;	226	El Rummynge	461
She] 'Some' Day 1560, Marshe 1568			
She was a cumly callet.	226	El Rummynge	462
She was ugly hypped, /And ugly thycke-lypped	226	El Rummynge	468
She had her so guyded	226	El Rummynge	472
That she was therewithall /Into a palsey fall;	226	El Rummynge	474
She dranke so of the dregges,	226	El Rummynge	480
dregges] 'dragges' †Lant 1545, Kynge & Marche 1554, Day 1560			
All foggy fat she was;	226	El Rummynge	483
She had also the gout	226	El Rummynge	484
She dranke on the mash fat.	226	El Rummynge	491
She halted of a kybe,	227	El Rummynge	493
She yelled lyke a calfe!	227	El Rummynge	500
And as she at her dyd pluck,	227	El Rummynge	504
And] not in Day 1560, Marshe 1568; pluck] 'pulck' †Lant 1545			
Up she stert, halfe lame,	227	El Rummynge	512
She had a wyde wesant;	227	El Rummynge	517
wyde] 'wyse' Kynge & Marche 1554			
She was nothynge plesant;	227	El Rummynge	518
And she brought a bore pygge.	228	El Rummynge	539
Yet, or she went, she dranke,	228	El Rummynge	542
Yet, or she went, she dranke,	228	El Rummynge	542
That she thyder bare /To pay for her share.	228	El Rummynge	545
She sat downe in the place,	228	El Rummynge	551
'This ale,' sayd she, 'is noppy;	228	El Rummynge	557
'Dame Elynour,' sayde she,	228	El Rummynge	562
And wyth that she begynnes	228	El Rummynge	565
She swynged up a quarte /At ones for her parte.	228	El Rummynge	568
swynged] 'swinge' Marshe 1568			
Had she not hyed apace,	229	El Rummynge	572
She had defoyled the place.	229	El Rummynge	573
And began to paynty /As though she would faynty.	229	El Rummynge	585
She made it as koye /As a lege-de-moy;	229	El Rummynge	586
lege-de-moy] 'lege moy' †Lant 1545, Kynge & Marche 1554			
She was not halfe so wyse	229	El Rummynge	588
As she was pevysshe nyse.	229	El Rummynge	589
She sayde never a worde,	229	El Rummynge	590
We supposed, iwys, /That she rose to pys;	229	El Rummynge	595
To paye,' sayde she, 'God wote,	229	El Rummynge	601
Our Thomasen she doth trip, our Jenet she doth shayle;	233	Speke Parott	83
Our Thomasen she doth trip, our Jenet she doth shayle;	233	Speke Parott	83
Melpomene, that fayre mayde, she burneshed his beke:	236	Speke Parott	209
Lucina she wadythe among the watry floddes,	239	Speke Parott	285
Racell, rulye ragged, she is like to cache colde;	242	Speke Parott	401

SHED —SHERYFHOTTEN   Page   Title   Line

	Page	Title	Line
My lady nowe she ronnes,	256	Collyn Clout	390
What may she do therto?'	281	Why Come Ye	87
As goddesse inmortall she dyd represente;	313	Garlande	47
Cupyde hath stryken so that she ne wolde	320	Garlande	291
Transformyd was she into the laurell grene.	320	Garlande	294
'There shal he here what she wyl to hym say	325	Garlande	451
wyl to hym] 'to hym will' Marshe 1568			
A cry anone forthwith she made proclame,	325	Garlande	453
With that on me she kest her goodly loke.	327	Garlande	531
Under her arme, me thought, she hade a boke.	327	Garlande	532
'Come on with me,' she sayd, 'let us not stonde';	328	Garlande	559
And with that worde she toke me by the honde.	328	Garlande	560
And then she sayd, 'Whylis we have tyme and space	328	Garlande	563
Into a felde she brought me wyde and large,	328	Garlande	568
To walke on this walle she bed I sholde not stint;	328	Garlande	571
'Go softly,' she sayd, 'the stones be full glint.'	328	Garlande	572
She went before, and bad me take good holde;	328	Garlande	573
Wherto she answeryd, and brevely me tolde	328	Garlande	576
'Theis yatis,' she sayd, 'which that ye beholde,	328	Garlande	579
And seryously she shewyd me ther denominacyons.	328	Garlande	581
'What yate call ye this?' And she sayd, 'Anglea'.	328	Garlande	588
yate] 'gate' Marshe 1568			
'Forsothe,' quod she, 'theys be haskardis and rebawdis,	329	Garlande	607
haskardis] 'hastardis' †Fakes 1523			
She bet up a fyre with the sparkis full kene	330	Garlande	669
Of somer, so formally she fotid the daunce.	331	Garlande	686
She brought me to a goodly chaumber of astate,	333	Garlande	768
to] 'into' MS Cotton Vitellius E.x			
Come forth, jentylwomen, I pray you,' she sayd,	334	Garlande	773
She to whowchesafe me to informe and ken;	335	Garlande	825
That of Aconcyus whan she founde the byll	337	Garlande	886
In her bosome, lorde, how she was afrayd!	337	Garlande	887
how] not in MS Cotton Vitellius E.x			
She wonderyd, me thought, at my laurell grene;	343	Garlande	1116
She loked hawtly, and gave on me a glum.	344	Garlande	1117
For eche man herkynde what she wolde to me say;	344	Garlande	1119
wolde to me] 'to me wold' MS Cotton Vitellius E.x			
Forthwith she commaundid I shulde take my place.	344	Garlande	1142
'Be mirry,' she sayd, 'be not afferde a whit,	344	Garlande	1145
So then commaundid she was upon this	344	Garlande	1147
To shew her boke; and she sayd, 'Here it is.'	344	Garlande	1148
Was wrytin; and so she did her spede,	345	Garlande	1168
Lorde, how she made moche of her gentyll birth!	346	Garlande	1202
Go she never so gingirly, her honesty is gone away.	346	Garlande	1204
Wonder is to wryte what wrenchis she wrowght,	346	Garlande	1207
With pitche she patchid her pitcher shuld not crase;	346	Garlande	1209
Why shulde she be afrayd?	348	Garlande	1276
Why shulde she take shame	348	Garlande	1277
She raysed up in that stede	350	Garlande	1345
What myght she say? What myght he do therto?	351	Garlande	1395
How Dame Minerva first found the Olyve Tre, she red	351	Garlande	1404
And wele wotith the cat whos berde she likkith.	352	Garlande	1438
'Nay, sir' she sayd, 'what so in this place	353	Garlande	1481
But when of the laurell she made rehersall,	354	Garlande	1503
Your madnesse she attamed;	376	Replycacion	61

SHED
His corage manly, yet ther he shed his bloode.	32	Dol Dethe	103

SHEDDYNGE
Here shalbe not great sheddynge of blode.	203	Magnyfycence	2207

SHELDE
He was your chyfteyne, your shelde, your chef defens,	30	Dol Dethe	57
For yf they had occupied ther spere and ther shelde	31	Dol Dethe	73
They say they had /And wan the felde /With spere and shelde!	116	Ag Scottes	16

SHELFE
'Moryshe myne owne shelfe,' the costermonger sayth;	233	Speke Parott	85

SHENE
With, 'my lady bryght and shene'.	304	Why Come Ye	1004
Luna that so bryght doth shene,	350	Garlande	1358

SHENT
For your untruth now ar ye shent.	118	Ag Scottes	124

SHEPE
Madionita Jetro, our Moyses kepyth his shepe;	234	Speke Parott	115
Howe they take no hede /Theyr sely shepe to fede,	248	Collyn Clout	77
Howe evyll theyr shepe fare.'	250	Collyn Clout	131
To wary and to kepe /From theyr goostly shepe,	250	Collyn Clout	155
Our shepe are shrewdly shorn,	281	Why Come Ye	92
Lyke a mayny of shepe	286	Why Come Ye	295
Youre carkas to kepe, /Lyke a sely shepe,	365	Albany	274
A shepe of Cottyswolde,	365	Albany	275

SHEPE COTE
As it were a gote /In a shepe cote,	365	Albany	266

SHEPIS TAYLYS
So braynles calvys hedes, so many shepis taylys;	245	Speke Parott	484

SHEPYS IE
When ye kyst a shepys ie,	125	Garnesche3	54

SHERYFHOTTEN
studyously dyvysed at Sheryfhotten Castell,	312	Garlande	1

SHERTES —SHYLL   Page   Title   Line

SHERTES
Your skynne that was wrapped in shertes of Raynes,   197   Magnyfycence   2016
SHET
Shet were the gatis; thei might wel knock and cal,   329   Garlande   604
SHETT
The Quene of Fame commaundid shett fast the boke,   354   Garlande   1510
SHEW
Thes sorowfulle ditis that I may shew expres.   29   Dol Dethe   21
Whos noble actis shew worsheply his name,   33   Dol Dethe   143
To shew me their devyse   74   Phy Sparrow   100
And shew now unto me   106   Phy Sparrow   1368
Ye shew ryght well what good ye can;   117   Ag Scottes   60
Alas, myn owne servauntys to shew me such reproche!   205   Magnyfycence   2277
And 'Da racionales' dare not shew his pate.   235   Speke Parott   175
'Of your demawnd shew me the content,   332   Garlande   721
And of your wyll the plainnes shew at large.'   332   Garlande   727
I coude shew you suche a presedent   342   Garlande   1083
   you] not in MS Cotton Vitellius E.x
To shew her boke; and she sayd, 'Here it is.'   344   Garlande   1148
And shew now unto me   350   Garlande   1361
Shew them that shall you rede   371   Albany   509
SHEWE
And ye nede ought, man, shewe to me your mynde,   50   Bowge   165
That I must shewe you moche of my counselle -   52   Bowge   207
To shewe you thynges that may not be disclosed.'   52   Bowge   217
Shewe me the ryght path   78   Phy Sparrow   246
Shewe forth, I pray you, here in what you intende.   141   Magnyfycence   40
To shewe parte of my wyt,   142   Magnyfycence   58
To shewe you playnly the trouth as I thynke.   147   Magnyfycence   253
Where was it delyvered you? Shewe unto me.   150   Magnyfycence   340
And shortly shewe you the hole substaunce.   158   Magnyfycence   638
'Though I shewe you curtesy, say not that I crave[d];   177   Magnyfycence   1351
   craved] 'crave' †Rastell & Treveris C 1530, B
Shewe us your mynde then, howe to do and what.   180   Magnyfycence   1435
Plesyth it your grace to shewe what I do shall?   182   Magnyfycence   1517
To shewe you my mynde myselfe I wyll avaunce,   182   Magnyfycence   1520
I wolde yet shewe you further of my consayte,   185   Magnyfycence   1591
Let se what ye say. Shewe it strayte.   185   Magnyfycence   1592
To shewe you my mynde I wolde have the lesse fere.   186   Magnyfycence   1646
For though we shewe you this in game and play,   195   Magnyfycence   1948
Herein I wyll aforse me to shewe you my mynde: 211   Magnyfycence   2483
Whan she goeth out /Her selfe for to shewe,   216   El Rummynge   81
And shewe hym that all the world dothe conjecte,   240   Speke Parott   327
He facithe owte at a flusshe with, 'Shewe, take all!'   243   Speke Parott   430
They shewe them polytyke   269   Collyn Clout   923
Or els wyll I /Evydently /Shewe as it is: 361   Albany   86
SHEWED
And shewed that in this arte I was not sure;   46   Bowge   19
   I] not in †Wynkyn de Worde 1510
And of his mynde he shewed me all and some.   52   Bowge   226
Unthryftynes in hym may well be shewed,   58   Bowge   416
   Unthryftynes] 'Unthryftnes' †Wynkyn de Worde 1499, 1510
And shewed your selfe dawes!   377   Replycacion   124
SHEWETH
Plinni sheweth all /In his Story Naturall,   85   Phy Sparrow   536
That sheweth yourselfe thus spedde in physyke?   156   Magnyfycence   556
SHEWID
Some shewid his salfe cundight, some shewid his charter,   326   Garlande   503
   salfe cundight] 'safeconduct' Marshe 1568;
   charter] 'chart' Marshe 1568
Some shewid his salfe cundight, some shewid his charter,   326   Garlande   503
   salfe cundight] 'safeconduct' Marshe 1568;
   charter] 'chart' Marshe 1568
SHEWYD
Now have I shewyd you part of your proud mynde;   38   Coystrowne1   67
So many bullys of pardon publysshed and shewyd;   246   Speke Parott   515
Why have the goddes shewyd me this cruelte,   321   Garlande   309
So finally, when they had shewyd there devyse,   324   Garlande   442
And seryously she shewyd me ther denominacyons.   328   Garlande   581
SHEWYNGE
Shewynge him Goddis lawis.   305   Why Come Ye   1060
SHEWYTH
Shewyth nowe adayes howe the worlde comberyd is,   213   Magnyfycence   2539
Shewyth wysdome to them that wysdome can take: 213   Magnyfycence   2554
SHIPPIS
What shippis are sailing to Scalis Malis,   139   Ven Tongues   65
SHYDERYD
With synnews wyderyd, /With bonys shyderyd,   39   Coystrowne3   13
SHYFT
Here was scant thryft /Whan they made suche shyft.   222   El Rummynge   302
SHYFTE
Shyfte now therwith, let see, as ye can,   48   Bowge   99
Nowe holde ye content, for there is none other shyfte.   180   Magnyfycence   1443
And all this shyfte they make   228   El Rummynge   533
SHYLDE
O goodly chyld /Of Mary mylde, /Then be oure shylde!   40   Coystrowne3   43
SHYLL
Or pescoddes they may shyll,   281   Why Come Ye   111

	Page	Title	Line
SHYN			
And had broken her shyn	227	El Rummynge	494
SHYNE			
In a trone whiche fer clerer dyde shyne	47	Bowge	60
clerer] 'clere' Marshe 1568			
Lyke Phebus beames shyne.	101	Phy Sparrow	1174
Luna that so bryght doth shyne,	105	Phy Sparrow	1365
And whan Lucina plenarly did shyne,	312	Garlande	6
plenarly] 'plenary' †Fakes 1523, Marshe 1568			
With balassis and charbuncles the borders did shyne;	345	Garlande	1166
SHYNED			
In that faculte which shyned as Phebus bright;	383	Replycacion	333
SHYP			
'Maysters', he sayde, 'the shyp that ye here see,	47	Bowge	48
She that styreth the shyp, make her your frende.'	49	Bowge	107
My shyp nowe wyll I stere	278	Collyn Clout	1259
stere] 'pere' Kele 1545.1, Marshe 1568, 'stere' MS Harley 2252			
Committyth all to God, and lettyth his shyp ryde;	335	Garlande	834
SHYPBORDE			
And as they came, the shypborde faste I hente,	61	Bowge	530
SHYPPE			
Me thoughte I sawe a shyppe, goodly of sayle,	47	Bowge	36
Fortune gydeth and ruleth all our shyppe.	49	Bowge	111
For, as me thoughte, in our shyppe I dyde see	49	Bowge	132
And, as she wyll, so shall our grete shyppe sayle.	50	Bowge	172
Than hath some shyppe that into Bordews sayle.	57	Bowge	406
Without our shyppe be sure, it is lykely to brast,	213	Magnyfycence	2562
The forecastell of my shyppe	277	Collyn Clout	1251
Your storme dryven shyppe I repared new,	327	Garlande	544
SHYPPED			
This royall chaffre that is shypped here	47	Bowge	54
SHYPPES			
Another tolde how shyppes wente to wrak.	326	Garlande	507
SHYRE			
From qui fuit aliquid to shyre shakynge nought.	176	Magnyfycence	1303
They are shyre shakyng nought!'	226	El Rummynge	466
SHYT			
Shyt thy purse, dawe, and do no cost.	174	Magnyfycence	1207
That inne, is now shyt up,	284	Why Come Ye	239
SHYTTEL-COCKE			
Nat worth a shyttel-cocke,	287	Why Come Ye	354
SHYTTELL			
They set nat by us a shyttell;	276	Collyn Clout	1185
shytell] 'whystell' Kele 1545.1, Marshe 1568, 'shetyll' MS Harley 2252			
SHO			
Here is nothynge but the bockyll of a sho,	171	Magnyfycence	1107
The gray goos for to sho?	251	Collyn Clout	197
And, 'Mocke hath lost her sho;	281	Why Come Ye	86
Though Jak sayd nay, yet Mok there loste her sho;	351	Garlande	1396
SHO CLOUT			
Some with a sho clout /Bynde theyr heddes about;	218	El Rummynge	143
SHODER			
Alas, they make me shoder,	248	Collyn Clout	68
SHOKE			
When thou shoke thi sword so noble a man to mar!	32	Dol Dethe	115
He shoke downe all the clothys,	63	Hauke	51
And with his forme foote he shoke forthe this wrytyng:	328	Garlande	595
The starry hevyn, me thought, shoke with the showte;	354	Garlande	1508
SHOLD			
To the right of his prince which shold not be withstand;	31	Dol Dethe	67
And he shold be bought /For golde and fee,	76	Phy Sparrow	195
Whych provyth well that measure shold have domnyon.	143	Magnyfycence	120
Dame Pallas commaundid that they shold me convay	325	Garlande	449
And where the two Trions a man shold aspy,	331	Garlande	699
Trions] 'Troons' †Fakes 1523			
SHOLDE			
Than sholde ye were there pressynge in a pace	47	Bowge	56
For and I studye sholde as ye doo nowe,	53	Bowge	242
What sholde I tell more of his rebaudrye?	56	Bowge	372
Sholde be set and sorted,	103	Phy Sparrow	1287
To tell you, syr, I dare not, leest I sholde be maskyd	141	Magnyfycence	30
God forbyd ye sholde be let	142	Magnyfycence	63
If lyberte sholde lepe and renne where he lyst	144	Magnyfycence	133
Measure with noblenesse sholde be alyde.	145	Magnyfycence	194
God forbede that it other wyse sholde be!	147	Magnyfycence	246
Largesse, that all lordes sholde love, syr, I hyght.	148	Magnyfycence	270
Sholde be your dwellynge, in my consyderacyon.	148	Magnyfycence	274
What! Sholde you pynche at a pecke of [gr]otes	151	Magnyfycence	384
grotes] 'otes' †Rastell & Treveris C 1530, B			
Monkys may not for drede that men sholde them se.	154	Magnyfycence	493
Crafty Conveyaunce, I sholde say, and I.	154	Magnyfycence	502
That we thre galauntes sholde be longe asonder.	154	Magnyfycence	511
And wolde that we sholde for hym go –	158	Magnyfycence	646
We had hym founde, we sholde hym brynge,	158	Magnyfycence	653
No, by the masse. What! Sholde I swere?	166	Magnyfycence	936
And teche them howe they sholde syt ydyll	174	Magnyfycence	1221

SHONE —SHOULD	Page	Title	Line

SHONE —SHOULD

```
What sholde a man do with you? Loke you under [k]ay?  . . . . .   180   Magnyfycence   1429
  kay]  'bay'  †Rastell & Treveris C 1530, B
Whether sholde welth be rulyd by lyberte, . . . . . . . . . . .   180   Magnyfycence   1431
Syr, as me semeth, ye sholde be rulyd be me. . . . . . . . . .    180   Magnyfycence   1433
For nowe, syrs, I am lyke as a prynce sholde be;  . . . . . . .   181   Magnyfycence   1457
What sholde ye do elles? Are not you a lorde? . . . . . . . . .   185   Magnyfycence   1606
I speke the softlyer because he sholde not wete. . . . . . . .    186   Magnyfycence   1654
So I wote not what he sholde do here. . . . . . . . . . . . . .   189   Magnyfycence   1741
Than is it done as it sholde be; . . . . . . . . . . . . . . .    189   Magnyfycence   1764
Flewe, I sholde say - in to an olde barne . . . . . . . . . . .   191   Magnyfycence   1808
Fy, fy, that ever I sholde be brought in this snare! . . . . .    196   Magnyfycence   1972
Alasse that ever I sholde be so shamed! . . . . . . . . . . . .   196   Magnyfycence   1982
Alasse! I wote not what I sholde pray. . . . . . . . . . . . .    196   Magnyfycence   1994
That ever noblenesse sholde lyve thus wretchydly! . . . . . . .   197   Magnyfycence   2021
With ye, mary, syrs, thus sholde it be: . . . . . . . . . . . .   198   Magnyfycence   2064
Thou sholde not scape, horson, but thou sholde dye. . . . . . .   202   Magnyfycence   2195
Thou sholde not scape, horson, but thou sholde dye. . . . . . .   202   Magnyfycence   2195
Redresse sholde be at the rekenynge in every accompte, . . . .    208   Magnyfycence   2413
That I sholde use largesse. Nay, syr, there a pause. . . . . .    209   Magnyfycence   2437
All thynges sholde be amended, . . . . . . . . . . . . . . . .    307   Why Come Ye    1111
That he so sholde be, me semith it sittyng, . . . . . . . . . .   316   Garlande        149
  it]  'it is' MS Cotton Vitellius E.x
With laureat tryumphe why Skelton sholde be crownde. . . . . .    318   Garlande        217
But what sholde I say? Ye wote what I entende, . . . . . . . .    324   Garlande        426
To walke on this walle she bed I sholde not stint; . . . . . .    328   Garlande        571
But if I sholde aquyte your kyndnes, . . . . . . . . . . . . .    342   Garlande       1062
SHONE
His eyen blereed, his face shone lyke a glas; . . . . . . . . .    56   Bowge           353
Her shone smered wyth talowe, . . . . . . . . . . . . . . . . .   216   El Rummynge      88
Some their hose, some their shone; . . . . . . . . . . . . . .    220   El Rummynge     248
Our royals that shone, . . . . . . . . . . . . . . . . . . . .    302   Why Come Ye     921
SHOO
Shoo the mockyssh mare; . . . . . . . . . . . . . . . . . . .     251   Collyn Clout    180
SHOP
Suche shredis of sentence, strowed in the shop . . . . . . . .    233   Speke Parott     92
SHOPPE
Ye, and when ye come out of the shoppe, . . . . . . . . . . .     204   Magnyfycence   2271
SHORN
Our shepe are shrewdly shorn, . . . . . . . . . . . . . . . .     281   Why Come Ye      92
SHORNE
Whan the noppe is rughe, it wolde be shorne. . . . . . . . . .    153   Magnyfycence    448
Shavyn and shorne, /And all threde bare worne! . . . . . . . .    304   Why Come Ye    1028
And whan ye were preestes shorne, . . . . . . . . . . . . . .     376   Replycacion      81
SHORT
With heles short and rounde. . . . . . . . . . . . . . . . . .    100   Phy Sparrow    1150
SHORTE
I herde her speke of you within shorte space, . . . . . . . .      50   Bowge           158
  shorte]  'a shorte' Wynkyn de Worde 1510
His gowne so shorte that it ne cover myghte . . . . . . . . .      56   Bowge           354
Of Kyrkeby Kendall was his shorte demye; . . . . . . . . . . .     56   Bowge           359
To claterynge, to chaterynge, to shorte, and to farre, . . . .    199   Magnyfycence   2096
And of their shorte nyghtes; he browght in his songe . . . . .    331   Garlande        703
The cheke and the nek but a shorte cast; . . . . . . . . . . .    351   Garlande       1401
For Sir William Lyle /Within shorte whyle, . . . . . . . . . .    360   Albany           39
In shorte sentens, /Of your pretens /What is the grounde . . .    361   Albany           79
Of your lande in shorte space. . . . . . . . . . . . . . . . .    371   Albany          502
SHORTELY
But to the poynte shortely to procede, . . . . . . . . . . . .     53   Bowge           246
Let us, therfore, shortely at a worde . . . . . . . . . . . .      54   Bowge           307
Your pleasure, syr shortely shall be done. . . . . . . . . . .    149   Magnyfycence    321
That thou shortely tell, . . . . . . . . . . . . . . . . . . .    350   Garlande       1360
SHORTEN
By myschefe to brevyate and shorten his dayes. . . . . . . . .    206   Magnyfycence   2338
SHORTLY
That thou shortly tell, . . . . . . . . . . . . . . . . . . .     105   Phy Sparrow    1367
I could make him shortly repent him for ever; . . . . . . . .     139   Ven Tongues      76
And shortly shewe you the hole substaunce. . . . . . . . . . .    158   Magnyfycence    638
We wyll se you shortly, one of us twayne. . . . . . . . . . .     159   Magnyfycence    686
SHO-SOLE
She cut of her sho-sole, . . . . . . . . . . . . . . . . . . .    224   El Rummynge     405
SHOT
To shote forthe his shot; . . . . . . . . . . . . . . . . . .     265   Collyn Clout    751
For we have spente our shot! . . . . . . . . . . . . . . . . .    282   Why Come Ye     127
SHOTE
Ye wante but a wylde flyeng bolte to shote at the buttes. . . .   148   Magnyfycence    294
To shote forthe his shot; . . . . . . . . . . . . . . . . . .     265   Collyn Clout    751
For to shote a crowe /At her tyrly tyrlowe; . . . . . . . . .     270   Collyn Clout    948
Shote anker, and lye at rode, . . . . . . . . . . . . . . . .     277   Collyn Clout   1255
They shote all at one marke: . . . . . . . . . . . . . . . . .    283   Why Come Ye     174
They shote all at that! . . . . . . . . . . . . . . . . . . .     283   Why Come Ye     176
  They]  'Thy'  †Kele 1545.3
They shote at him with crownes. . . . . . . . . . . . . . . .     283   Why Come Ye     178
SHOUER
Ageynst a stormy shouer. . . . . . . . . . . . . . . . . . . .    127   Garnesche3      147
SHOULD
Both worde and dede /Should be agrede /In noblenes: . . . . .     357   Garlande       1600
Full soone ye should miscary, . . . . . . . . . . . . . . . .     367   Albany          342
Trouthe should nat be subdude. . . . . . . . . . . . . . . . .    369   Albany          422
```

SHOULDE —SHULD

SHOULDE
	Page	Title	Line
But, whan they shoulde walke,	230	El Rummynge	613
For feare thou shoulde be slayne	365	Albany	247

SHOURE
Refresshyng myndys the Aprell shoure of rayne;	44	Balettys3	11
In every marciall shoure,	365	Albany	240

SHOVELAR
The shovelar with his brode bek;	82	Phy Sparrow	408

SHOVYNGE
With hevynge and shovynge, 'have in' and 'have oute';	319	Garlande	251

SHOVLL
The mattocke and the shovll	262	Collyn Clout	646

SHOWELL
That occupyed a showell,	293	Why Come Ye	560

SHOWER
Agaynst you gave so sharpe a shower,	119	Ag Scottes	133

SHOWLDER
from CRAFTY CONVEYAUNCE showlder.	173	Magnyfycence	SD

SHOWRE
Howe after a drought there fallyth a showre of rayne	141	Magnyfycence	12
Now clere wether, forthwith a stormy showre;	312	Garlande	12
After the Aprill showre;	340	Garlande	987

SHOWRES
Nowe must be storm ybeten with showres and raynes.	197	Magnyfycence	2017

SHOWRIS
What thynge occasionyd the showris of rayne,	331	Garlande	693

SHOWTE
With hogeous showte and cry.	63	Hauke	48
Thys fawconer then gan showte,	65	Hauke	119
then] not in Day 1560, Marshe 1568			
The starry hevyn, me thought, shoke with the showte;	354	Garlande	1508

SHREDIS
Suche shredis of sentence, strowed in the shop	233	Speke Parott	92

SHREUD
That is a shreud aray!	218	El Rummynge	163

SHREWDE
Est [suavis vago] with a shrewde face vilis imago.	172	Magnyfycence	1154
suavis vago] 'snaui snago' †Rastell & Treveris C 1530, B			
So myche crossyng and blyssyng and hym all be shrewde;	246	Speke Parott	516
They dyd us a shrewde turne,	285	Why Come Ye	269

SHREWDENES
I laughe at all shrewdenes, and lye at lyberte.	160	Magnyfycence	735

SHREWDLY
Redes shrewdly and spelles,	257	Collyn Clout	414
redes] 'rede' †Godfray 1531, Kele 1545.1, Marshe 1568			
Our shepe are shrewdly shorn,	281	Why Come Ye	92
Whiche shrewdly doth accorde!	294	Why Come Ye	621
This shrewdly accordis /To be a cupborde for lordys!	302	Why Come Ye	913
That speke fayre before the and shrewdly behynde.	329	Garlande	620

SHREWE
With dugges, dugges, dugges. /I shrewe thy Scottishe lugges,	366	Albany	292

SHREWED
That ye gyve shrewed counsell	255	Collyn Clout	358

SHREWES
Who deleth with shrewes hath nede to loke aboute!'	61	Bowge	525

SHRYMPES
For shrympes, and for pranys,	102	Phy Sparrow	1243
Ye pyke no shrympes nor pranes,	252	Collyn Clout	208

SHRYNE
And shryne your rotten bonys	255	Collyn Clout	346

SHRYNYD
Wher thou xulddst have bene shrynyd;	128	Garnesche3	175

SHRYNKE
And this the cause doth shrynke.	66	Hauke	159

SHRYVE
To you oonly, me thynke, I durste shryve me;	52	Bowge	215
To shryve, assoyle, and to reles	268	Collyn Clout	875

SHROUDLY
By God, there be some that be shroudly towchyd.	175	Magnyfycence	1277
It may wele ryme, but shroudly it doth accorde,	346	Garlande	1210

SHROW
Lerne or be lewde, I shrow thy face.	132	Garnesche5	127

SHROWDE
That I counterfeyted you underneth a shrowde?	155	Magnyfycence	532
In lyke maner of wyse a myst did us shrowde;	330	Garlande	647

SHROWDES
Le tonsan de Jason is lodgid among the shrowdes;	239	Speke Parott	287

SHUDDER
To shudder and to shake	303	Why Come Ye	980

SHULD
What, shuld I flatter? What, shulde I glose or paynt?	30	Dol Dethe	41
Where was your wit and reson ye shuld have had?	30	Dol Dethe	52
your] 'ys' †MS Royal 18 D.ii			
I wold you coud! Then shuld ye se, mastres,	44	Balettys3	40
Wherto shuld I rehers /The sentens of my vers?	68	Hauke	246
He shuld over the see	76	Phy Sparrow	197
My sparowe than shuld be quycke	77	Phy Sparrow	205
But whereto shuld I /Lenger morne or crye?	86	Phy Sparrow	594

SHULDE —SINGLAR   Page   Title   Line

	Page	Title	Line
Alas, what shuld I fayne?	97	Phy Sparrow	1011
Wherto shuld I disclose	101	Phy Sparrow	1175
Why shuld she be afrayde?	103	Phy Sparrow	1283
Why shuld she take shame	103	Phy Sparrow	1284
The Philistinis shuld hym ascry,	105	Phy Sparrow	1358
And the next day he shuld dye,	105	Phy Sparrow	1359
Regardyd ye shuld your lord, your brother.	118	Ag Scottes	106
ye] 'you' Day 1560, Marshe 1568			
Of him shuld men report,	121	Ag Scottes2	33
How shuld a fals lying tung then be rewarded?	137	Ven Tongues	2
Such tunges shuld be torne out by the harde rootes,	137	Ven Tongues	3
These words shuld be more weyed,	265	Collyn Clout	769
These words] 'Those words' Marshe 1568, 'This' MS Harley 2252			
But they wolde no man shuld them blame.	275	Collyn Clout	1142
With pitche she patchid her pitcher shuld not crase;	346	Garlande	1209
To fayre maistres Anne that shuld have be sent,	347	Garlande	1241
By Candelmes day what wedder shuld holde;	352	Garlande	1442
What shuld I do but take it in gre?	353	Garlande	1487
Wherto shuld I more speke	366	Albany	302
SHULDE			
What, shuld I flatter? What, shulde I glose or paynt?	30	Dol Dethe	41
His hawke shulde pray and fede /Upon a pigeons maw.	63	Hauke	56
But whereto shulde I note	100	Phy Sparrow	1145
Wherefore shulde I be blamed	103	Phy Sparrow	1255
Shulde be lanternes of lyght.	257	Collyn Clout	440
Shulde open the brode gates	263	Collyn Clout	691
The whiche shulde be /Bothe franke and free,	264	Collyn Clout	710
That wolde it shulde be noted	265	Collyn Clout	754
How scrypture shulde be coted,	265	Collyn Clout	755
Shulde be imprynted better	265	Collyn Clout	761
And better shulde remayne /Amonge the people playne,	265	Collyn Clout	772
Wherfore shulde I be blamed?	274	Collyn Clout	1112
be] not in Marshe 1568			
We shulde nat ryse agayne	277	Collyn Clout	1232
For that no man shulde se	277	Collyn Clout	1240
He shulde be hyder brought;	287	Why Come Ye	351
That of shulde go his hede,	288	Why Come Ye	358
The kynges courte /Shulde have the excellence;	289	Why Come Ye	407
Shulde this man of suche mode	293	Why Come Ye	579
All noble men shulde outface,	294	Why Come Ye	623
Whan they with hym shulde mell,	295	Why Come Ye	649
Such a casuelte shulde be sene	297	Why Come Ye	747
Or suche chaunce shulde fall /Unto our cardynall!	297	Why Come Ye	748
Any man shulde be /In perplexyte /Of dyspleasure;	300	Why Come Ye	843
That in my courte Skelton shulde have a place,	313	Garlande	59
Out of my bokis full sone I shulde hym rase;	314	Garlande	72
Or wherto shulde he have the prerogatyve,	315	Garlande	117
the] 'that' MS Cotton Vitellius E.x			
For how shulde Cato els be callyd wyse,	315	Garlande	123
Whiche soverenly in honoure shulde excell;	317	Garlande	199
Withoute deservynge shulde have the best game.	318	Garlande	221
All orators and poetis shulde thider go before,	325	Garlande	454
Forthwith she commaundid I shulde take my place.	344	Garlande	1142
Caliope poynted me where I shulde sit.	344	Garlande	1143
Item the Boke how Men Shulde Fle Synne;	345	Garlande	1173
Why shulde she be afrayd?	348	Garlande	1276
Why shulde she take shame	348	Garlande	1277
Shulde be set and sortyd, /To be matriculate	348	Garlande	1280
The Phillistinis shulde hym askry,	350	Garlande	1351
And the next day he shulde dye,	350	Garlande	1352
A jentyll hownde shulde never play the kur.	352	Garlande	1436
Shulde bring about that thing.	367	Albany	335
What shulde I prosecute,	378	Replycacion	158
What shulde I recken more?	379	Replycacion	181
Ye shulde take further payne /To resorte agayne	379	Replycacion	201
SHUREWLYE			
And the date of the Devyll dothe shurewlye accord.	244	Speke Parott	445
SHURVY			
Tawny, tannyd, and shurvy;	127	Garnesche3	132
SICULUS			
Diodorus Siculus of my translacyon	354	Garlande	1498
SIGH			
I wayle, I wepe, I sobbe, I sigh ful sore	29	Dol Dethe	1
SIGHT			
Treytory and treson he bannesht ought of sight.	33	Dol Dethe	151
That durst nat byde the sight	364	Albany	236
SILKE			
Whose name enrolde /With silke and golde	112	Calliope	10
The silke, the golde, the flowris fresshe to syght,	343	Garlande	1111
SILOGISME			
Neyther frame a silogisme in phrisesomorum	235	Speke Parott	148
SILOGISTICALL			
In your dialeticall /And principles silogisticall,	377	Replycacion	97
SIMONIA			
Welcome dame Simonia, /With dame Castrimergia,	284	Why Come Ye	215
SINGLAR			
Falsly to slo ther moste singlar goode lorde?	30	Dol Dethe	27
slo] 'slee' Marshe 1568			

	Page	Title	Line

SINGULAR
The bankis enturfid with singular solas, ... 330 Garlande 655
SINNES
God sende him sorowe for his sinnes! . . . . 309 Why Come Ye 1201
SINODALS
Or holy sinodals, /Or els provincyals, ... 65 Hauke 132
SION
Sion is in sadness, Rachell ruly doth loke; . . . . 234 Speke Parott 114
SIR
Sir dominus vobiscum, ... 69 Hauke 286
Ye wantyd wyt, sir, at a worde; . . . . 119 Ag Scottes 147
Dundas, sir knave, ... 136 Dundas 42
With a frere of Fraunce men call Sir Gagwyne, ... 322 Garlande 374
With, 'Sir, I pray you, a lytyll tyme stande backe, ... 326 Garlande 505
And, sir, amonge all me thought I saw twaine, ... 329 Garlande 633
'Nay, sir' she sayd, 'what so in this place . . . . 353 Garlande 1481
For Sir William Lyle /Within shorte whyle, ... 360 Albany 38
Sir Duke of Albany, /Right inconvenyently . . . . 363 Albany 188
Syr drake of the lake, sir ducke . . . . 364 Albany 223
Sir Dunkan, ye dared. . . . . 365 Albany 271
But hyde the, Sir Topias, ... 366 Albany 287
Adue, nowe, Sir Wrig-wrag! /Adue, Sir Dalyrag! . . . . 366 Albany 296
Adue, nowe, Sir Wrig-wrag! /Adue, Sir Dalyrag! . . . . 366 Albany 297
Harke yet, Sir Duke, a worde . . . . 367 Albany 318
Sir Dunkan, in the devill waye, ... 367 Albany 330
With Sir Fraunces of Fraunce . . . . 371 Albany 497
SIRUS
This Naman Sirus, /So fell and so irous, ... 308 Why Come Ye 1166
Sirus] 'tyrus' MS Rawlinson C. 813
SIT
I sawe maister Newton sit with his compas, ... 343 Garlande 1096
Caliope poynted me where I shulde sit. . . . . 344 Garlande 1143
SITH
But sith he hath tastid of the sugred pocioun . . . . 314 Garlande 73
Sith he is slaundred for defaut of konnyng?' . . . . 316 Garlande 140
Sith I contryvyd first princyples medycynable? . . . . 321 Garlande 310
But sith I have lost now that I entended, ... 321 Garlande 318
Sith ye must nedis afforce it by pretence . . . . 335 Garlande 817
Sith mistres Jane Haiset . . . . 339 Garlande 968
'My frende, sith ye ar before us here present . . . . 344 Garlande 1121
SITHE
Sithe ye have me chalyngyd, Master Garnesche, ... 121 Garneschel 1
SITTYNG
That he so sholde be, me semith it sittyng, ... 316 Garlande 149
it] 'it is' MS Cotton Vitellius E.x
SITTYNGE
It is sittynge that ye must hym correct.' . . . . 314 Garlande 77
SYAR
Syrus, that soleme syar of Babylon, ... 181 Magnyfycence 1473
SYB
The devyll and she be syb. . . . . 217 El Rummynge 100
SYBBYLL
'Soft,' quod one hyght Sybbyll, ... 228 El Rummynge 549
hyght] 'high' Day 1560, Marshe 1568
SYBLY
Dame Sybly our abbesse, ... 256 Collyn Clout 391
SYCKE
And feleth hymselfe sycke, ... 274 Collyn Clout 1123
SYCKYLL
And make hereof a syckyll or a saw, ... 71 Hauke 333
SYDE
He was envyronde aboute on every syde . . . . 32 Dol Dethe 99
Nay, naye, be sure, whyles I am on your syde . . . . 50 Bowge 169
He set the arme proudly under the syde, ... 55 Bowge 321
By Goddis syde, my sworde thy berde shall shave! . . . . . . 55 Bowge 339
And by his syde his whynarde and his pouche, ... 56 Bowge 363
Now renne muste I to the stewys syde . . . . 57 Bowge 400
His hode was syde, his cope was roset graye; . . . . 58 Bowge 440
Of cokoldry syde, ... 83 Phy Sparrow 475
On that syde, on thys syde thou dost gasy, ... 130 Garnesche5 29
On that syde, on thys syde thou dost gasy, ... 130 Garnesche5 29
Howe so? By God, at the see syde, ... 150 Magnyfycence 346
On this halfe and on every syde . . . . 168 Magnyfycence 1020
Some start in at the backe syde, ... 221 El Rummynge 263
Honowre with renowne wyll ren on that syde. . . . . 234 Speke Parott 140
on] 'of' Kynge & Marche 1554, Day 1560, Marshe 1568
Borne up on every syde . . . . 284 Why Come Ye 203
A wonderfull noyse, and on every syde . . . . 319 Garlande 247
There birdis on the brere sange on every syde, ... 330 Garlande 653
SYDED
Like an onyon syded, /Lyke tan ledder hyded. . . . . 226 El Rummynge 470
SYDES
By Goddis sydes, syns I her thyder broughte, ... 57 Bowge 404
With sydes longe and streyte; . . . . 100 Phy Sparrow 1129
Well argued and surely on bothe sydes. . . . . 176 Magnyfycence 1304
SYDE-SADELL
And with a syde-sadell; . . . . 224 El Rummynge 385

SYDONY —SYMKYN　　　　　　　　　　　　　　　　　　　　Page　　Title　　　　Line

SYDONY
From Sydony to the mount Olympyan, ...　327　Garlande　　　552
SYDRAKE
And sadlye salute owur solen Syre Sydrake, ...　240　Speke Parott　326
SYER
Sym Sadylgose was my syer, and Dawcocke my dame. . . . .　192　Magnyfycence　1834
He is suche a grym syer, ...　303　Why Come Ye　　987
SYERS
By my syers soule, I fele no rayne. . . . .　170　Magnyfycence　1087
SYGH
Well may thou sygh, well may thou grone, ...　 42　Balettys1　　　 26
But sygh, and sorowe, and wysshe my selfe dede. . . . .　205　Magnyfycence　2306
SYGHE
A, so! That syghe was farre fet! . . . .　199　Magnyfycence　2071
SYGHED
I syghed and I sobbed, ...　 73　Phy Sparrow　　 50
SYGHYNGE
O syghynge sorowe, O thoughtfull mysere! . . . .　198　Magnyfycence　2050
SYGHT
Our kynge of England for to syght, ...　117　Ag Scottes　　 53
　　syght] 'fight' Day 1560, Marshe 1568
That measure shall nevere departe from my syght. . . . .　145　Magnyfycence　 190
A lurdayne lyke a lorde to [s]yght, ...　152　Magnyfycence　 418
　　syght] 'fyght' †Rastell & Treveris C 1530, B
For as sone as you come in Magnyfycence syght . . . .　176　Magnyfycence　1314
Have hym hens, I say, out of my syght! . . . .　188　Magnyfycence　1723
That thou canst not have never mercy in his syght. . . . . . .　205　Magnyfycence　2303
And ever let the drede of God be in your syght, ...　211　Magnyfycence　2498
In the peoples syght, ...　264　Collyn Clout　 695
Arectyng my syght toward the zodyake, ...　312　Garlande　　　　1
What he hath done, let it be brought to syght. . . . .　318　Garlande　　　230
Then furthermore aboute me my syght I revolde, ...　330　Garlande　　　664
Castyng my syght the chambre aboute, ...　343　Garlande　　　1093
The silke, the golde, the flowris fresshe to syght, ...　343　Garlande　　　1111
Whiche redde on still, as it cam to her syght, ...　354　Garlande　　　1493
SYGHTE
That he loked pale as asshes to my syghte. . . . .　 54　Bowge　　　　　293
And as I stode and kyste asyde my syghte, ...　 58　Bowge　　　　　418
　　kyste] 'caste' Marshe 1568
SYGHTES
Wherwith the Sodomites /Lost theyr inward syghtes. . . . . . .　291　Why Come Ye　　471
SYGNE
Under a notaries sygne . . . .　266　Collyn Clout　 807
　　a] 'an' Kele 1545.1, 'a' MS Harley 2252
The Sygne of the Cardynall Hat, ...　284　Why Come Ye　　238
SYGNES
The sygnes xii for to beholde a farre, ...　312　Garlande　　　　2
SYKE
Cockys bonys! Herde ye ever syke another? . . . .　170　Magnyfycence　1090
If ever I herde syke another, God gyve me shame. . . . .　192　Magnyfycence　1833
SYKERNESSE
In her promyse there is no sykernesse, ...　197　Magnyfycence　2028
So in this worlde there is no sykernesse, ...　212　Magnyfycence　2522
SYLENCE
And putteth them to sylence . . . .　305　Why Come Ye　 1064
SYLK
Well gydyng ther glowtonn to kepe streit theyr sylk, ...　334　Garlande　　　795
　　ther] 'the' MS Cotton Vitellius E.x
With, 'Reche me that skane of tewly sylk'; . . . .　334　Garlande　　　798
SYLKE
Whiche sat behynde a tra[v]es of sylke fyne, ...　 47　Bowge　　　　　 58
　　traves] 'tranes' †Wynkyn de Worde 1499, 1510, Marshe 1568
To sowe with stytchis of sylke . . . .　 77　Phy Sparrow　　212
And handes soft as sylke, ...　 99　Phy Sparrow　 1119
With curteyns of sylke, ye were wonte to be drawe; . . . . . .　197　Magnyfycence　2014
　　curteyns of sylke] 'courtely sylkes' †Rastell & Treveris 1530B
Some brought a sylke lace, ...　227　El Rummynge　　528
Theyr tabertes of fyne sylke; . . . .　254　Collyn Clout　 316
With sylke and golde. . . . .　342　Garlande　　　1075
SYLKES
For sylkes are wane. . . . .　302　Why Come Ye　　920
SYLLORYM
Alumbek sodyldym syllorym ben! . . . .　 37　Coystrownel　　 16
SYLT
Ensowkid with sylt of the myry [w]ose, ...　312　Garlande　　　 23
　　sylt] 'fylt' †Fakes 1523; wose] 'mose' †Fakes 1523
SYLVER
As for his plate of sylver and suche trasshe, ...　201　Magnyfycence　2164
A cage curyowsly carven, with sylver pynne, ...　231　Speke Parott　　8
Men say, for sylver and golde, ...　254　Collyn Clout　 289
From sylver to brasse, ...　301　Why Come Ye　　903
SYM
Knowe hym, syr, quod he. Yes, by Saynt Sym! . . . .　156　Magnyfycence　 585
Sym Sadylgose was my syer, and Dawcocke my dame. . . . .　192　Magnyfycence　1834
Subtyle Sym Sly /With madde foly. . . . .　300　Why Come Ye　　856
　　Sym Sly] 'Symonye' †Kele 1545.3
SYMKYN
Symkyn Tytyvell and Pers Pykthanke. . . . .　175　Magnyfycence　1267

633

SYMONIAKE —SYNNYS   Page   Title   Line

SYMONIAKE
For a symoniake /Is but a hermoniake;   254   Collyn Clout   296
SYMONIDES
Pyndarus and [S]ymonides   90   Phy Sparrow   765
  Symonides] 'Dymonides' †Kele 1545.2, Wyght 1553,
  Kitson 1560.6, Marshe 1568
Resembled to Symonides, that poete lyricall   383   Replycacion   331
  Symonides] 'Symphonides' †Pynson 1528
SYMONY
Of symony, men say, ...   254   Collyn Clout   299
SYMPER-THE-COCKET
With symper-the-cocket.   215   El Rummynge   55
SYMPLENESSE
His symplenesse resytynge, /Remordynge and bytynge, ...   305   Why Come Ye   1057
SYMPLYCYTE
Farewell benygnyte, /Farewell symplycyte, ...   261   Collyn Clout   590
SYN
Which men the viii dedly syn call.   36   Coystrowne1   5
  syn] 'sins' Marshe 1568
He had forgoten all dedely syn.   42   Balettys1   11
God wot, we thought no syn -   76   Phy Sparrow   168
To forget deadly syn   98   Phy Sparrow   1081
And I bequethe hym sorowe for his syn.   204   Magnyfycence   2256
Fyrst, from your magnyfycence syn must be abjectyd;   211   Magnyfycence   2484
Was nevyr suche a senatour syn Crystes Incarnacion.   240   Speke Parott   337
Syn Dewcalyons flodde, I make the faste and sure.   246   Speke Parott   511
SYNAMUM
Swete synamum styckis and pleris cum musco!   235   Speke Parott   185
SYNG
To syng Sospitati dedit egros.   38   Coystrowne1   59
The versycles shall syng.   82   Phy Sparrow   431
He shall syng the grayle;   82   Phy Sparrow   441
She made hym to syng   89   Phy Sparrow   701
Ye syng allway the kukkowe songe.   129   Garnesche5   4
Ye may syng weleaway   376   Replycacion   78
Thus can harpe and syng   384   Replycacion   344
SYNGE
That neyther they synge wel prycke song nor playne.   38   Coystrowne1   54
'Pryncers of youghte', can ye synge by rote?   53   Bowge   253
For on the booke I can not synge a note, ...   53   Bowge   255
  I] not in †Wynkyn de Worde 1499
And lerne me to synge Re my fa sol!   53   Bowge   258
These be my querysters /To helpe me to synge, ...   65   Hauke   123
Some to synge, and some to say, ...   81   Phy Sparrow   392
The requiem masse to synge, /Softly warbelynge, ...   81   Phy Sparrow   401
  Softly] 'Loftly' Marshe 1568
He can not well fly, /Nor synge tunably;   83   Phy Sparrow   484
He shall synge the verse   85   Phy Sparrow   531
For your kynge may synge weleawaye.   114   Scot Kynge   20
That the Scottys may synge, /'Fy on the wynnynge!'   116   Ag Scottes   47
  synge] 'sin' Marshe 1568
So in theyr eyre I synge them a songe   174   Magnyfycence   1223
I synge of two partys without a mene.   181   Magnyfycence   1463
Well cannest thou helpe a preest to synge a songe.   187   Magnyfycence   1676
Howe some synge letabundus /At every ale stake, ...   253   Collyn Clout   248
And to synge from place to place, /Lyke apostataas.   256   Collyn Clout   385
He coude nat synge hymselfe therout   268   Collyn Clout   878
In the Latyne synge we, ...   291   Why Come Ye   476
SYNGES
With armony that synges   93   Phy Sparrow   866
SYNGETH
The woodhacke, that syngeth 'chur', ...   82   Phy Sparrow   418
So merely syngeth the nyghtyngale!   199   Magnyfycence   2077
SYNGGYS
Nec magis bestialis /That synggys with a chalys;   70   Hauke   327
SYNGYNGE
They occupy them so /With syngynge Placebo, ...   269   Collyn Clout   907
SYNGULAR
solacyous and ryght pregnant allectyues of syngular pleasure, . 312   Garlande   I
With syngular pleasurs to dryve away the tyme, ...   326   Garlande   524
Paradyce this place is of syngular pleasure.   332   Garlande   717
SYNGULER
Byd hym take good hede of you, my synguler tresure.   149   Magnyfycence   317
SYNKE
That naythyr pump nor synke   127   Garnesche3   145
Here is none forsyth whether you flete or synke.   147   Magnyfycence   254
SYNKYNG
Oure eyen synkyng, /Oure bodys stynkyng, ...   39   Coystrowne3   33
SYNNE
Howe be it of all synne he was innocent, ...   196   Magnyfycence   2002
Some have so moche lyberte that they fere no synne, ...   200   Magnyfycence   2143
There is no man may synne more mortally   206   Magnyfycence   2336
Vyce to revyle /And synne to exyle?   247   Collyn Clout   12
Item the Boke how Men Shulde Fle Synne;   345   Garlande   1173
SYNNEWS
With synnews wyderyd, /With bonys shyderyd, ...   39   Coystrowne3   12
SYNNYS
For though they stumble in the synnys sevyn, ...   36   Coystrowne1   3

634

SYNODALLES — SYR

	Page	Title	Line
It is to late nowe thy synnys to repent.	205	Magnyfycence	2292
No, no; for thy synnys be so excedynge farre,	205	Magnyfycence	2300

SYNODALLES

	Page	Title	Line
And also gratyfyed /By holy synodalles	264	Collyn Clout	716

SYNS

	Page	Title	Line
By Goddis sydes, syns I her thyder broughte,	57	Bowge	404
That were syns Noes flode;	78	Phy Sparrow	268
Syns Dewcalyons flodde there can no clerkes rede.	244	Speke Parott	455
Syns Dewcalyons flodde there can no clerkes fynde.	244	Speke Parott	462
Syns Dewcalions flodde, was nevyr sene nor shall.	245	Speke Parott	469
Syns Dewcalyons flodde, I trowe, was nevyr sene.	245	Speke Parott	476
Syns Dewcalyons flodde was nevyr, I dar sey.	245	Speke Parott	483
Syns Dewcalyons flodde, I trow, no man can tell.	245	Speke Parott	490
Syns Dewcalyons flodde the world was never so yll.	245	Speke Parott	497
the world] 'the world the world' †MS Harley 2252			
Syns Dewcalyons flodde was nevyr sene nor lyerd.	246	Speke Parott	504

SYPPE

	Page	Title	Line
Let us syppe and soppy, /And not spyll a droppy,	228	El Rummynge	558

SYPPET

	Page	Title	Line
And ye wyll gyve me a syppet /Of your stale ale,	223	El Rummynge	367

SYR

	Page	Title	Line
Than asked she me, 'Syr, so God the spede,	48	Bowge	76
'Syr, God you save, why loke you so sadde?	53	Bowge	239
Syr, pardone me, I am an homely knave	53	Bowge	264
And ye be welcome, syr, so God me save,	54	Bowge	279
'And, syr, in fayth, why comste not us amonge	57	Bowge	379
And I am your, syr, so have I blys,	60	Bowge	495
Nor yet Egeas, /Nor yet Syr Pherumbras;	67	Hauke	205
No, no, syr, hardely!	78	Phy Sparrow	272
Of Gawen, and Syr Guy,	87	Phy Sparrow	629
How Syr Launcelote de Lake	87	Phy Sparrow	638
And of Syr Lybius /Named Dysconius;	88	Phy Sparrow	649
Syr squyer-galyarde ye were to swyfte;	113	Scot Kynge	11
Trowe ye, Syr James, his noble grace	114	Scot Kynge	17
By your wanton wyll, syr, at a worde,	114	Scot Kynge	48
Adieu, syr sumner, cast of your crowne!	117	Ag Scottes	64
Syr skyrgalyard, ye were so skyt,	118	Ag Scottes	101
Trowyd ye, Syr Jemy, his nobull grace	118	Ag Scottes	107
From you, Syr Scot, wolde turne his face?	118	Ag Scottes	108
With, 'Gup, Syr Scot of Galaway!'	118	Ag Scottes	109
Syr sumner, now where is your crowne?	120	Ag Scottes	178
Syr sumner, now ye have lost your crowne.	120	Ag Scottes	180
But yf yt war Syr Tyrmagant that tyrnyd without nall;	121	Garnesche1	4
For Syr Frollo de Franko was never halfe so talle.	121	Garnesche1	5
But sey me now, Syr Satrapas, what autoryte ye have	121	Garnesche1	6
In your chalenge, Syr Chystyn, to cale me knave?	121	Garnesche1	7
What, have ye kythyd yow a knyght, Syr Dugles the dowty,	121	Garnesche1	8
Ye bere yow bolde as Barabas, or Syr Terry of Trac[e].	122	Garnesche1	11
Trace] 'Tracy' †MS Harley 367			
But sey me yet, Syr Satropas, what auctoryte ye have	122	Garnesche1	13
In yor chalenge, Syr Chesten, to calle me a knave?	122	Garnesche1	14
Ye fowle, fers and felle, as Syr Ferumbras the ffreke,	122	Garnesche1	15
Syr capten of Catywade, catacumbas of Cayre,	122	Garnesche1	16
Thow ye be lusty as Syr Lybyus, launces to breke,	122	Garnesche1	17
But sey me yet, Syr Satrapas, wat auctoryte ye have	122	Garnesche1	20
In yor chalenge, Syr Chesten, to cal me a knave?	122	Garnesche1	21
But sey me yet, Syr Satrapas, what auctoryte ye have	122	Garnesche1	27
In yor chalenge, Syr Chesten, to calle me a knave?	122	Garnesche1	28
But sey me yet, Syr Satrapas, what auctoryte ye have	122	Garnesche1	34
In yor chalenge, Syr Chesten, to calle me a knave?	122	Garnesche1	35
Howkyd as an hawkys beke, lyke Syr Topyas.	122	Garnesche1	40
Why holde ye on yer cap, syr, then? Yor pardone ys expyryd.	123	Garnesche2	9
Syr Gy, Syr Gawen, Syr Cayus, for and Syr Olyvere,	123	Garnesche2	22
Syr Gy, Syr Gawen, Syr Cayus, for and Syr Olyvere,	123	Garnesche2	22
Syr Gy, Syr Gawen, Syr Cayus, for and Syr Olyvere,	123	Garnesche2	22
Syr Gy, Syr Gawen, Syr Cayus, for and Syr Olyvere,	123	Garnesche2	22
Pyramus, nor Priamus, nor Syr Pyrrus the prowde,	123	Garnesche2	23
Your stondarde, Syr Olifranke, agenst me for to splay;	123	Garnesche2	30
She callyd yow Syr Gy of Gaunt,	126	Garnesche3	70
I say, Syr Dalyrag,	129	Garnesche3	186
Ye, syr, rayle all in deformite;	129	Garnesche5	7
Wyth, 'Knave, syr, knave, and knave agenne',	130	Garnesche5	19
Thou thynkyst thy selfe Syr Pers de Brasy,	130	Garnesche5	30
With, 'Gup, Syr Gy', ye gate a moke.	131	Garnesche5	56
Wytles, wayward, Syr Wrag-wrag,	133	Garnesche5	149
Syr, as ye say. I have harde of your fame.	141	Magnyfycence	26
Trewe you say, syr. Gyve me your hande.	141	Magnyfycence	28
To tell you, syr, I dare not, leest I sholde be maskyd	141	Magnyfycence	30
In dede, syr, that lyberte was not worthe a cue.	141	Magnyfycence	36
Ye, syr, passyng well.	142	Magnyfycence	56
Syr, yf any worde have past	143	Magnyfycence	92
Yes, syr, with ryght good chere.	143	Magnyfycence	112
Syr, though ye be a noble prynce of myght,	145	Magnyfycence	166
And, syr, this other mannys name is Lyberte.	145	Magnyfycence	168
Where as ye have, syr, to me them assygned,	145	Magnyfycence	177
Your ordenaunce, syr, I wyll not forsake.	145	Magnyfycence	181
Hem, syr, yet beware of 'Had I wyste!'	146	Magnyfycence	211
What, syr, wolde ye make me a poppynge fole?	146	Magnyfycence	232

635

	Page	Title	Line
Syr, without any longer delyaunce,	147	Magnyfycence	237
From whens come you, syr, that no man lokyd after?	147	Magnyfycence	255
Largesse, that all lordes sholde love, syr, I hyght.	148	Magnyfycence	270
Ye, syr, undoubted. Then, of very ryght,	148	Magnyfycence	272
Syr, hardely remembre what may your name avaunce.	148	Magnyfycence	277
Plucke up your mynde, syr, what ayle you to muse?	148	Magnyfycence	283
By God, syr, ye se but fewe wyse men of myne age.	148	Magnyfycence	289
Syr, yf I have offended your noble estate,	149	Magnyfycence	308
Syr, thanked be God, he hath his hele.	149	Magnyfycence	315
Your pleasure, syr shortely shall be done.	149	Magnyfycence	321
Nay, syr, it was nothynge but your mynde.	149	Magnyfycence	330
But nowe, syr, as touchynge this letter -	149	Magnyfycence	331
By lakyn, syr, it hathe cost me pence	150	Magnyfycence	338
By God, syr, beyonde the se.	150	Magnyfycence	341
By my trouthe, syr, at Pountesse.	150	Magnyfycence	343
Mary, syr, ye were afrayde.	150	Magnyfycence	362
And in dede, syr, I here men talke -	151	Magnyfycence	374
With ye, syr, so God me spede.	151	Magnyfycence	379
Ye, syr, a blaunched almonde is no bene.	151	Magnyfycence	381
I pray you, syr, I may so be;	151	Magnyfycence	391
Yes, yes, syr. He and I have met.	154	Magnyfycence	498
But, syr, howe counterfetyd ye?	155	Magnyfycence	524
Yes, syr, I gyve God avowe,	155	Magnyfycence	529
By God, syr, this is Fansy Small-Brayne;	156	Magnyfycence	583
Knowe hym, syr, quod he. Yes, by Saynt Sym!	156	Magnyfycence	585
A, syr, I pray God gyve you confusyon!	157	Magnyfycence	597
Cappe, syr. I say you be to bolde.	157	Magnyfycence	602
Tushe! It is Syr Johnn Double-[Cope].	157	Magnyfycence	605
Cope] 'cloke' †Rastell & Treveris C 1530, B			
Syr, and yf ye wolde not be wrothe -	157	Magnyfycence	606
Syr, it is so that these twayne	157	Magnyfycence	612
Syr, the playnesse you me tell.	158	Magnyfycence	630
you me tell] 'you tell me' †Rastell & Treveris C 1530, B			
Tell on, syr. Howe then?	158	Magnyfycence	651
Mary, syr, he told us, when	158	Magnyfycence	652
But then, syr, what shall I hyght?	159	Magnyfycence	669
Syr, ye shall hyght Good Demeynaunce.	159	Magnyfycence	674
By God, syr, what nede all this waste?	161	Magnyfycence	754
Dusty! Nay, syr, ye be all of the lusty;	161	Magnyfycence	760
Abyde, syr, quod he! Mary, so I do.	162	Magnyfycence	789
But, syr, I wyll have this man with me.	163	Magnyfycence	815
Mary, syr, Cokermowthe is a good way hens.	170	Magnyfycence	1061
By my faythe, syr, the frubyssher hath my sworde.	170	Magnyfycence	1063
By God, syr, Foly, myne owne sworne brother.	172	Magnyfycence	1159
Yes, by my faythe, good Syr Johnn.	173	Magnyfycence	1186
Syr, of my maner I shall tell you the playne:	174	Magnyfycence	1219
Ye, by God, syr. For a nede,	174	Magnyfycence	1237
And, 'This is not well done, syr; take hede';	175	Magnyfycence	1248
Mary, syr, ye may swere it on a boke.	176	Magnyfycence	1292
A, syr, a, a! Howe by that?	176	Magnyfycence	1296
Syr, as by my wyll, it shall be so no more.	178	Magnyfycence	1377
All that ye say, syr, is reason and skyll.	178	Magnyfycence	1381
In good faythe, syr, me semeth he had the more wronge.	178	Magnyfycence	1384
Mary, syr, so dyd he excede and passe,	178	Magnyfycence	1385
Syr, by lyberte and largesse I wyll that ye shall	179	Magnyfycence	1396
Syr, yet without sapyence your substaunce may be smal;	179	Magnyfycence	1407
Syr, I am here at your pleasure.	179	Magnyfycence	1409
Syr, ye shall folowe myne appetyte and intent.	180	Magnyfycence	1420
What! All by mesure, good syr, and none excesse?	180	Magnyfycence	1422
Syr, as I say, there was no faute in me.	180	Magnyfycence	1426
Syr, as me semeth, ye sholde be rulyd be me.	180	Magnyfycence	1433
Syr, we can do nothynge the one without the other.	180	Magnyfycence	1450
At your commaundement, syr, wyth all dew reverence.	182	Magnyfycence	1515
Syr, then, with the favour of your benynge sufferaunce,	182	Magnyfycence	1519
Yes, syr, so good man in you I se,	182	Magnyfycence	1522
A, syr, your grace me dothe extole and rayse;	183	Magnyfycence	1525
Syr, I am the better of your noble reporte;	183	Magnyfycence	1541
Howe lyke you? Ye lacke, syr, suche a lusty lasse.	183	Magnyfycence	1559
It is none abusyon, syr, in a noble man.	185	Magnyfycence	1626
Syr, Sober Sadnesse cometh. Wherfore it be?	186	Magnyfycence	1631
Stand up, syr. Ye are welcom to me.	186	Magnyfycence	1632
Of our blessyd Lorde, syr, at the reverence -	186	Magnyfycence	1636
Nay, syr. That affeccyon ought to be reserved,	186	Magnyfycence	1643
Stande a lytell abacke, syr, and let hym come hyder.	186	Magnyfycence	1647
With a good wyll, syr, God spede you bothe togyder.	186	Magnyfycence	1648
Syr, so it is: this man is here by,	186	Magnyfycence	1649
Yet, syr, reserved your better advysement,	187	Magnyfycence	1661
He telleth you trouth, syr, as I you ensure.	187	Magnyfycence	1679
This is a wyse man, syr, where so ever ye hym had.	187	Magnyfycence	1689
Syr, God rewarde you as ye have deserved.	188	Magnyfycence	1701
Syr, as ye say. Nay, come on with me.	188	Magnyfycence	1707
Syr, I beseche you let pety have some place	188	Magnyfycence	1712
For your selfe. Syr, yf I myght permytted be,	188	Magnyfycence	1720
Abyde, syr, abyde. Let me holde your hede.	189	Magnyfycence	1727
A good dryfte, syr, a praty fete!	189	Magnyfycence	1731
Syr, nowe me thynke your harte is well eased.	189	Magnyfycence	1737
Syr, of my counsayle this shall be the grounde:	190	Magnyfycence	1768
Syr, syth that in me ye have suche devocyon,	190	Magnyfycence	1790

SYRE —SYRS	Page	Title	Line
Nowe Jesu preserve you, syr, prynce most of myght.	190	Magnyfycence	1796
Who is this? Consayte, syr, your owne man.	191	Magnyfycence	1804
What tydynges with you, syr? I befole thy brayne pan.	191	Magnyfycence	1805
By our lakyn, syr, I have ben a hawkyng for the wylde swan.	191	Magnyfycence	1806
A, syr, thy jarfawcon and thou be hanged togyder!	191	Magnyfycence	1812
And, syr as I was comynge to you hyder,	191	Magnyfycence	1813
A, syr, tolde I not you howe I dyd fynde	191	Magnyfycence	1819
Se, syr, I beseche you, Largesse my brother.	192	Magnyfycence	1842
What tydynges with you, syr, that you loke so sad?	192	Magnyfycence	1843
Alasse, syr, ye are undone with stelyng and robbynge!	192	Magnyfycence	1852
What? Yes, by the rode, syr. It was I all this whyle	193	Magnyfycence	1870
Ryse up, syr, and welcom unto me.	195	Magnyfycence	1966
Syr, all this wolde have bene thought on before.	196	Magnyfycence	1970
Ye, syr, ye; leve all this rage,	196	Magnyfycence	1988
Remembre you better, syr. Beware what ye say,	196	Magnyfycence	1995
Ye, syr, nowe must ye lerne to lye harde,	197	Magnyfycence	2005
Syr, remembre the tourne of Fortunes whele,	197	Magnyfycence	2022
Ye, syr, yesterday wyll not be callyd agayne.	197	Magnyfycence	2031
But yet, syr, nowe in this case	197	Magnyfycence	2032
With ye, syr, by Jesu, that slayne was with Jewes!	201	Magnyfycence	2167
By our lakyn, syr, not by my wyll.	203	Magnyfycence	2208
Mary, syr, this gentylman caled me javell.	203	Magnyfycence	2211
Mary, syr, he sayd that he was the pratyer man	203	Magnyfycence	2225
Abyde, syr, abyde; I shall make hym to pysse.	204	Magnyfycence	2250
A, blessyd may ye be, syr! What shall you I call?	206	Magnyfycence	2327
Good Hope, syr, my name is; remedy pryncypall	206	Magnyfycence	2328
Alas, syr! So I am lapped in adversyte	206	Magnyfycence	2331
Syr, your fesycyan is the grace of God,	207	Magnyfycence	2349
And nowe ye have had, syr, a wonderous fall,	207	Magnyfycence	2375
Howe say you, syr? Can ye these wordys grope?	207	Magnyfycence	2377
Ye, syr, now am I armyd with good hope,	207	Magnyfycence	2378
Syr, is your pacyent any thynge amendyd?	208	Magnyfycence	2387
Ye, syr, he is sory for that he hath offendyd.	208	Magnyfycence	2388
A wrechyd man, syr, to my maker unkynde.	208	Magnyfycence	2390
Syr, the repentaunce I have no man can wryte.	208	Magnyfycence	2392
Than stande up, syr, in Goddys name!	208	Magnyfycence	2397
Syr, your requeste shall not be delayed.	208	Magnyfycence	2401
Syr, after your message I hyed me hyder streyght,	209	Magnyfycence	2419
Syr, to accompte you, the contynewe of my consayte	209	Magnyfycence	2421
Syr, the longe absence of you, Sad Cyrcumspeccyon,	209	Magnyfycence	2424
Without fayle, syr, that is no nay:	209	Magnyfycence	2429
But, syr, by me to rule fyrst ye began.	209	Magnyfycence	2431
My wylfulnesse, syr, excuse I ne can.	209	Magnyfycence	2432
That I sholde use largesse. Nay, syr, there a pause.	209	Magnyfycence	2437
Syr, this letter ye sent to me at Pountes was enclosed.	209	Magnyfycence	2439
Largesse, syr, by his credence was his name.	209	Magnyfycence	2441
Truth it is, syr; for after he wrought me moch shame,	209	Magnyfycence	2444
Syr, in good hope I am to amende.	210	Magnyfycence	2454
Well, syr, after your counsell my mynde I wyll set.	210	Magnyfycence	2457
Ye, syr, with adversyte I have bene vexyd;	210	Magnyfycence	2461
Ye, syr. From hym my corage shall never flyt.	210	Magnyfycence	2466
But, syr, amonge all /That sate in that hall,	229	El Rummynge	580
Let Syr Wrig-wrag wrastell with Syr Delarag:	233	Speke Parott	89
Let Syr Wrig-wrag wrastell with Syr Delarag:	233	Speke Parott	89
Avaunt, Syr Gye of Gaunt!	275	Collyn Clout	1155
Avaunt, syr doctour Deuyas!	275	Collyn Clout	1157
Deuyas] 'Denyas' †Godfray 1531, 'dyvers' Marshe 1568, 'Devias' MS Harley 2252			
Syr, ye must tary a stounde,	294	Why Come Ye	626
And syr, ye must daunce attendaunce,	294	Why Come Ye	628
To the devyll Syr Sathanas,	299	Why Come Ye	805
To Pluto and Syr Bellyall,	299	Why Come Ye	806
My lorde now and syr knyght,	302	Why Come Ye	915
now] not in MS Rawlinson C. 813			
For now, Syr Trestram,	302	Why Come Ye	917
Unto me sayd, 'Lo, syr, now ye may se	326	Garlande	518
Syr Duke, nay, syr ducke,	364	Albany	222
Syr Duke, nay, syr ducke,	364	Albany	222
Syr drake of the lake, sir ducke	364	Albany	223
SYRE			
It is a solempne syre and a solayne,	38	Coystrownel	51
His dame and his syre	165	Magnyfycence	905
And sadlye salute owur solen Syre Sydrake,	240	Speke Parott	326
That makys our syre to glum.	288	Why Come Ye	389
SYRS			
Cockes woundes! Se, syrs, se, se!	156	Magnyfycence	572
Knowe you not me, syrs? No, in dede.	157	Magnyfycence	594
Tell me, syrs, what is your wyll?	157	Magnyfycence	611
Thus can I lerne you, syrs, to bere the devyls sacke;	160	Magnyfycence	721
This was properly prated, syrs! What sayd a?	161	Magnyfycence	746
Gyve this gentylman rome, syrs. Stonde utter!	161	Magnyfycence	753
Ha, ha, ha! Herke, syrs, harke!	171	Magnyfycence	1109
For nowe, syrs, I am lyke as a prynce sholde be;	181	Magnyfycence	1457
Howe say ye, syrs? Herein what is best?	186	Magnyfycence	1659
Lo, syrs, thus I handell them all	194	Magnyfycence	1896
To take, syrs, example of that I you tell,	195	Magnyfycence	1944
With ye, mary, syrs, thus sholde it be:	198	Magnyfycence	2064
But yet, syrs, hardely one thynge lerne of me:	199	Magnyfycence	2087

SYRUS—SKAN   Page Title   Line

```
Cockes armes, syrs, wyll ye not se . . . . . . . . . . . . . . . .   200   Magnyfycence   2109
Adewe, syrs, for I thynke leyst that I come to late. . . . . . .    201   Magnyfycence   2152
For we be, syrs, but a fewe of the best. . . . . . . . . . . . .    202   Magnyfycence   2203
Ye, but trowe you, syrs, that this is he? . . . . . . . . . . . .   204   Magnyfycence   2242
Alasse, alasse, syrs, ye are to blame! . . . . . . . . . . . . . .   204   Magnyfycence   2245
Syrs, I am agreed to abyde your ordenaunce - . . . . . . . . .      210   Magnyfycence   2471
SYRUS
Syrus, that soleme syar of Babylon, . . . . . . . . . . . . . .    181   Magnyfycence   1473
SYSE
My persone prest /Beyonde all syse . . . . . . . . . . . . .      164   Magnyfycence    845
SYSMATICATE
Your sysmaticate sawes /Agaynst Goddes lawes, . . . . . . . . .    377   Replycacion     122
SYSMATYKE
He semeth a sysmatyke /Or els an heretike, . . . . . . . . . .      62   Hauke            17
A subtyll sysmatyke, /Ryght nere an heretyke, . . . . . . . . .    121   Ag Scottes2      27
SYSMATYKES
Suche maner of sysmatykes /And halfe heretykes, . . . . . . . .    264   Collyn Clout    700
Agaynst these sysmatykes, /Agaynst these heretykes, . . . . . .    385   Replycacion     402
SYSTER
Cadmus, that his syster sought, . . . . . . . . . . . . . . . . .   76   Phy Sparrow     194
'Soft, my good syster, and make there a pawse. . . . . . . . .     316   Garlande        134
    my good syster] 'goode my sister' MS Cotton Vitellius E.x
Let se, my syster, now spede you, go aboute. . . . . . . . .       319   Garlande        242
    you] not in MS Cotton Vitellius E.x
SYSTERS
O Atropos, of the fatall systers iij, . . . . . . . . . . . . .     32   Dol Dethe       120
Your Seven Systers, that gun so gay, . . . . . . . . . . . . .     119   Ag Scottes      162
SYT
And wold syt upon my lap, . . . . . . . . . . . . . . . . . . .     74   Phy Sparrow     121
He dyd nothynge, perde, /But syt upon my kne. . . . . . . . . .     76   Phy Sparrow     172
How pretely it wolde syt . . . . . . . . . . . . . . . . . . . .    80   Phy Sparrow     354
And howe styll she doth syt! . . . . . . . . . . . . . . . . .    168   Magnyfycence   1003
Somtyme I syt as I were solempe prowde; . . . . . . . . . . .     168   Magnyfycence   1011
And teche them howe they sholde syt ydyll . . . . . . . . . .     174   Magnyfycence   1221
That wyll syt ydyll all the day . . . . . . . . . . . . . . . .   174   Magnyfycence   1229
With the gowte I make them to grone where they syt; . . . . .     194   Magnyfycence   1903
By the fayth that I owe to God, and I wyll syt styll. . . . .     203   Magnyfycence   2209
And syt there by styll, /Erly and late. . . . . . . . . . . .     217   El Rummynge     116
With, 'Hey,' and with, 'Howe, /Syt we downe arowe . . . . . .     221   El Rummynge     290
Why syt ye prelates styll . . . . . . . . . . . . . . . . . .     263   Collyn Clout    688
Syt styll as they were dom. . . . . . . . . . . . . . . . . .     283   Why Come Ye     199
And thus they shall syt - . . . . . . . . . . . . . . . . . .     295   Why Come Ye     633
Chuse them syt or flyt, . . . . . . . . . . . . . . . . . . .     295   Why Come Ye     634
To syt in causa sanguinis. . . . . . . . . . . . . . . . . .      308   Why Come Ye    1161
To syt hym upon, and rede Jacke a thrummis bybille, . . . . .     318   Garlande        209
    hym] not in MS Cotton Vitellius E.x
He wyll set men a feightynge and syt hymselfe styll, . . . .      333   Garlande        761
    set] 'stir' MS Cotton Vitellius E.x; a feightynge]
    'to brawlyng' MS Cotton Vitellius E.x
'Syt downe, fayre ladys, and do your diligence! . . . . . . .     334   Garlande        772
SYTH
Syth all in substaunce of slumbrynge doth procede. . . . . .       61   Bowge           536
For, syth he dyed, largesse was lytell used. . . . . . . . .      148   Magnyfycence    282
Go shake the, dogge, hay, syth ye wyll nedys! . . . . . . . .     148   Magnyfycence    303
Syr, syth that in me ye have suche devocyon, . . . . . . . .      190   Magnyfycence   1790
Nowe, syth it wyll no nother be, . . . . . . . . . . . . . .      196   Magnyfycence   1978
Syth unto me formest this processe is erectyd, . . . . . . .      211   Magnyfycence   2482
SYTHE
And ever he sange, 'Sythe I am no thynge playne'. . . . . .        52   Bowge           235
SYTTE
A thre-foted stole /That he may downe sytte, . . . . . . . .      247   Collyn Clout     31
At home full softe doth sytte. . . . . . . . . . . . . . . .      255   Collyn Clout    328
Some say ye sytte in trones, . . . . . . . . . . . . . . . .      255   Collyn Clout    344
That shall sytte in a trone . . . . . . . . . . . . . . . . .     258   Collyn Clout    474
    shall sytte] 'syttys nowe' MS Lansdowne 762 'shuld sytte'
    MS Harley 2252
And whan he weneth to sytte . . . . . . . . . . . . . . . .       271   Collyn Clout    995
SYTTES
In the Chauncery where he syttes, . . . . . . . . . . . . .       287   Why Come Ye     326
SYTTYNG
It is not syttyng in tower and towne . . . . . . . . . . . .      120   Ag Scottes      174
    syttyng] 'fytting' Kynge & Marche 1554
Unto the pavylyon where Pallas was syttyng. . . . . . . . . .     324   Garlande        448
SYTTYNGE
It is not syttynge in tour nor towne . . . . . . . . . . . .      115   Scot Kynge       66
That Measure be mayster us semeth it is syttynge. . . . . . .     145   Magnyfycence    176
Nowe semyth us syttynge that ye then resorte . . . . . . . .      214   Magnyfycence   2566
SKABED
Dundas, dronken and drowsy, /Skabed, scurvy and lowsy, . . . .    136   Dundas           51
SKALES
Whose skales ensilvred again the son beames . . . . . . . . .     330   Garlande        662
SKALPE
I shall skelpe the on the skalpe; lo, seest thou that? . . . .    202   Magnyfycence   2180
SKAN
I coude it skan and ye wolde it reherse. . . . . . . . . . . .     53   Bowge           245
    skan] 'stan' †Wynkyn de Worde 1499, 1510;
    it] (2nd) not in Marshe 1568
```

SKANE —SKYN	Page	Title	Line

SKANE
With, 'Reche me that skane of tewly sylk'; . . . . 334 Garlande 798
SKANT
Plente of yll, of goodnes skant, ... 40 Coystrowne4 3
SKANTE
The warde with yow was skante. 125 Garnesche3 53
As skante thou had no nede of me. . . . . 163 Magnyfycence 806
SKANTLY
He skantly loveth our kyng, /That grudgeth at this thing: . . . 121 Ag Scottes2 35
Was skantly worthe a grote; 125 Garnesche3 45
And skantly could go /For payne and for wo. . . . . 227 El Rummynge 513
Can skantly the tensis of his conjugacyons; . . . . 235 Speke Parott 180
SKAR
In her vysage a skar . . . . 97 Phy Sparrow 1045
SKEYNE
Some for very nede /Layde downe a skeyne of threde, ... 222 El Rummynge 310
And some a skeyne of yarne. . . . . 222 El Rummynge 311
SKELLET
Some ranne a good trot /With a skellet or a pot; . . . . 220 El Rummynge 250
SKELPE
I shall skelpe the on the skalpe; lo, seest thou that? . . . . 202 Magnyfycence 2180
What! Wylte thou skelpe me? Thou dare not loke on a gnat. . . 202 Magnyfycence 2181
SKELTON
Skelton Laureat Upon the Dolorus Dethe . . . . 29 Dol Dethe I
Skelton Laureat Agaynste a Comely Coystrowne . . . . 36 Coystrowne I
Quod Skelton, laureat. . . . . 38 Coystrowne2 E
Skelton Laureat, uppon a deedmans hed, ... 39 Coystrowne3 I
devysyd by Master Skelton Laureat . . . . 41 Balettys I
Quod Skelton laureate. . . . . 42 Balettys1 E
Quod Skelton laureat. . . . . 43 Balettys2 E
Quod Skelton laureat. . . . . 45 Balettys3 E
Quod Skelton laureat. . . . . 45 Balettys4 E
Skelton laureat, at the instance of a nobyll lady. . . . . . . 46 Balettys5 E
per Skelton laureat . . . . 61 Hauke I
How I, Skelton laureat, ... 62 Hauke 33
Quod Skelton laureat. . . . . 71 Hauke E
compyled by Mayster Skelton, poete laureate . . . . 71 Phy Sparrow I
and her foloweth an addicyon made by Maister Skelton. . . . . 103 Phy Sparrow R
Skelton Laureate, Orator Regius, maketh this aunswere &c. . . 112 Calliope I
Skelton laureate Agaynst The Scottes . . . . 115 Ag Scottes I
Quod Skelton laureate, ... 120 Ag Scottes E
Skelton Lauriate Defender Agenst Master Garnesche Chalenger, . 121 Garnesche1 I
Skelton Lauryate Defender Agenst Master Garnesche Chalangar, . 122 Garnesche2 I
SKELTONIDIS
PROLOGUS SKELTONIDIS LAUREATI SUPER WARE THE HAWKE . . . . . . 61 Hauke R
SKELTONS
sum parte of Skeltons bokes and baladis with ditis of plesure, 345 Garlande R
SKER
The sker upon her chyn . . . . 98 Phy Sparrow 1077
SKEWED
Some be flybytten, /Some skewed as a kytten; . . . . 218 El Rummynge 142
SKIP
It made them to skip, to stampe, and to stare, ... 353 Garlande 1473
SKY
Above the sky /That is so hy, ... 40 Coystrowne3 55
That Phyllyp may fly /Above the starry sky, ... 86 Phy Sparrow 599
That from the starry sky . . . . 110 Lawde 16
In our collage above the sterry sky, ... 323 Garlande 403
SKYE
Hyest in the skye, ... 85 Phy Sparrow 551
The skye is clowdy, the coste is nothyng clere; . . . . 242 Speke Parott 397
As though they wolde flye /Aboute the sterry skye. . . . . . 248 Collyn Clout 74
  Aboute] 'Above' Kele 1545.1, Marshe 1568, MS Harley 2252
SKYES
Towarde the cloudy skyes; . . . . 72 Phy Sparrow 38
Among the scabbed skyes /Of Wycliffes flesshe flyes. . . . . 378 Replycacion 165
SKYL
Of your complaynt it shal nat skyl. . . . . 310 Why Come Ye2 32
SKYLL
And can but lytell skyll . . . . 90 Phy Sparrow 755
It is reason and skyll . . . . 143 Magnyfycence 105
But have ye not herde say that wyll is no skyll? . . . . . . 144 Magnyfycence 148
Why, thynkys thou he can no better skyll? . . . . 172 Magnyfycence 1172
But some man wolde convey, and can not skyll, ... 178 Magnyfycence 1361
All that ye say, syr, is reason and skyll. . . . . 178 Magnyfycence 1381
Be it reason or none, it shall not gretely skyll; . . . . . . 185 Magnyfycence 1596
And they never thryve in theyr age, it shall not gretly skyll. 200 Magnyfycence 2138
And judge it as they wyll, /For other mens skyll, ... 249 Collyn Clout 99
Without good reason or skyll; . . . . 276 Collyn Clout 1191
Good Reason and good Skyll, ... 281 Why Come Ye 108
Without reason or skyll. . . . . 291 Why Come Ye 488
Ovyde was bannisshed for suche a skyll, ... 314 Garlande 93
SKYLLE
Thowthe ye kan skylle of large and longe, ... 129 Garnesche5 3
So ys all thyng wrowghte wylfully withowte reson and skylle. . 245 Speke Parott 496
SKYN
Upon my naked skyn. . . . . 76 Phy Sparrow 167
Enhached on her fayre skyn, ... 98 Phy Sparrow 1078

SKYNNE—SLAYNE

	Page	Title	Line
SKYN			
Your skyn scabbyd and scurvy, ...	127	Garnesche3	131
Within thy skyn he xall remayne.	130	Garnesche5	22
Or I shal fawchyn thy flesshe and scrape the on the skyn. . . .	202	Magnyfycence	2189
SKYNNE			
Yet I solde his skynne to Mackemurre, ...	169	Magnyfycence	1056
What! Fleyest thou his skynne every yere?	169	Magnyfycence	1058
Your skynne that was wrapped in shertes of Raynes, ...	197	Magnyfycence	2016
Her skynne lose and slacke, /Greuyned lyke a sacke;	215	El Rummynge	31
Greuyned] 'Grained' Day 1560, Marshe 1568			
SKYNNES			
I were skynnes of conny, ...	224	El Rummynge	399
SKYP			
Whome she hateth shall over the see-boorde skyp.	49	Bowge	112
see-boorde] 'shyp borde' Marshe 1568			
Than he wold lepe and skyp, ...	75	Phy Sparrow	139
SKYPPE			
Alasse, where is youth that was wont for to skyppe?	195	Magnyfycence	1957
SKYPPED			
Maude Ruggy thyther skypped:	226	El Rummynge	467
SKYPPES			
But not worth thre skyppes of a pye.	113	Scot Kynge	10
Not worth thre skyppes of a pye.	118	Ag Scottes	100
SKYRE-GALYARD			
With, 'Skyre-galyard, prowde palyard, vaunte-parler, ye prate!'	244	Speke Parott	433
SKYRGALIARDE			
Suche a proude palyarde, /Suche a skyrgaliarde, ...	363	Albany	168
SKYRGALYARD			
Syr skyrgalyard, ye were so skyt, ...	118	Ag Scottes	101
SKYRT			
Gresed upon dyrt /That baudeth her skyrt.	216	El Rummynge	90
SKYT			
Syr skyrgalyard, ye were so skyt, ...	118	Ag Scottes	101
SKLAUNDERING			
With skolding and sklaundering make their tungs lame.	139	Ven Tongues	62
SKOLDE			
A sclaunderous tunge, a tunge of a skolde, ...	137	Ven Tongues	7
SKOLDING			
With skolding and sklaundering make their tungs lame.	139	Ven Tongues	62
SKOLES			
To mainteyne with your skoles, ...	378	Replycacion	144
SKOMMER			
Another brought a skommer, ...	224	El Rummynge	408
SKOMMETH			
And skommeth it into a tray	219	El Rummynge	198
into] 'in' Day 1560, Marshe 1568			
SKORNE			
Why so koy and full of skorne?	40	Coystrowne4	8
Ye wan nothyng there but a skorne;	131	Garnesche5	51
In fayth, so to suffer the, it is but a skorne.	202	Magnyfycence	2201
And thus to be facyd, I thynke it great skorne.	203	Magnyfycence	2217
I was your mayster, though ye thynke it skorne;	204	Magnyfycence	2246
Wysdom is laught to skorne, ...	281	Why Come Ye	94
Thus to be laughed to skorne, ...	376	Replycacion	82
SKORNYS			
Wyll ye se this gentylman is all in his skornys?	162	Magnyfycence	773
SKOTTYS			
Lo, these fond sottes /And tratlyng Skottys, ...	115	Ag Scottes	6
SKRYBE			
And your skrybe I have aspyed, ...	124	Garnesche3	3
SKULL			
He plucked the bull /By the horned skull, ...	104	Phy Sparrow	1319
SLACKE			
Her skynne lose and slacke, /Greuyned lyke a sacke;	215	El Rummynge	31
Greuyned] 'Grained' Day 1560, Marshe 1568			
To slacke in recompence, ...	279	Why Come Ye	7
SLAIIS			
With slaiis, with tavellis, with hedellis well drest;	334	Garlande	791
SLAIN			
They have slain our Englisshmen	288	Why Come Ye	372
SLAYN			
To suffre hym slayn of his mortall fo?	30	Dol Dethe	38
What man, remembring how shamfully he was slayn, ...	32	Dol Dethe	111
That was late slayn at Carowe	72	Phy Sparrow	8
Whan I remembre agayn /How mi Philyp was slayn, ...	72	Phy Sparrow	18
SLAYNE			
Whos lordshepe doutles was slayne lamentably	29	Dol Dethe	5
This noble man doutles had not be slayne.	31	Dol Dethe	74
be] 'bene' Marshe 1568			
For cruell[y] amonge them ther he was slayne.	32	Dol Dethe	105
cruelly] 'cruell' †MS Royal 18 D.ii, Marshe 1568			
This noble man that cruelly was slayne.	34	Dol Dethe	182
That other loked as he wolde me have slayne.	58	Bowge	430
me have] 'have me' Wynkyn de Worde 1510			
For forthwyth there I had him slayne, ...	61	Bowge	523
Whom Gyb our cat hath slayne.	72	Phy Sparrow	27
The false cat hath the slayne!	80	Phy Sparrow	330
That he is slayne me fro, ...	81	Phy Sparrow	364
An hart was slayne /With hornes twayne	104	Phy Sparrow	1298

	Page	Title	Line
SLAKE —SLEW			
Thrugh your counseyle your fader was slayne;	114	Scot Kynge	27
When the Scot was slayne	117	Ag Scottes	R
Though ye untruly your father have slayne,	118	Ag Scottes	119
I trowe, by our lady, I had ben slayne,	150	Magnyfycence	348
With ye, syr, by Jesu, that slayne was with Jewes!	201	Magnyfycence	2167
Thou arte not the fyrst hymselfe hath slayne.	206	Magnyfycence	2316
Some hanged, some slayne,	276	Collyn Clout	1210
And never a Scot slayne!	282	Why Come Ye	152
An hart was slayne	348	Garlande	1291
For feare thou shoulde be slayne	365	Albany	247
SLAKE			
But, how it is, Skelton is wonder slake,	314	Garlande	69
SLATY			
Some go streyght thyder, /Be it slaty or slyder;	221	El Rummynge	258
SLAUNDRED			
Sith he is slaundred for defaut of konnyng?'	316	Garlande	140
SLAUNDRYS			
Whose tong ys attayntyd with slaundrys obliqui.	241	Speke Parott	363
SLAVER			
Her lewde lyppes twayne, /They slaver, men sayne,	215	El Rummynge	23
SLAVERYNG			
Slaveryng lyke a slymy snayle.	130	Garnesche5	45
SLE			
And make eche man to sle other;	194	Magnyfycence	1913
To drowne or to sle themselfe with a knyfe –	194	Magnyfycence	1914
SLEE			
Came for to slee me of mortall entente.	61	Bowge	529
Whan Mesure is gone, we may slee care.	176	Magnyfycence	1324
Here MAGNYFYCENCE wolde slee hymselfe with a knyfe.	206	Magnyfycence	SD
SLEEST			
O homycide, whiche sleest all that thou kan,	32	Dol Dethe	123
SLEETH			
I am wery of the worlde, for unkyndnesse me sleeth.	205	Magnyfycence	2283
SLEY			
And let us sley care!'	217	El Rummynge	111
SLEYGHT			
Counterfet letters by the way of sleyght;	152	Magnyfycence	439
SLEYGHTES			
And suche sleyghtes dothe fynde,	290	Why Come Ye	438
SLEYTE			
By Goddis bones, but yf we have som sleyte,	54	Bowge	304
SLENDER			
And ryght slender connynge /Within theyr heedes wonnynge.	250	Collyn Clout	140
SLENDYR			
At Gynys when ye ware /But a slendyr spere,	125	Garnesche3	41
Was sowyd with slendyr thre[de].	129	Garnesche3	201
threde] 'thre' †MS Harley 367			
Ye get therby a slendyr laude	131	Garnesche5	74
SLEPE			
All drowsy, dremyng, dround in slepe,	41	Balettys1	6
Enforsed to take some reste,	47	Bowge	32
And wake all nyghte and slepe tyll it be none.	57	Bowge	382
This worlde is nothynge but ete, drynke and slepe,	57	Bowge	384
The dyvendop to slepe;	83	Phy Sparrow	452
No slepe can him catch,	95	Phy Sparrow	928
His foule desyre /Wyll suffre no slepe	95	Phy Sparrow	934
And forthwith fell on slepe.	224	El Rummynge	375
That Latinum fari may fall to rest and slepe,	235	Speke Parott	164
But slombre forth and slepe,	249	Collyn Clout	124
In slumbrynge I fell and halfe in a slepe;	313	Garlande	30
Some sluggysh slovyns, that slepe day and nyght;	317	Garlande	191
Is layd down to slepe,	358	Garlande2	4
SLEPYNG			
She left hym slepyng and stale away,	42	Balettys1	14
SLEPYST			
Thou slepyst to long, thou art begylde!	41	Balettys1	I
SLEPYSTE			
For slepyste thou, Besse,	237	Speke Parott	238
SLEPT			
That never more slept,	104	Phy Sparrow	1304
SLEPTE			
That never more slepte	349	Garlande	1297
SLETH			
Alas, myne hert it sleth	80	Phy Sparrow	351
SLEVE			
I saw a knyfe hyd in his one sleve,	58	Bowge	433
And in his other sleve, me thought I sawe	58	Bowge	435
And on that sleve these wordes were wrete:	58	Bowge	438
Beyonde measure /My sleve is wyde;	164	Magnyfycence	850
He caryeth a kyng in hys sleve, yf all the worlde fayle;	243	Speke Parott	429
SLEW			
Unkindly thei slew hym that help them oft at nede.	30	Dol Dethe	47
help] 'holp' Marshe 1568			
Yet shamfully thei slew hym; that sham most them befall.	30	Dol Dethe	49
For whos causis ye slew hym with your awne hande.	31	Dol Dethe	68
And slew many a Chrysten man;	67	Hauke	215
That slew so cruelly	78	Phy Sparrow	279
And slew him there starke dead.	81	Phy Sparrow	378

SLIPPER — SMALE

	Page	Title	Line
Whom Achylles slew,	88	Phy Sparrow	675
Slew of the Epidaures	104	Phy Sparrow	1293
And slew Gerion /With thre bodyes in one;	104	Phy Sparrow	1307
Slew all the floure /Of theyr honoure.	116	Ag Scottes	27
The White there slew the Red starke ded.	119	Ag Scottes	138
Slew of the Epidawris	348	Garlande	1286
And slew Gerione /With thre bodys in one;	349	Garlande	1300

SLIPPER
'A slipper holde the taile is of an ele' — 326 Garlande 501

SLY
Subtyle Sym Sly /With madde foly. — 300 Why Come Ye 856
 Sym Sly] 'Symonye' †Kele 1545.3

SLYCE
A fryenge pan, and a slyce. — 224 El Rummynge 409

SLYDDER
I trowe it be a frost, for the way is slydder; — 191 Magnyfycence 1816

SLYDE
What and he slyde downe, who shall hym save? — 46 Bowge 28
For welthe without measure sodenly wyll slyde. — 145 Magnyfycence 192

SLYDER
Some go streyght thyder, /Be it slaty or slyder; — 221 El Rummynge 258

SLYGHT
Liing, spying by suttelte and slyght, — 133 Garnesche5 151
What and I frame suche a slyght — 159 Magnyfycence 677
Howe so? By God, by a praty slyght, — 167 Magnyfycence 952
Yet for his name we must fynde a [slyght]. — 176 Magnyfycence 1308
 slyght] shyfte †Rastell & Treveris C 1530, B

SLYMY
Slaveryng lyke a slymy snayle. — 130 Garnesche5 45
Enflorid with flowris and slymy snaylis, — 345 Garlande 1160

SLYP
But let the matter slyp, — 66 Hauke 154

SLYPPE
Leste that his fote slyppe, — 263 Collyn Clout 666
Shall glyde and smothely slyppe — 277 Collyn Clout 1252

SLYPPERS
Thy slyppers they swap it, yet thou fotys it lyke a swanne. — 161 Magnyfycence 765

SLYVE
Within his slyve; — 165 Magnyfycence 906

SLO
Falsly to slo ther moste singlar goode lorde? — 30 Dol Dethe 27
 slo] 'slee' Marshe 1568
To slo ther owne lorde? God was not in ther mynde! — 30 Dol Dethe 35
What aylde you to slo your lord ageyn all right? — 31 Dol Dethe 63
 slo] 'sle' Marshe 1568
To slo suche a lord, alas, it was grete shame. — 33 Dol Dethe 154
 slo] 'sle' Marshe 1568
Alas, it wyll me slo, — 75 Phy Sparrow 141
Himself doth slo /With payne and wo. — 95 Phy Sparrow 947

SLOGYSH
Avaunt, avaunt, thow slogysh...... — 132 Garnesche5 112

SLOMBRE
But slombre forth and slepe, — 249 Collyn Clout 124

SLOO
Thyselfe that thou wolde sloo agaynst nature and kynde. — 206 Magnyfycence 2326
Who knoweth me, hymselfe may never sloo. — 206 Magnyfycence 2330

SLOUTH
And, for to say trouth, /A great parte is for slouth; — 250 Collyn Clout 137
 for] 'full' †Godfray 1531, 'for' MS Harley 2252

SLOUTHFULL
Slouthfull to do good, — 293 Why Come Ye 577

SLOVEN
Thou swety sloven seymy, — 128 Garnesche3 169
The follest sloven ondyr heven, — 133 Garnesche5 145

SLOVYNS
Some sluggysh slovyns, that slepe day and nyght; — 317 Garlande 191

SLOWTHFULL
To pas the tyme in slowthfull ydelnes, — 315 Garlande 120

SLUFFERD
Ye slufferd up sowse — 125 Garnesche3 32

SLUGGYSH
Some sluggysh slovyns, that slepe day and nyght; — 317 Garlande 191

SLUMBRYNGE
At Harwyche Porte, slumbrynge as I laye, — 47 Bowge 34
Syth all in substaunce of slumbrynge doth procede. — 61 Bowge 536
Halfe slumbrynge, in a sounde — 72 Phy Sparrow 35
In slumbrynge I fell and halfe in a slepe; — 313 Garlande 30

SLUT
But she was a foule slut, — 223 El Rummynge 340

SLUTTES
Another sorte of sluttes: — 225 El Rummynge 436

SMACKE
And some have a smacke /Of Luthers sacke, — 260 Collyn Clout 540

SMAL
Syr, yet without sapyence your substaunce may be smal; — 179 Magnyfycence 1407

SMALE
And this an other, I have but smale substaunce.' — 48 Bowge 94
 And] 'But' Marshe 1568

SMALL —SMYLE

	Page	Title	Line
Make the churche to be /In smale auctoryte;	65	Hauke	140
And not for byrdes smale.	80	Phy Sparrow	340
And with her fyngers smale,	99	Phy Sparrow	1118
With fingers smale, and handis whyte as mylk;	334	Garlande	797
whyte] 'as white' Marshe 1568			
And hath smale lust to paint?	339	Garlande	955
Smale flowres helpt to sett	339	Garlande	969
Amonge the byrdes smale,	340	Garlande	998
All orators and poetis, with other grete and smale,	354	Garlande	1504
And thought in hym smale grace	379	Replycacion	195

SMALL

	Page	Title	Line
Nay, jape not with hym, he is no small fole;	38	Coystrownel	50
Hys jentyll curtoy[l], and set nowght by small naggys!	43	Balettys2	16
curtoyl] 'curtoyt' †Rastell 1527.1			
And seke after small wormes,	74	Phy Sparrow	122
Her goodly myddell small	99	Phy Sparrow	1128
goodly] 'godly' †Kele 1545.2			
As wytles as a wylde goos, ye have but small remorrs	123	Garnesche2	18
That welthe and felicite is passynge small.	141	Magnyfycence	21
In fayth, and Lybertyes rome is there but small.	158	Magnyfycence	663
A maystres, I tell you, is but a small thynge.	184	Magnyfycence	1579
I may say to you I have but small devocyon.	186	Magnyfycence	1640
Largesse in wordes - for rewardes are but small.	189	Magnyfycence	1760
Small chaffer doth ease /Sometyme, now and than.	222	El Rummynge	314
How the maters he mellis in com to small effecte;	240	Speke Parott	328
So many swannes dede, and so small revell -	245	Speke Parott	489
So many howgye howsys byldyng, and so small howse-holdyng;	245	Speke Parott	494
Of the clergye all, /Bothe great and small.	249	Collyn Clout	118
Small housholdes woll kepe,	249	Collyn Clout	123
But the greatest parte /Is for they have but small arte	250	Collyn Clout	139
Theyr lernynge is so small,	252	Collyn Clout	240
Theyr rule is very small,	261	Collyn Clout	609
Small newes that true is	284	Why Come Ye	234
In hym was small fayth,	297	Why Come Ye	744
A small defaute in a great lorde,	310	Why Come Ye2	12
For small is your sadnesse	310	Why Come Ye2	24
But of my spede /Small sekernes;	356	Garlande	1597
Of the donghyll, for small lucke	364	Albany	224
My lernyng is to small	370	Albany	457
Howe ye have small contrycion	379	Replycacion	183

SMALL-BRAYNE

	Page	Title	Line
By God, syr, this is Fansy Small-Brayne;	156	Magnyfycence	583

SMALLE

	Page	Title	Line
Then nodypollys and gramatolys of smalle intellygens:	240	Speke Parott	318
So many complayntes, and so smalle redresse;	245	Speke Parott	470
So myche callyng on, and so smalle takyng hede;	245	Speke Parott	471
So myche papers weryng for ryghte a smalle exesse;	245	Speke Parott	479

SMALLER

	Page	Title	Line
There were many wordes smaller and gretter,	326	Garlande	508

SMARAGD

	Page	Title	Line
Relucent smaragd, objecte imcomperable;	44	Balettys3	21

SMARAGDIS

	Page	Title	Line
Jacinctis and smaragdis out of the florthe they grew.	325	Garlande	480

SMART

	Page	Title	Line
Persyd with payn, bleding with wondes smart,	45	Balettys5	2

SMARTID

	Page	Title	Line
With wordes that smartid,	341	Garlande	1040

SMATER

	Page	Title	Line
For they that wyll so bysely smater	175	Magnyfycence	1257
With Crafty Conveyaunce dothe smater and flater,	346	Garlande	1194

SMATYR

	Page	Title	Line
I wondyr that ye smatyr,	126	Garnesche3	106

SMATTER

	Page	Title	Line
He can nothynge smatter	267	Collyn Clout	814
For I abhore to smatter	297	Why Come Ye	714

SMATTERYNGE

	Page	Title	Line
To flatterynge, to smatterynge, to to out of harre,	199	Magnyfycence	2095

SMATTERS

	Page	Title	Line
He clyttreth and he clatters, /He medleth and he smatters,	247	Collyn Clout	24

SMELLE

	Page	Title	Line
And so puauntely dothe smelle	127	Garnesche3	143

SMELLED

	Page	Title	Line
And smelled all of ale.	226	El Rummynge	487

SMELLETH

	Page	Title	Line
Howe be it of scape thryfte your clokes smelleth musty.	161	Magnyfycence	761

SMELLID

	Page	Title	Line
Foo, foisty bawdias, sum smellid of the smoke.	330	Garlande	639

SMERED

	Page	Title	Line
Her shone smered wyth talowe,	216	El Rummynge	88

SMERY

	Page	Title	Line
Masyd, wytles smery smyth,	71	Hauke	331
For ye war smery, lyke a sele,	131	Garnesche5	58

SMERKE

	Page	Title	Line
And smerke, lyke a smythy kur, at sperkes of steile;	333	Garlande	762

SMYGHT

	Page	Title	Line
For he wyll as sone smyght	293	Why Come Ye	582

SMYLE

	Page	Title	Line
Sodenly thus Fortune can bothe smyle and frowne,	212	Magnyfycence	2529

	Page	Title	Line
SMYLED —SO			
Sodenly thus Fortune can bothe smyle and frowne,	213	Magnyfycence	2536
I sawe hir smyle, and I then did the same.	327	Garlande	530
I then] 'than I' Marshe 1568			
Gog gyve you good yere, ye make me to smyle.	332	Garlande	736
SMYLED			
The snyte snyveled in the snowte and smyled at the game.	192	Magnyfycence	1840
SMYLID			
Came towarde me, and smylid halfe in game;	327	Garlande	529
SMYLYNG			
Though angelyk be youre smylyng,	41	Coystrowne4	15
SMYLYNGE			
Of our pole artyke, smylynge halfe in scorne	46	Bowge	5
SMYTH			
Masyd, wytles smery smyth,	71	Hauke	331
SMYTHY KUR			
And smerke, lyke a smythy kur, at sperkes of steile;	333	Garlande	762
SMOCKE			
And wrapt in a maidenes smocke,	86	Phy Sparrow	590
To clothe the nakyd where is lackynge a smocke -	177	Magnyfycence	1345
Under her surfled smocke	252	Collyn Clout	218
SMOCKES			
Theyr smockes all to-ragged, /Wyth tytters and tatters,	217	El Rummynge	125
SMOKE			
Whiche kyndelde the wyld fyre that made all this smoke.	31	Dol Dethe	77
But I am lothe for to reyse a smoke,	59	Bowge	479
Foo, foisty bawdias, sum smellid of the smoke.	330	Garlande	639
SMOKES			
And from the smokes sowre /Of Proserpinas bowre;	73	Phy Sparrow	82
SMOTHELY			
Shall glyde and smothely slyppe	277	Collyn Clout	1252
Some lokyd full smothely, and had a fals quarter,	326	Garlande	504
quarter] 'quart' Marshe 1568			
SNAYLE			
Slaveryng lyke a slymy snayle.	130	Garnesche5	45
What can it avayle /To dryve forth a snayle,	246	Collyn Clout	2
SNAYLIS			
Enflorid with flowris and slymy snaylis,	345	Garlande	1160
SNAP			
A maunchet for morell thereon to snap.	37	Coystrowne1	11
SNAPPAR			
To snappar and to fall /Into this opyn cryme;	65	Hauke	142
SNAPPER			
In pevyshnes yet they snapper and fall,	36	Coystrowne1	4
they] 'the' †Rastell 1527			
And snapper in suche werkes?	381	Replycacion	274
SNARE			
Ye be nat cawte in an hempen snare.	133	Garnesche5	163
Fy, fy, that ever I sholde be brought in this snare!	196	Magnyfycence	1972
And sette suche a snare	361	Albany	111
SNATCHE			
Grimbaldus gredy snatche a puddyng tyl the rost be redy.	172	Magnyfycence	1155
SNATCHYNGE			
By God, for snatchynge of puddynges and wortes.	171	Magnyfycence	1128
SNEVELYNG			
Snevelyng in her nose, /As though she had the pose.	223	El Rummynge	364
SNEVYLL			
In the pott your nose dedde snevyll;	124	Garnesche3	27
Let him cough, rough or snevyll!	277	Collyn Clout	1221
SNYTE			
The feldefare and the snyte;	82	Phy Sparrow	412
The snyte snyveled in the snowte and smyled at the game.	192	Magnyfycence	1840
SNYVELED			
The snyte snyveled in the snowte and smyled at the game.	192	Magnyfycence	1840
SNORT			
Than wyll he rout and snort;	220	El Rummynge	232
SNOUT			
She spake thus in her snout,	223	El Rummynge	363
spake thus] 'speketh this' †Lant 1545, Kynge & Marche 1554, Day 1560, Marshe 1568			
Garnysshed was her snout	228	El Rummynge	554
SNOWE			
Drove clowdes together lyke dryftis of snowe.	319	Garlande	263
SNOWTE			
Your tethe teintyd with tawny; your semely snowte doth passe,	122	Garnesche1	39
For thow hast a long snowte,	133	Garnesche5	130
So semely a snowte	168	Magnyfycence	994
The snyte snyveled in the snowte and smyled at the game.	192	Magnyfycence	1840
SNUF			
That made sum to snurre and snuf in the wynde;	353	Garlande	1472
snurre] 'surt' †Fakes 1523			
SNURRE			
That made sum to snurre and snuf in the wynde;	353	Garlande	1472
snurre] 'surt' †Fakes 1523			
SO			
So noble a man, so valiaunt lorde and knyght	30	Dol Dethe	29
So noble a man, so valiaunt lorde and knyght	30	Dol Dethe	29
I say, ye commoners, why wer ye so stark mad?	30	Dol Dethe	50
When thou shoke thi sword so noble a man to mar!	32	Dol Dethe	115

	Page	Title	Line
So forcibly upon this Erle thow ran,	32	Dol Dethe	124
He whystelyth so swetely he makyth me to swete;	37	Coystrowne1	37
He techyth them so wysely to solf and to fayne	38	Coystrowne1	53
Above the sky /That is so hy,	40	Coystrowne3	56
Why so koy and full of skorne?	40	Coystrowne4	8
To dele wyth her so cowardly;	42	Balettys1	27
That Dame Menolope was never half so wyse;	42	Balettys2	11
Yet so it is that a rumer begynnyth for to ryse	42	Balettys2	12
And so with your servantys he fersly doth fyght.	43	Balettys2	28
So fersly he fytyth, hys mynde is so fell,	43	Balettys2	29
So fersly he fytyth, hys mynde is so fell,	43	Balettys2	29
And if ye lyst to know the cause why so,	44	Balettys3	38
How there nys thynge that I covet so fayne	44	Balettys3	41
But hatefull absens, to me so envyous,	45	Balettys3	45
To be so cruell and so overthwart,	45	Balettys5	5
To be so cruell and so overthwart,	45	Balettys5	5
To suffer me so carefull to endure,	45	Balettys5	6
I am content to all partys be pleasyd:	45	Balettys5	11
But Fortune enforsyth me so carefully to endure,	46	Balettys5	13
And not to wrythe, for he so wyll atteyne,	46	Bowge	22
wrythe] 'wryte' Wynkyn de Worde 1510, Marshe 1568			
To be so perte to prese so proudly uppe.	48	Bowge	71
To be so perte to prese so proudly uppe.	48	Bowge	71
That, so to saye, I had gyven her no cause.	48	Bowge	75
Than asked she me, 'Syr, so God the spede,	48	Bowge	76
Desyre her name was, and so she me tolde,	48	Bowge	85
What though our chaffer be never so dere,	48	Bowge	89
They coude not faile, thei thought, they were so sure.	50	Bowge	142
'Noo thynge erthely that I wonder so sore	50	Bowge	148
As of your connynge, that is so excellent;	50	Bowge	149
So vertuously that hath his dayes spente;	50	Bowge	151
And, as she wyll, so shall our grete shyppe sayle.	50	Bowge	172
For, but I trusted you, so God me save,	52	Bowge	213
I wolde noo thynge so playne be.	52	Bowge	214
'Syr, God you save, why loke you so sadde?	53	Bowge	239
I wyste never man that so soone coude wynne	53	Bowge	269
And ye be welcome, syr, so God me save,	54	Bowge	279
Hatred by the herte so had hym wrounge	54	Bowge	292
'Than,' quod Hervy, 'why arte thou so dysmayde?'	54	Bowge	299
'By God,' quod Hervy, 'and it so happen myghte!	54	Bowge	306
We be thy betters, and so thou shalte us take,	55	Bowge	342
His gowne so shorte that it ne cover myghte	56	Bowge	354
His rumpe, he wente so all for somer lyghte;	56	Bowge	355
His elbowe bare, he ware his gere so nye,	56	Bowge	361
I was ashamed so to here hym prate.	56	Bowge	373
'How do ye, mayster? Ye loke so soberly!	58	Bowge	442
Alas, I coude not dele so with a [J]ew.	59	Bowge	462
a Jew] 'on yew' †Wynkyn de Worde 1499, 'a yew' Wynkyn de Worde 1510, Marshe 1568			
I dare not speke, we be so layde awayte,	59	Bowge	468
And so I wolde it were, so God me spede,	59	Bowge	481
And so I wolde it were, so God me spede,	59	Bowge	481
And I am your, syr, so have I blys,	60	Bowge	495
He tolde me so, by God, ye maye truste me.	60	Bowge	514
That be so far abusyd /They cannot be excusyd	62	Hauke	5
That preest that hawkys so,	62	Hauke	15
She had flowyn so oft,	63	Hauke	68
But lyke a March harum /His braynes were so parum.	64	Hauke	105
And so the Scrybe was feed,	65	Hauke	151
That so far dyd excede;	67	Hauke	191
So payned and so strayned	73	Phy Sparrow	48
So payned and so strayned	73	Phy Sparrow	48
So fervently I shake,	74	Phy Sparrow	104
So urgently I am brought /Into carefull thought.	74	Phy Sparrow	106
It was so prety a fole,	74	Phy Sparrow	115
And fly so to and fro;	75	Phy Sparrow	160
fly] 'fle' Wyght 1553, Kitson 1560.6, Marshe 1568			
What though he crept so lowe?	76	Phy Sparrow	169
though] 'thought' †Kele 1545.2			
Was never none so good;	78	Phy Sparrow	269
That slew so cruelly.	78	Phy Sparrow	279
So thou, foule cat that thou arte,	79	Phy Sparrow	302
So trayterously my byrde to kyll	79	Phy Sparrow	322
How my byrde so fayre,	80	Phy Sparrow	343
So none be left behynde.	81	Phy Sparrow	389
The pecocke so prowde,	82	Phy Sparrow	438
The owle, that is so foule,	82	Phy Sparrow	442
is] not in Kitson 1560.6, Marshe 1568			
The heron so gaunce,	83	Phy Sparrow	444
gaunce] 'gaunte' Wyght 1553, Kitson 1560.6, Marshe 1568			
An horshowe so great,	83	Phy Sparrow	479
And of the love so hote	88	Phy Sparrow	677
Our language is so rusty,	91	Phy Sparrow	777
So cankered and so full	91	Phy Sparrow	778
So cankered and so full	91	Phy Sparrow	778
Of frowardes, and so dull,	91	Phy Sparrow	779
So as it is enprowed,	91	Phy Sparrow	793
Ryght so she doth excede	93	Phy Sparrow	883

	Page	Title	Line
So Jupiter me socour,	94	Phy Sparrow	895
He is so bete /With malyce, and frete	95	Phy Sparrow	930
So Jupyter me socoure,	96	Phy Sparrow	991
Myne hert doth so enbrace,	96	Phy Sparrow	1005
And so hath ravyshed me	96	Phy Sparrow	1006
So Jupiter me socoure,	97	Phy Sparrow	1024
The orient perle so clere,	97	Phy Sparrow	1033
So properly it is set:	98	Phy Sparrow	1049
So Jupiter me succour,	98	Phy Sparrow	1056
And set so womanly,	98	Phy Sparrow	1067
So Jupiter me socoure,	98	Phy Sparrow	1085
So sad and so demure,	99	Phy Sparrow	1097
So sad and so demure,	99	Phy Sparrow	1097
Behavynge her so sure,	99	Phy Sparrow	1098
My eyne were so dased;	99	Phy Sparrow	1106
So Jupyter me socoure,	99	Phy Sparrow	1109
That are so quyckely vayned,	99	Phy Sparrow	1121
So Jupiter me succoure,	100	Phy Sparrow	1138
Ne no tyger so wood,	100	Phy Sparrow	1157
So Jupiter me succour,	100	Phy Sparrow	1163
So goodly as she dresses,	101	Phy Sparrow	1170
So properly she presses	101	Phy Sparrow	1171
Of her heer so fyne,	101	Phy Sparrow	1173
So Jupiter me socoure,	101	Phy Sparrow	1187
Her kyrtell so goodly lased,	101	Phy Sparrow	1194
So Jupiter me succoure,	101	Phy Sparrow	1210
So Jupiter me socoure,	102	Phy Sparrow	1233
And so forth per cetera;	104	Phy Sparrow	1321
But whether it were so,	105	Phy Sparrow	1354
Luna that so bryght doth shyne,	105	Phy Sparrow	1365
Ye summoned our kynge. Why dyde ye so?	113	Scot Kynge	2
To be so scornefull to your alye	113	Scot Kynge	13
They are so stowre, /So frantyke mad,	115	Ag Scottes	12
They are so stowre, /So frantyke mad,	115	Ag Scottes	13
So prowde of hart, /So overthwart,	116	Ag Scottes	35
So prowde of hart, /So overthwart,	116	Ag Scottes	36
So out of frame, /So voyde of shame,	116	Ag Scottes	37
So out of frame, /So voyde of shame,	116	Ag Scottes	38
So that now I have devysed,	117	Ag Scottes	69
Ye summond our kyng, why dyd ye so?	118	Ag Scottes	92
ye] not in Kynge & Marche 1554, Day 1560, Marshe 1568			
Syr skyrgalyard, ye were so skyt,	118	Ag Scottes	101
Agaynst you gave so sharpe a shower,	119	Ag Scottes	133
In double delyng so he dyd dreme,	119	Ag Scottes	155
In] 'An' Day 1560, Marshe 1568			
Your beard as brym as bore at bay,	119	Ag Scottes	161
Your Seven Systers, that gun so gay,	119	Ag Scottes	162
For Syr Frollo de Franko was never halfe so talle.	121	Garneschel	5
So curryshly to beknave me in the kynges place?	121	Garneschel	9
Ye stronge sturdy stalyon, so sterne and stowty,	122	Garneschel	10
Nor no bore so brymly brystlyd ys with here,	122	Garneschel	25
Me for to chalenge that of your chalennge makyth so lytyll fors.	123	Garnesche2	19
So that sche wolde have kum	125	Garnesche3	63
To occupy so your mynde;	126	Garnesche3	103
So for a knave to clatyr;	126	Garnesche3	107
So suerly yt xall nat tarnishe.	127	Garnesche3	122
Your wyt ys so geson,	127	Garnesche3	129
So tranchaunt and so kene,	127	Garnesche3	138
So tranchaunt and so kene,	127	Garnesche3	138
Your brethe yt ys so felle	127	Garnesche3	142
And so puauntely dothe smelle	127	Garnesche3	143
And so haynnously doth stynke,	127	Garnesche3	144
Dothe savyr halfe so souer	127	Garnesche3	146
With hys brethe so stronge,	128	Garnesche3	151
And so thy selfe hovyr-wachyd	128	Garnesche3	179
Rayle not so far.	136	Dundas	63
But yet I may say safely, so many wel lettred,	138	Ven Tongues	38
And so little learning, so lewdly alowed,	138	Ven Tongues	40
And so little learning, so lewdly alowed,	138	Ven Tongues	40
But ye are so full of vertibilite,	138	Ven Tongues	42
Although he made it never so tough,	139	Ven Tongues	77
But men nowe a dayes so unhappely be uryd,	140	Magnyfycence	6
But wyll hath reason so under subjeccyon,	141	Magnyfycence	19
And so dysordereth this worlde over all,	141	Magnyfycence	20
It is so swete in all maner of kynde.	142	Magnyfycence	51
So it in measure be.	143	Magnyfycence	101
So that lyberte be not lefte behynde.	144	Magnyfycence	129
So wolde I, but I wolde be lothe,	144	Magnyfycence	143
So in his harte he may be glad of us.	145	Magnyfycence	158
So that welthe with measure shalbe conbyned,	145	Magnyfycence	179
There is no flaterer nor losyll so lyther,	146	Magnyfycence	200
Yet measure hath ben so longe from us absent,	146	Magnyfycence	221
Welth and wyt, I say, be so threde bare worne,	146	Magnyfycence	223
Or who made you so bolde to interrupe my tale?	147	Magnyfycence	256
Largesse is laudable so it be in measure.	148	Magnyfycence	278
'in measure be' †Rastell & Treveris C 1530, B			
But covetyse hath blowen you so full of wynde	148	Magnyfycence	290
That with your lorde and mayster so pertly can prate!	149	Magnyfycence	305

SO — SO	Page	Title	Line
Howe so? By God, at the see syde,	150	Magnyfycence	346
It dothe so sure nowe and than.	150	Magnyfycence	368
And say they so in very dede?	151	Magnyfycence	378
With ye, syr, so God me spede.	151	Magnyfycence	379
I pray you, syr, I may so be;	151	Magnyfycence	391
But Fansy, my frende, where have ye bene so longe?	154	Magnyfycence	500
Why, wenyst thou, horson, that I were so mad?	155	Magnyfycence	517
So large a man, and so lytell of stature!	155	Magnyfycence	523
So large a man, and so lytell of stature!	155	Magnyfycence	523
So he ruleth over all our place.	155	Magnyfycence	545
That we can no better than so.	155	Magnyfycence	550
Ryght so a sharp fansy must be founde	155	Magnyfycence	553
Syr, it is so that these twayne	157	Magnyfycence	612
Mary, so wyll we also.	157	Magnyfycence	616
So that we have no lyberte;	158	Magnyfycence	659
For then shall we so craftely cary	159	Magnyfycence	683
And though I be so odyous a geste,	160	Magnyfycence	703
I move them, I mase them, I make them so fonde,	161	Magnyfycence	742
And so, by these meanes, I brewe moche bale.	161	Magnyfycence	744
Ye, so I can devyse my gere after the cowrtly maner.	161	Magnyfycence	766
So thou arte personable to bere a prynces baner.	161	Magnyfycence	767
Abyde, syr, quod he! Mary, so I do.	162	Magnyfycence	789
Art thou so angry as thou semyst?	162	Magnyfycence	794
Ye, so I tell the.	162	Magnyfycence	800
And so they go out of the place.	163	Magnyfycence	SD
My heyre bussheth /So plesauntly;	163	Magnyfycence	836
My robe russheth /So ruttyngly;	163	Magnyfycence	838
I am so lyght /To daunce delyght;	164	Magnyfycence	840
A very pore /That so wyll do,	164	Magnyfycence	870
His gowne so wyde	165	Magnyfycence	903
Ye, for the, so I say.	166	Magnyfycence	930
Howe so? Tell me, I the pray.	166	Magnyfycence	931
With Crafty Convayaunce. Ye, dyd they so?	166	Magnyfycence	941
By Goddes body, so dyd I.	166	Magnyfycence	947
Howe so? By God, by a praty slyght,	167	Magnyfycence	952
So I am poynted after my consayte.	167	Magnyfycence	961
So semely a snowte	168	Magnyfycence	994
So farly fayre as it lokys!	168	Magnyfycence	999
And her becke so comely crokys!	168	Magnyfycence	1000
But, in faythe, I am so occupyed	168	Magnyfycence	1019
I wyll not have it so, I wyll have it this.	169	Magnyfycence	1042
A pylde curre? Ye, so I tell the, a pylde curre.	169	Magnyfycence	1055
That thou so hye fro me doth sprynge,	170	Magnyfycence	1069
And I so lytell alway styll.	170	Magnyfycence	1070
Thou art so feble-fantastycall,	170	Magnyfycence	1072
And so braynsyke therwithall,	170	Magnyfycence	1073
For so with fantasyes my wyt dothe flete	170	Magnyfycence	1080
What! Wenyst thou that I were so folysshe and so fonde?	170	Magnyfycence	1098
What! Wenyst thou that I were so folysshe and so fonde?	170	Magnyfycence	1098
And hath so mased a wandrynge wyt?	172	Magnyfycence	1144
It forseth not of reason, so it kepe ryme.	172	Magnyfycence	1150
Ye, so redely and so sone!	172	Magnyfycence	1157
Ye, so redely and so sone!	172	Magnyfycence	1157
What? Wolde ye have mo folys, and are so many?	172	Magnyfycence	1170
In faythe, I can do mastryes, so I can.	173	Magnyfycence	1190
Cockes armes! It is not so, I trowe.	173	Magnyfycence	1202
So in theyr eyre I synge them a songe	174	Magnyfycence	1223
And make them so longe to muse	174	Magnyfycence	1224
Anone he waxyth so hy and prowde,	174	Magnyfycence	1244
He dawnsys so long, 'hey, troly, loly',	175	Magnyfycence	1250
Thynkyst thou not so, by thy fayth?	175	Magnyfycence	1253
Thynke I not so, quod he. Ellys have I shame,	175	Magnyfycence	1254
For they that wyll so bysely smater	175	Magnyfycence	1257
So helpe me God, man, ever at the length	175	Magnyfycence	1258
For with foly so do I them lede	175	Magnyfycence	1260
So is all the remenaunt, I make God avowe;	175	Magnyfycence	1283
So how, I say, the hare is squat!	176	Magnyfycence	1299
Pryvy poyntmentys conveyed so properly;	177	Magnyfycence	1337
'As oft as ye lyst, so honeste be savyd.	177	Magnyfycence	1348
So that there knowe no man but I and she.	177	Magnyfycence	1353
Syr, as by my wyll, it shall be so no more.	178	Magnyfycence	1377
Mayster Survayour, where have ye ben so longe?	178	Magnyfycence	1382
Mary, syr, so dyd he excede and passe,	178	Magnyfycence	1385
I am content so it in measure be.	179	Magnyfycence	1390
Nay, nay; not so, my frende Felycyte.	179	Magnyfycence	1392
And what so we say, holde you content withall.	179	Magnyfycence	1406
So it be by mesure I am ryght well content.	180	Magnyfycence	1421
And so as ye se it wyll be no better,	180	Magnyfycence	1438
No man so hardy to worke agaynst my wyll.	181	Magnyfycence	1479
Were never halfe so rychely as I am drest.	181	Magnyfycence	1483
What man is so maysyd with me that dare mete,	182	Magnyfycence	1506
Nor none so hardy of them with me that durste crake,	182	Magnyfycence	1513
Yes, syr, so good man in you I se,	182	Magnyfycence	1522
And in your delynge so good assuraunce,	183	Magnyfycence	1523
Of your langage, it is so well devysed;	183	Magnyfycence	1530
A, I wolde to God that I were halfe so crafty	183	Magnyfycence	1532
Or in electe utteraunce halfe so eloquent,	183	Magnyfycence	1533
So as ye be a prynce of great myght,	183	Magnyfycence	1545

SO — SO   Page   Title   Line

Text	Page	Title	Line
Her eyen relucent as carbuncle so clere,	183	Magnyfycence	1556
So I myght hobby for suche a lusty larke.	184	Magnyfycence	1564
These wordes in myne eyre, they be so lustely spoken,	184	Magnyfycence	1565
They towche me so thorowly and tykyll my consayte,	184	Magnyfycence	1567
And that ye wyll not cast hym away so sone.	186	Magnyfycence	1638
Syr, so it is: this man is here by,	186	Magnyfycence	1649
For, so helpe me God, for you he is not mete.	186	Magnyfycence	1653
And he go to the devyll, so that I may have my fee,	187	Magnyfycence	1670
What force ye, so that [y]e be payde?	187	Magnyfycence	1672
ye be] 'he be' †Rastell & Treveris C 1530, B			
So it is all the maner nowe a dayes	187	Magnyfycence	1677
So that I may craftely be excused.	187	Magnyfycence	1684
So masterfully upon you for to take	188	Magnyfycence	1715
Nay, so God me helpe, it was no grete vexacyon;	189	Magnyfycence	1733
So to be ruled by measure, it is a payne.	189	Magnyfycence	1739
So I wote not what he sholde do here.	189	Magnyfycence	1741
For as thou sayst, ryght so shall it be,	190	Magnyfycence	1783
For as thou wylte, so shall the game go;	190	Magnyfycence	1786
A, Lorde, so I wolde halse her hartely!	190	Magnyfycence	1801
So I wolde clepe her! So I wolde kys her swete!	190	Magnyfycence	1802
So I wolde clepe her! So I wolde kys her swete!	190	Magnyfycence	1802
What tydynges with you, syr, that you loke so sad?	192	Magnyfycence	1843
What! Hath Sadnesse begyled me so?	192	Magnyfycence	1855
Lorde, so my flesshe trymblyth nowe for drede!	193	Magnyfycence	1875
He knewe not hymselfe, his harte was so hye;	193	Magnyfycence	1888
Lydderyns so lytell set by Goddes lawes.	194	Magnyfycence	1919
Alasse that ever I sholde be so shamed!	196	Magnyfycence	1982
Alasse that ever I was so harde happed	196	Magnyfycence	1984
Ye, mary, is it. Ye, so mote I goo.	198	Magnyfycence	2046
I bassed that baby with harte so free;	198	Magnyfycence	2069
A, so! That syghe was farre fet!	199	Magnyfycence	2071
So merely syngeth the nyghtyngale!	199	Magnyfycence	2077
But he abused so his free lyberte,	200	Magnyfycence	2113
And so shall a noble man nobly be servyd.	200	Magnyfycence	2120
But so longe they rekyn with theyr reasons amysse	200	Magnyfycence	2127
they] 'theyr' †Rastell & Treveris C 1530, B			
And some in the worlde, theyr brayne is so ydyll	200	Magnyfycence	2135
Some hath so moche lyberte of one thynge and other,	200	Magnyfycence	2141
Some have so moche lyberte that they fere no synne,	200	Magnyfycence	2143
I am so lusty to loke on, so freshe, and so fre,	201	Magnyfycence	2145
I am so lusty to loke on, so freshe, and so fre,	201	Magnyfycence	2145
I am so lusty to loke on, so freshe, and so fre,	201	Magnyfycence	2145
Freers, with foly I make them so fayne	201	Magnyfycence	2147
So he is the worste brawler that ever was borne.	202	Magnyfycence	2200
In fayth, so to suffer the, it is but a skorne.	202	Magnyfycence	2201
Mary, so ungoodly langage you me gave.	203	Magnyfycence	2213
In fay, man, some rybbys of the motton be so ranke	204	Magnyfycence	2269
So shamfully to me, theyr mayster, to aproche,	205	Magnyfycence	2279
Thou hast bene so waywarde, so wranglyng, and so wrothsome,	205	Magnyfycence	2293
Thou hast bene so waywarde, so wranglyng, and so wrothsome,	205	Magnyfycence	2293
Thou hast bene so waywarde, so wranglyng, and so wrothsome,	205	Magnyfycence	2293
And so fer thou arte behynde of thy rent,	205	Magnyfycence	2294
And so ungracyously thy dayes thou hast spent,	205	Magnyfycence	2295
For I have so ungracyously my lyfe mysusyd,	205	Magnyfycence	2298
No, no; for thy synnys be so excedynge farre,	205	Magnyfycence	2300
So innumerable, and so full of dyspyte,	205	Magnyfycence	2301
So innumerable, and so full of dyspyte,	205	Magnyfycence	2301
Alas, syr! So I am lapped in adversyte	206	Magnyfycence	2331
There was never so harde a storme of mysery,	207	Magnyfycence	2343
They molefy so easely my harte that was so harde.	207	Magnyfycence	2346
They molefy so easely my harte that was so harde.	207	Magnyfycence	2346
How fortuned you, Magnyfycence, so far to fal behynde?	209	Magnyfycence	2423
To gyve so hasty credence ye were moche to blame.	209	Magnyfycence	2443
It wolde be founde so yf it were well tryde.	210	Magnyfycence	2449
Yf you be so myndyd, we be ryght glad.	210	Magnyfycence	2473
So that your largesse be not to prodygall.	211	Magnyfycence	2488
So in this worlde there is no sykernesse,	212	Magnyfycence	2522
I am content, my frendys, that it so be.	214	Magnyfycence	2570
And so doth it apere,	216	El Rummynge	59
doth it] 'it dothe' Day 1560, Marshe 1568			
For, be there never so moche prese,	218	El Rummynge	174
Her lyppes are so drye,	221	El Rummynge	272
And some went so narrowe	222	El Rummynge	297
Theyr thrust was so great,	222	El Rummynge	303
And so was made the peace.	223	El Rummynge	350
the peace] 'the drunken peace' †Lant 1545, Kynge & Marche 1554, Day 1560, Marshe 1568			
That causeth I loke so donny.'	224	El Rummynge	400
She had her so guyded	226	El Rummynge	472
She dranke so of the dregges,	226	El Rummynge	480
dregges] 'dragges' †Lant 1545, Kynge & Marche 1554, Day 1560			
And fell so wyde open	227	El Rummynge	496
For so mote I hoppy, /It coleth well my croppy.'	228	El Rummynge	560
croppy] 'coppy' Day 1560, Marshe 1568			
Her paunche was so puffed	228	El Rummynge	570
And so with ale stuffed,	229	El Rummynge	571
She was not halfe so wyse	229	El Rummynge	588
I have wrytten so mytche	230	El Rummynge	619

	Page	Title	Line
Pawbe une aruer, so the Welche man sayes.	233	Speke Parott	91
But our Grekis theyr Greke so well have applyed,	234	Speke Parott	145
For Greci fari so occupyeth the chayre,	235	Speke Parott	163
Tryvyals and quatryvyals so sore now they appayre,	235	Speke Parott	166
Settyng theyr myndys so moche of eloquens,	235	Speke Parott	181
Except mannes soule, that Chryst so dere bought;	236	Speke Parott	215
My harte is so sore payned,	237	Speke Parott	254
So many morall maters, and so lytell usyd; many] 'many many' †MS Harley 2252	244	Speke Parott	449
So many morall maters, and so lytell usyd; many] 'many many' †MS Harley 2252	244	Speke Parott	449
So myche newe makyng, and so madd tyme spente;	244	Speke Parott	450
So myche newe makyng, and so madd tyme spente;	244	Speke Parott	450
So myche translacion into Englyshe confused;	244	Speke Parott	451
So myche nobyll prechyng, and so lytell amendment;	244	Speke Parott	452
So myche nobyll prechyng, and so lytell amendment;	244	Speke Parott	452
So myche consultacion, almoste to none entente;	244	Speke Parott	453
So myche provision, and so lytell wytte at nede -	244	Speke Parott	454
So myche provision, and so lytell wytte at nede -	244	Speke Parott	454
So lytyll dyscressyon, and so myche reasonyng;	244	Speke Parott	456
So lytyll dyscressyon, and so myche reasonyng;	244	Speke Parott	456
So myche hardy-dardy, and so lytell manlynes;	244	Speke Parott	457
So myche hardy-dardy, and so lytell manlynes;	244	Speke Parott	457
So prodigall expence, and so shamfull reconyng;	244	Speke Parott	458
So prodigall expence, and so shamfull reconyng;	244	Speke Parott	458
So gorgyous garmentes, and so myche wrechydnese,	244	Speke Parott	459
So gorgyous garmentes, and so myche wrechydnese,	244	Speke Parott	459
So myche portlye pride, with pursys penyles;	244	Speke Parott	460
So myche spente before, and so myche unpayd behynde -	244	Speke Parott	461
So myche spente before, and so myche unpayd behynde -	244	Speke Parott	461
So myche forcastyng, and so farre an after-dele;	244	Speke Parott	463
So myche forcastyng, and so farre an after-dele;	244	Speke Parott	463
So myche poletyke pratyng, and so lytell stondythe in stede;	244	Speke Parott	464
So myche poletyke pratyng, and so lytell stondythe in stede;	244	Speke Parott	464
So lytell secretnese, and so myche grete councell;	245	Speke Parott	465
So lytell secretnese, and so myche grete councell;	245	Speke Parott	465
So manye bolde barons, there hertes as dull as lede;	245	Speke Parott	466
So many nobyll bodyes, undyr on dawys hedd;	245	Speke Parott	467
So royall a kyng, as reynythe uppon us all -	245	Speke Parott	468
So many complayntes, and so smalle redresse;	245	Speke Parott	470
So many complayntes, and so smalle redresse;	245	Speke Parott	470
So myche callying on, and so smalle takyng hede;	245	Speke Parott	471
So myche callying on, and so smalle takyng hede;	245	Speke Parott	471
So myche losse of merchaundyse, and so remedyles;	245	Speke Parott	472
So myche losse of merchaundyse, and so remedyles;	245	Speke Parott	472
So lytell care for the comynweall, and so myche nede;	245	Speke Parott	473
So lytell care for the comynweall, and so myche nede;	245	Speke Parott	473
So myche dowghtfull daunger, and so lytell drede;	245	Speke Parott	474
So myche dowghtfull daunger, and so lytell drede;	245	Speke Parott	474
So myche pride of prelattes, so cruell and so kene -	245	Speke Parott	475
So myche pride of prelattes, so cruell and so kene -	245	Speke Parott	475
So myche pride of prelattes, so cruell and so kene -	245	Speke Parott	475
So many thevys hangyd, and thevys neverthelesse;	245	Speke Parott	477
So myche presonment, for matyrs not worth a hawe;	245	Speke Parott	478
So myche papers weryng for ryghte a smalle exesse;	245	Speke Parott	479
So myche pelory pajauntes undyr colowur of good lawe;	245	Speke Parott	480
So myche towrnyng on the cooke-stole for every guy-gaw;	245	Speke Parott	481
So myche mokkyshe makyng of statutes of array -	245	Speke Parott	482
So braynles calvys hedes, so many shepis taylys;	245	Speke Parott	484
So braynles calvys hedes, so many shepis taylys;	245	Speke Parott	484
So bolde a braggyng bocher, and flesshe sold so dere;	245	Speke Parott	485
So bolde a braggyng bocher, and flesshe sold so dere;	245	Speke Parott	485
So many plucte partryches, and so fatte quaylles;	245	Speke Parott	486
So many plucte partryches, and so fatte quaylles;	245	Speke Parott	486
So mangye a mastyfe curre, the grete greyhoundes pere;	245	Speke Parott	487
So bygge a bulke of brow-auntleres cabagyd that yere;	245	Speke Parott	488
So many swannes dede, and so small revell -	245	Speke Parott	489
So many swannes dede, and so small revell -	245	Speke Parott	489
So many trusys takyn, and so lytyll perfyte trowthe; perfyte] 'profyte' †MS Harley 2252	245	Speke Parott	491
So many trusys takyn, and so lytyll perfyte trowthe; perfyte] 'profyte' †MS Harley 2252	245	Speke Parott	491
So myche bely-joye, and so wastefull banketyng;	245	Speke Parott	492
So myche bely-joye, and so wastefull banketyng;	245	Speke Parott	492
So pynchyng and sparyng, and so lytell profyte growth;	245	Speke Parott	493
So pynchyng and sparyng, and so lytell profyte growth;	245	Speke Parott	493
So many howgye howsys byldyng, and so small howse-holdyng;	245	Speke Parott	494
So many howgye howsys byldyng, and so small howse-holdyng;	245	Speke Parott	494
So ys all thyng wrowghte wylfully withowte reson and skylle.	245	Speke Parott	496
Syns Dewcalyons flodde the world was never so yll. the world] 'the world the world' †MS Harley 2252	245	Speke Parott	497
So many vacabondes, so many beggers bolde,	245	Speke Parott	498
So many vacabondes, so many beggers bolde,	245	Speke Parott	498
So myche decay of monesteries and relygious places;	245	Speke Parott	499
So hote hatered agaynste the Chyrche, and cheryte so colde;	245	Speke Parott	500
So hote hatered agaynste the Chyrche, and cheryte so colde;	245	Speke Parott	500
So myche of my lordes grace, and in hym no grace ys;	245	Speke Parott	501
So many holow hartes, and so dowbyll faces;	245	Speke Parott	502

SO—SO   Page   Title   Line

	Page	Title	Line
So many holow hartes, and so dowbyll faces;	245	Speke Parott	502
So myche sayntuary brekyng, and prevylegidde barryd –	246	Speke Parott	503
So myche raggyd ryghte of a rammes horne;	246	Speke Parott	505
So rygorous revelyng, in a prelate specially;	246	Speke Parott	506
So bold and so braggyng, and was so baselye borne;	246	Speke Parott	507
So bold and so braggyng, and was so baselye borne;	246	Speke Parott	507
So bold and so braggyng, and was so baselye borne;	246	Speke Parott	507
So lordlye of hys lokes, and so dysdayneslye;	246	Speke Parott	508
So lordlye of hys lokes, and so dysdayneslye;	246	Speke Parott	508
So fatte a magott, bred of a flesshe-flye;	246	Speke Parott	509
So myche prevye wachyng in cold wynters nyghtes;	246	Speke Parott	512
So myche serchyng of loselles, and ys hym selfe so lewde;	246	Speke Parott	513
So myche serchyng of loselles, and ys hym selfe so lewde;	246	Speke Parott	513
So myche conjuracions for elvyshe myday sprettes;	246	Speke Parott	514
So many bullys of pardon publysshed and shewyd;	246	Speke Parott	515
So myche crossyng and blyssyng and hym all be shrewde;	246	Speke Parott	516
'His heed is so fat	247	Collyn Clout	16
It may well so be,	247	Collyn Clout	38
The prelates ben so haute /They say, and loke so hye	248	Collyn Clout	71
The prelates ben so haute /They say, and loke so hye	248	Collyn Clout	72
For sothe, they are to lewde /To say so, all beshrewde!	249	Collyn Clout	91
And sol fa so alamyre	249	Collyn Clout	107
sol fa] 'so fa' †Godfray 1531, 'solfe' MS Harley 2252			
Theyr lernynge is so small,	252	Collyn Clout	240
To kepe so harde a rule,	254	Collyn Clout	307
Ye have so overthwarted,	256	Collyn Clout	371
So that theyr founders soules	257	Collyn Clout	421
Whan Scorpyon descendynge, /Was so then pretendynge	258	Collyn Clout	472
Then to be so dysgysed.	261	Collyn Clout	580
Ye are so puffed with pryde,	261	Collyn Clout	593
Fortune so tourneth the ball	262	Collyn Clout	632
And ruleth so over all	262	Collyn Clout	633
And so they blere your eye	263	Collyn Clout	684
And so clerkely promoted,	265	Collyn Clout	756
Though it were never so playne,	265	Collyn Clout	765
So as they myght be /Compendyously conveyed,	265	Collyn Clout	767
So that in divynyte	266	Collyn Clout	789
Theyr hertes are so faynted,	269	Collyn Clout	899
And they be so attaynted	269	Collyn Clout	900
They occupy them so /With syngynge Placebo,	269	Collyn Clout	906
That ye kepe them so under;	271	Collyn Clout	1007
ye] 'we' Kele 1545.1, 'ye' MS Harley 2252			
Yet they mervayle so moche lesse,	271	Collyn Clout	1008
For ye play so at the chesse,	271	Collyn Clout	1009
Hath played so checkmate	271	Collyn Clout	1012
And nat so hardy on his hede	272	Collyn Clout	1023
nat] 'not' Marshe 1568, MS Harley 2252			
So hardy to make suete,	272	Collyn Clout	1031
Nat so hardy on theyr pates!	275	Collyn Clout	1152
Delay causes so longe	276	Collyn Clout	1196
And so it semeth they play,	277	Collyn Clout	1234
But /Helas! sage overage /So madly decayes,	279	Why Come Ye	42
So] 'To' Toy 1553, Kitson 1560.7, Marshe 1568			
So /That rage must make pyllage	280	Why Come Ye	49
The French men he hathe so mated,	282	Why Come Ye	161
They make him so amased,	283	Why Come Ye	180
And his eyen so dased,	283	Why Come Ye	181
He is set so hye /In his ierarchy	283	Why Come Ye	184
For Dame Philargerya /Hathe so his herte in holde,	284	Why Come Ye	207
Our barons be so bolde,	286	Why Come Ye	292
None so hardy to speke.	287	Why Come Ye	328
And bereth him there so stowte	287	Why Come Ye	340
That his berde is so longe.	288	Why Come Ye	391
And so to rest a whyle etc.	289	Why Come Ye	398
His wysdome is so dyscrete	289	Why Come Ye	423
He dyggeth so in the trenche	290	Why Come Ye	434
So he dothe undermynde,	290	Why Come Ye	437
And so streatly coarted	290	Why Come Ye	441
He is so ambicyous,	290	Why Come Ye	461
So shamles and so vicyous,	290	Why Come Ye	462
and] 'an' †Kele 1545.3			
So shamles and so vicyous,	290	Why Come Ye	462
and] 'an' †Kele 1545.3			
And so supersticyous,	290	Why Come Ye	463
And so moche oblivyous	290	Why Come Ye	464
That they are so wo	294	Why Come Ye	613
Thus he, borne so base,	294	Why Come Ye	622
He is so fyers and fell.	295	Why Come Ye	650
Is toward hym so mynded,	295	Why Come Ye	659
And so farre blynded,	295	Why Come Ye	660
So boldely dare controule	296	Why Come Ye	674
And so malapertly withstande	296	Why Come Ye	675
Of one so devyllysshe a matter.	297	Why Come Ye	715
With hym so wele apayd	297	Why Come Ye	731
But he was so payned in the hede	299	Why Come Ye	795
And brynge it so lowe	303	Why Come Ye	951
For with us he so mellys	303	Why Come Ye	961

	Page	Title	Line
He wyll drynke us so drye,	303	Why Come Ye	965
so] not in MS Rawlinson C. 813			
And suck us so nye,	303	Why Come Ye	966
For I undertake /He wolde so brag and crake	303	Why Come Ye	977
Together are bended, /And so condyscended,	304	Why Come Ye	1023
bendyd] 'wendyd' MS Rawlinson C. 813			
So braggynge all with bost	306	Why Come Ye	1074
He makith so proude pretens,	307	Why Come Ye	1133
This Naman Sirus, /So fell and so irous,	308	Why Come Ye	1167
Sirus] 'tyrus' MS Rawlinson C. 813			
This Naman Sirus, /So fell and so irous,	308	Why Come Ye	1167
Sirus] 'tyrus' MS Rawlinson C. 813			
So full of malencoly,	308	Why Come Ye	1168
He is so ambicious, /So elate and so vicious,	308	Why Come Ye	1176
He is so ambicious, /So elate and so vicious,	308	Why Come Ye	1177
He is so ambicious, /So elate and so vicious,	308	Why Come Ye	1177
And so cruell hertyd, /That he wyll nat be convertyd;	308	Why Come Ye	1178
That] not in MS Rawlinson C. 813			
He is nowe so overthwart,	308	Why Come Ye	1181
nowe] not in MS Rawlinson C. 813			
And so payned with pangis,	308	Why Come Ye	1182
A daucock ye be, and so shal be styll!	310	Why Come Ye2	34
So depely drownyd I was in this dumpe,	312	Garlande	15
Encraumpysshed so sore was my conceyte,	312	Garlande	16
Ran on the raunge so longe, that I suppose	313	Garlande	25
Faire fall that forster that so well can bate his hownde!	313	Garlande	27
well] not in MS Cotton Vitellius E.x			
So that there workis myght famously be sene,	314	Garlande	67
And if so hym fortune to wryte true and plaine,	314	Garlande	85
so] not in MS Cotton Vitellius E.x			
That he so sholde be, me semith it sittyng,	316	Garlande	149
it] 'it is' MS Cotton Vitellius E.x			
The cause why Demostenes so famously is brutid	316	Garlande	155
Few shall ye fynde or none that wyll do so.'	317	Garlande	168
Your mynde that can maynteyne so apparently;	317	Garlande	170
Be he never so lytell of substaunce,	317	Garlande	177
Eolus, your trumpet, that knowne is so farre,	319	Garlande	235
that] 'whiche' MS Cotton Vitellius E.x			
Whos hevenly armony was so passynge sure,	320	Garlande	274
So truely proporsionyd, and so well did gree,	320	Garlande	275
So truely proporsionyd, and so well did gree,	320	Garlande	275
So duly entunyd with every mesure,	320	Garlande	276
That in the forest was none so great a tre	320	Garlande	277
In so moche the stumpe, whereto I me lente	320	Garlande	281
Cupyde hath stryken so that she ne wolde	320	Garlande	291
Yet loke on me, that lovyd you have so longe,	320	Garlande	298
So close to kepe your cloyster virgynall,	320	Garlande	305
Alas, what ayle you to be so overthwart,	320	Garlande	307
None so ryche stones in Turkey to sell;	323	Garlande	396
So have ye done, that meretoryously	323	Garlande	401
To have so laudabyle a commendacion:	323	Garlande	408
Oure Englysshe rude so fresshely hath set out,	324	Garlande	422
'So am I preventid of my brethern tweyne	324	Garlande	428
'So have ye me far passynge my meretis extollyd,	324	Garlande	435
Bownte, and so gloryously ye have enrollyd	324	Garlande	437
So finally, when they had shewyd there devyse,	324	Garlande	442
So curiously, so craftely, so connyngly wroght,	325	Garlande	461
So curiously, so craftely, so connyngly wroght,	325	Garlande	461
So curiously, so craftely, so connyngly wroght,	325	Garlande	461
So ryally, so rychely, so passyngly ornate,	325	Garlande	487
So ryally, so rychely, so passyngly ornate,	325	Garlande	487
So ryally, so rychely, so passyngly ornate,	325	Garlande	487
So am I supprysyd with pleasure and delyght	327	Garlande	537
So well entakeled, what wynde that ever blowe,	327	Garlande	545
that] 'so' Marshe 1568			
So passyd we forthe into the forsayd place,	328	Garlande	561
And from the sowth unto the north so colde,	328	Garlande	578
Or gummis of Saby so derely that be solde.	331	Garlande	675
Of somer, so formally she fotid the daunce.	331	Garlande	686
Behynde the taile of Ursa so clere;	331	Garlande	696
And of the winter days that hy them so fast,	331	Garlande	700
And of the wynter nyghtes that tary so longe,	331	Garlande	701
And of the somer days so longe that doth last,	331	Garlande	702
So many, that longe it were to reherse.	331	Garlande	706
it] 'in' Marshe 1568			
That of your bounte so well have me assurid;	332	Garlande	729
But my request is not so great a thynge,	332	Garlande	730
So I beseke Jhesu now to be my gyde.	335	Garlande	835
So shall your name endure perpetually,	336	Garlande	861
Right so, madame, the roses redde of hew	337	Garlande	890
So I, iwus, /Endevoure me	338	Garlande	935
And so observe /That ye ne swarve	339	Garlande	964
So joyously, /So maydenly, /So womanly	341	Garlande	1011
So joyously, /So maydenly, /So womanly	341	Garlande	1012
So joyously, /So maydenly, /So womanly	341	Garlande	1013
So corteise, so kynde	341	Garlande	1033
So corteise, so kynde	341	Garlande	1033
I for to be so myndles,	342	Garlande	1065

SOBBE —SOCOURE

	Page	Title	Line
Was never halfe so fayre, as I wene,	342	Garlande	1077
Of this warke they had so great delyght,	343	Garlande	1110
And so largely to lay for myne indempnite,	344	Garlande	1136
Of what charge so ever ye lay ageinst me;	344	Garlande	1138
And so Occupacyon, your regester, me told.'	344	Garlande	1141
So then commaundid she was upon this	344	Garlande	1147
Was wrytin; and so she did her spede,	345	Garlande	1168
Go she never so gingirly, her honesty is gone away.	346	Garlande	1204
As so forthe per cetera;	349	Garlande	1314
But whether it were so,	350	Garlande	1347
Luna that so bryght doth shene,	350	Garlande	1358
Where the sank royall is, Crystes blode so rede,	353	Garlande	1463
'Nay, sir' she sayd, 'what so in this place	353	Garlande	1481
The grownde gronid and tremblid, the noyse was so stowte.	354	Garlande	1509
So moche the better	355	Garlande	1539
And so procede /In you to rede,	355	Garlande	1548
That so indede /Your fame may sprede	355	Garlande	1550
And the twayne last /Be withholde so fast	358	Garlande2	13
This Duke so fell /Of Albany, /So cowardly	359	Albany	6
This Duke so fell /Of Albany, /So cowardly	359	Albany	8
And so attaynted, /Lyke cowardes starke,	359	Albany	28
Ye Duke so doutty, /So sterne, so stoutty,	361	Albany	77
Ye Duke so doutty, /So sterne, so stoutty,	361	Albany	78
Ye Duke so doutty, /So sterne, so stoutty,	361	Albany	78
So hardy nor so bolde	367	Albany	338
So hardy nor so bolde	367	Albany	338
So madde a cordylar, /So madde a murmurar?	368	Albany	375
So madde a cordylar, /So madde a murmurar?	368	Albany	376
So noble a prince as he /In all actyvite	368	Albany	395
They fynde his grace so kynde;	371	Albany	483
We will so folowe in the chace	371	Albany	503
They tumble so in theology,	374	Replycacion	5
howbeit they were puffed so full	375	Replycacion	I
Sive sic, sive nat so,	376	Replycacion	71
Ye strynged so Luthers lute	379	Replycacion	167
And so ye wyll be styll,	379	Replycacion	179
His foly so to face.	379	Replycacion	196
Ye cobble and ye clout /Holy scripture so about,	380	Replycacion	223
So was there never another,	381	Replycacion	258
Ye saye that poetry /Maye nat flye so hye	382	Replycacion	307
For Davyd, our poete, harped so meloudiously	383	Replycacion	339

SOBBE
I wayle, I wepe, I sobbe, I sigh ful sore	29	Dol Dethe	1

SOBBED
I syghed and I sobbed,	73	Phy Sparrow	50

SOBBYNG
It semyth the sobbyng of an old sow!	37	Coystrowne1	32

SOBBYNGE
I pray the, Largesse, let be thy sobbynge.	192	Magnyfycence	1851

SOBER
Demure, sober and sad,	111	Lawde	54
Yf noblenesse were aquayntyd with sober dyreccyon.	141	Magnyfycence	18
And Sober Sadnesse shalbe your name?	159	Magnyfycence	681
Somtyme to sober, somtyme to sadde;	168	Magnyfycence	1009
Syr, Sober Sadnesse cometh. Wherfore it be?	186	Magnyfycence	1631
To sober, to sad, to subtell, to wyse,	199	Magnyfycence	2091
And also dame Prudence, /With sober Sapyence.	279	Why Come Ye	14
But as touchynge dystrectyon, /With sober dyrectyon	304	Why Come Ye	1009
dystrectyon] 'dyscrecyon' Marshe 1568, MS Rawlinson C. 813			

SOBERLY
And whan he came walkynge soberly,	51	Bowge	190
'How do ye, mayster? Ye loke so soberly!	58	Bowge	442
Senek full soberly with his tragediis;	322	Garlande	358
with] 'wit' †Fakes 1523			

SOBRE
Goodly maystres Jane, /Sobre, demure Dyane;	102	Phy Sparrow	1224
With sobre cyrcumstance, /Our myndes to avaunce	385	Replycacion	394

SOCCOURE
Our lorde be his soccoure!	282	Why Come Ye	160

SOCHE
Demaundinge soche dutes as nedis most acord	31	Dol Dethe	66
They browght them in soche paine.	111	Lawde	35
Soche an odyr chalyngyr cowde me no man wysch,	121	Garnesche1	3
Of soche a gresy knyght?	125	Garnesche3	35
Soche pelfry thou hast pachchyd,	128	Garnesche3	178
Soche pollyng pajaunttis ye pley,	129	Garnesche3	190
Soche pajantes with your fryndes ye play,	130	Garnesche5	37
Of harlottes to use soche an harres,	131	Garnesche5	77
Yet ther may falle soche caswelte	132	Garnesche5	121
I rayle to the soche as thow art.	133	Garnesche5	137
It ys nat mete for soche a knave.	133	Garnesche5	156

SOCKE
Trymme at her tayle or a man can turne a socke.	177	Magnyfycence	1346

SOCOUR
So Jupiter me socour,	94	Phy Sparrow	895
So Jupyter me socour,	99	Phy Sparrow	1109

SOCOURE
So Jupyter me socoure,	96	Phy Sparrow	991

SOCRATES —SOLACE   Page   Title   Line

	Page	Title	Line
So Jupiter me socoure,	97	Phy Sparrow	1024
So Jupiter me socoure,	98	Phy Sparrow	1085
So Jupiter me socoure,	101	Phy Sparrow	1187
So Jupiter me socoure,	102	Phy Sparrow	1233
SOCRATES			
Or Socrates the wyse,	74	Phy Sparrow	99
SODAYNLY			
Sodaynly, as he departed me fro,	60	Bowge	498
Then myschefe sodaynly I them sende;	194	Magnyfycence	1927
Sodaynly upstarte /From the donge carte,	262	Collyn Clout	644
SODEYNE			
Thenne I, astonyed of that sodeyne fraye,	60	Bowge	501
SODEYNLY			
But sodeynly at ones, as I me advysed,	313	Garlande	36
SODENLY			
For welthe without measure sodenly wyll slyde.	145	Magnyfycence	192
Sodenly set up and sodenly pluckyd downe;	197	Magnyfycence	2025
Sodenly set up and sodenly pluckyd downe;	197	Magnyfycence	2025
Sodenly avaunsyd, and sodenly subdude;	212	Magnyfycence	2526
Sodenly avaunsyd, and sodenly subdude;	212	Magnyfycence	2526
Sodenly ryches, and sodenly poverte;	212	Magnyfycence	2527
Sodenly ryches, and sodenly poverte;	212	Magnyfycence	2527
Sodenly comfort, and sodenly adversyte;	212	Magnyfycence	2528
Sodenly comfort, and sodenly adversyte;	212	Magnyfycence	2528
Sodenly thus Fortune can bothe smyle and frowne,	212	Magnyfycence	2529
Sodenly set up, and sodenly cast downe.	212	Magnyfycence	2530
Sodenly set up, and sodenly cast downe.	212	Magnyfycence	2530
Sodenly promotyd, and sodenly put backe;	212	Magnyfycence	2531
Sodenly promotyd, and sodenly put backe;	212	Magnyfycence	2531
Sodenly cherysshyd, and sodenly cast asyde;	212	Magnyfycence	2532
Sodenly cherysshyd, and sodenly cast asyde;	212	Magnyfycence	2532
Sodenly commendyd, and sodenly fynde a lacke;	213	Magnyfycence	2533
Sodenly commendyd, and sodenly fynde a lacke;	213	Magnyfycence	2533
Sodenly grauntyd, and sodenly denyed;	213	Magnyfycence	2534
Sodenly grauntyd, and sodenly denyed;	213	Magnyfycence	2534
Sodenly hyd, and sodenly spyed;	213	Magnyfycence	2535
Sodenly hyd, and sodenly spyed;	213	Magnyfycence	2535
Sodenly thus Fortune can bothe smyle and frowne,	213	Magnyfycence	2536
Sodenly set up, and sodenly cast downe.	213	Magnyfycence	2537
Sodenly set up, and sodenly cast downe.	213	Magnyfycence	2537
Howe sodenly worldly welth dothe dekay;	213	Magnyfycence	2555
Sodenly is eclipsid in the wynter night,	330	Garlande	646
With that I stode up, halfe sodenly afrayd,	353	Garlande	1477
And therwith, sodenly, out of my dreme I woke.	354	Garlande	1511
dreme] 'slepe' Marshe 1568			
SODYLDYM			
Alumbek sodyldym syllorym ben!	37	Coystrownel	16
SODOMITES			
Wherwith the Sodomites /Lost theyr inward syghtes.	290	Why Come Ye	470
SOFREYNE			
That creaunser was to thy sofre[yne] lorde;	132	Garnesche5	102
sofreyne] 'sofre' †MS Harley 367			
SOFT			
The tarsell gentyll, /They shall morne soft and styll	85	Phy Sparrow	559
Her lyppes soft and mery	97	Phy Sparrow	1037
Soft, and make no dyn,	99	Phy Sparrow	1092
And handes soft as sylke,	99	Phy Sparrow	1119
'Soft,' quod one hyght Sybbyll,	228	El Rummynge	549
hyght] 'high' Day 1560, Marshe 1568			
'Soft, my good syster, and make there a pawse.	316	Garlande	134
my good syster] 'goode my sister' MS Cotton Vitellius E.x			
There blew in that gardynge a soft piplyng colde	331	Garlande	676
SOFTE			
Betwene my brestes softe	74	Phy Sparrow	125
Softe, my frende. Herein your reason is but rawe.	142	Magnyfycence	70
Nowe must I make you a lectuary softe –	207	Magnyfycence	2355
At home full softe doth sytte.	255	Collyn Clout	328
Yet softe and fayre for swellynge,	271	Collyn Clout	986
SOFTER			
Had I never sene, some softer, some lowder;	320	Garlande	271
SOFTLY			
And I than softly answered to that clause,	48	Bowge	74
The requiem masse to synge, /Softly warbelynge,	81	Phy Sparrow	402
Softly] 'Loftly' Marshe 1568			
Softly bemole /For my sparowes soule.	85	Phy Sparrow	534
'Go softly,' she sayd, 'the stones be full glint.'	328	Garlande	572
Whereon theis ladys softly myght rest,	334	Garlande	788
SOFTLYER			
I speke the softlyer because he sholde not wete.	186	Magnyfycence	1654
SOILE			
Dryades there daunsid upon that goodly soile,	331	Garlande	679
SOJOURNS			
And sojourns with them and dwelles.	384	Replycacion	378
SOL			
And lerne me to synge Re my fa sol!	53	Bowge	258
SOLACE			
To sorowfull harttis chef comfort and solace,	34	Dol Dethe	206
Thorow bounte of hym that formed all solace,	35	Dol Dethe	214

SOLACIOUS — SOMDELE

	Page	Title	Line
And thy palace, /Full of solace,	40	Coystrowne3	54
Theyr sayll of solace most comfortably clad,	44	Balettys3	27
With them to make solace and pleasure;	50	Bowge	144
Confort, pleasure, and solace,	96	Phy Sparrow	1004
Thus, I say, I am envyronned with solace.	190	Magnyfycence	1797
Nowe shall ye be renewyd with solace.	208	Magnyfycence	2404
Of welth and solace no thynge left behynde;	332	Garlande	711
Vertu, conyng, solace, pleasure, comforte.	337	Garlande	898
Vertu, connyng, solace, pleasure, comforte.	337	Garlande	905
With solace and gladnes,	340	Garlande	1008
With a sawte of solace at the longe last;	351	Garlande	1398

SOLACIOUS

	Page	Title	Line
His mater is delectable, /Solacious and commendable;	91	Phy Sparrow	791

SOLACYOUS

	Page	Title	Line
Here folowythe Dyvers Balettys and Dyties Solacyous	41	Balettys	I
solacyous and ryght pregnant allectyues of syngular pleasure,	312	Garlande	I
Grene tre of laurell moche solacyous game	331	Garlande	683

SOLACYUSLY

	Page	Title	Line
Prosperyte [by] hym is gyven solacyusly to man;	207	Magnyfycence	2367

by] 'to' †Rastell & Treveris C 1530, B

SOLAYNE

	Page	Title	Line
It is a solempne syre and a solayne,	38	Coystrowne1	51

SOLAS

	Page	Title	Line
For my solas and sporte.	77	Phy Sparrow	218
My delyght is solas, pleasure, dysporte and pley;	233	Speke Parott	108
The bankis enturfid with singular solas,	330	Garlande	655

SOLD

	Page	Title	Line
'Myne horse is sold, I wene', you say;	40	Coystrowne4	9
So bolde a braggyng bocher, and flesshe sold so dere;	245	Speke Parott	485

SOLDE

	Page	Title	Line
Yet I solde his skynne to Mackemurre,	169	Magnyfycence	1056
Why, was not for money Troy bothe bought and solde?	184	Magnyfycence	1576
Today in surety, tomorowe bought and solde;	213	Magnyfycence	2548
Howe hyr ale is solde /To mawte and to molde.	218	El Rummynge	158
Myters are bought and solde;	254	Collyn Clout	290
How prelacye is solde and bought	261	Collyn Clout	583
I drede we are bought and solde.	283	Why Come Ye	172
Or gummis of Saby so derely that be solde.	331	Garlande	675

SOLE

	Page	Title	Line
God sende my sparoes sole good rest!	86	Phy Sparrow	574

SOLEYNE

	Page	Title	Line
'By Cryste,' quod Favell, 'Drede is soleyne freke!	51	Bowge	187
To owur soleyne Seigneour Sadoke, desire hym to cum home,	239	Speke Parott	304

SOLEM

	Page	Title	Line
I sey, ye solem Sarson, alle blake ys yor ble;	122	Garnesche1	36
My scole is more solem and somwhat more haute	137	Ven Tongues	24

SOLEME

	Page	Title	Line
Syrus, that soleme syar of Babylon,	181	Magnyfycence	1473

SOLEMPE

	Page	Title	Line
Somtyme I syt as I were solempe prowde;	168	Magnyfycence	1011

SOLEMPNE

	Page	Title	Line
It is a solempne syre and a solayne,	38	Coystrowne1	51
A solempne sumner for to be?	116	Ag Scottes	51
This is a solempne drynkynge.	228	El Rummynge	548
With, 'Aveto' in Greco, and such solempne salutacyons,	235	Speke Parott	179
At every solempne feest,	309	Why Come Ye	1215
Nor solempne Serenus, for all his armony	383	Replycacion	337

SOLEMPNELY

	Page	Title	Line
In the pulpyt solempnely —	266	Collyn Clout	811

SOLEMPNYTE

	Page	Title	Line
With all solempnyte, /For theyr indempnyte;	269	Collyn Clout	926

SOLEN

	Page	Title	Line
And sadlye salute owur solen Syre Sydrake,	240	Speke Parott	326

SOLF

	Page	Title	Line
He techyth them so wysely to solf and to fayne	38	Coystrowne1	53

SOLFE

	Page	Title	Line
His playne songe to solfe;	82	Phy Sparrow	415
To solfe above E-la – /Fa, lorell, fa, fa –	84	Phy Sparrow	487

Fa] 'Ga' †Kele 1545.2, Wyght 1553, Kitson 1560.6

SOLFYTH

	Page	Title	Line
He solfyth to haute, hys trybyll is to hy;	37	Coystrowne1	23

SOM

	Page	Title	Line
By Goddis bones, but yf we have som sleyte,	54	Bowge	304
Som be wrestyd there that they thynke on it forty dayes,	204	Magnyfycence	2274
Now pandes mory, wax frantycke som men sey;	232	Speke Parott	46

mory] 'mery' †MS Harley 2252; men] 'mad' †MS Harley 2252

	Page	Title	Line
Som trete of theyr tirykis, som of astrology,	234	Speke Parott	137
Som trete of theyr tirykis, som of astrology,	234	Speke Parott	137
Som pseudo-propheta with ciromancy;	234	Speke Parott	138
Som sey they cannot my parables expresse;	242	Speke Parott	386
Som sey I rayle att ryott recheles;	242	Speke Parott	387

SOMDELE

	Page	Title	Line
Though I waxe olde /And somdele sere,	112	Calliope	16
Her nose somdele hoked /And camously croked,	215	El Rummynge	27
She semed somdele seke,	225	El Rummynge	414
My mynde of the grete din was somdele amasid.	354	Garlande	1512

SOME —SOME   Page   Title   Line

SOME

	Page	Title	Line
Dyverse in style, some spared not vyce to wrythe,	46	Bowge	13
wrythe] 'wryte' Wynkyn de Worde 1510, Marshe 1568			
Some of moralyte nobly dyde endyte;	46	Bowge	14
moralyte] 'mortalyte' †Wynkyn de Worde 1499, Marshe 1568			
Enforsed to slepe and for to take some reste,	47	Bowge	32
'Forsoth,' quod I, 'to bye some of youre ware.'	48	Bowge	79
And of his mynde he shewed me all and some.	52	Bowge	226
Wolde to God it wolde please you some daye	53	Bowge	256
Fynde some mene to caste him over the borde.'	54	Bowge	308
There muste for hym be layde some prety beyte.	55	Bowge	312
Than hath some shyppe that into Bordews sayle.	57	Bowge	406
It is a worlde, I saye, to here of some –	59	Bowge	464
to] 'te' †Wynkyn de Worde 1499, 'to' Wynkyn de Worde 1510, Marshe 1568			
Yet wyll I saye some wordes for your sake	59	Bowge	474
For some shall wene be hanged by the throte.	59	Bowge	476
Some pleasure and comforte	77	Phy Sparrow	217
Let some poetes wryte	78	Phy Sparrow	252
Some to synge, and some to say,	81	Phy Sparrow	392
Some to synge, and some to say,	81	Phy Sparrow	392
Some to wepe, and some to pray,	81	Phy Sparrow	393
Some to wepe, and some to pray,	81	Phy Sparrow	393
Some sad storyes, some mery,	87	Phy Sparrow	615
Some sad storyes, some mery,	87	Phy Sparrow	615
Some say she was lyght,	87	Phy Sparrow	645
Yet some men fynde a faute,	92	Phy Sparrow	811
With pen and ynk /For to compyle /Some goodly style;	96	Phy Sparrow	988
goodly] 'godly' †Kele 1545.2			
The gyse now a dayes /Of some janglynge jayes	103	Phy Sparrow	1269
But ye had some wyl[d] sede to sowe,	114	Scot Kynge	52
wyld] 'wyle' †Fakes 1513			
To write some lytell tragedy,	117	Ag Scottes	72
This invectyve to make /For some peoples sake	120	Ag Scottes2	4
How some delite for to lye, thycke and threfolde.	137	Ven Tongues	11
For though some be lidder, and list for to rayle,	138	Ven Tongues	30
Some reason we must make.	143	Magnyfycence	99
Lyberte in some cause becomyth a gentyll mynde –	146	Magnyfycence	212
Nowe, benedicite, ye wene I were some hafter,	147	Magnyfycence	257
Or ellys some jangelynge Jacke of the Vale.	147	Magnyfycence	258
And some bade, 'Sere hym with a marke.'	150	Magnyfycence	360
And yet, I trowe, some of you be better sped than I	160	Magnyfycence	722
What! Then he is some good poore mannes curre?	171	Magnyfycence	1129
Tushe, man! I kepe some Latyn in store.	172	Magnyfycence	1145
That some of them renneth strayght to the stuse.	174	Magnyfycence	1225
To thefte and bryboury I make some fall,	174	Magnyfycence	1226
As some be not ferre and yf it were well sought –	174	Magnyfycence	1241
By God, there be some that be shroudly towchyd.	175	Magnyfycence	1277
But some man wolde convey, and can not skyll,	178	Magnyfycence	1361
And some wyll take upon them to conterfet letters,	178	Magnyfycence	1364
And some wyll convey by the pretence of sadnesse	178	Magnyfycence	1366
Well, get you hens than and sende me some other.	180	Magnyfycence	1451
Ye, but some be full koy and passynge harde harted.	184	Magnyfycence	1583
Then some occacyon or quarell ye must fynde,	185	Magnyfycence	1600
Syr, I beseche you let pety have some place	188	Magnyfycence	1712
Some I make lyppers and lazars full horse;	194	Magnyfycence	1904
And from that they love best some I devorse;	194	Magnyfycence	1905
Some with the marmoll to halte I them make;	194	Magnyfycence	1906
And some to cry out of the bone ake;	194	Magnyfycence	1907
And some I vysyte with brennynge of fyre;	194	Magnyfycence	1908
Of some I wrynge of the necke lyke a wyre;	194	Magnyfycence	1909
And some I make in a rope to totter and walter;	194	Magnyfycence	1910
And some for to hange themselfe in an halter;	194	Magnyfycence	1911
And some I vysyte [with] batayle, warre, and murther, with] 'to' †Rastell & Treveris C 1530, B	194	Magnyfycence	1912
Some I make lame, and some I do kyll,	194	Magnyfycence	1931
Some I make lame, and some I do kyll,	194	Magnyfycence	1931
And some I stryke with a franesy;	194	Magnyfycence	1932
Of some of theyr chyldren I stryke on the eye;	194	Magnyfycence	1933
For nowe go I wyll begge for you some mete.	197	Magnyfycence	2034
And some in the worlde, theyr brayne is so ydyll	200	Magnyfycence	2135
Some fall to foly, them selfe for to spyll,	200	Magnyfycence	2139
And some fall prechynge at the Toure Hyll;	200	Magnyfycence	2140
Some hath so moche lyberte of one thynge and other,	200	Magnyfycence	2141
Some have so moche lyberte that they fere no synne,	200	Magnyfycence	2143
To get us there some freshe mete.	204	Magnyfycence	2264
In fay, man, some rybbys of the motton be so ranke	204	Magnyfycence	2269
Some wenches come unlased, /Some huswyves come unbrased, unlased] 'unbrased' Day 1560, Marshe 1568	217	El Rummynge	133
Some wenches come unlased, /Some huswyves come unbrased, unlased] 'unbrased' Day 1560, Marshe 1568	217	El Rummynge	134
Some be flybytten, /Some skewed as a kytten;	218	El Rummynge	141
Some be flybytten, /Some skewed as a kytten;	218	El Rummynge	142
Some with a sho clout /Bynde theyr heddes about;	218	El Rummynge	143
Some have no herelace,	218	El Rummynge	145
Some loke strawry, /Some cawry-mawry;	218	El Rummynge	149
Some loke strawry, /Some cawry-mawry;	218	El Rummynge	150
Some have no mony /That thyder commy,	218	El Rummynge	160

SOME —SOME

	Page	Title	Line
In stede of coyne and monny /Some brynge her a conny,	220	El Rummynge	245
And some a pot with honny,	220	El Rummynge	246
Some a salt, and some a spone,	220	El Rummynge	247
Some a salt, and some a spone,	220	El Rummynge	247
Some their hose, some their shone;	220	El Rummynge	248
Some their hose, some their shone;	220	El Rummynge	248
Some ranne a good trot /With a skellet or a pot;	220	El Rummynge	249
Some fyll theyr pot full /Of good Lemster woll.	220	El Rummynge	251
Some go streyght thyder, /Be it slaty or slyder;	221	El Rummynge	257
Some lothe to be espyde,	221	El Rummynge	262
Some start in at the backe syde,	221	El Rummynge	263
Some renne tyll they swete,	221	El Rummynge	266
Some bryngeth her husbandis hood,	221	El Rummynge	283
And some brought sowre dowe:	221	El Rummynge	288
Some layde to pledge /Theyr hatchet and theyr wedge,	221	El Rummynge	293
And some went so narrowe	222	El Rummynge	297
Some for very nede /Layde downe a skeyne of threde,	222	El Rummynge	309
And some a skeyne of yarne.	222	El Rummynge	311
Some brought from the barne /Both benes and pease;	222	El Rummynge	312
Some brought walnuttes,	225	El Rummynge	437
Some apples, some peres,	225	El Rummynge	438
Some apples, some peres,	225	El Rummynge	438
Some brought theyr clyppyng sheres,	225	El Rummynge	439
Some brought this and that,	225	El Rummynge	440
Some brought I wote nere what,	225	El Rummynge	441
Some brought theyr husbands hat,	225	El Rummynge	442
Some podynges and lynkes,	225	El Rummynge	443
Some trypes that stynkes.	225	El Rummynge	444
stynkes] 'stynges' Kynge & Marche 1554			
Some brought a wymble,	227	El Rummynge	526
Some brought a thymble,	227	El Rummynge	527
Some brought a sylke lace,	227	El Rummynge	528
Some brought a pyncase,	227	El Rummynge	529
Some her husbandes gowne,	227	El Rummynge	530
Some a pyllowe of downe,	227	El Rummynge	531
Some of the napery;	227	El Rummynge	532
But some than sate ryght sad	229	El Rummynge	607
Some run to far before, some run to far behynde,	233	Speke Parott	76
Some run to far before, some run to far behynde,	233	Speke Parott	76
Some be to churlysshe, and some be to kynde.	233	Speke Parott	77
Some be to churlysshe, and some be to kynde.	233	Speke Parott	77
Some argue secundum quid ad simpliciter,	235	Speke Parott	155
And some make distinctions multipliciter,	235	Speke Parott	157
Yet some folys say ye arre furnysshyd with knakkes,	239	Speke Parott	292
Passe forthe, Parotte, towardes some passengere;	239	Speke Parott	301
Some say but lityll and thynke more in there thowghte,	242	Speke Parott	388
Yf ye take well therwith /It hath in it some pyth.	248	Collyn Clout	58
take] 'talke' Kele 1545.1, Marshe 1568			
Howebeit, some there be,	250	Collyn Clout	147
For some say ye hunte in parkes	251	Collyn Clout	192
ye] 'they' †Godfray 1531, 'ye' MS Harley 2252; in parkes] 'partrykes' †Godfray 1531			
Howe some of you dothe eate /In lenton season flesshe meate,	251	Collyn Clout	204
Some are insufficientes,	252	Collyn Clout	223
Some parum sapientes,	252	Collyn Clout	224
Some nichil intelligentes,	252	Collyn Clout	225
Some valde negligentes,	252	Collyn Clout	226
Some nullum sensum habentes,	252	Collyn Clout	227
Some bestyall and untaught.	252	Collyn Clout	228
Howe some synge letabundus /At every ale stake,	253	Collyn Clout	248
Some can nat declyne theyr name!	253	Collyn Clout	276
Some can nat scarsly rede,	253	Collyn Clout	277
Some hatted and some capped, /Rychly bewrapped,	254	Collyn Clout	311
Some hatted and some capped, /Rychly bewrapped,	254	Collyn Clout	311
Some say ye sytte in trones,	255	Collyn Clout	344
It may take some effecte!	257	Collyn Clout	436
Howebeit, per assimile, /Some men thynke that ye	258	Collyn Clout	460
And some there are that rave,	259	Collyn Clout	514
Some make epylogacyon /Of hygh predestynacyon;	259	Collyn Clout	519
And some have a smacke /Of Luthers sacke,	260	Collyn Clout	540
And some of them barke, /Clatter and carpe	260	Collyn Clout	546
And some be Hussians,	260	Collyn Clout	551
And some be Arryans,	260	Collyn Clout	552
And some be Pollegyans,	260	Collyn Clout	553
Howe some of them glenes	260	Collyn Clout	567
But mayster Damyan, /Or some other man	264	Collyn Clout	721
Some maysters of arte,	264	Collyn Clout	730
Some doctours of lawe,	264	Collyn Clout	731
Some lerned in other sawe, /As in divynyte,	264	Collyn Clout	732
Though some of them by lyres.	267	Collyn Clout	833
lyres] 'lyers' Kele 1545.1, Marshe 1568, 'lyars' MS Harley 2252			
Some to gather chese	267	Collyn Clout	840
Some walke about in melottes,	268	Collyn Clout	864
Some wyl neyther golde ne grotes;	268	Collyn Clout	866
Some plucke a partryche in remotes,	268	Collyn Clout	867
Howe some of you are mellynge.	271	Collyn Clout	985
That some of you but late	271	Collyn Clout	1011

SOMER —SOMER

	Page	Title	Line
Some shall be sawde,	276	Collyn Clout	1205
And some of you shall dye /Lyke holy Jeremy;	276	Collyn Clout	1208
Some hanged, some slayne,	276	Collyn Clout	1210
Some hanged, some slayne,	276	Collyn Clout	1210
Some beaten to the brayne;	276	Collyn Clout	1211
Nor of some wytles pates	277	Collyn Clout	1245
Some men may happely rew,	280	Why Come Ye	60
And some theyr hedes mew.	280	Why Come Ye	61
some] not in Toy 1553, Kitson 1560.7, Marshe 1568			
Some say 'yes', and some	283	Why Come Ye	198
Some say 'yes', and some	283	Why Come Ye	198
Some sayde they were afrayde	285	Why Come Ye	254
But, as some men sayne,	288	Why Come Ye	362
I drede of some false trayne	288	Why Come Ye	363
But there is some travarse	288	Why Come Ye	387
Bytwene some and some	288	Why Come Ye	388
Bytwene some and some	288	Why Come Ye	388
Before some prothonotory, /Imperyall or papall.	299	Why Come Ye	819
Some haute and some base.	301	Why Come Ye	880
Some haute and some base.	301	Why Come Ye	880
Some daunce the trace	301	Why Come Ye	881
Some men myght aske a question,	309	Why Come Ye	1202
aske] 'make' MS Rawlinson C. 813			
Some have a name for thefte and brybery;	317	Garlande	183
Some be called crafty that can pyke a purse;	317	Garlande	184
pyke] 'kit' MS Cotton Vitellius E.x			
Some men be made of for the mokery;	317	Garlande	185
the] 'their' Marshe 1568			
Some carefull cokwoldes, some have theyr wyves curs;	317	Garlande	186
Some carefull cokwoldes, some have theyr wyves curs;	317	Garlande	186
Some famous wetewoldis, and they be moche wurs;	317	Garlande	187
Some lidderons, some losels, some noughty packis;	317	Garlande	188
Some lidderons, some losels, some noughty packis;	317	Garlande	188
Some lidderons, some losels, some noughty packis;	317	Garlande	188
Some facers, some bracers, some make great crackis;	317	Garlande	189
some] 'and sum' MS Cotton Vitellius E.x			
Some facers, some bracers, some make great crackis;	317	Garlande	189
some] 'and sum' MS Cotton Vitellius E.x			
Some facers, some bracers, some make great crackis;	317	Garlande	189
some] 'and sum' MS Cotton Vitellius E.x			
Some dronken dastardis with their dry soules;	317	Garlande	190
Some sluggysh slovyns, that slepe day and nyght;	317	Garlande	191
They presid in faste; some thought they were to longe;	319	Garlande	248
Some whispred, some rownyd, some spake, and some cryde,	319	Garlande	250
Some whispred, some rownyd, some spake, and some cryde,	319	Garlande	250
Some whispred, some rownyd, some spake, and some cryde,	319	Garlande	250
Some ranne the nexte way, sume ranne abowte.	319	Garlande	252
Some tremblid, some girned, some gaspid, some gasid,	319	Garlande	265
Some tremblid, some girned, some gaspid, some gasid,	319	Garlande	265
Some tremblid, some girned, some gaspid, some gasid,	319	Garlande	265
Some tremblid, some girned, some gaspid, some gasid,	319	Garlande	265
Had I never sene, some softer, some lowder;	320	Garlande	271
Had I never sene, some softer, some lowder;	320	Garlande	271
Some were of Poyle, and sum were of Trace,	326	Garlande	493
Some from Flaunders, sum from the se coste,	326	Garlande	496
Some from the mayne lande, some fro the Frensche hoste;	326	Garlande	497
Some from the mayne lande, some fro the Frensche hoste;	326	Garlande	497
Some shewid his salfe cundight, some shewid his charter,	326	Garlande	503
salfe cundight] 'safeconduct' Marshe 1568;			
charter] 'chart' Marshe 1568			
Some shewid his salfe cundight, some shewid his charter,	326	Garlande	503
salfe cundight] 'safeconduct' Marshe 1568;			
charter] 'chart' Marshe 1568			
Some lokyd full smothely, and had a fals quarter,	326	Garlande	504
quarter] 'quart' Marshe 1568			
Some came to tell treuth, some came to lye,	326	Garlande	510
Some came to tell treuth, some came to lye,	326	Garlande	510
Some came to flater, some came to spye.	326	Garlande	511
Some came to flater, some came to spye.	326	Garlande	511
Some Romaine letters, as I understode;	328	Garlande	583
Some were olde wryten, sum were writen new,	328	Garlande	584
Some carectis of Caldy, sum Frensshe was full good;	328	Garlande	585
That for them some goodly conseyt be devysid,	335	Garlande	814
Sume praysed the perle, some the stones bryght.	343	Garlande	1108
Whether he rode to Swaffhamm or to Some,	352	Garlande	1416
Swaffhamm] 'Swasshamm' †Fakes 1523, Marshe 1568			
In some of their condicions,	364	Albany	198
With some Scotyshe [l]as,	366	Albany	290
las] 'as' †Marshe 1568			
Some of you had ten pounde,	378	Replycacion	146
And yet some men say,	379	Replycacion	176
Some juged in this case	379	Replycacion	197

SOMER

	Page	Title	Line
Of lusty somer the passyng goodly quene;	44	Balettys3	14
His rumpe, he wente so all for somer lyghte;	56	Bowge	355
But lyght for somer grene;	89	Phy Sparrow	719
Of lusty somer grene;	101	Phy Sparrow	1184

SOMERS — SOMWHAT

	Page	Title	Line
How all thynge passyth as doth the somer flower,	312	Garlande	9
Of somer, so formally she fotid the daunce.	331	Garlande	686
And of the somer days so longe that doth last,	331	Garlande	702

SOMERS

	Page	Title	Line
'Lyke as the larke, upon the somers day,	327	Garlande	533

SOMETYME

	Page	Title	Line
That was sometyme aflote,	78	Phy Sparrow	250
SOMETYME THE HOLY PATRIARKE OF DIS.	106	Epitaphe1	I
Yet sometyme I stryke where is none offence,	194	Magnyfycence	1916
Small chaffer doth ease /Sometyme, now and than.	222	El Rummynge	315
Sometyme, as it semyth, when the mone light	330	Garlande	644
Sometyme for sadde dyrection,	385	Replycacion	390
Sometyme for correction,	385	Replycacion	391
Sometyme under protection /Of pacient sufferance,	385	Replycacion	392

SOMEWHAT

	Page	Title	Line
And are somewhat suspecte /In Luthers secte.	260	Collyn Clout	544
It is somewhat wronge	288	Why Come Ye	390

SOME WHAT

	Page	Title	Line
I coulde say some what,	288	Why Come Ye	381

SOMME

	Page	Title	Line
To you rehersyng the somme of my proces.	117	Ag Scottes	90

SOMMON

	Page	Title	Line
To sommon our kynge your soverayne lorde.	113	Scot Kynge	4
Whom I nowe sommon and con[v]ent,	375	Replycacion	23
convent] 'content' †Pynson 1528			

SOMMONDE

	Page	Title	Line
And how they were sommonde	88	Phy Sparrow	652

SOMMONS

	Page	Title	Line
With sommons and citacyons /And excommunycacyons	254	Collyn Clout	324
To make sommons peremtory	299	Why Come Ye	818

SOMNER

	Page	Title	Line
A kynge a somner it is wonder;	113	Scot Kynge	5
A somner to were a kynges crowne.	115	Scot Kynge	67

SOMNYNGE

	Page	Title	Line
In your somnynge ye were to malaperte,	113	Scot Kynge	7

SOMTIME

	Page	Title	Line
HE WAS SOMTIME THE HOLY BAILLYVE OF DIS.	109	Epitaphe2	I
Somtime women were put in great blame,	139	Ven Tongues	59

SOMTYME

	Page	Title	Line
And somtyme white bred crommes;	74	Phy Sparrow	123
Somtyme he wolde gaspe	75	Phy Sparrow	128
Somtyme a presyous thyng,	88	Phy Sparrow	685
Somtyme a prety chayn,	88	Phy Sparrow	688
Of two knaves somtyme of Dis.	106	Epitaphe.	I
How be it, lyberte may somtyme be to large,	141	Magnyfycence	37
Somtyme to sober, somtyme to sadde;	168	Magnyfycence	1009
Somtyme to sober, somtyme to sadde;	168	Magnyfycence	1009
Somtyme to mery, somtyme to madde;	168	Magnyfycence	1010
Somtyme to mery, somtyme to madde;	168	Magnyfycence	1010
Somtyme I syt as I were solempe prowde;	168	Magnyfycence	1011
Somtyme I laughe over lowde;	168	Magnyfycence	1012
Somtyme I wepe for a gew gaw;	168	Magnyfycence	1013
Somtyme I laughe at waggynge of a straw,	168	Magnyfycence	1014
Somtyme, I say, behynde the dore for nede;	177	Magnyfycence	1341
Ye, Mary, somtyme - in a messe of vergesse,	189	Magnyfycence	1756
Somtyme without measure he trusted in golde;	193	Magnyfycence	1894
I vysyte them somtyme with blaynes and with sores;	194	Magnyfycence	1901
For thoughe you were somtyme a noble estate,	196	Magnyfycence	1980
I am Magnyfycence, that somtyme thy mayster was.	200	Magnyfycence	2107
That lustely they lepe somtyme theyr cloyster wall.	201	Magnyfycence	2150
That somtyme was a noble prynce of myght!	205	Magnyfycence	2280
Somtyme to fall, another tyme to beware:	207	Magnyfycence	2374
And somtyme she blennes	219	El Rummynge	201
The sonne somtyme to be	258	Collyn Clout	468
Somtyme in lousy beddes.	263	Collyn Clout	659
Somtyme meale and salte,	267	Collyn Clout	843
Somtyme a bacon flycke /That is thre fyngers thycke	267	Collyn Clout	844
And somtyme they provoke	268	Collyn Clout	854
Of an oke, that somtyme grew full streyghte,	312	Garlande	18
A poete somtyme may for his pleasure taunt,	315	Garlande	100
Somtyme for affection,	385	Replycacion	389

SOMTYMEPARDE

	Page	Title	Line
Yet somtyme,parde, I must use largesse.	189	Magnyfycence	1755

SOMWHAT

	Page	Title	Line
Was somwhat wanton I wene;	87	Phy Sparrow	637
Ye bere yourselfe somwhat to bolde,	114	Scot Kynge	34
Ye bare yourselfe somwhat to bold;	118	Ag Scottes	125
Yet somwhat to say I dare well be bolde,	137	Ven Tongues	10
My scole is more solem and somwhat more haute	137	Ven Tongues	24
Somwhat I coulde enferre	142	Magnyfycence	59
I may do somwhat, and more I thynke shall.	162	Magnyfycence	778
Ye, but I can somwhat more of the letter.	170	Magnyfycence	1066
With me no longer. Say somwhat nowe, let se,	188	Magnyfycence	1719
Nowe gyve me somwhat, for God sake, I crave.	204	Magnyfycence	2251
For she is somwhat sage	214	El Rummynge	7
But she spake somwhat thycke,	223	El Rummynge	338

	Page	Title	Line
SOMWHERE —SOONE			
She was somwhat foule, /Crokenebbed lyke an oule;	225	El Rummynge	426
Crokenebbed] 'Croke necked' †Lant 1545, Kynge & Marche 1554, Day 1560, Marshe 1568			
For logicions to loke on, somwhat sophistice;	236	Speke Parott	193
Somwhat there is amysse!	272	Collyn Clout	1050
May stande somwhat in stede.	298	Why Come Ye	765
It standeth somwhat on the west;	308	Why Come Ye	1189
Somwhat of your madnesse;	310	Why Come Ye2	23
To walke where we lyst, let us somwhat fynde	328	Garlande	564
Yet somwhat ye be lyke	364	Albany	197
With Englyshe somwhat base,	367	Albany	356
Ye muse somwhat to far;	368	Albany	377
SOMWHERE			
I wolde he were somwhere ellys;	303	Why Come Ye	963
SON			
Pray to thy son above the starris clere,	35	Dol Dethe	208
The Father, the Son, the Holy Goste,	35	Dol Dethe	216
SON BEAMES			
Whose skales ensilvred again the son beames	330	Garlande	662
SONDE			
To thanke God of his sonde; and comforte ye shal fynde.	207	Magnyfycence	2360
SONE			
His sone the lorde admyrall is full good,	115	Scot Kynge	70
I understand, to sone ye came.	118	Ag Scottes	130
For welthe wyll sone departe the froo.	132	Garnesche5	125
For clatering of me I would him sone quight;	139	Ven Tongues	74
Nothynge but fare you well tyll sone -	149	Magnyfycence	319
Ye wolde sone pynche at a pecke of otes.	151	Magnyfycence	385
otes] 'grotes' †Rastell & Treveris C 1530, B			
Farewell, my frende. Adue tyll sone.	167	Magnyfycence	966
Mary, as for that, thou shalte sone here myne.	172	Magnyfycence	1153
Ye, so redely and so sone!	172	Magnyfycence	1157
For as sone as you come in Magnyfycence syght	176	Magnyfycence	1314
But, blessyd be our Lorde, they wyll be sone converted.	184	Magnyfycence	1584
And that ye wyll not cast hym away so sone.	186	Magnyfycence	1638
I care not howe sone he be refused,	187	Magnyfycence	1683
Fare well tyll sone; adue tyll to morowe.	192	Magnyfycence	1850
Alas, dere sone, sore combred is thy mynde,	206	Magnyfycence	2325
Then shall you be sone delyvered from dystresse,	208	Magnyfycence	2383
For Jerico and Jerssey shall mete togethyr as sone	239	Speke Parott	306
For he wyll as sone smyght	293	Why Come Ye	582
Out of my bokis full sone I shulde hym rase;	314	Garlande	72
It shall be losyd ful sone out of the bandis	332	Garlande	725
It is sone aspyed where the thorne prikkith.	352	Garlande	1437
SONER			
But yf therof the soner amendys be made;	146	Magnyfycence	226
For had ye not the soner ben my refuge,	206	Magnyfycence	2333
SONESHYNE			
Of the soneshyne engladid with the lyght,	327	Garlande	536
SONG			
The song of lovers lay;	89	Phy Sparrow	702
An ende of an olde song:	281	Why Come Ye	88
SONGE			
Ye syng allway the kukkowe songe.	129	Garnesche5	4
So in theyr eyre I synge them a songe	174	Magnyfycence	1223
Well cannest thou helpe a preest to synge a songe.	187	Magnyfycence	1676
'O thoughtfull herte,' was evermore his songe!	320	Garlande	296
And of their shorte nyghtes; he browght in his songe	331	Garlande	703
SONGES			
With dolorous songes funerall,	81	Phy Sparrow	391
SONNE			
In autumpne, whan the sonne in Vyrgyne	46	Bowge	1
A carlys sonne /Brought up of nought	165	Magnyfycence	898
For burnynge of the sonne;	168	Magnyfycence	988
Not a better name under the sonne;	176	Magnyfycence	1310
I sende ofte tymes a fole to his sonne.	195	Magnyfycence	1935
But, my good sonne, lerne from dyspaire to flee;	206	Magnyfycence	2339
The sonne somtyme to be	258	Collyn Clout	468
Nor lyke his sonne Hanyball,	363	Albany	194
SONNES			
The naturall sonnes thre	78	Phy Sparrow	255
SONNYS			
Ye knaves, ye churles sonnys,	294	Why Come Ye	603
SOO			
Soo sore enwered that I was, at the laste,	47	Bowge	31
'Maystres,' quod I, 'I praye you tell me why soo,	49	Bowge	108
'Ye, soo,' quod Suspecte, 'he maye us bothe begyle.'	51	Bowge	189
Soo he departed. There he wolde be come,	52	Bowge	228
Soo greate pleasyre, or who to you it gave.	53	Bowge	263
Wyth that, as he departed soo fro me,	54	Bowge	281
And soo outface hym with a carde of ten.'	55	Bowge	315
Save hym that nought can: scrypture sayth soo.	58	Bowge	448
SOONE			
But Ignorance full soone dyde me dyscure	46	Bowge	18
dyscure] 'dysture' †Wynkyn de Worde 1499, 1510			
And to lye downe as soone as I m[e] dreste,	47	Bowge	33
me] 'my' †Wynkyn de Worde 1499, 1510, Marshe 1568			
Farewell tyll soone. But no word that I sayde!'	51	Bowge	175

SOORED — SOROWES

	Page	Title	Line
I wyste never man that so soone coude wynne	53	Bowge	269
Of my querell soone wolde I venged be.	55	Bowge	333
Adewe tyll soone, we shall speke more of this.	60	Bowge	492
I understonde to soone ye cam,	114	Scot Kynge	39
And soone may be perceyvid	298	Why Come Ye	782
Full soone ye should miscary,	367	Albany	342
Ye may soone make construction	378	Replycacion	154

SOORED

Ye soored over hye /In the ierarchy /Of Jovenyans heresy,	378	Replycacion	161

SOPHISTICATID

Sophisticatid craftely is many a confecture;	315	Garlande	110

SOPHY

In the church of Saynt Sophy;	67	Hauke	219

SOPHYSMS

Sette asyde all sophysms, and speke now trew and playne.	244	Speke Parott	448

SOPHYSTYCATE

of certayne sophystycate scolers	373	Replycacion	1

SOPHOCLES

Anacreon and Arion, /Sophocles and Philemon,	90	Phy Sparrow	764

SOPPY

Let us syppe and soppy, /And not spyll a droppy,	228	El Rummynge	558

SOPPYS

Tushe! These maters that ye move are but soppys in ale;	203	Magnyfycence	2233

SORE

	Page	Title	Line
I wayle, I wepe, I sobbe, I sigh ful sore	29	Dol Dethe	1
And under the fell oft festerd is the sore:	45	Balettys4	5
For whose sake my hart is sore dyseasyd;	45	Balettys5	9
I was sore moved to aforce the same,	46	Bowge	17
Soo sore enwered that I was, at the laste,	47	Bowge	31
'Noo thynge erthely that I wonder so sore	50	Bowge	148
Whan there were dyverse that sore dyde you manace.	50	Bowge	159
'I wonder sore he is in such conceyte.'	54	Bowge	310
Me, passynge sore, myne herte than gan aryse;	58	Bowge	425
Ye be malygned sore, I you ensure,	59	Bowge	451
She made me sore amased	99	Phy Sparrow	1103
Trust me, Lyberte, it greveth me ryght sore	178	Magnyfycence	1375
Sore sayde, I tell you, and well to the purpose.	180	Magnyfycence	1428
I vysyte them and stryke them with many sore plagys.	195	Magnyfycence	1943
A, my bonys ake! My lymmys be sore!	195	Magnyfycence	1955
He woteth not what welth is that never was sore.	196	Magnyfycence	1971
That I used the to moche sore may I rewe.	199	Magnyfycence	2104
Alas, dere sone, sore combred is thy mynde,	206	Magnyfycence	2325
And sore I repent me of my wylfulnesse;	207	Magnyfycence	2379
Tryvyals and quatryvyals so sore now they appayre,	235	Speke Parott	166
My harte is so sore payned,	237	Speke Parott	254
Lay salve to your owne sore,	258	Collyn Clout	480
Whiche pyncheth him sore!	302	Why Come Ye	948
Dyd Moyses sore manase	305	Why Come Ye	1067
sore] not in MS Rawlinson C. 813			
And Aron sore he thret,	305	Why Come Ye	1068
Encraumpysshed so sore was my conceyte,	312	Garlande	16
'Make rowme,' sayd another, 'ye prese all to sore,'	319	Garlande	256
Tyll at the last they forcyd me sore,	324	Garlande	446
sore] 'so sore' Marshe 1568			
Of that aventuris, whiche made me sore agast.	330	Garlande	649
Your hartes sore fayntned,	359	Albany	27

SORES

I vysyte them somtyme with blaynes and with sores;	194	Magnyfycence	1901

SORY

And never am I sory but whan that I se	160	Magnyfycence	732
Ye, syr, he is sory for that he hath offendyd.	208	Magnyfycence	2388
With a sory face /Whey-wormed about;	228	El Rummynge	552
I am sory for your sake!	253	Collyn Clout	252
Sory therfore am I,	258	Collyn Clout	484
Helas, my herte is sory	284	Why Come Ye	227

SOROUFULL

To soroufull weping thei ought to be constreynd,	34	Dol Dethe	187

SOROW

Eche man may sorow in his inward thought	34	Dol Dethe	177
Moderatly to take /This sorow that I make	74	Phy Sparrow	102
To se my sorow new.	80	Phy Sparrow	337
Even no morow; /But other mennes sorow	94	Phy Sparrow	925
But hailid they be homwarde with sorow and shame.	329	Garlande	622
God sende you sorow and care!	363	Albany	181

SOROWE

Great sorowe than ye myght se,	73	Phy Sparrow	56
God send them sorowe and shame!	78	Phy Sparrow	277
A, I have spyed ye can moche broken sorowe.	184	Magnyfycence	1587
What! Is all your myrthe nowe tourned to sorowe?	192	Magnyfycence	1849
For when I come, comyth sorowe and care;	195	Magnyfycence	1937
O syghynge sorowe, O thoughtfull mysere!	198	Magnyfycence	2050
And I bequethe hym sorowe for his syn.	204	Magnyfycence	2256
But sygh, and sorowe, and wysshe my selfe dede.	205	Magnyfycence	2306
God sende him sorowe for his sinnes!	309	Why Come Ye	1201
Ye shall have shame and sorowe.	371	Albany	507

SOROWES

And pray to God your sorowes to asswage.	196	Magnyfycence	1989

SOROWFULL —SOULE   Page   Title   Line

SOROWFULL
	Page	Title	Line
To sorowfull harttis chef comfort and solace,	34	Dol Dethe	206
For your jentyll husband sorowfull am I;	43	Balettys2	37
It can not be exprest /My sorowfull hevynesse,	72	Phy Sparrow	32
Of any sorowfull lamentacyon,	117	Ag Scottes	74
Of sorowfull servauntes I have many scores:	194	Magnyfycence	1900

SOROWFULLE
Thes sorowfulle ditis that I may shew expres.	29	Dol Dethe	21

SOROWIS
It was a new comfort of sorowis escapid.	330	Garlande	657

SORSERY
I dought, lest by sorsery	295	Why Come Ye	663

SORT
Upon suche a sort was ille bestowde and spent.	32	Dol Dethe	98
All the goodly sort /Of her fetures clere,	96	Phy Sparrow	999

SORTE
With all the hole sorte of that glorious place,	35	Dol Dethe	212
Your Englysche lew[d]ly ye sorte,	124	Garnesche3	19
lewdly] 'lewly' †MS Harley 367			
I have another maner of sorte	174	Magnyfycence	1238
Unto Magnyfycence a full ungracyous sorte,	178	Magnyfycence	1373
A sorte of foule drabbes /All scurvy with scabbes.	218	El Rummynge	139
Suche a lewde sorte /To Elynour resorte	218	El Rummynge	153
Another sorte of sluttes:	225	El Rummynge	436
Than began the sporte /Amonge that dronken sorte.	229	El Rummynge	575
Hath fresshely enbewtid with many a goodly sorte	336	Garlande	868
All the roiall sorte /Of his nobilyte,	370	Albany	445
Than ye be a knappishe sorte	370	Albany	475
There, lyke a sorte of sottes,	376	Replycacion	65

SORTED
Sholde be set and sorted,	103	Phy Sparrow	1287

SORTIS
There were, I say, of all maner of sortis,	326	Garlande	512

SORTYD
Shulde be set and sortyd, /To be matriculate	348	Garlande	1280

SOT
Dunde, Dunbar, /Walke, Scot, /Walke, sot,	136	Dundas	62

SOTH
By your soth? Ye, and there is suche a wache,	150	Magnyfycence	350

SOTHE
For sothe, they are to lewde /To say so, all beshrewde!	249	Collyn Clout	90

SOTHELY
Sothely to repent me I have grete cause;	209	Magnyfycence	2434

SOTHRAY
And, as men say, /She dwelt in Sothray,	217	El Rummynge	96

SOTTES
Lo, these fond sottes /And tratlyng Skottys,	115	Ag Scottes	5
They commune lyke sottes,	260	Collyn Clout	564
sottes] 'scottes' Marshe 1568, 'sottes' MS Harley 2252			
They make us all sottes,	285	Why Come Ye	263
There, lyke a sorte of sottes,	376	Replycacion	65

SOTTYS
Are nat these Scottys /Folys and sottys,	116	Ag Scottes	30

SOUER
Dothe savyr halfe so souer	127	Garnesche3	146

SOUGHT
All gyf Englond and Fraunce wer thorow sought.	34	Dol Dethe	179
Now have I fownd that I have sought,	36	Man Margery	23
Cadmus, that his syster sought,	76	Phy Sparrow	194
With every condycyon measure must be sought.	143	Magnyfycence	115
As some be not ferre and yf it were well sought -	174	Magnyfycence	1241
But and it were well sought,	287	Why Come Ye	352
On every halfe my reasons forthe I sought,	312	Garlande	10
On] 'One' †Fakes 1523			
That all the worde, I trowe, and it were sought,	325	Garlande	462
worde] 'worlde' Marshe 1568			
Far may be sought	341	Garlande	1031
I dare wele saye that ye and I be sought.	343	Garlande	1089
For, if it were well sought,	379	Replycacion	185

SOUGHTE
Her har[n]es easy ferre and nere is soughte.	57	Bowge	403
harnes] 'harmes' †Wynkyn de Worde 1499, 1510, 'armes' Marshe 1568			

SOULE
His soule mot receyve in to ther company,	35	Dol Dethe	213
Lacrymable, Profytable for the soule.	39	Coystrowne3	I
By Goddis soule, I wonder how ye gete	53	Bowge	262
And specyally to controule /Such as have cure of soule,	62	Hauke	4
Of God nothynge els crave I /But Phyllypes soule to kepe	73	Phy Sparrow	68
Is for his soule to pray:	77	Phy Sparrow	238
Upon my sparowes soule,	77	Phy Sparrow	241
(God send the soule good rest!)	78	Phy Sparrow	262
Our Lorde thy soule reskew!	80	Phy Sparrow	332
For Phylyp Sparowes soule	81	Phy Sparrow	382
Phylyp] 'Phyyp' †Kele 1545.2			
Softly bemole /For my sparowes soule.	85	Phy Sparrow	535
Dirige for Phyllyppes soule;	85	Phy Sparrow	562
On Phillips soule have pyte!	86	Phy Sparrow	587

SOULES —SOWING   Page   Title   Line

SOULE
Belsabub his soule save, ... 109   Epitaphe2   25
By my syers soule, I fele no rayne. 170   Magnyfycence   1087
Ye, for he hathe a full drye soule. 176   Magnyfycence   1320
Except mannes soule, that Chryst so dere bought; 236   Speke Parott   215
Dame Margeres soule out of hell. 268   Collyn Clout   876

SOULES
For that swete soules sake, ... 72   Phy Sparrow   10
And for all sparowes soules 72   Phy Sparrow   11
Of infernall posty /Where soules frye and rousty; 105   Phy Sparrow   1333
    rousty] 'rosty' Marshe 1568
Theyr soules lame and dull; 250   Collyn Clout   129
Yet take they cure of soules, ... 252   Collyn Clout   233
    cure] 'cures' Kele 1545.1, Marshe 1568
And thus they hurte theyr soules, ... 255   Collyn Clout   341
So that theyr founders soules 257   Collyn Clout   421
But where theyr soules dwell, ... 257   Collyn Clout   427
Nor of theyr sely soules, ... 277   Collyn Clout   1244
Some dronken dastardis with their dry soules; 317   Garlande   190

SOULIS
Of infernall posty, /Where soulis fry and rosty; 349   Garlande   1326

SOULYS
Oure gummys grynnyng, /Oure soulys brynnyng! 40   Coystrowne3   36

SOUNDE
Halfe slumbrynge, in a sounde 72   Phy Sparrow   35
I counterfet suger that is but *[s]ounde, ... 152   Magnyfycence   435
    *sounde] 'founde' †Rastell & Treveris C 1530, B,
    'sande' Scattergood

SOURE
Her breth was soure and stale 226   El Rummynge   486
Yet swete meate hath soure sauce, ... 258   Collyn Clout   448
After gloria, laus, /May come a soure sauce. 258   Collyn Clout   483
Be it soure, be it swete! 289   Why Come Ye   422

SOURMOUNTINGE
Sourmountinge in honour all erlis he did excede; 33   Dol Dethe   135

SOVERAYGNE
To summon our kyng, your soveraygne lorde. 118   Ag Scottes   94
Your soveraygne lorde most reverent, ... 118   Ag Scottes   113

SOVERAYN
And against his lorde soverayn! 297   Why Come Ye   738

SOVERAYNE
Condute of comforte and well most soverayne; 44   Balettys3   12
In doynge his homage /Unto his soverayne. 80   Phy Sparrow   327
As my soverayne /Moost of pleasure. 113   Calliope   23
To summon our kynge your soverayne lorde. 113   Scot Kynge   4
Your soverayne lord and presedent. 114   Scot Kynge   22
Your soverayne lord, our prynce of myght. 117   Ag Scottes   54
Of our soverayne lorde, ... 291   Why Come Ye   485
Our soverayne lord, chyfe grounde 291   Why Come Ye   502
Then to this lady and soverayne of this palace 326   Garlande   491
The ruddy rosary, /The soverayne rosemary, ... 340   Garlande   980
Of Vertu also the soverayne enterlude; 345   Garlande   1177

SOVERAYNST
The soveraynst thynge that ony man maye have 52   Bowge   211

SOVERAYNTE
And of Soveraynte a noble pamphelet; 346   Garlande   1191

SOVEREIGNE
A Lawde And Prayse Made for Our Sovereigne Lord the Kyng . . 110   Lawde   I

SOVEREINE
Thy loving sovereine lorde, ... 110   Lawde   9
As king moost sovereine 111   Lawde   52

SOVEREYGNE
No man to our sovereygne lorde 272   Collyn Clout   1030

SOVEREYN
The grounde of his quarell was for his sovereyn lord, . . . 31   Dol Dethe   64

SOVERENLY
Whiche soverenly in honoure shulde excell; 317   Garlande   199

SOW
It semyth the sobbyng of an old sow! 37   Coystrowne1   32
Grace the sede did sow. 110   Lawde   5
The saumpler to sow on, the lacis to enbraid; 334   Garlande   789

SOWDEN
Yet the Sowden, nor the Turke, ... 67   Hauke   216

SOWE
To sowe with stytchis of sylke 77   Phy Sparrow   212
But ye had some wyl[d] sede to sowe, ... 114   Scot Kynge   52
    wyld] 'wyle' †Fakes 1513
I sowe sedycyous sedes of dyscorde and debates. 160   Magnyfycence   737
With clothes upon her hed /That wey a sowe of led, ... 216   El Rummynge   72
    That wey] 'That they wey' Kynge & Marche 1554, Day 1560,
    Marshe 1568
The sowe with her pygges; 219   El Rummynge   176
To sowe corne in the see-sande, ther wyll no crope growe. . . 240   Speke Parott   342
To sowe the sede of graces. 269   Collyn Clout   898
    sowe] 'save' †Godfray 1531, 'sowe' MS Harley 2252

SOWING
But whan I was sowing his beke, ... 77   Phy Sparrow   219

	Page	Title	Line

SOWYD
Was sowyd with slendyr thre[de]. 129 Garnesche3 201
  threde] 'thre' †MS Harley 367
SOWLE
The sowle of this lorde from all daunger of hell, ... 34 Dol Dethe 200
For the sowle of Philip Sparowe, ... 72 Phy Sparrow 7
With, 'Fill the blak bowle /For Jayberdes sowle.' 108 Epitaphe1 74
And pray for Mewtas sowle; . . . . 300 Why Come Ye 832
SOWLLYS
For ij dronken sowllys. 129 Garnesche3 194
SOWRE
A swete suger lofe and sowre bayardys bun 36 Coystrowne1 8
And from the smokes sowre /Of Proserpinas bowre; . . . . 73 Phy Sparrow 82
Me thynke she frowneth and lokys sowre. . . . . 166 Magnyfycence 924
And some brought sowre dowe: . . . . 221 El Rummynge 288
Nor worth a sowre calstocke. . . . . 287 Why Come Ye 355
SOWSE
Ye slufferd up sowse 125 Garnesche3 32
SOWTER
I sawe a sowter go to supper, or ever he had dynde. . . . . . . 191 Magnyfycence 1825
SOWTH
With, 'How doth the north?' 'What tydingis in the sowth?' . . . 326 Garlande 498
And from the sowth unto the north so colde, ... 328 Garlande 578
To my Lady Anne Dakers of the Sowth . . . . 337 Garlande R
SOWTTERS
Nor sowtters to drynke wyne, ... 126 Garnesche3 87
SPACE
He can not fynd it in rule nor in space: 37 Coystrowne1 22
Corage wyth lust, convenient tyme and space; 43 Balettys3 3
I herde her speke of you within shorte space, ... 50 Bowge 158
  shorte] 'a shorte' Wynkyn de Worde 1510
That commaunde with you, me thought, a p[ra]ty space? . . . . . 51 Bowge 198
  commaunde] 'commened' Wynkyn de Worde 1510; 'party spake'
  †Wynkyn de Worde 1499, Marshe 1568, 'party space' WdeW 1510
Hath nowe no tyme nor space . . . . 295 Why Come Ye 631
And then she sayd, 'Whylis we have tyme and space . . . . 328 Garlande 563
Of your lande in shorte space. . . . . 371 Albany 502
SPADE
A mattoke and a spade, ... 293 Why Come Ye 561
SPAINYARDES
And the Spainyardes onyons? . . . . 288 Why Come Ye 371
SPAYNE
With, 'Jayst ye, Jenet of Spayne, for your tayll waggys,' . . . 43 Balettys2 18
Of Lymerik, of Loreine, of Spayne, of Portyngale, ... 326 Garlande 494
SPAYNYSHE
With Dowche, with Spaynyshe, my tonge can agree; . . . . 231 Speke Parott 32
SPAYNYSSHE
By the masse, a Spaynysshe moght with a gray lyste! . . . . . . 173 Magnyfycence 1200
SPAYRE
And go in at my spayre, ... 80 Phy Sparrow 345
  go in] 'often' Kitson 1560.6
SPAKE
'In fayth,' quod Suspecte, 'spake Drede no worde of me?' . . . 51 Bowge 183
Spake he, a fayth, no worde to you of me? . . . . 51 Bowge 204
To Hervy Ha[f]ter than he spake of me, ... 54 Bowge 295
  Hafter] 'Haster' †Wynkyn de Worde 1499, 1510, Marshe 1568
Ryghte now I spake with one, I trowe, I see — . . . . 59 Bowge 458
For his false lying, of that I spake never, ... 139 Ven Tongues 75
But are ye not avysed to dwell where ye spake? . . . . 162 Magnyfycence 774
What! Of Cokermowth spake I no worde. . . . . 170 Magnyfycence 1062
It were better he spake with you or he wente, ... 187 Magnyfycence 1662
But she spake somwhat thycke, ... 223 El Rummynge 338
She spake thus in her snout, ... 223 El Rummynge 363
  spake thus] 'speketh this' †Lant 1545, Kynge & Marche 1554,
  Day 1560, Marshe 1568
Some whispred, some rownyd, some spake, and some cryde, ... 319 Garlande 250
Of noble Dame Pallas, wherof I spake; . . . . 320 Garlande 284
Suche lewde langage ye spake. . . . . 367 Albany 329
SPANYARDES
And Spanyardes onyons, ... 302 Why Come Ye 924
SPAR
When the stede is stolyn, spar the stable dur. . . . . 352 Garlande 1435
SPARE
Spare for no coste; . . . . 165 Magnyfycence 891
When Mesure is gone, what nedest thou spare? . . . . 176 Magnyfycence 1323
Yet convey it craftely, and hardely spare not for me' – . . . . 177 Magnyfycence 1352
Spare for no cost to gyve them pounde and peny; . . . . 190 Magnyfycence 1771
Than from theyr chyldren to spare the rod . . . . 194 Magnyfycence 1929
Spare for the spence of a noble that his honour myght save, . . 200 Magnyfycence 2125
Spare not thy selfe, but boldly the murder. . . . . 206 Magnyfycence 2318
That wyll nothynge spare, ... 217 El Rummynge 107
Spende? Nay, but spare! . . . . 251 Collyn Clout 178
And for no man hardely let hym spare . . . . 319 Garlande 244
And for my sake spare neyther pen nor ynke; . . . . 327 Garlande 549
In metricall muses, his harpyng we may spare; . . . . 383 Replycacion 338
SPARED
Dyverse in style, some spared not vyce to wrythe, ... 46 Bowge 13
  wrythe] 'wryte' Wynkyn de Worde 1510, Marshe 1568

	Page	Title	Line
There may no cost be spared;	254	Collyn Clout	318
SPARETH			
Who spareth to speke, in fayth, he spareth to spede.'	48	Bowge	91
Who spareth to speke, in fayth, he spareth to spede.'	48	Bowge	91
Spareth neither mayde ne wyfe.	284	Why Come Ye	225
SPARYD			
She sparyd not to wete her fete.	42	Balettys1	16
SPARYNG			
So pynchyng and sparyng, and so lytell profyte growth;	245	Speke Parott	493
SPARYS			
For no reverens thou sparys	69	Hauke	280
reverens] 'revens' Kynge & Marche 1554, Day 1560, Marshe 1568			
SPARKE			
I kyndell in her suche a lyther sparke	174	Magnyfycence	1231
And a brennynge sparke /Of Luthers warke,	260	Collyn Clout	542
SPARKIS			
She bet up a fyre with the sparkis full kene	330	Garlande	669
SPARKYLL			
I make them to startyll and sparkyll lyke a bronde;	161	Magnyfycence	741
SPARKLYNGES			
And from her fyry sparklynges,	73	Phy Sparrow	80
SPAROES			
God sende my sparoes sole good rest!	86	Phy Sparrow	574
SPAROW			
My sparow dead and colde,	72	Phy Sparrow	40
My sparow whyte as mylke,	77	Phy Sparrow	213
Me thought my sparow did spek,	77	Phy Sparrow	220
With helpe of the red sparow	82	Phy Sparrow	403
And for her sparow prayd /In lamentable wyse.	93	Phy Sparrow	854
Thus endeth the boke of Philip Sparow,	103	Phy Sparrow	E
I conjure the, Phillip Sparow,	104	Phy Sparrow	1290
Of Phillip Sparow the lamentable fate,	348	Garlande	1254
I conjure the, Phillip Sparow,	348	Garlande	1283
SPAROWE			
Here after foloweth the boke of Phyllyp Sparowe.	71	Phy Sparrow	1
For the sowle of Philip Sparowe,	72	Phy Sparrow	7
Encreaseth my dedly wo, /For my sparowe is go.	74	Phy Sparrow	114
Whan I sawe my sparowe dye!	75	Phy Sparrow	146
My sparowe to commende,	75	Phy Sparrow	155
Of my sparowe royall.	75	Phy Sparrow	158
My sparowe than shuld be quycke	77	Phy Sparrow	205
As my sparowe was.	78	Phy Sparrow	265
But my sparowe dyd pas	78	Phy Sparrow	266
My lytell pretty sparowe	78	Phy Sparrow	280
With me in kepynge suche a Phylyp Sparowe.	184	Magnyfycence	1562
SPAROWES			
And for all sparowes soules	72	Phy Sparrow	11
For that I was robbed /Of my sparowes lyfe.	73	Phy Sparrow	52
For Phyllip Sparowes sake!	74	Phy Sparrow	103
Upon my sparowes soule,	77	Phy Sparrow	241
Any of my sparowes kynde,	78	Phy Sparrow	261
All sparowes of the wode	78	Phy Sparrow	267
For Phylyp Sparowes soule	81	Phy Sparrow	382
Phylyp] 'Phyyp' †Kele 1545.2			
Softly bemole /For my sparowes soule.	85	Phy Sparrow	535
But for my sparowes sake,	92	Phy Sparrow	819
What ayle them to deprave /Phillip Sparowes grave?	103	Phy Sparrow	1275
SPAROWS			
What ayle them to deprave /Phillippe Sparows grave?	348	Garlande	1268
SPARRE			
Of a spyndell I wyll make a sparre;	169	Magnyfycence	1035
SPARRED			
The church dores were sparred,	64	Hauke	91
SPATTYL			
And fed him with my spattyl,	80	Phy Sparrow	358
SPECEFYE			
Parte of there names I thynke to specefye:	321	Garlande	325
SPECHE			
Than Favell gan wyth fayre speche me to fede.	50	Bowge	147
My speche was taken away.	77	Phy Sparrow	229
My speche is all pleasure, but I stynge lyke a waspe.	160	Magnyfycence	730
Mary, your speche is as pleasant as though it were pend,	183	Magnyfycence	1538
No man dare come to the speche	294	Why Come Ye	615
SPECIALL			
Yet for a speciall laud	89	Phy Sparrow	720
SPECIALLY			
More specially barons, and thos knightis bold,	34	Dol Dethe	183
So rygorous revelyng, in a prelate specially;	246	Speke Parott	506
SPECYALL			
A curate in specyall	65	Hauke	141
But for the specyall consolacyon	117	Ag Scottes	75
Whiche conteyned in it a specyall clause	209	Magnyfycence	2436
SPECYALLY			
And specyally to controule /Such as have cure of soule,	62	Hauke	3
That cat specyally,	78	Phy Sparrow	278
Me to enbrace and love moost specyally.	190	Magnyfycence	1800
And specyally to redresse that were out of joynte.	208	Magnyfycence	2414

SPECTACLE —SPEKE

	Page	Title	Line
But one gate specyally, where as I stode,	328	Garlande	586
And specyally which glad was to devyse	342	Garlande	1071

SPECTACLE
That shall be a spectacle	293	Why Come Ye	568

SPECTACLE CASE
Wer thi nose spectacle case;	133	Garnesche5	134
A spectacle case /To cover thy face, /With, tray deux ase.	136	Dundas	37

SPECTACLES
His plummet, his pensell, his spectacles of glas,	343	Garlande	1097
of] 'with' †Fakes 1523			

SPECULACYON
That is a speculacyon	270	Collyn Clout	970

SPED
Wele sped in spyndels and turnyng of tavellys,	37	Coystrownel	34
Yet I am nothyng sped,	90	Phy Sparrow	754
In Chauser I am sped,	91	Phy Sparrow	788
And yet, I trowe, some of you be better sped than I	160	Magnyfycence	722
Nay, nay; for lesse I waraunt you to be sped,	184	Magnyfycence	1571
Recoverd whan the forster was gone, and sped	351	Garlande	1407
and transcendingly sped in moche high connyng,	374	Replycacion	I

SPEDDE
That sheweth yourselfe thus spedde in physyke?	156	Magnyfycence	556

SPEDE
Your hap was unhappy, to ill was your spede.	31	Dol Dethe	61
Than asked she me, 'Syr, so God the spede,	48	Bowge	76
Who spareth to speke, in fayth, he spareth to spede.'	48	Bowge	91
'God spede, broder,' to me quod he than,	51	Bowge	195
And so I wolde it were, so God me spede,	59	Bowge	481
How unfortunately he doth now spede;	115	Scot Kynge	57
God sende you wele good spede,	129	Garnesche3	202
In your crosse rowe nor Christ crosse you spede,	137	Ven Tongues	18
With ye, syr, so God me spede.	151	Magnyfycence	379
The devyll spede whyt!	168	Magnyfycence	1006
With a good wyll, syr, God spede you bothe togyder.	186	Magnyfycence	1648
All that I can his matter for to spede.	187	Magnyfycence	1664
'Cristecrosse and Saynt Nycholas, Parrot, be your good spede!'	236	Speke Parott	189
In this your journey to prospere and spede.	239	Speke Parott	314
The devyll spede whitte!	304	Why Come Ye	1017
Let se, my syster, now spede you, go aboute.	319	Garlande	242
you] not in MS Cotton Vitellius E.x			
God geve them good spede there warke to begin!	334	Garlande	793
Was wrytin; and so she did her spede,	345	Garlande	1168
Ye shall have nede /You for to spede	355	Garlande	1555
Ye] 'You' Marshe 1568			
But of my spede /Small sekernes;	356	Garlande	1596
Ye had evill spede.	359	Albany	32
And maketh in us suche spede	385	Replycacion	386

SPEED
Ungraciously how he doth speed.	119	Ag Scottes	154

SPEK
Me thought my sparow did spek,	77	Phy Sparrow	220

SPEKE
Yet I avyse you to speke, for ony drede:	48	Bowge	90
Who spareth to speke, in fayth, he spareth to spede.'	48	Bowge	91
'Pece,' quod Desyre, 'ye speke not worth a bene!	48	Bowge	95
I herde her speke of you within shorte space,	50	Bowge	158
shorte] 'a shorte' Wynkyn de Worde 1510			
'Why? What than? Wylte thou lete men to speke?	51	Bowge	184
He wyll begyle you and speke fayre to your face.	51	Bowge	200
I dare not speke; I promysed to be dome.	52	Bowge	229
I dare not speke, we be so layde awayte,	59	Bowge	468
Adewe tyll soone, we shall speke more of this.	60	Bowge	492
No man for them wil speke.	111	Lawde	32
As men dare speke it hugger mugger:	151	Magnyfycence	387
For to speke with Lyberte.	155	Magnyfycence	539
For he wyll speke to Magnyfycence thus.	172	Magnyfycence	1168
Tushe! Holde your peas; ye speke lyke a dawe.	178	Magnyfycence	1379
Tushe! Holde your peas; ye speke out of season.	178	Magnyfycence	1388
Speke, I beseche the. Leve nothynge behynde.	183	Magnyfycence	1544
I speke the softlyer because he sholde not wete.	186	Magnyfycence	1654
I may no more speke tyll I have wept my fyll.	198	Magnyfycence	2063
This letter ye speke of never dyd I wryte.	209	Magnyfycence	2442
Speke Parott	230	El Rummynge	I
With, 'Speke, Parott, I pray yow,' full curteslye they sey,	231	Speke Parott	13
In Greke tong Parott can bothe speke and sey,	231	Speke Parott	26
To lerne all langage and hyt to speke aptlye.	232	Speke Parott	45
I pray you, let Parot have lyberte to speke.	233	Speke Parott	98
I pray you, let Parrot have lyberte to speke.	236	Speke Parott	210
Speke, Parotte, I pray yow, for Maryes saake,	237	Speke Parott	233
Speke, Parotte, my swete byrde, and ye shall have a date,	243	Speke Parott	416
Nowe, Parott, my swete byrde, speke owte yet ons agayn,	244	Speke Parott	447
Sette asyde all sophysms, and speke now trew and playne.	244	Speke Parott	448
Or yf he speke playne, /Than he lacketh brayne:	247	Collyn Clout	26
I speke nat nowe of all,	252	Collyn Clout	244
I speke nat of the good wyfe,	253	Collyn Clout	253
And therof speke nothynge	255	Collyn Clout	355
Nor to speke to hym secretly, /Openly nor prevyly,	272	Collyn Clout	1040
That I speke out of the way.	273	Collyn Clout	1094

SPEKES —SPEWE   Page   Title   Line

	Page	Title	Line
Of no good bysshop speke I,	273	Collyn Clout	1095
No man dare speke a worde,	283	Why Come Ye	191
None so hardy to speke.	287	Why Come Ye	328
But speke ye no more of that,	288	Why Come Ye	382
To speke with you as yet.'	295	Why Come Ye	632
I speke by protestacion:	305	Why Come Ye	1043
Dare speke for his lyfe	306	Why Come Ye	1076
That speke fayre before the and shrewdly behynde.	329	Garlande	620
Item the Boke to Speke Well or be Styll;	345	Garlande	1175
Wherto shuld I more speke	366	Albany	302

SPEKES

	Page	Title	Line
Of suche paternoster pekes /All the worlde spekes.	253	Collyn Clout	263

SPEKEST

	Page	Title	Line
Spekest thou to me?	162	Magnyfycence	799
Nay, that is my parte that thou spekest of nowe.	175	Magnyfycence	1282

SPEKETH

	Page	Title	Line
He wottyth never what /Ne whereof he speketh.'	247	Collyn Clout	18
Of suche vacabundus /Speketh totus mundus:	253	Collyn Clout	247

SPEKYNG

	Page	Title	Line
Spekyng in paroblis, how the fox, the grey,	315	Garlande	101

SPEKYNGE

	Page	Title	Line
In spekynge and rebellynge	274	Collyn Clout	1103

SPEKYS

	Page	Title	Line
Wotyst thou, I say, to whom thou spekys?	172	Magnyfycence	1166

SPEKYTH

	Page	Title	Line
For when he spekyth fayrest, then thynketh he moost yll;	333	Garlande	759

SPELL

	Page	Title	Line
Loke that ye spell /Well thys gospell;	39	Coystrowne3	20
To rede or to spell /What these verses tell.	68	Hauke	237
Though I can rede and spell,	87	Phy Sparrow	612
Spell the remenaunt, and do togyder.	157	Magnyfycence	619
For drede and he lerne them there A B C to spell.'	353	Garlande	1476

SPELLE

	Page	Title	Line
The honor of Englond I lernyd to spelle,	132	Garnesche5	95

SPELLES

	Page	Title	Line
Redes shrewdly and spelles,	257	Collyn Clout	414
redes] 'rede' †Godfray 1531, Kele 1545.1, Marshe 1568			

SPENCE

	Page	Title	Line
Spare for the spence of a noble that his honour myght save,	200	Magnyfycence	2125
With Elynour in the spence,	229	El Rummynge	598

SPEND

	Page	Title	Line
And spend my tyme /In prose and ryme,	95	Phy Sparrow	954
Though they wold spend	103	Phy Sparrow	1272

SPENDE

	Page	Title	Line
Lewdely your tyme ye spende,	124	Garnesche3	15
Spende all his hyre	165	Magnyfycence	907
For, Goddes cope, thou wyll spende!	171	Magnyfycence	1115
Wyll ye spende ony money? Ye, a thousande pounde.	184	Magnyfycence	1570
And spende C s. for the pleasure of a knave.	200	Magnyfycence	2126
Spende moche of theyr share	251	Collyn Clout	176
Spende? Nay, but spare!	251	Collyn Clout	178
With, 'Spende,' and wast witlesse,	280	Why Come Ye	74
Though they wolde spende	348	Garlande	1265
And to spende their hart blode,	371	Albany	487

SPENDETH

	Page	Title	Line
Ye. But he spendeth it all in mesure.	157	Magnyfycence	621

SPENT

	Page	Title	Line
Upon suche a sort was ille bestowde and spent.	32	Dol Dethe	98
Where is nowe my golde upon them that I spent?	198	Magnyfycence	2058
And so ungracyously thy dayes thou hast spent,	205	Magnyfycence	2295
Spent among wanton lasses;	257	Collyn Clout	424
Our fagottes are all spent.	281	Why Come Ye	83
And mor madly spent.	282	Why Come Ye	144
Bycause that he his tyme studyously hath spent	314	Garlande	60
he his tyme] 'his tyme he' MS Cotton Vitellius E.x			
And how that it was wantonly spent;	347	Garlande	1244
That leudly have their tyme spent,	375	Replycacion	24

SPENTE

	Page	Title	Line
So vertuously that hath his dayes spente;	50	Bowge	151
Lest that he thought that his money were evyll spente,	187	Magnyfycence	1674
Muche money, men sey, there madly he hathe spente;	240	Speke Parott	335
So myche newe makyng, and so madd tyme spente;	244	Speke Parott	450
So myche spente before, and so myche unpayd behynde -	244	Speke Parott	461
For we have spente our shot!	282	Why Come Ye	127

SPERE

	Page	Title	Line
For yf they had occupied ther spere and ther shelde	31	Dol Dethe	73
Than Phebus in his spere celestyne,	47	Bowge	61
Many a spere brake /For his ladyes sake;	87	Phy Sparrow	639
They say they had /And wan the felde /With spere and shelde!	116	Ag Scottes	16
At Gynys when ye ware /But a slendyr spere,	125	Garnesche3	41
In faythe, Lyberte is nowe a lusty spere.	166	Magnyfycence	937
Of fyre elementar in his supreme spere,	331	Garlande	694

SPERYCALL

	Page	Title	Line
Then to the hevyn sperycall upwarde I gasid,	354	Garlande	1514

SPERKES

	Page	Title	Line
And smerke, lyke a smythy kur, at sperkes of steile;	333	Garlande	762

SPEWE

	Page	Title	Line
Ha, ha, ha! For sporte I am lyke to spewe and cast.	201	Magnyfycence	2161

SPIES —SPOKEN   Page   Title   Line

SPIES
But lering and lurking here and there like spies, ...   139   Ven Tongues   67
SPIRITIS
Wherewith your spiritis may be revyvid.'   332   Garlande   713
SPIRITUALL
Bothe temporall and spirituall for to complayne   34   Dol Dethe   181
Of what estate he be /Of spirituall dygnyte;   294   Why Come Ye   618
SPIRYTUAL
Agaynst the spirytual contradictyons, ...   249   Collyn Clout   113
SPIRYTUALL
But nowe every spiryptuall father, ...   251   Collyn Clout   174
And set in majeste /And spirytuall dygnyte, ...   261   Collyn Clout   588
For your spiryptuall charge, ...   264   Collyn Clout   692
Agaynst all spirytuall men.   272   Collyn Clout   1054
SPIRYTUALTE
For the temporalte /Accuseth the spirytualte;   248   Collyn Clout   62
The spiryptualte agayne   248   Collyn Clout   63
Of the spirytualte /Or of the temporalte, ...   274   Collyn Clout   1119
SPY
My purpose is to spy and to poynte every man;   160   Magnyfycence   726
And where I spy a nysot gay   174   Magnyfycence   1228
For as far as they can spy   308   Why Come Ye   1172
    they] 'the' †Kele 1545.3
If they can spy /Circumspectly   356   Garlande   1579
    they] 'thy' †Fakes 1523
SPYCE
Deyntely dyetyd with dyvers delycate spyce, ...   231   Speke Parott   3
SPYCKE
Another brought a spycke /Of a bacon flycke;   223   El Rummynge   335
SPYE
That all the warlde wyll spye your shame.   132   Garnesche5   111
They bare me in hande that I was a spye;   150   Magnyfycence   352
Some came to flater, some came to spye.   326   Garlande   511
SPYED
For drede, that we dare not ofte, lest we be spyed.   177   Magnyfycence   1339
A, I have spyed ye can moche broken sorowe.   184   Magnyfycence   1587
Sodenly hyd, and sodenly spyed;   213   Magnyfycence   2535
SPYES
Sum medelynge spyes, by craft to grope thy mynde, ...   329   Garlande   617
SPYGHT
In the spyght of his tethe   302   Why Come Ye   942
In spyght of thy cowardes face, ...   369   Albany   408
In spyght of kyng Fraunces, ...   369   Albany   409
In spyght of thy cowardes face, ...   371   Albany   492
SPYGHTFULL
And your spyghtfull despyghtyng, ...   127   Garnesche3   114
SPYING
Liing, spying by sutteltie and slyght, ...   133   Garnesche5   151
SPYLL
Surely it is I that all may save and spyll, ...   181   Magnyfycence   1478
Some fall to foly, them selfe for to spyll, ...   200   Magnyfycence   2139
Let us syppe and soppy, /And not spyll a droppy, ...   228   El Rummynge   559
SPYLT
Alas for pite that Percy thus was spylt, ...   32   Dol Dethe   106
SPYN
Suche a webbe can spyn, ...   221   El Rummynge   255
SPYNDELL
Of a spyndell I wyll make a sparre;   169   Magnyfycence   1035
Theyr rybskyn and theyr spyndell, ...   222   El Rummynge   299
SPYNDELS
Wele sped in spyndels and turnyng of tavellys, ...   37   Coystrownel   34
SPYNKE
The spynke and the martynet also;   82   Phy Sparrow   407
SPYNNYNG WHELE
Theyr rocke, theyr spynnyng whele.   222   El Rummynge   296
SPYNNYS
Gyll swetis and Cate spynnys!   302   Why Come Ye   926
    Cate] not in MS Rawlinson C. 813
SPYNT
My study myght be better spynt;   134   Garnesche5   176
SPYRITUALL
With his harpe of prophesy /And spyrituall poetry, ...   384   Replycacion   346
Howe there is a spyrituall, ...   384   Replycacion   365
By whose inflammacion /Of spyrituall instygacion   384   Replycacion   380
SPYRYTUALL
And of the spyrytuall law /They made but a gewgaw, ...   66   Hauke   156
And theyr spyrytuall lambes /Sequestred from rambes   250   Collyn Clout   156
SPYTELL
And Saynt Mary Spytell   276   Collyn Clout   1184
SPLAY
Your stondarde, Syr Olifranke, agenst me for to splay; . . .   123   Garnesche2   30
SPOYLYD
and spoylyd from all his goodys and rayment.   193   Magnyfycence   SD
SPOKEN
These wordes in myne eyre, they be so lustely spoken, ...   184   Magnyfycence   1565
What nede all this be spoken?   227   El Rummynge   499
Of our noble courte is ones spoken owte, ...   353   Garlande   1482

SPOKYN—STAFFE

	Page	Title	Line
SPOKYN			
Sume be moche spokyn of for makynge of frays;	317	Garlande	182
SPONE			
A spone of golde, full of hony swete,	58	Bowge	436
Some a salt, and some a spone,	220	El Rummynge	247
SPORES			
Ye have loste spores, cote armure and sworde.	114	Scot Kynge	49
Alasse! Where is my botes and my spores?	156	Magnyfycence	569
SPORNE			
And nowe on me ye gaure and sporne.	204	Magnyfycence	2247
SPORT			
Your welth, your joy, your sport, your play,	119	Ag Scottes	159
In ernest and in sport.	121	Ag Scottes2	34
Tell by thy trouth what sport can thou make.	172	Magnyfycence	1162
For, after all our sport,	220	El Rummynge	231
This joy excedith all wordly sport and play,	332	Garlande	716
wordly] 'worldly' Marshe 1568			
SPORTE			
For my solas and sporte.	77	Phy Sparrow	218
To sporte at your pleasure, to ryn, and to ryde?	142	Magnyfycence	79
Ha, ha, ha! For sporte I am lyke to spewe and cast.	201	Magnyfycence	2161
Than began the sporte /Amonge that dronken sorte.	229	El Rummynge	574
Made lusty sporte and joy	270	Collyn Clout	952
Toke it for a sporte,	379	Replycacion	191
SPRAY			
The blossom on the spray,	340	Garlande	989
How her ble was bryght as blossom on the spray,	351	Garlande	1412
SPRANGE			
With that I sprange up towarde the tent	320	Garlande	283
SPREDE			
As proud a pohen as ye sprede,	41	Coystrowne4	13
Whose fame by me shall sprede	93	Phy Sparrow	885
That agaynst preesthode /Theyr malyce sprede abrode,	260	Collyn Clout	535
agaynst] 'agayn' Marshe 1568			
That so indede /Your fame may sprede	355	Garlande	1551
Over all the world[e] to sprede.	371	Albany	511
worlde] 'worlds' †Marshe 1568			
SPRYNG			
From Scarpary to Tartary renoun therein doth spryng,	234	Speke Parott	131
How ryvers rin not tyll the spryng be full;	314	Garlande	81
SPRYNGE			
Which makyth my hart oft to lepe and sprynge	44	Balettys3	32
That thou so hye fro me doth sprynge,	170	Magnyfycence	1069
The red rose in honour to flowrysshe and sprynge!'	231	Speke Parott	35
Good Sprynge of Lanam	302	Why Come Ye	933
Downe this hye sprynge;	302	Why Come Ye	950
SPUR			
Spur up at the hynder gyrth with, 'Gup, morell, gup!'	43	Balettys2	17
Dun is in the myre, dame, reche me my spur.	352	Garlande	1433
SPURRES			
Lyke cankerd curres /Ye loste your spurres;	360	Albany	34
SPURRYS			
Ye lost your spurrys, ye lost you sworde.	119	Ag Scottes	148
SQUAT			
So how, I say, the hare is squat!	176	Magnyfycence	1299
SQUYER-GALYARDE			
Syr squyer-galyarde ye were to swyfte;	113	Scot Kynge	11
SQUYERS			
Knyghtis and squyers, at every season when	30	Dol Dethe	32
Barons, knightis, squyers, one and alle,	31	Dol Dethe	92
Of knightis, of squyers, chef lord of toure and toune,	33	Dol Dethe	132
SQUYRE			
Squyre, knyght and lorde	271	Collyn Clout	980
Whether he be knyght or squyre,	287	Why Come Ye	344
STABBE			
What! He hathe ben hurte with a stabbe?	171	Magnyfycence	1124
STABILITE			
His stabilite, /His humilite,	370	Albany	453
STABILLE			
Stabille thy mynde constant to be and fast,	34	Dol Dethe	170
STABYLL			
I wyl be ferme and stabyll, /And to yow servyceabyll,	237	Speke Parott	246
Of Diomedis stabyll /He brought out a rabyll	349	Garlande	1305
STABLE			
Of Penelope most stable,	89	Phy Sparrow	725
Of Dyomedes stable /He brought out a rable	104	Phy Sparrow	1312
Fyrst, I saye, with mynde fyrme and stable	208	Magnyfycence	2408
For Parrot to pyke upon, his brayne for to stable,	235	Speke Parott	184
Than, our processe for to stable,	292	Why Come Ye	536
Than shall ye fynde it fyrme and stable,	382	Replycacion	289
STABLE DUR			
When the stede is stolyn, spar the stable dur.	352	Garlande	1435
STACIUS			
Lucan, with Stacius in Achilliedos;	321	Garlande	337
STAFFE			
Cros, staffe, lectryne and banner,	64	Hauke	114
With, 'Get me a staffe, /The swyne eate my draffe!	218	El Rummynge	170

	Page	Title	Line
STAKE			
And bynde them to a stake,	303	Why Come Ye	984
And be brent at a stake,	382	Replycacion	295
STALE			
Gup, Cristian Clowte, your breth is stale,	36	Man Margery	27
She left hym slepyng and stale away,	42	Balettys1	14
It was a stale to take /The devyll in a brake.	222	El Rummynge	324
stale] 'stale' 1521 Fragment, 'stare' †Lant 1545, Kynge & Marche 1554, Day 1560, Marshe 1568			
And ye wyll gyve me a syppet /Of your stale ale,	223	El Rummynge	368
Her breth was soure and stale	226	El Rummynge	486
STALYON			
Ye stronge sturdy stalyon, so sterne and stowty,	122	Garnesche1	10
STALKYNGE			
And for stalkynge cranys;	102	Phy Sparrow	1244
stalkynge] 'stalke' †Kele 1545.2			
STALL			
That was cast out of a bochers stall!	291	Why Come Ye	494
STALWORTHY			
A stalworthy stryplyng.	287	Why Come Ye	349
stalworthy] 'tall worthy' Kitson 1560.7, Marshe 1568			
STAMERYNG			
Parrot is no stameryng stare, that men call a starlyng;	236	Speke Parott	207
STAMMER			
Her felowe dyd stammer and stut,	223	El Rummynge	339
STAMPE			
It made them to skip, to stampe, and to stare,	353	Garlande	1473
What though ye stampe and stare?	363	Albany	180
STAMPPED			
He frounde, he stared, he stampped where he stoode.	55	Bowge	319
STAND			
Nor stand long wrestyng there aboute;	41	Coystrowne4	25
Shall stand in their morning gounes;	85	Phy Sparrow	566
Stand up, syr. Ye are welcom to me.	186	Magnyfycence	1632
STANDE			
Nowe pleasyth you a lytell whyle to stande;	145	Magnyfycence	161
In stede of ryght that wronge may stande;	152	Magnyfycence	433
To se you thus ruled and stande in suche awe.	178	Magnyfycence	1376
Let your lust and lykynge stande for a lawe.	185	Magnyfycence	1607
Stande styll here, and ye shall se	186	Magnyfycence	1629
Stande a lytell abacke, syr, and let hym come hyder.	186	Magnyfycence	1647
Well were that lady myght stande in my grace,	190	Magnyfycence	1799
Than stande up, syr, in Goddys name!	208	Magnyfycence	2397
Of adversyte it is to stande in drede.	209	Magnyfycence	2428
'A strawe,' sayde Bele, 'stande utter,	228	El Rummynge	535
And yf ye stande in doute /Who brought this ryme aboute,	248	Collyn Clout	47
Therfore stande sure and fast.	273	Collyn Clout	1071
Stande sure and take good fotyng,	273	Collyn Clout	1072
Of those that stande in your grace.	273	Collyn Clout	1076
They must stande all afar	286	Why Come Ye	301
Stande, walke, or ryde –	295	Why Come Ye	635
May stande somwhat in stede.	298	Why Come Ye	765
Myght stande now by potters,	301	Why Come Ye	910
Myght] 'most' MS Rawlinson C. 813			
With, 'Sir, I pray you, a lytyll tyme stande backe,	326	Garlande	505
How daungerous it were to stande in his lyght,	333	Garlande	755
were to stande in his lyght] 'is to stop up his sight' MS Cotton Vitellius E.x			
Fortune to stande betwene you and the lyght.	344	Garlande	1134
STANDETH			
Of fortune this the chaunce /Standeth on varyaunce:	81	Phy Sparrow	367
Crafty Conveyaunce standeth in the strete	167	Magnyfycence	956
Howe standeth the wynde	168	Magnyfycence	985
A bagpype without blowynge standeth in no sted:	232	Speke Parott	75
bagpype] 'bagbyte' †Lant 1545, Kynge & Marche 1554			
It standeth in no stede:	247	Collyn Clout	35
That standeth yet awrye;	308	Why Come Ye	1187
It standeth somwhat on the west;	308	Why Come Ye	1189
STANDIS			
What it is, and where upon it standis;	332	Garlande	722
STANDITH			
With litell besynes standith moche rest; in bed	351	Garlande	1410
STANDYNGE			
Standynge in sadde communicacion.	58	Bowge	420
STANDYTH			
Non phanum, sed prophanum, standyth in lytyll sted:	234	Speke Parott	125
STANG			
More stinging then scorpions that stang Pharaotis.	138	Ven Tongues	52
STANKE			
Sche seyd your brethe stanke lyke a broke;	131	Garnesche5	55
And her brethe strongely stanke,	228	El Rummynge	541
STAR			
Radyent Esperus, star of the clowdy nyght,	44	Balettys3	24
Lyke to the radyant star,	98	Phy Sparrow	1047
To treate of any star	292	Why Come Ye	524
STARE			
With browes bente, and gan on me to stare	48	Bowge	81
Thou muste swere and stare, man, aldaye longe,	57	Bowge	381

STARED —STEDE   Page   Title   Line

	Page	Title	Line
That lyke a fende doth stare;	73	Phy Sparrow	77
Swere and stare, and byde therby,	152	Magnyfycence	414
But may I drynke therof whylest that I stare?	176	Magnyfycence	1322
But drynke tyll they stare	217	El Rummynge	108
Parrot is no stameryng stare, that men call a starlyng;	236	Speke Parott	207
To blowe bararag tyll bothe his eyne stare.'	319	Garlande	245
bararag] 'bararag brag' MS Cotton Vitellius E.x			
Wele was hym that thereupon myght stare.	343	Garlande	1109
It made them to skip, to stampe, and to stare,	353	Garlande	1473
What though ye stampe and stare?	363	Albany	180
STARED			
He frounde, he stared, he stampped where he stoode.	55	Bowge	319
STARES			
Howe all the worlde stares	270	Collyn Clout	960
STARYNG			
And iche man stode gasyng and staryng upon other.	319	Garlande	268
STARYNGE			
With swerynge and starynge,	281	Why Come Ye	103
STARK			
I say, ye commoners, why wer ye so stark mad?	30	Dol Dethe	50
Withe his enmys that were stark mad and wode;	32	Dol Dethe	100
STARKE			
And slew him there starke dead.	81	Phy Sparrow	378
Iam iacet hic starke deed,	108	Epitaphe1	60
The White there slew the Red starke ded.	119	Ag Scottes	138
Ye were starke mad to make a fray,	119	Ag Scottes	143
And wretchedly ye lay starke naked.	119	Ag Scottes	167
starke naked] 'starke your naked' Kynge & Marche 1554,			
Day 1560, 'starke all naked' Marshe 1568			
He wolde trotte gentylly, but he is to starke.	153	Magnyfycence	481
Nowe hast thou not a prowde mocke and a starke?	174	Magnyfycence	1208
Ulula, Esebon, for Jepte is starke ded!	234	Speke Parott	126
Wherfor your remorders ar madde or else starke blynde,	241	Speke Parott	369
remorders] 'remordes' †MS Harley 2252			
Now frantick, now starke wode!	293	Why Come Ye	578
And so attaynted, /Lyke cowardes starke,	359	Albany	29
Suche a starke cowarde,	363	Albany	169
Your lernyng is starke nought,	376	Replycacion	56
STARKEST			
The starkest knave, and lest good kan,	130	Garnesche5	23
STARLYNG			
The starlyng with her brablyng;	83	Phy Sparrow	461
Parrot is no stameryng stare, that men call a starlyng;	236	Speke Parott	207
STARRIS			
Pray to thy son above the starris clere,	35	Dol Dethe	208
STARRY			
That Phyllyp may fly /Above the starry sky,	86	Phy Sparrow	599
That from the starry sky	110	Lawde	16
The starry hevyn, me thought, shoke with the showte;	354	Garlande	1508
START			
By Goddes fote, and I dare well fyght, for I wyll not start.	161	Magnyfycence	768
Some start in at the backe syde,	221	El Rummynge	263
STARTE			
The locke of a casket to make to starte.	203	Magnyfycence	2229
STARTYLL			
I make them to startyll and sparkyll lyke a bronde;	161	Magnyfycence	741
STATE			
Of grace out of the state /And dyed excomunycate.	121	Ag Scottes2	29
But largesse becometh a state ryall,	151	Magnyfycence	383
With the also? What! He playeth the state?	166	Magnyfycence	945
Of that I se you nowe in the state of grace.	208	Magnyfycence	2403
Of frantycknes and folysshnes whyche ys the grett state?	243	Speke Parott	417
Nacion moost in hate, /Proude and poore of state.	362	Albany	144
STATHAM			
To mastres Geretrude Statham	341	Garlande	R
STATURE			
So large a man, and so lytell of stature!	155	Magnyfycence	523
STATUTES			
So myche mokkyshe makyng of statutes of array -	245	Speke Parott	482
Suche statutes apon diettes, suche pyllyng and pollyng -	245	Speke Parott	495
STED			
Her wyt stood her in sted	89	Phy Sparrow	729
A bagpype without blowynge standeth in no sted:	232	Speke Parott	75
bagpype] 'bagbyte' †Lant 1545, Kynge & Marche 1554			
Non phanum, sed prophanum, standyth in lytyll sted:	234	Speke Parott	125
STEDE			
They wandred ay and stode styll in no stede.	58	Bowge	423
In the stede of meate	83	Phy Sparrow	480
She raysed up in that stede	105	Phy Sparrow	1352
Thus thorow every stede	110	Lawde	3
Cowde hocupy ther no stede.	126	Garnesche3	69
In stede of ryght that wronge may stande;	152	Magnyfycence	433
That he shall have you in the stede of sadnesse,	159	Magnyfycence	680
In the stede of a budge furre.	169	Magnyfycence	1057
Nay, offer hym a counter in stede of a peny.	172	Magnyfycence	1171
In a certayne stede /Bysyde Lederhede.	217	El Rummynge	97
In stede of coyne and monny /Some brynge her a conny,	220	El Rummynge	244

	Page	Title	Line
STEDFAST —STINT			
Now pas furthe, good Parott, Owur Lorde be your s[t]ede, stede] 'spede' †MS Harley 2252	239	Speke Parott	313
So myche poletyke pratyng, and so lytell stondythe in stede;	244	Speke Parott	464
It standeth in no stede:	247	Collyn Clout	35
Then renne they in every stede,	252	Collyn Clout	231
May stande somwhat in stede.	298	Why Come Ye	765
Tell me nowe in this stede,	298	Why Come Ye	786
Now he is gone to another stede	299	Why Come Ye	797
She raysed up in that stede	350	Garlande	1345
When the stede is stolyn, spar the stable dur.	352	Garlande	1435
STEDFAST			
Stedfast of thought, /Wele made, wele wrought;	341	Garlande	1029
STEDFASTNESSE			
In Fortunys frendshyppe there is no stedfastnesse;	201	Magnyfycence	2156
STEILE			
And smerke, lyke a smythy kur, at sperkes of steile;	333	Garlande	762
STELE			
They thynke it no shame to robbe and stele;	198	Magnyfycence	2042
STELYNG			
Alasse, syr, ye are undone with stelyng and robbynge!	192	Magnyfycence	1852
STELLYFYE			
Yow for to stellyfye;	339	Garlande	963
STENCHE			
With, 'Fo, ther is a stenche!	219	El Rummynge	180
STEPE			
Her eyen gray and stepe	97	Phy Sparrow	1014
STEPLE			
Ware the wether cocke /Of the steple of Poules.	255	Collyn Clout	340
They renne agaynst the steple,	271	Collyn Clout	983
STEPPIS			
An hundred steppis mountyng to the halle,	325	Garlande	471
STER CHAMBRE			
In the Ster Chambre he noddis and beks,	287	Why Come Ye	339
STERE			
Holde up the helme, loke up and lete God stere:	53	Bowge	250
My shyp nowe wyll I stere stere] 'pere' Kele 1545.1, Marshe 1568, 'stere' MS Harley 2252	278	Collyn Clout	1259
STERNE			
Ye stronge sturdy stalyon, so sterne and stowty,	122	Garnesche1	10
Ye Duke so doutty, /So sterne, so stoutty,	361	Albany	78
STERRE			
Sterre of the morow gray,	340	Garlande	988
STERRES			
Stretchynge to the sterres,	270	Collyn Clout	938
That in the Chambre of Sterres	283	Why Come Ye	188
STERRY			
As though they wolde flye /Aboute the sterry skye. Aboute] 'Above' Kele 1545.1, Marshe 1568, MS Harley 2252	248	Collyn Clout	74
Renownyd lady above the sterry hevyn,	313	Garlande	51
In our collage above the sterry sky,	323	Garlande	403
STERRYS			
To nombyr all the sterrys in the fyrmament,	240	Speke Parott	332
From the seven sterrys!	267	Collyn Clout	827
STERT			
Up she stert, halfe lame,	227	El Rummynge	512
STERTE			
Sterte all at ones, I lyked no thynge his playe,	60	Bowge	502
Than sterte in made Kyt, /That had lytell wyt;	224	El Rummynge	412
Than sterte forth a fysgygge	228	El Rummynge	538
Sterte all at ones an hundrethe fote backe.	320	Garlande	282
STERVE			
The fynde of hell mot sterve the!	365	Albany	251
STEVYN			
They wolde the wryght, all with one stevyn,	133	Garnesche5	144
STEWED			
Or a stewed cocke	252	Collyn Clout	217
He eateth c[a]pons stewed, capons] 'copons' †Kele 1545.3	284	Why Come Ye	221
STEWES			
But at the naked stewes	284	Why Come Ye	236
STEWYS			
Now renne muste I to the stewys syde	57	Bowge	400
STIGIALL			
By the Stigiall flode,	349	Garlande	1327
STILE			
What though my stile be rude?	369	Albany	419
STILL			
Whiche redde on still, as it cam to her syght,	354	Garlande	1493
Contynew still /With there good wyll.	356	Garlande	1585
STINGING			
More stinging then scorpions that stang Pharaotis.	138	Ven Tongues	52
STINGYNG			
As it reprehendyng, /And venemously stingyng,	120	Ag Scottes2	10
STINT			
To walke on this walle she bed I sholde not stint;	328	Garlande	571

STY —STYNKINGLY   Page   Title   Line

STY
   Than swetely togither we ly, /As two pygges in a sty.' 220   El Rummynge   234
      Than swetely] 'Thus swete' 1521 Fragment
STYCK
   That all the dayes of ther lyfe shall styck by ther rybbis. . . 330   Garlande   638
STYCKE
   But nowe adayes as huksters they hucke and they stycke, ... 200   Magnyfycence 2121
STYCKIS
   Swete synamum styckis and pleris cum musco! 235   Speke Parott   185
STYCKYNGE
   In styckynge my selfe with this fayre knyfe.   206   Magnyfycence 2322
STYGYALL
   By the Stygyall flood, ...   105   Phy Sparrow   1334
STYL
   That day and night brenneth styl, ...   79   Phy Sparrow   314
STYLE
   Dyverse in style, some spared not vyce to wrythe, ... 46   Bowge   13
      wrythe] 'wryte' Wynkyn de Worde 1510, Marshe 1568
   My style as yet direct   91   Phy Sparrow   772
   And my style dres /To this prosses. 96   Phy Sparrow   968
   With pen and ynk /For to compyle /Some goodly style;   96   Phy Sparrow   988
      goodly] 'godly' †Kele 1545.2
   Wolde God myne homely style 101   Phy Sparrow   1204
   Or bokes to compyle /Of dyvers maner style, ... 247   Collyn Clout   10
   My style for to dyrecte, ... 257   Collyn Clout   435
   And make a pleasaunt style 267   Collyn Clout   851
   At my style rude and playne, ... 273   Collyn Clout 1088
   Thus wyll I conclude my style, ... 289   Why Come Ye   396
STYLL
   A proverbe of old, 'Say well or be styll':   38   Coystrowne1   64
   'Ly styll', quod she, 'my paramoure, ...   41   Balettys1   3
   Ly styll hardely, and take a nap.'   41   Balettys1   4
   They wandred ay and stode styll in no stede.   58   Bowge   423
   In my church hawke styll.   64   Hauke   99
   The tarsell gentyll, /They shall morne soft and styll 85   Phy Sparrow   559
   His tong never styll /For to say yll, ...   95   Phy Sparrow   941
   Ay to contynewe and styll to endure. 141   Magnyfycence   15
   But I say, kepest thou the olde name styll that thou had? . . . 155   Magnyfycence   516
   What! Shall we jangle thus all the day styll? 156   Magnyfycence   565
   Nay, lette us not clatter thus styll. 157   Magnyfycence   610
   But shall I have myne olde name styll? 158   Magnyfycence   647
   And howe styll she doth syt! 168   Magnyfycence 1003
   And I so lytell alway styll. 170   Magnyfycence 1070
   But yet thou shalt holde me a fole styll. 173   Magnyfycence 1184
   Ryot at lyberte russheth it out styll. 176   Magnyfycence 1317
   Why, wene you that I can kepe hym longe styll? 179   Magnyfycence 1412
   Stande styll here, and ye shall se 186   Magnyfycence 1629
   By the fayth that I owe to God, and I wyll syt styll. 203   Magnyfycence 2209
   Ly styll, ly styll nowe, with yll hayle! 204   Magnyfycence 2248
   Ly styll, ly styll nowe, with yll hayle! 204   Magnyfycence 2248
   Under good hope endurynge ever styll, ... 208   Magnyfycence 2381
   If that ye wyll /A whyle be styll, ... 214   El Rummynge   3
   And syt there by styll, /Erly and late. 217   El Rummynge   116
   But, 'Drynke,' styll, 'Drynke, /And let the cat wynke! 222   El Rummynge   305
   Why syt ye prelates styll 263   Collyn Clout   688
   But lyve styll out of facyon, ... 275   Collyn Clout 1139
   As it is, it shall be styll, ... 277   Collyn Clout 1218
   He ruleth alway styll. 281   Why Come Ye   107
   Syt styll as they were dom. 283   Why Come Ye   199
   A daucock ye be, and so shal be styll! 310   Why Come Ye2   34
   He wyll set men a feightynge and syt hymselfe styll, ... 333   Garlande   761
      set] 'stir' MS Cotton Vitellius E.x; a feightynge]
      'to brawlyng' MS Cotton Vitellius E.x
   As pacient and as styll, ... 341   Garlande   1023
   Item the Boke to Speke Well or be Styll; 345   Garlande   1175
   For a wyndmil /Therin to couche styll   365   Albany   263
   And so ye wyll be styll, ... 379   Replycacion   179
STYLLA
   And you wyll be stylla, ... 253   Collyn Clout   260
STYLLY
   She coulde not lye styllyl' 224   El Rummynge   391
STYNGE
   Myght stynge the venymously! 79   Phy Sparrow   291
   My speche is all pleasure, but I stynge lyke a waspe. 160   Magnyfycence   730
STYNGES
   Alas, my hert it stynges, ...   80   Phy Sparrow   349
STYNGYNG
   Full lyke a scorpyon styngyng   41   Coystrowne4   17
   Wrythyng and wringyng, /Bytyng and styngyng;   95   Phy Sparrow   944
STYNKE
   At bothe endes ye stynke; 126   Garnesche3   81
   And so haynnously doth stynke, ... 127   Garnesche3   144
   Of these yong heretikes, that stynke unbrent, ... 375   Replycacion   22
STYNKES
   Some trypes that stynkes. 225   El Rummynge   444
      stynkes] 'stynges' Kynge & Marche 1554
STYNKINGLY
   And dyed stynkingly marterd. 297   Why Come Ye   741

STYNKYNG —STONDE   Page   Title   Line

STYNKYNG
Oure eyen synkyng, /Oure bodys stynkyng, ...   39   Coystrowne3   34
Els with hys stynkyng jawys   128   Garnesche3   154
Thou rammysche, stynkyng gote, ...   128   Garnesche3   166
Thou fals, stynkyng serpent, ...   128   Garnesche3   171
STYNT
Holde thy hande, dawe, of thy dagger, and stynt of thy dyn; . .   202   Magnyfycence   2188
STYNTETH
For largesse stynteth all maner of stryfe.   150   Magnyfycence   367
Largesse stynteth grete debates;   150   Magnyfycence   371
STYRE
To styre up your stomake you must you forge, ...   185   Magnyfycence   1613
STYRETH
She that styreth the shyp, make her your frende.'   49   Bowge   107
STYROPS
Theyr styrops of myxt golde begared, ...   254   Collyn Clout   317
    begared] 'begarded' Marshe 1568, 'be gloryd' MS Harley 2252
STYTCH
To helpe withall a stytch;   226   El Rummynge   457
STYTCHED
And gyrdeth in her gytes /Stytched and pranked with pletes; . .   216   El Rummynge   69
STYTCHIS
To sowe with stytchis of sylke   77   Phy Sparrow   212
STYTH
Hampar with your hammer upon thy styth, ...   71   Hauke   332
STOBBURNE
Hercules the herdy, with his stobburne clobbyd mase, ...   182   Magnyfycence   1494
STOCKE
And came of a gentyll stocke, ...   86   Phy Sparrow   589
STOCKEDOWVE
The culver, the stockedowve, ...   82   Phy Sparrow   429
STOCKFYSSH
Saltfysshe, stockfyssh nor herynge, ...   252   Collyn Clout   209
STOCKYS
In a payre of fetters or a payre of stockys.   141   Magnyfycence   31
STODE
Of whom both Flaunders and Scotland stode in drede, ...   30   Dol Dethe   44
Yet whils he stode he gave them woundes wyde.   32   Dol Dethe   101
    Yet] 'Ye' Marshe 1568
And as I stode redynge this verse myselfe allone, ...   48   Bowge   68
But as I stode musynge in my mynde, ...   52   Bowge   230
And as I stode and kyste asyde my syghte, ...   58   Bowge   418
    kyste] 'caste' Marshe 1568
They wandred ay and stode styll in no stede.   58   Bowge   423
Anone Dyscymular came where I stode.   58   Bowge   427
There on he stode, and craked;   63   Hauke   50
Thus stode I in the frytthy forest of Galtres, ...   312   Garlande   22
Whylis I stode musynge in this medytatyon, ...   313   Garlande   29
And iche man stode gasyng and staryng upon other.   319   Garlande   268
If xii were let in, xii hundreth stode without.   326   Garlande   490
But one gate specyally, where as I stode, ...   328   Garlande   586
Wheron stode a lybbard, crownyd with golde and stones, ...   328   Garlande   590
With that I stode up, halfe sodenly afrayd, ...   353   Garlande   1477
STOICALL
and stoicall studiantes, and friscajoly yonkerkyns, ...   374   Replycacion   I
STOKYS
Pay Stokys hys fyve pownd.   128   Garnesche3   185
STOL
Twyse! set hym a chare, or reche hym a stol   318   Garlande   208
    Twyse] 'Twyshe' Marshe 1568, MS Cotton Vitellius E.x
STOLE
It wold set on a stole, ...   74   Phy Sparrow   116
    set] 'sit' Wyght 1553, Kitson 1560.6, Marshe 1568
Without an antetyme or a stole;   150   Magnyfycence   359
A thre-foted stole /That he may downe sytte, ...   247   Collyn Clout   30
STOLYN
When the stede is stolyn, spar the stable dur.   352   Garlande   1435
STOMAK
His stomak stuffed ofte tymes dyde reboke.   51   Bowge   180
STOMAKE
Such fervent heat /His stomake doth freat;   83   Phy Sparrow   482
    doth freat] 'so great' †Kele 1545.2, Wyght 1553, Kitson 1560.6
And make youer stomake seke   128   Garnesche3   156
To styre up your stomake you must you forge, ...   185   Magnyfycence   1613
A, howe my stomake wambleth! I am all in a swete.   185   Magnyfycence   1617
Alas! My stomake fareth as it wolde cast.   188   Magnyfycence   1726
STOMBYLL
To jumbyll, to stombyll, to tumbyll down lyke folys;   243   Speke Parott   425
STONDARDE
Your stondarde, Syr Olifranke, agenst me for to splay;   123   Garnesche2   30
STONDE
Is called Favore to stonde in her good grace.'   47   Bowge   55
That ye shall stonde in favoure and in grace.   49   Bowge   105
Ye stonde in favoure and Fortune is your gyde, ...   50   Bowge   171
It is lyke he wyll stonde in our lyghte!'   54   Bowge   305
    our] 'your' Marshe 1568
Gyve this gentylman rome, syrs. Stonde utter!   161   Magnyfycence   753
I can do nothynge but he stonde besyde.   180   Magnyfycence   1449

673

STONDETH —STORYES

	Page	Title	Line
Faythe and good hope I make asyde to stonde.	205	Magnyfycence	2288
'Come on with me,' she sayd, 'let us not stonde';	328	Garlande	559

STONDETH

Naye, see where yonder stondeth the teder man!	59	Bowge	484
The drevyll stondeth to herken, and he can.	59	Bowge	486

STONDYNGE

Levynge me stondynge as a mased man;	48	Bowge	83

STONDYTHE

So myche poletyke pratyng, and so lytell stondythe in stede;	244	Speke Parott	464

STONE

They have made me here to put the stone;	151	Magnyfycence	406
What! Then he may drynke out of a stone cruyse.	201	Magnyfycence	2166
Or elles go rost a stone!	281	Why Come Ye	112
Lyke urcheons in a stone wall,	283	Why Come Ye	166
urcheons] 'heons' †Kele 1545.3, Marshe 1568			
Under a stone on a golde ryng	296	Why Come Ye	700
Of golde, entachid with many a precyous stone;	325	Garlande	470

STONE-CASTE

Nay, to wrangle, I warant the, it is but a stone-caste.	201	Magnyfycence	2174

STONES

Are sharper then swordes, sturdier then stones.	138	Ven Tongues	50
Enhachyde with perle and stones preciously,	313	Garlande	40
None so ryche stones in Turkey to sell;	323	Garlande	396
'Go softly,' she sayd, 'the stones be full glint.'	328	Garlande	572
Wheron stode a lybbard, crownyd with golde and stones,	328	Garlande	590
Sume praysed the perle, some the stones bryght.	343	Garlande	1108

STONGE

His serpentes tonge /That many one hath stonge;	94	Phy Sparrow	921

STONY

Out of the stony wall,	254	Collyn Clout	304
Enwallyd aboute with the stony flint,	328	Garlande	569

STONYS

With perles and precyous stonys.	255	Collyn Clout	347

STOOD

Her wyt stood her in sted	89	Phy Sparrow	729
She pyst where she stood.	223	El Rummynge	373

STOODE

He frounde, he stared, he stampped where he stoode.	55	Bowge	319

STOP

Stop a tyd, and be welle ware	133	Garnesche5	162
The devyll can nat stop their mouthes	272	Collyn Clout	1051
Stop at lawe tancrete,	289	Why Come Ye	420

STOPPED

Well nye had stopped my breath.	73	Phy Sparrow	63
had] not in Wyght 1553, Kitson 1560.6, Marshe 1568			
And stopped therewith the hole.	224	El Rummynge	406
Your eeres they be stopped!	263	Collyn Clout	678
That wyse Harpocrates /Had your mouthes stopped,	377	Replycacion	116

STOPPELL

But she had lost the stoppell.	224	El Rummynge	404
Of a lether bottell /With a knavysshe stoppell,	262	Collyn Clout	651

STOPPYD

For lyberte at large is lothe to be stoppyd,	141	Magnyfycence	46

STOPPYNG

With drawttys of deth /Stoppyng oure breth;	39	Coystrowne3	32

STOPPYNGE

Never stoppynge /But ever droppynge;	215	El Rummynge	29

STOPPYNGE OYSTER

I have a stoppynge oyster in my poke,	59	Bowge	477

STORE

For one fals poynt she is wont to kepe in store,	45	Balettys4	4
Deynte to have with us suche one in store,	50	Bowge	150
With moch matter more, /That I kepe in store.	67	Hauke	221
That I kepe in store.	126	Garnesche3	77
Tushe, man! I kepe some Latyn in store.	172	Magnyfycence	1145
I have an hole armory of suche haburdashe in store;	175	Magnyfycence	1279
Thus must ye stuffe and store your treasure.	189	Magnyfycence	1754
Why, is there any store of rawe motton?	204	Magnyfycence	2265
And gathereth up in store	260	Collyn Clout	568
gathereth] 'gathered' Marshe 1568			
Of his golde in store.	302	Why Come Ye	945

STORIS

The poemis and storis auncient inbryngis	331	Garlande	689
Wherein many storis ar brevely contayned	347	Garlande	1224

STORY

The story of Arystobell, /And of Constantynopell,	67	Hauke	212
Whoso lyst the story to se.	76	Phy Sparrow	193
The story doth appere,	79	Phy Sparrow	300
Plinni sheweth all /In his Story Naturall,	85	Phy Sparrow	537
The story telleth playne,	89	Phy Sparrow	696
But now upon this story	284	Why Come Ye	229
Rede ye the story oute,	296	Why Come Ye	694
Cirus by name, as wrytith the story;	336	Garlande	858

STORYES

Some sad storyes, some mery,	87	Phy Sparrow	615
/The storyes by name	88	Phy Sparrow	660
With suche storyes bydene	270	Collyn Clout	954

STORKE —STRAWBERY   Page   Title   Line

STORKE
The storke also,	83	Phy Sparrow	469

STORME
There was never so harde a storme of mysery,	207	Magnyfycence	2343

STORME DRYVEN
Your storme dryven shyppe I repared new,	327	Garlande	544

STORMIS
This goodly flowre with stormis was untwynde.	352	Garlande	1445

STORMY
Ageynst a stormy shouer.	127	Garnesche3	147
And after a hete oft cometh a stormy colde.	141	Magnyfycence	13
No stormy rage agaynst me can pervayle.	181	Magnyfycence	1465
Today fayre wether, tomorowe a stormy rage;	213	Magnyfycence	2545
Of the stormy flodde,	277	Collyn Clout	1254
Now clere wether, forthwith a stormy showre;	312	Garlande	12
No stormy tempeste your barge shall overthrow.	327	Garlande	546
As a mariner that amasid is in a stormy rage,	335	Garlande	829
amasid] 'masid' MS Cotton Vitellius E.x			

STORM YBETEN
Nowe must be storm ybeten with showres and raynes.	197	Magnyfycence	2017

STORMYS
Gayne dangerous stormys theyr anker of supporte,	44	Balettys3	26
Beten with stormys of many a frowarde blast,	213	Magnyfycence	2560

STOULE
To weve in the stoule sume were full preste,	334	Garlande	790

STOUNDE
For within that stounde,	72	Phy Sparrow	34
Syr, ye must tary a stounde,	294	Why Come Ye	626

STOUNGE
His face was belymmed as byes had him stounge;	54	Bowge	289

STOUT
Howe gay and howe stout	163	Magnyfycence	832

STOUTTY
Ye Duke so doutty, /So sterne, so stoutty,	361	Albany	78

STOW
And cryed, 'Stow, stow, stow!'	63	Hauke	73
And cryed, 'Stow, stow, stow!'	63	Hauke	73
And cryed, 'Stow, stow, stow!'	63	Hauke	73
Here cometh in FANSY craynge 'Stow, stow!'	165	Magnyfycence	SD
Here cometh in FANSY craynge 'Stow, stow!'	165	Magnyfycence	SD
That cryest 'Stow, stow'?	166	Magnyfycence	917
That cryest 'Stow, stow'?	166	Magnyfycence	917

STOWE
Stowe, byrde, stowe, stowe!	167	Magnyfycence	967
Stowe, byrde, stowe, stowe!	167	Magnyfycence	967
Stowe, byrde, stowe, stowe!	167	Magnyfycence	967

STOWNDE
With hym to stryve a stownde.	367	Albany	344

STOWPE
All honour to me must nedys stowpe and lene.	181	Magnyfycence	1462
To lowre, to droupe, to knele, to stowpe and to play cowche-quale;	243	Speke Parott	426
With, 'Stowpe, thou havell! /Rynne thou javell!	294	Why Come Ye	607

STOWRE
They are so stowre, /So frantyke mad,	115	Ag Scottes	12

STOWTE
A semly nose and a stowte,	133	Garnesche5	131
And bereth him there so stowte	287	Why Come Ye	340
The grownde gronid and tremblid, the noyse was so stowte.	354	Garlande	1509

STOWTY
Ye stronge sturdy stalyon, so sterne and stowty,	122	Garnesche1	10

STRAYGHT
That some of them renneth strayght to the stuse.	174	Magnyfycence	1225

STRAYNED
So payned and so strayned	73	Phy Sparrow	48
Wherwyth my hand she strayned,	99	Phy Sparrow	1122

STRAYTE
And to mewarde the strayte waye he toke.	51	Bowge	194
He was trussed in a garmente strayte -	60	Bowge	505
Al of pleasure /My hose strayte tyde;	164	Magnyfycence	852
Let se what ye say. Shewe it strayte.	185	Magnyfycence	1592

STRAKE
Strake one with a birdbolt to the hart rote;	351	Garlande	1380

STRANGLE
And streitly strangle us	308	Why Come Ye	1155

STRAUGHT
For frantick faitours half mad and half straught;	138	Ven Tongues	27

STRAUNGE
And the floodes in straunge remes,	93	Phy Sparrow	882
Your workes, they say, are straunge -	257	Collyn Clout	420
To a straunge jurisdictyon /Called Dymingis Dale,	299	Why Come Ye	800
I made it straunge, and drew bak ones or twyse,	324	Garlande	444
Recountyng commoditis of many a straunge nacyon;	354	Garlande	1500

STRAW
Somtyme I laughe at waggynge of a straw,	168	Magnyfycence	1014

STRAWBERY
The praty strawbery;	340	Garlande	981
This delycate dasy, this strawbery pretely set,	352	Garlande	1449

STRAWE

	Page	Title	Line
Tully, valy, strawe, let be I say!	35	Man Margery	5
Strawe, Jamys foder, ye play the fode;	35	Man Margery	10
Naye, strawe for tales, thou shalte not rule us;	55	Bowge	341
But, what, a strawe! I maye not tell all thynge.	59	Bowge	459
Tushe, a strawe! It is a shame	155	Magnyfycence	549
Tushe, a strawe! I thought none yll.	156	Magnyfycence	564
Ye, bere me this strawe to a dawys nest.	170	Magnyfycence	1097
Yet Lyberte without rule is not worth a strawe.	178	Magnyfycence	1378
Nowe must ye lerne to lye on the strawe.	197	Magnyfycence	2015
'A strawe,' sayde Bele, 'stande utter,	228	El Rummynge	535
A strawe for Goddes curse!	254	Collyn Clout	294
Lodged in the strawe,	263	Collyn Clout	657
Strawe for lawe canon,	289	Why Come Ye	416

STRAWES

They make us to pyll strawes;	285	Why Come Ye	265

STRAWRY

Some loke strawry, /Some cawry-mawry;	218	El Rummynge	149

STREAMES

And the streames wood	105	Phy Sparrow	1335

STREATLY

And so streatly coarted	290	Why Come Ye	441

STREIGHT

Of kingis line moost streight,	110	Lawde	10

STREIT

Well gydyng ther glowtonn to kepe streit theyr sylk, ther] 'the' MS Cotton Vitellius E.x	334	Garlande	795

STREITLY

And streitly strangle us	308	Why Come Ye	1155

STREYGHT

Streyght to the sacrament	63	Hauke	46
Syr, after your message I hyed me hyder streyght,	209	Magnyfycence	2419
For they go to roust, /Streyght over the ale-joust,	219	El Rummynge	192
Some go streyght thyder, /Be it slaty or slyder;	221	El Rummynge	257

STREYGHTE

Of an oke, that somtyme grew full streyghte,	312	Garlande	18

STREYNES

The streynes of her vaynes as asure Inde blewe,	183	Magnyfycence	1553

STREYTE

With sydes longe and streyte;	100	Phy Sparrow	1129
By Goddys body, I come streyte.	151	Magnyfycence	399

STREYTES

Thorow the streytes of Marock of] not in Toy 1553, Kitson 1560.7, Marshe 1568	303	Why Come Ye	955

STREME

At the streme of Banockesburne	285	Why Come Ye	268
He is not wyse ageyne the streme that stryvith.	352	Garlande	1432

STREMES

With pypes of golde engusshing out stremes;	330	Garlande	659
And the stremes wode	349	Garlande	1328

STREMYS

Cosmography, and the stremys	93	Phy Sparrow	881
He wolde dry up the stremys	303	Why Come Ye	957

STRENGTH

By marcyall strength /He wan at length;	104	Phy Sparrow	1305
I make hym lese moche of theyr strength;	175	Magnyfycence	1259
Under strength of the great seale,	306	Why Come Ye	1102
With all our strength that we can brynge about,	324	Garlande	424
By merciall strength /He wan at length;	349	Garlande	1298

STRENGTHE

But blessyd Bachus, potenciall god of strengthe,	322	Garlande	348

STRETCHYNGE

Stretchynge to the sterres,	270	Collyn Clout	938

STRETE

That wonnes at the Key in Temmys Strete.	41	Coystrowne4	30
Ye have a fantasy to Fanchyrche strete,	130	Garnesche5	41
Crafty Conveyaunce standeth in the strete	167	Magnyfycence	956
And from thens to the halfe strete,	204	Magnyfycence	2263

STRYDYNGE

Naked boyes strydynge,	270	Collyn Clout	967

STRYFE

For whom was moch stryfe;	87	Phy Sparrow	644
For largesse stynteth all maner of stryfe.	150	Magnyfycence	367

STRYKE

No; for or we stryke, we wyll be advysed twyse.	163	Magnyfycence	810
Yet sometyme I stryke where is none offence,	194	Magnyfycence	1916
But nowe a dayes to stryke I have grete cause,	194	Magnyfycence	1918
And some I stryke with a franesy;	194	Magnyfycence	1932
Of some of theyr chyldren I stryke out the eye;	194	Magnyfycence	1933
For I stryke lordys of realmes and landys	195	Magnyfycence	1938
I vysyte them and stryke them with many sore plagys.	195	Magnyfycence	1943
It wyll stryke a man myschevously in a hete.	204	Magnyfycence	2268
Stryke the hogges with a clubbe,	218	El Rummynge	172

STRYKEN

Cupyde hath stryken so that she ne wolde	320	Garlande	291

STRYNGED

Ye strynged so Luthers lute	379	Replycacion	167

	Page	Title	Line
STRYNGES			
Warblynge with his strynges	384	Replycacion	349
STRYPE			
Nay, in faythe, it was but a strype	171	Magnyfycence	1125
STRYPLYNG			
A stalworthy stryplyng.	287	Why Come Ye	349
stalworthy] 'tall worthy' Kitson 1560.7, Marshe 1568			
STRYPTE			
The hy auter he strypte naked;	63	Hauke	49
STRYVE			
Upon artycles judicyall, /To contende and to stryve	299	Why Come Ye	815
With hym to stryve a stownde.	367	Albany	344
STRYVES			
And thus the loselles stryves,	261	Collyn Clout	574
STRYVITH			
He is not wyse ageyne the streme that stryvith.	352	Garlande	1432
STROKE			
The stroke of God, Adversyte, I hyght.	193	Magnyfycence	1882
And the stroke of God!	307	Why Come Ye	1138
With a pellit of pevisshenes they had suche a stroke,	330	Garlande	637
STROKES			
That hathe the strokes alone;	281	Why Come Ye	114
STRONG			
Full many a strong cyte and towne hath been wonne	184	Magnyfycence	1577
STRONGE			
Ye stronge sturdy stalyon, so sterne and stowty,	122	Garnesche1	10
Your brethe ys stronge and quike;	126	Garnesche3	78
With hys brethe so stronge,	128	Garnesche3	151
Save a stronge thefe and hange a trew man.	178	Magnyfycence	1360
With this halter good and stronge;	206	Magnyfycence	2313
And myghty stronge meate	225	El Rummynge	433
Oute of theyr stronge townes	283	Why Come Ye	177
Yet have compassyon upon my paynes stronge.'	320	Garlande	299
Against our st[r]onge captaine;	365	Albany	245
stronge] 'stonge' †Marshe 1568			
STRONGE-HERTED			
Stronge-herted lyke an hen.	285	Why Come Ye	276
STRONGELY			
And her brethe strongely stanke,	228	El Rummynge	541
STRONGLY			
Strongly enbateld, moche costious of charge.	328	Garlande	570
STROUDE			
From Stroude to Kent,	167	Magnyfycence	982
STROWED			
Suche shredis of sentence, strowed in the shop	233	Speke Parott	92
STUBBED			
But they were sturdy and stubbed,	225	El Rummynge	422
stubbed] 'stubbled' Kynge & Marche 1554, Day 1560, Marshe 1568			
STUDIANTES			
and stoicall studiantes, and friscajoly yonkerkyns,	374	Replycacion	1
STUDIOUS			
That causeth me /Studious to be	95	Phy Sparrow	960
in the moche studious scolehous of scrupulous philology,	373	Replycacion	1
STUDY			
My study myght be better spynt;	134	Garnesche5	176
Whan other men laughe, than study I and muse,	160	Magnyfycence	707
In their study abhomynable,	375	Replycacion	25
STUDYE			
For and I studye sholde as ye doo nowe,	53	Bowge	242
Thou mayste not studye or muse on the mone.	57	Bowge	383
STUDYOUS			
And studyous medytacion	93	Phy Sparrow	848
Of studyous doctryne when at the port salu	327	Garlande	541
STUDYOUSLY			
studyously dyvysed at Sheryfhotten Castell,	312	Garlande	1
Bycause that he his tyme studyously hath spent	314	Garlande	60
he his tyme] 'his tyme he' MS Cotton Vitellius E.x			
STUED			
Your gorge nat endued /Without a capon stued,	252	Collyn Clout	216
STUFFE			
Thus must ye stuffe and store your treasure.	189	Magnyfycence	1754
STUFFED			
His stomak stuffed ofte tymes dyde reboke.	51	Bowge	180
And so with ale stuffed,	229	El Rummynge	571
STUMBLE			
For though they stumble in the synnys sevyn,	36	Coystrowne1	3
STUMPE			
That, me to rest, I lent me to a stumpe	312	Garlande	17
In so moche the stumpe, whereto I me lente	320	Garlande	281
STURBRYDGE			
And silogisari was drowned at Sturbrydge Fayre;	235	Speke Parott	165
STURDIER			
Are sharper then swordes, sturdier then stones.	138	Ven Tongues	50
STURDY			
Ye stronge sturdy stalyon, so sterne and stowty,	122	Garnesche1	10
But they were sturdy and stubbed,	225	El Rummynge	422
stubbed] 'stubbled' Kynge & Marche 1554, Day 1560, Marshe 1568			

	Page	Title	Line
STUSE			
That some of them renneth strayght to the stuse.	174	Magnyfycence	1225
STUT			
Her felowe dyd stammer and stut,	223	El Rummynge	339
SUBDUDE			
I say there is no welthe where as lyberte is subdude.	142	Magnyfycence	73
Sodenly avaunsyd, and sodenly subdude;	212	Magnyfycence	2526
Trouthe should nat be subdude.	369	Albany	422
SUBJECCYON			
But wyll hath reason so under subjeccyon,	141	Magnyfycence	19
That all the oryent had in subjeccyon,	181	Magnyfycence	1467
Caused me of adversyte to fall in subjeccyon.	209	Magnyfycence	2425
SUBJECTES			
His subjectes he dothe supporte,	370	Albany	471
All his subjectes and he /Moost lovyngly agre	371	Albany	480
SUBJECTIS			
Unto thy subjectis be kurteis and beningne.	33	Dol Dethe	168
SUBJECTYON			
He kepeth them in subjectyon.	304	Why Come Ye	1010
To be under his subjectyon.	307	Why Come Ye	1126
SUBMYTTED			
humbly submytted unto the ryght discrete reformacyon	373	Replycacion	1
SUBSCRYBE			
Yes. With his hande I made hym to subscrybe	187	Magnyfycence	1666
SUBSTANCE			
For only the substance of that I entend,	323	Garlande	412
SUBSTAUNCE			
And this an other, I have but smale substaunce.' And] 'But' Marshe 1568	48	Bowge	94
Syth all in substaunce of slumbrynge doth procede.	61	Bowge	536
And shortly shewe you the hole substaunce.	158	Magnyfycence	638
Syr, yet without sapyence your substaunce may be smal;	179	Magnyfycence	1407
Take of his substaunce a sure inventory,	180	Magnyfycence	1445
Be he never so lytell of substaunce,	317	Garlande	177
With maters that amount the Romayns in substaunce;	321	Garlande	346
Wherof in substaunce I brought this away.	344	Garlande	1120
SUBSTYTUTE			
Or elles his substytute	272	Collyn Clout	1043
SUBTELL			
To sober, to sad, to subtell, to wyse,	199	Magnyfycence	2091
SUBTELLY			
Subtelly usynge counterfet weyght;	152	Magnyfycence	440
Subtelly wrought shall be	288	Why Come Ye	364
SUBTYLE			
Subtyle Sym Sly /With madde foly. Sym Sly] 'Symonye' †Kele 1545.3	300	Why Come Ye	856
SUBTYLL			
Full subtyll persones in nombre foure and thre.	49	Bowge	133
A subtyll sysmatyke, /Ryght nere an heretyke,	121	Ag Scottes2	27
SUBTYLLY			
Can touche a troughte and cloke it subtylly troughte] 'trouth' Wynkyn de Worde 1510, Marshe 1568; it] not in Marshe 1568	46	Bowge	11
SUBTYLTE			
Dysdayne, Ryotte, Dyssymuler, Subtylte.	50	Bowge	140
But to here the subtylte and the crafte,	61	Bowge	519
SUBVERTED			
That good lawes are subverted	256	Collyn Clout	372
By him is subverted;	290	Why Come Ye	440
SUCCOUR			
To the for succour, to the for helpe I kall,	29	Dol Dethe	12
So Jupiter me succour,	98	Phy Sparrow	1056
So Jupiter me succour,	100	Phy Sparrow	1163
Our paves, our succour,	111	Lawde	46
SUCCOURE			
So Jupiter me succoure,	100	Phy Sparrow	1138
So Jupiter me succoure,	101	Phy Sparrow	1210
SUCH			
Hys hed was hevy, such was his hap,	41	Balettys1	5
I am insuffycyent to make such enterpryse;	42	Balettys2	9
Ye cast all your corage uppon such courtly haggys!	43	Balettys2	19
Theyre browys all to-brokyn, such clappys they cach;	43	Balettys2	32
'I wonder sore he is in such conceyte.'	54	Bowge	310
With us olde servauntes such maysters to playe.	55	Bowge	329
And specyally to controule /Such as have cure of soule,	62	Hauke	4
Of such mysadvysed /Parsons and dysgysed,	62	Hauke	21
Such sacrificium laudis /He made with suche gambawdis.	63	Hauke	64
Dowtles such losels	65	Hauke	138
Wrought never such a worke,	67	Hauke	217
That they dyd such a dede,	70	Hauke	300
Such paynes dyd me frete	73	Phy Sparrow	58
If any such might be found!	76	Phy Sparrow	188
Had no such Phylyp as I,	78	Phy Sparrow	271
Such fervent heat /His stomake doth freat; doth freat] 'so great' †Kele 1545.2, Wyght 1553, Kitson 1560.6	83	Phy Sparrow	481
Or such other poetes mo,	90	Phy Sparrow	760
Such relucent grace /Is formed in her face;	100	Phy Sparrow	1159
Such pleasures that I may	101	Phy Sparrow	1196

SUCHE —SUCHE

	Page	Title	Line
Such boste to make, /To prate and crake,	116	Ag Scottes	31
Your pryde was pevysh to play such prankys:	119	Ag Scottes	150
Experiens hath brought you in such a brake.	119	Ag Scottes	158
That cast such overthwartes /Percase have hollow hartes.	121	Ag Scottes2	37
And takyn up in such a frame,	132	Garnesche5	110
Such tunges shuld be torne out by the harde rootes,	137	Ven Tongues	3
Than to be founde in any such faute.	137	Ven Tongues	25
Any such foly to rest or to be.	138	Ven Tongues	35
Such tunges unhappy hath made great division	139	Ven Tongues	55
With, 'I can tel you what such a man said,	139	Ven Tongues	71
What! Is thy harte pryckyd with such a prowde pynne?	162	Magnyfycence	785
Alas, myn owne servauntys to shew me such reproche!	205	Magnyfycence	2277
Such a bedfellaw /Wold make one cast his craw.	226	El Rummynge	488
Of auncyent Aristippus and such other mo,	233	Speke Parott	93
With, 'Aveto' in Greco, and such solempne salutacyons,	235	Speke Parott	179
Such a casuelte shulde be sene	297	Why Come Ye	747
And such as sell trotters, /Pytchars, potshordis.	302	Why Come Ye	911
potshordis] 'pouchers' MS Rawlinson C. 813			
May be brought forth, such as can be founde,	318	Garlande	216
And, 'Wynde me that botowme of such an hew',	334	Garlande	799
an] 'a' MS Cotton Vitellius E.x			
Then such that have disdaynyd	350	Garlande	1367
that] 'as' †Fakes 1523			
And such a mad ymage	365	Albany	254
And such after-clappes.	366	Albany	278

SUCHE

	Page	Title	Line
Kyndle in me suche plente of thy nobles,	29	Dol Dethe	20
Upon suche a sort was ille bestowde and spent.	32	Dol Dethe	98
To slo suche a lord, alas, it was grete shame.	33	Dol Dethe	154
slo] 'sle' Marshe 1568			
Yet have I knowen suche er this;	46	Bowge	25
Bone aventure may brynge you in suche case	49	Bowge	104
Deynte to have with us suche one in store,	50	Bowge	150
Ye never dwelte in suche an other place,	51	Bowge	201
It is greate scorne to see suche a hayne	55	Bowge	327
Yet on my backe I bere suche lewde delynge.	59	Bowge	457
I have not sene suche anothers page -	60	Bowge	506
But yet oftyme suche dremes be founde trewe.	61	Bowge	538
This worke devysed is /For suche as do amys,	61	Hauke	2
But suche dawes to amend,	62	Hauke	26
Such sacrificium laudis /He made with suche gambawdis.	63	Hauke	65
And was in suche a fray	77	Phy Sparrow	228
Than suche as have disdayned	106	Phy Sparrow	1374
Than in Englonde to playe ony suche prankes;	114	Scot Kynge	51
And sende the Frensshe kynge suche another fall.	115	Scot Kynge	73
Ye for to sende suche a cytacyon,	117	Ag Scottes	55
In realmes, in cities, by suche fals abusion.	139	Ven Tongues	56
Of fals fickil tunges suche cloked collusion	139	Ven Tongues	57
With, 'He wrate suche a bil withouten dout',	139	Ven Tongues	70
Suche order I trust with them for to take,	145	Magnyfycence	178
In whose attemperaunce I have suche delyght,	145	Magnyfycence	189
I trow I have brought you suche wrytynge of recorde,	149	Magnyfycence	309
By your soth? Ye, and there is suche a wache,	150	Magnyfycence	350
What and I frame suche a slyght	159	Magnyfycence	677
Put Magnyfycence in suche a madnesse	159	Magnyfycence	679
Amonge all suche persones as I well understonde	161	Magnyfycence	739
Made purveaunce /And suche ordenaunce,	165	Magnyfycence	881
For to excede /In suche aray.	165	Magnyfycence	896
Cockes harte! I love suche japes.	171	Magnyfycence	1133
I kyndell in her suche a lyther sparke	174	Magnyfycence	1231
What, horson! Arte thou suche a one?	174	Magnyfycence	1234
Suche dawys, what soever they be,	174	Magnyfycence	1242
All men beware of suche folys!	175	Magnyfycence	1265
I have an hole armory of suche haburdashe in store;	175	Magnyfycence	1279
For thou fourmest suche fantasyes in theyr mynde	175	Magnyfycence	1284
To se you thus ruled and stande in suche awe.	178	Magnyfycence	1376
Take it in worthe suche as ye fynde.	180	Magnyfycence	1439
Howe lyke you? Ye lacke, syr, suche a lusty lasse.	183	Magnyfycence	1559
With me in kepynge suche a Phylyp Sparowe.	184	Magnyfycence	1562
So I myght hobby for suche a lusty larke.	184	Magnyfycence	1564
That such a female my flesshe wolde be wroken.	184	Magnyfycence	1566
That weryed I wolde be on suche a bayte.	184	Magnyfycence	1568
A, Cockes armes! Where myght suche one be founde?	184	Magnyfycence	1569
Wolde money, trowest thou, make suche one to the call?	184	Magnyfycence	1573
I coude holde you with suche talke hens tyll to morowe.	184	Magnyfycence	1588
For ofte tymes suche a wamblynge goth over my harte;	185	Magnyfycence	1620
For suche abusyon I use nowe and than.	185	Magnyfycence	1625
Suche lustes at large may not be lefte behynde.	186	Magnyfycence	1628
For to use suche haftynge and crafty wayes.	187	Magnyfycence	1678
With my servauntys, and suche maystryes gan make,	188	Magnyfycence	1716
To chose out ii., iii., of suche as you love best,	190	Magnyfycence	1769
And suche as you wyll shall lacke no promocyon.	190	Magnyfycence	1789
Syr, syth that in me ye have suche devocyon,	190	Magnyfycence	1790
Cockes bones! Harde ye ever suche another?	192	Magnyfycence	1841
Why, who wolde have thought in you suche gyle?	193	Magnyfycence	1869
Lo, suche is this worlde! I fynde it wryt,	196	Magnyfycence	1974
Alasse, that ever I occupyed suche abusyon!	200	Magnyfycence	2129
As for his plate of sylver and suche trasshe,	201	Magnyfycence	2164

	Page	Title	Line
And agayne thy maker thou hast made suche warre,	205	Magnyfycence	2302
In your rewardys use suche moderacyon	211	Magnyfycence	2494
Suche a lewde sorte /To Elynour resorte	218	El Rummynge	153
Suche a webbe can spyn,	221	El Rummynge	255
Here was scant thryft /Whan they made suche shyft.	222	El Rummynge	302
Suche were there menny	230	El Rummynge	611
Suche shredis of sentence, strowed in the shop	233	Speke Parott	92
Suche malyncoly mastyvys and mangye curre dogges	240	Speke Parott	320
To suche thynges ympossybyll, reason cannot consente;	240	Speke Parott	334
Was nevyr suche a senatour syn Crystes Incarnacion.	240	Speke Parott	337
For drede ye darre not medyll with suche gere,	242	Speke Parott	394
The reste of suche reconyng may make a fowle fraye.	243	Speke Parott	403
Suche statutes apon diettes, suche pyllyng and pollyng -	245	Speke Parott	495
Suche statutes apon diettes, suche pyllyng and pollyng -	245	Speke Parott	495
Was nevyr suche a fylty gorgon, nor suche an epycure,	246	Speke Parott	510
Was nevyr suche a fylty gorgon, nor suche an epycure,	246	Speke Parott	510
Suche pollaxis and pyllers, suche mulys trapte with gold -	246	Speke Parott	517
Suche pollaxis and pyllers, suche mulys trapte with gold -	246	Speke Parott	517
Or suche laboure to take.	250	Collyn Clout	135
Of suche vacabundus /Speketh totus mundus:	252	Collyn Clout	246
Of suche paternoster pekes /All the worlde spekes.	253	Collyn Clout	262
Agayne all suche rebelles	259	Collyn Clout	492
Suche logyke men woll choppe,	259	Collyn Clout	528
Suche ye may well knowe and ken	260	Collyn Clout	533
And have suche a tryppe,	263	Collyn Clout	667
And fall in suche decay,	263	Collyn Clout	668
fall] 'false' Kele 1545.1, 'fall' MS Harley 2252			
Suche maner of sysmatykes /And halfe heretykes,	264	Collyn Clout	700
In suche maner of cases,	269	Collyn Clout	895
To occupye suche places,	269	Collyn Clout	897
Suche temporall warre and bate	269	Collyn Clout	913
With suche storyes bydene	270	Collyn Clout	954
With suche perfytenesse	271	Collyn Clout	976
And all suche holynesse.	271	Collyn Clout	977
After suche a rate,	271	Collyn Clout	1014
But they wyl talke of suche uncouthes,	272	Collyn Clout	1052
And through suche detractyon	273	Collyn Clout	1059
To use suche despytynge	274	Collyn Clout	1107
despytynge] 'despysyng' Kele 1545.1, Marshe 1568, 'dysputyng' MS Harley 2252			
Suche grace God them sende	274	Collyn Clout	1125
Suche grace that he us sende	278	Collyn Clout	1262
Through suche abusyon, /And by suche illusyon,	279	Why Come Ye	19
Through suche abusyon, /And by suche illusyon,	279	Why Come Ye	20
And with suche forage /Hunte the boskage,	280	Why Come Ye	52
And brynge[s] them in suche feare.	286	Why Come Ye	306
brynges] 'brynge' †Kele 1545.3, Toy 1553, Kitson 1560.7, Marshe 1568			
He wryngeth them suche a wrenche,	287	Why Come Ye	321
But suche as he admyttes,	287	Why Come Ye	327
And suche sleyghtes dothe fynde,	290	Why Come Ye	438
He hath in him suche fayth.	290	Why Come Ye	445
And useth suche abusyoun,	290	Why Come Ye	456
He is in suche elacyon /Of his exaltacyon,	291	Why Come Ye	482
To reche to suche degre,	292	Why Come Ye	538
Take him in suche conceyght	292	Why Come Ye	541
Suche is a kynges power	293	Why Come Ye	565
And worke suche a myracle,	293	Why Come Ye	567
Shulde this man of suche mode	293	Why Come Ye	579
Suche a madde bedleme	295	Why Come Ye	655
Or suche other loselry	295	Why Come Ye	664
Now suche a hoddy poule	296	Why Come Ye	673
To practique suche abolete sciens.	297	Why Come Ye	713
practique] 'practyve' †Kele 1545.3			
Or suche chaunce shulde fall /Unto our cardynall!	297	Why Come Ye	748
He is at suche takynge,	302	Why Come Ye	936
Suche a prelate, I trowe, /Were worthy to rowe	303	Why Come Ye	953
He is suche a grym syer,	303	Why Come Ye	987
And suche a potestolate,	303	Why Come Ye	988
And] 'And make' MS Rawlinson C. 813; potestate] 'prostrate' Toy 1553, Kitson 1560.7, Marshe 1568			
And suche a potestate,	303	Why Come Ye	989
Suche gredynesse, /Suche nedynesse,	305	Why Come Ye	1030
Suche gredynesse, /Suche nedynesse,	305	Why Come Ye	1031
With crakynge in suche wyse,	306	Why Come Ye	1073
For he hath suche a bull,	306	Why Come Ye	1078
And makith suche provisyon	306	Why Come Ye	1093
Of Rome to the see /Weth suche dygnyte.	307	Why Come Ye	1146
Ovyde was bannisshed for suche a skyll,	314	Garlande	93
Of suche an endarkid chapiter sum season.	315	Garlande	108
That gave Eschines suche a cordyall,	316	Garlande	131
That] 'Whiche' MS Cotton Vitellius E.x			
Men of suche maters make but mummynge,	318	Garlande	200
but] 'but a' MS Cotton Vitellius E.x			
And suche of my servauntes as I have promotyd,	318	Garlande	202
A murmer of mynstrels, that suche another	320	Garlande	270
Suche an other there coude no man fynde;	325	Garlande	463
With suche communycacyon as came to our mynde;	328	Garlande	562

SUCK —SUFFRE	Page	Title	Line
With a pellit of pevisshenes they had suche a stroke,	330	Garlande	637
For to his servyce I have suche regarde,	334	Garlande	778
I coude shew you suche a presedent	342	Garlande	1083
you] not in MS Cotton Vitellius E.x			
But suche evydence I thynke for to enduce,	344	Garlande	1135
for to] 'for me to' MS Cotton Vitellius E.x			
Ladyes and gentylwomen suche as deservyd,	346	Garlande	1189
And suche as be counterfettis they be reservyd;	346	Garlande	1190
To pyke out honesty of suche a potshorde.	346	Garlande	1211
Fynde no mo suche fro Wanflete to Walis.	347	Garlande	1218
To make suche trifels it asketh sum konnyng,	347	Garlande	1235
Suche problemis to paynt it longyth to his arte.	347	Garlande	1246
Suche trechery /And traytory /Is all your cast.	361	Albany	99
And sette suche a snare	361	Albany	111
By suche a dronken drane.	363	Albany	164
By suche a cowarde knyght,	363	Albany	166
Suche a proude palyarde, /Suche a skyrgaliarde,	363	Albany	167
Suche a proude palyarde, /Suche a skyrgaliarde,	363	Albany	168
Suche a starke cowarde,	363	Albany	169
Suche a proude pultrowne,	363	Albany	170
Suche a foule coystrowne,	363	Albany	171
Suche a doutty dagswayne.	363	Albany	172
That put the in suche fray.	365	Albany	242
No man hath harde /Of suche a cowarde,	365	Albany	253
Or of suche a mawment /Caryed in a tent.	365	Albany	257
Suche a captayne of [h]ors	366	Albany	281
hors] 'fors' †Marshe 1568			
Of suche a farly freke,	366	Albany	303
Of suche an horne keke	366	Albany	304
Of suche an bolde captayne	366	Albany	305
Suche lewde langage ye spake.	367	Albany	329
And set you in suche case	368	Albany	367
What, wold Fraunces, our friar, /Be suche a false lyar,	368	Albany	374
Of suche as be his foos	370	Albany	469
Ye suffred suche correction.	376	Replycacion	68
And suche wondringes many mo.	376	Replycacion	76
And to prove your selfe suche foles.	378	Replycacion	145
Suche apple tre, suche frute.	378	Replycacion	157
Suche apple tre, suche frute.	378	Replycacion	157
Why jangle you suche jestes,	381	Replycacion	264
Full of suche dottages,	381	Replycacion	272
And snapper in suche werkes?	381	Replycacion	274
To answere or reply /Agaynst suche heresy.	383	Replycacion	313
Of suche theologicall thynges,	384	Replycacion	350
Of suche an industry /And suche a pregnacy,	384	Replycacion	370
Of suche an industry /And suche a pregnacy,	384	Replycacion	371
We are kyndled in suche facyon	385	Replycacion	382
And maketh in us suche spede	385	Replycacion	386
SUCK			
And suck us so nye,	303	Why Come Ye	966
SUCKE			
I saw a foxe sucke on a kowes ydder;	191	Magnyfycence	1814
SUE			
Unto this place all poetis there did sue,	325	Garlande	481
SUERLY			
So suerly yt xall nat tarnishe.	127	Garnesche3	122
SUETE			
So hardy to make suete,	272	Collyn Clout	1031
SUFFER			
To suffer me so carefull to endure,	45	Balettys5	6
Then thus to you - Nay, suffer me yet ferther to say,	142	Magnyfycence	48
Yet suffer me to say the surpluse of my sawe.	142	Magnyfycence	71
That I shall suffer none impechment	179	Magnyfycence	1418
In fayth, so to suffer the, it is but a skorne.	202	Magnyfycence	2201
Among my recordes suffer hym namyd,	316	Garlande	160
SUFFERAYNE			
And tell to his sufferayne every whyt;	175	Magnyfycence	1270
Whiche shall be to you a sufferayne accessary,	326	Garlande	523
SUFFERANCE			
Sometyme under protection /Of pacient sufferance,	385	Replycacion	393
SUFFERAUNCE			
Syr, then, with the favour of your benynge sufferaunce,	182	Magnyfycence	1519
And take pacient sufferaunce,	294	Why Come Ye	629
'Madame, with favour of your benynge sufferaunce,	315	Garlande	113
But your benynge sufferaunce for my discharge I laid,	318	Garlande	213
SUFFERD			
How the grene coverlet sufferd grete pine;	351	Garlande	1378
SUFFERED			
And remembre he suffered moche more for your sake;	196	Magnyfycence	2001
SUFFICE			
Or suffice to wryght	341	Garlande	1018
SUFFYCE			
Of all your bewte I suffyce not to wryght:	336	Garlande	875
SUFFRAGE			
Support Parrot, I pray you, with your suffrage ornate,	236	Speke Parott	195
SUFFRE			
To suffre hym slayn of his mortall fo?	30	Dol Dethe	38
His foule desyre /Wyll suffre no slepe	95	Phy Sparrow	934

SUFFRED —SUMMOND   Page   Title   Line

SUFFRE
	Page	Title	Line
Wherfore I fere ye wyll suffre payne.	114	Scot Kynge	28
And I to suffre you lewdly to ly	138	Ven Tongues	47
And suffre theyr chyldren to have theyr entent,	194	Magnyfycence	1921
Nowe must ye suffre bothe hunger and colde.	197	Magnyfycence	2013
And suffre all this yll?	263	Collyn Clout	689
Nor wyll suffre this boke	277	Collyn Clout	1237

SUFFRED
Suffred and taken in gre	290	Why Come Ye	447
Wherfore he suffred payn,	297	Why Come Ye	739
Ye suffred suche correction.	376	Replycacion	68

SUGER
Knowe ye not salte and suger asonder?	113	Scot Kynge	6
Know ye not suger and salt asonder?	118	Ag Scottes	96
I counterfet suger that is but *[s]ounde;	152	Magnyfycence	435

*sounde] 'founde' †Rastell & Treveris C 1530, B, 'sande' Scattergood

SUGER LOFE
A swete suger lofe and sowre bayardys bun	36	Coystrownel	8

SUGGESTYON
By whose suggestyon /I toke on hand this warke,	309	Why Come Ye	1203

suggestyon] 'subjectyon' MS Rawlinson C. 813

SUGRED
Her sugred mouth to kysse.	97	Phy Sparrow	1040
But sith he hath tastid of the sugred pocioun	314	Garlande	73

SUGRYD
I yave hym drynke of the sugryd welle	132	Garnesche5	98

SUYNG
There was suyng to the Quene of Fame;	319	Garlande	253

SULPICIA
Dame Sulpicia at Rome,	75	Phy Sparrow	148

SUM
Of al good praiers God send him sum!	86	Phy Sparrow	584
Ye lernyd of sum py-bakar.	127	Garnesche3	111
Yf he wyst what sum wotte,	129	Garnesche3	199
Myxte with sum incommodite,	130	Garnesche5	10
I wold sum manys bake ink-horne	133	Garnesche5	133
With sum flyp-flap,	227	El Rummynge	508
And thowe sum dysdayne yow and sey how ye prate,	240	Speke Parott	315
Yet sum surgions put a dout	309	Why Come Ye	1198
'The sum of your purpose, as we ar advysid,	314	Garlande	78
Then sum wyll say he hath but lyttil brayne,	314	Garlande	87
Savynge he rubbid sum on the gall.	315	Garlande	97

on] 'upon' Marshe 1568

Of suche an endarkid chapiter sum season.	315	Garlande	108
Yet harde is to make but sum fawt be founde.'	315	Garlande	112
But if he had made sum memoryall,	315	Garlande	118
Some were of Poyle, and sum were of Trace,	326	Garlande	493
Some from Flaunders, sum from the se coste,	326	Garlande	496
They had wrytyng, sum Greke, sum Ebrew,	328	Garlande	582
They had wrytyng, sum Greke, sum Ebrew,	328	Garlande	582
Some were olde wryten, sum were writen new,	328	Garlande	584
Some carectis of Caldy, sum Frensshe was full good;	328	Garlande	585
Sum medelynge spyes, by craft to grope thy mynde,	329	Garlande	617
Sum dysdanous dawcokkis that all men dispyse,	329	Garlande	618
It made sum lympe-legged and broisid there bones;	329	Garlande	625
Sum were made pevysshe, porisshly pynk iyde,	329	Garlande	626
Foo, foisty bawdias, sum smellid of the smoke,	330	Garlande	639
Sum pirlyng of goldde theyr worke to encrese	334	Garlande	796
Avaunsynge my selfe sum thanke to deserve,	335	Garlande	822
sum parte of Skeltons bokes and baladis with ditis of plesure,	345	Garlande	R
To make suche trifels it asketh sum konnyng,	347	Garlande	1235
Yet sum there be therewith that take grevaunce	348	Garlande	1257
Of sum jangelyng jays	348	Garlande	1262
It made sum mens eye dasild and dasid;	351	Garlande	1389
But how it was, sum were to recheles,	351	Garlande	1393
That made sum to snurre and snuf in the wynde;	353	Garlande	1472

snurre] 'surt' †Fakes 1523

Welcome shall ye /To sum men be;	355	Garlande	1541
Yet now and then /Sum Latin men	355	Garlande	1545

SUMDELE
Be sumdele lyke in forme and shap,	36	Coystrownel	9

SUME
Sume be moche spokyn of for makynge of frays;	317	Garlande	182
Sume were to hasty and wold no man byde;	319	Garlande	249
Some ranne the nexte way, sume ranne abowte.	319	Garlande	252
Sume sayd, 'Holde thy peas, thou getest here no more.'	319	Garlande	257
Sume fayne themselfe folys, and wolde be callyd wyse,	329	Garlande	616
To weve in the stoule sume were full preste,	334	Garlande	790
Sume to enbrowder put them in prese,	334	Garlande	794
Sume praysed the perle, some the stones bryght.	343	Garlande	1108

SUMES
With armatycke gummes /That cost great sumes,	84	Phy Sparrow	521

SUMMON
To summon our kyng, your soveraygne lorde.	118	Ag Scottes	94

SUMMOND
Ye summond our kyng, why dyd ye so?	118	Ag Scottes	92

ye] not in Kynge & Marche 1554, Day 1560, Marshe 1568

SUMMONED
Ye summoned our kynge. Why dyde ye so? 113   Scot Kynge   2
SUMNER
A solempne sumner for to be? 116   Ag Scottes   51
Adieu, syr sumner, cast of your crowne! 117   Ag Scottes   64
A kyng, a sumner! It was great wonder: 118   Ag Scottes   95
Your sumner to saucy, to malapert; 118   Ag Scottes   97
A sumner to were a kynges crowne. 120   Ag Scottes   175
Syr sumner, now where is your crowne? 120   Ag Scottes   178
Syr sumner, now ye have lost your crowne. 120   Ag Scottes   180
SUMTYME
As sumtyme he must vyces remorde, ... 314   Garlande   86
Sumtyme with sadnes, sumtyme with play. 352   Garlande   1424
Sumtyme with sadnes, sumtyme with play. 352   Garlande   1424
SUMWHAT
Yet sumwhat wright supprisid with hartly lust, ... 33   Dol Dethe   145
    hartly] 'herty' Marshe 1568
........sat sumwhat to longe; 125   Garnesche3   57
But to do sumwhat iche man doth hym dres 315   Garlande   122
SUM WHAT
Is that our servaunt is sum what to dull; 314   Garlande   79
    that] 'for that' MS Cotton Vitellius E.x
Sum what wolde gadder in there conjecture 315   Garlande   107
    conjecture] 'convecture' †Fakes 1523
SUN
Of wandryng of the mone, the course of the sun, ... 331   Garlande   691
SUNNYNG
For wysdome and sadnesse be out a sunnyng; 318   Garlande   201
    be out] 'be set out' Marshe 1568, MS Cotton Vitellius E.x
SUP
He dynyd with delyte, with poverte he must sup. 195   Magnyfycence   1965
SUPERCILIUSLY
and whan they have ones superciliusly caught 374   Replycacion   1
SUPERFLUE
Or of humors superflue, that often wyll crepe 313   Garlande   32
SUPERSTICIOUNS
Of mervelous conclusiouns, /And by her supersticiouns 350   Garlande   1343
SUPERSTICYON
It is halfe a supersticyon 378   Replycacion   142
SUPERSTICYONS
And by her supersticyons, ... 105   Phy Sparrow   1350
SUPERSTICYOUS
And so supersticyous, ... 290   Why Come Ye   463
SUPERSTYCYON
With covytous ambycion /And other superstycyon, ... 269   Collyn Clout   902
    ambycyon] 'and ambycyon' Kele 1545.1, Marshe 1568,
    'ambyssyon' MS Harley 2252
SUPERVYSOUR
To be supervysour, and on Largesse also; 190   Magnyfycence   1785
Ye sent us a supervysour for to take hede; 192   Magnyfycence   1853
SUPPED
But supped it up at ones, ... 224   El Rummynge   380
SUPPER
I sawe a sowter go to supper, or ever he had dynde. 191   Magnyfycence   1825
SUPPLE
In Englysshe to God Parott can supple: 231   Speke Parott   33
    supple] 'shewe propyrlye' †MS Harley 2252
SUPPLEYNG
Suppleyng to Fame, I besought her grace, ... 353   Garlande   1478
SUPPLEMENT
Or that we beganne in the supplement, ... 323   Garlande   415
SUPPLY
With notable clerkes; supply to them, I pray, ... 241   Speke Parott   359
SUPPLYCACYON
Of my pore instance and supplycacyon, ... 186   Magnyfycence   1634
With harte contryte make your supplycacyon 196   Magnyfycence   1991
My supplycacyon to you I arrect, ... 313   Garlande   55
SUPPLYCACYONS
Sutys, and supplycacyons, ... 289   Why Come Ye   414
SUPPLYE
What sayst thou, man? Why dost thou not supplye, ... 162   Magnyfycence   797
SUPPLYED
That he knowe not but that I have supplyed 187   Magnyfycence   1663
To whome supplyed the royall Quene of Fame. 313   Garlande   49
SUPPORT
Support Parrot, I pray you, with your suffrage ornate, ... 236   Speke Parott   195
SUPPORTACYON
Under supportacyon /Of your pacyent tolleracyon, ... 62   Hauke   31
Under supportacyon /Of pacyent tolleracyon. 142   Magnyfycence   61
And the supportacyon 291   Why Come Ye   484
That any man under supportacyon 318   Garlande   220
With toleracyon /And supportacyon /Of reformacyon, ... 356   Garlande   1577
SUPPORTE
Gayne dangerous stormys theyr anker of supporte, ... 44   Balettys3   26
But of your pacyence under the supporte, ... 183   Magnyfycence   1542
The lynage of Lot toke supporte of Assur; 232   Speke Parott   66
You supporte and rescue, ... 257   Collyn Clout   434
    rescue] 'rescite' Marshe 1568

SUPPOSE — SURFET

	Page	Title	Line
But under your supporte,	259	Collyn Clout	505
Than lette reason you supporte,	271	Collyn Clout	1004
Me to supporte, to helpe, and to assist,	335	Garlande	827
His subjectes he dothe supporte,	370	Albany	471
His heresy to supporte;	379	Replycacion	192

SUPPOSE

Though ye suppose all jeperdys ar paste,	45	Balettys4	1
It is for to suppose	101	Phy Sparrow	1177
As they suppose and gesse,	271	Collyn Clout	1010
For I suppose that he is	308	Why Come Ye	1163
Ran on the raunge so longe, that I suppose	313	Garlande	25
Ye have reed them, I suppose,	381	Replycacion	276

SUPPOSED

We supposed, iwys, /That she rose to pys;	229	El Rummynge	594
In you the faute is supposed	253	Collyn Clout	264
And yet ye supposed /Respondere ad quantum,	377	Replycacion	109

SUPPOSICYON

But of that supposicyon that callyd is arte,	236	Speke Parott	197

SUPPOSYCIONS

Surrendring your supposycions,	377	Replycacion	112

SUPPOSYNGE

Wherfore men be supposynge	255	Collyn Clout	357

SUPPRISID

Yet sumwhat wright supprisid with hartly lust,	33	Dol Dethe	145
hartly] 'herty' Marshe 1568			

SUPPRYSYD

As I be saved, with pleasure I am supprysyd	183	Magnyfycence	1529
So am I supprysyd with pleasure and delyght	327	Garlande	537

SUPREME

Of fyre elementar in his supreme spere,	331	Garlande	694

SURCUDANT

of vaynglorious pompe and surcudant elacyon,	375	Replycacion	1

SURE

And shewed that in this arte I was not sure;	46	Bowge	19
I] not in †Wynkyn de Worde 1499, 1510			
'Alas,' quod I, 'how myghte I have her sure?'	49	Bowge	118
They coude not faile, thei thought, they were so sure.	50	Bowge	142
But this one thynge ye maye be sure of me,	50	Bowge	162
Nay, naye, be sure, whyles I am on your syde	50	Bowge	169
To kepe it hymselfe; for than he myghte be sure	52	Bowge	222
For sure he wrought amys	62	Hauke	41
He then, to be sure, /Callyd her with a lure.	63	Hauke	75
No man can be sure	81	Phy Sparrow	370
Of that name he is sure	89	Phy Sparrow	722
Behavynge her so sure,	99	Phy Sparrow	1098
He might be sure to have shame ynough.	139	Ven Tongues	78
It dothe so sure nowe and than.	150	Magnyfycence	368
Sure Surveyaunce I named me.	155	Magnyfycence	525
I am sure ye wolde have me excused.	156	Magnyfycence	581
Take of his substaunce a sure inventory,	180	Magnyfycence	1445
Of worldly welthe, alasse, who can be sure?	201	Magnyfycence	2155
How none estate lyvynge of hymselfe can be sure,	213	Magnyfycence	2557
Without our shyppe be sure, it is lykely to brast,	213	Magnyfycence	2562
Thus none estate lyvynge of hym[selfe] can be sure,	214	Magnyfycence	2564
hymselfe] 'hym' †Rastell & Treveris C 1530, B			
Syn Dewcalyons flodde, I make the faste and sure.	246	Speke Parott	511
In theyr pryncypall cure /They make but lytell sure,	249	Collyn Clout	103
And in nothynge is sure.	253	Collyn Clout	280
Therfore stande sure and fast.	273	Collyn Clout	1071
Stande sure and take good fotyng,	273	Collyn Clout	1072
Wherfore we make you sure,	276	Collyn Clout	1203
For I make you sure,	300	Why Come Ye	846
Whos hevenly armony was so passynge sure,	320	Garlande	274
O wele were hym that herof myght be sure,	332	Garlande	718
Wherfore, I make you sure,	340	Garlande	993
I make you sure] 'I yow assure' MS Cotton Vitellius E.x			
No man lyvyng, he sayth, can be sure;	351	Garlande	1403
I make you fast and sure,	380	Replycacion	232

SURELY

But of reproche surely he maye not mys	46	Bowge	26
Surely I am joyous that ye be myndyd thus;	144	Magnyfycence	156
And surely ye are to hym beholde,	149	Magnyfycence	333
But surely largesse saved my lyfe.	150	Magnyfycence	366
Well argued and surely on bothe sydes.	176	Magnyfycence	1304
Surely it is I that all may save and spyll,	181	Magnyfycence	1478
And surely, as I am nowe advysed,	186	Magnyfycence	1657
Put your wyll to his wyll, for surely it is he	196	Magnyfycence	1997
Now, surely, Magnyfycence, I am ryght well apayed	208	Magnyfycence	2402
Surely my welthe with them was overthrow.	210	Magnyfycence	2450
What, brother Perceveraunce, surely well met!	210	Magnyfycence	2458
And surely thus they sey:	249	Collyn Clout	121
And ye shall fynde surely	296	Why Come Ye	695

SURETY

Ye, for surety. Ofte peas is taken for frayes.	163	Magnyfycence	814
Today in surety, tomorowe bought and solde;	213	Magnyfycence	2548

SURFET

There is no surfet where measure rulyth the feste;	144	Magnyfycence	139

	Page	Title	Line
SURFETOUS			
Geyne surfetous suspecte the emeraud comendable;	44	Balettys3	20
SURFFILLYNG			
With burris rowth and bottons surffillyng,	334	Garlande	803
rowth] 'rowgh' Marshe 1568			
SURFLED			
Under her surfled smocke	252	Collyn Clout	218
SURGERY			
By the craft of surgery,	308	Why Come Ye	1173
SURGIONS			
Or els his surgions they lye;	308	Why Come Ye	1171
Yet sum surgions put a dout	309	Why Come Ye	1198
SURMYSED			
For in this processe, Parrot nothing hath surmysed,	236	Speke Parott	200
But they have enterprysed /And shamfully surmysed	261	Collyn Clout	582
surmysed unsurely in their perihermeniall principles,	374	Replycacion	1
Howe falsely ye had surmysed,	380	Replycacion	209
SURMOUNTYNG			
Transendyng plesure, surmountyng all dysporte;	43	Balettys3	7
SURMOUNTYNGE			
All erthely tresoure it is surmountynge.	50	Bowge	154
SURMOWNTYNGE			
Fayre Diianira surmowntynge in bewte;	337	Garlande	901
SURPLUSE			
Yet suffer me to say the surpluse of my sawe.	142	Magnyfycence	71
SURRAY			
Yet the good Erle of Surray,	282	Why Come Ye	153
SURREY			
Where the noble Cowntes of Surrey in a chayre	333	Garlande	769
To the ryght noble Countes of Surrey	335	Garlande	R
The noble Erle of Surrey,	365	Albany	241
SURRENDRED			
All be it grete parte he hath surrendred	316	Garlande	150
SURRENDRING			
Surrendring your supposycions,	377	Replycacion	112
SURVAYOUR			
Mayster Survayour, where have ye ben so longe?	178	Magnyfycence	1382
Mayster Survayour, Largesse to me call.	179	Magnyfycence	1398
And your Su[rvay]our, Crafty Conveyaunce,	192	Magnyfycence	1862
Survayour] 'supervysour' †Rastell & Treveris C 1530, B			
SURVEY			
Surveyaunce! Where ye survey,	155	Magnyfycence	526
SURVEYAUNCE			
Sure Surveyaunce I named me.	155	Magnyfycence	525
Surveyaunce! Where ye survey,	155	Magnyfycence	526
His name Largesse, Surveyaunce myne.	158	Magnyfycence	643
For in Pleasure and Surveyaunce and also in the,	190	Magnyfycence	1787
SUSPECTE			
Geyne surfetous suspecte the emeraud comendable;	44	Balettys3	20
The seconde was Suspecte, whiche that dayly	49	Bowge	136
'In fayth,' quod Suspecte, 'spake Drede no worde of me?'	51	Bowge	183
'Twyst,' quod Suspecte, 'goo playe; hym I ne reke!'	51	Bowge	186
Twyst] 'Whist' Wynkyn de Worde 1510, 'Twysshe' Marshe 1568			
'Ye, soo,' quod Suspecte, 'he maye us bothe begyle.'	51	Bowge	189
And are somewhat suspecte /In Luthers secte.	260	Collyn Clout	544
And in maner as abjecte, /For evermore suspecte,	380	Replycacion	241
SUSPICION			
Men have you in suspicion	379	Replycacion	182
SUSPYCYON			
Suspycyon, me thoughte, mette hym at a brayde,	51	Bowge	181
SUTE			
That ye dawns all in a sute	379	Replycacion	168
SUTER			
And suter to his parlyament.	118	Ag Scottes	123
SUTERS			
And suters to his parlyment.	114	Scot Kynge	31
Whyche cawsythe pore suters have many a hongry mele;	239	Speke Parott	311
SUTYS			
Sutys, and supplycacyons,	289	Why Come Ye	414
SUTTELTE			
Liing, spying by suttelte and slyght,	133	Garnesche5	151
SUWED			
Suwed to Fortune that she wold be theyre frynde.	49	Bowge	121
SWAFFHAMM			
Whether he rode to Swaffhamm or to Some,	352	Garlande	1416
Swaffhamm] 'Swasshamm' †Fakes 1523, Marshe 1568			
SWALLOW			
And the chattrynge swallow,	82	Phy Sparrow	404
SWAN			
The swan of Menander,	82	Phy Sparrow	434
Whyter than the swan,	98	Phy Sparrow	1079
By our lakyn, syr, I have ben a hawkyng for the wylde swan.	191	Magnyfycence	1806
The gray gose is no swan;	301	Why Come Ye	889
no] 'a' MS Rawlinson C. 813			
SWANNE			
But yf I coulde knowe a gose from a swanne.	148	Magnyfycence	299
Thy slyppers they swap it, yet thou fotys it lyke a swanne.	161	Magnyfycence	765

	Page	Title	Line
SWANNES			
So many swannes dede, and so small revell –	245	Speke Parott	489
SWAP			
Thy slyppers they swap it, yet thou fotys it lyke a swanne.	161	Magnyfycence	765
SWARE			
And sware horryble othes /Before the face of God,	63	Hauke	52
Sche sware with hyr ye xulde nat dele,	131	Garnesche5	57
And sware by Saynt Benet,	224	El Rummynge	393
SWART			
Of Martyn Swart and all hys mery men.	37	Coystrowne1	18
With vysage wan, /As swart as tan;	94	Phy Sparrow	911
swart] 'wart' †Kele 1545.2, Wyght 1553, Kitson 1560.6, 'swarte' Marshe 1568			
Tawny, swart and sallowe,	222	El Rummynge	321
sallowe] 'swallowe' Kynge & Marche 1554, Day 1560, Marshe 1568			
SWARTE			
The colour dedely, swarte, blo and wan	351	Garlande	1399
SWARVE			
And now wolde ye swarve from your owne ordynaunce?	147	Magnyfycence	234
And so observe /That ye ne swarve	339	Garlande	965
SWEARD			
Gentle Paule lie doune thy sweard,	358	Couplet	1
SWEAT			
That made the Romayns to s[wea]t:	90	Phy Sparrow	748
sweat] 'smart' †Kele 1545.2, Wyght 1553, Kitson 1560.6, Marshe 1568			
SWELL			
He bresyth theyr braynpannys and makyth them to swell,	43	Balettys2	31
Maketh his membres swell	284	Why Come Ye	210
SWELLYNGE			
Yet softe and fayre for swellynge,	271	Collyn Clout	986
SWELLYS			
All waters that swellys;	303	Why Come Ye	960
SWEPT			
How the Temple was swept,	66	Hauke	169
SWERD			
Nor Alerycus, that rulyd the Gothyaunce by swerd,	182	Magnyfycence	1504
SWERDE			
His swerde hath bathed in the Scottes blode.	115	Scot Kynge	71
Rule the swerde of myght?	293	Why Come Ye	580
Nor durst nat drawe his swerde	366	Albany	308
SWERE			
He frowned as he wolde swere by Cockes blode.	54	Bowge	287
Thou muste swere and stare, man, aldaye longe,	57	Bowge	381
Your sworde ye swere, I wene,	127	Garnesche3	137
Swere and stare, and byde therby,	152	Magnyfycence	414
No, by the masse. What! Sholde I swere?	166	Magnyfycence	936
Mary, syr, ye may swere it on a boke.	176	Magnyfycence	1292
I swere by all hallowe	222	El Rummynge	323
SWERED			
Elynour swered, 'Nay,	218	El Rummynge	164
She swered by the Rode of Rest,	221	El Rummynge	271
SWERYNGE			
With swerynge and starynge,	281	Why Come Ye	103
SWETE			
A swete suger lofe and sowre bayardys bun	36	Coystrowne1	8
He whystelyth so swetely he makyth me to swete;	37	Coystrowne1	37
But to swete Jesu /On us then for to rew?	40	Coystrowne3	39
To mastres Anne, that farly swete,	41	Coystrowne4	29
That halsyd her hartely and kyst her swete.	42	Balettys1	18
A spone of golde, full of hony swete,	58	Bowge	436
For that swete soules sake,	72	Phy Sparrow	10
Do mi nus, /Helpe nowe swete Jesus!	74	Phy Sparrow	96
Had I of his swete musse;	80	Phy Sparrow	362
his] 'this' †Kele 1545.2, Wyght 1553			
Swete of refla[yre]	84	Phy Sparrow	524
reflayre] 'reflary' †Kele 1545.2, Wyght 1553, Kitson 1560.6, Marshe 1568			
And swete Saynt George, our ladyes knyght!	119	Ag Scottes	141
Now upon thys hete /Rankely whan ye swete,	127	Garnesche3	134
It is so swete in all maner of kynde.	142	Magnyfycence	51
A byrde full swete,	167	Magnyfycence	975
A, howe my stomake wambleth! I am all in a swete.	185	Magnyfycence	1617
So I wolde clepe her! So I wolde kys her swete!	190	Magnyfycence	1802
I kyst her swete, and she kyssyd me;	198	Magnyfycence	2065
Some renne tyll they swete,	221	El Rummynge	266
I have as swete a breth	223	El Rummynge	345
Fresshely they dresse and make swete my bowur,	231	Speke Parott	12
Collustrum now for Parot, whyte bred and swete creme!	233	Speke Parott	82
With, 'Bas me, swete Parrot, bas me, swete swete;'	233	Speke Parott	104
With, 'Bas me, swete Parrot, bas me, swete swete;'	233	Speke Parott	104
With, 'Bas me, swete Parrot, bas me, swete swete;'	233	Speke Parott	104
Swete synamum styckis and pleris cum musco!	235	Speke Parott	185
Goddes blissyng lyght on thy lytell swete musse!	238	Speke Parott	266
Speke, Parotte, my swete byrde, and ye shall have a date,	243	Speke Parott	416
Nowe, Parott, my swete byrde, speke owte yet ons agayn,	244	Speke Parott	447
What care they thoughe Gyll swete,	254	Collyn Clout	321
But swete ypocras ye drynke,	258	Collyn Clout	456

SWETELY —TABULL	Page	Title	Line
And by swete saynt Marke,	272	Collyn Clout	1047
Nor basse her swete swete.	279	Why Come Ye	35
Nor basse her swete swete.	279	Why Come Ye	35
I drede, by swete Jesu,	280	Why Come Ye	64
Swete ypocrus and swete meate.	284	Why Come Ye	218
Be it soure, be it swete!	289	Why Come Ye	422
And his swete hart rote,	295	Why Come Ye	667
It wolde make the devyll to swete!	306	Why Come Ye	1088
'The devyll wold swete' MS Rawlinson C. 813			
With braunches and bowghis of the swete olyve,	330	Garlande	670
Colyaunder, /Swete pomaunder, /Good Cassaunder;	341	Garlande	1027
Your sermon was nat swete;	376	Replycacion	51

SWETELY

He whystelyth so swetely he makyth me to swete;	37	Coystrownel	37
Than swetely togither we ly, /As two pygges in a sty.'	220	El Rummynge	233
Than swetely] 'Thus swete' 1521 Fragment			

SWETE MEATE

Yet swete meate hath soure sauce,	258	Collyn Clout	448
Swete ypocrus and swete meate.	284	Why Come Ye	218

SWETER

| Your wordes be more sweter than ony precyous narde, | 207 | Magnyfycence | 2345 |

SWETERS

| To travellars, to tynkers, /To sweters, to swynkers, | 217 | El Rummynge | 105 |

SWETIS

| Gyll swetis and Cate spynnys! | 302 | Why Come Ye | 926 |
| Cate] not in MS Rawlinson C. 813 | | | |

SWETY

| Thou swety sloven seymy, | 128 | Garnesche3 | 169 |

SWETYNG

| His nobbes and his conny, /His swetyng and his honny, | 220 | El Rummynge | 226 |

SWETTER

| And bicause it is no swetter, | 220 | El Rummynge | 239 |

SWYFTE

| Syr squyer-galyarde ye were to swyfte; | 113 | Scot Kynge | 11 |

SWYLLYNG TUBBE

| They have dronke up my swyllyng tubbe!' | 218 | El Rummynge | 173 |

SWYNE

[Your] gronynge, yor grontynge, yor groinynge lyke a swyne?	123	Garnesche2	2
Yt fallyth for no swyne	126	Garnesche3	86
Here is no man that callyd the hogge nor swyne.	170	Magnyfycence	1084
With, 'Get me a staffe, /The swyne eate my draffe!	218	El Rummynge	171
These swyne go to the hye dese,	218	El Rummynge	175
As wyse as Robyn Swyne,	266	Collyn Clout	806
The Gruntyng and the Groynninge of the Gronnyng Swyne,	351	Garlande	1376
and the] 'a' †Fakes 1523; of the] not in †Fakes 1523			

SWYNE HERDE

| Ar mete for a swyne herde to hunte after hogges. | 240 | Speke Parott | 321 |

SWYNGED

| She swynged up a quarte /At ones for her parte. | 228 | El Rummynge | 568 |
| swynged] 'swinge' Marshe 1568 | | | |

SWYNKERS

| To travellars, to tynkers, /To sweters, to swynkers, | 217 | El Rummynge | 105 |

SWORD

| When thou shoke thi sword so noble a man to mar! | 32 | Dol Dethe | 115 |

SWORDE

Of knightly prowes the sworde, pomel, and hilt,	32	Dol Dethe	108
That with thy sworde enharpid of mortall drede	32	Dol Dethe	125
By Goddis syde, my sworde thy berde shall shave!	55	Bowge	339
Ye have loste spores, cote armure and sworde.	114	Scot Kynge	49
Ye lost your spurrys, ye lost you sworde.	119	Ag Scottes	148
Your sworde ye swere, I wene,	127	Garnesche3	137
By my faythe, syr, the frubyssher hath my sworde.	170	Magnyfycence	1063
Put up his sworde, for he cowde make no warre,	312	Garlande	5

SWORDE

| Hole ys your brow that ye brake with Deu[ra]ndall your awne sworde; Deurandall] 'Deundall' †MS Harley 367 | 123 | Garnesche2 | 8 |

SWORDES

Are sharper then swordes, sturdier then stones.	138	Ven Tongues	50
What the devyll! Use ye not to drawe no swordes?	163	Magnyfycence	811
Wordes be swordes, and hard to call ageine.'	328	Garlande	567

SWORDYS

| Go together by the heddys, and gyve me your swordys. | 202 | Magnyfycence | 2199 |

SWORNE

Sche wolde nat of yt thow had sworne.	131	Garnesche5	52
Falshode in felowshyp is my sworne brother.	160	Magnyfycence	713
By God, syr, Foly, myne owne sworne brother.	172	Magnyfycence	1159

TABERS

| With diamauntis and rubis there tabers were trasid, | 323 | Garlande | 395 |
| tabers] 'taberdes' Marshe 1568 | | | |

TABERTES

| Theyr tabertes of fyne sylke; | 254 | Collyn Clout | 316 |

TABLE

| Or Arturs rounde table, | 87 | Phy Sparrow | 634 |

TABLES

| Forever in tables of bras, | 75 | Phy Sparrow | 150 |

TABULL

| Then in a tabull playne /I wroute a verse or twayne, | 68 | Hauke | 222 |
| Loke on this tabull, /Whether thou art abull | 68 | Hauke | 235 |

	Page	Title	Line
TACKE			
A thousande pounde with lyberte may holde no tacke.	199	Magnyfycence	2084
TA HA			
With, 'Te he, ta ha, bo ho, bo ho!'	376	Replycacion	75
TAILE			
'A slipper holde the taile is of an ele'	326	Garlande	501
Behynde the taile of Ursa so clere;	331	Garlande	696
TAILES			
He rymes and railes /That Englishmen have tailes.	135	Dundas	10
TAYLE			
Yet is youre tong an adders tayle,	41	Coystrowne4	16
An eestryche fedder of a capons tayle	56	Bowge	366
An] 'And' Marshe 1568			
How ofte he hadde hit Jenet on the tayle,	56	Bowge	369
hadde] 'not' Marshe 1568			
She hath gote me more money with her tayle	57	Bowge	405
Set in thy tayle a blase	79	Phy Sparrow	315
And hath a glorious tayle,	82	Phy Sparrow	440
For youre owne tayle ye made a rod.	119	Ag Scottes	146
owne] not in Day 1560, Marshe 1568			
I wolde ye had kyst hyr on the tayle!	130	Garnesche5	46
Shake thy tayle, Scot, lyke a cur,	135	Dundas	25
Trymme at her tayle or a man can turne a socke.	177	Magnyfycence	1346
The bore his tayle wrygges,	219	El Rummynge	177
Or score on the tayle.	230	El Rummynge	616
Parrot hath a blacke beard and a fayre grene tayle.	233	Speke Parott	84
Or to make a sayle /Of a herynges tayle?	246	Collyn Clout	4
And by the barres of her tayle	268	Collyn Clout	868
of] 'if' Marshe 1568, 'of' MS Harley 2252			
With, 'Gingirly, go gingerly!' Her tayle was made of hay;	346	Garlande	1203
TAYLERS			
Ye have eten sauce I trowe, at the Taylers Hall.	179	Magnyfycence	1404
TAYLES			
With thy versyfyeng rayles /How they have tayles.	135	Dundas	31
TAYLIS			
With butterfllyis and fresshe pecoke taylis,	345	Garlande	1159
TAYLL			
With, 'Jayst ye, Jenet of Spayne, for your tayll waggys,'	43	Balettys2	18
TAYNE			
Huffa, huffa, taunderum, taunderum, tayne, huffa, huffa!	161	Magnyfycence	745
TAKE			
Take up whos wolde, for ther they let hym ly.	32	Dol Dethe	96
Take thys in worth, the best is behynde.	38	Coystrowne1	68
Ly styll hardely, and take a nap.	41	Balettys1	4
Wyth bound and rebound, bounsyngly take up	43	Balettys2	15
Enforsed to slepe and for to take some reste,	47	Bowge	32
But, an he can Bone aventure take,	48	Bowge	102
an] 'and' Wynkyn de Worde 1510, Marshe 1568			
He wente aboute to take me in a fawte:	55	Bowge	318
We be thy betters, and so thou shalte us take,	55	Bowge	342
I hate this wayes agayne you that they take!	59	Bowge	471
this] 'these' Wynkyn de Worde 1510			
Moderatly to take /This sorow that I make	74	Phy Sparrow	101
And take me by the lyp.	75	Phy Sparrow	140
And for to take him in	76	Phy Sparrow	166
Phillip wolde seke and take	76	Phy Sparrow	179
How hartely he dyd it take	89	Phy Sparrow	692
In worth I shall it take,	92	Phy Sparrow	817
Is to take this commendacyon	93	Phy Sparrow	849
Why shuld she take shame	103	Phy Sparrow	1284
Of the kynge of Naverne ye may take hede	115	Scot Kynge	56
At hym example ye wolde none take;	115	Scot Kynge	60
Of the kynge of Naverne ye might take heed,	119	Ag Scottes	153
And, for example [y]e wold none take,	119	Ag Scottes	157
ye] 'he' †Lant 1545, Kynge & Marche 1554, Day 1560, Marshe 1568			
Upon hym for to take	126	Garnesche3	92
To take upon the for to scryve;	132	Garnesche5	91
Take thys for that, bere thys in mynde,	134	Garnesche5	172
On Huntley bankes, /Take this our thankes;	136	Dundas	59
But men take upon theim nowe all the shame	139	Ven Tongues	61
Dyspleasure that you none take	143	Magnyfycence	98
Take sad dyreccyon, and leve this wantonnesse.	144	Magnyfycence	149
Well, I am content your wayes to take.	144	Magnyfycence	155
Suche order I trust with them for to take,	145	Magnyfycence	178
Wherfore, Measure, take Lyberte with you hence,	146	Magnyfycence	230
Take Lyberte to rule, and folowe myne entent.	147	Magnyfycence	238
Please it your grace to take no dysdayne.	147	Magnyfycence	252
Yet we wyll therin take good delyberacyon.	148	Magnyfycence	275
For whiche ende goth forwarde ye take lytell charge.	148	Magnyfycence	296
Byd hym take good hede of you, my synguler tresure.	149	Magnyfycence	317
And that he take good kepe to Lyberte.	149	Magnyfycence	320
Wolde take, in the way of counterfet charyte,	154	Magnyfycence	489
Take no dyspleasure of that we say.	156	Magnyfycence	561
Abyde. Lette me se. Take better hede.	157	Magnyfycence	595
A very fon, /A very asse /Wyll take upon /To compasse	164	Magnyfycence	865
And as for me, I take but one folysshe way,	170	Magnyfycence	1076

TAKELYNGE —TAKELYNGE

	Page	Title	Line
Nowe, by my truth, man, take, there is my purse;	171	Magnyfycence	1104
my] 'myne' †Rastell & Treveris C 1530, B			
Nowe take thou my dogge and gyve me thy fowle.	171	Magnyfycence	1116
Hay, chysshe, come hyder! Nay, torde! Take hym be tyme.	171	Magnyfycence	1117
Here FOLY maketh semblaunt to take a lowse	173	Magnyfycence	SD
to take money of CRAFTY CONVEYAUNCE, saynge to hym,	173	Magnyfycence	SD
And for a fole a man wolde hym take.	174	Magnyfycence	1212
And, 'This is not well done, syr; take hede';	175	Magnyfycence	1248
And some wyll take upon them to conterfet letters,	178	Magnyfycence	1364
Come hyther Largesse; take here Felycyte.	179	Magnyfycence	1411
Take it in worthe suche as ye fynde.	180	Magnyfycence	1439
Take of his substaunce a sure inventory,	180	Magnyfycence	1445
If it lyke your grace to take it in degre.	182	Magnyfycence	1521
Take your pleasure and use free lyberte;	185	Magnyfycence	1598
But do as ye lyst and take your owne way.	185	Magnyfycence	1604
So masterfully upon you for to take	188	Magnyfycence	1715
And therfore hye you hens, and take this oversyght.	190	Magnyfycence	1795
Ye sent us a supervysour for to take hede;	192	Magnyfycence	1853
Take hede of your selfe, for nowe ye have nede.	192	Magnyfycence	1854
To take, syrs, example of that I you tell,	195	Magnyfycence	1944
Take hede of this captyfe that lyeth here on grounde.	195	Magnyfycence	1946
And take myscheffe and vengeaunce of other mo	195	Magnyfycence	1951
Take this caytyfe to thy lore.	195	Magnyfycence	1954
All that God sendeth, take it in gre;	196	Magnyfycence	1979
Therefore poverte loke pacyently ye take,	196	Magnyfycence	2000
Take it mekely, and thanke God of his grace;	197	Magnyfycence	2033
Nay, horson, here is my glove. Take it up and thou dare.	202	Magnyfycence	2178
Take nowe upon you this abylyment,	208	Magnyfycence	2405
Shewyth wysdome to them that wysdome can take:	213	Magnyfycence	2554
Take up dyrt and all, /And bere out of the hall.'	219	El Rummynge	183
dyrt] 'drit' Kynge & Marche 1554, Day 1560, Marshe 1568			
It was a stale to take /The devyll in a brake.	222	El Rummynge	324
stale] 'stale' 1521 Fragment, 'stare' †Lant 1545,			
Kynge & Marche 1554, Day 1560, Marshe 1568			
Let every man after his merit take his parte;	236	Speke Parott	199
Prepayre yow, Parrot, brevely your passage to take,	240	Speke Parott	324
He facithe owte at a flusshe with, 'Shewe, take all!'	243	Speke Parott	430
Yf ye take well therwith /It hath in it some pyth.	248	Collyn Clout	57
take] 'talke' Kele 1545.1, Marshe 1568			
Howe they take no hede /Theyr sely shepe to fede,	248	Collyn Clout	76
Or suche laboure to take.	250	Collyn Clout	135
But this reason they take:	250	Collyn Clout	142
Take me as I entende,	251	Collyn Clout	185
Yet take they cure of soules,	252	Collyn Clout	233
cure] 'cures' Kele 1545.1, Marshe 1568			
Uppon hym for to take /A mattocke or a rake.	253	Collyn Clout	273
Yf he on hym dare take	254	Collyn Clout	306
And take a fyne meritorum, /Contra regulam morum,	256	Collyn Clout	379
It may take some effecte!	257	Collyn Clout	436
And upon you take	261	Collyn Clout	603
But yf ye wolde take payne	265	Collyn Clout	763
God wotte, they take great payne	268	Collyn Clout	860
For they must take in hande	268	Collyn Clout	888
To take sadde dyrections,	268	Collyn Clout	894
sadde] 'the sayd' Kele 1545.1, Marshe 1568			
And take theyr worldly ease	269	Collyn Clout	910
Than to take on hande	269	Collyn Clout	911
Nor upon them take,	272	Collyn Clout	1016
Stande sure and take good fotyng,	273	Collyn Clout	1072
Take upon me /Thus copyously to wryte,	273	Collyn Clout	1084
Take upon me] 'Take now upon' Kele 1545.1, 'I take now uppon'			
MS Harley 2252			
Wherfore, take no dysdayne	273	Collyn Clout	1087
Take him, wardeyn of the Flete,	275	Collyn Clout	1165
And let take all the rest!	277	Collyn Clout	1224
All noble men of this take hede,	278	Why Come Ye	1
of this] not in MS Rawlinson C. 813			
All noble men of this take hede,	279	Why Come Ye	15
Than the devyll take all!	279	Why Come Ye	26
All noble men of this take hede,	279	Why Come Ye	27
Dare take nothynge on hande.	286	Why Come Ye	291
Take peper in the nose;	288	Why Come Ye	384
Take him in suche conceyght	292	Why Come Ye	541
And take pacient sufferaunce,	294	Why Come Ye	629
He may take whom he wull,	306	Why Come Ye	1079
Let hym blowe now, that we may take a vewe	319	Garlande	237
a] 'the' MS Cotton Vitellius E.x			
He sange also how, the tre as he did take	320	Garlande	300
She went before, and bad me take good holde;	328	Garlande	573
Forthwith she commaundid I shulde take my place.	344	Garlande	1142
Yet sum there be therewith that take grevaunce	348	Garlande	1257
Why shulde she take shame	348	Garlande	1277
What shuld I do but take it in gre?	353	Garlande	1487
Take no dispare,	355	Garlande	1535
Ye shulde take further payne /To resorte agayne	379	Replycacion	201
Therefore no grevance, /I pray you, for to take,	385	Replycacion	398

TAKELYNGE

	Page	Title	Line
Her takelynge ryche and of hye apparayle;	47	Bowge	38

	Page	Title	Line
TAKEN			
How he is now taken in conceyte,	54	Bowge	302
My speche was taken away.	77	Phy Sparrow	229
From me was taken away	81	Phy Sparrow	374
This wrytynge was taken me there,	150	Magnyfycence	344
Ye, for surety. Ofte peas is taken for frayes.	163	Magnyfycence	814
I have taken it to Largesse and Lyberte.	189	Magnyfycence	1763
That hath taken degre /In the unyversyte	266	Collyn Clout	792
Suffred and taken in gre	290	Why Come Ye	447
And have taken ryght gret payne	295	Why Come Ye	644
TAKETH			
Than Elynour taketh	219	El Rummynge	195
Taketh his pyllyon and his cappe	266	Collyn Clout	803
TAKING			
Taking his course toward the west;	86	Phy Sparrow	573
TAKITH			
And takith no kepe;	358	Garlande2	5
takith] 'bidythe' Marshe 1568			
TAKYN			
And takyn up in such a frame,	132	Garnesche5	110
So many trusys takyn, and so lytyll perfyte trowthe;	245	Speke Parott	491
perfyte] 'profyte' †MS Harley 2252			
TAKYNG			
So myche callyng on, and so smalle takyng hede;	245	Speke Parott	471
TAKYNGE			
He is at suche takynge,	302	Why Come Ye	936
TAKYST			
To cal me knave thou takyst gret payne.	130	Garnesche5	20
TALE			
Wyth fables false, that well coude fayne a tale;	49	Bowge	135
Tellynge this pyteyus tale,	80	Phy Sparrow	342
The popyngay to tell her tale,	82	Phy Sparrow	421
Whan her tale is tolde	87	Phy Sparrow	620
And to amende her tale,	99	Phy Sparrow	1116
Who soever that tale unto you tolde,	137	Ven Tongues	20
Or who made you so bolde to interrupe my tale?	147	Magnyfycence	256
That they wyll here no man but the fyrst tale.	161	Magnyfycence	743
But to make up my tale,	217	El Rummynge	101
And of this tale to rest,	220	El Rummynge	236
This tale will be to trew:	280	Why Come Ye	65
Mustred ther amonge them with many a mad tale;	322	Garlande	373
Of pursevantis ther presid in with many a dyverse tale:	326	Garlande	492
a] not in Marshe 1568			
Yet, thoughe I say it, therby lyith a tale,	346	Garlande	1200
I] 'ye' †Fakes 1523			
TALES			
Naye, strawe for tales, thou shalte not rule us;	55	Bowge	341
Of the Tales of Caunterbury	87	Phy Sparrow	614
Of these historious tales,	90	Phy Sparrow	751
His tales I have red;	91	Phy Sparrow	789
For men be now tratlers and tellers of tales;	139	Ven Tongues	63
And she was full of tales,	223	El Rummynge	352
In credensynge his tales,	290	Why Come Ye	442
TALIS			
A good herynge of thes olde talis;	347	Garlande	1217
TALKE			
And thus to talke with me he began.	51	Bowge	196
He sayde of me, whan he with you dyde talke -	52	Bowge	209
'Fare well,' quod he, 'we wyll talke more of this.'	52	Bowge	227
And in dede, syr, I here men talke -	151	Magnyfycence	374
Togyder we wyll talke more of this.	151	Magnyfycence	393
To passe the tyme and order whyle a man may talke	159	Magnyfycence	689
I coude holde you with suche talke hens tyll to morowe.	184	Magnyfycence	1588
I here the people talke.	254	Collyn Clout	288
That the people talke this,	272	Collyn Clout	1049
But they wyl talke of suche uncouthes,	272	Collyn Clout	1052
TALKES			
And talkes lyke tytyvylles	257	Collyn Clout	416
talkes] 'talke' †Godfray 1531, Kele 1545.1, Marshe 1568			
TALKYD			
Ye and I talkyd therof to nyght.	159	Magnyfycence	670
TALKYNG			
Thus talkyng we went forth in at a postern gate.	333	Garlande	766
forth] not in MS Cotton Vitellius E.x			
TALKYNGE			
I dempte and drede theyr talkynge was not good.	58	Bowge	426
Thus is the talkynge of one and of oder,	151	Magnyfycence	386
Thus talkynge and tellynge	271	Collyn Clout	984
TALL			
For, 'Synke quater trey' /Is a tall man.	301	Why Come Ye	886
tall] 'toll' MS Rawlinson C. 813			
TALLE			
For Syr Frollo de Franko was never halfe so talle.	121	Garnesche1	5
TALLOWE			
Lyke a cake of tallowe;	222	El Rummynge	322
TALOWE			
Her shone smered wyth talowe,	216	El Rummynge	88

	Page	Title	Line
TALWOD			
Our talwod is all brent,	281	Why Come Ye	82
TAME			
Of cattes wylde and tame;	78	Phy Sparrow	276
TAN			
With vysage wan, /As swart as tan;	94	Phy Sparrow	911
swart] 'wart' †Kele 1545.2, Wyght 1553, Kitson 1560.6, 'swarte' Marshe 1568			
Like an onyon syded, /Lyke tan ledder hyded.	226	El Rummynge	471
TANCRETE			
Stop at lawe tancrete,	289	Why Come Ye	420
TANE			
If that ye had tane	366	Albany	283
TANGYD			
Your trymynge and tramynge by me must be tangyd,	203	Magnyfycence	2234
TANNYD			
Tawny, tannyd, and shurvy;	127	Garnesche3	132
TANTE			
To turney or to tante with me ye ar to fare to seke.	123	Garnesche2	37
TAPPET			
Bytwene the tap[pet] and the wall.	174	Magnyfycence	1233
tappet] 'tap' †Rastell & Treveris C 1530, B			
TAPPETT			
Betweyn the tappett and the walle;	131	Garnesche5	75
TAPPETTIS			
The carpettis within and tappettis of pall;	325	Garlande	474
With that the tappettis and carpettis were layd,	334	Garlande	787
TAPPID			
Theis titi[v]yllis with taumpinnis wer towchid and tappid;	330	Garlande	642
titivyllis] 'titinyllis' †Fakes 1523, 'titiuls' Marshe 1568			
TAPPYSTER			
A tappyster lyke a lady bryght:	152	Magnyfycence	420
TARY			
That Mesure shall not there longe tary.	159	Magnyfycence	684
For Cockys harte, tary whylyst that I come agayne.	159	Magnyfycence	685
Well, tary here tyll I for you sende.	163	Magnyfycence	817
Tary here. Wote ye what I say?	163	Magnyfycence	819
But I must tary here; go thou before.	167	Magnyfycence	954
At ones, and let hym not tary all day.	179	Magnyfycence	1400
Syr, ye must tary a stounde,	294	Why Come Ye	626
From you most we, but not longe to tary.	326	Garlande	520
And of the wynter nyghtes that tary so longe,	331	Garlande	701
TARNISHE			
So suerly yt xall nat tarnishe.	127	Garnesche3	122
TARQUINIUS			
Nor yet Tarquinius,	67	Hauke	208
TARRY			
For ye durst nat tarry	367	Albany	343
TARSELL GENTYLL			
The tarsell gentyll, /They shall morne soft and styll	85	Phy Sparrow	558
TART			
It was tart and punyete.	225	El Rummynge	435
TARTARY			
From Scarpary to Tartary renoun therein doth spryng,	234	Speke Parott	131
TARTE			
The Balade also of the Mustard Tarte.	347	Garlande	1245
TASTE			
For lyke as mustarde is sharpe of taste	155	Magnyfycence	552
TASTID			
But sith he hath tastid of the sugred pocioun	314	Garlande	73
TATTERD			
But tatterd and tuggyd, /Raggyd and ruggyd,	304	Why Come Ye	1026
tatterd] 'taxed' MS Rawlinson C. 813			
TATTERED			
For though my ryme be ragged, /Tattered and jagged,	248	Collyn Clout	54
TATTERS			
Theyr smockes all to-ragged, /Wyth tytters and tatters,	217	El Rummynge	126
TATTRED			
Thus tattred and thus torne,	376	Replycacion	83
TAUMPINNIS			
Theis titi[v]yllis with taumpinnis wer towchid and tappid;	330	Garlande	642
titivyllis] 'titinyllis' †Fakes 1523, 'titiuls' Marshe 1568			
TAUNDERUM			
Huffa, huffa, taunderum, taunderum, tayne, huffa, huffa!	161	Magnyfycence	745
Huffa, huffa, taunderum, taunderum, tayne, huffa, huffa!	161	Magnyfycence	745
TAUNT			
To taunt theim like liddrons, lewde as thei bee.	138	Ven Tongues	29
'Shall they taunt us prelates,	275	Collyn Clout	1150
taunt] 'daunt' Kele 1545.1, Marshe 1568, 'teche' MS Harley 2252			
A poete somtyme may for his pleasure taunt,	315	Garlande	100
TAUNTE			
Gave me a taunte, and sayde I was to blame	48	Bowge	70
TAUNTED			
Thus dayly they be decked, /Taunted and checked,	294	Why Come Ye	612
TAUNTES			
To touche them with tauntes of your armony,	117	Ag Scottes	86

TAUNTING —TELL   Page   Title   Line

TAUNTING
And of their taunting toies rest with il hayle.   138   Ven Tongues   33
TAUNTYD
Thow ye be tauntyd, Parotte, with tonges attayntyd, ...   240   Speke Parott   343
TAVELLIS
With slaiis, with tavellis, with hedellis well drest;   334   Garlande   791
TAVELLYS
Wele sped in spyndels and turnyng of tavellys, ...   37   Coystrownel   34
TAVERNARS
As malypert tavernars that checke with theyr betters, ...   178   Magnyfycence   1362
TAVERNE
And to the taverne let us drawe nere.   204   Magnyfycence   2262
TAWLE
By Saynt Mary, he is a tawle man.   163   Magnyfycence   821
TAWNY
Your tethe teintyd with tawny; your semely snowte doth passe, .   122   Garneschel   39
Tawny, tannyd, and shurvy;   127   Garnesche3   132
My colour is tawny, colouryd as a turffe;   195   Magnyfycence   1959
It wygges and it wagges /Lyke tawny saffron bagges;   218   El Rummynge   138
Tawny, swart and sallowe, ...   222   El Rummynge   321
    sallowe] 'swallowe' Kynge & Marche 1554, Day 1560, Marshe 1568
Grene, rede, tawny, whyte, purpill, and blew.   334   Garlande   800
    whyte] 'whyght blak' MS Cotton Vitellius E.x
TAX
He must tax for his wull   302   Why Come Ye   938
TAXES
The commonns renyyd ther taxes to pay   31   Dol Dethe   78
TAXYNGE
By taxynge and tollage, ...   255   Collyn Clout   362
TEACH
As provost pryncypall, /To teach them theyr ordynall;   85   Phy Sparrow   555
TEARYS
The tearys downe hayled;   72   Phy Sparrow   24
TECHE
And teche them howe they sholde syt ydyll   174   Magnyfycence   1221
To teche or to preche /As reason wyll reche?   247   Collyn Clout   13
For all that they preche and teche   374   Replycacion   12
TECHED
And your lollardy lernyng teched, ...   379   Replycacion   204
TECHYNGE
Nor no vertuous techynge, ...   274   Collyn Clout   1134
TECHYTH
He techyth them so wysely to solf and to fayne   38   Coystrownel   53
TECHYTHE
Vis consilii expers, as techythe me Orace, ...   232   Speke Parott   40
TEDER
Naye, see where yonder stondeth the teder man!   59   Bowge   484
TEENE
Whom he forsoke with teene, ...   90   Phy Sparrow   742
TEGGES
Full untydy tegges, /Lyke rotten egges.   218   El Rummynge   151
TEGGYS
Bryngges yow out of favyr with alle femall teggys: 122   Garneschel   31
TEHE
And Annot wolde be nyce, and laughes, 'tehe wehe.'   153   Magnyfycence   477
TE HE
With, 'Te he, ta ha, bo ho, bo ho!'   376   Replycacion   75
TEINTYD
Your tethe teintyd with tawny; your semely snowte doth passe, .   122   Garneschel   39
TEL
With, 'I can tel you what such a man said, ...   139   Ven Tongues   71
TELE
The puffyn and the tele, ...   83   Phy Sparrow   454
    puffyn] 'pussyn' †Kele 1545.2
TELL
Whoos name to tell is Dame Saunce-Pere.   47   Bowge   51
'Maystres,' quod I, 'I praye you tell me why soo, ...   49   Bowge   108
Tell me your mynde, me thynke ye make a verse, ...   53   Bowge   244
I tell the, I am of countenaunce.   55   Bowge   330
What sholde I tell more of his rebaudrye?   56   Bowge   372
But, what, a strawe! I maye not tell all thynge.   59   Bowge   459
Iwys I coude tell - but humlery, home, ...   59   Bowge   467
    tell] 'not tell' Wynkyn de Worde 1510
Ye muste be ruled, as I shall tell you howe.   60   Bowge   493
As I shall tell you, yf ye wyll harke agayne: 61   Bowge   520
To rede or to spell /What these verses tell.   68   Hauke   238
The popyngay to tell her tale, ...   82   Phy Sparrow   421
Must tell what is of the clocke   84   Phy Sparrow   496
Recounte, reporte and tell   87   Phy Sparrow   613
And tell can a great pece   87   Phy Sparrow   630
Of Marcus Marcellus /A proces I could tell us;   90   Phy Sparrow   735
To wryte and tell /How women excell /In noblenes;   96   Phy Sparrow   981
To tell you what conceyte   100   Phy Sparrow   1130
How be it to Saull dyd he tell   105   Phy Sparrow   1357
That thou shortly tell, ...   105   Phy Sparrow   1367
To tell you the cause me semeth it no nede.   140   Magnyfycence   8
To tell you, syr, I dare not, leest I sholde be maskyd   141   Magnyfycence   30
Nowe, I beseche the, tell me what is thy name?   148   Magnyfycence   269

TELLE —TELLETH	Page	Title	Line
Tell you where of my name dothe ryse.	151	Magnyfycence	409
Tell me, syrs, what is your wyll?	157	Magnyfycence	611
But tell me where aboute ye go.	157	Magnyfycence	617
I can not tell you. Why aske you me?	157	Magnyfycence	628
Syr, the playnesse you me tell.	158	Magnyfycence	630
you me tell] 'you tell me' †Rastell & Treveris C 1530, B			
Nay; eyther let me tell, or elles tell ye.	158	Magnyfycence	633
Nay; eyther let me tell, or elles tell ye.	158	Magnyfycence	633
I care not, I. Tell on for me.	158	Magnyfycence	634
Tell on, syr. Howe then?	158	Magnyfycence	651
Ye, so I tell the.	162	Magnyfycence	800
Cockes bones! I ne tell can	162	Magnyfycence	801
But nowe what tydynges can you tell? Let se.	166	Magnyfycence	928
Howe so? Tell me, I the pray.	166	Magnyfycence	931
Fyrst to tell you what were best:	168	Magnyfycence	1022
A pylde curre? Ye, so I tell the, a pylde curre.	169	Magnyfycence	1055
By God, I can tell the; and I wyll.	170	Magnyfycence	1071
Tell by thy trouth what sport can thou make.	172	Magnyfycence	1162
Nay, I tell the, he maketh no dowtes	174	Magnyfycence	1210
Syr, of my maner I shall tell you the playne:	174	Magnyfycence	1219
Forsothe, tell on. Hast thou any mo?	175	Magnyfycence	1262
mo] 'more' †Rastell & Treveris C 1530, B			
Yes. I shall tell you or I go	175	Magnyfycence	1263
And tell to his sufferayne every whyt;	175	Magnyfycence	1270
Ye. But tell me one thynge. What is that?	176	Magnyfycence	1318
Sore sayde, I tell you, and well to the purpose.	180	Magnyfycence	1428
Or lyberte by welth? Let se, tell me that.	180	Magnyfycence	1432
Money maketh marchauntes, I tell you, over all.	184	Magnyfycence	1574
A maystres, I tell you, is but a small thynge.	184	Magnyfycence	1579
An honest person, I tell you, and a sad.	187	Magnyfycence	1690
Nay, I tell you, I am not wonte to fode	188	Magnyfycence	1698
By my trouth, I can not tell you that.	188	Magnyfycence	1703
Ye, let be thy japes, and tell me howe	192	Magnyfycence	1846
I wolde tell you and yf I myght for wepynge.	192	Magnyfycence	1848
To take, syrs, example of that I you tell,	195	Magnyfycence	1944
A laudable largesse, I tell you, for a lorde,	200	Magnyfycence	2123
I can not well tell of your dysposycyons;	203	Magnyfycence	2218
By God, I tell you, I wyll not be out facyd.	203	Magnyfycence	2220
Tell me brefly where upon ye began.	203	Magnyfycence	2224
And I tell you, I dysdayne moche of his mockys.	203	Magnyfycence	2227
In Goddys mercy, I tell them, is but foly to truste;	205	Magnyfycence	2289
Tell you I chyll,	214	El Rummynge	1
For I may tell you, /I lerned it of a Jewe,	219	El Rummynge	207
For though ye can tell in Greke what is phormio,	235	Speke Parott	151
Syns Dewcalyons flodde, I trow, no man can tell.	245	Speke Parott	490
Set nought by golde ne grotes, /Theyr names yf I durst tell.	250	Collyn Clout	161
I tell you as men say.	251	Collyn Clout	188
Shall I tell you more? Ye, shall.	262	Collyn Clout	635
I am lothe to tell all;	262	Collyn Clout	636
And wyll preche and tell	267	Collyn Clout	822
And tell of other mo,	267	Collyn Clout	829
And can nat tell no cause why	274	Collyn Clout	1115
can nat] 'can' Marshe 1568, MS Harley 2252			
To tell of vayne glory;	284	Why Come Ye	228
Yet what here ye tell	288	Why Come Ye	379
To tell the trouth playnly,	290	Why Come Ye	460
They can nat well tell	295	Why Come Ye	648
But wele I can tell	296	Why Come Ye	686
Tell you the rest; for me they shal.	296	Why Come Ye	709
Tell me nowe in this stede,	298	Why Come Ye	786
Few men can tell where the hynde calfe gose.	313	Garlande	26
tell] 'telle now' MS Cotton Vitellius E.x			
I can not tell you what was the occasyon.	313	Garlande	35
not tell] 'not wele tell' MS Cotton Vitellius E.x			
But lytell or nothynge ye shall here tell	317	Garlande	197
ye shall] 'shall ye' MS Cotton Vitellius E.x			
There apparell farre passynge beyonde that I can tell;	323	Garlande	394
I can nat tell you, but that I was brought	325	Garlande	458
It is harde to tell of every mannes mouthe:	326	Garlande	500
Some came to tell treuth, some came to lye,	326	Garlande	510
But, goodly maystres, one thynge ye me tell.'	332	Garlande	720
To tell all his towchis it were to grete wonder;	333	Garlande	764
How be it to Saull he did tell	350	Garlande	1350
That thou shortely tell,	350	Garlande	1360
No man can tell whether.	358	Garlande2	9
Whan he herde tell /That my Lorde Amrell	360	Albany	54

TELLE

But I wolde telle you a thynge, and I durste.	51	Bowge	203
I wote, and he dyde, ye wolde me telle.	51	Bowge	205
And for to telle the gronde,	128	Garnesche3	184

TELLERS

For men be now tratlers and tellers of tales;	139	Ven Tongues	63

TELLES

Thus the people telles, /Rayles lyke rebelles,	257	Collyn Clout	412

TELLETH

The story telleth playne,	89	Phy Sparrow	696
He telleth you trouth, syr, as I you ensure.	187	Magnyfycence	1679

	Page	Title	Line
TELLYNGE			
Tellynge this pyteyus tale,	80	Phy Sparrow	342
Thus talkynge and tellynge	271	Collyn Clout	984
TEMMYS			
That wonnes at the Key in Temmys Strete.	41	Coystrowne4	30
TEMPESTE			
No stormy tempeste your barge shall overthrow.	327	Garlande	546
TEMPESTOUS			
Of that the tempestous wynde wyll aswage	335	Garlande	831
tempestous] 'tempeous' †Fakes 1523, 'tempestuows' MS Cotton Vitellius E.x			
TEMPLE			
How the Temple was kept,	66	Hauke	168
How the Temple was swept,	66	Hauke	169
Betwene Temple Bar /And the Crosse in Chepe,	223	El Rummynge	359
Nor how farre Temple Barre is	267	Collyn Clout	826
TEMPLES			
By the good Lorde, yet your temples bete.	189	Magnyfycence	1732
TEMPORALL			
Bothe temporall and spirituall for to complayne	34	Dol Dethe	181
Dothe grudge and complayne /Upon the temporall men.	248	Collyn Clout	65
Through temporall afflictyons.	249	Collyn Clout	111
For the lordes temporall,	261	Collyn Clout	608
Suche temporall warre and bate	269	Collyn Clout	913
With all temporall people	271	Collyn Clout	982
TEMPORALTE			
For the temporalte /Accuseth the spirytualte;	248	Collyn Clout	61
The temporalte say playne	250	Collyn Clout	132
Of the spirytualte /Or of the temporalte,	274	Collyn Clout	1120
TEMPORALTYE			
Bytwene the clergye /And the temporaltye:	260	Collyn Clout	556
TEN			
And soo outface hym with a carde of ten.'	55	Bowge	315
His benefyce worth ten pounde,	264	Collyn Clout	725
Above threscore and ten.	288	Why Come Ye	373
Some of you had ten pounde,	378	Replycacion	146
TENDE			
He wyll come, man, when he may tende to.	162	Magnyfycence	790
And I may tende therto for play;	168	Magnyfycence	1018
TENDER			
O yonge lyon, bot tender yet of age,	33	Dol Dethe	162
Whereof I beseche you to tender the effecte.	313	Garlande	56
Of womanly feturis, whos florysshyng tender age	336	Garlande	869
But, as I sayd, your florisshinge tender age	337	Garlande	876
TENDERLY			
Tenderly to consyder in your advertence -	186	Magnyfycence	1635
And that it wolde please her, full tenderly I prayd,	353	Garlande	1479
TENDYR			
With herte moste tendyr,	237	Speke Parott	226
TENE			
That vilane hastarddis in ther furious tene,	30	Dol Dethe	24
TENNYS			
In the tennys play,	301	Why Come Ye	884
TENOR			
He trymmyth in hys tenor to counter pyrdewy;	37	Coystrowne1	26
This is the tenor of my byl,	310	Why Come Ye2	33
TENOURS			
All trebyllys and tenours be rulyd by a meyne.	144	Magnyfycence	137
TENSIS			
Can skantly the tensis of his conjugacyons;	235	Speke Parott	180
TENT			
With that I sprange up towarde the tent	320	Garlande	283
Or of suche a mawment /Caryed in a tent.	365	Albany	258
In a tent? Nay. Nay.	365	Albany	259
TENTER-HOKYS			
Her naylys sharpe as tenter-hokys!	168	Magnyfycence	1001
TERE			
Myght tere out all thy trypes!	79	Phy Sparrow	308
The devill tere their tunges and pike out their ies!	139	Ven Tongues	68
For he wyll tere it asonder!	296	Why Come Ye	671
TERED			
To be tered thus and torne?	276	Collyn Clout	1201
TERENCE			
Mayster Terence, the famous comicar,	322	Garlande	353
comicar] 'conucar' †Fakes 1523			
TERESTRE			
Of the terestre [t]rechery we fall in the flode,	213	Magnyfycence	2559
trechery] 'rechery' †Rastell & Treveris C 1530, B			
TERMES			
Under as coverte termes as coude be,	46	Bowge	10
With pullysshed termes lusty;	91	Phy Sparrow	776
I wot not where to fynd /Termes to serve my mynde.	91	Phy Sparrow	783
His termes were not darke,	91	Phy Sparrow	801
With sentence fructuous and termes convenable.'	335	Garlande	821
TERMYS			
Yower termys ar to grose,	126	Garnesche3	96
TERRIBLE			
Terrible of countenaunce and passynge formydable,	328	Garlande	591

	Page	Title	Line
TERRY			
Ye bere yow bolde as Barabas, or Syr Terry of Trac[e].	122	Garnesche1	11
Trace] 'Tracy' †MS Harley 367			
TESSEW			
Of golde of tessew the fynest that myghte be,	47	Bowge	59
TESTALIS			
Phillis and Testalis, ther tressis with oyle	331	Garlande	681
TESTAMENTIS			
Of Lovers Testamentis and of There Wanton Wyllis,	354	Garlande	1496
TESTEFY			
As all his kuntrey kan testefy the same:	33	Dol Dethe	153
TESTIFYE			
All men can testifye.	376	Replycacion	64
TESTY			
But, Lorde, as she was testy, /Angry as a waspy!	222	El Rummynge	329
TETH			
Your teth whett on this bone	258	Collyn Clout	476
whett on] 'whetten' †Godfray 1531, 'whette on' MS Harley 2252			
TETHE			
Your tethe teintyd with tawny; your semely snowte doth passe,	122	Garnesche1	39
Ful of greet knavys tethe,	127	Garnesche3	126
In the spyght of his tethe	302	Why Come Ye	942
Of elephantis tethe were the palace gatis,	325	Garlande	468
TETRYCALL			
as touchyng the tetrycall theologisacion of these demy divines,	374	Replycacion	I
TETTER			
In faythe, Mesure is lyke a tetter	155	Magnyfycence	543
TEUYT			
Teuyt, teuyt! /Where is my wyt?	168	Magnyfycence	1004
Teuyt, teuyt! /Where is my wyt?	168	Magnyfycence	1004
TEUSDAY			
O dolorous Teusday, dedicate to thi name,	32	Dol Dethe	114
TEWYNE			
With neythyr of yow tewyne:	124	Garnesche3	7
The prowdyst knave yet of us tewyne	130	Garnesche5	21
TEWLY			
With, 'Reche me that skane of tewly sylk';	334	Garlande	798
TEWSDAY			
Of the Tewsday in the weke	225	El Rummynge	449
TEXT			
This is a trew text!	285	Why Come Ye	261
TEXTE			
Of the texte and the glose.	266	Collyn Clout	779
TEXTES			
And hys textes grounde -	264	Collyn Clout	724
hys] not in Kele 1545.1, Marshe 1568			
THAGUS			
Of Thagus, that golden flod,	93	Phy Sparrow	875
THALYA			
Thalya, my muse, for you also call I,	117	Ag Scottes	85
THAMAR			
Thamar also wrought with her goodly honde	336	Garlande	852
THAMARYS			
As dame Thamarys, whiche toke the kyng of Perce,	336	Garlande	857
THAN			
Than to beholde youre bewteouse countenaunce:	44	Balettys3	44
Excedynge ferther than his connynge is,	46	Bowge	23
That clymmeth hyer than he may fotynge have;	46	Bowge	27
But than I thoughte I wolde not dwell behynde;	47	Bowge	43
Than there coude I none aquentaunce fynde;	47	Bowge	45
Than sholde ye see there pressynge in a pace	47	Bowge	56
Than Phebus in his spere celestyne,	47	Bowge	61
And I than softly answered to that clause,	48	Bowge	74
Than asked she me, 'Syr, so God the spede,	48	Bowge	76
Favoure we have toughther than ony elme,	49	Bowge	129
toughther] 'tougher' Wynkyn de Worde 1510, Marshe 1568			
Than Favell gan wyth fayre speche me to fede.	50	Bowge	147
Than thanked I hym for his grete gentylnes.	51	Bowge	176
'Why? What than? Wylte thou lete men to speke?	51	Bowge	184
'God spede, broder,' to me quod he than,	51	Bowge	195
Than I assured hym my fydelyte,	52	Bowge	218
To kepe it hymselfe; for than he myghte be sure	52	Bowge	222
To Hervy Ha[f]ter than he spake of me,	54	Bowge	295
Hafter] 'Haster' †Wynkyn de Worde 1499, 1510, Marshe 1568			
'Than,' quod Hervy, 'why arte thou so dysmayde?'	54	Bowge	299
'By him that me boughte,' than quod Dysdayne,	54	Bowge	309
Than hath some shyppe that into Bordews sayle.	57	Bowge	406
Me, passynge sore, myne herte than gan aryse;	58	Bowge	425
Than, in his hode, I sawe there faces tweyne:	58	Bowge	428
As than befell to me.	72	Phy Sparrow	22
Great sorowe than ye myght se,	73	Phy Sparrow	56
Than he wold lepe and skyp,	75	Phy Sparrow	139
My sparowe than shuld be quycke	77	Phy Sparrow	205
Men se hym now and than	88	Phy Sparrow	657
than] 'then' Marshe 1568			
Than is he sad, /Frantyke and mad;	95	Phy Sparrow	939
Whyter than the swan,	98	Phy Sparrow	1079

THAN —THAN

	Page	Title	Line
Whyter than the mylke,	99	Phy Sparrow	1120
the] not in Kitson 1560.6, Marshe 1568			
I had than in a tryce,	100	Phy Sparrow	1131
Than suche as have disdayned	106	Phy Sparrow	1374
No worse than is contayned	106	Phy Sparrow	1377
Our kynge than beynge out of the waye;	114	Scot Kynge	45
Than in Englonde to playe ony suche prankes;	114	Scot Kynge	51
Your wyll than ran before your wyt.	118	Ag Scottes	102
Than with my poems for to melle.	132	Garnesche5	94
Worketh more mischiefe than can be tolde;	137	Ven Tongues	8
Than ye may commaunde me to gentil cok wat.	137	Ven Tongues	15
Than to be founde in any such faute.	137	Ven Tongues	25
That nothynge than welth may worse be enduryd.	140	Magnyfycence	7
Me semeth that ye have dronken more than ye have bled.	147	Magnyfycence	260
It dothe so sure nowe and than.	150	Magnyfycence	368
That we can no better than so.	155	Magnyfycence	550
Whan other men laughe, than study I and muse,	160	Magnyfycence	707
And yet, I trowe, some of you be better sped than I	160	Magnyfycence	722
Well, and I be a coward, there is mo than I.	162	Magnyfycence	770
Moche more than nede	165	Magnyfycence	894
Why? Is he crossed than with a chalke?	166	Magnyfycence	950
Than a butterflye of our lande.	169	Magnyfycence	1053
Than thou can in yerys seven.	170	Magnyfycence	1078
By the masse, yet art thou more fole than I.	171	Magnyfycence	1111
Than wyll I say that thou hast no pere.	173	Magnyfycence	1195
He wyll make it mykyll worse than it is;	175	Magnyfycence	1273
Than waste must be welcome, and fare well thryfte.	180	Magnyfycence	1444
Well, get you hens than and sende me some other.	180	Magnyfycence	1451
For suche abusyon I use nowe and than.	185	Magnyfycence	1625
And more than ever I dyd for ony man.	187	Magnyfycence	1694
Than is it done as it sholde be;	189	Magnyfycence	1764
Better to make iii. ryche than for to make many.	190	Magnyfycence	1772
Gyve them more than ynoughe, and let them not lacke;	190	Magnyfycence	1773
Than Rowlande the reve ran, and I began to rave,	192	Magnyfycence	1831
Than from theyr chyldren to spare the rod	194	Magnyfycence	1929
Nowe must your fete lye hyer than your crowne.	197	Magnyfycence	2007
Better it is to begge than to be hangyd with shame.	198	Magnyfycence	2039
For to lyve in mysery, it is herder than dethe.	205	Magnyfycence	2282
Ye, ryd thy selfe rather than this lyfe for to lede.	205	Magnyfycence	2307
Than of wanhope thrughe the unhappy wayes,	206	Magnyfycence	2337
Your wordes be more sweter than ony precyous narde,	207	Magnyfycence	2345
More delectable than your langage to me.	207	Magnyfycence	2348
Adversyte to hym therwith nowe and than;	207	Magnyfycence	2368
Than stande up, syr, in Goddys name!	208	Magnyfycence	2397
Than Elynour taketh	219	El Rummynge	195
It shall make you loke /Yonger than ye be	219	El Rummynge	214
Than wyll he rout and snort;	220	El Rummynge	232
Than swetely togither we ly, /As two pygges in a sty.'	220	El Rummynge	233
Than swetely] 'Thus swete' 1521 Fragment			
Than cometh an other gest;	221	El Rummynge	270
Small chaffer doth ease /Sometyme, now and than.	222	El Rummynge	315
And than came haltyng Jone	222	El Rummynge	326
Than Elynour sayde, 'Ye calettes,	223	El Rummynge	347
Than thydder came dronken Ales	223	El Rummynge	351
Than began she to wepe,	223	El Rummynge	374
An other than dyd hyche her,	224	El Rummynge	401
hyche] 'hye' 1521 Fragment			
Than sterte in made Kyt, /That had lytell wyt;	224	El Rummynge	412
Than Margery Mylkeducke /Her kyrtell she dyd uptucke	225	El Rummynge	418
Than sterte forth a fysgygge	228	El Rummynge	538
Than began the sporte /Amonge that dronken sorte.	229	El Rummynge	574
Than Elynour dyd them hyde /Within her beddes syde.	229	El Rummynge	605
But some than sate ryght sad	229	El Rummynge	607
Maters more precious than the ryche jacounce,	241	Speke Parott	366
Or yf he speke playne, /Than he lacketh brayne:	247	Collyn Clout	27
Than to be combred with care.	251	Collyn Clout	177
Than a thousande thousande other	266	Collyn Clout	776
Than to take on hande	269	Collyn Clout	911
Than lette reason you supporte,	271	Collyn Clout	1004
Ye knowe better than I.	273	Collyn Clout	1064
Why than /Wreke ye your anger on me?	273	Collyn Clout	1090
Than, without collusyon,	279	Why Come Ye	17
Than the devyll take all!	279	Why Come Ye	26
Than wyll age have a corage	279	Why Come Ye	38
Farewell, than, have good day!	280	Why Come Ye	57
Than have good daye. Adewe!	280	Why Come Ye	58
For than thyne heed of gose.	288	Why Come Ye	385
Than, 'Have him to the Towre /Saunz aulter remedy!	289	Why Come Ye	429
He regardeth lordes /No more than potshordes.	291	Why Come Ye	481
Than, our processe for to stable,	292	Why Come Ye	536
Than farewell to the, /Welthfull Felycite;	300	Why Come Ye	860
Welthfull] 'Welthe full of felycyte' MS Rawlinson C. 813			
For prosperyte /Away than wyll fle.	300	Why Come Ye	863
Than must we agre /With poverte;	300	Why Come Ye	864
That he wolde than make /The devyls to quake,	303	Why Come Ye	978
Than any other a thousand folde.	310	Why Come Ye2	16
any] 'yn any' MS Rawlinson C. 813			

THANKE —THEIM

	Page	Title	Line
Bete a dum mouthe than a brainles scull;	314	Garlande	82
Bete] 'Better' Marshe 1568, MS Cotton Vitellius E.x			
Goodly Creisseid, fayrer than Polexene,	336	Garlande	871
But if he wryte oftenner than ones or twyse.'	345	Garlande	1155
No wors than is contaynyd	350	Garlande	1370
than] 'and' †Fakes 1523			
How than lyke a man he wan the barbican	351	Garlande	1397
Than a chyldis birde and a knavis wyfe?	352	Garlande	1452
A pleasaunter place than Ashrige is, harde were to fynde,	353	Garlande	1465
were] 'where' †Fakes 1523			
Duke of Albany, /Than shamefuly	360	Albany	51
What losels than are ye	370	Albany	459
Than ye be a knappishe sorte	370	Albany	475
Than forthwith by and by	374	Replycacion	4
Is farther than their wytte wyll reche.	374	Replycacion	13
moche better bayned than brayned,	374	Replycacion	1
Your hertes than were hosed, /Your relacions reposed;	377	Replycacion	107
Oftnar than ones or twyse,	378	Replycacion	133
Than all your lytterature.	380	Replycacion	233
Than ye know what betokeneth dulia:	382	Replycacion	288
Than shall ye fynde it fyrme and stable,	382	Replycacion	289
Than, if this noble kyng,	384	Replycacion	343
Why have ye than disdayne /At poetes, and complayne	384	Replycacion	351

THANKE

	Page	Title	Line
Yes, in faythe, I thanke God I may here.	169	Magnyfycence	1059
Take it mekely, and thanke God of his grace;	197	Magnyfycence	2033
Ye, but thanke me therof every dele.	201	Magnyfycence	2171
Thanke the therof, in the devyls date!	201	Magnyfycence	2172
To thanke God of his sonde; and comforte ye shal fynde.	207	Magnyfycence	2360
And hartely thanke God of your adversyte;	207	Magnyfycence	2362
And gat her great thanke	228	El Rummynge	543
'A thanke to have, ye have well deservyd,	317	Garlande	169
'I thanke you, goodly maystres, to me most benynge,	332	Garlande	728
Avaunsynge my selfe sum thanke to deserve,	335	Garlande	822

THANKED

	Page	Title	Line
Than thanked I hym for his grete gentylnes.	51	Bowge	176
Thanked be saynte Gorge, our ladyes knythe,	114	Scot Kynge	42
Syr, thanked be God, he hath his hele.	149	Magnyfycence	315
I thanked her moche of her most noble offer,	327	Garlande	554

THANKEFULLYER

	Page	Title	Line
And better perceyved, /And thankefullyer receyved,	265	Collyn Clout	771

THANKES

	Page	Title	Line
On Huntley bankes, /Take this our thankes;	136	Dundas	59

THANKIS

	Page	Title	Line
To iche of them rendryng thankis commendable,	335	Garlande	820

THANKYD

	Page	Title	Line
Thankyd be God in trinyte,	119	Ag Scottes	140

THANKKIS

	Page	Title	Line
In rendrynge to you thankkis meritory,	324	Garlande	429

THEDER

	Page	Title	Line
But Phebus was formest of all that cam theder;	320	Garlande	287

THEE

	Page	Title	Line
Who that is ruled by us, it shalbe longe or he thee.	154	Magnyfycence	515
I pray God let you never to thee!	158	Magnyfycence	635
That useth me. /He can not thee.	164	Magnyfycence	862

THEEM

	Page	Title	Line
Moche mischefe, I hyght you, amonge theem ther happid.	330	Garlande	643

THEFE

	Page	Title	Line
Save a stronge thefe and hange a trew man.	178	Magnyfycence	1360

THEFFECT

	Page	Title	Line
Now, by your faith, is not this theffect	333	Garlande	737
by] 'be' †Fakes 1523			

THEFT

	Page	Title	Line
Ryot, reveler, railer, brybery, theft,	329	Garlande	614

THEFTE

	Page	Title	Line
To thefte and bryboury I make some fall,	174	Magnyfycence	1226
Thefte also and pety brybery	177	Magnyfycence	1354
Some have a name for thefte and brybery;	317	Garlande	183

THEI

	Page	Title	Line
And were not thei to blame, I say also,	30	Dol Dethe	36
Unkindly thei slew hym that help them oft at nede.	30	Dol Dethe	47
help] 'holp' Marshe 1568			
Yet shamfully thei slew hym; that sham most them befall.	30	Dol Dethe	49
Bot men say thei wer lynked with a double chayn	31	Dol Dethe	75
With one vice importune thei playnly said nay.	31	Dol Dethe	80
All kingis, all princis, all dukis, well thei ought	34	Dol Dethe	180
To soroufull weping thei ought to be constreynd,	34	Dol Dethe	187
As oft as thei call to ther remembrance	34	Dol Dethe	188
They coude not faile, thei thought, they were so sure.	50	Bowge	142
To taunt theim like liddrons, lewde as thei bee.	138	Ven Tongues	29
And wotteth never what thei rede, /Paternoster nor crede;	252	Collyn Clout	234
And say properly thei are sacerdotes	268	Collyn Clout	874
When thei agayn thyder shal come,	268	Collyn Clout	883
And through all the worlde thei go	268	Collyn Clout	885
Thei wantid nothynge but the laurell;	323	Garlande	397
Shet were the gatis; thei might wel knock and cal,	329	Garlande	604

THEIM

	Page	Title	Line
To taunt theim like liddrons, lewde as thei bee.	138	Ven Tongues	29

	Page	Title	Line
But men take upon theim nowe all the shame	139	Ven Tongues	61
THEIR			
For to let their hawkys fly	67	Hauke	218
To shew me their devyse	74	Phy Sparrow	100
The dragones with their tonges	79	Phy Sparrow	292
Shall stand in their morning gounes;	85	Phy Sparrow	566
Their husbandes to set at nought:	87	Phy Sparrow	627
Ever to be /Their true bedell	96	Phy Sparrow	980
At Englysh bowes have fetched their banes.	120	Ag Scottes	173
Agaynst this my makyng, /Their males therat shakyng,	120	Ag Scottes2	8
Then let them vale a bonet of their proud sayle,	138	Ven Tongues	32
And of their taunting toies rest with il hayle.	138	Ven Tongues	33
Men said they could not their tunges atame;	139	Ven Tongues	60
With skolding and sklaundering make their tungs lame.	139	Ven Tongues	62
The devill tere their tunges and pike out their ies!	139	Ven Tongues	68
The devill tere their tunges and pike out their ies!	139	Ven Tongues	68
Some their hose, some their shone;	220	El Rummynge	248
Some their hose, some their shone;	220	El Rummynge	248
That nothynge had /There of their awne,	229	El Rummynge	609
The devyll can nat stop their mouthes	272	Collyn Clout	1051
They were nat payde their hyre.	285	Why Come Ye	248
They play their olde pranckes /After Huntley Bankes.	285	Why Come Ye	266
Their hertes be in thyr hose!	286	Why Come Ye	289
To holde up their hande at the bar.	286	Why Come Ye	302
For all their noble blode,	286	Why Come Ye	303
Against their wylles, God wot.	306	Why Come Ye	1100
Some dronken dastardis with their dry soules;	317	Garlande	190
These orators and poetes refreshed their throtes.	321	Garlande	343
Their orators and poetis refresshed there throtis.	322	Garlande	357
And of their shorte nyghtes; he browght in his songe	331	Garlande	703
As dasid doterdis that dreme in their dumpis.'	332	Garlande	734
In some of their condicions,	364	Albany	198
And their false sedycions,	364	Albany	199
And their dealyng double,	364	Albany	200
And their weywarde trouble.	364	Albany	201
And manly manyfolde, /Their enemyes to assayle	364	Albany	204
And to spende their hart blode,	371	Albany	487
Their bodyes and their gode,	371	Albany	488
Their bodyes and their gode,	371	Albany	488
To magnifye their names.	374	Replycacion	10
Is farther than their wytte wyll reche.	374	Replycacion	13
Thus by demeryttes of their abusyon;	374	Replycacion	14
basked and baththed in their wylde burblyng and boyling blode,	374	Replycacion	I
of their rechelesse youthe and wytlesse wontonnesse,	374	Replycacion	I
of their insensate sensualyte,	374	Replycacion	I
surmysed unsurely in their perihermeniall principles,	374	Replycacion	I
That leudly have their tyme spent,	375	Replycacion	24
In their study abhomynable,	375	Replycacion	25
By way of their devocion	378	Replycacion	136
THEIRE			
Theire grevis to complaine;	111	Lawde	34
THEIS			
Maintenaunce and Mischefe, theis be men of myght;	317	Garlande	193
Theis people by me have none assignement,	317	Garlande	195
Theis orators and poetis refresshed there throtis.	322	Garlande	350
Theis orators and poetis refresshed there throtis.	322	Garlande	364
Theis orators and poetis refresshid there throtis.	322	Garlande	378
Theis notable poetis refresshid there throtis.	322	Garlande	385
Dane Johnn Lydgate. Theis Englysshe poetis thre,	323	Garlande	391
Tyll at the last theis noble poetis thre	326	Garlande	517
'Theis yatis,' she sayd, 'which that ye beholde,	328	Garlande	579
Theis titi[v]yllis with taumpinnis wer towchid and tappid; titivyllis] 'titinyllis' †Fakes 1523, 'titiuls' Marshe 1568	330	Garlande	642
Of cristall the clerenes theis waters far past,	330	Garlande	660
Whereon theis ladys softly myght rest,	334	Garlande	788
How theis ladys and gentylwomen all	335	Garlande	809
Gower, Chawcer, Lydgate, theis thre	343	Garlande	1101
God wote, theis wordes made me full sad;	353	Garlande	1484
THEY			
They bode not till the rekenyng were discust.	30	Dol Dethe	40
For yf they had occupied ther spere and ther shelde	31	Dol Dethe	73
They buskt them on a bushment them selfe in baile to bringe	31	Dol Dethe	81
They saide they forsede not nor carede not to dy.	31	Dol Dethe	84
They saide they forsede not nor carede not to dy.	31	Dol Dethe	84
Bot all they fled from hym for falshode or fere.	31	Dol Dethe	91
Of whos [life] they counteded not a fly. life] not in †MS Royal 18 D.ii or Marshe 1568	31	Dol Dethe	95
Take up whos wolde, for ther they let hym ly.	32	Dol Dethe	96
Of aureat poems they want ellumynynge;	32	Dol Dethe	128
For though they stumble in the synnys sevyn,	36	Coystrownel	3
In pevyshnes yet they snapper and fall, they] 'the' †Rastell 1527	36	Coystrownel	4
That neyther they synge wel prycke song nor playne.	38	Coystrownel	54
Theyre browys all to-brokyn, such clappys they cach;	43	Balettys2	32
By theyr conusaunce knowing how they serve a wily py;	43	Balettys2	34
Therein they founde royall marchaundyse,	47	Bowge	41
They thronge in fast and flocked her aboute,	49	Bowge	122
They coude not faile, thei thought, they were so sure.	50	Bowge	142

THEY—THEY	Page	Title	Line
They coude not faile, thei thought, they were so sure.	50	Bowge	142
But my dysporte they could not well endure:	50	Bowge	145
They sayde they hated for to dele with Drede.	50	Bowge	146
They sayde they hated for to dele with Drede.	50	Bowge	146
And I drewe nere to herke what they two sayde.	51	Bowge	182
His eyen rollynge, his hondes faste they quoke;	51	Bowge	193
And I drewe nere to harke what they two sayde.	54	Bowge	296
Yet at the knee they were broken, I wene.	56	Bowge	357
Fye on this dyce, they be not worth a turde!	57	Bowge	392
They wandred ay and stode styll in no stede.	58	Bowge	423
I hate this wayes agayne you that they take!	59	Bowge	471
this] 'these' Wynkyn de Worde 1510			
And by my trouthe, but yf an ende they make,	59	Bowge	473
And as they came, the shypborde faste I hente,	61	Bowge	530
That be so far abusyd /They cannot be excusyd	62	Hauke	6
But that they playe the daw	62	Hauke	8
They rangyd Hankyn Bovy /My churche all abowte.	65	Hauke	117
And of the spyrytuall law /They made but a gewgaw,	66	Hauke	157
That they dyd such a dede,	70	Hauke	300
And nowe they lye and rote;	78	Phy Sparrow	251
Money they shall dele	83	Phy Sparrow	455
The tarsell gentyll, /They shall morne soft and styll	85	Phy Sparrow	559
And how they were sommonde	88	Phy Sparrow	652
And how they rode eche one	88	Phy Sparrow	655
And what they wrote and sayd,	88	Phy Sparrow	680
They ar to diffuse for me:	90	Phy Sparrow	768
His Englyssh whereat they barke	91	Phy Sparrow	798
And mar all they warke;	91	Phy Sparrow	799
Is to discommende /That they cannot amend,	103	Phy Sparrow	1271
Though they wold spend	103	Phy Sparrow	1272
All the wyttes they have.	103	Phy Sparrow	1273
I pray God they be payned	106	Phy Sparrow	1376
Yet, where so ever they ly	106	Epitaphe	I
They shall wirry no mo,	111	Lawde	26
The law they shall not breke;	111	Lawde	30
They shall com to rekening,	111	Lawde	31
They browght them in soche paine.	111	Lawde	35
Therfor no more they shall	111	Lawde	36
Wan they the felde and lost theyr kynge?	115	Ag Scottes	3
They may well say, fye on that wynnynge!	115	Ag Scottes	4
How theyr are blynde /In theyr owne mynde,	115	Ag Scottes	7
They are so stowre, /So frantyke mad,	115	Ag Scottes	12
They say they had /And wan the felde /With spere and shelde!	116	Ag Scottes	14
They say they had /And wan the felde /With spere and shelde!	116	Ag Scottes	14
What ever they say, /Jemmy is ded /And closyd in led,	116	Ag Scottes	20
Cause have they none other /But for that he was brother,	120	Ag Scottes2	13
have they] 'they have' Day 1560, Marshe 1568			
brother] 'hys brother' Day 1560, Marshe 1568			
For, if they understood /His traytourly dispyght,	121	Ag Scottes2	24
Yor moth etyn mokkysh maneres, they be all to-myryd.	123	Garnesche2	12
Of naturys workys, how they be	130	Garnesche5	9
Haroldis they know thy cote-armur;	131	Garnesche5	68
If they wer lyveyng thys day,	133	Garnesche5	142
Of the wote I what they wolde say;	133	Garnesche5	143
They wolde the wryght, all with one stevyn,	133	Garnesche5	144
With thy versyfyeng rayles /How they have tayles.	135	Dundas	31
Yet to lie upon me they can not prevayle.	138	Ven Tongues	31
I care muche the lesse what ever they say,	138	Ven Tongues	36
Malicious tunges, though they have no bones,	138	Ven Tongues	49
Men said they could not their tunges atame;	139	Ven Tongues	60
Then ren they with lesinges, and blow them about,	139	Ven Tongues	69
For, when men by welth, they have lytell drede	140	Magnyfycence	10
Pleasyth, your grace, Felycyte they me call.	145	Magnyfycence	171
By me all persons worke what they lyste.	146	Magnyfycence	210
That no man can scape but they hym cache.	150	Magnyfycence	351
They bare me in hande that I was a spye;	150	Magnyfycence	352
And say they so in very dede?	151	Magnyfycence	378
They have made me here to put the stone;	151	Magnyfycence	406
But nowe wyll I, that they be gone,	151	Magnyfycence	407
To Tyburne, where they hange on hyght.	152	Magnyfycence	423
Wyth golde and grotes they grese my hande,	152	Magnyfycence	432
To counterfet thyr counsell they gyve me a fee.	154	Magnyfycence	491
Thy wordes be but wynde, never they have no wayght.	156	Magnyfycence	578
Se you not howe they prece	156	Magnyfycence	591
Knowe they not me? They are to blame.	157	Magnyfycence	593
Knowe they not me? They are to blame.	157	Magnyfycence	593
And there they wolde ha[v]e me to dwell.	157	Magnyfycence	614
have] 'hane' †Rastell & Treveris C 1530, B			
That they wyll here no man but the fyrst tale.	161	Magnyfycence	743
Thy slyppers they swap it, yet thou fotys it lyke a swanne.	161	Magnyfycence	765
And so they go out of the place.	163	Magnyfycence	SD
Tyll, as the devyll wolde, they fell a chydynge	166	Magnyfycence	940
With Crafty Convayaunce. Ye, dyd they so?	166	Magnyfycence	941
And teche them howe they sholde syt ydyll	174	Magnyfycence	1221
And those be they that come up of nought –	174	Magnyfycence	1240
Suche dawys, what soever they be,	174	Magnyfycence	1242
For they that wyll so bysely smater	175	Magnyfycence	1257
They drove me to lernynge lyke a dull asse.	178	Magnyfycence	1386

	Page	Title	Line
These wordes in myne eyre, they be so lustely spoken,	184	Magnyfycence	1565
They towche me so thorowly and tykyll my consayte,	184	Magnyfycence	1567
But, blessyd be our Lorde, they wyll be sone converted.	184	Magnyfycence	1584
Why, wyll they then be intreted, the most and the lest?	184	Magnyfycence	1585
Here no man what so ever they say	185	Magnyfycence	1603
They catche that catche may, kepe and holde fast,	189	Magnyfycence	1750
I sawe a losell lede a lurden, and they were bothe blynde.	191	Magnyfycence	1824
The bytter sayd boldly that they were to blame;	192	Magnyfycence	1837
Man or woman, of what estate they be,	194	Magnyfycence	1898
With the gowte I make them to grone where they syt;	194	Magnyfycence	1903
And from that they love best some I devorse;	194	Magnyfycence	1905
Theyr chyldren, bycause that they have no mekenesse,	194	Magnyfycence	1924
And yf I se therby they wyll not amende,	194	Magnyfycence	1926
That rule not be mesure that they have in theyr handys,	195	Magnyfycence	1939
Full fewe but they have envy of me.	195	Magnyfycence	1963
They thynke it no shame to robbe and stele;	198	Magnyfycence	2042
Yet were they better to begge, a great dele;	198	Magnyfycence	2043
For by robbynge they rynne to in manus tuas quecke;	198	Magnyfycence	2044
But nowe adayes as huksters they hucke and they stycke,	200	Magnyfycence	2121
But nowe adayes as huksters they hucke and they stycke,	200	Magnyfycence	2121
But so longe they rekyn with theyr reasons amysse	200	Magnyfycence	2127
they] 'theyr' †Rastell & Treveris C 1530, B			
That they lose theyr lyberte and all that there is.	200	Magnyfycence	2128
That they set theyr chyldren to rynne on the brydyll,	200	Magnyfycence	2136
And they never thryve in theyr age, it shall not gretly skyll.	200	Magnyfycence	2138
That nother they set by father and mother;	200	Magnyfycence	2142
Some have so moche lyberte that they fere no synne,	200	Magnyfycence	2143
Tyll, as ye se many tymes, they shame all theyr kynne.	201	Magnyfycence	2144
They cast up theyr obedyence to cache me agayne;	201	Magnyfycence	2148
That lustely they lepe somtyme theyr cloyster wall.	201	Magnyfycence	2150
But they say it is a queysy mete;	204	Magnyfycence	2267
That they wyll fyre one ungracyously in the flanke.	204	Magnyfycence	2270
Som be wrestyd there that they thynke on it forty dayes,	204	Magnyfycence	2274
They molefy so easely my harte that was so harde.	207	Magnyfycence	2346
And sad cyrcumspeccyon to me they have annexyd.	210	Magnyfycence	2463
Accordynge to treuth they be well devysyd.	210	Magnyfycence	2470
Her lewde lyppes twayne, /They slaver, men sayne,	215	El Rummynge	23
For they are blered;	215	El Rummynge	36
Lyke as they were with buckels /Togyder made fast.	215	El Rummynge	46
But drynke tyll they stare	217	El Rummynge	108
They have dronke up my swyllyng tubbe!'	218	El Rummynge	173
For they go to roust, /Streyght over the ale-joust,	219	El Rummynge	191
They holde the hye waye,	221	El Rummynge	259
They care not what men saye!	221	El Rummynge	260
Some renne tyll they swete,	221	El Rummynge	266
They layde to pledge theyr wharrowe,	222	El Rummynge	298
Here was scant thryft /Whan they made suche shyft.	222	El Rummynge	302
They asked never for mete	222	El Rummynge	304
But they were sturdy and stubbed,	225	El Rummynge	422
stubbed] 'stubbled' Kynge & Marche 1554, Day 1560, Marshe 1568			
'They be wretchockes thou hast brought,	226	El Rummynge	465
They] 'The' Day 1560			
They are shyre shakyng nought!'	226	El Rummynge	466
And all this shyfte they make	228	El Rummynge	533
'Dame Elynour,' sayde they,	229	El Rummynge	576
But, whan they shoulde walke,	230	El Rummynge	613
Fresshely they dresse and make swete my bowur,	231	Speke Parott	12
With, 'Speke, Parott, I pray yow,' full curteslye they sey,	231	Speke Parott	13
That they cannot say in Greke, rydynge by the way,	234	Speke Parott	146
Tryvyals and quatryvyals so sore now they appayre,	235	Speke Parott	166
For the cliffes of Scaloppe they rore wellaway,	238	Speke Parott	280
But lewdlye ar they lettyrd that your lernyng lackys,	239	Speke Parott	294
Your rudeness to pardon and also that they wolde	241	Speke Parott	360
Yow to remorde erste or they know your mynde.	241	Speke Parott	370
Som sey they cannot my parables expresse;	242	Speke Parott	386
The nebbis of a lyon they make to trete and trembyll,	243	Speke Parott	424
'The devyll,' they say, 'is dede, /The devyll is dede.'	247	Collyn Clout	36
Or elles they wolde se /Otherwyse,	247	Collyn Clout	39
Alas, they make me shoder,	248	Collyn Clout	68
The prelates ben so haute /They say, and loke so hye	248	Collyn Clout	72
As though they wolde flye /Aboute the sterry skye.	248	Collyn Clout	73
Aboute] 'Above' Kele 1545.1, Marshe 1568, MS Harley 2252			
Howe they take no hede /Theyr sely shepe to fede,	248	Collyn Clout	76
Unneth they leve a locke /Of wolle amongest theyr flocke.	248	Collyn Clout	80
They gaspe and they gape /All to have promocyon;	248	Collyn Clout	85
They gaspe and they gape /All to have promocyon;	248	Collyn Clout	85
For sothe, they are to lewde /To say so, all beshrewde!	249	Collyn Clout	90
What trowe ye they say more /Of the bysshoppes lore?	249	Collyn Clout	92
Howe in matters they ben rawe,	249	Collyn Clout	94
They lumber forth the lawe	249	Collyn Clout	95
To herken Jacke and Gyll /Whan they put up a byll;	249	Collyn Clout	97
And judge it as they wyll, /For other mens skyll,	249	Collyn Clout	98
In theyr pryncypall cure /They make but lytell sure,	249	Collyn Clout	103
Men say they have prescrypcyons	249	Collyn Clout	112
I wote never howe they warke,	249	Collyn Clout	119
And surely thus they sey:	249	Collyn Clout	121
'Bysshoppes, yf they may,	249	Collyn Clout	122
But the greatest parte /Is for they have but small arte	250	Collyn Clout	139

THEY —THEY	Page	Title	Line
But this reason they take:	250	Collyn Clout	142
Howe they are able to make /With theyr golde and treasure	250	Collyn Clout	143
But they are lothe to mell,	250	Collyn Clout	162
They are fayne to play deuz decke.	250	Collyn Clout	166
Howebeit they are good men,	251	Collyn Clout	167
Theyr lessons forgoten they have	251	Collyn Clout	169
Men say, they had rather	251	Collyn Clout	175
They make her wynche and kycke,	251	Collyn Clout	181
Lyke houndes of hell, /They crye and they yell	251	Collyn Clout	199
Lyke houndes of hell, /They crye and they yell	251	Collyn Clout	199
Thus they make theyr boost /Through every coost,	251	Collyn Clout	202
But whan they have ones caught	252	Collyn Clout	229
Then renne they in every stede,	252	Collyn Clout	231
Yet take they cure of soules,	252	Collyn Clout	233
cure] 'cures' Kele 1545.1, Marshe 1568			
For that they are nat apposed	253	Collyn Clout	265
They have none instructyon	253	Collyn Clout	268
What are they the worse?	254	Collyn Clout	295
What care they thoughe Gyll swete,	254	Collyn Clout	321
The poore people they yoke	254	Collyn Clout	323
Howe warely they wrangle!	255	Collyn Clout	331
Full falsely on you they lye,	255	Collyn Clout	334
And thus they hurte theyr soules,	255	Collyn Clout	341
And all the faute they lay	256	Collyn Clout	402
the faute] not in Kele 1545.1, Marshe 1568			
And all that they have elles.	257	Collyn Clout	411
Your workes, they say, are straunge -	257	Collyn Clout	420
Ye lyve, they say, in delyte, /Drowned in deliciis,	257	Collyn Clout	441
Or elles they are madde	259	Collyn Clout	503
Howe they are to blame	259	Collyn Clout	509
And of resyde[v]acyon /They make enterpretacyon	259	Collyn Clout	522
resydevacyon] 'resdenacyon' †Godfray 1531, Kele 1545.1, Marshe 1568			
And they have to lytell,	260	Collyn Clout	558
They commune lyke sottes,	260	Collyn Clout	564
sottes] 'scottes' Marshe 1568, 'sottes' MS Harley 2252			
Of parsons and vycaryes /They make many outcryes:	261	Collyn Clout	571
'They can nat kepe theyr wyves	261	Collyn Clout	572
They mought be better advysed	261	Collyn Clout	579
But they have enterprysed /And shamfully surmysed	261	Collyn Clout	581
Yf they well understode	262	Collyn Clout	616
understode] 'understand' Marshe 1568			
They wolde pype you another daunce.	262	Collyn Clout	618
But noble men borne, /To lerne they have scorne,	262	Collyn Clout	620
Of bysshoppes they chat,	263	Collyn Clout	672
Your eeres they be stopped!	263	Collyn Clout	678
They folowe your desyris,	263	Collyn Clout	683
And so they blere your eye	263	Collyn Clout	684
So as they myght be /Compendyously conveyed,	265	Collyn Clout	767
What they do in hell.	267	Collyn Clout	823
What they do in heven;	267	Collyn Clout	825
Lothe they are to lese	267	Collyn Clout	841
But they theyr tonges fyle,	267	Collyn Clout	850
Howe they have no fraude.	267	Collyn Clout	853
fraude] 'faude' †Godfray 1531, 'fawte' MS Harley 2252			
And somtyme they provoke	268	Collyn Clout	854
That they ought by the lawe	268	Collyn Clout	857
God wotte, they take great payne	268	Collyn Clout	860
Agaynst curates, they repyne,	268	Collyn Clout	873
They] not in Kele 1545.1, Marshe 1568, 'They' MS Harley 2252			
For they must take in hande	268	Collyn Clout	888
They say, to do corrections,	268	Collyn Clout	892
But they have no affections	268	Collyn Clout	893
affections] 'afflictions' Kele 1545.1, 'affeccions' Harley 2252			
Men say, they bere no faces	269	Collyn Clout	896
And they be so attaynted	269	Collyn Clout	900
That they be deefe and dum,	269	Collyn Clout	903
They occupy them so /With syngynge Placebo,	269	Collyn Clout	906
They wyll no farder go.	269	Collyn Clout	908
They had lever to please	269	Collyn Clout	909
As they were very sayntes.	269	Collyn Clout	921
They shewe them polytyke,	269	Collyn Clout	923
For they wyll have no losse	269	Collyn Clout	928
And as farre as they dare set,	269	Collyn Clout	932
Howe they ryde in goodly chares,	270	Collyn Clout	961
Howebeit they let downe fall	271	Collyn Clout	978
They renne agaynst the steple,	271	Collyn Clout	983
That they have great wonder	271	Collyn Clout	1006
Yet they mervayle so moche lesse,	271	Collyn Clout	1008
As they suppose and gesse,	271	Collyn Clout	1010
That they shall mell nor make,	271	Collyn Clout	1015
But they wyl talke of suche uncouthes,	272	Collyn Clout	1052
All that ever they ken	272	Collyn Clout	1053
They put you to your actyon.	273	Collyn Clout	1060
And whether they say trewly	273	Collyn Clout	1061
As they may byde therby,	273	Collyn Clout	1062
Or elles that they do lye,	273	Collyn Clout	1063

THEY —THEY	Page	Title	Line
They say they wyll you cast.	273	Collyn Clout	1070
They say they wyll you cast.	273	Collyn Clout	1070
Great ydeottes they be,	274	Collyn Clout	1130
And lytell grace they have	274	Collyn Clout	1131
To do shame, they have no shame;	275	Collyn Clout	1141
But they wolde no man shuld them blame.	275	Collyn Clout	1142
They have an evyll name,	275	Collyn Clout	1143
But yet they wyll occupye the same.	275	Collyn Clout	1144
They counte it for a raylynge	275	Collyn Clout	1147
'Shall they taunt us prelates,	275	Collyn Clout	1150
taunt] 'daunt' Kele 1545.1, Marshe 1568, 'teche' MS Harley 2252			
They set nat by us a shyttell;	276	Collyn Clout	1185
shytell] 'whystell' Kele 1545.1, Marshe 1568, 'shetyll' MS Harley 2252			
They counte us for lyars;	276	Collyn Clout	1187
They carpe of us lyke crakers;	276	Collyn Clout	1189
They say many matters be borne	276	Collyn Clout	1198
Lest they be Seduces,	277	Collyn Clout	1229
Seduces] 'Saducies' Marshe 1568, 'Adusayes' MS Harley 2252			
As they be sad sayne,	277	Collyn Clout	1230
sad] 'sayd' Kele 1545.1, Marshe 1568			
And so it semeth they play,	277	Collyn Clout	1234
Whan they be infected,	277	Collyn Clout	1236
They may garlycke pyll,	281	Why Come Ye	109
Or pescoddes they may shyll,	281	Why Come Ye	111
Wote ye whyther they went?	282	Why Come Ye	146
That they are but halfe men;	283	Why Come Ye	163
They kepe them in theyr holdes	283	Why Come Ye	167
But yet they over-shote us	283	Why Come Ye	169
They shote all at one marke:	283	Why Come Ye	174
They shote all at that!	283	Why Come Ye	176
They] 'Thy' †Kele 1545.3			
They shote at him with crownes.	283	Why Come Ye	178
They make him so amased,	283	Why Come Ye	180
Syt styll as they were dom.	283	Why Come Ye	199
They were nat payde their hyre.	285	Why Come Ye	248
They are fel as any fyre!	285	Why Come Ye	249
They have layde all in the myre.	285	Why Come Ye	251
They grugyd and sayde	285	Why Come Ye	252
Some sayde they were afrayde	285	Why Come Ye	254
They were, whan they were next.	285	Why Come Ye	260
they] 'the' †Kele 1545.3			
They were, whan they were next.	285	Why Come Ye	260
they] 'the' †Kele 1545.3			
They make us all sottes,	285	Why Come Ye	263
They make us to pyll strawes;	285	Why Come Ye	265
They play their olde pranckes /After Huntley Bankes.	285	Why Come Ye	266
They dyd us a shrewde turne,	285	Why Come Ye	269
To well they do agre,	286	Why Come Ye	278
Into a mouse hole they wolde	286	Why Come Ye	293
They must stande all afar	286	Why Come Ye	301
He sayth they have no brayne	286	Why Come Ye	310
He sayth, they are to seke	287	Why Come Ye	317
They have slain our Englisshmen	288	Why Come Ye	372
No better they agre!	288	Why Come Ye	375
Thus dayly they be decked, /Taunted and checked,	294	Why Come Ye	611
That they are so wo	294	Why Come Ye	613
They wot not whether to go.	294	Why Come Ye	614
And thus they shall syt –	295	Why Come Ye	633
They can nat well tell	295	Why Come Ye	648
Whan they with hym shulde mell,	295	Why Come Ye	649
Tell you the rest; for me they shal.	296	Why Come Ye	709
They have the full intellygence,	297	Why Come Ye	710
And beggers they ban,	301	Why Come Ye	891
And they cursed Datan	301	Why Come Ye	892
they cursed] 'the course' MS Rawlinson C. 813			
They are happy that wynnys,	302	Why Come Ye	927
They growwe very ranke	304	Why Come Ye	1001
They play nat all clene,	304	Why Come Ye	1006
Bycause they have proclamed	305	Why Come Ye	1055
Or els his surgions they lye;	308	Why Come Ye	1171
For as far as they can spy	308	Why Come Ye	1172
they] 'the' †Kele 1545.3			
In figure wherof they were the laurell grene.	314	Garlande	68
they were the] 'the were they' †Fakes 1523			
Some famous wetewoldis, and they be moche wurs;	317	Garlande	187
Yet they ryde and rinne from Carlyll to Kent.	317	Garlande	196
they ryde and rinne] 'ryde they and ryn they' MS Cotton Vitellius E.x			
Eyther they wyll say he is to wyse,	318	Garlande	204
wyll] 'shall' MS Cotton Vitellius E.x			
They presid in faste; some thought they were to longe;	319	Garlande	248
They presid in faste; some thought they were to longe;	319	Garlande	248
Lyke to the boryall wyndes whan they blowe,	319	Garlande	261
And of there bounte they made me godely chere	323	Garlande	398
So finally, when they had shewyd there devyse,	324	Garlande	442
And ever they presed on me more and more,	324	Garlande	445

	Page	Title	Line
Tyll at the last they forcyd me sore,	324	Garlande	446
sore] 'so sore' Marshe 1568			
That with them I went where they wolde me brynge,	324	Garlande	447
Dame Pallas commaundid that they shold me convay	325	Garlande	449
Jacinctis and smaragdis out of the florthe they grew.	325	Garlande	480
When they were past and wente forth on there way,	327	Garlande	526
They had wrytyng, sum Greke, sum Ebrew,	328	Garlande	582
And turne home ageyne, for they cam al to late.	329	Garlande	605
Pope holy ypocrytis, as they were golde and hole,	329	Garlande	612
Hither they come crowdyng to get them a name,	329	Garlande	621
But hailid they be homwarde with sorow and shame.	329	Garlande	622
Bowns, bowns, bowns! that all they out cryde.	329	Garlande	624
That ever more after by it they were aspyid;	329	Garlande	627
With a pellit of pevisshenes they had suche a stroke,	330	Garlande	637
They made, with chapellettes and garlandes grene;	331	Garlande	684
Of men and of bestis, and whereof they begone,	331	Garlande	692
But if they were counterfettes that women them call,	334	Garlande	785
And truly of theyr bownte thus were they bent	334	Garlande	806
And for your sake how fast to warke they fall:	335	Garlande	811
Into that place where as they left me,	343	Garlande	1103
But when they sawe my lawrell rychely wrought,	343	Garlande	1105
All other besyde were counterfete they thought	343	Garlande	1106
All ... counterfete] 'that they ware were counterfettis' MS Cotton Vitellius E.x			
Of this warke they had so great delyght,	343	Garlande	1110
They seyd my lawrell was the goodlyest	343	Garlande	1112
That ever they saw, and wrought it was the best.	343	Garlande	1113
Of Englande, his workis here they begynne:	345	Garlande	1171
And suche as be counterfettis they be reservyd;	346	Garlande	1190
Is to discommende /That they can not amende,	348	Garlande	1264
Though they wolde spende	348	Garlande	1265
All the wittis they have.	348	Garlande	1266
I pray God they be paynyd	350	Garlande	1369
Whiche, if they be happy, have cause to beware	353	Garlande	1474
'Triumpha, triumpha!' they cryid all aboute.	354	Garlande	1506
If they can spy /Circumspectly	356	Garlande	1579
they] 'thy' †Fakes 1523			
They can not come agayne.	358	Garlande2	15
But yet they were bolde	364	Albany	202
They fynde his grace so kynde;	371	Albany	483
They fledde full cowardly.	371	Albany	515
whan they have delectably lycked a lytell	373	Replycacion	I
and whan they have ones superciliusly caught	374	Replycacion	I
They tumble so in theology,	374	Replycacion	5
That they juge them selfe able to be	374	Replycacion	7
For all that they preche and teche	374	Replycacion	12
Finally they fall to carefull confusyon,	374	Replycacion	15
Thus are they undone and utterly shamed.	374	Replycacion	17
and yet they were but febly enformed	374	Replycacion	I
howbeit they were puffed so full	375	Replycacion	I
And feare leest they be out	380	Replycacion	225
They saye howe latria is an honour grete,	381	Replycacion	282

THEYM

	Page	Title	Line
Lete theym go lowse theym, in the devylles date.	59	Bowge	455
Lete theym go lowse theym, in the devylles date.	59	Bowge	455
How be it, mayden Meed /Made theym to be agreed;	65	Hauke	150
I have red theym poll by poll	67	Hauke	211

THEYR

	Page	Title	Line
He bresyth theyr braynpannys and makyth them to swell,	43	Balettys2	31
By theyr conusaunce knowing how they serve a wily py:	43	Balettys2	34
Lodestar to lyght these lovers to theyr porte,	44	Balettys3	25
Gayne dangerous stormys theyr anker of supporte,	44	Balettys3	26
Theyr sayll of solace most comfortably clad,	44	Balettys3	27
Wherby I rede theyr renome and theyr fame	46	Bowge	15
Wherby I rede theyr renome and theyr fame	46	Bowge	15
With other foure of theyr affynyte:	50	Bowge	139
Fortune theyr frende, with whome oft she dyde daunce:	50	Bowge	141
I dempte and drede theyr talkynge was not good.	58	Bowge	426
To let theyr hawkys fly	70	Hauke	301
The leopardes savage, /The lyons in theyr rage,	79	Phy Sparrow	287
Myght catche the in theyr pawes,	79	Phy Sparrow	288
And gnawe the in theyr jawes!	79	Phy Sparrow	289
That shall be theyr charge;	83	Phy Sparrow	457
As provost pryncypall, /To teach them theyr ordynall;	85	Phy Sparrow	555
In theyr amysse of gray;	85	Phy Sparrow	560
That was all theyr joye,	88	Phy Sparrow	674
And of theyr wanton wylles,	88	Phy Sparrow	681
Theyr names shall never dye.	106	Epitaphe	I
That never wyll leve theyr tratlynge:	115	Ag Scottes	2
Wan they the felde and lost theyr kynge?	115	Ag Scottes	3
How they are blynde /In theyr owne mynde,	115	Ag Scottes	8
And wyll not know /Theyr overthrow /At Branxton More?	115	Ag Scottes	10
That was theyr owne kynge. /Fy on that wynnyng!	116	Ag Scottes	23
Slew all the floure /Of theyr honoure.	116	Ag Scottes	28
By hole consent of theyr senate,	131	Garnesche5	83
And flatered them with fables fayre before theyr face,	160	Magnyfycence	717
And tolde all the myschef I coude behynde theyr backe,	160	Magnyfycence	718
This theyr desyre, /This newe atyre.	165	Magnyfycence	887

	Page	Title	Line
To pyke theyr fyngers all the day longe;	174	Magnyfycence	1222
So in theyr eyre I synge them a songe	174	Magnyfycence	1223
I make hym lese moche of theyr strength;	175	Magnyfycence	1259
For thou fourmest suche fantasyes in theyr mynde	175	Magnyfycence	1284
As malypert tavernars that checke with theyr betters,	178	Magnyfycence	1362
Theyr conveyaunce weltyth the worke all by wyll;	178	Magnyfycence	1363
Tyll all theyr conveyaunce is turnyd into madnesse.	178	Magnyfycence	1367
By theyr demenaunce, nor loss repryvable.	179	Magnyfycence	1419
That Israell releysyd of theyr captyvyte,	181	Magnyfycence	1474
Them that dare put theyr truste in me;	188	Magnyfycence	1699
And in theyr moste truste I make them overthrowe.	193	Magnyfycence	1885
That folowe theyr fansyes in foly to fall.	194	Magnyfycence	1897
An all is for theyr ungracyous lyfe.	194	Magnyfycence	1915
Bycause I wolde prove men of theyr pacyence.	194	Magnyfycence	1917
And suffre theyr chyldren to have theyr entent,	194	Magnyfycence	1921
And suffre theyr chyldren to have theyr entent,	194	Magnyfycence	1921
Them or theyr chyldren ofte tymes I dysmembre;	194	Magnyfycence	1923
Theyr children, bycause that they have no mekenesse,	194	Magnyfycence	1924
I vysyte theyr faders and moders with sekenesse;	194	Magnyfycence	1925
Than from theyr chyldren to spare the rod	194	Magnyfycence	1929
Of correccyon, but let them have theyr wyll.	194	Magnyfycence	1930
Of some of theyr chyldren I stryke out the eye;	194	Magnyfycence	1933
That rule not be mesure that they have in theyr handys,	195	Magnyfycence	1939
That sadly rule not theyr howsholde men.	195	Magnyfycence	1940
Because of theyr neglygence and of theyr wanton vagys,	195	Magnyfycence	1942
Because of theyr neglygence and of theyr wanton vagys,	195	Magnyfycence	1942
Then for to begge theyr mete for charyte.	198	Magnyfycence	2041
But so longe they rekyn with theyr reasons amysse they] 'theyr' †Rastell & Treveris C 1530, B	200	Magnyfycence	2127
That they lose theyr lyberte and all that there is.	200	Magnyfycence	2128
And some in the worlde, theyr brayne is so ydyll	200	Magnyfycence	2135
That they set theyr chyldren to rynne on the brydyll,	200	Magnyfycence	2136
In youth to be wanton, and let them have theyr wyll -	200	Magnyfycence	2137
And they never thryve in theyr age, it shall not gretly skyll.	200	Magnyfycence	2138
Tyll, as ye se many tymes, they shame all theyr kynne.	201	Magnyfycence	2144
That nonnes wyl leve theyr holynes and ryn after me;	201	Magnyfycence	2146
They cast up theyr obedyence to cache me agayne;	201	Magnyfycence	2148
That lustely they lepe somtyme theyr cloyster wall.	201	Magnyfycence	2150
So shamfully to me, theyr mayster, to aproche,	205	Magnyfycence	2279
Cysly and Sare, /With theyr legges bare,	217	El Rummynge	120
And also theyr fete /Hardely full unswete;	217	El Rummynge	121
Wyth theyr heles dagged, /Theyr kyrtelles all to-jagged,	217	El Rummynge	123
Wyth theyr heles dagged, /Theyr kyrtelles all to-jagged,	217	El Rummynge	124
Theyr smockes all to-ragged, /Wyth tytters and tatters,	217	El Rummynge	125
With all theyr myght runnynge /To Elynour Rummynge,	217	El Rummynge	128
Wyth naked pappes, /That flyppes and flappes,	217	El Rummynge	135
Some with a sho clout /Bynde theyr heddes about;	218	El Rummynge	144
Theyr lockes aboute theyr face,	218	El Rummynge	146
Theyr lockes aboute theyr face,	218	El Rummynge	146
Theyr tresses untrust, /All full of unlust;	218	El Rummynge	147
For theyr ale to pay;	218	El Rummynge	162
Some fyll theyr pot full /Of good Lemster woll.	220	El Rummynge	251
Some layde to pledge /Theyr hatchet and theyr wedge,	221	El Rummynge	294
Some layde to pledge /Theyr hatchet and theyr wedge,	221	El Rummynge	294
Theyr hekell and theyr rele,	222	El Rummynge	295
Theyr hekell and theyr rele,	222	El Rummynge	295
Theyr rocke, theyr spynnyng whele.	222	El Rummynge	296
Theyr rocke, theyr spynnyng whele.	222	El Rummynge	296
They layde to pledge theyr wharrowe,	222	El Rummynge	298
Theyr rybskyn and theyr spyndell,	222	El Rummynge	299
Theyr rybskyn and theyr spyndell,	222	El Rummynge	299
Theyr nedell and theyr thymbell:	222	El Rummynge	300
Theyr nedell and theyr thymbell:	222	El Rummynge	300
Theyr thrust was so great,	222	El Rummynge	303
Some brought theyr clyppyng sheres,	225	El Rummynge	439
Some brought theyr husbands hat,	225	El Rummynge	442
But reason and wytte wantythe theyr provynciall,	232	Speke Parott	53
Som trete of theyr tirykis, som of astrology,	234	Speke Parott	137
But our Grekis theyr Greke so well have applyed,	234	Speke Parott	145
Settyng theyr myndys so moche of eloquens,	235	Speke Parott	181
That of theyr scole maters lost is the hole sentens.	235	Speke Parott	182
Howe they take no hede /Theyr sely shepe to fede,	248	Collyn Clout	77
But plucke away and pull /Theyr fleces of wull.	248	Collyn Clout	79
Unneth they leve a locke /Of wolle amongest theyr flocke.	248	Collyn Clout	81
And as for theyr connynge, /A glommynge and a mommynge,	248	Collyn Clout	82
There is theyr hole devocyon,	248	Collyn Clout	87
Expoundynge out theyr clauses, /And leve theyr owne causes.	249	Collyn Clout	100
Expoundynge out theyr clauses, /And leve theyr owne causes.	249	Collyn Clout	101
In theyr pryncypall cure /They make but lytell sure,	249	Collyn Clout	102
In theyr jurysdictyons,	249	Collyn Clout	110
To fatte theyr bodyes full,	250	Collyn Clout	128
Theyr soules lame and dull;	250	Collyn Clout	129
Howe evyll theyr shepe fare.'	250	Collyn Clout	131
And ryght slender connynge /Within theyr heedes wonnynge.	250	Collyn Clout	141
Howe they are able to make /With theyr golde and treasure	250	Collyn Clout	144
As appereth by theyr werkes,	250	Collyn Clout	151
To wary and to kepe /From theyr goostly shepe,	250	Collyn Clout	155
And theyr spyrytuall lambes /Sequestred from rambes	250	Collyn Clout	156

	Page	Title	Line
And from the berded gotes /With theyr heery cotes;	250	Collyn Clout	159
Set nought by golde ne grotes, /Theyr names yf I durst tell.	250	Collyn Clout	161
Theyr lessons forgoten they have	251	Collyn Clout	169
Spende moche of theyr share	251	Collyn Clout	176
Thus they make theyr boost /Through every coost,	251	Collyn Clout	202
Theyr matyns madly sayde, /Nothynge devoutly prayde,	252	Collyn Clout	238
Theyr lernynge is so small,	252	Collyn Clout	240
Theyr prymes and houres fall	252	Collyn Clout	241
And lepe out of theyr lyppes	252	Collyn Clout	242
Some can nat declyne theyr name!	253	Collyn Clout	276
Theyr shall no clergye appose	254	Collyn Clout	291
God wotte, to theyr great paynes,	254	Collyn Clout	313
Theyr tabertes of fyne sylke;	254	Collyn Clout	316
Theyr styrops of myxt golde begared,	254	Collyn Clout	317
begared] 'begarded' Marshe 1568, 'be gloryd' MS Harley 2252			
Theyr moyles golde dothe eate,	254	Collyn Clout	319
Theyr neyghbours dye for meate.	254	Collyn Clout	320
And thus they hurte theyr soules,	255	Collyn Clout	341
And to forsake theyr corum	256	Collyn Clout	377
Out of theyr cloyster and quere /With an hevy chere,	256	Collyn Clout	394
Must cast up theyr blacke vayles	256	Collyn Clout	396
And set up theyr fucke sayles	256	Collyn Clout	397
fucke sayles] 'flucke sayles' †Godfray 1531, 'fulke saylys' MS Harley 2252			
To catche wynde with theyr ventayles.	256	Collyn Clout	398
Plucke away the leedes /Over theyr heedes,	257	Collyn Clout	409
And sell away theyr belles	257	Collyn Clout	410
So that theyr founders soules	257	Collyn Clout	421
Have lost theyr bedde roules;	257	Collyn Clout	422
bedde] 'beade' Kele 1545.1, 'bede' MS Harley 2252			
The money for theyr masses	257	Collyn Clout	423
Theyr dyriges are forgotten,	257	Collyn Clout	425
Theyr dyriges] 'The Diriges' Kele 1545.1, 'the dyrige' MS Harley 2252			
Theyr founders lye there rotten;	257	Collyn Clout	426
But where theyr soules dwell,	257	Collyn Clout	427
Presumyng on theyr owne wytte,	259	Collyn Clout	515
owne] not in Marshe 1568			
And in theyr fury hoppe,	259	Collyn Clout	529
Whan the good ale soppe /Dothe daunce in theyr foretoppe;	260	Collyn Clout	531
That agaynst preesthode /Theyr malyce sprede abrode,	260	Collyn Clout	535
agaynst] 'agayn' Marshe 1568			
Of preestly dygnytes /By theyr malygnytes.	260	Collyn Clout	539
By] 'But' Kele 1545.1, Marshe 1568			
As cometh to theyr lottes,	260	Collyn Clout	565
'They can nat kepe theyr wyves	261	Collyn Clout	572
From them for theyr lyves!'	261	Collyn Clout	573
Theyr rule is very small,	261	Collyn Clout	609
And mocke them to theyr face.	262	Collyn Clout	625
And breke theyr hose at the kne,	262	Collyn Clout	629
And have theyr lyberte,	264	Collyn Clout	712
Theyr covent to encrease.	267	Collyn Clout	847
But they theyr tonges fyle,	267	Collyn Clout	850
Theyr dewtyes to withdrawe,	268	Collyn Clout	856
Theyr curates to content	268	Collyn Clout	858
And by Dudum, theyr Clementyne,	268	Collyn Clout	872
Theyr hertes are so faynted,	269	Collyn Clout	899
And take theyr worldly ease	269	Collyn Clout	910
With all solempnyte, /For theyr indempnyte;	269	Collyn Clout	927
Of theyr predyall landes,	269	Collyn Clout	930
That cometh to theyr handes;	269	Collyn Clout	931
Buyldynge royally /Theyr mancyons curyously,	269	Collyn Clout	935
Theyr chambres well sene,	270	Collyn Clout	955
And by unycornes /With theyr semely hornes;	270	Collyn Clout	965
Theyr courage to abate	270	Collyn Clout	973
Theyr chambre thus to dresse	270	Collyn Clout	975
Theyr churches cathedrall.	271	Collyn Clout	979
Theyr tonges thus do clap;	273	Collyn Clout	1058
And put them out of theyr place.	273	Collyn Clout	1078
To refourme theyr neglygence,	275	Collyn Clout	1138
To theyr owne dampnacyon.	275	Collyn Clout	1140
That be theyr prymates?	275	Collyn Clout	1151
Nat so hardy on theyr pates!	275	Collyn Clout	1152
Of theyr dronken nolles,	277	Collyn Clout	1242
Nor of theyr noddy polles,	277	Collyn Clout	1243
Nor of theyr sely soules,	277	Collyn Clout	1244
And some theyr hedes mew.	280	Why Come Ye	61
some] not in Toy 1553, Kitson 1560.7, Marshe 1568			
And mad theyr hertes attaynted.	282	Why Come Ye	158
And theyr courage abated,	283	Why Come Ye	162
Lyke foxes in theyr denne,	283	Why Come Ye	164
They kepe them in theyr holdes	283	Why Come Ye	167
Oute of theyr stronge townes	283	Why Come Ye	177
That occupy theyr holys;	285	Why Come Ye	245
Theyr wages were nat payde.	285	Why Come Ye	253
For all theyr crack and bost,	285	Why Come Ye	256
crack] 'crake' †Kele 1545.3, Toy 1553, Marshe 1568			
Theyr wyttes, he saith, are dull;	286	Why Come Ye	309

THEYRE —THEM | Page | Title | Line

	Page	Title	Line
Theyr astate to mayntayne;	286	Why Come Ye	311
And maketh them to bow theyr kne /Before his majeste.	286	Why Come Ye	312
maketh them] 'make' Toy 1553, Kitson 1560.7, Marshe 1568			
In pletynge of theyr case	287	Why Come Ye	318
Dare nat set theyr penne	287	Why Come Ye	323
Wherwith the Sodomites /Lost theyr inward syghtes.	291	Why Come Ye	471
By theyr cyrcumspection,	298	Why Come Ye	768
And theyr sad dyrection,	298	Why Come Ye	769
Of theyr game it is sene	304	Why Come Ye	1005
Some carefull cokwoldes, some have theyr wyves curs;	317	Garlande	186
Well gydyng ther glowtonn to kepe streit theyr sylk,	334	Garlande	795
ther] 'the' MS Cotton Vitellius E.x			
Sum pirlyng of goldde theyr worke to encrese	334	Garlande	796
And truly of theyr bownte thus were they bent	334	Garlande	806
For all theyr boost,	359	Albany	11

THEYRE

	Page	Title	Line
Theyre browys all to-brokyn, such clappys they cach;	43	Balettys2	32
Suwed to Fortune that she wold be theyre frynde.	49	Bowge	121

THEYS

	Page	Title	Line
Theys lythers I lerne them for to lere,	175	Magnyfycence	1268
'Forsothe,' quod she, 'theys be haskardis and rebawdis,	329	Garlande	607
haskardis] 'hastardis' †Fakes 1523			
Now by theys names thre,	350	Garlande	1356

THEKE

	Page	Title	Line
Plucke down lede and theke with tyle;	169	Magnyfycence	1026

THEM

	Page	Title	Line
He calde upon them, as menyall houshold men:	30	Dol Dethe	33
Unkindly thei slew hym that help them oft at nede.	30	Dol Dethe	47
help] 'holp' Marshe 1568			
Yet shamfully thei slew hym; that sham most them befall.	30	Dol Dethe	49
Of them demaunded and asked by the kynge;	31	Dol Dethe	79
They buskt them on a bushment them selfe in baile to bringe	31	Dol Dethe	81
And lyke marciall Hector he faught them agayne	31	Dol Dethe	88
Vigorously upon them with myght and with mayne,	31	Dol Dethe	89
Yet whils he stode he gave them woundes wyde.	32	Dol Dethe	101
Yet] 'Ye' Marshe 1568			
For cruell[y] amonge them ther he was slayne.	32	Dol Dethe	105
cruell] 'cruell' †MS Royal 18 D.ii, Marshe 1568			
Bot by them to knoulege ye may attayne	32	Dol Dethe	129
He techyth them so wysely to solf and to fayne	38	Coystrowne1	53
That he dryvyth them doune with dyntys on ther day-wach.	43	Balettys2	30
He bresyth theyr braynpannys and makyth them to swell,	43	Balettys2	31
Whose jalawsy malycyous makyth them to lepe the hach!	43	Balettys2	33
And I with them prayed her to have in mynde.	49	Bowge	123
With them to make solace and pleasure;	50	Bowge	144
Were I as you, I wolde ryde them full nere;	59	Bowge	472
That shall them angre, I holde thereon a grote,	59	Bowge	475
In them be no scolys /For braynsycke frantycke folys:	68	Hauke	248
God send them sorowe and shame!	78	Phy Sparrow	277
Myght fede them on thy braynes!	79	Phy Sparrow	295
As provost pryncypall, /To teach them theyr ordynall;	85	Phy Sparrow	555
The sacre with them shall say	85	Phy Sparrow	561
And them to despyse	87	Phy Sparrow	624
What ayle them to deprave /Phillip Sparowes grave?	103	Phy Sparrow	1274
No man for them wil speke.	111	Lawde	32
They browght them in soche paine.	111	Lawde	35
To touche them with tauntes of your armony,	117	Ag Scottes	86
We have well eased them of the bottes.	120	Ag Scottes	171
With trechery ye them betray.	130	Garnesche5	38
Then let them vale a bonet of their proud sayle,	138	Ven Tongues	32
Then ren they with lesinges, and blow them about,	139	Ven Tongues	69
Where as ye have, syr, to me them assygned,	145	Magnyfycence	177
Suche order I trust with them for to take,	145	Magnyfycence	178
To gete me fro them I had moche warke.	150	Magnyfycence	361
Thus make I them wyth thryft to fyght.	152	Magnyfycence	421
Monkys may not for drede that men sholde them se.	154	Magnyfycence	493
And flatered them with fables fayre before theyr face,	160	Magnyfycence	717
I make them to startyll and sparkyll lyke a bronde;	161	Magnyfycence	741
I move them, I mase them, I make them so fonde,	161	Magnyfycence	742
I move them, I mase them, I make them so fonde,	161	Magnyfycence	742
I move them, I mase them, I make them so fonde,	161	Magnyfycence	742
This ladyes have, /I it them gave.	165	Magnyfycence	890
Fyrst I lay before them my bybyll	174	Magnyfycence	1220
And teche them howe they sholde syt ydyll	174	Magnyfycence	1221
So in theyr eyre I synge them a songe	174	Magnyfycence	1223
And make them so longe to muse	174	Magnyfycence	1224
That some of them renneth strayght to the stuse.	174	Magnyfycence	1225
For with foly so do I them lede	175	Magnyfycence	1260
Theys lythers I lerne them for to lere,	175	Magnyfycence	1268
And I Foly bryngeth them to qui fuit gadde;	176	Magnyfycence	1301
With qui fuit brayne seke I have them brought;	176	Magnyfycence	1302
And some wyll take upon them to conterfet letters,	178	Magnyfycence	1364
That ratyd the Romaynes and made them yll rest,	181	Magnyfycence	1481
I set not by the prowdest of them a prane,	181	Magnyfycence	1489
It wolde not become them with me for to mell;	182	Magnyfycence	1497
Nor none so hardy of them with me that durste crake,	182	Magnyfycence	1513
But I shall frounce them on the foretop and gar them to quake.	182	Magnyfycence	1514
But I shall frounce them on the foretop and gar them to quake.	182	Magnyfycence	1514

	Page	Title	Line
Them that dare put theyr truste in me;	188	Magnyfycence	1699
And let all your fansyes upon them rest.	190	Magnyfycence	1770
Spare for no cost to gyve them pounde and peny;	190	Magnyfycence	1771
Gyve them more than ynoughe, and let them not lacke;	190	Magnyfycence	1773
Gyve them more than ynoughe, and let them not lacke;	190	Magnyfycence	1773
And as for all other, let them trusse and packe;	190	Magnyfycence	1774
Let neyther patent scape them nor fee;	190	Magnyfycence	1776
For the[m] shall you have at lyberte to lowte.	190	Magnyfycence	1779
them] 'then' †Rastell & Treveris C 1530, B			
Let them have all, and the other go without;	190	Magnyfycence	1780
And with a lyme rodde I toke them bothe togyder.	191	Magnyfycence	1815
I rushe at them rughly and make them ly full lowe;	193	Magnyfycence	1884
I rushe at them rughly and make them ly full lowe;	193	Magnyfycence	1884
And in theyr moste truste I make them overthrowe.	193	Magnyfycence	1885
Lo, syrs, thus I handell them all	194	Magnyfycence	1896
I counsayle them beware of adversyte.	194	Magnyfycence	1899
I vysyte them somtyme with blaynes and with sores;	194	Magnyfycence	1901
With botches and carbuckyls in care I them knyt;	194	Magnyfycence	1902
With the gowte I make them to grone where they syt;	194	Magnyfycence	1903
Some with the marmoll to halte I them make;	194	Magnyfycence	1906
To gyde them vertuously that wyll not remembre,	194	Magnyfycence	1922
Them or theyr chyldren ofte tymes I dysmembre;	194	Magnyfycence	1923
Then myschefe sodaynly I them sende;	194	Magnyfycence	1927
Of correccyon, but let them have theyr wyll.	194	Magnyfycence	1930
I am Goddys preposytour; I prynt them with a pen;	195	Magnyfycence	1941
I vysyte them and stryke them with many sore plagys.	195	Magnyfycence	1943
I vysyte them and stryke them with many sore plagys.	195	Magnyfycence	1943
Where is nowe my golde upon them that I spent?	198	Magnyfycence	2058
I am presydent of pryncys; I prycke them with pryde.	199	Magnyfycence	2082
Largely rewardynge them that have deservyd;	200	Magnyfycence	2119
In youth to be wanton, and let them have theyr wyll -	200	Magnyfycence	2137
Freers, with foly I make them so fayne	201	Magnyfycence	2147
In Goddys mercy, I tell them, is but foly to truste;	205	Magnyfycence	2289
Surely my welthe with them was overthrow.	210	Magnyfycence	2450
Shewyth wysdome to them that wysdome can take:	213	Magnyfycence	2554
She leneth them on the same,	217	El Rummynge	131
on] 'of' Day 1560, Marshe 1568			
Brynge wyth them malte or whete,	221	El Rummynge	267
To byrle them of the best.	221	El Rummynge	269
But of all this thronge /One came them amonge,	225	El Rummynge	446
She brought them in a wallet;	226	El Rummynge	461
She] 'Some' Day 1560, Marshe 1568			
Bere them to your chamber.'	229	El Rummynge	604
Than Elynour dyd them hyde /Within her beddes syde.	229	El Rummynge	605
With ladyes I lerne and goe with them to scole.	231	Speke Parott	21
Goe, lytyll quayre, pray them that yow beholde,	239	Speke Parott	290
With notable clerkes; supply to them, I pray,	241	Speke Parott	359
He maketh them to bere babylles, and to bere a lowe sayle;	243	Speke Parott	428
Accomptynge them as fictyons.	249	Collyn Clout	114
And them all to-mangle?	255	Collyn Clout	333
to-mangle] 'mangle' †Godfray 1531, Kele 1545.1, Marshe 1568			
Ye do them wronge and no ryght	256	Collyn Clout	404
them] not in Marshe 1568			
To put them thus to flyght;	256	Collyn Clout	405
And some of them barke, /Clatter and carpe	260	Collyn Clout	546
Howe some of them glenes	260	Collyn Clout	567
From them for theyr lyves!'	261	Collyn Clout	573
Alas, and wellaway, /What eyles them thus to say?	261	Collyn Clout	578
Howe connynge myght them avaunce,	262	Collyn Clout	617
Therfore ye kepe them base,	262	Collyn Clout	624
And mocke them to theyr face.	262	Collyn Clout	625
And reherse them agayne,	266	Collyn Clout	775
Though some of them by lyres.	267	Collyn Clout	833
lyres] 'lyers' Kele 1545.1, Marshe 1568, 'lyars' MS Harley 2252			
They occupy them so /With syngynge Placebo,	269	Collyn Clout	906
The lay men call them barelles	269	Collyn Clout	917
In matters that them lyke	269	Collyn Clout	922
They shewe them polytyke,	269	Collyn Clout	923
By them to gette a name.	270	Collyn Clout	959
That ye kepe them so under;	271	Collyn Clout	1007
ye] 'we' Kele 1545.1, 'ye' MS Harley 2252			
Nor upon them take,	272	Collyn Clout	1016
And put them out of theyr place.	273	Collyn Clout	1078
But my recountynge is /Of them that do amys	274	Collyn Clout	1102
Suche grace God them sende	274	Collyn Clout	1125
But they wolde no man shuld them blame.	275	Collyn Clout	1142
With them the worde of God	275	Collyn Clout	1145
And vexeth them day by day	282	Why Come Ye	155
They kepe them in theyr holdes	283	Why Come Ye	167
Wold wyrry them lyke an hogge.	286	Why Come Ye	299
He pluckes them by the hode,	286	Why Come Ye	304
And shakes them by the eare,	286	Why Come Ye	305
And brynge[s] them in suche feare.	286	Why Come Ye	306
brynges] 'brynge' †Kele 1545.3, Toy 1553, Kitson 1560.7, Marshe 1568			
He bayteth them lyke a bere,	286	Why Come Ye	307

THEMSELFE —THEN   Page   Title   Line

And maketh them to bow theyr kne /Before his majeste.   286   Why Come Ye   312
   maketh them] 'make' Toy 1553, Kitson 1560.7, Marshe 1568
He countys them foles and dawes;   286   Why Come Ye   315
He wryngeth them suche a wrenche, ...   287   Why Come Ye   321
And cals them cankerd knaves.   287   Why Come Ye   335
And in the Checker he them cheks, ...   287   Why Come Ye   338
That he ruleth them all.   290   Why Come Ye   436
At them that be well borne;   294   Why Come Ye   600
He rebukes them and rayles, ...   294   Why Come Ye   601
Chuse them syt or flyt, ...   295   Why Come Ye   634
He calleth them doddy patis;   295   Why Come Ye   652
Brose them on a brake, ...   303   Why Come Ye   983
   Brose] 'bruse' Toy 1553, Kitson 1560.7, Marshe 1568
And bynde them to a stake, ...   303   Why Come Ye   984
And rule them echone /In Lucyfers trone.   304   Why Come Ye   992
He kepeth them in subjectyon.   304   Why Come Ye   1010
He counteth them for gygawis;   305   Why Come Ye   1063
And putteth them to sylence   305   Why Come Ye   1064
He hathe them in derisyon, ...   306   Why Come Ye   1092
To dryve them at divisyon, ...   306   Why Come Ye   1094
To bringe them to confusyon -   306   Why Come Ye   1096
Of them that have vertue by reason of cunnyng, ...   317   Garlande   198
One faute or other in them shalbe notyd.   318   Garlande   203
Mustred ther amonge them with many a mad tale;   322   Garlande   373
And as I thus sadly amonge them avysid   323   Garlande   386
The monke of Bury then after them ensuyd, ...   323   Garlande   390
That with them I went where they wolde me brynge, ...   324   Garlande   447
I her demaunded of them and ther astate.   329   Garlande   606
Hither they come crowdyng to get them a name, ...   329   Garlande   621
And of the winter days that hy them so fast, ...   331   Garlande   700
But if they were counterfettes that women them call, ...   334   Garlande   785
God geve them good spede there warke to begin!   334   Garlande   793
Sume to enbrowder put them in prese, ...   334   Garlande   794
That for them some goodly conseyt be devysid, ...   335   Garlande   814
To iche of them rendryng thankis commendable, ...   335   Garlande   820
There was amonge them no worde then but mum, ...   344   Garlande   1118
   amonge them no worde] 'not a worde amonge them' MS Cotton
   Vitellius E.x
What ayle them to deprave /Phillippe Sparows grave?   348   Garlande   1267
That in them comprisid consyderacyons;   352   Garlande   1422
It made them to skip, to stampe, and to stare, ...   353   Garlande   1473
For drede and he lerne them there A B C to spell.'   353   Garlande   1476
I wypid myne eyne for to make them clere.   354   Garlande   1513
Els ye shall pray /Them that ye may   356   Garlande   1584
God sende them bothe myschauns!   363   Albany   176
For to recount them all.   370   Albany   458
His noble baronage /He putteth them in corage   370   Albany   466
Maintayne them with comforte   370   Albany   472
Wherwith he dothe them bynde   371   Albany   484
Shew them that shall you rede   371   Albany   509
that popholy and pevysshe presumpcion provoked them to publysshe   375   Replycacion   I
And chase them thorowe the muse   380   Replycacion   212
To hunt them into hell, ...   380   Replycacion   214
Ye have reed them, I suppose, ...   381   Replycacion   276
And sojourns with them and dwelles.   384   Replycacion   378
THEMSELFE
Full fewe that can themselfe of me excuse.   160   Magnyfycence   706
Out of all measure themselfe to enryche;   189   Magnyfycence   1751
And some for to hange themselfe in an halter;   194   Magnyfycence   1911
To drowne or to sle themselfe with a knyfe -   194   Magnyfycence   1914
Themselfe to amende;   274   Collyn Clout   1126
Sume fayne themselfe folys, and wolde be callyd wyse, ...   329   Garlande   616
THEM SELFE
They buskt them on a bushment them selfe in baile to bringe . .   31   Dol Dethe   81
Some fall to foly, them selfe for to spyll, ...   200   Magnyfycence   2139
And brynge them selfe bare, ...   217   El Rummynge   109
Them selfe to embesy with all there holl corage, ...   314   Garlande   66
The huge myghty okes them selfe dyd avaunce, ...   320   Garlande   279
countyng them selfe clerkes exellently enformed   373   Replycacion   I
That they juge them selfe able to be   374   Replycacion   7
THEN
Then by my councell, ...   39   Coystrowne3   19
To whom then shall we sew /For to have rescew, ...   40   Coystrowne3   37
But to swete Jesu /On us then for to rew?   40   Coystrowne3   40
O goodly chyld /Of Mary mylde, /Then be oure shylde!   40   Coystrowne3   43
I wold you coud! Then shuld ye se, mastres, ...   44   Balettys3   40
Fyrste pycke a quarell and fall oute with hym then, ...   55   Bowge   314
The fauconer then was prest, ...   63   Hauke   71
   prest] 'priest' Kynge & Marche 1554, Day 1560
He then, to be sure, /Callyd her with a lure.   63   Hauke   75
Thys fawconer then gan showte, ...   65   Hauke   119
   then] not in Day 1560, Marshe 1568
His hawke then flew uppon /The rode, with Mary and Johnn. . . .   65   Hauke   126
And the Pharasay /Then durst nothynge say, ...   66   Hauke   153
Then moch more, by the rode, ...   66   Hauke   178
Then in a tabull playne /I wroute a verse or twayne, ...   68   Hauke   222
Whom now and then /He pluckteth by the hede   84   Phy Sparrow   510
That was engendred then;   105   Phy Sparrow   1329

THEN —THEN   Page   Title   Line

Phrase	Page	Title	Line
For then began our myrth and game.	117	Ag Scottes	68
Why holde ye on yer cap, syr, then? Yor pardone ys expyryd.	123	Garnesche2	9
How shuld a fals lying tung then be rewarded?	137	Ven Tongues	2
Then let them vale a bonet of their proud sayle,	138	Ven Tongues	32
Are sharper then swordes, sturdier then stones.	138	Ven Tongues	50
Are sharper then swordes, sturdier then stones.	138	Ven Tongues	50
Sharper then raysors, that shave and cut throtes,	138	Ven Tongues	51
More stinging then scorpions that stang Pharaotis.	138	Ven Tongues	52
Then any poysoned tode, or any serpent.	138	Ven Tongues	54
Then ren they with lesinges, and blow them about,	139	Ven Tongues	69
Then Cerberus the cur couching in the kenel of hel;	140	Ven Tongues	80
Then thus to you - Nay, suffer me yet ferther to say,	142	Magnyfycence	48
Wolde it please you then -	143	Magnyfycence	87
Then ye must bothe consent	143	Magnyfycence	107
What, lyberte to measure then wolde ye bynde?	144	Magnyfycence	131
Then may I say that ye be servauntys myne.	145	Magnyfycence	183
Then, Lyberte, se that Measure by your gyde,	146	Magnyfycence	195
Then shall you have with you prosperyte resydent.	146	Magnyfycence	197
Then noblenesse, I se well, is almoste undone,	146	Magnyfycence	225
Ye, syr, undoubted. Then, of very ryght,	148	Magnyfycence	272
This nonnes nowe and then, and it myght be,	154	Magnyfycence	488
Tell on, syr. Howe then?	158	Magnyfycence	651
But then, syr, what shall I hyght?	159	Magnyfycence	669
For then shall we so craftely cary	159	Magnyfycence	683
Now let us go, and we shall, then.	159	Magnyfycence	687
Then for the season that I here shall walke,	159	Magnyfycence	691
What! Then he is some good poore mannes curre?	171	Magnyfycence	1129
Then I pray the hartely,	172	Magnyfycence	1148
And then he is moche made of for his [wyt];	175	Magnyfycence	1271
wyt] 'whyt' †Rastell & Treveris C 1530, B			
Nowe then goo we hens. Away the mare.	177	Magnyfycence	1325
Then fare well thryfte, by hym that crosse kyst!	179	Magnyfycence	1416
Shewe us your mynde then, howe to do and what.	180	Magnyfycence	1435
Syr, then, with the favour of your benynge sufferaunce,	182	Magnyfycence	1519
Why, wyll they then be intreted, the most and the lest?	184	Magnyfycence	1585
Then some occacyon or quarell ye must fynde,	185	Magnyfycence	1600
Then feyne yourselfe dyseased, and make yourselfe seke.	185	Magnyfycence	1612
Then myschefe sodaynly I them sende;	194	Magnyfycence	1927
Then for to begge theyr mete for charyte.	198	Magnyfycence	2041
What! Then he may drynke out of a stone cruyse.	201	Magnyfycence	2166
Nay. Then thou wylte dynge the devyll and thou be not holde.	202	Magnyfycence	2183
Then trust I to God and the holy rode,	203	Magnyfycence	2206
Then I was in opynynge of lockys;	203	Magnyfycence	2226
Then shall you be sone delyvered from dystresse,	208	Magnyfycence	2383
Then ye of foly in tymes past you repent?	209	Magnyfycence	2433
'Then ye repent you of foly in tymes past' †Rastell & Treveris C 1530, B			
Then welthe with you myght in no wyse abyde.	210	Magnyfycence	2447
Use not then your countenaunce for to counterfet.	210	Magnyfycence	2455
And ye shall have more worshyp then ever ye had.	210	Magnyfycence	2474
Be gentyll, then, of corage, and lerne to be kynde;	211	Magnyfycence	2486
To the increse of your honour then arme you with ryght,	211	Magnyfycence	2496
Nowe semyth us syttynge that ye then resorte	214	Magnyfycence	2566
It had ben hers, I wene, /More then fourty yere;	216	El Rummynge	58
Then came in a genet,	224	El Rummynge	392
Then Parot moste have an almon or a date.	231	Speke Parott	7
And sette to a D, /And then hyt ys 'Amend',	238	Speke Parott	276
to] not in †MS Harley 2252			
Then nodypollys and gramatolys of smalle intellygens:	240	Speke Parott	318
Then renne they in every stede,	252	Collyn Clout	231
Whan Scorpyon descendynge, /Was so then pretendynge	258	Collyn Clout	472
Then to be so dysgysed.	261	Collyn Clout	580
Ye caste up then your bokes	261	Collyn Clout	596
For then ye wyll be wroken	261	Collyn Clout	598
Then all the freres letter.	265	Collyn Clout	762
Then yf any there be	274	Collyn Clout	1117
In place alone then musynge in my thought	312	Garlande	8
Then men wyll say how he doth but flatter.	314	Garlande	84
Then sum wyll say he hath but lyttil brayne,	314	Garlande	87
Unto your grace then make I this motyve:	315	Garlande	114
Wherfore then rasid ye not away	316	Garlande	137
Of that most folow then consequently,	317	Garlande	172
Then he that doth worste is as good as the best.	317	Garlande	175
Then he assurded into his exclamacyon	320	Garlande	302
his] 'this' Marshe 1568			
The monke of Bury then after them ensuyd,	323	Garlande	390
Then to this lady and soverayne of this palace	326	Garlande	491
I sawe hir smyle, and I then did the same.	327	Garlande	530
I then] 'than I' Marshe 1568			
Of worldly trust, then did I you rescu;	327	Garlande	543
And then she sayd, 'Whylis we have tyme and space	328	Garlande	563
Then questionyd I her what thos yatis ment;	328	Garlande	575
thos] 'these' Marshe 1568			
Then I me lent, and loked over the wall:	329	Garlande	602
Then furthermore aboute me my syght I revolde,	330	Garlande	664
For when he spekyth fayrest, then thynketh he moost yll;	333	Garlande	759
To Mercury also hertely prayed I then,	335	Garlande	826

THENCE —THER

	Page	Title	Line
There was amonge them no worde then but mum,	344	Garlande	1118
amonge them no worde] 'not a worde amonge them' MS Cotton Vitellius E.x			
So then commaundid she was upon this	344	Garlande	1147
That was engendred then;	349	Garlande	1322
Then such that have disdaynyd	350	Garlande	1367
that] 'as' †Fakes 1523			
Then to the hevyn sperycall upwarde I gasid,	354	Garlande	1514
Yet now and then /Sum Latin men	355	Garlande	1544
But then I drede	355	Garlande	1553
then] 'that' Marshe 1568			

THENCE
Reson is banysshed thence,	279	Why Come Ye	12

THENNE
Thenne I behelde how he dysgysed was:	56	Bowge	351
Thenne I, astonyed of that sodeyne fraye,	60	Bowge	501

THENS
Or that he thens yede,	63	Hauke	55
And from thens to the halfe strete,	204	Magnyfycence	2263
I saw dyvers that were cariid away thens in cribbis,	330	Garlande	640

THEOCRITUS
As Linus and Homerus, /Euphorion and Theocritus,	90	Phy Sparrow	762
Theocritus with his bucolycall relacyons;	321	Garlande	327

THEOLOGIA
Adew Philosophia, /Adew Theologia.	284	Why Come Ye	214

THEOLOGICALL
Of suche theologicall thynges,	384	Replycacion	350

THEOLOGISACION
as touchyng the tetrycall theologisacion of these demy divines,	374	Replycacion	1

THEOLOGY
They tumble so in theology,	374	Replycacion	5
In theology, /Nor analogy,	383	Replycacion	308

THEOLOGYS
Yf it please nat theologys	258	Collyn Clout	465
nat theologys] 'the not onely' MS Lansdowne 762 'not theologi' MS Harley 2252			

THER
	Page	Title	Line
That vilane hastarddis in ther furious tene,	30	Dol Dethe	24
Falsly to slo ther moste singlar goode lorde?	30	Dol Dethe	27
slo] 'slee' Marshe 1568			
To slo ther owne lorde? God was not in ther mynde!	30	Dol Dethe	35
To slo ther owne lorde? God was not in ther mynde!	30	Dol Dethe	35
Fy, fy, for shame, ther hartis wer to faynt.	30	Dol Dethe	42
He was ther bulwarke, ther paves and ther wall,	30	Dol Dethe	48
He was ther bulwarke, ther paves and ther wall,	30	Dol Dethe	48
He was ther bulwarke, ther paves and ther wall,	30	Dol Dethe	48
Bot ther was fals packinge or els I am begylde,	31	Dol Dethe	71
For yf they had occupied ther spere and ther shelde	31	Dol Dethe	73
For yf they had occupied ther spere and ther shelde	31	Dol Dethe	73
The commonns renyyd ther taxes to pay	31	Dol Dethe	78
Turnd ther backis and let ther master fall,	31	Dol Dethe	94
backis] 'backe' Marshe 1568			
Turnd ther backis and let ther master fall,	31	Dol Dethe	94
backis] 'backe' Marshe 1568			
Take up whos wolde, for ther they let hym ly.	32	Dol Dethe	96
His corage manly, yet ther he shed his bloode.	32	Dol Dethe	103
For cruell[y] amonge them ther he was slayne.	32	Dol Dethe	105
cruelly] 'cruell' †MS Royal 18 D.ii, Marshe 1568			
As oft as thei call to ther remembrance	34	Dol Dethe	188
Of ther good lord the fate and dedely chaunce.	34	Dol Dethe	189
His soule mot receyve in to ther company,	35	Dol Dethe	213
That he dryvyth them doune with dyntys on ther day-wach.	43	Balettys2	30
One ther is, and ever one shalbe,	45	Balettys5	8
Anone ther mette with him, as me thoughte,	54	Bowge	282
Ther is no beest savage,	100	Phy Sparrow	1156
........that ye ther prechyd,	125	Garnesche3	60
Cowde hocupy ther no stede.	126	Garnesche3	69
The nexte halter ther xall be	128	Garnesche3	176
That ther thou xuldyst be rachchyd	128	Garnesche3	180
Yet ther may falle soche caswelte	132	Garnesche5	121
With, 'Fo, ther is a stenche!	219	El Rummynge	180
For replicacion restles that he of late ther made;	239	Speke Parott	282
To sowe corne in the see-sande, ther wyll no crope growe.	240	Speke Parott	342
Yet dyverse ther be, industryous of reason,	315	Garlande	106
ther] 'that' MS Cotton Vitellius E.x			
These orators and poetis refresshid ther throtis.	322	Garlande	371
Mustred ther amonge them with many a mad tale;	322	Garlande	373
Of pursevantis ther presid in with many a dyverse tale:	326	Garlande	492
a] not in Marshe 1568			
And seryously she shewyd me ther denominacyons.	328	Garlande	581
I her demaunded of them and ther astate.	329	Garlande	606
And one ther was there, I wondred of his hap,	329	Garlande	628
That all the dayes of ther lyfe shall styck by ther rybbis.	330	Garlande	638
That all the dayes of ther lyfe shall styck by ther rybbis.	330	Garlande	638
Moche mischefe, I hyght you, amonge theem ther happid.	330	Garlande	643
Phillis and Testalis, ther tressis with oyle	331	Garlande	681
Of Pliades he prechid with ther drowsy chere,	331	Garlande	697
Ther names recountyng in the court of Fame;	334	Garlande	781

	Page	Title	Line
THERAT —THERE			
Well gydyng ther glowtonn to kepe streit theyr sylk,	334	Garlande	795
ther] 'the' MS Cotton Vitellius E.x			
THERAT			
Agaynst this my makyng, /Their males therat shakyng,	120	Ag Scottes2	8
Who so therat pyketh mood,	121	Ag Scottes2	21
whoso] 'but who so' Day 1560, Marshe 1568			
The crane and the curlewe therat gan to grame;	192	Magnyfycence	1839
And grudge therat with frownyng countenaunce;	348	Garlande	1258
THERBY			
Ye get therby a slendyr laude	131	Garnesche5	74
Swere and stare, and byde therby,	152	Magnyfycence	414
And yf I se therby they wyll not amende,	194	Magnyfycence	1926
As they may byde therby,	273	Collyn Clout	1062
Yet, thoughe I say it, therby lyith a tale,	346	Garlande	1200
I] 'ye' †Fakes 1523			
Therby I shall purchace /No displesaunt rewarde,	367	Albany	358
THERE			
Trustinge in noble men that wer with hym there;	31	Dol Dethe	90
There may no frauchys /Nor worldly blys	39	Coystrowne3	26
Good mastres Anne, there ye do shayle!	41	Coystrowne4	19
Nor stand long wrestyng there aboute;	41	Coystrowne4	25
How there nys thynge that I covet so fayne	44	Balettys3	41
She kyste an anker, and there she laye at rode,	47	Bowge	39
kyste] 'keste' Wynkyn de Worde 1510, 'kast' Marshe 1568			
Than there coude I none aquentaunce fynde;	47	Bowge	45
There was moche noyse, anone one cryed, 'Cese!'	47	Bowge	46
Than sholde ye see there pressynge in a pace	47	Bowge	56
But of eche thynge there as I toke hede,	47	Bowge	64
To whome there came another gentylwoman.	48	Bowge	84
For I dare saye that there nys erthly man	48	Bowge	101
There can no favour nor frendshyp hym forsake.	48	Bowge	103
Whan there were dyverse that sore dyde you manace.	50	Bowge	159
Soo he departed. There he wolde be come,	52	Bowge	228
And I dare saye there is no man hereinne	53	Bowge	267
There muste for hym be layde some prety beyte.	55	Bowge	312
But there was poyntynge and noddynge with the hede,	58	Bowge	421
Than, in his hode, I sawe there faces tweyne:	58	Bowge	428
By God, I saye, there is a grete herte-brennynge	59	Bowge	460
Par[d]e, remembre whan ye were there,	60	Bowge	515
Parde] 'Parte' †Wynkyn de Worde 1499, 1510, Marshe 1568			
There I wynked on you - wote ye not where?	60	Bowge	516
For forthwyth there I had him slayne,	61	Bowge	523
Me thoughte I see lewde felawes here and there	61	Bowge	528
There on he stode, and craked;	63	Hauke	50
And in the holy place /She mutyd there a chase	63	Hauke	62
To hunte there by lyberte	64	Hauke	108
And to halow there the fox.	64	Hauke	110
There he may se and reed	65	Hauke	147
he] 'her' Marshe 1568			
Pla ce bo, /Who is there, who?	71	Phy Sparrow	2
That he coulde there espye	76	Phy Sparrow	181
I kest downe that there was,	77	Phy Sparrow	230
And slew him there starke dead.	81	Phy Sparrow	378
Shall rede there the pystell	82	Phy Sparrow	425
No broken galles /May there abyde	83	Phy Sparrow	474
No] 'Nor' Kitson 1560.6			
And yet there is none /But one alone;	84	Phy Sparrow	516
Of whose incyneracyon /There ryseth a new creacyon	85	Phy Sparrow	541
Yet there was a thyng	89	Phy Sparrow	699
There is no Englysh voyd,	91	Phy Sparrow	795
And there agayne /Envy doth complayne, /And hath disdayne;	95	Phy Sparrow	963
And yet there was no vyce,	100	Phy Sparrow	1133
For a prysoner there now ye be	114	Scot Kynge	40
The White Lyon, there rampaunt of moode,	119	Ag Scottes	135
The White there slew the Red starke ded.	119	Ag Scottes	138
For when ye dwelt there,	125	Garnesche3	43
Ye wan nothyng there but a mow:	131	Garnesche5	50
Ye wan nothyng there but a skorne;	131	Garnesche5	51
And thus there ye lost yower pray;	131	Garnesche5	61
But behynd in our hose /We bere there a rose	136	Dundas	35
If there be none other mater but that,	137	Ven Tongues	14
There is no noble man wil judge in me	138	Ven Tongues	34
But lering and lurking here and there like spies,	139	Ven Tongues	67
Howe after a drought there fallyth a showre of rayne	141	Magnyfycence	12
Lyberte, I wote well, forbere no man there may;	142	Magnyfycence	50
I say there is no welthe where as lyberte is subdude.	142	Magnyfycence	73
Where drede ledyth the daunce, there is no joy nor blysse.	142	Magnyfycence	76
Or howe can you prove that there is felycyte,	142	Magnyfycence	77
Where measure is ruler, there is nothynge amysse.	144	Magnyfycence	124
There is no surfet where measure rulyth the feste;	144	Magnyfycence	139
There is no excesse where measure hath his helthe.	144	Magnyfycence	140
There is no prynce but he hath nede of us thre -	145	Magnyfycence	159
There is no flaterer nor losyll so lyther,	146	Magnyfycence	200
Is there ony thynge elles your grace wyll commaunde me?	149	Magnyfycence	318
This wrytynge was taken me there,	150	Magnyfycence	344
By your soth? Ye, and there is suche a wache,	150	Magnyfycence	350
And there they wolde ha[v]e me to dwell.	157	Magnyfycence	614
have] 'hane' †Rastell & Treveris C 1530, B			

THERE —THERE

	Page	Title	Line
Yet where we wonne, nowe there wonneth he.	157	Magnyfycence	624
Aske these two that there dothe dwell.	158	Magnyfycence	629
There dwelleth a mayster men calleth Mesure -	158	Magnyfycence	631
In fayth, and without lyberte there is no bydyng.	158	Magnyfycence	662
In fayth, and Lybertyes rome is there but small.	158	Magnyfycence	663
That Mesure shall not there longe tary.	159	Magnyfycence	684
There cometh and groweth of my comynge;	159	Magnyfycence	694
Well, and I be a coward, there is mo than I.	162	Magnyfycence	770
With whom shall I there mete.	167	Magnyfycence	955
There is many evyll faveryd, and thou be foule!	167	Magnyfycence	969
And thy wyt wanderynge here and there,	170	Magnyfycence	1074
In faythe, ellys is there none in all Englonde.	170	Magnyfycence	1099
By my trouth, there is myne.	171	Magnyfycence	1103
Nowe, by my trouth, man, take, there is my purse;	171	Magnyfycence	1104
my] 'myne' †Rastell & Treveris C 1530, B			
In faythe, there is not a better dogge for hogges,	171	Magnyfycence	1120
What hast thou founde there? By God, a lowse.	173	Magnyfycence	1198
There be two lyther, rude and ranke,	175	Magnyfycence	1266
By God, there be some that be shroudly towchyd.	175	Magnyfycence	1277
For there be other that foly dothe use	175	Magnyfycence	1280
Ye, tourne over the lefe, rede there, and loke	176	Magnyfycence	1293
So that there knowe no man but I and she.	177	Magnyfycence	1353
My inwyt delynge there can no man dyscry.	177	Magnyfycence	1356
Syr, as I say, there was no faute in me.	180	Magnyfycence	1426
Nowe holde ye content, for there is none other shyfte.	180	Magnyfycence	1443
Is there no horson that knave that wyll bete?'	185	Magnyfycence	1618
Where mennes belyes is mesured, there is no chere;	189	Magnyfycence	1742
With Mesure. Where as all noblenes is, there I have past:	189	Magnyfycence	1749
Ly there, losell, for all thy pompe and pryde;	193	Magnyfycence	1880
Nowe is there no man that wyll set by hym a flye.	193	Magnyfycence	1889
For there is nothynge that more dyspleaseth God	194	Magnyfycence	1928
In her promyse there is no sykernesse,	197	Magnyfycence	2028
That they lose theyr lyberte and all that there is.	200	Magnyfycence	2128
In Fortunys frendshyppe there is no stedfastnesse;	201	Magnyfycence	2156
And yf there were none to dysplease but thou and I,	202	Magnyfycence	2194
To get us there some freshe mete.	204	Magnyfycence	2264
Why, is there any store of rawe motton?	204	Magnyfycence	2265
Som be wrestyd there that they thynke on it forty dayes,	204	Magnyfycence	2274
For there be horys there at all assayes.	204	Magnyfycence	2275
For there be horys there at all assayes.	204	Magnyfycence	2275
What! Lyest thou there lyngrynge, lewdly and lothsome?	205	Magnyfycence	2291
But nowe I se well there is no better rede,	205	Magnyfycence	2305
There is no man may synne more mortally	206	Magnyfycence	2336
There was never so harde a storme of mysery,	207	Magnyfycence	2343
But thrughe good hope there may come remedy.	207	Magnyfycence	2344
There is no bawme ne gumme of Arabe	207	Magnyfycence	2347
Full many thynges there be that lacketh redresse,	209	Magnyfycence	2415
That I sholde use largesse. Nay, syr, there a pause.	209	Magnyfycence	2437
Well, I perceyve in you there is moche sadnesse,	210	Magnyfycence	2475
Howe in this worlde there is no seke[r]nesse,	212	Magnyfycence	2515
sekernesse] 'sekenesse' †Rastell & Treveris C 1530, B			
So in this worlde there is no sykernesse,	212	Magnyfycence	2522
Thus in this worlde there is no erthly truste.	213	Magnyfycence	2544
Thus in this worlde there is no erthly truste.	213	Magnyfycence	2551
There to indeuer with all felycyte.	214	Magnyfycence	2569
And syt there by styll, /Erly and late.	217	El Rummynge	116
For, be there never so moche prese,	218	El Rummynge	174
But let us turne playne, /There we lefte agayne.	219	El Rummynge	188
Another there was that ran /With a good brasse pan -	222	El Rummynge	316
There hath ben greate war	223	El Rummynge	358
And there began a fabell,	224	El Rummynge	386
There came an old rybybe;	227	El Rummynge	492
With here and there a puscull,	228	El Rummynge	555
There was a prycke-me-denty, /Sat lyke a seynty,	229	El Rummynge	582
That nothynge had /There of their awne,	229	El Rummynge	609
Suche were there menny	230	El Rummynge	611
In Palestina there is Jerusalem.	233	Speke Parott	81
With, 'Who is there? A mayd?' Nay, nay, I trow!	233	Speke Parott	100
In there remembraunce ye may be inrolde.	239	Speke Parott	291
There is none that your name woll abbrogate	240	Speke Parott	317
To rude ys there reason to reche to your sentence;	240	Speke Parott	319
Muche money, men sey, there madly he hathe spente;	240	Speke Parott	335
Some say but lityll and thynke more in there thowghte,	242	Speke Parott	388
To practise or postyll thys prosses here and there?	242	Speke Parott	393
Moloc, that mawmett, there darre no man withsay;	243	Speke Parott	402
Agayne Frentike Frenesy there dar no man sey nay,	243	Speke Parott	422
Syns Dewcalyons flodde there can no clerkes rede.	244	Speke Parott	455
Syns Dewcalyons flodde there can no clerkes fynde.	244	Speke Parott	462
So manye bolde barons, there hertes as dull as lede;	245	Speke Parott	466
There is theyr hole devocyon,	248	Collyn Clout	87
Howebeit, some there be,	250	Collyn Clout	147
There may no cost be spared;	254	Collyn Clout	318
What, Collyn, there thou shayles!	256	Collyn Clout	399
Theyr founders lye there rotten;	257	Collyn Clout	426
And some there are that rave,	259	Collyn Clout	514
Whan there is never a whytte,	259	Collyn Clout	516
Somwhat there is amysse!	272	Collyn Clout	1050
Then yf any there be	274	Collyn Clout	1117

THERE—THERE	Page	Title	Line
Who dare say there agayne,	276	Collyn Clout	1214
There hath ben moche excesse:	280	Why Come Ye	70
There vayleth no resonynge;	281	Why Come Ye	104
There is no man but one	281	Why Come Ye	113
There went the hare away;	281	Why Come Ye	120
All maters there he marres,	283	Why Come Ye	189
And bereth him there so stowte	287	Why Come Ye	340
There is a whyspring and a whipling	287	Why Come Ye	350
There] 'Her' Kitson 1560.7, Marshe 1568			
There goth many a lye	288	Why Come Ye	356
But there is some travarse	288	Why Come Ye	387
In there absolute consciens	297	Why Come Ye	712
That there wantys grace	300	Why Come Ye	849
For and he were there,	303	Why Come Ye	973
There is a dyversyte	307	Why Come Ye	1149
Them selfe to embesy with all there holl corage,	314	Garlande	66
So that there workis myght famously be sene,	314	Garlande	67
Sum what wolde gadder in there conjecture	315	Garlande	107
conjecture] 'convecture' †Fakes 1523			
'Soft, my good syster, and make there a pawse.	316	Garlande	134
my good syster] 'goode my sister' MS Cotton Vitellius E.x			
Forthwith there rose amonge the thronge	319	Garlande	246
There was suyng to the Quene of Fame;	319	Garlande	253
With that there come in wonderly at ones	319	Garlande	269
I helpe all other of there infirmite,	321	Garlande	311
Parte of there names I thynke to specefye:	321	Garlande	325
These orators and poetes refresshed there throtis.	321	Garlande	336
There Titus Lyvius hymselfe dyd avaunce	321	Garlande	344
Theis orators and poetis refresshed there throtis.	322	Garlande	350
But blessyd Bachus was in there company,	322	Garlande	355
Their orators and poetis refresshed there throtis.	322	Garlande	357
Theis orators and poetis refresshed there throtis.	322	Garlande	364
There came John Bochas with his volumys grete;	322	Garlande	365
Theis orators and poetis refresshid there throtis.	322	Garlande	378
Theis notable poetis refresshid there throtis.	322	Garlande	385
There apparell farre passynge beyonde that I can tell;	323	Garlande	394
With diamauntis and rubis there tabers were trasid,	323	Garlande	395
tabers] 'taberdes' Marshe 1568			
And of there bounte they made me godely chere	323	Garlande	398
That welny nothynge there doth remayne	324	Garlande	430
welny] 'welnere' Marshe 1568			
So finally, when they had shewyd there devyse,	324	Garlande	442
'There shal he here what she wyl to hym say	325	Garlande	451
wyl to hym] 'to hym will' Marshe 1568			
With all the prese that there was lesse and more.	325	Garlande	455
Suche an other there coude no man fynde;	325	Garlande	463
Unto this place all poetis there did sue,	325	Garlande	481
There were many wordes smaller and gretter,	326	Garlande	508
There were, I say, of all maner of sortis,	326	Garlande	512
When they were past and wente forth on there way,	327	Garlande	526
It made sum lympe-legged and broisid there bones;	329	Garlande	625
And one ther was there, I wondred of his hap,	329	Garlande	628
There birdis on the brere sange on every syde,	330	Garlande	653
There blew in that gardynge a soft piplyng colde	331	Garlande	676
All frutis and flowris grew there in there kynde.	331	Garlande	678
and] not in †Fakes 1523			
All frutis and flowris grew there in there kynde.	331	Garlande	678
and] not in †Fakes 1523			
Dryades there daunsid upon that goodly soile,	331	Garlande	679
There Cintheus sat twynklyng upon his harpe stringis;	331	Garlande	687
There was counteryng of carollis in meter and verse	331	Garlande	705
and] 'and in' Marshe 1568			
And if there be in it any thyng ment,	332	Garlande	723
That list of there lewdnesse with hym for to brall.'	334	Garlande	786
God geve them good spede there warke to begin!	334	Garlande	793
For your pleasure do there endevourment,	335	Garlande	810
Commensyng your proces after there degre,	335	Garlande	819
Yet shall there be no restraynt	339	Garlande	956
Where all the sayd poetis sat in there degre.	343	Garlande	1104
In her astate there sat the noble Quene	343	Garlande	1114
There was amonge them no worde then but mum,	344	Garlande	1118
amonge them no worde] 'not a worde amonge them' MS Cotton Vitellius E.x			
Yet sum there be therewith that take grevaunce	348	Garlande	1257
Of his pleasaunt paine there and his glad distres	351	Garlande	1391
Though Jak sayd nay, yet Mok there loste her sho;	351	Garlande	1396
And plantid it there where never before was none, unshred	351	Garlande	1405
it there where] 'yet wher' Marshe 1568			
By there phesik doth many a man ease,	352	Garlande	1427
For drede and he lerne them there A B C to spell.'	353	Garlande	1476
Of Lovers Testamentis and of There Wanton Wyllis,	354	Garlande	1496
Contynew still /With there good wyll.	356	Garlande	1586
There he putte backe	360	Albany	44
And lurke there lyke an as	366	Albany	289
There shalbe drawen a trayne	368	Albany	369
There, lyke a sorte of sottes,	376	Replycacion	65
For there ye myst you[r] quosshons.	377	Replycacion	113
your] 'you' †Pynson 1528			

THEREATT — THEROF	Page	Title	Line
And folysshly there fopped	377	Replycacion	120
One of you there was	379	Replycacion	186
And there to make relacion /In open predycacion,	379	Replycacion	205
So was there never another,	381	Replycacion	258
Rede what Jerome there dothe say/	383	Replycacion	328
Howe there is a spyrituall,	384	Replycacion	365

THEREATT

Lyacon lawghyth thereatt and berythe hym more bolde;	242	Speke Parott	400

THEREBY

That ye can nat byde thereby.	310	Why Come Ye2	28

THEREFORE

Ageynste you hardely; therefore be not afrayde.	51	Bowge	174
Therefore to make complaynte	62	Hauke	20
Therefore poverte loke pacyently ye take,	196	Magnyfycence	2000
Therefore, 'Fyll it by and by	221	El Rummynge	274
Therefore no grevance, /I pray you, for to take,	385	Replycacion	397

THEREIN

Therein they founde royall marchaundyse,	47	Bowge	41
And therein reed /Shall fynde indeed	116	Ag Scottes	43
She founde therein no bones.	224	El Rummynge	381
bones] 'bornes' Day 1560			
From Scarpary to Tartary renoun therein doth spryng,	234	Speke Parott	131

THEREOF

Thereof the fame dothe blow,	110	Lawde	4
And maketh thereof port-sale	217	El Rummynge	103
port-sale] 'pore sale' Kynge & Marche 1554, Day 1560			
The fleshe thereof was ranke,	228	El Rummynge	540

THEREON

A maunchet for morell thereon to snap.	37	Coystrownel	11
That shall them angre, I holde thereon a grote,	59	Bowge	475
The devyll thereon be wroken!	227	El Rummynge	498

THEREUPON

Wele was hym that thereupon myght stare.	343	Garlande	1109

THEREWITH

And stopped therewith the hole.	224	El Rummynge	406
Therewith I dare nat mell.	288	Why Come Ye	378
Yet sum there be therewith that take grevaunce	348	Garlande	1257

THEREWITHALL

Enbrasynge therewithall	99	Phy Sparrow	1127
That she was therewithall /Into a palsey fall;	226	El Rummynge	474

THERFOR

Therfor no more they shall	111	Lawde	36

THERFORE

But who wyll have it muste paye therfore dere.	47	Bowge	53
Let us, therfore, shortely at a worde	54	Bowge	307
Wherfore, as I be savyd, /Ye ar therfore beknavyd.	70	Hauke	310
Therfore ye have lost your copyholde.	114	Scot Kynge	35
Therfore ye be layde now full lowe.	114	Scot Kynge	53
Therfore ye lost your copyehold.	118	Ag Scottes	126
Fortune on you therfore dyd frowne;	120	Ag Scottes	176
Thy selfe therfore defende.	128	Garnesche3	161
Come of therfore, let se;	143	Magnyfycence	102
'And therfore shall my husbande pay'.	153	Magnyfycence	461
Nowe therfore, whylest we are togyder –	155	Magnyfycence	546
And therfore I growe more on one day	170	Magnyfycence	1077
It is no wonder, therfore, thoughe ye be wrothe	189	Magnyfycence	1748
And therfore hye you hens, and take this oversyght.	190	Magnyfycence	1795
And therfore our Lorde sende you a very wengaunce!	203	Magnyfycence	2237
Remembre you, therfore, howe late ye were low.	210	Magnyfycence	2451
Men call you therfore prophanes.	252	Collyn Clout	207
Sory therfore am I,	258	Collyn Clout	484
Therfore ye kepe them base,	262	Collyn Clout	624
Therfore stande sure and fast.	273	Collyn Clout	1071
Therfore I render of her the memory	339	Garlande	971
Therfore I vyse you to forsake	382	Replycacion	297

THERIN

The devyll myghte daunce therin for ony crowche.	56	Bowge	364
Causeth him to gryn /And rejoyce therin;	95	Phy Sparrow	927
Ye dyde not your dewty therin,	114	Scot Kynge	32
Yet we wyll therin take good delyberacyon.	148	Magnyfycence	275
Ales founde therin no thornes,	224	El Rummynge	379
A myrrour of glasse, that I may tote therin;	231	Speke Parott	10
Moche dowblenes of the worlde therin he may fynde.	346	Garlande	1197
Therin to rede, and to understande	347	Garlande	1230
For a wyndmil /Therin to couche styll	365	Albany	263
Therin, like a royle,	365	Albany	270

THEROF

The awnner therof is lady of estate,	47	Bowge	50
Whatsomever aventure therof fall.	55	Bowge	336
And moche therof dyd make;	89	Phy Sparrow	693
The amense therof is far to call agayne;	140	Magnyfycence	9
To you I arecte it, and cast /Therof the reformacyon.	143	Magnyfycence	95
But yf therof the soner amendys be made;	146	Magnyfycence	226
Ye and I talkyd therof to nyght.	159	Magnyfycence	670
But may I drynke therof whylest that I stare?	176	Magnyfycence	1322
And therof ye shall a larger profe se.	188	Magnyfycence	1700
Ye, but thanke me therof every dele.	201	Magnyfycence	2171
Thanke the therof, in the devyls date!	201	Magnyfycence	2172

THEROUT — THESE

	Page	Title	Line
And make therof a jape!	248	Collyn Clout	84
And therof speke nothynge	255	Collyn Clout	355
The beldynge therof was passynge commendable;	328	Garlande	589
He wrate therof many a praty lyne,	347	Garlande	1242

THEROUT

He coude nat synge hymselfe therout	268	Collyn Clout	878

THERTO

And I may tende therto for play;	168	Magnyfycence	1018
What may she do therto?'	281	Why Come Ye	87
Therto am I full insuffycyent;	313	Garlande	46
That but if my warkes therto be agreable,	324	Garlande	439
What myght she say? What myght he do therto?	351	Garlande	1395

THERUPON

Therupon must herke,	272	Collyn Clout	1026

THERWITH

Shyfte now therwith, let see, as ye can,	48	Bowge	99
I wolde therwith no man were myscontente;	61	Bowge	533
Adversyte to hym therwith nowe and than;	207	Magnyfycence	2368
Yf ye take well therwith /It hath in it some pyth. take] 'talke' Kele 1545.1, Marshe 1568	248	Collyn Clout	57
Therwith I wyll nat mell.	257	Collyn Clout	428
To fyll therwith your mawe –	263	Collyn Clout	656
That therwith can mell.	296	Why Come Ye	685
And therwith, sodenly, out of my dreme I woke. dreme] 'slepe' Marshe 1568	354	Garlande	1511
Therwith for to be founde /At the unyversyte,	378	Replycacion	147

THERWITHALL

And so braynsyke therwithall,	170	Magnyfycence	1073
And therwithall convey hymselfe into a payre of fetters;	178	Magnyfycence	1365

THES

Thes sorowfulle ditis that I may shew expres.	29	Dol Dethe	21
Were not thes commones uncurteis karlis of kynd not] 'no' †MS Royal 18 D.ii, 'not' Marshe 1568	30	Dol Dethe	34
For thes twayne whypslovens calle for a coke stole.	124	Garnesche2	38
A good herynge of thes olde talis;	347	Garlande	1217

THESBE

Was betwene you twayne, /Pyramus and Thesbe,	72	Phy Sparrow	21

THESE

These frantyke foolys I hate most of all;	36	Coystrownel	2
These feverous axys, the dedely wo and payne	44	Balettys3	9
Lodestar to lyght these lovers to theyr porte,	44	Balettys3	25
And on that sleve these wordes were wrete:	58	Bowge	438
'These be my gospellers,	65	Hauke	120
These be my pystyllers,	65	Hauke	121
These be my querysters /To helpe me to synge,	65	Hauke	122
To rede or to spell /What these verses tell.	68	Hauke	238
These vylanous false cattes	80	Phy Sparrow	338
Of these historious tales,	90	Phy Sparrow	751
These poetes of auncyente,	90	Phy Sparrow	767
Now by these names thre,	105	Phy Sparrow	1363
Lo, these fond sottes /And tratlyng Skottys,	115	Ag Scottes	5
Are nat these Scottys /Folys and sottys,	116	Ag Scottes	29
It is but a maddynge, these wayes that ye use.	148	Magnyfycence	285
For all these japes yet that [y]e make – ye] 'we' †Rastell & Treveris C 1530, B	156	Magnyfycence	558
I say, come hyder. What are these twayne?	156	Magnyfycence	582
Syr, it is so that these twayne	157	Magnyfycence	612
Aske these two that there dothe dwell.	158	Magnyfycence	629
But dyvysyon, dyssencyon, dyrysyon – these thre	159	Magnyfycence	700
I muster, I medle amonge these grete estates;	160	Magnyfycence	736
And so, by these meanes, I brewe moche bale.	161	Magnyfycence	744
Where the devyll gate he all these hurtes?	171	Magnyfycence	1127
I dryve downe these dastardys with a dynt of my fyste.	181	Magnyfycence	1486
These wordes in myne eyre, they be so lustely spoken,	184	Magnyfycence	1565
Wysely let these wordes in your mynde be wayed:	185	Magnyfycence	1593
And happe you the whyles with these homly raggys.	197	Magnyfycence	2037
What a very vengeaunce nede all these wordys?	202	Magnyfycence	2198
Tushe! These maters that ye move are but soppys in ale;	203	Magnyfycence	2233
Howe say you, syr? Can ye these wordys grope?	207	Magnyfycence	2377
With, 'Hey, dogge, hay, /Have these hogges away!' hogges] 'dogges' Day 1560, Marshe 1568	218	El Rummynge	169
These swyne go to the hye dese,	218	El Rummynge	175
These maydens full meryly with many a dyvers flowur a] not in †MS Harley 2252	231	Speke Parott	11
These words shuld be more weyed, These words] 'Those words' Marshe 1568, 'This' MS Harley 2252	265	Collyn Clout	769
Upon these beestes rydynge,	270	Collyn Clout	966
Where these kepe resydence,	279	Why Come Ye	11
These orators and poetes refresshed there throtis.	321	Garlande	336
These orators and poetes refreshed their throtes.	321	Garlande	343
These orators and poetis refresshid ther throtis.	322	Garlande	371
These tidinges newe,	359	Albany	3
as touchyng the tetrycall theologisacion of these demy divines,	374	Replycacion	I
Of these yong heretikes, that stynke unbrent,	375	Replycacion	22
Agaynst these frenetykes, /Agaynst these lunatykes,	385	Replycacion	400
Agaynst these frenetykes, /Agaynst these lunatykes,	385	Replycacion	401
Agaynst these sysmatykes, /Agaynst these heretykes,	385	Replycacion	402
Agaynst these sysmatykes, /Agaynst these heretykes,	385	Replycacion	403

THESEUS —THIS	Page	Title	Line

THESEUS
Whom Theseus dyd afraye,	74	Phy Sparrow	86
Duke Theseus, and Partelet;	87	Phy Sparrow	617

THESIUS
And Thesius, th[at] prowde was Pluto to face - that] 'the' †Rastell & Treveris C 1530, B	182	Magnyfycence	1496

THEVYS
Ye be the thevys, I say, away my goodys dyd cary.	203	Magnyfycence	2239
So many thevys hangyd, and thevys neverthelesse;	245	Speke Parott	477
So many thevys hangyd, and thevys neverthelesse;	245	Speke Parott	477

THEWDE
Malapert, medyllar, nothyng well thewde,	133	Garnesche5	147
Thy tonge is nat well thewde,	287	Why Come Ye	331

THI
O dolorous Teusday, dedicate to thi name,	32	Dol Dethe	114
When thou shoke thi sword so noble a man to mar!	32	Dol Dethe	115
Hevyn, hell and erth obey unto thi kall;	34	Dol Dethe	192
Which to thi resemblance wonderusly has wrought	34	Dol Dethe	193
With thi blode precious our fenaunce thou dyd pay	34	Dol Dethe	195
To pardon thi servant and brynge to savacioun.	35	Dol Dethe	210
Sayth, from thy to unto thi croune,	130	Garnesche5	26
Avaunt, rybawde, thi tung reclame!	132	Garnesche5	106
Wer thi nose spectacle case;	133	Garnesche5	134
Of thi lewdenes that may be tolde.	134	Garnesche5	175

THICKESTE
Amonge the thickeste of all the hole rowte,	319	Garlande	240

THIDER
All orators and poetis shulde thider go before,	325	Garlande	454

THING
That with one worde formd all thing of nought;	34	Dol Dethe	191
He skantly loveth our kyng, /That grudgeth at this thing:	121	Ag Scottes2	36
Shulde bring about that thing.	367	Albany	335

THINKE
Wherof hereafter, I thinke for to write,	140	Ven Tongues	81
But what his grace doth thinke,	296	Why Come Ye	683
And more paper I thinke to blot	299	Why Come Ye	826

THIRDE
The thirde, with hole affectyon	307	Why Come Ye	1125

THIS
This noble man doutles had not be slayne. be] 'bene' Marshe 1568	31	Dol Dethe	74
Whiche kyndelde the wyld fyre that made all this smoke.	31	Dol Dethe	77
The nobelnes of the northe, this valyant lorde and knyght,	31	Dol Dethe	85
So forcibly upon this Erle thow ran,	32	Dol Dethe	124
Of this lordis dethe and of his murdrynge;	32	Dol Dethe	130
This lordis dethe, whos pere is hard to fynd,	34	Dol Dethe	178
This noble man that cruelly was slayne.	34	Dol Dethe	182
The sowle of this lorde from all daunger of hell,	34	Dol Dethe	200
This wanton clarkis be nyse allway.	35	Man Margery	2
This pevysh proud, thys prendergest,	36	Coystrownel	6
To poynte this proude page a place and a rome,	37	Coystrownel	41
Devysyd this gostly medytacyon in Englysh:	39	Coystrowne3	I
Redeme us from this.	39	Coystrowne3	28
And shewed that in this arte I was not sure; I] not in †Wynkyn de Worde 1499, 1510	46	Bowge	19
Yet have I knowen suche er this;	46	Bowge	25
This royall chaffre that is shypped here	47	Bowge	54
In golde letters, this worde, whiche I dyde rede:	48	Bowge	66
And as I stode redynge this verse myselfe allone,	48	Bowge	68
And this an other, I have but smale substaunce.' And] 'But' Marshe 1568	48	Bowge	94
A precyous jewell, no rycher in this londe:	48	Bowge	97
But this one thynge ye maye be sure of me,	50	Bowge	162
'By God,' quod he, 'this and thus it is';	52	Bowge	225
'Fare well,' quod he, 'we wyll talke more of this.'	52	Bowge	227
Er this, whan that ye made me royall chere.	53	Bowge	249
Dysdayne, I wene, [t]his comerous car[k]es hyghte. this] 'his' editions; carkes] 'carbes' †Wynkyn de Worde 1499, 1510, 'crabes' Marshe 1568	54	Bowge	294
This Doctour Dawcocke, Drede, I wene he hyghte.	54	Bowge	303
And in this wyse he gan with me to chyde.	55	Bowge	322
'Forsothe,' quod I, 'in this courte I dwell nowe.'	56	Bowge	377
This worlde is nothynge but ete, drynke and slepe,	57	Bowge	384
Fye on this dyce, they be not worth a turde!	57	Bowge	392
Gone is this knave, this rybaude foule and leude.	58	Bowge	414
Gone is this knave, this rybaude foule and leude.	58	Bowge	414
Wheron was wryten this worde, Myscheve.	58	Bowge	434
It is a perylous vyce, this envy.	58	Bowge	444
For allbeit that this longe not to me,	59	Bowge	456
I hate this faynynge, fye upon it, fye!	59	Bowge	465
I hate this wayes agayne you that they take! this] 'these' Wynkyn de Worde 1510	59	Bowge	471
For this may brede to a confusyon,	59	Bowge	482
More coude I saye, but what this is ynowe.	60	Bowge	491
Adewe tyll soone, we shall speke more of this.	60	Bowge	492
Caughte penne and ynke, and wroth this lytell boke. wroth] 'wrote' Wynkyn de Worde 1510, Marshe 1568	61	Bowge	532
This worke devysed is /For suche as do amys,	61	Hauke	1

THIS —THIS	Page	Title	Line
This fonde frantyke fouconer,	63	Hauke	43
To snappar and to fall /Into this opyn cryme;	65	Hauke	143
To loke on this were tyme.	65	Hauke	144
And this the cause doth shrynke.	66	Hauke	159
To be polutyd this;	66	Hauke	181
And this he overthwartyd.	68	Hauke	230
Loke on this tabull, /Whether thou art abull	68	Hauke	235
This dowtless ye ravyd,	70	Hauke	307
Moderatly to take /This sorow that I make	74	Phy Sparrow	102
But all this is in vayne	77	Phy Sparrow	208
How commeth this to pas?'	77	Phy Sparrow	232
Tellynge this pyteyus tale,	80	Phy Sparrow	342
Of fortune this the chaunce /Standeth on varyaunce:	81	Phy Sparrow	366
Of this dolorous mater.	81	Phy Sparrow	398
This herse for to halow.	82	Phy Sparrow	405
Shall watche at this wake;	82	Phy Sparrow	437
At this Placebo	83	Phy Sparrow	466
A phenex it is /This herse that must blys	84	Phy Sparrow	519
This corse for to sence /With greate reverence,	85	Phy Sparrow	526
Of this phenyx kynde;	85	Phy Sparrow	539
This matter trew and playne,	85	Phy Sparrow	547
The kestrell in all this warke	86	Phy Sparrow	569
Is to take this commendacyon	93	Phy Sparrow	849
In this consyderacion;	93	Phy Sparrow	850
For this most goodly floure,	94	Phy Sparrow	893
This blossome of fresshe coulour,	94	Phy Sparrow	894
And thus this elf /Consumeth himself,	95	Phy Sparrow	945
This fals Envy /Sayth that I /Use great folly	95	Phy Sparrow	949
And my style dres /To this prosses.	96	Phy Sparrow	969
For this most goodly floure,	96	Phy Sparrow	989
This blossome of fresh coloure,	96	Phy Sparrow	990
For this most goodly floure,	97	Phy Sparrow	1022
This blossome of fresshe coloure,	97	Phy Sparrow	1023
This jelofer amyable;	98	Phy Sparrow	1053
[For] this most goodly floure,	98	Phy Sparrow	1054
For] not in †Kele 1545.2, Wyght 1553, Kitson 1560.6, Marshe 1568			
This blossom of fressh colour,	98	Phy Sparrow	1055
For this most goodly floure,	98	Phy Sparrow	1083
goodly] 'godly' †Kele 1545.2			
This blossom of fressh coloure,	98	Phy Sparrow	1084
For this most goodly flour,	99	Phy Sparrow	1107
This blossom of fressh colour,	99	Phy Sparrow	1108
This] 'The' Wyght 1553, Kitson 1560.6, Marshe 1568			
For this most goodly floure,	100	Phy Sparrow	1136
Th[is] blossom of fressh coloure,	100	Phy Sparrow	1137
This] 'The' editions			
For this most goodly floure,	100	Phy Sparrow	1161
This blossome of fressh coloure,	100	Phy Sparrow	1162
For this most goodly floure,	101	Phy Sparrow	1185
For] not in Kitson 1560.6, Marshe 1568			
This blossom of fressh coloure,	101	Phy Sparrow	1186
For this most goodly floure,	101	Phy Sparrow	1208
For this] 'The' †Kele 1545.2, Marshe 1568			
This blossome of fressh coloure,	101	Phy Sparrow	1209
This] 'Thus' †Kele 1545.2			
Jane this maystres hyght,	102	Phy Sparrow	1225
[For] this most goodly floure,	102	Phy Sparrow	1231
For] not in †Kele 1545.2, Wyght 1553, Kitson 1560.6, Marshe 1568; this] 'the' Wyght, Kitson, Marshe			
This blossome of fresshe colour,	102	Phy Sparrow	1232
With this psalme, Domine, probasti me,	102	Phy Sparrow	1239
This treatyse to despyse	103	Phy Sparrow	1252
Honour to this fayre mayd;	103	Phy Sparrow	1254
What the cause may be /Of this perplexite!	106	Phy Sparrow	1370
And of this worke complayned,	106	Phy Sparrow	1375
This tretise devysed it is	106	Epitaphe	I
Though this knaves be deade,	106	Epitaphe	I
Fratres, orate, /For this knavate,	108	Epitaphe1	65
And pray shall, /At this trentall	108	Epitaphe1	70
This hunderd yere scantly	111	Lawde	18
Of this our noble king	111	Lawde	29
Skelton Laureate, Orator Regius, maketh this aunswere &c.	112	Calliope	I
Within this quaire? /Who lyst repayre	116	Ag Scottes	41
lyst] 'lyst to' Kynge & Marche 1554, Day 1560, Marshe 1568			
UNTO DYVERS PEOPLE THAT REMORD THIS RYMYNG	120	Ag Scottes	R
This invectyve to make /For some peoples sake	120	Ag Scottes2	3
Agaynst this my makyng, /Their males therat shakyng,	120	Ag Scottes2	7
He skantly loveth our kyng, /That grudgeth at this thing:	121	Ag Scottes2	36
This Dundas, /This Scottishe as	135	Dundas	7
This Dundas, /This Scottishe as	135	Dundas	8
Skelton laureat /After this rate	135	Dundas	20
Why doste thow deprave /This royall reame,	136	Dundas	44
On Huntley bankes, /Take this our thankes;	136	Dundas	59
And so dysordereth this worlde over all,	141	Magnyfycence	20
Here you not howe this gentylman mockys?	141	Magnyfycence	32
Perceyve ye this parcell?	142	Magnyfycence	55
I trowe ye can not say nay moche to this:	142	Magnyfycence	74
Measure is treasure. Howe say ye, is it not this?	144	Magnyfycence	125

717

THIS —THIS

	Page	Title	Line
Take sad dyreccyon, and leve this wantonnesse.	144	Magnyfycence	149
But Measure, my frende, what hyght this mannys name?	145	Magnyfycence	165
Yet in this man you must set your delyght.	145	Magnyfycence	167
And, syr, this other mannys name is Lyberte.	145	Magnyfycence	168
This lynkyd chayne of love that can unbynde.	146	Magnyfycence	201
It is a wanton thynge, this Lyberte.	147	Magnyfycence	240
Now leve this jangelynge and to us expounde	147	Magnyfycence	262
With Magnyfycence, this noble prynce of myght,	148	Magnyfycence	273
Let se this checke yf ye voyde canne.	148	Magnyfycence	297
And sendeth you this wrytynge closed under sele.	149	Magnyfycence	312
This wrytynge is welcome with harty affeccyon!	149	Magnyfycence	313
I shall come to you myselfe, I trowe, this afternone.	149	Magnyfycence	322
Whylest I knowe that this letter dothe contayne.	149	Magnyfycence	324
But nowe, syr, as touchynge this letter -	149	Magnyfycence	331
This letter was wryten ferre hence.	150	Magnyfycence	337
This wrytynge was taken me there,	150	Magnyfycence	344
I had not been here with you this nyght.	150	Magnyfycence	365
And he that I came fro to this place	150	Magnyfycence	372
Togyder we wyll talke more of this.	151	Magnyfycence	393
I hate this blunderyng that thou doste make.	151	Magnyfycence	400
This noble man Magnyfycence,	151	Magnyfycence	404
This worlde is full of my foly.	152	Magnyfycence	411
To counterfet this freers have lerned me.	154	Magnyfycence	487
This nonnes nowe and then, and it myght be,	154	Magnyfycence	488
In all this hast whether wyll ye ryde?	156	Magnyfycence	570
By God, syr, this is Fansy Small-Brayne;	156	Magnyfycence	583
What call ye him, this?	156	Magnyfycence	588
Ye, by the masse, this is even the same,	157	Magnyfycence	599
That all this matter must under grope.	157	Magnyfycence	600
What is this he wereth? A cope?	157	Magnyfycence	601
All this ye may easely brynge aboute.	158	Magnyfycence	655
This was properly prated, syrs! What sayd a?	161	Magnyfycence	746
Gyve this gentylman rome, syrs. Stonde utter!	161	Magnyfycence	753
By God, syr, what nede all this waste?	161	Magnyfycence	754
What is this, a betell or a batowe or a buskyn lacyd?	161	Magnyfycence	755
Wyll ye se this gentylman is all in his skornys?	162	Magnyfycence	773
What the devyll! Where had we this joly jetter?	162	Magnyfycence	796
Why, is this the gyse nowe adays?	163	Magnyfycence	813
But, syr, I wyll have this man with me.	163	Magnyfycence	815
This newe fonne jet	165	Magnyfycence	877
All this nacyon /I set on fyre; /In my facyon	165	Magnyfycence	884
This theyr desyre, /This newe atyre.	165	Magnyfycence	887
This theyr desyre, /This newe atyre.	165	Magnyfycence	888
This ladyes have, /I it them gave.	165	Magnyfycence	889
That fell amonge us this same day?	166	Magnyfycence	933
Cockes bones! This is all of John de Gay.	167	Magnyfycence	960
Lo, this is /My fansy, iwys;	167	Magnyfycence	971
In all this rowte	168	Magnyfycence	992
Among this prese - /Even a hole mese	168	Magnyfycence	995
On this halfe and on every syde	168	Magnyfycence	1020
Nowe I wyll this, and nowe I wyll that -	169	Magnyfycence	1027
I wyll not have it so, I wyll have it this.	169	Magnyfycence	1042
What is this, an owle or a glede?	169	Magnyfycence	1047
Cockys armys! This is a warke, I trowe.	170	Magnyfycence	1094
Ye, bere me this strawe to a dawys nest.	170	Magnyfycence	1097
What! Canest thou all this Latyn yet,	172	Magnyfycence	1143
And, 'This is not well done, syr; take hede';	175	Magnyfycence	1248
My frende, as touchynge to this your mocyon,	186	Magnyfycence	1639
Syr, so it is: this man is here by,	186	Magnyfycence	1649
That he shall lyke the worse all this woke.	187	Magnyfycence	1682
This is a wyse man, syr, where so ever ye hym had.	187	Magnyfycence	1689
He can full craftely this matter brynge aboute.	187	Magnyfycence	1691
In your brest towardes this gentylman.	188	Magnyfycence	1713
For I am panged ofte tymes in this same facyon.	189	Magnyfycence	1734
Syr, of my counsayle this shall be the grounde:	190	Magnyfycence	1768
And therfore hye you hens, and take this oversyght.	190	Magnyfycence	1795
Who is this? Consayte, syr, your owne man.	191	Magnyfycence	1804
Why, is this the largesse that I have usyd?	193	Magnyfycence	1865
And is this the credence that I gave to the letter?	193	Magnyfycence	1867
What? Yes, by the rode, syr. It was I all this whyle	193	Magnyfycence	1870
Take hede of this captyve that lyeth here on grounde.	195	Magnyfycence	1946
For though we shewe you this in game and play,	195	Magnyfycence	1948
For nowe wyll I from this caytyfe go,	195	Magnyfycence	1950
Take this caytyfe to thy lore.	195	Magnyfycence	1954
Nowe must I this carcasse lyft up.	195	Magnyfycence	1964
Syr, all this wolde have bene thought on before.	196	Magnyfycence	1970
Fy, fy, that ever I sholde be brought in this snare!	196	Magnyfycence	1972
Lo, suche is this worlde! I fynde it wryt,	196	Magnyfycence	1974
Never had I bene brought in this case.	196	Magnyfycence	1977
Ye, syr, ye; leve all this rage,	196	Magnyfycence	1988
And ye have deserved this punysshment.	196	Magnyfycence	2003
Fye on this worlde, full of trechery,	197	Magnyfycence	2020
But yet, syr, nowe in this case	197	Magnyfycence	2032
This lurden that here lyeth had ben a noble man.	200	Magnyfycence	2112
This mysery, this carefull wrechydnesse?	201	Magnyfycence	2154
This mysery, this carefull wrechydnesse?	201	Magnyfycence	2154
Mary, syr, this gentylman caled me javell.	203	Magnyfycence	2211
A, shall we have more of this maters yet?	203	Magnyfycence	2214

THIS — THIS	Page	Title	Line
Ye, but trowe you, syrs, that this is he?	204	Magnyfycence	2242
Ye, ryd thy selfe rather than this lyfe for to lede.	205	Magnyfycence	2307
With this halter good and stronge;	206	Magnyfycence	2313
Or ellys with this knyfe cut out a tonge	206	Magnyfycence	2314
Nay; rather wyll I chose to ryd me of this lyve	206	Magnyfycence	2321
In styckynge my selfe with this fayre knyfe.	206	Magnyfycence	2322
Take nowe upon you this abylyment,	208	Magnyfycence	2405
Yet let us se this matter thorowly ingrosed.	209	Magnyfycence	2438
Syr, this letter ye sent to me at Pountes was enclosed.	209	Magnyfycence	2439
This letter ye speke of never dyd I wryte.	209	Magnyfycence	2442
What this man hath sayd, perceyve ye his sentence?	210	Magnyfycence	2465
Commensynge this processe at mayster Redresse.	211	Magnyfycence	2481
Syth unto me formest this processe is erectyd,	211	Magnyfycence	2482
Remember this lyfe lastyth but a whyle.	211	Magnyfycence	2502
Unto this processe brefly compylyd,	212	Magnyfycence	2510
Howe in this worlde there is no seke[r]nesse,	212	Magnyfycence	2515
sekernesse] 'sekenesse' †Rastell & Treveris C 1530, B			
So in this worlde there is no sykernesse,	212	Magnyfycence	2522
A myrrour incleryd is this interlude,	212	Magnyfycence	2524
This lyfe inconstant for to beholde and se:	212	Magnyfycence	2525
This treatyse, devysyd to make you dysporte,	213	Magnyfycence	2538
Thus in this worlde there is no erthly truste.	213	Magnyfycence	2544
Thus in this worlde there is no erthly truste.	213	Magnyfycence	2551
This mater we have movyd, you myrthys to make,	213	Magnyfycence	2552
For the welthe of this worlde can not indure.	213	Magnyfycence	2558
For the welthe of this worlde can not indure.	214	Magnyfycence	2565
And this comely dame,	216	El Rummynge	91
This ale shal be thycker,	219	El Rummynge	205
This make I my falyre fonny,	220	El Rummynge	229
And of this tale to rest,	220	El Rummynge	236
And for to leve this letter, /Bicause it is no better;	220	El Rummynge	237
We wyll no farther ryme /Of it at this tyme.	220	El Rummynge	241
'I dranke not this sennet /A draught to my pay.	224	El Rummynge	394
Some brought this and that,	225	El Rummynge	440
But of all this thronge /One came them amonge,	225	El Rummynge	445
What nede all this be spoken?	227	El Rummynge	499
And all this shyfte they make	228	El Rummynge	533
This is a solempne drynkynge.	228	El Rummynge	548
'This ale,' sayd she, 'is noppy;	228	El Rummynge	557
Of this mad mummynge /Of Elynour Rummynge	230	El Rummynge	620
Thus endeth the gest /Of this worthy fest.	230	El Rummynge	623
'Parott hathe not dyned of all this long day;'	231	Speke Parott	23
'Que pensez-voz, Parrot? What meneth this besynes?'	232	Speke Parott	58
'What is this to purpose?' Over in a whynnymeg!	232	Speke Parott	71
For in this processe, Parrot nothing hath surmysed,	236	Speke Parott	200
Poynt well this probleme that Parrot doth prate,	236	Speke Parott	220
Shall lepe from this lyfe, as mery as we be.	236	Speke Parott	222
In this your journey to prosper and spede.	239	Speke Parott	314
Sey this and sey that:	247	Collyn Clout	15
And yf ye stande in doute /Who brought this ryme aboute,	248	Collyn Clout	48
And whyles the heedes do this, /The remenaunt is amys	249	Collyn Clout	115
But this reason they take:	250	Collyn Clout	142
In this that I have pende.	251	Collyn Clout	187
This dominus vobiscum	253	Collyn Clout	281
Over this, the foresayd lay	254	Collyn Clout	301
This is a farly fytte	255	Collyn Clout	329
farly] 'fearfull' †Godfray 1531, Kele 1545.1, Marshe 1568, 'ffarly' MS Harley 2252			
Your teth whett on this bone	258	Collyn Clout	476
whett on] 'whetten' †Godfray 1531, 'whette on' MS Harley 2252			
Of this to reporte.	259	Collyn Clout	504
This is a pyteous case:	262	Collyn Clout	626
All this is out of mynde.	263	Collyn Clout	660
All] 'Alas' Kele 1545.1, Marshe 1568, 'All' MS Harley 2252			
And suffre all this yll?	263	Collyn Clout	689
For the wele publyke /Of preesthode in this case;	264	Collyn Clout	698
After this maner rates;	264	Collyn Clout	709
He must do this werke;	264	Collyn Clout	728
Farther in this broke,	266	Collyn Clout	782
In devysynge of this boke,	266	Collyn Clout	784
This can nat be brought about	267	Collyn Clout	849
Howe may this come to pas,	272	Collyn Clout	1021
And howe may this accorde,	272	Collyn Clout	1029
This is a wonderous warke!	272	Collyn Clout	1048
That the people talke this,	272	Collyn Clout	1049
In your convenire /Of this premenyre,	273	Collyn Clout	1068
Though I wryte after this facyon;	273	Collyn Clout	1080
This treatyse to deprave;	274	Collyn Clout	1132
Make this lurdeyne for to loure;	275	Collyn Clout	1168
And after this rate	276	Collyn Clout	1180
Is nat this a shamfull scorne	276	Collyn Clout	1200
Lo, this is the gyse noweadayes!	277	Collyn Clout	1227
Nor wyll suffre this boke	277	Collyn Clout	1237
All noble men of this take hede,	278	Why Come Ye	1
of this] not in MS Rawlinson C. 813			
All noble men of this take hede,	279	Why Come Ye	15
Marke well this conclusyon:	279	Why Come Ye	18
And yf ye thynke this shall	279	Why Come Ye	24

THIS—THIS

	Page	Title	Line
All noble men of this take hede,	279	Why Come Ye	27
This tale will be to trew:	280	Why Come Ye	65
This byll well over loked,	281	Why Come Ye	118
This is a postels lyfe.	284	Why Come Ye	226
But now upon this story	284	Why Come Ye	229
For all this worldly wonder,	285	Why Come Ye	258
This is a trew text!	285	Why Come Ye	261
For and this curre do gnar,	286	Why Come Ye	300
Now yet all this myght be	290	Why Come Ye	446
But this madde Amalecke,	291	Why Come Ye	478
Of all this prelacy,	291	Why Come Ye	503
But have ye nat harde this,	292	Why Come Ye	532
This man was full unable	292	Why Come Ye	537
And of this poore vassall	293	Why Come Ye	557
Shulde this man of suche mode	293	Why Come Ye	579
Of this gentell Jack Breche,	294	Why Come Ye	616
This daungerous dowsypere /Lyke a kynges pere!	295	Why Come Ye	639
And within this xvi yere	295	Why Come Ye	641
For to rewle this reame,	295	Why Come Ye	656
And is governed by this mad kote!	295	Why Come Ye	668
And] not in Marshe 1568			
This is no fable nor no lye;	296	Why Come Ye	705
Of this isagogicall colation,	297	Why Come Ye	717
All the rule of this lande,	298	Why Come Ye	762
Of this matter the grownde	298	Why Come Ye	780
Tell me nowe in this stede,	298	Why Come Ye	786
Upon this matter mistycall	299	Why Come Ye	821
Of this wanton scrowle.	300	Why Come Ye	831
That this warke began	301	Why Come Ye	894
This shrewdly accordis /To be a cupborde for lordys!	302	Why Come Ye	913
Fye on this wynnyng allway!	302	Why Come Ye	929
this] not in MS Rawlinson C. 813			
Downe this hye sprynge;	302	Why Come Ye	950
What a frensy is this,	305	Why Come Ye	1050
This maumet in lyke wyse	306	Why Come Ye	1070
Wherof this ungracyous lorde	306	Why Come Ye	1098
All this he dothe deale	306	Why Come Ye	1101
'Thys now he dothe meale' MS Rawlinson C. 813			
And yet, this gracelesse elfe,	307	Why Come Ye	1115
gracelesse] 'ungratyous' MS Rawlinson C. 813			
This Naman Sirus, /So fell and so irous,	308	Why Come Ye	1166
Sirus] 'tyrus' MS Rawlinson C. 813			
And yet this proude Antiochus,	308	Why Come Ye	1175
By whose suggestyon /I toke on hand this warke,	309	Why Come Ye	1204
suggestyon] 'subjectyon' MS Rawlinson C. 813			
To wryght of this glorious gest,	309	Why Come Ye	1212
glorious] 'gromys' MS Rawlinson C. 813			
Of this vayne gloryous best,	309	Why Come Ye	1213
This is the tenor of my byl,	310	Why Come Ye2	33
So depely drownyd I was in this dumpe,	312	Garlande	15
Whylis I stode musynge in this medytatyon,	313	Garlande	29
Wherin this answere for hym we have comprisid,	314	Garlande	80
How be it, it were harde to construe this lecture;	315	Garlande	109
Unto your grace then make I this motyve:	315	Garlande	114
Yet shall I answere your grace as in this,	316	Garlande	144
Anone, I sey, this trumpet were founde out,	319	Garlande	243
Why have the goddes shewyd me this cruelte,	321	Garlande	309
Odious Disdayne, why raist thou me on this facyon?	321	Garlande	317
This sayd, a great nowmber folowyd by and by	321	Garlande	323
To yow thre this honor shalbe reserved	323	Garlande	409
Envawtyd with rubies the vawte was of this place.	325	Garlande	476
Unto this place all poetis there did sue,	325	Garlande	481
Encrownyd as empresse of all this wordly fate,	325	Garlande	486
wordly] 'worldly' Marshe 1568			
This hous envyrowne was a myle about;	326	Garlande	489
Then to this lady and soverayne of this palace	326	Garlande	491
Then to this lady and soverayne of this palace	326	Garlande	491
Of this high courte the dayly besines;	326	Garlande	519
This gentilwoman, that callyd was by name	327	Garlande	527
To se this howre now, that I may say,	327	Garlande	538
How ye ar welcome to this court of aray.	327	Garlande	539
To walke on this walle she bed I sholde not stint;	328	Garlande	571
'What yate call ye this?' And she sayd, 'Anglea'.	328	Garlande	588
yate] 'gate' Marshe 1568			
And with his forme foote he shoke forthe this wrytyng:	328	Garlande	595
'How say ye? Is this after your appetite?	331	Garlande	707
May this contente you and your mirry mynde?	332	Garlande	708
Jupiter hymselfe this lyfe myght endure;	332	Garlande	715
This joy excedith all wordly sport and play,	332	Garlande	716
wordly] 'worldly' Marshe 1568			
Paradyce this place is of syngular pleasure.	332	Garlande	717
Now, by your faith, is not this theffect	333	Garlande	737
by] 'be' tFakes 1523			
Of your questyon ye make all this whyle	333	Garlande	738
To worke me this chapelet by goode advysemente.	334	Garlande	807
Cause me to cese, /Amonge this prese,	339	Garlande	958
To here this nightingale,	340	Garlande	997

	Page	Title	Line
As mirry Margarete, /This midsomer flowre,	341	Garlande	1035
This] 'The' MS Cotton Vitellius E.x			
To wryte of you this goodli clause,	341	Garlande	1042
To wryte of yow this goodly clause,	342	Garlande	1050
To wryte of you this goodly clause,	342	Garlande	1058
Set on your hede this laurell whiche is wrought.	343	Garlande	1087
Forthwith upon this, as it were in a thought,	343	Garlande	1100
Of this warke they had so great delyght,	343	Garlande	1110
Wherof in substaunce I brought this away.	344	Garlande	1120
To answere unto this noble audyence,	344	Garlande	1122
So then commaundid she was upon this	344	Garlande	1147
This fustiane maistres and this giggisse gase	346	Garlande	1206
This fustiane maistres and this giggisse gase	346	Garlande	1206
What the cause may be /Of this perplexyte.	350	Garlande	1363
And of this worke complaynyd,	350	Garlande	1368
Graund juir, of this Frenshe proverbe olde,	352	Garlande	1440
This goodly flowre with stormis was untwynde.	352	Garlande	1445
This jeloffer jentyll, this rose, this lylly flowre,	352	Garlande	1446
This jeloffer jentyll, this rose, this lylly flowre,	352	Garlande	1446
This jeloffer jentyll, this rose, this lylly flowre,	352	Garlande	1446
This primerose pereles, this propre vyolet,	352	Garlande	1447
This primerose pereles, this propre vyolet,	352	Garlande	1447
This columbyne clere and fresshest of coloure,	352	Garlande	1448
This delycate dasy, this strawbery pretely set,	352	Garlande	1449
This delycate dasy, this strawbery pretely set,	352	Garlande	1449
Thynke what ye wyll /Of this wanton byll;	353	Garlande	1454
'Nay, sir' she sayd, 'what so in this place	353	Garlande	1481
Good luk this new yere, the olde yere is past.	354	Garlande	1518
Though I you wrate /After this rate	355	Garlande	1537
This Duke so fell /Of Albany, /So cowardly	359	Albany	6
Of this cowarde knyght,	359	Albany	15
For the cause is this,	361	Albany	87
Of this, his realme royall /And lande imperiall,	368	Albany	393
This mater to credence	372	Albany	522
This lytel enterprise;	372	Albany	527
that this lytell pamphilet, called the Replicacion	373	Replycacion	I
Over this, for a more ample processe	374	Replycacion	I
Agaynst this horryble heresy	375	Replycacion	21
Or more of this to clatter?	378	Replycacion	159
Howe ye are this day,	379	Replycacion	177
Some juged in this case	379	Replycacion	197
To this ye nedes must agre.	381	Replycacion	284
agaynst Skelton laureate, devyser of this Replycacyon, etc.	382	Replycacion	R
I call to this rekenyng	383	Replycacion	316
Th[i]s may nat be remorded	383	Replycacion	323
This] 'Thus' †Pynson 1528			
Than, if this noble kyng,	384	Replycacion	343
In this that I do make	385	Replycacion	399

THY

	Page	Title	Line
By thy report ar wonte to be extolde	29	Dol Dethe	17
Of thy bounte after the usuall rate	29	Dol Dethe	19
Kyndle in me suche plente of thy nobles,	29	Dol Dethe	20
O grounde ungracious, unhappy be thy fame,	32	Dol Dethe	116
That with thy sworde enharpid of mortall drede	32	Dol Dethe	125
Unto thy subjectis be kurteis and beningne.	33	Dol Dethe	168
Stabille thy mynde constant to be and fast,	34	Dol Dethe	170
Thow bringe unto thy joye etermynable	34	Dol Dethe	199
Thow] 'how' †MS Royal 18 D.ii			
In thy palace above the orient,	34	Dol Dethe	202
Pray to thy son above the starris clere,	35	Dol Dethe	208
He to vouchesaf, by thy mediacioun,	35	Dol Dethe	209
But graunt us grace /To se thy face,	40	Coystrowne3	50
And thy palace, /Full of solace,	40	Coystrowne3	53
Thy lust and lykyng is from the gone;	42	Balettys1	23
Bewayle thy fortune, with vaynys wan and blo.	45	Balettys5	3
What is thy name?' and I sayde it was Drede.	48	Bowge	77
By Goddis syde, my sworde thy berde shall shave!	55	Bowge	339
We be thy betters, and so thou shalte us take,	55	Bowge	342
Or we shall the oute of thy clothes shake!'	55	Bowge	343
A brydelynge caste for that is in thy male!	57	Bowge	390
Domine concupisti, /With thy hawke on thy fysty?	69	Hauke	260
Domine concupisti, /With thy hawke on thy fysty?	69	Hauke	260
Hampar with your hammer upon thy styth,	71	Hauke	332
The fynde was in thy mynde	78	Phy Sparrow	283
Might poyson thy lyver and longes!	79	Phy Sparrow	293
Myght fede them on thy braynes!	79	Phy Sparrow	295
Myght byte asondre thy throte!	79	Phy Sparrow	306
Myght tere out all thy trypes!	79	Phy Sparrow	308
Byte asondre thy backe bone!	79	Phy Sparrow	312
Set in thy tayle a blase	79	Phy Sparrow	315
Our Lorde thy soule reskew!	80	Phy Sparrow	332
Thy loving sovereine lorde,	110	Lawde	9
Now Garnyche, garde thy gummys;	128	Garnesche3	158
Thou mokkyshe marmoset, /I will nat dy in [thy] det.	128	Garnesche3	173
thy] 'they' †MS Harley 367			
[Thy] myrrour may be the devyllys ars.	130	Garnesche5	18
Thy] 'They' †MS Harley 367			
Within thy skyn he xall remayne.	130	Garnesche5	22

	Page	Title	Line
Sayth, from thy to unto thi croune,	130	Garnesche5	26
Thy caytyvys carkes, cours and crasy;	130	Garnesche5	31
Moche of thy maneres I ca[n] blasy.	130	Garnesche5	32
can] 'cam' †MS Harley 367			
Haroldis they know thy cote-armur;	131	Garnesche5	68
It semyth nat thy pyllyd pate	132	Garnesche5	89
That creaunser was to thy sofre[yne] lorde;	132	Garnesche5	102
sofreyne] 'sofre' †MS Harley 367			
Thy tong untawte, with poyson infecte,	132	Garnesche5	108
Lerne or be lewde, I shrow thy face.	132	Garnesche5	127
Yt wold garnyche wyll thy face.	133	Garnesche5	135
Thy fonde face can me nat fray.	134	Garnesche5	171
Of thy lewdenes more ys behynde;	134	Garnesche5	173
Set in better /Thy pentameter.	135	Dundas	6
Shake thy tayle, Scot, lyke a cur,	135	Dundas	25
With thy versyfyeng rayles /How they have tayles.	135	Dundas	30
For thy Scottyshe nose,	136	Dundas	36
A spectacle case /To cover thy face, /With, tray deux ase.	136	Dundas	38
Nowe, I beseche the, tell me what is thy name?	148	Magnyfycence	269
For Cockys harte, gyve me thy hande.	154	Magnyfycence	512
Thy wordes be but wynde, never they have no wayght.	156	Magnyfycence	578
Thy slyppers they swap it, yet thou fotys it lyke a swanne.	161	Magnyfycence	765
Nay. Thou art a man good inough but for thy false hart.	162	Magnyfycence	769
What! Is thy harte pryckyd with such a prowde pynne?	162	Magnyfycence	785
And desyre me thy good mayster to be?	162	Magnyfycence	798
What the devyll hast thou on thy fyste? An owle?	166	Magnyfycence	922
Holde thy pease! Measure shall frome us walke.	166	Magnyfycence	949
What, fonnysshe Foly! I befole thy face.	169	Magnyfycence	1045
Tusshe! Thy lyppes hange in thyne eye;	169	Magnyfycence	1049
eye] 'eyen' †Rastell & Treveris C 1530, B			
What pylde curre ledest thou in thy hande?	169	Magnyfycence	1054
And thy wyt wanderynge here and there,	170	Magnyfycence	1074
That thou cannyst not growe out of thy boyes gere;	170	Magnyfycence	1075
Nowe, of good felowshyp, let me by thy [d]ogge.	170	Magnyfycence	1082
dogge] 'hogge' †Rastell & Treveris C 1530, B			
The devyls torde for thy brayne!	170	Magnyfycence	1086
Let me have thy dogge, what soever I pay.	171	Magnyfycence	1101
Yet gyve me thy dogge, and I am content;	171	Magnyfycence	1112
Nowe take thou my dogge and gyve me thy fowle.	171	Magnyfycence	1116
What callest thou thy dogge? Tusshe! His name is Gryme.	171	Magnyfycence	1118
Ye, for all thy mynde is on owles and apes.	171	Magnyfycence	1134
But I have thy pultre, and thou hast my catell.	171	Magnyfycence	1135
Tell by thy trouth what sport can thou make.	172	Magnyfycence	1162
A, holde thy peas! I have the tothe ake.	172	Magnyfycence	1163
What hast thou on thy fyst? A [k]esteryll?	173	Magnyfycence	1174
kesteryll] 'besteryll' †Rastell & Treveris C 1530, B			
Thou must have thy fansy and thy wyll,	173	Magnyfycence	1183
Thou must have thy fansy and thy wyll,	173	Magnyfycence	1183
That I shall laughe the out of thy cote.	173	Magnyfycence	1194
Put on thy gowne agayne, for thou hast lost nowe.	173	Magnyfycence	1203
thou ... nowe] 'nowe thou hast lost' †Rastell & Treveris C 1530, B			
Lo, Johnn a Bonam, where is thy brayne?	173	Magnyfycence	1204
Nowe put on, fole, thy cote agayne.	173	Magnyfycence	1205
Shyt thy purse, dawe, and do no cost.	174	Magnyfycence	1207
Thynkyst thou not so, by thy fayth?	175	Magnyfycence	1253
Holde thy tonge, and thou love thy helth.	179	Magnyfycence	1402
Holde thy tonge, and thou love thy helth.	179	Magnyfycence	1402
Thy wordes and my mynde well accorde.	185	Magnyfycence	1605
Well, for thy sake the better I may endure	187	Magnyfycence	1680
What tydynges with you, syr? I befole thy brayne pan.	191	Magnyfycence	1805
A, syr, thy jarfawcon and thou be hanged togyder!	191	Magnyfycence	1812
Thy wordes hange togyder as fethers in the wynde.	191	Magnyfycence	1818
Ye, let be thy japes, and tell me howe	192	Magnyfycence	1846
I pray the, Largesse, let be thy sobbynge.	192	Magnyfycence	1851
I am Adversyte, that for thy mysdede	193	Magnyfycence	1876
From God am sente to quyte the thy mede.	193	Magnyfycence	1877
Ly there, losell, for all thy pompe and pryde;	193	Magnyfycence	1880
Thy pleasure now with payne and trouble shalbe tryde.	193	Magnyfycence	1881
Take this caytyfe to thy lore.	195	Magnyfycence	1954
I am Magnyfycence, that somtyme thy mayster was.	200	Magnyfycence	2107
What hast thou gotted, in faythe, to thy share?	201	Magnyfycence	2162
Leve thy pratynge or els I shall lay the on the pate.	201	Magnyfycence	2173
By the messe, I shall cleve thy heed to the waste.	201	Magnyfycence	2175
Ye, wylte thou clenly cle[v]e me in the clyfte with thy nose?	202	Magnyfycence	2176
cleve] 'clene' †Rastell & Treveris C 1530, B			
Peas, or I shall wrynge thy be in a brake.	202	Magnyfycence	2187
Holde thy hande, dawe, of thy dagger, and stynt of thy dyn;	202	Magnyfycence	2188
Holde thy hande, dawe, of thy dagger, and stynt of thy dyn;	202	Magnyfycence	2188
Holde thy hande, dawe, of thy dagger, and stynt of thy dyn;	202	Magnyfycence	2188
Or I shal fawchyn thy flesshe and scrape the on the skyn.	202	Magnyfycence	2189
Mary, I defye thy best and thy worst.	202	Magnyfycence	2197
Mary, I defye thy best and thy worst.	202	Magnyfycence	2197
Cockys bonys! Thou begger, what is thy name?	203	Magnyfycence	2240
Ye, for thy langage can not the avayle.	204	Magnyfycence	2249
It is to late nowe thy synnys to repent.	205	Magnyfycence	2292
And so fer thou arte behynde of thy rent,	205	Magnyfycence	2294
And so ungracyously thy dayes thou hast spent,	205	Magnyfycence	2295

THYCKE —THYNE	Page	Title	Line

	Page	Title	Line
No, no; for thy synnys be so excedynge farre,	205	Magnyfycence	2300
And agayne thy maker thou hast made suche warre,	205	Magnyfycence	2302
Out of thy lyfe the for to lede.	205	Magnyfycence	2310
Of thy throte bole, and ryd the out of payne.	206	Magnyfycence	2315
Lo, here is thy knyfe and a halter, and or we go ferther,	206	Magnyfycence	2317
Alas, dere sone, sore combred is thy mynde,	206	Magnyfycence	2325
A grete mysadventure, thy maker to dysplease,	206	Magnyfycence	2341
'I beshrew the for thy cummyng!'	227	El Rummynge	503
With, 'Fy, cover thy shap	227	El Rummynge	507
thy] 'the' Kynge & Marche 1554, Day 1560, Marshe 1568			
Quod Parot, thy popagay royall.	238	Speke Parott	262a
Quod] 'Quid' †MS Harley 2252			
Goddes blissyng lyght on thy lytell swete musse!	238	Speke Parott	266
Prate of thy matens and thy mas,	275	Collyn Clout	1158
Prate of thy matens and thy mas,	275	Collyn Clout	1158
Ge heme! ge scour thy pot,	282	Why Come Ye	126
Thy lernynge is to lewde,	287	Why Come Ye	330
Thy tonge is nat well thewde,	287	Why Come Ye	331
'Nay, holde thy tunge,' quod another, 'let me have the name.'	319	Garlande	255
Sume sayd, 'Holde thy peas, thou getest here no more.'	319	Garlande	257
Sum medelynge spyes, by craft to grope thy mynde,	329	Garlande	617
Full gloryously can he glose, thy mynde for to fele;	333	Garlande	760
Gentle Paule lie doune thy sweard,	358	Couplet	1
For Peter of Westminster hath shaven thy beard.	358	Couplet	2
Twyt, Scot, go kepe thy den.	362	Albany	145
We shall breke thy bones	362	Albany	150
The fynde, Scot, breke thy necke.	363	Albany	156
Thy herte wolde nat serve the.	365	Albany	250
With dugges, dugges, dugges. /I shrewe thy Scottishe lugges,	366	Albany	292
Thy munpynnys, and thy crag,	366	Albany	293
Thy munpynnys, and thy crag,	366	Albany	293
Thy mellyng is but mockyng.	366	Albany	298
Thou mayst give up thy cocking.	366	Albany	299
In spyght of thy cowardes face,	369	Albany	408
In spyght of thy cowardes face,	371	Albany	492
Avaunt, cowarde recrayed! /Thy pride shalbe alayd,	371	Albany	496

THYCKE

	Page	Title	Line
How some delite for to lye, thycke and threfolde.	137	Ven Tongues	11
But she spake somwhat thycke,	223	El Rummynge	338
Was well a fote thycke,	225	El Rummynge	430
Somtyme a bacon flycke /That is thre fyngers thycke	267	Collyn Clout	845

THYCKE-LYPPED

	Page	Title	Line
She was ugly hypped, /And ugly thycke-lypped	226	El Rummynge	469

THYCKER

	Page	Title	Line
This ale shal be thycker,	219	El Rummynge	205

THYDDER

	Page	Title	Line
Than thydder came dronken Ales	223	El Rummynge	351

THYDER

	Page	Title	Line
By Goddis sydes, syns I her thyder broughte,	57	Bowge	404
By God, we wolde gete us all thyder,	157	Magnyfycence	618
When we have hym thyder convayed,	159	Magnyfycence	676
Hyder and thyder, I wote not whyder;	169	Magnyfycence	1033
Some have no mony /That thyder commy,	218	El Rummynge	161
Some go streyght thyder, /Be it slaty or slyder;	221	El Rummynge	257
And thyder came an hepe /Of mylstones in a route.'	223	El Rummynge	361
thyder] 'there' †Lant 1545, Kynge & Marche 1554, Day 1560, Marshe 1568			
That she thyder bare /To pay for her share.	228	El Rummynge	545
When thei agayn thyder shal come,	268	Collyn Clout	883
Have hym thyder by and by!	275	Collyn Clout	1172

THYDYR

	Page	Title	Line
Of owur clerke Cleros. Whythyr, thydyr and why not hethyr?	243	Speke Parott	412

THYMBELL

	Page	Title	Line
Theyr nedell and theyr thymbell:	222	El Rummynge	300

THYMBLE

	Page	Title	Line
Some brought a thymble,	227	El Rummynge	527

THYN

	Page	Title	Line
Grow and encrese, remembre thyn astate!	33	Dol Dethe	163
For harlottes hawnte thyn hatefull cors;	131	Garnesche5	72
Presumptuous pride ys all thyn hope;	133	Garnesche5	160
Her thryfte is full thyn.	221	El Rummynge	256

THYNE

	Page	Title	Line
God the assyst unto thyne heritage,	33	Dol Dethe	164
And to purchace /Thyne hevenly place	40	Coystrowne3	52
I wys, powle hachet, she bleryd thyne I!	42	Balettys1	28
Plucke up thyne herte upon a mery pyne,	57	Bowge	386
'Harken,' quod he, 'loo here myne honde in thyne;	60	Bowge	510
Might plucke away thyne eares!	79	Phy Sparrow	310
By God, man, bothe his pagent and thyne he can play.	154	Magnyfycence	505
Nowe what is his name? And what is thyne?	155	Magnyfycence	519
Cockes harte! Tourne the; let me se thyne aray.	167	Magnyfycence	959
Tusshe! Thy lyppes hange in thyne eye;	169	Magnyfycence	1049
eye] 'eyen' †Rastell & Treveris C 1530, B			
In faythe, man, my brayne is as good as thyne.	170	Magnyfycence	1085
Thou shalte have my purse, and I wyll have thyne.	171	Magnyfycence	1102
Nay, in fayth, fyrst let me here thyne.	172	Magnyfycence	1152
And was it his, and nowe it is thyne?	173	Magnyfycence	1182
Why, wenest thou that I forbere the for thyne owne sake?	202	Magnyfycence	2186

THYNG —THYNKE	Page	Title	Line

	Page	Title	Line
Thyselfe myschevynge to thyne endlesse dysease!	206	Magnyfycence	2342
Of thyne ale let us assaye,	224	El Rummynge	397
For than thyne heed of gose.	288	Why Come Ye	385
THYNG			
But one thyng is: that ye be lewde!	41	Coystrowne4	27
Somtyme a presyous thyng,	88	Phy Sparrow	685
Yet there was a thyng	89	Phy Sparrow	699
To you no thyng it dyde accorde	113	Scot Kynge	3
A trym-tram for an horse-myll it were a nyse thyng,	234	Speke Parott	128
That is another thyng.	287	Why Come Ye	347
But wele may ye thynk I was no thyng prowde	330	Garlande	648
Of broken warkis wrought many a goodly thyng,	334	Garlande	801
To se how duly ich thyng in ordre was,	343	Garlande	1094
But ye meane a thyng	361	Albany	91
THYNGE			
And to remember many a praty thynge;	44	Balettys3	33
How there nys thynge that I covet so fayne	44	Balettys3	41
But of eche thynge there as I toke hede,	47	Bowge	64
But of one thynge I werne you er I goo:	49	Bowge	106
werne] 'warne' Marshe 1568; er] 'or' Wynkyn de Worde 1510			
But this one thynge ye maye be sure of me,	50	Bowge	162
But I wolde telle you a thynge, and I durste.	51	Bowge	203
The soveraynst thynge that ony man maye have	52	Bowge	211
I wolde noo thynge so playne be.	52	Bowge	214
And ever he sange, 'Sythe I am no thynge playne'.	52	Bowge	235
What thynge is that I maye do for you?	53	Bowge	240
A wonder thynge that ye waxe not madde!	53	Bowge	241
For, and I knowe ony erthly thynge	54	Bowge	277
But, what, a strawe! I maye not tell all thynge.	59	Bowge	459
Sterte all at ones, I lyked no thynge his playe,	60	Bowge	502
Yet one thynge is behynde,	86	Phy Sparrow	603
And your harolde no thynge experte;	113	Scot Kynge	8
A mad rekenynge, /Consydrynge all thynge,	116	Ag Scottes	46
Lyberte without measure prove a thynge of nought.	143	Magnyfycence	117
It were no vertue, it were a thynge unblyst.	144	Magnyfycence	134
It is a wanton thynge, this Lyberte.	147	Magnyfycence	240
By measure eche thynge duly is tryde.	147	Magnyfycence	244
Of one thynge and other to occupy the place,	159	Magnyfycence	690
For clokyd colusyon is a perylous thynge.	159	Magnyfycence	695
Eche thynge is fayre when it is yonge; all hayle, owle!	167	Magnyfycence	970
I have a thynge for to say,	168	Magnyfycence	1017
But, broder Foly, I wonder moche of one thynge,	170	Magnyfycence	1068
A peryllous thynge, to cast a cat	176	Magnyfycence	1297
Ye. But tell me one thynge. What is that?	176	Magnyfycence	1318
A maystres, I tell you, is but a small thynge.	184	Magnyfycence	1579
But one thynge I warne you, prece forth and be bolde.	184	Magnyfycence	1582
By waywarde wylfulnes let eche thynge be convayed;	185	Magnyfycence	1594
As in a tryfyll or in a thynge of nought,	189	Magnyfycence	1757
As gyvynge a thynge that ye never bought.	189	Magnyfycence	1758
Of erthely thynge I have no care nor charge.	199	Magnyfycence	2081
But yet, syrs, hardely one thynge lerne of me:	199	Magnyfycence	2087
Some hath so moche lyberte of one thynge and other,	200	Magnyfycence	2141
Mele, salte or other thynge,	221	El Rummynge	279
To make all thynge cleane;	229	El Rummynge	578
It is a besy thynge	271	Collyn Clout	988
For Wyll dothe rule all thynge,	281	Why Come Ye	105
Thought to do a thynge	292	Why Come Ye	549
Desyring you above all thynge	299	Why Come Ye	828
What thynge occasionyd the showris of rayne,	331	Garlande	693
But, goodly maystres, one thynge ye me tell.'	332	Garlande	720
But my request is not so great a thynge,	332	Garlande	730
THYNGES			
To shewe you thynges that may not be disclosed.'	52	Bowge	217
Remembrynge prety thynges!	80	Phy Sparrow	350
And of all pleasaunt thynges,	93	Phy Sparrow	868
Craftely all thynges upryght to save:	158	Magnyfycence	642
By the menys of myschyef to bryng all thynges to nought.	159	Magnyfycence	702
For by crafty conveyaunce wonderful thynges are wrought.	178	Magnyfycence	1371
Full many thynges there be that lacketh redresse,	209	Magnyfycence	2415
To suche thynges ympossybyll, reason cannot consente;	240	Speke Parott	334
And rule all thynges alone.	258	Collyn Clout	475
Thynges that are amys,	278	Collyn Clout	1264
Bryngeth all thynges under cure.	286	Why Come Ye	284
All thynges sholde be amended,	307	Why Come Ye	1111
Of suche theologicall thynges,	384	Replycacion	350
THYNGIS			
Of Athlas astrology, and many noble thyngis,	331	Garlande	690
THYNGYS			
l thyngys contryvyd by mannys reason,	140	Magnyfycence	1
Shall se many thyngys donne craftely.	177	Magnyfycence	1334
THYNK			
As my maistres, /Of whom I thynk	96	Phy Sparrow	985
But wele may ye thynk I was no thyng prowde	330	Garlande	648
THYNKE			
That when ye thynke all daunger for to pas,	45	Balettys4	6
To you oonly, me thynke, I durste shryve me;	52	Bowge	215
Tell me your mynde, me thynke ye make a verse,	53	Bowge	244
No man can let me thynke,	101	Phy Sparrow	1199

THYNKEST —THYSE	Page	Title	Line
To thynke a mery thought	101	Phy Sparrow	1202
Ye wot what I thynke;	126	Garnesche3	80
For by measure I warne you we thynke to be gydyd;	145	Magnyfycence	184
Thynke you not thus my frende Felycyte?	147	Magnyfycence	245
To shewe you playnly the trouth as I thynke.	147	Magnyfycence	253
Counterfet kyndnesse, and thynke dyscayte;	152	Magnyfycence	438
He hawketh, me thynke, for a butterflye.	156	Magnyfycence	575
Frendshyp to fayne and thynke full lytherly.	160	Magnyfycence	723
I may do somwhat, and more I thynke shall.	162	Magnyfycence	778
Me thynke she frowneth and lokys sowre.	166	Magnyfycence	924
Thynke I not so, quod he. Ellys have I shame,	175	Magnyfycence	1254
But thynke you with Magnyfycence I shal be reserved?	188	Magnyfycence	1702
Syr, nowe me thynke your harte is well eased.	189	Magnyfycence	1737
Say on; me thynke your reasons be profounde.	190	Magnyfycence	1767
They thynke it no shame to robbe and stele;	198	Magnyfycence	2042
Adewe, syrs, for I thynke leyst that I come to late.	201	Magnyfycence	2152
Me thynke ye are not gretly acomberyd wyth wyt.	203	Magnyfycence	2215
And thus to be facyd, I thynke it great skorne.	203	Magnyfycence	2217
I was your mayster, though ye thynke it skorne;	204	Magnyfycence	2246
Som be wrestyd there that they thynke on it forty dayes,	204	Magnyfycence	2274
Some say but lityll and thynke more in there thowghte,	242	Speke Parott	388
Iche wotte what yche do thynke!'	258	Collyn Clout	458
yche do] 'eche other' Kele 1545.1, Marshe 1568			
Howebeit, per assimile, /Some men thynke that ye	258	Collyn Clout	460
And have no grace to thynke	262	Collyn Clout	648
That doth thynke or wene	274	Collyn Clout	1121
And yf ye thynke this shall	279	Why Come Ye	24
Parte of there names I thynke to specefye:	321	Garlande	325
Welcome to me as hertely as herte can thynke!	327	Garlande	547
But suche evydence I thynke for to enduce,	344	Garlande	1135
for to] 'for me to' MS Cotton Vitellius E.x			
Thynke what ye wyll /Of this wanton byll;	353	Garlande	1453
THYNKEST			
But is it not well? Howe thynkest thou?	155	Magnyfycence	528
THYNKETH			
For whan she *fronneth she thynketh to make a fray.	49	Bowge	116
*fronneth] 'frouneth' Wynkyn de Worde 1510, Marshe 1568			
And yet I dare saye /She thynketh her selfe gaye	216	El Rummynge	65
Wherfore, as thynketh me,	274	Collyn Clout	1129
For when he spekyth fayrest, then thynketh he moost yll;	333	Garlande	759
THYNKITH			
Lytill wotith the goslyng what the gose thynkith.	352	Garlande	1431
THYNKYNG			
Nowe trewely, to my thynkyng,	270	Collyn Clout	969
THYNKYNGE			
Nowe truly, to my thynkynge,	228	El Rummynge	547
THYNKYS			
Why, thynkys thou he can no better skyll?	172	Magnyfycence	1172
THYNKYST			
Thou thynkyst thy selfe Syr Pers de Brasy,	130	Garnesche5	30
Thynkyst thou not so, by thy fayth?	175	Magnyfycence	1253
THYNNE			
His wytte is thynne, his hode is threde-bare.	60	Bowge	490
THYR			
To counterfet thyr counsell they gyve me a fee.	154	Magnyfycence	491
Their hertes be in thyr hose!	286	Why Come Ye	289
THYS			
This pevysh proud, thys prendergest,	36	Coystrowne1	6
Thys Doctor Deuyas commensyd in a cart;	38	Coystrowne1	55
Deuyas] 'dellias' Marshe 1568			
Take thys in worth, the best is behynde.	38	Coystrowne1	68
Loke that ye spell /Well thys gospell;	39	Coystrowne3	21
Thys grevyth your husband, tha~ ryght jentyll knyght,	43	Balettys2	27
Thys boke we have devysed, /Compendyously comprysed,	62	Hauke	23
Thys rebell to behold,	64	Hauke	95
He hawked on thys facyon,	64	Hauke	101
Fell downe on thys manner.	64	Hauke	115
Thys fawconer then gan showte,	65	Hauke	119
then] not in Day 1560, Marshe 1568			
In thys preestly gydynge	65	Hauke	125
In] 'Is' †Lant 1545			
Or els is thys Goddis law,	65	Hauke	130
That thys is matter indeed.	65	Hauke	148
In the resydew of thys boke.	68	Hauke	234
I advyse yow beware of thys war, rannge yow in aray.	123	Garnesche2	33
Now upon thys hete /Rankely whan ye swete,	127	Garnesche3	133
On that syde, on thys syde thou dost gasy,	130	Garnesche5	29
In thys debate I the askry.	131	Garnesche5	66
Note and mark wyl thys parcele;	132	Garnesche5	97
If they wer lyveyng thys day,	133	Garnesche5	142
Take thys for that, bere thys in mynde,	134	Garnesche5	172
Take thys for that, bere thys in mynde,	134	Garnesche5	172
Thys losyll was a lorde and lyvyd at his lust;	193	Magnyfycence	1886
And ye that have harde thys dysporte and game,	214	Magnyfycence	2571
To rekyn with thys recule now	237	Speke Parott	227
THYSE			
Thyse lewde cok wattes shall nevermore prevayle	51	Bowge	173
wattes] 'witts' Marshe 1568			

THY SELF —THOSE   Page   Title   Line

THY SELF
Thyse were the wordes he to me dyde saye. 58   Bowge   441
  he] 'that he' Marshe 1568

THY SELF
Correct fyrst thy self; walk, and be nought! 38   Coystrowne1   62

THYSELFE
To name thyselfe. Come of, it were done. 167   Magnyfycence   965
Thyselfe that thou wolde sloo agaynst nature and kynde. 206   Magnyfycence   2326
Thyselfe myschevynge to thyne endlesse dysease! 206   Magnyfycence   2342

THY SELFE
Thy selfe therfore defende. 128   Garnesche3   161
And so thy selfe hovyr-wachyd 128   Garnesche3   179
Beholde thy selfe, and thou mayst se. 130   Garnesche5   16
Thou thynkyst thy selfe Syr Pers de Brasy, ... 130   Garnesche5   30
To know thy selfe yf thow lake grace, ... 132   Garnesche5   126
Ye, ryd thy selfe rather than this lyfe for to lede. 205   Magnyfycence   2307
Or that thy selfe thou go honge 206   Magnyfycence   2312
Spare not thy selfe, but boldly the murder. 206   Magnyfycence   2318
To put thy selfe to flyght. 364   Albany   233

THYSTELS
Ye pyke out many thystels, ... 380   Replycacion   220

THYTHER
For the passyon of God, let us go thyther. 204   Magnyfycence   2276
Thyther cometh Kate, ... 217   El Rummynge   118
Maude Ruggy thyther skypped: 226   El Rummynge   467

THO
Tho ye prate lyke prowde Pylate, beware of cheke mate. 123   Garnesche2   21

THOLOME
For Tholome tolde me 258   Collyn Clout   467

THOLOMYE
Tholomye and Haly were cunnyng and wyse 234   Speke Parott   134

THOM
Thus thwartyng over thom, ... 283   Why Come Ye   200

THOMAS
'Nowe have at all, by Saynte Thomas of Kente!' 56   Bowge   348
That Saynt Thomas of Canterbury gave. 251   Collyn Clout   170
  'That becket them gave' Kele 1545.1, Marshe 1568
Thomas manum mittit ad forcia, ... 251   Collyn Clout   171
And at Saynt Thomas of Akers 276   Collyn Clout   1188
Saynt Thomas de Aquyno, ... 381   Replycacion   279

THOMASEN
Our Thomasen she doth trip, our Jenet she doth shayle; 233   Speke Parott   83

THONDER
Wylde fyre and thonder; 285   Why Come Ye   257

THONGE
In Affryc tongue byrsa is a thonge of lether; 233   Speke Parott   80

THORNE
Counterfet haltynge without a thorne; 153   Magnyfycence   449
It is sone aspyed where the thorne prikkith. 352   Garlande   1437

THORNES
Ales founde therin no thornes, ... 224   El Rummynge   379

THOROW
Thorow treson, ageyn hym compassyd and wrought, ... 29   Dol Dethe   6
All gyf Englond and Fraunce wer thorow sought. 34   Dol Dethe   179
Thorow bounte of hym that formed all solace, ... 35   Dol Dethe   214
Thorow the grace dyvyne 93   Phy Sparrow   857
Thorow his godly myght; 93   Phy Sparrow   870
Thus thorow every stede 110   Lawde   3
Thorow the streytes of Marock 303   Why Come Ye   955
  of] not in Toy 1553, Kitson 1560.7, Marshe 1568

THOROWE
Not thorowe largesse of lyberall expence, ... 200   Magnyfycence   2115
I shall thrust in the my dagger - Thorowe the legge in to the . 202   Magnyfycence   2177
  hose.
How wysdom thorowe wantonnesse vanysshyth away; 213   Magnyfycence   2556
Thorowe your owne foly, ... 376   Replycacion   84
And chase them thorowe the muse 380   Replycacion   212

THOROWE OUT
Thorowe out every border. 380   Replycacion   228

THOROWE OUTE
His here was growen thorowe oute his hat. 56   Bowge   350

THOROWLY
They towche me so thorowly and tykyll my consayte, ... 184   Magnyfycence   1567
Yet let us se this matter thorowly ingrosed. 209   Magnyfycence   2438

THORUGH
I durse aventure to journey thorugh Fraunce; 57   Bowge   408

THOS
More specially barons, and thos knightis bold, ... 34   Dol Dethe   183
Then questionyd I her what thos yatis ment; 328   Garlande   575
  thos] 'these' Marshe 1568

THOSE
All those by whom ye have avayle. 41   Coystrowne4   18
Within those walles 83   Phy Sparrow   472
At those dayes moch commended; 91   Phy Sparrow   796
Those maters that he hath pende; 92   Phy Sparrow   810
And those be they that come up of nought - 174   Magnyfycence   1240
Those thre wyll be redy even at your bekenynge; 190   Magnyfycence   1778
Of those that stande in your grace. 273   Collyn Clout   1076
For those that vertuous be 273   Collyn Clout   1092

THOU —THOU | Page | Title | Line

	Page	Title	Line
Those wordes his grace dyd saye /Of an ammas gray.	372	Albany	530

THOU

	Page	Title	Line
O cruell Mars, thou dedly god of war!	32	Dol Dethe	113
When thou shoke thi sword so noble a man to mar!	32	Dol Dethe	115
O homycide, whiche sleest all that thou kan,	32	Dol Dethe	123
All mankynd, whom thou ful dere hast boght,	34	Dol Dethe	194
With thi blode precious our fenaunce thou dyd pay	34	Dol Dethe	195
As thou art of mercy and pite the well,	34	Dol Dethe	198
Deme what thou lyst, thou knowyst not my thought.	38	Coystrowne1	63
Deme what thou lyst, thou knowyst not my thought.	38	Coystrowne1	63
Thou slepyst to long, thou art begylde!	41	Balettys1	I
Thou slepyst to long, thou art begylde!	41	Balettys1	I
What dremyst thou, drunchard, drousy pate?	42	Balettys1	22
Thou blynkerd blowboll, thou wakyst to late;	42	Balettys1	24
Thou blynkerd blowboll, thou wakyst to late;	42	Balettys1	24
Behold, thou lyeste, luggard, alone!	42	Balettys1	25
Well may thou sygh, well may thou grone,	42	Balettys1	26
Well may thou sygh, well may thou grone,	42	Balettys1	26
Though thou withdraw me from her by long dystaunce,	45	Balettys3	46
Whyles I have ought, by God, thou shalt not lacke,	50	Bowge	167
'Why? What than? Wylte thou lete men to speke?	51	Bowge	184
'Than,' quod Hervy, 'why arte thou so dysmayde?'	54	Bowge	299
'Remembrest thou what thou sayd yesternyght?	55	Bowge	323
'Remembrest thou what thou sayd yesternyght?	55	Bowge	323
Wylt thou abyde by the wordes agayne?	55	Bowge	324
As thou arte, one that cam bat yesterdaye,	55	Bowge	328
What weneste I were? I trowe thou knowe not me.	55	Bowge	331
Trowest thou, drevyll, I saye, thou gawdy knave,	55	Bowge	337
Trowest thou, drevyll, I saye, thou gawdy knave,	55	Bowge	337
Well, ones thou shalte be chermed, iwus:	55	Bowge	340
Naye, strawe for tales, thou shalte not rule us;	55	Bowge	341
We be thy betters, and so thou shalte us take,	55	Bowge	342
And ay he sange, 'In fayth, Decon, thou crewe.'	56	Bowge	360
What arte thou? I sawe the nowe but late.'	56	Bowge	376
Thou muste swere and stare, man, aldaye longe,	57	Bowge	381
Thou mayste not studye or muse on the mone.	57	Bowge	383
Now wolde to God thou wolde leye money downe!	57	Bowge	395
To us welcome thou arte, by Saynte Quyntyne!'	60	Bowge	511
Loke on this tabull, /Whether thou art abull	68	Hauke	236
For no reverens thou sparys	69	Hauke	280
reverens] 'revens' Kynge & Marche 1554, Day 1560, Marshe 1568			
Thou shalt no where rede	70	Hauke	299
Whan thou my byrde untwynde!	79	Phy Sparrow	284
I wold thou haddest ben blynde!	79	Phy Sparrow	285
So thou, foule cat that thou arte,	79	Phy Sparrow	302
So thou, foule cat that thou arte,	79	Phy Sparrow	302
That thou shortly tell,	105	Phy Sparrow	1367
Adieu, Jayberd, adue. /I faith, dikkon, thou crue!	108	Epitaphe1'	63
Thou tode, thow scorpyon, /Thow bawdy babyone,	128	Garnesche3	162
Thow bere, thow brystlyd bore, /Thou Moryshe mantycore,	128	Garnesche3	165
Thow rammysche, stynkyng gote,	128	Garnesche3	166
Thou fowle, chorlyshe parote,	128	Garnesche3	167
Thou gresly gargone glaymy,	128	Garnesche3	168
Thou swety sloven seymy,	128	Garnesche3	169
Thou murrioun, thow mawment,	128	Garnesche3	170
Thou fals, stynkyng serpent,	128	Garnesche3	171
Thou mokkyshe marmoset, /I will nat dy in [thy] det.	128	Garnesche3	172
thy] 'they' †MS Harley 367			
Tyburne thou me assynyd	128	Garnesche3	174
Wher thou xulddst have bene shrynyd;	128	Garnesche3	175
Soche pelfry thou hast pachchyd,	128	Garnesche3	178
That ther thou xuldyst be rachchyd	128	Garnesche3	180
Beholde thy selfe, and thou mayst se.	130	Garnesche5	16
To cal me knave thou takyst gret payne.	130	Garnesche5	20
Thou art callyd of every man.	130	Garnesche5	24
On that syde, on thys syde thou dost gasy,	130	Garnesche5	29
Thou thynkyst thy selfe Syr Pers de Brasy,	130	Garnesche5	30
Thow claimist the jentyll, thou art a curre;	131	Garnesche5	67
Thow thou be a jantyll man borne,	131	Garnesche5	69
Withowte thou leve thou shalt be chekt,	132	Garnesche5	109
Withowte thou leve thou shalt be chekt,	132	Garnesche5	109
Thow callyst me scallyd, thou callydst me mad;	132	Garnesche5	116
Thow thou be pyllyd, thow ar nat sade.	132	Garnesche5	117
For thou beggest at every mannes dur.	135	Dundas	26
By Jesu Christ, /Fals Scot, thou lyest:	135	Dundas	33
Thou hast in despite, /Thou donghyll knyght?	136	Dundas	47
Thou hast in despite, /Thou donghyll knyght?	136	Dundas	48
But thou lakest might,	136	Dundas	49
I hate this blunderyng that thou doste make.	151	Magnyfycence	400
As longe as I lyve, thou haste an heyre parent.	154	Magnyfycence	507
But I say, kepest thou the olde name styll that thou had?	155	Magnyfycence	516
But I say, kepest thou the olde name styll that thou had?	155	Magnyfycence	516
Why, wenyst thou, horson, that I were so mad?	155	Magnyfycence	517
But is it not well? Howe thynkest thou?	155	Magnyfycence	528
I wote thou arte false ynoughe for one.	155	Magnyfycence	536
Thou hast made me play the jeu dehayte.	156	Magnyfycence	579
Tusshe! Fonnysshe Fansy, thou arte frantyke.	158	Magnyfycence	650

	Page	Title	Line
Howe sayst thou, man? Am not I a joly rutter?	161	Magnyfycence	752
What! Wenyst thou that I knowe the not, Clokyd Colusyon?	161	Magnyfycence	756
Cankard Jacke Hare, loke thou be not rusty;	161	Magnyfycence	758
For thou shalt well knowe I am nother durty nor dusty.	161	Magnyfycence	759
But whether art thou walkynge, in faythe unfaynyd?	161	Magnyfycence	762
By the masse, for the cowrte thou art a mete man;	161	Magnyfycence	764
Thy slyppers they swap it, yet thou fotys it lyke a swanne.	161	Magnyfycence	765
So thou arte personable to bere a prynces baner.	161	Magnyfycence	767
Nay. Thou art a man good inough but for thy false hart.	162	Magnyfycence	769
Beryst thou any rome? Or cannyst thou do ought?	162	Magnyfycence	776
Beryst thou any rome? Or cannyst thou do ought?	162	Magnyfycence	776
Cannyst thou helpe in faver that I myght be brought?	162	Magnyfycence	777
Nay, come away, man! Thou playst the cayser.	162	Magnyfycence	787
By the masse, thou shalt byde my leyser.	162	Magnyfycence	788
Here he is nowe, man. Mayst thou not se?	162	Magnyfycence	792
What the devyll, man, what thou menyst?	162	Magnyfycence	793
Art thou so angry as thou semyst?	162	Magnyfycence	794
Art thou so angry as thou semyst?	162	Magnyfycence	794
What sayst thou, man? Why dost thou not supplye,	162	Magnyfycence	797
What sayst thou, man? Why dost thou not supplye,	162	Magnyfycence	797
Spekest thou to me?	162	Magnyfycence	799
Rule the roste! Thou woldest, ye,	163	Magnyfycence	805
Thou woldest, ye] 'ye thou woldest' †Rastell & Treveris C 1530, B			
As skante thou had no nede of me.	163	Magnyfycence	806
Cockes ha[r]te! I trowe thou wylte make a fray.	163	Magnyfycence	808
harte] 'hate' †Rastell & Treveris C 1530, B			
But what the devyll art thou	166	Magnyfycence	916
What! Fansy, my frende! Howe dost thou fare?	166	Magnyfycence	920
What the devyll hast thou on thy fyste? An owle?	166	Magnyfycence	922
Why, harde thou not of the fray	166	Magnyfycence	932
As here after thou shalte knowe more.	167	Magnyfycence	953
But I must tary here; go thou before.	167	Magnyfycence	954
Mary, thou jettes it of hyght.	167	Magnyfycence	962
There is many evyll faveryd, and thou be foule!	167	Magnyfycence	969
What, Fansy! Arte thou here alone?	169	Magnyfycence	1044
What pylde curre ledest thou in thy hande?	169	Magnyfycence	1054
What! Fleyest thou his skynne every yere?	169	Magnyfycence	1058
What! Thou wylte coughe me a dawe for forty pens?	170	Magnyfycence	1060
That thou so hye fro me doth sprynge,	170	Magnyfycence	1069
Thou art so feble-fantastycall,	170	Magnyfycence	1072
That thou cannyst not growe out of thy boyes gere;	170	Magnyfycence	1075
Than thou can in yerys seven.	170	Magnyfycence	1078
In faythe, trouth thou sayst nowe, by God of heven!	170	Magnyfycence	1079
Cockys harte! Thou lyest; I am no [h]ogge.	170	Magnyfycence	1083
hogge] 'dogge' †Rastell & Treveris C 1530, B			
Mary, I knewe the when thou waste a ladde.	170	Magnyfycence	1089
Nay, but wotest thou what I do say?	170	Magnyfycence	1092
Why, sayst thou that I was here yesterday?	170	Magnyfycence	1093
What! Callyst thou me a donnyshe crowe?	170	Magnyfycence	1095
Nowe, in good faythe, thou art a fonde gest.	170	Magnyfycence	1096
What! Wenyst thou that I were so folysshe and so fonde?	170	Magnyfycence	1098
Thou shalte have my purse, and I wyll have thyne.	171	Magnyfycence	1102
By the masse, yet art thou more fole than I.	171	Magnyfycence	1111
And thou shalte have my hauke to a botchment.	171	Magnyfycence	1113
That ever thou thryve, God it forfende!	171	Magnyfycence	1114
For, Goddes cope, thou wyll spende!	171	Magnyfycence	1115
Nowe take thou my dogge and gyve me thy fowle.	171	Magnyfycence	1116
What callest thou thy dogge? Tusshe! His name is Gryme.	171	Magnyfycence	1118
Ye. But trowest thou that he be not maungey?	171	Magnyfycence	1122
Nowe thou hast done me a pleasure grete.	171	Magnyfycence	1131
In faythe, I wolde thou had a marmosete.	171	Magnyfycence	1132
But I have thy pultre, and thou hast my catell.	171	Magnyfycence	1135
Remembrest thou not the japes and the toyes –	171	Magnyfycence	1137
What! Canest thou all this Latyn yet?	172	Magnyfycence	1143
By Cockes harte, I wene thou hast no more.	172	Magnyfycence	1146
But wylte thou make another on Gryme?	172	Magnyfycence	1151
Mary, as for that, thou shalte sone here myne.	172	Magnyfycence	1153
Tell by thy trouth what sport can thou make.	172	Magnyfycence	1162
Ye, thou haste the four quarters of a knave.	172	Magnyfycence	1165
Wotyst thou, I say, to whom thou spekys?	172	Magnyfycence	1166
Wotyst thou, I say, to whom thou spekys?	172	Magnyfycence	1166
Why, thynkys thou he can no better skyll?	172	Magnyfycence	1172
What hast thou on thy fyst? A [k]esteryll?	173	Magnyfycence	1174
kesteryll] 'besteryll' †Rastell & Treveris C 1530, B			
In a cote thou can play well the dyser.	173	Magnyfycence	1176
Ye, but thou can play the fole without a vyser.	173	Magnyfycence	1177
Mary, as thou sayst, he gave me a blurre.	173	Magnyfycence	1179
But where gatte thou that mangey curre?	173	Magnyfycence	1180
Thou must have thy fansy and thy wyll,	173	Magnyfycence	1183
But yet thou shalt holde me a fole styll.	173	Magnyfycence	1184
Why, wenyst thou that I cannot make the play the fon?	173	Magnyfycence	1185
Why, wenyst thou that I were as moche a fole as thou?	173	Magnyfycence	1188
Why, wenyst thou that I were as moche a fole as thou?	173	Magnyfycence	1188
Nay, nay. Thou shalt fynde hym another maner of man.	173	Magnyfycence	1189
What canest thou do but play cocke wat?	173	Magnyfycence	1191
Than wyll I say that thou hast no pere.	173	Magnyfycence	1195
What hast thou founde there? By God, a lowse.	173	Magnyfycence	1198

THOU —THOU	Page	Title	Line
By Cockes harte, I trowe thou lyste.	173	Magnyfycence	1199
Put on thy gowne agayne, for thou hast lost nowe.	173	Magnyfycence	1203
thou ... nowe] 'nowe thou hast lost' †Rastell & Treveris C 1530, B			
Gyve me my grote, for thou hast lost.	173	Magnyfycence	1206
Nowe hast thou not a prowde mocke and a starke?	174	Magnyfycence	1208
Nay, wylte thou here nowe of his scoles,	174	Magnyfycence	1216
What, horson! Arte thou suche a one?	174	Magnyfycence	1234
Hast thou ony more? Let se, procede.	174	Magnyfycence	1236
Thynkyst thou not so, by thy fayth?	175	Magnyfycence	1253
Forsothe, tell on. Hast thou any mo?	175	Magnyfycence	1262
mo] 'more' †Rastell & Treveris C 1530, B			
But, I say, let se and yf thou have any more.	175	Magnyfycence	1278
Nay, that is my parte that thou spekest of nowe.	175	Magnyfycence	1282
For thou fourmest suche fantasyes in theyr mynde	175	Magnyfycence	1284
For, frantyke Fansy, thou makyst men madde;	176	Magnyfycence	1300
With Magnyfycence thou shalte wonne.	176	Magnyfycence	1311
Cockes armes! Thou shalte kepe the brewhouse boule.	176	Magnyfycence	1321
When Mesure is gone, what nedest thou spare?	176	Magnyfycence	1323
Holde thy tonge, and thou love thy helth.	179	Magnyfycence	1402
Wolde money, trowest thou, make suche one to the call?	184	Magnyfycence	1573
By Cockes woundes, a wonder felowe thou arte!	185	Magnyfycence	1619
Well cannest thou helpe a preest to synge a songe.	187	Magnyfycence	1676
What! Woldest thou, lurden, with me brawle agayne?	188	Magnyfycence	1722
Hens, thou haynyarde, out of dores fast!	188	Magnyfycence	1725
Thou sayst truthe, by the harte that God me gave!	190	Magnyfycence	1782
For as thou sayst, ryght so shall it be,	190	Magnyfycence	1783
For as thou wylte, so shall the game go;	190	Magnyfycence	1786
A, syr, thy jarfawcon and thou be hanged togyder!	191	Magnyfycence	1812
By Cockes harte, thou arte a fyne mery knave.	191	Magnyfycence	1826
What sayst thou? Mary, I pray God your mastershyp to save.	191	Magnyfycence	1828
What, brother braynsyke, how farest thou?	192	Magnyfycence	1845
Vyle velyarde, thou must not nowe my dynt withstande;	193	Magnyfycence	1878
Thou must not abyde the dynt of my hande.	193	Magnyfycence	1879
Howe, where art thou? Come hether, Poverte.	195	Magnyfycence	1953
A, woo worthe the, Lyberte, nowe thou sayst full trewe;	199	Magnyfycence	2103
What hast thou gotted, in faythe, to thy share?	201	Magnyfycence	2162
Ye, wylte thou clenly cle[v]e me in the clyfte with thy nose?	202	Magnyfycence	2176
cleve] 'clene' †Rastell & Treveris C 1530, B			
Nay, horson, here is my glove. Take it up and thou dare.	202	Magnyfycence	2178
Torde! Thou arte good to be a man of warre.	202	Magnyfycence	2179
I shall skelpe the on the skalpe; lo, seest thou that?	202	Magnyfycence	2180
What! Wylte thou skelpe me? Thou dare not loke on a gnat.	202	Magnyfycence	2181
What! Wylte thou skelpe me? Thou dare not loke on a gnat.	202	Magnyfycence	2181
By Cockes bones, I shall blysse the and thou be to bolde.	202	Magnyfycence	2182
Nay. Then thou wylte dynge the devyll and thou be not holde.	202	Magnyfycence	2183
Nay. Then thou wylte dynge the devyll and thou be not holde.	202	Magnyfycence	2183
But wottest thou, horson? I rede the to be wyse.	202	Magnyfycence	2184
Why, wenest thou that I forbere the for thyne owne sake?	202	Magnyfycence	2186
Ye, wylte thou, hangman? I say, thou cavell!	202	Magnyfycence	2190
Ye, wylte thou, hangman? I say, thou cavell!	202	Magnyfycence	2190
Nay, thou rude ravener, rayne beten javell!	202	Magnyfycence	2191
What! Thou Colyn Cowarde, knowen and tryde!	202	Magnyfycence	2192
Nay, thou false harted dastarde! Thou dare not abyde.	202	Magnyfycence	2193
Nay, thou false harted dastarde! Thou dare not abyde.	202	Magnyfycence	2193
And yf there were none to dysplease but thou and I,	202	Magnyfycence	2194
Thou sholde not scape, horson, but thou sholde dye.	202	Magnyfycence	2195
Thou sholde not scape, horson, but thou sholde dye.	202	Magnyfycence	2195
By the masse, man, thou shall fynde me resonable.	202	Magnyfycence	2204
Thou sawe never yet but I dyd my parte,	203	Magnyfycence	2228
What begger art thou, that thus doth banne and wary?	203	Magnyfycence	2238
Cockys bonys! Thou begger, what is thy name?	203	Magnyfycence	2240
Ye, in faythe; or ellys thou arte to great a glotton.	204	Magnyfycence	2266
What! Lyest thou there lyngrynge, lewdly and lothsome?	205	Magnyfycence	2291
Thou hast bene so waywarde, so wranglyng, and so wrothsome,	205	Magnyfycence	2293
And so fer thou arte behynde of thy rent,	205	Magnyfycence	2294
And so ungracyously thy dayes thou hast spent,	205	Magnyfycence	2295
That thou arte not worthy to loke God in the face.	205	Magnyfycence	2296
And agayne thy maker thou hast made suche warre,	205	Magnyfycence	2302
That thou canst not have never mercy in his syght.	205	Magnyfycence	2303
The worlde waxyth wery of the; thou lyvest to longe.	205	Magnyfycence	2308
Or that thy selfe thou go honge	206	Magnyfycence	2312
Thou arte not the fyrst hymselfe hath slayne.	206	Magnyfycence	2316
Thyselfe that thou wolde sloo agaynst nature and kynde.	206	Magnyfycence	2326
Gather up, thou wenche.	219	El Rummynge	181
Seest thou not what is fall?	219	El Rummynge	182
Thou art worth good and monny.'	220	El Rummynge	228
'By Chryst,' sayde she, 'thou lyest.	223	El Rummynge	344
As thou, wyth shamefull deth!'	223	El Rummynge	346
'They be wretchockes thou hast brought,	226	El Rummynge	465
They] 'The' Day 1560			
For slepyste thou, Besse,	237	Speke Parott	238
What, Collyn, there thou shayles!	256	Collyn Clout	399
How darest thou, daucocke, mell?	275	Collyn Clout	1160
Howe darest thou, losell,	275	Collyn Clout	1161
'In faythe, Dycken, thou krew,	280	Why Come Ye	66
In fayth, Dicken, thou krew, etc.'	280	Why Come Ye	67
Dicken, thou krew doutlesse!	280	Why Come Ye	68

729

THOUGH —THOUGH	Page	Title	Line
With, 'Do thou for me,	286	Why Come Ye	279
He sayth, 'Thou huddy peke!	287	Why Come Ye	329
With, 'Stowpe, thou havell! /Rynne thou javell!	294	Why Come Ye	607
With, 'Stowpe, thou havell! /Rynne thou javell!	294	Why Come Ye	608
Thou pevysshe pye pecked,	294	Why Come Ye	609
Thou losell longe necked!'	294	Why Come Ye	610
Yet sayst thou, per case	301	Why Come Ye	874
Sume sayd, 'Holde thy peas, thou getest here no more.'	319	Garlande	257
Odious Disdayne, why raist thou me on this facyon?	321	Garlande	317
With, 'I as good as thou, ifayth, and no better.'	326	Garlande	509
That thou shortely tell,	350	Garlande	1360
Thou dyd nothyng but barke	362	Albany	147
Twyt, Scot, thou ran away.'	363	Albany	160
Thou hast to lytell myght	364	Albany	230
Thou art a graceles wyght	364	Albany	232
Thou durst no felde derayne,	365	Albany	243
But thou ran home agayne	365	Albany	246
For feare thou shoulde be slayne	365	Albany	247
For thou can not but brag	366	Albany	294
Thou mayst give up thy cocking.	366	Albany	299
I say, thou lewde lurdayne,	367	Albany	336
I saye, thou madde Marche hare,	375	Replycacion	35
THOUGH			
For though they stumble in the synnys sevyn,	36	Coystrowne1	3
What though ye can cownter Custodi nos?	38	Coystrowne1	57
Though angelyk be youre smylyng,	41	Coystrowne4	15
Though thou withdraw me from her by long dystaunce,	45	Balettys3	46
Though ye suppose all jeperdys ar paste,	45	Balettys4	1
What though our chaffer be never so dere,	48	Bowge	89
And, though I say it, I was myselfe your frende,	50	Bowge	160
For though ye lyve a c. yere, ye shal dy a daw.	71	Hauke	334
As though I had ben racked,	73	Phy Sparrow	47
Though she wolde pretende	75	Phy Sparrow	154
What though he crept so lowe?	76	Phy Sparrow	169
though] 'thought' †Kele 1545.2			
Phyllyp, though he were nyse,	76	Phy Sparrow	173
Though I can rede and spell,	87	Phy Sparrow	612
And though that rede have I	87	Phy Sparrow	628
What though I can fram	88	Phy Sparrow	659
though] 'thought' †Kele 1545.2			
And though I can expounde	88	Phy Sparrow	672
Though his father were a kyng;	89	Phy Sparrow	698
Though I remembre the fable	89	Phy Sparrow	724
Though I have enrold	90	Phy Sparrow	749
Though it be refused,	92	Phy Sparrow	816
Though I regester her name	94	Phy Sparrow	891
Yet though I wryte not with ynke,	101	Phy Sparrow	1198
Though they wold spend	103	Phy Sparrow	1272
Though this knaves be deade,	106	Epitaphe	I
Though I waxe olde /And somdele sere,	112	Calliope	15
Though ye untruly your father have slayne,	118	Ag Scottes	119
For though some be lidder, and list for to rayle,	138	Ven Tongues	30
Malicious tunges, though they have no bones,	138	Ven Tongues	49
Syr, though ye be a noble prynce of myght,	145	Magnyfycence	166
Though Largesse ye hyght your langage is to large;	148	Magnyfycence	295
And though I be so odyous a geste,	160	Magnyfycence	703
'Though I shewe you curtesy, say not that I crave[d];	177	Magnyfycence	1351
craved] 'crave' †Rastell & Treveris C 1530, B			
Though al his conquestys were brought to rekenynge,	181	Magnyfycence	1468
Mary, your speche is as pleasant as though it were pend,	183	Magnyfycence	1538
For though we shewe you this in game and play,	195	Magnyfycence	1948
To grope a gardevyaunce, though it be well bandyd.	203	Magnyfycence	2231
I was your mayster, though ye thynke it skorne;	204	Magnyfycence	2246
Though I aske mercy I must nedys be refusyd.	205	Magnyfycence	2299
Snevelyng in her nose, /As though she had the pose.	223	El Rummynge	365
And began to paynty /As though she would faynty.	229	El Rummynge	585
For though ye can tell in Greke what is phormio,	235	Speke Parott	151
For though my ryme be ragged, /Tattered and jagged,	248	Collyn Clout	53
As though they wolde flye /Aboute the sterry skye.	248	Collyn Clout	73
Aboute] 'Above' Kele 1545.1, Marshe 1568, MS Harley 2252			
That though ye rounde your heere	263	Collyn Clout	673
Though it were never so playne,	265	Collyn Clout	765
Though some of them by lyres.	267	Collyn Clout	833
lyres] 'lyers' Kele 1545.1, Marshe 1568, 'lyars' MS Harley 2252			
Though I wryte after this facyon;	273	Collyn Clout	1080
Though I, Collyn Clout,	273	Collyn Clout	1081
Though his purs wax dull,	302	Why Come Ye	937
What though ye be namelesse,	309	Why Come Ye2	3
For though he were venquesshid, yet was he not shamyd:	316	Garlande	161
For] 'Sithe' MS Cotton Vitellius E.x			
That I ne force what though it be discurid.	332	Garlande	731
What though my penne wax faynt,	339	Garlande	954
Though ye wer hard hertyd,	341	Garlande	1038
Though they wolde spende	348	Garlande	1265
Though Jak sayd nay, yet Mok there loste her sho;	351	Garlande	1396
Though Galiene and Diascorides,	352	Garlande	1425
And though Albumasar can the enforme and ken	352	Garlande	1428

THOUGHE —THOUSAND	Page	Title	Line

	Page	Title	Line
Though I you wrate /After this rate	355	Garlande	1536
What though ye stampe and stare?	363	Albany	180
As though ye wolde parbrake /Your avauns to make, ...	367	Albany	322
Though insufficient am I	369	Albany	401
What though my stile be rude?	369	Albany	419
Though your Englishe be rude, ...	372	Albany	516

THOUGHE

	Page	Title	Line
It wolde be nyce, thoughe I say nay;	153	Magnyfycence	459
And frowne it and face it, as thoughe ye wolde fyght;	185	Magnyfycence	1601
That he wolde loke on hym, thoughe it were not longe.	187	Magnyfycence	1675
It is no wonder, therfore, thoughe ye be wrothe	189	Magnyfycence	1748
No force what thoughe his neyghbour dye in a dyche.	189	Magnyfycence	1752
For thoughe you were somtyme a noble estate, ...	196	Magnyfycence	1980
What care they thoughe Gyll swete, ...	254	Collyn Clout	321
Yet, thoughe I say it, therby lyith a tale, ...	346	Garlande	1200
I] 'ye' †Fakes 1523			
Thoughe I trym you thys trace	367	Albany	355

THOUGHT

	Page	Title	Line
Trew to his prince in word, in dede, and thought.	29	Dol Dethe	7
As perflyghtly as koude be thought or devysyd;	33	Dol Dethe	158
Eche man may sorow in his inward thought	34	Dol Dethe	177
Wed me or els I dye for thought!	36	Man Margery	26
Deme what thou lyst, thou knowyst not my thought.	38	Coystrownel	63
They coude not faile, thei thought, they were so sure.	50	Bowge	142
That commaunde with you, me thought, a p[ra]ty space?	51	Bowge	198
commaunde] 'commened' Wynkyn de Worde 1510; 'party spake'			
†Wynkyn de Worde 1499, Marshe 1568, 'party space' WdeW 1510			
And in his other sleve, me thought I sawe	58	Bowge	435
So urgently I am brought /Into carefull thought.	74	Phy Sparrow	107
God wot, we thought no syn –	76	Phy Sparrow	168
Me thought my sparow did spek, ...	77	Phy Sparrow	220
Me thought, of Phyllyps blode.	77	Phy Sparrow	226
Brynge other wyves in thought	87	Phy Sparrow	626
Me thought min hert was crased, ...	99	Phy Sparrow	1105
For thought hath lyberte, ...	101	Phy Sparrow	1200
Thought is franke and fre;	101	Phy Sparrow	1201
To thynke a mery thought	101	Phy Sparrow	1202
Ye thought ye dyde it full valyauntolye, ...	113	Scot Kynge	9
Ye thought ye dyd yet valyauntly;	118	Ag Scottes	99
But plenarly all thought from you must be dyschargyd, ...	146	Magnyfycence	207
With care and with thought howe Jacke shall have Gyl?	148	Magnyfycence	287
Me thought he called Fan[s]y.	149	Magnyfycence	327
fansy] 'fanfy' †Rastell & Treveris C 1530, B			
Me thought he called Fansy me behynde.	149	Magnyfycence	329
Tushe, a strawe! I thought none yll.	156	Magnyfycence	564
And I, am counterfet of one mynde and thought, ...	159	Magnyfycence	701
Lest that he thought that his money were evyll spente, ...	187	Magnyfycence	1674
Why, who wolde have thought in you suche gyle?	193	Magnyfycence	1869
Alasse, alasse, alasse! I dye for thought.	196	Magnyfycence	1969
Syr, all this wolde have bene thought on before.	196	Magnyfycence	1970
Ye com hether as well as can be thought.	210	Magnyfycence	2459
And that is all your thought.	261	Collyn Clout	607
Thought to do a thynge	292	Why Come Ye	549
In place alone then musynge in my thought	312	Garlande	8
They presid in faste; some thought they were to longe;	319	Garlande	248
Forthwith, I say, thus wandrynge in my thought, ...	325	Garlande	456
Under her arme, me thought, she hade a boke.	327	Garlande	532
And, sir, amonge all me thought I saw twaine, ...	329	Garlande	633
Stedfast of thought, /Wele made, wele wrought;	341	Garlande	1029
Forthwith upon this, as it were in a thought, ...	343	Garlande	1100
All other besyde were counterfete they thought	343	Garlande	1106
All ... counterfete] 'that they ware were counterfettis' MS			
Cotton Vitellius E.x			
She wonderyd, me thought, at my laurell grene;	343	Garlande	1116
The starry hevyn, me thought, shoke with the showte;	354	Garlande	1508
And thought in hym smale grace	379	Replycacion	195
And thought, if ye had right, ...	379	Replycacion	200

THOUGHTE

	Page	Title	Line
Me thoughte I sawe a shyppe, goodly of sayle, ...	47	Bowge	36
But than I thoughte I wolde not dwell behynde;	47	Bowge	43
For, as me thoughte, in our shyppe I dyde see	49	Bowge	132
But, as me thoughte, he ware on hym a cloke	51	Bowge	177
Me thoughte, of wordes that he had full a poke;	51	Bowge	179
Suspycyon, me thoughte, mette hym at a brayde, ...	51	Bowge	181
Me thoughte his hede was full of gelousy, ...	51	Bowge	192
Me thoughte his gowne was all furred wyth foxe.	52	Bowge	234
Me] 'My' †Wynkyn de Worde 1499			
Anone ther mette with him, as me thoughte, ...	54	Bowge	282
Me thoughte alwaye Dyscymulair dyde devyse;	58	Bowge	424
Me thoughte I see lewde felawes here and there	61	Bowge	528
And thoughte to lepe; and even with that woke, ...	61	Bowge	531

THOUGHTFULL

	Page	Title	Line
Of thoughtfull hertys plungyd in dystres;	44	Balettys3	10
O syghynge sorowe, O thoughtfull mysere!	198	Magnyfycence	2050
'O thoughtfull herte,' was evermore his songe!	320	Garlande	296

THOUSAND

	Page	Title	Line
A thousand myle of grounde, ...	76	Phy Sparrow	187
A thousand new and old	90	Phy Sparrow	750

THOUSANDE —THOWSANDE	Page	Title	Line

THOUSANDE
Ye be to her, yea, worth a thousande pounde.	50	Bowge	157
Wyll ye spende ony money? Ye, a thousande pounde.	184	Magnyfycence	1570
A thousande pounde with lyberte may holde no tacke.	199	Magnyfycence	2084
Than a thousande thousande other	266	Collyn Clout	776
Than a thousande thousande other	266	Collyn Clout	776
A thousande or twayne	302	Why Come Ye	944
Of a thousande poetes assembled togeder.	320	Garlande	286
The claspis and bullyons were worth a thousande pounde;	345	Garlande	1165
with an hundred thousande tratlande Scottes	359	Albany	1
Two thousande of Fraunce	360	Albany	43
Nat for a thousande poun[de]	367	Albany	346
pounde] 'pouned' †Marshe 1568			
Whereat a thousande gased,	379	Replycacion	193

THOUSAND FOLDE
Than any other a thousand folde.	310	Why Come Ye2	16
any] 'yn any' MS Rawlinson C. 813			

THOUTHE
Alas for routhe, what thouthe his mynde wer goode,	32	Dol Dethe	102
To me also all thouthe yt wer promysyde	33	Dol Dethe	159

THOW
So forcibly upon this Erle thow ran,	32	Dol Dethe	124
Thow kit asonder his perfight vitall threde.	32	Dol Dethe	126
Thow bringe unto thy joye etermynable	34	Dol Dethe	199
Thow] 'how' †MS Royal 18 D.ii			
Where thow art Lord and God omnipotent.	34	Dol Dethe	203
O Fortune unfrendly, Fortune unkynde thow art,	45	Balettys5	4
Thow ye be lusty as Syr Lybyus, launces to breke,	122	Garnesche1	17
Thow ye prate lyke prowde Pylate, beware yet of chek mate.	123	Garnesche2	7
Thow ye prate lyke prowde Pylate, beware of cheke mate.	123	Garnesche2	14
Thow ye prate lyke prowde Pylate, beware of cheke mate.	123	Garnesche2	28
Thow ye prate lyke prowde Pylate, beware of cheke mate.	123	Garnesche2	35
Thow mantycore, ye marmset, garnyshte lyke a Greke,	124	Garnesche2	39
Thow ye prate lyke prowde Pylate, beware of cheke mate.	124	Garnesche2	42
Thow a Sarsens hed ye bere,	127	Garnesche3	123
Thou tode, thow scorpyon, /Thow bawdy babyone,	128	Garnesche3	162
Thou tode, thow scorpyon, /Thow bawdy babyone,	128	Garnesche3	163
Thow bere, thow brystlyd bore, /Thou Moryshe mantycore,	128	Garnesche3	164
Thow bere, thow brystlyd bore, /Thou Moryshe mantycore,	128	Garnesche3	164
Thou murrioun, thow mawment,	128	Garnesche3	170
If thow war metely machchyd.	128	Garnesche3	181
Thow xalte beholde no wher a warse;	130	Garnesche5	17
Of all prowde knavys thow beryst the belle,	130	Garnesche5	27
Thow wolde have scoryd hys habarion;	130	Garnesche5	34
Sche wolde nat of yt thow had sworne.	131	Garnesche5	52
I sey, thow felle and fowle flessh fly,	131	Garnesche5	65
Thow claimist the jentyll, thou art a curre;	131	Garnesche5	67
Thow thou be a jantyll man borne,	131	Garnesche5	69
Me to beknave thow art to blame;	132	Garnesche5	107
Avaunt, avaunt, thow slogysh......	132	Garnesche5	112
Thow callyst me scallyd, thou callydst me mad;	132	Garnesche5	116
Thow thou be pyllyd, thow ar nat sade.	132	Garnesche5	117
Thow thou be pyllyd, thow ar nat sade.	132	Garnesche5	117
Thow ar frantyke and lakkyst wyt,	132	Garnesche5	118
Er thow beware, that in a throw	132	Garnesche5	122
Thow mayst fale downe and ebbe full lowe.	132	Garnesche5	123
To know thy selfe yf thow lake grace,	132	Garnesche5	126
Thow seyst I callyd the a pecok;	133	Garnesche5	128
Thow liist, I callyd the a wodcoke;	133	Garnesche5	129
For thow hast a long snowte,	133	Garnesche5	130
Thow demyst my raylyng ovyrthwarthe;	133	Garnesche5	136
I rayle to the soche as thow art.	133	Garnesche5	137
If thow war aquentyd with alle	133	Garnesche5	138
Thow wrythtyst I xulde let the go pley;	134	Garnesche5	166
I care nat what thow wryght or sey;	134	Garnesche5	168
Scrybbyl thow, scrybyll thow, rayle or wryght,	134	Garnesche5	179
Scrybbyl thow, scrybyll thow, rayle or wryght,	134	Garnesche5	179
Wryght what thow wylte, I xall the aquyte.	134	Garnesche5	180
Why doste thow deprave /This royall reame,	136	Dundas	43
And wenyst thow that I know not the, cankard Abusyon?	161	Magnyfycence	757
Or wakeste thow, Besse,	237	Speke Parott	239
Thow ye be tauntyd, Parotte, with tonges attayntyd,	240	Speke Parott	343

THOWE
And thowe sum dysdayne yow and sey how ye prate,	240	Speke Parott	315

THOWGH
Ye wolde not dele with hym, thowgh that ye myght,	333	Garlande	756
though] 'thought' Marshe 1568, 'thowth' MS Cotton Vit.E.x			

THOWGHE
Thowghe he pampyr not hys paunche with the grete seall;	239	Speke Parott	309

THOWGHTE
Some say but lityll and thynke more in there thowghte,	242	Speke Parott	388

THOWSANDE
A thowsande thowsande I sawe on a plumpe.	319	Garlande	258
A thowsande thowsande I sawe on a plumpe.	319	Garlande	258
I sawe a thowsande yatis new and olde.	328	Garlande	574
A thowsande, thowsande, I trow, to my dome,	354	Garlande	1505
A thowsande, thowsande, I trow, to my dome,	354	Garlande	1505

	Page	Title	Line
THOWSANDE FOLDE			
Whiche was extolde /A thowsande folde	342	Garlande	1079
THOWTH			
Thowth it be now ful tyde with the, ...	132	Garnesche5	120
THOWTHE			
Thowthe ye kan skylle of large and longe, ...	129	Garnesche5	3
THRE			
Full subtyll persones in nombre foure and thre.	49	Bowge	133
'But by that Lorde that is one, two and thre, ...	60	Bowge	512
With gastly hedes thre;	74	Phy Sparrow	91
The naturall sonnes thre	78	Phy Sparrow	255
And slew Gerion /With thre bodyes in one;	104	Phy Sparrow	1308
Now by these names thre, ...	105	Phy Sparrow	1363
In verses two or thre	106	Phy Sparrow	1378
But not worth thre skyppes of a pye.	113	Scot Kynge	10
Not worth thre skyppes of a pye.	118	Ag Scottes	100
Nothing to write, but hay the gy of thre, ...	138	Ven Tongues	46
There is no prynce but he hath nede of us thre -	145	Magnyfycence	159
Chanons can not counterfet but upon thre.	154	Magnyfycence	492
Why, shall we dwell togyder all thre?	154	Magnyfycence	509
That we thre galauntes sholde be longe asonder.	154	Magnyfycence	511
All thre, I say. Shall I go? Whyder?	158	Magnyfycence	666
But dyvysyon, dyssencyon, dyrysyon - these thre	159	Magnyfycence	700
I have not kept her yet thre wokys, ...	168	Magnyfycence	1002
Plucke from an hundred, and gyve it to thre;	190	Magnyfycence	1775
Those thre wyll be redy even at your bekenynge;	190	Magnyfycence	1778
Yeres two or thre, ...	219	El Rummynge	215
With clauses two or thre, ...	265	Collyn Clout	766
Somtyme a bacon flycke /That is thre fyngers thycke	267	Collyn Clout	845
But within monethes thre	288	Why Come Ye	366
In thre poyntes expressed:	307	Why Come Ye	1122
Dane Johnn Lydgate. Theis Englysshe poetis thre, ...	323	Garlande	391
To yow thre this honor shalbe reserved	323	Garlande	409
Tyll at the last theis noble poetis thre	326	Garlande	517
Gower, Chawcer, Lydgate, theis thre	343	Garlande	1101
And slew Gerione /With thre bodys in one;	349	Garlande	1301
Now by theys names thre, ...	350	Garlande	1356
In verses two or thre	350	Garlande	1371
At the Thre Cranes, ...	374	Replycacion	9
and have waded but weakly in his thre maner of clerkly workes,	374	Replycacion	1
THRED-BARE			
Yet jentylnes in the ys thred-bare worne.	131	Garnesche5	70
THREDE			
Thow kit asonder his perfight vitall threde.	32	Dol Dethe	126
My nedle and threde	77	Phy Sparrow	235
Was sowyd with slendyr thre[de].	129	Garnesche3	201
threde] 'thre' †MS Harley 367			
I knyt togyther many a broken threde.	177	Magnyfycence	1343
For the grene bare threde	216	El Rummynge	60
For] 'And' Day 1560, Marshe 1568			
Some for very nede /Layde downe a skeyne of threde, ...	222	El Rummynge	310
THREDE-BARE			
His wytte is thynne, his hode is threde-bare.	60	Bowge	490
THREDE BARE			
Welth and wyt, I say, be so threde bare worne, ...	146	Magnyfycence	223
For thrifte is threde bare worn, ...	281	Why Come Ye	91
Shavyn and shorne, /And all threde bare worne!	304	Why Come Ye	1029
THREE			
Almoost two or three, /Of that dygnyte, ...	250	Collyn Clout	148
THREFOLDE			
How some delite for to lye, thycke and threfolde.	137	Ven Tongues	11
THRE-FOTED			
A thre-foted stole /That he may downe sytte, ...	247	Collyn Clout	30
THRESCORE			
Above threscore and ten.	288	Why Come Ye	373
THRESHOLD			
At the threshold comyng in, ...	227	El Rummynge	495
THRESTYL			
The threstyl with her warblyng;	83	Phy Sparrow	460
THRET			
And Aron sore he thret, ...	305	Why Come Ye	1068
Juvenall was thret, parde, for to kyll	315	Garlande	95
THRETE			
The kynges colours to threte.	127	Garnesche3	141
THREWE			
And ever he threwe, and kyst I wote nere what;	56	Bowge	349
I threwe away for drede.	77	Phy Sparrow	236
THRIFTE			
For thrifte is threde bare worn, ...	281	Why Come Ye	91
THRIFTLES			
Careles and shamlesse, /Thriftles and gracelesse	304	Why Come Ye	1021
Careles] 'Marcyles' MS Rawlinson C. 813			
THRIVE			
God let you never thrive!	368	Albany	379
THRYFT			
It were more thryft he boughte him a newe cote;	60	Bowge	487
Thus make I them wyth thryft to fyght.	152	Magnyfycence	421
Here was scant thryft /Whan they made suche shyft.	222	El Rummynge	301

THRYFTE —THUS

	Page	Title	Line
THRYFTE			
Thryfte hathe lost her cofer kay.	155	Magnyfycence	527
Ye. But thryfte and we have made a batell.	171	Magnyfycence	1136
Then fare well thryfte, by hym that crosse kyst!	179	Magnyfycence	1416
Than waste must be welcome, and fare well thryfte.	180	Magnyfycence	1444
Her thryfte is full thyn.	221	El Rummynge	256
THRYFTLESSE			
With gambaudynge thryftlesse,	280	Why Come Ye	73
THRYVE			
That ever thou thryve, God it forfende!	171	Magnyfycence	1114
And they never thryve in theyr age, it shall not gretly skyll.	200	Magnyfycence	2138
THRONGE			
They thronge in fast and flocked her aboute,	49	Bowge	122
But of all this thronge /One came them amonge,	225	El Rummynge	445
Forthwith there rose amonge the thronge	319	Garlande	246
THROTE			
His throte was clere and lustely coude fayne.	52	Bowge	233
For some shall wene be hanged by the throte.	59	Bowge	476
Myght byte asondre thy throte!	79	Phy Sparrow	306
For wasshyng of my throte;	229	El Rummynge	602
THROTE BOLE			
Of thy throte bole, and ryd the out of payne.	206	Magnyfycence	2315
THROTES			
Sharper then raysors, that shave and cut throtes,	138	Ven Tongues	51
These orators and poetes refreshed their throtes.	321	Garlande	343
About your traytours throtes.	362	Albany	124
THROTIS			
These orators and poetes refresshed there throtis.	321	Garlande	336
Theis orators and poetis refresshed there throtis.	322	Garlande	350
Their orators and poetis refresshed there throtis.	322	Garlande	357
Theis orators and poetis refresshed there throtis.	322	Garlande	364
These orators and poetis refresshid ther throtis.	322	Garlande	371
Theis orators and poetis refresshid there throtis.	322	Garlande	378
Theis notable poetis refresshid there throtis.	322	Garlande	385
THROUGH			
Through temporall afflictyons.	249	Collyn Clout	111
Thus they make theyr boost /Through every coost,	251	Collyn Clout	203
And through all the worlde thei go	268	Collyn Clout	885
And through suche detractyon	273	Collyn Clout	1059
Through suche abusyon, /And by suche illusyon,	279	Why Come Ye	19
THROUGH OUT			
That all men it founde /Through out Englonde.	165	Magnyfycence	883
THROW			
Er thow beware, that in a throw	132	Garnesche5	122
He wrate of a muse throw a mud wall;	351	Garlande	1384
THRUGH			
Thrugh your counseyle your fader was slayne;	114	Scot Kynge	27
THRUGHE			
Than of wanhope thrughe the unhappy wayes,	206	Magnyfycence	2337
But thrughe good hope there may come remedy.	207	Magnyfycence	2344
THRUST			
I shall thrust in the my dagger - Thorowe the legge in to the hose.	202	Magnyfycence	2177
Theyr thrust was so great,	222	El Rummynge	303
THUMBED			
To se howe she is gumbed, /Fyngered and thumbed,	215	El Rummynge	41
THURIFYCATION			
The way of thurifycation	84	Phy Sparrow	522
THUS			
Alas for pite that Percy thus was spylt,	32	Dol Dethe	106
Thus after her cold she cought a hete.	42	Balettys1	19
For thus dare I say, without tradiccyon,	42	Balettys2	10
Thus up and down my mynde was drawen and cast	47	Bowge	29
Thus, in a rowe, of martchauntes a grete route	49	Bowge	120
Thus endeth the prologue.	49	Bowge	R
And thus to talke with me he began.	51	Bowge	196
'By God,' quod he, 'this and thus it is';	52	Bowge	225
To be with you thus perte and thus bolde;	53	Bowge	265
To be with you thus perte and thus bolde;	53	Bowge	265
That I have deynte to see the cheryssched thus?	55	Bowge	338
And thus with us good company to kepe.	57	Bowge	385
And as he rounded thus in myne ere rounded] 'roynded' †Wynkyn de Worde 1499	61	Bowge	526
Thus endeth the Bowge of Courte.	61	Bowge	E
Thus within the wals /Of holy church to deale,	65	Hauke	134
Thus to ryng a peale /Wyth his hawkys bels?	65	Hauke	136
The church is thus abusyd, /Reproched and pollutyd;	66	Hauke	160
Dys church ye thus depravyd;	70	Hauke	308
Thus for to complayne.	77	Phy Sparrow	209
And now the cause is thus,	80	Phy Sparrow	363
Thus in conclusyon,	89	Phy Sparrow	707
And thus this elf /Consumeth himself,	95	Phy Sparrow	945
Thus endeth the boke of Philip Sparow,	103	Phy Sparrow	E
Thus thorow every stede	110	Lawde	3
I dare be bolde /Thus for to were.	112	Calliope	12
Thus for your guerdon quyt ar ye,	119	Ag Scottes	139
Thus fortune hath tourned you, I dare well say,	119	Ag Scottes	164
Thus with yow sche ded wary,	126	Garnesche3	75

734

	Page	Title	Line
And thus there ye lost yower pray;	131	Garnesche5	61
Then thus to you - Nay, suffer me yet ferther to say,	142	Magnyfycence	48
Surely I am joyous that ye be myndyd thus;	144	Magnyfycence	156
Thynke you not thus my frende Felycyte?	147	Magnyfycence	245
Why kepte you it thus longe? Howe dothe he? Wele?	149	Magnyfycence	314
Who is that that thus dyd cry?	149	Magnyfycence	326
Thus is the talkynge of one and of oder,	151	Magnyfycence	386
Thus make I them wyth thryft to fyght.	152	Magnyfycence	421
Thus at the laste I brynge hym ryght	152	Magnyfycence	422
Thus am I occupyed at all assayes.	152	Magnyfycence	428
That sheweth yourselfe thus spedde in physyke?	156	Magnyfycence	556
What! Shall we jangle thus all the day styll?	156	Magnyfycence	565
Nay, lette us not clatter thus styll.	157	Magnyfycence	610
Thus can I lerne you, syrs, to bere the devyls sacke;	160	Magnyfycence	721
By Cloked Colusyon thus many one is begyled.	160	Magnyfycence	728
For he wyll speke to Magnyfycence thus.	172	Magnyfycence	1168
To se you thus ruled and stande in suche awe.	178	Magnyfycence	1376
What! Wyll ye waste wynde and prate thus in vayne?	179	Magnyfycence	1403
What! Can ye agree thus and appose?	180	Magnyfycence	1425
What nede you with hym thus prate and chat?	180	Magnyfycence	1434
Thus must ye stuffe and store your treasure.	189	Magnyfycence	1754
Thus joy without mesure you shall have.	190	Magnyfycence	1781
Thus, I say, I am envyronned with solace.	190	Magnyfycence	1797
Lo, syrs, thus I handell them all	194	Magnyfycence	1896
In mysery and wretchydnesse thus to be lapped!	196	Magnyfycence	1985
That ever noblenesse sholde lyve thus wretchydly!	197	Magnyfycence	2021
With ye, mary, syrs, thus sholde it be:	198	Magnyfycence	2064
Thus totum in toto groweth up, as ye may se,	199	Magnyfycence	2099
What! Is the worlde thus come to passe?	200	Magnyfycence	2108
And thus to be facyd, I thynke it great skorne.	203	Magnyfycence	2217
What begger art thou, that thus doth banne and wary?	203	Magnyfycence	2238
Thus to rebuke me and have me in dyspyght!	205	Magnyfycence	2278
Sodenly thus Fortune can bothe smyle and frowne,	212	Magnyfycence	2529
Sodenly thus Fortune can bothe smyle and frowne,	213	Magnyfycence	2536
Thus in this worlde there is no erthly truste.	213	Magnyfycence	2544
Thus in this worlde there is no erthly truste.	213	Magnyfycence	2551
Thus none estate lyvynge of hym[selfe] can be sure,	214	Magnyfycence	2564
hymselfe] 'hym' †Rastell & Treveris C 1530, B			
And thus begynneth the game.	217	El Rummynge	132
Thus and thus it is,	223	El Rummynge	357
Thus and thus it is,	223	El Rummynge	357
She spake thus in her snout,	223	El Rummynge	363
spake thus] 'speketh this' †Lant 1545, Kynge & Marche 1554, Day 1560, Marshe 1568			
Thus endeth the gest /Of this worthy fest.	230	El Rummynge	622
Thus dyvers of language by lernyng I grow:	233	Speke Parott	103
Thus Parott dothe pray yow,	237	Speke Parott	225
Thus myche Parott hathe opynlye expreste;	242	Speke Parott	381
Thus eche of other blother /The tone against the tother.	248	Collyn Clout	66
But thus the people carke,	249	Collyn Clout	120
And surely thus they sey:	249	Collyn Clout	121
Thus they make theyr boost /Through every coost,	251	Collyn Clout	202
Thus I, Collyn Cloute,	253	Collyn Clout	285
And thus they hurte theyr soules,	255	Collyn Clout	341
Yet thus with yll hayles	256	Collyn Clout	400
To put them thus to flyght;	256	Collyn Clout	405
Thus the people telles, /Rayles lyke rebelles,	257	Collyn Clout	412
With language thus poluted	258	Collyn Clout	486
You thus to dyffame.	259	Collyn Clout	510
And thus the loselles stryves,	261	Collyn Clout	574
Alas, and wellaway, /What eyles them thus to say?	261	Collyn Clout	578
Theyr chambre thus to dresse	270	Collyn Clout	975
Thus the churche remorde.	271	Collyn Clout	981
Thus talkynge and tellynge	271	Collyn Clout	984
Theyr tonges thus do clap;	273	Collyn Clout	1058
Take upon me /Thus copyously to wryte,	273	Collyn Clout	1085
Take upon me] 'Take now upon' Kele 1545.1, 'I take now uppon' MS Harley 2252			
To be tered thus and torne?	276	Collyn Clout	1201
Howe may we thus endure?	276	Collyn Clout	1202
Thus age, (a graunt domage)	280	Why Come Ye	45
a] not in Kitson 1560.7, Marshe 1568			
Thus thwartyng over thom,	283	Why Come Ye	200
Thus royally he dothe deale	287	Why Come Ye	336
Thus wyll I conclude my style,	289	Why Come Ye	396
Thus dayly they be decked, /Taunted and checked,	294	Why Come Ye	611
Thus he, borne so base,	294	Why Come Ye	622
And thus they shall syt -	295	Why Come Ye	633
Thus boldly for to barke?	309	Why Come Ye	1205
Thus stode I in the frytthy forest of Galtres,	312	Garlande	22
And as I thus sadly amonge them avysid	323	Garlande	386
Forthwith, I say, thus wandrynge in my thought,	325	Garlande	456
Thus passid we forth walkynge unto the pretory	325	Garlande	477
And all tyme wandred I thus to and fro,	326	Garlande	516
In derkenes thus dwelt we, tyll at the last	330	Garlande	650
Thus talkyng we went forth in at a postern gate.	333	Garlande	766
forth] not in MS Cotton Vitellius E.x			
And truly of theyr bownte thus were they bent	334	Garlande	806

THWARTID—TYLL   Page   Title   Line

Thus passyth he the tyme both nyght and day,	352	Garlande	1423
Thus ye have compast	361	Albany	102
And thus ye prepared	365	Albany	272
Thus in your cowardly castell	366	Albany	279
Thus he dothe disparage	369	Albany	414
And thus, Sainct George to borowe,	371	Albany	506
Thus by demeryttes of their abusyon,	374	Replycacion	14
Thus are they undone and utterly shamed.	374	Replycacion	17
Thus to be laughed to skorne,	376	Replycacion	82
Thus tattred and thus torne,	376	Replycacion	83
Thus tattred and thus torne,	376	Replycacion	83
Your selfe thus ye discured	377	Replycacion	92
Thus all thyng ye disorder	380	Replycacion	227
Thus can harpe and syng	384	Replycacion	344
Thus endeth the Replicacyon of Skelton Laureate, etc.	386	Replycacion	E

THWARTID
And I with you thwartid 341   Garlande   1039

THWARTYNG
Thus thwartyng over thom, ... 283   Why Come Ye   200

TIDINGES
These tidinges newe, ... 359   Albany   3

TIDINGS
What tidings at Tot[nam], what newis in Wales, ... 139   Ven Tongues   64
  Totnam] 'Totman' Marshe 1568

TILL
They bode not till the rekenyng were discust. 30   Dol Dethe   40
Till the chaunce ran ageyne hym of Fortuns double dyse. . 33   Dol Dethe   140

TIME
And let the other another [time] awayte. 180   Magnyfycence   1454
  time] not in †Rastell & Treveris C 1530, B
It is time for you to brydell 368   Albany   388

TIMOROUS
That longe tyme blewe a full timorous blaste, ... 319   Garlande   260

TIRIKKIS
He turnyd his tirikkis, his volvell ran fast, ... 354   Garlande   1517

TIRYKIS
Som trete of theyr tirykis, som of astrology, ... 234   Speke Parott   137

TISSEW
Encoverde over with golde of tissew fyne; 345   Garlande   1164

TITAN
Whan Titan radiant burnisshith his bemis bryght, ... 327   Garlande   534

TITILLE
His titille dothe recorde; 110   Lawde   11

TITIVYLLIS
Theis titi[v]yllis with taumpinnis wer towchid and tappid; . . 330   Garlande   642
  titivyllis] 'titinyllis' †Fakes 1523, 'titiuls' Marshe 1568

TITUS
There Titus Lyvius hymselfe dyd avaunce 321   Garlande   344

TYBORNE
For whome Tyborne groneth both daye and nyghte. 58   Bowge   417
  whome] 'home' †Wynkyn de Worde 1499
A Tyborne checke /Shall breke his necke. 165   Magnyfycence   910

TYBURNE
Tyburne thou me assynyd 128   Garnesche3   174
To Tyburne, where they hange on hyght. 152   Magnyfycence   423

TYD
Stop a tyd, and be welle ware 133   Garnesche5   162

TYDE
Thowth it be now ful tyde with the, ... 132   Garnesche5   120
Al of pleasure /My hose strayte tyde; 164   Magnyfycence   852
From tyde to tyde. 218   El Rummynge   155
From tyde to tyde. 218   El Rummynge   155
In open tyde and in lent. 268   Collyn Clout   859
  open tyde] 'open tyme' Kele 1545.1, Marshe 1568, 'Ester tyde'
  MS Harley 2252

TYDES
And nyghtly the tydes 84   Phy Sparrow   507
  nyghtly] 'nyghly' †Kele 1545.2

TYDINGIS
With, 'How doth the north?' 'What tydingis in the sowth?' . . 326   Garlande   498

TYDYNGES
But nowe what tydynges can you tell? Let se. 166   Magnyfycence   928
What tydynges with you, syr? I befole thy brayne pan. . . 191   Magnyfycence   1805
What tydynges with you, syr, that you loke so sad? . . . 192   Magnyfycence   1843
Of tydynges in Wales, ... 223   El Rummynge   353

TYGER
Ne no tyger so wood, ... 100   Phy Sparrow   1157

TYKYLL
They towche me so thorowly and tykyll my consayte, . . . 184   Magnyfycence   1567

TYL
Grimbaldus gredy snatche a puddyng tyl the rost be redy. . . 172   Magnyfycence   1155

TYLE
Plucke down lede and theke with tyle; 169   Magnyfycence   1026

TYLL
Tyll fykkill Fortune began on hym to frowne. 33   Dol Dethe   133
Farewell tyll soone. But no word that I sayde!' 51   Bowge   175
And wake all nyghte and slepe tyll it be none. 57   Bowge   382

TYLLBERY —TYMES

	Page	Title	Line
And tyll I come, have, here is myne hat to plege.'	57	Bowge	413
is] not in Marshe 1568			
Adewe tyll soone, we shall speke more of this.	60	Bowge	492
Tyll cruell fate made him to dy:	86	Phy Sparrow	592
Tyll more matyr may cum.	129	Garnesche3	205
Nothynge but fare you well tyll sone -	149	Magnyfycence	319
Well, tary here tyll I for you sende.	163	Magnyfycence	817
Tyll, as the devyll wolde, they fell a chydynge	166	Magnyfycence	940
Farewell, my frende. Adue tyll sone.	167	Magnyfycence	966
I daunce up and downe tyll I am dyssy.	169	Magnyfycence	1040
Tyll all theyr conveyaunce is turnyd into madnesse.	178	Magnyfycence	1367
I coude holde you with suche talke hens tyll to morowe.	184	Magnyfycence	1588
Tyll I be revenged on that horson knave.	185	Magnyfycence	1616
I was your good lorde tyll that ye beganne	188	Magnyfycence	1714
Fare well tyll sone; adue tyll to morowe.	192	Magnyfycence	1850
Fare well tyll sone; adue tyll to morowe.	192	Magnyfycence	1850
I may no more speke tyll I have wept my fyll.	198	Magnyfycence	2063
Tyll, as ye se many tymes, they shame all theyr kynne.	201	Magnyfycence	2144
But drynke tyll they stare	217	El Rummynge	108
Tyll that he dreme and dronny;	220	El Rummynge	230
Some renne tyll they swete,	221	El Rummynge	266
And drynke tyll we blowe, /And pype tyrly-tyrlowe!'	221	El Rummynge	291
Tyll Eufrates, that flodde, dryvythe me into Ynde,	231	Speke Parott	4
Tyll my dyenge day	259	Collyn Clout	506
Tyll the coost be clere	277	Collyn Clout	1257
I wyll no further ryme /Tyll another tyme;	284	Why Come Ye	231
Tyll another tyme etc.	284	Why Come Ye	232
Tyll better layser be founde;	294	Why Come Ye	627
Tyll he cheked at the fyst,	297	Why Come Ye	735
How ryvers rin not tyll the spryng be full;	314	Garlande	81
To blowe bararag tyll bothe his eyne stare.'	319	Garlande	245
bararag] 'bararag brag' MS Cotton Vitellius E.x			
Tyll at the last they forcyd me sore,	324	Garlande	446
sore] 'so sore' Marshe 1568			
Tyll at the last theis noble poetis thre	326	Garlande	517
In derkenes thus dwelt we, tyll at the last	330	Garlande	650

TYLLBERY

From Tyllbery fery /To the playne of Salysbery!	79	Phy Sparrow	320

TYLNEY

To mastres Margaret Tylney	338	Garlande	R

TYME

Redy to assyst you in every tyme of nede;	30	Dol Dethe	58
Corage wyth lust, convenient tyme and space;	43	Balettys3	3
The tyme whan Mars to werre hym dyd dres;	46	Bowge	7
It was no tyme with him to jape nor toye.	54	Bowge	290
To loke on this were tyme.	65	Hauke	144
Oft tyme after pleasaunce,	81	Phy Sparrow	368
Yet long tyme she ne knew	89	Phy Sparrow	727
And spend my tyme /In prose and ryme,	95	Phy Sparrow	954
Lewdely your tyme ye spende,	124	Garnesche3	15
My tyme, I trow, I xulde but lese	133	Garnesche5	154
To passe the tyme and order whyle a man may talke	159	Magnyfycence	689
Let us here of your pleasure, to passe the tyme withall.	182	Magnyfycence	1518
In tyme of dystresse I am redy at hande;	205	Magnyfycence	2285
Somtyme to fall, another tyme to beware:	207	Magnyfycence	2374
We wyll no farther ryme /Of it at this tyme.	220	El Rummynge	241
We have longyd and lokyd long tyme for that,	239	Speke Parott	310
So myche newe makyng, and so madd tyme spente;	244	Speke Parott	450
The tyme dothe fast ensew	280	Why Come Ye	62
I wyll no further ryme /Tyll another tyme;	284	Why Come Ye	231
Tyll another tyme etc.	284	Why Come Ye	232
Hath nowe no tyme nor space	295	Why Come Ye	631
And at more convenyent tyme	310	Why Come Ye2	21
Bycause that he his tyme studyously hath spent	314	Garlande	60
he his tyme] 'his tyme he' MS Cotton Vitellius E.x			
To pas the tyme in slowthfull ydelnes,	315	Garlande	120
That longe tyme blewe a full timorous blaste,	319	Garlande	260
With, 'Sir, I pray you, a lytyll tyme stande backe,	326	Garlande	505
And all tyme wandred I thus to and fro,	326	Garlande	516
With syngular pleasurs to dryve away the tyme,	326	Garlande	524
And then she sayd, 'Whylis we have tyme and space	328	Garlande	563
To pas the tyme with, but let us wast no wynde.	328	Garlande	565
Intentyfe ay /And dylygent, /No tyme myspent;	339	Garlande	944
'Withdrawe your hande, the tyme passis fast.	343	Garlande	1086
That unremembred longe tyme remayned.	347	Garlande	1225
Thus passyth he the tyme both nyght and day,	352	Garlande	1423
That leudly have their tyme spent,	375	Replycacion	24

TYMEROUS

But for I am a mayde, /Tymerous, halfe afrayde,	87	Phy Sparrow	608

TYMES

And many tymes and ofte	74	Phy Sparrow	124
Many tymes and ofte,	80	Phy Sparrow	355
For many tymes moche kyndnesse is denyed	177	Magnyfycence	1338
Tyll, as ye se many tymes, they shame all theyr kynne.	201	Magnyfycence	2144
Then ye of foly in tymes past you repent?	209	Magnyfycence	2433
'Then ye repent you of foly in tymes past' †Rastell & Treveris C 1530, B			
Of your acquefntaunce I was in tymes past,	327	Garlande	540

TYN —TOGETHER	Page	Title	Line
With vertu enbesid all tymes and howris;	334	Garlande	805
TYN			
To copper, to tyn, /To lede, or alcumyn?	301	Why Come Ye	906
TYNE			
From Tyne to Trent,	167	Magnyfycence	981
TYNED			
My tonge is with favell forked and tyned.	160	Magnyfycence	727
TYNKERS			
To travellars, to tynkers, /To sweters, to swynkers,	217	El Rummynge	104
TYPPET			
'Lo, here is an olde typpet,	223	El Rummynge	366
TYRAND			
Of no tyrand I rede,	67	Hauke	190
TYRE			
Your name recountynge beyonde the lande of Tyre,	327	Garlande	551
TYRYD			
The hawke tyryd on a *bonne,	63	Hauke	60
*bonne] 'bone' Scattergood			
TYRLY-TYRLOWE			
And drynke tyll we blowe, /And pype tyrly-tyrlowe!'	221	El Rummynge	292
TYRLY TYRLOWE			
For to shote a crowe /At her tyrly tyrlowe;	270	Collyn Clout	949
TYRMAGANT			
But yf yt war Syr Tyrmagant that tyrnyd without nall;	121	Garneschel	4
TYRNYD			
But yf yt war Syr Tyrmagant that tyrnyd without nall;	121	Garneschel	4
TYSE			
Ye dyde provoke and tyse,	378	Replycacion	132
TYSYKE			
Can you remedy for a tysyke	156	Magnyfycence	555
TYTAN			
Tytan hathe truste up hys tressys of fyne golde;	242	Speke Parott	398
TYTELL-TATTYLL			
I played with him tytell-tattyll,	80	Phy Sparrow	357
TYTYVELL			
Symkyn Tytyvell and Pers Pykthanke.	175	Magnyfycence	1267
TYTYVYLLES			
And talkes lyke tytyvylles	257	Collyn Clout	416
talkes] 'talke' †Godfray 1531, Kele 1545.1, Marshe 1568			
TYTLE			
His tytle is true in Fraunce to raygne;	118	Ag Scottes	120
TYTMOSE			
The semewe and the tytmose;	83	Phy Sparrow	458
TYTTERS			
Theyr smockes all to-ragged, /Wyth tytters and tatters,	217	El Rummynge	126
TYTUS			
Whom Tytus Lyvyus /In wrytynge doth enroll;	67	Hauke	209
For Tytus at Dover abydythe in the rode;	239	Speke Parott	284
TO-BROKYN			
Theyre browys all to-brokyn, such clappys they cach;	43	Balettys2	32
TODAY			
Today it is well, tomorowe it is all amysse;	213	Magnyfycence	2541
Today in delyte, tomorowe bare of blysse;	213	Magnyfycence	2542
Today a lorde, tomorowe ly in the duste;	213	Magnyfycence	2543
Today fayre wether, tomorowe a stormy rage;	213	Magnyfycence	2545
Today hote, tomorowe outragyous colde;	213	Magnyfycence	2546
Today a yoman, tomorowe made of page;	213	Magnyfycence	2547
Today in surety, tomorowe bought and solde;	213	Magnyfycence	2548
Today maysterfest, tomorowe he hath no holde;	213	Magnyfycence	2549
Today a man, tomorowe he lyeth in the duste:	213	Magnyfycence	2550
TODE			
Thou tode, thow scorpyon, /Thow bawdy babyone,	128	Garnesche3	162
Then any poysoned tode, or any serpent.	138	Ven Tongues	54
TOFORE			
For as I tofore have sayd,	90	Phy Sparrow	769
Under the forme as I sayd tofore,	324	Garlande	443
tofore] 'before' Marshe 1568			
TO-FRET			
With frowarde frostis, alas, was all to-fret!	352	Garlande	1450
TOGEDER			
Confeterd togeder of commoun concente	30	Dol Dethe	26
commoun] 'cominion' Marshe 1568			
Togeder with servauntis of his famuly,	31	Dol Dethe	93
His byrth and rowme togeder,	291	Why Come Ye	498
Of a thousande poetes assembled togeder.	320	Garlande	286
Togeder in armes, as brethern, enbrasid;	323	Garlande	393
TOGEDYR			
That hang togedyr as fethyrs in the wynde;	239	Speke Parott	293
TOGETHER			
Embraudred, enlasid together, and fettred,	138	Ven Tongues	39
I trowe good fortune hath annexyd us together,	146	Magnyfycence	198
Go together by the heddys, and gyve me your swordys.	202	Magnyfycence	2199
Together are bended, /And so condyscended,	304	Why Come Ye	1022
bendyd] 'wendyd' MS Rawlinson C. 813			
Drove clowdes together lyke dryftis of snowe.	319	Garlande	263
Sex volumis engrosid together it doth containe.	354	Garlande	1502
Gone to seke hallows, /With Reason together,	358	Garlande2	8

	Page	Title	Line
TOGETHYR			
For Jerico and Jerssey shall mete togethyr as sone	239	Speke Parott	306
Whate sequele shall folow when pendugims mete togethyr?	243	Speke Parott	415
TOGITHER			
Than swetely togither we ly, /As two pygges in a sty.'	220	El Rummynge	233
Than swetely] 'Thus swete' 1521 Fragment			
TOGYDER			
Togyder we wyll talke more of this.	151	Magnyfycence	393
We have bene togyder bothe erly and late.	154	Magnyfycence	499
Why, shall we dwell togyder all thre?	154	Magnyfycence	509
Nowe therfore, whylest we are togyder –	155	Magnyfycence	546
I say, whylest we are togyder in same –	155	Magnyfycence	548
Nay. Let us our heddes togyder cast.	156	Magnyfycence	566
Spell the remenaunt, and do togyder.	157	Magnyfycence	619
But, Counterfet Countenaunce, go we togyder,	158	Magnyfycence	665
Do and undo, bothe togyder;	169	Magnyfycence	1034
In faythe, trouthe ye say, we wente togyder to scole.	170	Magnyfycence	1065
To here you two rutters dyspute togyder.	176	Magnyfycence	1287
With a good wyll, syr, God spede you bothe togyder.	186	Magnyfycence	1648
A, syr, thy jarfawcon and thou be hanged togyder!	191	Magnyfycence	1812
And with a lyme rodde I toke them bothe togyder.	191	Magnyfycence	1815
Thy wordes hange togyder as fethers in the wynde.	191	Magnyfycence	1818
Lyke as they were with buckels /Togyder made fast.	215	El Rummynge	47
The donge of her hennes /And the ale togyder,	219	El Rummynge	203
TOGYTHER			
I knyt togyther many a broken threde.	177	Magnyfycence	1343
And get [y]ou home togyther; for Lyberte shall byde you] 'thou' †Rastell & Treveris C 1530, B	180	Magnyfycence	1446
I gader togyther and close in my crop,	233	Speke Parott	94
TOIES			
And of their taunting toies rest with il hayle.	138	Ven Tongues	33
TOYE			
It was no tyme with him to jape nor toye.	54	Bowge	290
TOYES			
Remembrest thou not the japes and the toyes –	171	Magnyfycence	1137
TOYLE			
Men call it a toyle.	365	Albany	269
TO-JAGGED			
Wyth theyr heles dagged, /Theyr kyrtelles all to-jagged,	217	El Rummynge	124
TO-JAGGID			
For a gun stone, I say, had all to-jaggid his cap, to-jaggid] 'to lagged' Marshe 1568	329	Garlande	629
TOKE			
That of hys love he toke no kepe,	41	Balettys1	7
But of eche thynge there as I toke hede,	47	Bowge	64
And to mewarde the strayte waye he toke.	51	Bowge	194
Lyghte lyme-fynger, he toke none other wage.	60	Bowge	509
And toke it oute in drynke,	66	Hauke	158
I toke my sampler ones	77	Phy Sparrow	210
And with a lyme rodde I toke them bothe togyder.	191	Magnyfycence	1815
Elynour toke her up	224	El Rummynge	376
The lynage of Lot toke supporte of Assur;	232	Speke Parott	66
Yet whan he toke first his hat, first] not in MS Rawlinson C. 813	306	Why Come Ye	1108
By whose suggestyon /I toke on hand this warke, suggestyon] 'subjectyon' MS Rawlinson C. 813	309	Why Come Ye	1204
And with that worde she toke me by the honde.	328	Garlande	560
As dame Thamarys, whiche toke the kyng of Perce,	336	Garlande	857
Toke it for a sporte,	379	Replycacion	191
Your penaunce toke no place,	379	Replycacion	198
TOKEN			
from an honorable Jentyllwoman for a token,	39	Coystrowne3	I
That token for her sake;	89	Phy Sparrow	691
That one might se her token.	227	El Rummynge	497
TOKENS			
The tokens ar not good /To be true Englysh blood;	121	Ag Scottes2	22
TOKYN			
Youre ugly tokyn /My mynd hath brokyn /From worldly lust;	39	Coystrowne3	1
TOLD			
Gowers Englysh is olde /And of no value told; told] 'is tolde' Wyght 1553, Kitson 1560.6, Marshe 1568	91	Phy Sparrow	785
Mary, syr, he told us, when	158	Magnyfycence	652
Sens Dewcalyons flodde, in no cronycle ys told.	246	Speke Parott	518
I have told you part, but nat all.	299	Why Come Ye	822
And so Occupacyon, your regester, me told.'	344	Garlande	1141
TOLDE			
Desyre her name was, and so she me tolde.	48	Bowge	85
He tolde me so, by God, ye maye truste me.	60	Bowge	514
Whan her tale is tolde	87	Phy Sparrow	620
As it is enrolde, /Wrytten and tolde	116	Ag Scottes	40
Of thi lewdenes that may be tolde.	134	Garnesche5	175
Worketh more mischiefe than can be tolde;	137	Ven Tongues	8
Who soever that tale unto you tolde,	137	Ven Tongues	20
And tolde all the myschyef I coude behynde theyr backe,	160	Magnyfycence	718
A, syr, tolde I not you howe I dyd fynde	191	Magnyfycence	1819
Abyde, abyde, /And to you shall be tolde	218	El Rummynge	157
For Tholome tolde me	258	Collyn Clout	467
A kynge, as I have tolde,	293	Why Come Ye	563

TOLE —TOP

	Page	Title	Line
Another tolde how shyppes wente to wrak.	326	Garlande	507
Wherto she answeryd, and brevely me tolde	328	Garlande	576

TOLE
And occupyed no better your tole,	127	Garnesche3	118

TOLERACYON
With toleracyon /And supportacyon /Of reformacyon,	356	Garlande	1576

TOLLAGE
By taxynge and tollage,	255	Collyn Clout	362

TOLLERACYON
Under supportacyon /Of your pacyent tolleracyon,	62	Hauke	32
And under pacyent tolleracyon	93	Phy Sparrow	851
Under supportacyon /Of pacyent tolleracyon.	142	Magnyfycence	62

TOLLERATE
How may I your mokery mekely tollerate,	123	Garnesche2	1

TOLMAN
A tolman to blot, /A rough foted Scot!	136	Dundas	40

TO-MANGLE
And them all to-mangle?	255	Collyn Clout	333
to-mangle] 'mangle' †Godfray 1531, Kele 1545.1, Marshe 1568			

TO-MYRYD
Yor moth etyn mokkysh maneres, they be all to-myryd.	123	Garnesche2	12

TOMOROWE
Today it is well, tomorowe it is all amysse;	213	Magnyfycence	2541
Today in delyte, tomorowe bare of blysse;	213	Magnyfycence	2542
Today a lorde, tomorowe ly in the duste:	213	Magnyfycence	2543
Today fayre wether, tomorowe a stormy rage;	213	Magnyfycence	2545
Today hote, tomorowe outragyous colde;	213	Magnyfycence	2546
Today a yoman, tomorowe made of page;	213	Magnyfycence	2547
Today in surety, tomorowe bought and solde;	213	Magnyfycence	2548
Today maysterfest, tomorowe he hath no holde;	213	Magnyfycence	2549
Today a man, tomorowe he lyeth in the duste:	213	Magnyfycence	2550

TO MOROWE
I coude holde you with suche talke hens tyll to morowe.	184	Magnyfycence	1588
Fare well tyll sone; adue tyll to morowe.	192	Magnyfycence	1850

TONE
Ye, a fole the tone, and a fole the tother.	170	Magnyfycence	1091
Thus eche of other blother /The tone against the tother.	248	Collyn Clout	67

TONG
Yet is youre tong an adders tayle,	41	Coystrowne4	16
Holde youre tong, now, all beshrewde!	41	Coystrowne4	28
Our naturall tong is rude,	91	Phy Sparrow	774
His tong never styll /For to say yll,	95	Phy Sparrow	941
Cicero with hys tong of golde.	130	Garnesche5	12
Thy tong untawte, with poyson infecte,	132	Garnesche5	108
In Greke tong Parott can bothe speke and sey,	231	Speke Parott	26
Whose tong ys attayntyd with slaundrys obliqui.	241	Speke Parott	363
Holde ye your tong, ye can no goode.	310	Why Come Ye2	20
ye] (1st) not in MS Rawlinson C. 813			

TONGE
His serpentes tonge /That many one hath stonge;	94	Phy Sparrow	920
My tonge is with favell forked and tyned.	160	Magnyfycence	727
Holde thy tonge, and thou love thy helth.	179	Magnyfycence	1402
Or ellys with this knyfe cut out a tonge	206	Magnyfycence	2314
Her tonge was very quycke	223	El Rummyng	337
With Dowche, with Spaynyshe, my tonge can agree;	231	Speke Parott	32
Myden agan in Grekys tonge we rede,	232	Speke Parott	52
Thy tonge is nat well thewde,	287	Why Come Ye	331
His Latyne tonge dothe hobbyll,	292	Why Come Ye	526

TONGES
The dragones with their tonges	79	Phy Sparrow	292
Thow ye be tauntyd, Parotte, with tonges attayntyd,	240	Speke Parott	343
But they theyr tonges fyle,	267	Collyn Clout	850
Theyr tonges thus do clap;	273	Collyn Clout	1058
Your tonges were to flete;	376	Replycacion	50
And your tonges cropped, /Whan ye logyke chopped,	377	Replycacion	117

TONGE-TAYDE
Men say ye are tonge-tayde,	255	Collyn Clout	354

TONGUE
In Affryc tongue byrsa is a thonge of lether;	233	Speke Parott	80

TONGUES
Against Venemous Tongues	136	Ven Tongues	I

TONNELL
A tonnell and a bottell,	224	El Rummynge	403

TONNYSH
She is a tonnysh gyb;	217	El Rummynge	99

TONSORS
And your tonsors be croppyd,	263	Collyn Clout	677
tonsors be croppyd] 'coursers betrapped' †Godfray 1531, Kele 1545.1, Marshe 1568			

TOO
To pyke my lytell too,	76	Phy Sparrow	176
A, Lord God, how the gowte wryngeth me by the too.	198	Magnyfycence	2047
With my beke I can pyke my lyttel praty too;	233	Speke Parott	107

TOOTE
With a balde face to toote;	82	Phy Sparrow	411

TOP
Above, in the top, a byrde of Araby,	330	Garlande	667

	Page	Title	Line
TOPAS			
The topas rych and precyouse in vertew;	44	Balettys3	15
TOPIAS			
But hyde the, Sir Topias,	366	Albany	287
TOPICALL			
analeticall, topicall, and logycall:	375	Replycacion	1
TOPYAS			
Howkyd as an hawkys beke, lyke Syr Topyas.	122	Garneschel	40
TO-RAGGED			
A rusty gallande, to-ragged and to-rente;	56	Bowge	345
Theyr smockes all to-ragged, /Wyth tytters and tatters,	217	El Rummynge	125
TORDE			
Do away, I say, the devylles torde!	151	Magnyfycence	397
Torde! Man, it is an hawke of the towre.	166	Magnyfycence	925
The devyls torde for thy brayne!	170	Magnyfycence	1086
Torde, I say! What have I do?	171	Magnyfycence	1106
Hay, chysshe, come hyder! Nay, torde! Take hym be tyme.	171	Magnyfycence	1117
The tothe ake! Lo, a torde ye have.	172	Magnyfycence	1164
Torde! Thou arte good to be a man of warre.	202	Magnyfycence	2179
TO-RENTE			
A rusty gallande, to-ragged and to-rente;	56	Bowge	345
TORNE			
Such tunges shuld be torne out by the harde rootes,	137	Ven Tongues	3
It is evyll patchynge of that is torne.	153	Magnyfycence	447
Ye, all thyng mortall shall torne unto nought	236	Speke Parott	214
Nowe torne agayne to me.	237	Speke Parott	245
My propyr Besse, /And torne agayne to me!	238	Speke Parott	262
To be tered thus and torne?	276	Collyn Clout	1201
Thus tattred and thus torne,	376	Replycacion	83
TOTE			
How often dyd I tote	100	Phy Sparrow	1146
A myrrour of glasse, that I may tote therin;	231	Speke Parott	10
The myrrour that I tote in, quasi diaphonum,	236	Speke Parott	190
TOTETH			
That toteth oft in a glasse,	82	Phy Sparrow	422
TOTH			
Never a toth in his heed.	108	Epitaphel	61
TOTHE AKE			
A, holde thy peas! I have the tothe ake.	172	Magnyfycence	1163
The tothe ake! Lo, a torde ye have.	172	Magnyfycence	1164
In faythe, and I bequethe hym the tothe ake.	204	Magnyfycence	2253
TOTHER			
Ye, a fole the tone, and a fole the tother.	170	Magnyfycence	1091
What, Fansy! Let me se who is the tother.	172	Magnyfycence	1158
Thus eche of other blother /The tone against the tother.	248	Collyn Clout	67
TOTYNGE			
Your gasynge and your totynge	273	Collyn Clout	1074
TOTNAM			
What tidings at Tot[nam], what newis in Wales, Totnam] 'Totman' Marshe 1568	139	Ven Tongues	64
TO-TORNE			
And trouthe is all to-torne;	281	Why Come Ye	93
TOT QUOT			
We shall have a tot quot	282	Why Come Ye	128
TOT QUOTTES			
Of tryalytes, /And of tot quottes;	260	Collyn Clout	563
TOTTER			
And some I make in a rope to totter and walter;	194	Magnyfycence	1910
TOUCHE			
Can touche a troughte and cloke it subtylly troughte] 'trouth' Wynkyn de Worde 1510, Marshe 1568; it] not in Marshe 1568	46	Bowge	11
For yf I had not quyckely fledde the touche,	60	Bowge	503
To touche them with tauntes of your armony,	117	Ag Scottes	86
Brefly to touche of my purpose the effecte:	142	Magnyfycence	67
As yf a man fortune to touche you on the quyke -	185	Magnyfycence	1611
TOUCHED			
Or touched on the quycke,	274	Collyn Clout	1124
TOUCHYNG			
as touchyng the tetrycall theologisacion of these demy divines,	374	Replycacion	1
TOUCHYNGE			
But nowe, syr, as touchynge this letter -	149	Magnyfycence	331
My frende, as touchynge to this your mocyon,	186	Magnyfycence	1639
But as touchynge dystrectyon, /With sober dyrectyon dystrectyon] 'dyscrecyon' Marshe 1568, MS Rawlinson C. 813	304	Why Come Ye	1008
TOUGH			
Although he made it never so tough,	139	Ven Tongues	77
TOUGHT			
Conceyved and cought, /And was never tought	84	Phy Sparrow	500
TOUGHTHER			
Favoure we have toughther than ony elme, toughther] 'tougher' Wynkyn de Worde 1510, Marshe 1568	49	Bowge	129
TOUNE			
Of knightis, of squyers, chef lord of toure and toune,	33	Dol Dethe	132
TOUR			
It is not syttynge in tour nor towne	115	Scot Kynge	66
TOURE			
Of knightis, of squyers, chef lord of toure and toune,	33	Dol Dethe	132

TOURES —TOWRIS   Page   Title   Line

	Page	Title	Line
And some fall prechynge at the Toure Hyll;	200	Magnyfycence	2140
I say, lieutenaunt of the Toure,	275	Collyn Clout	1167
TOURES			
With turrettes and with toures,	270	Collyn Clout	936
TOURNE			
For you and your Scottes wolde tourne his face?	114	Scot Kynge	18
Cockes harte! Tourne the; let me se thyne aray.	167	Magnyfycence	959
To tourne a fole out of his clowtes.	174	Magnyfycence	1211
Ye, tourne over the lefe, rede there, and loke	176	Magnyfycence	1293
Syr, remembre the tourne of Fortunes whele,	197	Magnyfycence	2022
Parrot sayth playnly, shall tourne all to dust.	236	Speke Parott	224
Relygyous men are fayne /For to tourne agayne	256	Collyn Clout	375
We tourne ryght into wronge,	276	Collyn Clout	1195
With, 'Tourne all home agayne!'	282	Why Come Ye	151
And cowardly tourne your backes	367	Albany	349
And never tourne agayne.	368	Albany	372
Shall tourne you to myschauns.	371	Albany	499
For to tourne your face;	371	Albany	505
TOURNED			
Thus fortune hath tourned you, I dare well say,	119	Ag Scottes	164
What! Is all your myrthe nowe tourned to sorowe?	192	Magnyfycence	1849
Is tourned to glasse.	301	Why Come Ye	902
TOURNETH			
Fortune so tourneth the ball	262	Collyn Clout	632
TOWARD			
Taking his course toward the west;	86	Phy Sparrow	573
Is toward hym so mynded,	295	Why Come Ye	659
Arectyng my syght toward the zodyake,	312	Garlande	1
TOWARDE			
Towarde the cloudy skyes;	72	Phy Sparrow	38
Towarde the porte salue /Of our Savyoure Jesu,	278	Collyn Clout	1260
With that I sprange up towarde the tent	320	Garlande	283
Came towarde me, and smylid halfe in game;	327	Garlande	529
Towarde the dore, as he were comyng oute,	343	Garlande	1095
TOWARDES			
In your brest towardes this gentylman.	188	Magnyfycence	1713
Passe forthe, Parotte, towardes some passengere;	239	Speke Parott	301
TOWCHE			
They towche me so thorowly and tykyll my consayte,	184	Magnyfycence	1567
TOWCHID			
Towchid, and hard for to be barrid.	316	Garlande	143
barrid] 'debarrid' MS Cotton Vitellius E.x			
Theis titi[v]yllis with taumpinnis wer towchid and tappid;	330	Garlande	642
titivyllis] 'titinyllis' †Fakes 1523, 'titiuls' Marshe 1568			
Envyvid picturis well towchid and quikly.	345	Garlande	1161
TOWCHIS			
To tell all his towchis it were to grete wonder;	333	Garlande	764
TOWCHYD			
By God, there be some that be shroudly towchyd.	175	Magnyfycence	1277
As quikly towchyd as it were flesshe and bones,	328	Garlande	592
TOWCHYNG			
As towchyng that Eschines is remembred,	316	Garlande	148
TOWE			
With flaxe and with towe;	221	El Rummynge	287
TOWER			
In Plut[o]s gastly tower;	104	Phy Sparrow	1323
Plutos] 'Plutus' editions			
It is not syttyng in tower and towne	120	Ag Scottes	174
syttyng] 'fytting' Kynge & Marche 1554			
TOWNE			
It is not syttynge in tour nor towne	115	Scot Kynge	66
Of Edyngeborrow and Saynt Jonys towne.	117	Ag Scottes	63
It is not syttyng in tower and towne	120	Ag Scottes	174
syttyng] 'fytting' Kynge & Marche 1554			
The corte, the contre, wylage, and towne,	130	Garnesche5	25
Full many a strong cyte and towne hath been wonne	184	Magnyfycence	1577
Borowgh, cyte, and towne!'	302	Why Come Ye	932
TOWNE CLARKE			
As well it becomyth yow, a parysh towne clarke,	38	Coystrowne1	58
TOWNES			
Oute of theyr stronge townes	283	Why Come Ye	177
That towres and townes and trees downe caste,	319	Garlande	262
TOWRE			
From Brytons Albion /To the towre of Babilon.	94	Phy Sparrow	888
To] 'Bo' †Kele 1545.2			
Torde! Man, it is an hawke of the towre.	166	Magnyfycence	925
Than, 'Have him to the Towre /Saunz aulter remedy!	289	Why Come Ye	429
Frome Babill towre to the hillis Caspian.'	327	Garlande	553
Caspian] 'Gaspian' †Fakes 1523			
Jentill as fawcoun /Or hawke of the towre;	340	Garlande	1007
Jentyll as fawcoun /Or hawke of the towre.	341	Garlande	1022
Jentyll as fawcoun /Or hawke of the towre.	341	Garlande	1037
In Plutos gastly towre;	349	Garlande	1316
TOWRES			
That towres and townes and trees downe caste,	319	Garlande	262
TOWRIS			
Into a palace with turrettis and towris,	325	Garlande	459

TOWRNYNG —TRATYSE

TOWRNYNG
So myche towrnyng on the cooke-stole for every guy-gaw; .... 245 Speke Parott 481
TRACE
Ye bere yow bolde as Barabas, or Syr Terry of Trac[e]. .... 122 Garneschel 11
    Trace] 'Tracy' †MS Harley 367
As good to be occupyed as up and downe to trace . . . . 159 Magnyfycence 692
And out of trace, ... 166 Magnyfycence 913
With fidasso de cosso in Turke and in Trace; . . . . 232 Speke Parott 39
Some daunce the trace . . . . 301 Why Come Ye 881
Some were of Poyle, and sum were of Trace, ... 326 Garlande 493
Thoughe I trym you thys trace . . . . 367 Albany 355
TRACIANE
Orpheus, the Traciane, herped meledyously . . . . 320 Garlande 272
TRADICCYON
For thus dare I say, without tradiccyon, ... 42 Balettys2 10
TRAGEDIIS
Senek full soberly with his tragediis; . . . . 322 Garlande 358
    with] 'wit' †Fakes 1523
TRAGEDY
To write some lytell tragedy, ... 117 Ag Scottes 72
TRAGEDYALL
Melpomone, O muse tragedyall, ... 117 Ag Scottes 77
TRAGYDESE
To wryght to the of tragydese, ... 133 Garnesche5 155
TRAY
And skommeth it into a tray . . . . 219 El Rummynge 198
    into] 'in' Day 1560, Marshe 1568
TRAYNE
As man that was innocent of trechery or trayne, ... 31 Dol Dethe 86
I drede of some false trayne . . . . 288 Why Come Ye 363
There shalbe drawen a trayne . . . . 368 Albany 369
TRAYSON
And agayne all reason /Commyted open trayson . . . . 297 Why Come Ye 737
TRAYTEROUSLY
So trayterously my byrde to kyll . . . . 79 Phy Sparrow 322
TRAYTORY
Suche trechery /And traytory /Is all your cast. . . . . 361 Albany 100
TRAYTOUR
Moost false attaynted traytour, ... 371 Albany 493
TRAYTOURLY
For, if they understood /His traytourly dispyght, ... 121 Ag Scottes2 25
TRAYTOURS
About your traytours throtes. . . . . 362 Albany 124
TRAMYNGE
Your trymynge and tramynge by me must be tangyd, ... 203 Magnyfycence 2234
TRANCHAUNT
So tranchaunt and so kene, ... 127 Garnesche3 138
TRANS
As one in a trans or in an extasy, ... 313 Garlande 37
TRANSCENDING
Transcending f[a]r myne homely Muse that must . . . . 33 Dol Dethe 144
    far] 'for' †MS Royal 18 D.ii, Marshe 1568
TRANSCENDINGLY
and transcendingly sped in moche high connyng, ... 374 Replycacion I
TRANSCENDYNG
All other transcendyng, of very congruence . . . . 313 Garlande 52
In famous glory all other transcendyng, ... 344 Garlande 1129
TRANSCENDYNGE
Transcendynge out of mesure, ... 292 Why Come Ye 548
All other transcendynge, the most rychely besene, ... 325 Garlande 483
TRANSENDYNG
Transendyng plesure, surmountyng all dysporte; 43 Balettys3 7
TRANSFORMACYON
Yet, in remembraunce of Daphnes transformacyon, ... 321 Garlande 320
TRANSFORMYD
Transformyd was she into the laurell grene. . . . . 320 Garlande 294
TRANSYTORY
Comprehendynge the worlde casuall and transytory, ... 212 Magnyfycence 2511
TRANSLACION
So myche translacion into Englyshe confused; . . . . 244 Speke Parott 451
TRANSLACYON
Diodorus Siculus of my translacyon . . . . 354 Garlande 1498
TRANSLACYOUN
Of Tullis Familiars the translacyoun; . . . . 346 Garlande 1185
TRANSLATE
He did translate, enterprete, and disclose; . . . . 347 Garlande 1222
TRAPTE
Suche pollaxis and pyllers, suche mulys trapte with gold – . . 246 Speke Parott 517
TRASID
With diamauntis and rubis there tabers were trasid, ... 323 Garlande 395
    tabers] 'taberdes' Marshe 1568
TRASSHE
As for his plate of sylver and suche trasshe, ... 201 Magnyfycence 2164
TRATYSE
A ryght delectable tratyse . . . . 312 Garlande I
The Tratyse of the Triumphis of the Rede Rose, ... 347 Garlande 1223
A tratyse he devysid and browght it to pas, ... 347 Garlande 1228
Here endith a ryght delectable tratyse . . . . 358 Garlande2 E

TRATLANDE—TRENTALL	Page	Title	Line

TRATLANDE
with an hundred thousande tratlande Scottes 359   Albany   1
TRATLERS
For men be now tratlers and tellers of tales; 139   Ven Tongues   63
TRATLYNG
Lo, these fond sottes /And tratlyng Skottys, ... 115   Ag Scottes   6
TRATLYNGE
That never wyll leve theyr tratlynge: 115   Ag Scottes   2
TRAVARSE
But there is some travarse 288   Why Come Ye   387
TRAVELL
Jack Travell and Cole Crafter, ... 281   Why Come Ye   98
TRAVELLARS
To travellars, to tynkers, /To sweters, to swynkers, ... 217   El Rummynge   104
TRAVES
Whiche sat behynde a tra[v]es of sylke fyne, ... 47   Bowge   58
     traves] 'tranes' †Wynkyn de Worde 1499, 1510, Marshe 1568
TRAVILLIAN
Gup, Guilliam Travillian!' 285   Why Come Ye   241
TRE
Chryst by cruelte /Was nayled upon a tre; 258   Collyn Clout   451
A myghty tre and of a noble heyght, ... 312   Garlande   19
That in the forest was none so great a tre 320   Garlande   277
He sange also how, the tre as he did take 320   Garlande   300
Shall were a garlande of the laurell tre.' 321   Garlande   322
Grene tre of laurell moche solacyous game 331   Garlande   683
How Dame Minerva first found the Olyve Tre, she red 351   Garlande   1404
TREADE
To treade the prety wren /That is our Ladyes hen. 86   Phy Sparrow   600
To se her treade the grounde 100   Phy Sparrow   1149
TREASURE
The well of worldly treasure; 102   Phy Sparrow   1228
Measure is treasure. Howe say ye, is it not this? 144   Magnyfycence   125
Thus must ye stuffe and store your treasure. 189   Magnyfycence   1754
Where is nowe my treasure, my landes, and my rent? 198   Magnyfycence   2056
Howe they are able to make /With theyr golde and treasure . . 250   Collyn Clout   144
Who wryteth wysely hath a grete treasure. 314   Garlande   91
TREATE
To treate of any star 292   Why Come Ye   524
TREATEE
Under a fayned treatee. 288   Why Come Ye   365
TREATINGE
Treatinge of trewse restlesse, ... 280   Why Come Ye   75
TREATYSE
Here begynneth a lytell treatyse named The Bowge of Courte . . 46   Bowge   1
This treatyse to despyse 103   Phy Sparrow   1252
This treatyse, devysyd to make you dysporte, ... 213   Magnyfycence   2538
This treatyse to deprave; 274   Collyn Clout   1132
TREBELLES
With sharp twynkyng trebelles 259   Collyn Clout   491
TREBYLLYS
All trebyllys and tenours be rulyd by a meyne. 144   Magnyfycence   137
TRECHERY
As man that was innocent of trechery or trayne, ... 31   Dol Dethe   86
By extort trechery. 111   Lawde   28
With trechery ye them betray. 130   Garnesche5   38
Fye on this worlde, full of trechery, ... 197   Magnyfycence   2020
Of the terestre [t]rechery we fall in the flode, ... 213   Magnyfycence   2559
     trechery] 'rechery' †Rastell & Treveris C 1530, B
The trechery and the prankes 288   Why Come Ye   368
From trechery and dysceyght, ... 298   Why Come Ye   773
Fals trechery, /Fals brybery, ... 300   Why Come Ye   854
     flatery] 'flatteryng' MS Rawlinson C. 813
Suche trechery /And traytory /Is all your cast. 361   Albany   99
TREDE
Whan he doth her trede. 84   Phy Sparrow   512
TREES
That towres and townes and trees downe caste, ... 319   Garlande   262
TREYTORY
Treytory and treson he bannesht ought of sight. 33   Dol Dethe   151
TREMBYLL
The nebbis of a lyon they make to trete and trembyll, ... 243   Speke Parott   424
TREMBLID
Some tremblid, some girned, some gaspid, some gasid, ... 319   Garlande   265
The grownde gronid and tremblid, the noyse was so stowte. . . 354   Garlande   1509
TREMELYNG
But absens, alas, wyth tremelyng fere and drede, ... 44   Balettys3   34
TREMLYNG
To gyde and to governe my dredfull tremlyng fist. 335   Garlande   828
TRENCHE
It is perlous for a horseman to dyg in the trenche. 43   Balettys2   26
He dyggeth so in the trenche 290   Why Come Ye   434
TRENT
From Tyne to Trent, ... 167   Magnyfycence   981
TRENTALE
A DEVOUTE TRENTALE FOR OLD JOHN CLARKE, ... 106   Epitaphe1   1
TRENTALL
And pray shall, /At this trentall 108   Epitaphe1   70

TRESON —TRIPPYNG   Page   Title   Line

TRESON
Thorow treson, ageyn hym compassyd and wrought,   29   Dol Dethe   6
Treytory and treson he bannesht ought of sight.   33   Dol Dethe   151
TRESOURE
All erthely tresoure it is surmountynge.   50   Bowge   154
TRESSES
The bryght golden tresses   101   Phy Sparrow   1172
Theyr tresses untrust, /All full of unlust;   218   El Rummynge   147
TRESSIS
Phillis and Testalis, ther tressis with oyle   331   Garlande   681
TRESSYS
Tytan hathe truste up hys tressys of fyne golde;   242   Speke Parott   398
TRESTRAM
For now, Syr Trestram,   302   Why Come Ye   917
TRESURE
Byd hym take good hede of you, my synguler tresure.   149   Magnyfycence   317
Hath Magnyfycence ony tresure?   157   Magnyfycence   620
Ye. And he hath rule of all his tresure.   158   Magnyfycence   632
In mesure is tresure, cum sensu maturato: 232   Speke Parott   62
TRETE
Som trete of theyr tirykis, som of astrology,   234   Speke Parott   137
The nebbis of a lyon they make to trete and trembyll,   243   Speke Parott   424
Wherof for to trete   306   Why Come Ye   1087
  for] not in Kele 1545.3, Marshe 1568
Of Alexander; and Macrobius that did trete   322   Garlande   367
Whiche de latria do trete.   381   Replycacion   281
TRETISE
This tretise devysed it is   106   Epitaphe   I
TREU
Of Scipions dreme what was the treu probate;   322   Garlande   368
TREUTH
Accordynge to treuth they be well devysd.   210   Magnyfycence   2470
Some came to tell truth, some came to lye,   326   Garlande   510
TREW
Trew to his prince in word, in dede, and thought.   29   Dol Dethe   7
Trew to his prince for to defende his right,   33   Dol Dethe   149
And have forgoten your old, trew, lovyng knyght.   42   Balettys2   14
Of my trew hart, to love her best of all!   45   Balettys3   49
With the turtyll most trew.   83   Phy Sparrow   465
This matter trew and playne,   85   Phy Sparrow   547
To her husband most trew,   89   Phy Sparrow   726
That is as trew /As blacke is blew /And grene is gray.   116   Ag Scottes   17
Save a stronge thefe and hange a trew man.   178   Magnyfycence   1360
And I have found it trew.   219   El Rummynge   210
Sette asyde all sophysms, and speke now trew and playne.   244   Speke Parott   448
This tale will be to trew: 280   Why Come Ye   65
This is a trew text!   285   Why Come Ye   261
To plete a trew tryall   287   Why Come Ye   324
Be faythfull, trew and just   298   Why Come Ye   753
TREWE
But yet oftyme suche dremes be founde trewe.   61   Bowge   538
Welth is of wysdome the very trewe probate.   140   Magnyfycence   4
Of that may come after; experyence trewe and playne,   141   Magnyfycence   11
Trewe you say, syr. Gyve me your hande.   141   Magnyfycence   28
All that ye say is as trewe as the crede.   146   Magnyfycence   218
A, woo worthe the, Lyberte, nowe thou sayst full trewe;   199   Magnyfycence   2103
To make a trewe constructyon.   253   Collyn Clout   269
Whiche be as trewe /As the gospell: 359   Albany   4
Of all trewe Englyshemen,   372   Albany   521
TREWELY
Nowe trewely, to my thynkyng,   270   Collyn Clout   969
TREWLY
Regestringe trewly every formare date;   29   Dol Dethe   18
And whether they say trewly   273   Collyn Clout   1061
But that I wryte trewly.   274   Collyn Clout   1116
For trewly to expresse,   280   Why Come Ye   69
For trewly and unfayned,   309   Why Come Ye   1209
TREWSE
Treatinge of trewse restlesse,   280   Why Come Ye   75
And mad a worthy trewse.   282   Why Come Ye   141
  mad] 'made' Toy 1553, Kitson 1560.7, Marshe 1568
TREWTH
For wrytynge of trewth   300   Why Come Ye   842
TRIED
As by myne auctor tried it was.   296   Why Come Ye   707
TRIFELS
To make suche trifels it asketh sum konnyng,   347   Garlande   1235
TRINITE
Eyther to the devyll or the trinite.   114   Scot Kynge   41
TRINYTE
Thankyd be God in trinyte,   119   Ag Scottes   140
TRIONS
And where the two Trions a man shold aspy,   331   Garlande   699
  Trions] 'Troons' †Fakes 1523
TRIP
Our Thomasen she doth trip, our Jenet she doth shayle;   233   Speke Parott   83
TRIPPYNG
How a do cam trippyng in at the rerewarde,   351   Garlande   1385

TRIUMPHANTLYE —TROYLUS   Page   Title   Line

TRIUMPHANTLYE
In a trone triumphantlye, ... 293   Why Come Ye   586
TRIUMPHAUNT
In joy triumphaunt the hevenly *gerarchy, ... 35   Dol Dethe   211
    *gerarchy] 'gerarchy' †MS Royal 18 D.ii, Marshe 1568,
    'yerarchy' Scattergood
TRIUMPHE
Of laureat triumphe, your place is here reservyd, ... 344   Garlande   1126
    triumphe] 'promocioun' MS Cotton Vitellius E.x
TRIUMPHIS
The Tratyse of the Triumphis of the Rede Rose, ... 347   Garlande   1223
TRIVIALS
Or yet of trivials; 292   Why Come Ye   515
TRYALYTES
Of tryalytes, /And of tot quottes; 260   Collyn Clout   562
TRYALL
To plete a trew tryall 287   Why Come Ye   324
It was not for hym to abyde the tryall. 315   Garlande   98
    abyde] 'byde' MS Cotton Vitellius E.x
TRYBYLL
He solfyth to haute, hys trybyll is to hy; 37   Coystrowne1   23
TRYCE
I had than in a tryce, ... 100   Phy Sparrow   1131
TRYDE
By measure eche thynge duly is tryde. 147   Magnyfycence   244
Thy pleasure now with payne and trouble shalbe tryde. 193   Magnyfycence   1881
What! Thou Colyn Cowarde, knowen and tryde! 202   Magnyfycence   2192
It wolde be founde so yf it were well tryde. 210   Magnyfycence   2449
But all must be tryde, ... 304   Why Come Ye   1013
TRYFYLL
As in a tryfyll or in a thynge of nought, ... 189   Magnyfycence   1757
TRYFYLS
As ever I was, and as full of tryfyls – 172   Magnyfycence   1141
TRYHUMFYTHE
He tryhumfythe, he trumpythe, he turnythe all up and downe, . 244   Speke Parott   432
TRYM
For you love to go trym, ... 262   Collyn Clout   641
Thoughe I trym you thys trace 367   Albany   355
TRYMBLYTH
Lorde, so my flesshe trymblyth nowe for drede! 193   Magnyfycence   1875
TRYMYNGE
Your trymynge and tramynge by me must be tangyd, ... 203   Magnyfycence   2234
TRYMME
Trymme at her tayle or a man can turne a socke. 177   Magnyfycence   1346
TRYMMYTH
He trymmyth in hys tenor to counter pyrdewy; 37   Coystrowne1   26
TRYM-TRAM
With a whym-wham /Knyt with a trym-tram 216   El Rummynge   76
A trym-tram for an horse-myll it were a nyse thyng, ... 234   Speke Parott   128
TRYNALL
Of Mercury undyr the trynall aspecte, ... 240   Speke Parott   325
TRYNYTE
Eternally /To beholde and se /The Trynyte! 40   Coystrowne3   59
TRYP
And made truth to tryp; 66   Hauke   155
TRYPE
That the horson had for etynge of a trype. 171   Magnyfycence   1126
TRYPES
Myght tere out all thy trypes! 79   Phy Sparrow   308
Some trypes that stynkes. 225   El Rummynge   444
    stynkes] 'stynges' Kynge & Marche 1554
TRYPPE
And have suche a tryppe, ... 263   Collyn Clout   667
TRYSYD
Ye wolde have trysyd hys trowle away. 130   Garnesche5   36
TRYSTRAM
Of Trystram, and Kynge Marke, ... 87   Phy Sparrow   641
TRYUMPHE
With laureate tryumphe in the courte of Fame. 314   Garlande   63
With laureat tryumphe why Skelton sholde be crownde. 318   Garlande   217
TRYUMPHES
With tryumphes of Cesar 270   Collyn Clout   956
TRYVYALS
Tryvyals and quatryvyals so sore now they appayre, ... 235   Speke Parott   166
TROILUS
Troilus, I trowe, if that he had you sene, ... 336   Garlande   873
TROY
Wherfore all Troy dyd rew; 88   Phy Sparrow   676
Our Priamus of Troy, ... 111   Lawde   48
Why, was not for money Troy bothe bought and solde? 184   Magnyfycence   1576
And howe Parys of Troy /Daunced a lege moy, ... 270   Collyn Clout   950
    lege moy] 'lege de moy' Kele 1545.1, Marshe 1568
In loyalte and foy /Lyke to Ector of Troy, ... 369   Albany   437
TROYE
Noble Hector of Troye; 74   Phy Sparrow   111
Of Hector of Troye 88   Phy Sparrow   673
TROYLUS
That made Troylus to dote 88   Phy Sparrow   678

TROLD —TROW   Page   Title   Line

	Page	Title	Line
Prayd Troylus for to were	89	Phy Sparrow	690
Troylus also hath lost	89	Phy Sparrow	714
He is named Troylus baud;	89	Phy Sparrow	721
TROLD			
How the rest of good lernyng is roufled up and trold.	235	Speke Parott	168
roufled] 'roulled' Day 1560, Marshe 1568			
TROLY			
He dawnsys so long, 'hey, troly, loly',	175	Magnyfycence	1250
TROLY-LOLY-LO			
Wyth, 'Hey, troly-loly-lo, whip here, Jak',	37	Coystrownel	15
TROLL			
Wyth, 'Troll, cytrace and trovy,'	65	Hauke	116
TROMPE			
With, 'Trompe up!' 'Alleluya!'	284	Why Come Ye	205
TRONE			
In a trone whiche fer clerer dyde shyne	47	Bowge	60
clerer] 'clere' Marshe 1568			
Amonge all other was wrytten in her trone,	47	Bowge	65
For al his pompe, for all his ryall trone,	181	Magnyfycence	1475
That shall sytte in a trone	258	Collyn Clout	474
shall sytte] 'syttys nowe' MS Lansdowne 762 'shuld sytte' MS Harley 2252			
In a trone triumphantlye,	293	Why Come Ye	586
And rule them echone /In Lucyfers trone.	304	Why Come Ye	993
TRONES			
Some say ye sytte in trones,	255	Collyn Clout	344
TROT			
Some ranne a good trot /With a skellet or a pot;	220	El Rummynge	249
TROTTE			
He wolde trotte gentylly, but he is to starke.	153	Magnyfycence	481
TROTTERS			
And such as sell trotters, /Pytchars, potshordis.	302	Why Come Ye	911
potshordis] 'pouchers' MS Rawlinson C. 813			
TROUBLE			
/Trouble and grevaunce.	81	Phy Sparrow	369
Comberaunce and trouble in Englande fyrst I began.	160	Magnyfycence	715
Thy pleasure now with payne and trouble shalbe tryde.	193	Magnyfycence	1881
Afflyccyon and trouble to prove his pacyence;	207	Magnyfycence	2371
And their weywarde trouble.	364	Albany	201
TROUBLED			
Vitulus in Oreb troubled Arons brayne;	232	Speke Parott	59
TROUGHTE			
Can touche a troughte and cloke it subtylly	46	Bowge	11
troughte] 'trouth' Wynkyn de Worde 1510, Marshe 1568; it] not in Marshe 1568			
TROUTE			
I am forthwith as hole as a troute.	185	Magnyfycence	1624
TROUTH			
Trouth doth me bynd /And loyalte	96	Phy Sparrow	977
To shewe you playnly the trouth as I thynke.	147	Magnyfycence	253
Mary, upon trouth my reason I grounde,	147	Magnyfycence	264
Say trouth? Yes, yes, by lakyn, I shall the warent,	154	Magnyfycence	506
In faythe, trouth thou sayst nowe, by God of heven!	170	Magnyfycence	1079
By my trouth, there is myne.	171	Magnyfycence	1103
Nowe, by my trouth, man, take, there is my purse;	171	Magnyfycence	1104
my] 'myne' †Rastell & Treveris C 1530, B			
Tell by thy trouth what sport can thou make.	172	Magnyfycence	1162
Yes, yes, by my trouth. I holde the a grote	173	Magnyfycence	1193
He telleth you trouth, syr, as I you ensure.	187	Magnyfycence	1679
By my trouth, I can not tell you that.	188	Magnyfycence	1703
And, for to say trouth, /A great parte is for slouth;	250	Collyn Clout	136
for] 'full' †Godfray 1531, 'for' MS Harley 2252			
But trouth can never lye.	258	Collyn Clout	485
To tell the trouth playnly,	290	Why Come Ye	460
Where trouth is abhorde,	300	Why Come Ye	847
Trouth ought to be rescude;	369	Albany	421
TROUTHE			
And by my trouthe, but yf an ende they make,	59	Bowge	473
By my trouthe, syr, at Pountesse.	150	Magnyfycence	343
By my trouthe, had I not payde and prayde,	150	Magnyfycence	363
By my trouthe, we had ben gone.	155	Magnyfycence	537
No, by my trouthe, but crake grete wordes.	163	Magnyfycence	812
By my trouthe, she hathe a grete hede.	169	Magnyfycence	1048
By my trouthe, I trowe well;	169	Magnyfycence	1051
In faythe, trouthe ye say, we wente togyder to scole.	170	Magnyfycence	1065
No, by my trouthe. It is but the scurfe and the scabbe.	171	Magnyfycence	1123
Nowe, by your trouthe, gave he you not a brybe?	187	Magnyfycence	1665
Ye, by my trouthe, I shall waraunt you for me,	187	Magnyfycence	1669
By my trouthe, we have ryfled hym metely well.	201	Magnyfycence	2170
All that he sayth of trouthe dothe procede;	209	Magnyfycence	2426
And trouthe is all to-torne;	281	Why Come Ye	93
With trouthe it is ennewde.	369	Albany	420
Trouthe should nat be subdude.	369	Albany	422
On trouthe under defence	372	Albany	520
TROVY			
Wyth, 'Troll, cytrace and trovy,'	65	Hauke	116
TROW			
My tyme, I trow, I xulde but lese	133	Garnesche5	154

TROWE —TRULY   Page   Title   Line

	Page	Title	Line
I trow I have brought you suche wrytynge of recorde,	149	Magnyfycence	309
With, 'Who is there? A mayd?' Nay, nay, I trow!	233	Speke Parott	100
Syns Dewcalyons flodde, I trow, no man can tell.	245	Speke Parott	490
I trow all wyll be nought,	287	Why Come Ye	353
'Now what ye mene, I trow I conject.	332	Garlande	735
A thowsande, thowsande, I trow, to my dome,	354	Garlande	1505

TROWE

	Page	Title	Line
For, as I trowe, I have sene you in dede	53	Bowge	248
We tweyne, I trowe, be not withoute dysceyte:	55	Bowge	313
What weneste I were? I trowe thou knowe not me.	55	Bowge	331
Ryghte now I spake with one, I trowe, I see -	59	Bowge	458
I trowe she coude not amende	75	Phy Sparrow	156
It was no hurt, I trowe.	76	Phy Sparrow	170
Trowe ye, Syr James, his noble grace	114	Scot Kynge	17
I trowe ye can not say nay moche to this:	142	Magnyfycence	74
I trowe good fortune hath annexyd us together,	146	Magnyfycence	198
I shall come to you myselfe, I trowe, this afternone.	149	Magnyfycence	322
I trowe, by our lady, I had ben slayne,	150	Magnyfycence	348
I trowe it shall not nede to abyde.	156	Magnyfycence	571
I trowe that he is -	156	Magnyfycence	589
And yet, I trowe, some of you be better sped than I	160	Magnyfycence	722
To come to me I trowe he shalbe fayne.	162	Magnyfycence	784
Cockes ha[r]te! I trowe thou wylte make a fray.	163	Magnyfycence	808
harte] 'hate' †Rastell & Treveris C 1530, B			
By my trouthe, I trowe well;	169	Magnyfycence	1051
A, I trowe ye shall coughe me a fole.	170	Magnyfycence	1064
Cockys armys! This is a warke, I trowe.	170	Magnyfycence	1094
By Cockes harte, I trowe thou lyste.	173	Magnyfycence	1199
Cockes armes! It is not so, I trowe.	173	Magnyfycence	1202
Ye have eten sauce I trowe, at the Taylers Hall.	179	Magnyfycence	1404
I trowe ye herde yourselfe what I sayd.	188	Magnyfycence	1695
I trowe it be a frost, for the way is slydder;	191	Magnyfycence	1816
Ye, but trowe you, syrs, that this is he?	204	Magnyfycence	2242
A ha, fansy and foly met with you, I trowe.	210	Magnyfycence	2448
Non sine postica sanna, as I trowe,	240	Speke Parott	339
Or elles ye pynche curtesy, trulye as I trowe,	242	Speke Parott	395
Syns Dewcalyons flodde, I trowe, was nevyr sene.	245	Speke Parott	476
What trowe ye they say more /Of the bysshoppes lore?	249	Collyn Clout	92
Suche a prelate, I trowe, /Were worthy to rowe	303	Why Come Ye	953
That all the worde, I trowe, and it were sought,	325	Garlande	462
worde] 'worlde' Marshe 1568			
Troilus, I trowe, if that he had you sene,	336	Garlande	873
Dunbar, Dunde, /Ye shall trowe me,	359	Albany	25
But, I trowe, your selfe ye overse	381	Replycacion	285

TROWED

	Page	Title	Line
She sayde she trowed that I had eten sause;	48	Bowge	72
had] not in †Wynkyn de Worde 1499, 1510			

TROWEST

	Page	Title	Line
Trowest thou, drevyll, I saye, thou gawdy knave,	55	Bowge	337
Ye. But trowest thou that he be not maungey?	171	Magnyfycence	1122
Wolde money, trowest thou, make suche one to the call?	184	Magnyfycence	1573

TROWYD

	Page	Title	Line
Trowyd ye, Syr Jemy, his nobull grace	118	Ag Scottes	107

TROWLE

	Page	Title	Line
Ye wolde have trysyd hys trowle away.	130	Garnesche5	36

TROWTH

	Page	Title	Line
With trowth to medelle was all his hole delight,	33	Dol Dethe	152
That for her trowth is in remembraunce had;	337	Garlande	900
Trowth with a drowsy hede;	358	Garlande2	2

TROWTHE

	Page	Title	Line
For trowthe in parabyll ye wantonlye pronounce,	241	Speke Parott	364
So many trusys takyn, so lytyll perfyte trowthe;	245	Speke Parott	491
perfyte] 'profyte' †MS Harley 2252			

TRU

	Page	Title	Line
Of all your feturs favorable to make tru discripcion,	42	Balettys2	8

TRUE

	Page	Title	Line
That she was true and just,	90	Phy Sparrow	730
Ever to be /Their true bedell	96	Phy Sparrow	980
His tytle is true in Fraunce to raygne;	118	Ag Scottes	120
The tokens ar not good /To be true Englysh blood;	121	Ag Scottes2	23
Small newes that true is	284	Why Come Ye	234
And if so hym fortune to wryte true and plaine,	314	Garlande	85
so] not in MS Cotton Vitellius E.x			
To owe her my servyce with true perseveraunce.	327	Garlande	558
Never true nor playne,	362	Albany	134
With hole hart and true mynde,	371	Albany	482
and of every true Christen man laudably to be enployed,	374	Replycacion	I

TRUELY

	Page	Title	Line
So truely proporsionyd, and so well did gree,	320	Garlande	275
Envyous Rancour truely he hight.	333	Garlande	753

TRULY

	Page	Title	Line
Truly reportinge his right noble astate,	33	Dol Dethe	146
For Welthfull Felicite truly is my name.	141	Magnyfycence	23
Nowe truly, to my thynkynge,	228	El Rummynge	547
To pronostycate truly the chaunce of fortunys dyse;	234	Speke Parott	136
Whiche, truly to expresse, /Is a forgetfulnesse,	290	Why Come Ye	467
And, my wordes marke truly,	310	Why Come Ye2	27
'And espetyally to make a lye' MS Rawlinson C. 813			

748

TRULYE—TULLIS   Page   Title   Line

	Page	Title	Line
For truly it were a pyte that he sat ydle'.	318	Garlande	210
And truly of theyr bownte thus were they bent	334	Garlande	806

TRULYE

	Page	Title	Line
Or elles ye pynche curtesy, trulye as I trowe, ...	242	Speke Parott	395

TRUMPE

	Page	Title	Line
The crane with his trumpe, ...	82	Phy Sparrow	433
With that I harde the noyse of a trumpe, ...	319	Garlande	259

TRUMPET

	Page	Title	Line
Eolus, your trumpet, that knowne is so farre, ...	319	Garlande	235
that] 'whiche' MS Cotton Vitellius E.x			
Anone, I sey, this trumpet were founde out, ...	319	Garlande	243

TRUMPETTIS

	Page	Title	Line
Of trumpettis and clariouns the noyse went to Rome;	354	Garlande	1507

TRUMPYTHE

	Page	Title	Line
He tryhumfythe, he trumpythe, he turnythe all up and downe, . .	244	Speke Parott	432

TRUSYS

	Page	Title	Line
So many trusys takyn, and so lytyll perfyte trowthe;	245	Speke Parott	491
perfyte] 'profyte' †MS Harley 2252			

TRUSSE

	Page	Title	Line
And as for all other, let them trusse and packe;	190	Magnyfycence	1774

TRUSSED

	Page	Title	Line
For she is trussed for to breke a launce.	57	Bowge	410
He was trussed in a garmente strayte -	60	Bowge	505

TRUST

	Page	Title	Line
That were aboute hym, his awne servauntis of trust, ...	30	Dol Dethe	37
By Crede, I trust to se the day, ...	41	Coystrowne4	12
I trust it is no shame, ...	94	Phy Sparrow	889
I have not offended, I trust, ...	102	Phy Sparrow	1249
Suche order I trust with them for to take, ...	145	Magnyfycence	178
Trust me, Lyberte, it greveth me ryght sore	178	Magnyfycence	1375
To trust in me he is but dyssayved;	186	Magnyfycence	1652
Your welthe and felycyte, I trust we shall optayne	190	Magnyfycence	1792
Then trust I to God and the holy rode, ...	203	Magnyfycence	2206
An huswyfe of trust /Whan she is athrust, ...	220	El Rummynge	253
A chaplayne of trust, /Layth all in the dust.	253	Collyn Clout	283
Allmyghty God, I trust, ...	298	Why Come Ye	750
That all his trust hangis	308	Why Come Ye	1183
trust] 'harte' MS Rawlinson C. 813			
Of worldly trust, then did I you rescu;	327	Garlande	543
In trust wherof comforte his hart doth grope, ...	335	Garlande	832
Trust me, ententifly, ...	339	Garlande	962
That I trust to make myne excuse	344	Garlande	1137
I trust, to lowe estate	368	Albany	385

TRUSTE

	Page	Title	Line
I truste to quyte you or I dy!	41	Coystrowne4	21
Ye maye not fall; truste me, ye maye not fayle.	50	Bowge	170
For here is none that dare well other truste;	51	Bowge	202
Yf he coude fynde in herte to truste me.	52	Bowge	220
Truste me, and yf it come to a nede;	59	Bowge	478
He tolde me so, by God, ye maye truste me.	60	Bowge	514
I truste your grace wyll be agreabyll	179	Magnyfycence	1417
Truste me, with you I am hyghly pleasyd;	183	Magnyfycence	1535
Them that dare put theyr truste in me;	188	Magnyfycence	1699
And in theyr moste truste I make them overthrowe.	193	Magnyfycence	1885
In Goddys mercy, I tell them, is but foly to truste;	205	Magnyfycence	2289
And I truste to ratyfye and amende your fame.	208	Magnyfycence	2398
Thus in this worlde there is no erthly truste.	213	Magnyfycence	2544
Thus in this worlde there is no erthly truste.	213	Magnyfycence	2551
Tytan hathe truste up hys tressys of fyne golde;	242	Speke Parott	398

TRUSTED

	Page	Title	Line
He trusted her payment and lost all hys pray.	42	Balettys1	13
For, but I trusted you, so God me save, ...	52	Bowge	213
Somtyme without measure he trusted in golde;	193	Magnyfycence	1894

TRUSTINGE

	Page	Title	Line
Trustinge in noble men that wer with hym there;	31	Dol Dethe	90

TRUSTYD

	Page	Title	Line
That you trustyd, and Fansy is my name;	193	Magnyfycence	1871

TRUTH

	Page	Title	Line
And made truth to tryp;	66	Hauke	155
Truth it is, syr; for after he wrought me moch shame, ...	209	Magnyfycence	2444

TRUTHE

	Page	Title	Line
By the good Lorde, truthe he sayth.	175	Magnyfycence	1252
Thou sayst truthe, by the harte that God me gave!	190	Magnyfycence	1782
In sclaundrynge you for truthe.	255	Collyn Clout	342

TUCKE

	Page	Title	Line
And wolde have made me Freer Tucke, ...	150	Magnyfycence	357

TUGGYD

	Page	Title	Line
But tatterd and tuggyd, /Raggyd and ruggyd, ...	304	Why Come Ye	1026
tatterd] 'taxed' MS Rawlinson C. 813			

TUGGYNG

	Page	Title	Line
Wrestlyng and tuggyng, ...	104	Phy Sparrow	1317
And with myghty luggyng, /Wrastelynge and tuggyng, ...	349	Garlande	1310

TUICYON

	Page	Title	Line
But under pacient tuicyon, ...	378	Replycacion	141

TULLIS

	Page	Title	Line
In Tullis faculte /Called humanyte.	292	Why Come Ye	528
Of Tullis Familiars the translacyoun;	346	Garlande	1185

	Page	Title	Line
TULLIUS			
Prynce of eloquence, Tullius Cicero,	321	Garlande	330
TULLY			
Tully, valy, strawe, let be I say!	35	Man Margery	5
TUMBYLL			
'Rumbyll downe, tumbyll downe, hey, go, now, now!'	37	Coystrownel	30
To jumbyll, to stombyll, to tumbyll down lyke folys;	243	Speke Parott	425
TUMBLAR			
The one was a tumblar, that afterwarde againe	330	Garlande	634
TUMBLARS			
Dysers, carders, tumblars with gambawdis,	329	Garlande	608
TUMBLE			
They tumble so in theology,	374	Replycacion	5
TUMRELL			
A dong cart or a tumrell	132	Garnesche5	93
TUNABLE			
His tunable harpe stryngges	93	Phy Sparrow	865
TUNABLY			
He can not well fly, /Nor synge tunably;	83	Phy Sparrow	484
TUNG			
Avaunt, rybawde, thi tung reclame!	132	Garnesche5	106
How shuld a fals lying tung then be rewarded?	137	Ven Tongues	2
TUNGE			
A fals lying tunge is harde to withholde;	137	Ven Tongues	6
A sclaunderous tunge, a tunge of a skolde,	137	Ven Tongues	7
A sclaunderous tunge, a tunge of a skolde,	137	Ven Tongues	7
'Nay, holde thy tunge,' quod another, 'let me have the name.'	319	Garlande	255
TUNGES			
Such tunges shuld be torne out by the harde rootes,	137	Ven Tongues	3
For tunges untayde be renning astray.	138	Ven Tongues	37
Malicious tunges, though they have no bones,	138	Ven Tongues	49
Such tunges unhappy hath made great division	139	Ven Tongues	55
Of fals fickil tunges suche cloked collusion	139	Ven Tongues	57
Men said they could not their tunges atame;	139	Ven Tongues	60
The devill tere their tunges and pike out their ies!	139	Ven Tongues	68
TUNGS			
With skolding and sklaundering make their tungs lame.	139	Ven Tongues	62
TUNNYNG			
The Tunnyng of Elynour Rummyng per Skelton Laureat.	214	El Rummynge	I
TUNNYNGE			
To have of her tunnynge.	217	El Rummynge	130
Also the Tunnynge of Elinour Rummyng,	347	Garlande	1233
TURDE			
'Turde,' quod Ha[f]ter, 'I wyll the nothynge layne, layne] 'sayne' †Wynkyn de Worde 1499, Marshe 1568	55	Bowge	311
Fye on this dyce, they be not worth a turde!	57	Bowge	392
TURFFE			
My colour is tawny, colouryd as a turffe;	195	Magnyfycence	1959
TURKE			
Yet the Sowden, nor the Turke,	67	Hauke	216
With fidasso de cosso in Turke and in Trace;	232	Speke Parott	39
What coude the Turke do more	257	Collyn Clout	429
Turke, Sarazyn or Jewe?	257	Collyn Clout	431
TURKEY			
None so ryche stones in Turkey to sell;	323	Garlande	396
TURKIS			
With turkis and grossolitis enpavyd was the grounde;	325	Garlande	466
TURKY			
Pocenya, the prowde provoste of Turky lande,	181	Magnyfycence	1480
TURND			
Turnd ther backis and let ther master fall, backis] 'backe' Marshe 1568	31	Dol Dethe	94
TURNE			
From you, Syr Scot, wolde turne his face?	118	Ag Scottes	108
Trymme at her tayle or a man can turne a socke.	177	Magnyfycence	1346
But let us turne playne, /There we lefte agayne.	219	El Rummynge	187
But we wyll turne playne /Where we left agayne.	220	El Rummynge	242
Turne ons agayne to me;	237	Speke Parott	237
My propyr Besse, /To turne agayne to me.	237	Speke Parott	251
Turne monasteries into water mylles,	257	Collyn Clout	418
They dyd us a shrewde turne,	285	Why Come Ye	269
But of my purpose now turne we to the grownde. purpose] 'proces' MS Cotton Vitellius E.x	313	Garlande	28
And turne home ageyne, for they cam al to late.	329	Garlande	605
That dare nat turne agayne,	366	Albany	306
TURNED			
Is turned into corage	85	Phy Sparrow	545
TURNEY			
To turney or to tante with me ye ar to fare to seke.	123	Garnesche2	37
TURNYD			
Tyll all theyr conveyaunce is turnyd into madnesse.	178	Magnyfycence	1367
He turnyd his tirikkis, his volvell ran fast,	354	Garlande	1517
TURNYNG			
Wele sped in spyndels and turnyng of tavellys,	37	Coystrownel	34
Turnyng on the ryght hande, by a windyng stayre, a] not in †Fakes 1523	333	Garlande	767
TURNYNGE			
In castyng, in turnynge, in florisshyng of flowris,	334	Garlande	802

TURNYTHE —TWYBYLL	Page	Title	Line

TURNYTHE
He tryhumfythe, he trumpythe, he turnythe all up and downe,	244	Speke Parott	432

TURRETTES
With turrettes and with toures,	270	Collyn Clout	936

TURRETTIS
Into a palace with turrettis and towris,	325	Garlande	459

TURTYLL
With the turtyll most trew.	83	Phy Sparrow	465

TUSCHE
Tusche, holde your pece! Your langage is vayne.	147	Magnyfycence	251

TUSHE
It i[s] no maystery. Tushe, let Measure procede,	144	Magnyfycence	150
is] 'it' †Rastell & Treveris C 1530, B			
Tushe, a strawe! It is a shame	155	Magnyfycence	549
Tushe, a strawe! I thought none yll.	156	Magnyfycence	564
Tushe! Holde your pece.	156	Magnyfycence	590
Tushe! It is Syr Johnn Double-[Cope].	157	Magnyfycence	605
Cope] 'cloke' †Rastell & Treveris C 1530, B			
Tushe! He that hathe nede, man, let hym rynne.	162	Magnyfycence	786
Tushe, man! I kepe some Latyn in store.	172	Magnyfycence	1145
Tushe! Holde your peas; ye speke lyke a dawe.	178	Magnyfycence	1379
Tushe! Holde your peas; ye speke out of season.	178	Magnyfycence	1388
Tushe, tushe! It is a great defaute;	203	Magnyfycence	2222
Tushe, tushe! It is a great defaute;	203	Magnyfycence	2222
Tushe! These maters that ye move are but soppys in ale;	203	Magnyfycence	2233

TUSSHE
Tusshe! Fonnysshe Fansy, thou arte frantyke.	158	Magnyfycence	650
Tusshe! Thy lyppes hange in thyne eye;	169	Magnyfycence	1049
eye] 'eyen' †Rastell & Treveris C 1530, B			
What callest thou thy dogge? Tusshe! His name is Gryme.	171	Magnyfycence	1118

TUT
Tut, Scot, I sey, /Go shake th[e], dog, hey!	135	Dundas	27
the] 'thy' Marshe 1568			
Measure? Tut, what the devyll of hell!	189	Magnyfycence	1745

TWAINE
And, sir, amonge all me thought I saw twaine,	329	Garlande	633
In his distichon made on verses twaine.	353	Garlande	1467
distichon] 'distincyon' †Fakes 1523			

TWAYN
The aunciont acquaintance, madam, betwen us twayn,	42	Balettys2	1

TWAYNE
As to enbrace you in myne armys twayne.	44	Balettys3	42
Then in a tabull playne /I wroute a verse or twayne,	68	Hauke	223
Was betwene you twayne, /Pyramus and Thesbe,	72	Phy Sparrow	20
With a charme or twayne,	77	Phy Sparrow	206
Deth hath departed us twayne;	80	Phy Sparrow	329
An hart was slayne /With hornes twayne	104	Phy Sparrow	1299
For thes twayne whypslovens calle for a coke stole.	124	Garnesche2	38
Or elles I had lost myne eres twayne.	150	Magnyfycence	349
I say, come hyder. What are these twayne?	156	Magnyfycence	582
Syr, it is so that these twayne	157	Magnyfycence	612
Fansy and I, we twayne,	158	Magnyfycence	639
To Magnyfycence with us twayne.	158	Magnyfycence	667
We wyll se you shortly, one of us twayne.	159	Magnyfycence	686
Ye. Let us here a worde or twayne.	174	Magnyfycence	1218
I wolde to you say a worde or twayne.	188	Magnyfycence	1721
Commyttynge to me and to my felowes twayne	190	Magnyfycence	1791
Her lewde lyppes twayne, /They slaver, men sayne,	215	El Rummynge	22
To preche a worde or twayne,	265	Collyn Clout	764
A thousande or twayne	302	Why Come Ye	944
With hornnis twayne /Of glitteryng golde;	348	Garlande	1292
The first twayne to wake;	358	Garlande2	11
And the twayne last /Be withholde so fast	358	Garlande2	12
With a worde or twayne /In sentence playne.	361	Albany	75
That neyther of you twayne	367	Albany	337
That bytwene you twayne	368	Albany	368

TWEDE
beside the water of Twede, etc	359	Albany	I
By the water of Twede,	359	Albany	31
Beside the water of Twede	371	Albany	514

TWEYNE
We tweyne, I trowe, be not withoute dysceyte:	55	Bowge	313
And lete us laugh a placke or tweyne at nale.	57	Bowge	387
placke] 'plucke' Marshe 1568			
Than, in his hode, I sawe there faces tweyne:	58	Bowge	428
'So am I preventid of my brethern tweyne	324	Garlande	428

TWENE
Twene hope and drede /My lyfe I lede,	356	Garlande	1594

TWENTY
And in my purse was twenty marke.	171	Magnyfycence	1108
Or scante worth twenty marke,	264	Collyn Clout	726

TWIT
Twit, Andrewe! Twit, Scot!	282	Why Come Ye	125
Scot] 'scote' †Kele 1545.3			
Twit, Andrewe! Twit, Scot!	282	Why Come Ye	125
Scot] 'scote' †Kele 1545.3			

TWYBYLL
A pykes or a twybyll;	126	Garnesche3	72

TWYCE —UNBYNDE   Page   Title   Line

TWYCE
Cockys armys! He hath callyd for the twyce.	162	Magnyfycence	782

TWYNKYNG
With sharp twynkyng trebelles	259	Collyn Clout	491

TWYNKLYNG
There Cintheus sat twynklyng upon his harpe stringis;	331	Garlande	687

TWYSE
No; for or we stryke, we wyll be advysed twyse.	163	Magnyfycence	810
Nowe I rede the beware. I have warned the twyse.	202	Magnyfycence	2185
Scorpione ascendynge degrees twyse nyne;	312	Garlande	7
Twyse! set hym a chare, or reche hym a stol	318	Garlande	208
Twyse] 'Twyshe' Marshe 1568, MS Cotton Vitellius E.x			
I made it straunge, and drew bak ones or twyse,	324	Garlande	444
But if he wryte oftenner than ones or twyse.'	345	Garlande	1155
Oftnar than ones or twyse,	378	Replycacion	133

TWYST
'Twyst,' quod Suspecte, 'goo playe; hym I ne reke!'	51	Bowge	186
Twyst] 'Whist' Wynkyn de Worde 1510, 'Twysshe' Marshe 1568			

TWYT
Twyt, Scot, go kepe thy den.	362	Albany	145
Twyt, Scot, yet agayne ones,	362	Albany	149
With, 'twyt Scot, twyt Scot, twyt.'	362	Albany	153
With, 'twyt Scot, twyt Scot, twyt.'	362	Albany	153
With, 'twyt Scot, twyt Scot, twyt.'	362	Albany	153
'Twyt, Scot,' agayne I saye,	363	Albany	157
'Twyt, Scot, of Galaway.	363	Albany	158
Twyt, Scot, shake th[e] dogge, hay.	363	Albany	159
the] 'thy' †Marshe 1568			
Twyt, Scot, thou ran away.'	363	Albany	160

TWO
And I drewe nere to herke what they two sayde.	51	Bowge	182
And I drewe nere to harke what they two sayde.	54	Bowge	296
'But by that Lorde that is one, two and thre,	60	Bowge	512
In verses two or thre	106	Phy Sparrow	1378
Of two knaves somtyme of Dis.	106	Epitaphe	I
In fayth, I set not by the worlde two Dauncaster cuttys.	148	Magnyfycence	293
What the devyll! Are ye two of aquayntaunce?	154	Magnyfycence	496
Why, dwelleth Mesure where ye two dwell?	157	Magnyfycence	622
Aske these two that there dothe dwell.	158	Magnyfycence	629
Two faces in a hode covertly I bere;	160	Magnyfycence	710
There be two lyther, rude and ranke,	175	Magnyfycence	1266
To here you two rutters dyspute togyder.	176	Magnyfycence	1287
I synge of two partys without a mene.	181	Magnyfycence	1463
With a payre of heles /As brode as two wheles.	216	El Rummynge	84
Yeres two or thre,	219	El Rummynge	215
Than swetely togither we ly, /As two pygges in a sty.'	220	El Rummynge	234
Than swetely] 'Thus swete' 1521 Fragment			
Another brought two goslynges	226	El Rummynge	459
Almoost two or three, /Of that dygnyte,	250	Collyn Clout	148
With clauses two or thre,	265	Collyn Clout	766
The mountenaunce of two houres.	288	Why Come Ye	361
Ye rebads nat worth two plummis!	294	Why Come Ye	604
Plutarke and Petrarke, two famous clarkis;	322	Garlande	379
And where the two Trions a man shold aspy,	331	Garlande	699
Trions] 'Troons' †Fakes 1523			
In verses two or thre	350	Garlande	1371
Two thousande of Fraunce	360	Albany	43

UDDERSALE
ADAM UDDERSALE, ALIAS DICTUS ADAM ALL A KNAVE,	109	Epitaphe2	I

UDDERSALL
Uddersall stratus	109	Epitaphe2	13

UGLY
He fumblyth in hys fyngeryng an ugly good noyse;	37	Coystrowne1	31
Youre ugly tokyn /My mynd hath brokyn /From worldly lust;	39	Coystrowne3	1
By the ugly Eumenides,	104	Phy Sparrow	1324
Rowlynge in yower holow hede, ugly to see;	122	Garnesche1	38
But ugly of chere,	214	El Rummynge	14
She is ugly fayre:	215	El Rummynge	26
She was ugly hypped, /And ugly thycke-lypped	226	El Rummynge	469
By the ugly Eumenides,	349	Garlande	1317

UGLY HYPPED
She was ugly hypped, /And ugly thycke-lypped	226	El Rummynge	468

ULIXES
To Ulixes her make,	90	Phy Sparrow	732

UMANYTE
Of your professyoun unto umanyte,	335	Garlande	818

UMBLIS
The umblis of venyson, the botell of wyne,	347	Garlande	1240

UMWHYLE
Ye countyr umwhyle to capcyously, and ar ye be dysiryd;	123	Garnesche2	11

UNABLE
My pen it is unable,	102	Phy Sparrow	1219
This man was full unable	292	Why Come Ye	537
Reputyng hym unable /To gainsay replycable	382	Replycacion	302

UNASSURED
As clerkes unassured, /With ignorance obscured:	377	Replycacion	93

UNBYNDE
This lynkyd chayne of love that can unbynde.	146	Magnyfycence	201

UNBLYST —UNDERSTANDE   Page   Title   Line

	Page	Title	Line
Is from adversyte Magnyfycence to unbynde.	209	Magnyfycence	2422
UNBLYST			
It were no vertue, it were a thynge unblyst.	144	Magnyfycence	134
UNBRASED			
Some wenches come unlased, /Some huswyves come unbrased,	217	El Rummynge	134
unlased] 'unbrased' Day 1560, Marshe 1568			
She ran in all the hast /Unbrased and unlast,	222	El Rummynge	320
UNBRENT			
Of these yong heretikes, that stynke unbrent,	375	Replycacion	22
UNCOUTHES			
But they wyl talke of suche uncouthes,	272	Collyn Clout	1052
UNCURTEIS			
Were not thes commones uncurteis karlis of kynd	30	Dol Dethe	34
not] 'no' †MS Royal 18 D.ii, 'not' Marshe 1568			
UNCURTESLY			
Iwiss, ye dele uncurtesly;	36	Man Margery	15
UNDER			
And held with the commonns under a cloke,	31	Dol Dethe	76
Of all nacyons under the hevyn,	36	Coystrownel	1
And under the fell oft festerd is the sore:	45	Balettys4	5
Under as coverte termes as coude be,	46	Bowge	10
But under hony ofte tyme lyeth bytter gall,	49	Bowge	131
He set the arme proudly under the syde,	55	Bowge	321
Under supportacyon /Of your pacyent tolleracyon,	62	Hauke	31
And under pacyent tolleracyon	93	Phy Sparrow	851
And under that is brased	101	Phy Sparrow	1195
But wyll hath reason so under subjeccyon,	141	Magnyfycence	19
Under supportacyon /Of pacyent tolleracyon.	142	Magnyfycence	61
To lyve under lawe, it is captyvyte.	142	Magnyfycence	75
Of to moche lyberte under the offence;	146	Magnyfycence	229
And sendeth you this wrytynge closed under sele.	149	Magnyfycence	312
Of Largesse under the pretence.	151	Magnyfycence	405
The grace of God under benedicite.	154	Magnyfycence	490
That all this matter must under grope.	157	Magnyfycence	600
Why, under whom was he abydynge?	166	Magnyfycence	938
Not a better name under the sonne;	176	Magnyfycence	1310
What sholde a man do with you? Loke you under [k]ay?	180	Magnyfycence	1429
kay] 'bay' †Rastell & Treveris C 1530, B			
Myght seme ryght wel under my proteccyon	181	Magnyfycence	1469
But of your pacyence under the supporte,	183	Magnyfycence	1542
Under good hope endurynge ever styll,	208	Magnyfycence	2381
Precely purposyd under pretence of play,	213	Magnyfycence	2553
Under her surfled smocke	252	Collyn Clout	218
But under your supporte,	259	Collyn Clout	505
Under a notaries sygne	266	Collyn Clout	807
a] 'an' Kele 1545.1, 'a' MS Harley 2252			
That ye kepe them so under;	271	Collyn Clout	1007
ye] 'we' Kele 1545.1, 'ye' MS Harley 2252			
Bryngeth all thynges under cure.	286	Why Come Ye	284
Under the kynges brode seale;	287	Why Come Ye	337
Under a fayned treatee.	288	Why Come Ye	365
A prelate potencyall /To rule under Bellyall,	294	Why Come Ye	592
Under a certayne constellacion,	296	Why Come Ye	698
Under a stone on a golde ryng	296	Why Come Ye	700
With a bull under lead,	299	Why Come Ye	798
Under strength of the great seale,	306	Why Come Ye	1102
To be under his subjectyon,	307	Why Come Ye	1126
Under the protectyon /Of the kynges great seale,	307	Why Come Ye	1128
great] 'brode' MS Rawlinson C. 813			
That any man under supportacyon	318	Garlande	220
How all that I do is under refformation,	323	Garlande	411
Under the forme as I sayd tofore,	324	Garlande	443
tofore] 'before' Marshe 1568			
Under a gloryous cloth of astate,	325	Garlande	484
Under her arme, me thought, she hade a boke.	327	Garlande	532
Your discharge here under myne arme is it.'	344	Garlande	1146
Under the banner /Of all good manner,	356	Garlande	1572
Under proteccyon /Of sad correccyon,	356	Garlande	1574
And hyde you under logges,	364	Albany	213
On trouthe under defence	372	Albany	520
But under pacient tuicyon,	378	Replycacion	141
Sometyme under protection /Of pacient sufferance,	385	Replycacion	392
UNDERMYNDE			
So he dothe undermynde,	290	Why Come Ye	437
UNDERNETH			
That I counterfeyted you underneth a shrowde?	155	Magnyfycence	532
UNDERSET			
An olde barne wolde be underset.	153	Magnyfycence	454
UNDERSTAND			
I understand, to sone ye came.	118	Ag Scottes	130
UNDERSTANDE			
Your name is Lyberte, as I understande.	141	Magnyfycence	27
For to understande your pleasure and also your mynde.	209	Magnyfycence	2420
I understande, her name /Is Elynour Rummynge,	216	El Rummynge	92
But now my mynde ye understande,	268	Collyn Clout	887
I understande how that	284	Why Come Ye	237
To understande who dwellyth in yone pile,	333	Garlande	739
yone] 'yonder' MS Cotton Vitellius E.x			

UNDERSTANDES — UNHAPPYEST

	Page	Title	Line
We wyll understande how ye have it deservyd.'	344	Garlande	1127
Therin to rede, and to understande	347	Garlande	1230
Rejoyse, Englande, /And understande	359	Albany	2
To envade Englande, /As I understande.	361	Albany	106

UNDERSTANDES

	Page	Title	Line
Who so that understandes	93	Phy Sparrow	880

UNDERSTODE

	Page	Title	Line
But whoso understode /Of Medeas arte,	76	Phy Sparrow	201
Yf they well understode	262	Collyn Clout	616
understode] 'understand' Marshe 1568			
Some Romaine letters, as I understode;	328	Garlande	583

UNDERSTONDE

	Page	Title	Line
I understonde to soone ye cam,	114	Scot Kynge	39
Amonge all suche persones as I well understonde	161	Magnyfycence	739

UNDERSTOOD

	Page	Title	Line
For, if they understood /His traytourly dispyght,	121	Ag Scottes2	24

UNDERTAKE

	Page	Title	Line
For I undertake /He wolde so brag and crake	303	Why Come Ye	976
No man wyll undertake	358	Garlande2	10
Howe ye wyll undertake	367	Albany	326

UNDERTOKE

	Page	Title	Line
Gedeon is gon, that Zalmane undertoke,	234	Speke Parott	116

UNDYR

	Page	Title	Line
Of Mercury undyr the trynall aspecte,	240	Speke Parott	325
Parott, ye may prate thys undyr protestacion,	240	Speke Parott	336
Langagys divers; yet undyr that dothe reste	241	Speke Parott	365
So many nobyll bodyes, undyr on dawys hedd;	245	Speke Parott	467
So myche pelory pajauntes undyr colowur of good lawe;	245	Speke Parott	480

UNDO

	Page	Title	Line
Do and undo, bothe togyder;	169	Magnyfycence	1034

UNDONE

	Page	Title	Line
Then noblenesse, I se well, is almoste undone,	146	Magnyfycence	225
Alasse, syr, ye are undone with stelyng and robbynge!	192	Magnyfycence	1852
Gone? Alasse, ye have undone me!	192	Magnyfycence	1858
Howe he is undone by the meanes of me?	200	Magnyfycence	2110
Thus are they undone and utterly shamed.	374	Replycacion	17

UNDOUBTED

	Page	Title	Line
Ye, syr, undoubted. Then, of very ryght,	148	Magnyfycence	272
Undoubted ye had lost yourselfe eternally.	206	Magnyfycence	2335

UNFAYNED

	Page	Title	Line
But the fawconer unfayned	64	Hauke	81
I pray the, Besse, unfayned, /Yet com agayne to me!	238	Speke Parott	255
For trewly and unfayned,	309	Why Come Ye	1209

UNFAYNYD

	Page	Title	Line
But whether art thou walkynge, in faythe unfaynyd?	161	Magnyfycence	762

UNFETHERED

	Page	Title	Line
A narrow unfethered and without an hed,	232	Speke Parott	74

UNFORTUNATELY

	Page	Title	Line
How unfortunately he doth now spede;	115	Scot Kynge	57

UNFRENDLY

	Page	Title	Line
O Fortune unfrendly, Fortune unkynde thow art,	45	Balettys5	4

UNGOODLY

	Page	Title	Line
Mary, so ungoodly langage you me gave.	203	Magnyfycence	2213

UNGRACIOUS

	Page	Title	Line
O grounde ungracious, unhappy be thy fame,	32	Dol Dethe	116
Of unhappy generacion /And most ungracious nacion.	136	Dundas	53

UNGRACIOUSLY

	Page	Title	Line
Ungraciously how he doth speed.	119	Ag Scottes	154
With wordes enbosed, /Ungraciously engrosed,	367	Albany	325

UNGRACYOUS

	Page	Title	Line
Unto Magnyfycence a full ungracyous sorte,	178	Magnyfycence	1373
An all is for theyr ungracyous lyfe.	194	Magnyfycence	1915
Wherof this ungracyous lorde	306	Why Come Ye	1098
But who may have a more ungracyous lyfe	352	Garlande	1451
a] not in Marshe 1568			

UNGRACYOUSLY

	Page	Title	Line
That they wyll fyre one ungracyously in the flanke.	204	Magnyfycence	2270
And so ungracyously thy dayes thou hast spent,	205	Magnyfycence	2295
For I have so ungracyously my lyfe mysusyd,	205	Magnyfycence	2298
Full ungracyously, /Fals flatery,	300	Why Come Ye	852

UNHAPLY

	Page	Title	Line
O Scottes parjured, /Unhaply ured,	362	Albany	126

UNHAPPELY

	Page	Title	Line
But men nowe a dayes so unhappely be uryd,	140	Magnyfycence	6
Ye are unhappely ured.	377	Replycacion	95
Now of late abjured, /Most unhappely ured;	385	Replycacion	405

UNHAPPY

	Page	Title	Line
Your hap was unhappy, to ill was your spede.	31	Dol Dethe	61
O grounde ungracious, unhappy be thy fame,	32	Dol Dethe	116
Ye are to unhappy occasyons to fynde	38	Coystrowne1	65
occasyons] 'occasion' Marshe 1568			
Of unhappy generacion /And most ungracious nacion.	136	Dundas	52
Such tunges unhappy hath made great division	139	Ven Tongues	55
For all hokes unhappy to me have resorte.	178	Magnyfycence	1374
Than of wanhope thrughe the unhappy wayes,	206	Magnyfycence	2337
Ye, and beware of unhappy abusyon.	210	Magnyfycence	2452

UNHAPPYEST

	Page	Title	Line
Nor Sardanapall, /Unhappyest of all;	67	Hauke	201

UNHURT — UNTAWTE

UNHURT
An hynde unhurt hit by casuelte, not bled . . . . 351 Garlande 1406
UNICORNE
Prickyd lyke an unicorne. 133 Garnesche5 132
UNIVERSYTE
At Oxforth, the universyte, ... 131 Garnesche5 81
But the poore degre /Of the universyte; . . . . 265 Collyn Clout 736
UNYCORNES
And by unycornes /With theyr semely hornes; . . . . 270 Collyn Clout 964
UNYVERSYTE
That hath taken degre /In the unyversyte . . . . 266 Collyn Clout 793
Therwith for to be founde /At the unyversyte, ... 378 Replycacion 148
UNKINDLY
Unkindly thei slew hym that help them oft at nede. . . . . . . 30 Dol Dethe 47
   help] 'holp' Marshe 1568
UNKYND
Well may ye be cald commons most unkynd. . . . . 30 Dol Dethe 56
   ye] 'you' Marshe 1568
UNKYNDE
O Fortune unfrendly, Fortune unkynde thow art, ... 45 Balettys5 4
For here be dyverse to you that be unkynde. . . . . 50 Bowge 161
Nowe to curteys, forthwith unkynde; . . . . 168 Magnyfycence 1008
A wrechyd man, syr, to my maker unkynde. . . . . 208 Magnyfycence 2390
And all overcast with cloudis unkynde, ... 352 Garlande 1444
UNKYNDNESSE
I am wery of the worlde, for unkyndnesse me sleeth. . . . . . . 205 Magnyfycence 2283
UNLASED
Some wenches come unlased, /Some huswyves come unbrased, . . . 217 El Rummynge 133
   unlased] 'unbrased' Day 1560, Marshe 1568
UNLAST
She ran in all the hast /Unbrased and unlast, ... 222 El Rummynge 320
UNLYKYNGE
I am lowsy and unlykynge and full of scurffe; . . . . 195 Magnyfycence 1958
UNLUST
Theyr tresses untrust, /All full of unlust; . . . . 218 El Rummynge 148
UNLUSTY
His gummes rusty /Are full unlusty; . . . . 94 Phy Sparrow 915
UNMETE
For the courte full unmete; . . . . 279 Why Come Ye 33
With baudy wordes unmete . . . . 376 Replycacion 49
UNNATURALL
Brother unnaturall /Unto our kyng royall, ... 120 Ag Scottes2 15
UNNETH
And yet unneth I can have my lyvynge; . . . . 53 Bowge 275
Unneth I kest myne eyes . . . . 72 Phy Sparrow 37
Unneth I me refrayned, ... 99 Phy Sparrow 1124
Unneth they leve a locke /Of wolle amongest theyr flocke. . . . 248 Collyn Clout 80
UNPAYD
So myche spente before, and so myche unpayd behynde - . . . . . 244 Speke Parott 461
UNPULLYSHT
Mi wordis unpullysht be nakide and playne, ... 32 Dol Dethe 127
UNREMEMBERED
Not unremembered it is unto your grace, ... 313 Garlande 57
UNREMEMBRED
That unremembred longe tyme remayned. . . . . 347 Garlande 1225
UNRESONABLE
remordyng dyvers recrayed and moche unresonable errours . . . . 373 Replycacion I
UNREVERENT
Wyth cry unreverent, /Before the sacrament, ... 62 Hauke 11
As preest unreverent, ... 63 Hauke 45
O pryeest unreverent. . . . . 67 Hauke 187
UNREWARDED
Can nat be unrewarded. . . . . 378 Replycacion 139
UNSET
Of the vertue of an unset leke; . . . . 225 El Rummynge 451
UNSHRED
And plantid it there where never before was none, unshred . . . 351 Garlande 1405
   it there where] 'yet wher' Marshe 1568
UNSOWNDY
Her eyen gowndy /Are full unsowndy, ... 215 El Rummynge 35
UNSTABLE
My hand it is unstable, ... 102 Phy Sparrow 1220
UNSTABLENESSE
Fyckell falsenesse, /Varyablenesse, /With unstablenesse. . . . 247 Collyn Clout 46
UNSTEDFASTNESSE
At our foly and our unstedfastnesse; . . . . 46 Bowge 6
UNSURELY
surmysed unsurely in their perihermeniall principles, ... 374 Replycacion I
UNSWETE
And also theyr fete /Hardely full unswete; . . . . 217 El Rummynge 122
UNTAYDE
For tunges untayde be renning astray. . . . . 138 Ven Tongues 37
UNTAUGHT
My scoles are not for unthriftes untaught, ... 138 Ven Tongues 26
Some bestyall and untaught. . . . . 252 Collyn Clout 228
UNTAWTE
Thy tong untawte, with poyson infecte, ... 132 Garnesche5 108

UNTHRIFTES —UNTRUST

	Page	Title	Line
UNTHRIFTES			
My scoles are not for unthriftes untaught,	138	Ven Tongues	26
UNTHRYFTYNES			
Unthryftynes in hym may well be shewed,	58	Bowge	416
Unthryftynes] 'Unthryftnes' †Wynkyn de Worde 1499, 1510			
UNTYDE			
The goslenges were untyde;	226	El Rummynge	463
UNTYDY			
Full untydy tegges, /Lyke rotten egges.	218	El Rummynge	151
UNTO			
Goddes mooste cruell unto the lyfe of man,	32	Dol Dethe	121
God the assyst unto thyne heritage,	33	Dol Dethe	164
Unto thy subjectis be kurteis and beningne.	33	Dol Dethe	168
Hevyn, hell and erth obey unto thi kall;	34	Dol Dethe	192
Thow bringe unto thy joye etermynable	34	Dol Dethe	199
Thow] 'how' †MS Royal 18 D.ii			
Unto the Iles of Orchady,	79	Phy Sparrow	319
In doynge his homage /Unto his soverayne.	80	Phy Sparrow	327
And shew now unto me	106	Phy Sparrow	1368
Is it come unto your lot	116	Ag Scottes	50
Unto our prince, anoynted kyng.	117	Ag Scottes	58
Unto your grace for grace now I call,	117	Ag Scottes	78
Unto the castell of Norram,	118	Ag Scottes	129
UNTO DYVERS PEOPLE THAT REMORD THIS RYMYNG	120	Ag Scottes	R
Brother unnaturall /Unto our kyng royall,	120	Ag Scottes2	16
Sayth, from thy to unto thi croune,	130	Garnesche5	26
Who soever that tale unto you tolde,	137	Ven Tongues	20
Unto that same I am ryght well agrede,	144	Magnyfycence	128
Unto your rule I wyll annex my mynde.	144	Magnyfycence	142
Welcome, frendys, ye are bothe unto me.	145	Magnyfycence	169
Where was it delyvered you? Shewe unto me.	150	Magnyfycence	340
Not from Anwyke unto Aungey.	171	Magnyfycence	1121
Unto Magnyfycence a full ungracyous sorte,	178	Magnyfycence	1373
He may not be comparyd unto me.	181	Magnyfycence	1476
Unto measure, I say, nowe a days.	189	Magnyfycence	1744
Ryse up, syr, and welcom unto me.	195	Magnyfycence	1966
Unto your maker that made bothe you and me;	196	Magnyfycence	1992
Me humbly commyttynge unto Goddys wyll.	208	Magnyfycence	2382
Syth unto me formest this processe is erectyd,	211	Magnyfycence	2482
Unto this processe brefly compylyd,	212	Magnyfycence	2510
Ye, all thyng mortall shall torne unto nought	236	Speke Parott	214
I compas the conveyaunce unto the capitall	243	Speke Parott	411
Unto great confusyon	279	Why Come Ye	21
Or suche chaunce shulde fall /Unto our cardynall!	297	Why Come Ye	749
Whiche madly he dothe apply /Unto an extravagancy,	306	Why Come Ye	1105
Not unremembered it is unto your grace,	313	Garlande	57
Unto your grace then make I this motyve:	315	Garlande	114
Unto the rowme of laureat promotyve?	315	Garlande	116
Unto your palas, our noble courte of Fame,	318	Garlande	219
Unto Diana, the goddes inmortall,	320	Garlande	303
Unto me; alas, that herbe nor gresse	321	Garlande	314
gresse] 'gras' †Fakes 1523			
As I ymagenyd, repayrid unto me,	323	Garlande	392
Arrectinge unto your wyse examinacion	323	Garlande	410
Unto the pavylyon where Pallas was syttyng.	324	Garlande	448
Thus passid we forth walkynge unto the pretory	325	Garlande	477
Unto this place all poetis there did sue,	325	Garlande	481
Unto me sayd, 'Lo, syr, now ye may se	326	Garlande	518
How from the est unto the occident,	328	Garlande	577
And from the sowth unto the north so colde,	328	Garlande	578
Of your professyoun unto umanyte,	335	Garlande	818
Unto you, madame, I make reconusaunce,	335	Garlande	838
Paregall in honour unto Penolepe,	337	Garlande	899
Unto the legend of fare Laodomi.	339	Garlande	972
To answere unto this noble audyence,	344	Garlande	1122
And shew now unto me	350	Garlande	1361
From the Scottish se /Unto Gabione.	362	Albany	131
In merciall prowes /Lyke unto Hercules.	369	Albany	431
In prudence and wysdom /Lyke unto Salamon,	369	Albany	433
In his goodly person /Lyke unto Absolon,	369	Albany	435
In royal mageste /Lyke unto Ptholome,	370	Albany	441
humbly submytted unto the ryght discrete reformacyon	373	Replycacion	I
Lyke unto Alcheus, he dothe hym magnify.	383	Replycacion	335
UNTREW			
And his untrew adversary?	298	Why Come Ye	789
UNTREWE			
And an untrewe knyght.	364	Albany	229
UNTREWLY			
And say as untrewly /As the butterfly,	255	Collyn Clout	336
UNTRUE			
Lyke that untrue rebell /Fals Kayn agaynst Abell.	121	Ag Scottes2	19
Adue, cowarde, adue! /Fals knight and mooste untrue,	366	Albany	315
UNTRULY			
Though ye untruly your father have slayne,	118	Ag Scottes	119
He saith untruly, to say that I would	137	Ven Tongues	21
UNTRUST			
Theyr tresses untrust, /All full of unlust;	218	El Rummynge	147

	Page	Title	Line
UNTRUTH			
For your untruth now ar ye shent.	118	Ag Scottes	124
UNTWYNDE			
Whan thou my byrde untwynde!	79	Phy Sparrow	284
Many one ye have untwynde	263	Collyn Clout	662
ye have untwynde] 'have but wynde' †Godfray 1531, Kele 1545.1, Marshe 1568			
This goodly flowre with stormis was untwynde.	352	Garlande	1445
UP			
Take up whos wolde, for ther they let hym ly.	32	Dol Dethe	96
Put up your purs, ye shall non pay!'	40	Coystrowne4	11
Wyth bound and rebound, bounsyngly take up	43	Balettys2	15
Spur up at the hynder gyrth with, 'Gup, morell, gup!'	43	Balettys2	17
Thus up and down my mynde was drawen and cast	47	Bowge	29
The sayle is up, Fortune ruleth our helme,	49	Bowge	127
What, lete us holde him up, man, for a whyle.'	51	Bowge	188
Holde up the helme, loke up and lete God stere:	53	Bowge	250
Holde up the helme, loke up and lete God stere:	53	Bowge	250
He set up fresshely upon his hat alofte.	56	Bowge	367
Plucke up thyne herte upon a mery pyne,	57	Bowge	386
That I brought up at Carowe.	78	Phy Sparrow	281
She raysed up in that stede	105	Phy Sparrow	1352
Gyve up your game, ye playe chek mate;	114	Scot Kynge	37
Cast of your crowne, cast up your crowne!	120	Ag Scottes	179
Ye slufferd up sowse	125	Garnesche3	32
Caste up your curyows wrytyng,	127	Garnesche3	112
And takyn up in such a frame,	132	Garnesche5	110
Yet lyberte hath ben lockyd up and kept in the mew.	141	Magnyfycence	35
Yet amonge noble men I was brought up and bred.	147	Magnyfycence	261
Plucke up your mynde, syr, what ayle you to muse?	148	Magnyfycence	283
As good to be occupyed as up and downe to trace	159	Magnyfycence	692
A carlys sonne /Brought up of nought	165	Magnyfycence	899
Plucke downe an house and set up a rafter,	169	Magnyfycence	1032
I daunce up and downe tyll I am dyssy.	169	Magnyfycence	1040
And those be they that come up of nought –	174	Magnyfycence	1240
By crafty conveyaunce many one is brought up of nought;	178	Magnyfycence	1369
To styre up your stomake you must you forge,	185	Magnyfycence	1613
Call for a ca[u]dell and cast up your gorge,	185	Magnyfycence	1614
caudell] 'candell' †Rastell & Treveris C 1530, B			
Stand up, syr. Ye are welcom to me.	186	Magnyfycence	1632
Nowe must I this carcasse lyft up.	195	Magnyfycence	1964
Ryse up, syr, and welcom unto me.	195	Magnyfycence	1966
Sodenly set up and sodenly pluckyd downe;	197	Magnyfycence	2025
Thus totum in toto groweth up, as ye may se,	199	Magnyfycence	2099
They cast up theyr obedyence to cache me agayne;	201	Magnyfycence	2148
Nay, horson, here is my glove. Take it up and thou dare.	202	Magnyfycence	2178
Than stande up, syr, in Goddys name!	208	Magnyfycence	2397
Sodenly set up, and sodenly cast downe.	212	Magnyfycence	2530
Sodenly set up, and sodenly cast downe.	213	Magnyfycence	2537
Gently joynted, /Gresed and anoynted /Up to the knockles:	215	El Rummynge	44
But to make up my tale,	217	El Rummynge	101
They have dronke up my swyllyng tubbe!'	218	El Rummynge	173
Gather up, thou wenche.	219	El Rummynge	181
Take up dyrt and all, /And bere out of the hall.	219	El Rummynge	183
dyrt] 'drit' Kynge & Marche 1554, Day 1560, Marshe 1568			
Elynour toke her up	224	El Rummynge	376
But supped it up at ones,	224	El Rummynge	380
'Ryse up, on Gods halfe,'	227	El Rummynge	501
Up she stert, halfe lame,	227	El Rummynge	512
She swynged up a quarte /At ones for her parte.	228	El Rummynge	568
swynged] 'swinge' Marshe 1568			
Jobab was brought up in the lande of Hus;	232	Speke Parott	65
Jobab] 'Iob' Day 1560, Marshe 1568			
How the rest of good lernyng is roufled up and trold.	235	Speke Parott	168
roufled] 'roulled' Day 1560, Marshe 1568			
Let se who dare make up the reste.	242	Speke Parott	382
Tytan hathe truste up hys tressys of fyne golde;	242	Speke Parott	398
He tryhumfythe, he trumpythe, he turnythe all up and downe,	244	Speke Parott	432
To herken Jacke and Gyll /Whan they put up a byll;	249	Collyn Clout	97
Must cast up theyr blacke vayles	256	Collyn Clout	396
And set up theyr fucke sayles	256	Collyn Clout	397
fucke sayles] 'flucke sayles' †Godfray 1531, 'fulke saylys' MS Harley 2252			
And wrest up my harpe	259	Collyn Clout	490
And gathereth up in store	260	Collyn Clout	568
gathereth] 'gathered' Marshe 1568			
And come up of nought;	261	Collyn Clout	584
Ye caste up then your bokes	261	Collyn Clout	596
Brought up of poore estate, /With pryde inordynate,	262	Collyn Clout	642
We have cast up our war,	282	Why Come Ye	140
Borne up on every syde	284	Why Come Ye	203
With, 'Trompe up!' 'Alleluya!'	284	Why Come Ye	205
That inne, is now shyt up,	284	Why Come Ye	239
To holde up their hande at the bar.	286	Why Come Ye	302
To make up one of nought,	293	Why Come Ye	551
Set up a wretche on hye,	293	Why Come Ye	585
Made up a great astate	297	Why Come Ye	723
He wolde dry up the stremys	303	Why Come Ye	957

UPON —UPON	Page	Title	Line
Put up his sworde, for he cowde make no warre,	312	Garlande	5
With that I sprange up towarde the tent	320	Garlande	283
She bet up a fyre with the sparkis full kene	330	Garlande	669
She raysed up in that stede	350	Garlande	1345
Item Apollo that whirllid up his chare,	353	Garlande	1471
With that I stode up, halfe sodenly afrayd,	353	Garlande	1477
And brake up all his hoost.	360	Albany	67
To be knytte up with knottes	362	Albany	122
Thou mayst give up thy cocking.	366	Albany	299
Gyve it up, and cry, 'creke', /Lyke an huddy peke.	366	Albany	300

UPON

	Page	Title	Line
Skelton Laureat Upon the Dolorus Dethe	29	Dol Dethe	I
He calde upon them, as menyall houshold men:	30	Dol Dethe	33
Vigorously upon them with myght and with mayne,	31	Dol Dethe	89
Upon suche a sort was ille bestowde and spent.	32	Dol Dethe	98
So forcibly upon this Erle thow ran,	32	Dol Dethe	124
Upon his breste he bare a versynge boxe:	52	Bowge	232
Counter he coude O lux upon a potte.	56	Bowge	365
He set up fresshely upon his hat alofte.	56	Bowge	367
Plucke up thyne herte upon a mery pyne,	57	Bowge	386
Now have at all that lyeth upon the burde.	57	Bowge	391
I hate this faynynge, fye upon it, fye!	59	Bowge	465
For he coude well upon a casket wayte,	60	Bowge	507
His hawke shulde pray and fede /Upon a pigeons maw.	63	Hauke	57
The blode ran downe raw /Upon the auter stone.	63	Hauke	59
Upon my corporas face.	63	Hauke	63
Full upon the gorge.	64	Hauke	87
Hampar with your hammer upon thy styth,	71	Hauke	332
No creature but that wolde /Have rewed upon me,	72	Phy Sparrow	42
And wold syt upon my lap,	74	Phy Sparrow	121
Upon my naked skyn.	76	Phy Sparrow	167
He dyd nothynge, perde, /But syt upon my kne.	76	Phy Sparrow	172
Upon my sparowes soule,	77	Phy Sparrow	241
And wonder upon the,	79	Phy Sparrow	317
Upon my fynger aloft!	80	Phy Sparrow	356
Upon a great payne,	88	Phy Sparrow	654
Upon fayre Cressyde,	88	Phy Sparrow	679
A warte upon her cheke,	97	Phy Sparrow	1043
The sker upon her chyn	98	Phy Sparrow	1077
Upon her whan I gased,	99	Phy Sparrow	1104
Upon her prety fote?	100	Phy Sparrow	1147
Upon us he doth reigne	111	Lawde	50
Ye grounde yow upon Godfrey, that grysly gargons face,	123	Garnesche2	29
A gose with the fete upon;	125	Garnesche3	31
........gynys upon a gonge,	125	Garnesche3	56
Upon hym for to take	126	Garnesche3	92
Now upon thys hete /Rankely whan ye swete,	127	Garnesche3	133
To take upon the for to scryve;	132	Garnesche5	91
Yet to lie upon me they can not prevayle.	138	Ven Tongues	31
But men take upon theim nowe all the shame	139	Ven Tongues	61
Wyll crepe upon us, and us to myschefe lede;	144	Magnyfycence	153
Mary, upon trouth my reason I grounde,	147	Magnyfycence	264
Chanons can not counterfet but upon thre.	154	Magnyfycence	492
A very fon, /A very asse /Wyll take upon /To compasse	164	Magnyfycence	865
Upon a naked man and yf she scrat.	176	Magnyfycence	1298
And some wyll take upon them to conterfet letters,	178	Magnyfycence	1364
And wayte upon me. And yet for a memory,	180	Magnyfycence	1447
To fasten your fansy upon a fayre maystresse	183	Magnyfycence	1550
As lyly whyte to loke upon her [l]eyre,	183	Magnyfycence	1555
leyre] 'heyre' †Rastell & Treveris C 1530, B			
So masterfully upon you for to take	188	Magnyfycence	1715
And let all your fansyes upon them rest.	190	Magnyfycence	1770
And here I make the upon Lyberte	190	Magnyfycence	1784
Where is nowe my golde upon them that I spent?	198	Magnyfycence	2058
Take nowe upon you this abylyment,	208	Magnyfycence	2405
Upon the holy daye, /Whan she doth her aray,	216	El Rummynge	66
With clothes upon her hed /That wey a sowe of led,	216	El Rummynge	71
That wey] 'That they wey' Kynge & Marche 1554, Day 1560, Marshe 1568			
Upon her brayne-pan, /Lyke an Egypcyan /Lapped about.	216	El Rummynge	77
Lapped] 'Capped' Kynge & Marche 1554, Day 1560, Marshe 1568			
Gresed upon dyrt /That baudeth her skyrt.	216	El Rummynge	89
For Parrot to pyke upon, his brayne for to stable,	235	Speke Parott	184
Dothe grudge and complayne /Upon the temporall men.	248	Collyn Clout	65
To ryde upon a mule	254	Collyn Clout	308
Chryst by cruelte /Was nayled upon a tre;	258	Collyn Clout	451
And upon you take	261	Collyn Clout	603
Upon Grenewytche border /Called Observaunce,	265	Collyn Clout	746
To postell upon a kyry,	265	Collyn Clout	753
Upon these beestes rydynge,	270	Collyn Clout	966
Nor upon them take,	272	Collyn Clout	1016
Take upon me /Thus copyously to wryte,	273	Collyn Clout	1084
Take upon me] 'Take now upon' Kele 1545.1, 'I take now uppon' MS Harley 2252			
But now upon this story	284	Why Come Ye	229
Upon artycles judicyall, /To contende and to stryve	299	Why Come Ye	814
Upon this matter mistycall	299	Why Come Ye	821
Upon every banke /Of his herbers grene,	304	Why Come Ye	1002

UPPE —US	Page	Title	Line
upon a goodly Garlande or Chapelet of Laurell	312	Garlande	1
To syt hym upon, and rede Jacke a thrummis bybille, hym] not in MS Cotton Vitellius E.x	318	Garlande	209
And iche man stode gasyng and staryng upon other.	319	Garlande	268
Yet have compassyon upon my paynes stronge.'	320	Garlande	299
'Lyke as the larke, upon the somers day,	327	Garlande	533
Dryades there daunsid upon that goodly soile,	331	Garlande	679
There Cintheus sat twynklyng upon his harpe stringis;	331	Garlande	687
Forthwith upon this, as it were in a thought,	343	Garlande	1100
So then commaundid she was upon this	344	Garlande	1147
May happely loke /Upon your boke,	355	Garlande	1547
upon a goodly Garlonde or Chapelet of Laurell,	358	Garlande2	R
And hang you upon polles	362	Albany	151
Ye argued argumentes, /As it were upon the elenkes,	377	Replycacion	126

UPPE

To be so perte to prese so proudly uppe.	48	Bowge	71

UPPON

Uppon me to clater or else to say yll.	38	Coystrowne1	66
Skelton Laureat, uppon a deedmans hed,	39	Coystrowne3	1
Ye cast all your corage uppon such courtly haggys!	43	Balettys2	19
Devysed and also wrate /Uppon a lewde curate,	62	Hauke	35
His hawke then flew uppon /The rode, with Mary and Johnn.	65	Hauke	126
Christi crucifixi /To fede uppon your fisty;	69	Hauke	291
So royall a kyng, as reynythe uppon us all -	245	Speke Parott	468
Uppon hym for to take /A mattocke or a rake.	253	Collyn Clout	273

UPRYGHT

Craftely all thynges upryght to save:	158	Magnyfycence	642

UPSTARTE

Sodaynly upstarte /From the donge carte,	262	Collyn Clout	644

UPSTODE

Myne hear ryght upstode,	77	Phy Sparrow	227

UPTUCKE

Than Margery Mylkeducke /Her kyrtell she dyd uptucke	225	El Rummynge	419

UPWARDE

Then to the hevyn sperycall upwarde I gasid,	354	Garlande	1514

UR

Aram was fyred with Caldies fyer called Ur;	232	Speke Parott	64

URCHEONS

Lyke urcheons in a stone wall, urcheons] 'heons' †Kele 1545.3, Marshe 1568	283	Why Come Ye	166

URE

Lyke Aron and Ure,	250	Collyn Clout	152
Wherfore he hath good ure	271	Collyn Clout	1001

URED

O Scottes parjured, /Unhaply ured,	362	Albany	126
Ye are unhappely ured.	377	Replycacion	95
Now of late abjured, /Most unhappely ured;	385	Replycacion	405

URGENTLY

So urgently I am brought /Into carefull thought.	74	Phy Sparrow	106

URYD

But men nowe a dayes so unhappely be uryd,	140	Magnyfycence	6

URSA

Behynde the taile of Ursa so clere;	331	Garlande	696

US

And us redemede from the fendys pray.	34	Dol Dethe	196
Deth wyll us quell /And with us mell.	39	Coystrowne3	23
Deth wyll us quell /And with us mell.	39	Coystrowne3	24
Redeme us from this.	39	Coystrowne3	28
But to swete Jesu /On us then for to rew?	40	Coystrowne3	40
But graunt us grace /To se thy face,	40	Coystrowne3	49
The auncient acquaintance, madam, betwen us twayn,	42	Balettys2	1
She promysed to us all she wolde be kynde;	49	Bowge	124
And we asked favoure, and favour she us gave.	49	Bowge	126
That wyll abyde and never frome us fall.	49	Bowge	130
Deynte to have with us suche one in store,	50	Bowge	150
To dwell with us and serve my ladyes grace.	50	Bowge	156
What, lete us holde him up, man, for a whyle.'	51	Bowge	188
'Ye, soo,' quod Suspecte, 'he maye us bothe begyle.'	51	Bowge	189
Let us, therfore, shortely at a worde	54	Bowge	307
With us olde servauntes such maysters to playe.	55	Bowge	329
Naye, strawe for tales, thou shalte not rule us;	55	Bowge	341
We be thy betters, and so thou shalte us take,	55	Bowge	342
'And, syr, in fayth, why comste not us amonge	57	Bowge	379
And thus with us good company to kepe.	57	Bowge	385
And lete us laugh a placke or tweyne at nale. placke] 'plucke' Marshe 1568	57	Bowge	387
To us welcome thou arte, by Saynte Quyntyne!'	60	Bowge	511
Deth hath departed us twayne;	80	Phy Sparrow	329
Let us now whysper /A Pater noster.	81	Phy Sparrow	384
The plover with us to wayle;	82	Phy Sparrow	417
Must helpe us to houle;	82	Phy Sparrow	443
Of Marcus Marcellus /A proces I could tell us;	90	Phy Sparrow	735
That right dwelt us among,	111	Lawde	20
Upon us he doth reigne	111	Lawde	50
The prowdyst knave yet of us tewyne	130	Garnesche5	21
Us to informe and ken -	143	Magnyfycence	88
Wyll crepe upon us, and us to myschefe lede;	144	Magnyfycence	153
Wyll crepe upon us, and us to myschefe lede;	144	Magnyfycence	153

	Page	Title	Line
For myschefe wyll mayster us yf measure us forsake.	144	Magnyfycence	154
For myschefe wyll mayster us yf measure us forsake.	144	Magnyfycence	154
So in his harte he may be glad of us.	145	Magnyfycence	158
There is no prynce but he hath nede of us thre -	145	Magnyfycence	159
That Measure be mayster us semeth it is syttynge.	145	Magnyfycence	176
I trowe good fortune hath annexyd us together,	146	Magnyfycence	198
Yet measure hath ben so longe from us absent,	146	Magnyfycence	221
Now leve this jangelynge and to us expounde	147	Magnyfycence	262
You are nothynge mete with us for to dwell,	149	Magnyfycence	304
Let us departe from hens home to my place.	151	Magnyfycence	394
Who that is ruled by us, it shalbe longe or he thee.	154	Magnyfycence	515
Nay. Let us our heddes togyder cast.	156	Magnyfycence	566
Nay, lette us not clatter thus styll.	157	Magnyfycence	610
By God, we wolde gete us all thyder,	157	Magnyfycence	618
Magnyfycence to us begynneth to enclyne,	158	Magnyfycence	644
Mary, syr, he told us, when	158	Magnyfycence	652
To Magnyfycence with us twayne.	158	Magnyfycence	667
We wyll se you shortly, one of us twayne.	159	Magnyfycence	686
Now let us go, and we shall, then.	159	Magnyfycence	687
That fell amonge us this same day?	166	Magnyfycence	933
Holde thy pease! Measure shall frome us walke.	166	Magnyfycence	949
Ye, but of my name let us be wyse.	167	Magnyfycence	963
Cockys armys, a mete man for us!	172	Magnyfycence	1169
Ye. Let us here a worde or twayne.	174	Magnyfycence	1218
Shewe us your mynde then, howe to do and what.	180	Magnyfycence	1435
Let us here of your pleasure, to passe the tyme withall.	182	Magnyfycence	1518
Well, call hym, and let us here hym reason;	187	Magnyfycence	1687
Ye sent us a supervysour for to take hede;	192	Magnyfycence	1853
Nay. He that ye sent us, Clokyd Colusyon,	192	Magnyfycence	1859
Or ever we were ware, brought us in adversyte,	193	Magnyfycence	1863
Now let us be all one, and let us lyve in rest	202	Magnyfycence	2202
Now let us be all one, and let us lyve in rest;	202	Magnyfycence	2202
Go we nere and let us se.	204	Magnyfycence	2243
But nowe let us make mery and good chere.	204	Magnyfycence	2261
And to the taverne let us drawe nere.	204	Magnyfycence	2262
To get us there some freshe mete.	204	Magnyfycence	2264
For the passyon of God, let us go thyther.	204	Magnyfycence	2276
Yet let us se this matter thorowly ingrosed.	209	Magnyfycence	2438
Nowe semyth us syttynge that ye then resorte	214	Magnyfycence	2566
And let us sley care!'	217	El Rummynge	111
But let us turne playne, /There we lefte agayne.	219	El Rummynge	187
Let us wasshe our gommes /From the drye crommes!'	222	El Rummynge	307
Of thyne ale let us assaye,	224	El Rummynge	397
Let us syppe and soppy, /And not spyll a droppy,	228	El Rummynge	558
So royall a kyng, as reynythe uppon us all -	245	Speke Parott	468
To redeme us with all.	258	Collyn Clout	455
That goostly can heale us;	265	Collyn Clout	742
'Shall they taunt us prelates,	275	Collyn Clout	1150
taunt] 'daunt' Kele 1545.1, Marshe 1568, 'teche' MS Harley 2252			
Agaynst us of the counsell?	275	Collyn Clout	1163
Agaynst us dothe prate.	276	Collyn Clout	1181
They set nat by us a shyttell;	276	Collyn Clout	1185
shytell] 'whystell' Kele 1545.1, Marshe 1568, 'shetyll' MS Harley 2252			
They counte us for lyars;	276	Collyn Clout	1187
They crakers of us lyke crakers;	276	Collyn Clout	1189
Suche grace that he us sende	278	Collyn Clout	1262
Wrang un the [m]ales!	280	Why Come Ye	78
males] 'wales' †Kele 1545.3, Toy 1553, Kitson 1560.7, Marshe 1568			
God sende us better luck!	282	Why Come Ye	123
God sende us better lucke, etc.	282	Why Come Ye	124
But yet they over-shote us	283	Why Come Ye	169
They make us all sottes,	285	Why Come Ye	263
They make us to pyll strawes;	285	Why Come Ye	265
They dyd us a shrewde turne,	285	Why Come Ye	269
He maketh us Jack Rakers;	285	Why Come Ye	273
He calleth us England men	285	Why Come Ye	275
For with us he so mellys	303	Why Come Ye	961
He wyll drynke us so drye,	303	Why Come Ye	965
so] not in MS Rawlinson C. 813			
And suck us so nye,	303	Why Come Ye	966
For amonge us is none	304	Why Come Ye	995
That wyll hed us and hange us,	308	Why Come Ye	1154
That wyll hed us and hange us,	308	Why Come Ye	1154
And streitly strangle us	308	Why Come Ye	1155
And he may fange us.	308	Why Come Ye	1156
And] 'That' Kitson 1560.7, Marshe 1568			
'Come on with me,' he sayd, 'let us not stonde';	328	Garlande	559
To walke where we lyst, let us somwhat fynde	328	Garlande	564
To pas the tyme with, but let us wast no wynde.	328	Garlande	565
In lyke maner of wyse a myst did us shrowde;	330	Garlande	647
'My frende, sith ye ar before us here present	344	Garlande	1121
With us for to compare.	363	Albany	179
With us, whan ever ye mell	363	Albany	182
That our Savyour bare, /Whiche us redemed from care.	375	Replycacion	34
And maketh in us suche spede	385	Replycacion	386

USAGE —VAYNE GLORIOUS | Page | Title | Line

USAGE
But, good madame, the accustome and usage . . . . 314 Garlande 64
USE
By myne avyse use not with him to walke. . . . . 52 Bowge 210
To use youre hawkys forica /In propitiatorio, ... 69 Hauke 271
This fals Envy /Sayth that I /Use great folly . . . . 95 Phy Sparrow 951
Of harlottes to use soche an harres, ... 131 Garnesche5 77
For I wyll use you by his advertysment. . . . . 146 Magnyfycence 196
It is but a maddynge, these wayes that ye use. . . . . 148 Magnyfycence 285
I wyll not use you to play with me checke mate. . . . . 149 Magnyfycence 307
What the devyll! Use ye not to drawe no swordes? . . . . 163 Magnyfycence 811
For there be other that foly dothe use . . . . 175 Magnyfycence 1280
Take your pleasure and use free lyberte; . . . . 185 Magnyfycence 1598
For suche abusyon I use nowe and than. . . . . 185 Magnyfycence 1625
For to use suche haftynge and crafty wayes. . . . . 187 Magnyfycence 1678
Yet somtyme, parde, I must use largesse. . . . . 189 Magnyfycence 1755
But use your largesse by the advyse of me, ... 189 Magnyfycence 1765
A prynce to use with all his hole intent, ... 200 Magnyfycence 2118
That I sholde use largesse. Nay, syr, there a pause. . . . . . 209 Magnyfycence 2437
And caused me also to use to moche lyberte, ... 209 Magnyfycence 2445
Use not then your countenaunce for to counterfet. . . . . 210 Magnyfycence 2455
In your rewardys use suche moderacyon . . . . 211 Magnyfycence 2494
To use suche despytynge . . . . 274 Collyn Clout 1107
  despytynge] 'despysyng' Kele 1545.1, Marshe 1568, 'dysputyng'
  MS Harley 2252
And dare use the experyens . . . . 297 Why Come Ye 711
It is no foly to use the Walshemannys hoos. . . . . 347 Garlande 1239
USED
For, syth he dyed, largesse was lytell used. . . . . 148 Magnyfycence 282
What, that we used whan we were boyes? . . . . 172 Magnyfycence 1138
To se what foly is used in every place; . . . . 177 Magnyfycence 1327
For I am a vertue yf I be well used, ... 199 Magnyfycence 2101
That I used the to moche sore may I rewe. . . . . 199 Magnyfycence 2104
Redresse my name is, that lytell am I used . . . . 208 Magnyfycence 2411
USETH
That useth me. /He can not thee. . . . . 164 Magnyfycence 861
For I knowe dyverse that useth the same. . . . . 175 Magnyfycence 1255
And useth suche abusyoun, ... 290 Why Come Ye 456
USYD
Why, is this the largesse that I have usyd? . . . . 193 Magnyfycence 1865
Nay. It was your fondnesse that ye have usyd. . . . . 193 Magnyfycence 1866
For where I am occupyed and usyd wylfully, ... 200 Magnyfycence 2131
So many morall maters, and so lytell usyd; . . . . 244 Speke Parott 449
  many] 'many many' †MS Harley 2252
USYNGE
Subtelly usynge counterfet weyght; . . . . 152 Magnyfycence 440
USSCHERES
Savynge your usscheres rod, ... 124 Garnesche3 5
USSHER
An ussher of the hall fayn wold I get 37 Coystrowne1 40
USUALL
Of thy bounte after the usuall rate . . . . 29 Dol Dethe 19
UTERAUNCE
In elect uteraunce to make memoryall! . . . . 29 Dol Dethe 11
UTTER
Gyve this gentylman rome, syrs. Stonde utter! . . . . 161 Magnyfycence 753
'A strawe,' sayde Bele, 'stande utter, ... 228 El Rummynge 535
Of Demostenes, that was his utter foo. . . . . 317 Garlande 167
To your great lacke /And utter shame . . . . 360 Albany 46
UTTERAUNCE
Wyth fresshe utteraunce full sentencyously; . . . . 46 Bowge 12
Or in electe utteraunce halfe so eloquent, ... 183 Magnyfycence 1533
UTTERLY
Thus are they undone and utterly shamed. . . . . 374 Replycacion 17
VACABONDES
So many vacabondes, so many beggers bolde, ... 245 Speke Parott 498
VAGYS
Because of theyr neglygence and of theyr wanton vagys, ... 195 Magnyfycence 1942
VAYLES
Must cast up theyr blacke vayles . . . . 256 Collyn Clout 396
VAYLETH
There vayleth no resonynge; . . . . 281 Why Come Ye 104
VAYNE
All left alone, alas, he fawte in vayne! . . . . 32 Dol Dethe 104
I shall the angre ones in every vayne! . . . . 55 Bowge 326
But all this is in vayne, ... 77 Phy Sparrow 208
And all that was in vayne, ... 89 Phy Sparrow 694
Ne worde he wrote in vayne. . . . . 91 Phy Sparrow 803
Tusche, holde your pece! Your langage is vayne. . . . . 147 Magnyfycence 251
Why that ye sayd our langage was in vayne. . . . . 147 Magnyfycence 263
What! Wyll ye waste wynde and prate thus in vayne? . . . . . . 179 Magnyfycence 1403
VAYNED
That are so quyckely vayned, ... 99 Phy Sparrow 1121
VAYNE GLORIE
And your vayne glorie . . . . 381 Replycacion 251
VAYNE GLORIOUS
of the moche vayne glorious pipplyng wynde, ... 373 Replycacion I

Term / Quotation	Page	Title	Line
VAYNE GLORY			
To tell of vayne glory;	284	Why Come Ye	228
Presumcyon and vayne glory,	293	Why Come Ye	574
VAYNE GLORYOUS			
Of this vayne gloryous best,	309	Why Come Ye	1213
VAYNES			
The Indy saphyre blew /Her vaynes doth ennew;	97	Phy Sparrow	1032
The streynes of her vaynes as asure Inde blewe,	183	Magnyfycence	1553
VAYNGLORIOUS			
of vaynglorious pompe and surcudant elacyon,	375	Replycacion	1
VAYNGLORY			
A playne example of worldly vaynglory,	212	Magnyfycence	2514
VAYNYS			
Bewayle thy fortune, with vaynys wan and blo.	45	Balettys5	3
VALE			
Then let them vale a bonet of their proud sayle,	138	Ven Tongues	32
Warbelynge in the vale	340	Garlande	999
VALERIUS			
Lucilius and Valerius Maximus by name;	322	Garlande	380
VALERY			
Nother Phalary, /Rehersyd in Valery,	67	Hauke	199
VALIANT			
Valiant as Hector in every marciall nede,	33	Dol Dethe	138
VALIAUNCE			
His valiaunce to expresse,	369	Albany	400
VALIAUNT			
So noble a man, so valiaunt lorde and knyght	30	Dol Dethe	29
That valiaunt knyght, /Putte you to flyght /By his valyaunce.	360	Albany	40
Lyke to Duke Josue /And the valiaunt Machube,	370	Albany	443
VALY			
Tully, valy, strawe, let be I say!	35	Man Margery	5
VALYANT			
The nobelnes of the northe, this valyant lorde and knyght,	31	Dol Dethe	85
VALYAUNCE			
That valiaunt knyght, /Putte you to flyght /By his valyaunce.	360	Albany	42
VALYAUNT			
Lyke a valyaunt man;	87	Phy Sparrow	633
VALYAUNTLY			
Ye thought ye dyd yet valyauntly;	118	Ag Scottes	99
VALYAUNTOLYE			
Ye thought ye dyde it full valyauntolye,	113	Scot Kynge	9
VALUE			
Gowers Englysh is olde /And of no value told;	91	Phy Sparrow	785
told] 'is tolde' Wyght 1553, Kitson 1560.6, Marshe 1568			
VANYSSHYTH			
How wysdom thorowe wantonnesse vanysshyth away;	213	Magnyfycence	2556
VANYTE			
and fle /From worldly vanyte	247	Collyn Clout	41
worldly] 'wordly' Kele 1545.1			
VANTONNESSE			
And with sad cyrcumspeccyon correcte my vantonnesse.	212	Magnyfycence	2509
VARY			
Frome that I have sayde in no poynt doth vary,	316	Garlande	163
VARYABLENESSE			
Fyckell falsenesse, /Varyablenesse, /With unstablenesse.	247	Collyn Clout	45
VARYANS			
And make moche varyans	260	Collyn Clout	554
VARYAUNCE			
Of fortune this the chaunce /Standeth on varyaunce:	81	Phy Sparrow	367
She dawnsyth varyaunce with mutabylyte,	197	Magnyfycence	2026
VARYETH			
How oftyn fortune varyeth in an howre,	312	Garlande	11
VARNYSHE			
Your face I wyse to varnyshe	127	Garnesche3	121
VARRY			
Lyst with you to varry	367	Albany	341
VASSAYLES			
'Ye horsons, ye vassayles,	294	Why Come Ye	602
VASSALL			
And of this poore vassall	293	Why Come Ye	557
VAUNTE-PARLER			
With, 'Skyre-galyard, prowde palyard, vaunte-parler, ye prate!'	244	Speke Parott	433
VAWTE			
Envawtyd with rubies the vawte was of this place.	325	Garlande	476
VELYARDE			
Vyle velyarde, thou must not nowe my dynt withstande;	193	Magnyfycence	1878
VELVET			
It had a velvet cap,	74	Phy Sparrow	120
Crimsin velvet for your bawdry.	130	Garnesche5	40
VENEMOUS			
And with a venemous arow	104	Phy Sparrow	1292
By the venemous serpent,	104	Phy Sparrow	1326
Against Venemous Tongues	136	Ven Tongues	1
More venemous and much more virulent	138	Ven Tongues	53
VENEMOUSLY			
As it reprehendyng, /And venemously stingyng,	120	Ag Scottes2	10
VENEMOWS			
By the venemows serpent	349	Garlande	1319

VENGEAUNCE —VERTEW   Page   Title   Line

VENGEAUNCE
That vengeaunce I aske and crye, ...   78   Phy Sparrow   273
And take myscheffe and vengeaunce of other mo   195   Magnyfycence 1951
What, a very vengeaunce, I say! Who is that?   199   Magnyfycence 2105
What a very vengeaunce nede all these wordys?   202   Magnyfycence 2198
A vengeaunce and dispight /On the must nedes lyght   364   Albany   234
VENGED
Of my querell soone wolde I venged be.   55   Bowge   333
VENYMOUSLY
Myght stynge the venymously!   79   Phy Sparrow   291
VENYSON
The umblis of venyson, the botell of wyne, ...   347   Garlande   1240
VENOMOWS
And with a venomows arow   348   Garlande   1285
VENQUESSHID
For though he were venquesshid, yet was he not shamyd: 316   Garlande   161
  For] 'Sithe' MS Cotton Vitellius E.x
VENTAYLES
To catche wynde with theyr ventayles.   256   Collyn Clout   398
VENUS
Dame Venus of all pleasure, ...   102   Phy Sparrow   1227
Howe lusty Venus quaked, ...   270   Collyn Clout   945
VERDURIS
A cronell of lawrell with verduris light and darke   334   Garlande   776
VERELY
But as verely as ye be   78   Phy Sparrow   254
As verely my hope is, ...   93   Phy Sparrow   874
VERGESSE
Ye, Mary, somtyme - in a messe of vergesse, ...   189   Magnyfycence 1756
VERY
Her mete was very crude, ...   63   Hauke   77
  mete] 'mere' Kynge & Marche 1554
Ye hobble very homly before the kynges borde;   123   Garnesche2   10
Welth is of wysdome the very trewe probate.   140   Magnyfycence   4
Ye, syr, undoubted. Then, of very ryght, ...   148   Magnyfycence   272
And say they so in very dede?   151   Magnyfycence   378
God gyve you a very myschaunce!   154   Magnyfycence   497
A very fon, /A very asse /Wyll take upon /To compasse   164   Magnyfycence   863
A very fon, /A very asse /Wyll take upon /To compasse   164   Magnyfycence   864
A very pore /That so wyll do, ...   164   Magnyfycence   869
What, a very vengeaunce, I say! Who is that?   199   Magnyfycence 2105
What a very vengeaunce nede all these wordys?   202   Magnyfycence 2198
And therfore our Lorde sende you a very wengaunce!   203   Magnyfycence 2237
Some for very nede /Layde downe a skeyne of threde, ...   222   El Rummynge   309
Her tonge was very quycke   223   El Rummynge   337
But the very grounde /Was for to compound   229   El Rummynge   596
And meddels very lyght /In the churches ryght.   249   Collyn Clout   104
Alas, for very shame, ...   253   Collyn Clout   275
Theyr rule is very small, ...   261   Collyn Clout   609
As they were very sayntes.   269   Collyn Clout   921
They growwe very ranke   304   Why Come Ye   1001
All other transcendyng, of very congruence   313   Garlande   52
And ye shall well fynde he is a very fole;   318   Garlande   207
  well fynde] 'fynde wele' MS Cotton Vitellius E.x
Of very dwte it may not well accorde, ...   318   Garlande   212
In very dede /How ye excede.   343   Garlande   1084
VERYE
Yett dates now are deynte, and wax verye scante, ...   244   Speke Parott   440
VERMYNE
Of vermyne and of lyce   364   Albany   220
VERS
Wherto shuld I rehers /The sentens of my vers?   68   Hauke   247
VERSE
And as I stode redynge this verse myselfe allone, ...   48   Bowge   68
Tell me your mynde, me thynke ye make a verse, ...   53   Bowge   244
Then in a tabull playne /I wroute a verse or twayne, ...   68   Hauke   223
He shall synge the verse   85   Phy Sparrow   531
Make a verse of my butterfly;   172   Magnyfycence 1149
That Pety Caton can scantly construe a verse, ...   235   Speke Parott   178
There was counteryng of carollis in meter and verse   331   Garlande   705
  and] 'and in' Marshe 1568
VERSES
To rede or to spell /What these verses tell.   68   Hauke   238
In verses two or thre   106   Phy Sparrow   1378
In verses two or thre   350   Garlande   1371
In his distichon made on verses twaine.   353   Garlande   1467
  distichon] 'distincyon' †Fakes 1523
VERSYCLES
The versycles shall syng.   82   Phy Sparrow   431
VERSYFY
No? Yes, in faythe; I can versyfy.   172   Magnyfycence 1147
VERSYFYENG
With thy versyfyeng rayles /How they have tayles.   135   Dundas   30
VERSYNGE BOXE
Upon his breste he bare a versynge boxe: 52   Bowge   232
VERTEW
The topas rych and precyouse in vertew;   44   Balettys3   15
In bewte and vertew.   94   Phy Sparrow   897

VERTIBILITE — VILLAYNS

	Page	Title	Line
In beaute and vertew:	96	Phy Sparrow	993
In beautye and vertew:	97	Phy Sparrow	1026
In beaute and vertew:	98	Phy Sparrow	1058
In beaute and vertew:	98	Phy Sparrow	1087
In beauty and vertew:	99	Phy Sparrow	1111
In beaute and vertew:	100	Phy Sparrow	1140
In beaute and vertew:	100	Phy Sparrow	1165
In beautye and vertew:	101	Phy Sparrow	1189
In beaute and vertew:	102	Phy Sparrow	1212
In beaute and vertew:	102	Phy Sparrow	1235

VERTIBILITE

	Page	Title	Line
But ye are so full of vertibilite,	138	Ven Tongues	42

VERTU

	Page	Title	Line
I knowe your vertu and your lytterkture lytterkture] 'lytterature' Wynkyn de Worde 1510	59	Bowge	449
That folowe fonde fantasyes and vertu refuse.	175	Magnyfycence	1281
With vertu enbesid all tymes and howris;	334	Garlande	805
Of vertu and konnyng the well and perfight grounde; and] (1st) not in MS Cotton Vitellius E.x	336	Garlande	866
Vertu, conyng, solace, pleasure, comforte.	337	Garlande	898
Vertu, connyng, solace, pleasure, comforte.	337	Garlande	905
With vertu well renwde.	341	Garlande	1045
With vertu well renude.	342	Garlande	1053
With vertu well renude.	342	Garlande	1061
Of Vertu also the soverayne enterlude;	345	Garlande	1177

VERTUE

	Page	Title	Line
It were no vertue, it were a thynge unblyst.	144	Magnyfycence	134
For I am a vertue yf I be well used,	199	Magnyfycence	2101
Of the vertue of an unset leke;	225	El Rummynge	451
To wyse is no vertue, to medlyng, to restles;	232	Speke Parott	61
Without his vertue be greatter,	253	Collyn Clout	271
And vertue is forgotten,	261	Collyn Clout	597
Of them that have vertue by reason of cunnyng,	317	Garlande	198

VERTUES

	Page	Title	Line
Reportynge the vertues all	75	Phy Sparrow	157
Dyscrecion ys modyr of nobyll vertues all;	232	Speke Parott	51
And what vertues be resydent	369	Albany	426

VERTUOUS

	Page	Title	Line
For I rebuke no man /That vertuous is.	273	Collyn Clout	1090
For those that vertuous be	273	Collyn Clout	1092
Nor no vertuous techynge,	274	Collyn Clout	1134
Of any vertuous wrytynge;	274	Collyn Clout	1136

VERTUOUSLY

	Page	Title	Line
So vertuously that hath his dayes spente;	50	Bowge	151
To gyde them vertuously that wyll not remembre,	194	Magnyfycence	1922

VERTUOWS

	Page	Title	Line
Madame regent /I may you call /Of vertuows all.	339	Garlande	953

VERTUS

	Page	Title	Line
Be vertus well comprysid.	338	Garlande	921

VESCA

	Page	Title	Line
And of Vesca his queene,	90	Phy Sparrow	741

VESPASYAN

	Page	Title	Line
Nor Vespasyan, that bare in his nose a waspe,	182	Magnyfycence	1510

VESTMENT

	Page	Title	Line
Is it not a vestment? A, ye wante a rope.	157	Magnyfycence	604

VEWE

	Page	Title	Line
Let hym blowe now, that we may take a vewe a] 'the' MS Cotton Vitellius E.x	319	Garlande	237

VEXACYON

	Page	Title	Line
Nay, so God me helpe, it was no grete vexacyon;	189	Magnyfycence	1733

VEXED

	Page	Title	Line
That Goddes grace hath vexed you sharply	207	Magnyfycence	2352

VEXETH

	Page	Title	Line
And vexeth them day by day	282	Why Come Ye	155

VEXYD

	Page	Title	Line
Ye, syr, with adversyte I have bene vexyd;	210	Magnyfycence	2461

VICAR GENERALL

	Page	Title	Line
When wylfulnes ys vicar generall.	232	Speke Parott	54

VICE

	Page	Title	Line
With one vice importune thei playnly said nay.	31	Dol Dethe	80

VICIOUS

	Page	Title	Line
He is so ambicious, /So elate and so vicious,	308	Why Come Ye	1177

VICYOUS

	Page	Title	Line
So shamles and so vicyous, and] 'an' †Kele 1545.3	290	Why Come Ye	462

VIGOROUSLY

	Page	Title	Line
Vigorously upon them with myght and with mayne,	31	Dol Dethe	89

VIIJ

	Page	Title	Line
Now Henry the viij, Kyng of Englonde,	347	Garlande	1227

VILANE

	Page	Title	Line
That vilane hastarddis in ther furious tene,	30	Dol Dethe	24

VILANY

	Page	Title	Line
Of me with your language full of vilany.	138	Ven Tongues	48

VILLAYN

	Page	Title	Line
What have ye, villayn, forged, /And virulently dysgorged	367	Albany	320

VILLAYNS

	Page	Title	Line
A maynny of rude villayns made hym for to blede.	30	Dol Dethe	46

VINCENCIUS —VOYCE   Page   Title   Line

VINCENCIUS
With Vincencius in Speculo, that wrote noble warkis; 322   Garlande   381
VINIS
Enrailid with rosers, and vinis engrapid; 330   Garlande   656
VIOLATE
To contaminate /And to violate /The dygnyte lauryate. 126   Garnesche3   99
VIRGILL
Virgill the Mantuan, with his Eneidos; 321   Garlande   339
VIRGYLL
Of Ovyd or Virgyll, /Or of Plutharke, ... 90   Phy Sparrow   756
VIRGYNALL
So close to kepe your cloyster virgynall, ... 320   Garlande   305
Of all pure clennesse virgynall, ... 375   Replycacion   32
VIRULENT
More venemous and much more virulent 138   Ven Tongues   53
VIRULENTLY
What have ye, villayn, forged, /And virulently dysgorged ... 367   Albany   321
VISAGE
Your goodly port, your bewteous visage, ... 42   Balettys2   6
VITALL
Thow kit asonder his perfight vitall threde. 32   Dol Dethe   126
VYCARE GENERALL
The devyls vycare generall, ... 299   Why Come Ye   807
VYCARYES
Of parsons and vycaryes /They make many outcryes: 261   Collyn Clout   570
VYCE
Dyverse in style, some spared not vyce to wrythe, ... 46   Bowge   13
    wrythe] 'wryte' Wynkyn de Worde 1510, Marshe 1568
It is a perylous vyce, this envy. 58   Bowge   444
And yet there was no vyce, ... 100   Phy Sparrow   1133
And I am a vyce where I am abused. 199   Magnyfycence   2102
Vyce to revyle /And synne to exyle? 247   Collyn Clout   11
And of all maner vyce? 364   Albany   221
VYCES
As sumtyme he must vyces remorde, ... 314   Garlande   86
VYENE
And of the love betwene /Paris and Vyene; 88   Phy Sparrow   664
VYLANOUS
These vylanous false cattes 80   Phy Sparrow   338
VYLE
Vyle velyarde, thou must not nowe my dynt withstande; 193   Magnyfycence   1878
VYLLAGE
By pollynge and pyllage /In cytes and vyllage; 255   Collyn Clout   361
VYLLAYNE
The vyllayne precheth openly 275   Collyn Clout   1173
VYLLANY
Nor yet no vyllany, /But only fantasy; 100   Phy Sparrow   1134
And declareth our vyllany; 275   Collyn Clout   1174
VYLLONY
To your great vyllony, ... 380   Replycacion   245
VYNTRE
Doctours of the chayre in the Vyntre 374   Replycacion   8
VYOLATE
That wolde contemminate, /And that wolde vyolate, ... 264   Collyn Clout   705
    contemminate] 'contaminate' Marshe 1568, MS Harley 2252
VYOLENCE
And with wordis of vyolence, ... 305   Why Come Ye   1065
VYOLET
She is the vyolet, ... 98   Phy Sparrow   1050
My vyolet amyabyll, /My joye inexplicabill, ... 237   Speke Parott   243
The jeloffer well set, /The propre vyolet; 340   Garlande   984
This primerose pereles, this propre vyolet, ... 352   Garlande   1447
VYSAGE
My vysage pale and dead, ... 73   Phy Sparrow   60
With vysage blacke and blo; 73   Phy Sparrow   75
With vysage wan, /As swart as tan; 94   Phy Sparrow   910
    swart] 'wart' †Kele 1545.2, Wyght 1553, Kitson 1560.6,
    'swarte' Marshe 1568
In her vysage a skar 97   Phy Sparrow   1045
For her vysage /It woldt aswage /A mannes courage. 214   El Rummynge   9
The ruddy shamefastnes in her vysage fyll, ... 337   Garlande   888
VYSE
In him it was no vyse; 76   Phy Sparrow   174
Yet be meanes of that vyse 378   Replycacion   131
Therfore I vyse you to forsake 382   Replycacion   297
VYSER
Ye, but thou can play the fole without a vyser. 173   Magnyfycence   1177
VYSYTACYON
It is foly to grudge agaynst his vysytacyon. 196   Magnyfycence   1990
VYSYTE
I vysyte them somtyme with blaynes and with sores; 194   Magnyfycence   1901
And some I vysyte with brennynge of fyre; 194   Magnyfycence   1908
And some I vysyte [with] batayle, warre, and murther, ... 194   Magnyfycence   1912
    with] 'to' †Rastell & Treveris C 1530, B
I vysyte theyr faders and moders with sekenesse; 194   Magnyfycence   1925
I vysyte them and stryke them with many sore plagys. 195   Magnyfycence   1943
VOYCE
Bycause his voyce is lowde, ... 82   Phy Sparrow   439

VOYD — WAY

Page | Title | Line

VOYD
There is no Englysh voyd,	91	Phy Sparrow	795
Is voyd of all good grace;	124	Garnesche3	10

VOYDE
Yet is she fayne, /Voyde of disdayn,	112	Calliope	18
To face, to brace, /All voyde of grace,	116	Ag Scottes	34
So out of frame, /So voyde of shame,	116	Ag Scottes	38
Let se this checke yf ye voyde canne.	148	Magnyfycence	297
Lyke Pharao, voyde of grace,	305	Why Come Ye	1066
Your chefe cheftayne, /Voyde of all brayne,	360	Albany	49

VOLUMES
For, as I have rede in volumes olde,	137	Ven Tongues	5

VOLUMIS
Sex volumis engrosid together it doth containe.	354	Garlande	1502

VOLUMYS
Oracius to recorde in his volumys olde,	143	Magnyfycence	114
There came John Bochas with his volumys grete;	322	Garlande	365

VOLVELL
In the volvell, in the quadrant and in the astroloby,	234	Speke Parott	135
He turnyd his tirikkis, his volvell ran fast,	354	Garlande	1517

VOUCHESAF
He to vouchesaf, by thy mediacioun,	35	Dol Dethe	209

VOUCHESAFE
Vouchesafe to defend yow agayne the brawlyng scolde	241	Speke Parott	361

VOWCHESAFE
She to vowchesafe me to informe and ken;	335	Garlande	825

WACHE
By your soth? Ye, and there is suche a wache,	150	Magnyfycence	350

WACHYNG
So myche prevye wachyng in cold wynters nyghtes;	246	Speke Parott	512

WADE
That I wyll nat wade	266	Collyn Clout	781

WADED
and have waded but weakly in his thre maner of clerkly workes,	374	Replycacion	I

WADYD
She wadyd over, she found a man	42	Balettys1	17

WADYTHE
Lucina she wadythe among the watry floddes,	239	Speke Parott	285

WAG
But moveatur terra, let the world wag,	233	Speke Parott	88

WAGE
Lyghte lyme-fynger, he toke none other wage.	60	Bowge	509

WAGES
Theyr wages were nat payde.	285	Why Come Ye	253

WAGGE
I sawe a wethercocke wagge with the wynde!	191	Magnyfycence	1821

WAGGES
It wygges and it wagges /Lyke tawny saffron bagges;	218	El Rummynge	137

WAGGYNGE
Somtyme I laughe at waggynge of a straw,	168	Magnyfycence	1014

WAGGYS
With, 'Jayst ye, Jenet of Spayne, for your tayll waggys,'	43	Balettys2	18

WAGTAYLE
The goldfynche, the wagtayle;	81	Phy Sparrow	395

WAY
'Walke forth your way, ye cost me nought;	36	Man Margery	22
By way of apostrofacyon	62	Hauke	30
By way of exclamacyon,	78	Phy Sparrow	274
The way of thurifycation	84	Phy Sparrow	522
His grace beyng out of the way;	119	Ag Scottes	144
Ye myght no better a way;	125	Garnesche3	49
Bycause course of measure - yf I be in the way:	146	Magnyfycence	213
By the way as I ryde and walke -	151	Magnyfycence	375
Counterfet eyrnest by way of playes.	152	Magnyfycence	427
Counterfet letters by the way of sleyght;	152	Magnyfycence	439
Wolde take, in the way of counterfet charyte,	154	Magnyfycence	489
Let se, fynde you a better way.	156	Magnyfycence	560
Mary, syr, Cokermowthe is a good way hens.	170	Magnyfycence	1061
And as for me, I take but one folysshe way,	170	Magnyfycence	1076
But do as ye lyst and take your owne way.	185	Magnyfycence	1604
I trowe it be a frost, for the way is slydder;	191	Magnyfycence	1816
But by the way of fansy insolence.	200	Magnyfycence	2116
For where sad cyrcumspeccyon is longe out of the way,	209	Magnyfycence	2427
But wyfull waywardnesse muste walke out of the way;	211	Magnyfycence	2490
Phronessys for frenessys may not hold her way.	232	Speke Parott	47
That they cannot say in Greke, rydynge by the way,	234	Speke Parott	146
'Come downe, on the devyll way.'	263	Collyn Clout	670
devyll] 'deuils' Marshe 1568, 'devyll' MS Harley 2252			
That I speke out of the way.	273	Collyn Clout	1094
The way to heven or to hell!'	277	Collyn Clout	1226
By way of commissyon	299	Why Come Ye	799
Some ranne the nexte way, sume ranne abowte.	319	Garlande	252
When they were past and wente forth on there way,	327	Garlande	526
Of a dysour, a devyl way, grew a jentilman,	330	Garlande	635
The myllar was loth to be out of the way,	351	Garlande	1414
And ryn your way apace.	367	Albany	354
By way of their devocion	378	Replycacion	136
That bringes you out of the way	379	Replycacion	170

WAYE —WALKE	Page	Title	Line

WAYE
And how I maye that waye and meanes fynde.'	49	Bowge	109
And to mewarde the strayte waye he toke.	51	Bowge	194
Our kynge than beynge out of the waye;	114	Scot Kynge	45
Sir Dunkan, in the devill waye,	367	Albany	330

WAYED
Wysely let these wordes in your mynde be wayed:	185	Magnyfycence	1593

WAYES
To have that connynge and wayes that ye have!	53	Bowge	261
I hate this wayes agayne you that they take!	59	Bowge	471
this] 'these' Wynkyn de Worde 1510			
Well, I am content your wayes to take.	144	Magnyfycence	155
It is but a maddynge, these wayes that ye use.	148	Magnyfycence	285
To counterfet I can by praty wayes:	152	Magnyfycence	424
Devysynge the meanes and wayes that I can,	160	Magnyfycence	708
For to use suche haftynge and crafty wayes.	187	Magnyfycence	1678
Than of wanhope thrughe the unhappy wayes,	206	Magnyfycence	2337
Every man after his maner of wayes,	233	Speke Parott	90
And all wayes to chase	264	Collyn Clout	699
For reporte ryseth many deverse wayes.	317	Garlande	181
For] not MS Cotton Vitellius E.x			
Moche better other wayes.	378	Replycacion	150

WAYGHT
Thy wordes be but wynde, never they have no wayght.	156	Magnyfycence	578

WAYLE
I wayle, I wepe, I sobbe, I sigh ful sore	29	Dol Dethe	1
The plover with us to wayle;	82	Phy Sparrow	417

WAYLED
I wept and I wayled,	72	Phy Sparrow	23

WAYTE
For he coude well upon a casket wayte,	60	Bowge	507
And wayte upon me. And yet for a memory,	180	Magnyfycence	1447
I am a mynyon to wayte apon a quene;	231	Speke Parott	19
a (2)] 'the' Lant 1545, Kynge & Marche 1554, Day 1560, Marshe 1568			

WAYWARD
Wytles, wayward, Syr Wrag-wrag,	133	Garnesche5	149

WAYWARDE
By waywarde wylfulnes let eche thynge be convayed;	185	Magnyfycence	1594
Thou hast bene so waywarde, so wranglyng, and so wrothsome,	205	Magnyfycence	2293
to all waywarde or frowarde altercacyons	382	Replycacion	R

WAYWARDLY
That lyst for to jangyll /And waywardly to wrangyll	120	Ag Scottes2	6
Waywardly wrowght she hath in the,	130	Garnesche5	15

WAYWARDNESSE
But wyfull waywardnesse muste walke out of the way;	211	Magnyfycence	2490

WAYWYRDE
Wranglynge, waywyrde, wytles, wraw, and nothyng meke.	124	Garnesche2	40

WAKE
And wake all nyghte and slepe tyll it be none.	57	Bowge	382
Me often for to wake	76	Phy Sparrow	165
Shall watche at this wake;	82	Phy Sparrow	437
How Scipion dyd wake	88	Phy Sparrow	668
The first twayne to wake;	358	Garlande2	11

WAKESTE
Or wakeste thow, Besse,	237	Speke Parott	239

WAKYST
Thou blynkerd blowboll, thou wakyst to late;	42	Balettys1	24

WALD
Hop Lobyn of Lowdeon wald have e byt of bred;	232	Speke Parott	72

WALES
What tidings at Tot[nam], what newis in Wales,	139	Ven Tongues	64
Totnam] 'Totman' Marshe 1568			
Of tydynges in Wales,	223	El Rummynge	353

WALIS
Fynde no mo suche fro Wanflete to Walis.	347	Garlande	1218

WALYS
From Wynchelsee to Walys, /Non est braynsycke talys,	70	Hauke	323

WALK
Correct fyrst thy self; walk, and be nought!	38	Coystrowne1	62

WALKE
'Walke forth your way, ye cost me nought;	36	Man Margery	22
By myne avyse use not with him to walke.	52	Bowge	210
Sche praiid yow walke, on Goddes halfe!	131	Garnesche5	60
Dunde, Dunbar, /Walke, Scot, /Walke, sot,	136	Dundas	61
Dunde, Dunbar, /Walke, Scot, /Walke, sot,	136	Dundas	62
By the way as I ryde and walke -	151	Magnyfycence	375
Then for the season that I here shall walke,	159	Magnyfycence	691
Holde thy pease! Measure shall frome us walke.	166	Magnyfycence	949
Ye, walke he must; it was no better worth.	189	Magnyfycence	1736
I wyll walke nowe with my beggers baggys,	197	Magnyfycence	2036
At lyberte to wander and walke over all,	201	Magnyfycence	2149
But wyfull waywardnesse muste walke out of the way;	211	Magnyfycence	2490
But, whan they shoulde walke,	230	El Rummynge	613
And wandrynge as I walke,	254	Collyn Clout	287
Some walke about in melottes,	268	Collyn Clout	864
Stande, walke, or ryde -	295	Why Come Ye	635
To walke where we lyst, let us somwhat fynde	328	Garlande	564

WALKYNGE — WANDRYNGE

	Page	Title	Line
To walke on this walle she bed I sholde not stint;	328	Garlande	571
Walke, Scot, go begge a byt	362	Albany	154

WALKYNGE

	Page	Title	Line
And whan he came walkynge soberly,	51	Bowge	190
But whether art thou walkynge, in faythe unfaynyd?	161	Magnyfycence	762
Thus passid we forth walkynge unto the pretory	325	Garlande	477

WALL

	Page	Title	Line
He was ther bulwarke, ther paves and ther wall,	30	Dol Dethe	48
For I have gravyd her wythin the secret wall	45	Balettys3	48
And pyke a locke and clyme a wall.	174	Magnyfycence	1227
Bytwene the tap[pet] and the wall.	174	Magnyfycence	1233
tappet] 'tap' †Rastell & Treveris C 1530, B			
That lustely they lepe somtyme theyr cloyster wall.	201	Magnyfycence	2150
Betwene the cup and the wall,	226	El Rummynge	473
shall be his protectyon, his pavys and his wall.	236	Speke Parott	203
Out of the stony wall,	254	Collyn Clout	304
Lyke urcheons in a stone wall,	283	Why Come Ye	166
urcheons] 'heons' †Kele 1545.3, Marshe 1568			
Enhardid adyment the sement of your wall!	320	Garlande	306
Of dyamauntis pointed was the wall;	325	Garlande	473
the] 'the rokky' Marshe 1568			
Then I me lent, and loked over the wall:	329	Garlande	602
He wrate of a muse throw a mud wall;	351	Garlande	1384

WALLE

	Page	Title	Line
Betweyn the tappett and the walle;	131	Garnesche5	75
To walke on this walle she bed I sholde not stint;	328	Garlande	571

WALLES

	Page	Title	Line
Within those walles	83	Phy Sparrow	472
In double w[a]lles now he dooth dreme.	115	Scot Kynge	58
walles] 'welles' †Fakes 1513			
And assay to crepe /Within the noble walles	249	Collyn Clout	126
Hangynge about the walles	270	Collyn Clout	940

WALLET

	Page	Title	Line
She brought them in a wallet;	226	El Rummynge	461
She] 'Some' Day 1560, Marshe 1568			

WALLYS

	Page	Title	Line
Aut sanguis vitulorum, /Was offryd within the wallys,	66	Hauke	172

WALNUTTES

	Page	Title	Line
Some brought walnuttes,	225	El Rummynge	437

WALOW

	Page	Title	Line
Our Grekys ye walow in the washbol Argolycorum;	235	Speke Parott	150

WALS

	Page	Title	Line
Thus within the wals /Of holy church to deale,	65	Hauke	134

WALSHEMANNYS

	Page	Title	Line
It is no foly to use the Walshemannys hoos.	347	Garlande	1239

WALTER

	Page	Title	Line
And some I make in a rope to totter and walter;	194	Magnyfycence	1910

WALTOMS

	Page	Title	Line
As wyse as Waltoms calfe,	266	Collyn Clout	809

WAMBLETH

	Page	Title	Line
A, howe my stomake wambleth! I am all in a swete.	185	Magnyfycence	1617

WAMBLYNGE

	Page	Title	Line
For ofte tymes suche a wamblynge goth over my harte;	185	Magnyfycence	1620

WAN

	Page	Title	Line
The ryvers rowth, the waters wan;	42	Balettys1	15
Bewayle thy fortune, with vaynys wan and blo.	45	Balettys5	3
Whych cytie myscreantys wan,	67	Hauke	214
How Jason it wan,	87	Phy Sparrow	632
With vysage wan, /As swart as tan;	94	Phy Sparrow	910
swart] 'wart' †Kele 1545.2, Wyght 1553, Kitson 1560.6, 'swarte' Marshe 1568			
By marcyall strength /He wan at length;	104	Phy Sparrow	1306
Wan they the felde and lost theyr kynge?	115	Ag Scottes	3
They say they had /And wan the felde /With spere and shelde!	116	Ag Scottes	15
Ye wan nothyng there but a mow:	131	Garnesche5	50
Ye wan nothyng there but a skorne;	131	Garnesche5	51
Her colour was full wan –	222	El Rummynge	318
Lost all his father wan.	285	Why Come Ye	271
all his] 'al that his' Toy 1553, Kitson 1560.7, Marshe 1568			
Whiche his lyvenge wan	293	Why Come Ye	554
The waters wax wan,	301	Why Come Ye	890
By merciall strength /He wan at length;	349	Garlande	1299
How than lyke a man he wan the barbican	351	Garlande	1397
The colour dedely, swarte, blo and wan	351	Garlande	1399

WANDER

	Page	Title	Line
At lyberte to wander and walke over all,	201	Magnyfycence	2149

WANDERYNGE

	Page	Title	Line
And thy wyt wanderynge here and there,	170	Magnyfycence	1074

WANDRED

	Page	Title	Line
They wandred ay and stode styll in no stede.	58	Bowge	423
And all tyme wandred I thus to and fro,	326	Garlande	516

WANDRING

	Page	Title	Line
Wytlesse wandring to and fro!'	376	Replycacion	74

WANDRYNG

	Page	Title	Line
Of wandryng of the mone, the course of the sun,	331	Garlande	691

WANDRYNGE

	Page	Title	Line
And hath so mased a wandrynge wyt?	172	Magnyfycence	1144
And wandrynge as I walke,	254	Collyn Clout	287

WANE—WAR

	Page	Title	Line
Forthwith, I say, thus wandrynge in my thought,	325	Garlande	456
WANE			
For sylkes are wane.	302	Why Come Ye	920
WANFLETE			
Fynde no mo suche fro Wanflete to Walis.	347	Garlande	1218
WANHOPE			
Than of wanhope thrughe the unhappy wayes,	206	Magnyfycence	2337
Wynde you from wanhope and aquaynte you with me.	206	Magnyfycence	2340
WANNE			
Wanne, and blewe as lead:	73	Phy Sparrow	61
Nor yet [C]ypyo, that noble Cartage wanne,	182	Magnyfycence	1512
Cypyo] 'Typyo' †Rastell & Treveris C 1530, B			
For worldly shame I wax bothe wanne and bloo.	198	Magnyfycence	2054
Hys wolvys hede, wanne, bloo as lede, gapythe over the crowne:	244	Speke Parott	434
WANT			
Of aureat poems they want ellumynynge;	32	Dol Dethe	128
Womanhod, wanton, ye want!	40	Coystrowne4	1
WANTE			
We wante no wynde to passe now over all;	49	Bowge	128
Your drapry ye ded wante	125	Garnesche3	52
Ye wante but a wylde flyeng bolte to shote at the buttes.	148	Magnyfycence	294
Is it not a vestment? A, ye wante a rope.	157	Magnyfycence	604
WANTID			
Thei wantid nothynge but the laurell;	323	Garlande	397
WANTYD			
He wantyd wyt her love to wyn:	42	Balettys1	12
Ye wantyd wyt, sir, at a worde;	119	Ag Scottes	147
WANTYS			
That there wantys grace	300	Why Come Ye	849
WANTYTH			
That wyt he wantyth when he hath moste nede.	175	Magnyfycence	1261
WANTYTHE			
But reason and wytte wantythe theyr provynciall,	232	Speke Parott	53
For he wantythe of hys wyttes that all wold rule alone;	240	Speke Parott	329
WANTON			
This wanton clarkis be nyse allway.	35	Man Margery	2
Womanhod, wanton, ye want!	40	Coystrowne4	1
Ware, ware, the mare wynsyth wyth her wanton hele!	43	Balettys2	22
With his wanton eye.	76	Phy Sparrow	182
Was somwhat wanton I wene;	87	Phy Sparrow	637
And of theyr wanton wylles,	88	Phy Sparrow	681
By your wanton wyll, syr, at a worde,	114	Scot Kynge	48
It is a wanton thynge, this Lyberte.	147	Magnyfycence	240
What! Wanton, wanton, nowe well ymet!	153	Magnyfycence	456
What! Wanton, wanton, nowe well ymet!	153	Magnyfycence	456
By me conveyed is wanton insolence;	177	Magnyfycence	1335
Because of theyr neglygence and of theyr wanton vagys,	195	Magnyfycence	1942
Alasse my foly! Alasse my wanton wyll!	198	Magnyfycence	2062
In youth to be wanton, and let them have theyr wyll –	200	Magnyfycence	2137
Determyne to amende all your wanton excesse;	208	Magnyfycence	2409
Wythe my beke bente, and my lytell wanton iye,	231	Speke Parott	15
and] not in Lant 1545, Kynge and Marche 1554, Day 1560, Marshe 1568			
Of my wanton conseyt, unde depromo	233	Speke Parott	95
Lyke a wanton, whan I wyll, I rele to and froo.	233	Speke Parott	109
And other wanton warkes /Whan the nyght darkes.	251	Collyn Clout	194
And her wanton wodicocke.	252	Collyn Clout	219
Spent among wanton lasses;	257	Collyn Clout	424
With wanton wenches wynkyng!	270	Collyn Clout	968
With Dalyda to mell, /That wanton damosell.	284	Why Come Ye	212
that] 'the' Kitson 1560.7, Marshe 1568			
Of this wanton scrowle.	300	Why Come Ye	831
A wanton wenche and wele coude bake a cake;	351	Garlande	1413
Thynke what ye wyll /Of this wanton byll;	353	Garlande	1454
Of Lovers Testamentis and of There Wanton Wyllis,	354	Garlande	1496
WANTONES			
From worldly wantones,	270	Collyn Clout	974
WANTONLY			
And nothynge wantonly,	98	Phy Sparrow	1068
That wantonly can wynke and wynche with her hele.	197	Magnyfycence	2023
And how that it was wantonly spent;	347	Garlande	1244
WANTONLYE			
For trowthe in parabyll ye wantonlye pronounce,	241	Speke Parott	364
WANTONNESSE			
Take sad dyreccyon, and leve this wantonnesse.	144	Magnyfycence	149
How wysdom thorowe wantonnesse vanysshyth away;	213	Magnyfycence	2556
WAR			
What movyd you agayn hym to war or to fight?	31	Dol Dethe	62
O cruell Mars, thou dedly god of war!	32	Dol Dethe	113
With our kyng royall war to mayntayne.	119	Ag Scottes	152
But yf yt war Syr Tyrmagant that tyrnyd without nall;	121	Garnesche1	4
I advyse yow beware of thys war, rannge yow in aray.	123	Garnesche2	33
Whan ye war yonger of age	124	Garnesche3	24
Ye war a kechyn page, /A dyshwasher, a dryvyll,	124	Garnesche3	25
In dud frese ye war schrynyd,	125	Garnesche3	46
If thow war metely machchyd.	128	Garnesche3	181
Sche seyd ye war coluryd with cole dust;	131	Garnesche5	53
For ye war smery, lyke a sele,	131	Garnesche5	58

WARANT —WARKE   Page   Title   Line

```
And ye war herey, lyke a calfe;                          131   Garnesche5      59
If thow war aquentyd with alle                           133   Garnesche5     138
There hath ben greate war                                223   El Rummynge    358
We have cast up our war,                                 282   Why Come Ye    140
Of the feytis of war                                     297   Why Come Ye    719
Enyus that wrate of mercyall war at lengthe;             321   Garlande       347
With the Romayns that made war,                          363   Albany         193
```
WARANT
```
It was a ronner; nay, fole, I warant her blode warme.    191   Magnyfycence  1811
Nay, to wrangle, I warant the, it is but a stone-caste.  201   Magnyfycence  2174
Goddys fote! I warant you I am a gentylman borne;        203   Magnyfycence  2216
By the masse, I warant the, I wyll not be bracyd.        203   Magnyfycence  2221
```
WARAUNT
```
I waraunt you I wyll not go away.                        163   Magnyfycence   820
Nay, nay; for lesse I waraunt you to be sped,            184   Magnyfycence  1571
Ye, by my trouthe, I shall waraunt you for me,           187   Magnyfycence  1669
And I shall waraunt you welth and lyberte.               190   Magnyfycence  1766
I waraunt you I have gyven it a lasshe.                  201   Magnyfycence  2165
```
WARBELYNGE
```
The requiem masse to synge, /Softly warbelynge,           81   Phy Sparrow    402
  Softly] 'Loftly' Marshe 1568
Warbelynge in the vale                                   340   Garlande       999
```
WARBLYNG
```
The threstyl with her warblyng;                           83   Phy Sparrow    460
```
WARBLYNGE
```
Warblynge with his stryngus                              384   Replycacion    349
```
WARDE
```
The warde with yow was skante.                           125   Garnesche3      53
```
WARDEYN
```
Take him, wardeyn of the Flete,                          275   Collyn Clout  1165
'Wardeyn of the Flete,                                   289   Why Come Ye    425
```
WARE
```
Ware, ware, the mare wynsyth wyth her wanton hele!        43   Balettys2       22
Ware, ware, the mare wynsyth wyth her wanton hele!        43   Balettys2       22
Ware gallyng in the widders, ware of that wrenche!        43   Balettys2       25
Ware gallyng in the widders, ware of that wrenche!        43   Balettys2       25
Ware yet, I rede you, of Fortunes double cast,            45   Balettys4        3
Ware of the lesard lyeth lurkyng in the gras.             45   Balettys4        7
'Forsoth,' quod I, 'to bye some of youre ware.'           48   Bowge           79
But, as me thoughte, he ware on hym a cloke               51   Bowge          177
His elbowe bare, he ware his gere so nye,                 56   Bowge          361
All that he wereth, it is borowed ware;                   60   Bowge          489
Er I was ware, behynde me he sayde 'Bo!'                  60   Bowge          500
Here after foloweth the boke entytuled Ware the Hauke    61   Hauke            I
PROLOGUS SKELTONIDIS LAUREATI SUPER WARE THE HAWKE        61   Hauke            R
Ware the hauke!                                           68   Hauke          252
Doctor Dawcocke? /Ware the hawke!                         69   Hauke          266
Domine Dawcocke? /Ware the hawke!                         69   Hauke          276
Doctor Dawkocke? /Ware the hawke!                         69   Hauke          285
  Ware] 'Whare' †Lant 1545
Domine Dawcocke? /Ware the hawke!                         70   Hauke          296
Doctor Dawcock! /Ware the hawke!                          70   Hauke          306
Domine Dawkock? /Ware the hawke!                          70   Hauke          319
  Ware] 'Whare' †Lant 1545
Doctor Dawcoke! /Ware the hawke!                          70   Hauke          330
At Gynys when ye ware /But a slendyr spere,              125   Garnesche3      40
Stop a tyd, and be welle ware                            133   Garnesche5     162
By me is conveyed mykyll praty ware -                    177   Magnyfycence  1340
Or ever we were ware, brought us in adversyte,           193   Magnyfycence  1863
Of Elynour for her ware,                                 228   El Rummynge    544
'But ware the cat, Parot, ware the fals cat!'            233   Speke Parott    99
'But ware the cat, Parot, ware the fals cat!'            233   Speke Parott    99
Ware, ryat, Parrot, ware ryot, ware that!                233   Speke Parott   101
Ware, ryat, Parrot, ware ryot, ware that!                233   Speke Parott   101
Ware, ryat, Parrot, ware ryot, ware that!                233   Speke Parott   101
Ware the wether cocke /Of the steple of Poules.          255   Collyn Clout   339
He ware a cardynals hat;                                 297   Why Come Ye    743
In comparyson of that whiche I ware.                     343   Garlande      1107
Be well ware what ye say.                                367   Albany         331
```
WARELY
```
Howe warely they wrangle!                                255   Collyn Clout   331
```
WARENT
```
Say trouth? Yes, yes, by lakyn, I shall the warent,      154   Magnyfycence   506
```
WARY
```
Thus with yow sche ded wary,                             126   Garnesche3      75
What begger art thou, that thus doth banne and wary?     203   Magnyfycence  2238
To wary and to kepe /From theyr goostly shepe,           250   Collyn Clout   154
```
WARK
```
At me, that medeled nothyng with youre wark.              38   Coystrownel     61
```
WARKE
```
Advertysyng you, madame, to warke more secretly,          43   Balettys2       39
The kestrell in all this warke                            86   Phy Sparrow    569
And all the hole warke                                    87   Phy Sparrow    642
And mar all they warke;                                   91   Phy Sparrow    799
To gete me fro them I had moche warke.                   150   Magnyfycence   361
A carter a courtyer, it is a worthy warke,               153   Magnyfycence   483
Cockys armys! This is a warke, I trowe.                  170   Magnyfycence  1094
And can not set herselfe to warke,                       174   Magnyfycence  1230
```

WARKES —WAS

	Page	Title	Line
I wolde hauke whylest my hede dyd warke,	184	Magnyfycence	1563
I wote never howe they warke,	249	Collyn Clout	119
And a brennynge sparke /Of Luthers warke,	260	Collyn Clout	543
This is a wonderous warke!	272	Collyn Clout	1048
It is a wonders warke.	283	Why Come Ye	173
That this warke began	301	Why Come Ye	894
By whose suggestyon /I toke on hand this warke, suggestyon] 'subjectyon' MS Rawlinson C. 813	309	Why Come Ye	1204
He can never leve warke whylis it is wele.	333	Garlande	763
'I have contryvyd for you a goodly warke,	334	Garlande	774
God geve them good spede there warke to begin!	334	Garlande	793
And for your sake how fast to warke they fall:	335	Garlande	811
In helpyng to warke my laurell grene	342	Garlande	1074
Of this warke they had so great delyght,	343	Garlande	1110
At the castell of Warke,	359	Albany	30
At the castell of Warke.	362	Albany	148
About hym a parke /Of a madde warke,	365	Albany	268

WARKES

And other wanton warkes /Whan the nyght darkes.	251	Collyn Clout	194
That but if my warkes therto be agreable,	324	Garlande	439

WARKIS

With Vincencius in Speculo, that wrote noble warkis;	322	Garlande	381
Of broken warkis wrought many a goodly thyng,	334	Garlande	801
For Latin warkis /Be good for clerkis,	355	Garlande	1542

WARKYS

In all your warkys more grace shall ye fynde;	211	Magnyfycence	2485
For whoo lokythe wyselye in your warkys may fynde	239	Speke Parott	296

WARLDE

That all the warlde wyll spye your shame.	132	Garnesche5	111
How the warlde is conveyed.	298	Why Come Ye	783

WARME

It was a ronner; nay, fole, I warant her blode warme.	191	Magnyfycence	1811

WARNE

For by measure I warne you we thynke to be gydyd;	145	Magnyfycence	184
But one thynge I warne you, prece forth and be bolde.	184	Magnyfycence	1582
To reche at a rat — I coude not her warne.	191	Magnyfycence	1809
I warne you beware of to moche lyberte,	199	Magnyfycence	2088
Beware of hym, I warne you; for and ye wist and] 'if' Marshe 1568	333	Garlande	754

WARNED

Nowe I rede the beware. I have warned the twyse.	202	Magnyfycence	2185

WARRE

Warre with our kynge to meyntayne.	114	Scot Kynge	55
Ay warre and warre /In every place.	166	Magnyfycence	914
Ay warre and warre /In every place.	166	Magnyfycence	914
And some I vysyte [with] batayle, warre, and murther, with] 'to' †Rastell & Treveris C 1530, B	194	Magnyfycence	1912
Torde! Thou arte good to be a man of warre.	202	Magnyfycence	2179
And agayne thy maker thou hast made suche warre,	205	Magnyfycence	2302
Suche temporall warre and bate	269	Collyn Clout	913
And of his Pompeyus warre,	270	Collyn Clout	957
Put up his sworde, for he cowde make no warre,	312	Garlande	5
That bararag blowyth in every mercyall warre,	319	Garlande	236
Ye have in feates of warre.	364	Albany	225

WARSE

Thow xalte beholde no wher a warse;	130	Garnesche5	17
All is warse and warse.	282	Why Come Ye	135
All is warse and warse.	282	Why Come Ye	135

WART

And whan I perceyved /Her wart and conceyved,	98	Phy Sparrow	1064

WARTE

A warte upon her cheke,	97	Phy Sparrow	1043

WAS

Whos lordshepe doutles was slayne lamentably	29	Dol Dethe	5
To slo ther owne lorde? God was not in ther mynde!	30	Dol Dethe	35
In Englande and Fraunce which gretly was redouted,	30	Dol Dethe	43
He was ther bulwarke, ther paves and ther wall,	30	Dol Dethe	48
Where was your wit and reson ye shuld have had? your] 'ys' †MS Royal 18 D.ii	30	Dol Dethe	52
He was your chyfteyne, your shelde, your chef defens,	30	Dol Dethe	57
Your hap was unhappy, to ill was your spede.	31	Dol Dethe	61
Your hap was unhappy, to ill was your spede.	31	Dol Dethe	61
The grounde of his quarell was for his sovereyn lord,	31	Dol Dethe	64
Bot ther was fals packinge or els I am begylde,	31	Dol Dethe	71
Howbeit the mater was evident and playne;	31	Dol Dethe	72
As man that was innocent of trechery or trayne,	31	Dol Dethe	86
Upon suche a sort was ille bestowde and spent.	32	Dol Dethe	98
He was envyronde aboute on every syde	32	Dol Dethe	99
For cruell[y] amonge them ther he was slayne. cruell] 'cruell' †MS Royal 18 D.ii, Marshe 1568	32	Dol Dethe	105
Alas for pite that Percy thus was spylt,	32	Dol Dethe	106
What man, remembring how shamfully he was slayn,	32	Dol Dethe	111
His noble blode never desteynyd was,	33	Dol Dethe	148
With trowth to medelle was all his hole delight,	33	Dol Dethe	152
To slo suche a lord, alas, it was grete shame. slo] 'sle' Marshe 1568	33	Dol Dethe	154
This noble man that cruelly was slayne.	34	Dol Dethe	182
He braggyth of hys byrth, that borne was full bace;	37	Coystrownel	24

WAS — WAS

	Page	Title	Line
For Jak wold be a jentylman, that late was a grome.	37	Coystrowne1	42
that was sent to hym	39	Coystrowne3	1
Hys hed was hevy, such was his hap,	41	Balettys1	5
Hys hed was hevy, such was his hap,	41	Balettys1	5
That he wyst never where he was;	42	Balettys1	10
That Dame Menolope was never half so wyse;	42	Balettys2	11
I was sore moved to aforce the same,	46	Bowge	17
And shewed that in this arte I was not sure;	46	Bowge	19
I] not in †Wynkyn de Worde 1499, 1510			
For to illumyne, she sayde, I was to dulle,	46	Bowge	20
Thus up and down my mynde was drawen and cast	47	Bowge	29
That I ne wyste what to do was beste;	47	Bowge	30
Soo sore enwered that I was, at the laste,	47	Bowge	31
There was moche noyse, anone one cryed, 'Cese!'	47	Bowge	46
Amonge all other was wrytten in her trone,	47	Bowge	65
Gave me a taunte, and sayde I was to blame	48	Bowge	70
What is thy name?' and I sayde it was Drede.	48	Bowge	77
Desyre her name was, and so she me tolde,	48	Bowge	85
The fyrste was Favell, full of flatery,	49	Bowge	134
The seconde was Suspecte, whiche that dayly	49	Bowge	136
And, though I say it, I was myselfe your frende,	50	Bowge	160
That lyned was with doubtfull doublenes.	51	Bowge	178
Me thoughte his hede was full of gelousy,	51	Bowge	192
His throte was clere and lustely coude fayne.	52	Bowge	233
Me thoughte his gowne was all furred wyth foxe.	52	Bowge	234
Me] 'My' †Wynkyn de Worde 1499			
To kepe him frome pykynge, it was a grete payne.	52	Bowge	236
Whan I loked on hym, my purse was half aferde.	52	Bowge	238
A man, but wonderly besene was he.	54	Bowge	283
His gawdy garment with Scornnys was all wrought;	54	Bowge	285
Scornnys] 'storunys' †Wynkyn de Worde 1499, 1510, 'scornes' Marshe 1568			
With Indygnacyon lyned was his hode;	54	Bowge	286
His face was belymmed as byes had hem stounge;	54	Bowge	289
It was no tyme with him to jape nor toye.	54	Bowge	290
His here was growen thorowe oute his hat.	56	Bowge	350
Thenne I behelde how he dysgysed was:	56	Bowge	351
His hede was hevy for watchynge overnyghte,	56	Bowge	352
His hose was garded with a lyste of grene,	56	Bowge	356
His cote was checked with patches rede and blewe;	56	Bowge	358
checked] 'checkered' Marshe 1568			
Of Kyrkeby Kendall was his shorte demye;	56	Bowge	359
I was ashamed so to here hym prate.	56	Bowge	373
What the devyll, man, myrthe was never one!	57	Bowge	388
was never one] 'is here within' Marshe 1568			
But there was poyntynge and noddynge with the hede,	58	Bowge	421
I dempte and drede theyr talkynge was not good.	58	Bowge	426
That one was lene and lyke a pyned goost,	58	Bowge	429
Whan that he was even at me almoost,	58	Bowge	432
Wheron was wryten this worde, Myscheve.	58	Bowge	434
His hode was syde, his cope was roset graye;	58	Bowge	440
His hode was syde, his cope was roset graye;	58	Bowge	440
Er I was ware, behynde me he sayde 'Bo!'	60	Bowge	500
He was trussed in a garmente strayte –	60	Bowge	505
And was with flyenge wery.	63	Hauke	67
The fauconer then was prest,	63	Hauke	71
prest] 'priest' Kynge & Marche 1554, Day 1560			
Her mete was very crude,	63	Hauke	77
mete] 'mere' Kynge & Marche 1554			
She was not clene ensaymed,	63	Hauke	79
She was not wel reclaymed;	63	Hauke	80
Was moch more febler brayned.	64	Hauke	82
And so the Scrybe was feed.	65	Hauke	151
How the Temple was kept,	66	Hauke	168
How the Temple was swept,	66	Hauke	169
Aut sanguis vitulorum, /Was offryd within the wallys,	66	Hauke	172
When it was polutyd	66	Hauke	174
Sentence was executyd,	66	Hauke	175
When consecratyd was /The blessyd sacrament.	67	Hauke	185
That was late slayn at Carowe	72	Phy Sparrow	8
Whan I remembre agayn /How mi Philyp was slayn,	72	Phy Sparrow	18
Was betwene you twayne, /Pyramus and Thesbe,	72	Phy Sparrow	20
For that I was robbed /Of my sparowes lyfe.	73	Phy Sparrow	51
Was wery of her lyfe,	74	Phy Sparrow	109
It was so prety a fole,	74	Phy Sparrow	115
It was propre and prest.	75	Phy Sparrow	127
Alas, I was evyll at ease!	75	Phy Sparrow	144
Whose name regystred was	75	Phy Sparrow	149
Whan I was aslepe,	75	Phy Sparrow	162
It was no hurt, I trowe.	76	Phy Sparrow	170
In him it was no vyse;	76	Phy Sparrow	174
But whan I was sowing his beke,	77	Phy Sparrow	219
And was in suche a fray	77	Phy Sparrow	228
My speche was taken away.	77	Phy Sparrow	229
I kest downe that there was,	77	Phy Sparrow	230
That was sometyme aflote,	78	Phy Sparrow	250
As my sparowe was.	78	Phy Sparrow	265
Was never none so good;	78	Phy Sparrow	269

	Page	Title	Line
The fynde was in thy mynde	78	Phy Sparrow	283
Was chaunged to an harte:	79	Phy Sparrow	301
Was never byrde in cage /More gentle of corage	80	Phy Sparrow	324
That was wont to repayre,	80	Phy Sparrow	344
It was my prety Phyppes!	80	Phy Sparrow	360
From me was taken away	81	Phy Sparrow	374
Conceyved and cought, /And was never tought	84	Phy Sparrow	500
For he was a prety cocke,	86	Phy Sparrow	588
Was somwhat wanton I wene;	87	Phy Sparrow	637
For whom was moch stryfe;	87	Phy Sparrow	644
Some say she was lyght,	87	Phy Sparrow	645
That was all theyr joye,	88	Phy Sparrow	674
And all that was in vayne,	89	Phy Sparrow	694
Yet there was a thyng	89	Phy Sparrow	699
For she was quyte gone;	89	Phy Sparrow	706
She was moch to blame;	89	Phy Sparrow	710
That she was true and just,	90	Phy Sparrow	730
Al floodes that ever was	93	Phy Sparrow	878
It cannot be denayd /But it was well convayd,	98	Phy Sparrow	1066
Me thought min hert was crased,	99	Phy Sparrow	1105
Lorde, how I was payned!	99	Phy Sparrow	1123
And yet there was no vyce,	100	Phy Sparrow	1133
An hart was slayne /With hornes twayne	104	Phy Sparrow	1298
That was engendred then;	105	Phy Sparrow	1329
Samuell that was dede;	105	Phy Sparrow	1353
HE WAS SOMTIME THE HOLY BAILLYVE OF DIS.	109	Epitaphe2	I
And that was the more wrong.	111	Lawde	21
Your counseyle was not worth a flye.	113	Scot Kynge	14
Thrugh your counseyle your fader was slayne;	114	Scot Kynge	27
That was theyr owne kynge. /Fy on that wynnyng!	116	Ag Scottes	23
When the Scot was slayne	117	Ag Scottes	R
A kyng, a sumner! It was great wonder:	118	Ag Scottes	95
Male uryd was your fals entent	118	Ag Scottes	111
Your pryde was pevysh to play such prankys:	119	Ag Scottes	150
For lacke of grace hard was your hap;	119	Ag Scottes	168
Cause have they none other /But for that he was brother, have they] 'they have' Day 1560, Marshe 1568 brother] 'hys brother' Day 1560, Marshe 1568	120	Ag Scottes2	14
He was a recrayed knyght,	121	Ag Scottes2	26
And for he was a kyng, /The more shamefull rekenyng	121	Ag Scottes2	31
For Syr Frollo de Franko was never halfe so talle.	121	Garnesche1	5
That mastres Punt put yow of, yt was nat alle causeles;	122	Garnesche1	32
At Orwelle hyr havyn your anggre was laules.	122	Garnesche1	33
Was skantly worthe a grote;	125	Garnesche3	45
The warde with yow was skante.	125	Garnesche3	53
Was sowyd with slendyr thre[de], thredel 'thre' †MS Harley 367	129	Garnesche3	201
Avaunsid I was to that degre;	131	Garnesche5	82
I was made poete lawreate.	131	Garnesche5	84
That creaunser was to thy sofre[yne] lorde; sofreyne] 'sofre' †MS Harley 367	132	Garnesche5	102
Mary, Welthe and I was apoynted to mete,	141	Magnyfycence	24
In dede, syr, that lyberte was not worthe a cue.	141	Magnyfycence	36
That wonte was to be formyst, now to come behynde.	144	Magnyfycence	144
As I was wonte ever, at my fre wyll.	144	Magnyfycence	147
Perceyve you not howe lothe he was to abyde	147	Magnyfycence	241
Yet amonge noble men I was brought up and bred.	147	Magnyfycence	261
Why that ye sayd our langage was in vayne.	147	Magnyfycence	263
For, syth he dyed, largesse was lytell used.	148	Magnyfycence	282
It was a Flemynge hyght Hansy.	149	Magnyfycence	328
Nay, syr, it was nothynge but your mynde.	149	Magnyfycence	330
This letter was wryten ferre hence.	150	Magnyfycence	337
Where was it delyvered you? Shewe unto me.	150	Magnyfycence	340
This wrytynge was taken me there,	150	Magnyfycence	344
But never was I in gretter fere.	150	Magnyfycence	345
They bare me in hande that I was a spye;	150	Magnyfycence	352
Sayd I was mete for your grace.	150	Magnyfycence	373
That with his whyp his mares was wonte to yarke;	153	Magnyfycence	484
Howe coulde ye do that, and [I] was away? I] not in †Rastell & Treveris C 1530, B	154	Magnyfycence	504
What sayst? Here was to lytell clothe.	157	Magnyfycence	607
Ye. My fansy was out of owle flyght,	159	Magnyfycence	671
This was properly prated, syrs! What sayd a?	161	Magnyfycence	746
That never was /Abusyd before.	164	Magnyfycence	867
Why, under whom was he abydynge?	166	Magnyfycence	938
That was before I set behynde;	168	Magnyfycence	1007
Why, sayst thou that I was here yesterday?	170	Magnyfycence	1093
And in my purse was twenty marke.	171	Magnyfycence	1108
Nay, in faythe, it was but a strype	171	Magnyfycence	1125
As ever I was, and as full of tryfyls –	172	Magnyfycence	1141
Mary, it was his, and nowe it is myne.	173	Magnyfycence	1181
And was it his, and nowe it is thyne?	173	Magnyfycence	1182
'What howe! Be ye mery! Was it not well conveyed?'	177	Magnyfycence	1347
Remembre ye not how my lyberte by mesure ruled was?	178	Magnyfycence	1383
That was by the menys of to moche lyberte.	180	Magnyfycence	1424
Syr, as I say, there was no faute in me.	180	Magnyfycence	1426
No, that I assure you; loke who was the best:	181	Magnyfycence	1484

Text	Page	Title	Line
And Thesius, th[at] prowde was Pluto to face -	182	Magnyfycence	1496
that] 'the' †Rastell & Treveris C 1530, B			
Why, was not for money Troy bothe bought and solde?	184	Magnyfycence	1576
I was your good lorde tyll that ye beganne	188	Magnyfycence	1714
Nay, so God me helpe, it was no grete vexacyon;	189	Magnyfycence	1733
Ye, walke he must; it was no better worth.	189	Magnyfycence	1736
It was a ronner; nay, fole, I warant her blode warme.	191	Magnyfycence	1811
And, syr as I was comynge to you hyder,	191	Magnyfycence	1813
Sym Sadylgose was my syer, and Dawcocke my dame.	192	Magnyfycence	1834
Howe a wodcocke wrastled with a larke that was lame;	192	Magnyfycence	1836
Nay. It was your fondnesse that ye have usyd.	193	Magnyfycence	1866
What? Yes, by the rode, syr. It was I all this whyle	193	Magnyfycence	1870
Thys losyll was a lorde and lyvyd at his lust;	193	Magnyfycence	1886
He knewe not hymselfe, his harte was so hye;	193	Magnyfycence	1888
He was wonte to boste, brage, and to brace;	193	Magnyfycence	1890
All worldly welth for hym to lytell was;	193	Magnyfycence	1892
Alasse, where is youth that was wont for to skyppe?	195	Magnyfycence	1957
He woteth not what welth is that never was sore.	196	Magnyfycence	1971
Alasse that ever I Magnyfycence was named!	196	Magnyfycence	1983
Alasse that ever I was so harde happed	196	Magnyfycence	1984
Howe be it of all synne he was innocent,	196	Magnyfycence	2002
That was wonte to lye on fetherbeddes of downe;	197	Magnyfycence	2006
Your skynne that was wrapped in shertes of Raynes,	197	Magnyfycence	2016
Your hede that was wonte to be happed moost drowpy and drowsy,	197	Magnyfycence	2018
A, so! That syghe was farre fet!	199	Magnyfycence	2071
I am Magnyfycence, that somtyme thy mayster was.	200	Magnyfycence	2107
With ye, syr, by Jesu, that slayne was with Jewes!	201	Magnyfycence	2167
So he is the worste brawler that ever was borne.	202	Magnyfycence	2200
Well sayd. But, in fayth, what was your quarell?	203	Magnyfycence	2210
Nay, by Saynt Mary, it was ye called me knave.	203	Magnyfycence	2212
Mary, syr, he sayd that he was the pratyer man	203	Magnyfycence	2225
Then I was in opynynge of lockys;	203	Magnyfycence	2226
Magnyfycence I was, whom ye have brought to shame.	204	Magnyfycence	2241
I was your mayster, though ye thynke it skorne;	204	Magnyfycence	2246
That somtyme was a noble prynce of myght!	205	Magnyfycence	2280
There was never so harde a storme of mysery,	207	Magnyfycence	2343
They molefy so easely my harte that was so harde.	207	Magnyfycence	2346
And love that Lorde that for your love was dede,	207	Magnyfycence	2363
Syr, this letter ye sent to me at Pountes was enclosed.	209	Magnyfycence	2439
Largesse, syr, by his credence was his name.	209	Magnyfycence	2441
Surely my welthe with them was overthrow.	210	Magnyfycence	2450
But, Perseveraunce, me semyth your probleme was best;	212	Magnyfycence	2505
Here was scant thryft /Whan they made suche shyft.	222	El Rummynge	301
Theyr thrust was so great,	222	El Rummynge	303
Another there was that ran /With a good brasse pan -	222	El Rummynge	316
Her colour was full wan	222	El Rummynge	318
It was a stale to take /The devyll in a brake.	222	El Rummynge	324
stale] 'stale' 1521 Fragment, 'stare' †Lant 1545, Kynge & Marche 1554, Day 1560, Marshe 1568			
And brought a gambone /Of bakon that was resty;	222	El Rummynge	328
But, Lorde, as she was testy, /Angry as a waspy!	222	El Rummynge	329
It was dere that was far fet!	223	El Rummynge	334
It was dere that was far fet!	223	El Rummynge	334
Her tonge was very quycke	223	El Rummynge	337
But she was a foule slut,	223	El Rummynge	340
And so was made the peace.	223	El Rummynge	350
the peace] 'the drunken peace' †Lant 1545, Kynge & Marche 1554, Day 1560, Marshe 1568			
And she was full of tales,	223	El Rummynge	352
And, as she was drynkynge,	223	El Rummynge	370
She was somwhat foule, /Crokenebbed lyke an oule;	225	El Rummynge	426
Crokenebbed] 'Croke necked' †Lant 1545, Kynge & Marche 1554, Day 1560, Marshe 1568			
Was well a fote thycke,	225	El Rummynge	430
It was huge and greate,	225	El Rummynge	432
It was tart and punyete.	225	El Rummynge	435
She was a cumly callet.	226	El Rummynge	462
She was ugly hypped, /And ugly thycke-lypped	226	El Rummynge	468
That she was therewithall /Into a palsey fall;	226	El Rummynge	474
The dropsy was in her legges;	226	El Rummynge	481
All foggy fat she was;	226	El Rummynge	483
Her breth was soure and stale	226	El Rummynge	486
She was nothynge plesant;	227	El Rummynge	518
It was a bullyfant, /A gredy cormerant.	227	El Rummynge	520
The fleshe thereof was ranke,	228	El Rummynge	540
Garnysshed was her snout	228	El Rummynge	554
Her paunche was so puffed	228	El Rummynge	570
There was a prycke-me-denty, /Sat lyke a seynty,	229	El Rummynge	582
She was not halfe so wyse	229	El Rummynge	588
As she was pevysshe nyse,	229	El Rummynge	589
But the very grounde /Was for to compound	229	El Rummynge	597
Aram was fyred with Caldies fyer called Ur;	232	Speke Parott	64
Jobab was brought up in the lande of Hus;	232	Speke Parott	65
Jobab] 'Iob' Day 1560, Marshe 1568			
In Popering grew peres, whan Parrot was an eg.	232	Speke Parott	70
The Jebet of Baldock was made for Jack Leg;	232	Speke Parott	73
And silogisari was drowned at Sturbrydge Fayre;	235	Speke Parott	165
Was nevyr suche a senatour syn Crystes Incarnacion.	240	Speke Parott	337

774

	Page	Title	Line
Syns Dewcalions flodde, was nevyr sene nor shall.	245	Speke Parott	469
Syns Dewcalyons flodde, I trowe, was nevyr sene.	245	Speke Parott	476
Syns Dewcalyons flodde was nevyr, I dar sey.	245	Speke Parott	483
Syns Dewcalyons flodde the world was never so yll.	245	Speke Parott	497
the world] 'the world the world' †MS Harley 2252			
Syns Dewcalyons flodde was nevyr sene nor lyerd.	246	Speke Parott	504
So bold and so braggyng, and was so baselye borne;	246	Speke Parott	507
Was nevyr suche a fylty gorgon, nor suche an epycure,	246	Speke Parott	510
Chryst by cruelte /Was nayled upon a tre;	258	Collyn Clout	451
Whan Scorpyon descendynge, /Was so then pretendynge	258	Collyn Clout	472
Whan mammockes was your meate,	263	Collyn Clout	652
As of antyquyte /It was ratyfyed,	264	Collyn Clout	714
As] 'And' †Godfray 1531, Kele 1545.1, Marshe 1568			
Was made a divyne;	266	Collyn Clout	808
The holy prophet, was;	276	Collyn Clout	1207
was] 'Ozeas' MS Harley 2252			
Chefe counselour was carlesse,	280	Why Come Ye	79
That was cast out of a bochers stall!	291	Why Come Ye	494
But, however he was borne,	291	Why Come Ye	495
For he was, parde,	291	Why Come Ye	508
This man was full unable	292	Why Come Ye	537
Before that he was made	293	Why Come Ye	562
But was ravysht with a rage	296	Why Come Ye	691
It was by nycromansy,	296	Why Come Ye	696
In Acon it was brought to pas,	296	Why Come Ye	706
As by myne auctor tried it was.	296	Why Come Ye	707
Johannes Balua was his name	297	Why Come Ye	726
Promoted was he /To a cardynalles dygnyte	297	Why Come Ye	728
Was hedyd, drawen, and quarterd,	297	Why Come Ye	740
In hym was small fayth,	297	Why Come Ye	744
That was a peryllous rekenyng!	299	Why Come Ye	793
But he was so payned in the hede	299	Why Come Ye	795
Your cupbord that was	301	Why Come Ye	901
He said he knew what was what.	306	Why Come Ye	1109
To whom he was professed	307	Why Come Ye	1121
Whan he was creat pope /First in Antioche.	307	Why Come Ye	1142
Saynt Dunstane, what was he?	307	Why Come Ye	1147
Domingos nose that was wheled.	308	Why Come Ye	1185
was] not in MS Rawlinson C. 813			
It was nat heled alderbest,	308	Why Come Ye	1188
I meane Domyngo Lomelyn /That was wont to wyn	309	Why Come Ye	1191
So depely drownyd I was in this dumpe,	312	Garlande	15
Encraumpysshed so sore was my conceyte,	312	Garlande	16
Whose bewte blastyd was with the boystors wynde,	312	Garlande	20
His levis loste, the sappe was frome the rynde.	312	Garlande	21
I can not tell you what was the occasyon.	313	Garlande	35
not tell] 'not wele tell' MS Cotton Vitellius E.x			
That passynge goodly it was to beholde:	313	Garlande	42
As I harde say, Dame Pallas was her name,	313	Garlande	48
Ovyde was bannisshed for suche a skyll,	314	Garlande	93
Juvenall was thret, parde, for to kyll	315	Garlande	95
It was not for hym to abyde the tryall.	315	Garlande	98
abyde] 'byde' MS Cotton Vitellius E.x			
That banisshed was he by his proposicyoun,	316	Garlande	132
by] 'through' Marshe 1568			
And was Eschines rebukid as ye say?	316	Garlande	135
To corage Demostenes was moche excitynge,	316	Garlande	152
Eschines, whiche was not shamefully confutid	316	Garlande	157
For though he were venquesshid, yet was he not shamyd:	316	Garlande	161
For] 'Sithe' MS Cotton Vitellius E.x			
Of Demostenes, that was his utter foo.	317	Garlande	167
There was suyng to the Quene of Fame;	319	Garlande	253
Anone all was whyste, as it were for the nonys,	319	Garlande	267
Whos hevenly armony was so passynge sure,	320	Garlande	274
That in the forest was none so great a tre	320	Garlande	277
But Phebus was formest of all that cam theder;	320	Garlande	287
Transformyd was she into the laurell grene.	320	Garlande	294
'O thoughtfull herte,' was evermore his songe!	320	Garlande	296
But blessyd Bachus was in there company,	322	Garlande	355
Of Scipions dreme what was the treu probate;	322	Garlande	368
That welny was loste when that we were gone.'	323	Garlande	406
welny] 'welnere' Marshe 1568			
Unto the pavylyon where Pallas was syttyng.	324	Garlande	448
With all the prese that there was lesse and more.	325	Garlande	455
How far it was, or ellis within what howris,	325	Garlande	457
far] not in †Fakes 1523			
I can nat tell you, but that I was brought	325	Garlande	458
With turkis and grossolitis enpavyd was the grounde;	325	Garlande	466
Of dyamauntis pointed was the wall;	325	Garlande	473
the] 'the rokky' Marshe 1568			
Envawtyd with rubies the vawte was of this place.	325	Garlande	476
Wherin was set of Fame the noble Quene,	325	Garlande	482
It was excedyng byyonde the commowne rate.	326	Garlande	488
This hous envyrowne was a myle about;	326	Garlande	489
This gentilwoman, that callyd was by name	327	Garlande	527
Of your acqueintaunce I was in tymes past,	327	Garlande	540
Ye fyrste aryvyd; whan broken was your mast	327	Garlande	542
Ye] 'The' †Fakes 1523			

WASHBOL —WASTE

	Page	Title	Line
Some carectis of Caldy, sum Frensshe was full good;	328	Garlande	585
The beldynge therof was passynge commendable;	328	Garlande	589
And one ther was there, I wondred of his hap,	329	Garlande	628
The one was a tumblar, that afterwarde againe	330	Garlande	634
But wele may ye thynk I was no thyng prowde	330	Garlande	648
The clowdis gan to clere, the myst was rarifiid;	330	Garlande	651
In an herber I saw, brought where I was,	330	Garlande	652
It was a new comfort of sorowis escapid.	330	Garlande	657
In the middis a coundight, that coryously was cast,	330	Garlande	658
Englisterd, that joyous it was to beholde.	330	Garlande	663
Whos flagraunt flower was chefe preservatyve	330	Garlande	671
How wronge was no ryght, and ryght was no wronge;	331	Garlande	704
How wronge was no ryght, and ryght was no wronge;	331	Garlande	704
There was counteryng of carollis in meter and verse	331	Garlande	705
and] 'and in' Marshe 1568			
The frame was browght forth with his wevyng pin.	334	Garlande	792
In her bosome, lorde, how she was afrayd!	337	Garlande	887
how] not in MS Cotton Vitellius E.x			
Of porturature which was the famous Greke,	337	Garlande	895
Was my fresshe coronell;	342	Garlande	1056
And specyally which glad was to devyse	342	Garlande	1071
Was never halfe so fayre, as I wene,	342	Garlande	1077
Whiche was extolde /A thowsande folde	342	Garlande	1078
To se how duly ich thyng in ordre was,	343	Garlande	1094
Wele was hym that thereupon myght stare.	343	Garlande	1109
They seyd my lawrell was the goodlyest	343	Garlande	1112
That ever they saw, and wrought it was the best.	343	Garlande	1113
Of Fame. Perceyvynge how that I was cum,	343	Garlande	1115
There was amonge them no worde then but mum,	344	Garlande	1118
amonge them no worde] 'not a worde amonge them' MS Cotton Vitellius E.x			
So then commaundid she was upon this	344	Garlande	1147
The margent was illumynid all with golden railles	345	Garlande	1157
To beholde how it was garnysshyd and bounde,	345	Garlande	1163
Was wrytin; and so she did her spede,	345	Garlande	1168
Item Bowche of Courte, where Drede was begyled;	346	Garlande	1183
With, 'Gingirly, go gingerly!' Her tayle was made of hay;	346	Garlande	1203
The Duke of Yorkis creauncer whan Skelton was,	347	Garlande	1226
And how that it was wantonly spent;	347	Garlande	1244
For he was ever ageynst Goddis hows;	347	Garlande	1251
All his delight was to braule and to barke	347	Garlande	1252
An hart was slayne	348	Garlande	1291
That was engendred then;	349	Garlande	1322
Samuell that was dede.	350	Garlande	1346
Whan the flye net was set for to catche a cote,	351	Garlande	1379
But, lorde, how the parker was wroth with all.	351	Garlande	1386
But how it was, sum were to recheles,	351	Garlande	1393
And plantid it there where never before was none, unshred	351	Garlande	1405
it there where] 'yet wher' Marshe 1568			
Recoverd whan the forster was gone, and sped	351	Garlande	1407
How her ble was bryght as blossom on the spray,	351	Garlande	1412
The myllar was loth to be out of the way,	351	Garlande	1414
But Marione Clarione was caught with a colde colde,	352	Garlande	1443
a colde colde] 'a colde' Marshe 1568			
This goodly flowre with stormis was untwynde.	352	Garlande	1445
With frowarde frostis, alas, was all to-fret!	352	Garlande	1450
The grownde gronid and tremblid, the noyse was so stowte.	354	Garlande	1509
My mynde of the grete din was somdele amasid.	354	Garlande	1512
Was comyng downe /To make hym frowne	360	Albany	56
howe it was idolatry to offre to ymages of our blessed lady,	375	Replycacion	1
Your sermon was nat swete;	376	Replycacion	51
One of you there was	379	Replycacion	186
Your penaunce was to lyght;	379	Replycacion	199
So was there never another,	381	Replycacion	258

WASHBOL

Our Grekys ye walow in the washbol Argolycorum;	235	Speke Parott	150

WASPE

Whan he sawe a waspe;	75	Phy Sparrow	129
My speche is all pleasure, but I stynge lyke a waspe.	160	Magnyfycence	730
Nor Vespasyan, that bare in his nose a waspe,	182	Magnyfycence	1510

WASPIS

And byse, enpicturid with gressoppes and waspis,	345	Garlande	1158

WASPY

But, Lorde, as she was testy, /Angry as a waspy!	222	El Rummynge	330

WASSHE

Let us wasshe our gommes /From the drye crommes!'	222	El Rummynge	307

WASSHYNG

For wasshyng of my throte;	229	El Rummynge	602

WAST

With, 'Spende,' and wast witlesse,	280	Why Come Ye	74
To pas the tyme with, but let us wast no wynde.	328	Garlande	565

WASTE

My wytte wolde waste, I make God avowe.	53	Bowge	243
By God, syr, what nede all this waste?	161	Magnyfycence	754
Mary, I knewe the when thou waste a ladde.	170	Magnyfycence	1089
What! Wyll ye waste wynde and prate thus in vayne?	179	Magnyfycence	1403
Than waste must be welcome, and fare well thryfte.	180	Magnyfycence	1444
By the messe, I shall cleve thy heed to the waste.	201	Magnyfycence	2175

WASTED —WE	Page	Title	Line
And the sandes of Cefas begyn to waste and fade,	239	Speke Parott	281
Cefas] 'Tefas' †MS Harley 2252			
And full of waste wynde,	364	Albany	208
WASTED			
Envye hathe wasted hys lyver and his lounge;	54	Bowge	291
WASTEFULL			
So myche bely-joye, and so wastefull banketyng;	245	Speke Parott	492
WAT			
But sey me yet, Syr Satrapas, wat auctoryte ye have	122	Garneschel	20
WATCH			
Go watch a bole, your bak is brode.	35	Man Margery	12
But ever doth watch,	95	Phy Sparrow	929
WATCHE			
Shall watche at this wake;	82	Phy Sparrow	437
WATCHYNGE			
His hede was hevy for watchynge overnyghte,	56	Bowge	352
WATER			
Water in the one hande and fyre in the other.	160	Magnyfycence	711
beside the water of Twede, etc	359	Albany	1
By the water of Twede,	359	Albany	31
Beside the water of Twede	371	Albany	514
WATER-LAG			
'Fate, fate, fate, ye Irysh water-lag.'	233	Speke Parott	86
WATER MYLLES			
Turne monasteries into water mylles,	257	Collyn Clout	418
WATERS			
With the freshe waters of Elyconys welle.	29	Dol Dethe	14
The ryvers rowth, the waters wan;	42	Balettysl	15
Of Eliconys waters crystallyne,	132	Garnesche5	99
The waters wax wan,	301	Why Come Ye	890
All waters that swellys;	303	Why Come Ye	960
Of cristall the clerenes theis waters far past,	330	Garlande	660
WATHER-HEN			
The wather-hen to wepe;	83	Phy Sparrow	453
WATRY			
Lucina she wadythe among the watry floddes,	239	Speke Parott	285
WAWES			
Out of the wawes wodde	277	Collyn Clout	1253
WAWYS			
Ensor[b]yd with the wawys savage and wode;	213	Magnyfycence	2561
ensorbyd] 'ensordyd' †Rastell & Treveris C 1530, B			
WAX			
Men sey ye wyll wax lowsy, /Drunkyn, drowpy, drowsy.	127	Garnesche3	135
Lyberte at large wyll oft wax reklesse.	142	Magnyfycence	54
For worldly shame I wax bothe wanne and bloo.	198	Magnyfycence	2054
Now pandes mory, wax frantycke som men sey;	232	Speke Parott	46
mory] 'mery' †MS Harley 2252; men] 'mad' †MS Harley 2252			
Yett dates now are deynte, and wax verye scante,	244	Speke Parott	440
The waters wax wan,	301	Why Come Ye	890
Though his purs wax dull,	302	Why Come Ye	937
What though my penne wax faynt,	339	Garlande	954
WAXE			
A wonder thynge that ye waxe not madde!	53	Bowge	241
Though I waxe olde /And somdele sere,	112	Calliope	15
WAXED			
With that my nedle waxed red,	77	Phy Sparrow	225
waxed] 'ware' Marshe 1568			
WAXETH			
Alas, my face waxeth pale,	80	Phy Sparrow	341
Our armye waxeth dull,	282	Why Come Ye	150
WAXYTH			
Anone he waxyth so hy and prowde,	174	Magnyfycence	1244
The worlde waxyth wery of the; thou lyvest to longe.	205	Magnyfycence	2308
WE			
To the pray we as Prince incomperable,	34	Dol Dethe	197
For I have dyscust /We ar but dust,	39	Coystrowne3	5
And dy we must.	39	Coystrowne3	6
For wherso we dwell,	39	Coystrowne3	22
To whom then shall we sew /For to have rescew,	40	Coystrowne3	37
That we be not exylyd	40	Coystrowne3	44
Youre key is redy, we nede not knok	41	Coystrowne4	24
Of Bowge of Court she asketh what we wold have,	49	Bowge	125
And we asked favoure, and favour she us gave.	49	Bowge	126
We wante no wynde to passe now over all;	49	Bowge	128
Favoure we have toughther than ony elme,	49	Bowge	129
toughther] 'tougher' Wynkyn de Worde 1510, Marshe 1568			
'Fare well,' quod he, 'we wyll talke more of this.'	52	Bowge	227
By Goddis bones, but yf we have som sleyte,	54	Bowge	304
We tweyne, I trowe, be not withoute dysceyte:	55	Bowge	313
We be thy betters, and so thou shalte us take,	55	Bowge	342
Or we shall the oute of thy clothes shake!'	55	Bowge	343
I dare not speke, we be so layde awayte,	59	Bowge	468
Adewe tyll soone, we shall speke more of this.	60	Bowge	492
Thys boke we have devysed, /Compendyously comprysed,	62	Hauke	23
To Jupyter pray we	74	Phy Sparrow	92
God wot, we thought no syn -	76	Phy Sparrow	168
We may not well forgo /The countrynge of the coe;	83	Phy Sparrow	467
The best that we can,	84	Phy Sparrow	491

	Page	Title	Line
All other of whom we rede,	93	Phy Sparrow	884
We have well eased you of the bottes.	115	Scot Kynge	63
We have well eased them of the bottes.	120	Ag Scottes	171
But behynd in our hose /We bere there a rose	136	Dundas	35
Fyrst, I say, we owght to have in consyderacyon	141	Magnyfycence	43
Some reason we must make.	143	Magnyfycence	99
We your pleasure fulfyll.	143	Magnyfycence	106
For by measure I warne you we thynke to be gydyd;	145	Magnyfycence	184
To se howe greable we are of one mynde;	146	Magnyfycence	199
Of his rekenynge, as evydently we may	146	Magnyfycence	215
The rule of Measure, notwithstandynge we	147	Magnyfycence	242
Yet we wyll therin take good delyberacyon.	148	Magnyfycence	275
Togyder we wyll talke more of this.	151	Magnyfycence	393
We have bene togyder bothe erly and late.	154	Magnyfycence	499
By God, we have made Magnyfycence to ete a flye.	154	Magnyfycence	503
Yet have we pycked out a rome for the.	154	Magnyfycence	508
Why, shall we dwell togyder all thre?	154	Magnyfycence	509
That we thre galauntes sholde be longe asonder.	154	Magnyfycence	511
By my trouthe, we had ben gone.	155	Magnyfycence	537
And yet, in fayth, man, we lacked the	155	Magnyfycence	538
Nowe therfore, whylest we are togyder -	155	Magnyfycence	546
I say, whylest we are togyder in same -	155	Magnyfycence	548
That we can no better than so.	155	Magnyfycence	550
We wyll remedy it, man, or we go;	155	Magnyfycence	551
We wyll remedy it, man, or we go;	155	Magnyfycence	551
Take no dyspleasure of that we say.	156	Magnyfycence	561
What! Shall we jangle thus all the day styll?	156	Magnyfycence	565
Mary, so wyll we also.	157	Magnyfycence	616
By God, we wolde gete us all thyder,	157	Magnyfycence	618
Yet where we wonne, nowe there wonneth he.	157	Magnyfycence	624
Fansy and I, we twayne,	158	Magnyfycence	639
And counterfeted our names we have	158	Magnyfycence	641
And wolde that we sholde for hym go -	158	Magnyfycence	646
We had hym founde, we sholde hym brynge,	158	Magnyfycence	653
We had hym founde, we sholde hym brynge,	158	Magnyfycence	653
And that we fayled not for nothynge.	158	Magnyfycence	654
So that we have no lyberte;	158	Magnyfycence	659
But, Counterfet Countenaunce, go we togyder,	158	Magnyfycence	665
When we hym thyder convayed,	159	Magnyfycence	676
For then shall we so craftely cary	159	Magnyfycence	683
We wyll se you shortly, one of us twayne.	159	Magnyfycence	686
Now let us go, and we shall, then.	159	Magnyfycence	687
What the devyll! Where had we this joly jetter?	162	Magnyfycence	796
No; for or we stryke, we wyll be advysed twyse.	163	Magnyfycence	810
No; for or we stryke, we wyll be advysed twyse.	163	Magnyfycence	810
What! Whom have we here, Jenkyn Joly?	166	Magnyfycence	918
Pease, man, pease! /I rede we sease.	168	Magnyfycence	998
In faythe, trouthe ye say, we wente togyder to scole.	170	Magnyfycence	1065
Ye. But thryfte and we have made a batell.	171	Magnyfycence	1136
What, that we used whan we were boyes?	172	Magnyfycence	1138
What, that we used whan we were boyes?	172	Magnyfycence	1138
Yet for his name we must fynde a [slyght].	176	Magnyfycence	1308
slyght] shyfte †Rastell & Treveris C 1530, B			
And shall we have lyberte to do what we wyll?	176	Magnyfycence	1316
And shall we have lyberte to do what we wyll?	176	Magnyfycence	1316
Whan Mesure is gone, we may slee care.	176	Magnyfycence	1324
Nowe then goo we hens. Away the mare!	177	Magnyfycence	1325
For drede, that we dare not ofte, lest we be spyed.	177	Magnyfycence	1339
For drede, that we dare not ofte, lest we be spyed.	177	Magnyfycence	1339
Alas, dere harte, loke that we be not perseyvyd!'	177	Magnyfycence	1349
And what so we say, holde you content withall.	179	Magnyfycence	1406
I am here redy. What! Shall we	179	Magnyfycence	1414
Have welth at our gydynge to rule as we lyst?	179	Magnyfycence	1415
Syr, we can do nothynge the one without the other.	180	Magnyfycence	1450
That we delyte gretly in your dalyaunce.	183	Magnyfycence	1524
And we wyll be comonynge in the mene season.	187	Magnyfycence	1688
Your welthe and felycyte, I trust we shall optayne	190	Magnyfycence	1792
Or ever we were ware, brought us in adversyte,	193	Magnyfycence	1863
For though we shewe you this in game and play,	195	Magnyfycence	1948
By my trouthe, we have ryfled hym metely well.	201	Magnyfycence	2170
For we be, syrs, but a fewe of the best.	202	Magnyfycence	2203
A, shall we have more of this maters yet?	203	Magnyfycence	2214
When we with Magnyfycence goodys made chevysaunce.	203	Magnyfycence	2236
Go we nere and let us se.	204	Magnyfycence	2243
Lo, here is thy knyfe and a halter, and or we go ferther,	206	Magnyfycence	2317
Alarum, alarum! To longe we abyde!	206	Magnyfycence	2323
Yf you be so myndyd, we be ryght glad.	210	Magnyfycence	2473
But frendly I wyll refrayne you ferther, or we flyt:	211	Magnyfycence	2478
This mater we have movyd, you myrthys to make,	213	Magnyfycence	2552
Of the terestre [t]rechery we fall in the flode,	213	Magnyfycence	2559
trechery] 'rechery' †Rastell & Treveris C 1530, B			
But let us turne playne, /There we lefte agayne.	219	El Rummynge	188
Whan we kys and play /In lust and in lykyng.	220	El Rummynge	221
Than swetely togither we ly, /As two pygges in a sty.'	220	El Rummynge	233
Than swetely] 'Thus swete' 1521 Fragment			
We wyll no farther ryme /Of it at this tyme.	220	El Rummynge	240
But we wyll turne playne /Where we left agayne.	220	El Rummynge	242
But we wyll turne playne /Where we left agayne.	220	El Rummynge	243

WE —WE	Page	Title	Line
With, 'Hey,' and with, 'Howe, /Syt we downe arowe	221	El Rummynge	290
And drynke tyll we blowe, /And pype tyrly-tyrlowe!'	221	El Rummynge	291
For we have egges and butter,	228	El Rummynge	536
Ye wote well what we meane.'	229	El Rummynge	579
We supposed, iwys, /That she rose to pys;	229	El Rummynge	594
Myden agan in Grekys tonge we rede,	232	Speke Parott	52
With, 'He sayd,' and 'We said.' Ich wot now what ich wot,	234	Speke Parott	132
Shall lepe from this lyfe, as mery as we be.	236	Speke Parott	222
We have longyd and lokyd long tyme for that,	239	Speke Parott	310
Or elles yf we may	265	Collyn Clout	743
He sayes that we are recheles,	275	Collyn Clout	1176
Howe we wyll rule all at wyll	276	Collyn Clout	1190
And say howe that we be /Full of parcyallyte;	276	Collyn Clout	1192
We tourne ryght into wronge,	276	Collyn Clout	1195
Howe may we thus endure?	276	Collyn Clout	1202
Wherfore we make you sure,	276	Collyn Clout	1203
And we wyll rule and rayne,	276	Collyn Clout	1212
We set nat a nutte shell	277	Collyn Clout	1225
We shulde nat ryse agayne	277	Collyn Clout	1232
We may blowe at the cole!	281	Why Come Ye	84
We shall here more herafter!	281	Why Come Ye	99
Clerely percevye we may	281	Why Come Ye	119
For we have spente our shot!	282	Why Come Ye	127
We shall have a tot quot	282	Why Come Ye	128
We have cast up our war,	282	Why Come Ye	140
I drede we are bought and solde.	283	Why Come Ye	172
He sayes we ar but crakers;	285	Why Come Ye	274
In the Latyne synge we,	291	Why Come Ye	476
In writynge as we fynde	292	Why Come Ye	545
Than must we agre /With poverte;	300	Why Come Ye	864
We can lacke no grace,	301	Why Come Ye	875
He rod, but we ran.	301	Why Come Ye	887
'He rode not but he ran' MS Rawlinson C. 813			
We nede never feere	303	Why Come Ye	974
'We nedyd never to feyre' MS Rawlinson C. 813			
He sayth we ar to blame!	305	Why Come Ye	1049
'Nothynge,' he sayth, 'lyke to We.	307	Why Come Ye	1148
to we] 'to mee' Toy 1553, Kitson 1560.7, Marshe 1568,			
'we' MS Rawlinson C. 813			
We passe hym in degre	308	Why Come Ye	1151
But of my purpose now turne we to the grownde.	313	Garlande	28
purpose] 'proces' MS Cotton Vitellius E.x			
And, as we dare, we fynde in hym grete lake:	314	Garlande	70
grete] 'a' Marshe 1568			
And, as we dare, we fynde in hym grete lake:	314	Garlande	70
grete] 'a' Marshe 1568			
'The sum of your purpose, as we ar advysid,	314	Garlande	78
Wherin this answere for hym we have comprisid,	314	Garlande	80
'To your request we be well condiscendid;	318	Garlande	232
Let hym blowe now, that we may take a vewe	319	Garlande	237
a] 'the' MS Cotton Vitellius E.x			
What poetis we have at our retenewe.	319	Garlande	238
That welny was loste when that we were gone.'	323	Garlande	406
welny] 'welnere' Marshe 1568			
Or that we beganne in the supplement,	323	Garlande	415
Enforcid ar we you to recompence,	323	Garlande	416
That we shall brynge you personally present	324	Garlande	418
That bounde ar we with all deu reverence,	324	Garlande	423
With all our strength that we can brynge about,	324	Garlande	424
To owe to yow our servyce, and more if we mowte!	324	Garlande	425
Thus passid we forth walkynge unto the pretory	325	Garlande	477
From you most we, but not longe to tary.	326	Garlande	520
And we shall se you ageyne or it be pryme.'	326	Garlande	525
So passyd we forthe into the forsayd place,	328	Garlande	561
And then she sayd, 'Whylis we have tyme and space	328	Garlande	563
To walke where we lyst, let us somwhat fynde	328	Garlande	564
In derkenes thus dwelt we, tyll at the last	330	Garlande	650
Thus talkyng we went forth in at a postern gate.	333	Garlande	766
forth] not in MS Cotton Vitellius E.x			
That of our bownte we wyll hym rewarde:	334	Garlande	779
We wyll understande how ye have it deservyd.'	344	Garlande	1127
'Yowre boke of remembrauns we will now that ye rede;	345	Garlande	1149
boke] 'bokes' †Fakes 1523			
We shall breke thy bones	362	Albany	150
We set nat a flye	363	Albany	161
We set nat a prane	363	Albany	163
We set nat a myght	363	Albany	165
Yet we bear away the bell,	363	Albany	183
We shall pype you a daunce	371	Albany	498
We will so folowe in the chace	371	Albany	503
Retourne we to our matter.	378	Replycacion	160
To whom we are bounde echone	381	Replycacion	260
In metricall muses, his harpyng we may spare;	383	Replycacion	338
Returne we to our former processe.	384	Replycacion	R
To whom we must gyve faythe,	384	Replycacion	348
We are kyndled in suche facyon	385	Replycacion	382
That forthwith we must nede	385	Replycacion	387

WEAKLY —WELCOME   Page   Title   Line

WEAKLY
    and have waded but weakly in his thre maner of clerkly workes,   374   Replycacion   1
WEALE
    To cause the commune weale   298   Why Come Ye   770
WEARE
    Ye must weare bukram, ...   302   Why Come Ye   918
    Ye may weare a cockes come, ...   310   Why Come Ye2   18
WEBBE
    Suche a webbe can spyn, ...   221   El Rummynge   255
    A webbe of lylse wulse, ...   282   Why Come Ye   131
WED
    Wed me or els I dye for thought!   36   Man Margery   26
    He may rynse a pycher, for his plate is to wed.   201   Magnyfycence   2168
WEDDER
    By Candelmes day what wedder shuld holde;   352   Garlande   1442
WEDDYNGE RYNGE
    Her hernest gyrdle, her weddynge rynge, ...   221   El Rummynge   280
    hernest] 'haruest' Day 1560, 1521 Fragment
WEDES
    Sepultus est amonge the wedes;   107   Epitaphe1   18
    /Loke lyke sere wedes, ...   216   El Rummynge   61
WEDGE
    Some layde to pledge /Theyr hatchet and theyr wedge, ...   221   El Rummynge   294
WEHE
    And Annot wolde be nyce, and laughes, 'tehe wehe.'   153   Magnyfycence   477
WEY
    By wey of expyacyon /For reconcylyacyon.   66   Hauke   176
    for reconcylyacyon] not in Day 1560, Marshe 1568
    With clothes upon her hed /That wey a sowe of led, ...   216   El Rummynge   72
    That wey] 'That they wey' Kynge & Marche 1554, Day 1560,
    Marshe 1568
WEYED
    These words shuld be more weyed, ...   265   Collyn Clout   769
    These words] 'Those words' Marshe 1568, 'This' MS Harley 2252
WEYGHT
    Subtelly usynge counterfet weyght;   152   Magnyfycence   440
WEYWARDE
    And their weywarde trouble.   364   Albany   201
WEKE
    My wyttys be weke, my braynys are lyght;   169   Magnyfycence   1024
    Of the Tewsday in the weke   225   El Rummynge   449
WEKES
    By the dayes and by the wekes.   293   Why Come Ye   556
WEL
    But had his nobillmen donn wel that day   31   Dol Dethe   69
    That neyther they synge wel prycke song nor playne.   38   Coystrowne1   54
    She had not wel endude;   63   Hauke   78
    She was not wel reclaymed;   63   Hauke   80
    Al maters wel pondred and wel to be regarded, ...   137   Ven Tongues   1
    Al maters wel pondred and wel to be regarded, ...   137   Ven Tongues   1
    But yet I may say safely, so many wel lettred, ...   138   Ven Tongues   38
    Wel, wyse men may ete the fysshe when ye shal draw the pole. .   148   Magnyfycence   300
    Myght seme ryght wel under my proteccyon   181   Magnyfycence   1469
    Mesure, ye knowe wel, with hym I can not be content; . . .   186   Magnyfycence   1656
    Bo-ho doth bark wel, Hough-ho he rulyth the ring;   234   Speke Parott   130
    Nether wise nor wel lernid, but like hermaphradita: 235   Speke Parott   159
    Shet were the gatis; thei might wel knock and cal, ...   329   Garlande   604
    I you assure, /Ful wel I know   338   Garlande   927
WELAWAYE
    For your kynge may synge welawaye.   114   Scot Kynge   20
WELCHE MAN
    Pawbe une aruer, so the Welche man sayes.   233   Speke Parott   91
WELCHMANS
    And make a Welchmans hose   266   Collyn Clout   778
WELCOM
    For whose love, welcom dysease to me!   45   Balettys5   10
    Nowe welcom, by the God holy!   166   Magnyfycence   919
    Welcom, Pleasure, to our magnyfycence.   182   Magnyfycence   1516
    Stand up, syr. Ye are welcom to me.   186   Magnyfycence   1632
    Ryse up, syr, and welcom unto me.   195   Magnyfycence   1966
    'Welcom Jacke and Gylla!'   253   Collyn Clout   258
WELCOME
    But ye be welcome to our housholde.   53   Bowge   266
    And ye be welcome, syr, so God me save, ...   54   Bowge   279
    'Welcome,' quod Ryote, 'I make God avowe.'   56   Bowge   378
    To us welcome thou arte, by Saynte Quyntyne!'   60   Bowge   511
    Welcome, frendys, ye are bothe unto me.   145   Magnyfycence   169
    This wrytynge is welcome with harty affeccyon!   149   Magnyfycence   313
    In faythe, Largesse, welcome to me.   151   Magnyfycence   390
    Than waste must be welcome, and fare well thryfte.   180   Magnyfycence   1444
    Nowe welcome, forsoth, Sad Cyrcumspeccyon.   209   Magnyfycence   2418
    With, 'Welcome, hake and make!'   253   Collyn Clout   250
    Welcome dame Simonia, /With dame Castrimergia, ...   284   Why Come Ye   215
    How ye ar welcome to this court of aray.   327   Garlande   539
    Welcome to me as hertely as herte can thynke!   327   Garlande   547
    Welcome to me with all my hole desyre!   327   Garlande   548
    Welcome shall ye /To sum men be;   355   Garlande   1540

WELE —WELL	Page	Title	Line

WELE

	Page	Title	Line
Wele sped in spyndels and turnyng of tavellys,	37	Coystrowne1	34
In whome dothe wele acorde	110	Lawde	12
As hevery man wele seethe,	127	Garnesche3	125
Ye may wele be bedawyd,	128	Garnesche3	182
God sende you wele good spede,	129	Garnesche3	202
Yt commyth the wele me to remorde,	132	Garnesche5	101
Why kepte you it thus longe? Howe dothe he? Wele?	149	Magnyfycence	314
But wele I can tell	296	Why Come Ye	686
With hym so wele apayd	297	Why Come Ye	731
Of auncient poetis, ye wote full wele, hath bene	314	Garlande	65
Remembre you wele, poynt wele that clause,	316	Garlande	136
Remembre you wele, poynt wele that clause,	316	Garlande	136
'Madame, your apposelle is wele inferrid,	316	Garlande	141
As wele foly as wysdome oft ye do avaunce,	317	Garlande	180
ye do] 'tyme ye' MS Cotton Vitellius E.x			
'The west is wyndy.' 'The est is metely wele.'	326	Garlande	499
But wele ye thynk I was no thyng prowde	330	Garlande	648
O wele were hym that herof myght be sure,	332	Garlande	718
He can never leve warke whylis it is wele.	333	Garlande	763
Whome dame Nature, as wele I may reporte,	336	Garlande	867
Phedra ye may /Wele represent;	338	Garlande	941
Stedfast of thought, /Wele made, wele wrought;	341	Garlande	1030
Stedfast of thought, /Wele made, wele wrought;	341	Garlande	1030
I dare wele saye that ye and I be sought.	343	Garlande	1089
Wele was hym that thereupon myght stare.	343	Garlande	1109
For in owr courte, ye wote wele, his name can not ryse	345	Garlande	1154
With Courtely Abusyoun; who pryntith it wele in mynde	346	Garlande	1196
It may wele ryme, but shroudly it doth accorde,	346	Garlande	1210
A wanton wenche and wele coude bake a cake;	351	Garlande	1413
And wele wotith the cat whos berde she likkith.	352	Garlande	1438
If ye wele can regarde	368	Albany	360
Ye count your selfe wele lettred:	376	Replycacion	55
Whose charite wele regarded	378	Replycacion	138
For it is wele recorded	383	Replycacion	324
For be ye wele assured,	385	Replycacion	406

WELEAWAY

	Page	Title	Line
Ye may syng weleaway	376	Replycacion	78

WELE PUBLYKE

	Page	Title	Line
For the wele publyke /Of preesthode in this case;	264	Collyn Clout	697

WELL

	Page	Title	Line
Well may ye be cald commons most unkynd.	30	Dol Dethe	56
ye] 'you' Marshe 1568			
All kingis, all princis, all dukis, well thei ought	34	Dol Dethe	180
As thou art of mercy and pite the well,	34	Dol Dethe	198
Well of pite, of mercy, and of grace,	35	Dol Dethe	215
When he is well, yet can he not rest.	36	Coystrowne1	7
As well it becomyth yow, a parysh towne clarke,	38	Coystrowne1	58
A proverbe of old, 'Say well or be styll':	38	Coystrowne1	64
I have well espyde	39	Coystrowne3	9
Loke that ye spell /Well thys gospell;	39	Coystrowne3	21
As well borne as ye full oft tyme beggys.	40	Coystrowne4	7
Well may thou sygh, well may thou grone,	42	Balettys1	26
Well may thou sygh, well may thou grone,	42	Balettys1	26
He rydyth well the horse, but he rydyth better the mare.	43	Balettys2	21
Wordys well set with good habylyte;	43	Balettys3	5
Condute of comforte and well moste soverayne;	44	Balettys3	12
Wyth fables false, that well coude fayne a tale;	49	Bowge	135
And Harvy Ha[f]ter that well coude picke a male;	50	Bowge	138
Hafter] 'Haster' †Wynkyn de Worde 1499, 1510, Marshe 1568			
But my dysporte they could not well endure:	50	Bowge	145
He sayth he can not well accorde with he.'	51	Bowge	185
For here is none that dare well other truste;	51	Bowge	202
Well, ones thou shalte be chermed, iwus:	55	Bowge	340
It is a curtel that well can wynche and praunce;	57	Bowge	411
curtel] 'curtet' †Wynkyn de Worde 1499, 1510			
Unthryftynes in hym may well be shewed,	58	Bowge	416
Unthryftynes] 'Unthryftnes' †Wynkyn de Worde 1499, 1510			
In no place well, but foles with hym fraye!	58	Bowge	446
hym] not in †Wynkyn de Worde 1499, Marshe 1568			
For he coude well upon a casket wayte,	60	Bowge	507
A parson benyfyced /But nothynge well advysed.	62	Hauke	37
That no lyfe well nye remayned.	73	Phy Sparrow	49
Well nye had stopped my breath.	73	Phy Sparrow	63
had] not in Wyght 1553, Kitson 1560.6, Marshe 1568			
From the marees depe /Of Acherontes well,	73	Phy Sparrow	70
As well perceyve ye maye	81	Phy Sparrow	372
We may not well forgo /The countrynge of the coe;	83	Phy Sparrow	467
He can not well fly, /Nor synge tunably;	83	Phy Sparrow	483
Yet at a brayde /He hath well assayde	84	Phy Sparrow	486
That never yet asayde /Of Elyconys well,	87	Phy Sparrow	610
His Englysh well alowed,	91	Phy Sparrow	792
If I have not well perused	92	Phy Sparrow	814
She may well represent	97	Phy Sparrow	1017
It cannot be denayd /But it was well convayd,	98	Phy Sparrow	1066
The well of worldly treasure;	102	Phy Sparrow	1228
Of Cocitus botumles well;	105	Phy Sparrow	1336
We have well eased you of the bottes.	115	Scot Kynge	63

WELL —WELL	Page	Title	Line
They may well say, fye on that wynnynge!	115	Ag Scottes	4
Ye shew ryght well what good ye can;	117	Ag Scottes	60
Thus fortune hath tourned you, I dare well say,	119	Ag Scottes	164
We have well eased them of the bottes.	120	Ag Scottes	171
And well I have yt perseyved,	124	Garnesche3	2
Well Be Seen Crystofer Chalangar, et cetera	129	Garnesche5	I
As provithe well, in hys rethorikys olde,	130	Garnesche5	11
Yower lothesum lypps love well to kyse,	130	Garnesche5	44
Malapert, medyllar, nothyng well thewde,	133	Garnesche5	147
Yet somwhat to say I dare well be bolde,	137	Ven Tongues	10
To that ye say I can well condyssende.	141	Magnyfycence	39
Lyberte, I wote well, forbere no man there may;	142	Magnyfycence	50
Ye, syr, passyng well.	142	Magnyfycence	56
I parceyve well howe eche of you doth reason.	142	Magnyfycence	83
Whych provyth well that measure shold have domynyon.	143	Magnyfycence	120
Unto that same I am ryght well agrede,	144	Magnyfycence	128
Well, I am content your wayes to take.	144	Magnyfycence	155
Then noblenesse, I se well, is almoste undone,	146	Magnyfycence	225
Nothynge but fare you well tyll sone -	149	Magnyfycence	319
For, in fayth, ye be well met.	151	Magnyfycence	402
To counterfet well is a good consayte.	152	Magnyfycence	444
Counterfet maydenhode may well be borne,	152	Magnyfycence	445
What! Wanton, wanton, nowe well ymet!	153	Magnyfycence	456
But is it not well? Howe thynkest thou?	155	Magnyfycence	528
By the masse, odly well alowde.	155	Magnyfycence	533
Nowe, by Cockes harte, well abyden!	156	Magnyfycence	576
By the armes of Calys, well conceyved.	159	Magnyfycence	675
Amonge all suche persones as I well understonde	161	Magnyfycence	739
For thou shalt well knowe I am nother durty nor dusty.	161	Magnyfycence	759
By Goddes fote, and I dare well fyght, for I wyll not start.	161	Magnyfycence	768
Well, and I be a coward, there is mo than I.	162	Magnyfycence	770
Well, tary here tyll I for you sende.	163	Magnyfycence	817
As well as me. I wolde, and I durste -	163	Magnyfycence	827
Well rounde aboute.	163	Magnyfycence	831
Methynke she is well becked to catche a rat.	166	Magnyfycence	927
By the masse, well done and boldely.	166	Magnyfycence	948
Her fethers donne; /Well faveryd bonne!	168	Magnyfycence	990
By my trouthe, I trowe well;	169	Magnyfycence	1051
By the harte of God, well done!	172	Magnyfycence	1156
Can he play well at the hoddypeke?	172	Magnyfycence	1161
In a cote thou can play well the dyser.	173	Magnyfycence	1176
As some be not ferre and yf it were well sought -	174	Magnyfycence	1241
And, 'This is not well done, syr; take hede';	175	Magnyfycence	1248
But all that he dothe, and yf he reken well	175	Magnyfycence	1274
Well argued and surely on bothe sydes.	176	Magnyfycence	1304
'What howe! Be ye mery! Was it not well conveyed?'	177	Magnyfycence	1347
Without crafte nothynge is well behavyd.	177	Magnyfycence	1350
So it be by mesure I am ryght well content.	180	Magnyfycence	1421
Sore sayde, I tell you, and well to the purpose.	180	Magnyfycence	1428
Well, get you hens than and sende me some other.	180	Magnyfycence	1451
Of your langage, it is so well devysed;	183	Magnyfycence	1530
Thy wordes and my mynde odly well accorde.	185	Magnyfycence	1605
And that your mynde can not well be eased -	185	Magnyfycence	1610
What care I? By the masse, well sayd.	187	Magnyfycence	1671
Well cannest thou helpe a preest to synge a songe.	187	Magnyfycence	1676
Well, for thy sake the better I may endure	187	Magnyfycence	1680
Well, call hym, and let us here hym reason.	187	Magnyfycence	1687
Syr, nowe me thynke your harte is well eased.	189	Magnyfycence	1737
In faythe, and your servyce ryght well shall I acquyte;	190	Magnyfycence	1794
Well were that lady myght stande in my grace,	190	Magnyfycence	1799
That hath deservyd it as well as he.	195	Magnyfycence	1952
Alas! Of Fortune I may well complayne.	197	Magnyfycence	2030
For I am a vertue yf I be well used,	199	Magnyfycence	2101
By my trouthe, we have ryfled hym metely well.	201	Magnyfycence	2170
Well sayd. But, in fayth, what was your quarell?	203	Magnyfycence	2210
I can not well tell of your dysposycyons;	203	Magnyfycence	2218
Nay, I know well inough ye are bothe well handyd	203	Magnyfycence	2230
Nay, I know well inough ye are bothe well handyd	203	Magnyfycence	2230
To grope a gardevyaunce, though it be well bandyd.	203	Magnyfycence	2231
But nowe I se well there is no better rede,	205	Magnyfycence	2305
That dyspayre well nyghe had myscheved me;	206	Magnyfycence	2332
Now, surely, Magnyfycence, I am ryght well apayed	208	Magnyfycence	2402
It wolde be founde so yf it were well tryde.	210	Magnyfycence	2449
Well, syr, after your counsell my mynde I wyll set.	210	Magnyfycence	2457
What, brother Perceveraunce, surely well met!	210	Magnyfycence	2458
Ye com hether as well as can be thought.	210	Magnyfycence	2459
Accordynge to treuth they be well devysyd.	210	Magnyfycence	2470
Well, I perceyve in you there is moche sadnesse,	210	Magnyfycence	2475
Yf it be regystryd well in memory;	212	Magnyfycence	2513
Nowe well, nowe wo, nowe hy, nowe lawe degre;	212	Magnyfycence	2517
Today it is well, tomorowe it is all amysse;	213	Magnyfycence	2541
And well worne in age,	214	El Rummynge	8
Was well a fote thycke,	225	El Rummynge	430
For so mote I hoppy, /It coleth well my croppy.'	228	El Rummynge	561
croppy] 'coppy' Day 1560, Marshe 1568			
Ye wote well what we meane.'	229	El Rummynge	579
But our Grekis theyr Greke so well have applyed,	234	Speke Parott	145
Poynt well this probleme that Parrot doth prate,	236	Speke Parott	220

WELLAWAY —WELTH

	Page	Title	Line
It may well so be,	247	Collyn Clout	38
Yf ye take well therwith /It hath in it some pyth.	248	Collyn Clout	57
take] 'talke' Kele 1545.1, Marshe 1568			
And bere it well away.	258	Collyn Clout	464
Suche ye may well knowe and ken	260	Collyn Clout	533
Yf they well understode	262	Collyn Clout	616
understode] 'understand' Marshe 1568			
Let hym well beware	263	Collyn Clout	665
That clerkely is, and can /Well scrypture expounde	264	Collyn Clout	723
And he dare nat well neven	267	Collyn Clout	824
But whan the frere fell in the well	268	Collyn Clout	877
Theyr chambres well sene,	270	Collyn Clout	955
As well as other men.	277	Collyn Clout	1247
Marke well this conclusyon:	279	Why Come Ye	18
This byll well over loked,	281	Why Come Ye	118
To well they do agre,	286	Why Come Ye	278
Thy tonge is nat well thewde,	287	Why Come Ye	331
But and it were well sought,	287	Why Come Ye	352
At them that be well borne;	294	Why Come Ye	600
They can nat well tell	295	Why Come Ye	648
As well calodemonyall /As to cacademonyall,	299	Why Come Ye	809
For he is well past and gone.	300	Why Come Ye	833
Were gone as well as he!	300	Why Come Ye	836
But Englande may well say	302	Why Come Ye	928
Faire fall that forster that so well can bate his hownde!	313	Garlande	27
well] not in MS Cotton Vitellius E.x			
Of Elyconis well, refresshid with your grace,	314	Garlande	74
Elyconis] 'Elycoms' †Fakes 1523, 'Heliconis' Marshe 1568			
'A thanke to have, ye have well deservyd,	317	Garlande	169
But whome that ye favoure, I se well, hath a name,	317	Garlande	176
And ye shall well fynde he is a very fole;	318	Garlande	207
well fynde] 'fynde wele' MS Cotton Vitellius E.x			
Of very dwte it may not well accorde,	318	Garlande	212
Or elles, ye know well, I can do no lesse	318	Garlande	226
'To your request we be well condiscendid;	318	Garlande	232
So truely proporsionyd, and so well did gree,	320	Garlande	275
My name, I know well, beyonde that I am able,	324	Garlande	438
So well entakeled, what wynde that ever blowe,	327	Garlande	545
that] 'so' Marshe 1568			
Be well assurid I shall aquyte your hyre,	327	Garlande	550
With other condycyons that well myght be left.	329	Garlande	615
That of your bounte so well have me assurid;	332	Garlande	729
With slaiis, with tavellis, with hedellis well drest;	334	Garlande	791
Well gydyng ther glowtonn to kepe streit theyr sylk,	334	Garlande	795
ther] 'the' MS Cotton Vitellius E.x			
Of vertu and konnyng the well and perfight grounde;	336	Garlande	866
and] (1st) not in MS Cotton Vitellius E.x			
Benynge, corteise, and meke, /With wordes well devysid;	338	Garlande	919
Be vertus well comprysid.	338	Garlande	921
The jeloffer well set, /The propre vyolet;	340	Garlande	983
With vertu well renwde.	341	Garlande	1045
With vertu well renude.	342	Garlande	1053
With vertu well renude.	342	Garlande	1061
Galathea, the made well besene,	342	Garlande	1076
Whiche in your recordes, I know well, be enrolde,	344	Garlande	1140
Envyvid picturis well towchid and quikly.	345	Garlande	1161
Item the Boke to Speke Well or be Styll;	345	Garlande	1175
Of Cochitos bottumles well;	349	Garlande	1329
Of chivalry the well,	365	Albany	238
Be well ware what ye say.	367	Albany	331
For, if it were well sought,	379	Replycacion	185
Wherfore ye are well checte,	380	Replycacion	238

WELLAWAY

	Page	Title	Line
For the cliffes of Scaloppe they rore wellaway,	238	Speke Parott	280
Alas, and wellaway, /What eyles them thus to say?	261	Collyn Clout	577

WELLE

	Page	Title	Line
With the freshe waters of Elyconys welle.	29	Dol Dethe	14
The welle concernyng of all the hole lande,	31	Dol Dethe	65
Welle Be Seyn Crysteovyr Chalannger, et cetera	124	Garnesche3	I
I yave hym drynke of the sugryd welle	132	Garnesche5	98
Stop a tyd, and be welle ware	133	Garnesche5	162

WELLYS

	Page	Title	Line
All ryvers and wellys,	303	Why Come Ye	959

WELL-SYGHTED

	Page	Title	Line
Well-syghted when /He is amonge blynde men?	292	Why Come Ye	534

WELNY

	Page	Title	Line
That welny was loste when that we were gone.'	323	Garlande	406
welny] 'welnere' Marshe 1568			
That welny nothynge there doth remayne	324	Garlande	430
welny] 'welnere' Marshe 1568			

WELTH

	Page	Title	Line
Our welth, our worldly joy,	111	Lawde	49
Your welth, your joy, your sport, your play,	119	Ag Scottes	159
Be it erly or late, welth hath a season.	140	Magnyfycence	3
Welth is of wysdome the very trewe probate.	140	Magnyfycence	4
A fole is he with welth that fallyth at debate.	140	Magnyfycence	5
That nothynge than welth may worse be enduryd.	140	Magnyfycence	7
For, when men by welth, they have lytell drede	140	Magnyfycence	10

WELTHE —WENE   Page   Title   Line

	Page	Title	Line
A man may have welth, but not as he wolde,	141	Magnyfycence	14
Welth and wyt, I say, be so threde bare worne,	146	Magnyfycence	223
Yet it is good wysdome to worke wysely by welth.	179	Magnyfycence	1401
Have welth at our gydynge to rule as we lyst?	179	Magnyfycence	1415
Why, welth hath made many a man braynlesse.	180	Magnyfycence	1423
I say it is foly to gyve all welth away.	180	Magnyfycence	1430
Whether sholde welth be rulyd by lyberte,	180	Magnyfycence	1431
Or lyberte by welth? Let se, tell me that.	180	Magnyfycence	1432
For welth without largesse is all out of kynde.	180	Magnyfycence	1441
And welth is nought worthe yf lyberte be behynde.	180	Magnyfycence	1442
I have welth at wyll, largesse and lyberte.	181	Magnyfycence	1458
And I shall waraunt you welth and lyberte.	190	Magnyfycence	1766
All worldly welth for hym to lytell was;	193	Magnyfycence	1892
He woteth not what welth is that never was sore.	196	Magnyfycence	1971
In welth to beware; and that is wyt.	196	Magnyfycence	1975
In welth to beware yf I had had grace,	196	Magnyfycence	1976
Nowe all in welth, forthwith in poverte;	197	Magnyfycence	2027
Where is nowe my welth and my noble estate?	198	Magnyfycence	2055
Howe sodenly worldly welth dothe dekay;	213	Magnyfycence	2555
Of welth and solace no thynge left behynde;	332	Garlande	711
It were an endeles welth,	340	Garlande	995

WELTHE

	Page	Title	Line
And welthe ar com agayne,	111	Lawde	41
Wherfore, in welthe beware of woo,	132	Garnesche5	124
For welthe wyll sone departe the froo.	132	Garnesche5	125
Welthe myght be wonne and made to the lure,	141	Magnyfycence	17
That welthe and felicite is passynge small.	141	Magnyfycence	21
But where wonnys welthe, and a man wolde wyt?	141	Magnyfycence	22
Mary, Welthe and I was apoynted to mete,	141	Magnyfycence	24
I say there is no welthe where as lyberte is subdude.	142	Magnyfycence	73
Where lyberte is absent, set welthe asyde.	142	Magnyfycence	80
Welthe without measure wolde bere hymselfe to bolde;	143	Magnyfycence	116
Measure contynwyth prosperyte and welthe.	144	Magnyfycence	141
Welthe, with Measure and plesaunt Lyberte.	145	Magnyfycence	160
Welthe with Lyberte, with me bothe dwell ye shall,	145	Magnyfycence	174
So that welthe with measure shalbe conbyned,	145	Magnyfycence	179
For welthe without measure sodenly wyll slyde.	145	Magnyfycence	192
For howe be it lyberte to welthe is convenyent,	146	Magnyfycence	219
Have ye not welthe here at your wyll?	148	Magnyfycence	284
Welthe, gete you home and commaunde me to Mesure.	149	Magnyfycence	316
In hynderaunce of welthe and prosperyte.	160	Magnyfycence	734
Ye shall be occupyed, Welthe, at my wyll.	178	Magnyfycence	1380
Your welthe and felycyte, I trust we shall optayne	190	Magnyfycence	1792
Welthe without lyberte gothe all to wrake.	199	Magnyfycence	2086
Of worldly welthe, alasse, who can be sure?	201	Magnyfycence	2155
In welthe to beware of herde adversyte.	201	Magnyfycence	2159
Then welthe with you myght in no wyse abyde.	210	Magnyfycence	2447
Surely my welthe with them was overthrow.	210	Magnyfycence	2450
For the welthe of this worlde can not indure.	213	Magnyfycence	2558
For the welthe of this worlde can not indure.	214	Magnyfycence	2565
But now in welthe, now in adversyte.	312	Garlande	14

WELTHFULL

	Page	Title	Line
For Welthfull Felicite truly is my name.	141	Magnyfycence	23
Than farewell to the, /Welthfull Felycite; Welthfull] 'Welthe full of felycyte' MS Rawlinson C. 813	300	Why Come Ye	861

WELTYTH

	Page	Title	Line
Theyr conveyaunce weltyth the worke all by wyll;	178	Magnyfycence	1363

WENCHE

	Page	Title	Line
Gather up, thou wenche.	219	El Rummynge	181
A wanton wenche and wele coude bake a cake;	351	Garlande	1413

WENCHES

	Page	Title	Line
Some wenches come unlased, /Some huswyves come unbrased, unlased] 'unbrased' Day 1560, Marshe 1568	217	El Rummynge	133
With wanton wenches wynkyng!	270	Collyn Clout	968

WENDE

	Page	Title	Line
I loked on hym, I wende he had be woode.	55	Bowge	320

WENE

	Page	Title	Line
'Myne horse is sold, I wene', you say;	40	Coystrowne4	9
Dysdayne, I wene, [t]his comerous car[k]es hyghte. this] 'his' editions; carkes] 'carbes' †Wynkyn de Worde 1499, 1510, 'crabes' Marshe 1568	54	Bowge	294
This Doctour Dawcocke, Drede, I wene he hyghte.	54	Bowge	303
Yet at the knee they were broken, I wene.	56	Bowge	357
For some wene be hanged by the throte.	59	Bowge	476
Was somwhat wanton I wene?	87	Phy Sparrow	637
Hath won nothing, I wene,	89	Phy Sparrow	718
Fayre Lucres, as I wene,	97	Phy Sparrow	1018
Your sworde ye swere, I wene,	127	Garnesche3	137
Nowe, benedicite, ye wene I were some hafter,	147	Magnyfycence	257
Ye wene that I am dronken bycause I loke pale.	147	Magnyfycence	259
By Cockes harte, I wene thou hast no more.	172	Magnyfycence	1146
Your grace sent for me, I wene. What is your wyll?	179	Magnyfycence	1410
Why, wene you that I can kepe hym longe styll?	179	Magnyfycence	1412
Mary, I wene he wolde not be glad to come agayne.	189	Magnyfycence	1740
It had ben hers, I wene, /More then fourty yere;	215	El Rummynge	57
That doth thynke or wene	274	Collyn Clout	1121
And it be as I wene.	304	Why Come Ye	1007

WENEST —WER

	Page	Title	Line
Men wene that he is pocky, wene that] 'say' MS Rawlinson C. 813	308	Why Come Ye	1170
Was never halfe so fayre, as I wene,	342	Garlande	1077
Wene ye, daucockes, to drive	368	Albany	380

WENEST
Why, wenest thou that I forbere the for thyne owne sake?	202	Magnyfycence	2186

WENESTE
What weneste I were? I trowe thou knowe not me.	55	Bowge	331

WENETH
And whan he weneth to sytte	271	Collyn Clout	995

WENGAUNCE
And therfore our Lorde sende you a very wengaunce!	203	Magnyfycence	2237

WENYD
I wenyd ones never to have knowen of care.	196	Magnyfycence	1973

WENYST
Why, wenyst thou, horson, that I were so mad?	155	Magnyfycence	517
What! Wenyst thou that I knowe the not, Clokyd Colusyon?	161	Magnyfycence	756
And wenyst thow that I know not the, cankard Abusyon?	161	Magnyfycence	757
What! Wenyst thou that I were so folysshe and so fonde?	170	Magnyfycence	1098
Why, wenyst thou that I cannot make the play the fon?	173	Magnyfycence	1185
Why, wenyst thou that I were as moche a fole as thou?	173	Magnyfycence	1188

WENT
Downe went my offerynge box,	64	Hauke	111
Pand[aer], that went betwene, Pandaer] 'pandara' †Kele 1545.2, Wyght 1553, Kitson 1560.6, Marshe 1568	89	Phy Sparrow	717
And some went so narrowe	222	El Rummynge	297
Yet, or she went, she dranke,	228	El Rummynge	542
There went the hare away;	281	Why Come Ye	120
Wote ye whyther they went?	282	Why Come Ye	146
Went with the pecok ageyne the fesaunt;	315	Garlande	103
He plucked hym backe, and he went afore.	319	Garlande	254
That with them I went where they wolde me brynge,	324	Garlande	447
She went before, and bad me take good holde;	328	Garlande	573
Thus talkyng we went forth in at a postern gate. forth] not in MS Cotton Vitellius E.x	333	Garlande	766
Where it became, and whether it went,	347	Garlande	1243
Of trumpettis and clariouns the noyse went to Rome;	354	Garlande	1507

WENTBRIDGE
From Wentbridge to Hull,	282	Why Come Ye	149

WENTE
He wente aboute to take me in a fawte:	55	Bowge	318
'Quater treye dews' he clatered as he wente.	56	Bowge	347
His rumpe, he wente so all for somer lyghte;	56	Bowge	355
In faythe, trouthe ye say, we wente togyder to scole.	170	Magnyfycence	1065
It were better he spake with you or he wente,	187	Magnyfycence	1662
But yet, lo, I wolde, or that he wente,	187	Magnyfycence	1673
Wherfor he may now come agayne as he wente,	240	Speke Parott	338
Another tolde how shyppes wente to wrak.	326	Garlande	507
When they were past and wente forth on there way,	327	Garlande	526

WENTWORTHE
To mastres Margery Wentworthe	337	Garlande	R

WEPE
I wayle, I wepe, I sobbe, I sigh ful sore	29	Dol Dethe	1
And lerne to wepe at me!	73	Phy Sparrow	57
To wepe with me loke that ye come,	81	Phy Sparrow	387
Some to wepe, and some to pray,	81	Phy Sparrow	393
The wather-hen to wepe;	83	Phy Sparrow	453
Somtyme I wepe for a gew gaw;	168	Magnyfycence	1013
Than began she to wepe,	223	El Rummynge	374
Ulula, Esebon, for Jeromy doth wepe!	234	Speke Parott	113

WEPING
To soroufull weping thei ought to be constreynd,	34	Dol Dethe	187

WEPINGE
From bitter wepinge hym self kan restrayne?	32	Dol Dethe	112

WEPYNGE
I wolde tell you and yf I myght for wepynge.	192	Magnyfycence	1848

WEPT
I wept and I wayled,	72	Phy Sparrow	23
I may no more speke tyll I have wept my fyll.	198	Magnyfycence	2063

WER
Fy, fy, for shame, ther hartis wer to faynt.	30	Dol Dethe	42
I say, ye commoners, why wer ye so stark mad?	30	Dol Dethe	50
Bot men say thei wer lynked with a double chayn	31	Dol Dethe	75
Trustinge in noble men that wer with hym there;	31	Dol Dethe	90
Alas for routhe, what thouthe his mynde wer goode,	32	Dol Dethe	102
In me all onely wer sett and comprisyde,	33	Dol Dethe	156
To me also all thouthe yt wer promysyde	33	Dol Dethe	159
All gyf Englond and Fraunce wer thorow sought.	34	Dol Dethe	179
It wer a plesaunt payne	97	Phy Sparrow	1012
That wont wer over all	111	Lawde	38
Wer thi nose spectacle case;	133	Garnesche5	134
If they wer lyveyng thys day,	133	Garnesche5	142
Of birrall enbosid wer the pyllers rownde;	325	Garlande	467
Where the postis wer enbulyoned with saphiris indy blew,	325	Garlande	478
Theis titi[v]yllis with taumpinnis wer towchid and tappid; titivyllis] 'titinyllis' †Fakes 1523, 'titiuls' Marshe 1568	330	Garlande	642
Though ye wer hard hertyd,	341	Garlande	1038

WERE —WERE   Page   Title   Line

WERE

	Page	Title	Line
Were not thes commones uncurteis karlis of kynd	30	Dol Dethe	34
not] 'no' †MS Royal 18 D.ii, 'not' Marshe 1568			
And were not thei to blame, I say also,	30	Dol Dethe	36
That were aboute hym, his awne servauntis of trust,	30	Dol Dethe	37
They bode not till the rekenyng were discust.	30	Dol Dethe	40
Withe his enmys that were stark mad and wode;	32	Dol Dethe	100
All were to litill for his magnyficence.	33	Dol Dethe	161
Yet, and God wold, I wold my payne were easyd!	45	Balettys5	12
They coude not faile, thei thought, they were so sure.	50	Bowge	142
Whan there were dyverse that sore dyde you manace.	50	Bowge	159
Whyles of his mynde it were lockte with the keye.	52	Bowge	224
What weneste I were? I trowe thou knowe not me.	55	Bowge	331
Yet at the knee they were broken, I wene.	56	Bowge	357
His nose a-droppynge, his lyppes were full drye;	56	Bowge	362
a-droppynge] 'droppynge' Marshe 1568			
And on that sleve these wordes were wrete:	58	Bowge	438
Thyse were the wordes he to me dyde saye.	58	Bowge	441
he] 'that he' Marshe 1568			
I wolde eche man were as playne as I.	59	Bowge	463
Were I as you, I wolde ryde them full nere;	59	Bowge	472
And so I wolde it were, so God me spede,	59	Bowge	481
It were more thryft he boughte him a newe cote;	60	Bowge	487
Par[d]e, remembre whan ye were there,	60	Bowge	515
Parde] 'Parte' †Wynkyn de Worde 1499, 1510, Marshe 1568			
I wolde therwith no man were myscontente;	61	Bowge	533
The church dores were sparred,	64	Hauke	91
But lyke a March harum /His braynes were so parum.	64	Hauke	105
To loke on this were tyme.	65	Hauke	144
The wordis were parvertyd;	68	Hauke	229
Phyllyp, though he were nyse,	76	Phy Sparrow	173
It were worth an hundreth pound	76	Phy Sparrow	189
That were syns Noes flode;	78	Phy Sparrow	268
And it were a Jewe,	80	Phy Sparrow	335
were] 'where' †Kele 1545.2			
Were made for myse and rattes,	80	Phy Sparrow	339
And how they were sommonde	88	Phy Sparrow	652
Prayd Troylus for to were	89	Phy Sparrow	690
Though his father were a kyng;	89	Phy Sparrow	698
Whether he were onlyve or ded;	89	Phy Sparrow	728
His termes were not darke,	91	Phy Sparrow	801
It were an hevenly blysse	97	Phy Sparrow	1039
My eyne were so dased;	99	Phy Sparrow	1106
The matter were to nyse,	100	Phy Sparrow	1132
How that she can were /Gorgiously her gere;	101	Phy Sparrow	1178
Were pullysshed with the fyle /Of Ciceros eloquence,	101	Phy Sparrow	1205
pullysshed] 'publysshed' †Kele 1545.2			
It were no gentle gyse	103	Phy Sparrow	1251
But whether it were so,	105	Phy Sparrow	1354
He were idem in numero,	105	Phy Sparrow	1355
Why were ye Calliope, embrawdred with letters of golde?	112	Calliope	1
I dare be bolde /Thus for to were.	112	Calliope	12
In your somnynge ye were to malaperte,	113	Scot Kynge	7
Syr squyer-galyarde ye were to swyfte;	113	Scot Kynge	11
Ye were beten weth your owne rod.	114	Scot Kynge	47
A somner to were a kynges crowne.	115	Scot Kynge	67
That late were discomfect with battayle marcyall.	117	Ag Scottes	84
Syr skyrgalyard, ye were so skyt,	118	Ag Scottes	101
And ye were disloyall Amalec.	118	Ag Scottes	116
Anoynted kyng, and ye were none.	118	Ag Scottes	118
Pardy, ye were his homager,	118	Ag Scottes	122
Ye were bonde tenent to his estate;	118	Ag Scottes	127
Ye were starke mad to make a fray,	119	Ag Scottes	143
Out of your robes ye were shaked,	119	Ag Scottes	166
your] not in Kynge & Marche 1554, Day 1560, Marshe 1568			
A sumner to were a kynges crowne.	120	Ag Scottes	175
Ye were to hye, ye ar cast downe.	120	Ag Scottes	177
Somtime women were put in great blame,	139	Ven Tongues	59
Yf noblenesse were aquayntyd with sober dyreccyon.	141	Magnyfycence	18
What ellys? For otherwyse it were agaynst kynde;	144	Magnyfycence	132
It were no vertue, it were a thynge unblyst.	144	Magnyfycence	134
It were no vertue, it were a thynge unblyst.	144	Magnyfycence	134
It were a myschefe, yf lyberte lacked a reyne	144	Magnyfycence	135
It were a shame, to God I make an othe,	144	Magnyfycence	145
Why, were not your selfe agreed to the same,	147	Magnyfycence	233
Endure? No, God wote, it were great payne.	147	Magnyfycence	248
But yf I were orderyd by just measure,	147	Magnyfycence	249
It were not possyble me longe to retayne.	147	Magnyfycence	250
Nowe, benedicite, ye wene I were some hafter,	147	Magnyfycence	257
Another wolde myne eye were blerde;	150	Magnyfycence	354
Mary, syr, ye were afrayde.	150	Magnyfycence	362
Why, man, it were to great a wonder	154	Magnyfycence	510
Why, wenyst thou, horson, that I were so mad?	155	Magnyfycence	517
That Mesure were cast out of the dores.	156	Magnyfycence	568
In faythe, he were better to dwell in hell.	157	Magnyfycence	623
Mary, the better and Mesure were out.	158	Magnyfycence	656
That I can were /Courtly my gere!	163	Magnyfycence	833
To name thyselfe. Come of, it were done.	167	Magnyfycence	965

WERE — WERE

	Page	Title	Line
Somtyme I syt as I were solempe prowde;	168	Magnyfycence	1011
Fyrst to tell you what were best:	168	Magnyfycence	1022
What! Wenyst thou that I were so folysshe and so fonde?	170	Magnyfycence	1098
What, that we used whan we were boyes?	172	Magnyfycence	1138
For you bothe it were inough.	173	Magnyfycence	1187
Why, wenyst thou that I were as moche a fole as thou?	173	Magnyfycence	1188
As some be not ferre and yf it were well sought –	174	Magnyfycence	1241
Though al his conquestys were brought to rekenynge,	181	Magnyfycence	1468
Were never halfe so rychely as I am drest.	181	Magnyfycence	1483
A, I wolde to God that I were halfe so crafty	183	Magnyfycence	1532
Mary, your speche is as pleasant as though it were pend,	183	Magnyfycence	1538
A, that were a baby to brace and to basse!	183	Magnyfycence	1560
It were better he spake with you or he wente,	187	Magnyfycence	1662
Lest that he thought that his money were evyll spente,	187	Magnyfycence	1674
That he wolde loke on hym, thoughe it were not longe.	187	Magnyfycence	1675
But, and I were as ye, I wolde not set a gnat.	188	Magnyfycence	1704
Well were that lady myght stande in my grace,	190	Magnyfycence	1799
I sawe a losell lede a lurden, and they were bothe blynde.	191	Magnyfycence	1824
The bytter sayd boldly that they were to blame;	192	Magnyfycence	1837
Or ever we were ware, brought us in adversyte,	193	Magnyfycence	1863
For thoughe you were somtyme a noble estate,	196	Magnyfycence	1980
Where you were wonte to have cawdels for your hede,	197	Magnyfycence	2008
And where that ye were pomped with what that ye wolde,	197	Magnyfycence	2012
With curteyns of sylke, ye were wonte to be drawe;	197	Magnyfycence	2014
curteyns of sylke] 'courtely sylkes' †Rastell & Treveris 1530B			
Yet were they better to begge, a great dele;	198	Magnyfycence	2043
And yf there were none to dysplease but thou and I,	202	Magnyfycence	2194
And specyally to redresse that were out of joynte.	208	Magnyfycence	2414
The whiche were to longe nowe to expresse;	209	Magnyfycence	2416
To gyve so hasty credence ye were moche to blame.	209	Magnyfycence	2443
It wolde be founde so yf it were well tryde.	210	Magnyfycence	2449
Remembre you, therfore, howe late ye were low.	210	Magnyfycence	2451
Whereto were most metely my corage to knyt?	211	Magnyfycence	2479
Lyke as they were with buckels /Togyder made fast.	215	El Rummynge	46
I were skynnes of conny,	224	El Rummynge	399
But they were sturdy and stubbed,	225	El Rummynge	422
stubbed] 'stubbled' Kynge & Marche 1554, Day 1560, Marshe 1568			
That were noughty froslynges;	226	El Rummynge	460
The goslenges were untyde;	226	El Rummynge	463
Suche were there menny	230	El Rummynge	611
Were fayne with a chalke /To score on the balke,	230	El Rummynge	614
'Peace, Parrot, ye prate as ye were ebrius!'	232	Speke Parott	68
A trym-tram for an horse-myll it were a nyse thyng,	234	Speke Parott	128
Tholomye and Haly were cunnyng and wyse	234	Speke Parott	134
Yf it were cond perfytely, and after the rate,	234	Speke Parott	143
Whether ita were before non, or non before ita,	235	Speke Parott	158
The progeny of Parrottis were fayre and favorable;	236	Speke Parott	187
Hyt ys to fere leste he wolde were the garland on hys pate,	244	Speke Parott	435
For grocers were grugyd at and groynyd at but late;	244	Speke Parott	441
Doutlesse were moche better	253	Collyn Clout	272
were] 'where' Kele 1545.1			
Howe [ye] were wonte to drynke	262	Collyn Clout	649
ye] 'thy' †Godfray 1531, 'they' Kele 1545.1, Marshe 1568, MS Harley 2252			
Though it were never so playne,	265	Collyn Clout	765
As they were very sayntes.	269	Collyn Clout	921
Syt styll as they were dom.	283	Why Come Ye	199
They were nat payde their hyre.	285	Why Come Ye	248
Theyr wages were nat payde.	285	Why Come Ye	253
Some sayde they were afrayde	285	Why Come Ye	254
They were, whan they were next.	285	Why Come Ye	260
they] 'the' †Kele 1545.3			
They were, whan they were next.	285	Why Come Ye	260
they] 'the' †Kele 1545.3			
But and it were well sought,	287	Why Come Ye	352
To any good ende were brought.	290	Why Come Ye	449
The Gommoryans also /Were brought to deedly wo,	291	Why Come Ye	473
As it were Jack Napis!	295	Why Come Ye	654
That were done in Fraunce,	297	Why Come Ye	720
Were gone as well as he!	300	Why Come Ye	836
It were great rewth	300	Why Come Ye	841
Suche a prelate, I trowe, /Were worthy to rowe	303	Why Come Ye	954
I wolde he were somwhere ellys;	303	Why Come Ye	963
For and he were there,	303	Why Come Ye	973
I wolde he were gone;	304	Why Come Ye	994
And whether it were of ymagynacyon,	313	Garlande	31
In figure wherof they were the laurell grene.	314	Garlande	68
they were the] 'the were they' †Fakes 1523			
For, ne were onely he hath your promocyon,	314	Garlande	71
How be it, it were harde to construe this lecture;	315	Garlande	109
For though he were venquesshid, yet was he not shamyd:	316	Garlande	161
For] 'Sithe' MS Cotton Vitellius E.x			
Wordes that were moch consolatory	317	Garlande	165
For truly it were a pyte that he sat ydle'.	318	Garlande	210
For elles it were to great a derogacyon	318	Garlande	218
Anone, I sey, this trumpet were founde out,	319	Garlande	243
They presid in faste; some thought they were to longe;	319	Garlande	248
Sume were to hasty and wold no man byde;	319	Garlande	249

WERETH—WERYED	Page	Title	Line
As people halfe pevysshe, or men that were masyd.	319	Garlande	266
Anone all was whyste, as it were for the nonys,	319	Garlande	267
Shall were a garlande of the laurell tre.'	321	Garlande	322
With diamauntis and rubis there tabers were trasid,	323	Garlande	395
tabers] 'taberdes' Marshe 1568			
That welny was loste when that we were gone.'	323	Garlande	406
welny] 'welnere' Marshe 1568			
That all the worde, I trowe, and it were sought,	325	Garlande	462
worde] 'worlde' Marshe 1568			
Of elephantis tethe were the palace gatis,	325	Garlande	468
If xii were let in, xii hundreth stode without.	326	Garlande	490
Some were of Poyle, and sum were of Trace,	326	Garlande	493
Some were of Poyle, and sum were of Trace,	326	Garlande	493
There were many wordes smaller and gretter,	326	Garlande	508
There were, I say, of all maner of sortis,	326	Garlande	512
When they were past and wente forth on there way,	327	Garlande	526
Some were olde wryten, sum were writen new,	328	Garlande	584
Some were olde wryten, sum were writen new,	328	Garlande	584
As quikly towchyd as it were flesshe and bones,	328	Garlande	592
Shet were the gatis; thei might wel knock and cal,	329	Garlande	604
Pope holy ypocrytis, as they were golde and hole,	329	Garlande	612
Sum were made pevysshe, porisshly pynk iyde,	329	Garlande	626
That ever more after by it they were aspyid;	329	Garlande	627
I saw dyvers that were cariid away thens in cribbis,	330	Garlande	640
It passid all bawmys that ever were namyd,	331	Garlande	674
Were newly enbybid; and rownd about the same	331	Garlande	682
So many, that longe it were to reherse.	331	Garlande	706
it] 'in' Marshe 1568			
O wele were hym that herof myght be sure,	332	Garlande	718
How daungerous it were to stande in his lyght,	333	Garlande	755
were to stande in his lyght] 'is to stop up his sight' MS			
Cotton Vitellius E.x			
To tell all his towchis it were to grete wonder;	333	Garlande	764
But if they were counterfettes that women them call,	334	Garlande	785
With that the tappettis and carpettis were layd,	334	Garlande	787
To weve in the stoule sume were full preste,	334	Garlande	790
And truly of theyr bownte thus were they bent	334	Garlande	806
You to devyse his crafte were to seke;	337	Garlande	893
It were an hevenly helth,	340	Garlande	994
It were an endeles welth,	340	Garlande	995
That in me were grete blyndnes,	342	Garlande	1064
Towarde the dore, as he were comyng oute,	343	Garlande	1095
Forthwith upon this, as it were in a thought,	343	Garlande	1100
All other besyde were counterfete they thought	343	Garlande	1106
All ... counterfete] 'that they ware were counterfettis' MS			
Cotton Vitellius E.x			
With that, of the boke losende were the claspis.	345	Garlande	1156
The claspis and bullyons were worth a thousande pounde;	345	Garlande	1165
in as moche as it were to longe a proces	345	Garlande	R
But whether it were so,	350	Garlande	1347
He were idem in numero,	350	Garlande	1348
Of Pajauntis that were played in Joyows Garde;	351	Garlande	1383
But how it was, sum were to recheles,	351	Garlande	1393
How men were wonte for to discerne	352	Garlande	1441
A pleasaunter place than Ashrige is, harde were to fynde,	353	Garlande	1465
were] 'where' †Fakes 1523			
Whan he were deed.	361	Albany	98
And falsest forsworne /That ever were borne.	362	Albany	118
But yet they were bolde	364	Albany	202
What an army were ye?	364	Albany	216
Caried in a cage, /As it were a cotage,	365	Albany	256
As it were a gote /In a shepe cote,	365	Albany	265
and yet they were but febly enformed	374	Replycacion	I
howbeit they were puffed so full	375	Replycacion	I
Your tonges were to flete;	376	Replycacion	50
Ye were nothyng discrete;	376	Replycacion	52
Ye were in a dronken hete.	376	Replycacion	53
For ye were worldly shamed, /At Poules Crosse openly,	376	Replycacion	62
Ye were fayne to beare fagottes;	376	Replycacion	66
Whan ye were bredde and borne,	376	Replycacion	80
And whan ye were preestes shorne,	376	Replycacion	81
Fayne ye were to reny	377	Replycacion	87
Your hertes than were hosed, /Your relacions reposed;	377	Replycacion	107
But ye were confuse tantum,	377	Replycacion	111
Ye argued argumentes, /As it were upon the elenkes,	377	Replycacion	126
But ye were folysshe nyse.	378	Replycacion	130
As ye were before.	379	Replycacion	180
For, if it were well sought,	379	Replycacion	185
WERETH			
All that he wereth, it is borowed ware;	60	Bowge	489
What is this he wereth? A cope?	157	Magnyfycence	601
WERY			
And was with flyenge wery.	63	Hauke	67
Was wery of her lyfe,	74	Phy Sparrow	109
I am wery of the worlde, for unkyndnesse me sleeth.	205	Magnyfycence	2283
The worlde waxyth wery of the; thou lyvest to longe.	205	Magnyfycence	2308
WERYED			
That weryed I wolde be on suche a bayte.	184	Magnyfycence	1568

	Page	Title	Line
WERYNG			
So myche papers weryng for ryghte a smalle exesse;	245	Speke Parott	479
WERYNGE			
It is nat for your werynge,	252	Collyn Clout	210
WERKE			
He must do this werke;	264	Collyn Clout	728
Nor of no good werke;	274	Collyn Clout	1100
WERKES			
As appereth by theyr werkes,	250	Collyn Clout	151
And snapper in suche werkes?	381	Replycacion	274
WERKIS			
Can lay any werkis that he hath compylyd,	318	Garlande	223
WERNE			
But of one thynge I werne you er I goo:	49	Bowge	106
werne] 'warne' Marshe 1568; er] 'or' Wynkyn de Worde 1510			
WERRE			
The tyme whan Mars to werre hym dyd dres;	46	Bowge	7
WERT			
Whiche wert endiyd with rede blode of the same	32	Dol Dethe	117
WESANT			
She had a wyde wesant;	227	El Rummynge	517
wyde] 'wyse' Kynge & Marche 1554			
WESAUNT			
Harke, howe the losell prates /With a wyde wesaunt!	275	Collyn Clout	1154
WESELY			
And wesely rede the Boke	384	Replycacion	360
WEST			
Taking his course toward the west;	86	Phy Sparrow	573
It standeth somwhat on the west;	308	Why Come Ye	1189
'The west is wyndy.' 'The est is metely wele.'	326	Garlande	499
WESTMINSTER			
For Peter of Westminster hath shaven thy beard.	358	Couplet	2
WESTMYNSTER			
Within Westmynster Hall.	287	Why Come Ye	325
WESTMYNSTERE			
Openly at Westmynstere	276	Collyn Clout	1183
WETE			
She sparyd not to wete her fete.	42	Balettys1	16
To wete yf Malkyn, my lemman, have gete oughte.	57	Bowge	401
To wete if he coulde brynge	76	Phy Sparrow	198
I speke the softlyer because he sholde not wete.	186	Magnyfycence	1654
WETEWOLDIS			
Some famous wetewoldis, and they be moche wurs;	317	Garlande	187
WETH			
Ye were beten weth your owne rod.	114	Scot Kynge	47
Of Rome to the see /Weth suche dygnyte.	307	Why Come Ye	1146
Weth Amphion, and other musis of Archady	320	Garlande	273
WETHER			
I have wynde and wether over all to sayle;	181	Magnyfycence	1464
Today fayre wether, tomorowe a stormy rage;	213	Magnyfycence	2545
Now clere wether, forthwith a stormy showre;	312	Garlande	12
WETHERCOCKE			
I sawe a wethercocke wagge with the wynde!	191	Magnyfycence	1821
WETHER COCKE			
Ware the wether cocke /Of the steple of Poules.	255	Collyn Clout	339
WETYNGE			
That is agayne you, you shall have wetynge;	54	Bowge	278
WEVE			
To weve all in one lome	282	Why Come Ye	130
To weve in the stoule sume were full preste,	334	Garlande	790
WEVYNG PIN			
The frame was browght forth with his wevyng pin.	334	Garlande	792
WEXYD			
His seconde hawke wexyd gery	63	Hauke	66
WHALIS BONE			
One of jasper, another of whalis bone;	325	Garlande	472
WHAN			
In autumpne, whan the sonne in Vyrgyne	46	Bowge	1
Whan Luna, full of mutabylyte,	46	Bowge	3
The tyme whan Mars to werre hym dyd dres;	46	Bowge	7
For whan she *fronneth she thynketh to make a fray.	49	Bowge	116
*fronneth] 'frouneth' Wynkyn de Worde 1510, Marshe 1568			
Whan there were dyverse that sore dyde you manace.	50	Bowge	159
And whan he came walkynge soberly,	51	Bowge	190
He sayde of me, whan he with you dyde talke –	52	Bowge	209
Whan I loked on hym, my purse was half aferde.	52	Bowge	238
Er this, whan that ye made me royall chere.	53	Bowge	249
And whan I fayle, bobbe me on the noll!	53	Bowge	259
Come whan it wyll, oppose the I shall,	55	Bowge	335
Whan that he was even at me almoost,	58	Bowge	432
Par[d]e, remembre whan ye were there,	60	Bowge	515
Parde] 'Parte' †Wynkyn de Worde 1499, 1510, Marshe 1568			
And whan I sawe the horsons wolde you hafte,	61	Bowge	521
Whan I remembre agayn /How mi Philyp was slayn,	72	Phy Sparrow	17
But whan I dyd beholde	72	Phy Sparrow	39
Whan she had lost her joye,	74	Phy Sparrow	110
Whan he sawe a waspe;	75	Phy Sparrow	129
Whan he saw an ant;	75	Phy Sparrow	133

	Page	Title	Line
And whan I sayd, 'Phyp, Phyp,'	75	Phy Sparrow	138
Whan I sawe my sparowe dye!	75	Phy Sparrow	146
Whan I was aslepe,	75	Phy Sparrow	162
But whan I was sowing his beke,	77	Phy Sparrow	219
Whan thou my byrde untwynde!	79	Phy Sparrow	284
Whan I remember it,	80	Phy Sparrow	353
Whan he doth her trede.	84	Phy Sparrow	512
Whan her tale is tolde	87	Phy Sparrow	620
Whan other ar glad,	95	Phy Sparrow	938
And whan I perceyved /Her wart and conceyved,	98	Phy Sparrow	1063
Upon her whan I gased,	99	Phy Sparrow	1104
Whan she lyst to avale,	99	Phy Sparrow	1117
Whan ye war yonger of age	124	Garnesche3	24
Whan hys grace ys fastynge,	126	Garnesche3	83
Now upon thys hete /Rankely whan ye swete,	127	Garnesche3	134
Whan the noppe is rughe, it wolde be shorne.	153	Magnyfycence	448
All thynge is worse whan it is worne.	153	Magnyfycence	451
Whan other men laughe, than study I and muse,	160	Magnyfycence	707
I am never glad but whan I may do yll,	160	Magnyfycence	731
And never am I sory but whan that I se	160	Magnyfycence	732
What, that we used whan we were boyes?	172	Magnyfycence	1138
And whan foly cometh, all is past.	176	Magnyfycence	1289
Whan Mesure is gone, we may slee care.	176	Magnyfycence	1324
And whan it pleaseth God, better may be.	196	Magnyfycence	1993
Upon the holy daye, /Whan she doth her aray,	216	El Rummynge	67
Whan she goeth out /Her selfe for to shewe,	216	El Rummynge	80
And donge, whan it commes, /In the ale tunnes.	219	El Rummynge	193
Whan I began to brewe,	219	El Rummynge	209
Whan we kys and play /In lust and in lykyng.	220	El Rummynge	221
An huswyfe of trust /Whan she is athrust,	220	El Rummynge	254
Here was scant thryft /Whan they made suche shyft.	222	El Rummynge	302
Whan the mare doth keke;	225	El Rummynge	450
But, whan they shoulde walke,	230	El Rummynge	613
In Popering grew peres, whan Parrot was an eg.	232	Speke Parott	70
Lyke a wanton, whan I wyll, I rele to and froo.	233	Speke Parott	109
To herken Jacke and Gyll /Whan they put up a byll;	249	Collyn Clout	97
Amende whan ye may,	251	Collyn Clout	189
And other wanton warkes /Whan the nyght darkes.	251	Collyn Clout	195
And howe whan ye gyve orders	252	Collyn Clout	220
But whan they have ones caught	252	Collyn Clout	229
Whan Scorpyon descendynge, /Was so then pretendynge	258	Collyn Clout	471
Whan there is never a whytte,	259	Collyn Clout	516
Whan the good ale soppe /Dothe daunce in theyr foretoppe;	260	Collyn Clout	530
Whan mammockes was your meate,	263	Collyn Clout	652
But whan the frere fell in the well	268	Collyn Clout	877
And whan he weneth to sytte	271	Collyn Clout	995
Whan they be infected,	277	Collyn Clout	1236
Whan that his pleasure is.	278	Collyn Clout	1265
But whan age seeth that rage	279	Why Come Ye	36
They were, whan they were next.	285	Why Come Ye	260
they] 'the' †Kele 1545.3			
Whan Edwarde of Karnarvan	285	Why Come Ye	270
Whan him lyst to lowre,	289	Why Come Ye	428
Whan they with hym shulde mell,	295	Why Come Ye	649
Whan ye fall to redynge	300	Why Come Ye	830
Yet whan he toke first his hat,	306	Why Come Ye	1108
first] not in MS Rawlinson C. 813			
Whan he was creat pope /First in Antioche.	307	Why Come Ye	1142
And whan Lucina plenarly did shyne,	312	Garlande	6
plenarly] 'plenary' †Fakes 1523, Marshe 1568			
Or elles he can nought bot whan he is at scole;	318	Garlande	205
Lyke to the boryall wyndes whan they blowe,	319	Garlande	261
Whan Titan radiant burnisshith his bemis bryght,	327	Garlande	534
Ye fyrste aryvyd; whan broken was your mast	327	Garlande	542
Ye] 'The' †Fakes 1523			
That of Aconcyus whan she founde the byll	337	Garlande	886
The Duke of Yorkis creauncer whan Skelton was,	347	Garlande	1226
Whan the flye net was set for to catche a cote,	351	Garlande	1379
Recoverd whan the forster was gone, and sped	351	Garlande	1407
Yet whan the rayne rayneth and the gose wynkith	352	Garlande	1430
Whan he herde tell /That my Lorde Amrell	360	Albany	54
Whan he were deed.	361	Albany	98
With us, whan ever ye mell	363	Albany	182
Whan ye cankerd knaves	363	Albany	184
whan they have delectably lycked a lytell	373	Replycacion	I
and whan they have ones superciliusly caught	374	Replycacion	I
Whan ye were bredde and borne,	376	Replycacion	80
And whan ye were preestes shorne,	376	Replycacion	81
Whan prelacy you opposed.	377	Replycacion	106
And your tonges cropped, /Whan ye logyke chopped,	377	Replycacion	118
That laughed whan he dyd pas	379	Replycacion	187

WHARROWE

	Page	Title	Line
They layde to pledge theyr wharrowe,	222	El Rummynge	298

WHAT

	Page	Title	Line
What, shuld I flatter? What, shulde I glose or paynt?	30	Dol Dethe	41
What, shuld I flatter? What, shulde I glose or paynt?	30	Dol Dethe	41
What frantyk frensy fyll in youre brayne?	30	Dol Dethe	51
What willfull foly made you to ryse agayn	30	Dol Dethe	53

	Page	Title	Line
What movyd you agayn hym to war or to fight?	31	Dol Dethe	62
What aylde you to slo your lord ageyn all right?	31	Dol Dethe	63
slo] 'sle' Marshe 1568			
Alas for routhe, what thouthe his mynde wer goode,	32	Dol Dethe	102
What man, remembring how shamfully he was slayn,	32	Dol Dethe	111
What nedethe me for to extoll his fame	33	Dol Dethe	141
'What, will ye do nothyng but play?'	35	Man Margery	4
What, wolde ye frompill me now? Fy, fy!	36	Man Margery	16
'What, and ye shal be my piggesnye?'	36	Man Margery	17
What though ye can cownter Custodi nos?	38	Coystrowne1	57
Deme what thou lyst, thou knowyst not my thought.	38	Coystrowne1	63
What prate ye, praty pyggys-ny?	41	Coystrowne4	20
What dremyst thou, drunchard, drousy pate?	42	Balettys1	22
What and he slyde downe, who shall hym save?	46	Bowge	28
That I ne wyste what to do was beste;	47	Bowge	30
Marchauntes her borded to see what she had lode.	47	Bowge	40
lode] not in Marshe 1568			
Fraghted with plesure to what ye coude devyse.	47	Bowge	42
What is thy name?' and I sayde it was Drede.	48	Bowge	77
'What movyd the,' quod she, 'hydder to come?'	48	Bowge	78
What though our chaffer be never so dere,	48	Bowge	89
Of Bowge of Court she asketh what we wold have,	49	Bowge	125
Loo, what it is a man to have connynge!	50	Bowge	153
And I drewe nere to herke what they two sayde.	51	Bowge	182
'Why? What than? Wylte thou lete men to speke?	51	Bowge	184
What, lete us holde him up, man, for a whyle.'	51	Bowge	188
But I wonder what the devyll of helle	52	Bowge	208
What thynge is that I maye do for you?	53	Bowge	240
Loo, what is to you a pleasure grete	53	Bowge	260
And I drewe nere to harke what they two sayde.	54	Bowge	296
'Remembrest thou what thou sayd yesternyght?	55	Bowge	323
What weneste I were? I trowe thou knowe not me.	55	Bowge	331
And ever he threwe, and kyst I wote nere what;	56	Bowge	349
'What, revell route!' quod he, and gan to rayle	56	Bowge	368
What sholde I tell more of his rebaudrye?	56	Bowge	372
What arte thou? I sawe the nowe but late.'	56	Bowge	376
What the devyll, man, myrthe was never one!	57	Bowge	388
was never one] 'is here within' Marshe 1568			
What, loo, man, see here of dyce a bale;	57	Bowge	389
But, what, a strawe! I maye not tell all thynge.	59	Bowge	459
More coude I saye, but what this is ynowe.	60	Bowge	491
Now constrewe ye what is the resydewe.	61	Bowge	539
What the sentence ment.	68	Hauke	227
To rede or to spell /What these verses tell.	68	Hauke	238
To behold and se /What hevynesse dyd me pange:	72	Phy Sparrow	44
Of what estate ye be, /Of hye or lowe degre,	73	Phy Sparrow	54
What though he crept so lowe?	76	Phy Sparrow	169
though] 'thought' †Kele 1545.2			
And do what he wolde;	76	Phy Sparrow	178
Must tell what is of the clocke	84	Phy Sparrow	496
What he doth fynde	85	Phy Sparrow	538
What though I can fram	88	Phy Sparrow	659
though] 'thought' †Kele 1545.2			
And what they wrote and sayd,	88	Phy Sparrow	680
Alas, what shuld I fayne?	97	Phy Sparrow	1011
To tell you what conceyte	100	Phy Sparrow	1130
What ayle them to deprave /Phillip Sparowes grave?	103	Phy Sparrow	1274
What the cause may be /Of this perplexite!	106	Phy Sparrow	1369
Ye shew ryght well what good ye can;	117	Ag Scottes	60
But sey me now, Syr Satrapas, what autoryte ye have	121	Garneschel	6
What, have ye kythyd yow a knyght, Syr Dugles the dowty,	121	Garneschel	8
But sey me yet, Syr Satropas, what auctoryte ye have	122	Garneschel	13
But sey me yet, Syr Satrapas, what auctoryte ye have	122	Garneschel	27
But sey me yet, Syr Satrapas, what auctoryte ye have	122	Garneschel	34
Ye wot what I thynke;	126	Garnesche3	80
Yf he wyst what sum wotte,	129	Garnesche3	199
What eylythe the, rebawde, on me to rave?	131	Garnesche5	79
Of the wote I what they wolde say;	133	Garnesche5	143
I care nat what thow wryght or sey;	134	Garnesche5	168
Wryght what thow wylte, I xall the aquyte.	134	Garnesche5	180
For ye said, that he said, that I said, wote ye what?	137	Ven Tongues	12
What fault find ye herein but may be avowed.	138	Ven Tongues	41
What tidings at Tot[nam], what newis in Wales,	139	Ven Tongues	64
Totnam] 'Totman' Marshe 1568			
What tidings at Tot[nam], what newis in Wales,	139	Ven Tongues	64
Totnam] 'Totman' Marshe 1568			
What shippis are sailing to Scalis Malis,	139	Ven Tongues	65
With, 'I can tel you what such a man said,	139	Ven Tongues	71
But if that I knewe what his name hight,	139	Ven Tongues	73
Ye, to knackynge ernyst what and it preve?	141	Magnyfycence	33
Why, to say what he wyll, Lyberte hath leve.	141	Magnyfycence	34
Shewe forth, I pray you, here in what you intende.	141	Magnyfycence	40
Say what ye wyll to me.	142	Magnyfycence	66
What wote ye where upon I wyll conclude?	142	Magnyfycence	72
What, lyberte to measure then wolde ye bynde?	144	Magnyfycence	131
What ellys? For otherwyse it were agaynst kynde;	144	Magnyfycence	132
But Measure, my frende, what hyght this mannys name?	145	Magnyfycence	165
By me all persons worke what they lyste.	146	Magnyfycence	210

	Page	Title	Line
What, syr, wolde ye make me a poppynge fole?	146	Magnyfycence	232
Nowe, I beseche the, tell me what is thy name?	148	Magnyfycence	269
Syr, hardely remembre what may your name avaunce.	148	Magnyfycence	277
Plucke up your mynde, syr, what ayle you to muse?	148	Magnyfycence	283
What avayleth lordshype, yourselfe for to kyll	148	Magnyfycence	286
What! I have aspyed ye are a carles page.	148	Magnyfycence	288
What, Fansy! Fansy!	149	Magnyfycence	325
Do what I coude to do you good.	150	Magnyfycence	335
At what place, nowe, as you gesse?	150	Magnyfycence	342
What! Sholde you pynche at a pecke of [gr]otes grotes] 'otes' †Rastell & Treveris C 1530, B	151	Magnyfycence	384
What! I say, herke a worde.	151	Magnyfycence	396
What! Wolde ye wyves counterfet	153	Magnyfycence	452
What! Wanton, wanton, nowe well ymet!	153	Magnyfycence	456
What! Margery Mylke Ducke, mermoset!	153	Magnyfycence	457
What! Counterfet Countenaunce!	154	Magnyfycence	494
What! Crafty Conveyaunce.	154	Magnyfycence	495
What the devyll! Are ye two of aquayntaunce?	154	Magnyfycence	496
Nowe what is his name? And what is thyne?	155	Magnyfycence	519
Nowe what is his name? And what is thyne?	155	Magnyfycence	519
But what became of the letter	155	Magnyfycence	531
What! Is Largesse without lyberte?	155	Magnyfycence	540
What! Is your conveyaunce no better.	155	Magnyfycence	542
What! Shall we jangle thus all the day styll?	156	Magnyfycence	565
Cockes armes! What is he?	156	Magnyfycence	573
I say, come hyder. What are these twayne?	156	Magnyfycence	582
What call ye him, this?	156	Magnyfycence	588
What is this he wereth? A cope?	157	Magnyfycence	601
What sayst? Here was to lytell clothe.	157	Magnyfycence	607
Tell me, syrs, what is your wyll?	157	Magnyfycence	611
What the devyll! Howe may that be?	157	Magnyfycence	627
What the devyll ayleth you? Can you not agree?	158	Magnyfycence	636
Pease! I have not yet sayd what I wyll.	158	Magnyfycence	648
But then, syr, what shall I hyght?	159	Magnyfycence	669
What and I frame suche a slyght	159	Magnyfycence	677
This was properly prated, syrs! What sayd a?	161	Magnyfycence	746
By God, syr, what nede all this waste?	161	Magnyfycence	754
What is this, a betell or a batowe or a buskyn lacyd?	161	Magnyfycence	755
What! Wenyst thou that I knowe the not, Clokyd Colusyon?	161	Magnyfycence	756
What! Is thy harte pryckyd with such a prowde pynne?	162	Magnyfycence	785
What the devyll! Who sent for the?	162	Magnyfycence	791
What the devyll, man, what thou menyst?	162	Magnyfycence	793
What the devyll, man, what thou menyst?	162	Magnyfycence	793
What the devyll! Can ye agre no better?	162	Magnyfycence	795
What the devyll! Where had we this joly jetter?	162	Magnyfycence	796
What sayst thou, man? Why dost thou not supplye,	162	Magnyfycence	797
What the devyll! Use ye not to drawe no swordes?	163	Magnyfycence	811
Tary here. Wote ye what I say?	163	Magnyfycence	819
What nowe? Let se /Who loketh on me	163	Magnyfycence	829
But what the devyll art thou	166	Magnyfycence	916
What! Whom have we here, Jenkyn Joly?	166	Magnyfycence	918
What! Fansy, my frende! Howe dost thou fare?	166	Magnyfycence	920
What the devyll hast thou on thy fyste? An owle?	166	Magnyfycence	922
But nowe what tydynges can you tell? Let se.	166	Magnyfycence	928
What the devyll! Never a whyt?	166	Magnyfycence	935
No, by the masse. What! Sholde I swere?	166	Magnyfycence	936
What neded that, in the dyvyls date?	166	Magnyfycence	943
With the also? What! He playeth the state?	166	Magnyfycence	945
Ye, but what shall I call my name?	167	Magnyfycence	958
Fyrst to tell you what were best:	168	Magnyfycence	1022
Nowe I wolde - and I wyst what -	169	Magnyfycence	1029
What, Fansy! Arte thou here alone?	169	Magnyfycence	1044
What, fonnysshe Foly! I befole thy face.	169	Magnyfycence	1045
What, frantyke Fansy, in a foles case?	169	Magnyfycence	1046
What is this, an owle or a glede?	169	Magnyfycence	1047
What pylde curre ledest thou in thy hande?	169	Magnyfycence	1054
What! Fleyest thou his skynne every yere?	169	Magnyfycence	1058
What! Thou wylte coughe me a dawe for forty pens?	170	Magnyfycence	1060
What! Of Cokermowth spake I no worde.	170	Magnyfycence	1062
Nay, but wotest thou what I do say?	170	Magnyfycence	1092
What! Callyst thou me a donnyshe crowe?	170	Magnyfycence	1095
What! Wenyst thou that I were so folysshe and so fonde?	170	Magnyfycence	1098
Torde, I say! What have I do?	171	Magnyfycence	1106
What callest thou thy dogge? Tusshe! His name is Gryme.	171	Magnyfycence	1118
What! He hathe ben hurte with a stabbe?	171	Magnyfycence	1124
What! Then he is some good poore mannes curre?	171	Magnyfycence	1129
What, that we used whan we were boyes?	172	Magnyfycence	1138
What! Canest thou all this Latyn yet,	172	Magnyfycence	1143
What, Fansy! Let me se who is the tother.	172	Magnyfycence	1158
Tell by thy trouth what sport can thou make.	172	Magnyfycence	1162
What? Wolde ye have mo folys, and are so many?	172	Magnyfycence	1170
What hast thou on thy fyst? A [k]esteryll? kesteryll] 'besteryll' †Rastell & Treveris C 1530, B	173	Magnyfycence	1174
What canest thou do but play cocke wat?	173	Magnyfycence	1191
What hast thou founde there? By God, a lowse.	173	Magnyfycence	1198
And what maner of people he maketh foles?	174	Magnyfycence	1217
What, horson! Arte thou suche a one?	174	Magnyfycence	1234
What he sayth and she sayth to lay good ere,	175	Magnyfycence	1269

	Page	Title	Line
And shall we have lyberte to do what we wyll?	176	Magnyfycence	1316
Ye. But tell me one thynge. What is that?	176	Magnyfycence	1318
When Mesure is gone, what nedest thou spare?	176	Magnyfycence	1323
To se what foly is used in every place;	177	Magnyfycence	1327
'What howe! Be ye mery! Was it not well conveyed?'	177	Magnyfycence	1347
Be governed and gyded; wote ye what I say?	179	Magnyfycence	1397
What! Wyll ye waste wynde and prate thus in vayne?	179	Magnyfycence	1403
And what so we say, holde you content withall.	179	Magnyfycence	1406
Your grace sent for me, I wene. What is your wyll?	179	Magnyfycence	1410
I am here redy. What! Shall we	179	Magnyfycence	1414
What! All by mesure, good syr, and none excesse?	180	Magnyfycence	1422
What! Can ye agree thus and appose?	180	Magnyfycence	1425
What sholde a man do with you? Loke you under [k]ay?	180	Magnyfycence	1429
kay] 'bay' †Rastell & Treveris C 1530, B			
What nede you with hym thus prate and chat?	180	Magnyfycence	1434
Shewe us your mynde then, howe to do and what.	180	Magnyfycence	1435
What the devyll, man, your name shalbe the greter;	180	Magnyfycence	1440
What man is so maysyd with me that dare mete,	182	Magnyfycence	1506
Plesyth it your grace to shewe what I do shall?	182	Magnyfycence	1517
Let se what ye say. Shewe it strayte.	185	Magnyfycence	1592
What sholde ye do elles? Are not you a lorde?	185	Magnyfycence	1606
Howe say ye, syrs? Herein what is best?	186	Magnyfycence	1659
What care I? By the masse, well sayd.	187	Magnyfycence	1671
What force ye, so that [y]e be payde?	187	Magnyfycence	1672
ye be] 'he be' †Rastell & Treveris C 1530, B			
I trowe ye herde yourselfe what I sayd.	188	Magnyfycence	1695
What! Woldest thou, lurden, with me brawle agayne?	188	Magnyfycence	1722
So I wote not what he sholde do here.	189	Magnyfycence	1741
Measure? Tut, what the devyll of hell!	189	Magnyfycence	1745
No force what thoughe his neyghbour dye in a dyche.	189	Magnyfycence	1752
To make fayre promyse, what are ye the worse?	189	Magnyfycence	1761
What tydynges with you, syr? I befole thy brayne pan.	191	Magnyfycence	1805
What sayst thou? Mary, I pray God your mastershyp to save.	191	Magnyfycence	1828
What tydynges with you, syr, that you loke so sad?	192	Magnyfycence	1843
What, brother braynsyke, how farest thou?	192	Magnyfycence	1845
What! Is all your myrthe nowe tourned to sorowe?	192	Magnyfycence	1849
What! Hath Sadnesse begyled me so?	192	Magnyfycence	1855
What? Yes, by the rode, syr. It was I all this whyle	193	Magnyfycence	1870
Man or woman, of what estate they be,	194	Magnyfycence	1898
He woteth not what welth is that never was sore.	196	Magnyfycence	1971
Alasse! I wote not what I sholde pray.	196	Magnyfycence	1994
Remembre you better, syr. Beware what ye say,	196	Magnyfycence	1995
And where that ye were pomped with what that ye wolde,	197	Magnyfycence	2012
What is he lyvynge that lyberte wolde lacke?	199	Magnyfycence	2083
What, a very vengeaunce, I say! Who is that?	199	Magnyfycence	2105
What brothell, I say, is yonder bounde in a mat?	199	Magnyfycence	2106
What! Is the worlde thus come to passe?	200	Magnyfycence	2108
What hast thou gotted, in faythe, to thy share?	201	Magnyfycence	2162
What! Then he may drynke out of a stone cruyse.	201	Magnyfycence	2166
What! Wylte thou skelpe me? Thou dare not loke on a gnat.	202	Magnyfycence	2181
What! Thou Colyn Cowarde, knowen and tryde!	202	Magnyfycence	2192
What a very vengeaunce nede all these wordys?	202	Magnyfycence	2198
Well sayd. But, in fayth, what was your quarell?	203	Magnyfycence	2210
What begger art thou, that thus doth banne and wary?	203	Magnyfycence	2238
Cockys bonys! Thou begger, what is thy name?	203	Magnyfycence	2240
What! Lyest thou there lyngrynge, lewdly and lothsome?	205	Magnyfycence	2291
A, blessyd may ye be, syr! What shall you I call?	206	Magnyfycence	2327
Who brought you that letter? Wote ye what he hyght?	209	Magnyfycence	2440
What, brother Perceveraunce, surely well met!	210	Magnyfycence	2458
What this man hath sayd, perceyve ye his sentence?	210	Magnyfycence	2465
Seest thou not what is fall?	219	El Rummynge	182
They care not what men saye!	221	El Rummynge	260
Some brought I wote nere what,	225	El Rummynge	441
What nede all this be spoken?	227	El Rummynge	499
Ye wote well what we meane.'	229	El Rummynge	579
'Que pensez-voz, Parrot? What meneth this besynes?'	232	Speke Parott	58
'What is this to purpose?' Over in a whynnymeg!	232	Speke Parott	71
With, 'He sayd,' and 'We said.' Ich wot now what ich wot,	234	Speke Parott	132
For though ye can tell in Greke what is phormio,	235	Speke Parott	151
What can it avayle /To dryve forth a snayle,	246	Collyn Clout	1
He wottyth never what /Ne whereof he speketh.'	247	Collyn Clout	17
What trowe ye they say more /Of the bysshoppes lore?	249	Collyn Clout	92
What have laye men to do	251	Collyn Clout	196
And wotteth never what thei rede, /Paternoster nor crede;	252	Collyn Clout	234
What are they the worse?	254	Collyn Clout	295
What care they thoughe Gyll swete?	254	Collyn Clout	321
What, Collyn, there thou shayles!	256	Collyn Clout	399
What coude the Turke do more	257	Collyn Clout	429
Iche wotte what yche do thynke!'	258	Collyn Clout	458
yche do] 'eche other' Kele 1545.1, Marshe 1568			
Nota what I say	258	Collyn Clout	463
'Note well what to say' MS Lansdowne 762 'Note whayte I say' MS Harley 2252			
And what ipostacis /Of Chrystes manhode is.	259	Collyn Clout	526
Alas, and wellaway, /What eyles them thus to say?	261	Collyn Clout	578
What they do in hell.	267	Collyn Clout	823
What they do in heven;	267	Collyn Clout	825
What may she do therto?'	281	Why Come Ye	87

WHAT — WHAT	Page	Title	Line
What newes? What news?	284	Why Come Ye	233
What newes? What news?	284	Why Come Ye	233
What here ye of Lancashyre?	285	Why Come Ye	247
What here ye of Chesshyre?	285	Why Come Ye	250
What here ye of the Scottes?	285	Why Come Ye	262
What here ye of the lorde Dakers?	285	Why Come Ye	272
What here ye of the lord Rose?	286	Why Come Ye	286
What say ye of the Scottysh kynge?	287	Why Come Ye	346
What here ye of Burgonyons	288	Why Come Ye	370
What here ye of Mutrell?	288	Why Come Ye	377
Yet what here ye tell	288	Why Come Ye	379
Of what estate he be /Of spirituall dygnyte;	294	Why Come Ye	617
For what is a man the better	295	Why Come Ye	669
And writeth he wottith nat what.	296	Why Come Ye	679
wottith] 'wot' Toy 1553, Kitson 1560.7, Marshe 1568			
But what his grace doth thinke,	296	Why Come Ye	683
Must counte what became	302	Why Come Ye	934
What a frensy is this,	305	Why Come Ye	1050
He said he knew what was what.	306	Why Come Ye	1109
He said he knew what was what.	306	Why Come Ye	1109
Saynt Dunstane, what was he?	307	Why Come Ye	1147
What though ye be namelesse,	309	Why Come Ye2	3
Complayne or do what ye wyll,	310	Why Come Ye2	31
I can not tell you what was the occasyon.	313	Garlande	35
not tell] 'not wele tell' MS Cotton Vitellius E.x			
And what estates to her did resorte,	313	Garlande	45
What he hath done, let it be brought to syght.	318	Garlande	230
What poetis we have at our retenewe.	319	Garlande	238
Alas, what ayle you to be so overthwhart,	320	Garlande	307
O fatall Fortune, what have I offendid?	321	Garlande	316
Of Scipions dreme what was the treu probate;	322	Garlande	368
But what sholde I say? Ye wote what I entende,	324	Garlande	426
But what sholde I say? Ye wote what I entende,	324	Garlande	426
'There shal he here what she wyl to hym say	325	Garlande	451
wyl to hym] 'to hym will' Marshe 1568			
How far it was, or ellis within what howris,	325	Garlande	457
far] not in †Fakes 1523			
With, 'How doth the north?' 'What tydingis in the sowth?'	326	Garlande	498
So well entakeled, what wynde that ever blowe,	327	Garlande	545
that] 'so' Marshe 1568			
Then questionyd I her what thos yatis ment;	328	Garlande	575
thos] 'these' Marshe 1568			
'What yate call ye this?' And she sayd, 'Anglea'.	328	Garlande	588
yate] 'gate' Marshe 1568			
What thynge occasionyd the showris of rayne,	331	Garlande	693
What it is, and where upon it standis;	332	Garlande	722
That I ne force what though it be discurid.	332	Garlande	731
'Now what ye mene, I trow I conject.	332	Garlande	735
And what blunderar is yonder that playth didil diddil?	333	Garlande	740
What though my penne wax faynt,	339	Garlande	954
For eche man herkynde what she wolde to me say;	344	Garlande	1119
wolde to me] 'to me wold' MS Cotton Vitellius E.x			
Of what charge so ever ye lay ageinst me;	344	Garlande	1138
What Skelton hath compilid and wryton in dede,	345	Garlande	1151
Rehersyng by ordre, and what is the grownde,	345	Garlande	1152
Wonder is to wryte what wrenchis she wrowght,	346	Garlande	1207
But what of that? Hard it is to please all men;	348	Garlande	1259
What ayle them to deprave /Phillippe Sparows grave?	348	Garlande	1267
What the cause may be /Of this perplexyte.	350	Garlande	1362
What myght she say? What myght he do therto?	351	Garlande	1395
What myght she say? What myght he do therto?	351	Garlande	1395
What constellacions ar good or bad for men,	352	Garlande	1429
Lytill wotith the goslyng what the gose thynkith.	352	Garlande	1431
By Candelmes day what wedder shuld holde;	352	Garlande	1442
Thynke what ye wyll /Of this wanton byll;	353	Garlande	1453
'Nay, sir' she sayd, 'what so in this place	353	Garlande	1481
What shuld I do but take it in gre?	353	Garlande	1487
I did what I cowde to scrape out the scrollis,	354	Garlande	1489
scrape] 'scarpe' Marshe 1568			
In shorte sentens, /Of your pretens /What is the grounde	361	Albany	81
What though ye stampe and stare?	363	Albany	180
What an army were ye?	364	Albany	216
Or what actyvyte /Is in you, beggars braules,	364	Albany	217
What have ye, villayn, forged, /And virulently dysgorged	367	Albany	320
Be well ware what ye say.	367	Albany	331
What, wold Fraunces, our friar, /Be suche a false lyar,	368	Albany	373
What though my stile be rude?	369	Albany	419
What noblenesse dothe abounde,	369	Albany	424
And what honour is founde	369	Albany	425
And what vertues be resydent	369	Albany	426
What losels than are ye	370	Albany	459
Ye heretykes recrayed, /Wotte ye what ye sayed	375	Replycacion	46
What may be ment hereby,	378	Replycacion	153
What shulde I prosecute,	378	Replycacion	158
What shulde I recken more?	379	Replycacion	181
What longeth to Christes humanyte.	381	Replycacion	286
Than ye know what betokeneth dulia:	382	Replycacion	288
Rede what Jerome there dothe say/	383	Replycacion	328

	Page	Title	Line
WHATE			
Whate mone he made when Pamphylus loste hys make.	237	Speke Parott	234
Whate sequele shall folow when pendugims mete togethyr?	243	Speke Parott	415
WHAT EVER			
What ever they say, /Jemmy is ded /And closyd in led,	116	Ag Scottes	20
I care muche the lesse what ever they say,	138	Ven Tongues	36
WHATSOEVER			
With a poore knyght, /Whatsoever he hyght!	295	Why Come Ye	646
Whatsoever your name be?	309	Why Come Ye2	2
WHAT SOEVER			
Let me have thy dogge, what soever I pay.	171	Magnyfycence	1101
Suche dawys, what soever they be,	174	Magnyfycence	1242
WHAT SO EVER			
What so ever I do, all men me prayse,	152	Magnyfycence	429
What so ever ye do, folowe your owne wyll,	185	Magnyfycence	1595
Here no man what so ever they say	185	Magnyfycence	1603
For your sake, what so ever befall;	188	Magnyfycence	1709
WHATSOMEVER			
Whatsomever aventure therof fall.	55	Bowge	336
WHEY-WORMED			
With a sory face /Whey-wormed about;	228	El Rummynge	553
WHELE			
Syr, remembre the tourne of Fortunes whele,	197	Magnyfycence	2022
To you that over the whele	262	Collyn Clout	627
WHELED			
Domingos nose that was wheled.	308	Why Come Ye	1185
was] not in MS Rawlinson C. 813			
WHELES			
With a payre of heles /As brode as two wheles.	216	El Rummynge	84
WHEN			
Knyghtis and squyers, at every season when	30	Dol Dethe	32
When thou shoke thi sword so noble a man to mar!	32	Dol Dethe	115
When he is well, yet can he not rest.	36	Coystrowne1	7
'My new furryd gowne, when it is worne -	40	Coystrowne4	10
That when ye thynke all daunger for to pas,	45	Balettys4	6
When it was polutyd	66	Hauke	174
When consecratyd was /The blessyd sacrament.	67	Hauke	185
To hawke when [you] lista	69	Hauke	257
you] 'your' editions			
When the Scotte lyved	116	Ag Scottes	R
When the Scot was slayne	117	Ag Scottes	R
At Gynys when ye ware /But a slendyr spere,	125	Garnesche3	40
For when ye dwelt there,	125	Garnesche3	43
When ye kyst a shepys ie,	125	Garnesche3	54
When Garnyche cummyth yow amonge	128	Garnesche3	150
For, when men by welth, they have lytell drede	140	Magnyfycence	10
Wel, wyse men may ete the fysshe when ye shal draw the pole.	148	Magnyfycence	300
Mary, syr, he told us, when	158	Magnyfycence	652
When we have hym thyder convayed,	159	Magnyfycence	676
He wyll come, man, when he may tende to.	162	Magnyfycence	790
Eche thynge is fayre when it is yonge; all hayle, owle!	167	Magnyfycence	970
Mary, I knewe the when thou waste a ladde.	170	Magnyfycence	1089
That wyt he wantyth when he hath moste nede.	175	Magnyfycence	1261
When Mesure is gone, what nedest thou spare?	176	Magnyfycence	1323
For go when ye shall, of you shall he mysse.	188	Magnyfycence	1706
When ye knowe that I knowe, ye wyll not be glad.	192	Magnyfycence	1844
For when I come, comyth sorowe and care;	195	Magnyfycence	1937
When we with Magnyfycence goodys made chevysaunce.	203	Magnyfycence	2236
Ye, when ye come out of the shoppe,	204	Magnyfycence	2271
Gave me a gyfte in my neste when I lay,	232	Speke Parott	44
I] 'he' †MS Harley 2252			
When wylfulnes ys vicar generall.	232	Speke Parott	54
When Parrot is ded, he dothe not putrefy;	236	Speke Parott	213
he] 'she' †Lant 1545, Kynge & Marche 1554, Day 1560, Marshe 1568			
Whate mone he made when Pamphylus loste hys make.	237	Speke Parott	234
Of Argus revengyd, recover when he may,	239	Speke Parott	288
Whate sequele shall folow when pendugims mete togethyr?	243	Speke Parott	415
When thei agayn thyder shal come,	268	Collyn Clout	883
Well-syghted when /He is amonge blynde men?	292	Why Come Ye	534
When Mars retrogradant reversed his bak,	312	Garlande	3
That welny was loste when that we were gone.'	323	Garlande	406
welny] 'welnere' Marshe 1568			
So finally, when they had shewyd there devyse,	324	Garlande	442
When he is callid to answere to his name.'	325	Garlande	452
When they were past and wente forth on there way,	327	Garlande	526
Of studyous doctryne when at the port salu	327	Garlande	541
Sometyme, as it semyth, when the mone light	330	Garlande	644
For when he spekyth fayrest, then thynketh he moost yll;	333	Garlande	759
But when they sawe my lawrell rychely wrought,	343	Garlande	1105
Item to Lerne You to Dye When ye Wyll;	345	Garlande	1176
to] 'do' †Fakes 1523			
When the stede is stolyn, spar the stable dur.	352	Garlande	1435
And when that I sawe it wolde no better be,	353	Garlande	1485
But when of the laurell she made rehersall,	354	Garlande	1503
WHENS			
And from whens come ye, and it myght be askyd?	141	Magnyfycence	29
From whens come you, syr, that no man lokyd after?	147	Magnyfycence	255

WHER — WHERE

	Page	Title	Line
From whens that he came,	290	Why Come Ye	465
From whens that mastyfe cam.	298	Why Come Ye	777

WHER

	Page	Title	Line
To ask wher he fyndyth among hys monacordys	37	Coystrownel	20
That wher I love best I dare not dyscure!	45	Balettys5	7
Wher Cerberus doth barke,	73	Phy Sparrow	85
Wher thou xulddst have bene shrynyd;	128	Garnesche3	175

WHERAT

	Page	Title	Line
Wherat moche I wonder	296	Why Come Ye	672

WHERBY

	Page	Title	Line
Wherby I rede theyr renome and theyr fame	46	Bowge	15
Wherby he myght have a name inmortall?	315	Garlande	119

WHERE

	Page	Title	Line
Where was your wit and reson ye shuld have had? your] 'ys' †MS Royal 18 D.ii	30	Dol Dethe	52
Where thow art Lord and God omnipotent.	34	Dol Dethe	203
That he wyst never where he was;	42	Balettys1	10
That where I love best I dare not dyscure.	46	Balettys5	14
Where hathe your dwellynge ben, er ye cam here?	53	Bowge	247
He frounde, he stared, he stampped where he stoode.	55	Bowge	319
Anone Dyscymular came where I stode.	58	Bowge	427
A man can not wote where to become.	59	Bowge	466
Naye, see where yonder stondeth the teder man!	59	Bowge	484
There I wynked on you - wote ye not where?	60	Bowge	516
Where sanguis taurorum,	66	Hauke	170
Where Crystis precyous blode /Dayly offryd is,	66	Hauke	179
Doctor Dialetica, /Where fynde you in Ypotetica,	69	Hauke	268
Where the muses dwell:	87	Phy Sparrow	611
I wot not where to fynd /Termes to serve my mynde.	91	Phy Sparrow	782
And where my pen hath offendyd,	102	Phy Sparrow	1245
Of infernall posty /Where soules frye and rousty; rousty] 'rosty' Marshe 1568	105	Phy Sparrow	1333
Syr sumner, now where is your crowne?	120	Ag Scottes	178
Get ye anothyr where ye may.	131	Garnesche5	62
But where wonnys welthe, and a man wolde wyt?	141	Magnyfycence	22
Where drede ledyth the daunce, there is no joy nor blysse.	142	Magnyfycence	76
Where lyberte is absent, set welthe asyde.	142	Magnyfycence	80
Where measure is mayster, plenty dothe none offence;	144	Magnyfycence	121
Where measure lackyth, all thynge dysorderyd is;	144	Magnyfycence	122
Where measure is absent, ryot kepeth resydence;	144	Magnyfycence	123
Where measure is ruler, there is nothynge amysse.	144	Magnyfycence	124
If lyberte sholde lepe and renne where he lyst	144	Magnyfycence	133
There is no surfet where measure rulyth the feste;	144	Magnyfycence	139
There is no excesse where measure hath his helthe.	144	Magnyfycence	140
Where was it delyvered you? Shewe unto me.	150	Magnyfycence	340
To Tyburne, where they hange on hyght.	152	Magnyfycence	423
But Fansy, my frende, where have ye bene so longe?	154	Magnyfycence	500
Surveyaunce! Where ye survey,	155	Magnyfycence	526
Alasse! Where is my botes and my spores?	156	Magnyfycence	569
But tell me where aboute ye go.	157	Magnyfycence	617
Why, dwelleth Mesure where ye two dwell?	157	Magnyfycence	622
Yet where we wonne, nowe there wonneth he.	157	Magnyfycence	624
But are ye not avysed to dwell where ye spake?	162	Magnyfycence	774
What the devyll! Where had we this joly jetter?	162	Magnyfycence	796
Teuyt, teuyt! /Where is my wyt?	168	Magnyfycence	1005
That I wote not where I may rest.	168	Magnyfycence	1021
Where is my cappe? I have lost my hat!	169	Magnyfycence	1030
I can fynde fantasyes where none is;	169	Magnyfycence	1041
Where the devyll gate he all these hurtes?	171	Magnyfycence	1127
But where gatte thou that mangey curre?	173	Magnyfycence	1180
Lo, Johnn a Bonam, where is thy brayne?	173	Magnyfycence	1204
And where I spy a nysot gay	174	Magnyfycence	1228
And maketh hym besy where is no nede.	175	Magnyfycence	1249
To put where he lyst, foly hath fre chace;	177	Magnyfycence	1329
Foly and fansy all where every man dothe face and brace.	177	Magnyfycence	1330
To clothe the nakyd where is lackynge a smocke -	177	Magnyfycence	1345
Mayster Survayour, where have ye ben so longe?	178	Magnyfycence	1382
For where is no mesure, howe may worshyp endure?	179	Magnyfycence	1408
A, Cockes armes! Where myght suche one be founde?	184	Magnyfycence	1569
Where is he? Mary, I made hym abyde	187	Magnyfycence	1685
Where mennes belyes is measured, there is no chere;	189	Magnyfycence	1742
With the gowte I make them to grone where they syt;	194	Magnyfycence	1903
Yet sometyme I stryke where is none offence,	194	Magnyfycence	1916
And where the fader by wysdom worshyp hath wonne,	195	Magnyfycence	1934
Howe, where art thou? Come hether, Poverte.	195	Magnyfycence	1953
Alasse, where is youth that was wont for to skyppe?	195	Magnyfycence	1957
Alasse! Where is nowe my golde and fe?	196	Magnyfycence	1967
Alasse, I say, where to am I brought?	196	Magnyfycence	1968
Where you were wonte to have cawdels for your hede,	197	Magnyfycence	2008
And where you had chaunges of ryche aray,	197	Magnyfycence	2010
And where that ye were pomped with what that ye wolde,	197	Magnyfycence	2012
Where is nowe my welth and my noble estate?	198	Magnyfycence	2055
Where is nowe my treasure, my landes, and my rent?	198	Magnyfycence	2056
Where is nowe all my servauntys that I had here a late?	198	Magnyfycence	2057
Where is nowe my golde upon them that I spent?	198	Magnyfycence	2058
Where is nowe all my ryche abylement?	198	Magnyfycence	2059
Where is nowe my kynne, my frendys, and my noble blood?	198	Magnyfycence	2060
Where is nowe all my pleasure and my worldly good?	198	Magnyfycence	2061

WHERE AS —WHEREUPON

	Page	Title	Line
And I am a vyce where I am abused.	199	Magnyfycence	2102
For where I am occupied and usyd wylfully,	200	Magnyfycence	2131
Out harowe! Hyll burneth! Where shall I me hyde?	206	Magnyfycence	2324
For where sad cyrcumspeccyon is longe out of the way,	209	Magnyfycence	2427
Where every thyng is ordenyd after your noble porte.	214	Magnyfycence	2568
But we wyll turne playne /Where we left agayne.	220	El Rummynge	243
She pyst where she stood.	223	El Rummynge	373
Where men of that contre by fortune me fynde,	231	Speke Parott	5
O connyng clergye, where ys your redynes	242	Speke Parott	392
But where theyr soules dwell,	257	Collyn Clout	427
And where the prelates be /Come of lowe degre	261	Collyn Clout	585
Where these kepe resydence,	279	Why Come Ye	11
In the Chauncery where he syttes,	287	Why Come Ye	326
Where trouth is abhorde,	300	Why Come Ye	847
Where hartis belluyng, embosyd with distres,	312	Garlande	24
Few men can tell where the hynde calfe gose.	313	Garlande	26
tell] 'telle now' MS Cotton Vitellius E.x			
Call forthe, let se where is your clarionar,	318	Garlande	233
Where I sawe come after, I wote, full lytell lake	320	Garlande	285
That with them I went where they wolde me brynge,	324	Garlande	447
Unto the pavylyon where Pallas was syttyng.	324	Garlande	448
Where the postis wer enbulyoned with saphiris indy blew,	325	Garlande	478
To walke where we lyst, let us somwhat fynde	328	Garlande	564
In an herber I saw, brought where I was,	330	Garlande	652
Where I saw growyng a goodly laurell tre,	330	Garlande	665
And where the two Trions a man shold aspy,	331	Garlande	699
Trions] 'Troons' †Fakes 1523			
Where the noble Cowntes of Surrey in a chayre	333	Garlande	769
Where ye must brevely answere to your name.'	343	Garlande	1092
Where all the sayd poetis sat in there degre.	343	Garlande	1104
Caliope poynted me where I shulde sit.	344	Garlande	1143
Item Bowche of Courte, where Drede was begyled;	346	Garlande	1183
Where it became, and whether it went,	347	Garlande	1243
Of infernall posty, /Where soulis fry and rosty;	349	Garlande	1326
And plantid it there where never before was none, unshred	351	Garlande	1405
it there where] 'yet wher' Marshe 1568			
It is sone aspyed where the thorne prikkith.	352	Garlande	1437
Where the sank royall is, Crystes blode so rede,	353	Garlande	1463
Where I saw Janus, with his double chere,	354	Garlande	1515
Se where the heretykes go,	376	Replycacion	73
To places where ye have preched,	379	Replycacion	203
Where worde for worde ye may	383	Replycacion	327

WHERE AS

	Page	Title	Line
I say there is no welthe where as lyberte is subdude.	142	Magnyfycence	73
Where as ye have, syr, to me them assygned,	145	Magnyfycence	177
With Mesure. Where as all noblenes is, there I have past:	189	Magnyfycence	1749
Where as the yeest is,	219	El Rummynge	199
But one gate specyally, where as I stode,	328	Garlande	586
Into that place where as they left me,	343	Garlande	1103

WHEREAT

	Page	Title	Line
Whereat he made dysdayne.	68	Hauke	224
His Englyssh whereat they barke	91	Phy Sparrow	798
Whereat a thousande gased,	379	Replycacion	193

WHERE EVER

	Page	Title	Line
Where ever he go or ryde	289	Why Come Ye	394
Where ever he rydes or goos.	370	Albany	470

WHEREFORE

	Page	Title	Line
Wherefore shulde I be blamed	103	Phy Sparrow	1255
Wherefore by and by /Nowe consequently	383	Replycacion	314

WHEREIN

	Page	Title	Line
wherein ar comprysyde many and dyvers	312	Garlande	1
Wherein he reporteth of the coragius	317	Garlande	164
Wherein] 'Where' MS Cotton Vitellius E.x			
Wherein many storis ar brevely contayned	347	Garlande	1224

WHEREOF

	Page	Title	Line
Whereof the elegy /Foloweth by and by.	92	Phy Sparrow	824
Sacro vatum, whereof to you I breke;	233	Speke Parott	97
He wottyth never what /Ne whereof he speketh.'	247	Collyn Clout	18
Whereof I beseche you to tender the effecte.	313	Garlande	56
Of men and of bestis, and whereof they begone,	331	Garlande	692

WHERE OF

	Page	Title	Line
Tell you where of my name dothe ryse.	151	Magnyfycence	409

WHEREON

	Page	Title	Line
Whereon theis ladys softly myght rest,	334	Garlande	788

WHERE SOEVER

	Page	Title	Line
And where soever you wyll fall to a rekenynge,	190	Magnyfycence	1777

WHERE SO EVER

	Page	Title	Line
Yet, where so ever they ly	106	Epitaphe	1
This is a wyse man, syr, where so ever ye hym had.	187	Magnyfycence	1689

WHERETO

	Page	Title	Line
But whereto shuld I /Lenger morne or crye?	86	Phy Sparrow	594
But whereto shulde I note	100	Phy Sparrow	1145
Whereto were most metely my corage to knyt?	211	Magnyfycence	2479
Whereto made ye me hym to avaunce	315	Garlande	115
In so moche the stumpe, whereto I me lente	320	Garlande	281

WHEREUPON

	Page	Title	Line
Whereupon he metrefyde after his mynde;	353	Garlande	1464

	Page	Title	Line
WHERE UPON			
What wote ye where upon I wyll conclude?	142	Magnyfycence	72
Tell me brefly where upon ye began.	203	Magnyfycence	2224
What it is, and where upon it standis;	332	Garlande	722
WHEREWITH			
Wherewith my handes I wrange /That my senaws cracked	72	Phy Sparrow	45
Wherewith he wolde make	76	Phy Sparrow	164
Wherewith your spiritis may be revyvid.'	332	Garlande	713
WHERE WITH			
Where with to rule hym with the wrythyng of a rest.	144	Magnyfycence	136
WHERFOR			
Wherfor he may now come agayne as he wente,	240	Speke Parott	338
Wherfor your remorders ar madde or else starke blynde, remorders] 'remordes' †MS Harley 2252	241	Speke Parott	369
WHERFORE			
Wherfore, as I be savyd, /Ye ar therfore beknavyd.	70	Hauke	309
Wherfore and why, why?	72	Phy Sparrow	6
Wherfore the bordes yet cry bordes] 'byrdes' Wyght 1553, Kitson 1560.6, Marshe 1568	78	Phy Sparrow	248
Wherfore all Troy dyd rew;	88	Phy Sparrow	676
Wherfore hold me excused	92	Phy Sparrow	813
Wherfore I fere ye wyll suffre payne.	114	Scot Kynge	28
Wherfore I wryght ageyne	124	Garnesche3	8
Wherfore, in welthe beware of woo,	132	Garnesche5	124
Wherfore at lyberte	142	Magnyfycence	65
Wherfore, Measure, take Lyberte with you hence,	146	Magnyfycence	230
Wherfore I preve,	165	Magnyfycence	909
Syr, Sober Sadnesse cometh. Wherfore it be?	186	Magnyfycence	1631
Wherfore I wyll that ye be resydent	188	Magnyfycence	1718
Wherfore, of adversyte loke ye be ware;	195	Magnyfycence	1936
Wherfore men be supposynge	255	Collyn Clout	357
Wherfore he hath good ure	271	Collyn Clout	1001
Wherfore, take no dysdayne	273	Collyn Clout	1087
Wherfore shulde I be blamed? be] not in Marshe 1568	274	Collyn Clout	1112
Wherfore, as thynketh me,	274	Collyn Clout	1129
Wherfore we make you sure,	276	Collyn Clout	1203
Wherfore he suffred payn,	297	Why Come Ye	739
Wherfore then rasid ye not away	316	Garlande	137
Whiche passid all other; wherfore I may	316	Garlande	159
Of scrupulus dout. Wherfore, your mynde discharge,	332	Garlande	726
To your remembraunce wherfore ye must call	335	Garlande	812
Wherfore delyght /I have to whryght.	339	Garlande	945
Wherfore, I make you sure, I make you sure] 'I yow assure' MS Cotton Vitellius E.x	340	Garlande	993
Wherfore doutles ye geve me cause	342	Garlande	1057
Wherfore to jeste /Is my delyght	359	Albany	13
Wherfore ye are well checte,	380	Replycacion	238
Wherfore make ye no mo restrayntes,	382	Replycacion	292
WHERIN			
Wherin he had apes and owles,	78	Phy Sparrow	258
Wherin it is necessary my pleasure you knowe:	145	Magnyfycence	185
Wherin this answere for hym we have comprisid,	314	Garlande	80
Wherin was set of Fame the noble Quene,	325	Garlande	482
WHEROF			
I have a favoure to you, wherof it be	52	Bowge	206
Wherof I hym controld; I hym] 'him I' Kynge & Marche 1554, Day 1560, Marshe 1568	64	Hauke	96
Wherof hereafter, I thinke for to write,	140	Ven Tongues	81
Wherof moche care began.	297	Why Come Ye	725
Wherof for to trete for] not in Kele 1545.3, Marshe 1568	306	Why Come Ye	1087
Wherof this ungracyous lorde	306	Why Come Ye	1098
In figure wherof they were the laurell grene. they were the] 'the were they' †Fakes 1523	314	Garlande	68
Of noble Dame Pallas, wherof I spake;	320	Garlande	284
Wherof partely I purpose to expounde,	325	Garlande	464
Wherof the answere restyth in my handis,	332	Garlande	724
In trust wherof comforte his hart doth grope,	335	Garlande	832
Wherof in substaunce I brought this away.	344	Garlande	1120
WHERON			
Wheron he gat his fynall dedely wounde.	32	Dol Dethe	119
Wheron was wryten this worde, Myscheve.	58	Bowge	434
Wheron stode a lybbard, crownyd with golde and stones,	328	Garlande	590
WHERSO			
For wherso we dwell,	39	Coystrowne3	22
WHERTO			
Wherto shuld I rehers /The sentens of my vers?	68	Hauke	246
Wherto shuld I disclose	101	Phy Sparrow	1175
Wherto xulde I wryght	125	Garnesche3	34
Or wherto shulde he have the prerogatyve, the] 'that' MS Cotton Vitellius E.x	315	Garlande	117
Wherto she answeryd, and brevely me tolde	328	Garlande	576
Wherto shuld I more speke	366	Albany	302
WHERWITH			
Wherwith Mesure to confounde.	155	Magnyfycence	554
Wherwith the Sodomites /Lost theyr inward syghtes.	290	Why Come Ye	470
Wherwith to geve you my regraciatory,	324	Garlande	431

WHERWYTH —WHICHE

	Page	Title	Line
Wherwith he dothe them bynde	371	Albany	484
WHERWYTH			
Wherwyth my hand she strayned,	99	Phy Sparrow	1122
WHESTON			
Esebon, Marybon, Wheston next Barnet;	234	Speke Parott	127
WHETE			
Brynge wyth them malte or whete,	221	El Rummynge	267
WHETHER			
Ask all your neybours whether that I ly.	43	Balettys2	35
Loke on this tabull, /Whether thou art abull	68	Hauke	236
Whether he were onlyve or ded;	89	Phy Sparrow	728
But whether it were so,	105	Phy Sparrow	1354
Here is none forsyth whether you flete or synke.	147	Magnyfycence	254
In all this hast whether wyll ye ryde?	156	Magnyfycence	570
But whether art thou walkynge, in faythe unfaynyd?	161	Magnyfycence	762
I wote not whether it cometh of the or of me,	176	Magnyfycence	1290
Yes, perde, man, whether that ye ryde or go.	176	Magnyfycence	1307
Whether sholde welth be rulyd by lyberte,	180	Magnyfycence	1431
Whether ita were before non, or non before ita,	235	Speke Parott	158
Whether it be wronge or ryght	272	Collyn Clout	1055
And whether they say trewly	273	Collyn Clout	1061
For whether he blesse or curse,	282	Why Come Ye	137
Whether he be knyght or squyre,	287	Why Come Ye	344
They wot not whether to go.	294	Why Come Ye	614
Whether God be pleased or wroth.	307	Why Come Ye	1132
And whether it were of ymagynacyon,	313	Garlande	31
Where it became, and whether it went,	347	Garlande	1243
But whether it were so,	350	Garlande	1347
Whether he rode to Swaffhamm or to Some,	352	Garlande	1416
Swaffhamm] 'Swasshamm' †Fakes 1523, Marshe 1568			
No man can tell whether.	358	Garlande2	9
WHETT			
Your teth whett on this bone	258	Collyn Clout	476
whett on] 'whetten' †Godfray 1531, 'whette on' MS Harley 2252			
WHICH			
In Englande and Fraunce which gretly was redouted,	30	Dol Dethe	43
To the right of his prince which shold not be withstand;	31	Dol Dethe	67
Which to thi resemblance wonderusly has wrought	34	Dol Dethe	193
Which men the viii dedly syn call.	36	Coystrownel	5
syn] 'sins' Marshe 1568			
Which makyth thy hart oft to lepe and sprynge	44	Balettys3	32
Worrowyd her on that /Which I loved best.	72	Phy Sparrow	30
Which by his mercyfull rage	88	Phy Sparrow	670
mercyfull] 'unmercifull' Wyght 1553, Kitson 1560.6, Marshe 1568			
which hath to name Why Come Ye Nat to Courte?	278	Why Come Ye	1
Which glad am to please, and lothe to offende.'	324	Garlande	441
'Theis yatis,' she sayd, 'which that ye beholde,	328	Garlande	579
Of honour and worshyp which hath the formar date:	336	Garlande	842
Of porturature which was the famous Greke,	337	Garlande	895
And specyally which glad was to devyse	342	Garlande	1071
The False Fayth that Now Goth, which dayly is renude;	346	Garlande	1179
Which is the most clere christall	375	Replycacion	31
In that faculte which shyned as Phebus bright;	383	Replycacion	333
Which is God of myghtes most,	385	Replycacion	384
WHICHE			
Adres the to me, whiche am bothe halt and lame,	29	Dol Dethe	10
At his commaundement whiche had both day and night	30	Dol Dethe	31
Whiche kyndelde the wyld fyre that made all this smoke.	31	Dol Dethe	77
Whiche wert endiyd with rede blode of the same	32	Dol Dethe	117
O homycide, whiche sleest all that thou kan,	32	Dol Dethe	123
Whiche whils he lyvyd had fuyson of every thing,	32	Dol Dethe	131
Immortally whiche is inmaculate?	33	Dol Dethe	147
And as the lyonne whiche is of bestis kinge	33	Dol Dethe	167
Whiche sat behynde a tra[v]es of sylke fyne,	47	Bowge	58
traves] 'tranes' †Wynkyn de Worde 1499, 1510, Marshe 1568			
In a trone whiche fer clerer dyde shyne	47	Bowge	60
clerer] 'clere' Marshe 1568			
In golde letters, this worde, whiche I dyde rede:	48	Bowge	66
The seconde was Suspecte, whiche that dayly	49	Bowge	136
Whiche gave to me /The high degre	112	Calliope	5
For whiche ende goth forwarde ye take lytell charge.	148	Magnyfycence	296
Whiche of you is the better man,	162	Magnyfycence	802
Or whiche of you can do most.	162	Magnyfycence	803
And be ruled by me, whiche am called Redresse.	208	Magnyfycence	2410
The whiche were to longe nowe to expresse;	209	Magnyfycence	2416
Whiche conteyned in it a specyall clause	209	Magnyfycence	2436
The whiche shulde be /Bothe franke and free,	264	Collyn Clout	710
Whiche determyne playne	277	Collyn Clout	1231
Whiche hate to be corrected	277	Collyn Clout	1235
Whiche, truly to expresse, /Is a forgetfulnesse,	290	Why Come Ye	467
Whiche he can nat se.	291	Why Come Ye	507
Whiche, of his royall mynde	292	Why Come Ye	546
Whiche his lyvenge wan	293	Why Come Ye	554
Whiche shrewdly doth accorde!	294	Why Come Ye	621
Whiche constrayned him forcebly	296	Why Come Ye	702
Whiche pyncheth him sore!	302	Why Come Ye	948
Whiche madly he dothe apply /Unto an extravagancy,	306	Why Come Ye	1104

	Page	Title	Line
In Balthasor, whiche heled	308	Why Come Ye	1184
But that his bokis, whiche he did devyse,	315	Garlande	124
From whiche Eschines had none evacyon.	316	Garlande	154
Eschines, whiche was not shamefully confutid	316	Garlande	157
Whiche passid all other; wherfore I may	316	Garlande	159
Whiche soverenly in honoure shulde excell;	317	Garlande	199
With decadis historious, whiche that he mengith	321	Garlande	345
Whiche glad am to please, and loth to offende'	324	Garlande	427
Whiche shall be to you a sufferayne accessary,	326	Garlande	523
Of that aventuris, whiche made me sore agast.	330	Garlande	649
And of that pole artike whiche doth remayne	331	Garlande	695
As dame Thamarys, whiche toke the kyng of Perce,	336	Garlande	857
Whiche maner of abasshement became her not yll;	337	Garlande	889
Whiche was extolde /A thowsande folde	342	Garlande	1078
Set on your hede this laurell whiche is wrought.	343	Garlande	1087
In comparyson of that whiche I ware.	343	Garlande	1107
Whiche in your recordes, I know well, be enrolde,	344	Garlande	1140
Whiche, if they be happy, have cause to beware	353	Garlande	1474
Whiche redde on still, as it cam to her syght,	354	Garlande	1493
Whiche be as trewe /As the gospell:	359	Albany	4
Agaynst whiche erronyous errours,	375	Replycacion	1
That our Savyour bare, /Whiche us redemed from care.	375	Replycacion	34
Employed whiche myght have be	378	Replycacion	149
Whiche de latria do trete.	381	Replycacion	281
In poetes whiche excelles,	384	Replycacion	377

WHIGHT

Be it blacke or whight	281	Why Come Ye	115

WHILOM

And assilum, whilom refugium miserorum,	234	Speke Parott	124

WHILS

Yet whils he stode he gave them woundes wyde. Yet] 'Ye' Marshe 1568	32	Dol Dethe	101
Whiche whils he lyvyd had fuyson of every thing,	32	Dol Dethe	131

WHIP

Wyth, 'Hey, troly-loly-lo, whip here, Jak',	37	Coystrowne1	15

WHIPLING

There is a whyspring and a whipling There] 'Her' Kitson 1560.7, Marshe 1568	287	Why Come Ye	350

WHIRLLID

Item Apollo that whirllid up his chare,	353	Garlande	1471

WHISPRED

Some whispred, some rownyd, some spake, and some cryde,	319	Garlande	250

WHIT

'Be mirry,' she sayd, 'be not afferde a whit,	344	Garlande	1145

WHITE

And somtyme white bred crommes;	74	Phy Sparrow	123
The rose both white and rede	110	Lawde	1
The White Lyon, there rampaunt of moode,	119	Ag Scottes	135
He the White, and ye the Red, ye] 'you' Day 1560, Marshe 1568	119	Ag Scottes	137
The White there slew the Red starke ded.	119	Ag Scottes	138
Agaynst the lyon white,	366	Albany	309

WHITTE

The devyll spede whitte!	304	Why Come Ye	1017
Of my laurell the proces every whitte.	343	Garlande	1099

WHY

I say, ye commoners, why wer ye so stark mad?	30	Dol Dethe	50
Why so koy and full of skorne?	40	Coystrowne4	8
And if ye lyst to know the cause why so,	44	Balettys3	38
'Maystres,' quod I, 'I praye you tell me why soo,	49	Bowge	108
'Why? What than? Wylte thou lete men to speke?	51	Bowge	184
'Syr, God you save, why loke you so sadde?	53	Bowge	239
'Than,' quod Hervy, 'why arte thou so dysmayde?'	54	Bowge	299
'And, syr, in fayth, why comste not us amonge	57	Bowge	379
Wherfore and why, why?	72	Phy Sparrow	6
Wherfore and why, why?	72	Phy Sparrow	6
Why shuld she be afrayde?	103	Phy Sparrow	1283
Why shuld she take shame	103	Phy Sparrow	1284
Why were ye Calliope, embrawdred with letters of golde?	112	Calliope	1
Ye summoned our kynge. Why dyde ye so?	113	Scot Kynge	2
Ye summond our kyng, why dyd ye so? ye] not in Kynge & Marche 1554, Day 1560, Marshe 1568	118	Ag Scottes	92
Why holde ye on yer cap, syr, then? Yor pardone ys expyryd.	123	Garnesche2	9
O Gabionyte of Gabyone, why do ye gane and gaspe?	123	Garnesche2	15
Why doste thow deprave /This royall reame,	136	Dundas	43
Why, to say what he wyll, Lyberte hath leve.	141	Magnyfycence	34
Why, have you harde of our dysputacyon?	142	Magnyfycence	82
Why, were not your selfe agreed to the same,	147	Magnyfycence	233
Why that ye sayd our langage was in vayne.	147	Magnyfycence	263
Why have ye hym named and all other refused?	148	Magnyfycence	281
Why kepte you it thus longe? Howe dothe he? Wele?	149	Magnyfycence	314
Why, shall we dwell togyder all thre?	154	Magnyfycence	509
Why, man, it were to great a wonder	154	Magnyfycence	510
Why, wenyst thou, horson, that I were so mad?	155	Magnyfycence	517
Why, dwelleth Mesure where ye two dwell?	157	Magnyfycence	622
I can not tell you. Why aske you me?	157	Magnyfycence	628
Why, can ye not put out that foule freke?	158	Magnyfycence	657
What sayst thou, man? Why dost thou not supplye,	162	Magnyfycence	797

	Page	Title	Line
Why, is this the gyse nowe adays?	163	Magnyfycence	813
Why, shall he be of your bende?	163	Magnyfycence	818
Why, harde thou not of the fray	166	Magnyfycence	932
Why, under whom was he abydynge?	166	Magnyfycence	938
Why? Is he crossed than with a chalke?	166	Magnyfycence	950
Why, sayst thou that I was here yesterday?	170	Magnyfycence	1093
Why, thynkys thou he can no better skyll?	172	Magnyfycence	1172
Why, wenyst thou that I cannot make the play the fon?	173	Magnyfycence	1185
Why, wenyst thou that I were as moche a fole as thou?	173	Magnyfycence	1188
Why, shall I not have Foly with me also?	176	Magnyfycence	1306
Why, wene you that I can kepe hym longe styll?	179	Magnyfycence	1412
Why, welth hath made many a man braynlesse.	180	Magnyfycence	1423
Why, wyl a maystres be wonne for money and for golde?	184	Magnyfycence	1575
Why, was not for money Troy bothe bought and solde?	184	Magnyfycence	1576
Why, wyll they then be intreted, the most and the lest?	184	Magnyfycence	1585
Why, is this the largesse that I have usyd?	193	Magnyfycence	1865
Why, coulde not your wyt serve you no better?	193	Magnyfycence	1868
Why, who wolde have thought in you suche gyle?	193	Magnyfycence	1869
Why, wenest thou that I forbere the for thyne owne sake?	202	Magnyfycence	2186
Why, is there any store of rawe motton?	204	Magnyfycence	2265
Of owur clerke Cleros. Whythyr, thydyr and why not hethyr?	243	Speke Parott	412
Alas, why do ye nat handle	255	Collyn Clout	332
Why syt ye prelates styll	263	Collyn Clout	688
Why than /Wreke ye your anger on me?	273	Collyn Clout	1090
And can nat tell no cause why	274	Collyn Clout	1115
can nat] 'can' Marshe 1568, MS Harley 2252			
which hath to name Why Come Ye Nat to Courte?	278	Why Come Ye	I
Why come ye nat to court?	279	Why Come Ye	31
Why come ye nat to court?	289	Why Come Ye	401
Perceyve the cause why:	290	Why Come Ye	459
To the court why I cam not,	299	Why Come Ye	827
Recorde the same? Or why is had in mynde	315	Garlande	125
His name? Or why is it, I you praye,	316	Garlande	138
The cause why Demostenes so famously is brutid	316	Garlande	155
With laureat tryumphe why Skelton sholde be crownde.	318	Garlande	217
'Daphnes, my derlynge, why do you me refuse?	320	Garlande	297
Why have the goddes shewyd me this cruelte,	321	Garlande	309
Odious Disdayne, why raist thou me on this facyon?	321	Garlande	317
Why shulde she be afrayd?	348	Garlande	1276
Why shulde she take shame	348	Garlande	1277
Ageyne envy, /And obloquy. /And wote ye why?	355	Garlande	1560
Why jangle you suche jestes,	381	Replycacion	264
Why fall ye at debate /With Skelton laureate,	382	Replycacion	300
Why have ye than disdayne /At poetes, and complayne	384	Replycacion	351
WHYCH			
Whych to behold makyth hevy hartys glad;	44	Balettys3	28
Whych cytie myscreantys wan,	67	Hauke	214
Of the whych proces /Ye may know more expres,	68	Hauke	231
Whych provyth well that measure shold have domynyon.	143	Magnyfycence	120
WHYCHE			
Of poetes olde, whyche, full craftely,	46	Bowge	9
Whyche cawsythe pore suters have many a hongry mele;	239	Speke Parott	311
Whyche of yow fyrste dare boldlye plucke the crowe.	242	Speke Parott	396
Of frantycknes and folysshnes whyche ys the grett state?	243	Speke Parott	417
To whyche court? /To the kynges courte?	289	Why Come Ye	402
Whyche he and ye? Let se;	367	Albany	333
WHYDER			
All thre, I say. Shall I go? Whyder?	158	Magnyfycence	666
Hyder and thyder, I wote not whyder;	169	Magnyfycence	1033
WHYLE			
What, lete us holde him up, man, for a whyle.'	51	Bowge	188
Nowe pleasyth you a lytell whyle to stande;	145	Magnyfycence	161
To passe the tyme and order whyle a man may talke	159	Magnyfycence	689
Mary, Mesure had hym a whyle in gydynge,	166	Magnyfycence	939
For it is I that other whyle	169	Magnyfycence	1025
What? Yes, by the rode, syr. It was I all this whyle	193	Magnyfycence	1870
Remember this lyfe lastyth but a whyle.	211	Magnyfycence	2502
If that ye wyll /A whyle be styll,	214	El Rummynge	3
Drinke now whyle it is new;	219	El Rummynge	211
And now a whyle to rest,	277	Collyn Clout	1249
And fall to rest a whyle;	289	Why Come Ye	397
And so to rest a whyle etc.	289	Why Come Ye	398
Of your questyon ye make all this whyle	333	Garlande	738
For Sir William Lyle /Within shorte whyle,	360	Albany	39
WHYLES			
Whyles she laugheth and hath luste for to playe.	49	Bowge	114
laugheth] 'laughed' †Wynkyn de Worde 1499			
Whyles I have ought, by God, thou shalt not lacke,	50	Bowge	167
Nay, naye, be sure, whyles I am on your syde	50	Bowge	169
Whyles of his mynde it were lockte with the keye.	52	Bowge	224
Whyles he senseth [the herse],	85	Phy Sparrow	530
the herse] not in †Kele 1545.2, Wyght 1553, Kitson 1560.6, Marshe 1568			
Whyles the world shall dure:	89	Phy Sparrow	723
And happe you the whyles with these homly raggys.	197	Magnyfycence	2037
And whyles the heedes do this, /The remenaunt is amys	249	Collyn Clout	115
For whyles he doth rule,	282	Why Come Ye	134
Whyles the red hat doth endure,	286	Why Come Ye	281

WHYLEST —WHYTTE

	Page	Title	Line
Whyles it remanyth fresshe in my mynde.	325	Garlande	465
WHYLEST			
Whylest I knowe that this letter dothe contayne.	149	Magnyfycence	324
Nowe therfore, whylest we are togyder -	155	Magnyfycence	546
I say, whylest we are togyder in same -	155	Magnyfycence	548
But may I drynke therof whylest that I stare?	176	Magnyfycence	1322
I wolde hauke whylest my hede dyd warke,	184	Magnyfycence	1563
Whylest I came to you, a lytell here besyde.	187	Magnyfycence	1686
Whylest I have hym, I nede nothynge doute.	187	Magnyfycence	1692
WHYLIS			
Whylis I stode musynge in this medytatyon,	313	Garlande	29
And then she sayd, 'Whylis we have tyme and space	328	Garlande	563
He can never leve warke whylis it is wele.	333	Garlande	763
WHYLYST			
For Cockys harte, tary whylyst that I come agayne.	159	Magnyfycence	685
Whylyst he hath ought.	165	Magnyfycence	901
WHYM-WHAM			
With a whym-wham /Knyt with a trym-tram	216	El Rummynge	75
WHYNARDE			
And by his syde his whynarde and his pouche,	56	Bowge	363
WHYNE			
You mantyca[re], ye maltaperte, ye can bothe wins and whyne; mantycare] 'mantyca' †MS Harley 367	123	Garnesche2	4
WHYNING			
Barkyng and whyning lyke churlysshe currys of kynde,	239	Speke Parott	295
WHYNNYMEG			
'What is this to purpose?' Over in a whynnymeg!	232	Speke Parott	71
WHYP			
That with his whyp his mares was wonte to yarke;	153	Magnyfycence	484
WHYPSLOVENS			
For thes twayne whypslovens calle for a coke stole.	124	Garnesche2	38
WHYRLED			
And on the borde he whyrled a payre of bones,	56	Bowge	346
WHYSKYNGE			
Of Jeremy the whyskynge rod,	308	Why Come Ye	1164
WHYSPER			
Let us now whysper /A Pater noster.	81	Phy Sparrow	384
WHYSPRING			
There is a whyspring and a whipling There] 'Her' Kitson 1560.7, Marshe 1568	287	Why Come Ye	350
WHYSTE			
Anone all was whyste, as it were for the nonys,	319	Garlande	267
WHYSTELYTH			
He whystelyth so swetely he makyth me to swete;	37	Coystrowne1	37
WHYSTELL			
The mavys with her whystell	82	Phy Sparrow	424
Construe nat worth a whystell	252	Collyn Clout	236
WHYT			
What the devyll! Never a whyt?	166	Magnyfycence	935
The devyll spede whyt!	168	Magnyfycence	1006
And tell to his sufferayne every whyt;	175	Magnyfycence	1270
Elynour made the pryce /For god ale eche whyt.	224	El Rummynge	411
WHYTE			
My sparow whyte as mylke,	77	Phy Sparrow	213
That noble erle, the Whyte Lyon,	115	Scot Kynge	68
As lyly whyte to loke upon her [l]eyre, leyre] 'heyre' †Rastell & Treveris C 1530, B	183	Magnyfycence	1555
As fayre and as whyte /As the fote of a kyte.	225	El Rummynge	424
Collustrum now for Parot, whyte bred and swete creme!	233	Speke Parott	82
Whyte as mares mylke; mares] 'morowes' Kele 1545.1, Marshe 1568, 'marys' Harley 2252	254	Collyn Clout	315
With fingers smale, and handis whyte as mylk; whyte] 'as white' Marshe 1568	334	Garlande	797
Grene, rede, tawny, whyte, purpill, and blew. whyte] 'whyght blak' MS Cotton Vitellius E.x	334	Garlande	800
With lillis whyte your bewte doth renewe. With lillis] 'The lylly' MS Cotton Vitellius E.x	337	Garlande	884
With lillys whyte your bewte dothe renewe.	337	Garlande	891
The whyte apperyth the better for the black,	347	Garlande	1237
WHYTENES			
The pullyshed perle youre whytenes doth declare;	44	Balettys3	18
WHYTER			
Whyter than the swan,	98	Phy Sparrow	1079
Whyter than the mylke, the] not in Kitson 1560.6, Marshe 1568	99	Phy Sparrow	1120
WHYTHER			
Wote ye whyther they went?	282	Why Come Ye	146
WHYTHYR			
Of owur clerke Cleros. Whythyr, thydyr and why not hethyr?	243	Speke Parott	412
WHYTYNG			
He calleth me his whytyng, /His mullyng and his [m]ytyng, mytyng] 'nytyng' †Lant 1545, Kynge & Marche 1554, 'nittinge' Day 1560, 'nittine' Marshe 1568	220	El Rummynge	223
WHYTNESSE			
The whytnesse of her lere;	97	Phy Sparrow	1034
WHYTTE			
Whan there is never a whytte,	259	Collyn Clout	516

WHO —WHOM   Page   Title   Line

WHO

	Page	Title	Line
In sesons past who hathe harde or sene	30	Dol Dethe	22
What and he slyde downe, who shall hym save?	46	Bowge	28
But who wyll have it muste paye therfore dere.	47	Bowge	53
Who spareth to speke, in fayth, he spareth to spede.'	48	Bowge	91
Soo greate pleasyre, or who to you it gave.	53	Bowge	263
Who rydeth on her, he nedeth not to care,	57	Bowge	409
Who deleth with shrewes hath nede to loke aboute!'	61	Bowge	525
Pla ce bo, /Who is there, who?	71	Phy Sparrow	2
Pla ce bo, /Who is there, who?	71	Phy Sparrow	2
Within this quaire? /Who lyst repayre	116	Ag Scottes	42
lyst] 'lyst to' Kynge & Marche 1554, Day 1560, Marshe 1568			
Who lyst to knowe, Magnyfycence I hyght.	145	Magnyfycence	164
Who county[th] without me is caste to fer behynde	146	Magnyfycence	214
countyth] 'countyd' †Rastell & Treveris C 1530, B			
Or who made you so bolde to interrupe my tale?	147	Magnyfycence	256
Who is that that thus dyd cry?	149	Magnyfycence	326
Who that is ruled by us, it shalbe longe or he thee.	154	Magnyfycence	515
Cockys harte! Who is yonde that for the dothe call?	162	Magnyfycence	780
What the devyll! Who sent for the?	162	Magnyfycence	791
What nowe? Let se /Who loketh on me	163	Magnyfycence	830
What, Fansy! Let me se who is the tother.	172	Magnyfycence	1158
Who is mayster of the masshe fat?	176	Magnyfycence	1319
No, that I assure you; loke who was the best:	181	Magnyfycence	1484
Who is this? Consayte, syr, your owne man.	191	Magnyfycence	1804
Why, who wolde have thought in you suche gyle?	193	Magnyfycence	1869
Alas, wh[o] is yonder that grymly lokys?	193	Magnyfycence	1873
who] 'why' †Rastell & Treveris C 1530, B			
What, a very vengeaunce, I say! Who is that?	199	Magnyfycence	2105
Of worldly welthe, alasse, who can be sure?	201	Magnyfycence	2155
Who knoweth me, hymselfe may never sloo.	206	Magnyfycence	2330
For who loveth God can ayle nothynge but good.	207	Magnyfycence	2365
Who brought you that letter? Wote ye what he hyght?	209	Magnyfycence	2440
Who lyst to consyder shall never be begylyd,	212	Magnyfycence	2512
To the pythe of the mater who lyst to resorte:	213	Magnyfycence	2540
Jereboseth is Ebrue, who lyst the cause dyscus.	232	Speke Parott	67
cause] 'law' Day 1560, Marshe 1568			
With, 'Who is there? A mayd?' Nay, nay, I trow!	233	Speke Parott	100
Let se who dare make up the reste.	242	Speke Parott	382
And yf ye stande in doute /Who brought this ryme aboute,	248	Collyn Clout	48
For let se who that dare	251	Collyn Clout	179
Who dare say there agayne,	276	Collyn Clout	1214
Or who dare dysdayne,	276	Collyn Clout	1215
Renne who may renne best,	277	Collyn Clout	1223
For who can best lye,	300	Why Come Ye	858
best] not in MS Rawlinson C. 813			
Who lyst to enquere,	307	Why Come Ye	1118
Who wryteth wysely hath a grete treasure.	314	Garlande	91
To understande who dwellyth in yone pile,	333	Garlande	739
yone] 'yonder' MS Cotton Vitellius E.x			
And who can worke beste now shall be asayde;	334	Garlande	775
In you, who list to seke,	338	Garlande	920
Who list to rede.	342	Garlande	1081
With Courtely Abusyoun; who pryntith it wele in mynde	346	Garlande	1196
Who list amende it, let hym set to his penne.	348	Garlande	1260
But who may have a more ungracyous lyfe	352	Garlande	1451
a] not in Marshe 1568			
Who redyth it ones wolde rede it agayne;	354	Garlande	1501

WHOM

	Page	Title	Line
Of whom both Flaunders and Scotland stode in drede,	30	Dol Dethe	44
Whom he as lorde worsheply manteynd,	34	Dol Dethe	186
All mankynd, whom thou ful dere hast boght,	34	Dol Dethe	194
To whom then shall we sew /For to have rescew,	40	Coystrowne3	37
All those by whom ye have avayle.	41	Coystrowne4	18
Wyth 'Whom' and 'Ha' and with a croked loke,	51	Bowge	191
Whom Tytus Lyvyus /In wrytynge doth enroll;	67	Hauke	209
Whom Gyb our cat hath slayne.	72	Phy Sparrow	27
Whom Theseus dyd afraye,	74	Phy Sparrow	86
Whom Hercules dyd outraye,	74	Phy Sparrow	87
Whom now and then /He plucketh by the hede	84	Phy Sparrow	510
For whom was moch stryfe;	87	Phy Sparrow	644
Whom Achylles slew,	88	Phy Sparrow	675
Whom he forsoke with teene,	90	Phy Sparrow	742
With whom he ledd a plesaunt life;	90	Phy Sparrow	744
To whom be the laude ascrybed	93	Phy Sparrow	871
All other of whom we rede,	93	Phy Sparrow	884
As my maistres, /Of whom I thynk	96	Phy Sparrow	985
Agaynst whom he dyd fyght /Falsly agaynst all right,	120	Ag Scottes2	17
What! Whom have we here, Jenkyn Joly?	166	Magnyfycence	918
Why, under whom was he abydynge?	166	Magnyfycence	938
With whom shall I there mete	167	Magnyfycence	955
Wotyst thou, I say, to whom thou spekys?	172	Magnyfycence	1166
Whom? Lusty Pleasure or mery Consayte?	180	Magnyfycence	1452
Galba, whom his galantys garde for agaspe,	182	Magnyfycence	1508
Magnyfycence I was, whom ye have brought to shame.	204	Magnyfycence	2241
He may take whom he wull,	306	Why Come Ye	1079
To whom he was professed	307	Why Come Ye	1121

WHOME —WHOSO   Page   Title   Line

	Page	Title	Line
Ye put to blame ye wot nere whom.	310	Why Come Ye2	17
nere] 'nott' MS Rawlinson C. 813			
Ageyne whom he cowde make no contradiccyoun?'	316	Garlande	133
Whom fortune and fate playnly have discust	337	Garlande	881
Whom I nowe sommon and con[v]ent,	375	Replycacion	23
convent] 'content' †Pynson 1528			
To whom we are bounde echone	381	Replycacion	260
Whom Hieronymus, /That doctour glorious,	383	Replycacion	318
To whom we must gyve faythe,	384	Replycacion	348
WHOME			
To whome grete astatis obeyde and lowttede,	30	Dol Dethe	45
To whome there came another gentylwoman.	48	Bowge	84
Whome she hateth shall over the see-boorde skyp.	49	Bowge	112
see-boorde] 'shyp borde' Marshe 1568			
Whome she loveth, of all plesyre is ryche	49	Bowge	113
Whome she hateth, she casteth in the dyche,	49	Bowge	115
hateth] 'hatch' †Wynkyn de Worde 1499, 'hateth' Wynkyn de Worde 1510, Marshe 1568			
Fortune theyr frende, with whome oft she dyde daunce:	50	Bowge	141
For ye have me whome faythfull ye shall fynde;	50	Bowge	166
For whome Tyborne groneth both daye and nyghte.	58	Bowge	417
whome] 'home' †Wynkyn de Worde 1499			
In whome dothe wele acorde	110	Lawde	12
Whome he wyll depute?	272	Collyn Clout	1044
To whome supplyed the royall Quene of Fame.	313	Garlande	49
And many mo whome I cowde enduce;	314	Garlande	94
For if ye laude hym whome honour hath opprest,	317	Garlande	174
But whome that ye favoure, I se well, hath a name,	317	Garlande	176
And whome ye love not ye wyll put to shame.	317	Garlande	178
Lamentyng Daphnes, whome with the darte of lede	320	Garlande	290
Sat honorably, to whome did repaire	334	Garlande	770
Prudent Rebecca, of whome remembraunce	336	Garlande	845
Whome ye represent and exemplify,	336	Garlande	854
Whome dame Nature, as wele I may reporte,	336	Garlande	867
WHOO			
For whoo lokythe wyselye in your warkys may fynde	239	Speke Parott	296
WHOOS			
Whoos name to tell is Dame Saunce-Pere.	47	Bowge	51
Whoos beaute, honoure, goodly porte,	47	Bowge	62
WHOS			
Whos lordshepe doutles was slayne lamentably	29	Dol Dethe	5
For whos causis ye slew hym with your awne hande.	31	Dol Dethe	68
Of whos [life] they countede not a fly.	31	Dol Dethe	95
life] not in †MS Royal 18 D.ii or Marshe 1568			
Take up whos wolde, for ther they let hym ly.	32	Dol Dethe	96
Whos noble actis shew worsheply his name,	33	Dol Dethe	143
This lordis dethe, whos pere is hard to fynd,	34	Dol Dethe	178
To whos astate all noblenes most leven,	313	Garlande	54
leven] 'lene' †Fakes 1523, MS Cotton Vitellius E.x			
Of his onour, whos dissuasyve in wrytyng	316	Garlande	151
Whos hevenly armony was so passynge sure,	320	Garlande	274
'O noble Chaucer, whos pullisshyd eloquence	324	Garlande	421
Whos flagraunt flower was chefe preservatyve	330	Garlande	671
The Byble makith; with whos chast lyvynge	336	Garlande	846
Whos passynge bounte, and ryght noble astate,	336	Garlande	848
Whos passynge bounte, and ryght noble astate,	336	Garlande	855
Whos passyng bounte, and ryght noble astate,	336	Garlande	862
Of womanly feturis, whos florysshyng tender age	336	Garlande	869
Whos lusty lokis make hevy hartis glad;	337	Garlande	903
By whos myght and maine	348	Garlande	1290
And wele wotith the cat whos berde she likkith.	352	Garlande	1438
WHOSE			
Whose jalawsy malycyous makyth them to lepe the hach!	43	Balettys2	33
For whose sake my hart is sore dyseasyd;	45	Balettys5	9
For whose love, welcom dysease to me!	45	Balettys5	10
Whose name regystred was	75	Phy Sparrow	149
Of whose incyneracyon /There ryseth a new creacyon	85	Phy Sparrow	540
Whose fame by me shall sprede	93	Phy Sparrow	885
By whose myght and mayne	104	Phy Sparrow	1297
Whose name enrolde /With silke and golde	112	Calliope	9
Whose radiant beame /And relucent light	136	Dundas	45
In whose attemperaunce I have suche delyght,	145	Magnyfycence	189
Mole ruit sua, whose dictes ar pregnaunte	232	Speke Parott	41
Whose tong ys attayntyd with slaundrys obliqui.	241	Speke Parott	363
To whose magnifycence /Is all the conflewence,	289	Why Come Ye	412
In whose place, /Dothe occupy,	300	Why Come Ye	850
By whose suggestyon /I toke on hand this warke,	309	Why Come Ye	1203
suggestyon] 'subjectyon' MS Rawlinson C. 813			
Whose bewte blastyd was with the boystors wynde,	312	Garlande	20
In whose court poynted is your place.'	324	Garlande	420
Whose skales ensilvred again the son beames	330	Garlande	662
Whose name over all	361	Albany	108
Whose charite wele regarded	378	Replycacion	138
By whose inflammacion /Of spyrituall instygacion	384	Replycacion	379
WHOSO			
Whoso lyst the story to se.	76	Phy Sparrow	193
But whoso understode /Of Medeas arte,	76	Phy Sparrow	201
Playne matter indede, /Whoso lyst to rede	85	Phy Sparrow	549

WHO SO —WITH   Page   Title   Line

WHO SO
  But who so that lokys /In the offycyallys bokys, ...   65   Hauke   145
  Who so that understandes   93   Phy Sparrow   880
  Who so lyst to seke   97   Phy Sparrow   1044
  Who so lyst beholde, ...   98   Phy Sparrow   1073
  Who so therat pyketh mood, ...   121   Ag Scottes2   21
    whoso] 'but who so' Day 1560, Marshe 1568
  Who so to me gyveth good advertence   177   Magnyfycence   1333
  Come who so wyll /To Elynoure on the hyll, ...   217   El Rummynge   113
  Who so dothe magnifye   381   Replycacion   255
WHO SOEVER
  Who soever that tale unto you tolde, ...   137   Ven Tongues   20
WHRYGHT
  Wherfore delyght /I have to whryght.   339   Garlande   946
WIDDERS
  Ware gallyng in the widders, ware of that wrenche!   43   Balettys2   25
WIL
  That evermore wil ly /And say cursedly;   94   Phy Sparrow   906
  No man for them wil speke.   111   Lawde   32
  There is no noble man wil judge in me   138   Ven Tongues   34
WILY
  By theyr conusaunce knowing how they serve a wily py: 43   Balettys2   34
WILL
  'What, will ye do nothyng but play?'   35   Man Margery   4
  I will not be japed bodely.   36   Man Margery   19
  Thou mokkyshe marmoset, /I will nat dy in [thy] det.   128   Garnesche3   173
    thy] 'they' †MS Harley 367
  This tale will be to trew: 280   Why Come Ye   65
  'Yowre boke of remembrauns we will now that ye rede;   345   Garlande   1149
    boke] 'bokes' †Fakes 1523
  My pen I will avaunce   369   Albany   406
  But nowe will I expounde   369   Albany   423
  We will so folowe in the chace   371   Albany   503
WILLE
  Ye armed you with wille and left your wit behynd;   30   Dol Dethe   55
WILLFULL
  What willfull foly made you to ryse agayn   30   Dol Dethe   53
WILLIAM
  For Sir William Lyle /Within shorte whyle, ...   360   Albany   38
WILLIAMS
  And Sainct Williams also.   360   Albany   64
WINDYNG STAYRE
  Turnyng on the ryght hande, by a windyng stayre, ...   333   Garlande   767
    a] not in †Fakes 1523
WINDMIL
  I made, he said, a windmil of an olde mat.   137   Ven Tongues   13
WINS
  You mantyca[re], ye malteperte, ye can bothe wins and whyne; .   123   Garnesche2   4
    mantycare] 'mantyca' †MS Harley 367
WINTER
  And of the winter days that hy them so fast, ...   331   Garlande   700
WIRRY
  They shall wirry no mo, ...   111   Lawde   26
WISE
  Adrastus wise and sage.   110   Lawde   14
  Nether wise nor wel lernid, but like hermaphradita: 235   Speke Parott   159
WIST
  That, if I wist not to be controlde, ...   137   Ven Tongues   9
  Beware of hym, I warne you; for and ye wist   333   Garlande   754
    and] 'if' Marshe 1568
WIT
  Where was your wit and reson ye shuld have had?   30   Dol Dethe   52
    your] 'ys' †MS Royal 18 D.ii
  Ye armed you with wille and left your wit behynd;   30   Dol Dethe   55
  Dyvysynge in pycture, by his industrious wit, ...   343   Garlande   1098
WITCHECRAFT
  To witchecraft her to dres, ...   350   Garlande   1339
WITH
  With the freshe waters of Elyconys welle.   29   Dol Dethe   14
  Fulfyld with malice of froward entente, ...   30   Dol Dethe   25
  Fulfilled with honour, as all the world dothe ken, ...   30   Dol Dethe   30
    world] 'wold' Marshe 1568
  Ye armed you with wille and left your wit behynd;   30   Dol Dethe   55
  For whos causis ye slew hym with your awne hande.   31   Dol Dethe   68
  Bot men say thei wer lynked with a double chayn   31   Dol Dethe   75
  And held with the commonns under a cloke, ...   31   Dol Dethe   76
  With one vice importune thei playnly said nay.   31   Dol Dethe   80
  Bluntly as bestis withe boste and with cry   31   Dol Dethe   83
  Vigorously upon them with myght and with mayne, ...   31   Dol Dethe   89
  Vigorously upon them with myght and with mayne, ...   31   Dol Dethe   89
  Trustinge in noble men that wer with hym there;   31   Dol Dethe   90
  Togeder with servauntis of his family, ...   31   Dol Dethe   93
  Whiche wert endiyd with rede blode of the same   32   Dol Dethe   117
  That with thy sworde enharpid of mortall drede   32   Dol Dethe   125
  With my rude pen enkankerd all with rust, ...   33   Dol Dethe   142
  With my rude pen enkankerd all with rust, ...   33   Dol Dethe   142
  Yet sumwhat wright supprisid with hartly lust, ...   33   Dol Dethe   145
    hartly] 'herty' Marshe 1568

	Page	Title	Line
With trowth to medelle was all his hole delight,	33	Dol Dethe	152
Enbrethed with the blast of influence dyvyne,	33	Dol Dethe	157
Wythe hevy chere, with dolorous hart and mynd,	34	Dol Dethe	176
And all other gentelmen with hym enterteynd	34	Dol Dethe	184
That with one worde formd all thing of nought;	34	Dol Dethe	191
With thi blode precious our fenaunce thou dyd pay	34	Dol Dethe	195
In endles blis with the to byde and dwell	34	Dol Dethe	201
With all the hole sorte of that glorious place,	35	Dol Dethe	212
With manerly Margery Mylk and Ale.	35	Man Margery	7
With manerly Margery Mylk and Ale.	36	Man Margery	14
With manerly Margery Mylk and Ale.	36	Man Margery	21
With manerly Margery Milk and Ale.	36	Man Margery	28
With manerly Margery Mylk and Ale.	36	Man Margery	30
He counteth in his countenaunce to checke with the best:	37	Coystrownel	44
Nay, jape not with hym, he is no small fole;	38	Coystrownel	50
At me, that medeled nothyng with youre wark.	38	Coystrownel	61
With synnews wyderyd, /With bonys shyderyd,	39	Coystrowne3	12
With synnews wyderyd, /With bonys shyderyd,	39	Coystrowne3	13
With hys worme-etyn maw /And hys gastly jaw	39	Coystrowne3	14
Deth wyll us quell /And with us mell.	39	Coystrowne3	24
With drawttys of deth /Stoppyng oure breth;	39	Coystrowne3	31
With 'Lullay, lullay', lyke a chylde,	41	Balettys1	I
With hey, lullay, &c.	41	Balettys1	R
With 'Ba, ba, ba', and 'bas, bas, bas',	42	Balettys1	8
With hey, lullay, &c.	42	Balettys1	Rub
Spur up at the hynder gyrth with, 'Gup, morell, gup!'	43	Balettys2	17
With, 'Jayst ye, Jenet of Spayne, for your tayll waggys,'	43	Balettys2	18
She kykyth with her kalkyns and keylyth with a clench;	43	Balettys2	23
She kykyth with her kalkyns and keylyth with a clench;	43	Balettys2	23
And so with your servantys he fersly doth fyght.	43	Balettys2	28
That he dryvyth them doune with dyntys on ther day-wach.	43	Balettys2	30
Or ells with gret shame your game wylbe sene.	43	Balettys2	42
Knolege, aquayntance, resort, favour, with grace;	43	Balettys3	1
Wordys well set with good habylyte;	43	Balettys3	5
Go, pytyous hart, rasyd with dedly wo,	45	Balettys5	1
Persyd with payn, bleding with wondes smart,	45	Balettys5	2
Persyd with payn, bleding with wondes smart,	45	Balettys5	2
Bewayle thy fortune, with vaynys wan and blo.	45	Balettys5	3
Fraghted with plesure to what ye coude devyse.	47	Bowge	42
And with that worde on me she gave a glome	48	Bowge	80
With browes bente, and gan on me to stare	48	Bowge	81
And I with them prayed her to have in mynde.	49	Bowge	123
Mysdempte eche man, with face deedly and pale;	50	Bowge	137
With other foure of theyr affynyte:	50	Bowge	139
Fortune theyr frende, with whome oft she dyde daunce:	50	Bowge	141
With them to make solace and pleasure;	50	Bowge	144
They sayde they hated for to dele with Drede.	50	Bowge	146
Deynte to have with us suche one in store,	50	Bowge	150
To dwell with us and serve my ladyes grace.	50	Bowge	156
That lyned was with doubtfull doublenes.	51	Bowge	178
He sayth he can not well accorde with the.'	51	Bowge	185
Wyth 'Whom' and 'Ha' and with a croked loke,	51	Bowge	191
And thus to talke with me he began.	51	Bowge	196
That commaunde with you, me thought, a p[ra]ty space?	51	Bowge	198
commaunde] 'commened' Wynkyn de Worde 1510; 'party spake' †Wynkyn de Worde 1499, Marshe 1568, 'party space' WdeW 1510			
He sayde of me, whan he with you dyde talke -	52	Bowge	209
By myne avyse use not with him to walke.	52	Bowge	210
Els, I prayed hym with all my besy cure,	52	Bowge	221
Whyles of his mynde it were lockte with the keye.	52	Bowge	224
He gased on me with his gotyshe berde;	52	Bowge	237
To be with you thus perte and thus bolde;	53	Bowge	265
The favoure that ye have with my lady.	53	Bowge	270
Anone ther mette with him, as me thoughte,	54	Bowge	282
His gawdy garment with Scornnys was all wrought;	54	Bowge	285
Scornnys] 'storunys' †Wynkyn de Worde 1499, 1510, 'scornes' Marshe 1568			
With Indygnacyon lyned was his hode;	54	Bowge	286
It was no tyme with him to jape nor toye.	54	Bowge	290
Fyrste pycke a quarell and fall oute with hym then,	55	Bowge	314
And soo outface hym with a carde of ten.'	55	Bowge	315
With scornfull loke mevyd all in moode.	55	Bowge	317
scornfull] 'scorfull' Marshe 1568			
And in this wyse he gan with me to chyde.	55	Bowge	322
With us olde servauntes such maysters to playe.	55	Bowge	329
But, no force, I shall ones mete with the;	55	Bowge	334
His hose was garded with a lyste of grene,	56	Bowge	356
His cote was checked with patches rede and blewe;	56	Bowge	358
checked] 'checkered' Marshe 1568			
And thus with us good company to kepe.	57	Bowge	385
She hath gote me more money with her tayle	57	Bowge	405
Dysdayne I sawe with Dyssymulacyon,	58	Bowge	419
But there was poyntynge and noddynge with the hede,	58	Bowge	421
In no place well, but foles with hym fraye!	58	Bowge	446
hym] not in †Wynkyn de Worde 1499, Marshe 1568			
With a clerke that connynge is to prate.	59	Bowge	454
Ryghte now I spake with one, I trowe, I see -	59	Bowge	458

	Page	Title	Line
Alas, I coude not dele so with a [J]ew.	59	Bowge	462
a Jew] 'on yew' †Wynkyn de Worde 1499, 'a yew' Wynkyn de Worde 1510, Marshe 1568			
Who deleth with shrewes hath nede to loke aboute!'	61	Bowge	525
And thoughte to lepe; and even with that woke,	61	Bowge	531
With hogeous showte and cry.	63	Hauke	48
Such sacrificium laudis /He made with suche gambawdis.	63	Hauke	65
And was with flyenge wery.	63	Hauke	67
Came runnynge with a dow,	63	Hauke	72
He then, to be sure, /Callyd her with a lure.	63	Hauke	76
The hawke with that clap /Fell downe with evyll hap.	64	Hauke	89
The hawke with that clap /Fell downe with evyll hap.	64	Hauke	90
His hawke then flew uppon /The rode, with Mary and Johnn.	65	Hauke	127
With Regum by and by;	66	Hauke	166
With moch matter more, /That I kepe in store.	67	Hauke	220
Domine concupisti, /With thy hawke on thy fysty?	69	Hauke	260
Nec magis bestialis /That synggys with a chalys;	70	Hauke	327
Hampar with your hammer upon thy styth,	71	Hauke	332
Pater noster qui, /With an Ave Mari,	72	Phy Sparrow	14
And with the corner of a Crede,	72	Phy Sparrow	15
With vysage blacke and blo;	73	Phy Sparrow	75
With gastly hedes thre;	74	Phy Sparrow	91
Amen, say ye with me!	74	Phy Sparrow	94
With, 'Phyllyp, kepe your cut!'	74	Phy Sparrow	119
With his wanton eye.	76	Phy Sparrow	182
With a charme or twayne,	77	Phy Sparrow	206
And playe with me agayne.	77	Phy Sparrow	207
To sowe with stytchis of sylke	77	Phy Sparrow	212
With that my nedle waxed red,	77	Phy Sparrow	225
waxed] 'ware' Marshe 1568			
The dragones with their tonges	79	Phy Sparrow	292
Flyckerynge with his wynges.	80	Phy Sparrow	348
I played with him tytell-tattyll,	80	Phy Sparrow	357
And fed him with my spattyl,	80	Phy Sparrow	358
With his byll betwene my lippes,	80	Phy Sparrow	359
To wepe with me loke that ye come,	81	Phy Sparrow	387
With dolorous songes funerall,	81	Phy Sparrow	391
With helpe of the red sparow	82	Phy Sparrow	403
The larke with his longe to;	82	Phy Sparrow	406
The shovelar with his brode bek;	82	Phy Sparrow	408
With a balde face to toote;	82	Phy Sparrow	411
The plover with us to wayle;	82	Phy Sparrow	417
The mavys with her whystell	82	Phy Sparrow	424
But with a large and a longe	82	Phy Sparrow	426
With Puwyt the lapwyng,	82	Phy Sparrow	430
The *better with his bumpe,	82	Phy Sparrow	432
*better] 'bitter' Wyght 1553, Kitson 1560.6, Marshe 1568			
The crane with his trumpe,	82	Phy Sparrow	433
And the cormoraunce, /With the fesaunte,	83	Phy Sparrow	446
cormoraunce] 'cormoraunte' Wyght 1553, Kitson 1560.6, Marshe 1568			
With the wylde mallarde;	83	Phy Sparrow	451
wylde] 'wynde' †Kele 1545.2			
The wodcocke with the longe nose;	83	Phy Sparrow	459
The threstyl with her warblyng;	83	Phy Sparrow	460
The starlyng with her brablyng;	83	Phy Sparrow	461
The roke, with the ospraye	83	Phy Sparrow	462
With the turtyll most trew.	83	Phy Sparrow	465
With Partlot his hen,	84	Phy Sparrow	509
With armatycke gummes /That cost great sumes,	84	Phy Sparrow	520
This corse for to sence /With greate reverence,	85	Phy Sparrow	527
Also the noble fawcon, /With the gerfawcon,	85	Phy Sparrow	557
The sacre with them shall say	85	Phy Sparrow	561
With his knightes commendable,	87	Phy Sparrow	635
In maner half with shame;	89	Phy Sparrow	713
Whom he forsoke with teene,	90	Phy Sparrow	742
With whom he ledd a plesaunt life;	90	Phy Sparrow	744
With bokes that I have red,	90	Phy Sparrow	753
With Englysh wordes elect;	91	Phy Sparrow	773
elect] 'clere' †Kele 1545.2, 'elect' Wyght 1553, Kitson 1560.6, Marshe 1568			
With pullysshed termes lusty;	91	Phy Sparrow	776
And with my pen to wryte;	93	Phy Sparrow	862
With armony that synges	93	Phy Sparrow	866
With the aureat droppes,	93	Phy Sparrow	873
With his golden sandes,	93	Phy Sparrow	879
With his ledder ey, /And chekes dry;	94	Phy Sparrow	908
With vysage wan, /As swart as tan;	94	Phy Sparrow	910
swart] 'wart' †Kele 1545.2, Wyght 1553, Kitson 1560.6, 'swarte' Marshe 1568			
His lyver, his longe /With anger is wronge;	94	Phy Sparrow	919
longe] 'longes' Wyght 1553, Kitson 1560.6, Marshe 1568			
He is so bete /With malyce, and frete	95	Phy Sparrow	931
With angre and yre,	95	Phy Sparrow	932
Himself doth slo /With payne and wo.	95	Phy Sparrow	948
With pen and ynk /For to compyle /Some goodly style;	96	Phy Sparrow	986
goodly] 'godly' †Kele 1545.2			

WITH —WITH	Page	Title	Line
Ennewed all with grace,	96	Phy Sparrow	1003
all with] 'with al' Wyght 1553, Kitson 1560.6, Marshe 1568			
With her aye to remayne.	97	Phy Sparrow	1013
With her browes bent	97	Phy Sparrow	1016
All with favour fret,	98	Phy Sparrow	1048
With wordes of pleasure	99	Phy Sparrow	1099
And with her fyngers smale,	99	Phy Sparrow	1118
With sydes longe and streyte;	100	Phy Sparrow	1129
With heles short and rounde.	100	Phy Sparrow	1150
Emportured with corage,	100	Phy Sparrow	1154
Her fresshe habylementes /With other implementes	101	Phy Sparrow	1181
Yet though I wryte not with ynke,	101	Phy Sparrow	1198
Were pullysshed with the fyle /Of Ciceros eloquence,	101	Phy Sparrow	1205
pullysshed] 'publysshed' †Kele 1545.2			
With this psalme, Domine, probasti me,	102	Phy Sparrow	1239
With, Tibi, Domine, commendamus.	102	Phy Sparrow	1241
With letters of golde.	103	Phy Sparrow	1259
With Phillyppes enterement.	103	Phy Sparrow	1281
To be matriculate /With ladyes of estate?	104	Phy Sparrow	1289
And with a venemous arow	104	Phy Sparrow	1292
An hart was slayne /With hornes twayne	104	Phy Sparrow	1299
And with a dragon kept	104	Phy Sparrow	1303
And slew Gerion /With thre bodyes in one;	104	Phy Sparrow	1308
With myghty corage /A[d]aunted the rage /Of a lyon savage;	104	Phy Sparrow	1309
Adaunted] 'Auaunted' editions			
With leapes and bounses;	104	Phy Sparrow	1315
And with myghty luggyng,	104	Phy Sparrow	1316
Caron with his beerd hore,	105	Phy Sparrow	1338
That roweth with a rude ore	105	Phy Sparrow	1339
And with his [frownsid] fore top	105	Phy Sparrow	1340
frownsid] not in †Kele 1545.2, Wyght 1553, Kitson 1560.6, Marshe 1568			
Gydeth his bote with a prope;	105	Phy Sparrow	1341
With, 'Fill the blak bowle /For Jayberdes sowle.'	108	Epitaphe1	73
Wit[h], 'Hey, howe, rumbelowe,' /Rumpopulorum,	108	Epitaphe1	80
With] 'Wit' Marshe 1568			
Why were ye Calliope, embrawdred with letters of golde?	112	Calliope	I
Whose name enrolde /With silke and golde	112	Calliope	10
With her certayne /I wyll remayne	112	Calliope	21
Warre with our kynge to meyntayne.	114	Scot Kynge	55
They say they had /And wan the felde /With spere and shelde!	116	Ag Scottes	16
Chryst sence you with a fryinge pan! –	117	Ag Scottes	62
sence] 'fence' †Lant 1545			
With the ix day of the same,	117	Ag Scottes	67
That with myxture of aloes and bytter gall	117	Ag Scottes	81
That late were discomfect with battayle marcyall.	117	Ag Scottes	84
To touche them with tauntes of your armony,	117	Ag Scottes	86
A medley to make of myrth with sadnes,	117	Ag Scottes	87
The hertes of England to comfort with gladnes.	117	Ag Scottes	88
With, 'Gup, Syr Scot of Galaway!'	118	Ag Scottes	109
With our kyng royall war to mayntayne.	119	Ag Scottes	152
I am now constrayned, /With wordes nothing fayned,	120	Ag Scottes2	2
Ye gyrne grymly with your gomys and with yor grysly face.	122	Garnesche1	12
Ye gyrne grymly with your gomys and with yor grysly face.	122	Garnesche1	12
Nor blake Baltazar with hys basnet routh as a bere,	122	Garnesche1	23
Nor no bore so brymly brystlyd ys with here,	122	Garnesche1	25
Bryngges yow out of favyr with alle femall teggys:	122	Garnesche1	31
Your tethe teintyd with tawny; your semely snowte doth passe,	122	Garnesche1	39
with Gresy, Gorbelyd Godfrey et cetera	122	Garnesche2	I
Hole ys your brow that ye brake with Deu[ra]ndall your awne sworde; Deurandall] 'Deundall' †MS Harley 367	123	Garnesche2	8
Cum Garnyche, cum Godfrey, with as many as ye may!	123	Garnesche2	32
To turney or to tante with me ye ar to fare to seke.	123	Garnesche2	37
With neythyr of yow tewyne:	124	Garnesche3	7
A gose with the fete upon;	125	Garnesche3	31
With haftynge and with polleynge,	125	Garnesche3	38
With haftynge and with polleynge,	125	Garnesche3	38
With lyenge and controlleynge,	125	Garnesche3	39
With better frese lynyd;	125	Garnesche3	47
The warde with yow was skante.	125	Garnesche3	53
Thus with yow sche ded wary,	126	Garnesche3	75
With moche mater more	126	Garnesche3	76
Had ye gonne with me to scole,	127	Garnesche3	117
With hys brethe so stronge,	128	Garnesche3	151
Els with hys stynkyng jawys	128	Garnesche3	154
With othyr menys charge;	129	Garnesche3	188
Was sowyd with slendyr thre[de].	129	Garnesche3	201
threde] 'thre' †MS Harley 367			
With 'Dominus vobyscum',	129	Garnesche3	203
Ye rayle, ye ryme, with, 'Hay, dog, hay!'	129	Garnesche5	5
Myxte with sum incommodite,	130	Garnesche5	10
Cicero with hys tong of golde.	130	Garnesche5	12
Soche pajantes with your fryndes ye play,	130	Garnesche5	37
With trechery ye them betray,	130	Garnesche5	38
Garnyshe, ye gate of Gorge with gaudry	130	Garnesche5	39
With Lumbardes lemmanns for to mete,	130	Garnesche5	42
With, 'Bas me, buttyng, praty Cys',	130	Garnesche5	43
Sche seyd ye war colluryd with cole dust;	131	Garnesche5	53

	Page	Title	Line
To daly with yow she had no lust.	131	Garnesche5	54
With, 'Gup, Syr Gy', ye gate a moke.	131	Garnesche5	56
Sche sware with hyr ye xulde nat dele,	131	Garnesche5	57
Than with my poems for to melle.	132	Garnesche5	94
Aqueintyng hym with the Musys nyne.	132	Garnesche5	100
Thy tong untawte, with poyson infecte,	132	Garnesche5	108
To rayle with me that the can hyt.	132	Garnesche5	119
Thowth it be now ful tyde with the,	132	Garnesche5	120
If thow war aquentyd with alle	133	Garnesche5	138
They wolde the wryght, all with one stevyn,	133	Garnesche5	144
Defendeth with his pen /All Englysh men	135	Dundas	21
With thy versyfyeng rayles /How they have tayles.	135	Dundas	30
A spectacle case /To cover thy face, /With, tray deux ase.	136	Dundas	39
enpoysoned with sclaunder and false detractions &c.	136	Ven Tongues	I
Either by language or with my pen.	137	Ven Tongues	23
And of their taunting toies rest with il hayle.	138	Ven Tongues	33
Of me with your language full of vilany.	138	Ven Tongues	48
With skolding and sklaundering make their tungs lame.	139	Ven Tongues	62
Then ren they with lesinges, and blow them about,	139	Ven Tongues	69
With, 'He wrate suche a bil withouten dout',	139	Ven Tongues	70
With, 'I can tel you what such a man said,	139	Ven Tongues	71
A fole is he with welth that fallyth at debate.	140	Magnyfycence	5
But yf prudence be proved with sad cyrcumspeccyon,	141	Magnyfycence	16
Yf noblenesse were aquayntyd with sober dyreccyon.	141	Magnyfycence	18
It askyth lesure with good advert[ence].	141	Magnyfycence	42
advertence] 'advertysment' †Rastell & Treveris 1530, B			
That lyberte be lynkyd with the chayne of countenaunce,	141	Magnyfycence	44
But with countenaunce your corage must be croppyd.	141	Magnyfycence	47
Can be content with Measure presence.	143	Magnyfycence	86
You to holde content /With myne argument;	143	Magnyfycence	109
Yes, syr, with ryght good chere.	143	Magnyfycence	112
With all my herte intere.	143	Magnyfycence	113
With every condycyon measure must be sought.	143	Magnyfycence	115
Ye, lyberte with measure nede never drede.	144	Magnyfycence	130
Where with to rule hym with the wrythyng of a rest.	144	Magnyfycence	136
Welthe, with Measure and plesaunt Lyberte.	145	Magnyfycence	160
Welthe with Lyberte, with me bothe dwell ye shall,	145	Magnyfycence	174
Welthe with Lyberte, with me bothe dwell ye shall,	145	Magnyfycence	174
Suche order I trust with them for to take,	145	Magnyfycence	178
So that welthe with measure shalbe conbyned,	145	Magnyfycence	179
And lyberte his large with measure shall make.	145	Magnyfycence	180
Measure with noblenesse sholde be alyde.	145	Magnyfycence	194
Then shall you have with you prosperyte resydent.	146	Magnyfycence	197
And not embracyd with pusyllanymyte.	146	Magnyfycence	206
All delectacyons aquayntyd is with me;	146	Magnyfycence	209
Wherfore, Measure, take Lyberte with you hence,	146	Magnyfycence	230
Ye coulde not ellys, I wote, with me endure.	147	Magnyfycence	247
With Magnyfycence, this noble prynce of myght,	148	Magnyfycence	273
With care and with thought howe Jacke shall have Gyl?	148	Magnyfycence	287
With care and with thought howe Jacke shall have Gyl?	148	Magnyfycence	287
You are nothynge mete with us for to dwell,	149	Magnyfycence	304
That with your lorde and mayster so pertly can prate!	149	Magnyfycence	305
I wyll not use you to play with me checke mate.	149	Magnyfycence	307
This wrytynge is welcome with harty affeccyon!	149	Magnyfycence	313
And some bade, 'Sere hym with a marke.'	150	Magnyfycence	360
I had not been here with you this nyght.	150	Magnyfycence	365
If you had with you largesse.	151	Magnyfycence	377
With ye, syr, so God me spede.	151	Magnyfycence	379
Counterfet sadnesse, with delynge full madly;	153	Magnyfycence	468
That with his whyp his mares was wonte to yarke;	153	Magnyfycence	484
A counterfet courtyer with a knaves marke.	154	Magnyfycence	486
For to speke with Lyberte.	155	Magnyfycence	539
With Magnyfycence in housholde do remayne;	157	Magnyfycence	613
With Magnyfycence in housholde do remayne;	158	Magnyfycence	640
To Magnyfycence with us twayne.	158	Magnyfycence	667
That Fansy with his fonde consayte	159	Magnyfycence	678
In faythe, yet am I occupyed with the best;	160	Magnyfycence	705
And flatered them with fables fayre before theyr face,	160	Magnyfycence	717
My tonge is with favell forked and tyned.	160	Magnyfycence	727
Mary, with Magnyfycence I wolde be retaynyd.	161	Magnyfycence	763
poyntyng with his fynger, and sayth,	162	Magnyfycence	SD
What! Is thy harte pryckyd with such a prowde pynne?	162	Magnyfycence	785
But, syr, I wyll have this man with me.	163	Magnyfycence	815
With Crafty Convayaunce. Ye, dyd they so?	166	Magnyfycence	941
Ye, by Goddes sacrament; and with other mo.	166	Magnyfycence	942
Yes, yes. He fell with me also at debate.	166	Magnyfycence	944
With the also? What! He playeth the state?	166	Magnyfycence	945
Why? Is he crossed than with a chalke?	166	Magnyfycence	950
With whom shall I there mete.	167	Magnyfycence	955
With a pere my love you may wynne,	168	Magnyfycence	1015
Plucke down lede and theke with tyle;	169	Magnyfycence	1026
For so with fantasyes my wyt dothe flete	170	Magnyfycence	1080
What! He hathe ben hurte with a stabbe?	171	Magnyfycence	1124
Est [suavis vago] with a shrewde face vilis imago.	172	Magnyfycence	1154
suavis vago] 'snaui snago' †Rastell & Treveris C 1530, B			
By the masse, a Spaynysshe moght with a gray lyste!	173	Magnyfycence	1200
With, yes, by the rode of Wodstocke Parke.	174	Magnyfycence	1209
To felowshyp with foly I can hym brynge.	174	Magnyfycence	1215

	Page	Title	Line
For with foly so do I them lede	175	Magnyfycence	1260
With qui fuit brayne seke I have them brought;	176	Magnyfycence	1302
Why, shall I not have Foly with me also?	176	Magnyfycence	1306
With Magnyfycence thou shalte wonne.	176	Magnyfycence	1311
As malypert tavernars that checke with theyr betters,	178	Magnyfycence	1362
Here cometh in MAGNYFYCENCE with LYBERTE and FELYCYTE.	178	Magnyfycence	SD
What sholde a man do with you? Loke you under [k]ay?	180	Magnyfycence	1429
kay] 'bay' †Rastell & Treveris C 1530, B			
What nede you with hym thus prate and chat?	180	Magnyfycence	1434
Bathyd with blysse, embracyd with comforte.	181	Magnyfycence	1472
Bathyd with blysse, embracyd with comforte.	181	Magnyfycence	1472
I dryve downe these dastardys with a dynt of my fyste.	181	Magnyfycence	1486
Hercules the herdy, with his stobburne clobbyd mase,	182	Magnyfycence	1494
It wolde not become them with me for to mell;	182	Magnyfycence	1497
What man is so maysyd with me that dare mete,	182	Magnyfycence	1506
Nor none so hardy of them with me that durste crake,	182	Magnyfycence	1513
Syr, then, with the favour of your benynge sufferaunce,	182	Magnyfycence	1519
As I be saved, with pleasure I am supprysyd	183	Magnyfycence	1529
Truste me, with you I am hyghly pleasyd;	183	Magnyfycence	1535
And to aqueynte you with carnall delectacyon;	183	Magnyfycence	1547
And to fall in aquayntaunce with every newe facyon,	183	Magnyfycence	1548
That quyckly is envyved with rudyes of the rose,	183	Magnyfycence	1551
Inpurtured with fetures after your purpose,	183	Magnyfycence	1552
Enbudded with beautye and colour fresshe of hewe,	183	Magnyfycence	1554
With me in kepynge suche a Phylyp Sparowe.	184	Magnyfycence	1562
May wynne with a sawte the fortresse of the holde.	184	Magnyfycence	1581
I coude holde you with suche talke hens tyll to morowe.	184	Magnyfycence	1588
And ye se a man that with hym ye be not pleased,	185	Magnyfycence	1609
With, 'Cockes armes! Rest shall I none have	185	Magnyfycence	1615
Here cometh in CLOKED COLUSYON with MESURE	186	Magnyfycence	SD
With a good wyll, syr, God spede you bothe togyder.	186	Magnyfycence	1648
Mesure, ye knowe wel, with hym I can not be content;	186	Magnyfycence	1656
By myne advyse, with you in fayth he shall not rest.	186	Magnyfycence	1660
It were better he spake with you or he wente,	187	Magnyfycence	1662
Yes. With his hande I made hym to subscrybe	187	Magnyfycence	1666
But thynke you with Magnyfycence I shal be reserved?	188	Magnyfycence	1702
Syr, as ye say. Nay, come on with me.	188	Magnyfycence	1707
The Holy Goost be with your grace.	188	Magnyfycence	1711
With my servauntys, and suche maystryes gan make,	188	Magnyfycence	1716
That holly my mynde with you is myscontente;	188	Magnyfycence	1717
With me no longer. Say somwhat nowe, let se,	188	Magnyfycence	1719
What! Woldest thou, lurden, with me brawle agayne?	188	Magnyfycence	1722
Scantly one with measure that wyll dwell.	189	Magnyfycence	1746
With Mesure. Where as all noblenes is, there I have past:	189	Magnyfycence	1749
With pollynge and pluckynge out of all measure,	189	Magnyfycence	1753
Thus, I say, I am envyronned with solace.	190	Magnyfycence	1797
What tydynges with you, syr? I befole thy brayne pan.	191	Magnyfycence	1805
And with a lyme rodde I toke them bothe togyder.	191	Magnyfycence	1815
I sawe a wethercocke wagge with the wynde!	191	Magnyfycence	1821
Howe a wodcocke wrastled with a larke that was lame;	192	Magnyfycence	1836
What tydynges with you, syr, that you loke so sad?	192	Magnyfycence	1843
Alasse, syr, we are undone with stelyng and robbynge!	192	Magnyfycence	1852
And your demenour with Counterfet Countenaunce,	192	Magnyfycence	1861
Thy pleasure now with payne and trouble shalbe tryde.	193	Magnyfycence	1881
I vysyte them somtyme with blaynes and with sores;	194	Magnyfycence	1901
I vysyte them somtyme with blaynes and with sores;	194	Magnyfycence	1901
With botches and carbuckyls in care I them knyt;	194	Magnyfycence	1902
With the gowte I make them to grone where they syt;	194	Magnyfycence	1903
Some with the marmoll to halte I them make;	194	Magnyfycence	1906
And some I vysyte with brennynge of fyre;	194	Magnyfycence	1908
And some I vysyte [with] batayle, warre, and murther,	194	Magnyfycence	1912
with] 'to' †Rastell & Treveris C 1530, B			
To drowne or to sle themselfe with a knyfe -	194	Magnyfycence	1914
I vysyte theyr faders and moders with sekenesse;	194	Magnyfycence	1925
And some I stryke with a fransey;	194	Magnyfycence	1932
I am Goddys preposytour; I prynt them with a pen;	195	Magnyfycence	1941
I vysyte them and stryke them with many sore plagys.	195	Magnyfycence	1943
I am baytyd with doggys at every mannys gate;	195	Magnyfycence	1961
He dynyd with delyte, with poverte he must sup.	195	Magnyfycence	1965
He dynyd with delyte, with poverte he must sup.	195	Magnyfycence	1965
With harte contryte make your supplycacyon	196	Magnyfycence	1991
Alasse! With colde my lymmes shall be marde.	197	Magnyfycence	2004
And where that ye were pomped with what that ye wolde,	197	Magnyfycence	2012
With curteyns of sylke, ye were wonte to be drawe;	197	Magnyfycence	2014
curteyns of sylke] 'courtely sylkes' †Rastell & Treveris 1530B			
Nowe must be storm ybeten with showres and raynes.	197	Magnyfycence	2017
That wantonly can wynke and wynche with her hele.	197	Magnyfycence	2023
She dawnsyth varyaunce with mutabylyte,	197	Magnyfycence	2026
I wyll walke nowe with my beggers baggys,	197	Magnyfycence	2036
And happe you the whyles with these homly raggys.	197	Magnyfycence	2037
Better it is to begge than to be hangyd with shame.	198	Magnyfycence	2039
With ye, mary, syrs, thus sholde it be:	198	Magnyfycence	2064
With daunce on the le, the le!	198	Magnyfycence	2068
I bassed that baby with harte so free;	198	Magnyfycence	2069
At my devyse I with her met;	199	Magnyfycence	2075
I am desyred with hyghest and lowest degre.	199	Magnyfycence	2079
I am presydent of prynces; I prycke them with pryde.	199	Magnyfycence	2082
A thousande pounde with lyberte may holde no tacke.	199	Magnyfycence	2084

	Page	Title	Line
A prynce to use with all his hole intent,	200	Magnyfycence	2118
But so longe they rekyn with theyr reasons amysse	200	Magnyfycence	2127
they] 'theyr' †Rastell & Treveris C 1530, B			
Freers, with foly I make them so fayne	201	Magnyfycence	2147
She hath dyssayvyd me with her doublenesse.	201	Magnyfycence	2157
with a lusty laughter.	201	Magnyfycence	SD
With ye, syr, by Jesu, that slayne was with Jewes!	201	Magnyfycence	2167
With ye, syr, by Jesu, that slayne was with Jewes!	201	Magnyfycence	2167
Ye, wylte thou clenly cle[v]e me in the clyfte with thy nose?	202	Magnyfycence	2176
cleve] 'clene' †Rastell & Treveris C 1530, B			
When we with Magnyfycence goodys made chevysaunce.	203	Magnyfycence	2236
Ly styll, ly styll nowe, with yll hayle!	204	Magnyfycence	2248
With never a peny in his purse.	204	Magnyfycence	2258
Ye shall be clappyd with a coloppe	204	Magnyfycence	2272
I make hevy hertys, with eyen full holowe.	205	Magnyfycence	2286
With this halter good and stronge;	206	Magnyfycence	2313
Or ellys with this knyfe cut out a tonge	206	Magnyfycence	2314
Shall I myselfe hange with an halter? Nay,	206	Magnyfycence	2320
In styckynge my selfe with this fayre knyfe.	206	Magnyfycence	2322
Here MAGNYFYCENCE wolde slee hymselfe with a knyfe.	206	Magnyfycence	SD
Wynde you from wanhope and aquaynte you with me.	206	Magnyfycence	2340
That you hath punysshed with his sharpe rod.	207	Magnyfycence	2350
And payned you with a purgacyon of odyous poverte,	207	Magnyfycence	2353
Myxed with bytter alowes of herde adversyte.	207	Magnyfycence	2354
With rubarbe of repentaunce in you for to rest;	207	Magnyfycence	2357
With drammes of devocyon your dyet must be drest,	207	Magnyfycence	2358
With gommes goostly of glad herte and mynde,	207	Magnyfycence	2359
Ye, syr, now am I armyd with good hope,	207	Magnyfycence	2378
Ye, but have ye repentyd you with harte contryte?	208	Magnyfycence	2391
Good Hope, I pray you with harty affeccyon	208	Magnyfycence	2399
Nowe shall ye be renewyd with solace.	208	Magnyfycence	2404
Fyrst, I saye, with mynde fyrme and stable	208	Magnyfycence	2408
Then welthe with you myght in no wyse abyde.	210	Magnyfycence	2447
A ha, fansy and foly met with you, I trowe.	210	Magnyfycence	2448
Surely my welthe with them was overthrow.	210	Magnyfycence	2450
I herde say that adversyte with Magnyfycence had fought.	210	Magnyfycence	2460
Ye, syr, with adversyte I have bene vexyd;	210	Magnyfycence	2461
Faythfull assuraunce with good peradvertaunce.	210	Magnyfycence	2472
Faythfull] 'Faythfully' †Rastell & Treveris C 1530, B			
To the increse of your honour then arme you with ryght,	211	Magnyfycence	2496
And fumously adresse you with magnanymyte;	211	Magnyfycence	2497
And with sad cyrcumspeccyon correcte my vantonnesse.	212	Magnyfycence	2509
But fallyble flatery enmyxyd with bytternesse.	212	Magnyfycence	2516
But fallyble flatery enmyxyd with bytternesse.	212	Magnyfycence	2523
Beten with stormys of many a frowarde blast,	213	Magnyfycence	2560
Ensor[b]yd with the wawys savage and wode;	213	Magnyfycence	2561
ensorbyd] 'ensordyd' †Rastell & Treveris C 1530, B			
Home to your paleys with joy and ryalte.	214	Magnyfycence	2567
There to indeuer with all felycyte.	214	Magnyfycence	2569
Brystled with here.	215	El Rummynge	21
With a croked backe.	215	El Rummynge	33
Lyke as they were with buckels /Togyder made fast.	215	El Rummynge	46
With symper-the-cocket.	215	El Rummynge	55
And gyrdeth in her gytes /Stytched and pranked with pletes;	216	El Rummynge	69
With clothes upon her hed /That wey a sowe of led,	216	El Rummynge	71
That wey] 'That they wey' Kynge & Marche 1554, Day 1560, Marshe 1568			
With a whym-wham /Knyt with a trym-tram	216	El Rummynge	75
With a whym-wham /Knyt with a trym-tram	216	El Rummynge	76
With a payre of heles /As brode as two wheles.	216	El Rummynge	83
She hobles as she gose /With her blanket hose	216	El Rummynge	86
she gose] 'a gose' Day 1560, Marshe 1568			
With, 'Now away the mare,	217	El Rummynge	110
With, 'Fyll the cup, fyll!'	217	El Rummynge	115
Cysly and Sare, /With theyr legges bare,	217	El Rummynge	120
With all theyr myght runnynge /To Elynour Rummynge,	217	El Rummynge	128
A sorte of foule drabbes /All scurvy with scabbes.	218	El Rummynge	140
Some with a sho clout /Bynde theyr heddes about;	218	El Rummynge	143
With, 'Hey, dogge, hay, /Have these hogges away!'	218	El Rummynge	168
hogges] 'dogges' Day 1560, Marshe 1568			
With, 'Get me a staffe, /The swyne eate my draffe!	218	El Rummynge	170
Stryke the hogges with a clubbe,	218	El Rummynge	172
The sowe with her pygges;	219	El Rummynge	176
With, 'Fo, ther is a stenche!	219	El Rummynge	180
With her maungy fystis.	219	El Rummynge	200
With, 'Bas, my prety bonny,	220	El Rummynge	227
And some a pot with honny,	220	El Rummynge	246
Some ranne a good trot /With a skellet or a pot;	220	El Rummynge	250
And with her doth brynge	221	El Rummynge	278
With flaxe and with towe;	221	El Rummynge	287
With flaxe and with towe;	221	El Rummynge	287
With, 'Hey,' and with, 'Howe, /Syt we downe arowe	221	El Rummynge	289
With, 'Hey,' and with, 'Howe, /Syt we downe arowe	221	El Rummynge	289
Another there was that ran /With a good brasse pan -	222	El Rummynge	317
She fyll in a wynkynge /With a barlyhood;	223	El Rummynge	372
And blessed her with a cup /Of newe ale in cornes.	224	El Rummynge	377
Another with a cradell,	224	El Rummynge	384
And with a syde-sadell;	224	El Rummynge	385

WITHALL — WITHIN	Page	Title	Line
Of [a] foles fylly /That had a fole with Wylly,	224	El Rummynge	389
a] not in †Lant 1545, Kynge & Marche 1554, Day 1560, Marshe 1568; fylly] 'silly' Marshe 1568			
With, 'Jast you, and gup, gylly,	224	El Rummynge	390
With the feders of a quale	226	El Rummynge	453
And with good ale barme /She could make a charme	226	El Rummynge	455
With that her hed shaked /And her handes quaked.	226	El Rummynge	476
With, 'Fy, cover thy shap	227	El Rummynge	507
thy] 'the' Kynge & Marche 1554, Day 1560, Marshe 1568			
With sum flyp-flap,	227	El Rummynge	508
In came another dant, /With a gose and a gant.	227	El Rummynge	516
'And let me with you bybyll.'	228	El Rummynge	550
With a sory face /Whey-wormed about;	228	El Rummynge	552
With here and there a puscull,	228	El Rummynge	555
And so with ale stuffed,	229	El Rummynge	571
With Elynour in the spence,	229	El Rummynge	598
Were fayne with a chalke /To score on the balke,	230	El Rummynge	614
Deyntely dyetyd with dyvers delycate spyce,	231	Speke Parott	3
A cage curyowsly carven, with sylver pynne,	231	Speke Parott	8
These maydens full meryly with many a dyvers flowur	231	Speke Parott	11
a] not in †MS Harley 2252			
With, 'Speke, Parott, I pray yow,' full curteslye they sey,	231	Speke Parott	13
With ladyes I lerne and goe with them to scole.	231	Speke Parott	21
With ladyes I lerne and goe with them to scole.	231	Speke Parott	21
With, 'Parlez byen, Parott, ow parles ryen.'	231	Speke Parott	31
With Dowche, with Spaynyshe, my tonge can agree;	231	Speke Parott	32
With Dowche, with Spaynyshe, my tonge can agree;	231	Speke Parott	32
'With Kateryne incomporabyll, owur royall quene also,	231	Speke Parott	36
With fidasso de cosso in Turke and in Trace;	232	Speke Parott	39
Aram was fyred with Caldies fyer called Ur;	232	Speke Parott	64
Let Syr Wrig-wrag wrastell with Syr Delarag;	233	Speke Parott	89
With, 'Who is there? A mayd?' Nay, nay, I trow!	233	Speke Parott	100
With, 'Bas me, swete Parrot, bas me, swete swete;'	233	Speke Parott	104
With my beke I can pyke my lyttel praty too;	233	Speke Parott	107
With, 'He sayd,' and 'We said.' Ich wot now what ich wot,	234	Speke Parott	132
Som pseudo-propheta with ciromancy:	234	Speke Parott	138
Honowre with renowne wyll ren on that syde.	234	Speke Parott	140
on] 'of' Kynge & Marche 1554, Day 1560, Marshe 1568			
With, 'Da causales,' is cast out of the gate,	235	Speke Parott	174
And medyll with Quintylyan in his Decla[m]acyons,	235	Speke Parott	177
Declamacyons] 'Declaracyons' †Lant 1545, Kynge & Marche 1554, Day 1560, Marshe 1568			
With, 'Aveto' in Greco, and such solempne salutacyons,	235	Speke Parott	179
Support Parrot, I pray you, with your suffrage ornate,	236	Speke Parott	195
With herte moste tendyr,	237	Speke Parott	226
To rekyn with thys recule now	237	Speke Parott	227

WITHALL

	Page	Title	Line
In hope that no man shall /Be myscontent withall.	62	Hauke	28
Be] 'By' Kynge & Marche 1554			
And that he wysshed withall	66	Hauke	182
His herte withall /Bytter as gall;	94	Phy Sparrow	916
To angre the Scottes and Irysh keterynges withall,	117	Ag Scottes	83
And what so we say, holde you content withall.	179	Magnyfycence	1406
Let us here of your pleasure, to passe the tyme withall.	182	Magnyfycence	1518
To lerne you hereafter for to beware withall.	207	Magnyfycence	2376
To helpe withall a stytch;	226	El Rummynge	457
But that metaphora, alegoria withall,	236	Speke Parott	202

WITHDRAW

	Page	Title	Line
Though thou withdraw me from her by long dystaunce,	45	Balettys3	46

WITHDRAWE

	Page	Title	Line
Theyr dewtyes to withdrawe,	268	Collyn Clout	856
Nowe to withdrawe my pen,	277	Collyn Clout	1248
'Withdrawe your hande, the tyme passis fast.	343	Garlande	1086

WITHE

	Page	Title	Line
Bluntly as bestis withe boste and with cry	31	Dol Dethe	83
Withe his enmys that were stark mad and wode;	32	Dol Dethe	100
Paregall to dukis, withe kingis he myght compare,	33	Dol Dethe	134

WITHHOLD

	Page	Title	Line
And the appels of gold /Of Hesperides withhold,	104	Phy Sparrow	1302

WITHHOLDE

	Page	Title	Line
A fals lying tunge is harde to withholde;	137	Ven Tongues	6
And the apples of golde /Of Hesperides withholde,	349	Garlande	1295
And the twayne last /Be withholde so fast	358	Garlande2	13

WITHIN

	Page	Title	Line
I herde her speke of you within shorte space,	50	Bowge	158
shorte] 'a shorte' Wynkyn de Worde 1510			
Thus within the wals /Of holy church to deale,	65	Hauke	134
Aut sanguis vitulorum, /Was offryd within the wallys,	66	Hauke	172
For within that stounde,	72	Phy Sparrow	34
Within those walles	83	Phy Sparrow	472
Within this quaire? /Who lyst repayre	116	Ag Scottes	41
lyst] 'lyst to' Kynge & Marche 1554, Day 1560, Marshe 1568			
Within thy skyn he xall remayne.	130	Garnesche5	22
Within his slyve;	165	Magnyfycence	906
And within an houre after,	169	Magnyfycence	1031
Than Elynour dyd them hyde /Within her beddes syde.	229	El Rummynge	606
And assay to crepe /Within the noble walles	249	Collyn Clout	126
And ryght slender connynge /Within theyr heedes wonnynge.	250	Collyn Clout	141

WITHOUT —WITHOUTEN   Page   Title   Line

	Page	Title	Line
Within Westmynster Hall.	287	Why Come Ye	325
But within monethes thre	288	Why Come Ye	366
To make within an hower,	293	Why Come Ye	566
And within this xvi yere	295	Why Come Ye	641
Within the cattes eare	298	Why Come Ye	758
For his prerogatyve, /Within that consystory	299	Why Come Ye	817
That within Englande dwellys.	303	Why Come Ye	962
Within that, a pryncess excellente of porte;	313	Garlande	43
that] 'it' MS Cotton Vitellius E.x			
How far it was, or ellis within what howris,	325	Garlande	457
far] not in †Fakes 1523			
The carpettis within and tappettis of pall;	325	Garlande	474
For Sir William Lyle /Within shorte whyle,	360	Albany	39

WITHOUT

	Page	Title	Line
For thus dare I say, without tradiccyon,	42	Balettys2	10
But all without redresse;	72	Phy Sparrow	33
Farewell without restore,	80	Phy Sparrow	333
Of the same facyon /Without alteracyon,	85	Phy Sparrow	543
That is a kynge without a realme.	115	Scot Kynge	59
That he is kyng without a reme;	119	Ag Scottes	156
But yf yt war Syr Tyrmagant that tyrnyd without nall;	121	Garneschel	4
Welthe without measure wolde bere hymselfe to bolde;	143	Magnyfycence	116
Lyberte without measure prove a thynge of nought.	143	Magnyfycence	117
Lyberte without measure is acountyd for a beste;	144	Magnyfycence	138
Without I myght cut it out of the brode clothe,	144	Magnyfycence	146
For, without measure, poverte and nede	144	Magnyfycence	152
For welthe without measure sodenly wyll slyde.	145	Magnyfycence	192
Who county[th] without me is caste to fer behynde	146	Magnyfycence	214
countyth] 'countyd' †Rastell & Treveris C 1530, B			
That all is without measure and fer beyonde the mone.	146	Magnyfycence	224
Without measure lyghtly may fade,	146	Magnyfycence	228
Syr, without any longer delyaunce,	147	Magnyfycence	237
That without largesse noblenesse can not rayne.	147	Magnyfycence	265
I say, without largesse worshyp hath no place,	148	Magnyfycence	267
Without an antetyme or a stole;	150	Magnyfycence	359
Counterfet haltynge without a thorne;	153	Magnyfycence	449
What! Is Largesse without lyberte?	155	Magnyfycence	540
In fayth, and without lyberte there is no bydyng.	158	Magnyfycence	662
Ye, but thou can play the fole without a vyser.	173	Magnyfycence	1177
Without crafte nothynge is well behavyd.	177	Magnyfycence	1350
Without me be full ofte aspyed.	177	Magnyfycence	1355
Yet Lyberte without rule is not worth a strawe.	178	Magnyfycence	1378
Syr, yet without sapyence your substaunce may be smal;	179	Magnyfycence	1407
For welth without largesse is all out of kynde.	180	Magnyfycence	1441
Syr, we can do nothynge the one without the other.	180	Magnyfycence	1450
I synge of two partys without a mene.	181	Magnyfycence	1463
I folowe in felycyte without reversse;	181	Magnyfycence	1491
By the meanes of money without ony gonne.	184	Magnyfycence	1578
Let them have all, and the other go without;	190	Magnyfycence	1780
Thus joy without mesure you shall have.	190	Magnyfycence	1781
Somtyme without measure he trusted in golde;	193	Magnyfycence	1894
And now without measure he shal have hunger and colde.	193	Magnyfycence	1895
Welthe without lyberte gothe all to wrake.	199	Magnyfycence	2086
Ye, have done at ones without delay.	206	Magnyfycence	2319
Without fayle, syr, that is no nay:	209	Magnyfycence	2429
That nothynge be gyven without consyderacyon.	211	Magnyfycence	2495
Without our shyppe be sure, it is lykely to brast,	213	Magnyfycence	2562
Without drynke she must dye;	221	El Rummynge	273
A narrow unfethered and without an hed,	232	Speke Parott	74
A bagpype without blowynge standeth in no sted:	232	Speke Parott	75
bagpype] 'bagbyte' †Lant 1545, Kynge & Marche 1554			
Your gorge nat endued /Without a capon stued,	252	Collyn Clout	216
A preest without a letter,	253	Collyn Clout	270
Without his vertue be greatter,	253	Collyn Clout	271
Without the assent /Of your presydent;	272	Collyn Clout	1034
Without	272	Collyn Clout	1037
....] blank in †Godfray 1531, 'your consentacyon' Kele 1545.1,			
'your assentacion' Marshe 1568, 'george gascone' Harley 2252			
Without his presydent be by,	272	Collyn Clout	1042
Without good reason or skyll;	276	Collyn Clout	1191
Than, without collusyon,	279	Why Come Ye	17
For he hathe all the sayenge /Without any renayenge.	283	Why Come Ye	193
Without reason or skyll.	291	Why Come Ye	488
Without all good reason.	304	Why Come Ye	997
If xii were let in, xii hundreth stode without.	326	Garlande	490
Recount, reporte, reherse without delay	336	Garlande	840

WITHOUTE

	Page	Title	Line
Of hym that is gone, alas, withoute restore,	29	Dol Dethe	3
Hys musyk withoute mesure, to sharp is hys my;	37	Coystrownel	25
Hys dyscant is besy, it is withoute a mene;	37	Coystrownel	27
We tweyne, I trowe, be not withoute dysceyte:	55	Bowge	313
Withoute God make a good conclusyon.	59	Bowge	483
Withoute deservynge shulde have the best game.	318	Garlande	221

WITHOUTEN

	Page	Title	Line
Of all women O floure withouten pere,	35	Dol Dethe	207
With, 'He wrate suche a bil withouten dout',	139	Ven Tongues	70
Withouten drede or feare!	298	Why Come Ye	759

WITHOWTE —WYLD   Page   Title   Line

WITHOWTE
	Page	Title	Line
Withowte ye have a confectioun	128	Garnesche3	152
Withowte thou leve thou shalt be chekt,	132	Garnesche5	109
So ys all thyng wrowghte wylfully withowte reson and skylle.	245	Speke Parott	496

WITHSAY
Moloc, that mawmett, there darre no man withsay;	243	Speke Parott	402
No man dare him withsay.	294	Why Come Ye	598

WITHSTAND
To the right of his prince which shold not be withstand;	31	Dol Dethe	67

WITHSTANDE
Nor Cesar July, that no man myght withstande,	181	Magnyfycence	1482
Vyle velyarde, thou must not nowe my dynt withstande;	193	Magnyfycence	1878
To preche, and withstande	268	Collyn Clout	889
Worshypfully to withstande	269	Collyn Clout	912
worshypfully] 'worshyp' †Godfray 1531, Kele 1545.1, Marshe 1568			
And so malapertly withstande	296	Why Come Ye	675

WITLESSE
With, 'Spende,' and wast witlesse,	280	Why Come Ye	74

WITSTAND
Presed forthe boldly to witstand the myght,	31	Dol Dethe	87

WITTIS
All the wittis they have.	348	Garlande	1266

WYCHECRAFT
As wychecraft or charmyng;	295	Why Come Ye	665

WYCKYDNESSE
Alasse, my wyckydnesse, that may I wyte!	205	Magnyfycence	2304

WYCLIFFES
Among the scabbed skyes /Of Wycliffes flesshe flyes.	378	Replycacion	166

WYDDERED
Wyddered lyke hay, /The woll worne away.	216	El Rummynge	62

WYDE
Yet whils he stode he gave them woundes wyde.	32	Dol Dethe	101
Yet] 'Ye' Marshe 1568			
She goyth wyde behynde and hewyth never a dele:	43	Balettys2	24
Garnyche, ye gape to wyde:	124	Garnesche3	21
Had I not opened my purse wyde,	150	Magnyfycence	347
Beyonde measure /My sleve is wyde;	164	Magnyfycence	850
My buskyn wyde, /Ryche to beholde	164	Magnyfycence	853
His gowne so wyde	165	Magnyfycence	903
And fell so wyde open	227	El Rummynge	496
She had a wyde wesant;	227	El Rummynge	517
wyde] 'wyse' Kynge & Marche 1554			
Harke, howe the losell prates /With a wyde wesaunt!	275	Collyn Clout	1154
Into a felde she brought me wyde and large,	328	Garlande	568

WYDERYD
With synnews wyderyd, /With bonys shyderyd,	39	Coystrowne3	12

WYDOW
O mayden, wydow, and wyfe,	73	Phy Sparrow	53

WYERFORE
Wyerfore ye may it now repent.	114	Scot Kynge	33

WYFE
O mayden, wydow, and wyfe,	73	Phy Sparrow	53
Like Andromach, Hectors wyfe,	74	Phy Sparrow	108
And of the Wyfe of Bath,	87	Phy Sparrow	618
Of Bele Isold his wyfe,	87	Phy Sparrow	643
And of Hester his other wyfe,	90	Phy Sparrow	743
I speke nat of the good wyfe,	253	Collyn Clout	253
Spareth neither mayde ne wyfe.	284	Why Come Ye	225
Of my lordis grace nor his wyfe!	306	Why Come Ye	1077
The noble wyfe of Polimites kynge;	336	Garlande	844
The millar durst not leve his wyfe at home.	352	Garlande	1417
Than a chyldis birde and a knavis wyfe?	352	Garlande	1452

WYFULL
But wyfull waywardnesse muste walke out of the way;	211	Magnyfycence	2490

WYGGES
It wygges and it wagges /Lyke tawny saffron bagges;	218	El Rummynge	137

WYGHT
Xall kyt both wyght and grene:	127	Garnesche3	139
Thou art a graceles wyght	364	Albany	232

WYL
He wyl cause yow caste your crawes,	128	Garnesche3	155
Note and mark wyl thys parcele;	132	Garnesche5	97
Why, wyl a maystres be wonne for money and for golde?	184	Magnyfycence	1575
That nonnes wyl leve theyr holynes and ryn after me;	201	Magnyfycence	2146
I wyl be ferme and stabyll, /And to yow servyceabyll,	237	Speke Parott	246
Some wyl neyther golde ne grotes;	268	Collyn Clout	866
But they wyl talke of suche uncouthes,	272	Collyn Clout	1052
'There shal he here what she wyl to hym say	325	Garlande	451
wyl to hym] 'to hym will' Marshe 1568			

WYLAGE
The corte, the contre, wylage, and towne,	130	Garnesche5	25

WYLBE
Or ells with gret shame your game wylbe sene.	43	Balettys2	42

WYLD
Whiche kyndelde the wyld fyre that made all this smoke.	31	Dol Dethe	77
But ye had some wyl[d] sede to sowe,	114	Scot Kynge	52
wyld] 'wyle' †Fakes 1513			

WYLDE—WYLL   Page   Title   Line

WYLDE
Of cattes wylde and tame;   78   Phy Sparrow   276
The wylde wolfe Lycaon   79   Phy Sparrow   311
With the wylde mallarde;   83   Phy Sparrow   451
     wylde] 'wynde' †Kele 1545.2
As wytles as a wylde goos, ye have but small remorrs .. 123   Garnesche2   18
And it is wonder that your wylde insolence   143   Magnyfycence   85
Ye wante but a wylde flyeng bolte to shote at the buttes. 148 Magnyfycence   294
By our lakyn, syr, I have ben a hawkyng for the wylde swan. 191 Magnyfycence 1806
Wylde fyre and thonder;   285   Why Come Ye   257
basked and baththed in their wylde burblyng and boyling blode, 374 Replycacion I
WYLFULL
Or wylfull blyndnesse, ...   290   Why Come Ye   469
Of his wylfull affectyon.   304   Why Come Ye   1015
     his] 'him' Toy 1553, Kitson 1560.7, Marshe 1568
WYLFULLY
For where I am occupied and usyd wylfully, ...   200   Magnyfycence   2131
So ys all thyng wrowghte wylfully withowte reson and skylle. 245 Speke Parott 496
WYLFULNES
By waywarde wylfulnes let eche thynge be convayed; .. 185   Magnyfycence   1594
When wylfulnes ys vicar generall.   232   Speke Parott   54
The enfatuate fantasies, the wytles wylfulnes   242   Speke Parott   384
Wylfulnes and Braynles no[w] rule all the raye.   243   Speke Parott   421
     now] 'no' †MS Harley 2252
For Frantiknes and Wylfulnes and Braynles ensembyll, .. 243   Speke Parott   423
And full of wylfulnes, ...   276   Collyn Clout   1177
WYLFULNESSE
And sore I repent me of my wylfulnesse;   207   Magnyfycence   2379
My wylfulnesse, syr, excuse I ne can.   209   Magnyfycence   2432
WYLY
Yet it is a wyly mouse   298   Why Come Ye   756
WYLL
Deth wyll us quell /And with us mell.   39   Coystrowne3   23
And not to wrythe, for he so wyll atteyne, ...   46   Bowge   22
     wrythe] 'wryte' Wynkyn de Worde 1510, Marshe 1568
But who wyll have it muste paye therfore dere.   47   Bowge   53
That wyll for me be medyatoure and mene;   48   Bowge   93
Yf ye have not, in fayth, I wyll you lene   48   Bowge   96
That wyll abyde and never frome us fall.   49   Bowge   130
And, as she wyll, so shall our grete shyppe sayle. ..   50   Bowge   172
He wyll begyle you and speke fayre to your face. ...   51   Bowge   200
'Fare well,' quod he, 'we wyll talke more of this.' .   52   Bowge   227
It is lyke he wyll stonde in our lyghte!'   54   Bowge   305
     our] 'your' Marshe 1568
'Turde,' quod Ha[f]ter, 'I wyll the nothynge layne, .. 55   Bowge   311
     layne] 'sayne' †Wynkyn de Worde 1499, Marshe 1568
Come whan it wyll, oppose the I shall, ...   55   Bowge   335
To her wyll I nowe all my poverte lege.   57   Bowge   412
Yet wyll I saye some wordes for your sake   59   Bowge   474
It wyll not be, his purse is not on-flote.   60   Bowge   488
As I shall tell you, yf ye wyll harke agayne: 61   Bowge   520
I wyll not saye it is mater in dede, ...   61   Bowge   537
I wyll not fayne nor forge;   64   Hauke   88
Agaynst my mynde and wyll   64   Hauke   98
(The Bybyll wyll not ly)   66   Hauke   167
Alas, it wyll me slo, ...   75   Phy Sparrow   141
Saynge, 'Mayd, ye are in wyll   77   Phy Sparrow   222
That never ought the evyll wyll!   79   Phy Sparrow   323
The estryge, that wyll eate   83   Phy Sparrow   478
Now wyll I enterpryse, ...   93   Phy Sparrow   856
If Arethusa wyll send   93   Phy Sparrow   860
If Apollo wyll promyse   93   Phy Sparrow   863
And no man wyll me blame, ...   94   Phy Sparrow   890
His foule desyre /Wyll suffre no slepe   95   Phy Sparrow   934
But yet certayne /I wyll be playne, ...   96   Phy Sparrow   967
     Be] 'me' †Kele 1545.2
For now I wyll begyn   99   Phy Sparrow   1093
I wyll my selfe dyscharge   105   Phy Sparrow   1360
With her certayne /I wyll remayne   112   Calliope   22
Your wyll renne before your wytte.   113   Scot Kynge   12
Wherfore I fere ye wyll suffre payne.   114   Scot Kynge   28
By your wanton wyll, syr, at a worde, ...   114   Scot Kynge   48
That never wyll leve theyr tratlynge: 115   Ag Scottes   2
And wyll not know /Theyr overthrow /At Branxton More? . 115   Ag Scottes   9
And now to begyn I wyll me adres, ...   117   Ag Scottes   89
Your wyll than ran before your wyt.   118   Ag Scottes   102
Your harte ys to hawte, iwys, yt wyll nat be alowde. .. 123   Garnesche2   26
And wyll never intende   124   Garnesche3   17
Yower knavery I wyll nat hyde, ...   124   Garnesche3   22
Men sey ye wyll wax lowsy, /Drunkyn, drowpy, drowsy. .. 127   Garnesche3   135
That all the warlde wyll spye your shame.   132   Garnesche5   111
For welthe wyll sone departe the froo.   132   Garnesche5   125
Yt wold garnyche wyll thy face.   133   Garnesche5   135
Inordynate pride wyll have a falle.   133   Garnesche5   159
A reme of papyr wyll nat holde   134   Garnesche5   174
But wyll hath reason so under subjeccyon, ...   141   Magnyfycence   19
Why, to say what he wyll, Lyberte hath leve.   141   Magnyfycence   34
Lyberte at large wyll oft wax reklesse.   142   Magnyfycence   54

	Page	Title	Line
Say what ye wyll to me.	142	Magnyfycence	66
What wote ye where upon I wyll conclude?	142	Magnyfycence	72
That wyll not I forsake,	143	Magnyfycence	100
Nay, ye shall begynne, by my wyll.	143	Magnyfycence	104
Unto your rule I wyll annex my mynde.	144	Magnyfycence	142
As I was wonte ever, at my fre wyll.	144	Magnyfycence	147
But have ye not herde say that wyll is no skyll?	144	Magnyfycence	148
Wyll crepe upon us, and us to myschefe lede;	144	Magnyfycence	153
For myschefe wyll mayster us yf measure us forsake.	144	Magnyfycence	154
Your ordenaunce, syr, I wyll not forsake.	145	Magnyfycence	181
And I my selfe hooly to you wyll inclyne.	145	Magnyfycence	182
Measure and I wyll never be devydyd,	145	Magnyfycence	186
For welthe without measure sodenly wyll slyde.	145	Magnyfycence	192
For I wyll use you by his advertysment.	146	Magnyfycence	196
I wyll endevour me to order every thynge	146	Magnyfycence	203
Yet we wyll therin take good delyberacyon.	148	Magnyfycence	275
As in that I wyll not be agaynst your pleasure.	148	Magnyfycence	276
Have ye not welthe here at your wyll?	148	Magnyfycence	284
In fayth, I wyll not say that ye shall prove a fole,	148	Magnyfycence	301
Go shake the, dogge, hay, syth ye wyll nedys!	148	Magnyfycence	303
I wyll not use you to play with me checke mate.	149	Magnyfycence	307
Is there ony thynge elles your grace wyll commaunde me?	149	Magnyfycence	318
Togyder we wyll talke more of this.	151	Magnyfycence	393
But nowe wyll I, that they be gone,	151	Magnyfycence	407
A knave wyll counterfet nowe a knyght,	152	Magnyfycence	417
To counterfet she wyll assay	153	Magnyfycence	462
Coll wolde go clenly, and it wyll not be,	153	Magnyfycence	476
A knokylbonyarde wyll counterfet a clarke;	153	Magnyfycence	480
We wyll remedy it, man, or we go;	155	Magnyfycence	551
In all this hast whether wyll ye ryde?	156	Magnyfycence	570
Tell me, syrs, what is your wyll?	157	Magnyfycence	611
But I wyll be ruled after your counsell.	157	Magnyfycence	615
Mary, so wyll we also.	157	Magnyfycence	616
I wyll passe over the cyrcumstaunce	158	Magnyfycence	637
Pease! I have not yet sayd what I wyll.	158	Magnyfycence	648
No. In every corner he wyll peke,	158	Magnyfycence	658
We wyll se you shortly, one of us twayne.	159	Magnyfycence	686
That they wyll here no man but the fyrst tale.	161	Magnyfycence	743
By Goddes fote, and I dare well fyght, for I wyll not start.	161	Magnyfycence	768
Wyll ye se this gentylman is all in his skornys?	162	Magnyfycence	773
He wyll come, man, when he may tende to.	162	Magnyfycence	790
No; for or we stryke, we wyll be advysed twyse.	163	Magnyfycence	810
But, syr, I wyll have this man with me.	163	Magnyfycence	815
I waraunt you I wyll not go away.	163	Magnyfycence	820
But nowe I wyll not say the worste.	163	Magnyfycence	828
A very fon, /A very asse /Wyll take upon /To compasse	164	Magnyfycence	865
A very pore /That so wyll do,	164	Magnyfycence	870
Wyth me wyll wonne	165	Magnyfycence	900
He wyll have wrought	165	Magnyfycence	902
Nowe I wyll this, and nowe I wyll that -	169	Magnyfycence	1027
Nowe I wyll this, and nowe I wyll that -	169	Magnyfycence	1027
Of a spyndell I wyll make a sparre;	169	Magnyfycence	1035
I wyll not have it so, I wyll have it this.	169	Magnyfycence	1042
I wyll not have it so, I wyll have it this.	169	Magnyfycence	1042
I wyll not gyve a halfepeny for to chose the better.	170	Magnyfycence	1067
By God, I can tell the; and I wyll.	170	Magnyfycence	1071
Thou shalte have my purse, and I wyll have thyne.	171	Magnyfycence	1102
For, Goddes cope, thou wyll spende!	171	Magnyfycence	1115
Ye. But he wyll in at every mannes dore.	171	Magnyfycence	1130
For he wyll speke to Magnyfycence thus.	172	Magnyfycence	1168
In fayth, I can make you bothe folys, and I wyll.	172	Magnyfycence	1173
Thou must have thy fansy and thy wyll,	173	Magnyfycence	1183
Yes, yet he wyll make the ete a gnat.	173	Magnyfycence	1192
Yes, yet] 'Yet yes' †Rastell & Treveris C 1530, B			
Than wyll I say that thou hast no pere.	173	Magnyfycence	1195
Nowe, by the rode, and he wyll go nere.	173	Magnyfycence	1196
That wyll syt ydyll all the day	174	Magnyfycence	1229
For they that wyll so bysely smater	175	Magnyfycence	1257
He wyll make it mykyll worse than it is;	175	Magnyfycence	1273
And shall we have lyberte to do what we wyll?	176	Magnyfycence	1316
And by crafty conveyaunce I wyll, and I can,	178	Magnyfycence	1359
Theyr conveyaunce weltyth the worke all by wyll;	178	Magnyfycence	1363
And some wyll take upon them to conterfet letters,	178	Magnyfycence	1364
And some wyll convey by the pretence of sadnesse	178	Magnyfycence	1366
Syr, as by my wyll, it shall be so no more.	178	Magnyfycence	1377
Ye shall be occupyed, Welthe, at my wyll.	178	Magnyfycence	1380
Syr, by lyberte and largesse I wyll that ye shall	179	Magnyfycence	1396
What! Wyll ye waste wynde and prate thus in vayne?	179	Magnyfycence	1403
Your grace sent for me, I wene. What is your wyll?	179	Magnyfycence	1410
I truste your grace wyll be agreabyll	179	Magnyfycence	1417
I say that I wyll ye have hym in gydynge.	180	Magnyfycence	1436
And so as ye se it wyll be no better,	180	Magnyfycence	1438
I have welth at wyll, largesse and lyberte.	181	Magnyfycence	1458
No man so hardy to worke agaynst my wyll.	181	Magnyfycence	1479
To shewe you my mynde myselfe I wyll avaunce,	182	Magnyfycence	1520
Wyll ye spende ony money? Ye, a thousande pounde.	184	Magnyfycence	1570
But, blessyd be our Lorde, they wyll be sone converted.	184	Magnyfycence	1584
Why, wyll they then be intreted, the most and the lest?	184	Magnyfycence	1585

	Page	Title	Line
What so ever ye do, folowe your owne wyll,	185	Magnyfycence	1595
Is there no horson that knave that wyll bete?'	185	Magnyfycence	1618
That for your sake I wyll fall on my kne.	186	Magnyfycence	1630
And that ye wyll not cast hym away so sone.	186	Magnyfycence	1638
Howe be it, at your instaunce I wyll the rather	186	Magnyfycence	1641
With a good wyll, syr, God spede you bothe togyder.	186	Magnyfycence	1648
I wyll have hym rehayted and dyspysed.	186	Magnyfycence	1658
And we wyll be comonynge in the mene season.	187	Magnyfycence	1688
Wherfore I wyll that ye be resydent	188	Magnyfycence	1718
Scantly one with measure that wyll dwell.	189	Magnyfycence	1746
And where soever you wyll fall to a rekenynge,	190	Magnyfycence	1777
Those thre wyll be redy even at your bekenynge;	190	Magnyfycence	1778
And suche as you wyll shall lacke no promocyon.	190	Magnyfycence	1789
I make God avowe ye wyll none other men have.	191	Magnyfycence	1827
When ye knowe that I knowe, ye wyll not be glad.	192	Magnyfycence	1844
Adewe, for I wyll not come in his clokys.	193	Magnyfycence	1874
Nowe is there no man that wyll set by hym a flye.	193	Magnyfycence	1889
To gyde them vertuously that wyll not remembre,	194	Magnyfycence	1922
And yf I se therby they wyll not amende,	194	Magnyfycence	1926
Of correccyon, but let them have theyr wyll.	194	Magnyfycence	1930
For nowe wyll I from this caytyfe go,	195	Magnyfycence	1950
Nowe, syth it wyll no nother be,	196	Magnyfycence	1978
Put your wyll to his wyll, for surely it is he	196	Magnyfycence	1997
Put your wyll to his wyll, for surely it is he	196	Magnyfycence	1997
Nowe she wyll laughe, forthwith she wyll frowne;	197	Magnyfycence	2024
Nowe she wyll laughe, forthwith she wyll frowne;	197	Magnyfycence	2024
Ye, syr, yesterday wyll not be callyd agayne.	197	Magnyfycence	2031
For nowe go I wyll begge for you some mete.	197	Magnyfycence	2034
I wyll walke nowe with my beggers baggys,	197	Magnyfycence	2036
Alasse my foly! Alasse my wanton wyll!	198	Magnyfycence	2062
To love that lovesome I wyll not let;	199	Magnyfycence	2072
Cockes armes, syrs, wyll ye not se	200	Magnyfycence	2109
In youth to be wanton, and let them have theyr wyll -	200	Magnyfycence	2137
In faythe, and I wyll be to reason agreable.	203	Magnyfycence	2205
By our lakyn, syr, not by my wyll.	203	Magnyfycence	2208
By the fayth that I owe to God, and I wyll syt styll.	203	Magnyfycence	2209
By God, I tell you, I wyll not be out facyd.	203	Magnyfycence	2220
By the masse, I warant the, I wyll not be bracyd.	203	Magnyfycence	2221
It wyll stryke a man myschevously in a hete.	204	Magnyfycence	2268
That they wyll fyre one ungracyously in the flanke.	204	Magnyfycence	2270
That wyll make you to halt and to hoppe.	204	Magnyfycence	2273
Nay; rather wyll I chose to ryd me of this lyve	206	Magnyfycence	2321
Me humbly commyttynge unto Goddys wyll.	208	Magnyfycence	2382
Well, syr, after your counsell my mynde I wyll set.	210	Magnyfycence	2457
But frendly I wyll refrayne you ferther, or we flyt:	211	Magnyfycence	2478
Herein I wyll aforse me to shewe you my mynde:	211	Magnyfycence	2483
But hooly to perseveraunce my selfe I wyll bynde,	212	Magnyfycence	2507
If that ye wyll /A whyle be styll,	214	El Rummynge	2
And yet she wyll jet, /Lyke a joyly fet	215	El Rummynge	51
That wyll nothynge spare,	217	El Rummynge	107
Come who so wyll /To Elynoure on the hyll,	217	El Rummynge	113
Than wyll he rout and snort;	220	El Rummynge	232
We wyll no farther ryme /Of it at this tyme.	220	El Rummynge	240
But we wyll turne playne /Where we left agayne.	220	El Rummynge	242
And ye wyll gyve me a syppet /Of your stale ale,	223	El Rummynge	367
Lyke a wanton, whan I wyll, I rele to and froo.	233	Speke Parott	109
Honowre with renowne wyll ren on that syde.	234	Speke Parott	140
on] 'of' Kynge & Marche 1554, Day 1560, Marshe 1568			
Hyt wyll not be refrayned:	238	Speke Parott	259
To sowe corne in the see-sande, ther wyll no crope growe.	240	Speke Parott	342
To teche or to preche /As reason wyll reche?	247	Collyn Clout	14
With money, yf it wyll happe /To catche the forked cappe.	249	Collyn Clout	88
And judge it as they wyll, /For other mens skyll,	249	Collyn Clout	98
Ye wyll neyther beanes ne peason.	252	Collyn Clout	212
And you wyll be stylla,	253	Collyn Clout	260
And yet he wyll nat drede	253	Collyn Clout	278
Therwith I wyll nat mell.	257	Collyn Clout	428
My penne nowe wyll I sharpe,	259	Collyn Clout	489
For then ye wyll be wroken	261	Collyn Clout	598
Ye wyll brynge all to nought,	261	Collyn Clout	606
Alas, for Goddes wyll,	263	Collyn Clout	687
That I wyll nat wade	266	Collyn Clout	781
And yet he wyll melle	267	Collyn Clout	820
And wyll preche and tell	267	Collyn Clout	822
Nowe wyll I go	267	Collyn Clout	828
Wyll charge and dyscharge,	267	Collyn Clout	835
Wyll knowe a raven from a rayle,	268	Collyn Clout	869
They wyll no farder go.	269	Collyn Clout	908
For they wyll have no losse	269	Collyn Clout	928
How fortune wyll endure.	271	Collyn Clout	1003
Whome he wyll depute?	272	Collyn Clout	1044
They say they wyll you cast.	273	Collyn Clout	1070
For I wyll nat pretende	274	Collyn Clout	1127
Nor wyll here no prechynge,	274	Collyn Clout	1133
Nor wyll have no resytynge	274	Collyn Clout	1135
Wyll knowe none intellygence	275	Collyn Clout	1137
But yet they wyll occupye the same.	275	Collyn Clout	1144
Howe we wyll rule all at wyll	276	Collyn Clout	1190

	Page	Title	Line
Howe we wyll rule all at wyll	276	Collyn Clout	1190
And we wyll rule and rayne,	276	Collyn Clout	1212
At our pleasure and wyll.	276	Collyn Clout	1216
our] 'your' Kele 1545.1, Marshe 1568, 'owur' MS Harley 2252			
Nor wyll suffre this boke	277	Collyn Clout	1237
My shyp nowe wyll I stere	278	Collyn Clout	1259
stere] 'pere' Kele 1545.1, Marshe 1568, 'stere' MS Harley 2252			
Than wyll age have a corage	279	Why Come Ye	38
That hartes wyll ronne away,	280	Why Come Ye	54
For Wyll dothe rule all thynge,	281	Why Come Ye	105
Wyll, Wyll, Wyll, Wyll, Wyll!	281	Why Come Ye	106
Wyll, Wyll, Wyll, Wyll, Wyll!	281	Why Come Ye	106
Wyll, Wyll, Wyll, Wyll, Wyll!	281	Why Come Ye	106
Wyll, Wyll, Wyll, Wyll, Wyll!	281	Why Come Ye	106
Wyll, Wyll, Wyll, Wyll, Wyll!	281	Why Come Ye	106
I wyll no further ryme /Tyll another tyme;	284	Why Come Ye	230
Wyll ye bere no coles?'	285	Why Come Ye	243
I trow all wyll be nought,	287	Why Come Ye	353
Thus wyll I conclude my style,	289	Why Come Ye	396
It shall be as he wyll.	289	Why Come Ye	419
He ruleth all at wyll	291	Why Come Ye	487
For he wyll as sone smyght	293	Why Come Ye	582
And he wyll play checke mate /With ryall majeste	293	Why Come Ye	588
For he wyll tere it asonder!	296	Why Come Ye	671
But I wyll make further relacion	297	Why Come Ye	716
For prosperyte /Away than wyll fle.	300	Why Come Ye	863
My lordis grace wyll brynge	302	Why Come Ye	949
He wyll drynke us so drye,	303	Why Come Ye	965
so] not in MS Rawlinson C. 813			
For in lent he wyll ete	306	Why Come Ye	1083
wyll] 'doeth' MS Rawlinson C. 813			
That wyll hed us and hange us,	308	Why Come Ye	1154
And so cruell hertyd, /That he wyll nat be convertyd;	308	Why Come Ye	1179
That] not in MS Rawlinson C. 813			
Lest he wyll put it clene out,	309	Why Come Ye	1199
I wyll answere lyke a clerke:	309	Why Come Ye	1208
Complayne or do what ye wyll,	310	Why Come Ye2	31
Or of humors superflue, that often wyll crepe	313	Garlande	32
And wyll not endevour hymselfe to purchase	314	Garlande	75
Then men wyll say how he doth but flatter.	314	Garlande	84
Then sum wyll say he hath but lyttil brayne,	314	Garlande	87
And how his wordes with reason wyll not accorde.	314	Garlande	88
Few shall ye fynde or none that wyll do so.'	317	Garlande	168
And whome ye love not ye wyll put to shame.	317	Garlande	178
Eyther they wyll say he is to wyse,	318	Garlande	204
wyll] 'shall' MS Cotton Vitellius E.x			
To se if Skelton wyll put hymselfe in prease	319	Garlande	239
wyll] 'dare' MS Cotton Vitellius E.x			
Powle hatchettis, that prate wyll at every ale pole,	329	Garlande	613
wyll] 'well' Marshe 1568			
And of your wyll the plainnes shew at large.'	332	Garlande	727
He wyll set men a feightynge and syt hymselfe styll,	333	Garlande	761
set] 'stir' MS Cotton Vitellius E.x; a feightynge] 'to brawlyng' MS Cotton Vitellius E.x			
That of our bownte we wyll hym rewarde:	334	Garlande	779
Of that the tempestous wynde wyll aswage	335	Garlande	831
tempestous] 'tempeous' †Fakes 1523, 'tempestuows' MS Cotton Vitellius E.x			
I wyll my selfe applye,	339	Garlande	961
And as full of good wyll, /As fayre Isaphill;	341	Garlande	1024
fayre] 'the fayre' MS Cotton Vitellius E.x			
I wyll that ye shall be /In all benyngnyte	341	Garlande	1046
We wyll understande how we have it deservyd.'	344	Garlande	1127
Item to Lerne You to Dye When ye Wyll;	345	Garlande	1176
to] 'do' †Fakes 1523			
I wyll myselfe discharge	350	Garlande	1353
Thynke what ye wyll /Of this wanton byll;	353	Garlande	1453
To Occupacyon I wyll agayne resorte,	354	Garlande	1492
Contynew still /With there good wyll.	356	Garlande	1586
No man wyll undertake	358	Garlande2	10
Or els wyll I /Evydently /Shewe as it is:	361	Albany	84
Howe ye wyll beres bynde	364	Albany	209
Howe ye wyll undertake	367	Albany	326
And nowe I wyll me dresse	369	Albany	399
Is farther than their wytte wyll reche.	374	Replycacion	13
And so ye wyll be styll,	379	Replycacion	179
Nor heresy wyll never dye.	385	Replycacion	408

WYLLA

	Page	Title	Line
You shall have your wylla!'	253	Collyn Clout	261

WYLLES

	Page	Title	Line
And of theyr wanton wylles,	88	Phy Sparrow	681
Howe ye breke the dedes wylles,	257	Collyn Clout	417
Against their wylles, God wot.	306	Why Come Ye	1100

WYLLIS

	Page	Title	Line
Of Lovers Testamentis and of There Wanton Wyllis,	354	Garlande	1496

	Page	Title	Line
WYLLY			
Of [a] foles fylly /That had a fole with Wylly,	224	El Rummynge	389
a] not in †Lant 1545, Kynge & Marche 1554, Day 1560, Marshe 1568; fylly] 'silly' Marshe 1568			
WYLT			
Wylt thou abyde by the wordes agayne?	55	Bowge	324
WYLTE			
'Why? What than? Wylte thou lete men to speke?	51	Bowge	184
Wryght what thow wylte, I xall the aquyte.	134	Garnesche5	180
Cockes ha[r]te! I trowe thou wylte make a fray.	163	Magnyfycence	808
harte] 'hate' †Rastell & Treveris C 1530, B			
What! Thou wylte coughe me a dawe for forty pens?	170	Magnyfycence	1060
But wylte thou make another on Gryme?	172	Magnyfycence	1151
Nay, wylte thou here nowe of his scoles,	174	Magnyfycence	1216
For as thou wylte, so shall the game go;	190	Magnyfycence	1786
Ye, wylte thou clenly cle[v]e me in the clyfte with thy nose?	202	Magnyfycence	2176
cleve] 'clene' †Rastell & Treveris C 1530, B			
What! Wylte thou skelpe me? Thou dare not loke on a gnat.	202	Magnyfycence	2181
Nay. Then thou wylte dynge the devyll and thou be not holde.	202	Magnyfycence	2183
Ye, wylte thou, hangman? I say, thou cavell!	202	Magnyfycence	2190
WYMBLE			
Some brought a wymble,	227	El Rummynge	526
WYN			
He wantyd wyt her love to wyn:	42	Balettys1	12
Her favour to wyn;	98	Phy Sparrow	1082
I meane Domyngo Lomelyn /That was wont to wyn	309	Why Come Ye	1191
WYNCHE			
It is a curtel that well can wynche and praunce;	57	Bowge	411
curtel] 'curtet' †Wynkyn de Worde 1499, 1510			
That wantonly can wynke and wynche with her hele.	197	Magnyfycence	2023
They make her wynche and kycke,	251	Collyn Clout	181
WYNCHELSEE			
From Wynchelsee to Walys, /Non est braynsycke talys,	70	Hauke	323
WYNCHELSEY			
From Wynchelsey to Rye	282	Why Come Ye	147
WYNDE			
'Forsothe,' quod she, 'how ever blowe the wynde,	49	Bowge	110
We wante no wynde to passe now over all;	49	Bowge	128
I wolde be mery that wynde that ever blowe,	53	Bowge	251
But covetyse hath blowen you so full of wynde	148	Magnyfycence	290
Thy wordes be but wynde, never they have no wayght.	156	Magnyfycence	578
Howe standeth the wynde	168	Magnyfycence	985
What! Wyll ye waste wynde and prate thus in vayne?	179	Magnyfycence	1403
I have wynde and wether over all to sayle;	181	Magnyfycence	1464
Thy wordes hange togyder as fethers in the wynde.	191	Magnyfycence	1818
I sawe a wethercocke wagge with the wynde!	191	Magnyfycence	1821
Wynde you from wanhope and aquaynte you with me.	206	Magnyfycence	2340
That hang togedyr as fethyrs in the wynde;	239	Speke Parott	293
To catche wynde with theyr ventayles.	256	Collyn Clout	398
Whose bewte blastyd was with the boystors wynde,	312	Garlande	20
So well entakeled, what wynde that ever blowe,	327	Garlande	545
that] 'so' Marshe 1568			
To pas the tyme with, but let us wast no wynde.	328	Garlande	565
Enbrethyng of Zepherus with his pleasant wynde;	331	Garlande	677
And, 'Wynde me that botowme of such an hew',	334	Garlande	799
an] 'a' MS Cotton Vitellius E.x			
Of that the tempestous wynde wyll aswage	335	Garlande	831
tempestous] 'tempeous' †Fakes 1523, 'tempestuows' MS Cotton Vitellius E.x			
That made sum to snurre and snuf in the wynde;	353	Garlande	1472
snurre] 'surt' †Fakes 1523			
And full of waste wynde,	364	Albany	208
of the moche vayne glorious pipplyng wynde,	373	Replycacion	I
WYNDES			
Lyke to the boryall wyndes whan they blowe,	319	Garlande	261
WYNDE-SCHAKYN			
Yor wynde-schakyn shankkes, yor longe *lothy legges,	122	Garnesche1	29
*lothy] 'lothly' Scattergood			
WYNDY			
'The west is wyndy.' 'The est is metely wele.'	326	Garlande	499
WYNDMIL			
For a wyndmil /Therin to couche styll	365	Albany	262
WYNDMYLL			
Make a wyndmyll of a mat –	169	Magnyfycence	1028
WYNDOWES			
With glasse wyndowes and barres;	270	Collyn Clout	939
WYNE			
Nor sowtters to drynke wyne,	126	Garnesche3	87
For lacke of good wyne;	266	Collyn Clout	805
But blessed Bacchus, the pleasant god of wyne,	321	Garlande	334
But blessed Bacchus, the pleasant god of wyne,	321	Garlande	341
The umblis of venyson, the botell of wyne,	347	Garlande	1240
WYNGES			
For burnynge of his wynges;	73	Phy Sparrow	81
Flyckerynge with his wynges.	80	Phy Sparrow	348
Men call a phenix; her wynges bytwene	330	Garlande	668
WYNKE			
That wantonly can wynke and wynche with her hele.	197	Magnyfycence	2023

WYNKED —WYSE   Page   Title   Line

	Page	Title	Line
But, 'Drynke,' styll, 'Drynke, /And let the cat wynke!	222	El Rummynge	306
With, 'Let the catte wynke!	258	Collyn Clout	457
WYNKED			
There I wynked on you – wote ye not where?	60	Bowge	516
WYNKITH			
Yet whan the rayne rayneth and the gose wynkith	352	Garlande	1430
WYNKYNG			
With wanton wenches wynkyng!	270	Collyn Clout	968
WYNKYNGE			
She fyll in a wynkynge /With a barlyhood;	223	El Rummynge	371
WYNNE			
I wyste never man that so soone coude wynne	53	Bowge	269
With a pere my love you may wynne,	168	Magnyfycence	1015
May wynne with a sawte the fortresse of the holde.	184	Magnyfycence	1581
Item Royall Demenaunce Worshyp to Wynne;	345	Garlande	1174
WYNNYNG			
That was theyr owne kynge. /Fy on that wynnyng!	116	Ag Scottes	24
Fye on this wynnyng allway!	302	Why Come Ye	929
this] not in MS Rawlinson C. 813			
WYNNYNGE			
They may well say, fye on that wynnynge!	115	Ag Scottes	4
That the Scottys may synge, /'Fy on the wynnynge!'	116	Ag Scottes	48
synge] 'sin' Marshe 1568			
WYNNYS			
They are happy that wynnys,	302	Why Come Ye	927
WYNSHED			
For Margery wynshed, and breke her hinder girth;	346	Garlande	1201
WYNSYTH			
Ware, ware, the mare wynsyth wyth her wanton hele!	43	Balettys2	22
WYNTER			
Sodenly is eclipsid in the wynter night,	330	Garlande	646
And of the wynter nyghtes that tary so longe,	331	Garlande	701
WYNTERS			
So myche prevye wachyng in cold wynters nyghtes;	246	Speke Parott	512
WYPID			
I wypid myne eyne for to make them clere.	354	Garlande	1513
WYRE			
Of some I wrynge of the necke lyke a wyre;	194	Magnyfycence	1909
WYRRY			
Wold wyrry them lyke an hogge.	286	Why Come Ye	299
WYSCH			
Soche an odyr chalyngyr cowde me no man wysch,	121	Garneschel	3
WYSDOM			
And where the fader by wysdom worshyp hath wonne,	195	Magnyfycence	1934
How wysdom thorowe wantonnesse vanysshyth away;	213	Magnyfycence	2556
Wysdom is laught to skorne,	281	Why Come Ye	94
In prudence and wysdom /Lyke unto Salamon,	369	Albany	432
WYSDOME			
Welth is of wysdome the very trewe probate.	140	Magnyfycence	4
Counterfet wysdome, and workes of foly;	153	Magnyfycence	471
That wysdome and I shall seldome mete.	170	Magnyfycence	1081
Yet it is good wysdome to worke wysely by welth.	179	Magnyfycence	1401
Shewyth wysdome to them that wysdome can take:	213	Magnyfycence	2554
Shewyth wysdome to them that wysdome can take:	213	Magnyfycence	2554
His wysdome is so dyscrete	289	Why Come Ye	423
As wele foly as wysdome oft ye do avaunce,	317	Garlande	180
ye do] 'tyme ye' MS Cotton Vitellius E.x			
For wysdome and sadnesse be out a sunnyng;	318	Garlande	201
be out] 'be set out' Marshe 1568, MS Cotton Vitellius E.x			
Devoyde of wysdome sage,	369	Albany	412
WYSE			
Provydent, discrete, circumspect and wyse,	33	Dol Dethe	139
Provydent] 'Prudent' Marshe 1568			
That Dame Menolope was never half so wyse;	42	Balettys2	11
And in this wyse he gan with me to chyde.	55	Bowge	322
And many wordes sayde in secrete wyse;	58	Bowge	422
Or Socrates the wyse,	74	Phy Sparrow	99
In the homylyest wyse,	87	Phy Sparrow	625
And for her sparow prayd /In lamentable wyse.	93	Phy Sparrow	855
As Nature cold devyse, /In most goodly wyse.	98	Phy Sparrow	1072
Of your wyse reformacyon;	102	Phy Sparrow	1248
Your face I wyse to varnyshe	127	Garnesche3	121
God forbede that it other wyse sholde be!	147	Magnyfycence	246
By God, syr, ye se but fewe wyse men of myne age.	148	Magnyfycence	289
Wel, wyse men may ete the fysshe when ye shal draw the pole.	148	Magnyfycence	300
But ofte tymes have I sene wyse men do mad dedys.	148	Magnyfycence	302
Ye, but of my name let us be wyse.	167	Magnyfycence	963
This is a wyse man, syr, where so ever ye hym had.	187	Magnyfycence	1689
To sober, to sad, to subtell, to wyse,	199	Magnyfycence	2091
For to be wyse all men may lerne of me,	201	Magnyfycence	2158
But wottest thou, horson? I rede the to be wyse.	202	Magnyfycence	2184
Then welthe with you myght in no wyse abyde.	210	Magnyfycence	2447
Wrythen in wonder wyse /After the Sarasyns gyse,	216	El Rummynge	73
in] 'in a' Day 1560, Marshe 1568			
As wyse as an hare!	217	El Rummynge	112
She was not halfe so wyse	229	El Rummynge	588
To wyse is no vertue, to medlyng, to restles;	232	Speke Parott	61
Tholomye and Haly were cunnyng and wyse	234	Speke Parott	134

WYSELY —WYTH	Page	Title	Line
As wyse as Jacke-a-Thrum,	253	Collyn Clout	282
Jacke] 'Tom' Kele 1545.1, Marshe 1568			
As wyse as Robyn Swyne,	266	Collyn Clout	806
As wyse as Waltoms calfe,	266	Collyn Clout	809
One wyse mannys hede	298	Why Come Ye	764
But the wyttys of many wyse	298	Why Come Ye	766
This maumet in lyke wyse	306	Why Come Ye	1070
With crakynge in suche wyse,	306	Why Come Ye	1073
For how shulde Cato els be callyd wyse,	315	Garlande	123
Eyther they wyll say he is to wyse,	318	Garlande	204
wyll] 'shall' MS Cotton Vitellius E.x			
Arrectinge unto your wyse examinacion	323	Garlande	410
Sume fayne themselfe folys, and wolde be callyd wyse,	329	Garlande	616
In lyke maner of wyse a myst did us shrowde;	330	Garlande	647
In humble wyse as lowly as I may,	335	Garlande	837
Her that is bothe womanly and wyse,	342	Garlande	1070
womanly] 'maydenly' MS Cotton Vitellius E.x			
He is not wyse ageyne the streme that stryvith.	352	Garlande	1432
In moost humble wyse,	372	Albany	524
That wyse Harpocrates /Had your mouthes stopped,	377	Replycacion	115
And ye wolde appere wyse	378	Replycacion	129
WYSELY			
He techyth them so wysely to solf and to fayne	38	Coystrownel	53
Yet it is good wysdome to worke wysely by welth.	179	Magnyfycence	1401
Wysely let these wordes in your mynde be wayed:	185	Magnyfycence	1593
Who wryteth wysely hath a grete treasure.	314	Garlande	91
WYSELYE			
For whoo lokythe wyselye in your warkys may fynde	239	Speke Parott	296
WYSSHE			
But sygh, and sorowe, and wysshe my selfe dede.	205	Magnyfycence	2306
WYSSHED			
And that he wysshed withall	66	Hauke	182
WYST			
He wold be made moch of and he wyst how;	37	Coystrownel	33
That he wyst never where he was;	42	Balettys1	10
Yf he wyst what sum wotte,	129	Garnesche3	199
Nowe I wolde - and I wyst what -	169	Magnyfycence	1029
Yet it is good to beware of 'had I wyst'.	179	Magnyfycence	1395
WYSTE			
That I ne wyste what to do was beste;	47	Bowge	30
I wyste never man that so soone coude wynne	53	Bowge	269
Hem, syr, yet beware of 'Had I wyste!'	146	Magnyfycence	211
WYT			
To fat is hys fantsy, hys wyt is to lene.	37	Coystrownel	28
He wantyd wyt her love to wyn:	42	Balettys1	12
Her wyt stood her in sted	89	Phy Sparrow	729
My wyt I shall assay	92	Phy Sparrow	821
Your wyll than ran before your wyt.	118	Ag Scottes	102
Ye wantyd wyt, sir, at a worde;	119	Ag Scottes	147
Lytyll wyt in your scrybys nolle	126	Garnesche3	90
Your wyt ys so geson,	127	Garnesche3	129
Thow ar frantyke and lakkyst wyt,	132	Garnesche5	118
But where wonnys welthe, and a man wolde wyt?	141	Magnyfycence	22
To shewe parte of my wyt,	142	Magnyfycence	58
Welth and wyt, I say, be so threde bare worne,	146	Magnyfycence	223
Ye, for your wyt is cloked for the rayne.	157	Magnyfycence	609
Teuyt, teuyt! /Where is my wyt?	168	Magnyfycence	1005
And thy wyt wanderynge here and there,	170	Magnyfycence	1074
For so with fantasyes my wyt dothe flete	170	Magnyfycence	1080
And hath so mased a wandrynge wyt?	172	Magnyfycence	1144
That wyt he wantyth when he hath moste nede.	175	Magnyfycence	1261
And then he is moche made of for his [wyt];	175	Magnyfycence	1271
wyt] 'whyt' †Rastell & Treveris C 1530, B			
Why, coulde not your wyt serve you no better?	193	Magnyfycence	1868
In welth to beware; and that is wyt.	196	Magnyfycence	1975
Me thynke ye are not gretly acomberyd wyth wyt.	203	Magnyfycence	2215
Gravyte of counsell, provydence, and wyt;	210	Magnyfycence	2476
Your comfortable advyse and wyt excedyth all gladnesse;	210	Magnyfycence	2477
Than sterte in made Kyt, /That had lytell wyt;	225	El Rummynge	413
WYTCH			
She semed to be a wytch.	226	El Rummynge	458
WYTCHCRAFT			
To wytchcraft her to dresse,	105	Phy Sparrow	1346
WYTCLYFTISTA			
Of that heresy arte /Called Wytclyftista,	260	Collyn Clout	549
Wytclyftista] 'Wicleuista' Marshe 1568			
WYTE			
Alasse, my wyckydnesse, that may I wyte!	205	Magnyfycence	2304
WYTEYNG			
A makerell nor a wyteyng:	127	Garnesche3	116
WYTH			
Wyth, 'Hey, troly-loly-lo, whip here, Jak',	37	Coystrownel	15
Wyth hey, lullay, &c.	42	Balettys1	Rub
To dele wyth her so cowardly;	42	Balettys1	27
Wyth bound and rebound, bounsyngly take up	43	Balettys2	15
Ware, ware, the mare wynsyth wyth her wanton hele!	43	Balettys2	22
Delyte, desyre, respyte, wyth lyberte;	43	Balettys3	2
Corage wyth lust, convenient tyme and space;	43	Balettys3	3

WYTHE—WYVES

	Page	Title	Line
Your ruddys wyth ruddy rubys may compare;	44	Balettys3	16
Saphyre of sadnes, envayned wyth Indy blew;	44	Balettys3	17
Illumynyd wyth feturys far passyng my reporte;	44	Balettys3	23
But absens, alas, wyth tremelyng fere and drede,	44	Balettys3	34
Wyth fresshe utteraunce full sentencyously;	46	Bowge	12
Wyth fables false, that well coude fayne a tale;	49	Bowge	135
Than Favell gan wyth fayre speche me to fede.	50	Bowge	147
Wyth 'Whom' and 'Ha' and with a croked loke,	51	Bowge	191
Me thoughte his gowne was all furred wyth foxe.	52	Bowge	234
Me] 'My' †Wynkyn de Worde 1499			
Or 'Shall I sayle wyth you' a felashyp assaye?	53	Bowge	254
Wyth that, as he departed soo fro me,	54	Bowge	281
Wyth that came Ryotte, russhynge all at ones,	56	Bowge	344
Wyth cry unreverent, /Before the sacrament,	62	Hauke	11
Wyth his polutyd pawtenar,	63	Hauke	44
Wyth that he gave her a bounce	64	Hauke	86
Yet wyth a prety gyn /I fortuned to come in,	64	Hauke	93
Wyth, 'Troll, cytrace and trovy,'	65	Hauke	116
Thus to ryng a peale /Wyth his hawkys bels?	65	Hauke	137
Wyth, 'Knave, syr, knave, and knave agenne',	130	Garnesche5	19
Thus make I them wyth thryft to fyght.	152	Magnyfycence	421
Wyth golde and grotes they grese my hande,	152	Magnyfycence	432
Wyth me wyll wonne	165	Magnyfycence	900
At your commaundement, syr, wyth all dew reverence.	182	Magnyfycence	1515
And wyth a brystell of a bore his berde dyd I shave.	192	Magnyfycence	1832
Me thynke ye are not gretly acomberyd wyth wyt.	203	Magnyfycence	2215
Her shone smered wyth talowe,	216	El Rummynge	88
Wyth theyr heles dagged, /Theyr kyrtelles all to-jagged,	217	El Rummynge	123
Theyr smockes all to-ragged, /Wyth tytters and tatters,	217	El Rummynge	126
Wyth theyr naked pappes, /That flyppes and flappes,	217	El Rummynge	135
Brynge wyth them malte or whete,	221	El Rummynge	267
As thou, wyth shamefull deth!'	223	El Rummynge	346
Wyth, 'Lo, gossyp, iwys,	223	El Rummynge	356
First one wyth a ladell,	224	El Rummynge	383
And wyth that she begynnes	228	El Rummynge	565
Wyth crownes and wyth scutus;	283	Why Come Ye	170
Wyth crownes and wyth scutus;	283	Why Come Ye	170
Wyth scutis and crownes of golde	283	Why Come Ye	171
Mell nat wyth Englyshe men.	362	Albany	146

WYTHE

	Page	Title	Line
Wythe hevy chere, with dolorous hart and mynd,	34	Dol Dethe	176
Wythe my beke bente, and my lytell wanton iye,	231	Speke Parott	15
and] not in Lant 1545, Kynge and Marche 1554, Day 1560, Marshe 1568			

WYTHIN

	Page	Title	Line
For I have gravyd her wythin the secret wall	45	Balettys3	48
Wythin the holy church bowndis,	62	Hauke	13

WYTHOUT

	Page	Title	Line
I shall breke your palettes, /Wythout ye now cease!'	223	El Rummynge	349

WYTLES

	Page	Title	Line
Masyd, wytles smery smyth,	71	Hauke	331
As wytles as a wylde goos, ye have but small remorrs	123	Garnesche2	18
Wranglynge, waywyrde, wytles, wraw, and nothyng meke.	124	Garnesche2	40
Wytles, wayward, Syr Wrag-wrag,	133	Garnesche5	149
The enfatuate fantasies, the wytles wylfulnes	242	Speke Parott	384
Nor of some wytles pates	277	Collyn Clout	1245
But braynsyk and braynlesse, /Wytles and rechelesse,	304	Why Come Ye	1019

WYTLESSE

	Page	Title	Line
of their rechelesse youthe and wytlesse wontonnesse,	374	Replycacion	1
Wytlesse wandring to and fro!'	376	Replycacion	74

WYTT

	Page	Title	Line
'Prove his wytt', sayth he, 'at cardes or dyce,	318	Garlande	206

WYTTE

	Page	Title	Line
My wytte wolde waste, I make God avowe.	53	Bowge	243
His wytte is thynne, his hode is threde-bare.	60	Bowge	490
Your wyll renne before your wytte.	113	Scot Kynge	12
But reason and wytte wantythe theyr provynciall,	232	Speke Parott	53
To rule ix realmes by one mannes wytte,	240	Speke Parott	333
So myche provision, and so lytell wytte at nede –	244	Speke Parott	454
For he lacketh wytte.'	247	Collyn Clout	32
Presumyng on theyr owne wytte,	259	Collyn Clout	515
owne] not in Marshe 1568			
By one mannes wytte.	271	Collyn Clout	993
For as for wytte,	304	Why Come Ye	1016
Is farther than their wytte wyll reche.	374	Replycacion	13

WYTTES

	Page	Title	Line
All the wyttes they have.	103	Phy Sparrow	1273
For he wantythe of hys wyttes that all wold rule alone;	240	Speke Parott	329
Theyr wyttes, he saith, are dull;	286	Why Come Ye	309

WYTTYS

	Page	Title	Line
My wyttys be weke, my braynys are lyght;	169	Magnyfycence	1024
But the wyttys of many wyse	298	Why Come Ye	766

WYVES

	Page	Title	Line
Brynge other wyves in thought	87	Phy Sparrow	626
What! Wolde ye wyves counterfet	153	Magnyfycence	452
'They can nat kepe theyr wyves	261	Collyn Clout	572
Some carefull cokwoldes, some have theyr wyves curs;	317	Garlande	186

	Page	Title	Line
WO			
These feverous axys, the dedely wo and payne	44	Balettys3	9
My dedely wo, my paynfull hevynes.	44	Balettys3	37
Go, pytyous hart, rasyd with dedly wo,	45	Balettys5	1
Heu, heu, me, /That I am wo for the!	73	Phy Sparrow	65
The prynce of endles wo;	73	Phy Sparrow	73
Encreaseth my dedly wo, /For my sparowe is go.	74	Phy Sparrow	113
To my great payne and wo.	81	Phy Sparrow	365
Himself doth slo /With payne and wo.	95	Phy Sparrow	948
And browght Englond in wo;	111	Lawde	25
Nowe well, nowe wo, nowe hy, nowe lawe degre;	212	Magnyfycence	2517
Jhesus preserve you frome endlesse wo and shame.	214	Magnyfycence	2572
And skantly could go /For payne and for wo.	227	El Rummynge	514
The Gommoryans also /Were brought to deedly wo,	291	Why Come Ye	473
That they are so wo	294	Why Come Ye	613
Helas, ye wreches, ye may be wo!	376	Replycacion	77
WODCOCKE			
The wodcocke with the longe nose;	83	Phy Sparrow	459
Howe a wodcocke wrastled with a larke that was lame;	192	Magnyfycence	1836
WODCOKE			
Thow liist, I callyd the a wodcoke;	133	Garnesche5	129
WODDE			
Out of the wawes wodde	277	Collyn Clout	1253
WODDIS			
Diana in the woddis grene,	350	Garlande	1357
WODE			
Withe his enmys that were stark mad and wode;	32	Dol Dethe	100
All sparowes of the wode	78	Phy Sparrow	267
Ensor[b]yd with the wawys savage and wode;	213	Magnyfycence	2561
ensorbyd] 'ensordyd' †Rastell & Treveris C 1530, B			
Now frantick, now starke wode!	293	Why Come Ye	578
And the stremes wode	349	Garlande	1328
WODICOCKE			
And her wanton wodicocke.	252	Collyn Clout	219
WODSTOCKE			
With, yes, by the rode of Wodstocke Parke.	174	Magnyfycence	1209
WOFULLY			
With Wofully Arayd and Shamefully Betrayd;	352	Garlande	1418
WOKE			
And thoughte to lepe; and even with that woke,	61	Bowge	531
That he shall lyke the worse all this woke.	187	Magnyfycence	1682
And therwith, sodenly, out of my dreme I woke.	354	Garlande	1511
dreme] 'slepe' Marshe 1568			
WOKYS			
I have not kept her yet thre wokys,	168	Magnyfycence	1002
WOLD			
Lo, Jak wold be a jentyl man!	37	Coystrownel	14
He wold be made moch of and he wyst how;	37	Coystrownel	33
An ussher of the hall fayn wold I get	37	Coystrownel	40
For Jak wold be a jentylman, that late was a grome.	37	Coystrownel	42
Jak wold jet and yet Jyll sayd nay;	37	Coystrownel	43
I wold you coud! Then shuld ye se, mastres,	44	Balettys3	40
Yet, and God wold, I wold my payne were easyd!	45	Balettys5	12
Yet, and God wold, I wold my payne were easyd!	45	Balettys5	12
Suwed to Fortune that she wold be theyre frynde,	49	Bowge	121
Of Bowge of Court she asketh what we wold have,	49	Bowge	125
But she wold not bow.	63	Hauke	74
He sayde he wold not let /His houndys for to fet,	64	Hauke	106
He sayd that he wold hunt	67	Hauke	188
It wold set on a stole,	74	Phy Sparrow	116
set] 'sit' Wyght 1553, Kitson 1560.6, Marshe 1568			
And wold syt upon my lap,	74	Phy Sparrow	121
Than he wold lepe and skyp,	75	Phy Sparrow	139
For it wold come and go,	75	Phy Sparrow	159
I wold thou haddest ben blynde!	79	Phy Sparrow	285
An epytaphe I wold have /For Phyllyppes grave.	86	Phy Sparrow	605
And never wold him forsake.	90	Phy Sparrow	733
And now men wold have amended	91	Phy Sparrow	797
It wold make any man	98	Phy Sparrow	1080
She wold make to the lure	99	Phy Sparrow	1100
Though they wold spend	103	Phy Sparrow	1272
And, for example [y]e wold none take,	119	Ag Scottes	157
ye] 'he' †Lant 1545, Kynge & Marche 1554, Day 1560, Marshe 1568			
I wold sum manys bake ink-horne	133	Garnesche5	133
Yt wold garnyche wyll thy face.	133	Garnesche5	135
Ones hed wold have aked /To se her naked.	226	El Rummynge	478
Such a bedfellaw /Wold make one cast his craw.	226	El Rummynge	489
For he wantythe of hys wyttes that all wold rule alone;	240	Speke Parott	329
Wold wyrry them lyke an hogge.	286	Why Come Ye	299
Sume were to hasty and wold no man byde;	319	Garlande	249
What, wold Fraunces, our friar, /Be suche a false lyar,	368	Albany	373
WOLDE			
Take up whos wolde, for ther they let hym ly.	32	Dol Dethe	96
What, wolde ye frompill me now? Fy, fy!	36	Man Margery	16
But than I thoughte I wolde not dwell behynde;	47	Bowge	43
Of one and other that wolde his lady see,	47	Bowge	57
She promysed to us all she wolde be kynde;	49	Bowge	124

WOLDE — WOLDE

	Page	Title	Line
And oftentymes I wolde myselfe avaunce	50	Bowge	143
But I wolde telle you a thynge, and I durste.	51	Bowge	203
I wote, and he dyde, ye wolde me telle.	51	Bowge	205
I wolde noo thynge so playne be.	52	Bowge	214
Soo he departed. There he wolde be come,	52	Bowge	228
My wytte wolde waste, I make God avowe.	53	Bowge	243
I coude it skan and ye wolde it reherse.	53	Bowge	245
skan] 'stan' †Wynkyn de Worde 1499, 1510; it] (2nd) not in Marshe 1568			
I wolde be mery that wynde that ever blowe,	53	Bowge	251
Wolde to God it wolde please you some daye	53	Bowge	256
Wolde to God it wolde please you some daye	53	Bowge	256
But wolde be glad of your company.	53	Bowge	268
He frowned as he wolde swere by Cockes blode.	54	Bowge	287
Of my querell soone wolde I venged be.	55	Bowge	333
Now wolde to God thou wolde leye money downe!	57	Bowge	395
Now wolde to God thou wolde leye money downe!	57	Bowge	395
Lorde, how that I wolde caste it full rounde!	57	Bowge	396
That other loked as he wolde me have slayne.	58	Bowge	430
me have] 'have me' Wynkyn de Worde 1510			
I wolde eche man were as playne as I.	59	Bowge	463
Were I as you, I wolde ryde them full nere;	59	Bowge	472
And so I wolde it were, so God me spede,	59	Bowge	481
And whan I sawe the horsons wolde you hafte,	61	Bowge	521
But that I drede mordre wolde come oute.	61	Bowge	524
I wolde therwith no man wolde be myscontente;	61	Bowge	533
But he sayde that he wolde	64	Hauke	97
No creature but that wolde /Have rewed upon me,	72	Phy Sparrow	41
Wolde God I had Zenophontes,	74	Phy Sparrow	98
It wolde lye and rest –	75	Phy Sparrow	126
Somtyme he wolde gaspe	75	Phy Sparrow	128
A fly, or a gnat, /He wolde flye at that;	75	Phy Sparrow	131
And prytely he wolde pant	75	Phy Sparrow	132
Lord, how he wolde pry /After the butterfly!	75	Phy Sparrow	134
Lorde, how he wolde hop /After the gressop!	75	Phy Sparrow	136
Though she wolde pretende	75	Phy Sparrow	154
And on me it wolde lepe	75	Phy Sparrow	161
Wherewith he wolde make	76	Phy Sparrow	164
And do what he wolde;	76	Phy Sparrow	178
Phillip wolde seke and take	76	Phy Sparrow	179
Alas, I wolde ryde and go	76	Phy Sparrow	186
I wolde I had a parte /Of her crafty magyke!	76	Phy Sparrow	203
I wolde have yet a nest	78	Phy Sparrow	263
have yet] 'yet have' Wyght 1553, Kitson 1560.6, Marshe 1568			
It wolde make one rew	80	Phy Sparrow	336
How pretely it wolde syt	80	Phy Sparrow	354
How she controlde /Her husbandes as she wolde,	87	Phy Sparrow	623
That if I wolde apply /To wryte ornatly,	91	Phy Sparrow	780
ornately] 'ordinately' Kitson 1560.6, Marshe 1568			
But she wolde chaunge his mood,	100	Phy Sparrow	1158
Wolde God myne homely style	101	Phy Sparrow	1204
For you and your Scottes wolde tourne his face?	114	Scot Kynge	18
At hym example ye wolde none take;	115	Scot Kynge	60
From you, Syr Scot, wolde turne his face?	118	Ag Scottes	108
Ye wolde have bassyd hyr bumme,	125	Garnesche3	62
So that sche wolde have kum	125	Garnesche3	63
Ye wolde be callyd a maker,	127	Garnesche3	108
Thow wolde have scoryd hys habarion;	130	Garnesche5	34
Ye wolde have trysyd hys trowle away.	130	Garnesche5	36
I wolde ye had kyst hyr on the tayle!	130	Garnesche5	46
Sche wolde nat of yt thow had sworne.	131	Garnesche5	52
Of the wote I what they wolde say;	133	Garnesche5	143
They wolde the wryght, all with one stevyn,	133	Garnesche5	144
A man may have welth, but not as he wolde,	141	Magnyfycence	14
But where wonnys welthe, and a man wolde wyt?	141	Magnyfycence	22
But and you wolde me permyt	142	Magnyfycence	57
Wolde it please you then –	143	Magnyfycence	87
Welthe without measure wolde bere hymselfe to bolde;	143	Magnyfycence	116
What, lyberte to measure then wolde ye bynde?	144	Magnyfycence	131
So wolde I, but I wolde be lothe,	144	Magnyfycence	143
So wolde I, but I wolde be lothe,	144	Magnyfycence	143
What, syr, wolde ye make me a poppynge fole?	146	Magnyfycence	232
And now wolde ye swarve from your owne ordynaunce?	147	Magnyfycence	234
I wolde be rulyd and I myght for shame.	147	Magnyfycence	235
And for his sake ryght gladly I wolde	149	Magnyfycence	334
Another wolde myne eye were blerde;	150	Magnyfycence	354
And wolde have made me Freer Tucke,	150	Magnyfycence	357
Ye wolde sone pynche at a pecke of otes.	151	Magnyfycence	385
otes] 'grotes' †Rastell & Treveris C 1530, B			
Whan the noppe is rughe, it wolde be shorne.	153	Magnyfycence	448
What! Wolde ye wyves counterfet	153	Magnyfycence	452
An olde barne wolde be underset.	153	Magnyfycence	454
It wolde be masked in my net!	153	Magnyfycence	458
It wolde be nyce, thoughe I say nay;	153	Magnyfycence	459
By crede, it wolde have fresshe aray,	153	Magnyfycence	460
Coll wolde go clenly, and it wyll not be,	153	Magnyfycence	476
And Annot wolde be nyce, and laughes, 'tehe wehe.'	153	Magnyfycence	477
He wolde trotte gentylly, but he is to starke.	153	Magnyfycence	481

	Page	Title	Line
Wolde take, in the way of counterfet charyte,	154	Magnyfycence	489
I am sure ye wolde have me excused.	156	Magnyfycence	581
Syr, and yf ye wolde not be wrothe –	157	Magnyfycence	606
And there they wolde ha[v]e me to dwell.	157	Magnyfycence	614
have] 'hane' †Rastell & Treveris C 1530, B			
By God, we wolde gete us all thyder,	157	Magnyfycence	618
And wolde that we sholde for hym go –	158	Magnyfycence	646
And every man gladly my company wolde refuse,	160	Magnyfycence	704
I wolde begyn all myschyef, but I wolde bere no lacke.	160	Magnyfycence	720
I wolde begyn all myschyef, but I wolde bere no lacke.	160	Magnyfycence	720
Mary, with Magnyfycence I wolde be retaynyd.	161	Magnyfycence	763
As well as me. I wolde, and I durste –	163	Magnyfycence	827
Tyll, as the devyll wolde, they fell a chydynge	166	Magnyfycence	940
Nowe I wolde – and I wyst what –	169	Magnyfycence	1029
In faythe, I wolde thou had a marmosete.	171	Magnyfycence	1132
What? Wolde ye have mo folys, and are so many?	172	Magnyfycence	1170
And for a fole a man wolde hym take.	174	Magnyfycence	1212
The knave wolde make it koy, and he cowde;	175	Magnyfycence	1246
Yet I wolde that ye had gone rather;	176	Magnyfycence	1313
But some man wolde convey, and can not skyll,	178	Magnyfycence	1361
Not and your grace wolde be ruled by me.	179	Magnyfycence	1393
It wolde not become them with me for to mell;	182	Magnyfycence	1497
Howe be it, I wolde be ryght gladde, I you assure,	183	Magnyfycence	1527
A, I wolde to God that I were halfe so crafty	183	Magnyfycence	1532
If it wolde lyke you to here my pore mynde –	183	Magnyfycence	1543
I wolde I had, by hym that hell dyd harowe,	184	Magnyfycence	1561
I wolde hauke whylest my hede dyd warke,	184	Magnyfycence	1563
That on suche a female my flesshe wolde be wroken.	184	Magnyfycence	1566
That weryed I wolde be on suche a bayte.	184	Magnyfycence	1568
Wolde money, trowest thou, make suche one to the call?	184	Magnyfycence	1573
I wolde yet shewe you further of my consayte.	185	Magnyfycence	1591
And frowne it and face it, as thoughe ye wolde fyght;	185	Magnyfycence	1601
To shewe you my mynde I wolde have the lesse fere.	186	Magnyfycence	1646
But yet, lo, I wolde, or that he wente,	187	Magnyfycence	1673
That he wolde loke on hym, thoughe it were not longe.	187	Magnyfycence	1675
But, and I were as ye, I wolde not set a gnat.	188	Magnyfycence	1704
I wolde to you say a worde or twayne.	188	Magnyfycence	1721
Alas! My stomake fareth as it wolde cast.	188	Magnyfycence	1726
Mary, I wene he wolde not be glad to come agayne.	189	Magnyfycence	1740
A, Lorde, so I wolde halse her hartely!	190	Magnyfycence	1801
So I wolde clepe her! So I wolde kys her swete!	190	Magnyfycence	1802
So I wolde clepe her! So I wolde kys her swete!	190	Magnyfycence	1802
The feldfare wolde have fydled, and it wolde not frame;	192	Magnyfycence	1838
The feldfare wolde have fydled, and it wolde not frame;	192	Magnyfycence	1838
I wolde tell you and yf I myght for wepynge.	192	Magnyfycence	1848
Why, who wolde have thought in you suche gyle?	193	Magnyfycence	1869
Bycause I wolde prove men of theyr pacyence.	194	Magnyfycence	1917
Syr, all this wolde have bene thought on before.	196	Magnyfycence	1970
And where that ye were pomped with what that ye wolde,	197	Magnyfycence	2012
What is he lyvynge that lyberte wolde lacke?	199	Magnyfycence	2083
Here MAGNYFYCENCE wolde slee hymselfe with a knyfe.	206	Magnyfycence	SD
Thyselfe that thou wolde sloo agaynst nature and kynde,	206	Magnyfycence	2326
It wolde be founde so yf it were well tryde.	210	Magnyfycence	2449
A man wolde have pytty	215	El Rummynge	39
And yet he wolde be rekenyd pro Ariopagita;	235	Speke Parott	156
Your rudeness to pardon and also that they wolde	241	Speke Parott	360
Hyt ys to fere leste he wolde were the garland on hys pate,	244	Speke Parott	435
Or elles they wolde se /Otherwyse,	247	Collyn Clout	39
As though they wolde flye /Aboute the sterry skye.	248	Collyn Clout	73
Aboute] 'Above' Kele 1545.1, Marshe 1568, MS Harley 2252			
They wolde pype you another daunce.	262	Collyn Clout	618
That wolde intoxicate, /That wolde conquinate,	264	Collyn Clout	702
intoxicate] 'intoxicall' †Godfray 1531, 'intrixicate' MS Harley 2252			
That wolde intoxicate, /That wolde conquinate,	264	Collyn Clout	703
intoxicate] 'intoxicall' †Godfray 1531, 'intrixicate' MS Harley 2252			
That wolde contemminate, /And that wolde vyolate,	264	Collyn Clout	704
contemminate] 'contaminate' Marshe 1568, MS Harley 2252			
That wolde contemminate, /And that wolde vyolate,	264	Collyn Clout	705
contemminate] 'contaminate' Marshe 1568, MS Harley 2252			
And that wolde derogate,	264	Collyn Clout	706
And that wolde abrogate,	264	Collyn Clout	707
That wolde it shulde be noted	265	Collyn Clout	754
But yf ye wolde take payne	265	Collyn Clout	763
That wolde your wordes retayne	266	Collyn Clout	774
But they wolde no man shuld them blame.	275	Collyn Clout	1142
Into a mouse hole they wolde	286	Why Come Ye	293
Ones yet agayne /Of you I wolde frayne	289	Why Come Ye	400
Men wolde have the lesse scorne	291	Why Come Ye	496
And ruled as he wolde.	293	Why Come Ye	564
He wolde have ben ryght fayne	295	Why Come Ye	642
That wolde God everychone /Of his affynyte	300	Why Come Ye	834
He wolde dry up the stremys	303	Why Come Ye	957
I wolde he were somwhere ellys;	303	Why Come Ye	963
For I undertake /He wolde so brag and crake	303	Why Come Ye	977
That he wolde than make /The devyls to quake,	303	Why Come Ye	978
That he wolde breke the braynes	304	Why Come Ye	990

	Page	Title	Line
WOLDEST — WON			
I wolde he were gone;	304	Why Come Ye	994
It wolde make the devyll to swete!	306	Why Come Ye	1088
'The devyll wold swete' MS Rawlinson C. 813			
All wronges he wolde redresse,	307	Why Come Ye	1112
All injuris he wolde represse,	307	Why Come Ye	1113
All perjuris he wolde oppresse,	307	Why Come Ye	1114
Sum what wolde gadder in there conjecture	315	Garlande	107
conjecture] 'convecture' †Fakes 1523			
For that I wolde not with you fall at discorde.	318	Garlande	214
Cupyde hath stryken so that she ne wolde	320	Garlande	291
How dotynge age wolde jape with yonge foly;	322	Garlande	361
That with them I went where they wolde me brynge,	324	Garlande	447
Sume fayne themselfe folys, and wolde be callyd wyse,	329	Garlande	616
Ye wolde not dele with hym, thowgh that ye myght,	333	Garlande	756
though] 'thought' Marshe 1568, 'thowth' MS Cotton Vit.E.x			
In you he wolde have set his hole delight.	336	Garlande	874
For eche man herkynde what she wolde to'me say;	344	Garlande	1119
wolde to me] 'to me wold' MS Cotton Vitellius E.x			
It wolde have made a man hole that had be ryght sekely,	345	Garlande	1162
Though they wolde spende	348	Garlande	1265
And that it wolde please her, full tenderly I prayd,	353	Garlande	1479
And when that I sawe it wolde no better be,	353	Garlande	1485
But that my peticyon wolde not be had,	353	Garlande	1486
Who redyth it ones wolde rede it agayne;	354	Garlande	1501
Thy herte wolde nat serve the.	365	Albany	250
As though ye wolde parbrake /Your avauns to make,	367	Albany	322
Ye wolde ryn away rounde	367	Albany	348
Ye wolde defoyle the place	367	Albany	353
That if I wolde reporte	370	Albany	444
And wolde have her defamed,	376	Replycacion	60
Wolde God, for your owne ease,	377	Replycacion	114
And ye wolde appere wyse	378	Replycacion	129
WOLDEST			
Rule the roste! Thou woldest, ye,	163	Magnyfycence	805
Thou woldest, ye] 'ye thou woldest' †Rastell & Treveris C 1530, B			
What! Woldest thou, lurden, with me brawle agayne?	188	Magnyfycence	1722
WOLDT			
For her vysage /It woldt aswage /A mannes courage.	214	El Rummynge	10
WOLFE			
The wylde wolfe Lycaon	79	Phy Sparrow	311
The wolfe from the dore	250	Collyn Clout	153
The wolfe from the lam;	298	Why Come Ye	776
WOLL			
Wyddered lyke hay, /The woll worne away.	216	El Rummynge	63
Some fyll theyr pot full /Of good Lemster woll.	220	El Rummynge	252
There is none that your name woll abbrogate	240	Speke Parott	317
Small housholdes woll kepe,	249	Collyn Clout	123
Suche logyke men woll choppe,	259	Collyn Clout	528
WOLLE			
Unneth they leve a locke /Of wolle amongest theyr flocke.	248	Collyn Clout	81
WOLVIS			
The wolvis, the beris also,	111	Lawde	23
WOLVYS			
Hys wolvys hede, wanne, bloo as lede, gapythe over the crowne:	244	Speke Parott	434
WOMAN			
Yet as a woman may,	92	Phy Sparrow	820
Maketh man and woman in foly to fall.	176	Magnyfycence	1295
Man or woman, of what estate they be,	194	Magnyfycence	1898
Many a good man /And many a good woman,	378	Replycacion	135
WOMANHOD			
Womanhod, wanton, ye want!	40	Coystrowne4	1
Of your bownte and of youre womanhod,	44	Balettys3	31
WOMANHODE			
Maydenly demure, /Of womanhode the lure;	340	Garlande	992
Maistres Geretrude, /With womanhode endue,	341	Garlande	1044
Maistres Geretrude, /With womanhode endue,	342	Garlande	1052
Maistres Geretrude /With womanhode endue,	342	Garlande	1060
WOMANKYND			
That I may say /Honour alway /Of womankynd!	96	Phy Sparrow	976
WOMANLY			
Demure demenaunce, womanly of porte;	43	Balettys3	6
And set so womanly,	98	Phy Sparrow	1067
Of womanly feturis, whos florysshyng tender age	336	Garlande	869
Demure Diana womanly and sad,	337	Garlande	902
So joyously, /So maydenly, /So womanly	341	Garlande	1013
Her that is bothe womanly and wyse,	342	Garlande	1070
womanly] 'maydenly' MS Cotton Vitellius E.x			
WOMEN			
Of all women O floure withouten pere,	35	Dol Dethe	207
To wryte and tell /How women excell /In noblenes;	96	Phy Sparrow	982
Somtime women were put in great blame,	139	Ven Tongues	59
Bothe women and men,	260	Collyn Clout	532
For yet of women he never sayd shame,	334	Garlande	784
But if they were counterfettes that women them call,	334	Garlande	785
WON			
Hath won nothing, I wene,	89	Phy Sparrow	718

WONDER

	Page	Title	Line
'Noo thynge erthely that I wonder so sore	50	Bowge	148
But I wonder what the devyll of helle	52	Bowge	208
A wonder thynge that ye waxe not madde!	53	Bowge	241
By Goddis soule, I wonder how ye gete	53	Bowge	262
As I be saved, it is a wonder case.	53	Bowge	273
'I wonder sore he is in such conceyte.'	54	Bowge	310
Came pressynge in one in a wonder araye.	60	Bowge	499
And wonder upon the,	79	Phy Sparrow	317
A kynge a somner it is wonder;	113	Scot Kynge	5
A kyng, a sumner! It was great wonder:	118	Ag Scottes	95
And it is wonder that your wylde insolence	143	Magnyfycence	85
Why, man, it were to great a wonder	154	Magnyfycence	510
But, broder Foly, I wonder moche of one thynge,	170	Magnyfycence	1068
It is wonder to se the worlde aboute,	177	Magnyfycence	1326
By Cockes woundes, a wonder felowe thou arte!	185	Magnyfycence	1619
It is no wonder, therfore, thoughe ye be wrothe	189	Magnyfycence	1748
Wrythen in wonder wyse /After the Sarasyns gyse, in] 'in a' Day 1560, Marshe 1568	216	El Rummynge	73
That they have great wonder	271	Collyn Clout	1006
For all this worldly wonder,	285	Why Come Ye	258
Wherat moche I wonder	296	Why Come Ye	672
But, how it is, Skelton is wonder slake,	314	Garlande	69
To tell all his towchis it were to grete wonder;	333	Garlande	764
Wonder is to wryte what wrenchis she wrowght,	346	Garlande	1207

WONDERFUL

	Page	Title	Line
For by crafty conveyaunce wonderful thynges are wrought.	178	Magnyfycence	1371

WONDERFULL

	Page	Title	Line
And wonderfull condityons,	105	Phy Sparrow	1351
A wonderfull noyse, and on every syde	319	Garlande	247
Of wonderfull condiciouns Of] 'And' Marshe 1568	350	Garlande	1344

WONDERYD

	Page	Title	Line
She wonderyd, me thought, at my laurell grene;	343	Garlande	1116

WONDERLY

	Page	Title	Line
A man, but wonderly besene was he.	54	Bowge	283
With that there come in wonderly at ones	319	Garlande	269

WONDEROUS

	Page	Title	Line
And nowe ye have had, syr, a wonderous fall,	207	Magnyfycence	2375
This is a wonderous warke!	272	Collyn Clout	1048

WONDEROWUS

	Page	Title	Line
By Nature devysed of a wonderowus kynde,	231	Speke Parott	2

WONDERS

	Page	Title	Line
A, ye be wonders men!	143	Magnyfycence	89
It is a wonders warke.	283	Why Come Ye	173
It is a wonders case: wonders] 'wonderous' Kitson 1560.7, Marshe 1568	295	Why Come Ye	657

WONDERSLY

	Page	Title	Line
I sawe a pavylyon wondersly disgysede,	313	Garlande	38

WONDERUSLY

	Page	Title	Line
Which to thi resemblance wonderusly has wrought	34	Dol Dethe	193

WONDES

	Page	Title	Line
Persyd with payn, bleding with wondes smart,	45	Balettys5	2

WONDYR

	Page	Title	Line
I wondyr that ye smatyr,	126	Garnesche3	106

WONDRE

	Page	Title	Line
I wondre howe ye dare	375	Replycacion	36

WONDRED

	Page	Title	Line
And one ther was there, I wondred of his hap,	329	Garlande	628

WONDRINGES

	Page	Title	Line
And suche wondringes many mo.	376	Replycacion	76

WONNE

	Page	Title	Line
Welthe myght be wonne and made to the lure,	141	Magnyfycence	17
Yet where we wonne, nowe there wonneth he.	157	Magnyfycence	624
Wyth me wyll wonne	165	Magnyfycence	900
With Magnyfycence thou shalte wonne.	176	Magnyfycence	1311
Why, wyl a maystres be wonne for money and for golde?	184	Magnyfycence	1575
Full many a strong cyte and towne hath been wonne	184	Magnyfycence	1577
And where the fader by wysdom worshyp hath wonne,	195	Magnyfycence	1934

WONNES

	Page	Title	Line
That wonnes at the Key in Temmys Strete.	41	Coystrowne4	30

WONNETH

	Page	Title	Line
Yet where we wonne, nowe there wonneth he.	157	Magnyfycence	624

WONNYNGE

	Page	Title	Line
At home in her wonnynge;	216	El Rummynge	94
And ryght slender connynge /Within theyr heedes wonnynge.	250	Collyn Clout	141

WONNYS

	Page	Title	Line
But where wonnys welthe, and a man wolde wyt?	141	Magnyfycence	22

WONT

	Page	Title	Line
For one fals poynt she is wont to kepe in store,	45	Balettys4	4
That was wont to repayre,	80	Phy Sparrow	344
That wont wer over all	111	Lawde	38
Alasse, where is youth that was wont for to skyppe?	195	Magnyfycence	1957
I meane Domyngo Lomelyn /That was wont to wyn	309	Why Come Ye	1191

WONTE

	Page	Title	Line
By thy report ar wonte to be extolde	29	Dol Dethe	17
That wonte was to be formyst, now to come behynde.	144	Magnyfycence	144
As I was wonte ever, at my fre wyll.	144	Magnyfycence	147

WONTONNESE — WORDES

	Page	Title	Line
That with his whyp his mares was wonte to yarke;	153	Magnyfycence	484
Nay, I tell you, I am not wonte to fode	188	Magnyfycence	1698
He was wonte to boste, brage, and to brace;	193	Magnyfycence	1890
That was wonte to lye on fetherbeddes of downe;	197	Magnyfycence	2006
Where you were wonte to have cawdels for your hede,	197	Magnyfycence	2008
With curteyns of sylke, ye were wonte to be draw;	197	Magnyfycence	2014
curteyns of sylke] 'courtely sylkes' †Rastell & Treveris 1530B			
Your hede that was wonte to be happed moost drowpy and drowsy,	197	Magnyfycence	2018
Howe [ye] were wonte to drynke	262	Collyn Clout	649
ye] 'thy' †Godfray 1531, 'they' Kele 1545.1, Marshe 1568, MS Harley 2252			
How men were wonte for to discerne	352	Garlande	1441

WONTONNESE

	Page	Title	Line
of their rechelesse youthe and wytlesse wontonnesse,	374	Replycacion	1

WOO

	Page	Title	Line
Woo is hym that is blynde and maye not see!	60	Bowge	518
Wherfore, in welthe beware of woo,	132	Garnesche5	124
Woo is that purse that ye shall share!	156	Magnyfycence	587
O odyous dystresse, O dedly payne and woo!	198	Magnyfycence	2053
A, woo worthe the, Lyberte, nowe thou sayst full trewe;	199	Magnyfycence	2103

WOOD

	Page	Title	Line
Ne no tyger so wood,	100	Phy Sparrow	1157
And the streames wood	105	Phy Sparrow	1335

WOODE

	Page	Title	Line
I loked on hym, I wende he had be woode.	55	Bowge	320

WOODECOCKE

	Page	Title	Line
Parrot is no woodecocke, nor no butterfly,	236	Speke Parott	206

WOODES

	Page	Title	Line
Diana in the woodes grene,	105	Phy Sparrow	1364

WOODHACKE

	Page	Title	Line
The woodhacke, that syngeth 'chur',	82	Phy Sparrow	418

WORD

	Page	Title	Line
Trew to his prince in word, in dede, and thought.	29	Dol Dethe	7
Farewell tyll soone. But no word that I sayde!'	51	Bowge	175

WORDE

	Page	Title	Line
Lyke to Eneas benygne in worde and dede,	33	Dol Dethe	137
That with one worde formd all thing of nought;	34	Dol Dethe	191
In golde letters, this worde, whiche I dyde rede:	48	Bowge	66
And with that worde on me she gave a glome	48	Bowge	80
And, yf nede be, a bolde worde I dare cracke.	50	Bowge	168
'In fayth,' quod Suspecte, 'spake Drede no worde of me?'	51	Bowge	183
Spake he, a fayth, no worde to you of me?	51	Bowge	204
But I requyre you no worde that I saye!	54	Bowge	276
Let us, therfore, shortely at a worde	54	Bowge	307
Wheron was wryten this worde, Myscheve.	58	Bowge	434
Ne worde he wrote in vayne.	91	Phy Sparrow	803
By your wanton wyll, syr, at a worde,	114	Scot Kynge	48
Ye wantyd wyt, sir, at a worde;	119	Ag Scottes	147
Syr, yf any worde have past	143	Magnyfycence	92
What! I say, herke a worde.	151	Magnyfycence	396
What! Of Cokermowth spake I no worde.	170	Magnyfycence	1062
Ye. Let us here a worde or twayne.	174	Magnyfycence	1218
I wolde to you say a worde or twayne.	188	Magnyfycence	1721
She sayde never a worde,	229	El Rummynge	590
To preche a worde or twayne,	265	Collyn Clout	764
With them the worde of God	275	Collyn Clout	1145
No man dare speke a worde,	283	Why Come Ye	191
But harke, my frende, one worde	298	Why Come Ye	784
The worde of God to let.	305	Why Come Ye	1069
worde] 'wordis', to] 'he' MS Rawlinson C. 813			
That all the worde, I trowe, and it were sought,	325	Garlande	462
worde] 'worlde' Marshe 1568			
And with that worde she toke me by the honde.	328	Garlande	560
There was amonge them no worde then but mum,	344	Garlande	1118
amonge them no worde] 'not a worde amonge them' MS Cotton Vitellius E.x			
Any worde defacid /That myght be rasid,	356	Garlande	1581
Both worde and dede /Should be agrede /In noblenes:	357	Garlande	1599
With a worde or twayne /In sentence playne.	361	Albany	75
Nor durst nat crak a worde,	366	Albany	307
Harke yet, Sir Duke, a worde	367	Albany	318
Where worde for worde ye may	383	Replycacion	327
Where worde for worde ye may	383	Replycacion	327

WORDES

	Page	Title	Line
Me thoughte, of wordes that he had full a poke;	51	Bowge	179
Wylt thou abyde by the wordes agayne?	55	Bowge	324
And many wordes sayde in secrete wyse;	58	Bowge	422
And on that sleve these wordes were wrete:	58	Bowge	438
Thyse were the wordes he to me dyde saye.	58	Bowge	441
he] 'that he' Marshe 1568			
Yet wyll I saye some wordes for your sake	59	Bowge	474
With Englysh wordes elect;	91	Phy Sparrow	773
elect] 'clere' †Kele 1545.2, 'elect' Wyght 1553, Kitson 1560.6, Marshe 1568			
And fewer wordes make.	92	Phy Sparrow	818
That in wordes playne	97	Phy Sparrow	1008
With wordes of pleasure	99	Phy Sparrow	1099
I am now constrayned, /With wordes nothing fayned,	120	Ag Scottes2	2

WORDIS —WORLD	Page	Title	Line

WORDIS (continued)

	Page	Title	Line
Thy wordes be but wynde, never they have no wayght.	156	Magnyfycence	578
No, by my trouthe, but crake grete wordes.	163	Magnyfycence	812
These wordes in myne eyre, they be so lustely spoken,	184	Magnyfycence	1565
Wysely let these wordes in your mynde be wayed:	185	Magnyfycence	1593
Thy wordes and my mynde odly well accorde.	185	Magnyfycence	1605
Largesse in wordes - for rewardes are but small.	189	Magnyfycence	1760
Thy wordes hange togyder as fethers in the wynde.	191	Magnyfycence	1818
Your wordes be more sweter than ony precyous narde,	207	Magnyfycence	2345
That wolde your wordes retayne	266	Collyn Clout	774
And my wordes marke,	309	Why Come Ye	1207
And, my wordes marke truly,	310	Why Come Ye2	27
'And espetyally to make a lye' MS Rawlinson C. 813			
And how his wordes with reason wyll not accorde.	314	Garlande	88
In generrall wordes, I say not gretely nay,	315	Garlande	99
Wordes that were moch consolatory	317	Garlande	165
There were many wordes smaller and gretter,	326	Garlande	508
Enpryntyng her wordes in my remembraunce,	327	Garlande	557
Wordes be swordes, and hard to call ageine.'	328	Garlande	567
In goodly wordes plesauntly comprysid,	335	Garlande	813
Benynge, corteise, and meke, /With wordes well devysid;	338	Garlande	919
With wordes that smartid,	341	Garlande	1040
With wordes devoute and sentence agerdows,	347	Garlande	1250
As Skelton rehersith, with wordes few and playne,	353	Garlande	1466
God wote, theis wordes made me full sad;	353	Garlande	1484
With wordes enbosed, /Ungraciously engrosed,	367	Albany	324
To rayle on his astate /With wordes inordinate?	370	Albany	462
Those wordes his grace dyd saye /Of an ammas gray.	372	Albany	530
With baudy wordes unmete	376	Replycacion	49

WORDIS

	Page	Title	Line
Mi wordis unpullysht be nakide and playne,	32	Dol Dethe	127
The wordis were parvertyd;	68	Hauke	229
And with wordis of vyolence,	305	Why Come Ye	1065
The favour of ladys with wordis electe,	314	Garlande	76

WORDYS

	Page	Title	Line
Wordys well set with good habylyte;	43	Balettys3	5
I am of fewe wordys. I love not to [crake].	162	Magnyfycence	775
crake] 'barke' †Rastell & Treveris C 1530, B			
Are not his wordys cursydly cowchyd?	175	Magnyfycence	1276
What a very vengeaunce nede all these wordys?	202	Magnyfycence	2198
Howe say you, syr? Can ye these wordys grope?	207	Magnyfycence	2377

WORDLY

	Page	Title	Line
Encrownyd as empresse of all this wordly fate,	325	Garlande	486
wordly] 'worldly' Marshe 1568			
This joy excedith all wordly sport and play,	332	Garlande	716
wordly] 'worldly' Marshe 1568			

WORDS

	Page	Title	Line
These words shuld be more weyed,	265	Collyn Clout	769
These words] 'Those words' Marshe 1568, 'This' MS Harley 2252			

WORKE

	Page	Title	Line
This worke devysed is /For suche as do amys,	61	Hauke	1
Wrought never such a worke,	67	Hauke	217
And of this worke complayned,	106	Phy Sparrow	1375
By me all persons worke what they lyste.	146	Magnyfycence	210
Theyr conveyaunce weltyth the worke all by wyll;	178	Magnyfycence	1363
Yet it is good wysdome to worke wysely by welth.	179	Magnyfycence	1401
No man so hardy to worke agaynst my wyll.	181	Magnyfycence	1479
And worke suche a myracle,	293	Why Come Ye	567
And who can worke beste now shall be asayde;	334	Garlande	775
Sum pirlyng of goldde theyr worke to encrease	334	Garlande	796
To worke me this chapelet by goode advysemente.	334	Garlande	807
And of this worke complaynyd,	350	Garlande	1368

WORKES

	Page	Title	Line
Counterfet wysdome, and workes of foly;	153	Magnyfycence	471
Your workes, they say, are straunge -	257	Collyn Clout	420
and have waded but weakly in thre maner of clerkly workes,	375	Replycacion	I

WORKETH

	Page	Title	Line
That worketh moch scath	87	Phy Sparrow	619
That] 'Thay' †Kele 1545.2, Wyght 1553, Kitson 1560.6			
Worketh more mischiefe than can be tolde;	137	Ven Tongues	8

WORKIS

	Page	Title	Line
So that there workis myght famously be sene,	314	Garlande	67
Of Englande, his workis here they begynne:	345	Garlande	1171

WORKYS

	Page	Title	Line
Of naturys workys, how they be	130	Garnesche5	9

WORLD

	Page	Title	Line
Fulfilled with honour, as all the world dothe ken,	30	Dol Dethe	30
world] 'wold' Marshe 1568			
Let not all the world make an owtcry;	43	Balettys2	40
That all the world may gase	79	Phy Sparrow	316
Whyles the world shall dure:	89	Phy Sparrow	723
The world [envyronn], of hygh and low estate.	140	Magnyfycence	2
envyronn] 'envyronnyd' †Rastell & Treveris C 1530, B			
But moveatur terra, let the world wag,	233	Speke Parott	88
And shewe hym that all the world dothe conjecte,	240	Speke Parott	327
Syns Dewcalyons flodde the world was never so yll.	245	Speke Parott	497
the world] 'the world the world' †MS Harley 2252			
And after conveyauns as the world goos,	347	Garlande	1238

WORLDE —WORSE | | Page | Title | Line

WORLDE

	Page	Title	Line
This worlde is nothynge but ete, drynke and slepe,	57	Bowge	384
It is a worlde, I saye, to here of some -	59	Bowge	464
to] 'te' †Wynkyn de Worde 1499, 'to' Wynkyn de Worde 1510, Marshe 1568			
A bawdy dyschyclowte, /That bryngyth the worlde abowte	125	Garnesche3	37
And so dysordereth this worlde over all,	141	Magnyfycence	20
S[e] at our eye the worlde day by day.	146	Magnyfycence	216
Se] 'so' †Rastell & Treveris C 1530, B			
In fayth, I set not by the worlde two Dauncaster cuttys.	148	Magnyfycence	293
This worlde is full of my foly.	152	Magnyfycence	411
It is wonder to se the worlde aboute,	177	Magnyfycence	1326
Not amonge noble men, as the worlde gothe.	189	Magnyfycence	1747
Lo, suche is this worlde! I fynde it wryt,	196	Magnyfycence	1974
Fye on this worlde, full of trechery,	197	Magnyfycence	2020
What! Is the worlde thus come to passe?	200	Magnyfycence	2108
And some in the worlde, theyr brayne is so ydyll	200	Magnyfycence	2135
I am wery of the worlde, for unkyndnesse me sleeth.	205	Magnyfycence	2283
The worlde waxyth wery of the; thou lyvest to longe.	205	Magnyfycence	2308
As the worlde requyreth, but rather I am refused.	208	Magnyfycence	2412
Comprehendynge the worlde casuall and transytory,	212	Magnyfycence	2511
Howe in this worlde there is no seke[r]nesse,	212	Magnyfycence	2515
sekernesse] 'sekenesse' †Rastell & Treveris C 1530, B			
So in this worlde there is no sykernesse,	212	Magnyfycence	2522
Shewyth nowe adayes howe the worlde comberyd is,	213	Magnyfycence	2539
Thus in this worlde there is no erthly truste.	213	Magnyfycence	2544
Thus in this worlde there is no erthly truste.	213	Magnyfycence	2551
For the welthe of this worlde can not indure.	213	Magnyfycence	2558
For the welthe of this worlde can not indure.	214	Magnyfycence	2565
He caryeth a kyng in hys sleve, yf all the worlde fayle;	243	Speke Parott	429
Of suche paternoster pekes /All the worlde spekes.	253	Collyn Clout	263
That all the worlde myght say,	263	Collyn Clout	669
And through all the worlde thei go	268	Collyn Clout	885
Howe all the worlde stares	270	Collyn Clout	960
But as the worlde now gose,	286	Why Come Ye	285
Moche dowblenes of the worlde therin he may fynde.	346	Garlande	1197
It must nedes after rin all the worlde aboute.'	353	Garlande	1483
Over all the world[e] to sprede.	371	Albany	511
worlde] 'worlds' †Marshe 1568			

WORLDLY

	Page	Title	Line
Youre ugly tokyn /My mynd hath brokyn /From worldly lust;	39	Coystrowne3	3
There may no fraunchys /Nor worldly blys	39	Coystrowne3	27
The well of worldly treasure;	102	Phy Sparrow	1228
Our welth, our worldly joy,	111	Lawde	49
All worldly welth for hym to lytell was;	193	Magnyfycence	1892
For worldly shame I wax bothe wanne and bloo.	198	Magnyfycence	2054
Where is nowe all my pleasure and my worldly good?	198	Magnyfycence	2061
Of worldly welthe, alasse, who can be sure?	201	Magnyfycence	2155
A playne example of worldly vaynglory,	212	Magnyfycence	2514
Howe sodenly worldly welth dothe dekay;	213	Magnyfycence	2555
Pompe, pryde, honour, ryches and worldly lust,	236	Speke Parott	223
and fle /From worldly vanyte	247	Collyn Clout	41
worldly] 'wordly' Kele 1545.1			
And take theyr worldly ease	269	Collyn Clout	910
From worldly wantones,	270	Collyn Clout	974
For all this worldly wonder,	285	Why Come Ye	258
Of renowme and worldly fame	293	Why Come Ye	569
Of worldly trust, then did I you rescu;	327	Garlande	543
For ye were worldly shamed, /At Poules Crosse openly,	376	Replycacion	62

WORME-ETYN

	Page	Title	Line
With hys worme-etyn maw /And hys gastly jaw	39	Coystrowne3	14

WORMES

	Page	Title	Line
And seke after small wormes,	74	Phy Sparrow	122

WORN

	Page	Title	Line
For thrifte is threde bare worn,	281	Why Come Ye	91

WORNE

	Page	Title	Line
'My new furryd gowne, when it is worne -	40	Coystrowne4	10
As emperes the dyademe hath worne	46	Bowge	4
Yet jentylnes in the ys thred-bare worne.	131	Garnesche5	70
Welth and wyt, I say, be so threde bare worne,	146	Magnyfycence	223
All thynge is worse whan it is worne.	153	Magnyfycence	451
And well worne in age,	214	El Rummynge	8
Wyddered lyke hay, /The woll worne away.	216	El Rummynge	63
Shavyn and shorne, /And all threde bare worne!	304	Why Come Ye	1029

WORROWYD

	Page	Title	Line
Worrowyd her on that /Which I loved best.	72	Phy Sparrow	29

WORS

	Page	Title	Line
No wors than is contaynyd	350	Garlande	1370
than] 'and' †Fakes 1523			

WORSE

	Page	Title	Line
No worse than is contayned	106	Phy Sparrow	1377
That nothynge than welth may worse be enduryd.	140	Magnyfycence	7
All thynge is worse whan it is worne.	153	Magnyfycence	451
And I beshrowe hym that hath the worse.	171	Magnyfycence	1105
He wyll make it mykyll worse than it is;	175	Magnyfycence	1273
That he shall lyke the worse all this woke.	187	Magnyfycence	1682
That day I se hym I shall be worse all nyght.	188	Magnyfycence	1724
To make fayre promyse, what are ye the worse?	189	Magnyfycence	1761

	Page	Title	Line
WORSHEPLY — WORTHY			
What are they the worse?	254	Collyn Clout	295
It can not be moche worse.	282	Why Come Ye	138
Ye are but lydder logici, /But moche worse isagogici,	380	Replycacion	235
WORSHEPLY			
Whos noble actis shew worsheply his name,	33	Dol Dethe	143
Whom he as lorde worsheply manteynd,	34	Dol Dethe	186
WORSHIP			
Your worship depended of his excellence.	31	Dol Dethe	59
Of honour and worship it hath the formar date.	336	Garlande	849
Of honour and worship it hath the formar date.	336	Garlande	856
Of honour and worship it hath the formar date.	336	Garlande	863
WORSHYP			
I say, without largesse worshyp hath no place,	148	Magnyfycence	267
Counterfet worshyp outwarde men may se;	153	Magnyfycence	473
For where is no mesure, howe may worshyp endure?	179	Magnyfycence	1408
And where the fader by wysdom worshyp hath wonne,	195	Magnyfycence	1934
And ye shall have more worshyp then ever ye had.	210	Magnyfycence	2474
Of honour and worshyp which hath the formar date:	336	Garlande	842
Item Royall Demenaunce Worshyp to Wynne;	345	Garlande	1174
Ye rage and ye rave, /And your worshyp deprave:	363	Albany	191
WORSHYPFULL			
Full worshypfull clerkes,	250	Collyn Clout	150
WORSHYPFULLY			
Worshypfully to withstande	269	Collyn Clout	912
worshypfully] 'worshyp' †Godfray 1531, Kele 1545.1, Marshe 1568			
WORSHYPPE			
To worshyppe none ymages, /Nor do pylgrymages?	381	Replycacion	269
To worshyppe ymages of sayntes.	382	Replycacion	291
WORST			
Nor Nero the worst, /Nor Clawdyus the curst;	67	Hauke	202
Mary, I defye thy best and thy worst.	202	Magnyfycence	2197
WORSTE			
But nowe I wyll not say the worste.	163	Magnyfycence	828
So he is the worste brawler that ever was borne.	202	Magnyfycence	2200
Then he that doth worste is as good as the best.	317	Garlande	175
WORTES			
By God, for snatchynge of puddynges and wortes.	171	Magnyfycence	1128
WORTH			
Take thys in worth, the best is behynde.	38	Coystrownel	68
'Pece,' quod Desyre, 'ye speke not worth a bene!	48	Bowge	95
Ye be to her, yea, worth a thousande pounde.	50	Bowge	157
Fye on this dyce, they be not worth a turde!	57	Bowge	392
It were worth an hundreth pound	76	Phy Sparrow	189
His mater is worth gold,	91	Phy Sparrow	786
In worth I shall it take,	92	Phy Sparrow	817
But not worth thre skyppes of a pye.	113	Scot Kynge	10
Your counseyle was not worth a flye.	113	Scot Kynge	14
Not worth thre skyppes of a pye.	118	Ag Scottes	100
Your frantyck fable not worth a fly,	118	Ag Scottes	104
And all is not worth a couple of nut shalis.	139	Ven Tongues	66
Counterfet reason is not worth a flye;	153	Magnyfycence	470
Yet Lyberte without rule is not worth a strawe.	178	Magnyfycence	1378
Ye, walke he must; it was no better worth.	189	Magnyfycence	1736
For totum in toto is not worth an hawe –	199	Magnyfycence	2089
Thou art worth good and monny.'	220	El Rummynge	228
So myche presonment, for matyrs not worth a hawe;	245	Speke Parott	478
But it is not worth a leke.	251	Collyn Clout	182
Construe nat worth a whystell	252	Collyn Clout	236
His benefyce worth ten pounde,	264	Collyn Clout	725
Or scante worth twenty marke,	264	Collyn Clout	726
And all nat worth a flye,	282	Why Come Ye	148
That be worth ii kues.	284	Why Come Ye	235
Nat worth a cockly fose!	286	Why Come Ye	288
Nat worth a shyttel-cocke,	287	Why Come Ye	354
Nor worth a sowre calstocke.	287	Why Come Ye	355
Not acquaynted worth a fly /With honorable Haly,	292	Why Come Ye	520
Ye rebads nat worth two plummis!	294	Why Come Ye	604
The claspis and bullyons were worth a thousande pounde;	345	Garlande	1165
WORTHE			
Was skantly worthe a grote;	125	Garnesche3	45
For alle ys nat worthe a myteyng,	127	Garnesche3	115
In dede, syr, that lyberte was not worthe a cue.	141	Magnyfycence	36
It is moche worthe that is ferre fet.	153	Magnyfycence	455
Take it in worthe suche as ye fynde.	180	Magnyfycence	1439
And welth is nought worthe yf lyberte be behynde.	180	Magnyfycence	1442
A, woo worthe the, Lyberte, nowe thou sayst full trewe;	199	Magnyfycence	2103
WORTHY			
And worthy to be enrold.	91	Phy Sparrow	787
She is worthy to be enrolde	103	Phy Sparrow	1258
Measure is worthy to have domynyon.	144	Magnyfycence	127
A carter a courtyer, it is a worthy warke,	153	Magnyfycence	483
That thou arte not worthy to loke God in the face.	205	Magnyfycence	2296
Thus endeth the gest /Of this worthy fest.	230	El Rummynge	623
And mad a worthy trewse.	282	Why Come Ye	141
mad] 'made' Toy 1553, Kitson 1560.7, Marshe 1568			
Suche a prelate, I trowe, /Were worthy to rowe	303	Why Come Ye	954

WOSE —WOUNDERSLY   Page   Title   Line

WOSE
	Page	Title	Line
Ensowkid with sylt of the myry [w]ose,	312	Garlande	23

sylt] 'fylt' †Fakes 1523; wose] 'mose' †Fakes 1523

WOT
	Page	Title	Line
God wot, we thought no syn –	76	Phy Sparrow	168
I wot not where to fynd /Termes to serve my mynde.	91	Phy Sparrow	782
Ye wot what I thynke;	126	Garnesche3	80
With, 'He sayd,' and 'We said.' Ich wot now what ich wot,	234	Speke Parott	132
With, 'He sayd,' and 'We said.' Ich wot now what ich wot,	234	Speke Parott	132
God wot, had lytell parte	292	Why Come Ye	513
They wot not whether to go.	294	Why Come Ye	614
Against their wylles, God wot.	306	Why Come Ye	1100
Ye put to blame ye wot nere whom.	310	Why Come Ye2	17

nere] 'nott' MS Rawlinson C. 813

WOTE
	Page	Title	Line
I wote, and he dyde, ye wolde me telle.	51	Bowge	205
And ever he threwe, and kyst I wote nere what;	56	Bowge	349
Betwene the persone ye wote of, you –	59	Bowge	461
A man can not wote where to become.	59	Bowge	466
A flaterynge knave and false he is, God wote.	59	Bowge	485
There I wynked on you – wote ye not where?	60	Bowge	516
Of the wote I what they wolde say;	133	Garnesche5	143
For ye said, that he said, that I said, wote ye what?	137	Ven Tongues	12
Lyberte, I wote well, forbere no man there may;	142	Magnyfycence	50
What wote ye where upon I wyll conclude?	142	Magnyfycence	72
Ye coulde not ellys, I wote, with me endure.	147	Magnyfycence	247
Endure? No, God wote, it were great payne.	147	Magnyfycence	248
I wote thou arte false ynoughe for one.	155	Magnyfycence	536
Tary here. Wote ye what I say?	163	Magnyfycence	819
That I wote not where I may rest.	168	Magnyfycence	1021
Hyder and thyder, I wote not whyder;	169	Magnyfycence	1033
I wote not whether it cometh of the or of me,	176	Magnyfycence	1290
Be governed and gyded; wote ye what I say?	179	Magnyfycence	1397
So I wote not what he sholde do here.	189	Magnyfycence	1741
Alasse! I wote not what I sholde pray.	196	Magnyfycence	1994
Who brought you that letter? Wote ye what he hyght?	209	Magnyfycence	2440
Some brought I wote nere what,	225	El Rummynge	441
Ye wote well what we meane.'	229	El Rummynge	579
To paye,' sayde she, 'God wote,	229	El Rummynge	601
I wote never howe they warke,	249	Collyn Clout	119
God wote, with dronken nolles.	252	Collyn Clout	232
As many a frere, God wote,	267	Collyn Clout	836
Wote ye whyther they went?	282	Why Come Ye	146
Of auncient poetis, ye wote full wele, hath bene	314	Garlande	65
Where I sawe come after, I wote, full lytell lake	320	Garlande	285
But what sholde I say? Ye wote what I entende,	324	Garlande	426
For in owr courte, ye wote wele, his name can not ryse	345	Garlande	1154
God wote, theis wordes made me full sad;	353	Garlande	1484
Ageyne envy, /And obloquy. /And wote ye why?	355	Garlande	1560

WOTEST
	Page	Title	Line
Nay, but wotest thou what I do say?	170	Magnyfycence	1092

WOTETH
	Page	Title	Line
He woteth not what welth is that never was sore.	196	Magnyfycence	1971

WOTITH
	Page	Title	Line
Lytill wotith the goslyng what the gose thynkith.	352	Garlande	1431
And wele wotith the cat whos berde she likkith.	352	Garlande	1438

WOTYST
	Page	Title	Line
Wotyst thou, I say, to whom thou spekys?	172	Magnyfycence	1166

WOTTE
	Page	Title	Line
Yf he wyst what sum wotte,	129	Garnesche3	199
God wotte, to theyr great paynes,	254	Collyn Clout	313
Iche wotte what yche do thynke!'	258	Collyn Clout	458

yche do] 'eche other' Kele 1545.1, Marshe 1568

	Page	Title	Line
God wotte, they take great payne	268	Collyn Clout	860
Ye heretykes recrayed, /Wotte ye what ye sayed	375	Replycacion	46

WOTTEST
	Page	Title	Line
But wottest thou, horson? I rede the to be wyse.	202	Magnyfycence	2184

WOTTETH
	Page	Title	Line
And wotteth never what thei rede, /Paternoster nor crede;	252	Collyn Clout	234

WOTTITH
	Page	Title	Line
And writeth he wottith nat what.	296	Why Come Ye	679

wottith] 'wot' Toy 1553, Kitson 1560.7, Marshe 1568

WOTTYTH
	Page	Title	Line
He wottyth never what /Ne whereof he speketh.'	247	Collyn Clout	17

WOULD
	Page	Title	Line
He saith untruly, to say that I would	137	Ven Tongues	21
That ye would coarte and enforce me	138	Ven Tongues	45
And you knew all ye would be ill apayd'.	139	Ven Tongues	72
For clatering of me I would him sone quight;	139	Ven Tongues	74
And began to paynty /As though she would faynty.	229	El Rummynge	585

WOUNDE
	Page	Title	Line
Wheron he gat his fynall dedely wounde.	32	Dol Dethe	119
Gave hym his mortall wounde,	79	Phy Sparrow	298

WOUNDED
	Page	Title	Line
Wounded from the fote to the crowne of the hede:	207	Magnyfycence	2364

WOUNDERSLY
	Page	Title	Line
Comely crynklyd, /Wounderslly wrynklyd,	215	El Rummynge	19

WOUNDES —WRETCHE

	Page	Title	Line
WOUNDES			
Yet whils he stode he gave them woundes wyde.	32	Dol Dethe	101
Yet] 'Ye' Marshe 1568			
By Goddis woundes, but for dysplesaunce,	55	Bowge	332
Cockes woundes! Se, syrs, se, se!	156	Magnyfycence	572
By Cockes woundes, a wonder felowe thou arte!	185	Magnyfycence	1619
WOUNDID			
I am not woundid but that I may be cured.	332	Garlande	732
WRAG-WRAG			
Wytles, wayward, Syr Wrag-wrag,	133	Garnesche5	149
WRAK			
Another tolde how shyppes wente to wrak.	326	Garlande	507
WRAKE			
Welthe without lyberte gothe all to wrake.	199	Magnyfycence	2086
WRANG			
Wrang us on the [m]ales!	280	Why Come Ye	78
males] 'wales' †Kele 1545.3, Toy 1553, Kitson 1560.7, Marshe 1568			
WRANGE			
Wherewith my handes I wrange /That my senaws cracked	72	Phy Sparrow	45
WRANGYLL			
Dremyng in dumpys to wrangyll and to wrest,	37	Coystrowne1	47
That lyst for to jangyll /And waywardly to wrangyll	120	Ag Scottes2	6
WRANGLE			
Nay, to wrangle, I warant the, it is but a stone-caste.	201	Magnyfycence	2174
Howe warely they wrangle!	255	Collyn Clout	331
WRANGLYNG			
Thou hast bene so waywarde, so wranglyng, and so wrothsome,	205	Magnyfycence	2293
WRANGLYNGE			
Wranglynge, waywyrde, wytles, wraw, and nothyng meke.	124	Garnesche2	40
WRAPPED			
Se howe he is wrapped for the colde.	157	Magnyfycence	603
Your skynne that was wrapped in shertes of Raynes,	197	Magnyfycence	2016
WRAPT			
And wrapt in a maidenes smocke,	86	Phy Sparrow	590
WRASTEL			
Agayne the kingis plesure to wrastel or to wringe.	31	Dol Dethe	82
WRASTELYNGE			
And with myghty luggyng, /Wrastelynge and tuggyng,	349	Garlande	1310
WRASTELL			
Let Syr Wrig-wrag wrastell with Syr Delarag:	233	Speke Parott	89
WRASTYNGE			
Be wrastynge and wrythynge, and away drawe.	185	Magnyfycence	1608
WRASTLED			
Howe a wodcocke wrastled with a larke that was lame;	192	Magnyfycence	1836
WRATE			
Devysed and also wrate /Uppon a lewde curate,	62	Hauke	34
With, 'He wrate suche a bil withouten dout',	139	Ven Tongues	70
Enyus that wrate of mercyall war at lengthe;	321	Garlande	347
Quintus Cursius, full craftely that wrate	322	Garlande	366
Cursius] 'Cursus' †Fakes 1523			
He wrate therof many a praty lyne,	347	Garlande	1242
He wrate an Epitaph for his grave stone,	347	Garlande	1249
He wrate of a muse throw a mud wall;	351	Garlande	1384
Though I you wrate /After this rate	355	Garlande	1536
That I wrate with my pen.	372	Albany	523
WRATH			
Envy, wrath, and lechery, /Covetys and glotony;	293	Why Come Ye	575
WRAW			
Wranglynge, waywyrde, wytles, wraw, and nothyng meke.	124	Garnesche2	40
WRECHES			
Helas, ye wreches, ye may be wo!	376	Replycacion	77
WRECHYD			
A wrechyd man, syr, to my maker unkynde.	208	Magnyfycence	2390
WRECHYDNESE			
So gorgyous garmentes, and so myche wrechydnese,	244	Speke Parott	459
WRECHYDNESSE			
This mysery, this carefull wrechydnesse?	201	Magnyfycence	2154
WREKE			
Why than /Wreke ye your anger on me?	273	Collyn Clout	1091
WREN			
To treade the prety wren /That is our Ladyes hen.	86	Phy Sparrow	600
WRENCHE			
Ware gallyng in the widders, ware of that wrenche!	43	Balettys2	25
He wryngeth them suche a wrenche,	287	Why Come Ye	321
WRENCHIS			
Wonder is to wryte what wrenchis she wrowght,	346	Garlande	1207
WREST			
Dremyng in dumpys to wrangyll and to wrest,	37	Coystrowne1	47
And wrest up my harpe	259	Collyn Clout	490
WRESTYD			
Som be wrestyd there that they thynke on it forty dayes,	204	Magnyfycence	2274
WRESTYNG			
Nor stand long wrestyng there aboute;	41	Coystrowne4	25
WRESTLYNG			
Wrestlyng and tuggyng,	104	Phy Sparrow	1317
WRETCHE			
Set up a wretche on hye,	293	Why Come Ye	585

	Page	Title	Line
WRETCHED			
Of his wretched originall,	291	Why Come Ye	490
A wretched poore man	293	Why Come Ye	553
O ye wretched Scottes, /Ye puaunt pyspottes,	362	Albany	119
In wretched beggary /And maungy misery,	362	Albany	137
WRETCHEDLY			
And wretchedly ye lay starke naked.	119	Ag Scottes	167
starke naked] 'starke your naked' Kynge & Marche 1554, Day 1560, 'starke all naked' Marshe 1568			
Are ye nat frantyke madde, /And wretchedly bestadde,	368	Albany	364
WRETCHEDNESSE			
And foule covytousnesse /And other wretchednesse,	247	Collyn Clout	43
WRETCHID			
Of a poore wretchid man,	297	Why Come Ye	724
WRETCHYDLY			
That ever noblenesse sholde lyve thus wretchydly!	197	Magnyfycence	2021
For mysery /With penury /Myserably /And wretchydly	300	Why Come Ye	869
WRETCHYDNESSE			
In mysery and wretchydnesse thus to be lapped!	196	Magnyfycence	1985
Myserablenesse, /With wretchydnesse,	305	Why Come Ye	1033
WRETCHOCKES			
'They be wretchockes thou hast brought,	226	El Rummynge	465
They] 'The' Day 1560			
WRETE			
And on that sleve these wordes were wrete:	58	Bowge	438
WRIGHT			
Yet sumwhat wright supprisid with hartly lust,	33	Dol Dethe	145
hartly] 'herty' Marshe 1568			
And for to wright /In the dispyght	359	Albany	16
Of poetes chefe poete, saint Jerome dothe wright,	383	Replycacion	330
WRIG-WRAG			
Let Syr Wrig-wrag wrastell with Syr Delarag:	233	Speke Parott	89
Adue, nowe, Sir Wrig-wrag! /Adue, Sir Dalyrag!	366	Albany	296
WRINGE			
Agayne the kingis plesure to wrastel or to wringe.	31	Dol Dethe	82
WRINGYNG			
Wrythyng and wringyng, /Bytyng and styngyng;	95	Phy Sparrow	943
WRIT			
By nature of a newe writ.	302	Why Come Ye	939
WRITE			
To write some lytell tragedy,	117	Ag Scottes	72
Nothing to write, but hay the gy of thre,	138	Ven Tongues	46
Wherof hereafter, I thinke for to write,	140	Ven Tongues	81
Dothe bothe write and call	383	Replycacion	320
WRITEN			
Some were olde wryten, sum were writen new,	328	Garlande	584
WRITETH			
And writeth he wottith nat what.	296	Why Come Ye	679
wottith] 'wot' Toy 1553, Kitson 1560.7, Marshe 1568			
(Myne auctor writeth the same);	297	Why Come Ye	727
WRITINGE			
Of formar writinge by any presidente	30	Dol Dethe	23
WRITYNGE			
In writynge as we fynde	292	Why Come Ye	545
For he sent in writynge	299	Why Come Ye	790
His madnesse by writynge,	305	Why Come Ye	1056
WRITTIN			
Yowr name to se /It be enrolde, /Writtin with golde.	338	Garlande	939
WRYE			
Howe the male dothe wrye.	263	Collyn Clout	686
wrye] 'wryte' Kele 1545.1, Marshe 1568, 'wrye' MS Harley 2252			
WRYGGES			
The bore his tayle wrygges,	219	El Rummynge	177
WRYGHT			
An epytaphe to wryght	92	Phy Sparrow	822
Wherfore I wryght ageyne	124	Garnesche3	8
Wherto xulde I wryght	125	Garnesche3	34
They wolde the wryght, all with one stevyn,	133	Garnesche5	144
To wryght to the of tragydese,	133	Garnesche5	155
I care nat what thow wryght or sey;	134	Garnesche5	168
Scrybbyl thow, scrybyll thow, rayle or wryght,	134	Garnesche5	179
Wryght what thow wylte, I xall the aquyte.	134	Garnesche5	180
To wryght of this glorious gest,	309	Why Come Ye	1212
glorious] 'gromys' MS Rawlinson C. 813			
Of all your bewte I suffyce not to wryght:	336	Garlande	875
Or suffice to wryght	341	Garlande	1018
And cowde not wryght /Of Isabell Knyght.	342	Garlande	1066
WRYNG			
That made the male to wryng;	89	Phy Sparrow	700
the] 'tha' †Kele 1545.2			
WRYNGE			
Of some I wrynge of the necke lyke a wyre;	194	Magnyfycence	1909
Peas, or I shall wrynge thy be in a brake.	202	Magnyfycence	2187
Nay, iche shall wrynge the, horson, on the wryst.	202	Magnyfycence	2196
WRYNGETH			
A, Lord God, how the gowte wryngeth me by the too.	198	Magnyfycence	2047
He wryngeth them suche a wrenche,	287	Why Come Ye	321

WRYNKLYD —WRYTYNGE	Page	Title	Line

WRYNKLYD
Comely crynklyd, /Woundersly wrynklyd,	215	El Rummynge	19

WRYST
Nay, iche shall wrynge the, horson, on the wryst.	202	Magnyfycence	2196

WRYT
Lo, suche is this worlde! I fynde it wryt,	196	Magnyfycence	1974

WRYTE
But that I must wryte for my plesaunt pastaunce	42	Balettys2	4
In poesy to endyte /And eloquently to wryte,	75	Phy Sparrow	153
Let some poetes wryte	78	Phy Sparrow	252
That if I wolde apply /To wryte ornatly,	91	Phy Sparrow	781
ornatly] 'ordinately' Kitson 1560.6, Marshe 1568			
And with my pen to wryte;	93	Phy Sparrow	862
For to endyte, /And for to wryte,	95	Phy Sparrow	953
To wryte and tell /How women excell /In noblenes;	96	Phy Sparrow	981
Neyther wryte nor say;	101	Phy Sparrow	1197
Yet though I wryte not with ynke,	101	Phy Sparrow	1198
Syr, the repentaunce I have no man can wryte.	208	Magnyfycence	2392
This letter ye speke of never dyd I wryte.	209	Magnyfycence	2442
To ryme or to rayle, /To wryte or to indyte,	247	Collyn Clout	6
For I abhorre to wryte	257	Collyn Clout	437
I shall bothe wryte and say,	259	Collyn Clout	507
Though I wryte after this facyon;	273	Collyn Clout	1080
Take upon me /Thus copyously to wryte,	273	Collyn Clout	1085
Take upon me] 'Take now upon' Kele 1545.1, 'I take now uppon' MS Harley 2252			
But that I wryte trewly.	274	Collyn Clout	1116
He sayth the kynge doth wryte,	296	Why Come Ye	678
But to wryte of his shame	305	Why Come Ye	1048
And if so hym fortune to wryte true and plaine,	314	Garlande	85
so] not in MS Cotton Vitellius E.x			
My lyfe endurynge I shall both wryte and say,	335	Garlande	839
To wryte of you this goodli clause,	341	Garlande	1042
To wryte of yow this goodly clause,	342	Garlande	1050
To wryte of you this goodly clause,	342	Garlande	1058
But if he wryte oftenner than ones or twyse.'	345	Garlande	1155
Wonder is to wryte what wrenchis she wrowght,	346	Garlande	1207
Now hereof it erkith me lenger to wryte,	354	Garlande	1491

WRYTEN
Wryten at Croydon by Crowland in the Clay,	38	Coystrowne1	69
Wheron was wryten this worde, Myscheve.	58	Bowge	434
Wryten in my bede roule!	77	Phy Sparrow	242
This letter was wryten ferre hence.	150	Magnyfycence	337
Some were olde wryten, sum were written new,	328	Garlande	584

WRYTETH
Wryteth after an hyer rate;	91	Phy Sparrow	805
Yet wryteth he in his kynd,	91	Phy Sparrow	808
And say he wryteth to haute.	92	Phy Sparrow	812
Of hym that wryteth to fast.	143	Magnyfycence	91
Wryteth how Charlemayn	296	Why Come Ye	689
Who wryteth wysely hath a grete treasure.	314	Garlande	91

WRYTHE
Dyverse in style, some spared not vyce to wrythe,	46	Bowge	13
wrythe] 'wryte' Wynkyn de Worde 1510, Marshe 1568			
And not to wrylle, for he so wyll atteyne,	46	Bowge	22
wrythe] 'wryte' Wynkyn de Worde 1510, Marshe 1568			

WRYTHEN
Wrythen in wonder wyse /After the Sarasyns gyse,	216	El Rummynge	73
in] 'in a' Day 1560, Marshe 1568			

WRYTHYNG
Wrythyng and wringyng, /Bytyng and styngyng;	95	Phy Sparrow	943
Where with to rule hym with the wrythyng of a rest.	144	Magnyfycence	136

WRYTHYNGE
Be wrastynge and wrythynge, and away drawe.	185	Magnyfycence	1608

WRYTHTYST
Thow wrythtyst I xulde let the go pley;	134	Garnesche5	166

WRYTIN
Was wrytin; and so she did her spede,	345	Garlande	1168

WRYTITH
Cirus by name, as wrytith the story;	336	Garlande	858

WRYTYNG
Caste up your curyows wrytyng,	127	Garnesche3	112
Beware, for wrytyng remayneth of recorde!	314	Garlande	89
Of his onour, whos dissuasyve in wrytyng	316	Garlande	151
They had wrytyng, sum Greke, sum Ebrew,	328	Garlande	582
And with his forme foote he shoke forthe this wrytyng:	328	Garlande	595

WRYTYNGE
Whom Tytus Lyvyus /In wrytynge doth enroll;	67	Hauke	210
I trow I have brought you suche wrytynge of recorde,	149	Magnyfycence	309
And sendeth you this wrytynge closed under sele.	149	Magnyfycence	312
This wrytynge is welcome with harty affeccyon!	149	Magnyfycence	313
This wrytynge was taken me there,	150	Magnyfycence	344
Is all my hole wrytynge;	274	Collyn Clout	1108
Of any vertuous wrytynge;	274	Collyn Clout	1136
For wrytynge of trewth	300	Why Come Ye	842
Plato, but for that he left wrytynge behynde,	315	Garlande	126
that] not in MS Cotton Vitellius E.x			

WRYTON
What Skelton hath compilid and wryton in dede, ... 345 Garlande 1151
WRYTTEN
Amonge all other was wrytten in her trone, ... 47 Bowge 65
Because I have wrytten and sayd . . . . 103 Phy Sparrow 1253
As it is enrolde, /Wrytten and tolde . . . . 116 Ag Scottes 40
I have wrytten so mytche . . . . 230 El Rummynge 619
WROKEN
That on suche a female my flesshe wolde be wroken. . . . . . . 184 Magnyfycence 1566
The devyll thereon be wroken! . . . . 227 El Rummynge 498
For then ye wyll be wroken . . . . 261 Collyn Clout 598
WRONG
And that was the more wrong. . . . . 111 Lawde 21
WRONGE
Right to maynten and to resist all wronge. . . . . 34 Dol Dethe 171
His lyver, his longe /With anger is wronge; . . . . 94 Phy Sparrow 919
   longe] 'longes' Wyght 1553, Kitson 1560.6, Marshe 1568
In stede of ryght that wronge may stande; . . . . 152 Magnyfycence 433
In good faythe, syr, me semeth he had the more wronge. . . . . 178 Magnyfycence 1384
Be it ryght or wronge, by the advyse of me, ... 185 Magnyfycence 1597
It is wronge with eche degre; . . . . 248 Collyn Clout 60
Ye do them wronge and no ryght . . . . 256 Collyn Clout 404
   them] not in Marshe 1568
Whether it be wronge or ryght . . . . 272 Collyn Clout 1055
We tourne ryght into wronge, ... 276 Collyn Clout 1195
'Do ryght and do no wronge.' . . . . 281 Why Come Ye 89
   do no] 'no' Kitson 1560.7, Marshe 1568
It is somewhat wronge . . . . 288 Why Come Ye 390
How wronge was no ryght, and ryght was no wronge; . . . . 331 Garlande 704
How wronge was no ryght, and ryght was no wronge; . . . . 331 Garlande 704
WRONGES
All wronges he wolde redresse, ... 307 Why Come Ye 1112
WROTE
And what they wrote and sayd, ... 88 Phy Sparrow 680
Ne worde he wrote in vayne. . . . . 91 Phy Sparrow 803
Nor wrote the rosary . . . . 111 Lawde 27
For certayne envectyfys, yet wrote he none ill, ... 315 Garlande 96
   certayne envectyfys] 'that he enveiyd' MS Cotton Vit.E.x
That wrote the history of Jugurta also; . . . . 321 Garlande 332
With Plautus, that wrote full many a comody; . . . . 322 Garlande 354
   full] not in Marshe 1568
With Vincencius in Speculo, that wrote noble warkis; . . . . . 322 Garlande 381
To her he wrote many maters of myrthe; . . . . 346 Garlande 1199
WROTES
Hoyning like hogges that groynis and wrotes. . . . . 137 Ven Tongues 4
WROTH
Caughte penne and ynke, and wroth this lytell boke. . . . . . 61 Bowge 532
   wroth] 'wrote' Wynkyn de Worde 1510, Marshe 1568
Whether God be pleased or wroth. . . . . 307 Why Come Ye 1132
But, lorde, how the parker was wroth with all. . . . . 351 Garlande 1386
WROTHE
Syr, and yf ye wolde not be wrothe - . . . . 157 Magnyfycence 606
It is no wonder, therfore, thoughe ye be wrothe . . . . . . 189 Magnyfycence 1748
WROTHSOME
Thou hast bene so waywarde, so wranglyng, and so wrothsome, . . 205 Magnyfycence 2293
WROUGHT
Thorow treson, ageyn hym compassyd and wrought, ... 29 Dol Dethe 6
Which to thi resemblance wonderusly has wrought . . . . 34 Dol Dethe 193
Yet, for his love that all hath wrought, ... 36 Man Margery 25
His gawdy garment with Scornnys was all wrought; . . . . . . 54 Bowge 285
   Scornnys] 'storunys' †Wynkyn de Worde 1499, 1510,
   'scornes' Marshe 1568
For sure he wrought amys . . . . 62 Hauke 41
Wrought never such a worke, ... 67 Hauke 217
I[n] ponder, by number, by measure all thynge is wrought, . . 143 Magnyfycence 118
   In] 'I' †Rastell & Treveris C 1530, B
He wyll have wrought . . . . 165 Magnyfycence 902
For by crafty conveyaunce wonderful thynges are wrought. . . . 178 Magnyfycence 1371
Truth it is, syr; for after he wrought me moch shame, ... 209 Magnyfycence 2444
God of his goodnes him framed and wrought; . . . . 236 Speke Parott 212
Subtelly wrought shall be . . . . 288 Why Come Ye 364
If that that he wrought . . . . 290 Why Come Ye 448
Wrought to Charlemayn the king, ... 296 Why Come Ye 701
Of broken warkis wrought many a goodly thyng, ... 334 Garlande 801
Thamar also wrought with her goodly honde . . . . 336 Garlande 852
Stedfast of thought, /Wele made, wele wrought; . . . . 341 Garlande 1030
Set on your hede this laurell whiche is wrought. . . . . . . 343 Garlande 1087
But when they sawe my lawrell rychely wrought, ... 343 Garlande 1105
That ever they saw, and wrought it was the best. . . . . . . 343 Garlande 1113
For shamefully ye have wrought, ... 376 Replycacion 57
WROUNGE
Hatred by the herte so had hym wrounge . . . . 54 Bowge 292
WROUTE
Then in a tabull playne /I wroute a verse or twayne, ... 68 Hauke 223
WROWGHT
That wrowght have moche care, ... 111 Lawde 24
That nature wrowght in yow and me, ... 130 Garnesche5 13
Waywardly wrowght she hath in the, ... 130 Garnesche5 15

	Page	Title	Line
So curiously, so craftely, so connyngly wrowght,	325	Garlande	461
Wonder is to wryte what wrenchis she wrowght,	346	Garlande	1207

WROWGHTE

	Page	Title	Line
So ys all thyng wrowghte wylfully withowte reson and skylle.	245	Speke Parott	496

WULL

	Page	Title	Line
But plucke away and pull /Theyr fleces of wull.	248	Collyn Clout	79
He must tax for his wull	302	Why Come Ye	938
He may take whom he wull,	306	Why Come Ye	1079

WURS

	Page	Title	Line
Some famous wetewoldis, and they be moche wurs;	317	Garlande	187

XALL

	Page	Title	Line
So suerly yt xall nat tarnishe.	127	Garnesche3	122
Xall kyt both wyght and grene:	127	Garnesche3	139
The nexte halter ther xall be	128	Garnesche3	176
Within thy skyn he xall remayne.	130	Garnesche5	22
I have red, and rede I xall,	133	Garnesche5	158
Wryght what thow wylte, I xall the aquyte.	134	Garnesche5	180

XALTE

	Page	Title	Line
Thow xalte beholde no wher a warse;	130	Garnesche5	17

XULDDST

	Page	Title	Line
Wher thou xulddst have bene shrynyd;	128	Garnesche3	175

XULDE

	Page	Title	Line
Wherto xulde I wryght	125	Garnesche3	34
Ye xulde have kowththyd me a fole.	127	Garnesche3	119
Sche sware with hyr ye xulde nat dele,	131	Garnesche5	57
My tyme, I trow, I xulde but lese	133	Garnesche5	154
Thow wrythtyst I xulde let the go pley;	134	Garnesche5	166

XULDYST

	Page	Title	Line
That ther thou xuldyst be rachchyd	128	Garnesche3	180

YALOWE

	Page	Title	Line
With heris encrisped yalowe as the golde,	320	Garlande	289
encrisped] 'enscrisped' †Fakes 1523			

YANE

	Page	Title	Line
She began to yane and gaspy,	222	El Rummynge	331
began] 'gan' 1521 Fragment			

YARKE

	Page	Title	Line
That with his whyp his mares was wonte to yarke;	153	Magnyfycence	484

YARNE

	Page	Title	Line
And some a skeyne of yarne.	222	El Rummynge	311

YATE

	Page	Title	Line
'What yate call ye this?' And she sayd, 'Anglea'.	328	Garlande	588
yate] 'gate' Marshe 1568			

YATIS

	Page	Title	Line
I sawe a thowsande yatis new and olde.	328	Garlande	574
Then questionyd I her what thos yatis ment;	328	Garlande	575
thos] 'these' Marshe 1568			
'Theis yatis,' she sayd, 'which that ye beholde,	328	Garlande	579

YAVE

	Page	Title	Line
I yave hym drynke of the sugryd welle	132	Garnesche5	98

YAWDE

	Page	Title	Line
Ye prechers shall be yawde:	276	Collyn Clout	1204

YCHE

	Page	Title	Line
Iche wotte what yche do thynke!'	258	Collyn Clout	458
yche do] 'eche other' Kele 1545.1, Marshe 1568			

YDDER

	Page	Title	Line
I saw a foxe sucke on a kowes ydder;	191	Magnyfycence	1814

YDELL

	Page	Title	Line
Your braynes are ydell;	368	Albany	387

YDELNES

	Page	Title	Line
To pas the tyme in slowthfull ydelnes,	315	Garlande	120

YDEOTTES

	Page	Title	Line
Great ydeottes they be,	274	Collyn Clout	1130

YDILNES

	Page	Title	Line
As he that aquentyth hym with ydilnes.	318	Garlande	228

YDYLL

	Page	Title	Line
And teche them howe they sholde syt ydyll	174	Magnyfycence	1221
That wyll syt ydyll all the day	174	Magnyfycence	1229
And some in the worlde, theyr brayne is so ydyll	200	Magnyfycence	2135

YDLE

	Page	Title	Line
For truly it were a pyte that he sat ydle'.	318	Garlande	210
For ydle jangelers have but lytill braine;	328	Garlande	566

YDOLLES

	Page	Title	Line
Ydolles of Babylon, /De terra Zabulon,	262	Collyn Clout	638

YE

	Page	Title	Line
I say, ye commoners, why wer ye so stark mad?	30	Dol Dethe	50
I say, ye commoners, why wer ye so stark mad?	30	Dol Dethe	50
Where was your wit and reson ye shuld have had?	30	Dol Dethe	52
your] 'ys' †MS Royal 18 D.ii			
Ye armed you with wille and left your wit behynd;	30	Dol Dethe	55
Well may ye be cald commons most unkynd.	30	Dol Dethe	56
ye] 'you' Marshe 1568			
Alas, ye madmen, to far ye did excede.	31	Dol Dethe	60
Alas, ye madmen, to far ye did excede.	31	Dol Dethe	60
For whos causis ye slew hym with your awne hande.	31	Dol Dethe	68
Ye had not ben hable to have saide hym nay.	31	Dol Dethe	70
Bot by them to knoulege ye may attayne	32	Dol Dethe	129
'What, will ye do nothyng but play?'	35	Man Margery	4
'Be Gad, ye be a praty pode,	35	Man Margery	8

YE —YE   Page   Title   Line

Strawe, Jamys foder, ye play the fode;	35	Man Margery	10
Iwiss, ye dele uncurtesly;	36	Man Margery	15
What, wolde ye frompill me now? Fy, fy!	36	Man Margery	16
'What, and ye shal be my piggesnye?'	36	Man Margery	17
Be Crist, ye shall not! No, no, hardely!	36	Man Margery	18
'Walke forth your way, ye cost me nought;	36	Man Margery	22
What though ye can cownter Custodi nos?	38	Coystrowne1	57
Yet bere ye not to bold to braule ne to bark	38	Coystrowne1	60
Ye are to unhappy occasyons to fynde	38	Coystrowne1	65
occasyons] 'occasion' Marshe 1568			
Loke that ye spell /Well thys gospell;	39	Coystrowne3	20
Womanhod, wanton, ye want!	40	Coystrowne4	1
Ye rayll at ryot, recheles.	40	Coystrowne4	4
As well borne as ye full oft tyme beggys.	40	Coystrowne4	7
Put up your purs, ye shall non pay!'	40	Coystrowne4	11
As proud a pohen as ye sprede,	41	Coystrowne4	13
Of me and other ye may have nede.	41	Coystrowne4	14
All those by whom ye have avayle.	41	Coystrowne4	18
Good mastres Anne, there ye do shayle!	41	Coystrowne4	19
What prate ye, praty pyggys-ny?	41	Coystrowne4	20
Of youre doregate ye have no doute.	41	Coystrowne4	26
But one thyng is: that ye be lewde!	41	Coystrowne4	27
Ye may be countyd comfort of all corage.	42	Balettys2	7
How in good horsmen ye set your hole delyght,	42	Balettys2	13
With, 'Jayst ye, Jenet of Spayne, for your tayll waggys,'	43	Balettys2	18
Ye cast all your corage uppon such courtly haggys!	43	Balettys2	19
Play fayre-play, madame, and loke ye play clene,	43	Balettys2	41
And if ye lyst to know the cause why so,	44	Balettys3	38
I wold you coud! Then shuld ye se, mastres,	44	Balettys3	40
Though ye suppose all jeperdys ar paste,	45	Balettys4	1
And all is done ye lokyd for before,	45	Balettys4	2
That when ye thynke all daunger for to pas,	45	Balettys4	6
Fraghted with plesure to what ye coude devyse.	47	Bowge	42
'Maysters', he sayde, 'the shyp that ye here see,	47	Bowge	48
Than sholde ye see there pressynge in a pace	47	Bowge	56
'Pece,' quod Desyre, 'ye speke not worth a bene!	48	Bowge	95
Yf ye have not, in fayth, I wyll you lene	48	Bowge	96
Shyfte now therwith, let see, as ye can,	48	Bowge	99
That ye shall stonde in favoure and in grace.	49	Bowge	105
Ye be an apte man, as ony can be founde	50	Bowge	155
Ye be to her, yea, worth a thousande pounde.	50	Bowge	157
But this one thynge ye maye be sure of me,	50	Bowge	162
And ye nede ought, man, shewe to me your mynde,	50	Bowge	165
For ye have me whome faythfull ye shall fynde;	50	Bowge	166
For ye have me whome faythfull ye shall fynde;	50	Bowge	166
Ye maye not fall; truste me, ye maye not fayle.	50	Bowge	170
Ye maye not fall; truste me, ye maye not fayle.	50	Bowge	170
Ye stonde in favoure and Fortune is your gyde,	50	Bowge	171
'Ye, soo,' quod Suspecte, 'he maye us bothe begyle.'	51	Bowge	189
'Ye remembre the gentylman ryghte nowe	51	Bowge	197
Ye never dwelte in suche an other place,	51	Bowge	201
I wote, and he dyde, ye wolde me telle.	51	Bowge	205
A wonder thynge that ye waxe not madde!	53	Bowge	241
For and I studye sholde as ye doo nowe,	53	Bowge	242
Tell me your mynde, me thynke ye make a verse,	53	Bowge	244
I coude it skan and ye wolde it reherse.	53	Bowge	245
skan] 'stan' †Wynkyn de Worde 1499, 1510; it] (2nd) not in Marshe 1568			
Where hathe your dwellynge ben, er ye cam here?	53	Bowge	247
Er this, whan that ye made me royall chere.	53	Bowge	249
'Prynces of youghte', can ye synge by rote?	53	Bowge	253
To have that connynge and wayes that ye have!	53	Bowge	261
By Goddis soule, I wonder how ye gete	53	Bowge	262
But ye be welcome to our housholde.	53	Bowge	266
The favoure that ye have with my lady.	53	Bowge	270
And ye be welcome, syr, so God me save,	54	Bowge	279
'How do ye, mayster? Ye loke so soberly!	58	Bowge	442
'How do ye, mayster? Ye loke so soberly!	58	Bowge	442
Ye be malygned sore, I you ensure,	59	Bowge	451
But ye have crafte your selfe alwaye to save.	59	Bowge	452
Betwene the persone ye wote of, you -	59	Bowge	461
Yf ye coude be otherwyse agrede;	59	Bowge	480
Ye muste be ruled, as I shall tell you howe.	60	Bowge	493
He tolde me so, by God, ye maye truste me.	60	Bowge	514
Par[d]e, remembre whan ye were there,	60	Bowge	515
Parde] 'Parte' †Wynkyn de Worde 1499, 1510, Marshe 1568			
There I wynked on you - wote ye not where?	60	Bowge	516
As I shall tell you, yf ye wyll harke agayne:	61	Bowge	520
Now construewe ye what is the resydewe.	61	Bowge	539
Of the whych proces /Ye may know more expres,	68	Hauke	232
Maister sophista, /Ye simplex silogista,	68	Hauke	254
[Y]e develysh dogmatista, /Your hawke on your fista,	69	Hauke	255
Ye] 'The' †Lant 1545, Kynge & Marche 1554, Day 1560, Marshe 1568			
Ye made your hawke to cum /Desuper candelabrum	69	Hauke	288
This dowtless ye ravyd,	70	Hauke	307
Dys church ye thus depravyd;	70	Hauke	308
Wherfore, as I be savyd, /Ye ar therfore beknavyd.	70	Hauke	310

	Page	Title	Line
For though ye lyve a c. yere, ye shal dy a daw.	71	Hauke	334
For though ye lyve a c. yere, ye shal dy a daw.	71	Hauke	334
Of what estate ye be, /Of hye or lowe degre,	73	Phy Sparrow	54
Great sorowe than ye myght se,	73	Phy Sparrow	56
Amen, say ye with me!	74	Phy Sparrow	94
Saynge, 'Mayd, ye are in wyll	77	Phy Sparrow	222
Ye prycke me in the head!'	77	Phy Sparrow	224
But as verely as ye be	78	Phy Sparrow	254
That if ye can fynde	78	Phy Sparrow	260
As well perceyve ye maye	81	Phy Sparrow	372
To wepe with me loke that ye come,	81	Phy Sparrow	387
To mornynge loke that ye fall	81	Phy Sparrow	390
Why were ye Calliope, embrawdred with letters of golde?	112	Calliope	1
Calliope, /As ye may se,	112	Calliope	2
Ye summoned our kynge. Why dyde ye so?	113	Scot Kynge	2
Ye summoned our kynge. Why dyde ye so?	113	Scot Kynge	2
Knowe ye not salte and suger asonder?	113	Scot Kynge	6
In your somnynge ye were to malaperte,	113	Scot Kynge	7
Ye thought ye dyde it full valyauntolye,	113	Scot Kynge	9
Ye thought ye dyde it full valyauntolye,	113	Scot Kynge	9
Syr squyer-galyarde ye were to swyfte;	113	Scot Kynge	11
Ye ought to honour your lorde and brother.	114	Scot Kynge	16
Trowe ye, Syr James, his noble grace	114	Scot Kynge	17
Now ye proude Scottes of Gelawaye	114	Scot Kynge	19
Now must ye knowe our kynge for your regent,	114	Scot Kynge	21
And ye be desolate as Armeleche.	114	Scot Kynge	24
A kynge anoynted, and ye be non.	114	Scot Kynge	26
Wherfore I fere ye wyll suffre payne.	114	Scot Kynge	28
And ye proude Scottes of Dunbar,	114	Scot Kynge	29
Parde ye be his homager.	114	Scot Kynge	30
Ye dyde not your dewty therin,	114	Scot Kynge	32
Wyerfore ye may it now repent.	114	Scot Kynge	33
Ye bere yourselfe somwhat to bolde,	114	Scot Kynge	34
Therfore ye have lost your copyholde.	114	Scot Kynge	35
Ye be bounde tenauntes to his estate;	114	Scot Kynge	36
Gyve up your game, ye playe chek mate;	114	Scot Kynge	37
I understonde to soone ye cam,	114	Scot Kynge	39
For a prysoner there now ye be	114	Scot Kynge	40
Ye have determyned to make a fraye,	114	Scot Kynge	44
Ye were beten weth your owne rod.	114	Scot Kynge	47
Ye have loste spores, cote armure and sworde.	114	Scot Kynge	49
Ye had be better to have busked to Huntley Bankes, be] 'bet' †Fakes 1513	114	Scot Kynge	50
But ye had some wyl[d] sede to sowe, wyld] 'wyle' †Fakes 1513	114	Scot Kynge	52
Therfore ye be layde now full lowe.	114	Scot Kynge	53
Of the kynge of Naverne ye may take hede	115	Scot Kynge	56
At hym example ye wolde none take;	115	Scot Kynge	60
Of the out yles ye rough foted Scottes	115	Scot Kynge	62
Ye rowe ranke Scottes and dronken Danes	115	Scot Kynge	64
Of our Englysshe bowes ye have fette your banes.	115	Scot Kynge	65
Joly Jemmy, ye scornefull Scot,	116	Ag Scottes	49
Ye for to sende suche a cytacyon,	117	Ag Scottes	55
Ye play Hop Lobbyn of Lowdean;	117	Ag Scottes	59
Ye shew ryght well what good ye can;	117	Ag Scottes	60
Ye shew ryght well what good ye can;	117	Ag Scottes	60
Ye may be lorde of Locryan -	117	Ag Scottes	61
Ye summond our kyng, why dyd ye so? ye] not in Kynge & Marche 1554, Day 1560, Marshe 1568	118	Ag Scottes	92
Ye summond our kyng, why dyd ye so? ye] not in Kynge & Marche 1554, Day 1560, Marshe 1568	118	Ag Scottes	92
Know ye not suger and salt asonder?	118	Ag Scottes	96
Ye thought ye dyd yet valyauntly;	118	Ag Scottes	99
Ye thought ye dyd yet valyauntly;	118	Ag Scottes	99
Syr skyrgalyard, ye were so skyt;	118	Ag Scottes	101
Your lege ye layd and your aly,	118	Ag Scottes	103
Regardyd ye shuld your lord, your brother. ye] 'you' Day 1560, Marshe 1568	118	Ag Scottes	106
Trowyd ye, Syr Jemy, his nobull grace	118	Ag Scottes	107
And ye were disloyall Amalec.	118	Ag Scottes	116
Anoynted kyng, and ye were none.	118	Ag Scottes	118
Though ye untruly your father have slayne,	118	Ag Scottes	119
And ye, proud Scot, Dunde, Dunbar	118	Ag Scottes	121
Pardy, ye were his homager,	118	Ag Scottes	122
For your untruth now ar ye shent.	118	Ag Scottes	124
Ye bare yourselfe somwhat to bold;	118	Ag Scottes	125
Therfore ye lost your copyhold.	118	Ag Scottes	126
Ye were bonde tenent to his estate;	118	Ag Scottes	127
Lost is your game, ye are checkmate.	118	Ag Scottes	128
I understand, to sone ye came.	118	Ag Scottes	130
That of Scotland ye lost the flower.	118	Ag Scottes	134
He the White, and ye the Red, ye] 'you' Day 1560, Marshe 1568	119	Ag Scottes	137
Thus for your guerdon quyt ar ye,	119	Ag Scottes	139
Ye were starke mad to make a fray,	119	Ag Scottes	143
For youre owne tayle ye made a rod. owne] not in Day 1560, Marshe 1568	119	Ag Scottes	146
Ye wantyd wyt, sir, at a worde;	119	Ag Scottes	147

	Page	Title	Line
Ye lost your spurrys, ye lost you sworde.	119	Ag Scottes	148
Ye lost your spurrys, ye lost you sworde.	119	Ag Scottes	148
Ye myght have buskyd you to Huntley Bankys;	119	Ag Scottes	149
Of the kynge of Naverne ye might take heed, ...	119	Ag Scottes	153
And, for example [y]e wold none take, ...	119	Ag Scottes	157
ye] 'he' †Lant 1545, Kynge & Marche 1554, Day 1560, Marshe 1568			
All have ye lost and cast away.	119	Ag Scottes	163
Out of your robes ye were shaked, ...	119	Ag Scottes	166
your] not in Kynge & Marche 1554, Day 1560, Marshe 1568			
And wretchedly ye lay starke naked.	119	Ag Scottes	167
starke naked] 'starke your naked' Kynge & Marche 1554, Day 1560, 'starke all naked' Marshe 1568			
Ye were to hye, ye ar cast downe.	120	Ag Scottes	177
Ye were to hye, ye ar cast downe.	120	Ag Scottes	177
Syr sumner, now ye have lost your crowne.	120	Ag Scottes	180
Sithe ye have me chalyngyd, Master Garnesche, ...	121	Garnesche1	1
But sey me now, Syr Satrapas, what autoryte ye have	121	Garnesche1	6
What, have ye kythyd yow a knyght, Syr Dugles the dowty, . . .	121	Garnesche1	8
Ye stronge sturdy stalyon, so sterne and stowty, ...	122	Garnesche1	10
Ye bere yow bolde as Barabas, or Syr Terry of Trac[e].	122	Garnesche1	11
Trace] 'Tracy' †MS Harley 367			
Ye gyrne grymly with your gomys and with yor grysly face. . . .	122	Garnesche1	12
But sey me yet, Syr Satrapas, what auctoryte ye have	122	Garnesche1	13
Ye fowle, fers and felle, as Syr Ferumbras the ffreke, ...	122	Garnesche1	15
Thow ye be lusty as Syr Lybyus, launces to breke, ...	122	Garnesche1	17
But sey me yet, Syr Satrapas, wat auctoryte ye have	122	Garnesche1	20
As ye ar brystlyd on the bake for alle your gay gere.	122	Garnesche1	26
But sey me yet, Syr Satrapas, what auctoryte ye have	122	Garnesche1	27
But sey me yet, Syr Satrapas, what auctoryte ye have	122	Garnesche1	34
I sey, ye solem Sarson, alle blake ys yor ble;	122	Garnesche1	36
You mantyca[re], ye maltaperte, ye can bothe wins and whyne; .	123	Garnesche2	4
mantycare] 'mantyca' †MS Harley 367			
You mantyca[re], ye maltaperte, ye can bothe wins and whyne; .	123	Garnesche2	4
mantycare] 'mantyca' †MS Harley 367			
Ye cappyd Cayface copious, your paltoke on your pate, ...	123	Garnesche2	6
Thow ye prate lyke prowde Pylate, beware yet of chek mate. . .	123	Garnesche2	7
Hole ys your brow that ye brake with Deu[ra]ndall your awne sworde; Deurandall] 'Deurandall' †MS Harley 367	123	Garnesche2	8
Why holde ye on yer cap, syr, then? Yor pardone ys expyryd. . .	123	Garnesche2	9
Ye hobble very homly before the kynges borde;	123	Garnesche2	10
Ye countyr umwhyle to capcyously, and ar ye be dysiryd;	123	Garnesche2	11
Ye countyr umwhyle to capcyously, and ar ye be dysiryd;	123	Garnesche2	11
Ye cappyd Cayface copyous, your paltoke on your pate, ...	123	Garnesche2	13
Thow ye prate lyke prowde Pylate, beware of cheke mate.	123	Garnesche2	14
O Gabionyte of Gabyone, why do ye gane and gaspe?	123	Garnesche2	15
Lusty Garnysche, lyke a lowse, ye jet full lyke a jaspe; . . .	123	Garnesche2	17
As wytles as a wylde goos, ye have but small remorrs	123	Garnesche2	18
Ye capyd Cayfas copyous, your paltoke on your pate, ...	123	Garnesche2	20
Tho ye prate lyke prowde Pylate, beware of cheke mate.	123	Garnesche2	21
Ye capyd Cayfas copyus, your paltoke on your pate, ...	123	Garnesche2	27
Thow ye prate lyke prowde Pylate, beware of cheke mate.	123	Garnesche2	28
Ye grounde yow upon Godfrey, that grysly gargons face, ...	123	Garnesche2	29
Cum Garnyche, cum Godfrey, with as many as ye may!	123	Garnesche2	32
Ye cappyd Cayfas copyous, your paltoke on your pate, ...	123	Garnesche2	34
Thow ye prate lyke prowde Pylate, beware of cheke mate.	123	Garnesche2	35
To turney or to tante with me ye ar to fare to seke.	123	Garnesche2	37
Thow mantycore, ye marmset, garnyshte lyke a Greke, ...	124	Garnesche2	39
Ye cappyd Cayfas copyous, your paltoke on your pate, ...	124	Garnesche2	41
Thow ye prate lyke prowde Pylate, beware of cheke mate.	124	Garnesche2	42
Ye have knavyche condycyonns.	124	Garnesche3	12
Gup, marmeset, jast ye morelle!	124	Garnesche3	13
Lewdely your tyme ye spende, ...	124	Garnesche3	15
Your Englysche lew[d]ly ye sorte, ...	124	Garnesche3	19
lewdly] 'lewly' †MS Harley 367			
And falsly ye me reporte.	124	Garnesche3	20
Garnyche, ye gape to wyde:	124	Garnesche3	21
Whan ye war yonger of age	124	Garnesche3	24
Ye war a kechyn page, /A dyshwasher, a dryvyll, ...	124	Garnesche3	25
Ye fryed and ye broylyd, ...	125	Garnesche3	28
Ye fryed and ye broylyd, ...	125	Garnesche3	28
Ye rostyd and ye boylyd, ...	125	Garnesche3	29
Ye rostyd and ye boylyd, ...	125	Garnesche3	29
Ye rostyd, lyke a fonne, ...	125	Garnesche3	30
Ye slufferd up sowse	125	Garnesche3	32
At Gynys when ye ware /But a slendyr spere, ...	125	Garnesche3	40
For when ye dwelt there, ...	125	Garnesche3	43
Ye had a knavysche cote	125	Garnesche3	44
In dud frese ye war schrynyd, ...	125	Garnesche3	46
Ye myght no better a way;	125	Garnesche3	49
The insyde ye ded calle	125	Garnesche3	50
Your drapry ye ded wante	125	Garnesche3	52
When ye kyst a shepys ie, ...	125	Garnesche3	54
........that ye ther prechyd, ...	125	Garnesche3	60
To hyr love ye nowte rechyd.	125	Garnesche3	61
Ye wolde have bassyd hyr bumme, ...	125	Garnesche3	62
Ye loste hyr favyr quyt!	125	Garnesche3	67
Sche seyd how ye ded brydell, ...	126	Garnesche3	73

	Page	Title	Line
Ye ar an eldyr steke;	126	Garnesche3	79
Ye wot what I thynke;	126	Garnesche3	80
At bothe endes ye stynke;	126	Garnesche3	81
Bolde bayarde, ye are to blynde,	126	Garnesche3	101
I wondyr that ye smatyr,	126	Garnesche3	106
Ye wolde be callyd a maker,	127	Garnesche3	108
Ye ar a comly crakar,	127	Garnesche3	110
Ye lernyd of sum py-bakar.	127	Garnesche3	111
Had ye gonne with me to scole,	127	Garnesche3	117
Ye xulde have kowththyd me a fole.	127	Garnesche3	119
Thow a Sarsens hed ye bere,	127	Garnesche3	123
Ye ryme yet owte of reson;	127	Garnesche3	128
Ye rayle all out of seson.	127	Garnesche3	130
Now upon thys hete /Rankely whan ye swete,	127	Garnesche3	134
Men sey ye wyll wax lowsy, /Drunkyn, drowpy, drowsy.	127	Garnesche3	135
Your sworde ye swere, I wene,	127	Garnesche3	137
Withowte ye have a confectioun	128	Garnesche3	152
Agenst ye now I bynde;	128	Garnesche3	160
Ye may wele be bedawyd,	128	Garnesche3	182
Ye ar a fole owtelauyd;	128	Garnesche3	183
Ye bere yow bold and brag	129	Garnesche3	187
Ye kyt your clothe to large,	129	Garnesche3	189
Soche pollyng pajaunttis ye pley,	129	Garnesche3	190
Rede and lerne ye may,	129	Garnesche3	195
Thowthe ye kan skylle of large and longe,	129	Garnesche5	3
Ye syng allway the kukkowe songe.	129	Garnesche5	4
Ye rayle, ye ryme, with, 'Hay, dog, hay!'	129	Garnesche5	5
Ye rayle, ye ryme, with, 'Hay, dog, hay!'	129	Garnesche5	5
Ye, syr, rayle all in deformite:	129	Garnesche5	7
Ye have nat red the properte	129	Garnesche5	8
Ye wolde have trysyd hys trowle away.	130	Garnesche5	36
Soche pajantes with your fryndes ye play,	130	Garnesche5	37
With trechery ye them betray.	130	Garnesche5	38
Garnyshe, ye gate of Gorge with gaudry	130	Garnesche5	39
Ye have a fantasy to Fanchyrche strete,	130	Garnesche5	41
I wolde ye had kyst hyr on the tayle!	130	Garnesche5	46
Ye pressyd pertely to pluk a crow:	130	Garnesche5	48
Ye lost your [h]olde, onbende your bow, holde] 'bolde' †MS Harley 367	131	Garnesche5	49
Ye wan nothyng there but a mow:	131	Garnesche5	50
Ye wan nothyng there but a skorne:	131	Garnesche5	51
Sche seyd ye war coluryd with cole dust;	131	Garnesche5	53
With, 'Gup, Syr Gy', ye gate a moke.	131	Garnesche5	56
Sche sware with hyr ye xulde nat dele,	131	Garnesche5	57
For ye war smery, lyke a sele,	131	Garnesche5	58
And ye war herey, lyke a calfe;	131	Garnesche5	59
And thus there ye lost yower pray;	131	Garnesche5	61
Get ye anothyr where ye may.	131	Garnesche5	62
Get ye anothyr where ye may.	131	Garnesche5	62
Dysparage ye myn auncetry?	131	Garnesche5	63
Ye ar dysposyd for to ly.	131	Garnesche5	64
Ye bere out brothells lyke a bawde;	131	Garnesche5	73
Ye get therby a slendyr laude	131	Garnesche5	74
To cal me lorell ye ar to lewde;	131	Garnesche5	85
Ye be nat cawte in an hempen snare.	133	Garnesche5	163
Harkyn herto, ye Harvy Ha[f]tar, Haftar] 'Hastar' †MS Harley 367	133	Garnesche5	164
Gup Scot, /Ye blot:	135	Dundas	2
For ye said, that he said, that I said, wote ye what?	137	Ven Tongues	12
For ye said, that he said, that I said, wote ye what?	137	Ven Tongues	12
Than ye may commaunde me to gentil cok wat.	137	Ven Tongues	15
What fault find ye herein but may be avowed.	138	Ven Tongues	41
But ye are so full of vertibilite,	138	Ven Tongues	42
That ye would coarte and enforce me	138	Ven Tongues	45
And you knew all ye would be ill apayd'.	139	Ven Tongues	72
And eyther I am dysseyved, or ye be the same.	141	Magnyfycence	25
Syr, as ye say. I have harde of your fame.	141	Magnyfycence	26
And from whens come ye, and it myght be askyd?	141	Magnyfycence	29
Ye, to knackynge ernyst what and it preve?	141	Magnyfycence	33
To that ye say I can well condyssende.	141	Magnyfycence	39
Perceyve ye this parcell?	142	Magnyfycence	55
Ye, syr, passyng well.	142	Magnyfycence	56
God forbyd ye sholde be let	142	Magnyfycence	63
Say what ye wyll to me.	142	Magnyfycence	66
What wote ye where upon I wyll conclude?	142	Magnyfycence	72
I trowe ye can not say nay moche to this:	142	Magnyfycence	74
A, ye be wonders men!	143	Magnyfycence	89
Shall I begynne or ye?	143	Magnyfycence	103
Nay, ye shall begynne, by my wyll.	143	Magnyfycence	104
Then ye must bothe consent	143	Magnyfycence	107
Measure is treasure. Howe say ye, is it not this?	144	Magnyfycence	125
Ye, lyberte with measure nede never drede.	144	Magnyfycence	130
What, lyberte to measure then wolde ye bynde?	144	Magnyfycence	131
But have ye not herde say that wyll is no skyll?	144	Magnyfycence	148
Surely I am joyous that ye be myndyd thus;	144	Magnyfycence	156
Syr, though ye be a noble prynce of myght,	145	Magnyfycence	166
Welcome, frendys, ye are bothe unto me.	145	Magnyfycence	169
Welthe with Lyberte, with me bothe dwell ye shall,	145	Magnyfycence	174

YE — YE

	Page	Title	Line
Where as ye have, syr, to me them assygned,	145	Magnyfycence	177
Then may I say that ye be servauntys myne.	145	Magnyfycence	183
Nowe that ye have me chefe ruler assygned,	146	Magnyfycence	202
If ye lyst to lyve after your fre lyberte.	146	Magnyfycence	208
All that ye say is as trewe as the crede.	146	Magnyfycence	218
What, syr, wolde ye make me a poppynge fole?	146	Magnyfycence	232
And now wolde ye swarve from your owne ordynaunce?	147	Magnyfycence	234
A, ye make me laughe at your inconstaunce.	147	Magnyfycence	236
Ye coulde not ellys, I wote, with me endure.	147	Magnyfycence	247
Nowe, benedicite, ye wene I were some hafter,	147	Magnyfycence	257
Ye wene that I am dronken bycause I loke pale.	147	Magnyfycence	259
Me semeth that ye have dronken more than ye have bled.	147	Magnyfycence	260
Me semeth that ye have dronken more than ye have bled.	147	Magnyfycence	260
Why that ye sayd our langage was in vayne.	147	Magnyfycence	263
Ye, syr, undoubted. Then, of very ryght,	148	Magnyfycence	272
Why have ye hym named and all other refused?	148	Magnyfycence	281
Have ye not welthe here at your wyll?	148	Magnyfycence	284
It is but a maddynge, these wayes that ye use.	148	Magnyfycence	285
What! I have aspyed ye are a carles page.	148	Magnyfycence	288
By God, syr, ye se but fewe wyse men of myne age.	148	Magnyfycence	289
Ye wante but a wylde flyeng bolte to shote at the buttes.	148	Magnyfycence	294
Though Largesse ye hyght your langage is to large;	148	Magnyfycence	295
For whiche ende goth forwarde ye take lytell charge.	148	Magnyfycence	296
Let se this checke yf ye voyde canne.	148	Magnyfycence	297
Wel, wyse men may ete the fysshe when ye shal draw the pole.	148	Magnyfycence	300
In fayth, I wyll not say that ye shall prove a fole,	148	Magnyfycence	301
Go shake the, dogge, hay, syth ye wyll nedys!	148	Magnyfycence	303
And surely ye are to hym beholde,	149	Magnyfycence	333
By your soth? Ye, and there is suche a wache,	150	Magnyfycence	350
Mary, syr, ye were afrayde.	150	Magnyfycence	362
With ye, syr, so God me spede.	151	Magnyfycence	379
Ye, syr, a blaunched almonde is no bene.	151	Magnyfycence	381
Ye wolde sone pynche at a pecke of otes.	151	Magnyfycence	385
otes] 'grotes' †Rastell & Treveris C 1530, B			
Ye, but how longe shall I here awayte?	151	Magnyfycence	398
For, in fayth, ye be well met.	151	Magnyfycence	402
What! Wolde ye wyves counterfet	153	Magnyfycence	452
What the devyll! Are ye two of aquayntaunce?	154	Magnyfycence	496
But Fansy, my frende, where have ye bene so longe?	154	Magnyfycence	500
Howe coulde ye do that, and [I] was away?	154	Magnyfycence	504
I] not in †Rastell & Treveris C 1530, B			
By the masse, for ye are able to dystroy an hole lande.	154	Magnyfycence	513
But, syr, howe counterfetyd ye?	155	Magnyfycence	524
Surveyaunce! Where ye survey,	155	Magnyfycence	526
For all these japes yet that [y]e make –	156	Magnyfycence	558
ye] 'we' †Rastell & Treveris C 1530, B			
Ye, and se howe it may be compast	156	Magnyfycence	567
In all this hast whether wyll ye ryde?	156	Magnyfycence	570
And yf ye knewe howe I have mased,	156	Magnyfycence	580
I am sure ye wolde have me excused.	156	Magnyfycence	581
Woo is that purse that ye shall share!	156	Magnyfycence	587
What call ye him, this?	156	Magnyfycence	588
Ye, by the masse, this is even the same,	157	Magnyfycence	599
Is it not a vestment? A, ye wante a rope.	157	Magnyfycence	604
Syr, and yf ye wolde not be wrothe –	157	Magnyfycence	606
Ye, for your wyt is cloked for the rayne.	157	Magnyfycence	609
But tell me where aboute ye go.	157	Magnyfycence	617
Ye. But he spendeth it all in mesure.	157	Magnyfycence	621
Why, dwelleth Mesure where ye two dwell?	157	Magnyfycence	622
Ye. But he is a captyvyte.	157	Magnyfycence	626
Ye. And he hath rule of all his tresure.	158	Magnyfycence	632
Nay; eyther let me tell, or elles tell ye.	158	Magnyfycence	633
All this ye may easely brynge aboute.	158	Magnyfycence	655
Why, can ye not put out that foule freke?	158	Magnyfycence	657
Ye and I talkyd therof to nyght.	159	Magnyfycence	670
Ye. My fansy was out of owle flyght,	159	Magnyfycence	671
Syr, ye shall hyght Good Demeynaunce.	159	Magnyfycence	674
Dusty! Nay, syr, ye be all of the lusty;	161	Magnyfycence	760
Ye, so I can devyse my gere after the cowrtly maner.	161	Magnyfycence	766
Ye, in faythe, a bolde man and a hardy.	162	Magnyfycence	771
Wyll ye se this gentylman is all in his skornys?	162	Magnyfycence	773
But are ye not avysed to dwell where ye spake?	162	Magnyfycence	774
But are ye not avysed to dwell where ye spake?	162	Magnyfycence	774
What the devyll! Can ye agre no better?	162	Magnyfycence	795
Ye, so I tell the.	162	Magnyfycence	800
Rule the roste! Thou woldest, ye,	163	Magnyfycence	805
Thou woldest, ye] 'ye thou woldest' †Rastell & Treveris C 1530, B			
What the devyll! Use ye not to drawe no swordes?	163	Magnyfycence	811
Ye, for surety. Ofte peas is taken for frayes.	163	Magnyfycence	814
Tary here. Wote ye what I say?	163	Magnyfycence	819
Ye, and do ryght good servyce he can.	163	Magnyfycence	822
Nay. Purchace ye a pardon for the pose,	163	Magnyfycence	825
Ye, for the, so I say.	166	Magnyfycence	930
With Crafty Convayaunce. Ye, dyd they so?	166	Magnyfycence	941
Ye, by Goddes sacrament; and with other mo.	166	Magnyfycence	942
Ye. But I bade hym pyke out of the gate;	166	Magnyfycence	946
Crossed? Ye, checked out of consayte.	166	Magnyfycence	951

	Page	Title	Line
Ye, but what shall I call my name?	167	Magnyfycence	958
Ye, but of my name let us be wyse.	167	Magnyfycence	963
And ye may lese it for a pynne.	168	Magnyfycence	1016
A pylde curre? Ye, so I tell the, a pylde curre.	169	Magnyfycence	1055
A, I trowe ye shall coughe me a fole.	170	Magnyfycence	1064
In faythe, trouthe ye say, we wente togyder to scole.	170	Magnyfycence	1065
Ye, but I can somwhat more of the letter.	170	Magnyfycence	1066
Cockys bonys! Herde ye ever syke another?	170	Magnyfycence	1090
Ye, a fole the tone, and a fole the tother.	170	Magnyfycence	1091
Ye, bere me this strawe to a dawys nest.	170	Magnyfycence	1097
Ye. But trowest thou that he be not maungey?	171	Magnyfycence	1122
Ye. But he wyll in at every mannes dore.	171	Magnyfycence	1130
Ye, for all thy mynde is on owles and apes.	171	Magnyfycence	1134
Ye. But thryfte and we have made a batell.	171	Magnyfycence	1136
Ye, by the rode, even the same.	172	Magnyfycence	1139
Ye, so redely and so sone!	172	Magnyfycence	1157
The tothe ake! Lo, a torde ye have.	172	Magnyfycence	1164
Ye, thou haste the four quarters of a knave.	172	Magnyfycence	1165
What? Wolde ye have mo folys, and are so many?	172	Magnyfycence	1170
Ye, but thou can play the fole without a vyser.	173	Magnyfycence	1177
Ye. Let us here a worde or twayne.	174	Magnyfycence	1218
Ye, by God, syr. For a nede,	174	Magnyfycence	1237
Mary, syr, ye may swere it on a boke.	176	Magnyfycence	1292
Ye, tourne over the lefe, rede there, and loke	176	Magnyfycence	1293
Yes, perde, man, whether that ye ryde or go.	176	Magnyfycence	1307
Yet I wolde that ye had gone rather;	176	Magnyfycence	1313
Ye. But tell me one thynge. What is that?	176	Magnyfycence	1318
Ye, for he hathe a full drye soule.	176	Magnyfycence	1320
'What howe! Be ye mery! Was it not well conveyed?'	177	Magnyfycence	1347
'As oft as ye lyst, so honeste be savyd.	177	Magnyfycence	1348
Tushe! Holde your peas; ye speke lyke a dawe.	178	Magnyfycence	1379
Ye shall be occupyed, Welthe, at my wyll.	178	Magnyfycence	1380
All that ye say, syr, is reason and skyll.	178	Magnyfycence	1381
Mayster Survayour, where have ye ben so longe?	178	Magnyfycence	1382
Remembre ye not how my lyberte by mesure ruled was?	178	Magnyfycence	1383
Tushe! Holde your peas; ye speke out of season.	178	Magnyfycence	1388
Syr, by lyberte and largesse I wyll that ye shall	179	Magnyfycence	1396
Be governed and gyded; wote ye what I say?	179	Magnyfycence	1397
It shall be done. Ye, but byd hym come away	179	Magnyfycence	1399
What! Wyll ye waste wynde and prate thus in vayne?	179	Magnyfycence	1403
Ye have eten sauce I trowe, at the Taylers Hall.	179	Magnyfycence	1404
To rule as ye lyst, lo, here is Lyberte.	179	Magnyfycence	1413
Syr, ye shall folowe myne appetyte and intent.	180	Magnyfycence	1420
What! Can ye agree thus and appose?	180	Magnyfycence	1425
Ye, of Jacke a Thrommys bybyll can ye make a glose.	180	Magnyfycence	1427
Ye, of Jacke a Thrommys bybyll can ye make a glose.	180	Magnyfycence	1427
Syr, as me semeth, ye sholde be rulyd be me.	180	Magnyfycence	1433
I say that I wyll ye have hym in gydynge.	180	Magnyfycence	1436
And so as ye se it wyll be no better,	180	Magnyfycence	1438
Take it in worthe suche as ye fynde.	180	Magnyfycence	1439
Nowe holde ye content, for there is none other shyfte.	180	Magnyfycence	1443
Make indentures how ye and I shal gyde.	180	Magnyfycence	1448
But loke that ye occupye the auctoryte that I you gave.	180	Magnyfycence	1456
And ferre beyond my merytys ye me commende and prayse.	183	Magnyfycence	1526
So as ye be a prynce of great myght,	183	Magnyfycence	1545
It is semynge your pleasure ye delyte,	183	Magnyfycence	1546
Howe lyke you? Ye lacke, syr, suche a lusty lasse.	183	Magnyfycence	1559
Wyll ye spende ony money? Ye, a thousande pounde.	184	Magnyfycence	1570
Wyll ye spende ony money? Ye, a thousande pounde.	184	Magnyfycence	1570
Ye, but some be full koy and passynge harde harted.	184	Magnyfycence	1583
Ye, for omnis mulier meretrix si celari potest.	184	Magnyfycence	1586
A, I have spyed ye can moche broken sorowe.	184	Magnyfycence	1587
Let se what ye say. Shewe it strayte.	185	Magnyfycence	1592
What so ever ye do, folowe your owne wyll,	185	Magnyfycence	1595
Then some occacyon or quarell ye must fynde,	185	Magnyfycence	1600
And frowne it and face it, as thoughe ye wolde fyght;	185	Magnyfycence	1601
But do as ye lyst and take your owne way.	185	Magnyfycence	1604
What sholde ye do elles? Are not you a lorde?	185	Magnyfycence	1606
And ye se a man that with hym ye be not pleased,	185	Magnyfycence	1609
And ye se a man that with hym ye be not pleased,	185	Magnyfycence	1609
Stande styll here, and ye shall se	186	Magnyfycence	1629
Stand up, syr. Ye are welcome to me.	186	Magnyfycence	1632
And that ye wyll not cast hym away so sone.	186	Magnyfycence	1638
Mesure, ye knowe wel, with hym I can not be content;	186	Magnyfycence	1656
Howe say ye, syrs? Herein what is best?	186	Magnyfycence	1659
Ye, by my trouthe, I shall waraunt you for me,	187	Magnyfycence	1669
What force ye, so that [y]e be payde?	187	Magnyfycence	1672
ye be] 'he be' †Rastell & Treveris C 1530, B			
What force ye, so that [y]e be payde?	187	Magnyfycence	1672
ye be] 'he be' †Rastell & Treveris C 1530, B			
This is a wyse man, syr, where so ever ye hym had.	187	Magnyfycence	1689
I trowe I herde yourselfe what I sayd.	188	Magnyfycence	1695
Nay, indede, but I sawe howe ye prayed,	188	Magnyfycence	1696
And therof ye shall a larger profe se.	188	Magnyfycence	1700
Syr, God rewarde you as ye have deserved.	188	Magnyfycence	1701
But, and I were as ye, I wolde not set a gnat.	188	Magnyfycence	1704
For go when ye shall, of you shall he mysse.	188	Magnyfycence	1706
Syr, as ye say. Nay, come on with me.	188	Magnyfycence	1707

	Page	Title	Line
I was your good lorde tyll that ye beganne	188	Magnyfycence	1714
Wherfore I wyll that ye be resydent	188	Magnyfycence	1718
Ye, walke he must; it was no better worth.	189	Magnyfycence	1736
It is no wonder, therfore, thoughe ye be wrothe	189	Magnyfycence	1748
Thus must ye stuffe and store your treasure.	189	Magnyfycence	1754
Ye, Mary, somtyme - in a messe of vergesse,	189	Magnyfycence	1756
As gyvynge a thynge that ye never bought.	189	Magnyfycence	1758
To make fayre promyse, what are ye the worse?	189	Magnyfycence	1761
Syr, syth that in me ye have suche devocyon,	190	Magnyfycence	1790
Mary, Cryst graunt ye catche no colde on your fete!	191	Magnyfycence	1803
I make God avowe ye wyll none other men have.	191	Magnyfycence	1827
Cockes bones! Harde ye ever suche another?	192	Magnyfycence	1841
When ye knowe that I knowe, ye wyll not be glad.	192	Magnyfycence	1844
When ye knowe that I knowe, ye wyll not be glad.	192	Magnyfycence	1844
Ye, let be thy japes, and tell me howe	192	Magnyfycence	1846
Alasse, syr, ye are undone with stelyng and robbynge!	192	Magnyfycence	1852
Ye sent us a supervysour for to take hede;	192	Magnyfycence	1853
Take hede of your selfe, for nowe ye have nede.	192	Magnyfycence	1854
Gone? Alasse, ye have undone me!	192	Magnyfycence	1858
Nay. He that ye sent us, Clokyd Colusyon,	192	Magnyfycence	1859
Nay. It was your fondnesse that ye have usyd.	193	Magnyfycence	1866
Wherfore, of adversyte loke ye be ware;	195	Magnyfycence	1936
Yet it proveth eyrnest, ye may se, every day.	195	Magnyfycence	1949
I am raggyd and rent, as ye may se;	195	Magnyfycence	1962
Ye, syr, ye; leve all this rage,	196	Magnyfycence	1988
Ye, syr, ye; leve all this rage,	196	Magnyfycence	1988
Remembre you better, syr. Beware what ye say,	196	Magnyfycence	1995
For drede ye dysplease the hygh deyte.	196	Magnyfycence	1996
Therefore poverte loke pacyently ye take,	196	Magnyfycence	2000
And ye have deserved this punysshment.	196	Magnyfycence	2003
Ye, syr, nowe must ye lerne to lye harde,	197	Magnyfycence	2005
Ye, syr, nowe must ye lerne to lye harde,	197	Magnyfycence	2005
And where that ye were pomped with what that ye wolde,	197	Magnyfycence	2012
And where that ye were pomped with what that ye wolde,	197	Magnyfycence	2012
Nowe must ye suffre bothe hunger and colde.	197	Magnyfycence	2013
With curteyns of sylke, ye were wonte to be drawe; curteyns of sylke] 'courtely sylkes' †Rastell & Treveris 1530B	197	Magnyfycence	2014
Nowe must ye lerne to lye on the strawe.	197	Magnyfycence	2015
Now shal ye be scabbed, scurvy, and lowsy.	197	Magnyfycence	2019
Ye, syr, yesterday wyll not be callyd agayne.	197	Magnyfycence	2031
Ye, mary, is it. Ye, so mote I goo.	198	Magnyfycence	2046
Ye, mary, is it. Ye, so mote I goo.	198	Magnyfycence	2046
With ye, mary, syrs, thus sholde it be:	198	Magnyfycence	2064
Thus totum in toto groweth up, as ye may se,	199	Magnyfycence	2099
Cockes armes, syrs, wyll ye not se	200	Magnyfycence	2109
Ye, for nowe it hath brought the to confusyon;	200	Magnyfycence	2130
As evydently in retchlesse youth ye may se	200	Magnyfycence	2133
Tyll, as ye se many tymes, they shame all theyr kynne.	201	Magnyfycence	2144
With ye, syr, by Jesu, that slayne was with Jewes!	201	Magnyfycence	2167
Ye, but thanke me therof every dele.	201	Magnyfycence	2171
Ye, wylte thou clenly cle[v]e me in the clyfte with thy nose? cleve] 'clene' †Rastell & Treveris C 1530, B	202	Magnyfycence	2176
Ye, wylte thou, hangman? I say, thou cavell!	202	Magnyfycence	2190
Nay, by Saynt Mary, it was ye called me knave.	203	Magnyfycence	2212
Me thynke ye are not gretly acomberyd wyth wyt.	203	Magnyfycence	2215
And ye be a gentylman, ye have knavys condycyons.	203	Magnyfycence	2219
And ye be a gentylman, ye have knavys condycyons.	203	Magnyfycence	2219
Tell me brefly where upon ye began.	203	Magnyfycence	2224
Nay, I know well inough ye are bothe well handyd	203	Magnyfycence	2230
Tushe! These maters that ye move are but soppys in ale;	203	Magnyfycence	2233
For had I not bene, ye bothe had bene hangyd,	203	Magnyfycence	2235
Ye be the thevys, I say, away my goodys dyd cary.	203	Magnyfycence	2239
Magnyfycence I was, whom ye have brought to shame.	204	Magnyfycence	2241
Ye, but trowe you, syrs, that this is he?	204	Magnyfycence	2242
Alasse, alasse, syrs, ye are to blame!	204	Magnyfycence	2245
I was your mayster, though ye thynke it skorne;	204	Magnyfycence	2246
And nowe on me ye gaure and sporne.	204	Magnyfycence	2247
Ye, for thy langage can not the avayle.	204	Magnyfycence	2249
Ye, for requiem eternam groweth forth of his nose.	204	Magnyfycence	2260
Ye, in faythe; or ellys thou arte to great a glotton.	204	Magnyfycence	2266
Ye, and when ye come out of the shoppe,	204	Magnyfycence	2271
Ye, and when ye come out of the shoppe,	204	Magnyfycence	2271
Ye shall be clappyd with a coloppe	204	Magnyfycence	2272
Ye, ryd thy selfe rather than this lyfe for to lede.	205	Magnyfycence	2307
Ye, have done at ones without delay.	206	Magnyfycence	2319
A, blessyd may ye be, syr! What shall you I call?	206	Magnyfycence	2327
For had ye not the soner ben my refuge,	206	Magnyfycence	2333
Undoubted ye had lost yourselfe eternally.	206	Magnyfycence	2335
To thanke God of his sonde; and comforte ye shal fynde.	207	Magnyfycence	2360
And nowe ye have had, syr, a wonderous fall,	207	Magnyfycence	2375
Howe say you, syr? Can ye these wordys grope?	207	Magnyfycence	2377
Ye, syr, now am I armyd with good hope,	207	Magnyfycence	2378
Ye, syr, he is sory for that he hath offendyd.	208	Magnyfycence	2388
Ye, but have ye repentyd you with harte contryte?	208	Magnyfycence	2391
Ye, but have ye repentyd you with harte contryte?	208	Magnyfycence	2391
Ye, holly to good hope I have made my repare.	208	Magnyfycence	2394
Nowe shall ye be renewyd with solace.	208	Magnyfycence	2404
But, syr, by me to rule fyrst ye began.	209	Magnyfycence	2431

	Page	Title	Line
Then ye of foly in tymes past you repent?	209	Magnyfycence	2433
'Then ye repent you of foly in tymes past' †Rastell & Treveris C 1530, B			
Syr, this letter ye sent to me at Pountes was enclosed.	209	Magnyfycence	2439
Who brought you that letter? Wote ye what he hyght?	209	Magnyfycence	2440
This letter ye speke of never dyd I wryte.	209	Magnyfycence	2442
To gyve so hasty credence ye were moche to blame.	209	Magnyfycence	2443
Remembre you, therfore, howe late ye were low.	210	Magnyfycence	2451
Ye, and beware of unhappy abusyon.	210	Magnyfycence	2452
Ye com hether as well as can be thought.	210	Magnyfycence	2459
Ye, syr, with adversyte I have bene vexyd;	210	Magnyfycence	2461
What this man hath sayd, perceyve ye his sentence?	210	Magnyfycence	2465
Ye, syr. From hym my corage shall never flyt.	210	Magnyfycence	2466
And ye shall have more worshyp then ever ye had.	210	Magnyfycence	2474
And ye shall have more worshyp then ever ye had.	210	Magnyfycence	2474
In all your warkys more grace shall ye fynde;	211	Magnyfycence	2485
Nowe semyth us syttynge that ye then resorte	214	Magnyfycence	2566
And ye that have harde thys dysporte and game,	214	Magnyfycence	2571
If that ye wyll /A whyle be styll,	214	El Rummynge	2
Ye shall not bere awaye /Myne ale for nought,	218	El Rummynge	165
myne] 'my' Kynge & Marche 1554, Day 1560, Marshe 1568			
And ye may it broke,	219	El Rummynge	212
It shall make you loke /Yonger than ye be	219	El Rummynge	214
For ye may prove it by me.'	219	El Rummynge	216
Than Elynour sayde, 'Ye calettes,	223	El Rummynge	347
I shall breke your palettes, /Wythout ye now cease!'	223	El Rummynge	349
And ye wyll gyve me a syppet /Of your stale ale,	223	El Rummynge	367
Her legges that ye myght se;	225	El Rummynge	421
ye] 'he' 1521 Fragment			
Ye wote well what we meane.'	229	El Rummynge	579
'Heghe, ha, ha, Parott, ye can lawghe pratylye!'	231	Speke Parott	22
'Peace, Parrot, ye prate as ye were ebrius!'	232	Speke Parott	68
'Peace, Parrot, ye prate as ye were ebrius!'	232	Speke Parott	68
'Fate, fate, fate, ye Irysh water-lag.'	233	Speke Parott	86
Our Grekys ye walow in the washbol Argolycorum;	235	Speke Parott	150
For though ye can tell in Greke what is phormio,	235	Speke Parott	151
Yet ye seke out your Greke in Capricornio;	235	Speke Parott	152
For [ye] scrape out good scrypture, and set in a gall:	235	Speke Parott	153
ye] 'they' †Lant 1545, Kynge & Marche 1554, Day 1560, Marshe 1568			
Ye go about to amende, and ye mare all.	235	Speke Parott	154
Ye go about to amende, and ye mare all.	235	Speke Parott	154
Ye, all thyng mortall shall torne unto nought	236	Speke Parott	214
And remembre amonge how Parrot and ye	236	Speke Parott	221
And also prophytabyll, /Yf ye be agreabyll,	237	Speke Parott	249
In there remembraunce ye may be inrolde.	239	Speke Parott	291
Yet some folys say ye arre furnysshyd with knakkes,	239	Speke Parott	292
And thowe sum dysdayne yow and sey how ye prate,	240	Speke Parott	315
Parott, ye may prate thys undyr protestacion,	240	Speke Parott	336
Thow ye be tauntyd, Parotte, with tonges attayntyd,	240	Speke Parott	343
For trowthe in parabyll ye wantonlye pronounce,	241	Speke Parott	364
For drede ye darre not medyll with suche gere,	242	Speke Parott	394
Or elles ye pynche curtesy, trulye as I trowe,	242	Speke Parott	395
Speke, Parotte, my swete byrde, and ye shall have a date,	243	Speke Parott	416
With, 'Skyre-galyard, prowde palyard, vaunte-parler, ye prate!'	244	Speke Parott	433
And yf ye stande in doute /Who brought this ryme aboute,	248	Collyn Clout	47
Yf ye take well therwith /It hath in it some pyth.	248	Collyn Clout	57
take] 'talke' Kele 1545.1, Marshe 1568			
What trowe ye they say more /Of the bysshoppes lore?	249	Collyn Clout	92
Amende whan ye may,	251	Collyn Clout	189
Men say, ye can nat appare;	251	Collyn Clout	191
For some say ye hunte in parkes	251	Collyn Clout	192
ye] 'they' †Godfray 1531, 'ye' MS Harley 2252; in parkes] 'partrykes' †Godfray 1531			
Howe that ye sell /The grace of the Holy Goost.	251	Collyn Clout	200
Ye pyke no shrympes nor pranes,	252	Collyn Clout	208
Ye wyll neyther beanes ne peason.	252	Collyn Clout	212
But ye loke to be let lose	252	Collyn Clout	213
And howe whan ye gyve orders	252	Collyn Clout	220
And no more ye make	254	Collyn Clout	298
Alas, why do ye nat handle	255	Collyn Clout	332
Some say ye sytte in trones,	255	Collyn Clout	344
Men say ye are tonge-tayde,	255	Collyn Clout	354
That ye gyve shrewed counsell	255	Collyn Clout	358
Ye make monkes to have the colerage	255	Collyn Clout	363
make] 'haue' Kele 1545.1, Marshe 1568, 'make' MS Harley 2252; colerage] 'culerage' Kele 1545.1, 'colerage' Harley 2252			
Ye have so overthwarted,	256	Collyn Clout	371
Ye do them wronge and no ryght	256	Collyn Clout	404
them] not in Marshe 1568			
Howe ye breke the dedes wylles,	257	Collyn Clout	417
Of an abbey ye make a graunge	257	Collyn Clout	419
ye] 'they' Kele 1545.1, 'to' MS Harley 2252			
Ye lyve, they say, in delyte, /Drowned in deliciis,	257	Collyn Clout	441
But swete ypocras ye drynke,	258	Collyn Clout	456
Howebeit, per assimile, /Some men thynke that ye	258	Collyn Clout	460
As ye may dayly se /Howe the lay fee	259	Collyn Clout	495
And eyther ye be to badde,	259	Collyn Clout	502

YE — YE   Page   Title   Line

Entry	Page	Title	Line
And ye shall do the same,	259	Collyn Clout	508
Suche ye may well knowe and ken	260	Collyn Clout	533
Ye are so puffed with pryde,	261	Collyn Clout	593
Ye caste up then your bokes	261	Collyn Clout	596
For then ye wyll be wroken	261	Collyn Clout	598
A knyght a knave ye make.	261	Collyn Clout	601
ye] 'to' Kele 1545.1, Marshe 1568, 'ye' MS Harley 2252			
Ye boost, ye face, ye crake,	261	Collyn Clout	602
Ye boost, ye face, ye crake,	261	Collyn Clout	602
Ye boost, ye face, ye crake,	261	Collyn Clout	602
And yf ye may have layser,	261	Collyn Clout	605
ye] 'you' Kele 1545.1, Marshe 1568, 'ye' MS Harley 2252			
Ye wyll brynge all to nought,	261	Collyn Clout	606
Men say howe ye appalle	262	Collyn Clout	611
Ye are the lesse to blame,	262	Collyn Clout	614
Therfore ye kepe them base,	262	Collyn Clout	624
Shall I tell you more? Ye, shall.	262	Collyn Clout	635
But the communalte ye call	262	Collyn Clout	637
Howe [ye] were wonte to drynke	262	Collyn Clout	649
ye] 'thy' †Godfray 1531, 'they' Kele 1545.1, Marshe 1568, MS Harley 2252			
Ye coude none other gette	263	Collyn Clout	654
coude] 'wolde' Kele 1545.1, Marshe 1568, 'cowde' MS Harley 2252			
Ye growe nowe out of kynde.	263	Collyn Clout	661
Many one ye have untwynde	263	Collyn Clout	662
ye have untwynde] 'have but wynde' †Godfray 1531, Kele 1545.1, Marshe 1568			
That though ye rounde your heere	263	Collyn Clout	673
That ye can nat espye	263	Collyn Clout	685
Why syt ye prelates styll	263	Collyn Clout	688
Ye bysshoppes of estates	263	Collyn Clout	690
But yf ye wolde take payne	265	Collyn Clout	763
But now my mynde ye understande,	268	Collyn Clout	887
That ye kepe them so under;	271	Collyn Clout	1007
ye] 'we' Kele 1545.1, 'ye' MS Harley 2252			
For ye play so at the chesse,	271	Collyn Clout	1009
Ye knowe better than I.	273	Collyn Clout	1064
But olde servauntes ye chase	273	Collyn Clout	1077
Make ye no murmuracyon	273	Collyn Clout	1079
Why than /Wreke ye your anger on me?	273	Collyn Clout	1091
Ye ought to be ashamed	274	Collyn Clout	1113
Ye prechers shall be yawde:	276	Collyn Clout	1204
which hath to name Why Come Ye Nat to Courte?	278	Why Come Ye	I
And yf ye thynke this shall	279	Why Come Ye	24
Why come ye nat to court?	279	Why Come Ye	31
Wote ye whyther they went?	282	Why Come Ye	146
He sayth, 'How saye ye, my lordes?	283	Why Come Ye	195
Wyll ye bere no coles?'	285	Why Come Ye	243
What here ye of Lancashyre?	285	Why Come Ye	247
What here ye of Chesshyre?	285	Why Come Ye	250
What here ye of the Scottes?	285	Why Come Ye	262
What here ye of the lorde Dakers?	285	Why Come Ye	272
What here ye of the lord Rose?	286	Why Come Ye	286
What say ye of the Scottysh kynge?	287	Why Come Ye	346
What here ye of Burgonyons	288	Why Come Ye	370
What here ye of Mutrell?	288	Why Come Ye	377
Yet what here ye tell	288	Why Come Ye	379
But speke ye no more of that,	288	Why Come Ye	382
Why come ye nat to court?	289	Why Come Ye	401
But have ye nat harde this,	292	Why Come Ye	532
'Ye horsons, ye vassayles,	294	Why Come Ye	602
'Ye horsons, ye vassayles,	294	Why Come Ye	602
Ye knaves, ye churles sonnys,	294	Why Come Ye	603
Ye knaves, ye churles sonnys,	294	Why Come Ye	603
Ye rebads nat worth two plummis!	294	Why Come Ye	604
Ye raynbetyn beggers rejagged,	294	Why Come Ye	605
Ye recrayed ruffyns all ragged!'	294	Why Come Ye	606
Syr, ye must tary a stounde,	294	Why Come Ye	626
And syr, ye must daunce attendaunce,	294	Why Come Ye	628
Rede ye the story oute,	296	Why Come Ye	694
And ye shall fynde surely	296	Why Come Ye	695
Whan ye fall to redynge	300	Why Come Ye	830
Amen, amen, say ye	300	Why Come Ye	837
Ye must weare bukram,	302	Why Come Ye	918
Now mayster doctor, howe say ye,	309	Why Come Ye2	1
What though ye be namelesse,	309	Why Come Ye2	3
Ye shall nat escape blamelesse,	309	Why Come Ye2	4
escape] 'be' MS Rawlinson C. 813			
Yourselfe madly ye overse!	309	Why Come Ye2	7
Ye put to blame ye wot nere whom.	310	Why Come Ye2	17
nere] 'nott' MS Rawlinson C. 813			
Ye put to blame ye wot nere whom.	310	Why Come Ye2	17
nere] 'nott' MS Rawlinson C. 813			
Ye may weare a cockes come,	310	Why Come Ye2	18
Holde ye your tong, ye can no goode.	310	Why Come Ye2	20
ye] (1st) not in MS Rawlinson C. 813			

YE—YE

	Page	Title	Line
Holde ye your tong, ye can no goode.	310	Why Come Ye2	20
ye] (1st) not in MS Rawlinson C. 813			
That ye can nat byde thereby.	310	Why Come Ye2	28
Complayne or do what ye wyll,	310	Why Come Ye2	31
A daucock ye be, and so shal be styll!	310	Why Come Ye2	34
Of auncient poetis, ye wote full wele, hath bene	314	Garlande	65
It is sittynge that ye must hym correct.'	314	Garlande	77
Whereto made ye me hym to avaunce	315	Garlande	115
And was Eschines rebukid as ye say?	316	Garlande	135
Wherfore then rasid ye not away	316	Garlande	137
Few shall ye fynde or none that wyll do so.'	317	Garlande	168
'A thanke to have, ye have well deservyd,	317	Garlande	169
But a grete parte yet ye have reservyd	317	Garlande	171
But...yet] 'Bot yit a grete parte' MS Cotton Vitellius E.x			
Or els ye demeane you inordinatly;	317	Garlande	173
For if ye laude hym whome honour hath opprest,	317	Garlande	174
But whome that ye favoure, I se well, hath a name,	317	Garlande	176
And whome ye love not ye wyll put to shame.	317	Garlande	178
And whome ye love not ye wyll put to shame.	317	Garlande	178
Ye counterway not evynly your balaunce;	317	Garlande	179
As wele foly as wysdome oft ye do avaunce,	317	Garlande	180
ye do] 'tyme ye' MS Cotton Vitellius E.x			
But lytell or nothynge ye shall here tell	317	Garlande	197
ye shall] 'shall ye' MS Cotton Vitellius E.x			
And ye shall well fynde he is a very fole;	318	Garlande	207
well fynde] 'fynde wele' MS Cotton Vitellius E.x			
'To make repugnaunce agayne that ye have sayde,	318	Garlande	211
Or elles, ye know well, I can do no lesse	318	Garlande	226
'Make rowme,' sayd another, 'ye prese all to sore,'	319	Garlande	256
In maner and forme as ye shall after here.	323	Garlande	399
So have ye done, that meretoryously	323	Garlande	401
Ye have deservyd to have an enplement	323	Garlande	402
Bycause that ye encrese and amplyfy	323	Garlande	404
ye] not in †Fakes 1523			
But what sholde I say? Ye wote what I entende,	324	Garlande	426
'So have ye me far passynge my meretis extollyd,	324	Garlande	435
Bownte, and so gloryously ye have enrollyd	324	Garlande	437
Unto me sayd, 'Lo, syr, now ye may se	326	Garlande	518
How ye ar welcome to this court of aray.	327	Garlande	539
Ye fyrste aryvyd; whan broken was your mast	327	Garlande	542
Ye] 'The' †Fakes 1523			
'Theis yatis,' she sayd, 'which that ye beholde,	328	Garlande	579
'What yate call ye this?' And she sayd, 'Anglea'.	328	Garlande	588
yate] 'gate' Marshe 1568			
But wele may ye thynk I was no thyng prowde	330	Garlande	648
'How say ye? Is this after your appetite?	331	Garlande	707
Contynuall comfort here ye may fynde,	332	Garlande	710
'Questionles no dowte of that ye say;	332	Garlande	714
But, goodly maystres, one thynge ye me tell.'	332	Garlande	720
'Now what ye mene, I trow I conject.	332	Garlande	735
Gog gyve you good yere, ye make me to smyle.	332	Garlande	736
Of your questyon ye make all this whyle	333	Garlande	738
His name for to know if that ye lyst,	333	Garlande	752
Beware of hym, I warne you; for and ye wist	333	Garlande	754
and] 'if' Marshe 1568			
Ye wolde not dele with hym, thowgh that ye myght,	333	Garlande	756
though] 'thought' Marshe 1568, 'thowth' MS Cotton Vit.E.x			
Ye wolde not dele with hym, thowgh that ye myght,	333	Garlande	756
though] 'thought' Marshe 1568, 'thowth' MS Cotton Vit.E.x			
To your remembraunce wherfore ye must call	335	Garlande	812
Sith ye must nedis afforce it by pretence	335	Garlande	817
Whome ye represent and exemplify,	336	Garlande	854
Ye be, as I devyne,	338	Garlande	911
Phedra ye may /Wele represent;	338	Garlande	940
And so observe /That ye ne swarve	339	Garlande	965
Erst that ye can fynde	341	Garlande	1032
that] 'than' MS Cotton Vitellius E.x			
Though ye wer hard hertyd,	341	Garlande	1038
Yet nowe doutles ye geve me cause	341	Garlande	1041
I wyll that ye shall be /In all benyngnyte	341	Garlande	1046
For nowe dowtles ye geve me cause	342	Garlande	1049
Wherfore doutles ye geve me cause	342	Garlande	1057
Els saye ye myght	342	Garlande	1063
In very dede /How ye excede.	343	Garlande	1085
I dare wele saye that ye and I be sought.	343	Garlande	1089
Make no delay, for now ye must be brought	343	Garlande	1090
Where ye must brevely answere to your name.'	343	Garlande	1092
'My frende, sith ye ar before us here present	344	Garlande	1121
Of that shalbe resonde you ye must be content;	344	Garlande	1123
you] not in Marshe 1568			
That ye have now by the preemynence	344	Garlande	1125
by the] 'thorow' MS Cotton Vitellius E.x			
We wyll understande how ye have it deservyd.'	344	Garlande	1127
Of what charge so ever ye lay ageinst me;	344	Garlande	1138
For of my bokis parte ye shall se,	344	Garlande	1139
'Yowre boke of remembrauns we will now that ye rede;	345	Garlande	1149
boke] 'bokes' †Fakes 1523			
Let se now for hym how ye can expounde;	345	Garlande	1153

	Page	Title	Line
For in owr courte, ye wote wele, his name can not ryse	345	Garlande	1154
Item to Lerne You to Dye When ye Wyll; to] 'do' †Fakes 1523	345	Garlande	1176
That folowe as ye may se:	350	Garlande	1372
Thynke what ye wyll /Of this wanton byll;	353	Garlande	1453
Welcome shall ye /To sum men be;	355	Garlande	1540
Ye shall have nede /You for to spede Ye] 'You' Marshe 1568	355	Garlande	1554
Ageyne envy, /And obloquy. /And wote ye why?	355	Garlande	1560
Els ye shall pray /Them that ye may	356	Garlande	1583
Els ye shall pray /Them that ye may	356	Garlande	1584
Dunbar, Dunde, /Ye shall trowe me,	359	Albany	25
False Scottes are ye.	359	Albany	26
Ye had evill spede.	359	Albany	32
Lyke cankerd curres /Ye loste your spurres;	360	Albany	34
For in that fraye /Ye ranne awaye	360	Albany	36
Ye Duke so doutty, /So sterne, so stoutty,	361	Albany	77
Howe ye pretende /For to defende	361	Albany	88
But ye meane a thyng	361	Albany	91
And ye coude bryng /The matter about	361	Albany	92
Thus ye have compast	361	Albany	102
That knowen ye shall be	361	Albany	114
O ye wretched Scottes, /Ye puaunt pyspottes,	362	Albany	119
O ye wretched Scottes, /Ye puaunt pyspottes,	362	Albany	120
Ye may be assured /Your falshod discured	362	Albany	127
For ye be false echone,	362	Albany	132
Ye Scottes all the rable,	363	Albany	177
Ye shall never be hable,	363	Albany	178
What though ye stampe and stare?	363	Albany	180
With us, whan ever ye mell	363	Albany	182
Whan ye cankerd knaves	363	Albany	184
For ye dare nat abyde.	363	Albany	187
Ye rage and ye rave, /And your worshyp deprave:	363	Albany	190
Ye rage and ye rave, /And your worshyp deprave:	363	Albany	190
Yet somwhat ye be lyke	364	Albany	197
But ye and your hoost,	364	Albany	206
Howe ye wyll beres bynde	364	Albany	209
Yet ye dare do nothynge	364	Albany	211
What an army were ye?	364	Albany	216
Ye have in feates of warre.	364	Albany	225
Ye make nought but ye marre.	364	Albany	226
Ye make nought but ye marre.	364	Albany	226
Ye are a fals entrusar, /And a fals abusar,	364	Albany	227
Sir Dunkan, ye dared.	365	Albany	271
And thus ye prepared	365	Albany	272
Ye decte you to dwell;	366	Albany	280
If that ye had tane	366	Albany	283
What have ye, villayn, forged, /And virulently dysgorged	367	Albany	320
As though ye wolde parbrake /Your avauns to make,	367	Albany	322
Howe ye wyll undertake	367	Albany	326
Suche lewde langage ye spake.	367	Albany	329
Be well ware what ye say.	367	Albany	331
Ye saye that he and ye –	367	Albany	332
Ye saye that he and ye –	367	Albany	332
Whyche he and ye? Let se;	367	Albany	333
Ye meane Fraunces, French kyng,	367	Albany	334
Full soone ye should miscary,	367	Albany	342
For ye durst nat tarry	367	Albany	343
Ye durst byde on the grounde.	367	Albany	347
Ye wolde ryn away rounde	367	Albany	348
Ye wolde defoyle the place	367	Albany	353
If ye wele can regarde	368	Albany	360
Are ye nat frantyke madde, /And wretchedly bestadde,	368	Albany	363
To flye ye shalbe fayne	368	Albany	371
Ye muse somwhat to far;	368	Albany	377
All out of joynt ye jar.	368	Albany	378
Wene ye, daucockes, to drive	368	Albany	380
What losels than are ye	370	Albany	459
Lyke cowardes as ye be	370	Albany	460
Than ye be a knappishe sorte	370	Albany	475
That ye shall have no grace	371	Albany	504
Ye shall have shame and sorowe.	371	Albany	507
How that ye are lykely	371	Albany	510
I wondre howe ye dare	375	Replycacion	36
Ye heretykes recrayed, /Wotte ye what ye sayed	375	Replycacion	45
Ye heretykes recrayed, /Wotte ye what ye sayed	375	Replycacion	46
Ye heretykes recrayed, /Wotte ye what ye sayed	375	Replycacion	46
With baudrie at her ye brayed;	376	Replycacion	48
Ye were nothyng discrete;	376	Replycacion	52
Ye were in a dronken hete.	376	Replycacion	53
Ye count your selfe wele lettred:	376	Replycacion	55
For shamefully ye have wrought,	376	Replycacion	57
Bycause ye her mysnamed,	376	Replycacion	59
For ye were worldly shamed, /At Poules Crosse openly,	376	Replycacion	62
Ye were fayne to beare fagottes;	376	Replycacion	66
Ye suffred suche correction.	376	Replycacion	68
Ye are brought to, 'Lo, Lo, Lo!	376	Replycacion	72
Helas, ye wreches, ye may be wo!	376	Replycacion	77

	Page	Title	Line
Helas, ye wreches, ye may be wo!	376	Replycacion	77
Ye may syng weleaway	376	Replycacion	78
Whan ye were bredde and borne,	376	Replycacion	80
And whan ye were preestes shorne,	376	Replycacion	81
Fayne ye were to reny	377	Replycacion	87
Confessyng howe ye dyde lye /In prechyng shamefully.	377	Replycacion	90
Your selfe thus ye discured	377	Replycacion	92
Ye are unhappely ured.	377	Replycacion	95
If ye to remembrance call	377	Replycacion	98
Ye coude nat corde tenus, /Nor answere verbo tenus,	377	Replycacion	104
And yet ye supposed /Respondere ad quantum,	377	Replycacion	109
But ye were confuse tantum,	377	Replycacion	111
For there ye myst you[r] quosshons.	377	Replycacion	113
your] 'you' †Pynson 1528			
And your tonges cropped, /Whan ye logyke chopped,	377	Replycacion	118
Ye argued argumentes, /As it were upon the elenkes,	377	Replycacion	125
And ye wolde appere wyse	378	Replycacion	129
But ye were folysshe nyse.	378	Replycacion	130
Ye dyde provoke and tyse,	378	Replycacion	132
Ye may soone make construction	378	Replycacion	154
Ye soored over hye /In the ierarchy /Of Jovenyans heresy,	378	Replycacion	161
Ye strynged so Luthers lute	379	Replycacion	167
That ye dawns all in a sute	379	Replycacion	168
Ye shayle inter enigmata	379	Replycacion	172
Howe ye are this day,	379	Replycacion	177
And so ye wyll be styll,	379	Replycacion	179
As ye were before.	379	Replycacion	180
Howe ye have small contrycion	379	Replycacion	183
Of that ye have myswrought;	379	Replycacion	184
And thought, if ye had right,	379	Replycacion	200
Ye shulde take further payne /To resorte agayne	379	Replycacion	201
To places where ye have preched,	379	Replycacion	203
Howe falsely ye had surmysed,	380	Replycacion	209
Ye pyke out many thystels,	380	Replycacion	220
Ye cobble and ye clout /Holy scripture so about,	380	Replycacion	222
Ye cobble and ye clout /Holy scripture so about,	380	Replycacion	222
Thus all thyng ye disorder	380	Replycacion	227
Ye had never lerned letter,	380	Replycacion	230
Ye are but lydder logici, /But moche worse isagogici,	380	Replycacion	234
For ye have enduced a secte	380	Replycacion	236
Wherfore ye are well checte,	380	Replycacion	238
Bycause ye have eaten a flye,	380	Replycacion	244
Come forthe, ye pope holy, /Full of melancoly!	381	Replycacion	247
I saye, ye braynlesse beestes,	381	Replycacion	263
I saye, ye devyllysshe pages	381	Replycacion	271
Count ye your selfe good clerkes,	381	Replycacion	273
Ye have reed them, I suppose,	381	Replycacion	276
To this ye nedes must agre.	381	Replycacion	284
But, I trowe, your selfe ye overse	381	Replycacion	285
If ye have reed de hyperdulia,	382	Replycacion	287
Than ye know what betokeneth dulia:	382	Replycacion	288
Than shall ye fynde it fyrme and stable,	382	Replycacion	289
Wherfore make ye no mo restrayntes,	382	Replycacion	292
Or els doutlesse ye shalbe blased,	382	Replycacion	294
If further busynesse that ye make.	382	Replycacion	296
Why fall ye at debate /With Skelton laureate,	382	Replycacion	300
Ye saye that poetry /Maye nat flye so hye	382	Replycacion	306
Where worde for worde ye may	383	Replycacion	327
Why have ye than disdayne /At poetes, and complayne	384	Replycacion	351
Ye do moche great outrage,	384	Replycacion	354
For if ye sadly loke,	384	Replycacion	359
With me ye must consent	384	Replycacion	362
For be ye wele assured,	385	Replycacion	406

YEA

	Page	Title	Line
Ye be to her, yea, worth a thousande pounde.	50	Bowge	157

YEDE

Or that he thens yede,	63	Hauke	55

YEEST

Where as the yeest is,	219	El Rummynge	199

YELL

Lyke houndes of hell, /They crye and they yell	251	Collyn Clout	199

YELLED

She yelled lyke a calfe!	227	El Rummynge	500

YELLYNGE

Beware of a quenes yellynge!	271	Collyn Clout	987

YER

Why holde ye on yer cap, syr, then? Yor pardone ys expyryd.	123	Garnesche2	9

YERE

For though ye lyve a c. yere, ye shal dy a daw.	71	Hauke	334
This hunderd yere scantly	111	Lawde	18
What! Fleyest thou his skynne every yere?	169	Magnyfycence	1058
It had ben hers, I wene, /More then fourty yere;	216	El Rummynge	58
So bygge a bulke of brow-auntleres cabagyd that yere;	245	Speke Parott	488
Parchaunce halfe a yere;	295	Why Come Ye	637
And within this xvi yere	295	Why Come Ye	641
Lorde of the yere in his orbicular,	312	Garlande	4
Gog gyve you good yere, ye make me to smyle.	332	Garlande	736
Dug, dug, /Jug, jug, /Good yere and good luk,	340	Garlande	1002

YERES —YET   Page   Title   Line

	Page	Title	Line
Makynge his almanak for the new yere;	354	Garlande	1516
Good luk this new yere, the olde yere is past.	354	Garlande	1518
Good luk this new yere, the olde yere is past.	354	Garlande	1518

YERES

Yeres two or thre,	219	El Rummynge	215

YERIS

For now the yeris of grace	111	Lawde	40

YERYS

Than thou can in yerys seven.	170	Magnyfycence	1078

YERNE

The howndes began to yerne and to quest; and dred	351	Garlande	1409

YERTHLY

Nothynge yerthly to me more desyrous	44	Balettys3	43

YES

Yes, syr, with ryght good chere.	143	Magnyfycence	112
Yes, questyonlesse, in myne opynyon;	144	Magnyfycence	126
Yes, yes, syr. He and I have met.	154	Magnyfycence	498
Yes, yes, syr. He and I have met.	154	Magnyfycence	498
Say trouth? Yes, yes, by lakyn, I shall the warent,	154	Magnyfycence	506
Say trouth? Yes, yes, by lakyn, I shall the warent,	154	Magnyfycence	506
Yes, syr, I gyve God avowe,	155	Magnyfycence	529
Knowe hym, syr, quod he. Yes, by Saynt Sym!	156	Magnyfycence	585
Nede? Yes, Mary. I say not nay.	163	Magnyfycence	807
Yes, yes. He fell with me also at debate.	166	Magnyfycence	944
Yes, yes. He fell with me also at debate.	166	Magnyfycence	944
Yes, in faythe, I thanke God I may here.	169	Magnyfycence	1059
Yes, yes! I am yet as full of game	172	Magnyfycence	1140
Yes, yes! I am yet as full of game	172	Magnyfycence	1140
No? Yes, in faythe; I can versyfy.	172	Magnyfycence	1147
Yes, by my faythe, good Syr Johnn.	173	Magnyfycence	1186
Yes, yet he wyll make the ete a gnat.	173	Magnyfycence	1192
Yes, yet] 'Yet yes' †Rastell & Treveris C 1530, B			
Yes, yes, by my trouth. I holde the a grote	173	Magnyfycence	1193
Yes, yes, by my trouth. I holde the a grote	173	Magnyfycence	1193
With, yes, by the rode of Wodstocke Parke.	174	Magnyfycence	1209
Yes. I shall tell you or I go	175	Magnyfycence	1263
Yes, perde, man, whether that ye ryde or go.	176	Magnyfycence	1307
Yes, syr, so good man in you I se,	182	Magnyfycence	1522
Yes. With his hande I made hym to subscrybe	187	Magnyfycence	1666
What? Yes, by the rode, syr. It was I all this whyle	193	Magnyfycence	1870
Some say 'yes', and some	283	Why Come Ye	198

YESTERDAY

Why, sayst thou that I was here yesterday?	170	Magnyfycence	1093
Ye, syr, yesterday wyll not be callyd agayne.	197	Magnyfycence	2031

YESTERDAYE

To see Johan Dawes, that came but yesterdaye,	54	Bowge	301
As thou arte, one that cam but yesterdaye,	55	Bowge	328

YESTERNYGHT

'Remembrest thou what thou sayd yesternyght?	55	Bowge	323

YET

Yet shamfully thei slew hym; that sham most them befall.	30	Dol Dethe	49
Yet whils he stode he gave them woundes wyde.	32	Dol Dethe	101
Yet] 'Ye' Marshe 1568			
His corage manly, yet ther he shed his bloode.	32	Dol Dethe	103
Yet sumwhat wright supprisid with hartly lust,	33	Dol Dethe	145
hartly] 'herty' Marshe 1568			
O yonge lyon, bot tender yet of age,	33	Dol Dethe	162
Yet, for his love that all hath wrought,	36	Man Margery	25
In pevyshnes yet they snapper and fall,	36	Coystrowne1	4
they] 'the' †Rastell 1527			
When he is well, yet can he not rest.	36	Coystrowne1	7
Jak wold jet and yet Jyll sayd nay;	37	Coystrowne1	43
Yet bere ye not to bold to braule ne to bark	38	Coystrowne1	60
For all your 'Draffe' yet and your 'Dreggys',	40	Coystrowne4	6
Yet is youre tong an adders tayle,	41	Coystrowne4	16
Yet so it is that a rumer begynnyth for to ryse	42	Balettys2	12
Yet shall she never oute of remembraunce,	45	Balettys3	47
Ware yet, I rede you, of Fortunes double cast,	45	Balettys4	3
Yet, and God wolde, I wold my payne were easyd!	45	Balettys5	12
Yet have I knowen suche er this;	46	Bowge	25
Yet I avyse you to speke, for ony drede:	48	Bowge	90
And yet unneth I can have my lyvynge;	53	Bowge	275
Yet at the knee they were broken, I wene.	56	Bowge	357
Yet on my backe I bere suche lewde delynge.	59	Bowge	457
Yet wyll I saye some wordes for your sake	59	Bowge	474
But yet oftyme suche dremes be founde trewe.	61	Bowge	538
Yet wyth a prety gyn /I fortuned to come in,	64	Hauke	93
Neither yet Dyoclesyan, /Nor yet Domysyan;	67	Hauke	192
Neither yet Dyoclesyan, /Nor yet Domysyan;	67	Hauke	193
Nother crokyd Cacus, /Nor yet dronken Bacus;	67	Hauke	195
Nother] 'Nor yet' Kynge & Marche 1554, Day 1560, Marshe 1568			
Nor yet Egeas, /Nor yet Syr Pherumbras,	67	Hauke	204
Nor yet Egeas, /Nor yet Syr Pherumbras,	67	Hauke	205
Nor yet Tarquinius,	67	Hauke	208
Yet the Sowden, nor the Turke,	67	Hauke	216
Apostata Julianus /Nor yet Nestorianus,	70	Hauke	298
Wherfore the bordes yet cry	78	Phy Sparrow	248
bordes] 'byrdes' Wyght 1553, Kitson 1560.6, Marshe 1568			

YET —YET	Page	Title	Line
I wolde have yet a nest	78	Phy Sparrow	263
have yet] 'yet have' Wyght 1553, Kitson 1560.6, Marshe 1568			
Yet at a brayde /He hath well assayde	84	Phy Sparrow	485
Nor yet by Haly;	84	Phy Sparrow	505
And yet he croweth dayly	84	Phy Sparrow	506
And yet there is none /But one alone;	84	Phy Sparrow	516
Yet one thynge is behynde,	86	Phy Sparrow	603
That never yet asayde /Of Elyconys well,	87	Phy Sparrow	609
Yet there was a thyng	89	Phy Sparrow	699
Yet for a speciall laud	89	Phy Sparrow	720
Yet long tyme she ne knew	89	Phy Sparrow	727
Yet I am nothyng sped,	90	Phy Sparrow	754
My style as yet direct	91	Phy Sparrow	772
Yet wryteth he in his kynd,	91	Phy Sparrow	808
Yet some men fynde a faute,	92	Phy Sparrow	811
Yet as a woman may,	92	Phy Sparrow	820
But yet certayne /I wyll be playne,	95	Phy Sparrow	966
Be] 'me' †Kele 1545.2			
And yet there was no vyce,	100	Phy Sparrow	1133
Nor yet no vyllany, /But only fantasy;	100	Phy Sparrow	1134
Yet though I wryte not with ynke,	101	Phy Sparrow	1198
Yet, where so ever they ly	106	Epitaphe	1
Yet is she fayne, /Voyde of disdayn,	112	Calliope	17
Your harrold in armes not yet halfe expert.	118	Ag Scottes	98
Ye thought ye dyd yet valyauntly;	118	Ag Scottes	99
But sey me yet, Syr Satropas, what auctoryte ye have	122	Garnesche1	13
Yet your contenons oncomly, yor face ys nat fayer.	122	Garnesche1	18
But sey me yet, Syr Satrapas, wat auctoryte ye have	122	Garnesche1	20
But sey me yet, Syr Satrapas, what auctoryte ye have	122	Garnesche1	27
But sey me yet, Syr Satrapas, what auctoryte ye have	122	Garnesche1	34
Thow ye prate lyke prowde Pylate, beware yet of chek mate.	123	Garnesche2	7
Ye ryme yet owte of reson;	127	Garnesche3	128
The prowdyst knave yet of us tewyne	130	Garnesche5	21
Yet jentylnes in the ys thred-bare worne.	131	Garnesche5	70
Yet ther may falle soche caswelte	132	Garnesche5	121
Yet somwhat to say I dare well be bolde,	137	Ven Tongues	10
Yet to lie upon me they can not prevayle.	138	Ven Tongues	31
But yet I may say safely, so many wel lettred,	138	Ven Tongues	38
Yet lyberte hath ben lockyd up and kept in the mew.	141	Magnyfycence	35
Then thus to you - Nay, suffer me yet ferther to say,	142	Magnyfycence	48
Yet suffer me to say the surplus of my sawe.	142	Magnyfycence	71
Yet in this man you must set your delyght.	145	Magnyfycence	167
Hem, syr, yet beware of 'Had I wyste!'	146	Magnyfycence	211
Yet measure hath ben so longe from us absent,	146	Magnyfycence	221
Yet amonge noble men I was brought up and bred,	147	Magnyfycence	261
And that I sayd ones yet I say agayne:	147	Magnyfycence	266
Yet we wyll therin take good delyberacyon.	148	Magnyfycence	275
Yet mesure is a mery mene.	151	Magnyfycence	380
Yet counterfet chafer is but evyll corne.	153	Magnyfycence	450
Yet have we pycked out a rome for the.	154	Magnyfycence	508
By God, yet it muste begynne moche of the.	154	Magnyfycence	514
Yet Fansy had ben dysc[r]yved.	155	Magnyfycence	535
dyscryved] 'dysceyved' †Rastell & Treveris C 1530, B			
And yet, in fayth, man, we lacked the	155	Magnyfycence	538
By Mesure mastered yet is he.	155	Magnyfycence	541
For all these japes yet that [y]e make -	156	Magnyfycence	558
ye] 'we' †Rastell & Treveris C 1530, B			
Yet where we wonne, nowe there wonneth he.	157	Magnyfycence	624
Pease! I have not yet sayd what I wyll.	158	Magnyfycence	648
In faythe, yet am I occupyed with the best;	160	Magnyfycence	705
And yet, I trowe, some of you be better sped than I	160	Magnyfycence	722
Thy slyppers they swap it, yet thou fotys it lyke a swanne.	161	Magnyfycence	765
And yet in dede	165	Magnyfycence	892
No, Mary; not yet.	166	Magnyfycence	934
I have not kept her yet thre wokys,	168	Magnyfycence	1002
Yet I solde his skynne to Mackemurre,	169	Magnyfycence	1056
Yet for my fansy sake, I say,	171	Magnyfycence	1100
By the masse, yet art thou more fole than I.	171	Magnyfycence	1111
Yet gyve me thy dogge, and I am content;	171	Magnyfycence	1112
Yes, yes! I am yet as full of game	172	Magnyfycence	1140
What! Canest thou all this Latyn yet,	172	Magnyfycence	1143
But yet thou shalt holde me a fole styll.	173	Magnyfycence	1184
Yes, yet he wyll make the ete a gnat.	173	Magnyfycence	1192
Yes, yet] 'Yet yes' †Rastell & Treveris C 1530, B			
Yet for his name we must fynde a [slyght].	176	Magnyfycence	1308
slyght] shyfte †Rastell & Treveris C 1530, B			
Yet I wolde that ye had gone rather;	176	Magnyfycence	1313
Yet convey it craftely, and hardely spare not for me' -	177	Magnyfycence	1352
Yet Lyberte without rule is not worth a strawe.	178	Magnyfycence	1378
It is good yet that lyberte be ruled by reason.	178	Magnyfycence	1387
Yet it is good to beware of 'had I wyst'.	179	Magnyfycence	1395
Yet it is good wysdome to worke wysely by welth.	179	Magnyfycence	1401
Syr, yet without sapyence your substaunce may be smal;	179	Magnyfycence	1407
And wayte upon me. And yet for a memory,	180	Magnyfycence	1447
Nor yet [C]ypyo, that noble Cartage wanne,	182	Magnyfycence	1512
Cypyo] 'Typyo' †Rastell & Treveris C 1530, B			
I wolde yet shewe you further of my consayte.	185	Magnyfycence	1591
Yet I am not harte seke, but that me lyst.	185	Magnyfycence	1621

YET — YET

	Page	Title	Line
Yet, syr, reserved your better advysement,	187	Magnyfycence	1661
But yet, lo, I wolde, or that he wente,	187	Magnyfycence	1673
By Magnyfycence nor yet none of his;	188	Magnyfycence	1705
Yet ones agayne I shall fall on my kne	188	Magnyfycence	1708
By the good Lorde, yet your temples bete.	189	Magnyfycence	1732
Yet somtyme, parde, I must use largesse.	189	Magnyfycence	1755
Yet sometyme I stryke where is none offence,	194	Magnyfycence	1916
Yet it proveth eyrnest, ye may se, every day.	195	Magnyfycence	1949
But yet, syr, nowe in this case	197	Magnyfycence	2032
Yet many had lever hangyd to be	198	Magnyfycence	2040
Yet were they better to begge, a great dele;	198	Magnyfycence	2043
But yet, syrs, hardely one thynge lerne of me:	199	Magnyfycence	2087
A, shall we have more of this maters yet?	203	Magnyfycence	2214
Thou sawe never yet but I dyd my parte,	203	Magnyfycence	2228
I am the better yet in a bowget. And I the better in a male.	203	Magnyfycence	2232
Yet let us se this matter thorowly ingrosed.	209	Magnyfycence	2438
Yet of magnyfycence oft made is the mast:	213	Magnyfycence	2563
And yet she wyll jet, /Lyke a joyly fet	215	El Rummynge	51
And yet I dare saye /She thynketh her selfe gaye	216	El Rummynge	64
And yet she brought her fees,	225	El Rummynge	428
But yet, for all that,	226	El Rummynge	490
Yet, or she went, she dranke,	228	El Rummynge	542
Yet ye seke out your Greke in Capricornio;	235	Speke Parott	152
And yet he wolde be rekenyd pro Ariopagita;	235	Speke Parott	156
I pray the, Besse, unfayned, /Yet com agayne to me!	238	Speke Parott	256
Yet some folys say ye arre furnysshyd with knakkes,	239	Speke Parott	292
Yet your problemes ar preignaunte and with loyalte acquayntyd.	240	Speke Parott	344
Langagys divers; yet undyr that dothe reste	241	Speke Parott	365
Yet, aftyr the sagacite of a popagay,	243	Speke Parott	419
Ryn God, rynne Devyll! Yet the date of Owur Lord	244	Speke Parott	444
Nowe, Parott, my swete byrde, speke owte yet ons agayn,	244	Speke Parott	447
And yet that is a pleasure.	250	Collyn Clout	146
Yet take they cure of soules,	252	Collyn Clout	233
cure] 'cures' Kele 1545.1, Marshe 1568			
And yet he wyll nat drede	253	Collyn Clout	278
Yet thus with yll hayles	256	Collyn Clout	400
Yet swete meate hath soure sauce,	258	Collyn Clout	448
Yet over all that,	263	Collyn Clout	671
And yet a noble clerke -	264	Collyn Clout	727
And yet the frere doted!	265	Collyn Clout	757
And yet he wyll melle	267	Collyn Clout	820
Yet softe and fayre for swellynge,	271	Collyn Clout	986
Yet may he mysse the quysshon!	271	Collyn Clout	996
Yet they mervayle so moche lesse,	271	Collyn Clout	1008
But yet they wyll occupye the same.	275	Collyn Clout	1144
Yet the good Erle of Surray,	282	Why Come Ye	153
But yet they over-shote us	283	Why Come Ye	169
Yet what here ye tell	288	Why Come Ye	379
Ones yet agayne /Of you I wolde frayne	289	Why Come Ye	399
Now yet all this myght be	290	Why Come Ye	446
Or yet of trivials;	292	Why Come Ye	515
Yet proudly he dare pretende	292	Why Come Ye	530
Yet with lewde condicyons cotyd	293	Why Come Ye	572
cotyd] 'noted' Kitson 1560.7, Marshe 1568			
To speke with you as yet.'	295	Why Come Ye	632
And yet never the nere!	295	Why Come Ye	638
And yet, for all that,	296	Why Come Ye	680
Lo, yet for all that	297	Why Come Ye	742
Yet it is a wyly mouse	298	Why Come Ye	756
Yet sayst thou, per case	301	Why Come Ye	874
And yet he payde before	302	Why Come Ye	946
And yet he is ashamed	305	Why Come Ye	1052
Yet whan he toke first his hat,	306	Why Come Ye	1108
first] not in MS Rawlinson C. 813			
And yet, this gracelesse elfe,	307	Why Come Ye	1115
gracelesse] 'ungratyous' MS Rawlinson C. 813			
But yet beware the rod	307	Why Come Ye	1137
And yet this proude Antiochus,	308	Why Come Ye	1175
That standeth yet awrye;	308	Why Come Ye	1187
Yet sum surgions put a dout	309	Why Come Ye	1198
Nor yet shall scape shamlesse.	309	Why Come Ye2	5
shall] not in MS Rawlinson C. 813			
For certayne envectyfys, yet wrote he none ill,	315	Garlande	96
certayne envectyfys] 'that he enveiyd' MS Cotton Vit.E.x			
Yet dyverse ther be, industryous of reason,	315	Garlande	106
ther] 'that' MS Cotton Vitellius E.x			
Yet harde is to make but sum fawt be founde.'	315	Garlande	112
Yet shall I answere your grace as in this,	316	Garlande	144
For though he were venquesshid, yet was he not shamyd:	316	Garlande	161
For] 'Sithe' MS Cotton Vitellius E.x			
But a grete parte yet ye have reservyd	317	Garlande	171
But...yet] 'Bot yit a grete parte' MS Cotton Vitellius E.x			
Yet they ryde and rinne from Carlyll to Kent.	317	Garlande	196
they ryde and rinne] 'ryde they and ryn they' MS Cotton Vitellius E.x			
But yet I beseche your grace that good recorde	318	Garlande	215
good] not in MS Cotton Vitellius E.x			
Yet loke on me, that lovyd you have so longe,	320	Garlande	298

YETT—YF	Page	Title	Line

	Page	Title	Line
Yet have compassyon upon my paynes stronge.'	320	Garlande	299
Yet, in remembraunce of Daphnes transformacyon,	321	Garlande	320
For yet of women he never sayd shame,	334	Garlande	784
Yet shall there be no restraynt	339	Garlande	956
Yet nowe doutles ye geve me cause	341	Garlande	1041
Hath bene full often and yet is entendyng	344	Garlande	1131
Yet, thoughe I say it, therby lyith a tale,	346	Garlande	1200
I] 'ye' †Fakes 1523			
Yet sum there be therewith that take grevaunce	348	Garlande	1257
Though Jak sayd nay, yet Mok there loste her sho;	351	Garlande	1396
But yet for all that, be as be may,	352	Garlande	1415
Yet whan the rayne rayneth and the gose wynkith	352	Garlande	1430
Yet now and then /Sum Latin men	355	Garlande	1544
Twyt, Scot, yet agayne ones,	362	Albany	149
Yet we bear away the bell,	363	Albany	183
Yet somwhat ye be lyke	364	Albany	197
But yet they were bolde	364	Albany	202
Yet ye dare do nothynge	364	Albany	211
Harke yet, Sir Duke, a worde	367	Albany	318
Yet, sav[e] voster grace,	367	Albany	357
save] 'sava' †Marshe 1568			
Yet, brevely to conclude,	372	Albany	518
and yet they were but febly enformed	374	Replycacion	I
And yet ye supposed /Respondere ad quantum,	377	Replycacion	109
Yet be meanes of that vyse	378	Replycacion	131
And yet some men say,	379	Replycacion	176
YETT			
Yett dates now are deynte, and wax verye scante,	244	Speke Parott	440
YF			
For yf they had occupied ther spere and ther shelde	31	Dol Dethe	73
She asked yf ever I dranke of saucys cuppe.	48	Bowge	73
Yf ye have not, in fayth, I wyll you lene	48	Bowge	96
And, yf nede be, a bolde worde I dare cracke.	50	Bowge	168
Yf he coude fynde in herte to truste me.	52	Bowge	220
By Goddis bones, but yf we have som sleyte,	54	Bowge	304
To wete yf Malkyn, my lemman, have gete oughte.	57	Bowge	401
And by my trouthe, but yf an ende they make,	59	Bowge	473
Truste me, and yf it come to a nede;	59	Bowge	478
Yf ye coude be otherwyse agrede;	59	Bowge	480
For yf I had not quyckely fledde the touche,	60	Bowge	503
As I shall tell you, yf ye wyll harke agayne:	61	Bowge	520
But yf yt war Syr Tyrmagant that tyrnyd without nall;	121	Garnesche1	4
Yf he wyst what sum wotte,	129	Garnesche3	199
To know thy selfe yf thow lake grace,	132	Garnesche5	126
But yf prudence be proved with sad cyrcumspeccyon,	141	Magnyfycence	16
Yf noblenesse were aquayntyd with sober dyreccyon.	141	Magnyfycence	18
But yf reason be regent and ruler of your barge.	141	Magnyfycence	38
Syr, yf any worde have past	143	Magnyfycence	92
It were a myschefe, yf lyberte lacked a reyne	144	Magnyfycence	135
For myschefe wyll mayster us yf measure us forsake.	144	Magnyfycence	154
Bycause course of measure - yf I be in the way:	146	Magnyfycence	213
But yf therof the soner amendys be made;	146	Magnyfycence	226
But yf I were orderyd by just measure,	147	Magnyfycence	249
Let se this checke yf ye voyde canne.	148	Magnyfycence	297
But yf I coulde knowe a gose from a swanne.	148	Magnyfycence	299
Syr, yf I have offended your noble estate,	149	Magnyfycence	308
And yf ye knewe howe I have mused,	156	Magnyfycence	580
Syr, and yf ye wolde not be wrothe -	157	Magnyfycence	606
Yf I can fynde out	168	Magnyfycence	993
As some be not ferre and yf it were well sought -	174	Magnyfycence	1241
But all that he dothe, and yf he reken well	175	Magnyfycence	1274
But, I say, let se and yf thou have any more.	175	Magnyfycence	1278
Upon a naked man and yf she scrat.	176	Magnyfycence	1298
And welth is nought worthe yf lyberte be behynde.	180	Magnyfycence	1442
But yf it lyke your grace more at large	185	Magnyfycence	1589
And yf you se ony thynge agaynst your mynde,	185	Magnyfycence	1599
As yf a man fortune to touche you on the quyke -	185	Magnyfycence	1611
But yf it lyke you that I myght rowne in your eyre,	186	Magnyfycence	1645
For your selfe. Syr, yf I myght permytted be,	188	Magnyfycence	1720
I wolde tell you and yf I myght for wepynge.	192	Magnyfycence	1848
And yf I se therby they wyll not amende,	194	Magnyfycence	1926
In welth to beware yf I had had grace,	196	Magnyfycence	1976
For I am a vertue yf I be well used,	199	Magnyfycence	2101
For yf Measure had ruled Lyberte as he began,	200	Magnyfycence	2111
And yf there were none to dysplease but thou and I,	202	Magnyfycence	2194
It wolde be founde so yf it were well tryde,	210	Magnyfycence	2449
Yf you be so myndyd, we be ryght glad.	210	Magnyfycence	2473
Yf it be regystryd well in memory;	212	Magnyfycence	2513
Yf fortune be frendly, and grace be the guyde,	234	Speke Parott	139
Yf it were cond perfytely, and after the rate,	234	Speke Parott	143
And also prophytabyll, /Yf ye be agreabyll,	237	Speke Parott	249
He caryeth a kyng in hys sleve, yf all the worlde fayle;	243	Speke Parott	429
Or yf he speke playne, /Than he lacketh brayne:	247	Collyn Clout	26
And yf that he hytte /The nayle on the hede	247	Collyn Clout	33
And yf ye stande in doute /Who brought this ryme aboute,	248	Collyn Clout	47
Yf ye take well therwith /It hath in it some pyth.	248	Collyn Clout	57
take] 'talke' Kele 1545.1, Marshe 1568			
With money, yf it wyll happe /To catche the forked cappe.	249	Collyn Clout	88

853

YLKE — YONDE

	Page	Title	Line
'Bysshoppes, yf they may,	249	Collyn Clout	122
Set nought by golde ne grotes, /Theyr names yf I durst tell.	250	Collyn Clout	161
Yf he on hym dare take	254	Collyn Clout	306
Yf it please nat theologys	258	Collyn Clout	465
nat theologys] 'the not onely' MS Lansdowne 762 'not theologi' MS Harley 2252			
And yf ye may have layser,	261	Collyn Clout	605
ye] 'you' Kele 1545.1, Marshe 1568, 'ye' MS Harley 2252			
Yf they well understode	262	Collyn Clout	616
understode] 'understand' Marshe 1568			
Or elles yf we may	265	Collyn Clout	743
But yf ye wolde take payne	265	Collyn Clout	763
Then yf any there be	274	Collyn Clout	1117
And yf ye thynke this shall	279	Why Come Ye	24

YLKE

Of brede at ylke mannes hecke.	363	Albany	155

YLL

Uppon me to clater or else to say yll.	38	Coystrowne1	66
Plente of yll, of goodnes skant,	40	Coystrowne4	3
His tong never styll /For to say yll,	95	Phy Sparrow	942
Tushe, a strawe! I thought none yll.	156	Magnyfycence	564
I am never glad but whan I may do yll,	160	Magnyfycence	731
And, be the mater yll more or lesse,	175	Magnyfycence	1272
That ratyd the Romaynes and made them yll rest,	181	Magnyfycence	1481
Ly styll, ly styll nowe, with yll hayle!	204	Magnyfycence	2248
God gyve it yll prevynge,	219	El Rummynge	185
For, as yll a patch as that,	219	El Rummynge	189
God gyve it yll hap!'	227	El Rummynge	509
God gyve it yll hayle,	230	El Rummynge	617
Syns Dewcalyons flodde the world was never so yll.	245	Speke Parott	497
the world] 'the world the world' †MS Harley 2252			
Yet thus with yll hayles	256	Collyn Clout	400
And suffre all this yll?	263	Collyn Clout	689
For, be it good, be it yll,	276	Collyn Clout	1217
And say yll behynde his back,	310	Why Come Ye2	26
For when he spekyth fayrest, then thynketh he moost yll;	333	Garlande	759
Whiche maner of abasshement became her not yll;	337	Garlande	889
And be nowe as yll,	379	Replycacion	178

YMAGE

And such a mad ymage	365	Albany	254
The ymage of her grace	381	Replycacion	261

YMAGENYD

As I ymagenyd, repayrid unto me,	323	Garlande	392

YMAGES

howe it was idolatry to offre to ymages of our blessed lady,	375	Replycacion	I
or to make oblacions to any ymages of sayntes,	375	Replycacion	I
To worshyppe none ymages, /Nor do pylgrymages?	381	Replycacion	269
To worshyppe ymages of sayntes.	382	Replycacion	291

YMAGYNACYON

And whether it were of ymagynacyon,	313	Garlande	31

YMAGYNACYOUN

Item his Diologgis of Ymagynacyoun;	346	Garlande	1180

YMET

What! Wanton, wanton, nowe well ymet!	153	Magnyfycence	456

YMPOSSYBYLL

To suche thynges ympossybyll, reason cannot consente;	240	Speke Parott	334

YN

Yn Latyn, in Ebrue, and in Caldee,	231	Speke Parott	25
and] 'Araby and' Lant 1545, Kynge and Marche 1554, Day 1560, Marshe 1568			

YNCHE

An ynche above her kne,	225	El Rummynge	420
An ynche above your eere,	263	Collyn Clout	674

YNDE

Tyll Eufrates, that flodde, dryvythe me into Ynde,	231	Speke Parott	4

YNK

With pen and ynk /For to compyle /Some goodly style;	96	Phy Sparrow	986
goodly] 'godly' †Kele 1545.2			

YNKE

Caughte penne and ynke, and wroth this lytell boke.	61	Bowge	532
wroth] 'wrote' Wynkyn de Worde 1510, Marshe 1568			
Yet though I wryte not with ynke,	101	Phy Sparrow	1198
And for my sake spare neyther pen nor ynke;	327	Garlande	549
With penne and ynke procede,	385	Replycacion	388

YNOUGH

He might be sure to have shame ynough.	139	Ven Tongues	78

YNOUGHE

I wote thou arte false ynoughe for one.	155	Magnyfycence	536
Gyve them more than ynoughe, and let them not lacke;	190	Magnyfycence	1773

YNOWE

More coude I saye, but what this is ynowe.	60	Bowge	491

YOKE

The poore people they yoke	254	Collyn Clout	323

YOMAN

Today a yoman, tomorowe made of page;	213	Magnyfycence	2547

YONDE

Cockys harte! Who is yonde that for the dothe call?	162	Magnyfycence	780
Farre by yonde Portyngale,	299	Why Come Ye	802

YONDER —YOU	Page	Title	Line

YONDER
Naye, see where yonder stondeth the teder man!	59	Bowge	484
Alas, wh[o] is yonder that grymly lokys?	193	Magnyfycence	1873
who] 'why' †Rastell & Treveris C 1530, B			
What brothell, I say, is yonder bounde in a mat?	199	Magnyfycence	2106
Yonder is a horson for me doth rechate;	201	Magnyfycence	2151
And what blunderar is yonder that playth didil diddil?	333	Garlande	740

YONE
To understande who dwellyth in yone pile,	333	Garlande	739
yone] 'yonder' MS Cotton Vitellius E.x			

YONG
I am but a yong mayd,	91	Phy Sparrow	770
A Replycacion Agaynst Certayne Yong Scolers Abjured of Late,	373	Replycacion	I
Howe yong scolers nowe a dayes enbol[n]ed	373	Replycacion	I
enbolned] 'enbolmed' †Pynson 1528			
Of these yong heretikes, that stynke unbrent,	375	Replycacion	22

YONGE
O yonge lyon, bot tender yet of age,	33	Dol Dethe	162
Alexis yonge of age,	110	Lawde	13
Eche thynge is fayre when it is yonge; all hayle, owle!	167	Magnyfycence	970
How dotynge age wolde jape with yonge foly;	322	Garlande	361
The yonge Scottyshe kyng,	361	Albany	90
and rechelesse yonge heretykes lately abjured, etc.	373	Replycacion	I

YONGER
Whan ye war yonger of age	124	Garnesche3	24
It shall make you loke /Yonger than ye be	219	El Rummynge	214

YONGLYNG
He is but an yonglyng,	287	Why Come Ye	348

YONKERKYNS
and stoicall studiantes, and friscajoly yonkerkyns,	374	Replycacion	I

YOR
Ye gyrne grymly with your gomys and with yor grysly face.	122	Garnesche1	12
In yor chalenge, Syr Chesten, to calle me a knave?	122	Garnesche1	14
Yet your contenons oncomly, yor face ys nat fayer.	122	Garnesche1	18
For alle your proude prankyng, yor pride may apayere.	122	Garnesche1	19
In yor chalenge, Syr Chesten, to cal me a knave?	122	Garnesche1	21
In yor chalenge, Syr Chesten, to calle me a knave?	122	Garnesche1	28
Yor wynde-schakyn shankkes, yor longe *lothy legges,	122	Garnesche1	29
*lothy] 'lothly' Scattergood			
Yor wynde-schakyn shankkes, yor longe *lothy legges,	122	Garnesche1	29
*lothy] 'lothly' Scattergood			
In yor chalenge, Syr Chesten, to calle me a knave?	122	Garnesche1	35
I sey, ye solem Sarson, alle blake ys yor ble;	122	Garnesche1	36
[Your] gronynge, yor grontynge, yor groinynge lyke a swyne?	123	Garnesche2	2
[Your] gronynge, yor grontynge, yor groinynge lyke a swyne?	123	Garnesche2	2
Why holde ye on yer cap, syr, then? Yor pardone ys expyryd.	123	Garnesche2	9
Yor moth etyn mokkysh maneres, they be all to-myryd.	123	Garnesche2	12

YORKES
And Yorkes Place, /With, 'My lordes grace',	289	Why Come Ye	410

YORKIS
The Duke of Yorkis creauncer whan Skelton was,	347	Garlande	1226

YOR SELFE
Chalenge yor selfe for a fole, call me no more knave.	122	Garnesche1	42

YOU
What willfull foly made you to ryse agayn	30	Dol Dethe	53
Ye armed you with wille and left your wit behynd;	30	Dol Dethe	55
Redy to assyst you in every tyme of nede;	30	Dol Dethe	58
What movyd you agayn hym to war or to fight?	31	Dol Dethe	62
What aylde you to slo your lord ageyn all right?	31	Dol Dethe	63
slo] 'sle' Marshe 1568			
And I love you an hole cart lode.'	35	Man Margery	9
Now have I shewyd you part of your proud mynde;	38	Coystrowne	67
'Myne horse is sold, I wene', you say;	40	Coystrowne4	9
I truste to quyte you or I dy!	41	Coystrowne4	21
Advertysyng you, madame, to warke more secretly,	43	Balettys2	39
You I assure, absens is my fo,	44	Balettys3	36
I wold you coud! Then shuld ye se, mastres,	44	Balettys3	40
As to enbrace you in myne armys twayne.	44	Balettys3	42
Ware yet, I rede you, of Fortunes double cast,	45	Balettys4	3
Abasshe you not, but hardely be bolde,	48	Bowge	87
Yet I avyse you to speke, for ony drede:	48	Bowge	90
Yf ye have not, in fayth, I wyll you lene	48	Bowge	96
Bone aventure may brynge you in suche case	49	Bowge	104
But of one thynge I werne you er I goo:	49	Bowge	106
werne] 'warne' Marshe 1568; er] 'or' Wynkyn de Worde 1510			
'Maystres,' quod I, 'I praye you tell me why soo,	49	Bowge	108
Fortune to you gyftes of grace hath lente:	50	Bowge	152
I herde her speke of you within shorte space,	50	Bowge	158
shorte] 'a shorte' Wynkyn de Worde 1510			
Whan there were dyverse that sore dyde you manacé.	50	Bowge	159
For here be dyverse to you that be unkynde.	50	Bowge	161
Ageynste you hardely; therefore be not afrayde.	51	Bowge	174
That commaunde with you, me thought, a p[ra]ty space?	51	Bowge	198
commaunde] 'commened' Wynkyn de Worde 1510; 'party spake' †Wynkyn de Worde 1499, Marshe 1568; 'party space' WdeW 1510			
He wyll begyle you and speke fayre to your face.	51	Bowge	200
But I wolde telle you a thynge, and I durste.	51	Bowge	203
Spake he, a fayth, no worde to you of me?	51	Bowge	204

YOU —YOU

	Page	Title	Line
I have a favoure to you, wherof it be	52	Bowge	206
That I must shewe you moche of my counselle -	52	Bowge	207
He sayde of me, whan he with you dyde talke -	52	Bowge	209
For, but I trusted you, so God me save, ...	52	Bowge	213
To you oonly, me thynke, I durste shryve me;	52	Bowge	215
To shewe you thynges that may not be disclosed.'	52	Bowge	217
'Syr, God you save, why loke you so sadde?	53	Bowge	239
'Syr, God you save, why loke you so sadde?	53	Bowge	239
What thynge is that I maye do for you?	53	Bowge	240
For, as I trowe, I have sene you in dede	53	Bowge	248
Or 'Shall I sayle wyth you' a felashyp assaye?	53	Bowge	254
Wolde to God it wolde please you some daye	53	Bowge	256
Loo, what is to you a pleasure grete	53	Bowge	260
Soo greate pleasyre, or who to you it gave.	53	Bowge	263
To be with you thus perte and thus bolde;	53	Bowge	265
But I requyre you no worde that I saye!	54	Bowge	276
That is agayne you, you shall have wetynge;	54	Bowge	278
That is agayne you, you shall have wetynge;	54	Bowge	278
I hope here after a frende of you to have.'	54	Bowge	280
Ye be malygned sore, I you ensure, ...	59	Bowge	451
Betwene the persone ye wote of, you -	59	Bowge	461
I hate this wayes agayne you that they take!	59	Bowge	471
this] 'these' Wynkyn de Worde 1510			
Were I as you, I wolde ryde them full nere;	59	Bowge	472
Ye muste be ruled, as I shall tell you howe.	60	Bowge	493
There I wynked on you - wote ye not where?	60	Bowge	516
As I shall tell you, yf ye wyll harke agayne:	61	Bowge	520
And whan I sawe the horsons wolde you hafte, ...	61	Bowge	521
Besechynge you that shall it see or rede, ...	61	Bowge	534
I shall you make relacyon	62	Hauke	29
If it please you to loke	68	Hauke	233
To hawke when [you] lista	69	Hauke	257
you] 'your' editions			
Doctor Dialetica, /Where fynde you in Ypotetica, ...	69	Hauke	268
Was betwene you twayne, /Pyramus and Thesbe, ...	72	Phy Sparrow	20
To tell you what conceyte	100	Phy Sparrow	1130
I pray you it may be amendyd	102	Phy Sparrow	1246
That folowe as you may se.	106	Phy Sparrow	1379
you] 'ye' Wyght 1553, Kitson 1560.6, Marshe 1568			
I pray you all, ...	108	Epitaphe1	68
To you no thyng it dyde accorde	113	Scot Kynge	3
For you and your Scottes wolde tourne his face?	114	Scot Kynge	18
Experyence hath brought you in the same brake.	115	Scot Kynge	61
We have well eased you of the bottes.	115	Scot Kynge	63
Chryst sence you with a fryinge pan! -	117	Ag Scottes	62
sence] 'fence' †Lant 1545			
Thalya, my muse, for you also call I, ...	117	Ag Scottes	85
To you rehersyng the somme of my proces.	117	Ag Scottes	90
To you nothing it dyd accorde	118	Ag Scottes	93
From you, Syr Scot, wolde turne his face?	118	Ag Scottes	108
Agaynst you gave so sharpe a shower, ...	119	Ag Scottes	133
Ye lost your spurrys, ye lost you sworde.	119	Ag Scottes	148
Ye myght have buskyd you to Huntley Bankys;	119	Ag Scottes	149
Experiens hath brought you in such a brake.	119	Ag Scottes	158
Thus fortune hath tourned you, I dare well say, ...	119	Ag Scottes	164
The Popes cur[se] gave you that clap.	119	Ag Scottes	169
curse] 'cures' †Lant 1545, Kynge & Marche 1554, Day 1560, Marshe 1568			
Fortune on you therfore dyd frowne;	120	Ag Scottes	176
Boldly bend you to batell, and buske your selfe to save. . . .	122	Garnesche1	41
You mantyca[re], ye maltaperte, ye can bothe wins and whyne; .	123	Garnesche2	4
mantycare] 'mantyca' †MS Harley 367			
God sende you wele good spede, ...	129	Garnesche3	202
In your crosse rowe nor Christ crosse you spede, ...	137	Ven Tongues	18
Who soever that tale unto you tolde, ...	137	Ven Tongues	20
And I to suffre you lewdly to ly	138	Ven Tongues	47
With, 'I can tel you what such a man said, ...	139	Ven Tongues	71
And you knew all ye would be ill apayd'.	139	Ven Tongues	72
To tell you the cause me semeth it no nede.	140	Magnyfycence	8
Trewe you say, syr. Gyve me your hande.	141	Magnyfycence	28
To tell you, syr, I dare not, leest I sholde be maskyd	141	Magnyfycence	30
Here you not howe this gentylman mockys?	141	Magnyfycence	32
Shewe forth, I pray you, here in what you intende.	141	Magnyfycence	40
Shewe forth, I pray you, here in what you intende.	141	Magnyfycence	40
Then thus to you - Nay, suffer me yet ferther to say, ...	142	Magnyfycence	48
But and you wolde me permyt	142	Magnyfycence	57
Or howe can you prove that there is felycyte, ...	142	Magnyfycence	77
And you have not your owne fre lyberte	142	Magnyfycence	78
Cryst you assyste in your altrycacyon!	142	Magnyfycence	81
Why, have you harde of our dysputacyon?	142	Magnyfycence	82
I parceyve well howe eche of you doth reason.	142	Magnyfycence	83
Mayster Measure, you be come in good season.	143	Magnyfycence	84
Wolde it please you then -	143	Magnyfycence	87
To you I arecte it, and cast /Therof the reformacyon.	143	Magnyfycence	94
Dyspleasure that you none take	143	Magnyfycence	98
You to holde content /With myne argument;	143	Magnyfycence	108
And I muste you requyre	143	Magnyfycence	110
Nowe pleasyth you a lytell whyle to stande;	145	Magnyfycence	161

YOU —YOU   Page   Title   Line

To assure you of my noble porte and fame,	145	Magnyfycence	163
Yet in this man you must set your delyght.	145	Magnyfycence	167
To the gydynge of my measure you bothe commyttynge;	145	Magnyfycence	175
And I my selfe hooly to you wyll inclyne.	145	Magnyfycence	182
For by measure I warne you we thynke to be gydyd;	145	Magnyfycence	184
Wherin it is necessary my pleasure you knowe:	145	Magnyfycence	185
For I wyll use you by his advertysment.	146	Magnyfycence	196
Then shall you have with you prosperyte resydent.	146	Magnyfycence	197
Then shall you have with you prosperyte resydent.	146	Magnyfycence	197
But plenarly all thought from you must be dyschargyd,	146	Magnyfycence	207
Wherfore, Measure, take Lyberte with you hence,	146	Magnyfycence	230
Perceyve you not howe lothe he was to abyde	147	Magnyfycence	241
Thynke you not thus my frende Felycyte?	147	Magnyfycence	245
To shewe you playnly the trouth as I thynke.	147	Magnyfycence	253
Here is none forsyth whether you flete or synke.	147	Magnyfycence	254
From whens come you, syr, that no man lokyd after?	147	Magnyfycence	255
Or who made you so bolde to interrupe my tale?	147	Magnyfycence	256
But hyght you, Largesse, encreace of noble fame?	148	Magnyfycence	271
Plucke up your mynde, syr, what ayle you to muse?	148	Magnyfycence	283
But covetyse hath blowen you so full of wynde	148	Magnyfycence	290
That colyca passyo hath gropyd you by the guttys.	148	Magnyfycence	291
In fayth, broder Largesse, you have a mery mynde.	148	Magnyfycence	292
You are nothynge mete with us for to dwell,	149	Magnyfycence	304
Gete you hens, I say, by my counsell.	149	Magnyfycence	306
I wyll not use you to play with me checke mate.	149	Magnyfycence	307
I trow I have brought you suche wrytynge of recorde,	149	Magnyfycence	309
That I shall have you agayne my good lorde.	149	Magnyfycence	310
To you recommendeth Sad Cyrcumspeccyon,	149	Magnyfycence	311
And sendeth you this wrytynge closed under sele.	149	Magnyfycence	312
Why kepte you it thus longe? Howe dothe he? Wele?	149	Magnyfycence	314
Welthe, gete you home and commaunde me to Mesure.	149	Magnyfycence	316
Byd hym take good hede of you, my synguler tresure.	149	Magnyfycence	317
Nothynge but fare you well tyll sone –	149	Magnyfycence	319
I shall come to you myselfe, I trowe, this afternone.	149	Magnyfycence	322
I pray you, Larges, here to remayne,	149	Magnyfycence	323
Do what I coude to do you good.	150	Magnyfycence	335
I pray God kepe you in that mood!	150	Magnyfycence	336
Where was it delyvered you? Shewe unto me.	150	Magnyfycence	340
At what place, nowe, as you gesse?	150	Magnyfycence	342
I had not been here with you this nyght.	150	Magnyfycence	365
No. But for you grete estates	150	Magnyfycence	370
Say howe you excede in noblenesse,	151	Magnyfycence	376
If you had with you largesse.	151	Magnyfycence	377
If you had with you largesse.	151	Magnyfycence	377
What! Sholde you pynche at a pecke of [gr]otes	151	Magnyfycence	384
grotes] 'otes' †Rastell & Treveris C 1530, B			
I pray you, syr, I may so be;	151	Magnyfycence	391
And of my servyce you shall not mysse.	151	Magnyfycence	392
Tell you where of my name dothe ryse.	151	Magnyfycence	409
God gyve you a very myschaunce!	154	Magnyfycence	497
That I counterfeyted you underneth a shrowde?	155	Magnyfycence	532
Can you remedy for a tysyke	156	Magnyfycence	555
Let se, fynde you a better way.	156	Magnyfycence	560
Nay, and you be angry and overwharte,	156	Magnyfycence	562
For had you not come I had ryden.	156	Magnyfycence	577
And Crafty Conveyaunce, knowe you not hym?	156	Magnyfycence	584
Se you not howe they prece	156	Magnyfycence	591
Knowe you not me, syrs? No, in dede.	157	Magnyfycence	594
A, syr, I pray God gyve you confusyon!	157	Magnyfycence	597
Cappe, syr. I say you be to bolde.	157	Magnyfycence	602
And have you not amonge you Lyberte?	157	Magnyfycence	625
And have you not amonge you Lyberte?	157	Magnyfycence	625
I can not tell you. Why aske you me?	157	Magnyfycence	628
I can not tell you. Why aske you me?	157	Magnyfycence	628
Syr, the playnesse you me tell.	158	Magnyfycence	630
you me tell] 'you tell me' †Rastell & Treveris C 1530, B			
I pray God let you never to thee!	158	Magnyfycence	635
What the devyll ayleth you? Can you not agree?	158	Magnyfycence	636
What the devyll ayleth you? Can you not agree?	158	Magnyfycence	636
And shortly shewe you the hole substaunce.	158	Magnyfycence	638
That he shall have you in the stede of sadnesse,	159	Magnyfycence	680
We wyll se you shortly, one of us twayne.	159	Magnyfycence	686
Nowe let se. Quyte you lyke praty men!	159	Magnyfycence	688
Thus can I lerne you, syrs, to bere the devyls sacke;	160	Magnyfycence	721
And yet, I trowe, some of you be better sped than I	160	Magnyfycence	722
Whiche of you is the better man,	162	Magnyfycence	802
Or whiche of you can do most.	162	Magnyfycence	803
Well, tary here tyll I for you sende.	163	Magnyfycence	817
I waraunt you I wyll not go away.	163	Magnyfycence	820
But nowe what tydynges can you tell? Let se.	166	Magnyfycence	928
With a pere my love you may wynne,	168	Magnyfycence	1015
Fyrst to tell you what were best:	168	Magnyfycence	1022
In fayth, I can make you bothe folys, and I wyll.	172	Magnyfycence	1173
Howe rode he by you? Howe put he to you?	173	Magnyfycence	1178
Howe rode he by you? Howe put he to you?	173	Magnyfycence	1178
For you bothe it were inough.	173	Magnyfycence	1187
Syr, of my maner I shall tell you the playne:	174	Magnyfycence	1219
Yes. I shall tell you or I go	175	Magnyfycence	1263

YOU — YOU	Page	Title	Line
To here you two rutters dyspute togyder.	176	Magnyfycence	1287
For as sone as you come in Magnyfycence syght	176	Magnyfycence	1314
'Though I shewe you curtesy, say not that I crave[d]; craved] 'crave' †Rastell & Treveris C 1530, B	177	Magnyfycence	1351
To se you thus ruled and stande in suche awe.	178	Magnyfycence	1376
Must mesure, in the mares name, you furnysshe and dresse?	179	Magnyfycence	1391
Be not to bolde my frende; I counsell you, bere a brayne.	179	Magnyfycence	1405
And what so we say, holde you content withall.	179	Magnyfycence	1406
Why, wene you that I can kepe hym longe styll?	179	Magnyfycence	1412
Sore sayde, I tell you, and well to the purpose.	180	Magnyfycence	1428
What sholde a man do with you? Loke you under [k]ay? kay] 'bay' †Rastell & Treveris C 1530, B	180	Magnyfycence	1429
What sholde a man do with you? Loke you under [k]ay? kay] 'bay' †Rastell & Treveris C 1530, B	180	Magnyfycence	1429
What nede you with hym thus prate and chat?	180	Magnyfycence	1434
And get [y]ou home togyther; for Lyberte shall byde you] 'thou' †Rastell & Treveris C 1530, B	180	Magnyfycence	1446
Well, get you hens than and sende me some other.	180	Magnyfycence	1451
But loke that ye occupye the auctoryte that I you gave.	180	Magnyfycence	1456
No, that I assure you; loke who was the best:	181	Magnyfycence	1484
To shewe you my mynde myselfe I wyll avaunce,	182	Magnyfycence	1520
Yes, syr, so good man in you I se,	182	Magnyfycence	1522
Howe be it, I wolde be ryght gladde, I you assure,	183	Magnyfycence	1527
Truste me, with you I am hyghly pleasyd;	183	Magnyfycence	1535
For in my favour I have you feffyd and seasyd.	183	Magnyfycence	1536
If it wolde lyke you to here my pore mynde -	183	Magnyfycence	1543
And to aqueynte you with carnall delectacyon;	183	Magnyfycence	1547
Howe lyke you? Ye lacke, syr, suche a lusty lasse.	183	Magnyfycence	1559
Nay, nay; for lesse I waraunt you to be sped,	184	Magnyfycence	1571
Money maketh marchauntes, I tell you, over all.	184	Magnyfycence	1574
A maystres, I tell you, is but a small thynge.	184	Magnyfycence	1579
But one thynge I warne you, prece forth and be bolde.	184	Magnyfycence	1582
I coude holde you with suche talke hens tyll to morowe.	184	Magnyfycence	1588
I wolde yet shewe you further of my consayte.	185	Magnyfycence	1591
And yf you se ony thynge agaynst your mynde,	185	Magnyfycence	1599
What sholde ye do elles? Are not you a lorde?	185	Magnyfycence	1606
As yf a man fortune to touche you on the quyke -	185	Magnyfycence	1611
To styre up your stomake you must you forge,	185	Magnyfycence	1613
To styre up your stomake you must you forge,	185	Magnyfycence	1613
Remembre the good servyce that Mesure hath you done,	186	Magnyfycence	1637
I may say to you I have but small devocyon.	186	Magnyfycence	1640
But yf it lyke you that I myght rowne in your eyre,	186	Magnyfycence	1645
To shewe you my mynde I wolde have the lesse fere.	186	Magnyfycence	1646
With a good wyll, syr, God spede you bothe togyder.	186	Magnyfycence	1648
Notwithstandynge to you be it sayde	186	Magnyfycence	1651
For, so helpe me God, for you he is not mete.	186	Magnyfycence	1653
Come hyder, Pleasure; you shall here myne entent.	186	Magnyfycence	1655
By myne advyse, with you in fayth he shall not rest.	186	Magnyfycence	1660
It were better he spake with you or he wente,	187	Magnyfycence	1662
Nowe, by your trouthe, gave he you not a brybe?	187	Magnyfycence	1665
Ye, by my trouthe, I shall waraunt you for me,	187	Magnyfycence	1669
He telleth you trouth, syr, as I you ensure.	187	Magnyfycence	1679
He telleth you trouth, syr, as I you ensure.	187	Magnyfycence	1679
Whylest I came to you, a lytell here besyde.	187	Magnyfycence	1686
An honest person, I tell you, and a sad.	187	Magnyfycence	1690
Nay, I tell you, I am not wonte to fode	188	Magnyfycence	1698
Syr, God rewarde you as ye have deserved.	188	Magnyfycence	1701
But thynke you with Magnyfycence I shal be reserved?	188	Magnyfycence	1702
By my trouth, I can not tell you that.	188	Magnyfycence	1703
For go when ye shall, of you shall he mysse.	188	Magnyfycence	1706
Syr, I beseche you let pety have some place	188	Magnyfycence	1712
So masterfully upon you for to take	188	Magnyfycence	1715
That holly my mynde with you is myscontente;	188	Magnyfycence	1717
I wolde to you say a worde or twayne.	188	Magnyfycence	1721
And I shall waraunt you welth and lyberte.	190	Magnyfycence	1766
To chose out ii., iii., of suche as you love best,	190	Magnyfycence	1769
And where soever you wyll fall to a rekenynge,	190	Magnyfycence	1777
For the[m] shall you have at lyberte to lowte. them] 'then' †Rastell & Treveris C 1530, B	190	Magnyfycence	1779
Thus joy without mesure you shall have.	190	Magnyfycence	1781
And suche as you wyll shall lacke no promocyon.	190	Magnyfycence	1789
To do you servyce after your appetyte.	190	Magnyfycence	1793
And therfore hye you hens, and take this oversyght.	190	Magnyfycence	1795
Nowe Jesu preserve you, syr, prynce most of myght.	190	Magnyfycence	1796
What tydynges with you, syr? I befole thy brayne pan.	191	Magnyfycence	1805
And, syr as I was comynge to you hyder,	191	Magnyfycence	1813
A, syr, tolde I not you howe I dyd fynde	191	Magnyfycence	1819
I shall gyve you a gaude of a goslynge that I gave,	191	Magnyfycence	1829
I coude, and I lyst, garre you laughe at a game:	192	Magnyfycence	1835
Se, syr, I beseche you, Largesse my brother.	192	Magnyfycence	1842
What tydynges with you, syr, that you loke so sad?	192	Magnyfycence	1843
What tydynges with you, syr, that you loke so sad?	192	Magnyfycence	1843
I wolde tell you and yf I myght for wepynge.	192	Magnyfycence	1848
Nay. Madnesse hath begyled you and many mo;	192	Magnyfycence	1856
And had robbyd you quyte from all felycyte.	193	Magnyfycence	1864
Why, coulde not your wyt serve you no better?	193	Magnyfycence	1868
Why, who wolde have thought in you suche gyle?	193	Magnyfycence	1869
That you trustyd, and Fansy is my name;	193	Magnyfycence	1871

YOU—YOU

	Page	Title	Line
And Foly, my broder, that made you moche game.	193	Magnyfycence	1872
To take, syrs, example of that I you tell,	195	Magnyfycence	1944
For though we shewe you this in game and play,	195	Magnyfycence	1948
For thoughe you were somtyme a noble estate,	196	Magnyfycence	1980
Nowe must you lerne to begge at every mannes gate.	196	Magnyfycence	1981
Unto your maker that made bothe you and me;	196	Magnyfycence	1992
Remembre you better, syr. Beware what ye say,	196	Magnyfycence	1995
That may restore you agayne to felycyte,	196	Magnyfycence	1998
And brynge you agayne out of adversyte.	196	Magnyfycence	1999
Where you were wonte to have cawdels for your hede,	197	Magnyfycence	2008
Nowe must you monche mamockes and lumpes of brede;	197	Magnyfycence	2009
And where you had chaunges of ryche aray,	197	Magnyfycence	2010
Nowe lap you in a coverlet, full fayne that you may;	197	Magnyfycence	2011
Nowe lap you in a coverlet, full fayne that you may;	197	Magnyfycence	2011
For nowe go I wyll begge for you some mete.	197	Magnyfycence	2034
And happe you the whyles with these homly raggys.	197	Magnyfycence	2037
I warne you beware of to moche lyberte,	199	Magnyfycence	2088
A laudable largesse, I tell you, for a lorde,	200	Magnyfycence	2123
I waraunt you I have gyven it a lasshe.	201	Magnyfycence	2165
Mary, so ungoodly langage you me gave.	203	Magnyfycence	2213
Goddys fote! I warant you I am a gentylman borne;	203	Magnyfycence	2216
By God, I tell you, I wyll not be out facyd.	203	Magnyfycence	2220
The one of you is to proude, the other is to haute.	203	Magnyfycence	2223
And I tell you, I dysdayne moche of his mockys.	203	Magnyfycence	2227
And therfore our Lorde sende you a very wengaunce!	203	Magnyfycence	2237
Ye, but trowe you, syrs, that this is he?	204	Magnyfycence	2242
That wyll make you to halt and to hoppe.	204	Magnyfycence	2273
A, blessyd may ye be, syr! What shall you I call?	206	Magnyfycence	2327
Wynde you from wanhope and aquaynte you with me.	206	Magnyfycence	2340
Wynde you from wanhope and aquaynte you with me.	206	Magnyfycence	2340
That you hath punysshed with his sharpe rod.	207	Magnyfycence	2350
That Goddes grace hath vexed you sharply	207	Magnyfycence	2352
And payned you with a purgacyon of odyous poverte,	207	Magnyfycence	2353
Nowe must I make you a lectuary softe -	207	Magnyfycence	2355
I to mynyster it, you to receyve it ofte -	207	Magnyfycence	2356
With rubarbe of repentaunce in you for to rest;	207	Magnyfycence	2357
Put fro you presumpcyon and admyt humylyte,	207	Magnyfycence	2361
He may helpe you. He may mende your mode.	207	Magnyfycence	2366
To lerne you hereafter for to beware withall.	207	Magnyfycence	2376
Howe say you, syr? Can ye these wordys grope?	207	Magnyfycence	2377
Then shall you be sone delyvered from dystresse,	208	Magnyfycence	2383
Cryst be amonge you, and the Holy Goste!	208	Magnyfycence	2385
How fele you your selfe, my frend? How is your mynde?	208	Magnyfycence	2389
Ye, but have ye repentyd you with harte contryte?	208	Magnyfycence	2391
And have you banyshed from you all dyspare?	208	Magnyfycence	2393
And have you banyshed from you all dyspare?	208	Magnyfycence	2393
Good Hope, I pray you with harty affeccyon	208	Magnyfycence	2399
Of that I se you nowe in the state of grace.	208	Magnyfycence	2403
Take nowe upon you this abylyment,	208	Magnyfycence	2405
Syr, to accompte you, the contynewe of my consayte	209	Magnyfycence	2421
How fortuned you, Magnyfycence, so far to fal behynde?	209	Magnyfycence	2423
Syr, the longe absence of you, Sad Cyrcumspeccyon,	209	Magnyfycence	2424
Then ye of foly in tymes past you repent?	209	Magnyfycence	2433
'Then ye repent you of foly in tymes past' †Rastell & Treveris C 1530, B			
Howe be it, from you I receyved a letter [sent], sent] not in †Rastell & Treveris C 1530, B	209	Magnyfycence	2435
Who brought you that letter? Wote ye what he hyght?	209	Magnyfycence	2440
Then welthe with you myght in no wyse abyde.	210	Magnyfycence	2447
A ha, fansy and foly met with you, I trowe.	210	Magnyfycence	2448
Remembre you, therfore, howe late ye were low.	210	Magnyfycence	2451
And kepe you from counterfaytynge of clokyd colusyon.	210	Magnyfycence	2453
And from crafters and hafters I you forfende.	210	Magnyfycence	2456
Yf you be so myndyd, we be ryght glad.	210	Magnyfycence	2473
Well, I perceyve in you there is moche sadnesse,	210	Magnyfycence	2475
But frendly I wyll refrayne you ferther, or we flyt:	211	Magnyfycence	2478
Your myndys I beseche you here in to expresse,	211	Magnyfycence	2480
Herein I wyll aforse me to shewe you my mynde:	211	Magnyfycence	2483
To the increse of your honour then arme you with ryght,	211	Magnyfycence	2496
And fumously adresse you with magnanymyte;	211	Magnyfycence	2497
This treatyse, devysyd to make you dysporte,	213	Magnyfycence	2538
This mater we have movyd, you my myrthys to make,	213	Magnyfycence	2552
Jhesus preserve you frome endlesse wo and shame.	214	Magnyfycence	2572
Tell you I chyll,	214	El Rummynge	1
Abyde, abyde, /And to you shall be tolde	218	El Rummynge	157
For I may tell you, /I lerned it of a Jewe	219	El Rummynge	207
It shall make you loke /Yonger than ye be	219	El Rummynge	213
God sende you good sale!'	223	El Rummynge	369
With, 'Jast you, and gup, gylly,	224	El Rummynge	390
'And let me with you bybyll.'	228	El Rummynge	550
Sacro vatum, whereof to you I breke;	233	Speke Parott	97
I pray you, let Parot have lyberte to speke.	233	Speke Parott	98
Let Parrot, I pray you, have lyberte to prate,	234	Speke Parott	141
Support Parrot, I pray you, with your suffrage ornate,	236	Speke Parott	195
I pray you, let Parrot have lyberte to speke.	236	Speke Parott	210
He made you of nothynge by his magistye;	236	Speke Parott	219
I tell you as men say.	251	Collyn Clout	188
Howe some of you dothe eate /In lenton season flesshe meate,	251	Collyn Clout	204

859

YOU—YOU

	Page	Title	Line
Men call you therfore prophanes.	252	Collyn Clout	207
And you wyll be stylla,	253	Collyn Clout	260
You shall have your wylla!'	253	Collyn Clout	261
In you the faute is supposed	253	Collyn Clout	264
Full falsely on you they lye,	255	Collyn Clout	334
And shamfully you ascrye,	255	Collyn Clout	335
In sclaundrynge you for truthe.	255	Collyn Clout	342
In you prelates, and say	256	Collyn Clout	403
In] 'On' Marshe 1568, 'In' MS Harley 2252			
I reporte me to you.	257	Collyn Clout	432
You supporte and rescue,	257	Collyn Clout	434
rescue] 'rescite' Marshe 1568			
You prelates, that of ryght	257	Collyn Clout	439
Amongest you everychone	258	Collyn Clout	477
You thus to dyffame.	259	Collyn Clout	510
And upon you take	261	Collyn Clout	603
They wolde pype you another daunce.	262	Collyn Clout	618
To you that over the whele	262	Collyn Clout	627
Shall I tell you more? Ye, shall.	262	Collyn Clout	635
For you love to go trym,	262	Collyn Clout	641
I put you out of dout,	267	Collyn Clout	848
Howe some of you are mellynge.	271	Collyn Clout	985
Than lette reason you supporte,	271	Collyn Clout	1004
That some of you but late	271	Collyn Clout	1011
They put you to your actyon.	273	Collyn Clout	1060
They say they wyll you cast.	273	Collyn Clout	1070
Of you that clerkes be,	273	Collyn Clout	1083
Wherfore we make you sure,	276	Collyn Clout	1203
And some of you shall dye /Lyke holy Jeremy;	276	Collyn Clout	1208
Not rubbe you on the gall,	279	Why Come Ye	25
you] 'hym' MS Rawlinson C. 813			
With, 'Jast you, I say, Jullian!	285	Why Come Ye	242
Ones yet agayne /Of you I wolde frayne	289	Why Come Ye	400
To speke with you as yet.'	295	Why Come Ye	632
Tell you the rest; for me they shal.	296	Why Come Ye	709
I have told you part, but nat all.	299	Why Come Ye	822
Desyring you above all thynge	299	Why Come Ye	828
To kepe you from laughynge	299	Why Come Ye	829
For I make you sure,	300	Why Come Ye	846
I can not tell you what was the occasyon.	313	Garlande	35
not tell] 'not wele tell' MS Cotton Vitellius E.x			
My supplycacyon to you I arrect,	313	Garlande	55
Whereof I besechne you to tender the effecte.	313	Garlande	56
How you gave me a ryall commaundement	313	Garlande	58
you] 'ye' Marshe 1568, MS Cotton Vitellius E.x;			
a] 'in' MS Cot. Vit. E.x			
Remembre you wele, poynt wele that clause,	316	Garlande	136
His name? Or why is it, I you praye,	316	Garlande	138
Or els ye demeane you inordinatly;	317	Garlande	173
Extorcyon is counted with you for a knyght;	317	Garlande	194
For that I wolde not with you fall at discorde.	318	Garlande	214
Graunt my petycyon, I aske you but ryght.'	318	Garlande	231
Let se, my syster, now spede you, go aboute.	319	Garlande	242
you] not in MS Cotton Vitellius E.x			
'Daphnes, my derlynge, why do you me refuse?	320	Garlande	297
Yet loke on me, that lovyd you have so longe,	320	Garlande	298
Alas, what ayle you to be so overthwhart,	320	Garlande	307
Enforcid ar we you to recompence,	323	Garlande	416
That we shall brynge you personally present	324	Garlande	418
In rendrynge to you thankkis meritory,	324	Garlande	429
Wherwith to geve you my regraciatory,	324	Garlande	431
But that I poynt you to be prothonotary	324	Garlande	432
I can nat tell you, but that I was brought	325	Garlande	458
With, 'Sir, I pray you, a lytyll tyme stande backe,	326	Garlande	505
From you most we, but not longe to tary.	326	Garlande	520
Whiche shall be to you a sufferayne accessary,	326	Garlande	523
And we shall se you ageyne or it be pryme.'	326	Garlande	525
Of worldly trust, then did I you rescu;	327	Garlande	543
Moche mischefe, I hyght you, amonge theem ther happid.	330	Garlande	643
May this contente you and your mirry mynde?	332	Garlande	708
'I thanke you, goodly maystres, to me most benynge,	332	Garlande	728
Gog gyve you good yere, ye make me to smyle.	332	Garlande	736
Beware of hym, I warne you; for and ye wist	333	Garlande	754
and] 'if' Marshe 1568			
Come forth, jentylwomen, I pray you,' she sayd,	334	Garlande	773
'I have contryvyd for you a goodly warke,	334	Garlande	774
Unto you, madame, I make reconusaunce,	335	Garlande	838
Troilus, I trowe, if that he had you sene,	336	Garlande	873
In you he wolde have set his hole delight.	336	Garlande	874
But to do you servyce nedis now I must;	337	Garlande	879
to do you] 'do her' MS Cotton Vitellius E.x			
Compare you I may to Cidippes, the mayd,	337	Garlande	885
You to devyse his crafte were to seke;	337	Garlande	893
In you, who list to seke,	338	Garlande	920
I you assure, /Ful wel I know	338	Garlande	926
Madame regent /I may you call /Of vertuows all.	339	Garlande	952
Wherfore, I make you sure,	340	Garlande	993
I make you sure] 'I yow assure' MS Cotton Vitellius E.x			

YOUER — YOUR

	Page	Title	Line
And I with you thwartid	341	Garlande	1039
To wryte of you this goodli clause,	341	Garlande	1042
To wryte of you this goodly clause,	342	Garlande	1058
I coude shew you suche a presedent	342	Garlande	1083
you] not in MS Cotton Vitellius E.x			
Here you not Eolus for you blowyth a blaste?	343	Garlande	1088
you (1st)] 'ye' MS Cotton Vitellius E.x			
Here you not Eolus for you blowyth a blaste?	343	Garlande	1088
you (1st)] 'ye' MS Cotton Vitellius E.x			
Of that shalbe resonde you ye must be content;	344	Garlande	1123
you] not in Marshe 1568			
Fortune to stande betwene you and the lyght.	344	Garlande	1134
Item to Lerne You to Dye When ye Wyll;	345	Garlande	1176
to] 'do' †Fakes 1523			
Go, litill quaire, /Demene you faire.	355	Garlande	1534
Though I you wrate /After this rate	355	Garlande	1536
And so procede /In you to rede,	355	Garlande	1549
Ye shall have nede /You for to spede	355	Garlande	1555
Ye] 'You' Marshe 1568			
Nor for to chyde, /Nor for to hyde /You cowardly;	356	Garlande	1568
That valiaunt knyght, /Putte you to flyght /By his valyaunce.	360	Albany	41
That shall cast you in care,	361	Albany	112
And hang you upon polles	362	Albany	151
And byrne you all to colles,	362	Albany	152
God sende you sorow and care!	363	Albany	181
And hyde you under logges,	364	Albany	213
Or what actyvyte /Is in you, beggars braules,	364	Albany	218
Ye decte you to dwell;	366	Albany	280
With a gon stone, /To make you to grone.	366	Albany	286
That neyther of you twayne	367	Albany	337
Lyst with you to varry	367	Albany	341
If he on you but frounde	367	Albany	345
Thoughe I trym you thys trace	367	Albany	355
That shall bring you full bace	368	Albany	366
And set you in suche case	368	Albany	367
That bytwene you twayne	368	Albany	368
God let you never thrive!	368	Albany	379
Our mayster shall you brynge,	368	Albany	384
And mate you with chek mate.	368	Albany	386
It is time for you to brydell	368	Albany	388
For you to bring about	368	Albany	391
We shall pype you a daunce	371	Albany	498
Shall tourne you to myschauns.	371	Albany	499
I rede you, loke about;	371	Albany	500
For you shalbe driven out	371	Albany	501
Shew them that shall you rede	371	Albany	509
That caused you to devise	372	Albany	526
Whan prelacy you opposed.	377	Replycacion	106
To helpe you to promocion,	378	Replycacion	137
To gyve you exhibycion	378	Replycacion	143
Some of you had ten pounde,	378	Replycacion	146
That bringes you out of the way	379	Replycacion	170
Men have you in suspicion	379	Replycacion	182
One of you there was	379	Replycacion	186
I make you fast and sure,	380	Replycacion	232
Have made you eate the fly,	381	Replycacion	252
Why jangle you suche jestes,	381	Replycacion	264
Therfore I vyse you to forsake	382	Replycacion	297
Therefore no grevance, /I pray you, for to take,	385	Replycacion	398

YOUER

	Page	Title	Line
And make youer stomake seke	128	Garnesche3	156

YOUGHTE

	Page	Title	Line
'Prynces of youghte', can ye synge by rote?	53	Bowge	253

YOUR

	Page	Title	Line
Where was your wit and reson ye shuld have had?	30	Dol Dethe	52
your] 'ys' †MS Royal 18 D.ii			
Your naturall lord? Alas, I kan not fayne.	30	Dol Dethe	54
Ye armed you with wille and left your wit behynd;	30	Dol Dethe	55
He was your chyfteyne, your shelde, your chef defens,	30	Dol Dethe	57
He was your chyfteyne, your shelde, your chef defens,	30	Dol Dethe	57
He was your chyfteyne, your shelde, your chef defens,	30	Dol Dethe	57
Your worship depended of his excellence.	31	Dol Dethe	59
Your hap was unhappy, to ill was your spede.	31	Dol Dethe	61
Your hap was unhappy, to ill was your spede.	31	Dol Dethe	61
What aylde you to slo your lord ageyn all right?	31	Dol Dethe	63
slo] 'sle' Marshe 1568			
For whos causis ye slew hym with your awne hande.	31	Dol Dethe	68
I am no hakney for your rode;	35	Man Margery	11
Go watch a bole, your bak is brode.	35	Man Margery	12
'Walke forth your way, ye cost me nought;	36	Man Margery	22
Gup, Cristian Clowte, your breth is stale,	36	Man Margery	27
Now here I shewyd you part of your proud mynde;	38	Coystrowne1	67
To prayse your porte it is nedeles;	40	Coystrowne4	5
For all your 'Draffe' yet and your 'Dreggys',	40	Coystrowne4	6
For all your 'Draffe' yet and your 'Dreggys',	40	Coystrowne4	6
Put up your purs, ye shall non pay!'	40	Coystrowne4	11
Let me', quod he, 'ly in your lap.'	41	Balettys1	2
Remembryng your passyng goodly countenaunce,	42	Balettys2	5

Text	Page	Title	Line
Your goodly port, your bewteous visage,	42	Balettys2	6
Your goodly port, your bewteous visage,	42	Balettys2	6
Of all your feturs favorable to make tru discripcion,	42	Balettys2	8
How in good horsmen ye set your hole delyght,	42	Balettys2	13
And have forgoten your old, trew, lovyng knyght.	42	Balettys2	14
With, 'Jayst ye, Jenet of Spayne, for your tayll waggys,'	43	Balettys2	18
Ye cast all your corage uppon such courtly haggys!	43	Balettys2	19
Thys grevyth your husband, that ryght jentyll knyght,	43	Balettys2	27
And so with your servantys he fersly doth fyght.	43	Balettys2	28
Ask all your neybours whether that I ly.	43	Balettys2	35
For your jentyll husband sorowfull am I;	43	Balettys2	37
Or ells with gret shame your game wylbe sene.	43	Balettys2	42
Your ruddys wyth ruddy rubys may compare;	44	Balettys3	16
Of your bownte and of youre womanhod,	44	Balettys3	31
Bone aventure have here now in your honde.	48	Bowge	98
She that styreth the shyp, make her your frende.'	49	Bowge	107
As of your connynge, that is so excellent;	50	Bowge	149
And, though I say it, I was myselfe your frende,	50	Bowge	160
And ye nede ought, man, shewe to me your mynde,	50	Bowge	165
Nay, naye, be sure, whyles I am on your syde	50	Bowge	169
Ye stonde in favoure and Fortune is your gyde,	50	Bowge	171
He wyll begyle you and speke fayre to your face.	51	Bowge	200
Tell me your mynde, me thynke ye make a verse,	53	Bowge	244
Where hathe your dwellynge ben, er ye cam here?	53	Bowge	247
But wolde be glad of your company.	53	Bowge	268
It is your fortune for to have that grace;	53	Bowge	272
I knowe your vertu and your lytterkture lytterkture] 'lytterature' Wynkyn de Worde 1510	59	Bowge	449
I knowe your vertu and your lytterkture lytterkture] 'lytterature' Wynkyn de Worde 1510	59	Bowge	449
Yet wyll I saye some wordes for your sake	59	Bowge	474
And I am your, syr, so have I blys,	60	Bowge	495
Gyve me your honde, fare well and have good daye.'	60	Bowge	497
I have an errande to rounde in your ere.	60	Bowge	513
Under supportacyon /Of your pacyent tolleracyon,	62	Hauke	32
[Y]e develysh dogmatista, /Your hawke on your fista, Ye] 'The' †Lant 1545, Kynge & Marche 1554, Day 1560, Marshe 1568	69	Hauke	256
[Y]e develysh dogmatista, /Your hawke on your fista, Ye] 'The' †Lant 1545, Kynge & Marche 1554, Day 1560, Marshe 1568	69	Hauke	256
Ye made your hawke to cum /Desuper candelabrum	69	Hauke	288
Christi crucifixi /To fede uppon your fisty;	69	Hauke	291
Hampar with your hammer upon thy styth,	71	Hauke	332
The more shal be your mede.	72	Phy Sparrow	16
With, 'Phyllyp, kepe your cut!'	74	Phy Sparrow	119
Of your fathers bote,	78	Phy Sparrow	249
All maner of byrdes in your kynd;	81	Phy Sparrow	388
Of your wyse reformacyon;	102	Phy Sparrow	1248
Kynge Jamy, Jomy your joye is all go.	113	Scot Kynge	1
To sommon our kynge your soverayne lorde.	113	Scot Kynge	4
In your somnynge ye were to malaperte,	113	Scot Kynge	7
And your harolde no thynge experte;	113	Scot Kynge	8
Your wyll renne before your wytte.	113	Scot Kynge	12
Your wyll renne before your wytte.	113	Scot Kynge	12
To be so scornefull to your alye	113	Scot Kynge	13
Your counseyle was not worth a flye.	113	Scot Kynge	14
Ye ought to honour your lorde and brother.	114	Scot Kynge	16
For you and your Scottes wolde tourne his face?	114	Scot Kynge	18
For your kynge may synge welawaye.	114	Scot Kynge	20
Now must ye knowe our kynge for your regent,	114	Scot Kynge	21
Your soverayne lorde and presedent.	114	Scot Kynge	22
Thrugh your counseyle your fader was slayne;	114	Scot Kynge	27
Thrugh your counseyle your fader was slayne;	114	Scot Kynge	27
Ye dyde not your dewty therin,	114	Scot Kynge	32
Therfore ye have lost your copyholde.	114	Scot Kynge	35
Gyve up your game, ye playe chek mate;	114	Scot Kynge	37
Your pryd is paste, adwe, good nycht.	114	Scot Kynge	43
Ye were beten weth your owne rod.	114	Scot Kynge	47
By your wanton wyll, syr, at a worde,	114	Scot Kynge	48
Your power coude no lenger attayne	114	Scot Kynge	54
Of our Englysshe bowes ye have fette your banes.	115	Scot Kynge	65
Your pompe and pryde hath layde a downe.	115	Scot Kynge	69
Is it come unto your lot	116	Ag Scottes	50
It greyth nought for your degre	116	Ag Scottes	52
Your soverayne lord, our prynce of myght.	117	Ag Scottes	54
It shameth all your noughty nacyon,	117	Ag Scottes	56
Adieu, syr sumner, cast of your crowne!	117	Ag Scottes	64
Unto your grace for grace now I call,	117	Ag Scottes	78
Illumyn me, your poete and your scrybe,	117	Ag Scottes	80
Illumyn me, your poete and your scrybe,	117	Ag Scottes	80
To touche them with tauntes of your armony,	117	Ag Scottes	86
To summon our kyng, your soveraygne lorde.	118	Ag Scottes	94
Your sumner to saucy, to malapert;	118	Ag Scottes	97
Your harrold in armes not yet halfe expert.	118	Ag Scottes	98
Your wyll than ran before your wyt.	118	Ag Scottes	102
Your wyll than ran before your wyt.	118	Ag Scottes	102
Your lege ye layd and your aly,	118	Ag Scottes	103

YOUR —YOUR   Page   Title   Line

Entry	Page	Title	Line
Your lege ye layd and your aly,	118	Ag Scottes	103
Your frantyck fable not worth a fly,	118	Ag Scottes	104
Regardyd ye shuld your lord, your brother.	118	Ag Scottes	106
ye] 'you' Day 1560, Marshe 1568			
Regardyd ye shuld your lord, your brother.	118	Ag Scottes	106
ye] 'you' Day 1560, Marshe 1568			
Now is your pryde fall to decay.	118	Ag Scottes	110
Male uryd was your fals entent	118	Ag Scottes	111
For to offend your presydent,	118	Ag Scottes	112
Your soveraygne lorde most reverent,	118	Ag Scottes	113
Your lorde, your brother, and your regent.	118	Ag Scottes	114
Your lorde, your brother, and your regent.	118	Ag Scottes	114
Your lorde, your brother, and your regent.	118	Ag Scottes	114
Though ye untruly your father have slayne,	118	Ag Scottes	119
For your untruth now ar ye shent.	118	Ag Scottes	124
Therfore ye lost your copyehold.	118	Ag Scottes	126
Lost is your game, ye are checkmate.	118	Ag Scottes	128
He ragyd and rent out your hart bloode;	119	Ag Scottes	136
Thus for your guerdon quyt ar ye,	119	Ag Scottes	139
Ye lost your spurrys, ye lost you sworde.	119	Ag Scottes	148
Your pryde was pevysh to play such prankys:	119	Ag Scottes	150
Your welth, your joy, your sport, your play,	119	Ag Scottes	159
Your welth, your joy, your sport, your play,	119	Ag Scottes	159
Your welth, your joy, your sport, your play,	119	Ag Scottes	159
Your welth, your joy, your sport, your play,	119	Ag Scottes	159
Your braggyng bost, your royall aray,	119	Ag Scottes	160
Your braggyng bost, your royall aray,	119	Ag Scottes	160
Your beard so brym as bore at bay,	119	Ag Scottes	161
Your Seven Systers, that gun so gay,	119	Ag Scottes	162
Out of your robes ye were shaked,	119	Ag Scottes	166
your] not in Kynge & Marche 1554, Day 1560, Marshe 1568			
For lacke of grace hard was your hap;	119	Ag Scottes	168
Syr sumner, now where is your crowne?	120	Ag Scottes	178
Cast of your crowne, cast up your crowne!	120	Ag Scottes	179
Cast of your crowne, cast up your crowne!	120	Ag Scottes	179
Syr sumner, now ye have lost your crowne.	120	Ag Scottes	180
In your chalenge, Syr Chystyn, to cale me knave?	121	Garneschel	7
Ye gyrne grymly with your gomys and with yor grysly face.	122	Garneschel	12
Yet your contenons oncomly, yor face ys nat fayer.	122	Garneschel	18
For alle your proude prankyng, yor pride may apayere.	122	Garneschel	19
As ye ar brystlyd on the bake for alle your gay gere.	122	Garneschel	26
At Orwelle hyr havyn your anggre was laules.	122	Garneschel	33
As a glede glowynge, your ien glyster as glasse,	122	Garneschel	37
Your tethe teintyd with tawny; your semely snowte doth passe,	122	Garneschel	39
Your tethe teintyd with tawny; your semely snowte doth passe,	122	Garneschel	39
How may I your mokery mekely tollerate,	123	Garnesche2	1
[Your] gronynge, yor grontynge, yor groinynge lyke a swyne?	123	Garnesche2	2
[Your] pride ys alle to peviche, your porte importunate;	123	Garnesche2	3
[Your] pride ys alle to peviche, your porte importunate;	123	Garnesche2	3
Your lothesum lere to loke on, lyke a gresyd bote dothe schyne.	123	Garnesche2	5
Ye cappyd Cayface copious, your paltoke on your pate,	123	Garnesche2	6
Ye cappyd Cayface copious, your paltoke on your pate,	123	Garnesche2	6
Hole ys your brow that ye brake with Deu[ra]ndall your awne sworde; Deurandall] 'Deundall' †MS Harley 367	123	Garnesche2	8
Hole ys your brow that ye brake with Deu[ra]ndall your awne sworde; Deurandall] 'Deundall' †MS Harley 367	123	Garnesche2	8
Ye cappyd Cayface copyous, your paltoke on your pate,	123	Garnesche2	13
Ye cappyd Cayface copyous, your paltoke on your pate,	123	Garnesche2	13
Huf, a galante, Garnesche, loke on your comly cors!	123	Garnesche2	16
Me for to chalenge that of your chalennge makyth so lytyll fors.	123	Garnesche2	19
Ye capyd Cayfas copyous, your paltoke on your pate,	123	Garnesche2	20
Ye capyd Cayfas copyous, your paltoke on your pate,	123	Garnesche2	20
In Arturys auncyent actys nowhere ys provyd your pere;	123	Garnesche2	24
The facyoun of your fysnamy the devyl in a clowde;	123	Garnesche2	25
Your harte ys to hawte, iwys, yt wyll nat be alowde.	123	Garnesche2	26
Ye capid Cayfas copyus, your paltoke on your pate,	123	Garnesche2	27
Ye capid Cayfas copyus, your paltoke on your pate,	123	Garnesche2	27
Your stondarde, Syr Olifranke, agenst me for to splay;	123	Garnesche2	30
Ye cappydd Cayfas copyous, your paltoke on your pate,	123	Garnesche2	34
Ye cappydd Cayfas copyous, your paltoke on your pate,	123	Garnesche2	34
Ye cappydd Cayfas copyous, your paltoke on your pate,	124	Garnesche2	41
Ye cappydd Cayfas copyous, your paltoke on your pate,	124	Garnesche2	41
I have your lewde letter receyvyd,	124	Garnesche3	1
And your skrybe I have aspyed,	124	Garnesche3	3
That your mad mynde contryved.	124	Garnesche3	4
Savynge your usscheres rod,	124	Garnesche3	5
How the favyr of your face	124	Garnesche3	9
For alle your carpet cousshons	124	Garnesche3	11
Lewdely your tyme ye spende,	124	Garnesche3	15
Your awne lewdnes to amende.	124	Garnesche3	18
Your Englysche lew[d]ly ye sorte,	124	Garnesche3	19
lewdly] 'lewly' †MS Harley 367			
For to aswage your pride.	124	Garnesche3	23
In the pott your nose dedde snevyll;	124	Garnesche3	27
Dekkyd lewdly in your gere.	125	Garnesche3	42
Your beste gowne festyvalle.	125	Garnesche3	51
Your drapry ye ded wante	125	Garnesche3	52
On to your lowsy den;	125	Garnesche3	64

	Page	Title	Line
Your pyllyd garleke hed	125	Garnesche3	68
Your brethe ys stronge and quike;	126	Garnesche3	78
Yt ys to your reproche.	126	Garnesche3	85
Lytyll wyt in your scrybys nolle	126	Garnesche3	90
That scrybblyd your fonde scrolle,	126	Garnesche3	91
To occupy so your mynde;	126	Garnesche3	103
Caste up your curyows wrytyng,	127	Garnesche3	112
And your dyrty endytyng,	127	Garnesche3	113
And your spyghtfull despyghtyng,	127	Garnesche3	114
And occupyed no better your tole,	127	Garnesche3	118
Your face I wyse to varnyshe	127	Garnesche3	121
Your wyt ys so geson,	127	Garnesche3	129
Your skyn scabbyd and scurvy,	127	Garnesche3	131
Your sworde ye swere, I wene,	127	Garnesche3	137
Your foly ys to grett	127	Garnesche3	140
Your brethe yt ys so felle	127	Garnesche3	142
He wyl cause yow caste your crawes,	128	Garnesche3	155
Ye kyt your clothe to large,	129	Garnesche3	189
And he that scryblyd your scrolles,	129	Garnesche3	192
I have receyvyd your secunde ryme.	129	Garnesche5	2
Your chorlyshe chauntyng ys all o lay.	129	Garnesche5	6
Soche pajantes with your fryndes ye play,	130	Garnesche5	37
Crimsin velvet for your bawdry.	130	Garnesche5	40
Ye lost your [h]olde, onbende your bow, holde] 'bolde' †MS Harley 367	131	Garnesche5	49
Ye lost your [h]olde, onbende your bow, holde] 'bolde' †MS Harley 367	131	Garnesche5	49
Sche seyd your brethe stanke lyke a broke;	131	Garnesche5	55
That all the warlde wyll spye your shame.	132	Garnesche5	111
For before on your brest, and behind on your back	137	Ven Tongues	16
For before on your brest, and behind on your back	137	Ven Tongues	16
In your crosse rowe nor Christ crosse you spede,	137	Ven Tongues	18
Your Pater noster, your Ave, nor your Crede.	137	Ven Tongues	19
Your Pater noster, your Ave, nor your Crede.	137	Ven Tongues	19
Your Pater noster, your Ave, nor your Crede.	137	Ven Tongues	19
Of me with your language full of vilany.	138	Ven Tongues	48
Syr, as ye say. I have harde of your fame.	141	Magnyfycence	26
Your name is Lyberte, as I understande.	141	Magnyfycence	27
Trewe you say, syr. Gyve me your hande.	141	Magnyfycence	28
But yf reason be regent and ruler of your barge.	141	Magnyfycence	38
But with countenaunce your corage must be croppyd.	141	Magnyfycence	47
And peradventure I shall content your mynde.	142	Magnyfycence	49
Your consayte to debarre,	142	Magnyfycence	60
Your reasons forth to fet.	142	Magnyfycence	64
Softe, my frende. Herein your reason is but rawe.	142	Magnyfycence	70
And you have not your owne fre lyberte	142	Magnyfycence	78
To sporte at your pleasure, to ryn, and to ryde?	142	Magnyfycence	79
Cryst you assyste in your altrycacyon!	142	Magnyfycence	81
And it is wonder that your wylde insolence	143	Magnyfycence	85
Your langage is lyke the penne	143	Magnyfycence	90
We your pleasure fulfyll.	143	Magnyfycence	106
Unto your rule I wyll annex my mynde.	144	Magnyfycence	142
Well, I am content your wayes to take.	144	Magnyfycence	155
Magnyfycence to mayntayne, your promosyon shalbe.	144	Magnyfycence	157
Yet in this man you must set your delyght.	145	Magnyfycence	167
But nowe let me knowe of your conversacyon.	145	Magnyfycence	170
Pleasyth, your grace, Felycyte they me call.	145	Magnyfycence	171
Your ordenaunce, syr, I wyll not forsake.	145	Magnyfycence	181
Laudable your consayte is to be acountyd,	145	Magnyfycence	191
As your grace full nobly hath recountyd,	145	Magnyfycence	193
Then, Lyberte, se that Measure by your gyde,	146	Magnyfycence	195
Your noblenesse and honour conservnynge.	146	Magnyfycence	204
In joy and myrthe your mynde shalbe inlargyd	146	Magnyfycence	205
If ye lyst to lyve after your fre lyberte.	146	Magnyfycence	208
And rule hym after the rule of your scole.	146	Magnyfycence	231
And now wolde ye swarve from your owne ordynaunce?	147	Magnyfycence	234
A, ye make me laughe at your inconstaunce.	147	Magnyfycence	236
It shalbe done at your commaundement.	147	Magnyfycence	239
Tusche, holde your pece! Your langage is vayne.	147	Magnyfycence	251
Tusche, holde your pece! Your langage is vayne.	147	Magnyfycence	251
Please it your grace to take no dysdayne,	147	Magnyfycence	252
Sholde be your dwellynge, in my consyderacyon.	148	Magnyfycence	274
As in that I wyll not be agaynst your pleasure.	148	Magnyfycence	276
Syr, hardely remembre what may your name avaunce.	148	Magnyfycence	277
Plucke up your mynde, syr, what ayle you to muse?	148	Magnyfycence	283
Have ye not welthe here at your wyll?	148	Magnyfycence	284
Though Largesse ye hyght your langage is to large;	148	Magnyfycence	295
That with your lorde and mayster so pertly can prate!	149	Magnyfycence	305
Syr, yf I have offended your noble estate,	149	Magnyfycence	308
Is there ony thynge elles your grace wyll commaunde me?	149	Magnyfycence	318
Your pleasure, syr shortely shall be done.	149	Magnyfycence	321
Nay, syr, it was nothynge but your mynde.	149	Magnyfycence	330
And grotes many one or I came to your presence.	150	Magnyfycence	339
By your soth? Ye, and there is suche a wache,	150	Magnyfycence	350
Sayd I was mete for your grace.	150	Magnyfycence	373
But largesse may amende your name.	151	Magnyfycence	389
I folow even after your noble grace.	151	Magnyfycence	395
Your counterfet countenaunce is all of nysyte,	153	Magnyfycence	478

Text	Page	Title	Line
What! Is your conveyaunce no better.	155	Magnyfycence	542
Your fansy maketh myne elbowe to ake.	156	Magnyfycence	559
A man may beshrowe your angry harte.	156	Magnyfycence	563
Tushe! Holde your pece.	156	Magnyfycence	590
For to knowe your name?	157	Magnyfycence	592
Cockes armes! Is that your name?	157	Magnyfycence	598
Ye, for your wyt is cloked for the rayne.	157	Magnyfycence	609
Tell me, syrs, what is your wyll?	157	Magnyfycence	611
But I wyll be ruled after your counsell.	157	Magnyfycence	615
And Sober Sadnesse shalbe your name?	159	Magnyfycence	681
Decke your hofte and cover a lowce.	161	Magnyfycence	749
Howe be it of scape thryfte your clokes smelleth musty.	161	Magnyfycence	761
Why, shall he be of your bende?	163	Magnyfycence	818
Tushe! Holde your peas; ye speke lyke a dawe.	178	Magnyfycence	1379
Tushe! Holde your peas; ye speke out of season.	178	Magnyfycence	1388
Not and your grace wolde be ruled by me.	179	Magnyfycence	1393
Syr, yet without sapyence your substaunce may be smal;	179	Magnyfycence	1407
Syr, I am here at your pleasure.	179	Magnyfycence	1409
Your grace sent for me, I wene. What is your wyll?	179	Magnyfycence	1410
Your grace sent for me, I wene. What is your wyll?	179	Magnyfycence	1410
I truste your grace wyll be agreabyll	179	Magnyfycence	1417
Shewe us your mynde then, howe to do and what.	180	Magnyfycence	1435
Mayster Felycyte, let be your chydynge;	180	Magnyfycence	1437
What the devyll, man, your name shalbe the greter;	180	Magnyfycence	1440
At your commaundement, syr, wyth all dew reverence.	182	Magnyfycence	1515
Plesyth it your grace to shewe what I do shall?	182	Magnyfycence	1517
Let us here of your pleasure, to passe the tyme withall.	182	Magnyfycence	1518
Syr, then, with the favour of your benynge sufferaunce,	182	Magnyfycence	1519
If it lyke your grace to take it in degre.	182	Magnyfycence	1521
And in your delynge so good assuraunce,	183	Magnyfycence	1523
That we delyte gretly in your dalyaunce.	183	Magnyfycence	1524
A, syr, your grace me dothe extole and rayse;	183	Magnyfycence	1525
Any thynge to do that myght be to your pleasure.	183	Magnyfycence	1528
Of your langage, it is so well devysed;	183	Magnyfycence	1530
Pullyshyd and fresshe is your ornacy.	183	Magnyfycence	1531
As that I myght your noble grace content!	183	Magnyfycence	1534
He is not lyvynge your maners can amend;	183	Magnyfycence	1537
Mary, your speche is as pleasant as though it were pend,	183	Magnyfycence	1538
To here your comon, it is my hygh comforte.	183	Magnyfycence	1539
Poynt devyse, all pleasure is your porte.	183	Magnyfycence	1540
Syr, I am the better of your noble reporte;	183	Magnyfycence	1541
But of your pacyence under the supporte,	183	Magnyfycence	1542
It is semynge your pleasure ye delyte,	183	Magnyfycence	1546
And quyckely your appetytes to sharpe and adresse;	183	Magnyfycence	1549
To fasten your fansy upon a fayre maystresse	183	Magnyfycence	1550
Inpurtured with fetures after your purpose,	183	Magnyfycence	1552
And brought home and layde in your bed.	184	Magnyfycence	1572
But yf it lyke your grace more at large	185	Magnyfycence	1589
Wysely let these wordes in your mynde be wayed:	185	Magnyfycence	1593
What so ever ye do, folowe your owne wyll,	185	Magnyfycence	1595
Take your pleasure and use free lyberte;	185	Magnyfycence	1598
And yf you se ony thynge agaynst your mynde,	185	Magnyfycence	1599
But do as ye lyst and take your owne way.	185	Magnyfycence	1604
Let your lust and lykynge stande for a lawe.	185	Magnyfycence	1607
And that your mynde can not well be eased -	185	Magnyfycence	1610
To styre up your stomake you must you forge,	185	Magnyfycence	1613
Call for a ca[u]dell and cast up your gorge,	185	Magnyfycence	1614
caudell] 'candell' †Rastell & Treveris C 1530, B			
That for your sake I wyll fall on my kne.	186	Magnyfycence	1630
Please it your grace at the contemplacyon	186	Magnyfycence	1633
Tenderly to consyder in your advertence -	186	Magnyfycence	1635
My frende, as touchynge to this your mocyon,	186	Magnyfycence	1639
Howe be it, at your instaunce I wyll the rather	186	Magnyfycence	1641
For of your grace I have it nought deserved.	186	Magnyfycence	1644
But yf it lyke you that I myght rowne in your eyre,	186	Magnyfycence	1645
Yet, syr, reserved your better advysement,	187	Magnyfycence	1661
Nowe, by your trouthe, gave he you not a brybe?	187	Magnyfycence	1665
For your sake, what so ever befall;	188	Magnyfycence	1709
The Holy Goost be with your grace.	188	Magnyfycence	1711
In your brest towardes this gentylman.	188	Magnyfycence	1713
I was your good lorde tyll that ye beganne	188	Magnyfycence	1714
Abyde, syr, abyde. Let me holde your hede.	189	Magnyfycence	1727
By the good Lorde, yet your temples bete.	189	Magnyfycence	1732
Syr, nowe me thynke your harte is well eased.	189	Magnyfycence	1737
Thus must ye stuffe and store your treasure.	189	Magnyfycence	1754
Let me have the rule of your purse.	189	Magnyfycence	1762
But use your largesse by the advyse of me,	189	Magnyfycence	1765
Say on; me thynke your reasons be profounde.	190	Magnyfycence	1767
And let all your fansyes upon them rest.	190	Magnyfycence	1770
Those thre wyll be redy even at your bekenynge;	190	Magnyfycence	1778
Your welthe and felycyte, I trust we shall optayne	190	Magnyfycence	1792
To do you servyce after your appetyte.	190	Magnyfycence	1793
In faythe, and your servyce ryght well shall I acquyte;	190	Magnyfycence	1794
Mary, Cryst graunt ye catche no colde on your fete!	191	Magnyfycence	1803
Who is this? Consayte, syr, your owne man.	191	Magnyfycence	1804
What sayst thou? Mary, I pray God your mastershyp to save.	191	Magnyfycence	1828
What! Is all your myrthe nowe tourned to sorowe?	192	Magnyfycence	1849
And your payntyd Pleasure, Courtly Abusyon,	192	Magnyfycence	1860

| YOUR — YOUR | Page | Title | Line |

And your demenour with Counterfet Countenaunce,	192	Magnyfycence	1861
And your Su[rvay]our, Crafty Conveyaunce,	192	Magnyfycence	1862
Survayour] 'supervysour' †Rastell & Treveris C 1530, B			
Nay. It was your fondnesse that ye have usyd.	193	Magnyfycence	1866
Why, coulde not your wyt serve you no better?	193	Magnyfycence	1868
And pray to God your sorowes to asswage.	196	Magnyfycence	1989
With harte contryte make your supplycacyon	196	Magnyfycence	1991
Unto your maker that made bothe you and me;	196	Magnyfycence	1992
Put your wyll to his wyll, for surely it is he	196	Magnyfycence	1997
And remembre he suffered moche more for your sake;	196	Magnyfycence	2001
Nowe must your fete lye hyer than your crowne.	197	Magnyfycence	2007
Nowe must your fete lye hyer than your crowne.	197	Magnyfycence	2007
Where you were wonte to have cawdels for your hede,	197	Magnyfycence	2008
Your skynne that was wrapped in shertes of Raynes,	197	Magnyfycence	2016
Your hede that was wonte to be hawped moost drowpy and drowsy,	197	Magnyfycence	2018
Go together by the heddys, and gyve me your swordys.	202	Magnyfycence	2199
Well sayd. But, in fayth, what was your quarell?	203	Magnyfycence	2210
I can not well tell of your dysposycyons;	203	Magnyfycence	2218
Your trymynge and tramynge by me must be tangyd,	203	Magnyfycence	2234
I was your mayster, though ye thynke it skorne;	204	Magnyfycence	2246
Agaynst all [s]autes of your goostly foo.	206	Magnyfycence	2329
sautes] 'fautes' †Rastell & Treveris C 1530, B, Douce Fragment d.7			
Your wordes be more sweter than ony precyous narde,	207	Magnyfycence	2345
More delectable than your langage to me.	207	Magnyfycence	2348
Syr, your fesycyan is the grace of God,	207	Magnyfycence	2349
Good Hope, your potecary, assygned am I,	207	Magnyfycence	2351
With drammes of devocyon your dyet must be drest,	207	Magnyfycence	2358
And hartely thanke God of your adversyte;	207	Magnyfycence	2362
And love that Lorde that for your love was dede,	207	Magnyfycence	2363
He may helpe you. He may mende your mode.	207	Magnyfycence	2366
He be your conducte, the Lorde of myghtys moste!	208	Magnyfycence	2386
Syr, is your pacyent any thynge amendyd?	208	Magnyfycence	2387
How fele you your selfe, my frend? How is your mynde?	208	Magnyfycence	2389
And I truste to ratyfye and amende your fame.	208	Magnyfycence	2398
Syr, your requeste shall not be delayed.	208	Magnyfycence	2401
To your requeste I shall be confyrmable.	208	Magnyfycence	2407
Determyne to amende all your wanton excesse;	208	Magnyfycence	2409
Syr, after your message I hyed me hyder streyght,	209	Magnyfycence	2419
For to understande your pleasure and also your mynde.	209	Magnyfycence	2420
For to understande your pleasure and also your mynde.	209	Magnyfycence	2420
Use not then your countenaunce for to counterfet.	210	Magnyfycence	2455
Well, syr, after your counsell my mynde I wyll set.	210	Magnyfycence	2457
Syrs, I am agreed to abyde your ordenaunce –	210	Magnyfycence	2471
Your comfortable advyse and wyt excedyth all gladnesse;	210	Magnyfycence	2477
Your myndys I beseche you here in to expresse,	211	Magnyfycence	2480
Fyrst, from your magnyfycence syn must be abjectyd;	211	Magnyfycence	2484
In all your warkys more grace shall ye fynde;	211	Magnyfycence	2485
So that your largesse be not to prodygall.	211	Magnyfycence	2488
Measure of your lustys must have the oversyght,	211	Magnyfycence	2491
Let never nygarshyp your noblenesse affray;	211	Magnyfycence	2493
In your rewardys use suche moderacyon	211	Magnyfycence	2494
To the increse of your honour then arme you with ryght,	211	Magnyfycence	2496
And ever let the drede of God be in your syght,	211	Magnyfycence	2498
And knowe your selfe mortal for all your dygnyte;	211	Magnyfycence	2499
Set not all your affyaunce in Fortune full of gyle;	211	Magnyfycence	2501
Redresse, in my remembraunce your lesson shall rest;	211	Magnyfycence	2503
But, Perseveraunce, me semyth your probleme was best;	212	Magnyfycence	2505
Home to your paleys with joy and ryalte.	214	Magnyfycence	2567
Where every thyng is ordenyd after your noble porte.	214	Magnyfycence	2568
I shall breke your palettes, /Wythout ye now cease!'	223	El Rummynge	348
And ye wyll gyve me a syppet /Of your stale ale,	223	El Rummynge	368
Bere them to your chamber.'	229	El Rummynge	604
Yet ye seke out your Greke in Capricornio,	235	Speke Parott	152
'Cristecrosse and Saynt Nycholas, Parrot, be your good spede!'	236	Speke Parott	189
Support Parrot, I pray you, with your suffrage ornate,	236	Speke Parott	195
But lewdlye ar they lettyrd that your lernyng lackys,	239	Speke Parott	294
For whoo lokythe wyselye in your warkys may fynde	239	Speke Parott	296
Muche frutefull mater. But now for your defence,	239	Speke Parott	297
Now pas furthe, good Parott, Owur Lorde be your s[t]ede,	239	Speke Parott	313
stede] 'spede' †MS Harley 2252			
In this your journey to prospere and spede.	239	Speke Parott	314
And howe your poemys arre barayne of polyshed eloquens,	240	Speke Parott	316
There is none that your name woll abbrogate	240	Speke Parott	317
To rude ys there reason to reche to your sentence;	240	Speke Parott	319
Prepayre yow, Parrot, brevely your passage to take,	240	Speke Parott	324
Yet your problemes ar preignaunte and with loyalte acquayntyd.	240	Speke Parott	344
Your rudeness to pardon and also that they wolde	241	Speke Parott	360
Wherfor your remorders ar madde or else starke blynde,	241	Speke Parott	369
remorders] 'remordes' †MS Harley 2252			
Yow to remorde erste or they know your mynde.	241	Speke Parott	370
O connyng clergye, where ys your redynes	242	Speke Parott	392
It is nat for your werynge,	252	Collyn Clout	210
Your gorge nat endued /Without a capon stued,	252	Collyn Clout	215
In your provyncyall borders,	252	Collyn Clout	221
I am sory for your sake!	253	Collyn Clout	252
You shall have your wylla!'	253	Collyn Clout	261
And shryne your rotten bonys	255	Collyn Clout	346

YOUR —YOUR	Page	Title	Line
Your workes, they say, are straunge -	257	Collyn Clout	420
Shall have penalte /For your iniquite.	258	Collyn Clout	462
Your teth whett on this bone	258	Collyn Clout	476
whett on] 'whetten' †Godfray 1531, 'whette on' MS Harley 2252			
Lay salve to your owne sore,	258	Collyn Clout	480
But under your supporte,	259	Collyn Clout	505
Your hygh and lordely lokes.	261	Collyn Clout	595
Ye caste up then your bokes	261	Collyn Clout	596
And that is all your thought.	261	Collyn Clout	607
Whan mammockes was your meate,	263	Collyn Clout	652
To fyll therwith your mawe -	263	Collyn Clout	656
Couchynge your drousy heddes	263	Collyn Clout	658
That though ye rounde your heere	263	Collyn Clout	673
An ynche above your eere,	263	Collyn Clout	674
And your tonsors be croppyd,	263	Collyn Clout	677
tonsors be croppyd] 'coursers betrapped' †Godfray 1531, Kele 1545.1, Marshe 1568			
Your eeres they be stopped!	263	Collyn Clout	678
They folowe your desyris,	263	Collyn Clout	683
And so they blere your eye	263	Collyn Clout	684
For your spirytuall charge,	264	Collyn Clout	692
But men say your auctoryte	265	Collyn Clout	758
But men say] 'Men say but' †Godfray 1531, Kele 1545.1, Marshe 1568			
And your noble se /And your dygnyte	265	Collyn Clout	759
se] 'fee' Marshe 1568, 'see' MS Harley 2252			
And your noble se /And your dygnyte	265	Collyn Clout	760
se] 'fee' Marshe 1568, 'see' MS Harley 2252			
That wolde your wordes retayne	266	Collyn Clout	774
Without the assent /Of your presydent;	272	Collyn Clout	1035
They put you to your actyon.	273	Collyn Clout	1060
In your convenire /Of this premenyre,	273	Collyn Clout	1067
And let be all your motynge,	273	Collyn Clout	1073
Your gasynge and your totynge	273	Collyn Clout	1074
Your gasynge and your totynge	273	Collyn Clout	1074
And your parcyall promotynge	273	Collyn Clout	1075
Of those that stande in your grace.	273	Collyn Clout	1076
Why than /Wreke ye your anger on me?	273	Collyn Clout	1091
And beleve it as your crede.	278	Why Come Ye	2
To scarce of your expence,	278	Why Come Ye	5
And beleve it as your crede.	279	Why Come Ye	16
And beleve it as your crede.	279	Why Come Ye	28
Of your inward charyte;	300	Why Come Ye	838
Amen, /Of your inward charyte.	300	Why Come Ye	840
Your cupbord that was	301	Why Come Ye	901
But the chefe of your fayre	301	Why Come Ye	909
Whatsoever your name be?	309	Why Come Ye2	2
Mayster doctor, in your degre,	309	Why Come Ye2	6
Your fonde hed in your furred hode!	310	Why Come Ye2	19
your] (2nd) 'a' MS Rawlinson C. 813			
Your fonde hed in your furred hode!	310	Why Come Ye2	19
your] (2nd) 'a' MS Rawlinson C. 813			
Holde ye your tong, ye can no goode.	310	Why Come Ye2	20
ye] (1st) not in MS Rawlinson C. 813			
Somwhat of your madnesse;	310	Why Come Ye2	23
For small is your sadnesse	310	Why Come Ye2	24
Of your complaynt it shal nat skyl.	310	Why Come Ye2	32
Not unremembered it is unto your grace,	313	Garlande	57
In your servyce; and, to the accomplysshement	314	Garlande	61
Of your request, regestred is his name	314	Garlande	62
For, ne were onely he hath your promocyon,	314	Garlande	71
Of Elyconis well, refresshid with your grace,	314	Garlande	74
Elyconis] 'Elycoms' †Fakes 1523, 'Heliconis' Marshe 1568			
'The sum of your purpose, as we ar advysid,	314	Garlande	78
'Madame, with favour of your benynge sufferaunce,	315	Garlande	113
Unto your grace then make I this motyve:	315	Garlande	114
Of your royall palace it is not the gyse,	315	Garlande	121
That he to your courte is goyng and commynge,	316	Garlande	139
'Madame, your apposelle is wele inferrid,	316	Garlande	141
And at your avauntage quikly it is	316	Garlande	142
Yet shall I answere your grace as in this,	316	Garlande	144
With your reformacion, if I say amis,	316	Garlande	145
For, but if your bounte did me assure,	316	Garlande	146
Your mynde that can maynteyne so apparently;	317	Garlande	170
Ye counterway not evynly your balaunce;	317	Garlande	179
Ryot and Revell be in your courte rowlis;	317	Garlande	192
But your benynge sufferaunce for my discharge I laid,	318	Garlande	213
But yet I beseche your grace that good recorde	318	Garlande	215
good] not in MS Cotton Vitellius E.x			
Unto your palas, our noble courte of Fame,	318	Garlande	219
'To your request we be well condiscendid;	318	Garlande	232
Call forthe, let se where is your clarionar,	318	Garlande	233
Eolus, your trumpet, that knowne is so farre,	319	Garlande	235
that] 'whiche' MS Cotton Vitellius E.x			
'O mercyles madame, hard is your constellacyon,	320	Garlande	304
So close to kepe your cloyster virgynall,	320	Garlande	305
Enhardid adyment the sement of your wall!	320	Garlande	306
'Brother Skelton, your endevorment	323	Garlande	400

YOUR —YOUR	Page	Title	Line
Arrectinge unto your wyse examinacion	323	Garlande	410
'Counterwayng your besy delygence	323	Garlande	414
In whose court poynted is your place.'	324	Garlande	420
Mayster Lidgate, of your accustomable	324	Garlande	436
Of your acqueintaunce I was in tymes past,	327	Garlande	540
Ye fyrste aryvyd; whan broken was your mast	327	Garlande	542
Ye] 'The' †Fakes 1523			
Your storme dryven shyppe I repared new,	327	Garlande	544
No stormy tempeste your barge shall overthrow.	327	Garlande	546
Be well assurid I shall aquyte your hyre,	327	Garlande	550
Your name recountynge beyonde the lande of Tyre,	327	Garlande	551
'How say ye? Is this after your appetite?	331	Garlande	707
May this contente you and your mirry mynde?	332	Garlande	708
Wherewith your spiritis may be revyvid.'	332	Garlande	713
'Of your demawnd shew me the content,	332	Garlande	721
Of scrupulus dout. Wherfore, your mynde discharge,	332	Garlande	726
And of your wyll the plainnes shew at large.'	332	Garlande	727
That of your bounte so well have me assurid;	332	Garlande	729
Now, by your faith, is not this theffect	333	Garlande	737
by] 'be' †Fakes 1523			
Of your questyon ye make all this whyle	333	Garlande	738
'Syt downe, fayre ladys, and do your diligence!	334	Garlande	772
'Beholde and se in your advertysement	335	Garlande	808
For your pleasure do there endevourment,	335	Garlande	810
And for your sake how fast to warke they fall:	335	Garlande	811
To your remembraunce wherfore ye must call	335	Garlande	812
Ornatly pullysshid after your faculte,	335	Garlande	816
Of your professyoun unto umanyte,	335	Garlande	818
Commensyng your proces after there degre,	335	Garlande	819
The passynge bounte of your noble astate,	336	Garlande	841
Your noble demenour is counterwayng,	336	Garlande	847
So shall your name endure perpetually,	336	Garlande	861
To be your remembrauncer, madame, I am bounde,	336	Garlande	864
Of all your bewte I suffyce not to wryght:	336	Garlande	875
But, as I sayd, your florisshinge tender age	337	Garlande	876
With lillis whyte your bewte doth renewe.	337	Garlande	884
With lillis] 'The lylly' MS Cotton Vitellius E.x			
With lillys whyte your bewte dothe renewe.	337	Garlande	891
And if Apelles your countenaunce had sene,	337	Garlande	894
He coude not devyse the lest poynt of your cheke;	337	Garlande	896
Enbrowdred the mantill /Is of your maydenhede.	338	Garlande	909
maydenhede] 'maydenhode' †Fakes 1523			
Your mammy and your dady	339	Garlande	974
Your mammy and your dady	339	Garlande	974
Enuwyd your colowre /Is lyke the dasy flowre	340	Garlande	985
your] 'her' MS Cotton Vitellius E.x			
Partly by your councell,	342	Garlande	1054
But if I sholde aquyte your kyndnes,	342	Garlande	1062
'Withdrawe your hande, the tyme passis fast.	343	Garlande	1086
Set on your hede this laurell whiche is wrought.	343	Garlande	1087
Where ye must brevely answere to your name.'	343	Garlande	1092
Of laureat triumphe, your place is here reservyd,	344	Garlande	1126
triumphe] 'promocioun' MS Cotton Vitellius E.x			
Of your bounte the accustomable rate	344	Garlande	1130
Whiche in your recordes, I know well, be enrolde,	344	Garlande	1140
And so Occupacyon, your regester, me told.'	344	Garlande	1141
Your discharge here under myne arme is it.'	344	Garlande	1146
'Of your oratour and poete laureate	345	Garlande	1170
May happely loke /Upon your boke,	355	Garlande	1547
That so indede /Your fame may sprede	355	Garlande	1551
Your hartes sore faynted,	359	Albany	27
Lyke cankerd curres /Ye loste your spurres;	360	Albany	34
To your great lacke /And utter shame	360	Albany	45
Of your Scottysshe name.	360	Albany	47
Your chefe cheftayne, /Voyde of all brayne,	360	Albany	48
Your capitayne ranne to go,	360	Albany	65
But now must I /Your Duke ascry /Of Albany	360	Albany	73
In shorte sentens, /Of your pretens /What is the grounde	361	Albany	80
And set hys crowne /On your owne heed	361	Albany	97
Suche trechery /And traytory /Is all your cast.	361	Albany	101
It shalbe your lottes	362	Albany	121
About your traytours throtes.	362	Albany	124
Ye may be assured /Your falshod discured	362	Albany	128
By your Duke of Albany.	363	Albany	162
Must crepe in to your caves	363	Albany	185
Your heedes for to hyde	363	Albany	186
Ye rage and ye rave, /And your worshyp deprave:	363	Albany	191
But ye and your hoost,	364	Albany	206
Thus in your cowardly castell	366	Albany	279
Your last deedly bane	366	Albany	284
As though ye wolde parbrake /Your avauns to make,	367	Albany	323
And cowardly tourne your backes	367	Albany	349
For all your comly crackes.	367	Albany	350
And ryn your way apace.	367	Albany	354
Your cankarde cowardnesse /And your shamfull doublenesse.	368	Albany	361
Your cankarde cowardnesse /And your shamfull doublenesse.	368	Albany	362
That shalbe to your payne?	368	Albany	370
Your braynes are ydell;	368	Albany	387

YOURE —YOUR SELFE

	Page	Title	Line
With your enbosed jawes	370	Albany	477
The fende scrache out your mawes!	371	Albany	479
Of your lande in shorte space.	371	Albany	502
For to tourne your face;	371	Albany	505
Though your Englishe be rude,	372	Albany	516
Grounded is your sentence	372	Albany	519
With your lyppes polluted	375	Replycacion	29
Open your janglyng jawes,	375	Replycacion	37
Your tonges were to flete;	376	Replycacion	50
Your sermon was nat swete;	376	Replycacion	51
Your lernyng is starke nought,	376	Replycacion	56
Your madnesse she attamed;	376	Replycacion	61
Thorowe your owne foly,	376	Replycacion	84
In your dialeticall /And principles silogisticall,	377	Replycacion	96
Your hertes than were hosed, /Your relacions reposed;	377	Replycacion	107
Your hertes than were hosed, /Your relacions reposed;	377	Replycacion	108
Surrendring your supposycions,	377	Replycacion	112
For there ye myst you[r] quosshons.	377	Replycacion	113
your] 'you' †Pynson 1528			
Wolde God, for your owne ease,	377	Replycacion	114
That wyse Harpocrates /Had your mouthes stopped,	377	Replycacion	116
And your tonges cropped, /Whan ye logyke chopped,	377	Replycacion	117
Your sysmaticate sawes /Agaynst Goddes lawes,	377	Replycacion	122
To mainteyne with your skoles,	378	Replycacion	144
Your names to magnifye,	378	Replycacion	164
Marked in your cradels	379	Replycacion	174
Your penaunce toke no place,	379	Replycacion	198
Your penaunce was to lyght;	379	Replycacion	199
And your lollardy lernyng teched,	379	Replycacion	204
And knowledge your offence /Before open audyence,	380	Replycacion	207
Of your noughty counsell,	380	Replycacion	213
With blowyng out your hornes,	380	Replycacion	215
And your busy pratyng.	380	Replycacion	218
And bremely with your bristels	380	Replycacion	221
For your ignorance is gretter,	380	Replycacion	231
Than all your lytterature.	380	Replycacion	233
To your great vyllony,	380	Replycacion	245
Your madde ipocrisy, /And your idiosy,	381	Replycacion	249
Your madde ipocrisy, /And your idiosy,	381	Replycacion	250
And your vayne glorie	381	Replycacion	251
In your divynite /Of Luthers affynite,	381	Replycacion	265
Raylyng in your rages	381	Replycacion	268
But mende your myndes that are mased;	382	Replycacion	293
YOURE			
What frantyk frensy fyll in youre brayne?	30	Dol Dethe	51
At me, that medeled nothyng with youre wark.	38	Coystrownel	61
Youre ugly tokyn /My mynd hath brokyn /From worldly lust;	39	Coystrowne3	1
Youre medelyng, mastres, is manerles;	40	Coystrowne4	2
Though angelyk be youre smylyng,	41	Coystrowne4	15
Yet is youre tong an adders tayle,	41	Coystrowne4	16
Youre key is mete for every lok,	41	Coystrowne4	22
Youre key is commen and hangyth owte;	41	Coystrowne4	23
Youre key is redy, we nede not knok	41	Coystrowne4	24
Of youre doregate ye have no doute.	41	Coystrowne4	26
Holde youre tong, now, all beshrewde!	41	Coystrowne4	28
The pullyshed perle youre whytenes doth declare;	44	Balettys3	18
Remorse have I of youre most goodlyhod,	44	Balettys3	29
Of youre behavoure curtes and benynge,	44	Balettys3	30
Of your bownte and of youre womanhod,	44	Balettys3	31
Than to beholde youre bewteouse countenaunce:	44	Balettys3	44
'Forsoth,' quod I, 'to bye some of youre ware.'	48	Bowge	79
To use youre hawkys forica /In propitiatorio,	69	Hauke	271
Youre eye is out; adew, good nyght!	119	Ag Scottes	142
For youre owne tayle ye made a rod.	119	Ag Scottes	146
owne] not in Day 1560, Marshe 1568			
Youre poverte cowde not attayne	119	Ag Scottes	151
For all youre amyte,	288	Why Come Ye	374
A goldsmyth youre mayre:	301	Why Come Ye	908
Youre carkas to kepe, /Lyke a sely shepe,	365	Albany	273
YOURSELFE			
Ye bere yourselfe somwhat to bolde,	114	Scot Kynge	34
Ye bere yourselfe somwhat to bold;	118	Ag Scottes	125
What avayleth lordshype, yourselfe for to kyll	148	Magnyfycence	286
That sheweth yourselfe thus spedde in physyke?	156	Magnyfycence	556
Convey yourselfe fyrst, let se.	163	Magnyfycence	816
Yourselfe shall be ruled by lyberte and largesse.	179	Magnyfycence	1389
Frete yourselfe for anger and for dyspyte;	185	Magnyfycence	1602
Then feyne yourselfe dyseased, and make yourselfe seke.	185	Magnyfycence	1612
Then feyne yourselfe dyseased, and make yourselfe seke.	185	Magnyfycence	1612
I trowe ye herde yourselfe what I sayd.	188	Magnyfycence	1695
Undoubted ye had lost yourselfe eternally.	206	Magnyfycence	2335
Yourselfe madly ye overse!	309	Why Come Ye2	7
YOUR SELFE			
Avaunce your selfe to aproche and come nere.	48	Bowge	88
But ye have crafte your selfe alwaye to save.	59	Bowge	452
Boldly bend you to batell, and buske your selfe to save.	122	Garnesche1	41
And after his mynde herdely your selfe adresse,	144	Magnyfycence	151
Why, were not your selfe agreed to the same,	147	Magnyfycence	233

YOUTH — YOWTHE

	Page	Title	Line
For your selfe. Syr, yf I myght permytted be,	188	Magnyfycence	1720
Take hede of your selfe, for nowe ye have nede.	192	Magnyfycence	1854
How fele you your selfe, my frend? How is your mynde?	208	Magnyfycence	2389
And knowe your selfe mortal for all your dygnyte;	211	Magnyfycence	2499
Addressyng your selfe, lyke a sadde messengere,	239	Speke Parott	303
Ye count your selfe wele lettred;	376	Replycacion	55
And to shame your selfe have brought.	376	Replycacion	58
Your selfe thus ye discured	377	Replycacion	92
And shewed your selfe dawes!	377	Replycacion	124
And to prove your selfe suche foles.	378	Replycacion	145
Count ye your selfe good clerkes,	381	Replycacion	273
But, I trowe, your selfe ye overse	381	Replycacion	285

YOUTH

	Page	Title	Line
Of fresshe youth agayne;	85	Phy Sparrow	546
Alasse, where is youth that was wont for to skyppe?	195	Magnyfycence	1957
As evydently in retchlesse youth ye may se	200	Magnyfycence	2133
In youth to be wanton, and let them have theyr wyll -	200	Magnyfycence	2137
Her youth is farre past;	215	El Rummynge	48
Princes of youth, and flowre of goodly porte,	337	Garlande	904

YOUTHE

	Page	Title	Line
of their rechelesse youthe and wytlesse wontonnese,	374	Replycacion	1

YOUWARDE

	Page	Title	Line
For nowe I se comynge to youwarde Redresse.	208	Magnyfycence	2384

YOW

	Page	Title	Line
Ay, beshrewe yow! Be my fay	35	Man Margery	1
As well it becomyth yow, a parysh towne clarke,	38	Coystrownel	58
What, have ye kythyd yow a knyght, Syr Dugles the dowty,	121	Garneschel	8
Ye bere yow bolde as Barabas, or Syr Terry of Trac[e]. Trace] 'Tracy' †MS Harley 367	122	Garneschel	11
Bryngges yow out of favyr with alle femall teggys:	122	Garneschel	31
That mastres Punt put yow of, yt was nat alle causeles;	122	Garneschel	32
Ye grounde yow upon Godfrey, that grysly gargons face,	123	Garnesche2	29
Baile, baile at yow bothe, frantyke folys! Follow on the chase!	123	Garnesche2	31
I advyse yow beware of thys war, rannge yow in aray.	123	Garnesche2	33
I advyse yow beware of thys war, rannge yow in aray.	123	Garnesche2	33
With neythyr of yow tewyne:	124	Garnesche3	7
The warde with yow was skante.	125	Garnesche3	53
Had yow most in despyght;	125	Garnesche3	66
She callyd yow Syr Gy of Gaunt,	126	Garnesche3	70
Thus with yow sche ded wary,	126	Garnesche3	75
When Garnyche cummyth yow amonge	128	Garnesche3	150
He wyl cause yow caste your crawes,	128	Garnesche3	155
Ye bere yow bold and brag	129	Garnesche3	187
To poynt yow fresche and gay.	129	Garnesche3	191
I rekyn yow in my rowllys,	129	Garnesche3	193
That nature wrowght in yow and me,	130	Garnesche5	13
To daly with yow she had no lust.	131	Garnesche5	54
Sche praiid yow walke, on Goddes halfe!	131	Garnesche5	60
With, 'Speke, Parott, I pray yow,' full curteslye they sey,	231	Speke Parott	13
Thus Parott dothe pray yow,	237	Speke Parott	225
Speke, Parotte, I pray yow, for Maryes saake,	237	Speke Parott	233
I wyl be ferme and stabyll, /And to yow servyceabyll,	237	Speke Parott	247
Be love I am constreyned /To be with yow retayned,	238	Speke Parott	258
I pray yow be reclaymed,	238	Speke Parott	260
Goe, lytyll quayre, pray them that yow beholde,	239	Speke Parott	290
Agayne all remordes arme yow with paciens.	239	Speke Parott	298
Require hym to convey yow ovyr the salte fome;	239	Speke Parott	302
And thowe sum dysdayne yow and sey how ye prate,	240	Speke Parott	315
Prepayre yow, Parrot, brevely your passage to take,	240	Speke Parott	324
Vouchesafe to defend yow agayne the brawlyng scolde	241	Speke Parott	361
Yow to remorde erste or they know your mynde.	241	Speke Parott	370
Whyche of yow fyrste dare boldlye plucke the crowe.	242	Speke Parott	396
Now, Galathea, lett Parrot, I pray yow, have hys date -	244	Speke Parott	439
To yow thre this honor shalbe reserved	323	Garlande	409
To owe to yow our servyce, and more if we mowte!	324	Garlande	425
My besy cure /To yow I owe;	338	Garlande	929
Yow for to stellyfye;	339	Garlande	963
To wryte of yow this goodly clause,	342	Garlande	1050

YOWER

	Page	Title	Line
Rowlynge in yower holow hede, ugly to see;	122	Garneschel	38
Yower knavery I wyll nat hyde,	124	Garnesche3	22
Yower termys ar to grose,	126	Garnesche3	96
Nor good ryme in yower mater.	126	Garnesche3	105
Yower lothesum lypps love well to kyse,	130	Garnesche5	44
And thus there ye lost yower pray;	131	Garnesche5	61

YOWR

	Page	Title	Line
Enbrawderid the mantill /Is of yowr maydenhede.	338	Garlande	925
Yowr name to se /It be enrolde, /Writtin with golde.	338	Garlande	937

YOWRE

	Page	Title	Line
Enbrawderyd the mantyll /Is of yowre maydenhede.	338	Garlande	917
Humbly and low /Commendynge me /To yowre bownte.	338	Garlande	932
For to encrese /Yowre goodly name.	339	Garlande	960
'Yowre boke of remembrauns we will now that ye rede; boke] 'bokes' †Fakes 1523	345	Garlande	1149

YOWTH

	Page	Title	Line
Princes of yowth, and flowre of goodly porte,	337	Garlande	897

YOWTHE

	Page	Title	Line
Of yowthe the godely flour,	111	Lawde	44

YPOCRAS —ZALMANE

	Page	Title	Line
YPOCRAS			
But swete ypocras ye drynke,	258	Collyn Clout	456
YPOCRYSY			
Counterfet holynes is called ypocrysy;	153	Magnyfycence	469
Full of glotony /And of ypocrysy,	269	Collyn Clout	919
YPOCRYTIS			
Pope holy ypocrytis, as they were golde and hole,	329	Garlande	612
YPOCRUS			
Swete ypocrus and swete meate.	284	Why Come Ye	218
YRE			
With angre and yre,	95	Phy Sparrow	932
YS			
All merciles in the ys no pite!	32	Dol Dethe	122
Yet your contenons oncomly, yor face ys nat fayer.	122	Garneschel	18
Nor no bore so brymly brystlyd ys with here,	122	Garneschel	25
I sey, ye solem Sarson, alle blake ys yor ble;	122	Garneschel	36
[Your] pride ys alle to peviche, your porte importunate;	123	Garnesche2	3
Hole ys your brow that ye brake with Deu[ra]ndall your awne sworde; Deurandall] 'Deundall' †MS Harley 367	123	Garnesche2	8
Why holde ye on yer cap, syr, then? Yor pardone ys expyryd.	123	Garnesche2	9
In Arturys auncyent actys nowhere ys provyd your pere;	123	Garnesche2	24
Your harte ys to hawte, iwys, yt wyll nat be alowde.	123	Garnesche2	26
Your brethe ys stronge and quike;	126	Garnesche3	78
Whan hys grace ys fastynge,	126	Garnesche3	83
Yt ys to your reproche.	126	Garnesche3	85
For alle ys nat worthe a myteyng,	127	Garnesche3	115
Your wyt ys so geson,	127	Garnesche3	129
Your foly ys to grett	127	Garnesche3	140
Your brethe yt ys so felle	127	Garnesche3	142
That byrd ys nat honest	129	Garnesche3	197
Your chorlyshe chauntyng ys all o lay.	129	Garnesche5	6
Irrevocable ys her decre;	130	Garnesche5	14
Yet jentylnes in the ys thred-bare worne.	131	Garnesche5	70
It ys for no bawdy knave	132	Garnesche5	114
It ys nat mete for soche a knave.	133	Garnesche5	156
Presumptuous pride ys all thyn hope;	133	Garnesche5	160
Of thy lewdenes more ys behynde;	134	Garnesche5	173
My name ys Parott, a byrde of Paradyse,	231	Speke Parott	1
'Parott ys a goodlye byrde and a pratye popagay.' and] not in Lant 1545, Kynge and Marche 1554, Day 1560, Marshe 1568	231	Speke Parott	14
My fethyrs fresshe as ys the emerawde grene,	231	Speke Parott	16
In Salve festa dyes, toto ys the beste. ys the] 'theyr doth' Lant 1545, Kynge & Marche 1554, Day 1560, Marshe 1568	232	Speke Parott	49
Dyscrecion ys modyr of nobyll vertues all;	232	Speke Parott	51
When wylfulnes ys vicar generall.	232	Speke Parott	54
Myne herte hyt ys with the.	237	Speke Parott	240
And sette to a D, /And then hyt ys 'Amend', to] not in †MS Harley 2252	238	Speke Parott	276
To rude ys there reason to reche to your sentence;	240	Speke Parott	319
Hyt ys no lytyll bordon to bere a grete mylle stone.	240	Speke Parott	330
Whose tong ys attayntyd with slaundrys obliqui.	241	Speke Parott	363
How thys prosses I prate of, hyt ys not all for nowghte.	242	Speke Parott	389
O connyng clergye, where ys your redynes	242	Speke Parott	392
For passe-a-Pase apase ys gone to cache a molle,	243	Speke Parott	413
Of frantycknes and folysshnes whyche ys the grett state?	243	Speke Parott	417
Difficille hit ys to ansswere thys demaunde;	243	Speke Parott	418
Of Pope Julius cardys, he ys chefe Cardynall.	243	Speke Parott	431
Hyt ys to fere leste he wolde were the garland on hys pate,	244	Speke Parott	435
So ys all thyng wrowghte wylfully withowte reson and skylle.	245	Speke Parott	496
So myche of my lordes grace, and in hym no grace ys;	245	Speke Parott	501
So myche serchyng of loselles, and ys hym selfe so lewde;	246	Speke Parott	513
Sens Dewcalyons flodde, in no cronycle ys told.	246	Speke Parott	518
YT			
To me also all thouthe yt wer promysyde	33	Dol Dethe	159
But yf yt war Syr Tyrmagant that tyrnyd without nall;	121	Garneschel	4
That mastres Punt put yow of, yt was nat alle causeles;	122	Garneschel	32
Your harte ys to hawte, iwys, yt wyll nat be alowde.	123	Garnesche2	26
And well I have yt perseyved,	124	Garnesche3	2
Yt ys to your reproche.	126	Garnesche3	85
Yt fallyth for no swyne	126	Garnesche3	86
So suerly yt xall nat tarnishe.	127	Garnesche3	122
Your brethe yt ys so felle	127	Garnesche3	142
I bequeth yt hole to the.	128	Garnesche3	177
Sche wolde nat of yt thow had sworne.	131	Garnesche5	52
Yt bredth mothys in clothe of Arres.	131	Garnesche5	78
Yt commyth the wele me to remorde,	132	Garnesche5	101
Yt wold garnyche wyll thy face.	133	Garnesche5	135
YTCHE			
For my fyngers ytche. fyngers] 'fynger' Kynge & Marche 1554	230	El Rummynge	618
YVELL			
Clenly as yvell chevynge!	219	El Rummynge	186
ZABULON			
Ydolles of Babylon, /De terra Zabulon,	262	Collyn Clout	639
ZALMANE			
Gedeon is gon, that Zalmane undertoke,	234	Speke Parott	116

ZEB — ZOROBABELL

	Page	Title	Line
ZEB			
Oreb et Zeb, of Judicum rede the boke.	234	Speke Parott	117
ZENOPHONTES			
Wolde God I had Zenophontes,	74	Phy Sparrow	98
ZEPHERUS			
Enbrethyng of Zepherus with his pleasant wynde;	331	Garlande	677
ZEUXES			
Zeuxes, that enpicturid fare Elene the quene,	337	Garlande	892
ZODYAKE			
Arectyng my syght toward the zodyake,	312	Garlande	1
ZOROBABELL			
Nother Zorobabell, /Nor cruell Jesabell;	67	Hauke	206

APPENDIX A
Frequency Index

Word	Count	Word	Count	Word	Count	Word	Count
AND	2826	GRACE	106	WYTH	45	WHERFORE	31
THE	2267	NEVER	106	DOWNE	44	BERE	30
TO	2148	THEN	102	GOLDE	44	BEWARE	30
OF	1935	NAT	101	THOUGHT	44	BOLDE	30
I	1596	NOBLE	101	BOTHE	43	FOLE	30
A	1500	ARE	100	CALL	43	KYNGES	30
THAT	1264	DO	99	FALL	43	KNOWE	30
IN	1099	ONE	97	ROYALL	43	MANER	30
FOR	973	MORE	96	RULE	43	NOUGHT	30
YE	964	WHAN	96	SHOLDE	43	SAYDE	30
WITH	955	LYBERTE	94	SHULDE	43	SAYE	30
IS	857	TELL	92	WYSE	43	SORE	30
HE	784	OTHER	90	YOW	43	WORTH	30
BE	717	MUST	88	ALAS	42	ELS	29
YOUR	641	NAME	88	FAME	42	FALS	29
SO	620	MANY	85	GRETE	42	OWNE	29
HIS	574	MOCHE	85	HOLDE	42	SODENLY	29
ALL	568	NAY	85	KYNG	42	WELTHE	29
BUT	565	UPON	84	LARGESSE	42	COMETH	28
IT	565	UP	81	MARY	42	CRAFTY	28
MY	537	DOTH	80	OVER	42	FAYTH	28
ME	536	SET	80	GYVE	41	GONE	28
AS	514	MYNDE	79	SHAME	41	HALFE	28
YOU	495	COME	78	SUCH	41	HAWKE	28
HAVE	462	MYGHT	77	SWETE	41	HELL	28
BY	459	GO	76	ANY	40	KNYGHT	28
THIS	412	WHY	74	BEFORE	40	ONES	28
WAS	398	LORDE	73	MAGNYFYCENCE	40	QUENE	28
THEY	384	BROUGHT	72	ANOTHER	39	SCOT	28
NOT	344	SKELTON	70	AR	39	WELTH	28
NO	333	AGAYNE	69	DREDE	39	ALASSE	27
WHAT	333	DOTHE	69	FANSY	39	LAUREAT	27
HER	297	EVERY	69	KEPE	39	LOST	27
OR	290	AFTER	68	PARROT	38	SAME	27
WYLL	289	YF	68	PLAY	38	SMALL	27
THOU	271	HIM	65	WANTON	38	WANTON	27
SHALL	261	BETTER	64	WORDES	38	WRYTE	27
SHE	261	GOODLY	64	COUDE	37	BEN	26
AT	245	MEASURE	64	FAYTHE	37	LUSTY	26
THERE	233	THOUGH	64	NEDE	37	PRATE	26
SOME	229	GREAT	63	CAN NOT	36	YES	26
WERE	228	IF	62	FORTUNE	36	ABYDE	25
MAY	227	UNTO	61	HARTE	36	ABOUTE	25
SYR	218	MYNE	60	HEDE	36	ARTE	25
HYM	217	LOKE	58	HOLE	36	CAUSE	25
MAN	215	RYGHT	58	KNAVE	36	ELLES	25
ON	214	WITHOUT	58	NEW	36	FAYNE	25
YET	214	PLEASURE	57	STYLL	36	GAVE	25
THEYR	207	DYD	56	SUM	36	HARDE	25
MAKE	201	HYS	55	TYLL	36	HAST	25
WOLDE	195	WHICHE	55	HOLY	35	MAKETH	25
SAY	191	ALSO	54	PUT	35	NE	25
THEM	187	DARE	54	REASON	35	SAD	25
SUCHE	184	MOST	54	TYME	35	SAYNT	25
WE	184	LYTELL	53	TROWE	35	SAWE	25
LYKE	183	NONE	53	WARE	35	SEY	25
WELL	182	PRAY	53	WHOM	35	TWAYNE	25
CAN	181	AGAYNST	51	CAME	34	TWO	25
GOD	181	NOTHYNGE	51	CAST	34	WYT	25
GOOD	176	PLACE	51	DAY	34	ALE	24
NOWE	162	FYNDE	50	LYST	34	BOKE	24
OUR	160	LONGE	50	MYCHE	34	BRYNGE	24
NOR	159	QUOD	50	THYNKE	34	CARE	24
NOW	158	THOW	50	WELE	34	COCKES	24
THY	150	UNDER	50	WORDE	34	DID	24
HATH	146	WHO	50	WOTE	34	FOUNDE	24
HAD	144	EVER	49	AMONGE	33	LADY	24
HERE	139	WHEN	49	BEHYNDE	33	LYE	24
HOW	135	FOLY	48	LOVE	33	PROWDE	24
FROM	134	KYNGE	48	OLDE	33	SHULD	24
AN	132	O	48	PLAYNE	33	VERY	24
THAN	131	REDE	48	THRE	33	WARKE	24
AM	128	SAYD	48	WOLD	33	YOURE	24
LET	127	COUNTERFET	47	WORLDE	33	CONVEYAUNCE	23
FULL	126	DAME	47	INTO	32	GUP	23
THUS	124	THEIR	47	MESURE	32	HATHE	23
OUT	123	AWAY	46	REST	32	HYGHT	23
MEN	121	FACE	46	SOMTYME	32	KYNDE	23
HOWE	120	THER	46	SURE	32	LARGE	23
TAKE	117	THESE	46	WAY	32	SAYTH	23
MADE	113	YS	46	BEST	31	SAVE	23
US	113	DEVYLL	45	FAYRE	31	SEE	23
SE	112	SPEKE	45	MAYSTER	31	SHEWE	23
WHERE	112	THYNGE	45	METE	31	WITHIN	23
				THYS	31		

Word	Count	Word	Count	Word	Count	Word	Count
WONDER	23	SOULE	18	WELCOME	15	BRYGHT	12
ABOUT	22	THYNE	18	WO	15	CAM	12
ADVERSYTE	22	TRUST	18	ABOVE	14	CAT	12
DUKE	22	WAR	18	ARMES	14	CHERE	12
ELYNOUR	22	WORLDLY	18	BARE	14	CONSAYTE	12
ESTATE	22	AMENDE	17	BENE	14	DYGNYTE	12
FALSE	22	BORNE	17	CLERE	14	DOCTOR	12
GRENE	22	COLDE	17	COCKYS	14	DOGGE	12
HONOUR	22	CONTENT	17	CONNYNGE	14	DURST	12
LERNE	22	ENDURE	17	DATE	14	FACYON	12
LYFE	22	FELYCYTE	17	FARRE	14	FAMOUS	12
LYGHT	22	FELL	17	FOULE	14	FAVOUR	12
PAYNE	22	FLYE	17	FRANTYKE	14	FEDE	12
SHALBE	22	GODDES	17	FRERE	14	FETE	12
SOMWHAT	22	HOPE	17	GYSE	14	FLODDE	12
SPEDE	22	LAUREATE	17	LADYES	14	FORTHE	12
THERFORE	22	LAWE	17	LEPE	14	FROME	12
USE	22	LETTER	17	LORDES	14	GAN	12
WHETHER	22	LY	17	MAYSTRES	14	HEY	12
WYNDE	22	MATTER	17	MANNES	14	HYDER	12
ART	21	MOOST	17	NERE	14	HORSON	12
ASTATE	21	PARTE	17	NEWE	14	HOWE BE IT	12
BEHOLDE	21	PAS	17	NYGHT	14	JENTYLL	12
COUNTENAUNCE	21	PRYNCE	17	NOTHYNG	14	LANGAGE	12
COURTE	21	REPORTE	17	OFT	14	LONG	12
DYDE	21	RODE	17	OUTE	14	LOTHE	12
DWELL	21	SHAL	17	PALLAS	14	MAISTER	12
FAR	21	SIR	17	PLEASE	14	MARGERY	12
FORTH	21	SYDE	17	POVERTE	14	MARKE	12
GAME	21	TOGYDER	17	RYME	14	MYSELFE	12
GROUNDE	21	TROUTHE	17	SEKE	14	MUSE	12
HANDE	21	WAN	17	SYGHT	14	PAST	12
LATE	21	WHICH	17	TALE	14	POETE	12
LEWDE	21	YOUR SELFE	17	TOLDE	14	PRECHE	12
LO	21	AGE	16	WEL	14	PRINCE	12
MAD	21	BLODE	16	WHYLE	14	PURSE	12
MAYE	21	CALLED	16	YOR	14	RECORDE	12
PEOPLE	21	CHURCHE	16	YT	14	REMEMBRAUNCE	12
SAKE	21	COURT	16	AVAUNCE	13	RENNE	12
SENDE	21	FRENDE	16	BYRDE	13	ROME	12
SONE	21	FRO	16	BONES	13	RUDDY	12
STANDE	21	HERTE	16	BREKE	13	SAYLE	12
WENE	21	HYE	16	COUNSELL	13	SAW	12
WHOSE	21	LEDE	16	DAUNCE	13	SORTE	12
WROUGHT	21	LORD	16	DELYGHT	13	SPARE	12
ALONE	20	MADDE	16	DEVYSE	13	THOUGHTE	12
BEGAN	20	NOSE	16	DYSDAYNE	13	THOUSANDE	12
BRAYNE	20	ONY	16	FLY	13	TUSHE	12
DEGRE	20	POETES	16	FONDE	13	VERTEW	12
FYRST	20	PRETY	16	FRAUNCE	13	WAYES	12
MERY	20	PURPOSE	16	GOSE	13	WHEROF	12
RAN	20	RAGE	16	HART	13	WONTE	12
SLAYNE	20	REMEMBRE	16	HED	13	WORKE	12
STEDE	20	RIGHT	16	LACKE	13	WRYGHT	12
WHOME	20	RYCHE	16	LAURELL	13	YOURSELFE	12
YLL	20	TAYLE	16	LYVE	13	AY	11
DEDE	19	THEI	16	MATERS	13	ALLE	11
DYE	19	TROUTH	16	MELL	13	ANSWERE	11
FAST	19	WER	16	NEYTHER	13	ARAY	11
FRESSHE	19	CALLYD	15	PAY	13	BYCAUSE	11
HA	19	CAN NAT	15	PLUCKE	13	BLOWE	11
HYMSELFE	19	CASE	15	POORE	13	BROTHER	11
LEVE	19	DERE	15	RYDE	13	CATCHE	11
MASSE	19	DRYNKE	15	RULED	13	CYRCUMSPECCYON	11
PAROTT	19	DRONKEN	15	SENTENCE	13	COLUSYON	11
PRATY	19	FLOURE	15	SHEW	13	COULDE	11
SCOTTES	19	FORTHWITH	15	SKYLL	13	CRAFTELY	11
SYRS	19	HOME	15	SLEPE	13	CROWNE	11
SYT	19	LUST	15	SLEW	13	DELE	11
WALKE	19	MATER	15	SOLACE	13	EYE	11
WHOS	19	MONEY	15	SPAKE	13	ENGLYSH	11
BLAME	18	OUGHT	15	STARKE	13	ERLE	11
CORAGE	18	PASSYNGE	15	STRAWE	13	EVYLL	11
DONE	18	PORTE	15	SURELY	13	FAREWELL	11
ECHE	18	RED	15	THYNGES	13	FYLL	11
GLAD	18	REDRESSE	15	TOURNE	13	FLOWRE	11
HELPE	18	RUDE	15	WALL	13	FOLOWE	11
KNOW	18	SENE	15	WENT	13	GRAY	11
LAY	18	STODE	15	WRONGE	13	HAY	11
MO	18	THEIS	15	YERE	13	HERESY	11
PEN	18	THEROF	15	ABUSYON	12	HY	11
POETIS	18	TOKE	15	AMEN	12	HYDE	11
RAYLE	18	TREW	15	BOTH	12	ITEM	11
SYNGE	18	TRUSTE	15	BOUGHT	12	LANDE	11

LESSE	11	SOULES	10	SHORTE	9	LEST	8
MADAME	11	SPAROWES	10	SPAROW	9	LYETH	8
MERCY	11	SPENDE	10	SPENT	9	LYPPES	8
MOCH	11	STYLE	10	STRYKE	9	MAYD	8
PAROT	11	STORE	10	STRONGE	9	MIGHT	8
PATE	11	TALKE	10	SUPPORTE	9	NATURE	8
RAYNE	11	THANKE	10	TAKEN	9	OPEN	8
RATE	11	THERIN	10	TARY	9	PALACE	8
ROD	11	THI	10	THERWITH	9	PERE	8
ROSE	11	THYDER	10	THY SELFE	9	PHEBUS	8
SAYST	11	THYNG	10	THOSE	9	PHILLIP	8
SCOLE	11	TRUE	10	THOUGHE	9	PHYLLYP	8
SERVYCE	11	UNDERSTANDE	10	TODAY	9	PLAYE	8
SOCHE	11	VERTU	10	TOMOROWE	9	POYNT	8
SOUGHT	11	WYSDOME	10	TONG	9	PRELATES	8
SOVERAYNE	11	AGEYNE	9	TONGE	9	PRYNCES	8
SPAROWE	11	AGRE	9	TRECHERY	9	PROCES	8
STARE	11	AL	9	TREWE	9	PROPERLY	8
TURNE	11	AUCTORYTE	9	TWYT	9	QUYTE	8
WARRE	11	AVAUNT	9	WENTE	9	RANKE	8
WHYLES	11	BYDE	9	WITHALL	9	RECHE	8
WHYTE	11	BLESSYD	9	WYLDE	9	REDY	8
WYDE	11	BOTE	9	WORLD	9	REGENT	8
WYFE	11	CERTAYNE	9	WOT	9	RESORTE	8
WYLTE	11	CHAUNCE	9	WRATE	9	RYSE	8
WYTTE	11	CLERKES	9	WRYTYNGE	9	ROUNDE	8
WORSE	11	CLOKED	9	AGAYN	8	SHARPE	8
ACCORDE	10	COLOUR	9	ALBANY	8	SHEPE	8
AMONG	10	COMFORTE	9	AMYS	8	SHYPPE	8
BACKE	10	COTE	9	ANONE	8	SYN	8
BESY	10	CRAKE	9	ASYDE	8	SOBER	8
BETWENE	10	CREDE	9	ASSURE	8	SOLDE	8
BLYNDE	10	CURRE	9	AWAYE	8	SOM	8
BOUNTE	10	DED	9	BARKE	8	SOMETYME	8
BRAKE	10	DESYRE	9	BAS	8	SONNE	8
CHEFE	10	DEVYSED	9	BEAUTE	8	SOO	8
COWARDE	10	DEWCALYONS	9	BEYONDE	8	STONDE	8
COWDE	10	EYEN	9	BERDE	8	STORY	8
DELYTE	10	ELLYS	9	BESSE	8	STORMY	8
DYVERS	10	ENGLANDE	9	BLACKE	8	SUBSTAUNCE	8
DULL	10	EXPOUNDE	9	BROKEN	8	SUFFRE	8
ENGLYSSHE	10	EXPRESSE	9	CANNOT	8	SUME	8
EVEN	10	FATE	9	CASTE	8	SWORDE	8
EXCEDE	10	FERE	9	CASTELL	8	TOWRE	8
FOLYS	10	FY	9	CHARGE	8	TRULY	8
HARDELY	10	FYRE	9	CLERKE	8	UGLY	8
HARDY	10	GATE	9	COLOURE	8	UNHAPPY	8
HEVY	10	GET	9	CONFUSYON	8	UPPON	8
JOHNN	10	GYDE	9	COST	8	VAYNE	8
JUPITER	10	GODDIS	9	CREDENCE	8	WASTE	8
LAUGHE	10	GOWNE	9	CRY	8	WAX	8
LEFT	10	HARKE	9	DAYE	8	WEPE	8
LIKE	10	HAT	9	DAYLY	8	WHO SO	8
LYTYLL	10	HENS	9	DEDELY	8	WILL	8
LOKED	10	HERDE	9	DEMURE	8	WYL	8
LOSTE	10	HETE	9	DYVERSE	8	WORNE	8
LOWE	10	HEVEN	9	DOCTOUR	8	WORSHYP	8
MADLY	10	HYR	9	DRYVE	8	WORTHY	8
MARE	10	HYT	9	EASE	8	WROTE	8
MASTRES	10	HODE	9	EATE	8	ADUE	7
MYGHTY	10	HOSE	9	EYTHER	8	AGAINST	7
MUSTE	10	JOY	9	FARE	8	ALL THYNGE	7
NAKED	10	LAYDE	9	FAVOURE	8	ALWAY	7
NAMES	10	LAST	9	FYGHT	8	AMEND	7
NOBLENESSE	10	LENT	9	FYNE	8	ASKE	7
OCCUPACYON	10	MENE	9	FOLES	8	ASONDER	7
OCCUPYED	10	MOSTE	9	FORSAKE	8	AVOWE	7
OWUR	10	NAMED	9	FOTE	8	BEHOLD	7
PYKE	10	NOTHER	9	FRAY	8	BESECHE	7
POPAGAY	10	OFTE	9	FRAUNCES	8	BEWTE	7
POUNDE	10	ORATORS	9	FRESSH	8	BYLL	7
PREEST	10	OURE	9	GAY	8	BYNDE	7
PRYDE	10	PASSE	9	GALL	8	BYSSHOPPES	7
PROUDE	10	PENNE	9	GENTYLMAN	8	BLOSSOM	7
REMAYNE	10	PRIDE	9	GERE	8	BODY	7
RULETH	10	PROVE	9	GLORIOUS	8	BONYS	7
SCORNE	10	REVERENCE	9	GOTH	8	BORDE	7
SEASON	10	SADNESSE	9	GREKE	8	BOUNDE	7
SEMETH	10	SAID	9	HANGE	8	BREDE	7
SHAKE	10	SAT	9	HAP	8	BREVELY	7
SYNS	10	SCHE	9	HYGH	8	CAREFULL	7
SMALE	10	SENT	9	IN DEDE	8	CHALENGE	7
SOONE	10	SHALTE	9	LAME	8	CHARYTE	7
SOROWE	10	SHAMFULLY	9	LERNYNG	8	CHASE	7

CHURCH	7	REHERSE	7	DUNDAS	6	PRETENCE	6
CLENE	7	RELUCENT	7	DUST	6	PROUD	6
CLUSTERS	7	RYNNE	7	ENROLDE	6	RATHER	6
COM	7	SAVAGE	7	ENVY	6	REKENYNGE	6
COMFORT	7	SERVE	7	ER	6	REPENT	6
COMPLAYNE	7	SHALT	7	ESCHINES	6	RESON	6
CONVEY	7	SHOTE	7	ESEBON	6	RYALL	6
COULD	7	SITH	7	ESTATES	6	RYOT	6
COWARDES	7	SYLKE	7	EVERMORE	6	SADDE	6
CREPE	7	SYNG	7	FEE	6	SAGE	6
CROSSE	7	SKORNE	7	FELDE	6	SAYES	6
CRUELL	7	SOFT	7	FET	6	SEMYTH	6
CUM	7	SOMER	7	FEWE	6	SEND	6
CURE	7	SOWE	7	FYE	6	SYTH	6
CUT	7	SPACE	7	FLESSHE	6	SLO	6
DAYES	7	SPED	7	FLODE	6	SOLEMPNE	6
DAWES	7	SPERE	7	FOLOWETH	6	SORY	6
DY	7	STANDETH	7	FORMAR	6	SOROW	6
DRANKE	7	STOW	7	FORSOTHE	6	SPECYALLY	6
DREME	7	SUMNER	7	FRAYE	6	SPENTE	6
DRYE	7	SUSPECTE	7	FRE	6	SPORTE	6
DROWSY	7	SWERE	7	FRESSHELY	6	STABLE	6
ERTHLY	7	SWYNE	7	GARDE	6	STATE	6
ETE	7	TALES	7	GASTLY	6	STONE	6
FATHER	7	THEM SELFE	7	GENTYLL	6	STONES	6
FAUTE	7	THOROW	7	GEVE	6	SUFFER	6
FIRST	7	THROTIS	7	GODDYS	6	SUPPOSE	6
FLOTIS	7	TYMES	7	GOLDEN	6	TAWNY	6
FORCE	7	TOGETHER	7	GORGE	6	TEMPORALL	6
FOWLE	7	TORDE	7	GREATE	6	THEMSELFE	6
FRAME	7	TORNE	7	GROPE	6	THERBY	6
FROWNE	7	TRACE	7	GROTE	6	THREDE	6
FUL	7	TRE	7	HAFTER	6	TONGES	6
FURTHER	7	TROW	7	HARTELY	6	TOWNE	6
GARNYCHE	7	TUNGES	7	HAWKYS	6	TREASURE	6
GETE	7	TWYSE	7	HEED	6	TRONE	6
GOSPELL	7	VERSE	7	HELAS	6	USED	6
HALL	7	VERTUE	7	HERTES	6	VYCE	6
HARD	7	WHYLEST	7	HEVYN	6	VYSAGE	6
HARE	7	WYTLES	7	HOGGES	6	VOYDE	6
HATE	7	WONNE	7	IWYS	6	WATERS	6
HAUTE	7	WORTHE	7	JOYE	6	WELCOM	6
HENRY	7	ABLE	6	KAN	6	WENYST	6
HERT	7	ADVYSE	6	KING	6	WHERE AS	6
HEVENLY	7	AGENST	6	KYLL	6	WHERTO	6
HONDE	7	AN OTHER	6	KYST	6	WHITE	6
HOW BE IT	7	ANSWERYTH	6	KNAVES	6	WHYCHE	6
JESU	7	ARME	6	KNYFE	6	WITHOUTE	6
JET	7	BACHUS	6	KNOWEN	6	WYLFULNES	6
JOLY	7	BEGGE	6	LAKE	6	WOMANLY	6
KEN	7	BENYNGE	6	LANGUAGE	6	WOMEN	6
KNE	7	BESTE	6	LETE	6	WRYTETH	6
LADYS	7	BETE	6	LYVYNGE	6	XALL	6
LERNED	7	BYTWENE	6	MAKER	6	YONGE	6
LETTERS	7	BLAKE	6	MANNYS	6	YOUTH	6
LYON	7	BLESSED	6	MEANE	6	YOWER	6
LOWSY	7	BLYSSE	6	MET	6	ADVYSED	5
MADNESSE	7	BLOSSOME	6	MYRTH	6	AFRAYDE	5
MAISTRES	7	BOT	6	MORTALL	6	AGEYNST	5
MAKYTH	7	BOWGE	6	NACYON	6	AYLE	5
MANERLY	7	BRODE	6	NECKE	6	ALEXANDER	5
MASTER	7	CALLE	6	NEVYR	6	AMYSSE	5
MEANES	7	CHYLDREN	6	NOBLY	6	ANGRY	5
MYGHTE	7	CLAUSE	6	NON	6	ANKER	5
MYSCHEFE	7	COMELY	6	NOTHING	6	ARMYS	5
MY SELFE	7	COMPANY	6	OFTE TYMES	6	ARMONY	5
MONE	7	CONJURE	6	OLD	6	ASKED	5
NYNE	7	CONVEYED	6	OPENLY	6	ASSE	5
NYSE	7	COUNTE	6	OWTE	6	AWNE	5
NOYSE	7	COURTLY	6	PAGE	6	BAD	5
OCCUPY	7	COWARDLY	6	PAYDE	6	BALE	5
OFFENCE	7	CRYE	6	PALTOKE	6	BASE	5
PAYNED	7	CRYST	6	PASSYNG	6	BEAUTYE	5
PAYRE	7	DAUNGER	6	PEASE	6	BEGYN	5
PALE	7	DAWE	6	PECE	6	BEGYNNE	5
PEAS	7	DEDLY	6	PENY	6	BEGYNNETH	5
PHYLYP	7	DEPRAVE	6	PERCEYVE	6	BEKE	5
PLAYNLY	7	DESERVYD	6	PEVYSSHE	6	BESYDE	5
POPE	7	DETH	6	PYLATE	6	BYTTER	5
PRESE	7	DEVYSYD	6	PLESAUNT	6	BLEW	5
PROCEDE	7	DYSPORTE	6	PLUCKED	6	BOLD	5
PROCESSE	7	DOLOROUS	6	POMPE	6	BOLDLY	5
QUAKE	7	DOUBLE	6	PORE	6	BORE	5
RANNE	7	DRAWE	6	PRAYSE	6	BOST	5

BOWNTE	5	HERE AFTER	5	SCOTTYSHE	5	ANNE	4
BRED	5	HEREIN	5	SCRYPTURE	5	ANOYNTED	4
BRETH	5	HERETYKES	5	SCURVY	5	APOLLO	4
BRETHE	5	HIGH	5	SELY	5	APPERE	4
BRODER	5	HIMSELFE	5	SERVAUNTES	5	ASPYED	4
BROWGHT	5	HYLL	5	SHEWYD	5	ASWAGE	4
BULL	5	HONEST	5	SHYNE	5	ATTAYNE	4
CACHE	5	HOOST	5	SHOLD	5	ATTAYNTED	4
CALLETH	5	HUNTE	5	SHREWDLY	5	AUNCIENT	4
CARDYNALL	5	HUNTLEY	5	SYNNE	5	BADE	4
CHECKE	5	HUSBAND	5	SYTTE	5	BANKES	4
CHEKE MATE	5	HUSBANDES	5	SKYN	5	BARONS	4
CHRYST	5	ICHE	5	SLEVE	5	BECAME	4
CHURCHES	5	JACKE	5	SOCOURE	5	BECAUSE	4
CLARKE	5	JAYBERD	5	SOFTE	5	BED	4
CLENLY	5	JAK	5	SOFTLY	5	BEGYLED	4
CLOKYD	5	JANE	5	SONGE	5	BELL	4
CLOUT	5	JAPES	5	SOROWFULL	5	BENCHE	4
CLOWTE	5	JAVELL	5	SOWRE	5	BENT	4
COLLYN	5	JEMMY	5	SPECHE	5	BEQUETHE	4
COMMAUNDE	5	JEROME	5	SPELL	5	BETEN	4
COMMAUNDEMENT	5	JUPYTER	5	SPORT	5	BYBYLL	4
COMMENDABLE	5	JUST	5	SPREDE	5	BYRDES	4
COMPARE	5	LAW	5	SPRYNGE	5	BLAST	4
CONSYDERACYON	5	LEGGES	5	STALE	5	BLASTE	4
COPE	5	LEWDLY	5	STOMAKE	5	BODYES	4
CRAFTE	5	LIST	5	STRAUNGE	5	BOYES	4
CRISTIAN	5	LORDIS	5	STRENGTH	5	BOKES	4
CROWE	5	LOSELL	5	SUPPORTACYON	5	BOKIS	4
CURSE	5	LOVERS	5	TERMES	5	BOOST	4
DE	5	LULLAY	5	THEREFORE	5	BRACE	4
DEBATE	5	LURE	5	THERTO	5	BRAYNES	4
DEFAUTE	5	LUTHERS	5	THOMAS	5	BRAYNLES	4
DEFENDE	5	MAYDE	5	THOROWE	5	BRAYNLESSE	4
DELECTABLE	5	MAYNTAYNE	5	THOWSANDE	5	BRING	4
DEVYLS	5	MAKYNG	5	THRYFTE	5	BRYBERY	4
DYSTRESSE	5	MALE	5	THROUGH	5	BUTTERFLY	4
DOCTOURS	5	MATTERS	5	TYDE	5	CAGE	4
DOUT	5	MIRRY	5	TOGEDER	5	CAYFAS	4
DRESSE	5	MYLK	5	TOLD	5	CAL	4
DWELT	5	MYSERY	5	TOUCHE	5	CALLID	4
EYRE	5	MOTHER	5	TOWARDE	5	CANKERD	4
ELOQUENCE	5	NEXT	5	TRETE	5	CAP	4
ENDETH	5	NOBYLL	5	TREWLY	5	CAPPE	4
ENGLAND	5	NOBLENES	5	TRYDE	5	CAPPYD	4
ENTENT	5	NOBLES	5	TROY	5	CAPTYVYTE	4
ERNEST	5	ODYOUS	5	TROUBLE	5	CATTES	4
EXCELLENCE	5	OFTEN	5	UNDYR	5	CAUGHT	4
EXCESSE	5	ORDER	5	UNDONE	5	CAUSETH	4
EXPRES	5	OWE	5	UNKYNDE	5	CHAPELET	4
FARE WELL	5	PARDE	5	VENGEAUNCE	5	CHAUCER	4
FARLY	5	PARDON	5	VYSYTE	5	CHAUNGED	4
FARTHER	5	PAROTTE	5	WAKE	5	CHEKE	4
FAT	5	PERLE	5	WARAUNT	5	CHESTEN	4
FATALL	5	PYE	5	WARNE	5	CHUK	4
FAVELL	5	PLESURE	5	WELLE	5	CLERGYE	4
FEARE	5	POYNTE	5	WHEREOF	5	CLOKE	4
FERRE	5	POT	5	WHERETO	5	CLOTHE	4
FYNGERS	5	POWER	5	WITHSTANDE	5	CLOTHES	4
FLATERY	5	PRECYOUS	5	WYNE	5	COLE	4
FLETE	5	PRESYDENT	5	WYST	5	COMYNGE	4
FLOWRIS	5	PRINCES	5	WODE	5	COMMAUNDID	4
FOLYSSHE	5	PROSPERYTE	5	WOLL	5	COMPAS	4
FREE	5	QUARELL	5	WONT	5	COMPLYD	4
FRENSHE	5	QUYCKE	5	WOO	5	CONCEYTE	4
FRESHE	5	RAGGED	5	WORDYS	5	CONCLUSYON	4
GARNESCHE	5	RAYLES	5	WOTTE	5	CONFOUNDE	4
GASPE	5	REALME	5	WOULD	5	CONSENT	4
GYDYNGE	5	REASONS	5	WRYTEN	5	CONTRYVYD	4
GYLL	5	RECHELESSE	5	WRYTYNG	5	CONVENYENT	4
GLASSE	5	RECRAYED	5	WROWGHT	5	COOST	4
GLOSE	5	REFORMACYON	5	XULDE	5	COPYOUS	4
GOWER	5	REFRAYNE	5	YONDER	5	CORNE	4
GRAUNT	5	REKENYNG	5	ABOWTE	4	COUNTER	4
GREW	5	REMEDY	5	ABUSYD	4	COVER	4
GRYME	5	RENT	5	ADEW	4	CRYSTE	4
GRONE	5	RETAYNE	5	ADEWE	4	CROKED	4
GROTES	5	RYGHTE	5	AFFECCYON	4	CROWNES	4
HALF	5	RYN	5	AFRAYD	4	CRUELTE	4
HALTER	5	ROWE	5	AGEINST	4	CUR	4
HARTES	5	RULYD	5	AGREED	4	DARKE	4
HAUKE	5	RUSTY	5	ALL THYNG	4	DAWCOCKE	4
HELE	5	SAYNTE	5	AMONGEST	4	DEAD	4
HERCULES	5	SAVED	5	ANGRE	4	DEALE	4

DELAY	4	GOLD	4	LOWSE	4	ROUTE	4
DEPARTED	4	GOO	4	LURDEN	4	ROWTE	4
DESERVED	4	GOODE	4	MAYDEN	4	RULER	4
DETHE	4	GOOS	4	MAYST	4	SACRAMENT	4
DEVILL	4	GOOSTLY	4	MAYSTERS	4	SADLY	4
DEVYSID	4	GRAVE	4	MAKITH	4	SAYNE	4
DEVOCYON	4	GRESY	4	MARCIALL	4	SALTE	4
DEVOUTE	4	GRET	4	MEATE	4	SAMUELL	4
DIANA	4	GRETLY	4	MEMORY	4	SANGE	4
DIS	4	GROW	4	MENT	4	SATRAPAS	4
DISCHARGE	4	GROWE	4	METELY	4	SCANTLY	4
DISCRETE	4	GROWETH	4	MI	4	SCAPE	4
DISDAYNE	4	GROWNDE	4	MYLKE	4	SCORNEFULL	4
DISPYGHT	4	HAYLE	4	MYN	4	SCOTTYSSHE	4
DIVYNE	4	HAND	4	MYRROUR	4	SEYD	4
DYCE	4	HANDES	4	MYRTHE	4	SELFE SAME	4
DYSCURE	4	HANGYD	4	MOCKE	4	SELL	4
DYSEASE	4	HARTIS	4	MOYSES	4	SERPENT	4
DYSPYTE	4	HARVY	4	MONY	4	SERVAUNTYS	4
DYSPLEASE	4	HASTY	4	MOOSTE	4	SETTE	4
DOGGES	4	HATEFULL	4	MUCHE	4	SHAMEFULLY	4
DONGE	4	HECTOR	4	MUSES	4	SHARE	4
DORE	4	HEEDES	4	MUSIS	4	SHAVE	4
DOUTLES	4	HEM	4	NACION	4	SHEWED	4
DOWN	4	HEN	4	NACYONS	4	SHYP	4
DRAWEN	4	HENNES	4	NATURALL	4	SHO	4
DRES	4	HERKE	4	NEDES	4	SHOKE	4
DREST	4	HYNDER	4	NEST	4	SHONE	4
DRY	4	HYRE	4	NIGHT	4	SHORTELY	4
DUCKE	4	HOMELY	4	NYE	4	SHORTLY	4
DULY	4	HONOURE	4	NOUGHTY	4	SYLVER	4
DUNBAR	4	HORSE	4	NOWE A DAYES	4	SYRE	4
DURSTE	4	HOUSHOLDE	4	OFFENDE	4	SKANTLY	4
EASED	4	HOWEBEIT	4	OFFER	4	SKY	4
EASY	4	HUFFA	4	ORATOUR	4	SKYNNE	4
EFFECTE	4	HUMANYTE	4	ORIENT	4	SLAYN	4
ENCRESE	4	HUNDRED	4	OWLE	4	SLYGHT	4
ENDE	4	ICH	4	PACIENT	4	SLUMBRYNGE	4
ENDYTE	4	INDURE	4	PACYENT	4	SMALLE	4
ENDUDE	4	INMORTALL	4	PARROTT	4	SMYLE	4
ENGLOND	4	INTENDE	4	PERELES	4	SNOWTE	4
ENGLONDE	4	IN TO	4	PHILOSOPHY	4	SOMDELE	4
ENGROSED	4	INWARD	4	PITE	4	SOTTES	4
ENGROSYD	4	ISABELL	4	PYGGES	4	SOURE	4
ENTENTE	4	JACK	4	PYNCHE	4	SOWLE	4
EXAMPLE	4	JAK OF THE VALE	4	PYPE	4	SPIRYTUALL	4
EXCUSE	4	JAPE	4	PYSTELL	4	SPY	4
EXPENCE	4	KEY	4	PYTE	4	SPYGHT	4
FACES	4	KENT	4	PLACES	4	STERTE	4
FACULTE	4	KEPT	4	PLEASANT	4	STYNKYNG	4
FAYLE	4	KINGIS	4	PLEY	4	STOPPED	4
FANTASY	4	KNEWE	4	POEMS	4	STRAYTE	4
FANTASYES	4	KNYT	4	POETA	4	STREYGHT	4
FASTE	4	LAYE	4	POETRY	4	STRETE	4
FATTE	4	LAY FEE	4	POLE	4	SUCCOUR	4
FELE	4	LAYSER	4	POSE	4	SUFFERAUNCE	4
FER	4	LAKYN	4	PRAYED	4	SURMYSED	4
FERTHER	4	LAMENTABLE	4	PREEMYNENCE	4	SURVEYAUNCE	4
FETHERS	4	LAP	4	PRESED	4	SWAN	4
FYND	4	LARKE	4	PREST	4	TEMPLE	4
FYRSTE	4	LATYN	4	PRETENDE	4	TEN	4
FYST	4	LAUDABLE	4	PROPYR	4	TENDER	4
FLATER	4	LAUDE	4	PROPRE	4	TETHE	4
FLATTER	4	LAWES	4	PROUDLY	4	THANKED	4
FLEDDE	4	LAWRELL	4	PRUDENCE	4	THEYM	4
FLOURYSSHETH	4	LENE	4	PUTTETH	4	THERAT	4
FLOWER	4	LENGTH	4	QUAYRE	4	THEREIN	4
FO	4	LERE	4	RASE	4	THES	4
FOLOW	4	LERNYNGE	4	RAVE	4	THYCKE	4
FOO	4	LESE	4	RAWE	4	THYN	4
FORME	4	LETTE	4	RECHELES	4	THYNKETH	4
FOUND	4	LYDGATE	4	REED	4	THROTE	4
FREKE	4	LYEST	4	REFRESSHED	4	TYDYNGES	4
FURRED	4	LYGHTE	4	REFRESSHID	4	TRATYSE	4
GALAWAY	4	LYSTE	4	REFUSED	4	TREATYSE	4
GANDER	4	LYTHER	4	REMORDE	4	TRESURE	4
GARNYSHE	4	LOGYKE	4	REQUEST	4	TROYLUS	4
GERETRUDE	4	LOKYD	4	RESERVED	4	TUNGE	4
GEST	4	LOKYS	4	RESTE	4	TURKE	4
GYB	4	LOO	4	REW	4	TWEYNE	4
GYVEN	4	LORDYS	4	RYCHELY	4	UNGRACYOUS	4
GLORYOUSLY	4	LOT	4	RYNG	4	UNGRACYOUSLY	4
GNAT	4	LOVETH	4	ROBYN	4	UNNETH	4
GODFREY	4	LOW	4	ROST	4	USYD	4

UTTER	4	BEESTES	3	CONVENABLE	3	FALLYTH	3
VENEMOUS	4	BEGANNE	3	CORRECCYON	3	FALSLY	3
VERSES	4	BEGGERS	3	CORRECTE	3	FAMOUSLY	3
VERTUOUS	4	BELEVE	3	CORRECTION	3	FANSYES	3
VYOLET	4	BESENE	3	COSTE	3	FAVYR	3
WAYE	4	BESYNES	3	COUNCELL	3	FAWCOUN	3
WALLES	4	BESTIS	3	COUNSEYLE	3	FELLE	3
WANNE	4	BET	3	COUNTED	3	FELOWE	3
WANTE	4	BYSY	3	COURAGE	3	FELOWSHYP	3
WARANT	4	BYSSHOP	3	COURSE	3	FENDE	3
WATER	4	BLAMED	3	CRANE	3	FENDYS	3
WERY	4	BLE	3	CRYED	3	FERSLY	3
WETE	4	BLEWE	3	CROKYD	3	FEW	3
WHAT SO EVER	4	BLYS	3	CRUELLY	3	FYSSHE	3
WHENS	4	BLO	3	CUP	3	FLE	3
WHER	4	BLOODE	3	CURYOWSLY	3	FLED	3
WHERIN	4	BLOT	3	DAYS	3	FLYGHT	3
WHERWITH	4	BLOTHER	3	DALYAUNCE	3	FLYT	3
WHYCH	4	BLOW	3	DAPHNES	3	FLORYSSHETH	3
WHYT	4	BOSTE	3	DARRE	3	FON	3
WYNNE	4	BOW	3	DAW	3	FOREST	3
WYSDOM	4	BOWES	3	DAWYS	3	FORGOTEN	3
WYSELY	4	BOWNS	3	DECAY	3	FORMEST	3
WYVES	4	BRAG	3	DEEDLY	3	FORSWORNE	3
WOMAN	4	BRAGGYNG	3	DEFENDER	3	FORTUNATE	3
WOMANHODE	4	BRAINLES	3	DEYNTE	3	FORTUNES	3
WORDIS	4	BREFLY	3	DELIGHT	3	FOURE	3
WORSHIP	4	BRENNYNGE	3	DELYNGE	3	FOX	3
WOUNDES	4	BRENT	3	DEMENAUNCE	3	FRANTYCKE	3
WRETCHED	4	BRINGE	3	DEMENOUR	3	FRENCH	3
WRITE	4	BRYNG	3	DEMOSTENES	3	FRENCHE	3
WRYTTEN	4	BRYNGETH	3	DEPARTE	3	FRENDYS	3
YMAGES	4	BRYSTLYD	3	DESTENY	3	FRENESY	3
YNKE	4	BROKE	3	DEVYLLES	3	FRENSY	3
YONG	4	BUTTERFLYE	3	DEVYLLYSSHE	3	FRENSSHE	3
YOWRE	4	CALFE	3	DEVOYDE	3	FRETE	3
ABJURED	3	CALLIOPE	3	DEVOUTLY	3	FROUNDE	3
ABSENS	3	CANNYST	3	DIFFUSE	3	FROWARDE	3
ABSENT	3	CARY	3	DIVYNYTE	3	GAPE	3
ACOUNTYD	3	CARTAGE	3	DYCHE	3	GARNYSSHED	3
ADAM	3	CAUSED	3	DYED	3	GASED	3
ADRESSE	3	CERBERUS	3	DYNT	3	GAWDY	3
ADVERTENCE	3	CESAR	3	DYS	3	GE	3
ADVYSEMENT	3	CHAFFER	3	DYSCHARGE	3	GENTYLWOMEN	3
AFFYNYTE	3	CHAYRE	3	DYSCUST	3	GENTLE	3
AFORE	3	CHALYS	3	DYSGYSED	3	GETTE	3
AGAYNSTE	3	CHAMBRE	3	DYSPLEASURE	3	GY	3
AGREABLE	3	CHARE	3	DYVYSED	3	GLAS	3
AGREDE	3	CHECKED	3	DOLEFULL	3	GLORY	3
AGREE	3	CHEF	3	DOME	3	GLUM	3
ALLWAY	3	CHEK MATE	3	DOST	3	GODELY	3
ALMOOST	3	CHYDE	3	DOUBLENESSE	3	GOODYS	3
ALMOST	3	CHOSE	3	DOUTE	3	GOODLYHEDE	3
ALOWDE	3	CHRIST	3	DOUTLESSE	3	GOOST	3
AMASED	3	CHRISTEN	3	DRAUGHT	3	GOTE	3
ANGER	3	CHURLYSSHE	3	DRESTE	3	GOTHE	3
APACE	3	CLAP	3	DROVE	3	GOWTE	3
APPETYTE	3	CLATTER	3	DROWNED	3	GRACELESSE	3
APROCHE	3	CLERKELY	3	DUGGES	3	GRAYE	3
AQUYTE	3	CLOYSTER	3	DUNDE	3	GREDY	3
ARABY	3	CLOUTE	3	DUSTE	3	GREKES	3
ASHAMED	3	COCKE	3	ECHONE	3	GREKIS	3
ASKRY	3	COLD	3	EFFECT	3	GRETTER	3
ASSAY	3	COLLAGE	3	EYGHT	3	GRUDGE	3
ASSYST	3	COLUMBYNE	3	EYNE	3	GUYDE	3
ASSURAUNCE	3	COMYNG	3	ENBRACE	3	GUMMYS	3
ASSURED	3	COMLY	3	ENDLESSE	3	HAFTYNGE	3
ASTROLOGY	3	COMMENDE	3	ENGLYSHE	3	HALY	3
AUCTOR	3	COMMETH	3	ENGLYSSH	3	HANGED	3
AUNCYENT	3	COMMYTH	3	ENGROSID	3	HAPPE	3
AVAYLE	3	COMMYTTYNGE	3	EOLUS	3	HAPPED	3
AWAYTE	3	COMMONS	3	ERE	3	HAPPELY	3
BA	3	COMMUNE	3	ERLY	3	HAPPY	3
BABY	3	COMPYLED	3	ERTHELY	3	HARPE	3
BAILE	3	CONCEYVED	3	ETEN	3	HAWTE	3
BAK	3	CONCLUDE	3	EVERYCHONE	3	HEDDES	3
BAKE	3	CONNY	3	EVYDENTLY	3	HELES	3
BANNER	3	CONNYNG	3	EVYN	3	HELLE	3
BARNE	3	CONSCYENCE	3	EXCUSED	3	HELTH	3
BATAYLE	3	CONSYDER	3	FABLE	3	HEME	3
BAWDY	3	CONSTRAYNED	3	FABLES	3	HERAFTER	3
BEARD	3	CONSTRUE	3	FAGOTTES	3	HERSE	3
BEARE	3	CONVAYAUNCE	3	FAYNTED	3	HERVY	3
BEEN	3	CONVAYED	3	FAYTHFULL	3	HEVYNESSE	3

HEW	3	MAYDENLY	3	PLUTO	3	SAULL	3
HIGHT	3	MAYNTEYNE	3	POCKY	3	SCABBED	3
HIT	3	MAJESTE	3	POYNTED	3	SCOLERS	3
HYER	3	MAKYNGE	3	POLLYNGE	3	SCOLES	3
HYGHTE	3	MALES	3	POLUTYD	3	SCORPYON	3
HYLLES	3	MANNER	3	POUCHE	3	SCOTTISHE	3
HOGGE	3	MAR	3	POULES	3	SCOTTYS	3
HOLLY	3	MARCHAUNTES	3	POWRE	3	SCRAPE	3
HOMLY	3	MARCHE HARE	3	PRAYD	3	SEALE	3
HONOR	3	MARCYALL	3	PRAYDE	3	SECONDE	3
HONORABLE	3	MARGARET	3	PRAYE	3	SEDE	3
HONORABLY	3	MARGERAIN	3	PRANKES	3	SEMBLAUNT	3
HORE	3	MARRE	3	PRATYNGE	3	SEMED	3
HORNES	3	MARS	3	PRECE	3	SEMELY	3
HORRYBLE	3	MASE	3	PRECHYNGE	3	SENTENS	3
HORS	3	MASED	3	PRELATE	3	SERE	3
HOTE	3	MAT	3	PRESENCE	3	SEVEN	3
HOURES	3	MAUNGY	3	PRESERVE	3	SHAYLE	3
HOWBEIT	3	MEDE	3	PRESID	3	SHAKED	3
HUMBLY	3	MEMORYALL	3	PRYNCYPALL	3	SHAMED	3
HUNDRETH	3	MENYALL	3	PROBLEME	3	SHAMEFULL	3
HUNT	3	MENYS	3	PROBLEMES	3	SHAMFULL	3
HURTE	3	MERCIALL	3	PROMYSE	3	SHARP	3
IGNORANCE	3	MERCYFULL	3	PROMOCYON	3	SHELDE	3
ILL	3	MERCYLES	3	PROMOTED	3	SHYFTE	3
INDEDE	3	MYLE	3	PROSSES	3	SHORNE	3
INOUGH	3	MYNDES	3	PROTECTYON	3	SHOULD	3
INSOLENCE	3	MYNDYS	3	PROTESTACION	3	SHOWRE	3
INSTANCE	3	MYRE	3	PROTESTACYON	3	SHOWTE	3
INTENT	3	MYSCHYEF	3	PROVERBE	3	SHREWDE	3
JANGLE	3	MYSCONTENT	3	PUFFED	3	SYDES	3
JAST	3	MYSSE	3	PURCHACE	3	SYM	3
JAWES	3	MYST	3	PUTTE	3	SYNGULAR	3
JENET	3	MOOD	3	QUERE	3	SYNNYS	3
JEWE	3	MOUTHE	3	QUIKLY	3	SYSTER	3
JOHN	3	MOVYD	3	QUYCKELY	3	SYTTYNGE	3
KAYSER	3	MUSYNGE	3	RAGGYD	3	SKYE	3
KENE	3	MUSYS	3	RAY	3	SLEE	3
KEST	3	NAYE	3	RAYLYNG	3	SLENDYR	3
KYND	3	NAMYD	3	RAYNES	3	SMOCKE	3
KYRTELL	3	NEDIS	3	RAYSED	3	SMOKE	3
KYS	3	NEDYS	3	RAKE	3	SNARE	3
KYSSE	3	NEGLYGENCE	3	REALMES	3	SOBERLY	3
KYT	3	NYCE	3	REAME	3	SODAYNLY	3
KNAVYS	3	NYGHTES	3	RECLAYMED	3	SOLACYOUS	3
KNEW	3	NONNES	3	RECONYNG	3	SOLAS	3
KNIGHT	3	NORTHUMBERLANDE	3	RECORDES	3	SOW	3
KNIGHTIS	3	NOTABLE	3	RECULE	3	SOWTH	3
KOY	3	NOTE	3	REFUSE	3	SPARETH	3
KONNYNG	3	NOTWITHSTANDYNGE	3	REYNE	3	SPECYALL	3
KREW	3	OCCUPYE	3	REKYN	3	SPIRYTUALTE	3
KUS	3	OFFEND	3	REME	3	SPYE	3
LABOURE	3	ONELY	3	REMEMBER	3	SPYED	3
LACK	3	OPYNYON	3	REMENAUNT	3	SPYLL	3
LACKETH	3	ORDENAUNCE	3	RENUDE	3	SPYRITUALL	3
LADIES	3	OTHERWYSE	3	REPORT	3	SPOKEN	3
LAYD	3	OVERTHROW	3	REPRESENT	3	SQUYERS	3
LAPPED	3	OVERTHWART	3	REPROCHE	3	STAND	3
LATYNE	3	PACYENCE	3	REQUYRETH	3	STAR	3
LAUGH	3	PAYE	3	RESERVYD	3	STARRY	3
LAURYATE	3	PAYNES	3	RESYDENT	3	STED	3
LEFTE	3	PARCEYVE	3	RESONS	3	STERRY	3
LENGER	3	PAREGALL	3	RESTORE	3	STYNKE	3
LETTRED	3	PARSONS	3	REWARDE	3	STOLE	3
LEWES	3	PARTRYCHE	3	RIN	3	STOP	3
LIGHT	3	PASSID	3	RYCHES	3	STORYES	3
LYING	3	PEACE	3	RYD	3	STOWE	3
LYVER	3	PECKE	3	RYVERS	3	STOWPE	3
LOCKE	3	PENDE	3	ROIALL	3	STOWTE	3
LOYALTE	3	PERFIGHT	3	ROMAYNS	3	STROKE	3
LONGER	3	PERPLEXYTE	3	ROPE	3	STUDY	3
LORE	3	PERS	3	ROTE	3	SUBDUDE	3
LORELL	3	PERSEVERAUNCE	3	ROTTEN	3	SUBJECCYON	3
LOSE	3	PETRARKE	3	ROW	3	SUFFRED	3
LOSELS	3	PHILOLOGY	3	ROWME	3	SUGER	3
LOSSE	3	PHYLLYPPES	3	RUMMYNG	3	SUMTYME	3
LOTH	3	PYLDE	3	RUMMYNGE	3	SUMWHAT	3
LOWDE	3	PYLGRIMAGE	3	SACKE	3	SUPPLYCACYON	3
LOWRE	3	PYLL	3	SADNES	3	SUPPOSED	3
LUCKE	3	PYLLYD	3	SAINCT	3	SURREY	3
LUNA	3	PYNNE	3	SAYENGE	3	SURVAYOUR	3
LUSTELY	3	PLAYED	3	SAYNTES	3	SWARE	3
MAGNIFYE	3	PLEASAUNT	3	SAPYENCE	3	SWART	3
MAYDENHEDE	3	PLEASED	3	SAUCE	3	SWERDE	3

SWORDES	3	WYN	3	ASPY	2	BONNE	2
SWORNE	3	WYNCHE	3	ASSAYE	2	BORDER	2
TALKYNGE	3	WYNGES	3	ASSAYES	2	BORDERS	2
TAUNT	3	WYNKE	3	ASSENT	2	BOTELL	2
TECHE	3	WYSTE	3	ASSYGNED	2	BOTTELL	2
TELLE	3	WYTTES	3	ASSURID	2	BOTTES	2
TEMPORALTE	3	WOKE	3	ASTRAY	2	BOUGHTE	2
TENT	3	WOLFE	3	ASTRONOMY	2	BOWE	2
TERE	3	WONDERFULL	3	ATTAYNTYD	2	BOWRE	2
THEE	3	WONDERS	3	ATTEYNE	2	BOWRIS	2
THEFTE	3	WORKES	3	AUDYENCE	2	BRAGE	2
THEYS	3	WORSTE	3	AUREAT	2	BRAGGYNGE	2
THENS	3	WRIGHT	3	AUSTEN	2	BRAYDE	2
THEREOF	3	WRITYNGE	3	AUTER	2	BRAYNED	2
THEREON	3	WRYNGE	3	AVENT	2	BRAYNSYCKE	2
THEREWITH	3	WROKEN	3	AVENTURE	2	BRAYNSYKE	2
THEVYS	3	WROTH	3	AVYSE	2	BRALL	2
THING	3	WULL	3	BABYLON	2	BRANXTON	2
THINKE	3	YATIS	3	BACCHUS	2	BRASSE	2
THYSELFE	3	YDYLL	3	BACE	2	BRAST	2
THYTHER	3	A B C	2	BACK	2	BRAULE	2
THOUGHTFULL	3	ABYDES	2	BACON FLYCKE	2	BRAWLER	2
THREDE BARE	3	ABYLYMENT	2	BAYARDE	2	BREST	2
THRYFT	3	ABRODE	2	BAYTE	2	BRETHERN	2
THRONGE	3	ABUSED	2	BALDOCK	2	BREWE	2
THROTES	3	ABUSYONS	2	BALTHASOR	2	BRIGHT	2
TOGYTHER	3	ABUSYOUN	2	BANES	2	BRYDELL	2
TOKEN	3	ACCOMPTE	2	BANYSSHED	2	BRYMLY	2
TOLLERACYON	3	ACCUSTOMABLE	2	BANKE	2	BRONDE	2
TOO	3	ACTIS	2	BAR	2	BROWES	2
TOTE	3	ADIEU	2	BARARAG	2	BROWYS	2
TOTHE AKE	3	ADRES	2	BARGE	2	BRUTID	2
TOTHER	3	ADVERTYSEMENT	2	BARK	2	BULLY	2
TOUCHYNGE	3	AFAR	2	BARRES	2	BURGONYONS	2
TOURE	3	AFFECTION	2	BARRYD	2	BURNYNGE	2
TOURNED	3	AFFECTYON	2	BASSE	2	BUSKYN	2
TOWARD	3	AGEYN	2	BATE	2	CAYFACE	2
TOWCHID	3	AGREABYLL	2	BATELL	2	CAYSER	2
TRAYNE	3	AKE	2	BATTAYLE	2	CAYTYFE	2
TROWEST	3	ALARUM	2	BEANES	2	CAKE	2
TROWTH	3	ALBION	2	BECOME	2	CALDE	2
TRUSTED	3	ALBUMASAR	2	BECOMYTH	2	CALIOPE	2
TRUTHE	3	ALCHEUS	2	BEDES	2	CALYS	2
TUSSHE	3	ALES	2	BEEST	2	CALLYST	2
TWEDE	3	ALL A KNAVE	2	BEFALL	2	CANE	2
UNABLE	3	ALMON	2	BEFOLE	2	CANEST	2
UNDERSTODE	3	ALMOSTE	2	BEGGER	2	CANKARD	2
UNDERTAKE	3	ALOWED	2	BEGYLDE	2	CANON	2
UNFAYNED	3	ALWAYE	2	BEGYLE	2	CAPYD	2
UNHAPPELY	3	AMASID	2	BEHYND	2	CAPONS	2
UNREVERENT	3	AMENDED	2	BEKNAVE	2	CAPTAYNE	2
UNTWYNDE	3	AMENDYD	2	BELE	2	CARDYNALS HAT	2
URED	3	AMPLE	2	BELLYALL	2	CARDYS	2
USETH	3	AMRELL	2	BENIGNITE	2	CARKES	2
VALIAUNT	3	ANY THYNGE	2	BENTE	2	CARON	2
VERTUES	3	ANNEXYD	2	BERETH	2	CAROWE	2
VYSE	3	ANNUALL	2	BERYST	2	CARPE	2
WAYTE	3	A PACE	2	BESHREWDE	2	CARPET	2
WAYWARDE	3	APAYD	2	BESHROWE	2	CARPETTIS	2
WALKYNGE	3	APAYED	2	BESIDE	2	CASKET	2
WANDRYNGE	3	APERE	2	BETTERS	2	CASTYNG	2
WANTONLY	3	APES	2	BICAUSE	2	CASUELTE	2
WARY	3	APON	2	BITTER	2	CATE	2
WARKIS	3	APPETITE	2	BYD	2	CATO	2
WARSE	3	APPLES	2	BYLEVE	2	CAUNTERBURY	2
WASPE	3	APPLY	2	BYLLES	2	CAUSELES	2
WEST	3	APPOSE	2	BYRD	2	CAUSES	2
WETH	3	AQUAYNTAUNCE	2	BYRDIS	2	CEASE	2
WETHER	3	AQUAYNTYD	2	BYRTH	2	CESE	2
WHEREAT	3	AQUENTAUNCE	2	BYT	2	CHACE	2
WHEREIN	3	ARGUED	2	BYTE	2	CHAYN	2
WHERE UPON	3	ARGUMENT	2	BYTTERNESSE	2	CHAYNE	2
WHEREWITH	3	ARGUMENTES	2	BLED	2	CHALANGAR	2
WHERON	3	ARON	2	BLOO	2	CHALKE	2
WHYLIS	3	ARONS	2	BLOOD	2	CHAMBRES	2
WHOSO	3	AROW	2	BLOWEN	2	CHARLEMAYN	2
WIL	3	ARRE	2	BLOWYTH	2	CHARME	2
WIT	3	ARSE	2	BOCHERS	2	CHARTER	2
WITHDRAWE	3	ASAYDE	2	BODELY	2	CHAST	2
WITHE	3	ASCRY	2	BODYS	2	CHAT	2
WITHHOLDE	3	ASHRIGE	2	BO HO	2	CHAUNTYNG	2
WITHOUTEN	3	ASK	2	BOLDELY	2	CHECKE MATE	2
WITHOWTE	3	ASKETH	2	BOLE	2	CHECKMATE	2
WYLLES	3	ASONDRE	2	BONE AKE	2	CHEMERAS	2

CHEPE	2	COURTYER	2	DYRECTION	2	ENTERPRYSED	2
CHERY	2	COVERLET	2	DYRT	2	ENVYE	2
CHERYSSHED	2	CRADELL	2	DYSCEYTE	2	ENVYOUS	2
CHESE	2	CRAFT	2	DYSCYMULAR	2	EPITAPH	2
CHEVYSAUNCE	2	CRAKERS	2	DYSCORDE	2	EPYTAPHE	2
CHYDYNGE	2	CRANES	2	DYSE	2	ERROURS	2
CHYLD	2	CRAVE	2	DYSPARE	2	ESPYDE	2
CHYN	2	CREACYON	2	DYSTRES	2	ESPYE	2
CHYRCHE	2	CREKE	2	DYVYNE	2	EST	2
CHORLYSHE	2	CRYDE	2	DOG	2	ETERNALLY	2
CHOWGH	2	CRYME	2	DOYNGE	2	EUMENIDES	2
CICERO	2	CRYSTES	2	DOMINGOS	2	EVERY THYNGE	2
CYTE	2	CROYDON	2	DOMYNYON	2	EXCEDYNGE	2
CYVYLL	2	CRONELL	2	DONGHYLL	2	EXCELL	2
CLAY	2	CROPPYD	2	DONNE	2	EXCELLENT	2
CLARIONE	2	CROS	2	DORES	2	EXCLAMACYON	2
CLARKIS	2	CROSSED	2	DOSTE	2	EXYLYD	2
CLASPIS	2	CROW	2	DOTAGE	2	EXPERYENCE	2
CLATER	2	CUNNYNG	2	DOTTAGE	2	EXPLOYTE	2
CLATERYNGE	2	CUPYDE	2	DOUBLENES	2	EXTOLDE	2
CLAUSES	2	CURATE	2	DOUGHTY	2	EXTOLL	2
CLEMENTYNE	2	CURATES	2	DOUNE	2	FADE	2
CLEVE	2	CURYOUSLY	2	DOUTTY	2	FADER	2
CLOSE	2	CURLEWE	2	DOWCHE	2	FADERS	2
CLOUDY	2	CURRYSHLY	2	DOWTLES	2	FAGOT	2
CLOWDE	2	CURTEISLY	2	DOWTLESSE	2	FAIRE	2
CLOWDY	2	CURTESY	2	DRAFFE	2	FAITH	2
COFERS	2	DAGGER	2	DRAGON	2	FAY	2
COYNE	2	DAKERS	2	DRAKE	2	FAYNED	2
COYSTROWNE	2	DALE	2	DRED	2	FAYNT	2
COLYN	2	DALYRAG	2	DREDEFULL	2	FALLE	2
COLLEGE	2	DAMPNACYON	2	DREDFULL	2	FALLYBLE	2
COLLUSYON	2	DANES	2	DREGGES	2	FALSELY	2
COMBRED	2	DAR	2	DREMYNG	2	FALSHODE	2
COMENDABLE	2	DAREST	2	DREVYLL	2	FAMES	2
COMMANDEMENNT	2	DASED	2	DREWE	2	FAVORABLE	2
COMMAUNDMENT	2	DASID	2	DRIVEN	2	FAWCONER	2
COMMENDACION	2	DASY	2	DRYNKYNGE	2	FAWTE	2
COMMENDACYON	2	DAUCOCK	2	DRYVYLL	2	FEBLE	2
COMMONNS	2	DAUNCED	2	DRONKE	2	FEES	2
COMMUNALTE	2	DAUNGEROUS	2	DROWPY	2	FEEST	2
COMPARYSON	2	DAVYD	2	DUG	2	FELICITE	2
COMPASSYD	2	DAWCOKE	2	DUKIS	2	FELOWES	2
COMPAST	2	DAWNCE	2	DUM	2	FEN	2
COMPENDYOUSLY	2	DEBATES	2	DUN	2	FERCE	2
COMPYLE	2	DECKE	2	DUNKAN	2	FERYMAN	2
COMPRISID	2	DECLARE	2	DUR	2	FERVENT	2
COMPRYSID	2	DECRE	2	DUSTY	2	FERVENTLY	2
CONCENTE	2	DEDES	2	DWELLETH	2	FESAUNT	2
CONCRETE	2	DEED	2	DWELLYNGE	2	FETHYRS	2
CONDYCYONS	2	DEFENCE	2	EARE	2	FETTERS	2
CONSEYT	2	DELYCATE	2	EASELY	2	FETURES	2
CONSEQUENTLY	2	DELYVERED	2	EBBE	2	FINALLY	2
CONSOLACYON	2	DELT	2	EBRUE	2	FYER	2
CONTAYNED	2	DEMAUNDED	2	EGGES	2	FYLE	2
CONTEYNED	2	DEME	2	EYES	2	FYNGER	2
CONTYNEW	2	DEMEANE	2	EYRNEST	2	FYRME	2
CONTYNEWE	2	DEN	2	ELACYON	2	FYSTE	2
CONTYNUALL	2	DENYED	2	ELBOWE	2	FLAMES	2
CONTYNUALLY	2	DEPE	2	ELECT	2	FLATTERYNGE	2
CONTRE	2	DERAYNE	2	ELECTE	2	FLAUNDERS	2
CONTRYTE	2	DEROGACYON	2	ELENKES	2	FLERY	2
CONTRYVED	2	DESERVE	2	ELYCONYS	2	FLYBLOWEN	2
CONTROLDE	2	DESPYGHT	2	ELLS	2	FLYE NET	2
CONTROLLE	2	DESPYSE	2	ELOQUENS	2	FLOODES	2
CONTROULE	2	DESPYTE	2	ELSE	2	FLORA	2
CONVERSACYON	2	DETERMYNE	2	EMBRACYD	2	FLORISHETH	2
CORDYALL	2	DETESTABLE	2	ENBOSED	2	FLOUR	2
CORNER	2	DEUYAS	2	ENCREASE	2	FLOWE	2
CORNUCOPIA	2	DEVYL	2	ENDEVOUR	2	FODE	2
CORRECT	2	DEVYSYNGE	2	ENDLES	2	FOLOWYNGE	2
CORRECTYON	2	DEW	2	ENDUCE	2	FONNE	2
CORS	2	DICKEN	2	ENDURYNGE	2	FONNYSSHE	2
CORTEISE	2	DISCLOSE	2	ENFORMED	2	FORBERE	2
COTES	2	DISCOMMENDE	2	ENFORSED	2	FORCEBLY	2
COUGHE	2	DISCURED	2	ENGENDRED	2	FORFENDE	2
COUGHT	2	DISCUST	2	ENMYXYD	2	FORGE	2
COUNSAYLE	2	DISPARAGE	2	ENNEWED	2	FORGET	2
COUNT	2	DISPLESAUNT	2	ENPICTURID	2	FORGOTTEN	2
COUNTERFETYNGE	2	DISTRES	2	ENROLD	2	FORKED	2
COUNTERWAYNG	2	DITIS	2	ENSURE	2	FORMED	2
COUNTETH	2	DYN	2	ENTENDE	2	FORMER	2
COUNTRYNGE	2	DYNGE	2	ENTEREMENT	2	FORS	2
COURSERS	2	DYRECCYON	2	ENTERPRYSE	2	FORSOTH	2

FORSTER	2	GRYSLY	2	ILES	2	LEWDENES	2
FORTY	2	GRONYNGE	2	IMAGE	2	LEWDNESSE	2
FORTUNED	2	GRUGYD	2	INDEED	2	LIE	2
FORTUNYS	2	GUMMES	2	INDY BLEW	2	LIFE	2
FORTUNS	2	HABLE	2	INFECTE	2	LITELL	2
FOUNDERS	2	HALLES	2	INFERNALL	2	LITILL	2
FOUR	2	HALOW	2	INFORME	2	LYACON	2
FOXE	2	HALT	2	INNOCENT	2	LYBERALL	2
FRANKE	2	HAMPTON	2	INNUMERABLE	2	LYFT	2
FRANTICK	2	HANDIS	2	INORDINATE	2	LYKELY	2
FRANTIKNES	2	HANG	2	INORDINATLY	2	LYKYNG	2
FREERS	2	HANYBALL	2	INORDYNATE	2	LYKYNGE	2
FRENCH MEN	2	HARLOTTES	2	INSPYRACION	2	LYMMYS	2
FRENDLY	2	HAROW	2	INSUFFYCYENT	2	LYNE	2
FRENDSHYP	2	HAROWE	2	INTELLYGENCE	2	LYNED	2
FRERES	2	HARPED	2	IRYSH	2	LYNKYD	2
FRESCHE	2	HARRE	2	I WYS	2	LYTEL	2
FRESE	2	HARTY	2	IWUS	2	LYTILL	2
FRESSHEST	2	HARTLY	2	JAY	2	LYVYD	2
FRET	2	HART ROTE	2	JAMES	2	LYVYNG	2
FRYGGES	2	HASTE	2	JAMY	2	LOCRYAN	2
FROO	2	HATETH	2	JANGELYNGE	2	LODESTERRE	2
FROUNCE	2	HAVELL	2	JANGLYNGE	2	LOKES	2
FROWNETH	2	HAWE	2	JANTILL	2	LOKETH	2
FROWNSID	2	HEAD	2	JELOFFER	2	LONDE	2
FULFYLL	2	HEALE	2	JEREMY	2	LORDLY	2
FUNERALL	2	HEDES	2	JOYOUS	2	LOSELLES	2
FUNT	2	HEERY	2	JONE	2	LOSYLL	2
GAYE	2	HEYGHT	2	JOURNEY	2	LOTHESUM	2
GALATHEA	2	HELED	2	JUDAS	2	LOTTES	2
GALTRES	2	HELME	2	JUDGE	2	LOUSY	2
GAMBAWDIS	2	HELTHE	2	JUG	2	LOVED	2
GARDED	2	HENCE	2	JUSTYCE	2	LOVYD	2
GARGONE	2	HERBER	2	JUVENALL	2	LOWEST	2
GARLANDE	2	HERD	2	JUVINALL	2	LOWLY	2
GARNISSHED	2	HEREAFTER	2	KALL	2	LOWTE	2
GARNYSCHE	2	HERE IN	2	KEYE	2	LUCINA	2
GASE	2	HEREOF	2	KENTE	2	LUGGYNG	2
GASID	2	HERYNGE	2	KEPETH	2	LUK	2
GAT	2	HERKEN	2	KEPTE	2	LURDAYNE	2
GATES	2	HER SELFE	2	KYNDELL	2	MACEDONY	2
GATHER	2	HERTELY	2	KYNDNESSE	2	MAGESTE	2
GATIS	2	HERTYS	2	KYNNE	2	MAGNANYMYTE	2
GAUNT	2	HESPERIDES	2	KYSTE	2	MAGNIFY	2
GAWEN	2	HETHER	2	KYTE	2	MAGNIFYCENCE	2
GENERALL	2	HIMSELF	2	KNELE	2	MAISTERS	2
GENTYLWOMAN	2	HISTORIAR	2	KNOWETH	2	MAYDENS	2
GEORGE	2	HISTORIOUS	2	KOUDE	2	MAYNE	2
GESON	2	HITHER	2	KUSSE	2	MAYNY	2
GESSE	2	HYD	2	LACKED	2	MALAPERT	2
GINGIRLY	2	HYED	2	LAYE MEN	2	MALAPERTE	2
GYDETH	2	HYM SELFE	2	LAMENTABLY	2	MALYCE	2
GYDYNG	2	HYNDE	2	LANDES	2	MALTE	2
GYLE	2	HOBBY	2	LANTERNES	2	MANERES	2
GYN	2	HOLD	2	LARGELY	2	MANGYE	2
GYNYS	2	HOLYNES	2	LARGER	2	MANLY	2
GLADLY	2	HOLL	2	LASTE	2	MANTILL	2
GLADNES	2	HOLOW	2	LATIN	2	MANTYCORE	2
GLE	2	HOMAGER	2	LAUGHED	2	MANTUAN	2
GLEDE	2	HOMERUS	2	LAUGHETH	2	MARCHAUNDYSE	2
GLENT	2	HONESTY	2	LAUGHYNGE	2	MARES	2
GLOTONY	2	HONY	2	LAUGHTER	2	MARGARETE	2
GNAWE	2	HONNY	2	LAWGHYTH	2	MARIONE	2
GODDESSE	2	HONOWRE	2	LE	2	MARSHALSY	2
GODLY	2	HOOLY	2	LEAD	2	MAS	2
GOE	2	HOPPE	2	LEARNING	2	MASYD	2
GOETH	2	HORSONS	2	LED	2	MAST	2
GOMMES	2	HOUNDE	2	LEDDER	2	MASTYFE	2
GONNE	2	HOUNDES	2	LEDYTH	2	MATYNS	2
GOODNES	2	HOUSE	2	LEEST	2	MATRICULATE	2
GOSSYP	2	HOUSHOLD	2	LEFE	2	MATTOCKE	2
GOSTE	2	HOWARDE	2	LEGE	2	MAUDE	2
GOVERNE	2	HOWNDE	2	LEYSER	2	MAW	2
GOVERNED	2	HOWRE	2	LEKE	2	MAWMENT	2
GRACELES	2	HOWRIS	2	LENTE	2	MEDYLL	2
GRAUNTE	2	HUDDY PEKE	2	LENTON	2	MEDLER	2
GRAVYTE	2	HUGE	2	LERNA	2	MEKE	2
GRE	2	HUMBLE	2	LERNYD	2	MEKELY	2
GREKYS	2	HUMYLYTE	2	LESTE	2	MELANCOLY	2
GRESED	2	HUNDERD	2	LETHER	2	MELE	2
GRETELY	2	HUNGER	2	LEUDLY	2	MELLE	2
GRETT	2	HUSWYVES	2	LEVER	2	MENDE	2
GREVAUNCE	2	IDOLATRY	2	LEVIS	2	MENNES	2
GRYMLY	2	IERARCHY	2	LEWDELY	2	MENS	2

MERCYALL	2	ONLY	2	PLAUTUS	2	QUAKED	2
MERCURY	2	ONS	2	PLEASYD	2	QUARTERS	2
MERELY	2	OPENED	2	PLEASYTH	2	QUENES	2
MERVAYLE	2	OPTAYNE	2	PLEDGE	2	QUESTYONLESSE	2
MESSE	2	ORACE	2	PLENARLY	2	QUYT	2
METTE	2	ORDRE	2	PLENTE	2	RABLE	2
MEW	2	ORE	2	PLESAUNTLY	2	RADIANT	2
MEWARDE	2	OREB	2	PLESYTH	2	RAGES	2
MEWTAS	2	ORNATE	2	PLETE	2	RAYLYNGE	2
MIDSOMER	2	ORNATLY	2	PLUCKYNGE	2	RAM	2
MISCHEFE	2	OTHE	2	PLUCTE	2	RAMMES HORNE	2
MYDSOMER	2	OUTFACE	2	PLUTOS	2	RASID	2
MYKYLL	2	OVERAGE	2	POHEN	2	RAT	2
MYND	2	OVERSE	2	POYSON	2	RATIS	2
MYNDED	2	OVERSYGHT	2	POKE	2	RAVEN	2
MYNDYD	2	OVYDE	2	POLEXENE	2	REBELL	2
MYNSTRELL	2	OVYR	2	POLYTYKE	2	REBELLES	2
MYSCHAUNS	2	OWLE FLYGHT	2	POLL	2	REBUKE	2
MYSCHEFFE	2	OWLES	2	POPPYNGE	2	RECEYVE	2
MYSCONTENTE	2	OWT	2	PORISSHLY	2	RECEYVED	2
MYTER	2	PACYENTLY	2	PORPOSE	2	RECEYVYD	2
MOCKYS	2	PAINE	2	PORTIS	2	RECOMPENCE	2
MODE	2	PAYMENT	2	PORTYNGALE	2	RECORDIS	2
MODERS	2	PAYN	2	POSTY	2	RECOUNT	2
MOKERY	2	PAYNFULL	2	PRAYER	2	RECOUNTE	2
MOKKYSHE	2	PAYNT	2	PRANE	2	RECOUNTYNG	2
MOLDE	2	PAYNTYD	2	PRATES	2	RECOUNTYNGE	2
MOLOC	2	PAN	2	PRATYE	2	REDDE	2
MONKE	2	PANDAER	2	PRATYNG	2	REDEME	2
MONNY	2	PARADYCE	2	PREASE	2	REDYNESSE	2
MOODE	2	PARDONE	2	PRECHERS	2	REDYNGE	2
MORELL	2	PARIS	2	PRECHYNG	2	REFRAYNED	2
MORYSHE	2	PARKE	2	PRECHOUR	2	REGARDE	2
MORNE	2	PARSON	2	PRECHOURS	2	REGARDED	2
MOROW	2	PART	2	PRECIOUS	2	REGENTE	2
MOT	2	PARTYS	2	PREESTHODE	2	REGESTER	2
MOTE	2	PASSYTH	2	PREESTLY	2	REHERSALL	2
MOTTON	2	PASTAUNCE	2	PRELACY	2	REHERSYNG	2
MOUSE	2	PASTE	2	PREMENYRE	2	REYSONS	2
MOUTH	2	PATCHYNGE	2	PREPENSED	2	RELACION	2
MOUTHES	2	PATER NOSTER	2	PREROGATYVE	2	RELE	2
MOVE	2	PATES	2	PRESEDENT	2	REMAYNED	2
MUM	2	PATRYARKE	2	PRESENT	2	REMEMBRANCE	2
MUMMYNGE	2	PAULE	2	PRESSYNGE	2	REMEMBRED	2
MUSED	2	PAUNCHE	2	PRESTE	2	REMEMBREST	2
MUSSE	2	PAVES	2	PRETELY	2	REMORDYNG	2
MUSTARDE	2	PAVYLYON	2	PRETENDYNGE	2	REN	2
MUTABYLYTE	2	PEASON	2	PRETENS	2	RENDER	2
NACYOUN	2	PECOK	2	PREVAYLE	2	RENDRYNGE	2
NAKYD	2	PENAUNCE	2	PREVE	2	RENEWE	2
NAVERNE	2	PENNY	2	PRIAMUS	2	RENOWNE	2
NEDLE	2	PEOPLES	2	PRINCELY	2	REPAYRE	2
NEITHER	2	PERCE	2	PRINCIPLES	2	REPENTAUNCE	2
NERO	2	PERCEYVED	2	PRINCIS	2	REPLICACION	2
NET	2	PERCIUS	2	PRINCYPALL	2	REPLY	2
NEWES	2	PERDE	2	PRYCKE	2	REPRESSE	2
NEXTE	2	PERES	2	PRYETH	2	REQUESTE	2
NYGHTE	2	PERYLLOUS	2	PROBATE	2	REQUYRE	2
NYGHTYNGALE	2	PERYLOUS	2	PROCLAMED	2	RESCEW	2
NYS	2	PERLYS	2	PROFESSED	2	RESYDENCE	2
NOBLE MEN	2	PERMYT	2	PROFYTABLE	2	RESYTYNGE	2
NOLLES	2	PERMYTTED	2	PROGENY	2	RESTLES	2
NONES	2	PERSON	2	PROMYSED	2	RETAYNED	2
NONNE	2	PERSONE	2	PROMOTYD	2	REVELL	2
NOO	2	PERSONES	2	PRONGE	2	REVERENT	2
NOPPY	2	PERSONS	2	PROPER	2	REVYLE	2
NORTH	2	PERSUACYON	2	PROPERTE	2	RYDETH	2
NOTYD	2	PERTE	2	PROPHETE	2	RYDYNGE	2
NOWE ADAYES	2	PETER	2	PROPHETES	2	RYDYTH	2
NOWE ADAYS	2	PETY	2	PROSE	2	RYNGE	2
NUTMEG	2	PEVICHE	2	PROTECCYON	2	RYOTTE	2
OBEDYENCE	2	PEVYSH	2	PROVISION	2	RYSETH	2
OBJECTED	2	PHILIP	2	PROVYD	2	ROBBYNGE	2
OCCUPACIOUN	2	PHILLIPPE	2	PROVYNCYALL	2	ROYALLY	2
OCCUPACYOUN	2	PHILLIPS	2	PROVOKE	2	ROMAINE	2
ODLY	2	PHILLIS	2	PROWES	2	ROMAYNES	2
OFFENDED	2	PHYP	2	PRUDENT	2	ROSARY	2
OFFENDYD	2	PYLERY	2	PTHOLOMY	2	ROSES	2
OFFRED	2	PYLLAGE	2	PULLYSSHED	2	ROSTE	2
OFFRYD	2	PYLLERS	2	PURCHASE	2	ROSTYD	2
OLYVE	2	PYNDARUS	2	PURE	2	ROUGH FOTED	2
OMNIPOTENT	2	PYRAMUS	2	PURS	2	ROUT	2
ONYONS	2	PLAYNE SONGE	2	QUAIRE	2	ROWTH	2
ONY THYNGE	2	PLATE	2	QUAYLE	2	RUBYE	2

886

RUDELY	2	SYSMATYKES	2	STOPPELL	2	TYTUS	2
RULYTH	2	SYSTERS	2	STORIS	2	TODE	2
RUMPE	2	SYTTYNG	2	STORMYS	2	TOFORE	2
RUN	2	SKANTE	2	STOUNDE	2	TOGETHYR	2
RUNNYNGE	2	SKEYNE	2	STRAYNED	2	TO MOROWE	2
RUSSET	2	SKELPE	2	STRAWBERY	2	TONE	2
RUSSHE	2	SKYES	2	STREYTE	2	TO-RAGGED	2
RUSSHETH	2	SKYLLE	2	STREME	2	TOWARDES	2
SAIDE	2	SKYP	2	STREMES	2	TOWCHYD	2
SAINT	2	SKYPPES	2	STREMYS	2	TOWER	2
SAITH	2	SLACKE	2	STRYFE	2	TOWNES	2
SAYNGE	2	SLE	2	STRYVE	2	TRANSCENDYNG	2
SALT	2	SLYDE	2	STUDIOUS	2	TRANSCENDYNGE	2
SAMPLER	2	SLYMY	2	STUDYE	2	TREADE	2
SANDES	2	SLYPPE	2	STUDYOUS	2	TREMBLID	2
SANK ROYALL	2	SLOO	2	STUDYOUSLY	2	TRENCHE	2
SAPHYRE	2	SLOVEN	2	STUFFED	2	TRESON	2
SARE	2	SMATER	2	STUMPE	2	TRESSES	2
SATE	2	SMATTER	2	STURDY	2	TREUTH	2
SAVYD	2	SMERY	2	SUBJECTES	2	TREWSE	2
SAVYNGE	2	SMOTHELY	2	SUBJECTYON	2	TRYALL	2
SAVYOUR	2	SNAYLE	2	SUBTELLY	2	TRYM	2
SAWTE	2	SNAPPER	2	SUBTYLL	2	TRYM-TRAM	2
SCABBES	2	SNEVYLL	2	SUBTYLTE	2	TRYPES	2
SCABBYD	2	SNYTE	2	SUBVERTED	2	TRYUMPHE	2
SCANTE	2	SNOUT	2	SUCCOURE	2	TROYE	2
SCARPARY	2	SOBRE	2	SUFFERAYNE	2	TROWTHE	2
SCOLE MATTER	2	SOCOUR	2	SUGRED	2	TRUELY	2
SCOLYS	2	SOLD	2	SUM WHAT	2	TRUMPE	2
SCORE	2	SOLEYNE	2	SUPERVYSOUR	2	TRUMPET	2
SCORNFULL	2	SOLEM	2	SUPPLYED	2	TRUSSED	2
SCOTLAND	2	SOLFE	2	SUPPRYSYD	2	TRUTH	2
SCRYBE	2	SOMEWHAT	2	SURETY	2	TUGGYNG	2
SCROLLES	2	SOMMON	2	SURGIONS	2	TULLIS	2
SCULL	2	SOMMONS	2	SUTERS	2	TUMBYLL	2
SECRETE	2	SOMNER	2	SWANNE	2	TUNG	2
SECRETLY	2	SOMTIME	2	SWARVE	2	TUNNYNGE	2
SECTE	2	SON	2	SWELL	2	TURDE	2
SEEST	2	SONER	2	SWERED	2	TURNYD	2
SEKENESSE	2	SONG	2	SWETELY	2	TURNYNG	2
SELDOME	2	SORT	2	SWETE MEATE	2	TUT	2
SELE	2	SOUNDE	2	TABULL	2	TWAINE	2
SEM	2	SOVERAYGNE	2	TAILE	2	TWENTY	2
SEME	2	SOVEREINE	2	TAKETH	2	TWIT	2
SENATE	2	SPAYNE	2	TAKYN	2	UNBYNDE	2
SENCE	2	SPARED	2	TAN	2	UNBRASED	2
SENDETH	2	SPARKE	2	TAPPETTIS	2	UNDERSTONDE	2
SERVAUNTIS	2	SPECIALLY	2	TAUNDERUM	2	UNDOUBTED	2
SETT	2	SPECTACLE CASE	2	TELLETH	2	UNGRACIOUS	2
SETTETH	2	SPEKEST	2	TELLYNGE	2	UNGRACIOUSLY	2
SETTYNG	2	SPEKETH	2	TENDE	2	UNIVERSYTE	2
SEVYN	2	SPENCE	2	TENDERLY	2	UNYVERSYTE	2
SHAKYNG	2	SPEND	2	TENOR	2	UNMETE	2
SHAMELES	2	SPIRITUALL	2	TEUYT	2	UNTAUGHT	2
SHAMLESSE	2	SPYNDELL	2	TEWYNE	2	UNTRUE	2
SHAP	2	SPYRYTUALL	2	THEIM	2	UNTRULY	2
SHARPER	2	SPONE	2	THEYRE	2	URE	2
SHENE	2	SPORES	2	THENNE	2	UTTERAUNCE	2
SHEWETH	2	SPRAY	2	THEOCRITUS	2	VAYNE GLORY	2
SHEWID	2	SPRYNG	2	THEOLOGY	2	VAYNES	2
SHEWYTH	2	SPUR	2	THEREWITHALL	2	VALE	2
SHYRE	2	SQUYRE	2	THERWITHALL	2	VARYAUNCE	2
SHYT	2	STABYLL	2	THESEUS	2	VELVET	2
SHOT	2	STAFFE	2	THEWDE	2	VENUS	2
SHOULDE	2	STAKE	2	THYNGYS	2	VERELY	2
SHOURE	2	STAMPE	2	THYNK	2	VERTUOUSLY	2
SHRYMPES	2	STANKE	2	THYNKYST	2	VIRGYNALL	2
SHRYVE	2	STARK	2	THYR	2	VYLLANY	2
SHROUDLY	2	STARLYNG	2	THYSE	2	VOYD	2
SHROWDE	2	START	2	THORNE	2	VOLUMYS	2
SIGHT	2	STATUTES	2	THOROWLY	2	VOLVELL	2
SILKE	2	STEPLE	2	THOS	2	WAYLE	2
SIT	2	STERE	2	THOUSAND	2	WAYWARDLY	2
SYER	2	STERNE	2	THOUTHE	2	WALES	2
SYGH	2	STERRES	2	THRET	2	WALLE	2
SYGHTE	2	STERRYS	2	THREWE	2	WANDRED	2
SYGNE	2	STEWED	2	THRYVE	2	WANHOPE	2
SYKE	2	STILL	2	THROW	2	WANT	2
SYKERNESSE	2	STYNGE	2	THRUGHE	2	WANTYD	2
SYLK	2	STYNGYNG	2	THRUST	2	WANTYTHE	2
SYMONIDES	2	STYNTETH	2	TILL	2	WANTONNESSE	2
SYNGETH	2	STONDETH	2	TIME	2	WARBELYNGE	2
SYNKE	2	STONY	2	TYBORNE	2	WARDEYN	2
SYSMATYKE	2	STOOD	2	TYBURNE	2	WARKES	2

Word	Count	Word	Count	Word	Count	Word	Count
WARKYS	2	WROTHE	2	ADDICYON	1	ALYE	1
WARLDE	2	YDLE	2	ADDRESSYNG	1	ALYS	1
WAST	2	YESTERDAY	2	ADYMENT	1	ALLBEIT	1
WATCH	2	YESTERDAYE	2	ADMYRALL	1	ALLECTYUES	1
WAXE	2	YMAGE	2	ADMYRELL	1	ALLECTUARY	1
WAXETH	2	YNCHE	2	ADMYT	1	ALLEGYAUNCE	1
WAXYTH	2	YNOUGHE	2	ADMYTTES	1	ALLELUYA	1
WEARE	2	YONDE	2	ADONIS	1	ALL HALLOWE	1
WEBBE	2	YONGER	2	ADRASTUS	1	ALLYGATE	1
WED	2	YOWR	2	A-DROPPYNGE	1	ALLMYGHTY	1
WEDES	2	YPOCRYSY	2	ADVERSARY	1	ALLONE	1
WEY	2	ABACKE	1	ADVERTYSYNG	1	ALL WAY	1
WEKE	2	ABANDUNE	1	ADVERTYSMENT	1	ALMANAK	1
WELLAWAY	2	ABASHYTH	1	ADVYSEMENTE	1	ALMESSE	1
WELNY	2	ABASSHE	1	ADVYSID	1	ALMIGHTY	1
WELTHFULL	2	ABASSHEMENT	1	ADWE	1	ALMONDE	1
WENCHE	2	ABATE	1	AFERD	1	ALOES	1
WENCHES	2	ABATED	1	AFERDE	1	ALOFT	1
WEPT	2	ABBEY	1	AFFABILITE	1	ALOFTE	1
WERETH	2	ABBESSE	1	AFFECTIONS	1	ALOWES	1
WERKE	2	ABBOT	1	AFFERDE	1	ALTERACYON	1
WERKES	2	ABBROGATE	1	AFFYAUNCE	1	ALTERCACYONS	1
WEVE	2	ABELL	1	AFFYAUNSYNGE	1	ALTHOUGH	1
WHATE	2	ABHOMINACION	1	AFFYNITE	1	ALTRYCACYON	1
WHAT EVER	2	ABHOMYNABLE	1	AFFLICTYONS	1	ALUMBEK	1
WHATSOEVER	2	ABHOR	1	AFFLYCCYON	1	AMALEC	1
WHAT SOEVER	2	ABHORDE	1	AFFORCE	1	AMALECKE	1
WHELE	2	ABHORE	1	AFFRAY	1	AMALOCH	1
WHERBY	2	ABHORRE	1	AFFRYC	1	AMBER	1
WHERE EVER	2	ABYDEN	1	AFYRE	1	AMBICIOUS	1
WHEREFORE	2	ABYDYNGE	1	AFLOTE	1	AMBICYOUS	1
WHERE SO EVER	2	ABYDYTHE	1	AFORCE	1	AMBYCYON	1
WHERFOR	2	ABYLEMENT	1	AFORESAYD	1	AMBROSE	1
WHILS	2	ABJECTE	1	AFORSE	1	AMBROSIUS	1
WHITTE	2	ABJECTIONS	1	AFRAYE	1	AMENDIS	1
WHYDER	2	ABJECTYD	1	AFTER-CLAPPES	1	AMENDYS	1
WHYLYST	2	ABOLETE	1	AFTER-DELE	1	AMENDMENT	1
WHYSTELL	2	ABOUNDE	1	AFTERNONE	1	AMENSE	1
WHYTER	2	ABROGATE	1	AFTERWARDE	1	AMIS	1
WHOOS	2	ABSENCE	1	AFTYR	1	AMYABYLL	1
WISE	2	ABSOLON	1	AGAIN	1	AMYABLE	1
WIST	2	ABSOLUTE	1	AGAINE	1	AMYTE	1
WITHSAY	2	ABSTRACT	1	AGASPE	1	AMMAS	1
WYGHT	2	ABSTRACTE	1	AGAST	1	AMON	1
WYLD	2	ABULL	1	AGEINE	1	AMOUNT	1
WYLFULL	2	ABUSAR	1	AGEYNSTE	1	AMPHION	1
WYLFULLY	2	ABUSE	1	AGENYST	1	AMPLYFY	1
WYLFULNESSE	2	ABUSION	1	AGENNE	1	ANACREON	1
WYNNYNG	2	ABUSIOUNS	1	AGENNST	1	ANALETICALL	1
WYNNYNGE	2	ACCESSARY	1	AGERDOWS	1	ANALOGY	1
WYNTER	2	ACCOMPLYSSHE	1	AGO	1	ANDREWE	1
WYTHE	2	ACCOMPLYSSHEMENT	1	AGREAMENT	1	ANDROMACH	1
WYTHIN	2	ACCOMPTYNGE	1	AGRIPPINA	1	ANGELYK	1
WYTLESSE	2	ACCORD	1	AYE	1	ANGERLY	1
WYTTYS	2	ACCORDIS	1	AYLDE	1	ANGGRE	1
WODCOCKE	2	ACCORDYNG	1	AYLETH	1	ANGLEA	1
WOLDEST	2	ACCORDYNGE	1	AKED	1	ANIMOSITE	1
WOMANHOD	2	ACCUSETH	1	AKERS	1	ANY THYNG	1
WONDERLY	2	ACCUSTOME	1	AKUSE	1	ANNEX	1
WONDEROUS	2	ACHADEMIOS	1	ALAYD	1	ANNOT	1
WONNYNGE	2	ACHERONTES	1	ALBEIT	1	AN ODYR	1
WOOD	2	ACHEVE	1	ALBERTUS	1	ANOYANCE	1
WORD	2	ACHILLIEDOS	1	ALBYAN	1	ANOTHERS	1
WORDLY	2	ACHYLLES	1	ALBONS	1	ANOTHYR	1
WORKETH	2	ACOMBERYD	1	ALBUMAZER	1	ANSSWERE	1
WORKIS	2	ACON	1	ALCUMYN	1	ANSWERED	1
WORSHEPLY	2	ACONCYUS	1	ALDAYE	1	ANSWERYD	1
WORSHYPPE	2	ACORD	1	ALDERBEST	1	ANT	1
WORST	2	ACORDE	1	ALE BARME	1	ANTEOCUS	1
WOTITH	2	ACQUAINTANCE	1	ALECTO	1	ANTETYME	1
WOUNDE	2	ACQUAYNTED	1	ALE DRYNKERS	1	ANTIOCHE	1
WRANGYLL	2	ACQUAYNTYD	1	ALE HOUSE	1	ANTIOCHUS	1
WRANGLE	2	ACQUEINTAUNCE	1	ALE-JOUST	1	ANTYQUYTE	1
WRAPPED	2	ACQUYTE	1	ALE-POLE	1	ANWYKE	1
WRENCHE	2	ACTEON	1	ALE POLE	1	APAYERE	1
WREST	2	ACTES	1	ALERYCUS	1	APART	1
WRETCHEDLY	2	ACTYON	1	ALE SOPPE	1	APARTE	1
WRETCHYDLY	2	ACTYS	1	ALE STAKE	1	APASE	1
WRETCHYDNESSE	2	ACTYVITE	1	ALE TAP	1	APELLES	1
WRIG-WRAG	2	ACTYVYTE	1	ALE TAPPE	1	APHRIKE	1
WRITETH	2	ADAME	1	ALE TUNNES	1	APOYNTED	1
WRYNGETH	2	ADAUNTED	1	ALEXIS	1	APOSTATA	1
WRYTHE	2	ADAUNTID	1	ALY	1	APOSTATAAS	1
WRYTHYNG	2	ADDERS	1	ALYDE	1	APOSTELS	1

APOSTYLL	1	ASE	1	AXES	1	BASKED	1
APOSTROFACYON	1	ASKYD	1	AXYS	1	BASNET	1
APPAYRE	1	ASKYNGE	1	BABELL	1	BASSED	1
APPALL	1	ASKYTH	1	BABI	1	BASSYD	1
APPALLE	1	ASKRYE	1	BABILL	1	BASTARDE	1
APPARAYLE	1	ASLEPE	1	BABILON	1	BASTYNG	1
APPARE	1	ASMODEUS	1	BABYLLES	1	BATH	1
APPARELL	1	ASPECTE	1	BABYLS	1	BATHED	1
APPARENTLY	1	ASPYID	1	BABYONE	1	BATHYD	1
APPELS	1	ASSAYDE	1	BABLE	1	BATHTHED	1
APPERETH	1	ASSAYLE	1	BABVELL	1	BATOWE	1
APPERYTH	1	ASSAWTE	1	BACHELER	1	BAUD	1
APPETYTES	1	ASSEMBLED	1	BACHELERS	1	BAUDETH	1
APPLE TRE	1	ASSENCE	1	BACKE BONE	1	BAUDY	1
APPLYE	1	ASSENTE	1	BACKES	1	BAUDRIE	1
APPLYED	1	ASSHES	1	BACKIS	1	BAUDRY	1
APPOSED	1	ASSIGNEMENT	1	BACUS	1	BAUMBEROW	1
APPOSELLE	1	ASSIST	1	BADDE	1	BAWDE	1
APPROCHE	1	ASSYNGNED	1	BADNES	1	BAWDIAS	1
APRELL	1	ASSYNYD	1	BAGGE	1	BAWDYAS	1
APRILL	1	ASSYSTE	1	BAGPYPE	1	BAWDRY	1
APTE	1	ASSYSTENCE	1	BAILLYVE	1	BAWME	1
APTLYE	1	ASSOYLE	1	BAY	1	BAWMYS	1
AQUAYNTANCE	1	ASSUERUS	1	BAYARDYS BUN	1	BEAME	1
AQUAYNTE	1	ASSUR	1	BAYNED	1	BEAMES	1
AQUEINTED	1	ASSURDED	1	BAYTETH	1	BEAR	1
AQUEINTYNG	1	ASSWAGE	1	BAYTYD	1	BEARES	1
AQUEYNTE	1	ASTATIS	1	BAKON	1	BEATEN	1
AQUENTYD	1	ASTONYED	1	BALADE	1	BEAUTY	1
AQUENTYTH	1	ASTREA	1	BALADE BOKE	1	BECHREWDE	1
AQUYNO	1	ASTROLOBY	1	BALADIS	1	BECKE	1
ARABE	1	ASTROLOGYS	1	BALAK	1	BECKED	1
ARACE	1	ASTRONOMER	1	BALAM	1	BECOMETH	1
ARAYD	1	ASURE	1	BALAS	1	BEDAWYD	1
ARAYE	1	ATAME	1	BALASSIS	1	BEDDE ROULES	1
ARAYES	1	ATHLAS	1	BALAUNCE	1	BEDDES	1
ARAYSE	1	ATHRUST	1	BALDE	1	BEDDES SYDE	1
ARAM	1	ATYRE	1	BALES	1	BEDELL	1
ARCADY	1	ATROPOS	1	BALETTYS	1	BEDE ROLLE	1
ARCET	1	ATT	1	BALKE	1	BEDE ROLLES	1
ARCHADY	1	ATTALUS	1	BALL	1	BEDE ROULE	1
ARDEN	1	ATTAMED	1	BALLADE	1	BEDFELLAW	1
ARECTE	1	ATTEINTID	1	BALLYVIS	1	BEDLEME	1
ARECTYNG	1	ATTEMPERAUNCE	1	BALTAZAR	1	BEE	1
ARERAGE	1	ATTENDAUNCE	1	BALUA	1	BEERD	1
ARETHUSA	1	AUCTORITE	1	BAN	1	BEFELL	1
ARGYVA	1	AUDELBY	1	BANDIS	1	BEFOULE	1
ARGUE	1	AUGMENT	1	BANDYD	1	BEGARED	1
ARGUS	1	AUGUSTINUS	1	BANE	1	BEGGARY	1
ARION	1	AULTER	1	BANER	1	BEGGARS	1
ARISTIPPUS	1	AULUS	1	BANISSHED	1	BEGGERS BAGGYS	1
ARISTOTILLE	1	AUNCETRY	1	BANYSHED	1	BEGGEST	1
ARYNA	1	AUNCYENTE	1	BANYSSHE	1	BEGGYNGE	1
ARYSE	1	AUNCYENTLY	1	BANKETYNG	1	BEGGYS	1
ARYSTOBELL	1	AUNGEY	1	BANKETYNGE	1	BEGIN	1
ARYVYD	1	AUNGELL	1	BANKIS	1	BEGYLYD	1
ARKE	1	AUNSWERE	1	BANKYS	1	BEGYNNES	1
ARMATYCKE	1	AUQUARDE	1	BANNE	1	BEGYNNYTH	1
ARMED	1	AUTENTYKE	1	BANNESHT	1	BEGON	1
ARMELECHE	1	AUTER STONE	1	BANNISSHED	1	BEGONE	1
ARMY	1	AUTOMEDON	1	BANNYSSHE	1	BEHAVYD	1
ARMYD	1	AUTORYTE	1	BANOCKESBURNE	1	BEHAVYNGE	1
ARMYE	1	AUTUMPNE	1	BARABAS	1	BEHAVOURE	1
ARMORY	1	AVAYLED	1	BARAYNE	1	BEHELDE	1
AROWE	1	AVAYLETH	1	BARATOWS	1	BEHIND	1
ARRAY	1	AVAYLYNGE	1	BARBELLIS	1	BEHINDE	1
ARRECT	1	AVALE	1	BARBICAN	1	BEYGHT	1
ARRECTINGE	1	AVAUNCED	1	BARBYD	1	BEYNG	1
ARRECTYD	1	AVAUNS	1	BARELLES	1	BEYNGE	1
ARRECTYNG	1	AVAUNSID	1	BARKAMSTEDE	1	BEYOND	1
ARRES	1	AVAUNSYD	1	BARKYNG	1	BEYTE	1
ARRYANS	1	AVAUNSYNGE	1	BARLYHOOD	1	BEK	1
ARS	1	AVAUNTAGE	1	BARNACLE	1	BEKENYNGE	1
ARTHUR	1	AVE	1	BARNET	1	BEKNAVYD	1
ARTIKE	1	AVENTURIS	1	BARON	1	BEKS	1
ARTYCLES	1	AVYCEN	1	BARONAGE	1	BELAPPED	1
ARTYKE	1	AVYSED	1	BARONES	1	BELDYNGE	1
ARTURIS	1	AVYSID	1	BARRE	1	BELY	1
ARTURYS	1	AVYSYNGE	1	BARREYNE	1	BELYES	1
ARTURS	1	AVOYDYNGE	1	BARRID	1	BELY-JOYE	1
ASCENDENT	1	AVOWED	1	BASAN	1	BELYMMED	1
ASCENDYNGE	1	AWE	1	BASELYE	1	BELLE	1
ASCRYBED	1	AWNNER	1	BASYAN	1	BELLES	1
ASCRYE	1	AWRYE	1	BASYN	1	BELLYS	1

889

BELLUYNG	1	BLABER	1	BOTES	1	BRYNGGES	1
BELMAN	1	BLACK	1	BOTHOMBAR	1	BRYNGYTH	1
BELONGYNG	1	BLAYNES	1	BOTOWME	1	BRYNNYNG	1
BELONGYTH	1	BLAK	1	BOTTOMS	1	BRYNSTON	1
BELS	1	BLAMELES	1	BOTTONS	1	BRYSTELL	1
BELSABUB	1	BLAMELESSE	1	BOTTUMLES	1	BRYSTLED	1
BEME	1	BLANKET	1	BOTUMLES	1	BRYSTOWE RED	1
BEMIS	1	BLASE	1	BOUGETS	1	BRYTONS	1
BEMOLE	1	BLASED	1	BOULE	1	BRODE CLOTHE	1
BEND	1	BLASY	1	BOUNCE	1	BROISID	1
BENDE	1	BLASTYD	1	BOUND	1	BROISIOURS	1
BENDED	1	BLAUNCHED	1	BOUNDE TENAUNTES	1	BROYLYD	1
BENEFYCE	1	BLEDE	1	BOUNSES	1	BROKYN	1
BENES	1	BLEDING	1	BOUNSIS	1	BROOD	1
BENET	1	BLEMYSSHED	1	BOUNSYNGLY	1	BROSE	1
BENEVOLENCE	1	BLENKARDIS	1	BOURES	1	BROTHELL	1
BENINGE	1	BLENNER-HAISET	1	BOURNE	1	BROTHELLS	1
BENINGNE	1	BLENNES	1	BOWCHE	1	BROUGHTE	1
BENYFYCED	1	BLERDE	1	BOWER	1	BROW	1
BENYGNE	1	BLERE	1	BOWGET	1	BROW-AUNTLERES	1
BENYGNYTE	1	BLERED	1	BOWGHIS	1	BROWDE	1
BENYNGNYTE	1	BLEREED	1	BOWGY	1	BROWNE	1
BEQUETH	1	BLERYD	1	BOWYS	1	BRUTE	1
BERDED	1	BLESSE	1	BOWLE	1	BRUTED	1
BERES	1	BLIS	1	BOWNDIS	1	BRUTUS	1
BERIS	1	BLISSED	1	BOWSY	1	BUCK	1
BERY	1	BLISSYNG	1	BOWUR	1	BUCKELL	1
BERYTH	1	BLYNDED	1	BRABLYNG	1	BUCKELS	1
BERYTHE	1	BLYNDNES	1	BRACELET	1	BUCOLYCALL	1
BESECHYNGE	1	BLYNDNESSE	1	BRACERS	1	BUDGE FURRE	1
BESEKE	1	BLYNKERD	1	BRACYD	1	BUYLDYNGE	1
BESEME	1	BLYSSYNG	1	BRAGGE	1	BUKRAM	1
BESHREW	1	BLYST	1	BRAGGYTH	1	BULKE	1
BESHREWE	1	BLOMMER	1	BRAINE	1	BULLES	1
BESINES	1	BLOSSOMS	1	BRAYED	1	BULLYFANT	1
BESYNESSE	1	BLOWBOLL	1	BRAYNE-PAN	1	BULLYONS	1
BESOUGHT	1	BLOWYNG	1	BRAYNE PAN	1	BULLYS	1
BESTAD	1	BLOWYNGE	1	BRAYNE SEKE	1	BULWARKE	1
BESTADDE	1	BLUNDER	1	BRAYNYS	1	BUMME	1
BESTYALL	1	BLUNDERAR	1	BRAYNPANNYS	1	BUMPE	1
BESTOWDE	1	BLUNDERYNG	1	BRAYNSYK	1	BUNGLER	1
BETAKE	1	BLUNTLY	1	BRALLE	1	BURBLYNG	1
BETELL	1	BLURRE	1	BRANDE	1	BURDE	1
BE TYME	1	BLUSTER	1	BRAS	1	BURDEOU	1
BETOKENETH	1	BO	1	BRASED	1	BURGEIS	1
BETRAY	1	BOBBE	1	BRASY	1	BURY	1
BETRAYD	1	BOCHAS	1	BRAULES	1	BURNESHED	1
BETRAPPED	1	BOCHER	1	BRAUNCHES	1	BURNETH	1
BETWEYN	1	BOCKYLL	1	BRAWLE	1	BURNISSHITH	1
BETWEN	1	BODE	1	BRAWLYNG	1	BURRIS	1
BEVE	1	BOGHT	1	BREATH	1	BUSHMENT	1
BEWAYLE	1	BO-HO	1	BRECHE	1	BUSY	1
BE WARE	1	BOYCE	1	BRED CROMMES	1	BUSYNESSE	1
BEWRAPPED	1	BOYLING	1	BREDDE	1	BUSKE	1
BEWREYE	1	BOYLYD	1	BREDTH	1	BUSKED	1
BEWTEOUS	1	BOYSTORS	1	BREED	1	BUSKYD	1
BEWTEOUSE	1	BOKYS	1	BREKES	1	BUSKT	1
BIL	1	BOLDENES	1	BREMELY	1	BUSSARDE	1
BIRDBOLT	1	BOLDLYE	1	BREMIS	1	BUSSHETH	1
BIRDE	1	BOLLE	1	BRENDE	1	BUTE	1
BIRDIS	1	BOLTE	1	BRENNETH	1	BUTTER	1
BIRRALL	1	BOLTYD	1	BRENTE	1	BUTTERFLLYIS	1
BIRTH	1	BONAM	1	BRERE	1	BUTTES	1
BYBILLE	1	BONDE TENENT	1	BRESYTH	1	BUTTYNG	1
BYBYLL CLARKE	1	BONE	1	BRESTE	1	CABAGYD	1
BYBLE	1	BONEHOMS	1	BRESTES	1	CACADEMONYALL	1
BYDENE	1	BONET	1	BREVYATE	1	CACH	1
BYDYNG	1	BONNY	1	BREW	1	CACHYD	1
BYE	1	BOOKE	1	BREWETH	1	CACUS	1
BYES	1	BORDED	1	BREWHOUSE	1	CADMUS	1
BYGGE	1	BORDES	1	BREWSYS	1	CAYRE	1
BYYONDE	1	BORDEWS	1	BRINGES	1	CAYTYVYS	1
BYL	1	BORDON	1	BRINGETH	1	CAYUS	1
BYLDE	1	BORE PYGGE	1	BRISTELS	1	CALCYDONY	1
BYLDYNG	1	BORYALL	1	BRITONS	1	CALD	1
BYLLYS	1	BOROWE	1	BRYBAUNCE	1	CALDEE	1
BYND	1	BOROWED	1	BRYBE	1	CALDIES	1
BYRLE	1	BOROWGH	1	BRYBOURY	1	CALDY	1
BYRNE	1	BOROWYNGE	1	BRYDELYNGE CASTE	1	CALE	1
BYSE	1	BOSKAGE	1	BRYDYLL	1	CALED	1
BYSELY	1	BOSOME	1	BRYGE	1	CALES	1
BYSYDE	1	BOTCHES	1	BRYM	1	CALETTES	1
BYTYNG	1	BOTCHMENT	1	BRYMME	1	CALFLES	1
BYTYNGE	1	BOTELES	1	BRYNGES	1	CALYCE	1

CALLEST	1	CASWELTE	1	CHESSE	1	CLEROS	1
CALLET	1	CATACUMBAS	1	CHESSHYRE	1	CLIFFES	1
CALLYDST	1	CATCH	1	CHEVALRY	1	CLYFTE	1
CALLYING	1	CATCHED	1	CHEVYNGE	1	CLYME	1
CALLYNGE	1	CATELYNE	1	CHEWE	1	CLYMMETH	1
CALODEMONYALL	1	CATELL	1	CHIVALRY	1	CLYO	1
CALS	1	CATHEDRALL	1	CHYDDER	1	CLYPPYNG SHERES	1
CALSTOCKE	1	CATYWADE	1	CHYDETH	1	CLYTTRETH	1
CALVYS HEDES	1	CATTE	1	CHYDYNG	1	CLOBBYD	1
CAMAMELL	1	CATULLUS	1	CHYEF	1	CLOCKE	1
CAMMOCKE	1	CAUDELL	1	CHYFE	1	CLOKES	1
CAMOKE	1	CAUGHTE	1	CHYFTEYNE	1	CLOKYS	1
CAMOUSLY	1	CAUSIS	1	CHYLDE	1	CLOSED	1
CANACE	1	CAUSYTH	1	CHYLDES	1	CLOSYD	1
CANCOUR	1	CAVELL	1	CHYLDIS	1	CLOSTERS	1
CANDELMAS	1	CAVES	1	CHYLDYS	1	CLOT	1
CANDELMES	1	CAWDELS	1	CHYLL	1	CLOTH	1
CANDYLL	1	CAWGHTE	1	CHYMNEYES	1	CLOTHE MAKYNGE	1
CANKARDE	1	CAWRY-MAWRY	1	CHYNCHERDE	1	CLOTHYNGE	1
CANKERED	1	CAWSYTHE	1	CHYPPES	1	CLOTHYS	1
CANNAT	1	CAWTE	1	CHYSSHE	1	CLOUDIS	1
CANNE	1	CEFAS	1	CHYSTYN	1	CLOWDES	1
CANNEST	1	CELESTYNE	1	CHOPPE	1	CLOWDIS	1
CANONICALL	1	CENTAURES	1	CHOPPED	1	CLOWT	1
CANONICALLY	1	CENTAWRIS	1	CHRISTALL	1	CLOWTES	1
CANST	1	CERCULETT	1	CHRIST CROSSE	1	CLUBBE	1
CANTELL	1	CEREMONIALLYS	1	CHRISTES	1	CLUBBED	1
CANTERBURY	1	CERTEYNTE	1	CHRYSTEN	1	COARTE	1
CANTORBURY	1	CHAFER	1	CHRYSTES	1	COARTED	1
CANVES	1	CHAFFRE	1	CHUR	1	COBBILL	1
CAPCYOUSLY	1	CHAYNES	1	CHURCH DORES	1	COBBLE	1
CAPITAYNE	1	CHALANNGER	1	CHURLES	1	COCHITOS	1
CAPITALL	1	CHALENGER	1	CHURLISH	1	COCITUS	1
CAPYTAYNES	1	CHALENNGE	1	CHUSE	1	COCKES COME	1
CAPYTALL	1	CHALYNGYD	1	CICEROS	1	COCKE WAT	1
CAPON	1	CHALYNGYR	1	CIDIPPES	1	COCKING	1
CAPPED	1	CHAMBER	1	CINTHEUS	1	COCKLY	1
CAPTACYONS	1	CHAMPYON	1	CIRCUMSPECT	1	COCK SURE	1
CAPTAINE	1	CHANON	1	CIRCUMSPECTLY	1	COE	1
CAPTEN	1	CHANONS	1	CIROMANCY	1	COFER KAY	1
CAPTYFE	1	CHAPELLETTES	1	CIRUS	1	COGNISAUNCE	1
CARBUCKYLS	1	CHAPITER	1	CITACYONS	1	COYE	1
CARBUNCLE	1	CHAPLAYNE	1	CITIES	1	COYFE	1
CARCASSE	1	CHAPLEYNE	1	CY-AND-SLIDDYR	1	COYNES	1
CARDE	1	CHARBUNCLES	1	CYATYCA	1	COKE	1
CARDERS	1	CHARES	1	CYPYO	1	COKERMOWTH	1
CARDES	1	CHARITE	1	CYRCUMSPECTION	1	COKERMOWTHE	1
CARDINALS	1	CHARLEMAYNE	1	CYRCUMSTANCE	1	COKE STOLE	1
CARDYNALLES	1	CHARMYNG	1	CYRCUMSTAUNCE	1	COKKES	1
CARDYNALL HAT	1	CHASETH	1	CYS	1	COKOLDES	1
CARDYNALS	1	CHATERYNGE	1	CYSLY	1	COKOLDRY	1
CARECTES	1	CHATYNG	1	CYTACYON	1	COK WAT	1
CARECTIS	1	CHATTER	1	CYTES	1	COK WATTES	1
CAREDE	1	CHATTERS	1	CYTIE	1	COKWOLDES	1
CAREFULLY	1	CHATTRYNGE	1	CYTYE	1	COLATION	1
CARELES	1	CHAUMBER	1	CYTRACE	1	COLE DUST	1
CARIED	1	CHAUNCELAR	1	CLAD	1	COLERAGE	1
CARIID	1	CHAUNCERY	1	CLAIMIST	1	COLE RAKE	1
CARYED	1	CHAUNGE	1	CLAPPYD	1	COLES	1
CARYETH	1	CHAUNGES	1	CLAPPYNG	1	COLETH	1
CARKAS	1	CHAUNTECLERE	1	CLAPPYS	1	COLYAUNDER	1
CARKE	1	CHAUNTERS	1	CLAPPYTH	1	COLL	1
CARLE	1	CHAUSER	1	CLARIONAR	1	COLLES	1
CARLES	1	CHAWCER	1	CLARIOUNS	1	COLLUCYOUN	1
CARLESSE	1	CHAWNTYD	1	CLATERARS	1	COLLUSION	1
CARLYLL	1	CHECKER	1	CLATERED	1	COLOPPE	1
CARLYNG	1	CHECKYNGES	1	CLATERING	1	COLOURYD	1
CARLYS	1	CHECTE	1	CLATYR	1	COLOURS	1
CARLYSHE	1	CHEFTAYN	1	CLATTERYNGE	1	COLOWRE	1
CARMELLUS	1	CHEFTAYNE	1	CLATTERS	1	COLOWUR	1
CARNALL	1	CHEYNES	1	CLAVYCORDYS	1	COLUMBYN	1
CAROLLIS	1	CHEKED	1	CLAWDYUS	1	COLURYD	1
CARP	1	CHEKES	1	CLAWES	1	COMBERAUNCE	1
CART	1	CHEKMATE	1	CLEANE	1	COMBERYD	1
CARTER	1	CHEKMATYD	1	CLEMENCY	1	COMEDIES	1
CART LODE	1	CHEKS	1	CLENCH	1	COMEROUS	1
CARVEN	1	CHEKT	1	CLENNESSE	1	COMFORTABLE	1
CASES	1	CHERYSHED	1	CLEPE	1	COMFORTABLY	1
CASPIAN	1	CHERYSSHETH	1	CLERELY	1	COMICAR	1
CASSAUNDER	1	CHERYSSHYD	1	CLERENES	1	COMINALTE	1
CASSETH	1	CHERYSTON PYTTE	1	CLERER	1	COMYN	1
CASTETH	1	CHERYTE	1	CLERE STORY	1	COMYNE HALL	1
CASTRIMERGIA	1	CHERLEMAYNE	1	CLERKIS	1	COMYNWEALL	1
CASUALL	1	CHERMED	1	CLERKLY	1	COMYTH	1

Word	Count	Word	Count	Word	Count	Word	Count
COMMANDEMENT	1	CONFETRYD	1	COPYHOLDE	1	COWRTE	1
COMMAUNDYNGE	1	CONFETTRED	1	COPYOUSLY	1	COWRTLY	1
COMME	1	CONFYRMABLE	1	COPYUS	1	CRACK	1
COMMEDY	1	CONFLEWENCE	1	COPPER	1	CRACKE	1
COMMEMORACION	1	CONFORT	1	CORAGIUS	1	CRACKED	1
COMMEN	1	CONFUSED	1	CORDYLAR	1	CRACKES	1
COMMENDABYLL	1	CONFUSION	1	CORYED	1	CRACKIS	1
COMMENDACIONS	1	CONFUTACION	1	CORYOUSLY	1	CRADELS	1
COMMENDACIOUN	1	CONFUTED	1	CORMERANT	1	CRAFTER	1
COMMENDACYOUN	1	CONFUTID	1	CORMORAUNCE	1	CRAFTERS	1
COMMENDATION	1	CONGRUENCE	1	CORNES	1	CRAFTYNGE	1
COMMENDED	1	CONGRUENTLY	1	CORNYS	1	CRAG	1
COMMENDYD	1	CONYNG	1	CORONELL	1	CRAYNGE	1
COMMENDYNGE	1	CONJECT	1	CORPORAS	1	CRAK	1
COMMENSYD	1	CONJECTE	1	CORRAGE	1	CRAKAR	1
COMMENSYNG	1	CONJECTURE	1	CORRECTED	1	CRAKED	1
COMMENSYNGE	1	CONJUGACYONS	1	CORRECTIONS	1	CRAKYNGE	1
COMMES	1	CONJURACIONS	1	CORSE	1	CRANYS	1
COMMISSYON	1	CONJURACYON	1	CORTE	1	CRASE	1
COMMITTYTH	1	CONNYNGLY	1	COSMOGRAPHY	1	CRASED	1
COMMY	1	CONQUESTYS	1	COSTERMONGER	1	CRASY	1
COMMYNGE	1	CONQUINATE	1	COSTIOUS	1	CRAVED	1
COMMYTED	1	CONSCIENS	1	COTAGE	1	CRAVYNGE	1
COMMYTTED	1	CONSECRATYD	1	COTE-ARMUR	1	CRAW	1
COMMODITIS	1	CONSENTE	1	COTE ARMURE	1	CRAWES	1
COMMON	1	CONSERNYNGE	1	COTED	1	CREACYOUN	1
COMMONERS	1	CONSYDERACION	1	COTYD	1	CREAT	1
COMMONES	1	CONSYDERACYONS	1	COTTAGE	1	CREATE	1
COMMOUN	1	CONSYDRYNGE	1	COTTYSWOLDE	1	CREATURE	1
COMMOUNS	1	CONSYSTORY	1	COUCHE	1	CREAUNCER	1
COMMOWNE	1	CONSOLACYOUN	1	COUCHING	1	CREAUNSER	1
COMMUNEWELL	1	CONSOLATORY	1	COUCHYNGE	1	CREDENSYNGE	1
COMMUNEWELTH	1	CONSTANT	1	COUD	1	CREISSEID	1
COMMUNE WELTH	1	CONSTANTYNOPELL	1	COUGH	1	CREKETH	1
COMMUNICACION	1	CONSTANTLY	1	COULOUR	1	CREME	1
COMMUNYCACYON	1	CONSTELLACION	1	COUNDIGHT	1	CREPT	1
COMODY	1	CONSTELLACIONS	1	COUNFORTE	1	CRESSYDE	1
COMON	1	CONSTELLACYON	1	COUNSEL	1	CRESUS	1
COMONYNGE	1	CONSTYTUCYON	1	COUNSELLE	1	CREWE	1
COMPARYD	1	CONSTREYND	1	COUNSELOUR	1	CRIBBIS	1
COMPASSE	1	CONSTREYNED	1	COUNTEDE	1	CRIMSIN	1
COMPASSYON	1	CONSTREWE	1	COUNTERFAYTYNGE	1	CRIST	1
COMPETENT	1	CONSTRUCTION	1	COUNTERFEYTED	1	CRISTALL	1
COMPILID	1	CONSTRUCTYON	1	COUNTERFEYTES	1	CRISTECROSSE	1
COMPLAINE	1	CONSULTACION	1	COUNTERFETE	1	CRYEST	1
COMPLAYNED	1	CONSUMETH	1	COUNTERFETED	1	CRYETH	1
COMPLAYNYD	1	CONTAINE	1	COUNTERFETYD	1	CRYID	1
COMPLAYNT	1	CONTAYNE	1	COUNTERFETTES	1	CRYNKLYD	1
COMPLAYNTE	1	CONTAYNYD	1	COUNTERFETTIS	1	CRYSTALLYNE	1
COMPLAYNTES	1	CONTAMINATE	1	COUNTERYNG	1	CRYSTEOVYR	1
COMPOUND	1	CONTEMMINATE	1	COUNTERWAY	1	CRYSTIS	1
COMPOUNDE	1	CONTEMPLACYON	1	COUNTES	1	CRYSTYS	1
COMPREHENDYNGE	1	CONTEMPLACYONS	1	COUNTYD	1	CRYSTOFER	1
COMPRISE	1	CONTEMPLACYOUN	1	COUNTYNAUNCE	1	CROKE	1
COMPRISED	1	CONTENDE	1	COUNTYNG	1	CROKENEBBED	1
COMPRISYDE	1	CONTENONS	1	COUNTYR	1	CROKYS	1
COMPRYSED	1	CONTENTE	1	COUNTYS	1	CROMMES	1
COMPRYSYDE	1	CONTERFET	1	COUNTYTH	1	CRONYCLE	1
COMSTE	1	CONTYNUED	1	COUPLE	1	CROP	1
CONBYNED	1	CONTYNWYTH	1	COURS	1	CROPE	1
CONCEYGHT	1	CONTRADICCYOUN	1	COURTELY	1	CROPPED	1
CONCEPCION	1	CONTRADICTYONS	1	COURTE ROWLIS	1	CROPPY	1
CONCERNYNG	1	CONTRADYCCYON	1	COURTESY	1	CROSE	1
CONCLUSIOUNS	1	CONTRARY	1	COUSSHONS	1	CROSSE ROWE	1
CONCLUSYONS	1	CONTRYCION	1	COVENT	1	CROSSYNG	1
CONCLUSYOUN	1	CONTROLD	1	COVERYNGE	1	CROUCHE	1
COND	1	CONTROLL	1	COVERTE	1	CROUNE	1
CONDICIONS	1	CONTROLLEYNGE	1	COVERTLY	1	CROWCHE	1
CONDICIOUNS	1	CONUSAUNCE	1	COVERTURE	1	CROWDYNG	1
CONDICYONS	1	CONVAY	1	COVET	1	CROWETH	1
CONDISCENDID	1	CONVAYD	1	COVETYS	1	CROWLAND	1
CONDISCENDYNG	1	CONVEYAUNS	1	COVETYSE	1	CROWNDE	1
CONDITYONS	1	CONVEYDE	1	COVYTOUS	1	CROWNYCLER	1
CONDYCYON	1	CONVENIENT	1	COVYTOUSNESSE	1	CROWNYD	1
CONDYCYONNS	1	CONVENYENTLY	1	COWARD	1	CRUDE	1
CONDYSCENDED	1	CONVENT	1	COWARDNESSE	1	CRUE	1
CONDYSSENDE	1	CONVENTUALL	1	COWCHE-QUALE	1	CRUELL HERTYD	1
CONDUCTE	1	CONVERT	1	COWCHYD	1	CRUYSE	1
CONDUTE	1	CONVERTED	1	COWGHE	1	CUCKOLDES	1
CONFECTIOUN	1	CONVERTYD	1	COWNTENAUNCE	1	CUCKOUE	1
CONFECTURE	1	COOKE-STOLE	1	COWNTER	1	CUE	1
CONFECTURES	1	COOTE	1	COWNTERFET	1	CULE	1
CONFESSYNG	1	COPIOUS	1	COWNTES	1	CULVER	1
CONFETERD	1	COPYEHOLD	1	COWNTRED	1	CUMYS	1

892

CUMLY	1	DAWNSYS	1	DENOMINACYONS	1	DIODORUS	1
CUMMYNG	1	DAWNSYTH	1	DENTY	1	DIOGENES	1
CUMMYTH	1	DAWPATE	1	DEPELY	1	DIOLOGGIS	1
CUNNYNGLY	1	DEADE	1	DEPENDED	1	DIOMEDIS	1
CUNTREIS	1	DEADLY	1	DEPRAVYD	1	DIRECT	1
CUPBORD	1	DEALYNG	1	DEPUTE	1	DISABLE	1
CUPBORDE	1	DEALL	1	DEPUTYD	1	DISCEYVE	1
CUPPE	1	DEANES	1	DERELY	1	DISCERNE	1
CURED	1	DEATH	1	DERISYON	1	DISCLOSED	1
CURIOUSLY	1	DEBARRE	1	DERKE	1	DISCOMFECT	1
CURYOWS	1	DECACORDE	1	DERKENES	1	DISCORAGE	1
CURRANT	1	DECADIS	1	DERLING	1	DISCORDE	1
CURRES	1	DECAYDE	1	DERLYNG	1	DISCRIPCION	1
CURRYS	1	DECAYES	1	DERLYNGE	1	DISCURID	1
CURS	1	DECKED	1	DEROGACYOUN	1	DISDAYN	1
CURSED	1	DECLAMACYONS	1	DEROGATE	1	DISDAYNED	1
CURSEDLY	1	DECLARETH	1	DERTMOUTH	1	DISDAYNYD	1
CURSIUS	1	DECLYNE	1	DESCANT	1	DISGYSEDE	1
CURSYDLY	1	DECOLLACYON	1	DESCENDINGE	1	DISLOYALL	1
CURST	1	DECON	1	DESCENDYNGE	1	DISORDER	1
CURTEYNS	1	DECREES	1	DESE	1	DISPARAGED	1
CURTEYS	1	DECRETALL	1	DESERVYNGE	1	DISPARE	1
CURTEYSE	1	DECRETALS	1	DESIRE	1	DISPIGHT	1
CURTEL	1	DECTE	1	DESYER	1	DISPITE	1
CURTES	1	DEDDE	1	DESYRED	1	DISPYSE	1
CURTESLYE	1	DEDICATE	1	DESYRING	1	DISPLAYD	1
CURTOYL	1	DEDYS	1	DESYRIS	1	DISPLEASE	1
CUSTOME	1	DEEDMANS	1	DESYROUS	1	DISPORTE	1
CUSTRELL	1	DEEFE	1	DESYTE	1	DISPUTED	1
CUTBERDES	1	DEFACES	1	DESOLATE	1	DISSUASYVE	1
CUTTYS	1	DEFACID	1	DESOLATION	1	DISTICHON	1
D	1	DEFAMED	1	DESPENSYTH	1	DISTINCTIONS	1
DADY	1	DEFAUT	1	DESPITE	1	DITIIS	1
DAGGED	1	DEFEND	1	DESPYGHTYNG	1	DIVERS	1
DAGGESWANE	1	DEFENDAR	1	DESPYTYNGE	1	DIVINITE	1
DAGGID	1	DEFENDETH	1	DESTEYNYD	1	DIVISION	1
DAGMATISTA	1	DEFENS	1	DESTENNY	1	DIVISIS	1
DAGSWAYNE	1	DEFFEND	1	DESTYNY	1	DIVISYON	1
DAYNNOUSLY	1	DEFYE	1	DET	1	DIVYNITE	1
DAYNTELY	1	DEFOYLE	1	DETERMYNED	1	DYADEME	1
DAYSY	1	DEFOYLED	1	DETERMYNYD	1	DYAMAND	1
DAYSY FLOURE	1	DEFORMITE	1	DETRACCION	1	DYAMAUNTIS	1
DAY-WACH	1	DEGREE	1	DETRACTIONS	1	DYAMOUNDE	1
DALY	1	DEGREES	1	DETRACTYON	1	DYANA	1
DALYDA	1	DEITE	1	DETRAXION	1	DYANE	1
DAM	1	DEYNTELY	1	DEU	1	DYCKEN	1
DAMYAN	1	DEYNTES	1	DEUCALYONS	1	DYENGE	1
DAMMOYSELS	1	DEYSY	1	DEURANDALL	1	DYET	1
DAMNABLE	1	DEYTE	1	DEUZ	1	DYETYD	1
DAMOSELL	1	DEKAY	1	DEVELYSH	1	DYFFAME	1
DAMPNABLE	1	DEKKYD	1	DEVELLYSSHE	1	DYFFUSE	1
DANE	1	DELAYDE	1	DEVERSE	1	DYG	1
DANGEROUS	1	DELAYED	1	DEVINYTE	1	DYGGETH	1
DANT	1	DELARAG	1	DEVISE	1	DYGNYTES	1
DARED	1	DELATED	1	DEVISIS	1	DYKES	1
DARYUS	1	DELECTABYLL	1	DEVYDYD	1	DYLECTABLE	1
DARKES	1	DELECTABLY	1	DEVYLYSHE	1	DYLYGENT	1
DARLYNG	1	DELECTACYON	1	DEVYLLYS	1	DYMINGIS	1
DARLYNGE	1	DELECTACYONS	1	DEVYLLYSSHELY	1	DYMOSTENES	1
DART	1	DELETH	1	DEVYNE	1	DYNDE	1
DARTE	1	DELITE	1	DEVYSER	1	DYNE	1
DASILD	1	DELYAUNCE	1	DEVYSION	1	DYNED	1
DASYNG	1	DELYBERACION	1	DEVOCION	1	DYNYD	1
DASSHED	1	DELYBERACYON	1	DEVORS	1	DYNTES	1
DASTARDE	1	DELYCATELYE	1	DEVORSE	1	DYNTYS	1
DASTARDIS	1	DELYGENCE	1	DEWCALIONS	1	DYOCLESYAN	1
DASTARDYS	1	DELYVER	1	DEWE	1	DYOMEDES	1
DATAN	1	DELL	1	DEWTY	1	DYONYSYUS	1
DATES	1	DEMAUNDE	1	DEWTYES	1	DYRECTE	1
DATYD	1	DEMAUNDINGE	1	DIALETICALL	1	DYRECTIONS	1
DAUCOCKE	1	DEMAWND	1	DIAMAUNTIS	1	DYRECTYON	1
DAUCOCKES	1	DEMEYNAUNCE	1	DIAMOUNDE	1	DYRIGES	1
DAUNCASTER	1	DEMENE	1	DIASCORIDES	1	DYRYSYON	1
DAUNS	1	DEMENYNG	1	DICTES	1	DYRTY	1
DAUNSED	1	DEMENSY	1	DIDIL DIDDIL	1	DYSAVAYLYNGE	1
DAUNSID	1	DEMERYTTES	1	DIETTES	1	DYSCAYTE	1
DAUPATUS	1	DEMY DIVINES	1	DIFFICILLE	1	DYSCANT	1
DAVID	1	DEMYE	1	DIGNITE	1	DYSCEYGHT	1
DAWCOCK	1	DEMYST	1	DIGNYTE	1	DYSCHARGYD	1
DAWCOKKIS	1	DEMONSTRACYON	1	DIIANIRA	1	DYSCHECLOWTE	1
DAWIS	1	DEMPTE	1	DIKKON	1	DYSCONIUS	1
DAWKOCK	1	DENAYD	1	DILIGENCE	1	DYSCORDES	1
DAWKOCKE	1	DENNE	1	DIN	1	DYSCREASE	1
DAWNS	1	DENNES	1	DINNE	1	DYSCRECION	1

893

Word	Count	Word	Count	Word	Count	Word	Count
DYSCRESSYON	1	DORMOWS	1	DUD	1	EMPEROUR	1
DYSCRETE	1	DOROTHE	1	DUGLES	1	EMPLOYED	1
DYSCRY	1	DOSEN	1	DULLE	1	EMPORTURED	1
DYSCRYVE	1	DOTE	1	DUMPE	1	EMPRESSE	1
DYSCRYVED	1	DOTED	1	DUMPIS	1	ENBATELD	1
DYSCUS	1	DOTERDIS	1	DUMPYS	1	ENBAWMED	1
DYSDAYNED	1	DOTERELL	1	DUNSTANE	1	ENBESID	1
DYSDAYNESLYE	1	DOTERYLL	1	DURE	1	ENBEWTID	1
DYSDAYNOUS	1	DOTYNGE	1	DURSE	1	ENBYBE	1
DYSDAYNOUSLY	1	DOTRELLIS	1	DURTY	1	ENBYBED	1
DYSDAYNS	1	DOTTAGES	1	DUTES	1	ENBYBID	1
DYSDANOUS	1	DOUBLE-COPE	1	DWELLE	1	ENBLASED	1
DYSEASED	1	DOUBLE DELINGE	1	DWELLES	1	ENBOLNED	1
DYSEASYD	1	DOUBLE DELYNG	1	DWELLINGE HOUSE	1	ENBOSID	1
DYSEYTE	1	DOUBLE DELYNGE	1	DWELLITH	1	ENBRAID	1
DYSER	1	DOUBLE TUNGE	1	DWELLYS	1	ENBRASED	1
DYSERS	1	DOUBLE TUNGES	1	DWELLYTH	1	ENBRASID	1
DYSGORGED	1	DOUBTFULL	1	DWELTE	1	ENBRASYNGE	1
DYSH	1	DOUGHT	1	DWTE	1	ENBRAWDERID	1
DYSHWASHER	1	DOUGHTYEST	1	E	1	ENBRAWDERYD	1
DYSIRYD	1	DOULFULL	1	EARES	1	ENBRETHED	1
DYSMAYDE	1	DOUTY	1	EASYD	1	ENBRETHYNG	1
DYSMEMBRE	1	DOUTTED	1	EATEN	1	ENBROWDER	1
DYSORDERETH	1	DOVER	1	EATETH	1	ENBROWDRED	1
DYSORDERYD	1	DOVYR	1	EBREW	1	ENBUDDED	1
DYSOUR	1	DOW	1	EBRON	1	ENBUDDID	1
DYSPAIRE	1	DOWBYLL	1	ECATES	1	ENBULYONED	1
DYSPAYRE	1	DOWBLE	1	ECLIPSID	1	ENCANKRYD	1
DYSPARAGE	1	DOWBLENES	1	ECTOR	1	ENCLERYD	1
DYSPYGHT	1	DOWE	1	EDDERS	1	ENCLYNE	1
DYSPYSE	1	DOWGHTFULL	1	EDYNGEBORROW	1	ENCLOSED	1
DYSPYSED	1	DOWSYPERE	1	EDWARDE	1	ENCOVERDE	1
DYSPLEASETH	1	DOWTE	1	EERE	1	ENCRAUMPYSSHED	1
DYSPLESAUNCE	1	DOWTES	1	EERES	1	ENCREACE	1
DYSPORT	1	DOWTY	1	EESTRYCHE FEDDER	1	ENCREASETH	1
DYSPOSED	1	DOWTLESS	1	EG	1	ENCREST	1
DYSPOSYCYONS	1	DOWVES	1	EGEAS	1	ENCRISPED	1
DYSPOSYD	1	DRABBES	1	EGERIA	1	ENCROWNYD	1
DYSPUTACYON	1	DRAGONES	1	EGYPCYAN	1	ENDARKID	1
DYSPUTE	1	DRAMMES	1	EGLE	1	ENDARKYD	1
DYSSAYVED	1	DRANE	1	EIGHT	1	ENDELES	1
DYSSAYVYD	1	DRANES	1	EITHER	1	ENDES	1
DYSSEYVED	1	DRAPRY	1	EY	1	ENDEVORMENT	1
DYSSEMBLE	1	DRAW	1	EYLES	1	ENDEVOURE	1
DYSSENCYON	1	DRAWTTYS	1	EYLYTHE	1	ENDEVOURMENT	1
DYSSHES	1	DREGGYS	1	EYNDYE	1	ENDIYD	1
DYSSY	1	DREMES	1	EYSELL	1	ENDITH	1
DYSSYMULACYON	1	DREMYST	1	EKE	1	ENDYGHT	1
DYSSYMULER	1	DRESSES	1	E-LA	1	ENDYTYNG	1
DYSSYMULYNGE	1	DREW	1	ELATE	1	ENDUCED	1
DYSTAUNCE	1	DRIBBIS	1	ELDYR STEKE	1	ENDUED	1
DYSTRECTYON	1	DRIFT	1	ELE	1	ENDURYD	1
DYSTROY	1	DRIGHNES	1	ELECTUARY	1	ENEAS	1
DYTIES	1	DRINKE	1	ELEGY	1	ENEIDOS	1
DYVENDOP	1	DRIVE	1	ELEMENTAR	1	ENEMYES	1
DYVERSYTE	1	DRYADES	1	ELENE	1	ENERGIALL	1
DYVYLS	1	DRYFTE	1	ELEPHANTIS	1	ENFAYNTYD	1
DYVYSYNGE	1	DRYFTIS	1	ELF	1	ENFATUATE	1
DYVYSYON	1	DRYNK	1	ELFE	1	ENFERRE	1
DOCTRYNE	1	DRYNKYNG	1	ELICONYS	1	ENFLAMED	1
DODDY PATIS	1	DRYVEN	1	ELINOUR	1	ENFLAMYD	1
DOGGYS	1	DRYVETH	1	ELISABETH	1	ENFLORID	1
DOGMATISTA	1	DRYVITH	1	ELYCONIS	1	ENFLUENCE	1
DOGRELL	1	DRYVYTH	1	ELYNOR	1	ENFORCE	1
DOLEFULLE	1	DRYVVYTHE	1	ELYNOURE	1	ENFORCID	1
DOLOROUSLY	1	DROMADARY	1	ELLIS	1	ENFORME	1
DOLORUS	1	DRONNY	1	ELLUMYNYNGE	1	ENFORSYTH	1
DOLOWRE	1	DROPPES	1	ELME	1	ENGLADID	1
DOLOWRS	1	DROPPY	1	ELOQUENT	1	ENGLASID	1
DOM	1	DROPPYNG	1	ELOQUENTLY	1	ENGLISHE	1
DOMAGE	1	DROPPYNGE	1	ELSEWHERE	1	ENGLISHMEN	1
DOMESDAY	1	DROPSY	1	ELSWHERE	1	ENGLISSHMEN	1
DOMINYK	1	DROUGHT	1	ELVYSHE	1	ENGLISTERD	1
DOMYNGO	1	DROUND	1	EMBASSADES	1	ENGLYSCHE	1
DOMYSYAN	1	DROUPE	1	EMBESY	1	ENGLYSHEMEN	1
DONATUS	1	DROUPY	1	EMBLOMED	1	ENGLYSHE MEN	1
DONG CART	1	DROUSY	1	EMBOSYD	1	ENGOLERID	1
DONGE CARTE	1	DROUSY PATE	1	EMBRAUDRED	1	ENGRAPID	1
DONN	1	DROWNE	1	EMBRAWDRED	1	ENGUSSHING	1
DONNY	1	DROWNYD	1	EMERAUD	1	ENHACHED	1
DONNYSHE	1	DRUNCHARD	1	EMERAWDE	1	ENHACHYDE	1
DOO	1	DRUNKARDIS	1	EMPERES	1	ENHARDID	1
DOOTH	1	DRUNKYN	1	EMPERYALL	1	ENHARPID	1
DOREGATE	1	DUCK	1	EMPERYALLE	1	ENYUS	1

ENJOY	1	ERST	1	FAINE	1	FELYCITE	1
ENKANKERD	1	ERSTE	1	FAINT HARTED	1	FELT	1
ENLASID	1	ERTH	1	FAITHE	1	FEMALE	1
ENLOSENGED	1	ESCAPE	1	FAITOURS	1	FEMALL	1
ENMYS	1	ESCAPID	1	FAYER	1	FENAUNCE	1
ENNEUDE	1	ESCRYE	1	FAYLED	1	FENESTRALL	1
ENNEW	1	ESIODUS	1	FAYN	1	FERY	1
ENNEWDE	1	ESPERUS	1	FAYNYNGE	1	FERME	1
ENOUGHE	1	ESSEX	1	FAYNTE	1	FERS	1
ENPAVYD	1	ESTRYCH	1	FAYNTY	1	FERUMBRAS	1
ENPLEMENT	1	ESTRYGE	1	FAYRE-PLAY	1	FESAUNTE	1
ENPLOYD	1	ETERMYNABLE	1	FAYRER	1	FESAUNTES	1
ENPLOYED	1	ETETH	1	FAYREST	1	FESYCYAN	1
ENPOYSONED	1	ETHNA	1	FAYRLY	1	FEST	1
ENPRYNTYNG	1	ETYNGE	1	FAYTES	1	FESTE	1
ENPROWED	1	EUFRATES	1	FAYTORS	1	FESTERD	1
ENQUERE	1	EUPHORION	1	FAYTOUR	1	FESTYVALLE	1
ENRAILID	1	EVACYON	1	FAL	1	FETCHE	1
ENRYCHE	1	EVANDER	1	FALE	1	FETCHED	1
ENRYPED	1	EVERITHING	1	FALYRE	1	FETEWSE	1
ENROLL	1	EVERY THING	1	FALLETH	1	FETHER	1
ENROLLYD	1	EVERY THYNG	1	FALLOWS	1	FETHER BED	1
ENSAYMED	1	EVIDENT	1	FALOWE	1	FETHERBEDDES	1
ENSANDID	1	EVILL	1	FALSE HARTED	1	FETTE	1
ENSEMBYLL	1	EVYDENCE	1	FALSEHODE	1	FETTRED	1
ENSEW	1	EVYLL FAVERYD	1	FALSENESSE	1	FETURIS	1
ENSHRYNED	1	EVYNLY	1	FALSEST	1	FETURYS	1
ENSILVRED	1	EVYR	1	FALSHOD	1	FETURS	1
ENSORBYD	1	EXALTACYON	1	FALS QUARTER	1	FEVEROUS	1
ENSOWKID	1	EXAMINACION	1	FAMILIARS	1	FEWER	1
ENSUYD	1	EXAMYNACYON	1	FAMYLYARYTE	1	FFREKE	1
ENSUYNGE	1	EXCEDITH	1	FAMYS	1	FICKIL	1
ENSWYMMYNG	1	EXCEDYNG	1	FAMULY	1	FICTYONS	1
ENTACHID	1	EXCEDYTH	1	FAMUS	1	FIDDILL	1
ENTAKELED	1	EXCELLE	1	FANCHYRCHE	1	FIERS	1
ENTEND	1	EXCELLENTE	1	FANGE	1	FIGHT	1
ENTENDED	1	EXCELLES	1	FANSY-SERVYCE	1	FIGURE	1
ENTENDYNG	1	EXCEPT	1	FANTASIES	1	FIGURED	1
ENTENTES	1	EXCITYNGE	1	FANTASTICALL	1	FILL	1
ENTENTIFLY	1	EXCLUDE	1	FANTSY	1	FIND	1
ENTERLASED	1	EXCOMMUNYCACYONS	1	FARDER	1	FINGERS	1
ENTERLUDE	1	EXCOMUNYCATE	1	FAREST	1	FIST	1
ENTERPRETACYON	1	EXCUSYD	1	FARETH	1	FISTA	1
ENTERPRETE	1	EXECRABLE	1	FAR-FET	1	FISTY	1
ENTERPRISE	1	EXECUTE	1	FARLE	1	FYCKELL	1
ENTERPRYSYD	1	EXECUTYD	1	FARRE FET	1	FYDELYTE	1
ENTERTEYND	1	EXEDE	1	FARTE	1	FYDLED	1
ENTYTULED	1	EXELLENTLY	1	FARVENT	1	FYDLER	1
ENTRETE	1	EXEMPLIFY	1	FASTEN	1	FYER DRAKE	1
ENTRUSAR	1	EXEMPLYFYENGE	1	FASTYNGE	1	FYERS	1
ENTUNYD	1	EXESSE	1	FATHERS	1	FYERSLY	1
ENTURFID	1	EXHIBYCION	1	FAUCON	1	FYEST	1
ENUWYD	1	EXIONE	1	FAUCONER	1	FYGHTYNG	1
ENVADE	1	EXYLE	1	FAUGHT	1	FYGURED	1
ENVAYNED	1	EXYLIDE	1	FAULT	1	FYKKELLE	1
ENVAWTYD	1	EXPELLE	1	FAVER	1	FYKKILL	1
ENVECTYFYS	1	EXPERIENS	1	FAVERYD	1	FYLYTHE	1
ENVERDURID	1	EXPERYENS	1	FAVORE	1	FYLLY	1
ENVERDURYD	1	EXPERT	1	FAWCHYN	1	FYLTY	1
ENVI	1	EXPERTE	1	FAWCON	1	FYNALL	1
ENVYRONDE	1	EXPYACYON	1	FAWNE	1	FYNALLY	1
ENVYRONN	1	EXPYRYD	1	FAWT	1	FYNDETH	1
ENVYRONNED	1	EXPOUNDYNGE	1	FE	1	FYNDITH	1
ENVYROWNE	1	EXPOUNDYTH	1	FEATES	1	FYNDYTH	1
ENVYVE	1	EXPRESSED	1	FEBLE-FANTASTYCALL	1	FYNEST	1
ENVYVED	1	EXPREST	1	FEBLER	1	FYNGERED	1
ENVYVID	1	EXPRESTE	1	FEBLY	1	FYNGERYNG	1
ENWALLYD	1	EXTASY	1	FED	1	FYRED	1
ENWERED	1	EXTENDID	1	FEDERIS	1	FYRY	1
EPIDAURES	1	EXTOLE	1	FEDERS	1	FYRMAMENT	1
EPIDAWRIS	1	EXTOLLYD	1	FEED	1	FYSGYGGE	1
EPITOMIS	1	EXTORCYON	1	FEERE	1	FYSNAMY	1
EPYCURE	1	EXTORT	1	FEE SYMPLENES	1	FYSSHES	1
EPYLOGACYON	1	EXTRAVAGANCY	1	FEFFYD	1	FYSTIS	1
EQUIPOLENS	1	EXTREME	1	FEIGHTYNGE	1	FYSTY	1
EQUIVALENT	1	FA	1	FEYNE	1	FYTYTH	1
EQUIVALENTLY	1	FABELL	1	FEYTIS	1	FYTTE	1
ERECTYD	1	FABIAN	1	FEL	1	FYVE	1
ERES	1	FACERS	1	FELASHYP	1	FYXT	1
ERKITH	1	FACION	1	FELAWES	1	FLACCUS	1
ERLIS	1	FACITHE	1	FELDEFARE	1	FLAGRANT	1
ERNYST	1	FACYD	1	FELDFARE	1	FLAGRAUNT	1
ERRANDE	1	FACYOUN	1	FELETH	1	FLAYLE	1
ERRONYOUS	1	FAILE	1	FELYCE	1	FLAMYS	1

FLANDERKYNS	1	FOND	1	FREDOME	1	GALBA	1
FLANKE	1	FONDNESSE	1	FREER	1	GALES	1
FLAP	1	FONGE	1	FRENCHEMEN	1	GALIENE	1
FLAPPE	1	FONNY	1	FRENCHE MEN	1	GALYS	1
FLAPPES	1	FOOLE	1	FREND	1	GALLANDE	1
FLATERED	1	FOOLYS	1	FRENDSHYPPE	1	GALLES	1
FLATERER	1	FOOS	1	FRENESSYS	1	GALLYNG	1
FLATERERS	1	FOOTE	1	FRENETYKE	1	GAMBAUDYNGE	1
FLATERYNGE	1	FOPPED	1	FRENETYKES	1	GAMBONE	1
FLATYRYNG	1	FORAGE	1	FRENSCHE	1	GAMUT	1
FLATRINGE	1	FORBEDE	1	FRENTIKE	1	GANE	1
FLATTERS	1	FORBYD	1	FRESH	1	GANT	1
FLATTRYNG	1	FORBORNE	1	FRIAR	1	GAPIS	1
FLAXE	1	FORCASTYNG	1	FRISCAJOLY	1	GAPYTHE	1
FLECE	1	FORCIBLY	1	FRY	1	GAR	1
FLECES	1	FORCYD	1	FRYARS	1	GARDEVYAUNCE	1
FLECKYD	1	FOR-DREDE	1	FRYE	1	GARDYNGE	1
FLEE	1	FORECASTELL	1	FRYED	1	GARGONS	1
FLEES	1	FORESAYD	1	FRYENGE	1	GARLAND	1
FLEYEST	1	FORESTE	1	FRYINGE PAN	1	GARLANDES	1
FLEKYD	1	FORETOP	1	FRYNDE	1	GARLANTES	1
FLEMYNGE	1	FORE TOP	1	FRYNDES	1	GARLEKE HED	1
FLEMMYNGE	1	FORETOPPE	1	FRYTTHY	1	GARLYCKE	1
FLERIING	1	FOREVER	1	FROGGES	1	GARLYKE HEDDES	1
FLESH	1	FORGATE	1	FROLLO	1	GARLONDE	1
FLESHE	1	FORGED	1	FROMPILL	1	GARMENT	1
FLESSH	1	FORGERS	1	FRONNETH	1	GARMENTE	1
FLESSHE-FLYE	1	FORGETFULNESSE	1	FROSLYNGES	1	GARMENTES	1
FLESSHE FLYES	1	FORGEVE	1	FROST	1	GARNATE	1
FLESSHE MEATE	1	FORGO	1	FROSTIS	1	GARNYSHTE	1
FLESSHE METE	1	FORMALLY	1	FROWARD	1	GARNYSSHYD	1
FLESSH FLY	1	FORMARE	1	FROWARDES	1	GARRE	1
FLEW	1	FORMD	1	FROWNED	1	GARTERYNGE	1
FLEWE	1	FORMYDABLE	1	FROWNYD	1	GASY	1
FLINGANDE	1	FORMYST	1	FROWNYNG	1	GASYNG	1
FLINT	1	FORSAYD	1	FROWNYNGE	1	GASYNGE	1
FLYBYTTEN	1	FORSEDE	1	FROWNYTH	1	GASPID	1
FLYCKERYNGE	1	FORSETH	1	FRUBYSSHER	1	GASPY	1
FLYENG	1	FORSYTH	1	FRUCTUOUS	1	GASPYNG	1
FLYENGE	1	FORSOKE	1	FRUGALITE	1	GATHERETH	1
FLYP-FLAP	1	FORTHWYTH	1	FRUTE	1	GATTE	1
FLYPPES	1	FORTOP	1	FRUTEFULL	1	GAUDE	1
FLYTYNGE	1	FORTRESSE	1	FRUTIS	1	GAUDY	1
FLYTTE	1	FORTUNIS	1	FUCKE SAYLES	1	GAUDRY	1
FLOCKE	1	FORWARDE	1	FUYSON	1	GAUNCE	1
FLOCKED	1	FOSE	1	FULFILLED	1	GAUNTE	1
FLOCKET	1	FOTEBALL	1	FULFYLD	1	GAURE	1
FLOD	1	FOTED	1	FUMBLYTH	1	GAW	1
FLODDEN	1	FOTID	1	FUME	1	GEBALL	1
FLODDES	1	FOTYNG	1	FUMIGATION	1	GEDEON	1
FLODDON	1	FOTYNGE	1	FUMYGACION	1	GEYNE	1
FLOOD	1	FOTYS	1	FUMOUSLY	1	GELAWAYE	1
FLORENTINE	1	FOTYTH	1	FURDRERS	1	GELIUS	1
FLORISSHINGE	1	FOUCONER	1	FURIOUS	1	GELOUSY	1
FLORISSHYNG	1	FOUGHT	1	FURY	1	GELT	1
FLORYSHETH	1	FOULES	1	FURYOUS	1	GENEALOGY	1
FLORYSSHYNG	1	FOUNDACYONS	1	FURNISSHE	1	GENERACION	1
FLORTHE	1	FOURME	1	FURNYSSHE	1	GENERRALL	1
FLOTES	1	FOURMEST	1	FURNYSSHYD	1	GENET	1
FLOURISSHETH	1	FOURTY	1	FURRYD	1	GENTELL	1
FLOURS	1	FOWND	1	FURST	1	GENTELMEN	1
FLOWYN	1	FOXES	1	FURTHE	1	GENTIL	1
FLOWR	1	FOXIS	1	FURTHERMORE	1	GENTILWOMAN	1
FLOWRES	1	FRAGHTED	1	FUSTIANE	1	GENTYLLY	1
FLOWRYSSHE	1	FRAYES	1	FUSTY	1	GENTYLNES	1
FLOWUR	1	FRAYNE	1	GABIONE	1	GENTLY	1
FLUSSHE	1	FRAYS	1	GABIONYTE	1	GERARCHY	1
FOGGY	1	FRAM	1	GABYLL ROPE	1	GERFAWCON	1
FOISTY	1	FRAMED	1	GABYONE	1	GERION	1
FOY	1	FRAMES	1	GAD	1	GERIONE	1
FOYNES	1	FRANESY	1	GADDE	1	GERY	1
FOLABILITE	1	FRANKO	1	GADDER	1	GESTE	1
FOLAM	1	FRANTYCK	1	GADDIR	1	GETEST	1
FOLYSHE	1	FRANTYCKNES	1	GADER	1	GEW	1
FOLYSSHLY	1	FRANTYK	1	GAGLYNGE	1	GEWGAW	1
FOLYSSHNES	1	FRAUDE	1	GAGUINE	1	GIGGISSE	1
FOLKE	1	FRAUNCEYS	1	GAGUYNE	1	GINGERLY	1
FOLLEST	1	FRAUNCHYS	1	GAGWYNE	1	GIPCY	1
FOLLY	1	FRAUNCIS	1	GAINSAY	1	GIRNED	1
FOLLOW	1	FRAUNCYS	1	GAYNE	1	GIRTH	1
FOLOWYD	1	FRAUNS	1	GAYNOUR	1	GIVE	1
FOLOWYTHE	1	FRAWARD	1	GALANTE	1	GYBBET	1
FOME	1	FREAT	1	GALANTYS	1	GYDED	1
FOMYD	1	FREDERYK	1	GALAUNTES	1	GYDITH	1

GYDYD	1	GOWNDY	1	GUMBED	1	HARLOTRYE	1
GYE	1	GRACES	1	GUMME	1	HARME	1
GYF	1	GRAY-HERED	1	GUMMIS	1	HARMYS	1
GYFTE	1	GRAYLE	1	GUMMY	1	HARNES	1
GYFTES	1	GRAMATOLYS	1	GUN	1	HARNNES	1
GYGAWIS	1	GRAME	1	GUNNIS	1	HAROLDE	1
GYGLYNGE	1	GRAMED	1	GUNNYS	1	HAROLDES	1
GYL	1	GRAMER	1	GUN STONE	1	HAROLDIS	1
GYLLA	1	GRANADO	1	GUTTYS	1	HARPE STRINGIS	1
GYLLY	1	GRAS	1	HABARION	1	HARPE STRYNGGES	1
GYRDETH	1	GRASYNGE	1	HABILLIMENTIS	1	HARPYNG	1
GYRDLE	1	GRATYFYED	1	HABYLEMENTES	1	HARPOCRATES	1
GYRNE	1	GRAUNDE	1	HABYLYTE	1	HARRES	1
GYRTH	1	GRAUNDEPOSE	1	HABYTACION	1	HARRY	1
GYTES	1	GRAUNGE	1	HABYTE	1	HARROLD	1
GYVETH	1	GRAUNTYD	1	HABURDASHE	1	HART BLODE	1
GYVYNGE	1	GRAVE STONE	1	HACH	1	HART BLOODE	1
GLADDE	1	GRAVIN	1	HADDE	1	HARTE SEKE	1
GLADNESSE	1	GRAVYD	1	HADDEST	1	HARTYS	1
GLAYMY	1	GREABLE	1	HADE	1	HARTLES	1
GLAYRE	1	GREATEST	1	HAFTAR	1	HARTTIS	1
GLARIS	1	GREATTER	1	HAFTE	1	HARWYCHE	1
GLASID	1	GRECE	1	HAFTERS	1	HAS	1
GLENES	1	GREDYNESSE	1	HAG	1	HASARDE	1
GLETTERYNGE	1	GREE	1	HAGGE	1	HASDRUBALL	1
GLINT	1	GREET	1	HAGGYS	1	HASERDYNGE	1
GLISTRYNG	1	GREGORIE	1	HAILID	1	HASKARDIS	1
GLITTERING	1	GREY	1	HAISET	1	HASTARDDIS	1
GLITTERYNG	1	GREYHOUNDES	1	HAYLED	1	HASTYVE	1
GLITTRYNG	1	GREYHOWNDE	1	HAYLES	1	HATCHET	1
GLYDE	1	GREYTH	1	HAYLYNGE	1	HATED	1
GLYSTER	1	GRENEWYTCHE	1	HAYNE	1	HATERED	1
GLYSTRYNG	1	GRESE	1	HAYNYARDE	1	HATINGE	1
GLYTTERYNG	1	GRESYD	1	HAYNNOUSLY	1	HATRED	1
GLOME	1	GRESLY	1	HAYNOUSLY	1	HATTED	1
GLOMMYNGE	1	GRESSE	1	HAY THE GY	1	HAUNTYTH	1
GLORYOUS	1	GRESSOP	1	HAY THE GYE	1	HAVEN	1
GLOSETH	1	GRESSOPPES	1	HAKE	1	HAVYN	1
GLOSYNGE	1	GRETER	1	HAKNEY	1	HAWKED	1
GLOTTON	1	GREUYNED	1	HALFE-ABUSED	1	HAWKES	1
GLOVE	1	GREVANCE	1	HALFE HERETYKES	1	HAWKETH	1
GLOWYNGE	1	GREVETH	1	HALFE-MAYMED	1	HAWKYNG	1
GLOWTONN	1	GREVIS	1	HALFE MEN	1	HAWNTE	1
GNAR	1	GREVYTH	1	HALFEPENY	1	HAWTLY	1
GODE	1	GRIMBALDUS	1	HALLE	1	HEAR	1
GODFATHER	1	GRIMLY	1	HALLIS	1	HEAT	1
GODS	1	GRYLL	1	HALLOWS	1	HECATES	1
GOG	1	GRYM	1	HALPENY	1	HECKE	1
GOYNG	1	GRYN	1	HALSE	1	HECTORS	1
GOYTH	1	GRYNNES	1	HALSYD	1	HEDD	1
GOLDDE	1	GRYNNYNG	1	HALTE	1	HEDDYS	1
GOLDFYNCHE	1	GRYPES	1	HALTED	1	HEDELLIS	1
GOLDSMYTH	1	GROCERS	1	HALTERS	1	HEDGE	1
GOMYS	1	GROINYNGE	1	HALTITH	1	HEDYD	1
GOMMORYANS	1	GROYNIS	1	HALTYNG	1	HEER	1
GON	1	GROYNYD	1	HALTYNGE	1	HEERE	1
GONGE	1	GROYNNINGE	1	HAMYLCAR	1	HEGHE	1
GON STONE	1	GROME	1	HAMMER	1	HEYDA	1
GOODLI	1	GRONDE	1	HAMPAR	1	HEYNOUSLY	1
GOODLYE	1	GRONED	1	HANDELL	1	HEYRE	1
GOODLYEST	1	GRONETH	1	HANDYD	1	HEYRE PARENT	1
GOODLYHOD	1	GRONID	1	HANDY-DANDY	1	HEKELL	1
GOOSE	1	GRONIS	1	HANDYLL	1	HEL	1
GORBELYD	1	GRONYS	1	HANDYS	1	HELD	1
GORBELLYD	1	GRONNYNG	1	HANDLE	1	HELYD	1
GORE	1	GRONTYNGE	1	HANGID	1	HELYN	1
GORGIOUSLY	1	GROPYD	1	HANGIS	1	HELL-HOUNDE	1
GORGYOUS	1	GROSE	1	HANGYNGE	1	HELP	1
GORGON	1	GROSELY	1	HANGYTH	1	HELPYNG	1
GOSHAUKE	1	GROSSOLITIS	1	HANGMAN	1	HELPT	1
GOSLENGES	1	GROUCHYNG	1	HANKYN BOVY	1	HEMPEN	1
GOSLYNG	1	GROUNDED	1	HANNYBALL	1	HEN-HERTED	1
GOSLYNGE	1	GROUNDLY	1	HANSY	1	HENTE	1
GOSLYNGES	1	GROWEN	1	HAPPEN	1	HEPE	1
GOSPELLERS	1	GROWYNG	1	HAPPID	1	HERBE	1
GOST	1	GROWND	1	HARDE HARTED	1	HERBERS	1
GOSTLY	1	GROWWE	1	HARD HERTYD	1	HERDELY	1
GOTES	1	GRUDGETH	1	HARDY-DARDY	1	HERDER	1
GOTHYAUNCE	1	GRUNTYNG	1	HARDYNES	1	HERDY	1
GOTYSHE	1	GUERDON	1	HARDYSON	1	HEREBY	1
GOTTED	1	GUILLIAM	1	HARDLY	1	HEREINNE	1
GOUT	1	GUY	1	HARYS	1	HEREY	1
GOVERNYNGE	1	GUYDED	1	HARKEN	1	HERELACE	1
GOWERS	1	GUY-GAW	1	HARKYN	1	HERETIKE	1

HERETIKES	1	HOMYLYEST	1	ILLE	1	INTELLEGENCE	1
HERETYKE	1	HOMWARDE	1	ILLUMYN	1	INTELLYGENS	1
HERETYKIS	1	HONDES	1	ILLUMYNE	1	INTENTYFE	1
HERIS	1	HONESTE	1	ILLUMYNID	1	INTERE	1
HERITAGE	1	HONGE	1	ILLUMYNYD	1	INTERLUDE	1
HERITYKES	1	HONGRY	1	ILLUSIOUNS	1	INTERRUPE	1
HERYNGES	1	HONOROUS	1	ILLUSYON	1	INTOXICATE	1
HERKYNDE	1	HOOD	1	ILLUSYONS	1	INTRETE	1
HERMONIAKE	1	HOOLL	1	IMAGINACION	1	INTRETED	1
HERNEST	1	HOOS	1	IMCOMPERABLE	1	INVECTYVE	1
HEROF	1	HOP	1	IMMEDIATLY	1	INVENTORY	1
HERON	1	HOP LOBBYN	1	IMMOYSTURID	1	INWYT DELYNGE	1
HERPED	1	HOP LOBYN	1	IMMORTALLY	1	IOLLAS	1
HERRY	1	HOPPED	1	IMPECHMENT	1	IOPAS	1
HERS	1	HOPPY	1	IMPERIALL	1	IPOCRAS	1
HERSELFE	1	HORACE	1	IMPERYALL	1	IPOCRISY	1
HERTE-BRENNYNGE	1	HORYBLE	1	IMPLEMENTES	1	IPOSTACIS	1
HERTED	1	HORYS	1	IMPORTE	1	IROUS	1
HERTIS	1	HORNE	1	IMPORTUNATE	1	IRREVOCABLE	1
HERTO	1	HORNED	1	IMPORTUNE	1	ISAGOGICALL	1
HERT ROTE	1	HORNE KEKE	1	IMPOSSIBLE	1	ISAIAS	1
HESTER	1	HORNID	1	IMPRYNTED	1	ISAPHILL	1
HETHYR	1	HORNIS	1	IMPRUDENT	1	ISOLD	1
HEVE	1	HORNNIS	1	INBRYNGIS	1	ISRAELL	1
HEVERY	1	HORSEMAN	1	INCARNACION	1	ISSUIS	1
HEVYNES	1	HORSE-MYLL	1	INCYNERACYON	1	IVE	1
HEVYNGE	1	HORSHOWE	1	INCLERYD	1	IWISS	1
HEWE	1	HORSLY	1	INCLYNE	1	JACINCTIS	1
HEWYTH	1	HORSMEN	1	INCOMMODITE	1	JACKE A THROMMYS	1
HIERONYMUS	1	HOSE	1	INCOMPERABLE	1	JACKE-A-THRUM	1
HIH	1	HOSED	1	INCOMPORABYLL	1	JACKE A THRUMMIS	1
HILL	1	HOSTE	1	INCONSTANT	1	JACKE AT NOKE	1
HILLIS	1	HOSTELER	1	INCONSTAUNCE	1	JACKENAPES	1
HILT	1	HOSTES	1	INCONVENYENTLY	1	JACKE OF THE NOCKE	1
HINDER	1	HOTHYR	1	INCORRIGIBLE	1	JACKE OF THE VALE	1
HIPOCENTAURES	1	HOUGH-HO	1	INCREASE	1	JACK NAPIS	1
HIPPOCENTAURIS	1	HOULE	1	INCRES	1	JACK RAKER	1
HIR	1	HOUNDYS	1	INCRESE	1	JACK RAKERS	1
HISTORY	1	HOURE	1	INDE	1	JACOUNCE	1
HYCHE	1	HOUS	1	INDE BLEWE	1	JAGGED	1
HYDDER	1	HOUSHOLDES	1	INDEMPNITE	1	JAGGYNGE	1
HYDED	1	HOVYR-WACHYD	1	INDEMPNYTE	1	JAYBERDE	1
HYEST	1	HOWEEVER	1	INDENTURES	1	JAYBERDES	1
HYE WAYE	1	HOWER	1	INDEUER	1	JAYES	1
HYGHEST	1	HOWEVER	1	INDY	1	JAYS	1
HYGHLY	1	HOWGYE	1	INDYFFERENTE	1	JAYST	1
HYLLARY	1	HOWKYD	1	INDYGNACYON	1	JAKE A THRUM	1
HYLLYS	1	HOWNDES	1	INDYTE	1	JAKE RAKAR	1
HYM SELF	1	HOWS	1	INDUSTRIOUS	1	JALAWSY	1
HYNDE CALFE	1	HOWSE	1	INDUSTRIOUSLY	1	JAMYS	1
HYNDERAUNCE	1	HOWSE-HOLDYNG	1	INDUSTRY	1	JAMYS FODER	1
HYNDES	1	HOWSHOLDE	1	INDUSTRYOUS	1	JANGELERS	1
HYNDRYNGE	1	HOWSYS	1	INEVYTABLY	1	JANGELYNG	1
HYPPE	1	HOWST	1	INEXPLICABILL	1	JANGYLL	1
HYSTORIALL	1	HUCKE	1	INFALLIBLY	1	JANGLYNG	1
HYTHER	1	HUCKELS	1	INFATUATE	1	JANTYLL	1
HYTTE	1	HUDGE	1	INFECCIOUN	1	JANUAY	1
HOBBY LARKES	1	HUF	1	INFECCYONS	1	JANUS	1
HOBBYLL	1	HUGGER MUGGER	1	INFECTED	1	JAPED	1
HOBBLE	1	HUGULINUS	1	INFERRID	1	JAPHET	1
HOBY	1	HUKE	1	INFIRMITE	1	JAPHETH	1
HOBLES	1	HUKSTERS	1	INFLAMMACION	1	JAR	1
HOCUPY	1	HULL	1	INFLUENCE	1	JARFAWCON	1
HODDYPEKE	1	HUMILITE	1	INGROSED	1	JASON	1
HODDY POULE	1	HUMLERY	1	INHABITE	1	JASPE	1
HODER-MODER	1	HUMORS	1	INHATETH	1	JASPER	1
HOFTE	1	HUNDRETHE	1	INIQUITE	1	JAW	1
HOG	1	HUNGRE	1	INJURIS	1	JAWED	1
HOGEOUS	1	HURT	1	INKE	1	JAWYS	1
HOYNING	1	HURTES	1	INK-HORNE	1	JEBET	1
HOKE	1	HUS	1	INLARGYD	1	JELOFER	1
HOKED	1	HUSBANDE	1	INMACULATE	1	JELOFFER FLOWRE	1
HOKES	1	HUSBANDIS	1	INNE	1	JELOUSY	1
HOLDES	1	HUSBANDS	1	INPURTURED	1	JEMY	1
HOLY DAYE	1	HUSSEY	1	INROLDE	1	JENKYN	1
HOLYNESSE	1	HUSSIANS	1	INSACIATE	1	JENTILL	1
HOLYS	1	HUSWYFE	1	INSENSATE	1	JENTILMAN	1
HOLY WATER	1	ICONOMICAR	1	INSYDE	1	JENTYLLWOMAN	1
HOLY WATHER	1	IDIOSY	1	INSTAUNCE	1	JENTYLMAN	1
HOLLOW	1	IEN	1	INSTYGACION	1	JENTYL MAN	1
HOLOWE	1	IES	1	INSTRUCTION	1	JENTYLNES	1
HOLOW-EYED	1	IFAYTH	1	INSTRUCTYON	1	JENTYLWOMEN	1
HOMAGE	1	IYE	1	INSTRUMENT	1	JEPERDYS	1
HOMYCIDE	1	IL	1	INSUFFICIENT	1	JEPTE	1

JEREBOSETH	1	KESTERYLL	1	LAYNE	1	LENGTHE	1
JERICO	1	KESTRELL	1	LAYTH	1	LEOPARDES	1
JEROBESETHE	1	KETERYNG	1	LAYTHE	1	LEPES	1
JEROMY	1	KETERYNGES	1	LAKES	1	LEPYNG	1
JERSSEY	1	KINGE	1	LAKEST	1	LEPYNGE	1
JERUSALEM	1	KINGES	1	LAKKYST	1	LERING	1
JESABELL	1	KIS	1	LAM	1	LERNID	1
JESSE	1	KIT	1	LAMBES	1	LESARD	1
JESTE	1	KYBE	1	LAMENTACYON	1	LESARDE	1
JESTES	1	KYBY	1	LAMENTE	1	LESINGES	1
JESUS	1	KYCKE	1	LAMENTYNG	1	LESSON	1
JETRO	1	KYKYTH	1	LAMPATRAMS	1	LESSONS	1
JETTER	1	KYNDELDE	1	LANAM	1	LESURE	1
JETTES	1	KYNDLE	1	LANCASHYRE	1	LETT	1
JETTY	1	KYNDLED	1	LAND	1	LETTERD	1
JETTYNGE	1	KYNDNES	1	LANDYS	1	LETTYRD	1
JEW	1	KYNGYS	1	LANGAGYS	1	LETTYTH	1
JEWELL	1	KYRY	1	LANNERS	1	LETTRE	1
JEWES	1	KYRKEBY	1	LAODOMI	1	LEUDE	1
JHESU	1	KYRTELLES	1	LAPWYNG	1	LEVELL SUSE	1
JHESUS	1	KYSE	1	LARDE	1	LEVEN	1
JYLL	1	KYSSYD	1	LARG	1	LEVETH	1
JO	1	KYTHYD	1	LARGES	1	LEVYNGE	1
JOBAB	1	KYTTEN	1	LARKYS	1	LEWDLYE	1
JOCKY	1	KLYCKED GATE	1	LAS	1	LEWDNES	1
JOFORTH	1	KNACKYNGE	1	LASED	1	LEWTE	1
JOHAN	1	KNAK	1	LASSE	1	LIBYK	1
JOHANNES	1	KNAKKES	1	LASSES	1	LIBRARY	1
JOYLY	1	KNAPPISHE	1	LASSHE	1	LIDDER	1
JOYNT	1	KNAVATE	1	LASTYTH	1	LIDDERONS	1
JOYNTE	1	KNAVERY	1	LATELY	1	LIDDYRNES	1
JOYNTED	1	KNAVIS	1	LATINE	1	LIDDRONS	1
JOYNTES	1	KNAVYCHE	1	LAUD	1	LIDGATE	1
JOYOUSLY	1	KNAVYSCHE	1	LAUDABYLE	1	LIEUTENAUNT	1
JOYOWS	1	KNAVYSSHE	1	LAUDABLY	1	LIING	1
JOYSE	1	KNEE	1	LAUGHES	1	LIIST	1
JOMY	1	KNEES	1	LAUGHT	1	LIKKITH	1
JONYS	1	KNIGHTES	1	LAULES	1	LILLIS	1
JORGE	1	KNIGHTHODE	1	LAUNCE	1	LILLYS	1
JOSEPHUS	1	KNIGHTLY	1	LAUNCELOTE	1	LIMBIS	1
JOSUE	1	KNYGHTIS	1	LAUNCES	1	LIMYTERS	1
JOVENYANS	1	KNYTHE	1	LAURELLE	1	LIMMES	1
JUDICYALL	1	KNYTTE	1	LAURELL LEVIS	1	LINE	1
JUDICUM	1	KNOCK	1	LAURELL TRE	1	LINUS	1
JUDYCYALL	1	KNOCKED	1	LAURIATE	1	LIPPES	1
JUGE	1	KNOCKLES	1	LAURYAT	1	LISTA	1
JUGED	1	KNOK	1	LAWDE	1	LITELLE	1
JUGES	1	KNOKYLBONYARDE	1	LAWGHE	1	LITYLL	1
JUGETH	1	KNOLEGE	1	LAWIS	1	LITTLE	1
JUGYTH	1	KNOTTES	1	LAWYS	1	LYAR	1
JUGURTA	1	KNOULEGE	1	LAWREAT	1	LYARS	1
JULIANUS	1	KNOUTE	1	LAWRYAT	1	LYBANY	1
JULIOUS	1	KNOWING	1	LAWRYATE	1	LYBBARD	1
JULIUS	1	KNOWYST	1	LAZARS	1	LYBERALITE	1
JULY	1	KNOWLEDGE	1	LEANE	1	LYBERALYTE	1
JULLIAN	1	KNOWNE	1	LEAPES	1	LYBERTYES	1
JUMBYLL	1	KOYE	1	LEASURE	1	LYBIUS	1
JUPPITER	1	KOPPYNGE	1	LECHE	1	LYBYUS	1
JURISDICTYON	1	KOTE	1	LECHERY	1	LYCAON	1
JURYDICCYON	1	KOWD	1	LECTRYNE	1	LYCE	1
JURYSDICTYONS	1	KOWE	1	LECTUARY	1	LYCENCE	1
JUSTE	1	KOWES	1	LECTURE	1	LYCKED	1
JUSTICE	1	KOWNNAGE	1	LEDD	1	LYCLYHOD	1
JUSTIFYED	1	KOWTHTHYD	1	LEDERHEDE	1	LYCON	1
JUVYNALL	1	KUES	1	LEDEST	1	LYCOROUS	1
JUVYNALS	1	KUKKOWE	1	LEEDES	1	LYCOUR	1
KAY	1	KUM	1	LEG	1	LYDDER	1
KAYES	1	KUNTREY	1	LEGACY	1	LYDDERYNS	1
KAYN	1	KUR	1	LEGE-DE-MOY	1	LYDDYR	1
KALENDAS	1	KURRIS	1	LEGE MOY	1	LYDY	1
KALKYNS	1	KURTEIS	1	LEGEND	1	LYENGE	1
KARLIS	1	KUTTYTH	1	LEGGE	1	LYERD	1
KARNARVAN	1	LACE	1	LEGGED	1	LYESTE	1
KAST	1	LACIS	1	LEY	1	LYF	1
KATE	1	LACYD	1	LEYE	1	LYGHTLY	1
KATERYNE	1	LACKYNGE	1	LEYRE	1	LYITH	1
KECHYN PAGE	1	LACKYS	1	LEYSSHE	1	LYKED	1
KEYLYTH	1	LACKYTH	1	LEYST	1	LYKELYHOD	1
KEKE	1	LACRYMABLE	1	LEKES	1	LYKEWYSE	1
KENDALL	1	LADDE	1	LEMMAN	1	LYKYS	1
KENEL	1	LADELL	1	LEMMANNS	1	LYLE	1
KEPEST	1	LADYN	1	LEMSTER	1	LYLY	1
KEPYNGE	1	LAID	1	LENDE	1	LYLLY FLOWRE	1
KEPYTH	1	LAY MEN	1	LENETH	1	LYLSE WULSE	1

LYME-FYNGER	1	LOURE	1	MAKERELL	1	MASHE BOLLE	1
LYMERIK	1	LOUTE	1	MAKETHE	1	MASHFAT	1
LYME RODDE	1	LOVES	1	MAKYS	1	MASH FAT	1
LYMMES	1	LOVESOME	1	MAKYST	1	MASID	1
LYMPE-LEGGED	1	LOVING	1	MAKYTHE	1	MASKED	1
LYNAGE	1	LOVYNG	1	MALAPERTLY	1	MASKYD	1
LYNCOLE GRENE	1	LOVYNGLY	1	MALARDE	1	MASSES	1
LYNDE	1	LOWCE	1	MALCHUS	1	MASSHE FAT	1
LYNGRYNGE	1	LOWDEAN	1	MALENCOLY	1	MASTERED	1
LYNYD	1	LOWDEON	1	MALE URYD	1	MASTERFULLY	1
LYNKED	1	LOWDER	1	MALICE	1	MASTERS	1
LYNKES	1	LOWDYAN	1	MALICIOUS	1	MASTERSHYP	1
LYONNE	1	LOWTTEDE	1	MALIS	1	MASTYVE	1
LYONS	1	LUCAN	1	MALYCYOUS	1	MASTYVYS	1
LYOUN	1	LUCIFER	1	MALYGNED	1	MASTRIS	1
LYP	1	LUCILIUS	1	MALYGNYTES	1	MASTRYES	1
LYPPE	1	LUCIUS	1	MALYNCOLY	1	MATE	1
LYPPERS	1	LUCYFER	1	MALYPERT	1	MATED	1
LYPPS	1	LUCYFERS	1	MALKYN	1	MATENS	1
LYRES	1	LUCK	1	MALLARDE	1	MATERYALYTES	1
LYRICALL	1	LUCRES	1	MALLE	1	MATHEMATICAL	1
LYSTYN	1	LUGE	1	MALTAPERTE	1	MATYR	1
LYTELTON	1	LUGGARD	1	MAMELEK	1	MATYRS	1
LYTHE	1	LUGGES	1	MAMMY	1	MATRYCULAT	1
LYTHERLY	1	LUKE	1	MAMMOCKES	1	MATRYCULATE	1
LYTHERS	1	LUMBARDES	1	MAMOCKES	1	MATTENS	1
LYTTEL	1	LUMBARDY	1	MANACE	1	MATTOKE	1
LYTTERATURE	1	LUMBER	1	MANASE	1	MAUMET	1
LYTTERKTURE	1	LUMBERDES	1	MANCYONS	1	MAUNCHET	1
LYTTIL	1	LUMBRYTH	1	MANDE	1	MAUNGEY	1
LYTTYL	1	LUMPE	1	MANERLES	1	MAVYS	1
LYVED	1	LUMPES	1	MANERS	1	MAWE	1
LYVEYNG	1	LUMPIS	1	MANES	1	MAWES	1
LYVENGE	1	LUNATYKE	1	MANGEY	1	MAWMETT	1
LYVES	1	LUNATYKES	1	MANHOD	1	MAWTE	1
LYVEST	1	LURDEYNE	1	MANHODE	1	MAXIMUS	1
LYVIUS	1	LURKE	1	MANYE	1	MAXYMYANE	1
LYVYUS	1	LURKING	1	MANYFOLDE	1	MEALE	1
LOCKES	1	LURKYNG	1	MANYS	1	MEANYS	1
LOCKYD	1	LUSKE	1	MANKYND	1	MEDDELYD	1
LOCKYS	1	LUSTE	1	MANKYNDE	1	MEDDELS	1
LOCKTE	1	LUSTES	1	MANLES	1	MEDEAS	1
LODE	1	LUSTYS	1	MANLYNES	1	MEDECYNE	1
LODESTAR	1	LUTE	1	MANS	1	MEDELED	1
LODE STARE	1	MACHABEUS	1	MANTEYND	1	MEDELYD	1
LODGE	1	MACHAREUS	1	MANTENYD	1	MEDELYNG	1
LODGED	1	MACHCHYD	1	MANTYCARE	1	MEDELYNGE	1
LODGID	1	MACHUBE	1	MANTYCORS	1	MEDELLE	1
LOGGES	1	MACKEMURRE	1	MANTYLL	1	MEDIACIOUN	1
LOGICIONS	1	MACROBIUS	1	MANTRYBLE	1	MEDITACYON	1
LOGYCALL	1	MADAM	1	MAPELY ROTE	1	MEDITACYOUN	1
LOYALLY	1	MADD	1	MARCELLUS	1	MEDYACYON	1
LOK	1	MADDYNGE	1	MARCH HARUM	1	MEDYATOURE	1
LOKIS	1	MADIONITA	1	MARCUS	1	MEDYCYNABLE	1
LOKYTHE	1	MADMEN	1	MARDE	1	MEDYLLAR	1
LOLY	1	MADNES	1	MARDOCHEUS	1	MEDYTACION	1
LOLLARDY	1	MAGISTYE	1	MAREES	1	MEDYTACYON	1
LOME	1	MAGYKE	1	MAREFOLES	1	MEDYTACYONS	1
LOMELYN	1	MAGNYFICENCE	1	MARES MYLKE	1	MEDYTATYON	1
LONDON	1	MAGNYFYED	1	MARGARITE	1	MEDLE	1
LONGE NECKED	1	MAGOTT	1	MARGENT	1	MEDLEY	1
LONGES	1	MAGOTTES	1	MARGERES	1	MEDLETH	1
LONGETH	1	MAHOUNDE	1	MARINER	1	MEDLYNG	1
LONGYD	1	MAIDEN	1	MARYBON	1	MEDUSA	1
LONGYTH	1	MAIDENES	1	MARYES	1	MEED	1
LONYS	1	MAIDENHODE	1	MARK	1	MEGERAS	1
LORDELY	1	MAINE	1	MARKED	1	MEYNE	1
LORDLYE	1	MAINTAYNE	1	MARKET	1	MEYNTAYNE	1
LORDSHEPE	1	MAINTEYNE	1	MARLYONS	1	MEKENESSE	1
LORDSHYPE	1	MAINTEYNED	1	MARMESET	1	MEKYLL	1
LOREINE	1	MAINTENAUNCE	1	MARMOLL	1	MELANCHATES	1
LOS	1	MAYDENHODE	1	MARMOSET	1	MELCHISEDEC	1
LOSELRY	1	MAYED	1	MARMOSETE	1	MELCHISEDECHE	1
LOSENDE	1	MAYNE LANDE	1	MARMSET	1	MELCHISEDECK	1
LOSYD	1	MAYNNY	1	MARO	1	MELEDYOUSLY	1
LOSS	1	MAYNTEN	1	MAROCK	1	MELLES	1
LOTHELY	1	MAYNTENANCE	1	MARQUES	1	MELLIS	1
LOTHY	1	MAYRE	1	MARRES	1	MELLYNG	1
LOTHLY	1	MAYSYD	1	MARTCHAUNTES	1	MELLYNGE	1
LOTHSOME	1	MAYSTE	1	MARTERD	1	MELLYS	1
LOTHSUM	1	MAYSTERFEST	1	MARTIS	1	MELODIOUS	1
LOTHSUMNESSE	1	MAYSTERY	1	MARTYN	1	MELODYOUSLY	1
LOUDLY	1	MAYSTRESSE	1	MARTYNET	1	MELOTTES	1
LOUNGE	1	MAYSTRYES	1	MARVEYLUS	1	MELOUDIOUSLY	1

MELPOMENE	1	MYSDEDE	1	MOURNYNG	1	NESTORIANUS	1
MELPOMONE	1	MYSDEDES	1	MOUSE HOLE	1	NETHER	1
MEMBRES	1	MYSDEMPTE	1	MOVED	1	NETTE	1
MENANDER	1	MYSDONE	1	MOW	1	NEVEN	1
MENANDERS	1	MYSE	1	MOWYNGE	1	NEVERE	1
MENDYD	1	MYSELF	1	MOWTE	1	NEVERMORE	1
MENES	1	MYSERABLENESSE	1	MUCH	1	NEVERTHELESSE	1
MENETH	1	MYSERABLY	1	MUD	1	NEW-FOUNDE	1
MENGITH	1	MYSERACION	1	MULE	1	NEWIS	1
MENYST	1	MYSERE	1	MULYS	1	NEWLY	1
MENNY	1	MYSNAMED	1	MULLYNG	1	NEWS	1
MENOLOPE	1	MYSPENT	1	MUNPYNNYS	1	NEWTER	1
MERCHAUNDYSE	1	MYSPROUDE	1	MUR	1	NEWTON	1
MERCILES	1	MYSSE USE	1	MURDER	1	NIGHTINGALE	1
MERETIS	1	MYSTERIALL	1	MURDRYNGE	1	NYCHOLAS	1
MERETORYOUSLY	1	MYSTICALL	1	MURMER	1	NYCHT	1
MERIT	1	MYSURYD	1	MURMURACYON	1	NYCROMANSY	1
MERITORY	1	MYSUSYD	1	MURMURAR	1	NYFYLS	1
MERYLY	1	MYSWROUGHT	1	MURNYNG	1	NYGARDE	1
MERYTYS	1	MYTCHE	1	MURNYNGE	1	NYGHE	1
MERMOSET	1	MYTE	1	MURRE	1	NYGHTYS	1
MERVELOUS	1	MYTEYNG	1	MURRIOUN	1	NYGHTLY	1
MESE	1	MYTERS	1	MURRYON	1	NYSYTE	1
MESSAGE	1	MYTYNG	1	MURTHER	1	NYSOT	1
MESSENGERE	1	MYXED	1	MUSCULL	1	NOBBES	1
MESURED	1	MYXT	1	MUSYK	1	NOBELLY	1
MESURIS	1	MYXTE	1	MUSYKKYS	1	NOBELNES	1
METER	1	MYXTURE	1	MUSYNG	1	NOBIL	1
METHYNKE	1	MOBYLL	1	MUSKETTE	1	NOBILYTE	1
METYNGE	1	MOCYON	1	MUSTER	1	NOBILLMEN	1
METREFYDE	1	MOCKYNG	1	MUSTY	1	NOBULL	1
METRICALL	1	MOCKYNGE	1	MUSTRED	1	NODDIS	1
METRIFYDE	1	MOCKYSSH	1	MUTABILITE	1	NODDYNGE	1
MEVYD	1	MOCKYSSHE	1	MUTYD	1	NODDY POLLES	1
MEWED	1	MODER	1	MUTRELL	1	NODY POLLE	1
MEWTE	1	MODERACYON	1	NAGGYS	1	NODYPOLLYS	1
MIDDIS	1	MODERATLY	1	NAYLE	1	NOE	1
MILK	1	MODYR	1	NAYLED	1	NOES	1
MILLAR	1	MOGHT	1	NAYLYS	1	NOLL	1
MIN	1	MOYLES	1	NAYTHYR	1	NOLLE	1
MINERVA	1	MOK	1	NAKID	1	NOMBER	1
MIRRIELL	1	MOKE	1	NAKIDE	1	NOMBYR	1
MIRTHE	1	MOKKYNG	1	NALE	1	NOMBRE	1
MISCARY	1	MOKKYSH	1	NALL	1	NONYS	1
MISCHIEFE	1	MOKKYSHLY	1	NAMAN	1	NOO THYNGE	1
MISERACYON	1	MOLEFY	1	NAMELES	1	NOPPE	1
MISERY	1	MOLYS	1	NAMELESSE	1	NORHAM	1
MISLYNG	1	MOLLE	1	NAMETH	1	NORMAN	1
MISTYCALL	1	MOMMYNGE	1	NAMYS	1	NORRAM	1
MISTRES	1	MONACORDYS	1	NAP	1	NORTHE	1
MYDAY SPRETTES	1	MONASTERIES	1	NAPERY	1	NOSYD	1
MYDDELL	1	MONCHE	1	NAPULS	1	NOTARIES	1
MYDNYGHT	1	MONE LIGHT	1	NARDE	1	NOTED	1
MYGHTES	1	MONESTERIES	1	NARROW	1	NO THYNGE	1
MYGHTIS	1	MONETH	1	NARROWE	1	NOUGHTE	1
MYGHTYS	1	MONETHES	1	NATURALLY	1	NOUMBYR	1
MYKELL	1	MONYS	1	NATURYS	1	NOWADAYES	1
MYKKYLLE	1	MONKES	1	NAVERN	1	NOW A DAYES	1
MYLDE	1	MONKYS	1	NEBBIS	1	NOWADAYS	1
MYLKEDUCKE	1	MONSYRE	1	NECESSARY	1	NOWEADAYES	1
MYLL	1	MONTAYNES	1	NECESSYTE	1	NOWE A DAYS	1
MYLLAR	1	MOR	1	NECKED	1	NOWGHT	1
MYLLER	1	MORALYTE	1	NECLYGENT	1	NOWGHTE	1
MYLLE STONE	1	MORALL	1	NEDED	1	NO WHER	1
MYLSTONES	1	MORDRE	1	NEDELES	1	NOWHERE	1
MYNDLES	1	MORELLE	1	NEDELL	1	NO WHERE	1
MYNERVE	1	MORNETH	1	NEDER	1	NOWMBER	1
MYNYON	1	MORNING GOUNES	1	NEDEST	1	NOWTE	1
MYNYSTER	1	MORNYNGE	1	NEDETH	1	NUTSHALES	1
MYNSTRELS	1	MORTAL	1	NEDETHE	1	NUT SHALIS	1
MYRACLE	1	MORTALLY	1	NEDILL WARK	1˙	NUTTE SHELL	1
MYRY	1	MOTHE-EATEN	1	NEDYNESSE	1	OBEISAUNCE	1
MYRROURE	1	MOTH ETYN	1	NEGARDE	1	OBEY	1
MYRTHYS	1	MOTHYS	1	NEGARSHYP	1	OBEYDE	1
MYS	1	MOTYNGE	1	NEGLYGESSE	1	OBJECTE	1
MYSADVENTURE	1	MOTYVE	1	NEYBOURS	1	OBJECTYON	1
MYSADVYSED	1	MOUGHT	1	NEYGHBOUR	1	OBLACIONS	1
MYSCHAUNCE	1	MOULDE	1	NEYGHBOURS	1	OBLIQUI	1
MYSCHEVE	1	MOUNT	1	NEYTHYR	1	OBLIVYOUS	1
MYSCHEVED	1	MOUNTAYNE	1	NEK	1	OBLOQUY	1
MYSCHEVYNGE	1	MOUNTALBON	1	NEPTALYM	1	OBSCURED	1
MYSCHEVOUSLY	1	MOUNTENAUNCE	1	NEPTE	1	OBSEQUIOUS	1
MYSCHIEFE	1	MOUNTITH	1	NEPTUNE	1	OBSERVAUNCE	1
MYSCREANTYS	1	MOUNTYNG	1	NESTE	1	OBSERVE	1

Word	Count	Word	Count	Word	Count	Word	Count
OCCACYON	1	OUTCRYES	1	PARDY	1	PERCEYVID	1
OCCASIONYD	1	OUTESYDE	1	PARGAME	1	PERCEYVYNGE	1
OCCASYON	1	OUT FACYD	1	PARYS	1	PERCEVERAUNCE	1
OCCASYONS	1	OUT YLES	1	PARYSH	1	PERCEVYE	1
OCCIDENT	1	OUTRAGE	1	PARYSSHE CLERKE	1	PERCHAUNCE	1
OCCYAN	1	OUTRAGYOUS	1	PARJURED	1	PERCY	1
OCCUPIED	1	OUTRAY	1	PARKER	1	PERDURABLE	1
OCCUPYETH	1	OUTRAYE	1	PARKES	1	PEREGRYNACIOUN	1
OD	1	OUTWARDE	1	PARLYAMENT	1	PERELESSE	1
ODER	1	OVERBACE	1	PARLYMENT	1	PEREMTORY	1
ODIOUS	1	OVERCAST	1	PAROBLIS	1	PERFIGHTLY	1
OFFENDID	1	OVERGROWETH	1	PAROTE	1	PERFYTE	1
OFFERYNGE BOX	1	OVERNYGHTE	1	PARROTTIS	1	PERFYTELY	1
OFFYCYALLYS	1	OVER-SHOTE	1	PARTELET	1	PERFYTENESSE	1
OFFRE	1	OVERTHROWE	1	PARTELY	1	PERIHERMENIALL	1
OFSPRYNGE	1	OVERTHWARTED	1	PARTLY	1	PERILOUSLY	1
OFTENNER	1	OVERTHWARTES	1	PARTLOT	1	PERJURED	1
OFTENTYMES	1	OVERTHWARTYD	1	PARTRICHE	1	PERJURIS	1
OFTE TYME	1	OVERTHWHART	1	PARTRYCHES	1	PERKE	1
OFTYME	1	OVERWHARTE	1	PARTRYDGE	1	PERKYD	1
OFTYN	1	OVYD	1	PARVERTYD	1	PERKYN	1
OFTNAR	1	OVYRTHWARTHE	1	PASIPHE	1	PERLES	1
OFT TYME	1	OWERS	1	PASPORT	1	PERLESSE	1
OG	1	OWGHT	1	PASSAGE	1	PERLOUS	1
OYLE	1	OWR	1	PASSE-A-PASE	1	PERPETUALLY	1
OKE	1	OWRE	1	PASSENGERE	1	PERPETUYTE	1
OKES	1	OWTCRY	1	PASSETH	1	PERPLEXITE	1
OLIFRANKE	1	OWTELAUYD	1	PASSIS	1	PERSE	1
OLIPHAUNT	1	OXE	1	PASSYD	1	PERSEYVED	1
OLYBRYUS	1	OXFORTH	1	PASSYNGLY	1	PERSEYVYD	1
OLYFANT	1	PACHCHYD	1	PASSYON	1	PERSIUS	1
OLYFAUNT	1	PACIENS	1	PATCH	1	PERSYD	1
OLYFAUNTES	1	PACKE	1	PATCHE	1	PERSONABLE	1
OLYMPYAN	1	PACKINGE	1	PATCHES	1	PERSONALLY	1
OLYVERE	1	PACKIS	1	PATCHID	1	PERSPECTYVE	1
ONBENDE	1	PAGENT	1	PATENT	1	PERSWADE	1
ONCOMLY	1	PAGES	1	PATERNOSTER	1	PERTEYNETH	1
ONDYR	1	PAINT	1	PATERNOSTER PEKES	1	PERTELY	1
ONE-EYED	1	PAYED	1	PATH	1	PERTLY	1
ON-FLOTE	1	PAYNYD	1	PATLET	1	PERUSED	1
ONYON	1	PAYNTE	1	PATRIARKE	1	PERVAYLE	1
ONYWHERE	1	PAYNTES	1	PATRIARKES	1	PERVERTED	1
ONLYVE	1	PAYNTY	1	PATTERS	1	PESCODDES	1
ONOCENTAURES	1	PAJANTES	1	PAULES	1	PESON	1
ONOCENTAURIS	1	PAJAUNTIS	1	PAUNCHYS	1	PESTELS	1
ONOUR	1	PALAMON	1	PAUSE	1	PETICYON	1
OONLY	1	PALAS	1	PAVYS	1	PETYCYON	1
OPINYONS	1	PALEYS	1	PAWES	1	PETRONYLLA	1
OPYN	1	PALESTINA	1	PAWNE	1	PEVISSHENES	1
OPYNIONS	1	PALETTES	1	PAWSE	1	PEVYSHNES	1
OPYNYNGE	1	PALYARD	1	PAWTENAR	1	PEWTER	1
OPYNLYE	1	PALYARDE	1	PEALE	1	PHALARY	1
OPPOSE	1	PALL	1	PEASLESSE	1	PHARAO	1
OPPOSED	1	PALSEY	1	PECKED	1	PHARAOTIS	1
OPPRESSE	1	PAMFLETT	1	PECOCKE	1	PHARASAY	1
OPPREST	1	PAMPERDE	1	PECOKE	1	PHEDRA	1
ORACIUS	1	PAMPHELET	1	PEK	1	PHENEX	1
ORATOURS	1	PAMPHILA	1	PEKE	1	PHENIX	1
ORBICULAR	1	PAMPHILET	1	PEKYSH	1	PHENYX	1
ORCHADY	1	PAMPHYLUS	1	PELFRY	1	PHERUMBRAS	1
ORDENYD	1	PAMPYR	1	PELLIT	1	PHESIK	1
ORDERYD	1	PANDARUS	1	PELORY PAJAUNTES	1	PHILARGERYA	1
ORDERS	1	PANGE	1	PENALTE	1	PHILEMON	1
ORDYNALL	1	PANGED	1	PENCE	1	PHILISTINIS	1
ORDYNAUNCE	1	PANGES	1	PENCYON	1	PHILISTION	1
ORDRED	1	PANGIS	1	PEND	1	PHILYP	1
ORDRES	1	PANT	1	PENDUGIMS	1	PHILLIPPIS	1
ORGULYOUS	1	PAPALL	1	PENDUGUM	1	PHILLISTINIS	1
ORIGINALL	1	PAPALLES	1	PENELOPE	1	PHILLYP	1
ORYENT	1	PAPER	1	PENY CHEKE	1	PHILLYPPES	1
ORYENTE	1	PAPERS	1	PENYLES	1	PHILOSOPHIA	1
ORYGYNALL	1	PAPYR	1	PENNELL	1	PHITONES	1
ORNACY	1	PAPPES	1	PENOLEPE	1	PHITONESSE	1
ORPHEUS	1	PARABYLL	1	PENOLOPE	1	PHYLLIP	1
ORWELLE	1	PARABLES	1	PENS	1	PHYLLYPES	1
OSPRAYE	1	PARADYSE	1	PENSELL	1	PHYLLYPS	1
OTES	1	PARAMOURE	1	PENTAMETER	1	PHYLOLOGY	1
OTHES	1	PARATO	1	PENURY	1	PHYLOSOPHERS	1
OTHYR	1	PARBRAKE	1	PEPER	1	PHYLOSOPHY	1
OUCHE	1	PARCELE	1	PEPIL	1	PHYPPES	1
OUGHTE	1	PARCELL	1	PERADVENTURE	1	PHYSYKE	1
OULE	1	PARCHAUNCE	1	PERADVERTAUNCE	1	PHOROCIDES	1
OUTCRI	1	PARCYALL	1	PERCASE	1	PHRONESSYS	1
OUTCRY	1	PARCYALLYTE	1	PER CASE	1	PICKE	1

PICTURIS	1	PLATTERS	1	POPERING	1	PREGNAUNTE	1
PIERIDES	1	PLEASAUNCE	1	POPES	1	PREIGNAUNTE	1
PIGEONS	1	PLEASAUNTER	1	POPHOLY	1	PREYE	1
PIGGES	1	PLEASETH	1	POPIGAY	1	PREKETH	1
PIGGESNYE	1	PLEASYRE	1	POPINGAY	1	PRELACYE	1
PIKE	1	PLEASURES	1	POPYNGAY	1	PRELATTES	1
PIKYS	1	PLEASURS	1	POPPED	1	PRENDERGEST	1
PILE	1	PLEGE	1	POPPYNG	1	PREORDINATE	1
PINE	1	PLENARELY	1	PORCENA	1	PREPAYRE	1
PIPLYNG	1	PLENTY	1	PORPHIRIS	1	PREPARED	1
PIPPLYNG	1	PLESANT	1	PORT	1	PREPOSYCYON	1
PIRLYNG	1	PLESAUNTE	1	PORTE SALUE	1	PREPOSYTOUR	1
PISANDROS	1	PLESYRE	1	PORTISMOUTH	1	PRESCYENCE	1
PITCHE	1	PLETES	1	PORTYNGALES	1	PRESCRYPCYONS	1
PITCHER	1	PLETYNGE	1	PORTLYE	1	PRESENS	1
PY	1	PLIADES	1	PORT-SALE	1	PRESERVATYVE	1
PY-BAKAR	1	PLINNI	1	PORT SALU	1	PRESERVED	1
PYCHER	1	PLOVER	1	PORTURATURE	1	PRESIDENT	1
PYCKE	1	PLUCK	1	POSSYBLE	1	PRESIDENTE	1
PYCKED	1	PLUCKES	1	POST	1	PRESYOUS	1
PYCTURE	1	PLUCKETH	1	POSTELL	1	PRESONMENT	1
PYGEONS	1	PLUCKID	1	POSTELS	1	PRESSES	1
PYGGE	1	PLUCKYD	1	POSTERN GATE	1	PRESSYD	1
PYGGES EARE	1	PLUK	1	POSTIS	1	PRESTES	1
PYGGYS-NY	1	PLUMMED	1	POSTYKE	1	PRESUMCYON	1
PYGYONS	1	PLUMMET	1	POSTYIL	1	PRESUMYNG	1
PYKED	1	PLUMMIS	1	POTECARY	1	PRESUMPCION	1
PYKER	1	PLUMMOUTH	1	POTENCIALL	1	PRESUMPCYON	1
PYKES	1	PLUMPE	1	POTENCYALL	1	PRESUMPTUOUS	1
PYKETH	1	PLUNGYD	1	POTENCYALLY	1	PRETENDED	1
PYKYNGE	1	PLURALYTES	1	POTESTATE	1	PRETENDITH	1
PYKTHANKE	1	PLUTARKE	1	POTESTOLATE	1	PRETENDYD	1
PYLCHE	1	PLUTHARKE	1	POT SHARDE	1	PRETORY	1
PYLGRIMAGES	1	POCENYA	1	POTSHORDE	1	PREVENTID	1
PYLGRYMAGES	1	POCIOUN	1	POTSHORDES	1	PREVYE	1
PYLLYNG	1	PODDYNGE PRYCKE	1	POTSHORDIS	1	PREVYLEGIDDE	1
PYLLYON	1	PODE	1	POTT	1	PREVYLY	1
PYLLORY	1	PODYNGES	1	POTTE	1	PREVYNGE	1
PYLLOWE	1	POEMIS	1	POTTELL-PYCHER	1	PRICKYD	1
PYNCASE	1	POEMYS	1	POTTERS	1	PRIKKITH	1
PYNCHED	1	POESY	1	POUND	1	PRIMEROSE	1
PYNCHETH	1	POETE LAWREATE	1	POUNSED	1	PRIMORDIALL	1
PYNCHYNG	1	POETTES	1	POUNTES	1	PRIMORDYALL	1
PYNE	1	POETTYS	1	POUNTESSE	1	PRIMROSE	1
PYNED	1	POGGEUS	1	POWERS	1	PRINCESSE	1
PYNYON	1	POINTED	1	POWLE HACHET	1	PRINCIPALL	1
PYNK IYDE	1	POINTYD	1	POWLE HATCHETTIS	1	PRINCYPLES	1
PYNNES	1	POYETE	1	POWND	1	PRISIANS	1
PYPES	1	POYET LAWREAT	1	PRACTIQUE	1	PRIVILEGED	1
PYRDEWY	1	POYLE	1	PRACTISE	1	PRY	1
PYRRUS	1	POYNT DEVYSE	1	PRAIERS	1	PRYCE	1
PYS	1	POYNTES	1	PRAIID	1	PRYCKE-ME-DENTY	1
PYSPOTTES	1	POYNTYD	1	PRAYETH	1	PRYCKE SONG	1
PYSSE	1	POYNTYNG	1	PRAYSED	1	PRYCKE SONGE	1
PYST	1	POYNTYNGE	1	PRANCKES	1	PRYCKYD	1
PYSTELS	1	POYNTMENTYS	1	PRANES	1	PRYD	1
PYSTYLLERS	1	POYSOND	1	PRANYS	1	PRYEEST	1
PYTCHARS	1	POYSONED	1	PRANKED	1	PRYK	1
PYTEYUS	1	POLETYKE	1	PRANKYNG	1	PRYMATES	1
PYTEOUS	1	POLIMITES	1	PRANKYS	1	PRYME	1
PYTH	1	POLYS	1	PRASE	1	PRYMEROSE	1
PYTHE	1	POLYSHED	1	PRATED	1	PRYMES	1
PYTYE	1	POLYTYKES	1	PRATER	1	PRYNCELY	1
PYTYOUS	1	POLLAXIS	1	PRATYER	1	PRYNT	1
PYTTY	1	POLLEGYANS	1	PRATYLYE	1	PRYNTED	1
PLACIS	1	POLLEYNGE	1	PRAUNCE	1	PRYNTITH	1
PLACKE	1	POLLES	1	PREAMBLE	1	PRYORESSE	1
PLAGYS	1	POLLYCY	1	PREBENDARIES	1	PRYSONER	1
PLAINE	1	POLLYNG	1	PRECELY	1	PRYSTE	1
PLAINLY	1	POLLYNG PAJAUNTTIS	1	PRECHED	1	PRYTELY	1
PLAINNES	1	POLLUTED	1	PRECHES	1	PRYVY	1
PLAYES	1	POLLUTYD	1	PRECHETH	1	PRYVYLEGYD	1
PLAYETH	1	POLUTED	1	PRECHID	1	PROBLEMIS	1
PLAYN	1	POMAUNDER	1	PRECHYD	1	PROCEDID	1
PLAYNE DELYNGE	1	POMEGARNAT	1	PRECIOUSLY	1	PROCEDYD	1
PLAYNESSE	1	POMEL	1	PRECYOUSE	1	PROCERPINA	1
PLAYST	1	POMPED	1	PREDESTYNACYON	1	PROCESSYON	1
PLAYTH	1	POMPEYUS	1	PREDICAMENTES	1	PROCLAME	1
PLANE	1	PONDER	1	PREDYALL	1	PRODIGALL	1
PLANTID	1	PONDRED	1	PREDYCACION	1	PRODYGALL	1
PLANTYNG	1	PONTIFYCALL	1	PREESTES	1	PROFE	1
PLANTYNGE	1	PONTYFICALL	1	PREFERMENT	1	PROFER	1
PLATIS	1	POPEGAY	1	PREGNACY	1	PROFESSYOUN	1
PLATO	1	POPE HOLY	1	PREGNANT	1	PROFYTE GROWTH	1

Word	Count	Word	Count	Word	Count	Word	Count
PROFYTETH	1	PURSEVANTIS	1	RAMBES HORNE	1	REFRESHED	1
PROFOUNDE	1	PURSYS	1	RAMMYSCHE	1	REFRESSHYNG	1
PROLOGUE	1	PURVEAUNCE	1	RAMMYSSHE	1	REFUGE	1
PROMISED	1	PURVEY	1	RAMPAUNT	1	REFUSYD	1
PROMYSYDE	1	PUSANT	1	RANCOUR	1	REGARDETH	1
PROMOCION	1	PUS CATT	1	RANGYD	1	REGARDYD	1
PROMOSYON	1	PUSCULL	1	RANKELY	1	REGESTARY	1
PROMOTYNGE	1	PUSYLLANYMYTE	1	RANKIS	1	REGESTERDE	1
PROMOTYVE	1	PUSKYLDE	1	RANNGE	1	REGESTRED	1
PRONOSTYCATE	1	PUTREFY	1	RAPPES	1	REGESTRINGE	1
PRONOUNCE	1	PUWYT	1	RARIFIID	1	REGIMENT	1
PRONOWNSYNG	1	QUADRANT	1	RASYD	1	REGYSTRED	1
PROP	1	QUAYLLES	1	RATCHES	1	REGYSTRYD	1
PROPE	1	QUALE	1	RATES	1	REGRACIATORY	1
PROPERCIUS	1	QUALYFYED	1	RATYD	1	REGSTRY	1
PROPHANES	1	QUALYTES	1	RATYFYE	1	REHAYTED	1
PROPHESY	1	QUARELLES	1	RATYFYED	1	REHERS	1
PROPHET	1	QUARELLYS	1	RATTES	1	REHERSED	1
PROPHYTABYLL	1	QUARILLIS	1	RAUNGE	1	REHERSITH	1
PROPIR	1	QUARTE	1	RAVENER	1	REHERSYD	1
PROPORCYON	1	QUARTERD	1	RAVES	1	REHERSSE	1
PROPORSIONYD	1	QUATRIVIALS	1	RAVYD	1	REIGNE	1
PROPOSICYOUN	1	QUATRYVYALS	1	RAVYN	1	REYGNE	1
PROSCRIPCYON	1	QUECKE	1	RAVYNGE	1	REYNYTHE	1
PROSECUTE	1	QUEED	1	RAVYSHED	1	REYSE	1
PROSERPINA	1	QUEENE	1	RAVYSHT	1	REJAGGED	1
PROSERPINAS	1	QUEYSY	1	RAW	1	REJOYCE	1
PROSPERE	1	QUELL	1	RE	1	REJOYSE	1
PROSPERYOUSLY	1	QUENCHE	1	REALMYS	1	REKE	1
PROSPEROUS	1	QUERELL	1	REASONYNG	1	REKEN	1
PROTECTION	1	QUERESTERS	1	REBADS	1	REKENED	1
PROTECTIONS	1	QUERYSTERS	1	REBAUDRYE	1	REKENING	1
PROTESTACYOUN	1	QUEST	1	REBAWDE	1	REKENYD	1
PROTHONATORY	1	QUESTION	1	REBAWDIS	1	REKLESSE	1
PROTHONOTORY	1	QUESTIONYD	1	REBECCA	1	REKNYNG	1
PROVED	1	QUESTIONLES	1	REBELLE	1	RELACIONS	1
PROVERBYS	1	QUESTYON	1	REBELLYNGE	1	RELACYON	1
PROVETH	1	QUIBYBLE	1	REBELLYON	1	RELACYONS	1
PROVINCYALL	1	QUICKLY	1	REBELLYONNS	1	RELATION	1
PROVINCYALS	1	QUIGHT	1	REBOYLED	1	RELEYSYD	1
PROVISYON	1	QUIKE	1	REBOKE	1	RELES	1
PROVITHE	1	QUINTILIANE	1	REBOUND	1	RELYGION	1
PROVYDENCE	1	QUINTYLYAN	1	REBUKES	1	RELYGIOUS	1
PROVYDENT	1	QUINTUS	1	REBUKID	1	RELYGYOUS	1
PROVYNCIALL	1	QUYCKER	1	REBUKYD	1	REMAYNETH	1
PROVYTH	1	QUYCKLY	1	REBUKYNG	1	REMANYTH	1
PROVOKED	1	QUYGHT	1	RECH	1	REMEDELES	1
PROVOST	1	QUYKE	1	RECHATE	1	REMEDYLES	1
PROVOSTE	1	QUYNTYNE	1	RECHATYNG	1	REMEMBYR	1
PROWDEST	1	QUYSSHON	1	RECHYD	1	REMEMBRAUNCER	1
PROWDYST	1	QUOKE	1	RECKEN	1	REMEMBRAUNS	1
PSALME	1	QUOSSHONS	1	RECKYS	1	REMEMBRING	1
PSAUTRY	1	RABELL	1	RECLAME	1	REMEMBRYNG	1
PTHOLOME	1	RABYLL	1	RECOMMENDETH	1	REMEMBRYNGE	1
PUAUNT	1	RACELL	1	RECONCYLYACYON	1	REMES	1
PUAUNTELY	1	RACHCHYD	1	RECONED	1	REMORD	1
PUBLISSHE	1	RACHELL	1	RECONYNGE	1	REMORDED	1
PUBLYSSHE	1	RACKED	1	RECONUSAUNCE	1	REMORDERS	1
PUBLYSSHED	1	RADYANT	1	RECORDED	1	REMORDES	1
PUDDYNG	1	RADYANTE	1	RECOUNFORTYD	1	REMORDYNGE	1
PUDDYNGES	1	RADYENT	1	RECOUNTYD	1	REMORRS	1
PUFFYN	1	RAFTER	1	RECOVER	1	REMORSE	1
PUFTE	1	RAGGE	1	RECOVERD	1	REMOTES	1
PULL	1	RAGGID	1	RECRAYD	1	RENAYENGE	1
PULLE	1	RAGGYS	1	RECTYFYE	1	RENDRYNG	1
PULLISSHYD	1	RAGYD	1	RECULED	1	RENEWYD	1
PULLYSHED	1	RAGMAN ROLLIS	1	REDBREST	1	RENY	1
PULLYSHYD	1	RAILER	1	REDELY	1	RENYYD	1
PULLYSSHID	1	RAILES	1	REDEMED	1	RENNETH	1
PULPETE	1	RAILLES	1	REDEMEDE	1	RENNING	1
PULPYT	1	RAIST	1	REDEMPCYON	1	RENNYNGE	1
PULPYTTES	1	RAYE	1	REDES	1	RENOME	1
PULTRE	1	RAYGNE	1	REDITH	1	RENOUN	1
PULTROWNE	1	RAYLL	1	REDYNES	1	RENOWME	1
PUMP	1	RAYMENT	1	REDYTH	1	RENOWNYD	1
PUNYETE	1	RAYNBETYN	1	REDLESSE	1	RENTE	1
PUNYSSHED	1	RAYNE-BEATEN	1	REDOLENT	1	RENWDE	1
PUNYSSHMENT	1	RAYNE BETEN	1	REDOUTED	1	REPAIRE	1
PUNT	1	RAYNETH	1	REDRES	1	REPAYRID	1
PURCHASER	1	RAYNNING	1	REFFORMATION	1	REPARE	1
PURGACYON	1	RAYSE	1	REFLAYRE	1	REPARED	1
PURPILL	1	RAYSYNG	1	REFLARING	1	REPAST	1
PURPLE	1	RAYSORS	1	REFORMACION	1	REPENTYD	1
PURPOSYD	1	RAMBES	1	REFOURME	1	REPETE	1

REPYNE	1	RINNE	1	ROWND	1	SATHANAS	1
REPLICACYON	1	RY	1	ROWNDE	1	SATIRRAY	1
REPLYCABLE	1	RYALLY	1	ROWNE	1	SATROPAS	1
REPLYCACION	1	RYALTE	1	ROWNYD	1	SATURICALL	1
REPLYCACYON	1	RYAT	1	ROWTYTH	1	SATURNE	1
REPORTED	1	RYBAUDE	1	RUBARBE	1	SAUCY	1
REPORTETH	1	RYBAWDE	1	RUBBE	1	SAUCYS	1
REPORTID	1	RYBBIS	1	RUBBED	1	SAUL	1
REPORTINGE	1	RYBBYS	1	RUBBID	1	SAUMPLER	1
REPORTYNG	1	RYBYBE	1	RUBIES	1	SAUNCE-PERE	1
REPORTYNGE	1	RYBON	1	RUBIS	1	SAUSE	1
REPOSED	1	RYBSKYN	1	RUBY	1	SAUTES	1
REPREHENDE	1	RYCH	1	RUBYS	1	SAVACIOUN	1
REPREHENDYNG	1	RYCHER	1	RUDDES	1	SAVYNG	1
REPRESENTACYON	1	RYCHLY	1	RUDDYS	1	SAVYOURE	1
REPRESENTE	1	RYDEN	1	RUDENESS	1	SAVYR	1
REPRYVABLE	1	RYDES	1	RUDYES	1	SAWDE	1
REPROBITANTE	1	RYDLESSE	1	RUDNES	1	SAWDUST	1
REPROCHED	1	RYE	1	RUFFYNS	1	SAWES	1
REPUGNAUNCE	1	RYFLED	1	RUFFLYNGE	1	SAWIS	1
REPUTYNG	1	RYGOROUS	1	RUGGY	1	SCABBE	1
REQUIEM	1	RYGOURE	1	RUGGYD	1	SCALIS	1
REQUIRE	1	RYMES	1	RUGHE	1	SCALLYD	1
REREWARDE	1	RYMING	1	RUGHLY	1	SCALOPPE	1
RESAYTE	1	RYMYNG	1	RULES	1	SCANT	1
RESCU	1	RYNDE	1	RULY	1	SCAPE THRYFTE	1
RESCUDE	1	RYNSE	1	RULYE	1	SCARCE	1
RESCUE	1	RYOTE	1	RULYTHE	1	SCARIOTH	1
RESEMBLANCE	1	RYOTYNGE	1	RUMBELOWE	1	SCARSLY	1
RESEMBLAUNCE	1	RYOTT	1	RUMBYLL	1	SCATH	1
RESEMBLE	1	RYPEST	1	RUMER	1	SCAULES	1
RESEMBLED	1	ROBBE	1	RUMPOPULORUM	1	SCHAME	1
RESIST	1	ROBBED	1	RUNE	1	SCHYNE	1
RESYDEVACYON	1	ROBBYD	1	RUSH	1	SCHRYNYD	1
RESYDEW	1	ROBE	1	RUSHE	1	SCIENS	1
RESYDEWE	1	ROBES	1	RUSSHYNGE	1	SCIPIADES	1
RESKEW	1	ROBYS	1	RUST	1	SCIPION	1
RESONABLE	1	ROCHIS	1	RUTHE	1	SCIPIONE	1
RESONDE	1	ROCKE	1	RUTTER	1	SCIPIONS	1
RESONYNGE	1	ROCKET	1	RUTTERKYN	1	SCYENCE	1
RESORT	1	RODE LOFT	1	RUTTERS	1	SCYLENCE	1
RESPYTE	1	ROYAL	1	RUTTY	1	SCLAUNDER	1
RESPONSYVE	1	ROYALS	1	RUTTYNGLY	1	SCLAUNDEROUS	1
RESSEYTE	1	ROYLE	1	SAAKE	1	SCLAUNDRYNGE	1
RESTY	1	ROKE	1	SABY	1	SCOLDE	1
RESTYTH	1	ROLE	1	SACERDOTES	1	SCOLEHOUS	1
RESTLESSE	1	ROLFE	1	SACKES	1	SCOLE MATERS	1
RESTRAYNE	1	ROLLETH	1	SACRAMENTES	1	SCORES	1
RESTRAYNT	1	ROLLYNGE	1	SACRE	1	SCORFFYNESSE	1
RESTRAYNTES	1	ROMBELOW	1	SACRYNGE	1	SCORYD	1
RESURRECTION	1	RON	1	SADE	1	SCORNES	1
RETAYNYD	1	RONNE	1	SADYLGOSE	1	SCORNIS	1
RETCHLESSE	1	RONNER	1	SADLYE	1	SCORNNYS	1
RETENEWE	1	RONNES	1	SADNESS	1	SCORPIONE	1
RETHORIKE	1	ROOTES	1	SADOKE	1	SCORPIONS	1
RETHORIKYS	1	ROPES	1	SAFELY	1	SCOTYSHE	1
RETORICYONS	1	ROPY	1	SAFFRON BAGGES	1	SCOTLANDE	1
RETOURNE	1	RORE	1	SAGACITE	1	SCOTTE	1
RETROGRADANT	1	ROSABELL	1	SAILING	1	SCOTTISH	1
RETURNE	1	ROSE BUDDES	1	SAYED	1	SCOTTYSH	1
REVE	1	ROSEMARY	1	SAYLYNGE	1	SCOUR	1
REVELER	1	ROSERS	1	SAYLL	1	SCOURGE	1
REVELYNG	1	ROSET	1	SAYNTUARY BREKYNG	1	SCRACHE	1
REVELL ROUTE	1	ROSIAR	1	SAYTHE	1	SCRAT	1
REVENGED	1	ROSTY	1	SALAMON	1	SCRIPTURE	1
REVENGYD	1	ROTCHETTES	1	SALE	1	SCRIPTURES	1
REVERENDE	1	ROTY	1	SALFE CUNDIGHT	1	SCRYBBYL	1
REVERENS	1	ROUFLED	1	SALYSBERY	1	SCRYBBLYD	1
REVERSED	1	ROUGH	1	SALLOWE	1	SCRYBYLL	1
REVERSSE	1	ROUGH-FOTED	1	SALTFYSSHE	1	SCRYBYS	1
REVILYNG	1	ROUNCEVALL	1	SALUSTY	1	SCRYBLYD	1
REVYNGE	1	ROUNDED	1	SALUTACYONS	1	SCRYVE	1
REVYVID	1	ROUNSES	1	SALUTE	1	SCROLLE	1
REVOLDE	1	ROUNSIS	1	SALVE	1	SCROLLIS	1
REWARDED	1	ROUST	1	SANDE	1	SCROWLE	1
REWARDES	1	ROUSTY	1	SAPHER	1	SCRUPULOUS	1
REWARDYNGE	1	ROUTH	1	SAPHIRIS	1	SCRUPULUS	1
REWARDYS	1	ROUTHE	1	SAPHO	1	SCRUTENY	1
REWE	1	ROWETH	1	SAPPE	1	SCURFE	1
REWED	1	ROWGH	1	SARASYNS	1	SCURFFE	1
REWLE	1	ROWYTH	1	SARAZYN	1	SCUT	1
REWTH	1	ROWLANDE	1	SARDANAPALL	1	SCUTIS	1
REWTHE	1	ROWLYNGE	1	SARSENS	1	SCUTUS	1
RING	1	ROWLLYS	1	SARSON	1	SEALL	1

905

Word	Count	Word	Count	Word	Count	Word	Count
SEASE	1	SHAMYD	1	SYDED	1	SLEPYSTE	1
SEASYD	1	SHAMLES	1	SYDE-SADELL	1	SLEPT	1
SECHE	1	SHANKKES	1	SYDONY	1	SLEPTE	1
SE COSTE	1	SHARPELY	1	SYDRAKE	1	SLETH	1
SECRET	1	SHARPLY	1	SYERS	1	SLIPPER	1
SECRETARY	1	SHAVEN	1	SYGHE	1	SLY	1
SECRETNESE	1	SHAVYN	1	SYGHED	1	SLYCE	1
SECTES	1	SHAVYNGE	1	SYGHYNGE	1	SLYDDER	1
SECUND	1	SHED	1	SYGHTES	1	SLYDER	1
SECUNDE	1	SHEDDYNGE	1	SYGNES	1	SLYP	1
SEDEANE	1	SHELFE	1	SYLENCE	1	SLYPPERS	1
SEDES	1	SHENT	1	SYLKES	1	SLYVE	1
SEDICION	1	SHEPE COTE	1	SYLLORYM	1	SLOGYSH	1
SEDYCIONS	1	SHEPIS TAYLYS	1	SYLT	1	SLOMBRE	1
SEDYCYOUS	1	SHEPYS IE	1	SYMKYN	1	SLOUTH	1
SEDUCE	1	SHERYFHOTTEN	1	SYMONIAKE	1	SLOUTHFULL	1
SEDUCES	1	SHERTES	1	SYMONY	1	SLOVYNS	1
SEE-BOORDE	1	SHET	1	SYMPER-THE-COCKET	1	SLOWTHFULL	1
SEEN	1	SHETT	1	SYMPLENESSE	1	SLUFFERD	1
SEE-SANDE	1	SHEWYNGE	1	SYMPLYCYTE	1	SLUGGYSH	1
SEETH	1	SHIPPIS	1	SYNAMUM	1	SLUT	1
SEETHE	1	SHYDERYD	1	SYNGES	1	SLUTTES	1
SEIGNEOUR	1	SHYFT	1	SYNGGYS	1	SMACKE	1
SEYGNYORYTE	1	SHYLDE	1	SYNGYNGE	1	SMAL	1
SEYGNOURS	1	SHYLL	1	SYNGULER	1	SMALL-BRAYNE	1
SEYMY	1	SHYN	1	SYNKYNG	1	SMALLER	1
SEYN	1	SHYNED	1	SYNNEWS	1	SMARAGD	1
SEYNTY	1	SHYPBORDE	1	SYNODALLES	1	SMARAGDIS	1
SEYST	1	SHYPPED	1	SYPPE	1	SMART	1
SEKELY	1	SHYPPES	1	SYPPET	1	SMARTID	1
SEKERNES	1	SHYTTEL-COCKE	1	SYRUS	1	SMATYR	1
SEKERNESSE	1	SHYTTELL	1	SYSE	1	SMATTERYNGE	1
SEMENT	1	SHO CLOUT	1	SYSMATICATE	1	SMATTERS	1
SEMEWE	1	SHODER	1	SYTHE	1	SMELLE	1
SEMITH	1	SHOO	1	SYTTES	1	SMELLED	1
SEMYNGE	1	SHOP	1	SKABED	1	SMELLETH	1
SEMYST	1	SHOPPE	1	SKALES	1	SMELLID	1
SEMLY	1	SHORN	1	SKALPE	1	SMERED	1
SENATOUR	1	SHORT	1	SKAN	1	SMERKE	1
SENAWS	1	SHORTEN	1	SKANE	1	SMYGHT	1
SENEK	1	SHO-SOLE	1	SKANT	1	SMYLED	1
SENNET	1	SHOUER	1	SKAR	1	SMYLID	1
SENS	1	SHOVELAR	1	SKELLET	1	SMYLYNG	1
SENSERS	1	SHOVYNGE	1	SKELTONIDIS	1	SMYLYNGE	1
SENSETH	1	SHOVLL	1	SKELTONS	1	SMYTH	1
SENSUALYTE	1	SHOWELL	1	SKER	1	SMYTHY KUR	1
SENTE	1	SHOWER	1	SKEWED	1	SMOCKES	1
SENTENCYOUSLY	1	SHOWLDER	1	SKIP	1	SMOKES	1
SEON	1	SHOWRES	1	SKYL	1	SNAYLIS	1
SEPTEMBER	1	SHOWRIS	1	SKYNNES	1	SNAP	1
SEQUELE	1	SHREDIS	1	SKYPPE	1	SNAPPAR	1
SEQUESTRED	1	SHREUD	1	SKYPPED	1	SNATCHE	1
SERCHYNG	1	SHREWDENES	1	SKYRE-GALYARD	1	SNATCHYNGE	1
SERENUS	1	SHREWE	1	SKYRGALIARDE	1	SNEVELYNG	1
SERGEAUNT FERROUR	1	SHREWED	1	SKYRGALYARD	1	SNYVELED	1
SERGYANTES	1	SHREWES	1	SKYRT	1	SNORT	1
SERYOUSLY	1	SHRYNE	1	SKYT	1	SNOWE	1
SERMON	1	SHRYNYD	1	SKLAUNDERING	1	SNUF	1
SERMONS	1	SHRYNKE	1	SKOLDE	1	SNURRE	1
SERPENS	1	SHROW	1	SKOLDING	1	SOBBE	1
SERPENTES	1	SHROWDES	1	SKOLES	1	SOBBED	1
SERPENTINS	1	SHUDDER	1	SKOMMER	1	SOBBYNG	1
SERVANT	1	SHUREWLYE	1	SKOMMETH	1	SOBBYNGE	1
SERVANTYS	1	SHURVY	1	SKORNYS	1	SOCCOURE	1
SERVAUNT	1	SICULUS	1	SKOTTYS	1	SOCKE	1
SERVED	1	SIGH	1	SKRYBE	1	SOCRATES	1
SERVETH	1	SILOGISME	1	SKULL	1	SODEYNE	1
SERVITURE	1	SILOGISTICALL	1	SLAIIS	1	SODEYNLY	1
SERVYCEABYLL	1	SIMONIA	1	SLAIN	1	SODYLDYM	1
SERVYD	1	SINGLAR	1	SLAKE	1	SODOMITES	1
SESON	1	SINGULAR	1	SLATY	1	SOFREYNE	1
SESONS	1	SINNES	1	SLAUNDRED	1	SOFTER	1
SETTYS	1	SINODALS	1	SLAUNDRYS	1	SOFTLYER	1
SEW	1	SION	1	SLAVER	1	SOILE	1
SEWE	1	SIRUS	1	SLAVERYNG	1	SOJOURNS	1
SEX	1	SITHE	1	SLEEST	1	SOL	1
SHAYLES	1	SITTYNG	1	SLEETH	1	SOLACIOUS	1
SHAKES	1	SITTYNGE	1	SLEY	1	SOLACYUSLY	1
SHAKETH	1	SYAR	1	SLEYGHT	1	SOLAYNE	1
SHAKYNGE	1	SYB	1	SLEYGHTES	1	SOLE	1
SHAM	1	SYBBYLL	1	SLEYTE	1	SOLEME	1
SHAMEFASTNES	1	SYBLY	1	SLENDER	1	SOLEMPE	1
SHAMEFULY	1	SYCKE	1	SLEPYNG	1	SOLEMPNELY	1
SHAMETH	1	SYCKYLL	1	SLEPYST	1	SOLEMPNYTE	1

SOLEN	1	SPEKES	1	STY	1	STRONGLY	1
SOLF	1	SPEKYNG	1	STYCK	1	STROUDE	1
SOLFYTH	1	SPEKYNGE	1	STYCKE	1	STROWED	1
SOMERS	1	SPEKYS	1	STYCKIS	1	STUBBED	1
SOME WHAT	1	SPEKYTH	1	STYCKYNGE	1	STUDIANTES	1
SOMME	1	SPELLE	1	STYGYALL	1	STUED	1
SOMMONDE	1	SPELLES	1	STYL	1	STUFFE	1
SOMNYNGE	1	SPENDETH	1	STYLLA	1	STUMBLE	1
SOMTYMEPARDE	1	SPERYCALL	1	STYLLY	1	STURBRYDGE	1
SOMWHERE	1	SPERKES	1	STYNGES	1	STURDIER	1
SON BEAMES	1	SPEWE	1	STYNKES	1	STUSE	1
SONDE	1	SPIES	1	STYNKINGLY	1	STUT	1
SONESHYNE	1	SPIRITIS	1	STYNT	1	SUBJECTIS	1
SONGES	1	SPIRYTUAL	1	STYRE	1	SUBMYTTED	1
SONNES	1	SPYCE	1	STYRETH	1	SUBSCRYBE	1
SONNYS	1	SPYCKE	1	STYROPS	1	SUBSTANCE	1
SOORED	1	SPYES	1	STYTCH	1	SUBSTYTUTE	1
SOPHISTICATID	1	SPYGHTFULL	1	STYTCHED	1	SUBTELL	1
SOPHY	1	SPYING	1	STYTCHIS	1	SUBTYLE	1
SOPHYSMS	1	SPYLT	1	STYTH	1	SUBTYLLY	1
SOPHYSTYCATE	1	SPYN	1	STOBBURNE	1	SUCK	1
SOPHOCLES	1	SPYNDELS	1	STOCKE	1	SUCKE	1
SOPPY	1	SPYNKE	1	STOCKEDOWVE	1	SUE	1
SOPPYS	1	SPYNNYNG WHELE	1	STOCKFYSSH	1	SUERLY	1
SORES	1	SPYNNYS	1	STOCKYS	1	SUETE	1
SOROUFULL	1	SPYNT	1	STOICALL	1	SUFFERANCE	1
SOROWES	1	SPYTELL	1	STOKYS	1	SUFFERD	1
SOROWFULLE	1	SPLAY	1	STOL	1	SUFFERED	1
SOROWIS	1	SPOYLYD	1	STOLYN	1	SUFFICE	1
SORSERY	1	SPOKYN	1	STOMAK	1	SUFFYCE	1
SORTED	1	SPORNE	1	STOMBYLL	1	SUFFRAGE	1
SORTIS	1	SPRANGE	1	STONDARDE	1	SUGER LOFE	1
SORTYD	1	SPURRES	1	STONDYNGE	1	SUGGESTYON	1
SOT	1	SPURRYS	1	STONDYTHE	1	SUGRYD	1
SOTH	1	SQUAT	1	STONE-CASTE	1	SUYNG	1
SOTHE	1	SQUYER-GALYARDE	1	STONGE	1	SULPICIA	1
SOTHELY	1	STABBE	1	STONYS	1	SUMDELE	1
SOTHRAY	1	STABILITE	1	STOODE	1	SUMES	1
SOTTYS	1	STABILLE	1	STOPPYD	1	SUMMON	1
SOUER	1	STABLE DUR	1	STOPPYNG	1	SUMMOND	1
SOUGHTE	1	STACIUS	1	STOPPYNGE	1	SUMMONED	1
SOULIS	1	STALYON	1	STOPPYNGE OYSTER	1	SUN	1
SOULYS	1	STALKYNGE	1	STORKE	1	SUNNYNG	1
SOURMOUNTINGE	1	STALL	1	STORME	1	SUP	1
SOVERAYN	1	STALWORTHY	1	STORME DRYVEN	1	SUPERCILIUSLY	1
SOVERAYNST	1	STAMERYNG	1	STORMIS	1	SUPERFLUE	1
SOVERAYNTE	1	STAMMER	1	STORM YBETEN	1	SUPERSTICIOUNS	1
SOVEREIGNE	1	STAMPPED	1	STOULE	1	SUPERSTICYON	1
SOVEREYGNE	1	STANDIS	1	STOUNGE	1	SUPERSTICYONS	1
SOVEREYN	1	STANDITH	1	STOUT	1	SUPERSTICYOUS	1
SOVERENLY	1	STANDYNGE	1	STOUTTY	1	SUPERSTYCYON	1
SOWDEN	1	STANDYTH	1	STOWNDE	1	SUPPED	1
SOWING	1	STANG	1	STOWRE	1	SUPPER	1
SOWYD	1	STARED	1	STOWTY	1	SUPPLE	1
SOWLLYS	1	STARES	1	STRAYGHT	1	SUPPLEYNG	1
SOWSE	1	STARYNG	1	STRAKE	1	SUPPLEMENT	1
SOWTER	1	STARYNGE	1	STRANGLE	1	SUPPLY	1
SOWTTERS	1	STARKEST	1	STRAUGHT	1	SUPPLYCACYONS	1
SPADE	1	STARRIS	1	STRAW	1	SUPPLYE	1
SPAINYARDES	1	STARTE	1	STRAWES	1	SUPPORT	1
SPAYNYSHE	1	STARTYLL	1	STRAWRY	1	SUPPOSICYON	1
SPAYNYSSHE	1	STATHAM	1	STREAMES	1	SUPPOSYCIONS	1
SPAYRE	1	STATURE	1	STREATLY	1	SUPPOSYNGE	1
SPANYARDES	1	STEDFAST	1	STREIGHT	1	SUPPRISID	1
SPAR	1	STEDFASTNESSE	1	STREIT	1	SUPREME	1
SPARYD	1	STEILE	1	STREITLY	1	SURCUDANT	1
SPARYNG	1	STELE	1	STREYGHTE	1	SURFET	1
SPARYS	1	STELYNG	1	STREYNES	1	SURFETOUS	1
SPARKIS	1	STELLYFYE	1	STREYTES	1	SURFFILLYNG	1
SPARKYLL	1	STENCHE	1	STRENGTHE	1	SURFLED	1
SPARKLYNGES	1	STEPE	1	STRETCHYNGE	1	SURGERY	1
SPAROES	1	STEPPIS	1	STRYDYNGE	1	SURMOUNTYNG	1
SPAROWS	1	STER CHAMBRE	1	STRYKEN	1	SURMOUNTYNGE	1
SPARRE	1	STERRE	1	STRYNGED	1	SURMOWNTYNGE	1
SPARRED	1	STERT	1	STRYNGES	1	SURPLUSE	1
SPATTYL	1	STERVE	1	STRYPE	1	SURRAY	1
SPECEFYE	1	STEVYN	1	STRYPLYNG	1	SURRENDRED	1
SPECIALL	1	STEWES	1	STRYPTE	1	SURRENDRING	1
SPECTACLE	1	STEWYS	1	STRYVES	1	SURVEY	1
SPECTACLES	1	STIGIALL	1	STRYVITH	1	SUSPICION	1
SPECULACYON	1	STILE	1	STROKES	1	SUSPYCYON	1
SPEDDE	1	STINGING	1	STRONG	1	SUTE	1
SPEED	1	STINGYNG	1	STRONGE-HERTED	1	SUTER	1
SPEK	1	STINT	1	STRONGELY	1	SUTYS	1

SUTTELTE	1	TAVELLIS	1	THESBE	1	TYRAND	1
SUWED	1	TAVELLYS	1	THESIUS	1	TYRE	1
SWAFFHAMM	1	TAVERNARS	1	THICKESTE	1	TYRYD	1
SWALLOW	1	TAVERNE	1	THIDER	1	TYRLY-TYRLOWE	1
SWANNES	1	TAWLE	1	THIRDE	1	TYRLY TYRLOWE	1
SWAP	1	TAX	1	THYCKE-LYPPED	1	TYRMAGANT	1
SWARTE	1	TAXES	1	THYCKER	1	TYRNYD	1
SWEARD	1	TAXYNGE	1	THYDDER	1	TYSE	1
SWEAT	1	TEACH	1	THYDYR	1	TYSYKE	1
SWELLYNGE	1	TEARYS	1	THYMBELL	1	TYTAN	1
SWELLYS	1	TECHED	1	THYMBLE	1	TYTELL-TATTYLL	1
SWEPT	1	TECHYNGE	1	THYNGIS	1	TYTYVELL	1
SWERD	1	TECHYTH	1	THYNKEST	1	TYTYVYLLES	1
SWERYNGE	1	TECHYTHE	1	THYNKITH	1	TYTLE	1
SWETER	1	TEDER	1	THYNKYNG	1	TYTMOSE	1
SWETERS	1	TEENE	1	THYNKYNGE	1	TYTTERS	1
SWETIS	1	TEGGES	1	THYNKYS	1	TO-BROKYN	1
SWETY	1	TEGGYS	1	THYNNE	1	TO-FRET	1
SWETYNG	1	TEHE	1	THY SELF	1	TOGEDYR	1
SWETTER	1	TE HE	1	THYSTELS	1	TOGITHER	1
SWYFTE	1	TEINTYD	1	THO	1	TOIES	1
SWYLLYNG TUBBE	1	TEL	1	THOLOME	1	TOYE	1
SWYNE HERDE	1	TELE	1	THOLOMYE	1	TOYES	1
SWYNGED	1	TELLERS	1	THOM	1	TOYLE	1
SWYNKERS	1	TELLES	1	THOMASEN	1	TO-JAGGED	1
SWORD	1	TEMMYS	1	THONDER	1	TO-JAGGID	1
SWORDYS	1	TEMPESTOUS	1	THORNES	1	TOKYN	1
TABERS	1	TEMPLES	1	THOROWE OUT	1	TOLE	1
TABERTES	1	TEMPORALTYE	1	THOROWE OUTE	1	TOLERACYON	1
TABLE	1	TENDYR	1	THORUGH	1	TOLLAGE	1
TABLES	1	TENE	1	THOUSAND FOLDE	1	TOLLERATE	1
TACKE	1	TENNYS	1	THOWE	1	TOLMAN	1
TA HA	1	TENOURS	1	THOWGH	1	TO-MANGLE	1
TAILES	1	TENSIS	1	THOWGHE	1	TO-MYRYD	1
TAYLERS	1	TENTER-HOKYS	1	THOWGHTE	1	TONGE-TAYDE	1
TAYLES	1	TERED	1	THOWSANDE FOLDE	1	TONGUE	1
TAYLIS	1	TERENCE	1	THOWTH	1	TONGUES	1
TAYLL	1	TERESTRE	1	THOWTHE	1	TONNELL	1
TAYNE	1	TERMYS	1	THRED-BARE	1	TONNYSH	1
TAKELYNGE	1	TERRIBLE	1	THREDE-BARE	1	TONSORS	1
TAKING	1	TERRY	1	THREE	1	TOOTE	1
TAKITH	1	TESSEW	1	THREFOLDE	1	TOP	1
TAKYNG	1	TESTALIS	1	THRE-FOTED	1	TOPAS	1
TAKYNGE	1	TESTAMENTIS	1	THRESCORE	1	TOPIAS	1
TAKYST	1	TESTEFY	1	THRESHOLD	1	TOPICALL	1
TALIS	1	TESTIFYE	1	THRESTYL	1	TOPYAS	1
TALKES	1	TESTY	1	THRETE	1	TO-RENTE	1
TALKYD	1	TETH	1	THRIFTE	1	TOTETH	1
TALKYNG	1	TETRYCALL	1	THRIFTLES	1	TOTH	1
TALL	1	TETTER	1	THRIVE	1	TOTYNGE	1
TALLE	1	TEUSDAY	1	THRYFTLESSE	1	TOTNAM	1
TALLOWE	1	TEWLY	1	THROTE BOLE	1	TO-TORNE	1
TALOWE	1	TEWSDAY	1	THROUGH OUT	1	TOT QUOT	1
TALWOD	1	TEXT	1	THRUGH	1	TOT QUOTTES	1
TAME	1	TEXTE	1	THUMBED	1	TOTTER	1
TANCRETE	1	TEXTES	1	THURIFYCATION	1	TOUCHED	1
TANE	1	THAGUS	1	THWARTID	1	TOUCHYNG	1
TANGYD	1	THALYA	1	THWARTYNG	1	TOUGH	1
TANNYD	1	THAMAR	1	TIDINGES	1	TOUGHT	1
TANTE	1	THAMARYS	1	TIDINGS	1	TOUGHTHER	1
TAPPET	1	THANKEFULLYER	1	TIMOROUS	1	TOUNE	1
TAPPETT	1	THANKES	1	TIRIKKIS	1	TOUR	1
TAPPID	1	THANKIS	1	TIRYKIS	1	TOURES	1
TAPPYSTER	1	THANKYD	1	TISSEW	1	TOURNETH	1
TARNISHE	1	THANKKIS	1	TITAN	1	TOWCHE	1
TARQUINIUS	1	THEDER	1	TITILLE	1	TOWCHIS	1
TARRY	1	THEEM	1	TITIVYLLIS	1	TOWCHYNG	1
TARSELL GENTYLL	1	THEFE	1	TITUS	1	TOWE	1
TART	1	THEFFECT	1	TYD	1	TOWNE CLARKE	1
TARTARY	1	THEFT	1	TYDES	1	TOWRES	1
TARTE	1	THEIRE	1	TYDINGIS	1	TOWRIS	1
TASTE	1	THEKE	1	TYGER	1	TOWRNYNG	1
TASTID	1	THENCE	1	TYKYLL	1	TRACIANE	1
TATTERD	1	THEOLOGIA	1	TYL	1	TRADICCYON	1
TATTERED	1	THEOLOGICALL	1	TYLE	1	TRAGEDIIS	1
TATTERS	1	THEOLOGISACION	1	TYLLBERY	1	TRAGEDY	1
TATTRED	1	THEOLOGYS	1	TYLNEY	1	TRAGEDYALL	1
TAUMPINNIS	1	THEREATT	1	TYMEROUS	1	TRAGYDESE	1
TAUNTE	1	THEREBY	1	TYN	1	TRAY	1
TAUNTED	1	THEREUPON	1	TYNE	1	TRAYSON	1
TAUNTES	1	THERFOR	1	TYNED	1	TRAYTEROUSLY	1
TAUNTING	1	THEROUT	1	TYNKERS	1	TRAYTORY	1
TAUNTYD	1	THERUPON	1	TYPPET	1	TRAYTOUR	1

Word	Count	Word	Count	Word	Count	Word	Count
TRAYTOURLY	1	TROLL	1	UNYCORNES	1	VASSAYLES	1
TRAYTOURS	1	TROMPE	1	UNKINDLY	1	VASSALL	1
TRAMYNGE	1	TRONES	1	UNKYND	1	VAUNTE-PARLER	1
TRANCHAUNT	1	TROT	1	UNKYNDNESSE	1	VAWTE	1
TRANS	1	TROTTE	1	UNLASED	1	VELYARDE	1
TRANSCENDING	1	TROTTERS	1	UNLAST	1	VENEMOUSLY	1
TRANSCENDINGLY	1	TROUBLED	1	UNLYKYNGE	1	VENEMOWS	1
TRANSENDYNG	1	TROUGHTE	1	UNLUST	1	VENGED	1
TRANSFORMACYON	1	TROUTE	1	UNLUSTY	1	VENYMOUSLY	1
TRANSFORMYD	1	TROVY	1	UNNATURALL	1	VENYSON	1
TRANSYTORY	1	TROWED	1	UNPAYD	1	VENOMOWS	1
TRANSLACION	1	TROWYD	1	UNPULLYSHT	1	VENQUESSHID	1
TRANSLACYON	1	TROWLE	1	UNREMEMBERED	1	VENTAYLES	1
TRANSLACYOUN	1	TRU	1	UNREMEMBRED	1	VERDURIS	1
TRANSLATE	1	TRULYE	1	UNRESONABLE	1	VERGESSE	1
TRAPTE	1	TRUMPETTIS	1	UNREWARDED	1	VERYE	1
TRASID	1	TRUMPYTHE	1	UNSET	1	VERMYNE	1
TRASSHE	1	TRUSYS	1	UNSHRED	1	VERS	1
TRATLANDE	1	TRUSSE	1	UNSOWNDY	1	VERSYCLES	1
TRATLERS	1	TRUSTINGE	1	UNSTABLE	1	VERSYFY	1
TRATLYNG	1	TRUSTYD	1	UNSTABLENESSE	1	VERSYFYENG	1
TRATLYNGE	1	TUCKE	1	UNSTEDFASTNESSE	1	VERSYNGE BOXE	1
TRAVARSE	1	TUGGYD	1	UNSURELY	1	VERTIBILITE	1
TRAVELL	1	TUICYON	1	UNSWETE	1	VERTUOWS	1
TRAVELLARS	1	TULLIUS	1	UNTAYDE	1	VERTUS	1
TRAVES	1	TULLY	1	UNTAWTE	1	VESCA	1
TRAVILLIAN	1	TUMBLAR	1	UNTHRIFTES	1	VESPASYAN	1
TREATE	1	TUMBLARS	1	UNTHRYFTYNES	1	VESTMENT	1
TREATEE	1	TUMBLE	1	UNTYDE	1	VEWE	1
TREATINGE	1	TUMRELL	1	UNTYDY	1	VEXACYON	1
TREBELLES	1	TUNABLE	1	UNTREW	1	VEXED	1
TREBYLLYS	1	TUNABLY	1	UNTREWE	1	VEXETH	1
TREDE	1	TUNGS	1	UNTREWLY	1	VEXYD	1
TREES	1	TUNNYNG	1	UNTRUST	1	VICAR GENERALL	1
TREYTORY	1	TURFFE	1	UNTRUTH	1	VICE	1
TREMBYLL	1	TURKEY	1	UPPE	1	VICIOUS	1
TREMELYNG	1	TURKIS	1	UPRYGHT	1	VICYOUS	1
TREMLYNG	1	TURKY	1	UPSTARTE	1	VIGOROUSLY	1
TRENT	1	TURND	1	UPSTODE	1	VIIJ	1
TRENTALE	1	TURNED	1	UPTUCKE	1	VILANE	1
TRENTALL	1	TURNEY	1	UPWARDE	1	VILANY	1
TRESOURE	1	TURNYNGE	1	UR	1	VILLAYN	1
TRESSIS	1	TURNYTHE	1	URCHEONS	1	VILLAYNS	1
TRESSYS	1	TURRETTES	1	URGENTLY	1	VINCENCIUS	1
TRESTRAM	1	TURRETTIS	1	URYD	1	VINIS	1
TRETISE	1	TURTYLL	1	URSA	1	VIOLATE	1
TREU	1	TUSCHE	1	USAGE	1	VIRGILL	1
TREWELY	1	TWAYN	1	USYNGE	1	VIRGYLL	1
TREWTH	1	TWENE	1	USSCHERES	1	VIRULENT	1
TRIED	1	TWYBYLL	1	USSHER	1	VIRULENTLY	1
TRIFELS	1	TWYCE	1	USUALL	1	VISAGE	1
TRINITE	1	TWYNKYNG	1	UTERAUNCE	1	VITALL	1
TRINYTE	1	TWYNKLYNG	1	UTTERLY	1	VYCARE GENERALL	1
TRIONS	1	TWYST	1	VACABONDES	1	VYCARYES	1
TRIP	1	UDDERSALE	1	VAGYS	1	VYCES	1
TRIPPYNG	1	UDDERSALL	1	VAYLES	1	VYENE	1
TRIUMPHANTLYE	1	UGLY HYPPED	1	VAYLETH	1	VYLANOUS	1
TRIUMPHAUNT	1	ULIXES	1	VAYNED	1	VYLE	1
TRIUMPHE	1	UMANYTE	1	VAYNE GLORIE	1	VYLLAGE	1
TRIUMPHIS	1	UMBLIS	1	VAYNE GLORIOUS	1	VYLLAYNE	1
TRIVIALS	1	UMWHYLE	1	VAYNE GLORYOUS	1	VYLLONY	1
TRYALYTES	1	UNASSURED	1	VAYNGLORIOUS	1	VYNTRE	1
TRYBYLL	1	UNBLYST	1	VAYNGLORY	1	VYOLATE	1
TRYCE	1	UNBRENT	1	VAYNYS	1	VYOLENCE	1
TRYFYLL	1	UNCOUTHES	1	VALERIUS	1	VYSER	1
TRYFYLS	1	UNCURTEIS	1	VALERY	1	VYSYTACYON	1
TRYHUMFYTHE	1	UNCURTESLY	1	VALIANT	1	VOYCE	1
TRYMBLYTH	1	UNDERMYNDE	1	VALIAUNCE	1	VOLUMES	1
TRYMYNGE	1	UNDERNETH	1	VALY	1	VOLUMIS	1
TRYMME	1	UNDERSET	1	VALYANT	1	VOUCHESAF	1
TRYMMYTH	1	UNDERSTAND	1	VALYAUNCE	1	VOUCHESAFE	1
TRYNALL	1	UNDERSTANDES	1	VALYAUNT	1	VOWCHESAFE	1
TRYNYTE	1	UNDERSTOOD	1	VALYAUNTLY	1	WACHE	1
TRYP	1	UNDERTOKE	1	VALYAUNTOLYE	1	WACHYNG	1
TRYPE	1	UNDO	1	VALUE	1	WADE	1
TRYPPE	1	UNFAYNYD	1	VANYSSHYTH	1	WADED	1
TRYSYD	1	UNFETHERED	1	VANYTE	1	WADYD	1
TRYSTRAM	1	UNFORTUNATELY	1	VANTONNESSE	1	WADYTHE	1
TRYUMPHES	1	UNFRENDLY	1	VARY	1	WAG	1
TRYVYALS	1	UNGOODLY	1	VARYABLENESSE	1	WAGE	1
TROILUS	1	UNHAPLY	1	VARYANS	1	WAGES	1
TROLD	1	UNHAPPYEST	1	VARYETH	1	WAGGE	1
TROLY	1	UNHURT	1	VARNYSHE	1	WAGGES	1
TROLY-LOLY-LO	1	UNICORNE	1	VARRY	1	WAGGYNGE	1

WAGGYS	1	WENGAUNCE	1	WITHDRAW	1	WORDS	1
WAGTAYLE	1	WENYD	1	WITHHOLD	1	WORKYS	1
WAYED	1	WENTBRIDGE	1	WITHSTAND	1	WORME-ETYN	1
WAYGHT	1	WENTWORTHE	1	WITLESSE	1	WORMES	1
WAYLED	1	WEPING	1	WITSTAND	1	WORN	1
WAYWARD	1	WEPINGE	1	WITTIS	1	WORROWYD	1
WAYWARDNESSE	1	WEPYNGE	1	WYCHECRAFT	1	WORS	1
WAYWYRDE	1	WERYED	1	WYCKYDNESSE	1	WORSHYPFULL	1
WAKESTE	1	WERYNG	1	WYCLIFFES	1	WORSHYPFULLY	1
WAKYST	1	WERYNGE	1	WYDDERED	1	WORTES	1
WALD	1	WERKIS	1	WYDERYD	1	WOSE	1
WALIS	1	WERNE	1	WYDOW	1	WOTEST	1
WALYS	1	WERRE	1	WYERFORE	1	WOTETH	1
WALK	1	WERT	1	WYFULL	1	WOTYST	1
WALLET	1	WESANT	1	WYGGES	1	WOTTEST	1
WALLYS	1	WESAUNT	1	WYLAGE	1	WOTTETH	1
WALNUTTES	1	WESELY	1	WYLBE	1	WOTTITH	1
WALOW	1	WESTMINSTER	1	WYLY	1	WOTTYTH	1
WALS	1	WESTMYNSTER	1	WYLLA	1	WOUNDED	1
WALSHEMANNYS	1	WESTMYNSTERE	1	WYLLIS	1	WOUNDERSLY	1
WALTER	1	WETEWOLDIS	1	WYLLY	1	WOUNDID	1
WALTOMS	1	WETHERCOCKE	1	WYLT	1	WRAG-WRAG	1
WAMBLETH	1	WETHER COCKE	1	WYMBLE	1	WRAK	1
WAMBLYNGE	1	WETYNGE	1	WYNCHELSEE	1	WRAKE	1
WANDER	1	WEVYNG PIN	1	WYNCHELSEY	1	WRANG	1
WANDERYNGE	1	WEXYD	1	WYNDES	1	WRANGE	1
WANDRING	1	WHALIS BONE	1	WYNDE-SCHAKYN	1	WRANGLYNG	1
WANDRYNG	1	WHARROWE	1	WYNDY	1	WRANGLYNGE	1
WANE	1	WHATSOMEVER	1	WYNDMIL	1	WRAPT	1
WANFLETE	1	WHEY-WORMED	1	WYNDMYLL	1	WRASTEL	1
WANTID	1	WHELED	1	WYNDOWES	1	WRASTELYNGE	1
WANTYS	1	WHELES	1	WYNKED	1	WRASTELL	1
WANTYTH	1	WHERAT	1	WYNKITH	1	WRASTYNGE	1
WANTONES	1	WHERE OF	1	WYNKYNG	1	WRASTLED	1
WANTONLYE	1	WHEREON	1	WYNKYNGE	1	WRATH	1
WARBLYNG	1	WHERE SOEVER	1	WYNNYS	1	WRAW	1
WARBLYNGE	1	WHEREUPON	1	WYNSHED	1	WRECHES	1
WARDE	1	WHERE WITH	1	WYNSYTH	1	WRECHYD	1
WARELY	1	WHERSO	1	WYNTERS	1	WRECHYDNESE	1
WARENT	1	WHERWYTH	1	WYPID	1	WRECHYDNESSE	1
WARK	1	WHESTON	1	WYRE	1	WREKE	1
WARME	1	WHETE	1	WYRRY	1	WREN	1
WARNED	1	WHETT	1	WYSCH	1	WRENCHIS	1
WART	1	WHIGHT	1	WYSELYE	1	WRESTYD	1
WARTE	1	WHILOM	1	WYSSHE	1	WRESTYNG	1
WASHBOL	1	WHIP	1	WYSSHED	1	WRESTLYNGE	1
WASPIS	1	WHIPLING	1	WYTCH	1	WRETCHE	1
WASPY	1	WHIRLLID	1	WYTCHCRAFT	1	WRETCHEDNESSE	1
WASSHE	1	WHISPRED	1	WYTCLYFTISTA	1	WRETCHID	1
WASSHYNG	1	WHIT	1	WYTE	1	WRETCHOCKES	1
WASTED	1	WHYM-WHAM	1	WYTEYNG	1	WRETE	1
WASTEFULL	1	WHYNARDE	1	WYTHOUT	1	WRINGE	1
WAT	1	WHYNE	1	WYTT	1	WRINGYNG	1
WATCHE	1	WHYNING	1	WODCOKE	1	WRIT	1
WATCHYNGE	1	WHYNNYMEG	1	WODDE	1	WRITEN	1
WATER-LAG	1	WHYP	1	WODDIS	1	WRITINGE	1
WATER MYLLES	1	WHYPSLOVENS	1	WODICOCKE	1	WRITTIN	1
WATHER-HEN	1	WHYRLED	1	WODSTOCKE	1	WRYE	1
WATRY	1	WHYSKYNGE	1	WOFULLY	1	WRYGGES	1
WAWES	1	WHYSPER	1	WOKYS	1	WRYNG	1
WAWYS	1	WHYSPRING	1	WOLDT	1	WRYNKLYD	1
WAXED	1	WHYSTE	1	WOLLE	1	WRYST	1
WEAKLY	1	WHYSTELYTH	1	WOLVIS	1	WRYT	1
WEALE	1	WHYTENES	1	WOLVYS	1	WRYTHEN	1
WEDDER	1	WHYTHER	1	WOMANKYND	1	WRYTHYNGE	1
WEDDYNGE RYNGE	1	WHYTHYR	1	WON	1	WRYTHTYST	1
WEDGE	1	WHYTYNG	1	WONDERFUL	1	WRYTIN	1
WEHE	1	WHYTNESSE	1	WONDERYD	1	WRYTITH	1
WEYED	1	WHYTTE	1	WONDEROWUS	1	WRYTON	1
WEYGHT	1	WHOO	1	WONDERSLY	1	WRONG	1
WEYWARDE	1	WHO SOEVER	1	WONDERUSLY	1	WRONGES	1
WEKES	1	WHRYGHT	1	WONDES	1	WROTES	1
WELAWAYE	1	WIDDERS	1	WONDYR	1	WROTHSOME	1
WELCHE MAN	1	WILY	1	WONDRE	1	WROUNGE	1
WELCHMANS	1	WILLE	1	WONDRED	1	WROUTE	1
WELEAWAY	1	WILLFULL	1	WONDRINGES	1	WROWGHTE	1
WELE PUBLYKE	1	WILLIAM	1	WONNES	1	WURS	1
WELLYS	1	WILLIAMS	1	WONNETH	1	XALTE	1
WELL-SYGHTED	1	WINDYNG STAYRE	1	WONNYS	1	XULDDST	1
WELTYTH	1	WINDMIL	1	WONTONNESE	1	XULDYST	1
WENDE	1	WINS	1	WOODE	1	YALOWE	1
WENEST	1	WINTER	1	WOODECOCKE	1	YANE	1
WENESTE	1	WIRRY	1	WOODES	1	YARKE	1
WENETH	1	WITCHECRAFT	1	WOODHACKE	1	YARNE	1

YATE	1
YAVE	1
YAWDE	1
YCHE	1
YDDER	1
YDELL	1
YDELNES	1
YDEOTTES	1
YDILNES	1
YDOLLES	1
YEA	1
YEDE	1
YEEST	1
YELL	1
YELLED	1
YELLYNGE	1
YER	1
YERES	1
YERIS	1
YERYS	1
YERNE	1
YERTHLY	1
YESTERNYGHT	1
YETT	1
YLKE	1
YMAGENYD	1
YMAGYNACYON	1
YMAGYNACYOUN	1
YMET	1
YMPOSSYBYLL	1
YN	1
YNDE	1
YNK	1
YNOUGH	1
YNOWE	1
YOKE	1
YOMAN	1
YONE	1
YONGLYNG	1
YONKERKYNS	1
YORKES	1
YORKIS	1
YOR SELFE	1
YOUER	1
YOUGHTE	1
YOUTHE	1
YOUWARDE	1
YOWTH	1
YOWTHE	1
YPOCRAS	1
YPOCRYTIS	1
YPOCRUS	1
YRE	1
YTCHE	1
YVELL	1
ZABULON	1
ZALMANE	1
ZEB	1
ZENOPHONTES	1
ZEPHERUS	1
ZEUXES	1
ZODYAKE	1
ZOROBABELL	1

APPENDIX B

Modern Spelling Index

This index will help readers find spelling variants of any word in the concordance. The modern spelling of a word, given at the beginning of each entry, has been taken from *The Oxford English Dictionary*. When homographic lemmata (i.e. two or more headwords spelled the same but with different derivation) occur, the *OED* order of numbering has been adopted; for example, "bale(s *n1*" corresponds to *OED* "bale *sb.*[1]," and "bale *n3*" to *OED* "bale *sb.*[3]." If no grammatical marker is provided for a word, readers may assume that the word is a noun.

Modern spellings shown in roman type and not followed by a square bracket and a suffix occur in the concordance. Those in italic do not occur —only the archaic spellings that follow them are attested.

The presence of a parenthesis or a square bracket in a word reveals which forms of the word occur in the concordance. "Abate(d" indicates that both "abate" and "abated" can be found in the concordance, whereas "abound]e" indicates that the modern spelling "abound" does not occur except as suffixed by a final "e." Common inflectional suffixes are not always listed exhaustively. Thus the verb form "amend(-" is shorthand for "amend amende amended amendyd," and "compass]-" is shorthand for "compasse compassyd." The noun form "blossom(-" stands for "blossom blossome blossoms."

Participial adjectives are sometimes included within finite verb entries; those unaccompanied by finite verb forms are marked *p.a.* Past tense forms and irregular forms of verbs are listed under the infinitive form.

Morphologically related synonyms that appear under two or more headwords in the *OED* are often cross-referenced. See "account" and "accompt," for example.

With the exception of proper names, the index is as complete a record of concordance spellings as we could make it. Readers should appreciate, however, that Skelton's deliberate and extensive use of wordplay, nonce words, dialect forms, and other kinds of rare or nonstandard language made it difficult at times to assign forms to a particular headword with complete confidence.

ABBREVIATIONS

a	adjective
av	adverb
cj	conjunction
comp	comparative
def. art	definite article
indef. art	indefinite article
int	interjection
n	noun
num	numeral
p.a	participial adjective
poss.	possessive
prep	preposition
pron	pronoun
v	verb
v.n	verbal noun (gerund)

a e an *indef.art*
aback]e av
abandon abandune *v*
abash]yth abasshe *v*
abashment abasshement
abate(d v
abbey
abbess]e
abbot
abhor(r(e abhorde *v*
abide abyd- *v*
abiliment abyle- abyly-
   (*cf* habiliment)
ability habylyte
abject]e a
abject]yd v
abjection]s
abjure]d v
able abull hable *a*
abolete a
abominable abhomynable *a*
abomination abhominacion
abound]e v
about(e abowte *av, prep*
above av, prep
abroad abrode *av*
abrogate abbrogate *v*
absence absens
absent a
absolute a
abstract(e a, n
abuse(d -yd v
abuser abusar
abusion -ioun*s* -yo(u)n(s
access axes axys
accessary
accomplish accomplysshe *v*
accomplishment
   accomplysshement
accompt]e n
accompt]- v (cf account)
accord(- acord(e *v*
account n (see accompt)
account acountyd *v*
accumber acomberyd *v*
accuse]th akuse *v*
accustom]e *n*
accustomable *a*
ace ase *n*
ache ake(d *v*
achieve acheve *v*
acquaint aquaynt- aqueint-
   aque(y)nt- *v*
acquaintance acqueint- aquaynt-
   aquent-
acquit a(c)quyte *v*
act]- *n*
action actyon
activity actyvity actyvyty
adamant adyment

adaunt]- *v*
adder]s edders *n2*
addition addicyon
address]yng adres(se *v*
adieu adew(e adue adwe *int*
admiral admyrall admyrell amrell
admit admyt(tes *v*
adropping a-droppynge *p.a*
advance avaunc- avauns- *v*
advantage avauntage
adventure aventure
adversary
adversity adversyte
advertence
advertise advertysyng *v*
advertisement advertys(e)ment
advice a(d)vyse
advise a(d)vys- *v*
advisement advysement(e
afar *av*
afeard aferd(e afferde *p.a*
affability affabilite
affection(s -cyon -tyon
affiance affyaunce *n*
affiance affyaunsynge *v*
affinity affynite -yte
affliction afflictyons afflyccyon
afforce aforce aforse *v*
affray afraye afrayde *v (cf* fray)
afire afyre *av, a*
afloat aflote on-flote *av, a*
afore *av, prep*
aforesaid -sayd *p.a*
afraid afrayd(e *p.a*
Afric Affryc *a*
after aftyr *av, prep*
afterclap]pes
afterdeal after-dele
afternoon afternone
afterward]e *av*
again(e agayn(e ageine ageyn(e
   agenne *av, prep*
against -ayn- -ein- -eyn-
   -en(n)- *prep*
agasp]e *v(?)*
age
agerdows (*i.e.* aigre-doux) *a*
aghast agast *a*
ago *av*
agree(d agre(de *v (cf* gree)
agreeable agreabyll -able *a*
   (*cf* greable)
agreement agreament
aigre-doux (see agerdows)
ail ayl- eyl- *v*
air eyre
alarum *int*
alas(se helas *int*
albeit allbeit *cj*
alcamyne alcumyn

alday]e *av*
alderbest *a (i.e.* allerbest)
ale nale
ale-barm]e
ale-drinker ale drynkers
ale-house
ale-joust
ale-pole
ale-sop[pe
ale-stake
ale-tap(pe
ale-tun]nes
alive onlyve *a*
all(e al *a, n, av*
allay alayd *v*
allective allectyves
allegate allygate *v*
allege lege *v2*
allegiance allegyaunce
alleluia alleluya *int*
allerbest (see alderbest)
alley alys
all-hallow]e
allow alowde alowed *v*
ally alyde *v*
ally aly(e *n*
almanac almanak
almighty allmyghty *a, n*
almond]e almon
almost(e almoost *av*
alms almesse
aloe]s alowes
aloft(e av
alone allone *av*
also av
altar aulter auter
altar-stone auter stone
alteration alteracyon
altercation altercacyons
   altrycacyon
although *cj*
alway(e all- *av*
am *(see* be)
Amalec(ke
amaze amased -id *v*
amber
ambition ambycyon
ambitious ambicious -cyous *a*
amen *av, int, sb*
amend(- v
amendment
amends amendis amendys amense
amiable amyabyll amyable *a*
amice amysse ammas
amiss amis amys(se *av, a*
amity amyte
among(e *prep, (av)*
amongst amongest *prep*
amount v
ample a

amplify amplyfy *v*
amrell *(see* admiral*)*
an *indef.art*
analogy
analytical analetycall *a*
ancestry auncetry
anchor anker *n1,2*
ancient auncient auncyent(e *a, (n)*
anciently auncyently *av*
and *cj*
angelic angelyk *a*
anger angre *v*
anger ang(g)re *n*
angerly *av*
angry *a*
animosity animosite
annex(yd *v*
annual]l *a*
annoyance anoyance *n*
anointed anoynted *p.a*
anon]e *av*
another(s anothyr anodyr *a, pron*
answer]e aunswere *n*
answer]- answere *v*
ant
antetheme antetyme
Antiochus
antiquity antyquyte
any ony *a, pron*
anything -thyng(e ony- *pron, n, av*
anywhere ony- *av*
apace apase *av*
apaid apay(e)d *p.a*
apart(e *av*
ape]s
apostate apostata(as
apostle apostyll -els *(cf* postle*)*
apostrophation -facyon
apothecary (see pothecary*)*
appair apayere appa(y)re *v*
appall(e *v*
apparel]l apparayle
apparently *av*
appear apere apper- *v*
appetite appetyte(s
apple(s appels
apple-tree apple tre
apply(e(d *v*
appoint apoynted *v (cf* point*)*
appointment (see pointment*)*
appose(d *v*
apposal apposelle
approach ap(p)roche *v*
apt]e *a*
aptly]e *av*
arbour herber(s
arctic artike artyke *a, n*
are *(see* be*)*
argue(d *v*
argument(es

Arian Arryans
arise aryse *v*
ark]e
arm]es armys *n1,2*
arm]- *v1*
Armenian hermoniake
armoury armory *n (cf* armory *n2)*
army(e
aromatic armatycke *a*
a-row]e *av*
arras arace arayse Arres
array arayd *v*
array aray(e(s *n (cf* ray *n3)*
arrearage arerage
arrect(- arect- *v (cf* erect*)*
arrive aryvyd *v*
arrow arow narrow
arse ars
art]e *n*
article artycles
as *av, cj*
ascend]ynge *v*
ascendent a
ascribe ascrybed *v*
ascry(e askry escrye *v*
ascry askrye *n*
ash asshes
ashamed p.a
aside asyde *av*
ask(- *v*
asleep aslepe *a*
aspect]e
aspy(- *v (cf* espy*)*
ass]e
assail assayle *v*
assault assawte *(cf* sault*)*
assay]- asayde *v*
assay]es *n*
assemble]d *v*
assent(e
assign assygn- assyn- *v*
assignment assignement
assist assyst(e *v*
assistance assystence
assoil assoyle *v*
assuage as(s)wage *v*
assurance assuraunce
assurd]ed *v*
assure(- *v*
astate astatis *(cf* estate*)*
astonied astonyed *p.a*
astray *a,av*
astrolabe astroloby
astrolog]ys *n*
astrology
astronomer
astronomy
asunder asonder asondre *av*
at att *prep*
atame attamed *v*

athirst athrust *a*
attain attayne -eyne *v*
attainted attaynted atteintid *p.a*
attemperance attemperaunce
attendance attendaunce
attire atyre
audience audyence
aught oughte
augment v
aureate aureat *a*
Austin Austen *a*
author auctor
authority au(c)tority
autumn autumpne
authentic autentyke *a*
avail avayl- avale *v*
avaunt avauns *n1*
avaunt avent *v*
Ave *n*
avoid avoydynge *v*
avow]e *n*
avow]ed *v*
away(e *av*
await awayte *v, n*
awe
awkward auquarde *a*
awl nall
awry]e *a*
ay(e *av*
aye ay *int*
azure asure
ba *v (cf* bass, buss*)*
babble bable *v*
babble babell *n*
babion (baboon) babyone
baby babi
bachelor -eler(s
back(- bak(e *n, (av)*
back-bone backe bone
bacon bakon
bacon-flitch bacon flycke
bad(de *a*
badness badnes
bag]ge
bagpipe bagpype
bail]e *v(?)*
bail]e *n*
bailiff baillyve ballyvis
bait bayt- bate *v*
bait bayte beyght beyte *n*
bake *v*
balas(sis *n*
balance balaunce *n*
bald]e *a*
bale(s *n1*
bale *n3*
balk]e *n*
ball *n1*
ballad]e balad- balettys
ballad-book balade boke

balm bawm- *n*
ban(ne *v*
band]is *n1* (*cf* bond)
band n3 (*see* bend *n3*)
band]yd bended *v*
bane(s *n1*
banish bannesht bannisshed
　　ban(n)y(s)sh- *v*
bank]- *n1*
banner baner
banqueting banketyng(e *v.n*
bar]rid -yd *v*
bar(re(s *n1*
bararag
barbel]lis *n*
barbed barbyd *p.a*
barbican
bare *a*
barge
bark(- *v1*
barley-hood barlyhood
barn]e
barnacle *n2*
baron(e)s
baronage
barratous baratows *a*
barrel barelles
barren barayne barreyne *a*
base bace *a*
basely]e *av*
basin basyn
basinet basnet
bask]ed *v*
bass bas *n3*
bass]- bas *v1* (*cf* ba, buss)
bastard]e *a*
basting bastyng *v.n1*
bate *n1*
bathe]d -yd baththed *v*
battle batayle batell battayle
bauble babyl(le)s
bawd]e baud *n1*
bawd baudeth *v1*
bawdias bawdyas
bawdry baudry *n1*
bawdry *n2*
bawdy baudy *a1,2(?)*
bay *n4*
bayard]e
bayard's bun bayardys bun
be bee(n ben(e beyng(e am
　　ar(r)e art(e is was wer(e wert
　　ys nys *v*
bead bedes
beadle bedell
bead-roll bed(d)e roule(s
　　bede rolle(s
beak becke bek(e
beaked becked *a*
beam]e(s bemis

bean]es bene(s
bear(e ber(- bare borne *v1*
bear]es bere(s beris *n1*
beard beerd berde *n*
bearded berded *a*
beast beest(es best(e bestis
beat bet(e beaten beten *v1*
beauteous bewteous(e *a*
beauty(e beaute bewte
because bi- by- *av, cj*
beck beks *v*
beckoning bekenynge *v.n*
become(th -yth became *v*
bed(des
bedaw]yd *v*
bedene bydene *av*
bedfellow bedfellaw
bedlam bedleme
bee byes byse(?) *n1*
beetle betell *n1*
befall befell *v*
befool befo(u)le *v*
before *av, prep*
beg begg- *v*
begair begared *v*
beggar]s begger(s
beggars bag beggers baggys
beggary
begging beggynge *v.n*
begin begyn(- began(n)e
　　begon(e *v*
beguile begyl- *v*
behave behavyd -ynge *v*
behaviour behavoure
behind(e behynd(e *av, prep*
behold(e behelde *v*
beknave beknavyd *v*
bel]e *a*
belapped p.a
belief byleve
believe beleve byleve *v*
belim belimn(?) belymmed *v*
bell belle(s bellys bels
bellman belman
bellow belluyng *v*
belly bely(es
belly-joy bely-joye
belong]- *v*
bemol]e *n*
bench]e
bend bent(e *v*
bend]e *n3*
benefice benefyce *n*
beneficed benyfyced *p.a*
benevolence
benign bening(n)e benygne
　　benynge *a*
benignity benignite beny(n)gnyte
bequeath bequeth(e *v*
beryl birall

beseech besech- beseke
　　besought *v*
beseem beseme *v*
beseen besene *p.a*
beshrew(- beshrowe bechrewde *v*
beside besyde bysyde *av, prep*
best(e *a, av*
bested, bestead bestad(de *p.a*
bestial bestyall *a*
bestow]de *v*
betake *v*
betime be tyme *av*
betoken]eth *v*
betrap]ped *v2*
betray(d *v*
better *a, av*
better(s *n*
between betweyn betwen(e
　　bytwene *av, prep*
bevy beve
bewail bewayle *v*
beware *v*
bewrapped *p.a*
bewray bewreye *v*
beyond(e byyonde *av, prep*
bibble bybyll *v*
bible byble bybille bybyll
bible-clerk bybyll clarke
bice byse *a, n*
bid byd bad(e bed *v*
bide byde bode *v*
biding bydyng *v.n*
big bygge *a*
bill bil byl(- *n1,2,3*
bind bynd(e bounde *v*
bird]e birdis byrd(e(s
bird-bolt
birle byrle *v*
birth byrth
bishop bysshop(p)es
bit byt *n2*
bite byt(- bote *v*
bitter bytter *a*
bittern better
bitterness bytternesse
blabber blaber *v*
black(e blak(e *a, n*
blain blaynes
blame *n*
blame(d *v*
blameless]e -les *a*
blanched blaunched *p.a*
blanked blanket *p.a* (*cf* blunket)
blast(e *n*
blast]yd *v*
blaze blase *n1*
blaze blased *v1*
blaze blasy *v2*
blear bler- *v1*
blee ble

bleed bled(- *v*
blemish blemysshed *v*
blend blennes *v2*
bless]- blys(- *v1*,2
blessed -yd blissed *p.a*
blessing blissyng blyssyng *v.n*
blether (see bluther)
blind blynde *a*
blinded blynded *p.a*
blindness blyndnes(se
bliss blis blys(se
blinkard blenkardis blynkerd(?)
blinkered blynkerd(?) *p.a*
blommer
blood(e blode
blossom(- *n*
blot *v*
blow(- blew(e *v1*
blow-bowl blowboll
blowing blowyng *v.n*
blue blew(e blo(o *a, n*
blunder *v*
blunderer blunderar
blundering -yng *v.n*
blunket blanket *a*
bluntly *av*
blur (?) blurre
bluster *v*
bluther blother *v*
boar bore
boar-pig bore pygge
board borde(s burde *n*
board borded *v*
boast boost bost(e *n*
boast boost boste *v1*
boat bote
bob]be *v2*
bodily bodely *av, a*
body(e)s
boil boyl- *v*
boistous boystors *a*
bold(e *a*
boldly(e -ely *av*
boldness boldenes
bolt]e *n1*
bolted boltyd *p.a*
bondtenant bonde tenent
    bounde tenauntes
bone(s -ys
bone-ache bone ake
boned bayned(?) *a*
bonnet bonet
bonne a, n
bonny a, n
boo bo *int*
boohoo bo-ho *int*
book]e boke(s bokys
boot bote *n1*
boot bote(s *n3*
bootless boteles *a1*

border(s
boreal boryall *a*
born]e *p.a*
borough borowgh
borrow borowe(d *v1*
borrowing borowynge *v.n*
boscage boskage
bosom]e
bot]tes
botch]es *n1*
botchment
botew batowe
both(e *a, av*
bottle bot(t)ell *n2,3*
bottom]s botowme
bottomless bot(t)umles *a*
bouge bowche bowge *n2*
bough bowghis
bounce bouns- bowns *n*
bouncingly bounsyngly *av*
bound]e bonde *p.a*
bound bowndis *n1*
bound *n2*
bounty bounte bownte
bousy bowsy *a*
bow *v1*
bow(- *n1*
bower boures bowr- bowur *n1*
bowl]e bol(l)e boule *n1*
box(e *n2*
boy]es
brabbling brablyng *v.n*
brace brased *v1 (cf* embrace)
brace bracyd *v2*
bracelet
bracer]s
brag(- *v*
brag]ge *n1*
bragging braggynge *v.n*
braid brayde
brain]e brayn-
brained brayned *a*
brainless -les braynles(se *a*
brain-pan brayne-pan
    braynpannys
brainsick braynsy(c)k(e
    brayne seke *a*
brake *n3,6*
branch braunches
brand]e bronde
brass]e bras
brawl]- brall(e braule *v*
brawler braules(?)
bray]ed *v1*
bread bred(e breed
bread-crumb bred crommes
break breke(s brake broken
    brokyn *v*
bream bremis
breast brest(e(s

breath breth(e
brede n2 (cf breadth)
breed brede bredth bred(de *v*
breme brym(me *a*
bremely brymly *av*
brethren brethern
breviate brevyate *v*
brew(e(th *v*
brewhouse
briar brere
bribance brybaunce
bribe brybe *n*
bribery brybery bryboury
bridge bryge
bridle brydyll *n*
bridle brydell *v*
bridling-cast brydelynge caste
briefly brefly brevely *av*
bright bryght *a, av*
brimstone brynston
bring(- bryng(- brought(e
    browght *v*
bristle bristels brystell
bristled brystled *p.a*
Bristol-red Brystowe red
Briton]s
broad brode brood *a*
broadcloth brode clothe
brock broke *n1*
broil broylyd *v1*
brook broke *n*
brook broke *v*
brothel]l(s
brother broder
brow(es -ys
brow-antler brow-auntleres
browed browde *a*
brown]e *a*
bruise broisiours *n*
bruise bresyth broisid brose *v*
bruit brute *n*
bruit bruted -id *v*
buck *n1*
buckle bockyll buckel-
buckram bukram
bucolical bucolycall *a*
budge-fur]re
budget bougets bowget
build byld- buyld- *v*
building beldyng *v.n*
bulk]e *n1*
bull bole(?) *n1*
bull]es -ys *n2*
bullifant bullyfant
bullion bullyons *n3*
bulwark]e
bum]me *n1*
bump]e *n2*
bun *n2*
bungler

burbling -yng *p.a*
burden bordon
burgess burgeis
burn]- byrne bren- bryn- *v1*
burn bourne *v2, (p.a?)*
burnish burneshed burnissheth *v1*
burr]is *n1?4?*
burst brast *v*
bush bussheth *v1*
bushment
busily bysely *av*
business busy-ness besines
    besynes(se
busk]- *v1*
buskin buskyn
busy besy bysy *a*
but bute bot *cj (prep)*
butcher bocher(s
butt]es *n4*
butter
butterfly(e -flyis
butting buttyng *n*
button bottons
buy bye boght bought(e *v*
buzzard bussarde
by be *prep*
by(r)lakin (see lakin)
cabbage cabagyd *v1*
cable-rope (cf gable-rope)
cacodemonial cacademonyall *a*
cage
Caiaphas Cayface Cayfas
cain cane *n1*
caitiff caytyfe -yvys
cake
calends kalendas
calf]e *n1*
calfless calfles *a2*
calf's head calvys hedes
calkin kalkyns
call(- cal(- kall *v*
callet calettes
calodemonial calodemonyall *a*
calstock]e (*i.e.* kale-stock)
cammock]e camoke *n2*
camoisly camously *av*
camomile camamell
can(- kan koude kowd coud(e
    cowde cold *v1 (cf* con *v1)*
candle candyll
Candlemas Candelmas -mes
canker cancour
canker(e)d cankard(e *p.a*
cannot cannat (*cf* can *v1*)
canon *n1*
canon chanon(s *n2*
canonical]l *a*
canonically av
cantle cantell
canvas canves

cap(pe *n1*
capital capytall *a*
capital]l *n2*
capon(s
capped cap(p)yd *p.a*
captain]e capitayne -(y)tayne(s
    -ten
captation captacyons
captiously capcyously *av*
captive captyfe
captivity captyvyte
carbuncle carbuckyls charbuncles
carcass]e carkas carkes *n*
card]- *n2*
carder]s *n2*
cardinal]s cardynall(es -ynals
cardinal-hat cardynal-
care *n1*
care carede *v*
careful]l *a*
carefully av
careless careles carles(se *a*
cark]e *v*
carl]- karlis *n*
carline carlyng *n1*
carlish carlyshe *a*
carnal]l *a*
carol]lis
carp(e *v*
carpet(tis *n*
carry cary(- cariid caried *v*
cart *n*
carter *n1*
cart-load cart lode
carven *p.a*
case(s *n1,2*
casket *n1*
cass]eth *v*
cast *n*
cast(- kast kest kyste *v*
casting castyng *v.n*
castle castell
casual]l *a*
casualty casuelte caswelte
cat(t(e(s *n1*
catacomb catacumbas
catch(- cach(- caught(e caw(gh)te
    cought *v*
cateran keteryng(es
cathedral]l *a*
cattle catell
caudle caudell cawdels
caury-maury cawry-mawry
cause(- causyth cawsythe *v*
cause(s -is *n*
causeless causeles *a*
cave]s *n1*
cavel]l *n2*
cease cese sease *v*
celestine celestyne *a*

cement sement
cense sence senseth *v*
censer sensers *n1*
Centaur]es -awris
ceremonial]lys *n*
certain certayne *av*
certain certayne *a*
certainty certeynte
chaffer chafer chaffre *n1*
chain chayn(e(s cheynes
chair chayre chare(s *n1,2*
chalcedony calcydony
chalice chalys
chalk]e
challenge chalenge *n*
challenge chalen(n)ge
    chalyngyd *v*
challenger chalanger
    chalen- chalyn-
chamber chambre(s chaumber
champion champyon
chance chaunce *n*
chance chaunce *v*
chancellor chauncelar
chancery chauncery
change chaunge(d *v*
change chaunges *n*
chanter chaunters
chanticleer chaunteclere
chant chawntyd chauntyng *v*
chanting chauntyng *v.n*
chaplain chaplayne -eyne
chaplet chapelet -ellettes
chapter chapiter
char]e(s *n2 (cf* chair *n2)*
charact carect-
chare *v*
charge *n*
charge *v*
charity charite -yte cheryte
charm]e *n1*
charm chermed *v*
charming charmyng *v.n*
charter *n1*
chase chace *n1*
chase(th *v1*
chaste chast *a*
chat *v1*
chatter(- chater- *v*
chating -yng *v.n*
cheap chepe *n*
check]e *n1*
check]e(d chek- checte *v1,2*
check-mate che(c)k(e)- *int, n, v*
cheek cheke(s
cheer chere
cheese chese
chequer checker
cherish cherys(s)h- *v*
cherry chery

921

cherry-stone cheryston
chess]e *n1*
cheving chevynge
chevisance chevysaunce *n1*
chew]e *v*
chick cheke
chicken checkynges
chide chyd- *v*
chief chefe *n*
chief chef(e chyef chyfe *a*
chieftain cheftayn(e chyfteyne
child chyld(-
chimney chymneyes
chin chyn
chincherd chyncherde
chip chyppes *n1*
chiromancy ciromancy
chivalry chevalry
choir quere
choose chose chuse *v*
chop]pe(d *v2*
chorister queresters querysters
chough chowgh
Christ-cross]e Cristecrosse
Christian Christen Chrysten *a*
chronicle cronycle
chronicler crownycler
chrysolite grossolitis
chuck chuk *n1*
church(e(s chyrche
church-door church dores
churl]es
churlish -ysshe chorlyshe *a*
cinnamon synamum
circlet cerculett
circumspect a
circumspection cyrcumspection -cyon
circumspectly av
circumstance cyrcumstance -staunce
citation citacyons cytacyon
cite syght *v*
city cities cyte(s cytie cytye
civil cyvyll *a*
clad p.a
claim]ist *v*
clap(pys *n1*
clap(p- *v1*
clarion clariouns
clarioner clarionar
clasp]is *n*
clatter(s clater(- clatyr *v*
clatterer claterars
clattering clat(t)erynge
clause(s clawes
clavichord clavycordys
clay
clean]e clene *a*
clean clene *av*

cleanly clenly *av*
cleanness clennesse
clear clere *a*
clearer clerer *comp.av*
clearly clerely *av*
clearness clereness
cleave cleve *v1*
cleft clyfte *n*
clemency
clench
clepe *v*
clerestory
clergy]e
clerk]- clark-
clerkly clerkely *a*
clerkly clerkely *av*
clicket-gate klycked gate
cliff]es
climb clyme clymmeth *v*
clipping-shears clyppyng sheres
clitter clyttreth *v*
cloak clok(e(s -ys *n*
cloak cloke(d -yd *v*
clock]e *n1*
cloister cloyster
close *av*
close(d -yd *v*
clot
cloth(-
clothe clad *v*
clothes
clothing -ynge *v.n*
cloth-making clothe makynge
cloud]is clowd-
cloudy clowdy *a*
clout(e clowtes *n1*
clout(e *v*
club]be
clubbed clobbyd *p.a*
cluster]s closters
co]e *n1*
coal cole(s colles
coal-dust cole dust
coal-rake cole rake
coarct coarte(d *v*
coarse cours *a*
coast coost coste *n*
coast coost *v*
coat cote(s
coat-armour cote-armur(e
cobble -ill *v1*
cock]- cok- *n1,2,8*
cocking v.n1
cockly a1
cock's-comb cockes come
cock-sure a
coffer cofer(s
coffer-key cofer kay
cognizance cognisaunce conu-
coif coyfe

coin coyne(s
coinage kownnage
coinquinate conquinate *v*
cold(e *a*
cold(e *n*
coliander colyaunder
collation colation
college collage
collop coloppe
collusion -syon collucyoun colusyon
colour(- colowre colowur coulour
colour]yd coluryd *v*
columbine columbyn(e *n2*
combine conbyned *v*
come com(- cam- cum- kum- *v*
comedy comedies commedy comody
comely comly cumly *a*
comely *av*
comfort(e con- coun- *n*
comfort *v*
comfortable *a*
comfortably *av*
comicar
command commaund- *v*
commandment comma(u)ndemen(n)t
commemoration commemoracion
commence commens- *v*
commend]- commaunde(?) *v*
commendable -byll comendable *a*
commendation -acio(u)n -acyo(u)n
commission commissyon *n1*
commit]tyth commyt(t)- *v*
commodity commoditis
common]- -ouns *n1*
common comon *n2*
common -oun -owne *a*
commonalty cominalte communalte
commoner]s
common hall comyne hall
common pleas commune place
commonweal comyn- commune-
commonwealth commune welth
commune commaunde comonynge *v*
commune common *n2*
communication communicacion communycacyon
company
compare -yd *v1*
comparison comparyson
compass compas *n1*
compass]- compas(t *v1*
compassion compassyon
compendiously compendyously *av*

competent *a*
compile -id compyl- *v*
complain]e complayn- *v*
complaint complaynt(e(s
compound(e *v*
comprehend]ynge *v*
comprise(d -id -yde comprys- *v*
con]d *v1* (*cf* can *v1*)
conceit -ceyght -ceyte -sayte -seyt
conceive conceyved *v*
conception concepcion
concerning -yng consernynge
conclude *v*
conclusion -ious -yo(u)n(s
concrete *a*
condescend condiscend
condyscend
condition condityons
condicion -ycion
conduct]e *n1*
conduit condute coundight
cundight
confection confectioun
confecture(s
confeder confet(t)- *v*
confess]yng *v*
confirmable confyrmable *a*
confluence conflewence
confound]e *v*
confused *p.a*
confusion confusyon
confutation confutacion
confute]d -id *v*
congruence
congruently *av*
conject(e *v*
conjecture
conjugation conjugacyons
conjuration conjuracions -cyon
conjure *v*
conquest]ys
conscience consciens conscyence
consecrate -yd *v*
consent concente *n*
consent(e concente *v*
consequently *av*
consider consyder *v*
consideration consyderacion
-cyon(s
consistory consystory
consolation consolacyo(u)n
consolatory *a*
constant *a*
constantly *av*
constellation constellacion(s
-cyon
constitution constytucyon
constrain constrayn- constreyn- *v*
construction -tyon
construe constrewe *v*

consultation -cion
consume]th *v1*
contain]e contayn- conteyn- *v*
contaminate contemminate *v*
contemplation -cyo(u)n(s
contend]e *v*
content *n1*
content *a*
content(e *v*
contenu contynewe *n*
continence countenaunce
continue contynued contyn(e)w(- *v*
continual contynuall *a*
continually -y- *av*
contradiction -yons -dicc- -dycc-
contrary *n*
contrite contryte *a*
contrition contrycion
contrive contryv- *v1*
control]- controule *v*
conusance -aunce *v*
(*cf* cognizance)
convenable *a*
convenient -yent *a*
conveniently convenyently *av*
convent *v*
convent covent *n*
conventual conventuall *a*
conversation -cyon
convert(- *v*
convey(- convay(e)d *v*
conveyance -aunce -auns convay-
cony conny
cool coleth *v*
coot]e cote kote *n1*
cope *n1*
copious copy(o)us *a*
copiously copyously *av*
copper *n1*
copyhold]e copyehold
cordelier cordylar
cordial cordyall
coriander (*see* coliander)
cormorant -erant -oraunce
corn]- *n1*
corner *n1*
Cornucopia
coronal c(o)ronell
corporas
corpse (*see* corse)
correct(e(d *v*
correction(s -cyon -tyon
corse cors
cosmography
cost(e *n2*
cost *v*
costermonger
costious *a*
cottage cotage
couch]- cowchyd *v*

couch-quail cowche-quale
cough(e *v1*
cough cowghe *n*
could (*see* can)
counsel(l(e -cell -sayle -seyle *n*
counsel]l counsayle *v*
counsellor counselour
count]e *n1*
count]e *n2(?)*
count(- *v*
countenance countenaunce
-ynaunce contenons
cowntenaunce
counter(- -yr cownt(e)r(ed *v2*
counter *n3*
counterfeit
counterfayt- counterfe(y)t-
conter- cownter- *v*
counterfeit -fet- *a, n*
counterfeiting -faytynge *v.n*
countering countrynge *v.n1*
countering counteryng *v.n2*
counterweigh -way(ng *v*
countess countes cowntes
country contre cuntreis kuntrey
couple
courage cor(r)age
courageous coragius *a*
course
courser]s *n2*
court(e corte cowrte *n1*
courteous corteise curte(y)s(e
kurteis *a*
courteously curteisly curteslye
courtesy curtesy
courtier courtyer
courtly courtely cowrtly *a*
court roll courte rowlis
covering -ynge *v.n1*
coverlet
covert]e *a*
covertly *av*
coverture
covet *v*
covetise covetys(e
covetous covytous *a*
covetousness covytousnesse
cow kowe(s
coward(e(s *n*
coward]e *a*
cowardly *a*
cowardly *av*
cowardness]e
coy]e koy(e *a*
crack(- crake *n*
crack]e(d crak- *v*
cracker crakar crakers
cradle cradel-
craft(e
crafter]s

craftily craftely *av*
crafting craftynge *v.n*
crafty *a*
crag *n2*
crane(s -ys *n1*
crave(d -ynge *v*
craving -ynge *v.n*
craw(es
craze crase(d *v*
crazy crasy *a*
creak creke(th *v*
cream creme
creancer creauncer creaunser
create creat *v*
creation creacyo(u)n
creature
credence *n*
credence credensynge *v*
creed crede
creep crepe crept *v*
crib]bis
crime cryme
crimson crimsin *a*
crinkled crynklyd *p.a*
croak v (see creak)
crook croke *n*
crook crokys *v1*
crooked croked -yd *a*
crook-nebbed crokenebbed *a*
crop(e croppy(?) *n*
crop]ped -yd *v*
croppy
crose
cross]e cros *n (cf* crouch *n1)*
cross]ed *v*
crossing -yng *v.n*
cross-row crosse rowe
crouch]e *v1*
crouch crowche *n1*
crow(e *n1*
crow(e(th crewe crue krew *v*
crowd]yng *v1*
crown]e(s croune *n*
crown]de -yd *v*
crude *a*
cruel]l *a*
cruel-hearted cruell hertyd *a*
cruelly *av*
cruelty cruelte
crumb crommes
cruse cruyse
cry *n*
cry(- craynge(?) *v*
crystal christall cristall
crystalline crystallyne *a*
cuck(ing)-stool cooke-stole
cuckold]es cok(w)oldes
co(c)k(e wat(tes
cuckoo cuckoue kukkowe
cue kues *n1*

cule
culrage colerage
culver
cumber combred -eryd *v*
cumbrance comberaunce
cumbrous comerous *a*
cunning cunnynge con(n)yng(e konnyng *v.n*
cunning cunnyng connyng(e *a*
cunningly cunnyngly connyngly *av*
cup(pe
cupboard cupbord(e
cur curr kur kurris
curate(s
cure *n1*
cure]d *v1*
curious curyows *a*
curiously cury- coryously curiowsly *av*
curlew]e
current -ant *a*
currishly curryshly *av*
curry coryed *v1*
curse curs *n*
curse(d curst *v*
cursedly cursydly *av*
curtain curteyns
curtal curtel curtoyl
cushion cousshons quysshon quosshons
custom]e
custrel]l
custron coystrowne
cut(tys *n2*
cut kit kyt kuttyth *v*
cuckoldry cokoldry
daddy dady
dagged daggid *p.a1,2*
dagger
dagswain daggeswane dagswayne
daily dayly *a, av*
daintily dayntely deyntely *av*
dainty deynte(s *n*
dainty deynte denty *a*
dais dese
daisy da(y)sy deysy
daisy-flower daysy floure
dale *n1*
dalliance dalyaunce delyaunce
dally daly *v*
Dallyrag Dalyrag Delarag
dam *n2*
damage domage
dame
damnable dampnable *a*
damnation dampnacyon
damsel dammoysels damosell
dan dane *n1*
dance daunce dawnce *n*

dance daunce(d dauns(- dawnce dawns(- *v*
Dane]s
danger daunger
dangerous daungerous *a*
dant *n1*
dare dar(- darre durse durst(e *v*
dark]e *a*
dark derke *n*
dark]es *v*
darkness derkenes
darling darlyng(e derl- *a, n*
dart(e
dash dasshed *v*
dastard]e
date(s *n1*
date *n2*
date datyd *v*
daw(-
dawcock(e daucocke(s Dawcok- Dawkock(e
dawpate
day(-
day-watch day-wach
daze das- *v*
dazzle dasild *v*
dead(e ded(e deed *a*
deadly ded(e)ly deedly *a*
deadman deedmans
deaf deefe *a*
deal]e deall dele dell *n*
deal]- dele(th -ynge delt *v*
dean]es *n1*
dear dere *a*
dear dere *av*
dearly derely *av*
death deth(e
debar]re *v*
debate(s *n*
debt det
decachord decacorde
decade decadis
decay *n*
decay]- dekay *v*
deceit dyscayte -ceyght -(c)eyte
deceive disceyve dyssayv- disseyved *v*
deck]e *n*
deck]e(d decte dekkyd *v*
declamation declamacyons
declare(th *v*
decline declyne *v*
decollation decollacyon
decrease (see discrease)
decree]s decre
decretal]-
dedicate *v*
deed dede(s dedys
deem dem- dempte *v*
deep depe *a*

deeply depely *av*
deer dere
deface]s -id *v*
defame]d dyffame *v*
default defaut(e
defence defens
defend(e(th deffend *v*
defender defendar
defile (see file *v*2)
deformity deformite
defoul defoyle(d *v*
defy]e *vl*
degree(s degre
deignously daynnously *av*
deity deite deyte
delay *n*
delay(- *v*
delectable -abyll dylectable *a*
delectably *av*
delectation -cyon(s
deliberation delyberacion -cyon
delicate delycate *a*
delicately delycatelye *av*
delight delyght delyte *n*
delight delite delyte *v*
deliver delyver(ed *vl*
demand demaunde demawnd *nl*
demand demaund- *v*
demean]e demen- *vl*
demeanance deme(y)naunce
demeaning demenyng *v.n*
demeanour demenour
demency demensy
demerit demeryttes
demi-divine demy divines
demonstration demonstracyon
demure *a*
demy]e *n*
den(ne(s *nl*
denomination denominacyons
deny]ed denayd *v*
depart]e(d *v*
depend]ed *v*
deprave -yd *v*
depute -yd *v*
deraign derayne *vl*
derision derisyon dyrysyon
derogate *v*
derogation derogacyo(u)n
descant dyscant
descend]- *v*
description discripcion
descrive dyscryve(d *v*
descry dyscry *v*
deserve(d -yd *v*
deserving deservynge *v.n*
desire desyer desyre desyris *n*
desire desyr- dysiryd *v*
desirous desyrous *a*
desolate *a*

desolation
despair dispare dyspaire
    dyspa(y)re
despise despyse dispyse
    dyspyse(d *v*
despite despy(gh)t(e dis- dys-
despiting despytynge
    dispytynge *v.n*
destiny desten(n)y destyny *n*
destroy dystroy *v*
desyte *v*
determine determyn- *v*
detestable *a*
detraction]s detraccion detractyon
    detraxion
deuce deuz *nl*
device devisis devyse divisis *n*
devil]l devyl(l)(- dyvyls
devilish devyl(l)ys(s)he devel- *a*
devilishly devyllysshely *av*
devise devys- dyvys- *v*
deviser devyser
devising devysynge *v.n*
devoid devoyde
devotion devocion devocyon
devout]e *a*
devoutly *av*
dew]e
diadem dyademe
dialectical dialeticall *n*
dialogue diologgis
diamond diamauntis diamounde
    dy(a)mand dyamounde *n*
dicer dyser(s dysour
dict]es
diddle-diddle didil diddil
die dyce dyse *n*
die dy(- *vl*
diet]tes dyet *nl*
diet dyetyd *v*
difficile difficille *a*
diffuse dyffuse *a*
dig dyg(geth *v*
dignity dignite dignyte dygnyte(s
dike dykes
dilate delated *v*
diligence delygence *nl*
diligent dylygent *a*
din(ne dyn
dine dyn- *v*
ding dynge *v*
dint dynt(-
direct dyrecte *v*
direct *a*
direction dyreccyon
    dyrection(s -tyon
dirge dyriges
dirt dyrt
dirty dyrty durty *a*
disable *v*

disavail(ing) dysavaylynge *v*
discern]e *v*
discharge dyscharg- *v*
discharge *n*
disclose(d *v*
discomfect *p.a*
discommend](e *v*
discord]e dyscorde(s
discourage discorage *v*
discover discured discurid
    dyscure *v*
discrease dyscrease
discreet discrete dyscrete *a*
discretion dyscrecion -ssyon
discure (see discover)
discuss discust dyscus(t *v*
disdain disdayn(e dysdayn- *n*
disdain disdayn- dysdayne(d *v*
disdainous dysda(y)nous *a*
disdainously dysdayneslye
    -ously *av, a*
disease dyesease *n*
disease dyseased -yd *v*
disgorge dysgorged *v*
disguise disgysede dysgysed *v*
dish dysh dysshes
dish-clout dyscheclowte
dish-washer dyshwasher
disloyal]l *a*
dismay dysmayde *v*
dismember dysmembre *v*
disorder dysorder- *v*
disparage(d dys- *v*
dispense despensyth *v*
display]d *v*
displeasance dyspleasaunce
displeasant displeasaunt *a*
displease dysplease(th *v*
displeasure dyspleasure
disport]e dysport(e
disposed dysposed -yd *p.a*
disposition dysposycyons
disputation dysputacyon
dispute]d dyspute *v*
dissemble dyssemble *v*
dissension dyssencyon
dissimulation dyssymulacyon
dissimuler dyscymular
    dyssymuler
dissimuling dyssymulynge *v.n*
dissuasive dissuasyve *n*
distain desteynyd *v*
distance dystaunce
distich]on
distinction]s
distress distres dystres(se
ditch dyche
ditty diti(i)s dyties
dive-dap dyvendop
divers deverse dyvers(e *a, n*

925

diversity dyversyte
divide devydyd *v*
divine devyne *v*
divine divyne dyvyne *a*
divinity divinite devinyte divyn-
division -syon devysion dyvysyon
divorce devors(e *v*
dizzy dyssy *a*
do(- dedde did dyd(e *v*
doctor doctour(s
doctrine doctryne
doddy-pate doddy patis
dog(ge(s doggys
doggerel dogrell
dogmatist]a dagmatista
doleful]l(e doulfull *a*
dolorous dolorus *a*
dolorously *av*
dolour dolowr-
dominion domynyon
doom dome
Doomsday Domesday
door dore(s dur
door-gate doregate
dormouse dormows
dotage dottage(s
dotard doterdis
dote(d dotynge *vI*
dotterel doterell -yll dotrellis
double dowbyll dowble *a*
double-cope
double-dealing -delinge -delyng(e
doubleness]e -nes dowblenes
double-tongue double tunge(s
doubt dought dout(t)- *v*
doubt dout(e dowte(s *n*
doubtful]l dowghtfull *a*
doubtless doutles(se
dowtles(s(e *av*
dough dowe
doughty(est dout(t)y dowty *a*
douzepers dowsypere
dove dow(ves
down(e doune *av*
dozen dosen
drab]bes *nl*
draff]e
dragon(es
drake *n2*
dram]mes *nl*
drapery drapry
draught drawttys
draw(e(n drew(e *v*
dread dred(e *n*
dread drede *v*
dreadful dred(e)full *a*
dream dreme(s *n2*
dream drem- *v2*
dreg]ges -gys
dress]e(s dres(t(e *v*

drib]bis *v*
drift dryfte -is
drink]e drynk(- dranke
 dronke(n *vl*
drink drynke *n*
drive(n dryv- drove *v*
drivel drevyll dryvyll *nl*
dromedary dromadary
drone drane(s *nl*
drone dronny *v2*
droop droupe *v*
droopy droupy drowpy *a*
drop]pes droppy(?)
dropping -yng(e *p.a*
dropsy
drought
drown]- dround *v*
drowsy *a*
drowsy-pate drousy pate
drunk dronke *p.a*
drunkard]is drunchard
drunken dronken drunkyn *p.a*
dry(e *a*
dry *v*
dryad]es
dryness drighnes
duck(e *nl*
dud
due deu dew *a*
dug]ges *nl*
duke dukis
dull(e *a*
duly *av*
dumb dom(e dum *a*
dump]- *nl*
dun *nl*
dun dyne donn(- *a*
dung donge
dung-cart dong(e cart(e
dung-hill donghyll
dunnish donnyshe *a*
dure *v*
dust(e
dusty *a*
Dutch Dowche
duty dewty(es dutes dwte
dwell(- dwelt(e *v*
dwelling -ynge *v.n*
dwelling-house dwellinge house
each eche ich(e yche *a, pron*
each one echone
eagle egle
ear]e(s e(e)re(s eyre *nl*
earl erle erlis
early erly *av*
earnest e(y)rnest *a, n*
earth erth *nl*
earthly erth(e)ly yerthly *a*
ease *n*
ease(d -yd *v*

easily easely *av*
east est
easy *a*
eat]e(- ete(- etynge *v*
ebb]e *v*
ebb]e *n*
eclipse eclipsid *v*
economicer iconomicar
ecstasy extasy
eel ele
effect(e theffect
egg]es eg
Egyptian Egypcyen
eight(h) eyght *num*
eisell eysell
either eyther *av*
eke *av*
elate *a*
elation elacyon
elbow]e
elder-stick eldyr steke
elect(e *a*
electuary (al)lectuary
elegy
elementary elementar
elench elenkes
elephant]is (*cf* oliphant)
elf]e
elm]e
eloquence eloquens
eloquent *a*
eloquently *av*
else ell(e)s ellis -ys els *av*
elsewhere elswhere *av*
elvish elvyshe *a*
embalm enbawmed *v*
embassade]s
embattled enbateld *p.a*
embeauty enbewtid *v*
emblaze enblased *v2*
embloom emblomed *v*
emboss enbosed -id *vl*
emboss embosyd enbosed *v2*
embrace embracyd enbrace
 enbras- *v2*
embraid en- *v2*
embreathe enbreth- *v*
embroider embraudred enbrawd-
 enbrowd- *v*
embud enbudded -id *v*
embullion enbulyoned *v*
embusy embesy enbesid *v*
emerald emeraud -awde
empave enpavyd *v*
emperor emperour
empicture enpicturid *v*
employ]ed enploy(e)d *v*
empoison enpoysoned *v*
emporture]d *v*
empress]e emperes *nl*

enboln]ed *v*
encanker encankryd enkankerd *v*
enclear encleryd incleryd *v*
enclose]d *v*
encover]de *v*
encrampish encraumpysshed *v*
encrisp]ed *v*
encrown]yd *v*
end]e(s *n*
end]eth -ith *v1*
endarked endarkid -yd *p.a*
endeavour endevour(e *n*
endeavourment endevourment
endless]e end(e)les *a*
endue]d endude *v*
endure endur- indeuer indure *v*
endye endiyd *v*
enemy]es enmys
energial]l *a*
enfaint enfayntyd *v*
enflower enflorid *v*
enforce -id enfors- *v*
engalared engolerid *v*
engender engendred *v*
englad]id *v*
englaze englasid *v*
English]e Englys(s)h(e
Englishman -men Englissh-
    Englyshe-
englister]d *v*
engrape engrapid *v*
engross engros- ingrosed *v*
engush engusshing *v*
enhach]- *v*
enhard]id *v*
enharped enharpid *p.a*
enjoy *v*
enlace enlasid *v*
enlarge inlargyd *v*
enlozenge enlosenged *v*
enmix enmyxyd *v*
ennew(- enneude enuwyd *v1*
enough]e inough ynough(e
    ynowe *a, av*
enrail]id *v*
enrich enryche *v*
enripe enryped *v*
enrol]- inrolde *v*
ensand]id *v*
enseam ensaymed *v1*
ensemble ensembyll *av*
enshrine enshryned *v*
ensilver ensilvred *v*
ensorb]yd *v*
ensoak ensowked *v*
ensue ensu- ensew *v*
ensure *v*
enswimming enswymmyng *a*
entach]id *v*
entackle entakeled *v*

enterprise -yse *n*
enterprise -yse(d -ysyd *v*
entertain enterteynd *v*
entire intere *a*
entitle entytuled *v*
entreat entrete intrete(d *v*
entune entunyd *v*
enturf]id *v*
envault envawtyd *v*
enverdure enverdurid -yd *v*
envious envyous *a*
environ envyronn envyrowne *av*
environ envyronde -ned *v*
envive envyv- *v*
envy(e envi *n*
enwall]yd *v*
enweary enwered *v*
epicure epycure
epilogation epylogacyon
epistle (*see* pistle)
epistler (*see* pistler)
epitaph epytaphe
epitome epitomis
equipollence equipolens
equivalent *n*
equivalently *av*
ere er *prep, av*
erect]yd (*cf* arrect) *v*
errand]e
erroneous erronyous *a*
error errours
erst(e *av*
escape escapid (*cf* scape) *v*
escry]e *v* (*cf* ascry)
espy]e espyde *v* (*cf* aspy)
essence assence
estate(s (*cf* astate)
eterminable etermynable *a*
eternally *av*
eure ure *n1*
eure ured -yd *v*
evasion evacyon
even evyn *n*
even *a, av*
evenly evynly *av*
ever evyr *av*
evermore *av*
every hevery *a*
everyone everychone
everything everi- -thyng(e
evidence evydence
evident *a*
evidently evydently *av*
evil]l evyll yvell a, av
evil-favoured evyll faveryd *a*
exaltation exaltacyon
examination -cion examynacyon
example
exceed exced- exede *v*
exceeding excedynge *av*

excell(e(s *v*
excellence
excellent(e *a*
excellently exellently *av*
except *prep*
excess]e exesse
exchequer checker
excite excitynge *v*
exclamation exclamacyon
exclude *v*
excommunication
    excommunycacyons
excommunicate excomunycate *p.a*
excuse(d -yd *v*
excuse *n*
execrable *a*
execute -yd *v*
exemplify exemplyfyenge *v*
exhibition exhibycion
exile exyl- *v*
expel]le *v*
expense expence (*cf* spense)
experience -iens -yence -yens
expert(e *a*
expiation expyacyon
expire expyryd *v*
exploit exployte *v*
expound]- *v*
express]e expres *a, av*
express]ed expres(t(e *v*
extend]id *v*
extol]- *v*
extort *p.a*
extortion extorcyon
extravagancy
extreme *a*
eye eyen eyes ey(ne I iye ien ies
fable(s fabell
face(s *n*
face facithe facyd *v*
facer]s
faculty faculte
fade *v1*
faggot fagot(tes
fail fayle *n2*
fail]e fayle(d *v*
fain]e fayn(e *a, av*
faint faynt(e *a*
faint faynt- *v*
faint-hearted faint harted *a*
fair fayer fayr- fare *a*
fair]e fayre *av*
fairly fayrly *av*
fair-play fayre-play
faith(e fayth(e ifayth
faithful faythfull
faitour]s faytors -our
falchion fawchyn *v*
falcon faucon fawco(u)n
falconer fauconer fawconer

fouconer
fall(e *n1*
fall(- fal(e fell fyll *v*
fallible fallyble *a*
fallow]s falowe
false(st fals *a, av*
false-hearted false harted *a*
falsehood -hode falshod(e
falsely falsly *av*
falseness]e
false quarter fals quarter
fame(s -ys
familiarity famylyaryte
family famuly
famous famus *a*
famously *av*
fancy fansy(es fantsy
fang]e fonge *v1*
fantastical]l fantastycall *a*
fantasy(es -ies
far(r)e fer(re *av*
far(re *a*
fare(- *v*
farewell *int, n*
far-fet farre- *a*
fart]e
farther farder ferther *av*
  (*cf* further)
fashion facion facyo(u)n
fast(e *a*
fast(e *av*
fast]ynge *v2*
fasten *v*
fat(te *a*
fat]te *v*
fatal]l *a*
fate
father(s fader(s
fault faute fawt(e
favel]l
favour(e faver -yr *n*
favour]e faveryd *v*
favourable favorable *a*
fawn]e *v1*
fay *n* (*cf* foy)
fear]e fere *n*
fear]e fe(e)re *v*
feast feest fest(e fyest
feat]es fay[c]tes feytis fet
feat fete *a*
feather feder(i)s fether(s -yrs
feather-bed fether bed(des
featous fetewse *a*
feature fetur-
fee(s fe *n1*
fee]d *v1*
feeble feble *a, av*
feebly febly *av*
feed fede fed *v*
feel fele(th felt *v*

fee-simpleness fee symplenes
feign fayne(d feyne *v*
feigning faynynge *v.n*
felicity felicite -ycite -ycyte
fell *n1*
fell(e fel *a*
fellow felawes felowe(s
fellowship felashyp felowshyp
female femall *a, n*
fen *n1*
fenestral]l *n*
feoff feffyd *v*
ferly farly farle *a*
ferly farly *av*
ferry fery *n1*
ferryman feryman
fervent farvent *a*
fervently *av*
festered festerd *p.a*
festival festyvalle *a*
fetch]e(d fet(te *v*
fetter]s *n*
fetter fettred *v*
feverous *a*
few(e(r *a, n*
fickle fickil fyckell fykkelle -ill *a*
fiction fictyons
fiddle fiddill *n*
fiddle fydled *v*
fiddler fydler
fidelity fydelyte
fie fy(e *int*
field felde
fieldfare feld(e)fare
fiend fende fendys fynd(e
fierce ferce f(i)ers fyers *a*
fiercely f(y)ersly *av*
fiery fyry *a*
fight fy(gh)t(- feight- faught
  fought fawte *v*
figure *n*
figure]d fygured *v*
file fyle *n1*
file fyle *v1*
file fylythe *v2* (*cf* defile)
fill fyll *v*
fill fyll *n1*
filly fylly
filthy fylty *a*
final fynall a
finally fynally *av*
finance fenaunce
find fynd(- found(e fownd *v*
fine fyne(st *a*
finger]s fynger(s
finger fynger- *v*
fire fyer fyre *n*
fire fyre(d *v*
fire-drake fyer drake
firm ferme fyrme *a*

firmament fyrm-
first fyrst(e furst *a, n, av*
fish fysshe(s *n*
fish fysshe *v*
fist(- fyst(-
fit fytte *n2*
five fyve *num*
fixed fyxt *p.a*
fizgig fysgygge
flagrant flagraunt *a*
flail flayle
flame]s flamys
Flanderkin Flanderkyns
flank]e
flap *n*
flap]pe(s *v*
flatter(- flater(- flat(y)r- *v*
flatterer flaterer(s
flattery flatery
flax]e
flay fleyest *v*
flea flees
flecked fle(c)kyd *p.a*
flee fle(d(de *v*
fleece flece(s
fleer flery *v*
fleering fleriing *p.a*
fleet flete *v1* (*cf* float)
fleet flete *a1*
fleet flete *n1*
Flemming Flem(m)ynge
flesh(e flessh(e
flesh-fly flessh(e)-fly(e(s
flesh-meat flesshe me(a)te
flicker flyckerynge *v*
flight flyght
flinging flingande *p.a*
flint
flip-flap flyp-flap
flip flyppes *v*
flit flyt(te *v*
fliting flytynge *v.n*
float flotes -is *n*
float *v* (*cf* fleet)
flock]e *n*
flock]ed *v*
flocket
flood(es flod(-
floorth florthe
Florentine
flourish -is(s)h- -ys(s)h- flo(w)r- *v*
flow]e *v*
flower flour(- flowr- flowur
flush flusshe *n3*
fly(e flew(e flowyn flyeng(e *v1*
fly(e *n*
fly-bitten -bytten *p.a*
fly-blown -blowen *p.a*
fly-net flye-
foal fole

foam fome *n*
foam fomyd *v*
fodder foder
fode *v*
fode *n*
foe fo(o(s
foggy a
foin foynes *v*
foison fuyson
foisty a (cf fusty)
folability folabilite
folk]e
follow folow(- *v*
follower falyre (?)
folly foly
fon(ne -ny *a, n*
fond(e *a*
fondness]e
fonnish fonnysshe *a*
font funt
fool]- fole(s folys
foolish folys(s)he *a*
foolishly folysshly *av*
foolishness folysshnes
foos fose
foot]e fote fete
footed foted *a*
football fote-
footing fotyng(e *v.n*
fop]ped *v*
for *prep, cj*
forage
forbear forbere forborne *v*
forbid forbede forbyd *v*
force fors *n*
force -yd fors- *v*
forcibly forcebly *av*
fordread fordrede *v*
forecasting forcastyng *v.n*
forecastle forecastell
fore-foot forme foote(?)
foremost formest formyst *a, av*
foresaid for(e)sayd *p.a*
forest(e
forester forster
foretop(pe fortop
forever *av*
forfend]e *v*
forge(d *v1*
forger]s
forget forgate forgot(t)en *v*
forgetfulness]e
forgive forgeve *v*
forgo *v*
forked *p.a*
form]e fourme *n*
form]- fourmest *v1*
formally *av*
former -ar(e *a*
form-foot forme foote (*i.e.* fore-

foot?)
formidable formydable *a*
forsake forsoke *v*
forsooth forsoth(e *av*
forsworn]e *p.a*
forth(e furthe *av*
forthwith -wyth *av*
fortress]e
fortunate *a*
fortune(s -is -ys fortuns
fortune]d *v*
forty fourty *num*
forward]e *av*
foul]e felle follest fowle *a*
foundation foundacyons
founder]s *n2*
four(e *num*
fowl]e foules
fox(-
foy *n1* (*cf* fay)
fragrant (see flagrant)
frame *n*
frame(- *v*
franchise fraunchys
frank]e *a2*
frantic]k franty(c)k(e frentike *a*
franticness frantiknes -ycknes
fraud]e
fraught fraghted *v*
fray(- *n1*
fray(e *v1* (*cf* affray)
frayne *v*
free fre *a*
freedom fredome
freke ffreke
French(e Frens(s)he
Frenchman Frenchemen
frenzy franesy fren(e)sy frenessys
fresh(e fresche fressh(e(st *a*
freshly fresshely *av*
fret]e freat *v1*
fret *v2*
friar freer(s frere(s fryars
friend frend(- frynde(s
friendly frendly *a, av*
friendship frendshyp(pe
frieze frese *n1*
frig frygges *v*
friscajoly a
frithy frytthy *a*
fro(o *prep, av* (*cf* from)
frog]ges
from(e *prep*
frosling -lynges
frost(is
frounce *n2*
frounce *v*
frounced frownsid *p.a*
froward(e(s fraward *a, n*
frown]- frounde fronneth *v*

fructuous a
frugality frugalite
fruit frute -is
fruitful frutefull a
frumple frompill *v*
fry(e(d *v*
frying-pan fryenge- fryinge-
fuk-sail fucke sayles
fulfil]led fulfyl- *v*
full ful *a, av, n*
fumble fumblyth *v*
fume *n*
fumigation fumygacion
fumously av
funeral]l *a*
furbisher frubyssher
furious furyous *a*
furnish furnisshe furnyssh- *v*
furred -yd *p.a*
further *a, av* (*cf* farther)
further *v*
furtherer furdrers *n*
furthermore *av*
fury
fustian]e *a*
fusty foisty *a*
gable-rope gabyll rope
gad]de *n1?2?*
gad *n5*
gaggling gaglynge *p.a*
gain gayne geyne *prep*
gainsay *v*
gall *n1*
gall(es *n2*
gallant galant- galauntes gallande
galling gallyng *v.n*
gambol gambawdis
gambolling gambaudynge *v.n*
game
gammon gambone *n1*
gamut
gander gan(?) gant(?) gaunte(?)
gane *v*
gannet gant gaunte
gape gapis -ythe *v*
gar(re garde *v*
garden gardynge
gardeviance gardevyaunce
garland(e(s garlonde garlantes
garlic garlycke
garlic-head garleke hed
garlyke heddes
garment(e(s
garnet garnate
garnish garnissh- -y(s)sh- *v*
gartering -ynge *v.n*
gasp]- *v*
gate(s gatis yate -is
gather(eth ga(d)der -ir *v*
gaud]e *n2*

gaudery gaudry
gaudy gawdy *a2*
gaunt gaunce *a*
gaure v
gay(e *a*
gaze gas- *v*
gaze gase *n*
gazing gasynge *v.n*
gear gere
geason geson *a*
gelt *n2*
genealogy
general]l generrall *a, n*
generation generacion
Genoway January
gentle gentell -til -tyll jan- jen- *a*
gentleman gentelmen gentyl- jent-
gentleness gentylnes jent-
gentlewoman gentil- gentyl- jentyl(l)-
gently gentylly *av*
gerfalcon gerfawcon jarfawcon
gery a
gest n1
get(- gat(- got- *v*
gew-gaw gygawis guygaw
ghastly gastly *a*
ghost goost gost(e
ghostly go(o)stly *a*
gib gyb *n1*
gibbet gybbet jebet *n1*
Gibeonite Gabionyte
gif gyf conj
gift gyft(e(s
giggish giggisse *a*
giggling gyglynge *p.a*
gill gyll *n4*
gillie gylly *n3*
gillyflower jelof(f)er
gin gyn *n1*
gin gan gynys(?) *v1*
gingerly gingirly *av*
gipsy Gipcy
gird gyrdeth *v*
girdle gyrdle
girn]ed gyrne *v (cf* grin)
girth gyrth
gite gytes *n1*
give gave geve gyv- yave *v*
glad(de *a*
gladly *av*
gladness]e gladnes
glair glayre *n1*
glare glaris *v*
glass]e glas *n1*
glazed glasid *p.a*
glean glenes *v*
glee gle *n*
glee gle *v*
gleed glede *n*

gleimy glaymy *a*
glent n
glent a
glide glyde *v*
glint a
glister glyster glystryng *v*
glittering -yng gletter- glittr- glytter- *p.a*
glorious gloryous *a*
gloriously gloryously *av*
glory
gloss glose
glove
gloze glose(th *v*
glozing glosynge *v.n*
glowing -ynge *p.a*
glum glome *n*
glum *v*
glumming glommynge *v.n*
glutton glotton glowtonn
gluttony glotony
gnar *v*
gnat
gnaw]e *v*
go(- ge yede went(e *v*
goat gote(s
goatish gotyshe *a*
god(- (cf* gog)
goddess]e goddes
godfather
godly *a*
gog *n1*
gold(d)e
golden *a*
goldfinch goldfynche
goldsmith goldsmyth
Gomorr(h)ean Gommoryans
gong]e *n1*
good(e *a*
good]ys gode *n*
goodlihead goodlyhede -hod
goodly(- god(e)ly goodli *a*
goodness goodnes
goose goos gose
gorbellied gorbel(l)yd *a*
gore *n2*
gorge *n1*
gorgeous gorgyous *a*
gorgeously gorgiously *av*
gorgon gargon-
goshawk goshauke
gosling goslenges goslyng(e(s
gospell
gospeller]s
gossip gossyp
Gothian(ce) Gothyaunce
goundy gowndy *a*
gout gowte
govern]e(d *v*
governing -ynge *v.n*

gown]e gounes
grace(s
graceless]e graceles
grail grayle *n1*
grained greuyned *p.a*
grame(d *v*
grammar gramer
grammatol gramatolys
grampus graundepose
grand graunde *a*
grange graunge
grant graunt(- *v*
grass gras gresse
grasshopper gressop(pes
gratify gratyfyed *v*
grave *n1*
grave gravin gravyd *v1*
grave-stone
gravity gravyte
graze grasynge *v1*
greable a (cf agreeable)
grease grece *n*
grease grese(d *v*
greased gresyd *a*
greasy gresy *a*
great(- greet gret(- *a*
greatly gret(e)ly *av*
gree gre *n2*
gree greyth *v (cf* agree)
greediness gredynesse
greedy gredy *a*
Greek Grek- *a, n*
green grene *a, n*
grey gray(e *a, n*
grey-haired gray-hered *a*
greyhound]es -hownde
grief grevis
grievance greva(u)nce
grieve grev- *v*
grill gryll *a*
grim grym(e *a*
grimly grymly *av*
grin gryn(- *v (cf* girn)
gripe grypes *n3*
grisly gresly grysly *a*
groan gron- *v*
groaning gronynge *v.n*
groat grote(s
groats grotes (?)
grocer]s
groin groyn- *v1*
groining groinynge groynninge *v.n*
groom grome *n1*
grope gropyd *v*
gross grose *a*
grossly grosely *av*
grossolite (see chrysolyte)
ground]e gro(w)nd(e *n*
ground]e(d *v*

groundly *av*
grow(- grew *v*
grudge(th grugyd *v*
grunting gruntyng grontynge *v.n*
grutching grouchyng *v.n*
guard garde(d *v*
guerdon
guess gesse *v*
guest gest(e
guide gyde *n*
guide gyd- guyde(d *v*
guiding gydyng(e *v.n*
guile gyle
guise gyse
gum]- gommes gomys *n1*
gum]- gommes *n2*
gummed gumbed *a2*
gummy *a*
gun gon(ne gunn-
gun-stone gon-
gup *int*
gut]tys *n*
ha *int*
haberdash haburdashe
habergeon habarion
(*h*)*abiliment* abylyment
    h)abylement(es habillimentis
hability (*see* ability)
habit habyte
habitation habytacion
hackney hakney
haft]e *v2*
hafter(s haftar *n2*
hafting -ynge *v.n*
hag(- *n1*
hail hayle(s *n2* (*cf* heal)
hail hayle *n3*
hailing haylynge *v.n*
hair hear heer(e he(y)r-
hair-lace herelace
hairy heery herey *a*
hake *n5*
hale hailid hayled *v1*
half(e *a, av, n*
half-abused halfe- *a*
half-heretic halfe heretykes
half-maimed halfe-maymed *a*
half-man halfe men
halfpenny hal(fe)peny
hall(-
hallow]s *n1*
hallow halow *v1*
hallow halow *v2*
halse halsyd *v2*
halt *a*
halt(- *v1*
halter(s *n1*
hammer
hamper hampar *v2*
hand(- honde(s

handed -yd *a*
handle handell -yll *v*
handy-dandy *av*
hang(- honge *v*
hangman
hap(pe *n1*
hap(- hoppy(?) *v1*
hap]pe(d *v2*
haply (*see* happily)
happen *v*
happily happely *av*
happy *a*
haras harres *n*
hard(e herde herder *a, av*
hard-hearted hard hertyd
    harde harted *a*
hardily hardely herdely *av*
hardiness hardyness
hardly hardely *av*
hardy herdy *a*
hardy-dardy
hare
hark]e herk- *v*
harlot]tes
harlotry]e
harm]-
harmony armony
harness harn(n)es
harnessed hernest *p.a*
harp]e *n*
harp]- herped *v*
harp-string harpe stringis
    -stryngges
harre
harrow harow(e *v2*
harrow harowe *int*
hart(-
haskard]is hastarddis
haste hast
hastive hastyve *a*
hasty *a*
hat
hatch hach *n1*
hatchet
hate *n1*
hate(- hatinge *v*
hateful]l *a*
hatred hatered
hatted *p.a*
haught haute hawte *a*
haughtly hawtly *av*
haunt]yth hawnte *v*
have has hast(e hath(e had(- *v*
havel]l *n1*
haven havyn
haw]e *n2*
hawk]- hauke *n1*
hawk]- hauke *v1*
hawk's-bell hawkys bels
hay hey n1

hay (hey) *n4*
hay-de-guy hay the gy(e
hayne *n1*
hayniard haynyarde
hazard hasarde
hazarding haserdynge *v.n*
he *pron*
head hed(d)- heed(es
head hed(yd *v*
heal]e hele(d helyd *v*
heal]e hele *n* (*cf* hail, hale)
health helth(e
heap hepe
hear here harde herd(e *v*
hearken harken -yn herken *v*
hearse herse
heart hart(- harttis hert(-
heart-blood hart blo(o)de
heart-burning herte-brennynge
hearted herted *a*
heartily hartely hertely *av*
heartless hartles *a*
heartly hartly *a*
heart-root hart rote hert rote
heart-sick harte seke *a*
hearty harty *a*
heat hete
heave heve hevynge *v*
heaven heven hevyn
heavenly hevenly *a*
heaviness hevynesse -nes
heavy hevy *a*
Hebrew Ebrew Ebrue
heck]e
heckle hekell
heddle hedellis
hedge
heed hede *n*
heel hele(s *n1*
height heyght hyght
heinously hayn(n)ously heyn- *av*
heir apparent heyre parent
hell(e hel hyll
hell-hound]e
helm]e *n2*
help]e *n*
help(- helpt *v*
hem *int*
hempen *a*
hen(nes
hence hens *av*
hen-hearted hen-herted *a*
hent]e *v*
her(s hir hyr(e *pron*
herald har(r)old(-
herb]e
herd *n1*
here her *av*
hereafter herafter *av*
hereby *av*

herein(ne *av*
hereof herof *av*
heresy
heretic heretike(s -tyke(- heritykes
hereto herto *av*
heritage
heron
herring herynge(s
herself]e *pron*
hew]yth yawde *v*
hey hay heghe *int*
hide hyde *n1*
hide hyd(e *v1*
hided hyded *a*
hie hy(- *v*
hierarchy ierarchy gerarchy
high hih hygh(- hy(e(- *a*
highly hyghly *av*
hight hyght(e *v*
hill(is hyll(-
hilt
him hym *pron*
himself(e hym- *pron*
hind hynde(s *n1*
hind-calf hynde calfe
hinder hynder *a1*
hinder hynder *v*
hindering hyndrynge *v.n*
hindrance hynderaunce
hip hyppe *n1*
hipped hypped *a1*
Hippocentaur]is Hipocentaures
hippocras ypocras ypocrus
hire hyre *n*
his hys *poss.pron*
historial hystoriall *a*
historier historiar
historious *a*
history
hit hyt(te *v*
hitch hyche *v*
hither hether -yr hyd(d)er
  hyther *av*
ho hough *int*
hoar hore *a*
hoarsely horsly *av*
hobble hobbyll hobles *v*
hobby hoby *n2*
hobby *v*
hobby-lark]es
hoddypeak hoddypeke
  huddy peke
hoddypoll hoddy poule
hofte
hog(ge(s
hoine hoynyng *v*
hold(e held *v*
hold]e(s *n1*
hole holys
holiday holy daye

holiness holynes(se
hollow holow(e *a*
hollow-eyed holow-eyed *a*
holy *a*
holy water -wather
homage
homager
home heme
homely homylyest homly *a*
homely homly *av* (*cf* humbly?)
homeward homwarde *av*
homicide homycide *n1*
honest *a*
honesty honeste
honey hon(n)y
honorous *a*
honour(e honor honowre onour
honour *v*
honourable honorable *a*
honourably honorably *av*
hood hode
hook hoke(s
hooked hoked howkyd *a*
hop(pe(d *v*
hope *n*
hope (hoppy?) *v*
horn]- hornnis
horned hornid *a*
hornkeck horne keke
horrible hor(r)yble *a*
horse hors
horseman horsmen
horse-mill horse-myll
horseshoe horshowe
hose hoos
hose]d *v*
host]e hoost *n1*
host]es *n2*
host(e)ler
hot]e *a, av*
hound]- hownde(s *n1*
hour]e(s hower howre -is
house hoos hous hows-
household housholde(s hows- *n, a*
house-holding howse-holdyng
housewife huswyfe -wyves
how(e *av*
howbeit howebeit *av, cj*
however howe- *av*
howl houle *v*
huck]e *v*
huckle huckels
huckster huksters
hudder-mudder hoder-moder
hue hew(e *n1*
huff(a huf *int*
huge howgye hudge *a*
hugeous hogeous *a*
hugger-mugger *av*
huke

humanity (h)umanyte
humble *a*
humbly homly(?) *av*
humility humilite -yte
humlery
humour humors
hundred hunderd hundreth(e
hunger
hungry hongry hungre *a*
hunt(e *v*
hurt(es *n1*
hurt]e *v*
husband(-
hush howst *imp.v*
hypocrisy ipocrisy ypocrysy
hypocrite ypocrytis
hypostasis ipostacis
I ich(e *pron*
iconomicar
idiocy idiosy
idiot ydeottes
idle ydell ydyll ydle *a*
idleness ydelnes ydilnes
idol ydolles
idolatry
if yf *cj*
ignorance
ilk ylke *a2*
ill(e il yll *a, av, n*
illumine ellumynge illumyn(- *v*
illusion illusiouns illusyon(s
image ymage(s
imagination -cion
  ymagynacyo(u)n
imagine ymagenyd *v*
imbibe enbyb- *v*
immaculate inmaculate *a*
immediately immediatly *av*
immoisture immoysturid *v*
immortal inmortall *a*
immortally *av*
impeachment impechment
imperial]l -yall emperyall(e *a*
implement]es enplement(?)
import]e
importure (*see* emporture)
importunate *a*
importune *a*
impossible ympossybyll *a*
imprint imprynted enpryntyng *v*
improve enprowed *v*
imprudent *a*
in yn *av, prep*
inbring inbryngis *v*
incarnation incarnacion
inch ynche
incineration incyneracyon
incline enclyne inclyne *v*
incommodity incommodite
incomparable im- incomperable

incomporabyll *a*
inconstance inconstaunce
inconstant *a*
inconveniently inconvenyently *av*
incorrigible *a*
increase incres
    encre(a)s- *v*
increase increse encreace
    encrease *n*
indeed indede *av*
indemnity indempnite -yte
indenture]s
India Eyndye Inde Indy Ynde *a, n*
indifferent indyfferente *a*
indignation indygnacyon
indite -dyte endy(gh)t(e *v*
inditing enydytyng *v.n*
induce enduce(d *v*
industrious industryous *a*
industriously *av*
industry
inevitably inevytably *av*
inexplicable inexplicabill *a*
infallibly *av*
infatuate enfatuate *p.a*
infect]e(d *v*
infection infeccioun -yons
infer]rid enferre *v*
infernal]l *a*
infirmity infirmite
inflame enflam- *v*
inflammation inflammacion
influence enfluence
inform]e enforme *v*
inhabit]e *v*
inhate]th *v*
iniquity iniquite
injury injuris
ink]e ynk(e
ink-horn]e
inn]e
innocent *a*
innumerable *a*
inordinate -ynate *a*
inordinately inordinatly *av*
inpurtured *p.a*
inquire enquere *v*
insatiate insaciate *a*
insensate *a*
inside insyde *n*
insolence
inspiration inspyracion
instance instaunce
instigation instygacion
instruction -tyon
instrument
insufficient insuffycyent *a*
intelligence intellegence
    intellygence -ygens
intend]e entend(- *v*

intent entent(-
intentive intentyfe *a*
intentively ententifly *av*
interlace enterlased *v*
interlude enterlude
interment enterement
interpret enterprete *v*
interpretation enterpretacyon
interrupt interrupe *v*
into *prep*
intoxicate *v*
intruder entrusar(?)
invade envade *v*
invective invectyve envectyfys
invein envayned *v*
inventory
inward *a*
inwit-dealing inwyt delynge
ire yre
Irish Irysh *a*
irk erkith *v*
irous *a*
irrevocable *a*
isagogical]l *a*
isle iles
issue issuis
it yt hit hyt *pron*
itch ytche *vl*
item *av*
iwis]s iwys iwus *av*
jacinth -ctis
jackanapes -en-
jacounce
jagged *a*
jagging -ynge *v.nl*
James' fodder Jamys foder
jangle jangyll *v*
jangler jangelers
jangling jang(e)lyng(e *p.a*
jangling jangelynge *v.n*
jape]s *n*
jape(d *v*
jar *v*
jasp]e
jasper
javel]l *nl*
jaw(- *nl*
jawed *a*
jay(-
jealousy gelousy jalawsy jelousy
jennet jenet genet
jeopardy jeperdys
jest]es *n*
jest]e *v*
jet *nl*
jet get *n2*
jet(tes *vl*
jetter *nl*
jetting -ynge *p.a1*
jetty

Jew(e(s
jewel]l
jo
joint joynt(e(s *n*
jointed joynted *a*
jolly joly joyly(?) *a*
jolly joly *av*
journey *n*
journey *v*
joy(e
joyous joyows *a*
joyously *av*
judge jug- *v*
judicial judicyall judycyall *a*
jug *n3*
jumble jumbyll *v*
jurisdiction -tyon jury(s)dic-
just(e *a*
justice justyce
justify]ed *v*
kaiser kayser cayser
kale-stock calstocke
keel keylyth *vl*
keen kene *a*
keep kepe *n*
keep kep- kept(e *v*
ken *vl*
Kendal]l
kennel kenel *nl*
kestrel]l kesteryll
key(e kay(es *nl*
kibe kybe
kiby kyby *a*
kick kycke kykyth keke *v*
kill kyll *v*
kin kynne
kind kynd(e *n*
kind kynde *a*
kindle kyndelde -dell -dle(d *v*
kindness kyndnes(se
king(- kyng(-
kirtle kyrtell(es
kiss kusse *n*
kiss kis kus(- kys(- *v*
kitchen-page kechyn page
kite kyte
kithe kythyd kowththyd *v*
kitten kytten
knack knak *v*
knack knakkes *n*
knacking -ynge *p.a*
knappish]e *a*
knavate
knave(s -is -ys
knavery
knavish knavyche knavys(s)che *a*
knee]s kne
kneel knele *v*
knife knyfe
knight(- knyght(is knythe

knighthood knighthode
knightly *a*
knit knyt(te *v*
knock(ed knok *v*
knot]tes *n1*
knot knoute *n2*
know(- knew(e knowne *v*
knowledge kno(u)lege
knuckle knockles
knuckle-boneyard
    knokylbonyarde
kyrie kyry
labour]e *n*
labour]e *v*
lace lacis *n*
laced lacyd lased *p.a*
lachrymable lacrymable *a*
lack]- lak- *v1*
lack(e lake *n1*
lad]de *n1*
lade ladyn *v*
ladle ladell *n*
lady(e)s -ies
laggard (*see* luggard)
lain layne *v*
lake(s *n4*
lakin lakyn *n2*
lamb]es lam
lame *a*
lament]- *v*
lamentable *a*
lamentably *av*
lamentation lamentacyon
lampatram]s
lance launce(s *n1*
land(- londe
language langage -ys
lanner]s
lantern]es
lap *n1*
lap(ped *v2*
lapwing lapwyng
lard]e
large(r larg *a, n*
largely *av*
largesse larges
lark]- *n1*
lash lasshe *n1(?)*
lass]e(s las
last(e *a, av, n6*
last]yth *v1*
latch laught *v*
late *av, n2*
lately *av*
Latin(e Latyn(e *a, n*
laud(e *n1*
laud]e *v*
laudable -abyle *a*
laudably *av*
laugh(- lawgh- *v*

laughter
laureat(e -iate -yat(e lawr- *a, n*
laurel]l(e lawrell *n1*
laurel-leaf laurell levis
laurel-tree laurell tre
law(- *n1*
lawless laules *a*
lay(- laid ley(e *v1*
lay *n3*
lay(e *n4*
lay-fee
layman lay(e) men
lazar]s
lea le *n1*
lead led- ledd *v1*
lead led(e leedes *n1*
leaf lefe levis
lean]e lene *a*
lean lene *v1*
leap lep- *v*
leap]es lepes *n1*
learn lern- *v*
learned lerned -id -yd *p.a*
learning lernyng(e *v.n*
leash leysshe
leasing lesinges *n*
least lest *a, av, n*
leather ledder lether
leave leve *n*
leave lev- left(e *v1*
lechery
lectern -ryne
lectuary (*see* electuary)
lecture
leech leche *n1*
leek leke(s
leer le(y)re *n1*
leer lering *v*
leese lese *v1* (*cf* lose)
leg]ge(s
legacy
lege (de) moy
legend
legged *a*
leisure layser leyser le(a)sure
leman lemman(ns
lend]e lene(th lent(e *v2*
lenger *av* (*cf* longer)
length(e
lent *n1*
lenten lenton *a*
leopard]es lybbard
leper lyppers *n2*
lere lyerd *v*
less]e *a, av, n*
lesson(s
lest(e leest leyst *cj*
let(t(- *v1*
let(e *v2*
letter(s lettre *n1*

lettered letterd -yrd -red *p.a*
level-sice levell suse
lewd]e leude *a*
lewdly(e lewdely leudly *av*
lewdness]e lewd(e)nes
liar lyar(s lyres
liberal lyberall *a*
liberality lyberalite -yte
liberty lyberte lybertyes
library
licence lycence
lick likkith lycked *v*
lickerous lycorous *a*
lidderon]s liddrons lydderyns
lie lye *n1*
lie ly(- lay(e *v1*
lie liist ly(- *v2*
lief lefe lever *av, n*
liege lege
lieutenant lieutenaunt
life lyf(e lyve(s
lift lyft *v*
light lyght(e *n*
light lyght(e *al*
light *a2*
light lyght *v1*
light lyght *v2*
lightly lyghtly *av*
like lyk- *v1*
like lyke *a, av*
likelihood lykelyhod lyclyhod
likely lykely *a, av*
likewise lykewyse *av*
liking lykyng(e *v.n1*
lily lillis -ys lyl(l)y
lily-flower lylly flowre
limb]is limmes lymm- *n1*
limiter limyters
lime-finger lyme-fynger
lime-rod lyme rodde
limp-legged lympe-legged *a*
lineage lynage
Lincoln Green Lyncole grene
lind lynde
line lyne *n2*
line lyn- *v1*
linger lyngrynge *v*
link lynkes *n2*
link lynk- *v1*
linsey-woolsey lylse wulse
lion lyon(ne lyons lyoun
lip]pes lyp(p-
liquor lycour
list]a lyst(e *v1*
list lyste *n3*
list lyst *n4*
listen lystyn *v*
literature lytterture lytterkture
lithe lythe *v3*
lither ledder lidder lyddyr

lyther(s *a, n*
litherly lytherly *av*
litherness liddyrnes
little litell(e -ill -yll lyt- *a, av, n*
Little-Ease Lytell Ease
live lyve(- lyvyd *vl*
liver lyver *nl*
living lyvenge -yng(e *v.n*
living lyvyng(e *p.a*
lizard lesard(e
lo(o *int*
load lode *v*
loan lonys *nl*
loath loth *a*
loathly loth(e)ly *a*
loathsome loth(e)sum lothsome *a*
loathsomeness lothsumnesse
loathy lothy *a*
lock]- loke *vl*
lock]e(s *nl*
lock]- lok *n2*
lodestar -sterre lode stare
lodge luge
lodge(d -id *v*
log]ges *nl*
logic logyke
logical logycall *a*
logician logicions
lollardy *a*
long(e *a, av*
long]yd *vl*
long]- *v2* (*cf* belong)
longer *a, av* (*cf* lenger)
long-necked longe- *a*
look lok- *v*
look lok- *n*
loom lome *nl*
loose lose *a, av*
loose losyd *v*
loosen losende *v*
lord(-
lordly(e -ely *a, av*
lordship lordshepe -shype
lore *nl*
lorel]l
lose lost(e *vl*
losel]l(- losyll
loselry
loss(e los
lot(tes
loth(e *a*
loud lowde(r *a*
loud lowde *av*
loudly *av*
lour]e lowre *v*
louse lowce lowse lyce
louse lowse *v*
lousy lowsy *a*
lout]e lowt(- *vl*
love(s

love(d lov- *vl*
lover]s *nl*
lovesome *a*
lovingly lovyngly *av*
low(e(st lawe *a*
lowly *av*
loyally *av*
loyalty loyalte
luck(e luk
lug]ges *n2*
luggard
lugging -yng *v.n*
lulla]y *int*
lumber lumbryth *vl*
lump]- *nl*
Luna
lunatic lunatyke *a*
lunatic lunatykes *n*
lung lo(u)nge(s
lurdan lurdayne -den -deyne
lure *n2*
lurk]- *v*
lusk]e
lust(-
lustily lustely *av*
lusty *a*
lute lewte *nl*
lying liing *p.a2*
lying -enge *v.n2*
lyrical]l *a*
mace mase *nl*
mackerel makerell *nl*
mad(d(e *a*
madam(e
madding -ynge *v.n*
madly *av*
madman madmen
madness]e madnes
maggot magott(es *nl*
magic magyke
magnanimity magnanymyte
magnificence magnifycence
  magnyf-
magnify(e magnyfyed *v*
Mahound]e
maid mayd(e mayed
maiden(es mayden(s
maidenhead maydenhede *nl*
maidenhood maidenhode
  mayden-
maidenly maydenly *a, av*
mail male(s *n3*
main]e mayne *nl*
mainland mayne lande
maintain maintayne
  -eyne ma(y)nt- meynt- *v*
maintenance maintenaunce
  mayntenance
majesty majeste mageste magistye
make(th(e mak- mad(e *v*

make *nl*
maker
making makyng(e *v.nl*
malapert(e malypert
  maltaperte *a, n*
malapertly malapertly *av*
male(s *n3*
maleured male uryd *a*
malice malyce
malicious malycyous *a*
malign malygned *v*
malignity malygnytes
malkin malkyn
mallard]e malarde
malt]e mawte *n, (a?)*
Mameluke Mamelek
mammock]es mamockes
mammy
man(- men- *nl*
man]de *v*
manchet maunchet
mangy]e mangey maung(e)y *a*
manhood manhod(e
manifold manyfolde *a*
mankind mankynd(e
manless *a*
manliness manlynes
manly *a*
manner maner(e)s *nl*
mannerless manerles *a*
mannerly *a*
mansion mancyons
manticore mantycare
  -ycore -ycors
mantle mantill mantyll
Mantuan *n*
many(e menny *a, n*
maple-root Mapely Rote
mar marre(s marde *v*
March hare Marche hare -harum
mare(s *nl*
mare *n2*
mare-foal marefoles
mare's milk mares mylke
margarite
margent (*cf* margin)
mariner
marish marees
marjoram margerain
mark(e(d *v*
mark]e *nl*
mark]e *n2*
market
marmoset(e marm(e)set mermoset
marquis marques
marry mary *int*
marsh (see marish)
Marshalsea -sy (*cf* marshalcy)
martial marciall -yall merc- *a*
martinet martynet *nl* (*cf* martin)

martyr marterd *v*
marvel mervayle *n*
marvel mervayle *v*
marvellous marveylus
　　mervelous *a*
mash-bowl mashe bolle
mash-vat masshe fat mash-fat
mask]- *v1*
mass]e(s mas messe *n1*
mast *n1*
master(s maister(s mayster(s *n1*
master]ed *v*
masterfast maysterfest *a*
masterfully *av*
mastership mastershyp
mastery maystery -ryes
　　mastris -ryes
mastiff mastyfe -yvys
mastiff-cur mastyfe curre
　　mastyve curre
mat *n1*
match machchyd *v1*
mate(d *v1*
materiality materyalytes
mathematical *a*
matin mat(t)ens -yns
matriculate matryculate *a*
matter(s mater(s -yr(s *n1*
mattock(e mattoke
maumet mawment mawmett
maun man *v1* (*cf* must)
mavis mavys
maw(e(s *n1*
May *n3*
may(e mayst(e might myght(e *v1*
mayor mayre
maze mase(d maysyd *v*
maze mase *n*
me *pron*
meal]e mele *n1*
meal mele *n2*
mean]e mene(th menyst ment *v1*
mean]- meyne mene(s menys *n2*
mean mene *a2*
measure mesure -is *n*
measure mesured *v*
meat]e mete
meddle meddel- med(e)l- medyll *v*
meddler medler -yllar
meddling medelyng *v.n*
mediation mediacioun -yacyon
mediator medyatoure
medicinable medycynable *a*
medicine medecyne
meditation meditacyo(u)n medyt-
medley meed mede
meek meke *a*
meekly mekely *av*
meekness mekenesse

meet mete *a*
meet met((t)e *v*
meeting metynge *v.n*
meetly metely *av*
meinie mayn(n)y
melancholy melancoly malen-
　　malyn- *a*, *n*
mell(- *v* (*cf* meddle)
melling -yng *v.n*
melodious *a*
melodiously meledyously
　　melo(u)d- *av*
melote melottes
member membres
memorial memoryall
memory
menace manace -ase *v*
mend]- *v*
meng]ith *v*
menial menyall *a*
merchandise merchaundyse mar-
merchant marchauntes mart-
merciful mercyfull *a*
merciless merciles mercyles *a*
mercy
merit meretis merytys
meritoriously meretoryously *av*
meritory *a*
merlin marlyons *n1*
merrily merely meryly *av*
merry mery mirry *a*
mess]e mese
message
messenger]e
met *n*
methinks methynke *impers.v*
metre meter *n1*
metrical]l *al*
metrify metrefyde metrifyde *v*
meuse muse
mew *n2*
mew(ed *v2*
mewt]e *v*
mi my *n*
mickle mekyll mykell
　　myk(k)yll(e *a*
midday sprite myday sprettes
middle myddell
midnight mydnyght
mids middis
midsummer midsomer myd- *a*, *n*
might myght(-
mighty myghty *a*
mild mylde *a*
mile myle
milk mylk(e
mill myll *n1*
miller millar myllar -er
millstone mylle stone mylstones
mind mynd(-

minded mynded -yd *p.a*
mindless myndles *a*
mine min myn(e *poss.pron*
minion mynyon *n1*
minister mynyster *v*
minstrel mynstrell -els
miracle myracle
mire myre *n1*
mirror myrrour(e
mirth]e myrth(-
miry myry *a*
misadventure mysadventure
misadvised mysadvysed *p.a*
miscarry miscary *v*
mischance myschaunce -chauns
mischief]e mischefe mys-
mischieve myscheved -ynge *v*
mischievously myschev- *av*
miscontent myscontent *v*
miscontent myscontent(e *a*
miscreant myscreantys
misdeed mysdede(s
misdeem mysdempte *v*
misdo mysdone *v*
miserableness myserablenesse
miserably myserably *av*
miseration miseracyon
　　myseracion
misery mysery mysere
miseured mysuryd *a*
misname mysnamed *v*
misproud mysproude *a*
miss mys(se myst *v1*
misspend myspent *v*
mistress mistres maistres
　　ma(y)stres(se
mist myst *n1*
misuse mysse use mysusyd *v*
miswork myswrought *v*
mite myte myght *n2*
miting myt(e)yng
mitre myter(s *n1*
mix myxed myxt(e *v*
mixture myxture
mizzling mislyng *v.n*
mo *a*, *av* (*cf* more)
moan mone monys *v*
mobile mobyll *a*
mock]e mok(e *n1*
mock]- mokk- *v*
mockery mokery
mocking -yng *v.n*
mockish -yssh(e mokkysh(e *a*
mockishly mokkyshely *av*
moderately moderatly *av*
moderation moderacyon
mole molys *n1*
mole molle *n2*
mollify molefy *v*
mompyns munpynnys

monastery -ies monesteries
money mon(n)y
monk]-
monochord monacordys
monsieur monsyre
month moneth(es
mood(e mode
moon mone
moonlight mone light
moor more *n1*
Moorish Moryshe *a*
mooting motynge *v.n*
moral]l *a*
morality moralyte
more mor *a, av (cf* mo)
morel]l(e *n4*
Morian murrioun Murryon
mormal marmoll
morrow morow
mortal(l *a*
mortally *av*
most(e moost(e *a, av*
mote mo(ugh)t mowte *v1*
moth]ys moght
moth-eaten mothe-eaten
    moth etyn *a*
mother moder(s modyr
motion mocyon
motive motyve
mould molde *n1*
mouldy mo(u)lde *a2*
mount *n1*
mount]- *v*
mountain mountayne montaynes
mountenance mountenaunce
mourn(yng morne(th *v*
mourning momynge
    murnyng(e *v.n*
mourning-gown morning gounes
mouse myse
mouse-hole
mouth(e(s
move(d mevyd movyd *v*
mow *n2*
mowing -ynge *p.a*
much(e my(t)che moch(e *a, av*
mud
mule moyles mulys *n1*
mulling mullyng
mum *n1, int*
mumming mummynge
    mommynge *v.n*
munch monche *v*
murder mordre murther *n*
murder *v*
murdering murdrynge *v.n*
murmur murmer
murmuration murmuracyon
murmurer murmurar
murr mur murre

muse(s musis -ys *n1*
muse(- *v*
music musyk(kys
musket]te *n1*
muss]e *n2*
mussel muscull
must(e most(e *v1*
mustard]e
muster mustred *v1*
musty *a2*
mutability mutabilite -ylyte
mute mutyd *v1*
mutton motton
my mi *poss. pron*
myself(e *pron*
mysterial]l *a*
mystical]l mistycall *a*
nag]gys *n1*
nail nayle -ys *n*
nail nayled *v*
naked nakid(e -yd *a*
name(s -ys *n*
name]- namyd *v*
nameless(e -les *a*
nap *n2*
nap noppe *n3*
napery
nappy noppy *a2*
nard]e
narrow]e *av*
nation nacion nacyo(u)n(s
natural]l *a*
naturally *av*
nature naturys
nay(e *av*
ne *av*
near nere *av*
neb]bis
necessary a
necessity necessyte
neck]e nek
necked *a*
necromancy nycromansy
need ned- *v*
need nede *n*
neediness nedynesse
needle nedell nedle
needless nedeles *a*
needle-work nedill wark
negligence neglygence -ygesse
negligent neglygent *a*
neighbour ney(gh)bour(s
neither naythyr ne(y)ther -yr *a, av*
    (cf nother)
nept]e
nest(e
net(te *n1*
nether neder *a*
neuter newter *n*
neven *v*

never(e nevyr nere *av*
nevermore *av*
nevertheless]e *av*
new(e *a*
new-found]e *a*
newly *av*
news newes newis
next(e *a, av*
nice nyce nyse *a*
nicety nysyte
nifle nyfyls
niggard negarde nygarde
niggardship negarshyp
nigh ny(gh)e *av*
night nycht nyght(e(s -ys
nightingale nyghtyngale *n1*
nightly nyghtly *av*
nine nyne *num*
nis nys *v (cf* be)
no(o *a, av*
nobility nobilyte
noble nobil -yll -ull *a*
noble]s *n*
nobleman noblemen nobillmen
nobleness]e nobelnes noblenes
noblesse nobles
nobly nobelly *av*
nobs nobbes
nock]e noke
nod]dis *v*
nodding -ynge *v.n*
noddypoll]es nodypoll-
noise noyse
noll(e(s
none non *a, pron*
nor *cj*
north(e
nose
nosed nosyd *a*
not nat *av*
notable *a*
notary notaries
note *n2*
note(d -yd *v*
nother *pron*
nother *av, cj (cf* neither)
nothing nothyng(e noo-
notwithstanding -ynge *av, cj*
nought(e nowght(e nowte
noughty *a*
now(e *av, cj*
nowaday(e)s noweaday(e)s *av*
nowhere nowher *av*
number nombyr *v*
number nomber -re no(u)mbyr
    nowmber *n*
nun non- *n1*
nutmeg
nutshell nutshales -is nutte-
    nysot

937

o *int*
oak oke(s noke nock(?)
oar ore
oat otes
oath othe(s
obedience obedyence
obeisance obeisaunce
obey(de *v*
object]e *n*
object]ed *v*
objection objectyon
oblation oblacions
oblivious oblivyous *a*
obloquy obliqui
obscure]d *v*
obsequious *a*
observance observaunce
observe *v*
obtain optayne *v*
occasion]yd *v*
occasion occasyon(s -cyon *n*
occident *n*
occupation occupacioun -cyo(u)n
occupy(- hocupy *v*
ocean occyan
odd od *a*
oddly odly *av*
odious odyous *a*
of *prep*
offence
offend(- *v*
offer *n*
offer offred -yd *v*
offering box offerynge box
official offycyallys *n*
offspring ofsprynge
oft(e *a, av*
often(ner oftyn oftnar *av*
oftentimes oftentymes *av*
oft-time oft(e) tyme oftyme *av*
oft-times ofte tymes *av*
oil oyle *n1*
old *n*
old(e *a*
oliphant oliphaunt olyfa(u)nt(es
olive olyve
Olympian Olympyan *a*
omnipotent *a*
on *prep, av*
once on(e)s *av*
one *num*
one(s *pron*
one-eyed *a*
onion onyon(s
only onely oonly *a, av*
Onocentaur]es -is
ooze wose *n2*
open opyn *a*
open(ed opynynge *v*
openly opynlye *av*

opinion opinyons opynions -yon
oppose(d *v (cf* appose)
oppress]e opprest *v*
or *cj, av*
orator]s oratour(s
orbicular
ordain ordenyd *v*
order(yd *v*
order(s ordre(s *n*
ordered ordred *p.a*
ordinal ordynall *n2*
ordinance ordenaunce ordyn-
orgulous orgulyous *a*
orient oryent(e *a, n*
original]l orygynall *n*
ornacy
ornate *a*
ornately ornatly *av*
osprey ospraye
ostrich estrych estryge
ostrich feather eestryche fedder
other (h)othyr odyr oder *a, n, pron*
otherwise otherwyse *av*
ouch]e *n*
ought owght *v*
our(e owr(e owur owers *poss.pron*
out]e ought owt(e *av*
outcry(es outcri owtcry
outface outfacyd *v*
out-isle outyles
outlawed owtelauyd *p.a*
outrage
outrageous outragyous *a*
outray(e *v*
outside outesyde *n*
outward]e *av*
over ovyr *av, prep*
overage *n*
overcast *p.a*
overgrow]eth *v*
overlook overloked *v*
overnight overnyghte *av*
oversee overse *v*
over-shoot overshote *v*
oversight oversyght
overthrow *n*
overthrow(e *v*
overthwart]- *v*
overthwart]es *n*
overthwart(e -wharte
 ovyrthwarte *a*
over-watch hovyr-wachyd *v*
owe *v*
owle(s oule
owl-flight owle flyght
own]e awne *a*
owner awnner
ox]e
oyster
pack]is *n1*

pack]e *v1*
packing]e v.*n2*
page(s *n1*
pageant pagent paja(u)nt(t)-
pain]e payn(e(s *n1*
pain]ed payned -yd *v*
painful paynfull *a*
paint paynt(- *v1*
pair payre
palace palas paleys *n1*
pale *a*
pale *n1*
pall paule(s *n1*
pallet palettes *n1*
palliard palyard(e
palsy palsey
paltock paltoke
pamper]de pampyr *v*
pamphlet pamphelet -ilet pamflett
pan *n1*
pang]e(d *v1*
pang]es -is *n*
pant paynty(?) *v*
pap]pes *n1*
papal]l(es *a*
paper(s papyr
parable]s parabyll paroblis
Paradise Paradyce -dyse
paramour]e
parbreak parbrake *v*
parcel]e parcell
pardie parde pardy perde *int*
pardon(e *n*
pardon(e *v*
paregal]l *a, n*
parish parysh
parish-clerk parysshe clerke *n*
park]e(s
parker
parliament parly(a)ment
parrot(t(is parot(e -ott(e
parson(s
part(e -ys
partial parcyall *a*
partiality parcyallyte
partly partely *av*
partridge partriche -yche(s -ydge
pass]- pas past(e *v*
pass pas *n2*
passage
passenger]e
passing -yng(e *p.a, av*
passingly -yngly *av*
passion passyon
passport pasport
pastance pastaunce
patch(e(s *n1*
patch]id pachchyd *v*
patching -ynge *v.n*
pate(s *n1*

patent
Paternoster
paternoster-peeks -pekes
path
patience paciens pacyence
patient pacyent *a*
patiently pacyently *av*
patlet
patriarch patriarkes patryarke
patter]s *v1*
paunch]e -ys *n1*
pause pawse
pautener pawtenar *n2*
pavilion pavylyon
pavis paves -ys
paw]es *n1*
pawn]e *n2*
pay(e(d payde *v1*
payment
peace peas(e pece *n1*
peace peas(e pece *imp.v*
peaceless peaslesse *a*
peacock peco(c)k(e
peahen pohen
peak pek *n3*
peakish pekysh *a1*
peal]e *n1*
pear pere(s
pearl perle(s -ys *n1*
pease pe(a)son
peasecod pescoddes
peck]e *n1*
pecked *p.a*
peek peke *v1*
peer pere *n*
peerless pereles(se perlesse *a*
peevish peviche pevys(s)h(e *a*
peevishness pevissheness pevyshnes
Pelagian Pollegyans *n*
pelfry
pellet pellit *n1*
pen(ne *n2*
pen]d(e *v3*
penalty penalte
penance penaunce
pence pens
pencil pensell
pendugum pendugims
penniless penyles *a*
penny peny
penny-chick peny cheke
pension pencyon
pentameter
penury
people(s pepil
pepper peper
peradventure *av*
peradvertence -aunce
percase

perceive perceyv- perseyv- parceyve *v*
perch *v* (*see* perk)
perchance parchaunce *av*
perdurable *a*
peregrination peregrynacioun
peremptory peremtory *a*
perfect perfight perfyte *a*
perfectly perfightly perfytely *av*
perfectness perfytenesse
perihermenial]l *a*
perilous peryl(l)ous perlous *a*
perilously *av*
perjured parjured *p.a*
perjury perjuris
perk]yd *v2*
perk]e *n1*
permit permyt(ted *v*
perpetually *av*
perpetuity perpetuyte
perplexity perplexite -yte
perseverance -aunce perceveraunce
person person(e)s
personable *a*
personally *av*
perspective perspectyve
persuade perswade *v*
persuasion persuacyon
pert]e *a*
pertain perteyneth *v*
pertly pertely *av*
peruse]d *v*
pervert]ed parvertyd *v*
pestle pestels
petition peticyon -ycyon
petty pety *a*
pewit puwyt
pewter
Pharaoh Pharao
Pharisee Pharasay
pheasant fesaunt(e(s
philargyry philargerya
Philistine Phil(l)istinis
philology phylology
philosopher phylosophers
philosophy phylosophy
phip Phyp
phoenix phenex -ix -yx
phrenetic frenetyke(s *a, n*
phronesis phronessys
phthisic tysyke
physic phesik physyke
physician fesycyan
physiognomy fysnamy
pick]e pike pycke(d pyk- *v1*
pickax pykes
picker pyker *n1*
picking pykynge *v.n*
pickthank pykthanke

picture picturis pycture
pie py(e *n1*
pie-baker py-bakar
piece pece
pierce persyd *v*
pig]ges pygge(s *n1*
pigeon]s pygeons -yons
pigs-ear pygges eare
pigsney piggesnye pyggys-ny
pike pikys *n4*
pike pyke *v3*
pilch pylche
pile *n2*
pilgrimage pylgrimage pylgrymages
pill pyll *v1*
pillage pyllage *v*
pillar pyllers
pilled pylde pyllyd *p.a*
pilling pyllyng *v.n*
pillion pyllyon *n2*
pillory pylery pyllory
pillory-pageant pelory pajauntes
pillow pyllowe
pin pyn(n)e(s *n1*
pin-case pyncase
pinch pynch- *v*
pine *n1*
pined pyned *p.a*
pinion pynyon *n1*
pink-eyed pynk iyde *a*
pipe pype *v1*
pipe pypes *n1*
pippling pip(p)lyng *p.a*
pirling -yng *v.n*
piss pys(se pyst *v*
piss-pot pyspottes
pistle pystell pystels
pistler pystyllers
pit pytte *n2*
pitch]e *n1*
pitcher pycher pytchars *n1*
piteous pyteyus -eous -yous *a*
pith pyth(e
pity pite pyt(y)e pytty pety
place(s placis
plack]e (*see* pluck *n*)
plague plagys
plain]e playn(e *a, av*
plain playne *n1*
plain-dealing playne delynge *v.n*
plainly playnly *av*
plainness plainnes playnesse
plain-song playne songe
plane *n2*
plant]id *v*
planting -yng(e *v.n*
plate platis
platter]s *n1*
play(e(s pley *n*

play(- pley *v*
plead plete *v*
pleading pletynge *v.n*
pleasance pleasaunce
pleasant pleasaunt(e(r plesa(u)nt(e *a*
pleasantly plesauntly *av*
please(- plesyth *v*
pleasure(s -urs -yre plesure -yre
pleat pletes
pledge plege
Pleiades Pliades
plenarly plenarely *av*
plenty plente
plover
pluck(- plucte pluk plyckyd *v*
pluck placke (*v.r.* plucke)
plucking -ynge *v.n*
plum]mis
plumed plummed *p.a*
plummet
plump]e *n1*
plunge plungyd *v*
plurality pluralytes
pocky *al*
pode
poem]-
poesy
poet]- poyete
poet-laureate poete lawreate poyet lawreat
poetry
poignant (*see* pungent)
point poynte(s *n1*
point]e -yd -yng *v1,2*
pointing poyntynge *v.n1*
pointment poyntmentys
poison poyson *n*
poison poyson *v*
poisoned poyson(e)d *p.a*
poke *n1*
pole polys polles *n1*
pole *n2*
pole-ax pollaxis
pole-hatchet powle ha(t)chet(tis
policy pollycy *n1*
polished polyshed pullisshyd pullys(s)h- *p.a*
politic poletyke polytyke *a*
politic polytykes *n*
poll *n1*
polling poll(e)yng(e *v.n*
polling-pageant pollyng pajaunttis
polluted -yd poluted -yd *p.a*
poltroon pultrowne
pomander pomaunder
pomegranate pomegarnat
pommel pomel
pomp]e *n*

pomp]ed *v2*
ponder *n1*
ponder pondred *v*
pontifical pontifycall -yficall *a*
pool pole polys *n1*
poor]e pore *a*
pop]ped *v1*
pope(s
pope-holy popholy *a, n*
popinjay -gay popagay -eg- -ig- -yng-
popping -yng(e *p.a*
porishly porisshley *av*
porpoise porpose
port]e -is *n1*
port(e *n4*
portly]e *a*
portraiture porturature
port-sale
port salut port(e) salu(e
pose *n1*
possible possyble *a*
post(is *n1*
postern gate
postic postyke(?) *n*
postil postell postyll *v*
postle postels
pot pott potte *n1*
potential potenciall -cyall *a*
potentially potencyally *av*
potestate
potestolate
pothecary potecary
potion pocioun
potsherd pot sharde -shorde(s -is
potter]s
pottle-pitcher pottell-pycher
pouch]e
poultry pultre
pounced pounsed *p.al*
pound(e pownd *n1*
poustie posty
poverty poverte
power(s powre
practic practique *v*
practise *v*
praemunire premenyre
praetory pretory
praise prayse(d prase *v*
praise prayse *n*
prance praunce *v*
prank]- pranckes *n2*
prank]es *v3*
pranking -yng *v.n2*
pranked *p.a* (*cf* prank *v1*)
prate(- *v*
prater
prating -yng(e *v.n*
prawn prane(s -ys
pray(- praiid *v*

prayer praiers *n1*
preach prech- *v*
preacher prechers -our(s
preaching prechyng(e *v.n*
preamble
prebendary prebendaries
precedent presedent presidente
precious precyous(e presyous *a*
preciously *av*
predestination predestynacyon
predial predyall *a*
predicament]es
predication predycacion
pre-eminence preemynence
preferment
pregnancy pregnacy
pregnant pre(i)gnaunte *al*
prelacy(e
prelate(s prelattes
prendergest
preordinate *p.a*
prepare]d prepayre *v*
prepense]d *v*
preposition (*see* proposition)
prepositor prepositour *n1*
prerogative prerogatyve
prescience prescyence
prescription prescrypcyons
presence presens
present *a*
preservative preservatyve
preserve(d *v*
president presedent presydent
press pre(a)se prece *n1*
press]- prease prece pres- *v1*
pressly precely *av*
prest]es *n1*
prest(e *a*
presume -yng *v*
presumption presumpcion presum(p)cyon
presumptuous *a*
pretence pretens
pretend]- *v*
prettily pratylye pretely prytely *av*
pretty praty(e(r prety *a*
prevail prevayle pervayle *v*
prevent]id *v*
prey pray *n*
prey]e *v*
price pryce
prick]- prek- prikk- pry(c)k(- *v*
prick-me-dainty prycke-me-denty
prick-song prycke song(e
pride pryd(e *n1*
priest pryeest(es prest(e(s pryste
priesthood preesthode
priestly preestly *a*
primate prymates *n1*
prime pryme(s *n1*

primordial]l *a*
primordial primordyall *n*
primrose primerose prymerose
prince(s -is prynce(s
princely pryncely *av*
princess]e
principal princypall *n*
principal]l pryncypall *a*
principle]s princyples
print prynt(- *v*
prioress pryoresse
prisoner prysoner *n2*
prisonment presonment
privileged prevylegidde
    pryvylegyd *p.a*
privily prevyly *av*
privy prevye pryvy *a*
probate
problem]-
proceed proced- *v*
process]e proces prosses *n*
procession processyon
proclaim proclame(d *v*
prodigal]l prodygall *a*
profane prophanes *n*
profess]ed *v*
profession professyoun
proffer profer *n*
profit profyteth *v*
profitable profytable
    prophytabyll *a*
profit-growth profyte growth
profound]e *a*
progeny
prognosticate pronostycate *v*
prologue
promise promyse *n*
promise]d promys- *v*
promote]d -yd *v*
promoting -ynge *v.n*
promotion promocion -cyon -syon
promotive promotyve *a*
prong]e *nl*
pronounce pronownsyng *v*
proof profe
prop(e *nl*
proper propire propyr propre *a*
properly *av*
property properte
prophecy prophesy
prophet(e(s
proportion proporcyon
proportioned proporsionyd *p.a*
proposition preposycyon
    proposicyoun
proscription proscripcyon
prose
prosecute *v*
prosper]e *v*
prosperity prosperyte

prosperous *a*
prosperously prosperyously *av*
protection(s -tyon proteccyon
protestation -cion -cyo(u)n
protonotary prothonatory -otory
proud(e prowd- *a*
proudly *av*
prove(- prov- preve *v*
proverb]e -ys
providence -y-
provident provydent *a*
provincial -yall -ials provync- *a, n*
proving prevynge *v.n*
provision provisyon
provoke *v*
provost(e
prowess prowes
prudence
prudent *a*
pry(eth *vl*
psalm]e
psaltery psautry
puant puaunt *a*
puantly puauntely *av*
publish publisshe -ysshed *v*
pudding puddyng(es podynges
pudding-prick poddynge-prycke
puffed pufte *p.a*
puffin puffyn
puissant pusant *a*
pull(e *v*
pulpit pulpete pulpyt(tes
pump *n*
pungent punyete *a*
punish punysshed *v*
punishment punysshment
purchase -ace *v*
purchaser
pure *a*
purgation purgacyon
purling (see pirlyng)
purple purpill *a*
purpose porpose *n*
purpose -yd *v*
purse purs(ys
pursuivant pursevantis
purvey *v*
purveyance purveaunce
pusillanimity pusyllanymyte
puss-cat pus catt
pustule puscull
pustuled puskylde *a*
put(te(th *vl*
putrefy *v*
pyrdewy *n*
pythoness phitones(se
quack quake *int*
quadrant *nl*
quadrivial quatrivials -yvyals
quail qua(y)le quaylles

quake(ed quoke *vl*
qualified qualyfyed *p.a*
quality qualytes *n*
quarrel quarell(- quarillis
    querell *n3*
quart]e *n2*
quarter(s *n*
quarter]d *v*
queasy queysy *a*
qued queed *n*
queen]e quene(s
quell *vl*
quench]e *v*
querele (see quarrel)
quest *vl*
question -yon *n*
question]yd *v*
questionless -les -yonlesse *av*
quibible quibyble
quick quike quycke(r *a*
quick quy(c)ke *n*
quickly quikly quyck(e)ly *av*
quire quaire quayre *nl*
quit quight quyt(e *v*
quite quyght quyte *av*
quote coted -yd *v*
quoth quod
rabble rabell rabyll rable *nl*
rache ratches *nl*
rack]ed rachchyd(?) *v3*
radiant radyant(e radyent *a*
rafter *nl*
rag]ge raggys *nl*
rage(s *n*
rage(s ragyd *v*
ragged -id -yd *al*
ragman roll]is
rail]les *n2?3?*
rail rayle *n3*
rail rayles *n4*
rail]es rayle(s rayll raylyng(e *v4*
railer *nl*
railing raylynge(?) *v.nl*
raiment rayment
rain rayne(s *nl*
rain rayne(th raynning *v*
rain-beaten rayn(e) beten -yn *p.a*
raines raynes
raise rayse(d -yng reyse *vl*
raisin reysons
rake *nl*
ram(bes *nl*
ramage a (see rammish al)
rammish rammysche *al*
rammish rammysshe *a2*
rampant rampaunt *a*
ram's-horn rambes- rammes-
rancour
range rangyd rannge *vl*
range raunge *nl*

941

rank]e *a*
rank]is *v3*
rankly -ely *av*
rap]pes *n1*
rarefy rarifiid *v*
rase -id -yd *v1* (*cf* erase, raze)
rat(tes *n1*
ratch rachchyd *v1*
rate -is -yd *v2*
rate(s *n1*
rather av
ratify ratyfye(d *v*
rave(s ravyd -ynge *v1*
raven ravyn
ravener
ravish ravysh- *v*
raw(e *a*
ray raist *v2*
ray(e *n3* (*cf* array)
ray *n6*
razor raysors
reach rech(- *v1*
read red(- reed *v*
readily redely *av*
readiness redynes(se
ready redy *a*
realm]- reame reme(s
ream reme *n3*
rearward rerewarde
reason(s reson(s *n1*
reason resonde *v*
reasonable reson- *a*
reasoning reasonyng
    resonynge *v.n*
reasty a (*see* resty *a2*)
reaving revynge *v.n*
†ebeck (*cf* ribibe)
rebel rebell(e(s
rebelling rebellynge *v.n*
rebellion rebellyon(ns *n1,2?*
reboil reboyled *v*
reboke *v*
rebound
rebuke(s -id -yd -yng *v*
receipt resayte resseyte
receive receyve(d -yd *v*
recheat rechat- *v*
recidivation resydevacyon
recite resytynge *v*
reck]ys reke *v*
reckless recheles(se retch- rek- *a*
reckon re(c)ken(- reconed
    rekyn(ng *v*
reckoning reconyng(e rek- v.n
reclaim reclaymed reclame *v*
recognizance reconusaunce
recoil reculed *v*
recomfort recounfortyd *v*
recommend]eth *v*
recompense recompence *n*

recompense recompence *v*
reconciliation reconcylyacyon
record]- *n*
record]- *v*
recount(- *v1*
recover(d *v1*
recrayed recrayd *p.a*
rectify rectyfye *v*
recueil recule
red red(d)e *a*
redbreast redbrest
rede(s *v1*
redeem redeme(d(e *v*
redeless redlesse rydlesse *a*
redemption redempcyon
redolent a
redoubt redouted *v*
redress]e redres *v1*
redress]e *n*
reel rele *n1*
reel rele *v1*
reeve reve *n1*
reflair reflayre *n*
reflairing reflaring *p.a*
reform refourme *v*
reformation reformacion -cyon
    refformation
refrain refrayne(d *v*
refresh]ed refressh- *v*
refuge
refuse(d -yd *v*
regard]e *n*
regard]- *v*
regent(e
regestary (*cf* registrary)
regiment
register regest(e)r(-
    regystred -yd *v*
register regester *n2*
registry regstry (*cf* registery)
regratiatory regraciatory
rehayte]d *v1*
rehearsal rehersall
rehearse rehers(- *v*
rehete rehayte(?) *v2*
reign]e raygne rey(g)n- *v*
rein reyne *n1*
rejagged *p.a*
rejoice rejoyce rejoyse *v*
relation -cion(s -cyon(s *n*
release releysyd reles *v*
religion relygion
religious relygious -yous *a*
relucent *a*
remain remayne(d -eth remanyth *v*
remediless remedeles remedyles *a*
remedy *n*
remedy *v*
remember remembyr remembr- *v*
remembrance -aunce -auns

remembrancer -auncer
rem(e)nant remenaunt
remord]es *n*
remord]- *v*
remorder]s
remorse remorrs
remote]s *n*
renay reny(yd *v*
renaying -enge *v.n*
rend rent *v1*
render rendryng(e *v*
renew]- renude renwde *v1*
renome (*cf* renown)
renown]e renoun renowme
renowned -yd *p.a*
rent(e *n1*
repair]e repayr- *v1*
repair repare *n1*
repair repared *v2*
repast
repeat repete
repent(yd *v*
repentance repentaunce
repine repyne *v*
replicable replycable *a*
replication replicacion
    -cyon reply-
reply *v*
report(e *n*
report(- *v*
repose]d *v*
reprehend]- *v*
represent(e *v*
representation representacyon
repress]e *v1*
reproach reproche *n*
reproach reproched *v*
reprobitant]e *a*
reprovable repryvable *a*
repugnance repugnaunce
repute reputyng *v*
request(e
requiem *a, n*
require requyre(th *v*
rescue rescew *n*
rescue rescu(de reskew *v*
resemblance -aunce
resemble(d *v1*
reserve]d -yd *v*
residence resydence *n1*
resident resydent *a*
residue resydew(e
resist *v*
resort(e *n*
resort]e *v*
respite respyte
responsive responsyve *a*
rest(e *n1*
rest(e *n2*
rest *n3*

942

rest(e -yth *vl*
restless]e -les *a*
restore *n*
restore *v*
restrain restrayne *v*
restraint restraynt(es *n*
resty *a2*
resurrection
retain retayne(d -yd *v*
retinue retenewe
retrogradant *a*
return]e retourne *v*
revel revell *nl*
reveller reveler
revelling revelyng *v.n*
revel-rout revell route
revenge]d -yd *v*
reverence reverens *n*
reverence *v*
reverend]e *a*
reverent *a*
reverse reversse *n*
reverse]d *v*
revile revilyng revyle *v*
revive revyvid *v*
revolve revolde *v*
reward]- *v*
reward]e(s -ys *n*
rhetoric rethorik- *nl*
rhetorician retoricyons
rhubarb rubarbe
rhyme n (*see* rime)
rhyme v (*see* rime)
rial nl (*see* royal)
rib rybbis -ys *nl*
ribald rybaude rybawde reba(w)d-
ribaldry rebaudrye
ribbon rybon
ribibe rybybe
ribskin rybskyn
rich rych(e(r *a*
riches ryches
richly rych(e)ly *av*
rid ryd *v*
ride ryd- rod(e *v*
rifle ryfled *vl*
right ryght(e *nl*
right ryght *a*
right ryght(e wright *av*
rigorous rygorous *a*
rigour rygoure
rime ryme *nl*
rime ryme(s -ing *vl*
riming rymyng *v.n*
rind rynde *nl*
ring ryng(e *nl*
ring ryng(e *v2*
rinse rynse *v*
riot ryat ryot(t(e
rioting ryotynge *v.n*

ripe rypest *a*
rise ryse(th rose *v*
river ryvers *nl*
roach rochis *nl*
road rode
roar rore *v*
roast rost(e *n*
roast rost(- rousty *v*
rob]b- *v*
robe(s robys
Robin Hood Robyn Hode
Robin Redbreast Redbrest
rock]e *n2*
rochet rotchettes rocket *nl*
rod nl
roil royle *nl*
role nl?
roll]eth rowe (?) *vl*
roll]ynge rowlynge *v2*
roll]is rowl- role(?) *nl*
Roman Romaine -ayn(e)s *a, n*
rood rode
rood-loft rode loft
rook roke *nl*
room ro(w)me *nl*
roost ro(u)st *nl*
root]es rote
rope(s *nl*
ropy a
rosabell
rosary
rose(s
rosebud rose buddes
rosemary
roser]s
rosier rosiar
rot]e rotten *v*
rote n2
rough routh row(e rowth rughe *a*
rough v2
rough-footed -foted *a*
roughly rughly *av*
rouncy rounses -is *n*
round]e rownde *a*
round]e rownd *av, prep*
round]e *vl*
round]e(d rowne -yd rune *v2*
rout(e rowte *nl*
rout rowt- *vl*
row]e *nl*
row(eth -yth *vl*
royal(l ryall roiall *a*
royal]s *n*
royally ryally *av*
royalty ryalte
rub]be(d -id *vl*
ruby(e(s rubi(e)s
rud]des ruddys rudyes n1
ruddy a
rude a

rudely av
rudeness rudnes
rue rew(e(d *vl*
ruff rowgh *n4*
ruffian ruffyns
ruffle roufled *vl*
ruffling -ynge *v.nl*
rugged -yd *al*
rule *n*
rule rul- rewle *v*
ruler
ruly al
ruly rulye *av*
rumbelow rombelow rumbelowe
rumble rumbyll *vl*
rumour rumer
rump]e *nl*
run(n)- ran(ne ren(n- rin(ne
   ron(ne(s ryn(ne *v*
runner ronner
rush(e russhe(th -russhynge *v2*
russet roset *a, n*
rust nl
rusty al
ruth rewth(e r(o)uthe *nl*
rutter(s
rutterkin rutterkyn
ruttingly ruttyngly *av*
rye ry *nl*
sacerdote]s
sack]e(s *nl*
sack]e *n3*
sacrament(es
sacring sacrynge *v.n*
sad(d)e *a*
sad *av*
saddle-goose sadylgose
Sadducee Seduces
sadly(e *av*
sadness(e -nes
safe-conduct salfe cundight
safely *av*
saffron-bag saffron bagges
sagacity sagacite
sage *a, n2*
sail]ing sayle saylynge *v*
sail sayle sayll *nl*
saint sainct saynt(e(s seynty
sake saake
saker sacre *nl*
sale n2
sallow]e *a*
salt(e *nl*
salt-fish saltfysshe
salutation salutacyons
salute v
salvation savacioun
salve nl
same a, pron
sampler saumpler *nl*

943

sanctuary-breaking
    sayntuary brekyng
sand sonde *n1*
sand]e(s *n2*
sang royal sank royall
sans-peer saunce-pere
sap]pe *n1*
sapience sapyence
sapphire sapher saphiris -yre
Saracen Sarasyns -zyn Sarsens Sarson
satire satirray
satirical saturicall *a*
satrap]as satropas
sauce sause sowse
saucy *a*
sault sautes sawte *n1* (*cf* assault)
savage *a*
save(d savyd -yng(e *v*
Saviour Savyour(e
savour savyr *v*
saw *n1*
saw(e(s -is *n2*
saw]de *v1*
sawdust
say(- sai- sey(- *v1*
scab]be(s
scabbed -yd skabed *a*
scale skales *n2*
scall scaules
scalled scallyd *a*
scalp skalpe *n1*
scan skan *v*
scant(e ska(u)nt(e *a, av*
scantly skantly *av*
scape *v1* (*cf* escape)
scapethrift scape thryfte
scar skar sker *n2*
scarce *a*
scarcely scarsly *av*
scathe scath *n*
schismatic sysmatyke(s *n*
schismaticate sysmaticate *a*
scholar scolers
school scole(s scolys skoles
school-house scolehous
school-matter scole mat(t)er(s
sciatica cyatyca
science sciens scyence
scold]e skolde *n*
scolding skolding *v.n*
score]s *n*
score scoryd *v*
scorn]e *v*
scorn]- skorn- *n*
scornful]l scornefull *a*
scorpion]- scorpyon
Scot(tes -ys Skottys *n1*
scot *n2*
Scottish(e Scot(t)ys(s)h(e *a*

scour *v2*
scourge
scrape *v*
scrat *v*
scratch scrache *v*
scribble scrybbyl scrybblyd scrybyll scryblyd *v*
scribe scryb- skrybe *n1*
scripture(s scrypture
scrive scryve *v*
scroll]- scrowle
scrupulous scrupulus *a*
scrutiny scruteny
scum skommeth *v*
scummer skommer
scurf]e scurffe *n1*
scurfiness scorffynesse
scurvy *a*
scut *n1*
scute scutis scutus
sea se(e
sea-board see-boorde
sea-coast se coste
seal sele *n1*
seal]e seall sele *n2*
seamew semewe
seamy seymy *al*
sear *a1* (*see* sere)
sear sere *v*
searching serchyng *v.n*
sea-sand see-sande
season seson(s
second]e secund(e *a, n2*
secret(e *a, n*
secretary *n1*
secretly *av*
secretness secretnese
sect]e(s *n1*
sedition sedicion sedycions
seditious sedycyous *a*
seduce *v*
see *n1*
see(- se sene saw(e *v*
seed sede(s
seek seke sought(e *v*
seely *a* (*see* silly)
seem sem- *v2*
seemly sem(e)ly *a*
seen sene seyn *p.a* (*cf* beseen)
seignior seigneour seygnours
seigniority seygnyoryte
seise seasyd *v* (*cf* seize)
seldom]e *av*
self shelfe
selfsame selfe same *a*
sell sold(e *v*
semblant semblaunt
senate
senator senatour
send(e(th sent(e *v1*

sennight sennet *n*
sensuality sensualyte
sentence sentens
sententiously sentencyously *av*
September
sequel]e
sequester sequestred *v*
sere *a1*
sergeant sergyantes
sergeant-ferrer sergeaunt ferrour
seriously seryously *av1*
sermon(s
serpent(es serpens
serpentine serpentins *n*
servant(ys servaunt(-
serve(d -eth -yd *v1*
service servyce *n1*
serviceable servyceabyll *a*
servitor serviture
set sett(- *v*
seven sevyn *num*
sew sow- *v1*
shail shayle(s *v2*
shake(- shakyng(e shoke *v*
shall shal(t(e sho(u)ld(e shuld(e xall xalte xuld- *v* (*cf* chyll)
shame schame sham *n*
shame]- -yd *v*
shamefastness shamefastnes
shameful]l *a*
shamefully shamefuly shamfully *av*
shameless shameles shamles(se *a*
shank]kes
shape shap *n*
shard]e *n1*
share *n3*
share *v1?2?*
sharp(e(r *a*
sharp]e *v*
sharply sharpely *av*
shave(n shavyn(ge *v*
she sche *pron*
shear sheres *n1*
shear shorn(e *v*
shedding -ynge *v.n*
sheel *v* (*see* shell)
sheen shene *a*
sheep shepe
sheepcote (coat?) shepe cote
sheep's eye shepys ie
sheep's tail shepis taylys
sheer *a* (*see* shire)
shell shyll *v*
shend shent *v1*
shidered shyderyd *p.a*
shield shelde shylde
shift shyft(e *n*
shift shyfte *v*
shilling s.

shin shyn
shine s(c)hyne(d shone *v*
shine shyne *nl*
ship]pis shyp(pe(s *n*
ship shypped *v*
shipboard shypborde
shire shyre *a*
shirt shertes
shoe sho(ne *n*
shoe sho(o *v*
shoe-clout sho clout
shoe-sole sho-sole
shoot shot(e *v*
shop(pe
short(e *a*
shorten *v*
shortly shortely *av*
shot *nl*
shoulder showlder
shout showte *v*
shout showte *n2*
shovel shovll showell
shovelard, shoveller shovelar
shoving shovynge *v.n*
show shew(- *v*
shower shouer shoure
    showre(s -is *n*
shred]is *n*
shrew]e shrow *v*
shrew]es *n2*
shrewd]e shrewed shreud *a*
shrewdly shroudly *av*
shrewdness shrewdenes
shrewly shurewlye *av*
shrimp shrympes
shrine shryn- schryn- *v*
shrink shrynke *v*
shrive shryve *v*
shroud shrowde(s *nl*
shroud shrowde *vl*
shudder shoder chydder *v*
shurvy *a*
shut shet(t shyt *v*
shuttle shyttell *nl*
shuttlecock shyttel-cocke
sib syb *a, n2*
sick sycke seke *a*
sickerness sekernes(se sykernesse
sickle syckyll
sickly sekely *a*
sickness sekenesse
side syde(s
sided syded *a*
side-saddle syde-sadell
sigh syghe *n*
sigh sygh(ed *v*
sighing syghynge *p.a*
sight syght(e(s *nl*
sign sygne(s
signiority (*see* seigniority)

silence scylence
silk]e sylk(e(s
silly sely *a*
silt sylt
silver sylver
simoniac symoniake
simony symony
simper-de-cocket
    symper-the-cocket
simpleness symplenesse
simplicity symplycyte
sin synne *v*
sin]nes syn(ne -ys *n*
since sens syn(s *av, prep*
sinew senaws synnews
sing syng- sange songe *v*
singular singlar syngular -er *a*
sink synk- *v*
sip syppe *v*
sippet syppet *nl*
sir syr(s
sire syar syer(s syre
sister syster(s
sit sat(e syt(t- *v*
sith(e sythe *av, cj*
sitting -yng(e syttyng(e *p.a*
six sex *num*
size syse *nl*
skein skane skeyne *nl*
skelp]e *vl*
skewed a*l*
skill skyl(l(e
skillet skellet
skin skyn(ne(s
skip skyp(pe(- *vl*
skirt skyrt
skit skyt *a*
skull scull *nl*
sky(e(s *nl*
skyrgaliard]e skyr(e)galyard
    squyer-
slack]e *a*
slake *a*
slander sclaunder *n*
slander slaundred sclaund- *v*
slandering sklaundering *v.n*
slanderous sclaunderous
    slaundrys *a*
slaty *a*
slaver slaveryng *v*
slay slaiis *nl*
slay]n(e slain sle(- slo(o *v*
sleep slepe *n*
sleep slep- *v*
sleeve sleve slyve
sleight sl(e)yght(es sleyte *nl*
slender slendyr *a*
slice slyce *nl*
slidder sly(d)der *a*
slide slyde *v*

slimy slymy *a*
slip slyp(pe *vl*
slipper *a*
slipper slyppers *n*
sloth slouth *nl*
slothful slouthfull slowthfull *a*
sloven slovyns *n*
sluffer]d *v*
sluggish sluggysh slogysh *a*
slumber slumbrynge slombre *v*
slut(tes
sly *a*
smack]e *nl*
small(e(r smal(e *a*
small-brain small-brayne
smaragd(is *n*
smart *a*
smart]id *v*
smatter(- smater -yr *v*
smear smered *v*
smeary smery *a*
smell]- smellid *v*
smile smyle(d -id -ynge *v*
smiling smylyng *v.n*
smirk smerke *v*
smite smyght *v*
smith smyth
smithy-cur smythy kur
smock]e(s
smoke(s
smoothly smothely *av*
snail snayle snaylis
snap *v*
snapper snappar *vl*
snare
snatch]e *v*
snatching -ynge *v.n*
snite snyte *nl*
snivel snevyll snevelyng
    snyveled *v*
snort *v*
snout snowte
snow]e *nl*
snuff snuf *v2*
snur]re *v*
so(o *av, cj*
soar soored *v*
sob]be(d *vl*
sobbing -yng(e *v.n*
sober sobre *a*
soberly *av*
sock]e *nl*
Sodomite]s
soft *av*
soft(e(r *a*
softly(er *av*
soil]e *nl*
sojourn]s *v*
solace solas *nl*
solacious solacyous *a*

945

solaciously solacyusly *av*
soldan (*see* sultan)
solein solayne soleyne solen *a*
solemn solem(e solempne *a*
solemnity solempnyte
solemnly solempnely *av*
solf(e -yth *v*
some som sum(e *a, pron*
somedeal somdele sumdele *av*
sometime sometyme sumtyme *av*
somewhat somwhat sumwhat *av*
somewhere somwhere *av*
son sonne(s sonnys
song(e(s
soon]e sone(r *av*
sooth soth(e *n*
soothly sothely *av*
sop]pys *n1*
sop]py *v*
sophism -ysms
sophisticate sophisticatid
    sophystycate *v*
sorcery sorsery
sore *av*
sore(s *n1*
sore *a1*
sorrow sorow(e(s -is *n*
sorrow sorow *v*
sorrowful soroufull sorowfull(e *a*
sorry sory *a*
sort(e -is *n2*
sort]e(d -yd *v1*
sot(tes sottys *n1*
soul]- sole sowl-
sound]e *n4*
sour]e souer sowre *a*
souter sowter sowtters
south sowth
sovereign]e -ay(g)n(e -aynst
    -ey(g)n(e sofreyne
    sufferayne *a, n*
sovereignly soverenly *av*
sovereignty soveraynte
sow(e *n1*
sow(e sawe *v1*
space *n1*
spade *n1*
Spaniard Spanyardes Spainyardes
Spanish Spayny(s)she *a*
spar]re *n1*
spar(red *v1*
spare spar- *v1*
spare spayre *n2*
spark]e -is sperkes *n1*
sparkle sparkyll *v1*
sparkling -ynges *v.n*
sparrow sparoes sparow(e)s
spattle spattyl *n1*
speak spake spek(- spok- *v*
spear spere *n1,3*

special]l specyall *a, av*
specially specyally *av*
specify specefye *v*
spectacle(s *n1*
spectacle-case
speculation speculacyon
speech speche
speed sped(d(e *v*
speed spede *n*
spell *v1*
spell(e(s *v2*
spence *n1*
spend(e(th spent(e spynt *v1*
spense *n* (*cf* expense)
spew]e *v*
spherical sperycall *a*
spill spyll spylt *v*
spin spyn(nys *v*
spindle spyndell spyndels
spink spynke *n1*
spinning-wheel spynnyng whele
spirit]is
spiritual]l spiryt- spyrit- spyryt- *a*
spiritualty spirytualte
    (*cf* spirituality)
spital (*see* spittle)
spite spyght (*cf* despite)
spiteful spyghtfull *a*
spittle spytell n1
splay *v1*
spoil spoylyd *v*
spoon spone
sport(e *n1*
spray *n1*
spread sprede *v*
spring sprange -yng(e *v*
spring spryng(e *n1*
spur *v1*
spur(res spurrys spores *n1*
spurn sporne *v1*
spy(e(d -ing *v*
spy]es spies *n*
squat a
squire squyers squyre
stab]be *n1*
stability stabilite
stable stabyll *n1*
stable stabille -yll *a*
stable stabille *v1*
stable-door stable dur
staff]e *n1*
stair stayre
stake *n1*
stale *a*
stale *n3*
stalking -ynge *p.a*
stall *n1*
stallion stalyon
stalworthy *a*
stammer *v*

stammering stameryng *p.a*
stamp]e stampped *v*
stand]- stond- sto(o)d(e *v*
standard stondarde
star(ris sterre(s -ys *n1*
Star-Chamber Ster Chambre
stare *n1*
stare star- *v*
staring -ynge *v.n*
stark(e *av*
stark]e(st *a*
starling starlyng *n1*
starry sterry *a*
start(e stert(e *v*
startle startyll *v*
starve sterve *v*
state
stature
statute]s
stead sted(e *n*
steadfast stedfast *a*
steadfastness stedfastnesse
steal stale stele stolyn *v1*
stealing stelyng *v.n*
steed stede
steel steile *n1*
steep stepe *a*
steeple steple *n1*
steer stere styreth *v*
stellify stellyfye *v*
stench]e
step]pis
stern]e *a*
steven stevyn *n1*
stew]es -ys stuse *n2*
stewed stued *p.a*1
stick styck(- *v1*
stick styckis *n1*
still styl(l *av*
still styll *a*
stilly *av*
sting stang sto(u)nge stynge(s *v1*
stinging -yng styngyng *p.a*
stink stynk- stanke *v*
stinkingly stynkingly *av*
stint stynt(eth *v*
stir styre *v*
stirrup styrops
stitch stytch(is *n1*
stitched stytched *p.a*
stith styth
stock]e -ys *n1*
stock-dove stockedowve
stock-fish stockfyssh
stoical]l *a*
stomach stomak(e
stone(s stonys
stone-cast]e *n*
stony *a*
stool stol(e stoule

stoop stowpe *vl*
stop stopp- *v*
stopping-oyster stoppynge oyster
stopple stoppell *nl*
store *n*
store *v*
stork]e
storm]- *n*
storm-beaten storm ybeten *a*
storm-driven storme dryven *a*
stormy *a*
story(es storis *nl*
stound]e stownde *nl*
stour stowre *a*
stout stowte *a*
stout stowte *av*
stouty stoutty stowty *a*
stow(e *int*
straight stray(gh)t(e
    strey(gh)t(e *av*
straight strayte strei(gh)t
    strey(gh)te *a*
straightly streatly streitly *av*
strain streynes *n3*
strain strayned *vl*
strait streytes *n*
strait a, av (*cf* straight)
strange straunge *a*
strangle *v*
straught *a*
straw(e(s *nl*
strawberry strawbery
straw(r)y *a*
stream]es streme(s -ys
street strete
strength(e
stretch]ynge *v*
strew strowed *v*
stride strydynge *v*
strife stryfe
strike strake stryke(n *v*
string strynged *v*
string strynges *n*
strip strypte *vl*
stripe strype *n2*
stripling stryplyng
strive stryve(s stryvith *v*
stroke(s *nl*
strong(e *a*
strong-hearted stronge-herted *a*
strongly strongely *av*
stubbed *p.a*
stubborn stobburne *a*
student studiantes
studious studyous *a*
studiously studyously *av*
study *n*
study(e *v*
stuff]e(d *vl*
stumble stombyll *v*

stump]e *n*
sturdy sturdier *a*
stut *vl*
sty *n3*
Stygial Stygyall Stigiall *a*
style stile
subdean sedeane
subdue subdude *v*
subject]es -is
subjection subjectyon -ccyon
submit submytted *v*
subscribe subscrybe *v*
substance substaunce
substitute substytute *n*
subtle subtell subtyle -yll *a*
subtlety subtylte suttelte
subtly subtelly subtylly *av*
subvert]ed *v*
succour soccoure *n*
succour(e socour(e *v*
such(e seche soche
    syke *dem.a, pron*
suck(e *v*
sudden sodeyne *a*
suddenly sodaynly sode(y)nly *av*
sue sew(e suwed *v*
suffer(e)d suffre(d *v*
sufferance -aunce
suffice suffyce *v*
suffrage
sugar suger
sugared sugred -yd *p.a*
sugar-loaf suger lofe
suggestion suggestyon
suing suyng *v.n*
suit su(e)te sutys
suitor suter(s
sullen (*see* solein)
sultan sowden
sum]es somme *nl*
summer somer(s *nl*
summon(e)d sommon(de *v*
summoner somner sumner
summoning somnynge *v.n*
summons sommons
sun sonne
sunbeam sonbeames
sunning sunnyng *v.n*
sunshine soneshyne
sup(ped soppy(?) *vl*
superciliously superciliusly *av*
superflue *a*
superstition supersticiouns
    supersticyon(s -ycyon
superstitious supersticyous *a*
supervisor supervysour
supper *nl*
supplement *nl*
supplication supplycacyon(s
supply(e(d supple(yng *vl,2*

support(e *v*
support]e *n*
supportation supportacyon
suppose(d -ynge *v*
supposition supposicyon -ycions
supreme *a*
sure *a*
surely suerly *av*
surety
surfeit surfet
surfetous *a*
surfled *p.a*
surfling surfillyng *v.n*
surgeon surgions
surgery
surmise surmysed *v*
surmount]ynge (-mownt- sour- *v*
surplus]e
surprise supprisid suprysyd *v*
surquidant surcudant *a*
surrender surrendr- *v*
survey *v*
surveyance surveyaunce
surveyor survayour
suspect]e *nl*
suspect]e *a*
suspicion suspycyon
swallow *nl*
swan(ne(s
swap *v*
swart(e *a*
swear sware swere(d sworne *v*
swearing swerynge *v.n*
sweat swete *n*
sweat swete swetis *v*
sweater sweters
sweaty swety *a*
sweep swept *v*
sweet swete(r swetter *a*
sweet swete *av*
sweeting swetyng *nl*
sweetly swetely *av*
sweetmeat swete meate
swell(ys *v*
swelling -ynge *v.n*
swerve swarve *v*
swift swyfte *a*
swilling-tub swyllyng tubbe
swine swyne
swineherd swyne herde
swing swynged *vl* (*cf* swig?)
swinker swynkers
sword(e(s -ys swe(a)rd(e
sworn]e *p.a*
syllogism silogisme
syllogistical silogisticall *a*
synodal]les sinodals
tabard taber(te)s
table(s tabull
tack]e *nl*

tackling takelynge *v.n*
ta ha *int*
tail]e(s tayl- *nl*
tailor taylers
taint teintyd *v*
take(- tak- tane toke *v*
taking -ynge *v.n*
tale(s -is tailes tayles
talk]e *n*
talk]- *v*
talking -ynge *v.n*
tall(e tawle *a*
tallow]e talowe
talwood talwod
tame *a*
tampion taumpinnis
tan
tan *a*
tancred tancrete *a*
tang]yd *vl*
tanned tannyd *p.a*
tap]pid *vl*
tapet tappet(t(is
tapster tappyster
tarnish]e *v*
tarry tary *v*
tart]e *n*
tart *a*
taste tastid *v*
taste *n*
tatter]s
tattered tatterd -red *p.a*
taunt]e(s *nl*
taunt(- tante *v*
taunting *p.a*
tavell]is tavellys
tavern]e
taverner tavernars
tawny *a*
tawny *n*
tax]es *nl*
tax *v*
taxing -ynge *v.n*
teach teche(d -yth(e tought *v*
teaching techynge *v.n*
teal tele *n*
tear]ys *nl*
tear tere(d torne *vl*
teen]e tene *nl*
teeth teth(e
teg]ges teggys *n*
tehee tehe *int*
tell(- tel told(e *v*
teller]s
tempest]e
tempestous *a*
temple *nl*
temple]s *n2*
temporal]l *al*
temporalty]e temporalte

ten *a, n*
tend]e *vl,2*
tender *v2*
tender tendyr *a*
tenderly *av*
tennis tennys
tenor tenours *nl*
tense tensis *n*
tent *nl*
tenter-hook tenter-hokys
tercel-gentle tarsell gentyll *n*
term]es termys
termagant Tyrmagant
terrestre terestre *a*
terrible *a*
testament]is
testify]e testefy *v*
testy *a*
tetrical tetrycall *a*
tetter tytters(?)
te-wit teuyt
text(e(s
than then *cj*
thank]e(s thank(k)is *n*
thank]e(d -yd *v*
thankfully thankefullyer *av*
that *pron, a , av, cj*
the *def.art*
thee thy *pron*
thee *vl*
theek theke *v*
theft(e
their(e ther(e theyr(e
    thyr *poss.pron*
them theem theim theym
    thom *pron*
themselves themselfe *pron*
then(ne than *av*
thence thens *av*
theological]l *a*
theologization theologisacion
theologue theologys
theology
theoric tirikkis tirykis *n*
there ther *av*
thereat]t therat *av*
thereby therby *av*
therefore therfor(e *av*
therein therin *av*
thereof therof *av*
thereon *av*
thereout therout *av*
thereto therto *av*
thereupon therupon *av*
therewith therwith *av*
therewithal]l therwithall *av*
these the(i)s theys this
    thyse *pron, a*
thewed thewde *p.a*
they thei *pron*

thick]este thycke(r *a*
thick thycke *av*
thick-lipped thycke-lypped *a*
thief thefe thevys
thimble thymbell thymble
thin thyn(ne *a*
thine thyn(e *pron*
thing thyng(-
think]e thynk(- thought(e *v*
thinking thynkyng(e *v.n*
third]e *n*
thirst thrust
this thys *pron, a*
thistle thystels
thither thyther theder thider
    thyd(d)er *av*
thong]e
thorn]e(s
thorough (see through)
thoroughly thorowly *av*
those thos *pron, a*
thou thow *pron*
though(e thouthe tho(w(gh)e
    thowth(e *cj*
thought thowghte *nl*
thoughtful]l *a*
thousand(e thow- *a, n*
thousandfold]e
    thowsande folde *av*
thread threde(s
threadbare thred(e)-bare *a*
threat thret(e *v*
three thre *num*
threefold threfolde *av*
three-footed thre-foted *a*
threescore threscore *a*
threshold
thrift]e thryft(e *nl*
thriftless thrifltes thryftlesse *a*
thrive thryve *v*
throat throte(s throtis
throat-boll throte bole
throne trone(s
throng]e *n*
throng]e *v*
throstle threstyl
through thrugh(e throw thorow(e
    thorugh *prep, av*
throughout thorowe out(e *prep, av*
throw *nl*
throw threwe *vl*
thrust *v*
thumbed *a*
thunder thonder
thurification thurifycation
thus *av*
thwart]- *v*
thy thi *poss.pron*
thyself(e thy selfe *pron*
tice tyse *v*

948

tickle tykyll *v*
tide tyd(e(s
tiding](e)s tydingis tydynges
tied tyde *p.a*
tiger tyger
tile tyle
till tyl(l *av, prep*
tilly-vally tully valy *int*
time tyme(s *n*
timorous tymerous *a*
tin tyn
tine tyned *v3*
tinker tynkers
tippet typpet
tire tyryd *v2*
tirly-tirlow tyrly tyrlowe
tissue tissew tessew
titivish titivyllis tytyvell tytyvylles *n*
title titille tytle
titmouse tytmose
titter tytters
tittle-tattle tytell-tattyll
to *prep*
toad tode
to-broken to-brokyn *p.a*
today *av*
toe to(o
tofore *av*
to-fret v
together -yr toged- togith-
   togyd- togyth- *av*
toil toyle *n2*
to-jag]ged tojaggid *v*
token(s tokyn
tolerate v
toleration tol(l)eracyon
tollage
to-mangle v
to-mired to-myryd *p.a*
tomorrow tomorowe *av*
tone *pron*
tongue tong(e(s tung(-
tongue-tied tonge-tayde *p.a*
tonnel]l
tonsure tonsors
too to *av*
tool tole
toolman tolman(?)
toot]e tote(th *v1*
tooth toth teth(e
toothache tothe ake
tooting totynge *v.n*
top *n1*
topaz topas
topical]l
to-ragged p.a
to-rent]e p.a
tother tedder *pron*
tot-quot tot quottes
totter v

to-torn]e p.a
touch]e towchis *n*
touch]e(d towch- *v*
touching touchyng(e
   towchyng *prep*
tough(ther *a*
tourney turney tyrnyd *v*
tow]e n1
toward(e prep
towards -es *prep*
tower tour(e(s towre(s -is *n1*
town]e(s toune
town-clerk towne clarke
toy]es toies *n*
toy]e v
trace trasid *v1*
tradiction(?) tradiccyon
tragedial tragedyall *a*
tragedy tragediis tragydese
train trayne *n2*
traitor traytour(s
traitorly traytourly *a*
traitorously trayterously *av*
traitory traytory treytory
tramming tramynge *v.n*
trance trans *n1*
tranchant tranchaunt *a*
transcend]- transendyng v
transcendingly av
transform]yd v
transformation transformacyon
transitory transytory *a*
translate v
translation translacion -cyo(u)n
trapped trapte *p.a*
trash trasshe *n1*
trattler tratlers
trattling tratlyng(e tratlande *p.a*
traveller travellars
traverse travarse traves *n*
tray *n2*
treachery trechery
tread]e trede *v*
treason trayson treson
treasure tres(o)ure
treat]- trete v
treatise treatyse tratyse tretise
treaty treatee
treble trebelles trebyllys trybyll
tree]s tre
tremble trembyll tremblid
   trymblyth trem(e)lyng *v*
trench]e
trental]e trentall
tress]es -is -ys
trial tryall *n1*
triality tryalytes
trice trysyd *v*
trice tryce *n2*
trifle trifels tryfyll tryfyls

trim trym *a*
trim trym(me trymmyth *v*
trimming trymynge *v.n*
trim-tram trym-tram
trinal trynall *a*
trinity trinite trinyte Trynyte
Triones Trions
trip(pyng tryp *v*
trip tryppe *n1*
tripe trype(s *n1*
triumph]e -is tryumphe(s *n*
triumph tryhumfythe *v*
triumphant triumphaunt *a*
triumphantly]e av
trivial]s tryvyals *n*
troll trold *v*
trolly-lolly troly loly *int*
trot]te v
trot *n1*
troth trouth(e
trotter]s
trouble *n*
trouble]d v
trout]e n1
trovy int
trow(- v
truce trewse trusys
true tr(e)u trew(e *a*
trull trowle
truly truely trulye trew(e)ly *av*
trump]e *n1*
trump]ythe trompe *v1,3?*
trumpet(tis *n*
truss]e(d *v*
trust(e *n*
trust(e(d -inge -yd *v*
truth(e treuth trewth troughte
   trouth(e trowth(e
try]de tried *v*
Tuesday Teusday Tewsday
tugged tuggyd *p.a*
tugging tyggyng *v.n*
tuition tuicyon
tuly tewly *a*
tumble tumbyll *v*
tumbler tumblar(s
tumbrel tumrell *n1*
tunable *a*
tunably *av*
tunnel (see tonnel)
tunning -ynge *v.n*
tunnish tonnysh *a*
turd]e torde
turf]fe *n1*
Turk]e
turn]e tourne *n*
turn]- torne tourne- *v*
turning turnyng(e towrnyng *v.n*
turquoise turkis
turret]tes turrettis

949

turtle turtyll *n1*
tush]e tusche tusshe *int*
tut *int*
twain]e tewyne twayn(e tweyne *num, n*
tween twene *prep*
twenty *num*
twibill twybyll
twice twyce twyse *av*
twink twynkyng *v2*
twinkle twynklyng *v2*
twist twyst *int*
twit twyt *int*
two *num*
tyrant tyrand
udder ydder
ugly *a*
umbles umblis
umwhile umwhyle *av*
unable *a*
unassured *p.a*
unbend onbende *v*
unbind unbynde *v*
unblest unblyst *p.a*
unbraced unbrased *p.a*
unburnt unbrent *p.a*
uncomely oncomly *a*
uncourteous uncurteis *a*
uncourteously uncurtesly *a*
uncouth]es *n*
under undyr ondyr *prep*
undermine undermynde *v*
underneath underneth *prep*
underset *v*
understand(e(s -stonde -st(o)d(e *v*
undertake undertoke *v*
undo undone *v*
undoubted *av*
uneath unneth *av*
unfeathered unfethered *p.a*
unfeigned unfayned -yd *a*
unfortunately *av*
unfriendly unfrendly *a*
ungoodly *a*
ungracious ungracyous *a*
ungraciously ungracyously *a*
unhappily unhap(pe)ly *av*
unhappy(est *a*
unhurt *p.a*
unicorn]e unycornes
university universyte unyversyte
unkind unkynd(e *a*
unkindly *av*
unkindness unkyndnesse
unlaced unlased unlast *p.a*
unliking unlykynge *p.a*
unlust
unlusty *a*
unmeet unmete *a*
unnatural]l *a*

unpaid unpayd *p.a*
unpolished unpullysht *p.a*
unreasonable unresonable *a*
unremembered unbred *p.a*
unreverent *a*
unrewarded *p.a*
unset *p.a*
unshred *p.a*
unsound(y) unsowndy *a*
unstable *a*
unstableness]e
unsteadfastness unstedfastnesse
unsurely *av*
unsweet unswete *a*
untaught untawte *a*
unthrift]es
unthriftiness unthryftynes
untidy untydy *a*
untied untayde untyde *p.a*
unto *prep*
untrue untrew(e *a*
untruly untrewly *av*
untrussed untrust *p.a*
untruth
untwine untwynde *v*
up(pe *av*
upon uppon apon *prep*
upright upryght *a*
upstand upstode *v*
upstart]e *v*
uptuck]e *v*
upward]e *av*
urchin urcheons
ure (*see* eure)
urgently *av*
us *pron*
usage
use(- usyd usynge *v*
usher usscheres ussher
usual]l *a*
utter *av*
utter *a*
utterance ut(t)eraunce *n1*
utterly *av*
vagabond vacabondes
vague vagys *n1*
wail vayleth *v1*
wail vale *v2*
vain vayne *a, n*
vainglorious vayne gloryous *a*
vainglory vayn(e)glorie -glory
vale *n1*
valiance valiaunce valyaunce
valiant valiaunt valya(u)nt *a*
valiantly valyaunt(o)ly(e *av*
value
vanish vanysshyth *v*
vanity vanyte
vanquish venquesshid *v*
variableness varyablenesse

variance varyans varyaunce
varnish varnyshe *v*
vary(eth varry *v*
vassal]l vassayles
vat (*cf* mash-fat)
vault vawte *n1*
vauntparler vaunte-parler
veil vayles *n1*
vein vayne(s -ys
veined vayned *a*
velvet
velyard]e
venge]d *v*
vengeance vengeaunce wengaunce
venison venyson
venomous venomows venemous venemows *a*
venomously venemously venymously *av*
ventail ventayles
verdure verduris
verily verely *av*
verjuice vergesse
vermin vermyne
verse(s vers
versicle versycles
versify versyfy *v*
versifying versyfyeng *v.n*
versing box versynge boxe
vertibility vertibilite
very(e *av*
very *a*
vestment
vex]- *v*
vexation vexacyon
vicar vycaryes
vicar general]l vycare generall
vice vyce(s vyse *n1*
vicious vicyous *a*
view vewe
vigorously *av*
vile vyle *a*
village vyllage wylage
villain vilane *a*
villain villayn(s vyllayne *n*
villainous vylanous *a*
villainy vilany vyllany vyllony
vine vinis
violate vyolate *v*
violence vyolence
violet vyolet *n1*
virginal virgynall *a*
virtue vertew vertu(e)s
virtuous vertuous virtuows *a*
virtuously vertuously *av*
virulent *a*
virulently *av*
visage vysage
visit vysyte *v*

visitation vysytacyon
visor vyser
vital]l *a*
voice voyce vice
void voyd(e *a, n*
void voyde *v*
volume]s -is -ys
volvelle volvell
vouchsafe vouchesaf(e vowchsafe *v*
vow (*see* avow)
wade wadyd -ythe *v*
wag(ge(s waggys *v*
wage(s
wagging -ynge *v.n*
wagtail wagtayle
wail wayle(d *v*
wait wayte *vl*
wake *nl*
wake(ste wakyst woke *v*
wale v (*see* wheal)
walk(e -ynge *v*
wall(e(s -ys wals
wallet
wallow walow *vl*
walnut]tes
walter *vl*
wamble]th *v*
wambling -lynge *v.n*
wan(ne *a*
wander(ynge wandred -rynge *v*
wandering wandring -ryng *v.n*
wane *a*
wanhope
want(- *v*
wanton *a, n*
wantonly(e *av*
wantonness]e vantonnesse
   wantones wontones
war wary(?) *vl*
war(re werre *n*
warble warbelynge warblynge *v*
warbling warblyng *v.n*
ward]e *n2*
warden wardeyn *nl*
ware *vl*
warely *av*
waring weryng(e *v.n*
warm]e *a*
warn]e(d werne *v*
warrant wara(u)nt warent *v*
warray wary(?) *v*
wart(e
wary *v*
wash wasshe *v*
wash-bowl washbol
washing wasshyng *v.n*
wasp]e waspis
waspy
waste(d *v*

wasteful]l *a*
watch wache *n*
watch(e *v*
watching -ynge wachyng *v.n*
water(s
water-hen wather-hen
waterlag
water-mill water mylles
watery watry *a*
waw]es wawys
wax(- wexyd *vl*
way(e(s wey *nl*
wayward(e waywyrde weywarde *a*
waywardly *av*
waywardness]e
we *pron*
weak weke *a*
weakly *av*
weal-public wele publyke
wealth welth(e
wealthful welthfull *a*
wear]e were(th worn(e *vl*
weary wery *a*
weasand wesa(u)nt
weather wedder wether
weathercock wethercocke
weave weve *vl*
weaving-pin wevyng pin
web]be
wed *n*
wed *v*
wedding-ring weddynge rynge
wedge
weed wedes *nl*
week weke(s woke wokys
ween wen- *v*
weep wepe wept *v*
weeping weping(e -ynge *v.n*
wehee wehe *int*
weigh waye(d wey(ed *v*
weight wayght weyght *nl*
welcome welcom *v*
welcome *a, int*
well wel(e *av, a*
well(e -ys *nl*
wellaway wel(e)away(e *int*
well-handed well handyd *a*
well-nigh welny *av*
well-sighted well-syghted *p.a*
Welshman Walshemannys Welch-welt]yth *v2*
wench]e(s
wery]ed *v*
west *n*
wet]e *v*
whalebone whalis bone
wharrow]e
what(e wat *a, pron, etc*
whatever *pron*
whatsoever *pron*

whatsomever *pron*
wheal wheled *vl*
wheat whete
wheel whele(s
when whan *av*
whence whens *av*
where wher *av*
whereas *av, cj*
whereat wherat *av*
whereby wherby *av*
wherever *av*
wherefore wherfor(e wyerfore *av*
wherein wherin *av*
whereof wherof *av*
whereon wheron *av*
whereso wherso *av*
wheresoever *av*
whereto wherto *av*
whereupon *av*
wherewith wherwith wherwyth *av*
whet]t *v*
whether *cj*
whey-wormed *a*
which(e whych(e *a, pron*
while whyle *cj*
while whyle *n*
whiles whils whyles -is *n, cj, av*
whilom *av*
whilst whylest whylyst *av, cj*
whim-wham whym-wham
whine whyn- *v*
whinnymeg whynnymeg *n*
whinyard whynarde
whip *v*
whip whyp *n*
whipling *v.n*
whip-sloven whypslovens
whirl]lid whyrled *v*
whisking whyskynge *p.a*
whisper whispred whysper *v*
whispering whyspryng *v.n*
whist whyste *a*
whistle whystelyth *v*
whistle whystell *n*
whit(te whyt(te *nl*
white whight whyte(r wyght *a*
whiteness whyt(e)nes(se
whither whyder whyther whythyr *av*
whiting whytyng wyteyng
who(o *pron*
whole hole ho(o)ll *a*
wholly holly hooly *av*
whom(e *pron*
whore horys
whoreson horson(s
whose who(o)s *pron*
whoso *pron*
whosoever *pron*
why *av*

wickedness wyckydnesse
wide wyde *a, av*
widow wydow
wife wyfe wyves
wig wygges *v1*
wild wyld(e *a*
wilful willfull wy(l)full *a*
wilfully wylfully *av*
wilfulness wylfulnes(se
will]e wyll- *n1*
will wil wyl(l wylt(e wold(- would wald woll *v1*
wily wyly *a*
wimble wymble
win wyn- wan(ne won(ne *v1*
wince wins wynsyth *v1* (*cf* winch)
winch wynche wynshed *v1* (*cf* wince)
wind wynde(s *n*
wind wynde *v1*
winding-stair windyngstayre
windmill windmil wyndmil wyndmyll
window wyndowes
wind-shaken wynde-schakyn *p.a*
windy wyndy *a*
wine wyne *n1*
wing wynges
wink wynk- *v1*
winning wynnyng(e *v.n1*
winter wynter(s *n, a*
wipe wypid *v*
wire wyre
wisdom wysdom(e
wise wyse *a*
wise wyse *n1*
wise wyse vyse *v1*
wisely wysely(e wesely *av*
wish wysch wysshe(d *v*
wit(tis wyt(- *n*
wit wete wist wyst(e *v1*
witch wytch *n2*
witchcraft witchecraft wy(t)ch(e)craft
wite wyte *v1*
with(e wyth(e weth *prep*
withdraw(e v
withers widders *n*
withered wyddered wyderyd *p.a*
withhold(e v
within wythin *prep*
without(e(n -owte wyth- *av, prep, cj*
withsay *v*
withstand(e witstand *v*
witless]e wytles(se *a*
witting wetynge *v.n1*
wittol wetewoldis
woe wo(o *n, a*
woefully wofully *av*

wolf]e wolvis -ys
woman women
womanhood womanhod(e
womankind womankynd
womanly *a*
won(n- *v*
wonder *n*
wonder *a*
wonder(yd wondyr wondre(d *v*
wonderful(l *a*
wondering wondringes *v.n*
wonderly *av*
wondersly wounderly *av* (*cf* wondrously)
wondrous wondero(w)us wonders *a*
wondrously wonderusly *av*
wonning -ynge *v.n*
wont(e *p.a*
wood]es woddis *n1*
wood(e wod(d)e *a*
woodcock wodco(c)ke wodi- woode-
woodhack]e
wool woll(e wull
word(-
work]- wark(- werk- *n*
work]e(th warke wrou(gh)t(e wrowght(e *v*
world(e warlde
worldly wordly *a*
worm]es
worm-eaten worme-etyn *p.a*
worry wirry wyrry worrowyd weryed(?) *v*
worse wors warse wurs *a, av*
worse warse *n*
worship worshyp *n*
worship worshyppe *v*
worshipful worshypfull *a*
worshipfully worshypfully *av*
worshiply worsheply *av*
worst(e *a, n*
wort]es *n1*
worth]e *v1*
worth *n1*
worth(e *a*
worthy *a*
wot(- wott- *v*
wound]e(s wondes *n*
wound]ed -id *v*
wrack wrak(e *n1*
wrangle wrangyll wranglyng(e *v*
wrap]ped wrapt *v*
wrath
wraw *a*
wreak wreke wroken *v*
wren
wrench]e wrenchis *n1*
wrench]e *n2*

wrest(yd -yng wrast- *v*
wrestle wrastel(l wrastled *v*
wrestling wrestlyng wrastelynge *v.n*
wretch]e wreches
wretched -id wrechyd *a*
wretchedly wretchydly *av*
wretchedness]e wre(t)chyd- wretchock]es
wrig wrygges *v*
wrig-wrag wrag-wrag
wring]- wryng(- wrang(e wro(u)nge *v*
wrinkled wrynklyd *p.a*
wrist wryst
writ
write writ- wryt(h)- wright w(h)ryght wrate wrete wro(u)te wroth *v*
writing]e -ynge *v.n*
writhen wrythen *p.a*
writhing wrythyng(e *v.n*
wrong]e(s
wrong(e *a*
wroot wrote(s *v*
wroth(e *a*
wrothsome *a*
wry]e *v2*
Wycliffist Wytclyftista
yarn]e
yaw]de *v*
yawn yane *v*
ye *pron*
yea ye *av*
year yer-
yearn yerne *v*
yeast yeest
yell(ed *v*
yelling yellynge *v.n*
yellow yalowe *a*
yeoman yoman
yerk]e *v*
yes *av*
yesterday(e av
yesternight -nyght *av*
yet(t *av, cj*
ymete ymet *v*
yoke *v*
yon]e *a*
yond]e *a, av*
yonder *av*
yonkerkin yonkerkyns
you yow *pron*
young yong(e(r *a*
youngling yonglyng
your(e yor youer yowr(e yower yer *pron*
yourself]e yorselfe *pron*
youth yowth(e youghte
youward]e *av*
zodiac zodyake

APPENDIX C

Index of Compounds

This index provides a complete list of the second elements of compounds in Skelton's poetry. Elements that are typographically separate words in Scattergood's edition but that we have treated as second elements of compounds in the concordance are preceded by an asterisk. The index does not include prefixed elements (e.g. *to-mangle*) or ablaut combinations (e.g. *whym-wham*).

-abuse	halfe-	*-cocke	wether-
-adays	(see -days)	-cockes	dau-
-after	her-, here-	-cocket	symper-the-
*-after	here-	-coddes	pes-
*-ake	bone-, tothe-	-coke	daw-, pe-, wod-
-all	with-	-cokkis	daw-
-a-Pase	passe-	*-come	cockes-
-armur	cote-	-Cope	Double-
*-armure	cote-	*-coste	se-
*-as	where-	*-cote	shepe-
-at	ther-, wher-, where-	-craft	witche-, wyche-, wytch-
-att	there-	-cri	out-
-auntleres	brow-	-cry	out-, owt-
*-bagges	saffron-	-cryes	out-
*-baggys	beggers-	*-crommes	bred-
-bakar	py-	*-crosse	Christ-
-ball	fote-	-crosse	Criste-
-bare	thred-, threde-	*-cundight	salfe-
*-bare	threde-	-day	Domes-, myd-, yester-
*-barme	ale-	-daye	yester-
-be	shal-, wyl-	*-daye	holy-
*-be	shal-, shall-	-dayes	nowa-, nowea-
*-beames	son-	*-dayes	nowa-, nowea-
-beaten	rayne-	-days	nowa-
*-bed	fether-	*-days	nowea-
-beddes	fether-	-dandy	handy-
*-be it	How-, Howe-	-dardy	hardy-
-beit	all-, how-, howe-	-dede	in-
*-bels	hawkys-	*-dede	in-
-bery	straw-	-deed	in-
*-beten	rayne- (cf -ybeten)	-dele	after-
-betyn	rayn-	*-delinge	double-
-by	here-, there-, wher-	*-delyng	double-
-bytten	fly-	*-delynge	Double-, inwyt-, Playne-
*-blew	Indy-	-denty	prycke-me-
*-blewe	Inde-	*-dores	church-
*-blode	hart-	-dowve	stocke-
*-bloode	hart-	*-drake	fyer-
-blowen	fly-	-drede	For-
*-boke	balade-	*-drynkers	ale-
-bol	wash-	*-dryven	storme-
*-bole	throte-	-ducke	mylke-
-boll	blow-	*-dur	stable-
*-bolle	mashe-	-dust	saw-
-bolt	bird-	*-dust	cole-
*-bone	backe-, whalis-	*-eare	pygges-
-bonyarde	knokyl-	*-Ease	Lytell-
-boorde	see-	-eaten	mothe-
-bord	cup-	-eyed	holow-, one-
-borde	cup-, shyp-	-etyn	worme-
-bowl	(see -bol(l(e)	*-etyn	moth-
*-box	offerynge-	-ever	how-, howe-, so-
*-boxe	versynge-	*-ever	What-, whatso-, whatsom-, Where-
-Brayne	Small-	-eye	(see -ie, -iyde, -ny(e))
*-brekyng	sayntuary-	-face	out-
-brennynge	herte-	*-facyd	out-
-brest	red-	-fare	feld-, felde-
-bryngis	in-	-fast	sted-
*-buddes	rose-	-fast	(see -fest)
*-bun	bayardys-	-father	god-
*-calfe	hynde-	-fat	mash-
*-cart	dong-	*-fat	mash-, masshe-
*-carte	donge-	*-faveryd	evyll-
*-case	per-	-fawcon	ger-, jar-
-case	pyn-	*-fedder	eestryche-
*-case	spectacle-	-fee	lay-
-cast	over-	-fellaw	bed-
-caste	stone-	*-ferrour	sergeaunt-
*-caste	brydelynge-	-fest	mayster-
*-catt	pus-	-fet	far-
*-Chambre	Ster-	*-fet	farre-
*-cheke	peny-	-fynche	gold-
-clappes	after-	-fynger	lyme-
*-clarke	bybyll-, towne-	-fyssh	stock-
*-clerke	parysshe-	-fysshe	salt-
*-clothe	brode-	-fly	butter-
*-clout	sho-	*-fly	flessh-
-clowte	dysche-	*-flycke	bacon-
-cock	dau-, daw- (cf -kock(e)	-flye	butter-, flesshe-
-cocke	dau-, daw-, shyttel-, wether-, wod-, wodi-, woode-	*-flyes	flesshe-

*-flyght	owle-	-hownde	grey-
-fllyis	butter-	*-ie	shepys-
-flote	on-	*-iyde	pynk-
*-floure	daysy-	-in	here-, ther-, there-, wher-, where-, with-, wyth-
*-flowre	jeloffer-, lylly-		
*-foder	Jamys-	*-in	here-
*-folde	thousand-, thowsande-	-inne	here-
-foles	mare-	*-ybeten	storm-
*-foote	forme-	*-yles	out-
-for	ther-, wher-	-joye	bely-
-fore	ther-, there-, wher-, where-, wyer-	-joust	ale-
		*-kay	cofer-
-foted	rough-, thre-	*-keke	horne-
*-foted	rough-	-kynd	man-, woman-
-founde	new-	-kynde	man-
-fret	to-	-kock	daw-
*-furre	budge-	-kocke	daw-
-galiard	squyer-	*-kur	smythy-
-galiarde	skyr-	-lace	here-
-galyarde	squyer-	-lag	water-
-galyard	skyr-, Skyre-	*-lande	mayne-
-gate	dore-	*-larkes	hobby-
*-gate	klycked-, postern-	-lauyd	owte-
-gaw	guy-	*-lawreate	poete-
*-generall	vicar-, vycare-	*-lawreat	poyet-
*-gentyll	tarsell-	-legged	lympe-
*-gy	hay the-	-lesse	neverthe-
*-gye	Hay the-	*-levis	laurell-
*-glorie	vayne-	*-light	mone-
-glorious	vayn-	-lypped	thycke-
*-glorious	vayne-	*-Lobbyn	Hop-
*-gloryous	vayne-	*-Lobyn	Hop-
-glory	vayn-	*-lode	cart-
*-glory	vayne-	*-lofe	suger-
-gose	sadyl-	*-loft	rode-
*-gounes	morning-	-loked	over-
-grene	Lyncole-	-loly-lo	troly-
-groweth	over-	-maymed	halfe-
*-growth	profyte-	*-makynge	clothe-
*-hachet	powle-	-man	fery-, gentyl-, hang-, horse-, jentil-, jentyl-, rag-
-hacke	wood-		
-haired	(see -hered)	*-man	jentyl-, Welche-
*-hall	comyne-	-mannys	Walshe-
*-hallowe	all-	-mans	deed-
-handyd	well-	-mas	Candel-
*-hare	Marche-	*-mate	checke-, chek-, cheke-
*-harted	faint-, false-, harde-	*-maters	scole-
*-harum	March-	*-matter	scole-
*-hat	Cardynall-, Cardynals-	*-meate	flesshe-, swete-
*-hatchettis	Powle-	-me-denty	prycke-
-hauke	gos-	-men	English-, Englissh-, Englyshe-, gentel-, horse-, mad-, nobill-
*-hed	garleke-		
*-heddes	garlyke-		
*-hedes	calvys-	*-men	Englyshe-, French-, Frenche-, halfe-, lay-, Laye-, noble-
-hen	po-, wather-		
*-herde	swyne-	-mes	candel-
-hered	gray-	*-mete	flesshe-
*-heretykes	halfe-	-mewe	se-
-herted	hen-, Stronge-	-mighty	al-
*-hertyd	cruell-, hard-	-mil	wind-, wynd-
-hyll	dong-	-myghty	all-
*-hypped	ugly-	*-mylke	mares-
-ho	Bo-, Hough-	-myll	horse-, wynd-
*-ho	bo-	*-mylles	water-
-hokys	tenter-	-mynde	under-
-hold	copye-, hous-	-moder	hoder-
-holde	copy-, hous-, hows-	-monger	coster-
-holdes	hous-	-moost	al-
-holdyng	howse-	-more	ever-, never-
-hole	mouse-	*-morowe	to-
-holy	pop-	-most	al-
*-holy	pope-	-moste	al-
-hood	barly-	*-nat	can-
-hope	wan-	-nebbed	croke-
-horne	ink-	*-necked	longe-
*-horne	rambes-, rammes-	-net	flye-
-hounde	hell-	-ny	pyggys-
-houndes	grey-	-nye	pigges-
-hous	scole-	-nyght	yester-, myd-
*-house	ale-, dwellinge-	-nyghte	over-
-house	brew-	-none	after-

-not	can-	*-salue	porte-
*-not	can-	*-salu	port-
*-odyr	an-	*-same	selfe-
-of	her-, here-, ther-, there-, wher-, where-	-sande	see-
		-schakyn	wynde-
*-of	where-	-score	thre-
*-oyster	stoppynge-	-se	over-
-on	there-, upp-, wher-, where-	*-seke	brayne-, harte-
-one	everych-	-self	him-, my-
-other	an-	*-self	hym-, thy-
*-other	an-	-selfe	her-, him-, hym-, my-, them-, thy-, your-
-otherys	an-		
-others	an-	*-selfe	her-, Hym-, my-, them-, thy, yor-, your-
-out	ther-, with-, wyth-		
*-out	Thorowe-, Through-	-Servyce	Fansy-
-oute	with-	-set	under-
*-oute	thorowe-	-shales	nut-
-outen	with-	*-shalis	nut-
-owte	with-	-sharde	pot-
*-pace	a-	*-shell	nutte-
*-page	kechyn-	*-sheres	clyppyng-
*-pajauntes	pelory-	-shyne	sone-
*-pajaunttis	pollyng-	-shoe	(see -showe)
-pan	brayne-	-shorde	pot-
*-pan	brayne-, fryinge-, fryenge-	-shordes	pot-
-pannys	brayn-	-shordis	pot-
*-parent	heyre-	-shote	over-
-Pase	passe-a-	-showe	hors-
-pate	daw-	-sycke	brayn-
*-pate	drousy-	-syde	in-, oute-
*-patis	doddy-	*-syde	beddes-
-peke	hoddy-	-syghted	Well-
*-peke	huddy-	-syght	over-
*-pekes	paternoster-	-syk	brayn-
-peny	hal-, halfe-	-syke	brayn-
*-pin	wevyng-	*-symplenes	fee-
-pycher	pottell-	-skyn	ryb-
*-pygge	bore-	-slovens	whyp-
-pynnys	mun-	-smyth	gold-
*-pype	bag-	-so	al-, wher-, who-
*-pytte	cheryston-	*-so	who-
*-place	commune-	-soever	what-
-play	fayre-	*-soever	what-, where-, who-
-pleas	(see -place)	-sole	sho-
-pole	ale-	-somer	mid-, myd-
*-polle	nody-	-somever	what-
*-polles	noddy-	-son	hor-
-pollys	nody-	-song	prycke-
-pottes	pys-	*-songe	playne-, prycke-
*-poule	hoddy-	-soppe	ale-
*-prest	persone-	*-sprettes	myday-
*-prycke	poddynge-	-sprynge	of-
*-publyke	wele-	*-stayre	windyng-
-quale	cowche-	*-stake	ale-
*-quarter	fals-	-stand	under-
*-quottes	tot-	-stande	under-
-rage	out-	-standes	under-
*-rake	cole-	*-standynge	notwith-
*-red	Brystowe-	-star	lode-
-ryght	up-	*-stare	lode-
*-rynge	weddynge-	-starte	up-
*-rodde	lyme-	*-steke	eldyr-
*-royall	sank-	-sterre	lode-
*-rolle	bede-	-stocke	cal-
*-rolles	bede-	-stode	under-, up-
*-rollis	ragman-	-stole	cooke-
-rope	gabyll-	*-stole	coke-
-rose	prim-, prime-, pryme-	-ston	bryn-, chery-
*-rote	hart-, hert-, Mapely-	-stonde	under-
*-roule	bede-	-stone	gon-, grave-, gun-, mylle-
*-roules	bedde-	-stones	myl-
*-route	revell-	-stood	under-
*-rowe	crosse-	-story	clere-
*-rowlis	courte-	*-stringis	harpe-
-sadell	syde-	*-stryngges	harpe-
-saf	vouche-	-sure	cock-
-safe	vouche-, vowche-	-tayde	tonge-
-sayd	afore-	-tayle	wag-
-say	gain-	*-taylys	shepis-
*-sayles	fucke-	-take	under-
-sale	port-	*-tap	ale-

```
*-tappe          ale-                      -wyse        lyke-, other-
*-tenauntes      bounde-                   -wyth        forth-
*-tenent         bonde-                    -wyves       hus-
 -thanke         pik-                      -wod         tal-
 -thing          everi-, no-               -woman       gentil-, gentyl-, jentyll-
*-thing          every-                    -women       gentyl-, jentyl-
 -thyng          no-                       -wormed      Whey-
*-thyng          all-, any-, every-        -worthy      stal-
 -thynge         no-                      *-wulse       lylse-
*-thynge         all-, Any-, every-, no-, Noo-,
                 ony-
 -thynke         me-
*-thryfte        scape-
 -throwe         over-
 -throw          over-
 -thwarted       over-
 -thwartes       over-
 -thwarthe       ovyr-
 -thwartyd       over-
 -thwart         over-
 -thwhart        over-
 -time           som-
 -tyme           oft-, som-, some-
*-tyme           be-, oft-, ofte-
 -tymes          often-
*-tymes          ofte-
 -tyrlowe        tyrly-
*-tyrlowe        tyrly-
 -to             her-, in-, ther-, wher-,
                 where-
*-to             in-
 -toke           under-
*-top            fore-
*-tre            apple-, laurell-
*-tubbe          swyllyng-
 -tucke          up-
*-tunge          double-
*-tunges         double-
*-tunnes         ale-
 -upon           ther-, there-, where-
*-upon           where-
*-uryd           Male-
*-use            mysse-
*-Vale           Jack of the-
 -vat            (see -fat)
 -wach           day-
 -wachyd         hovyr-
 -way            al-, all-
*-way            All-
 -way            counter-
 -waye           al-
*-waye           hye-
 -wayng          counter-
*-ware           be-
*-wark           nedill-
 -washer         dysh-
*-wat            cocke-, cok-
*-water          holy-
*-wather         holy-
*-wattes         cok-
 -weall          comyn-
 -weigh          (see -way)
 -well           commune-
 -well           fare-
*-well           Fare-
 -welth          commune-
*-welth          commune-
 -wharte         over-
 -what           som-, some-
*-what           some-, sum-
*-whele          spynnyng-
*-wher           no-
 -where          els-, no-, ony-, som-
*-where          no-
 -with           forth-, ther-, there-, wher-,
                 where-
*-with           Where-
 -withall        ther-, there-
 -withstandyng   not-
 -wyfe           hus-
 -wyng           lap-
```

APPENDIX D

Transcript of Collyn Clout, British Library MS Harley 2252

Quis resurgat ad malyngna*n*tes, aut quis
stabit mecu*m* adu*er*sus op*er*antes
iniquitate*m*? Nemo d*omi*ne!

Whate can hyt avayle
To dryve forthe a snayle
Or to make a sayle
Of an heryng tayle
To ryme or to rayle
To wryte or to endyte
Eythyr for to endyte
Or else for to desyte
Or bok*es* co*m*pyle
10   Of dyv*ers* man*er* of style
Vyce to revyle
And syn for to exile
To teche or to preche
As reason wold reherse
Say thus or say that
Hys hede ys so fatte
And saythe he wott not whate
Nor whereof he spekythe
He cryethe he crekythe
20   He p*r*yethe he p*r*ekythe
He chydethe he chat*ers*
He pratythe he patyrs
He cleteryth he clat*ers*
He medelythe he smat*ers*
He glosythe he fflat*ers*
Or yf he speke playne
Then he lackythe brayne
He ys but a foole
Lett hym go to scole
30   On a iij fotyd stole
Th*at* he may downe sytte
For he lackythe wytte
And yff th*at* he hytte
The nayle on the hed
Hyt stondydythe in no stede
The devyll they say ys dede
Hyte may so well be
Or else they wold see
Hoth*er*wyse *and* flee
40   From worldly vanyte
And fowlle covetosnes
And hoth*er* wrechydnes
And fykyll falsenes
And varyabulnes
W*ith* vnstedfastnes
And yf they stonde in dowte
Whoo browghte thys ryme abowte
My name ys Colyn Clowte

	And purpose to shake owte
50	All my connyng bagge
	Lyke a clarkely hagge
	For thowe my ryme be ragge
	Tateryd *and* jaggyd
	Rvdely rayne betyn
	Rusty *and* mothe etyn
	And yf thow take well th*er* wythe
	Hyt hathe in hyt s*om* pythe
	For as fer as I can see
	Hyt ys wronge w*ith* eche degre
60	For the temporalte
	Accusythe the spyrytualte
	The spiritualte agayne
	Dothe groge *and* complayne
	Vppon the temporall men
	Thys eche w*ith* hothyr blen
	The tone ayenste th*at* hother
	Alas they make me shodyr
	For in hodyr modyr
	The chyrche ys put in fawte
70	The p*re*la*te*s be so hawte
	They sey *and* loke so hye
	As thow they wold flye
	Above the sterry skyee
	Lay men sey in dede
	How they take none hede
	There sely shepe to fede
	But plucke away *and* pull
	Th*er* flesys of wolle
	Scantly they leve a locke
80	Of wolle amonge the flocke
	And as for th*er* connyng
	A glommyng *and* a mo*m*myng
	And make thereof a jape
	They gaspe *and* they gape
	All to have p*ro*mocion
	There ys all th*er* devocion
	W*ith* money yf hyt wyll happe
	To cache them a forkyd cappe.
	For sothe they ar lewde
90	To sey soo al beshrewde
	Whate trow yow they sey more
	Of the bysshopp*es* lore
	How in ma*ter*s they be rawe
	They labor forth*e* so in the lawe
	To harkyn Jacke *and* Gyll
	When they put vp a byll
	And juge all as they wyll
	For hother menn*es* skyll
	Expownyng owte there clawsys
100	And leve th*er* owne cawsys

147v1

In the provynciall cure
They make but lytell sure
And medlythe verrey lyte
In the chyrche ryghte
But yre and venery
And solfe so alamyre
That the premenire
Ys lyke to sett a fire
Yn theyr juridiccion
110 Throwe temporall afflyccion
Men sey they have prescripcion
Agaynste spirituall contradiccion
Accomptyng them as affeccions
And whyles the hedes do thys
The remynaunte ys amys
Of the clergye all
Bothe the grete and smalle
I wotte not howe they werke
But thys the pepyll barke
120 And surely thus they sey
Bysshoppes yf they may
Smalle howsoldes woll kepe
But slumbyr forthe and slepe
And assay to crepe
Within the nobyll walles
Of the kynges halles
To fatte there bodyse full
There sowlys lene and dull
And hathe but lytell cure
130 Howe yll ther shepe fare
The temporalte sathe playne 147^{v2}
Howe bysshoppes dysdayne
Sermons for to make
Or suche labour to take
And for to sey trowthe
A grete parte ys for slowthe
But the grettyste parte
Ys they haue lytell arte
And ryghte slendyr connyng
140 With in ther heddes wonnyng
But thys reason they take
Howe they ar abyll to make
With theyre golde and treasure
Clerkes withowte measu[r]e
And yette that ys a pleasure
How be hyt som ther be
Allmoste ij or iij
Of that dyngnyte
Full worsshypfull clerkes
150 As hyte aperythe by ther werkes
Lyke Aron and Ure
The wolfe from the dore

    To werryn *and* to kepe
    From theyre gostly shepe
    And sp*iritu*all lambys
    Sequest*er* fro*m* rammys
    And from thyse berdyd got*es*
    W*ith* there hery cot*es*
    Sette nowght by golde ne grot*es*
160 There namys yf I durste tell
    But they be lothe to mell
    And lothe to hange the bell
    Abowte the catt*es* necke
    For drede to haue a checke
    They ar fayne to play decke
    They ar made for the becke
    How be hyt they ar good men
    Myche hartyd lyke a hen
    Th*er* lessons forgoton they haue
170 th*at* Saynt Thom*as* of C*an*terbury gave
    Thom*as* manu*m* mittit ad forcia
    Spernit da*m*pna spernit obp*ro*bria
    Nulla Thoma*m* frangit iniuria
    But now ev*er*y sp*iritu*all fadyr
    Me*n* say th*at* they had rathyr
    Spende myche of th*er* share   148^{r1}
    Then to be co*m*bryd w*ith* care
    Spende nay nay but spare
    For lette see whoo dare
180 Shoo the mockyshe mare
    They make hyr wynche *and* keke
    Boldnes ys seke
    The chyrche for to defende
    Take me as I entende
    In thys th*at* I have pende
    I tell yow as men sey
    Amende when th*at* ye may
    For usq*ue* ad Monte*m* Sair
    Me*n* sey ye cannot payre
190 For som sey ye hunte p*ar*k*es*
    And hawke on hoby lark*es*
    And hoth*er* wanton wark*es*
    When the nyghte dark*es*
    Whate hathe ley me*n* to doo
    The grey gose for to shoo
    Lyke hound*es* of hell
    They crye *and* they yell
    How th*at* yow sell
    The grace of the holy gooste
200 Th*us* they make th*er* boste
    Throw owte ev*er*y coste
    Howe som of yow do ete
    In lente so myche flesshe mete
    Fesaunt*es* partryche *and* cran*us*

Men call yow therfor prophanus
Thus pyke ne shrympes ne crevus
Saltfysshe stocfyshe ne heryng
Hyt ys not for your weryng
Nor in holy lente season
210 They wyll neythyr benes nor pesyon
But ye loke to be lett lose
To ete eythyr pygge or gose
Your gorge not endewyd
With owte a capon stewyd
Or a stewyd cocke
To knowe whate ys a clocke
Vndyr hyr surfuld smocke
And hyr wanton wedycoke
And when they geve ordyrs   148r2
220 In your provynciall bordyrs
At all citientes
Som ad sufficientes
Som parum sapientes
Som nichill intelligentes
Som valde necligentes
Som nullum sensim habentes
But bestiall and vntawghte
But when they have ons cawghte
Dominus vobiscum by the hede
230 Then ron they in every stede
God wotte with dronkyn nolles
Yet they take cure of sowlys
And wot not whate they rede
Pater noster Ave nor crede
Constrew not worthe a whystyll
Nother gospell nor pystyll
There matens madly sayd
Nothyng devoutly prayd
Ther lernyng ys so lewde
240 Ther pryme and owrys fall
But the moste parte in generall
Of suche vacabondes
Spekythe totus mondus
How som syng letabundes
At every ale stake
With welcom hake and make
By the bred that God brake
I am seke for your sake
I speke not of every good wyfe
250 But of ther postylles lyffe
Cum ipso vell cum ipsa
Que in venitur villi[s]
Est vxor vell ancella
Welcum Jacke and Gylla
My praty Petronylla
And ye can be stylla

>
> Ye shall haue yo*ur* wylla
> Of soche pa*ter* nost*er* pek*es*
> All the worlde spekys
> Yn yow y[our] fawte y[s] supposyd (MS ys fawte *your*)
261 For th*at* they ar nat aposyd
> By fyrste examynac[i]o*u*n
> In connyng c*on*versacion
> They have none ynstruxion   148^v1
> To make trewe construccion
> A preste wi*th*owte hys let*ter*
> wi*th*owte hys *ver*tu be gret*ter*
> Dowtles we were myche bet*ter*
> Vppon hym for to take
270 A mattocke or a rake
> Alas for verrey shame
> Som cannot declyne th*er* owne name
> Some scantlye rede
> And yete wyl not drede
> For to kepe a cure
> And in nothyng ys sure
> Thys d*omi*n*us* vobyscom
> As wyse as Jacke a Thrum
> A chapeleyne of truste
280 Leythe all in the duste
> Th*us* I Colyn Clowte
> As I goe abowte
> *And* wanderyng as I walke
> I here the pepyll talke
> Men sey for money *and* golde
> Myters ar bowghte *and* solde
> They shall no clergy appose
> A myter or a crose
> But a full purse.
290 A strawe for Godd*es* curse
> Whate ar ye the worse
> For a symyniake
> Hyt ys but a harma*n*iake
> And no more they make
> Of symony me*n* sey
> But a chyld*es* playe
> Also the forsayd lay
> Reportythe how the pope maye
> An holy ankyr call
300 Owte of a stone wall
> *And* hym a bysshoppe make
> Yf he on hym can take
> To kepe so harde a rule
> To ryde apon a mvle
> Wi*th* golde all be trappyd
> In purpull *and* pall belappyd
> Some hattyd *and* som cappyd
> Rychely *and* warme wrappyd

       God wotte to th*er* grete payn*us*
310 Yn rechett*es* of fyne reynes
       Whyte as marys mylke
       Th*er* tabard*es* of fyne sylke
       Th*er* styropp*us* *with* golde be gloryd
       Th*er* may no coste be sparyd
       Th*er* mvles golde doth*e* ete
       Ther neybors dye for mete
       Whate care they thow Gyll swete
       Or else Jacke of the Noke
       The pore pepyll they choke
320 W*ith* somners *and* sytacons
       And extermynacions
       Abowte chyrche and m*er*kett
       The bysshoppe on hys carpett
       At home full softe doth*e* sytte
       Thy*s* ys a ffarly fytte
       To here the pepyll jangyll
       And them all to mangyll
       For falsely on yow they lye
       And as shamfully yow ascrye
330 *And* say vtt*er*ly
       Th*at* a butt*er*flye
       Was a weth*er*cocke
       Of the stepyll of Pawl*us*
       And thus they hurte th*er* sowl*us*
       In slaunderyng yow of truthe
       Alas hyt ys grete ruthe
       Som sey yow syt in tron*us*
       As p*r*ynopes aquilones
       And shryne yo*ur* rotyn bonys
340 W*ith* p*er*le *and* p*re*ciuse ston*us*
       But how the com*on*s gron*us*
       And the pepyll mornys
       For prest*es* *and* for loonys
       Lente *and* nevyr payd
       But fro*m* day to day delayd
       The comyn welthe decayed
       Men sey yowe ar tong tyed
       And thereof spekys nothyng
       But dyssymulyng *and* glosyng
350 Wherfore me*n* ar supposyng
       That ye geve shrewde councell
       Ayenste the comyn wele
       By pollyng *and* pyllage
       In cetes *and* vyllage
       By taxing and tollyng
       Ye make monkys haue the colerage
       For coveryng of an olde cotage
       That vnnethe ys a colage
       In the chart*er* of dotage
360 Religio*us* men ar fayne

For to returne agayne
In to secula seculor*um*
Contra p*re*septa mor*um*
And the selfe same game
Begon ys now *with* shame
Among the selye nonnys
My lady nonne she ronnys
Dan Dorothe *and* lady Besse
Dame Sybylle o*ur* p*r*yoresse
370   Owte of the cloyst*er and* quere
With an hevy chere
Moste caste vp th*er* blacke vaylys
And sette vppe th*er* fulke saylys
To cache wynde *with* th*er* ventaylys
Th*us* the lay peepyll rayll
And all the fawte they laye
In yo*ur* p*r*esepte *and* saye
Ye do them wronge *and* no ryghte
To put them thus to flyghte
380   No matens at mydnyghte
Boke *and* chalys gon quyte
And plucke away th*er* led*es*
Evyn ovyr there hed*es*
And sell away there bell*es*
And all th*at* they haue ell*es*
Thus the pepyll tell*es*
Raylys and rebell*es*
Redys shrewdly *and* spell*es*
And *with* foundacion mell*es*
390   And talkys lyke tetevyll*es*
How th*at* he brek*es* the deths wyll*es*
To torne monestarys to wat*er* myll*es*
Of an abay to make a graunge
Yo*ur* worke they sey ys v*e*raye strau*n*ge
So th*at* there found*er*s sowl*es*   149r2
Haue loste there bede roll*es*
The money for there massys
Spend among wanton lassys
The dyrige forgoton
400   There founders lye th*er* rotyn
Whate can the turke do more
With all hys hole lore
Howe be hyt *par* assimile
So*m* me*n* thynke th*at* ye
Shall haue penalte
For yo*ur* iniquite
Note whate I say
And bere hyt well awaye
Yf hyt pleas not theologi
410   Hyt ys good for astrologi
For Tholomye told me
The son somtyme to be

In aryete
Assendente a dextre
Whan scorpion dessendyng
A fatall fall of on
That shuld sytte in a trone
And rule all thynge alone
Your teethe whette on thys bone
420 Among yow every chone
And lette Colyn Clowte alon[e]
Som sey holy chyrche haue to mykyll
Som sey they haue tryalytes
And some sey they bryng pluralites
And qualifie qualites
And also tot cotte
They talke lyke sottes
Makyng many owtecryes
That they cannot kepe ther wyfes
430 And thus the loselles stryvys
And lewdly sayes be Cryste
Agaynste the sely preste
Alas and wellawaye
Whate eylythe them thus to sey
They myghte be better avysed   149v1
Then to be so dysgwysed
But they haue enterprysed
And shamfullye surmysed
How the prelacye ys solde and bowghte
440 And com vp of nowghte
And whan they prellattes be
Comyn vp of lowe degre
And sette in ther mageste
And spirituall dyngnyte
Farwell benyngnyte
Farwell humilite
Farwell good charite
Theyse ar so puffyd with pryde
That no man may abyde
450 Your hye and lordly lokes
They caste then vp your bokes
And vertue ys forgoton
For then ye wol be wrokyn
Of every lyghte quarell
And call a lorde javell
A knyghte a knave ye make
Ye boste ye face ye crake
And apon yow ye take
To rule bothe kyng and keyser
460 And yff ye may haue leyser
Ye wyll bryng all to nowghte
And that hyt ys your thowghte
For the lordes temporall
Ther rule ys verray smalle

Almoste nothyng at all
Men sey that they appall
That nobyll blode royall
In ernyste and in game
Ye ar the lesse to blame
470 For lordes of nobyll blode
Yf they well vndyrstode
Howe connyng myghte them avayle
They wolde pype yow a new daunce
But nobyllmen borne
To lerne they haue grete scorne
But hunte and blow an horne   149v2
Kepe vnnethe lakes and dykes
And sette nowghte by polytykes
Therfor ye kepe them base
480 And mocke them to ther face
Thys ys a petous cace
To yow that be on the whele
Grete lordes moste cruche and [knele]
And breke ther hose at the kne
As dayly men may see
And to remembrans I have calle
Fortune so tornythe the ball
And rulythe so overall
That honour hathe a grete fall
490 Shall I tell more ye shall
I am lothe to tell all
But the commynalte yow call
Idolles of Babylon
De terra Zabulon
De terra Neptalim
For ye love to goe trym
Browghte vp of pore estate
With pryde inordynate
Sodenlye vpsterte
500 From the donge carte
The mactocke and the shovyll
To rayne and to rule
And hathe no grace to thynke
How they were wonte to drynke
Of a ledyr botell
With a knavyshe stopyll
When mammockes was your mete
With moldy brede to ete
Ye cowde no nother gete
510 To chewe and to gnawe
To fyll therwith your mawe
Loggyng in fayre strawe
Cowchyng your drowsy hedes
Somtyme in a lowsy bed
All thys ys owte of mynde (MS owte owte)
Ye grow now owte of kynde

	Many on ye have vntwynde	
	And made the comons blynde	
	But *qui* existimat stare	
520	Let hym be well ware	
	Leste t*ha*t hys fote slyppe	150^r1
	And haue suche a tryppe	
	And fall in suche decay	
	Th*at* all the worlde may say	
	Com downe in the devyll way	
	And yete ov*er* that	
	Of bysshopp*es* th*us* they chatte	
	Th*at* thowe ye rounde yo*ur* here	
	An ynche above the here	
530	*And* haue aures pate*n*tes	
	And pa*rum* inte*n*dentes	
	And yo*ur* tonsors be croppyd	
	Yo*ur* erys they sey byn stoppyd	
	For m*aister* adulator	
	And docto*ur* assentator	
	And blandor blandiers	
	W*ith* mecier me*n*tirers	
	They folow yo*ur* desyris	
	And so they blere yo*ur* yee	
540	Th*at* ye cannot esspye	
	How the male dothe wrye	
	Alas for Godd*es* wyll	
	Why syte yow so styll	
	And suffyr all thys yll	
	The bysshopp*us* of estate	
	Shuld opyn the brode gate	
	Of yo*ur* sp*iri*tuall charge	
	And co*m* forthe at large	
	Lyke lanternys of lyghte	
550	In the pepyll*es* syghte	
	In pulpyt awte*n*tyke	
	For the wele publycke	
	Suche ma*n*er of sysmatyk*es*	
	And halfe eretyk*es*	
	Th*at* wolde intrixicate	
	Th*at* wold co*n*quinate	
	Th*at* wold co*n*taminate	
	And wolde violate	
	And th*at* wolde dirogate	
560	And wolde abrogate	
	The chyrchys hye estate	
	Aft*er* thy*s* ma*n*er of rate	
	The whyche shulde be	
	Bothe francke *and* fre	
	And haue her lyberte	
	As of antyquite	
	Hyt was ratyfied	150^r2
	And also gratyfyed	

	By holye synodalys
570	And bulles papall
	As hyt ys res carta
	Conteyned in Magna Carta
	But Damian
	Or som hother man
	That clarkely ys and can
	Well scripture expownde
	And hys textes grounde
	Hys benefice worth x. li.
	Or scante worthe xxti marke
580	And ys a nobyll clerke
	He moste do thys werke
	As I knowe a parte
	Som maister of arte
	Som doctours of lawe
	Som lerid in hother sawe
	As in devinite
	That hathe no dygnyte
	But the pore degre
	Of the vniversite
590	Or else frere Frederyke
	Or frere Dominicke
	Or frere Hugulius
	Or frere Augustinus
	Or frere Carmelinus
	That gostlye can hele vs
	Or else yf we may
	Gete a ffrere grey
	Or elles of the ordyr
	Of Grenwyche bordyr
600	Callyd observuaunce
	Or a frere of Fraunce
	Or else the pore Scotte
	Hyt moste com to hys lotte
	To shote forthe thys shotte
	Or of Babwell Besyde Bury
	To postyll apon thys kery
	That wolde hyt shulde be notyd
	How scripture shuld be cotyd
	And so clerely promotyd
610	And yet the frere dotyd
	But men sey your auctoryte
	And your nobyll see
	And your hye dyngnyte
	Shuld be impryntyd better
	For yf ye wolde take payne
	To preche a worde or twayn
	Thowe hyt were nevyr so playne
	With clawsys ij or iij
	So as they myghte be
620	Compendiously conveyde

150^{v1}

          Thys shuld be now more weyed
          And bet*ter* p*er*seyvid
          And tha*n*kfullerlye reseyvyd
          And bet*ter* shuld rettayne
          The peopyll playne
          Th*at* wolde reherse these word*es* agayn
          Then a thowsand hother
          Th*at* babyll barke *and* blondyr
          And make a Walsoma[n]*us* hose
630   Of the texte *and* glose
          For p*ro*testacion made
          Th*at* I wyll not wade
          Forth*er* in thys boke
          Nor forth*er* to loke
          In devysyng th*ys* boke
          But to ansswere th*at* I may
          For myselfe alway
          Eythyr anolegie
          Or cathegory
640   So th*at* dyngnite
          Doct*ours* that lernyd be
          Nor bachelers of th*at* faculte
          Shall not be obiecte at by me
          But docto*ur* bullat*us*
          Par*um* litterat*us*
          D*omi*nus doctorat*us*
          Docto*ur* dawepat*us*
          And bachelar bagalat*us*
          Dronken as a mowse
650   At an ale howse
          Take hys pillion *and* hys cuppe
          At the good ale tappe
          For lacke of good wyne
          As wyse as a swyne
          Vndyr a notarys syne
          Was made a devyne
          As wyse as Walta*ms* calfe
          Moste preche a Godd*es* halfe
          In the pulpyt solemly   150^{v2}
660   More mete in the pyllery
          For by saynte Illary
          He can no thyng smatyr
          Of logyke *and* scole matyr
          Nothir foly silogizare
          Nor entimemare
          Nor know*ith* not hys ele*n*kes
          Nor hys p*re*dictame*nt*tes
          And yet he wyll medyll
          To amend the gospell
670   *And* wyll p*r*eche *and* tell
          Whate they do in hell
          And wyll newyn

            Whate they do in hevyn
            And how farre Tempyll Barre ys
            From the vij starrys
            Now I wyll goe
            And tell of other mo
            Semper protestando
            De non impugnando
680   The iij ordyrs of frerys
            There som of them be lyars
            As lymyters at large
            Wyll charge and dyscharge
            As many a frere God wott
            Prechy[t]he for hys grote (MS prechyche)
            And flatyrs for a new cote
            And for to haue hys fees
            Som to gadyr chese
            Lothe they ar to lese (MS the they)
690   Eythyr corne or salte
            Somtyme mele and malte
            Somtyme a bakon flycke
            That ys iij fyngers thycke
            Of lard and of grece
            There covente to encrese
            I put yow owte of dowte
            Thys cannot be browghte
            But they ther tonges fyle
            And make a plesante style
700   To Mergery and Mawde
            How they haue no fawte
            And somtym they provoke
            Bothe Gyll and Jacke at Noke
            Ther dutes to withdrawe
            That they owghte by the lawe
            There curate to contente (MS to to)   151^{r1}
            In Ester tyde and lente
            God wotte they take grete payne
            To flater and to fayne
710   Hyt ys an old sayd sawe
            That nede hyt hathe no lawe
            Som walke abowte in flockes
            In grey russet and hery cotes
            Som wyll take neythyr gold ne grotes
            Som plucke a partryche in romotes
            And by the barrys of hyr tayle
            Wyll knowe a rewen or a rayle
            A quayle a rayle an old rowen
            Sed libera nos a malo amen
720   And Bidudum the Clementyne
            Ayenste curates they repyne
            And sey they ar properli sacerdotes
            To shewe assoyle and to releas
            Dame Mergaretes sowle owte of hell

But when the frere fyll in the well
He cowde not syng hym selfe owte
But by the helpe of Crystyan Clowte
A nother Clementyn how frere Faby *and* mo
Exiuit de paradiso
730　When they agayne thedyr shall com
De hoc petymus concilium
And throw all the world they goe
With dyrige and placebo
But now my mynde ye vnderstond
For they moste take in hande
To preche and to withstande
Suche maner of subieccions
For bysshoppus haue proteccions
They sey to do coreccions
740　But they haue no affeccions
To take sadde direccions
In suche maner of cawsys
Men sey they bere no fases
To ocupye suche places
To sowe sede of grace
Ther hartes ar so faynted
And they be so attaynted
With couetus ambyssyon
And hother supersticion　　　　　　　151r2
750　That they be bothe defe and dome
And play sylens and mome
They ocupy them soo
With syngyng placebo
They wyll no fardyr goe
They had levyr to pleas
And take ther wordly ease
Then to take on hande
Worsshepfully to withstande
Suche temporall warre and bate
760　As nowe ys made of late
Ayenste holy chyrche estate
Or to mayntayne quarelles
The lay men call them barelles
Full of glotonye
And of ypocrecie
That conterfetes and payntes
As they were very seyntes
In maters that they lyke
They shewe them polytyke
770　Pretendyng grauite
And senyoryte
With all solemnite
For there indemnyte
For they wyll haue no losse
Of peny nor of crosse
Of ther perdyall londes

977

That comyth to ther handes
As far as they dar sett
All ys fysshe that comythe to nett
780   Byldyng ryally
Ther mancions curyowusly
With torrettes and with towrys
With hattes and with bowyrs
So recchyng to the sterrys
With glasse wyndowus and barrys
Hangyng apon the walles
Clothys of golde and pallys
Arras of ryche array
As fresshe as flowrys in May
790   With dame Dyana nakyd
How lusty Venus quakyd
Howe god Cupyde shakyd
Hys darte and bente a bowe
For to shote a crowe   151^{v1}
At hyr tyrly tyrlow
And how Parys of Troy
Daunsyd a lege moy
Made lusty sporte and joy
With dame Elyn the quene
800   With suche storys be dene
Ther chambyrs wel be sene
With tryhumphes of Cesar
And of Pompeus warre
Of renowne and fame
By them to gete a name
How all the worlde starys
Howe they ryde in goodly charys
Conveyd by olyfauntes
With lawryat garlondes
810   And by vnycornus
With ther semelye hornus
Apon these bestes rydyng
Nakyd boyes strydyng
With wanton wenchys wynkyng
Now truly to my thynkyng
Thys ys a speculacion
And a mete medytacion (MS medytacacion)
For prelattes of estate
There corage to abate
820   From wordlye wantones
Ther chambyrs thus to drese
With suche perfytenes
And all suche holynes
How be hyt they let downe fall
Ther chyrchys cathedrall
Squyre knyghte and lorde
Thus the chyrche remorde
With all temporall pepyll

	The ron ayenste the stepyll
830	Thus talkyng *and* yellyng
	Thus softe *and* fayre for swellyng
	Beware of a co*m*myn yellyng
	Hyt ys a besy thyng
	For on to rule a kyng
	Alone to make rekenyng
	To gov*er*ne ovyr all 151ᵛ²
	And rule a realm royall
	By on ma*n*nys verrey wyll
	Fortune may chaunce to flyte
840	Yet may he mys the quyssh[on]
	I rede by *p*reposyssyon
	Cu*m* regibus amicare
	Et om*n*ibus dominare
	Et supra te grassari
	Th*er*for he hathe good vre
	Th*at* can hym sylfe assure
	How fortune wyll endure
	Then let reason yow supporte
	For the co*mm*on*al*te doth*e* reporte
850	How they haue grete wo*n*dyr
	Th*at* ye kepe them so vndyr
	And yet they m*er*vayle myche lesse
	As they suppose *and* gesse
	Ye play so at the chesse
	Th*at* som of yow but late
	Hathe played so checkmate
	Wi*th* lord*es* of grete estate
	Aft*er* suche a rate
	Th*at* they shall neyther melle nor make
860	Nor apon them to take
	More for kyng nor keysar sake
	But at the pleasure all of one
	Th*at* rulythe the roste alone
	O alas I say alas
	How may thy*s* co*m* to passe
	Th*at* a man shall here mas
	And not soo hardy on hys hed[e]
	To loke on God in forme of [brede]
	But yet the *p*arysshe clerke
870	There apon moste harte
	And graunte hym all hys [askyng]
	For to se the sacryng
	Or how may thy*s* acorde
	No man to ow*ur* soverayn lord
	So hardy to make sute
	Nor yet to execute
	Hys co*m*maundmente
	Wi*th*owte the assente
	Of ow*ur* p*r*esydente
880	Not to prese to hys p*ar*son

Withowte George Gascone 152r1
Graunte hym hys lycens
To prese to hys presens
Nor to speke secretly
Opynly or preuyly
Withowte thys presydent be by
Or else hys substytute
Whom he wyll depute
Nowther erle nor duke
890   Now by Saynte Luke
And by swete Saynt Marke
Thys ys a wonder warke
That the peopyll talke thys
Somwhate ther ys amys
The devyll cannot stoppe ther mouthys
But they wyll tell veritatem
All that ever they ken
Ayenste spirituall men
Whether hyt be wrong or ryght
900   Or else for dysspyte
Or how ever hyt dothe happe
Ther tonges thus they clappe
And throw suche detraccyon
They put yow to your accion
Whether they sey trulye
As they may abyde therbye
Or else that they do lye
Ye knowe bettyr then I
But now debetis scire
910   And groundlye audyre
Of thys premvnire
Or else in the myre
They sey they wyll yow caste
Therfor stonde faste
Stonde sure and make good fotyng
And let be all your motyng
Your gasyng and your totyng
Your parciall promotyng
Of thyse that stondyng in your grace
920   But as for old servauntes ye chase
And put them owte of ther place
Make ye no murmuracion
Thowe I write on thys fassyon 152r2
Thowe I Colyn Clowte
Amonge the hole rowte
Of yow that clarkes be
I take nowe vppon me
Thys copyously to write
I do hyt for no dyspyte
930   Wherfor take no dysdayne
At my style bothe rude and playne
For I rebuke no man

That vertu ys whye then
Wreke ye your angyr on me
For they that vertuous be
Haue no cawse to sey
That I do speke owte of the wey
Of no good bysshope speke I
Nor no good preste I askrye
940 Good frere nor good chanon
Good nonne nor good canon
Good monke nor good clerke
Nor yette of no good werke
But my recountyng ys
Of suche as dothe amys
In spekyng and in raylyng
In hynderyng and dyssauaylyng
Holy chyrche owur modyr
Oon agayne another
950 To cawse suche dysputyng
Ys all my hole wrytyng
To hyndyr no man
As nere as I can
For no man have I namyd
Wherfor shuld I be blamyd
Ye owghte to be ashamyd
Ayenste me to be grevyd
And can tell no cawse why
But that I wryte trulye
960 Then yf ony therbe
Of hye and lowe degre
Of the spiritualte
Or the temporalte
That dothe thynke or wene
Hys conciens be not clene
Or fele hym selfe seke
Or towchyd on the quycke
Suche grace God them sende
Them selfe for to amende
970 For I wyll not pretente
Any man to offende
Wherfor as thynkes me
Grete idolles they be
And lytyll grace they haue
Thys tretes to deprave
Nor wyll here no prechyng
Nor noo vertuous techyng
Nor wyll haue no resytyng
Of no vertuous wrytyng
980 Wyll knowe none intellygens
To reforme theyre neclygens
But lyve stylle owte of fascion
To ther awne damnacion
To do shame they haue no shame

But yet they wolde haue no blame
And yet they woll ocupye the same
With them the worde of God
Ys countyd for no rede
They count hyt for a raylyng
990 Whyche ys nothyng avaylyng
The prechers with yll haylyng
Shall they teche vs prelattes
That be ther grete prymates
Not so hardy on ther pates
Harke how the pollshorne prates
With a wyde wesante
Avaunte Sir Gwye of Gawnte
Avaunte lewde preste avaunte
Avaunte Sir Doctour Deuias
1000 Prate on thy matens and thy mas
And let owur medlyng passe
How dar thow dawcoke melle
How dar thow lorell
Allegate the gospell
Ayenste vs of the prevy councell 152ᵛ2
Avante avante to the devyll of hell
Take him warden of the Flete
Sett hym faste by the fete
I say lefetenaunte of the Towur
1010 Make thus lorden for to lowur
Loge hym in lytell ease
Fede hym with benus and pese
The Kynges Benche or Merchalse
Haue them thedyr by and by
The polshorne prechy[t]he opynly (MS prechyche
And declaryth owur velany
And of owur sympylnes
He seythe we be recheles
And full of wylfullnes
1020 Shamles and graceles
Incorrigibyll and incessant
And after thys rate
Ayenste vs he dothe prate
At Powlus Crosse or elsewhere
Openly at Westmynster
Or at Saynte Marys Spetyll
Sett nowghte by vs a shetyll
At the Awstyn frerys
They counte vs all lyars
1030 At Saynt Thomas of Acrys
They clacke of vs lyke crakers
How we ren all at wyll
Withowte good reson and skyll
And sey how that we be
Full of parcialite
And how at a pronge

	We torne ryghte to wronge
	Delay cawsys so longe
	That ryghte no man can fonge
1040	They say many maters ar borne
	Be hyt ryghte as a ramse horne
	Ys not thys a shamfull scorne
	Howe may we thys endure
	Wherfor we make yow sure
	The prechars shalbe yawyd
	And som shalbe sawyd
	As nobyll Isay was 153^r1
	The holye prophete Ozeas
	And some of yow shall dye
1050	Lyke holye Jeremy
	Som hangyd and som slayne
	Som betyn to the brayne
	And we wyll rayle and rayne
	And owur maters mayntayne
	Who dar say there agayn
	Or who dar dysdayn
	At owur pleasu[r]e and wyll
	For be hyt good or be hyt yll
	As hyt ys hyt shal be stylle
1060	For all maister doctour wyll
	Or of Domynicke or doctour Oryll
	Let hym cowgh or snevyll
	Ryn God or ryn devyll
	Ryn whoo may ryn beste
	And let them take there reste
	Ffor we sette not a not shell
	The way to hevyn or hell
	Lo thys ys the gyse now a dayes
	Hyt ys to drede men sayes
1070	Leste they be Adusayes
	Wyttes determyned playne
	We sholde not ryse agayne
	At dredfull domysday
	And soe hyt semys they play
	Whyche hate to be corectyd
	When they be ynfectyd
	Nor wyll not suffyr thys boke
	By hoke nor yet by croke
	Pryntyd for to be
1080	Ffor that no man shuld see
	Nor rede in ony
	Of theyre dronkyn nollys
	Nor of there nody pollys
	Nor of there sowlys (MS there there)
	Nor of som wytles pattys
	Off dyverse grete esstates
	Now to withdrawe my pen
	And now a whyle to reste

	Me semythe for the beste	
1090	The forcastell of my shyppe	153r2
	Shall glyde *and* smothely slyppe	
	Owte of the wawys wode	
	And the stormy flode	
	Shote ankyr *and* lye at rode	
	And sayle not ferre a brode	
	Tyll the coste be clere	
	And the lode sterre apere	
	My shyppe now wyll I stere	
	Towarde the porte salve	
1100	Of ow*u*r savyo*u*r Jh*e*su	
	Such grace th*at* he vs sende	
	To rectifye *and* to amend	
	Thyng*es* th*at* ar amys	
	When hys pleasure ys	
	Amen	
	Quod Collyn Clowte	
	In op*ere* imp*er*fecto	
	In op*ere* semp*er* *per*fecto	
	Et in op*ere* plusquam *per*fecto	
	Qu*o*d Sceltony*us* lawreat*us*.	

APPENDIX E

Word Index to Collyn Clout, British Library MS Harley 2252

A 2, 3, 28, 30, 51, 79, 82, 82, 83, 88, 96, 108, 136, 145, 164, 168, 214, 215, 216, 235, 266, 270, 270, 275, 279, 288, 288, 289, 290, 292, 293, 296, 300, 301, 303, 304, 325, 331, 332, 358, 393, 416, 417, 455, 456, 473, 481, 489, 505, 506, 514, 522, 580, 582, 597, 601, 616, 627, 629, 649, 654, 655, 656, 658, 684, 686, 692, 699, 715, 717, 717, 718, 718, 728, 793, 794, 797, 805, 816, 817, 832, 833, 834, 837, 858, 866, 892, 989, 996, 1027, 1036, 1041, 1042, 1066, 1068, 1088, 1095

ABAY 393

ABATE 819

ABYDE 449, 906

ABYLL 142

ABOVE 73, 529

ABOWTE 47, 163, 282, 322, 712

ABROGATE 560

ACCION 904

ACCOMPTYNG 113

ACCUSYTHE 61

ACORDE 873

ACRYS 1030

ADUSAYES 1070

AFFECCIONS 113, 740

AFFLYCCION 110

AFTER 562, 858, 1022

AGAYN 626, 1055

AGAYNE 62, 361, 730, 949, 1072

AGAYNSTE 112, 432

AYENSTE 66, 352, 721, 761, 829, 898, 957, 1005, 1023

AL 90

ALAS 67, 271, 336, 433, 542, 864, 864

ALE 245

ALE HOWSE 650

ALE TAPPE 652

ALL 50, 85, 86, 97, 116, 221, 259, 280, 305, 327, 376, 385, 402, 418, 461, 465, 491, 515, 524, 544, 732, 772, 779, 806, 823, 828, 836, 862, 871, 897, 916, 951, 1029, 1032, 1060

ALLEGATE 1004

ALLMOSTE 147

ALMOSTE 465

ALONE 418, 421, 835, 863

ALSO 297, 426, 568

ALWAY 637

AM 248, 491

AMBYSSYON 748

AMEN 1105

AMEND 669, 1102

AMENDE 187, 969

AMYS 115, 894, 945, 1103

AMONG 366, 398, 420

AMONGE 80, 925

AN 4, 299, 357, 371, 393, 476, 529, 650, 710, 718

AND 12, 17, 33, 39, 41, 42, 43, 44, 46, 49, 53, 55, 56, 63, 71, 77, 81, 82, 83, 84, 95, 97, 100, 103, 105, 106, 114, 117, 120, 123, 124, 128, 129, 135, 139, 143, 145, 151, 153, 155, 157, 162, 181, 191, 192, 197, 204, 218, 219, 227, 233, 240, 246, 254, 256, 274, 276, 283, 285, 286, 294, 301, 306, 307, 308, 320, 321, 322, 327, 329, 330, 334, 339, 340, 342, 343, 344, 348, 349, 353, 354, 355, 364, 368, 370, 373, 376, 377, 378, 381, 382, 384, 385, 387, 388, 389, 390, 408, 418, 421, 424, 425, 426, 430, 431, 433, 438, 439, 440, 441, 443, 444, 450, 452, 455, 458, 459, 460, 462, 468, 476, 477, 478, 480, 483, 484, 486, 488, 501, 502, 503, 510, 518, 522, 523, 526, 530, 531, 532, 535, 536, 539, 544, 548, 554, 558, 559, 560, 564, 565, 568, 570, 575, 577, 580, 609, 610, 612, 613, 622, 623, 624, 628, 629, 630, 648, 651, 663, 668, 670, 670, 672, 674, 677, 683, 686, 687, 691, 694, 699, 700, 702, 703, 707, 709, 713, 716, 720, 722, 723, 728, 732, 733, 736, 747, 749, 750, 751, 751, 756, 759, 765, 766, 771, 782, 783, 785, 787, 793, 796, 798, 803, 804, 810, 817, 823, 826, 830, 831, 837, 852, 853, 867, 871, 891, 903, 910, 915, 916, 917, 921, 931, 946, 947, 958, 961, 974, 986, 1000, 1001, 1012, 1014, 1016, 1017, 1019, 1020, 1021, 1022, 1033, 1034, 1036, 1046, 1049, 1051, 1053, 1053, 1054, 1057, 1065, 1074, 1088, 1091, 1093, 1094, 1095, 1097, 1102

ANGYR 934

ANY 971

ANKYR 299, 1094

ANOLEGIE 638

ANOTHER 949

ANSSWERE 636

ANTYQUITE 566

APERE 1097

APERYTHE 150

APON 304, 458, 606, 786, 812, 860, 870

APOSYD 261

APPALL 466

APPOSE 287

AR 89, 142, 165, 166, 167, 261, 286, 291, 347, 350, 360, 448, 469, 689, 722, 746, 1040, 1103

ARYETE 413

ARON 151

ARRAY 788

ARRAS 788

ARTE 138, 583

AS 14, 58, 58, 72, 81, 97, 113, 150, 184, 186, 278, 278, 282, 283, 311, 329, 338, 485, 566, 571, 582, 586, 619, 649, 654, 654, 657, 657, 682, 684, 760, 767, 778, 778, 789, 789, 853, 906, 920, 945, 953, 953, 972, 1041, 1047, 1059

ASCRYE 329

ASHAMYD 956

ASKYNG 871

ASKRYE 939

ASSAY 124

ASSENTE 878

ASSOYLE 723

ASSURE 846

ASTROLOGI 410

AT 221, 245, 324, 380, 465, 484, 548, 643, 650, 652, 682, 795, 854, 862, 931, 1024, 1025, 1026, 1028, 1030, 1032, 1036, 1057, 1073, 1094

ATTAYNTED 747

AUCTORYTE 611

AUGUSTINUS 593

AVAYLE 1, 472

AVAYLYNG 990

AVANTE 1006, 1006

AVAUNTE 997, 998, 998, 999

AVE 234

AVYSED 435

AWAY 77, 382, 384

AWAYE 408

AWNE 983

AWSTYN 1028

AWTENTYKE 551

BABYLL 628

BABYLON 493

BABWELL BESYDE BURY 605

BACHELAR 648

BACHELERS 642

BAGGE 50

BAKON FLYCKE 692

BALL 487

BARELLES 763

BARKE 119, 628

BARRE 674

BARRYS 716, 785

BASE 479

BATE 759

BE 37, 52, 70, 93, 146, 146, 161, 167, 177, 211, 256, 267, 305, 313, 314, 403, 412, 431, 435, 436, 441, 453, 482, 520, 532, 563, 607, 608, 614, 619, 621, 641, 643, 681, 697, 747, 750, 800, 801, 824, 886, 899, 916, 926, 935, 955, 956, 957, 965, 973, 993, 1018, 1034, 1041, 1058, 1058, 1059, 1070, 1075, 1076, 1079, 1096

BECKE 166

BED 514

BEDE ROLLES 396

BEGON 365

BELAPPYD 306

BELL 162

BELLES 384

BENCHE 1013

BENEFICE 578

BENES 210

BENYNGNYTE 445

BENTE 793

BENUS 1012

BERDYD 157

BERE 408, 743

BESHREWDE 90

BESY 833

BESSE 368

BESTE 1064, 1089

BESTES 812

BESTIALL 227

BETYN 54, 1052

BETTER 268, 435, 614, 622, 624

BETTYR 908

BEWARE 832

BIDUDUM 720

BY 150, 159, 229, 247, 262, 353, 355, 478, 569, 643, 661, 705, 716, 727, 805, 808, 810, 838, 841, 886, 890, 891, 1008, 1014, 1014, 1027, 1078, 1078

BYLDYNG 780

BYLL 96

BYN 533

BYSSHOPE 938

BYSSHOPPE 301, 323

BYSSHOPPES 92, 121, 132, 527

BYSSHOPPUS 545, 738

BLACKE 372

BLAME 469, 985

BLAMYD 955

BLEN 65

BLERE 539

BLYNDE 518

BLODE 467, 470

BLONDYR 628

BLOW 476

BODYSE 127

BOYES 813

BOKE 381, 633, 635, 1077

BOKES 9, 451

BOLDNES 182

BONE 419

BONYS 339

BORDYR 599

BORDYRS 220

BORNE 474, 1040

BOSTE 200, 457

BOTELL 505

BOTHE 117, 459, 564, 703, 750, 931

BOWE 793

BOWGHTE 286, 439

BOWYRS 783

BRAYNE 27, 1052

BRAKE 247

BRED 247

BREDE 508, 868

BREKE 484

BREKES 391

BRYNG 424, 461

BRODE 546, 1095

BROWGHTE 47, 497, 697

BULLES 570

BUT 28, 77, 102, 105, 119, 123, 129, 137, 141, 161, 174, 178, 211, 227, 228, 241, 250, 289, 293, 296, 341, 345, 349, 437, 474, 476, 492, 519, 573, 588, 611, 636, 644, 698, 725, 727, 734, 740, 855, 862, 869, 896, 909, 920, 944, 959, 982, 985

BUTTERFLYE 331

CACE 481

CACHE 88, 374

CALFE 657

CALL 205, 299, 455, 492, 763

CALLE 486

CALLYD 600

CAN 1, 58, 256, 302, 401, 575, 595, 662, 846, 953, 958, 1039

CANNOT 189, 272, 429, 540, 697, 895

CANON 941

CANTERBURY 170

CAPON 214

CAPPE 88

CAPPYD 307

CARE 177, 317

CARMELINUS 594

CARPETT 323

CASTE 372, 451, 913

CATHEDRALL 825

CATHEGORY 639

CATTES 163

CAWGHTE 228

CAWSE 936, 950, 958

CAWSYS 100, 742, 1038

CESAR 802

CETES 354

CHAMBYRS 801, 821
CHANON 940
CHAPELEYNE 279
CHARGE 547, 683
CHARITE 447
CHARYS 807
CHARTER 359
CHASE 920
CHATERS 21
CHATTE 527
CHAUNCE 839
CHECKE 164
CHECKMATE 856
CHERE 371
CHESE 688
CHESSE 854
CHEWE 510
CHYDETHE 21
CHYLDES 296
CHYRCHE 69, 104, 183, 322, 422, 761, 827, 948
CHYRCHYS 561, 825
CHOKE 319
CHONE 420
CLACKE 1031
CLAPPE 902
CLARKELY 51, 575
CLARKES 926
CLATERS 23
CLAWSYS 99, 618
CLEMENTYN 728
CLEMENTYNE 720
CLENE 965
CLERE 1096
CLERELY 609
CLERGY 287
CLERGYE 116
CLERKE 580, 942
CLERKES 144, 149
CLETERYTH 23
CLOCKE 216
CLOYSTER 370
CLOTHYS 787
CLOWTE 48, 281, 421, 727, 924

COCKE 215
COLAGE 358
COLERAGE 356
COLYN 48, 281, 421, 924
COM 440, 525, 548, 603, 730, 865
COMBRYD 177
COMYN 346, 442
COMYN WELE 352
COMYTH 777
COMYTHE 779
COMMAUNDMENTE 877
COMMYN 832
COMMYNALTE 492
COMMONALTE 849
COMONS 341, 518
COMPENDIOUSLY 620
COMPYLE 9
COMPLAYNE 63
CONCIENS 965
CONNYNG 50, 81, 139, 263, 472
CONQUINATE 556
CONSTREW 235
CONSTRUCCION 265
CONTAMINATE 557
CONTEYNED 572
CONTENTE 706
CONTERFETES 766
CONTRADICCION 112
CONVEYD 808
CONVEYDE 620
CONVERSACION 263
COPYOUSLY 928
CORAGE 819
CORECCIONS 739
CORECTYD 1075
CORNE 690
COSTE 201, 314, 1096
COTAGE 357
COTE 686
COTES 158, 713
COTYD 608
COUETUS 748
COUNCELL 351, 1005

COUNT 989
COUNTE 1029
COUNTYD 988
COVENTE 695
COVERYNG 357
COVETOSNES 41
COWCHYNG 513
COWDE 509, 726
COWGH 1062
CRAKE 457
CRAKERS 1031
CRANUS 204
CREDE 234
CREKYTHE 19
CREPE 124
CREVUS 206
CRYE 197
CRYETHE 19
CRYSTE 431
CRYSTYAN 727
CROKE 1078
CROPPYD 532
CROSE 288
CROSSE 775, 1024
CROWE 794
CRUCHE 483
CUPYDE 792
CUPPE 651
CURATE 706
CURATES 721
CURE 101, 129, 232, 275
CURYOWUSLY 781
CURSE 290
DAY 345, 345
DAYES 1068
DAYLY 485
DAME 369, 724, 790, 799
DAMIAN 573
DAMNACION 983
DAN 368
DAR 778, 1002, 1003, 1055, 1056
DARE 179
DARKES 193

DAUNCE 473
DAUNSYD 797
DAWCOKE 1002
DAWEPATUS 647
DECAY 523
DECAYED 346
DECKE 165
DECLARYTH 1016
DECLYNE 272
DEDE 36, 74
DEFE 750
DEFENDE 183
DEGRE 59, 442, 588, 961
DELAY 1038
DELAYD 345
DENE 800
DEPRAVE 975
DEPUTE 888
DESYRIS 538
DESYTE 8
DESSENDYNG 415
DETERMYNED 1071
DETHS 391
DETRACCYON 903
DEUIAS 999
DEVINITE 586
DEVYLL 36, 525, 895, 1006, 1063
DEVYNE 656
DEVYSYNG 635
DEVOCION 86
DEVOUTLY 238
DIRECCIONS 741
DIROGATE 559
DYANA 790
DYE 316, 1049
DYGNYTE 587
DYKES 477
DYNGNITE 640
DYNGNYTE 148, 444, 613
DYRIGE 399, 733
DYSCHARGE 683
DYSDAYN 1056
DYSDAYNE 132, 930
DYSGWYSED 436

DYSPYTE 929
DYSPUTYNG 950
DYSSAUAYLYNG 947
DYSSYMULYNG 349
DYSSPYTE 900
DYVERS 10
DYVERSE 1086
DO 114, 202, 378, 401, 581, 671, 673, 739, 907, 929, 937, 984
DOCTOUR 535, 644, 647, 999, 1060, 1061
DOCTOURS 584, 641
DOME 750
DOMINICKE 591
DOMYNICKE 1061
DOMYSDAY 1073
DONGE CARTE 500
DOO 194
DORE 152
DOROTHE 368
DOTAGE 359
DOTHE 63, 315, 324, 541, 849, 901, 945, 964, 1023
DOTYD 610
DOWNE 31, 525, 824
DOWTE 46, 696
DOWTLES 268
DREDE 164, 274, 1069
DREDFULL 1073
DRESE 821
DRYNKE 504
DRYVE 2
DRONKEN 649
DRONKYN 231, 1082
DROWSY 513
DUKE 889
DULL 128
DURSTE 160
DUSTE 280
DUTES 704
EASE 756, 1011
ECHE 59, 65
EYLYTHE 434
EYTHYR 7, 212, 638, 690
ELENKES 666

ELYN 799
ELLES 385, 598
ELSE 8, 38, 318, 590, 596, 602, 887, 900, 907, 912
ELSEWHERE 1024
ENCRESE 695
ENDEWYD 213
ENDYTE 6, 7
ENDURE 847, 1043
ENTENDE 184
ENTERPRYSED 437
ENTIMEMARE 665
ERETYKES 554
ERYS 533
ERLE 889
ERNYSTE 468
ESSPYE 540
ESSTATES 1086
ESTATE 497, 545, 561, 761, 818, 857
ESTER 707
ETE 202, 212, 315, 508
ETYN 55
EVER 897, 901
EVERY 174, 201, 230, 245, 249, 420, 454
EVYN 383
EXAMYNACIOUN 262
EXECUTE 876
EXILE 12
EXPOWNDE 576
EXPOWNYNG 99
EXTERMYNACIONS 321
FABY 728
FACE 457, 480
FACULTE 642
FADYR 174
FAYNE 165, 360, 709
FAYNTED 746
FAYRE 512, 831
FALL 240, 416, 489, 523, 824
FALSELY 328
FALSENES 43
FAME 804
FAR 778

FARDYR 754

FARE 130

FARRE 674

FARWELL 445, 446, 447

FASCION 982

FASES 743

FASSYON 923

FASTE 914, 1008

FATALL 416

FATTE 16, 127

FAWTE 69, 260, 376, 701

FEDE 76, 1012

FEES 687

FELE 966

FER 58

FERRE 1095

FESAUNTES 204

FETE 1008

FFARLY 325

FFLATERS 25

FFOR 1066, 1080

FFRERE 597

FIRE 108

FYKYLL 43

FYLE 698

FYLL 511, 725

FYNE 310, 312

FYNGERS 693

FYRSTE 262

FYSSHE 779

FYTTE 325

FLATER 709

FLATYRS 686

FLEE 39

FLESYS 78

FLESSHE 203

FLETE 1007

FLYE 72

FLYGHTE 379

FLYTE 839

FLOCKE 80

FLOCKES 712

FLODE 1093

FLOWRYS 789

FOLY 664

FOLOW 538

FONGE 1039

FOOLE 28

FOR 7, 8, 12, 32, 52, 58, 60, 68, 81, 89, 98, 133, 135, 136, 164, 166, 179, 183, 188, 190, 195, 208, 248, 261, 269, 271, 275, 285, 290, 292, 316, 328, 343, 343, 357, 361, 397, 406, 410, 411, 453, 463, 470, 496, 534, 542, 552, 615, 631, 637, 653, 661, 685, 686, 687, 735, 738, 773, 774, 794, 818, 831, 834, 849, 861, 872, 900, 920, 929, 932, 935, 954, 969, 970, 988, 989, 1010, 1058, 1060, 1079, 1089

FORCASTELL 1090

FORGOTON 169, 399, 452

FORKYD 88

FORME 868

FORSAYD 297

FORTHE 2, 94, 123, 548, 604

FORTHER 633, 634

FORTUNE 487, 839, 847

FOTE 521

FOTYD 30

FOTYNG 915

FOUNDACION 389

FOUNDERS 395, 400

FOWLLE 41

FRANCKE 564

FRAUNCE 601

FRE 564

FREDERYKE 590

FRERE 590, 591, 592, 593, 594, 601, 610, 684, 725, 728, 940

FRERYS 680, 1028

FRESSHE 789

FROM 40, 152, 154, 156, 157, 345, 500, 675, 820

FULKE SAYLYS 373

FULL 127, 149, 289, 324, 764, 1019, 1035

GADYR 688

GAME 364, 468

GAPE 84

GARLONDES 809

GASCONE 881

GASYNG 917

GASPE 84

GATE 546

GAVE 170

GAWNTE 997

GENERALL 241

GEORGE 881

GESSE 853

GETE 509, 597, 805

GEVE 219, 351

GYLL 95, 317, 703

GYLLA 254

GYSE 1068

GLASSE 785

GLYDE 1091

GLOMMYNG 82

GLORYD 313

GLOSE 630

GLOSYNG 349

GLOSYTHE 25

GLOTONYE 764

GNAWE 510

GO 29

GOD 231, 247, 309, 684, 708, 792, 868, 968, 987, 1063

GODDES 290, 542, 658

GOE 282, 496, 676, 732, 754

GOLD 714

GOLDE 143, 159, 285, 305, 313, 315, 787

GON 381

GOOD 167, 249, 410, 447, 652, 653, 845, 915, 938, 939, 940, 940, 941, 941, 942, 942, 943, 1033, 1058

GOODLY 807

GOOSTE 199

GORGE 213

GOSE 195, 212

GOSPELL 236, 669, 1004

GOSTLY 154

GOSTLYE 595

GOTES 157

GOVERNE 836

GRACE 199, 503, 745, 919, 968, 974, 1101

GRACELES 1020

GRATYFYED 568

GRAUITE 770

GRAUNGE 393

GRAUNTE 871, 882

GRECE 694

GREY 195, 597, 713

GRENWYCHE 599

GRETE 117, 136, 309, 336, 475, 483, 489, 708, 850, 857, 973, 993, 1086

GRETTER 267

GRETTYSTE 137

GREVYD 957

GROGE 63

GRONUS 341

GROTE 685

GROTES 159, 714

GROUNDE 577

GROUNDLYE 910

GROW 516

GWYE 997

HAD 175, 755

HAGGE 51

HAYLYNG 991

HAKE 246

HALFE 554, 658

HALLES 126

HANDE 735, 757

HANDES 777

HANGE 162

HANGYD 1051

HANGYNG 786

HAPPE 87, 901

HARDE 303

HARDY 867, 875, 994

HARKE 995

HARKYN 95

HARMANIAKE 293

HARTE 870

HARTES 746

HARTYD 168

HATE 1075

HATHE 57, 129, 194, 489, 503, 587, 711, 845, 856

HATTES 783

HATTYD 307

HAUE 138, 164, 169, 257, 356, 385, 396, 405, 422, 423, 437, 460, 475, 522, 530, 565, 687, 701, 738, 740, 774, 850, 936, 974, 978, 984, 985, 1014

HAVE 85, 111, 185, 228, 264, 486, 517, 954

HAWKE 191

HAWTE 70

HE 17, 18, 19, 19, 20, 20, 21, 21, 22, 22, 23, 23, 24, 24, 25, 25, 26, 27, 28, 31, 32, 33, 302, 391, 581, 662, 668, 726, 840, 845, 888, 1018, 1023, 1101

HED 34

HEDDES 140

HEDE 16, 75, 229, 867

HEDES 114, 383, 513

HELE 595

HELL 196, 671, 724, 1006, 1067

HELPE 727

HEN 168

HER 565

HERE 284, 326, 528, 529, 866, 976

HERY 158, 713

HERYNG 4, 207

HEVY 371

HEVYN 673, 1067

HIM 1007

HYE 71, 450, 561, 613, 961

HYM 29, 269, 301, 302, 520, 726, 846, 871, 882, 966, 1008, 1011, 1012, 1062

HYNDERYNG 947

HYNDYR 952

HYR 181, 217, 218, 716, 795

HYS 16, 266, 267, 323, 402, 521, 577, 578, 603, 651, 651, 666, 667, 685, 687, 793, 867, 871, 877, 880, 882, 883, 887, 965, 1104

HYT 1, 35, 57, 57, 59, 87, 146, 167, 208, 293, 336, 403, 408, 409, 410, 462, 567, 571, 603, 607, 617, 710, 711, 824, 833, 899, 901, 929, 989, 1041, 1058, 1058, 1059, 1059, 1069, 1074

HYTE 37, 150

HYTTE 33

HOBY 191

HODYR 68

HOKE 1078

HOLE 402, 925, 951

HOLY 199, 209, 299, 422, 761, 948

HOLYE 569, 1048, 1050

HOLYNES 823

HOME 324

HONOUR 489

HORNE 476

HORNUS 811

HOSE 484, 629

HOTHER 42, 66, 98, 192, 574, 585, 627, 749

HOTHERWYSE 39

HOTHYR 65

HOUNDES 196

HOW 75, 93, 146, 167, 198, 244, 298, 341, 391, 439, 504, 541, 608, 674, 701, 728, 791, 796, 806, 824, 847, 850, 865, 873, 901, 995, 1002, 1003, 1032, 1034, 1036

HOWE 118, 130, 132, 142, 202, 403, 472, 792, 807, 1043

HOWSOLDES 122

HUGULIUS 592

HUMILITE 446

HUNTE 190, 476

HURTE 334

I 58, 118, 160, 184, 185, 186, 248, 249, 281, 282, 283, 284, 407, 486, 490, 491, 582, 632, 636, 676, 696, 841, 864, 908, 923, 924, 927, 929, 932, 937, 938, 939, 953, 954, 955, 959, 970, 1009, 1098

IDOLLES 493, 973

ILLARY 661

IMPRYNTYD 614

IN 35, 46, 57, 68, 69, 74, 93, 94, 101, 104, 140, 185, 203, 209, 220, 230, 241, 263, 276, 280, 306, 335, 337, 354, 359, 362, 377, 413, 417, 443, 468, 468, 512, 514, 523, 525, 550, 551, 572, 585, 586, 633, 635, 659, 660, 671, 673, 707, 712, 713, 715, 725, 735, 742, 768, 789, 807, 868, 912, 919, 946, 946, 947, 1011, 1081

INCESSANT 1021

INCORRIGIBYLL 1021

INDEMNYTE 773

INIQUITE 406
INORDYNATE 498
INTELLYGENS 980
INTRIXICATE 555
ISAY 1047
JACKE 95, 254
JACKE A THRUM 278
JACKE AT NOKE 703
JACKE OF THE NOKE 318
JAGGYD 53
JANGYLL 326
JAPE 83
JAVELL 455
JEREMY 1050
JHESU 1100
JOY 798
JUGE 97
JURIDICCION 109
KEYSAR 861
KEYSER 459
KEKE 181
KEN 897
KEPE 122, 153, 275, 303, 429, 477, 479, 851
KERY 606
KYNDE 516
KYNG 459, 834, 861
KYNGES 126, 1013
KNAVE 456
KNAVYSHE 506
KNE 484
KNELE 483
KNYGHTE 456, 826
KNOWE 216, 582, 717, 908, 980
KNOWITH 666
LABOR 94
LABOUR 134
LACKE 653
LACKYTHE 27, 32
LADY 367, 368
LAY 74, 297, 375, 763
LAYE 376
LAKES 477
LAMBYS 155

LANTERNYS 549
LARD 694
LARGE 548, 682
LARKES 191
LASSYS 398
LATE 760, 855
LAWE 94, 584, 705, 711
LAWRYAT 809
LEDES 382
LEDYR 505
LEFETENAUNTE 1009
LEGE MOY 797
LEY 194
LEYSER 460
LEYTHE 280
LENE 128
LENTE 203, 209, 344, 707
LERID 585
LERNE 475
LERNYD 641
LERNYNG 239
LESE 689
LESSE 469, 852
LESSONS 169
LESTE 521, 1070
LET 520, 824, 848, 916, 1001, 1062, 1065
LETT 29, 211
LETTE 179, 421
LETTER 266
LEVE 79, 100
LEVYR 755
LEWDE 89, 239, 998
LEWDLY 431
LYARS 681, 1029
LYBERTE 565
LYCENS 882
LYE 328, 400, 907, 1094
LYFFE 250
LYGHTE 454, 549
LYKE 51, 108, 151, 168, 196, 390, 427, 549, 768, 1031, 1050
LYMYTERS 682
LYTE 103
LYTELL 102, 129, 138, 1011

LYTYLL 974
LYVE 982
LO 1068
LOCKE 79
LODE 1097
LOGE 1011
LOGGYNG 512
LOGYKE 663
LOKE 71, 211, 634, 868
LOKES 450
LONDES 776
LONGE 1038
LOONYS 343
LORD 874
LORDE 455, 826
LORDEN 1010
LORDES 463, 470, 483, 857
LORDLY 450
LORE 92, 402
LORELL 1003
LOSE 211
LOSELLES 430
LOSSE 774
LOSTE 396
LOTHE 161, 162, 491, 689
LOTTE 603
LOVE 496
LOWE 442, 961
LOWSY 514
LOWUR 1010
LUKE 890
LUSTY 791, 798
MACTOCKE 501
MADE 166, 518, 631, 656, 760, 798
MADLY 237
MAGESTE 443
MAGNA CARTA 572
MAISTER 534, 583, 1060
MAY 31, 37, 121, 187, 314, 449, 460, 485, 524, 596, 636, 789, 839, 840, 865, 873, 906, 1043, 1064
MAYE 298
MAYNTAYNE 762, 1054
MAKE 3, 67, 83, 102, 133, 142, 181, 200, 246, 265, 294, 301, 356, 393, 456, 629, 699, 835, 859, 875,

915, 922, 1010, 1044

MAKYNG 428

MALE 541

MALTE 691

MAMMOCKES 507

MAN 449, 574, 866, 874, 932, 952, 954, 971, 1039, 1080

MANCIONS 781

MANER 10, 553, 562, 737, 742

MANGYLL 327

MANY 428, 517, 684, 1040

MANNYS 838

MARE 180

MARYS 311, 1026

MARKE 579, 891

MAS 866, 1000

MASSYS 397

MATENS 237, 380, 1000

MATERS 93, 768, 1040, 1054

MATYR 663

MATTOCKE 270

MAWDE 700

MAWE 511

ME 67, 184, 411, 643, 927, 934, 957, 972, 1089

MEASURE 144

MEDELYTHE 24

MEDYLL 668

MEDYTACION 817

MEDLYNG 1001

MEDLYTHE 103

MELE 691

MELL 161

MELLE 859, 1002

MELLES 389

MEN 64, 74, 111, 167, 175, 186, 189, 194, 205, 285, 295, 347, 350, 360, 404, 466, 485, 611, 743, 763, 898, 1069

MENNES 98

MERCHALSE 1013

MERGARETES 724

MERGERY 700

MERKETT 322

MERVAYLE 852

METE 203, 316, 507, 660, 817

MY 48, 50, 52, 255, 367, 734, 815, 931, 944, 951, 1087, 1090, 1098

MYCHE 168, 176, 203, 268, 852

MYDNYGHTE 380

MYGHTE 435, 472, 619

MYKYLL 422

MYLKE 311

MYLLES 392

MYNDE 515, 734

MYRE 912

MYS 840

MYSELFE 637

MYTER 288

MYTERS 286

MO 677, 728

MOCKE 480

MOCKYSHE 180

MODYR 68, 948

MOLDY 508

MOME 751

MOMMYNG 82

MONEY 87, 285, 397

MONESTARYS 392

MONKE 942

MONKYS 356

MORE 91, 294, 401, 490, 621, 660, 861

MORNYS 342

MOSTE 241, 372, 483, 581, 603, 658, 735, 870

MOTHE 55

MOTYNG 916

MOUTHYS 895

MOWSE 649

MURMURACION 922

MVLE 304

MVLES 315

NAY 178, 178

NAYLE 34

NAKYD 790, 813

NAME 48, 272, 805

NAMYD 954

NAMYS 160

NAT 261

NE 159, 206, 206, 207, 714

NECKE 163

NECLYGENS 981

NEDE 711

NEYBORS 316

NEYTHER 859

NEYTHYR 210, 714

NERE 953

NETT 779

NEVYR 344, 617

NEW 473, 686

NEWYN 672

NYGHTE 193

NO 35, 287, 294, 314, 378, 380, 449, 503, 509, 587, 662, 701, 711, 740, 743, 754, 774, 874, 922, 929, 930, 932, 936, 938, 939, 943, 952, 954, 958, 976, 978, 979, 984, 985, 988, 1039, 1080

NOBYLL 125, 467, 470, 580, 612, 1047

NOBYLLMEN 474

NODY POLLYS 1083

NOLLES 231

NOLLYS 1082

NONE 75, 264, 980

NONNE 367, 941

NONNYS 366

NOO 977

NOR 18, 209, 210, 234, 236, 634, 642, 665, 666, 667, 775, 859, 860, 861, 876, 884, 889, 939, 940, 941, 942, 943, 976, 977, 978, 1077, 1078, 1081, 1083, 1084, 1085

NOT 17, 118, 208, 213, 233, 235, 249, 274, 409, 632, 643, 666, 726, 867, 880, 965, 970, 994, 1042, 1066, 1072, 1077, 1095

NOTARYS 655

NOTE 407

NOTHER 236, 509, 728

NOTHIR 664

NOTHYNG 238, 276, 348, 465, 990

NOTYD 607

NOT SHELL 1066

NOW 174, 365, 516, 621, 676, 734, 815, 890, 909, 1068, 1087, 1088, 1098

NOWE 760, 927

NOWGHT 159

NOWGHTE 440, 461, 478, 1027

NOWTHER 889

O 864

OBIECTE 643

OBSERUAUNCE 600

OCUPY 752

OCUPYE 744, 986

OF 4, 10, 10, 78, 80, 92, 116, 126, 148, 170, 176, 196, 199, 202, 232, 242, 249, 250, 258, 279, 295, 300, 310, 312, 333, 333, 335, 357, 359, 370, 393, 416, 440, 442, 454, 470, 493, 497, 505, 515, 516, 527, 545, 547, 549, 553, 562, 566, 583, 584, 589, 598, 599, 601, 605, 630, 642, 653, 663, 677, 680, 681, 694, 694, 696, 716, 724, 727, 737, 742, 745, 760, 764, 765, 775, 775, 776, 787, 788, 796, 802, 803, 804, 818, 832, 855, 857, 862, 868, 879, 911, 919, 921, 926, 937, 938, 943, 945, 961, 962, 979, 982, 987, 997, 1005, 1006, 1007, 1009, 1017, 1019, 1030, 1031, 1035, 1049, 1061, 1082, 1083, 1084, 1085, 1090, 1092, 1100

OFF 1086

OFFENDE 971

OLD 710, 718, 920

OLDE 357

OLYFAUNTES 808

ON 30, 34, 191, 302, 323, 328, 416, 419, 482, 517, 757, 834, 838, 867, 868, 923, 934, 967, 994, 1000

ONE 862

ONY 960, 1081

ONS 228

OON 949

OPENLY 1025

OPYN 546

OPYNLY 885, 1015

OR 3, 5, 6, 8, 9, 13, 15, 26, 38, 134, 147, 212, 215, 270, 288, 318, 574, 579, 590, 591, 592, 593, 594, 596, 598, 601, 602, 605, 616, 618, 639, 690, 717, 762, 873, 885, 887, 899, 900, 901, 907, 912, 963, 964, 966, 967, 1013, 1024, 1026, 1056, 1058, 1061, 1061, 1062, 1063, 1067

ORDYR 598

ORDYRS 219, 680

ORYLL 1061

OTHER 677

OUR 369

OVER 526

OVERALL 488

OVYR 383, 836

OWGHTE 705, 956

OWNE 100, 272

OWRYS 240

OWTE 49, 99, 214, 300, 370, 515, 516, 696, 724, 726, 921, 937, 982, 1092

OWTECRYES 428

OWUR 874, 879, 948, 1001, 1016, 1017, 1054, 1057, 1100

OZEAS 1048

PAYD 344

PAYNE 615, 708

PAYNTES 766

PAYNUS 309

PAYRE 189

PALL 306

PALLYS 787

PAPALL 570

PARCIALITE 1035

PARCIALL 918

PARYS 796

PARYSSHE CLERKE 869

PARKES 190

PARSON 880

PARTE 136, 137, 241, 582

PARTRYCHE 204, 715

PASSE 865, 1001

PATER NOSTER 234

PATER NOSTER PEKES 258

PATES 994

PATYRS 22

PATTYS 1085

PAWLUS 333

PEEPYLL 375

PEN 1087

PENALTE 405

PENDE 185

PENY 775

PEOPYLL 625, 893

PEPYLL 119, 284, 319, 326, 342, 386, 828

PEPYLLES 550

PERDYALL 776

PERFYTENES 822

PERLE 340

PERSEYVID 622

PESE 1012

PESYON 210

PETOUS 481

PETRONYLLA 255

PILLION 651

PYGGE 212

PYKE 206

PYLLAGE 353

PYLLERY 660

PYPE 473

PYSTYLL 236

PYTHE 57

PLACE 921

PLACEBO 733, 753

PLACES 744

PLAY 165, 751, 854, 1074

PLAYE 296

PLAYED 856

PLAYNE 26, 131, 617, 625, 931, 1071

PLEAS 409, 755

PLEASURE 145, 862, 1057, 1104

PLESANTE 699

PLUCKE 77, 382, 715

PLURALITES 424

POLYTYKE 769

POLYTYKES 478

POLLYNG 353

POLLSHORNE 995

POLSHORNE 1015

POMPEUS 803

POPE 298

PORE 319, 497, 588, 602

PORTE 1099

POSTYLL 606

POSTYLLES 250

POWLUS 1024

PRAYD 238	PROPHETE 1048	RECTIFYE 1102
PRATE 1000, 1023	PROTECCIONS 738	REDE 233, 273, 841, 988, 1081
PRATES 995	PROTESTACION 631	REDYS 388
PRATY 255	PROVYNCIALL 101, 220	REFORME 981
PRATYTHE 22	PROVOKE 702	REHERSE 14, 626
PRECHARS 1045	PUFFYD 448	REYNES 310
PRECHE 13, 616, 658, 670, 736	PULL 77	REKENYNG 835
PRECHERS 991	PULPYT 551, 659	RELEAS 723
PRECHYNG 976	PURPOSE 49	RELIGIOUS 360
PRECHYTHE 685, 1015	PURPULL 306	REMEMBRANS 486
PRECIUSE 340	PURSE 289	REMYNAUNTE 115
PREDICTAMENTTES 667	PUT 69, 96, 379, 696, 904, 921	REMORDE 827
PREKYTHE 20	QUAYLE 718	REN 1032
PRELACYE 439	QUAKYD 791	RENOWNE 804
PRELATES 70	QUALIFIE 425	REPYNE 721
PRELATTES 818, 992	QUALITES 425	REPORTE 849
PRELLATTES 441	QUARELL 454	REPORTYTHE 298
PREMENIRE 107	QUARELLES 762	RESEYVYD 623
PREMVNIRE 911	QUENE 799	RESYTYNG 978
PREPOSYSSYON 841	QUERE 370	RESON 1033
PRESCRIPCION 111	QUYCKE 967	RESTE 1065, 1088
PRESE 880, 883	QUYSSHON 840	RETTAYNE 624
PRESENS 883	QUYTE 381	RETURNE 361
PRESEPTE 377	RAGGE 52	REVYLE 11
PRESYDENT 886	RAYLE 5, 717, 718, 1053	REWEN 717
PRESYDENTE 879	RAYLYNG 946, 989	RYALLY 780
PRESTE 266, 432, 939, 998	RAYLYS 387	RYCHE 788
PRESTES 343	RAYLL 375	RYCHELY 308
PRETENDYNG 770	RAYNE 54, 502, 1053	RYDE 304, 807
PRETENTE 970	RAKE 270	RYDYNG 812
PREUYLY 885	RAMMYS 156	RYGHT 899
PREVY 1005	RAMSE HORNE 1041	RYGHTE 104, 139, 378, 1037, 1039, 1041
PRYDE 448, 498	RATE 562, 858, 1022	RYME 5, 47, 52
PRYETHE 20	RATHYR 175	RYN 1063, 1063, 1064, 1064
PRYMATES 993	RATYFIED 567	RYSE 1072
PRYME 240	RAWE 93	RODE 1094
PRYNTYD 1079	REALM 837	ROYALL 467, 837
PRYORESSE 369	REASON 14, 141, 848	ROMOTES 715
PROMOCION 85	REBELLES 387	RON 230, 829
PROMOTYD 609	REBUKE 932	RONNYS 367
PROMOTYNG 918	RECCHYNG 784	ROSTE 863
PRONGE 1036	RECHELES 1018	ROTYN 339, 400
PROPERLI 722	RECHETTES 310	ROUNDE 528
PROPHANUS 205	RECOUNTYNG 944	

ROWEN 718

ROWTE 925

RUDE 931

RULE 303, 418, 459, 464, 502, 834, 837

RULYTHE 488, 863

RUSSET 713

RUSTY 55

RUTHE 336

RVDELY 54

SACERDOTES 722

SACRYNG 872

SADDE 741

SAY 15, 15, 36, 175, 330, 407, 524, 864, 1009, 1040, 1055

SAYD 237, 710

SAYE 377

SAYES 431, 1069

SAYLE 3, 1095

SAYNT 170, 891, 1030

SAYNTE 661, 890, 1026

SAYTHE 17

SAKE 248, 861

SALTE 690

SALTFYSSHE 207

SALVE 1099

SAME 986

SATHE 131

SAVYOUR 1100

SAWE 585, 710

SAWYD 1046

SCANTE 579

SCANTLY 79

SCANTLYE 273

SCOLE 29, 663

SCORNE 475, 1042

SCORPION 415

SCOTTE 602

SCRIPTURE 576, 608

SE 872

SEASON 209

SECRETLY 884

SEDE 745

SEE 38, 58, 179, 485, 612, 1080

SEY 71, 74, 90, 91, 111, 120, 135, 186, 189, 190, 285, 295, 337, 347, 394, 422, 423, 424, 434, 466, 533, 611, 722, 739, 743, 905, 913, 936, 1034

SEYNTES 767

SEYTHE 1018

SEKE 182, 248, 966

SELFE 726, 966, 969

SELFE SAME 364

SELY 76, 432

SELYE 366

SELL 198, 384

SEMELYE 811

SEMYS 1074

SEMYTHE 1089

SENDE 968, 1101

SENE 801

SENYORYTE 771

SEQUESTER 156

SERMONS 133

SERVAUNTES 920

SETT 108, 778, 1008, 1027

SETTE 159, 373, 443, 478, 1066

SHAKE 49

SHAKYD 792

SHAL 1059

SHALBE 1045, 1046

SHALL 257, 287, 405, 490, 490, 643, 730, 859, 866, 992, 1049, 1091

SHAME 271, 365, 984, 984

SHAMFULL 1042

SHAMFULLY 329

SHAMFULLYE 438

SHAMLES 1020

SHARE 176

SHE 367

SHEPE 76, 130, 154

SHETYLL 1027

SHEWE 723, 769

SHYPPE 1090, 1098

SHODYR 67

SHOLDE 1072

SHOO 180, 195

SHOTE 604, 794, 1094

SHOTTE 604

SHOVYLL 501

SHREWDE 351

SHREWDLY 388

SHRYMPES 206

SHRYNE 339

SHULD 417, 546, 608, 614, 621, 624, 955, 1080

SHULDE 563, 607

SILOGIZARE 664

SIR 997, 999

SYBYLLE 369

SYGHTE 550

SYLENS 751

SYLFE 846

SYLKE 312

SYMYNIAKE 292

SYMONY 295

SYMPYLNES 1017

SYN 12

SYNE 655

SYNG 244, 726

SYNGYNG 753

SYNODALYS 569

SYSMATYKES 553

SYT 337

SYTACONS 320

SYTE 543

SYTTE 31, 324, 417

SKYEE 73

SKYLL 98, 1033

SLAYNE 1051

SLAUNDERYNG 335

SLENDYR 139

SLEPE 123

SLYPPE 521, 1091

SLOWTHE 136

SLUMBYR 123

SMALLE 117, 122, 464

SMATERS 24

SMATYR 662

SMOCKE 217

SMOTHELY 1091

SNAYLE 2

SNEVYLL 1062

SO 16, 37, 70, 71, 94, 106, 203, 239, 303, 395, 436, 448, 487, 488, 539, 543, 609, 617, 619, 640, 746, 747, 784, 851, 854, 856, 875, 994, 1038

SOCHE 258

SODENLYE 499

SOE 1074

SOFTE 324, 831

SOLDE 286, 439

SOLEMLY 659

SOLEMNITE 772

SOM 57, 146, 190, 202, 222, 223, 224, 225, 226, 244, 272, 307, 337, 404, 422, 423, 574, 583, 584, 585, 681, 688, 712, 714, 715, 855, 1046, 1051, 1051, 1052, 1085

SOME 273, 307, 424, 1049

SOMNERS 320

SOMTYM 702

SOMTYME 412, 514, 691, 692

SOMWHATE 894

SON 412

SOO 90, 752, 867

SOTHE 89

SOTTES 427

SOVERAYN 874

SOWE 745

SOWLE 724

SOWLES 395

SOWLYS 128, 232, 1084

SOWLUS 334

SPARE 178

SPARYD 314

SPECULACION 816

SPEKE 26, 249, 884, 937, 938

SPEKYNG 946

SPEKYS 259, 348

SPEKYTHE 18, 243

SPELLES 388

SPEND 398

SPENDE 176, 178

SPETYLL 1026

SPIRITUAL 898

SPIRITUALL 112, 155, 174, 444, 547

SPIRITUALTE 62, 962

SPYRYTUALTE 61

SPORTE 798

SQUYRE 826

STAKE 245

STARYS 806

STARRYS 675

STEDE 35, 230

STEPYLL 333, 829

STERE 1098

STERRE 1097

STERRY 73

STERRYS 784

STEWYD 214, 215

STYLE 10, 699, 931

STYLL 543

STYLLA 256

STYLLE 982, 1059

STYROPPUS 313

STOCFYSHE 207

STOLE 30

STONDE 46, 914, 915

STONDYDYTHE 35

STONDYNG 919

STONE 300

STONUS 340

STOPYLL 506

STOPPE 895

STOPPYD 533

STORYS 800

STORMY 1093

STRAUNGE 394

STRAWE 290, 512

STRYDYNG 813

STRYVYS 430

SUBIECCIONS 737

SUBSTYTUTE 887

SUCH 1101

SUCHE 134, 242, 522, 523, 553, 737, 742, 744, 759, 800, 822, 823, 858, 903, 945, 950, 968

SUFFYR 544, 1077

SUPERSTICION 749

SUPPORTE 848

SUPPOSE 853

SUPPOSYD 260

SUPPOSYNG 350

SURE 102, 276, 915, 1044

SURELY 120

SURFULD 217

SURMYSED 438

SUTE 875

SWELLYNG 831

SWETE 317, 891

SWYNE 654

TABARDES 312

TAYLE 4, 716

TAKE 56, 75, 134, 141, 184, 232, 269, 302, 458, 615, 651, 708, 714, 735, 741, 756, 757, 860, 927, 930, 1007, 1065

TALKE 284, 427, 893

TALKYNG 830

TALKYS 390

TATERYD 53

TAXING 355

TECHE 13, 992

TECHYNG 977

TEETHE 419

TELL 160, 186, 490, 491, 670, 677, 896, 958

TELLES 386

TEMPYLL 674

TEMPORALL 64, 110, 463, 759, 828

TEMPORALTE 60, 131, 963

TETEVYLLES 390

TEXTE 630

TEXTES 577

THANKFULLERLYE 623

THAT 15, 31, 33, 66, 107, 145, 148, 170, 175, 185, 187, 198, 247, 261, 331, 351, 358, 385, 391, 395, 404, 417, 429, 449, 462, 466, 467, 482, 489, 521, 524, 526, 528, 540, 555, 556, 557, 559, 575, 587, 595, 607, 626, 628, 632, 636, 640, 641, 642, 693, 705, 711, 750, 766, 768, 777, 779, 846, 851, 855, 859, 863, 866, 893, 897, 907, 919, 926, 933, 935, 937, 959, 964, 993, 1034, 1039, 1080, 1101, 1103

THE 34, 34, 36, 60, 61, 62, 64, 66, 69, 70, 73, 80, 92, 94, 101, 104, 107, 114, 115, 116, 117, 119, 125, 126, 131, 137, 152, 152, 162, 163, 166, 180, 183, 193, 195, 199, 199, 229, 241, 247, 259, 280, 284, 291, 297, 298, 319, 323,

326, 333, 341, 342, 346, 352, 356, 359, 364, 366, 370, 375, 376, 386, 391, 397, 399, 401, 412, 430, 432, 439, 463, 469, 482, 484, 487, 492, 500, 501, 501, 518, 524, 525, 529, 541, 545, 546, 550, 552, 561, 563, 588, 589, 598, 602, 610, 625, 630, 652, 659, 660, 669, 675, 680, 705, 716, 720, 725, 725, 727, 732, 763, 784, 786, 799, 806, 827, 829, 829, 840, 849, 854, 862, 863, 869, 872, 878, 893, 895, 912, 925, 937, 962, 963, 967, 986, 987, 991, 995, 1004, 1005, 1006, 1007, 1008, 1009, 1013, 1015, 1028, 1045, 1048, 1052, 1067, 1068, 1089, 1090, 1092, 1093, 1096, 1097, 1099

THEDYR 730, 1014

THEY 36, 38, 46, 67, 71, 72, 75, 79, 84, 84, 89, 91, 93, 94, 96, 97, 102, 111, 118, 120, 121, 138, 141, 142, 161, 165, 166, 167, 169, 175, 181, 197, 197, 200, 210, 219, 228, 230, 232, 233, 261, 264, 287, 294, 317, 319, 328, 334, 376, 385, 394, 423, 424, 427, 429, 435, 437, 441, 451, 466, 471, 473, 475, 504, 527, 533, 538, 539, 619, 671, 673, 689, 698, 701, 702, 705, 708, 721, 722, 730, 732, 735, 739, 740, 743, 747, 750, 752, 754, 755, 767, 768, 769, 774, 778, 807, 824, 850, 852, 853, 859, 896, 897, 902, 904, 905, 906, 907, 913, 913, 935, 973, 974, 984, 985, 986, 989, 992, 1029, 1031, 1040, 1070, 1074, 1076

THEYR 109

THEYRE 143, 154, 981, 1082

THEYSE 448

THEM 88, 113, 327, 378, 379, 434, 472, 479, 480, 681, 752, 763, 769, 805, 851, 860, 921, 968, 969, 987, 1014, 1065

THEN 27, 177, 230, 436, 451, 453, 627, 757, 848, 908, 933, 960

THEOLOGI 409

THER 56, 78, 81, 86, 100, 130, 140, 146, 150, 169, 176, 200, 239, 240, 250, 272, 309, 312, 313, 314, 315, 316, 334, 372, 373, 374, 382, 400, 429, 443, 464, 480, 484, 698, 704, 746, 756, 776, 777, 781, 801, 811, 821, 825, 894, 895, 902, 921, 983, 993, 994

THERBE 960

THERBYE 906

THERE 76, 86, 99, 127, 128, 158, 160, 237, 383, 384, 395, 396, 397, 400, 681,

695, 706, 773, 819, 870, 1055, 1065, 1083, 1084

THEREOF 83, 348

THERFOR 205, 479, 845, 914

THERWITH 511

THESE 626, 812

THY 1000, 1000

THYCKE 693

THYNG 662, 833

THYNGE 418

THYNGES 1103

THYNKE 404, 503, 964

THYNKES 972

THYNKYNG 815

THYS 47, 65, 114, 119, 141, 185, 277, 325, 419, 481, 515, 544, 562, 581, 604, 606, 621, 633, 635, 697, 816, 865, 873, 886, 892, 893, 911, 923, 928, 975, 1022, 1042, 1043, 1068, 1077

THYSE 157, 919

THOLOMYE 411

THOMAS 170, 1030

THOW 56, 72, 317, 1002, 1003

THOWE 52, 528, 617, 923, 924

THOWGHTE 462

THOWSAND 627

THROW 732, 903

THROWE 110

THROW OWTE 201

THUS 15, 120, 200, 206, 281, 334, 375, 379, 386, 430, 434, 527, 821, 827, 830, 831, 902, 1010

TYDE 707

TYLL 1096

TYRLY TYRLOW 795

TO 2, 3, 5, 5, 6, 6, 7, 8, 11, 12, 13, 13, 29, 49, 76, 85, 88, 90, 95, 108, 124, 127, 133, 134, 135, 142, 153, 153, 161, 162, 164, 165, 177, 183, 194, 195, 211, 212, 216, 265, 269, 275, 303, 304, 309, 326, 327, 345, 361, 362, 374, 379, 379, 392, 392, 393, 412, 422, 434, 436, 459, 461, 469, 475, 480, 482, 486, 491, 496, 502, 502, 503, 504, 508, 510, 510, 511, 603, 604, 606, 616, 634, 636, 669, 687, 688, 689, 695, 700, 704, 706, 709, 709, 723, 723, 736, 736, 739, 741, 744, 745, 755, 757, 758, 762, 777, 779, 784, 794, 805, 815,

819, 821, 834, 835, 836, 839, 860, 865, 868, 872, 874, 875, 876, 880, 880, 883, 883, 884, 904, 928, 936, 950, 952, 956, 957, 969, 971, 975, 981, 983, 984, 1006, 1010, 1037, 1052, 1067, 1069, 1075, 1079, 1087, 1088, 1102, 1102

TOLD 411

TOLLYNG 355

TONE 66

TONGES 698, 902

TONG TYED 347

TONSORS 532

TORNE 392, 1037

TORNYTHE 487

TORRETTES 782

TOT COTTE 426

TOTYNG 917

TOWARDE 1099

TOWCHYD 967

TOWRYS 782

TOWUR 1009

TRAPPYD 305

TREASURE 143

TRETES 975

TREWE 265

TRYALYTES 423

TRYHUMPHES 802

TRYM 496

TRYPPE 522

TROY 796

TRONE 417

TRONUS 337

TROW 91

TROWTHE 135

TRULY 815

TRULYE 905, 959

TRUSTE 279

TRUTHE 335

TURKE 401

TWAYN 616

URE 151

VACABONDES 242

VAYLYS 372

VANYTE 40

VARYABULNES 44

VELANY 1016

VENERY 105

VENTAYLYS 374

VENUS 791

VERAYE 394

VERY 767

VERRAY 464

VERREY 103, 271, 838

VERTU 267, 933

VERTUE 452

VERTUOUS 935, 977, 979

VIOLATE 558

VYCE 11

VYLLAGE 354

VNDERSTOND 734

VNDYR 217, 655, 851

VNDYRSTODE 471

VNIVERSITE 589

VNYCORNUS 810

VNNETHE 358, 477

VNSTEDFASTNES 45

VNTAWGHTE 227

VNTWYNDE 517

VOBISCUM 229

VP 96, 372, 440, 442, 451, 497

VPPE 373

VPPON 64, 269, 927

VPSTERTE 499

VRE 845

VS 595, 992, 1005, 1023, 1027, 1029, 1031, 1101

VTTERLY 330

WADE 632

WAY 525, 1067

WALKE 283, 712

WALL 300

WALLES 125, 786

WALSOMANUS 629

WALTAMS 657

WANDERYNG 283

WANTON 192, 218, 398, 814

WANTONES 820

WARDEN 1007

WARE 520

WARKE 892

WARKES 192

WARME 308

WARRE 759, 803

WAS 332, 507, 567, 656, 1047

WATER 392

WAWYS 1092

WE 268, 596, 1018, 1032, 1034, 1037, 1043, 1044, 1053, 1066, 1072

WEDYCOKE 218

WEY 937

WEYED 621

WEL 801

WELCOM 246

WELCUM 254

WELE PUBLYCKE 552

WELL 37, 56, 408, 471, 520, 576, 725

WELLAWAYE 433

WELTHE 346

WENCHYS 814

WENE 964

WERE 268, 504, 617, 767

WERYNG 208

WERKE 118, 581, 943

WERKES 150

WERRYN 153

WESANTE 996

WESTMYNSTER 1025

WETHERCOCKE 332

WHAN 415, 441

WHATE 1, 17, 91, 194, 216, 233, 291, 317, 401, 407, 434, 671, 673

WHELE 482

WHEN 96, 187, 193, 219, 228, 507, 725, 730, 1076, 1104

WHEREOF 18

WHERFOR 930, 955, 972, 1044

WHERFORE 350

WHETHER 899, 905

WHETTE 419

WHY 543, 958

WHYCHE 563, 990, 1075

WHYE 933

WHYLE 1088

WHYLES 114

WHYSTYLL 235

WHYTE 311

WHO 1055, 1056

WHOM 888

WHOO 47, 179, 1064

WITH 45, 59, 65, 87, 140, 143, 158, 177, 214, 231, 246, 305, 313, 320, 340, 365, 371, 374, 389, 402, 448, 498, 506, 508, 537, 618, 733, 748, 753, 772, 782, 782, 783, 783, 785, 790, 799, 800, 802, 809, 811, 814, 822, 828, 857, 987, 991, 996, 1012

WITHDRAWE 704, 1087

WITHIN 125

WITHOWTE 144, 266, 267, 878, 881, 886, 1033

WITHSTANDE 736, 758

WYDE 996

WYFE 249

WYFES 429

WYL 274

WYLFULLNES 1019

WYLL 87, 97, 210, 461, 542, 632, 668, 670, 672, 676, 683, 714, 717, 754, 774, 838, 847, 888, 896, 913, 970, 976, 978, 980, 1032, 1053, 1057, 1060, 1077, 1098

WYLLA 257

WYLLES 391

WYNCHE 181

WYNDE 374

WYNDOWUS 785

WYNE 653

WYNKYNG 814

WYSE 278, 654, 657

WYTHE 56

WYTLES 1085

WYTTE 32

WYTTES 1071

WODE 1092

WOL 453

WOLD 14, 38, 72, 556, 557

WOLDE 473, 555, 558, 559, 560, 607, 615, 626, 985

WOLFE 152

WOLL 122, 986

WOLLE 78, 80

WONDER 892

WONDYR 850

WONNYNG 140

WONTE 504

WORDE 616, 987

WORDES 626

WORDLY 756

WORDLYE 820

WORKE 394

WORLD 732

WORLDE 259, 524, 806

WORLDLY 40

WORSE 291

WORSSHEPFULLY 758

WORSSHYPFULL 149

WORTH 578

WORTHE 235, 579

WOT 233

WOTT 17, 684

WOTTE 118, 231, 309, 708

WRAPPYD 308

WRECHYDNES 42

WREKE 934

WRITE 923, 928

WRYE 541

WRYTE 6, 959

WRYTYNG 951, 979

WROKYN 453

WRONG 899

WRONGE 59, 378, 1037

YAWYD 1045

YE 187, 189, 190, 211, 256, 257, 291, 351, 356, 378, 404, 453, 456, 457, 457, 457, 458, 460, 461, 469, 479, 490, 496, 509, 516, 517, 528, 540, 615, 734, 851, 854, 908, 920, 922, 934, 956

YEE 539

YELL 197

YELLYNG 830, 832

YET 232, 610, 668, 840, 852, 869, 876, 985, 986, 1078

YETE 274, 526

YETTE 145, 943

YF 26, 46, 56, 87, 121, 160, 302, 409, 471, 596, 615, 960

YFF 33, 460

YLL 130, 544, 991, 1058

YN 109, 260, 310

YNCHE 529

YNFECTYD 1076

YNSTRUXION 264

YOUR 208, 213, 220, 248, 257, 260, 339, 377, 394, 406, 419, 450, 451, 462, 507, 511, 513, 528, 532, 533, 538, 539, 547, 611, 612, 613, 904, 916, 917, 917, 918, 919, 934

YOW 91, 186, 198, 202, 205, 260, 328, 329, 335, 337, 420, 458, 473, 482, 492, 543, 696, 848, 855, 904, 913, 926, 1044, 1049

YOWE 347

YPOCRECIE 765

YRE 105

YS 16, 28, 36, 48, 59, 69, 86, 108, 115, 136, 138, 145, 182, 208, 216, 239, 260, 276, 293, 325, 336, 358, 365, 394, 410, 439, 452, 462, 464, 481, 515, 571, 575, 580, 674, 693, 710, 760, 779, 816, 833, 892, 894, 933, 944, 951, 988, 990, 1042, 1059, 1068, 1069, 1104

1001

Library of Congress Cataloging-in-Publication Data

Fox, Alistair.
  A concordance to the complete English poems of John Skelton.

  (Cornell concordances)
  "Based on John Skelton, the complete English poems / edited by John Scattergood. New Haven : Yale University Press, 1983"—Verso t.p.
  1. Skelton, John, 1460?–1529—Concordances. I. Waite, Gregory, 1954–
II. Skelton, John, 1460?–1529. Selections. 1983. III. Title. IV. Series.
PR2348.A3   1987   821'.2   87-47552
ISBN 0-8014-1944-1